KU-307-545

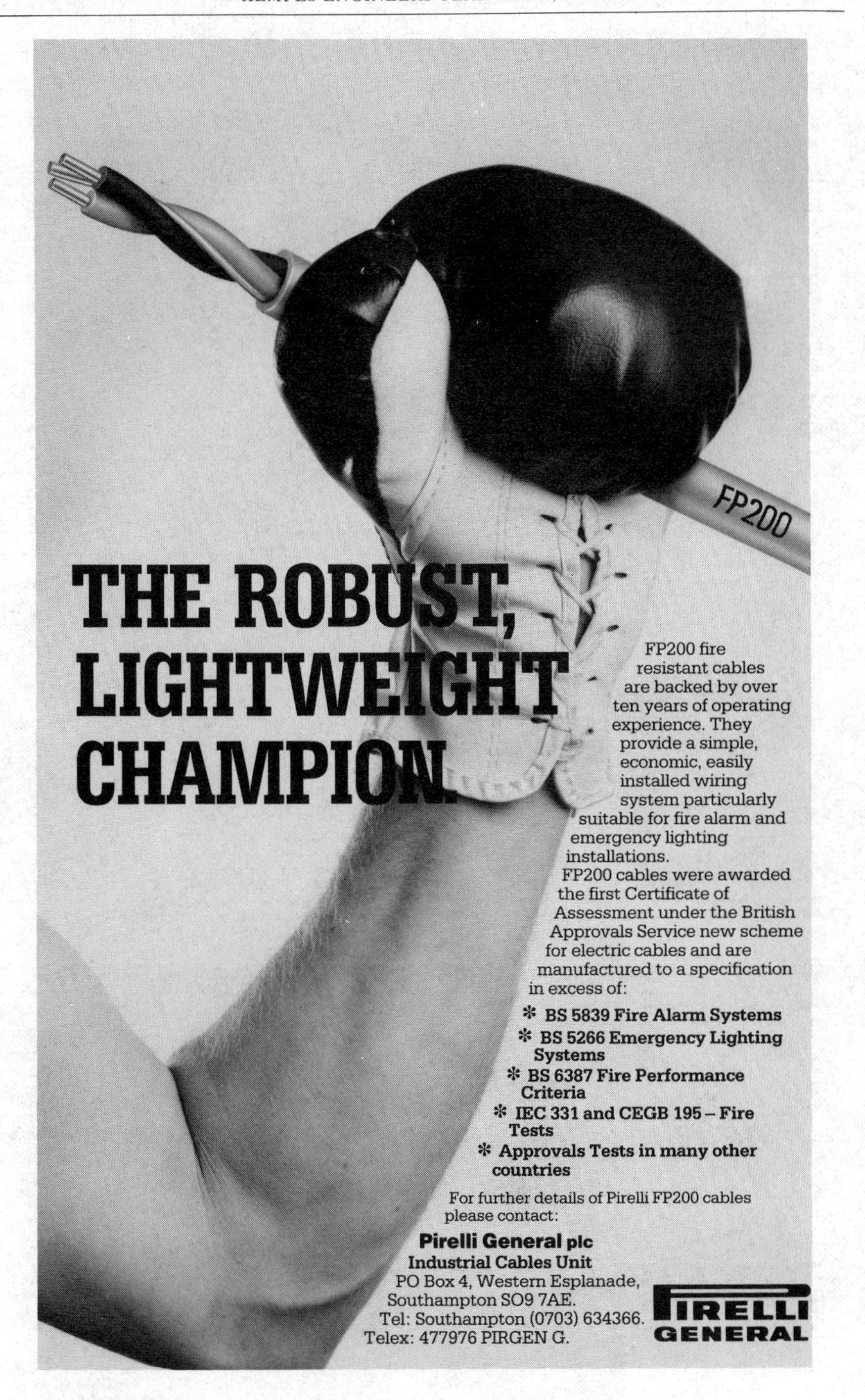
FP200
THE ROBUST, LIGHTWEIGHT CHAMPION.
FP200 fire resistant cables are backed by over ten years of operating experience. They provide a simple, economic, easily installed wiring system particularly suitable for fire alarm and emergency lighting installations.
FP200 cables were awarded the first Certificate of Assessment under the British Approvals Service new scheme for electric cables and are manufactured to a specification in excess of:
* BS 5839 Fire Alarm Systems
* BS 5266 Emergency Lighting Systems
* BS 6387 Fire Performance Criteria
* IEC 331 and CEGB 195 – Fire Tests
* Approvals Tests in many other countries
For further details of Pirelli FP200 cables please contact:
Pirelli General plc
Industrial Cables Unit
PO Box 4, Western Esplanade,
Southampton SO9 7AE.
Tel: Southampton (0703) 634366.
Telex: 477976 PIRGEN G.
PIRELLI GENERAL

KEMPE'S ENGINEERS YEAR-BOOK 1989

94th EDITION

VOLUME 2

Edited by
CARILL SHARPE

MORGAN-GRAMPIAN BOOK PUBLISHING CO. LTD
ROYAL SOVEREIGN HOUSE, 40 BERESFORD STREET,
LONDON SE18 6BQ

ISBN 0 86213 096 4

VOLUME 2
CONTENTS (Alphabetical)

CONTENTS

CHAPTER

CHAPTER

CHAPTER

REGULATIONS FOR ELECTRICAL INSTALLATIONS

The IEE Wiring Regulations—Isolation and Switching—Overcurrent Protection—Selection of Live Conductors—Shock Protection—Protective Conductors and Earthing—Wiring Systems and Circuits—Protection against Thermal Effects—Inspection and Testing—Conclusion and Further Reading—Tables.

By J. F. Whitfield

THE IEE WIRING REGULATIONS

HISTORY AND BACKGROUND.—In 1882 the Society of Telegraph Engineers and Electricians published their 'rules and Regulations for the prevention of fire risks arising from electric lighting'. The Society became the Institution of Electrical Engineers, which has continued to publish the 'IEE Regs.' as they have come to be known. The Regulations have sought to keep pace with the rapidly-changing technology of electical installations, and have also moved towards the ultimate aim of world-wide acceptance.

Two international bodies are concerned with the regulations. First, the International Electrotechnical Commission (IEC), which is world-wide, and second the European Committee for Electrotechnical Standardization (CENELEC). IEC committee TC64 was set up in 1968 to formulate international rules for the electrical installations of buildings and it soon became apparent that a return to basic fundamentals would be necessary. The 15th Edition of the IEE Wiring Regulations, published March 1981 amended in February 1983, May 1984, January 1985, January 1986 and June 1987, incorporates much of the IEC work. In some cases, international work is incomplete, and then the 15th Edition repeats (in updated form) the rules of the 14th Edition.

It should be stressed that the Regulations are intended for the professional electrical installation designer and installer. They are not a set of simple rules to be followed by the working electrician, although he will need to have some understanding of them. Unlike its predecessors, the 15th Edition takes the form of a 'design manual'. As such it allows much greater freedom to the designer, and is more useful, particularly for the larger and more complex industrial or commercial installation.

It will be appreciated that to summarise a major publication like the Regulations for Electrical Installations (IEE Wiring Regulations, 15th Edition) in a comparatively small section of the Year Book is extremely difficult. For those who need to refer to the Regulations for more detailed study, references are given to the relevant sections of the IEE Regulations in the text of the chapter, eg Earth Electrodes 542-10.

PLAN AND STRUCTURE OF THE REGULATIONS.—The 15th Edition of the IEE Regulations is divided into six parts, with further information in seventeen appendices.

Part 1 gives the overriding requirements, which cover the scope of the Regulations, their object, and the fundamental requirements for safety.

Part 2 consists of definitions, where the precise meanings of the terms used are clarified.

Part 3 concerns the assessment of general characteristics. This information dealing with the source of energy (the supply) and the installation itself, is important to the designer before he can begin.

Part 4 covers protection for safety, taking into account protection against electric shock, thermal effects and overcurrent.

Part 5 deals with the selection and erection of equipment, giving common rules as well as precise requirements for cables, conductors and wiring materials, and for switchgear, earthing and other equipment.

Part 6 covers the important requirements of testing and inspection, including the necessary certification.

The seventeen appendices occupy more space than the rest of the regulations, and include much vital information, such as the characteristics of fuses and circuit breakers, as well as current rating tables.

The layout of the 15th Edition and an excellent index facilitate identification of the correct material.

Each of the six parts is divided into chapters and each chapter into sections. The regulations themselves then make up the sections. For example, Regulation 553-11 (spoken five five three dash eleven) is in Part 5 (selection and erection of equipment), Chapter 55 (other equipment), Section 553 (accessories), Regulation 553-11 (cable couplers).

In previous editions of the Year Book, each Regulation has been taken in turn and its contents explained. The layout of the 15th Edition prevents this simple approach, because closely allied matters will be found in different parts of the Regulations. For example, earthing of the supply neutral is referred to five times, in three different parts and in an appendix.

A particular subject (eg protective conductors and earthing) is considered in its entirety, and the relevant regulations from various parts, as well as information from the appendices, are brought together.

ASSESSMENT OF GENERAL CHARACTERISTICS.—Before planning or completing an electrical installation, a number of factors which will affect its operation must be considered.

Purposes, Supplies and Structure (Regs. Chap 31 & Sec 512).—The factors to be assessed are:

(1) *Maximum demand.*—Estimation of the value is important so that there is no doubt that the supply is capable of feeding the proposed installation.
(2) *Diversity.*—Smaller cables may be used if it can safely be assumed that not all connected equipment will be used simulataneously. Regs Appendix 4 gives guidance.
(3) *Number and type of live conductor.*—Whether the circuits are single- or three-phase and so on. It should be noticed that in the 15th Edition, the term 'live' applies to all conductors normally carrying current (including the neutral). The non-neutral conductors are now called 'phase conductors'.
(4) *Type of earthing arrangement.*—Designation letters are now used, and these are described later, in the section headed 'protective conductors and earthing'.
(5) *Nature of the supply.*—Including voltage, frequency, fault level, main protective device, and earth fault loop impedance at the supply intake position.
(6) *Safety and standby circuits.*
(7) *Arrangement of main circuits.*—The design must ensure that convenience and safety are taken into account. For example, a fire sprinkler pump must be fed by a circuit as separate as possible from others to assure as far as is possible that it will remain operational in the event of a fire.
(8) *Arrangement of final circuits* (used to be called 'final sub-circuits').—Standard arrangements are given in appendix 5. Table 35 shows the permissible arrangements for BS 1363 (13A) socket outlets.

External Influences.—An electrical installation may be affected by its surroundings. Effects which may need to be taken into account fall under three headings.

(1) *Environmental Conditions.*—Factors including ambient temperature, humidity, altitude, presence of water (see Table 1) and of foreign bodies (eg dust), corrosive or polluting substances, impact, vibration, flora and/or mould growth, fauna, electric and magnetic fields, solar radiation, earthquakes, lightning, and wind are included and classified. Future editions of the Regulations may make concrete proposals.
(2) *Type of Utilization of Premises.*—Classifications include:
(a) Capability of persons: eg skilled, instructed, children, handicapped.
(b) Contact of persons with earth potential, eg none, low, frequent, continuous.
(c) Conditions of evacuation in an emergency, eg low density, and high density, low and high-rise buildings.
(d) Nature of processed or stored materials in terms of fire, explosion or contamination risks.
(3) *Construction of Buildings.*—Listed in terms of combustibility of materials, propagation of fire, building settlement and movement, and oscillation.

Full details of classifications appear in Appendix 6 of the IEE Regs. 15th Edition.

Compatibilty.—Assessment must be made (Reg. 331-1) of the electrical characteristics of equipment which might have a harmful effect on other equipment or services or on the supply.

Maintainability.—Regulation 341-1 requires that an assessment be made of the frequency and quality of the maintenance that the installation can reasonably be expected to receive during its life. Thus, it should be possible to carry out maintenance and repairs safely, the protective measures for safety should remain effective during the intended life of the installation, and the reliability of installed equipment is appropriate to the intended life.

Compliance with Standards.—To comply with section 511 of the Regs. all equipment should comply, where possible, with the appropriate standard. A list of relevant British Standards forms Appendix 1 of the Regulations.

ISOLATION AND SWITCHING.—The Regulations recognise four functions:
Isolation, functional switching, switching-off for mechanical maintenance and emergency switching. Some switches will be arranged so that they can fulfill more than one of these functions.

Part of the Regulations includes the fundamental requirements, Chapter 47 covers the need for isolation and switching, and Chapter 46 gives details as to how the functions must be carried out. Devices used are dealt with in Section 537.

Isolation.—Isolation is defined as cutting off an electrical installation, a circuit, or an item of equipment from every source of electrical energy. It is applied to ensure that conductive parts which are live in normal operation, are safely separated from their sources of energy to enable work to be undertaken. Isolated parts should be tested to ensure that they are dead; operating the isolator is not sufficient.

Devices for isolation are covered by Regulations 537-2 to 537-7. They stipulate that all live supply conductors must be disconnected, the isolator must prevent unintentional reclosure and must be arranged to clearly indicate when the supply is off. Semiconductor devices such as thyristors and triacs must *not* be used as isolators.

The poles to be switched are indicated in Fig. 1. Note that in the 15th Edition the neutral is considered to be a live conductor, and must be isolated except in three-phase systems and where a combined neutral and earth (one example is earthed concentric wiring) is used. Isolation may be carried out using specialised isolators, switch disconnectors, plugs and sockets, fuse links, isolating links or circuit breakers having the required contact separation. It is acceptable to remove conductors from terminals and insulate their ends, but the practice is limited by the wear and tear on conductor ends if used too frequently.

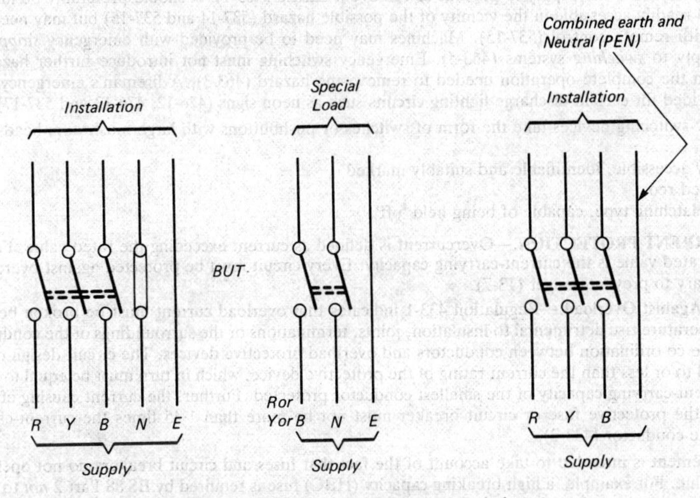

FIG. 1.—Supply Poles Broken by Switches.

Isolation must be (i) provided at the origin of every installation (476-2), (ii) for every circuit or group of circuits (461-1), (iii) for every motor and associated control gear (476-5), (iv) for every high voltage discharge lighting circuit (476-6), (v) for maintenance of main switchgear (476-3), and (vi) if primary isolation is remote from equipment protected, it must be duplicated adjacent to the equipment, *or* be operable only by skilled persons with a lock or removable handle to prevent unauthorised reclosure (476-4).

No isolator or means of isolation must be provided in the protective (earth) conductor.

Isolators cannot all be operated by unskilled persons. Where isolating switches, plugs and sockets and other load-breaking devices are concerned, there need be no limitations. However, off-load isolators, neutral links and so on should only be disconnected by skilled persons or instructed persons under direct supervision.

Functional Switching.—Functional switching can be defined as switching necessary for the normal control of electrical equipment. Requirements include (i) A main switch is required for every installation (476-15) (ii) Every circuit must be provided, singly or in groups, with a switching device (476-16), (iii) Every appliance and lighting fitting not connected by a plug and socket must be controlled by a switch (476-17), (iv) Each cooking appliance must be provided with a switch situated within 2 m of it (476-20), (v) Plugs and sockets of rating not more than 16A may be used as switches (not emergency switches (537-18)) and (vi) Switches controlling discharge lighting must be rated at twice the normal value of steady current—this takes account of control gear losses and the possibility of higher current due to poor power factor (537-19).

Switching-off for Mechanical Maintenance.—Mechanical maintenance is defined in the Regulations as the replacement, refurbishment or cleaning of lamps or non-electrical parts of equipment, plant and machinery. Switching-off in this case is to protect against physical injury as a result of contact with moving parts of machinery, electrically-heated equipment, etc. For example, lamp replacement and cleaning is considered to be mechanical maintenance. The switches used must be suitably placed (462-2), readily identifiable, convenient for their intended use and with a means to prevent unintentional or inadvertant reclosing (462-3).

Devices suitable are switches, circuit breakers, control switches, operating contactors and plugs and sockets. They must be capable of cutting off full load current, must be hand operated, clearly indicate that they are 'off', and must be arranged so that they prevent unintentional reclosure (eg by mechanical shock or vibration).

Functional switches may be suitable for switching-off for mechanical maintenance. For example, a one-way lighting switch will be suitable. A two-way switch will NOT be suitable, because the 'off' position cannot be clearly shown and the circuit can be energised from the second (remote) switch.

Emergency Switching.—Emergency switching is defined as the rapid cutting off of electrical energy to remove any hazard to persons, livestock or property which may occur unexpectedly. The requirements of the 15th Edition correlate with those of the Electricity (Factories Act) Special Regulations.

Emergency switching will be necessary whenever an installation, or part of an installation, must be disconnected rapidly from the supply to prevent or remove a hazard (463-1). It should preferably be manually operated and readily accessible in the vicinity of the possible hazard (537-14 and 537-15) but may need to be duplicated with remote control (537-15). Machines may need to be provided with emergency *stopping*, as opposed simply to *switching* systems (463-5). Emergency switching must not introduce further hazards or interfere with the complete operation needed to remove the hazard (463-3). A fireman's emergency switch must be provided for certain discharge lighting circuits such as neon signs (476-12, 476-13 and 537-17).

Emergency switching devices take the form of switches or pushbuttons with large mushroom heads. They must be:

(i) readily accessible, identifiable and suitably marked
(ii) coloured red
(iii) of the latching type, capable of being held 'off'.

OVERCURRENT PROTECTION.—Overcurrent is defined as current exceeding the rated value. For conductors, the rated value is the current-carrying capacity. Every circuit must be protected against overcurrent where necessary to prevent danger (13-7).

Protection Against Overload.—Regulation 433-1 indicates that overload current must be broken before it causes a temperature rise detrimental to insulation, joints, terminations or the surroundings of the conductors. There must be co-ordination between conductors and overload protective devices. The circuit design current must be equal to or less than the current rating of the protective device, which in turn must be equal to or less than the current-carrying capacity of the smallest conductor protected. Further, the current causing effective operation of the protective fuse or circuit breaker must not be more than 1·45 times the current-carrying capacity of the conductor (433-2).

This requirement is intended to take account of the fact that fuses and circuit breakers do not operate at their rated value. For example, a high breaking capacity (HBC) fuse is required by BS 88 Part 2 *not* to 'blow' within one hour when it carries 1·2 times its rated current. The time/current characteristics for fuses and circuit breakers will be considered in more detail in the next section.

When designing an installation, advantage must *not* be taken of the fact that protection rating is greater than the current rating of the cable it protects.

Circuit design should ensure that small overloads of long duration do not occur (433-2), although overloads of short duration (eg motor starting currents) may be acceptable.

The 1·45 factor between the protection and cable ratings does *not* apply to semi-enclosed (rewirable) fuses, because they often require more than twice their rated current to operate them. In these cases, the fuse rating must not exceed 0·725 times the current-carrying capacity of the smallest conductor protected. This is a new departure in the 15th Edition. In the 14th, a similar provision was made by defining rewirable fuses as 'coarse protection'. The only exception to the de-rating factor of 0·725 is when the circuit concerned is wired completely in mineral-insulated cable.

If a reduction occurs in the current-carrying capacity of the conductors of an installation, a fuse or circuit breaker must be placed at the point of reduction (473-1). The reduction in current-carrying capacity may occur due to (i) a change in conductor cross-sectional area, (ii) a change in the type of cable or conductor, (iii) a change in the method of installation, (iv) an increase in the number of conductors grouped together, and (v) a change in environmental conditions, such as higher ambient temperature or enclosure in thermally insulating material.

The overload protective device at the reduction in current-carrying capacity may be omitted (473-3) if (a) the overload protection already installed in the larger circuit adequately protects the smaller, (b) the characteristics of the load are such that overloads are unlikely to occur, (c) the unexpected opening of the circuit would cause greater danger than the overload, (d) the circuit is the secondary circuit of a current transformer.

Protection Against Short-Circuit Currents.—Regulation 434-1 requires that any short-circuit current shall be broken before it causes danger due to thermal and mechanical effects produced in conductors and connections. Short-circuit currents are often in the order of thousands of amperes, and it is necessary to limit the time for which they are allowed to persist to keep the energy released within acceptable limits.

To ensure that a protective device is capable of breaking short-circuit current, its prospective value must first be ascertained (Reg. 434-2). The prospective short-circuit current at the supply intake should have been already ascertained from the Electricity Board (Reg. 313-1) or may be assessed after measurement by a prospective short circuit current tester. If this value is less than the breaking capacity of the smallest rated protective device in the installation. No further action is necessary (Reg. 434-2).

The breaking capacity of a fuse or circuit breaker is the maximum current which that device can break safely within an acceptable time. The breaking capacity of a protective device must not be less than the prospective short-circuit current at the point at which it is installed (Reg. 434-4) unless another device of suitable capacity is installed on the supply side and the characteristics of the two devices are co-ordinated so that the energy let-through will not allow damage to the smaller device or the conductors (Reg. 434-5).

When an overload protective device has a rating greater than that of the cable it protects, clearly overload protection is not provided. In such cases, the effectiveness of short-circuit protection must be checked by applying the *adiabatic equation* (Reg. 434-6). This assumes that no heat leaves the system and that all the heat produced in the cables by the fault current remains and raises the conductor temperature to a point where insulation degradation is still tolerable for that period of time.

The adiabatic equation is:

$$t = \frac{k^2 S^2}{I^2}$$

where

t = the duration of short-circuit current in seconds
S = conductor cross-sectional area in mm^2
I = fault current in amperes
k = a factor depending on conductor and insulation materials, as well as on initial and final temperature

Some k values from Reg. 434-6 are shown in Table 2.

Having substituted the values of k, S and I for the particular circumstances, the calculated value of t must be no greater than the time taken for the protective device to clear the fault current. This time can be found from the IEE protective device characteristics which will be given in the next section (Figs 3 to 10).

Short-circuit protective devices may only be omitted (Reg. 473-6) where (*a*) the length of unprotected conductors does not exceed 3 m and (*b*) the risk of short circuit is reduced to a minimum, and (*c*) the risk of fire or danger is reduced to a minimum.

This relaxation of requirements can be useful in the case of interconnections at switchgear, which are short and well protected by their enclosures.

Discrimination.—In most installations, the loads will have at least two protective devices in series to feed the loads. For example, the Electricity Board main protection, the installation main protective device and circuit protection devices.

To prevent unnecessary interruption of supplies, the protective devices must have discrimination in operation (Reg. 533-6). This means that a fault or overload at a particular point in a circuit should operate *only* the protective device next in line between that point and the supply. If a device nearer the supply operates before one closer to the fault or overload, other parts of the installation may be unnecessarily disconnected causing inconvenience and possible danger.

In simple terms, this means that the rating of protective devices must reduce through an installation from the supply intake. However, since operation of devices is related to time as well as current, operating characteristics must be consulted to ensure proper discrimination of protective devices.

SELECTION OF LIVE CONDUCTORS.—In the 15th Edition the term 'live' is taken to mean all conductors normally carrying current. The old term 'live' meaning the conductor(s) *not* at earth potential, is replaced by 'phase'. The neutral, as well as the phase, is now a live conductor. This section is therefore concerned with the selection of all conductors except protective conductors, previously known as earth continuity conductors.

The purpose of the section is to give guidance on how the right size cable is selected to comply with the Regulations. There is a fundamental change from the 14th Edition, where the nominal current rating was selected from a table and then subjected to derating to allow for factors such as grouping, ambient temperature and coarse protection. The method of the 15th Edition is to start with the rating of the *protective device* (fuse or circuit breaker) and then to apply the correction factors to *increase* the rating before selecting a suitable cable from the tables.

Grouping Factor.—A number of cables run together will mutually prevent cooling and will become hotter than if they were separated. Table 9B1 from Appendix 9 of the Regulations lists the correction factors for groups of more than one single-core or multi-core cables when in 'enclosed' or 'clipped direct' conditions. The factors in the Table, which is reproduced here as Table 3, are divided into, not multiplied by, the rating value. For example, a single-phase circuit protected by a 60 A circuit breaker which is run with four other fully-loaded single-phase circuits (five circuits in all) encosed in trunking will have a grouping factor of 0.65, and the cable would be selected on a current-carrying capacity of 60/0·60 or 100 A. Individual current rating tables sometimes give individual limitations on the factors in the main table (see Tables 5 to 13).

Table 3 gives an approximate value for a rating factor for grouping which is easily applied. Some more complicated formulae are given in Appendix 9, and if these are applied it is probable that a smaller cable size may be used. The formulae are divided into two groups, the first of which covers all types of circuit protection other than the semi-enclosed (rewirable) fuse. The three formulae in the first group are:-

$$I_T = \frac{In}{C_g} \quad (1)$$

$$I_T = \frac{I_B}{C_g} \quad (2)$$

$$I_T = \sqrt{In^2 + 0{\cdot}48\, I_B^2 \frac{(1 - C_g^2)}{C_g}} \quad (3)$$

The formulae in the second group, dealing with circuits protected by semi-enclosed (rewirable) fuses, are as follows:-

$$I_T = \frac{In}{0{\cdot}725\, C_g} \quad (4)$$

$$I_T = \frac{I_B}{C_g} \quad (5)$$

$$I_T = \sqrt{1{\cdot}9\, In^2 + 0{\cdot}48\, I_B^2 \frac{(1 - C_g^2)}{C_g}} \quad (6)$$

The symbols used in the six formulae have the following meanings:-

I_T is the current-carrying capacity of the circuit under design,
C_g is the group rating factor (from Table 3),
In is the current rating of the circuit protective device (A),
I_B is the circuit design current (A).

The designer now has a choice. He can use the size of cable calculated from formula (1) or formula (4) depending on the type of circuit protection. Alternatively, he can carry out calculations using the other formulae ((2) and (3) for HBC fuses or miniature circuit breakers, or (4) and (5) for semi-enclosed fuses). The larger of the two results obtained must be used. Considerable savings can often be made by using the more complicated formulae.

It should be noted that the "alternative" formulae given above (numbers (2), (3), (5) and (6)), can only be applied when there is no possibility of simultaneous overloads occurring on the grouped cables.

Ambient Temperature Factor.—This factor allows for reduced dissipation of heat from cables if surrounding temperatures are high. Tables 4A and 4B give the ambient temperature factors for circuits protected by semienclosed fuses and all other types of protection respectively.

For example, the single-phase 60 A circuit mentioned under the grouping correction factor heading above will, if subject to an ambient temperature of 50°C and if wired in single-core PVC cables in trunking, need a rating of 60/0·71 (correction factor from Table 4A), or 84·5 A. Note that this assumes that the ambient temperature and the grouping do not occur at the same point (see below).

It is most important that figures from Table 4A are selected when the circuit protection is a semienclosed (rewirable) fuse and that Table 4B is used in situations where HBC fuses on circuit breakers provide protection.

It has become standard building practice (and is a requirement of the Building Regulations) to reduce the heat loss by filling wall cavities, roof spaces, etc, with thermal insulation. Cables buried in, or in contact with, such insulation, clearly will be less able to dissipate heat than others, so their cable rating must be reduced to take account of this fact. In the tables of current carrying capacities (see Tables 5 to 13 inclusive) provision is made for the ratings of cables run in insulated walls or ceilings. In the absence of more precise information, the current carrying capacity of a cable run within thermal insulation should be halved. This can be done by applying a thermal insulation correction factor (C_i) of 0.5.

Semi-enclosed (Rewirable) Fuse Factor.—If this form of protection is used, a further factor of 0·725 is applied. Effectively, this takes the place of 'coarse protection' rating factor of the 14th Edition (Reg. 433-2).

Application of all correction Factors.—

$$Iz = In \times \frac{1}{C_g} \times \frac{1}{C_a} \times \frac{1}{C_i} \times \frac{1}{C_f}$$

where

Iz = required current-rating of cable (A)
In = nominal current rating of protective device (A)

C_g = grouping factor
C_a = ambient temperature factor
C_i = thermal insulation factor
C_f = semi-enclosed fuse factor

It must be stressed that *all* of the correction factors are only applied if they *all* apply to the cable at the same place. For example, if cables are grouped at one point of their run, and then separated before entering an area with a high ambient temperature, separate rating calculations are used for the two cases and the most onerous is applied. The formula given for application of the correction factors is modified by application of the alternative formula for grouping given above.

It should be stressed that economies are often possible by changing a proposed installation. For example, it may be less expensive to run circuits in separate conduits, rather than in a common trunking. Again, the use of HBC, rather than a rewirable, fuse protection, may lead to the use of smaller cables.

Voltage Drop.—The voltage drop allowed at any point in an installation must not exceed 2½% of the nominal voltage of the installation (6V for a 240 V supply and 10·38 V for a 415 V supply) (Reg. 522-8). Where a final circuit is protected by a device with a current rating not exceeding 100 A, the volt drop calculations may exclude the main cables provided that the equipment fed will not have its operation impaired by the volt drop.

The volt drop depends on five factors:

(i) The size and material of the conductor
(ii) The circuit length
(iii) The current carried
(iv) The cable operating temperature
(v) The self-inductance of the cable. For cables of up to 16mm² in cross section, the self inductance may be ignored.

These smaller cables are provided in the current rating and volt drop tables with columns of volt drop in millivolts per ampere carried per metre length of run, shown as mV/A/m. (Strictly this is incorrect and should be expressed as mV/A·m). If the figure from the table for a particular case is multiplied by the current carried (not the rated current) and by the length of run, the actual volt drop can be calculated. For example, if four 4mm² single core mineral insulated cables having pvc covering with a length of run of 25 m feed a 415 V motor taking a current of 40 A, the volt drop can be calculated as

$$9.1 \times 40 \times 25 = 9100 \text{ mV or } 9.1 \text{ V}.$$

The figure of 9.1 mV/A/m comes from Table 13. Since the allowable volt drop for a 415 V supply is 2.5% of 415 V or 10.375 V the circuit complies with the Regulations. If it had not done so, a larger cable with a lower mV/A/m figure would have been necessary.

The actual volt drop in a cable is due to current flowing in its impedance, rather than simply in its resistance. Smaller cables have resistance and impedance values which are practically the same because they have virtually no self inductance, but for larger cables, the inductive reactance of the cable increases the impedance and the volt drop. Resistance and inductive reactance add at right angles to give the impedance.

Thus, $Z = \sqrt{R^2 + X_L^2}$

where Z is circuit impedance in ohm
R is circuit resistance in ohm and
X_L is circuit inductive reactance in ohm.

Voltage drop tables for cables of 25 mm² cross sectional area and above give r, x and z components of drop, representing the resistance, reactive and impedance drops respectively. The position is complicated by the fact that impedance drops in cables calculated using z values are strictly only correct when the load power factor is equal to the cable power factor (both have the same resistance to reactance ratios or phase angles). If they are not the same, a more correct z value is given by the formula

$$z = (\cos\phi \times r) + (\sin\phi \times x)$$

where $\cos\phi$ is the power factor of the load.

The tabulated values of r and z assume that the cable is at its highest permissble temperature, and thus the resistance value and the volt drop are overestimated for cases where the cable is cooler. In such cases the r value for large cables or the total mV/A/m value for smaller cables can be found by application of a factor C_t to either. This is found from the formula

$$C_t = \frac{230 + t_p - (C_a^2 C_g^2 - (I_b^2/I_t^2))(t_p - 30)}{230 + t_p}$$

where t_p is the maximum permitted cable temperature, °C
C_a is the ambient temperature correction factor,
C_g is the grouping correction factor
I_b is the design current
I_t is the tabulated current.

The equation does not apply where protection is by a semienclosed (rewirable) fuse and can only be used where the ambient temperature is 30°C or greater.

For larger cables, the z value for the lower cable operating temperature is found by adding the modified r value at right angles to the tabulated x value,

$$\text{i.e. } z = \sqrt{r^2 + x^2}$$

Current Rating Tables.—The current rating tables in Appendix 9 of the Regulations give current carrying capacities and volt drop data for most types of cable when installed in various ways. Tables 5 to 13 reprint the most important of these tables.

Capacities of Conduits and Trunking (529-7). Appendix 12 of the 15th Edition provides a much more comprehensive method than its predecessor for determining the capacity of conduits and trunkings. It allows for mixed cable sizes, as well as for the difficulty of drawing-in cables because of conduit lengths and the number of bends and sets. Each size of single-core pvc insulated cable up to 10 mm² is allocated a factor as shown in Table 14 for short straight runs (up to 3 m), in Table 17 for long straight runs, or those incorporating bends. Other tables (16 for short, straight runs, 15 for runs with bends) given conduit factors. For each cable, the appropriate factor is found from Tables 14 and 17, and all the factors added. The conduit size which will satisfactorily accommodate the cables is that with a factor exceeding or equal to the sum of the cable factors. In the same way, Tables 18 and 19 give cable factors and factors for trunking.

Where the cable and/or trunking sizes required are not covered in the tables, the space factor (amount of space in trunking taken up by cables) must not exceed 45%.

SHOCK PROTECTION.—The 15th Edition goes much further than earlier regulations in seeking to prevent electric shock. Shock will occur due to contact with live parts, and two types of contact are defined.

DIRECT CONTACT.—is defined as contact of persons or livestock with live parts which may result in electric shock—i.e, direct contact only occurs due to a failure of insulation or of barriers and enclosures.

INDIRECT CONTACT.—is defined as contact of persons or livestock with exposed conductive parts made live by a fault and which may result in electric shock. Indirect contact is with conductors which should normally be safely at earth potential.

Protection Against Direct Contact.—Four basic protective measures are outlined in Section 412 of the Regulations. They are:

(1) Insulation of live parts (412-2). This is the basic insulation of live conductors to prevent contact.

(2) Barriers or enclosures (412-3 to 412-6).

The IP Classification is used to indicate the degree of protection, and is indicated by the letters IP followed by two numbers, the first of which indicates protection of persons against contact and second the ingress of water. If either type of protection is not considered, the numeral is replaced by the letter X.

Two classifications are considered in the Regulations.

IP2X: Solid objects not exceeding 80 mm long and exceeding 12 mm in diameter are excluded. This is intended to prevent finger contact.

IP4X: Wires, strips or solid objects of thickness greater than 1 mm are excluded.

(3) Obstacles, to prevent unintentional contact with live parts, but not deliberate circumvention of the obstacles (412-7 and 412-8).

(4) Placing out of reach. The definition of 'arm's reach' is shown in diagrammatic form in Fig. 2 (412-13). The possible zone of contact should be extended where bulky or long conducting objects are normally handled. These protective measures, new in the 15th Edition, are an example of how the Regulations are becoming more directly applicable to industrial and commercial installations (471-22 to 471-25).

Protection Against Indirect Contact.—There are five methods of complying with the requirements of the Regulations. The first two are widely used, whilst the last three have very limited application.

(1) EARTH EQUIPOTENTIAL BONDING AND AUTOMATIC SUPPLY DISCONNECTION.—This is the most common form of protection, and consists of bonding together and to earth all exposed conducting parts (non-current-carrying metalwork associated with an installation. such as conduits, machine enclosures, etc.) and all extraneous conductive parts (non-electrical materials which may, nevertheless, conduct a live or earth potential, such as gas and water services, structural steelwork, ventilation ducting, etc.).

Having ensured that all this metalwork is bonded to earth, the presence of a dangerous potential on it must automatically disconnect the supply before a shock is likely to prove fatal. To ensure effective disconnection, the characteristics of the protective devices, the earthing arrangements and the relevant circuit impedances must be co-ordinated so that during an earth fault, voltages between simultaneously accessible parts are of such magnitude and duration as not to cause danger (413-2 and 413-3). The regulations do not *prevent* the appearance of potential differences, rather they limit their magnitude and duration.

There are two maximum time periods within which automatic disconnection must occur (413-4).

(1) For socket outlets or in bathrooms–0·4s. Contact with conducting parts is likely to be better in a bathroom, and where the equipment is portable, eg, kettle, drill, etc, so the disconnection time is short.

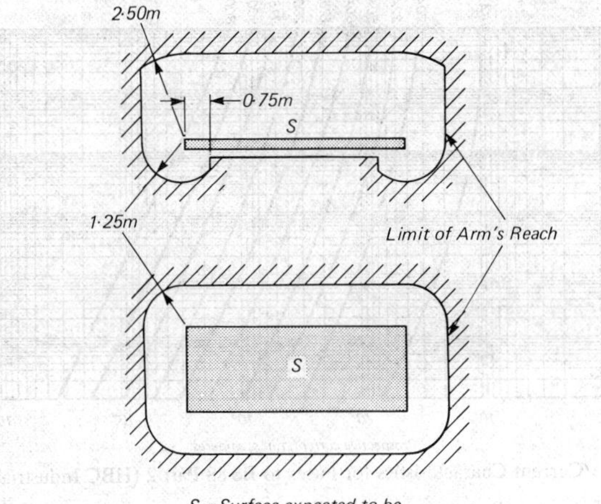

FIG. 2.—Limit of Arm's Reach.

(2) For circuits feeding fixed equipment—5s. Contact with equipment such as motors and cookers is limited because they would not normally be grasped—hence the longer disconnection time.

There are three methods of achieving the required disconnection times:

(1) Limiting earth-fault loop impedance (413-5) so that enough current flows in the event of a fault to operate the protective device quickly. Tables of maximum earth-fault loop impedance for socket outlet circuits (20) and fixed appliance circuits (21) are shown.

(2) The use of a residual current device (previously called a current earth leakage circuit breaker) (413-6). *N.B.* The amendment dated January, 1985 came into effect on January 1st, 1986, and deleted all reference to fault-voltage operated devices (voltage earth leakage circuit breakers) from the Regulations. Such circuit breakers installed before that date may be left in service, but no new fault-voltage operated devices may be installed. A household installation where the Supply Authority does not provide an earth (TT system) must have all socket outlets protected by one or more residual current devices with operating current not exceeding 30 mA (471-13). Where, in any installation, a socket is intended to feed equipment outside the equipotential earthing zone, it must be protected by a residual current device with an operating current not exceeding 30 mA and must be marked 'For Equipment Outdoors' (514-8).

(3) Limiting the impedance of the circuit protective conductor (formerly called the earth continuity conductor) to a value depending on the type and rating of the protective device (Regs. appendix 7). The values of maximum impedance in this case are shown in Table 22.

Note that the overall earth loop impedance of Table 21 must still be met, but this effectively extends the disconnection time for socket-outlet circuits (and bathrooms) to 5s, because of the lower voltages available.

(2) USE OF CLASS II EQUIPMENT (Sections 413 & 471). Class II is a term normally used to describe appliances with double insulation which have no exposed conductive parts and therefore do not require connecting to earth. It must be stressed, however, that where fixed Class II equipment is used, a circuit protective conductor (earth wire) is still required in case changes occur—e.g. replacement of insulated plate accessories by the metal plate type. There is nothing to give a shock in this case, so there is no question of stating a disconnection time. Because of its technical simplicity and safety, Class II equipment is becoming more widely used.

(3) NON-CONDUCTING LOCATION.—Specialised industrial situations such as electrical and electronic test bays, test rooms, etc. (413-27 to 413-31 and 471-19).

(4) EARTH-FREE LOCAL EQUIPOTENTIAL BONDING.—Again, a rare and specialised situation, such as a conductive floor insulated from earth for test purposes. (413-32 to 413-34 and 471-20).

(5) ELECTRICAL SEPARATION.—Isolating transformers or equivalent energy sources with the secondary non-earthed are used. For example, a television set in a testing bay, or the socket in a bathroom for the sole use of a shaver. (413-35 to 413-39 and 471-21).

Of the five methods of providing safety from shock as a result of indirect contact, the first, earth equipotential bonding and automatic disconnection of the supply, is by far the most important. An alternative approach to reducing impedance where reduced body resistance or confined conditions are involved (building sites, working inside boilers, etc.) is to reduce the voltage of the system. There are three types:

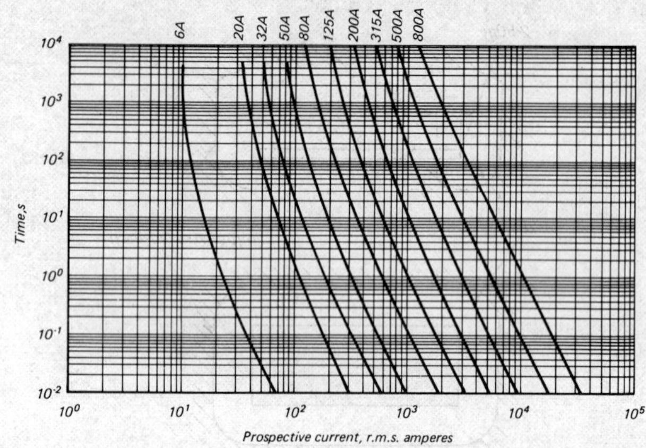

FIG. 3.—Time/Current Characteristics for Fuses to BS 88 Part 2 (HBC Industrial Fuses)

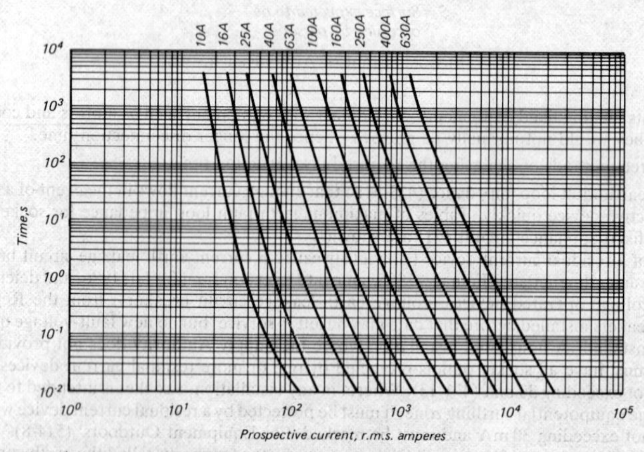

FIG. 4. Time/Current Characteristics for Fuses to BS 88 Part 2 (HBC Industrial Fuses)

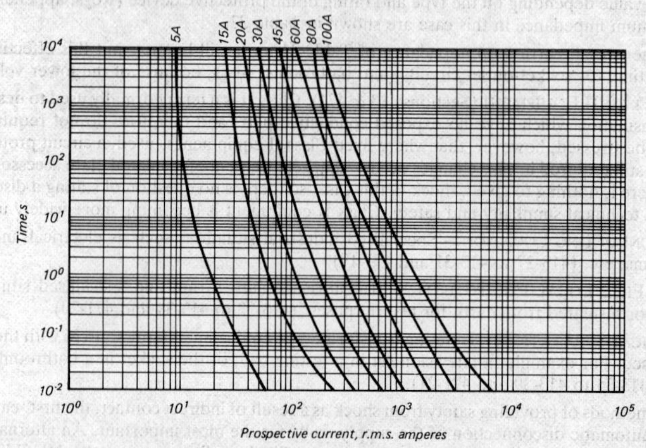

FIG. 5.—Time/Current Characteristics for Fuses to BS 1361 (HBC Domestic Fuses)

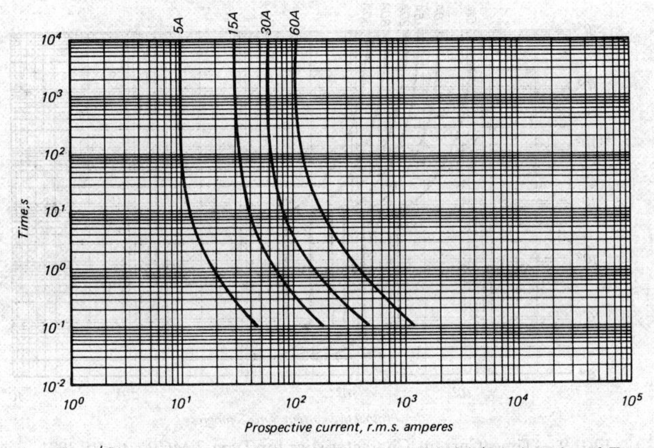

FIG. 6.—Time/Current Characteristics for Fuses to BS 3036 (Semi-enclosed Fuses)

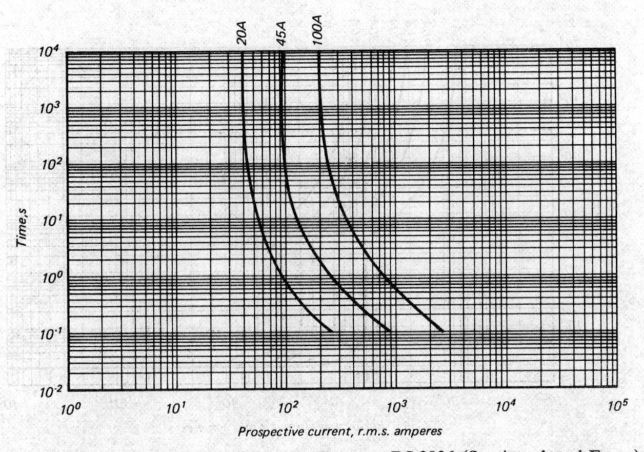

FIG. 7.—Time/Current Characteristics for Fuses to BS 3036 (Semi-enclosed Fuses)

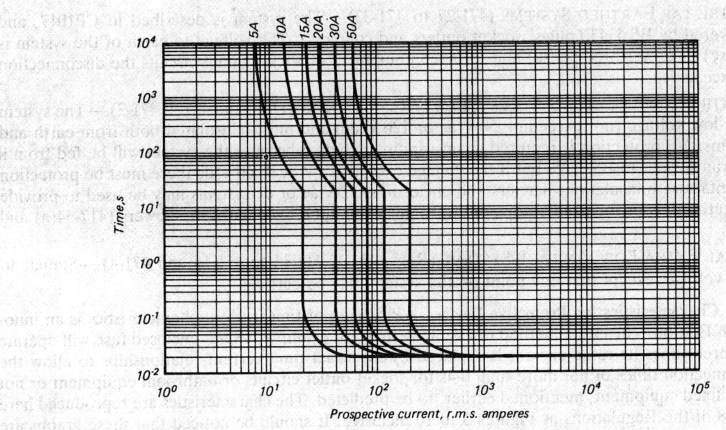

FIG. 8.—Time/Current Characteristics for Type 1 MCB's to BS 3871

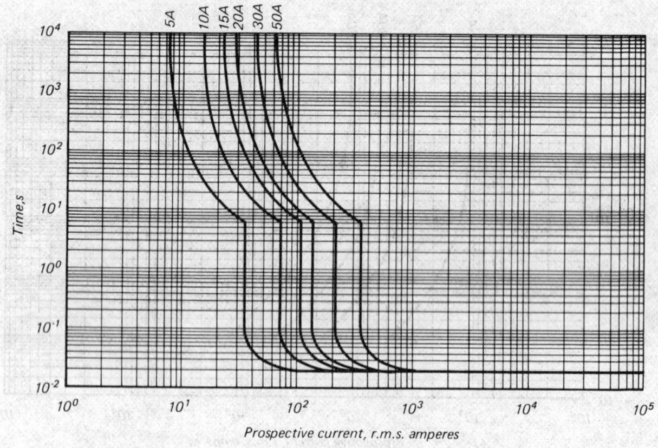

FIG. 9.—Time/Current Characteristics for Type 2 MCB's to BS 3871

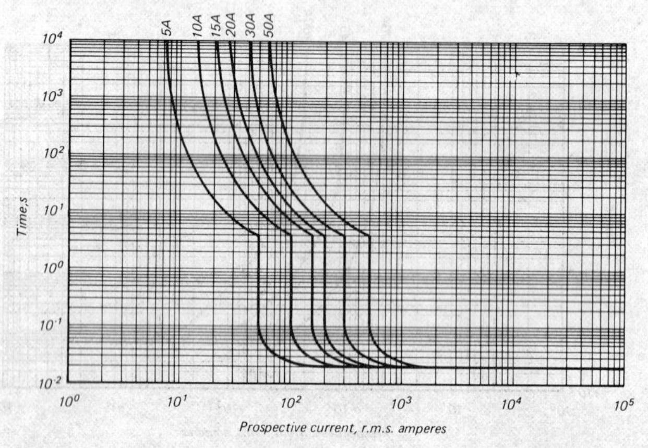

FIG. 10.—Time/Current Characteristics for Type 3 MCB's to BS 3871

(1) 110 V CENTRE-TAP EARTHED SYSTEMS (471-27 to 471-33).—The system is described in CP1017, and equipment is covered by BS 4343 (plugs, socket outlets and couplers). The voltage to earth of the system is 55 V (single-phase) or 65 V (three-phase) and for fixed equipment or socket outlet circuits the disconnection time must not exceed 5s.

(2) SAFETY EXTRA-LOW VOLTAGE SYSTEMS (SELV) (Regs. 411-2 to 411-10 and 471-2, 471-3),—The system must be at extra-low voltage (not exceeding 50 V ac or 120 V dc) and must be isolated both from earth and from other systems. No protection is required against indirect contact because the system will be fed from a safety isolating transformer to BS 3535, but if the voltage exceeds 25 V ac or 60 V dc there must be protection against direct contact with insulation, barriers and enclosures. 12 V ac or dc systems may be used to provide supplies for socket outlets or for fixed equipment in rooms containing fixed baths or showers (417-34(a) and 417-39(a).

(3) FUNCTIONAL EXTRA-LOW VOLTAGE SYSTEMS (Regs. 411-1, 411-11 to 411-15 and 471-4).—Similar to safety extra-low voltage, except that one point on the system may be earthed.

Time/Current Characteristics for Protective Devices.—Provision of time/current characteristics is an innovation in the 15th Edition. The crude method of assuming that, for example, a semi-enclosed fuse will operate when carrying three times its rated current is replaced by the exact time/current relationships to allow the maximum disconnection times of not more than 0·4s for socket outlet circuits or bathroom equipment or not more than 5s for fixed equipment, mentioned earlier, to be predicted. The characteristics are reproduced here from Appendix 8 of the Regulations as Figures 3 to 10 inclusive. It should be noticed that these graphs are plotted on log/log scales to allow reasonably accurate estimation of both low and high times and currents.

Particular Locations.—Some locations have specific requirements.

BATHROOMS AND SHOWERS

(1) Supplementary equipotential bonding is mandatory (471-35)
(2) 0·4s disconnection time for fixed equipment (473-36)
(3) No provision (socket outlets) for portable equipment (471-34) except that they may be installed where they form part of a 12 volt safety extra-low voltage (SELV) system, the source of which is out of reach of a person using the bath or shower (417-34(a)).
(4) Shaver sockets must be to BS3052 (471-37)
(5) Totally-enclosed luminaires or shrouded lampholders must be used (471-38)
(6) All switches, other than those for shaver sockets, controls for instantaneous water heaters and 12 V equipment fed from SELV systems, must be out of reach of a person using a fixed bath or shower (471-39 and 471-39(a)). An exception to this rule is where the switches are part of a 12 V SELV system (471–39a).

AGRICULTURAL INSTALLATIONS

(1) Class II equipment must be used where possible (471-40)
(2) Since livestock is particularly susceptible to electric shock, impedance for automatic disconnection should be lower (25% recommended) than the tabulated values (471-40)
(3) Reduced voltages also apply to safety extra-low voltage (471-41)

MOBILE CARAVANS AND THEIR SITES

(1) These special requirements apply to touring caravans with a maximum demand of 16A or less.
(2) Automatic disconnection must be the method for protection from indirect contact (471-42)
(3) Special earthing arrangements exist for sites, with requirements for duplicated overhead or protected underground earth connections, or the use of residual current devices (471-43)
(4) Groups of not more than six caravans to be protected by residual current devices with an operating current not exceeding 30mA (471-44)
(5) The metalwork of the caravan itself and all the electrical equipment within it must be protected by equipotential bonding (471-45 and 471-46)

PROTECTIVE CONDUCTORS AND EARTHING.—It is perhaps in earthing requirements and terms that the 15th Edition differs most from its predecessors.

Connections to Earth.—Appendix 3 of the Regulations introduces a new method for defining systems of earthing, using a series of designation letters.

The first letter denotes the earthing arrangement at the supply:

T =direct connection of one or more points to earth
I =all live parts isolated from earth or connected to it through an impedance.

The second letter denotes the relationship of the exposed conductive parts of the installation to earth.

T = direct connection of exposed conductive parts to earth independently of the supply earthing.
N=direct connection of exposed conductive parts to the earth connection of the supply.

The designation *TN* is further subdivided using the letters:

S =neutral and protective functions use separate conductors
C =neutral and protective functions combined in a single conductor

The Appendix indicates the following five types of system.

(1) IT SYSTEM (Fig. 11) (542-4).—Because the neutral point of the supply is not earthed, or only through an impedance, this method is not permitted for public supplies in the United Kingdom.

(2) TT SYSTEM (Fig. 12) (542-4)—An example of this system is an installation fed from an overhead supply with no earthing provided, so that the installation has to be earthed to an electrode.

(3) TN-S SYSTEM (Fig. 13) (542-2).—Probably a majority of installations in the United Kingdom are TN-S systems, with the sheath of the supply cable providing the separate earth path.

(4) TN-C-S SYSTEM (Fig. 14) (542–3).—This is the 'protective multiple earth' (PME) system, where the neutral and earth are combined in the supply system (PEN conductor), but separate in the installation itself.

(5) TN-C SYSTEM (Fig. 15) (542–5).—This method uses a combined protective and neutral (PEN) conductor throughout both the supply and the installation. It is not often used, but an example is earthed concentric wiring.

Earth Electrodes.—The following types of earth electrode are recognised by Regulations 542-10.

(1) Earth rods or pipes.
(2) Earth tapes or wires.
(3) Earth plates.
(4) Earth electrodes embedded in foundations.
(5) Metallic reinforcement of concrete.

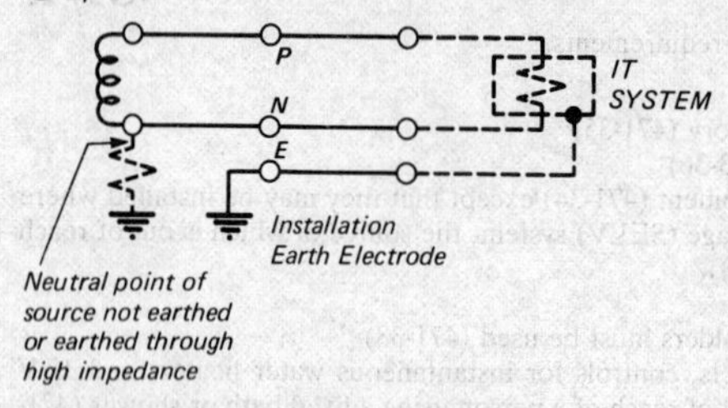

FIG. 11.—IT Earthing System

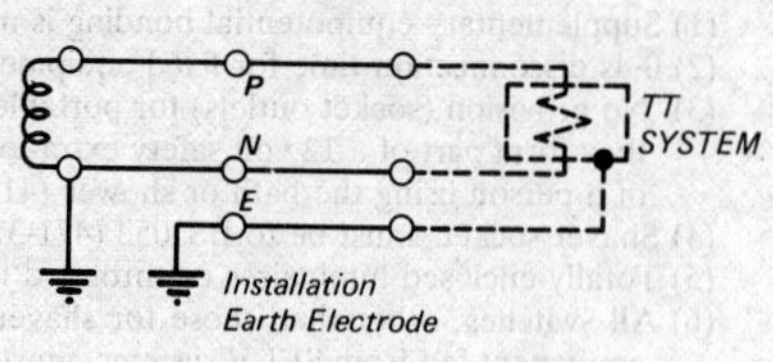

FIG. 12.—TT Earthing System

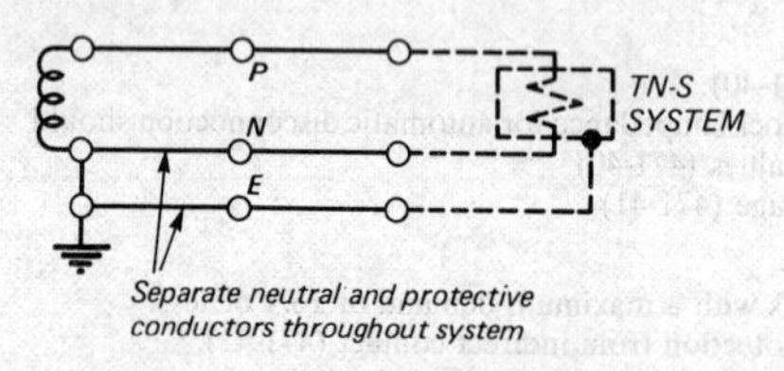

FIG. 13.—TN-S Earthing System

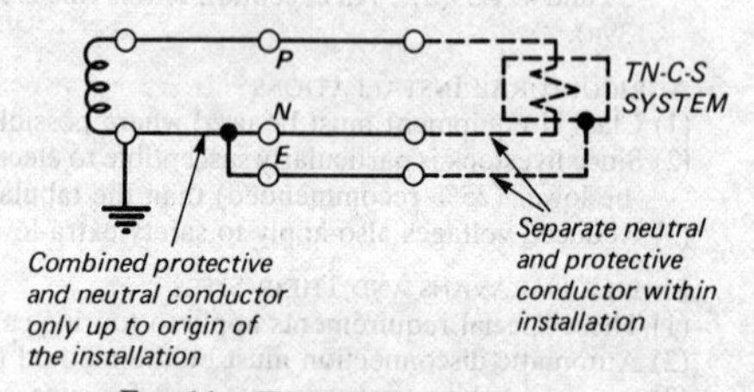

FIG. 14.—TN-C-S Earthing System

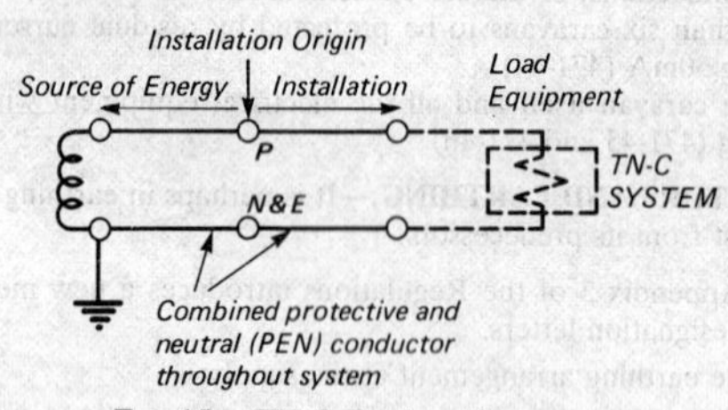

FIG. 15.—TN-C Earthing System

(6) Metallic pipe systems—but they must not be used as the sole protective earth (522-14).
(7) Lead sheaths and other metallic cable coverings if not subject to corrosion (542-15).

Other requirements for earth electrodes are:

(*a*) their type and length must maintain the required earth electrode resistance allowing for soil drying and freezing (542-11)
(*b*) they must withstand corrosion (542-12)
(*c*) allowance must be made for increased resistance due to the effects of corrosion (542-13)
(*d*) public gas and water systems *must* be bonded but must *not* be used as the sole earth electrode (542-14)
(*e*) lead sheaths of cables may be used under certain conditions with the cable owner's permission (542-15)

Protective Conductors.—This term has replaced 'earth continuity conductor'. There are four main types of protective conductor.

(*a*) EARTHING CONDUCTOR.—This conductor connects the protective conductors, which are collected at a main earthing terminal or bar (542-19) to the earth electrode or supply earthing terminal.

To prevent corrosion, earthing conductors connected to earth electrodes must *not* be aluminium. All connections of earthing conductors must be soundly made (542-18) and labelled 'Safety Electrical Earth—DO NOT Remove' (514-7).

(*b*) CIRCUIT PROTECTIVE CONDUCTORS.—These conductors may consist of any combination of

(1) bare conductors
(2) single-core cables
(3) one core of a cable
(4) cable sheath or armour
(5) metallic enclosures of fuseboards, etc
(6) enclosures of bus-bar trunking
(7) rigid metallic conduits
(8) cable ducting and trunking

Detailed requirements for protective conductors are quoted in Regs. 543-4 to 543-14.

(*c*) MAIN EQUIPOTENTIAL BONDING CONDUCTOR.—These conductors connect the main earthing terminal and the main extraneous conductive parts (eg sinks, baths, taps, etc) (413-2). All incoming services, (gas, water, electricity) must be bonded together on the consumer's side of the meter (547-3).

(*d*) SUPPLEMENTARY EQUIPOTENTIAL BONDING CONDUCTOR.—Additional (supplementary) bonding is required in bathrooms (471-35) as well as to certain other extraneous conductive parts, such as central heating systems, structural steelwork, etc (413-7).

Sizing of Protective Conductors.—Four factors affect the sizes of protective conductors.

(*a*) Adequate physical strength and protection against mechanical damage and corrosion.
(*b*) Ability to carry earth fault currents without thermal damage to adjacent insulating materials.
(*c*) Ability to comply with conductor impedance requirements for shock protection.
(*d*) Voltage drop limits on live conductors where the protective conductor is a core in the same cable or conduit.

Factors (*b*), (*c*) and (*d*) will limit the maximum length of a protective conductor of a given size. In the majority of cases, the 2½% voltage drop limit (*d*) will be the most onerous. Dealing with the four factors in turn:

(*a*) PHYSICAL STRENGTH AND MECHANICAL PROTECTION.—If a protective conductor is separate (does not form part of a cable or is not enclosed), the minimum sizes are $2{\cdot}5\text{mm}^2$ if protected and $4{\cdot}0\text{mm}^2$ if unprotected (543-1). In many cases, the requirement (*b*), (*c*) and (*d*) will require larger sizes.

(*b*) THERMAL CONSTRAINTS.—The aim is to select the cross-section of the protective conductor so that its temperature rise under fault conditions is limited. There are two methods:

(1) The Adiabatic Equation

$$S = \frac{\sqrt{I^2 t}}{k}$$

where S = cross-sectional area (mm^2)

I = earth fault current (A)

t = disconnection time (s)

k = a factor depending on the conductor uses.

Tables of values for k are given in the Regulations and are reproduced here as Tables 23 to 26. This is the same adiabatic equation encountered earlier, but expressed in a different way. Appendix 8 of the Regulations simplifies the designer's calculations by providing tables of maximum earth fault loop impedance for various types of protection with various sizes of protective conductor up to 16mm^2. They are reproduced here as Tables 27 to 29. Also included is a table of resistances of combined live and protective conductors (Table 31).

(2) Use of Table 54F of the Regulations (543-3).—This table is reproduced here as Table 32, and it will be seen that for all live conductors up to 16mm^2, the protective and live conductors must have the same size. In most cases this results in larger protective conductors than would be required using the adiabatic equation, and for some types of cable, is impossible. For example, for twin and earth cables to BS6004, only the 1mm^2 size has protective and live conductors of equal cross-sections.

(*c*) IMPEDANCE REQUIREMENTS FOR SHOCK PROTECTION.—For shock protection, earth faults on socket outlet circuits and in bathrooms must clear within 0·4s, and for other circuits within 5s.

This means that earth-fault loop impedances must not exceed those given in Tables 20 and 21 (Reg. 413-5). Maximum cable lengths for compliance can be calculated and checked against the lengths of run.

(*d*) VOLTAGE DROP LIMITATIONS.—Although the 2½% maximum volt drop stipulated in Reg. 522-8 apply only to live conductors (phase and neutral), the protective conductor will have the same length as the live conductor. As stated previously, this is usually the most onerous of the four limiting factors on the length of the cable run.

Protective Bonding Conductors.—Main bonding conductors must have a cross-sectional area of not less than half that of the installation earthing conductor, subject to a minimum of 6mm^2 and a maximum of 25 mm^2 if copper. Both limits may need to be increased where a PME service is provided (547-2).

Supplementary bonding conductors require minimum cross-sections of $2{\cdot}5\text{ mm}^2$ where mechanically protected, or $4{\cdot}0\text{ mm}^2$ if not (547-4 and 547-6). If the supplementary conductor connects directly or indirectly to an exposed conductive part which is itself protected by a circuit protective conductor, its cross-sectional area must be no less than that of the circuit protective conductor.

WIRING SYSTEMS AND CIRCUITS

Cable Types and Cable Enclosures.—Types of cables and conductors are listed in Regulations 521-1 to 521-8, extracts from which comprise Table 33. Conduits, trunking, ducting and fittings (521-9 to 521-12) must be erected completely before drawing-in cables. Supports must ensure protection from mechanical damage. The internal bending radius of cables (Table 34) determines in turn the radii of conduit and trunking bends.

Segregation of Circuits.—Electrical, and sometimes physical, segregation is required (525-3 to 525-9) between three categories of circuit.

Category 1. Most normal main circuits
Category 2. Telecommunication circuits
Category 3. Fire alarm or emergency lighting circuits

Standard Circuit Arrangements.—The 15th Edition gives greater freedom to the designer, but Appendix 5 lists certain standard circuit arrangements which are helpful. For example, Table 35 shows the arrangements for BS 1363 (13 A flat pin) socket outlets, taking diversity into account.

PROTECTION AGAINST THERMAL EFFECTS.—This section excludes thermal effects due to overcurrent, which have been considered earlier. Where electrical services pass through fire barrier walls, openings made must be sealed to maintain the fire protection (528-1).

Chapter 42 of the Regulations contains the requirements to prevent fire hazards by overheated equipment, and includes Fig. 16 to show the required spacings around equipment (other than lamps or luminaries) to provide safety.

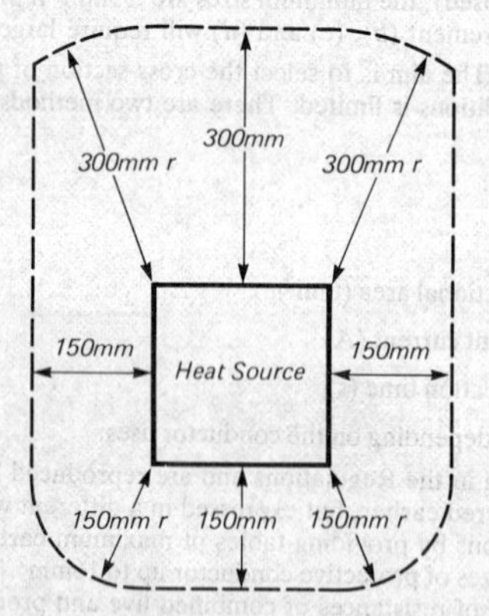

FIG. 16.—Required Distances of Materials Constituting a Fire Hazard from Fixed Equipment with a Surface Temperature ⩾90°C

When an electrical device (transformer, switchgear, etc) contains more than 25 litres of flammable liquid (oil, etc), extra fire precautions are necessary (422-5). Vertical channels and ducts containing cables must have barriers at each floor, or at 5 m intervals, whichever is less, to prevent the air at the top of the enclosure from becoming excessively hot (523-6).

INSPECTION AND TESTING.—Increased emphasis is placed on inspecting, testing and certification in the 15th Edition.

Initial Inspection.—This inspection must be carried out to verify that not only are workmanship and hardware in compliance with the Regulations, but also that the basic design meets the requirements. The installer must provide design data for the inspector. All equipment must comply with the relevant British Standard (511-1), and must be in good order. Appendix 14 provides a check-list for initial inspection (Table 36).

Testing.—SEQUENCE OF TESTS (613-1).—The required sequence is shown in Table 37. Adherence to this sequence is important to ensure safety, both of the installation and for the tester. The method of testing, and the required results, for *some* of these tests is given below.

RING CIRCUIT CONTINUITY (613-2).—The continuity of *each* conductor is measured. Appendix 15 suggests a method where the resistance of the complete opened ring conductor is measured from its supply position. This should be about four times to measurement of the closed ring from the supply position to a point near the centre of the ring.

INSULATION RESISTANCE (613-5 to 613-8).—Test voltage minimum is 500 V dc, and will need to be 1000 V if installation voltage is between 500 V and 1,000 V. Large installations may be tested in groups of not less than 50 outlets, when insulation resistance between live parts, or from live parts to earth, should not be less than 1 MΩ. For equipment, from live parts to earth, a value of 0·5 MΩ is acceptable. Note that electronic devices may be damaged by these tests, and should be isolated while they take place (613-7).

POLARITY (613-14).—Tests, not visual inspections, must be carried out to ensure that fuses and single-pole switches are connected in the phase, not the neutral conductor, and that the phase is connected to the centre cap of edison screw lampholders.

EARTH-FAULT LOOP IMPEDANCE (613-15).—A phase-earth (live-earth) loop tester must be used. Neutral-earth loop testers do not comply. The required value will depend on the design method of ensuring safety from shock (see earlier), but typical values are shown in Tables 20 and 21.

OPERATION OF RESIDUAL-CURRENT DEVICES (613-16). A special tester must be used which makes sure that the device operates within 0·2 s or at any delay time declared by the manufacturer of the device. Effectively, this means that the actual operating time must be measured. A device which applies a fault current for a specified period, resulting in operation, will not comply because it will not establish that operation was not delayed. Where a residual-current circuit breaker with a rating not exceeding 30 mA has been installed to prevent shock due to direct contact, application of a residual current of 150 mA must cause the breaker to open within 40 ms.

Certification.—The Inspection Certificate in Appendix 16 of the Regulations has new requirements in terms of testing the earth fault loop impedance external to the installation and the prospective short-circuit current at its origin, although values do not need to be entered. The Completion Certificate certifies inspection and testing, as well as giving particulars of the installation and details of departures (if any) from the Regulations. It also indicates the recommended interval at which the installation should be re-tested and re-inspected. A notice drawing attention to the need for periodic test and inspection, and giving the next date on which it should be carried out, is required to be fixed near the main distribution board (514-5).

The recommended periods between re-inspection are:

Installations, general 5 years
Temporary installations on construction sites 3 months
Agricultural premises 3 years
Caravan sites between 1 and 3 years

Alterations to Installations (621-1).—Any alterations, no matter how small, must be inspected and tested, and the correct certificates provided. Any defects found in related parts of the existing installation have to be notified by the person doing the new work to the person ordering the work.

REFERENCES

Regulations for Electrical Installations, 15th Edition; Institution of Electrical Engineers.

JENKINS, B. D. *Commentary on the 15th Edition of the IEE Wiring Regulations,* Second Edition, Peter Peregrinus Ltd (on behalf of the IEE).

WHITFIELD, J. F. *A Guide to the 15th Edition of the IEE Wiring Regulations*, Second Edition, Peter Peregrinus Ltd (on behalf of the IEE).

(In event of difficulty the above publications can be obtained from the publishers, Peter Peregrinus Ltd, Station House, Nightingale Rd, Hitchin, Herts. SG6 1RJ.)

LIST OF TABLES

TABLE 2.—VALUES OF k FOR COMMON MATERIALS, FOR CALCULATION OF THE EFFECTS OF SHORT CIRCUIT CURRENT

Conductor material	Insulation material	Assumed initial temperature °C	Limiting final temperature °C	k
Copper	pvc	70	160/140	115/103
	60°C rubber	60	200	141
	85°C rubber	85	220	134
	90°C thermosetting	90	250	143
	Impregnated paper	80	160	108
	mineral—conductor	70	160	115
	mineral—sleeves and seals	105	250	135
Aluminium	pvc	70	160/140	76/68
	60°C rubber	60	200	93
	85°C rubber	85	220	89
	90°C thermosetting	90	250	94
	Impregnated paper	80	160	71

NOTE: Where two values of limiting final temperature and of k are given the lower value relates to cables having conductors of greater than 300 mm² cross-sectional area.

TABLE 1.—CLASSES OF EXTERNAL INFLUENCE—PRESENCE OF WATER

Code	Class Designation	Characteristics	Applications and Examples
AD1	Negligible	Probability of presence of water is negligible.	Locations in which the walls do not generally show traces of water but may do so for short periods, for example in the form of vapour which good ventilation dries rapidly.
AD2	Free-falling drops	Possibility of vertically falling drops	Locations in which water vapour occasionally condenses as drops or where steam may occasionally be present.
AD3	Sprays	Possibility of water falling as a spray at an angle up to 60° from the vertical.	Locations in which sprayed water forms a continuous film on floors and/or walls.
AD4	Splashes	Possibility of splashes from any direction.	Locations where equipment may be subjected to splashed water; this applies, for example, to certain external lighting fittings, construction site equipment.
AD5	Jets	Possibility of jets of water from any direction.	Locations where hosewater is used regularly (yards, car-washing bays).
AD6	Waves	Possibility of water waves.	Seashore locations such as piers, beaches, quays, etc
AD7	Immersion	Possibility of intermittent partial or total covering by water.	Locations which may be flooded and/or where water may be at least 150 mm above the highest point of equipment, the lowest part of equipment being not more than 1 m below the water surface.
AD8	Submersion	Possibility of permanent and total covering by water.	Locations such as swimming pools where electrical equipment is permanently and totally covered with water under a pressure greater than 0·1 bar.

TABLE 3.—CORRECTION FACTORS FOR GROUPS OF MORE THAN ONE CIRCUIT OF SINGLE-CORE CABLES OR MORE THAN ONE MULTICORE CABLE.

Reference method of installation (see Table 9A)		Correction factor (C_g) Number of circuits or multicore cables													
		2	3	4	5	6	7	8	9	10	12	14	16	18	20
Enclosed (Method 3 or 4) or bunched and clipped direct to a non-metallic surface (Method 1)		0·80	0·70	0·65	0·60	0·57	0·54	0·52	0·50	0·48	0·45	0·43	0·41	0·39	0·38
Single layer clipped to a non-metallic surface (Method 1)	Touching	0·85	0·79	0·75	0·73	0·72	0·72	0·71	0·70	—	—	—	—	—	—
	Spaced*	0·94	0·90	0·90	0·90	0·90	0·90	0·90	0·90	0·90	0·90	0·90	0·90	0·90	0·90
Single layer *multicore* on a perforated metal cable tray, vertical or horizontal (Method 11)	Touching	0·86	0·81	0·77	0·75	0·74	0·73	0·73	0·72	0·71	0·70	—	—	—	—
	Spaced*	0·91	0·89	0·88	0·87	0·87	—	—	—	—	—	—	—	—	—
Single layer *single core* on a perforated metal cable tray, touching (Method 11)	Horizontal	0·90	0·85	—	—	—	—	—	—	—	—	—	—	—	—
	Vertical	0·85	—	—	—	—	—	—	—	—	—	—	—	—	—
Single layer multicore touching on ladder suports		0·86	0·82	0·80	0·79	0·78	0·78	0·78	0·77	—	—	—	—	—	—

* 'Spaced' means a clearance between adjacent surfaces of at least one cable diameter (D_e). Where the horizontal clearances between adjacent cables exceeds $2D_e$, no correction factor need be applied.

NOTES: 1. The factors in the table are applicable to groups of cables all of one size. The value of current derived from application of the appropriate factors is the maximum continuous current to be carried by any of the cables in the group.

2. If, due to known operating conditions, a cable is expected to carry not more than 30% of its *grouped* rating, it may be ignored for the purpose of obtaining the rating factor for the rest of the group.

For example, a group of N loaded cables would normally require a group reduction factor of C_g applied to the tabulated I_t. However, if M cables in the group carry loads which are not greater than 0.3 $C_g I_t$ amperes the other cables can be sized by using the group rating corresponding to (N-M) cables.

TABLE 4A. FACTORS FOR AMBIENT TEMPERATURE WHERE THE OVERLOAD PROTECTIVE DEVICE IS A SEMI-ENCLOSED FUSE TO BS 3036.

Type of insulation	Ambient temperature °C														
	25	30	35	40	45	50	55	60	65	70	75	80	85	90	95
60°C rubber (flexible cables only)	1·04	1·0	0·96	0·91	0·87	0·79	0·56	—	—	—	—	—	—	—	—
General purpose p.v.c.	1·03	1·0	0·97	0·94	0·91	0·87	0·84	0·69	0·48	—	—	—	—	—	—
Paper	1·02	1·0	0·97	0·95	0·92	0·90	0·87	0·84	0·76	0·62	0·43	—	—	—	—
85°C rubber	1·02	1·0	0·97	0·95	0·93	0·91	0·88	0·86	0·83	0·71	0·58	0·41	—	—	—
Thermosetting	1·02	1·0	0·98	0·95	0·93	0·91	0·89	0·87	0·85	0·79	0·69	0·56	0·39	—	—
Mineral: Bare and exposed to touch, or p.v.c. covered (70° sheath)	1·03	1·0	0·96	0·93	0·89	0·86	0·79	0·62	0·42	—	—	—	—	—	—
Bare and not exposed to touch (105°C sheath)	1·02	1·0	0·98	0·96	0·93	0·91	0·89	0·86	0·84	0·82	0·79	0·77	0·64	0·55	0·43

TABLE 4B.–CORRECTION FACTORS FOR AMBIENT TEMPERATURE

Note: This table is not applicable where overload protection is afforded by a semi-enclosed fuse to BS 3036, see TABLE 4A

Type of insulation	Ambient temperature °C														
	25	30	35	40	45	50	55	60	65	70	75	80	85	90	95
60°C rubber (flexible cables only)	1·04	1·0	0·92	0·82	0·71	0·58	0·41	—	—	—	—	—	—	—	—
General purpose pvc	1·03	1·0	0·94	0·87	0·79	0·71	0·61	0·50	0·35	—	—	—	—	—	—
Paper	1·02	1·0	0·95	0·89	0·84	0·77	0·71	0·63	0·55	0·45	0·32	—	—	—	—
85°C rubber	1·02	1·0	0·95	0·90	0·85	0·80	0·74	0·67	0·60	0·62	0·43	0·30	—	—	—
Thermosetting	1·02	1·0	0·96	0·91	0·87	0·82	0·76	0·71	0·65	0·58	0·50	0·41	0·29	—	—
Mineral: 70° sheath	1·03	1·0	0·93	0·85	0·77	0·67	0·57	0·45	—	—	—	—	—	—	—
Mineral: 105°C sheath	1·02	1·0	0·96	0·92	0·88	0·84	0·80	0·75	0·70	0·65	0·60	0·54	0·47	0·40	0·32

TABLE 5A.—SINGLE-CORE PVC-INSULATED CABLES, NON-ARMOURED, WITH OR WITHOUT SHEATH
COPPER CONDUCTORS

Current-Carrying Capacities (Amps)

Ambient temperature: 30°C
Conductor operating temperature: 70°C

	Conductor cross-sectional area	Reference Method 4 (enclosed in conduit in thermally insulating wall etc)		Reference Method 3 (enclosed in conduit on a wall or in trunking etc)		Reference Method 1 ('clipped direct')		Reference Method II (on a perforated cable tray horizontal or vertical)		Reference Method 12 (free air)		
										Horizontal flat spaced,	Vertical flat spaced,	
		2 cables, single-phase ac or dc	3 or 4 cables three-phase ac	2 cables, single-phase ac or dc	3 or 4 cables three-phase ac	2 cables, single-phase ac or dc	3 or 4 cables three-phase ac	2 cables, single-phase ac or dc flat and touching	3 cables, three-phase ac flat and touching or trefoil	2 cables, single-phase ac or dc or 3 cables three-phase ac	2 cables, single-phase ac or dc or 3 cables three-phase ac	3 cables, trefoil three-phase ac
	1	2	3	4	5	6	7	8	9	10	11	12
	mm²	A	A	A	A	A	A	A	A	A	A	A
BS 6004	1	11	10·5	13·5	12	15·5	14	—	—	—	—	—
BS 6004	1·5	14·5	13·5	17·5	15·5	20	18	—	—	—	—	—
BS 6004	2·5	19·5	18	24	21	27	25	—	—	—	—	—
BS 6004	4	26	24	32	28	37	33	—	—	—	—	—
BS 6004	6	34	31	41	36	47	43	—	—	—	—	—
BS 6004	10	46	42	57	50	65	59	—	—	—	—	—
BS 6004	16	61	56	76	68	87	79	—	—	—	—	—
BS 6004	25	80	73	101	89	114	104	126	112	146	130	110
BS 6004	35	99	89	125	110	141	129	156	141	181	162	137
BS 6346	50	119	108	151	134	182	167	191	172	219	197	167
BS 6346	70	151	136	192	171	234	214	246	223	281	254	216
BS 6346	95	182	164	232	207	284	261	300	273	341	311	264
BS 6346	120	210	188	269	239	330	303	349	318	396	362	308
BS 6346	150	240	216	300	262	381	349	404	369	456	419	356
BS 6346	185	273	245	341	296	436	400	463	424	521	480	409
BS 6346	240	320	286	400	346	515	472	549	504	615	569	485
BS 6346	300	367	328	458	394	594	545	635	584	709	659	561
BS 6346	400	—	—	546	467	694	634	732	679	852	795	656
BS 6346	500	—	—	626	533	792	723	835	778	982	920	749
BS 6346	630	—	—	720	611	904	826	953	892	1138	1070	855
BS 6346	800	—	—	—	—	1030	943	1086	1020	1265	1188	971
BS 6346	1000	—	—	—	—	1154	1058	1216	1149	1420	1337	1079

Table 5B.—Single-core PVC Insulated Cables

Volt Drops (mV/A/m)

Conductor cross-sectional area	2 cables dc	2 cables—single-phase ac									3 or 4 cables—three-phase ac											
		Reference Methods 3 & 4 (Enclosed in conduit etc in or on a wall)			Reference Methods 1 & 11 (Clipped direct or on trays, touching)			Reference Method 12 (Spaced*)			Reference Methods 3 & 4 (Enclosed in conduit etc in or on a wall)			Reference Methods 1, 11 & 12 (In trefoil)			Reference Methods 1 & 11 (Flat touching)			Reference Method 12 (Flat spaced*)		
1	2	3			4			5			6			7			8			9		
mm²	mV		mV			mV			mV			mV			mV			mV			mV	
1	44		44			44			44			38			38			38			38	
1·5	29		29			29			29			25			25			25			25	
2·5	18		18			18			18			15			15			15			15	
4	11		11			11			11			9·5			9·5			9·5			9·5	
6	7·3		7·3			7·3			7·3			6·4			6·4			6·4			6·4	
10	4·4		4·4			4·4			4·4			3·8			3·8			3·8			3·8	
16	2·8		2·8			2·8			2·8			2·4			2·4			2·4			2·4	
		r	x	z	r	x	z	r	x	z	r	x	z	r	x	z	r	x	z	r	x	z
25	1·75	1·80	0·33	1·80	1·75	0·20	1·75	1·75	0·29	1·80	1·50	0·29	1·55	1·50	0·175	1·50	1·50	0·25	1·55	1·50	0·32	1·55
35	1·25	1·30	0·31	1·30	1·25	0·195	1·25	1·25	0·28	1·30	1·10	0·27	1·10	1·10	0·170	1·10	1·10	0·24	1·10	1·10	0·32	1·15
50	0·93	0·95	0·30	1·00	0·93	0·190	0·95	0·93	0·28	0·97	0·81	0·26	0·85	0·80	0·165	0·82	0·80	0·24	0·84	0·80	0·32	0·86
70	0·63	0·65	0·29	0·72	0·63	0·185	0·66	0·63	0·27	0·69	0·56	0·25	0·61	0·55	0·160	0·57	0·55	0·24	0·60	0·55	0·31	0·63
95	0·46	0·49	0·28	0·56	0·47	0·180	0·50	0·47	0·27	0·54	0·42	0·24	0·48	0·41	0·155	0·43	0·41	0·23	0·47	0·40	0·31	0·51
120	0·36	0·39	0·27	0·47	0·37	0·175	0·41	0·37	0·26	0·45	0·33	0·23	0·41	0·32	0·150	0·36	0·32	0·23	0·40	0·32	0·30	0·44
150	0·29	0·31	0·27	0·41	0·30	0·175	0·34	0·29	0·26	0·39	0·27	0·23	0·36	0·26	0·150	0·30	0·26	0·23	0·34	0·26	0·30	0·40
185	0·23	0·25	0·27	0·37	0·24	0·170	0·29	0·24	0·26	0·35	0·22	0·23	0·32	0·21	0·145	0·26	0·21	0·22	0·31	0·21	0·30	0·36
240	0·180	0·195	0·26	0·33	0·185	0·165	0·25	0·185	0·25	0·31	0·17	0·23	0·29	0·160	0·145	0·22	0·160	0·22	0·27	0·160	0·29	0·34
300	0·145	0·160	0·26	0·31	0·150	0·165	0·22	0·150	0·25	0·29	0·14	0·23	0·27	0·130	0·140	0·190	0·130	0·22	0·25	0·130	0·29	0·32
400	0·105	0·130	0·26	0·29	0·120	0·160	0·20	0·115	0·25	0·27	0·12	0·22	0·25	0·105	0·140	0·175	0·105	0·21	0·24	0·100	0·29	0·31
500	0·086	0·110	0·26	0·28	0·098	0·155	0·185	0·093	0·24	0·26	0·10	0·22	0·25	0·086	0·135	0·160	0·086	0·21	0·23	0·081	0·29	0·30
630	0·068	0·094	0·25	0·27	0·081	0·155	0·175	0·076	0·24	0·25	0·08	0·22	0·24	0·072	0·135	0·150	0·072	0·21	0·22	0·066	0·28	0·29
800	0·053		—		0·068	0·150	0·165	0·061	0·24	0·25		—		0·060	0·130	0·145	0·060	0·21	0·22	0·053	0·28	0·29
1000	0·042		—		0·059	0·150	0·160	0·050	0·24	0·24		—		0·052	0·130	0·140	0·052	0·20	0·21	0·044	0·28	0·28

TABLE 6A.—MULTICORE PVC-INSULATED CABLES, NON-ARMOURED (COPPER CONDUCTORS)

Ambient temperature: 30°C
Conductor operating temperature: 70°C

Current-Carrying capacities (Amperes):

Conductor cross-sectional area	Reference Method 4 (enclosed in an insulated wall, etc)		Reference Method 3 (enclosed in conduit on a wall or ceiling, or in trunking)		Reference Method 1 (clipped direct)		Reference Method 11 (on a perforated cable tray), or Reference Method 13 (free air)	
	1 two-core cable single-phase ac or dc	1 three-core cable, or 1 four-core cable, three phase ac	1 two-core cable, single phase ac or dc	1 three-core cable, or 1 four-core cable, three phase ac	1 two-core cable single-phase ac or dc	1 three-core cable, or 1 four-core cable, three-phase ac	1 two-core cable, single-phase ac or dc	1 three-core cable, or 1 four-core cable, three-phase ac
1	2	3	4	5	6	7	8	9
mm²	A	A	A	A	A	A	A	A
1	11	10	13	11·5	15	13·5	17	14·5
1·5	14	13	16·5	15	19·5	17·5	22	18·5
2·5	18·5	17·5	23	20	27	24	30	25
4	25	23	30	27	36	32	40	34
6	32	29	38	34	46	41	51	43
10	43	39	52	46	63	57	70	60
16	57	52	69	62	85	76	94	80
25	75	68	90	80	112	96	119	101
35	92	83	111	99	138	119	148	126
50	110	99	133	118	168	144	180	153
70	139	125	168	149	213	184	232	196
95	167	150	201	179	258	223	282	238
120	192	172	232	206	299	259	328	276
150	219	196	258	225	344	299	379	319
185	248	223	294	255	392	341	434	364
240	291	261	344	297	461	403	514	430
300	334	298	394	339	530	464	593	497
400	—	—	470	402	634	557	715	597

Table 6B.—Multi-core PVC Insulated Cables

Volt Drops (mv/A/m)

Conductor cross-sectional area	Two-core cable dc	Two-core cable single phase ac			Three- or four-core cable three phase ac		
1	2	3			4		
mm²	mV	mV			mV		
1	44	44			38		
1·5	29	29			25		
2·5	18	18			15		
4	11	11			9·5		
6	7·3	7·3			6·4		
10	4·4	4·4			3·8		
16	2·8	2·8			2·4		
		r	x	z	r	x	z
25	1·75	1·75	0·170	1·75	1·50	0·145	1·50
35	1·25	1·25	0·165	1·25	1·10	0·145	1·10
50	0·93	0·93	0·165	0·94	0·80	0·140	0·81
70	0·63	0·63	0·160	0·65	0·55	0·140	0·57
95	0·46	0·47	0·155	0·50	0·41	0·135	0·43
120	0·36	0·38	0·155	0·41	0·33	0·135	0·35
150	0·29	0·30	0·155	0·34	0·26	0·130	0·29
185	0·23	0·25	0·150	0·29	0·21	0·130	0·25
240	0·180	0·190	0·150	0·24	0·165	0·130	0·21
300	0·145	0·155	0·145	0·21	0·135	0·130	0·185
400	0·105	0·115	0·145	0·185	0·100	0·125	0·160

Table 12.—Volt Drops for Single Phase Operation (in mV/A/m) for Mineral Insulated Cables Bare and Exposed to Touch or Having an Overall Covering of PVC: BS 6207 Copper Conductors and Sheath

Ambient temperature: 30°C
Sheath operating temperature: 70°C

Nominal cross-sectional area of conductors	Two single-core cables Touching			Multicore cables		
mm²	mV/A/m_r	mV/A/m_x	mV/A/m_z	mV/A/m_r	mV/A/m_x	mV/A/m_z
1	2	3	4	5	6	7
1	42	—	—	42	—	—
1·5	28	—	—	28	—	—
2·5	17	—	—	17	—	—
4	10	—	—	10	—	—
6	7	—	—	7	—	—
10	4·2	—	—	4·2	—	—
16	2·6	—	—	2·6	—	—
25	1·65	0·200	1·65	1·65	1·145	1·65
35	1·20	0·195	1·20	—	—	—
50	0·89	0·185	0·91	—	—	—
70	0·62	0·180	0·64	—	—	—
95	0·46	0·175	0·49	—	—	—
120	0·37	0·170	0·41	—	—	—
150	0·30	0·170	0·34	—	—	—
185	0·25	0·165	0·29	—	—	—
240	0·190	0·160	0·25	—	—	—

TABLE 7A.—MULTICORE ARMOURED PVC-INSULATED CABLES: BS 6540 COPPER CONDUCTORS

Current-Carrying Capacities (Amperes)

Ambient temperature: 30°C
Conductor operating temperature: 70°C

Conductor cross-sectional	Reference Method 1 (clipped direct)		Reference Method 11 (on a perforated horizontal cable tray, or Reference Method 13 (free air))	
	1 two-core cable, single-phase ac or dc	1 three- or four-core cable, three-phase ac	1 two-core cable, single-phase ac or dc	1 three- or four-core cable, three-phase ac
1	2	3	4	5
mm²	A	A	A	A
1·5	21	18	22	19
2·5	28	25	31	26
4	38	33	41	35
6	49	42	53	45
10	67	58	72	62
16	89	77	97	83
25	118	102	128	110
35	145	125	157	135
50	175	151	190	163
70	222	192	241	207
95	269	231	291	251
120	310	267	336	290
150	356	306	386	332
185	405	348	439	378
240	476	409	516	445
300	547	469	592	510
400	621	540	683	590

TABLE 7B.—MULTICORE ARMOURED PVC INSULATED CABLES

Volt Drops (mV/A/m)

Conductor cross-sectional area	Two-core cable dc	Two-core single-phase ac			Three- or four-core cable three-phase ac		
1	2		3			4	
mm²	mV		mV			mV	
1·5	29		29			25	
2·5	18		18			15	
4	11		11			9·5	
6	7·3		7·3			6·4	
10	4·4		4·4			3·8	
16	2·8		2·8			2·4	
		r	x	z	r	x	z
25	1·75	1·75	0·170	1·75	1·50	0·145	1·50
35	1·25	1·25	0·165	1·25	1·10	0·145	1·10
50	0·93	0·93	0·165	0·94	0·80	0·140	0·81
70	0·63	0·63	0·160	0·65	0·55	0·140	0·57
95	0·46	0·47	0·155	0·50	0·41	0·135	0·43
120	0·36	0·38	0·155	0·41	0·33	0·135	0·35
150	0·29	0·30	0·155	0·34	0·26	0·130	0·29
185	0·23	0·25	0·150	0·29	0·21	0·130	0·25
240	0·180	0·190	0·150	0·24	0·165	0·130	0·21
300	0·145	0·155	0·145	0·21	0·135	0·130	0·185
400	0·105	0·115	0·145	0·185	0·100	0·125	0·160

TABLE 8A.—MULTICORE ARMOURED CABLES HAVING THERMOSETTING INSULATION: BS 5467
COPPER CONDUCTORS

Current-Carrying capacities (Amperes):

Ambient temperature: 30°C
Conductor operating temperature: 90°C

Conductor cross-sectional	Reference Method 1 (clipped direct)		Reference Method 11 (on a perforated cable tray) or reference Method 13 (free air)	
	1 two-core cable, ac or dc	1 three- or four-core cable, balanced three-phase ac	1 two-core cable, single-phase ac or dc	1 three- or four-core cable, three-phase ac
1	2	3	4	5
mm²	A	A	A	A
16	110	94	115	99
25	146	124	152	131
35	180	154	188	162
50	219	187	228	197
70	279	238	291	251
95	338	289	354	304
120	392	335	410	353
150	451	386	472	406
185	515	441	539	463
240	607	520	636	546
300	698	599	732	628

TABLE 8B.—MULTICORE CABLES HAVING THERMOSETTING INSULATION; BS 5467
COPPER CONDUCTORS

Volt Drops (mV/A/m)

Conductor cross-sectional area	Two-core cable dc	Two-core cable single-phase ac			Three or four-core cable three-phase ac		
1	2	3			4		
mm²	mV	mV			mV		
16	2·9	2·9			2·5		
		r	x	z	r	x	z
25	1·85	1·85	0·160	1·90	1·60	0·140	1·65
35	1·35	1·35	0·155	1·35	1·15	0·135	1·15
50	0·98	0·99	0·155	1·00	0·86	0·135	0·87
70	0·67	0·67	0·150	0·69	0·59	0·130	0·60
95	0·49	0·50	0·150	0·52	0·43	0·130	0·45
120	0·39	0·40	0·145	0·42	0·34	0·130	0·37
150	0·31	0·32	0·145	0·35	0·28	0·125	0·30
185	0·25	0·26	0·145	0·29	0·22	0·125	0·26
240	0·195	0·200	0·140	0·24	0·175	0·125	0·21
300	0·155	0·160	0·140	0·21	0·140	0·120	0·185

TABLE 9A.—CURRENT-CARRYING CAPACITIES AND MASSES SUPPORTABLE FOR FLEXIBLE CORDS; BS 6500

Nominal cross-sectional area of conductor	Maximum diameter of wires forming conductor	Current-carrying capacity		Maximum mass supportable by twin flexible cord
		Single-phase ac	Three-phase ac	
1	2	3	4	5
mm²	mm	A	A	kg
0·5	0·21	3	3	2
0·75	0·21	6	6	3
1	0·21	10	10	5
1·25	0·26	13	—	5
1·5	0·26	16	16	5
2·5	0·26	25	20	5
4	0·31	32	25	5

CORRECTION FACTOR FOR AMBIENT TEMPERATURE

60°C rubber pvc cords

Ambient temperature	35°C	40°C	45°C	50°C	55°C
Correction factor	0·92	0·82	0·71	0·58	0·41

85°C rubber cords having a h.o.f.r. sheath or a heat-resisting pvc sheath

Ambient temperature	35°C to 50°C	55°C	60°C	65°C	70°C
Correction factor	1·0	0·96	0·83	0·67	0·47

150°C rubber cords

Ambient temperature	35°C to 120°C	125°C	130°C	135°C	140°C	145°C
Correction factor	1·0	0·96	0·85	0·74	0·60	0·42

Glass-fibre cords

Ambient temperature	35°C to 150°C	155°C	160°C	165°C	170°C	175°C
Correction factor	1·0	0·92	0·82	0·71	0·57	0·40

TABLE 9B.—FLEXIBLE CORDS

Volt Drops (mV/A/m)

Conductor cross-sectional area	dc or single-phase ac	three-phase ac
1	2	2
mm²	mV	mV
0·5	93	80
0·75	62	54
1	46	40
1·25	37	32
1·5	32	27
2·5	19	16
4	12	10

Note: The tabulated values above are for 60°C rubber insulated and PVC-insulated flexible cords and for other types of flexible cords they are to be multiplied by the following factors:
For 85°C rubber insulated 1.085
150°C rubber insulated 1.306
185°C glass fibre 1.425

TABLE 10.—MINERAL INSULATED CABLES BARE AND EXPOSED TO TOUCH OR HAVING AN OVERALL COVERING OF PVC
COPPER CONDUCTORS AND SHEATH CLIPPED DIRECT

Ambient temperature: 30°C
Sheath operating temperature: 70°C

Current-Carrying Capacities (Amperes):

Nominal cross-sectioal area of conductor	2 single-core cables or 1 two-core cable, single-phase ac or dc	3 single-core cables in trefoil or 1 three-core cable, three-phase ac	3 single-core cables in flat formation, three-phase ac	1 four-core cable 3 cores loaded three-phase ac	1 four-core cable all cores loaded	1 seven-core cable all cores loaded	1 twelve-core cable all cores loaded	1 nineteen-core cable all cores loaded
1	2	3	4	5	6	7	8	9
mm²	A	A	A	A	A	A	A	A
Light duty 500 V								
1	18·5	15	17	15	13	10	—	—
1·5	23	19	21	19.5	16.5	13	—	—
2·5	31	26	29	26	22	17·5	—	—
4	40	35	38	—	—	—	—	—
Heavy duty 750 V								
1	19·5	16	18	16·5	14·5	11·5	9·5	8·5
1·5	25	21	23	21	18	14·5	12·0	10·0
2·5	34	28	31	28	25	19·5	16·0	—
4	45	37	41	37	32	26	—	—
6	57	48	52	47	41	—	—	—
10	77	65	70	64	55	—	—	—
16	102	86	92	85	72	—	—	—
25	133	112	120	110	94	—	—	—
35	163	137	147	—	—	—	—	—
50	202	169	181	—	—	—	—	—
70	247	207	221	—	—	—	—	—
95	296	249	264	—	—	—	—	—
120	340	286	303	—	—	—	—	—
150	388	327	346	—	—	—	—	—
185	440	371	392	—	—	—	—	—
240	514	434	457	—	—	—	—	—

Notes: 1. For single-core cables, the sheaths of the circuit are assumed to be connected together at both ends.
2. For bare cables exposed to touch, the tabulated values should be multiplied by 0·9.

TABLE 11.—MINERAL INSULATED CABLES BARE AND EXPOSED TO TOUCH OR IN CONTACT WITH COMBUSTIBLE MATERIALS; BS 6207 COPPER CONDUCTORS AND SHEATH CLIPPED DIRECT

Current-Carrying Capacities (Amperes):

Ambient temperature: 30°C
Sheath operating temperature: 105°C

Nominal cross-sectioal area of conductor	2 single-core cables or 1 two-core cable, single-phase ac or dc	3 single-core cables in trefoil or 1 three-core cable, three-phase ac	3 single-core cables in flat formation, three-phase ac	1 four-core cable 3 cores loaded three-phase ac	1 four-core cable all cores loaded	1 seven-core cable all cores loaded	1 twelve-core cable all cores loaded	1 nineteen-core cable all cores loaded
1	2	3	4	5	6	7	8	9
mm²	A	A	A	A	A	A	A	A
Light duty 500 V								
1	22	19	21	18·5	16·5	13	—	—
1·5	28	24	27	24	21	16·5	—	—
2·5	38	33	36	33	28	22	—	—
4	51	44	47	—	—	—	—	—
Heavy duty 750 V								
1	24	20	24	20	17·5	14	12	10·5
1·5	31	26	30	26	22	17·5	15·5	13
2·5	42	35	41	35	30	24	20	—
4	55	47	53	46	40	32	—	—
6	70	59	67	58	50	—	—	—
10	96	81	91	78	68	—	—	—
16	127	107	119	103	90	—	—	—
25	166	140	154	134	117	—	—	—
35	203	171	187	—	—	—	—	—
50	251	212	230	—	—	—	—	—
70	307	260	280	—	—	—	—	—
95	369	312	334	—	—	—	—	—
120	424	359	383	—	—	—	—	—
150	485	410	435	—	—	—	—	—
185	550	465	492	—	—	—	—	—
240	643	544	572	—	—	—	—	—

Notes: 1. For single-core cables, the sheaths of the circuit are assumed to be connected together at both ends.
2. No correction factor for grouping need be applied.

TABLE 13.—VOLT DROPS FOR THREE PHASE OPERATION (mV/A/m) FOR MINERAL INSULATED CABLES BARE AND EXPOSED TO TOUCH OR HAVING AN OVERALL COVERING OF PVC: BS 6207

COPPER CONDUCTORS AND SHEATH

Ambient temperature: 30°C
Sheath operating temperature: 70°C

Nominal cross-sectional area of conductors	Three single-core cables									Multicore cables		
	Trefoil Touching			Flat Formation								
				Touching			Spaced 1 cable diameter apart					
mm^2 1	$mV/A/m_r$ 2	$mV/A/m_x$ 3	$mV/A/m_z$ 4	$mV/A/m_r$ 5	$mV/A/m_x$ 6	$mV/A/m_z$ 7	$mV/A/m_r$ 8	$mV/A/m_x$ 9	$mV/A/m_z$ 10	$mV/A/m_r$ 11	$mV/A/m_x$ 12	$mV/A/m_z$ 13
1	36	—	—	36	—	—	36	—	—	36	—	—
1·5	24	—	—	24	—	—	24	—	—	24	—	—
2·5	14	—	—	14	—	—	14	—	—	14	—	—
4	9·1	—	—	9·1	—	—	9·1	—	—	9·1	—	—
6	6·0	—	—	6·0	—	—	6·0	—	—	6·0	—	—
10	3·6	—	—	3·6	—	—	3·6	—	—	3·6	—	—
16	2·3	—	—	2·3	—	—	2·3	—	—	2·3	—	—
25	1·45	0·170	1·45	1·45	0·25	1·45	1·45	0·32	1·50	1·45	0·125	1·45
35	1·05	0·165	1·05	1·05	0·24	1·10	1·05	0·31	1·10	—	—	—
50	0·78	0·160	0·80	0·79	0·24	0·83	0·82	0·31	0·87	—	—	—
70	0·54	0·155	0·56	0·55	0·23	0·60	0·58	0·30	0·65	—	—	—
95	0·40	0·150	0·43	0·41	0·22	0·47	0·44	0·29	0·53	—	—	—
120	0·32	0·150	0·36	0·33	0·22	0·40	0·36	0·28	0·46	—	—	—
150	0·26	0·145	0·30	0·29	0·21	0·36	0·32	0·27	0·42	—	—	—
185	0·21	0·140	0·26	0·25	0·21	0·32	0·28	0·26	0·39	—	—	—
240	0·165	0·140	0·22	0·21	0·20	0·29	0·26	0·25	0·36	—	—	—

TABLES 14 TO 16

TABLE 14.—CABLE FACTORS FOR SHORT STRAIGHT RUNS

Type of conductors	Conductor cross-sectional area mm²	Factor
Solid	1	22
	1·5	27
	2·5	39
Stranded	1·5	31

Type of conductors	Conductor cross-sectional area mm²	Factor
Stranded	2·5	4·3
	4	58
	6	88
	10	146

TABLE 15.—CABLE FACTORS FOR LONG STRAIGHT RUNS OR RUNS INCORPORATING BENDS

Type of conductor	Conductor cross-sectional area mm²	Factor
Solid or stranded	1	16
	1·5	22
	2·5	30
	4	43
	6	58
	10	105

TABLE 16.—CONDUIT FACTORS FOR SHORT STRAIGHT RUNS

Conduit dia mm	Factor
16	290
20	460
25	800
32	1400

TABLE 17.—CONDUIT FACTORS FOR RUNS INCORPORATING BENDS

Length of run m	Straight				One bend				Two bends				Three bends				Four bends			
Conduit diameter, mm	16	20	25	32	16	20	25	32	16	20	25	32	16	20	25	32	16	20	25	32
1	Covered				188	303	543	947	177	286	514	900	158	256	463	818	130	213	388	692
1·5	by				182	294	528	923	167	270	487	857	143	233	422	750	111	182	333	600
2	Tables 14				177	286	514	900	158	256	463	818	130	213	388	692	97	159	292	529
2·5	and 16				171	278	500	878	150	244	442	783	120	196	358	643	86	141	260	474
3					167	270	487	857	143	233	422	750	111	182	333	600				
3·5	179	290	521	911	162	263	475	837	136	222	404	720	103	169	311	563				
4	177	286	514	900	158	256	463	818	130	213	388	692	97	159	292	529				
4·5	174	282	507	889	154	250	452	800	125	204	373	667	91	149	275	500				
5	171	278	500	878	150	244	442	783	120	196	358	643	86	141	260	474				
6	167	270	487	857	143	233	422	750	111	182	333	600								
7	162	263	475	837	136	222	404	720	103	169	311	563								
8	158	256	463	818	130	213	388	692	97	159	292	529								
9	154	250	452	800	125	204	373	667	91	149	275	500								
10	150	244	442	783	120	196	358	643	86	141	260	474								

TABLE 18.—CABLE FACTORS FOR TRUNKING

Type of conductor	Conductor cross-sectional area mm^2	Factor
Solid	1·5	7·1
	2·5	10·2
Stranded	1·5	8·1
	2·5	11·4
	4	15·2
	6	22·9
	10	36·3

TABLE 19.—FACTOR FOR TRUNKING

Dimensions of trunking mm × mm	Factor
50 × 37·5	767
50 × 50	1037
75 × 25	738
75 × 37·5	1146
75 × 50	1555
75 × 75	2371
100 × 25	993
100 × 37·5	1542
100 × 50	2091
100 × 75	3189
100 × 100	4252

TABLE 20.—MAXIMUM EARTH FAULT LOOP IMPEDANCE (Z_s) FOR SOCKET OUTLETS CIRCUITS

(*a*) Fuses to BS 88 Part 2

Rating (amperes)	6	10	16	20	25	32	40	50
Z_s (ohms)	8·7	5·3	2·8	1·8	1·5	1·1	0·8	0·6

(*b*) Fuses to BS 1361

Rating (amperes)	5	15	20	30	45
Z_s (ohms)	11·4	3·4	1·8	1·2	0·6

(*c*) Fuses to BS 3036

Rating (amperes)	5	15	20	30	45
Z_s (ohms)	9·6	2·7	1·8	1·1	0·6

(*d*) Fuse to BS 1362

Rating (amperes)	13
Z_s (ohms)	2·5

(*e*) Type 1 miniature circuit breakers to BS 3871

Rating (amperes)	5	10	15	20	30	50	I_n
Z_s (ohms)	12	6	4	3	2	1·2	$60/I_n$

(*f*) Type 2 miniature circuit breakers to BS 3871

Rating (amperes)	5	10	15	20	30	50	I_n
Z_s (ohms)	6·8	3·4	2·3	1·7	1·1	0·68	$34/I_n$

(*g*) Type 3 miniature circuit breakers to BS 3871

Rating (amperes)	5	10	15	20	30	50	I_n
Z_s (ohms)	4·8	2·4	1·6	1·2	0·8	0·48	$24/I_n$

Note When U_o, the nominal voltage to Earth, is other than 240 V the tabulated impedance values are to be multiplied by $U_o/240$.

TABLE 21.—MAXIMUM EARTH FAULT LOOP IMPEDANCE (Z_s) FOR CIRCUITS SUPPLYING FIXED EQUIPMENT

(*a*) fuses to BS 88 Part 2

Rating (amperes)	6	10	16	20	25	32	40	50
Z_s (ohms)	13·0	7·7	4·4	3·0	2·4	1·8	1·4	1·1

Rating (amperes)	63	80	100	125	160	200	250
Z_s (ohms)	0·86	0·6	0·45	0·34	0·27	0·19	0·16

Rating (amperes)	315	400	500	630	800
Z_s (ohms)	0·11	0·096	0·065	0·054	0·034

(*b*) Fuses to BS 1361

Rating (amperes)	5	15	20	30	45	60	80	100
Z_s (ohms)	17	5·3	2·9	2·0	1·0	0·6	0·48	0·28

(*c*) Fuses to BS 3036

Rating (amperes)	5	15	20	30	45	60	100
Z_s (ohms)	20	5·6	4·0	3·2	1·6	1·2	0·55

(*d*) Type 1 miniature circuit breakers to BS 3871

Rating (amperes)	5	10	15	20	30	50	I_n
Z_s (ohms)	12	6	4	3	2	1·2	$60/I_n$

(*e*) Type 2 miniature circuit breakers to BS 3871

Rating (amperes)	5	10	15	20	30	50	I_n
Z_s (ohms)	6.8	3·4	2·3	1·7	1·1	0·68	$34/I_n$

(*f*) Type 3 miniature circuit breakers to BS 2871

Rating (amperes)	5	10	15	20	30	50	I_n
Z_s (ohms)	4.8	2·4	1·6	1·2	0·8	0·48	$24/I_n$

Note When U_o, the nominal voltage to Earth, is other than 240 V the tabluated impedance values are to be multiplied by $U_o/240$.

TABLE 22.—MAXIMUM IMPEDANCE OF PROTECTIVE CONDUCTOR

(*a*) Fuses to BS 88 Part 2

Rating (amperes)	6	10	16	20	25	32	40	50
Z_2 (ohms)	2·78	1·61	0·92	0·65	0·5	0·39	0·29	0·24

(*b*) Fuses to BS 1361

Rating (amperes)	5	15	20	30	45
Z_2 ohms	3·57	1·08	0·63	0·42	0·21

(*c*) Fuses to BS 3036

Rating (amperes)	5	15	20	30	45
Z_2 (ohms)	2·0	0·55	0·38	0·24	0·125

(*d*) Fuse to BS 1362

Rating (amperes)	13
Z_2 (ohms)	0·83

(*e*) Type 1 miniature circuit breakers to BS 3871

Rating (amperes)	5	10	15	20	30	50	I_n
Z_2 (ohms)	2·5	1·25	0·83	0·63	0·41	0·25	$12{\cdot}5/I_n$

(*f*) Type 2 miniature circuit breakers to BS 3871

Rating (amperes)	5	10	15	20	30	50	I_n
Z_2 (ohms)	1·42	0·71	0·47	0·35	0·24	0·14	$7{\cdot}1/I_n$

(*g*) Type 3 miniature circuit breakers to BS 3871

Rating (amperes)	5	10	15	20	30	50	I_n
Z_2 (ohms)	1·06	0·53	0·35	0·26	0·17	0·10	$5\text{-}3/I_n$

TABLE 23.—VALUES OF *k* FOR INSULATED PROTECTIVE CONDUCTORS NOT INCORPORATED IN CABLES, OR BARE PROTECTIVE CONDUCTORS IN CONTACT WITH CABLE COVERING

Material of conductor	Insulation of protective conductor or cable covering		
	PVC	85°C rubber	90°C thermosetting
Copper	143	166	176
Aluminium	95	110	116
Steel	52	60	64
Assumed initial temperature	30°C	30°C	30°C
Final temperature	160°C	220°C	250°C

TABLE 24.—VALUES OF k FOR PROTECTIVE CONDUCTOR AS A CORE IN A CABLE

	PVC	85°C rubber	90°C thermosetting
Copper	115	134	143
Aluminium	76	89	94
Assumed inial temperature	70°C	85°C	90°C
Final temperature	160°C	220°C	250°C

TABLE 25.—VALUES OF k FOR PROTECTIVE CONDUCTOR AS A SHEATH OR ARMOUR OF A CABLE

Material of conductor	Insulation material		
	PVC	85°C rubber	90°C thermosetting
Steel	44	51	54
Aluminium	81	93	98
Lead	22	26	27
Assumed initial temperature	60°C	75°C	80°C
Final temperature	160°C	220°C	250°C

TABLE 26.—VALUES OF k FOR BARE CONDUCTORS WHERE THERE IS NO RISK OF DAMAGE TO ANY NEIGHBOURING MATERIAL BY THE TEMPERATURES INDICATED

Material of conductor	Conditions		
	Visible and in restricted areas*	Normal conditions	Fire risk
Copper	228	159	138
Aluminium	125	105	91
Steel	82	58	50
Assumed initial temperature	30°C	30°C	30°C
Final temperatures:			
Copper conductors	500°C	200°C	150°C
Aluminium conductors	300°C	200°C	150°C
Steel conductors	500°C	200°C	150°C

* The temperatures are valid only where they do not impair the quality of the connections.

TABLE 27.—MAXIMUM EARTH FAULT LOOP IMPEDANCE (Ω) WHEN OVERCURRENT PROTECTIVE DEVICE IS A FUSE TO BS 3036

(i) For circuits feeding socket outlets

Protective conductor mm²	Fuse rating, amperes				
	5	15	20	30	45
1	9·6	2·7	1·8	1·2(−)	—
1·5	9·6	2·7	1·8	1·1	—
2·5	9·6	2·7	1·8	1·1	0·6
4	9·6	2·7	1·8	1·1	0·6
6	9·6	2·7	1·8	1·1	0·6
10	9·6	2·7	1·8	1·1	0·6
16	9·6	2·7	1·8	1·1	0·6

(ii) For circuits feeding fixed equipment

Protective conductor mm²	Fuse rating, amperes				
	5	15	20	30	45
1	20	5·6	4·0 (3·4)	1·2 (−)	—
1·5	20	5·6	4·0	2·8 (2·5)	—
2·5	20	5·6	4·0	2·8	1·6 (1·4)
4	20	5·6	4·0	2·8	1·6
6	20	5·6	4·0	2·8	1·6
10	20	5·6	4·0	2·8	1·6
16	20	5·6	4·0	2·8	1·6

The values given in brackets apply when the protective conductor is incorporated in the same pvc-insluated cable as the associated phase conductor(s).

TABLE 28.—MAXIMUM EARTH FAULT LOOP (Ω) WHEN OVERCURRENT PROTECTIVE DEVICES IS A FUSE TO BS 88 PART. 2

(i) For circuits feeding socket outlets

Protective conductor mm²	Fuse rating, amperes							
	6	10	16	20	25	32	40	50
1	8·7	5·3	2·8	1·8	1·5	1·1 (0·92)	0·63 (0·5)	0·34 (0·28)
1·5	8·7	5·3	2·8	1·8	1·5	1·1	0·8 (0·77)	0·54 (0·43)
2·5	8·7	5·3	2·8	1·8	1·5	1·1	0·8	0·6
4	8·7	5·3	2·8	1·8	1·5	1·1	0·8	0·6
6	8·7	5·3	2·8	1·8	1·5	1·1	0·8	0·6
10	8·7	5·3	2·8	1·8	1·5	1·1	0·8	0·6
16	8·7	5·3	2·8	1·8	1·5	1·1	0·8	0·6

(ii) For circuits feeding fixed equipment

Protective conductor mm²	Fuse rating, amperes							
	6	10	16	20	25	32	40	50
1	13·0	7·7	4·4	2·5 (2·2)	1·7 (1·5)	1·1 (0·9)	0·63 (0·6)	0·34 (0·28)
1·5	13·0	7·7	4·4	3·0 (2·9)	2·2 (2·0)	1·6 (1·4)	0·95 (0·8)	0·55 (0·44)
2·5	13·0	7·7	4·4	3·0	2·4	1·8	1·3 (1·1)	0·86 (0·75)
4	13·0	7·7	4·4	3·0	2·4	1·8	1·4	1·1
6	13·0	7·7	4·4	3·0	2·4	1·8	1·4	1·1
10	13·0	7·7	4·4	3·0	2·4	1·8	1·4	1·1
16	13·0	7·7	4·4	3·0	2·4	1·8	1·4	1·1

The values given in brackets apply where the protective conductor is incorporated in the same pvc-insulated cable as the associated phase conductor(s).

TABLE 29.—MAXIMUM EARTH FAULT LOOP IMPEDANCE (Ω) WHEN OVERCURRENT PROTECTIVE DEVICE IS A FUSE TO BS 1361

(i) For circuits feeding socket outlets

Protective conductor mm^2	Fuse rating, amperes				
	5	15	20	30	45
1	11·4	3·4	1·8	1·2 (1·1)	0·34 (0·28)
1·5	11·4	3·4	1·8	1·2	0·53 (0·44)
2·5	11·4	3·4	1·8	1·2	0·6
4	11·4	3·4	1·8	1·2	0·6
6	11·4	3·4	1·8	1·2	0·6
10	11·4	3·4	1·8	1·2	0·6
16	11·4	3·4	1·8	1·2	0·6

(ii) For circuits feeding fixed equipment

Protective conductor mm^2	Fuse rating, amperes				
	5	15	20	30	45
1	17	5·3	2·5 (2·4)	1·4 (1·1)	0·34 (0·28)
1·5	17	5·3	2·9	1·7 (1·5)	0·53 (0·44)
2·5	17	5·3	2·9	2·0	0·75 (0·65)
4	17	5·3	2·9	2·0	1·0 (0·90)
6	17	5·3	2·9	2·0	1·0
10	17	5·3	2·9	2·0	1·0
16	17	5·3	2·9	2·0	1·0

The values given in brackets apply when the protective conductor is incorporated in the same pvc-insulated cable as the associated phase conductor(s).

TABLE 32.—MINIMUM CROSS-SECTIONAL AREA OF PROTECTIVE CONDUCTORS IN RELATION TO THE AREA OF ASSOCIATED PHASE CONDUCTORS

Cross-sectional of phase conductor (S)	Minimum cross-sectional area of the corresponding protective conductor (Sp)
mm^2	mm^2
$S \leq 16$	S
$16 < S \leq 35$	16
$S \leq 35$	S/2

TABLE 33.—NON-FLEXIBLE CABLES AND CONDUCTORS FOR LOW VOLTAGE

(i) Non-armoured pvc-insulated cables (BS 6004, BS 6231 Type B, or BS 6346).
(ii) Armoured pvc-insulated cables (BS 6346).
(iii) Split-concentric copper-conductor pvc-insulated cables (BS 4553).
(iv) Rubber insulated cables (BS 6007).
(v) Impregnated-paper-insulated cables, lead-sheathed (BS 6480).
(vi) Armoured cables with thermosetting insulation (BS 5467).
(vii) Mineral-insulated cables (BS 6207, Part 1 or Part 2), with, where appropriate, fittings to BS 6081.
(viii) Consac cables (BS 5593).
(ix) Cables approved under Regulation 12 of the Electricity Supply Regulations.

TABLE 30.—VALUES OF RESISTANCE/METRE FOR COPPER AND ALUMINIUM CONDUCTORS AND OF $(R_1 + R_2)$/METRE AT 20°C IN MILLIOHMS/METRE

Cross-sectional area, mm²		Resistance/metre or $(R_1 + R_2)$/metre	
Phase Conductor	Protective Conductor	Plain Copper	Aluminium
1	—	18·10	
1	1	36·20	—
1·5	—	12·10	—
1·5	1	30·20	—
1·5	1·5	24·20	—
2·5	—	7·41	—
2·5	1	25·51	—
2·5	1·5	19·51	—
2·5	2·5	14·82	—
4	—	4·61	—
4	1·5	16·71	—
4	2·5	12·02	—
4	4	9·22	—
6	—	3·08	—
6	2.5	10·49	—
6	4	7·69	—
6	6	6·16	—
10	—	1·83	—
10	4	6·44	—
10	6	4·91	—
10	10	3·66	—
16	—	1·15	1·91
16	6	4·23	—
16	10	2·98	—
16	16	2·30	3·82
25	—	0·727	1·2
25	10	2·557	—
25	16	1·877	—
25	25	1·454	2·4
35	—	0·524	0·868
35	16	1·674	2·778
35	25	1·251	2·068
35	35	1·048	1·736

TABLE 31.—MULTIPLIERS TO BE APPLIED TO TABLE 30

Insulation Material	p.v.c.	85°C rubber	90° thermosetting
Multiplier	1·38 (1·30)	1·53 (1·42	1·60 (1·48)

Note—The values in brackets are applicable to the resistance of circuit protective conductors where Table 23 applies.

TABLE 34.—MINIMUM INTERNAL RADII OF BENDS IN CABLES FOR FIXED WIRING

Insulation	Finish	Overall diameter	Ractor to be applied to overall diameter† of cable to detemine minimum internal radius of bend.
Rubber or pvc (circular, or circular stranded copper or aluminium conductors)	Non-armoured	Not exceeding 10 mm	3(2)*
		Exceeding 10 mm but not exceeding 25 mm	4(3)*
		Exceeding 25 mm	6
	Armoured	Any	6
PVC (solid aluminium or shaped copper conductors)	Armoured or non-armoured	Any	8
Impregnated paper	Lead sheath	Any	12
Mineral	Copper or aluminium sheath with or without pvc covering	Any	6

† For flat cables the factor is to be applied to the major axis.

* The figure in brackets relates to single-core circular conductors of stranded construction installed in conduit, ducting or trunking.

TABLE 36.—CHECK LIST FOR INITIAL INSPECTION OF INSTALLATIONS

Visual inspection as required by Regulation 612-1 should include a check of the following items, as relevant to the installation:

(i) — connections of conductors,
(ii) — identification of conductirs,
(iii) — selection of conductors for current-current capacity and voltage drop,
(iv) — connection of single-pole devices for protection or switching in phase conductors only,
(v) — correct connection of socket outlets and lampholders,
(vi) — presence of fire barriers and protection against thermal effects,
(vii) — methods of protection against direct contact (including measurement of distances where appropriate), ie:
— protection by insulation of live parts,
— protection by barriers or enclosures,
— protection by obstacles,
— protection by placing out of reach,
— protection by non-conducting location.
(viii) — presence of appropriate devices for isolation and switching.
(ix) — choice and settling of protective and monitoring devices,
(x) — labelling of circuits, fuses, switches, and terminals,
(xi) — selection of equipment and protective measures appropriate to external influences,
(xii) — presence of danger notices and other warning notices,
(xiii) — presence of diagrams, instructions and similar information.

TABLE 35.—FINAL CIRCUITS USING BS 1363 SOCKET OUTLETS

Type of circuit	Overcurrent protective device		Minimum conductor size*			Maximum floor area served
			Copper conductor rubber- or pvc-insulated cables	Copperclad aluminium conductor pvc insulated cables	Copper conductor mineral-insulated cables	
	Rating	Type				
1	2	3	4	5	6	7
	A		mm^2	mm^2	mm^2	m^2
A1 Ring	30 or 32	Any	2·5	4	1·5	100
A Radial	30 or 32	Cartridge fuse or circuit breaker	4	6	2·5	50
A3 Radial	20	Any	2·5	4	1·5	20

* The tabulated values of conductor size may be reduced for fused spurs.

TABLE 37.—SEQUENCE OF TESTING

(1) — Continuity of ring final circuit conductors,
(2) — Continuity of protective conductors, including main and supplementary equipotential bonding.
(3) — Earth electrode resistance,
(4) — Insulation resistance,
(5) — Insulation of site-built assemblies,
(6) — Protection by electrical separation,
(7) — Protection by barriers or enclosures provided during erection,
(8) — Insulation of non-conducting floors and walls,
(9) — Polarity,
(10) — Earth fault loop impedance,
(11) — Operation of residual current devices and fault-voltage operated protective devices.

ELECTRICAL POWER TRANSMISSION AND DISTRIBUTION

Energy Sources—AC Transmission and Distribution—Frequency and Choice of Voltage—AC Insulation Co-ordination and Insulation Levels—Transmission System and Equipment Design—Transmission System Planning and Practice—Distribution System and Equipment Design—Distribution System Planning and Practice—Substation, Busbar and Switching Arrangements—Lightning Protection—Station and Equipment Earthing—Switchgear—Circuit Breakers—Auto-reclosers—Isolators—Earthing Switches—Busbars and Connections—Power Transformers and Reactors—Reactive Compensation—Current and Voltage Transformers—Bushings—Power and Auxiliary Multicore Cables—Electrical Protection—BS, IEC and ESI Standards

By A. Allan, CEng, MIEE

ENERGY SOURCES.—The fuel or energy sources available at present for the large scale generation of electricity in thermal electric power stations using steam are:—

Thermal-electric with the prime mover driven by steam produced from:

(1) coal and lignite
(2) fuel oil
(3) natural gas
(4) peat
(5) atomic fission (nuclear)
(6) geothermal steam and hot water

The potential energy of an elevated volume of water may be used in a hydro-electric power station to drive a water turbine and hence an electricity generator.

Various grades of fuel oil may be burnt in a diesel engine to drive an electricity generator.

Gaseous fuel, or distillate oil, may be burnt in a gas turbine used to drive an electricity generator, and the use of poorer qualities of oil in gas turbines is the subject of much study.

The obtaining of oils from coal, shale and vegetable matter is also being pursued as is the obtaining of energy from the sun, from the winds, from waves, from the ebb and flow of tides, and from atomic fusion.

All of these sources are thought of mainly as power station inputs for the large scale generation of electricity. The electricity so generated must be transmitted to the place of usage and there distributed among the several users.

AC TRANSMISSION AND DISTRIBUTION.—The purpose of these systems is to transmit bulk electricity power supplies from primary generating sources to load centres and thereafter to distribute these supplies safely and reliably at the appropriate declared voltages to the various purchasers/consumers as economically as possible. Also for the interconnection of and transfer of power between substantially separate power supply systems.

Although the lines of demarcation are not always clearly defined, in general an AC power system may be sub-divided as follows for those systems where power supplies are transmitted at higher than generator voltage.

Generation		Transmission			Distribution		
Power station	Voltage step-up generator transformers	Switching stations	Transmission lines	Voltage step-down transmission transformers	Primary distribution network	Voltage step-down distribution transformers	Secondary distribution network

and as shown in Fig. 1.

Types of Supply System Networks.—The system connections are invariably one of three basic types or combinations of these for both transmission and distribution networks. They are:

(1) Radial system
(2) Ring main system (loop system)
(3) Interconnected system

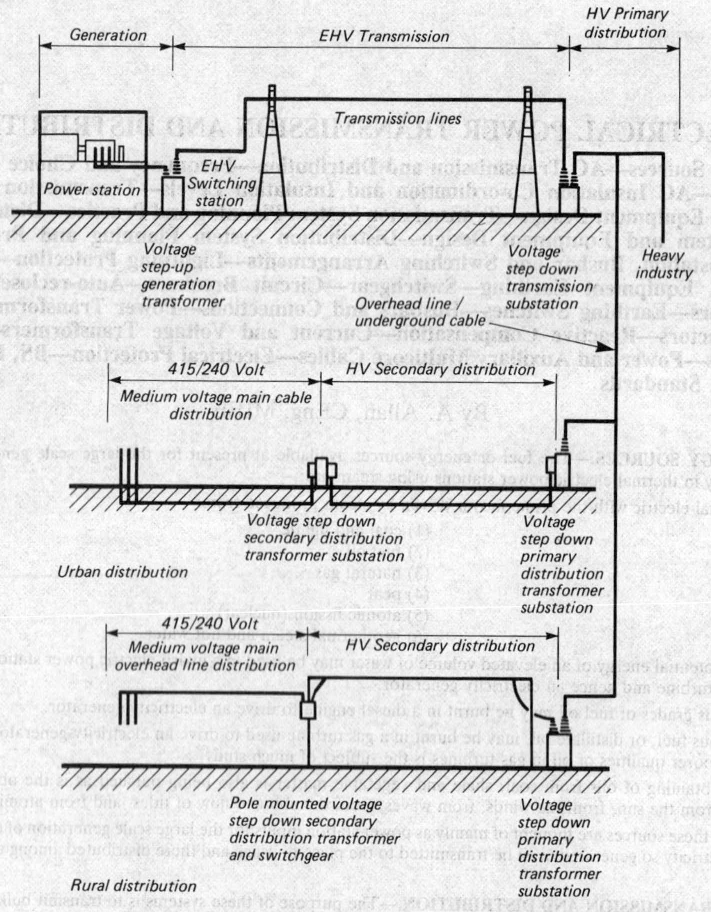

FIG. 1.—Typical AC Transmission and Urban and Rural Distribution Systems.

(1) The radial feeder type of system is shown in simple single line diagram form in Fig. 2. With this system the feeders (overhead lines or cables) and substations are connected in series and the lower voltage transmission or distribution systems are supplied from step-down power transformers connected to the substation busbars.

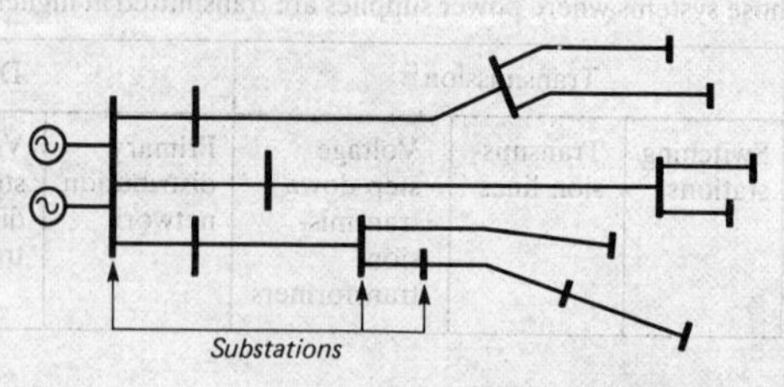

FIG. 2.—Radial System Network.

This is a simple, low cost system but is unsuitable where continuity of supply is essential. For example, where an overhead line is out of service due to a fault or for maintenance, this results in loss of supply to all substations and overhead lines beyond the out of service equipment. Duplicate feeders may however be used to supply important loads.

(2) The ring main (loop) system is illustrated in Fig. 3. With this system the feeders and substations are connected in a complete ring and again the lower voltage transmission or distribution systems are supplied from step-down transformers at appropriate points in the ring.

With this system any one feeder can be isolated from the system due to fault or for maintenance without loss of supply to any of the substations in the ring. This system provides greater security of supply than the radial feeder system, based on single circuit feeders, but is more expensive.

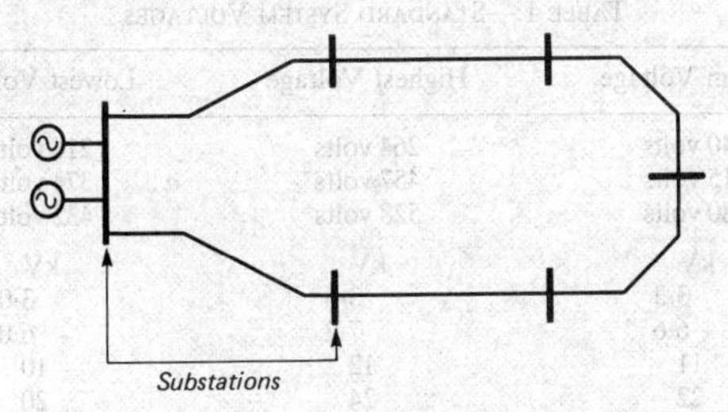

FIG. 3.—Ring Main System Network.

(3) A simple interconnected network system is shown in Fig. 4. In general the interconnected network system is much more extensive than either the radial or ring main system. In normal operation it may be sectionalised by opening circuit breakers at various points so as to divide the system into a number of separate networks. Under emergency or maintenance conditions or to improve voltage regulation under heavy load flow conditions, two or more separate parts of the network may be connected together by closing the appropriate circuit breakers.

An interconnected system properly designed and protected offers the greatest degree of security of supply and flexibility of operation but is invariably more expensive than the radial and ring main systems.

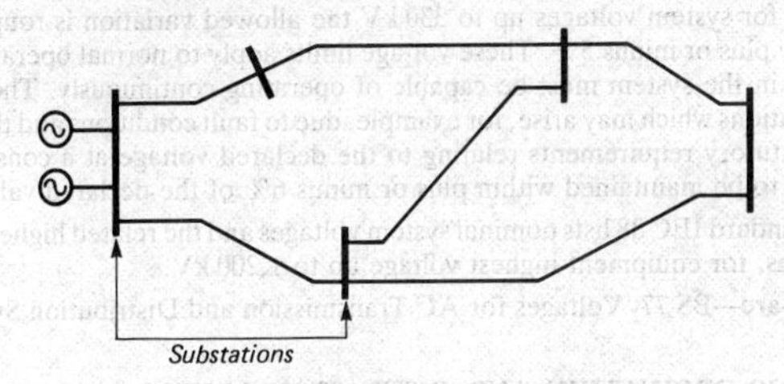

FIG. 4—Interconnected System Network.

FREQUENCY AND CHOICE OF VOLTAGE.—Most countries throughout the world which utilise electricity have adopted a standard supply frequency. This has been established in most countries at 50 Hz with some notable exceptions including North America where the standard is 60 Hz. The choice of transmission system voltage depends on both economic and technical considerations.

Economic considerations include:

(1) The initial capital cost of the necessary substation equipment including land acquisition and civil works costs and overhead line equipment including land and wayleave costs.

(2) Transmission operating costs including I^2R and constant energy losses.

(3) Present value of capital and operating costs of equipment to be provided at a future date to cater for future load growth.

Usually the known transmission distances and line lengths and initial and future power levels to be transmitted together with the voltage, normal and short circuit current ratings available for substation and transmission line equipment, will allow an approximate voltage level to be selected. The final choice based on detailed economic and technical studies can therefore usually be confined to three voltage levels spread one on either side of the initial approximate voltage level selected. The final choice will be based on the selection of suitable substation and line equipment capable of transmitting the initial and future load requirements in accordance with the established design criteria including operational flexibility and at the lowest overall average annual cost during the expected life of the system. The system should cater for any possible future developments with minimum of alteration and cost. The need to adopt a higher voltage for new or existing systems in order to achieve the required power transfer levels may be avoided by providing voltage regulation and power factor improvement in the form of reactive compensation equipment. The choice of voltage level based purely on economic/technical considerations may also on occasions be overriden by other factors such as existing transmission system voltage levels and/or the necessity to tie into these systems. These factors would in general apply to distribution systems voltage levels.

BS 77 lists the standard system voltages and the corresponding highest and lowest voltages as shown in Table 1.

TABLE 1.—STANDARD SYSTEM VOLTAGES.

System Voltage	Highest Voltage	Lowest Voltage
240 volts	264 volts	216 volts
415 volts	457 volts	374 volts
480 volts	528 volts	432 volts
kV	kV	kV
3·3	3·6	3·0
6·6	7·2	6·0
11	12	10
22	24	20
33	36	30
66	72·5	60
88	100	80
110	123	100
132	145	120
220	245	200
275	300	250
330	360	300
400	420	380

It will be noted that for system voltages up to 330 kV the allowed variation is roughly plus or minus 10% and at 400 kV is exactly plus or minus 5%. These voltage limits apply to normal operating conditions and with which equipment used in the system must be capable of operating continuously. The limits do not apply to temporary voltage variations which may arise, for example, due to fault conditions and the sudden disconnection of large loads or to statutory requirements relating to the declared voltage at a consumer's terminals which in Britain requires this to be maintained within plus or minus 6% of the declared value.

The International Standard IEC 38 lists nominal system voltages and the related highest voltage for equipmen for use on these systems, for equipment highest voltage up to 1,200 kV.

Reference standards are—BS 77 'Voltages for AC Transmission and Distribution Systems and IEC 38 'IEC Standard Voltages'.

AC INSULATION CO-ORDINATION AND INSULATION LEVELS.—Appropriate International and National Standards are—IEC 71 'Insulation Co-ordination', Part 1 'Terms, Definitions, Principles and Rules' (6th edn); Part 2 'Application Guide' (2nd edn); and the equivalent BS 5622 Parts 1 and 2. These standards apply to equipment for three-phase ac systems and in general cover only phase to earth insulation.

The equipment insulation must satisfactorily withstand continuous operation at the system highest voltage and externally and internally produced overvoltages. Depending on the system the increased insulation levels required to withstand all overvoltage conditions may not be economic, particularly in the case of the expensive insulation systems associated with power transformers and reactors which in themselves amplify at their terminals any incoming overvoltages. In these cases it may be more economic to provide overvoltage protective devices for example, surge diverters (lightning arresters) mounted close to the equipment and avoid the increased cost of insulation whilst retaining an acceptable level of reliability of service.

The equipment insulation level must be greater than the break-down voltage of the protective device which in turn must not have too low a break-down level causing excessive repeated operation. Corelation or co-ordination of the equipment and protective device insulation levels involves the economic and technical selection of appropriate insulation and protective device characteristics. IEC 71 gives a full statement on ne basic principles of insulation co-ordination as follows:

'Insulation co-ordination comprises the selection of the electric strength of equipment and its app ca-tion, in relation to the voltages which can appear on the system for which the equipment is intended and taking into account the characteristics of available protective devices, so as to reduce to an economically and operationally acceptable level the probability that the resulting voltage stresses imposed on the equipment will cause damage to equipment insulation or affect continuity of service.'

Voltage and Stresses on Insulation Dielectrics.—The dielectric stresses which may be imposed on the equipment insulation during service are:

(1) Power frequency voltages during normal operation which will not exceed the highest voltage rating for the equipment.
(2) Temporary overvoltages
(3) Switching overvoltages
(4) Lightning overvoltages.

(1), (2), and (3) are overvoltages produced internally in the system and (4), overvoltages of atmospheric origin, produced externally to the system.

Temporary Overvoltages usually originate from:

(1) System switching operations or faults which produce sudden changes in load such as load rejection.
(2) Earth faults on one phase of a connected three-phase system which is not solidly earthed give rise to an appreciable overvoltage at power frequency on the sound phases, the value of which will depend upon the method of system neutral earthing adopted, ie earthed through a resistance or high impedance or resonant earthed through an arc-suppression coil (Petersen coil) or with the neutral completely isolated from earth (except through indicating, measuring and protective devices of very high impedance).
    In addition to the method of earthing of the system where, for example, the highest increase in voltage on the sound phases with a phase to earth fault would occur on a fully insulated neutral system where the phase to earth voltage on the sound phases would be increased to line voltage, ie 1·7321 times the normal phase to earth voltage, much greater and particularly high overvoltages may occur with earth faults on an isolated neutral system due to arcing earth faults where persistent restriking of the arc may set up dangerously high voltage surges.
    Also with arc-suppression coil neutral earthed systems much higher overvoltages than those determined solely by the method of earthing may occur when the circuit is under-compensated.
(3) Temporary overvoltages due to resonance. FERRO-RESONANCE and harmonic oscillations may occur when energising or as a result of sudden changes of load in systems comprising lines, cables and series capacitors (with relatively large values of capacitance) and inductive equipment such as transformers and shunt reactors having non-linear magnetising characteristics. A typical example of ferro-resonance is that which can occur when switching in a wound type voltage transformer with an iron-cored inductive secondary load.

Switching overvoltages usually occur as a result of:

(1) Energising and re-energising lines
(2) Clearance of system faults
(3) Switching of capacitive and inductive circuits
(4) Load rejection
(5) Operation of high voltage fuses.

These overvoltages are dependent on the characteristics of the equipment including the circuit breakers, transformers and shunt reactors and may usually be reduced by the use of circuit breaker closing and/or opening resistors and protected against by the application of surge arrestors or rod gaps as close as possible to the terminals of the equipment to be protected.

Lightning Overvoltages are caused either by direct lightning strokes to overhead line phase conductors, strokes to overhead line towers or earth wires resulting in back flashovers or induced lightning surges resulting from strokes to earth in the close vicinity of the line.

IEC 71 specifies the short duration performance (1 min) power frequency dielectric test as a check on the equipment performance under power-frequency operating voltage, temporary overvoltages and switching overvoltages and a lightning impulse test as a check on lightning performance for equipment with voltage ratings above 1 kV and less than 300 kV. For equipment rated at 300 kV and above lightning and switching overvoltage performance of the insulation is checked by lightning impulse and switching surge tests.

Checking of pollution of external insulation in air and ageing of internal insulation generally requires long duration power frequency tests.

The standard lightning impulse test wave form is specified as having a front time of 1·2 μs and a time-to-half value of 50 μs, ie 1·2/50 wave.

The standard switching surge test wave form is specified as having a time-to-crest of 250 μs and a time-to-half value of 2,500 μs, ie 250/2,500 wave. IEC 71 tabulates standard insulation levels for various voltage ranges of equipment and is based on the proposition that for equipment having a highest voltage range up to 245 kV lightning overvoltages should have first consideration in the selection of insulation levels and that for equipment highest voltage in the range 300 kV and above, switching overvoltages become predominant in the selection of insulation level. For equipment with a highest voltage rating of 123 kV and above more than one insulation level is given. Guidance on the selection of appropriate insulation levels of equipment and of surge arrestors or protective spark gaps and the usefulness of controlling overvoltages with a view to obtaining rational and economic solutions are given in the second edition of the Application Guide (IEC 71-2).

The overvoltages to be expected on a system are influenced by the method of earthing the system neutral, system design and configuration, the characteristics of the equipment and operating practices and the type of line construction. They can usually be assessed from experience on existing systems supplemented if need be by switching tests and where technically and economically justified (usually for the higher voltages) from system studies.

The application guide also includes a section on natural pollution of external insulation and provisional indication of insulator creepage distances related to pollution levels.

Applicable IEC and BS Standards.—

IEC 71 'Insulation Co-ordination', Part 1 'Terms, Definitions, Principles and Rules (equivalent to BS 5622 Parts 1 and 2); Part 2 'Application Guide'.

IEC 60 'High Voltage Test Techniques', Parts 1 to 4 (equivalent to BS 925).

IEC 99 'Lightning Arrestors', Part 1 'Non-linear Resistor Type Arrestors for ac Systems (IEC 99-1 equivalent to BS 2914 'Surge Diverters for ac Systems'); Part 1A 'Application Guide'; Part 2 'Expulsion-type Lightning Arrestors'.

IEC282 'High Voltage Fuses, Part 1 'Current Limiting Fuses' (BS2692 'Fuses for Voltages Exceeding 1,000V ac'; Part 1 'Current Limiting Fuses; Part 2 'Expulsion Fuses').

IEC664 'Insulation Co-ordination Within Low Voltage Systems Including Clearances and Creepage Distances (up to 1,000V)'.

TRANSMISSION SYSTEM AND EQUIPMENT DESIGN, PLANNING AND PRACTICE

Transmission System and Equipment Design.—The essential feature of transmission system and equipment design is to determine the most advantageous selection both economically and technically of the transmission equipment (including overhead lines/power cables, transformers, switchgear and reactive compensation equipment) necessary to transmit the required amount of power within prescribed limits of voltage variation, frequency and power factor, with the required degree of reliability, operational flexibility, ease of maintenance and operation and future expansion all at the lowest overall average annual capital and operational costs taken over the expected life of the system.

Design factors to be considered and established to achieve this object include electrical, mechanical, electro-mechanical, structural and others, for example:

Electrical.—

(1) Load flows, maximum demand and energy pattern
(2) Type of supply system network
(3) Choice of system frequency, voltage, phasing and phase rotation
(4) Method of earthing the system neutral
(5) Choice and size of primary conductor material and for multi-conductor bundle arrangements, configuration
(6) Power factor, voltage and frequency regulation and control
(7) System losses, ie, line, transformer and reactive compensation losses
(8) Radio interference voltage (RIV) and corona levels involving voltage stress at surface of conductor or bundle conductor arrangement
(9) System steady state performance
(10) System steady state and transient stability
(10a) Voltage fluctuations due to disturbing loads
(10b) Propogation of harmonics generated by loads
(11) Reliability analysis
(12) Short circuit fault levels
(13) Switching and substation arrangements
(14) Equipment ratings and duties
(15) Line transpositions
(16) Control, protection, alarm, indication and metering systems
(17) Insulation co-ordination and insulation levels, overvoltage protection and insulator creepage distances
(18) Phase-to-phase, phase-to-earth and safety air clearances under conductor maximum swing and sag conditions
(19) Substation and overhead line tower earthing and earth resistivity
(20) Overhead earth wires, shielding angles and lightning protection
(21) Induced voltages on other equipment and voltage stress and electric fields on operating personnel and the public
(22) System operating rules and procedures. Commissioning and operational tests.

Mechanical.—

(1) Conductor swing, sag and stress. Maximum sag will normally occur with maximum current and ambient temperature.
Maximum swing will usually occur under maximum sag, wind and short circuit conditions and maximum stress normally with minimum ambient temperature and maximum wind, ice and short circuit loads.
(2) Ice (if applicable) and maximum wind loads. Light steady wind conditions may also give rise to mechanical resonance of tubular conductors depending on the span, method of support and physical characteristics of the tubular beam.

(3) Conductor or conductor bundle spacing. The electrical design will establish the minimum spacing required between conductors and fittings under maximum conductor swing and sag conditions.
(4) Mechanical strength of equipment including support insulation under maximum wind, ice and short circuit loads.
(5) Selection of suitable suspension, tension and post insulators to withstand (with a suitable factor of safety) the mechanical stress imposed under service, maintenance and access conditions.

Electro-mechanical.—

(1) Determination of maximum electro-mechanical loads under maximum short circuit conditions on all equipment, conductors and support insulation.

Structural.—

(1) Types of structure to be determined, eg open lattice or tubular, welded or bolted, steel or aluminium, reinforced concrete or wood construction.
(2) Mechanical stress and deflection calculations.
(3) Structure foundations including for overhead line structures guy ropes and fittings and anchor block foundations where applicable.

Other considerations.—

(1) Selection of suitable substation and control centre sites and land acquisition (to include for future development).
(2) Selection of suitable routes for overhead lines/cables (including river crossings) and acquisitions of right of way. Line and structure location and conductor profiling.
(3) Auxiliary supplies and ancillary equipment.
(4) Effect and visual impact on the landscape and existing amenities and environmental problems such as electric and magnetic fields, radio and telephone interference and audible noise.
(5) Study of ground conditions and slopes at the proposed substation sites and overhead line tower positions. The soil mechanics may show spread foundations, piles or pilotines to be necessary where ground conditions are poor.
(6) Determination and effect of altitude and climatic conditions including atmospheric pollution and siesmic (ie equipment resistance to earthquakes) considerations where appropriate throughout the entire system. These may vary particularly if the system is extensive.

Transmission System Planning and Practice.—Factors to be taken into account in transmission system planning include:

(1) Probable development of future load demand and power generation. Future load demand will usually be based on past load growth during earlier years and forecasts as to whether this load growth will continue at the same rate or increase or decrease. For the industrialised nations this in turn will in general, depend on the forecast rate of growth of the Gross National Product and the corresponding growth of energy requirements. Of the total future energy requirements, the proportion to be provided by electric energy will depend largely on the likely type and amount of energy required by, for example, future industry and on the future public and private domestic housing demand.
(2) The probable location and seasonal variation of future load growth.
(3) Possible difficulties in obtaining wayleaves for future lines and locations for future substations and power stations.
(4) Economic and technical assessment of the probable reliability performance of the system with the object of minimising the risk of interruption in supply consistent with reasonable cost. It is not economically viable nor is it technically possible to attempt to achieve 100% security of supply and reliability. Considerations are usually based on established practice and past experience, bearing in mind that as distinct from distribution, faults on the transmission system can result in loss of supply to complete areas and affect many consumers. Supply authorities normally compile failure statistics usually on a yearly basis for system faults on various transmission system components and arrangements such as overhead lines and cables, transformers, switchgear, busbars, reactive compensation equipment etc, for the purpose of assessing the reliability performance of their existing systems and this may be used as a basis and indication of reliability performance for extensions to the system and for new systems. The system design and selection of reliable equipment is also influenced by the necessity to have speedy restoration of supply following a fault.
(5) Inherent uncertainty in forecasting future load trends and growth make it desirable to plan as much flexibility as economically justified into the system to cater for possible changes in development trends.

System Design Studies.—Transmission networks are either radial, ring main, interconnected or a combination of these systems. Except for the simplest of systems and relatively short feeders the majority of calculations included in system design studies are now carried out by computer. For example, System Short Circuit Fault Current calculations in general involving balanced faults, ie symmetrical short circuits across all three phases and unbalanced faults, ie faults to earth or between two phases only.

For balanced faults on a radial system the calculation is simply based upon the impedance of the system up to the point at which the fault is assumed to occur. For a ring main system the balanced fault current resolves itself simply into the calculation of the two parallel impedances of the ring from the fault to the generating source. However, for an interconnected system the solution is more complex as it is frequently not possible to determine the total circuit impedance to the fault by the simple calculation of series and parallel impedances. It is possible to resolve these circuits by means of Kirchoff's laws but these calculations are cumbersome and rarely used. An alternative method, the star-delta transposition of network impedances allows the total fault current and branch currents throughout the network to be determined for all balanced fault conditions. This method basically involves the simplification and reduction of the network to a single equivalent reactance and by the replacement of delta-groups of impedances by equivalent star-groups or vice-versa.

For unbalanced faults the Method of Symmetrical Components or Co-ordinates may be used where any unbalanced three-phase system of vectors may be represented by three separate three-phase balanced systems, the standard vector rotation in Britain being taken as anti-clockwise.

The various established methods for the full analytical solution of network fault currents are given in various literature (see Bibliography).

For all but the simplest of networks or the solution of specific network conditions, the above methods of fault current calculation are time consuming and laborious and are not suited for network investigation or for exploring the effects of network extensions. For this reason ac network analysers were developed. Fundamentally, they are simply a miniature analogue model of the actual system in which the various items of plant are represented in the model by their corresponding impedances. In addition to short circuit calculations the ac network analyser may be used to solve other power system problems.

For complex networks all of the above methods previously used for power system analysis have largely been superseded or are extensively supplemented by digital computer programmes and calculations and in addition to system short circuit fault levels extensive use is made of the digital computer in other areas of system studies including:

(*a*) System load flow studies in order to establish and optimise the best ways of operating the initial system and planning for possible future extensions. This requires investigation of the steady state performance of the system for various generation and load conditions in the individual branches of the network. These load flow studies include confirmation that the system is stable, that no circuits (transmission lines or cables) are overloaded both under normal operation and with selected items and component parts of the system out of service, that all busbar voltages are within design limits and that the flow of reactive power throughout the system is acceptable.

(*b*) Steady State Stability studies of the system with the object of confirming that after a relatively small disturbance the system can regain and maintain synchronous speed. These types of disturbance result from all normal load fluctuations and include the action of the automatic voltage regulators and turbine governors.

(*c*) Transient Stability System studies to confirm that following a large sudden system distrubance the system can regain and maintain synchronous speed. Large sudden disturbances may be caused by faults and switching operations. For these studies the action of automatic voltage regulators and turbine governors are usually included.

Both steady state and transient stability limits may be improved by the use of reactive compensation equipment, generator high speed excitation control, high speed circuit breakers and protection systems and reducing the impedances of circuit connections between generators.

(*d*) Voltage Drop and for long lines Inherent Voltage Regulation studies to determine busbar voltage levels, load control and current distribution for both initial and future system design and various system operating conditions, under both normal and emergency conditons.

(*e*) The penetration of harmonic currents, sub-synchronous oscillations and voltage and current resonance effects for series and parallel connected capacitive and inductive reactance equipment etc.

Where possible it is prudent to carry out a factual check on all computer calculations by comparing the results with information available on disturbances and field tests on existing systems.

System Earthing, Frequency and Voltage Variation.—In three-phase star-connected high voltage systems the neutral point is earthed to (*a*) maintain the system at a definite safe voltage above earth and to comply with the requirements of insulation coordination, and (*b*) to enable earth faults to operate the protection and be automatically isolated by the appropriate circuit breakers.

For systems of 132 kV and above it is common practice to SOLIDLY EARTH the neutral point, ie to earth the neutral directly without the intentional insertion of impedance in the neutral earth connection. This has the advantage that under all conditions including fault the system is 'effectively earthed' (see System Earthing, page G2/12) and the voltage of all phase conductors is limited substantially to line-to-neutral voltage or to an acceptable level above this voltage. This results in economies in the cost of expensive high voltage insulation and in particular in the cost of equipment employing wound type insulation. The principal disadvantage of solid earthing is that the system is subjected to the short circuit current for every earth fault that occurs but at these high voltage levels the increased cost, if any, of providing for this condition, is outweighed by the savings in insulation costs.

In Britain solidly earthed transformer neutrals are adopted for the 132 kV, 275 kV and 400 kV systems. The standard frequency is 50 Hz and the Central Electricity Generating Board (CEGB) is responsible for the generation and transmission of electrical power to the consumer supply and purchase point, ie to the various Electricity Boards or large industrial consumers.

The transmission system is not subject to the same legal requirements that apply to the distribution system, ie that power should be supplied to the domestic consumer within ±6% of the declared rated voltage. The transmission voltage may vary typically by ±10%, the restriction being technical and not legal.

The distinction between transmission and distribution systems is not always clear cut and depends on function rather than voltage level. In Britain the 132 kV grid system used to be included in the CEGB transmission system but now in general this is classed as a sub transmission or high voltage primary distribution voltage and several large consumer distribution systems are being supplied direct at 132 kV from the CEGB higher voltage transmission system via step-down transformers.

DISTRIBUTION SYSTEM AND EQUIPMENT DESIGN, PLANNING AND PRACTICE

As indicated earlier the distinction between transmission and distribution is not always clear and depends on function rather than voltage level. In Britain the CEGB's function may be classed as the manufacturer and wholesaler transmitting and selling electric power to the Area Boards as the retailer who in turn distributes and sells power at the required voltage to the individual consumers. In the case of the very large consumer the CEGB may sell direct to the consumer who in turn would distribute and transform the supplies as required to the various items of plant within his industrial complex or factory.

The majority of the subjects referred to in the transmission system section also require consideration with respect to distribution systems and their equipment. Exceptions are that in general system stability problems are confined to transmission systems involving the transfer of large bulk power supplies over relatively long distances and for example, voltage stresses on equipment and personnel and switching surges only become significant at the higher voltage levels.

Apart from the design and planning considerations which are substantially common to both transmission and distribution systems the following factors apply mainly to distribution networks.

Distribution System and Equipment Design.—Typical voltage levels for distribution systems in Britain are a 415 V three-phase, 240 V single-phase, medium voltage main for domestic consumer supplies fed from a secondary distribution step-down transformer connected to a high voltage main usually at 6·6 kV or 11 kV and forming the Area Board's secondary distribution system. This in turn is fed from the Board's primary distribution system at 33 kV, 66 kV or 132 kV via primary distribution step-down transformers, the primary distribution networks being connected to and supplied from the CEGB transmission bulk supply points. There are many variations of this typical example, particularly so where supplies to large consumers are involved. The requirements of electricity distribution in industry vary to suit the requirements of the factory works concerned with the result that in general no two installations are the same.

In Britain the majority of the supply industry's customers are domestic consumers the supplies for which are covered by Statute Law which requires that the supply voltage and frequency be within defined limits: generally 240 V ±6% and 50 Hz ±1% for the domestic consumer. The statutory requirements for voltage do not apply to the transmission system where limits are generally determined on purely technical/economic grounds rather than legal. The domestic consumer is usually supplied from a medium voltage 415/240 V overhead line or underground cable main via a consumer service line fused at the intake point to provide protection against excess current and voltage. The individual domestic consumer may typically have a service line capacity of 60 A or 100 A and the connected individual load may well approach this higher value if, for example, electric heating is installed. However, it is unlikely (though not impossible) that all electric equipment will be connected and in use at the same time and the demand on the system can be expected to be be less than the total load possible if all equipment was in use. Similarly, the total load demand required by a number of domestic consumers can be expected to be less than the sum of the individual demands due to their varying requirements at any one time, ie there is diversity of load requirements between them resulting in an after-diversity maximum demand (admd) which is less than the theoretical maximum demand possible. This enables each phase of a distribution main rated at 300–400 A to satisfactorily supply more than three or four consumers. There is further diversity between different classes of users, the load requirements for industrial, commercial and domestic load in general differing in type and occurring at varying times of day and night. Diversity factors reflect throughout the power supply system right back to the generation source and accurate assessment of these at the various levels is essential in order to achieve a technically acceptable and economic system design.

The tapered-radial-main medium-voltage system is adopted over most of Britain as standard. With this system several single-phase domestic service connections may be connected to a small section medium voltage (415/240 V) main. This main will increase in cross sectional area towards the supply distribution transformer and this larger section main may have further small section mains jointed to it, ie the radial main feeders will increase in section with increase in load towards the supply transformer where they will usually be protected by suitable fuses. The layout, cross sectional area and conductor material of the mains are selected to give a voltage drop at full load, not exceeding 5% to the furthest consumer with an additional voltage drop not exceeding 2% in the consumer service connection, ie a maximum overall voltage drop of 7%. Distribution transformers usually have a standard secondary voltage of 433 V/250 V so as to ensure that the consumer single phase supply voltage remains within the declared voltage limit of 240 ± 6% under both full load and no load conditions. Where mains distribution is to be by cable it is usual to include for any expected future load as cable replacement can be expensive, whereas modification of overhead distribution is usually less expensive to modify if required, to cater for future load growth. Similarly, the transformer can be rated to suit little more than the initial and immediate future firm load requirement as it is usually relatively simple to replace this transformer at a future date if required.

It is now common practice to provide automatic on-load tap-changing gear controlled by an automatic voltage control relay for transformers at bulk supply points and primary distribution substations. This is arranged to maintain the transformer secondary voltage typically within ±2% of the nominal no-load voltage for all load conditions. Additionally, line-drop compensation equipment (LDC) may be provided at these locations to vary the transformer secondary voltage in proportion to the transformer load and to offset voltage drop by means of the tap-change equipment. It is not usual to provide LDC equipment for urban networks but it is an important method of voltage control on rural networks.

Master/Follower Control may be provided for transformers operating in parallel and where circulating current resulting from a single tap discrepancy is not a problem, the scheme may allow the transformers to be out of step by not more than one tap so as to reduce the total number of tap-change operations. Similarly, to reduce the number of operations due to small voltage fluctuations on transformers operating singly or in parallel, it may be acceptable to arrange that tap-change does not take place until the control indicates a change of more than one tap to be necessary.

Secondary distribution transformers have a standard secondary single phase no-load voltage of 250 V, ie an increase of 4·17% on the declared voltage of 240 V and are provided with off-load taps on the primary side which allow variation of the secondary voltage by ±2½% and ±5%.

These various arrangements are adopted to provide satisfactory voltage regulation of the distribution network.

Figure 5 illustrates in single line form, a typical primary and secondary distribution network with maximum permitted volt drops and typical tap-change arrangements for compensating voltage drop.

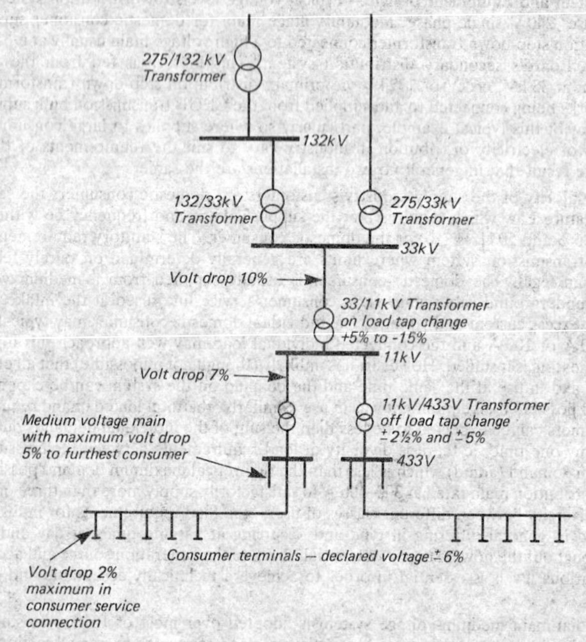

Fig. 5.—Typical Primary and Secondary Distribution Network Volt Drops and Tap Change Arrangements.

To facilitate maintenance of distribution transformers, interconnection of adjacent medium voltage networks should be provided where possible (usually for urban networks) so that approximately one-third of the load in either network can be provided from the other. This allows a distribution transformer to be switched out for maintenance during light load periods and may also provide some measure of support during a fault on either network.

Rural distribution networks are likely to have a wide range of power requirements varying from a few kilowatts for remote and widely dispersed cottages, farms and the like to a few hundred or thousand kilowatts for villages and small townships. Additionally, isolated industrial developments may require to be supplied in some rural areas. Small drift-mining operations, quarries, small open-cast coal sites and the lighter industrial estates can often be supplied by a relatively inexpensive connection to an existing high voltage rural distribution network. The larger power supplies required for deep mining or the more extensive open-cast mining operations and the larger heavy industrial estate are normally beyond the capacity of the distribution network and separate high power supplies at a higher voltage have usually to be provided. Typically, the electrical loading in a sample rural area of approximately 2,000 km^2 showed that 78% of the total area had a loading density of 0–25 kW/km^2 and 91% had a loading range of 0–100 kW/km^2. This compares with typical loading densities of 6,000 kW/km^2 for urban areas and much higher densities for cities of say 100,000 kW/km^2. Urban industrial estates may have values in the order of 10,000 kW/km^2 and industrial and commercial premises 161·5 kW/km^2 (15 W/ft^2). A typical rural distribution network is shown in Fig. 6.

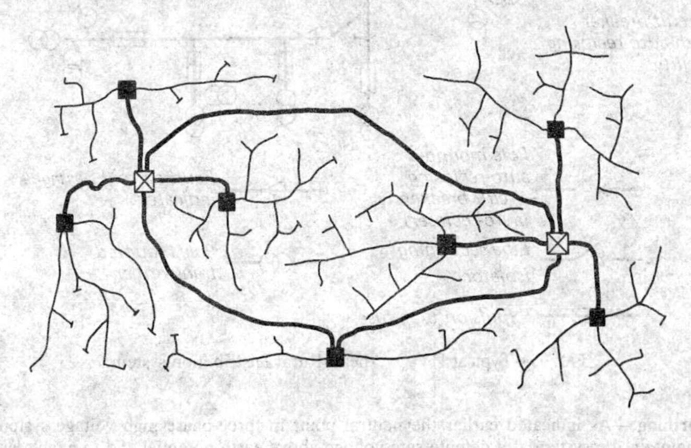

FIG. 6—Typical Rural Overhead Line Distribution Network.

In Britain distribution system development is seldom completely new and in the vast majority of cases consists of extensions and reinforcements to existing rural and urban networks, in which the voltage levels and distribution layout and practice are already established.

High voltage rural secondary distribution in Britain is commonly carried out at 11 kV with 33 kV as the primary distribution voltage with some 20 kV secondary and 66 kV primary distribution in certain parts of the country. A single wood pole with unearthed metal cross arms supporting porcelain or toughened glass insulators with insulated stay wires are mainly used for secondary distribution overhead line construction. Where pole mounted switchgear or transformers are supported on the metal cross-arms these are earthed and dual wood pole construction may be used at these locations to support the larger items of equipment.

Automatic voltage control of on-load tap-change equipment is provided for the primary supply source ground mounted transformers (typically 33 kV/11 kV) usually with line drop compensation compounding with off-load tapping arrangements for pole-mounted 250 V distribution transformers within general a volt drop of 7% in the 11 kV network and a further 7% in the supply to the consumer being permitted, ie except for LDC the voltage control arrangements are similar for both urban and rural networks. A typical overhead line rural distribution system is shown in Fig. 7.

Again both urban and rural distribution networks as for transmission are either radial, ring-main, inter-connected or a combination of these, various inter-connected arrangements being provided particularly in the more densely loaded areas such as cities where the MV networks can be readily more closely interconnected. Various MV and HV switching arrangements are also employed to provide firm supplies where economically and technically justified so that a fault or maintenance on one part of the system can occur without loss of supplies.

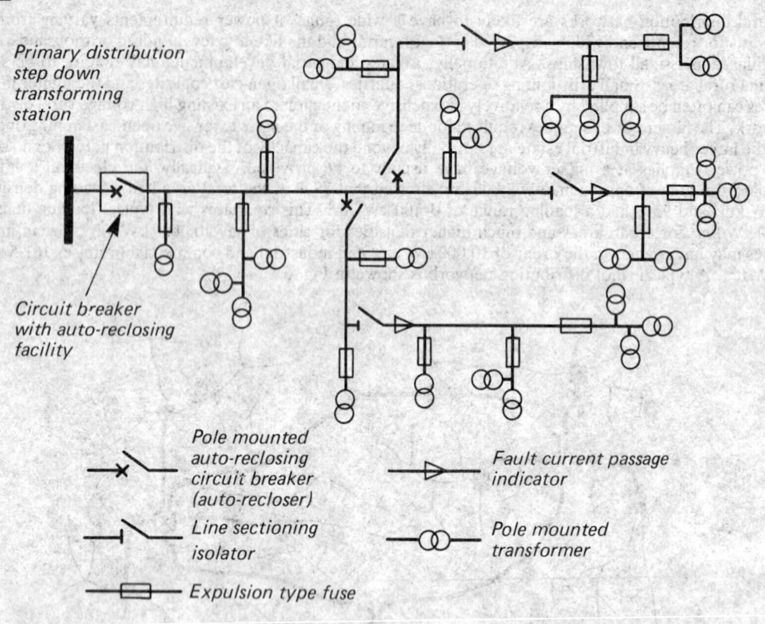

FIG. 7.—Typical HV Overhead Rural Distribution system.

System Earthing.—As indicated earlier the neutral point in three-phase high voltage systems is usually earthed to maintain the system at a definite safe voltage above earth potential and to enable earth faults to be automatically isolated.

There are three main methods of earthing the neutral, viz:

(*a*) solid earthing
(*b*) resistance earthing
(*c*) arc-suppression (Petersen) coil earthing.

In Britain solid earthing is provided for the 132 kV and higher voltage systems and (*b*) or (*c*) usually for the lower voltage systems to limit the earth fault current. If the system is either solidly earthed or earthed through a resistor or reactor of low impedance and the maximum voltage to earth on the sound phases during an earth fault on one phase does not exceed 80% of the line voltage the system is said to be effectively earthed, whereas systems in which the voltage can exceed this value are said to be non-effectively earthed. An effectively earthed system generally requires solid earthing of all transformer neutrals.

With Resistance Earthing the transformer neutral is earthed through a metallic grid or liquid resistance. The resistance is usually rated to pass the full load current of the transformer, which subjects the healthy part of the system to about 70% voltage increase during a single phase earth fault, but only for a short time and during which the fault current is restricted to a reasonable value.

Figure 8 illustrates diagrammatically the Arc-Suppression Coil method of earthing. An earth fault on one phase results in two currents in the fault consisting of I_L between line and neutral, lagging the line-to-neutral voltage by almost 90 degrees and a resulting capacity current Ic from the two sound phases (equal to three times the normal line-to-earth capacity current) leading the line-to-neutral voltage by 90 degrees. These currents are in the same direction through the fault and their resultant current is small and by adjusting the neutral reactance via the arc-suppression coil so that it resonates with the system capacitance, the resultant fault current becomes almost zero. If the fault is a flashover in air and does not involve failure of insulation (which would occur in the case of cable insulation) the system would probably return to normal as soon as the fault arc in air is extinguished. On overhead line networks where a large proportion of faults are in air and transient this is a very important advantage resulting in restoration of normal supply without circuit breaker operation. If however, the fault causes permanent damage to insulation and the fault-arc is extinguished, the system does not become normal again as one phase is permanently earthed. It would therefore be necessary to design the line-to-earth insulation for continuous operation at some 70% overvoltage. The preferred arrangement, however, is to short circuit the coil if the fault persists for more than say 5 seconds thereby allowing full earth fault current to flow and clearance of the fault by the appropriate device. Alternatively,

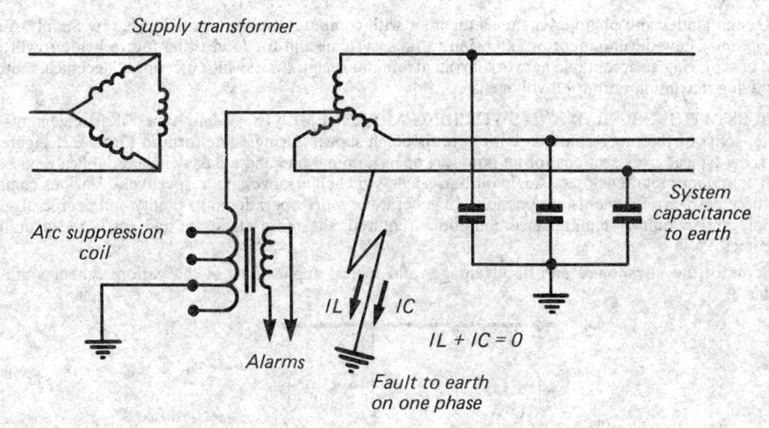

FIG. 8.—Arc-suppression (Petersen) Coil Method of Earthing System Neutral.

under certain conditions the system may be operated for limited periods with a fault on one phase until it is convenient to disconnect the circuit. This method is particularly suited to overhead line distribution in low density rural areas where for reasons of cost radial feeder systems are used.

Normally the system neutral is earthed via the starter point of a star-connected system. However, the lower voltage windings of some transformers are frequently delta-connected and an artificial neutral must be created, commonly by the use of an earthing transformer the star point of which is usually earthed through a neutral earthing resistor.

Distribution System Planning and Practice.—As for transmission systems accurate forecasting of future loads is an essential factor in distribution system planning, over-estimates lead to over-expenditure on non-revenue earning capital, under-estimates and under-investment may lead to reduced standards of security of supply and require premature reinforcement.

Past trends can be a useful aid to future load forecasting, for example, short term load forecasts may be based on load growth trends over the previous 5 year period whereas long term forecasts may take into account the load trend over the previous 10 year period.

In addition to load growth trends, load forecasting will take into account known firm load requirements but where these are not available electrical loading densities for typical rural and urban areas, industrial estates and premises may be used as a basis for planning purposes.

Table 2 indicates various standards of supply security related to supply demand which may be adopted by the Supply Authorities where the nature and size of the load does not warrant the provision of firm supplies.

TABLE 2.—SUPPLY SECURITY STANDARDS.

Range of Group Demand (MW)	Target Time for Restoration of Supply	Notes
0 to 1*	No maximum target time	Restoration after repair of single circuit. No alternative supply required.
1 to 8	2 hours	Restoration by switching alternative by direct or supervisory control from normally *unattended* control points.
8 to 24	15 minutes	Restoration by switching alternative by direct or supervisory control from *attended* control points.
24 to 80		If it is necessary to operate the lower voltage busbars in two sections, due to fault levels, restoration of supply should not exceed 30 secs after the loss of one transformer.

* Where the demand is supplied by a single 1,000 kVA transformer the ‘Range of Demand’ may be extended to cover the overload capacity of that transformer.

Design guides and planning manuals together with computer programmes are used by Supply Authorities to optimise new development or extension to their systems and for forecasting future load growth, with the aim of achieving an acceptable network layout at minimum capital cost whilst meeting all technical requirements including maximum permitted voltage drop.

SUBSTATION, BUSBAR AND SWITCHING ARRANGEMENTS.—Many types of arrangements are possible, some of the more common basic layouts being shown in single line form in Figs 9–22. Figures 23 and 24 show typical cross sections for an outdoor, open terminal one and a half switched duplicate busbar layout and an indoor metal-enclosed, single busbar, single switched arrangement respectively. Various combinations of these basic arrangements are possible. In general the more operational flexibility and degree of security of supply under fault or maintenance conditions required, the more elaborate and costly the overall scheme becomes.

Some of the advantages and disadvantages and typical applications of the various schemes are given in Table 3.

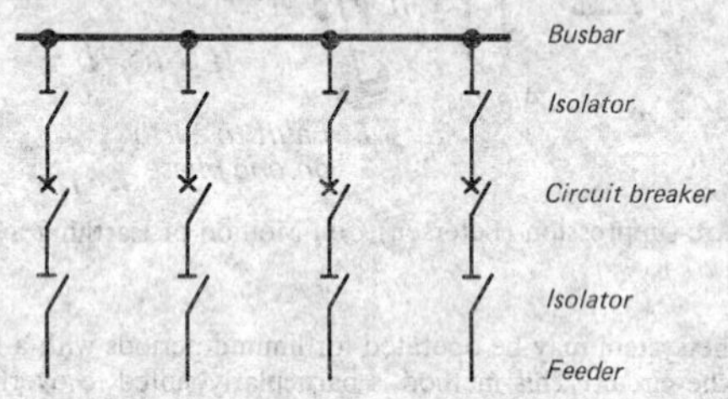

FIG. 9.—Single Busbar.

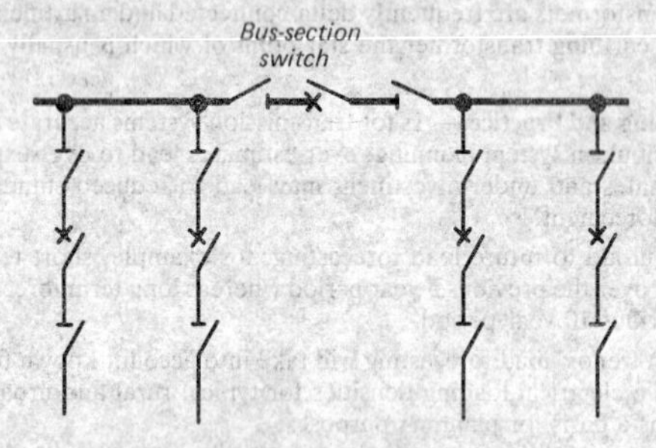

FIG. 10.—Single Busbar Sectionalised.

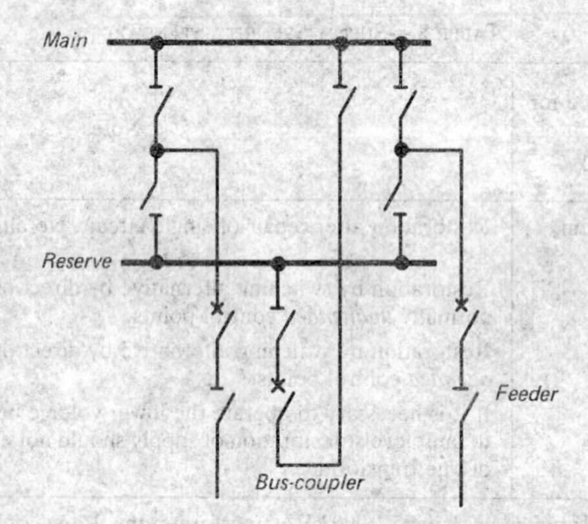

FIG. 11.—Duplicate Busbar and One Bus-Coupler.

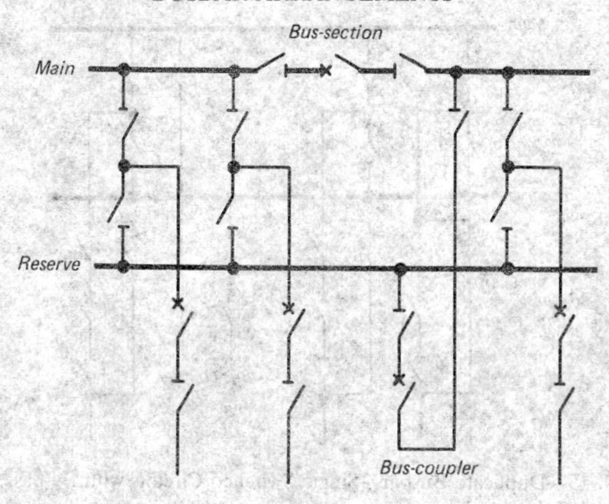

FIG. 12.—Duplicate Busbar-Main Busbar Sectionalised and One Bus-Coupler.

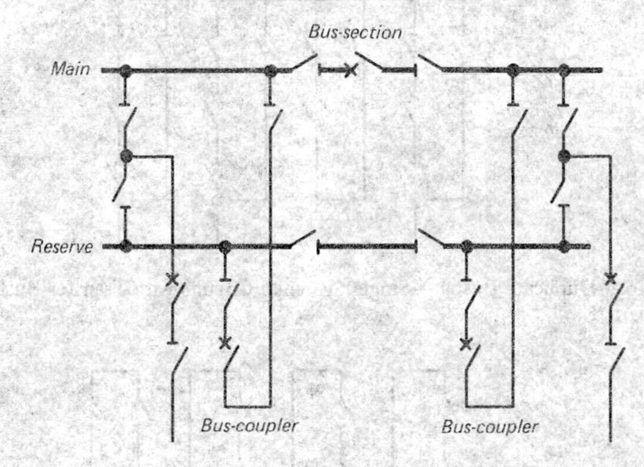

FIG. 13.—Duplicate Busbar—Main Busbar Sectionalised and One Bus-coupler on Each Section.

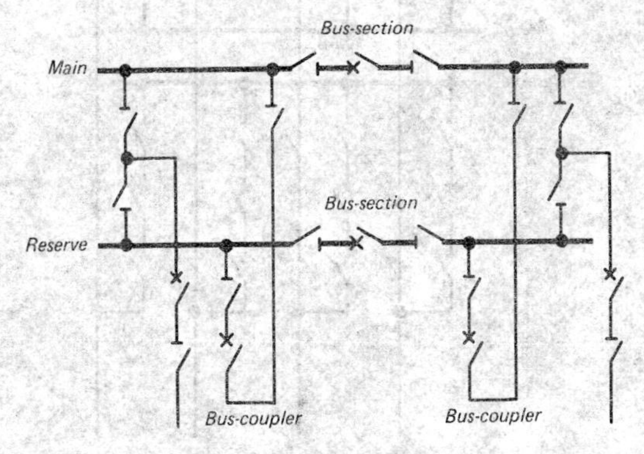

FIG. 14—Duplicate Busbar—both Busbars Sectionalised and One Bus-Coupler on Each Section.

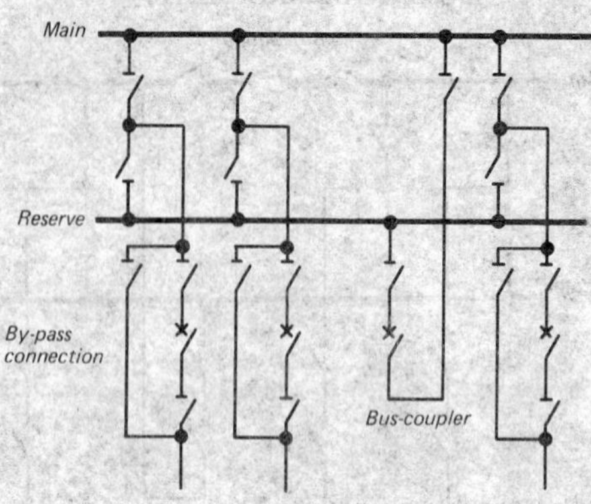

FIG. 15—Duplicate Busbar—Single Switched Circuits with By-pass.

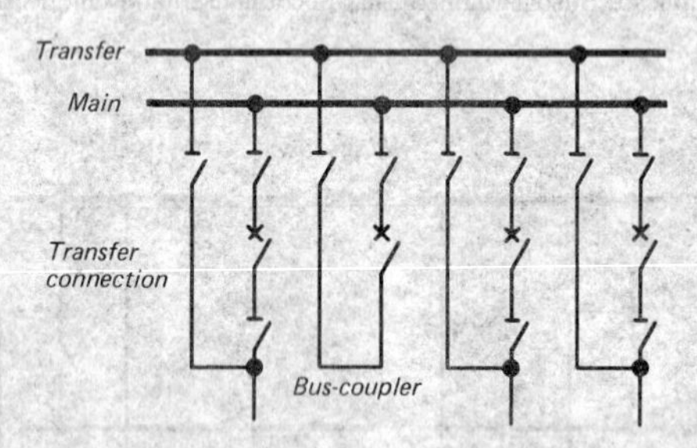

FIG. 16.—Duplicate Busbar—Single Switched Circuits with Transfer Busbar.

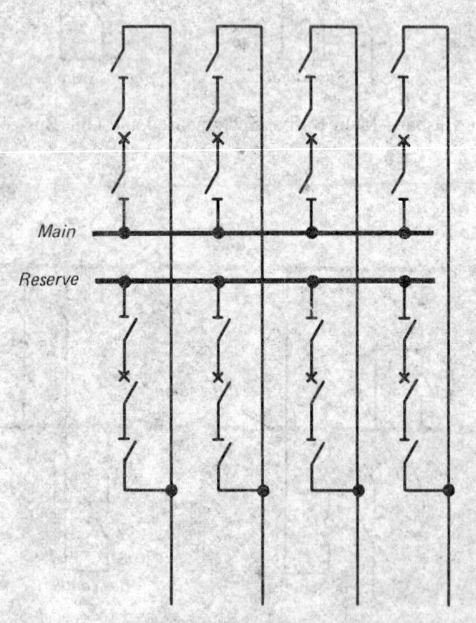

FIG. 17.—Duplicate Busbar—Double Switched Circuits.

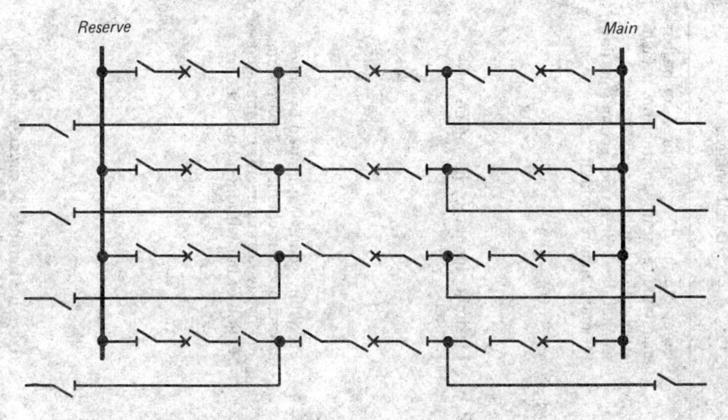

FIG. 18.—Duplicate Busbar 1½ Circuit Breaker.

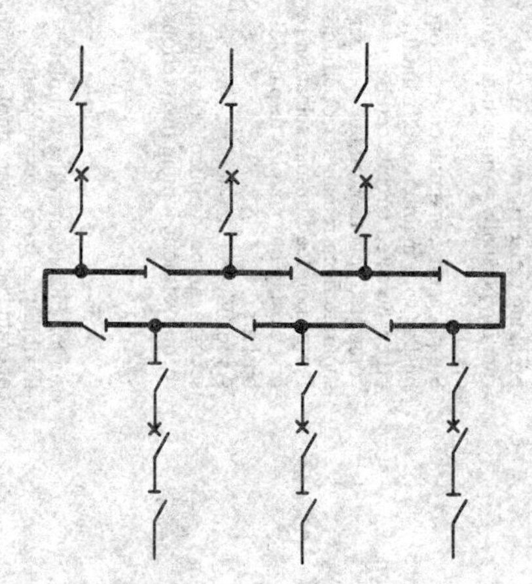

FIG. 19.—Ring Busbar.

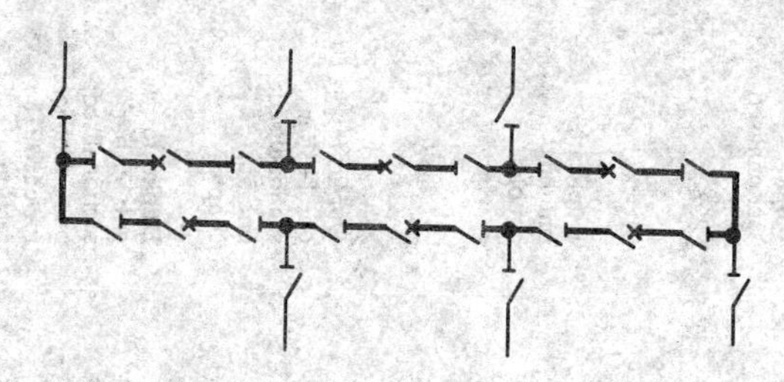

FIG. 20.—Mesh Busbar.

TABLE 3.—BUSBAR AND SWITCHING ARRANGEMENTS.

Fig. No.	Busbar Arrangement	Typical Application	Advantages	Disadvantages
9	Single	Minor substations	Simple: requires minimum number of circuit breakers.	Complete shutdown required for busbar maintenance, testing, extension or fault. Application limited.
10	Single sectionalised	Substations	Simple: greater flexibility than Fig. 9, especially if there are duplicate supplies, one to each section of busbar. Circuit breakers of lower breaking capacity may be used by running normally with section switch open.	Limited flexibility: one section shut down for maintenance or fault.
11	Duplicate: one bus coupler	More important substations	Supply can be maintained from one busbar with maintenance or fault on other. Selected circuits can be connected together on one bus bar separate from remainder of circuits. Permits on load busbar selection by first closing bus coupler to parallel busbars.	Flexibility limited by having no bus-section.
12	Duplicate: one busbar sectionalised: one bus-coupler	Major substations	As for Fig. 11, feeders on one section can be supplied from another section without joining the sections.	Flexibility somewhat limited by only having one bus-coupler. Synchronising and bypass arrangements complicated on section of bar without a bus-coupler.
13	Duplicate: one busbar sectionalised: bus-coupler for each section	Major important substations	As for Fig. 12 provides complete flexibility as each section can be operated as a separate duplicate busbar system. Essential for full flexibility with on-load busbar selection schemes.	
14	Duplicate both busbars sectionalised: bus-coupler for each section	Major important and special substations	As for Fig. 13. Circuits can be distributed between 4 sections of busbar, each operating as a main busbar. This allows duplicate circuits to be physically located adjacent to one another.	Excessive number of circuit breakers: usually unnecessary unless required to meet unusual circumstances.

15	Duplicate: single switched circuits with bypass	Substations provided with bus-coupler(s)	Allows supply to circuit to be maintained via bus-coupler with circuit breaker out of service for maintenance or fault.	
16	Duplicate: single switched circuits: transfer bus	Substations provided with bus-coupler	As for Fig. 15 with savings in isolators and connections.	Less flexible than Fig. 15 as circuit can only be connected to one (main) busbar through its own circuit breaker.
17	Duplicate: Double switched circuits	Major substations Special applications	Does not require a bus-coupler. Maximum operational and circuit breaker maintenance flexibility.	Excessive number of circuit breakers: only used for major stations and for special applications.
18	Duplicate: 1½ breaker switched circuits	Major substations	Does not require a bus-coupler. Approximately 25% fewer circuit breakers than Fig. 17. Flexibility approaching that provided by Fig. 17.	Busbar connected circuit breakers require increased normal current rating to cater for two circuits.
19	Ring	Limited application for distribution substations	Ease of busbar maintenance and can have flexibility approaching duplicate busbar schemes with economy in switchgear.	Busbar fault results in complete shut down.
20	Mesh	Major substations in large inter-connected networks	Circuit breaker can be maintained without interruption to any circuit. Saving in circuit breakers compared with equivalent duplicate bus scheme by elimination of bus-coupler.	A fault on a circuit trips two circuit breakers: more than one fault splits mesh into separate sections: all circuit breakers require increased normal current rating equivalent to maximum normal current in mesh.
21	Duplicate: single switched circuits with wrap-round U busbar	Major substations	Allows circuits to be arranged back-to-back and thereby reduces length of busbars and outdoor site or indoor switchhouse.	Increases width of outdoor site or indoor switch-house.
22	Any type: single switched transformer feeder circuit	Any type of substation	Economy in circuit breakers as one is used to switch both transformer and feeder	A fault on either transformer or feeder results in loss of both.

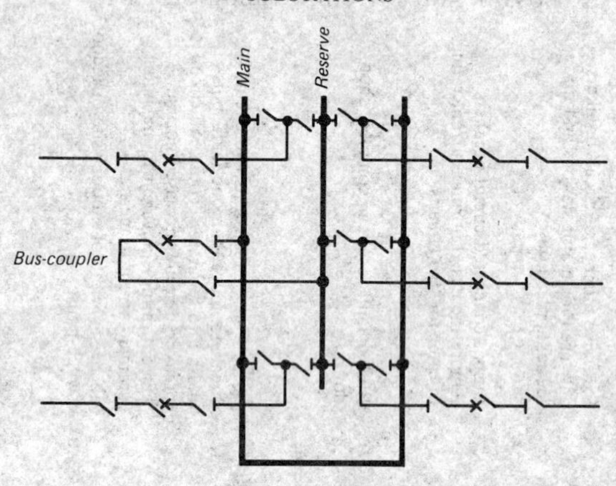

FIG. 21.—Duplicate Busbar—with Wrap-round Main Busbar.

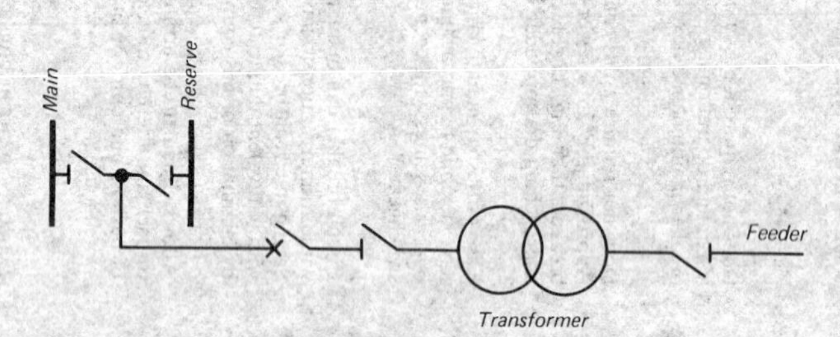

FIG. 22.—Single Switched Transformer Feeder Circuit.

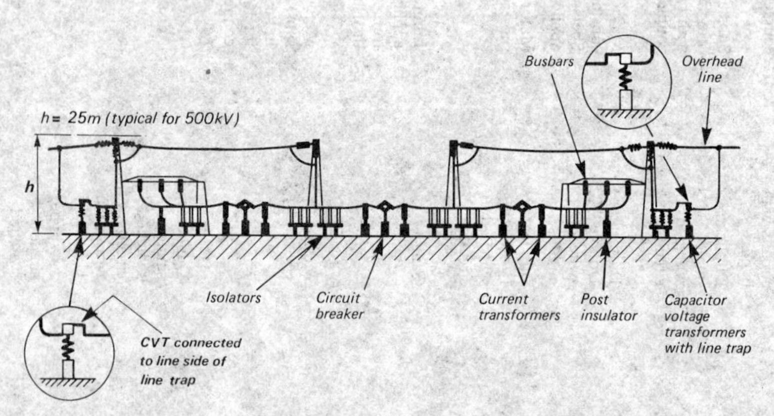

FIG. 23.—Typical Section Through Outdoor 1½ Switch Substation.

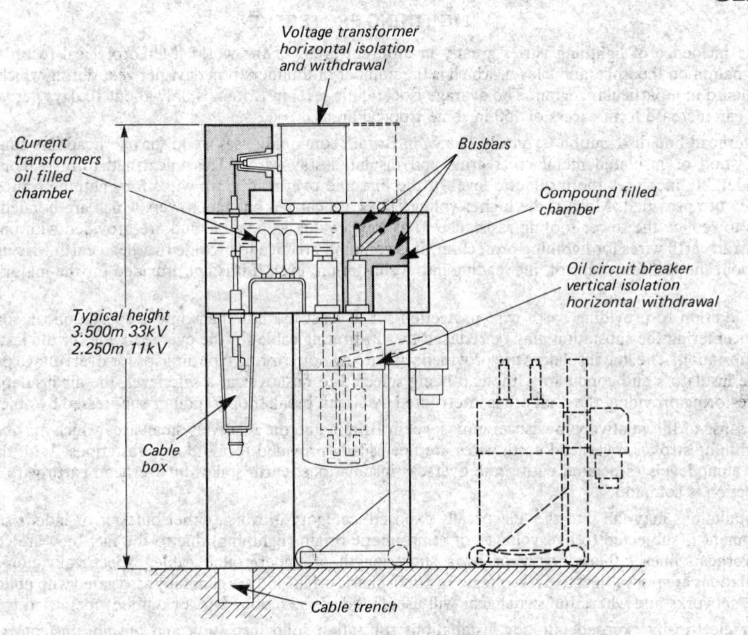

FIG. 24.—Typical Cross-section of Indoor Metal-clad Single Busbar Switchgear.

There are many other busbar arrangements, normally used outside Britain, including triplicate busbar schemes.

For distribution networks 'non-extensible' or 'extensible' ring main units may be used employing load-breaking, fault making switches, with or without high rupturing capacity (hrc) fuses so as to economise in the use of fully rated fault breaking circuit breakers, variations of which are shown in single line form in Fig. 25.

Either 'off-load' or 'on-load' methods of busbar selection are used for multi-busbar arrangements.

With sectionalised busbar schemes current limiting reactors may be connected in series between busbar sections when required in order to reduce the system fault level to an acceptable value.

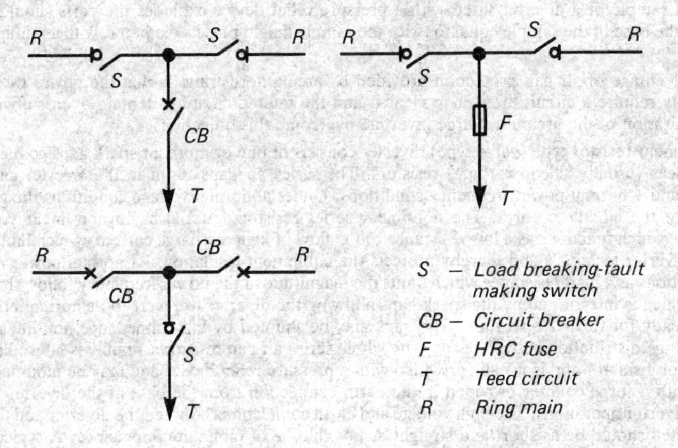

FIG. 25.—Typical Alternative Ring Main Unit Arrangements for Distribution Networks.

LIGHTNING PROTECTION

The incidence of lightning varies greatly in different areas of the world. Meteorological records provide information on the isoceraunic level, which is the number of thunderstorm days per year during which thunder was heard in a particular region. The average isoceraunic level in Britain is only about 10 days per year. This level can increase to in excess of 150 in some tropical areas.

Overhead line distribution (typically 11 kV) in Britain commonly uses wood for overhead line construction with wood or insulated metal cross arms and insulated stay wires. This unearthed form of construction considerably increases the insulation level of the line and overhead earth wires for lightning protection are usually not provided. Most of the higher voltage lines are carried on steel towers which are bonded to earth so as to reduce the tower footing resistance to as low a value as possible and are provided with one or two overhead earth wires for lightning protection. It is common practice to provide overhead earth wire protection on about the last few spans of line leading into a substation, even if it is not provided for the majority of the line.

In addition to providing earth wire protection for at least the last spans into a substation, in some cases surges entering the substation may be reduced by substituting cable for the overhead line for the last run into the substation. The line insulators are provided with arcing horn or ring type air gaps for overvoltage protection of the insulators and conductors, the gap being selected to flashover at a safe level, the air insulation being self-restoring providing the fault arc is interrupted by circuit breaker operation or suppressed by other means.

Because of the relatively low isoceraunic level in Britain and the relatively small area which may be subject to lightning strokes, overhead earth wires are not usually provided for outdoor substations. With the higher isoceraunic levels associated with some overseas installations, earth spikes or overhead earth wire lightning protection is common.

Installations may fall into the 'electrically exposed' category in which either outdoor or indoor substation equipment is subjected to overvoltages of atmospheric origin (lightning) due to the fact they are connected to overhead lines either directly or by a short length of underground cable. 'Electrically non-exposed' installations are not subject to overvoltages of atmospheric origin and are generally associated with underground cable networks and where the switchgear will usually be of the indoor type or outdoor metalclad type.

For electrically exposed outdoor installations substation solid insulation and bushing insulators may be protected by arcing horn or ring type air gaps.

Power transformers and reactors represent an appreciable change in surge impedance to incoming waves causing reflection of the waves and producing overvoltages at the equipment terminals. The more vulnerable wound transformer and reactor insulation may be protected by co-ordinating rod gaps mounted on or near the equipment, but in view of the cost of repair and outage time the extra expense of providing the improved protection afforded by means of surge diverters (lightning arresters) is usually considered warranted for this class of equipment.

Surge diverters may also be required at cable to overhead line junction points and in the neutral connection of star (Y) connected transformers where the neutral is isolated or earthed through a high impedance. BS 2914 Appendix C gives guidance on the application and selection of surge diverters for various basic applications.

The surge diverter should be located as close as possible to the equipment to be protected but vulnerable equipment such as insulation and particularly equipment which is expensive in both cost of dismantling and repair and outage time, such as transformer bushings, should be outside the explosion envelope of the diverter, ie if the test sample of a diverter fitted with a pressure relief device explodes the parts should fall within a diameter at the base of the sample equal to twice the sample height plus its diameter, with a minimum diameter of 1·8 m.

One disadvantage of air gap protection provided by arcing horns/rings is that the power frequency arc at flashover may require a circuit breaker to clear it and the faulted circuit to remain open sufficiently long to allow de-ionisation of the arc path. Surge diverters overcome this objection.

The non-linear resistor type (valve type) diverter consists of one or more air spark gaps connected in series with non-linear (usually silicon carbide) resistors. The series air gaps result in the arrester circuit to earth being open under normal power frequency conditions. Under abnormal voltage conditions the gaps flashover and complete the circuit to earth. The non-linear series resistor material has a non-linear voltage-current characteristic which functions as a low resistance to the flow of high discharge currents which limits the voltage across the diverter terminals and thereby protects the equipment insulation. At normal power frequency the resistor functions as a high resistance which limits the magnitude of the power frequency follow through current to a value which is interrupted by the spark gaps allowing the diverter to revert to its normal non-conducting condition, ready for further operation. The gaps may be shunted by high impedance non-linear resistors to improve voltage distribution between gaps. The whole series air gap resistor assembly is housed in an outdoor weather-proof insulator and is usually provided with a pressure relief device and may be mounted on nominal insulation with a surge counter provided in the earth connection from the base of the diverter to record the number of diverter operations. The high voltage and earth connections between the diverter and the equipment to be protected should be as short and straight as possible, ie of minimum impedance. A typical application for transformer protection is shown in Fig. 26.

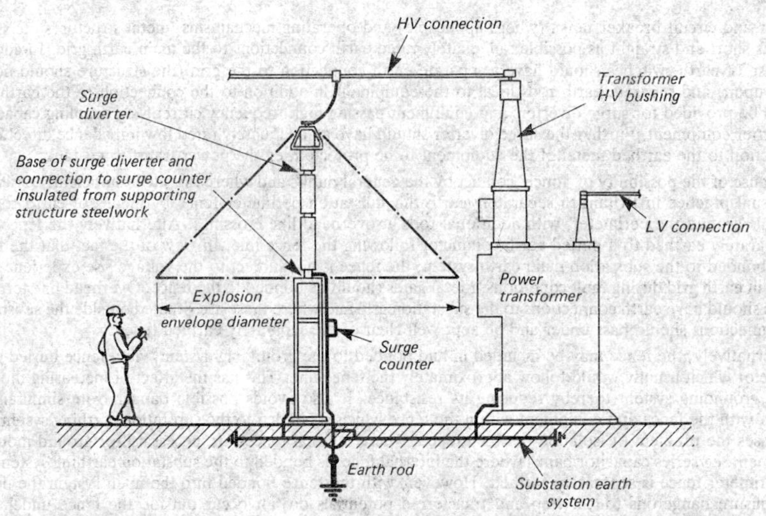

FIG. 26.—Typical Application of Surge Diverters for Overvoltage Protection of Power Transformer.

Solid state zinc oxide surge diverters are now also available which completely eliminate the series air gaps and parallel voltage grading components required for the valve type diverter. The very dense ceramic zinc oxide resistor material has superior non-linear characteristics and as these diverters are solid state devices they have a faster response during steep overvoltage conditions. They are appreciably smaller and lighter than the valve type.

Standards.—

BS 2914 'Surge Diverters for ac Systems' (equivalent to IEC 99-1).
BS 5622 'Guide for Insulation Co-ordination' (equivalent to IEC 71).
BS Code of Practice CP 326 'the protection of structures against lightning'.
CP 326C 'Map showing the annual number of thunderstorm days in England, Scotland and Wales'.

STATION AND EQUIPMENT EARTHING (TRANSMISSION AND DISTRIBUTION)

Electrical earthing should be provided for all transmission and distribution substations for the purpose of:

(*a*) earthing the system neutral so that the voltage on the system current carrying conductors is limited and consistent with the insulation levels adopted for the equipment.

(*b*) earthing all non-current carrying metalwork for the safety of personnel, animals and property.

Typically, for outdoor substations a fixed earthing system should be provided comprising a continuous ring of main copper earth bar around the site with interconnecting copper earth bar to form a grid and positioned as conveniently as possible to take the system and equipment earth connections. The earth bar should be buried horizontally direct in the ground. Where the soil characteristics are particularly hostile to copper; i.e. acidic (pH less than 6) or extremely alkaline (pH greater than 10) the grid should be surrounded by non-corrosive soil. If the soil is of reasonably good conductivity this system in itself can often provide an excellent grounding system particularly for the larger substations occupying an appreciable ground area. However, this network may be supplemented with earth electrodes, eg earth rods which can be of particular benefit where the upper layer of ground in which the grid is buried has a much higher resistivity than the deeper layers reached by the earth rods. They are also of value where the resistivity of the upper soil layer can become high due to drying out or freezing.

The resistance of the grounding system is largely influenced by the ground area enveloped by the grid and for this reason the overall area occupied by the grid should be kept as large as practicable. Danger to personnel within the substation may arise from '*touch potential*' that is hand-to-both-feet contact with earthed metal, 'step potential' that is foot-to-foot contact with the site surface and '*transferred potential*' contact which may be considered as a special case of 'touch' contact. These potential differences are of significance during short circuit fault conditions and their value will depend on the magnitude of fault current passing from the grid into the surrounding soil and thereby returning to the system neutral, the soil resistivity, the resistance of the grounding system and the extent of inter-connecting earth bar forming the grid (which will influence site surface voltage gradients within the substation). The safety of personnel will also be affected by other factors such as body and skin resistance, type of footwear, speed of fault clearing and resistance of site surfacing.

All non-current carrying metalwork including isolator and earth switch operating handles, transformer, reactor and circuit breaker tanks (where applicable) and operating mechanisms, metal structures etc should have as short and straight as possible, adequately rated earth connections to the main earth grid. In addition the base of earth switches should have a separate earth connection to the grid (the structure should not be relied upon) and separate earth rods local to the equipment in addition to the connection to the earth grid should be provided for surge diverters and equipment passing high frequency current, eg coupling capacitors for carrier equipment. Further the surge diverter should have an adequately rated low impedance direct earth connection to the earthed metal of the equipment to be protected, eg the power transformer tank.

Because of the possibility of 'touch' contact by the general public and where the site is sufficiently extensive it is usual practice in Britain to separately earth the substation perimeter fence by means of earth rods at intervals around the perimeter, with additional rods at overhead line crossings. Alternatively the fence may be separately earthed to a buried earth conductor following the fence line. In view of the fact that the fence is not bonded to the substation main earth system, the fence is not subject to the voltage rise experienced by the main earth grid during fault conditions. Metal gates should be bonded to the fence. Overhead line terminal towers should have earth connections to the substation grid and where these are situated outside the substation the connections should pass under and be kept well clear of the separately earthed fence.

Alternatively, the fence may be included in and bonded to the grounding system, via a fence buried earth conductor which usually would follow approximately the fence line. This has the affect of increasing the area of the grounding system thereby reducing its resistance. It also avoids possible danger from simultaneous contact with the fence and equipment within the fence which is bonded to the substation earthing system and also eases the problem of isolation between fences where internal fences are necessary for ground mounted equipment, eg series capacitor banks where the internal fence is bonded to the substation earthing system and the perimeter fence is separately earthed. However, with the fence bonded into the main system the design must ensure dangerous touch, step and transferred potentials do not occur outside the fence under fault conditions.

For indoor substations an internal main earth bar should be provided in each room for equipment earthing. This should be connected to the buried earthing system associated with outdoor substation equipment where applicable or if not to its own earth electrodes. Branch connections should be provided from the main internal earth bar to all indoor switchgear metalwork, cable sheaths and armouring, control and relay panels, fire fighting equipment, structural steelwork etc.

Where leakage-to-frame busbar zone protection is provided for indoor metalclad switchgear two earth bars are required, viz a switchgear bonding bar for earthing all switchgear metalwork within the protected zone and a true earth bar run separately from the switchgear metalwork or where it is mounted on the switchgear insulated from it by insulation with a test withstand level of 4 kV rms ac for one minute. The main and auxiliary cable glands are connected to the true earth bar and are insulated from the switchgear metalwork with insulation capable of withstanding the same test level.

It is recommended that the cable gland insulation should include a 'metallic island' test layer to facilitate testing of the gland insulation. These arrangements are shown in Fig. 27.

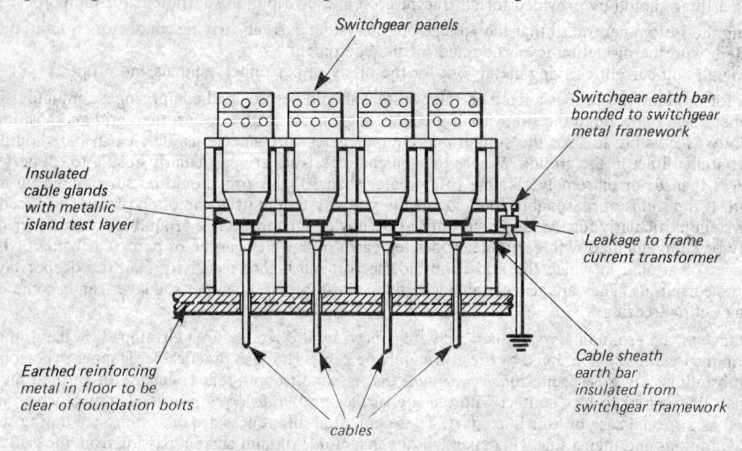

FIG. 27.—Earthing Arrangement for Metal Enclosed Switchgear with 'leakage to frame' Bus Zone Protection.

Where two stations adjoin one another the extremities of their individual earthing systems should be joined to encompass the whole area. These interconnections between sites should include test links to assist maintenance checking of the resistance of the individual earthing systems.

Where an appreciable rise in potential can occur in the station earthing system under fault conditions any services which enter the station such as water pipes, communication circuits etc may require insulating sections in the pipework, isolating transformers in the communication circuits and insulated glands for the pilot cables to avoid danger to personnel and damage to equipment which may arise from transferred potentials.

It is recommended that fully rated earth connections be provided for resistance or arc-suppression coil neutral earthed systems and that no distinction is made between these systems (in which the restriction of fault current provided by these methods of earthing does not apply for certain types of fault) and solidly earthed neutral systems. The tertiary windings of power transformers which are not loaded or are brought out for test purposes, should have one corner of the delta earthed.

Although not so widespread, earthing conductors other than copper may be used, eg aluminium conductor, which with a conductance equivalent to a given copper conductor will have an approximately equal short time current rating.

In addition to fixed earthing switches, maintenance earthing equipment is provided for application at the point of work for maintenance purposes and both outdoor and depending upon the type of switchgear, indoor main earth bars should be accessible and include provision for the connection of the temporary maintenance earths.

Recommendations, design procedures and calculations for substation earthing are given in BS Code of Practice CP1013: 'Earthing'; BS 162: 'Electric Power Switchgear'; IEEE Standard 80: 'Guide for Safety of Substation Grounding'; and Electra No. 71 July 1980, 'Station Earthing; Safety and Interference Aspects'.

AC TRANSMISSION AND DISTRIBUTION EQUIPMENT

Switchgear.—This term embraces basically assemblies of busbars and connections, circuit breakers, means of isolation and earthing and associated ancillary equipment for control, protection, instrumentation and metering.

Circuit Breakers.—These devices are required to carry, make and break normal load current and short circuit fault current and these duties may be performed by oil, air or gas blast, free air break, or vacuum circuit breakers.

Conventional Indoor Metalclad Switchgear may have air, compound or oil filled and insulated busbars and connections and bulk oil circuit breakers for distribution voltages up to 33 kV. The breaker may be isolated from its fixed portion either by withdrawing horizontally or vertically, most of the present designs being of the vertical isolation type. Designs using interchangeable plugs for busbar selection (alternatively busbar selection switches) and extensible plugs for busbar or circuit earthing are available but many modern designs use the transfer breaker scheme for busbar selection and busbar and circuit earthing. With both extensible plug and transfer breaker methods of earthing, the earth is applied by closing the fully rated circuit breaker. Typical vertical isolation, double break bulk oil, transfer breaker arrangements for single and duplicate compound filled busbar metalclad switchgears are shown in Fig. 28.

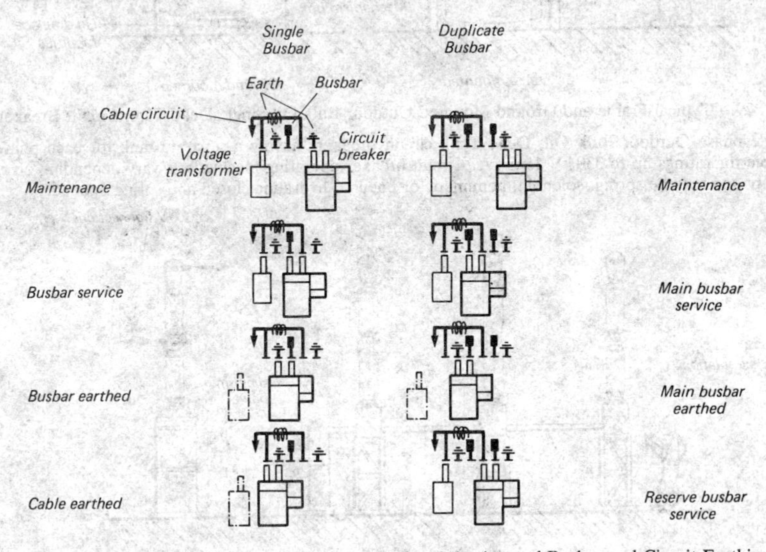

Fig. 28.—Typical Transfer Breaker Scheme for Busbar Selection and Busbar and Circuit Earthing.

With some indoor metalclad switchgear arrangements, it is necessary, when extending the substation, to shut down all or part of the substation during the whole of the time taken to erect and test the new equipment as it is impossible physically to remove the existing busbar end cap once the new extension panel is in position. The preferred design allows the extension to be completed with the existing substation live, thereby reducing the outage time to that required to remove the existing busbar end cap, inserting the busbar connecting links and fitting, and, where appropriate, filling the busbar band joint.

With indoor sectionalised busbar schemes employing oil circuit breakers, fire risks may be reduced by housing the bus-section and bus-coupler switchgear within fire-proof walls, often with self-closing, fire-proof sliding doors for access between sections.

Single break low oil content circuit breakers employing a self-compensating arc control interrupter and free air circuit breakers employing an arc chute interrupter, both commonly of the horizontal draw-out isolation type, are available as an alternative to the schemes using double break bulk oil circuit breakers. More recently metalclad switchgear employing vacuum circuit breakers for ratings typically up to 11 kV 250 MVA (13·1 kA rms symmetrical fault level) have become available. Mechanisms for circuit breaker operation are normally spring or solenoid closed, spring opened.

Conventional three phase Outdoor Bulk Oil, Single Dead Tank circuit breakers with three phases in one tank are usually frame mounted for ratings up to 66 kV 2,500 MVA which permits the circuit breaker tank with oil to be lowered for maintenance and alternatively ground mounted for 132 kV with suitable man access to the tank for maintenance. Mechanisms are normally spring, solenoid or pneumatic closed, spring opened. Typical frame and ground mounted arrangements are shown in Fig. 29. With both arrangements the height of the live bushing top cap is such as to provide the necessary safety clearance to ground.

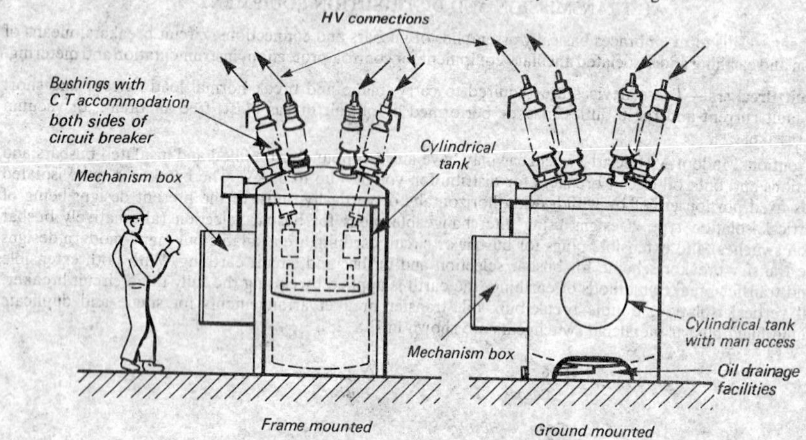

FIG. 29.—Typical Frame and Ground Mounted Outdoor Bulk Oil Single Dead Tank Circuit Breakers.

Single phase Outdoor Bulk Oil, Dead Tank circuit breakers having a separate tank for each phase are available for ratings up to 330 kV 15 GVA. Circuit breaker operating mechanisms vary depending on rating and duty and may be spring, solenoid, penumatic or pneumo-hydraulic closed and spring opened.

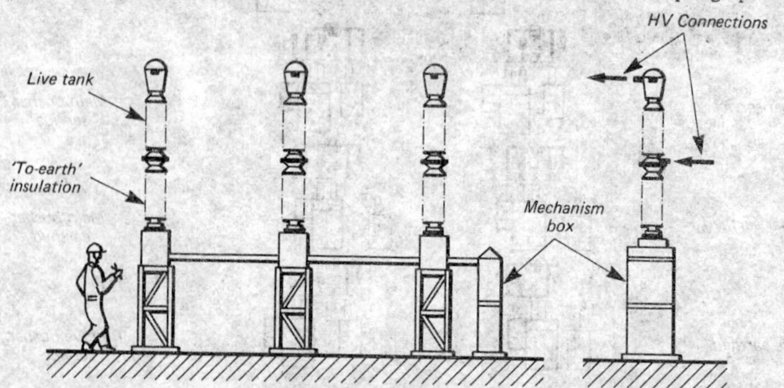

FIG. 30.—Typical Outdoor Open Type, Live Tank, Single Break, Reduced Oil Content, Circuit Breaker.

One advantage of all dead tank circuit breakers is that bushing type current transformers can be included within the circuit breaker and on both sides of the break, ie on all six bushings.

Outdoor Open Type, Live Tank Oil circuit breakers in which the contacts and interruptors are contained in oil filled tanks insulated from earth normally have much less oil than their dead tank equivalent. A separate tank is provided for each phase of these reduced oil (low or small oil) content breakers, ie they are of single phase construction and usually for voltages up to 132 kV are single break. For higher voltages and ratings they may have more than one break with resistors and or capacitors connected in parallel across each break to control the voltage distribution across the breaks during circuit interruption. Mechanisms are spring, solenoid, pneumatic, pneumo-hydraulic closed and spring opened or pneumo-hydraulic closed and opened. A typical single break arrangement is shown in Fig. 30.

Outdoor Open Type, Live Tank Air-Blast circuit breakers utilise dry compressed air for circuit interruption, insulation and breaker operation. Some of the early designs had the air receiver(s) and blast valves located at ground level with a normally non-pressurised insulated blast tube feeding compressed air to the interruptors during circuit interruption, the various chamber insulating surfaces having a continuous supply of dry low pressure conditioning air. For the higher voltages with long 'to earth' insulation this inherently introduces a delay in circuit interruption and this non-pressurised interruptor head design has been largely superseded and this disadvantage overcome by pressurised head designs in which the blast valves are located in the live interrupting chambers, which are permanently pressurised. The pilot air valves for blast valve and contact operation are controlled from the ground mounted mechanism by light, insulated (fibreglass) pull rods. The rapid discharge of high pressure air can be a problem due to noise and designs with silencers added to the interruptor exhaust or included in the interruptor design have been developed. Circuit breaker operation is by compressed air. A typical air blast circuit breaker arrangement is shown in Fig. 31.

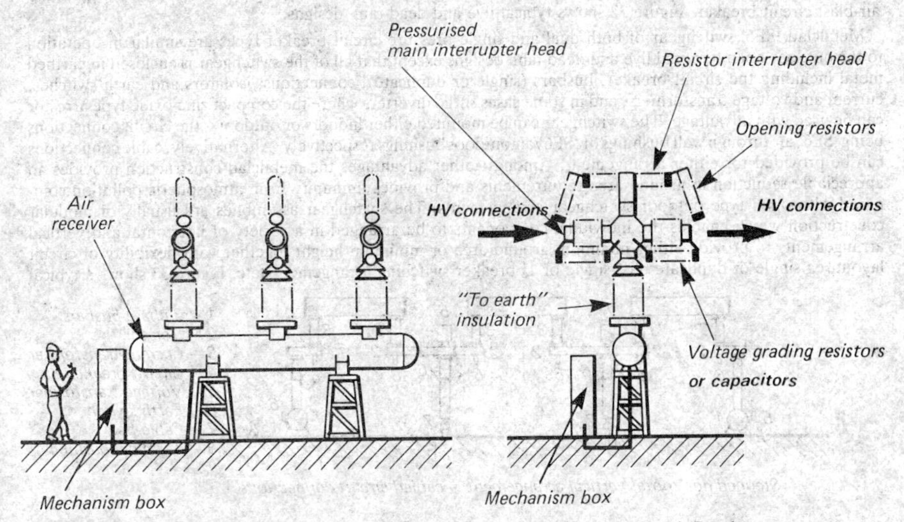

FIG. 31.—Typical Outdoor, Open Type, Live tank, Air-blast Circuit Breaker.

Outdoor Open Terminal, 'SF6' (sulphur hexafloride) circuit breakers use 'SF6' gas for both insulating and circuit interruption and are of both live and dead tank designs. For circuit interruption dual pressure and single pressure (puffer) 'SF6' arrangements are currently available. The dual pressure system utilises higher pressure 'SF6' for circuit interruption and lower pressure gas for insulation purposes, the higher pressure gas being discharged into the lower pressure chamber during circuit interruption, the pressure differential being restored by a gas compressor. This design may require heaters depending on operating temperature and pressure to prevent the gas stored at the higher pressure becoming liquid as for example, at sixteen atmospheres absolute the gas liquefies at about 10°C whereas at five atmospheres absolute, liquification occurs at about −30°C.

With the single pressure system, the 'SF6' gas is contained at the one low pressure throughout the breaker, except during circuit interruption. During the interruption process only, the necessary gas pressure is built up in the interruptor by means of a piston operating in conjunction with the moving contact forcing gas past and de-ionising the arc via usually a ptfe (poly-tetrafluoro-ethylene) nozzle. This arrangement is self-acting and requires no external gas compressor but the energy requirements for opening are considerably increased. Both dual and single pressure designs are closed gas systems, ie there is no discharge of 'SF6' gas to atmosphere during operation. Mechanisms for circuit breaker operation include pneumatic and pneumo-hydraulic. The

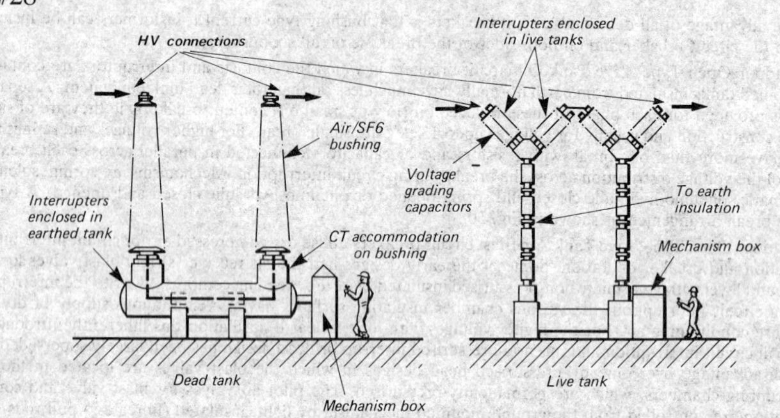

FIG. 32.—Typical Live and Dead Tank 'SF6' Circuit Breakers (Single Pole Units Shown; Three Pole Units Would Form a 3 Phase CB).

single pressure (puffer) design in particular is simple and has much fewer moving parts than the corresponding air-blast circuit breaker. Figure 32 shows typical live and dead tank designs.

Metalclad 'SF6' switchgear of both dual and single pressure circuit breaker types are similar in operation to the outdoor open terminal live and dead tank designs except that all of the switchgear is enclosed in earthed metal including the circuit breaker, busbars (single or duplicate), connections, isolators and earth switches, current and voltage transformers, and in some cases surge diverters where the compact zinc-oxide type arrestor can be used with advantage. The switchgear can be mounted either indoors or outdoors, the circuit connections being 'SF6'/air through wall bushings or 'SF6'/air outdoor bushings respectively. Alternatively, cable connections can be provided for either arrangement. Amongst other advantages the metalclad construction provides an appreciable reduction in ground area requirements and provides immunity from atmospheric pollution compared with open type outdoor switchgear arrangements. The switchgear assemblies are usually of modular construction which enables the individual components to be arranged in a variety of horizontal and vertical arrangements to provide either minimum ground area or minimum height together with flexibility of circuit layout, eg single or duplicate bus, single or 1½ breaker switching arrangements etc. Figure 33 shows a typical

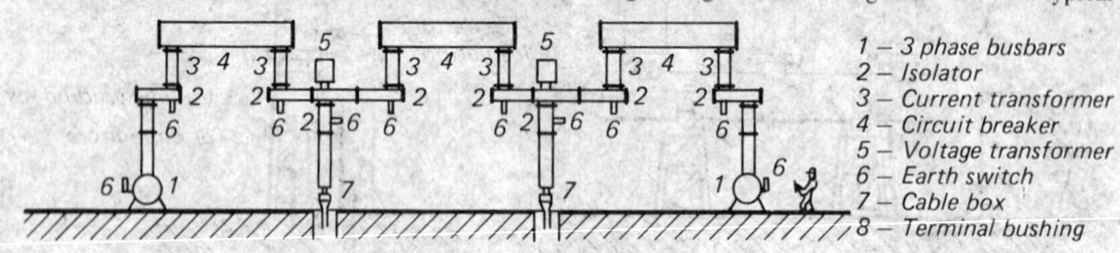

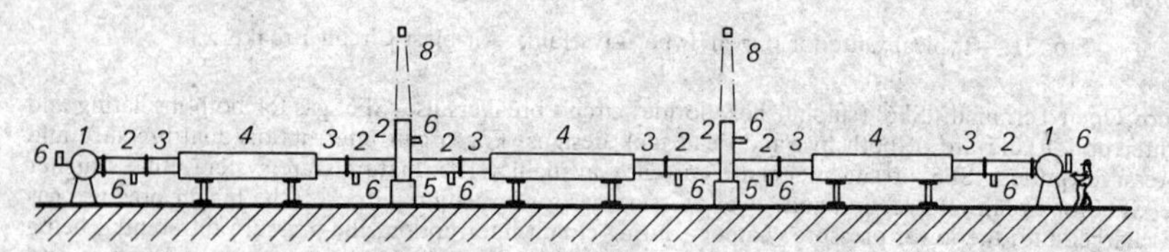

FIG. 33.—SF6 Metalclad 1½ Circuit Breaker Arrangements.

$1\frac{1}{2}$ breaker layout for an in-line horizontal arrangement and a stepped horizontal/vertical arrangement.

Both dual and single pressure 'SF6' circuit breakers rely on the gas being forced past the arc during circuit interruption. Alternative 'rotating-arc' designs are available for the lower voltages in which instead of the gas moving with respect to the arc, the arc is rotated through the 'SF6' gas.

In addition Outdoor Hybrid arrangements combining some 'SF6' metalclad modules including the circuit breakers with conventional outdoor open type busbar arrangements are available.

Conventional outdoor open type switchgear may be installed indoors, typical examples being the CEGB 'open-hall' 132 kV and 275 kV layouts and their 400 kV switch-house arrangements in which the equipment is frequently housed in relatively simple steel-framed, clad buildings in order to overcome amenity, noise (from air-blast circuit breakers) or atmospheric pollution problems. Even when full advantage is taken of indoor construction and clearances are reduced to a minimum the saving in space with these arrangements is limited because of the open construction which still requires equipment and safety clearances in air to be maintained.

Indoor Cubicle Type Free Air Break Switchgear in which the three-phase switchgear assembly is enclosed within a metal cubicle but without separate metal casings for the individual components has similar means of isolating the air break circuit breakers as that available for indoor metalclad bulk oil switchgear, ie horizontal or vertical isolation. Horizontal isolation is most common covering ratings up to 11 kV 750 MVA. Vertical isolation allows the transfer breaker method of earthing to be used and present designs cover ratings up to 11 kV 250 MVA. Circuit interruption is usually by means of arc chutes assisted by air puffers.

Low voltage air break units for service voltages up to 600 V are usually hand withdrawable from the cubicle and employ steel splitter plates or cold cathode arc chutes without air puffers. They are of compact design enabling multi-tier arrangements to be readily achieved.

This type of switchgear is classed as 'air-insulated' but most have provision for the busbars and connections to be insulated with PVC sleeving, resin bonded paper or cast epoxy resin.

Mechanisms generally used for this type of air breaker are manual, spring or solenoid closed but some designs include for pneumatic closing. The spring mechanisms are either manually re-charged or motor and manual re-charged.

Metalclad and cubicle switchgear designs employing low oil content, vacuum, or 'SF6' rotating-arc circuit breakers instead of bulk oil or air circuit breakers but having similar features are also commercially available.

Cellular gear in which the various switchgear components are housed in separate fire-proof insulating cells, usually employ fixed circuit breakers and separate isolators commonly with segregation between individual component assemblies and circuits, connections between busbars and equipment being by through bushings.

Package type substations with provision for internal access and operation and Kiosk type substations without internal access or operating space both provide a light shelter type low-cost enclosure for the switchgear and where appropriate transformer equipments.

Ring Main Units are commonly used for ring main distribution systems as a means of providing teed feeder circuits from the distribution ring main and may combine circuit breakers, switches and switch fuse units with busbars to form an extensible switchboard, or alternatively to form a composite non-extensible arrangement without busbars. Designs are available for indoor or outdoor service. They may be combined with a transformer to form a ring main connected transformer substation, a typical arrangement being shown in Fig. 34.

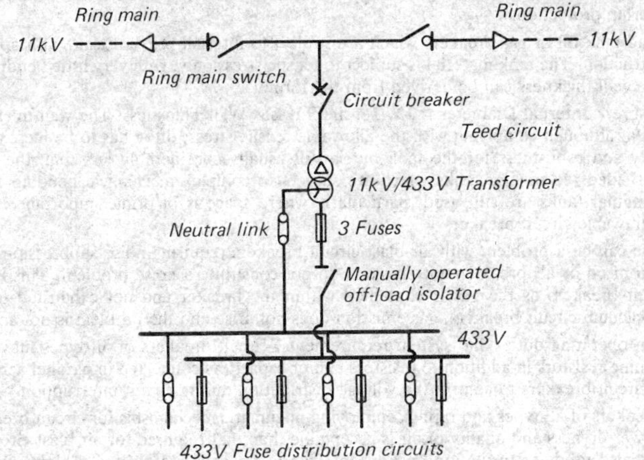

FIG. 34.—Typical Ring Main Connected Transformer Substation.

Automatic Reclosers are used on rural distribution systems which in general, employ overhead line radial feeders controlled by a circuit breaker at a main distribution substation supplying spur lines protected by fuses. The lines are vulnerable to transient faults due to air blown debris, birds and lightning and phase to phase conductor flashover under high wind conditions.

The recloser which operates in conjunction with slow acting fuses, is a circuit breaker. As such it has a rated breaking and making capacity and its automatic reclosing feature may, for example, include two instantaneous trips followed by two delayed trips by which time if the fault has not cleared will lock out. The fault if transient is cleared by the circuit breaker and if persistent by the slow acting fuse during the delayed close cycle. In both cases the main supply will be restored or maintained by the recloser. If the fault is persistent and on the supply side of the fuses (ie on the main radial feeder) this will be cleared by the recloser finally tripping and locking out. The main object of the scheme is to ensure security of supply to the maximum number of consumers at minimum equipment cost. Figure 35 shows a typical application.

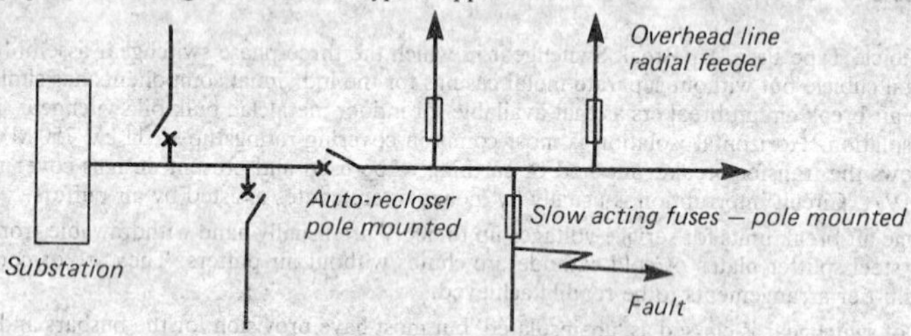

FIG. 35.—Auto-recloser with Slow-acting Fuses for Rural Distribution.

Sectionalising Switches capable of breaking load current and making and carrying fault current may be used instead of slow acting fuses. If a fault on the consumer side of the sectionaliser persists the sectionaliser is arranged to open during a delayed open cycle of the auto-recloser.

With both schemes proper co-ordination of the time/current characteristics of the fuses or sectionaliser protection and the auto-recloser is essential to achieve satisfactory discrimination in operation of the devices.

Auto-reclosers are suitable for pole mounting and the energy for multi-shot reclosure on some earlier designs was provided for example by a falling weight mechanism but more recent designs include spring close mechanisms, spring charging being by means of an electro-magnet connected across two phases on the incoming supply side of the recloser.

CIRCUIT BREAKERS (GENERAL COMMENTS).—All circuit breakers of both live and dead tank construction and where each phase is housed in a separate tank may be readily arranged for single pole as well as three pole auto-reclosing by providing a separate mechanism for each phase. Three phases in one tank constructions in which all three phases are operated from one mechanism are only suitable for three pole auto-reclose duty.

As distinct from dead tank circuit breakers all live tank (oil, air-blast and 'SF6') circuit breakers normally require current transformers mounted separate from and usually on line side of the breaker and therefore do not provide overlap protection.

Tanks for dead tank oil or gas breakers which are subject to internal pressure can, with advantage, be of cylindrical construction. The tank material is subject to tensile stress only, with very little bending and for thin walled tubes the wall thickness can be derived from the formula.

Internal Pressure × Internal Diameter = 2 × Tensile Stress × Wall Thickness. The wall thickness obtained from this formula, although complying with the allowable tensile stress, often has to be increased to provide adequate rigidity and robustness for the tank but is still usually considerably less than the wall thickness required for flat sided rectangular tanks which are subject to complex mechanical bending and deflection. However, rectangular tanks are still used, particularly where space is of prime importance, eg for indoor metalclad withdrawable circuit breakers.

Whereas noise can be a problem with air-blast circuit breakers requiring noise suppression measures, the exhaust gases from oil or air break circuit breakers do not constitute a noise problem. This is also the case with 'SF6' circuit breakers as the gas is contained within the breaker and not exhausted to atmosphere. Likewise, with vacuum circuit breakers, gas emission does not arise and the problem is not applicable.

Depending on operating duties and system requirements, circuit breakers of all types may be fitted with closing and opening resistors in addition to resistors and/or capacitors connected in parallel across each break of multi-break circuit breakers to control the voltage distribution during circuit interruption.

For circuit breakers of all types and ratings employing pneumatic mechanisms for circuit breaker operation only, a much lower dryness and quality of air is acceptable than that required for air-blast circuit breakers in which the air is also used for insulation and arc interruption purposes requiring a high quality and more complex compressed air system. All breakers with spring close mechanisms in which the closing spring can be re-charged with the breaker in the closed position (thereby providing single-shot auto-reclose) should be provided with a 'slow-opening' interlock to ensure that if the breaker makes satisfactory contact but does not latch closed, re-winding of the spring does not cause the contacts to open slowly (and dangerously) under the action of the opening springs.

CIRCUIT BREAKER THEORY AND DESIGN.—This subject including the theory of circuit making and breaking and arc characteristics, network and special switching conditions, oil, air-break, air-blast, SF6 and vacuum type power circuit breakers and circuit breaker insulation and design, is extensively covered in detail in various reference books including those listed in the bibliography.

ISOLATORS.—As indicated earlier with draw-out types of switchgear in which the circuit breaker may be withdrawn either horizontally or vertically, isolation in air is achieved by this action without the necessity of separate isolators. Where the breaker is not withdrawable, separate busbar and circuit isolators are required. Except for some special applications such as metalclad gas (air or SF6) fixed breaker equipment where the isolators operate in gas, most isolators are of the air break type. For rural distribution consisting of overhead line circuits, pole mounted isolators operating outdoors in air are commonly used for isolating sections of line, spur connections, small transformers etc, manual operation being direct from ground level or at high level by means of a hook stick.

Isolators are usually capable of dealing with, for example, the small charging currents associated with busbars and connections and on double busbar schemes, with load current shared by parallel circuits but other than this light duty they operate off-load. Basically isolators establish either a horizontal or vertical isolating air gap when in the open position. Typical examples of these two types are shown diagramatically in Fig. 36.

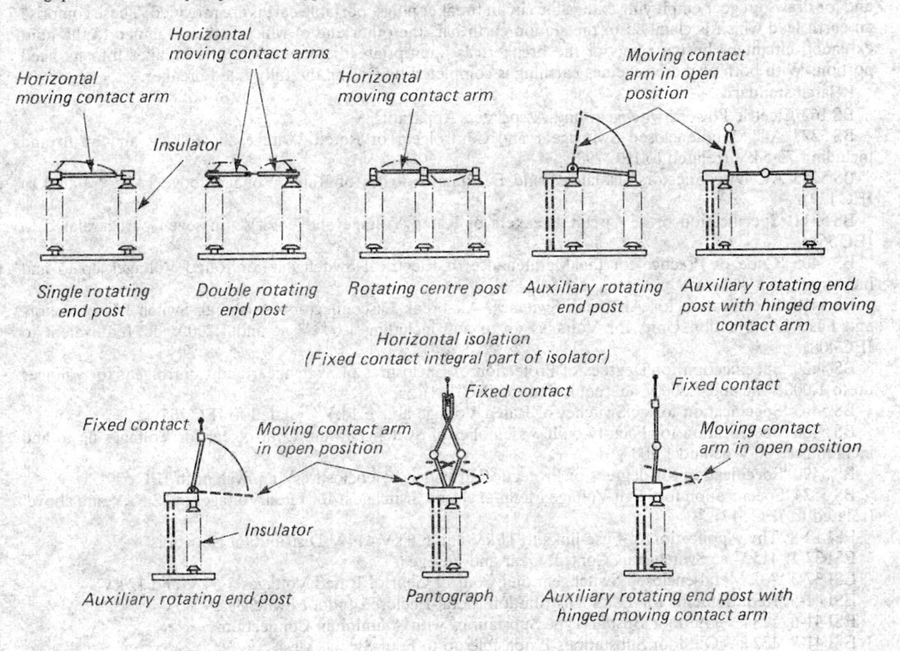

FIG. 36.—Single Phase Isolators Shown in Closed Position—Horizontal and Vertical Isolation.

Isolators with hinged moving contact arms (both horizontal and vertical isolation) and pantograph types are usually only employed in extra high voltage outdoor installations. Manual operation is common for the lower voltage range and requires the operator to attend the equipment. Power operation is required for the higher voltages with a manual standby operation facility and for any voltage where the isolator needs to be controlled remotely.

Special isolators employing swinging or rotating bushings for indoor use and load breaking switches and switching isolators capable of handling normal full load current and in the case of the latter, additionally capable of fault making, are commercially available.

Fixed Earthing Switches are commonly mounted on one or both sides of an isolator where they can be mechanically interlocked with the isolator supplemented with electrical bolt interlocking when the isolator is power operated. Additionally, they may be separately mounted on conductor support insulators or other equipment when either key type mechanical interlocking or electrical bolt interlocking may be necessary. At the highest voltages it may be advantageous to adopt a hinged earth arm as used by the CEGB for the 400 kV transmission system substations.

Earthing switches are provided as a safety device for maintanance and are usually manually operated as they do not form part of the system operation.

Maintenance Earthing Devices are applied at the point of work for maintenance and safety purposes. The portable types for outdoor substations usually consist of a translucent plastic covered copper or aluminium cable, one end of which is clamped to the substation earth bar, the other end being raised and clamped to the isolated equipment conductor system by means of an insulated pole. Taking into account the height of the equipment to be earthed and the weight and size of the portable maintenance earth this method is practical for voltages up to 132 kV, becomes increasingly difficult at about 275 kV and is impractical for voltages of 400 kV and above, bearing in mind that for outdoor installations, they may have to be applied under adverse weather conditions. At these higher voltages assistance for raising and guiding during application of the earth is required. Alternatively, the CEGB have developed semi-permanent and interlocked devices through which the earth arms can be manually and satisfactorily applied. Inevitably, these means are somewhat more expensive than the portable earths used at the lower voltages but they are still considerably cheaper than providing fixed earthing switches throughout the substation.

For indoor switchgear the transfer breaker schemes have integral busbar and circuit earthing arrangements and for draw-out gear employing extensible circuit breaker plugs, portable earths are provided. These comprise an earth lead which is clamped to the station earth bar, the other end of which is then clamped to the non-extended circuit or busbar plugs of the breaker, as appropriate, before racking the breaker into its fixed portion. With both of these schemes earthing is completed by closing the fully rated breaker.

Related standards.—

BS 162 Electric Power Switchgear and Associated Apparatus.

BS 5227 AC Metal-enclosed Switchgear and Controlgear of Rated Voltage above 1 kV and up to and including 72·5 kV (related to IEC 298).

BS 5253 AC Disconnectors (Isolators) and Earthing Switches of Rated Voltage above 1 kV. (related to IEC 129).

BS 5311 'Specification of ac Circuit Breakers of Rated Voltage above 1 kV' (in seven parts; related to IEC 56).

BS 5405 'Code of Practice for the Maintenance of Electrical Switchgear for Rated Voltages up to and including 145 kV'

BS 5419 'Specification for Air-break Switches, Air-break Disconnectors, Air-break Switch Disconnectors and Fuse Combination Units for Voltages up to and including 1,000 V ac and 1,200 V dc' (equivalent to IEC 408).

BS 5420 'Specification for Degrees of Protection of Enclosures of Switchgear and Controlgear for voltages up to 1,000 V ac and 1,200 V ac' (equivalent to IEC 144).

BS 5463 'Specification for ac Switches of Rated Voltage above 1 kV' (related to IEC 265).

BS 5486 'Specification for Factory-built Assemblies of Switchgear and Controlgear for Voltages up to and including 1,000 V ac and 1,200 V dc'

BS 5490 'Specification for degrees of Protection Provided by enclosures' (equivalent to IEC 529).

BS 5524 'Specification for High Voltage Metal-enclosed Switchgear for rated Voltages of 72·5 kV and above' (related to IEC 517).

ESI 12-8 'The Application of Fuse-links to 11 kV and 6·6 kV/415 V Distribution Networks'

ESI 37-1 '415 V ac Switchgear, Control Gear and Fusegear'

ESI 37-3 'AC Metal-enclosed Switchgear and Control Gear of Rated Voltages 3·6 kV and 12 kV'

ESI 41-5 'Requirements for 12 kV Distribution Metal-Enclosed Indoor Switchgear'

ESI 41-6 '123 kV Outdoor Busbar Type Substations with Aluminium Connections'

ESI 41-7 '132 kV Outdoor Substations Extensible up to Four-Switch Mesh'

ESI 41-8 '132 kV Compact Transformer Feeder Substations'

ESI 41-10 'Open Type Switchgear for Use on 66 and 132 kV Systems'

ESI 41-12 'Non-Extensible Ring Main Equipments'

ESI 41-19 'Open Type Switchgear for Use on 33 kV Systems'

BUSBARS AND CONNECTIONS.—Both copper and aluminium and their alloys are commonly used in switchgear installations for busbars and connections. Table 4 gives the relative properties of aluminium and copper. Aluminium is less than one third the density of copper and has an electrical conductivity 61% that of copper and therefore for equal conductivity is lighter but larger in dimension than copper.

Where the conductors are enclosed for example, in metalclad switchgear, physical dimensions are important as they affect the size of the enclosure, quantity of filling medium and conductor insulation as well as the overall size of the installation which is particularly important for indoor switchgear and copper is the common conductor material for these applications.

TABLE 4.—RELATIVE PROPERTIES OF COPPER AND ALUMINIUM.

	Copper	Aluminium
Weight per unit length for equal conductivity	1·00	0·50
Conductivity for equal areas:		
Electrical	1·00	0·61
Thermal	1·00	0·56
Tensile strength (hard drawn)	1·00	0·40
Hardness (hard drawn)	1·00	0·44
Modulus of elasticity	1·00	0·55
Coefficient of thermal expansion	1·00	1·39
Melting point	1·00	0·61

Copper for Busbars. Copper Development Association.

Electrical purity (99·5% pure) aluminium to BS 2898 Specification EIE and fully heat-treated aluminium alloy which includes additions of magnesium and silicon to BS 2898 Specification E91E are commonly used for high voltage outdoor open-type switchgear installations. E91E alloy has much superior mechanical properties with only a small reduction in electrical conductivity compared with EIE and is generally considered as providing the best combination of electrical and mechanical properties particularly for sections such as rectangular bar, channel and tube which may have to withstand large electro-mechanical forces due to high short circuit fault currents. Flexible aluminium and steel-cored aluminium conductors and hard drawn copper and hard drawn cadmium copper conductors are also used for busbar connections.

Some of the factors to be considered in selecting the material for and the size and arrangement of both busbars and connections are:

Thermal Rating for both normal and short circuit currents.—BS 159 specifies that the temperature rise of busbars and connections above the ambient temperature, when continuously carrying rated normal current at rated frequency, shall not exceed 50°C. This is based on an ambient temperature having a peak value not exceeding 40°C and an average value not exceeding 35°C measured over a 24-hour period. This represents a conductor maxiumum average operating temperature of 85°C. Where the ambient temperature exceeds that specified the permissible temperature rise of 50°C shall be reduced by an amount equal to the excess ambient temperature. When busbars and connections intended for service at high altitudes are tested near sea level, the limits of temperature rise shall be reduced one percent for each 300 m in excess of 1000 m above sea-level at which the busbars and connections are intended for service. Where conductors are enclosed in metal casings, eg metalclad switchgear, non-magnetic enclosures or inserts are necessary for the higher current ratings in order to comply with the temperature rise limitations.

The short-time short circuit current test shall not produce any mechanical damage, such as permanent distortion or burning of parts and shall not cause a temperature rise that, added to the maximum temperature attained at rated normal current, would damage the insulation of the current carrying parts. After the test the busbars and connections shall be in a condition to comply with their specified rating when they are again at the ambient temperature.

Skin and Proximity Effects.—Skin effect arises due to the conductor self-induced back emf which causes the current to flow largely in the outer skin of the conductor. The most electrically efficient (though not necessarily mechanically) conductor section is one in which the metal is positioned equidistant and as far as possible from the magnetic centre of the conductor, ie a thin walled tube.

Proximity effect arises due to mutual induction between conductors causing current density distortion in each of the conductors. This effect can be minimised by increasing the spacing between conductors and to a lesser extent by the conductor shape.

Both skin and proximity effects can influence the current rating of single conductor and multi-conductor phase arrangements.

Electro-Magnetic Forces.—May arise for a very short time but can be of considerable magnitude, either attracting or repelling adjacent conductors during short circuit fault currents, particularly at the lower voltages where spacing between conductors is small or at high fault levels.

Self Weight and Wind and Ice-Loads.—The weight of the conductor, with ice if appropriate and maximum wind loads need to be taken into account.

Resonant vibration of tubular conductors may also occur under steady light wind conditions and means of overcoming this need to be catered for during the design of the system. This critical condition may be avoided by limiting the mechanical deflection of the supporting beam by reducing the conductor unsupported span length, adopting fixed end supports at one or both ends of the span instead of freely supported ends and/or changing the physical characteristics and dimensions of the tube.

Electrical Clearances.—BS 159 specifies minimum air clearances between phases and to earth for voltages up to 275 kV and minimum clearances for oil or compound immersed conductors for voltages up to 33 kV.

Minimum clearances in air are repeated in BS 162 which also includes Safety Clearances to enable operation, inspection and maintenance work to be carried out. The 'Section Clearance' is the minimum Safety Clearance from the nearest unscreened live conductor in air to where a man may be required to stand either on the ground or on an established working platform, measured from the feet. Where an established working platform is not provided then the section clearance shall be taken as applying from the actual point of work, ie from the position of the hands to the nearest live conductor. The between phases and to earth air clearances apply to non-impulse tested equipment and for conductor maximum swing and sag conditions.

Creepage Distances in Air.—For indoor insulation BS 159 gives *for guidance only* creepage distances to earth in air for open and enclosed busbars of indoor-type switchgear.

For outdooor insulation reference is made to BS 223 which gives creepage distances in inches for normally and heavily polluted atmospheres for each voltage level, which for the voltage range 33 kV to 275 kV works out at 1" (25.4 mm) per kV of line voltage for heavily polluted and 0·67" (17 mm) per kV of line voltage for normally polluted atmospheres. Where marine or industrial pollution can be expected to be extremely severe and where the frequency with which the equipment can be taken out of service for cleaning without undue risk to the maintenance of supplies is limited, greater creepage distances may be required, typically 31·7 mm per kV line voltage. A draft IEC guide, at present under discussion, for the dimensioning of outdoor insulators related to pollution levels, includes insulator creepage distances for four categories of pollution. Consideration should also be given to the frequency and effectiveness of natural washing by rain, which may influence the weatherproof shed shape of the insulation and to 'live line washing' of equipment and in extreme cases to greasing of the insulators.

Corona and Radio Interference.—Visual Corona and Radio Interference Electrical Discharges can occur in air from live equipment and may be significant, particularly at the higher voltages when visual corona (VC) and radio interference voltage (RIV) tests would be specified. The VC test is very dependent on the sensitivity and training of the observers eyes but it is useful as it assists in locating the exact source of radio interference voltage generated by conductors, fittings and insulators, enabling modifications where necessary, to be made to the shape and smoothness of the equipment to improve the VC and hence the RIV performance. The RIV test is less subjective than the VC test and in general provides a more quantitative assessment of the discharge level of a particular piece of apparatus. Methods of calculating discharge levels in air for individual conductors and multi-conductor bundles are detailed in various reference books including those listed in the bibliography.

Thermal expansion and contraction.—Thermal expansion and contraction of conductors occurs with changes in ambient temperature and load and short circuit current. With long span rigid conductors expansion joints are required to prevent damage to the conductors, fittings, supports, insulators, structures and foundations. With flexible conductors maximum sag and minimum mechanical stress will occur at maximum conductor temperature. Maximum mechanical stress will occur in the conductors, fittings, insulators, structures and foundations due to increased conductor pull arising from minimum conductor sag as a result of minimum conductor temperature, short circuit and ice and wind loadings.

Joints in busbars and connections shall also comply with the temperature rise requirements and be so arranged to prevent deterioration in service. Mechanical joints between conductors require ample contact pressure to be maintained and preparation of the surfaces for copper to copper conductors include tinning, silver plating or coating with petroleum jelly before jointing and after removing the high resistance black copper oxide surface. Mechanical jointing of aluminium to aluminium conductors requires removal of the aluminium oxide film and to exclude air and miosture before making the joint, typically by vigorous scratch brushing under neutral grease. The same procedures may be used for aluminium to copper mechanical joints. In this case dissimilar metals having different electro-chemical potentials are in electrical contact and it is essential to permanently exclude moisture to ensure deterioration of the joint does not occur due to electrolytic action.

Special jointing compounds and bi-metallic joints and connectors are also available. The latter may include types where the bi-metallic joint carrying the current is made inside the fitting which is protected against the ingress of moisture by rubber or plastic. Alternatively, a rolled copper/aluminium bimetallic sheet is inserted (copper to copper and aluminium to aluminium) between the conductors or is manufactured in the form of a bi-metallic connector.

Where joints are to be permanent and are not to be dismantled, welding (correctly carried out) provides a very satisfactory method of jointing. Aluminium busbar systems commonly use inert (argon) gas shielded arc welding using the TIG (tungsten inert gas) or MIG (metal inert gas) or oxy-acetylene gas welding or brazing processes. With the long spans associated with the higher voltage transmission stations (400, 500 kV and above) and where the number of joints is sufficient to justify the relatively high cost of the welding equipment and trained operators, inert gas shielded arc welding of aluminium busbars and connections is frequently carried out on site.

Reference standards.—

BS 125 'Hard Drawn Copper and Copper-Cadium Conductors for Overhead Power Transmission Purposes'

BS 159 'Busbars and Busbar Connections' Covers current ratings of 200 A and above for voltages up to 275 kV for both copper and aluminium connections operating in air, oil, solid and semi-solid insulation.

BS 215 'Aluminium Conductors and Aluminium Conductors, Steel-reinforced, for Overhead Power Transmission' (includes code names for use when ordering), Part 1 'Aluminium Stranded Conductors' (equivalent to IEC 207); Part 2 'Aluminium Conductors, Steel-reinforced' (equivalent to IEC 209).

BS 223 'High Voltage Bushings'

BS 2898 'Wrought Aluminium and Aluminium Alloys for Electrical Purposes. Bars, extruded Round Tubes and Sections'

BS 5049 'Methods of Measurement of Radio Noise from Power Supply Apparatus for operation at 1 kV and above'

IEC 59 'IEC Standard Current Ratings (up to 10,000 A)'

ESI 41-11 'Tubular Aluminium Busbars, Connections and Terminal Fittings for 132 kV Outdoor Substations'

POWER TRANSFORMERS AND REACTORS

Power transformers for electrical transmission and distribution fall within the following types:

(i) Ground mounted, indoor or outdoor
(ii) Pole mounted outdoor, commonly used for rural distribution
(iii) Underground, indoor

They are of three-phase construction, ie all three phases within one tank for the lower ratings (even at the higher voltages), for example, 500 kV, 200 MVA and due to transport limitations single-phase construction, ie each of the three phases in a separate tank for the higher ratings, eg 500 kV, 800 MVA. Single-phase construction is more expensive than three-phase but offers the advantage of a cheaper spare, when required, in the form of a single-phase unit.

Another approach to overcome the transport limitations of weight and size for large transmission transformers is to adopt site re-assembled three-phase construction in which the transformer is broken down into discreet sub-assemblies for transport commonly with two vertical joins in the tank to form three single-phase units for transport, the yolk joining plates being interleaved on site. Alternatively, the tank assemblies are split horizontally. Unusually some designs break down the three-phase factory assembly into even smaller units for transport.

Transformer Filling.—Conventionally the filling is mineral insulating oil to BS 148 'Insulating Oil for Transformers and Switchgear' (equivalent to IEC 296) and additionally for the highest voltages a very low moisture content in the order of 5 to 10 parts per million (ppm) is required. To reduce the fire risk in high risk locations askarel filled transformers have been widely used, however, the polychlorinated biphenyls (pcb) contained in askarels are highly toxic and non-biodegradable requiring special measures for disposal such as very high temperature incineration. To overcome the objections to askarel filling, high fire point silicone and to a lesser extent modified hydro-carbon oil fillings are being increasingly used and for the lower rated distribution type transformers, conventional dry type, air-cooled and cast-in-resin, air-cooled units are available as alternatives to liquid filled units.

Core and Winding Construction.—The transformer core and winding construction may be CORE type in which a laminated iron core (commonly cold rolled grain orientated sheet steel for the higher ratings) is surrounded by the windings or SHELL type in which the windings are surrounded by the core. Fundamentally, there is no difference between the two types but the physical appearance of the core and winding assemblies differs considerably. For example, in the shell type the windings are more or less completely surrounded by the iron. Clamping of the core limb laminations is by insulated bolt or insulated bands, ('banded core').

Windings.—Two winding transformers consist of primary and secondary windings. Multi-winding transformers have one or more windings in addition to the primary and secondary windings having rated voltage the same as or intermediate between the primary and secondary winding rated voltages.

An auto-transformer has at least two of its windings common. Usually part of its primary and secondary windings.

A stabilising winding is a delta connected tertiary winding provided, for example, on star-star-connected transformers to reduce the zero-sequence impedance of the star connected winding which may for instance be necessary to reduce the magnitude of third harmonic voltages. Two points of the winding forming the same corner of the delta may be brought out for earthing and be connected together by a link which may be removed to open the delta for testing purposes. Alternatively, all three corners of the winding may be brought out to provide an external auxiliary load.

A zigzag star connected winding has one end of each phase connected to a common neutral point and each phase consists of two parts in which phase-displaced voltages are induced. These two parts normally have the same number of turns.

Winding Connections and Phase Displacement.—Vector Diagrams and Symbols to National Standard BS 171 and International Standard IEC 76: Star, delta or zigzag connected windings of three-phase transformers are identified by the letters Y, D or Z for the high voltage (HV) winding and y, d or z for the intermediate and low voltage (LV) windings respectively. Where the neutral point of star or zigzag connected windings is brought out these are indicated by YN or ZN or yn or zn respectively.

For auto-transformers the winding with the lower rated voltage is indicated by the letter a.

In representing phase displacement between windings the clock hour figure is used, the reference vector being that relating to the HV winding which is given first and the vector rotation being taken as counter-clockwise. Other symbols follow the HV vector symbol in diminishing sequence of rated voltages of the lower voltage windings. Typical vector diagrams, symbols and winding connections are shown in Fig. 37.

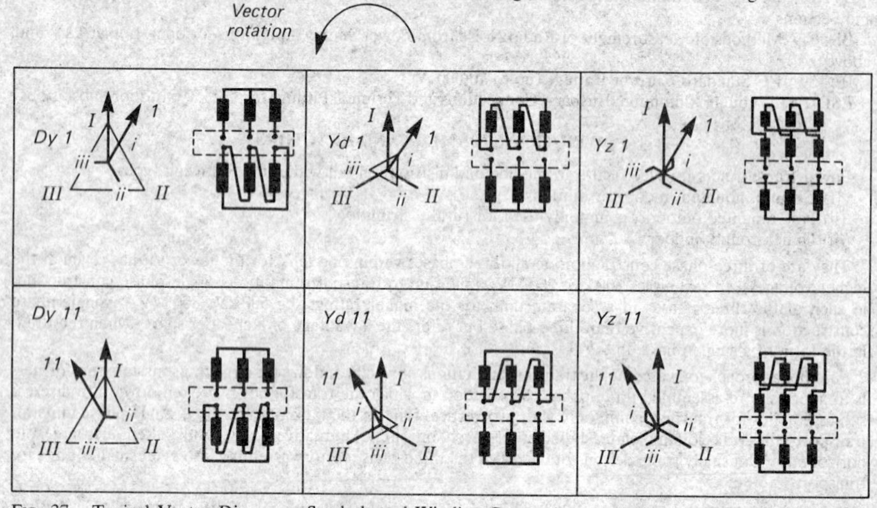

FIG. 37.—Typical Vector Diagrams, Symbols and Winding Connections for Three-Phase Separate Winding Transformers.

Phase displacements different from clock hour figures 0, 4 and 8 are not suitable for use with star-connected auto-transformers.

Parallel operation of some transformers with similar characteristics but of selected different vector groups is possible by transposing the external connections to one of the transformers. Parallel operation of transformers of certain vector groups is not possible without altering the internal connections to one of them. Parallel operation of any pair of transformers requires careful consideration.

Cooling Methods and Identification.—In accordance with BS 171 and IEC 76 identification letters for use with various cooling methods are given in Table 5 and the order of symbols in Table 6.

TABLE 5.—LETTER SYMBOLS.

Kind of Cooling Medium	Symbol
Mineral oil or equivalent flammable synthetic insulating liquid	O
Non-flammable synthetic insulating liquid	L
Gas	G
Water	W
Air	A
Kind of circulation	
Natural	N
Forced (oil not directed)	F
Forced-directed oil	D

TABLE 6.—ORDER OF SYMBOLS.

1st letter	2nd letter	3rd letter	4th letter
Indicating the cooling medium that is in contact with the windings		Indicating the cooling medium that is in contact with the external cooling system	
Kind of cooling medium	Kind of circulation	Kind of cooling medium	Kind of circulation

Typical designations for oil-immersed transformers having natural or forced cooling as alternatives with non-directed oil flow are.

ONAN/ONAF ONAN/OFAF

and for a dry-type transformer in a non-ventilated protective enclosure with natural air cooling inside and outside the enclosure—ANAN.

In an oil-filled water cooled transformer the water pressure should be less that the oil pressure so in the event of a leak this will be oil to water. Frequently this requires an oil to water and water to raw cooling water heat exchanger arrangement.

BS 171 specifies temperature rise limits for dry-type and oil-immersed type transformers for windings and cores and other parts and where appropriate, top oil temperature. Manufacturing tolerances on guaranteed values are also given for the transformer losses, voltage ratio, impedance voltage at rated current, short circuit impedance and no-load current and these tolerances may need to be taken into account in the system design.

Tappings.—When required tappings may be specified to provide small changes in voltage ratio. These may be off-circuit or on-load tap changers. In their simplest form off-circuit facilities can be provided (usually for distribution class transformers) by a system of removable links or switches. On-load tap changers require that the circuit must not be opened, even momentarily during tap changing as dangerous sparking may occur and equally, temporary short circuiting of a part of the winding must not take place. With automatic on-load tap change gear loss of the driving force should not allow the equipment to stop between taps and in the past various means have been adopted to prevent this including the use of energy stored in a flywheel so that once a tap change has commenced it is completed irrespective of whether or not the drive remains healthy. Present designs are commonly of the 'high speed resistor transition' type in which tapping selector and high speed spring operated diverter switches are housed in oil compartments separated from the transformer main tank. The selector switches do not interrupt any current and the diverter switches only the resistor transition current. The diverter switch contacts are capable of in the order of 200,000 operations and although they need very infrequent attention it is important to maintain the oil in the diverter switch tank in good condition. Voltage control schemes ensure that only one tap change is performed at one time even though for instance, the 'raise' or 'lower' pushbutton is still depressed. Automatic cooler control schemes are provided for forced cooled transformers.

The larger transformers usually have accommodation for current transformers on the bushings and where the transformer connections are by cable, a dis-connecting link box is provided as well as a cable box for cable testing.

Fittings include tank lifting, haulage and earthing facilities, oil conservators gauges and breathers, filter, drain valves and oil sampling devices, pressure relief devices, co-ordinating rod gaps, temperature indicating devices and alarms, gas and oil actuated relays, rating, diagram and property plates, marshalling kiosks and anti-vibration pads between tank and foundation. Close fitting enclosures may be necessary for noise suppression. For the larger units dwarf oil retaining walls should be provided the height and enclosed area of which should at least accept the transformer oil volume in the event of a burst tank. Air safety clearances should be maintained to the transformer terminals and connections with a man standing on the wall and when provided, earth clearances to fire fighting equipment pipework must be observed. The foundations should include reinforced pockets to accept hauling-in bollards.

Loading Guide.—British Standard Code of Practice CP 1010 'Loading Guide for Oil Immersed Transformers' substantially agrees with IEC 354 and gives guidance on overloading related to time on the basis that there may be some reduction in useful insulation life of the transformer.

Earthing Transformers and Auxiliary Transformers.—Where it is necessary to create an artificial neutral for earthing a lower voltage delta connecting winding (usually not exceeding 66 kV) of a main transformer an earthing transformer is provided which commonly includes an auxiliary winding for auxiliary supplies. The earthing and auxiliary supplies transformer is usually of the oil-immersed ONAN type having a main inter-connected zig-zag star winding connected directly to the lower voltage windings of the main transformer and an auxiliary star-connected winding arranged to provide a 415/240 V three-phase four-wire auxiliary supply. The neutral point of the interconnected star winding is usually either earthed directly or through an impedance. When an earthing transformer is not required a separate oil-immersed ONAN type auxiliary supplies transformer may be provided.

The much smaller earthing and auxiliary transformers should be provided with similar (but smaller) fittings to those supplied for the main transformers. Where auxiliary supplies are obtained from a main transformer delta connected tertiary, a simple automatic voltage control (AVC) scheme may be required for control of the auxiliary supplies voltage.

Power Reactors.—These are either series connected current limiting reactors for the limitation of short circuit fault current or shunt connected reactors for reactive (inductive) compensation, a typical application being on large long line transmission systems as a means of compensating for the overhead line capacitance under light load conditions. Fundamentally, series reactors are current dependent and shunt reactors voltage dependent devices, their reactive power absorption depending on current or voltage respectively. Because their function is not as for transformers which are for the purpose of voltage and current transformation, reactors are basically single primary winding devices, the three-phase series reactor having six terminals for series connection in the circuit and the shunt reactor, three terminals for parallel connection in the circuit as shown in Fig. 38.

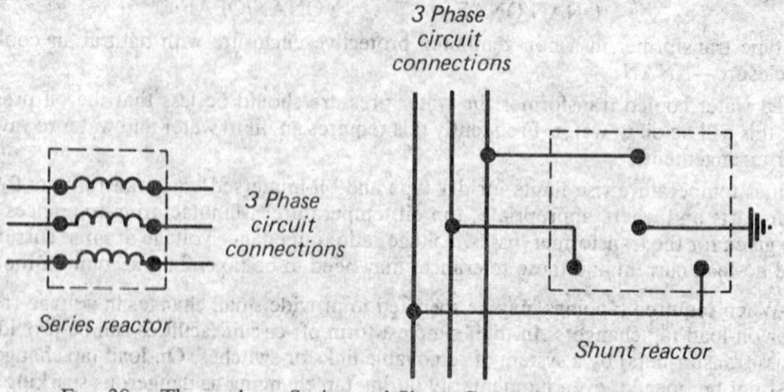

FIG. 38.—Three-phase Series and Shunt Connected Power Reactors.

For voltages of 132 kV and above shunt reactors are commonly star connected with their neutrals solidly earthed. Unusually reactors may be provided with auxiliarly supplies windings for substations in which no other means of providing a lower voltage supply is available and in these cases off-load or simple on-load tap changing facilities are usually necessary. Typically oil immersed reactors have ONAN type cooling but forced cooling may be necessary for the higher ratings. Fittings are similar to those provided for oil-immersed power transformers with CT accommodation in the bushing turrets. Noise levels not exceeding 5 db above that allowed for corresponding transformers based on continuous maximum ratings and impedance for series reactors and maximum system voltage for shunt reactors are usually expected and anti-vibration mountings between the reactor tank and its foundation are provided for the higher ratings.

Dissolved Gas in Oil Analysis (DGA).—Any form of fault within an oil filled transformer or reactor which produces heat causes the decomposition of the insulating oil and any insulation directly involved, resulting in the formation of various gases related to the type of fault. Where the rate of gas production is high, free gas will be collected in the gas and oil actuated (Buchholz) relay. When the rate of gas production is very small it is re-dissolved in the oil and does not appear as free gas. DGA involves the removal from the oil under vacuum of the dissolved gas and its subsequent analysis by gas chromatography, and is now commonly used for fault analysis. Regular DGA monitors the condition of the oil filled equipment and is a useful aid to diagnosing incipient faults such as under oil arcing, local overheating and insulation degradation.

Applicable national and international standards for transformers and reactors are:

BS 171 'Power Transformers', Part 1 'General' (related to IEC 76-1); Part 2 'Specification for Temperature Rise Requirements' (related to IEC 76-2); Part 4 'Specification for Tappings and Connections' (equivalent to IEC 76-4); Part 5 'Specification for Ability to Withstand Short Circuit' (related to IEC 76-5); Part 3 'Awaiting publication, meanwhile BS 171 1970 applies to Insulation Levels and Dielectric Tests. Expected Part 3 will follow closely IEC 76-3

BS 5953 'Guide to Power Transformers' (equivalent to IEC 606).

BS 4944 'Reactors, Arc-suppression Coils and Earthing Transformers for Electric Power Systems' (related to IEC 289).

BS 148 'Insulating Oil for Transformers and Switchgear' (equivalent to IEC 296).

BS 2511 'Methods for the Determination of Water (Karl Fischer Method)'.

BS 5730 'Code Practice for Maintenance of Insulating Oil' (related to IEC 422).

BS 5574 'Guide for Sampling of Gases and of Oil-filled Electrical Equipment and for the Analysis of Free and Dissolved Cases' (equivalent to IEC 567).

BS 5800 'Guide for the Interpretation of the Analysis of Gases in Transformers and Other Electrical Equipment in Service' (equivalent to IEC 599).

BS Code of Practice CP 1010 'Loading Guide for Oil-immersed Transformers' (substantially agrees with IEC 354).

BS 4571 'Specification for On-load Tap-changers' (equivalent to IEC 214).

BS 5611 'Application Guide for On-load Tap-changers' (equivalent to IEC 542).

ESI 53-1 'Distribution Transformers (from 16 kVA to 1,000 kVA).

REACTIVE COMPENSATION.—Reactive compensation may be required for transmission and distribution systems to improve power factor and voltage regulation and thereby reduce the losses and increase the power transfer capability of the system and additionally in the case of long transmission systems to limit switching surges and to improve their steady state and transient stability. Transmission capacity can often be improved by 1 to 2 MW per installed MVAr. At distribution voltages the consumer loads are largely inductive and the transmission and distribution equipment itself such as transformers, overhead lines, underground cables and compensation equipment either consume or generate reactive power the former predominating at high load transfer and the latter at low load transfer. For example, transformers and reactors consume reactive power, capacitors generate reactive power and long overhead transmission lines both consume and generate reactive power. With constant operating voltages at the line ends the line generates reactive power due to its capacitance and this is practically independent of the power transmitted. The line also consumes reactive power due to the line inductance and this varies with the power transferred. When one of a number of heavily loaded parallel lines is out of service for maintenance or fault, the generation of reactive power of the lines is reduced due to fewer lines being in service, and the consumption of reactive power is increased due to the remaining lines being more heavily loaded.

The following types of reactive equipment are commonly used for compensation purposes:

Shunt Reactors.—Are an economic means of compensating the reactive power generated by EHV overhead lines and large underground cable systems. Additionally, they can reduce the temporary overvoltages under open circuit conditions during line energising or load shedding and assist in the reduction of line switching overvoltages. During heavy load operation some or all of the reactors may be switched out of service to avoid over-compensation of the system and unnecessary voltage drop. Compensating reactors are usually directly connected at line voltage and unusually for present day practice via transformers unless required primarily for operational voltage control.

Shunt Capacitors.—Are most widely used for power factor correction in distribution systems but may be installed at some transmission substations where these supply sub-transmission and distribution systems as a means of economic generation of reactive power. As they are shunt connected they are voltage dependent for VAR power generation.

Series Capacitors.—The use of series connected capacitors is an effective and economic means for compensating the reactance of lines to improve and optimise their power transfer capability. A series capacitor is to some extent self-regulating as the reactive power generated in the capacitor increases with increase in load through the capacitor, ie they are current dependent for VAR generation.

The capacitor banks may be switched as part of the lines and located as unattended banks out on the lines or at the line ends at the substations. Alternatively, they may be connected and switched at the substations. A typical arrangement is shown in Fig. 39 in which the equipment is platform mounted on line-to-earth insulation with platform to ground signalling means.

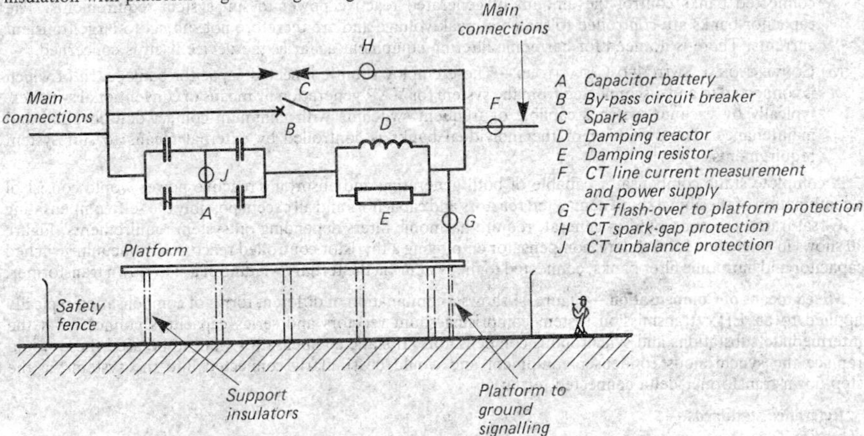

FIG. 39.—Typical Arrangement of Platform Mounted Series Capacitor Bank.

Synchronous Compensators.—Synchronous compensators have been the traditional means for generating and absorbing reactive power, particularly where better voltage control is required than that provided by switched lumped shunt reactors or shunt capacitors. Synchronous compensators are located at the receiving ends of long transmission networks or at important network substations and also at HVDC terminal stations. Their reactive generating and absorbing capability can be regulated by over and under exciting the synchronous machines and their short time overload generating ability may be of value to system operation. In general, they involve high capital and maintenance costs and introduce an additional infeed to the system which may represent an increase in short circuit fault level and switchgear duty.

Static compensators.—Comprise one or more static shunt connected reactive devices in which the reactive power generated by capacitor banks or absorbed by reactor banks is controlled either by their inherent voltage/current characteristics or controlled separately by external means typically employing thyristor (phase-angle) controlled reactors and thyristor switched or alternatively, vacuum switched capacitors in conjunction with high speed control equipment. For application to transmission systems they would typically be connected to the system via a lower voltage winding of a step down transformer.

The various types of reactor and capacitor equipment used in static compensator schemes are as follows:

(1) A.C. SATURATED REACTOR.—This depends upon its inherent voltage/current characteristics to achieve control of reactive power (VAR). An increase in supply voltage automatically increases the current taken by the reactor depending on its degree of saturation and no high speed control equipment is required. The voltage/current characteristic of the equipment is dependent on its natural reactance which may have to be modified by the introduction of slope compensating capacitors connected in series with the reactors to provide the necessary voltage control as determined by system requirements.

The A.C.-saturated reactor saturates every half cycle and therefore inherently will generate harmonics. By the use of some special iron core arrangements and suitably interconnected windings the compensator may be designed to be self-compensating for a range of harmonics which may eliminate or considerably reduce the need for harmonic filtering equipment.

(2) DC PRE-SATURATED REACTOR.—With this type of iron cored shunt reactor a dc winding is provided which enables the degree of saturation and the resulting VAR absorption of the reactor to be controlled. Thyristor rectifiers generally supply the dc current from the system via step-down transformers and by the use of modern techniques the control of the reactor can be made a function of system voltage, system real and reactive power flows or any combination of these. This type of iron cored reactor will also generate harmonics and with present designs, separate harmonic filtering equipment is usually necessary.

(3) THYRISTOR CONTROLLED REACTORS.—The rms value of current taken by this type of reactor can be made a function of the firing angle of a switch consisting of thyristors connected in anti-parallel thereby controlling the VAR absorption of the reactor which again can be made a function of the system voltage, system real and reactive power or a combination of these functions. In common with other forms of separately controlled shunt reactors this type invariably generates harmonics and harmonic filters are usually necessary.

(4) THYRISTOR CONTROLLED CAPACITORS.—These employ shunt connected capacitor banks each of which is connected to and disconnected from the system by means of a thyristor switch. The number of connected banks control the amount of generated reactive power to suit system requirements. The capacitor banks are controlled to switch at peak voltage and are therefore not subject to large transient currents. There is no need for harmonic filtering equipment as far as the device itself is concerned.

(5) CONVENTIONAL SWITCHED CAPACITORS.—These employ shunt connected capacitor banks each of which is connected to and disconnected from the system for VAR generation by means of conventional switches, typically by vacuum switches capable of frequent switching with minimum contact deterioration and maintenance. The switching of the individual banks is controlled by external means to suit system requirements.

A complete static compensator capable of both generating and absorbing reactive power would consist of a combination of the above shunt connected reactors and capacitors and all except possibly the self-compensating A.C. saturated reactor would in general, require harmonic filters depending on system requirements. Figure 40 shows in single line form a static compensator employing a thyristor controlled reactor with vacuum switched capacitor and harmonic filter banks, connected to the system via the tertiary winding of a step-down transformer.

Mixed means of Compensation.—Figure 41 shows a combination of different forms of compensation typically applied to an EHV transmission system comprising shunt reactors and series capacitors connected at the intermediate substations and synchronous compensators. If static compensators were to be used these would replace the synchronous condenser equipment and would be similarly connected into the system via the step-down transformer delta connected tertiary.

Reference standards.—

BS 1650 'Capacitors for Connection to Power Frequency Systems' (equivalent to IEC 70).
IEC 143 'Series Capacitors for Power Systems'.
BS 4296 'Methods of Test for Determining Synchronous Machine Quantities' (related to IEC 34).
BS 4999 'General Requirements for Rotating Electrical Machines' (related to IEC 34).
IEC 289 'Reactors (related to BS 4944').

CURRENT AND VOLTAGE TRANSFORMERS.—Wound type current and voltage transformers employ the same basic transforming principles as power transformers except that they have much reduced outputs rated in VA rather than the kVA/MVA ratings associated with power transformers. Current and voltage transformers are used for measurement (instrumentation and metering) and protective purposes the requirements for each in the case of current transformers in particular being entirely different as regards accuracy. For example, measuring current transformers need to be accurate throughout their normal and overload working range of rated current, whereas a protective current transformer is not normally required to be accurate at currents below the rated value, their accuracy being important at the higher values of current associated with short circuit fault currents. These differing requirements mean that apart from the use of single

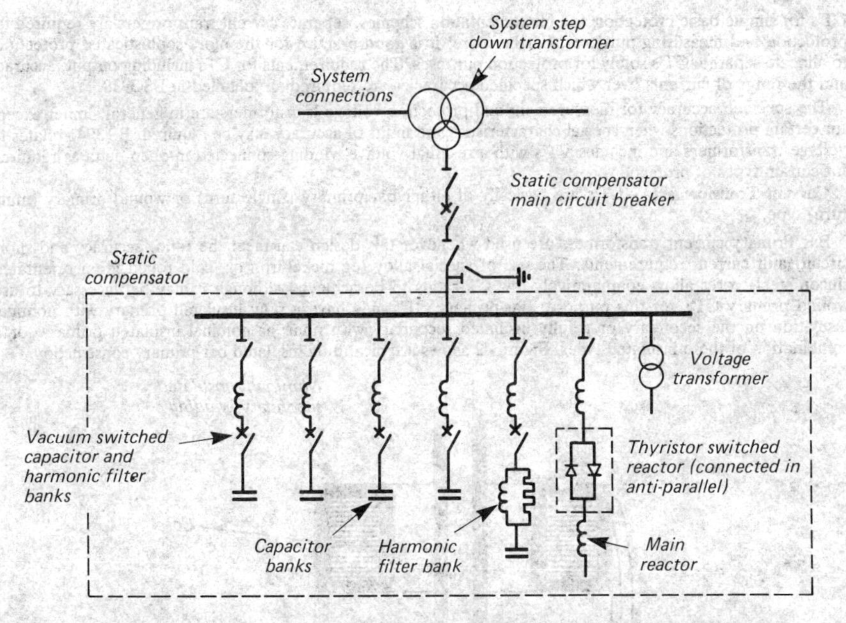

FIG. 40.—Complete Static Compensator for Generating and Absorbing Reactive Power.

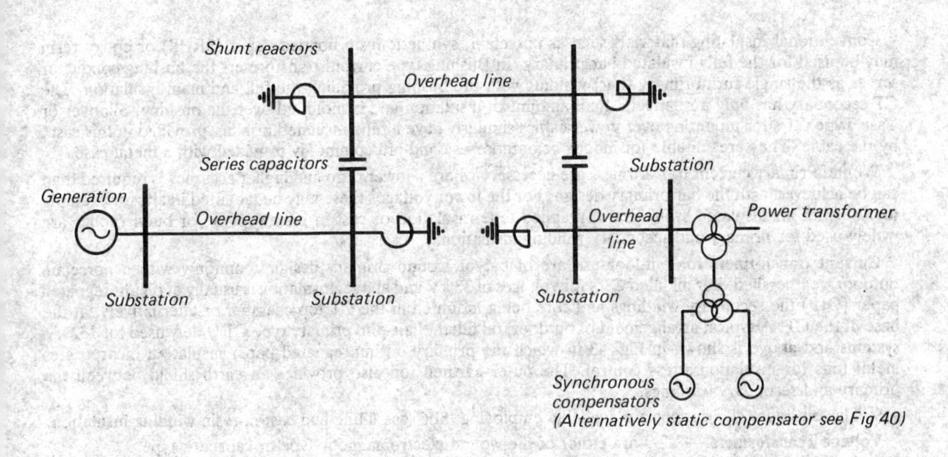

FIG. 41.—Mixed Means of Reactive Compensation for EHV Transmission System.

CT's for simple basic protection and instrumentation schemes, separate current transformers are required for protection and measuring purposes. Furthermore, it is good practice for the more sophisticated protections to allocate separate CT's solely for protection purposes. The requirements for CTs including output, accuracy and the range of currents over which specified accuracies are required are detailed in BS 3938.

The specified accuracy for measurement and protection voltage transformers are in general similar except for certain protections when special characteristics and limits of accuracy may be required. BS 3941 relates to voltage transformers and includes VT's with a residual voltage winding connected in open delta as required for certain types of protection.

Current Transformers.—'CT's are basically of either bar primary (single turn) or wound primary (multi turn) type.

Bar Primary current transformers are used whenever this design can meet the ratio, accuracy and short circuit fault current requirements. The use of special alloy (eg nickel-iron or, cold rolled grain orientated silicon steel) cores allow comparatively low CT ratios to be achieved although it may be necessary to use wound primary CT's for this purpose. Bar-primary CT's may have a fully insulated primary with nominal insulation on the secondary or a fully insulated secondary with none or nominal insulated primary, or a combination of these insulated types. Figure 42 shows a typical fully insulated bar primary construction.

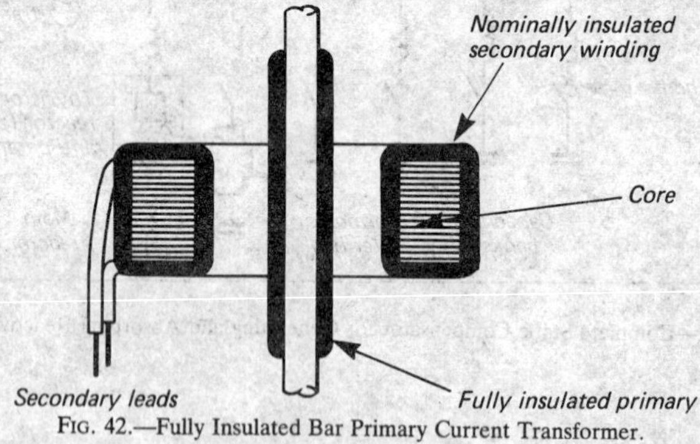

FIG. 42.—Fully Insulated Bar Primary Current Transformer.

Conventional insulating materials such as porcelain, synthetic-resin bonded paper (SRBP) or epoxy resin may be used for the fully insulated bar primary. In Bushing type current transformers the bushing conductor serves as the single turn primary (bar) winding with the bushing providing the full and main insulation. The CT secondary has only a relatively small amount of insulation and is mounted over the bushing. Slipover or Case Type CT's for mounting over power cables similarly have a fully insulated primary provided in this case, by the cable. They are suitable for indoor or outdoor use and are commonly provided with a metal case.

Wound Primary current transformers are necessary where a lower ratio and higher accuracy is required than can be achieved with the bar primary design. For the lower voltages these may be mounted in air, for example for use with air-insulated switchgear. Wrapped tape insulation or cast in resin (epoxy) or butyl rubber are widely used for primary and secondary winding insulation.

Current transformers for outdoor use are of bar or wound primary design commonly with a porcelain outdoor weathershed. For oil filled CT's for voltages of 33 kV and above, insulation is usually of oil impregnated paper (OIP) the secondary windings and core being mounted in the CT top chamber or alternatively, at the base of the CT. A typical arrangement of outdoor, oil filled, 'hair-pin' primary type CT widely used for 132 kV systems and above is shown in Fig. 43 in which the primary oil impregnated paper insulation incorporates metal foils for insulation stress control. The outer earthed foil also provides an earth shield between the primary and secondary windings.

Similar outdoor CT's designs are available employing 'SF6' gas filling and cast-in-resin winding insulation.

Voltage Transformers.—'VT's are either of the wound electromagnetic type or capacitor type.

Electromagnetic Voltage Transformers.—These are wound primary transformers and for indoor cubicle or cellular switchgear arrangements are fixed without withdrawable isolating features. For use in horizontal or vertical isolation metalclad switchgear the associated three phase voltage transformers would have a similar withdrawable feature for isolation. They may be mounted in air or oil with wrapped tape or cast-in-resin insulation and for the lower voltages may incorporate HV fuses.

Oil filled wound type VT's for system voltages above 33kV would usually include a gas actuated relay for protection and the HV primary fuses would be omitted.

Capacitor Voltage Transformers.—'CVT's are available as an economical alternative to the electromagnetic type for voltages of 132kV and above, a typical example for outdoor use being shown in Fig. 44. Figure 45

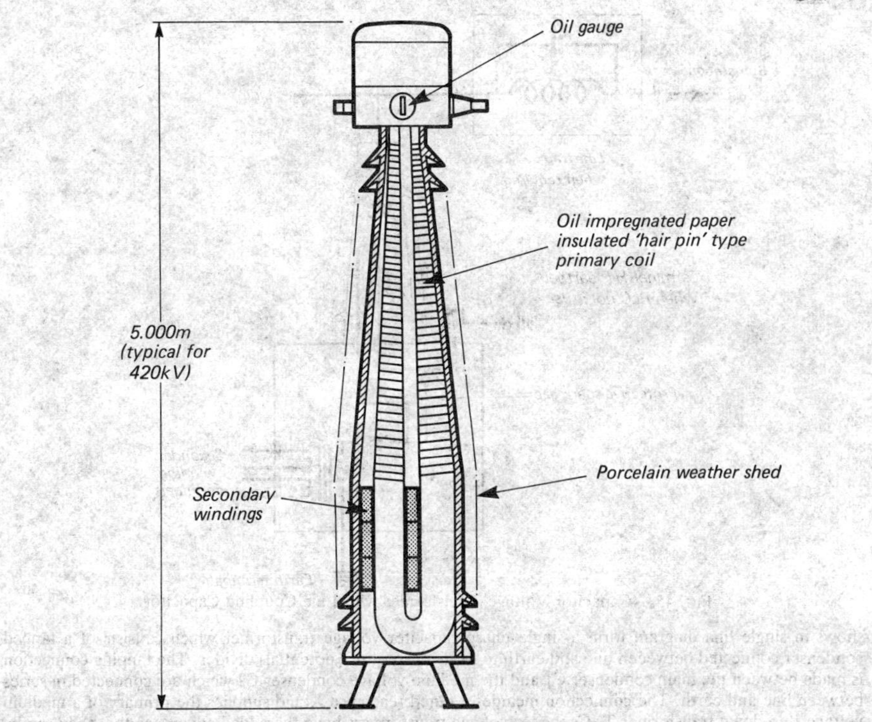

FIG. 43.—Outdoor Oil Filled 'Hair-pin' Primary Type Current Transformer.

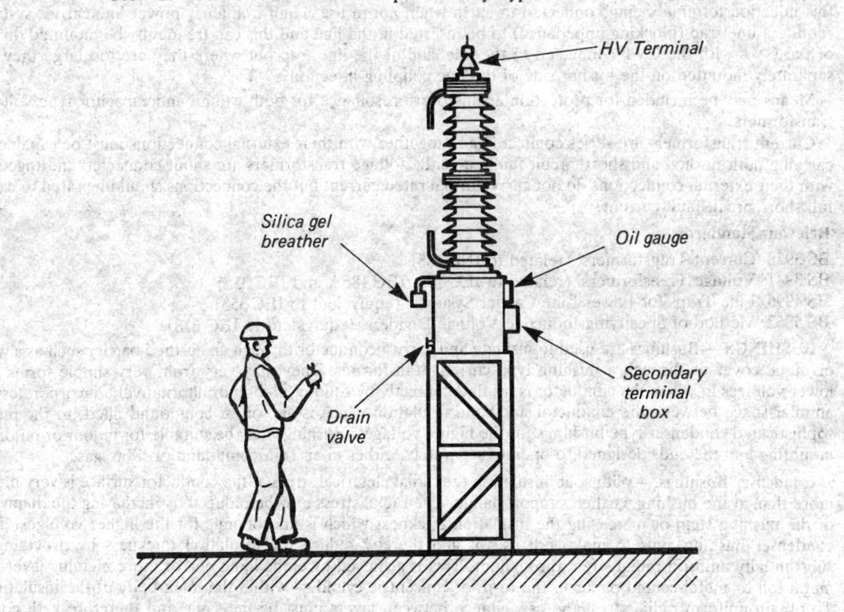

FIG. 44.—Outdoor, Single Phase, Capacitor Voltage Transformer.

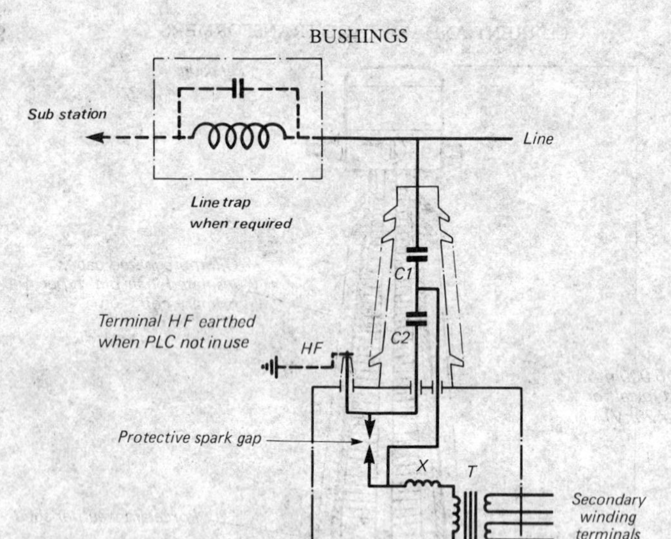

FIG. 45.—Capacitor Voltage Transformer with Line Coupling Capacitor.

shows in single line diagram form a single phase capacitor voltage transformer which consists of a tapped condenser connected betweeen line and earth to form a capacitor (potential) divider. The tapping connection is made between the main condenser C1 and the medium voltage condenser C2 which are connected in series between line and earth. The connection includes a tuned reactance X and supplies the primary of a medium voltage step-down transformer T. Capacitor voltage transformers have the added advantage that they can be used for injecting high frequency current for powerline carrier (PLC) systems via terminal HF when required, this injection terminal being connected to earth when not in use. High frequency power line carrier systems require a line trap (blocking impedance) to be inserted in the line and this can frequently be mounted on top of the CVT with the CVT connected to the line side of the line trap but where they are too large they are separately mounted on the busbar side of the line coupling injection CVT.

Means may be included for protection against ferro-resonance for both wound and capacitor type voltage transformers.

Current transformers are series connected and together with their external connections must be capable of carrying both normal and short circuit fault current. Voltage transformers are shunt connected and together with their external connections do not carry normal rated current but the connections should be rated to carry full short circuit fault current.

Relevant Standards.—

BS 3938 'Current Transformers' (related to IEC 185)
BS 3941 'Voltage Transformers' (related to IEC 186, IEC 186A and IEC 358)
BS 4996 'Line Traps for Power Line Carrier Systems' (equivalent to IEC 353).
BS 5862 'Method of Specifying Inductive Voltage Dividers' (equivalent to IEC 618)

BUSHINGS.—Bushings are used to insulate and carry a conductor through an earthed barrier such as a wall or metal cover or through a bushing type current transformer. They may vary from very simple forms for lower voltages in which the conductor is insulated directly by solid insulation or alternatively, incorporates an annular space between the conductor and solid insulation which is air, oil or compound filled, to the more sophisticated condenser type bushings for the higher voltages. Bushings may be suitable for indoor or outdoor mounting and the ends designed to operate separately, either in air, oil, compound or 'SF6' gas.

Condenser Bushings.—With solid insulation the radial electrical stress at the conductor surface is very much more than at the bushing earthed support flange. The radial stress may be reduced by increasing the diameter of the bushing stem or increasing the insulation thickness which is uneconomic for the higher voltages. The condenser bushing aims to make full use of and thereby reduce the insulation thickness by providing a substantially uniform radial stress throughout. This is achieved by embedding one or more metallic layers of metal foil or metal-coated paper in the form of concentric cylinders within the main body of the insulation. To obtain uniform radial stress the capacitance between layers must be the same and therefore with equal radial spacing the area of each conducting layer must be the same, ie the smallest diameter layer next to the conductor is the longest and conversely the outer layer next to the earthed flange has the largest diameter and shortest length. The embedded layers also control the axial electrical stress over the ends of the bushing operating in either air, oil, compound or 'SF6'. The outer layer is usually connected to the bushing earthed metal flange to confine the stress within the main insulation and may have means for disconnection for insulation power factor test purposes. The bushing may also be used as a capacitor voltage divider by tapping one of the outer layers to provide a voltage source for a small external supply. The permissible radial design stress, based on design function value, is considerably greater than that allowed for the axial design stress. The axial stress in clean oil is some 2½ times that allowed in air based on the design oil and air flashover values and oil circuit breaker bushings operating in carbonised oil require a greater length at the oil end than bushings operating in clean oil. Deposition of carbon on the oil end of the bushing can be reduced by providing the insulator surface in contact with the carbonised oil with a finish having a lower dielectric constant (permittivity or specific inductive capacity) than that of switch-oil, ie 2·25 or by arranging parts of the insulator surface to be normal to the electric field direction, for example, by using shedded insulators particularly towards the 'earthy' end of the bushing. Typical SRBP bushing design stresses are: radial 125 kV/cm, axial in air 3.5 kV/cm, in clean oil 8·5 kV/cm, and in dirty oil 6·5 kV/cm.

Re-entrant type bushings may be used to reduce the axial length of the end under oil for oil-filled power transformers and reactors by arranging the axial clearances between condenser layers not to be continuous in one direction as for a conventional bushing, but to reverse direction towards the conductor end of the bushing. Because of the difference in voltage between the condenser foils and the primary connection at the re-entry position, the transformer winding connection needs to be adequately insulated at this point.

Where the condenser bushings operate in conjunction with one another, for example, on metalclad withdrawable switchgear in which the circuit breaker 'spout' bushings are plugged into the busbar and circuit 'orifice' bushings when in the service position, care must be taken to ensure that the design voltage and relative positions of the condenser foils on each bushing are matched to one another to avoid overstressing the small air gap between the bushings under impulse or continuous working voltage conditions.

Bushing insulation may be synthetic resin bonded paper (SRBP), oil impregnated paper (OIP), epoxy resin paper, cast epoxide resin or porcelain. Metallic layers for stress control can be included in all but the porcelain insulators. Bushings are fitted with porcelain weathersheds on the outdoor end for outdoor service. The small annular gap between the porcelain and the bushing insulation is filled with compound or oil. Porcelain is considerably mechanically stronger in compression than in tension and to maintain the porcelain in compression and to make the oil seals, compression springs are frequently inserted in the bushing top cap between the bushing stalk (conductor) and the porcelain.

A typical oil-immersed, oil-filled bushing is shown in Fig. 46.

The following standards apply:

BS 223 'High Voltage Bushings'.
IEC 137 'Bushings for Alternating Voltages above 1,000 V.

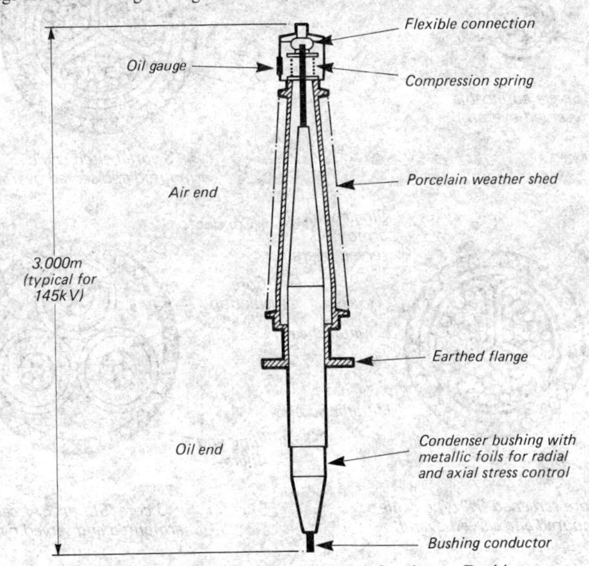

FIG. 46.—Outdoor Oil Immersed Oil-Filled Condenser Bushing.

POWER AND AUXILIARY MULTICORE CABLES

High Voltage Power Cables for power transmission and distribution have traditionally employed impregnated paper for the copper core (conductor) insulation with a lead, lead alloy or aluminium sheath of which the following types are typical.

Solid Paper Insulated Cables.—These employ a viscous resin-oil compound for mass impregnation of the paper insulation without special means of maintaining the paper under pressure. They may be single or multicore construction for voltages up to 33 kV. Multicore cables include the following types:

Belted Type Construction.—Multicore power cables in which the paper insulation is in two parts consisting of insulation applied to the individual cores and an additional belt of insulation wrapped around the laid up cores, before the sheath is applied. Commonly used for voltages up to 22 kV.

Screened or 'H' Type Multicore Power Cables.—Named after the inventor M. Hochstadter, in which each insulated core is surrounded by a metallic conducting screen which provides better stress control in the paper dielectric than the belted type. The screens are in electrical contact with one another and with the earthed metal sheath of the cable.

'SL' and 'SA' Type Multicore Power Cables.—These comprise single core paper insulated cables each with its own lead or lead alloy sheath for type 'SL' or aluminium sheath for type 'SA'. The insulated and sheathed cores are laid-up together and bound overall with layers of suitable material to form the bedding for the armour on armoured cables or the serving on unarmoured cables. Armoured and unarmoured cables would usually have a final overall outer serving. The bedding and serving materials may include fibrous materials such as jute yarn, hessian tapes and natural cotton or synthetic fibre tapes and when required impermeable layers of thermoplastic or natural or synthetic rubber compound.
Type 'H' 'SL' and 'SA' cables are invariably used for system voltages of 33 kV. The core for single core cables is circular and for multicore cables they may be circular or shaped. Typical examples of single core, three core belted and three core 'H', 'SL' or 'SA' cables are shown in Fig. 47.

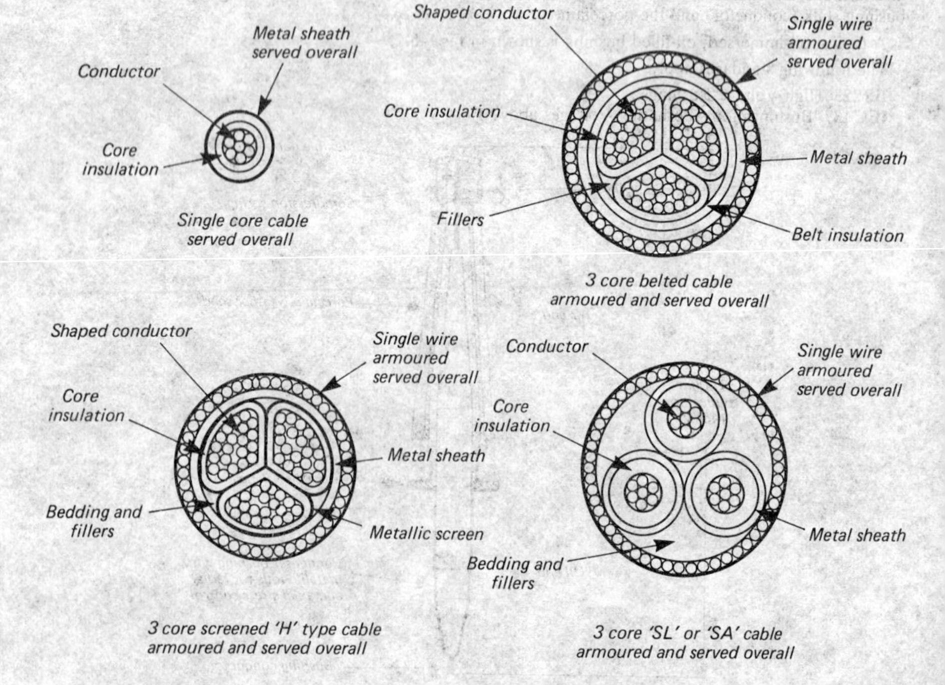

Fig. 47.—Typical Solid Paper Insulated Cables.

Conductor Material.—The most widely used conductor material is copper but aluminium may be used where this shows a saving in the overall cable cost.

Dielectric Strength.—Solid type cables have no external means of increasing the dielectric strength of the insulation by maintaining the paper dielectric under pressure thereby reducing the occurrence of voids in the insulation under cyclic loads or the possibility of compound migration. The following cable types employ external means of maintaining the paper dielectric under pressure.

Oil Filled Paper Insulated Cables.—These employ a viscous oil compound for impregnating the insulation and are oil filled with free flowing low viscosity insulating oil fed by means of internal oil ducts connected to oil reservoir tanks to form a closed oil system in which the oil pressure is maintained above atmospheric pressure under all conditions of loading and installation. For single core cables the conductor is hollow to accept a central oil duct and in three core cables three oil ducts are accommodated in the inter-core spaces. The oil ducts are in the form of an open helix. Pressure tanks usually take the form of sealed and air filled flexible bellows which are immersed in oil filled sealed containers, changes in oil volume due to temperature being accommodated by the flexible bellows. This system also prevents the cable oil coming into contact with air. Typical sections of single core and three core oil filled cables are shown in Fig. 48.

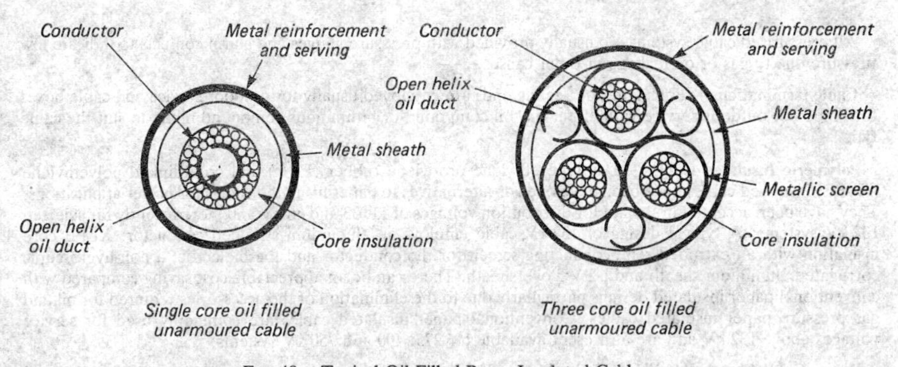

FIG. 48.—Typical Oil-Filled Paper Insulated Cables.

The pressure tank feed points are normally located at the cable end termination points and for longer cable route lengths additionally at intermediate points feeding self contained sections, oil flow between sections being prevented by the insertion of stop joints. The preferred positions for oil pressure tanks at terminations is above ground, at ground level or mounted on an overhead line terminal tower and for intermediate points, above ground. Where this is not possible for intermediate feed tanks and it is necessary to bury them below ground, the tanks should be accommodated in a buried pit with easy access to connections, valves and gauges.

Gas Filled Paper Insulated Cables.—These also employ a viscous oil compound for impregnating the core insulation which is kept under pressure by charging the cable internally with high pressure inert gas. For these gas filled cable systems the gas used is dry nitrogen stored at high pressure which is fed to the cable via reducing valves at suitably disposed gas feeding points. For long route lengths the cable is sectionalised by gas stop joints, each section having its own gas supply. As the gas pressure medium is compressible additional pressure tanks are unnecessary as is the case with oil filled cables which use a substantially non compressible pressure medium.

Gas Compression Paper Insulated Cables.—These are commonly but not exclusively of the Pipeline Type in which pressure on the insulation dielectric is maintained by inserting the three-core impregnated paper insulated cable in a steel pipe filled with high pressure nitrogen which exerts external pressure on a lead diaphragm which envelopes the cable core insulation. No external gas reservoir is permanently connected, ie it is a closed system in which changes in gas temperature are accommodated by small changes in the gas system pressure. Expansion and contraction of the oil in the oil-filled cable terminations is accommodated by compensator units which balance the cable termination oil pressure with the cable system gas pressure.

Oil Compression Pipe Line Cables.—These are similar to the gas compression pipe line type except that the pipe is filled with high pressure oil instead of high pressure nitrogen.

There are many variations of compression type cables, a typical example of a three core gas compression pipe line design being shown in Fig. 49.

Pipeline cables may be provided with skid wires overall to protect the cable during pulling into the pipe.

Impregnated paper insulated cables of oil-filled, gas filled and gas compression types are suitable for use up to the highest system voltages including in Britain 33, 66, 132, 275 and 400 kV.

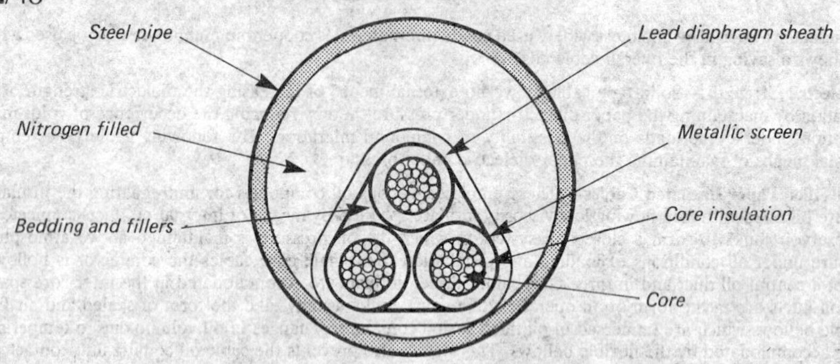

FIG. 49.—Typical Three Core Gas Compression Pipeline Cable.

All pressurised cable systems are usually provided with presssure gauges and alarm contacts to indicate low pressure due to gas or oil leakage or other causes.

Cable terminations.—Porcelain clad sealing ends are employed usually for outdoor service and cable boxes for indoor or outdoor service with either oil, oil compound or bituminous compound filling to suit the cable type.

Polymeric Insulated Cables.—Dry type ethylene propylene rubber (EPR) and cross linked polyethylene (XLPE) insulated cables have been developed as alternatives to paper insulated cables for power applications. They have been accepted in Britain for distribution voltages of 11, 33 and 66 kV and more recently for selected 132 kV systems. A typical design of 132 kV cable employs an aluminium stranded conductor, XLPE core insulation with an extruded semi-conducting screen for the conductor and the dielectric, a non-hygroscopic corrugated aluminium sheath and a PVC oversheath. There can be an appreciable cost saving compared with conventional paper insulated designs particularly due to the elimination of the accessories required for oil and gas pressure paper insulated cables. Conventional paper insulated cables are commonly used for service voltages above 132 kV and are at present available for 275, 400 and 750 kV systems.

Power Cable Sheath Bonding and Earthing.—The metal sheaths of three core cables may be bonded and earthed at each end of the route and at each joint depending on the supply authorities and design requirements. Cable box terminations are usually earthed but where outdoor sealing ends are used the three core cable is divided into three separate single core cables by means of a splitter trifurcating joint box and to avoid circulating currents, the cable sheaths may be bonded and earthed at the point where the cables separate and insulated at the terminations either by insulated glands or by mounting the sealing ends on porcelain insulators or wood blocks. When the length of cable tails between the splitter box and the sealing ends is appreciable it may be necessary to earth the sheath at the insulated sealing ends to limit the sheath standing voltage, care being taken to pass the earth bonding lead back through slipover current transformers when these are fitted.

When the installation consists of insulated sheath single core cables throughout and a solidly bonded and earthed system would give rise to excessive sheath circulating currents special Single Point Bonding or Cross Bonding methods of bonding and earthing the cable sheaths may be necessary to eliminate or substantially reduce the sheath circulating currents.

Single Point Bonding may be applied on relatively short runs of single core insulated sheath cable. The system involves bonding and earthing the sheaths at one end only so that the cable sheaths do not provide a path for the flow of circulating currents either under normal or through earth fault current conditions, ie with faults outside the cable system.

Cross Bonded Systems typically divide the cable route length into three or multiples of three equal length sections with the sheaths and core screens of each section insulated from one another at the cable joint positions. At each third section joint position the sheaths are solidly bonded together and earthed and at the two intermediate joint positions the sheaths are cross connected to provide a complete phase rotation of each of the sheaths at completion of the three section lengths. Providing the lengths of the sections are equal and the cables are laid symmetrical with one another in close trefoil formation, the resulting circulating current in the sheaths will be nil. Where the cables are not laid symmetrical with one another, eg in horizontal flat formation the induced voltages on the outer cable sheaths are greater than on the central cable sheath and to overcome this and provide a balanced arrangement the cable cores are transposed at each joint position and the sheath cross connections are made with an opposite rotation to that of the core transpositions, the resulting sheath voltages and circulating currents over three successive sections again being nil.

Cables with an insulated sheath anti-corrosion overall serving usually have the earth bonding connections made disconnectable via link boxes to permit insulation testing of the sheath.

Sheath Voltage Limiters may be included in the sheath earthing system in the form of non-linear resistors to limit the rise in sheath voltage and protect the sheath section insulation and cable insulated serving under transient voltage conditions.

Armouring.—This is commonly in the form of galvanised steelwires for three core cables but if required for single core cables should be non-ferrous. Armouring is not normally required for oil or gas pressure type cables, the non-magnetic reinforcement applied over the lead sheath being adequate for all normal installations. Where the cables are unarmoured and laid direct in the ground it is usual to provide additional protection by laying earthenware or concrete cable covers above the cables.

AUXILIARY MULTICORE AND MULTIPAIR CABLES.—These are used in general for cabling within transmission and distribution substations and are usually installed in the ground either direct or in cable troughs, or within the substation buildings.

Multicore Cables are used in substations for remote operation of tap changers and the protection circuits of transformers etc. Present practice employs thermoplastic or impregnated paper core insulation which have largely superseded the older traditional forms of insulation and are suitable for cable systems with working voltages up to and including 600/1,100 V, ie to earth and between phase voltages.

Sizes and number of cores in common use for multicore cables are:

7/0·67 mm cores with 2, 3, 4, 7, 12, 19, 27 or 37 cores per cable.

A common construction for thermoplastic insulated cables is PVC insulated, PVC inner sheathed, single wire armoured (SWA) consisting of a single layer of galvanised steelwire and an extruded PVC outer sheath and for paper insulated cables, impregnated paper insulated, lead sheathed, SWA and a lapped serving or extruded PVC oversheath.

Multipair Cables of the telephone type are used for speech and data transmission and for certain types of feeder protection circuits and employ twisted pairs of cores laid up to reduce cross-talk to a minimum and with controlled technical characteristics relating to the mutual capacitance between the two cores of each pair, pair to pair capacitance imbalance at audio frequencies etc.

Common sizes and number of cores for thermoplastic and impregnated paper insulated multipair cables are:

1/0·9 mm cores with 4, 7, 19, 37 or 61 pairs per cable, the cable typical make-ups being polythene insulated, polythene inner sheathed, SWA and an extruded PVC oversheath for thermoplastic insulated cables and impregnated paper insulated, lead sheathed, SWA and a lapped serving or extruded PVC oversheath for paper insulated cables.

Where steelwire armouring does not provide sufficient screening against induced voltages due to magnetic saturation, non-ferrous, eg aluminium wire armour may be used.

Thermoplastic Insulated Light Current Control Cables employing PVC insulated and sheathed cables are used for connecting the control, indication and alarm equipment of power apparatus such as switchgear and operate at circuit nominal voltages typically not exceeding 150 V dc or 110 V ac. The cables are normally unarmoured when installed indoors and armoured for outdoor use.

Common sizes for thermoplastic insulated light current control cables are:

1/0·9 mm cores with 2, 5, 10, 15, 20, 25, 30, 40, 50, 75 or 100 pairs per cable a typical armoured cable make-up being PVC insulated and sheathed, SWA, extruded PVC oversheath.

Pilot Cables consisting of multicore or multipair cables running between sites may be subject to high transient voltages under fault conditions in the power system and the pilot wire insulation and barrier equipment in the form of interposing transformers and relays must be capable of withstanding these overvoltages. The barrier equipment is located at each end of the pilot cables with the object of preventing these overvoltages being transferred to the lower insulated substation cables and equipment.

600/1,100 v Single and Three Phase Service Cables employing a combined neutral and earth (CNE) conductor may have copper or aluminium phase conductors, PVC, impregnated paper or polymeric (XLPE or EPR) core insulation, a concentric copper or aluminium CNE, anti-corrosive serving and PVC oversheath.

Submarine Cables.—In general Submarine Cables may have similar insulation and make up to land laid cables except special attention is paid to the mechanical strength of sheaths, minimum number and reliability of joints and in some cases, flexible joints are necessary. Submarine cables are invariably single wire armoured (SWA) to provide adequate strength during laying etc. and may be double wire armoured where the action of tidal waters, rocky bottoms which often occur where the cables leave the deeper water towards the ends of the crossing and possibility of damage from ships anchors may arise. For the same current rating the land power cables may have a larger core size than the submarine cable in which case special joints will be required. Submarine cables can be supplied for the highest voltages and in order to reduce the weight of the cable and allow the longest manufactured lengths to be produced and therefore for long route lengths to minimise the number of joints, single core cable installations are common for voltages of 33 kV and above where long crossings are involved. Depending on the length and type of water crossing, vessels for cable laying may vary from barge to specially designed ocean going laying ships.

OF GENERAL INTEREST.—

Where a fire hazard exists low voltage cables with special flame resisting finishes or fireproof mineral insulated metal sheathed cables (typically copper conductors, magnesium oxide insulant, bare copper sheath) may be used.

Co-Axial screened type cables are available typically for power line carrier applications, eg for cable connections to PLC capacitor couplers.

Water cooled cables may be used to provide an increase in cable rating, typically in the form of plastic water pipes laid adjacent to conventional power cables.

Fibre Optic cables are available in which electrical signals are converted to light pulses by means of photo-diodes at the sending end of the cable which transmit the light pulses to photo-detectors at the receiving end where they are re-converted to electrical signals. Fibre-optic cables are not subject to the effects of external electrical interference including induced voltages and are suitable for light current and telephone type applications. They may also be used to transmit electrical signals from equipment at high voltage to ground, the fibre optic cable (typically housed in an oil filled porcelain for outdoor application) providing the necessary 'to ground' insulation.

INSTALLATION

Methods of installing transmission and distribution power and auxiliary cables in general fall within the following categories:

Laid Direct in the Ground.—Single core power cables may be laid in a trench in close trefoil or flat horizontal formation with specified minimum spacing between groups of three single core cables or three core cables and between power and auxiliary cables, to suit design requirements. The cables should be laid in the trench and usually 'blinded', ie completely surrounded with a layer of sand or soft fill. Cable protection and warning earthenware or reinforced concrete covers are laid above the blinded cables before back filling the trench. Low voltage and auxiliary cables laid in the same trench as high voltage cables would normally be protected by a common run of covers.

Drawn into Pipes or ducts.—Pipes or ducts may be required for road crossings, in buildings or foundations and where these take one single core cable the pipe should be non-magnetic. Improvement in the cable thermal rating and constraint against thermal expansion and contraction can be achieved by completely filling the pipes and ducts with a mixture of Bentonite clay, sand and cement after drawing-in the cables.

Laid in Troughs.—Troughs are sunk in the ground and are usually of pre-cast reinforced concrete or cast-in-situ construction with close fitting lids. To meet design requirements the troughs may be ventilated, may have special backfills, eg a weak sand/cement mix or be designed to take water cooled cables. Power cables which are subject to thermal expansion and contraction under varying load conditions and are installed in unfilled troughs should be run in cable cleats or hangers. Auxiliary cables may be laid directly on the floor of the trough or on trough cable bearers.

Laid on Trays, Racks, Hangers or in Cleats.—These are used to support cables run inside buildings, in troughs, up equipment structure legs etc. Where the support completely surrounds a single core ac cable, eg a cable cleat they should be of non-magnetic material.

Joint Bays for working access at cable joint positions for laid direct in the ground installations, may have supports for the joint in the form of a cast-in-situ concrete raft with the excavated walls of the bays close timbered and tents or supported weatherproof sheetings being required during jointing. The cable contractor should usually record and provide 'as laid' route record drawings of the cable installation.

To avoid damage to the cable during laying a minimum radius of bend and minimum ambient temperature (typically 0°C) are specified for each type and size of cable.

CABLE CURRENT RATINGS.—Current Ratings depend on a number of factors such as conductor maximum permitted operating temperature, ground thermal resistivity, ground temperature, ambient air temperature, method of installation, ie laid direct in the ground, in ducts or in air and cable grouping and spacing, depth of laying etc. Various ERA (The Electrical Research Association), Cable Makers' Association and cable manufacturers publications and literature give cable current ratings for different types of cables with de-rating and up-rating factors for differing installation conditions. IEC 287 also deals with the calculation of continuous current ratings for all voltages and for different methods of installation and reference ambient temperatures and thermal resistivities of soils in various countries. Some of the applicable standards are:

BS 4066 'Tests on Electric Cables under Fire Conditions' (equivalent to IEC 332).

BS 5372 'Specification for Cable Terminations for Electrical Equipment'.

BS 5467 'Specification for Armoured Cables with Thermosetting Insulation for Electric Supply—related to IEC 502 and IEC 540'.

BS 6004 'PVC Insulated Cables (Non-armoured) for Electrical Power and Lighting' (equivalent to IEC 227).

BS 6081 'Specification for Terminations for Mineral Insulated Cables'.

BS 6207 'Mineral Insulated Cables'.

BS 6231 'Specification for PVC Insulated Cables for Switchgear and Control Gear Wiring'.

BS 6346 'PVC Insulated Cables for Electricity Supply'.
BS 6387 'Performance Requirements for Cables Required to Maintain Circuit Integrity under Fire Conditions'.
BS 6480 'Impregnated Paper Insulated Cables for Electricity Supply' (equivalent to IEC 55).
IEC 78 'Characteristic Impedances and Dimensions for Radio-frequency Co-axial Cables'.
IEC 287 'Calculation of the Continuous Current Rating of Cables'.
ESI 09-2 'The Installation of Transmission and Distribution Power and Auxiliary Cables'.
ESI 09-4 '66 kV and 132 kV Impregnated Paper Insulated Oil-filled and Gas-pressure Type Power Cable Systems'.
ESI 09-5 '275 kV and 400 kV Impregnated Paper Insulated, Oil-filled and Gas-compression Type Power Cable Systems'.
ESI 09-6 'Auxiliary Multicore and Multipair Cables'.
ESI 09-7 'PVC Insulated Concentric Service Cables with Stranded Copper or Solid Aluminium Phase Conductors and Copper Concentric Conductors'.
ESI 09-9 'Polymeric Insulated, Combined Neutral/Earth (CNE) Cables with Solid Aluminium Phase Conductors and Concentric Aluminium Wire Waveform Neutral/Earth Conductor'.
ESI 09-12 'Impregnated Paper Insulated Corrugated Aluminium Sheathed 6,350/11,000 V Cable'.
ESI 09-14 'Cross Linked Polyethylene Insulated Power Cables for 6,350/11,000 V.
ESI 09-15 'Jointing Instructions and Procedures for Mass-impregnated and Mass-impregnated Non-draining Paper Insulated 19/33 kV Cables'.
ESI 12-4 'Terminating Equipment for Pilot Cables Subjected to Induced Transient Voltages exceeding 650 V rms'.

ELECTRICAL PROTECTION

The method of earthing the system neutral and the use of surge diverters together with the gas actuated element of Buchholz relays all protect the power system and equipment against potentially dangerous conditions. Other protective devices such as relays (and fuses) do not prevent a fault or dangerous condition arising but once this has occurred detect and operate to isolate the fault, as speedily as possible, by tripping the appropriate circuit breakers with the object of retaining system stability and continuity of supply, limiting the extent of damage, and reducing the possible danger to human life.

To this end the power supply system is divided into individual protection zones covering feeders, transformers, busbars etc, the zones arranged to overlap where possible. The protection requires to be discriminative ie, operate only for an internal fault within its own zone, speedy in operation, reliable, stable, ie, remain inoperative for all external faults, sensitive, ie, certain to operate down to its minimum internal fault level.

In general the more costly the power system and plant, the more expensive and sophisticated is the protection required and justified (as insurance) to protect it.

Simple distribution systems may employ very basic forms of a.c. protection for direct operation of circuit breaker a.c. trip coils. The more sophisticated forms of relay protection employ both a.c. and d.c. circuits and components for operation of circuit breaker d.c. trip coils under fault conditions. Usual practice is to provide a single d.c. trip coil for circuit breakers up to and including 132 kV. For more important higher voltage transmission systems duplicate trip coils and protections for each circuit breaker and duplicate station d.c. battery supplies are increasingly being employed and justified to ensure security of supply. Modern practice is to employ static rather than the previously widely used electro-mechanical relays.

THE PROTECTION OF FEEDERS.—Commonly used feeder protections are of three different basic types. (1) Time/current graded eg, over-current (non-unit). (2) End to end comparison eg, differential and phase comparison (unit). (3) Ratio measurement eg, distance (non-unit).

Time/Current Graded Protection.—These systems employ protective devices individually installed at selected points throughout the primary network. To achieve discrimination they are graded so that the device nearest to and on the source side of the fault operates to clear the fault before the other devices operate.

Fuses.—The simplest graded protection schemes employ fuses, typically for low voltage 415/240 V distribution systems and also to a limited extent on higher voltage systems eg, 11 kV. Alternatively time/current graded relays may be used as main protection at these voltages and for back-up protection for the higher voltage systems. A fuse combines the fault detection function of a protective device and the circuit interruption function of a circuit breaker and can therefore provide a simple cheap form of graded protection for rural and urban distribution but they are subject to deterioration in service, give no protection between their rated current and minimum fusing current, require replacement after operation and at prescribed maintenance intervals. They do not provide the operational flexibility, high speed operation and fault breaking capacity afforded by modern protections and circuit breakers, required by some distribution and all transmission systems. Fuses operating in conjunction with automatic reclosers are shown in Fig. 35.

Instantaneous Overcurrent Relays.—These may be used to provide time or current graded overcurrent protection, the time or current settings increasing towards the fault current source. With time grading all relays are set to operate at the same current setting and on operation each relay starts a timing relay. For current grading the relays are set to operate at different instantaneous current settings. Systems with relatively high levels of fault current may employ time grading and those with low fault levels, current grading.

Inverse Definite Minimum Time Lag (I.D.M.T.L.) Overcurrent Relays.—These induction type relays have combined inverse and definite minimum time lag characteristics and may be employed where fault levels lie between the extremes covered by time or current graded instantaneous overcurrent relays. Directional and/or non-directional relays may be used for time graded discriminative protection of distribution networks. The relay definite minimum operating time settings selected provide discrimination as typically shown in Fig. 50.

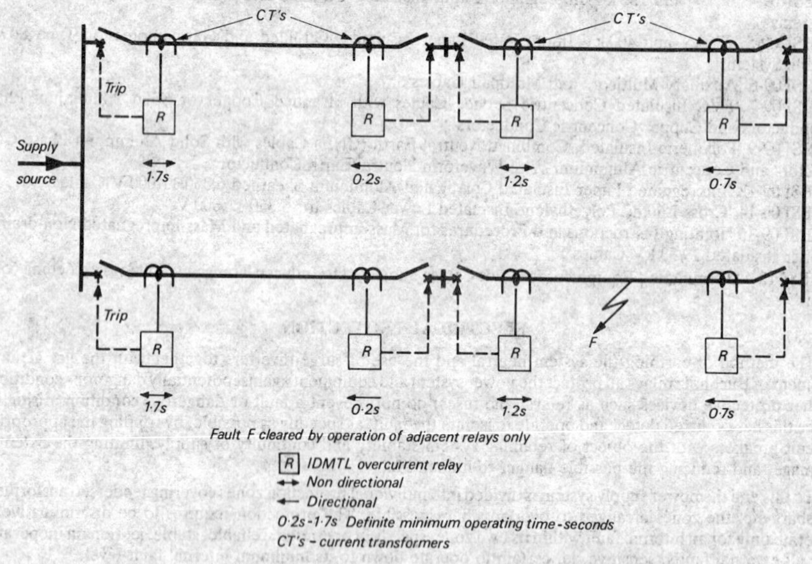

FIG. 50.—IDMTL Overcurrent Protection Applied to Ring Main System.

Relays which need to operate with fault power flows away from the source of supply are non-directional and those required to operate only with power flows towards the supply, directional. The typical time grading margin between adjacent relays of 0·4 to 0·5s is made up of the c.b. total break time and the relay operating time plus a safety margin including equipment tolerances. Line c.t. operated overcurrent relays for phase to phase and phase to earth faults must be set to operate above maximum load current including overload. To detect faults less than full load an earth fault overcurrent relay is supplied from a neutral c.t. in the residual circuit of the three line c.t.s.

Unit Protection Systems.—Discrimination is achieved by applying separate independent protections to each network unit or zone eg, feeder, transformer or busbar. They compare electrical quantities entering and leaving their zone, operate only for internal faults and remain unaffected by external faults.

Feeder Differential Pilot Wire Unit Protection.—Typically this system compares the primary currents entering and leaving its zone. These are substantially equal for normal through load and external faults and the zone is healthy. Conversely for internal faults the currents are not equal and the zone is faulty. Differential pilot wire systems may be of the current balance or voltage balance type employing biased relays (ie with restraining windings) to ensure stability under through fault conditions. In the former (suitable only for short pilot lengths) the biasing winding is operated by pilot current and in the latter (for longer lengths) by pilot voltage. Figure 51. It is usual to provide continuous pilot supervision where the integrity of the pilot protection circuits is outside the control of the supply authority eg, rented pilots. Various factors limit the distance pilot wire unit protection schemes can be used in some instances to about 30 kM and as a maximum approaching 50 kM.

Phase Comparison Power Line Carrier (P.L.C.) Protection.—A high speed unit system for long important overhead line feeders. It is basically similar to pilot wire differential protection. P.L.C. schemes are used for the end to end comparison signalling channel when unit protections are required over distances exceeding the limits imposed by pilot wire length. Various technical factors determine the maximum distance over which P.L.C. channels can be satisfactorily applied and limit this to about five times that of pilot wires ie, in the order of 150–250 kM. The pilot wire circuit is provided by two of the O.H.L. conductors over which a modulated H.F. signal is transmitted for end to end comparison. The long lines (and inclement weather) attenuate the signal preventing comparison of current magnitudes. Current phase angles have to be compared to detect an internal or external fault. Line voltage coupling capacitors and line traps (see Fig. 45) are necessary to inject and confine the signal to the appropriate two phases of the power line. Continuous transmission of the carrier signal may interfere with other services and in many countries including Britain the signal is only transmitted during fault conditions (or routine testing) via starting relays. The protection includes channel supervision

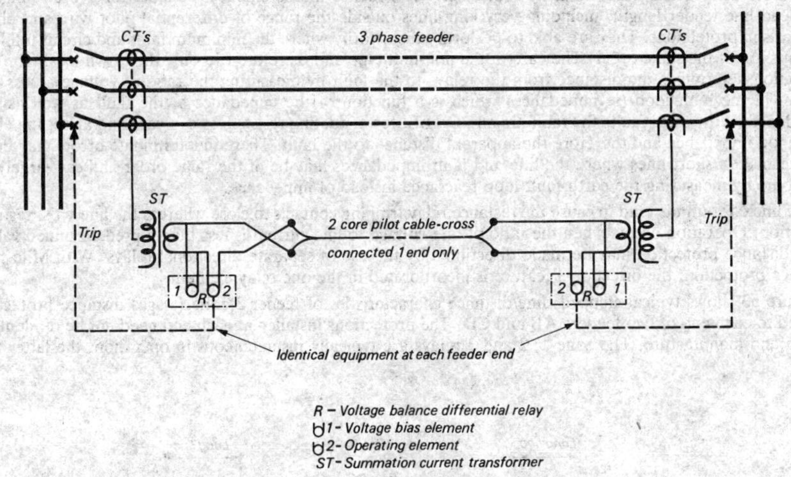

FIG. 51.—Voltage Balance Differential Pilot Wire Unit Feeder Protection.

facilities. The signal frequency allocated is chosen to minimise interference with other carrier systems etc. To reduce signal attenuation, lower frequencies (necessitating larger coupling capacitors) are required for longer lines. Figure 52 shows a single line end set of equipment, two of which are required for each protected feeder. Each line end set compares the remote and local H.F. signals and for an internal fault trips its local c.b. and if external remains stable.

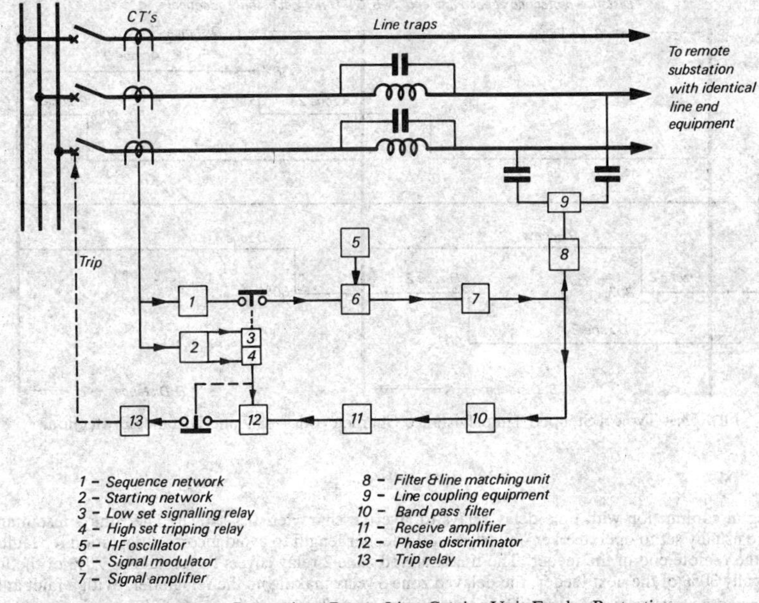

FIG. 52.—Phase Comparison Power Line Carrier Unit Feeder Protection.

Power Direction Comparison P.L.C. Unit Feeder Protection.—This depends on the principle that if fault current direction is towards the busbars at *either* end of the protected feeder then the feeder is healthy and a lockout signal is transmitted to the protection at the remote end to prevent operation. In general, other suitable protections eg, phase comparison P.L.C. are replacing this type.

Distance (Impedance Measurement) Protection.—Impedence measurement is suitable for a wide range of overhead line feeder lengths including very long lines outside the range of differential pilot wire and phase comparison protections. They are able to perform satisfactorily where the minimum fault and circuit full load currents are of the same order. They are of the non-unit type and therefore trip only their own local c.b. The protection determines the distance from the relays to the fault by measuring the ratio of voltage across and current in the fault loop (ie impedance) which is a function of the impedance at the fault as well as line impedance. With earth faults the fault arc and O.H.L. tower footing resistances can vary and affect the earth fault loop impedance and therefore the apparent distance to the fault. These indeterminate errors may be of significance on short lines where the line and fault impedances may be of the same order and can largely be overcome by measuring the earth fault loop reactance instead of impedance.

The line c.t. outputs tend to cause the distance relay tripping contacts to close whereas the line v.t's. restrain operation. Operation occurs when the ratio of line voltage to line current is less than a predetermined value. Plain distance protection may be made directional by the use of separate directional relays. With Mho type distance protection, the directional feature is incorporated in the one relay element.

Figure 53 shows typical stepped time/distance characteristics of feeder 3 zone (stage) distance protection applied to each end of two feeders AB and CD. The protections installed at each end need not be of identical design and manufacture. The zone 1, 2 and 3 relays are typically instantaneous in operation, the latter two

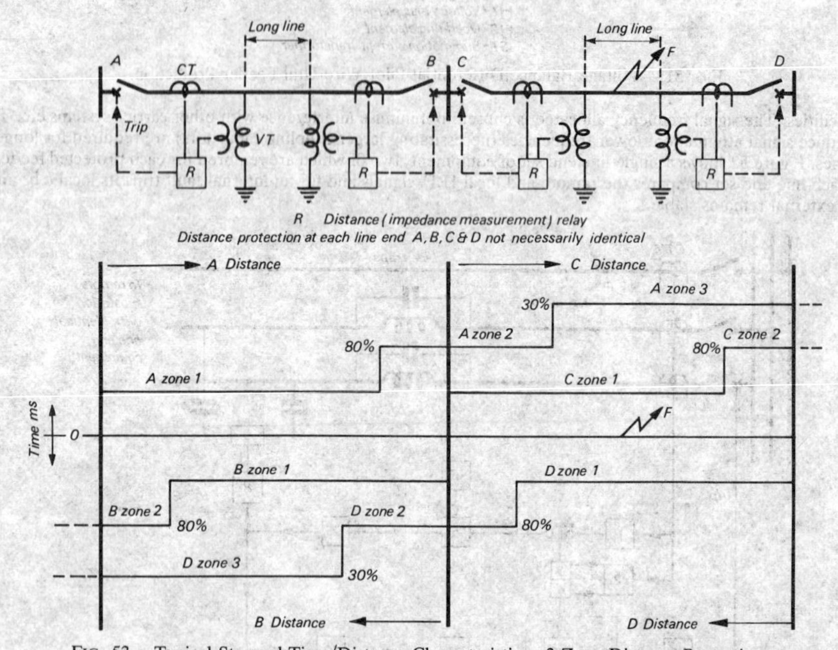

FIG. 53.—Typical Stepped Time/Distance Characteristics—3 Zone Distance Protection.

operating in conjunction with time delay relays to give the characteristics shown. The zone 1 instantaneous relays are usually set to operate over only 80% of the feeder length to avoid incorrect operation for faults just beyond the remote end of the feeder. The time delayed zone 2 relay covers the remaining 20% of the feeder and typically 30% of the next feeder, the delayed zone 3 relay making up the remainder. With a fault at F the zone 1 instantaneous relays at C and D operate before zone 3 relay at A operates. The relays are similarly graded in both directions and the faulted feeder is disconnected at both ends without affecting other feeders. Failure of zone 1 relays to operate is covered by operation of zone 2 or 3 relays on adjacent feeders.

Compensation of Distance Measuring Relays.—Distance protections are commonly used on multiple earthed systems ie, 132 kV and above resulting in *Errors in Earth Fault Measurement* which can be corrected by means of residual compensation to take into account the difference in faulted phase and earth return path currents. Appreciable *Mutual Coupling* can occur between adjacent circuits on double circuit O.H.L.'s. causing the protection to overreach or underreach with a fault on one line or to overreach with one line out of service and earthed for maintenance.

Mho distance relays are inherently directional. Offset Mho relays incorporate a reverse reach in the third zone relays to provide back-up protection for the associated busbars.

Accelerated Distance Protection.—From Fig. 53 faults occurring within the central 60% of feeder length are cleared at both ends by instantaneous operation of zone 1 relays. Faults occurring within 20% of the feeder ends are cleared by only one of the zone 1 relays and the slower zone 2 relay at the remote end. Speeding up or acceleration of the zone 2 relay may be achieved by arranging for operation of zone 1 relay to transmit a signal to the remote end to cause the zone 2 (or 3) relay to clear in a time approaching that of zone 1. A high integrity signalling channel is essential to prevent incorrect tripping due for example to interference on the channel.

Blocked Distance Protection.—This may be used as an alternative to accelerated schemes for the fast clearance of faults occurring at feeder ends. The zone 2 and 3 relays are arranged for instantaneous operation but for external faults are prevented from tripping by a blocking signal received from the feeder remote end. An internal fault also initiates the end to end blocking signals but these are cancelled immediately and the circuit is cleared at both ends by zone 2 (or 3) protections in a time approaching that of zone 1. Again a high integrity signalling channel is required. The scheme is also suitable for other than plain feeder protection eg, feeder with a transformer solidly teed to the line via a motorised isolator.

Application examples.—Feeder protections for 132kV and higher voltage circuits may typically be:— each 132kV feeder equipped with one main high speed, discriminative protection eg, phase comparison P.L.C., differential pilot wire or distance protection with I.D.M.T.L. overcurrent protection as back-up. Each higher voltage feeder equipped with two main high speed, discriminative protections of phase comparison P.L.C., differential pilot wire or accelerated or blocked distance protection. The protections may be of the same or different type/manufacture depending on the protection philosophy adopted. Each should operate separate tripping systems associated with the c.b. duplicate trip coils and preferably employ different signalling channels eg, pilot wire and P.L.C., alternatively the two channels should follow physically separate routes.

POWER TRANSFORMER PROTECTION.—Transformer winding arrangements and methods of earthing (see $G_2$8, 12, 35 and 37) as well as their size and importance determine the types of protection employed to detect such faults as overheating, phase, earth, winding interturn and core faults.

Gas and Oil Actuated (Buchholz) Relay.—Apart from some smaller distribution transformers this protection is fitted to most oil filled power transformers and reactors. The relay is inserted in a straight sloping run of pipe work between the transformer (reactor) tank and its oil conservator and is arranged to collect any gas generated by an internal incipient electrical fault to cause operation of a non-sinkable gas alarm float. A heavier under oil fault operates a separate non-sinkable oil surge float which trips the transformer c.b.s. A test pipe from the relay to ground level enables analysis of gas (or air) collected in the relay without removing the unit from service. The oil surge float may be slow to operate for small fault currents and the relay gives no protection for faults external to the transformer tank. For larger transformers additional protection schemes are justified, supplemented by Buchholz protection.

Tank Pressure Relief.—Devices are provided on the tanks of large oil filled transformers and reactors for the rapid release of abnormal pressure. Selfsealing, spring operated, pressure relief valve types (with auxiliary trip contacts) mounted directly on the tanks offer a faster release of excess pressure than the previously widely used bursting diaphragm types mounted at the end of an oil pipe extended above the maximum oil level.

Winding Temperature Protection.—Winding temperature indicators are provided for large oil filled transformers and reactors to indicate winding temperature and to provide an alarm and eventually a trip signal with progressive overheating. For force cooled units they also start and stop the coolers.

Tank Earth Fault Alarm.—A relay is provided for each unit where for example two auto-transformers are operated as pairs (banked) within one overall protection zone. For an earth fault within a transformer the relay indicates which of the two units is faulty. Insulated cable glands and tank fixings clear of earthed metal are required. The relay is not required when separate suitable protections are provided for each transformer.

Restricted Earth Fault Protection.—This is a current balance differential scheme which protects against earth faults occurring within a restricted zone limited to the transformer H.V. (or L.V.) windings. A set of residually connected H.V. (or L.V.) three phase c.t's. is balanced against the current from its neutral c.t. (H.V. or L.V.) so that the only current flowing in the restricted earth fault relay would be that due to an earth fault on the winding covered by the protection. This together with I.D.M.T.L. overcurrent protection applied to each

winding covered by the protection. This together with I.D.M.T.L. overcurrent protection applied to each winding provides phase and earth fault protection, typically for smaller two winding distribution type transformers as shown in Fig. 54.

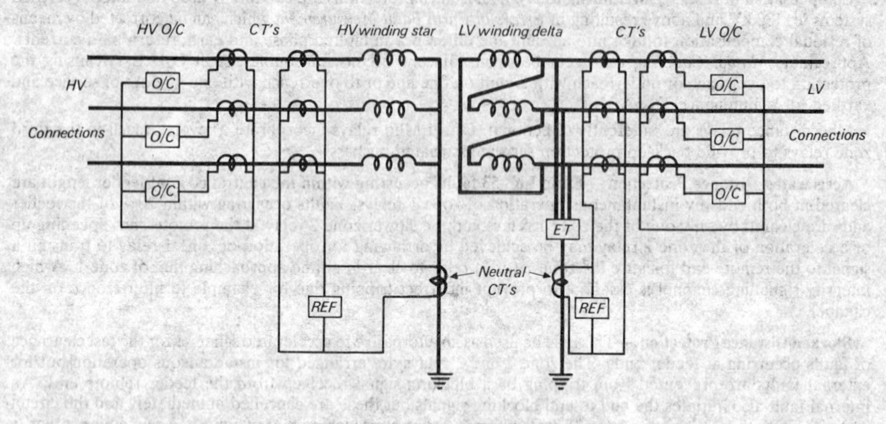

FIG. 54.—2 Winding Power Transformer Instantaneous Restricted Earth Fault and IDMTL Overcurrent Protections.

Overall Differential Protection.—The current balance type provides faster phase to phase main protection for large two winding transformers than I.D.M.T.L. overcurrent protection. Both H.V. and L.V. windings are included in the one overall single zone of protection. The scheme is similar to the current balance protection applied to feeders, the H.V. and L.V. current transformer connections local to the transformer being equivalent to very short pilot circuits. To achieve current balance the transformer winding arrangement and transformation

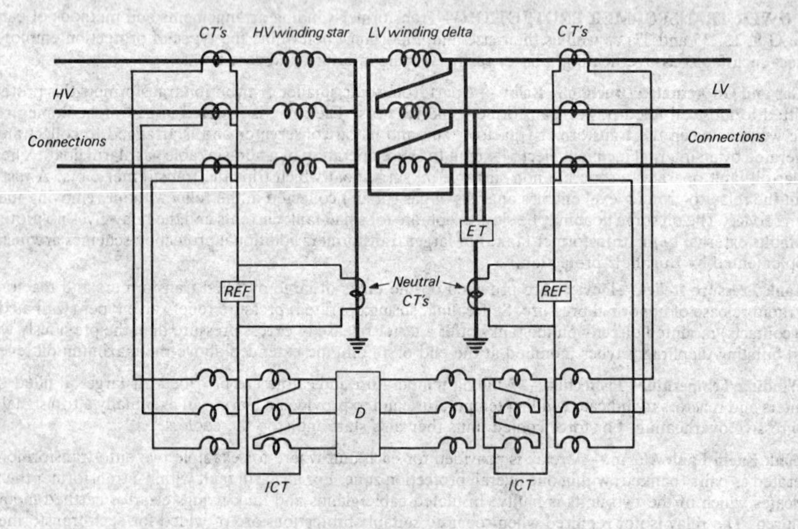

FIG. 55.—2 Winding Power Transformer Overall Differential and Restricted Earth Fault Protections.

ratio are corrected by selecting appropriate c.t. ratios and method of connecting ie either directly or via interposing c.t's. for example when restricted earth fault is required in addition to differential protection. For H.V. star and L.V. delta connected transformers the H.V. interposing c.t. secondaries are delta connected and the L.V. secondaries star connected to achieve balance. Load biased differential relays are used for transformers with on load tap change gear to compensate for out of balance current which flows in the relay during normal load and external fault conditions for tap positions other than mid tap upon which the c.t. ratios are fixed. The relay may also include a high harmonic biasing feature to avoid incorrect operation due to initial magnetizing inrush current when switching on an unloaded transformer. Harmonic restraint is preferred to time lag relays which introduce an unwanted delay in clearing a true transformer fault. Typical schemes are shown in Fig. 55.

Auto-Transformers.—For auto-transformers, simple current balance unbiased differential (circulating current) protection with high impedance relays provides phase and earth fault main protection. Biasing is not required as the protection problems regarding magnetizing inrush current and tap position change do not arise.

The larger transformer main protections are backed up by Buchholz, winding temperature, pressure relief and overcurrent protections.

BUSBAR PROTECTION.—Busbar protection protects busbars, associated connections and switchgear. Because of the serious consequences of incorrect tripping two independent protections are commonly provided, both of which must operate before the busbar is removed from service.

Frame Earth (Leakage to Frame) Bus Zone Protection for Metal Enclosed Switchgear.—The basic scheme shown in Fig. 27 may operate incorrectly caused for example by secondary wiring faults. This is guarded against by an independent check relay supplied from a neutral c.t. in all local incoming supply transformers or by a core balance c.t. on all incoming feeders (to accommodate an incoming circuit being out of service). Both frame earth and check protections must operate before the busbar is tripped. The scheme provides main phase to earth fault protection only for small distribution substations or as back-up to other protections.

Circulating Current Busbar Protection.—A current balance unbiased differential scheme employing high impedance relays and short pilots (in the form of local secondary wiring). It provides both phase and earth fault protection. Typically two completely independent protections are employed, each with their own c.t's. and operating one of the c.b. duplicate trip coils where applicable. On sectionalised busbar schemes one system discriminates between faulted bus bar sections. The second constitutes a check system operating usually over the whole installation except for special applications when more than one check system may be used for individual zones. Both discriminating and check systems must operate before the relevant busbar connected circuit breakers trip. See Fig. 56.

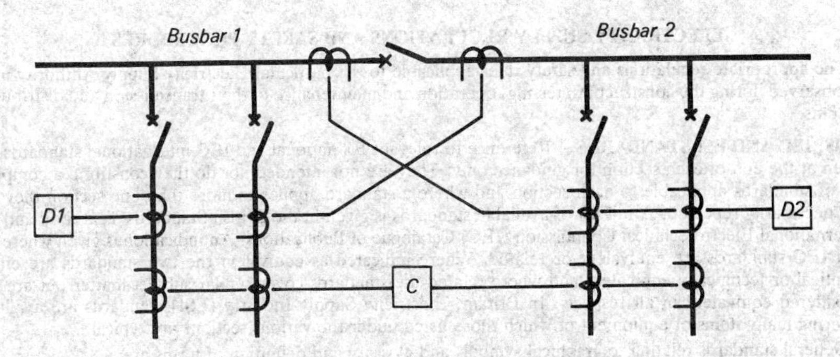

FIG. 56.—2 Zone Differential Circulating Current Busbar Protection.

Circuit Breaker Overlap Protection.—For practical and economic reasons live tank c.b's. normally have c.t's. mounted separate from the breaker, typically on the line side. From Fig. 57 a fault F between the c.b. and

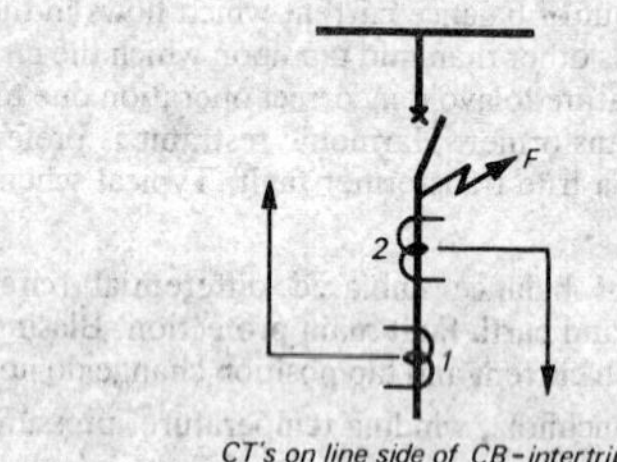

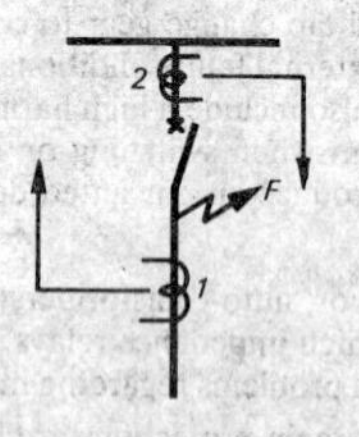

1-Busbar protection CT 2-Circuit protection CT

FIG. 57.—Circuit Breaker Overlap Protection.

c.t's. is isolated from the busbars by the busbar protection but as the fault is outside the circuit protection zone, intertripping of the remote c.b. is required to clear the fault. With dead tank c.b's. bushing type c.t's. can conveniently be accommodated on both sides of the break providing overlap protection and both busbar and circuit protections operate to clear the fault without intertripping.

Circuit Breaker Fail Protection.—This trips all c.b's. necessary to clear a fault having detected the appropriate c.b. has failed to open. It is inoperative for other than failure to trip on fault. Typically provided for important E.H.V. busbar stations.

Intertripping.—Affected by operation of the protection at one end of a circuit transmitting a signal to trip the remote end circuit breaker.

References:—

B.S. 142 Electrical Protective Relays.

B.S. 2692 Fuses for Voltages Exceeding 1,000V a.c. (related to I.E.C. 282)

B.S. 5992 Electrical Relays (equivalent to I.E.C. 255)

Power System Protection Handbook, Vol. 1. Principles and Components, Vol. 2. Systems and Models, Vol. 3. Application.

ELECTRICITY SUPPLY REGULATIONS AND SAFETY PROCEDURES

The appropriate regulations and safety rules applicable to the particular Electricity Supply Authority must be observed during the construction, testing, operation and maintenance of their transmission and distribution systems.

BS, IEC AND ESI STANDARDS.—Reference to relevant BS national and IEC international standards are given at the end of each section for guidance only. They are not intended nor do they constitute a complete list of standards applicable to each section and where a standard applies to more than one section they are not necessarily repeated. A full list of available standards is given in the British Standards Yearbook and the International Electrotechnical Commission (IEC) Catalogue of Publications. An indication is given where BS and IEC standards are equivalent or related. Where indicated as equivalent the two standards are either identical or technically equivalent and where related the standards cover similar subject matter but are not considered equivalent in all respects. In Britain, Electricity Supply Industry (ESI) standards are available covering many items of equipment of which those listed under the various sections are typical.

General standards relating to graphical symbols and glossary and definition of terms are:

BS 3939 'Graphical Symbols for Electrical Power, Telecommunications and Electronic Diagrams' (equivalent to IEC 117 'Recommended Graphical Symbols; Graphical Symbols').

BS 4727 'Glossary of Electrotechnical, Power, Telecommunications, Electronics, Lighting and Colour Terms'.

BS 661 'Glossary of Accoustical Terms' (BS 4727 and BS 661 related to IEC 50 'International Electrotechnical Vocabulary').

ESI 99-3 'Definitions of Terms used when Predicting or Measuring Electricity Transmission and Distribution Reliability'.

BIBLIOGRAPHY—REFERENCES

WESTINGHOUSE, Ed. Electrical Transmission and Distribution Reference Book; Westinghouse Electric Corporation, Pennsylvania, USA.

GUILE, A. E. and PATERSON, W., *Electrical Power Systems*, Vol 1 and 2; Oliver & Boyd, Edinburgh.

FINK, D. G. and CARROL, J. M., Ed., *Standard handbook for Electrical Engineers*; McGraw-Hill Book Company, New York and London.

LAUGHTON, M. A. and SAY, M. G., Ed., *Electrical Engineers' Reference Book*; Newnes-Butterworths, London.

STARR, A. T., *Generation, Transmission and Utilization of Electrical Power*; Pitman, London.

COTTON, H., *Transmission and Distribution of Electrical Energy;* English Universities Press, London.

GRIDLEY, J. H., Ed., *High Voltage Distribution Practice*; Ernest Benn.

TAYLOR, E. O. and BOAL, G. A., *Electrical Power Distribution,* Edward Arnold, London.

BROSAN A. S. and HAYDEN, J. T., *Advanced Electrical Power and Machines*; Pitman, London.

KEMP, P. *Alternating Current Electrical Engineering*; MacMillan, London.

WILSON, W. *The Calculation and Design of Electrical Apparatus*; Chapman and Hall, London.

MORTLOCK, J. R. and HUMPHREY DAVIES, M. W., *Power System Analysis*; Chapman and Hall, London.

GILES, R. L., *Layout of E.H.V. Substations*; IEE Monograph Series 5. Cambridge University Press, London.

LYTHALL, R. T., *The J and P Switchgear Book;* Newnes-Butterworths, London.

FLURSCHEIM, C. H., Ed., *Power Circuit Breaker Theory and Design*, IEE Monograph Series 17; Peter Peregrinus, Stevenage.

AUSTEN STIGANT, S. and FRANKLIN, A. C., *The J and P Transformer Book;* Newnes-Butterworths, London.

BARNES, C. C., *Power Cables: Their Design and Installation*; Chapman and Hall, London.

HUNTER, P. V. and TEMPLE HAZELL, J., *Development of Power Cables*; George Newnes, London.

PULSFORD, J. A. and KNOX, C. C. Ed., *Underground Systems Reference Book*; Edison Electric Institute, New York.

THOMAS, A. G. and RATA, P. J. H., *Aluminium Busbar*; Hutchinson Scientific and Technical, London, for Alcan Industries.

THE ELECTRICITY COUNCIL (Ed.), *Power System Protection Handbook*, Peter Peregrinus, Stevenage.

Publications:

Copper for Busbars Pub. No. 22; Copper Development Association, London.

Copper for Earthing Pub. No. 30; Copper Development Association, London.

Copper Cables Pub. No. 56; Copper Development Association, London.

Aluminium Busbars, Pub. No. L4; British Aluminium Co. Ltd.

Aluminium for Busbars, Earthing and Lightning Conductors, Pub. No M4; British Aluminium Co. Ltd.

Aluminium Busbars; Aluminium Federation, London.

Aluminium Federation Information Bulletins. No. 5, *The Gas Welding of Aluminium;* No. 19, *The Arc Welding of Aluminium*.

BANBURY, J. C., *Distribution—The Final Link in the Electricity Supply Chain*; IEE Electronics and Power, 17 July 1975.

BILLINGTON, R. and ALLAN, R. N., *Power System Reliability in Perspective*, IEE Electronics and Power, March 1984.

CAKEBREAD, R. J. and BROWN, H. J., *Integrated Mechanical Loading for Open Type EHV Substation Structures and Equipment*; Electra (CIGRE) Paper No. 60 (1978).

CIGRE paper 23-12 (1976), *Design of Substations for Systems Operating at 765 and 1050 kV.*

Buckling Strength Analysis of large Power Transformer Windings subjected to Electromagnetic force under Short Circuit; IEEE Trans. Vol. PAS-99. No. 3. 1980.

CIGRE Paper 23-10 (1976), *Behaviour of Rigid Conductors and their supports under Short Circuit Conditions, Comparison of Calculated and Measured Values.*

CIGRE Paper 23-06 (1972), *Influence of the Electric Field in 500 and 750 kV Switchyards on Maintenance Staff and means for its Protection.*

CIGRE Paper 31-05 (1976), *Influence of Electric Field Effects on 500 kV System Design.*

CIGRE Paper 36-08 (1976), *Electric Field Measurement in the vicinity of H.V. Equipment and assessment of its Bio-Physiological Perturbing Effects.*

CIGRE Paper 36-09 (1976), *Investigation into Interference in Substation and Power Station Auxiliary Cabling.*

CIRED (Congrès International des Reseaux Electriques de Distribution) International Conference on Electricity Distribution, London, 1977.

CRONSHAW, K., *Electricity Distribution in Rural Areas*; IEE Electronics and Power, October 1981.

CRONSHAW, K. CUNNINGHAM, C. DEUSE, M. and MESSAGER, P., *A Distribution System for Rural Zones with Low Consumption Rates*; CIRED, 1981. Discussion Paper 6.10.

Herriot-Watt University Edinburgh. *Distribution System Developments. Paper No. 1 Design and Performance.*

IEE/ERA Conference on Distribution, Edinburgh, 1970.

IEE International Conference on Thyristor and Variable Static Equipment for ac and dc Transmission, London, December 1981.

THOREN, H. B. and CARLSSON, K. L., *A Digital Computer Programme For the Calculation of Switching and Lightning Surges on Power Systems;* IEEE Trans. Vol. PAS-89, No. 2, 1970.

Olwegard, A. et al., *Thyristor-controlled Shunt Capacitors for improving System Stability*; CIGRE Paper No. 32-20, 1976.
Fahlen, N. T., E.H.V. Series Capacitor Equipment Protection and Control; IEE Proceedings Part C, November 1981. Generation, Transmission and Distribution.
Torseng, S., *Shunt connected Reactors and Capacitors controlled by Thyristors*; ibid.
Adami, H. and Batch, B. A., *Aeolian Vibrations of Tubular Busbars in Outdoor Substations*; Electra (CIGRE) Paper No. 75, March 1981.
Electrical Review, 12 September 1980, *Toroids give Added Protection against Transient Overvoltages.*
Kelsey, T. and Besford, S. J., *The use of Auto-reclosers and Sectionalisers in Rural Distribution Networks*, IEE Electronics and Power, October 1983.
Tedford, D. J., Campbell, L. C., and Pender, J. T., *Modern Research and Development in SF6 Switchgear.* IEE Electronics and Power, October 1983.
Lawson, W. G., Rechowicz, M. and Rigby, S. J., *Developing Cross Linked Polyethylene Cables for High Voltage power Transmission,* IEE Electronics and Power, February 1978.
Electrical Times, 6 November 1981, *Area Board Now Installs XLPE at 132 kV.*
Baker, H., and Wilson, I. O., *Mineral Insulated Cable—the Inorganic Solution.* IEE Electronics and Power, April 1987.
Stewart, J. S., *SF6 Circuit Breaker Design and Performance*, IEE Electronics and Power, February 1979.
Parry, J., *Mechanical Aspects in the Design of Distribution Switchgear.*, ibid.
Rees, D. W., *Silicone Liquid Filled Transformers.*, ibid.
BS Code of Practice CP3, *Code of Basic Data for the Design of Buildings.* Chapter V *Loading.* Part 2. *Wind Loads.*
BS Code of Practice CP1014 'The Protection of Electric Power Equipment against Climatic Conditions'.
BS 2011 Basic Environmental Testing Procedures (Cold, Heat, Solar Radiation, Corrosion, Salt, Bump, Free Fall, Mould etc.) (equivalent to IEC 68).
BS 9530 'Code of Practice for Site Investigations'.
BS 6031 'Code of Practice for Earthworks'.
IEE Wiring Regulations. Regulations for Electrical Installations. Fifteenth Edition 1981.

Considerable literature is available from the various equipment manufacturers relating to several aspects of power transmission and distribution, together with comprehensive details of the individual manufacturer's equipment, and it is recommended this literature be consulted for further information.

ELECTRIC HEATING PROCESSES

Electric Heat Treatment — Furnaces — Direct Resistance Heating — Induction Heating — Salt Baths — Glow Discharge Nitriding — Surface Hardening using Lasers — Surface Heating — Metal Sheathed Resistance Heaters — Heating Tapes — Electrode Boilers — Infra-Red and Ultra-Violet Processes — Dielectric Heating — Resistance Melting — Channel Induction Furnaces — Coreless Furnaces — Direct Arc Furnaces — Submerged Arc Processes — Electron Beam Furnaces — Electroslag Melting — Glass Melting — Plasma Processes for Chemical Synthesis — Bibliography.

By H. Barber, BSc(Eng) and J. E. Harry, BSc(Eng), PhD, MIEE, CEng
Department of Electronic and Electrical Engineering,
University of Technology Loughborough

Electric heating processes are finding ever increasing application in spite of being in direct competition with other heating methods. A wide range of techniques is available. Frequencies vary from dc to microwave frequencies and power levels from a few watts to over 100 MW (Table 1). Although direct cost comparisons between fuel-fired and electric heating processes are not always favourable to electricity, nevertheless overall savings in energy and production costs can be made in many applications. Examples are the use of induction surface hardening in which only the outer surface of a component is heated, through heating in which the component is heated in a fraction of the time required by conventional processes (so minimising heat losses), heat treatment during the final stages of manufacture of a component where the reduced rejection rate arising from the use of electricity outweighs the increased energy costs and in melting processes where reduction in the loss of volatile constituents again outweighs the increase in energy costs. Although most of these factors are difficult to quantify it is necessary to make a balanced assessment of the alternative processes which are available and their effect on the cost of each manufacturing stage as well as on the total cost of the product.

ELECTRIC HEAT TREATMENT.—Heat treatment processes are extensively used in the manufacture of metal components. They range from through-heating prior to rolling of ingots and slabs to, finally, the case hardening of bearing surfaces of manufactured components. Some examples of electric heat treatment processes together with the temperature at which they are carried out are listed in Table 2. Similar applications also exist in other industries e.g. fusing sintered ceramics, glass annealing and vitreous enamelling. Fuel-fired furnaces are directly competitive with electric heating techniques in many applications and the final choice can only be made on economic grounds taking into account the overall process cost.

TABLE 1.—EXAMPLES OF ELECTRIC PROCESSES.

Frequency	Technique	Typical power range
dc–50 Hz	direct resistance	10 kW–30 MW
50 Hz	indirect resistance	5 W–5 kW
50 Hz	ovens and furnaces	100 kW–1 MW
dc–50 Hz	arc melting	1 MW–100 MW
50 Hz–450 kHz	induction melting	20 kW–10 MW
1 MHz–100 MHz	rf dielectric heating	1 kW–500 kW
500 MHz–2·5 GHz	microwave heating	1 kW–100 kW
dc–50 Hz, 4 MHz	plasma torches	1 kW–1 MW
30 THz	lasers	100 W–60 kW
	electron beams	10kW–500 kW
2–3 THz	infra-red	1 kW–12 kW
1–1.5 THz	ultra-violet	1 kW

TABLE 2.—COMMON HEAT TREATMENT PROCESSES.

Metal	Process
Aluminium and aluminium alloys	annealing 250°C–520°C forging 350°C–540°C solution heat treatment 400°C–500°C precipitation hardening 100°C–200°C stress relieving 100°C–200°C
Copper	annealing 200°C–650°C
Brass	annealing 400°C–760°C
Magnesium and magnesium alloys	annealing 205°C–450°C solution heat treatment 400°C–570°C precipitation hardening 100°C–1,100°C–250°C
Nickel and nickel alloys	annealing 650°C–1,190°C
Carbon steels (0·6%–1·5%)	full annealing 900°C–960°C forging 800°C–950°C tempering 200°C–650°C hardening 760°C–820°C
Stainless steels	hardening 950°C–1,050°C tempering 175°C–750°C
Cast iron	full annealing 500°C

ELECTRIC FURNACES FOR HEAT TREATMENT.—Electric furnaces are used for through-heating prior to forging, for example, to change the metallurgical structure of a component as in annealing, and for surface heat treatment by either exposure of the surface of the component to a chemically reactive environment (carburising, bright finishing, etc) or to produce a metallurgical change at the surface by rapid cooling in a quenching medium after heating. Process temperatures vary from about 550°C to more than 1,800°C although the majority of heat treatment furnaces operate in the range of 550°C to 900°C. Size and power ratings vary from less than 0·1 m^3 to more than 200 m^3 and from a few kW to over 1 MW.

The selection of a furnace is dependent on the method of work handling required, the operating temperature, the dimensions of the workpieces and the throughput.

Unlike fuel-fired furnaces, where the fuel burners are localised and the optimisation of heating by convection plays a key role in furnace design, temperature uniformity is not normally a severe problem. A number of different examples of batch furnaces for heat treatment are shown in Fig. 1.

The heating elements are arranged around the sides of the furnace and, where a very high degree of temperature uniformity is required in the roof, door and hearth. Methods of work handling include bogie hearths and elevator hearths which can be loaded prior to charging the furnace. The sealed quench furnace is used where it is necessary to avoid exposure to air during the quenching process. Forced convection furnaces allow high heating rates, and with careful design, good temperature uniformity can be achieved at temperatures up to about 600°C, operation up to 900°C is possible. The pit furnace, which depends on radiation as the principal mechanism of heat transfer, works at higher temperatures and, by using a sealed retort, can operate with a controlled atmosphere. The bell furnace allows unimpeded access to the hearth and is particularly suitable for large workpieces and in one form it is used as a hot-retort vacuum-furnace for bright annealing. Convection losses during cooling are reduced when the retort is evacuated and consequently one bell can be used to heat several retorts. The cold-retort vacuum-furnace is used where very high temperatures are required and for heat treatment and brazing in controlled low pressure atmospheres. Vacuum interlocks may be used to achieve high throughputs. Muffle furnaces can be used both for inline processes, such as wire annealing, and high temperature batch processes.

The various forms of conveyor mechanisms in continuous furnaces are shown in Fig. 2. Controlled cooling and heating cycles are possible and heat treatment can be carried out in-line with other processes. The choice of conveyor mechanism depends on the type of workpiece and the process which may vary from bright annealing small fasteners using a shaker hearth mechanism, in which a net forward motion is combined with rotation of the component so that it is uniformly exposed to the furnace atmosphere, to large roller hearth furnaces for normalising steel billets.

Heating elements used in electric furnaces.—The principal requirements of a heating element are a high creep resistance at the rated temperature, good resistance to thermal shock, resistance to corrosion or oxidisation due to ambient gases and vapours, good ductility, mechanical strength at high temperatures, a high resistivity

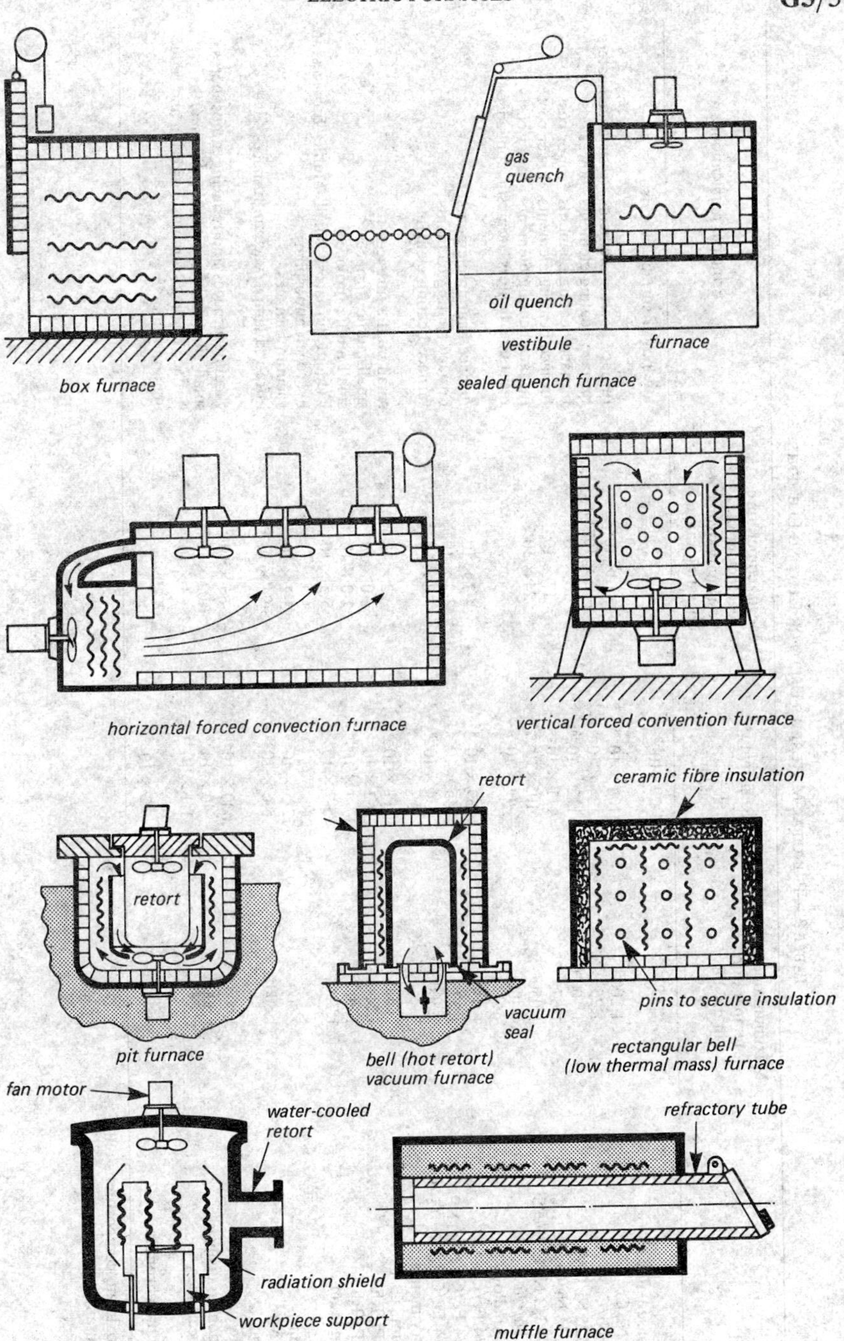

FIG. 1.—Examples of batch furnaces used for heat treatment.

TABLE 3.—PRINCIPAL MATERIALS USED FOR HEATING ELEMENTS.

Material	Maximum operating temperature in dry air, °C	Resistivity at 20°C, Ωm	Mean temperature coefficient of resistivity over operating range	Principal applications
Copper	350	$1{\cdot}29\times10^{-8}$		low power surface heaters
Nickel based alloys*				
80/20 Ni/Cr	1,200	108×10^{-8}	6×10^{-5}	furnace heating elements resistance heaters
80/20 Ni/Cr + Al	1,250	124×10^{-8}	-2×10^{-5}	furnace heating elements lower cost
60/15/25 Ni/Cr/Fe	1,100	112×10^{-8}	13×10^{-5}	furnace heating elements lower cost
50/18/32 Ni/Cr/Fe	1,075	111×10^{-8}	17×10^{-5}	furnace heating elements lower cost
37/18/43/2 Ni/Cr/Fe/Si	1,050	105×10^{-8}	24×10^{-5}	furnace heating elements lower cost
44/56 Ni/Cu	400	49×10^{-8}		resistance heaters, domestic appliances
Iron based alloys*				
72/22/4 Fe/Cr/Al	1,050	139×10^{-8}	$4{\cdot}7\times10^{-5}$	furnace heating elements
72/22/4 Fe/Cr/Al + Co	1,375	145×10^{-8}	$3{\cdot}2\times10^{-5}$	furnace heating elements
78/16/4 Fe/Cr/Al + Yt, C	1,300	134×10^{-8}	12×10^{-5}	furnace heating elements
Refractory metals				
platinum	1,300	11×10^{-8}	$3{\cdot}92\times10^{-3}$	small muffle furnaces
90/10 Pt/Rh	1,550	$19{\cdot}2\times10^{-8}$	$2{\cdot}0\times10^{-3}$	small muffle furnaces
60/40 Pt/Rh	1,800	$17{\cdot}4\times10^{-8}$	$2{\cdot}0\times10^{-3}$	small muffle furnaces
molybdenum	1,750†	$5{\cdot}7\times10^{-8}$	$5{\cdot}5\times10^{-3}$	vacuum furnaces, small muffle furnaces in hydrogen atmosphere
tantalum	2,500	$12{\cdot}5\times10^{-8}$	$3{\cdot}2\times10^{-3}$	vacuum furnaces
tungsten	1,800†	$5{\cdot}6\times10^{-8}$	$5{\cdot}94\times10^{-3}$	infra-red lamps; vacuum furnaces
Non-metals				
graphite	3,000†	$1{,}000\times10^{-8}$	$-2{\cdot}66\times10^{-4}$	vacuum furnaces and reducing atmospheres
molybdenum disilicide	1,800	40×10^{-8}	$1{\cdot}02\times10^{-2}$	small glass melting furnaces; forehearths
silicon carbide	1,600	$1{\cdot}1\times10^{-3}$	$-2{\cdot}63\times10^{-4}$	furnace heating elements; oxidising and reducing atmosphers
lanthanum chromite	1,800	2×10^{-5}		

* approximate compositions only
† not in air

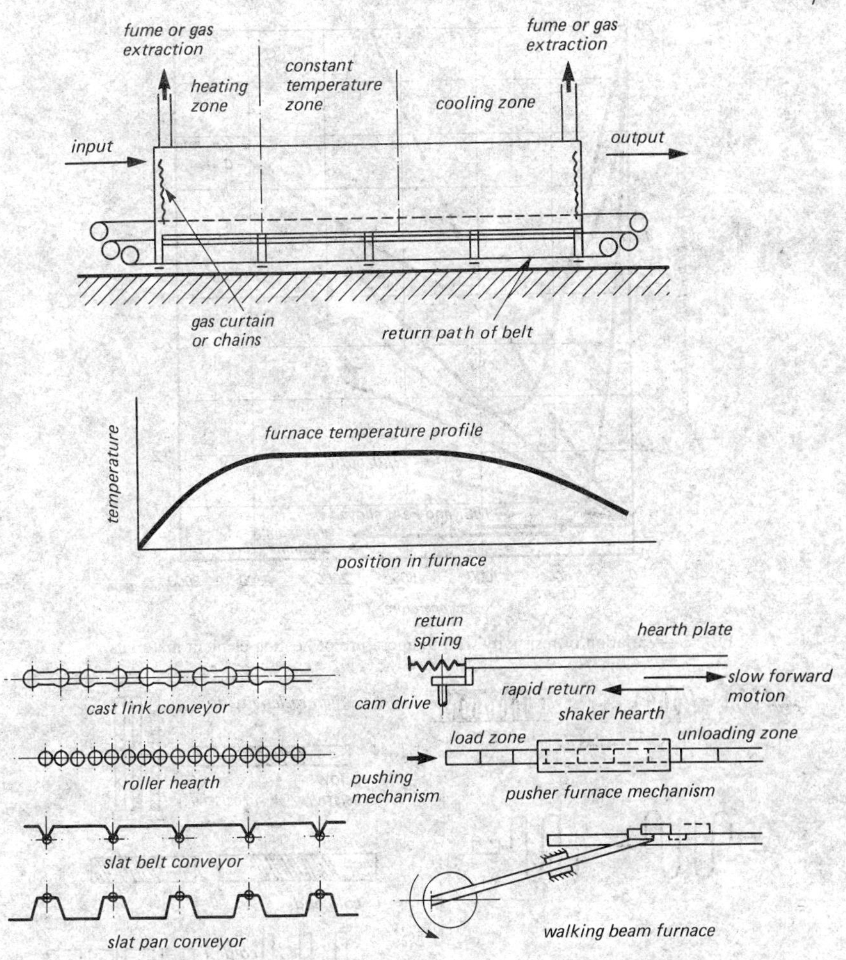

FIG. 2.—Different types of conveyor mechanisms used in furnaces.

so that the adequate cross section needed for mechanical strength can be used and a low temperature-coefficient of resistivity. Only a small number of materials satisfy even a few of these requirements. The principal heating element materials are listed in Table 3 and their variations of resistivity with temperature are shown in Fig. 3.

The most commonly encountered heating element materials for use up to temperatures of about 1,150°C are the nickel-chromium and iron-chromium alloys. These materials rely on the formation of a tenacious protective oxide surface layer, which can be improved by the addition of small amounts of alloying constituents, and have a relatively low temperature-coefficient of resistance. They are available in wire, rod, strip or tubular form and can be manufactured so as to be suitable for use in ovens and furnaces (Fig. 4). The maximum operating temperature is limited by the environment in which the element is used, however the vapour pressure of both nickel chrome and iron chrome alloys is relatively high (Fig. 5), and this restricts their use in furnaces operating at low pressures. Platinum and platinum-rhodium alloys are capable of operation at higher temperatures and have a low temperature-coefficient of resistance but they are very expensive whilst molybdenum and tungsten, which oxidise rapidly in air at high temperatures, can be used in protective atmospheres. Molybdenum, tungsten and tantalum have low vapour pressures and can be used in vacuum furnaces but they do have a very high positive temperature-coefficient of resistance (Fig. 3) which must be taken into account during furnace design.

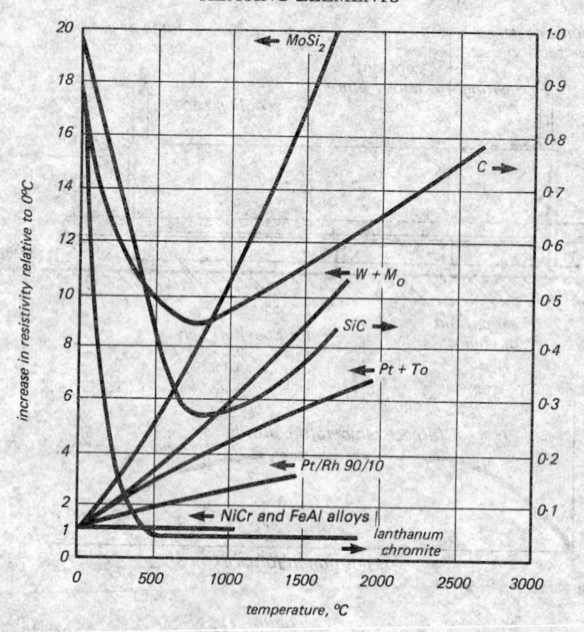

FIG. 3.—Variation of resistivity with temperature of heating element materials.

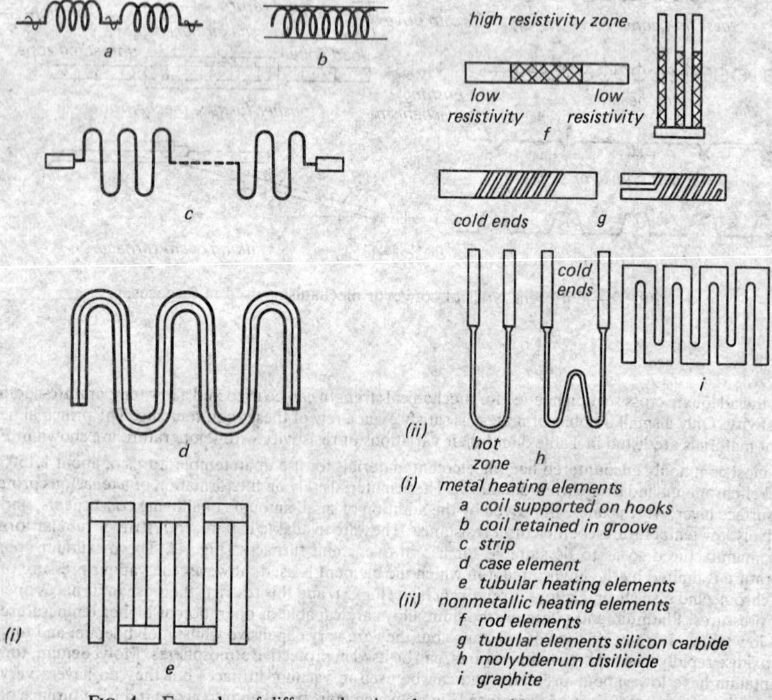

FIG. 4.—Examples of different heating elements used in ovens and furnaces.

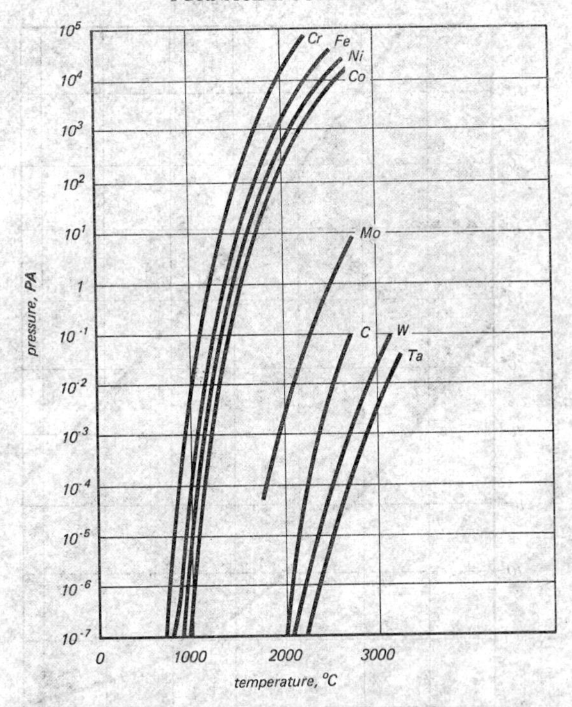

FIG. 5.—Variation of vapour pressure with temperature of some commonly used heating element materials.

Silicon carbide, in either rod or tubular form, is the most extensively used of the non-metals up to temperatures in excess of 1,500°C in both oxidising and reducing atmospheres. The resistivity decreases as the temperature increases above room temperature and then increases again above about 700°C. There is also an increase in resistivity, due to ageing, during the operating life of the element but these changes can be compensated by using SCR controlled power supplies. Molybdenum disilicide is capable of operation up to 1,800°C in both oxidising and reducing environments but is very brittle and is only available in a limited range of shapes. It has a high positive temperature coefficient of resistivity; at 1,800°C the resistance is about twenty times that at room temperature. Originally restricted to high temperature applications, the ability to operate in reducing atmospheres has resulted in growing application in carburising furnaces at lower temperatures. Lanthanum chromite is a recently developed heating element material also capable of operation in oxidising and reducing atmospheres. It has a high negative temperature coefficient of resistivity which at 600°C is about 5% of its room temperature value. Graphite also has a high negative temperature coefficient of resistivity up to 500°C. It oxidises rapidly in air above about 800°C but can be used in non-oxidising atmospheres up to about 3,000°C. Because of the relatively high vapour pressure of graphite its operation at low pressures is limited to 2,000°C.

Furnace insulation.—Insulation is required to minimise heat losses and since it must provide load bearing support it must have satisfactory mechanical as well as thermal properties. Refractory materials for electric ovens and furnaces are based on oxides of silicon, aluminium, magnesium and zirconium, which may be combined with other materials such as calcium and chromium. Carbon can also be used alone or in combination with silicon in the form of silicon carbide. The most common materials for this purpose are the alumino-silicates which are mixtures of silica (melting point 1,730°C) and alumina (melting point 2,050°C) in various proportions (Table 4). The electrical resistance of refractory materials is significant in furnace design since adequate electrical insulation strength is important. The electrical resistivity of some refractory materials is shown in Fig. 6. In general the resistivity decreases as the temperature increases. At temperatures above about 1,500°C the range of electrically insulating materials available is restricted to high purity alumina and zirconia.

The most common material used for linings and load-bearing surfaces in electric furnaces is high-grade alumino-silicate brick. The alumina content should preferably be greater than 50% in order to obtain a satisfactory electrical resistivity, the iron oxide content is also important where reducing amospheres are involved. High-density refractory bricks or silicon carbide tiles are also used for load-bearing and structural

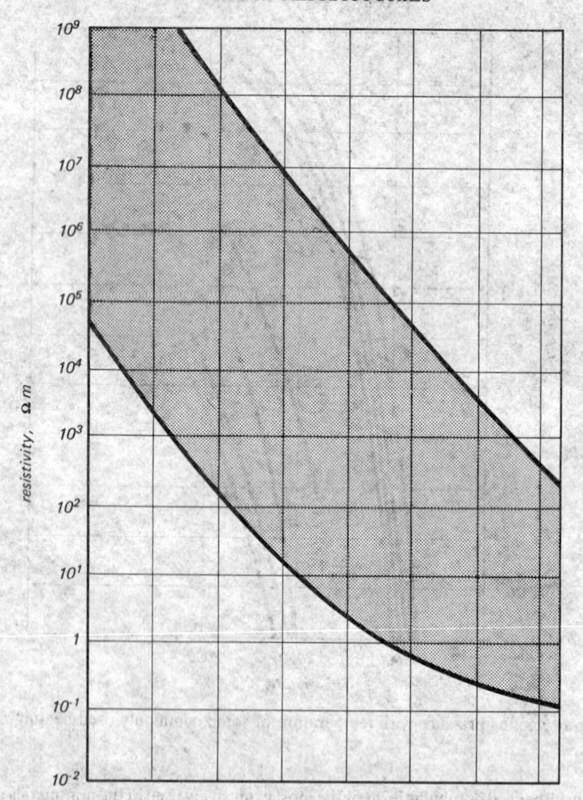

FIG. 6.—Typical variation of resistivity of refractory materials with temperature.

parts of the furnace and specially shaped refractory blocks, in the form of grooved tiles and ledges, can be used to support the heating elements.

Fibre insulation has a very low thermal mass and is particularly suitable where batch processes, with controlled heating and cooling cycles, are involved. The overall effect is a considerable reduction in the amount of energy needed to raise the temperature of the furnace structure. Alumina fibre is available either compressed in layers to form a brick or as a blanket which is held in place by ceramic or temperature resistant metal fasteners attached to the wall or roof.

TABLE 4.—PROPERTIES OF REFRACTORY AND INSULATING MATERIALS USED IN THE CONSTRUCTION OF ELECTRIC FURNACES.

Material	Max operating temp (°C)	Bulk density (kg/m³)	Typical thermal conductivity (W/mK)
Mineral Wool (slab)	750	144	0·01
Vermiculite	870	140	0·19
Calcium silicate fibre (slab)	800	200	0·09
Alumina fibre	1,600	100	0·22
Fireclay brick	1,400	2,000	1·29
Silica brick	1,600	1,740	1·44
Alumino silicate brick (79% Al_2O_3)	1,700	2,900	1·88
High alumina HTI brick (66% porosity)	1,600	910	0·28
Silicon carbide	1,750	2,640	16

Furnace atmospheres.—Examples of gas atmospheres used in heat treatment furnaces are given in Table 5. Many of these are reducing and therefore tend to destroy the protective oxide layer on the heating element surface so resulting in progressive deterioration. As a result the maximum allowable temperature of heating elements used under these conditions is lower than that in air (Table 6). The furnace atmosphere may be supplied directly from gas cylinders or, in the case of nitrogen or hydrogen, by cracking liquid ammonia.

DIRECT RESISTANCE HEATING.—Direct resistance heating, in which an electric current is passed through the component to be heated to raise its temperature, is used for heating billets prior to forging and for annealing wire. Important advantages of this technique are speed and flexibility. Large billets can be heated in very few minutes and only one component is heated at a time. The process is confined to components of uniform cross-section if uniform heating is required and to materials of relatively high resistivity if the bulk of the available power is to be dissipated in the component rather than the supply circuit so enabling a high efficiency to be achieved. In practice these considerations limit the process mainly to ferrous billets and to ferrous and non-ferrous wire and rod.

The resistance of metals increases rapidly with temperature. For steel there is a six-fold increase between the value at room temperature and that at 1,200°C. With magnetic materials, when the Curie temperature is reached the material becomes non-magnetic (Table 7) and the inductance and the overall impedance decrease.

TABLE 5.—GAS ATMOSPHERES COMMONLY USED IN FURNACES FOR HEAT TREATMENT.

Atmosphere	Typical analysis, % (excluding water vapour content) H_2	CO	CO_2	NH_2	CH_4	N_2
Hydrogen	100	—	—	—	—	—
Cracked ammonia	75	—	—	—	—	25
Endothermic gas						
(a) from natural gas feedstock	40	20	<1	—	<1	bal
(b) from propane feedstock	30	22	<1	—	<1	bal
Ammonia (at 20% dissociation)	25	—	—	67	—	8
Rich exothermic gas	17	12	4	—	—	bal
Forming gas	10	—	—	—	—	90
Lean exothermic gas	2	2	10	—	—	bal
Inert gases	Nitrogen, argon, etc.					

TABLE 6.—MAXIMUM OPERATING TEMPERATURES (°C) OF HEATING ELEMENTS IN DIFFERENT ATMOSPHERES.

	Ni/Cr	Fe/Cr/Al/Co	Molybdenum Disilicide	Molybdenum	Silicon Carbide
Air	1,200	1,350	1,700	400–700	1,350–1,500
Nitrogen	1,200	950	1,600	1,750	—
Hydrogen	1,200	1,350	1,350	1,750	—
Water-vapour	1,100	1,300	1,460	—	—
Hydrocarbons	1,050	1,050	1,350–1,500	1,100	1,100–1,250
CO_2 and CO	1,000	1,100	1,200–1,400	1,200–1,400	1,250–1,350
Vacuum*	900	900	1,750	1,700	—

* Dependent on partial pressure (Fig. 5)

TABLE 7.—CURIE TEMPERATURES OF MAGNETIC MATERIAL.

Material	Temperature °C
Iron	775
Cobalt	1,150
Nickel	360
Nickel-iron (30/70)	70
Permalloy (78/22)	550
Nickel-copper	16–70
Carbon steel (medium)	730

Process control can be achieved by timing the input power cycle or by weighing the billet before the process is started so as to determine the precise energy requirement. Alternatively an optical pyrometer in conjunction with a closed loop control system may be used to measure the surface temperature. In the case of wire and strip heating where the wire or strip passes over rotating contacts the controlled variable is the rate of throughput.

Direct resistance heating presents a single-phase load to the supply system. Furthermore it is a load which is switched at frequent intervals. This may result in voltage unbalance and transient voltage disturbances on the public electricity system. A balanced three-phase load can be obtained by using a static balancer consisting of inductors and capacitors connected across the other phases of the supply. High transient starting currents can be avoided by using semiconductor soft-start circuits. Where continuous heating of wire and strip is involved the contact arrangement can be arranged to present a balanced three-phase load to the supply.

INDUCTION HEATING.—Induction heating makes use of the transformer effect to produce circulating eddy currents in a workpiece which is then heated by I^2R losses. The technique is used for through heating metal billets prior to forging and for surface heat treatment. The current density in the component is a maximum at the surface and decreases with the distance from the surface. The depth to which a dc current (of uniform current density) equivalent, in heating terms, to the non uniform ac current distribution would flow, is defined as the skin depth δ and is given by

$$\delta = \sqrt{\frac{2\rho}{\omega\mu_o\mu_r}}$$

where ρ is the resistivity, ω the angular frequency and μ_o and μ_r the absolute and relative permeabilities respectively. The relative permeability of non-ferrous magnetic materials is 1. With ferromagnetic materials it falls to 1 above the Curie temperature (Table 7) but at lower temperatures it is much higher. For a cylindrical load where δ is very much less than the diameter D the decrease in current is exponential. Values of δ for different materials at different frequencies are given in Table 8, and the variation of current density with diameter for a solid cylinder is shown in Fig. 7 for the condition $D/\delta > 10$. As this ratio decreases the current distribution is no longer exponential and decreases more rapidly so that the heating rate falls. The power induced in a workpiece is a complex function of shape and skin depth but may be plotted in terms of the ratio of the normalised principal dimension to the skin depth as shown in Fig. 8 for a cylindrical workpiece. The curve indicates that for maximum power density (power/unit volume) to be developed in the cylinder a ratio

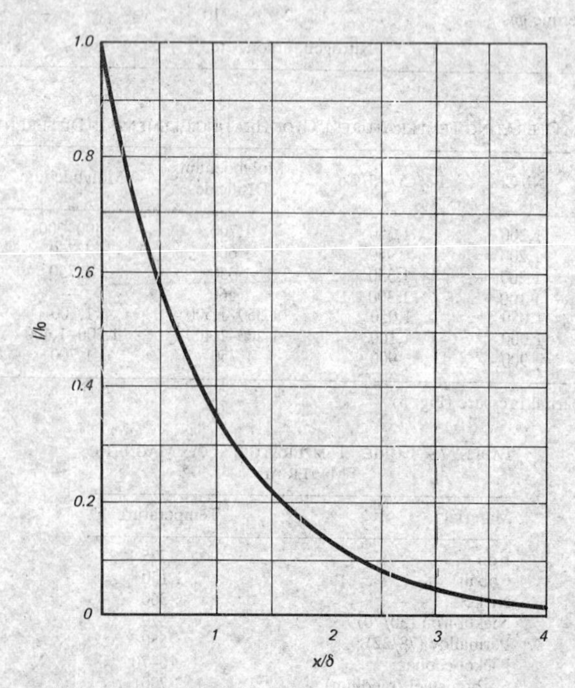

FIG. 7.—Variation of normalised current I/I_0 in a solid cylinder with the radius normalised in terms of x/δ.

TABLE 8.—TYPICAL VALUES OF SKIN DEPTH AT DIFFERENT FREQUENCIES.

Metal	Skin depth (mm)				
	50 Hz	150 Hz	1 kHz	10 kHz	450 kHz
Copper	9·2	5·3	2·1	0·65	0·096
Aluminium	11·69	6·7	2·6	0·82	0·12
Grey iron*	2·2	1·3	0·51	0·16	0·023
Grey iron†	62·0	37·0	14·0	4·5	0·89
Steel*	0·78	0·46	0·18	0·057	0·008
Steel†	22·0	13·0	5·1	1·60	0·23
Nickel*	0·65	0·38	0·15	0·05	0·007
Nickel†	18·0	11·0	4·3	1·3	0·19

* below the Curie temperature (μ_r assumed as 800)
† above the Curie temperature

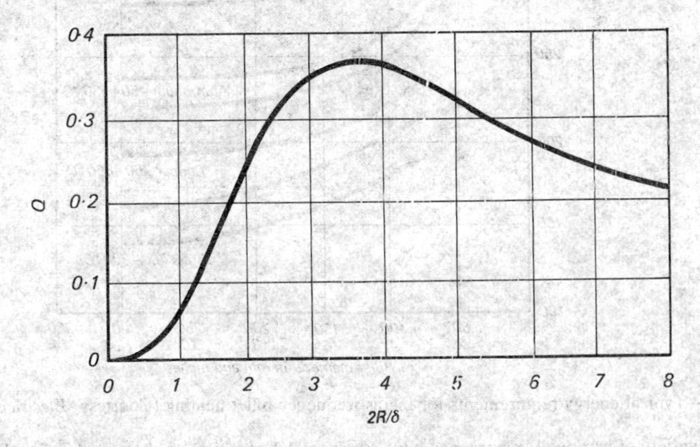

FIG. 8.—Relation between Q and skin depth δ normalised in terms of the diameter for a solid cylinder.

of D/δ of about 3·5 is required. For surface hardening D/δ must be much greater than 10 and the skin depth is normally less than 1 mm which is achieved by using frequencies between 3 kHz and 450 kHz.

Through heating of billets and slabs.—The through heating of ferrous and non-ferrous billets and slabs prior to hot forming processes such as rolling and forging using induction heating is a well established process. The rapid heating rates which can be obtained result in low heat losses and negligible scale formation. There are minimal stand-by losses and a high degree of control can be achieved. The billet, which may have either a circular or rectangular cross-section, is passed on metal skids through a series of current carrying water-cooled coils. Frequencies ranging from 50 Hz to several kHz, obtained from static inverters, are used depending on the material and the diameter of the billet. The energy requirements for mains frequency billet heating are shown in Fig. 9 and the variation of heating time with billet diameter for through heating at 50 Hz for different billet materials is given in Fig. 10. The efficiency and effectiveness of mains frequency through heating, particularly where large diameter billets are involved, have been improved by using multi-layer heating coils. The use of transverse flux heating in which the magnetic flux is passed through a sheet enables such workpieces to be processed. Induction heating, employing the above techniques, is also used for annealing.

Surface heat treatment.—Induction heating at medium and high frequencies is widely used for the surface hardening of low carbon (0·3–0·6%C) steel by heating a surface layer which is then quenched. The process results in a hard surface layer combined with a ductile core of unhardened material. The hardened depth, which is normally required to be less than 0·1 mm, is achieved by using a 450 kHz power source, the load forming part of the oscillatory circuit of a radio frequency oscillator. The very rapid heating rates, corresponding short cycle times and high throughputs, result in a high overall efficiency since only the outer surface of the component is heated. Recent developments in the maximum operating frequency of high power transistors and the gate-turn-off thyristor are likely to result in these replacing valves for many future applications.

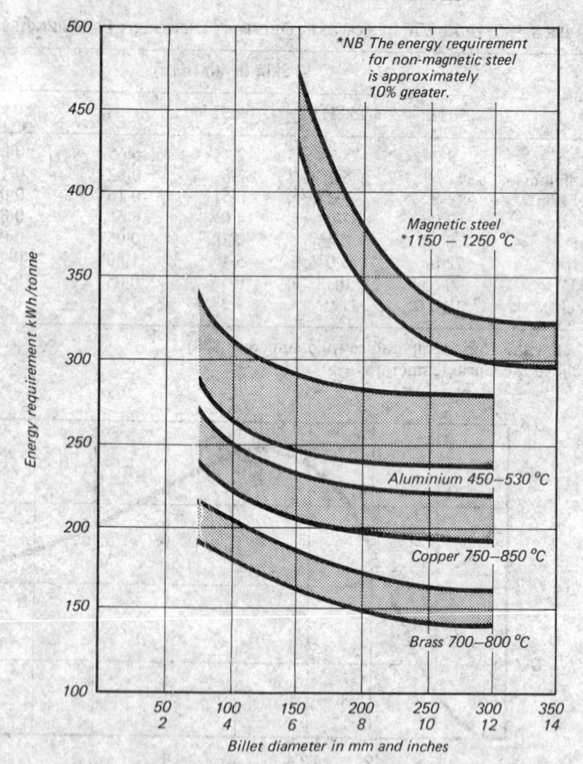

FIG. 9.—Typical energy requirements for mains frequency billet heating (Courtesy: *Electricity Council*).

A wide variety of work coil designs may be used, examples of which are illustrated in Fig. 11. The loaded work coil and the source must be matched to optimise the performance of the latter. A work-head transformer may also be used to assist in matching the high impedance output of the power supply to a low impedance load. This is particularly useful when the workpiece demands that a coil with only a few turns be used.

In addition to surface heat treatment, induction heating may also be used for soldering and brazing the flux pattern being modified using a suitable ferrite core concentrator. Ferrite concentrators are also used in the seam welding of steel tubes manufactured from flat strip bent into shape so that the field, and therefore the heat input, is concentrated at the interface of the joint to be welded. High throughput rates are achieved by using power sources with ratings up to 750 kW at 450 kHz.

SALT BATHS.—Salt baths are used for the heat treatment of metal components either by using the salt as a heat transfer medium to heat the component rapidly and uniformly to the required temperature or, by choice of a suitable salt, to carry out the required thermo-chemical reaction at the surface of the component. Applications of salt baths are limited to relatively small components and low throughputs but they are very versatile and, in some cases, are capable of carrying out thermo-chemical processes which would not be possible by any other method. The operating conditions in the bath tend to be corrosive and this action is further exacerbated by the presence of hot spots on the crucible surface which occur when it is heated externally by fuel fired burners. The use of electric immersion heaters (see p G3/15) enables refractory lined crucibles to be employed so giving indefinite crucible life and the process is inherently very efficient. At temperatures above about 800°C and up to about 1,400°C, depending upon the application, direct resistance heating using immersed graphite electrodes is used. The molten salt is a good electrical conductor at these temperatures although an auxiliary starting electrode is required to draw a localised arc when starting from cold. Single and three phase arrangements with currents up to 3,000 A at voltages of 30 V are available. Circular and rectangular crucibles with electrodes inserted from the top or through the sides are used.

GLOW DISCHARGE (PLASMA) CARBURISING AND NITRIDING.—Glow discharges are used to form a nitride layer on ferrous components at low pressures without heating and consequent thermal distortion. A low pressure glow discharge produces a stream of positive ions which bombards the workpiece connected

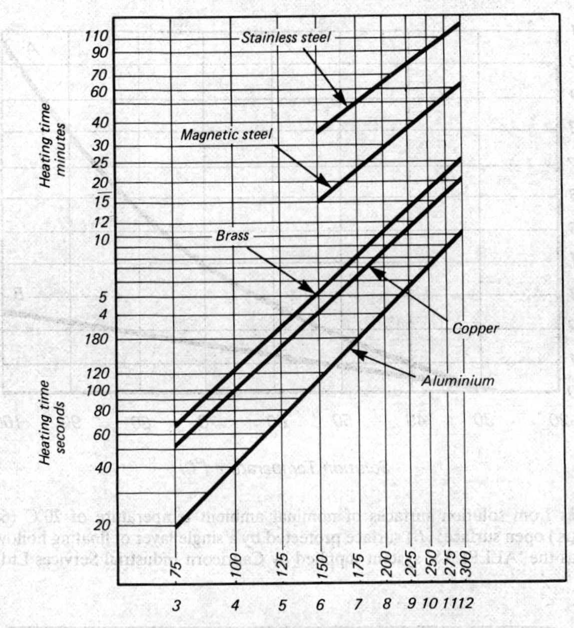

FIG. 10.—Typical times for mains frequency through heating of cylindrical billets of various materials and diameters to forging or extrusion temperatures (Courtesy: *Electricity Council*).

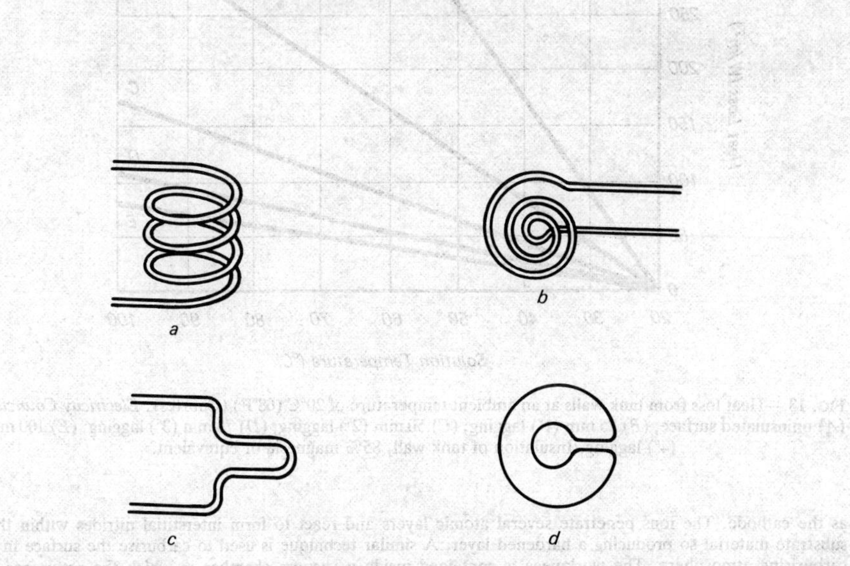

FIG. 11.—Different types of coils used for induction heating and their applications. (*a*) cylindrical coil for shaft hardening. (*b*) pancake coil for heating flat surfaces. (*c*) hair pin coil for localised heating. (*d*) current concentrator for use with (*a*).

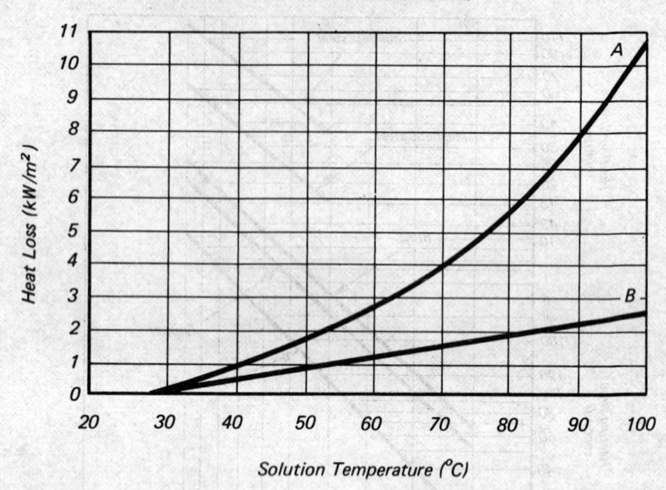

FIG. 12.—Heat losses from solution surfaces of nominal ambient temperature of 20°C (68°F) (Courtesy: *Electricity Council*). (*A*) open surface; (*B*) surface protected by a single layer of floating hollow plastic spheres such as the 'ALLPLAS' system supplied by Capricorn Industrial Services Ltd.

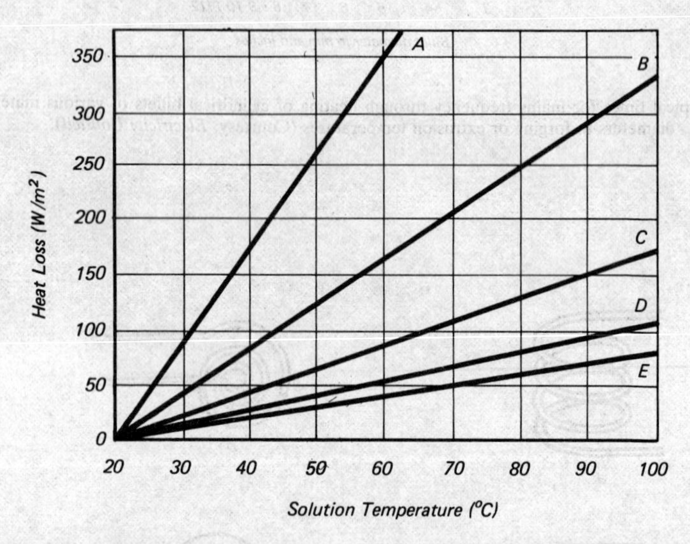

FIG. 13.—Heat loss from tank walls at an ambient temperature of 20°C (68°F) (Courtesy: *Electricity Council*). (*A*) uninsulated surface; (*B*) 25 mm (1″) lagging; (*C*) 50 mm (2″) lagging; (*D*) 75 mm (3″) lagging; (*E*) 100 mm (4″) lagging. Insulation of tank wall, 85% magnesia or equivalent.

as the cathode. The ions penetrate several atomic layers and react to form interstitial nitrides within the substrate material so producing a hardened layer. A similar technique is used to carburise the surface in a carburising atmosphere. The workpiece is contained inside a vacuum chamber in which the active gas is maintained at a pressure of about 100–1,000 Pa. The process is slow and capital intensive but reduces the workpiece distortion which can occur in thermal nitriding processes.

SURFACE HARDENING USING LASERS.—The carbon dioxide laser produces a high power (100 W–5 kW) focussed beam of infra-red radiation at 10,600 nm with a power density of more than 10^{13} W/m² at 10 kW, and is used selectively to heat treat the surface of a metal, to fuse surface coatings and claddings or to diffuse alloys into a surface.

Carbon dioxide lasers are in use in the automobile industry for selective hardening components which would be difficult or impossible to harden by alternative methods. CO_2 lasers are also used extensively for automated profile cutting and welding processes. The capital and running costs of the process are high although the total energy requirements are relatively low due to the selective nature of the heating.

ELECTRICAL INDIRECT RESISTANCE HEATING

Electric resistance heaters are used for heating by direct contact with a solid workpiece, immersed in a fluid or as a radiative heat source in an enormous variety of applications in industry including surface heating, the heating of liquids, localised heat sources in plastic sealing machines, melting of soft metals, pipe tracing and the annealing *in situ* of large welded structures.

The power rating required is established in the same way as many other heating processes as follows:

The maximum power input required is governed by either:

(1) The power required to reach the operating temperature, starting from the ambient temperature, in a specified time.
(2) The power required for a given throughput.

Whichever is the larger determines the maximum installed power required.

The power required to reach the operating temperature in a given time t, if no change of state occurs, is given by

$$W_1 = \frac{(T_1 - T_0) \times M \times C_p + L_1}{t}$$

Where M is the mass, C_p is the specific heat (J/kg°C) of the material, L_1 is the energy loss (J) during heating, and $(T_1 - T_0)$ the temperature rise required (°C). The thermal capacity may include the specific heat of the container and the latent heat of the material if applicable.

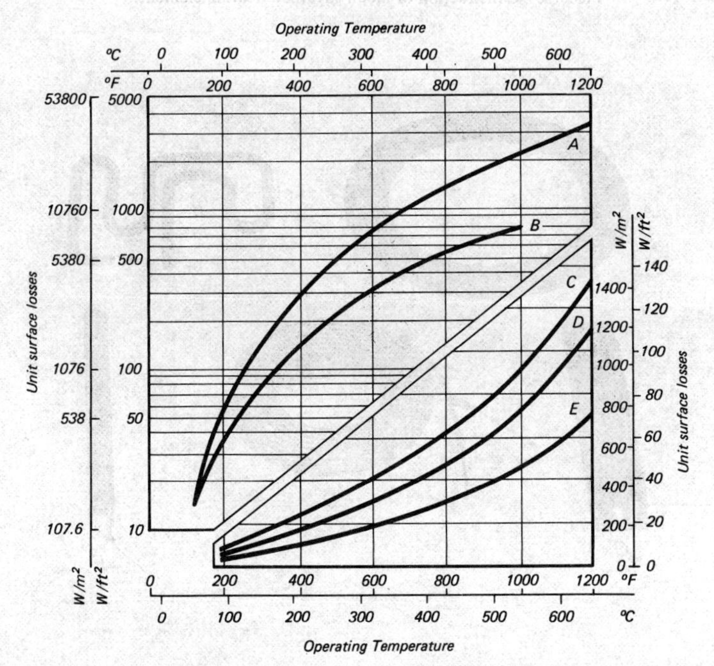

FIG. 14.—Heat losses from uninsulated platen surfaces (top graph). (Courtesy: *Electricity Council*). (*A*) oxidised steel; (*B*) oxidised aluminium. Heat losses from insulated platen surfaces (bottom graph) (*C*) 50 mm (2″) thick insulation; (*D*) 100 mm (4″); (*E*) 150 mm (6″) (*Courtesy:* Electricity Council).

If the temperature rise is small compared with $(T_F - T_0)$ where T_F is the final temperature that would eventually be reached, or if the heating-up time is short compared with the time t then the mean rate of heat loss can be approximated to half that which would occur at the operating temperature.

The power to achieve the desired throughput is given by

$$W_2 = \frac{(T_1 - T_0) \times M \times C_p + L_2}{t}$$

Where $M \times C_p$ is the thermal capacity of the throughput in a time t and the losses, L_2, are the energy losses at the operating temperature.

Heat losses should include those from the surface of the liquid (Fig. 12) and from the side walls of the vessel (Fig. 13). These will depend on the thickness and quality of thermal insulation used. Heat losses for uninsulated and insulated platen surfaces are given in Fig. 14.

METAL SHEATHED RESISTANCE HEATERS.—One of the most versatile forms of resistance heaters is the metal-sheathed mineral-insulated heating element (Fig. 15). The coiled heating element is located on the

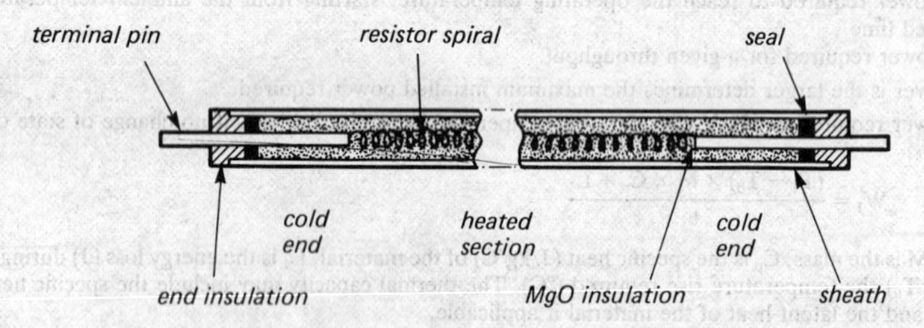

FIG. 15.—Construction of metal sheathed heating element.

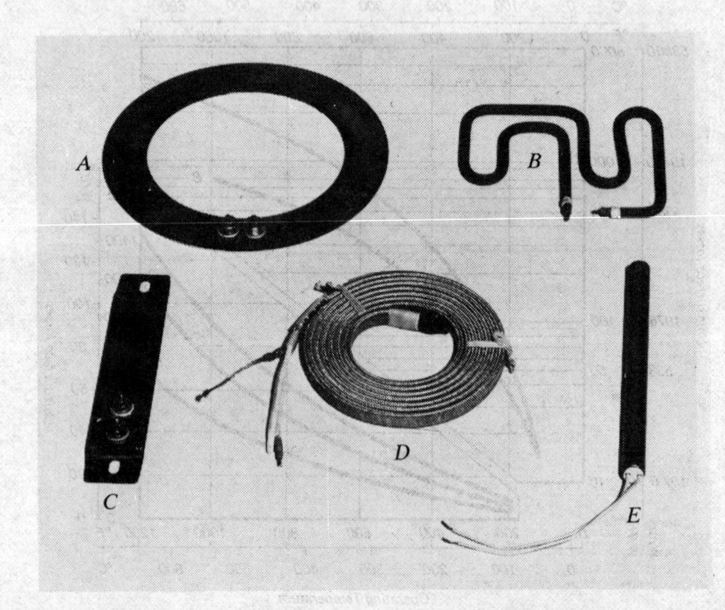

FIG. 16.—Resistance heating elements; (*A*) metal sheathed ring heating element; (*B*) mineral insulated heating element with rhomboid section; (*C*) flat mineral insulated heating element; (*D*) flexible surface heater; (*E*) cartridge heater.

axis of a seamless metal tube and electrically insulated from it by magnesium oxide powder which has a high electrical resistivity. A number of geometries are possible including linear, cartridge, strip and ring heaters (Fig. 16). After manufacture the heating elements can if required be shaped to conform to a given surface. Various methods of electrical connection are possible including single-ended and three-phase (Fig. 17).

The maximum temperature at the surface of a metal sheathed heating elements is limited by the thermal conductivity of the electrical insulation to about 750°C. The power density is governed by the thermal conductivity of the insulation and by the heat transfer coefficient at the surface of the heater which will depend on the application. The choice of sheath materal depends on the operating temperatures and environment. Different sheath materials are listed in Table 10.

The tubular metal-sheathed heating elements is extensively used for heating liquids and gases. The operating requirements are dependent on the maximum power density at the surface of the heater (Table 9) which in turn, determines the overall length and resistance of the heater required for a given application.

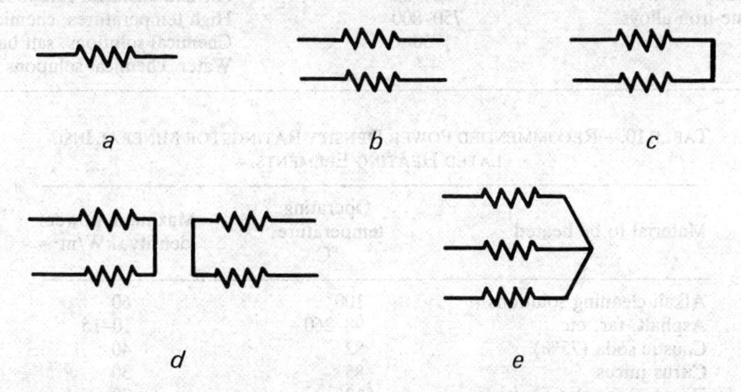

FIG. 17.—Different methods of electrical connection of metal sheathed heating elements. (*a*) single element; (*b*) double element; (*c*) single ended connection; (*d*) twin single ended connection; (*e*) three phase star connection

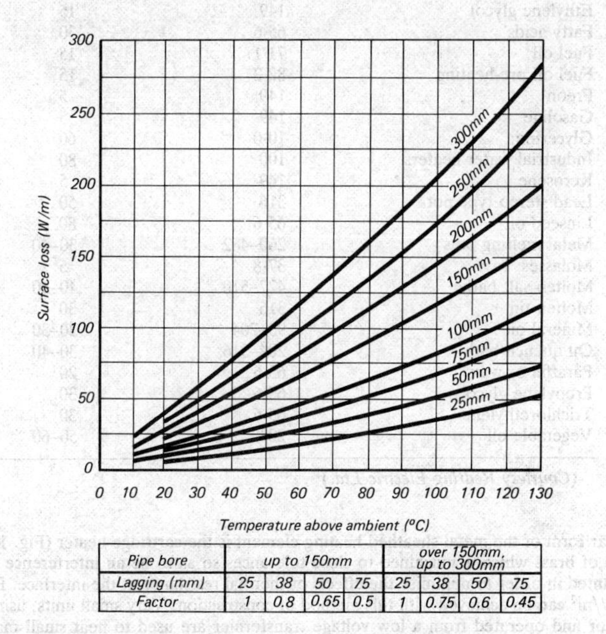

Pipe bore	up to 150mm				over 150mm, up to 300mm			
Lagging (mm)	25	38	50	75	25	38	50	75
Factor	1	0.8	0.65	0.5	1	0.75	0.6	0.45

FIG. 18.—Heat loss per unit length of exposed horizontal pipelines (Courtesy: *Electricity Council*).

TABLE 9.—DIFFERENT SHEATH MATERIALS USED FOR METAL SHEATHED HEATING ELEMENTS AND THEIR APPLICATIONS.

Sheath material	Maximum sheath temperature, °C	Applications
Copper	250	Water
Mild steel	450	Air, non-corrosive gases and liquids, contact heating and cast elements.
Aluminium/brass	500	Humid air
Aluminium bronze	600	
Copper-nickel alloys	500	Vegetable oils
Stainless steels	700–750	Air and chemical solutions
Nickel-chrome-iron alloys	750–800	High temperatures, chemical solutions
Nickel	750	Chemical solutions, salt baths
Titanium	—	Water, chemical solutions

TABLE 10.—RECOMMENDED POWER DENSITY RATINGS FOR MINERAL INSULATED HEATING ELEMENTS.

Material to be heated	Operating temperature, °C	Maximum power density, kW/m²
Alkali cleaning solutions	100	60
Asphalt, tar, etc.	98–260	10–15
Caustic soda (75%)	82	40
Citrus juices	85	30
Degreasing solution vapour	135	30
Dowtherm A	316	30
Elements cast into—		
Aluminium	260–399	80
Iron	399–538	85
Ethylene glycol	149	15
Fatty acids	65·6	30
Fuel oil	71·1	15
Fuel oil pre-heating	82·2	15
Freon	149	5
Gasoline	149	5
Glycerine	10·0	60
Industrial water heaters	100	80
Kerosene	149	5
Lead stereo type pot	316	50
Linseed oil	65·6	80
Metal melting pots	260–482	30–40
Molasses	37·8	5
Molten salt baths	427–510	40–50
Molten tin	316	30
Mineral oil	93–204	20–30
Oil quench bath	204–316	30–40
Paraffin or wax	65·6	20
Propylene glycol	65·6	30
Trichlorethylene	65·6	30
Vegetable oil	204	50–60

(*Courtesy Redring Electric Ltd.*)

One particular form of the metal sheathed heating element is the cartridge heater (Fig. 16(*e*)). The case is normally made of brass which is machined to close tolerances so as to be an interference fit in the body in which it is mounted in order to minimise the effects of thermal resistance at the interface. Power densities in excess of 1 MW/m² can be achieved with this method of construction. Very small units, using the sheath as a return conductor and operated from a low voltage transformer are used to heat small machine parts. The principal application of cartridge heaters is to provide controlled localised heating at high power densities.

One example of the use of electric resistance heating is for the surface heating of pipes containing a viscous fluid; ie pipe tracing. The power required is equivalent to the heat loss from the pipe which will normally be insulated. The thermal resistance of the pipe will usually be small compared with the resistance of the insulation so that the heat loss, W, per unit length of pipe is

$$W = (T_1 - T_2)\frac{2\pi k}{\ln(r_0/r_i)}$$

where T_1 is the temperature of the liquid, T_2 the temperature the external surface of the insulation and k is the thermal conductivity of the insulation which has inner and outer radii of r_i and r_0 respectively.

The relationship between temperature and heat loss from horizontal uninsulated pipes is shown in Fig. 18 together with correction factors which can be used to take different thicknesses of insulation into account.

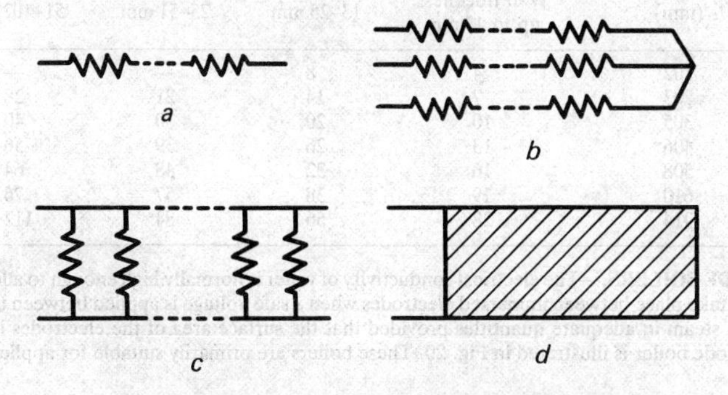

FIG. 19.—Different methods of construction used for surface heaters. (*a*) Surface heater with external return conductor; (*b*) Single-ended 3-phase star-connected surface heater; (*c*) Surface heater with parallel resistance paths; (*d*) Surface heater using distributed conductor

TABLE 11.—MATERIALS USED FOR INSULATING AND SUPPORTING FLEXIBLE HEATING ELEMENTS.

Support material	Temperate limit, °C
Polyethylene (film)	80–120
Paper	90–120
Polyester (film)	110
Polypropylene (film)	120
Asbestos paper	400
Glass fibre	425
PTFE	170
Silicone rubber	200
Mineral insulation (MgO)	
copper nickel sheath	350
stainless-steel sheath	600
Stainless-steel mesh	600
Quartz fibre	800
Ceramic beads	1,000

In many applications a more flexible construction than that of the metal sheathed element is required which is able to conform to the surface of a three-dimensional shape. Such heaters are available and various different methods of insulating and supporting the heating element are used depending on the operating temperature required (Table 11). The heating element may be woven onto a flexible insulating support to enable complex shapes such as retorts and valves to be heated although for pipe-tracing, in locations such as oil refineries and chemical plants flexible heating tapes are more commonly used.

A number of different types of heating tape are available using either series or parallel connection (Fig. 19). The series type suffers from the limitation that it cannot be cut to length and thus requires a separate specification for each application. The parallel heating tape is more versatile but on long runs a voltage drop occurs along its length and this results in lower power densities at the end remote from the supply.

Flexible surface heaters are also used to stress-relieve large welded structures and pipes. Some typical power requirements for such applications are given in Table 12. Temperatures up to 1,100°C can be achieved using a nickel-chrome or iron-chrome wire heating element insulated by an interlocking matrix of ceramic beads which provides a limited amount of flexibility in three dimensions.

TABLE 12.—SUGGESTED POWER RATINGS FOR STRESS-RELIEVING BUTT WELDS IN PIPES.
(Electricity Council)

Outside diameter of pipe (mm)	[Rating kW]			
	Wall thickness up to 13 mm	13–25 mm	25–51 mm	51–102 mm
102	4	8	—	—
203	7	14	21	28
305	10	20	30	40
406	13	26	39	56
508	16	32	48	64
610	19	38	57	76
914	28	56	84	112

ELECTRODE BOILERS.—The electrical conductivity of water is normally high enough to allow for sufficient conduction to take place between immersed electrodes when a safe voltage is applied between them to produce hot water and steam in adequate quantities provided that the surface area of the electrodes is large enough. Such an electrode boiler is illustrated in Fig. 20. These boilers are primarily suitable for application where the

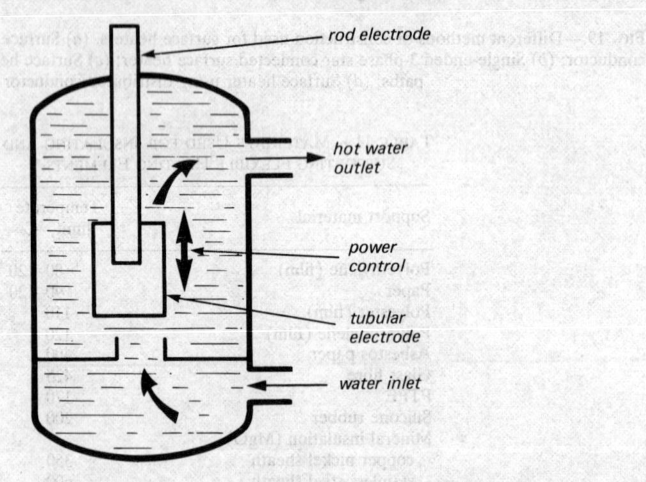

FIG. 20.—Electrode boiler.

demand for hot water or steam is intermittent and thus where the high capital and standby costs of a fuel fired boiler are uneconomic. Electrode boilers range in size from a few kW up to several MW. Where large outputs of steam are required in the brewing industry, for example, high capacity units in which the water is sprayed on to cast iron electrodes are used. These operate at voltages up to 6 kV. The heating rate can be varied by raising or lowering the electrodes by screening part of their surface area with an insulating shield or by varying the electrical conductivity of the water.

INFRA-RED AND ULTRA-VIOLET PROCESSES.—Infra-red technology is extensively used for surface heating, the drying and curing of coatings, pre-heating of plastics and rubbers, moisture removal and many other applications. Infra-red heating can be used as a localised heat source without the need for an enclosure or the heaters can be mounted in banks to form reflecting-wall ovens or furnaces which since no thermal insulation is required, have a very low thermal capacity and a correspondingly high efficiency.

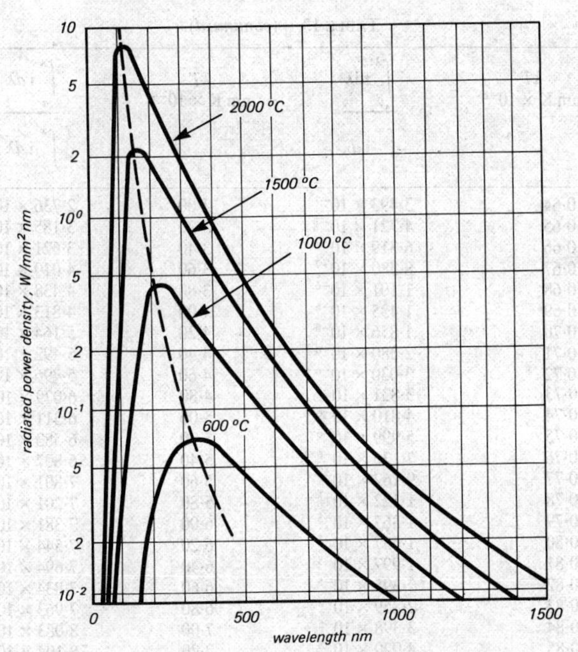

FIG. 21.—Variation of intensity of radiated power from a black-body source with wavelength at different temperature.

The proportion of the radiated power from an infra-red source emitted at short wavelengths increases with the temperature as shown in Fig. 21 for a black body source. The absorption of most materials varies with wavelength hence the effectiveness of an infra-red process varies with temperature.

It is often necessary to determine the radiated energy at a given temperature between different wavelengths. This can be calculated using a table (Table 13) in which the total radiated energy between a given wavelength and infinity is given as a ratio of the total black body radiated energy in terms of normalised values of the wavelength and absolute temperature.

TABLE 13.—BLACK-BODY RADIATION FUNCTIONS IN TERMS OF NORMALISED WAVELENGTH AND TEMPERATURE.

λT nm K × 10^{-6}	$\frac{\int_0^\lambda i d\lambda}{\int_0^\infty i d\lambda}$	λT nm K × 10^{-6}	$\frac{\int_0^\lambda i d\lambda}{\int_0^\infty i d\lambda}$
0·50	$1{\cdot}316 \times 10^{-9}$	1·55	$1{\cdot}610 \times 10^{-2}$
0·51	$2{\cdot}181 \times 10^{-9}$	1·60	$1{\cdot}979 \times 10^{-2}$
0·52	$3{\cdot}552 \times 10^{-9}$	1·65	$2{\cdot}396 \times 10^{-2}$
0·53	$5{\cdot}665 \times 10^{-9}$	1·70	$2{\cdot}862 \times 10^{-2}$
0·54	$8{\cdot}871 \times 10^{-9}$	1·75	$3{\cdot}379 \times 10^{-2}$
0·55	$1{\cdot}366 \times 10^{-8}$	1·80	$3{\cdot}946 \times 10^{-2}$
0·56	$2{\cdot}098 \times 10^{-8}$	1·85	$4{\cdot}561 \times 10^{-2}$
0·57	$3{\cdot}081 \times 10^{-8}$	1·90	$5{\cdot}225 \times 10^{-2}$
0·58	$4{\cdot}532 \times 10^{-8}$	1·95	$5{\cdot}535 \times 10^{-2}$
0·59	$6{\cdot}568 \times 10^{-8}$	2·00	$6{\cdot}690 \times 10^{-2}$
0·60	$9{\cdot}395 \times 10^{-8}$	2·20	$1{\cdot}011 \times 10^{-1}$
0·61	$1{\cdot}327 \times 10^{-7}$	2·40	$1{\cdot}405 \times 10^{-1}$
0·62	$1{\cdot}853 \times 10^{-7}$	2·60	$1{\cdot}834 \times 10^{-1}$
0·63	$2{\cdot}558 \times 10^{-7}$	2·80	$2{\cdot}282 \times 10^{-1}$

TABLE 13.—(*continued*).

λT nm K × 10⁻⁶	$\dfrac{\int_0^\lambda i d\lambda}{\int_0^\infty i\,d\lambda}$	λT nm K × 10⁻⁶	$\dfrac{\int_0^\lambda i\,d\lambda}{\int_0^\infty i\,d\lambda}$
0·64	$3{\cdot}493 \times 10^{-7}$	3·00	$2{\cdot}736 \times 10^{-1}$
0·65	$4{\cdot}721 \times 10^{-7}$	3·20	$3{\cdot}185 \times 10^{-1}$
0·66	$6{\cdot}319 \times 10^{-7}$	3·40	$3{\cdot}621 \times 10^{-1}$
0·67	$8{\cdot}380 \times 10^{-7}$	3·60	$4{\cdot}010 \times 10^{-1}$
0·68	$1{\cdot}101 \times 10^{-6}$	3·80	$4{\cdot}438 \times 10^{-1}$
0·69	$1{\cdot}435 \times 10^{-6}$	4·00	$4{\cdot}813 \times 10^{-1}$
0·70	$1{\cdot}856 \times 10^{-6}$	4·20	$5{\cdot}164 \times 10^{-1}$
0·71	$2{\cdot}380 \times 10^{-6}$	4·40	$5{\cdot}492 \times 10^{-1}$
0·72	$3{\cdot}030 \times 10^{-6}$	4·60	$5{\cdot}796 \times 10^{-1}$
0·73	$3{\cdot}831 \times 10^{-6}$	4·80	$6{\cdot}079 \times 10^{-1}$
0·74	$4{\cdot}810 \times 10^{-6}$	5·00	$6{\cdot}311 \times 10^{-1}$
0·75	$5{\cdot}999 \times 10^{-6}$	5·20	$6{\cdot}583 \times 10^{-1}$
0·76	$7{\cdot}136 \times 10^{-6}$	5·40	$6{\cdot}807 \times 10^{-1}$
0·77	$9{\cdot}162 \times 10^{-6}$	5·60	$7{\cdot}801 \times 10^{-1}$
0·78	$1{\cdot}122 \times 10^{-5}$	5·80	$7{\cdot}201 \times 10^{-1}$
0·79	$1{\cdot}367 \times 10^{-5}$	6·00	$7{\cdot}381 \times 10^{-1}$
0·80	$1{\cdot}657 \times 10^{-5}$	6·20	$7{\cdot}544 \times 10^{-1}$
0·81	$1{\cdot}997 \times 10^{-5}$	6·40	$7{\cdot}694 \times 10^{-1}$
0·82	$2{\cdot}395 \times 10^{-5}$	6·60	$7{\cdot}834 \times 10^{-1}$
0·83	$2{\cdot}859 \times 10^{-5}$	6·80	$7{\cdot}963 \times 10^{-1}$
0·84	$3{\cdot}398 \times 10^{-5}$	7·00	$8{\cdot}083 \times 10^{-1}$
0·85	$4{\cdot}020 \times 10^{-5}$	7·20	$8{\cdot}194 \times 10^{-1}$
0·86	$4{\cdot}735 \times 10^{-5}$	7·40	$8{\cdot}297 \times 10^{-1}$
0·87	$5{\cdot}555 \times 10^{-5}$	7·60	$8{\cdot}392 \times 10^{-1}$
0·88	$6{\cdot}491 \times 10^{-5}$	7·80	$8{\cdot}481 \times 10^{-1}$
0·89	$7{\cdot}556 \times 10^{-5}$	8·00	$8{\cdot}564 \times 10^{-1}$
0·90	$8{\cdot}763 \times 10^{-5}$	8·20	$8{\cdot}641 \times 10^{-1}$
0·91	$1{\cdot}013 \times 10^{-4}$	8·40	$8{\cdot}713 \times 10^{-1}$
0·92	$1{\cdot}166 \times 10^{-4}$	8·60	$8{\cdot}780 \times 10^{-1}$
0·93	$1{\cdot}339 \times 10^{-4}$	8·80	$8{\cdot}843 \times 10^{-1}$
0·94	$1{\cdot}532 \times 10^{-4}$	9·00	$8{\cdot}901 \times 10^{-1}$
0·95	$1{\cdot}747 \times 10^{-4}$	9·20	$8{\cdot}956 \times 10^{-1}$
0·96	$1{\cdot}986 \times 10^{-4}$	9·40	$9{\cdot}007 \times 10^{-1}$
0·97	2.252×10^{-4}	9·60	$9{\cdot}055 \times 10^{-1}$
0·98	$2{\cdot}546 \times 10^{-4}$	9·80	$9{\cdot}100 \times 10^{-1}$
0·99	$2{\cdot}870 \times 10^{-4}$	10.00	$9{\cdot}143 \times 10^{-1}$
1·00	$3{\cdot}228 \times 10^{-4}$	11·00	$9{\cdot}310 \times 10^{-1}$
1·05	$5{\cdot}591 \times 10^{-4}$	12·00	$9{\cdot}451 \times 10^{-1}$
1·10	$9{\cdot}162 \times 10^{-4}$	13·00	$9{\cdot}551 \times 10^{-1}$
1·15	$1{\cdot}431 \times 10^{-3}$	14·00	$9{\cdot}629 \times 10^{-1}$
1·20	$2{\cdot}145 \times 10^{-3}$	15·00	$9{\cdot}690 \times 10^{-1}$
1·25	$3{\cdot}000 \times 10^{-3}$	16·00	$9{\cdot}738 \times 10^{-1}$
1·30	$4{\cdot}336 \times 10^{-3}$	17·00	$9{\cdot}777 \times 10^{-1}$
1·35	$5{\cdot}897 \times 10^{-3}$	18·00	$9{\cdot}808 \times 10^{-1}$
1·40	$7{\cdot}822 \times 10^{-3}$	19·00	$9{\cdot}834 \times 10^{-1}$
1·45	$1{\cdot}015 \times 10^{-2}$	20·00	$9{\cdot}856 \times 10^{-1}$
1·50	$1{\cdot}290 \times 10^{-2}$		

Adapted from Am. Inst. Physics Handbook, Ed. D. E. Gray, McGraw Hill Inc., New York, 1972.

Thus for example, to determine the power radiated by a black body at a temperature of 2,000°C (2,273 K) between 800 nm and 2,000 nm as a proportion of the total radiated power:

At 2,000 nm, $\lambda T = 4{\cdot}6 \times 10^6$ nmK
At 800 nm, $\lambda T = 1{\cdot}8 \times 10^6$ nmK

and hence from from Table 13 the proportion of the total radiated power density between 800 nm and 2,000 nm is

$$\frac{\int_0^{\lambda_1} \mathrm{i}d\lambda - \int_0^{\lambda_2} \mathrm{i}d\lambda}{\int_0^{\infty} \mathrm{i}d\lambda} = 5{\cdot}8 \times 10^{-1} - 3{\cdot}95 \times 10^{-2}$$

Non-metals, including water and other liquids, absorb infra-red radiation effectively at wavelengths beyond about 2,000 nm while metals tend to reflect in this region and absorb at shorter wavelengths up to about 600 or 700 nm depending on the condition of the surface.

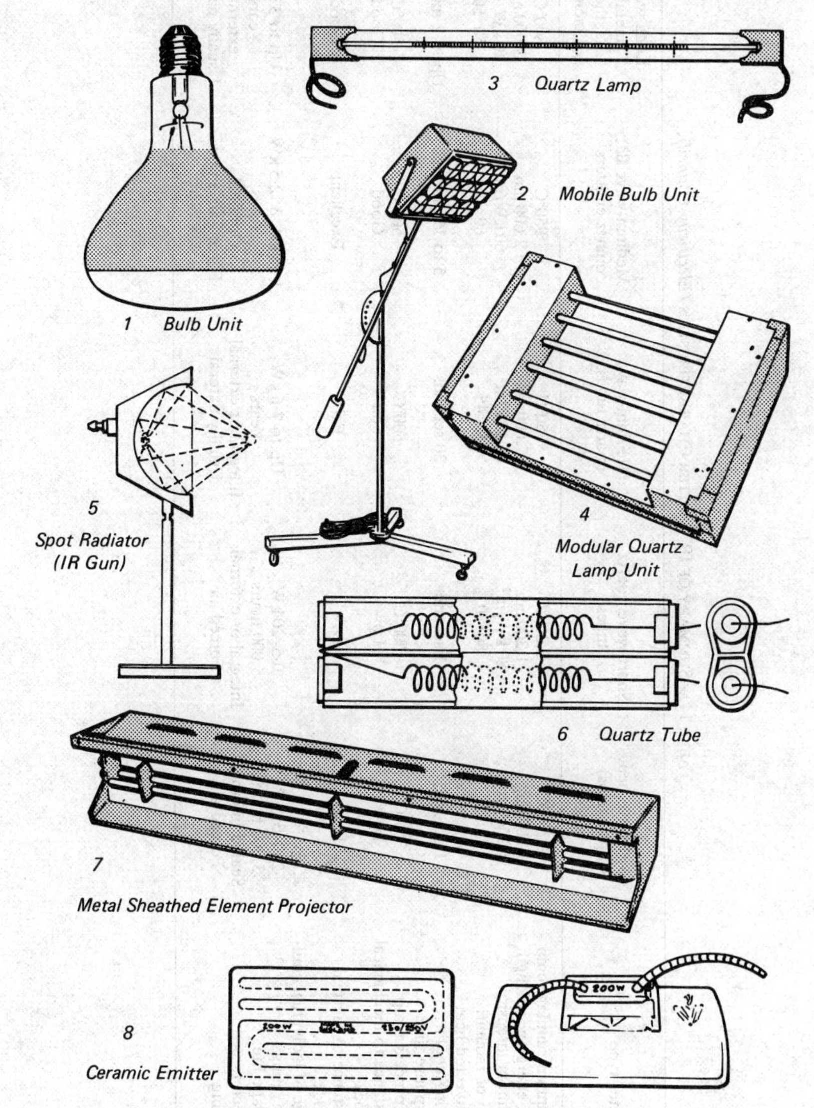

FIG. 22.—Different types of infra-red heaters (Courtesy: *Electricity Council*).

TABLE 14.—SUMMARY OF IR EMITTER CHARACTERISTICS *(Electricity Council)*.

Emitter type	Short-wave heat lamps (bulbs)	Short-wave quartz tubes	Medium-wave quartz tubes:	Medium-wave flat quartz emitters	Long-wave metal sheathed elements	Long-wave ceramic emitters
Maximum running temp	2,200°C	2,200°C	950°C	950°C	800°C	700°C
Peak energy wavelength	1,200 nm	1,200 nm	2,600 nm	2,600 nm	3,000 nm	4,000 nm
Maximum intensity	10 kW/m²	80 kW/m²	60 kW/m²	60 kW/m²	40 kW/m²	40 kW/m²
Ratio of radiant: convected heat	75:25	80:20	55:45	60:40	50:50	50:50
Heating/cooling response time	1 second	1 second	30 seconds	5 to 15 minutes	Up to 2 minutes	Up to 2 minutes
Max process temp	300°C	600°C	500°C	500°C	500°C	400°C
Resistance to mechanical shock	Low	Low	Fair	Good	Good	Fair
Resistance to thermal shock	Low	Low	Fair	Excellent	Good	Good
Range of individual emitter ratings	250–375 W	0·5–20 kW	Up to 7·6 kW	1·25 kW & 2·5 kW	Up to 3 kW	Up to 1 kW
Average life	5,000 hours	5,000 hours	Years	Years	Years	Years
Reflectors	Sealed internal	Integral or external	Integral or external	Optional	external	External
Cooling	Forced air	Forced air	Usually natural	Forced air above 40 kW/m²	Usually natural	Usually natural

Some examples of infra-red heaters are shown in Fig. 22. Three principal types are available: long, medium and short wavelength, the classification being related to the wavelength at which the radiation is a maximum. The characteristics of the different units are given in Table 14. Long-wavelength heaters are most suitable for heating non-metallic materials up to temperatures approaching 600 or 700°C whilst the short-wavelength units are used for the heating metals. If the required temperature is higher than that obtainable from a long wavelength unit the medium or short wavelength type may be used, depending on the application.

The aspect ratio, *ie* the effective radiating area of the heat source divided by the overall surface area of the heater, is an important factor. In the case of the embedded-ceramic heater this ratio is almost unity whereas with short wavelength heaters it is less than 0·1 so that the total mean radiated powers of the two are comparable despite the very much higher operating temperature of the short wavelength unit.

The embedded ceramic heater referred to above uses a nickel-chrome heating element contained within a refractory matrix which protects the element from oxidation and corrosion and increases the effective surface area. Some degree of focussing can be obtained by shaping the heater and a reflector can be incorporated within the ceramic. Another method uses flat mineral insulated strip heating elements assembled to form a panel. The effective radiating surface of the heater is relatively high and power densities up to 33 kW/m^2 at temperatures in the region of 600°C can be obtained. The heaters can be mounted close together so as to give very high aspect ratios. Applications include the preheating of plastics and rubber and the drying of paper, textiles, paint, plastic coatings, and ceramic glazes.

Metal sheathed heating elements are used for low temperatures, up to 700°C, in applications such as drying. The elements are mounted in aluminium reflectors to give an approximately uniform power density but the aspect ratio is very much lower than that of the ceramic heater and the power output obtainable is relatively low.

The medium wavelength quartz sheathed heating element is capable of operating up to about 1,100°C. The compact construction incorporates a reflector at the back of the heater and the heaters can be mounted in close proximity to each other so enabling high power densities to be achieved at higher temperatures than is possible with long-wave units. The heating element is a spiral coil of nickel-chrome wire protected and supported by the fused-quartz sheath.

Short-wavelength infra-red heaters use a tungsten filament, operating at about 2,200°C, enclosed in a borosilicate glass bulb filled with a low pressure protective gas. The infra-red transmission of the glass envelope is limited to below 2,000 nm; energy emitted by the filament above this wavelength is absorbed by the glass and reradiated at longer wavelengths. The internal surface of the circular lamp is silvered to reflect the radiation and an external reflector is not required. Linear lamps use an external reflector which may be either parabolic, to obtain a beam which is approximately parallel or elliptical to give a line source. Circular heat lamps are simple to mount and use, but the aspect ratio is low, therefore so also is the net radiated power. This ratio is considerably increased if several linear lamps mounted in an array are used to provide high power levels over large areas. These heaters are used where a high source temperature or a focussed heat source is required such as for the rapid drying of surface coatings. In such applications the drying mechanism is either by direct absorption of the energy by the coating or where the coating transmits the radiation by heating the substrate and using the conductive transfer of the heat to the coating. The latter has the advantage of preventing the formation of a hardened skin at the surface until the final stages of the process since earlier formation of this skin inhibits the drying action.

Some ink and plastic coatings contain monomers and photoactivators which polymerise rapidly when exposed to ultra-violet radiation; hence they can be cured using electric discharge lamps which emit ultra-violet light. This is not strictly a drying process and the overall energy requirement is often much less than that involved in other thermal methods.

DIELECTRIC HEATING AND DRYING

High frequency heating uses the high dielectric loss of certain materials to dissipate power within the material which acts as the dielectric of a capacitor (Fig. 23). Dielectric heating also has the advantage of moisture levelling in materials such as paper, woods and food since most heat is dissipated where the relative permittivity and the moisture content are highest. Various other electrode arrangements are possible (Fig. 24) as well as parallel-plate configurations. These enable rapid removal of the water-vapour and the incorporation of dielectric heating installations in inline processes such as paper making or ink drying.

The power dissipated in a dielectric heating process is given by

$$W = 2\pi f \epsilon_0 \epsilon_r E^2 \tan\delta \ W/m^3$$

where f is the frequency (Hz), E the voltage gradient (V/m), and ϵ_0 the absolute and relative permittivity. The product ($\epsilon_r \tan\delta$) is the loss factor.

The power loss is proportional to the loss factor, the relative permittivity and the square of the applied voltage. In practice, since the applied voltage is limited by the break-down voltage of the medium in which the heating takes place, usually air containing impurities, it is the relative permittivity and loss factor which are the important parameters in determining process viability. Table 15 lists these characteristic values for some common materials. The heating effect also increases with frequency but only a limited number of frequency

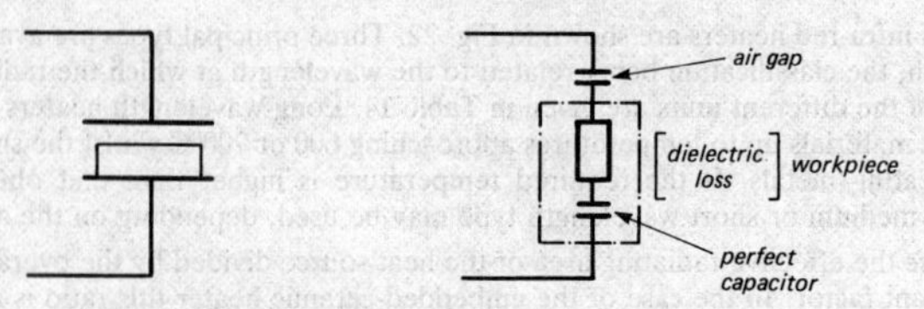

FIG. 23.—Parallel plate applicator with equivalent circuit.

TABLE 15.—LOSS FACTORS OF SOME INSULATING MATERIALS AT DIFFERENT FREQUENCIES.

Material	T, °C	10^6 Hz	10^7 Hz	10^8 Hz	3×10^9 Hz
water	65	5·61			4·89
water	95	7·87	0·725	0·174	2·44
porcelain	25	0·015	0·013	0·016	0·028
borosilicate glass	25	0·002	0·003	0·004	0·004
soda-silica glass	25	0·07		0·051	0·066
nylon 610	25	0·068	0·063	0·060	0·033
nylon 610	84	0·757	0·426	0·228	0·105
p.v.c. QYNA	20	0·046	0·033	0·023	0·016
p.v.c. QYNA	96	0·244	0·140	0·086	
p.v.c. VG 5904	25	0·602	0·407	0·22	0·10
p.v.c. VU 1900	25	0·29	0·165	0·087	0·035
araldite E134	25	0·339	0·410	0·481	0·147
araldite adhesive	25	0·111	0·121	0·111	0·072
natural rubber	25	0·004	0·008	0·012	0·006
neoprene GN	25	0·541	0·940	0·544	0·136
wool (fir)	25	0·05	0·06	0·062	0·049
paper (royal grey)	25	0·113	0·163	0·183	0·235
paper	82	0·076	0·138	0·194	0·235
leather (dry)	25	0·089	0·093	0·118	
leather (15% H_2O)	25	0·784	0·49	0·45	

TABLE 16.—PRINCIPAL FREQUENCIES FOR RADIO FREQUENCY HEATING IN THE UK.

Frequency, MHz	Wavelength, m	Tolerance, +/−
13·56*	22	0·05%
27·12*	11	0·6%
40·68*	7·5	0·05%
42, 49, 56, 61, 68	7·1, 6·1, 5·9, 4·9, 4·4	0·02%
84, 168	3·6, 1·8	0·005%
896	0·33	10 MHz
2450*	0·12	50 MHz
5800*	0·052	75 MHz
24125*	0·012	125 MHz
40680	0·0073	—

* International ISM frequency bands

bands are available (Table 16). The electric properties are frequency dependent and in some cases an optimum frequency exists which for water is around 10 MHz. Many other materials containing water, including a wide range of foods, can also be heated using dielectric techniques.

Radio-frequency (rf) heating is normally used to heat materials in laminar form but microwave frequencies may be used with either laminar or bulk objects. An example of a tuned microwave cavity for heating a material

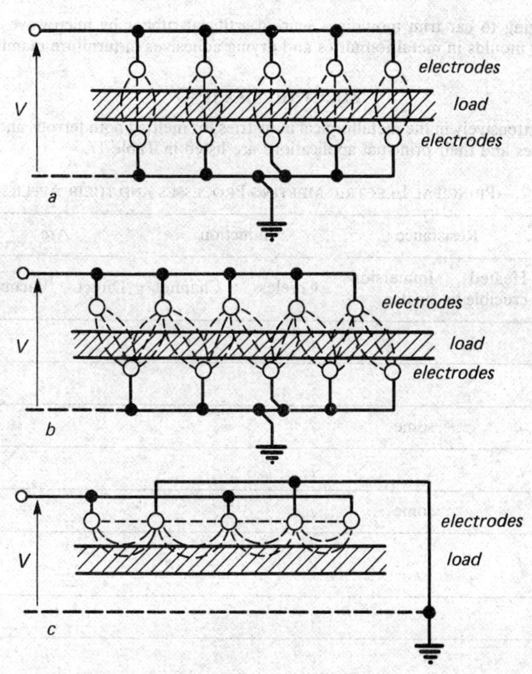

FIG. 24.—Examples of applicators used for dielectric heating. (*a*) through field; (*b*) staggered through field; (*c*) stray field.

in sheet form is shown in Fig. 25. Potential safety hazards exist at the high frequencies used but the electromagnetic radiation can be kept to acceptable limits by good design and continuous processes are possible.

A number of other processes can be carried out using rf and microwave dielectric heating although the range of materials of adequate loss factor is small. Examples are the use of rf heating for welding PVC in applications

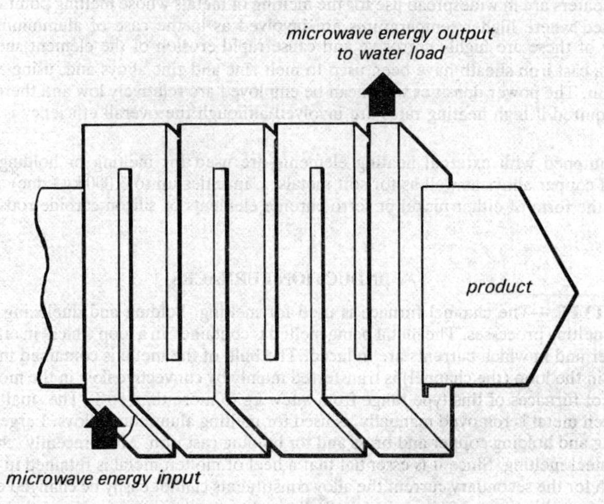

FIG. 25.—Microwave serpentine applicator for continuous heating proceses.

ranging from packaging to car trim mouldings, curing artificial rubber by microwave heating, curing resin coated sand used for moulds in metal foundries and drying adhesives in furniture manufacture.

ELECTRIC MELTING

Electricity is used extensively in the metallurgical industries for melting both ferrous and non-ferrous metals. The different processes and their principal applications are listed in Table 17.

TABLE 17.—PRINCIPAL ELECTRIC MELTING PROCESSES AND THEIR APPLICATIONS.

Metal	Resistance		Induction		Arc		Other processes
	Heated crucible	Immersion heater	Coreless	Channel	Direct	Vacuum	
White Metals	√	√	√	√			
Zinc Alloys	√	√	√	√			
Aluminium alloys	√	some	√	√			
Magnesium alloys	√	√	√	√			
Copper alloys	√	some	√	√			
Nickel alloys	√		√			√	electroslag electron beam
Cast iron			√	√	√		
Carbon steels			√		√		
Alloy steels			√		√	√	electroslag electron beam
Super alloys			√		√	√	electroslag electron beam

RESISTANCE FURNACES

Immersion heaters are in widespread use for the melting of metals whose melting point is below 650°C. They can also be used where higher temperatures are involved as in the case of aluminium alloys for example although many of these are highly corrosive and cause rapid erosion of the element sheath. Silicon carbide elements with a cast iron sheath have been used to melt zinc and zinc alloys and, using a ceramic sheath, for melting cast iron. The power densities which can be employed are relatively low and therefore a large number of units are required if high heating rates are involved although the overall efficiency is high and the capital cost low.

Crucibles equipped with external heating elements are used for melting or holding small quantities of aluminium and copper alloys as well as for soft metals. Capacities up to 3,000 kg (zinc) are available and the elements take the form of either nickel or ferro-chrome elements or silicon carbide rods.

INDUCTION FURNACES

CHANNEL TYPE.—The channel furnace is used for melting, holding and duplexing in conjunction with other primary melting processes. The metal being melted is contained in a loop which, in effect, is the secondary of a transformer and in which currents are induced. The bulk of the metal is contained in a bath to which the heat produced in the loop (the channel) is transferred mainly by convective flow in the molten metal (Fig. 26). The capacities of furnaces of this type range from a few kg to more than 30 T. The small bale-out type, from which the molten metal is removed manually, is used for melting aluminium alloys. Larger tilting furnaces are used for melting and holding copper and brass and for holding cast iron. More recently, channel furnaces have been used for steel melting. Since it is essential that a heel of molten metal is retained in the furnace in order to ensure a path for the secondary current the alloy constituents cannot easily be changed except within narrow limits and therefore this type of furnace is usually limited to continuous operation involving a single alloy.

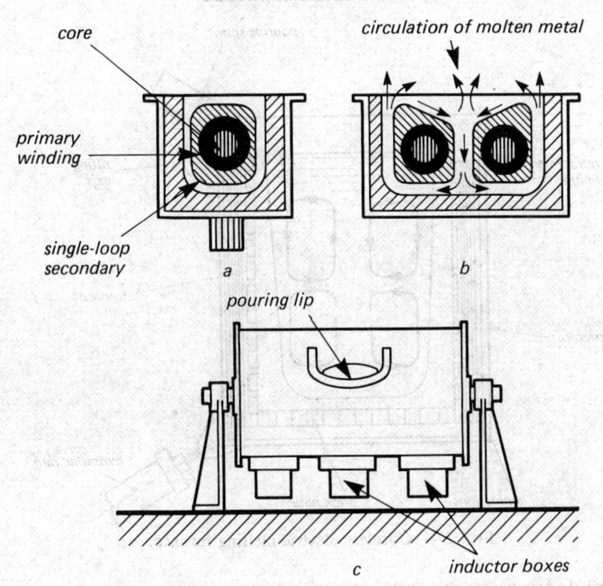

FIG. 26.—Examples of different induction melting furnaces. (*a*) Wyatt furnace with integral inductor; (*b*) Channel furnace with inductor box; (*c*) Drum channel furnace.

The power input is limited by the acceptable power density in the channel, which in turn is limited by the rate at which heat transfer occurs from the molten metal in this channel to the bath. Although convection in the molten metal assists the circulation the heat transfer can be greatly increased by utilising the motor effect that occurs due to the divergence of the current flow at the entrance of the channel and a number of different channel designs which utilise this effect have been developed for use at high powers. Single inductor single phase, twin inductor two phase (Scott transformer) and three phase (using one, two and three inductor boxes) are possible.

CORELESS TYPE.—In its simplest form (Fig. 27) the coreless furnace consists of a refractory crucible surrounded by a coil supplied from an ac source. The crucible material is chosen to suit the application. Small furnaces use pre-formed alumina or silicon-bonded-graphite. In the larger furnaces the crucibles are formed *in situ* from rammed refractory powders and the inside surfaces are subsequenty fritted by the molten metal during the first melt. The skin-depth of the molten metal at the operating frequency governs the choice of diameter and this in turn fixes the optimum dimensions. The minimum desirable frequency also depends on the size of the metal charge used when starting from cold since, if this is small compared with the skin-depth, insufficient power will be generated to enable the process to start (Table 8). Figure 29 shows the relationship between power and frequency for a given capacity of a furnace used for melting cast iron. If this is not acceptable the furnace may be started either by pouring in a small amount of molten metal, by using large specially selected scrap or a pre-formed starting charge from a previous melt. The interaction between the currents and magnetic fields in the charge produces stirring forces in the melt which increase as the frequency decreases. Although this stirring results in crucible erosion it does have the advantage, particularly at low frequencies, of moving solid scrap and particulate material, such as fluxes and alloy constituents, from the top of the furnace to the body of the melt. If the stirring is inadequate then additional low frequency stirring coils, used during only part of the melting cycle, can be incorporated.

Coreless furnaces are used for melting virtually all metals in quantities from less than a few kg of rare metals, at frequencies of 450 kHz, to more than 30 T of iron at 50 Hz. The main advantages, as compared with the channel furnace, are the stirring action, which assists in refining and alloying, and the ability to melt suitable scrap from cold so that the crucible can be completely emptied between melts and, if necessary, an alloy change to be made. For most foundry applications the choice is usually between a small unit, in which only limited stirring occurs, supplied at medium frequency (1–10 kHz) from an inverter, or a large furnace supplied at 50 Hz directly from the public electricity network. Static frequency multipliers, producing low harmonics of the 50 Hz mains supply, can also be used.

The furnace can be emptied by using a simple tilting mechanism, or alternatively the crucible can be removed from the coil when melting is complete (Fig. 28). In the latter case it is possible to employ several crucibles

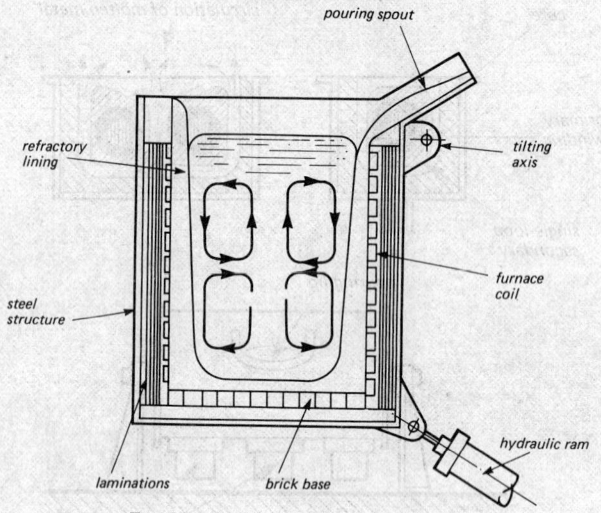

FIG. 27.—Coreless electric melting furnace.

serviced by one coil. In larger units it may be advantageous to use a pair of switched coils connected to the same power supply in order to achieve continuous melting.

THE DIRECT ARC FURNACE.—The direct arc furnace is used today principally for melting steel, special alloys and cast iron where large throughputs are required. There are also a limited number of specialised

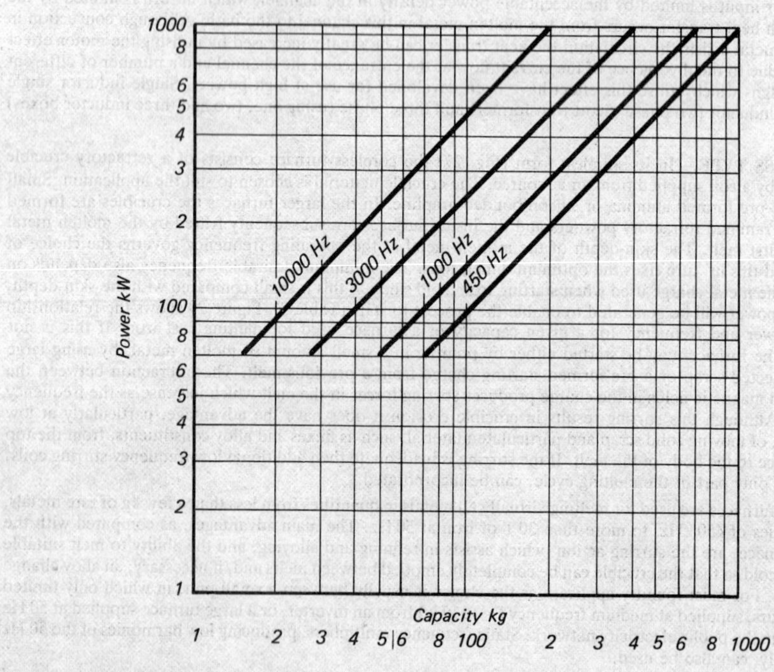

FIG. 28.—Typical power/capacity ratios at selected frequencies (based on cast iron) (Courtesy: *Electricity Council*).

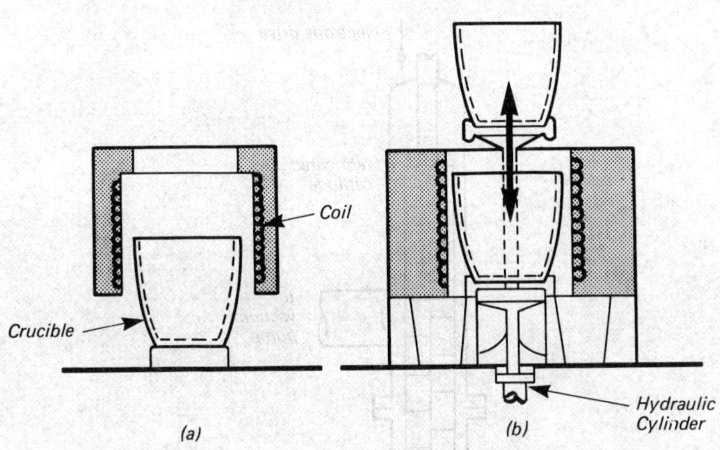

FIG. 29.—Examples of coreless crucible furnaces. (*a*) lift off furnace; (*b*) pop-up furnace.

applications. Although this type of furnace is unique in its ability to melt large quantities of high melting point metal with high efficiency it has been replaced in many applications by the channel and coreless furnaces referred to above.

The furnace is shown schematically in Fig. 30. Typically capacities range from 30 tonnes to 400 tonnes, the majority being less than 100 tonnes. The construction is robust with a shallow dish shaped hearth to give a large surface area enabling high heat transfer rates and effective slag reactions to be obtained. The arc current produces relatively little electromagnetic stirring and, if special alloys are to be produced, it may be necessary to incorporate a coil carrying a 5 Hz current in the hearth and using a non-magnetic steel shell for the bath. Although melting rates are similar to those obtained with the coreless furnace the capacity is much larger and the arc furnace is capable of producing very large outputs, unlike the coreless furnace its operation is largely independent of the quality of scrap used.

The furnace presents a rapidly fluctuating load to the supply, especially at the beginning of the melting cycle, and this results in voltage fluctuations at the point of common coupling. These fluctuations occur in the range 0.1 Hz to 10 Hz and are particularly objectionable in the way in which they affect the output of tungsten filament lamps. The maximum acceptable level of such fluctuations is 0·25% of the mains frequency voltage. The effects can be reduced by connecting the furnace to the supply system at as high a voltage as possible, in some cases 132 kV or even 275 kV. Various semiconductor and capacitor compensating devices have also been developed to overcome the problem.

At present there is considerable interest in the use of dc arc furnaces as well as the use of dc and ac plasma torches in steel melting furnaces and several installations are in operation. Advantages claimed include reduced

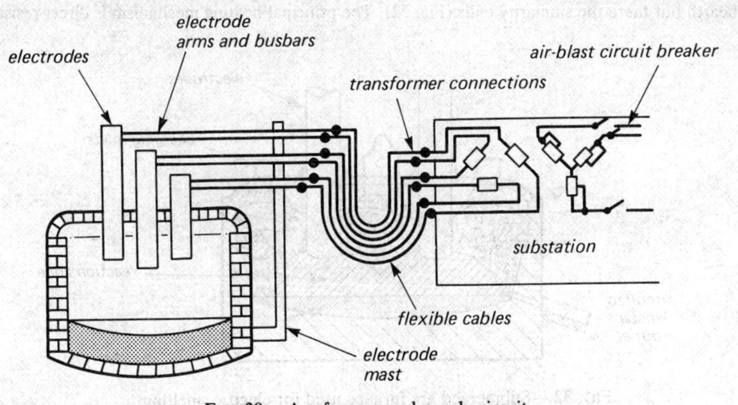

FIG. 30.—Arc furnace and supply circuit

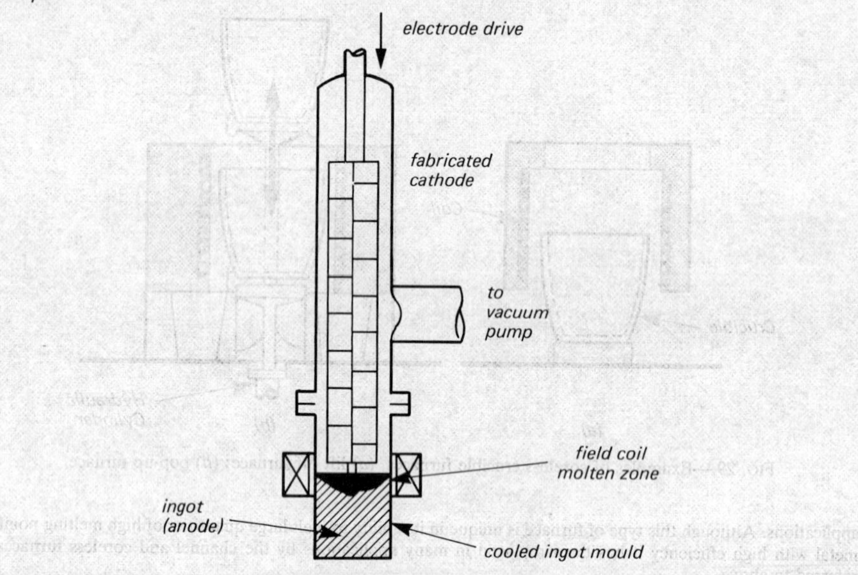

FIG. 31.—Vacuum arc furnace.

electrode costs, reduction of flicker and a smaller loss of alloying elements. Plasma torches are also being used for preheating hot blast cupolas so reducing the demand for high-cost metallurgical coke and increasing throughput.

THE VACUUM ARC FURNACE.—The vacuum arc furnace, Fig. 31, uses a low voltage, high current, dc arc to melt a preformed electrode. It is used chiefly to melt metals which react with air at high temperatures, e.g. titanium, and/or where gas inclusions need to be minimised, in steel or nickel alloys for example.

Inclusions from refractory linings are eliminated and the hemispherical molten pool at the top of the ingot, the 'skull' minimises temperature gradients and hence thermally induced stresses during cooling as well as piping at the end of the ingot. It also tends to concentrate impurities on the meniscus. The water-cooled ingot mould results in the process being highly energy intensive and this furnace is generally used where no alternative method is possible.

ELECTRIC ARC REDUCTION PROCESSES.—The submerged arc reduction process is not primarily a melting technique but is a method of reducing both metals and non-metals including ferro-alloys, copper, phosphorus and calcium-carbide. As with the arc furnace, the unit incorporates three electrodes and a saucer-shaped hearth but there the similarity ends (Fig. 32). The principal heating mechanism is direct resistance by

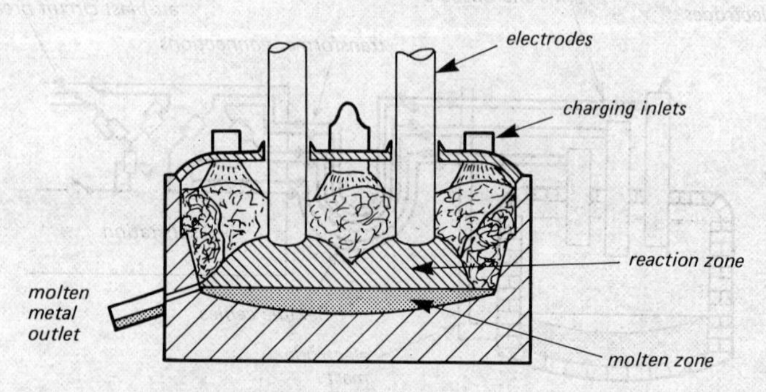

FIG. 32.—Submerged arc furnace used for electric smelting.

currents through the ore, slag and reducing agents in a similar way to the electroslag furnace. Discontinuities in the conducting path result in additional heating from localised arcs. The furnace is static and, as a result, the design is simple, the electrode is formed above the surface. The unit is normally limited to high temperature, highly energy intensive processes. Recent developments are the use of dc with a hollow electrode for reducing ore and fines and the use, in the USA, of plasma furnaces for reclaiming platinum from spent automobile exhaust catalyst.

ELECTRON BEAM FURNACES.—Electron beam furnaces are used for melting metals that react with air at elevated temperatures or where gas inclusions are to be prevented and low vapour pressure impurities evaporated. The process is similar in both operation and application to the vacuum-arc furnace, the ingot being formed in a water-cooled crucible. Ingots, slabs, tubes, castings and powder can be produced. One example is shown in Fig. 33, this consists of two electron beam guns arranged round a consumable electrode. Individual

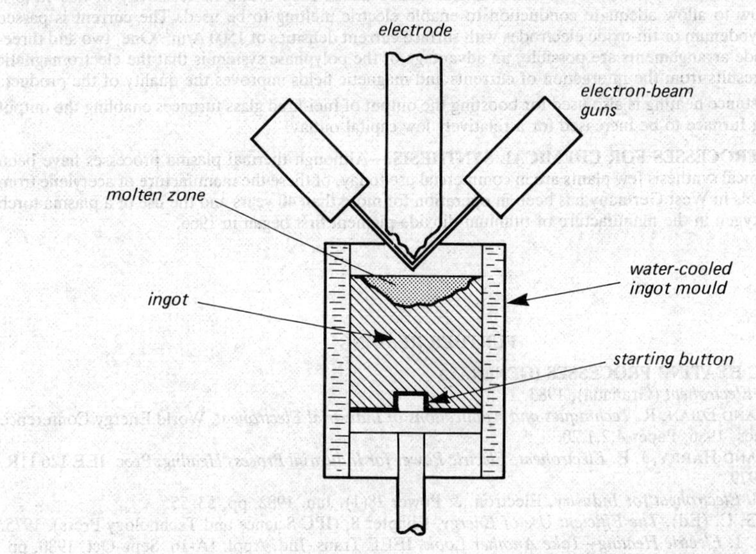

FIG. 33.—Electron beam melting furnace for refining.

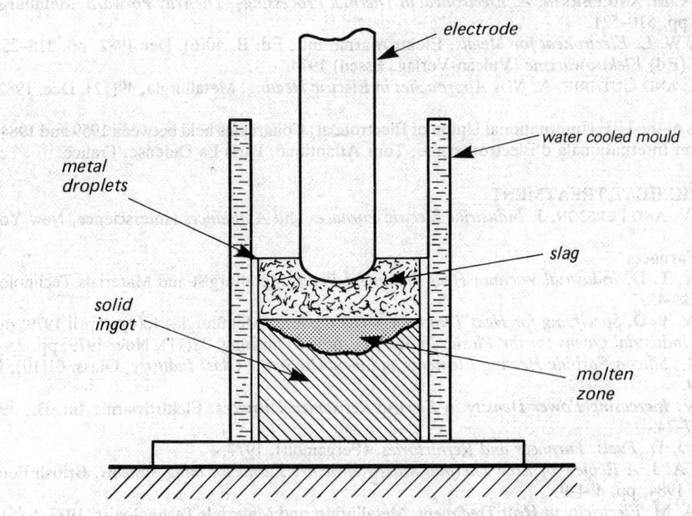

FIG. 34.—Electroslag furnace for melting and refining.

gun ratings up to 400 kW are possible thus giving total three-phase power inputs up to 1·2 MW which results in melting rates of 500 kg/h.

ELECTROSLAG MELTING.—Electroslag melting is used in the production of high purity alloys. A high degree of refining of the molten metal is obtained since small droplets of the metal from the preformed electrode pass through the molten slag. The process is very energy intensive and is only used where the highest properties of the material are required. The principle of operation is one of ionic conduction between the consumable electrode through the pre-melted slag on to the surface of the ingot (Fig. 34). The unit is similar to the vacuum-arc furnace in that it is a skull process, however it is carried out at atmospheric pressure relying on a protective covering of molten slag to screen the metal from the surrounding air. Ingots up to 15 T can be produced in single or three-phase furnaces.

ELECTRIC GLASS MELTING.—Glass is molten above about 1100°C and its resistivity in this state is sufficiently low to allow adequate conduction to enable electric melting to be used. The current is passed between molybdenum or tin-oxide electrodes with surface current densities of 1500 A/m^2. One, two and three-phase electrode arrangements are possible, an advantage of the polyphase system is that the electromagnetic stirring that results from the interaction of currents and magnetic fields improves the quality of the product.

Direct resistance heating is also used for boosting the output of fuel-fired glass furnaces enabling the output of an existing furnace to be increased for a relatively low capital outlay.

PLASMA PROCESSES FOR CHEMICAL SYNTHESIS.—Although thermal plasma processes have been used for chemical synthesis few plants are in commercial use today, of these the manufacture of acetylene from naptha at Huels in West Germany has been in operation for more than 40 years and the use of a plasma torch to preheat oxygen in the manufacture of titanium dioxide pigment first began in 1966.

FURTHER READING

ELECTRIC HEATING PROCESSES (GENERAL)

BARBER, H. *Electroheat* (Granada), 1983.
BARBER, H. AND DJIAN, R. *Techniques and Applications of Industrial Electroheat*, World Energy Conference (Paris), Cannes, 1986, Paper 4.2.1.20.
BARBER, H. AND HARRY, J. E. *Electroheat: Electric Power for Industrial Process Heating*. Proc. IEE 126 11R, 1126–1148, 1979.
DAVIES, E. J. *Electroheat for Industry*, Electron. & Power 28(1), Jan. 1982, pp. 53–55.
DRYDEN, I. G. C. (Ed), *The Efficient Use of Energy*, Chapter 8, (IPC Science and Technology Press), 1975.
ERICKSON, C. J. *Electric Heating—Take Another Look*, IEEE Trans. Ind. Appl. IA-16. Sept–Oct. 1980, pp. 641–8.
GUTHRIE, A. M. AND PERKIN, A. *Electroheat in Thermal Processing—The Way Forward*, Metallurgia, 51(12), Dec. 1984, pp. 510–521.
HARRISON, W. L. *Electroheat for Metals*, Elektrowarme Int., Ed. B, 40(6), Dec 1982, pp. 318–25.
KEGEL, K. (Ed) *Elektrowaerme* (Vulcan-Verlag, Essen) 1974.
PERKINS, A. AND GUTHRIE, A. *New Approaches in Electric Heating*, Metallurgia, 49(12), Dec. 1982, pp. 605–621.
Proceedings of the UIE (International Union of Electroheat) Congresses held between 1959 and 1984 published by the Union Internationale d'Electrothermie, Tour Atlantique, Paris La Defense, France.

ELECTRIC HEAT TREATMENT

PASCHKIS, V. AND PERSSON, J. *Industrial Electric Furnaces and Appliances* (Interscience, New York, 1960).

Electric Furnaces

ATTERBURY, T. D. *Industrial Vacuum Heat Treatment Plant*, Metallurgist and Materials Technologist, 5(5), 1973, pp. 238–45.
ATTERBURY, T. D. *Specifying for Heat Treatment—The Options*, Metallurgia, 46(4), April 1979, pp. 262—6.
DAVEY, S. *Industrial Ovens for the Plastic Industry*, Product Finishing, 32(11), Nov. 1979, pp. 23–5.
DAVIS, J. R., *Silicon Carbide Heating Elements and their Use in the Glass Industry*, Glass, 61(10), Oct. 1984, pp. 347–349.
ENDRESS, V. *Increasing Power Density in Electric Resistance Furnaces*, Elektrowarme Int. B., 39(2), April 1981, pp. 67–74.
GILCHRIST, J. D. *Fuels, Furnaces and Refractories*, (Pergamon), 1977.
GRIFFITHS, A. J. *A Review of Low Thermal Mass Refractory Furnace Lining Systems*, British Foundryman, 77(9), Nov. 1984, pp. 484–9.
GUTHRIE, A. M. *Electricity in Heat Treatment*, Metallurgist and Materials Technologist, 1973, 5 (5), pp. 246–251.

LUITEN, C. H. AND LIMQUE, F. *Developments in Vacuum Furnaces*, Metallurgia, 47(3), Mar. 1980, pp. 119–26.
MASTERS, C. F. *Electric Vacuum Furnaces for Heat Treating Steel*, Ind. Heating (USA), 1978, Sept., pp. 23–28.
NICKELS, R. G. AND HOLT, H. *Electricity in the Heat Treatment of Glass*, Glass (Int), 57(3), Mar. 1980, pp. 14–8.
OTTO, C. A.: *'Electric Furnaces'* (Newnes, London 1958).
PALETHORPE, L. G. W. *Economics and Automation in Heat Treatment*, Metallurgist and Materials Technologist, 1973, 5, (5), pp. 232–237.
REYNOLDSON, R. W. *Analysis of the Costs of Heat Treatment*, Metallurgia and Metal Forming, 1973, 40, (4), pp. 108–113 and 40 (5), pp. 143–147.
SEVERS, M. J. AND KUYSER, W. C. *Vacuum and Inert Gas Furnace Elements*. Proceedings of the 6th International Congress on Electroheat, Brighton, 1968. International Union for Electroheat (Paris), paper N316, pp. 1–6.
TRINKS, W. *Industrial Furnaces—Vol. I.* J. Wiley, New York, 1950, 3rd edn.
TRINKS, W. *Industrial Furnaces—Vol. II.* J. Wiley, New York, 1955, 3rd edn.

Direct Resistance Heating

GEIGER, R. *Conductive Heating of Steel Rods*, Elektrowarme Int. Ed. B. 42(3), June 1984, pp. 153–4.
HERBERT, T. M. *High Speed Wire Annealing Solved by Resistance Heating*, Electr. Times 1976, 4398, p. 7.
HEINE, H. G. *Electric Conductive Billet Heaters*, Iron & Steel Eng., 54(2), Feb. 1977, pp. 38–46.
KARUNASENA, W. G., GREENE, G. W., AND CHEN, N. N. S. *Direct Resistance Heating Characteristics of Rectangular Sheet Blanks*, IEEE Trans Ind. Appl., 1978, 1A-14, (3), May–June, pp. 282–288.
LLANDIS, G. N. AND TRACKMAN, J. C. *Direct Resistance Heating of Billets.* Presented at the 6th Biennial IEEE Conference on Electric Heating, 9th–10th April 1963.
SCHIFFARTH, J. *Heating Billets and Plates by the Direct Passage of Current*, Brown Boveri Rev., 1964, 51, (10–11), Oct–Nov., pp. 659–668.

Induction Heating

ANNEN, W. *Inductive Heating of Ingots and Bars in High-performance Forges*, Brown Boveri Rev., 1975, (1/2), Jan–Feb, 62, pp. 47–51.
BNCE, *Guide to Induction Heating Equipment*, BNCE, The Electricity Council, EC4519, 1983.
BOBART, G. F. *Energy Saving Considerations in Mass Induction Heating*, IEEE Trans. Ind. Appl., IA-15(5), Sept/Oct. 1978, pp. 438–442.
COX, E. R. *Developments in Induction Heat Treatment*, Metallurgia, 51(2), Feb. 1984, pp. 44–9.
CRAIG, R. H. *Induction Heating of Slabs at McLouth Steel*, Iron & Steel Eng., 56(9), Sept. 1979, pp. 50–5.
CUVELIER, M. *Continuous Pipe Welding Using a Static Frequency Multiplier*. Proceedings of the 8th International Congress on Electroheat, Liege 1976. International Union for Electroheat (Paris) paper IIa14, pp. 1–14.
DAVIES, E. J. AND SIMPSON, P. G. *Induction Heating*. McGraw Hill, 1979.
DI PIERI, C. *Modern Induction Heating Units for Steel Billets*, Elektrowarme Int. B, 38(1), Feb. 1980, pp. 22–8.
DUSSELDORK, M. *Special Applications of Induction Heating*, Elektrowarme Int. B, 42(3), June 1984, pp. 137–9.
GOLLOTTNISCH, T. AND ANNEN, W. *Technical Advances in High-Frequency and Medium-Frequency Heating in the Tube Industry*, Brown Boveri Rev. 65, Feb. 1978, pp. 96–102.
Induction Heating for Aluminium Extrusion, Elec. Rev., 1977, 198, 25 Nov., pp. 38–41.
JAMESON, F. R. *British Steel Saves Power and Space with Induction Heating*, Electr. Rev., 209(13), Oct. 1981, pp. 31–3.
LOSINSKI, M. G. *Industrial Applications of Induction Heating* Pergamon Press 1965.
MOLL, W. *Induction Heating of Steel Pipes*, Elektrowarme Int. B, 42(3), June 1984, p. 142.
NIGG, F. *Induction Annealing Plant for Heat Treating Welded Joints*, Brown Boveri Rev., 1973, 16(1), Jan., pp. 30–4.
PERKINS, A. *Rapid Electroheating of Steel Billets for Forging and Rolling*, Electr. Rev. 197, 5 Dec. 1975, pp. 739–41.
PERKINS, A. *Electrical Heating of Billets for Extrusion, Rolling and Forging*, Metallurgia and Metal Forming, 1977, 44, (April), pp. 164–172.
ROSS, N. V. *A system for Induction Heating of Large Steel Slabs*, IEEE Trans., 1970, *IGA-6*, (5) Sept–Oct., pp. 449–54.
SCHAUFLER, K. *Rationalizing Industrial Soldering and Brazing Processes with Induction Heating Plant.* Brown Boveri Rev., 1972, *59*, (5), May, pp. 231–5.
YOUNG, F. J. *Induction Heating for Case Hardening Applications*, IEEE Trans., 1977, MAG-13, pp. 1776–1785.
ZANDSTRA, K. A. *Zone Refining and Crystal Growing of Semi-conductor Materials.* Proceedings of the 5th International Congress on Electroheat, Wiesbaden, 1963. International Union for Electroheat (Paris) paper N316, pp. 1–8.

Salt Baths

ANDERSON, G. W. *Salt Bath Furnaces*, IEEE Trans., IA-10, 1974, pp. 340–346.

Glow Discharge Nitriding

BOOTH, M., FARRELL, T. AND JOHNSON, R. H. *The Theory and Practice of Plasma Carburising*, Heat Treatment of Metals, 10(2), 1983, pp. 45–52.

KOROTCHENKO, V. AND BELL, T. *Applications of Plasma Nitriding in UK Manufacturing Industries*, Heat Treatment of Metals, 5(4), 1978, pp. 88–94.

WAREING, J. B. *Application of Glow Discharge Heating to Continuous Metal Processing; Electricity for Materials Processing and Conservation*. IEE Conf. Publ., 149, 1977, pp. 101–106.

Surface Hardening using Lasers

GREGSON, V. G. ET AL, *Basics of Laser Material Processing*, Electro-Opt. Syst. Des., 8(11), Nov. 1976, pp. 25–8.

HARRY, J. E. *Industrial Lasers and Their Applications* McGraw Hill, Maidenhead, 1974.

KOEBNER, H. *Industrial Applications of Lasers* (John Wiley & Sons) 1984.

MILNE, W. I. *Lasers and Their Industrial Applications*, Electricity Council (London), 1983.

SEAMAN, F. D. AND GANAMTHU, D. S. *Using the Industrial Laser to Surface Harden and Alloy*, Metal Progress 1975, pp. 67–74.

STANFORD, K. *Lasers in Metal Surface Modification*, Metallurgia, 47(3), Mar. 1980, pp. 109–116.

SURFACE HEATING

Surface Heating of Liquids and Solids

ANGEL, F. *The Technology of Electric Trace Heating*, Executive Engineer, Vol. 61(3), 1979, pp. 15–17.

ANGEL, F. *Electric Trace Heating for Long Pipe Lines*, Elec. Rev., 1979, 204, (11), pp. 45–46.

COOPER, P. J. *Electroheat Gives Strength to Welded Constructions*. Proceedings of the 6th International Congress on Electroheat, Brighton 1968. International Union for Electroheat (Paris), paper N324, pp. 1–6.

COTTRELL, D. J. AND PARKER, G. F. *Electric Heating Eases Stress in Welded Structures*, Electr. Rev., 206(13), March 1980, pp. 23–5.

DOBIES, W. C. *Metal Sheathed Elements for Process Heating*,Energy Digest, Oct/Nov. 1972, pp. 2–8.

DOBIE, W. C. *Producing Process Steam and Hot Water Economically*, Elec. Rev., 1975, 197, (23), 5th Dec., pp. 748–50.

HAMMACK, T. J. AND JIKUKLINKA, S. *Self-limiting Electrical Heat Tracing: New Solutions to Old Problems*, IEEE Trans. Ind. Appl., 1977, IA-13, (2), March/April, pp. 134–138.

HEMPHILL, D. F. *The Use of Electric Boilers in Today's Market*, IEEE Conf. Electric Process Heating in Industry, April 1971, pp. 109–112.

LEAVINES, J. E. *Electrical Heaters for Use in Class 1 Division 2 Locations*, IEEE Trans. ind. Appl. 1973, IA-9, (4), July/Aug. pp. 467–72.

LONDON, A. *Electric Resistance Heating Elements*, Ind. Proc. Heating, 12(12), 1972, pp. 26–29.

MYERS, L. W. *A Users Experience with Electric Heat Tracing*, IEEE Trans. Ind. Appl. IA-16(6), Nov–Dec. 1980, pp. 840–4.

NICHOLS, C. AND REIK, M. *Elements of Electric Process Heating*, Process Eng Jan. 1981, pp. 59–61.

RESON, J. *How Electrode Boilers can Cut the Cost of Steam Generation*, Power, Vol. 128(5), May 1984, pp. 87–9.

REIK, P. H. *Electric Pipe Tracing,* Engineering 1972, 212, (11), Nov., pp. 1094–6.

Safety Guidelines for Industrial Electric Immersion Heaters, BNCE Electricity Council EC4729, 1985.

STUCHELI, A. *Economic Application of Electric Boilers for Steam and Hot Water Supplies,* Sulzer Tech. Rev., Vol. 57(2), pp. 103–111.

TURNER, B. *Industrial Heating Applications met by Rugged Sheathed Elements*, Electr. Times, 4564, March 1980, pp. 10–11.

WALLACE, D. AND SPIELVOGEL, L. G. *Field Performance of Steam and Hot Water Electric Boilers*, IEEE Trans. Ind. Appl. 1974, IA-10, (6) Nov–Dec. pp. 761–9.

Infra-red and Ultra-violet Processes

AITKEN, D. W. *Hybrid Circuit Manufacture Using an Infra-Red Source*, Hybrid Circuits, 3, Autumn 1983, pp. 27–32.

The Application of Electric Infra-Red Heating to Industrial Processes, BNCE, Electricity Council EC4114, 1981.

HANKINS, W. C. *Electric Infra-red Process Heating*, Product Finishing, 1979, 32, (12), pp. 28–33.

HOGARTH, G. M. *Infra-Red Heating—An Economic Technique for Industry*, IEEE Conf. Electricity for Materials Processing and Conservation, March 1977, pp. 39–42.

LAMBERT, J. L. *Infra-Red—A Worthwhile Investigation for Paint and Powder Coatings*, Product Finishing, 32(11), 1979, pp. 26–31.

LA TOISON, M. *Infra-red and its Thermal Applications*, Philips Technical Library (Macmillan, London 1964).

MARSHALL, P. W. *Electric Infra-red—a Worthwhile Investigation for Paint and Powder Coatings*, Product Finishing, 1979, 32, (11), pp. 26–31.

MILLER, N. *Ultra-violet Provides Quick Cure for Printing Inks*, Elec. Rev., 1974, 194, (19), 24th May, pp. 583–5.
PALMER, P. J. *Developments in Infra-Red Drying*, Paper 183(6), March 1976, pp. 331–8.
ROTH, R. *Improve Drying Efficiency*, Pulp and Paper (Canada), 1975, *76*, (4), April, pp. 85–88.
SUMMERS, W. *Ultra-violet and Infra-red Engineering* (Pitman, London, 1962).
UDUPA, K. G. *Mould Drying with Infra-red Bulbs*, Indian Foundry Journal, 1978, 24, April, pp. 1–3.

DIELECTRIC HEATING AND DRYING

BARBER, H. *Developments in the Industrial Application of Radio Frequency and Microwave Heating of Dielectric Materials in the UK*. World Electrotechnical Conf., Moscow June 1977, Paper 4A–82.
BARBER, H. *Microwaves for Cooking and Heating*, Electron. & Power, 27(5), May 1981, pp. 401–2.
BENGTSSON, N. AND OHLSSON, T. *Microwave Heating in the Food Industry*, Proc. IEEE, 1974, 62, pp. 44–55.
COPSON, D. A. *Microwave Heating* (Avi Publ. Co.) 1975.
ELECTRICITY COUNCIL, *Dielectric Heating for Industrial Processes*, 1983.
GIBSON, R. *Dielectric Heating and Drying in the Textile Industry* Electricity for materials processing and conservation, IEE Conf. Publ. 149, 1977, pp. 56–60.
HAFNER, T. *High Frequency Heating for Curing Glued Assemblies*, Brown Boveri Rev., 1972, 59, pp. 294–296.
HAFNER, T. *Tunnel Ovens for High Frequency Heat Treatment*, Brown Boveri Rev, 59(6), 1972, pp. 297–301.
HAIM, G. AND ZADE, H. P. *Welding of Plastics*, (Crosby Lockwood, London, 1969).
HARRISON, W. L., *Industrial Processing Using Dielectric Heating*, Elektrowarme Int. Ed. B., 41(4), Aug. 1983, pp. 180–6.
HODGETT. D. L. ET AL, *Drying by means of Radio Frequency Power*, Conf. on Electricity for Materials Processing and Conservation, IEE, March 1977, pp. 52–55.
HOLLAND, J. M., *Energy Efficient Radio Frequency Drying*, Conf. on Heating and Processing 1–3000 MHz, British National Committee for Electroheat (London), Cambridge 1986, Paper 2.4.
HULLS, P. J., *Development of the Industrial use of Dielectric Heating in the UK*, J. Microwave Power, 17(1), March 1982, pp. 29–38.
JONES, P. L., LAWTON, J., AND PARKER, I. M. *Paper Drying in Radio and Microwave Frequency Fields*, Trans. Inst. Chem. Eng., 1974, 52, pp. 121–131.
KASHYAP, S. C. *A Waveguide Applicator for Sheet Material Microwave Heating*, IEEE Trans Microwave Theory and Tech (USA), 1976, 24, (2) pp. 125–6.
LAWTON, J. *High Frequency Paper Drying: the Effect of Non-uniform Field Distributions*, Trans. Inst. Chem. Eng., 1974, 52, pp. 132–135.
JOLLY, J. A. *Economics and Energy Utilisation Aspects of the Application of Microwaves*, J. Microwave Power. 11(3), 1976, pp. 233–45.
JONES, P. L. AND HART, K. *Radio Frequency Air Flotation Drying*, 10th UIE Congress, Stockholm (Interntional Union for Electroheat, Paris), June
LAWTON, J. *Radio Frequency Drying of Non-metallic Materials*, Radio and Electronic Eng., 46(3), 1976, pp. 117–20.
MCLACHLAN, A. S. *Radio Interference from rf Heating Equipment*, Radio & Electron. Eng., 1976, 46, pp. 267–276.
MEISEL, N. *Microwave Applications to Food Processing and Food Systems in Europe*, J. Microwave Power, 8(4), 1973, pp. 143–8.
MEREDITH, R. J. *Recent Advances in Industrial Microwave Processing in the 896/915 MHz Frequency Band*, Conf. on Heating and processing 1–3000 MHz, Cambridge 1986, British National Committee for Electroheat, Paper 7.5.
METAXAS, A. C. *The Future of Electrical Techniques in the Production of Printed Tufted Carpets*, J. Microwave Power, 16(1), March 1981, pp. 43–55.
METAXAS, A. C. AND MEREDITH, R. J. *Industrial Microwave Heating* (Peter Peregrinus) 1983.
MINETT, P. J. *Microwave and RF Heating in Plastics and Rubber Processes*, Plastics and Rubber, 1(5), 1976, pp. 197–200.
MORROW, R. *Applications of Radio Frequency Power to the Drying of Timber*, IEE Proc. A, 127(6) July 1980, pp. 394–8.
OKRESS, F. C. *Microwave Power Engineering* (Academic Press) 1966.
POUND, J. *Practical rf Heating for the Wood Industry* Heywood, London, 1957.
PUSCHNER, H. *Heating with Microwaves*, Phillips Technical Libr., 1966.
SCHWARTZ, H. F., ET AL., *Microwave Curing of Synthetic Rubbers*, J. Microwave Power (Canada), 1973, *8*, (3), pp. 303–322.
VON HIPPELL, A. R. (Ed.) *Dielectric Materials and Applications* MIT Press, Massachusetts, 1954.

ELECTRIC MELTING

PASCHKIS, V. AND PERSSON, J. *Industrial Electric Furnaces and Appliances* Interscience, New York, 1960.
ROBIETTE, A. G. *Electric Melting Practice* Griffin, London, 1972.
SIMS, C. F. (ED), *Electric Furnace Steelmaking—Design, Operation and Practice*, Vol. 1, Interscience, 1962.

SIMS, C. E. (ED), *Electric Furnace Steelmaking—Theory and Practice*. Vol. 2, (Interscience) 1962.

Resistance Melting

RAMSELL, P. G. *Metal Melting using Resistance Furnaces (Aluminium and other Non-ferrous Metals)*, Conf. on Electricity for Materials Processing and Conservation, IEE Conf. Publ. No. 149, 1977, section V, paper 116, pp. 107–110. IEE, 1977.

SPECKMANN, C. *Melting of Non-Ferrous Metals in Electric Crucible Furnaces*, Elektrowarme Int. Ed. B, 42(3), June 1984, pp. 151–2.

The Channel Induction Furnace

AHMAD, M. A. *Channel Induction Furnaces in Iron foundries*. Brown Boveri Rev., 1975, 62, (1/2), Jan–Feb., pp. 27–34.

ANTOINE, J., BONIS, P. AND SHIVDASANI, C. *Channel Induction Furnaces for Holding, Superheating and Storing Steel*, Elektrowarme Int. B, 35(B4), Aug. 1977, pp. 200–6.

SHIVDASANI, C. *Channel Induction Furnaces for Holding, Superheating and Storing Steel*. Brown Boveri Rev., 1975, 62, (1/2), Jan–Feb., pp. 34–41.

SOMMER, R. A. *Channel Furnace Melting with Jet Flow Inductors*, IEEE Trans., 1976, 1A–12, pp. 540–545.

TAMA, M. *Development of Channel-type Induction Furnaces*, Elektrowaerme Int. B, 1973, 31, pp. 231–235.

TAMA, S. *Development of Channel Induction Furnaces for Melting Copper and Brass*, J. Metals, 26(1), Jan. 1974, pp. 18–25.

Coreless Furnace

DAVIES, I. *Coreless Induction Furnaces—Their Roles in the Iron Foundry*, British Foundryman, 71(10), Oct. 1978, pp. 49–53.

DOTSCH, E. *The Melting of Steel in Large Coreless Induction Furnaces*, IEE Conf. Publ. 149, (London), 1977, pp. 34–8.

EDGERLEY, C. J. *Improvements in the Melting Efficiency of Coreless Furnaces*, IEE Conf. Publ. 149 (London), 1977, pp. 28–33.

GUTHRIE, A. M. AND WILFORD, C. F. *The Production of Engineering Grey Iron Castings—A Review with Particular Reference to Electric Melting*, Metallurgist and Materials Technologist, 1977, 9, pp. 491–493.

HARRISON, W. L. *Application of Electroheat in the Iron Foundry*. Foundry Trades Jnl., 135(2959), 1973, pp. 225–230.

HARRISON, W. L. *Engineering and Installation of Coreless Induction Furnace Plant*, Elektrowaerme Int., 1979, 37, (B4), Aug., pp. 209–14.

ITURRIOZ, D. *Application of Modern Vacuum Techniques in the Metallurgical Industry—Steel Degasification*, Met. & Elec., 1972, 36, pp. 84–90.

LYCETT, J. D., AND KENDON, R. D. *Supplies to Induction Furnaces*, IEE Conf. Publ. No. 110, (London 1974), pp. 57–61.

SCHAUB, H. P. *Concept of an Induction-melting Installation for a Large Foundry*. Brown Boveri Rev., 1975, 62, (1/2), Jan–Feb., pp. 60–2.

SCHAUB, H. P. *Induction Furnaces for Melting and Holding in the Aluminium Industry*. Brown Boveri Rev., 1972, 59, (6), Jun., pp. 271–82.

SCHLATTER, R. *Vacuum Induction Melting Technology of High Temperature Alloys*, J. Met., 1972, 24, pp. 17–25.

SUNDBERG, Y. *Heat Recovery in Induction Melting Plants for Iron and Steel*, ASEA J., 52(3), 1979, pp. 57–63.

WANNER, P. *Melting Installation with Mains Frequency Coreless Induction Furnaces and Scrap Preheating in an Iron Foundry*, Foundry Trade J. 136(2990), Mar. 1974, pp. 337–41.

Direct Arc Furnaces

BOWMAN, B. *Trends in Electrical Parameters of Arc Steelmaking Furnaces*, Elektrowarme Int. Ed. B, 37(2), 1979, pp. 80–86.

BUHLER, K. AND HABERT, D. *Technical and Economic Advantages of the New BBC Arc Furnace for Direct Current*, Brown Boveri Rev., 71(6–7), Jun. 1984, pp. 288–293.

CAINE, K. E. *A Review of New Electric Arc Furnace Technologies*, Iron & Steel Eng., 60(10), Oct. 1983 pp. 45–7.

HEFFERMAN, G. R. *Two Routes to Steel*, IEEE Trans., IA-13(1), Jan–Feb. 1977, pp. 58–61.

HOWARD, E. C. *Arc Furnace Power: Existing and Future Installations*, Iron & Steel Eng., 60(10), Oct. 1983, pp. 42–4.

MORRIS, A. S. *Developments in Arc Furnaces*, Iron & Steel Int. 57(1), Feb. 1984, pp. 22–26.

SALOMON, P. J. *The Electric Arc Furnace System*, Elektrowarme Int. Ed. B. 42(2), 1984, pp. 81–3.

SCHNEIDER, R. *The New Generation of Electric Furnaces*, Iron & Steel Int. 531(6), Dec. 1980, pp. 349–55.

SWINDEN, D. J. *The Arc Furnace*, Electroproduction Teaching Monograph, Electricity Council, EC 4600/3, 1986.

Vacuum Arc Furnaces

BARRACLOUGH, K. C. *The Newer Specialist Steelmaking and Steel Refining Processes*, J. Iron and Steel Inst. June 1969, pp. 94–104.

CHILD, H. C. *The Choice of Vacuum Melting Plant for Special Alloy Production*. Proceedings of the 5th International Congress on Electroheat, Wiesbaden, 1963. International Union for Electroheat (Paris), paper N163, pp. 1–7.
JARVIS, E. *Vacuum Arc Remelting Furnaces*, Elec. Rev., 1977, 201, (21), 25th Nov., pp. 33–35.

Submerged Arc Processes
ROBIETTE, A. G. *Electric Melting and Smelting Practice*, Griffin, London 1955.

Plasma Furnaces
Alloy Steelmaking with Plasma Technology Promises High Efficiency and Environmental Advantages, Industrial Heating, Oct., 32, 1980.
HARRY, J. E. *The Use of Plasma and dc Arcs in Steelmaking*, Electric Arc Steelmaking for the 1980's, Institute of Steel Conference Report, 22–27, 1980.
HARRY, J. E. *Gentle Progress on DC Plasma Systems*, Metal Bulletin Monthly, 37(189), 1986, pp. 39–41.
LABROT, M., TALANDER, F. AND MONEUSE, M. *Applications of Plasma Torches in Industry*, Rev. Gen. Electr., 12, Dec. 1981, pp. 916–25.
THUNBERG, S. L., REED, W. H. AND MELLI, W. J. *Plasma Torches as Replacements for Oil Burners*, Iron & Steel Int., 56(6), Dec. 1983, pp. 107–211.

Electron Beam Processes
HUNT, C., AND HARRISON, C. V. *Airco's Facility for Steel Refining and Casting with Induction Furnaces and Electron Beams*, Iron and Steel Eng. (USA), 1971, 48, (8), Aug., p. 85.
OTTO, G. *Vacuum Sintering of Stainless Steel*, J. Vac. Science and Technology, 11(6), 1974, pp. 1110–3.
STEPHAN, H. *Present Position of Electron Beam Melting and Casting Technology*. Proceedings of the 8th International Congress on Electro-heat, Liege, 1976 (International Union for Electroheat, Paris) paper 1d-1, pp. 1–12.

Electroslag Remelting
DUCKWORTH, W. E., AND HOYLE, G. *Electroslag Refining* (Chapman & Hall, London 1969).
ELLIOTT, F., DANJOU, E. L., AND BLACKMOND, R. C. *Superalloy Melting in an ac Electroslag Remelt Furnace with Automatic Melt Control and rms Current Regulation*, IEEE Trans., 1976, IA-12, pp. 545–551.
PEOVER, M. E. *Electroslag Remelting: A Review of Electrical and Electrochemical Aspects*. J. Inst. Metals, 100, April 1972, pp. 97–106.
VOLKHONSKII, L. A., EFREMOV, V. I. AND NIKULIN, A. A. *Electrical and Thermal Processes in Electroslag Furnaces*. Sov. Electr. Eng. (USA), 50(8), 1979, pp. 46–53.

Direct Resistance Melting of Glass
DOYLE, J. P. *Electricity in the Glass Industry*, Glass, 59(5), May 19823, pp. 193–201.
FINCH, D. F. *Crusilite and the Electrically Heated Forehearth*, Glass, 52(6), June 1975, pp. 206–9.
GELL, P. A. M. *An Appreciation of some of the General Principles of Electric Melting of Glass and their Widening Application to Larger Tonnage Facilities*, IEEE Trans., Ind. Appl., 1973, IA-9, (3), pp. 338–42.
HYND, D. F. *Melting Practice and Electricity*, Glass, 54(2), Feb. 1977, pp. 35–37.
PATEMAN, K. H. *Electric Boosting and Mixed Melting*, Glass, 1974, 51, (5), May, pp. 181–188.
SCARFE, F. *Glass Melting and Heating Practice*, Glass, 1979, 56 (8), pp. 311–316.
SCARFE, F. *Electric Melting, a Review,* Glass Technol., 21(1), 1980, pp. 37–50.

STANDARDS, RECOMMENDATIONS AND GUIDELINES

IEC Recommendation 239 1967; Characteristics of Infra-Red Emitters for Heating Purposes.
BS 6462 1970; Glossary of Industrial Furnace Terms.
IEC Recommendation 396 1972; Test Methods for Induction Furnaces with Submerged Channels.
IEC Recommendation 397 1972; Test Methods for Batch Furnaces with Metallic Heating Resistors.
IEC Recommendation 398 1972; General Test Conditions for Industrial Electroheating Equipment.
IEC Recommendation 110 2nd. Edition; Recommendations for Capacitors for Inductive Heat Generating Plants Operating at Frequencies Between 40 and 24 kHz.
IEC Standard 479 1974; Effects of Current Passing Through the Human Body.
BS 2771 1974; Electrical Equipment of Machine Tools. General Purpose Mass-Produced Machines and their Electrical Equipment.
IEC Standard 397A 1975 (Supplement to IEC 397 (1972)); Test Methods for Batch Furnaces with Metallic Heating Resistors.
IEC Report 519-2, 1975; Safety in Electroheat Installations Part 2; Particular Requirements for Resistance Heating Applications.
BS 4727 1975; Glossary of Terms Used in Electrical Engineering (General and Physics).
IEC Report 519-4 1077; Safety in Electroheat Installations, Part 4; Particular Requirements for Arc Furnace Installations.
IEC Standard 364-3-312 1977; Types of Distribution Systems.
IEC Standard Standard 364-4-41 1977; Electrical Installations of Buildings, Part 4: Protection for Safety Chapter 41: Protection Against Electric Shock.
IEC Standard Standard 364-4-471 1977; Measures for Protection Against Electric Shock.

IEC Standard 364-4-43 1977; Protection against Overcurrent.
IEC Standard 364-4-477 1977; Measure of Protection Against Overcurrent.
IEC Standard 364-4-46 1977; Isolation and Switching.
IEC Standard 364-5-537 1977; Devices for Isolation and Switching.
IEC Standard 364-5-54 1977; Earthing Arrangements and Protective Conductors.
BS 800 1977; Specification for Radio Interference Limits and Measurements for Equipment Employing Small Motors, Contacts, Controls and Devices Causing Similar Interference.
IEC Standard 646 1979; Test Methods for Crucible Induction Furnaces.
BS 415 1979; Specification for Safety Requirements for Mains Operating Electronic and Related Apparatus.
IEC Standard 364-4-42 1980; Protection against Thermal Influences.
IEC Standard 676 1980; Test Methods for Direct Arc Furnaces.
IEC Standard 680 1980; Test Methods for Plasma Equipment for Electroheat Applications.
IEC Standard 683 1980; Test Methods for Submerged Arc Furnaces.
IEC Standard 519-5 1980, Safety in Electroheat Installations Part 5; Specifications for Safety in Plasma Installations.
IEC Standard 703 1981; Test Methods for Electroheat Installations with Electron Guns.
IEC Standard 519-6 1982; Safety in Electroheat Installations Part 6; Specifications for Safety in Industrial Microwave Heating Equipment.
International Electrotechnical Vocabulary, 2nd Edition 1983; Group 40 Electroheating Applications.
IEC Standard 779 1983; Test Methods for Electroslag Remelting Furnaces.
IEC Standard 519-7 1983; Safety in Electroheat Installations—Safety Requirements for Electro-Heating Installations with Electron Guns.
IEC Standard 519-8 1983; Safety in Electroheat Installations—Safety Requirements for Electro-Slag Resmelting Furnaces.
BS 6351 Part 1 1983; Electric Surface Heating Part 1; Specification for Electric Surface Heating Devices.
BS 6351 Part 2 1983; Electric Surface Heating Part 2; Guide to the Design of Electric Surface Heating Systems.
BS 6351 Part 3 1983; Electric Surface Heating Part 3; Code of Practice for the Installation, Testing and Maintenance of Electric Surface Heating Systems.
IEC Standard 800 1984; Heating Cables with a Rated Voltage of 300/500V for Comfort Heating and Prevention of Ice Formation.
IEC Report 519-1 (2nd Ed.) 1984, Safety in Elecctroheat Installtions Part 1; General Requirements.
BS 4727 Part 2, Group 10 1985; British Standard Glossary of Electrotechnical, Power, Telecommunication, Electronics, Lighting and Colour Terms. Part 2; Terms Particular to Power Engineering, Group 10 Industrial Electroheating Terminology.
IEC Report 519-3 (2nd. Ed.) 1986; Safety in Electroheat Equipment Part 3; Particular Requirements for Induction and Conduction Heating Installations and Induction Melting Installations.
IEC Standard 239 1986; Nominal Dimensions of Cylindrical Machined Graphite Electrodes with Threaded Sockets and Nipples for use in Arc Furnaces.

ELECTRIC MOTORS CHARACTERISTICS AND APPLICATIONS

Load Categories—Referred Loads—D.C. Motors—Induction Motors—Torque/Slip Relationship—Synchronous and Reluctance Motors—Choice of Motor—Starting and Run-up—Braking—Starting and Braking Energy Loss—Speed Control—Thyristor Control—Industrial Applications—Servo Motors—Fractional Horse Power Motors—Summary of Motor Types and Applications—Bibliography.

By R. W. Whitehead, BSc, PhD, MSc(Tech), CEng, MIEE

Load Character.—When selecting an electrical motor for a particular application it is essential to know the torque, speed, and duty cycle of the load to be driven, and if gear boxes or belts are to be used it is convenient to 'refer' the mechanical requirements to the output shaft of the motor.

In general load torques fall into two categories:

(*a*) those which remain unidirectional even though the driving motor may reverse, eg lifts, hoists, etc; and

(*b*) those which change direction such that they always oppose the direction of the driving motor, eg all friction loads, fans, pumps, etc

Because both categories of load may be present in any drive system the driving motor may be required to operate as a motor, a generator, or as a brake, and to incorporate the performance of either the load or the motor on one diagram it is necessary to use all four quadrants of the torque-speed plane. The best method of interpreting the four quadrant diagram is to consider a motor driving a hoist with a counter balance weight. A load torque may or may not be included. The counter balance weight is considered heavier than the unloaded cage, but lighter than the loaded cage, Fig. 1. Conventionally motoring occurs when the torque of the motor

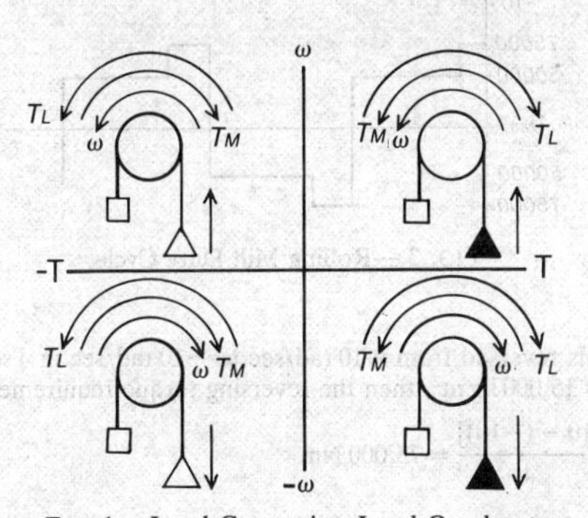

FIG. 1.—Load Categories; Load Quadrants.

is greater than the load torque, $T_m > T_L$, and the speed and the motor torque are in the same direction, quadrants 1 and 3. Generating and braking occur when the torque and the speed are in opposite directions, quadrants 2 and 4.

Typical category (*a*) loads which occur in practice are shown in Fig. 2. These occur in quadrants 1 and 3 opposing the motor torque. Category (*b*) loads are typically inertial and may occur in any quadrant.

Some load torques depend on the position of the motor shaft and, in particular, any motor driving a load having a crank shaft will experience a load torque which is a function of the position of the crank, eg rocking pumps in the oil industry, reciprocating pumps, weaving looms, etc. Alternatively there are loads which exhibit a torque dependent on the position of the load itself. For instance, a locomotive on an uphill climb will require more torque than when on the level. The torque required by cranes and hoists will depend on the height of the lift, and hence the weight of the rope.

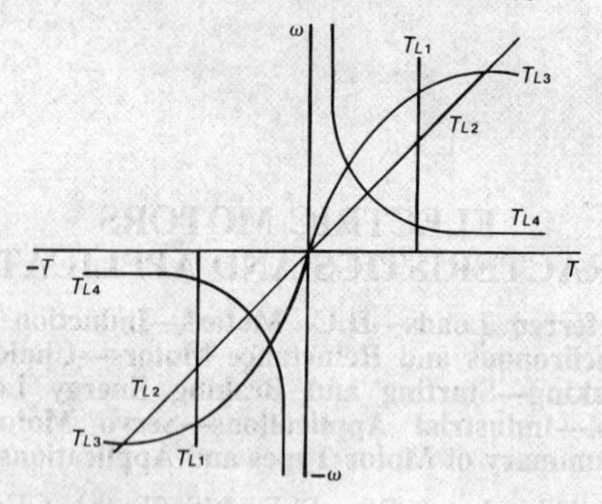

T_{L1}—constant torque
T_{L2}—viscous friction—eddy current brakes, calendering machines
T_{L3}—torque is proportional to some power of speed—fans, pumps, propellors
T_{L4}—constant power load, i.e. torque is inversely prop to speed—milling machines, boring machines, lathes, coilers.

FIG. 2.—Typical Load Curves occurring in Practice.

Duty Cycle.—In many applications the load may be applied intermittently or cyclically, in which case the *duty cycle* must be specified in order to determine the rating of the driving motor. For instance, the main motor on a rolling mill might have a duty cycle as shown (Fig. 3) where the rolling torque demand is 50,000 Nm for

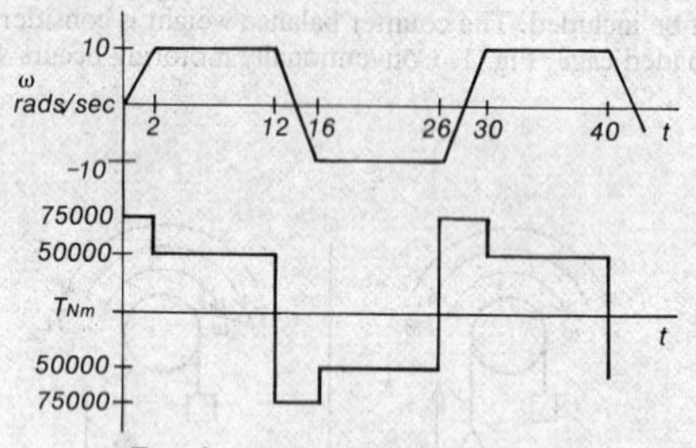

FIG. 3.—Rolling Mill Duty Cycle.

10 secs and the motor speed is reversed from +10 rad/sec to −10 rad/sec in 4 secs. If the effective inertia J referred to the motor shaft is 15,000 kg m², then the reversing torque requirement is

$$J\frac{d\omega}{dt} = 15000\frac{[10-(-10)]}{4} = 75{,}000 \text{ Nm}$$

and the rms torque is

$$T_{rms} = \sqrt{\frac{[(50{,}000^2 \times 10) + (75{,}000^2 \times 4)] \times 2}{28}} = 58{,}250 \text{ Nm}$$

and the motor power rating is $\omega T_{rms} = 10 \cdot 58250 = 582 \cdot 5$ kW.

The motor must be capable of withstanding the peak torque and current demand.

On the other hand the torque demand from a flying shear is impulsive, requiring a large torque for a short time, with a relatively long no-load period.

REFERRED LOADS.—If the load consists of a load torque T_L and has an interia J_L and is coupled to the driving motor through a gear box, then the 'referred' load is obtained as follows.

The referred load torque T'_L is obtained by equating the power at either side of the gear box, ie

$$T_L\omega_L = T'_L\omega_m$$

where ω_m and ω_L are the speeds of the motor and load respectively, hence

$$T'_L = T_L \frac{\omega_L}{\omega_m}$$

ie load torque × gear ratio.

The referred inertia J'_L is obtained by equating the stored kinetic energy, ie

$$\tfrac{1}{2} J_L \omega_L^2 = \tfrac{1}{2} J'_L \omega_m^2$$

hence

$$J'_L = J_L \left(\frac{\omega_L}{\omega_m}\right)^2$$

ie load inertia × gear ratio squared.

ELECTRIC MOTORS

Although it is outside the scope of this chapter to rigorously analyse the performance of all electrical machines, it is necessary to discuss briefly the operating characteristics and equations of the more commonly used electric motors.

DC Motor.—The dc motor consists of an armature with a conventional commutator winding rotating within a uni-directional electromagnetic field. The field can be connected

(*a*) separately from the armature—separate excitation
(*b*) in parallel with the armature—shunt excitation
(*c*) in series with the armature—series excitation.

The schematic representation of these methods of excitation is shown in Fig. 4.

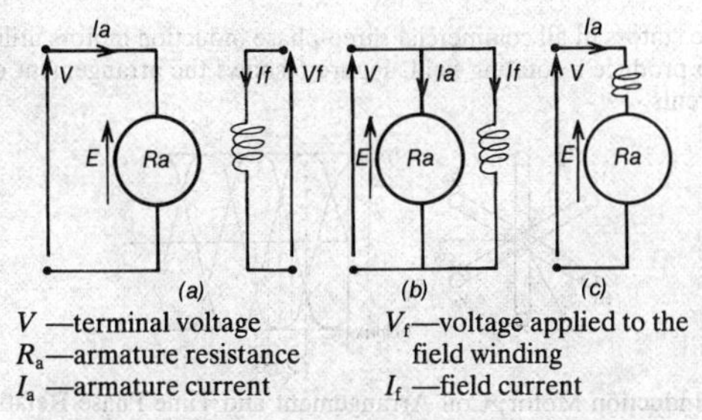

V —terminal voltage
R_a—armature resistance
I_a —armature current
V_f—voltage applied to the field winding
I_f —field current

FIG 4.—DC Motor Excitation.

The induced voltage E is proportional to the speed of rotation of the armature ω, and the amount of magnetic flux Φ produced by the field winding, ie

$$E = k\omega\Phi \tag{1}$$

For any given machine

$$k = 2pZ_s$$

where $2p$ is the number of magnetic poles on the field winding and Z_s is the number of armature conductors connected in series.

The terminal equation of the dc motor is

$$V = E + I_a R_a \tag{2}$$

multiplying through by I_a gives

$$VI_a = EI_a + I_a^2 R_a$$

where

VI_a —is the input power
$I_a^2 R$ —is the power loss in the armature resistance
EI_a —is the electrical power converted into mechanical power

Therefore, if T_m is the torque produced by the motor, then

$$EI_a = T_m \omega$$

or

$$T_m = \frac{EI_a}{\omega} = k\Phi I_a = 2pZ_s\Phi I_a \tag{3}$$

The relationship between the speed and the torque can be obtained from equations 1, 2 and 3, ie

$$\omega = \frac{E}{k\Phi} = \frac{V - I_aR_a}{k\Phi} = \frac{V}{k\Phi} - \frac{T_mR_a}{k^2\Phi^2} \tag{4}$$

Using equation (4) and assuming that for separate and shunt excitation Φ is constant, and that for series excitation $\Phi \propto I_a$, the speed-torque curves can be plotted, Fig. 5. These curves and the equations they were obtained from assume that there is no saturation of the iron circuit, ie that the flux varies linearly with the current producing it. This is not the case in practice, as the *armature reaction* effect reduces the nett flux as load is applied to the machine. However, the curves shown in Fig. 5 are only slightly modified.

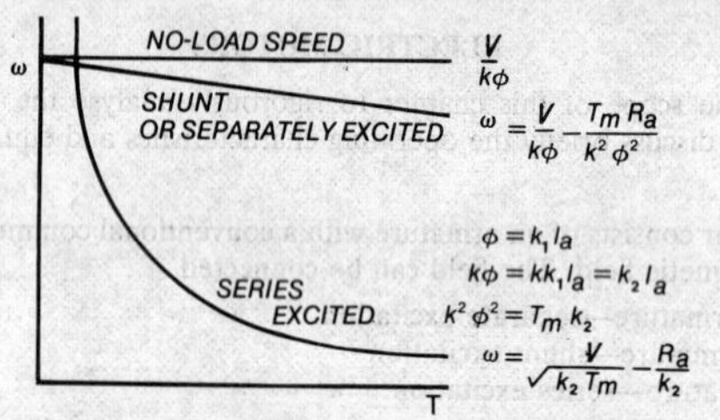

FIG. 5.—Speed-Torque Curves for DC Motor.

Induction Motors.—The stators of all commercial three-phase induction motors utilise a conventional three-phase winding in order to produce a rotating field. Figure 6 shows the arrangement of the coils and the time phase relation of the currents.

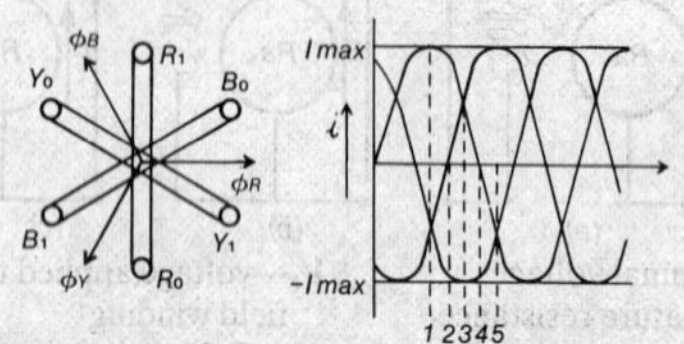

FIG. 6.—Induction Motor; Coil Arrangement and Time Phase Relationship.

Consider the position and magnitude of the resultant flux produced by the three coils at the instants in time shown, using the positive direction of the fluxes as shown below.

Instant in time	Magnitude of currents	Phasor diagram	Resultant flux $\phi_R + \phi_Y + \phi_B$
1	$i_R = I_{max}$ $i_y = i_B = -\frac{I_{max}}{2}$	ϕ_Y ϕ_R ϕ_B	$\frac{3}{2}\ \phi_{PHASE}$
2	$i_R = \frac{\sqrt{3}}{2} I_{max}$ $i_B = \frac{\sqrt{3}}{2} I_{max}$ $i_y = 0$	ϕ_R ϕ_B	$\frac{3}{2}\ \phi_{PHASE}$
3	$i_R = i_y = \frac{1}{2} I_{max}$ $i_B = -I_{max}$	ϕ_R ϕ_Y ϕ_B	$\frac{3}{2}\ \phi_{PHASE}$
4	$i_R = 0$ $i_y = \frac{\sqrt{3}}{2} I_{max}$ $i_B = \frac{\sqrt{3}}{2} I_{max}$	ϕ_Y ϕ_B	$\frac{3}{2}\ \phi_{PHASE}$

It can be seen that the magnitude of the resulting flux is 3/2 times the magnitude of the phase flux and it rotates at the frequency of the supply currents. If the coils were arranged to give a four-pole system as opposed to the two-pole one shown, then the speed of the rotating field would be halved (ie it would rotate through 180° for one cycle of the alternating current). In general, the speed of the field is,

$$N\,\text{r.p.m.} = \frac{\text{Supply Frequency} \times 60}{\text{Number of pole pairs}}$$

The speed of the rotating field is normally termed the *synchronous speed.*

There are two significant types of rotors used in induction motors, viz the *Squirrel Cage* and the *Slip Ring*. The rotor of the squirrel cage motor is very simple and robust and requires very little maintenance. The rotor core is constructed from laminated iron stampings with peripheral slots into which the rotor winding of copper or aluminium bars is cast. The rotor bars are then brazed on to end rings thus forming a completely short circuited set of conductors. The rotor of the slip ring motor consists of a three-phase rotor winding the ends of which are brought out to slip rings. Brushes are fitted so that the rotor winding may be connected to external circuitry.

The rotor of an induction motor receives power by induction as it is not normally connected to the supply. It can, therefore, be likened to a transformer and in fact at standstill with the rotor open circuit it behaves exactly like a three-phase transformer. However because of the air gap which exists between the stator and rotor winding, they are not as closely coupled magnetically as the primary and secondary of a transformer. The magnetising current of the induction motor is therefore larger than that in a transformer.

Slip.—Consider then an open circuited rotor coil at standstill. A voltage is induced in this coil by the rotating field produced by the stator winding, because there is a rate of change of flux linking the coil. If the coil is now short circuited this induced voltage will cause a current to flow and there will be a force produced ($F = BIl$) in the conductors of the coil which will cause the rotor to move in the direction of the field. The rotor speed will increase until the torque produced by the motor is equal to the load torque. The induction motor will never reach synchronous speed because at synchronous speed there would be no relative movement between the rotor and rotating field, therefore, no induced voltage and consequently no torque produced. The ratio of the difference in speed of the rotating field and the rotor to the speed of the rotating field is termed the *slip* (s), an important parameter in the analysis of induction motors.

$$s = \frac{N_s - N}{N_s}$$

where N_s is the speed of the rotating field or synchronous speed and N is the speed of the rotor.

Considering per phase quantities let E_1, be the induced voltage in the stator and E_2 be the induced voltage in the rotor at standstill. If f_1 is the frequency of the stator applied voltage, then when the rotor is rotating the frequency of the rotor voltage and current is sf_1 and the magnitude of the rotor induced voltage is reduced to sE_2. The magnitude of the rotor current is,

$$I_2 = \frac{sE_2}{\sqrt{R_2^2 + (sx_2)^2}} \qquad (5)$$

Where R_2 is the rotor resistance and x_2 is the rotor leakage reactance. Dividing equation (5) by s gives

$$I_2 = \frac{E_2}{\sqrt{\left(\frac{R_2}{s}\right)^2 + (x_2)^2}} = \frac{E_2}{\sqrt{\left[R_2 + R_2\left(\frac{1}{s} - 1\right)\right]^2 + x_2^2}} \qquad (6)$$

Using the transformer analogy the equivalent circuit of the induction motor, using the referred notation for rotor (secondary) quantities is shown in Fig. 7.

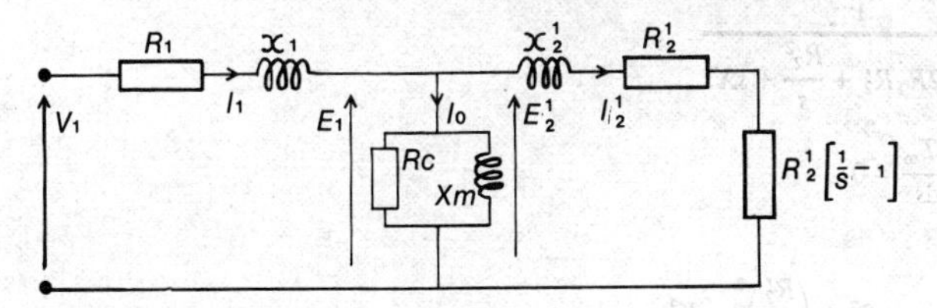

FIG. 7.—Equivalent Circuit of an Induction Motor.

where

R_1 = stator resistance/phase

R_2' = rotor resistance/phase referred to the stator

$$\left(R_2' = R_2\left[\frac{N_1}{N_2}\right]^2\right)$$

x_1 = stator leakage reactance/phase

x_2' = rotor leakage reactance/phase referred to the stator

$$\left(x_2' = x_2\left[\frac{N_1}{N_2}\right]^2\right)$$

R_c = resistance to represent the iron losses

X_m = magnetising reactance

I_1 = stator current

I_2' = rotor current referred to the stator

$$\left(I_2' = I_2\left[\frac{N_2}{N_1}\right]\right)$$

V_1 = voltage applied to the stator

TORQUE AND SLIP RELATIONSHIPS.—Consider the power distribution in the equivalent circuit of Fig. 7. The power input to the motor is $V_1 I_1 \cos\theta$ per phase. The stator and rotor copper losses are $I_1^2 R_1$ and $I_2'^2 R_2'$, and the iron losses are $I_c^2 R_c$.

The power dissipated in the other resistive term corresponds to the only other power sink, ie the mechanical load. The mechanical power output per phase is therefore

$$P_m = I_2'^2 R_2\left(\frac{1}{s} - 1\right)$$

The power supplied to the rotor, per phase, is

$$P_2 = I_2'^2 \frac{R_2}{s}$$

Thus:

$$P_m = P_2 - sP_2 = (1 - s)P_2$$

The torque for an '*m*' phase machine is given by:

$$T_m = \frac{mP_m}{2\pi N} = \frac{mP_2(1-s)}{2\pi N_s(1-s)} = \frac{mP_2}{2\pi N_s} = \frac{m}{2\pi N_s} I_2'^2 \frac{R_2'}{s}$$

$$T_m = \frac{m}{2\pi N_s}\frac{R_2'}{s}\frac{V_1^2}{\left(R_1 + \frac{R_2'}{s}\right)^2 + (x_1 + x_2')^2} \quad (7)$$

Maximum torque.—Assuming the stator applied voltage, the machine impedances and the frequency to be constant, and the slip '*s*' to be variable, also write X for $x_1 + x_2'$.

$$T_m = K\frac{1}{sR_1^2 + 2R_1R_2' + \frac{R_2'^2}{s} + sX^2}$$

$$\frac{dT_m}{ds} = 0$$

when

$$0 = -R_1^2 + \left(\frac{R_2'}{s}\right)^2 - X^2$$

from which

$$s = \pm \frac{R_2'}{\sqrt{R_1^2 + (x_1 + x_2')^2}} \text{ for maximum torque} \tag{8}$$

The negative sign is for supersynchronous speeds giving a negative (generating torque).

Substituting this value in the equation for torque, the maximum value for the torque 'T_{max}' is given by:

$$T_{max} = \frac{m}{2\pi N_s} \frac{V_1^2}{2(\pm\sqrt{R_1^2 + (x_1 + x_2')^2} + R_1)} \tag{9}$$

This expression is independent of R_2' which only determines the position at which the maximum torque occurs.

Starting torque.—At standstill $s = 1$, therefore the starting torque T_s is given by:

$$T_s = \frac{m}{2\pi N_s} V_1^2 \frac{R_2'}{(R_1 + R_2')^2 + (x_1 + x_2')^2} \tag{10}$$

If the machine is of the slip ring type, then the starting torque can be increased by adding external rotor resistance via the slip rings.

Torque-slip characteristic.—The approximate shape of the torque-slip curve of an induction motor can be obtained by considering the variation of torque when the slip approaches zero, and when the slip approaches unity. From the expression for torque, $s \to 0$.

$$T_m \simeq \frac{m}{2\pi N_s} \left(\frac{R_2'}{s}\right) \frac{V_1^2}{\frac{R_2'^2}{s^2}}$$

hence

T_m is proportional to s.

Also, when $s \to 1$

$$T_m \simeq \frac{m}{2\pi N_s} \left(\frac{R_2'}{s}\right) \frac{V_1^2}{(R_1 + R_2')^2 + (x_1 + x_2')^2}$$

hence

T_m is proportional to $\frac{1}{s}$.

The complete torque-slip curve is shown in Fig. 8.

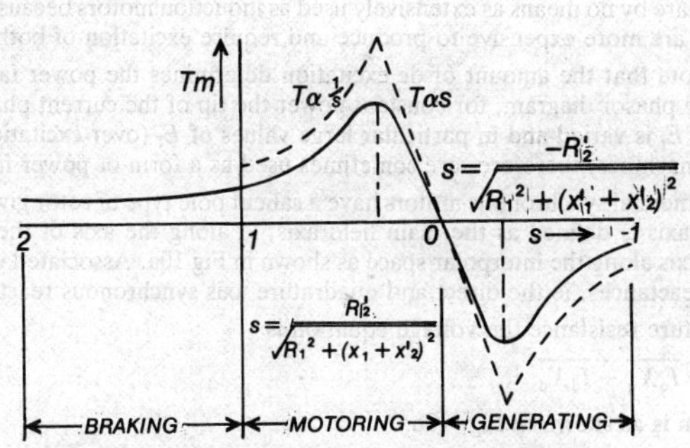

FIG. 8.—Torque-Slip Curve for Induction Motor.

The steady-state operating range is typically between $s = 0.01$ to $s = 0.05$, hence the induction motor is said to have a shunt characteristic, with small speed regulation from no-load to full-load.

Synchronous and Reluctance Motors.—A synchronous motor consists of a three-phase stator winding, similar to that of the induction motor, which produces a rotating magnetic field. The rotor is supplied with direct current and so produces a unidirectional magnetic field. Let the stator be initially disconnected from the mains supply and the dc energised rotor driven up to a speed approaching that of the rotating field. If the stator is now energised the two magnetic fields *lock* and the rotor runs in *synchronism* with the stator rotating field. At this stage it is assumed that the rotor is similar in construction to that of a slip ring induction motor and the dc current is fed to the winding via slip rings, ie a round rotor construction. For analytical purposes the synchronous motor is best represented by an induced voltage E_f at the back of an impedance Z_s which is termed the synchronous impedance, Fig. 9. The magnitude of the voltage E_f is dependent on the level of dc excitation in

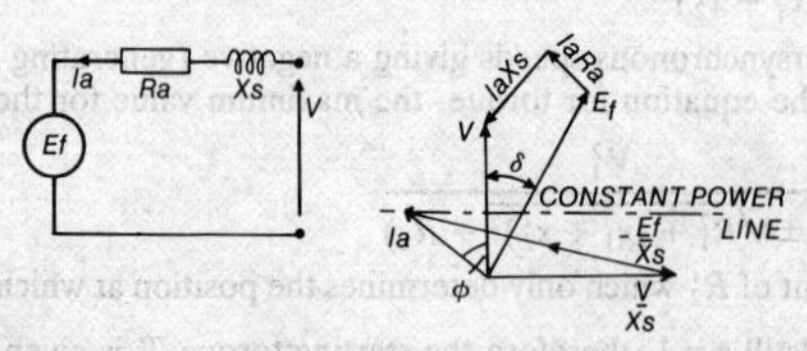

FIG. 9.—Phasor Diagram for Starting Synchronous Motor.

the rotor, and the synchronous impedance Z_s consists of the armature resistance R_a and the synchronous reactance X_s where $X_s \gg R_a$.

The defining voltage equation is,

$$\overline{V} = \overline{E_f} + \overline{I_a R_a} + \overline{I_a X_s} \tag{11}$$

If R_a is neglected and the equation is divided by X_s, then

$$\frac{\overline{V}}{X_s} - \frac{\overline{E_f}}{X_s} = \overline{I_a}$$

These equations are represented by phasor diagrams as shown in Fig. 9.

Neglecting R_a the input and output powers are equal and are given by:

$$P = VI_a \cos \phi$$

or substituting for $I_a \cos \phi$

$$P = V\frac{E_f}{X_s} \sin \delta$$

and the torque is

$$T_m = \frac{V}{\omega_s}\frac{E_f}{X_s} \sin \delta \tag{12}$$

where ω_s is the synchronous speed.

Synchronous motors are by no means as extensively used as induction motors because, although they provide a constant speed, they are more expensive to produce and require excitation of both stator and rotor.

It is interesting to note that the amount of dc excitation determines the power factor of operation of the motor. Considering the phasor diagram, for constant power the tip of the current phasor will move along the constant power line as E_f is varied and in particular large values of E_f (over excitation) will produce leading power factors. These machines, therefore, are sometimes used as a form of power factor correction.

The majority of commercial synchronous motors have a salient pole type of rotor giving two axes of magnetic symmetry. The direct axis is defined as the main field axis, ie along the axis of the salient pole, whilst the quadrature axis is the axis along the interpolar space as shown in Fig 10a. Associated with these two axes there are two synchronous reactances, ie the direct and quadrature axis synchronous reactances, X_d and X_q.

Neglecting the armature resistance the voltage equation is

$$\overline{V} = \overline{E_f} + \overline{I_q X_q} + \overline{I_d X_d}$$

and the phasor diagram is as shown in Fig. 10b.

The power is $VI_a \cos \phi$, thus

$$P = V[I_q \cos \delta + I_d \sin \delta]$$

$$= V\left[\frac{V \sin \delta}{X_q} \cos \delta + \frac{(E_f - V \cos \delta)}{X_d} \sin \delta\right]$$

$$= \frac{VE_f}{X_d} \sin \delta + V^2 \frac{(X_d - X_q)}{2X_d X_q} \sin 2\delta \tag{13}$$

The second term in the power equation is termed the *Reluctance Power*, and arises from the magnetic dissymmetry.

Reluctance motors are based on this effect and are built with a standard three-phase stator producing a rotating field, and a rotor which exhibits magnetic dissymmetry. No rotor excitation is required. (Note the absence of E_f in the reluctance power.) A squirrel cage winding is incorporated in the rotor so that it will run up to about 95% synchronous speed as an induction motor and then pull into synchronism and run as a reluctance motor at synchronous speed. The use of reluctance motors has increased over the last decade as their efficiencies have been improved by better designs which have increased the difference between X_d and X_q. The more usual applications involve machines with ratings of about 10 kW. It is uncommon for large reluctance motors to be used as the operating power factor is of the order of 0·5 lagging, as seen from the phasor diagram (Fig. 10c).

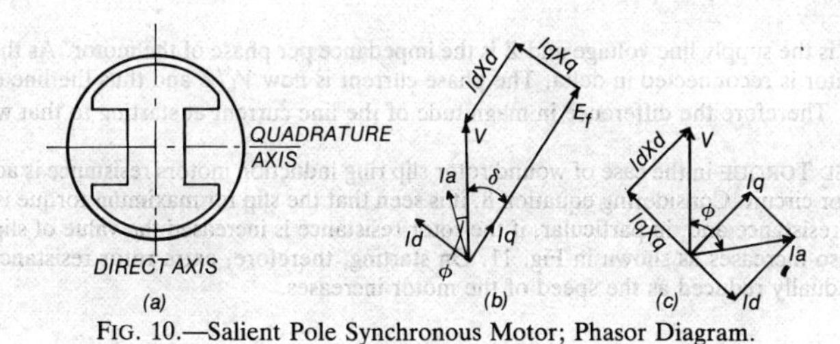

FIG. 10.—Salient Pole Synchronous Motor; Phasor Diagram.

CHOICE OF MOTOR

Before the final decision as to which type of motor is to be used for a particular application, it is essential that all the relevant factors are considered.

(*a*) The Torque-Speed Requirement (with special reference to the starting, braking, and stalling torque of the drive motor), provides the first basis on which motor selection is made. For fairly constant speed drives, that is a speed regulation of about 5–10% drop from no-load to full-load speed, the squirrel cage induction motor is invariably the first choice. For absolutely constant speeds synchronous or reluctance motors would be used and, if some measure of speed control is required, the choice will lie between induction and dc motors.

(*b*) The overall economy of the drive will depend on the initial cost, the maintenance cost (machines with commutators require regular maintenance), special starting or speed control gear, the efficiency and power factor of operation.

(*c*) The effect on the distribution system to which the motor is to be connected must also be considered. For instance, induction motors switched directly onto the mains will demand a large starting current and may cause a momentary voltage drop and light flicker to adjacent consumers.

(*d*) Environmental conditions in general determine the type of enclosure, eg open, drip proof or totally enclosed. Hazardous atmospheres prohibit motors with commutators and, in some cases, motor noise must be taken into consideration.

(*e*) The rating of the motor is determined from the load demand and the duty cycle. Continuous rating means that a given load torque can be delivered indefinitely without the temperature rising beyond the prescribed limits. For periodic or intermittent duty cycles the motor rating is determined from the rms value of the load torque.

STARTING.—On starting, the motor will take an excessive current. It may also be necessary that the motor is run up and stopped repeatedly over a short time interval (motors driving roller tables in steel mills have such a duty cycle) and it is essential to take these requirements into consideration when determining the size of a motor for a particular drive. With dc motors the commutation process may also cause a limitation in the magnitude of the starting current. Local Area Electricity Authorities have certain restrictions on the starting of motors, and often the equipment connected to the motor imposes its own constraints. For instance, discomfort to passengers in lifts and trains may well set the upper limits to the rate of acceleration.

METHODS OF STARTING

(i) FULL VOLTAGE STARTING, or direct on line starting, which, as the name suggests, in simply switching the supply directly on to the motor. This is the most arduous form of starting on both the motor and the supply and is limited to machines of less than about 20 kW.

(ii) REDUCED VOLTAGE STARTING, with dc motors a resistance is connected in series with the armature, so that the effective armature voltage is reduced. The resistance is cut out as the motor speed and induced emf increase, until at rated speed all the added resistance has been eliminated. This is normally done with the aid of a commercial *face plate* starter, which incorporates several other safety features.

With induction motors reduced voltage is achieved by (a) external stator resistance, (b) external stator reactance, (c) star-delta starter, or (d) an auto transformer. Many induction motors are now supplied via an energy saver which has a built-in soft start facility (see Section 'Open-loop speed control' p. G4/17).

The star-delta starter is by far the most common method of starting squirrel cage induction motors as it produces a three-to-one reduction in starting current.

At standstill the stator winding is connected in star and the line current taken from the supply is

$$I_L = \frac{V_L}{\sqrt{3}} \frac{1}{Z},$$

where V_L is the supply line voltage and Z is the impedance per phase of the motor. As the motor speeds up the stator is reconnected in delta. The phase current is now V_L/Z and thus the line current is $I_L = \sqrt{3}V_L/Z$. Therefore the difference in magnitude of the line current at starting to that when running is threefold.

(iii) INCREASED TORQUE in the case of wound rotor slip ring induction motors resistance is added externally to the rotor circuit. Considering equation 8, it is seen that the slip for maximum torque is dependent on the rotor resistance and, in particular, if the rotor resistance is increased the value of slip at which T_{max} occurs, also increases as shown in Fig. 11. On starting, therefore, extra rotor resistance is added and this is gradually reduced as the speed of the motor increases.

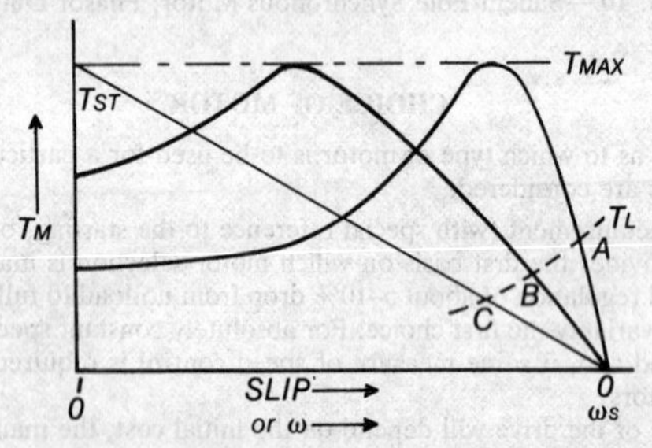

FIG. 11.—Wound Rotor Slip Ring Induction Motor; Rotor Resistance/Slip/Torque Characteristic.

(iv) THE GRADUAL VARIATION OF VOLTAGE AND FREQUENCY may be obtained when induction motors are fed from inverters, in which case the starting current and acceleration time can be set to any value.

ACCELERATION TIME.—The time required for a motor to run up to speed from standstill is determined from the equation of motion,

$$T_m = T_L + J\frac{d\omega}{dt} \tag{14}$$

where T_m and T_L may both be functions of the speed ω.

If T_m and T_L can be defined by algebraic equations the resulting differential equation may be solved analytically.

Two simple examples which might occur in practice are:

(*a*) The acceleration of a load which exhibits a constant load torque by a motor which develops a constant torque during starting. This type of motor characteristic is possible with a double cage induction motor. As the name suggests, a double cage induction motor has two squirrel cages housed in deep rotor slots. The cage nearest the periphery has a high resistance producing a large starting torque, whereas the inner cage has a high leakage reactance at mains frequency, so contributing little at starting but making a significant contribution at small slips when the reactance is reduced (Fig. 12).

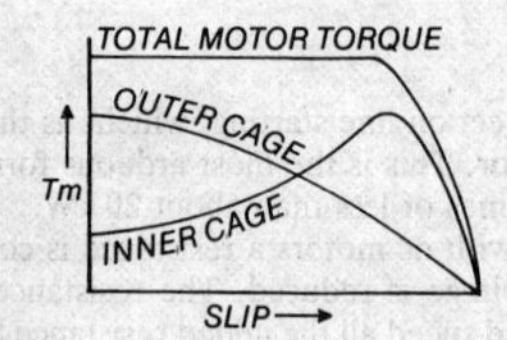

FIG. 12.—Double Cage Induction Motor; Torque/Slip Characteristics.

From Equation (14) if $(T_m - T_L)$ is constant, then $\dfrac{d\omega}{dt}$ is constant and the speed will increase linearly with time.

(*b*) The acceleration of a constant torque load by a motor which develops a linear torque-slip curve. This type of torque-slip curve could be obtained from a slip ring motor with added rotor resistance (Fig. 11).
At $\omega = 0$, slip $= 1$, T_m corresponds to the starting torque T_{ST}
At $\omega = \omega_{SYNC}$, $s = 0$, T_m equals zero.

Therefore $\dfrac{T_{ST}}{1} = \dfrac{T_m}{s}$

From equation (14)

$$sT_{ST} = T_L = J\frac{d\omega}{dt}$$

$$s = 1 - \frac{\omega}{\omega_s}, \text{ therefore}$$

$$\frac{d\omega}{dt} = \frac{T_{ST} - T_L}{J} - \frac{\omega}{\omega_s}\frac{T_{ST}}{J}$$

If $\dfrac{J\omega_s}{T_{ST}}$ be termed the starting time constant t_{ST}, then

$$\frac{d\omega}{dt} + \frac{\omega}{t_{st}} = \frac{T_{ST} - T_L}{J}$$

which is a standard first order differential equation, the solution of which is:

$$\omega = \omega_s\left(1 - \frac{T_L}{T_{ST}}\right)(1 - e^{-t/t_{st}})$$

and the response of ω is the standard first order response.

However, if, as is often the case, T_m may not be represented by an algebraic equation, the run up curve must be obtained graphically, as shown in Fig. 13.

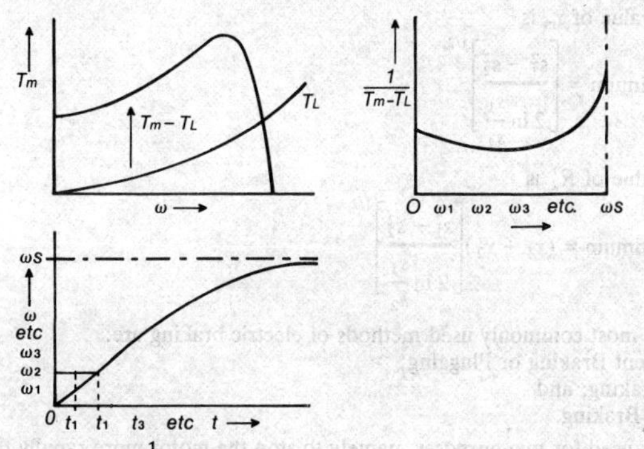

Given T_m and T_L versus ω plot $\dfrac{1}{T_m - T_L}$ versus ω, up to 95% ω_s and calcualte t for the various increments $0 - \omega_1$, $\omega_1 - \omega_2$, etc; hence plot ω versus t up to 95% of synchronous speed.

FIG. 13.—Graphical Construction of Run-up Curve.

From equation (14) the time required to change speed from ω_1 to ω_2 is

$$t = J\int_{\omega_1}^{\omega_2} \frac{d\omega}{T_m - T_L} \qquad (15)$$

Optimum rotor resistance for minimum starting or braking time.—It can be seen from Equation (8) and Fig. 11 that the rotor resistance influences the shape of the torque-slip curve and, in particular, changes the point at which the slip for maximum torque occurs. It follows, therefore, that there will be one value of rotor resistance which produces the fastest acceleration or deceleration times.

Neglecting the stator resistance, which is small compared to the combined reactance $x_1 + x_2'$, Equations (7), (8) and (9) become

$$T_m = \frac{m}{\omega_s}\frac{R_2'}{s}\frac{V_1^2}{\left(\frac{R_2'}{s}\right)^2 + (x_1 + x_2')^2} \tag{16}$$

$$s_m = \pm\frac{R_2'}{(x_1 + x_2')} \tag{17}$$

$$T_{max} = \pm\frac{m}{\omega_s}\frac{V_1^2}{2(x_1 + x_2')} \tag{18}$$

On no load the dynamic equation becomes:

$$T_m = J\frac{d\omega}{dt} = J\frac{d\omega_s(1-s)}{dt} = -J\omega_s\frac{ds}{dt} \tag{19}$$

From equations 16 and 19

$$t = -\frac{J\omega_s^2}{mV_1^2}\left\{\int_{s_1}^{s_2}\frac{R_2'}{s}\,ds + \int_{s_1}^{s_2}\frac{s(x_1 + x_2')^2}{R_2'}\,ds\right\}$$

and hence

$$t = \frac{J\omega_s^2}{mV_1^2}(x_1 + x_2')\left[s_m \ln\frac{s_1}{s_2} + \frac{(s_1^2 - s_2^2)}{2s_m}\right]$$

$$t = \frac{J\omega_s}{2T_{max}}\left[s_m \ln\frac{s_1}{s_2} + \frac{(s_1^2 - s_2^2)}{2s_m}\right] \tag{20}$$

Now differentiate equation (20) with respect to s_m and equate to zero to find the minimum value of t, ie

$$\frac{J\omega_s}{2T_{max}}\left[\ln\frac{s_1}{s_2} - \frac{(s_1^2 - s_2^2)}{2s_m^2}\right] = 0$$

Thus the optimum value of s_m is

$$s_m \text{ optimum} = \left[\frac{s_1^2 - s_2^2}{2\ln\frac{s_1}{s_2}}\right]^{1/2}$$

and the optimum value of R_2' is

$$R_2' \text{ optimum} = (x_1 + x_2')\left[\frac{s_1^2 - s_2^2}{2\ln\frac{s_1}{s_2}}\right]^{1/2} \tag{21}$$

BRAKING.—The most commonly used methods of electric braking are:

(i) Reverse Current Braking or Plugging;

(ii) Rheostatic Braking; and

(iii) Regenerative Braking.

Electric braking is used for two purposes, namely to stop the motor more rapidly than by simply switching off the supply (second and fourth quadrant operation), and to control the speed of a load which is overhauling the motor (fourth quadrant operation).

Reverse current braking involves reconnecting the supply to the motor so that it tends to drive in the reverse direction.

Rheostatic braking implies operating the motor as a generator which is generating into a resistance load. Regenerative braking also involves operating the motor as a generator, but in this case whilst it is still connected to the supply. The mechanical energy of the load (usually inertial) is converted into electrical energy, part of which is fed back into the supply and part is dissipated as heat in the windings. Most electrical machines move smoothly from motoring to generating when overdriven by the load.

Reverse Current Braking of dc Motors.—In order to reverse the torque developed it is necessary to reverse either the field or the armature connections. The field winding has a much greater time constant than the armature, so it is usual to reverse the armature. It is also necessary to include extra external armature resistance to reduce the braking current. Figure 14 shows the torque speed curves of a dc shunt and a dc series motor for normal motoring and reverse current braking.

Consider the shunt motor driving a load torque T_L at some speed ω_1, point A on Fig. 14. If the armature voltage is reversed and resistance is added to the armature circuit the motor will operate on the plugging characteristic at point B in Fig. 14. The motor speed will then change from ω_1 at point B to standstill at point C.

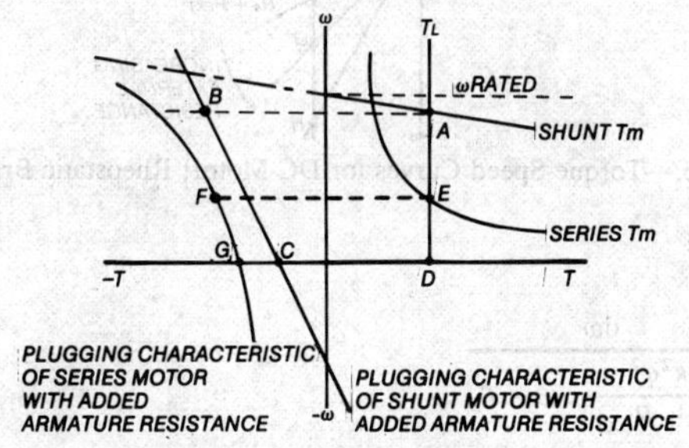

FIG. 14.—Torque-Speed Curves for DC Shunt and DC Series Motors for Normal Running and Reverse Current Braking.

The dynamic equation is

$$T_m = T_L + J\frac{d\omega}{dt}$$

but in this case both the load torque T_L and the braking torque T_m oppose the motion and decleration occurs; therefore the dynamic equation becomes

$$T_m + T_L = -J\frac{d\omega}{dt}$$

and

$$t = -J\int_{\omega_1}^{0}\frac{d\omega}{T_m + T_L} = J\int_{0}^{\omega_1}\frac{d\omega}{T_m + T_L}$$

To evaluate t, plot $1/(T_m + T_L)$ versus ω and multiply the area under the curve by J, the inertia of the motor load combination.

For a series motor driving a load torque T_L at point E, on reversing the armature voltage and increasing the armature circuit resistance, the operating point moves to point F and the motor runs down to standstill at G. The braking time is obtained as before.

Rheostatic Braking of dc Motors.—To brake rheostatically a dc motor, the armature is disconnected from its supply and connected across a resistance, whilst the field winding remains connected. For a shunt (or separately excited motor) under these conditions equations (2) and (4) become

$$E = -I_a(R_a + R_{EXTERNAL})$$

and

$$\omega = -\frac{T_m(R_a + R_{EXTERNAL})}{k^2\varphi^2}$$

If the flux is assumed to be constant the torque-speed curves for rheostatic braking are as shown in Fig. 15.

If the motor is driving a load torque T_L at point A in Fig. 15 and rheostatic braking is applied the operating point moves to either B, C or D, depending on the value of the external resistance. Assuming the characteristics are linear the dynamic equation for this condition is as before:

$$T_m + T_L = -J\frac{d\omega}{dt}$$

where

$$T_m = -\frac{k^2\varphi^2}{(R_A + R_{EXT})}\omega$$

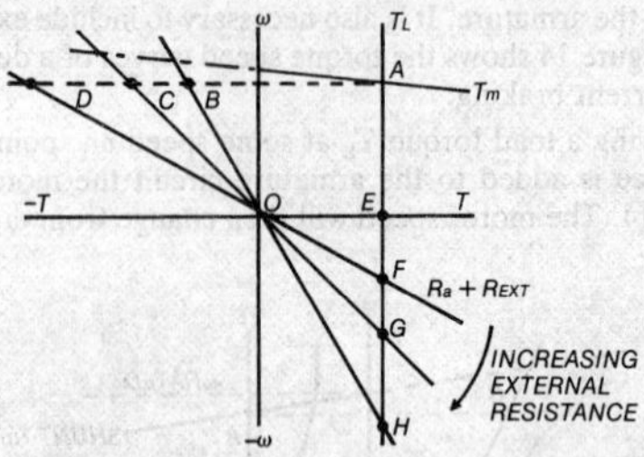

FIG. 15.—Torque-Speed Curves for DC Motor; Rheostatic Braking.

If T_m is negative then

$$t = -J \int_{\omega_1}^{0} \frac{d\omega}{\dfrac{k^2\varphi^2}{(R_a + R_{EXT})} \cdot \omega + T_L}$$

and

$$t = J \ln \frac{k^2\varphi^2\omega_1 + T_L(R_a + R_{EXT})}{T_L(R_L + R_{EXT})}$$

If the motor is being used to lower a hoist exhibiting a constant load torque T_L, rheostatic braking can be used to produce a constant lowering speed which will depend on the amount of external resistance added to the armature circuit, points F, G and H.

Rheostatic braking is possible with series motors, but care should be taken that the external resistance does not exceed the critical field resistance value when the machine would fail to excite and operate as a generator.

Regenerative Braking.—This is possible with shunt or separately excited motors when the load drives the motor above its rated speed. In this case the induced voltage E exceeds the applied voltage V, the current reverses and power is fed back into the supply. Steady-state is achieved when the braking (or generating) torque is just equal to the load torque.

It is not possible to produce regenerative braking with a series motor, because as the speed increases the torque and current reduces, and hence the flux and induced voltage is reduced. The induced voltage can never exceed the applied voltage, therefore the condition of regenerative braking cannot be achieved.

Reverse Current Braking of Induction Motors.—Plugging of induction motors is produced by reversing the direction of the rotating field which is obtained by switching any two connections to the stator. The slip for this condition is

$$s = \frac{-\omega_s - \omega}{-\omega_s} \quad [-\omega_s \text{ indicates reversal of the rotating field}]$$

For a pre-plugging slip of 0·05 the slip immediately after reversal of the rotating field is 1·95. In some applications, with slip ring motors, extra resistance is included to reduce the plugging current.

Plugging is the fastest method of stopping an induction motor, but it also demands the largest currents from the supply, and any motor that is to be continually started and plugged must be specially designed.

Rheostatic Braking of Induction Motors.—This is often called dc dynamic braking, and is obtained by disconnecting the stator from the ac mains and reconnecting it across a dc supply. The rotating field is now replaced by a unidirectional static field, and thus the machine behaves as an alternator on short circuit, the load inertia being the prime mover. The frequency of the rotor currents when motoring is sf_1 and when braking $(1-s)f_1$, thus the braking torque for an m phase motor can be obtained by replacing s by $(1-s)$ in equation (7) and using the negative sign to indicate a generating torque,

$$T_m = -\frac{m}{\omega_s}\frac{R_2'}{(1-s)} \frac{V_1^2}{\left(R_1 + \dfrac{R_2'}{(1-s)}\right)^2 + (x_1 + x_2')^2}$$

Regenerative Braking of Induction Motors.—Regenerative braking of induction motors is obtained when the rotor speed becomes greater than the synchronous speed, which will occur when (a) the supply frequency is reduced, a condition that can apply with inverter fed machines; (b) the pole number is increased, on machines with a pole changing capability; and (c) the load overhauls the motor.

ENERGY LOST IN STARTING AND BRAKING.—For a dc shunt or separately excited motor starting on no-load the dynamic equation is,

$$T_m = J\frac{d\omega}{dt}$$

If the field current is constant so that the flux φ can be condsidered constant then from equation (3), $T_m = kI_a$, and from equation (2)

$$I_a R_a = V - k\omega$$

therefore

$$I_a^2 R_a = J\frac{V}{k}\cdot\frac{d\omega}{dt} - J\omega\frac{d\omega}{dt}$$

On no load the rated speed ω_o is nearly equal to V/k therefore

$$I_a^2 R_a\, dt = J\omega_o\, d\omega - J\omega\, d\omega$$

Hence the energy lost on starting is

$$W = \int_0^t I_a^2 R_a\, dt = J\omega_o\int_0^{\omega_o} d\omega - J\int_0^{\omega_o}\omega\, d\omega = \tfrac{1}{2}J\omega_o^2$$

The energy dissipated in the armature during rheostatic braking is obtained in the same way, except that in this case the applied voltage V is zero, thus

$$W = \int_0^t I_a^2 R_a\, dt = -J\int_{\omega_0}^{0}\omega\frac{d\omega}{dt} = \tfrac{1}{2}J\omega_o^2$$

During reverse current braking the sign of the applied voltage is changed and therefore in this case,

$$W = \int_0^t I_a^2 R_a\, dt = -J\omega_o\int_{\omega_0}^{0} d\omega - J\int_{\omega_0}^{0}\omega\, d\omega = \tfrac{3}{2}J\omega_o^2$$

For the induction motor, if the magnetising current is neglected, the energy dissipated during starting is

$$W = \int_0^t I_2'^2 (R_1 + R_2)\, dt$$

on no-load the dynamic equation is

$$T_m = J\frac{d\omega}{dt} = -J\omega_s\frac{ds}{dt}$$

The torque is given by

$$T_m = \frac{m}{\omega_s} I_2'^2 \frac{R_2'}{s}$$

and therefore

$$I_2'^2 = -\frac{J\omega_s^2}{mR_2'} s\frac{ds}{dt}$$

and the energy lost during run up to a slip which approaches zero is

$$W = m\int_0^t I_2'^2 (R_1 + R_2)\, dt = -J\omega_s^2\int_1^0 \frac{R_1}{R_2'} s\, ds - J\omega_s^2\int_1^0 s\, ds$$

$$W = \tfrac{1}{2}J\omega_s^2\left(1 + \frac{R_1}{R_2'}\right)$$

During reverse current braking the slip changes from nearly 2 to 1, therefore the energy lost is given by,

$$W = -J\omega_s^2\int_2^1 \frac{R_1}{R_2'} s\, ds - J\omega_s^2\int_2^1 s\, ds = \tfrac{3}{2}J\omega_s^2\left(1 + \frac{R_1}{R_2'}\right)$$

EXAMPLE 1

A 30 kW, 200 V dc shunt motor driving a constant torque load at a speed of 500 rpm is to be braked by plugging. Calculate the value of resistance to be added to the armature circuit to limit the braking current to 250 A. Calculate the initial and final values of braking torque and the time it takes the motor to stop if the moment of inertia of the motor and load is 5 kg m^2.

The armature resistance of the motor is 0·1 Ω, and the full load current is 175 A, at the full load speed of 500 rpm.

The induced voltage at 500 rpm is $E = 220 - 175 \times 0{\cdot}1 = 202{\cdot}5$ V. The total voltage on commencement of reverse current braking is 220 + 202·5 = 422·5 V.

The resistance required to limit the current to 250 A is 422·5/250 = 1·69 Ω, therefore the external resistance requried is 1·59 Ω.

The torque is proportional to the current if the flux is assumed constant, therefore the initial braking torque is

$$T_{BI} = T_{FL} \times \frac{250}{175}$$

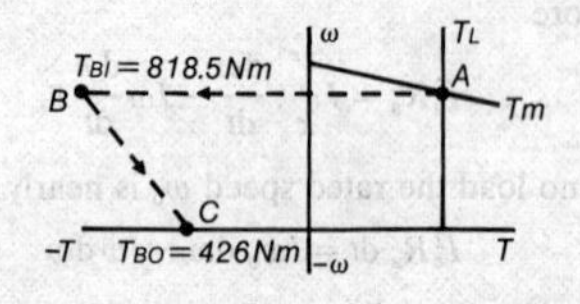

The full load torque

$$T_{FL} = \frac{\text{Power}}{\omega} = \frac{30{,}000}{500\,\dfrac{2\pi}{60}} = 572{\cdot}95 \text{ Nm}$$

Therefore $T_{BI} = 818{\cdot}5$ Nm.

When motoring at full load the operating point is A where $T_m = T_L = 572{\cdot}95$ Nm.

Immediately the armature voltage is reversed the operating point moves to B. The motor-load now decelerates to zero speed at point C.

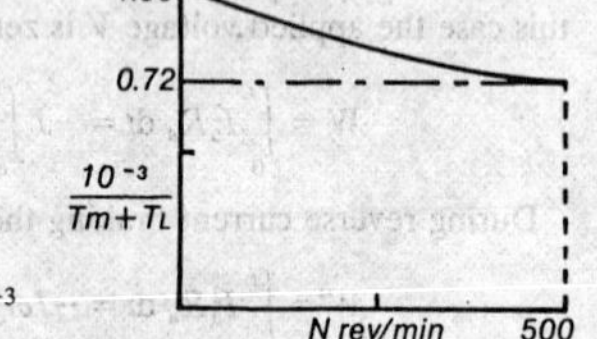

Area under the curve of $1/(T_m + T_L)$ versus ω is approximately:

$$500 \times \frac{2\pi}{60} \times 0{\cdot}72 \times 10^{-3} + \frac{1}{2} \times 500 \times \frac{2\pi}{60} \times 0{\cdot}28 \times 10^{-3} = 45 \times 10^{-3}$$

At zero speed the induced voltage is zero, therefore the voltage for braking is 220 V, and the current is 220/1·69 = 130·18 A, thus the braking torque at zero speed is

$$T_{BO} = 572{\cdot}95 \frac{130{\cdot}18}{175} = 426 \text{ Nm}$$

The dynamic equation during braking is

$$T_m + T_L = J\frac{d\omega}{dt}$$

The time taken to come to rest is

$$t = J\int_0^{52{\cdot}4} \frac{1}{T_m + T_L}\, d\omega$$

Therefore the time taken to brake to standstill is

$$t = 5 \times 45 \times 10^{-3} = 0{\cdot}225 \text{ secs}$$

EXAMPLE 2.

A 415 V, 3 phase, 4 pole, 60 kW squirrel cage induction motor has a full load rated speed of 1440 rpm. The total motor plus load inertia is 0·3 kg m². Assuming $R_1 = R_2'$, determine the number of direct on line starts and plug stops that the motor can make per minute without overheating.

$$\text{Full load slip} = \frac{15000 - 1440}{1500} = 0{\cdot}04$$

$$\text{Output power} = I_2'^2 R_2' \left(\frac{1}{s} - 1\right) = 24 I_2'^2 R_2' = 20 \text{ kW}$$

Therefore $I_2'^2 R_2' = 833$ W

Total loss $= I_2'^2 (R_1 + R_2') = 1666$ W

Permissible Energy dissipated per minute = 1666.60
= 99960 joules

Energy lost in starting $= \frac{1}{2} J\omega_s^2 \left(1 + \frac{R_1}{R_2'}\right)$

Energy lost in plugging $= \frac{3}{2} J\omega_s^2 \left(1 + \frac{R_1}{R_2'}\right)$

The energy lost in starting and plugging is

$$\tfrac{4}{2} J\omega_s^2 \left(1 + \frac{R_1}{R_2'}\right) = 2 \times 0{\cdot}3 \times \left(\frac{1500 \times 2\pi}{60}\right)^2 \times 2 = 29608{\cdot}8$$

Therefore the total number of starts and stops is

$$\frac{99960}{29608{\cdot}8} = 3{\cdot}37$$

Say 3 per minute.

OPEN LOOP SPEED CONTROL.—Open loop speed control falls broadly into two categories.

(i) Marginal Speed Control, where the speed can be changed by up to about 20% of rated speed; and

(ii) Overall Speed Control, where the speed can be varied from positive rated speed through zero to negative rated speed, ie a speed change of 200%.

Obviously the extra equipment required to produce overall speed control is far more expensive than that required for marginal speed control, so it is essential to establish the mechanical requirements of the drive at the outset.

Marginal speed control of dc motors is easily and cheaply obtained by incorporating rheostats or potential dividers in the field circuits, (Fig. 16). Normally the extra power loss in these resistors is small and the efficiency of the system is not impaired.

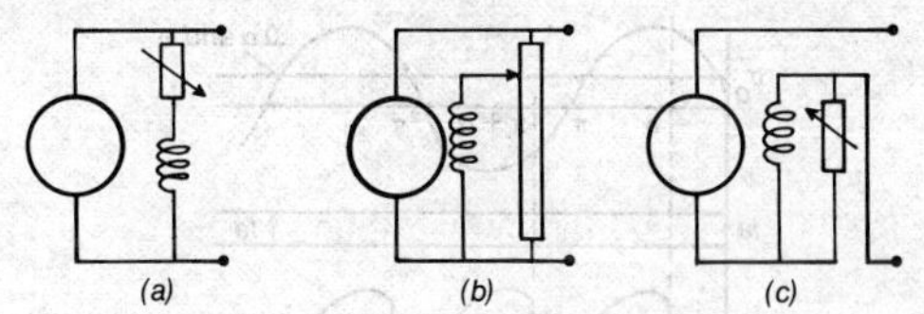

FIG. 16.—Speed Control of DC Motor by 'Field Weakening'.

The three circuits shown (Fig. 16) produce *field weakening*, because no matter what position the series rheostat in (a), the potential divider in (b) or the diverter resistence in (c) is set, the field current can only be reduced from its rated value. This means that the working flux is reduced and as the speed is inversely proportional to the flux the speed can only be increased by this technique. Unfortunately as the flux is reduced so too is the torque ($T_m \alpha I_a \varphi$) and it is this torque reduction that limits the speed control by field weakening to about 20% above rated speed.

Overall speed control of dc motors is obtained by varying the voltage applied to the armature ($\omega \alpha E/\varphi$). In the past this variable dc voltage was obtained by using the Ward Leonard Drive, which consisted of an induction motor driving a separately excited dc generator whose output voltage could be varied from $+V_{max}$ to $-V_{max}$ by variation of its field current. The output from this generator was then used to supply the armature of the main drive motor. Although the Ward Leonard Drive produced excellent speed control, with inherent regenerative braking, its capital cost was high. With the advent of fairly cheap, high powered, semiconductor devices, static converters and *chopper* circuits are now being widely used to produce the variable dc voltage required for the overall speed control of dc motors.

There are three types of semiconductor controlled rectifiers currently in use. These are:

(a) the Thyristor

(b) the Gate Turn Off Thyristor (GTO); and

(c) the Field Effect Transistor or Power FET.

In most of the power electronic circuits the device is used as an ON/OFF switch and the power dissipated within the device is small. The important factors are the rated maximum voltage in the OFF position, and the rated maximum current in the ON position. The thyristor is a three terminal device (ie anode, cathode and gate) and can be switched on by a pulse or preferably a train of pulses on the gate, which make the gate positive with respect to the cathode. The thyristor goes off when the cathode is negative with respect to the anode. The GTO thyristor is also a three terminal device which can be switched off as well as on by appropriate pulses on the gate. The FET, again a three terminal device, is controlled like a normal transistor by a continuous signal on the base. The GTO and FET require no auxiliary commutating circuits and may well surplant the use of thyristors in power electronic circuits of the future, but whatever the device the basic circuitry is unlikely to change radically.

For motors up to about 20 kW a single-phase, full wave thyristor bridge converter would be used, as shown in Fig. 17. Small letters are used to indicate instantaneous values, whilst capitals represent average values.

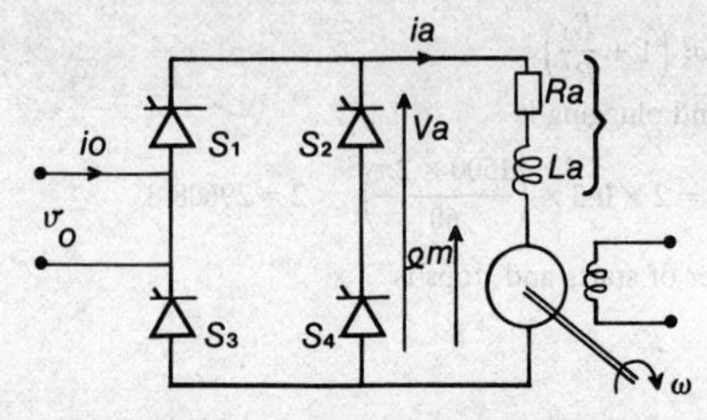

FIG. 17.—Full Wave Thyristor Bridge for Speed Control of DC Motor.

In considering the operation of the bridge it is generally assumed that the armature inductance is large enough to produce a ripple free armature current. Let the thyristors s_1 and s_4 be switched on at some angle α (firing angle or delay angle) so the current is conducted from the ac supply via s_1, the motor armature and s_4. At $\pi + \alpha$ thyristors s_2 and s_3 are switched on and the supply voltage appears across s_1 and s_4 as a reverse bias voltage and turns them off. This is called *natural* or *line* commutation. The current is now conducted through the motor armature via thyristors s_2 and s_3.

From Fig. 18 it is seen that during the period α to π the supply voltage v_0 and current i_0 are positive and the

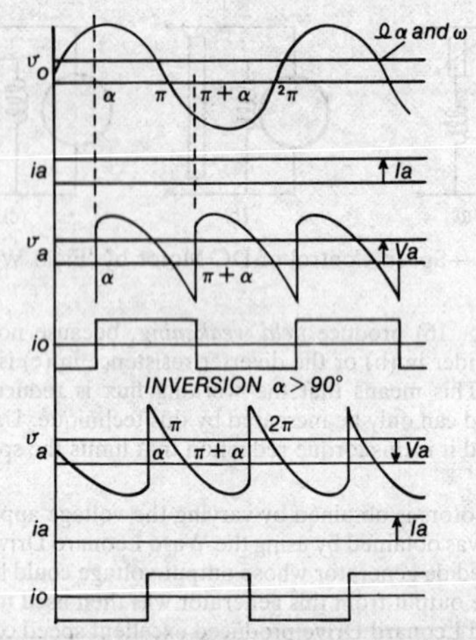

FIG. 18.—Thyristor Speed Control of DC Motor; Indicating Positive and Negative Power Flow.

armature voltage v_a and current i_a are positive, signifying positive power flow. However, from π to $\pi + \alpha$ some of the motor energy is fed back into the supply, v_0 and i_0 have opposite polarities and so too do v_a and i_a, signifying reverse power flow. For delay angles up to 90° the power flow, averaged over one cycle, is positive, indicating motoring operation. However, for firing angles greater than 90° the average motor terminal voltage V_a is negative. If the motor induced voltage is reversed, by reversing the armature connections, it will behave as a generator as shown in Fig. 19, and power will be fed back into the ac supply. This condition is known as

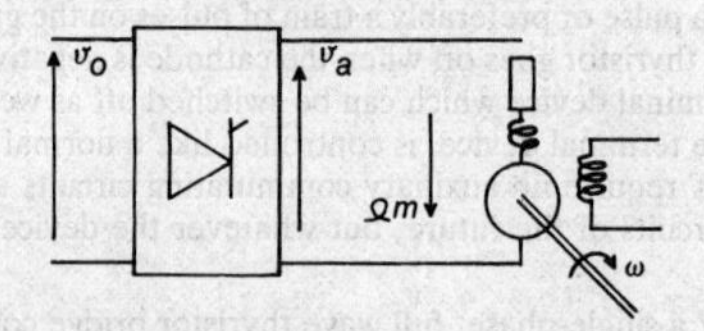

FIG. 19.—Inversion Condition of Thyristor Controlled DC Motor.

inversion and is used in regenerative braking. It is interesting to note that the current from the bridge has not reversed, and, in fact, cannot reverse, as current is unidirectional through the thyristors.

The theoretical average dc voltage V_a for the circuit shown in Fig. 17 is given by:

$$V_a = \frac{1}{\pi}\int_{\alpha}^{\pi+\alpha} \sqrt{2}V_0 \sin \omega t \, d(\omega t) = \frac{2\sqrt{2}}{\pi} V_0 \cos \alpha$$

With the circuit of Fig. 17 the motor can operate in the first and second quadrants, ie

1st Quad.	Motoring	$E_m I_a$ positive	$V_a I_a$ positive	converter is rectifying
2nd Quad.	Generating	$E_m I_a$ negative	$V_a I_a$ negative	converter is inverting
2nd Quad.	Plugging	$E_m I_a$ negative	$V_a I_a$ positive	converter is rectifying

In each case the direction of rotation is the same.

To change the direction of rotation and produce four quadrant operation a dual converter must be used, as shown (Fig. 20).

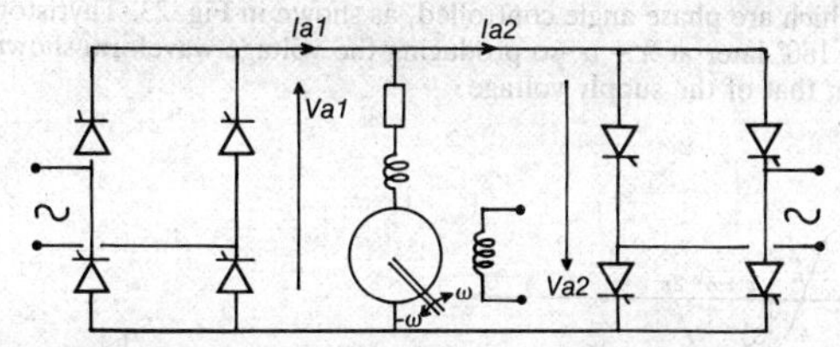

FIG. 20.—Use of dual Converter to produce Four Quadrant Operation with DC Motor.

For motors above 20 kW, three-phase bridge converters would be used, which are obtained by simply adding another pair of thyristors.

For electric transport applications the simple *chopper* circuit is now universally adopted. The dc power, usually from a battery, is switched ON and OFF through a controlled rectifier at an operating frequency of about 100 Hz. The mark-space ratio (ON to OFF time) can be changed by the firing circuit, and hence the average dc armature voltage V_a can be varied. Figure 21 shows the basic circuit, the firing and commutation

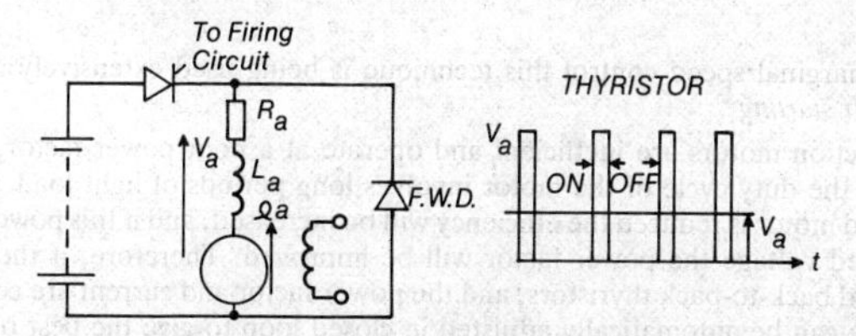

FIG. 21.—Basic 'Chopper' Circuit.

circuitry which are outside the scope of this test, have been omitted. The free wheeling diode, (FWD), is used to provide a path for the current as the inductance discharges its stored energy during the OFF period. There is no detectable speed change due to the current and torque fluctuations as the electrical transients are much faster than the mechanical ones.

Starting dc motors supplied from converter or chopper circuits is achieved by suitably adjusting the firing angle so as to provide a gradually increasing armature voltage as the machine speed increases. This can be done manually or automatically, depending on the application.

Marginal speed control of induction motors is obtained by (a) varying the slip at which the maximum torque occurs; or (b) varying the magnitude of the maximum torque.

It can be seen in Fig. 11 that if the rotor resistance is increased then, for a load torque T_L, the operating point changes from A to B to C. Speed variations of about 10% can be obtained by this method, but unfortunately there is considerable I^2R loss in the external resistance and the efficiency of the drive will be reduced. The addition of external rotor resistance is only possible with slip ring motors.

Equation (7) shows that the torque developed by an induction motor is proportional to the square of the stator applied voltage V_1, so that if the applied voltage is reduced so too is the torque. Figure 22 shows how the operating point is changed from A to B to C as the voltage is reduced.

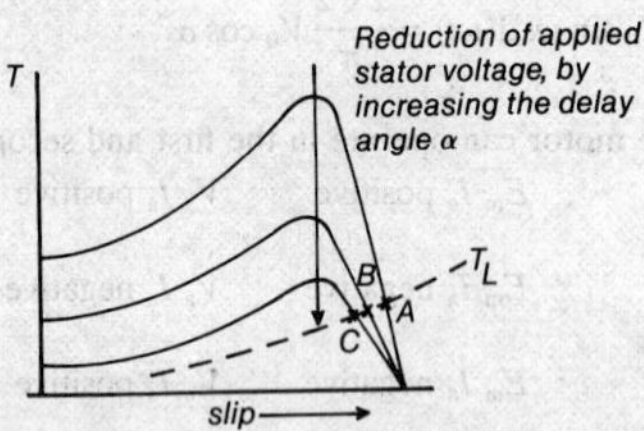

FIG. 22.—Change in Operating Point on Torque-Slip Plot with Change in Stator Applied Voltage.

To vary the applied stator voltage the induction motor is supplied via inverse parallel (back-to-back) connected thyristors, which are phase angle controlled, as shown in Fig. 23. Thyristor s_1 is fired at an angle α and thyristor s_2 is fired 180° later at $\pi + \alpha$, so producing the voltage waveform shown. The rms value of this wave is clearly less than that of the supply voltage.

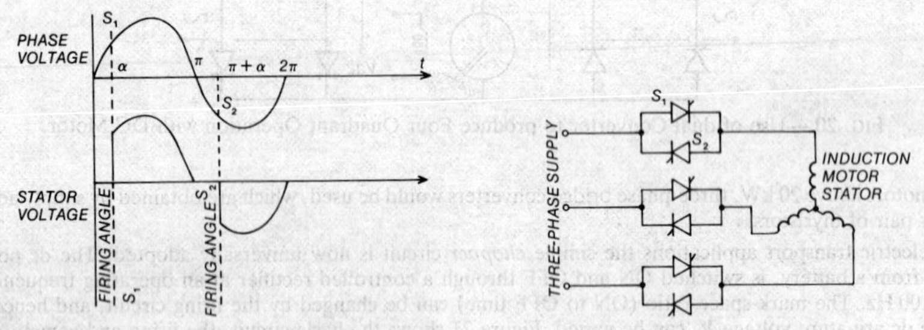

FIG. 23.—Control of Stator Voltage using Inverse Parallel Connected Thyristors.

Besides providing marginal speed control this technique is being used extensively as a method of energy saving and also for *soft starting*.

Lightly loaded induction motors are inefficient and operate at a poor power factor, and it is economic to compensate for this if the duty cycle of the motor involves long periods of light load. If the electrical power input to a lightly loaded motor is reduced the efficiency will be increased, and if this power reduction is achieved by reducing the applied voltage the power factor will be improved. Therefore, if the motor is supplied via phase angled controlled back-to-back thyristors, and the power factor and current are continuously monitored, then the stator voltage can be automatically adjusted in closed loop to give the best operating conditions.

Soft starting, which simply means starting at a reduced current, can be obtained by suitable adjustment of the firing angle. This can be done manually or automatically, depending on the application.

It was shown (p. G4/5) that the synchronous speed of an induction motor is given by:

$$N_s = \frac{\text{Supply Frequency} \times 60}{\text{Number of Pole Pairs}}$$

Therefore, Overall Speed Control can be obtained by varying (a) the supply frequency, or (b) the number of pole pairs.

In the past frequency converting machines were used to provide the variable frequency supply to the induction motor, but more recently semiconductor *inverters* have been widely introduced. The most common form of inverter is the dc link inverter (Fig. 24).

The thyristors of the inverter are switched in such a way as to route the current through the stator winding in the same sequence as would be experienced if it were connected to the three-phase mains. If the filter is predominantly inductive the stator current waveform will be as shown in Fig. 24. The frequency can be varied by the timing of the pulses applied to the thyristors, and a typical frequency range would be 5–100 Hz, giving

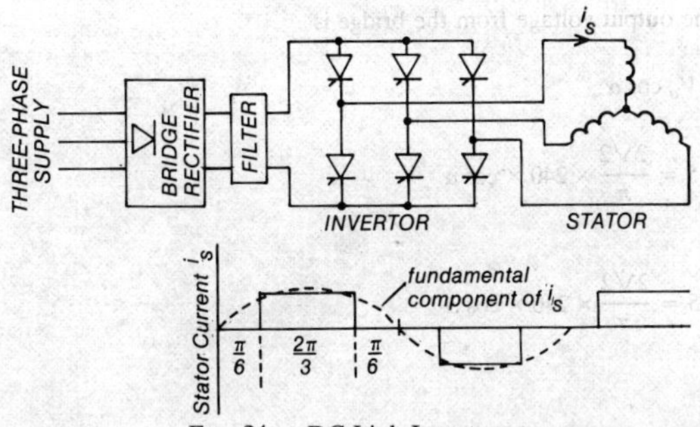

FIG. 24. —DC Link Inverter.

a speed range of almost twice synchronous speed. With this type of circuit there are clearly current, and hence torque harmonics introduced, which may cause vibration and noise.

Changing the number of poles of a motor will only produce a discrete speed change, for example, changing from 2 poles to 4 poles on a 50 Hz supply would reduce the operating speed (assuming a slip of 5%) from 2,850 rpm to 1,425 rpm. To effect a pole change requires a reconnection of the stator windings; therefore the ends of all the windings have to be brought out to a changeover switch and normally, because of the complexity of the switching, this technique is limited to just two pole numbers, and therefore two discrete speeds. It is very useful for two speed drives such as fans and blowers, etc.

Speed control of synchronous and reluctance motors can be achieved using inverter drives or pole changing techniques in the same way as induction motors.

EXAMPLE

A 10 kW, 220 V dc separately excited motor drives a load at a speed of 900 rpm. The armature of the motor is fed by a single-phase full thyristor bridge converter from the 240 V ac mains, whilst the field of the motor is fed from a constant dc supply. The motor takes a current of 40 A from the converter under these conditions, and the motor constant $k\varphi$ is 2·0 volts/rad/sec and the armature resistance is 0·3 Ω. If the load torque varies as the square of the speed, calculate

(i) The firing angle of the converter for operation at 900 rpm and 450 rpm.
(ii) The power factor at both speeds, assuming the current is continuous and ripple free.
(iii) The firing angle to produce regenerative braking from half speed without exceeding the rated current of 40 A.

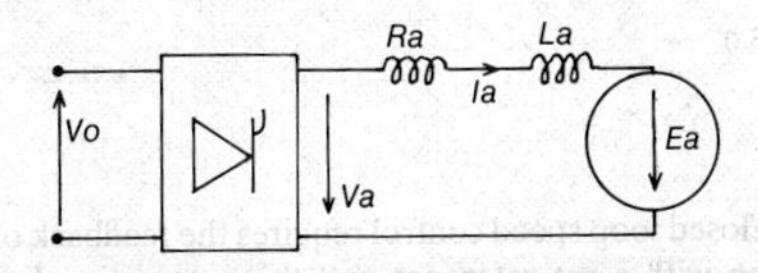

At 900 rpm $T_m = k\varphi I_a = 2{\cdot}0 \times 40 = 80$ Nm

$$\text{and } E_a = k\varphi\omega = 2{\cdot}0 \times 900 \times \frac{2\pi}{60} = 188{\cdot}5 \text{ V}$$

$$\therefore V_a = 188{\cdot}5 + 40 \times 0{\cdot}3 = 200{\cdot}5 \text{ V}$$

Now the load torque T_L varies as the square of the speed N, therefore

$$\frac{T_{L2}}{T_{L1}} = \left[\frac{N_2}{N_1}\right]^2 = \left[\frac{450}{900}\right]^2 = \tfrac{1}{4}$$

hence $T_{L2} = 20$ Nm.

At 450 rpm $T_m = 20$ Nm $\therefore I_a = 10$ A

$$\text{and } E_a = 2{\cdot}0 \times 450 \times \frac{2\pi}{60} = 94.25 \text{ V}$$

$$\therefore V_a = 94.25 + 10 \times 0{\cdot}3 = 97{\cdot}25 \text{ V}$$

For a full converter the output voltage from the bridge is

$$V_a = \frac{2\sqrt{2}}{\pi} V_o \cos\alpha$$

(i) At 900 rpm $200{\cdot}5 = \frac{2\sqrt{2}}{\pi} \times 240 \times \cos\alpha$

$\alpha = 21{\cdot}9°$

At 450 rpm $97{\cdot}25 = \frac{2\sqrt{2}}{\pi} \times 240 \times \cos\alpha$

$\alpha = 63{\cdot}3°$

(ii) The power factor for this type of drive is defined as

$$\text{pf} = \frac{\text{The fundamental power supplied } (V_o I_o \cos\varphi)}{V_{rms} I_{rms}}$$

or if the loss in the converter is neglected the power factor may be obtained from

$$\text{pf} = \frac{\text{Power supplied to the dc motor}}{V_{rms} I_{rms}}$$

Assuming the dc current is continuous and ripple free the current taken from the supply is a square wave, (Fig. 18), and the rms value of a square wave is the height of the square wave, which in this example is 40 A at 900 rpm and 10 A at 450 rpm.

At 900 rpm the pf $= \frac{200{\cdot}5 \times 40}{240 \times 40} = 0{\cdot}835$

At 450 rpm the pf $= \frac{97{\cdot}25 \times 10}{240 \times 10} = 0{\cdot}4$

(iii) For regenerative braking the induced voltage is reversed by reversing the armature connections, and the output from the bridge is made to go negative by increasing the firing angle beyond 90°. The effective circuit is as shown below. Note the current does not change direction, neither does the rotation.

At 450 rpm $E_a = 94.25$ V

$V_a = 94{\cdot}25 - 40.03 = 82{\cdot}25$ V

and $-82{\cdot}25 = \frac{2\sqrt{2}}{\pi} \times 240 \times \cos\alpha$

$\alpha = 112{\cdot}4°$

Closed-loop speed control.—Closed loop speed control requires the feedback of a signal which is proportional to the motor speed, comparision with a set reference and the automatic adjustment, in the case of power electronic circuits, of the firing angle. Figure 25 shows a simple speed control system using a separately excited dc motor with armature voltage control from a thyristor converter.

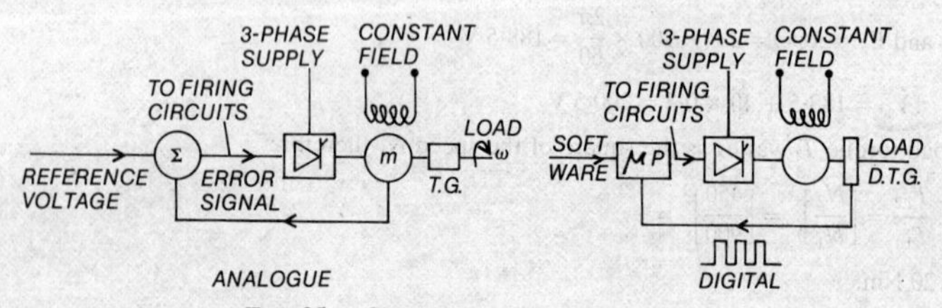

FIG. 25.—Closed Loop Speed Control.

The dc voltage from the tacho-generator (TG) is fed back into a comparator. The reference voltage is set such that the firing angle produced by the difference in reference and feedback voltages gives the required motor speed. Should the speed drop due to increased load on the shaft, the voltage difference from the comparator increases and the firing angle decreases, producing an increase in armature voltage with the attendant increase in speed back to the required value. It is now common practice to replace the analogue tacho-generator with a digital one, and the comparator and reference voltage with a microprocessor. Software can be written to define the duty cycle of motor, together with any constant speed requirements. Digital control systems using microprocessors are very versatile in that new software can be written for different applications as opposed to changing the circuitry of the analogue system.

INDUSTRIAL APPLICATIONS.—The requirements for electric motors in industry are many and varied, and it is impossible to devise hard and fast rules for using a particular type of machine. For medium and large kW drives requiring a fairly constant speed the first choice is always the squirrel cage induction motor because of its simplicity, low cost and relatively low maintenance. Drives such as ventilation fans, hydraulic pumps, compressors, etc, are suitable applications for the squirrel cage motor.

For applications where (a) the starting current cannot be permitted to exceed a specific value (b) a high starting torque is required (c) the average accelerating torque is to be large and (d) the motor is to have a fixed preset full-load regulation a slip ring motor would be used. The slip-ring induction motor is more expensive than the equivalent squirrel cage machine and requires extra maintenance because of the brushes. If wide speed control is required the choice lies between dc motors with armature voltage control and induction motors with frequency control.

The factor which determines the speed response of a drive is the torque-speed envelope as outlined in Fig. 13, and it is useful to compare the performance of dc motors and induction motors in respect of their maximum torque-speed envelopes. Figure 26 is a simplistic look at the general limits of these machines.

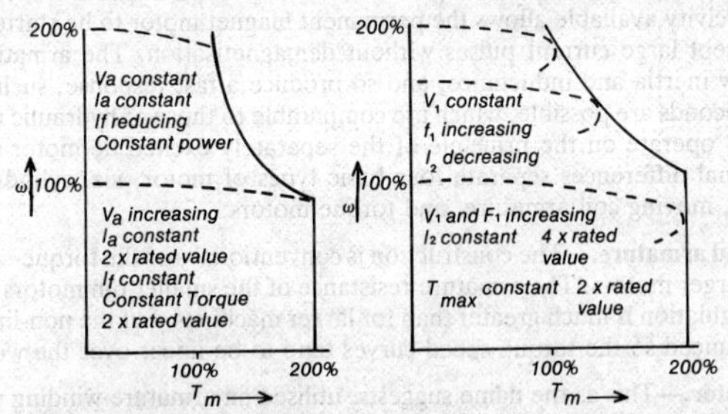

FIG. 26.—Maximum Torque-Speed Envelope for DC Motors and Induction Motors.

It has been shown (p G4/4) that for a dc motor

$$\omega = \frac{E}{k\varphi} \text{ and } T_m = k\varphi I_a \text{ ie } \omega = \frac{EI_a}{T_m}$$

Considering a separately excited motor with voltage control and rated field current, if the armature current is maintained at twice rated value the torque produced will also be twice the rated value. Therefore as the armature voltage is increased the torque will remain constant at 200% as the speed increases. At rated voltage any further increase in speed will require field weakening, and if E and I_a are assumed constant at 100% and 200% of their rated values the speed is inversely proportional to the torque, producing a constant power curve. Further increase in speed is limited by commutation and torque demand.

It is not quite so easy to develop simple relationships for the equivalent induction motor fed from a variable frequency supply. However, if it is assumed that the magnitude and frequency of the applied stator voltage are increased in the same proportion such that the flux per pole remains constant, then, if the stator parameters are neglected, certain simplified equations can be obtained. The maximum torque given by equation (9) (p. G4/7) can be reduced to:

$$T_{max} = \frac{m}{\omega_s} \times \frac{V_1^2}{2x_2'}$$

and the slip at which the maximum torque occurs given by equation (8), reduces to:

$$s = R_2'/x_2'.$$

The referred value of the rotor current at which the maximum torque occurs is obtained from equation (5),

$$I_2' = \frac{V_1}{\sqrt{\left(\frac{R_2'}{s}\right)^2 + (x_2')^2}} = \frac{V_1}{\sqrt{2}x_2'}$$

Therefore for proportional increases in V_1 and f_1 the maximum torque and referred rotor current remain constant.

For a normal induction motor the ratio of maximum torque to rated torque is about 2 to 3. The ratio of current for maximum torque to rated current is about 4 to 5. Selecting the lower values a current of about 400% is required to produce 200% torque.

Having increased the magnitude and frequency of the applied stator voltage to their rated values, any further increase in speed is obtained by increasing only the frequency. The torque developed is then inversely proportional to the frequency and hence the speed, and again the torque-speed variation follows the constant power line.

Servo motors are broadly defined as those motors used in remote control applications. They fall into the categories of motor previously discussed (p. G4/3) ie direct current, induction and synchronous, but the variation in performance and the type of construction is as great as the number of applications that are now presenting themselves. There was extensive development of servo motors for military applications in the 1940's, and more recently the space research programme has stimulated the development of special machines. The control motors used in industry, and more particularly in robotics, have ratings of about 25–250 W and are designed to run continuously, maintenance free, and be economically priced. The main requirement of a control motor is that its torque-speed or torque-angle characteristic is linear and that it operates identically in both directions.

DIRECT CURRENT SERVO MOTORS.—A dc motor will provide a higher output than an ac motor of the same rating, will be easier to stabilise and will be more efficient, especially in variable speed applications. The majority of dc servo motors use permanent magnets which have been improved over the years to such an extent that the high coercivity available allows the permanent magnet motor to be started and reversed on full voltage, and also to accept large current pulses without demagnetisation. The armature circuits have been developed to exhibit low inertia and inductance, and so produce a fast response, such that mechanical time constants of a few milliseconds are possible, which are comparable to those of hydraulic motors. All permanent magnet dc servo motors operate on the principle of the separately excited dc motor with armature voltage control, but constructional differences separate four basic types of motor, viz, cylindrical wound armature, printed circuit armature, moving coil armature, and torque motors.

The cylindrically wound armature.—The construction is conventional and the torque-speed curves are similar to those obtained with larger motors. The armature resistance of the smaller pm motors is, however, relatively high so that the speed regulation is much greater than for larger machines, but the non-linear armature reaction effects are not as pronounced so the torque-speed curves tend to be linear over the working range.

The printed circuit motor.—This as the name suggests, utilised an armature winding which was etched onto a pc board, as shown in Figure 27. The printed circuit armatures have now been superseded by a stamped armature disc of about one hundred effective conductors. The absence of iron in the armature ensures very low inertias and inductances, and results in a fast response. Pulsed operation of pc motors is often used to produce very fast response times, and it is common to use current pulses of 5 to 10 times the rated value to develop large peak torques. Typical torque-speed curves for a 250 W printed circuit motor are shown in Fig. 28.

The small moving coil motor.—These are widely used in battery operated audio and video equipment. The moving coil is housed in between the stationary permanent magnet field system in a similar way to the coil of a loudspeaker, as shown in Fig. 27. The moving coil armature is, of course, iron free, and hence of low inertia and inductance. This type of motor is normally used in the 0–10 W range.

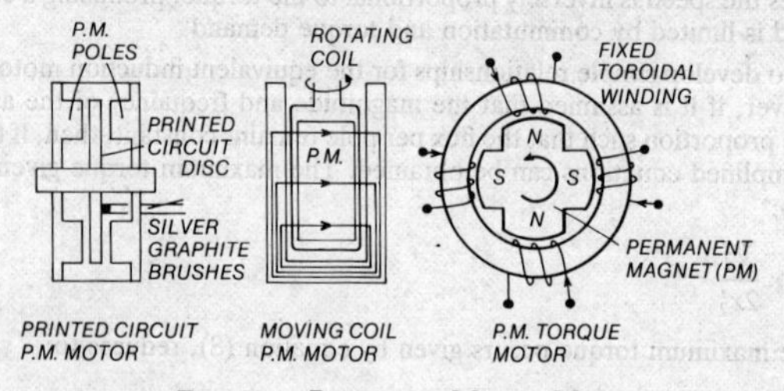

FIG. 27.—Permanent Magnet Motors.

DC torque motors.—In general these are designed for high torque standstill operation in position control systems. Brushless dc torque motors employ a constant reluctance magnetic circuit and a precision toroidally distributed armature winding, thus eliminating undesirable slot ripple or varying torque effects as the motor rotates (Fig. 27). Used over its defined angular range the motor is capable of providing extremely high linearity, resolution, efficiency and reliability.

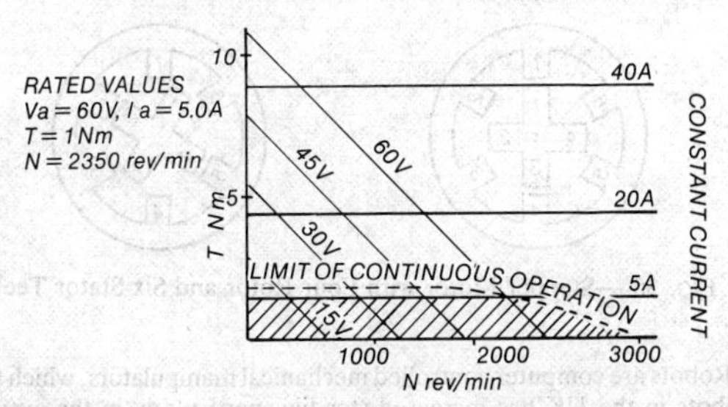

FIG. 28.—Speed-Torque Characteristics of printed circuit motor.

AC SERVO MOTORS.—These are normally two-phase induction motors with high resistance, low inertia, squirrel cage rotors. The high resistance rotor is an attempt to linearise the torque-speed curve and to provide large standstill torques, (see Fig. 11). It can be shown that as with the induction motor, (see p. G4/4), a two-phase stator will produce a rotating field with a synchronous speed related to the supply frequency as before. Normally one of the two phases is permanently connected whilst the other is connected to the control system. The magnitude of the voltage supplied to the 'control' phase will determine the torque and in turn the speed of the motor. In most applications the ac servo motor has been replaced by the dc permanent magnet motor—however, the use of *selsyns* still warrants a mention.

Selsyn is a reduction of the term *self synchronous system*, but it is used generally to describe a wide range of motors, all working on the induction motor principle, used to drive shafts of conveyors in absolute synchronism. Figure 29 shows two identical three-phase induction motors whose rotors are connected together and whose stators are connected to the three-phase mains.

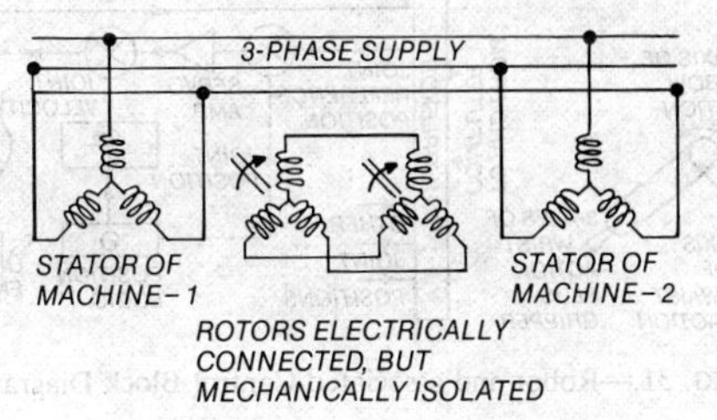

FIG. 29.—'Selsyn'; Self Synchronous System.

If the rotors of both machines are in exactly the same physical position with respect to their stators, then the voltage induced across equivalent rotor phases will be identical (and opposed) and no rotor current will flow, and therefore no torque will be produced. If one rotor is now moved from its original position current will flow and produce a torque in such a direction so as to realign the rotors. Furthermore, if one of the rotors is driven by some other machine, the other rotor will run in synchronism with it. More induction motors may be connected in parallel with the two originals so that a system can be produced whereby several motors (called *Receiver Selsyns*) which are mechanically isolated are controlled by one motor (called the *Transmitter Selsyn*).

Stepper Motors.—These have become widely used over the last decade because of the increasing use of digital control. The area which has had the most impact on the use of stepper motors is computer peripherals. Applications such as floppy disc head positioning, matrix printer, paper and print head positioning all employ stepper motor drives. There are three main types of stepper motor, namely, permanent magnet, variable reluctance and hybrid (a combination of the first two). The motion of the rotor, as the name suggests, is in a sequence of steps, the size of the step being dependent on the motor design, ie on the number of stator and rotor teeth. For instance, Fig. 30 shows a motor with six stator teeth and four rotor teeth. Each stator tooth has a coil wound around it which is energised by a dc current. When stator teeth 1S and 4S are energised the rotor teeth 1R and 3R align with them. If stator teeth 2S and 5S are next energised rotor teeth 2R and 4R will align with 2S and 4S, ie the rotor has moved anticlockwise by 30°. Similarly, for an eight-tooth rotor and a twelve-tooth stator the step angle would be 15°. The computer equipment market demands a high resolution and a basic step size of 1·8°, which is obtainable with permanent magnet stepper motors. Because of the precise nature of operation of the stepper motor users may take advantage of the possibility of open loop control, thus eliminating shaft position encoders.

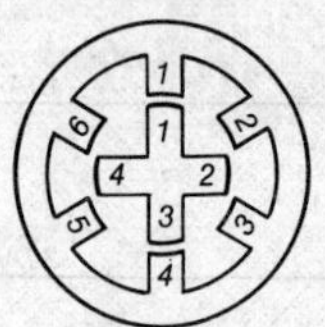

FIG. 30.—Stepper Motor with Four Rotor and Six Stator Teeth.

Robots.—Industrial Robots are computer controlled mechanical manipulators, which are basically positioning devices. The use of robots in the UK has increased steadily, particularly in the automobile industry where heavy duty robots are used extensively for welding and paint spraying. In the majority of cases the workpiece is brought to the robot and it is essential that positioning of the workpiece is accurate. The two types of drive used for the movement and accurate location of the workpiece are either ac frequency controlled induction motors or dc shunt motors supplied from static converters. Both systems offer individual advantages and are economically compatible up to about 50 kW.

The most familiar robots are hydraulically or electrically driven jointed arm structures. The advantage of hydraulic systems is that they can generate large powers with small actuators, but they do require regular maintenance. For small scale assembly robots electrical drives are adequate. The drive motor may be either a dc permanent magnet servo motor or a stepper motor.

Precise operations such as the assembly of electronic components on a printed circuit board require highly accurate positioning of the robot arm. In order to improve the accuracy, software servoing, in which the computer is located in the feedback loop of the servo system, has been employed. A hypothetical robot and a block diagram of a system that might be used to control the motor driving one of the joints are shown in Fig. 31.

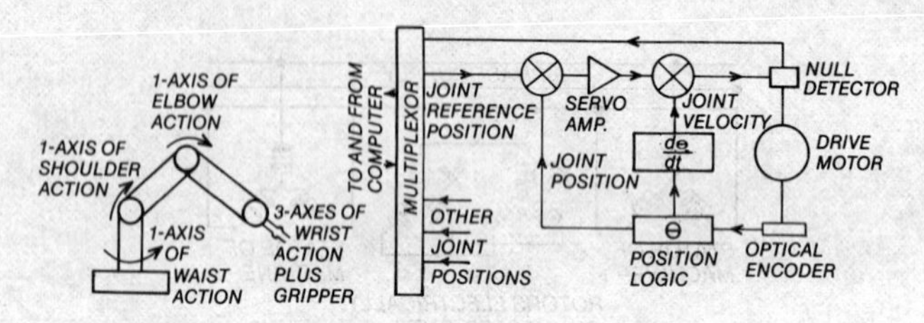

FIG. 31.—Robot and associated Control Block Diagram.

Differential positional feedback is used to provide velocity damping. The null detector informs the computer when the final position has been reached. The computer will provide data defining the incremental position of each robot joint and by checking the null detectors will determine when the robot has reached its predefined position.

FRACTIONAL HORSE POWER MOTORS.—FHP motors constitute a large proportion of the total number of motors manufactured in the UK. They are used extensively in domestic appliances and consequently are designed to operate from a single-phase supply. The most commonly used machines are capacitor motors and universal commutator motors.

The Capacitor Motor.—The stator has two windings displaced by 90°. Both windings are supplied from the single-phase supply, but a capacitor is connected in series with one of the windings so that the current in that winding leads the current in the other by nearly 90°, and a two-phase rotating field is thus produced. The rotor is normally squirrel cage and the performance is similar to that of a three-phase induction motor. Some capacitor motors are fitted with a centrifugal switch, which open circuits the capacitor winding when the motor reaches full speed. The motor then runs as a true single-phase machine. The capacitor is used to produce a starting torque, as single winding, single phase motors do not produce any starting torque.

Universal Series Motors.—These motors can operate from either ac or dc supplies. They are of similar construction to the normal dc series motor except that the iron core is totally laminated to reduce the iron losses when the motor is used on an ac supply. They exhibit the typical series torque-speed characteristic of high starting torque and relatively high running speed. Their full load efficiency is about 60–70% and on ac the operating power factor is usually better than 0.9.

SUMMARY OF THE MORE COMMONLY USED MOTORS

AC POLYPHASE

Induction

CAGE ROTOR
- Cheap
- Shunt Characteristic
- Low starting torque
- Easy starting and braking
- No speed flexibility
- Low pf on light loads
- Efficient

DOUBLE CAGE ROTOR
- More expensive
- Shunt Characteristic
- Good starting torque
- Fast starting and braking
- No speed flexibility
- Efficient

SLIP RING ROTOR
- Expensive
- Shunt Charactersitic
- Good starting torque
- Control of starting and braking currents
- Optimum starting and braking times obtainable
- Marginal speed control can be obtained simply using external resistors
- Efficient

Synchronous

SYNCHRONOUS MOTOR
- Expensive
- Constant speed
- No inherent starting torque
- Started by external motor or by squirrel cage built into the field system
- Possible to operate at a leading power factor
- Efficient

RELUCTANCE MOTOR
- Expensive
- Constant speed
- Same starting torque as a cage rotor
- Moderate operating pf
- Very low pf on light load
- Moderately efficient

PERMANENT MAGNET SYNCHRONOUS MOTOR
- Expensive
- No inherent starting torque
- Constant speed
- Efficient

AC SINGLE PHASE AND FRACTIONAL HORSE POWER MOTORS

Induction Type

CAPACITOR START

CAPACITOR RUN
- Not expensive
- Shunt Characteristic
- Low starting torque
- No speed flexibility
- Fairly efficient

CAPACITOR START
- As above but with good starting torque

SPLIT PHASE
- Inexpensive
- Shunt Characteristic
- Poor starting torque
- No speed flexibility
- Fairly efficient
- Low power factor

SHADED POLE
- Cheap
- Shunt Characteristic
- Poor starting torque
- No speed flexibility
- Inefficient
- Poor pf

Commutator type

UNIVERSAL MOTOR
- AC or DC operation
- More expensive than induction type motors
- Series Characteristic
- Good starting torque
- Good power-to-weight ratio
- Moderately efficient
- Reasonable Power Factor
- Requires maintenance of bushgear

Synchronous Type

RELUCTANCE
- Expensive
- Constant Speed
- Moderately efficient
- Poor pf

PERMANENT MAGNET
- Expensive
- Constant Speed
- Good starting torque and smooth accelerating torque
- Moderately efficient

DIRECT CURRENT MOTORS

SERIES MOTOR
- Expensive
- Series Characteristic
- Good starting torque
- Marginal speed control is easily obtained with field diverter resistance
- Efficient

PERMANENT MAGNET TYPE

CONVENTIONAL CYLINDRICAL ROTOR
- Limited to small ratings
- Fairly cheap
- Almost linear shunt characteristic
- Good starting torque
- Moderately efficient

cont. on **G4**/28

DIRECT CURRENT MOTORS (cont.)

SHUNT MOTOR
- Expensive
- Shunt Characteristic
- Good starting torque
- Marginal speed control is easily obtained with field rheostats
- Efficient

COMPOUND MOTOR
- Expensive
- Combination of shunt and series characteristics
- Good starting torque
- Marginal speed control is easily achieved
- Efficient

Note: The motors in this column require regular commutator and brushgear maintenance

PRINTED CIRCUIT MOTOR
- Limited to very small ratings
- Almost line shunt characteristic
- Good starting torque
- Low inertia rotor gives very fast reponse
- Moderately efficient

STEPPER MOTOR
- Limited to small ratings
- Fairly cheap
- Power electronics required may be more expensive than the motor
- Used extensively in digital control and open loop circuits

MOTORS TO PROVIDE WIDE SPEED CONTROL

DC Motors

SEPARATELY EXCITED MOTOR
- (with variable armature voltage obtained from a Ward Leonard Drive, a Static converter or a Chopper circuit)
- Good speed control
- Good inching control
- Regenerative braking possible
- Easy to operate in closed-loop
- Expensive

SERIES MOTOR
- (with chopper control mainly used for battery powered vehicles)
- Good speed control
- Regenerative braking possible
- Moderate cost

Note: Both dc motors require regular commutator and brushgear maintenance

AC Motors

INDUCTION MOTOR
- (with variable frequency, variable voltage supply, Inverter fed)
- Good speed control from 10 Hz to 100 Hz
- Regenerative braking possible
- Expensive

SWITCHED RELUCTANCE MOTOR
- Robust machines
- Torque pulsations
- Expensive control electronics
- Moderately cheap motor

SYNCHRONOUS MOTOR
- (Inverter fed)
- Can operate at leading pf
- Good speed control
- Regenerative braking possible
- The electronics may be simpler than for induction motor
- Expensive

BIBLIOGRAPHY

ACARNLEY, P. P., *Stepping Motors; A Guide to Modern Theory and Practice;* Peter Peregrins Ltd, 1982.
HINDMARSH, J., *Electrical Machines and their Applications;* Pergamon Press, 1970.
HINDMARSH, J., *Electrical Machines and Drives; worked examples;* Pergamon Press, 1985.
WERNINCK, E. H., *Electric Motor Handbook;* McGraw-Hill, 1978.

MICROPROCESSORS

Definition—Development—Use of Microprocessors—Components—Input/Output Interfaces—Microprocessor Operation—Programming—Programming PROMS—Peripherals—Glossary of Terms—References.

By F. G. A. Coupe, BSc, PhD, AMIEE

INTRODUCTION

This chapter seeks to explain the significance, design, programming and applications of microprocessors in general. The chapter is necessarily generalised although the internal operation of one type of microprocessor is explained in some detail by way of illustration. Because of the great diversity in the make and design of microprocessors this chapter cannot explain the intricate workings of every type. Thus it is intended as a general primer to explain what to expect in the way of hardware, instructions, software and ability in a typical microprocessor.

The power of a microprocessor depends on the number of basic instructions it can execute in a given time, its addressing modes and range as well as the internal word length, which these days may be 4, 8, 16 or 32 bits. The complexity of a microprocessor ranges from the very simple single chip mask programmed varieties used in high volume production to microprocessors which are to all intents and purposes minicomputers but for the use of Large Scale Integration (LSI) integrated circuits in the Central Processing Unit (CPU). Indeed the latest ranges of 32-bit microprocessors are significantly more powerful than quite large minicomputers of only a few years ago.

References 1 to 6 are included as general texts on microprocessors which enlarge on the text here.

MICROPROCESSOR DEFINITION

A microprocessor may be defined as a small computer constructed mainly from a few Large Scale or Very Large Scale Integrated Circuits. At the smallest scale all the necessary components of the microprocessor are integrated onto one chip whereas the largest microprocessors are almost indistinguishable from mini-computers, the only difference being that the physical size of the microprocessor is less than a mini-computer of the same power.

As the microprocessor is a type of computer it may also be defined as a stored–program list–processing machine, which executes the instructions stored in its memory sequentially. Furthermore it contains the ability to skip to different parts of the list according to tests performed on its data.

DEVELOPMENT OF MICROPROCESSORS

INTEGRATED CIRCUITS.—All microprocessors are constructed using one or more integrated circuits. The introduction of microprocessors was as a result of the development of Large Scale Integration. There has been a very strong tendancy to increase the complexity and packing density of integrated circuits, in order to introduce more and more complicated functions for the same cost, but in a smaller size and consuming less power. An integrated circuit is much more reliable than the equivalent circuit made with discrete components.

SSI and MSI circuits are very often used in conjunction with microprocessors wherever simple boolean logic functions are needed, such as in interfaces.

Small Scale Integration (SSI).—Small Scale Integration was the result of a successful attempt by Texas Instruments in 1961 to make a complete but small digital circuit on one wafer of monocrystalline silicon containing bipolar transistors and their interconnections. This in turn opened the way for integrated Resistor Transistor Logic (RTL), Diode Transistor Logic (DTL) and finally TTL.

SSI circuits are now available in 2 main technologies, TTL and CMOS, the latter offering lower speed but much smaller power dissipation. TTL circuits are available in a number of variations and in particular as Low Power Schottky (LSTTL) where the speed of standard TTL is retained but with a significantly reduced power dissipation.

Medium Scale Integration (MSI).—Medium Scale Integration was the logical development from SSI as processing techniques improved and the number of active elements in one circuit was increased significantly.

The MSI circuit functions available are extremely varied and fill in the gap between the simple SSI circuits and the very complicated and specialised LSI and VLSI circuits. They are also available in TTL and CMOS, though the former is the more extensive range.

Large Scale Integration (LSI).—Large Scale Integration was partly the next logical development from Medium Scale Integration, but was also brought about by the development of integration of Metal Oxide Silicon (MOS) transistors where it was found that a significantly higher packing density (greater than 10,000 transistors) could be achieved with only a moderate decrease in operating speed. Subsequently, LSI circuits using bipolar technologies were developed.

LSI circuits have been designed to replace large numbers of SSI and MSI circuits where the design costs can be justified. It was after the introduction of LSI fabrication techniques that INTEL designed a 4-bit LSI chip (in 1971) with all the elements necessary for a very basic computer integrated onto one chip. It was designated the 4004 and was constructed using PMOS technology.

Very Large Scale Integration (VLSI).—Very Large Scale Integration (VLSI) is an upward extension of LSI where the number of active components in a single integrated circuit exceeds about 100,000. MOS technology is used to make VLSI. VLSI circuits are also used for specialised functions (such as memories) in order to justify the cost of their design.

MICROPROCESSOR SEMICONDUCTOR TECHNOLOGY.—Microprocessors are LSI circuits and as such may be constructed by a number of different technologies. The individual gates and flip–flops making up the microprocessor circuit have a delay and power dissipation associated with them which is dependent on the fabrication technology used. Thus for a given technology there is a speed/power product which is constant (measured in Joules). This speed–power product is dependent on bias current in Integrated Injection Logic (IIL).

Bipolar transistor (BIPOLAR).—Bipolar technology is used to make TTL LSI integrated circuits. The gate delay of standard TTL is less than 10 nanoseconds, though LSTTL has a gate delay of less than 3 nanoseconds.

P-channel metal oxide semiconductor (PMOS).—PMOS technology is only used to make simple 4-bit microprocessors because its usefulness is restricted by the PMOS technology whose speed/power product is intrinsically greater than the NMOS technology, and which therefore produces gates with significantly higher delays than NMOS gates and with no power dissipation advantages.

N-channel metal oxide semiconductor (NMOS).—NMOS technology is used (in a variety of forms) to make the majority of the current generation of microprocessors.

NMOS integrated circuits are fabricated on p-type substrate which then has n-channel MOSFET transistors diffused into it. The speed of the MOSFETs is inversely proportional to the width of the gate region and thus increased speeds in NMOS microprocessors are to be expected as the gate widths are reduced towards 1 micron.

Complementary metal oxide semiconductor (CMOS).—More advanced techniques are now being used to make much faster CMOS circuits. The maximum number of gates that can be integrated into the one circuit is increasing and thus large LSI CMOS circuits are becoming a reality. Many microprocessors made in NMOS are also available in CMOS.

Integrated Injection Logic (IIL).—IIL technology is used by only one manufacturer. The main advantage of IIL is that the resulting integrated circuit is very easily radiation hardened and that the speed of the gates is proportional to the injected current.

Emitter coupled logic (ECL).—ECL technology is used to make special high speed components for microprocessors, such as fast multiplier/accumulators rather than microprocessors themselves. ECL LSI is normally arranged to have TTL compatible inputs and outputs as this makes interconnection of such devices much easier. The high-speed-power product and short gate delays of ECL (less than 1 nanosecond) causes a great deal of power to be dissipated by each LSI chip.

USE OF MICROPROCESSORS

The use of microprocessors is extremely extensive and though not a panacea of all industrial technical problems, it offers a degree of flexibility in machine operation which is without mechanical parallel.

A microprocessor may be used to make the operation of a machine by a man much easier and at the same time the quality of the manufactured item can be improved by the microprocessor monitoring the manufacturing process. For instance, the application of microprocessors to typesetting has made it much easier for large quantities of text to be set, and corrections applied to each line as it is entered.

The sophisticated instructions offered by microprocessors allow complicated control algorithms to be implemented which are quite beyond the scope of mechanical or hydraulic systems, and at the same time there is the flexibility to change the program more or less easily.

The use of a microprocessor can also bring increased funtionality to a machine by giving it the ability to perform complicated operations both accurately and repeatedly.

The incorporation of a microprocessor can also make a machine much easier to use, when it is said to be 'user-friendly', without necessarily augmenting the functionality of the machine. This can be achieved, for instance, by presenting numbers in the form most easily understood by the machine operator.

Some of the typical applications of microprocessors outside their immediate use in development systems, VDUs and other computer orientated applications are:

(i) Process Control
(ii) Process Monitoring
(iii) Robotics
(iv) Automatic data logging
(v) Man-machine Interfaces
(vi) Intelligent Displays
(vii) Automatic Testing
(viii) Optimisation of mechanical operations on-line, such as in car engines and jet engines
(ix) Point-of-sale terminals and cash registers
(x) Remote control of equipment (rather than local manual control)
(xi) Adding sophisticated commands to a test instrument
(xii) Games

It can be observed from the above table that the use of microprocessors is often associated with electronics in general and thus not only will software need developing, but hardware as well. Reference 1 addresses itself to the total problem of the design of digital systems.

MICROPROCESSOR COMPONENTS

The functional blocks which go to make up a microprocessor are basically the same for all computers, the microprocessor being the least sophisticated. By the definition of a microprocessor many or all of these functional blocks are colocated in the one integrated circuit.

CENTRAL PROCESSOR

Central Processor Architecture.—The internal design of all microprocessors is based around the use of buses, that is many parts of the CPU are daisy-chained together to make the passing of data easy. Any data to be passed is moved as a parallel word, the actual passing of the data creating bus signals, which can be passed in either direction along the bus, which is then said to be bi-directional. The parts connected to the bus are able to input or output data (if both are logical), but not at the same time. In order that the connection of many outputs does not stop the operation of the bus, each output is arranged to be Tri-state. A Tri-state output has the normal binary output states, but it can also be connected to or disconnected from the bus by the simple expedient of a separate control line. Only one control line is needed for each output, not for each bit, and only one output is allowed to be active at any one time. The multiplicity of inputs connected to the line does not upset the active output provided that its fan-out capability is great enough, though with MOS transistor gates this is not a problem.

This internal data bus is often brought out to pins on the integrated circuit so that external data may be similarly treated. Thus in principal it is possible to pass data from any part connected to the bus to any other part. An internally generated address bus is also brought out to pins on the integrated circuit so that external devices may be addressed, in particular memory.

The number of bits used in the internal data bus, that is the width, defines the internal word size of the microprocessor. Some microprocessors are available where the external data bus width is less than the internal data bus width. The width of the external address bus defines the addressing range of the microprocessor, and with microprocessors of limited data bus width (8 or less) it is normal to have an address bus increased to 16 bits in order to be able to address directly enough memory. 16-bit microprocessors have an external and internal data bus width of 16 bits, though the address bus width is sometimes increased to 18 or 22 bits to expand the addressing range beyond 64 kilobytes. 32-bit microprocessors have an external and internal data bus width of 32 bits, but the address bus width does not need to be 32 bits wide as this would define a memory of 4,294 megabytes which could not possibly be serviced by one microprocessor apart from the fact that it would be enormously expensive.

In order to control and sequence the moving of data along the bus control lines are necessary.

The various funtional blocks which make up the Central Processor Unit (CPU) are as follows:

Arithmetic Logic Unit.—The Arithmetic Logic Unit is used within the CPU for all the bit manipulations, that is addition, subtraction, shifting, complementing and the Boolean Logic functions.

Registers.—The register(s) in a CPU are used for the storage of the Program Counter, the Stack Pointer, and data. Some CPU's are constructed to have general access to all the registers (8 or 16). Other CPUs are constructed around a single data Accumulator (often with an auxilliary register for double length working).

Instruction Decoder.—The Instruction Decoder in a CPU is central to the whole operation and interprets the bits in each instruction into the exact internal operations and then sequences them. Thus the instruction decoder is the hardware implementation of the instruction set.

Timing and Control.—All the operations within the CPU have to be correctly sequenced and thus timing and control circuitry is necessary.

8080 CPU Functional Block Diagram.—As an example of the architecture of a microprocessor, Fig. 1 shows the Intel 8080 CPU functional block diagram. The CPU is based around an 8-bit Internal Data Bus which is connected to the outside world through a bidirectional Data Bus Buffer Latch. This data bus is multiplexed when passing 16-bit numbers to or from the Register Array. The Address Buffer is 16 bits wide and is also made externally available to enable it to address memory and peripherals.

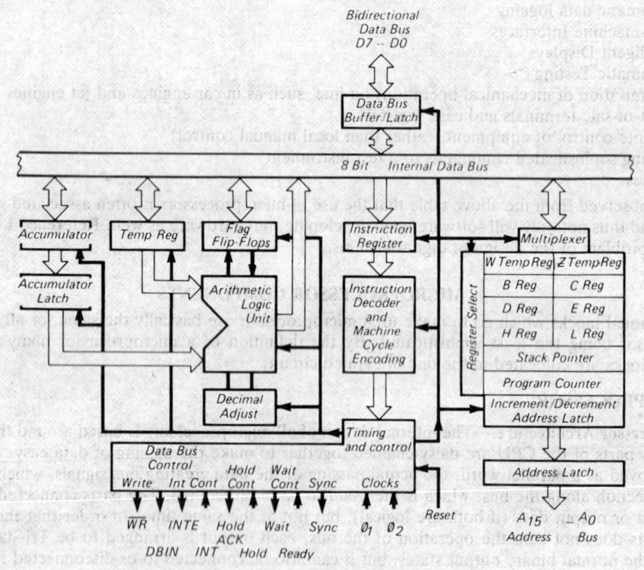

FIG. 1.—Block Diagram of a CPU.

Mathematical operations are executed by the Accumulator and Arithmetic Logic Unit (ALU), which is also connected to the Internal Data Bus. The 8080 operates by the Program Counter pointing to the next instruction to be executed. The memory address is passed out through the Address Buffer and the instruction itself returned through the Data Bus Buffer Latch to the Instruction Register, then Decoded into the various Machine Cycles in order to generate all the Timing and Control signals.

If the instruction is to fetch an Operand and load it into a register then it is fetched using a similar process, but one of the other registers (often the Accumulator) is loaded with the value returned. If the instruction is to operate on the contents of the Accumulator then that is performed. If the instruction is to return a value to memory from a register then the result is returned to its destination. All the data passes by way of the Internal Data Bus.

Instruction Decoding.—The Central Processing Unit (CPU) contains the means to fetch each instruction from memory and interpret it into the necessary actions such as fetching data from memory, modifying registers, etc. These instructions are often sub-divided into what is called 'micro-coded' instructions by a simple look-up table which is accessed for execution.

The CPU contains the logic to locate and interpret each field in the instruction, to calculate any indexed addresses and to fetch addresses in the case of indirect addressing. The resulting operands are then operated upon according to the Op Code which defines the basic type of instruction. If the type of instruction demands it, then the address in which to store the resulting operand has also to be calculated.

General Purpose Registers.—The simplest CPU is based around one general purpose register and there are explicit instructions to load and unload this register which is often called an Accumulator.

Such a CPU often has an auxiliary register for double length working. The disadvantage of such a method of working is that one or two registers provide very little room for storing numerical values while operating on them. Thus the logical development from these was the Processor with many general purpose registers.

Multi-register Processor.—The Multi-register Processor has a number of totally general purpose registers and numerical values can be moved into them, out of them and between them with the same basic MOVE instruction rather than having to use a special instruction for each register. The number of registers is normally 8 or 16 (a power of 2), depending on the manufacturer and type of microprocessor.

Some of the general purpose registers are often assigned special roles. Thus the Program Counter may be accessible as any other register, though its contents always point to the next instruction to be executed. The

Stack Pointer is normally assigned to another register. As the use of the Program Counter and Stack Pointer is involved in the actual execution of instructions, the general purpose nature of all the registers is somewhat lost.

Stack.—A Stack is an ordinary area of memory used for temporary storage of any numerical values or addresses. A microprocessor can have only one stack in use at any one time, that is one stack per program, but if a multitasking operating system is in use then there has to be one stack for each program.

The simplest method of implementing a stack is to reserve one register in a Multi-register CPU for the sole use of the Stack Pointer. The Stack Pointer holds the next free address on the Stack and temporary values are moved through this address onto the Stack, at the same time adjusting the Stack Pointer by Incrementing or Decrementing as chosen.

Address Double Word.—The basic addressing range of a microprocessor is limited by the intrinsic word length and is particularly restrictive for 8-bit microprocessors. This argument also applies to the storage of numerical values. For most 8-bit microprocessors the addressing range has to be extended by using two bytes for the address, which is called an Address Double Word, giving an address range of 64 kilobytes (65,536 bytes). This is the same as the natural addressing range of a 16-bit microprocessor but requires calculation every time a location more than 256 bytes away is accessed. More than 2 bytes may of course be used.

Extended Addressing.—The addressing range of a microprocessor may be extended beyond that specified by the basic word length by adding extra address lines to the address bus, controlled by Memory Management hardware. Thus 16-bit microprocessors may have their address bus width increased from 16 to 18, 22 or 24 bits which extends the memory from 64 kilobytes to 256, 4096 or 16384 kilobytes respectively.

Memory Management.—Memory Management is necessary partly as an adjunct to Extended Address calculation and partly as a means of implementing Relative Addressing. The technique of Relative Addressing can be used when Memory Management is available to enable the program counter to use the address specified in the program and not the physical address in memory. This is achieved by the Memory Management hardware adding the correct offset address between the physical address in memory and the program address. It is often the case that the starting address of a program is set to zero. The offset address is normally held in a memory management register. If more than one memory management register is provided then various absolute addresses can be mapped to appear as contiguous portions of the one program. This then gives the microprocessor the ability to share the areas of program and data between different programs by merely adjusting the contents of the memory management registers.

The contents of the memory management registers may also be adjusted by a program while it is executing in order to make use of more memory than is directly addressable from one program. This is particularly true of 16-bit microprocessors which are limited to running programs of no more than 64 kilobytes in length. By using and adjusting the memory management registers, programs larger than 64 kilobytes can be executed without resorting to overlays.

Paged Memory.—The memory of a microprocessor may be designed to be divided into 'pages', with the length of each page equal to the addressing range of the microprocessor (say 64 kilobytes). Thus different programs are run in different 'pages', possibly more than one page. Hence memory management may be replaced with memory paging.

Virtual Memory.—Virtual Memory is a technique to increase the apparent size of directly addressable memory far beyond the limit set by physical considerations such as the cost of memory. The extra memory is achieved by the use of an external mass storage device (a disk) to extend the size of physical memory very considerably. The whole memory is then treated as being directly addressable and special hardware is incorporated to interpret every address and retrieve those addresses (in blocks) from disk into physical memory. Actual program execution is always performed in physical memory. However, this technique is too complicated for anything but the most sophisticated microprocessors, which are virtually mini-computers.

Cache Memory.—A Cache Memory (Scratch-Pad) is an area of very rapid access memory which is used to store an area of physical memory which has been copied by special hardware monitoring the Program Counter position. The special hardware loads the Cache Memory with repeatedly used instructions. The microprocessor itself collects its instructions from this 'Scratch-pad', for which the access time is much reduced. Thus when the microprocessor is executing frequently repeated instructions a very significant decrease in execution time is observable. However, when the Cache Memory contents are no longer required, the whole Cache Memory has to be refilled which causes a slight pause.

Pipeline.—A pipeline is a technique to speed the execution of instructions by allowing the next instruction to be fetched and decoded whilst the present one is being executed. If decoding is likely to take a long time then the pipeline can work further ahead. By this technique the time it takes for a processor to execute instructions is reduced significantly. The decoded instructions are stored in a simple First-In First-Out store (FIFO). This overlapping of instructions effectively halves the instruction time except when Branching instructions are encountered, as was the case with the Cache Memory.

MEMORY.—Memory is all important to the operation of any computer (including a microprocessor) because by definition they are all stored program devices, and the memory is that store. The memory is constructed to store individual bits which are grouped up into bytes or words. Each memory location normally contains the same number of bits as the nominal word length of the particular type of microprocessor used.

Random Access Memory (RAM) is required in all microprocessors for the storage of the transient data being processed. Read Only Memory (ROM) is not necessarily required but is often used for the storage of the program to be executed and any data constants.

Memory size is normally measured in kilo-bytes or kilo-words, though the latter can cause confusion unless the word length is defined. The kilo above denotes 1,024 and not the more normal 1,000. This is because 1,024 is the tenth power of 2 and a much more convenient value than a power of 10 in a Binary machine.

Each particular memory location is given a unique Address on a byte or word basis, and there are normally thousands of locations. Memory locations are normally designed to be contiguous. The maximum size of memory that can be attached to a given microprocessor depends on the address bus width, that is the number of bits used to address memory, and other techniques used such as paging and memory management. However, it is clear that an 8-bit microprocessor can only directly address 256 locations (2^8) which will not be enough memory except for the most trivial applications. Thus, short word length microprocessors usually address double words to extend their effective addressing range to 65,536 locations. Clearly, a 16-bit microprocessor has an intrinsic advantage here in that it can directly address 65,536 locations (2^{16}), though even that is often not enough. The latest generation of large microprocessors have a word length of 32 bits giving a theoretical memory size of 4,294,967,304 bytes. The address bus is normally restricted to either 22 or 24 bits wide giving a 4 or 16 mega-byte addressing capability which is more than adequate for any microprocessor because it requires an enormously powerful processor to make effective use of even that much memory.

The periods during which memory is being written to and read from are called the Write Cycle and Read Cycle. The speed of a computer is governed by the time taken for the Read and Write Cycles which in turn depends on the access time of the integrated circuits used to make the memory.

Comparisons can be made between different types of memory by calculating the cost-per-bit. In general MOS memory is much cheaper than core memory. Furthermore, the cost-per-bit drops steeply as larger and larger memories are integrated onto single chips.

Random Access Memory (RAM).—Random Access Memory is found in every type of computer in large or small amounts. The RAM is able to store temporary values because it is capable of being addressed for reading or writing. It is also often used to store the instructions being executed. There are several different types of RAM.

CORE MEMORY.—Magnetic core memory used to be used very extensively in computers but the ability of semiconductor manufacturers to make microprocessors using LSI also brought with it the ability to make very large arrays of bit storage elements which have come to be known as MOS memory.

However, Core memory has the advantage that it is non-volatile when power is removed from the microprocessor and thus was useful for preventing the loss of information due to power failures. In recent years PROMs have overcome this disadvantage of MOS memory.

The cost-per-bit of core memory is very high and this speeded the development of MOS memory. Hence core memory is used only rarely in microprocessors.

MOS MEMORY.—MOS memory is made using standard IC semiconductor technology and consists of arrays of groups of transistors using one of a number of possible techniques to store a bit. The bit may be stored by the charge held on an integrated capacitor (as in dynamic MOS memory) or by the setting or resetting of a latch (as in static MOS memory).

However, MOS memory is normally manufactured to be either a bit wide, half a byte wide (4 bits) or a byte wide (8 bits). If larger word lengths than a byte are required then it is possible to arrange the bytes in parallel to make the longer word lengths.

64 kilo-bit MOS Memory integrated circuit are now available and 256 kilo-bit chips will be available shortly with 1 mega-bit chips coming later. The cost per bit of memory is reduced dramatically as the level of integration moves from LSI to VLSI. Simultaneously, the size of a complete memory of a given number of bits drops allowing more bits to be stored in the same physical space. MOS RAM memory has the disadvantage that the memory contents are volatile when power is removed and thus precautions have to be taken to prevent the loss of information due to power failures. In recent years battery back-up has become available for MOS memory which enables the data to be retained.

The first type of MOS memory to be designed was dynamic, that is to say the bits are held as charge in integrated capacitors and have to be periodically refreshed. If the memory is not continually refreshed every few milliseconds then too much charge will leak away and the state of the bit will be lost. The memory is circulated between refreshing and it is during this process that reading and writing can take place. The memory is organised to allow for the refreshing and yet give reasonably quick access to a specified location.

Static MOS memory is designed using a multiple MOS transistor latch for each bit. Thus providing that power is kept on the latch, its state will not be lost. It does not require periodic refreshing. However, the technology to make thousands of latches on one intergrated circuit has meant that large dynamic MOS memories were available before static MOS memory. The maximum size of Static MOS memory is 16 kbits at present, and rather less for Bipolar and CMOS memories. Advances in semiconductor technology have now brought static MOS memory access times down to 100 ns.

Read Only Memory (ROM).—Read Only Memory (ROM) is used to store the instructions and data constants for any fixed program microprocessor. These instructions and data are then totally inviolate, there being no way in which the microprocessor can alter this type of memory.

PROGRAMMABLE ROM (PROM).—Mask Programmable ROMs (PROMs) have their bit patterns fixed in them during manufacture and therefore there is no way of altering their contents. Such PROMs are useful for very simple programs such as Bootstraps but the cost of mask programming is very high unless the quantity is large and thus the cost of any program changes is prohibitive.

Fusible PROMs may be user programmed quite easily (with the appropriate PROM fuser or 'blaster') and once programmed there is no way again of altering their contents. Hence, unless a PROM fuser is available this is an expensive way of developing a program. The advent of EPROMs has greatly simplified the problem.

ERASABLE PROGRAMMABLE ROM (EPROM).—An EPROM has to be pre-programmed using a PROM programmer with the required data, such as the instructions for the execution of a program. More than one EPROM may be used to hold a program and 2 or more EPROMs may be used in parallel to increase the word length. EPROMs are normally byte-wide rather than bit-wide which is much more common with RAMs.

The programming process itself is done in one or more cycles, that is the bit patterns are written to each EPROM location sequentially. Some types of EPROM can be programmed in one cycle, while others take several hundred cycles, the difference being according to the integrated circuit technology used to fabricate it.

An EPROM has the enormous advantage that it can be erased by Ultra-Violet light when no longer required and re-programmed. The time taken for the erasing of an EPROM also depends on the technology used to fabricate it, but can be as much as 45 minutes. The number of re-programs possible with one chip may be as low as 10, but it is nevertheless a much more economical process than using Fusible PROMS.

ELECTRICALLY ALTERABLE ROM (EAROM).—Electrically Alterable ROM may have the contents of any one location changed at any time by the application of a signal (often a higher than normal voltage) which then enables writing to the EAROM. In all other respects the EAROM acts just like normal ROM. This technique provides a convenient way to perform occasional modifications but there is a significant overhead in providing the special power supply voltages and logic signals. EAROM's can be used in place of set of mechanical switches to store parameter settings, thereby providing an increased reliability.

ELECTRICALLY ERASABLE ROM (EEROM).—Electrically Erasable ROM may have the whole memory contents erased by the application of a higher voltage to a special erase line. New data may then be written to the EEROM. In all other respects the EEROM acts just like normal ROM. EEROM is similar to EAROM except in the ability to erase the whole memory electrically.

Because an EEROM may be erased electrically rather than with Ultra-Violet light (as is the case with an EPROM), an even quicker programming cycle is possible. Furthermore, large amounts of data may be stored almost indefinitely by a microprocessor, but still altered whenever required.

INTERRUPTS.—Interrupts are required in order that an external process of any given sort may interrupt the execution of a program by a microprocessor and optionally interchange data with that microprocessor. Thus an interrupt normally occurs asynchronously compared with the program execution.

In order for the microprocessor to respond to the interrupt it is necessary for the microprocessor to identify the source of the interrupt, store any current but transient numerical values and jump to a separate program to handle the interrupt logically. There are two techniques for identifying the source of an interrupt, to 'Poll' all sources of interrupt or to use a Vectored Interrupt.

Polling.—Polling is a sequential testing of all the possible sources of an interrupt. For handling normal interrupt this is very time consuming and is not normally used in microprocessors.

Vectored Interrupts.—Vectored Interrupts are a much faster method for the CPU to determine the source of an interrupt. In this method, when the interrupt occurs the first response (in hardware) by the CPU is to request the interrupting interface to put its Vector Address onto the address bus. This is read by the CPU, which then stores all current temporary values and jumps through this Vector Address to the interrupt handling program. However, although this technique is very efficient it requires that the Vector Address be filled beforehand with the address of the entry point of the interrupt handling program. Furthermore, it requires that the CPU has efficient instructions to store rapidly its current working values and switch to the new program, as well as reverse the process. Finally it requires that the CPU has the necessary hardware to ascertain the Vector Address from the interface.

Priority Vectored Interrupt.—A Priority Vectored Interrupt operates in the same manner as an ordinary Vectored Interrupt except that when the interrupt is generated, there is logic attached to the Vector Interrupt handling logic to determine the priority of the interrupt. Thus if 2 or more Priority Vectored Interrupts are received at the same time but with different priorities then the arbitration logic causes the interfaces to be handled in priority order.

A further level of complication is the use of software priority whereby there are instructions available to allow the CPU to alter its own state. Thus it is possible on the larger and more sophisticated microprocessors to have the priority state raised after an interrupt at a particular hardware priority level to lock out any more interrupts at that level or lower until the code vital to the interrupt has been executed. The priority can then be dropped to allow in any outstanding interrupts. Any interrupts at a higher priority level than that currently set by the processor will interrupt the current process.

Trap Vectors.—Trap Vectors are an alternative use of vectors whereby a detectable error, such as an illegal instruction, a Halt instruction, numerical overflow, and so on, does not cause the microprocessor to stop but merely to jump to a predetermined and appropriate error handling routine.

Direct Memory Access (DMA).—Direct Memory Access (DMA) is used to input or output data from the memory of a microprocessor with the minimum of CPU intervention. The microprocessor is required to fill a register with the address of a contiguous series of memory locations containing the data to be output or reserved for the data to be input, and a second register with the number of bytes or words (as appropriate) to be transferred. The microprocessor must then start the DMA transfers, normally by setting a bit in another register in the same interface. The data is passed at a rate determined by the external equipment but no faster than the maximum transfer speed set by the microprocessor's own fundamental speed. In order to achieve the transfer of each word, the CPU action is broken into between instructions and frozen and a memory fetching cycle (output) or a memory storing cycle (input) are executed without the assistance or intervention of the CPU itself. When all the data has been passed then the CPU is interrupted and the transfer completed.

Real Time Clock.—The purpose of a Real Time Clock is to allow the microprocessor to have an accurate and up to date record of the time (and date). A Real Time Clock can be implemented as a Line Clock or a Crystal Clock. The calendar portion of the clock requires human intervention to set its value when the microprocessor program is started. A Line Clock is a special piece of hardware which has an input from the AC mains supply running the equipment. The hardware logic counts the cycles of the AC mains and updates registers with the current time. It is important to note that the mains frequency has to be taken into account and appropriate switch settings are normally included to accommodate a 50 Hz or 60 Hz mains supply. This method is excellent provided that an AC mains supply is available, but if it is not then a Crystal Clock must be used.

A Crystal clock is based on the natural frequency stability of an oscillator when controlled by a quartz crystal. It operates in exactly the same manner as the Line Clock by updating registers which can be read by the microprocessor.

Calendar Card.—Calendar Cards are now available for use with various types of microprocessors. The card contains a clock integrated circuit (similar to those used in digital watches and clocks) and battery back-up. The date and time can be read through registers and thus may be read very easily by a program.

FLOATING POINT UNIT.—Floating Point operations may be performed in a microprocessor either entirely in software or alternatively with a piece of hardware called a Floating Point Unit. The number of software instructions necessary to perform floating point operations depends on the numerical precision required, but for division it is often the case that many tens of instructions are required for each operation.

Thus a Floating Point Unit is very advantageous in a microprocessor if a significant number of Floating Point calculations are to be used by a program. A Floating Point Unit may be implemented as microcoded instructions or as an actual piece of hardware. The former technique is faster than letting the microprocessor attempt the operations directly but not as fast as the latter technique.

PROCESSOR CONSTRUCTION

It is normal now for microprocessors to be purchased as a card containing all the relevant integrated circuits, rather than as individual integrated circuits.

Single Chip Microprocessor.—A microprocessor can be made up in a number of different ways, the simplest of which is the Single Chip microprocessor. This Single Chip microprocessor contains all the CPU and all the memory required, both RAM and ROM. The ROM is mask programmed and thus the expected usage of that particular version of the microprocessor has to be very high to warrant the cost of masking. However the costs of production with a single integrated circuit are low. The range of applications for a Single Chip microprocessor are restricted to fairly simple control operations.

Chip Set.—A special purpose microprocessor based around a Chip Set is a very flexible method of construction. A Chip Set allows the designer great freedom to construct special processors, but this can be of mixed benefit as a lot of software has also to be written, starting with an assembler. However, in certain applications this technique is attractive, though as the power and speed of general purpose microprocessors increases the need for special processors may diminish.

NUMERICAL REPRESENTATION

All general purpose microprocessors use binary numbers internally because binary logic is very much easier to design than multilevel logic. However, it is more convenient to represent these multibit words by several Octal (base 8) or Hexadecimal (base 16) digits. Octal or Hexadecimal conversion to binary is very quick because each Octal digit equates exactly to 3 bits, whereas each Hexadecimal digit equates to 4 bits.

However it is often the case that a decimal number has to be input or output.

Integers.—The simplest type of number that can be stored and manipulated numerically in a microprocessor is an integer. The numerical resolution of an integer depends whether it is signed or unsigned and the number of bits assigned to represent it which is equal normally to the microprocessor word length. 16 bit numbers are normally required, though this implies multiple words if the microprocessor has a word length less than 16 bits.

It is sometimes possible for double length integers to be used even with 16 bit microprocessors, though this facility is restricted to the most sophisticated microprocessors. Furthermore, any multi-word operations are considerably slower than single precision operations.

Fixed Point Numbers.—Fixed Point Numbers are stored in the same way as integers but are scaled by an implied but invisible decimal point. They are used where the advantages of working with single precision numbers are required but where decimal representation is also imperative. However, the instructions to handle Fixed Point Numbers are not often to be found in microprocessors.

Floating Point Numbers.—A Floating Point Number is the normal way a non-integer number is represented in a microprocessor. It is normally thought of as a decimal number, though it is stored and operated on as a binary floating point number. The number to be stored is held as a signed Mantissa and signed Exponent (Fig. 2).

237·85 =	0·23785	x	10^2
	Decimal Mantissa		Decimal Exponent
=	0·9291016	x	2^8
	Decimal Mantissa		Base 2 Exponent
≡	11101101	x	$2^{100000000}$
	Binary Mantissa		Binary Exponent

FIG. 2.—Floating Point Numbers.

The Mantissa of a floating point number is the numerical representation of the significant digits but adjusted in scale to lie in the range 0.1 to 0.999999....., recurring. The Exponent of a floating point number is a power of ten (normally) necessary to scale the Mantissa to represent the original number.

The exact layout of the bits for the Mantissa and Exponent depends on the make and type of the microprocessor. The resolution of the Mantissa portion depends on the number of bits assigned to it but the total number of bits needed is normally at least 32 so that the Mantissa represents 6 to 7 decimal figures. Hence, Floating Point Numbers require double or quadruple length operations on anything but the most sophisticated microprocessors with the attendant reduction in calculating speed.

2's Complement Arithmetic.—2's Complement Arithmetic is an almost universal technique for representing signed numbers in a microprocessor, be they integer or floating point. The basic advantage of 2's Complement Arithmetic is that subtraction is made almost as simple as addition.

In 2's Complement Arithmetic it is normal for the sign bit of a positive number to be set low, whereas it is set high for a negative number. Furthermore, the numerical magnitude can to be 2's complemented according to the following rules.

(1) Calculate the 1's complement by inverting each bit in turn
(2) Add 1 to the answer (with a modulo of the word length)

The above algorithm is implemented as an instruction inside a microprocessor. The following is an example of negation by the above process for a 16 bit microprocessor.

Integer = decimal 587

= hexadecimal 246

= 0000 0010 0100 0110

Now take the 1's complement:

= 1111 1101 1011 1001

and add 1:

= 1111 1101 1011 1010

As a cross check this number can be added to the original positive integer with a modulo of the word length and the result is zero.

2's Complement Arithmetic is also applied to the mantissa and exponent of floating point numbers.

NUMBER CONVERSION.—Conversion between Decimal (base 10), Octal (base 8) and Hexadecimal (base 16) is often necessary when programming microprocessors. If a great deal of manual number conversion is necessary then a Decimal/Octal/Hexadecimal calculator is very useful.

INPUT/OUTPUT INTERFACES

A computer is used to accept information, process the data in a program and output the results. Thus Input and Output of information is central to any computer operation and is conducted through interfaces.

ASYNCHRONOUS SERIAL INTERFACES.—An asynchronous serial interface is the most common form of interface on a microprocessor, and is used to send and receive data from peripherals such as Printers and Visual Display Units (VDUs). Serial interfaces transmit their data one bit at a time thus the speed of data transmission (the baud rate) is measured in bits-per-second (baud). The word baud is derived from the name of an early worker in telegraphic signalling, Baudot.

Asynchronous serial interfaces transmit the data bits in sequence from the least significant bit upwards and preceded by a start bit and terminated by one or more stop bits. The start and stop bits are necessary for correct reception of the transmitted data bits. The general structure of the data is shown in Fig 3. As well as data bits a single parity bit may be included optionally for single error detection.

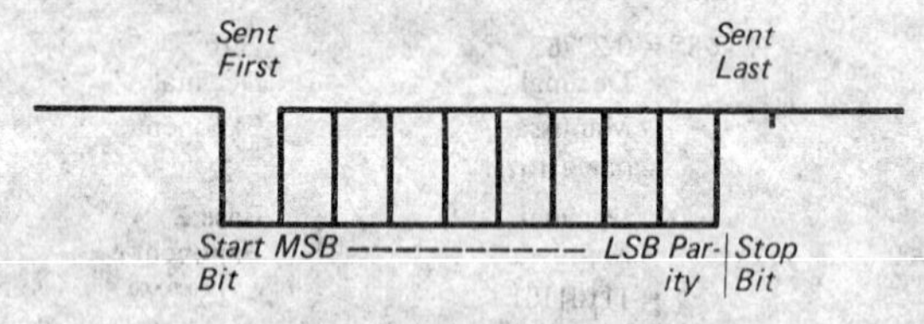

FIG. 3.—Asynchronous Data Structure.

Asynchronous byte transmission requires that the baud rate (bits-per-second of the transmitter and receiver be closely adjusted, the accuracy depending on the number of bits passed with each byte. The maximum practical baud rate depends on the integrated circuit technology used to make the UART. However, each bit being received has to be able to be sampled at typically one of sixteen possible points and thus a clock source is required to be 16 times the baud. This constraint limits the present asynchronous serial interfaces to no more than 38400 baud as the next highest standard baud rate would be 76800 baud. Table 1 lists all the standard asynchronous baud rates used with microprocessors.

TABLE 1.—ASYNCHRONOUS SERIAL BAUD RATES

Baud Rate bits/sec	Data Rate bytes/sec
110	10
150	15
300	30
600	60
1200	120
2400	240
4800	480
9600	960
19200	1920
38400	3840

By the definition of asynchronous interfaces, there is no explicit or implicit clocking signal passed with the data and thus the receiver has to be expecting data at a prearranged baud rate. However, as the clock signal is not passed, there is no guarantee that the generator and receiver baud rates are in phase and thus start and stop bits are needed to introduce the data and allow the receiver to synchronise itself. Furthermore, the maximum number of bits which can be sent is related to the baud rate accuracy, and must be correct to within about 2·5% for 8 data bits.

Universal Asynchronous Receiver Transmitters (UARTs).—Asynchronous serial interfaces are normally implemented using Integrated Circuits called Universal Asynchronous Receiver Transmitters (UARTS), which contain all the logic necessary to send and receive the data bits.

UARTs may normally send 5, 6, 7 or 8 data bits and this is controlled by connections to several of their pins.

Parity may be generated internally (optionally) from the data bits before the start and stop bits are added. If parity is specified then the UART will check the received bits for parity errors. The UART is also designed to check for Framing Errors in a complete set of data bits and stop bits, and if these are not received then an error is flagged.

TABLE 2.—7-BIT ASCII CODE

Control Characters			Punctuation and Figures			Upper Case			Lower Case		
Char	Octal	Hex	Char	Octal	Hex	Char	Octal	Hex	Char	Octal	Hex
NUL	0	0	Space	40	20	@	100	40	‘	140	60
SOH	1	1	!	41	21	A	101	41	a	141	61
STX	2	2	″	42	22	B	102	42	b	142	62
ETX	3	3	£	43	23	C	103	43	c	143	63
EOT	4	4	$	44	24	D	104	44	d	144	64
ENQ	5	5	%	45	25	E	105	45	e	145	65
ACK	6	6	&	46	26	F	106	46	f	146	66
BEL	7	7	’	47	27	G	107	47	g	147	67
BS	10	8	(	50	28	H	110	48	h	150	68
HT	11	9	)	51	29	I	111	49	i	151	69
LF	12	A	*	52	2A	J	112	4A	j	152	6A
VT	13	B	+	53	2B	K	113	4B	k	153	6B
FF	14	C	,	54	2C	L	114	4C	l	154	6C
CR	15	D	—	55	2D	M	115	4D	m	155	6D
SO	16	E	.	56	2E	N	116	4E	n	156	6E
SI	17	F	/	57	2F	O	117	4F	o	157	6F
DLE	20	10	0	60	30	P	120	50	p	160	70
DC1	21	11	1	61	31	Q	121	51	q	161	71
DC2	22	12	2	62	32	R	122	52	r	162	72
DC3	23	13	3	63	33	S	123	53	s	163	73
DC4	24	14	4	64	34	T	124	54	t	164	74
NAK	25	15	5	65	35	U	125	55	u	165	75
SYN	26	16	6	66	36	V	126	56	v	166	76
ETB	27	17	7	67	37	W	127	57	w	167	77
CAN	30	18	8	70	38	X	130	58	x	170	78
EM	31	19	9	71	39	Y	131	59	y	171	79
SUB	32	1A	:	72	3A	Z	132	5A	z	172	7A
ESC	33	1B	;	73	3B	[	133	5B	{	173	7B
FS	34	1C	<	74	3C	\	134	5C	|	174	7C
GS	35	1D	=	75	3D	]	135	5D	}	175	7D
RS	36	1E	>	76	3E	^	136	5E	”	176	7E
US	37	1F	?	77	3F	—	137	5F	DEL	177	7F

CONTROL CHARACTER ABBREVIATIONS.

NUL Null (Nothing)
SOH Start of Header
STX Start of Text
ETX End of Text
EOT End of Transmission
ENQ Enquiry
ACK Acknowledge
BEL Ring Bell
BS Back Space
HT Horizontal Tabulation
LF Line feed
VT Vertical Tabulation
FF Form Feed
CR Carriage Return
SO Shift Out
SI Shift In
DLE Data Link Escape
DC1 Device Control 1 (X-On)
DC2 Device Control 2
DC3 Device Control 3 (X-Off)
DC4 Device Control 4
NAK Negative acknowledge
SYN Synchronous Idle
ETB End of Transmission Block
CAN Cancel
EM End of Medium
SUB Substitute
ESC Escape
FS File Separator
GS Group Separator
RS Record Separator
US Unit Separator
DEL Delete

The data passed through the UART is normally double buffered in both directions, that is there is an intermediate register between its input or output connections and the internal shift register used to transmit the data serially. This is intended to allow one byte to be held while a second byte is being received, or to hold one byte while an earlier byte is being transmitted.

SYNCHRONOUS SERIAL INTERFACES.—Synchronous Serial Interfaces are used when higher baud rates are necessary but bit serial transmission is still acceptable. Such an interface is required to send a clock signal as well as the data signal, either explicitly or implicitly. Synchronous Serial Interfaces are normally implemented using Integrated Circuits called Universal Synchronous Receiver Transmitters (USRTS), which contain all the logic necessary to send and receive the data bits. The transmission of data synchronously requires that the transmitter clock be fed to the receiver (explicit clock transmission) or that the data carry an intrinsic clock, as follows. An Implicit Clock Transmission has the data and its clock signal encoded together, so that only one signal path is necessary. It is often implemented using a Manchester code, of which there are several variations, but they all ensure that a data transition occurs during the time of each bit.

The advantage of an implicit clock is that only one cable is needed, as in the case of asynchronous transmission. The disadvantage is that in carrying both clock and data in the one transmission, the maximum data rate is halved, or the bandwidth occupied is doubled.

DATA SYNCHRONISATION.—In order that bytes (that is characters) being sent at the higher rates are not lost, it is often necessary to protect an interface from being flooded by the peripheral, and similarly for the peripheral. There are a number of different techniques for achieving this but the most common is X-ON/X-OFF synchronisation. X-ON is equivalent to ASCII Control Q and X-OFF to ASCII Control S and are otherwise known as DC1 and DC3 respectively (see Table 3).

If a peripheral is getting full because the selected data rate is perhaps greater than its printing rate, then the peripheral is designed to send X-OFF to the microprocessor to tell it to pause in sending data. Similarly, if the peripheral is sending data too fast to the microprocessor then the microprocessor will send X-OFF to the peripheral device. X-ON is sent to resume transmission.

ASCII CODE.—The ASCII code is defined in the American National Standard (ANSI) Code for Information Interchange (7). The ASCII code defines 128 characters using 7 data bits, so that 7 upper and lower case letters are specified separately together with numerals, punctuation, and 32 control characters. See Table 3.

SERIAL DATA TRANSMISSION STANDARDS.—There are various international standards in use for the transmission of serial data, the ones mentioned here being applicable to microprocessors. It should be clearly noted that the adoption of a particular standard of interchange circuit does not necessarily imply adoption of a data structure standard. Many standards define the interchange circuits without reference to the data structure, either synchronous or asynchronous, and thus great care should be taken to check for compatibility when incorporating equipment with a microprocessor.

Serial data is normally generated and received with the aid of a Universal Asynchronous Receiver/Transmitter (UART). The output of a UART must be converted to a suitable voltage or current before being transmitted to the receiving UART which in turn needs the appropriate circuitry to correctly interpret the voltage or current. Most interface circuit types use voltage transmission nowadays, though current loop transmission is found, particularly in association with Telex type equipment.

As most serial interconnections are bi-directional, it is necessary to clearly define the terminology used in the standards. Thus the Transmitter which generates a signal becomes the Data Terminal Equipment (DTE) for that interface circuit. The Receiver is called the Data Communications Equipment (DCE) for that interface circuit.

Most digital interface circuit standards have been written with the assumption that they will be required to work with a Modem (short for Modulator/Demodulator). However, these standards are capable of application to microprocessors.

V24.—The CCITT standard V24 (8) defines suitable digital interface circuits for transmitting serial synchronous and asynchronous data along unbalanced lines, together with interface circuits to control the transmission. The actual signalling voltages are not defined. The standard describes a considerable number of Interchange Circuits, but for local connection of a terminal or equivalent device only a subset are required.

Microprocessors and terminals are often quoted as having a V24 interface, and this is normally taken to mean that they have a serial interface capable of transmitting and receiving asynchronous data in Full Duplex, with the serial data organised into bytes, typically following the ASCII code. However, reference to V24 shows that this is not strictly true.

V24 is also referenced in EIA standard RS-232C (10), though the former is a more extensive standard, and in particular defines the signalling voltages. However, both V24 and RS-232C are now being superceded by more modern standards (described later). For a fuller description see the CCITT standard (3).

V28.—V28 is a CCITT standard which specifies the equivalent electrical signalling characteristics to RS-232C (see below).

For a fuller description see the CCITT standard (9).

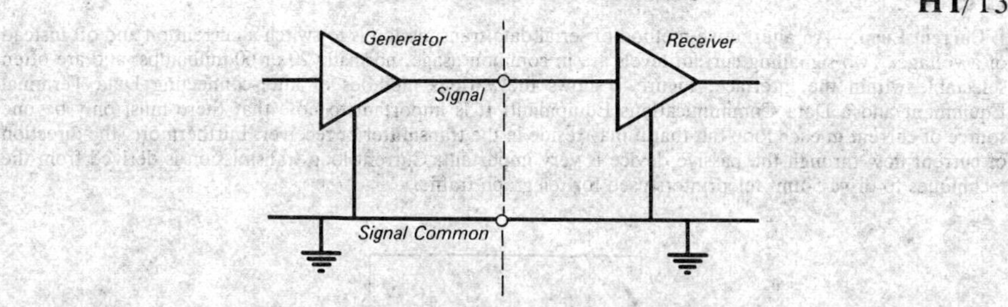

FIG. 4.—RS-232C Unbalanced Digital Interface Circuit.

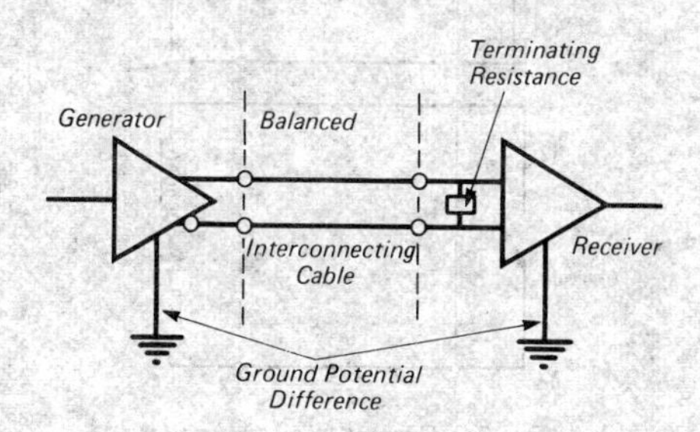

FIG. 5.—RS-422 Balanced Digital Interface Circuit.

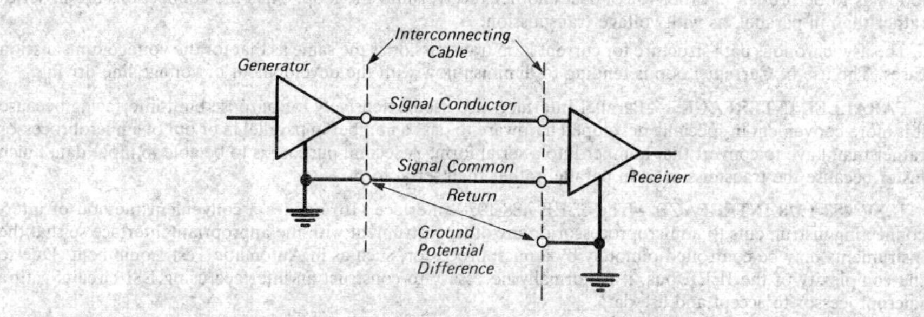

FIG. 6.—RS-423 Unbalanced Digital Interface Circuit.

EIA STANDARDS.—The American organisation, the Electrical Industries Association (EIA) has set 4 standards which are commonly used with microprocessors. RS-232C, RS-422, RS-422A, RS-423, RS-423A and RS-449 are tabulated in Table 3. Figures 4, 5 and 6 show the methods of interconnection for the various standards.

TABLE 3.—EIA STANDARDS

Standard	Max Baud Rate	Max Length (feet)	Transmission Type	Mark	Space	References
RS-232C	20 k	50	Unbalanced Voltage	−3 v −25 v	+3 v +25 v	10
RS-422	10 M 100 k	40 4000	Balanced Voltage	2–6 v diff		11, 12
RS-423	100 k 6k	30 1200	Unbalanced Voltage	200 mV diff		13, 14
RS-449	10 M		Balanced or Unbalanced			15

Current Loop.—An alternative method of serial data transmission is to switch a current on and off instead of a voltage. Two signalling current levels are in common usage, normally 20 or 60 milliamps, and are often selectable within the interface. Figure 7 shows the various methods of inter-connecting Data Terminal Equipment and a Data Communications Equipment. It is important to note that there must only be one source of current in each loop but that it may reside in the transmitter or receiver. Furthermore, the direction of current flow through the passive device is very important. Current loop transmission is derived from the techniques to drive 5-unit teleprinters used for telegraph traffic.

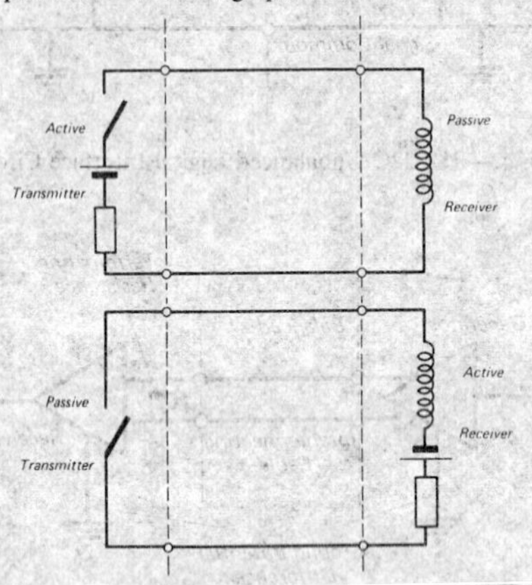

FIG. 7.—Current Loop Operation.

The use of more than one receiver with current loop transmission is made more difficult because the current loop has to be broken in order to connect another receiver into the loop. Thus the connections are in series rather than in parallel, as with voltage transmission.

The asynchronous data structure for current loop transmission is the same as that for the voltage transmission cases. The use of Current Loop is tending to diminish now with the development of voltage line driving.

PARALLEL INTERFACES.—Parallel Interfaces are used extensively for purpose built interfacing because it is more convenient in specially developed hardware to pass a number in parallel in or out of a microprocessor rather than have to convert that number into a serial form. A second purpose is to be able to input data much faster because the transmission is in parallel rather than serial form.

IEEE 488-1978 INTERFACE.—The IEEE 488-1978 Interface (16) defines a convenient method of inter-connecting instruments to a microprocessor or any other instrument with the appropriate interface so that the instruments may be controlled remotely by a microprocessor, such as in Automatic Test Equipment. Due to the complexity of the IEEE bus, it is normally necessary to construct an interface using LSI circuits with a microprocessor to accept and use data.

The following is not an exhaustive description of the IEEE bus but may serve as a simple reference source.

The IEEE 488-1978 interface bus standard, which was originally developed by Hewlett-Packard in 1968, is also described in an IEC standard (625-1) (17) and is variously known as the IEEE, IEC, General Purpose Interface Bus (GPIB), Hewlett-Packard Interface Bus (HPIB) and ASCII bus.

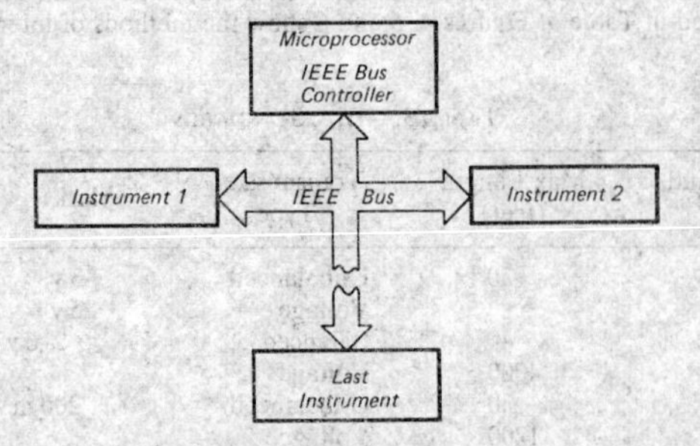

FIG. 8.—IEEE Bus System.

Up to 15 IEEE instruments (including the controller) can be connected to the bus at any one time. The limit is set by the electrical load introduced by each extra interface. The general arrangement of instruments is shown in Fig. 8. The maximum data rate achievable using an IEEE bus is dependent on the length of that bus. The standard defines that 1 Mbyte per second may be used with a bus of up to 6 m in length, but this rate is restricted to 250 kbyte per second for bus lengths up to 20 m, which is also the maximum recommended length for the bus. Thus the IEEE bus is very much a local link between instruments and cannot be considered as a means of linking very widely scattered instruments together.

An IEEE bus consists of 16 signal lines and 8 ground return lines.

The operation of the IEEE bus is controlled completely by the Controller, which assigns Talkers and Listeners as required by its program and answers service requests as appropriate to each instrument.

Apart from the 16 lines referred to by their 3 character mnemonics, there are a considerable number of command bytes referred to by trigraphs which can be sent over the bus for various purposes.

The properties of any IEEE 488 bus interface may be defined by Function Allowable Subsets, that is a list of the exact capabilities of the specified interface.

IEEE bus Handshake Lines.—The 3 handshake lines are DAV (Data Available), NRFD (Not Ready For Data) and NDAC (Not Data Accepted). The sequence of asserting and unasserting the handshake lines is shown in Fig. 9. The bus makes no distinction in the handshaking process for data or command bytes.

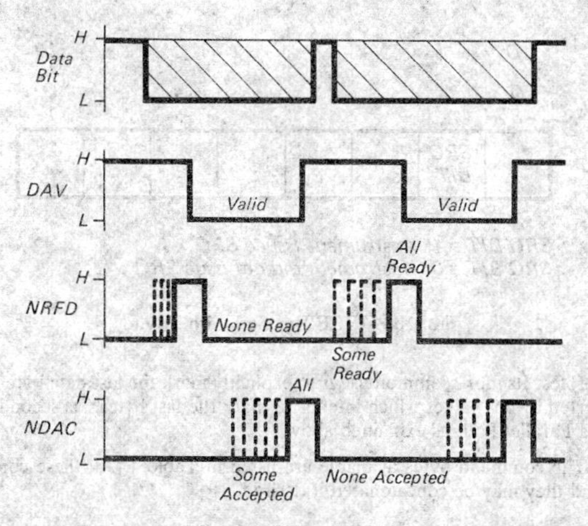

FIG. 9.—IEEE Bus Handshaking.

DAV.—The DAV line is asserted when a talker wants to send a byte but after NRFD line is unasserted, implying that a listener is ready to receive data.

NRFD.—NRFD is asserted whenever an instrument is not ready for data, which is normally just after it has accepted a data byte.

NDAC.—NDAC is asserted whenever an instrument is awaiting a byte.

IEEE bus Control Lines.—The 5 bus control lines are IFC (Interface Clear), REN (Remote Enable), ATN (Attention), EOI (End Or Identify) and SRQ (Service Request). The first 3 IEEE bus control lines are asserted by the controller only, EOI can be asserted by any talker (including the controller) to mark the last data byte being sent and also by the controller in conjunction with ATN during a parallel polling sequence. SRQ is asserted by any instrument requiring servicing by the controller.

IFC.—IFC is asserted by the controller to reset the IEEE bus interfaces in every instrument back to their initial conditions. Note that this is not the same as resetting the operation of the instrument which requires the command bytes DCL or SDC. When IFC is asserted all handshaking must cease and any talker relinquish that role together with every listener. Any service requests in progress must be cancelled. After IFC none of these conditions must continue until the controller assigns a Talker and more Listeners as required.

ATN.—The ATN line is used to alert every instrument that the byte being sent is a command byte and not a data byte. ATN must be asserted for the full duration of the transmission of any command bytes.

A second use of ATN is in association with EOI to achieve Parallel Polling of the instruments. (See EOI).

REN.—The REN line is used to control the Remote/Local operation of the instruments on the bus. The REN line does not have to be implemented on each instrument but when it is implemented then to gain remote control of an instrument REN has to be asserted and that instrument addressed once as a listener.

SRQ.—The SRQ line is asserted by one or more instruments simultaneously to inform the controller of some asynchronous external event with which they are involved, such as having data ready for transmission. The Controller monitors the SRQ line all the time and when it is asserted it Polls the bus to find out which instrument(s) issued the SRQ. In this respect the operation of the SRQ is analogous to a non-vectored interrupt. There are 2 methods to Poll the bus, Parallel Poll and Serial Poll.

PARALLEL POLLING.—Parallel Polling is a quick means of ascertaining which instrument or instruments issued the SRQ by a data line being assigned uniquely to each instrument capable of issuing SRQ either by hardware or software. In order to Parallel Poll, the ATN and EOI control lines are asserted simultaneously and the data lines read by the controller. A Serial Poll then has to be conducted to cause the instrument(s) to unassert SRQ and optionally acquire more data from that instrument on the cause of the SRQ. Action is then taken according to what asserted SRQ.

SERIAL POLLING.—Serial Polling has to be conducted on every instrument which has asserted SRQ because SRQ will only be removed by that instrument as a result of a Serial Poll. The command byte SPE (Serial Poll Enable) is sent first under ATN, the instrument set up as a talker and the controller as a listener. A single byte giving status information is then transferred from the instrument to the controller. The structure of that byte is shown in Fig. 10. If the seventh bit is set then that instrument asserted SRQ. The remaining bits can be used to convey user information. The Serial Poll is completed by the controller sending SPD (Serial Poll Disable) under ATN. The only information that can be returned when SPE has been issued are status bytes.

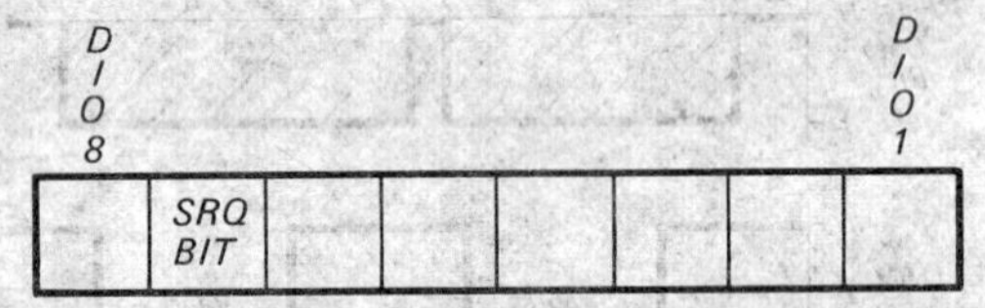

SRQ BIT = 1 Instrument Issued SRQ
SRQ BIT = 0 Instrument did not issue SRQ

Fig. 10.—IEEE Bus Serial Poll Byte.

The EOI line has 2 roles. Its more common use is to explicitly mark the last data byte being transferred and may therefore be asserted by any talker which intends to mark the last bytes. Its second use is in conjunction with ATN to initiate a Parallel Poll, as explained above.

Command Bytes.—The command bytes available are listed in Table 4. All these command bytes are sent with ATN asserted and they may be concatenated if desired.

Table 4.—IEEE Command Bytes

Mnemonic		DIO 8	7	6	5	4	3	2	DIO 1	Oct	Hex
DCL	Device Clear	0	0	0	1	0	1	0	0	24	14
GET	Group Execute Trigger	0	0	0	0	1	0	0	0	10	8
GTL	Go To Local	0	0	0	0	0	0	0	1	1	1
LLO	Local Lockout	0	0	0	1	0	0	0	1	21	11
MLA	My Listen Address	0	0	1	L	L	L	L	L	40 + L	20 + L
MTA	My Talk Address	0	1	0	T	T	T	T	T	100 + T	40 + T
MSA	My Secondary Address	0	1	1	S	S	S	S	S	140 + S	60 + S
PPC	Parallel Poll Configure	0	0	0	0	0	1	0	1	5	5
PPE	Parallel Poll Enable	1	1	1	0	S	P	P	P		
PPD	Parallel Poll Disable	1	1	1	1	D	D	D	D		
PPU	Parallel Poll Unconfigure	0	0	0	1	0	1	0	1	25	15
SDC	Selected Device Clear	0	0	0	0	0	1	0	0	4	4
SPD	Serial Poll Disable	0	0	0	1	1	0	0	1	31	19
SPE	Serial Poll Enable	0	0	0	1	1	0	0	0	30	18
UNL	Unlisten	0	0	1	1	1	1	1	1	77	3F
UNT	Untalk	0	1	0	1	1	1	1	1	137	5F

MICROPROCESSOR OPERATION

A Microprocessor (and indeed any computer) operates by executing a list of stored instructions. The method of interpreting and implementing these instructions has already been described. However it is necessary to explain the purpose of the different basic sorts of instruction in order to understand their programming at the lowest level.

INSTRUCTION EXECUTION.—Each instruction in a microprocessor occupies one or more contiguous memory locations. The current instruction is pointed to by the Program Counter.

In order to execute an instruction it must first be fetched from memory, then decoded to find out what is required, any OPERANDs fetched and the operation required actually performed, and concluded by storing away any OPERANDs as necessary. (Fig 11.) The period needed to complete the execution of an instruction is called an Instruction Cycle.

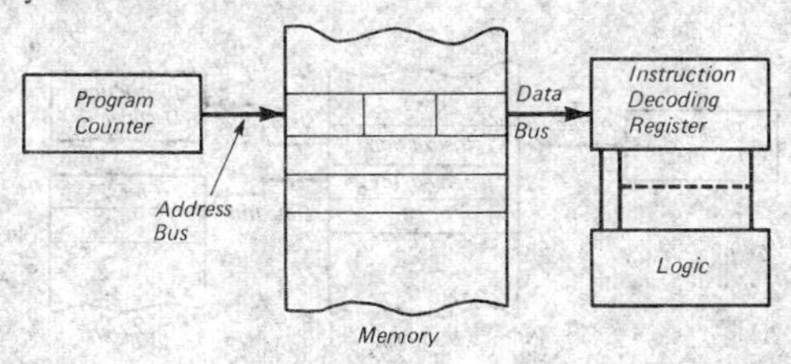

FIG. 11.—Fetch Phase.

Thus there are 2 phases in an Instruction Cycle, the Fetch Phase and the Execution Phase. The Fetch Phase collects the instruction from the address pointed to by the Program Counter and decodes the instruction. The Execution Phase fetches the OPERANDs by the specified addressing mode and operates upon them.

The Fetching and Execution Phases require a number of Machine Cycles, depending on the type of instruction and the method of addressing. Thus the duration of different instructions, or of the same instruction with different addressing modes will vary making the calculation of the exact time to execute a specified sequence of instructions very tedious to calculate. Within each Machine Cycle the microprocessor is normally required to progress through a number of operations, or States, whose duration is controlled by the clock period chosen.

INSTRUCTION ORGANISATION.—An instruction in a microprocessor can take up one or more words (8 or 16 bit), with the first word being the instruction proper and the succeeding words being OPERANDs (that is addresses or numerical values). (Fig 12.) The number of bits needed to fully specify an instruction and the location(s) and values to be used very often exceed the length of one word, and it is then easier to organise the instructions to have a first word to specify the basic operation and the way to treat the OPERANDs, followed by as many words as necessary for the OPERANDs themselves. Normally, no more than 3 words are necessary in a 16-bit microprocessor. From the instruction type, the microprocessor instruction decoder has to deduce the total number of words in order to advance the program counter to point to the next instruction after executing the present one.

The bits going to make up the instruction are divided into notional fields, that is different groups of bits are treated differently.

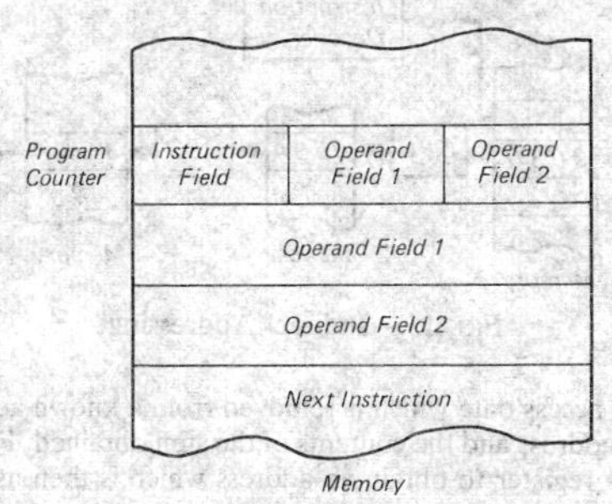

FIG. 12.—Instruction Storage.

Instruction Field.—The Instruction field contains the OPERATION CODE (or OP CODE). This OP CODE is required to operate on one or more OPERANDs. The OPERAND specifies the register or memory location required and the method of addressing. Accumulator based machines use the accumulator as an implied

OPERAND. The number of bits reserved for the OP CODE defines the number of basic types of instructions available in a microprocessor.

OPERAND FIELD(S).—The OPERAND Field(s) specify which objects are to be operated upon by defining a register or a value as well as specifying the method of addressing. The OPERANDs themselves normally are stored after the instruction word.

Addressing Mode. The following examples show the various methods of addressing a data source, the destination always being a register in these examples. However, all these methods are equally applicable to accessing destinations. Hexadecimal numbers are used.

Data may be accessed either by reference to a register, or by a combination of the 4 basic methods of addressing, REGISTER REFERENCE, ABSOLUTE, INDIRECT and INDEXED ADDRESSING.

Reference to a Register is shown in figure 13 where a numerical value (3A16) held as an OPERAND and is moved to a register.

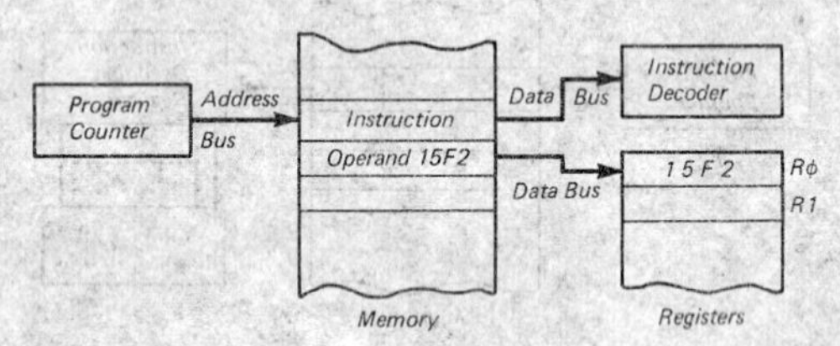

FIG. 13.—Data Transfer.

Absolute addressing is shown in figure 14 where a numerical value (30) is held as an OPERAND used as an address which is accessed and the contents (21A5) moved to a register.

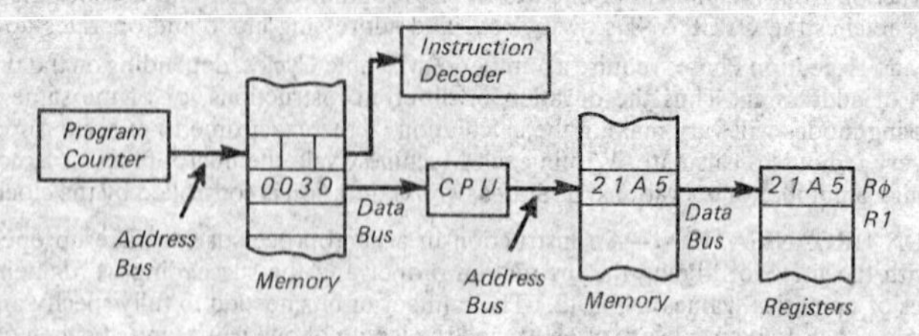

FIG. 14.—Absolute Addressing.

Indirect Addressing is used to access data through a known address which could be stored in a register or in another memory location which is known about by the program in the microprocessor. Figure 15 shows an OPERAND being used as an address which is then assessed to obtain the address of the required entity, which is in turn accessed and moved to a register.

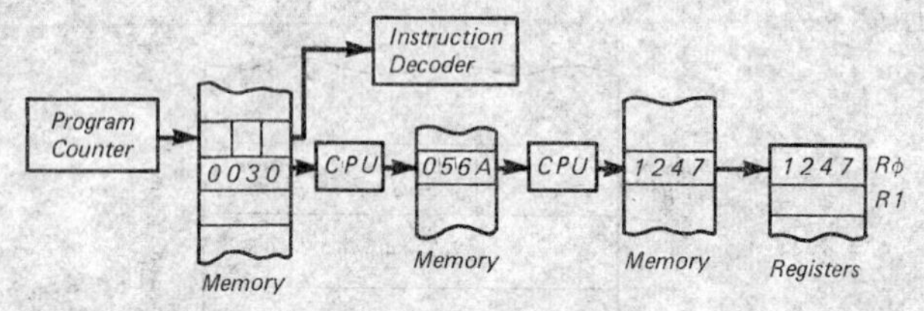

FIG. 15.—Indirect Addressing.

Indexed Addressing is used to access data which is removed from a known address by a known offset. Thus the index is added to the known address and the contents of the sum obtained. Figure 16 shows an OPERAND being added to the contents of a register to obtain an address which is then used to access the data which is moved to a register.

Note that this addition process is implied in the one instruction and does not have to be written out as a sequence of instructions by the programmer. This method is used to access arrays of data.

It is permissable to use Indirect and Indexed addressing in the one instruction. (Fig. 17.)

Auto-Incrementing and Auto-Decrementing are means of automatically incrementing or decrementing the

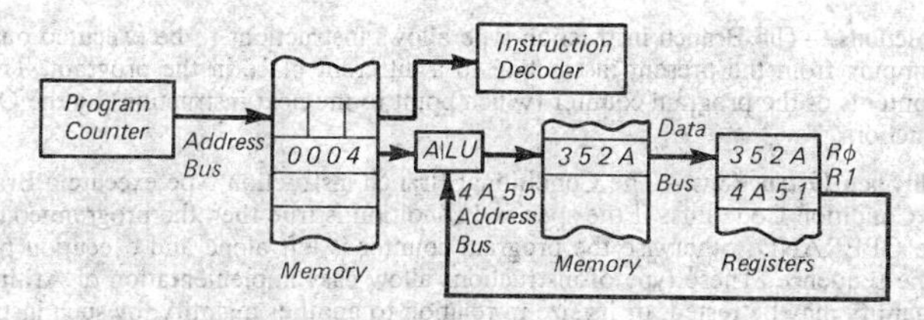

FIG. 16.—Indexed Addressing.

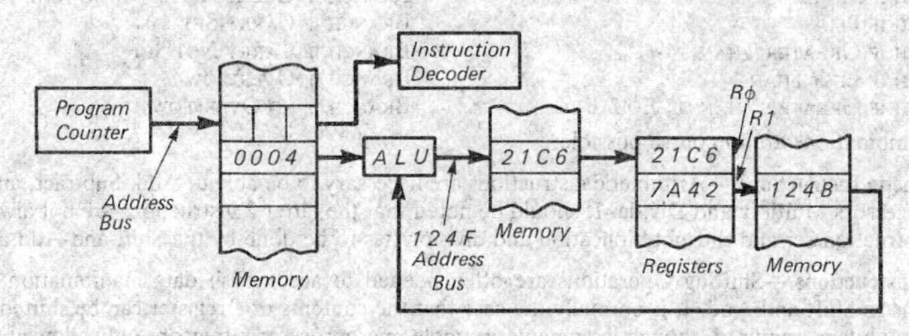

FIG. 17.—Inirect and Indexed Addressing.

address stored in a register. Thus if an address is being used to point to an array of data, this address may be incremented (or decremented) automatically by choosing the appropriate instruction and without the need for a separate instruction to operate on the address. Thus either before or after the execution of the instruction (depending on the microprocessor in use) the address stored in a memory location or register is incremented or decremented by one. If an instruction set incorporates this instruction then one complete instruction is saved every time incrementing or decrementing is used.

A Single Source OPERAND is used when the purpose of an instruction is to modify the contents of one register or memory location by Clearing, Incrementing, Decrementing it, etc. The Source OPERAND must specify the addressing mode to be employed.

Source/Destination. A Source OPERAND is used to specify a register, along with the addressing mode, or a value from which to obtain data for the OP CODE to operate upon before returning that data to the Destination. This type of instruction is very useful when executing arithmetic and boolean instructions, but is restricted to 16 or 32 bit microprocessors.

Two Source and Destination. A Two Source and Destination OPERAND is used to specify 2 registers or values from which to obtain data for the OP CODE to operate upon before returning that data to the Destination and is restricted to the few 32 bit microprocessors.

CONDITION CODES.—A Condition Code is a pattern of bits which are adjusted whenever a numerical quantity if operated upon in any way. The number of bits and their exact meaning depends on the manufacturer. However, there are often Condition Code bits with the following meanings:

Carry Bit	Detects when the carry bit is set
Sign Bit	Detects positive or negative
Zero Bit	Detects zero
Overflow Bit	Detects numerical overflow

INSTRUCTION TYPES

MOVE.—The MOVE type of instruction is implemented in one of 2 ways, depending on whether the microprocessor is accumulator or register orientated. Thus in an Accumulator based microprocessor the MOVE instruction only allows data to be transferred to or from memory. Often, different OP CODES are used to specify whether the Accumulator or one of the other registers (such as an address register) is to be used. INDIRECT and/or INDEXED addressing may be used. Thus MOVE operations between 2 memory locations are not possible directly and require the data to be copied to the accumulator before being written to another memory location.

In a register orientated microprocessor only one MOVE type OP CODE is used to give register to register transfers, memory to register transfers (and the reverse), and memory to memory transfers. INDIRECT and/or INDEXED addressing may be used. This technique is more versatile and is used in all the latest microprocessors.

Branch Instructions.—The Branch instruction type allows instructions to be executed out of their storage sequence by jumping from the present instruction to a different place in the program. This is achieved by replacing the ~~contents of the~~ program counter (which point to the next instruction) by the OPERAND of the branching instruction.

Conditional Branch Instructions.—The Conditional Branch instruction type execute a Branch as the result of a test of the Condition Code bits. If the specified condition is true then the program counter contents are replaced by the OPERAND, otherwise the program counter is left alone and execution passes to the next instruction in the sequence. These type of instructions allow easy implementation of Arithmetic tests. Thus the sign of a quantity may be tested, or its size in relation to another quantity, by such instructions as:

BRANCH IF ZERO
BRANCH IF MINUS
BRANCH IF PLUS
BRANCH IF GREATER THAN
BRANCH IF LESS THAN
BRANCH IF GREATER THAN OR EQUAL TO
BRANCH IF LESS THAN OR EQUAL TO
BRANCH IF GREATER THAN OR EQUAL TO
BRANCH IF CARRY SET
BRANCH IF CARRY NOT SET
BRANCH IF OVERFLOW
BRANCH IF NO OVERFLOW

Other combinations are of course possible.

Arithmetic Instructions.—Arithmetic instructions are necessary to be able to Add, Subtract, and with some microprocessors Multiply and Divide. It should be noted that the latter 2 instructions are not always included in the instruction set and thus multiplication and division has to be done by the Shift-and-Add algorithm.

Shift Instructions.—Shifting Operations are often needed to accomplish data manipulation and in such algorithms as Shift-and-Add. It is normally the case that the contents of a register can be shifted left or right by as many bits as required, though in some very simple microprocessors they are only allowed to be shifted one bit at a time. The register contents may also be rotated, that is the MSB is shifted into the LSB or vice-versa depending on the direction of rotation. The operations can often be performed on Double length words as well.

Boolean Logic Instructions.—Boolean Logic Instructions are needed to manipulate bit patterns within data words and they consist of instructions to INVERT, 2's COMPLEMENT, AND, INCLUSIVE-OR and EXCLUSIVE-OR the specified OPERAND. The Boolean Logic functions may be defined by means of truth tables where A and B are binary inputs and R is the output thus (Table 5).

TABLE 5. TRUTH TABLES

A	B	R (AND)	R (INC-OR)	R (EX-OR)
0	0	0	0	0
0	1	0	1	1
1	0	0	1	1
1	1	1	1	0

If a great number of bit manipulations are expected to be needed then care should be taken to select a microprocessor with a sophisticated enough instruction set to handle the requirement in the specified time.

MAPPING.—Mapping is a technique whereby a number of separated areas of memory are made to appear as one contiguous block of memory by using Mapping Registers. (Fig 18.) In order to make Mapping work

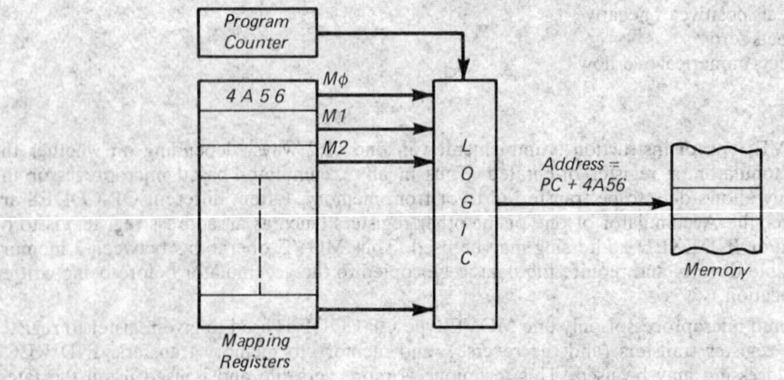

FIG. 18.—Mapping Register Operation.

efficiently at least 8 Mapping Registers are needed. Each register is assigned a particular role within a program so that the different parts of the program automatically access the correct memory locations by the relative address in the program being translated by the Mapping Hardware using the values in the appropriate register.

SOFTWARE HANDLING OF INTERRUPTS.—An interrupt is used to inform the program software within a microprocessor of the need to respond to an external event, and is generated in response to that external event.

Software Polling works well for a small number of separate interfaces, but if the number of interfaces requiring servicing is increased the microprocessor must spend more of its time just checking to see if there is work to do. Furthermore, because of the sequential action of polling there are delays before interfaces are serviced which can well be unacceptable.

If vectored interrupts are used in a microprocessor, then the need to check each interface periodically is removed. (See above). However, it is necessary to fill the Vector Location with the address to which the processor is to jump on receipt of a Vectored Interrupt. If an interface is not required then it is normal to fill its Vector Locations with dummy entry points in order that Unsolicited Interrupts from that interface can be ignored.

Interrupts divide into 2 classes, solicited interrupts and unsolicited interrupts. An alternative method of responding to external events is to include code in the microprocessor to poll every possible interface in case anything needs to be output or input.

Solicited Interrupts.—Solicited Interrupts are expected by the microprocessor and are generated by a microprocessor interface whenever data has to be passed into or out of the interface as a result of a previous operation. Thus, if a string of characters is to be printed on a terminal then the microprocessor software will be aware of this in the sense that it has set up an array of bytes to be output and merely awaits each interrupt in order to know when to send each byte. When data is to be input through an interface, Solicited Interrupts can occur for example as a response to a question. Thus the microprocessor will be expecting characters to be input through the interface.

Unsolicited Interrupts.—Unsolicited Interrupts are clearly not expected by the microprocessor but must nevertheless be handled correctly. Thus characters typed on a terminal, but not in response to a question, are unsolicited and require careful handling.

BOOTSTRAPPING.—Bootstrapping is a necessary technique to allow a microprocessor to start executing software, and is in itself a very simple program. Thus if a disk based microprocessor development system were started then its first operation would be to read a predefined track from a predetermined disk drive. The contents of that disk track would be loaded into memory as it is being read and control transferred to that code in memory. Thus a very simple program has been just sufficient to read a more complicated program from the disk, and this program in turn will read down the operating system of the development system. Thus the microprocessor can be said to have pulled itself up by its own bootstraps.

DOWN-LINE LOADING.—Down-line loading is a method of passing a program into a target microprocessor from a host computer (or microprocessor) and setting that program running. It assumes that the target microprocessor is capable of automatically starting and running a short program to accept data down the line and store it correctly, then to recognise the end of data (by counting the data entities – words or bytes) as they are received and to start executing this fresh code.

One possible use of this technique is in the rapid testing of new versions of programs. However, it relies on the target microprocessor already running a down-line loading bootstrap which in itself may be a not insignificant program. However, this technique avoids the need to program a new set of PROMs for each program revision.

Down-Line loading may also be used to allow the one target microprocessor to run several totally different programs.

PROGRAMMING MICROPROCESSORS

The programming of microprocessors is described in general and is not to restricted to any particular programming language. The appropriate software manuals should be consulted to understand the rules of any particular language. The constructions to be found in programming languages in general are described in order to give a clear overall picture of program preparation. The software is described generally and should not be taken as applying exactly to any particular programming language as there are always variations from the rule.

A microprocessor is designed to execute a list of instructions generally stored as binary numbers. To prepare this list, these instructions could be calculated directly by a human being and stored in sequential memory by one of the techniques previously described. However, it is far more efficient and far easier to use that microprocessor or a similar machine to calculate the exact instructions needed and let the human being specify the operation. Thus the first level of simplification for the programmer is to use a symbolic assembler so that the required instructions can be written without having to worry about the actual binary pattern required. The next programming level is to use a compiler which converts instructions written in a stylised language either directly into machine instructions or into mnemonic instructions ready for assembly. This again eases the programming operation. These higher level languages are based normally on English.

In general, the lower the level of software tools used then the higher is the skill required from the programmer. The higher the level of programming adopted then the more rapidly can the program be written. Furthermore, a high level program should be easier to understand. However, it is quite often necessary to write parts of programs in assembly language.

It is not always possible to write every program using a high level language. Thus if speed of execution has to be maximised or if a complicated Input/Output program (a driver or handler) has to be written then the programmer must resort to the assembly language of the microprocessor concerned. There is no advantage in writing these sort of operations in machine code as the complete instructions may be exactly specified at an assembly level.

PROGRAMMING DEFINITIONS

File Structure.—The creation of the various programs described hereafter depends on the availability and use of a development system. Such a system will have some sort of mass storage device on which all the files are kept. The naming of files is very important and inevitably depends on the nature of the operating system being run on the development system. If a generic file naming structure is available then the Source, Object, List, Map, Binary and any other associated files can all have the same generic name, differing only in their file name extensions.

Source Program.—A Source Program or Source Code normally consists of a sequence of statements arranged according to the syntactic rules of the particular language to be used. The Source Program is created on the development computer or microprocessor either by direct entry into a disk file or by using a text editor to achieve the same end. The latter is a simpler option as it allows any errors (beyond simple rubbing out) to be corrected then and there. The content of the Source Program is entirely up to the programmer.

If the chosen programming language is interpretative then the only other operation required is to Run the program (see below). If not then the Source Code must be submitted to an assembler or compiler to produce an Object Program.

Object Program.—An Object Program consists of one or more Object Modules which contain all the necessary instructions and sub-program calls to execute the Source Program statements and may be capable of running as they stand, though the Object Program normally contains unresolved references, that is calls to sub-programs which are not contained within the Object Program itself. The calls to sub-programs may be the result of statements in the Source Program and duly compiled, but may also be derived from the calls produced by the compiler to standard sub-programs contained in an Object Library in order to execute the high level commands.

The compiler will have constructed the Object Program to call as many standard Object Modules as possible. However it is not the job of the compiler to resolve the references by including the Object Modules of these sub-programs in the Object Program. To achieve this they must be 'Linked' to the Object program.

Object Libraries.—The facility to convert an Object Module or collection modules into an Object Library is provided as part of some development systems and is often called a Librarian. The purpose of a Librarian is to make each Object Module available separately for Linking so that only those modules that are actually required will be linked which helps to reduce the size of the Binary Program. Without this facility most Linkers will link all the Object Modules in an Object Program irrespective of whether they are called by anything or not.

Linking.—Linking is the process of combining many different Object Modules or Object Libraries into one executable program, at the same time resolving all references. It is sometimes known as Loading or Task Building. If an Object Library has been created then the Binary Program resulting from Linking will be no larger than is absolutely necessary.

Furthermore, Linking an Object Library is normally slightly quicker than an Object Program which has to be scanned to find out its contents whereas the Library contains an index. Normally, Main Programs cannot be turned into Libraries because there is no advantage as it consists of only one Object Module.

The Linking Process on a development system normally has the facility to create a Map of the Binary Program so that the various elements which go to make up that Binary Program can be 'found' in memory at run time when debugging the program.

Binary Program.—A Binary Program is constructed by the Linker to contain all the Object Modules from the specified Object Programs and some or all of the Object Modules from the specified Object Libraries. These various Modules may come in any mixture from standard Libraries written by the manufacturer or from user written libraries.

Program Installation.—The process of actually running a Binary Program appears simple but in a development system involves the executive reading it down from a mass storage device into memory and then starting its execution.

PROGRAM EDITING

Source Text Editing.—The process of Source Text Editing is the method used to correct and augment a Source Program before re-submitting it to a compiler as well as being the method normally used to create the Source Program. The operation of a Source Text Editor depends entirely on the make, type and operating system of the microprocessor development system in use. However, it is found in practice that a VDU based editor is much quicker ano easier to use because the cursor may be used to point to the exact position in the text where the next operation is to be performed.

Object Library Editing.—Object Library Editing is quite different from Source Text Editing because it involves the addition, removal or replacement of one or more Object Modules from an Object Library. It is therefore often to be found as a facility within a Librarian program.

PROGRAMMING LANGUAGES

Machine Code Programming.—At the lowest level a microprocessor may be programmed at the Machine Code level. This is generally possible on all computers and not just microprocessors by using microcoded Debug and Trace programs permanently resident in the computer. It is also possible on computers with display panels to program them directly from the front panel.

Machine Code programming involves calculating manually the exact binary pattern needed in each sequential location of the program memory space. This is very tedious and an extremely inefficent programming method. It is made more complicated by the Branching Instructions because the exact range of the branch has to be calculated and will be changed if instructions within the branching range are added or taken away from the list. Thus program modification of any kind is very difficult. With Machine Code Instructions any specific instructions which need to be directly accessed as in Branching must have their addresses carefully calculated manually.

Symbolic Assembler.—A Symbolic Assembler is used to overcome the disadvantages of Machine Code Programming and is available for every standard type of microprocessor. Mnemonics are used to represent Machine Code Instructions and addresses and are interpreted by the Assembler. Furthermore, because mnemonics can be used for addresses (that is for labels) with which to refer to specific instructions there is no need to calculate their absolute addresses. Thus Branching and Jumping become much easier, particularly when the program is modified, because the Assembler calculates the actual address for the particular instruction required. This makes the job of program writing much easier.

The purpose of the Assembler is to parse every statement line and extract every mnemonic and then interpret the meaning of that statement. The assembler then has to create the actual machine instruction required from a look-up table.

This type of object code produced depends very heavily on the make of microprocessor and the purpose for which the code is being created. However, there are a number of capabilities which are generally available.

RELOCATABLE CODE is the normal output of most assemblers and consists of instructions referencing one anothers addresses in relation to their own position. Thus the actual address that the code is to run at can be decided at Linking time or in some cases postponed until the actual running of the program.

RESERVED PROGRAM AREAS are used to separate data from code and from other data. Thus a program may be assembled to allow the code to be run anywhere and any data areas to be allocated later. The programming of an EPROM becomes much easier if the code is separated from the data.

RE-ENTRANT CODE is used as a means to make the same set of instructions able to be executed by more than one program, but not necessarily synchronously. This is often used when a number of identical external processes have to run separately, thereby requiring identical internal processes which would be very wasteful of memory if large portions could not be shared. In the case of using Re-Entrant Code it is necessary to separate the constants and variables very carefully and to keep the constants in memory but the variables referenced through the stack. This process is fairly easy to manage in a high level language.

Re-entrant code is best used with a multitasking operating system. Thus two programs may share any common sub-programs quite independently. Although the program code in the sub-programs are identical, the separate programs have different stacks and when a task is not being executed, the registers are stored within the program. Hence the programs and the sub-programs may be picked up and dropped without affecting one another.

Re-Entrant Code also requires a special and formalised method for calling the sub-program. Thus the current Program Counter and Stack pointer values must be stored on the stack before calling the Re-Entrant Sub-program and restored again after completing execution. The exact technique for achieving this in a particular microprocessor depends on the instructions available in that microprocessor.

Macro Assembler.—A Macro Assembler contains all the facilities of a normal Symbolic Assembler together with the ability to recognise a string within the Source program as a pseudonym for some previously declared set of instruction(s). This facility can be used to improve the readibility of an Assembler list file, but its most important advantage is that by careful construction of the Macros themselves, a complete operation requiring a number of instructions may be included using a single unique reference which is much easier to follow. Furthermore, by using Macros it is sometimes possible to write a cross-assembler for another microprocessor without actually having to write a native assembler. Thus if a special purpose microprocessor is being developed, perhaps using a chip set, an assembler may be constructed reasonably quickly using any readily available microprocessor development system.

Dis-assembly.—It is sometimes necessary to reverse the process of assembly or compilation and this may be done by using a Dis-assembler. Any Object Module may be returned to its equivalent assembler level source text by this process, but without any comments of course. Furthermore, the assembler level program labels are assigned arbitrary titles.

This process may be used to convert the Object program from a high level compiler back to its Assembly level equivalent in order that the exact technique chosen by the compiler to implement a particular set of statements can be deduced. This can be very useful in checking logical errors, particularly if a compiler error is suspected. However, such a technique should be used with caution because the output of a compiler is very often highly stylised and difficult to follow.

Cross-Assemblers.—Cross-Assemblers are designed to assemble the program for a specific microprocessor on a machine of a different type and/or make, which is very often a Mini-computer or a Mainframe computer. This technique has some advantages if a special purpose microprocessor is to be used for which a development system is not conveniently available. It is nevertheless a complicated and time consuming operation as the code to actually run in the target microprocessor has to be extracted from the host development computer by (perhaps) programming EPROMS, or by Down-Line Loading.

Higher Level Languages.—A High Level Language can be used to speed program development because it is easier to formulate a complicated set of statements for the microprocessor to execute and let the compiler determine how to implement these statements at instruction level. It is generally true that the efficiency of the Object Code produced by a compiler is not quite as high as could be achieved by a good programmer writing in the assembly language of that microprocessor, but it takes considerably less time to develop and debug using the high level language, perhaps one third of the time.

The second virtue of a High Level Language is portability, that is the ability to develop and test the program on one make and/or type of microprocessor but run it on another make and/or type. Although this is a useful property of a High Level Language it should be approached with caution because a great number of programs, particularly on microprocessors, are very machine dependent and the transferring of a program to another make and/or type of microprocessor can be difficult.

A Source Program in a high level language is converted into an Object Program by using a compiler which produces the required list of machine instructions. However, the higher level language also imposes a structure on the required instructions which may not yield the fastest possible method for achieving the desired aim which can be a serious disadvantage in time critical applications.

A complication of using a higher level language is the need to submit the Source code to the compiler for even the most minor of changes.

COMPILER.—A Compiler is used to convert a Source Program written in a high level language into an Object Program. The speed and complexity of such a compiler depends entirely on the nature of the high level language, though the block structured languages (such as PASCAL and CORAL) take longer to compile than the unstructured languages.

The Object Code output of a Compiler normally has the same format as that output from an Assembler. There is normally a List File output available from a compiler which contains a complete copy of the Source Program with a number of useful annotations and any syntactic errors marked. The List File is normally used during program development for reference to the Source Program as it contains more information, though it is the Source Program which is edited and compiled.

CROSS-COMPILERS are the high level language equivalent to cross-assemblers.

OPTIMISING COMPILERS.—Certain high level language compilers (such as CORAL) often include optional optimisation so that the Object code produced will be executed in the minimum possible time. This facility is particularly useful when writing programs for real time operation.

Interpretative Languages.—In order to overcome the delays involved in editing and compiling a source program an Interpretative Language may be used (such as BASIC). In such a language each statement is analysed and if syntactically correct is interpreted into machine instructions directly. The process of interpretation involves parsing the whole statement and organising the calls to the correct sub-programs as well as retrieving the correct data to actually execute the statement.

Furthermore, even if the statement lies within a loop it will be interpreted every time it is encountered rather than being interpreted once and for all. Thus interpretation takes far longer to run a program and the time taken is far from the minimum necessary on any particular type of microprocessor. However, a great deal of time can be saved in debugging a program because the time taken waiting for a compilation and linking is avoided. It is sometimes the case that a compiler is available as a substitute for the interpreter so that when the program has been thoroughly debugged in its interpretative form it can be compiled, thereby vastly increasing the speed of execution.

Most Interpretative Languages have their own mechanism for entering and editing their Source Code and do not rely on the methods used for compiler/assembler languages.

PROGRAM ELEMENTS

Data Storage.—In order to store an entity in a computer memory and be able to retrieve it using a high level language it is necessary to use '*Variables*'. Variables are used by a compiler to give a name to a particular location or set of locations in memory, and whenever that variable is referenced in the source program then it implies a reference to that particular entity. By this technique the programmer is freed from concern about the exact positioning of the entity in memory. This is particularly useful as for many operations it is immaterial where a particular value is stored, rather it is the contents of the address that matters. '*Constants*' are normally treated as a special case of a variable that needs only to be read.

Variable names normally consist of alphanumeric sequences of characters with the first character being alphabetic, which is simply to make it easier for the statement parser in the compiler to recognise the sequence of characters as a variable rather than a simple number.

In order to handle a sequence of related variables an '*Array*' is used which consists of a block of contiguous memory locations. Any element may be indexed, that is accessed separately, by a scheme of calculating the offset from the base address of the array and reading from or writing to that location. The speed of accessing any particular location in an array depends on the power of the instructions in a given microprocessor. However, operating on an array element is bound to be somewhat slower than operating on a simple variable because the offset has to be calculated and added to the base address of the array.

High level languages implement accessing of array elements by requiring the programmer to specify the array name and index value. The exact address required is calculated by code inserted by the compiler.

In general, arrays must have dimensions to specify their size so that sufficient storage may be allocated to that array and not overlap with another array except by deliberate design.

Most of the high level language compilers are capable of handling 2-dimensional arrays, and some can handle 3-dimensional arrays, but access to any particular array element is even slower.

Declarations.—In general, it is necessary to inform the compiler, assembler or interpreter of the nature of each type of variable and array to be used in a program, as well as the size of each array. This is so that the correct number of bytes can be reserved for storage of that variable and the correct type of arithmetic used when operating on it. Many languages reserve certain types of variable name for certain types of variable and hence declarations are by default (such as FORTRAN). It is also true that the block structured languages require far more careful declaration but scoping (see below) is a protection against the accidental reuse of the same variable.

Keywords.—A Keyword in a high-level language has a specific meaning, and is either an alphabetic string reserved for special use or appears in parentheses. The Keywords are recognised by the compiler and the statement translated into instructions.

Labels.—Labels are used in all non-block structured languages (and are available in most block structured languages) to act as a convenient way of marking a particular point in the program, for instance by allowing the program to jump back and repeat a section. A Label normally consists of a string of alphanumeric characters (like a variable) and delimited (often by a colon).

Although Labels provide a very simple means to organise the flow of a program, their use can cause considerable problems because of the ability to jump absolutely anywhere in the program which can cause obscure errors.

Statements.—A program in a high level language is made up of statements which in turn consist of the required mixture of Labels, Keywords and Variable names which are used to specify the operations. The statements are recognised by the compiler in order to operate on the data specified.

Main Programs.—The purpose of a main program is to organise the logical flow of the problem being programmed. This is achieved by executing statements and calling sub-programs.

Sub-programs.—Sub-programs are variously known as Subroutines or Procedures depending on the high level language being used. The simplest purpose of a Sub-program is to allow a collection of statements which need to be executed more than once to be repeated without having to repeat all those statements themselves. If a program is written which deliberately misses out opportunities to use Sub-programs then it is said to use In-Line programming. Sub-programs may also be used to clarify the operation being performed, that is for the purposes of improving the program structure.

Sub-Program Calling.—The execution of a Sub-program may be started by calling it from the Main Program or another Sub-program. The successive calling of Sub-programs by other Sub-programs is an example of nesting and requires a carefully constructed and stylised calling sequence. It is normally the case in modern microprocessors that Sub-program calls may be nested to any depth limited only by the maximum size of the Binary Program.

Dummy Arguments.—Sub-programs do not have to be used with exactly the same data every time they are called unless all the data they use is in common memory and thus shared by the calling program and the called sub-program. However, sharing all the data for a Sub-program in common memory is not good programming practice because it is difficult to be certain that values used and modified in one Sub-program are not being modified somewhere else in the Program, perhaps by accident. Instead, dummy arguments are used when specifying the Sub-program in the Source text and they are equated to actual values when the program is running and the Sub-program is called. Thus the same Sub-program may be called many times with changing values for each argument. Dummy arguments are also known as Parameters (ALGOL, CORAL).

Dummy arguments may have various number types and be numerical values or variables. Alternatively, they may be arrays of various number types. It is possible to pass a variable as an argument in one of several ways.

PASSING BY VALUE.—The value of a variable may be passed into a sub-program by copying that value onto the stack along with any other arguments and calling the Sub-program. The value is then available in the Sub-program but if it is changed it only affects the value as it appears in the Sub-program. The external value of the variable remains unchanged because the Sub-program did not have access to the address where the actual variable was stored and could not therefore modify the actual variable value.

PASSING BY ADDRESS.—The address of the variable may be passed into a sub-program as a argument on the stack and in this case any change made to the value of the variable from within the Sub-program will change the external value of that variable.

These two alternatives may be used to advantage in keeping a good program structure. It should be noted that not every language supports the option to pass variables by value (such as FORTRAN).

Functions.—It is possible for Sub-programs to be designed to return a value that may be regarded as a mathematical function operating on the input arguments. This is useful in many applications, not just in mathematical programs and such sub-programs are called Functions or Typed Procedures.

It is a prerequisite of Functions that the result of the operations on the arguments is a single value (be it a byte, integer, floating point number or whatever). This value could be returned as the new value of an argument but for Functions this value is better returned as the apparent value of the Sub-program. In reality the value is returned in a register (normally). Some languages require a Function to have at least one argument, but the more recent languages have removed this constraint.

Common Data Areas.—Common data areas may be used within a program to hold any amount of data which has to be accessed by many different Sub-programs, or to hold constants needed throughout the program. A further use of Common Data Areas is to allow different Object Programs linked together into one Binary Program to share data. The Linking process will check for Common Data Areas with the same name and only insert one Common Data Area in the final Binary Program. (see Fig. 19)

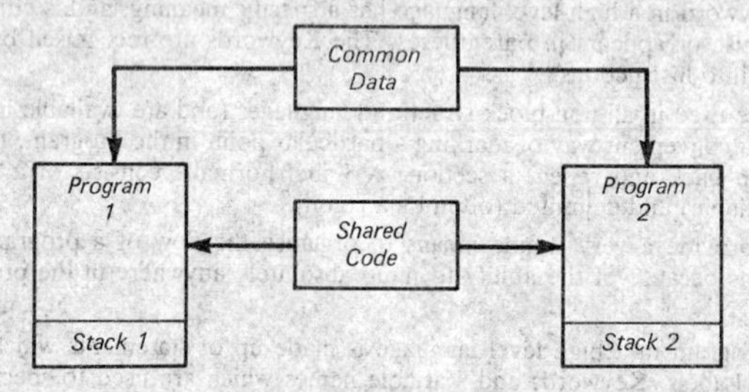

FIG. 19.—Data and Code Sharing.

Shared Data Areas.—Shared Data Areas in a program are a convenient method of treating the same contiguous locations as representing different number types, or of one array offset from another but accessing the same data. Such a technique is variously known as Overlaying (CORAL) and Equivalence (FORTRAN).

Comments.—It is normal practice to include comments in the Source program to clarify the various stages. These comments are not assembled, compiled or interpreted, as the case may be, because they are only there for the benefit of other programmers. Each statement in the source program in a high level language can be commented though this is not always necessary. However, each statement of an assembly level source program should contain a comment in the appropriate place, which is often at the end of the line, as well as comments before any significant operation.

PROGRAM DEVELOPMENT

Program development should proceed in a number of well defined steps.

Functional Specification.—The functional specification for the microprocessor program should be drawn up before the program for that microprocessor is written otherwise the capabilities of that program when written will generate more requirements and the programming will be poorly structured and take a long time.

In order to write a program at Assembler level or higher, the first stage is to create the 'Source Program' or 'Source Code'.

Coding and Desk Checking.—The program code should be written by hand and checked on paper before being typed up on a Microprocessor Development System according to the syntactic rules of the particular language to be used, unless the programmer is very confident of success using Terminal Development only, that is the typing up of the Source Program at a VDU. Neither technique should be scorned.

Terminal Development.—The first process in developing a program on a terminal is to remove all syntactic errors found by the compiler as well as any logical errors found by the programmer. Linking cannot proceed until all the syntactic errors have been eliminated. The compiler output will be an 'Object Program' and, optionally a 'List File' containing the Source Program suitably annotated. The List File is optionally obtained as a hard copy (a paper copy) in order to make the understanding of a program much easier, whereas the 'Editing' of the 'Source Text' is often done on a VDU. The List File is generally more useful than the actual Source Program in written form when attempting to correct or augment a program because it often contains details of variable and array storage as well as line numbers. When using an assembler it is sometimes possible to obtain a cross-reference table containing all the page and line numbers of the labels and sub-program calls and this is very valuable in following an assembler level program.

It should be noted that the errors detected by a compiler or assembler are syntactic rather than logical, that is they are a report of the breaking of the structural rules of the language concerned and not a means of detecting logical errors, which are errors due to the incorrect coding of the desired algorithm by the programmer. In order to detect these logical errors the final Binary Program has to be run under test conditions until the program response is exactly as predicted and desired. This process of testing programs for errors should not be underestimated as it constitutes a very important part of the writing process. The correction of a software error in the program of a microprocessor in production, particularly one in volume production, is to be avoided at all costs.

The Object Program may then be linked with other Object Modules and Object Libraries to make a Binary Program, which must be run and checked for logical errors.

Program Debugging and Testing.—Program Debugging may proceed in a number of different ways according to the development system in use and the type of program. After all the obvious logical errors have been eliminated from a program, the program should be tested either in the development system which has been set up to emulate as closely as possible the target environment, or in the target microprocessor itself. Testing a program under emulation conditions can be very helpful but it is not often possible to reproduce exactly the environment of the target microprocessor. Thus before finally passing the program as working correctly it must be tried in the prototype target microprocessor.

One very convenient way of debugging the program in a target microprocessor is to be able to down-line load the target microprocessor with the required program and a small monitor program which allows the host microprocessor to interrogate the target microprocessor and read and modify memory locations. This facility is similar to an On-Line Debug and Trace (ODT) program which can be used in the host development system.

A second very convenient method of debugging the program in a target microprocessor is to use 'In Circuit Emulation' (sometimes called ICE). In this method the microprocessor chip in the target machine is removed from its socket and a multipin plug inserted instead connected through a suitable interfacing box to the development system which can then run the desired program using all the hardware normally surrounding the target microprocessor. This process involves special software being run in the development system which then allows the programmer to control the execution of the program step by step, or set break points, and generally analyse the complete execution of the program. If the development system is used to intervene to analyse the program operation then the target microprocessor software will not run at full speed.

Drivers.—Drivers (Handlers) are a means of structured access to Input/Output ports on the microprocessor. However, in simple programs it is not always necessary to provide drivers handle the ports, but where multi-tasking is envisaged it is imperative to use drivers to allow queued access to the ports and to relieve each Binary program of the need to contain all the code to access the ports.

PROGRAMMING DISCIPLINES.—The programming disciplines described in this section are not absolutely necessary to the preparation of a program for a microprocessor, particularly if the program is required only briefly. However, for any more substantial program they will make the subsequent correction of errors or introduction of new capabilities (software servicing) into a program.

Program Description and Commenting.—At the first convenient position in the Source text of the program the exact purpose of the program should be described in fairly fine detail. The author, date of writing and a version number should be added together with any copyright information. Furthermore, the author and date of any corrections and amendments should be added at the time they are done, together with the exact reason for the change.

Comments should be added at each significant stage of the program to describe the operation at that point. At the beginning of each Sub-program there should be a description of the exact purpose of that Sub-program and a description of the use of each argument.

STRUCTURED PROGRAMMING.—Structured Programming is a methodology which appears at first to be arbitrary, but which is in fact intended to simplify the writing of programs, minimise the chances of making subtle errors which can be very difficult to find, and make the software much easier to service at a later date. Reference 28 is a standard text on Structured Programming. Structured Programming is a term which covers both the hierarchical structure of a program and the structure of data.

Structured Programming techniques are best applied to programs written in high level languages, and the so-called Block Structured Languages are designed to take advantage of Structured Programming techniques.

Block Structured Language.—A block structured language is based on the tenet that the instructions which necessarily make up a program can be placed in small self-contained units (blocks) with at least some of the variables declared within the block, so making them available only locally. This helps to clarify the use of a variable, and further makes sure that the value of that variable is not changed by some accidental reference to it elsewhere in the program, possibly by an accident of naming.

Furthermore, program blocks may be contained within program blocks so that the range over which any given variable is valid (often called the SCOPE) is limited to that range which it necessarily needs.

The use of self-contained blocks is based on the concept of modularity, so that each block can be tested with the knowledge that operations on local variables will not affect variables outside that block, thus making both programming more disciplined and rigorous, and debugging much simpler and quicker.

Program Labels are a particular case in point because the SCOPE over which they are valid is normally very wide when in fact they can be replaced (in an appropriate block structured language) by using statements with structures as follows.—

IF condition THEN statement(s) ELSE statement(s)

and

FOR expression WHILE condition DO statement(s)

The former structure enables a branching set of decisions to be implemented easily, while the latter structure enables a set of instructions to be repeated until a particular condition is met, rather than for a fixed number of times.

The use of labels in a block structured language should be avoided because it often breaks the modularity which is possible and also because it does not allow optimisation of the instructions (by the compiler).

Some Rules for Structured Programming.—It is advantageous to implement Structured Programming for every program but the simplest, because of the modularity that is imposed. Some of the rules of Structured Programming are.—

VARIABLES IN COMMON.—The number of variables held in any COMMON area should be restricted to only those absolutely necessary.

GOTO STATEMENTS.—All types of 'GOTO' statements should be eliminated from the program, being replaced by the structures mentioned above.

ARGUMENT PASSING.—All external variables required by a sub-program (procedure) should be passed as arguments (parameters). This can make the calling of sub-programs a little tedious, but helps greatly when actually designing a program. The use of Common areas for sharing data between program and sub-program should be avoided.

FUNCTIONS (TYPED PROCEDURES) should be used to pass status values back from a sub-program (procedure), except in the case of mathematical functions (where status values are normally not needed anyway). Thus the '*Function*' can then be used directly in a conditional expression.

SUB-PROGRAM USE.—Sub-programs (procedures) should be used not only to cater for repeated operations, but also to clarify program operation. Thus Main programs should be constructed mainly of sub-program (procedure) calls rather than statements.

Hierarchical Program Structure.—Where input data has to be processed through a number of stages, '*Bottom-up programming*' can be used. Bottom-up programming consists of the main program sequencing the operations on the input data right through to the output. This may seem a natural method of processing, but the obtaining of data and its subsequent manipulation becomes very awkward because all the data for each stage of processing has to be held in the Main Program.

As an alternative, '*Top-down programming*' may be used whereby the main program calls a sub-program which obtains data as necessary from the next lower sub-program and processes it. The next lower sub-program when called also obtains data and manipulates it, and this pattern is repeated back from the data output to the data input through as many sub-program calls and manipulations as required. Any intermediate data is held in its sub-program and thus the manipulations at any particular stage may be tested and the data flow regulated much more easily than with a Bottom-up program.

Modular Testing.—Each complete program should be treated as a Module and developed and tested separately if at all possible. Theoretically, all the possible values of input to a program should be generated sequentially and the program made to operate on them. In practice, the total number of times the program would have to run becomes extremely large very rapidly and thus testing often has to follow more realistic lines. Hence, by careful choice of input values, much redundant testing work can be eliminated. However, testing cannot be by-passed entirely.

OPERATING SYSTEMS

Single Job Operating System.—An operating system is an intrinsic part of a microprocessor development system and normally exists entirely as Software. A simple operating system allows a single user to edit, compile, assemble or whatever is required. It contains code to access whatever mass-storage system is in use on the development system using drivers; it can handle interrupts but it is not required to Schedule any programs because only one program can be executed at any one time.

Multi-Tasking Operating System.—A Multi-Tasking Operating System allows more than one program to be running simultaneously, though of course at any one instant in time the CPU can only be executing one instruction. Multi-Tasking is achieved by the Operating System having a list of all the current tasks, whether active or not, and an algorithm to Schedule each program in order to give it some running time if required.

A particular advantage of Multi-tasking is the capability to handle more than one operating terminal at a time, and this can help considerably to reduce the cost of a development system by greatly increasing its availability.

There are 2 types of Scheduling which can be used, Round Robin and Priority.

Round Robin Scheduling.—A Multi-tasking operating system which operates a Round Robin Scheduler contains a list of all programs currently to be executed and in its simplest form allocates a fixed time slice to each program provided that the program requires some time. Round Robin Scheduling has the advantage that every program has a time slot in which to run, but the disadvantage that if any program requires a very fast response then it may have to wait until it is its turn again in the sequence before being allowed to execute. Thus Real Time Programs cannot be scheduled by Round Robin techniques.

Priority Scheduling.—A Multi-tasking operating system which operates a Priority Scheduler contains a list of all programs currently to be executed and in its simplest form allocates a time slice according to the priority of the program so as to give the more important programs more time. Thus time critical programs can have as much time as they require, and Real Time Programs are therefore very suited to Priority Scheduling.

A disadvantage of this technique that if there are 2 or more time critical programs then there is a contention problem. This is normally obviated by only allowing a program to run for a predetermined maximum time and not allowing it to be restarted before other programs have had a chance to run. This latter technique is achieved by manipulating the instantaneous priority of the program in order to allow it to run or to lock it out.

It is normally necessary to allocate some time for the remaining programs which are not time critical to have a chance to execute otherwise they can be locked out for very long periods and make no progress at all.

Software Servicing.—Software Servicing is a specialised area of software writing when a program needs attention either because of an occasional malfunction or because enhancements to the program are envisaged. If the original programmer(s) is still available then the servicing is very easy, otherwise it will be necessary for someone else to study the program before taking any action. If the program is properly structured and documented then this job is much easier, and hence much cheaper.

PROGRAMMING PROMS

USE OF PROM PROGRAMMERS.—If PROMS are to be used in any target microprocessor then it is normally necessary to have the facility on the development system to program PROMs, and these are normally EPROMS.

The PROM programmer itself is normally treated as a peripheral of the development system, and a convenient means of connection is through a standard serial line (such as RS-232C) which is run at a reasonably high baud rate (typically 9,600 baud). Such a connection is normally available so that a PROM can be read from as well as being programmed. This allows one previously programmed PROM to be read, and its contents retained in the memory of the development system, and then as many PROMS as required programmed from this data. Although this technique is feasible, it is a slow means to replicate the program in PROMS.

The contents of an EPROM may be read on a PROM programmer to verify that the contents matches the requirement. This may be done by a byte by byte comparison of the actual PROM contents with the desired contents. This operation is normally necessary as some varieties of Ultra Violet EPROMS require several hundred programming cycles on each bit to fix the bit pattern.

The correct programming hardware has to be used with each type of EPROM and this is normally catered for by having 'Personality Cards', one per EPROM type. This is necessary to cater for the variations in pin connections and supply voltages used in EPROMS. The 'Personality Card' can also be designed to take into account the ability of some EPROMS to be programmed in a single pass, whilst others require up to 300 passes before the state of each bit is thoroughly fixed.

EPROM Eraser.—An EPROM eraser is a very worthwhile investment allowing EPROMS with old program versions to be erased and reprogrammed. The Eraser is a small self contained unit (normally mains powered) which uses an intense Ultra Violet light source to erase the EPROMS. The EPROMS have to be mounted on a tray (or similar arrangement), possibly into electrically conducting foam rubber, and the tray is then inserted into the eraser. The erasing process may take from 5 minutes to nearly an hour depending on the type of EPROM and the exact IC fabrication technique used to make them. Thus different makes of the supposedly same EPROM may take different times to erase.

PROM Copying.—In order to make multiple copies of EPROMS, PROM copiers are available which have a holder for the master PROM and typically 10 sockets for the PROMS to be programmed. This is clearly a much more efficient way to replicate the program in new PROMS than programming them one at a time on the development system.

MICROPROCESSOR PERIPHERALS

A microprocessor is only of use if it receives an input, processes that input and then generates an output. Thus the devices connected to the input(s) and output(s) of a microprocessor are all important. Peripherals may be divided conveniently into 2 classes, mass storage devices and non-mass storage devices. The former class consists of devices which are capable of storing a considerable quantity of data in the form of files internally and is therefore said to be a file structured device. The latter class consists of devices which can store minimal quantities of data internally and is therefore said to be a non-file structured device.

NON-MASS STORAGE DEVICES.—The simplest peripherals such as printers and Visual Display Units (VDUs) are Non-Mass Storage Devices. They normally contain only enough storage to facilitate their operation.

Printers.—There are a number of different printer types in common usage using a variety of printing techniques.

PRINTING TECHNIQUES.—Probably the most common is the '*Needle Printer*' where 7 needles (normally) are arranged in a print head in a vertical line to span about 3 to 4 millimetres. Printing is achieved by moving the print head across the paper and activating the appropriate needles to form each character. Thus a character is normally formed from a 7×5 dot matrix, the exact shape being defined by the contents of an internal ROM. Thus a wide range of characters are available within the constraint of a 7×5 dot matrix. A carbon ribbon is required, but no special paper is required. Needle Printers may be made to type at up to 180 characters per second. The quality of printing is acceptable for general use but not normally for correspondence. The Needle Printer is not intrinsically quiet in operation.

The '*Daisy Wheel Printer*' uses a plastic or metal wheel with the individual characters embossed on the ends of radial fronds. The wheel is normally mounted vertically and rotated to the correct position before the required frond is hit from behind by a hammer. The wheel itself may be changed so that a variety of fonts are available, though not simultaneously. A carbon ribbon is required, but no special paper is required. Daisy Wheel printers are made which can type at up to 60 characters per second. The quality of printing is very good for both general use and for correspondence. The Daisy Wheel Printer is not intrinsically quiet in operation.

The '*Golf Ball Printer*' carries its print font on an interchangeable metal hemisphere which is rotated and raised or lowered to index the character. The Golf Ball is then pressed against the carbon ribbon and the paper. The Golf Ball itself may be changed so that a variety of fonts is available, though not simultaneously. Golf Ball Printers are made which can type at up to 30 characters per second. A carbon ribbon is required, but no special paper is required. The quality of printing is very good for both general use and for correspondence. The Golf Ball Printer is not intrinsically quiet in operation.

The '*Ink Jet Printer*' sprays an electrically charged stream of ink onto ordinary paper to form the required characters. Because of the electrical charge on each of the droplets of ink, the spray may be deflected laterally and vertically by applied voltages so forming the characters. The exact character shape drawn is controlled from within the printer and is stored in a ROM. Thus a very wide range of fonts is available. The Ink Jet Printer can print very quickly, but is also more expensive than the other printer types. Thus its use is restricted to the faster line-printers. The quality of printing is very good and no carbon ribbon is required. The Ink Jet Printer is also intrinsically quiet, the only noise coming during the return of the carriage.

The '*Electrostatic Printer*' uses the mark made by an electrical spark on special paper to form the characters. An electrically conducting paper is required for these types of printer. A number of electrodes arranged in a column like a needle printer is used scan the special paper. To form the character sparks are made to jump from the appropriate electrodes at the right time, so burning a tiny dot on the paper. No carbon ribbon is needed, but a special paper is required. The Electrostatic Printer can print characters at up to 30 characters per second, its speed being limited by the time it takes to mark a discernable mark on the paper. The quality of printing is equivalent to the needle printer, and is acceptable for general use though not for correspondence.

Electrostatic printers can be made very compact and for this reason are often used wherever miniature printers are required. The Electrostatic Printer is also intrinsically quiet.

The *Thermal Printer* uses 7 heat generating spots arranged vertically on its print head and in contact with special thermally sensitive paper to print the characters. The Thermal Printer thus uses a dot matrix like the needle printer. No carbon ribbon is needed, but a special heat sensitive paper is required. The cost of the heat sensitive paper increases the cost of this printing technique. The quality of printing is equivalent to the needle printer, and is acceptable for general use though not for correspondence. However, the Thermal Printer is intrinsically quiet.

The *Drum Printer* is used in line printers to speed printing. The drum consists of as many rings mounted coaxially as there are columns required. To print a line the drum is spun and each ring stopped at the required character for that position. When all the rings have stopped then the drum is pressed rapidly against the carbon ribbon and the paper. No special paper is required, but a carbon ribbon is required. The type font is extremely difficult to change by any technique as it requires the complete replacement of the whole print drum. The quality of the printing is acceptable for general use but not for correspondence. However, the drum printer is not quiet and generally needs housing in a noise reducing cabinet.

PRINTER TERMINALS.—Printers are often used as terminals on computers of all sizes, their advantage is the production of a hard copy. Printers may be connected to serial lines and operated in Half or Full Duplex.

Half Duplex is a technique whereby the printer receives characters quite normally from the microprocessor but when a key on the keyboard is pressed that character is forwarded to the microprocessor as well as being printed locally. Thus the sending and receiving of a character is not separate.

Full Duplex is a technique whereby the printer receives characters quite normally from the microprocessor but when a key on the keyboard is pressed that character is forwarded to the microprocessor only. If that character is required to be printed locally then the microprocessor must echo it back again when it will be treated like any other received character and printed. Thus the sending and receiving processes are completely separate.

Half Duplex operation is slightly less demanding on the microprocessor but does not give the flexibility of Full Duplex operation where the response returned by the microprocessor does not need to be an exact echo of the character received but can be a totally different string. An example of this is that a microprocessors might echo Carriage Return followed by Line Feed in response to a single Carriage Return character.

PRINTER TYPES.—Receive Only (RO) printers do not have any form of keyboard and are equipped to accept characters only. Thus a fast RO printer may be used as a substitute for a Line-printer.

Keyboard Send Receive (KSR) printers have both a keyboard for sending characters and are equipped to accept and print characters, but in Full or Half Duplex.

Automatic Send Receive (ASR) printers have both a keyboard for sending characters and are equipped to accept and print characters, in Full or Half Duplex as well as paper tape reader and punch.

If the time taken for a carriage return and a line feed is more than a few characters then this may be reduced considerably if the printer is bidirectional, that is the first line is printed from left to right and the second line from right to left with the characters in reverse sequence. In order to obtain the characters in reverse sequence it is necessary to have already receive the whole line of text.

Any of the above types of printer may be speeded up by using bidirectional printing.

If a large quantity of data has to be passed to or from a terminal, in order not to overload the receiving device (terminal or microprocessor) it is normal now to include synchronisation. With this technique the device about to be overloaded sends a warning message to the transmitting device not to send any more data. When it has cleared the backlog then it sends another message to tell the transmitting device to continue. The most common scheme based on this technique is called X-ON/X-OFF synchronisation. X-OFF is sent to stop further transmission and X-ON sent to cause transmission to be resumed. It should be noted that this technique requires Full Duplex operation.

By the use of X-ON/X-OFF synchronisation it is possible to operate a printer at any baud rate in excess of ten times the printing rate with no fear of lost characters.

Line Printers can be used on serial or parallel interfaces and are invariably receive only, their purpose being to print textual material as quickly as possible. Any of the above printing techniques may be used, though the most common up to about 200 characters per second is the needle printer. In the case of using a needle printer a RO version could be used but it is often more useful to use a full ASR version, mainly for printing but occasionally for input as well.

Above the speed of a needle printer, a drum printer can be used, although Ink Jet printers are also capable of high speeds but at relatively high cost.

Visual Display Unit (VDU).—A Visual Display Unit (VDU) operates in many ways as KSR printer except the characters are displayed on the screen of a cathode ray tube (CRT). In order to display the current printing position the VDU displays a cursor on the screen. The use of a CRT saves a great deal of paper and furthermore, the screen of a CRT may be written upon very much faster than paper. The speed which data may be sent to a VDU is only limited by the speed at which the human operator can assimilate the data.

Modern VDUs normally display at least 24 lines of characters, and perhaps as many as 30, with at least 80 characters per line, though some have the option to display 132 characters. The maximum number of characters which can be displayed is limited by the VDU memory size.

It is also possible to obtain intelligent VDUs which not only store the current picture but the previous n lines of data sent to that VDU, and offer the facility to edit any of the data in any part of its memory, followed by returning that information to the microprocessor. This can be very useful for taking the load off the main microprocessor.

Various other facilities are available on some VDUs.

VDUs may be used in Half or Full Duplex. but for purposes of X-ON/X-OFF they are normally used in Full Duplex mode.

MASS STORAGE DEVICES.—Mass Storage Devices are used to store programs and data. Their method of access divides into 2 categories, Random Access and Sequential Access. Disks of all types are Random Access devices, whereas Tapes of all types use Sequential Access.

Disks.—The storage capacity of disks is normally quoted in bytes. For most character codes a byte is equivalent to a character. Disks are necessary to a microprocessor development system in order that programs may be operated upon with ease. The storage of information on the surface of a disk is not chaotic but is instead organised into concentric tracks and the tracks into sectors (a segment of a track). The exact layout depends on the disk type and manufacturer. Some disk type are factory formatted and are said to be Hard Sectored whereas other disks can be formatted by the user to his needs and these are said to be Soft Sectored.

The storage density on a Hard Sectored Disk is fixed whereas the storage density on a Soft Sectored disk is variable up to a maximum set by the magnetic material.

Some disks may be written on both sides and are said to be Double Sided whereas other disks may only be written on one side.

The time taken to access data at a known position on a disk depends on the time it takes to position the head over the correct track and the waiting time until the start of that block comes around. This total time is known as the latency time. The difference between the average latency times of two disks may be used to determine if there is any advantage of one disk over another. In general, the latency of a floppy disk is much greater than that of a hard disk.

Floppy Disks are a cheap and convenient method of storing a moderate amount of data. They consist of a circular sheet of plastic coated with a magnetic material. They come in several sizes, from 3 up to 8 inches in diameter. The floppy disk is made to revolve at about 300 rpm and a retractable head is lowered into contact with the disk. Thus the head actually touches the disk whenever there is a need to read from or write to the disk and this will cause wear in time. Hence it is advisable to keep spare copies of important floppy disks because of their finite life.

The storage capacity of a floppy disk is limited by the low rotational speed and the relatively poor magnetic material used for the surface. However floppy disks are attractive because of their low cost.

Floppy disks may be single or double density, and single or double sided. Storage capacities from 250 kbyte to 1 Mbyte are possible with 8 inch floppy disks and now with some smaller disks.

The layout of floppy disks varies from one manufacturer to another. Therefore if transportability of disks is important great care must be taken to ensure compatibility between different makes of system.

Hard disks work on almost the same principle as floppy disks except that the retractable head flies above the disk surface. Hard disks can be used to store far more bytes at the expense of a higher cost. Apart from being single or double density, and single or double sided, Hard disks may have more than one platter. The storage capacity of hard disks ranges from about 1 Mbyte to 600 Mbyte, though the upper limit is still increasing.

The read/write retractable head of a hard disk should never actually come in contact with the disk but instead 'flies' on a very thin layer of air above the disk surface. This entails the disk rotating at a significantly higher speed than with a floppy disk and this has the advantage that the writing speed can be much higher.

Magnetic Tape.—Magnetic tape is used for storing large quantities of data, and for archiving disks except in a few special cases.

A Cassette Tape Deck is sometimes used to input test programs to a computer and is also the cheapest form of bulk storage for small microprocessors. In the latter case an ordinary domestic cassette deck is used and although this is very cheap to operate the recording rate has to be very low in order to minimise the error rate. Thus if cost is critical or program loading time unimportant then a cassette deck is a possible option.

A Cartridge Tape Deck is sometimes used as an electronic replacement for paper tape. Although the writing speed is significantly greater than the cassette deck it offers minimal advantage over that type of recording.

CONCLUSIONS

The use of microprocessors in modern manufactured equipment is now becoming very important, and this chapter has sought to describe the use, construction, structure and programming of microprocessors and their interfacing to the real world. Although microprocessors have come from a blend of Electronic Engineering, Computer Science and Semiconductor Physics, their application is almost universal today and it is not possible to ignore their presence. Indeed, it would be unwise to avoid them as they offer so many advantages when once understood and applied.

GLOSSARY OF COMMON TERMS

2's Complement Arithmetic.—The technique used in virtually all computers to represent data such that mathematical operations can be easily realised.

Accumulator.—A register within the CPU of some microprocessors which is used for general data manipulation.

Address.—A number representing the sequential position of an entity in the memory of a microprocessor.

Addressing Range.—The Addressing Range of a microprocessor is the maximum address that can be referenced directly using all the bits of the address bus of the microprocessor.

Argument.—An address or value passed to a subprogram. The variable as used in the subprogram is a dummy value and is replaced by the actual value which is passed as an Argument.

Arrays.—A mechanism for storing lists of data in (normally) contiguous sections of memory within a microprocessor.

ASCII.—American Standard Code for Information Interchange (ASCII) is the code normally used by microprocessors for representing printing and non-printing characters, particularly when operating between a terminal and the microprocessor.

Baud Rate.—The Baud Rate of a terminal is the number of contiguous bits per second which are being passed in or out of that terminal, whether by synchronous or asynchronous means. Therefore the spasmodic transmission of characters is still at a fixed baud rate. Table 2 lists the standard asynchronous Baud Rates in use with terminals and microprocessors.

Binary.—A number convention using the base 2. Thus binary digits can only take the values 0 and 1, and the digit weightings are 1, 2, 4, 8, etc. Hence a considerable number of digits are required to represent large numbers.

Binary Program.—The result of Compiling/Assembling and Linking a program. The Binary Program is in a form whereby it can be executed directly, and all addresses in the program have been resolved, that is all addresses point to the correct places within the program.

Block Structured Language.—A class of computer languages which are specifically designed to implement structured programming. Such languages are PASCAL, PL/M, PL/Z, CORAL, and many others.

Boolean Logic.—The mathematical tool upon which the design of AND, OR, NAND, NOR etc gates are based. The Boolean Logic relationships are necessary to the design of digital hardware and also to the programming of complicated 'IF' . . . 'THEN' . . . 'ELSE' . . . statements.

Bootstrap.—A means of starting a microprocessor whereby a very small program is made resident in the microprocessor which can (say) read one specific track off the disk of a microprocessor development system and then execute the code which it has just read. This can in turn be another bootstrap. Hence Bootstraps can be nested.

Bottom-up programming.—A method of organising data processing in a microprocessor, and the opposite of Top-down Programming.

Branching.—A general description of the type of microprocessor instructions which cause modification of the Program Counter contents in order to break the sequential accessing of instructions and jump to another part of the same program.

Cache Memory.—A high speed memory sometimes used in the largest and fastest microprocessors (though not generally available for all microprocessors). The particular advantage of a cache memory is that frequently used instructions are copied into the cache from main memory and executed from the cache. As the cache memory is much faster than main memory, the speed of instruction execution is much increased.

Central Processor.—The Central Processor (CPU) of a microprocessor contains all the registers, Arithmetic Logic Unit, instruction decoder, etc to actually execute instructions.

Common Data Area.—A Common Data Area within a program is an area of memory reserved for storing data, and made available at Compile/Assembly time for linking to other programs. Thus separate programs may share the same data area using this technique, or separately compiled/assembled parts of one program can reference the one Common Data Area.

Compiler.—A special program to convert a user written program in the specific high level language into instructions for that type of microprocessor to execute. A different Compiler is needed for each high level language used.

Core Memory.—A type of memory which uses the magnetic state of magnetic rings to record the bits. It has now been superceded by MOS memory.

Cross-Assembler.—A program run on one type of computer (not necessarily a microprocessor) which converts mnemonic instructions for a different type of microprocessor into the equivalent machine instructions.

Cross-Compiler.—A program run on one type of computer (not necessarily a microprocessor) which converts high-level language statement into the equivalent machine instructions for a different type of microprocessor.

Declarations.—Declarations are obligatory in some high level languages but partly optional in others to inform the compiler of the exact nature of the data to be stored, and in particular the number of words to reserve for each variable and array, and furthermore the type of arithmetic to use on those variables and arrays.

Direct Memory Access.—DMA is a technique used to pass data in or out of memory without that data having to pass through the CPU. As there is no CPU intervention during the DMA transfer, that transfer can take place very rapidly, and up to almost the maximum access speed of the memory.

Dis-assembly.—A technique sometimes available on a microprocessor development system to reverse the process of compilation/assembly in order to reconstruct the instructions (in mnemonic form) which were actually produced. It is sometimes useful in finding compiler faults (bugs) and in modifying standard software from libraries.

Down Line Loading.—A technique whereby a program is not loaded into the memory of a microprocessor by a disk transfer or through an EPROM, but instead is sent to that microprocessor over a line (normally serial). This has the advantage that the memory contents can be replaced fairly easily, and is particularly useful during program development.

Driver.—A special program to give orderly access to an interface. Drivers are necessary with a multi-tasking operating system.

Dynamic MOS Memory.—A type of memory where the data bits are held in cells as charge, which has to be recirculated in order to regenerate the charge. Hence the title 'dynamic'.

EAROM.—Electrically alterable ROM (EAROM) is a type of ROM memory which can have bits cleared and re-written under electrical control. This is not the same as ordinary MOS RAM as the data is non-volatile.

EEROM.—Electrically erasable ROM (EEROM) is similar to EAROM in that the data can be modified under electrical control. However, with EEROM all the data bits have to be cleared simultaneously. The stored data are non-volatile.

EPROM.—Erasable Programmable ROM (EPROM) is a form of ROM memory which can be programmed electrically but erased optically using Ultra-violet light. It is also non-volatile.

EPROM Eraser.—An EPROM Eraser is used to erase an EPROM and consists of an Ultra-violet light source in a closed box with provision for the insertion of EPROMs for erasure.

Extended Addressing.—Extended Addressing is used to increase the basic Addressing Range of a microprocessor so that a larger memory can be used. The address extension is normally only by a few bits as every bit doubles the addressing range.

First-In First-Out (FIFO).—A First-In First-Out (FIFO) store is a type of buffer store that can accept data at its input at any time (unless full) and which advances that data up the empty part of the buffer to the back of the queue of data. The data is extracted from the FIFO in the same sequence as it was input.

Floating Point Numbers.—Floating Point Numbers are used to represent numbers as a Mantissa and Exponent.

Floppy Disks.—The simplest sequential mass storage devices available. They consist of a flexible circular plastic disk with an oxide coating on which the data is recorded. They are supplied in a square jacket and are made to revolve at about 300 rpm. The maximum storage capacity of Floppy Disks is up to 1 Megabyte depending on whether they are single or double sided, single or double density.

Functions.—A variety of sub-program whereby a value is returned as the apparent value of the sub-program. They are the computing equivalent of a mathematical function of one or more variables.

GPIB.—see IEEE bus.

Hard Disks.—Hard Disks consist of a circular metal disk (often aluminium) with an oxide coating on which data is recorded. As they are metallic, their speed of rotation is much greater than Floppy Disks, and their storage capacity commensurately larger. Hard disks can also be made with more than one actual disk concentrically mounted. Most hard disks have at least 1 megabyte of storage capacity, but as much as 600 megabyte is available on the largest disks. The access to data on hard disks is also much more rapid than for data on Floppy disks.

Hard Sectoring.—Hard Sectoring is sometimes used for Floppy Disks and consists of concentric pre-punched holes near the centre of the disk to mark the sectors on the disk. The format of data on the disk cannot be altered, though the data itself can of course be changed.

Hexadecimal.—A means of numerical representation with each digit having 16 possible values, and the digit weightings being 1, 16, 256, 4,096, etc.

HPIB.—see IEEE bus.

ICE.—see In-Circuit Emulator.

IEC 625-1.—see IEEE bus.

IEEE Bus.—The IEEE bus (IEEE 488-1978) is used to control instrumentation, and consists of byte serial, bit parallel transfers. It is variously known as the HPIB, GPIB, IEC 625-1 and ASCII bus.

In Circuit Emulator.—An In Circuit Emulator is used to help debug the program in a microprocessor by allowing the CPU in a development system to operate the target microprocessor directly. This is done by replacing the target microprocessor CPU chip with a special connection from the development system. Special software is also required in the development system in order to run the required software in the target microprocessor.

Indexed Addressing.—Indexed Addressing is used to access data which is at a known offset in a table from the reference address to that table. The action of indexing is to add the known offset to the basic address to obtain the data.

Indirect Addressing.—Indirect Addressing is used to access data when all that is known is that the address of the data is stored in another location. Thus the location containing the address is fetched, and the contents used as an address to obtain the data.

Instruction Cycle.—The Instruction Cycle of a microprocessor is the time taken to execute a complete instruction, and consists of various fetch cycles. It is not normally constant for different types of instruction.

Instruction Decoding.—The process of Instruction Decoding is done by the CPU after the instruction has been fetched from memory. The instruction has to be decoded and the correct sequence of operations started to fetch operands and perform any arithmetic operations, obtain address offsets etc.

Integers.—Integers as stored in a microprocessor normally occupy one data word. They represent positive or negative integral quantities. Often as many as 16 bits are needed to encompass a large enough numerical range to be useful, and this can mean that an 8-bit microprocessor has to use double length arithmetic.

Interpretive Language.—An Interpretive Language (such as BASIC) parses every statement as it is encountered and translates it into a sequence of operations which it then executes.

Interrupts.—A means for an external event to interrupt the operation of a program(s) in a microprocessor. The action of the microprocessor in response to an interrupt is to break off from the current program and go to some predefined code and execute it. A typical source of interrupt is the typing of a character on a terminal which is then forwarded to the microprocessor.

Latency.—A measure of the time taken to access information on a disk. As the disk is divided into surfaces, tracks, sectors and blocks, it takes time to align the read/head over the correct track and up to one revolution to find the beginning of the block before reading that block.

Librarian.—A Librarian is used to convert Object Modules into an Object Library so that linking may be done selectively rather than a reference to one object in an object module causing the whole module to be linked in. Thus a Librarian helps in reducing the eventual size of a binary program.

Line Clock.—A Line Clock is used to update a register in a microprocessor containing the time (and often the data as well). A line clock in particular receives its input from the mains frequency via the mains power supply of the microprocessor.

Linking.—The process of joining all specified object modules or objects from libraries into one homogeneous binary program. In particular, it can link standard libraries.

Listing.—A Listing can be produced by a compiler or assembler and consists of an annotated version of the source code. It is generally more useful than the source code itself when debugging a program.

Loading.—see Linking.

Location.—A Locaton is the same as an address.

Machine Code Programming.—Machine code Programming is the most basic form of programming possible and consists of inserting the actual binary patterns into memory as required. It is very labour intensive and slow.

Machine Cycle.—A Machine Cycle is the same as an Instruction Cycle.

Macro.—A sequence of statements or mnemonic instructions which is represented by a single phrase. Inclusion of that phrase invokes the compiler/assembler to expand the macro into the sequence of statements/instructions before processing them. Note that not every high level language has the capability for using macros.

Macro Assembler.—An assembler capable of interpreting macros.

Mantissa.—The magnitude portion of a floating point number.

Mapping.—A technique used to extend the size of the memory of a microprocessor without necessarily needing to use extended addressing. In particular, it allows different segments of a program which are not contiguous to appear to be so for the purposes of that program. Furthermore, the segments can be shared between several programs by virtue of mapping. Mapping is not normally available on the smallest microprocessors.

Mask Programmable ROM.—A type of ROM which is programmed at the last stage in its manufacture. It is a very cheap way of programming a large number of microprocessors, but great care is necessary as it is not possible to change the program afterwards. The stored data are non-volatile.

Memory.—The Memory of a microprocessor contains the list of instructions to be executed, as well as any data. It is arranged as a set of contiguous locations and is accessed by an address.

Modular Programming.—A technique in structured programming whereby the program to be written is broken down into separate operations (modules) and programmed accordingly.

Multi-Tasking Operating System.—A Multi-Tasking Operating System is used in a microprocessor when programs have to be executed in parallel. Thus, it allows more than one user to use a development system, and more than one program to be run by each person. It also allows a target microprocessor to handle separate processes with only a loose relationship between them without having to produce a very complicated program which is full of conflicting requirements. It is not normally available on small microprocessors.

Object Library.—An Object Library is created by a Librarian, and consists of one or more object modules each containing one or more actual object programs with an index to every object program added at the beginning of the library.

Object Program.—An Object Program is the result of compiling/assembling a source program. It consists of the machine instructions to execute the source program, but is very likely to contain calls to sub-programs which are not part of that actual object program.

Octal.—A means of numerical representation with each digit having eight possible values.

On-line Debug and Trace.—An On-line Debug and Tracer facility is used to debug a program in the course of it being run. It normally provides facilities to read the contents of any location in the program and change that location if necessary.

Operation Code (OP CODE).—An Operation Code (OP CODE) is the name of the field in the microprocessor instruction specifying the actual action to be taken.

Operand.—An Operand is the value or address on which the Operand Code operates.

Optimising Compiler.—An Optimising Compiler not only converts the source program into object form, but also tries to minimise the number of instructions necessary to execute any given set of statements. The rules of the optimisation are set by the writer of the compiler. Optimisation can give a useful improvement in execution speed.

Paged Memory.—Paged Memory is used as a means of extending the size of memory on a microprocessor by allowing a program to operate in a number of 'pages' rather than in ordinary memory. These pages may be loaded and unloaded from a disk so giving a significant increase in the useful memory size.

Parallel Interfaces.—Parallel Interfaces are used to transfer multibit words in parallel rather than serially.

Parameters.—see arguments.

Personality Card.—A printed circuit card used with EPROM programmers to define the connections and programming method of the particular EPROM.

Pipeline.—A technique to speed the execution of instructions by allowing one instruction to be decoded while the next one is being fetched.

Polling.—Polling is used to find the source of an interrupt if a vectored interrupt is not implemented on the microprocessor being used. It consists of scanning round all the possible sources of interrupt and handling that interrupt if anything is found. It is a very inefficient way of using a microprocessor and it has no advantages over a vectored interrupt.

Priority Scheduling.—A technique used with a multi-tasking operating system to decide on which program requires running next according to priority only. It is an alternative to Round-Robin scheduling.

Priority Vectored Interrupt.—A Priority Vectored Interrupt not only passes the address of the interrupt handling routine to the microprocessor, but it also has a fixed priority which is used by priority arbitration logic to decide when to allow that interrupt according to the priority status of the microprocessor at that time. Thus a priority vectored interrupt only occurs when the microprocessor priority is low enough to allow in that priority.

Procedure.—Another name for a sub-program which is often used in block structured languages.

Program Counter.—A register which contains the address of the next instruction to be executed.

Programmable ROM.—Any ROM which is capable of being programmed after manufacture, even if only once.

Quantisation Noise.—The inevitable result of converting an analogue quantity into the nearest digital quantity. The error between the analogue value and the digital value is the quantisation error, and when considered over many samples it appears as noise.

Quantising Error.—The difference between as analogue level and the nearest digital level as decided by an Analogue-to-Digital converter.

Random Access Memory (RAM).—Random Access Memory (RAM) is used for storing temporary values during the execution of a program, and also for the storage of the program code itself if necessary. It is needed in some quantity in all microprocessors, and in development systems in particular it will be the largest single type of memory.

Re-Entrant Code.—Re-Entrant Code is written when it is known that the same program should be executed more than once but out of step as a result of some event external to the program. It requires a proper sub-program calling structure to work efficiently.

Read Cycle.—The Read Cycle of a memory is the time during which a value is being read from the memory.

Real Time Clock.—A Real Time Clock is used to keep track of the time (and sometimes the date). It can be driven from a crystal controlled oscillator or from the mains, when it is called a Line Clock.

Real Time Program.—A Real Time Program is designed to run in real time, that is it accepts data as it appears at its input and processes it without getting behind time. It requires that the minimum amount of code be executed commensurate with obtaining the right answer. Thus, for example, disk accesses are kept to a minimum or eliminated altogether and array bounds are not checked.

Register.—A set of Flip-Flops used to store related data bits.

Relative Addressing.—A technique used with programs to allow the program to be loaded into memory at any arbitary location and run. Thus all Branching instructions are executed relative to the current program counter value rather than to some absolute value. Relative Addressing is a prerequisite of a multi-tasking operating system.

Relocatable Code.—The type of instructions produced by a compiler/assembler to allow relative addressing to occur.

Round Robin Scheduling.—An alternative technique to Priority Scheduling in a multi-tasking operating system. With Round Robin Scheduling each active program is allowed a fixed, though not necessarily identical, time slot in which to execute.

RS-232C.—An EIA standard for unbalanced serial data communication.

RS-422.—RS-422 and RS-422A are EIA standards for balanced serial data communication.

RS-423.—RS-423 and RS-423A are EIA standards for unbalanced serial data communication. They are more up to date than RS-232C.

RS-449.—RS-449 is an EIA standard for unbalanced or balanced serial data communication. It combines RS-422 and RS-423.

Serial Poll.—An action related to the operation of an IEEE bus. The bus is serial polled to determine which instrument issued the Service Request.

Service Request.—The mechanism used by an instrument on the IEEE bus to request servicing.

Shared Data Areas.—Shared Data Areas are sometimes needed so that 2 or more programs in a micro-processor can share the same data. In order to achieve this the microprocessor needs to have a mapping capability.

Single Job Operating System.—A Single Job Operating System is used when it is known that only one program is required to be run at any one time. Such an operating system is intrinsically smaller and simpler than a multi-tasking operating system.

Solicited Interrupts.—Solicited Interrupts occur in a microprocessor whenever the microprocessor is expecting data to be input. It is the opposite of the unsolicited interrupt.

Source Program.—The sequence of statements which go to form the program created by the programmer. It is also the input to a compiler/assembler.

Stack.—A Stack is used as an organised method of temporary storage of data in a program. There is normally one stack to each program. The current position is pointed to by the stack pointer.

Stack Pointer.—A register whose contents are used as the current address of the stack.

Structured Programming.—A methodology for creating programs with the intention of increasing the probability of the resulting code being accurate.

Sub-program.—The portion of a program which can be called from anywhere in the main program or other sub-programs (subject to the semantic rules of the language concerned) and which uses dummy variables (arguments or parameters) to pass values and addresses in and out of the sub-program.

Synchronous Serial Interfaces.—Synchronous Serial Interfaces are used to pass data at fairly high speeds into or out of a microprocessor. Transmission and reception is normally done with integrated circuits (USRTs).

Task Building.—An alternative name for Linking.

Top-down programming.—A technique for structuring the data flow through a program.

Universal Asynchronous Receiver Transmitter (UART).—An integrated circuit used to transmit and receive asynchronous serial data.

Unsolicited Interrupt.—An Unsolicited Interrupt occurs when a microprocessor receives an interrupt from an external device without it being expected, such as the typing of characters on a terminal.

V24.—A CCITT standard for interchange circuits and is similar to parts of the EIA standards.

V28.—A CCITT standard for the interconnections of interchange circuits and corresponds closely to RS-232C.

Vector Address.—A Vector Address is returned by a microprocessor interface after it has interrupted the microprocessor in order to say which interface caused the interrupt.

Virtual Memory.—A technique used in very large microprocessors to increase the apparent size of the memory of the microprocessor beyond the end of physical memory. The information not stored in physical memory is written to a disk, and thus such techniques are only feasible on very large systems.

Write Cycle.—The Write Cycle refers to the time during which a value is being written to memory.

ACKNOWLEDGEMENTS

The author would like to thank the Intel Corporation for permission to use some of their published information on the 8080 CPU.

REFERENCES

(1) BYWATER, R. E. H., *Hardware/Software Design of Digital Systems,* Prentice Hall, 1981.
(2) WOOD, A., *Microprocessors—Your Questions Answered*, Newnes, 1982.
(3) WOOLARD, B. G., *Microprocessors and Microcomputers for Engineering Students and Technicians*, McGraw Hill, 1981.
(4) RAO, G. V., *Microprocessors and Microcomputer Systems*, Van Nostrand Reinhold, 1978.
(5) TOCCI, R. J., LASKOWSKI, L. P., *Microprocessors and Microcomputers: Hardware and Software*, Prentice-Hall, 1982.
(6) MORGAN, E., *Microprocessors: A Short Introduction*, HMSO, 1980.
(7) ASCII, *American National Standard Code for Information Interchange,* X3, 4—1977, American National Standard Institute, 1977.
(8) Recommendation V24, *List of Definitions for Interchange Circuits between Data Terminal Equipment and Data Circuit-Terminating Equipment,* International Telegraph and Telephone Consultative Committee, CCITT, 1980.
(9) Recommendation V28, *Electrical Characteristics for Unbalanced Double-current Interchange Circuits,* International Telegraph and Telephone Consultative Committee, CCITT, 1980.
(10) Standard RS-232C, *Interface between Data Terminal Equipment and Data Communication Equipment employing Serial Binary Data Interchange,* Electronic Industries Association, 1969.
(11) Standard RS-422, *Electrical Characteristics of Balanced Voltage Digital Interface Circuits,* Electronic Industries Association, 1975.
(12) Standard RS-422A, *Electrical Characteristics of Balanced Voltage Digital Interface Circuits,* Electronic Industries Association, 1978.
(13) Standard RS-423, *Electrical Characteristics of Unbalanced Voltage Digital Interface Circuits,* Electronic Industries Association, 1975.
(14) Standard RS-423A, *Electrical Characteristics of Unbalanced Voltage Digital Interface Circuits,* Electronic Industries Association, 1978.
(15) Standard RS-449, *General Purpose 37-Position and 9-Position Interface for Data Terminal Equipment and Data Circuit-Terminating Equipment employing Serial Binary Data Interchange,* Electronic Industries Association, 1977.
(16) Standard 488-1978, *IEEE Standard Digital Interface for Programmable Instrumentation,* Institution of Electrical and Electronic Engineers, 1978.
(17) IEC Publication 625-1, *Interface System for Programmable Instruments (byte serial, bit parallel), Part 1: Functional Specification, Mechanical Specification, System Applications and Requirements for the Designer and User,* IEC 1979.
(18) KEMENY, J. G., KURTZ, T. E., *Basic Programming* (2nd Ed), Wiley, 1971.
(19) CRYER, N., CRYER, P., *Basic Programming on the BBC Microcomputer*, Prentice-Hall, 1982.
(20) WEBB, J. T., *Coral 66 Programming*, National Computing Centre, 1978.
(21) MCCRACKEN, D. D., *Simplified Guide to Fortran Programming*, Wiley, 1974.
(22) GROGONO, P., *Programming in Pascal*, Addison Wesley, 1980.
(23) BEER, M. D., *Programming Microcomputers with Pascal*, Granada, 1982.
(24) TIBERGHIEN, J., *Pascal Handbook*, Sybex, 1981.
(25) CHERRY, G. W., *Pascal Programming Structures: An Introduction to Systematic Programming*, Reston Publishing, 1980.
(26) ATKINSON, L. V., *Pascal Programming*, John Wiley, 1980.
(27) WILSON, I. R., ADDYMAN, A. M., *A Practical Introduction to Pascal*, Macmillan, 1978.
(28) DAHL, O.-J., DYKSTRA, E. W., HOARE, C. A. R., *Structured Programming*, Academic Press, 1972.

COMPUTER PROGRAMMING LANGUAGES

Introduction—Computer systems—Interpreters and Compilers—BASIC—Programming techniques—FORTRAN—Structured Software—Pascal—FORTH—C—Lisp—Prolog.

by J. D. Turner, BSc, PhD, C.Eng, MIEE

INTRODUCTION

For many users it is sufficient simply to regard the computer as a black box, and to ask no questions about how the black box operates. This can be a satisfactory starting point, but for the benefit of those who wish to know how it is done this introduction gives a brief description of the relationship between high level languages, machine codes, and the hardware they both control.

At its simplest level, a computer is a device which automatically executes a series of pre-defined instructions. The process of generating these instructions is known as programming. A program is "run" by supplying the instructions to the computer's central processing unit (or CPU) in the correct order, and carrying them out. Thus, a complicated calculation may for example be broken down into a series of simple calculations, with the answer obtained at each stage being supplied to the next until the final result is produced. Once the program to carry out such a calculation has been written, it can of course be run as many times as required with various numerical inputs.

The difference between a computer and a hardwired controller (which also carries out pre-determined instructions) lies in the computer's generality. A computer may be programmed to carry out a number of different tasks, and can switch between these tasks very rapidly. To illustrate this point, consider a hardwired digital process controller such as that shown in figure 1. Sensors supply the controller with information about

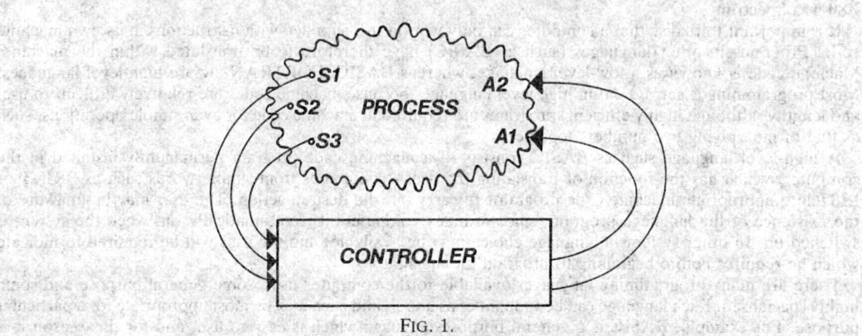

FIG. 1.

forces, temperatures, pressures etc. Actuators may be used to operate valves or to regulate motor speeds, so that the process is maintained at its optimum condition. The controller relating the sensory inputs to the output actuators is usually constructed from electronic components such as logic gates. The inputs are converted from analogue to digital form using A/D converters, and the outputs are reconverted where necessary using D/A converters. This type of construction is called hardwired, because the control functions are totally embodied in the components and their interconnections. The control functions of such a system can only be changed by reconstructing it.

If the process described above is computer controlled a different internal arrangement is used. The controller is still connected to the process by sensors and actuators, and the signals must still be converted to and from digital form where necessary. The controller circuitry however now has only a few parts, which are arranged so that they can carry out a series of functions in sequence. When the controller has carried out all the functions once, it loops back and executes them again, and so on continuously. Each control function may be executed many hundreds of times a second, giving a close approximation to the continuous control obtained from a hardwired system. The control functions are stored as a series of instructions (the program) in a store attached to the control system. As soon as it has finished executing one function, the system fetches the instructions governing the next function from the store. Figure 2 shows the structure of a computer-based controller. The important feature of a computer based controller (such as a microprocessor) is that this structure is the same for any control task. Different functions are obtained simply by changing the instructions held in the store.

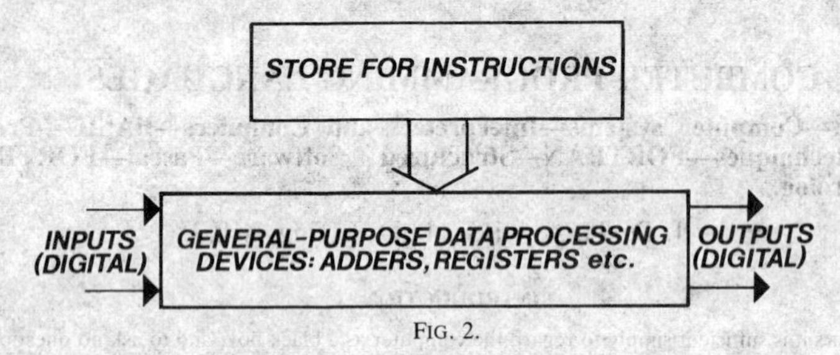

FIG. 2.

The part of a computer responsible for fetching and carrying out stored instructions is the CPU (Central Processing Unit). It is here that all the work is done; not only the retrieving of stored instructions but all the calculations. In a simple computer such as a microprocessor, all calculations are based on the arithmetical operations of add and subtract. Multiplication is therefore repeated addition, and a subtraction algorithm is used for division. More complicated computers use hardware for carrying out multiplication and division, and even for operations such as evaluating square roots. Microcomputers may therefore be slower in operation than minicomputers or mainframes, but can nevertheless carry out many hundreds or thousands of calculations per second.

When a program is run the CPU is responsible for retrieving an instruction from the store, collecting relevant data from other parts of the system, executing the instruction, and returning the results to the store before collecting the next instruction and repeating the cycle. This process typically occurs several million times a second. The CPU instructions have therefore to be very efficient and capable of rapid execution, so a special language called machine code is used. Machine code is specific to the computer being used. Thus, for example, the machine code used by the 6502 microprocessor in a BBC computer will be different from that used by the Z80 in a Spectrum.

It is important to realise that a computer can only work if it is supplied with instructions in its own machine code. Programs in other languages (such as BASIC) have therefore to be translated within the machine. Machine code is known as a low-level language, whereas BASIC, FORTRAN etc are high-level languages. Most programming is carried out in high level languages because machine codes are relatively difficult to use, and lengthy (although highly efficient) programs are required in machine code for even simple operations, such as that of multiplying two numbers together.

A high-level language such as BASIC consists of a machine code program permanently installed in the computer, which has the function of translating the user's commands from simple words such as PRINT or LIST into appropriate machine code programs to carry out the desired action. The user may be unaware of the existence of the language program, since in many computers it is automatically run when the system is switched on. In other systems a language choice may be available, and the user will be required to indicate which he requires before beginning to program the machine.

There are many programming languages available to the computer user, some general purpose and some highly specialised. Each language can be thought of as a tool, and each may be most appropriate for a particular purpose. For example, BASIC is a general purpose language which is easy to use, and for this reason it is deservedly popular with beginners and with programmers who want to write relatively simple programs. However, it is slow in execution, so if speed is required it may be preferrable to use PASCAL. If large amounts of numerical work are to be carried out FORTRAN may be best, and so on.

It was noted above that BASIC is generally slow in execution. This brings us to a fundamental division in the way that the translation programs which underly any high-level language act. There are two ways in which a high-level program can be translated into machine code and executed. The program can be translated and acted on line by line each time the program is run, or a "once and for all" translation of the complete program may be made, and stored for use each time the program is required.

The first option, line-by-line translation and execution, is used by most versions of BASIC, and is called interpreting. The reason for BASIC's slowness therefore becomes apparent, as each line has first to be translated into machine code before it can be executed. When running a BASIC program the computer may be spending as much as 90% of its time on translation, and only 10% in actually carrying out the program. However, interpreting languages can be easier to use than compiling languages, since the computer can be made to report any errors in each line of program as it is run. This makes de-bugging a BASIC program relatively straightforward.

The second option, once-and-for-all translation, is known as compilation. The user writes his program in a high-level language such as FORTRAN, and in so doing produces a file of instructions called the source code.

The translation program or compiler acts on the source code to produce a machine code version of the program, known as the object code. Where standard operations are required, such as finding the cosine of an angle for example, the compiler fetches appropriate segments of machine code from a library, and incorporates these into the object code. Compiled programs run very quickly since they are already in machine code. If changes to the program are required these are made on the source file which then has to be re-compiled. Program de-bugging may be more difficult with a compiling language, since errors can appear in the object file which are not apparent in the source code. It can also be difficult to relate an error which appears on running the object code to the source code instruction in which it originated.

Early computer services and some large installations are arranged in such a way that they can only deal with one program at a time. Programs are presented in groups or "batches", and the machine processes them one after the other. The programmer using such a system presents his program to a computing service, who run it for him and return the result sometime later. The disadvantages of batch processing for small programs and for learning is that the "turnround" time is unlikely to be less than a few hours and may be measured in days.

To circumvent this problem interactive systems were developed, in which the programmer is put into direct communication with the computer by means of a terminal. On a mainframe or minicomputer with a number of users this is achieved by a process known as timesharing, where the computer rapidly switches from terminal to terminal so rapidly that the user is unaware of any delay.

Obviously, with a desktop computer where there is only one user the arrangements described above do not apply. For this reason, many programmers start their training on a dedicated microcomputer, as many of the complexities inherent in the use of large systems are thereby avoided.

Instructions in a language such as FORTRAN or BASIC are stored as text, with each symbol occupying one byte according to the ASCII code. This code makes use of the numbers between 0 and 255 (which corresponds to the range available using 8-bit binary) to represent upper and lower case letters, numbers, and other keyboard symbols as shown in Table 1. Each eight-bit binary number is known as a byte, and can be represented in writing either as a three-digit denary number or as a two-digit hexadecimal (base 16) value. Hexadecimal code uses the symbols 0 to 9 followed by A to F to represent the denary numbers 0 to 15. To convert binary into hexadecimal, each 8-bit byte is split into two 4-bit parts. Each 4-bit group then corresponds to one hexadecimal digit. Thus, decimal 109 can be represented as binary 01101101 or hexadecimal 6D. This number represents the letter m in ASCII code. A typical BASIC program line will occupy around 50 bytes in text. After translation into machine code it will also occupy 50 bytes. Each machine code instruction occupies between one and three bytes. Variables (numbers) occupy around 5 bytes, depending on their format (integer, floating point, or exponential).

The fundamental techniques of computer programming are described in the sections on BASIC and FORTRAN. The use of structured languages is described in the Pascal section. Each section builds on the information contained by its predecessors, and the newcomer to computing will find it helpful to read through from the start. Those who are familiar with the fundamentals of programming will be able to turn directly to the languages of interest. References are given for further reading on each language.

The observant reader will note that the rapidly growing area of computer graphics has not been discussed. This is because as yet there are no standardised graphics program instructions within any of the languages described. The graphics instructions applicable at each user's installation will (if graphics are available) be described by a user manual. In general graphics programs are not portable, i.e. they cannot be transferred from one machine to another.

BASIC

The name BASIC stands for Beginners All-purpose Symbolic Instruction Code, and the inclusion of the word "Beginners" is the key to its special use as a language for learning the fundamentals of computing. However, in addition to being an excellent teaching tool BASIC is a very good general purpose language, with some unique features.

Most versions of BASIC are interpreting, but recently compiling versions have become available. At the same time hardware speeds have increased dramatically during the last few years, and BASIC software running on a modern desktop computer can now achieve speeds that a few years ago were only obtained by mainframe computer systems.

All programming languages have rules of syntax or grammar. These rules have very precise meanings in computing, and to a large extent it is the syntax of a line of BASIC (or of any other high level language) that tells the interpreter or compiler what the programmer intends. The syntax of BASIC has intentionally been kept very simple, so that programming can begin after only a few rules have been mastered. Despite this simplicity all the facilities offered by "professional" languages such as FORTRAN are included in BASIC, albeit sometimes in a less efficient form. When programming is being taught through the medium of BASIC the simple grammar means that the emphasis can be on the style and on computational methods. Once the techniques of computing have been mastered in BASIC it is easy to convert to the traditional languages of large-scale computing such as FORTRAN, since their structure is closely related to that of BASIC.

Line Numbering

All BASIC program lines are prefaced by an integer line number. The purpose of this is to tell the computer

TABLE 1.—ASCII* CODES FOR COMMON KEYBOARD CHARACTERS

Decimal	Hexadecimal	Character	Obtained from CONTROL with:	Decimal	Hexadecimal	Character	Decimal	Hexadecimal	Character	Decimal	Hexadecimal	Character
0	0	NUL	@	32	20	Space	64	40	@	96	60	\
1	1	SOH	A	33	21	!	65	41	A	97	61	a
2	2	STX	B	34	22	″	66	42	B	98	62	b
3	3	EXT	C	35	23	£	67	43	C	99	63	c
4	4	EOT	D	36	24	$	68	44	D	100	64	d
5	5	ENQ	E	37	25	%	69	45	E	101	65	e
6	6	ACK	F	38	26	&	70	46	F	102	66	f
7	7	BEL	G	39	27	'	71	47	G	103	67	g
8	8	BS	H	40	28	(	72	48	H	104	68	h
9	9	HT	I	41	29	)	73	49	I	105	69	i
10	A	LF	J	42	2A	*	74	4A	J	106	6A	j
11	B	VT	K	43	2B	+	75	4B	K	107	6B	k
12	C	FF	L	44	2C	,	76	4C	L	108	6C	l
13	D	CR	M	45	2D	–	77	4D	M	109	6D	m
14	E	SO	N	46	2E	″	78	4E	N	110	6E	n
15	F	SI	O	47	2F	/	79	4F	O	111	6F	o
16	10	DLE	P	48	30	0	80	50	P	112	70	p
17	11	DC1	Q	49	31	1	81	51	Q	113	71	q
18	12	DC2	R	50	32	2	82	52	R	114	72	r
19	13	DC3	S	51	33	3	83	53	S	115	73	s
20	14	DC4	T	52	34	4	84	54	T	116	74	t
21	15	NAK	U	53	35	5	85	55	U	117	75	u
22	16	SYN	V	54	36	6	86	56	V	118	76	v
23	17	ETB	W	55	37	7	87	57	W	119	77	w
24	18	CAN	X	56	38	8	88	58	X	120	78	x
25	19	EM	Y	57	39	9	89	59	Y	121	79	y
26	1A	SUB	Z	58	3A	:	90	5A	Z	122	7A	z
27	1B	ESC	[	59	3B	;	91	5B	[	123	7B	{
28	1C	FS	\	60	3C	<	92	5C	\	124	7C	|
29	1D	GS	]	61	3D	=	93	5D	]	125	7D	}
30	1E	RS	^	62	3E	>	94	5E	^	128	7E	~
31	1F	US	–	63	3F	?	95	5F	–	129	7F	DEL

* American Standard Code for Information Interchange. The table is in fact the so-called 7-bit subset of the code, as the first of the eight bits is zero.

the order in which the lines are to be processed. If a command like:

PRINT "HELLO" ⟨Return⟩

is typed in without a line number it is immediately acted on, and in this example the word HELLO will be printed. If however we type:

10 PRINT "HELLO" ⟨Return⟩

nothing happens until the command RUN is given, when this simple one-line program again causes HELLO to be printed. Note that a line of BASIC in either immediate or program mode is input from the keyboard and is terminated by pressing the ⟨Return⟩ or ⟨Endline⟩ key. Throughout this chapter ⟨Return⟩ (or ⟨Endline⟩ on some systems) will be assumed at the end of each program line or command.

Line numbers can have any increment from 1 upwards, although increments of 5 or 10 are common. If 1 is used it makes it very difficult to insert extra lines when this becomes necessary. Most computers have an upper limit for line numbers—for example, the largest line number allowed in a BBC model B is 32767.

The END statement

Some versions of BASIC will not allow a program to be run unless its last statement is END. Our simple demonstration would in such a case take the following form:

```
10 PRINT "HELLO"
20 END
```

LET, Arithmetic and precedence of operators

In addition to dealing with text, BASIC has powerful arithmetical facilities. The operations add, subtract, multiply, divide, and exponentiation are provided, together with trigonometric and other functions. Numerical values can be assigned to a variable, and the variable may then be used in calculations as shown by the following example:

```
10 LET A = 4.7
20 LET B = 5.2
30 LET C = A + B
40 PRINT C
50 END
```

In most versions of BASIC the LET statement is optional and can be omitted. Note that this program will cause the numerical value of C (which is 9.9) to be printed, rather than the character C, since C is not enclosed in quotation marks. We shall return to the subtleties of PRINT statements later.

An important use of the LET statement (or of an implied LET) is the self-replacement of a previously used variable. For example, we can write:

```
     10 LET A = A * 5
(or  10 A = A * 5 on some systems).
```

Although this may at first seem ambiguous, the meaning is simple. The statement requires the value of variable A to be replaced by its old value multiplied by five.

There was no ambiguity in the program example earlier, where C was evaluated as the sum of A and B. However, consider the following case:

```
10 A = 4.7
20 B = 5.2
30 C = A + B * 6
```

Is C going to be (A + B) * 6 = 59.4, or A + (B * 6) = 35.9? It may come as a surprise that the correct answer in this case is 35.9, which appears to contradict the general rule that expressions are evaluated by reading from left to right. The reason is that in BASIC arithmetical operators have strict rules of precedence. The user must be aware of this hierarchical arrangement, and must use brackets where necessary if the computer is to do what is expected of it. The overall order of operator precedence is as follows:

Group 1: Functions (e.g. SIN, SQR, etc.), NOT (logical operation), and brackets.
Group 2: ∧ (raise to a power)
Group 3: * (multiply) and / (divide).
Group 4: + (addition) and − (subtraction)
Group 5: = (equals), < > (not equal to), > (greater than), < (less than), >= (greater than or equal to), and <= (less than or equal to).
Group 6: AND (logical operation)
Group 7: OR (logical operation) and EOR (logical operation).

Group 1 has the highest priority, group 7 the lowest. The operators within each group have equal priority, and will be dealt with on a left to right basis—in other words, in order in each line.

RUN and LIST

As discussed earlier, a BASIC program is fed into a computer by typing each line on a keyboard and pressing ⟨Return⟩. Execution of a BASIC program is initiated by the command RUN. When RUN is entered the computer begins to execute the instructions given by the program. While a program is running the keyboard is normally deactivated. A program terminates and returns control of the computer to the user when an END or STOP statement is encountered, when a programming error is detected, or when the last line in a program has been executed.

It is all too easy for typing mistakes to occur in entering a BASIC program, so it is important to be able to examine a program as it is known to the computer. The command LIST is provided for this purpose, and it causes the current version of the program to be printed to the user's terminal.

RUN and LIST are examples of system commands, and are not prefaced with a line number since they cannot be used within a program. They should be distinguished from commands like PRINT, which can act alone as system commands or can be used within a program.

Editing

If a program is listed and is found to contain errors, some means of editing out the mistakes will be required. BASIC (in common with other computing languages) provides editing facilities. The sophistication of these will depend upon the computer system being used, but as a minimum the following facilities should be available:

a) To replace a faulty line, type in a replacement in full and press ⟨Return⟩. For example, if the program reads:

```
10 PRONT A
20 END
```

The mistake may be corrected by typing:

```
10 PRINT A ⟨Return⟩
```

b) To insert a new line into a program, assign it a suitable line number between the existing line numbers at the point where you wish to make the insertion. For example, a line numbered 15 can be inserted into the program above by typing:

```
15 PRINT B
```

The program listing will then be:

```
10 PRINT A
15 PRINT B
20 END
```

c) To remove an unwanted line simply type its line number followed by ⟨Return⟩. For instance, in the program above typing

```
15 ⟨Return⟩
```

would produce the following listing:

```
10 PRINT A
20 END
```

LOAD and SAVE

It would be very tedious if programs had to be typed into a computer from a listing each time they were required. To avoid this all computer systems provide some means of storing programs and data. The storage medium may be a tape cassette, a tape cartridge, a floppy disk or a hard disk. Generally, programs are stored using the SAVE command, e.g.

```
SAVE MYPROG
```

and are retrieved by the LOAD command, e.g.

```
LOAD MYPROG
```

Some systems require that the program name be enclosed in quotation marks. With disk systems both programs and data may be stored as files, and these files may be accessed both by the user's commands in immediate mode and by program instructions. It is not possible to give any detailed guidance on the use of file storage systems, since the syntax of file handling instructions varies from system to system.

Data input and the INPUT statement

In order to see the effect of carrying out a calculation using different inputs, all programming languages provide facilities to allow the user to input data while a program is running. This is done by using symbols to represent variable quantities, and the INPUT statement causes the program to pause and request that values be typed in which are assigned to these variables. The following example demonstrates the use of the INPUT statement, and also shows how variables may be used instead of numerical values:

```
10 INPUT A,B
20 PRINT (A+B)/5
30 END
```

When this program is run, line 10 will cause it to pause and indicate (usually by printing a question mark) that values for the variables A and B are required. When this occurs the user types in the two numerical values, separated by a comma, and execution of the program continues. In this case the output will be one-fifth of the sum of the two numbers.

In some versions of BASIC the INPUT statement can be made to print a message before the computer pauses for the user's response. This can be very helpful, and is often used to indicate what response is required. For example, in the program above we could have:

```
10 INPUT "Type in values of A and B now:"; A,B
```

This example is in the format used by the BASIC in an Apple computer, and the exact syntax may be different for other versions. In the example program it would cause the message "Type in the values of A and B now:" to be printed, and the computer will then wait for the user's response.

A second method of feeding in data is to use the READ and DATA statements, which are dealt with in the next section.

The DATA, READ and RESTORE statements

An INPUT statement is a good way of supplying a limited amount of data to a BASIC program, but it quickly becomes tiresome when dealing with larger amounts of data. BASIC allows a list of data values to be specified within a program using the DATA statement, and these are supplied to the program when required by the READ statement.

An example of a data statement is:

```
50 DATA 3,5,7.89,2E4
```

A data statement has no immediate effect on the running of a program, but causes the numerical values it contains to be stored for later assignment to a variable. Data values are retrieved by a READ statement, an example of which would be:

```
110 READ A,B,C,D
```

When a BASIC program encounters the first READ statement, values from the list previously defined in a DATA statement are assigned to the named variables. This process of equating variables with data is carried out in order and in one-to-one correspondence with the requirements of the READ. Successive READ statements in a program carry on the process of reading data into variables through the DATA list. Thus if only part of a DATA list is used by a given READ, the next READ will continue where the last stopped. It is as if a pointer were moved along the DATA statement as values are used by READ statements. The following example demonstrates the use of READ and DATA:

```
10 DATA 1,2,5,6,8,4,10
20 READ A,B
30 PRINT A,B
40 READ A,B,C
50 PRINT (A+B+C)
60 READ A,B
70 PRINT A*B
```

The output obtained from this program would be 1, 2, 19, and 40.

It may be necessary to return the imaginary pointer to the first value given in the first DATA statement, so that all the given values can be re-used. This is achieved by the command RESTORE. If an extra line were inserted into the program above:

```
55 RESTORE
```

The output would then be 1,2,19,2.

The E format

It is possible to supply either very small or very large numbers to the computer, using the E format recognised by BASIC. Any number can be represented as a figure between 0 and 10 multiplied by 10 raised to a power, as for example 3×10^8. The exponential form is nEm, where n and m are numbers (which may be signed) and E is the letter E. Thus, nEm is interpreted by BASIC as $n \times 10^m$. Most versions of BASIC have thresholds below or above which numbers are printed in E format, because they would contain too many characters if they were printed in the ordinary way. For example,

300000000 or 3×10^8 would be printed as 3E8
0.0000008 or 8×10^{-7} would be printed as 8E−7

Thus a valid response to:

```
40 INPUT "Type in the values of A and B now: ";A,B
```

would be:

```
Type in the values of A and B now: 3E8,5E9
```

Variable names

In the previous sections A and B have been used as variable names. All versions of BASIC allow at least 260 variable names; the letters A to Z and the combinations produced by a single letter followed by a single figure, e.g. A6, S9 etc. To avoid confusion between the letter O and the figure Ø (zero), the convention of crossing the zero is adopted.

Many versions of BASIC allow more complicated variable names to be used. For instance, in a BBC computer the variables COUNTER or sample-number could be used. This allows the user to write such lines as:

```
10 COUNTER = COUNTER + 1
```

or

```
560 INPUT sample-number
```

These can be very helpful when a program has to be read by persons other than the original programmer. As a general rule, variables must begin with a letter rather than a number. The variable 5G for example is not allowed by almost all versions of BASIC.

The IF. . . . .THEN and GOTO statements:

In a program it is often necessary to repeat an operation until some test criterion is satisfied. Testing the value of a variable is achieved using the IF. . . . THEN statement, and the result may be used to redirect the computer to various parts of a program by means of the GOTO statement. For example, consider a program to calculate the average age of a group of people. The number of pieces of data (how many people there are) can itself be a variable, in addition to their ages. A flow diagram of the required program is shown in figure 3,

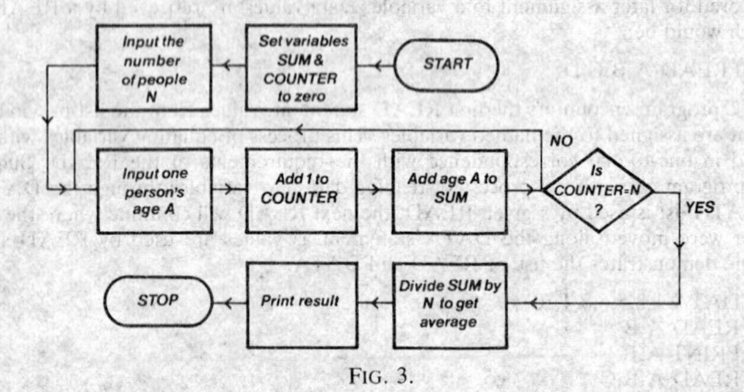

FIG. 3.

and its implementation in BASIC is shown below:

```
5 SUM = 0: C = 0
10 INPUT "HOW MANY PEOPLE ARE THERE?"; N
20 INPUT "TYPE IN AGE:"; A
30 C = C + 1
40 SUM = SUM + A
50 IF C = N THEN GOTO 100
60 GOTO 20
100 AVG = SUM/N
110 PRINT AVG
120 END
```

It will be noted that a counter C (which is initially set to zero) is incremented and tested after each piece of data has been entered, to see whether C equals the number of data points defined by N. So long as C is less than N data can be typed in, and the total of all the ages is maintained in the variable SUM. When C equals N SUM is divided by the number of people N to produce the required average AVG, which is printed out and the program ends. The value of C is tested by an IF. . . . . .THEN statement (line 50), and the action taken as a result of the outcome of the test is determined by the GOTO statements in lines 50 and 60.

GOTO statements should be used with caution, since it is possible to create an "endless loop" through their use. This is the case in the following example program:

```
10 PRINT "TRY AND STOP THIS!"
20 GOTO 10
30 END
```

The computer never reaches line 30, and in the absence of any intervention will continue to execute lines 10 and 20 forever. Methods of breaking out of a continuous loop vary from system to system, but pressing the RESET, BREAK or ESCAPE keys, or CONTROL and C together, are common.

Further discussion of the use of IF. . . . .THEN statements may be found in the later section on relational operators.

Output PRINT:

In a running program it can be very difficult to interpret what is going on unless explanatory messages appear. When a result has been calculated it is usually required as printed output. The output of both numerical and textual information is achieved using the PRINT command. The following examples demonstrate what can be done using PRINT statements:

```
10 PRINT A
20 PRINT
30 PRINT B$
40 PRINT "WELCOME TO MY PROGRAM"
50 PRINT A; "Newtons per square metre"
```

Line 10 will output the current value of variable A. Line 20 simply prints a linefeed or blank line. Line 30 prints the character string contained in B$ — note the $ suffix which denotes a character string rather than a numerical variable. Anything contained within quotation marks, such as the example in line 40, is literal information and is printed without the computer making any attempt to interpret it. Line 50 shows two printing features: first, the use of a semicolon as a delimiter between two items of printout causes them to be printed without a gap on the same line. If the semicolon were replaced by a comma the effect would be tabulation every 15 columns. Secondly, the words "Newtons per square metre" are faithfully reproduced since they are enclosed in quotes. Note that the same effect as that produced by line 50 would be obtained by:

```
50 PRINT A;B$
```

if B$ were previously defined as the character string "Newtons per square metre".

Library functions

The power of a computing language is greatly enhanced by the provision of a library of routines which evaluate commonly used functions. For example in BASIC the command SQR evaluates square roots. The range of functions available depends on which version of BASIC is used, but the following should be available on all systems:

Function:	*Meaning:*
SIN(x)	The sine of x, where x is an angle expressed in radians.
COS(x)	The cosine of x where x is in radians.
TAN(x)	The tangent of x where x is in radians.
ATN(x)	The arctangent of an angle x in the range $-\pi/2$ to $+\pi/2$ radians.
EXP(x)	The value of e^x.
LOG(x)	The natural logarithm of x.
INT(x)	The largest integer not greater than x.
ABS(x)	The absolute value of x.
SGN(x)	The sign of x. This function returns +1 if x is positive, −1 if x if negative, and 0 if x is zero.
SQR(x)	The square root of x.
RND(x)	Returns a random number between 0 and 1.

In the above list x represents any expression, which can include other functions.

The user is also able to define his own special-purpose functions in BASIC using the DEF FN command, which will be discussed in a later section.

Relational operators and the IF. . . . THEN statement

So far in this discussion, the example programs have used the simple arithmetic operators +, −, *, / and ∧. However, if a program is to make decisions it must in some way compare two quantities and test whether a stated relationship between them is TRUE or FALSE. For example, the relational expression:

```
A > B−1
```

will be TRUE if A is greater than the value of B minus 1, and FALSE otherwise. TRUE and FALSE are the only possible outcomes of a relational expression. In some versions of BASIC TRUE and FALSE are given the numerical values 1 and 0. The result of a relational expression can then be used as part of another expression. Many versions of BASIC additionally provide the relational operators AND, OR and EOR (exclusive-or), so that expressions such as:

```
10 IF (A > B−1) OR (A = 0) THEN GOTO 100
```

may be built up. In this example an IF. . . . .THEN statement has been used to alter the course of a BASIC program while it is being executed. When an IF. . . . .THEN statement is encountered the computer makes a decision about which line number to execute next. If the relational expression at the heart of the IF. . . . .THEN statement is TRUE, execution jumps to the line number given at the end of the IF. . . .THEN statement. If the result is FALSE, execution continues with the next line in sequence after the IF. . . . .THEN statement. As an example, consider the program below which evaluates square roots, the flow diagram for which is given in figure 4. A computer (unlike a mathematician) cannot evaluate the square root of a negative number, so

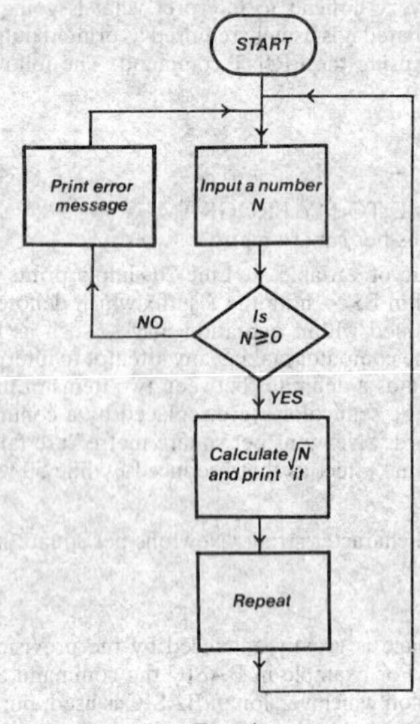

FIG. 4.

some means of rejecting negative inputs must be provided. An IF. . . . .THEN statement together with the relational operator >= can be used for this purpose:

```
10 PRINT "Type in a positive number to obtain its square root:"
20 INPUT N
30 IF N >= 0 then 60
40 PRINT "That was negative - I can't do those! Try again."
50 GOTO 20
60 PRINT "Square root = "; SQR(N)
70 GOTO 20
80 END
```

Notice that although this program does not contain a runaway loop, because it pauses for input during each cycle, it never reaches the END statement which is only there to satisfy the computer's operating system. The only way to stop this program as it stands is to press BREAK, ESCAPE, RESET or whatever is appropriate to the computer being used. The program could be modified to avoid this problem by adding/modifying the following lines:

```
70 INPUT "Do you want to continue?"; A$
75 IF A$ = "YES" THEN GOTO 20
```

The REM statement

Many programs are not self-explanatory to anyone other than the programmer (or even to the programmer after a time lapse!). All good software should be readily understandable, so that programs written by one person can continue to be used and modified when necessary long after the original programmer has moved on. A program of any complexity should include a generous number of comments or remarks which explain its operation. This is achieved using the REM statement, whose syntax is:

```
150 REM any remark, comment or explanation.
```

Any program line starting with the word REM is disregarded in execution, but is always included when a program is listed. The combination of a flow diagram and REM statements within a program are essential to any software documentation.

Program loops: The FOR and NEXT statements

We have already seen an example of a program loop in figure 3, where it was shown that the number of times a loop is executed may be controlled by the use of a counter, and completion tested by the use of an IF. . . . .THEN statement. However, this technique is rather clumsy, and there are simpler ways of controlling BASIC loops.

Looping is a common requirement in computer programming, and all high level languages provide some means of automatically initialising a counter, incrementing it and testing for completion of a loop. In BASIC loop control is achieved by FOR and NEXT statements. Suppose a calculation is to be carried out 50 times. A variable J (or any other convenient name) is used as a counter, and is automatically initialised by the FOR statement and incremented by the NEXT statement. The FOR and NEXT statements appear in a program as shown below:

```
100 FOR J = 1 TO 50
110
120 (Rest of program, which may include INPUT, PRINT,
130 calculations, and even other loops).
140
150
160 NEXT J
```

The FOR statement defines the number of times the loop is to be executed, 50 in this case, and initialises J to the value 1. A FOR. . .NEXT loop does not have to start with J = 1, line 100 could equally well have been:

```
      100 FOR J = 181 TO 230
or    100 FOR J = −20 to 20
```

The counter in a FOR. . .NEXT loop does not have to be incremented by one each time the loop is executed, although this is the default condition. Line 100 in the example above will result in an increment of one. However, if an increment of five were needed line 100 would be:

```
100 FOR I = 0 TO 50 STEP 5
```

In general, the FOR statement specifies the name of the variable which is to be used as loop counter, initialises the loop counter, and determines the amount by which the counter is incremented each time the loop is executed. The NEXT statement locates the end of a loop and restates the variable name, so that both the programmer and the computer are in no doubt as to which loop is being terminated.

In the discussion above it was implied that a program can contain a number of loops, often "nested" one within the other. For example a program may instruct the computer to evaluate a function of two variables I and J over a range of values of I and J. In BASIC, loops must be entirely contained one within another, and must never be allowed to cross. Correctly structured multiple loops are known as nested loops, and the example below shows the correct and incorrect use of multiple loops:

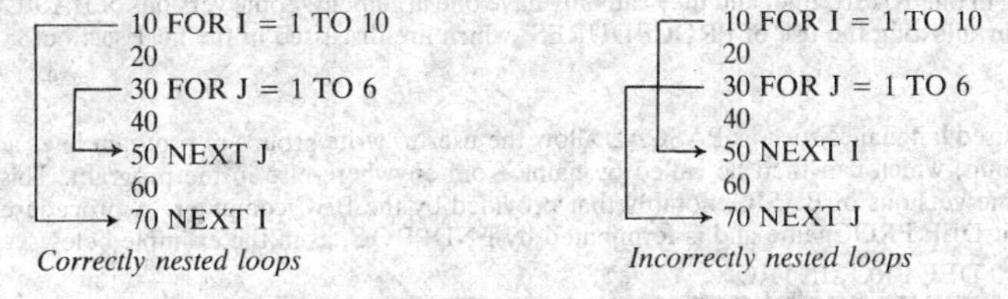

Correctly nested loops *Incorrectly nested loops*

Another common mistake made by programmers using multiple loops is to use the same variable name as a counter in more than one loop, as shown by the example below:

```
10 FOR I = 1 TO 10
20
30 FOR I = 1 TO 6
40
50 NEXT I
60
70 NEXT I
```

Multiple branching — ON. . . . . .GOTO

In the discussion of branching using relational operators the IF. . . . .THEN statement was used to provide a two-way branch. It is often useful to provide a multiple branch to one of several destinations within a program, and this is achieved using the ON. . . . .GOTO statement. The form of the command is:

```
300 ON X GOTO 1000, 2000, 3000, 4000
```

When this statement is encountered the variable (X in this case, although it can be an expression) is evaluated and is truncated to an integer. If X = 1 the program will jump to the first line number listed, 1000 in this example. If X = 2 a jump to line 2000 occurs, and so on. If X was found to be negative, zero or larger than the number of destinations given an error has occurred, and the computer will print an appropriate message and bring program execution to a stop.

The following program segment illustrates the use of multiple branching:

```
10 PRINT "CHOOSE ONE OF THE FOLLOWING:"
20 PRINT "1)INPUT DATA"
30 PRINT "2) ANALYSE DATA"
40 PRINT "3) OUTPUT DATA"
50 PRINT "4) STOP"
60 INPUT A
70 ON A GOTO 100,200,300,400
```

A is an integer between 1 and 4. If A=1 the program continues at line 100, if A=2 at line 200, and so on. If A is less than 1 or greater than 4 an error message is printed.

Defining functions—the DEF FNname statement

In an earlier section we saw how the power of BASIC was enhanced by the provision of a library of standard functions. Although these cover the most important requirements, it is often useful to be able to define new functions for arithmetic expressions which occur repeatedly. The statement DEF FNname is used for this purpose. Each user-defined function must be given a name, and the syntax of the name will depend on the version of BASIC being used. At least 26 single-letter function names are available in all versions of BASIC, corresponding to the letters of the alphabet i.e. FNA, FNB, FNC etc.

An example of the use of DEF FN is:

```
150 DEF FNC(X) = 0.5*(EXP(X) + EXP(-X))
```

which calculates the value of cosh(x), the hyperbolic cosine of x. Another example is:

```
200 DEF FNA(R) = 4*ATN(1)*R ∧ 2
```

which calculates the area of a circle of radius R. A statement like:

```
520 SUM = FNA(5) + FNA(12)
```

makes the value of the variable SUM equal to the sum of the areas of a circle of radius 5 and a circle of radius 12.

When a function is defined by DEF FNname(argument), such as in line 200 above, the variable in brackets (R in this case) is known as the argument of the function. Even if the argument used in defining a function has been assigned a value, it is not used by the function (unless of course the program calls for FNA(R)). An argument used but not evaluated in this way is known as a dummy argument.

A function can be defined anywhere in a BASIC program, and does not necessarily have to be defined at a lower line number than that which first uses it. The main limitations of functions are that they must be capable of being defined in one BASIC line, and they can only have one argument. Some versions of BASIC get around this limitation by allowing the use of PROCEDURES, which are discussed in the next section.

PROCEDURES

Highly structured languages such as PASCAL allow the user to write groups of program lines and assign a name to the group, which can then be called by name from anywhere else in the program. This feature is available on some versions of BASIC, notably that provided by the BBC computer. A procedure is defined by the statement DEF PROCname and is terminated by ENDPROC, as in the example below:

```
200 DEF PROCINTRO
210 PRINT "THIS PROGRAM WAS WRITTEN BY FRED SMITH"
220 INPUT "PRESS RETURN TO CONTINUE:";A$
230 ENDPROC
```

Another example of a procedure is:

```
300 DEF PROCMENU
310 PRINT "SELECT FROM THE FOLLOWING:"
320 PRINT "1) INPUT NEW DATA"
330 PRINT "2) ANALYSE DATA"
340 PRINT "3) QUIT"
```

```
350 INPUT "TYPE 1, 2 OR 3 NOW:"; N
360 ENDPROC
```

The main program might then begin:

```
10 PROCINTRO
20 PROCMENU
```

Whenever PROCINTRO is encountered in this example lines 200–230 are executed. The program then returns to the instruction after the PROCINTRO statement, which in this case is PROCMENU. The use of procedures allows a program to be broken into a number of small manageable sections. Each section can be given a name which assists program documentation, and the main part of a program then simply consists of a number of procedure calls.

Subroutines—The GOSUB statement

The GOSUB statement allows a program to temporarily jump to another part of a program, execute the program lines at that location, and return to the instruction following the GOSUB statement. A subsection of a program used in this way is known as a subroutine, and it will be noted that it has many features in common with a procedure. Procedures are usually more flexible and easier to use than subroutines, but they are not available in all versions of BASIC. Just as when using procedures, the use of subroutines allows a program to be broken up into recognisable modules.

The syntax of a GOSUB statement is:

```
150 GOSUB 2000
```

The first line of a subroutine is usually a REM statement giving information about the purpose of the subroutine. A subroutine is terminated with a RETURN statement, which causes program execution to resume immediately after the GOSUB instruction. A simple example of a program using a subroutine is given below:

```
10 PRINT "THIS PROGRAM CALCULATES THE AREAS OF TRIANGLES"
20 PRINT "FROM DIMENSIONS TYPED IN AT THE KEYBOARD."
30 PRINT
40 INPUT "WHAT IS THE LENGTH OF THE BASE?";L
50 INPUT "WHAT IS THE PERPENDICULAR HEIGHT?";H
60 GOSUB 1000
70 PRINT "AREA IS:"; A
80 INPUT "MORE (1) OR QUIT (2)?"; B
90 ON B GOTO 30, 100
100 STOP
1000 REM SUBROUTINE FOR CALCULATION OF AREA
1010 A = L * (H/2)
1020 RETURN
```

The STOP statement

In many versions of BASIC the END instruction has to be the statement with the largest line number. Thus, line 100 in the program above cannot be an END statement. It could have been a GOTO statement redirecting execution to an END statement at the end of the program, but this would be rather clumsy. Instead the STOP statement is provided, which has the same effect as END but which can be placed anywhere in the program. Note that in versions of BASIC where an END statement is required by the system at the end of a program something like:

```
9999 END
```

will be needed. However it will not neccesarily be executed during a program run, and is often only there to satisfy the computer's operating system that the whole program has been loaded.

Arrays

In the previous sections of this chapter labels such as A, B, C, or X have been used to represent variables, as in ordinary algebra. The name of a variable can be thought of as a label for the address containing the value of the variable.

If a list of values is to be supplied to a program, it is very wasteful to use a separate variable name for each value, since the computer then not only has to store all the data in the list but also the variable names. In addition, using a separate name for each value will quickly exhaust the set of allowed variable names in most versions of BASIC!

Most computing languages provide an array facility, which is a means of organising a list of data values under one variable name. A computer program can extract a value from the list by specifying the variable name together with a subscript. By altering the value of the subscript, for instance using a FOR. . .NEXT loop, a common operation may be carried out on all the elements in a list. In BASIC any allowed variable can be used as the name of a list or array, and the subscript specifying which array element is required is enclosed in brackets, as for example:

```
1500 PRINT A(53)
```

The subscript can take the form of an expression as well as a numerical value, i.e.

```
100 PRINT A(I+J)
```

A subscript can be any integer numerical value, or any expression which when evaluated yields a numerical value, but it should be obvious that it must not be negative. In BASIC the lowest allowed subscript value is 0. If a subscript is not integer it will be truncated, for example

```
150 PRINT X(8.56)
```

will print the value contained in X(8).

When running a BASIC program the computer needs to know in advance the size of any arrays it will be required to process. Before any reference is made to an array name therefore it is necessary to specify its size using the DIM (short for dimension) command. Several arrays may be dimensioned using a single DIM statement. An example DIM statement might be:

```
10 DIM A(10),B(100),C(6)
```

which sets up arrays A, B and C to store 11, 101 and 7 pieces of data respectively. Notice that since the lowest array subscript is 0, an array dimensioned with the value N will be able to store N+1 values.

Arrays can be used to store character strings as well as numerical data. The rules governing the use of string arrays are similar to those for numeric arrays. For example, the command DIM C$(10) will allocate memory space for 10 character strings to be stored under the label C$. The allowed length of a string depends upon the computer system, but in most machines the maximum length is 255 characters.

The following example illustrates the use of arrays in a program to store and retrieve the ages of named people:

```
5 DIM A(50),N$(50)
7 INPUT "DO YOU WANT TO INPUT (1) OR EXAMINE (2) DATA?";B
10 IF B = 2 THEN 60
20 FOR I = 1 TO 50
30 INPUT "NAME?";N$(I)
40 INPUT "AGE?";A(I)
50 NEXT I
55 STOP
60 REM DATA EXAMINATION
70 INPUT "GIVE THE NAME YOU ARE INTERESTED IN:"; M$
80 LET J = 1
90 IF N$(J) = M$ THEN 200
100 J = J +1
110 GOTO 90
200 PRINT "AGE OF";M$;" IS ";A(J)
210 GOTO 70
```

There are several points of interest in this program. Note that the arrays A and N$ are dimensioned in line 5, to allow 50 names and ages to be stored. A variable B is used with an IF. . .THEN statement to allow the user to indicate which half of the program is required. To input data a FOR. . .NEXT loop is used. In the retrieval part of the program a FOR. . .NEXT loop is not suitable, since we do not know how many searches the computer must undertake before it finds a match between the input name and stored data (line 90). The slightly more tedious approach of initialising (at line 80) and incrementing (line 100) a counter is used, with a GOTO statement at line 110. Finally, the required data is printed out at line 200.

The extension of the use of arrays from one to several dimensions is straightforward. The use of two dimensions for example is very common, since this form of data representation readily lends itself to matrix algebra. If an array in one dimension is a list (or a vector), and array of two dimensions forms a table or matrix as shown below:

$$A = \begin{pmatrix} A_1 \\ A_2 \\ A_3 \end{pmatrix} \qquad A = \begin{pmatrix} A_{11} & A_{12} & A_{13} \\ A_{21} & A_{22} & A_{23} \\ A_{31} & A_{32} & A_{33} \end{pmatrix}$$

which has double subscripts. In BASIC the subscripts are separated by a comma. For example, the matrix element A_{21} in BASIC is represented as A(2,1). Similarly a three dimensional array is available, in which A_{ijk} is represented by A(I,J,K).

As in the one-dimensional case, any subscripted variable is treated by BASIC as an array element. The number of subscripts must be constant throughout a program. If no DIM statement is provided some versions of BASIC assume that the size of an array will be 10 in as many dimensions as there are subscripts. For example, a program reference to an element of a previously undeclared array such as B(5,1) will cause a default DIMension statement B(10,10) to be executed.

Matrix operations

Some versions of BASIC include matrix manipulating instructions, which are very convenient and save considerable programming effort by replacing the many lines of software otherwise required. As mentioned earlier, a one-dimensional array can be used to represent a vector, and a two-dimensional array represents a matrix. In matrix algebra it is important to distinguish between two kinds of one-dimensional array, the column vector:

$$C = \begin{pmatrix} C_{11} \\ C_{21} \\ C_{31} \end{pmatrix}$$

and the row vector:

$$R = (R_{11}\ R_{12}\ R_{13})$$

To define a column vector having n elements the statement DIM (n,1) is required, and to define a row vector DIM (1,n). Note that although these are both one-dimensional arrays they have two subscripts. It is good practice to retain explicit control by dimensioning vectors in this way for matrix algebra, since whether a row or column vector results from a statement like DIM A(3) depends on the version of BASIC used.

If the ordinary PRINT and INPUT statements are used for matrix input and output a proliferation of loops results. The BASIC instructions MAT PRINT and MAT INPUT avoid this difficulty. MAT INPUT asks for data to be typed in one row at a time, separated by commas, and MAT PRINT causes a matrix to be printed out one row at a time. For example:

```
10 DIM A(5,5)
20 MAT INPUT A
30 MAT PRINT A
```

Line 20 requires five lines of five values to be typed in, with the values on each line separated by commas. Line 30 will cause to five lines of five values to be printed out as a table.

Three special matrices can be defined automatically. These are the zero matrix (all values are zero), the identity matrix (a square matrix in which all values are zero except the leading diagonal, which contains ones), and a matrix in which all elements are ones. The BASIC instructions are:

```
MAT A = ZER
MAT A = IDN
```

and MAT A = CON respectively.

The addition, subtraction and multiplication of matrices requires complicated FOR. . .NEXT loops if matrix instructions are not available. Matrix algebra is only meaningful if the matrices concerned conform for each operation. The meaning of conformability depends on the particular operation being undertaken, and will be explained for each operation.

Matrix addition is achieved by the instruction:

```
MAT A = B + C
```

The corresponding elements of the matrices **B** and **C** in this example are added together, and the result forms an element of the new matrix (which must previously be dimensioned) **A**.

Matrix subtraction is a similar process, with element-by-element subtraction being used to produce a new matrix which contains the results. In the case of addition and subtraction therefore, conformability means that all three matrices (**A**,**B**,**C** in our example) must have the same dimensions.

Each element of a matrix can be multiplied by a scalar, which may be a constant or may be an expression, using an instruction of the form: 50 MAT A = (5) * A

In this example each element of matrix **A** is multiplied by five.

Matrix multiplication is supported by the statement:

```
MAT A = B * C
```

For matrix multiplication to be meaningful conformability requires that, in this example, the number of elements in a row of matrix **B** is the same as the number of elements in a column of **C**. Matrix **A** will have dimensions r × s, where r is the number of elements in a column of **B** and s is the number of elements in a row of **C**.

If a system of simultaneous equations is expressed as a matrix A, the solution is contained in a matrix A^{-1} which is the inverse of **A**, i.e. $\mathbf{A}.\mathbf{A}^{-1}$ equals the identity matrix. Thus finding the inverse of a matrix is a valuable way to solve sets of equations. The MAT. . .INV statement is provided by BASIC as a means of inverting matrices. An example of its use is:

```
200 MAT B = INV A
```

where matrix **A** is inverted and the result placed in matrix **B**.

It is often necessary to exchange elements between the rows and columns of a matrix, so that for example element A(1,3) becomes element A(3,1) and so on. This process is known as transposing a matrix, and BASIC provides the instruction TRN to achieve it. An example of the use of TRN is:

```
200 MAT D = TRN (A)
```

Conformability requires that both matrices (**D** and **A** in the example) are square and of the same size.

MAT INPUT becomes tedious if large matrices have to be filled repeatedly, so BASIC provides the statement MAT READ which is used in conjunction with DATA (and RESTORE) instructions. When a MAT READ statement is encountered, an array is filled from the DATA list in row order. The following example illustrates the use of MAT READ:

```
.10 DIM A(2,2),B(2,2) C(2,2)
20 DATA 1,2,3,4,5,6,5,4
30 MAT READ A
40 MAT READ B
50 MAT C = A + B
```

Line 30 causes matrix A and B to be read in as:

$$\begin{pmatrix} 1 & 2 \\ 3 & 4 \end{pmatrix} \quad \begin{pmatrix} 5 & 6 \\ 5 & 4 \end{pmatrix}$$

respectively. Line 50 performs matrix addition of A and B, and the result (in C) is:

$$\begin{pmatrix} 6 & 8 \\ 8 & 8 \end{pmatrix}$$

FORTRAN

FORTRAN is an abbreviation of FORmula TRANslation. It is a language especially suited to algebraic manipulation (hence the "formula" part of the name). FORTRAN is a compiling language, and was first introduced in the mid-1950s. Since the first versions appeared many improvements have been made, and in its early years this inevitably led to the production of several incompatible versions of the language. To limit the proliferation of different versions of FORTRAN, the American National Standards Institute (ANSI) defined a standard version of FORTRAN in 1966, known as FORTRAN IV. Eleven years later a revised specification was prepared describing the current form of the language, which is known as FORTRAN 77. Any FORTRAN IV program should be acceptable to a FORTRAN 77 system, but not vice versa since the later version has some additional features. It is interesting to note in passing that despite several attempts no standard version of BASIC has been adopted. As a result, programs written in many of the common versions of BASIC are mutually incompatible!

Particular versions of FORTRAN may differ from FORTRAN 77 in that they provide non-standard extensions to the language to increase its power and flexibility. However, as a general rule a program written in FORTRAN 77 should run on any FORTRAN system. For this reason programmers writing software which is intended to be portable (i.e. which is intended for use on a number of different computers) should beware of using any extensions to the language provided by their particular version of FORTRAN.

As discussed in the introduction to this chapter, instructions written in a compiling language such as FORTRAN constitute the source code or source file. In early computer systems each program line or statement was punched onto a card, with the complete program forming a deck of cards. In modern systems the source code is usually typed into a terminal and stored as a disk file. The compiler has the function of translating the source code into a file of machine instructions known as the object code. This translating function contributes the second syllable of the name FORTRAN.

One of the obvious differences between BASIC and FORTRAN programs is that FORTRAN statements are only assigned a number by the programmer when it is necessary to label a statement. The sequence in which instructions are executed is dictated either by the statement order, or by commands which alter the flow of control in program execution, such as the IF instruction.

Integer and real numbers

Unlike BASIC, where the computer can (usually) be relied upon to make intelligent use of numbers regardless of their format, FORTRAN requires the programmer to declare whether a variable is real (also called floating point) or integer. Although the integer 1 and the real number 1.0 have the same value, FORTRAN deals with these two number types in a totally different way, and the type specified can seriously affect the result of a computation.

A FORTRAN integer is any positive or negative whole number having (typically) up to 12 digits. The limits to the size of an integer depend on the computer used. Integers are normally reserved for special purposes such as loop control. Real numbers are much more common, since a FORTRAN integer can only have an integer value, but a real variable can have either an integer or a real value. Most of the numbers used in a FORTRAN program are real for this reason. As discussed in the next section, FORTRAN examines a constant, and if it finds a decimal point or an E (denoting exponential format), the constant is classified as real.

Constants and variables

Just as in BASIC, any number (or in certain circumstances text string) that appears in explicit form is called a constant. Any quantity that is given a label or name and which is allowed to vary by assigning different values to it is called a variable. For example, in the arithmetic assignment statements:

```
I = 100
Z = A + B + 5.78
```

A,B,I and Z are variables, while 100 and 5.78 are constants. FORTRAN distinguishes between real and integer constants by examining them for a decimal point or the letter E, which as in BASIC denotes an exponent. If a constant contains a decimal point or an exponent, the FORTRAN compiler will classify it as real.

A constant may if desired be preceded by a plus (+) sign to show that it is positive. A negative constant must be preceded by a minus (−) sign.

The decimal point in a real constant must be a stop (.) not a comma (,). Most FORTRAN systems limit the user to 8 or 12 digits when specifying the value of a real constant. Many versions allow the programmer to specify that a variable or constant is to be treated as a double precision number. This is a number with (approximately) twice as many digits as an ordinary real number. This extra precision is often necessary to guard against the build-up of numerical errors in repeated or lengthy calculations.

As in BASIC, the letter E is used in a constant to signify that the number which it follows is to be multiplied by 10 raised to the power of the figure following the E. This simplifies the writing of very large or very small numbers. The following table gives examples of real and integer constants with an acceptable FORTRAN format:

TABLE 2.—FORTRAN FORMAT FOR REAL AND INTEGER CONSTANTS

Real	*Integer*
0.5	0
.5	9
3.0	−9
3.	+400
−5.0	−123456789
−0.00000789	987654321
+6.78	
209E9	
3.0E−17	
3.E−17	
−.5E5	
0.0	

Variable names

The first letter of a variable name in FORTRAN tells the compiler whether the variable is to have integer or real values.

Integer variables can have up to six digits and must begin with the letters I, J, K, L, M, or N. Thus, the following are examples of allowed integer variable names:

INDIA, K100, NUMBER, I5

The limit of six digits is typical, although some systems may allow more.

Real variables have names composed of (typically) up to six digits, the first of which is a letter but not I, J, K, L, M or N. The following are examples of allowed real variable names:

COUNT, ANSWER, A1, X77

A real value can never be stored in an integer variable. If an integer value is stored in a real variable it will become real.

As mentioned above, the FORTRAN compiler uses the first letter of a variable name to determine whether the variable is to be treated as real or integer. However, this default classification (the classification which would apply in the absence of a type statement) can be overridden by the statements REAL and INTEGER. These are examples of type statements, which will be dealt with in more detail later. A type statement consists of a type declaration followed by a list of variable names, separated by commas. Examples of REAL and INTEGER declarations are:

```
REAL A,B,J
INTEGER I,K,COUNT
```

Operators, precedence and algebraic expressions

There are five basic operators in FORTRAN, corresponding to the arithmetic operations of addition, subtraction, multiplication, division and exponentiation (or raising a number to a power). Each of these operations is represented as shown in table 3:

TABLE 3.—ARITHMETIC OPERATORS IN FORTRAN.

Operation:	*Symbol:*
Add	+
Subtract	−
Multiply	*
Divide	/
Exponentiate	**

Apart from exponentiation, the symbols are the same as those used in BASIC. (The BASIC equivalent of ** is ∧). FORTRAN considers the combination of two asterisks ** denoting exponentiation to be one symbol.

Just as in BASIC, the arithmetic operators may be used to build up FORTRAN expressions. Examples of FORTRAN expressions are given below. It will be noted that, apart from the omission of line numbers, they bear a strong resemblance to BASIC instructions:

```
J = J + 1
PI = 3.141593
X = (−B + (B**2 − 4.0*A*C)**0.5)/2.0*A)
```

When writing FORTRAN expressions the programmer must obey the following rules to correctly convey his intentions to the compiler:

(a) Two operation symbols cannot be adjacent to each other. Thus A*−B is not a valid FORTRAN expression. The correct version should be A*(−B). The exception to this rule is ** denoting exponentiation, which FORTRAN treats as though it were one symbol.

(b) Brackets must be used to clarify the programmers intention. Thus the expression $(A + B)^2$ would be written (A + B)**2 in FORTRAN, and not A + B **2. This last expression is of course perfectly valid, but it has the meaning $A + B^2$, which is not what was intended by the programmer.

(c) If the order in which operations are to be carried out is not completely specified by brackets, the following rules of operator precedence apply:

   Group 1: Functions (SIN, COS etc.) and brackets.
   Group 2: ** (raising to a power).
   Group 3: * (multiply) and / (divide).
   Group 4: + (addition) and − (subtraction).

   Just as in BASIC, group 1 has the highest priority and group 4 the lowest. The operators within each group have equal priority and will usually be dealt with on a left to right basis — in other words, in order in each line. However this cannot be relied upon as it is somewhat system dependent. As a general rule, the free use of brackets is to be encouraged even if this occasionally leads to the programmer writing more than is strictly necessary.

(d) Brackets are used in an expression to indicate grouping not multiplication. Thus the expression (A+1) (B+2) has no meaning; the correct version is (A+1)*(B+2).

(e) As a general rule integer and real quatitites must not be mixed in an expression. The exception to this is exponentiation, as a real quantity can obviously be raised to an integer power. Some versions of FORTRAN relax this rule, but the programmer should beware of taking advantage of this relaxation since surprising and undesired results may sometimes be obtained.

(f) As mentioned earlier, a real quantity can be raised to an integer power. However the converse is not true, as only a real quantity can be raised to a real power. An exponent can itself be an expression. It is never permissible to raise a negative value to a real power, or to raise zero to a zero power.

Library functions

FORTRAN includes a library of routines which evaluate commonly used mathematical functions. The exact contents of the function library will depend upon the version of FORTRAN used, but the following are commonly available:

Function:	*Meaning:*
SIN(X)	Calculates the sine of X, where X is an angle expressed in radians.
COS(X)	The cosine of X, where X is in radians.
TAN(X)	The tangent of X, where X is in radians.
ATAN(X)	The arctangent of X, where the result is in the range $-\pi/2$ to $+\pi/2$ radians.
EXP(X)	The value of e^x
ALOG(X)	The natural logarithm of X.
ALOG10(X)	The logarithm to the base 10 of X.
ABS(X)	The absolute value of X.
SQRT(X)	The square root of X

In the above list X can represent a constant, a variable or an expression. Note that X must be enclosed in brackets. There are three further functions which are usually available, in which X represents a list of variable names. These are:

IFIX X	Converts declaration of variable type from real to integer.
FLOAT X	Converts declaration of variable type from integer to real.
DOUBLE PRECISION X	Specifies that the list of variables X are to be double precision.

Structure of a FORTRAN statement

A FORTRAN statement has three parts; a line number, an indicator specifying the purpose of the statement, and finally the FORTRAN instruction. The general format is:

(1) Line number.	(2) Indicator for comment (C) or continuation (+).	(3) FORTRAN instruction.

The line number (1) is a positive non-zero integer of (usually) up to five digits. Line numbers are usually generated by the computer rather than typed in by the programmer. It is important to distinguish between line numbers, which are used by the system, and statement numbers, which as discussed later are supplied by the programmer.

The indicator (2) consists of a single character, which may be a space (i.e. it is blank), may be the letter C, or may be a plus sign. The character C tells the compiler that whatever follows is a comment for program documentation. It will not be compiled, but will appear whenever the program is listed. This is the FORTRAN equivalent of the REM statement in BASIC.

If the compiler finds a plus sign in position (2) the line is treated as a continuation of the preceding line. This enables the programmer to write long statements.

If (2) is blank (a space), the compiler expects to find the start of a new FORTRAN statement.

Part (3) contains the FORTRAN instruction itself. It may also contain a statement number, used to identify a particular instruction (for instance, the end of a loop).

The following example FORTRAN program demonstrates some of these points. The meaning of some of the statements used may be unclear at this stage and will be explained later.

```
00010 PROGRAM AVERAGE
00020C THE AVERAGE OF FIVE VALUES
00030 READ (*,*) VALUE1, VALUE2, VALUE3, VALUE4,
00040+VALUE5
00050 MEAN = (VALUE1 + VALUE2 + VALUE3 + VALUE4 +
00060+VALUE5)/5
00070 STOP
00080 END
```

The PROGRAM statement

Line 00010 in the example above illustrates the use of the PROGRAM statement. On some systems its use is not essential, but it is good practice to always begin with a PROGRAM instruction. The statement consists of the word PROGRAM, followed by a user-specified name. The name can have up to eight characters, depending on the system, and the first character must be a letter. It is helpful if a name is chosen which reflects the purpose of the program, so that when the user's file directory (list of programs) is printed it is easy to select the required program. The name of a program must not be used as a variable within the program.

Free-format input and output commands

Any computer system needs to be able to put data into memory and retrieve it as required. In BASIC, the INPUT and PRINT statements perform this function. The FORTRAN equivalents are READ and WRITE.

READ: When the FORTRAN compiler encounters the keyword READ, the system expects data to be input from some external source. In FORTRAN 77 the statement READ (*,*) is known as a free-format read, and it will have the effect of making the system pause and request the user to type in data from the keyboard. Usually the computer indicates that it is expecting some input by printing a question mark on the screen as a prompt. A typical read statement is:

```
READ (*,*) A1, A2, A3
```

Note that after the read statement there is a bracket containing two asterisks separated by a comma, and a list of variable names. In this example the computer would expect the user to type in three numerical values, which would be assigned to the variables A1, A2 and A3.

The asterisks within the bracket tell the system to expect the input to come from the default device, i.e. the keyboard, and to have a default or free format. The asterisks can be replaced by characters which specify alternative input devices and formats. The syntax for doing this will be discussed later.

WRITE: The keyword WRITE makes the FORTRAN compiler print data, to the user's terminal if the free format (*,*) is used. Both numbers and text can be output, as shown by the following example:

```
00010 PROGRAM READ/WRITE DEMONSTRATION
00020 WRITE (*,*) "TYPE IN 1 REAL, A COMMA THEN 1 INTEGER."
00030 READ (*,*) R1, I1
00040 WRITE (*,*) "INPUT DATA WAS:", R1, I1
00050 STOP
00060 END
```

The first WRITE statement (line 00020) contained only text, which was enclosed in quotations. The second WRITE statement (line 00040) prints a message and then the values of the variables R1 and I1. Note that in this case the text (enclosed in quotation marks) is separated from the variables by a comma. The use of a message as part of a WRITE statement helps to make a program's output more comprehensible. A message cannot however form part of a READ statement, so line 00030 is prefaced by line 00020 which explains to the user what input the program expects.

Input and output from other devices

In the examples above the characters (*,*) were used to specify a default input device (the keyboard) and a default output device (the user's terminal). However, the user may want data to be output to other devices, for example magnetic storage, or to be input from a disk rather than having to type it manually. The first * character within the bracketed part of a READ or WRITE statement can be replaced by an integer number, which specifies a particular input or output device. For example:

```
READ (3,*) A, B, C
WRITE (6,*) A, B, C
```

might be used to direct the computer to take data from magnetic disk and output it to a line printer. The correspondence between particular numbers and input/output devices is system dependent.

It is probable that a given input device will contain a number of files of data, so the name of the required input file must be specified in addition to the number of the device it is to be obtained from. The statement OPEN is provided in FORTRAN for this purpose. An example of the syntax is:

```
OPEN (3, FILE=DATA1)
READ (3,*) NUM1, NUM2, NUM3
```

In this case file DATA1 has been selected on device 3, and three values from the file are assigned to variables NUM1, NUM2, and NUM3.

The OPEN statement can also be used to create a data file on a storage device. For instance, in the following statements:

```
OPEN (5, FILE=DATA2)
WRITE (5,*) A1,B1,C1
CLOSE (5, STATUS="KEEP")
```

a file called DATA2 is created on device 5, which contains the values of A1, B1 and C1. The final statement has the effect of closing DATA2 and keeping it for future use. The reserved word (or keyword) STATUS can have one of two values, KEEP or DELETE. Note that the filename (DATA2 in the example) does not appear in a CLOSE command, but only the device number. CLOSE terminates all the open files on a particular device.

Fixed format input and output

In the READ and WRITE statements used up to this point, a * character or an integer number has been used to specify the input or output device. The observant reader will have noted that the parentheses contain a second * character, which tells the system to use a default format for input and output. It is often necessary to explicitly control or format the way in which information is laid out on the screen or printer. When reading in data from a device other than the keyboard, it may also be necessary to define the format before data can be read. The second * character can be replaced by an integer number, which is the label of a statement defining the format to be used. For example, in the statements

```
    WRITE (3,100) NUMBER
100 FORMAT (I6)
```

the integer value of the variable NUMBER is being output. The figure 100 within the bracket tells the system that it is to get the required format from statement 100, which is a FORMAT instruction containing I6. This tells the computer that a six-digit integer is to be printed.

The character I inside the brackets of a FORMAT statement must not be confused with any variable I used elsewhere in a program. When it is inside parentheses in a FORMAT statement it simply indicates an integer value.

As shown in the example, the figure following the I tells the system how many character spaces are to be used in printing out the number. Thus if NUMBER had the value 123456, line 100 would ensure that it was printed out as six characters. If NUMBER had the value 123, the effect would be to output 123, where three leading spaces are printed before the value. If NUMBER had the value 12345678 the computer would signal an error and stop. Line 100 would have to be

```
100 FORMAT (I8)
```

in such a case.

If several values are to be output, their values must be listed inside the bracket of the FORMAT statement and separated by commas, as for example:

```
    WRITE (3,200) NUM1, NUM2, NUM3
200 FORMAT (I3, I4, I5)
```

If the values of NUM1, NUM2 and NUM3 were 100, 9999 and 10500 respectively the output format would be:

```
100999910500
```

This is difficult to interpret because no spaces have been printed between the values. To include spaces in a FORMAT statement the symbol X is used, preceded by the number of spaces required. For example, an acceptable format for the example above might be:

```
    WRITE (3,200) NUM1, NUM2, NUM3
200 FORMAT (I3,5X,I4,5X,I5)
```

which would result in: 100   9999   10500

A comment may be included in a FORMAT statement by enclosing it in quotes, as for example:

```
500 FORMAT ("THE RESULT IS:", 5X, I5)
```

In this case the message is printed in the first 14 spaces, then 5 blank spaces and finally a 5-digit integer value are output.

When real (floating point) numbers are to be output, an F is used instead of I to tell the computer that a real value is to be formatted. For example, we might have:

```
    WRITE (2,200) VAR1
200 FORMAT (F10.3)
```

This lets the system know that the real value to be output has 10 characters, including its sign and the decimal point, and that 3 characters are to be printed after the decimal point. Thus if the value of VAR1 was −12500.345 the FORMAT statement would produce a correct output. Note that if VAR1 equals +12500.345 it does not matter whether the plus sign is printed or not, since if it is omitted there will be one less character than the ten specified by the FORMAT statement, and a leading space will be printed. When a value has less digits than specified by the I or F in a FORMAT statement, leading spaces are always printed to fill the unused characters.

The various features of the FORMAT statement can be mixed to produce more complicated format instructions, such as the example below:

```
500 FORMAT (5X, "FIRST VALUE:",1X,I5,5X,"SECOND VALUE:",1X,F7.2)
```

The STOP and END statements

The reader will have noted that some of the program examples were terminated by the following pair of statements:

```
STOP
END
```

These statements may appear alike, but they have quite different functions. The STOP command tells the computer that it has executed the last object code instruction, while the END statement tells the compiler that there are no more source code statements to translate. END must therefore be the last statement in any program. STOP is often found just before END, but it can appear in any position and may occur more than once in a program.

Branch instructions: GOTO and IF-THEN-ELSE

FORTRAN, like BASIC, provides the programmer with instructions that alter the flow of control within a program. The simplest branch instruction is GOTO, often called an unconditional branch, since its execution does not depend on the result of any test. The syntax of GOTO is the keyword GOTO followed by a statement number, as shown by the following example:

```
    I = 1
100 WRITE (*,*) "COUNT IS", I
    I = I +1
    GOTO 100
    STOP
    END
```

In this case an infinite loop has been set up, which will run until either the user intervenes or the value of I exceeds the limits allowed for an integer. A GOTO statement cannot be used to pass control to a non-executable statement, e.g. PROGRAM.

No numerical order is necessary when assigning numbers to statements, although most programmers try to keep some sort of order for the sake of tidiness.

GOTO statements should be used with caution, just as in BASIC, since as was shown above it is possible to set up an infinite loop. Conditional branch instructions are more often used, in which a pair of quantities are tested to see whether a state relationship between them is TRUE or FALSE. For example, the relational expression A > 5 will be TRUE if the value of A is more than 5, and FALSE otherwise.

FORTRAN, like BASIC, has six relational operators. The symbols used by FORTRAN are shown together with the BASIC equivalents by table 4:

TABLE 4.—RELATIONAL OPERATORS IN FORTRAN AND BASIC.

MEANING:	BASIC:	FORTRAN:
equals	=	.EQ.
greater than	>	.GT.
less than	<	.LT.
not equal to	<>	.NE.
greater or equal	>=	.GE.
less than or equal	<=	.LE.

In FORTRAN77 relational tests are controlled by the keywords IF-THEN-ELSE. Just as in BASIC, the programmer puts a question to the computer, and one of two possible courses of action is taken depending on the outcome. The syntax of the IF-THEN-ELSE statement in FORTRAN is rather different from that of the equivalent FOR-NEXT command in BASIC. A group of FORTRAN statements form an IF-THEN-ELSE block, as shown by the following example:

```
      PROGRAM CONBRANCH
  100 READ (*,*) NUMBER
      IF (NUMBER.GT.0) THEN
        WRITE (*,*) "POSITIVE"
        GOTO 100
      ELSE
        WRITE (*,*) "NOT POSITIVE"
        GOTO 100
      ENDIF
      STOP
      END
```

This program (which is given the name CONBRANCH) uses a free-format read to input an integer number from the keyboard. The relational operator .GT. is used to test whether the number is greater than zero. If the result of the test is TRUE, the message POSITIVE is printed. If the result is FALSE, NOT POSITIVE is printed. An ENDIF statement is used to terminate the IF-THEN-ELSE block. Indentation has been used in the example to make the program easier to read. Many programmers adopt this convention to assist program documentation, but the indentations are ignored by the compiler.

IF-THEN-ELSE statements can be extended in FORTRAN77 by means of the ELSE-IF construction to allow complex decision-making structures to be built up. This allows the programmer to select one of many possible courses of action as the outcome of a relational expression. The following example demonstrates the use of the ELSE-IF statement:

```
IF (relational expression) THEN
  . . . .(statements). . . .
  . . . .(      "      ). . . .
ELSE IF (relational expression) THEN
  . . . .(statements). . . .
  . . . .(      "      ). . . .
ELSE IF (relational expression) THEN
  . . . .(statements). . . .
              "

              "

      and so on as desired
              "

              "

ELSE
  . .(what to do if all the ELSE-IF's have proved FALSE). .
ENDIF
```

There is no limit to the number of ELSE-IF's the programmer can use with this construction. The computer makes each relational test in turn, and if the result is false continues on to the next. If they all prove to be false it will execute the instructions following the final ELSE statement, before the construction is terminated by the ENDIF statement and the program continues with the instruction following ENDIF.

IF-THEN statements may be nested to any depth with the structure shown below:

```
IF (. . . . .) THEN
. . . . . . . .
  IF (. . . . .) THEN
  . . . . . . .
  ELSE
  . . . . . . .
  ENDIF
ELSE
. . . . . . . .
ENDIF
```

Very complicated logical expressions result from nesting IF-THEN statements, and generally it is bad programming practice to use this technique.

If the programmer requires the computer to take no specific action when the result of a relational expression is FALSE, the ELSE statement may be omitted from the construction. The syntax in this case is:

```
IF (relational expression) THEN
  . . .(statements executed when TRUE). . .
  . . . . . . . . . . . . . . . . . . . . . . . . . . . . . .
ENDIF
```

Logical operators

In the discussion of conditional branch statements above the six relational operators available in FORTRAN were described. Just as in BASIC, logical operators are also provided. There are five logical operators in most versions of FORTRAN77, and they are described below in table 5:

TABLE 5. LOGICAL OPERATORS IN FORTRAN

Logical expression:	FORTRAN version:
and	.AND.
or	.OR.
not	.NOT.
equivalent (of two logical outcomes)	.EQV.
not equivalent	.NEQV.

The CHARACTER statement

A string of characters (which can be alphabetic or numeric) enclosed by quotation marks forms a character constant in FORTRAN. Character strings are often used to insert messages into WRITE statements, as discussed earlier. Just as when dealing with numeric variables, a character variable with a given name can be assigned to as many character strings as the programmer wishes. The only difference between a character variable name and a numerical variable name is that the first letter of a character variable has no type (real or integer) implication.

The maximum length (number of characters) of a string depends on the particular computer system being used, although a limit of 255 characters is common. When counting how many characters make up a string, a common error is to forget that spaces must be counted as well as characters.

Without instructions from the programmer, a computer has no way of knowing whether to interpret data as characters, as numbers or as variable names. The user has to provide this information by using the CHARACTER statement, which appears at the start of a program immediately after the PROGRAM statement. The CHARACTER statement tells the computer two things; first the names of all the character variables used within the program, and second the length (the number of characters) of each character variable. This is another example of a non-executable statement, like PROGRAM, which is used to give the compiler information. The form of the CHARACTER statement is

CHARACTER *n variable name, where

*n is the maximum length of the character variable(s). The final part of the statement is a list of the character variable names. An example CHARACTER statement might be:

CHARACTER *1 LENGTH

This statement is taken from a program in which a length can be input in feet or metres. The character variable LENGTH contains a single character, which is either F (for feet) or M (for metres). The contents of LENGTH can then be used to indicate the type of measurement involved, as shown by the following example:

```
      PROGRAM CHARDEMO
      CHARACTER *1 LENGTH
  100 READ (*,*) L, LENGTH
C     IF LENGTH IS IN FEET CONVERT TO METRES
      IF (LENGTH .EQ. "F" THEN)
        L = L * 0.3048
      ENDIF
```

The rest of the program then proceeds to use the value of L in calculations, secure in the knowledge that L has been converted to metres if necessary.

A number of character variables can be defined in one CHARACTER statement:

```
CHARACTER *4 LENGTH, WIDTH, HEIGHT
```

If the character variables are to contain different numbers of characters there are two ways to proceed. Either several CHARACTER statements may be used, as in the following example:

```
PROGRAM DEMO2
CHARACTER *1 LENGTH, FORCE
CHARACTER *6 PRESSURE, STRAIN
```

or a single CHARACTER statement can define several lengths as in the following:

```
PROGRAM DEMO2
CHARACTER *1 LENGTH, FORCE, PRESSURE *6, STRAIN *6
```

However, mistakes are easy to make when defining several lengths in one statement. For example, in

```
CHARACTER *1 A, B, C, D *4, E, F, G
```

only character variable D will have a length of 4. E, F and G (and of course A,B,C) will have length 1. For this reason it is good programming practice to use multiple CHARACTER statements, and it makes reading a program much easier.

If a character string is shorter than the specification in the CHARACTER statement, the trailing end of the string will be filled with spaces. If a character string is longer than its specification trailing characters will be ignored. The following example demonstrates this behaviour:

```
PROGRAM CHARS
CHARACTER *4 A,C,D
A = "CAT"
B = "CROW"
C = "CROCODILE"
WRITE (*,*) A,B,C
STOP
END
```

The output from this program would be:

```
CAT (space)      CROW      CROC
```

Loop control—the DO instruction

In the discussion of loops in BASIC we saw that it was unecessary for the programmer to manually control looping. The BASIC FOR. . .NEXT statement is provided for this purpose. In FORTRAN the equivalent statements are DO and CONTINUE, and a FORTRAN loop is often called a DO-loop.

A loop in FORTRAN begins with a DO statement, which names the variable acting as loop counter, defines the number of times the loop is to be executed, and gives the line number of the CONTINUE statement marking the end of the loop. An example of a FORTRAN loop is given by the following program:

```
      PROGRAM LOOPDEMO
      CHARACTER *12 C
      C = "ROUND WE GO!"
      DO 200 J = 1, 10
      WRITE (*,*) C
  200 CONTINUE
      STOP
      END
```

In this case the loop is executed 10 times under control of variable J which acts as a counter (the J=1,10 part of the statement). The end of the loop is statement 200, the CONTINUE instruction, which is specified by DO 200. Each time the loop is executed, the message ROUND WE GO! is printed.

The CONTINUE statement has no effect on a program, and indeed is not really necessary at all. In our example we could omit it altogether and give the preceding WRITE statement the number 200. However, this makes the program hard to read, and it is good (and almost universal) programming practice to end a DO loop with a CONTINUE statement.

The example above used a default value of 1 for the counter increment. Other increments can be specified by adding a third number to the list following the counter name, e.g.

```
DO 1000 I=0,100,5
```

In this case variable I will take the values 0, 5, 10 etc, up to I=100.

Unlike BASIC, it is permissible in FORTRAN to leave a DO loop before it has been completed, although it makes for rather inelegant programming. Consider the following example:

```
      PROGRAM LOOP2
      DO 100 K = 1,100,1
      READ (*,*) NUMBER
      IF (NUMBER .EQ. 999) THEN
           GOTO 200
      ELSE
  100 CONTINUE
  200 STOP
      END
```

This program will demand 100 inputs, unless 999 is typed before the value of K reaches 100.

Just as in BASIC, a number of DO loops can be "nested" one within another. However, in common with all programming languages FORTRAN demands that loops are correctly nested, as discussed in the section on BASIC. Failure to observe this rule will cause a program to fail.

The final rule that must be observed when using DO loops is that they must be entered "legally". It is perfectly possible to write a program in which a GOTO instruction is used to jump into the middle of a loop, as shown below:

```
      PROGRAM BADLOOP
      GOTO 100
      DO 500 I = 1,20
  100 . .(any statement). . .
  500 CONTINUE
      STOP
```

This program will fail, since the loop has been entered illegally by the GOTO command. A loop can only be entered by executing the DO statement.

Arrays

Before an array can be used in FORTRAN, its size must be declared by a DIMENSION statement (which has the same function as DIM in BASIC). The DIMENSION statement is a non-executable statement (like PROGRAM and CHARACTER), and it must be placed at the top of a program, after the PROGRAM and any CHARACTER statement. All the arrays used in a program can be declared in one DIMENSION statement, as for example in

```
DIMENSION A(100), B(50), C(10)
```

In this case the compiler will set aside 100 memory locations labelled A, 50 labelled B, and 10 labelled C.

Array names obey the same rules as variable names. Unless a type declaration is present, an array with a name beginning with I, J, K, L, M or N contains integer values. Arrays with names beginning with other letters contain floating-point numbers.

Some programmers find that it is helpful to dimension real and integer arrays separately, rather than all in one DIMENSION statement. This has no effect on the program but can be helpful in documentation. An example of this technique is:

```
PROGRAM ARR1
DIMENSION A(50), B(50), C(4)
DIMENSION NUMBER(100), KOUNT(50)
```

Arrays can also be used to store character strings. A string array may be dimensioned in two ways. In the first method, the name of the array is declared to be of type CHARACTER, and the array is then DIMENSIONED as usual, i.e.

```
PROGRAM ARR2
CHARACTER *5 A, B, C, D
DIMENSION B(100)
```

A, C and D in this example are character strings of length 5, while B is a character array with room for 100 strings each having at most 5 characters.

The second method of dimensioning string arrays uses the CHARACTER instruction. An array may be dimensioned within the CHARACTER instruction itself, as shown by the following example (which has the same effect as that above):

```
PROGRAM ARR3
CHARACTER *5 A, B(100), C, D
```

Arrays having up to seven dimensions can be used in FORTRAN, although it is rare that more than three are used in practice. The dimension statement for (for example) a three dimensional array would have the form:

```
DIMENSION A(100,100,20)
```

However, the programmer should beware of declaring large multi-dimensional arrays such as this example. Here 200,000 memory locations are being requested, and on many systems this will exceed the amount of memory available to the user!

Once a FORTRAN array has been DIMENSIONed, subscripts are used to refer to specific elements of the array just as in BASIC. Obviously, subscripts must have an integer value, and failure to observe this will lead to program failure. In FORTRAN IV array subscripts must be positive and non-zero. In FORTRAN 77 negative and zero subscripts are allowed. The default range (positive and non-zero) of subscripts is specified by DIMENSION statements like DIMENSION A(50). If for some reason a different range of subscripts is required, FORTRAN 77 allows initial and final subscripts to be specified within the DIMENSION statement, separated by a colon. For example, the FORTRAN 77 statement:

```
DIMENSION A(-49:50)
```

reserves 100 locations with name A which may be accessed by subscripts in the range −49 to +50, including zero.

Just as in BASIC, subscripts may be constants, variables or expressions, so long as when they are evaluated integer values are produced within the range specified for the array in question. Failure to observe this will usually cause a program to fail, although the results on some systems can be unpredictable.

Arrays can be dynamically dimensioned in FORTRAN. A statically dimensioned array is one in which the size is explicitly defined by the dimension statement — in other words, the dimension bounds are fixed by numerical constants. Dynamic dimensioning produces arrays of variable size, where the dimension bounds are given by the value of a variable or by the result of evaluating an expression. Thus, DIMENSION statements such as:

```
PARAMETER (J=5)
DIMENSION A(2,7*J)
```

can be written. Since the amount of memory required by an array is reserved by the compiler before a program is run, a PARAMETER (non-executable) statement is used to give the compiler the information it needs. The effect of a parameter statement (which can be used for purposes other than array dimensioning) is to assign specified constant values to the parenthesised variable names following the keyword PARAMETER each time the name is encountered in the program. In our example, J will be given the value 5 each time it appears.

Subroutines

Any complex programming task can be broken down into a series of simple steps, and in the discussion of BASIC it was shown how subroutines or procedures may be used to facilitate this process. Amongst programmers there is much discussion about the value of "structured programming", which essentially means that a program should be broken up into subroutines, each performing a set task, which are called as they are needed by a "master" program. Notice that with this approach the use of GOTO statements is avoided.

In FORTRAN, as in most other languages, a program can be written in modular form by means of subroutines. A subroutine is created by the keyword SUBROUTINE. The statements following this keyword make up the subroutine, which is terminated by the keyword RETURN.

Each subroutine is given a unique name, specified in the SUBROUTINE statement thus:

```
SUBROUTINE INPUT
```

The maximum length of a subroutine name depends on the system, however 8 characters is common. Subroutine names must begin with a letter, but carry no type (i.e. real or integer) implication.

A subroutine is called from the main program by the statement CALL, followed by the name of the required subroutine. A typical program using subroutines might look like this:

```
PROGRAM SUBDEMO1
......(statements)......
........................
CALL INPUT
CALL ANALYSE
CALL OUTPUT
STOP
END
SUBROUTINE INPUT
  ......(statements)......
  ........................
RETURN
END
```

```
SUBROUTINE ANALYSE
..........................
..........................
RETURN
END
SUBROUTINE OUTPUT
..........................
..........................
RETURN
END
```

A subroutine may be CALLed from the main program as in the example above, or from within another subroutine. RETURN may be at any position within a subroutine, and multiple RETURN statements can be used. This is frequently the case when subroutines are written which involve the IF-THEN-ELSE-IF construction.

The STOP statement can appear within a subroutine. However, this is bad programming practice since it stops the whole program, and may leave the user's hardware in an undefined state. It is much better to RETURN from a subroutine and execute a STOP statement in the main program.

It will be noted that the RETURN statement at the end of each subroutine in the example is followed by an END statement.

This seems odd at first, since the purpose of the END statement is to tell the compiler that no more instructions are to be translated. However, the FORTRAN compiler translates each subroutine separately, hence the need for each subroutine to have its own END statement. This means that each subroutine occupies its own area of memory after compilation, and, more importantly for the programmer, means that variable names and statement numbers used by a subroutine have "local" meanings which are not shared by the main program. Thus, the instruction GOTO 100 within a subroutine will cause line 100 of that subroutine to be executed, and not any other line 100's that may occur in other subroutines or the main program. The programmer does not therefore need to worry about duplicating variable names or statement numbers in different subroutines.

However, suppose the programmer does want to pass the value of a particular variable from one subroutine to another. Consider the following example:

```
PROGRAM SUBDEMO2
CALL INPUT
CALL OUTPUT
STOP
END
SUBROUTINE INPUT
  READ (*,*) A
RETURN
END
SUBROUTINE OUTPUT
  WRITE (*,*) A
RETURN
END
```

When this program is compiled and run, the user may for example type in the number 5 when prompted by the subroutine INPUT. Control then returns to the main program, which proceeds to call the next subroutine, OUTPUT. However, variable A has only local meaning within a subroutine, and it has not been assigned any value within OUTPUT. What happens next will depend on the system, either the program will fail or zero will be printed.

There are two ways to solve this problem, the use of the COMMON statement, or the use of arguments with CALL. The use of COMMON is more elegant and is better programming practice, and is considered first.

The COMMON statement appears first at the start of a program, usually after the PROGRAM, DIMENSION and CHARACTER statements (if used). The exact position is to some extent machine dependent. It consists of the keyword COMMON, followed by an optional user-defined block name delineated by slashes, followed by a list of variable names. An example COMMON statement is:

```
COMMON /BLOCK1/ A, B, C, D
```

The purpose of the block name, which need not be used if it is not required, is to let the programmer define several lists of common variables under different names within one statement. The appropriate COMMON statement is repeated at the beginning of a subroutine, and this has the effect of making the listed variable names available for reference by both the subroutine and the main program.

A frequent source of errors when using COMMON statements is illustrated by the following example. Suppose the first COMMON statement at the beginning of a program is

```
COMMON A,B,C,D
```

Suppose that in a later subroutine only variable B is required. It would be tempting to begin the subroutine with

```
COMMON B
```

However, the first COMMON statement tells the compiler to allocate whatever name it finds first to the address labelled A, the second name to area B and so on. It therefore becomes apparent that the effect of the subroutine's COMMON B statement will be to assign B to the first common memory location. Variables A and B will then have the same location in memory, with confusing results. The only way to avoid this is to ensure that once a COMMON statement has been written it is repeated in full each time any of its variables are required, even if they are not all wanted.

The second way in which variables can be passed between program modules is to give the CALL statement arguments. The arguments can consist of constants or variables, and appear in the SUBROUTINE statement as well as in the CALL instruction. The following example demonstrates the technique:

```
PROGRAM SUBDEMO3
READ (*,*)A
B = A + 5
CALL OUTPUT (B)
STOP
END
SUBROUTINE OUTPUT (X)
  WRITE (*,*) X
RETURN
END
```

In this example the value of A (typed in by the user) is increased by five and the result assigned to B. The value of B is then passed to the subroutine OUTPUT. Note that the argument in the SUBROUTINE statement is X rather than B. This is an example of the use of a "dummy argument". The value of B is placed in the common memory location locally (inside the subroutine) labelled X, and is output. If a CALL statement has several arguments, the first value is placed in the address of the first dummy argument, the second in the address of the next dummy argument, and so on.

The above discussion shows how a value may be passed to a subroutine, but not how a value is sent back from a subroutine. In fact the procedure is straightforward:

```
PROGRAM SUBDEMO4
READ (*,*) A
CALL SUB1 (A,B)
WRITE (*,*) B
STOP
END
SUBROUTINE SUB1 (Y,Z)
  Z = Y +5
RETURN
END
```

The program calls subroutine SUB1 with the value of variable A. At this stage the value of B is undefined. The subroutine assigns A to dummy argument Y, and on return B has the value of dummy argument Z. Therefore, a value has been passed back to the main program.

Using a large number of arguments looks messy and is prone to error. If more than a few arguments are needed, it is better to use COMMON.

An excellent introduction to FORTRAN 77 programming is provided by *Essentials of FORTRAN 77*, by J. Shelley, published by Wiley.

PASCAL

Pascal is a powerful, general-purpose language, which was derived in the late 1960's by Professor Wirth of Zurich Technical University. The language is named in honour of Blaise Pascal, the well-known 17th century mathematician. Professor Wirth published a definition of so-called standard Pascal in 1971, and relatively few changes have been made since that date.

The reason for introducing Pascal, and one of the reasons for its continued popularity, is that it encourages a systematic approach to program design and makes it easy to produce structured programs. Structured programming is a topic which was mentioned in the earlier discussion of BASIC and FORTRAN. This approach allows the programmer to write complex programs in such a way that many of the errors to which the older languages such as BASIC and FORTRAN are liable can be avoided. In simple terms, structured programming means that the task to be programmed is broken down by means of functions and procedures or subroutines into simple blocks, each of which can be tested in isolation. Procedures first appeared in Pascal, and are now recognised as being so useful that they have been included in some versions of BASIC.

The remarkable success of Pascal has come about solely because programmers chose to use the language, rather than as a result of any commercial pressure. However, Pascal is not the only block-structured language available. Other popular contenders include BCPL, C, ADA and Modula-2.

Pascal, like FORTRAN, is a compiling language. It is therefore usually faster than BASIC for any given application. In some cases Pascal may be slightly faster than FORTRAN, but the difference in speed is minor. The user may therefore ask what the advantages are of using Pascal rather than FORTRAN. The answer lies in Pascal's block structure. Although perfectly good structured programs can be written in FORTRAN, the programmer has to be very self disciplined if this is to be achieved. One of the strengths of Pascal is that it forces the user to think about his problem in a systematic way, and a well-structured program is almost always the result. Pascal also handles records, files and text better than FORTRAN, and can be used to generate recursive and tree structures.

Pascal programs are usually (though not always) written using lower case letters. This can make explanatory material consisting of a mixture of text and programs hard to read. Accordingly, the convention adopted in this section is to print Pascal statements in **bold** characters whenever there is a danger of confusion. This does not, of course, mean that Pascal programs have to be bold!

Example Pascal program

The following short example is written in Pascal to introduce the structure of Pascal statements:

```
program total (input, output);
{calculates the sum of five numbers from the keyboard}
var
    j:integer;
    sum:real;
    x:real;
begin
sum: =0;
for j:= 1 to 5 do;
begin
    readln(input,x);
    sum:=sum + x
end;
writeln (output, 'total = ',sum);
end.
```

This program calculates the sum of five numbers typed in from the keyboard. The first point to note is that just as in BASIC, extra spaces can be added between the parts of a Pascal statement to aid readability. The following are both acceptable Pascal lines:

```
for count:=   1 to 10   do
for count  := 1 to 10 do
```

It is necessary to have at least one space between adjacent words.

Like FORTRAN, Pascal does not require every statement to be numbered. Again just as in FORTRAN, a statement can be assigned a number, but this is normally only necessary when **goto** instructions are used. It is good Pascal programming practice to avoid using **goto** whenever possible. Generally any situation that seems to require **goto** can use a procedure call or repeat-loop instead. A program that uses **goto** cannot be said to be structured, and as discussed in the introduction structuring is the chief strength of Pascal.

If there is not alternative to using **goto**, the syntax is as follows. A statement like

```
goto 100;
```

redirects execution to a statement labelled as follows:

```
100: {now this line is executed};
```

At the beginning of the program all the statement numbers or labels used have to be listed in a **label** statement:

```
label 100,200,300......;
```

The first line in the example is the **program** statement. All Pascal programs should begin thus. Just as in FORTRAN it assigns a name to the program for cataloguing purposes, but more importantly it specifies the external files needed by the program. In this example the names input and output are specified. These are Pascal names for the default input device (the keyboard) and the default output device (the screen or printer).

The program line is followed by Pascal's version of a comment, which is surrounded by curly brackets {thus} or plain parentheses and asterisks (*thus*) on some systems.

Next comes the declaration of variables. In our example j is of integer data type, and sum and x are of real type. (Data types are discussed more fully in the next section).

So far, the statements in the example have been non-executable, i.e. they either supply information to the compiler or are comments. The first executable statement is sum:=0, where the value 0 is assigned to the variable sum. Note the use of := which is the equivalent of = in BASIC or FORTRAN, and which should be read as "becomes". It is important to distinguish Pascal's arithmetic assignment symbol := from the relational operator =, which is discussed later.

The Pascal equivalent of BASIC's FOR...NEXT or FORTRAN's DO construction is Pascal's **for** loop. The **for** instruction in Pascal is a clause rather than a statement; it comes before the statement(s) to be repeated. If several statements are to be repeated they must be made into a compound by being enclosed with **begin** and **end**. This is an example of a structuring construct, of which Pascal has several. Most of these constructs are enclosed by the statements **begin** and **end**, as in the example earlier. The enclosed statement(s) are treated as a single compound statement.

The executable body of a Pascal program is also enclosed by **begin** and **end** statements. However, note that the final end is written **end.** with a full stop, to tell the compiler that it has reached the end of the program.

Input to a Pascal program is provided by the **read** or **readln** statements, which have the same function as INPUT in BASIC. **Read** is normally used to get data from a file, while **readln** is used for keyboard input. The **program** line defines where the input data is to come from. In this example, it is the default input device or keyboard.

Output to the default device is provided by the statement **writeln**, which is a contraction of writeline. (A second means of output is provided by **write**, which does the same as **writeln** without forcing a line-feed at the end of the output. The BASIC equivalents are PRINT A and PRINT A;).

In Pascal a carriage return and line feed (which terminates a BASIC or FORTRAN line) is treated as a space. A semicolon (;) is used to terminate a Pascal line. To emphasise this point consider the following three lines:

```
y:=
a +
5; x:= b + 6;
```

which are equivalent to the single Pascal line:

```
y:= a + 5; x:= b + 6;
```

Both are perfectly acceptable to the compiler, although they are rather inelegant and it is best to place each instruction on a separate line. Generally, a semicolon should be placed at the end of each executable statement. The exception to this is that a semicolon must not precede an **else** statement. This point will be discussed later. A semicolon is not strictly required before an **end** statement, although it will not cause any harm if it is included.

Declaration of data types and variable names

Pascal requires the programmer to declare all variables before they are used in a program. Pascal variable names begin with any letter, and continue with any upper or lower case character. Upper and lower case letters are distinguished by the compiler, so for example the variables Count and count are different. The length of a variable name is determined by the compiler, but a limit of 8 characters is common. A variable name must not contain any spaces. Keywords that form part of the Pascal language such as **var, type** etc. must not be used as variable names.

Before a variable can be declared, its data type must be specified. The ability to define data types is one of the most powerful features of Pascal. There are four built-in data types: real, integer, Boolean and character. In addition, the programmer is free to define others as convenient.

A data type specifies the allowed set of values which a variable may take. For example, if the built-in integer data type is specified, a variable can obviously only take integer values. Likewise, if the data type char is specified for a variable only character strings can be assigned to that variable, and so on.

So far, this discussion of data types could equally well describe FORTRAN, or even some versions of BASIC where an implied data type is specified by appending % or $ to the name of a variable. However, Pascal extends the use of data types by allowing the user to define his own. Thus, a data type may for example represent the allowed set of states of a traffic light (i.e. red, red and amber, green, amber). This new data type would be defined within a Pascal program as follows:

```
type
    trafficlight = (green, amber, red, red-and-amber);
```

The variable lampstate can be declared as being of type trafficlight, and can then only take on the values defined in the type statement:

```
var
    lampstate:trafficlight;
begin
    lampstate := red; (and on with the rest of the program)
```

If this example were written in BASIC, the lack of user-definable data types would force the programmer to assign arbitrary numbers to the four possible states of a traffic light. (Obviously, only relational operators can be applied to char and user-defined data types. This point is discussed later).

Data types which are a subset of a previously defined type can also be specified. For example, it is often convenient to define the set of positive integers as a data type:

```
plusint = 1. .maxint
```

This statement declares plusint to be a new data type, which is a subset of the existing built-in integer type. The constant maxint is a built-in feature of Pascal which specifies the largest integer available on a given system.

In Pascal, everything can be assigned a name, and all names must be declared to the compiler before use. Unlike FORTRAN, Pascal allows any name (except a reserved word) to be assigned to any variable, procedure, constant or function. The statement **var** is used to declare variable names, and this is done at the start of a program after any **label**, **const** (see later) or **type** declarations. The following example demonstrates the format of name declarations:

```
program traffic(input,output);
label
    100,200,300;
const
    inchtocm = 2.54; {see later}
type
    trafficlight = (red, green, amber, red-and-amber);
var
    lampstate:trafficlight;
    x:real;
    y:real;
    j:integer;
procedure
{see later}
function
{see later}
```

A "program header" of this form should appear at the start of any Pascal program. Lines which are not required can be omitted.

Operators

As mentioned earlier, Pascal contains four built-in data types (real, integer, Boolean, char), and in addition user-defined types can be specified. Associated with each data type is a number of operators that can be applied to variables of that type. The operators applicable to built-in data types are given in table 6:

TABLE 6.—OPERATORS ASSOCIATED WITH BUILT-IN DATA TYPES.

Data type	Allowed operators
real	*, /, +, −
integer	*, **div**, **mod**, +, −
char(acter)	none
Boolean	**and**, **or**, **not**

In addition to the arithmetic and logical operators, Pascal contains relational operators. These are written identically in Pascal and BASIC, i.e.

=, <>, >, <, >=, <=

The relational operators can be applied to any data type and will give a Boolean result (i.e. true or false). Any operator which can be applied to a number of data types is known as polymorphic. Thus, the entry "none" against the char(acter) data type in table 6 does not mean that no operators can be applied to character data, but rather that only relational operators can be used. Any attempt to use the wrong kind of operator on a given data type will lead to program error.

As a general rule it is unsafe to rely on operator precedence when using Pascal. Good programming practice dictates that any complicated expression should contain as many parentheses as are necessary to make the meaning clear.

Constants

The format used for numeric constants in Pascal is almost identical to that found in BASIC. The exception is that in Pascal there must always be at least one digit before a decimal point. As an example, the constant .5 would be perfectly acceptable in BASIC, but must be written 0.5 in Pascal.

It is often necessary to change the values of constants used by a program before it is run, and Pascal contains a facility to do this. Constants may be grouped together into a **const** section at the start of the declarations (but after any **label** declaration). Each constant is given a name or label, and is therefore easy to find when changes are required. The label of the constant, rather than its value, is then used throughout the program. An example

const declaration is:

```
const
     inchtocm = 2.54;
     g = 9.81;
```

Library functions

Pascal incorporates a library of functions, some of which are listed in Table 7. Many versions of Pascal add to the list, but the following should be available on all systems:

TABLE 7.—PASCAL FUNCTION LIBRARY

Function	Meaning	
abs(x)	absolute value of x	Functions returning a real result
arctan (x)	arctangent of x	
cos(x)	cosine of x	
sin(x)	sine of x	
exp(x)	the value of e^x	
ln(x)	natural logarithm of x	
sqr(x)	the value of x^2	
sqrt(x)	the square root of x	
abs(x)	absolute value of x	Functions returning an integer result
ord(x)	ordinal number* of x	
round(x)	nearest integer to x	
sqr(x)	the value of x^2	
trunc(x)	integer obtained by removing the fractional part of x.	
chr(x)	returns the character whose ordinal number* is x.	Functions returning a character

* The data type of x defines all the possible values of x. The first value has ordinal number 0, the second number 1, and so on. Thus in the earlier example where we had:

```
type
     trafficlight = (red, green, amber, red-and-amber);
```

red has ordinal number 0, green number 1, amber 2, and so on.

Input and output

The use of the **program** line to direct output to the user's terminal and to specify input from the user's keyboard was discussed earlier. When input or output from other devices is required, the required device has to be specified. In FORTRAN this is done by device numbers. In Pascal devices are given names rather than numbers. The names are known as file variables, or simply files. These are declared in the **var** section of a program in the usual way, as in the following example:

```
var
     file1: file of char;
     file2: file of integer;
     file3: file of real;
     file4: text;
```

A file contains a series of elements all having the same data type. The data type used for a file is called the component data type. Files of data type char (like file1 in the example) contain text. If the data type is anything else the file contains binary values, and the compiler automatically converts the values of constants to and from binary as necessary. Text files are the most frequently used type, and for this reason Pascal contains the built-in data type **text**, which means **file of** char. In the example above file4 and file1 are both text files.

File variables are used in input and output statements just like device numbers in FORTRAN. A file variable is written as an optional first argument to the Pascal statements **read** and **write**. (If the file variable is omitted, the compiler assumes **input** or **output** as appropriate, i.e. to the user's terminal). For example, the file variables declared above might be used as follows:

```
read (file1, x, y); {read two characters from text file}
read (file2, x, y); {read 2 integers from binary file}
write (file3, a, b, c); {write 3 reals to a binary file}
write (file4, a); {write one character to a text file}
```

If a file contains text then data of real, integer or char type can be read from it. Items of numerical data held in a textfile must be separated by a space or placed on separate lines. When numerical data is read, leading spaces and linefeed characters are ignored. When a character (with data type char) is read a single character is taken from the file and spaces, linefeeds or carriage returns each count as one character.

File variables are labels attached to a particular storage or output device, rather than the names of actual files. If a storage device is, for instance, a disc drive, it will probably contain many files. Some way of telling the compiler the actual names of the files needed for input and output is required. The information is supplied in two parts. First, the **program** line tells the compiler which external devices are to be used, as for example in:

```
program model1 (input,output,file1);
```

which specifies that the device labelled file1 is to be used in addition to the user's terminal. Second, the operating system command RUN (used to compile and run the program on many systems) has optional arguments, as in the following example:

```
RUN model1 file1=TESTDATA
```

The effect of the pair of commands above is to tell the compiler to use the device labelled file1 when an appropriate read or write statement is encountered, and to use the file named TESTDATA on that device.

This description of file handling is typical, but the operating system is a non-standard feature of any Pascal system. It is essential therefore to consult the system manual before anything more than the simplest input or output is programmed.

Most Pascal files are sequential. In other words, the contents of a file have to be accessed by proceeding through the file element by element. New material can only be appended at the end of a file. Old data cannot be overwritten, other than by deleting the whole file and rewriting it.

Associated with every file is a file pointer, or in Pascal terminology a window, which indicates the file element currently being accessed. The window of file1 is referred to as file1 ^. The value of file1 ^ is the same as the value of the current component of the file.

Some Pascal systems also allow the use of random-access files. In these a file pointer is used to indicate the point at which data is to be read or written. The length of each record (i.e. the number of characters used) has to be specified before random-access files can be used.

Branch instructions 1: if-then-else

Any programming language needs to have some means of carrying out a test and using the result to change the flow of control within a program. In FORTRAN the IF-THEN-ELSE statement performs this function, and a similar statement is used by Pascal. The following example demonstrates the syntax:

```
if count > total then
    a:=1 (with no semicolon here!)
else
begin
    a:=0;
    writeln ('count has not reached total')
end;
```

As mentioned earlier, a semicolon cannot be used before an else statement. With this exception, extra semicolons do not matter. Otherwise, **if-then-else** in Pascal is similar to FORTRAN. Notice once again that whenever Pascal expects a single statement, a compound consisting of several statements enclosed by **begin** and **end** can be used instead if necessary. This is a further example of structuring.

The **else** statement can be omitted if required, just as in FORTRAN, when no specific action is required should the result of a relational expression be false. In the next example **else** and the statements following it have been omitted:

```
if count > total then
    a:=1;
```

Notice that this time the line a:=1 must be terminated by a semicolon, since there is no **else** statement.

Branch instructions 2: case of

Pascal also contains the **case** statement, which behaves like ON. . .GOTO in BASIC. A variable which can take several values is used to control which statement (or compound statement) is executed next. The controlling variable can be of any type, and is known as the case selector. Thus, for example:

```
read(a);
case a of
    1: datain {call data input procedure};
    2: analyse {call analysis procedure};
    3: stop {call program stop procedure}
end;
```

The numbers 1, 2 and 3 are called case labels, and are not accessible to **goto** statements. Case labels must be of the same type as the case selector (a in this example is of integer type). The case selector can be of any type, or it can be an expression. In the traffic light example at the start of this section, we might have written the following:

```
case lampstate of
     red: stop;
     green: continue;
     amber: slowup;
     red-and-amber; getready
end;
```

Where the colours red, green etc. are case labels and stop, continue, slowup and getready are procedure calls. (Procedures are akin to subroutines in BASIC, and will be discussed later).

Loops: for, while and repeat

Pascal contains three looping constructions, **for**, **while** and **repeat**. These are described in turn:

for: Pascal's **for** statement is similar to FOR in BASIC, with two restrictions. First, the variable used as a loop counter (i in the example below) must be integer. This is because real arithmetic is inexact in Pascal (and in all other languages), and if for instance something like

```
for a:= 1 to 50 do
```

is attempted and a has been declared as real, 50 additions of 1 may well result in 50.00000001 rather than 50. Thus, the loop would only be executed 49 times, not 50 as the programmer intends.

The second restriction is that the loop counter can only be incremented or decremented by 1 each time the loop is executed. In other words, there is no equivalent of BASIC's STEP instruction. If a loop counter is to be decremented rather than incremented **to** is replaced by **downto**, as in

```
for b:= 50 downto 1 do
```

while: The use of **for** is restricted as described above. The **while** statement is in some ways more flexible, as it allows a loop to be continually executed as long as a specified condition remains true. As shown below, the syntax of **while** is similar to that of **if** when **else** is absent:

```
while count < total do
begin
     a:=0;
     writeln ('count has not reached total')
end;
```

The difference between the **if** and **while** instructions is that **if** causes a statement (or a compound statement) to be executed once if a specified condition is true, but **while** causes repeated execution so long as the condition remains true. This is demonstrated by the following example:

```
program loopdemo (input,output);
var
     count, total:integer;
     a, b:real;
begin
count:=0;
total:=10;
if count < total then
begin
     writeln(count);
     count := count + 1
end;
while count < total do
begin
     writeln(count);
     count := count + 1
end;
end.
```

The **if** prints out the initial value of count, which is zero, and increments count by 1. The **while** loop is executed 9 times, and prints out the values 1,2,3,4,5,6,7,8 and 9, corresponding to the value of count each time the loop is carried out. When count reaches a value of 10 the relational test fails, and the program stops.

repeat-until: The final looping construct available in Pascal is the **repeat** statement. The syntax is demonstrated by the following example:

```
total:=10;
count:=0;
```

```
repeat
    writeln(count);
    count:=count +2
until count > total;
```

This loop will be executed six times, and will produce the outputs 0,2,4,6,8 and 10. Notice that the difference between a **repeat** loop and a **while** loop is that in a **repeat** loop the relational test comes after rather than before the loop. The effect of this is that a **repeat** loop is always executed at least once, but a **while** loop is not executed if the relational test fails.

All of Pascal's loop instructions can be nested, just as in BASIC and FORTRAN. As usual, correct nesting must be observed.

Arrays

Before an array can be used in Pascal the compiler must known how much memory the array will require. Arrays are declared in the **var** section at the beginning of a program, using square brackets to specify the array size as shown in the following example:

```
var
    a:array[1. .10] of real;
    b:array[−9. .10] of integer;
    c:array[0. .3,0. .5] of real;
```

(Pascal literature often uses the term index instead of subscript when discussing arrays. However, for the sake of consistency with the earlier sections, subscript is used here). Three arrays are declared in the example above. Array a has space for 10 real values, which are accessed by integer subscripts between 1 and 10. Array b stores 20 integer values, under subscripts from −9 to +10 including zero. Array c has two dimensions and can contain 24 (=4×6) real values. All Pascal compilers allow an array to have at least three dimensions, and some systems allow more.

In the example integer array subscripts are used. However Pascal allows any data type to be used as an array subscript. Thus, a Pascal array has two associated data types, which must both be declared, i.e. the array element type and the subscript type. The array element type is called the component data type, and the subscript type is called the index data type. So, for example, it is possible to write statements such as:

```
var
    a:array['a'. .'z'] of integer;
```

in which the component data type is integer, and the subscript type or index data type is a subrange of char. An element of this array can be accessed by a statement like:

```
x:= a[p];
```

which assigns the 16th integer value held in the array to the variable x.

The index type of an array must as mentioned earlier be declared, and this is done in the **type** section at the start of a program. For example,

```
type
    alphabet = 'a'. .'z'
```

If it subsequently becomes necessary to restrict the array subscripts to the letters a - m for example, changing the **type** declaration will automatically change the array size.

Subroutines and procedures

Pascal's equivalent of a subroutine is the procedure. A procedure consists of a number of statements grouped under a name, which are executed following a call to that name. The first line of a procedure consists of a declaration of its name, together with any arguments used by the procedure and their type. This is followed by the statements which are executed when the procedure is called. Both procedures and functions, which are discussed next, have to be declared at the start of a program, after the **var**'s. The following example demonstrates the use of a simple procedure:

```
procedure countdown (start:integer)
{counts down from start to zero}
var
    i:integer;
begin
for i:= start downto 0 do
    write(i);
    writeln('and counting');
end;
```

The name of a procedure, such as countdown in the example, is itself a Pascal statement, i.e.

```
countdown(10);
```

would be used to call the example procedure, assign the value 10 to the variable start, and generate a countdown from 10 to zero.

It should be noted that declarations made in a procedure only have a local scope or effect, so that variable names and values used within a procedure do not affect usage outside the procedure. **labels, consts, types** and **vars** can be declared after the **procedure** statement. In Pascal, any declaration is said to have an associated *scope*. Anything declared in the main program has the whole program as its scope. A variable declared in a procedure has that procedure as its scope, together with any procedures or functions called from within that procedure. Outside its scope, a variable is unknown. This is another example of a structuring construct in Pascal, and its purpose is to assist a method of structuring known as stepwise refinement. In this approach, the programmer first specifies very powerful procedures to solve his problems. Each of those powerful routines is in turn broken up into simpler routines, which are encoded using procedures which are still simpler. This process is continued until routines are arrived at which are so small that they can be written directly. The result is that any program, no matter how complex, is broken down into small, easily tested components.

Functions

Pascal functions resemble procedures with one important difference: a function returns a result. Functions are used as part of an expression, which means that a function has a type and the result it returns is of the same type. The type associated with a function is declared in the function header statement, which otherwise resembles a procedure header.

The observant reader will have noted from the table of library functions earlier that most Pascals lack a built-in function to raise a number to a power. (Only **sqr** and **sqrt** are provided). The following example carries out this calculation, and is often useful. It returns the value of x^y where x is positive. If x is negative an error message is produced. Both x and y are of real type.

```
function power(x,y:real);
begin
    if x <= 0.0 then
        begin
        power:=0.0;
        writeln('x has negative value');
        writeln('x = ', x);
        end
    else
        power:=exp(y*ln(x))
end;
```

The name of the function, once declared, becomes a Pascal statement. The example shows how it might be used:

```
begin
    writeln('input x and y');
    read (x,y);
    z:=power(x,y);
    writeln(x,y,z);
end.
```

Dynamic variables and pointers

In a structured language such as Pascal a nested block structure is used to allocate memory locations to variables. Each time a procedure is called the computer sets aside memory for the variables local to that procedure, which is released following completion of the procedure. Any variables declared in the main program are given memory space which is reserved for the whole of the time the program is resident. This is called global storage, and it exists throughout the "life" of the program.

All the variables described to this point have been what are known as *static objects*, defined by **var** declarations. Within its scope, only one version of each object exists.

Pascal also allows the programmer to create *dynamic objects*. Dynamic objects exist throughout the working of a program, i.e. they are global, and they can be thought of as lists which elements can be added to or removed from at any time. A dynamic object has no name, but is referenced by means of a *pointer variable* which is nothing other than the address in memory of the dynamic object. Dynamic objects can only be referred to by pointer variables, and pointer variables can only be used with dynamic objects, so the two are closely bound together. A pointer variable can be either a static or a dynamic object, and the **type** of a pointer is declared using the statement ∧ typename. For example, the declaration

```
type A = ∧ B;
```

creates a pointer of type A which is used to point at the elements of a dynamic object B. The symbol ∧ may be translated as "points at". A static pointer variable is declared in a **var** statement, such as:

var points:A;

which declares a pointer called points which is of type A.

A pointer type such as A consists of a set of values of A which point at the elements of a dynamic object B. A is said to be *bound* to B. The value nil is always an element of A, and is defined to mean "point at nothing". A dynamic object itself can contain pointers, and this enables the programmer to create complicated and flexible data structures. For example, supposing a series of records has been created where each record is a dynamic object. These may be used to form a *linked list* of records, where a pointer is used to access the first element of the list. The end of the first record can be a pointer to the second, the end of the second record is a pointer to the third, and so on. Obviously, the end of the last record must be a pointer which has been given the value nil.

The topic of dynamic storage is one which is of considerable importance to the programmer who has to deal with large amounts of data. However, for many applications dynamic storage is not necessary, and arrays can be used instead. There is insufficient space in this chapter to deal fully with pointers and dynamic objects, and the interested reader is referred to the *Pascal User Manual and Report* by K. Jensen and N. Wirth for further details.

FORTH

FORTH is a very compact and efficient high-level language. It enjoys considerable popularity among control engineers, because programs written in FORTH run very fast. Speeds approaching those of assembly-level programs can be achieved, and this means that FORTH software can be used for real-time control of engineering systems.

FORTH was developed in the USA in the mid 1960's by C. H. Moore. Much of its early use was for instrument control, but it is now much more widespread and has been used for many industrial applications.

FORTH is usually referred to as an environment rather than a language. The FORTH environment contains a high-level language, an assembly language, an operating system, and a number of utilities. The language part of FORTH consists of a "dictionary" of about 100 command words, which can be used to construct other commands as necessary. This allows structured programs to be built up, with simple commands being used to define more powerful statements, these statements being used to produce yet more powerful instructions, and so on. The highest level of a FORTH program resembles a conversational description of the problem in English. A FORTH program is rather like a Pascal program which uses a series of nested procedures.

As an example, consider the process of taking a photograph. This might consist of the following series of actions:

(1) Get the camera.
(2) Put a film in it if necessary.
(3) look through the viewfinder and focus.
(4) adjust the exposure.
(5) release the shutter.
(6) wind on the film.

Each of these actions can be further broken down. For instance, action number 5, "release the shutter", could be described as follows:

(a) move finger to button.
(b) exert downward pressure until click is heard.
(c) remove finger.

Thus, simple instructions are used to build up more complex instructions, which themselves become building blocks, until at the highest level a powerful instruction (like "photograph" in the example) sets the whole sequence in motion.

When a FORTH command word is executed, the operating system refers to a dictionary. Each dictionary entry for a word contains pointers to the words by which it was defined. These in turn contain pointers to the words by which they were defined, and so on until the FORTH "core" words are reached. Each word is executed as soon as it is found in the dictionary, so that FORTH neither interprets or compiles in the traditional sense. FORTH therefore enforces the development of structured software, and the stepwise refinement of programs. FORTH is often termed a "meta-application language", or in other words a language which is used to create other languages, which can be specifically aimed at a particular problem.

As mentioned earlier, FORTH programs can be very fast, and may achieve around half the speed of the equivalent program written in machine code. (Machine or assembly code is obviously best as far as speed is concerned, but unfortunately machine code is much harder to write than high-level code).

Programs written in FORTH occupy much less memory than the equivalent program written in other high-level languages. For this reason FORTH has become very popular for use by single-card microprocessor controllers, where the software has to be contained within the limited amount of memory available on such a system. A FORTH program listing consists of a series of definitions of new words (each of which can be independently tested), leading up to the final and most powerful instructions. Anything not needed by a program, such as unused dictionary entries, can be stripped away leaving the minimum necessary for the program to run. Typically a FORTH control program will occupy as little as 1kbyte.

Forth offers a compromise between the advantages of software written in machine code (speed, compactness) and the advantages which are gained by using easily understood source code, such as that produced by Pascal or BASIC. Many of the facilities taken for granted by BASIC or FORTRAN programmers, such as the ability to handle strings or arrays, are not initially present in FORTH. They can, of course, be built up by the user from simpler FORTH instructions.

One of the advantages of FORTH is that the FORTH operating system is itself written in FORTH. Any new command words defined by the user are treated in exactly the same way as the built-in words. A FORTH program may therefore be considered to be an extension of the operating system, designed to provide the commands and facilities necessary to solve a given problem.

The main drawback of FORTH is that, since the operating system is completely accessible to the user, it is very easy to "crash" the system, which usually means that the program is lost and the operating system has to be re-established. The other difficulty most users experience is that arithmetic is carried out in Reverse Polish notation. However, this last disadvantage is more imagined than real — with practice Reverse Polish notation soon seems quite natural!

In summary, FORTH is not a language for newcomers to programming. However, it has many advantages over BASIC, Pascal and FORTRAN, and deserves serious consideration for applications where either the program's speed of execution or the amount of memory it occupies are critical.

A good introduction to programming in FORTH is provided by *Discover FORTH* by T. Hogan, published by McGraw-Hill.

C

C was mainly developed by D. Ritchie of the Bell Laboratories in the 1970's, as a means of implementing the Unix operating system on Digital Equipment Corporation's PDP11 minicomputers. Although they are closely linked, C in in no way tied to Unix. Like other languages that are the product of one person rather than the result of a committee's deliberations, C is remarkably free of unexpected quirks and bugs. In recent years C has become very popular for general systems programming. (Systems programming is the term usually used to denote the process of writing compilers, interpreters, editors, utilities or complete operating systems). There are many implementations of C, but they are all quite consistent and C software is in general very portable, i.e. a C program will run on almost any C system without modification.

The main structural unit used in C is the function. An argument is passed to a function by copying its value, rather than by referring to a name. It is impossible for a called function to change the argument in the "caller". If it is wished to call by reference to a name, C allows a pointer to be passed explicitly, and the function is used to change the object to which the pointer points.

C compilers have now been produced for almost all of the popular computer systems, including many microcomputers. Many programmers now use C because it is a very well-structured language, which can be used to produce software which requires very little memory compared to the more traditional languages such as FORTRAN. In many cases a single C statement will replace two or three BASIC or Pascal statements. As an example, consider the instructions used to control a loop. In BASIC, a variable is used for loop control, and its start value, final value and the amount by which it is incremented each time the loop is executed must all be defined. In C, any data type may be used to initialise a loop, any condition used to terminate a loop, and any actions may be carried out within a loop. Initialisation, termination and activity inside a loop need not involve the same variable. To illustrate this consider the following example (a shell-sorting routine):

```
shell (v,n)      /*shell sorting routine, with
                   acknowledgements to Kernighan & Ritchie*/
int v[], n;
{
  int gap, i, j, temp;
    for (gap=n/2; gap>0; gap/=2)
        for (i=gap; i<n; i++)
          for (j=i−gap; j>=0 && v[j]>v[j+gap]; j−=gap) {
            temp=v[j]
            v[j]=v[j+gap]
            v[j+gap]=temp;
          }
}
```

In BASIC at least six instructions would be needed to control the three loops, rather than the three used here.

The other instructions which alter the flow of control within a program are equally efficient. C, like FORTRAN and Pascal, has versions of **if-then-else**, **while** and **do-while**. There is also a **case switch** instruction, which resembles BASIC's ON-GOTO or Pascal's **case of** statements. C does include a version of GOTO, but (as usual) it is good practice to avoid using GOTO's.

C's operators include the usual add, subtract, multiply and divide for artihmetic, symbolically represented +, −, *, and /. Relational operators are also included, and the Boolean operators AND, OR and NOT. C also includes four more unusual operator types: assignment, incremental, bitwise, and conditional.

The assignment operator allows a variable to be assigned a new value based on itself. In the example program earlier, the statement gap/=2 uses the assignment operator to halve the value of the variable gap.

The incremental operator is symbolically represented ++, and is used for loop control as follows:

x = i++ means set x equal to i, and then increment i
x = ++i means increment i, *then* set x equal to i

The bitwise operators are used for manipulating data at the binary level, and include the logical bit operations AND, OR and EXCLUSIVE-OR. Left and right shifts, and a complement (i.e. replace all ones by zeroes, and vice versa) operation are also available.

The conditional operator == can in some circumstances replace if-then-else, and has the advantage of compactness. For example,

```
x=(i==10)? 0:1
```

means that if i equals 10 the value 0 is assigned to x. Otherwise, x equals 1.

C can produce very efficient and compact programs. However, a program written in C is often very difficult to understand, and good program documentation is an essential part of any C software. C, like FORTH, provides the user with almost complete access to the operating system, which is itself usually written in C. The same disadvantage therefore occurs, i.e. it is very easy to "crash" a C system.

C can be difficult to learn, and is not recommended for the newcomer to programming. However, experienced programmers who need to do things that are impossible in the traditional languages, but who do not want to resort to machine code programming, often find that C is ideal.

The best guide to C is *The C Programming Language* by B. Kernighan and D. Ritchie, published by Prentice-Hall.

Lisp

Lisp is a language designed for manipulating symbolic expressions, which is mainly used by programmers working in the artificial intelligence areas such as expert systems programming. (An expert system is a computer program containing the knowledge of one or more human experts, which makes "intelligent" deductions on a probabalistic basis). Another term for symbolic manipulation is list processing, and it is this phrase that gives Lisp its name.

The data used by Lisp is, at its most fundamental level, binary digits or bits. Lisp uses bits to form word-like objects called atoms, and groups of atoms form lists. Lists themselves can be linked together to form higher level lists. An analogy for this process is given by the books in a library, where groups of characters form words, groups of words form chapters, groups of chapters form books, groups of books form shelf sections, and so on. The ability to group data in a hierarchical fashion is one of the most important features of Lisp. Atoms and lists are collectively known as symbolic expressions. The manipulation of symbolic expressions, or list processing, is the purpose of Lisp.

The simplest object in Lisp is, as mentioned above, an atom. There are several types of atom, of which the simplest is the integer. Most versions of Lisp restrict integers to the range −32768 to +32767. A second type is the real atom, although these are infrequently used. Lisp is more often used for mathematics (which involves symbol manipulation) than for calculations.

The most interesting data type in Lisp is the character atom. A character atom has a name and an associated value, and to that extent resembles a BASIC variable. Thus, a Lisp program might contain the following:

```
(SETQ A 100)
(PRINT A)
```

which is equivalent to the BASIC lines

```
10 LET A=100
20 PRINT A
```

In both cases the value of A, which is 100, is printed.

However, in Lisp the program can legitimately continue:

```
(SETQ A 'HELLO')
(PRINT A)
```

which is equivalent to the BASIC lines

```
30 LET A = "HELLO"
40 PRINT A
```

The BASIC program would fail at this stage and give an error message, since A has been implicitly defined as a numeric variable in line 10. However, in Lisp a character atom can be of any data type.

Lisp character atoms have two further features which are of interest. First, the name of a character atom is itself a string, and can be output or manipulated by Lisp. Second, a character atom can have associated *properties*, as well as a name and a value. Thus, statements such as:

```
(PUT 'A'ISIN'OCTAL)
```

adds the fact that the value of A is in octal without disturbing the value of A.

Items of data are grouped together to form lists by surrounding them with parentheses. For example,

```
(TIMES GUARDIAN TELEGRAPH INDEPENDENT)
```

is a list of the national daily newspapers which are printed on large sheets of paper. (Parentheses are a feature of any Lisp software, and it has been suggested that Lisp should stand for "Lots of Irritating Single Parentheses!).

Lisp is extensively used for writing "expert system" software, and the following example is taken from an expert system for recognising animals, with acknowledgements to Winston & Horn. It demonstrates symbolic manipulation in Lisp by the use of a *rule*:

```
(RULE IDENTIFY6
    (IF (ANIMAL HAS POINTED TEETH)
        (ANIMAL HAS CLAWS)
        (ANIMAL HAS FORWARD EYES))
    (THEN (ANIMAL IS CARNIVORE)))
```

This piece of software establishes a *rule*. Using such a rule amounts to checking whether any of the assertions following the IF are true, and if appropriate adding the statement after THEN to a list of believed assertions.

Lisp programs and data structures are both built from lists. Programs are based on functions, some of which (like PRINT) are predefined. Writing a Lisp program is a matter of adding new functions, which have to be defined by the user. A Lisp function resembles a Pascal procedure. It is called by specifying the function's name and passing parameters to it, and a value is returned. The variables used within a function have only local scope, and do not affect variables used by other functions. Thus, the Lisp programmer is forced to write structured programs.

Since Lisp functions and Lisp data have the same syntactic form, one Lisp function may be used to analyse another. A Lisp function can also be used to create a second function and use it.

A new function is defined in Lisp using a DEFUN statement. Thus, a function which converts temperatures in Farenheit to degrees Centigrade is created as follows:

```
(DEFUN F-TO-C (X)
    (QUOTIENT (DIFFERENCE X 32) 1.8))
  F-TO-C
```

To use the function F-TO-C, a two element list must be specified. The first element of the list is the function's name, F-TO-C. The second item is the argument of F-TO-C, the temperature value to be converted. After the argument is evaluated it becomes the temporary value of the parameter used by the function (X in the example). Suppose for example the variable A is assigned a (Farenheit) value of 75. The function F-TO-C is then called by

```
(F-TO-C A)
```

A is evaluated and passes the value 75 to the function F-TO-C. On entry to the function, 75 becomes the temporary value of X. The value returned by the function is 23.9 degrees Centrigrade.

The greatest advantage of Lisp is its flexibility, which allows it to be used for writing symbolic manipulation programs that are almost as efficient as machine code. Self-modifying programs can be created, which can generate other programs and immediately use them as subroutines. For the data base manipulation necessary when writing expert system software, Lisp probably has no equal.

A good introduction to Lisp programming is *Lisp*, by P. H. Winston and B. K. P. Horn, published by Addison-Wesley.

Prolog

Prolog resembles Lisp (and is its closest competitor), in that it is not a number processing language but one designed for the manipulation of symbols. The variables in a Prolog program are symbols or structures formed from symbols, such as lists. Instead of being structured around procedures and subroutines, a Prolog program is based on *inference steps*. This means that when a program is run, logically related program statements are compared by the operating system, and deductions are made based on the facts available to the software.

Prolog has only become popular amongst artificial intelligence programmers in the last few years. It has been used with success in several expert system applications.

Prolog is distinguished from other languages in that it can be read declaratively, in the form of a logical specification. The traditional languages such as BASIC etc. are referred to as procedural. This means that the only way to understand a program written in such a language is to follow its sequence of actions. Prolog software can be understood procedurally, but a declarative reading is often more informative. The same information is carried, but a declarative reading gives a description of what is meant by a program, rather than a description of how a particular task is to be carried out. Amongst other advantages this means that Prolog programs can be used to control many processors simultaneously. The Japanese research project aimed at the production of a fifth-generation computer, which will probably use parallel processing, is being carried out in Prolog.

A useful introduction to Prolog is given by *Programming in Prolog*, by Clocksin & Mellish, published by Springer-Verlag.

BIBLIOGRAPHY

BASIC:

Basic BASIC, by J. S. Coan, published by Heyden (1978).
Structured programming in BASIC, by P. Bishop, published by Nelson, 1984.
30 hour BASIC, by C. Pingmore. Published by the National Extension College Trust in 1981.

Fortran:

Computing with FORTRAN, by D. M. Munro. Published by Edward Arnold, 1974.
Essentials of FORTRAN 77, by J. Shelley. Published by Wiley, 1984.
A guide to FORTRAN IV programming, by D. McCracken. Published by Wiley, 1972.
A standard approach to FORTRAN 77, by T. M. R. Ellis. Published by Addison-Wesley, 1982.

Pascal:

The Pascal User Manual and Report, by K. Jensen and N. Wirth.
A student's guide to programming in Pascal, by L. V. Atkinson. Published by Wiley, 1982.
Pascal — A considerate approach, by D. Price. Published by Prentice-Hall, 1984.
Pascal programming, by L. V. Atkinson. Published by Wiley, 1980.

FORTH

FORTH fundamentals, by C. Kevin McCabe. Published by dilithium Press (Oregon), 1983.
Discover FORTH, by T. Hogan, published by McGraw-Hill, 1983.

C

The C programming language, by B. Kernighan and D. Ritchie, published by Prentice-Hall in 1983.
The C primer, by Hancock and Krieger. Published by McGraw-Hill, 1986.
Mastering C, by C. Bohr. Published by Symbex, 1986.
A book on C, by A. Ketley and I. Pohl. Published by Benjamin Cummings, 1984.

Lisp

Lisp, by P. H. Winston and B. K. P. Horn. Published by Addison-Wesley in 1984.
Essential Lisp, by Anderson, Corbett & Reiser. *Published by Addison-Wesley, 1987.*

Prolog

Programming in Prolog, by Clocksin & Mellish. Published by Springer-Verlag, 1983.
Prolog programming for artificial intelligence, by I. Bratco. Published by Addison-Wesley, 1986.

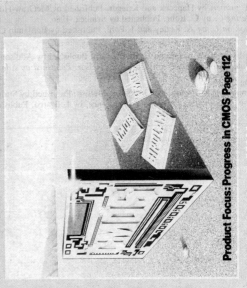

RADIO COMMUNICATION

Information Transfer—Wave Propagation—Modulation—Applications—Broadcasting—Radiodetermination

By G. L. Grisdale, B.Sc., Ph.D.

INFORMATION TRANSFER

Telecommunications embraces all methods of transferring information between people who are too far apart to speak to each other, or between machines. In many European countries the wider term 'communication' also includes ways of transporting people and goods, but here the information aspect only is considered. Electrical means are nearly always used, but there is increasing application of optical methods.

Information is transmitted by a series of changes, which have to be applied to a carrier of the information; modulation is the process of applying the information to the carrier, and demodulation is the rather inappropriate term for recovering the information at the distant terminal. When people use ordinary sound to talk to each other, the carrier is the air pressure, the changes due to the voice amounting to only about a millionth of the static air pressure. In the early telephone transmitters the sound pressure changes the electrical resistance of a capsule of carbon granules, thereby modulating a direct current flowing through the granules and acting as the carrier. Although the steady component of the current may be suppressed at the transmitting terminal to improve the efficiency of transmission, either the direct current or its equivalent in the form of a permanent magnet must be re-introduced at the receiving earpiece, otherwise the received sound would be severely distorted.

The transmitted information may be the sound of a voice or music (telephony), printed matter on a page (facsimile), a photograph with shades from black to white or in colour (telephotography) or a series of pictures sent sufficiently rapidly to represent a changing scene (television). All this information can be directly perceived by human ears or eyes; machines can exchange information in other forms (data transmission). The information is initially converted into electrical form by modulating a direct current in proportion to the intensity of the sound or light stimulus; such proportional control of the carrier is called analogue modulation, because the carrier is changed as a direct analogue of the applied sound or other stimulus.

For the first electrical communication apparatus it was possible only to interrupt a current or to reverse it, and analogue modulation was not introduced until the telephone was invented in 1877. Similarly, effective radio telephony had to await the development of the amplifying triode valve. In recent years there has been a return to on-off or digital modulation, even for transmitting telephony and television, mainly because transistors and other semi-conductor devices have made such methods advantageous in cost, equipment size, information capacity and freedom from distortion.

An essential feature of digital modulation is that information is transmitted by patterns of successive changes, or codes. An early example of digital transmission was the lighting of beacon fires which signalled the sighting of the Spanish armada; the single fire lighting could convey only one bit of information that ships had arrived; many more fire-lightings would have been required to indicate more information such as the number of ships or their course. The American Indian smoke signals were supposed to transmit more information by dividing the smoke column into separate bits; the smoke was the carrier and the blanket was the modulator. In radio telegraphy, the information is applied to the radio transmitter by an interrupting switch consisting of a morse key or a teleprinter machine, forming code patterns representing the letters or figures of the message; the codes are recognised at the distant end by a human listener or a machine to produce the message.

Radio communication uses a high-frequency electrical oscillation as the carrier, which is modulated by the amplified analogue current from the information source. The modulation produces changes to the amplitude, frequency or phase of the radio-frequency power, which is transmitted as an electro-magnetic wave through space, as Clerk Maxwell predicted it could be, as Hertz confirmed in the laboratory and as Marconi and others developed for practical communication over greater and greater distances.

WAVE PROPAGATION

Electrical conductors carrying rapidly changing currents radiate electro-magnetic waves into the space around the conductors. The amount of energy radiated and the directions in which it is radiated depend on the amplitude of the current, the frequency or wavelength of the oscillation, and the size and shape of the radiating conductor or antenna (aerial). Some of the energy of the current heats the conductor and surrounding objects including the earth; this is known as the resistance loss and the earth loss of the antenna, and must be kept as low as possible so that the generated energy is usefully radiated. The radiation from the conductors may be concentrated in a required direction by reflecting from shaped screens of sheet conducting material or from curtains of wires which are regarded as part of the complete antenna.

Electro-magnetic waves travel through a vacuum with velocity $2{\cdot}99793 \times 10^8$ m/s, with little difference in air; for most purposes a figure 3×10^8 is used. The basic characteristic of the radiation is the frequency, which is the same at all points which are fixed in relation to each other; if the distance between transmitter and receiver is changing there is a small difference between transmitted and received frequencies (Doppler effect):

$$f_d = f_o \times v/c \tag{1}$$

where f_d = change of the radiated frequency f_o,
v = velocity in metres per second of receiver towards transmitter,
c = velocity of electro-magnetic radiation (3×10^8 m/s).

For example, an aircraft flying at 670 m.p.h. towards a transmitter receives a frequency one part in a million above that radiated. The Doppler effect may present problems in certain communication systems to mobile stations but has been applied usefully in radio navigation.

The concept of wavelength is important in the design of antennae, since the ability of a structure to radiate energy and to concentrate the radiation in a desired direction is related to the size of the structure in wavelengths. A circular reflector which produces a radiation beam only 1° wide has a diameter of about 70 wavelengths, or 10.5 metres at 2,000 MHz frequency. Narrow beam radiators are therefore practical only at microwave frequencies (see p. H3/20). Wavelength is related to frequency by:

$$\text{Wavelength in metres} = \frac{\text{Velocity in metres per second } (3 \times 10^8)}{\text{Frequency in hertz (cycles per second)}}$$

The strength of an electro-magnetic wave may be expressed as the power flux density (PFD) at any place, measured in watts per square metre. In free space the PFD would decrease as the square of the distance from the radiating source. The strength of the wave may also be given as the field strength E volts per metre, which is related to PFD by

$$P = \frac{E^2}{120\pi} \tag{2}$$

The design of a radio system is based on a power budget which enables the power of the required transmitter to give a defined quality of communication to be calculated. Many factors must be included in the budget, including the power required at the receiver, the attenuation of the path between transmitting and receiving antennae, and the antenna efficiencies. The output quality of the received signal also depends on several factors, such as the bandwidth needed for transmitting the information, the noise level at the receiver, and the modulation method used.

The radio path between the transmitter and the receiver is through unobstructed free space in only a few applications, the main example being between an earth station and a satellite positioned well above the horizon. In most situations the propagation path is near to the ground or the sea, or to solid objects on them, which obstruct or reflect the waves so that the received signal is generally below the strength it would have if there were unobstructed free space between the antennae. Nevertheless, the basis for the power budget calculation is the free space attenuation between isotropic antennae, which are theoretical antennae which radiate equally in all directions and which may be related to the performance of practical antennae by gain factors.

The attenuation between isotropic antennae in free space is given by:

$$P_r = P_t \frac{5.7 \times 10^{14}}{d^2 f^2} = \frac{P_t \lambda^2}{16\pi^2 d^2} \tag{3}$$

where P_r and P_t are the powers received and transmitted in watts, f and λ are the frequency in hertz and the wavelength in metres, and d is the distance in metres between the antennae.

Multiplication factors are often large in radio calculations, so that it is more convenient to express these factors in logarithmic form (decibels) which can be added instead of multiplying the large numbers. Thus,

Path attenuation L_p between isotropic antennae in free space in decibels

$$= 10 \log_{10} \frac{P_t}{P_r} = -147.56 + 20 \log_{10}(df)$$

$$= 22 + 20 \log_{10}(d/\lambda) \tag{4}$$

Decibels are based on logarithms to the base 10 and will be used throughout; some engineers use nepers, based on natural logarithms; the attenuation in decibels is 8·685 times the attenuation in nepers.

Terrestrial radio links have antennae mounted close to a rough, spherical earth with a range of reflecting properties from those of salt water to those of dry sand, and under a surrounding gaseous atmosphere, both of which may obstruct, deflect or weaken the waves, either assisting or hindering the desired communication.

Some of the higher frequency links span short distances where the path between the antennae is unobstructed so that line-of-sight conditions are achieved. For propagation beyond the horizon there must be some means for deflecting the waves round the curvature of the earth; four physical mechanisms enable this to occur:

(i) *Diffraction* allows a diminished signal to be received beyond the horizon of a smooth curved earth, or over a sharp ridge like a mountain. Diffraction occurs independently of the presence of an atmosphere and the lower the frequency the greater is the energy deflected in this way.

(ii) *Reflection* occurs at boundaries between media with differing electrical properties, as at the surface of the earth or sea.

(iii) *Refraction* is bending of the ray paths at places where the velocity changes. There is a gradient in the refractive index of air with height which produces a slight bending downwards of a horizontally projected wave; the path curvature is normally allowed for by assuming that the waves travel in straight paths over an earth that is 4/3 times its real diameter. Important refraction also occurs in the ionised layers of air between 80 and 500 km above the earth, permitting very long distance communication at some frequencies.

(iv) *Scattering* takes place when a wave passes through discontinuities of refractive index; the air is not homogeneous, but has irregularities with changes over a few metres. The energy scattered is a small fraction of what passes straight on; typically only one millionth of the incident power might be scattered, and the angle through which the ray is deflected is only a degree or two.

All these mechanisms are used to achieve radio communication beyond the horizon; they also produce interference between stations at similar distances. Except for diffraction, the atmosphere is the essential medium in long-range communication.

Multipath Propagation.—The physical mechanisms which increase the range of radio signals also limit the type of information that can be transmitted through the radio links, and may produce severe distortion of the signal modulation. This is caused by multipath propagation, the signal being received over several paths which differ in length. Just as sound waves are reflected from walls or from solid objects in a room to give echoes of the directly received wave, so can radio waves take several paths from transmitter to receiver. Three examples are illustrated in Fig. 1, in which it can be seen that the arrival time of signals passing

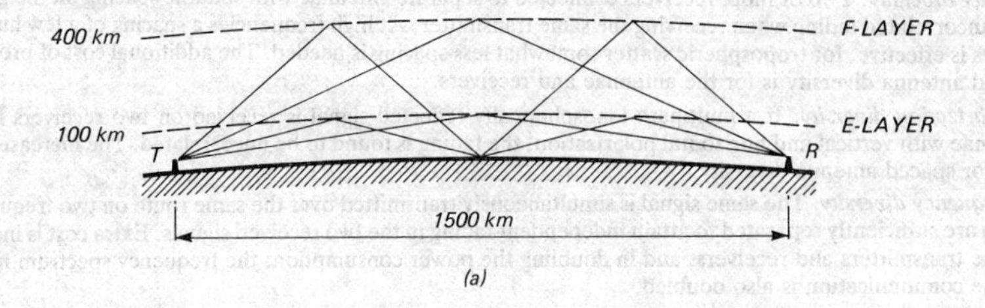

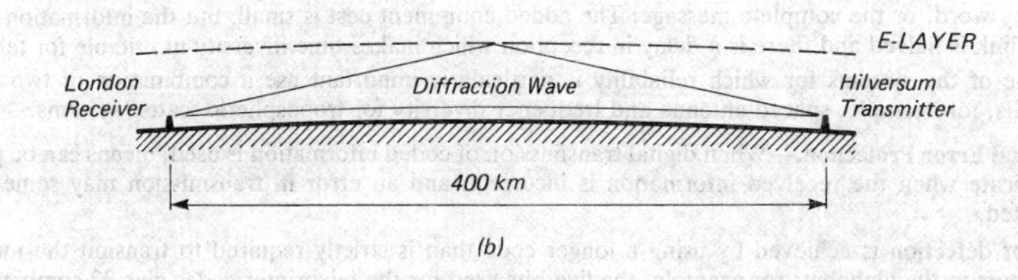

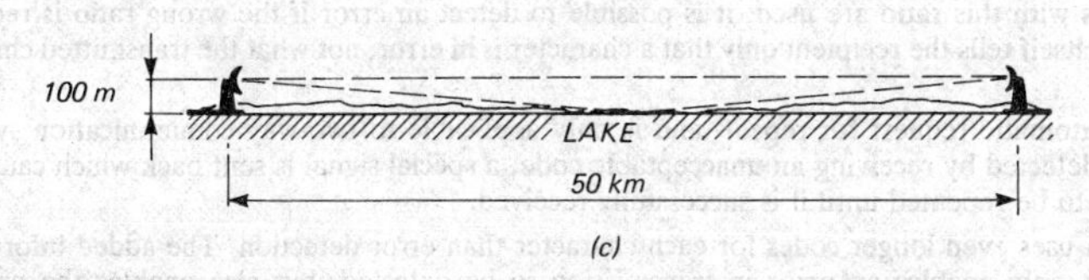

FIG. 1.—Radio transmissions with multipath interference. (a) Long-range short-wave (2–25 MHz) link with reflection at E and F ionised layers. (b) Medium-wave (500–1500 kHz) reception after dark of a medium distance broadcaster. (c) Microwave radio link over water. The differences in propagation time over the different paths might be (a) 1 millisecond (b) 0.2 millisecond (c) 1 nanosecond.

through the longer and shorter paths constitutes a delay which can vary over a range of more than a million to one, depending on the geometry of the paths.

The ionisation produced by radiations from the sun plays an important part in providing very long range communication between stations on the earth at frequencies below about 25 MHz. [23]At long wavelengths (up to 300 kHz) the waves are trapped between the E-layer and the earth surface; at higher frequencies several layers of the ionosphere provide possibility of reflection back to the ground. The atmosphere is a very irregular and changing medium, and radio communication depending on such propagation modes may have a performance that varies from one frequency band to another, and from second to second, or over longer periods up to years.

The effect of receiving the same signal through more than one route may be that the strength is either increased or decreased, depending on the multipath delay time and the frequency used. As the path length changes, the signal strength varies to produce fading and the modulation may suffer severe distortion. Medium-wave broadcasting stations suffer from severe distortion after dark because of such interference between the direct ground wave and the rays reflected from the ionosphere. Multipath propagation is also the cause of poor quality of long distance short-wave broadcasts, although interference between stations using the same frequencies is also a severe problem in the short-wave bands.

Diversity Reception.—It is easy to see that if a message is sent through several separate channels the probability of its correct reception is greater than if a single channel is relied upon. When wave interference between signal components arriving simultaneously through several paths causes fading, bad reception occurs when the signal falls to a low level. If the same signal can be received through several different routes which do not fade at the same time, the best signal at any time can be selected for use; this is known as diversity reception, and is widely used where fading occurs in long-range high-frequency communication and in tropospheric scatter installations. It is particularly effective with digital communication, and rather less so with analogue telephony modulation because of the inbuilt redundancy of speech. Two- to four-path diversity is used. At any instant the best output may be selected or the signals may be suitably combined to give the best signal to detect the information.

The main diversity reception methods are:—[22]

Space diversity. Two or more receivers connected to separate antennae with suitable spacing on the ground give uncorrelated fading when receiving the same transmitter. At high frequencies a spacing of a few hundred metres is effective; for tropospheric scatter somewhat less spacing is needed. The additional cost of providing spaced antenna diversity is for the antennae and receivers.

Polarization diversity. If a multipath ionospherically reflected signal is received on two receivers fed by antennae with vertical and horizontal polarization, the fading is found to be uncorrelated. The increased cost is as for spaced antenna diversity.

Frequency diversity. The same signal is simultaneously transmitted over the same route on two frequencies which are sufficiently separated to attain independent fading in the two received signals. Extra cost is incurred for the transmitters and receivers, and in doubling the power consumption; the frequency spectrum needed for the communication is also doubled.

Time diversity. If a message is sent twice through a single channel, the parts which are lost through fading or interference may not be the same in the two editions received. The repetition may be letter by letter, word by word, or the complete message. The added equipment cost is small, but the information capacity of the link is halved and there is a delay in reception which makes time diversity unsuitable for telephony.

Some of the systems for which reliability is particularly important use a combination of two diversity methods, for example, spaced antenna and frequency diversity for tropospheric scatter systems.

Digital Error Protection.—When digital transmission of coded information is used, means can be provided to indicate when the received information is incorrect, and an error in transmission may sometimes be corrected.

Error detection is achieved by using a longer code than is strictly required to transmit the number of characters in the alphabet; for example, the five bits used for the teleprinter codes give 32 combinations to represent characters, but a seven-bit code gives 128 combinations, of which 35 include four zeros and three ones; if only codes with this ratio are used, it is possible to detect an error if the wrong ratio is received. Error detection by itself tells the recipient only that a character is in error, not what the transmitted character was.

ARQ means 'automatic request for repeat' and is only applicable to two-way communication systems. When an error is detected by receiving an unacceptable code, a special signal is sent back which causes the rejected character to be repeated until it is successfully received.

Error correction uses even longer codes for each character than error detection. The added information in these codes not only enables an error in transmission to be detected, but also enables the probable character to be ascertained without asking for a repeated transmission. It is sometimes called 'forward error correction' (fec).

Both diversity and error protection are means of combating the defficiencies of some radio propagation paths. They cannot make very bad circuits good, but they can make poor circuits workable and make good

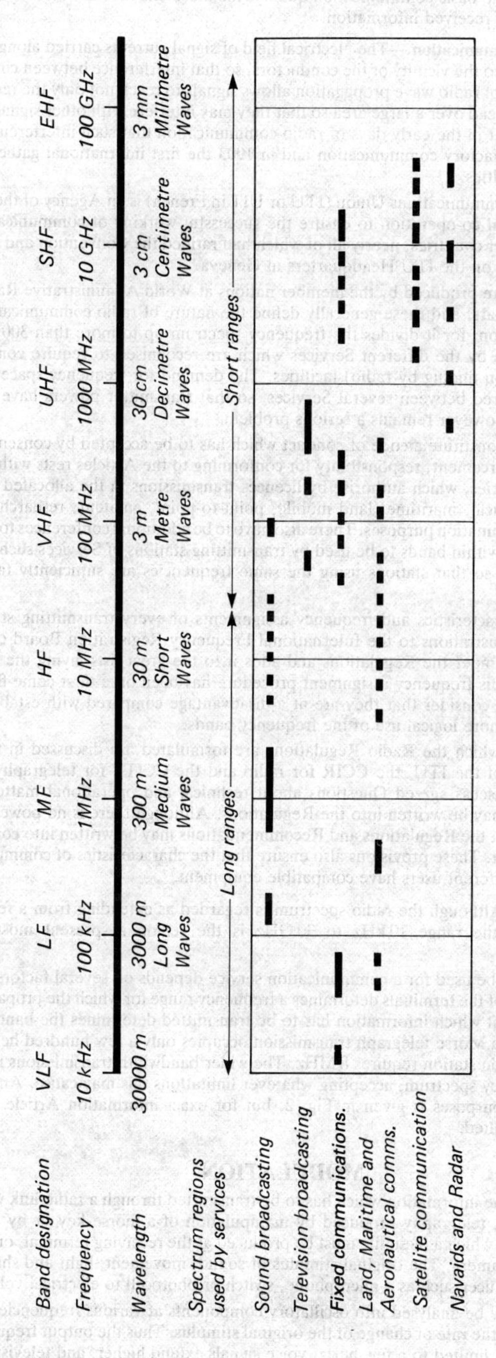

FIG. 2—The radio frequency spectrum, with an indication of its application. Frequencies above 1000 MHz are generally known as microwaves. The long and short ranges apply to terrestrial application; space services use microwaves for very long ranges. Precise allocations of frequency bands to services can be found in Article N7 of the Radio Regulations.

circuits better. The better the basic communication quality, the more effective are these systems in reducing the number of errors in the received information.

Regulation of Radio Communication.—The electrical field of signal currents carried along lines and cables may be largely constrained to the vicinity of the conductors, so that interference between circuits is generally small. However the nature of radio wave propagation allows signals to reach not only the receivers for which they are intended but to spread over a large area so that they may interfere with other signals using the same frequencies. It was apparent in the early days of radio communication that such interference posed serious problems in achieving satisfactory communication and in 1903 the first international gathering was held in Berlin to discuss the difficulties.

The International Telecommunications Union (ITU or UIT in French) is an Agency of the United Nations responsible for international co-operation to ensure the successful working of communication systems. In 1979 there were 154 member countries, nearly all of which had ratified the Convention and contribute to the activities which are centred on the ITU Headquarters in Geneva.

The Radio Regulations are produced by the member nations at World Administrative Radio Conferences held about every twenty years, and these generally define the nature of radio communications. Article N7 is the most important section, for it divides the frequency spectrum up to more than 300 GHz into bands which are allocated for use by the different Services which are recognised to require communication and radiodetermination (position finding by radio) facilities. The demand for frequency space has led to some frequency bands being shared between several Services, so that transmitter powers have to be limited to avoid interference, which however remains a serious problem.

The Radio Regulations constitute a code of conduct which has to be accepted by consent, for there is no international power of enforcement; responsibility for conforming to the Articles rests with the Administrations of the ratifying countries, which authorise by licences transmissions in the allocated frequency bands for broadcasting, aeronautical, maritime, land mobile, point-to-point, amateur, research and other communication and radiodetermination purposes. There also have to be additional conferences to reach agreement on the frequency channels within bands to be used by transmitting stations of Services such as broadcasting, aeronautical and maritime so that stations using the same frequencies are sufficiently far apart to avoid interference.

Details of technical characteristics and frequency assignments of every transmitting station have to be notified by national Administrations to the International Frequency Registration Board of the ITU which examines its acceptability under the Regulations and adds it to the great lists giving the characteristics of every registered station. This frequency assignment procedure has been on a 'first-come-first-served' basis, but the developing nations consider that they are at a disadvantage compared with established users, and would like to introduce a more logical use of the frequency bands.

The technical bases on which the Radio Regulations are formulated are discussed in the International Consultative Committees of the ITU, the CCIR for radio and the CCITT for telegraphy and telephony. Their Study Groups (2) discuss agreed Questions about technical and operational matters, and produce Recommendations which may be written into the Regulations. Although there is no power of enforcement internationally, the terms of the Regulations and Recommendations may be written into contract documents for the supply of equipment. These provisions also ensure that the characteristics of communication systems are standardised so that different users have compatible equipment.

The Radio Spectrum.—Although the radio spectrum is regarded as extending from a few hertz to above 500 GHz (500×10^9 Hz), the range 10 kHz to 30 GHz is the region at present most used for radio communication.

The frequency that may be used for a communication service depends on several factors. The distance to be covered and the height of the terminals determines a frequency range for which the propagation conditions are satisfactory. The rate at which information has to be transmitted determines the bandwidth demanded by the modulated carrier; a Morse telegraph transmission occupies only a few hundred hertz of bandwidth, but a single colour television station requires 8 MHz. The wider bandwidth transmissions must therefore be placed high in the frequency spectrum, accepting whatever limitations this may cause. An indication of the bands used for different purposes is given in Fig. 2, but for exact information Article N7 of the Radio Regulations must be consulted.

MODULATION

Modulating Signals.—The information which has to be transmitted through a radio link will be in the form of speech or music sound, telegraphy produced by manipulation of a morse key or by a machine coder, matter printed on paper of which a facsimile must be produced at the receiving terminal, or a moving picture output from a television camera. The original stimulus of sound, movement, light and shade or colour will be transformed in a transducer such as a microphone, switch or photocell to electrical voltage or current.[3]

The electrical signal may be analysed into oscillatory components at various frequencies from zero to an upper limit determined by the rate of change of the original stimulus. Thus the output frequency components of a morse key motion are limited to a few hertz, voice signals extend higher, and television signals extend to over a million hertz. The frequency band which must be transmitted through the radio link is one factor in selecting the radio frequency at which the communication must be achieved, and will determine the number of transmissions which may be simultaneously made in a given area of the earth.

The sound of the voice is composed of a spectrum of frequencies from below 100 Hz to above 10,000 Hz, but perfect intelligibility, if not realism, is produced if 200 to 6,000 Hz components are transmitted, and practical public telephony systems use only 300 to 3,400 Hz. High quality sound such as is used for music transmission may require 20 to 15,000 Hz, which is the range that can be heard by a healthy young human ear. The kind of pressure variation for a human voice is shown in Fig. 3 (a), with typical spectrum components, which vary from moment to moment. The minimum sound level at a frequency of 1,000 Hz which can be heard is 2×10^{-5} newtons per square metre, which is the reference level used for expressing sound levels in decibels. The barometric air pressure is about 10^5 newtons per square metre, so that even the loudest sound produces only a small change of static pressure.

The digital waveform which is used in coded transmissions consists of a series of pulse elements of nearly rectangular waveform as shown in Fig. 3(b). This can be analysed into spectral components from zero up to fundamental frequency equal to half the reciprocal of the element duration, together with a number of harmonics of this frequency. As with voice transmission, not all the higher frequency components are required for the correct transmission of the coded message; in fact it may be reconstructed from little more than the range from zero up to the fundamental frequency. Thus a digital data stream of 2400 bits per second should theoretically require a frequency band from zero to 1200 Hz for accurate transmission; in practice a margin must be added to allow for transmission deficiencies and to avoid digital errors. These bandwidths apply to communication over metal conductors using direct current; for radio frequency transmission the bandwidth may be doubled, as will be explained.

The appreciation of a picture image in the human eye involves the simultaneous detection in separate cells of many thousands of stimuli from different parts of the area seen, and their transmission along separate nerve connections to the brain. Such transmission through many separate channels in an electrical communication system would be uneconomical, so that in a television camera a screen of light sensitive cells is scanned by a beam of electrons which constitutes a rapid multi-way switch, the output from which is applied

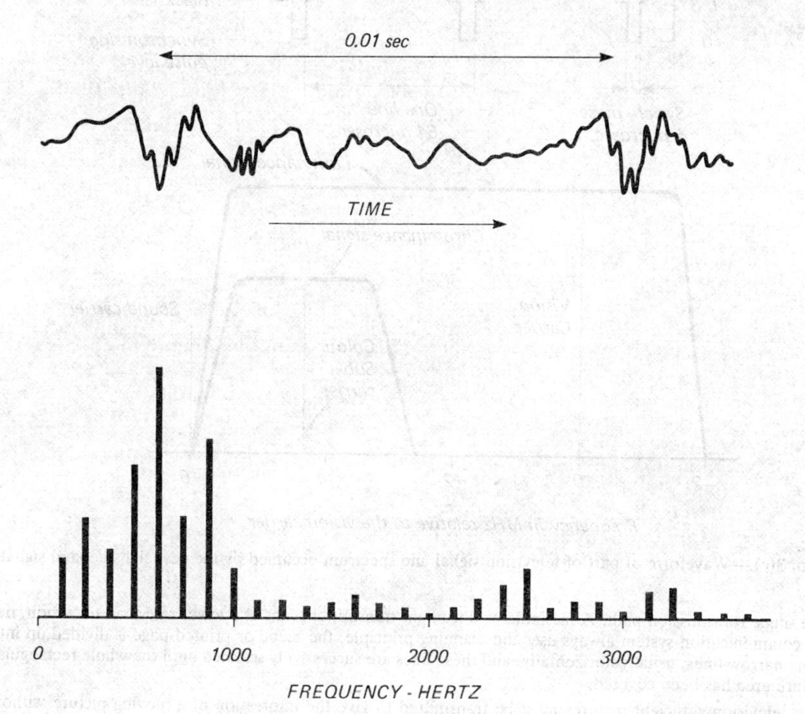

FIG. 3(a).—Voice pressure waveform for round 'O' sound, with its spectral components (from Harvey Fletcher).

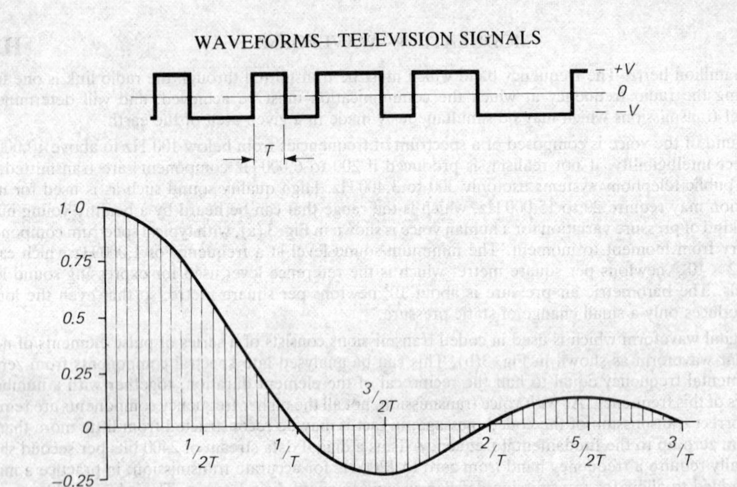

FIG. 3(b).—Waveform of a digital modulation of direct current and the spectral distribution of its frequency components. Removal of the higher frequencies would round the corners of the waveform.

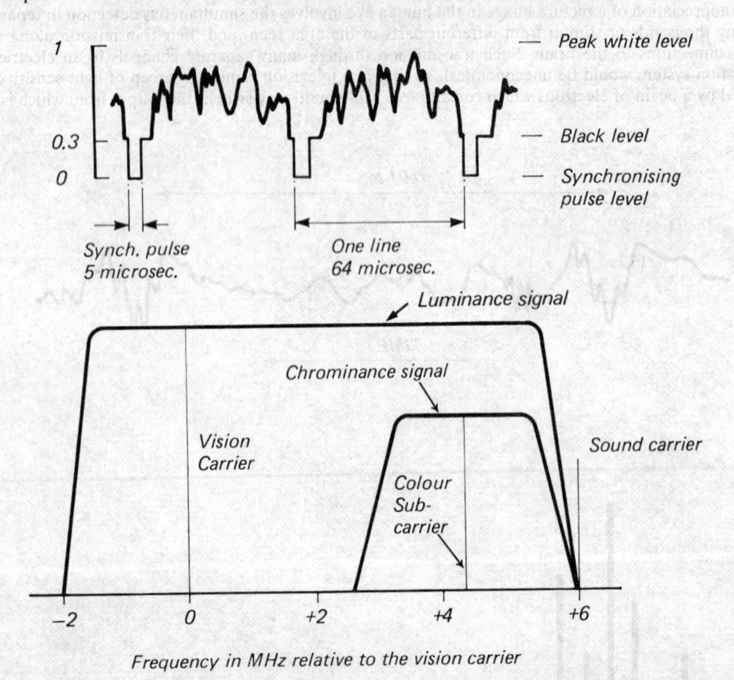

FIG. 3(c).—Waveform of part of television signal and spectrum occupied by the vestigial sideband signal.

to a single transmission path. A facsimile or document transmitter scans at a lower rate than television, but the communication system always uses the scanning principle; the scene or printed page is divided up into many narrow lines, usually horizontally, and these lines are successively scanned until the whole rectangular picture area has been covered.

In television sufficient pictures must be transmitted to give the impression of a moving picture without flicker; the CCIR standard adopted by many countries, but not USA and Japan, uses for broadcast television 25 picture frames per second each frame consisting of 625 lines and each line having 700 or more picture elements; it is therefore necessary to transmit 11 million picture elements in each second, requiring a frequency spectrum of more than 5.5 mHz. Because television requires such a wide frequency channel, many complexities have been introduced in the interests of bandwidth economy, particularly for colour systems. In addition to the picture elements, the modulation must include recognizable pulse shapes to enable the receiver picture scanning to be synchronised with that at the transmitter, so that the received picture elements are placed in their correct relative positions. For colour transmission the relative strength of the three colour components must also be transmitted through a separate channel in the spectrum; some details of the television waveform are shown in Fig. 3(c).

The waveforms and spectra which have been described are basically the modulation of a direct current or voltage, which may be the amplified output from a microphone, telegraph transmitter or television camera. This is known as a baseband signal, and to be transmitted by radio a suitable carrier oscillation must be generated and modulated with the baseband signal. The frequency of the carrier will depend on the nature of the radio path over which transmission is required and also the frequency range of the baseband; the carrier frequency is normally more than ten times the modulation bandwidth.

Modulation Methods.—Some baseband waveforms such as television and some digital signals have a constant or zero frequency component, the amplitude of which must be transmitted for correct reproduction of the signal; for sound, however, the ear requires only the audio frequency components to be reproduced.

Successful radio communication requires that the transmission frequency should be suitable for transmission through the propagation path provided. The baseband signal may change the carrier in amplitude, frequency or phase as in Fig. 4, these changes being detected in the demodulator of the receiving terminal to recover

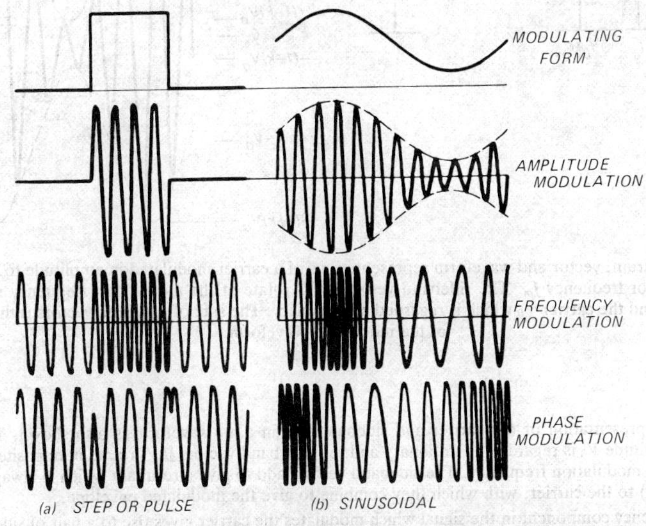

FIG. 4.—Comparison of Amplitude, Frequency and Phase Modulation.

the transmitted information. For accurate reproduction the whole transmission system must be linear, that is, the receiver output signal must be directly proportional to the transmitter input signal; departures from linearity, unless corrected, introduce distortion or noise, and linearity specifications are essential for analogue radio equipment. To attain this linearity the minimum carrier frequency should be about 10 kHz for telegraphy, 100 kHz for sound broadcasting and 50 MHz for television; propagation or frequency allocation requirements may dictate higher frequencies.

Even where analogue signals such as speech, television or facsimile are to be transmitted, the waveforms may be converted into digital codes and transmitted as binary digital signals. This is not a matter of fashion; there must be thorough examination of the technical and economic advantages of each method when making the choice, particularly when the new system has to be compatible with an established one.

Amplitude Modulation.—The early line communication systems transmitted the baseband and used direct current carriers, which could be changed only in amplitude. For many years this was thc method applied in radio communication, the amplitude of the radio oscillation being varied in proportion to the baseband signal.

The amplitude modulated waveform shown in Fig. 4(a) for sinusoidal modulation may be expressed algebraically:

$$V = V_0 \sin \omega t\,(1 + k \cos pt)$$
$$= V_0 \sin \omega t + \tfrac{1}{2} kV_0 \sin(\omega + p)t + \tfrac{1}{2}kV_0 \sin(\omega - p)t \tag{5}$$

where V_0 is the peak voltage of the carrier wave
ω is 2π times the carrier frequency f_c
p is 2π times the frequency of the sinusoidal modulation f_m
k is the modulation index, which may not be greater than 1.

The modulated wave can therefore be resolved into a carrier component and two smaller sidebands which are symmetrically disposed above and below the carrier by the modulation frequency (Fig. 5).

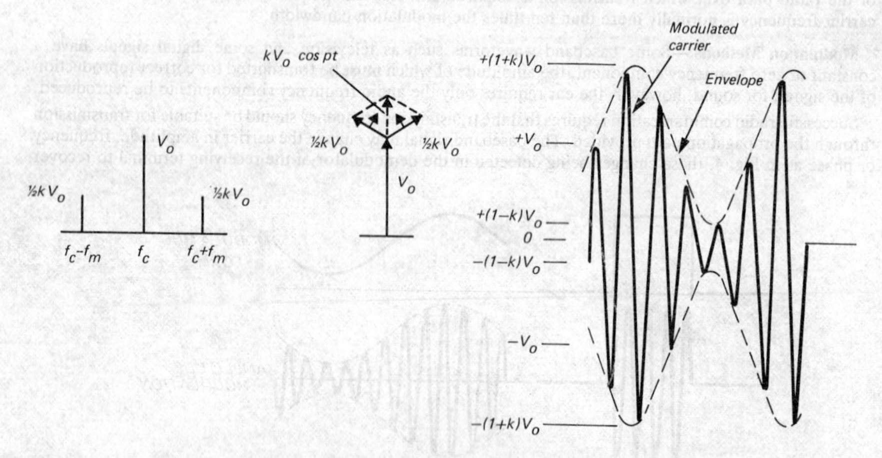

FIG. 5.—Spectrum, vector and waveform representations of a carrier modulated in amplitude to depth k by a single tone of frequency f_m. The sideband vectors $\tfrac{1}{2}kV_0$ rotate at the modulation frequency in opposite directions round the carrier V_0 which is regarded as stationary. The sum of the three vectors is the envelope of the modulated waveform.

A vector representation of the carrier and sidebands of an a.m. waveform is also shown. The carrier vector of amplitude V_0 is regarded as stationary and the side band vectors $\tfrac{1}{2}kV_0$ rotate in opposite directions about it at the modulation frequency. The sideband vectors add to give a resultant which is always in phase (or opposition) to the carrier, with which they combine to give the modulated envelope.

Each frequency component in the signal which modulates the carrier gives rise to a pair of sidebands; the frequency band which must be transmitted by radio is therefore at least double the highest modulation frequency. A speech signal for commercial telephony transmission extends from 300 to 3,400 Hz and therefore needs a 6,800 Hz width in the radio spectrum when amplitude modulated.

The transmitter powers needed for radio transmission are much greater than for line systems, so that the methods of keying them rapidly on and off for telegraphy, or of modulating the power proportionally for telephony pose much greater engineering problems. The designer must take into account the capital cost of such high power equipment and the buildings to house it, as well as the maintenance and the power costs to run it; the modulation method is an important factor in determining these costs.

The basic amplitude modulation methods are high level and low level (Fig. 6).[4] For high level modulation the radio frequency carrier is amplified to the high power needed for transmission and the audio or television modulation is also amplified to a similar level and applied to the final radio frequency power amplifier of the transmitter; the linearity requirement is that the radio frequency instantaneous power output should be directly proportional to the modulating power at all times.

In low-level modulation the modulation is done at an early stage in the transmitter and the modulated signal is then amplified to a high power in a linear amplifier. Thus the radio frequency power output of the final amplifier must be proportional to the modulated driving power at its input up to the maximum power at peaks of modulation.

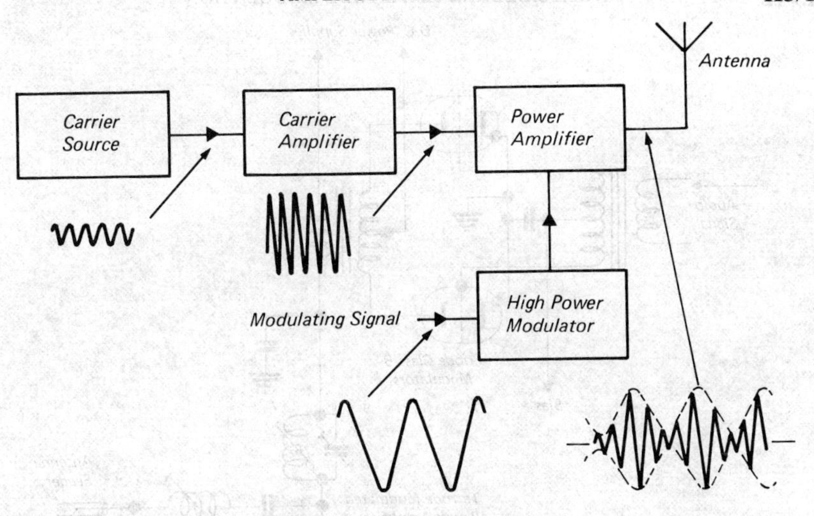

FIG. 6(a).—High level Modulation.

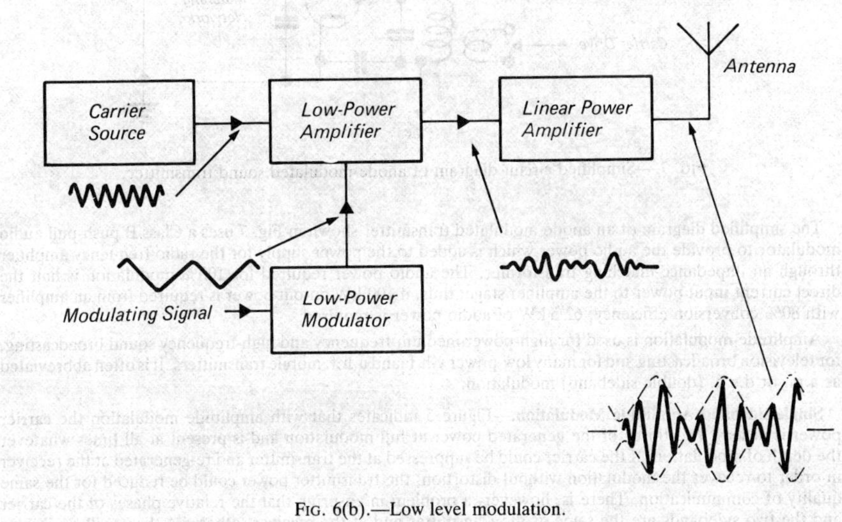

FIG. 6(b).—Low level modulation.

The main difference between these modulation systems lies in the efficiency and power capability of the final amplifiers. Although the low-level modulator requires very little modulating power, the linear radio frequency power amplifier operates at lower efficiency than the high-power modulated amplifier. A low efficiency means that not only is less output power produced, but that a higher fraction of the supplied power is converted into heat losses, which have to be removed. Therefore, to obtain a given power output, larger valves have to be used for a linear power amplifier than for high-level modulation. The high audio frequency power from the high-level modulator must of course be taken into account.

Amplitude modulation transmitters use the audio frequency power from the modulator to vary the anode power supply to a valve or the collector power supply to a transistor. Valves are essential for transmitters having power outputs above about one kilowatt. Modulated valve power amplifiers can attain 85% efficiency if operated in the Class D mode.[5]

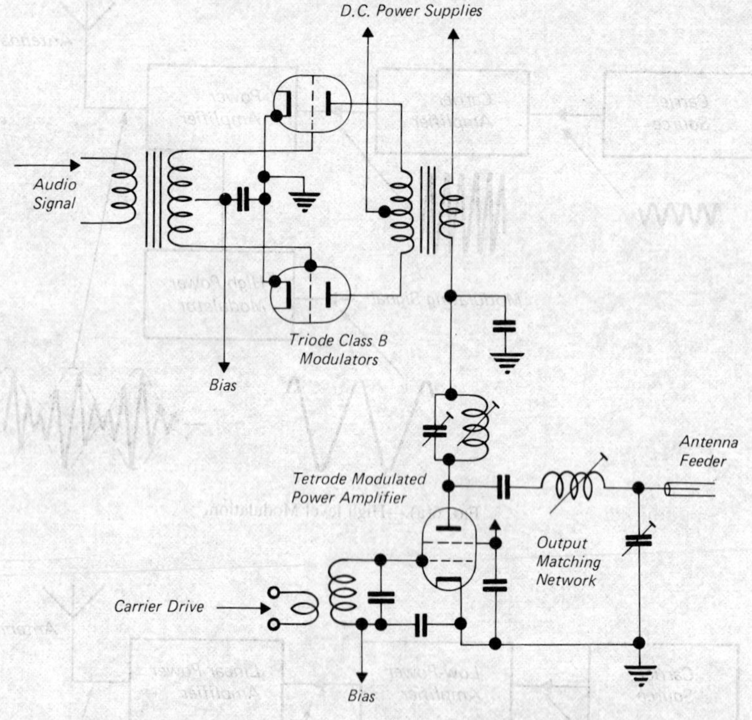

FIG. 7.—Simplified circuit diagram of anode-modulated sound transmitter.

The simplified diagram of an anode modulated transmitter shown in Fig. 7 uses a Class B push-pull audio modulator to provide the audio power which is added to the power supply for the radio frequency amplifier through an impedance-matching transformer. The audio power required for 100% modulation is half the direct current input power to the amplifier stage; thus, if 100 kW output power is required from an amplifier with 80% conversion efficiency, 62·5 kW of audio power is required.

Amplitude modulation is used for high-power medium-frequency and high-frequency sound broadcasting, for television broadcasting and for many low-power v.h.f. and u.h.f. mobile transmitters. It is often abbreviated as a.m. or d.s.b. (double sideband) modulation.

Single-sideband Amplitude Modulation.—Figure 5 indicates that with amplitude modulation the carrier power is at least two thirds of the generated power at full modulation and is present at all times whatever the depth of modulation. If the carrier could be suppressed at the transmitter and re-generated at the receiver in order to recover the modulation without distortion, the transmitter power could be reduced for the same quality of communication. There is, however, a problem in ensuring that the relative phases of the carrier and the two sidebands are the same at the transmitter and at the receiver, otherwise there will be serious distortion.

A second factor is that the two sidebands contribute the same information in the signal; if one sideband were removed only amplitude would be lost, and the bandwidth required for the communication would be halved. Using only one sideband also reduces the frequency stability requirement because the ear can tolerate a minor frequency displacement of the received sound.

Single-sideband suppressed-carrier transmission therefore improves the effective use of transmitter power and increases the number of transmissions that can be accommodated in a given band in the spectrum. The removal of the carrier also reduces the interference when transmitters attempt to use the same frequency channel. The penalty for s.s.b. is more complex equipment and operation, particularly in respect to frequency adjustment. The main application is in the high-frequency band 2–30 MHz for long distance communication between land stations, and more particularly for ships and aircraft where power is limited; there are both telephony and telegraphy applications. S.S.B. is proposed but not yet applied for v.h.f. mobile communication, where spectrum economy is not yet so pressing, transmitter powers are less, and the frequency stability

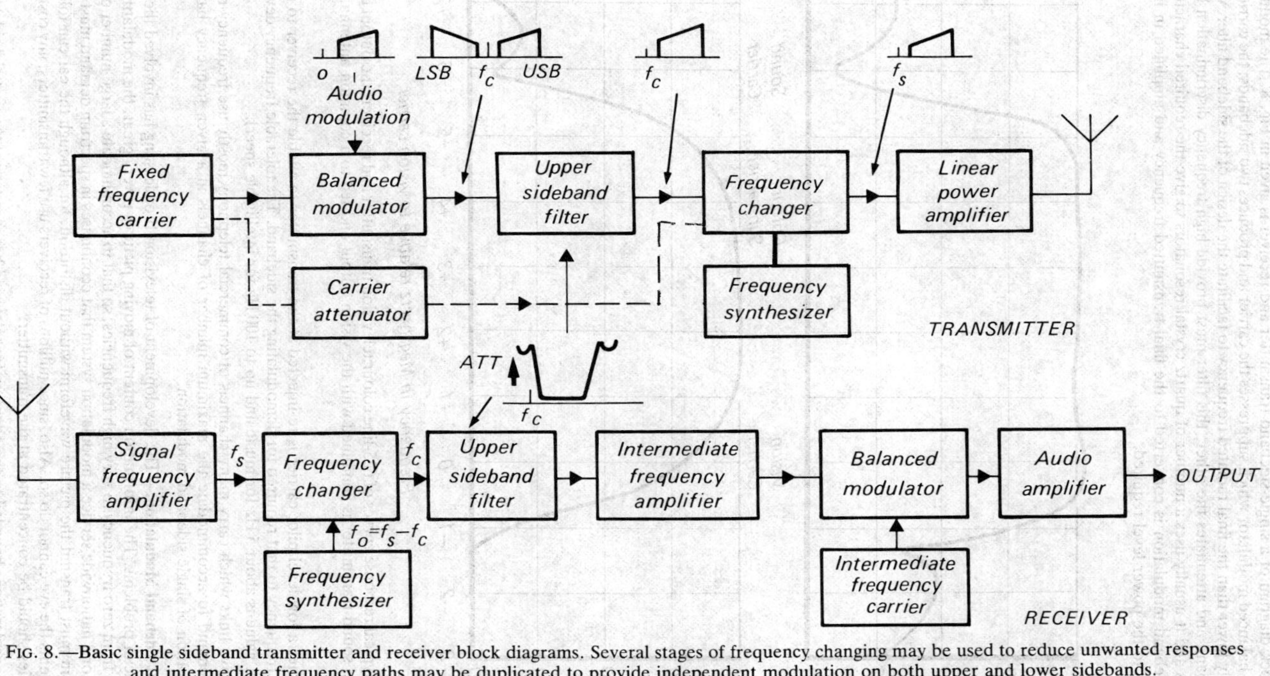

FIG. 8.—Basic single sideband transmitter and receiver block diagrams. Several stages of frequency changing may be used to reduce unwanted responses and intermediate frequency paths may be duplicated to provide independent modulation on both upper and lower sidebands.

required presents a more severe problem. It is also not yet applied in broadcasting where receiver complexity and cost are unwelcome.

The block diagram of a single-sideband transmitter and receiver is given in Fig. 8. The modulation takes place in a balanced modulator which suppresses the carrier and produces two sidebands; the carrier frequency is normally lower than the final radiated frequency to facilitate the design of the sideband filter, which passes one sideband and attenuates the other; this filter must provide high frequency discrimination between the sidebands and it usually uses a number of quartz crystal resonators to give the required characteristics. The single sideband modulation is converted to the final transmitted frequency and amplified in linear power amplifiers to the power level required.

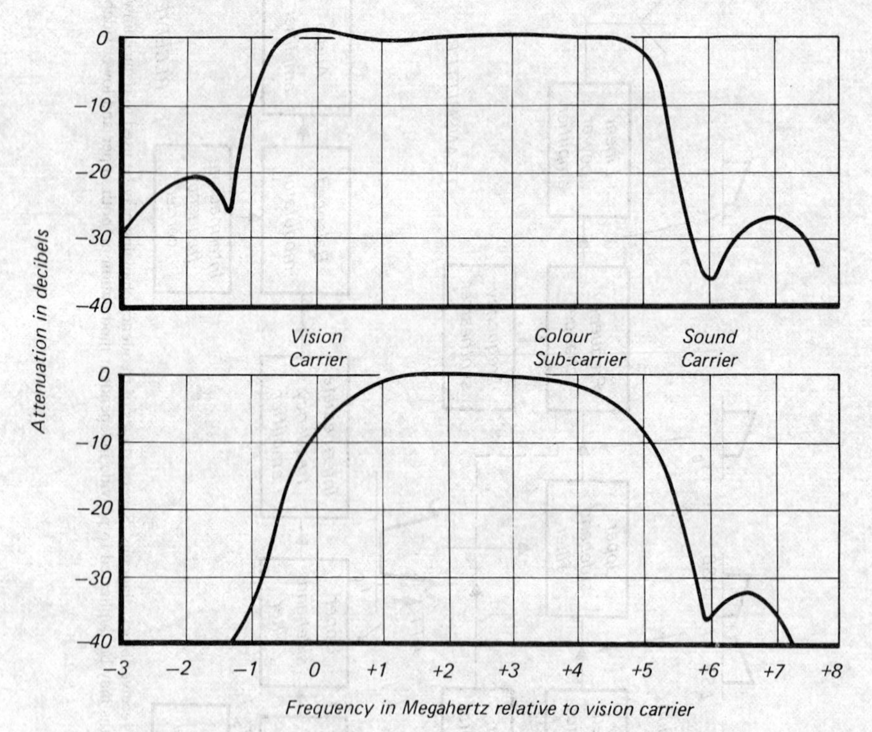

FIG. 9.—Typical response curves of 625-line colour television transmitter and receiver; the output of a separate sound transmitter is combined with the vision output and fed to a common antenna.

Sometimes a low-level pilot carrier is re-injected at the transmitter to enable the receiver to synchronise its carrier frequency to that required for demodulating the sideband. The tolerable frequency deviation from the correct value is about 5 Hz for music and up to 100 Hz for intelligible speech.

Microwave links which carry many channels of commercial telephony mostly use frequency modulation, but the demand to accommodate the maximum number of channels in a given frequency band leads to reconsideration of single-sideband modulation.

Vestigial-sideband Modulation.—The development of television broadcasting has involved the solution of many difficult problems. The information content of moving pictures is very great, the modulating spectrum extending from zero frequency to very high frequencies, so that to accommodate a large number of frequency channels for a nationwide service a modulation system that economises in spectrum demand must be devised. This system must transmit the picture waveform without distortion, for although the ear can tolerate phase displacements the eye cannot do so. Also, since millions of receivers use few transmitters, any costly technical complexities should be concentrated at the transmitter.

These considerations have led to the adoption for television broadcasting of the vestigial sideband system, which combines features of double and single sideband modulation. The television is first amplitude modulated onto a carrier to produce a double sideband signal, which is passed through a filter with the characteristics shown in Fig. 9, passing the upper sidebands up to 5 MHz above the carrier and the lower sidebands down to 1·25 MHz below the carrier. The receiver filter has a gradual attenuation from +1·25 to −1·25 MHz, and these filters together produce a signal with an amplitude envelope suitable for recovery in a simple rectifier circuit.

The vestigial sideband modulation system allows television channels in the European u.h.f. band to be spaced 8 MHz apart, whilst modulation components up to 5 MHz are received with the precision needed to produce good pictures.

Frequency Modulation.—The frequency of the carrier is changed in proportion to the applied modulating waveform, the amplitude being constant (Fig. 4). This is one form of angle modulation, so called because the phase angle varies in relation to the unmodulated carrier phase. For a single sinusoidal modulating frequency f_m both phase- and frequency-modulated waves are similar in form and may be written algebraically:

$$V = V_0 \cos(\omega_c t + m_f \sin pt) \tag{6}$$

where m_f is the phase deviation in radians and also the frequency-modulation index
ω_c is 2π times the carrier frequency f_c
other symbols are as in the amplitude-modulation analysis (eq. 5).

Angular frequency ω is defined as the rate of variation of the phase angle of the wave and therefore the instantaneous angular frequency may be written:

$$\omega = \frac{d}{dt}(\omega_c t + m_f \sin pt) = \omega_c + m_f p \cos pt,$$

$$\text{or } f = f_c + m_f f_m \cos pt \tag{7}$$

The peak frequency deviation is $f_d = m_f f_m$, or $m_f = f_d/f_m$

In frequency-modulation the frequency deviation f_d is constant for a given modulating voltage, and therefore m_f must be inversely proportional to the modulating frequency. It can be seen from equation (6) that m_f is also the phase deviation in radians, which for phase modulation is independent of the modulation frequency. In practice, analogue angle modulation is regarded as frequency modulation, and phase-modulation is only used in the circuits of transmitters as a step in producing frequency-modulation with improved frequency stability.

The expression for a frequency-modulated wave in equation 6 may be analysed into a series of frequency components:

$$V = V_0 \sum_{n=-\infty}^{n=+\infty} J_n(m_f) \cos(\omega_c + np)t \tag{8}$$

where the coefficients $J_n(m_f)$ are Bessel functions the value of which depends on the frequency deviation. The meaning of this equation is that a sinusoidally frequency-modulated signal consists of a carrier and a number of sidebands spaced at harmonics of the modulation frequency, the number depending on the frequency deviation. Only for very small deviations do the outer sidebands become insignificant so that the spectrum approaches the two-sideband amplitude-modulated spectrum. Fig. 10 shows the spectra with

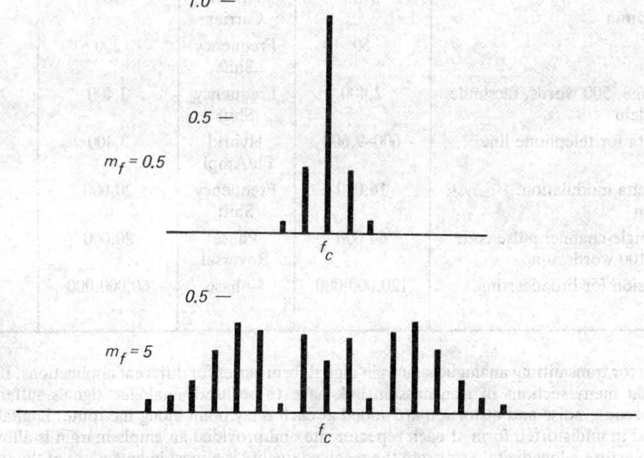

FIG. 10.—Spectra for frequency modulation with modulation indices 0·5 and 5, for a single tone frequency. The spacing of the sidebands is the modulation frequency.

modulation indices 0.5 and 5; in the latter case the occupied bandwidth is 16 times the modulation frequency.

For a given signal strength at the receiver, frequency-modulation with wide deviation can offer a higher output signal-to-noise ratio than amplitude-modulation. However, the penalty for this is that the received signal must be above a threshold level; below this level with f.m. there is a great increase of noise which obliterates the signal. Frequency-modulation is therefore used for sound broadcasting in the v.h.f. band, where the high carrier frequency allows a wide channel-bandwidth to be used, where the interference is low, and where a steady high signal strength can be maintained within the limited service area of the transmitter.

Frequency-modulation is also used in the low-power transmitters for mobile communications to ships and land vehicles at frequencies above 50 MHz; civil aviation finds amplitude-modulation advantageous in allowing area coverage by several overlapping transmitters in the same frequency channel. The performances of f.m. and a.m. for mobile communications are very similar.

For short-range microwave links between land stations and for long-range satellite communications frequency modulation has been the standard method; however, the increased number of microwave links is causing congestion in highly developed areas, and is leading to consideration of s.s.b. amplitude modulation which is more economical in the use of the spectrum.

Digital Modulation.—Most digital signals are in binary form, which means that they change at regular intervals between two states, which might be current-on and current-off, or frequency-one and frequency-two. The two states may be called 'mark' and 'space' (from telegraphy) or '0' and '1' (from mathematics and computers). The pulses of information are 'signalling elements' and the rate at which they occur is the 'information rate'.

Digital signals arise either from information produced in coded form, as with telegraphy and the output from machines such as computers, or from analogue waveforms from sources such as speech or pictures which have been converted to codes representing the amplitude of the analogue waveform at regular sampling times. The coded output from machines is called 'data' and the process of sending digital information of any form over communication links is often somewhat inaccurately called 'data transmission'.

The information rates for various sources originating in, or converted to digital streams are given in Table 1. It is clear that the information rates, and therefore the bandwidths necessary to transmit them, vary greatly according to the nature of the source. For speech and telegraphy the efficiency of using the spectrum may be expressed by the ratio of required bandwidth to the words per minute transmitted; it can be seen that telegraph methods give more efficient transmission of words than does telephony, with facsimile in an intermediate position.

TABLE 1.—INFORMATION RATES AND BANDWIDTHS FOR DIGITAL STREAMS.

Source of Information	Digital Information Rate, bits/sec	Modulation Method	Approximate Bandwidth Needed, Hertz	Communication Efficiency, Words per min per Hertz
Morse key 5 to 30 words/min	5–30	On-off Carrier	100	0·05–0·3
Teleprinter 66 words/min	50	Frequency Shift	200	0·33
Typescript page, 500 words, facsimile with line modem	2,400	Frequency Shift	3,400	0.04
Computer data for telephone line	600–9,600	Hybrid Ph/Ampl.	3,400	0.18–2.8
Voice with delta modulation. 100 words/min	16,000	Frequency Shift	20,000	0.005
Voice with single-channel pulse-code modulation. 100 words/min	64,000	Phase Reversal	80,000	0.0016
Colour television for broadcasting. Pulse coded	120,000,000	4-phase	60,000,000	

The reasons for transmitting analogue signals in digital form varies for different applications. If the distance is so great that many sections of transmission link have to be used, analogue signals suffer progressive degradation because noise and distortion are added at each relay point along the route. Digital signals may be regenerated in undistorted form at each repeater site and provided an ample margin is allowed by good engineering to assure a low digital error rate the received quality is almost independent of the total distance. For this reason the sound and television organisations are introducing digital modulation in the distribution of material from studios to broadcasting transmitters.

In military communications digital methods offer secrecy, because digital signals may be encrypted in ways which are believed to be absolutely immune from enemy observation and interception.

Digital modulation methods are being introduced in civil satellite communication because they can give more channels through costly satellites simultaneously from earth stations in many countries.

Where radio links are used in association with other transmission systems such as cables, there may be advantages in accepting digital transmission throughout the network, to avoid conversion at junction points. It is planned to convert whole national telephone systems to digital switching and transmission, and this will include the radio links in the network. Nevertheless, in an isolated radio link there must be good economic, technical or operational reasons for a decision to use either analogue or digital modulation.

Two methods are used for converting analogue waveforms into digital streams of information; although they are labelled 'modulation' they are in fact coding systems. They are:—

Pulse-code-modulation (p.c.m.).—Samples of the amplitude of the waveform are taken at least twice in each cycle of the highest frequency component of the waveform; each sample is converted into a code accurately representing the sample amplitude. The standard system for commercial quality speech samples 8,000 times per second and uses 8-bit codes to represent 128 voltage levels for each polarity. Thus each speech channel requires a digital transmission rate of 64,000 bits per second. P.C.M. is used in radio systems associated with public telephone networks, particularly for satellite communication, and it affords excellent speech quality.

Delta-modulation (d.m.).—is a simpler coding system than p.c.m. in which each amplitude sample is compared with the one before; if there is an increase a '1' is sent, and for decrease a '0' is sent. Delta modulation has been adopted in military radio communication with land vehicles at v.h.f. and has also been proposed for some satellite systems providing communication to ships. Acceptable speech quality is obtained with digital modulation rates of 16,000 bits per second or less; delta-modulation therefore needs less bandwidth than pulse-code-modulation and the equipment is less complex.

The methods used to modulate digital information such as pulse-code-modulation, delta-modulation and data information with radio carriers are:

Phase-shift-keying (p.s.k.)—uses the phase of the carrier to represent the two digital states. At the receiver a reference phase must be established so that the received signal may be compared in phase to determine the state of each modulation element.

Quadrature phase-shift-keying (q.p.s.k.)—uses four phase states at 90° intervals which can transmit two bits of information for each modulation symbol; it therefore doubles the information rate for a given modulation rate and bandwidth, but needs about twice the transmitter power to achieve a specified digital error rate.

Differential-phase-shift-keying (d.p.s.k.)—compares the phase of each signalling element with that of the preceding element to differentiate between a '0' or '1' bit. It therefore eliminates the need to establish a reference phase at the receiver, and may be applied to both phase reversal and quadrature phase systems. It is proposed for digital satellite links now being introduced.

Frequency-shift-keying (f.s.k.) is a digital frequency modulation in which the change of signal state is indicated by shifting from one frequency to another. It is widely applied in radio telegraphy links, particularly over long distances where the propagation path is variable in performance.

Frequency-exchange-keying (f.e.k.) is a variant of f.s.k. in which two frequencies are keyed on and off instead of modulating a single oscillator in frequency; the main advantages are obtained in the receiver detection circuit, particularly in reducing the adverse effects of signal distortion caused by multipath propagation on long-range links.

On-off keying (c.w. or w.t.) was the original radio telegraphy system and is still used for hand-speed Morse applications, where the signal is converted to an interrupted audible tone at the receiver so that the codes are easily interpreted by the listener.

Spread-spectrum (s.s.) is a modulation method which spreads the signal over a much larger bandwidth than is required by the modulation frequencies of the signal to be transmitted.[7] This appears to be contrary to concepts of economy in the use of the available frequency band, but spread spectrum systems are now being implemented to give immunity from electronic counter measures (e.c.m. or jamming) in aeronautical and satellite defence systems.

The normally modulated signal is subjected to a second digital modulation process which applies a high modulation-rate code, which has to be removed at the receiver by remodulating with a further identical and synchronous code so that the wanted signal can be recovered. By using different codes at different transmitters the same frequency band may be used simultaneously by several transmitters, so long as the received signal levels are not too different. The spread-spectrum method is used with success in the precision position-finding system using satellites called Navstar.

Frequency Hopping.—For defence communications it is obviously important to prevent an enemy from intercepting transmitted messages. If the message can be sent in a short time on a pre-arranged frequency, it is unlikely that the intercepting receiver can be adjusted to receive it, and so security may be achieved. An application of this principle divides the message stream into short sections, each of which is transmitted on a different frequency; the receiver must hop at the same rate and to the same frequency as the transmitter. High hopping rates are achieved by using one or more digital frequency synthesiser controlled by code generators similar to those used for digital encryption.

Noise.—The ability to receive intelligible signals through a communication system ultimately depends on the relative strengths of the wanted signal and the unwanted interference or noise accompanying it, the signal-to-noise ratio (S/N).

An irreducible basic noise is produced in all electrical conductors by the thermal agitation of free electrons, which produces noise power covering all frequencies from electrical circuits. The power of the noise produced is proportional to the width of the frequency band in which the noise is measured, and also to the absolute temperature of the source of the noise. The thermal noise may therefore be reduced by narrowing the bandwith of a communication channel, with a proportional loss in the information rate that can be transmitted through it. The source noise can also be reduced by lowering the temperature of the source in some conditions.

The thermal noise power that can be obtained from a resistive source is:

$$N = 1{\cdot}37 \times 10^{-23}\ TB \text{ watts} \qquad (9)$$

where T is the absolute temperature of the source in degrees Kelvin

B is the bandwidth in hertz in which the noise is measured.

At normal room temperature (290 K or 17 C) and 1 Hz bandwidth the noise power becomes:

$$N = 4 \times 10^{-21} \text{ watts} = -204 \text{ dBW}$$

In the case of a radio receiving station the basic thermal noise source is the radiation resistance of the antenna itself, which depends on the temperature of the space from which the antenna can receive radiation. For terrestrial radio communication the received radio wave arrives at a low elevation angle, so the antenna receives a part of its noise from the ground at normal temperature, but for a narrow-beam satellite ground station antenna it may be directed only at a cold area of space, and will receive a low level of galactic noise. The effective temperature of a satellite ground station antenna will be increased by any attenuation in the waveguide or cable from the antenna to the receiver input, and the noise will be increased by the contribution of the initial amplifier of the receiver. In such an expensive satellite system it pays to use a 'front-end' amplifier cooled by liquified helium or nitrogen and mounted as near to the antenna as possible.

At the lower frequencies which are used for terrestrial communication the noise may be above that corresponding to normal earth temperatures; this is atmospheric or route noise, largely derived from atmospheric electric discharges and from man-made electrical interference. Such noise is greater the lower the frequency, and at medium and high frequencies it is propagated thousands of kilometres from equatorial centres of high atmospheric noise near Indonesia, Africa and South America, reaching a maximum in the day at each centre. Such noise is composed of a continuous series of noise impulses, or atmospherics.

The signal-to-noise ratio produced in a radio receiving system cannot be greater than that in the source itself, the antenna. However, this is further degraded by the noise produced in the circuits, valves and transistors of the receiver itself, and receivers may be given a 'noise factor' which is a measure of how far the output signal-to-noise ratio is degraded by receiver noise below that of a resistive source at normal temperature. The attainment of a low receiver noise factor is important at frequencies above about 25 MHz; at lower frequencies the high source noise usually masks the noise of a well designed receiver.

Intermodulation interference is produced when strong signals outside the required signal band reach a level where the valves or transistors no longer behave linearly, that is, they begin to overload. To take this into account in the receiver design there must be a compromise between the sensitivity of the receiver and its ability to deal with large unwanted signals.

Multiplexing.—A single radio link is often required to carry simultaneously a number of separate channels of information; this varies from two to twenty channels of telegraphy on long-range radio paths to more than a thousand channels of telephony over line-of-sight microwave links. Multiplexing is the arrangement for combining the channels for transmission and for separating them at the receiving terminal. The combined signals from the separate channels are called the 'baseband' which is then applied as modulation to the radio carrier.[8]

The most used system is frequency-division-multiplex (f.d.m.) in which each channel of traffic is modulated onto a different sub-carrier, spaced normally at equal frequency intervals. This is applied for telegraphy with up to 20 sub-carriers at 110 or 170 Hz intervals in the audio frequency spectrum, and for telephony with a single-sideband modulation on sub-carriers at 4 kilohertz intervals up to frequencies of several megahertz.

Figure 11 shows how telephony channels are combined to form groups of 12 channels; the tops of the triangles indicate the high frequency end of the audio spectrum of each channel. Such groups of 12 channels may be further grouped by s.s.b. modulation onto higher frequency carriers to form 60-channel supergroups, 300-channel mastergroups and 900-channel super-mastergroups, according to the traffic requirements of the route.

A characteristic of f.d.m. is that all channel signals are present simultaneously and therefore the power of the radio transmitter is less for each channel than if it were devoted to a single communication. The level at which each channel is applied in the multiplex is specified in various CCIR and CCITT recommendations, for both telephony and telegraphy systems.

Digital information streams can use time-division-multiplex (t.d.m.) which is becoming more important as telephone networks are converted to all-digital operation. Single digits or groups of digits from separate information sources are sent over the radio link in time sequence at a higher rate than that of the input channels (Fig. 11). Each channel uses the full power of the radio transmitter, but for a fraction of the time. T.D.M. requires synchronisation of the digital information patterns of the input channels before they are combined so that some message storage method must be used in the multiplexer. Recent advances in solid-state technology have enabled t.d.m. systems to be implemented at lower cost than the equivalent f.d.m. arrangements, sometimes with improved performance and capacity for traffic.

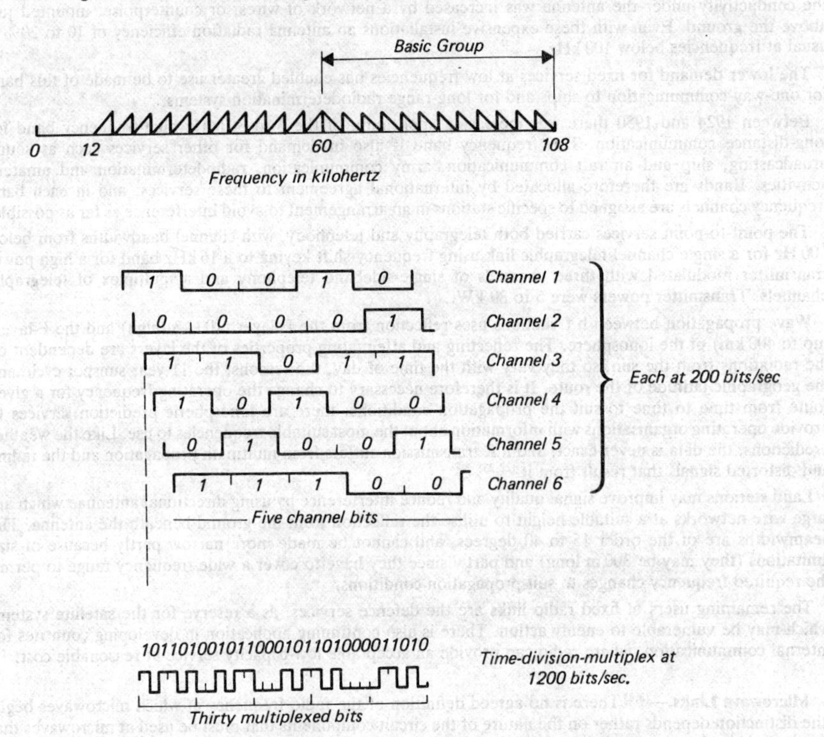

FIG. 11.—Multiplexing methods. Above, 24 telephony channels combined as 2 groups in frequency division multiplex. Below, 6 digital channels combined in time division multiplex; five bits from each of 6 channels are re-arranged into thirty shorter bits by sequentially sampling the six channels.

APPLICATIONS

Fixed Terrestrial Services.—Following the initial pressing requirement for radio communication to ships in the interests of safety and efficient operation, attention was given to long-distance radio services between fixed land stations. Such communication was possible between some places using undersea cables carrying telegraphic messages at very low keying rates, and radio links offered the possibility of both higher traffic capacity and greater flexibility of routes. After thirty years during which the most important method of communication over long distances was short-wave radio, the successful laying of transoceanic submarine cables from 1956 and the achievement of satellite communication in 1965, both carrying many channels of telephony and telegraphy, led to a decline in the use of radio. Fixed radio links are however still used for tails or short extension of satellite links and for internal communications in the less developed countries; radio also provides very high quality services of high capacity through microwave links.

Long-range Communication.[9]—Before the discovery in the early 1920s that frequencies above 2 MHz could be received at very long distances from the transmitter, a few point-to-point services were operated at much lower frequencies; indeed it was generally accepted that the longer the wavelength the longer the distance that it would be possible to cover.

In the first two decades of the century transatlantic communication was established using wavelengths of about 5,000 m, and a radio network of long-wave stations had been started. In 1923 this scheme was abandoned in favour of the newly discovered short-wave communication. A few long-wave international radio telegraphy circuits survived until 1960, being replaced by facilities available over the international telephone network.

Long-waves are propagated between the E-layer of the ionosphere, 85 to 100 km above the earth, and the earth surface; the ionised layer behaves like a conducting shell at these frequencies. The antennae consisted of high towers supporting a network of wires to give a high capacitance to earth, fed through a vertical wire; the conductivity under the antenna was increased by a network of wires, or counterpoise, mounted just above the ground. Even with these expensive installations an antenna radiation efficiency of 10 to 20% is usual at frequencies below 100 kHz.

The lower demand for fixed services at low frequencies has enabled greater use to be made of this band for one-way communication to ships and for long-range radiodetermination systems.

Between 1924 and 1950 there was increasing application of the 3 to 30 MHz high-frequency band for long-distance communication. This frequency band is also in demand for other services such as sound broadcasting, ship and aircraft communication, army communication, radiodetermination and amateur activities. Bands are therefore allocated by international agreement to these services, and in each band frequency channels are assigned to specific stations in an arrangement to avoid interference as far as possible.

The point-to-point services carried both telegraphy and telephony, with channel bandwidths from below 500 Hz for a single channel telegraphic link using frequency-shift keying to a 16 kHz band for a high power transmitter modulated with three channels of single-sideband telephony and a multiplex of telegraphy channels. Transmitter powers were 5 to 80 kW.

Wave propagation between h.f. stations uses reflection from the E-layer (100 km high) and the F-layers (up to 400 km) of the ionosphere. The reflecting and attenuating properties of the layers are dependent on the radiations from the sun, so they vary with the time of day, the seasons, the 11 year sunspot cycle and the geographic latitude of the route. It is therefore necessary to change the operating frequency for a given route from time to time to suit the propagation conditions; there are ionospheric prediction services to provide operating organisations with information about the most suitable frequencies to use. Like the weather predictions, the data is never exact, and h.f. transmission suffers from multipath propagation and the fading and distorted signals that result from it.[22,23]

Land stations may improve signal quality and reduce interference by using directional antennae which are large wire networks at a suitable height to utilise the reflection from the ground beneath the antenna. The beamwidths are of the order 15 to 40 degrees, and cannot be made more narrow partly because of size limitations (they may be 300 m long) and partly since they have to cover a wide frequency range to permit the required frequency changes to suit propagation conditions.

The remaining users of fixed radio links are the defence services, as a reserve for the satellite systems which may be vulnerable to enemy action. There is also continuing application in developing countries for internal communication, where radio can provide an acceptable low-capacity service at reasonable cost.

Microwave Links.—[3,8] There is no agreed definition of the radio frequency at which microwaves begin; the distinction depends rather on the nature of the circuit components that must be used at microwaves than on the length of the wave. Above some point in the u.h.f. band, frequency selectivity is provided by resonant lines and cavities rather than the coils and condensers which are used at lower frequencies and it is this change which characterises microwaves; at 1,000 MHz (30 cm wavelength) these techniques are already required.

Except in unusual propagation conditions, radio transmissions at frequencies above 30 MHz are not reflected by the ionosphere, so that the range over which radio communication can be used is limited by the obstruction of the earth's surface. The disadvantage of the restricted range over which communication can be effective is compensated by the reduction of interference from distant transmitters and the absence of long delay echo signals, which allows much wider bandwidths to be used so that radio links can be designed to carry very large amounts of information.

At these short wavelengths antenna beams only a few degrees wide can be formed with parabolic reflectors of acceptable size; a 3 m diameter dish radiating at 2,000 MHz would give about 4° beamwidth and more than 30 decibels greater signal strength than a simple dipole antenna. So long as the terrain allows the antennae to be mounted on elevated sites which keep the direct path between them well away from the surface of the ground serious multipath reflections can be prevented and a highly reliable service is attained. The short ranges covered by microwave links and the substantial antenna gains used allow ample margins to be allowed for unusual propagation conditions in the atmosphere even with transmitters of power output in the 10 W region. Such beamed microwave links using wide bandwidths can transmit many hundreds of telephony channels or a television signal over distances of tens of kilometres, the total transmission distance being extended by amplifying the signal at repeater stations along the route; in this way it is possible to cover transcontinental distances in a series of hops.

Although interference beyond the horizon is not a serious problem, it is desirable to have international agreement about the frequencies to be used so that links may cross national frontiers, equipment manufacture may be standardised and interference from other services such as radar may be minimised by separating the frequency bands used. The International Telecommunications Union therefore allocates bands of frequencies to be used for fixed microwave communication links, and the CCIR and CCITT issue recommendations how these bands are to be divided into a number of communication channels and the types of modulation to be used. Some of the bands used for fixed terrestrial services are also used for links to satellites, so that great attention must be paid to the radiated power levels from stations of the different services, and their locations, to make this sharing possible without interferences; such power limitation procedures are called 'co-ordination'.

The most used frequency bands for civil microwave link are centred around 2, 4, and 6 GHz. The 1979 ITU conference allocated spectrum up to 400 GHz for various applications, looking towards development of equipment at ever higher frequencies in the next 20 years to reduce the demands on existing lower frequency bands.

To carry a large number of separate telephony conversations over a single radio channel they must be combined in one of the multiplexing systems described earlier. Frequency division multiplex is the established system, groups of 12 telephony channels being further combined to form basebands of 60 to 2700 channels, according to the traffic capacity required on a particular route. A common grouping arranges 960 telephony channels in a baseband covering frequencies between 60 and 4287 kHz.

It is established practice to use frequency modulation to apply the multi-channel baseband to the carrier of a microwave link. The bandwidth of such a transmission is up to 20 MHz, and one standard arrangement of frequency channels in the allocated band spaces the transmissions 29 MHz apart, as shown in Fig. 12; in this arrangement six frequency channels are provided for each direction of transmission, so that the whole band could accommodate six times 1,800 two-way telephony communications over a single route. On routes carrying several separate transmissions, adjacent sections are arranged with different frequency channels to avoid possible interference as indicated in Fig. 13. Interference is also reduced by using both vertical and horizontal polarization for transmitting and receiving, changing between adjacent sections of the route. With care in the channel combining network it is also possible to use a single antenna for transmitting and receiving in a single direction.

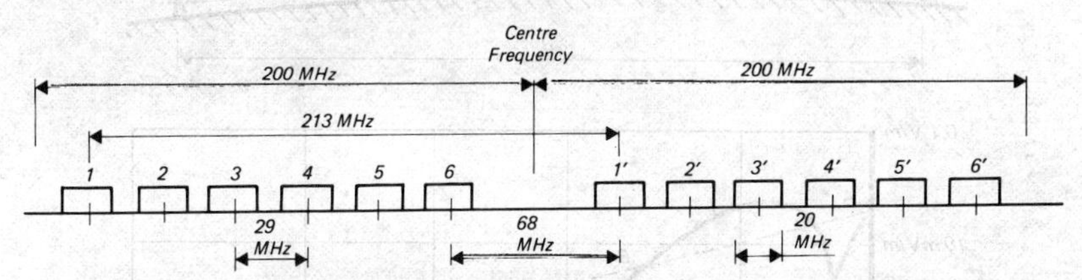

FIG. 12.—One internationally approved arrangement of 12 radio frequency channels each carrying 600 to 1800 telephony channels in the frequency bands around 2000 and 4000 MHz allocated for fixed microwave links. At any terminal the transmitting channels are in one half of the band and the receiving channels are in the other half. Adjacent channels use orthogonal antenna polarisation. Centre frequencies are 1903 or 2101 or 4003.5 MHz.

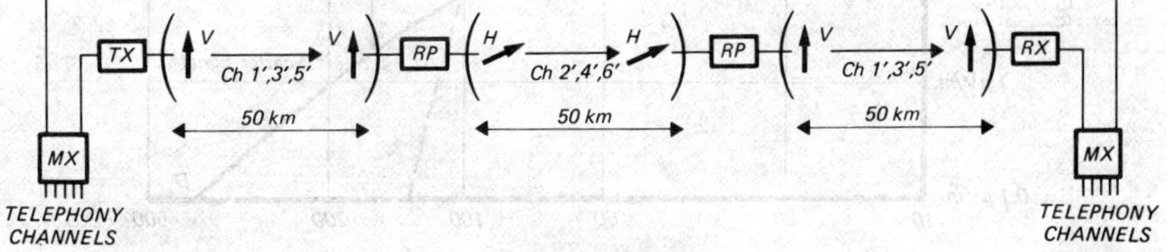

RX H Ch 1,3,5 H RP V Ch 2,4,6 V RP H Ch 1,3,5 H TX

TX V Ch 1',3',5' V RP H Ch 2',4',6' H RP V Ch 1',3',5' V RX

50 km 50 km 50 km

MX TELEPHONY CHANNELS MX TELEPHONY CHANNELS

FIG. 13.—Arrangement of microwave links over three hops, using alternate horizontal and vertical polarisation. The twin antennae may be combined into a single transmit/receive reflector. MX is telephony channel multiplexer. TX and RX are microwave transmitters and receivers. RP is frequency-changing and amplifying repeater.

The main advantage of frequency modulation for multichannel microwave links is that the transmitter power amplifiers may be driven to saturation without distortion so that changes in path attenuation can be accommodated without degrading communication quality. However, the higher frequency deviation that must be used to achieve high signal-to-noise ratios required for signals that are connected to the national public telephone networks lead to high channel bandwidths. Better economy in using the available frequency spectrum could be achieved by using single-sideband modulation, and in areas of high traffic this method is being reconsidered for microwave links, with the acceptance of accurate level control to avoid over-modulation and ensure equal performance in all channels.

At the present time the conversion of many national telephone systems to all digital operation is being actively pursued; the time division multiplexing method shown in principle in Fig. 11 would result in very high rate digital streams to be offered for transmission through microwave links; an 1800 channel digital baseband of 120 megabits per second might require 120 MHz bandwidth, as against 29 MHz using analogue FDM and only 10 MHz for single-sideband modulation. For this reason digital transmission will be introduced mainly in the bands above 10 GHz where the available bandwidth is wider. A digital microwave transmission method would not only be compatible with the general change to digital methods of switching and transmission in the future telephone system, but would afford lower noise transmission on long-distance routes; this is because digital signals can be regenerated at each repeater point, whereas in analogue systems the noise of each hop in the route is added to the finally received signal.

Tropospheric Scatter Links.—[9] Tropospheric scatter is a wave propagation mechanism which extends the range that can be covered by a direct microwave link to 300 to 500 km. The application is for routes over stretches of sea or desert where repeater stations cannot easily be installed. High power transmitters and large antennae are required so that the equipment is expensive to instal and maintain; it is justified in military applications and for oil platform communications.

If a microwave beam is directed at a distant receiving station as in Fig. 14, and the distance between the antennae is increased the received signal strength decreases as shown by the curve. Over the section AB the

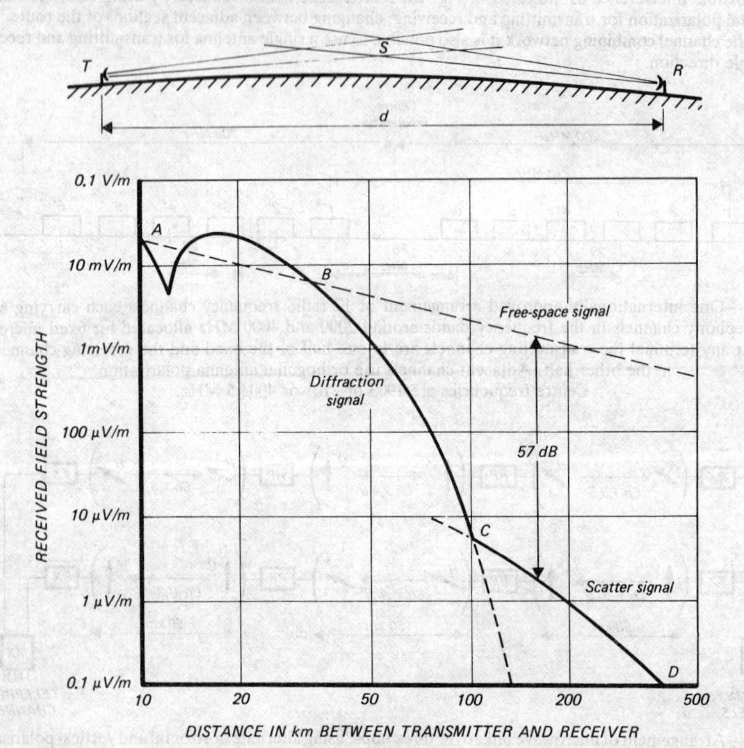

FIG. 14.—Signal field strength received at distance *d* from *a* transmitter radiating 1 kW at a frequency of 1000 MHz over a sea path.
Transmitting antenna height 100 m; receiving antenna height 20 m.

antennae are within line-of-sight distance and the received signal falls according to the free-space inverse square law, except for a small variation due to the proximity of the ground. Over the range BC the signal is due to diffraction round the curved earth or to ground wave; the received signal falls rather rapidly with increased distance, the slope of section BC being greater at higher frequencies. Over the section CD the signal decreases at a slower rate, and this is caused by scatter in the air a few thousand feet above the ground. If the power of the transmitter and the antenna size can be increased sufficiently to overcome the steep loss in section BC, communication may be possible up to several hundred kilometres.

Radio waves are scattered in the atmosphere because the air is not a homogeneous layer of gas; there are pockets of high and low refractive index, the variations taking place over tens of metres distance. The magnitude of the changes is small, but sufficient for a radio beam of suitable frequency to be scattered, much as a car headlight beam is scattered by fog. Fig. 14 shows how such scattering from the region *S* of the atmosphere where the transmitter and receiver antenna beams intersect enables signals transmitted from *T* to be received at *R*. Scatter can take place anywhere in the atmosphere; the volume *S* which is effective for the *TR* path is determined by the intersection of the two narrow antenna beams.

The scattered wave consists of many components from different scatter centres and interference between the components causes fading similar to that occurring in long-range ionospheric propagation. However, the average signal for a given path can be predicted with some accuracy, and the extra attenuation due to scattering that must be added to the free-space loss for the path can be stated:

$$L_{OH} = 57 + 0{\cdot}08(d - 160) \text{ decibels} \qquad (10)$$

where L_{OH} is called the 'over-horizon' loss and d is the distance between the transmitter and receiver in kilometres. It can be seen on Fig. 14 that at 160 km range the extra loss is 57 dB. This is the average performance between antennae near the ground on a level earth; if the terminals can be raised on hills or mountains the attenuation is less, and there is a worthwhile benefit if there are no obstructions in the horizon direction. An allowance must be made for fading in addition to the average loss.

For a 200 miles (320 km) over-horizon path the received average signal is about 70 dB less than it would be in free-space. To provide a high-quality service this large additional loss must be overcome by using high-power transmitters (1 to 10 kW carrier output) and transmitting and receiving antennae with large reflecting surfaces (10 to 30 m diameter). The equipment combination to be adopted is settled by the relative capital costs of the items and the maintenance and power costs which have become a more important factor in recent years.

The quality of the received signal is improved if several antennae are used to provide a diversity system to reduce the noise disturbances produced by signal fading. Tropospheric scatter links use frequency modulation and multiplexing arrangements similar to those of line-of-sight microwave links; there is a demand for digital modulation on military links, not because it gives any power advantage, but for the security which digital encryption offers.

A well engineered tropospheric scatter communication system may provide between 12 and 120 channels of telephony with quality suitable for connection into national telephone systems, over routes which cannot be economically bridged in any other way.

Satellite Communication.—[10] The idea of using an earth satellite as a platform to carry a radio relay equipment to receive and retransmit signals for radio communication stations on the earth was foretold with remarkable accuracy by Arthur Clarke in 1945, and was established as a working system in 1965, since when it has rapidly developed to provide the majority of long-distance communication links. Present day communication satellites can relay up to thousands of telephony channels, data links, telegraphy and document facsimile transmissions, in addition to television programmes, between nearly 100 countries equipped with large ground stations.

An earth satellite travels in an elliptical orbit with the earth centre at its focus; a circular orbit is a particular form of ellipse. The size of the orbit and the time taken to complete one orbit depend on the velocity and direction given to the satellite by its launching rockets. For communication purposes a circular orbit is often advantageous, particularly one in which the satellite takes 24 hours to complete one rotation. Such a satellite must be about 36,000 km (22,300 miles) above the earth surface, and if the orbit is in the plane of the equator and it travels from west to east it will appear to be stationary above a point on the equator; this is known as a geostationary satellite, and each satellite can be seen over about one third of the earth surface but not in polar latitudes. Three satellites suitably located round the orbit can cover most of the populated countries. The advantage of the geostationary satellite is that the earth station antenna beam can point constantly in much the same direction and there is no need to transfer the ground station beam from one satellite to another as they pass over. A minor disadvantage is the time delay of about a quarter second for the radio wave to travel to the satellite and back; telephone subscribers accept the delay from one satellite link, but notice that from two links in series.

The amount of communication traffic which a satellite can relay is limited by the power that the satellite can radiate down to the earth and the bandwidth that can be provided for the signal. Power is provided by the energy from the sun falling on panels of silicon cells which produce electrical power with an efficiency of 10 to 20 per cent; when the satellite passes into the earth's shadow power must be derived from storage batteries.

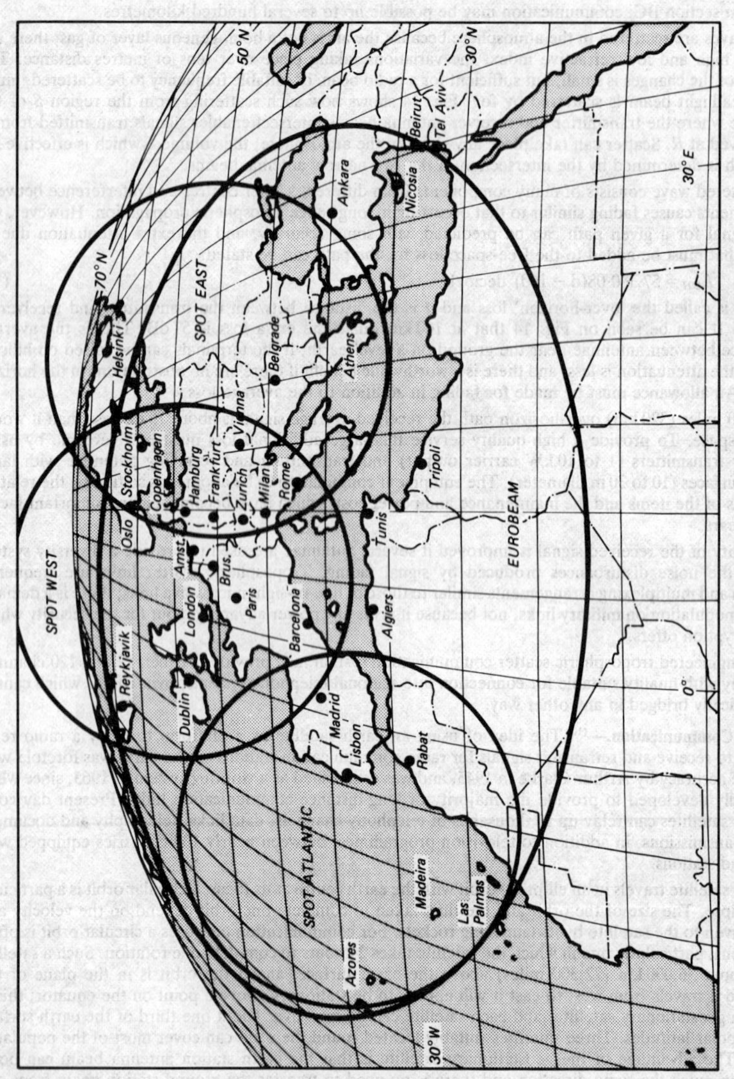

FIG. 15.—Planned antenna beam coverage for the European Communication Satellite, with ground stations.

The radio power produced by a geostationary satellite can be concentrated on the visible one-third of the earth by a parabolic dish antenna with a 17° beam, each watt transmitted producing on average about 7×10^{-15} watts per square metre power flux density at the earth. Some satellites now use narrower beams, giving a stronger signal over a limited area of the earth where the served earth stations are situated; for example, the new European Space Agency satellites ECS will have one elliptically shaped beam covering from Iceland to Turkey, and from Norway to North Africa, and three more powerful beams concentrated on smaller areas (Fig. 15). These improvements have been achieved because antenna techniques have improved and because the satellite attitude can now be accurately stabilised in relation to the earth.

The signal strength received from satellite transmissions can be predicted with great accuracy at frequencies between 1 and 10 GHz because the atmosphere does not cause significant variations of signal, and the beam is normally sufficiently elevated for the ground surface to be neglected. At lower frequencies passage through the ionosphere introduces attenuation and at higher frequencies the effect of rain attenuation must be allowed for. Established satellite services use the 4 GHz band for downward links and the 6 GHz band for the upwards links, and the 11 and 14 GHz bands will shortly be brought into service.

The same frequency bands are used for both the satellite communications and the fixed microwave links on the surface. To avoid interference between transmissions there are strict limits on the powers that may be used in both services and the location of antennae; this regulatory procedure is known as co-ordination.

The improvement to the quality of long-distance public telephone calls that has resulted from the use of satellites and submarine cables has led to a large increase in the demand for calls, so that consideration has been given to the number of channels that can be transmitted through a satellite in the available frequency band and the number of satellites that can be accommodated round the geostationary orbit. There is a difference also in the requirements of highly populated and developed countries which require links carrying many telephony channels between them, and the developing countries which require only small communication capacity to each of a large number of countries. Attention has therefore been given to modulation methods which will economically provide the required increase of capacity and flexibility, and new systems are using digital modulation methods rather than the frequency division multiplexing which was inherited from the terrestrial microwave links. It is also now possible to use the same frequency band twice through the same satellite, the two channels being separated by using special antennae giving two orthogonal linear polarisations instead of the original circular polarisation.

In the early 1960s several satellites carrying radio relay equipment were launched in the United States, with which practical international radio communication was proven to be practical. The international collaboration needed to establish the system was provided in 1964 by forming the International Telecommunication Satellite Consortium (Intelsat) in which 94 nations participated in 1977[10]. Intelsat is responsible for providing the satellites for the global system, and the actual provision and control of the satellites is managed on its behalf by the U.S. Communication Satellite Corporation (Comsat). Ground stations are provided by national administrations using the satellite service, but such ground stations must conform to the performance standards laid down by Intelsat. About 80% of the world's overseas communications now pass through communication satellites.

As well as the Intelsat Global System there are now several international, national and private organisations which operate their own satellites, such as Inmarsat (for services to ships), Eutelsat, Intersputnik, Arabsat and Insat. Companies like Western Union are mainly concerned with data transmission, and television companies run earth stations for programme distribution (see section on Broadcasting).

Although successive generations of communications satellites have become larger and more powerful, so that the number of telephony channels that can be relayed through a single satellite has increased from 240 to more than 10,000, the power available in the satellite from received solar radiation is limited and very sensitive earth stations must be used. The ability of the earth station to produce high quality signals from the low power-flux-density produced on the earth by the satellite radiation depends on the signal power collected by the earth station antenna and the sensitivity of the receiver, which can be expressed as its equivalent noise temperature. For the Global System the ratio of antenna gain to receiver noise temperature in degrees Kelvin is specified by Intelsat to be about 10,000 (40 dB), which leads to a ground antenna reflector 30 m in diameter, with a beamwidth of only 1/6°, and a receiver amplifier cooled with liquid helium. For countries which require intermittent use of single channels to communicate with many destinations, a new single-channel-access system has been introduced which allows smaller earth station antennae to be used, with the penalty of more satellite power needed for each channel, and therefore higher charges paid by the administration for the use of the satellite.

Maritime Communication.—Transmission of messages to ships was the main application seen for wireless communication at the end of the 19th century. No other method can provide such communication once the ship is beyond the land horizon; the radio link is therefore vital in the distress situations which occur all too frequently. Except on small ships, radio officers skilled in morse key operation must be carried for safety purposes, and their availability favours the maintenance of manual morse transmission for other traffic.

Two-way communication between ships and land stations uses internationally allocated frequency bands in the range 300 kHz to 1000 MHz. The frequency used depends on the propagation conditions at the time for the route between the ship and the land station. Nations with a coast have stations near the sea to communicate with local shipping; the long-established frequency band for morse working is between 400 and 535 kHz, with a calling and distress channel at 500 kHz. This 600 metre wavelength is guarded at regular intervals free of other traffic so that distress calls may be heard, and ships are also equipped with automatic alarm receivers which detect the agreed distress signal. Telephony distress calls use the higher frequency 2,182 kHz.

For ships beyond the approximately 300 km medium-frequency daytime range of the coast station the bands between 1,600 and 30,000 kHz are used, many nations having land stations working in these bands to communicate with ships by both telephony and telegraphy. In this range a total bandwidth of 4·749 MHz is now allocated for maritime communication. A band around 160 MHz is also used for telephony calls within a limited horizon range of coast stations.

Within the maritime frequency bands channels are specified for telegraphy and telephony communications; high frequency telegraphy channels are spaced 500 Hz apart, and for single sideband telephony 3,100 Hz is needed. Requests for calls are made by the ship on a calling channel, and a working channel is assigned for the call. Land stations send out lists of call-signs of stations for which they have calls at regular times.

Frequencies below 150 kHz are used by large land transmitting stations to broadcast morse messages such as weather forecasts, news and time signals to ships. These low frequencies are not used in the ship-to-shore direction because the required power could not be radiated from a ship antenna. A few stations in the world operate at frequencies between 15 and 30 kHz where almost world-wide coverage is possible.

Skilled operators transmit morse code at 15 to 25 wpm; calling time to set up the call must be allowed for. Direct-printing telegraphy using teleprinters, which is well established on lines and in fixed radio services, allows messages to be printed out at 66 wpm; however, a stronger signal is required for machine telegraphy than for aural reception, so that a morse message may be received at times when conditions are not good enough for teleprinter working. Direct printing telegraphy is associated with a selective calling system by which the message can be directed to the addressed ship alone, with the object of printing out the message on the ship even when the equipment is unattended. Special codes are also used to detect and correct errors caused by poor transmission conditions.

Larger ships carry radio telephony equipment through which simultaneous two-way telephony calls can be passed through shore stations and connected to the public telephone network. Long-distance calls must be set up and monitored by operators because radio propagation in the high frequency bands sometimes produces distortion and noise which is not acceptable for public correspondence.

For ships within about 100 km of a coast station the v.h.f. and u.h.f. bands provide telephone calls with quality and reliability which could enable calls to be made by the public to ships through the national automatic telephone system; the technical methods to be used for such a system are now being discussed internationally; the method of routing a call through the coast station nearest to the ship is one problem.

Smaller ships such as fishing vessels and yachts which need not carry a radio officer use telephony for routine communication. The amplitude modulation first used for maritime services has now been mostly replaced by single-sideband suppressed-carrier methods which give an improved signal-to-noise ratio.

In the face of development of satellite methods, the established terrestrial systems are likely to retain the majority of maritime traffic despite the variable quality of radio transmission, because the charges for calls are likely to remain lower than for the satellite service for many years.

Aeronautical Communication.—Messages to and from aircraft are concerned almost exclusively with the safe movement of the aircraft; with few exceptions calls from passengers are not a requirement. Ships attend to their own safe passage, but the speed of aircraft makes it essential to have an air-traffic-control organisation on the ground to regulate the movement of aircraft in a defined area. Communication between the air-traffic-controller and the pilot must be provided to establish the aircraft position and identity, and to pass information about future intentions and to give instructions to ensure safe operation. Messages must also be passed between the aircraft and its airline about the management of flights, destinations, passengers, fuel, and so on. The third part of the message is about weather conditions.

The heights at which aircraft normally fly enables v.h.f. communication between ground and aircraft to be maintained at longer distances than between two ground terminals. For an aircraft flying at 30,000 ft a communication range of 400 km is possible; this also applies to radar coverage. Over developed countries therefore, networks of radar and communication stations on the ground, linked to the air-traffic-control centres by lines or microwave links, enable radar surveillance of aircraft movement and high-quality pilot-to controller radio telephony communication to be maintained over a large area. The frequency channels for such communication are between 118 and 136 MHz, with channels spaced 50 or 100 kHz apart.

For long flights over oceans or undeveloped territory radio telephony in the bands between 2 and 25 MHz allocated to aeronautical communication is used. Morse operation ceased more than twenty years ago for civil aircraft. The performance of these long-range air-to-ground links is very variable, because aircraft transmitters have limited power of some 400 W and above all because the aircraft antenna is an inefficient radiator, particularly at the lower frequencies in the band which have to be used for night communication. Such weak signals from the aircraft suffer in the noise and interference of the high-frequency band.

Long-range aeronautical radio messages are received at the ground station by a skilled communicator who assembles the aircraft messages with any necessary confirmatory repeats into a standard teleprinter message which is forwarded to the air-traffic-controller, the airline and the weather bureau. The text of a standard message is shown, with its interpretation, in Fig. 16. For the eastern side of the north atlantic area the communication station is at Shannon, Eire, and the air-traffic-control centre is at Prestwick, Scotland.

```
PK707  59N 20W 1416 FL350 59N 30W
1456 106430 KIDL 1932
TMS 43 270/30 58N 15W DMS 760
```

FIG. 16.—A typical air-to-ground routine message, printed as a data message in teleprinter type. The above message as transmitted from the pilot in plain language by telephony would be:

"This is Pakistan Airways Flight 707 Present position 59°N 20°W at 14.16 G.M.T. Altitude 35,000 feet. Estimate arriving at 59°N 30°W at 14.56 G.M.T.	A.T.C. Information
106430 pounds of fuel remaining Estimating at Kennedy at 19.32 G.M.T.	Airline Information
Temperature Minus 43° Centigrade Wind 30 knots at 270° at 58°N 15°W Diversity factor minus 760 millibars."	Weather Information

There are no long-range navigational aids of the radar type to enable the ground controller to ascertain the positions of aircraft from the ground; each aircraft must therefore report its position frequently enough to maintain the separation between aircraft required for safety.

As in the maritime service, h.f. radio telephony uses single-sideband suppressed-carrier modulation for the aeronautical service. A multi-tone selective calling system enables the ground communicator to call a specific aircraft, so that the pilot does not have to listen to a noisy radio channel all the time.

Communication to Mobile Stations through Satellites.—Having achieved high quality communication through satellite relay between large ground stations, the possibility of applying similar methods with ships, aircraft and land vehicles was explored, so that the deficiencies of long-range mobile communication might be avoided.

The international satellite links of most countries concentrate the channels to pass through a single large earth station, but for a mobile system there are hundreds or thousands of independent small mobile terminals, each requiring communication on demand for short periods with national earth stations; the equipment at the mobile terminal should not be costly, and the antenna must be suitable for mounting on the mobile structure. These factors, and lack of enthusiasm from the airlines for a system which they felt did not give sufficient improvement to justify the cost, led to the abandonment after many years of planning and experiment, of the aeronautical satellite system. Except for certain military requirements there is also little justification for a land mobile satellite system, so that only in the maritime case has significant progress been made. The Marisat system introduced by Comsat in the mid-1970s offered communication to merchant ships, and in 1979 the international organisation INMARSAT came into operation with similar functions in the maritime field to INTELSAT in the global fixed service. Several satellites provided by the European Space Agency and by Intelsat are used to provide communications with ships in three world-wide zones; in 1985 there were already 3500 ships equipped to give high-quality telephone and data communication suitable for connection to national telephone networks through eight earth stations, with a dozen more to be installed by 1985.

The maritime satellite system provides a useful example of a communication power budget on which radio system design is based, shown in Table 2. Only the links in both directions between the satellite and the ship are considered here, the links between the satellite and the ground station not being a significant limitation on the performance of the whole system.

Frequency bands near 1500 MHz have been allocated for aeronautical and maritime satellite use; a lower frequency would have been preferred but the demands of other services, including television, with established services, prevailed. The balance of the factors in the power budget must be adjusted to give a practical, economic solution, with a signal-to-noise ratio adequate to maintain the minimum acceptable communication quality for the number of channels required to operate simultaneously. The satellite-to-earth direction gives the lower margin of carrier-to-noise ratio, satellite radiated power being as usual the limiting factor. The noise level −157·9 dBW in a 30 kHz bandwidth corresponds to equivalent noise temperature of 407°K (26·1

TABLE 2.—POWER BUDGET EXAMPLE.
Example of a power budget for both directions of a radio communication link between a ship and a satellite in synchronous orbit 40,700 km from the ship. The bandwidth and the carrier to noise ratios received would indicate that frequency modulation should be used.

	Gains	Losses
1. Ship-to-satellite link at 1·64 GHz		
Ship transmitter power (dBW)	+14	
Ship antenna gain (dB)	+23	
Free-space loss (dB)		+188·9
Atmospheric absorption (dB)		+0·2
Margin for random losses (dB)		+1·1
Satellite antenna gain (dB)	+17	
Satellite receiver noise in assumed 30 kHz bandwidth (dBW)		−154·7
	+54	+35.5
Carrier-to-noise ratio received in satellite (dB)	+18.5	
2. Satellite-to-ship link at 1·54 GHz		
Satellite transmitter power (dBW) (per channel)	+1·6	
Satellite antenna gain (dB)	+17	
Free-space path loss (dB)		+188·4
Atmospheric absorption (dB)		+0·2
Margin for random losses (dB)		+1·1
Ship antenna gain (dB)	+22·4	
Ship receiver noise in 30 kHz bandwidth (dBW)		−157·9
	+41·0	+31·8
Carrier-to-noise ratio received in ship (dB)	+9·2	

dB ref. 1°K) which combines with antenna gain 22·4 dB to give $10 \log_{10}(G/T) = -3{\cdot}7$ dB. The specified figure for the maritime satellite system is −4 dB, compared with the global system figure of 40·7 dB. The steerable ship antenna is about 1 m diameter and it must be mounted in a position to give an unobstructed view in all directions above the horizon.

A working maritime satellite system is now established, but increased use depends on reducing the costs so that the maritime interests are satisfied that the improved service justifies the cost of calls.

Land Mobile Communication.—[9] These services provide communication, almost always by voice modulation, between a fixed base station and a land vehicle or a person on foot. Apart from the military applications, the main users are the police, public utility services (ambulance, transport, telephones, gas, water, electricity), industry and limited public telephone service to vehicles and pedestrians.

A few countries with large distances between centres of population use medium-distance high-frequency systems, but most land-mobile systems are restricted to distances of about 50 km from the base station; frequency bands in the v.h.f./u.h.f. range are allocated by international agreement to mobile services and frequency channels in these bands may be assigned by national administrations to land-mobile stations. Except in border regions the ground wave propagation limitation confines the transmission to the country concerned. Many of the frequency bands are allocated to the mobile services in general, sometimes with a recommendation that in certain bands administrations should give priority to a particular service, for example, maritime. Countries with large land areas may give more frequencies to land mobile use, such as railways, than to maritime; the normal restriction in range of v.h.f./u.h.f. transmissions reduces the incidence of interference between stations using the same frequency.

Powers for mobile transmitters rarely exceed 50 W for vehicle sets and 1 or 2 W for personal sets, the battery weight setting a limit. The battery might have to sustain transmission with a personal radio for six minutes in the hour over an eight hour period with chargeable batteries; several days of such transmission should be obtained from non-chargeable batteries of similar weight. Vehicle equipment is usually powered from the vehicle battery.

Since the mobile station uses an antenna of limited size mounted near to the ground in a situation which is often surrounded by screening objects, its radiating and receiving effectiveness is poor; the base station must therefore have an antenna with as much gain as possible in the required directions, mounted high above surrounding obstructions, and in as quiet a situation as can be found in the required service area. When many different users wish to share the best site, as at the heights of Hampstead Heath in London, there are problems in erecting many transmitting and receiving antennae in a restricted area without causing unacceptable interference between base transmitters and receivers. When several high level signals are applied to the non-linear components of transmitters and receivers, intermodulation produces interference at frequencies other than those utilised for communication. Filters with large cavity resonators are used between transmitter and antenna to reduce these problems. Receiver radio-frequency selectivity has been improved by using helical tuned circuits to reduce unwanted signal levels before they reach the non-linear transistors and valves. Inter-modulation may also be produced by poor connections in the high field regions of the antenna structure; this has for many years been known as the rusty bolt effect.

The sensitivity of the mobile radio is limited by the level of man-made noise, contributed by ignition systems, electrical machinery, contacts and lighting around the receiving antenna. This becomes less important at the higher frequencies, for example, the 450 MHz band. The service range can only be predicted on a probability basis, taking into account the nature of the terrain and built-up areas; screening and reflection cause pockets of generally low signal strength and also rapid fading of the signal as the receiver moves through a wave-interference field caused by reflections. The time scale of the rapid fluctuations depends on the speed of the vehicle and the wavelength of the signal and may be less than 0.1 second; this effect produces less deterioration with telephony than with digital services in which bursts of errors may be produced.

Systems should be designed to give about the same communication range in the two directions; the high noise level and poor antenna at the mobile station are compensated by using a higher power transmitter and the more sensitive receiving installation at the base station. In rural areas with flat terrain 50 km communication range should be obtained.

Simplex operation, in which the mobile user has to operate a transmit/receive switch, is usually used because of the difficulty of transmitting and receiving simultaneously, sometimes with a single antenna. Duplex operation, with which simultaneous two-way communication is provided, is necessary when the public use the radio link to connect into the national telephone network, but simultaneous operation of a transmitter and receiver in the same equipment requires adequate radio filtering at the mobile equipment, and separation of the transmit and receive frequencies sufficient to prevent interference.

A public mobile radio telephone system is now being introduced in the United Kingdom, with subscriber equipment available for fitting into vehicles and for carrying by people on foot.[24,25] The fixed base stations are installed on the cellular principle, in which the country is divided into a large number of hexagonal areas, each of which is covered by a central base station. The nationwide network is now being completed, starting with the larger towns and the motorway routes; in towns a smaller cell may be used to give a greater density of base stations to deal with the heavier traffic. Frequencies around 900 MHz are used, with frequency modulation for speech transmission and frequency shift keying at 8000 bits/second for control channels. Moving subscribers are automatically transferred from cell to cell according to the relative signal strengths, without interruption of the communication. In addition to providing ordinary telephone calls, there are plans for storing messages for absent subscribers, and to transmit short data messages over the radio network.

A mobile radio telephone system requires many radio channels in a spectrum that will become increasingly congested. To avoid delays and to improve the channel utilisation, the system must give the user a choice of frequency channels; such sharing is known as trunking. The cellular arrangement of base stations also enables frequency channels to be re-used at regularly spaced cells.

Paging is a one-way radio selective calling system in which a coded signal composed of a number of tones or a digital combination is sent from a central transmitter to users with pocket receivers responding to the assigned personal code, giving an alarm to indicate that a call is waiting at the nearest telephone. Most such systems have been used to cover only the plant or office where the user is normally located. An area system associated with the public telephone network is being rapidly implemented, with facilities for short message storage for both telephone and short data messages. These developments have been made possible by modern electronic technology.

Land mobile radio communication becomes ineffective as soon as the vehicle enters a tunnel, since radio waves at normal communication frequencies will not propagate in such environments beyond a hundred metres or so. In the same way, radio systems engineered specially for wholly underground applications have to use special assisted-propagation techniques to be practicable. The general solution to these problems is to employ what is known as 'leaky feeder' technology. The subject is explained and discussed fully in Chapter K3 under RADIO COMMUNICATION IN MINES (q.v.) but briefly it involves laying through the tunnels a specially-designed coaxial cable that is designed to be imperfect in its screening. This will allow reliable two-way communication between a base station connected to it and any number of mobile or personal sets in its vicinity along its length.

Linear ranges of up to a kilometre or more may be achieved by this simple technique with no further active equipment involved. Beyond this range, it becomes necessary to include series amplifiers or 'repeaters' in the feeder at intervals of a half-kilometre or so to compensate for the inevitable losses which occur in the copper conductors and in the dielectric between them. Techniques exist by which full two-way communication may be achieved even though the repeaters themselves are very simple one-way devices—often containing but a single transistor each—and direct communication between mobile sets in talk-through mode is equally possible. The favoured principle uses small frequency converters at the extreme ends of the feeder to achieve this objective, but these may be avoided if a telephone line linking the two ends is acceptable.

Where the tunnel or underground system is to be served exclusively of any surface cover the entire system can be optimized for that purpose in terms of choice of frequency band and modulation. But where the requirement is to extend into a tunnel the service area of an existing land-mobile system there is usually no such freedom; moreover, careful planning is often necessary to avoid degradation of the communication, or even complete interruption, in the transition between surface and tunnel modes of propagation. Sometimes—as in the comprehensive schemes in the very long Swiss road tunnels—the underground section is served by its own base station, albeit necessarily on the same channel and using the same modulation at the main surface system. In more modest cases—as in the far shorter road tunnels in the city of Brussels—signals are taken 'off air' for relay through the tunnel, and vice versa.

The engineering of all such systems is still a very specialist matter which the major suppliers of land mobile radio equipment do not usually undertake beyond the simple non-repeated requirements, but consultancy in the field is now available.

Hand-held personal radios, or transceivers, are limited in power by battery size and ranges of one mile are typical; applications are to provide two-way voice communication on building construction sites, in survey operations, on board ships and oil rigs, and in the armed services.

Some administrations, including UK, permit free operation of radio equipment as citizens radio in a narrow frequency band round 27 MHz, which is also available for industrial, scientific and medical equipment. A similar band is now available above 460 MHz. These frequencies are used by car and truck drivers to talk to each other, and apart from providing a demand for cheap communication equipment the application may be regarded as an amusement facility.

Either frequency- or amplitude-modulation may be used for voice communication in mobile systems. There have been lengthy arguments about their merits and shortcomings, about the channel bandwidth required, the degradation due to impulsive noise and fading, the range and intelligibility; most countries have chosen frequency-modulated systems. One widely used method of improving the signal-to-noise ratio of frequency-modulated speech is to raise the modulation level at the upper end of the audio band; this pre-emphasis at the transmitter is compensated by a corresponding de-emphasis at the receiver, which reduces the high noise level at the higher frequencies with these receivers.

There is no doubt that the rapid growth of mobile communication and the limited bandwidth available in the spectrum allocated to these services will lead to renewed efforts to use single-sideband amplitude-modulation, which would operate in narrower channels than frequency-modulation. The frequency stability of crystal oscillators operating in mobile equipment is not normally sufficient for narrow-band s.s.b. operation at v.h.f./u.h.f.

Spread-spectrum modulation is an apparent contradiction of normal frequency spectrum economy principles, in that an additional high rate modulation is applied to the signal, increasing the bandwidth and identifying the separate signals. Several operators can then use the same frequency channel simultaneously without interference. The method has been considered for land-mobile operation alone, and for its possibilities in allowing television broadcasting to share the same frequency band with the mobile stations; the general conclusion is that such methods would not be beneficial.

Digital communication of messages in printed or displayed form has not yet been extensively applied in land-mobile communication, for technical, operational and cost reasons. The police and transport users have requirements for such information transfer, and experimental systems have been explored in recent years. The effect of signal fading on digital coded transmissions limits the range for reliable transmission, and a reliable and cheap printing or display device suitable for any background illumination under vehicle conditions remains a problem. Nevertheless, the requirement to determine the positions of many vehicles at regular intervals could best be satisfied with a digital system operated on a rollcall basis with short fixed-format coded messages.

The development of semi-conductor devices has reduced the size and improved the reliability of mobile communication equipment. Valves need additional power to heat the filaments, and also a higher voltage source for power valves, obtained from battery-powered vibrators or rotary converters.

The use of land-mobile communications grows every year, so that the provision of sufficient frequency channels to offer interference-free service to all users is a recurring problem. More bandwidth may be allocated if v.h.f. television channels are given up; it is argued that television could be distributed in town areas through cables, whereas radio is essential for mobile communication. Each television channel transferred could provide about 500 land-mobile channels.

Amateur Radio Communication.—Almost all nations have long recognised that radio transmission by amateurs should be permitted, whether the aim is technical experimenting, international friendship or simply a hobby. The I.T.U. has therefore always recognised Amateur Radio as a Service, and has allocated bands of frequencies which may be used by amateurs (Table 3); Administrations issue licences to allow transmission in these bands, but in most countries the technical competence and proficiency in morse code of the applicant must be proven by examination.[11]

The main activity is long-distance communication using relatively low transmitting power, either by morse or by telephony; the amateur strives to pass messages under adverse conditions, taking advantage of any

TABLE 3.—FREQUENCY BANDS UP TO 1000 MHz ALLOCATED BY ITU TO THE AMATEUR SERVICE.

Region 1 Europe, Africa	Region 2 Americas	Region 3 Asia, Australasia
kHz	kHz	kHz
1,810–1,850	1,800–1,850 1,850–2,000*	1,800–2,000*
3,500–3,800*	3,500–3,750 3,750–4,000*	3,500–3,900*
	7,000–7,100	
Broadcasting	7,100–7,300	Broadcasting
	10,100–10,150* 14,000–14,350 18,068–18,168 21,000–21,450 24,890–24,990 28,000–29,700	
MHz Broadcasting	MHz 50–54	MHz 50–54
	144–146	
	146–148 220–225*	146–148
	430–440*	
	902–928*	

Notes. * Shared with other services, which may have primary use.
There are bands allocated to Amateur Service above 1000 MHz.
The new bands at 18 and 25 MHz may not be available until mid-80s.
Some bands are also used for Amateur Satellite Service.
Where there is no vertical bar between region columns, the allocation is worldwide.

anomalous propagation conditions that may arise. Under natural disaster conditions any amateur stations on the spot can provide a valuable service, but such occasions are fortunately rare.

In the first half of this century the equipment was mostly home constructed but in recent years commercially-made transmitters and receivers have predominated; these are obtained either from surplus sales or from a number of companies manufacturing specially for the amateur.

Transmitters now use tunable, stable oscillators so that a frequency in an interference-free part of the allocated band may be selected. The call "CQ" may be sent as an invitation for any station to reply, the replying station normally adjusting his frequency to that of the heard station. Telegraphy transmission uses on-off keying of a continuous wave carrier; telephony in the high-frequency bands now uses mostly single-sideband modulation, to reduce the effect of interference between transmissions and make best use of limited transmitter powers. Such transmission requires accurate setting of transmitter and receiver frequency, and the higher the frequency the more acute does this problem become. The power amplifiers, using either transistors or valves, give output of 1 W to 1 kW to the antenna, according to the resources of the owner.

BROADCASTING

In its wider sense the term 'broadcasting' describes any distribution of information from central transmitting stations to a large number of receiving stations, but the ITU definition of the Broadcasting Service is limited to transmission of sound, television and other information to the general public. The frequency bands allocated from January 1982 for this service are indicated in Table 4; some of the short-wave bands are restricted to use in the tropical zones about the equator[1]. Within the allocated bands the division into frequency channels and the assignment of these channels to stations is settled at World or Regional Broadcasting Conferences.

TABLE 4.—FREQUENCY BANDS ALLOCATED BY THE ITU TO THE BROADCASTING SERVICE.

Band	Region 1 Europe, Africa	Region 2 Americas	Region 3 Asia, Australasia
	kHz	kHz	kHz
Long-wave (sound)	148·5–255 255–283·5*	— —	— —
Medium-wave (sound)	526·5–1,606·5	525–535* 535–1,625 1,625–1,705*	526·5–535* 535–1,606·5
Short-wave (sound)	2,300–2,498* 3,200–3,400* 3,950–4,000*	2,300–2,495* 3,200–3,400* —	2,300–2,495* 3,200–3,400* 3,950–4,000*
		4,750–4,850* 4,850–4,995* 5,005–5,060* 5,950–6,200	
	7,100–7,300	—	7,100–7,300
		9,500–9,900 11,650–12,050 13,600–13,800 15,100–15,600 17,550–17,900 21,450–21,850 25,670–26,100	
	MHz	MHz	MHz
VHF (sound)	87·5–100 100–108	76–88* 88–100 100–108	87–100* 100–108
VHF (television)	47–68 174–223 223–230*	54–72* 174–216*	47–50* 54–68* 174–230*
UHF (television)	470–790 790–960*	470–512* 512–608 608–890*	470–960*

Notes. * Shared with other services.
Where there is no vertical bar between region columns, the allocation is worldwide.

Sound Broadcasting.—Medium and long-wave transmitters use amplitude modulation with high-power Class-B modulating valves applying the power through a large audio transformer to the final Class-D radio-frequency amplifier anode. The increasing cost of fuel and the expense of buildings and cooling equipment have led to a search for transmitters with higher power conversion efficiency, even at the cost of more complex circuits and adjustment procedures. Pulsewidth modulation, the Doherty system and Ampliphase are the main contenders.[4]

Frequency channels in these bands are 9 kHz apart, but the large demand leads to several stations in each region sharing the same channel, and despite planning to separate sharing stations by as great a distance as possible interference between stations is a major problem. During the day the low D-layer of the ionosphere acts as an attenuating blanket which prevents medium- and long-wave transmissions from reaching the higher reflecting layers; an undistorted signal is received over a limited area by means of the groundwave component alone, free of interference from distant stations. After the sun has set, this absorbing D-layer disappears and distant signals are reflected from the upper layers to interfere with the local station, and at medium distances high-angle reflected signals interfere with the ground-wave to cause fading and distortion.

Some of the harm caused by co-channel transmissions is reduced by the 10 Hz frequency tolerance allowed for the carrier frequencies of sound broadcasting stations[1, App. 3]; this avoids the audible beat note caused by the interference between the carriers. Medium- and long-wave transmitting antennae are also designed to radiate as little as possible at high elevation angles so as to reduce the strength of ionospherically reflected signals relative to the ground wave; a vertical antenna about 0·6 wavelength high is optimum, but this criterion leads to excessive height at long wavelength.

Transmission in the v.h.f. band avoids the long-range interference troubles of the lower frequencies, but gives a reduced service area for each station; at these frequencies the atmospheric noise is far less, and the width of the allocated frequency band allows a larger channel bandwidth to be used with frequency modulation. V.H.F. transmission therefore offers higher quality sound reproduction than the old medium- and long-wave methods, but more stations are required to cover a large area. Because the signal strength decreases rapidly beyond line-of-sight distance from the transmitter (Fig. 14), the antenna must be designed to radiate at low angles of elevation, using a vertical stack of elements raised as high as possible above the ground so as to penetrate as far as possible into obstructed pockets. It is economical to cover small concentrations of population with local low-power transmitters, but large built-up areas require radiated powers up to 200 kW[12].

In the tropical areas where the noise level is very high at the lower frequencies it is advantageous to broadcast locally in the 2–6 MHz band, where restricted allocations have been made.

Transmissions between 6 and 26 MHz penetrate to longer distances by successive reflections between the ionospheric layers and the earth surface and are therefore used for international broadcasting. Interference between stations is at times serious and although there are proposals[2] for using single-sideband modulation or provide more frequency channels, the problem of devising simple receivers for this mode has discouraged implementation. The distortion and fading caused by multipath propagation on long-range ionospheric paths prevent a reliable and satisfying service to be obtained, but short-waves offer the only possibility for the distant listener until a satellite service is devised.

Short-wave broadcasting stations use antennae composed of curtains of wire radiating elements and reflectors to concentrate the power in the general direction of the region to be covered, and these antennae must be raised to the correct height above the ground to give maximum radiation at an elevation angle to be reflected from the ionosphere. Frequency must be changed to suit the propagation conditions at the season and time of day, so that transmitters and antennae must be designed for rapid frequency changes to be made without losing valuable programme time.

Television Broadcasting.—The detail needed to define a visual scene, and the number of pictures needed to convey the impression of continuous movement lead to a very high rate of information transmission. The first television stations used double-sideband amplitude modulation, but the need to accommodate more stations in a limited frequency band led to the vestigial-sideband system after 1946 (page H3/14). In most American countries and Japan 30 pictures per second with 525 lines per picture are transmitted; apart from a few early stations using obsolescent arrangements, the rest of the world uses variations of the European and African Broadcasting Union 25 pictures per second 625 line system in the u.h.f. band, the main differences lying in the sound and colour techniques[12] which make international standardisation of receivers impractical.

Some of the original v.h.f. television stations are still transmitting, particularly in less populated countries, but in more developed countries where land- and maritime-mobile services have a pressing need for more frequency channels, some v.h.f. television services have been transferred to the u.h.f. band. Where mobile services are introduced in the former television bands, any remaining television services in neighbouring countries must be protected from interference.

Colour television transmission in the u.h.f. band has been achieved with no increase in the 8 MHz channel bandwidth needed for black and white pictures. This is done by transmitting the supplementary colour information on a sub-carrier in the upper part of the vision sideband, the frequency being so chosen as to cause minimum interference to the picture luminence information; in the PAL (phase alternating line) method the colour carrier is 4,433,618·75 Hz above the vision carrier (Fig. 3c).

There are three colour television systems in operation, NTSC (America, Japan), PAL (FGR, UK) and SECAM (France, USSR). Conversion of television programmes using different line frequencies for simultaneous transmission or for international exchange is possible with electronic converters, at first using image storage tubes and now using digital storage on large-scale integrated circuits.

There are three different applications of television transmission through satellites (H3/23). For more than twenty years one of the services offered by Intelsat with the global satellite system has been to transmit a television picture from one large earth station to another, although such a moving picture communication occupies far more of the satellite's transmission capacity than a single sound channel; in fact, when a number of countries require television coverage of the same event, they use the same picture and accompany it with their individual sound commentary in their own language.

The second use of satellites is for distributing television programs to widely separated centres of population, the received pictures being displayed on community receivers or distributed to homes by a local low power transmitter or through a cable network. The receiving antennae for this application are much smaller than are used in the global system, so that more satellite power is required for each programme. This method of programme distribution is used in large countries such as U.S.S.R., India and Canada; recently it has been used in U.S.A. for the multi-programme cable television network.

A third use of satellites is now being developed for transmitting directly from the satellite to domestic receivers. Evidently the home receiver must not be costly, and it must be easy to maintain. In particular, neither the immense antennae of the global system earth stations or the medium size dishes used for community reception, with their accurate beam steering requirements can be used at homes. The receiver must work with antenna beamwidth of about 22°, so that the satellite must have a powerful transmitter and a narrow antenna beam to give sufficient signal in the small receiving antenna.

The cost of such satellites is high, so broadcasting organisations must compare the cost of numerous television transmitters on the ground with the satellite costs. The terrain of the country is important, a mountainous country where valley populations are difficult to reach by terrestrial television transmitters is more likely to find the satellite system advantageous; Switzerland is one of the first European countries to set up a satellite direct broadcasting channel.

Frequencies for satellite television relay have been given bands in the range 600 MHz to 13 GHz; the original 4/6 GHz band of the global system is still used for international programme exchange. Some countries may still use the lower frequency bands for internal distribution, but future applications, including direct broadcasting, are concentrated on 11/13 GHz.

RADIODETERMINATION

Radiodetermination is defined as the determination of the position, velocity or other characteristics of an object by means of the properties of radio waves. In association with radio communication it is of primary importance to navigation and safety of mobile stations at sea, in the air and nowadays also in space, and for surveying purposes.

The position-finding apparatus may be on the moving object, to find the position or velocity with respect to fixed points on land or on other moving objects, or it may be on land to find the positions of many mobile stations, in which case it is known as surveillance. The latter may be used with radio communication links to convey the determined position information to the mobile stations for navigation purposes.

Direction Finding.—If the direction of arrival of a radio wave from a station of known position can be found, a line of position for the receiver may be drawn. Two such lines from separated stations will intersect at the position of the receiver. Similarly, two separated receiving stations on land can fix the position of a mobile transmitter. A third direction determination should confirm the intersection position. This direction-finding system has been in use for ships since before 1920.

Almost all radio direction finders operate by adjusting a rotating receiving antenna until the output falls to a minimum, because this gives greater discrimination than using the maximum. The simplest form of directional antenna is a loop pivoted on a vertical axis, minimum signal being obtained when the plane of the loop is perpendicular to the direction of arrival of the wave; since the loop is symmetrical, there are two positions of minimum output, giving 180° ambiguity in the direction; this may be resolved by combining the output of a short vertical antenna with that of the loop. Modern direction-finders use two fixed loops arranged at right angles; the bearing indication is obtained from the angle of the rotating coil of a goniometer set for minimum signal, the loops being connected to the two orthogonal fixed coils (Fig. 17) In automatic direction finders the goniometer may be continuously rotated, or may be driven to the position of minimum signal by a servo system controlled by the receiver output; in either case the direction is displayed by a pointer against a 360° scale.

The main application of radio direction-finding is in ships and aircraft using the crossed loop and goniometer method. Servo operation controls the goniometer angle, the direction of the incoming signal being transmitted to a separate indicator near the operator or pilot. The angular accuracy of direction-finders under good conditions is better than 3° but wave propagation effects can cause serious errors.

Ships determine their positions by taking bearings on fixed medium-frequency radio beacons sited round the coasts. Aircraft also use specially installed beacons, or known broadcasting transmitters; the airborne radio direction finder is known as a radio-compass, and remains one of the main navigational aids in aircraft.

V.H.F. direction-finders are often installed at smaller airfields to find the direction of aircraft from their communication transmissions. This is an economical way to give the aircraft the direction to fly to reach the airfield; it has particular value in test flying.

Radar.—The principal method for 'Radio Detection and Ranging'[15] is by transmitting and receiving short pulses of microwave energy from a wide antenna giving a narrow beam of radiation and rotating 3 to 60

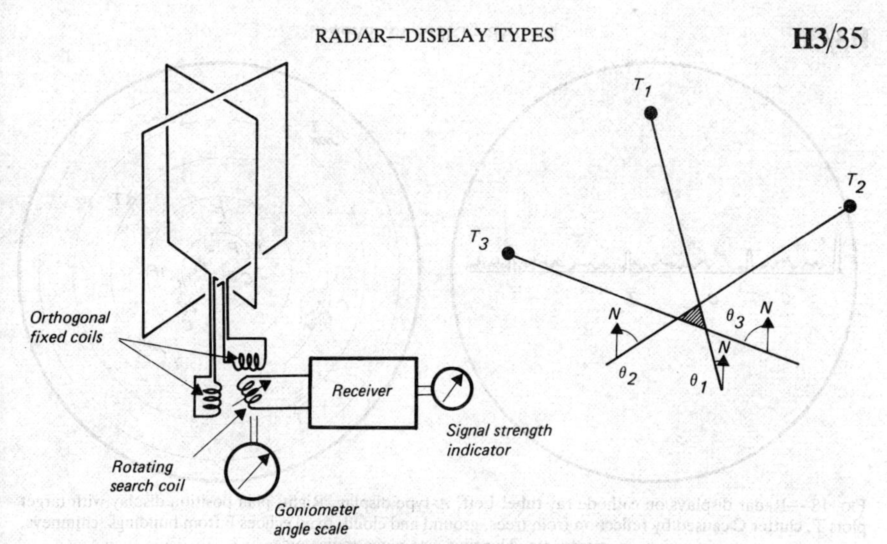

FIG. 17.—Radio direction finding. Left, fixed crossed-loops antenna with hand-turned radiogoniometer. Right, position fixing with mobile direction-finder using bearings on three transmitters T. Shaded triangle includes the area of location according to the three bearings θ.

times in a minute. A solid object in the beam reflects some of the energy back to the antenna, and by measuring the time between the emission of the pulse and its return the distance to the target may be calculated. The direction of the antenna at the time of the maximum reflected signal gives the bearing of the target. This is the R,θ method of position fixing, and the system is primary radar in that the target is quite passive. For secondary radar the target must carry a radio responder in which the received pulse triggers a responding pulse, usually on a different frequency. Secondary radar needs less power than primary, but only targets fitted with responders in working order can be seen. The principal uses for radar are for ship and aircraft navigation, and for defence purposes.

The radar equation gives the maximum range of primary radar in free space:

$$R^4_{max} = \frac{P_t G^2 A}{(4\pi)^3 S_{min}} \qquad (11)$$

where R_{max} = the maximum range in metres
S_{min} = the minimum peak pulse signal power in watts that can be detected.
P_t = the peak pulse transmitter power to the antenna in watts
G = the power gain of the antenna referred to an isotropic antenna
A = the effective reflecting area of the target in square metres.

The received pulses have to be detected against a background of noise generated in the antenna, the receiver circuits (page H3/18) and the clutter or reflections from objects on the ground and clouds. A cathode-ray tube display allows the pulses to be observed and the range to be accurately determined. In the A-type display (Fig. 18) the spot travels from left to right, starting when the transmitter pulse is emitted; the pulses received and the noise give vertical deflections, so that the picture changes as the antenna rotates. A more usual display is the plan position indicator (PPI) in which the range line travels outwards from the centre of the screen and the direction of the line rotates synchronously with the antenna. The receiver output brightens the spot, so that returns from targets appear as short bright arcs of circles and noise and clutter appear as a misty background. In Fig. 18, the Ts are moving targets (ships or aircraft), several 'paints' being retained by using a screen with a long after-glow. C is clutter caused by reflection from clouds and the Fs are fixed echoes from ground, trees and buildings in the inner area of the coverage. The receiver gain is usually varied as the spot traces outwards to give increased sensitivity at the longer ranges where the returns are weaker. The PPI thus gives a map of the whole area covered by the radar, a succession of responses giving an indication of the movement of targets.

The discrimination of the radar depends on the duration of the pulse and the beamwidth of the antenna; a 10 microsecond pulse from a ½° antenna covers about 1·5 km in each direction at 150 km range, so that targets 1 km apart are not likely to be seen as separate objects. For a given width of antenna the beamwidth and gain increase with frequency, so that it might be concluded that the chance of detection would increase with frequency; other factors such as reflection and attenuation by clouds and sea, and equipment consider-

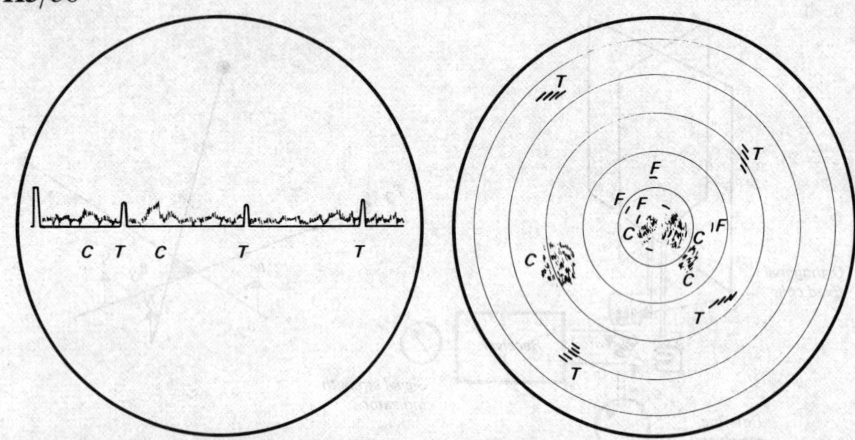

FIG. 18.—Radar displays on cathode ray tube. Left, A-type display. Right, plan position display with target plots T, clutter C caused by reflection from trees, ground and cloud, fixed echoes F from buildings, chimneys, masts, etc. The rings are range indicators.

ations may modify this conclusion. Some long-range surveillance radar uses 600 MHz and at the other extreme airport surface movement indicators may work above 30 GHz. Forward looking radars on aircraft are used to detect bad weather ahead, so that sensitivity to cloud and rain reflection is an advantage.

Radar with short pulses to give high range discrimination needs a receiver with large bandwidth to pass the short pulses, increasing the noise output. Assuming that the receiver bandwidth is the reciprocal of the pulse length, the radar range equation may be written

$$R^4_{max} = \frac{3{\cdot}68 \times 10^{19} P_t G^2 dA}{T(S/N)} \qquad (12)$$

where d = the duration of the transmitted pulse in seconds
T = the receiving system operating temperature
(S/N) = the lowest allowed signal pulse to noise power ratio for detection on the display

Practical figures for a large radar might be P_t = 1 MW, G = 2,000 (33 dB), d = 2 μs, A = 10m^2 (large aircraft), T = 1,000°K, (S/N) = 100 (20 dB). Applying these values in equation 12 gives maximum range 414 km. This result makes no allowance for parameter variations; the ground affects the antenna gain in some directions, the reflecting area of the aircraft depends on the aspect presented to the incident wave[15,16] and the cloud and rain attenuate the wave passing through them. On the other hand, during the rotation of the radar antenna the beam may rest on the target for some ten pulses, which increases the chance of seeing the reflected signal on the screen.

Moving target indication (MTI) decreases the displayed brightness of fixed objects relative to that from moving objects; when the reflecting object moves a fraction of a wavelength between successive pulses there is a change of the phase shift between transmitted and received waves. By using transmitters with high frequency stability and providing storage of received signals from pulse to pulse in quartz delay lines, the signals from fixed objects can be reduced by cancellation and those from moving targets allowed to remain.

To improve the probability of detecting a target the rate of antenna rotation should be as slow as is allowed by the required rate of revision of target position; the pulse repetition rate should also be as high as is allowed by the maximum range at which targets give a detectable signal.

If the practical limit to transmitter power, antenna gain and receiver sensitivity (system temperature) have been reached, only an increase of pulse length can increase the range. This results normally in reduced range discrimination, but by varying the frequency linearly during the pulse (chirp) it can be compressed in time by using a suitable filter at the receiver and an enhanced shorter pulse is obtained. This chirp system has been used in defence radar.

Secondary Surveillance Radar (SSR) obtains a return signal by installing on the targets transponders which emit responses when they receive pulses from the interrogating radar. In the aeronautical service the frequencies are 1,030 MHz for interrogation and 1,090 MHz for the responders. Several pulses may be used for interrogation, the pulse spacing being a form of code to prevent unwanted responses or to excite certain modes in the responders. The return signal may also consist of a train of pulses coded to give the aircraft identity or its height; the system was developed out of the wartime IFF system. Secondary radar needs a smaller radar transmitter and antenna, but of course it sees only those targets which carry a working

TABLE 5.—FREQUENCIES UP TO 40 HGz USED FOR NAVIGATION.

Band	Application
kHz	
9–14	Omega long-range continuous-wave phase-comparison location
70–90, 110–130	Decca continuous-wave hyperbolic system
90–110	Loran-C long-range pulse time-comparison location system
190–526*	Aeronautical and maritime direction finding; fixed beacons
1,600–2,000*	Loran-A medium-range pulse time-comparison location system
MHz	
75	Instrument landing distance fan-markers
108–112	Instrument landing localiser beams
112–118	VHF omni range
328–336	Instrument landing glide-slope beams
150 & 400	Transit satellite position fixing
582–606*	Air-traffic-control primary radar
960–1,215*	Aeronautical secondary radar. Aero distance measuring equipment. Tacan.
1,215–1,240	Navstar satellite position fixing system
1,300–1,350	Primary and secondary aeronautical radar
1,559–1,626*	Navstar satellite system and radio altimeters
2,700–3,100*	Aeronautical and maritime radar
4,200–4,400	Radio altimeters
5,000–5,250	Future microwave landing system
5,350–5,650*	Airborne and shipborne radar, beacons and transponders
8,750–8,850	Airborne doppler navigation
8,850–9,800	Aeronautical and maritime radar
GHz	
13·25–13·4	Airborne doppler navigation
14·0 –14.3*	Docking radar for ships
15·4 –15.7	Aeronautical navigation
24·25–25·25	Navigation generally
31·8 –33·4	Airfield surface movement indicator (radar)

* There are restrictions on the use of some parts of these bands for some types of navigation aid. See reference 1, Radio Regulations, Article N7.

responder, and so may not be as effective as primary radar for safety purposes. The Maritime Service also uses ship radars to interrogate beacons (Racons) for navigation.

Continuous wave (CW) radar systems in which the transmitter emits only a single frequency can measure only the radial velocity of a target by measuring the doppler frequency shift of the reflected signal. Since the transmitter is radiating at the same time as the reflected signal is to be received, only low-power short-range systems are possible. The main application is in police radar where only the speed of a vehicle is to be determined.

Range may be found with CW radar if the transmitter is linearly frequency modulated; the reflected signal differs in frequency from that transmitted, the difference being proportional to the distance to the target. Such a method has been used for aircraft radio-altimeters, working at a frequency near 1,600 MHz.

The most used frequencies for radar are included in Table 5 and the letter signs often used to label bands is shown in Table 6.

Aircraft En-route Navigation.—[17] Aircraft preferably fly under ground control along fixed air-routes at defined heights; this ensures that aircraft are safely separated. The aircraft location, determined by the aircrew, is notified by radio to the air-traffic-controller, who sometimes has a direction-finder or radar to confirm the reported position. This procedural control from air-traffic-control centres is the basis for safe navigation.

The aircraft radio instruments which are used to determine its position are:

(a) Automatic direction finder (ADF) or radio-compass which finds the direction of a medium frequency radio transmitter in relation to the heading of the aircraft. The direction is indicated by a pointer mounted in front of a rotating card linked to the magnetic compass. The ground stations used may be broadcasting stations or beacons located along the airways.

(b) VHF Omni-directional Range (VOR) is a ground transmitter in the band 112 to 118 MHz radiating a rotating pattern from a special antenna, which is received in the aircraft to give an automatic indication of its bearing from the range.

TABLE 6.—LETTER DESIGNATIONS OF FREQUENCY BANDS.

Frequency bands are identified by defence organisations by capital letters, and these are often found in radar documents. In 1972 the bands indicated by the letters were changed, leading to confusion. The system is not internationally standardised, but the lists are given here because it is so often used.

Old System		New System	
Letter	Frequency band	Letter	Frequency band
	Megahertz	*	Megahertz
P	80–390	A	0–250
		B	250–500
L	390–2,500	C	500–1000
	Gigahertz		Gigahertz
		D	1–2
S	2·5–4·1	E	2–3
		F	3–4
C	4·1–7	G	4–6
		H	6–8
X	7–11·5	I	8–10
J	11·5–18	J	10–20
K	18–33	K	20–40
O	33–40		
O	40–60	L	40–60
V	60–90	M	60–100

*** A figure from 1 to 10 may be added to the letter to indicate a more exact frequency, each band being divided into ten equal parts.**

(c) Distance Measuring Equipment (DME) is a ground station with a responder which receives pulses in the 1,000 MHz frequency band and emits reply pulses to give indication in the aircraft of its distance from the ground station.

VOR and DME equipment may be co-sited and so give both direction and range to aircraft. Tactical Air Navigation (TACAN) is a military system working in the 962 to 1213 MHz band and giving both range and direction to aircraft.

(d) Hyperbolic systems locate the position of a mobile station by comparing the time of arrival of signals transmitted by three fixed stations. LORAN C transmits simultaneous pulses timed by atomic clocks from groups of stations. The receiving station measures the difference of the arrival times of the pulses, each pair of stations giving a line of position which is hyperbolic in shape. The three sets of hyperbolae corresponding to equal increments of time difference (Fig. 19) are usually printed in colour on maps of the area covered by one chain of three stations. Location is established at the intersection of the three lines indicated by the time difference measurements, for which a cathode ray tube indication may be used. The LORAN-C stations transmit near to 100 kHz and may be used up to 2000 km from a station. LORAN-A stations still operate near 2 MHz, but the covered area is limited and position fixing may be inaccurate due to propagation complications.

The Decca navigation system[17] compares the phases of signals received from chains of three continuous wave transmitters radiating phase-locked carriers at frequencies between 70 and 130 kHz related in a simple ratio such as 5:8:9, and locked to a central master station. Uninterrupted reception at a mobile station enables change of position to be accurately determined by integration of the phase differences over ranges up to 400 km.

Omega is the latest terrestrial phase comparison system[20] covering the whole world from eight large transmitters radiating bursts of continuous waves at frequencies between 10 and 14 kHz. Both ships and aircraft use the system with location accuracy of about 2 km.

(e) The doppler system is an 8·8 or 13·3 GHz airborne equipment in which narrow beams of radiation are directed obliquely downwards, the reflection from the ground or sea giving ground speed and direction. In association with a gyrocompass and computer, the distance covered and the geographical position may be found. On a long flight accuracy of about 0·3% is possible, independent of any ground facilities.

Instrument Landing System (ILS).—Surveillance radar can be used to guide aircraft to positions where they may make a visual approach to the runway. Precision approach radar (PAR) has been installed at the ends of runways at some large airports, giving indication on cathode-ray displays of both the location and

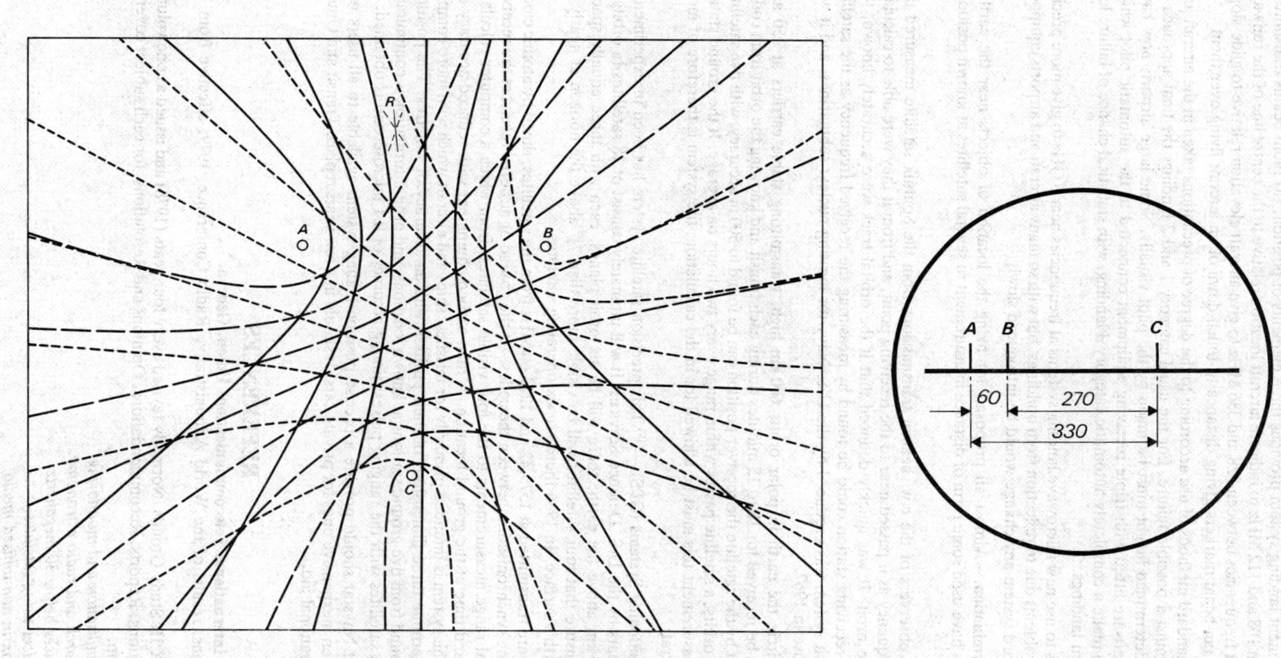

FIG. 19.—Equal time difference lines for three stations A, B, C, where AB = 240 km, AC = 265 km, BC = 270 km. Only the lines for 100 microseconds delay are shown for clarity.

—— Equal delay lines for stations A and B.
— — Equal delay lines for stations A and B.
- - - - Equal delay lines for stations B and C.

The cathode ray tube display on the right illustrates three pulses arriving at the time differences shown; these would give the position R on the plan.

elevation of the aircraft relative to the runway, so that radio telephony talk-down could be used until the aircraft descended to 300 feet above the ground, after which the pilot had to make a visual landing or overshoot. An instrument landing system uses radio beams directed along the approach path to give the pilot continuous indication on crossed-needle instruments in the cockpit of his position relative to the runway.

The standard instrument landing system provides three elements of position, (a) radio beams transmitted at frequencies between 108 and 112 MHz to indicate aircraft location relative to the centre line of the runway, (b) elevation beams at frequencies between 328 and 336 MHz to give aircraft elevation relative to glide-slope path, and (c) vertical fan-beam markers giving distance to touch-down of an aircraft flying over them.

There are several standard methods of use according to the degree of precautions taken in the aircraft and airport installation against a possible failure. For the usual category 1 and 2 landings the final approach to the runway below a determined height must be made by the pilot visually. Some large airports now have equipment, and aircraft are fitted with triple receiving equipment connected to the automatic pilot which enables the aircraft to make a completely automatic category 3 landing, with statistical chance of failure less than one in ten million landings.

There are proposals to use new microwave landing systems at frequencies near 5 GHz to give more precise guidance and avoid problems due to reflection from buildings, but with so many aircraft and airports equipped for the present standard system any change would be introduced slowly.

Satellite Radiodetermination.—Almost all proposals for fixing the location of objects near the earth's surface using satellites have used some form of distance measurement to several satellites at known positions relative to the earth.

Transit.—[18] Early observers of the c.w. beacon transmissions from the Sputnik satellite measured the doppler change of frequency as it passed near to the receiving point, and from it they were able to calculate the parameters of the orbit. It was quickly deduced that if the orbital track were accurately known, the position of a ground receiving station could be found by measuring the received frequency as the satellite passed by. The Transit system was produced by the U.S. Navy for locating nuclear submarines, and it was released for general use in 1967.

Transit satellites circle the earth in polar orbits 600 km high, transmitting stable carriers at 150 and 400 MHz. Signals can be received for 10 to 15 minutes during each transit and knowing the orbit from coded information broadcast by the satellite the receiver position can be found to 500 m accuracy; with five satellites in co-ordinated polar orbits, a satellite passes within range every two hours on average. If the ground station moves during the measurement this must be allowed for in the calculation; the system is therefore of more use to ships than aircraft.

Navstar Global Positioning Systems (GPS).—[19] This precision satellite system has been in experimental use in the past ten years by the U.S. Defence Services. It will ultimately consist of 18 satellites in orbits at 55° inclination 20169 km above the earth; there will be six orbit planes, each with three equally spaced satellites. This will ensure that four satellites will be visible more than 7½° above the horizon at nearly all times all over the earth's surface. In 1986 there are six operating satellites.

Coded pulse trains are transmitted at 1575.42 and 1227.60 MHz from the satellites, timed by atomic clocks to ensure accurate time synchronisation between the codes. At the ground or airborne receivers the received codes give differential range measurements to the four visible satellites, from which a computer calculates the location, height and time at the ground location. A man-carried equipment with reduced accuracy has been produced, but the system is intended primarily for missiles, ships and aircraft which with more complex equipment could determine three dimensions of their position with an accuracy of 7 metres. The positions of the satellites are found from five ground stations at known locations, and orbit information is continuously transmitted from the satellites with the ranging pulses; timing accuracy of 0.1 microsecond is obtained.

It is proposed that Navstar should provide a precise position-finding system available to all users with suitable receivers, even inexpensive ones for private cars. It should in a few years replace Transit and Omega as a worldwide navigational aid.

REFERENCES

Publications of the International Telecommunications Union, Geneva.

(1) Radio Regulations, results of the World Administrative Radio Conference, 1979, effective from 1st January, 1982.

(2) Documents of CCIR Study Groups. Normally revised every four years (1978) and issued as one volume containing Questions, Reports, Recommendations, Opinions and Resolutions, for each subject covered by a Study Group.

SG1. Spectrum utilisation and monitoring.
SG2. Space research and radio astronomy.
SG3. Fixed services below 30 megahertz.
SG4. Fixed services using satellites.
SG5. Propagation in non-ionised media.

SG6. Ionospheric propagation.
SG7. Frequency standards and time signals.
SG8. Mobile services.
SG9. Fixed services using radio relay.
SG10. Sound broadcasting.
SG11. Television.
CMTT. Joint CCIR/CCITT on television transmission.
CMV. Joint CCIR/CCITT on vocabulary.

Books and Journals.

(3) J. Brown and E. V. D. Glazier, *Telecommunications,* Chapman and Hall, 1964.
(4) S. W. Amos, *Radio, TV and Audio Reference Book,* Newnes-Butterworths, 1977.
(5) V. O. Stokes, *Radio Transmitters,* Van Nostrand, 1970.
(6) W. R. Bennett and J. R. Davey, *Data Transmission,* McGraw-Hill, 1965.
(7) R. C. Dixon, *Spread Spectrum Systems,* Wiley, 1976.
(8) B. J. Halliwell, *Advanced Communication Systems,* Newnes-Butterworths, 1974.
(9) D. H. Hamsher, *Communication Systems Engineering Handbook,* McGraw-Hill, 1967.
(10) W. L. Pritchard and other contributors. Satellite Communication, Proc. IEEE, Vol. 65, No. 3, March 1977.
Special Issue on Satellite Communication Networks, Proc. IEEE, Vol. 72, No. 11, Nov. 1984
(11) *Radio Amateurs Handbook.* American Radio Relay League.
(12) World Radio TV Handbook. Cardfont Publishers Ltd. (Annual).
(13) IBA Technical Reference Book, May 1977.
(14) D. W. Watson and H. E. Wright, Radio Direction Finding. Van Nostrand, 1971.
(15) M. I. Skolnok, *Introduction to Radar Systems.* McGraw-Hill, 1980.
(16) L. W. Turner, *Electronic Engineers' Reference Book.* Newnes-Butterworths, 1976.
(17) R. F. Hansford, *Radio Aids to Civil Aviation.* Heywood 1960.
(18) T. A. Stansell, *The Many Faces of Transit.* Navigation, Vol. 25, No. 2, Summer 1978.
(19) Microwave Systems News, Vol. 14, No. 12, Nov. 1984.
(20) E. R. Voss, *Omega Navigation System.* Navigation, Vol. 25, No. 1, p. 40, Spring 1978.
(21) H. Jasik, *Antenna Engineering Handbook*, McGraw-Hill, 1961.
A. W. Rudge, K. Milne, A. D. Olver and P. Knight (ed.) *The Handbook of Antenna Designl, Peter Perigrinus/IEE, 1982.*
(22) M. Schwartz, W. R. Bennett and S. Stein, *Communication Systems and Techniques.* McGraw-Hill, 1966.
(23) Kenneth Davies, *Ionospheric Radio Propagation.* National Bureau of Standards Monograph 80, 1965.
(24) M. S. Appleyard and J. Garrett, *The Cellnet Radio Network*, Journal of British Telecommunication Engineers Vol. 4, Part 2, July 1985.
(25) *Special Issue on Mobile Radio.* Proc. IEE Vol. 132, Part F, Aug. 1985.

LINE COMMUNICATION

History—Audio frequency—Cable characteristics—Equalisation—Modulation—Electrical Filters—Coaxial Systems—Power Transfer—Resistance/Impedance Matching—Decibel and Neper—Radio Waveguides—Optical Fibre Systems—P.C.M. Code and Sampling—Waveform Distortion—Switching Systems—Time Division Switching—Time/Space/Time Switching—British Telecom Transmission Plan—Traffic Measurement—Integrated Services Network—Bibliography.

by S. F. Luther, BSc, CEng, FIEE

GLOSSARY OF TERMS

Attenuation.—Loss experienced in sending a signal over a transmission line.

Cable balancing.—The selection of pairs in the lengths forming a cable and their connection together in an endeavour to produce a uniformity of the electrical characteristics pairs in the cable to limit cross-talk.

Cross-talk.—Unavoidable imperfections in the line which cause the transfer by electro-magnetic induction of some of the alternating current power in one transmission circuit to other circuits in close physical association. The quantity of power transferred is very small compared with that transmitted but it is nevertheless significant.

Equalisers.—The addition of reactive elements, capacitive and inductive, to a cable to reduce the slope of the frequency/attenuation response.

Loading.—The addition of inductance to a transmission line to decrease the attenuation suffered by higher frequency signals.

Exchange Types.

Strowger.—Electro-mechanical telephone exchanges working on a step by step system. Many Strowger exchanges are still working but they are being replaced by electronic exchanges which are faster in operation and less fault prone.

Crossbar.—A later developed electro-mechanical system which utilises a crossbar switch as the connecting agent. These are coded TXK 1 and 3 by British Telecom.

Reed Relay Exchanges.—Usually semi-electronic utilising a space divided matrix of reed relays as the switch point. They are coded TXE2 and 4 by British Telecom.

Electronic Exchanges.—These are now being installed in many countries. Switching is normally effected by a cascade of electronic switches arranged in Space/Time/Space configuration. System X is the British Telecom developed system.

HISTORY

Development of Audio Cables. The Telecommunications world can now look back upon a hundred years of history. The commonly known design and discovery of the telephone by Alexander Graham Bell has heralded in a new era of instant communication, person to person, across the globe. From a very simple beginning mankind has created the biggest machine, involving the greatest investment that this world has known.

Growth at the beginning in Britain was very slow and indeed it was impeded by powerful voices in both the Government and Post Office of the day who had invested significant sums of money in the telegraph system and therefore did not wish to see that investment jeopardised.

Now the essential purpose of the telephone network was and is, to carry information instantly from point A to point B. During the late 19th and early 20th centuries the network was limited to the environs of larger towns and cities and there were no interconnecting links. Uninsulated copper wires, often supported on roof top gantries, formed the transmission media and the calls were switched manually at a central exchange, in the first instance by boys and young men and later, in the main, by girl operators. The earliest manual systems used one wire and earth return for the transmission path as did the Army in the field in the first World War.

The first World War itself gave a great impetus to development and the need to interconnect towns and cities together. This was done by erecting heavy gauge overhead open copper wires attached to insulators and with soldered joints. Since the thermionic valve had not, at that stage, been invented there was no means of amplification. A pair of wires was necessary to form a circuit. This form of construction is still in use in many countries of the world today both in the local and trunk networks.

Even in the early days of the 20th century, when telephony was taking its first hesitant steps, a considerable telegraph network had been built up in this country. Both international and long distance telegraph underground cables had been laid, Bristol to Plymouth is but one example. In the 1930s some of these very heavy gauge copper conductor telegraph cables were re-utilised to provide trunk circuits.

The between wars decades of the 1920s and 1930s saw the development of the thermionic valve and its use as amplifiers or repeaters on trunk circuits. These were installed on either two wire or four wire circuits. To this end terminating networks had to be constructed since amplifiers are essentially unidirectional devices. The early two wire amplifiers were notoriously unstable. The two wire/four wire terminating units work in the following way.

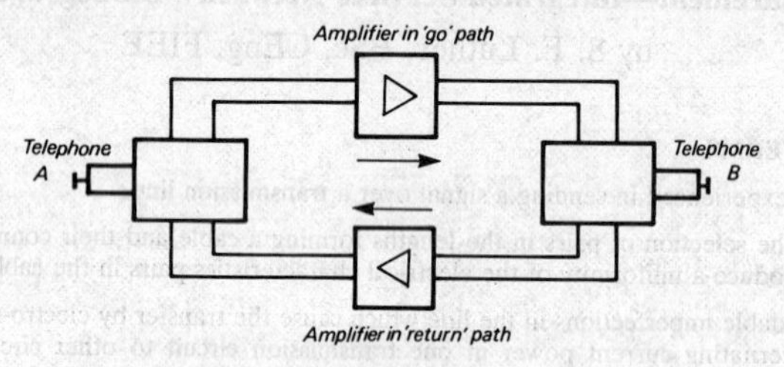

FIG. 1.—A 4-Wire Circuit.

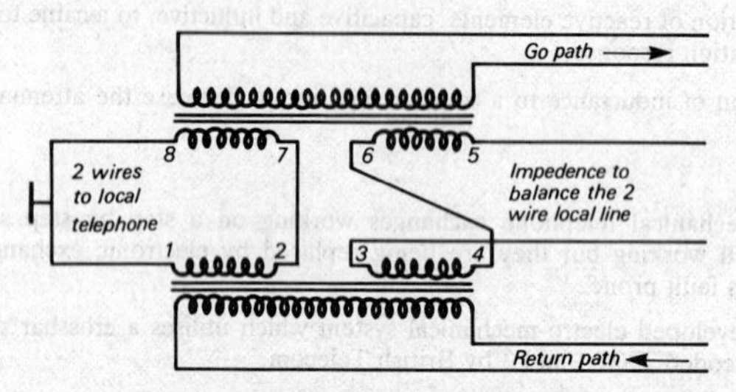

FIG. 2.—2-Wire/4-Wire Terminating Unit.

A signal received over the 'return' path of the four wire circuit will induce emfs into both windings 12 and 34 of equal size. Thus the power is shared between them creating a loss of 3 db between 2 wire (local telephone) and receive 4 wire. In addition, transformer losses amount to 1 db, creating a total loss of 4 db. The loss between 'return' and 'go' is very high (>60 db) since the emfs induced into the go path are, virtually, cancelled out in coils 87 and 65, provided that the impedance of the two wire balance reasonably equates to that of the two wire local telephone line.

With the introduction of repeaters as amplifiers came the inception of junction and trunk underground cables. These cables had a lead sheath and paper insulation on the conductors which were twisted in quads to reduce the effect of induction and 'cross-talk'.

AUDIO FREQUENCY CABLES

Trunk & Junction Cable.—No further trunk or junction audio cables are now being laid in Britain, although their use is continuing in countries overseas. Trunk and junction audio cables are almost invariably of star quad construction. This means that they are laid up in two pairs, twisting round one another to reduce interference and cross-talk.

The attenuation/frequency response to be expected from a pair in such a cable is given in Fig. 4.

The characteristic impedance of such a cable pair is dependent upon frequency and is expected to vary from 600 to 800 ohms at lower frequencies and 200 to 300 ohms at higher frequencies (about 3 kHz).

Earlier cables were lead sheathed. Later cable would be polythene sheathed with an aluminium tape barrier inside the sheath to provide a moisture barrier.

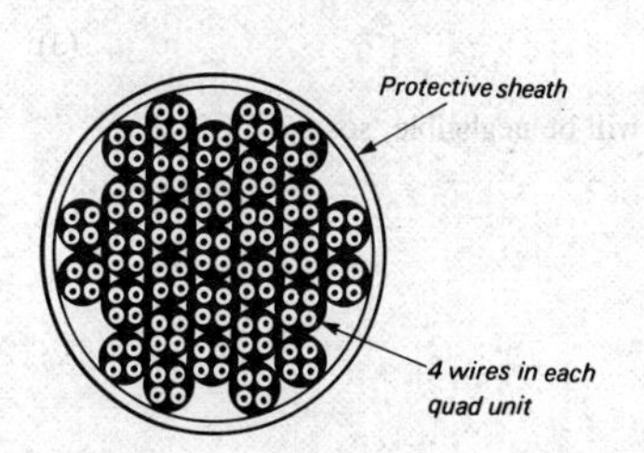

FIG. 3.—Cross-section of Audio Frequency Quad. Cable.

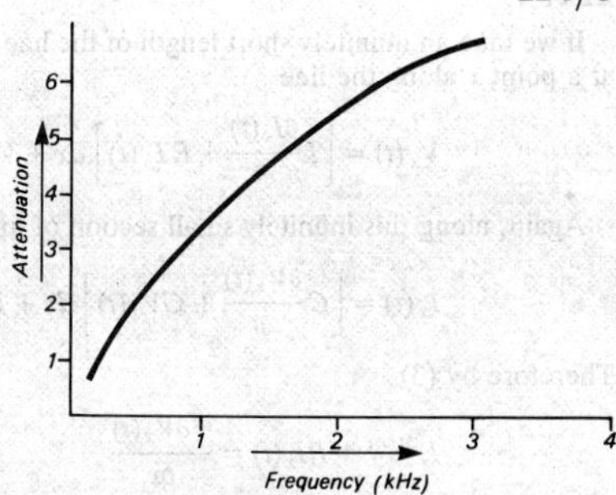

FIG. 4.—Audio Cable Attenuation/Frequency Response.

Junction and trunk cables are balanced by test selecting and jointing pairs at chosen joints throughout the length of cables.

Local Cable.—Local cable is laid up in pairs and is polythene/polythene. That is, polythene insulant for each wire and polythene sheath with an aluminium tape to limit moisture ingress. Cables of under 100 pairs have a water barrier wax filler between wires. Larger cables, as also with junction and trunk cables, are air filled under pressure. Very large, small conductor cables are now manufactured for use in dense parts of the network.

Aluminium came into use as a conductor material in local cables in the 1970s, but its non-malleable characteristic and its liability to crack and break at joints has tended to discourage its use.

The Primary Coefficients of a Telephone Cable.—The transmission characteristics of a pair in a telephone cable depend upon the primary coefficients of that line where these coefficients are resistance (R), capacitance between wire and wire, wire and sheath and wire and earth (C), inductance between wire and wire (L) and leakance between wire and wire (G).

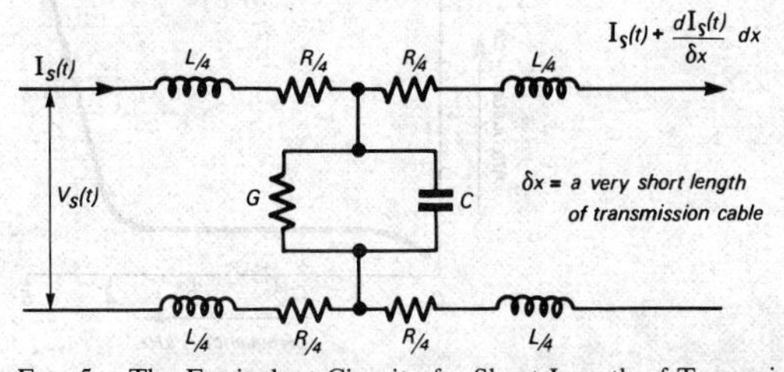

FIG. 5.—The Equivalent Circuit of a Short Length of Transmission.

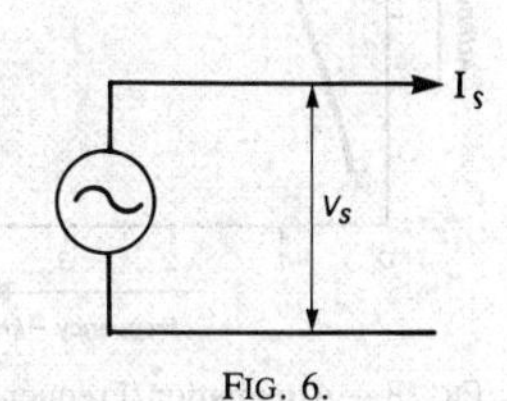

FIG. 6.

The characteristic impedance Z_0 of a transmission line is defined as the imput impedance of an infinite length of that line

$$Z_0 = \frac{V_s}{I_s} \text{ ohms} \tag{1}$$

Similarly at any point along the line the same ratio is sustained.

$$Z_0 = \frac{V}{I} \text{ ohms}$$

Now if the line is then terminated with its characteristic impedance the impedance looking into the line will still be Z_0.

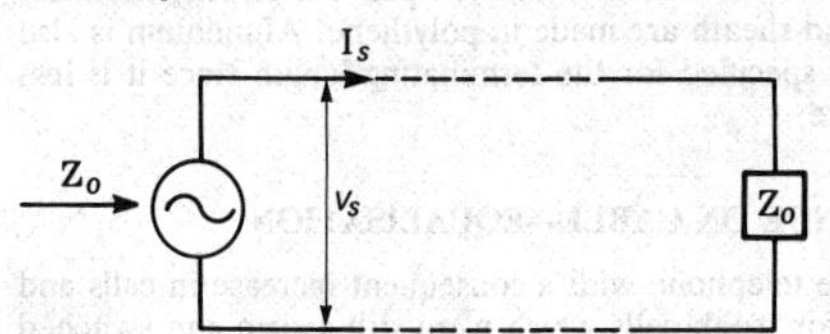

FIG. 7.—The Developed Impedance of a Transmission Line.

If we take an infinitely short length of the line δx then the leakance G is sufficiently small to be ignored and at a point x along the line

$$V_x(t) = \left[L\frac{\partial I_x(t)}{\partial t} + RT_x(t)\right] dx + V_x(t) + \frac{\partial V_x(t)}{\delta x} \cdot \partial x \qquad (3)$$

Again, along this infinitely small section of line the voltage drop will be negligible, so—

$$I_x(t) = \left[C\frac{\partial V_x(t)}{\partial t} + GV_x(t)\right] dx + I_x(t) + \frac{\partial I_x(t)}{\delta x} \cdot \delta x \qquad (4)$$

Therefore by (3)

$$L^{\partial I_x(t)} + RI_x(t) = \frac{-\partial V_x(t)}{\delta x}$$

and (4)

$$C\frac{\partial V_x(t)}{\delta t} + GV_x(t) = \frac{-\delta I_x(t)}{\delta x}$$

Applying Fourier

$$\frac{V_x}{I_x} = Z_0 = \sqrt{\frac{R + j\omega L}{G + j\omega C}} \text{ ohms} \qquad (5)$$

Audio Telephone Cable—'Loading'.—For the human voice to be recognised a telephone transmission line needs to be able to carry the frequency range 300–3400 Hz. The problem with an ordinary twisted cable pair is that it has a poor frequency/characteristic (Fig. 8).

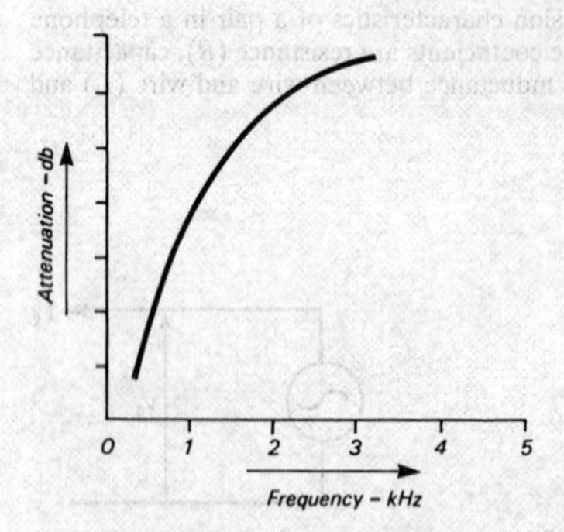

FIG. 8.—Attenuation/Frequency of Audio Telephone Cable.

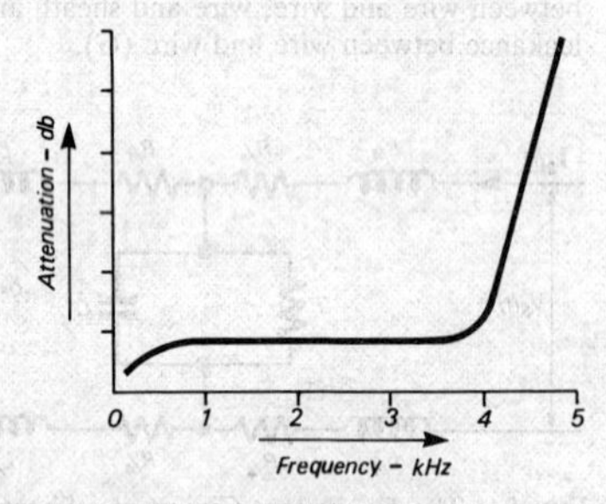

FIG. 9.—Attenuation/Frequency of Audio 'Lump Loaded' Telephone Cable.

The low inductance of the cable pair compared with the between wire capacitance is the main reason for the poor attenuation characteristic. If however the inductance of the cable pair is increased by introducing additional inductance at fixed intervals in the length of the cable (this is termed lump loading) then the frequency/attenuation characteristic is significantly improved (Fig. 9).

One thing which will be noted is that a sharp rise in attenuation will occur, normally at about 4 kHz.

At about this cut-off frequency of 4 kHz the phase characteristic of the line will demonstrate serious non-linear results. As a consequence of this a 'lump-loaded' audio cable pair is not suitable for digital data transmission because of the signal dispersion. This can only be dealt with by the introduction of phase equalisation to the pair.

The materials used in modern telephone cables have altered radically. Twisted pair cables only normally now find use in the local network where both insulant and sheath are made in polythene. Aluminium is also employed in the conductor although copper is normally specified for the terminating length since it is less brittle than aluminium, and hence is less likely to fracture.

UTILISING A WIDER FREQUENCY RANGE ON CABLE—EQUALISATION

The 1930s saw a significant increase in demand for the telephone with a consequent increase in calls and traffic carried. Delay was the normal order of the day for trunk calls which were still set up and switched manually. To cater for additional trunk traffic a new Star Quad cable was designed with a much wider frequency range than that of a 'lump loaded' cable. In order to overcome interference and cross-talk the 'go' direction of transmission was put in a separate cable to the 'return' direction of transmission. Each cable had 24 pairs and line equalisers were installed to ensure a flat frequency/attenuation response over the frequency band which was utilised.

Now, considering the equation.

$$Z_0 = \sqrt{\frac{R + j\omega L}{G + j\omega C}} \text{ ohms} \tag{6}$$

As the frequencies increase then ωL becomes increasingly greater than R and ωC becomes increasingly greater than G.

Under these circumstances

$$Z_0 \simeq \sqrt{L/C} \text{ ohms} \tag{7}$$

By increasing the capacitance at the beginning or end of the transmission line the frequency/attenuation curve can be flattened. Equalisation has been said to have taken place. Modern equalisers are more complex than this since phase equalisation can be important on digital circuits.

Exploitation of the band width, which thus became available, followed. A speech channel needs a band width of 4 kHz. The Star Quad cable with special loose packing and a characteristic impedance of 140 ohms demonstrated a potential band width of up to 250 kHz. By taking a speech channel and mixing it with a different carrier frequency for each channel, then the speech channels were stacked, one above another in the available transmission circuit frequency spectrum (Fig. 10).

The mixing is carried out in a modulator.

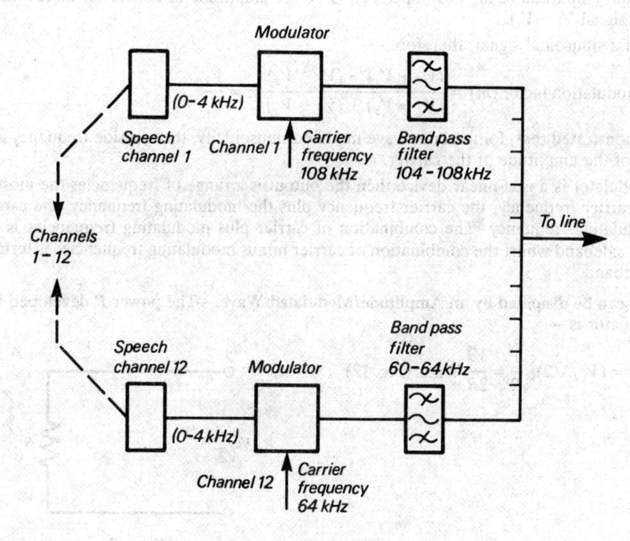

FIG. 10.—A 12 Channel Carrier System.

Modulation.—There are various types of modulation—amplitude—frequency—phase. In the case of frequency division multiplex (fdm) telephony, amplitude modulation is employed. During modulation one of the characteristics of a carrier wave is taken and modified to conform with the characteristics of the usually complex modulating signal. For modulation to take place both the carrier and the modulating signal are injected into a non-linear device. The modulated signal appears at the output. In the case of the carrier telephony system now being described, metal rectifiers form the non-linear device in a piece of equipment termed the Cowan modulator.

The reverse process, that is the retrieving of the former carrier frequency plus the former complex modulating signal, is called de-modulation.

Modulation Factor.—The definition of the Modulation Factor (m) in the case of an amplitude modulated wave is the maximum amplitude minus minimum amplitude divided by the maximum amplitude plus minimum amplitude.

$$\text{Modulation factor } (m) = \frac{\text{max. amplitude} - \text{min. amplitude}}{\text{max. amplitude} + \text{min. amplitude}}$$

Expressed as a percentage, m is described as the percentage modulation or depth of modulation.

Taking the modulated signal as shown in Fig. 11 since the envelope of the carrier frequency (V_c) must vary

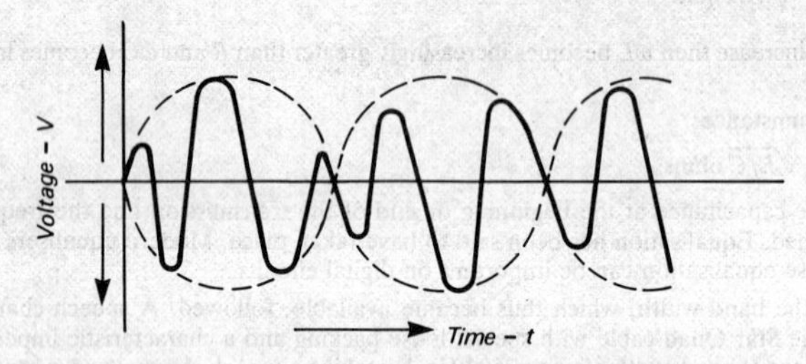

FIG. 11.—A Carrier Modulated by a Single Modulating Frequency.

to comply with the modulating signal (V_s) then the maximum amplitude of the envelope is equal to the summation of the amplitude of the carrier plus the amplitude of the modulating signal ($V_c + V_s$). Contrarywise the minimum amplitude of the envelope is equal to the amplitude of the carrier minus the amplitude of the modulating signal $V_c - V_s$).

In the case of a sinusoidal signal, therefore,

$$\text{Modulation factor } (m) = \frac{(V_c + V_s) - (V_c - V_s)}{(V_c + V_s) + (V_c - V_s)} \; m = \frac{V_s}{V_c} \tag{8}$$

It can be demonstrated that, for a carrier wave modified sinusoidally, the two side frequency amplitudes are equal and half of the amplitude of the carrier.

Since the modulator is a non-linear device then the output is a range of frequencies the most important of which are the carrier frequency, the carrier frequency plus the modulating frequency, the carrier frequency minus the modulating frequency. The combination of carrier plus modulating frequencies is known as the Upper or Erect sideband whilst the combination of carrier minus modulating frequencies is termed the Lower or Inverted sideband.

Power which can be disipated by an Amplitude/Modulated Wave.—The power P developed by a carrier at output of modulator is.—

$$P = (V_c/\sqrt{2})^2 \frac{1}{R} = \frac{V_c^2}{2R} \text{ Watts (Fig. 12)} \tag{9}$$

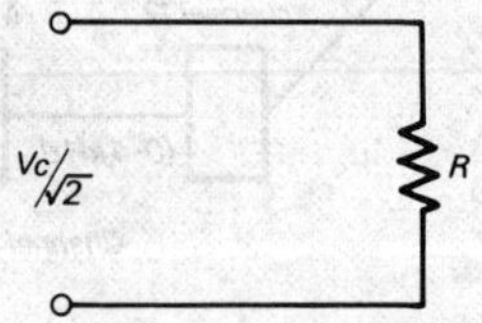

Vc/√2
R

FIG. 12.

The power P developed by upper and lower sideband components at output of modulator is—

$$P = \left(\frac{V_s}{2\sqrt{2}}\right)^2 \frac{1}{R} = \left(\frac{mV_c}{2\sqrt{2}}\right)^2 \frac{1}{R}$$

$$= \frac{\mathrm{m}^2 \mathrm{V}_c^2}{8\mathrm{R}} \tag{10}$$

The total power consumed in R is therefore the addition of the carrier plus upper and lower sidebands

$$P_T = \frac{V_c^2}{2R} + 2\left(\frac{m^2 V_c^2}{8R}\right) \text{ Watts} \tag{11}$$

Therefore

$$P_T = \frac{V_c^2}{2R}\left(1 + \frac{m^2}{2}\right) \text{ Watts} \tag{12}$$

Suppression of Carrier and Upper sideband.—There is advantage, in line telephony, to suppress and thus not transmit to line, all but the lower sideband. To do this a filter has to be fitted across the output of the modulator.

The advantages to be gained by carrying out this suppression are.—

(i) Only half the band width will be required over the line circuit.

(ii) Since noise is proportional to band width and also since the ratio sideband power/total power is increased, the signal to noise ratio is greater than is the case with a double sideband system.

(iii) Modulation takes place in a multi-channel line system if non-linearity is encountered in any device. The output stages of line amplifiers connected in circuit are dealing with high amplitude signals. Eliminating all but the lower sideband reduces the signal amplitudes which the line amplifiers have to handle.

The main disadvantage with Single (Lower) sideband working is that it complicates the equipment which has to be installed in the receiving terminal station. Oscillators are necessary to generate the carrier frequencies which are needed to de-modulate the incoming channel signals. These carriers must also be locked in frequency with the distant end.

Electrical Filters.—Electrical filters are employed in a carrier telephony system to block frequencies other than the Lower sideband. Filters can be constructed from inductances and capacitances to provide High Pass (i), Low Pass (ii), Band Pass (iii) and Band Stop (iv). (See Fig. 13).

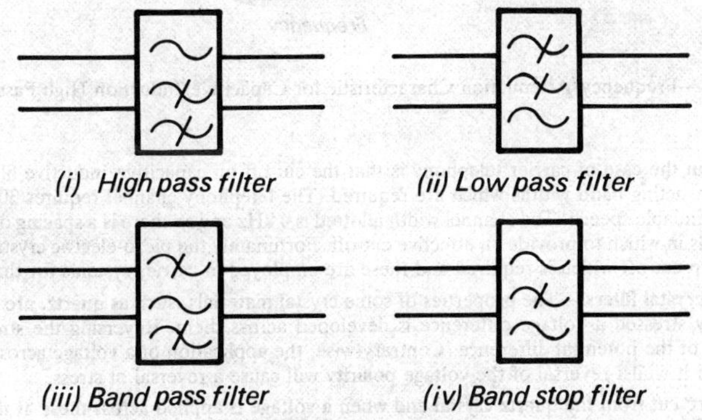

FIG. 13.—Electrical Filters.

Taking the High Pass Filter as a typical example of a capacitive/inductive filter, the components are arranged as in Figs. 14 and 15.

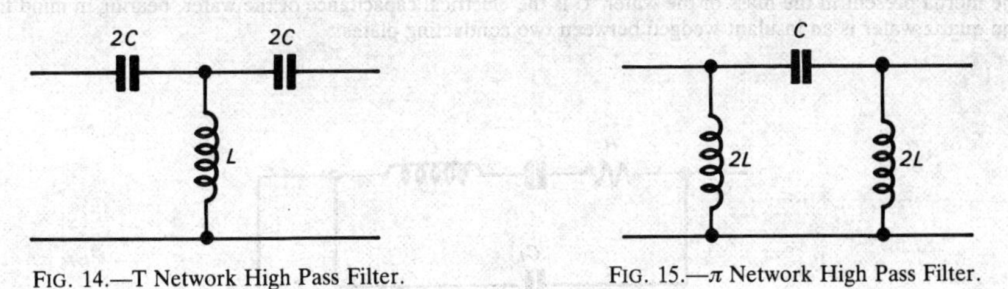

FIG. 14.—T Network High Pass Filter.

FIG. 15.—π Network High Pass Filter.

T network High Pass Filter.—The High Pass filter is intended to heavily attenuate lower frequencies and, at the same time, present a low loss path to higher frequencies. In this case the series capacitance presents a high reactance to applied voltages whilst the shunting inductive path presents a low reactance path. In consequence signals presented to the filter at lower frequencies will be heavily attenuated whilst high frequencies will pass through with little loss. The consequent attenuation/frequency curve demonstrates the result of the insertion of the High Pass Filter (Fig. 16).

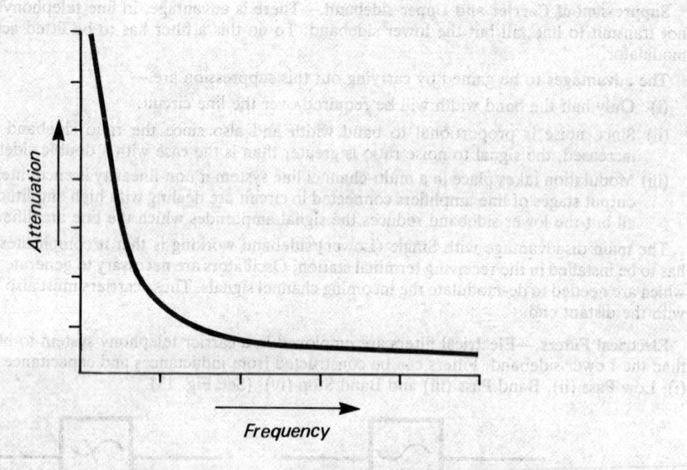

FIG. 16.—Frequency/Attenuation Characteristic for Capacitive/Induction High Pass Filter.

The problem in the case of carrier telephony is that the cut off on capacitive/inductive filters is not sharp enough for the exacting band widths which are required. The telephony channel requires 300 Hz to 3400 Hz to carry understandable speech. The channel width allotted is 4 kHz and so there is a spacing of less than 1 kHz between channels in which to provide an effective cut-off. Fortunately the piezo-electric crystal filter is able to provide the sharp cut-off which is required and these are employed in carrier systems for that purpose.

Piezo-electric crystal filters.—The properties of some crystal materials, such as quartz, are such that if they are mechanically stressed a voltage difference is developed across them. Reversing the stressing force will cause a reversal of the potential difference. Contrary-wise, the application of a voltage across the crystal will create a stress in it whilst reversal of the voltage polarity will cause a reversal of stress.

Thin wafers are cut from the quartz crystal and when a voltage is applied across these at their own natural frequency then the wafer will vibrate strongly. A progressive reduction of wafer thickness will produce higher natural frequencies of vibration and by utilising the facility that the crystal will vibrate to higher harmonics of its natural frequency it is possible to extend the range of operation of piezo-electric crystal filters to in excess of 100 MHz.

The typical circuit equivalent of a piezo-electric crystal is shown in Fig. 17. In the equivalent circuit R equals the functional losses introduced by the vibrating wafers, C the inverse factor for the stiffness of the wafer, L the inertia present in the mass of the wafer. C is the electrical capacitance of the wafer, bearing in mind that the quartz wafer is an insulant wedged between two conducting plates.

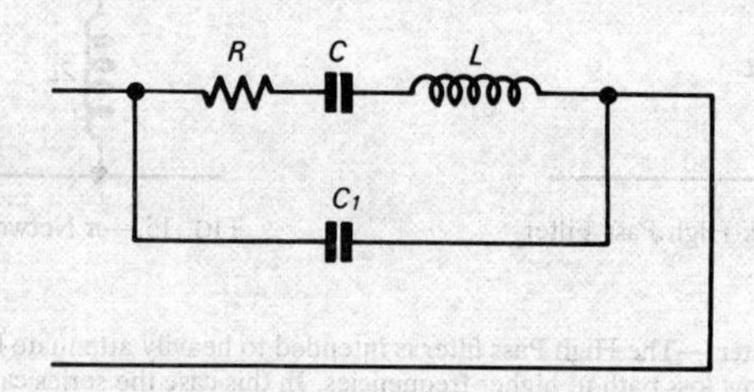

FIG. 17.—Circuit Equivalent of Piezo-electric Crystal.

12 and 24 Channel Carrier Systems.—Fig. 10 demonstrates the basic building blocks present in a Frequency Division Multiplex (FDM) telephony transmission system. The first systems introduced to service transmitted to line in the total frequency range 60 MHz–108 MHz. This provides band-width for twelve channels each working the following frequency range (Table 1).

TABLE 1.—BAND WIDTHS FOR FREQUENCY RANGE 60–108 MHz

Channels (Band-widths 300 Hz–3400 Hz)	Frequency range (kHz)	(Suppressed) Carrier frequency (kHz)
1	107.7–104.6	108
2	103.7–100.6	104
3	99.7– 96.6	100
4	95.7– 92.6	96
5	91.7– 88.6	92
6	87.7– 84.6	88
7	83.7– 80.6	84
8	79.7– 76.6	80
9	75.7– 72.6	76
10	71.7– 68.6	72
11	67.7– 64.6	68
12	63.7– 60.6	64

For early systems the frequency range chosen to transmit to line (60 kHz–108 kHz) facilitated filter and equipment design. Later the 12 kHz–60 kHz, which was still potentially available over the cable, was brought into use by introducing a second stage of modulation and demodulation for the whole system. The lower side-band of frequencies was taken and this shifted the frequency range of the second system to 12 kHz–60 kHz and doubled the circuit capacity of the cable in one stroke (Fig. 2.9).

These basic groups formed the building blocks on which much higher capacity Frequency Division Multiplex Systems were built when coaxial cable systems were introduced in the late 1930s.

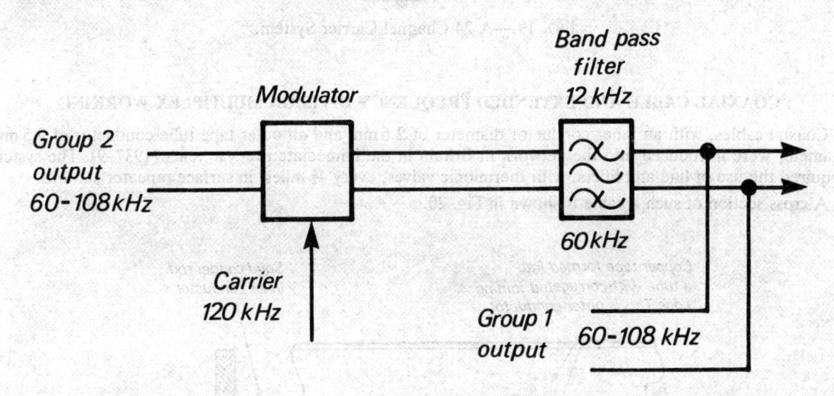

FIG. 18.—Second Stage Modulation and Demodulation to Increase Circuit Capacity.

One other factor requires mention before the full carrier system block schematic is drawn. The filters on the outputs of the channel modulators have their outputs commoned together (Fig. 10 refers). Each channel filter (other than channels 1 and 12) has filters on either side of its pass frequency range and so these filter outputs are terminated in the receive end load parallelled with the impedance of flanking filters. To compensate for this in the case of the filters on channels 1 and 12 an additional, compensating network is added. The block schematic diagram for a 12/24 channel group is therefore as is shown in Fig. 19.

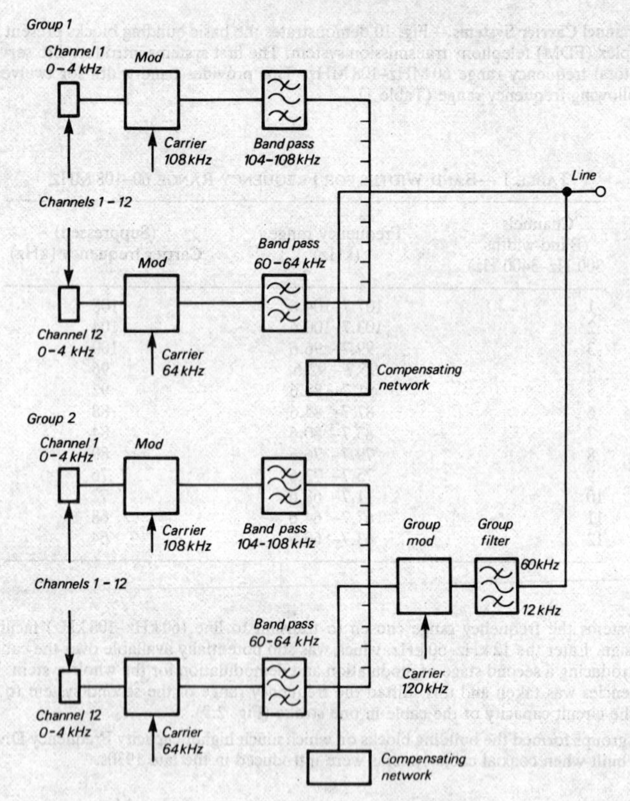

FIG. 19.—A 24 Channel Carrier System.

COAXIAL CABLE AND EXTENDED FREQUENCY DIVISION MULTIPLEX WORKING

Coaxial cables, with an inner conductor diameter of 2.6 mm and an outer tape tube conductor of 9.5 mm diameter were introduced into the network in Britain in the immediate pre-war years (1937–9). The system required the use of line amplifiers, with thermionic valves, every 4½ miles, in surface repeater stations.

A cross section of such a cable is shown in Fig. 20.

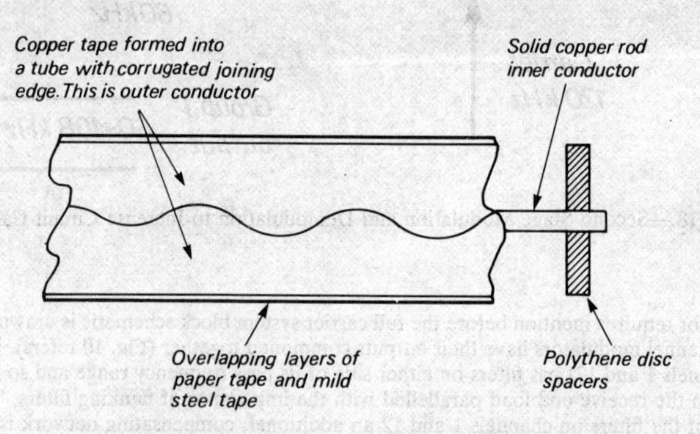

FIG. 20.—Cross-section of a 2·6/9·5 mm Coaxial Cable.

The 2.6/9.5 mm Coaxial Cable.—The inner conductor is a solid copper rod of 2.6 mm diameter. The outer conductor is a copper tube constructed from a tape with corrugated edges. The two conductors are held apart by polythene disc spacers 33 mm apart. Mild steel tape is wound over the whole to give the cable mechanical strength and to act as a barrier to low frequency interference (Fig. 16). The characteristic impedance of such a cable is 140 ohms.

Multi-tube coaxial cables are now extensively in service and in the case of vital, heavy density 'spine' routes in Britain, 64 tube coaxial cable has been laid over specially protected routes.

The typical attenuation/frequency response for 2.6/9.5 mm coaxial cable is given in Fig. 21.

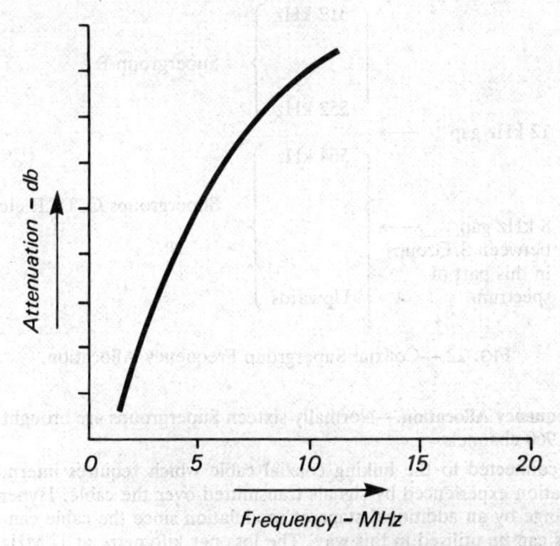

FIG. 21.—Typical Attenuation/Frequency Response for 2·6/9·5 mm Coaxial Cable.

Since a very wide frequency band of operation is being considered (up to 12 MHz) the response of the transmission line is complicated. At high frequencies the signals tend to remain on the surface or 'skin' of the conductors. The result is that the resistance of the conductors rises in proportion to the square root of the signal frequency.

The way in which the coaxial cable is constructed tends to produce significant inequalities in line constants.

$$2\pi f \gg R/L \gg \frac{G}{C}$$

This simplifies equations so that

$$Z_0 \simeq L/C$$

The cable offers relatively low attenuation per kilometre.

Small bore coaxial cable was introduced into the network in Britain in the 1960s and early 1970s.

The cable is constructed in similar manner to the larger coaxial cable. Its inner conductor is again copper with a diameter of 1.2 mm. The outer conductor is again a tape formed into a tube and this has a diameter of 4.4 mm. Characteristic impedance of this cable is 75 ohms.

Coaxial systems.—The group, as described in Carrier System working, is the basic building block of a Coaxial System. The twelve channel group in the frequency range 60–108 kHz is subjected to further stages of modulation. Five twelve channel groups are each modulated with a carrier in the range 420–612 kHz, at interval steps of 48 kHz. The lower sidebands are selected by use of filters and so the sixty channels which result occupy the frequency band 312–552 kHz. These are termed a Supergroup.

Next, a third stage of modulation is entered into. Supergroups are subjected to modulation with carriers in the frequency range of 1116 kHz upwards, in steps of 248 kHz. Again, lower sidebands are selected, placing the Supergroups in the range 564 kHz upwards.

Since there is space in the frequency range below 564 kHz for further communication channels, another Supergroup is taken and modulated by a carrier of 612 kHz frequency. Again, the lower sideband is selected resulting in a Supergroup in the transmission frequency range 60–300 kHz.

The remaining space between the upper end of this Supergroup (300 kHz) and the lower end of the frequency range of the already modulated Supergroups (564 kHz upwards) is filled by taking another Supergroup unmodulated (312–552 kHz); see Fig. 22.

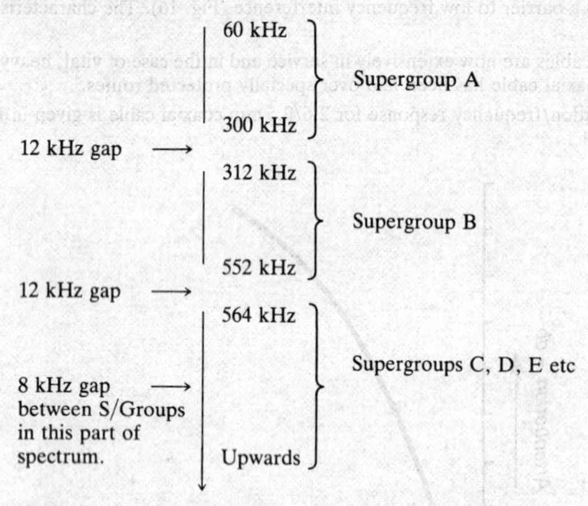

FIG. 22.—Coaxial Supergroup Frequency Allocation.

Coaxial System—Frequency Allocation.—Normally sixteen Supergroups are brought together in this way to form a Hypergroup of 960 channels.

The Hypergroup is connected to the linking coaxial cable which requires intermediate amplification to compensate for attenuation experienced by signals transmitted over the cable. Hypergroups can be built up further in frequency range by an additional stage of modulation since the cable can be used successfully to 12 MHz. 2700 channels can be utilised in this way. The loss per kilometre at 12 MHz is of the order of 7.5/8.0 db. Since a 12 MHz intermediate line amplifier can be expected to provide an amplification of about 36 db, repeater spacing of roughly 4½ miles is required.

Major repeater stations along the route feed power over the cable to intermediates and so a careful control system is essential to protect the safety of those working on the cable. The limit to the amplification which an intermediate repeater will provide is governed by the harmonic distortion generated in the repeater.

The attenuation experienced by the system is temperature dependent. Some intermediate repeaters are designed automatically to adjust gain against temperature variation.

The small bore coaxial cable of 1.2/4.4 millimetre construction suffers greater attenuation than the large cable and requires amplification at roughly 2000 yard spacing. This is provided by repeaters which are built in sealed containers and installed in underground jointing chambers. Power for the repeaters is fed over the cable and so, again, great care must be taken to control access by staff to work on the cable.

SUBMARINE CABLE SYSTEMS

Traffic offered to international telecommunications links increases roughly at the rate of 30% per annum compound. Demand for new circuits increases at a corresponding rate and is met either by the provision of new submarine cables or by new satellite systems. Inter-continental traffic is split roughly half and half between cable and satellite.

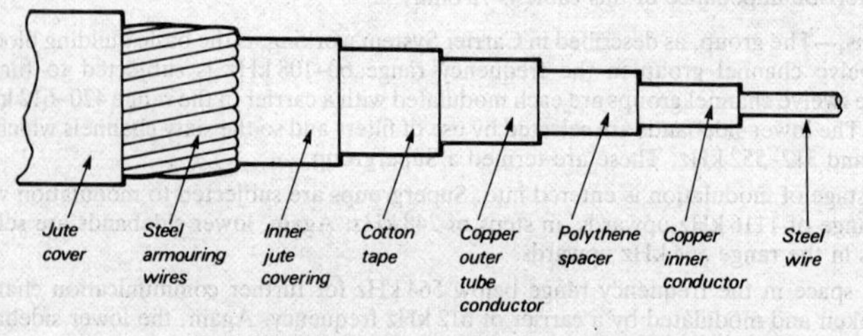

FIG. 23.—Typical Submarine Coaxial Cable.

Wideband cables are essential to give the circuit capacity which is needed and a modified form of coaxial cable is used for this purpose (Fig. 23).

In the case of submarine systems the same cable provides both way transmission by dividing the frequency range in two. Power is fed over the cable to, in the case of oceanic cables, what can be hundreds of submerged repeaters, the components for which have been specially selected for long life. A voltage dropping device enables each repeater to take its allocation of power.

Since it is important to both make maximum use of cable capacity available and to hold down costs the frequency width of each channel is halved compared with inland networks. This is done by sampling the traffic on each channel and only opening a channel to traffic when a signal is offered. The terminal equipment is expensive but warranted in the case of oceanic links where the cable systems themselves involve very heavy investment.

POWER TRANSFER AND POWER MEASUREMENT

At points of connection in electronic circuits it is important to ensure that a maximum transfer of power takes place. That it can be a variable can be determined by setting up the following simple experiment (Fig. 24).

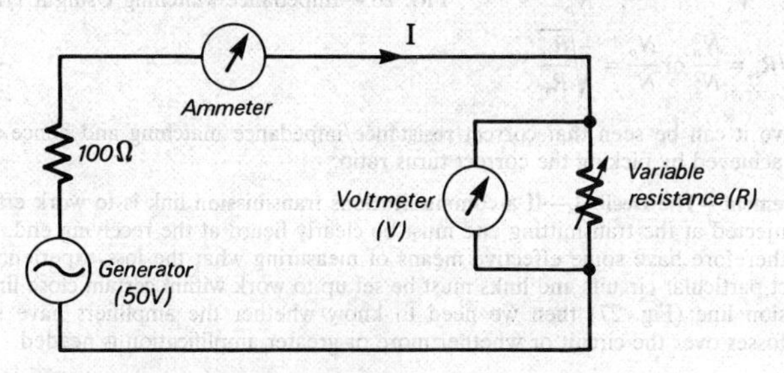

FIG. 24.—Variable Power Transfer Experimental Circuit.

The variable resistance (R) is adjusted in steps from zero upwards and the current (I) and voltage across the variable resistor (R) is plotted.

The power consumed in the variable resistance (R) is VI and so the power used can be calculated at the various resistance values. The result, plotted on a graph, is shown in Fig. 25.

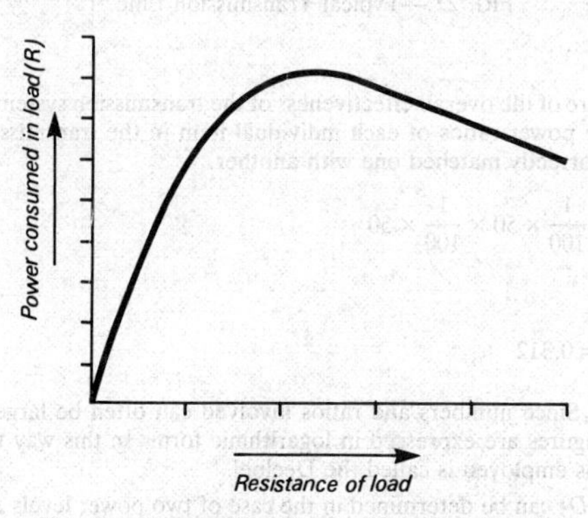

FIG. 25.—Power Transfer in a Transmission Line.

The experiment will demonstrate that the maximum power consumption occurs in the load when the load resistance equals the generator resistance.

Resistance/Impedance matching in a transmission line.—In a transformer which has a soft iron core there is good linkage between primary and secondary windings. Under these circumstances there is very little loss in the transfer and the ratio input/output voltage equals ratio primary/secondary windings equals ratio secondary current/primary current (Fig. 26).

ie

$$V_p/V_s = N_p/N_s = \frac{I_s}{I_p} \qquad (13)$$

Now $N_p/N_s = \frac{I_s}{I_p}$

From Ohm's Law $I = E/R$ or V/R

$$\therefore N_p/N_s = \frac{V_s/R_s}{V_p/R_p} = \frac{V_sR_p}{V_pR_s}$$

But from (13)

$$\frac{N_p}{N_s} = \frac{V_p}{V_s} \text{ or } V_s/V_p = \frac{N_s}{N_p}$$

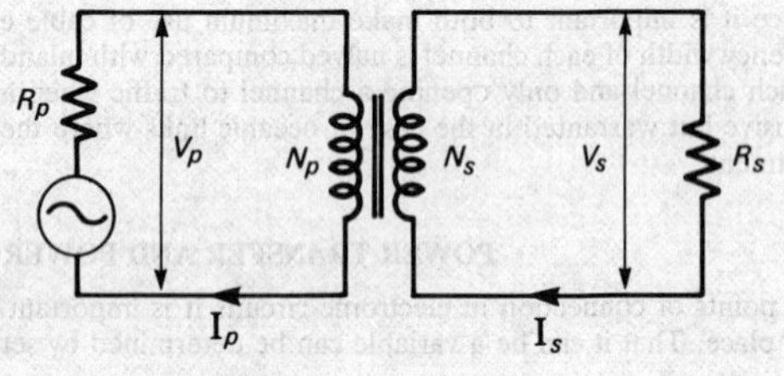

FIG. 26.—Impedance Matching Using a Transformer.

$$\therefore R_p/R_s = \frac{N_p^2}{N_s^2} \text{ or } \frac{N_p}{N_s} = \sqrt{\frac{R_p}{R_s}} \qquad (14)$$

From the above it can be seen that correct resistance/impedance matching and hence maximum power transfer, can be achieved by picking the correct turns ratio.

Power measurement—The Decibel.—If a communications transmission link is to work effectively then the signal which is injected at the transmitting end must be clearly heard at the receiving end. Communications engineers must therefore have some effective means of measuring what the loss experienced over a circuit really is. In effect particular circuits and links must be set up to work within certain close limits. If we take a typical transmission line (Fig. 27) then we need to know whether the amplifiers have sufficient gain to compensate for losses over the circuit or whether more or greater amplification is needed.

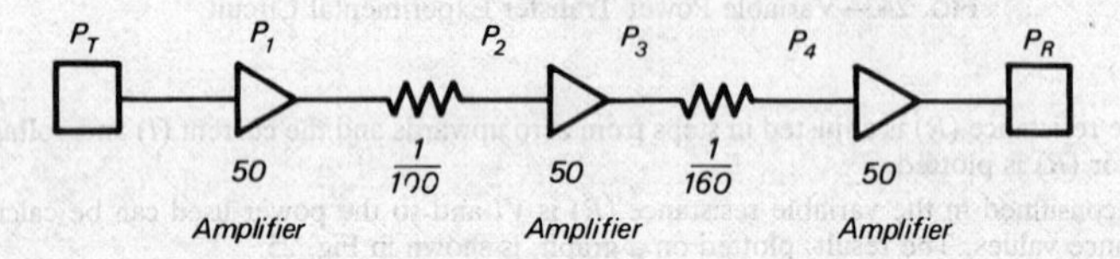

FIG. 27.—Typical Transmission Line.

The ratio P_R/P_T is a measure of the overall effectiveness of the transmission system and this can be calculated by taking the product of the power ratios of each individual item in the transmission line provided that the impedance of each item is correctly matched one with another.

$$P_R/P_T = 50 \times \frac{1}{100} \times 50 \times \frac{1}{100} \times 50$$

or

$$P_R/P_T = \frac{100}{320} = 0.312$$

This is a simple example. Since numbers and ratios involved can often be large and/or complex in these calculations the ratios and figures are expressed in logarithmic form. In this way they can simply be added. The logarithmic unit which is employed is called the Decibel.

The number of Decibels (D) can be determined in the case of two power levels $P1$ and $P2$ by the equation

$$D = 10\log_{10} P_1/P_2 \qquad (15)$$

The power which is taken up in a resistance R equals I^2R or V^2/R (Fig. 28).
So from equation (13)

$$D = 10\log_{10}\frac{V_1^2/R_1}{V_2^2/R_2} \qquad (16)$$

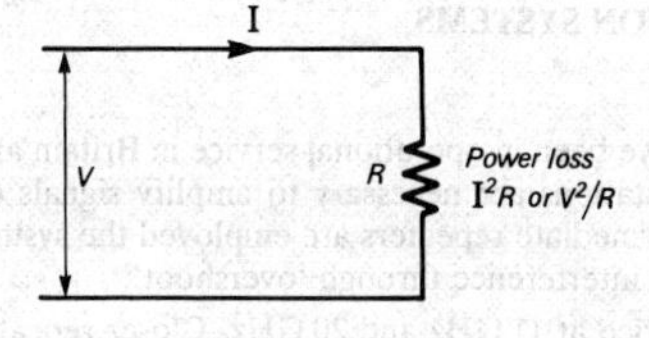

FIG. 28.

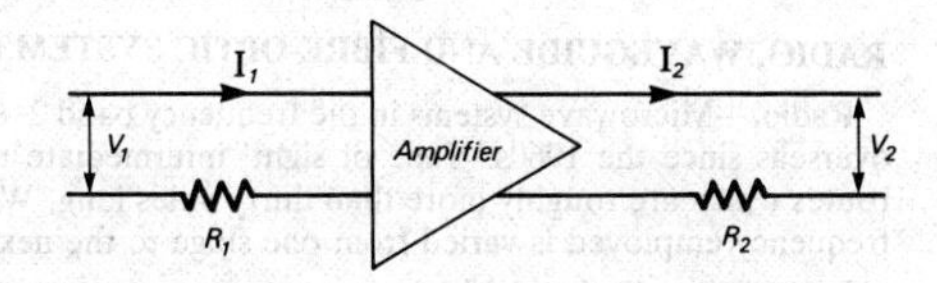

FIG. 29.—Loss or Gain in a Transmission Line.

Again from (13)

$$D = 10 \log_{10} \frac{I_1^2 R_1}{I_2^2 R_2} \quad (17)$$

From (14)

$$D = 10[\log_{10}(V_1^2/V_2^2) + \log_{10}(R_2/R_1)]$$

$$\therefore D = 20 \log_{10} V_1/V_2 + \log_{10} R_2/R_1 \quad (18)$$

From (15)

$$D = 10[\log_{10}(I_1^2/I_2^2) + \log_{10} R_1/R_2]$$

$$\therefore D = 20 \log_{10} I_1/I_2 + \log_{10} R_1/R_2 \quad (19)$$

Now, when $R_1 = R_2$ equations (18) and (19) can be reduced to

$$D = 20 \log_{10} V_1/V_2 \quad (20)$$

$$D = 20 \log_{10} I_1/I_2 \quad (21)$$

Transmission engineers, when checking the gain or loss along a circuit, find that a standard impedance reference point is usually available at the input and output of each separate stage. In the case of audio circuits this is normally 600 ohms and so a direct voltage reference across these points can be checked with a meter.

It can be seen from this that the Decibel is not an absolute measure but is, rather, a power ratio or, in the case of standard impedance measuring points, a voltage ratio.

If it is to have meaning, the decibel measurement must be related to a particular level. In the case of communication engineering this is normally *one milliwatt* and it could be stated that a particular amplifier has a gain of 40 db with reference to 1 milliwatt.

It has been established that the human ear responds to increasing and decreasing sounds logarithmically. The Decibel notation is therefore suitable when measuring levels of sound as they affect the human being.

The Neper and the Decibel.—It has already been mentioned that, for the convenience of transmission/communication engineers the impedance and output impedances of particular items of equipment are constant. In audio equipment it is usually 600 ohms; in fdm equipment 140 ohms. Under these circumstances a relationship can be established as between the Decibel and the Neper.

If an amplifier has a gain of N nepers

$$N = \log_e I_1/I_2$$

$$\therefore I_1/T_2 = e^N \quad (22)$$

The gain D in decibels, for the same amplifier, is

$$D = 20 \log_{10} I_1/I_2 \text{ (from)} \quad (19)$$

$$\therefore D = 20 \log_{10} e^N$$

$$= 20\,N(\log_{10} e)$$

$$= 20\,N(0.4343)$$

$$= 8.6867\,N.$$

If therefore we have identical impedance measuring points it can be stated that

$$1 \text{ Neper} = 8.6867 \text{ Decibels} \ldots\ldots \quad (23)$$

OTHER WIDEBAND TRANSMISSION SYSTEMS

RADIO, WAVEGUIDE AND FIBRE-OPTIC SYSTEMS

Radio.—Microwave systems in the frequency band 2–6 GHz have been in operational service in Britain and overseas since the 1960s. 'Line of sight' intermediate repeater stations are necessary to amplify signals on routes which are roughly more than thirty miles long. Where intermediate repeaters are employed the system frequency employed is varied from one stage to the next to limit interference through 'overshoot'.

New systems, in the higher frequency, are now coming into service at 11 GHz and 20 GHz. Closer repeater spacing is necessary at higher frequencies; about 30 km for 11 GHz and as low as 10 km for 20 GHz. One of the problems at higher frequencies is the attenuation/distortion created by heavy rain/snow.

Waveguide.—Development of a new method for wide-band transmission took place in the 1960s and 1970s. In waveguide systems a circular metal tube is employed. A tube of 5 cm diameter will act as a transmitting medium for a tremendously wide range of frequencies from roughly 30 to 100 GHz. This provides the potential for a massive communication link which could carry 600,000 communication channels.

TE01 Mode.—If a particular mode of propagation is employed, the TE01 mode, then attenuation over the guide tends to fall with increase in frequency and in the frequency band which has been mentioned (30–100 GHz) the loss is less than 3 decibels per kilometre. Regenerators would be required at about 20 km spacing to maintain signal strength. The TE01 Mode is but one of a number of possible transmitting modes. The TE family of modes are meridional rays and the equation defining them is complex. The TE01 mode is utilised as the transmission mode for mono-mode fibre.

Such a system as this would only be suitable for very dense traffic routes.

One of the problems with waveguide systems if that the tube can only deviate marginally from a straight line. The advent of the motorway network in Britain appeared to be a suitable opportunity to lay the duct for a waveguide network and provision was made of duct-lines in some of the motorways constructed in the 1970s. Outline planning was also undertaken to lay such systems on some spinal trunk routes in Britain.

Before any systems could be provided, however, work on development of fibre-optic systems indicated their greater potential and flexibility, and further work on waveguide systems was discontinued.

Fibre-optic systems.—There is little doubt that telecommunications is entering a new era in both transmission and switching systems. British Telecom, in the early 1980s, had virtually ceased placing contracts for copper trunk and junction cables of any type and were installing, in their place, both junction and trunk fibre optic cables.

Research in fibre optics had continued at a great pace during the 1970s and had reached the point where optic cable was being manufactured with no greater attenuation than its copper equivalent.

The advantages of the new transmission medium are:—

(1) total freedom from electrical/magnetic interference.
(2) Wide potential bandwidth.
(3) Cost now reducing below equivalent copper cable.
(4) Much greater intermediate repeater spacing. A spacing of 30 km or more is envisaged compared with less than 2 km for intermediate buried repeaters on small bore coaxial systems.
(5) Works at much lower signal/noise ratio when employed in ditial working.

Two different sorts of fibre have developed. Multi-mode working is employed over a fibre which is about 50 micro-metres in diameter and which has a stepped index glass core. The fibre has a glass cladding (Fig. 30).

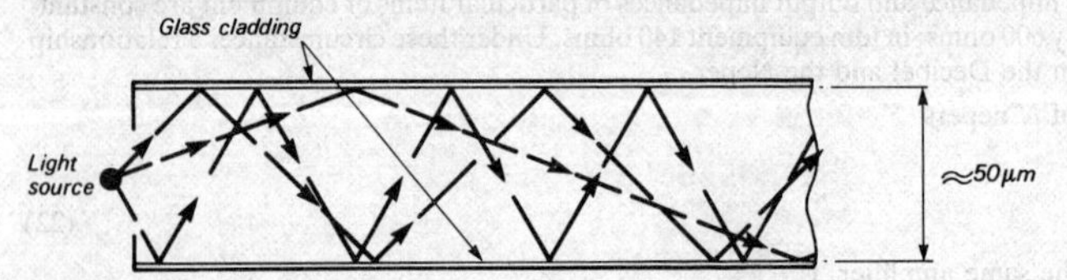

FIG. 30.—Multi-mode Fibre.

Mono-mode transmission employs a much smaller diameter fibre in the order of 2 to 10 micro-metres diameter. The fibre has a thicker glass cladding (Fig. 31), and the glass fibre is 'doped' with germanium to improve its transmission characteristics.

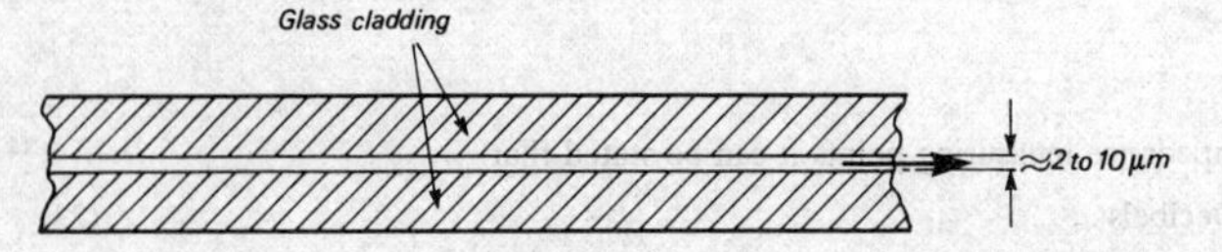

FIG. 31.—Mono-mode Fibre.

A characteristic which affects fibre-optic systems is dispersion. This causes different light frequencies to be transmitted at different group velocities. If very broadband signals are to be transmitted then this factor is bound to have an ill-effect, distorting the signal wave-form. Fibre design can limit the effect.

The quantity and type of doping employed will determine the refractive index of the media and affect the mode paths in the fibre. The spreading of pulses is affected by the dispersion factor and spreading tends to increase with distance. The bandwidth which can be utilised is therefore dependent upon system lengths.

A fibre system requires a light creating source at the transmitter and light sensitive detectors at the receiver. Many options have been tried but at the present time the normal sources at the transmitter are either gallium arsenide (GaAs) light emitting diodes (LEDs) or injection lasers. The LEDs should produce a power output range of 0.1 to 10 m Watts whilst the injection laser should produce an output range of 1.0 to 100 m Watts. The injection laser has been found to be more suitable for longer distance circuits of up to about 60 km when used for digital working. The LEDs for their part, tend to be used for short distance junction traffic of up to about 10 km, again when used for digital working. If an analogue link is required then because of the much higher signal to noise ratio necessary, the junction route distance would be greatly reduced.

The receiver detection is carried out by means of photo diodes and, at present, two types in the main will be found to be used. These are the avalanche diode and the p.i.n. diode. The avalanche diode needs a high voltage to operate in the avalanche mode. The p.i.n. diode, which receives its name from its construction of a lightly doped p or n layer (called the i layer) which is sandwiched between more heavily doped layers of p or n type materials. Silicon and germanium are other materials which are being developed for receiver detection purposes.

The Manufacture of Optical Fibres.—Certain essential conditions must be satisfied in optical fibre manufacture. The dielectric material used in the core must have a higher refractive index than the surrounding sheath to satisfy the need to create a guiding structure and the dielectric materials must have a low loss (less than 10 db/km) in the infrared region of the optical spectrum to utilise economical semi-conductor light sources.

Fabricated high silica glass preforms are manufactured by a variety of vapour phase processes. The preform itself is composed of a high index core with a surrounding cladding. Two processes are employed in their manufacture, *inside* or *outside* deposition. In the first method, deposition occurs on the inside surface of a fused silica tube. In the second method the materials are deposited on what is termed a *bait rod.*

The modified chemical deposition process was developed in Bell Laboratories and is an inside deposition method in which layers of doped silica are deposited on the inside of a silica tube. Intense heat is then applied to shrink these layers into a rod which becomes the preform to be drawn into a fibre.

Corning Glass Works, for their part, have developed a lateral deposition method in which glass soot is deposited on a bait rod. When the deposition is completed, the porous preform is slipped off the bait rod. Large preforms are formed in this way which can create in excess of 10 km of fibre.

A third and different method has been developed in Japan by Nippon Telephone and Telegraph Corporation, known as the Vapour-phase Axial Deposition process (VAD) which involves the simultaneous flame deposition of both core and cladding glass soots onto a rotating bait rod. This is drawn through a carbon heater where it becomes a transparent glass preform.

Manufacture of Multi-component Glass Fibres.—These are fabricated by first producing separate glass feed rods from purified glass melts of the core and cladding. These rods can then be used as feed stock in a double crucible drawing apparatus from which the composite fibre is drawn. The feed rods are produced by commencing with purified powders which are premixed and then heated in a crucible until they fuse. Then the feed rod is formed by dipping a seed rod into the molten glass and pulling it through a cooling ring. Graded index fibres can be drawn from the feed rods by utilising a double crucible.

DIGITAL WORKING—PCM (PULSE CODE MODULATION)

A form of digital working has been in use for many years in telegraphy. Here a square or rectangular waveform is transmitted and the line is in a state of either current/no current or positive/negative. The waveform is corrupted or distorted by the line characteristics so that the original signal has to be re-created at the receiver. Letters and numbers are turned into a code.

The Morse code represents each letter of the alphabet by a sequence of 'dots' and 'dashes', where the 'dash' is three times the length of the 'dot' (Fig. 32).

The system is essentially intended for manual operation.

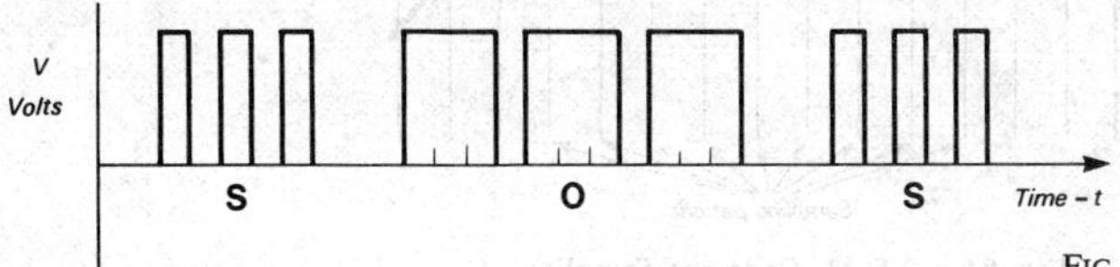

FIG. 32.—The Morse Code.

An alternative system is the Murray code which is utilised in teleprinter/telegraph working. In this system each letter in the alphabet is represented by a five unit code and the units can either be a positive voltage or negative voltage connected to line. A mark is a negative potential or connection of a tone whilst a space is a positive potential or no tone (Fig. 33).

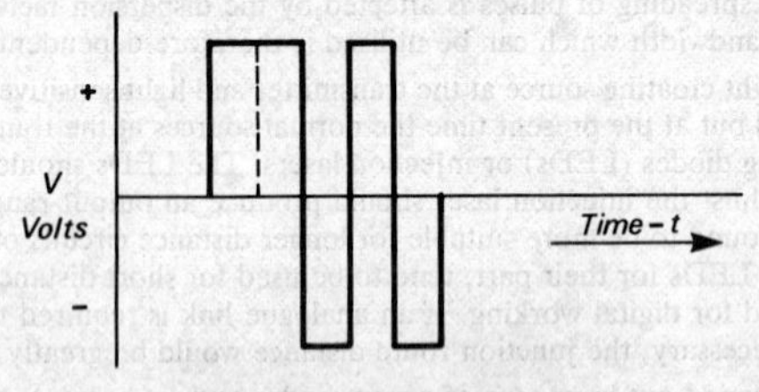

FIG. 33.—The Murray Code.

The speed at which the system is operating is measured in BAUD where it is defined as the reciprocal of the duration of time occupied by the shortest signal unit. The Murray code is used in teleprinter working and if the speed of a particular machine is 80 band then each individual unit will occupy 1/80 second or 0.012 seconds. The channel bandwidth which is required to carry such telegraph line is of the order of 40 Hz.

The great advantage in digital working, as opposed to analogue working, is that a much lower signal to noise ratio is possible for digital working. Digital systems therefore tend to be immune to interference.

Noise producing sources, such as line amplifiers, tend to have an output of noise which is directly proportional to bandwidth. The wider the bandwidth employed, the greater the problems which are encountered in the signal to noise ratio.

Advantage was seen, in the 1930s, in the development of a system which would convert analogue speech circuits into coded pulsed signals. Immediately telephone, telegraph and data circuits could be routed over the same sort of links which would be much more immune to a poor signal to noise ratio. The original work was done by A. H. Reeves of Standard Telephones and Cables Laboratories but failed to be brought into operational system use because fast speed devices which are essential to such a system, had not then been designed. The term Pulse Code Modulation (PCM) was given to such systems.

The arrival of inexpensive transistors in the 1960s provided the means for effective, economic development of PCM and many systems are now in use. Indeed the 30 channel system has become the 'building block' for modern digital telephone exchange systems.

The concept behind PCM is to sample an audio telephony channel, which operates in the frequency range of 300 to 3400 Hz at the rate of 8 kHz. The samples have then to be converted into digital form in two stages. In the first stage each sample is given a particular value from a set number of values. The second stage is the coding of this information about values (Fig. 34).

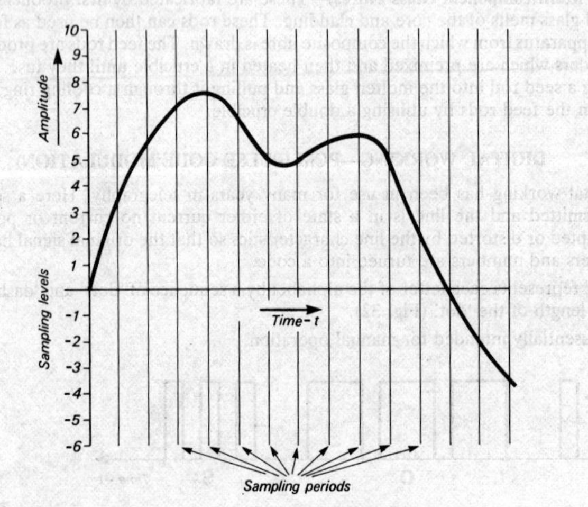

FIG. 34.—P.C.M. Code and Sampling.

A significant increase in channel carrying capacity can then be achieved by utilising Time Division Multiplex. A simple block schematic of a TDM system which could be applicable to PCM system is shown in Fig. 35.

Providing that the sample rate in such a system is right, and can be determined to be at least $2xf$, where x is the number of channels and f is the maximum frequency present on each channel, then the original analogue signal can be recreated at the receiver. Since, in the case of PCM, the traffic carried is in digital form and the binary digits can be timed to be midsampled, then the line speed can be calculated to be x (channels) multiplied by the speed of each channel.

From the basic block schematic (Fig. 35) it can be seen that synchronisation is essential as between sender and receiver to ensure that both ends are stepped into the same channel at the same time.

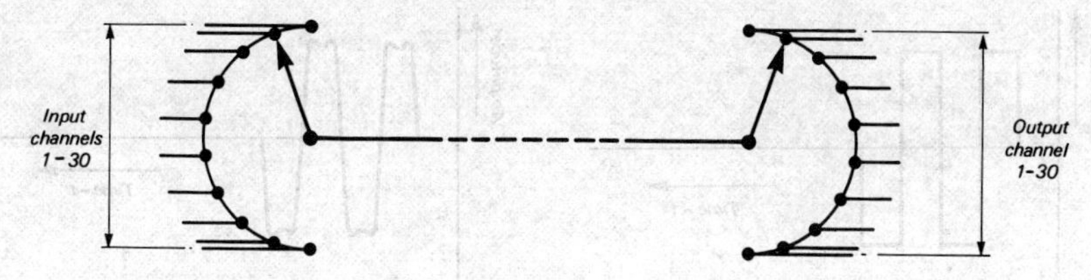

FIG. 35.—Basic Block Schematic.

The name TDM was given to the system from the fact that the signal amplitude was being constantly sampled and the information so gained turned into digital form.

Distortion.—The characteristics of a communications transmission line are such that a non-linear response is present when a signal is sent.

The signal will firstly change in phase because it moves at a finite speed (3×10^8 m/s) and so the receive voltage or current vector will have moved on from that of the send voltage or current vector. The phase change coefficient is defined as the change β (measured in radians) which occurs over one metre of line.

Now β is a variable which increases with frequency and so greater phase change is experienced at higher frequencies (Fig. 36).

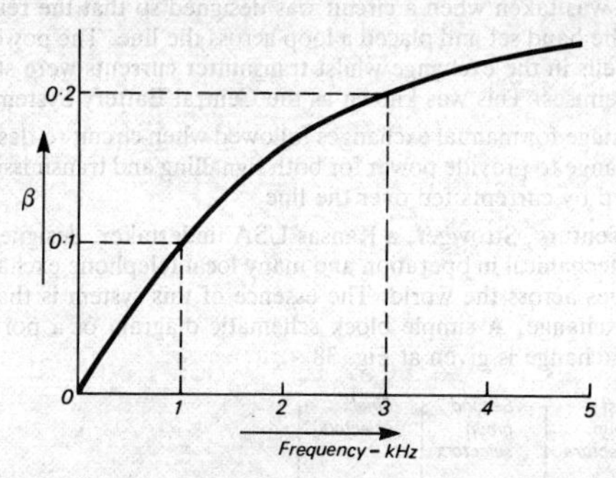

FIG. 36.—Phase change Response for an Audio Cable Pair.

But the phase velocity of transmission over the line is represented by ω/β (where $\omega = 2\pi f$).

So for higher frequencies the displacement may be less than for lower frequencies. Taking an example:

Two signals, one at 1 kHz the other at 3 kHz are applied to an audio cable pair.

$$\text{Phase velocity of 1 kHz} = \omega/\beta = \frac{2\pi + 10^3}{0.08 \times 10^{-3}}$$

$$= 78.5 \times 10^6 \text{ milliseconds—(1)}$$

$$\text{Phase velocity of 3 kHz} = \omega/\beta = \frac{2\pi \times 3 \times 10^3}{0.17 \times 10^{-3}}$$

$$= 110.8 \times 10 \text{ milliseconds—(2)}$$

But this is for sinusoidal (single frequency) signals. When a complex waveform is transmitted, as is the case in human speech, then *group delay* can take place.

'Group delay' is defined as the product of the length of the line and the reciprocal of its group velocity.

$$\text{Where Group velocity} = \frac{2\pi f_2 - 2\pi f_1}{\beta_2 - \beta_1} \qquad (24)$$

where f_1 and f_2 is the range of transmitted frequencies.

Now a square digital unit or waveform can be analysed (by Fouriers Theorem) into an infinite number of frequencies or harmonies. When it is passed over a line pair then distortion can occur. The original signal (Fig. 37(a)) can be distorted into the signal at the receive end (Fig. 37(b)).

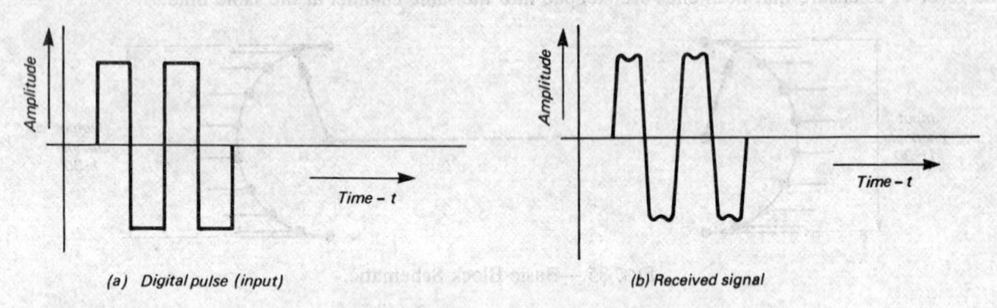

FIG. 37.—Waveform Distortion in Transmission.

Received signal.—More severe distortion could result in loss of ability of the repeater or receiver to re-construct the correct signal.

TELECOMMUNICATIONS SWITCHING SYSTEMS

Development.—The first, faltering steps, were taken in telephone switching in the late 1800s. The exchange operator was called by turning a hand generator. This energised a relay and indicator in the exchange. Power for the transmitter was provided by a local battery installed at the customer's premises.

The next move forward was taken when a circuit was designed so that the relay in the exchange operated when the customer lifted the hand set and placed a loop across the line. The power required for signalling was provided by a battery of cells in the exchange whilst transmitter currents were still provided by primary cells fitted in the customer's premises. This was known as the Central Battery System (CBS).

A further development stage for manual exchanges followed when circuit re-design made it possible to locate secondary cells in the exchange to provide power for both signalling and transmission purposes. The customer's transmitters were energised by currents fed over the line.

At the end of the 19th century, Strowger, a Kansas USA undertaker, designed the first automatic system. This was, and is, electro-mechanical in operation and many local telephone exchanges are still working on this principle in many exchanges across the world. The essence of this system is that the calling line sets up the connection through the exchange. A simple block schematic diagram of a portion of a basic Strowger ten thousand line automatic exchange is given at Fig. 38.

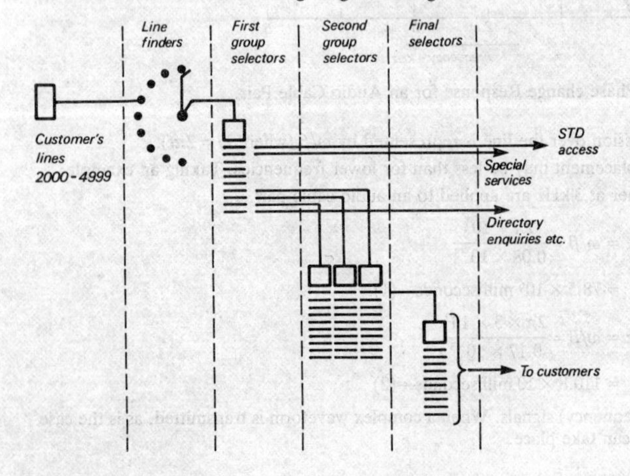

FIG. 38.—Part of Trunking Diagram for a 10,000 Line Exchange.

Operation of Strowger System.—The customer, in lifting the receiver, places a calling loop across the line. This will start the line-finder hunting for it. In the block schematic diagram, a uniselector is shown as fulfilling that function, as would be the case for business lines with a high calling rate. Two motion selectors normally fulfil that function for residential customers since the expected peak traffic is much lower.

Having seized a line-finder, dial tone is returned and the customer commences to send dialled impulses into the exchange equipment. The first digits will step the First group selector vertically and having reached, say, level 4, the wipers will cut into the bank searching for a disengaged outlet to level 4 second group selectors. The next digits will pulse the seized second group selector vertically and having reached, say, level eight will cut in looking for a spare outlet to a spare final selector serving 4800 to 4899.

The final selector has to be pulsed both vertically and horizontally, so the third lot of digits will cause vertical stepping, say 8. Then the final digits will cause the wipers to cut into the bank to the required number, say 6. So customer 4886 will be connected, if disengaged and ringing current extended to the line.

Metering of the calling customer's meter takes place when the called customer lifts his receiver.

This quite simple, basic local automatic exchange has been extended by the design and installation of 200 outlet two motion selectors.

The connections through the switching units are three wires. Two wires carry the transmission path whilst the third wire, called the private, carries the guard signal when the trunk or line concerned has been taken into use.

A more complex version of Strowger exchanges can be found in the multi-exchange areas of big cities like London. The network and dialling codes which would be necessary to permit inter-exchange dialling between the many exchanges led to the design and introduction of coders or registers in the 1930s. These coders take the simple code dialled to route the call and convert them to the complex of digits which are required to route the call. The coders or registers are based on relay sets with a series of relays, as were the early installations of registers in the STD trunk exchanges.

The 1960s in Britain saw the trunk network converted from manual working to automatic just as, earlier, the local exchanges had been converted from manual to automatic.

FIG. 39.—Two motion Strowger Switches.

Subscriber Trunk Dialling (STD) received its first installation in Bristol in the early 1960s and was quickly installed in other major centres. The inland STD network is now complete so that any customer or any exchange in Britain can set up their own call to any other customer or any exchange in Britain.

The principle on which STD is structured is that, if exchange X is required then the same code will be dialled to reach it over the trunk network independent of where the originating exchange may be. This means that, invariably, the code dialled has to be translated in the sending STD trunk exchange into the digits which are necessary to route the call to its destination. The call may well have to be set up through several switching centres and thus could well involve the translation of the dialled digits into a string of digits to carry out the necessary switching sequences.

The 1960s also witnessed a brave attempt to make a great leap forward in local exchange design in the, then, British Post Office. Design work developed to the field trial stage of a common control exchange which, in the absence of transistors at that stage was based upon diodes. The switching was space divided, a term applied to switch points which are separated in space.

Compromise technology exchanges were developed to fill the gap in Britain, but their design and technology lagged on that of other countries and this became one of the significant reasons as to why Britain lost most of its overseas markets in telecommunications equipment. The two types developed and brought into service were Crossbar (which were first seen in the 1930s) and Reed Relay exchanges.

The Crossbar design known as TXK1 was intended and used in non-director exchange areas whilst the design known as TXK3 was introduced for deployment in director exchange areas. The Crossbar system is essentially mechanical with a mechanical matrix operated by electro-magnets (Fig. 40).

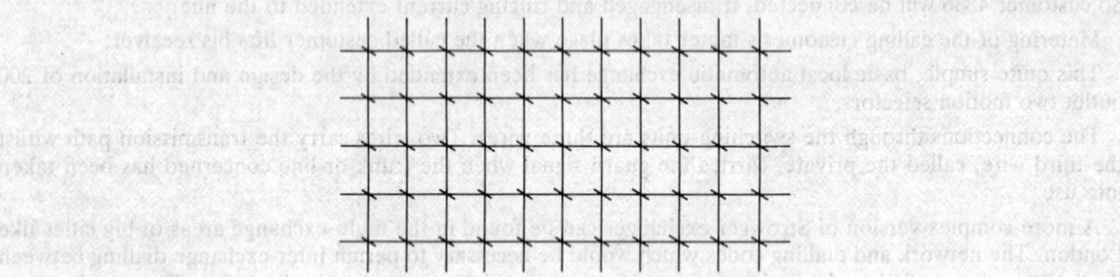

FIG. 40.—Schematic of Crossbar Switch.

It is a space divided switch and these are arranged in cascade to limit the size of the switching array. This can be done because all incoming links to a switch are not going to be in use at the same time and so, in Fig. 40, five outlets are serving the inlets. Under operational conditions, particularly in a residential district, ten outlets could well provide an effective grade of service for one hundred lines.

The Reed relay exchanges TXE2, 4 and 4A in British Telecom employ a hard wired memory for information about customer status. The technology of the common control equipment has been enhanced in the TXE4A exchanges. The space divided switching matrices are cascaded to limit switch size and the switch points are reed relays (Figs. 41 and 42).

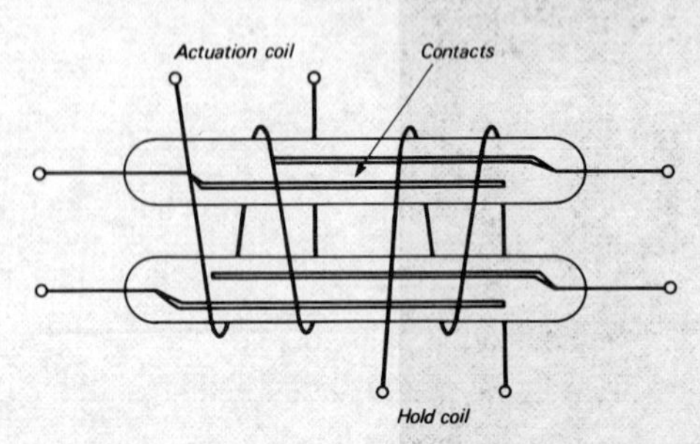

FIG. 41.—Reed Relay.

FIG. 42.—Reed switches and Set of Mounted Reed Switches.

In these exchanges, when the customer places a calling loop across the line, by lifting the receiver, the line unit in the exchange (see Fig. 8.4) sends a 'set up connection' signal to the exchange control unit. This is a programmable computer of increased complexity in the 4A design. The control sets up a path through the exchange and checks it before offering it to the calling customer. The reed relay has gold plated contacts and the contacts close and make contact when an energizing current passes through the activation coil.

All of the exchanges so far described have space division switching and are intended for analogue traffic. The vast majority of exchanges in the world are space divided switching units.

Radically new designs are, however, now emerging. The Bell ESS No. 4 switch in the USA and System X in Britain are but two examples of exchanges in which the concept of time division switching is used.

Time-division switching.—The great advantages of this concept are

(*a*) The exchange can switch all types of traffic whether it be speech or data.

(*b*) It fits in with developments in the transmission field where fibre optic cables offer a very wide band width of digital links.

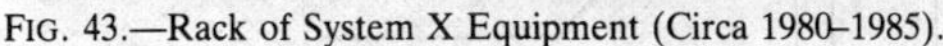

FIG. 43.—Rack of System X Equipment (Circa 1980–1985).

FIG. 44.—Card taken from System X Rack.

(*c*) It enhances the concept of the integrated services digital network.
(*d*) It significantly reduces maintenance costs.

The principle of the sharing of time in a time switch is similar to that which is used in the technology of PCM (Pulse Code Modulated) systems. Two synchronised switches are connected to a unit called a time slot interchanger which delays the PCM coded digits on the input until they are in synchronisation with the PCM output (Fig. 46). The switches are electronic in operation and design.

For large public exchanges a cascade of switches is necessary. These are a combination of time and space

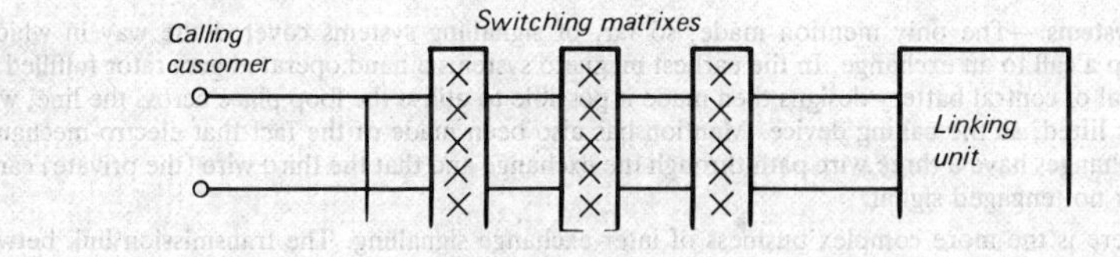

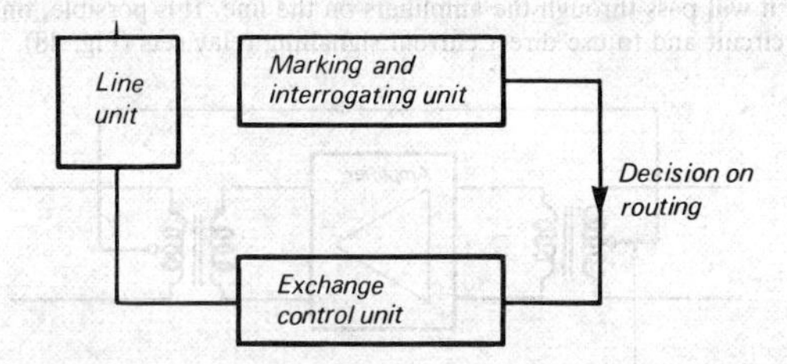

FIG. 45.—Block Schematic of Reed Relay Exchange.

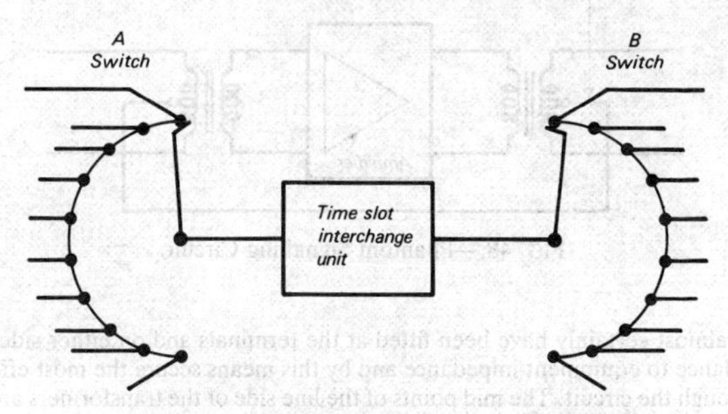

FIG. 46.—Time Division Switching Concept.

division. Different designs in different countries use a combination of these but Time/Space/Time is a fairly usual combination (Fig. 47).

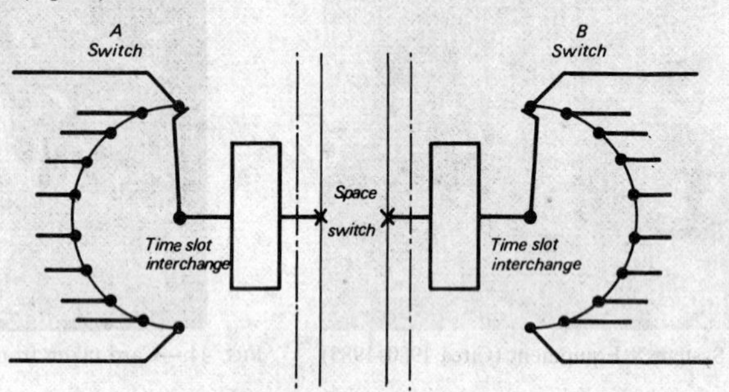

FIG. 47.—Time/Space/Time Switching Concept.

It is possible to cut a new electronic Space/Time/Space exchange into an existing analogue network by converting incoming analogue routes to PCM routes before connecting them to the exchange. This is obviously a great advantage when one bears in mind the quantity of analogue equipment which must continue to give service for a number of years. Data links can also be tied into the new exchange through an interface unit.

SIGNALLING SYSTEMS AND BRITISH TELECOM TRANSMISSION PLAN

Signalling systems.—The only mention made, so far, of signalling systems covered the way in which a customer set up a call to an exchange. In the earliest magneto systems a hand operated generator fulfilled this role. The arrival of central battery designs then made it possible to utilise the loop place across the line, when the hand set is lifted, as the calling device. Mention has also been made of the fact that electro-mechanical (Strowger) exchanges have a three wire path through the exchange and that the third wire (the private) carries the engaged or not engaged signal.

But then there is the more complex business of inter exchange signalling. The transmission link between exchanges (unless the distance is short and the circuit not amplified) will not normally carry direct current and so the direct current has to be put into an interface unit which will convert the signal to alternating current at such a frequency that it will pass through the amplifiers on the line. It is possible, on 4 wire circuits, to make use of the 'phantom' circuit and to use direct current signalling relay sets (Fig. 48).

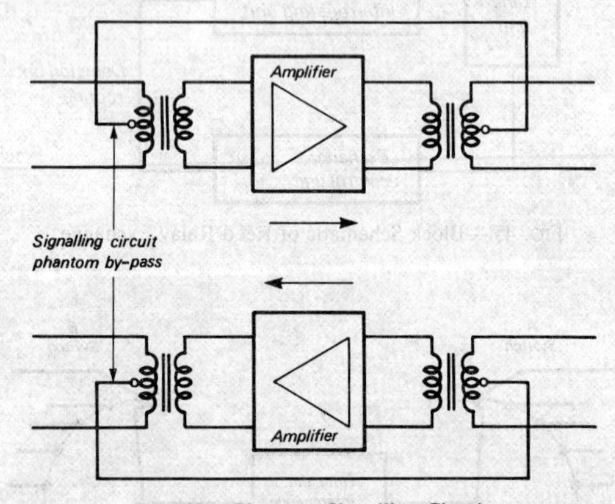

FIG. 48.—Phantom Signalling Circuit.

Transformers will almost certainly have been fitted at the terminals and on either side of line amplifiers to match the line impedance to equipment impedance and by this means secure the most effective and maximum transfer of power through the circuit. The mid points of the line side of the transformers are connected together as shown in Fig. 48.

The systems which have commonly been in use in British Telecom are DC2, which uses battery pulses over the signalling phantom; AC9, which converts loop disconnect pulses to a single frequency tone pulse and AC11, which converts into multi-tones.

Setting up call information, dialled pulses to switch the call at the distant end and clear down call information, must be passed over analogue transmission links; this is normally carried out over the speech channel which has been selected for the call. To speed the passage of the signalling information several tones, at different frequencies, can be utilised. These would be interrupted to 'code in' the necessary information.

This method is wasteful of overall channel use and one of the further advantages of digital working is that it facilitates 'out of band' signalling. Even in the case of the local customer end high speed input of call data can be introduced by using digital tone signals instead of direct current impulses from dial or key-pad.

In 'out of band' working a data or digital link between main centres will carry the signalling information for all channels. Much expensive terminal equipment which is provided at present on a per circuit basis will be saved.

'British Telecom' Transmission Plan.—The telecommunications network now offers direct, and almost worldwide, connection of any customer to any customer. The network has been laid down with this in mind and if a satisfactory grade of service is to be given then customers must be able to speak and hear clearly. The attenuation suffered on a call must therefore, if possible, be held within close limits. With this in mind telephone administrations lay down standards for particular links in the network.

The local network from exchange to customer is planned so that the loss suffered over this part of the link should not be greater than 10 db. This is achieved by carefully planning the type and weight of conductor employed in the local cable network.

Junction circuits between local exchanges are planned so that the loss experienced over the junction circuit will not exceed 6 db. A call from one local customer, connected over a junction to a local customer on another exchange should not therefore experience a loss of greater than 26 db.

If the call has to pass over the STD trunk network it will firstly be routed to a primary trunk exchange. The primary exchange may well have a direct route to another primary trunk exchange when there is sufficient community of interest. An alternative route could be from the primary trunk centre through transit trunk centres. In these cases 4 wire zero loss switching is utilised at the transit trunk centres.

A loss of about 1 db will be experienced in each terminal end on local trunk circuits.

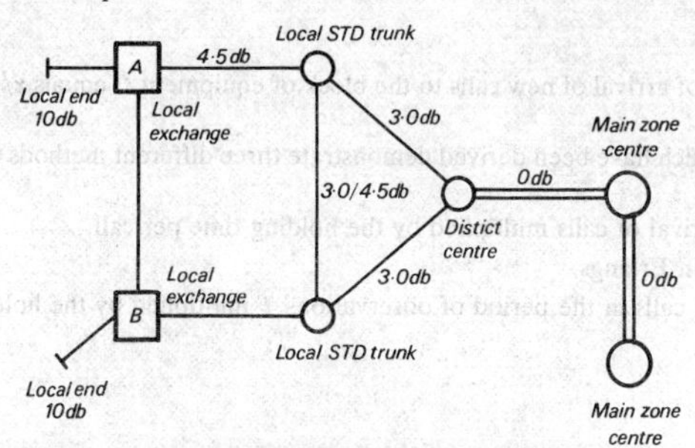

FIG. 49.—British Telecom Transmission Plan.

The greatest loss likely to be experienced on a call, providing that all circuits are working correctly, will be on a call routed local exchange—STD trunk exchange—District—distant STD trunk exchange—distant local exchange. From customer to customer, bearing in mind that there will be four two wire switching centres, with a loss in excess of 1 db in each, the total loss will amount to 39 db.

For STD coding purposes Britain is broken down into about 650 groups with about 10 exchanges in each group. These are served by over 350 local STD trunk exchanges which are called Group Switching Centres. Digitalisation will lead to a reduction in their numbers since economy of scale in the provision of common control equipment is achieved by combination of existing Group Centres. Their number in Britain is likely to be reduced to about 60. District and Main (Zone) Trunk exchanges in Britain are at present in Crossbar technology but will eventually be replaced by digital common control exchanges.

Backing up the great web of the trunk network is the Trunk Transit Network. Circuits in this supplementary network are 4 wire switched and are set up for zero overall loss.

TRAFFIC MEASUREMENT

Telecommunications switching and line plant is expensive and so care must be taken to ensure that, whilst adequate provision is made, plant and capital is not wasted. There are several key points in the network where a caller's wish to establish a link can be frustrated. Mention was made (Fig. 38) that uniselectors or 2 motion line-finders are utilised in Strowger local exchanges to identify a calling customer and to connect him to the switching plant. Now circuits out of line-finders may be, say, only 10 in number and so if more than 10 customers try and initiate calls at the same time then some will, at first attempt, receive no dial tone. Again, at sequential switching points, there will be a limit to the number of outlets provided so at particularly busy times some customers will fail to pick up a link, at least on the first occasion.

The grade of service being given to customers is therefore specified in terms of lost calls per hundred calls.

A careful watch is maintained by telecommunications authorities to ensure that the grade of service is maintained and this is done by connecting traffic recorders to monitor traffic at key points in the network.

If a block of equipment is found by traffic recorders to be carrying an average fifty calls over the period of review then this is termed by traffic engineers to be fifty Erlangs of traffic.

Now if during a period of T seconds when observations have been taken x calls have been made and if the duration of these calls is t_1 t_2 t_3 etc seconds then the total use made of that block of equipment is given by

$$\sum_{i=1}^{i=x} t_1$$

and the average amount of traffic being carried by the block of equipment for each time unit is given by

$$E = \frac{\sum_{i=1}^{i=x} t_1}{T} \text{ erlangs} \qquad (23)$$

From this can be deduced the average holding time for the equipment

$$\text{The average holding time } t = \frac{\sum_{i=x}^{i=x} t_1}{x} \text{ seconds} \ldots\ldots \qquad (24)$$

From (23) the average traffic E carried by the block of equipment over the period of time T is given by

$$\frac{xt}{T} \qquad (25)$$

Since the average rate of arrival of new calls to the block of equipment C equals x/T, E can be alternatively stated to equal Ct . . . . . (26)

The three equations which have been derived demonstrate three different methods of determining the traffic carried.

(26) $E = Ct$ or rate of arrival of calls multiplied by the holding time per call.

Where E is measured in Erlangs.

(25) $E = xt$ or number of calls in the period of observations T multiplied by the holding time per call.

(25)

$$E = \frac{\sum_{i=1}^{i=x} t_1}{T}$$

or the volume of traffic which is experienced during the period of observation T, divided by T.

THE INTEGRATED SERVICES DIGITAL NETWORK

It has been demonstrated that the great movement forward in the telecommunications industry is towards a digital network. The nature of the traffic which is carried is changing from solely speech analogue to a great variety of traffic with an increasingly significant content which is data.

Digital line systems, whether they be wideband coaxial cable or fibre optic, offer the great advantage of greater immunity to noise. Fibre optic cable, in particular, carries with it the great advantage of much greater regenerator spacing than the demand for intermediate repeaters in a coaxial system.

Digital exchanges will carry all forms of digital traffic amd will offer a better grade of service at much lower maintenance costs.

There is another new concept which demands to take its full place in the hierarchy of needs and that is Packet Switching. This is totally different from Message Switching which has been the normal way of operating a communications network. Packet Switching is applicable to data traffic where short delay between transmission and receipt of the block of information is not very material or significant. Storage facilities are available to hold part or all of the block of information when it is in transit. The information is given a coding tag to identify it and transmission takes place as and when a communication channel is available to it.

The concept of Cablevision brings with it the possibility that wideband cable, and this will be fibre-optic as system development takes place, will be in position in every street passing every door. The channel capacity which this will offer will greatly exceed the needs of the entertainment world and could be taken into use for wider communications purposes.

The arrival of the mini-computer and micro-processor also presents an opportunity of re-thinking the way in which telephone exchanges are provided. Instead of a copper pair to each customer in the local telephone network the sharing of a wideband facility under the control of remote micro-processors becomes a future possibility.

The network could develop to a number of configurations.

The Star System.—This system (Fig. 50) is being adopted by the most recent designs for cable vision. It must be borne in mind that customers are going to demand much more than the basic telephone in the near future.

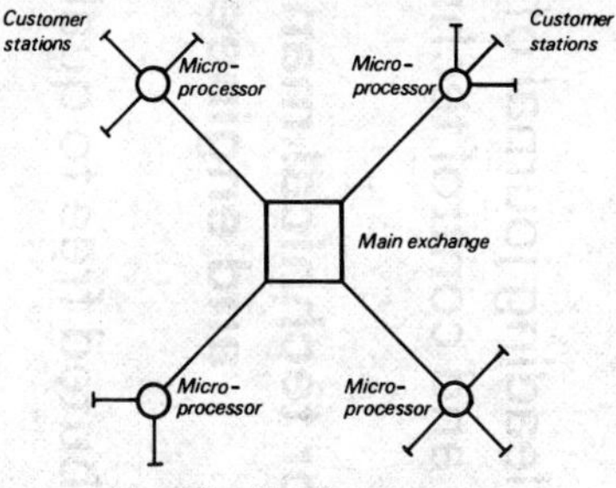

FIG. 50.—The Star System.

They will be looking for facilities to carry out home banking, home shopping and information interrogation to name but a few. The local micro-processor could act as a local switch selecting the sort of channel or facility that the customer is requesting.

The Ring System.—This system (Fig. 51) is akin to the ring main in an electrical system. In this case it is a very large capacity communication channel with local micro-processors connected across it to provide switching and other facilities to its local group of customers.

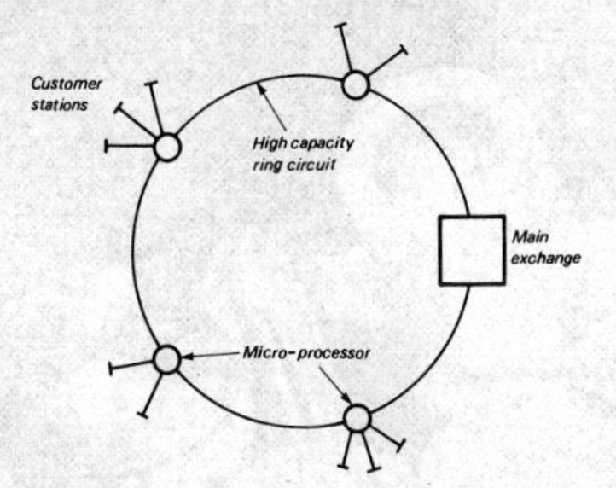

FIG. 51.—The Ring System.

BIBLIOGRAPHY

BALAKRISHNAN, A. V. *Advances in Communications Systems: Theory and Applications.*
ARMITAGE, M. D. *Basic Principles of Electronics and Telecommunications.*
CATTERMOLE, K. W. *Principles of Pulse Code Modulation Telecommunications Networks*, Peter Peregrinus Ltd. (for Institution of Electrical Engineers).
HAMER, M. P. and SMOL, G. (ed) *Telecommunications Systems.*
HILLS, M. T. and EVANS, B. J. *Telecommunications Systems Design.*
KARBOWIAK, A. *Trunk Waveguide Communications.*
MARSHALL, G. J. *Principles of Digital Communications.*
SCHWARZ, M. *Information Transmission, Modulation and Noise.*
CARLSON, A. B. *Communication Systems, and Introduction to Signals and Noise.*
WELCH, S. *Signalling in Telecommunications Networks.*
SMITH, S. F., *Telephony and Telegraphy, an Introduction to Instruments and Exchanges*, Proceedings of the Institution of British Telecom Engineers.

CONTROL SYSTEMS

Control—Differential Equation to Transfer Function—Second Order System—Closed Loop—Stability—System Specification, Performance and Compensation—Root Locus Technique—Laplace Transforms—Design Examples—Non-linear Elements—Sampled Data Systems—Modern Control Theory—References—Appendices.

By B. J. Cooper, BSc, CEng, FIEE, and I. Watts, MInst.MC

Automatic control systems form an ever increasing part of the modern engineering scene, whether it is the control of a domestic central heating system or the control of such complex engineering systems as high performance aircraft, nuclear reactors or prime movers, engines, turbines etc. There are very few aspects of modern engineering plant that do not in some way involve the use of the control sciences.

The history of control goes back many years, but perhaps the earliest form of control from which automatic control theory developed was the speed control of steam engines. The so-called 'hit and miss' speed governors were one of the first forms of modern speed control which now would be called an 'unstable' control system. It was Maxwell who first attempted to apply some theoretical foundation to the dynamics of 'hit and miss' governors. The section attempts to encapsulate the basic classical theory of control for the practical engineer who possesses some knowledge of differential equations.

THE CONCEPT OF A CLOSED CONTROL LOOP

One of the basic aspects of a controller is that it is either open or closed-loop. An example of an open-loop control system is the accelerator pedal on a car. This is used to demand a vehicle speed but the preciseness of the speed achieved depends upon adjustments by the driver. A closed-loop system is defined as an assembly of functional components designed to produce a specific output in response to an input, in which the control is determined by the difference between the demanded output and the actual output. This introduces the concept of negative feedback, where the control action is a function of the error between the output demanded and the actual output of the system. In the case of the motor vehicle (assuming an automatic gearbox) if the speed as demanded by the accelerator was subtracted from the actual vehicle speed, the engine, and hence the vehicle, would respond to the error between the two variables. If the system is sufficiently sensitive this error would be very small thus giving close control of speed.

MOTOR VEHICLE

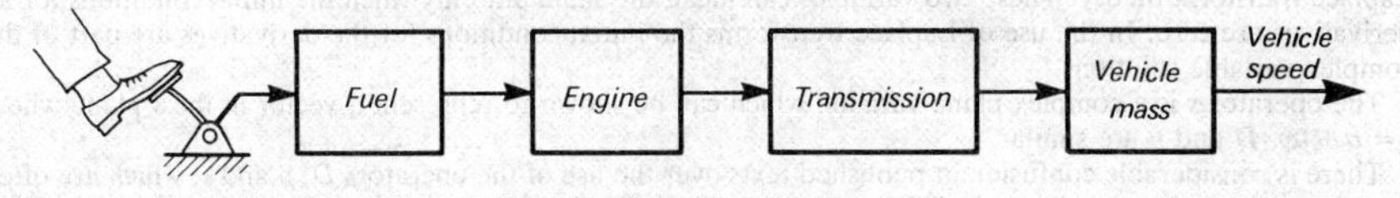

FIG. 1.—Open Loop Control.

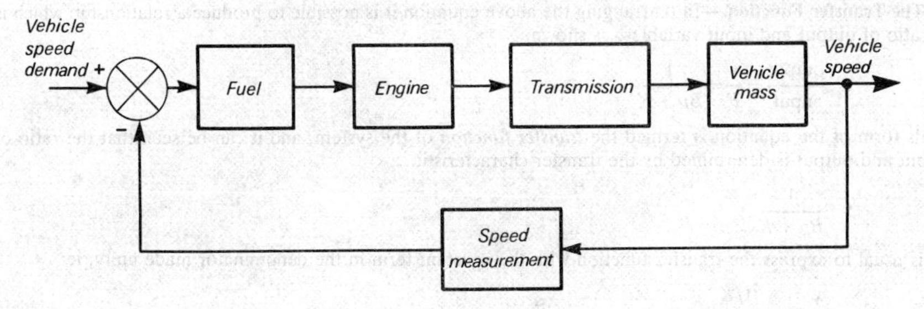

FIG. 2.—Closed Loop System.

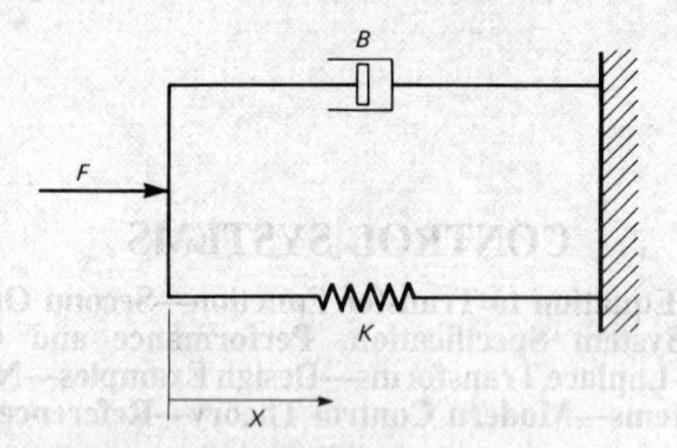

FIG. 3.—Parallel Spring and Damper System.

FROM DIFFERENTIAL EQUATION TO TRANSFER FUNCTION

Dependent and Independent Variables as Inputs and Outputs.—Looking at the equation of motion for a parallel spring and damper system as shown (Fig. 3)

where F = force (N), X = displacement (m), K = rate of spring (N/m), B = damper constant (Ns/m) the equation of motion is,

$$B\frac{dx}{dt} + Kx = F$$

or more correctly since all the variables are functions of time,

$$B\frac{dx(t)}{dt} + Kx(t) = F(t)$$

B and K are constant coefficients and $x(t)$ and $F(t)$ are the dependent and independent variables respectively. Since the disturbance $F(t)$ can be an arbitrary function of time, this is normally regarded as the input variable and $x(t)$ as the output variable. This is the differential equation of the system.

The D, p and s Operators.—Because the differential equation is linear with constant coefficients the principles of superposition and proportionality apply and therefore d/dt can be substituted by an operator p enabling differential equations to be manipulated as algebraic functions. The symbols D and s are also sometimes used.*

The spring damper mechanism equation above can therefore be represented in operator form as:

$$(Bp + K)x = F$$

* The difference between the operators p and s is that s has a specific meaning as the complex variable in Laplace transform theory. These two variables can mean the same but only when the initial conditions for all derivatives are zero. In the use of Laplace transforms the initial conditions for the derivatives are part of the complex variable solutions.

The operator s is a complex plane variable which can be shown to represent a vector in the s plane where $s = \sigma + j\omega$. D and p are similar.

There is considerable confusion in published texts over the use of the operators D, p and s, which are often used interchangeably despite their different mathematical significance. From a practical point of view in most control applications this does not cause problems—but the reader should be aware of the differences and examine the context in which they are used.

The Transfer Function.—In rearranging the above equation it is possible to produce a relationship which is a ratio of output and input variables, as shown.

$$\frac{\text{output}}{\text{input}} = \frac{x}{F} = \frac{1}{Bp + K}$$

This form of the equation is termed the *transfer function* of the system, and it can be seen that the ratio of input and output is determined by the transfer characteristic

$$\frac{1}{Bp + K}$$

It is usual to express the transfer function with the constant term in the denominator made unity, ie:

$$\frac{x}{F} = \frac{1/K}{(B/K)p + 1}$$

Under steady state conditions $p = 0$ and hence the transfer function becomes,

$$\frac{x}{F} = \frac{1}{K}$$

The term $1/K$ is defined as the *sensitivity* or *gain* of the system and the coefficient B/K in this form of transfer function has the dimension of time and is defined as the time constant of the system.

The general form of transfer function is:

$$\frac{\text{output}}{\text{input}} = \frac{C}{R} = \frac{G(b_m p^m + b_{m-1} p^{m-1} + \ldots + 1)}{a_n p^n + a_{n-1} p^{n-1} + \ldots + 1}$$

Since the denominator and numerator are polynomials in p they can be factorised. The steady state relationship between C and R is obtained when $p = 0$

ie. $$\frac{C}{R} = G$$

There are two forms of the factorial transfer function as follows,

$$\frac{C}{R} = \frac{G(1 + pT_q)(1 + pT_{q+1}) \ldots (1 + pT_m)}{(1 + pT_d)(1 + pT_{d+1}) \ldots (1 + pT_n)}$$

or, $$\frac{C}{R} = \frac{G \times T_q \times T_{q+1} \ldots \times T_m}{T_d \times T_{d+1} \ldots \times T_n} \cdot \frac{\left(p + \frac{1}{T_q}\right)\left(p + \frac{1}{T_{q+1}}\right) \ldots \left(p + \frac{1}{T_m}\right)}{\left(p + \frac{1}{T_d}\right)\left(p + \frac{1}{T_{d+1}}\right) \ldots \left(p + \frac{1}{T_n}\right)}$$

The use of either of these two forms depends upon the type of solution being attempted and their uses will become more evident as the text proceeds.

The Integrating Element.—If an element of control system has an output whose value increases linearly with time for a constant input then this element is defined as an integrator. Consider a system comprising a frictionless flywheel of inertia J driven by a torque τ.

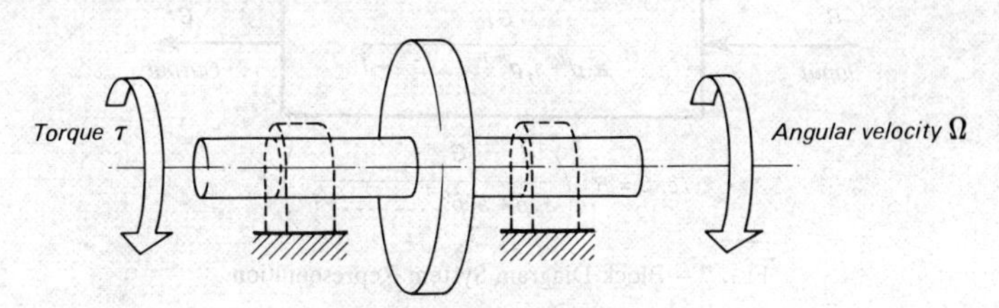

FIG. 4.—Flywheel in Frictionless Bearings.

The equation of motion is

$$\tau = J\frac{d\Omega}{dt} \quad \text{or using the } p \text{ operator } \tau = Jp\Omega$$

The transfer function

$$\frac{\Omega}{\tau} = \frac{1}{Jp}$$

Since

$$p = \frac{d}{dt} \qquad \frac{1}{p} = \int dt$$

ie. an integration w.r.t. time

A system as above is termed *an integrator*, ie for a constant input (τ) the output (Ω) increases linearly with time. The following are examples of integrating elements (Figs. 5 and 6)

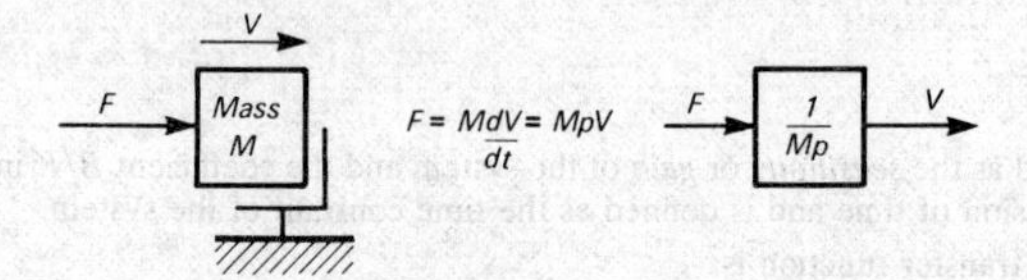

FIG. 5.—Integrating Element.

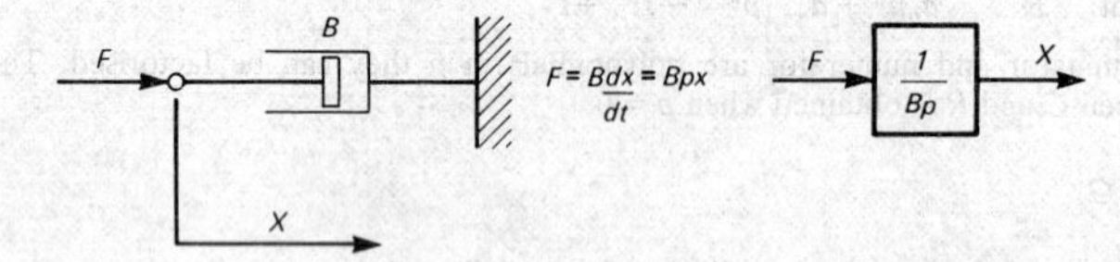

FIG. 6.—Integrating Element.

The Type and Order of a System.—*The order* of a control system is defined as the power of the highest derivative in the denominator of the expanded polynomial. *The type* of system is defined as number of integrators in the open-loop transfer function. The system represented by the following transfer function:

$$\frac{C}{R} = \frac{G}{p^n(a_0p^m + a_1p^{m-1} + a_2p^{m-2} + \ldots + 1)}$$

is of order m and type n.

The Block Diagram System Representation.—It is evident from the description of a transfer function that the transfer characteristic can be regarded as a multiplier of the input variable and can be depicted in block diagram form thus:

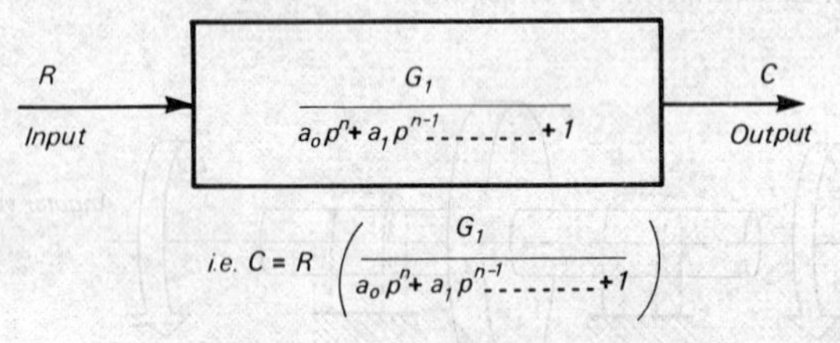

FIG. 7.—Block Diagram System Representation.

This representation is a useful technique for the intuitive understanding of a system. The variables shown entering the block can be regarded as being operated on by the transfer function in the block, the output variable being the result of this operation.

The Response of a System.—One of the fundamental characteristics of a control system is its response to a time-varying input signal.

There are three forms of input that are normally used to characterise a system:

(1) *Sinusoidal Inputs.* Constant amplitude sinusoidal signals over a range of frequencies.

(2) *Transient Inputs.* Consisting of a single disturbance which may be a step function, a single impulse, or a ramp function.

(3) *Random Inputs.* A signal whose amplitude and frequency vary in a statistically defined random manner. This type of input is termed stochastic and will not be covered in this text.

Mathematically the response of a system is the solution of the characteristic differential equation with the appropriate input function.

As an illustration let us consider the simple spring-damper system (Fig. 3) and determine its response to various inputs.

$$x(t) = \frac{G}{1 + pT} f(t)$$

where $G = 1/K$ and $T = B/K$

Step Input.—For a step input $f(t) = 1$, giving as the solution

$$x(t) = G(1 + \exp.(-t/T))$$

which may be represented graphically as shown in Fig. 8.

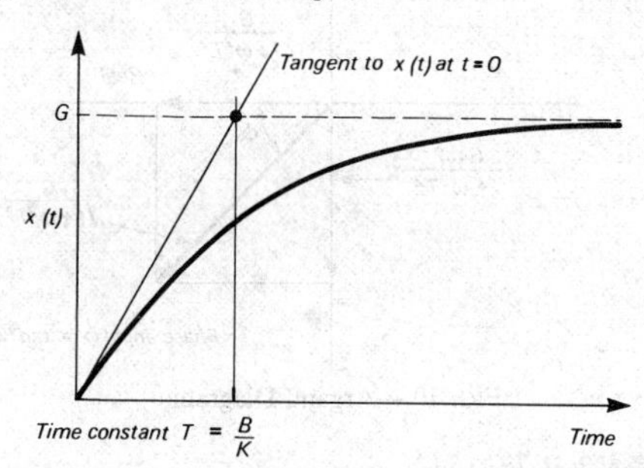

FIG. 8.—Graphical Representation of Step Input to Spring–damper System.

Sinusoidal Inputs.—For a sinusoidal signal $f(t) = A \sin \omega t$, where ω is the radian frequency

$$\therefore \frac{df(t)}{dt} = pf(t) = \omega A \cos \omega t$$
$$= \omega A \sin(\omega t + 90°)$$
$$= j\omega A \sin \omega t$$

Since the effect of the operator j is to move the vector through 90°

$$pf(t) = j\omega f(t)$$

hence $p = j\omega$.

Thus, for a sinusoidal input, the operator p may be replaced by $j\omega$.

Thus putting $p = j\omega$ in the Transfer Function the response to sinusoidal inputs may be determined.

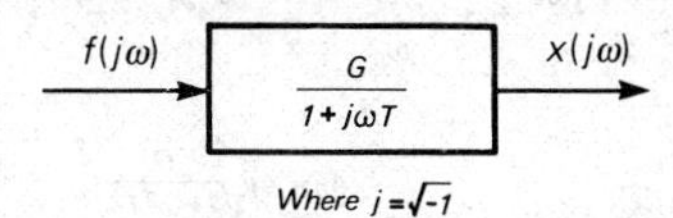

FIG. 9.—Block Representation–Sinusoidal Input.

Since the system is linear, for a sinusoidal input of amplitude A_i the output will be a sinusoid of amplitude A_0 phase shifted by an angle ϕ relative to the input.

$$\frac{x}{f}(j\omega) = \frac{G}{1 + j\omega T} = \frac{G(1 - j\omega T)}{1 + \omega^2 T^2}$$

$$= \frac{G}{1 + \omega^2 T^2} - j\frac{G\omega T}{1 + \omega^2 T^2}$$

Real Part Imaginary Part

This may be represented on an Argand Diagram (Fig. 10.)

Thus if $f(j\omega) = A_0 \sin \omega t$

$$x(j\omega) = \frac{A_0 G \sin(\omega t - \phi)}{\sqrt{(1 + \omega^2 T^2)}}$$

Both the gain

$$\frac{G}{\sqrt{(1 + \omega^2 T^2)}}$$

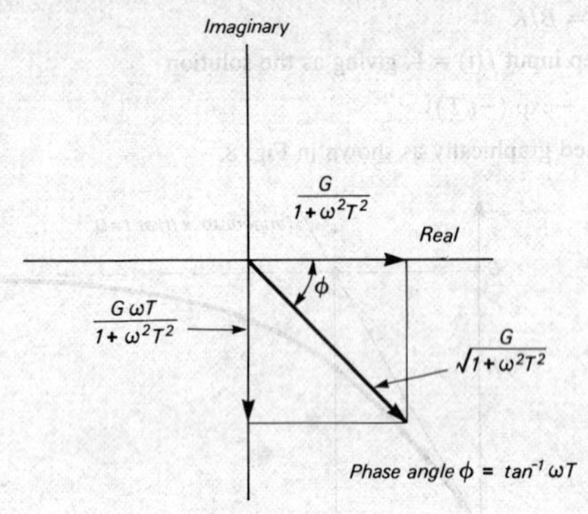

FIG. 10.—Argand Diagram.

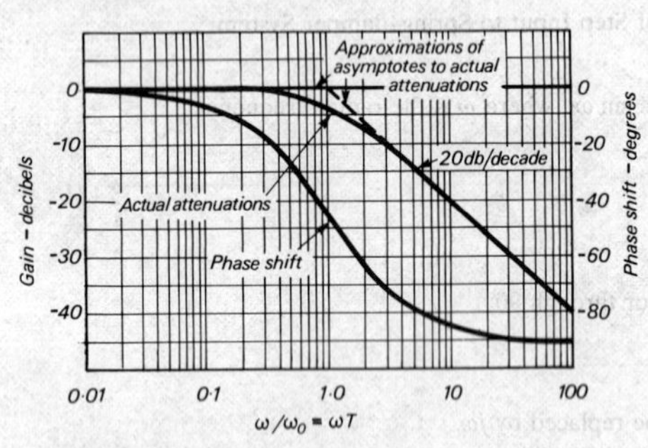

FIG. 11—Non-dimensional Plot of $\dfrac{1}{1+j\omega T} = \dfrac{1}{1+\dfrac{j\omega}{\omega_0}}$ $T = \dfrac{1}{\omega_0}$.

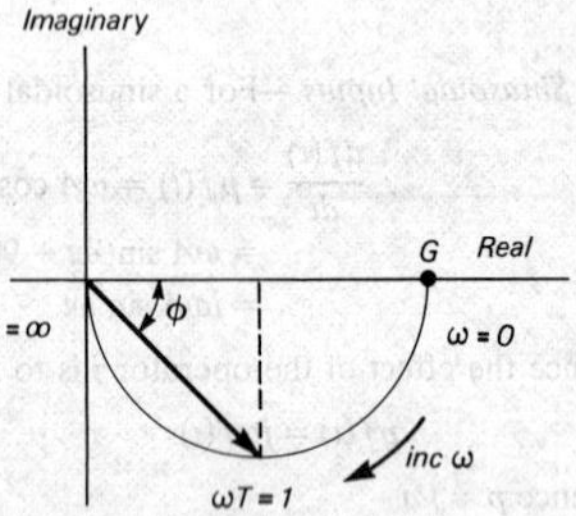

FIG. 12.—Polar Diagram Representation of Gain and Phase.

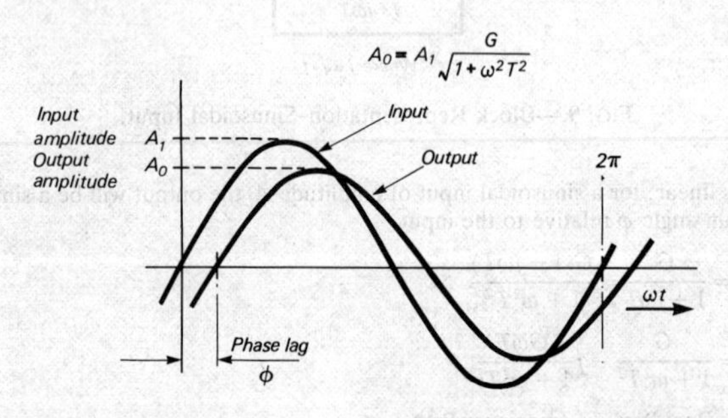

FIG. 13.—Time Response of $\dfrac{G}{1+j\omega T}$ to a Sine Wave Input $A_1 \sin \omega t$.

and phase angle ϕ ($\tan^{-1} \omega T$) vary with frequency and may be represented graphically on a BODE DIAGRAM: (see page H5/15)

In an alternative representation Gain and Phase may be combined to give a polar diagram: Fig. 12 is a form of Argand diagram showing the locus of the gain vector G with varying frequency ω. The variation of input and output with time at any frequency ω is shown in Fig. 13.

THE SECOND ORDER SYSTEM

Second Order Mechanical System.—Before proceeding with the analysis of closed loop systems it is informative to discuss a second order system, since this embodies a number of important aspects of control system theory.

The following mechanical system will be used as an example.

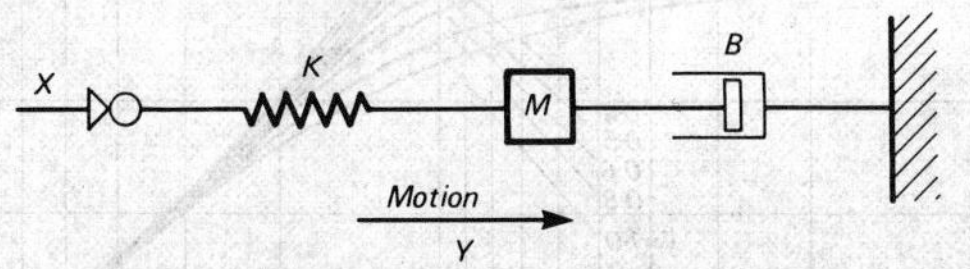

FIG. 14.—Spring–Mass–Damper System.

The transfer function of this system is

$$\frac{y}{x}(t) = \frac{K}{Mp^2 + Bp + K}$$

dividing by K

$$\frac{y}{x}(t) = \frac{1}{\frac{M}{K}p^2 + \frac{B}{K}p + 1}$$

This may be written as

$$\frac{y}{x}(t) = \frac{1}{\frac{p^2}{\omega_0^2} + \frac{2\zeta p}{\omega_0} + 1}$$

where $\omega_0 = \sqrt{\frac{K}{M}}$, $\quad \frac{2\zeta}{\omega_0} = \frac{B}{K}$,

The coefficient of p is $2\zeta/\omega_0$ where ζ is termed the damping factor, and ω_0 is the undamped natural frequency. ie the frequency at which the system will resonate when the damping factor is zero. At other damping factors the resonant frequency is given by,

$$\omega = \omega_0\sqrt{1 - \zeta^2}$$

The original equation can be seen to be quadratic equation in p. The roots of which are the values of p which make the denominator zero.

$$p = \frac{-2\zeta}{\omega_0} \pm \sqrt{\frac{4\zeta^2}{\omega_0^2} - \frac{4}{\omega_0^2}}$$

$\therefore$ if $\zeta < 1$ the roots are complex (oscillatory)

if $\zeta > 1$ the roots are real (over damped)

if $\zeta = 1$ the roots are real and equal (critical damping)

The step response of a second order system for these three conditions is as shown (Fig. 15).

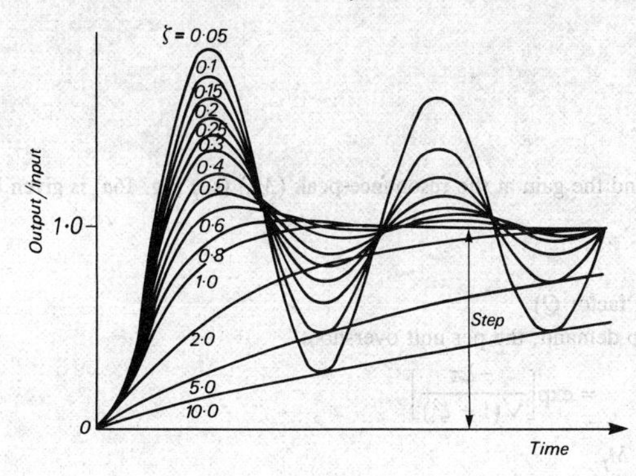

FIG. 15.—Second-order System Step-function Response.

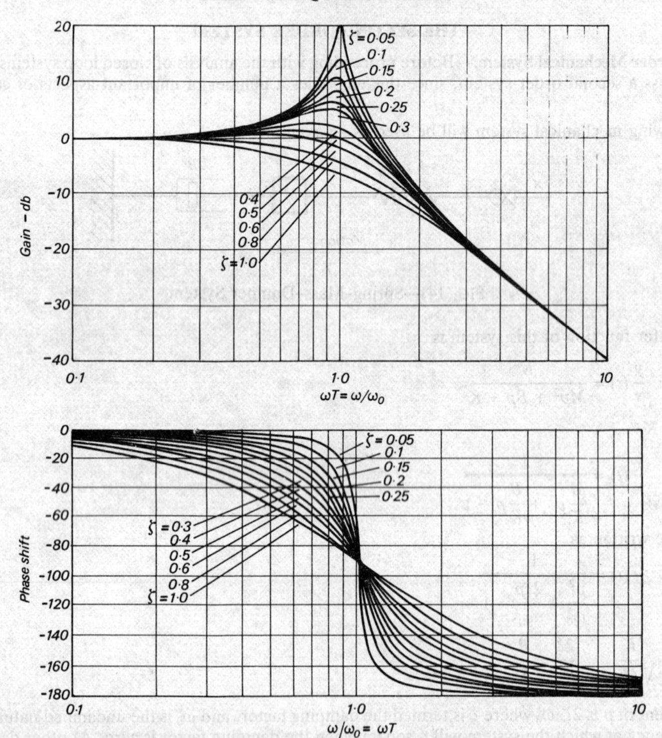

FIG. 16.(a).—Gain vs. Frequency Ratio ω/ω_0 and (b) Phase-shift vs. Frequency Ratio ω/ω_0 of $\dfrac{1}{\left(1-\dfrac{\omega^2}{\omega_0^2}\right)+j2\zeta\dfrac{\omega}{\omega_0}}$ for various values of $\zeta \leqslant 1$.

The corresponding Bode diagram is shown in Fig. 16.

For an underdamped system, damping factor ζ, the magnitude of the resonance peak M_p and the transient response are related by the following equations:

If the roots are $-\sigma + j\omega$

$$\zeta = \sqrt{\frac{1}{1+\left(\frac{\omega}{\sigma}\right)^2}}$$

The time to the first peak

$$t = \frac{\pi}{\omega_0\sqrt{1+\zeta^2}}$$

The ratio between the steady state gain and the gain at the resonance peak (M_p) (see Fig. 16*a*) is given by

$$M_p = \frac{1}{2\zeta}$$

(M_p is sometimes known as magnification factor Q)

In the transient response to a unity step demand, the per unit overshoot

$$= \exp\left[\frac{-\zeta\pi}{\sqrt{(1-\zeta^2)}}\right]$$

and the number of oscillations to settle $= M_p$.

The relationship between the per-unit overshoot and the number of oscillations to fall to within 5% of the final value is given in Fig. 17.

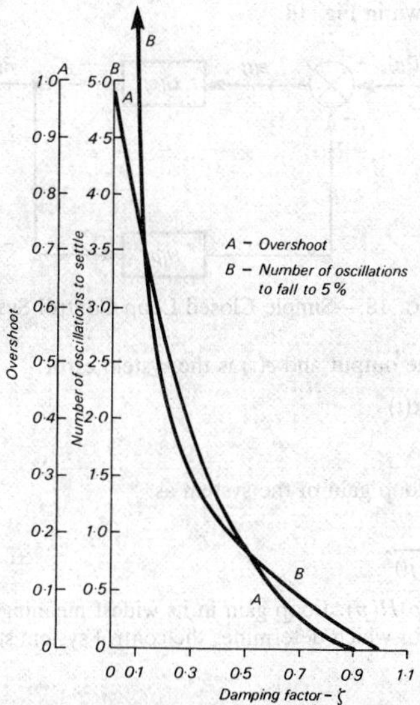

FIG. 17.—Relationship between Overshoot, Number of Oscillations and ζ.

More About Roots.—The denominator of the transfer function of a control system is, in terms of the classical solutions of differential equations, called the characteristic equation. Using a similar transfer function to that shown on page 3.

$$\frac{y}{x} = \frac{b_0 p^m + b_1 p^{m-1} + \ldots + b_m}{a_0 p^n + a_1 p^{n-1} + \ldots + a_n}$$

This is equivalent to the following differential equation with constant coefficients.

$$a_0 \frac{d^n y}{dt^n} + a_1 \frac{d^{n-1} y}{dt^{n-1}} + a_n y = b_0 \frac{d^m x}{dt^m} + b_1 \frac{d^{m-1} x}{dt^{m-1}} + \ldots + b_m x$$

The normal classical methods of solution give the characteristic equation of the system as

$$a_0 p^n + a_1 p^{n-1} + \ldots + a_n = 0$$

with n, possible solutions.

The general solution is

$$y = C_1 e^{P_1 t} + C_2 e^{P_2 t} + \ldots + C_n e^{P_n t}$$

where p_1, p_2, p_n may be real or complex.

If we factorise numerator and denominator of the transfer function then

$$\frac{x}{y} = \frac{(p + \alpha_1)(p + \alpha_2) \ldots (p + \alpha_m)}{(p + \beta_1)(p + \beta_2) \ldots (p + \beta_n)}$$

It follows that $\beta_1, \beta_2, \ldots, \beta_m$ are the roots of the characteristic equation, they are also termed the poles of the transfer function since these are the values which make the function equal to infinity. By similar reasoning $\alpha_1, \alpha_2, \ldots, \alpha_n$ are called the zeros. The poles and zeros of a transfer function can be used to define the complete details of a systems' response and stability. They can be plotted on diagram called a *pole-zero plot* or a *root locus*. If they are complex they must occur in conjugate pairs and will have a real and an imaginary part. For a stable solution the real part of the roots must always be negative (see page 21).

THE CLOSED LOOP

Negative Feedback.—The concept of a closed-loop control system is based on the principle that a system is 'error actuated'. In essence, this means that the output variable is fed-back and compared with the demand variable. The resulting error acts on the plant or system in such a way as to reduce the error. This is the concept of negative feedback.

Consider a simple loop as shown in Fig. 18.

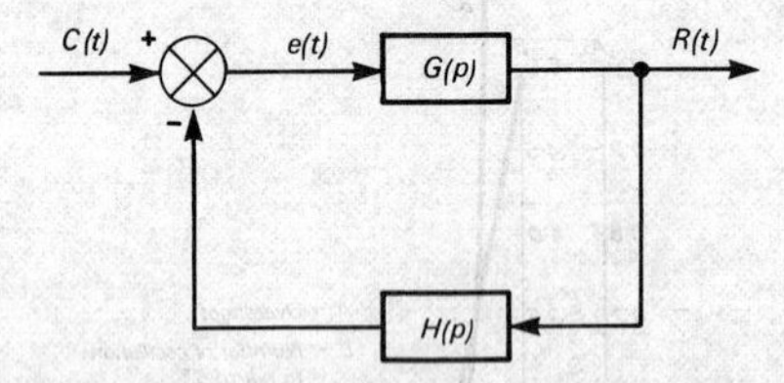

FIG. 18.—Simple Closed Loop Control System.

$C(t)$ is the input variable, $R(t)$ the output and $e(t)$ is the system error.

$$e(t) = C(t) - H(p)R(t) \tag{1}$$

$$R(t) = G(p)e(t) \tag{2}$$

eliminating $e(t)$ gives the closed-loop gain of the system as

$$\frac{R}{C}(t) = \frac{G(p)}{1 + G(p)H(p)} \tag{3}$$

The 'loop gain' is given by $G(p)H(p)$. Loop gain in its widest meaning involving all the dynamic terms in $G(p)$ and $H(p)$ is the critical factor which determines the control system stability. The characteristic equation is

$$1 + G(p)\,H(p) = 0$$

and for limiting stability $G(p)\ H(p) = -1$.

STABILITY

In the preceding section the benefits of feedback in improving system performance were illustrated. This process cannot be extended indefinitely, however, as increasing the loop-gain beyond a certain value produces instability. The determination of stability and techniques for modifying systems to improve stability are essential parts of control system design.

Mathematically, stability is determined by the roots of the characteristic equation of the system

$$GH = -1$$

There are several techniques for assessing system stability and these are briefly described in the following sections.

Routh–Hurwitz Criterion.—The Routh Criterion is a useful relationship for checking the stability of a control system without the necessity of finding the roots of the characteristic equation.

Suppose the characteristic equation of a linear system is written in general form;

$$F(p) = 1 + G(p)\,H(p) = a_0p^n + a_1p^{n-1} + a_2p^{n-2} + \ldots + a_{n-1}p + a_n = 0 \tag{1}$$

In order that there be no roots of this equation with positive real parts (unstable roots) it is necessary but not sufficient that;

(1) all the coefficients of the polynomial have the same sign

(2) none of the coefficients vanish

The Hurwitz determinants of equation (1) are given by

$$D_1 = a_1 \qquad D_2 = \begin{vmatrix} a_1 & a_3 \\ a_0 & a_2 \end{vmatrix} \qquad D_3 = \begin{vmatrix} a_1 & a_3 & a_5 \\ a_0 & a_2 & a_4 \\ 0 & a_1 & a_3 \end{vmatrix} \qquad D_n = \begin{vmatrix} a_1 & a_3 & a_5 \ldots a_{2n-1} \\ a_0 & a_2 & a_4 \ldots a_{2n-2} \\ 0 & a_1 & a_3 \ldots a_{2n-3} \\ 0 & a_0 & a_2 \ldots a_{2n-4} \\ 0 & 0 & a_1 \ldots a_{2n-5} \\ \cdot & & \\ \cdot & & \\ 0 & 0 & 0 \ldots a_n \end{vmatrix} \tag{2}$$

Routh–Hurwitz criteria states: The necessary and sufficient condition that all roots of the polynomial $F(p) = 0$ of equation (1) be in the left-hand half of the p plane is that $a_0 > 0$, $D_1 > 0$, $D_2 > 0, \ldots, D_n > 0$, where $D_1, D_2, D_3, \ldots, D_n$, are defined in equation (2). This is a formidable task for high order polynomials because of the labour involved in evaluating the determinants. However, the rule can be applied without actually working out the high order determinants given in equation (2), by the use of simplified standard procedures (Refs. 1, 4, 11).

A disadvantage of the Routh criterion is the lack of indication of any degree of stability or instability. It is essentially a go/no-go test and as such is difficult to use to assess the efficiency of system modifications made to improve stability, except for crude variations in loop gain.

Nyquist Stability Criterion.—In contrast with the Routh criterion the Nyquist Stability criterion gives a more physical insight into system stability and enables effects of modifications to be readily assessed. In essence the Nyquist criterion states that when a control system is excited with a sinusoidal input, if at any frequency the feedback signal is in-phase with and equal in amplitude to the input signal, then the system is unstable. The Nyquist criterion expresses this intuitively simple rule in a precise mathematical form which may be applied to all systems however complex. Extensions of the basic Nyquist rules enable the determination of the magnitude of the real parts of the roots thus giving an indication of damping factors or decrements.

In the previous section (page 10) it was seen that

$$\text{the closed-loop gain} = \frac{G(j\omega)}{1 + G(j\omega)H(j\omega)}$$

$G(j\omega)$ and $H(j\omega)$ being complex vector quantities.

Thus if $G(j\omega)\ H(j\omega) = -1$ the closed-loop gain becomes infinite. This is the condition of limiting stability as expressed above.

The Nyquist diagram is the locus of $G(j\omega)\ H(j\omega)$ over the range of ω from zero to ∞. A typical locus for type 0 system is shown.

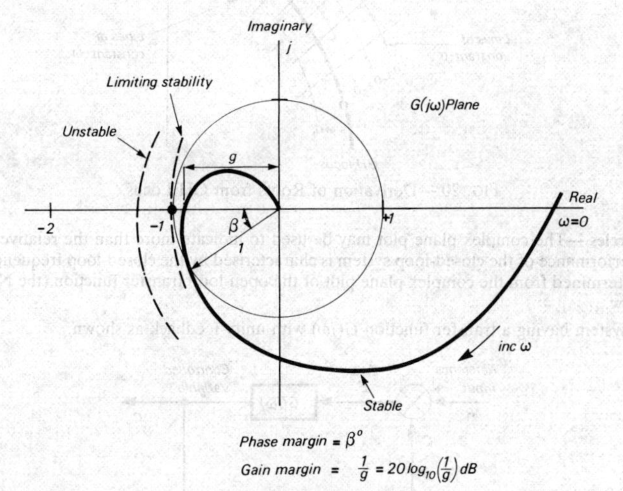

FIG. 19.—Typical Nyquist Diagram.

The locus starts at the steady state value of $G(j\omega)\ H(j\omega)$ when $\omega = 0$. The proximity of the locus to the $(-1, j0)$ point indicates relative stability. Obviously if the locus passes through the $(-1, j0)$ point then the above condition $(GH = -1)$ is satisfied and the system is at limiting stability. If the locus crosses the negative real axis to the left of the -1 point the system is unstable $(GH > 1)$. If it crosses to the right $(GH < -1)$ the system is stable. The rigorous application of the Nyquist criterion necessitates the plotting of the complete locus from $\omega = -\infty$ to $+\infty$. In practice this is not necessary, however, provided the following rule is applied: The locus is plotted for ω values from 0 to ∞ and the system is stable provided the $(-1, j0$ point) is on the left when the locus is transversed in the direction of increasing ω.

A more quantitative measure of stability is given by the measurement of the GAIN AND PHASE MARGINS.

The GAIN MARGIN is the reciprocal of the gain at the frequency at which the phase shift is π radians (180°). It is usually expressed in decibels (db).

The PHASE MARGIN is 180° minus the phase angle at the frequency at which the gain is unity.

Typical values for gain and phase margins in a well behaved control system would be 10 db and 35°–45° respectively.

If we consider the characteristic equation $GH + 1 = 0$ the system stability is indicated by the roots. Depending upon the order of the system there will be a number of roots which may be real or complex. The complex roots, which occur in conjugate pairs of the form $s = \sigma \pm j\omega$ determine the system stability.

For limiting stability $\sigma = 0$

For stability $\sigma = -ve$

For instability $\sigma = +ve$

If we construct the family of loci of GH for both imaginary and complex roots and determine the value of $s = \sigma + j\omega$ for the locus that intersects the -1 point then the relative stability of the closed loop system may be determined.

The basic Nyquist locus is the $\sigma = 0$ line.

In the figure shown the locus passing through the $(-1, j0)$ point gives the root as $-\sigma_2 + j\omega$.

From these roots the stability, damping factor, decrement etc. may be determined (see page 26).

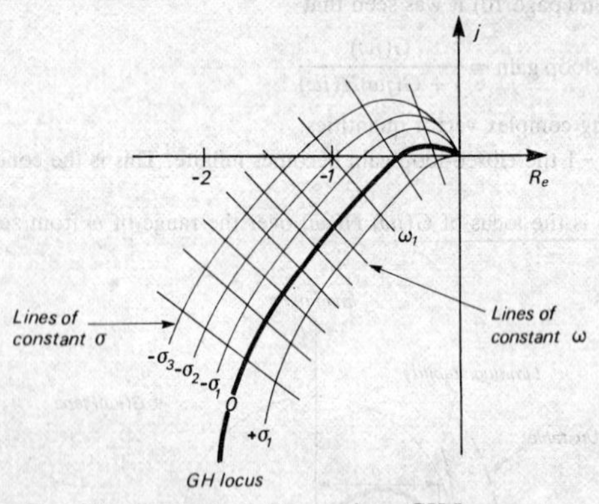

FIG. 20.—Derivation of Roots from GH Locus.

M and α Circles.—The complex plane plot may be used to indicate more than the relative stability of the system. The performance of the closed-loop system is characterised by the closed-loop frequency response and this may be determined from the complex plane plot of the open-loop transfer function (the Nyquist locus) as described below.

Consider a system having a transfer function $G(j\omega)$ with unity feedback as shown.

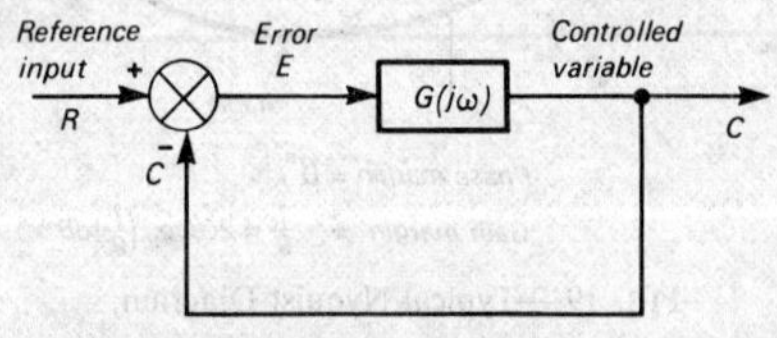

FIG. 21.—System with Transfer Frunction $G(j\omega)$ and unity feedback.

With sinusoidal input of frequency ω

$$\frac{C}{E} = G(j\omega) = |G(j\omega)|\, e^{-j\phi}$$

where $|G(j\omega)|$ is the magnitude of $G(j\omega)$ at frequency ω and ϕ is the phase angle of $G(j\omega)$.

Also $R - C = E$

Another relationship of interest is the *error response*

i.e.
$$\frac{\text{error}}{\text{input}} = \frac{E}{R} = \frac{1}{1 + G(j\omega)}$$

Constructing the Nyquist locus in the complex plane and marking point P at frequency ω.

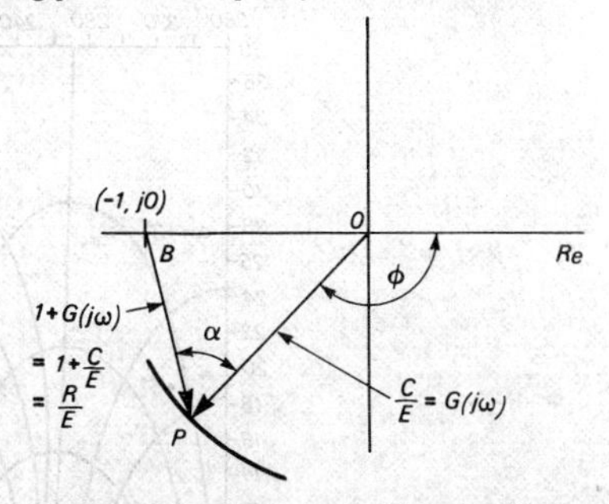

FIG. 22.—Nyquist Locus in Complex Plane.

The vector $OP = G(j\omega) = \dfrac{C}{E}$

Hence $BP = 1 + G(j\omega) = 1 + \dfrac{C}{E} = \dfrac{R}{E}$

and $BO = +1$

Thus the ratio $\dfrac{\text{output}}{\text{input}} = \dfrac{C}{R} = \dfrac{OP}{BP} = M\,e^{j\alpha}$

and the ratio of $\dfrac{\text{error}}{\text{input}} = \dfrac{E}{R} = \dfrac{1}{BP}$

Thus from the above relationship it is possible to obtain the error response from the Nyquist plot by taking the reciprocal of the distance from the $(-1, j0)$ point to the point on the $G(j\omega)$ locus at the desired frequency.

$$\text{The closed-loop transfer function} = \frac{C}{R} = \frac{G(j\omega)}{1 + G(j\omega)}$$
$$= Me^{j\alpha}$$

where $M = |C/R|$ = magnitude of ratio, and α = phase angle between C and R.

Thus for each point on the complex plane there is a definite value of M and α and it is possible to construct curves of constant M and α which, in fact, are circles. Such a plot is shown (Fig. 23) and is termed an $M - \alpha$ chart. If Nyquist loci are plotted directly on such a chart the closed-loop frequency response may be read off directly at each value of frequency.

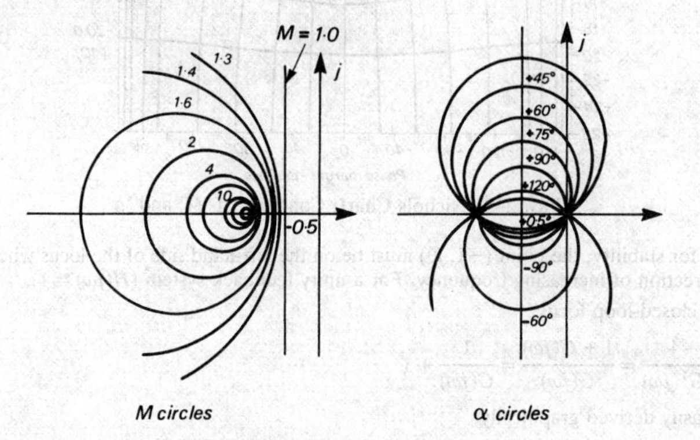

FIG. 23.—M and α Contours.

A development of the $M - \alpha$ chart by N. B. Nichols (Ref. 11) is known as the *Nichols Chart* and is a useful design aid. In the Nichols Chart open loop gain $|G\,j\omega|$, expressed in db, is plotted against phase angle ϕ on rectangular axes. Contours of M and α are superimposed and at each frequency values may be read off (Fig. 24). The Nichols chart contains identical information to the complex plane plots and may thus also be used to determine stability.

The use of the complex plane loci as described above have certain drawbacks particularly in cases in which the controlled variable is not compared directly with the input and/or when there are internal feedback loops. An alternative approach to counter these difficulties is the use of the inverse transfer function locus to investigate system performance and stability.

With the Inverse Nyquist locus:

$\dfrac{1}{G(j\omega)H(j\omega)}$ is plotted on the complex plane.

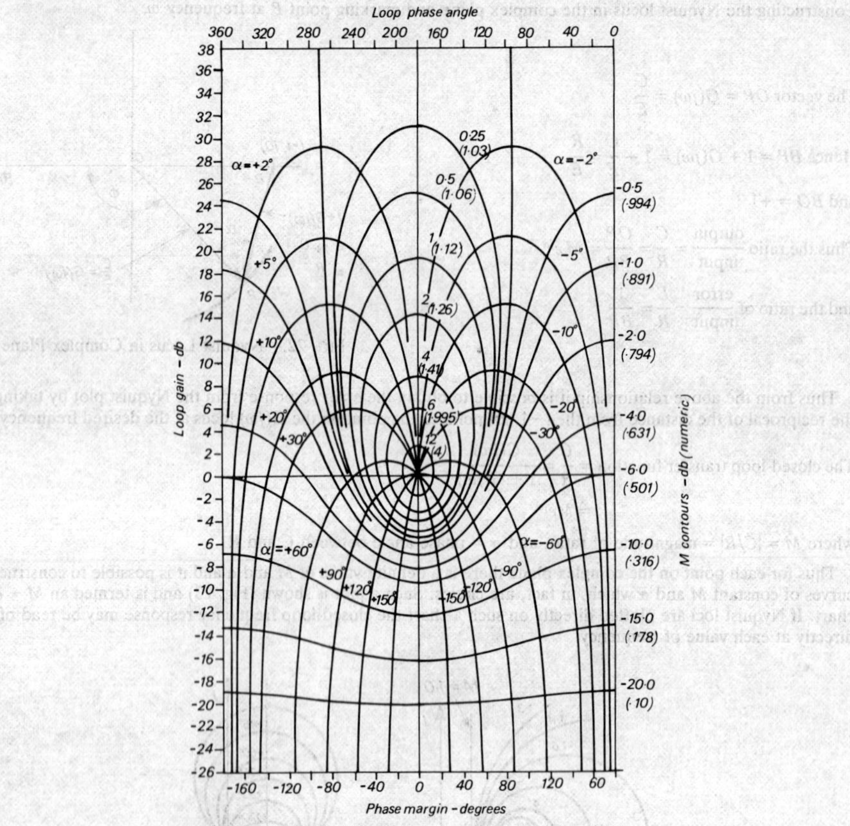

FIG. 24.—Nichols Chart; Contours of 'M' and 'α'.

In this case, for stability, the point $(-1, j0)$ must be on the left-hand side of the locus when transversing the locus in the direction of increasing frequency. For a unity feedback system $(H(j\omega) = 1)$.

The inverse closed-loop locus

$$\frac{1}{G^1(j\omega)} = \frac{1 + G(j\omega)}{G(j\omega)} = \frac{1}{G(j\omega)} + 1$$

may thus be easily derived graphically.

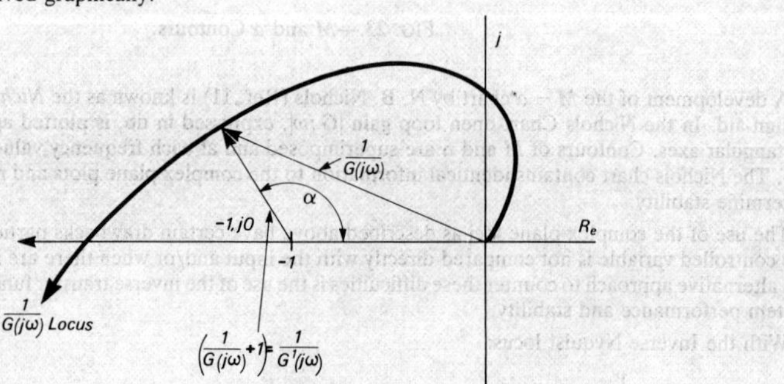

FIG. 25.—Inverse Nyquist Locus $1/G(j\omega)$.

In systems where there is not direct feedback, ie $H(j\omega) \neq 1$

$$\frac{1}{G^1(j\omega)} = \frac{1}{G(j\omega)} + H(j\omega)$$

If $H(j\omega)$ is real, ie has no complex terms then a similar locus may be constructed replacing the '1' vector by $|H|$. If $H(j\omega)$ is complex the construction becomes more complicated.

M and α have a similar significance with the inverse locus except that circles of radius $1/M$ are now used with lines of constant α as shown.

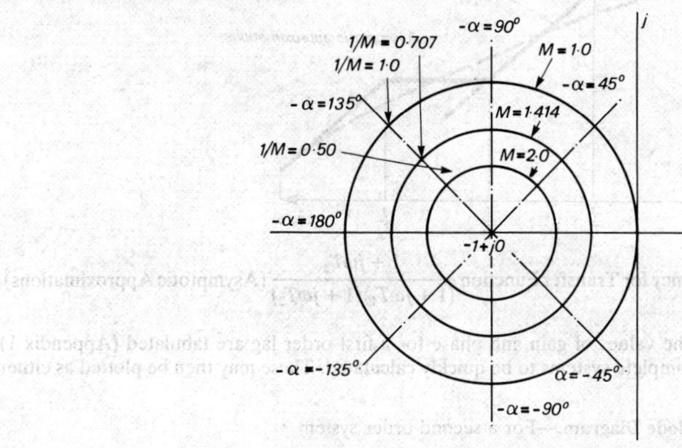

FIG. 26.—Loci of Constant $1/M$ and $-\alpha$.

COMPARISON BETWEEN THE DIRECT AND INVERSE PLOTS.—Both systems have their advocates and advantages. With systems consisting mainly of series connected elements then the direct plot is slightly more convenient. With systems involving the manipulation of the feedback characteristics to achieve stability then the inverse plot is preferred.

One advantage of the inverse locus is the fact that the locus increases in size with frequency and hence the higher frequency regions, that are normally of interest in determining stability, are more easily examined.

BODE DIAGRAMS.—Instead of plotting open-loop frequency responses as polar diagrams on the complex plane they can be studied by plotting $|G(j\omega)|$ and arg $G(j\omega)$ against frequency. When logarithmic scales are used for $|G(j\omega)|$ and frequency the plots are known as Bode Diagrams.

It is usual to employ a scale of decibels (db) = $20 \log_{10}|G(j\omega)|$ for the amplitude. The frequency may be either F_{Hz} (c/s) or ω (rad/s) on a logarithmic scale.

The advantages of logarithmic scales are:

(*a*) The multiplication of transfer functions becomes a simple additive process.

(*b*) The amplitude response may be approximated by straight lines on the Bode diagram thus enabling multiple series transfer functions to be combined and overall performance to be quickly assessed.

On page 5 it was shown that a first-order lag having a transfer function

$$G(j\omega) = \frac{1}{1 + j\omega T}$$

has an amplitude $|G(j\omega)| = \dfrac{1}{\sqrt{1 + \omega^2 T^2}}$

and argument arg $G(j\omega) = \tan^{-1} \omega T$

At low frequencies $1 \gg \omega T$ $\quad |G(j\omega)| = 1$ and arg $G(j\omega) = 0$

At high frequencies $1 \ll \omega T$ $\quad |G(j\omega)| = \dfrac{1}{\omega T}$ and arg $G(j\omega) = 90°$.

The corresponding Bode Diagram is shown in Fig. 11.

The high frequency gain falls off at a constant slope of 6 db/octave, ie the gain is halved for each doubling of frequency.

Using the asymptotic approximations the gain of more complex transfer functions may be sketched (Fig. 27).

ie $$G(j\omega) = \frac{(1 + j\omega T_2)}{(1 + j\omega T_1)(1 + j\omega T_3)}$$

where $T_1 > T_2 > T_3$

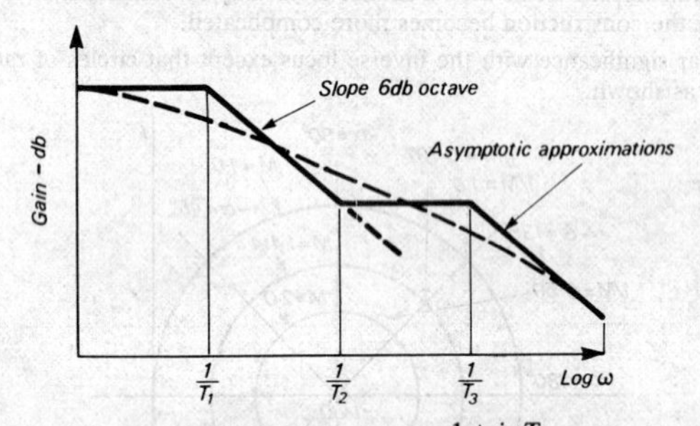

FIG. 27.—Amplitude and Frequency for Transfer Function $\frac{1 + j\omega T_2}{(1 + j\omega T_1)(1 + j\omega T_2)}$ (Asymptotic Approximations).

For more precise evaluation the values of gain and phase for a first order lag are tabulated (Appendix 1) enabling the gain and phase of complete systems to be quickly calculated. These may then be plotted as either Nyquist or Bode diagrams.

Second Order System on the Bode Diagram.—For a second order system

$$G(j\omega) = \frac{1}{\frac{(j\omega)^2}{\omega_0^2} + \frac{2\zeta j\omega}{\omega_0} + 1}$$

Amplitude $|G(j\omega)| =$

$$\frac{1}{\sqrt{\left(1 - \left(\frac{\omega}{\omega_0}\right)^2\right)^2 + \left(\frac{2\zeta\omega}{\omega_0}\right)^2}}$$

which at high frequency approximates to $\left(\frac{\omega_0}{\omega}\right)^2$

ie for a doubling of the frequency the gain falls by $\frac{1}{4}$. This corresponds to an asymptote having a slope of -12 db/octave. Similarly arg $G(j\omega) = 180°$ at high frequencies.

At ω_0 the amplitude depends upon the damping factor ζ and the argument is 90°. The frequency response of a second order system is shown in Fig. 16.

A large scale graph of this form is an invaluable aid in conjunction with Appendix 1 for evaluation of system frequency responses.

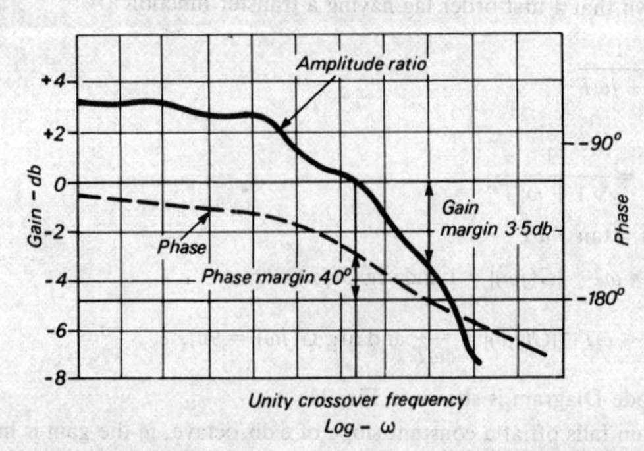

FIG. 28.—Calculation of Gain and Phase Margins on the Bode Diagram.

Higher Order Transfer Functions.—Transfer functions of higher order than 2 cannot easily be sketched on the Bode diagram, but the following rules are useful:

For a system of order n the high frequency gain has a slope of $n \times 6$ db/octave and the phase approaches $n \times 90°$.

STABILITY ON THE BODE DIAGRAM.—The gain and phase margin may be readily found from a Bode diagram by reading across between the gain and phase curves at the frequencies at which the gain = 1 (0 db) and the phase = 180° as shown.

SYSTEM SPECIFICATION, PERFORMANCE AND COMPENSATION

The design of any control system normally starts from a specification of the required performance. As well as factors such as output power ratings, operating conditions etc, the specification will normally cover the following points:

(1) The steady-state accuracy. The maximum permissible error between the input demand(s) and the corresponding outputs in the steady-state when all transients have died down. The steady-state accuracy is determined by the open loop-gain of the system in a type 0 system.

(2) The transient response of the system. This may be specified in several ways. Possible alternatives include:

(*a*) The response of the system to a step demand of a given amplitude, in terms of time to settle, maximum overshoot, number of oscillations etc.

(*b*) The closed-loop frequency response which may in turn be specified as (i) band-width (frequency at which the gain has fallen by a specified amount, usually 3 db); (ii) resonant frequency and damping factor.

(*c*) The response of the system to a ramp input, usually in terms of following error at a given input rate.

Implicit in the above specifications is the form of the complex-plane plot of the system open-loop transfer function. The steady-state accuracy determines the open-loop the gain of the system at low frequencies and the required transient response dictates the behaviour of the locus in the vicinity of the $(-1, j0)$ point as described in an earlier section.

The system designer must thus modify the transfer functions of the individual system elements to force the resultant locus to follow the required path. In general the transfer functions of the major system components are determined by factors such as power-rating etc and cannot be easily modified. Changes must therefore be made either by adding series or feedback compensating elements as described below.

Series Network Compensation.—The required form of system complex plane locus may be determined by using the $M - \alpha$ plots or Nichols charts. The difference between the required locus and that of the basic system indicates the contribution required from the series compensation network. By comparing the magnitude and phase of the two loci at each frequency the characteristics of the required compensating network may be determined.

In practice the limitations of physically realisable control system elements and electrical networks mean that it is difficult to achieve the desired compensation characteristic over a wide range of frequencies. This is not normally a serious problem, however, since compensation is normally only required over a limited frequency range and it is usually possible to achieve an acceptable solution.

The physical form of the compensating networks depends upon the system. The majority of modern control systems incorporate electronic signal processing and amplification and in analogue systems it is normally at the low power-end of such circuits that compenstion is applied. These may be as passive R, C, L electrical networks or more usually, networks in conjunction with operational amplifiers which enable complex transfer functions to be realised. With digital systems the necessary compensating transfer functions can be achieved in software by relatively simple algorithms.

In non-electrical systems the problem is more severe. It is difficult to realise anything more than very simple transfer functions in mechanical or fluid power systems and this together with inherent non-linearities etc make compensation very much more difficult.

Series compensation networks in general introduce phase-lag or phase-lead characteristics.

PHASE-LAG COMPENSATION (Fig. 29)

Phase-lag compensation may be used to reduce the system gain of type 0 and 1 systems at high frequencies. This enables the low frequency gain to be increased to give the necessary accuracy. At high frequency the gain is reduced without any increase in phase shift.

The electrical network designed to give phase-lag is shown below

$$\frac{E_0}{E_{in}} = \frac{1 + pR_2C_2}{1 + p(R_1 + R_2)C_2}$$

$$= \frac{1 + pT_2}{1 + pT_1}$$

where $T_1 > T_2$.

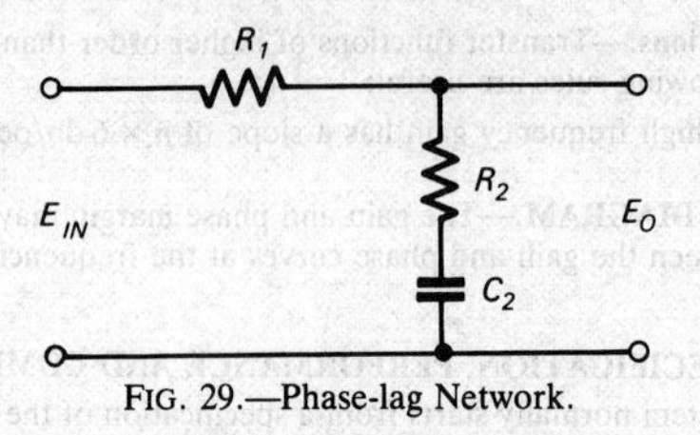

FIG. 29.—Phase-lag Network.

The frequency response of the phase-lag network is shown (Fig. 30(*a*)), typically $T_1 = 10\ T_2$ for a reasonable phase shift, giving a high frequency gain of 0.1

The complex plane plot is a semi-circle as shown (Fig. 30(*b*).)

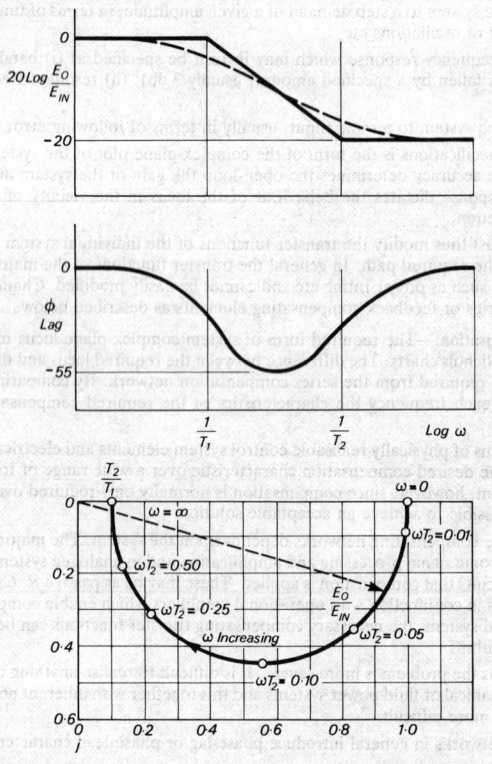

FIG. 30.—E_0/E_{IN} as a Function of Frequency for Phase-lag Network

$$\frac{E_0}{E_{IN}} = \frac{1 + j\omega T_2}{1 + j\omega T_1} \qquad \frac{T_2}{T_1} = 0{\cdot}1$$

The application of a phase-lag compensator to a typical type 0 system is shown in the example below which shows the modification of both the complex plane plot and the Bode diagram.

The benefit from phase-lag compensation arises from the attenuation at high frequencies (T_2/T_1) and not from the phase-lag which is an embarrassment in most systems. For this reason the network is designed to have its maximum phase shift at a frequency below that at which the system locus approaches the negative real axis.

PHASE-LEAD COMPENSATION (Fig. 31)

A phase-lead network introduces leading phase shift over a range of frequencies and also has a gain that increases with frequency.

A typical electrical network giving a phase lead characteristic is shown in Fig. 31.

$$=\frac{E_0}{E_{in}}=\frac{R_2}{R_1+R_2}\times\frac{1+pR_1C_1}{1+\dfrac{pR_1R_2C_1}{R_1+R_2}}$$

$$=\frac{T_2(1+pT_1)}{T_1(1+pT_2)}$$

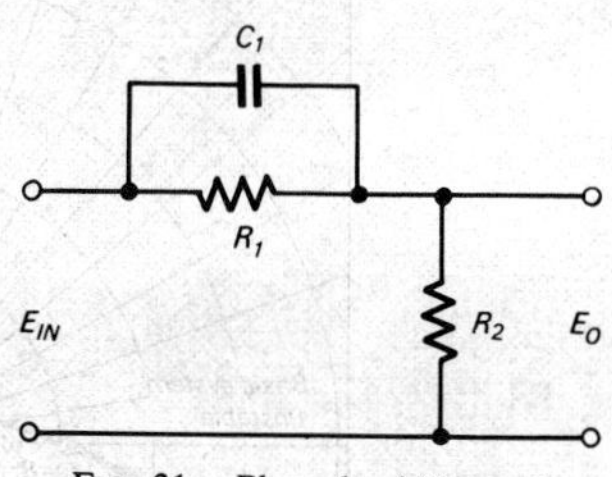

FIG. 31.—Phase-lead Network.

where $T_1 = R_1C_1$.

$$T_2 = R_1R_2C_1/(R_1+R_2) = R_2T_1/(R_1+R_2)$$

A typical value of $R_2/(R_1+R_2) = T_2/T_1 = 1/10$ giving a maximum phase angle of approx 55° lead

low frequency gain = 0.1
high frequency gain = 1

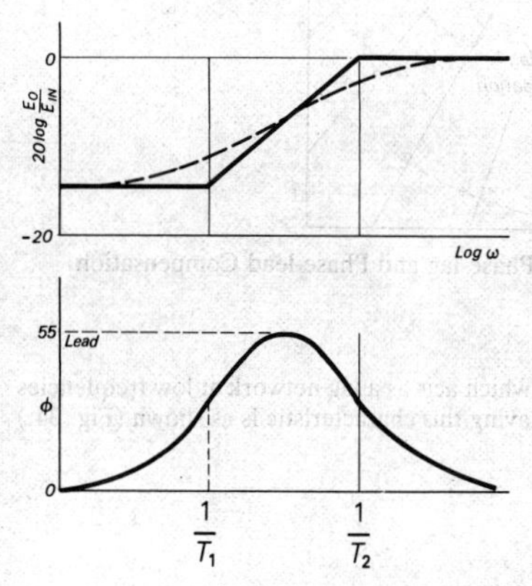

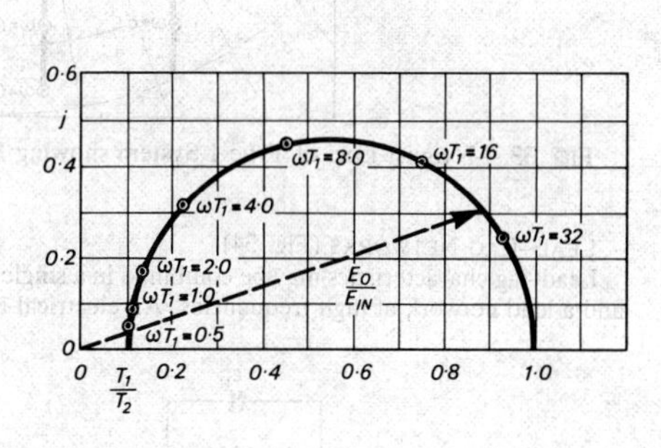

FIG. 32.—E_0/E_{IN} as a Function Frequency for Phase-lead Network

$$\frac{E_0}{E_{IN}}=\frac{T_2}{T_1}\left[\frac{1+j\omega T_1}{1+j\omega T_2}\right] \qquad \frac{T_2}{T_1}=0{\cdot}1$$

Phase-lead compensation may be used with advantages in both type 1 and 2 systems. The benefit with phase-lead compensation arises from the leading phase shift. The corresponding increase in gain is in general de-stabilising.

It is normally necessary to increase the system gain to compensate for the attenuation of the compensating network at low frequencies. With a type 1 system there is frequently a choice between the use of phase lag or phase lead compensation. The locus in Fig. 33 shows a unstable type 1 locus system and the effects of both phase lag and phase lead compensation.

From the loci it is seen that with phase-lag compensation the frequency at which the locus crosses the negative real axis is significantly reduced. Thus the frequency response of the system will be reduced. The converse appears with phase-lead compensation, the frequency at which the locus crosses the axis is increased thus improving the system frequency response. Thus depending upon the required performance, the form of compensation is determined. A further example is given below.

For systems of higher order (type 2 and above) satisfactory stability normally necessitates the use of phase lead compensation.

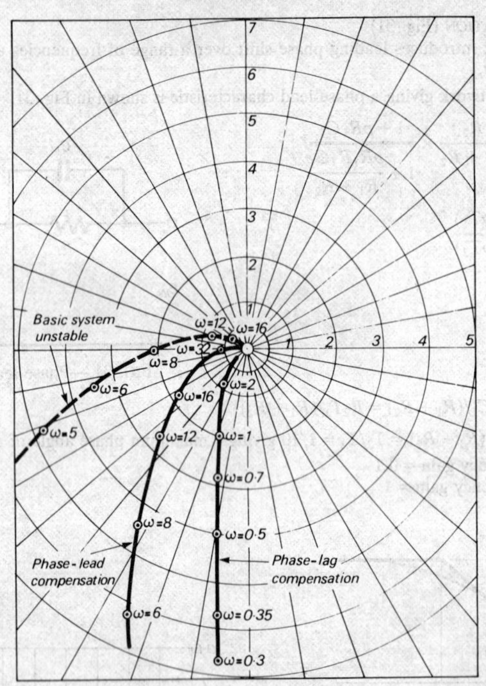

FIG. 33.—Nyquist Loci of Type 1 System showing Effect of Phase-lag and Phase-lead Compensation.

LEAD–LAG NETWORKS (Fig. 34)

Lead–lag characteristics may be combined in a single network which acts as a lag network at low frequencies and a lead network at high frequencies. An electrical network having this characteristic is as shown (Fig. 34.)

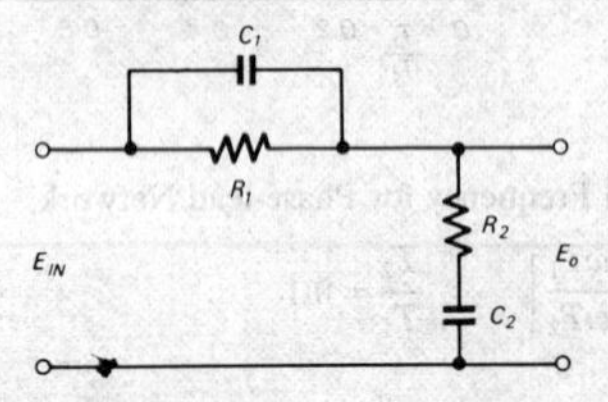

FIG. 34.—Lead-lag Network.

It is possible to synthesise many complex transfer functions with R C networks. A table showing the more commonly used networks is given in Appendix 2 (Ref. 10). The use of an operational amplifier in conjunction with R C neworks gives greater flexibility and enables more complex transfer functions to be synthesised.

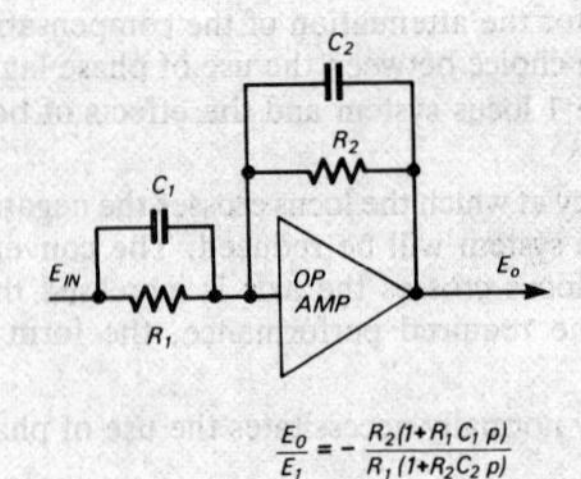

FIG. 35.—Use of Operational Amplifier to give Compensation.

Feedback Compensation.—With series compensation as described above the transfer function of the compensating network multiplies that of the basic system so that the resultant gain is the product of the gain of the compensator and that of the basic system and the net phase is the sum of that of the basic system and the compensator. With feedback compensation the situation is more complex and involves the use of additional subsidiary feedback loops to modify the transfer functions of loop elements.

It was shown earlier that the transfer function G becomes $G(1 + GH)$ if a negative feedback element having a transfer function H is added. Thus the transfer function of forward loop elements may be modified to meet the requirements of stability by local feedback connections having appropriate forms of H. This may be illustrated by the example shown in figure 36.

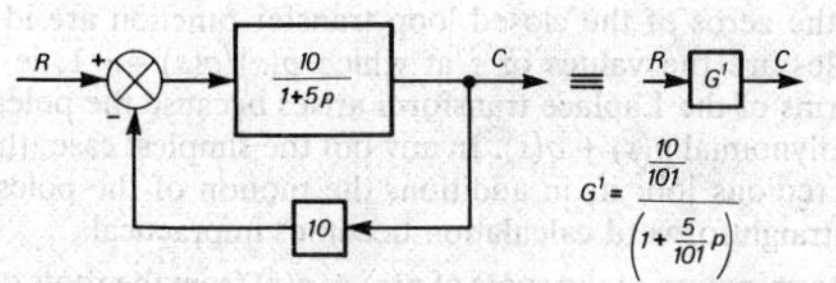

FIG. 36.—Use of Feedback to Modify Transfer Functions.

Thus the gain and time constant are both reduced by a factor of (1/101).

A common application of feedback compensation is the use of velocity feedback in position control systems as a method of stabilisation which introduces a damping term. An example of feedback compensation is given on page H5/32.

THE ROOT LOCUS TECHNIQUE

In the frequency domain study of linear feedback control systems, the Nyquist criterion, the Bode plot, and the Nichols chart are all useful tools of analysis.

If the specifications on system performance are given in terms of gain and phase margin, peak of resonance *Mp*, band-width etc, these techniques lead to the design of control systems from the frequency response view point. However, it is equally important to consider time domain specifications, ie the time response of the system, specified by factors such as overshoot, damping ratio, settling time etc. Although, there is a theoretical correlation between frequency response and transient response, simple direct relationships can be obtained only for systems of the order of two or less.

The root locus technique can be regarded as a graphical technique using the s plane ($s = \sigma + j\omega$) for determining the roots of the characteristic equation of a single loop feedback system, and deriving the system time response from these roots. (Refs 2, 3, 7).

The advantage of working in the s plane is that the roots of the characteristic equation not only give information concerning the transient behaviour directly but also indicate the behaviour of the system to sinusoidal inputs. The root locus technique is based on the relationship between the poles and zeros of the closed and open loop system functions. Once the relation is established for the system configuration under consideration, design is accomplished by adjusting the poles and zeros* and the multiplicative gain factor of the open-loop transfer function in such a way as to yield a closed-loop system function with satisfactory poles and zeros. Consider Fig. 37.

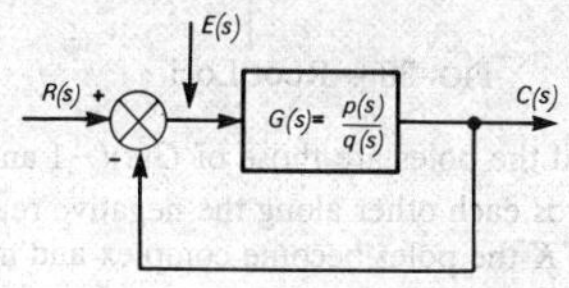

FIG. 37.—Closed Loop System.

* The poles are the values of s that make the function = ∞ and the zeros are the values of s that make the function = 0.

The closed-loop system function is given by the relation,

$$\frac{C}{R}(s) = \frac{G(s)}{1 + G(s)}$$

where, $G(s)$ is normally a rational algebraic function, the ratio of two polynomials in s:

ie $$G(s) = \frac{p(s)}{q(s)}$$

which gives

$$\frac{C}{R}(s) = \frac{p(s)/q(s)}{1 + p(s)/q(s)}$$

$$= \frac{p(s)}{q(s) + p(s)}$$

Thus, for the system shown, the zeros of the closed loop transfer function are identical with the open-loop zeros and the closed-loop poles are the values of s at which $p(s)/q(s) = -1$, ie $q(s) + p(s) = 0$. The basic difficulty with the design in terms of the Laplace transform arises because the poles of the closed loop system function are the roots of the polynomial $p(s) + q(s)$. In any but the simplest case, the evaluation of these poles for a given $p(s)$ and $q(s)$ is a tedious job; if, in addition, the motion of the poles with changes in a system design parameter is desired, straightforward calculation becomes impractical.

The root locus allows the determination of the roots of $p(s) + q(s)$ from the roots of $p(s)$ and $q(s)$, individually for a variation of the system open-loop gain parameter K.

For example, assume the open-loop system is second order, with

$$G(s) = \frac{K}{s(s+1)}$$

In this case the closed-loop transfer function is

$$\frac{C}{R}(s) = \frac{K}{s^2 + s + K}$$

The root loci are plots of the roots of the polynominal $s^2 + s + K$ as a function of K. For this example, the loci are shown in Fig. 38, which also illustrates the form of the root-locus plot. The figure is constructed in the following three steps.

(1) In the complex plane, the open-loop poles are marked by $\times$, the open-loop zeros by $\bigcirc$.

(2) On the basis of the relation that the closed-loop poles are the roots of the equation $G(s) = -1$, the loci of these poles are plotted as a function of K.

(3) Appropriate values of K are marked along the loci.

In the example of Fig. 38 the root loci take such a simple form that they can be drawn by inspection.

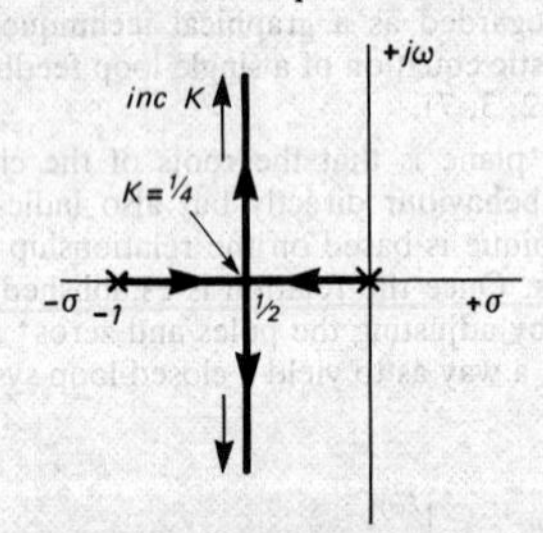

FIG. 38.—Root Loci.

At $K = 0$ the system is open-loop and the poles are those of $G(s)(-1$ and $0)$.

As K increases the poles move towards each other along the negative real axis until they meet at the point $-\frac{1}{2}$ when $K = \frac{1}{4}$. For further increase in K the poles become complex and move outwards as a conjugate pair along the vertical line as shown.

Construction of Root Loci.—It has been seen that the root loci are the roots of the equation $G(s) = -1$, as a function of the open-loop gain. In other words the root-loci constitute all s-plane points at which

$$\arg G(s) = 180° + k\,360°$$

where k is any integer including zero. The above equation is the basis for all techniques for the construction of root loci.

Arg $G(s)$ at any specific point on the s-plane is measured in terms of the angles contributed by the various poles and zeros.

Written in factored form, a typical $G(s)$ for a feedback control system is:

$$G(s) = \frac{K(s + z_1)(s + z_2)}{s(s + p_1)(s + p_2)(s + p_3)}$$

at the point s_i, $G(s)$ takes the value

$$G(s_i) = \frac{K(s_i + z_1)(s_i + z_2)}{s_i(s_i + p_1)(s_i + p_2)(s_i + p_3)(s_i + p_4)}$$

the value of $G(s_i)$ can be expressed in term of the vectors shown in Fig. 39.

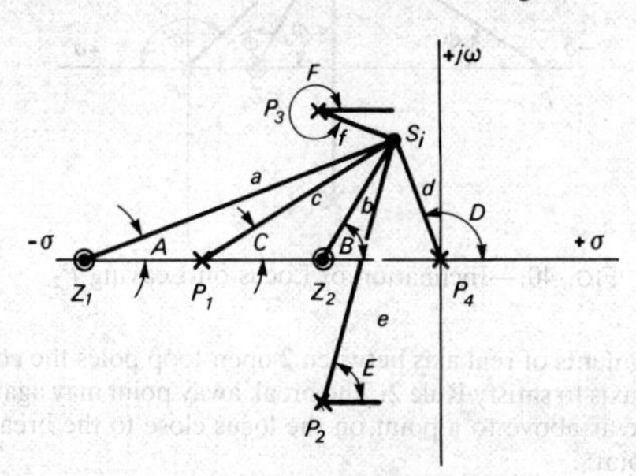

FIG. 39.—s_i Point Determination.

$$|G(s_i)| = K\frac{a \times b}{c \times d \times e \times f}$$

The argument of $G(s_i)$ is simply determined by the angles of the vector:

$$\angle G(s_i) = \angle A + \angle B - \angle C - \angle D - \angle E - \angle F$$

Thus the construction of the root loci involves the determination of those points, s_i, in the s-plane at which

$$\Sigma \text{ angles of vectors from zeros to } s_i - \Sigma \text{ angles of vectors from poles to } s_i = 180° + k\,360°$$

The actual location of points on the root locus can be obtained by a few simple rules and relationships.

Rules for the Construction of Root Loci.—

(1) Loci start on open-loop poles ($K = 0$)

(2) Loci terminate on open-loop zeros ($K = \infty$).

(3) Loci appear in distinct segments. The number of segments is equal to the number of open-loop poles (n) or the number of open-loop zeros (m) whichever is the greater.

(4) Loci occur in conjugate pairs, ie diagram is symmetrical about the real axis.

(5) For large values of s the open-loop transfer function may be approximated by taking only the highest order terms in the numerator and denominator.

ie $$G(s) = \frac{K(s^m + \ldots + a_m)}{qs^n + \ldots + b_n} \rightarrow \frac{K}{qs^{n-m}} \quad \text{as} \quad s \rightarrow \infty$$

Thus asymptotes to the loci make angles $\dfrac{(180 + k\,360)}{n - m}$ deg. With positive real axis

(6) Asymptotes radiate from a point on the real axis s_1 given by:

$$s_1 = \frac{\Sigma \text{ open-loop poles} - \Sigma \text{ open-loop zeros}}{(n - m)}$$

(n and m defined as in Rule 3.)

(7) On the negative real axis, loci lie only in sections to the left of an odd number of open-loop poles and zeros.

(8) Point of intersection of loci with imaginary axis can often be easily determined directly by substituting $s = j\omega$ in the characteristic equation and solving directly. The corresponding value of K is simply determined by Rouths criterion.

(9) Angles of departure and arrival. The angles at which the loci arrive at a zero or depart from a pole are easily evaluated from the 'sum of angles rule' above.

For example, inclination of locus leaving pole P_2 is given by

$$\gamma + (\phi_2 - \phi_1 - \phi_3 - \phi_4) = 180 + k\,360.$$

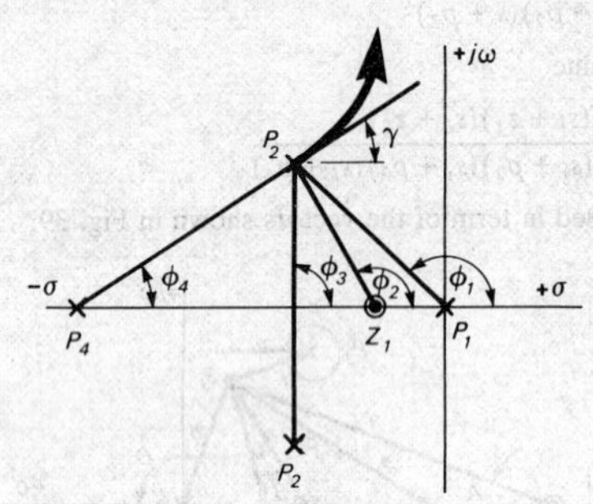

FIG. 40.—Inclination of Locus on Leaving P_2.

(10) Where loci exist on segments of real axis between 2 open-loop poles the contour must split away in two branches from the real axis to satisfy Rule 2. The break away point may again be determined by applying the 'sum of angles' rule as above to a point on the locus close to the break-away point, eg for point x close to break away point:

$$\phi_3 + \phi_2 + \phi_1 = 180 + k\,360$$

If δ is small:

$$\frac{\delta}{\alpha_3 - \alpha_x} + \frac{\delta}{\alpha_2 - \alpha_x} + 180 - \frac{\delta}{\alpha_x} = 180$$

ie

$$\frac{1}{\alpha_3 - \alpha_x} + \frac{1}{\alpha_2 - \alpha_x} = \frac{1}{\alpha_x}$$

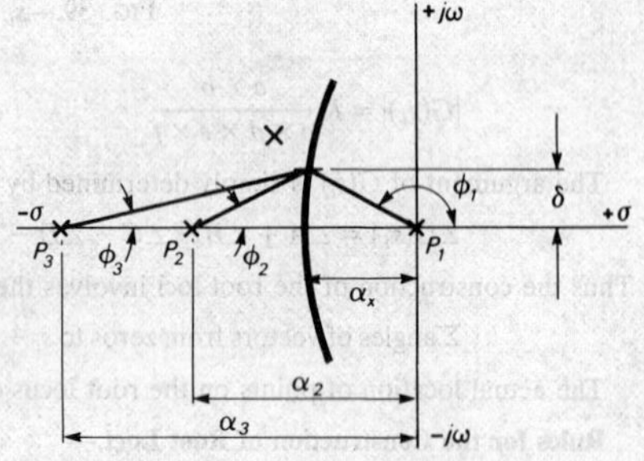

FIG. 41.—Determination of Break-away Point.

from which α_x may be determined by trial and error.

Further rules exist and are extensively treated in references (Refs 2, 3).

As a simple example illustrating the application of these rules consider:

$$G(s) = \frac{K(1 + 4s)}{s(1 + 2s)(1 + 1.6s + s^2)}$$

Open-loop poles are at 0, −0.5, (−0.8 ± j0.6) ie $n = 4$

Open-loop zero is at −0.25 ie $m = 1$

Therefore:

$$n - m = 3.$$

Thus asymptotes are at angles of $(180 + k360)/3 = 60°$, 180° and 300° to the positive real axis as shown.

From rule 6 the asymptotes radiate from the point

$$(0 - 0.5 - 0.8 \times 2 + 0.25)/3 = (-0.616, 0) \tag{3}$$

From Rule 8 the characteristic equation is:

$$2s^4 + 4.2s^3 + 3.6s^2 + (1 + 4K)s + K = 0$$

Substituting $s = j\omega$ and collecting real and imaginary parts

$$2\omega^4 - 3.6\omega^2 + K = 0$$

$$1 + 4K - 4.2\omega^2 = 0$$

which gives $\omega = +1.17$ for the intersection with the $j\omega$ axis

At this point $K = 1.19$.

Rule 9 gives the angle at which the locus leaves the complex poles as 35°.

From Rule 3 the loci has 4 segments, one of which must finish on the zero.

From Rule 7 the disposition of the segments on the real axis can be determined as shown.

The above enable the general form of the locus to be determined.

The application of Rules 1, 2, and 4 now enable the full locus to be sketched as shown in Fig. 42. With

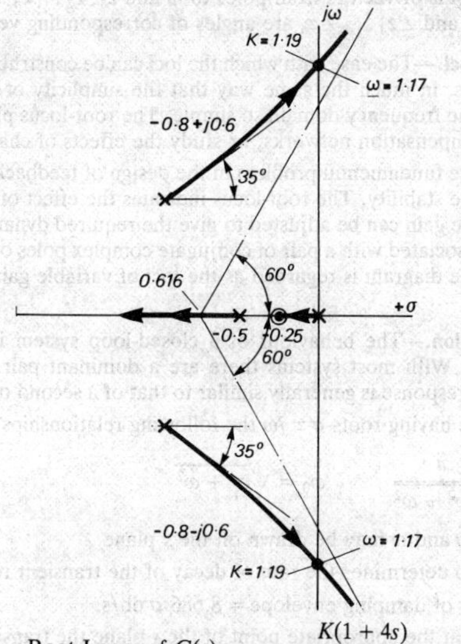

FIG. 42.—Root Locus of $G(s) = \dfrac{K(1 + 4s)}{s(s^2 + 1{\cdot}6s + 1)((1 + 2s)}$.

practice this process can be carried out with rapidity as familiarity with the general shapes of loci associated with various pole/zero configurations is gained.

Determination of Frequency Response from Roots.—Along the imaginary axis $s = j\omega$, ie the value of the function along this axis gives the frequency response of the function. This gives the direct connection between the pole-zero pattern and frequency response. The magnitude of the function is given by the distances between the poles and zeros and the corresponding value of ω (frequency) and the argument is given by the angle between the real axis and the vectors.

For example, consider a first order transfer function

$$G(s) = 1/(1 + sT) \text{ which has a single pole at } s = -1/T$$

At the frequency ω the gain is given by $1/a$ and the phase angle by ϕ. It can thus clearly be seen that at the break frequency $\omega = 1/T$ the phase angle is 45°. and the gain $(1/\sqrt{2})$ (−3 db) (Fig. 43).

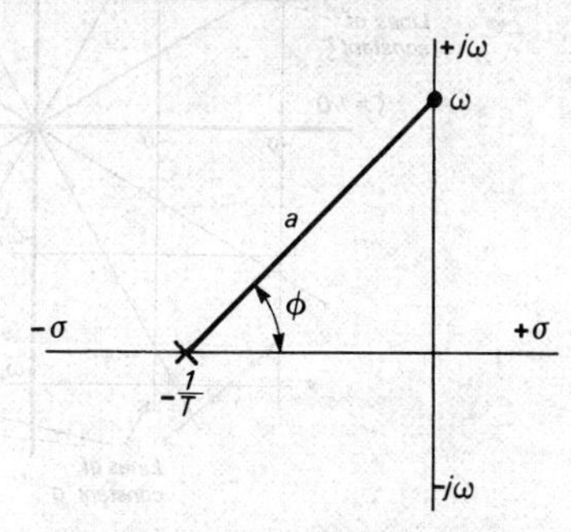

FIG. 43.—Root-locus of First Order Lag.

With multiple poles and zeros the gain at frequency ω is given by:

$$\frac{z_1 \times z_2 \ldots z_n}{p_1 \times p_2 \ldots p_m}$$

and phase angle by

$$(\angle p_1 + \angle p_2 \ldots \angle p_m) - (\angle z_1 + \angle z_1 \ldots \angle z_n)$$

where p_1, $p_2 \ldots p_m$ are lengths of vectors from poles to ω and z_1, $z_2 \ldots z_n$ are lengths of vectors from zeros to ω. Similarly $\angle p_1 \ldots \angle p_m$ and $\angle z_1 \ldots \angle z_n$ are angles of corresponding vectors.

Design in Terms of Root Loci.—The ease with which the loci can be constructed form the basis for the success of root-locus design methods, in much the same way that the simplicity of the gain and phase plots (Bode diagrams) makes design in the frequency domain so simple. The root-locus plots can be used to adjust system gain, guide the design of compensation networks, or study the effects of changes in system parameters.

ADJUSTMENT OF GAIN. The fundamental problem in the design of feedback control systems is the setting of the loop gain to yield suitable stability. The root-locus indicates the effect of gain variation on both transient and frequency responses. The gain can be adjusted to give the required dynamic performance as measured by the relative damping ratio associated with a pair of conjugate complex poles or by the dominant time constants of the system response. If the diagram is regarded as the loci of variable gain, the effects of gain adjustment becomes apparent.

Significance of Pole Location.—The behaviour of a closed-loop system is in general determined by the dominant closed-loop roots. With most systems there are a dominant pair of complex roots and to a first approximation the transient response is generally similar to that of a second order system having similar roots.

For a second order system having roots $\sigma \pm j\omega$ the following relationships exist

$$\zeta = \cos\theta = \frac{a}{\sqrt{\sigma^2 + \omega^2}} \qquad \omega_0 = \sqrt{\sigma^2 + \omega^2}$$

Thus lines of constant ζ, σ and ω may be drawn on the s plane.

The real part of the root σ determines the rate of decay of the transient response.

Rate of decay of damping envelope = 8.686 σ db/s.

Thus by positioning poles at the appropriate point of the s plane the transient response may be completely specified in terms of both frequency and damping.

The system specification in terms of natural frequency (response time) and damping factor (settling time) may thus be defined in terms of forbidden areas on the s plane.

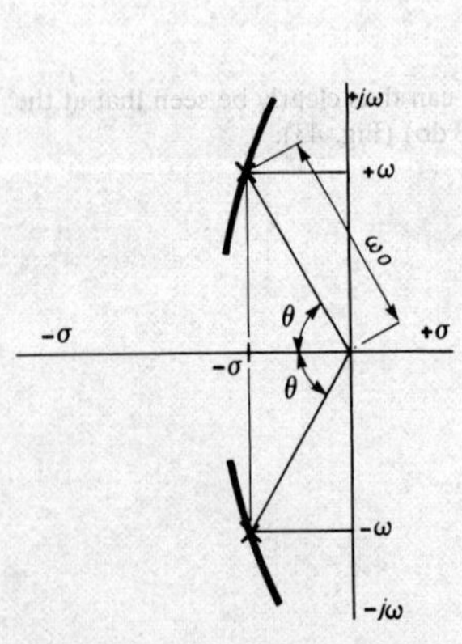

FIG. 44.—Second Order System with Roots $\sigma = \pm j\omega$.

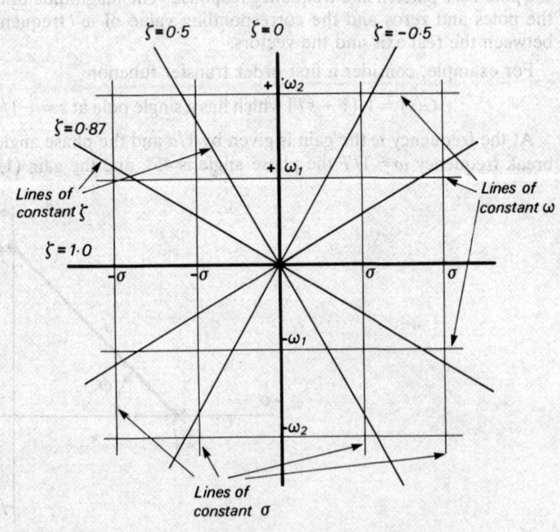

FIG. 45.—Lines of constant ζ, σ and ω on the s plane.

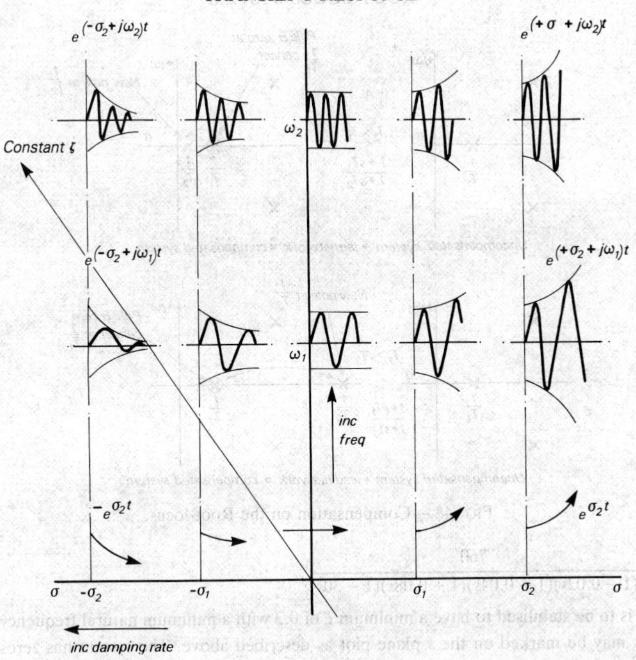

FIG. 46.—Rate of Decay of Transient Response Determined by Real Root σ.

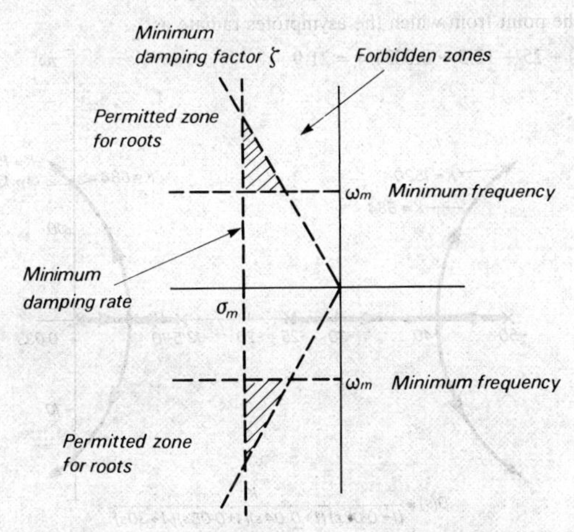

FIG. 47.—Forbidden Zones defining 'Response Time' and 'Settling Time'.

Compensation.—Compensation involves modifying the pole-zero pattern in order to achieve the required form of locus. With series compensation addition of the basic lag and lead compensation networks discussed above introduces one extra pole and one extra zero. If the zero is positioned over one of the existing system poles then this is cancelled and the net effect is to move the original pole—towards the origin with lag compensation, away from the origin with lead compensation.

Feedback compensation involves modifying the existing system poles or zeros by local feedback loops. In this case the local feedback enables complex poles to be introduced if required.

For example, consider the system having an open-loop transfer function:

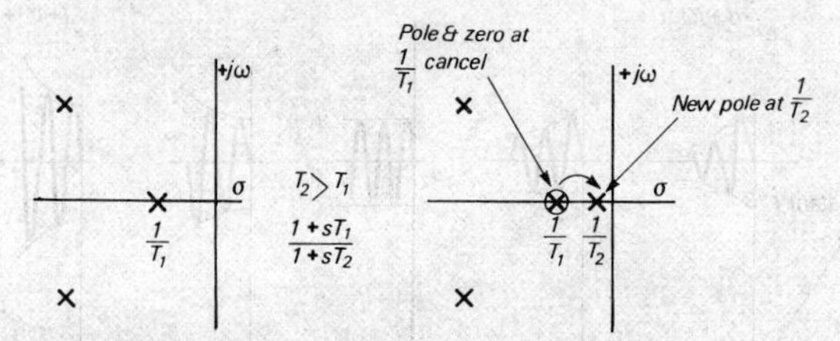

Uncompensated system + lag network = compensated system

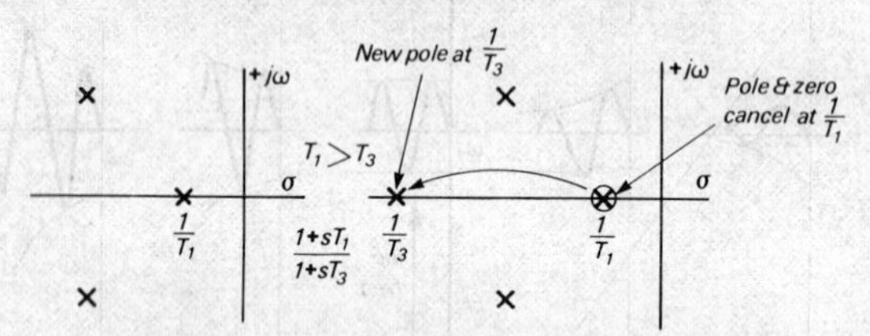

Uncompensated system + lead network = compensated system

FIG. 48.—Compensation on the Root-locus.

$$\frac{760}{(1 + 0.02s)(1 + 0.04s)(1 + 0.08s)(1 + 30s)}$$

This system is to be stabilised to have a minimum ζ of 0.3 with a minimum natural frequency of 20 rad/sec.

These limits may be marked on the s plane plot as described above. The system has zeros at -50, -25, -12.5, -0.033.

Rule 5 gives the angle of the asymptotes as $(180)/4 = 45°$.

Rule 6 gives the point from which the asymptotes radiate as

$$(50 + 25 + 12.5 + 0.033)/4 = 21.9$$

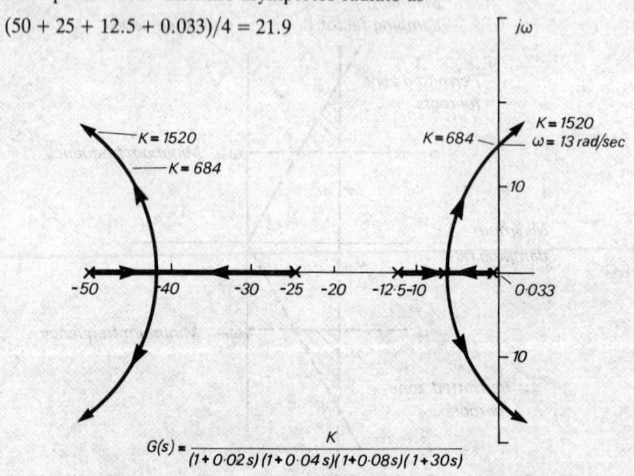

FIG. 49.—Root-locus of Basic System; $G(s) = \dfrac{K}{(1 + 0{\cdot}02s)(1 + 0{\cdot}04s)(1 + 0{\cdot}08s)(1 + 30s)}$.

The point of intersection with the real axis is 13.2 at a gain of 684. The second pair of complex roots are highly damped $\sigma/\omega \gg 1$ and well away from the real axis. They will thus exert little influence, and for preliminary design purposes, may be ignored.

Thus the basic system is unstable since the loop gain (760) is greater than that for limiting stability (684).

To stabilise the system consider the effect of a series lead network having a transfer function $(1 + 0.08\,s)/(1 + 0.008s)$. This has the effect of cancelling out the original pole at $-1/0.08$ (12·5) and replacing it with one at $-1/0.008$ (-125).

The system transfer function is now

$$\left[\frac{760}{(1 + 0.02s)(1 + 0.04s)(1 + 0.008s)(1 + 30s)}\right]$$

the new root locus is shown in Fig 50. The effect of the adjusted pole is to move the locus as shown giving a crossing of the real axis at $\omega = 28$ at a gain of 1500.

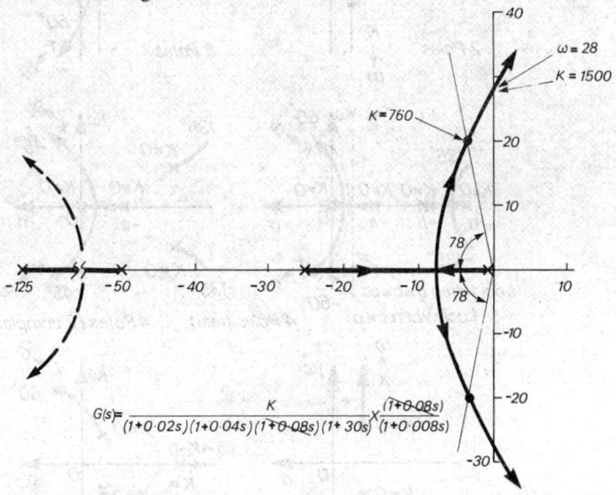

FIG. 50.—Root-locus of Basic System with Lead Compensation.

At the loop gain of 750 the system is stable with a $\zeta = \cos 78° = 0.21$. This gives insufficient stability margin and a further compensating network is necessary. Adding another lead network having a transfer function $(1 + 0.04s)/(1 + 0.004s)$ will move the pole at -25 to -250.

The resulting root locus is shown in Fig. 51.

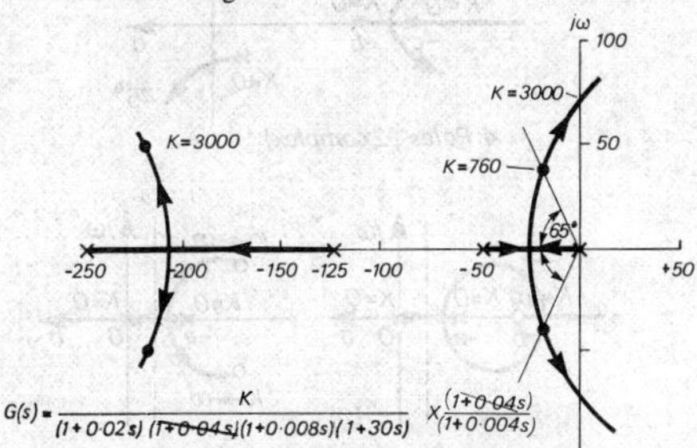

FIG. 51.—Root Locus with Second Compensating Network.

It is seen that the closed-loop roots at the loop gain of 760 have a damping factor of $\cos 65° = 0.42$ which is within the design specification.

This example is covered in more detail on page 32.

The design process using the root-locus is made easier if a familiarity is developed for the form of root-locus which applies to the more commonly occurring pole-zero configurations. This can only be gained by experience. Loci for the basic configurations are given in Fig 52, and illustrate the effects of adding poles and zeros.

From Fig. 52 the following basic conclusions may be drawn.

(1) The addition of poles moves the locus to the right and is in general de-stabilising.

(2) The addition of zeros moves the locus to the left and is stabilising.

LAPLACE TRANSFORMS.—Laplace transforms are used to evaluate the time solution of differential equations, using algebraic methods and are an invaluable aid to the control system designer.

The Laplace transform is formally defined by the equation

$$G(s) = g(t)\, e^{-st}\, dt$$

This is the direct Laplace transformation giving the Laplace transform $G(s)$ in terms of the time function $g(t)$.

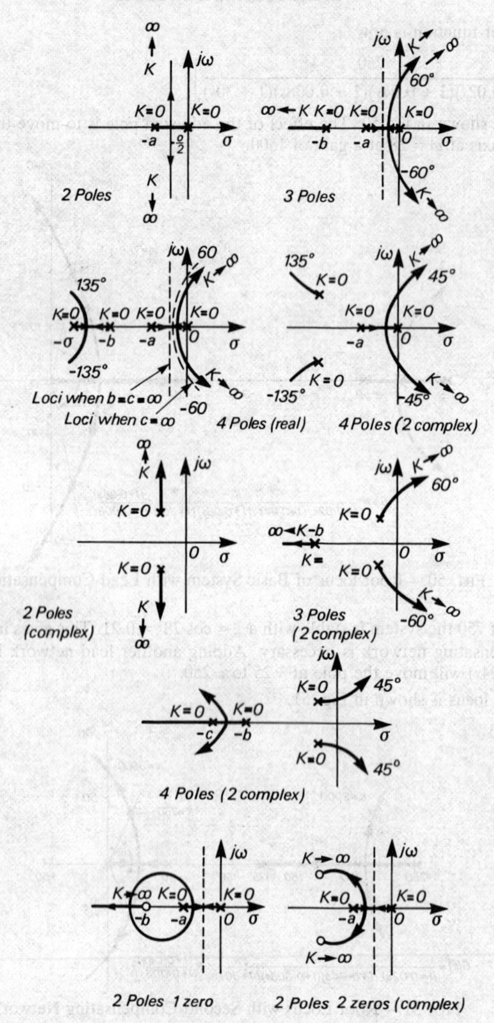

FIG. 52.—Root Loci for Various Pole-Zero Configurations.

The inverse transformation is given by

$$g(t) = \frac{1}{2\pi j} \int_{C-j\infty}^{C+j\infty} G(s)\, e^{ts}\, ds \qquad t > 0$$

where C is larger than σ the real parts of the singularities of $F(s)$.

The transformation permits consideration of analysis and design in terms of functions of the complex variable $s = \sigma + j\omega$ rather than as time functions. The usefulness of the Laplace transform stems primarily from the fact that differentiation of the time function corresponds to the multiplication of the transform by s. Thus differential equations become algebraic equations in s.

The theorems and properties of Laplace transforms are discussed at length in the literature and will not be dealt with here.

If it were necessary to carry out the above integrations for every application, there would obviously be little point in using them. However tables of transform pairs—the functions $g(t)$ and their transforms $G(s)$ have been built up and are available in the literature to make the operation simple.

A table of the basic transform pairs is given in Appendix 3.

Consider as an example a transfer function:

$$G(s) = \frac{10}{(s+2)(s+3)}$$

If we consider a unit step input $V_{in(s)} = 1/s$.

The response will be given by:

$$V_0(s) = \frac{10}{s(s+2)(s+3)}$$

which may be expanded as partial fractions to give

$$\frac{A}{s} + \frac{B}{s+2} + \frac{C}{s+3}$$

Solving gives

$$A = \frac{10}{6} = 1.67 \qquad B = -5 \qquad C = \frac{10}{3} = 3.33$$

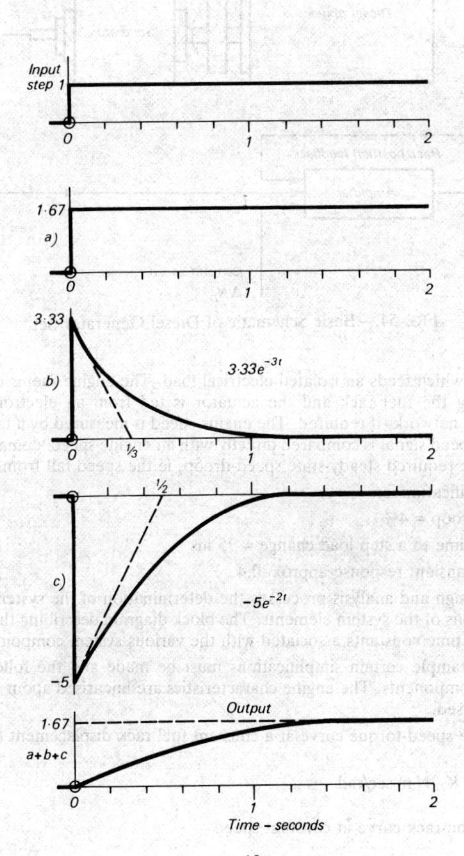

FIG. 53.—Response of $\frac{10}{(s+2)(s+3)}$ to Unit Step Input.

Thus

$$V_0(s) = \frac{1.67}{s} - \frac{5}{s+2} + \frac{3.33}{s+3}$$

from transform tables this gives the time response as

$$V_0(t) = 1.67 - 5e^{-2t} + 3.33\, e^{-3t}$$

This response is as shown in Fig. 53

AN EXAMPLE OF SYSTEM DESIGN AND COMPENSATION

Consider the speed control of a diesel generating set.

The mechanical arrangement of the set is shown in Fig. 54 and consists of a diesel engine directly coupled

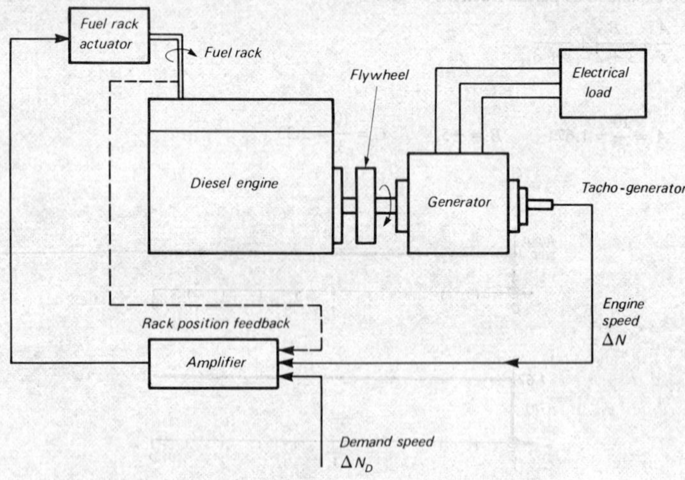

FIG. 54.—Basic Schematic of Diesel Generator Set.

to an electrical generator which feeds an isolated electrical load. The engine fuel is controlled via an electromagnetic actuator moving the fuel rack and the actuator is fed from an electronic amplifier which may incorporate compensation networks if required. The engine speed is measured by a tachogenerator coupled to the output shaft and the speed signal is compared directly with an engine speed 'demand' signal. The loop gain of the system is set by the required steady-state speed-droop, ie the speed fall from no-load to full-load.

The required system specification is:

Steady state speed droop = 4%

Maximum response time to a step load change = 75 ms

Damping factor of transient response approx. 0.4

The first step in the design and analysis process is the determination of the system parameters in order to derive the transfer functions of the system elements. The block diagram describing the system is shown in Fig. 55 showing the gains and time constants associated with the various system components.

For purposes of the example certain simplifications must be made and the following characteristics are assumed for the system components. The engine characteristics are linearised about the working point, ie the slopes of the curves are used.

The slope of the engine speed-torque curve at a constant fuel rack displacement (Fig. 56)

$$\left.\frac{\partial \tau}{\partial N}\right|_{(x=\text{const})} = K_D \text{ N m sec/rad}$$

and the slope of the torque-rack curve at constant speed

$$\left.\frac{\partial \tau}{\partial x}\right|_{(N=\text{const})} = K_M \text{ N m/mm}$$

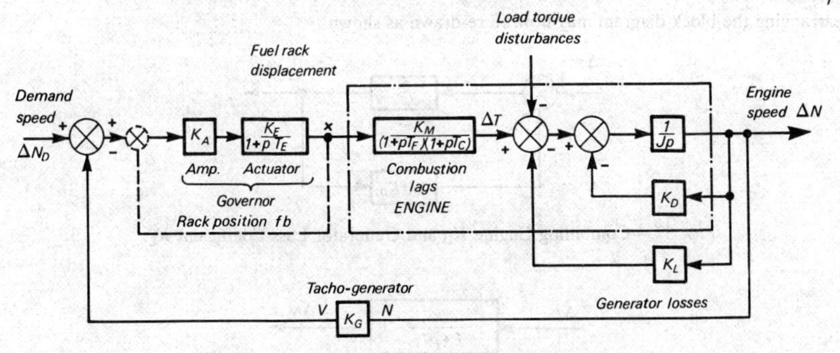

FIG. 55.—Block Diagram of Engine/Generator System.

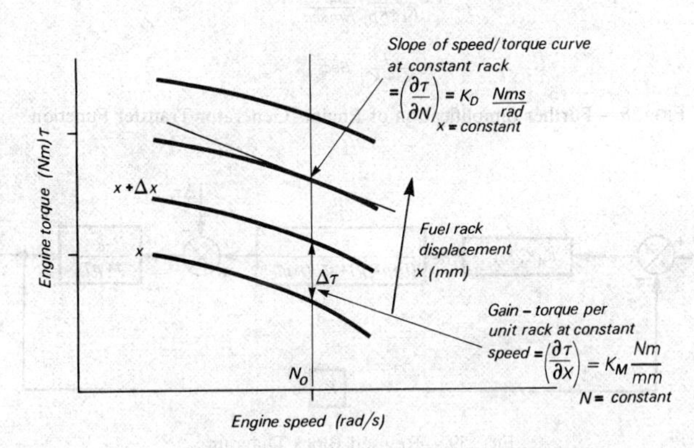

FIG. 56.—Engine Speed/Torque/Fuel Rack Characteristics.

These gains will change with operating point for an actual engine, and in practice stability analyses may be necessary at several points throughout the operating range. Due to the linearisation of engine characteristics the equations are only valid for small perturbations about the assumed working point. For this reason the input and output variables are designated ΔN_D $\Delta\tau_L$, $\Delta\tau$ etc.

The equivalent input to the engine is the movement of the fuel rack. This controls the fuel input and, following the firing stroke, produces torque. There are thus delays between the movement of the rack and the production of torque. This is a complex process and a considerable amount of study has been carried out on the dynamics of combustion. A range of dynamic models have been postulated, but for the purposes of this example we will assume that the delay due to the "sampled-data" nature of the process, ie the discrete firing strokes may be represented by a time constant of T_F sec and the combustion delay by a time constant of T_C sec.

The other engine parameter of interest is the moment of inertia of its rotating parts—the crankshaft and flywheel. As the engine and generator are solidly coupled the engine and generator inertias may be combined—giving an inertia of J kg m^2.

GENERATOR AND LOAD CHARACTERISTICS.—It will be assumed that the load is constant, independent of speed and the generator losses are assumed to be proportional to speed, ie loss torque $(Nm) = K_L \times$ speed (rad/sec).

GOVERNOR.—An electronic governor is assumed comprising an amplifier of gain K_A amp/V driving an electromagnetic actuator moving the fuel rack and having a gain $K_E$mm/amp and a time constant T_E sec.

SPEED MEASUREMENT.—The engine speed is measured by tachogenerator having a gain K_G volts . sec/rad.

BLOCK DIAGRAM.—The block diagram of the system is shown in Fig. 55. The engine/generator load blocks may be simplified by combined K_L and K_D which may be further simplified.

Rearranging the block diagram may now be re-drawn as shown.

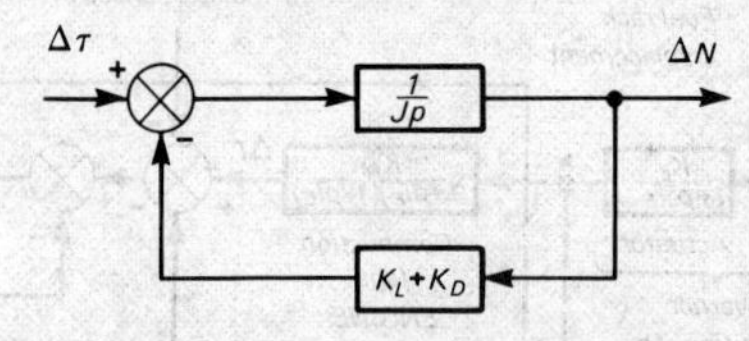

FIG. 57.—Combining Engine K_D and Generator Loss Coefficient K_L.

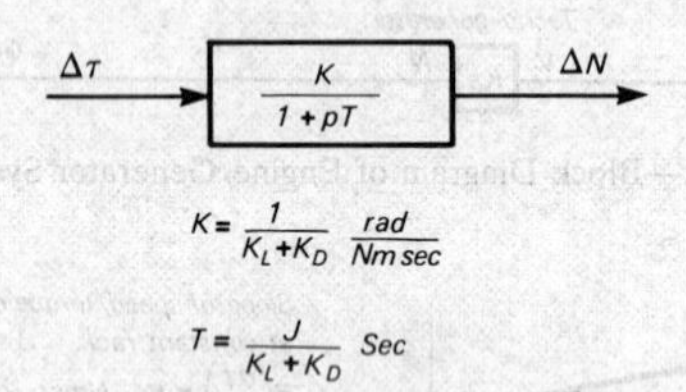

FIG. 58.—Further Simplification of Engine–Generator Transfer Function.

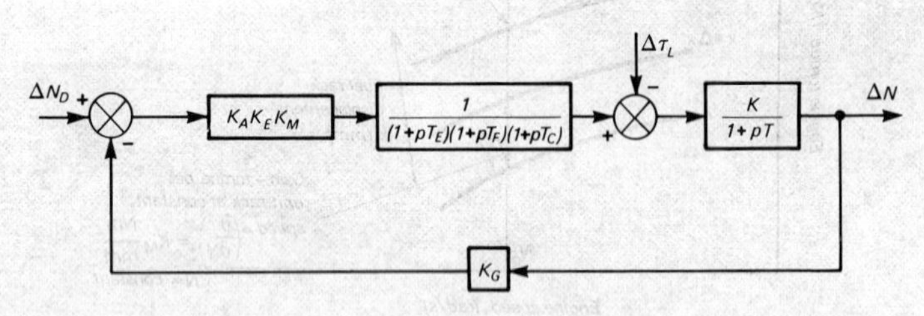

FIG. 59.—Revised Block Diagram.

Open loop transfer function

$$\frac{K_A K_E K_M K_G K}{(1 + pT_E)(1 + pT_F)(1 + pT_C)(1 + pT)}$$

Closed loop transfer function

$$\frac{\Delta N}{\Delta N_D} = \frac{K_A K_E K_M K_G K}{(1 + pT_E)(1 + pT_F)(1 + pT_C)(1 + pT) + K_A K_E K_M K_G K}$$

COEFFICIENT VALUES.—Stability is normally most critical at low loads, when the engine damping is small and the engine gain is high. The values given below correspond with the low load condition:

Speed droop = 4%

Full-load engine speed 180 rpm = 18.85 rad/sec

No-load—full-load engine fuel rack 0–6 mm

K_D	Slope of the engine speed torque characteristic at a constant rack = 11 Nm . sec/rad
K_L	Generator loss coefficient 2.7 Nm . sec/rad
K_M	Slope of engine torque/rack characteristic at a constant speed = 1300 Nm/mm
J	Combined inertia of engine and generator = 410 kg . m^2
T_C	Combustion time constant = 0.04 sec
T_F	Firing time constant = 0.02 sec
K_E	Actuator gain = 0.6 mm/V
T_E	Actuator time constant = 0.08 sec
K_G	Tachogenerator gain = 1 V rad/sec

$$\text{Thus } K = \frac{1}{K_D + K_L} = \frac{1}{11 + 2.7} \qquad T = \frac{J}{K_D + K_L} = \frac{410}{11 + 2.7} = 30 \text{ sec.}$$

The loop gain and hence K_A is determined by the required speed-droop. Assuming a 4% droop, ie the speed falls by 4% for a 100% increase in load torque, ie a change speed of $(4/100) \times 18{\cdot}85 = 0{\cdot}754$ rad/sec must produce 6 mm fuel rack motion.

Thus

$$\text{gain from speed to fuel rack} = K_M \times K_A \times K_E = \frac{6}{0{\cdot}754} \frac{\text{mm . sec}}{\text{rad}} = 8 \frac{\text{mm sec}}{\text{rad}}$$

Therefore

$$\begin{aligned} \text{loop-gain} &= K_G \times K_A \times K_E \times K_M \times K \\ &= 1 \times 8 \times K_m \times K \\ &= 8 \times 1300 \times \frac{1}{(11 + 2{\cdot}7)} = 760 \end{aligned}$$

Also

$$K_A = \frac{8}{K_G K_E} = \frac{8}{1 \times 0{\cdot}6} = 13{\cdot}3\ V/V$$

Thus, assuming for the moment that there are no load disturbances, ie $\Delta\tau_L = 0$, the block diagram may be drawn

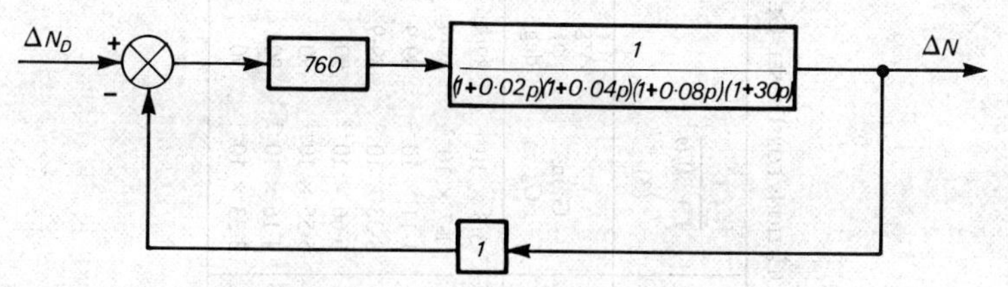

FIG. 60.—Block Diagram with Numerical Values.

giving an open-loop transfer function

$$G(p) = \frac{760}{(1 + 0{\cdot}02p)\,(1 + 0{\cdot}04p)\,(1 + 0{\cdot}08p)\,(1 + 30p)}$$

STABILITY—The stability of the system may now be investigated by calculating the gain and phase of the above, transfer function blocks and combining to form the complete system transfer function. This may be determined using tables as given in Appendix 1 or alternatively the calculation may be easily automated on a calculator or desk-top computer.

Sample calculations illustrating the process are given in Table 1.

This frequency response is illustrated on 4 plots, where the effects of the various forms of compensation are also shown. (a) Bode Diagram (Fig. 61), (b) Nyquist Plot (Fig. 62), (c) Inverse Nyquist Plot (Fig. 63) and (d) Nichols Chart (Fig. 64).

In each case it can be seen that the basic system is unstable having a gain of approximately 1·2 at the frequency at which the open-loop phase shift is 180°.

To stabilise the system it is necessary to introduce frequency compensation, either by connecting networks in series with the amplifier or by adding extra feed-back loops.

To design the series networks the above calculations are repeated to find the gain and phase of the chosen network over the frequency range of interest. The system frequency response is then modified by adding the network characteristics and the loci replotted.

For purposes of illustration the effects of both lag and lead series compensating networks are investigated and the results are plotted on the Bode, Nyquist and Nichols charts.

LAG COMPENSATION.—The effect of a series lag compensating network having a transfer function $(1 + p)/(1 + 5p)$ is shown. These values were chosen to give a gain reduction of 1/5 at high frequencies. To avoid exacerbating the instability the phase lag must occur at frequencies below 10 rad/sec.

This network gives a stable system having gain and phase margins of 12·5 db and 45° as shown. Although

TABLE 1.—STABILITY CALCULATIONS FOR DIESEL GENERATING SET

Frequency	$\frac{1}{1+0{\cdot}04j\omega}$ (1)			$\frac{1}{1+0{\cdot}08j\omega}$ (2)			$\frac{1}{1+30j\omega}$ (3)			$\frac{1}{1+0{\cdot}02j\omega}$ (4)			Complete system	
ω rad/sec.	$0{\cdot}04\omega$	Gain G_1	Arg ϕ_1 deg	$0{\cdot}08\omega$	Gain G_2	Arg ϕ_2 deg	30ω	Gain G_3	Arg ϕ_3 deg	$0{\cdot}02\omega$	Gain G_4	Arg ϕ_4 deg	Gain $G_1G_2G_3G_4$ $\times 760$	Arg $\phi_1+\phi_2+\phi_3+\phi_4$
1	0·04	1	2·3	0·08	1	4·6	30	$3{\cdot}3 \times 10^{-2}$	89·8	0·02	1	1	25·1	98
2	0·08	1	4·6	0·16	0·99	9·1	60	$1{\cdot}7 \times 10^{-2}$	89·9	0·04	1	2·3	12·7	106
3	0·12	1	6·8	0·24	0·97	13·4	90	$1{\cdot}11 \times 10^{-2}$	89·9	0·06	1	3·4	8·2	113
4	0·16	0·99	9·1	0·32	0·95	17·7	120	$8{\cdot}33 \times 10^{-3}$	89·9	0·08	1	4·6	5·9	121
5	0·2	0·98	11·3	0·4	0·93	21·8	150	$6{\cdot}66 \times 10^{-3}$	90	0·1	1	5·7	4·6	129
6	0·24	0·97	13·5	0·48	0·9	25·6	180	$5{\cdot}55 \times 10^{-3}$	90	0.12	1	6·8	3·7	135
8	0·32	0·95	17·7	0·64	0·84	32·6	240	$4{\cdot}16 \times 10^{-3}$	90	0·16	1	9·9	2·5	150
10	0·4	0.93	21·8	0·8	0·78	39	300	$3{\cdot}33 \times 10^{-4}$	90	0·2	1	11·3	1·8	162

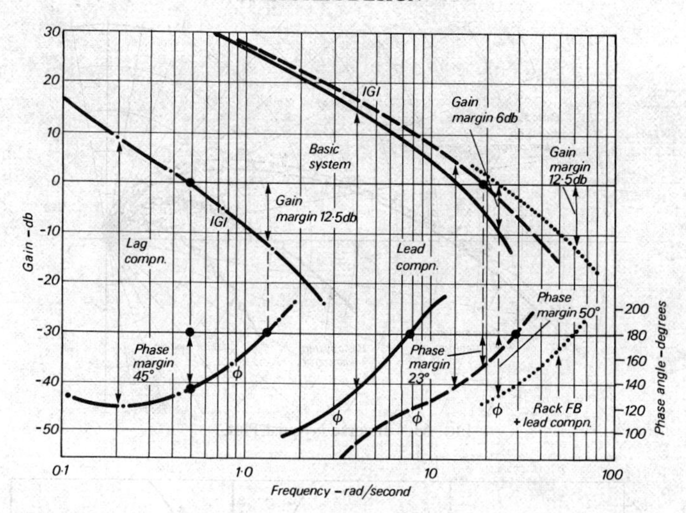

FIG. 61.—Bode Diagram for (a) Basic System ——; (b) Basic System + Lead Compensation – – –; (c) Basic System + Lag Compensation ·–·–·; (d) Basic System + Rack Feed-back + Lead Compensation ·····.

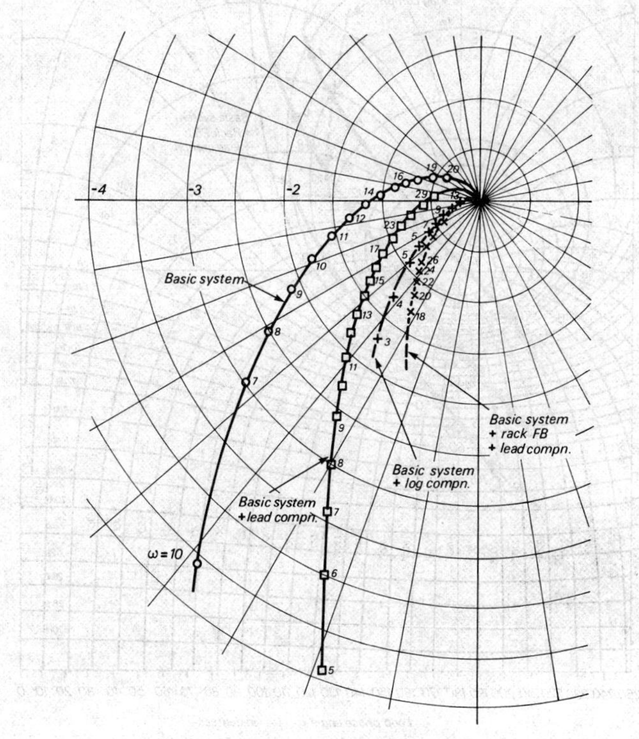

FIG. 62.—Nyquist Plot.

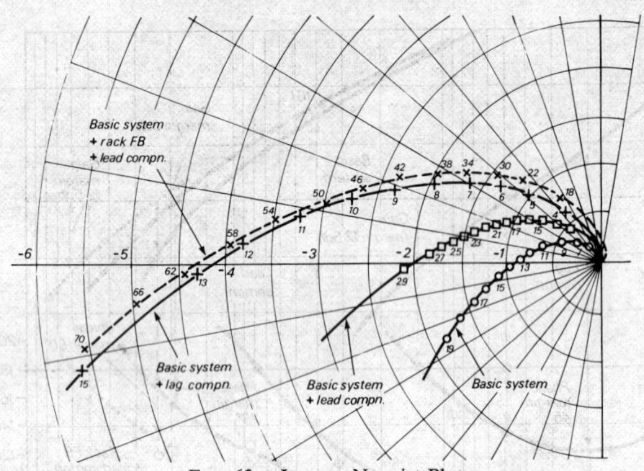

FIG. 63.—Inverse Nyquist Plot.

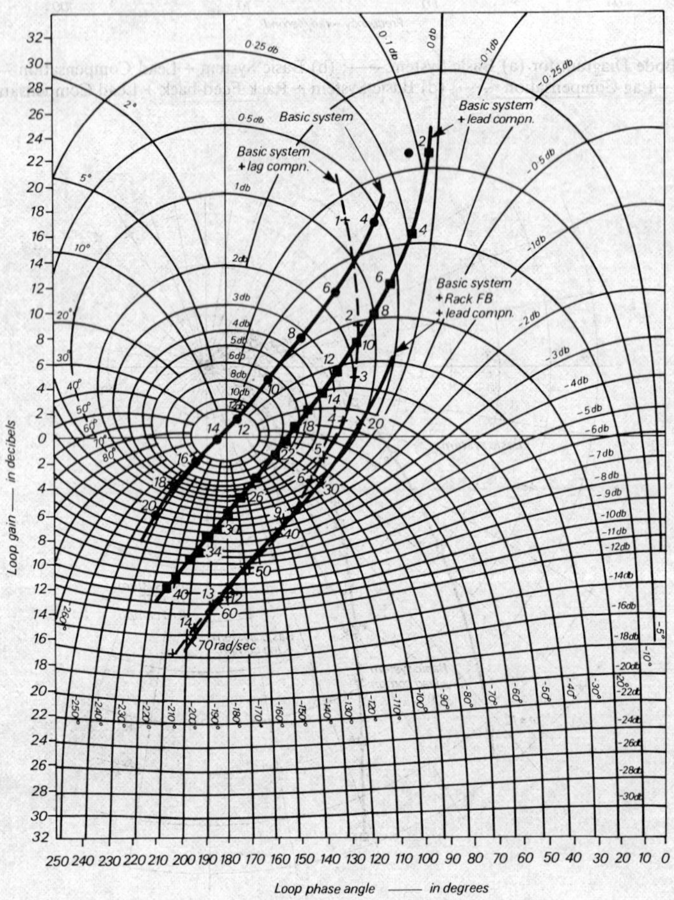

FIG. 64.—Nichols Chart.

this system is stable the critical frequency is approximately 2 rad/sec which is significantly less than that of the original system and which will not give the required time response.

LEAD COMPENSATION.—The effect of a series lead compensating network having a transfer function (1 + 0·08p)/(1 + 0·008p) is shown.

These values were chosen having a T_1/T_2 ratio of 10 which gives a maximum phase lead of approximately 55°. The break frequency of the lead-term is usually set at a frequency slightly below that at which the Nyquist locus crosses the negative real axis (ie phase shift = 180°). In this case the cross-over frequency is 13 rad/sec and the break frequency is set to 12·5 rad/sec (1/12·5 = 0·08 sec).

Larger values of phase lead are possible but give a greater increase in the high frequency gain of the system. As noise is present in all practical systems the effect of such gain increases can seriously degrade system performance as the higher frequency noise components are amplified and may cause saturation in the later amplifier stages. For a similar reason care must be taken in employing more than one phase lead network. In this case although the compensated system is now stable the gain and phase margins (6 db and 23°) are insufficient. As additional lead-networks could cause problems as detailed above, feedback compensation is investigated as an alternative method of improving stability.

FEEDBACK COMPENSATION.—If a position transducer is connected to the fuel rack it is possible to introduce an additional feed-back around the amplifier and actuator as shown dotted in Figs. 54 and 55. By adjustment of the gain within this subsidiary loop the effective time constant of the actuator may be reduced as shown in Fig. 65.

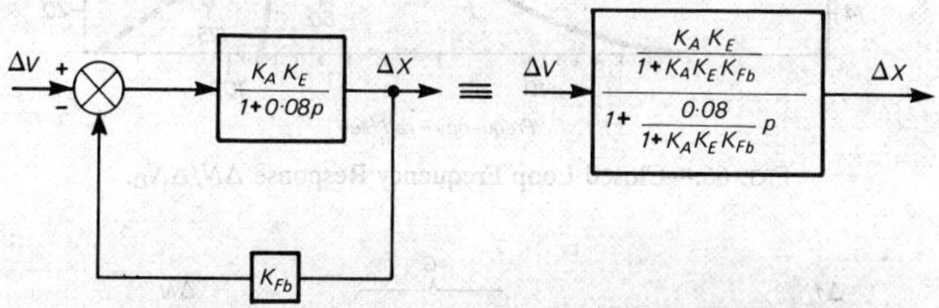

FIG. 65.—Effect of Fuel-rack Position Feed-back on Actuator Transfer Function.

Thus if $(K_A K_E K_{fb} + 1)$ is made equal to 10 then the actuator time constant is reduced from 0·08 to 0·008. The gain $K_A K_E$ will be reduced by the same factor and a pre-amplifier must be introduced to restore the lost gain to maintain the required loop gain and hence speed droop. The effect of this feedback is identical to that of the phase lead compensator $(1 + 0{\cdot}08p)/(1 + 0{\cdot}008p)$ examined above and, as it was seen, is insufficient in itself to give adequate stability. If we now introduce a further series lead network having a transfer function $(1 + 0{\cdot}04p)/(1 + 0{\cdot}004p)$ in addition to the subsidiary feedback, the modified Nyquist locus and Bode diagrams show that the system is adequately stable. The gain and phase margins are now 12·5 db and 50° which are satisfactory. The critical frequency is approximately 24 rad/sec which ensures that the time response specification will be met.

The root loci for the various forms of compensation were given in the previous section and are shown on Figs. 49, 50 and 51. It was seen in the root-locus design that the effect of the lead compensation $(1 + 0{\cdot}04p)/(1 + 0{\cdot}004p)$ is to cancel out the $(1 + 0{\cdot}04p)$ term in the denominator giving a transfer function.

$$G(p) = \frac{760}{(1 + 0{\cdot}02p)(1 + 0{\cdot}008p)(1 + 0{\cdot}004p)(1 + 30p)}$$

Comparison with the original system shows that the two original denominator time constants (0·08 sec. and 0·04 sec.) have been decreased by a factor of 10.

Closed Loop Response.—If we now take the Nichols Plot (Fig. 64) of the compensated system the values of closed-loop gain and phase may be read off and are shown plotted in Fig. 66. This gives the response in engine speed to a 'set speed' demand. Of more interest with a generating set of this type is the change in engine speed response to changes in load. For sudden changes in load the speed response should be rapid (specified as within 0·075 sec) and the resulting transient, well damped. To determine the response to load changes we must re-arrange the original block diagram (including compensation), to present the load torque ($\Delta\tau_L$), as the demanded input and engine speed as the output. For zero 'set speed' demand this is shown in Fig. 67.

The resulting closed-loop transfer function $G'(p)$ is given by

$$\frac{\Delta N}{\Delta \tau_L} = \frac{G}{1 + GH}$$

$$= \frac{K(1 + 0{\cdot}02p)(1 + 0{\cdot}008p)(1 + 0{\cdot}004p)}{(1 + 0{\cdot}02p)(1 + 0{\cdot}008p)(1 + 0{\cdot}004p)(1 + 30p) + K_G K_M K_E K_M K}$$

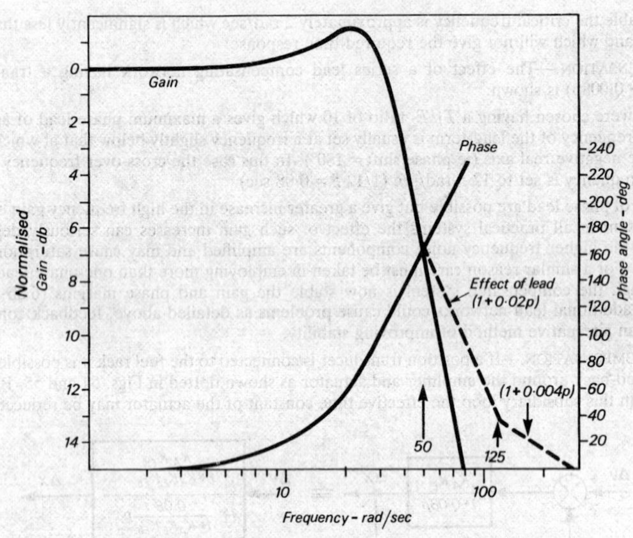

FIG. 66.—Closed Loop Frequency Response $\Delta N/\Delta N_D$.

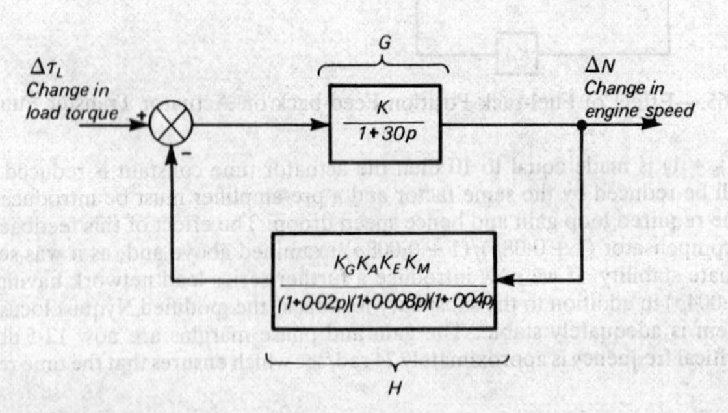

FIG. 67.—Block Diagram showing Response in Engine Speed (ΔN) to Changes in Load ($\Delta\tau_L$).

Comparing this with that of the transfer function $\Delta N/\Delta N_D$ above it is seen that the gain is reduced by a factor $(K_A K_E K_M K_G)$ and three phase-lead terms $(1 + 0{\cdot}02p)$ $(1 + 0{\cdot}008p)$ $(1 + 0{\cdot}004p)$ are added in the numerator.

We may thus obtain the desired frequency response $\Delta N/\Delta\tau_D$ by adjustment of the response $\Delta N/\Delta N_D$ given in Fig. 66.

The dynamic terms may be obtained by adding asymptotes of slope + 6 db/octave at the points

$$\omega_1 = 1/0{\cdot}02 = 50, \qquad \omega_2 = 1/0{\cdot}008 = 125, \qquad \omega_3 = 1/0{\cdot}004 = 250$$

on Fig. 66 and rescaling the gain axis.

It is seen that apart from the gain change the response is unaltered around the 20 rad/sec region and hence the transient response will be unchanged. [This effect may also be seen on the root-locus (Fig. 51). If the 3 poles at -50, -125 and -500 are added. The effect on the frequency response will still be dominated by the pair of complex poles close to the real axis].

From Fig. 66 it is seen that the frequency response peaks at a frequency of 23 rad/sec and the magnification Mp is 1·5 db (×1·2).

From the relationships given in above and in Fig. 17 this corresponds with a damping factor of $\zeta = 1/2{\cdot}4 = 0{\cdot}42$.

This implies an overshoot of approximately 25% to a step response with a rise time of approximately 0.1 sec, and 1 cycle of oscillation before settling.

These values correspond with those obtained from the root locus design (page 29) and the compensated system meets the required specification.

The computed time response of the system for a step input in load torque is given in Fig. 68 and confirms the above predictions.

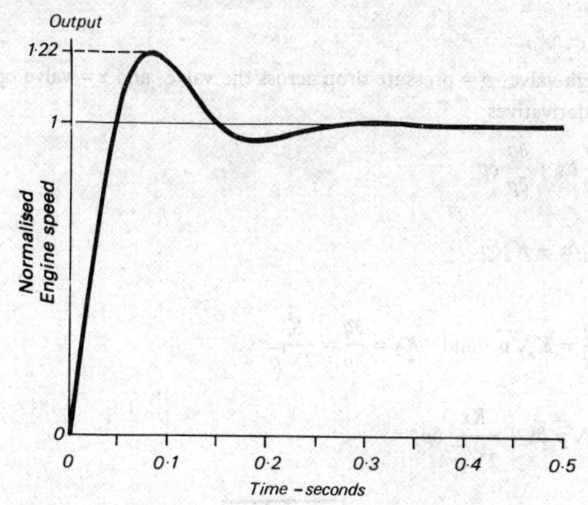

FIG. 68.—Engine Speed Response to Step Load Change.

It should be noted that this step-response is only valid for small changes in load torque/engine speed due to the linearisation of the engine characteristics. It could not therefore be used to predict the response to a large load change.

NON-LINEAR ELEMENTS IN CONTROL SYSTEMS

All the techniques described in previous sections are based upon the representation of the system by linear equations.

In practice, few systems are linear and in many hydraulic and mechanical systems major non-linearities occur arising from factors such as static friction, saturation, square-law pressure/flow relationships etc. If the design and analysis is to adequately represent the real system then the effects of the various non-linear elements must be included.

Non-linear elements may be classified into two basic groups:

(i) Non-linearities arising from non-linear relationships, ie square-law orifice characteristics, magnetisation curve effects, 'soft' saturation effects etc.

These effects are normally dealt with by linearising the characteristic about the particular working point. Then assuming that the signal level is small the local slope of the non-linear characteristic is taken as the gain. This is illustrated in Fig. 69.

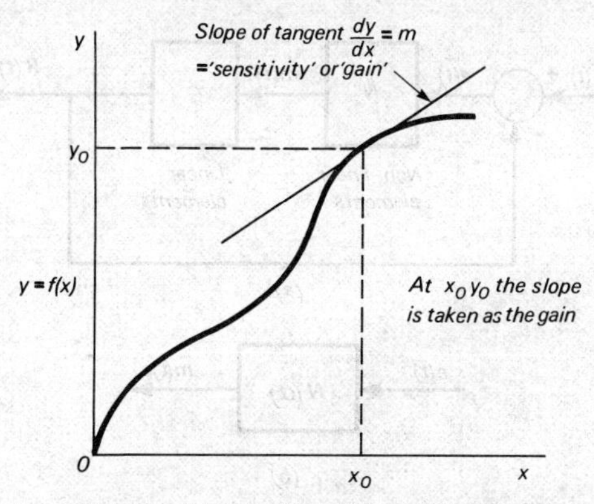

FIG. 69.—Linearisation of Characteristics.

With analytic functions the slope is found by differentiation of the function. With non-analytic functions the slope may be found by measurement.

With non-linear functions of two variables partial derivatives are used to determine the two incremental slopes. For example the flow/pressure relationship in a hydraulic spool valve, having spool displacement x is given by the equation.

$$q = K \, . \, x \, . \sqrt{p}$$

where q = flow through valve, p = pressure drop across the valve, and x = valve opening.

Taking the partial derivatives

$$\delta q = \frac{\partial q}{\partial x}\delta x + \frac{\partial q}{\partial p}\delta p$$

ie

$$\delta q = K_1 \delta x + K_2 \delta p$$

where

$$K_1 = \frac{\partial q}{\partial x} = K\sqrt{p} \quad \text{and} \quad K_2 = \frac{\partial q}{\partial p} = \frac{Kx}{2\sqrt{p}}$$

$$\delta q = K\sqrt{p}\,\delta x + \frac{Kx}{2\sqrt{p}}\delta p$$

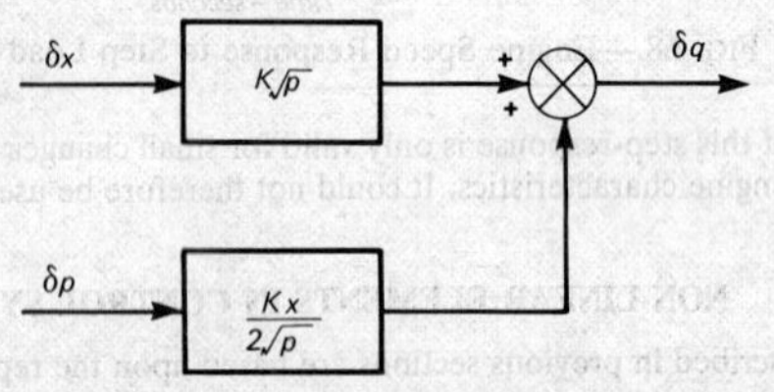

FIG. 70.—Linearisation of Hydraulic Spool Valve Characteristics.

(ii) Non-linearities arising from 'hard' saturation, dead-band, double-valued relationships such as hysteresis and backlash may be approximated using the *Describing Function Technique.*

Describing Function Technique.—This technique is employed in the frequency domain to evaluate the effect of amplitude dependent non-linearities. If a non-linear element is fed with a sinewave input the output will be a distorted signal including both the fundamental and harmonics of the input sinewave. The *Describing Function Technique* is based on the assumption that the output harmonics may be neglected, because they will be attenuated by other elements in the control loop, and the fundamental component only may be considered.

With single valued non-linearities no phase shift is introduced by the non-linear element, merely an attenuation or gain.

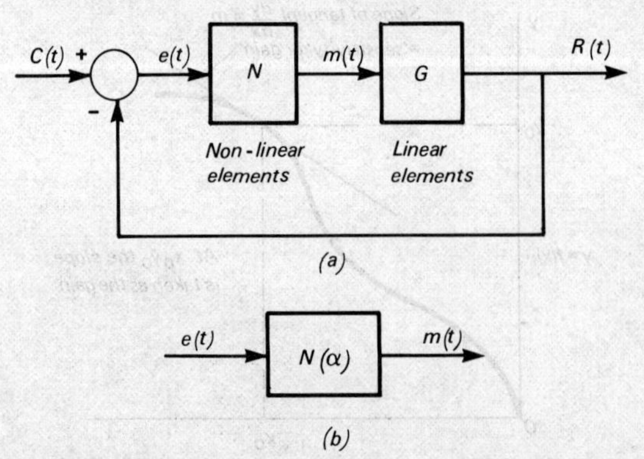

FIG. 71.—(a) Servo System with Non-linear Elements, (b) Single Non-linear Element.

The characteristics of some common non-linearities are shown in Appendix 4. The describing function N is given by:

$$N = \frac{\text{Fundamental component of output from Fourier Analysis}}{\text{Amplitude of sinusoidal input signal}}$$

It can be shown that N is a non-linear function which may be a function of amplitude or frequency or both. The method is based on the assumption that a control system contains only one non-linear element as shown:

If the input to the non-linear element $N(\alpha)$ is assumed to be

$$e(t) = E \sin \omega t$$

The output of the non-linear element $m(t)$ is a periodic function and may be represented by the Fourier series

$$m(t) = \sum_{n=1}^{n=\infty} (A_n \cos_n \omega t + B_n \sin_n \omega t)$$

where

$$A_n = \frac{1}{\pi}\int_{-\pi}^{+\pi} m(t) \cos n\omega t \, \mathrm{d}\omega t$$

$$B_n = \frac{1}{\pi}\int_{-\pi}^{+\pi} m(t) \sin n\omega t \, \mathrm{d}\omega t$$

The constant term in the Fourier series has been omitted since it assumed that the average valve of $m(t)$ is zero. This is true providing the non-linear element possesses symmetrical characteristics.

Taking the fundamental components of the Fourier series

$$\begin{aligned} m(t) &= A_1 \cos \omega t + B_1 \sin \omega t \\ &= \sqrt{A_1^2 + B_1^2} \sin(\omega t + \phi) \\ &= M_1 \sin(\omega t + \phi) \end{aligned}$$

where

$$\phi = \tan^{-1} A_1/B_1 \quad \text{and} \quad M_1 = \sqrt{A_1^2 + B_1^2}$$

The describing function is then defined according to the previous definition of N

$$N = \frac{M_1}{E} e^{-j\phi}$$

Therefore N is complex where ϕ is not zero. Thus the describing function N generally has the magnitude M_1/E and a phase angle ϕ.

Considering the Nyquist Diagram it is now possible to deal with a single non-linearity in the frequency domain with a non-linear function defined as $N(\alpha)$ in a control loop.

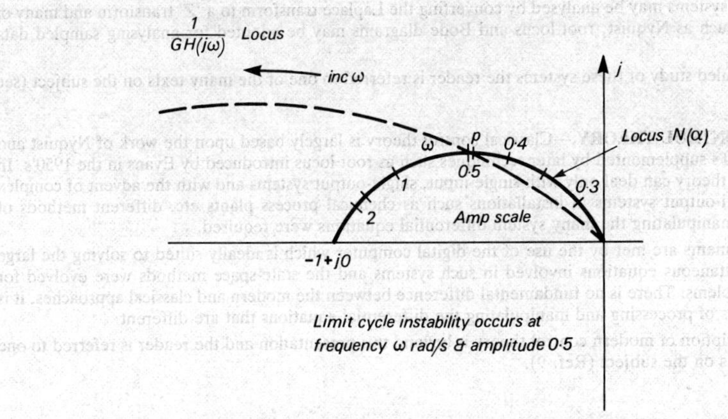

FIG. 72.—Describing Function for Hysteresis used with the Inverse Nyquist Locus.

The loop transfer function is $G(j\omega)H(j\omega)N(\alpha)$ and the condition for stability is:

$$G(j\omega)H(j\omega)N(\alpha) = -1$$

or

$$G(j\omega)H(j\omega) = \frac{-1}{N(\alpha)}$$

It is more convenient when considering most non-linearities in the frequency domain to employ the inverse Nyquist solution as follows

$$\frac{1}{G(j\omega)H(j\omega)} = -N(\alpha)$$

Thus stability is now determined not by the point $(-1, j0)$ but by the locus $-N(\alpha)$. In the case of the backlash non-linearity, $N(\alpha)$ is a cycloid, having amplitude as parameter. With the inverse Nyquist locus shown limiting stability occurs at point p at a frequency given by the inverse Nyquist locus and an amplitude given by the $N(\alpha)$ locus.

Similar techniques may be used on a root locus plot by modifying the basic system root locus to include the gain and phase of the non-linear element $N(\alpha)$.

SAMPLED-DATA SYSTEMS

Conventional feedback control systems have variables that are continuous with time. The advent of digital computers has led to the development of a field of control systems known as sampled-data or digital control systems. Usually 'sampled-data systems' refer to a more general class of systems while 'digital control systems' implies the use of digital computer or digital sensing devices in a control system.

Sampled-data systems pass information from element to element intermittently at specific instants of time. This means that the information is in the form of pulse amplitudes, when there is no pulse, no information is conveyed. If the information is conveyed at fixed intervals of time then the sampling is called '*periodic*'. If the time between pulses in time varying it is termed '*aperiodic*' or '*random*'.

There are many control systems in which the input signal is only available in sampled or discrete form. In modern control systems the applications of sampled-data systems are wide but generally they fall into the following two classes:

Control Systems with Inherent Sampling.—For example a radar tracking system employing digital computer control where the digital computer performs a series of operations on the input sampled-data and supplies an output in digital form to a hold circuit for reconstruction into data that is continuous with time.

Control Systems with Intentional Sampling.—Sometimes sampling is introduced into an otherwise continuous system, and under certain conditions this can, with varying sampling periods, produce a system which has a better performance than the equivalent continuous system. For example, it is possible to stabilise a continuous system which has a dominant transportation lag by the introduction of sampling. Adaptive control systems are also examples where the control parameters are required to change because of the change in plant parameters, this can be more easily achieved if sampling is introduced.

Sampled data systems may be analysed by converting the Laplace transform to a '*Z*' transform and many of the techniques such as Nyquist, root-locus and Bode diagrams may be adopted for analysing sampled data systems.

For more detailed study of these systems the reader is referred to one of the many texts on the subject (see Refs 2, 6, 11).

MODERN CONTROL THEORY.—Classical control theory is largely based upon the work of Nyquist and Bode in the 1930's supplemented by later techniques such as root locus introduced by Evans in the 1950's. In general classical theory can deal only with single-input, single-output systems and with the advent of complex multi-input/multi-output systems in installations such as chemical process plants etc, different methods of processing and manipulating the many system differential equations were required.

These requirements are met by the use of the digital computer which is ideally suited to solving the large number of simultaneous equations involved in such systems and the state-space methods were evolved for solving such problems. There is no fundamental difference between the modern and classical approaches, it is only the methods of processing and manipulating the differential equations that are different.

Detailed description of modern control theory is beyond this presentation and the reader is referred to one of the many texts on the subject (Ref. 9).

APPENDIX 1

TABLES 1(a), 1(b) and 1(c)

MODULUS AND ARGUMENT of $1 + j\omega T$.

$$K = \sqrt{1 + \omega^2 T^2} \quad \phi = \tan^{-1} \omega T$$

TABLE 1(a)

$1 + j\omega T$	K	ϕ deg	$1 + j\omega T$	K	ϕ deg	$1 + j\omega T$	K	ϕ deg
$1 + j0$	1	0	$1 + j4$	4·12	76	$1 + j8$	8·06	82·9
0·1	1·005	5·7	4·1	4·22	76·3	8·1	8·16	83
0·2	1·02	11·3	4·2	4·32	76·6	8·2	8·26	83·1
0·3	1·04	16·7	4·3	4·42	76·9	8·3	8·36	83·15
0·4	1·08	21·8	4·4	4·51	77·2	8·4	8·46	83·2
0·5	1·12	26·6	4·5	4·61	77·5	8·5	8·56	83·3
0·6	1·17	31	4·6	4·71	77·7	8·6	8·66	83·4
0·7	1·22	35	4·7	4·81	78	8·7	8·76	83·45
0·8	1·28	38·7	4·8	4·90	78·3	8·8	8·86	83·5
0·9	1·34	43	4·9	5·00	78·5	8·9	8·95	83·6
$1 + j1$	1·41	45	$1 + j5$	5·10	78·7	$1 + j9$	9.055	83·7
1·1	1·49	47·7	5·1	5·20	78·9	9.1	9·15	83·75
1·2	1·56	50·2	5·2	5·30	79·1	9·2	9·25	83·8
1·3	1·64	52·4	5·3	5·39	79·3	9·3	9·35	83·85
1·4	1·72	54·5	5·4	5·49	79·5	9·4	9·45	83·95
1·5	1·80	56·3	5·5	5·59	79·7	9·5	9·55	84
1·6	1·89	58	5·6	5·69	79·9	9·6	9·65	84·05
1·7	1·97	59·5	5·7	5·79	80·1	9·7	9·75	84·1
1·8	2·06	61	5·8	5·89	80·2	9·8	9·85	84·15
1·9	2·15	62·2	5·9	5·98	80·4	9·9	9·95	84·2
$1 + j2$	2·23	63·5	$1 + j6$	6·08	80·6	$1 + j10$	10·05	84·3
2·1	2·32	64·5	6·1	6·18	80·7	11	11·04	84·8
2·2	2·42	65·6	6·2	6·28	80·9	12	12·04	85·2
2·3	2·51	66·5	6·3	6·38	81	13	13·04	85·6
2·4	2·60	67·4	6·4	6·48	81·1	14	14·03	85·9
2·5	2·69	68·2	6·5	6·58	81·3	15	15·03	86·2
2·6	2·79	69	6·6	6·68	81·4	16	16·03	86·4
2·7	2·88	69·7	6·7	6·78	81·5	17	17·03	86·6
2·8	2·97	70·4	6·8	6·87	81·6	18	18·03	86·8
2·9	3·07	71	6·9	6·97	81·8	19	19·03	87
$1 + j3$	3·16	71·6	$1 + j7$	7·07	81·9	20	20·02	87·1
3·1	3·26	72·1	7·1	7·17	82	30	30·02	88·1
3·2	3·35	72·6	7·2	7·27	82·1	40	40	88·6
3·3	3·45	73·1	7·3	7·37	82·2	50	50	88·9
3·4	3·54	73·6	7·4	7·47	82·3	60	60	89
3·5	3·64	74·1	7·5	7·57	82·4	70	70	89·2
3·6	3·74	74·5	7·6	7·67	82·5	80	80	89·3
3·7	3·83	74·9	7·7	7·77	82·6	90	90	89·4
3·8	3·94	75·3	7·8	7·87	82·7	100	100	89·5
3·9	4·02	75·6	7·9	7·96	82·8	$1 + j\infty$	∞	90

TABLE 1(b)

$1 + j\omega T$	K	ϕ deg	$1 + j\omega T$	K	ϕ deg	$1 + j\omega T$	K	ϕ deg
$1 + j0{\cdot}0087$	1·000	0·5	0·3739	1·068	20·5	0·8693	1·324	41
0·0175	1	1	0·3839	1·070	21	0·8847	1·334	41·5
0·0262	1	1·5	0·3939	1·074	21·5	$1 + j0{\cdot}9001$	1·35	42
0·0349	1	2	$1 + j0{\cdot}4040$	1·080	22	0·9163	1·36	42·5
0·0437	1	2·5	0·4142	1·082	22·5	0·9325	1·37	43
0·0524	1	3	0·4245	1·086	23	0·9490	1·38	43·5
0·0612	1	3·5	0·4348	1·090	23·5	0·9657	1·39	44
0·0699	1	4	0·4452	1·095	24	0·9827	1·40	44·5
0·0787	1	4·5	0·4557	1·099	24·5	$1 + j1{\cdot}000$	1·414	45
0·0875	1	5	0·4663	1·102	25			
0·0963	1	5·5	0·4770	1·108	25·5			
$1 + j0{\cdot}1051$	1·005	6	0·4877	1·110	26			
0·1139	1·007	6·5	0·4986	1·117	26·5			
0·1228	1·008	7	$1 + j0{\cdot}5095$	1·120	27			
0·1317	1·009	7·5	0·5206	1·127	27·5			
0·1405	1·010	8	0·5317	1·130	28			
0·1495	1·011	8·5	0·5430	1·138	28·5			
0·1584	1·012	9	0·5543	1·142	29			
0·1673	1·013	9·5	0·5658	1·150	29·5			
0·1763	1·015	10	0·5774	1·155	30			
0·1853	1·018	10·5	0·5890	1·160	30·5			
0·1944	1·020	11	$1 + j0{\cdot}6009$	1·166	31			
$1 + j0{\cdot}2035$	1·021	11·5	0·6128	1·172	31·5			
0·2126	1·022	12	0·6249	1·180	32			
0·2217	1·025	12·5	0·6371	1·185	32·5			
0·2309	1·028	13	0·6491	1·190	33			
0·2101	1·029	13·5	0·6619	1·200	33·5			
0·2493	1·030	14	0·6745	1·205	34			
0·2586	1·032	14·5	0·6873	1·212	34·5			
0·2679	1·035	15	$1 + j0{\cdot}7002$	1·220	35			
0·2773	1·038	15·5	0·7133	1·228	35·5			
0·2867	1·040	16	0·7265	1·240	36			
0·2962	1·042	16·5	0·7400	1·244	36·5			
$1 + j0{\cdot}3057$	1·046	17	0·7536	1·250	37			
0·3153	1·048	17·5	0·7673	1·260	37·5			
0·3249	1·050	18	0·7843	1·270	38			
0·3346	1·055	18·5	0·7954	1·278	38·5			
0·3443	1·060	19	$1 + j0{\cdot}8098$	1·285	39			
0·3541	1·061	19·5	0·8243	1·297	39·5			
0·3640	1·063	20	0·8391	1·303	40			
			0·8541	1·315	40·5			

TABLE 1(c)

$1 + j\omega T$	K	ϕ deg	$1 + j\omega T$	K	ϕ deg	$1 + j\omega T$	K	ϕ deg
$1 + j$1·0000	1·414	45	1·7675	2·03	60·5	4·0108	4·13	76
1·0176	1·43	46·5	1·8040	2·06	61	4·1653	4·28	76·5
1·0355	1·44	46	1·8448	2·10	61·5	4·3315	4·45	77
1·0538	1·45	46·5	1·8807	2·13	62	4·5107	4·62	77·5
1·0724	1·47	47	1·9210	2·17	62·5	4·7046	4·81	78
1·0913	1·48	47·5	1·9626	2·20	63	4·9152	5·02	78·5
1·1106	1·495	48	$1 + j$2·0057	2·24	63·5	5·1446	5·25	79
1·1303	1·51	48·5	2·0503	2·28	64	5·3955	5·48	79·5
1·1504	1·525	49	2·0965	2·32	64·5	5·6713	5·76	80
1·1708	1·51	49·5	2·1445	2·37	65	5·9758	6·06	80·5
1·1918	1·556	50	2·1943	2·41	65·5	6·3138	6·40	81
1·2131	1·572	50·5	2·2460	2·46	66	6·6912	6·77	81·5
1·2349	1·590	51	2·2998	2·51	66·5	7·1154	7·18	82
1·2572	1·610	51·5	2·3559	2·56	67	7·5958	7·66	82·5
1·2799	1·625	52	2·4142	2·62	67·5	8·1443	8·20	83
1·3032	1·643	52·5	2·4751	2·67	68	8·7769	8·85	83·5
1·3270	1·662	53	2·5386	2·73	68·5	9·5144	9·56	84
1·3514	1·672	53·5	2·6051	2·79	69	$1 + j$10·39	10·4	84·5
1·3764	1·702	54	2·6746	2·86	69·5	11·43	11·44	85
1·4019	1·723	54·5	2·7475	2·92	70	12·71	12·71	85·5
1·4281	1·745	55	2·8239	3·00	70·5	14·30	14·30	86
1·4550	1·768	55·5	2·9042	3·07	71	16·35	16·35	86·5
1·4826	1·790	56	2·9887	3·15	71·5	19·08	19·08	87
1·5108	1·812	56·5	3·0777	3·24	72	22·90	22·90	87·5
1·5399	1·840	57	3·1716	3·33	72·5	28·64	28·64	88
1·5697	1·860	57·5	3·2709	3·42	73	38·19	38·19	88·5
1·6003	1·890	58	3·3759	3·52	73·5	57·29	57·29	89
1·6319	1·915	58·5	3·4874	3·63	74	114·6	114·6	89·5
1·6643	1·94	59	3·6059	3·74	74·5	$1 + j\infty$	∞	90
1·6977	1·97	59·5	3·7321	3·86	75			
1·7321	2·00	60	3·8667	4·00	75·5			

APPENDIX 2

TABLE 2(a). STABILIZING NETWORKS: LEAD NETWORKS WITH 20 db DECADE SLOPE

	Network	Attenuation characteristic	Transfer function	T_1	T_2
2-1	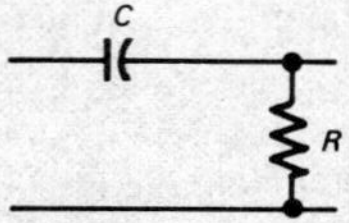 C, R	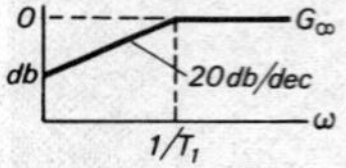 $G_0 = 0 \quad G_\infty = 1$	$\dfrac{T_1 s}{T_1 s + 1}$	RC	
2-2	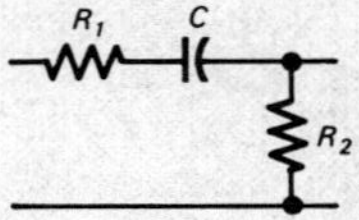 R_1, C, R_2	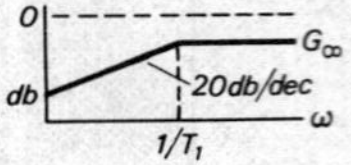 $G_0 = 0 \quad G_\infty = \dfrac{1}{1 + R_1/R_2}$	$\dfrac{T_2 s}{T_1 s + 1}$	$(R_1 + R_2)C$	R_2C
2-3	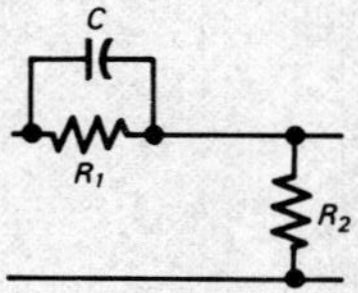 C, R_1, R_2	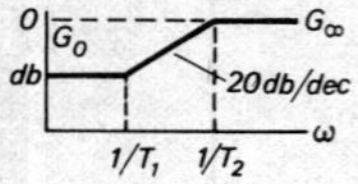 $G_0 = \dfrac{1}{1 + R_1/R_2} \quad G_\infty = 1$	$G_0 \dfrac{(T_1 s + 1)}{(T_2 s + 1)}$	R_1C	$\dfrac{R_2}{R_1 + R_2} T_1$
2-4	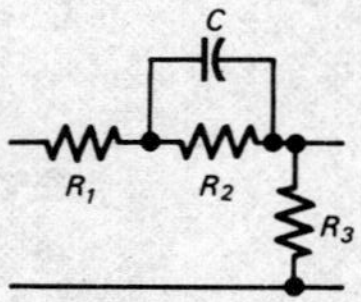 C, R_1, R_2, R_3	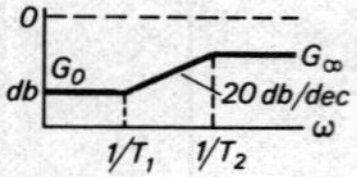 $G_0 = \dfrac{1}{1 + (R_1 + R_2)/R_3} \quad G_\infty = \dfrac{1}{1 + R_1/R_3}$	$G_0 \dfrac{(T_1 s + 1)}{(T_2 s + 1)}$	R_2C	$\left[\dfrac{R_3 + R_1}{R_1 + R_2 + R_3}\right] T_1$
2-5	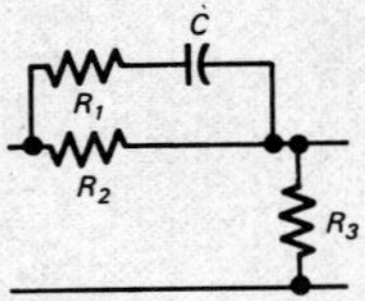 C, R_1, R_2, R_3	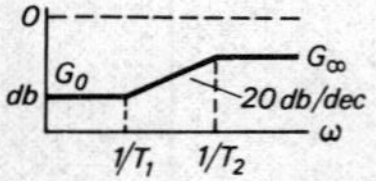 $G_0 = \dfrac{1}{1 + \dfrac{R_2}{R_3}} \quad G_\infty = \dfrac{1}{1 + \dfrac{R_1 R_2}{R_3(R_1 + R_2)}}$	$G_0 \dfrac{(T_1 s + 1)}{(T_2 s + 1)}$	$(R_1 + R_2)C$	$\left[\dfrac{R_3 + \dfrac{R_1 R_2}{R_1 + R_2}}{R_2 + R_3}\right] T_1$

	Network	Attenuation characteristic	Transfer function	T_1	T_2
2-6		$G_0 = \dfrac{1}{1 + \dfrac{R_1 + R_3}{R_4}}$ $\quad G_\infty = \dfrac{1}{1 + \dfrac{R_1}{R_4} + \dfrac{R_2 R_3}{R_4(R_2 + R_3)}}$	$G_0 \dfrac{(T_1 s + 1)}{(T_2 s + 1)}$	$(R_2 + R_3)C$	$\left[\dfrac{R_1 + R_4 + \dfrac{R_2 R_3}{R_2 + R_3}}{R_1 + R_3 + R_4}\right] T_1$
2-7		$G_0 = \dfrac{R_4}{R_2 + R_4}$ $\quad G_\infty = \dfrac{R_4(R_1 + R_2 + R_3) + R_2 R_3}{(R_2 + R_4)(R_1 + R_3) + R_2 R_4}$	$G_0 \dfrac{(T_1 s + 1)}{(T_2 s + 1)}$	$\left[(R_1 + R_2 + R_3) + \dfrac{R_2 R_3}{R_4}\right] C$	$\left[(R_1 + R_3) + \dfrac{R_2 R_4}{R_3 + R_4}\right] C$

* The tables in Appendix 2 are adapted, by permission, from Grabbe, E. M., Simon Ramo, and D. E. Wooldridge, *Handbook of Automation, Computation and Control*, Vol. 1, John Wiley & Sons, Inc., 1958.

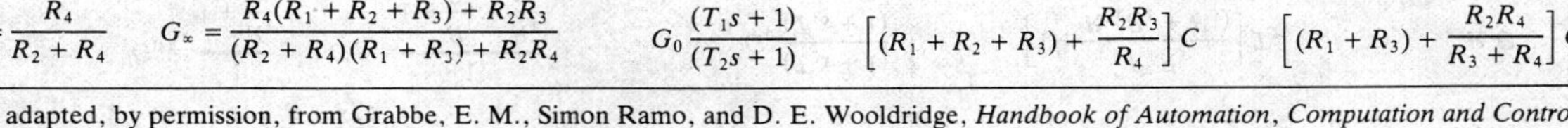

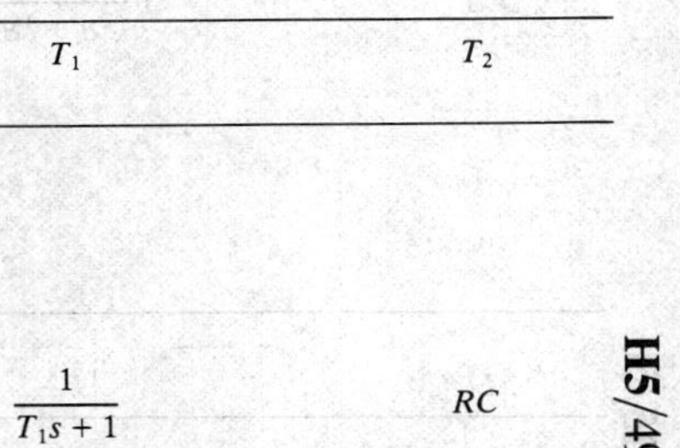

TABLE 2(b) STABILIZING NETWORKS: LAG NETWORKS WITH 20 db DECADE SLOPE

	Network	Attenuation characteristic	Transfer function	T_1	T_2
2-13	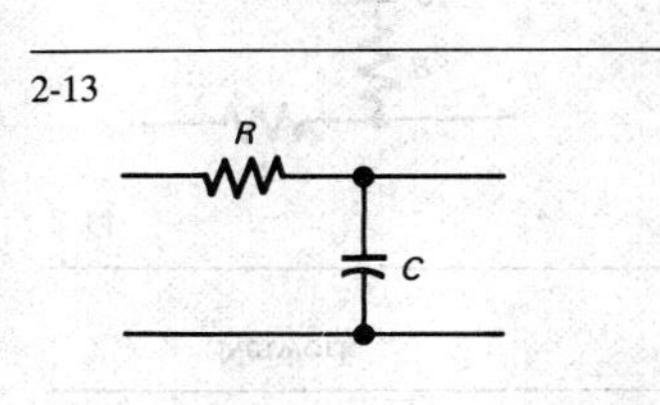	$G_0 = 1 \quad G_\infty = 0$		$\dfrac{1}{T_1 s + 1}$	RC

TABLE 2(b)—(*continued*)

	Network	Attenuation characteristic	Transfer function	T_1	T_2
2-14	R_1, R_2, C	$G_0 = 1 \quad G_\infty = \dfrac{1}{1 + \dfrac{R_1}{R_2}}$	$\dfrac{T_2 s + 1}{T_1 s + 1}$	$\dfrac{(R_1 + R_2)}{R_2} T_2$	$R_2 C$
2-15	R_1, R_2, C, R_3	$G_0 = \dfrac{1}{1 + \dfrac{R_1}{R_3}} \quad G_\infty = \dfrac{1}{1 + \dfrac{R_1}{R_2} + \dfrac{R_1}{R_3}}$	$G_0 \dfrac{(T_2 s + 1)}{(T_1 s + 1)}$	$\left[1 + \dfrac{R_1 R_3}{R_2(R_1 + R_3)}\right] T_2$	$R_2 C$
2-16	R_1, R_2, R_4, C, R_3	$G_0 = \dfrac{1}{1 + \dfrac{R_1}{R_2 + R_4} + \dfrac{R_1}{R_3}} \quad G_\infty = \dfrac{1}{1 + \dfrac{R_1}{R_2} + \dfrac{R_1}{R_3}}$	$G_0 \dfrac{(T_2 s + 1)}{(T_1 s + 1)}$	$\left[\dfrac{1 + \dfrac{R_1}{R_2} + \dfrac{R_1}{R_3}}{1 + \dfrac{R_1}{R_2 + R_4} + \dfrac{R_1}{R_3}}\right] T_2$	$\left(\dfrac{R_2 R_4}{R_2 + R_4}\right) C$

APPENDIX 3

BASIC LAPLACE TRANSFORM PAIRS.—$L[g(t)]$ is defined by $\int_0^\infty g(t)\exp(-st),\,dt$ and is written as $G(s)$.

$g(t)$ from $t = 0$	$G(s) = L[g(t)]$
$\frac{d}{dt}f(t)$	$sF(s) - f(0)$
$\frac{d^n}{dt^n}f(t)$	$s^nF(s) - s^{n-1}f(0) - s^{n-2}f'(0)\ldots - f^{(n-1)}(0)$
$\int_0^t f(t)\,dt$	$\frac{1}{s}F(s)$
$\exp(-\alpha t)\,f(t)$	$F(s+\alpha)$
Unit impulse δ	1
Unit function 1 or $H(t)$	$\frac{1}{s}$
Delayed unit function	$\frac{\exp(-sT)}{s}$
Rectangular pulse	$\frac{1-\exp(-sT)}{s}$
Ramp function t	$\frac{1}{s^2}$
$t^{n-1}/(n-1)!$	$\frac{1}{s^n}$
$\frac{t^{n-1}}{(n-1)!}\exp(-\alpha t)$	$\frac{1}{(s+\alpha)^n}$
$\exp(-\alpha t)$	$\frac{1}{(s-\alpha)}$
$1-\exp(-\alpha t)$	$\frac{\alpha}{s(s+\alpha)}$
$t\exp(-\alpha t)$	$\frac{1}{(s+\alpha)^2}$
$\exp(-\alpha t)-\exp(-\beta t)$	$\frac{\beta-\alpha}{(s+\alpha)(s+\beta)}$
$\sin\omega t$	$\frac{\omega}{s^2+\omega^2}$
$\cos\omega t$	$\frac{s}{s^2+\omega^2}$
$1-\cos\omega t$	$\frac{\omega^2}{s(s^2+\omega^2)}$
$\omega t\sin\omega t$	$\frac{2\omega^2 s}{(s^2+\omega^2)^2}$
$\sin\omega t-\omega t\cos\omega t$	$\frac{2\omega^3}{(s^2+\omega^2)^2}$
$\exp(-\alpha t)\sin\omega t$	$\frac{\omega}{(s+\alpha)^2+\omega^2}$
$\exp(-\alpha t)\cos\omega t$	$\frac{s+\alpha}{(s+\alpha)^2+\omega^2}$

APPENDIX 3 (*continued*)

Basic Laplace Transform Pairs.—$L[g(t)]$ is defined by $\int_0^x g(t)\exp(-st),\, dt$ and is written as $G(s)$.

$\exp(-\alpha t)\left(\cos \omega t - \dfrac{\alpha}{\omega}\sin \omega t\right)$	$\dfrac{s}{(s+\alpha)^2+\omega^2}$
$\sin(\omega t + \phi)$	$\dfrac{s \sin \phi + \omega \cos \phi}{s^2+\omega^2}$
$\exp(-\alpha t) + (\alpha/\omega)\sin \omega t - \cos \omega t$	$\dfrac{\alpha^2+\omega^2}{(s+\alpha)(s^2+\omega^2)}$
$\sinh \beta t$	$\dfrac{\beta}{s^2-\beta^2}$
$\cosh \beta t$	$\dfrac{s}{s^2-\beta^2}$

APPENDIX 4. (Ref. 11)

CHARACTERISTICS AND DESCRIBING FUNCTIONS OF NONLINEAR ELEMENTS

Type of nonlinearity	Input–output transfer characteristic	Output waveform corresponding to sinusoidal input	Describing function N
(a) Saturation	Output m(f) A Slope = k 0 Input e(t) −A	m(t) A 0 α π 2π ωt −AE	$N = k \quad E < A$ $N = \frac{M_1}{E} = \frac{2k}{\pi}\left(\alpha + \frac{\sin 2\alpha}{2}\right) \quad E > A$ where $\alpha = \sin^{-1}\frac{A}{E}$
(b) Saturation with dead zone	Output m(t) A −D Slope = k O D Input e(t) −A	m(t) A 0 α β π ωt	$N = 0 \qquad E < D$ $N = \frac{M_1}{E} = \frac{2k}{\pi}\left(\beta - \alpha - \frac{\sin 2\alpha - \sin 2\beta}{2}\right) \qquad E > \frac{A}{k}$ $N = \frac{2k}{\pi}\left(\frac{\pi}{2} - \alpha - \frac{\sin 2\alpha}{2}\right) \qquad A > E > d$ where $\alpha = \sin^{-1}\frac{D}{E} \qquad \beta = \sin^{-1}\frac{A}{E}$
(c) Dead zone but no saturation	Output m(t) −D Slope = k O D Input e(t)	m(t) 0 α π ωt	$N = 0 \qquad E < D$ $N = \frac{2k}{\pi}\left(\frac{\pi}{2} - \alpha - \frac{\sin 2\alpha}{2}\right) \qquad E > D$
(d) Ideal relay	Output m(t) Tm 0 Input e(t) -Tm	m(t) Tm 0 π 2π ωt	$N = \frac{4T_m}{\pi E}$

APPENDIX 4. (*continued*)

CHARACTERISTICS AND DESCRIBING FUNCTIONS OF NONLINEAR ELEMENTS

Type of nonlinearity	Input-output transfer characteristic	Output waveform corresponding to sinusoidal input	Describing function N
(h) Coulomb friction plus viscous friction	Frictional torque (output); Slope = f; A; −A; Velocity (input)	A+fE; A; 0; π; 2π; ωt; −A−fE	$N = \frac{4A}{\pi E} + f$
(i) Backlash element with viscous friction	Ouput m(t); b; Slope=1; $-\frac{b}{2}$; $\frac{b}{2}$; Input e(t)	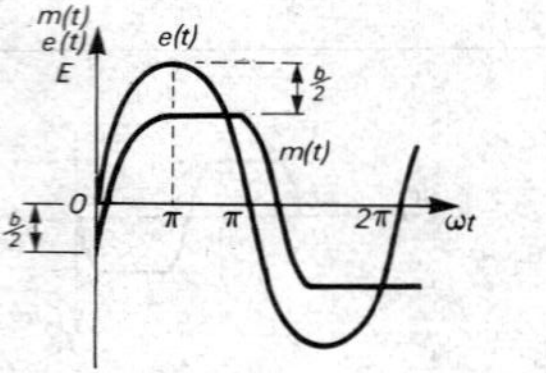	$\bar{N} = \frac{\bar{M}_1}{E} = \lvert N\rvert e^{i\phi}$ $\lvert N\rvert = \sqrt{A_1^2 + B_1^2}$ $\phi = \tan^{-1}\frac{A_1}{B_1}$ $A_1 = \frac{E}{\pi}\left[\left(\frac{\pi}{2} + \beta\right) + \frac{\sin 2\beta}{2}\right]$ $B_1 = \frac{2}{\pi}\left[\left(\frac{b}{E}\right)^2 - \left(\frac{b}{E}\right)\right]$ $\beta = \sin^{-1}\left(1 - \frac{b}{E}\right)$

(j) Backlash element with inertia

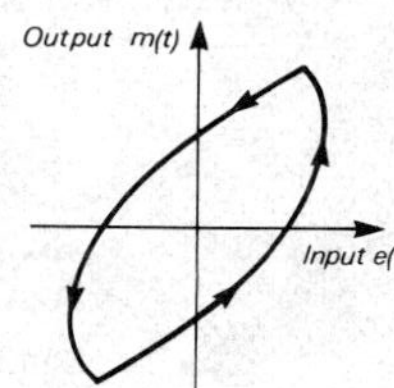
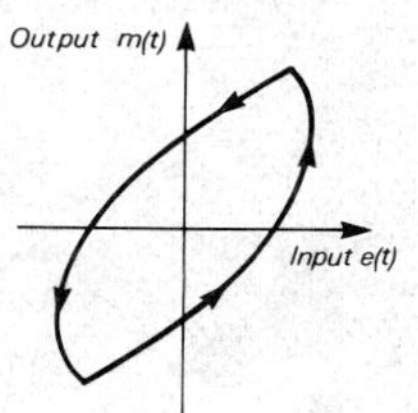

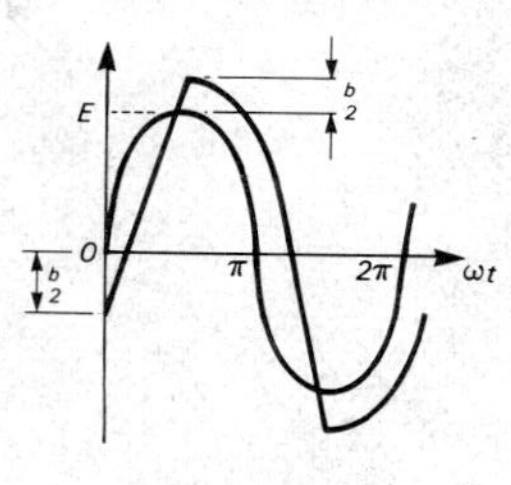

$$\bar{N} = \frac{\bar{M}_1}{E} = |N|\, e^{i\phi}$$

$$|N| = \sqrt{A_1^2 + B_1^2} \qquad \phi = \tan^{-1}\frac{A_1}{b_1}$$

$$A_1 = \frac{2E}{\pi}\left(-\frac{3}{4} + \cos\alpha - \frac{\cos 2\alpha}{4}\right)$$

$$B_1 = \frac{2E}{\pi}\left(\sin\alpha + \frac{\pi}{2} - \frac{\sin 2\alpha}{4} - \frac{\alpha}{2}\right)$$

$$\alpha = \sin\alpha + b/E$$

(e) Relay with dead zone

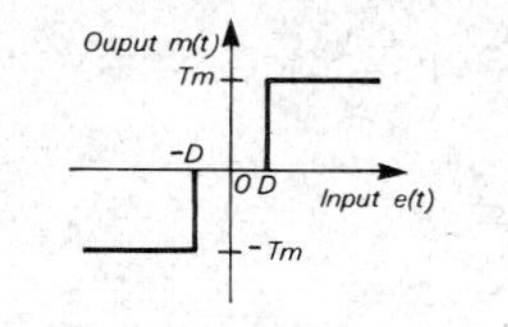

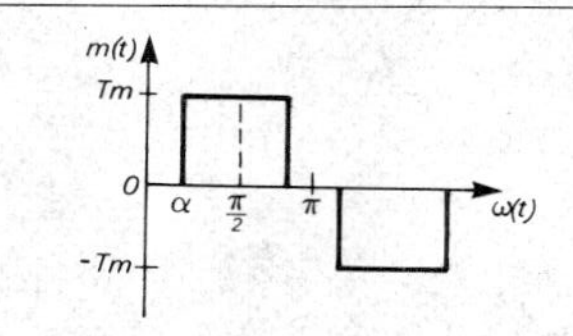

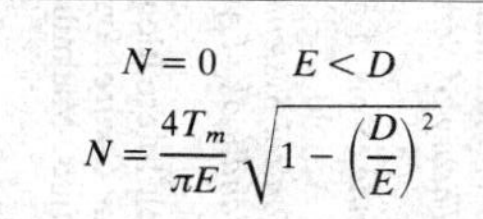

$$N = 0 \qquad E < D$$

$$N = \frac{4T_m}{\pi E}\sqrt{1 - \left(\frac{D}{E}\right)^2}$$

(f) Relay with dead zone and hysteresis

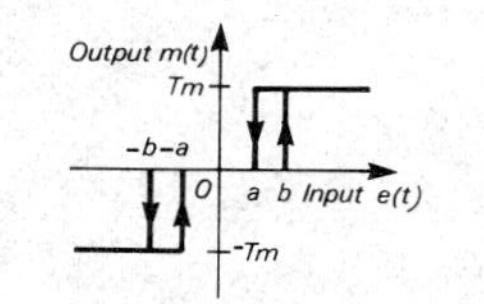

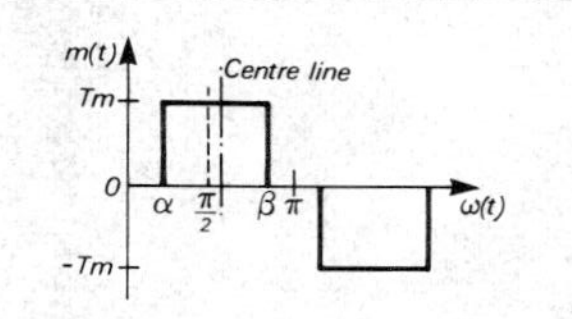

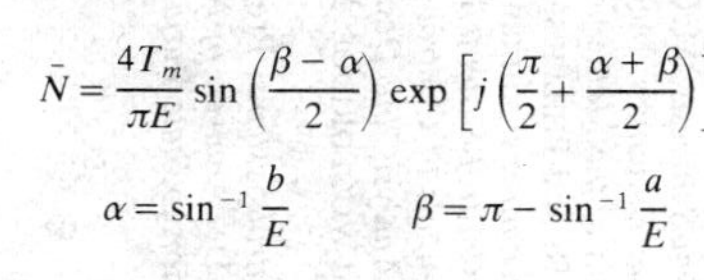

$$\bar{N} = \frac{4T_m}{\pi E}\sin\left(\frac{\beta - \alpha}{2}\right)\exp\left[j\left(\frac{\pi}{2} + \frac{\alpha + \beta}{2}\right)\right]$$

$$\alpha = \sin^{-1}\frac{b}{E} \qquad \beta = \pi - \sin^{-1}\frac{a}{E}$$

(g) Dead zone with linear transfer characteristic

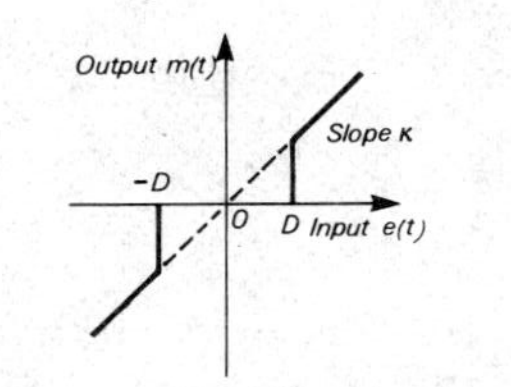

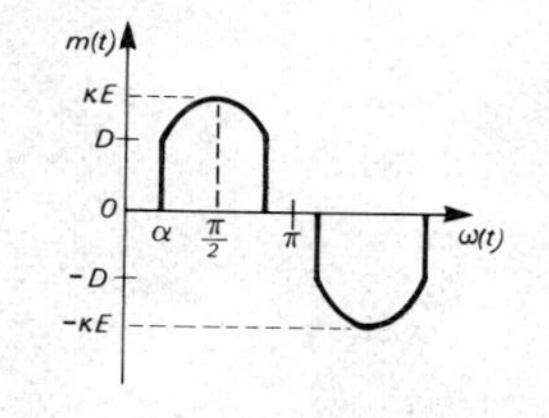

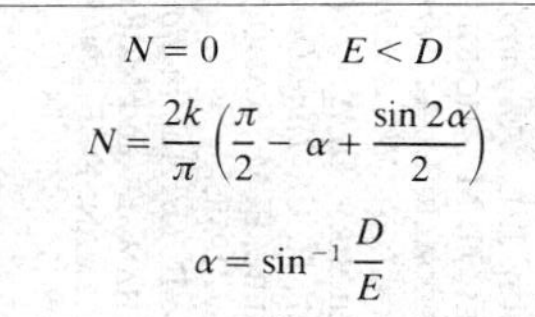

$$N = 0 \qquad E < D$$

$$N = \frac{2k}{\pi}\left(\frac{\pi}{2} - \alpha + \frac{\sin 2\alpha}{2}\right)$$

$$\alpha = \sin^{-1}\frac{D}{E}$$

REFERENCES

(1) CHESTNUT and MAYER, *Servomechanisms and Regulating System Design,* Vols. 1 and 2. Wiley.
(2) TRUXAL, J. G., *Control System Synthesis.* McGraw Hill, 1955.
(3) EVANS, W. R., *Control System Dynamics.* McGraw Hill, 1954.
(4) DOUCE, J. L., *An Introduction to the Mathematics of Servomechanisms,* E.U.P.
(5) JAMES, H. M., NICHOLS, N. B. and PHILLIPS, R. S., *Theory of Servomechanisms.* McGraw Hill, 1947.
(6) STOCKDALE, L. A., *Servomechanisms.* Pitman, 1960.
(7) LANGILL, A. W., *Automatic Control Systems Engineering,* Vols. 1 and 2. Prentice Hall.
(8) WELBOURN, D. A., *The Essentials of Control Theory.* Arnold.
(9) DORF, R. C., *Time Domain Analysis and Design of Control Systems.* Addison Wesley.
(10) GRABBE, E. M., RAMO, S. and WOOLDRIDGE, D. E., *Handbook of Automation Computation and Control.* Wiley, 1958.
(11) KUO, B. C., *Automation Control Systems.* Prentice-Hall International, 1962.
(12) GRAHAM, D. and MCRUER, D., *Analysis of Non-linear Control Systems.* Wiley, 1961.
(13) BLACKMAN, D. F., *Introduction to State Variable Analysis.* Macmillan.

COMPUTER-AIDED DESIGN

Introduction—History and Origins—Application Areas of CAD/CAM—Structural Options for CAD Systems—Effect of Price Decline on Suppliers—Specialised Hardware—Computer Memory—Input Devices—Output Devices—CAD Software (Levels 1 to 6) including Operating Systems, Standards, Data Transfer Methods, Applications, Simulation, Kinematics, Artificial Intelligence and User-Specific Software—Implementation of CAD/CAM.

By Andrew Pye, MA (Cantab), Editor, *Design Engineering*

INTRODUCTION

In design engineering, particularly in the high technology industries, computers have long been used to solve design problems and to model designs mathematically for performance analysis. In the mid-1960s, the US National Aeronautics and Space Administration (NASA) developed a general-purpose computer program for the analysis of field continua, using finite element methods, called NASTRAN. Many of the ingredients of CAD/CAM, including graphics displays, pen plotters, digitisers and light pens, were developed in the late 1950s/early 1960s. By the mid-1960s, experimental CAD systems were in development at General Motors (DAC/1), Lockheed, McDonnell Douglas, Boeing, North American Rockwell and elsewhere. All were purpose-built proprietary systems based on large mainframe computers and were developed in partnership with computer manufacturers such as IBM and Control Data. As recently as the mid-seventies, away from the 'technology-breeder' industries, such as aerospace and automotive, computer-aided design and manufacture (CAD/CAM) was limited by the costs of the necessary hardware and the consequent absence of a CAD industry infrastructure. The option for any company to buy an off-the-shelf 'turnkey' system simply was not available.

This situation has been altered radically by the silicon chip, the microprocessor and a dramatic and on-going fall in the price/performance ratio of computer hardware. A central processing unit (CPU) can now be squeezed onto a single large scale integrated (LSI) circuit chip of several millimetres square. The design of many small 'micro' computers is based on these chips, together with some input and output devices.

Two features which distinguish CAD/CAM from traditional engineering computing are its use of interactive graphics techniques, rather than batch techniques, and its potential to re-use information, such as part data, in the computer, both within an application area and across the boundaries of different application areas (*eg* finite element analysis, vibration analysis, heat transfer analysis, facilities management, circuit simulation and similar data requiring graphical descriptions). The requirement to re-use part data leads to two further distinguishing features: the first of these is the need to model in the computer the geometry of the part in such a way that sufficient information is available for re-use later; the other feature is the need to be able to store, transmit and retrieve part data.

ACRONYMS.—Concurrent with the mushrooming of CAD/CAM technology, associated systems, and with vendors, there have been more-than-sufficient claims, promises and advice, not to mention an intimidating dictionary of acronyms, many of which are ambiguous, or even downright misleading. A list of acronyms, which are meaningful to design engineers is shown on pages H6/8 and 9.

The term CAD was originally used to mean *computer-aided design* and is still sometimes used in this sense, in that it is the use of the computer in the conceptual design/engineering design part of the process and includes analysis and simulation, rather than draughting. The term CAD has nevertheless also been used to mean *computer-aided draughting*: in fact, for the vast majority of firms which use CAD, the 'D' stands for draughting—and that is as far as it goes. CAM was originally used to mean *computer-aided manufacture* and could be applied equally well to programming an NC machine tool as to scheduling use of the tool, or as to the use of the tool to manufacture a part. The term *NC programming* is not ambiguous, but does not refer to the entire manufacturing engineering activity. *Computer-aided production (CAP), computer-aided production planning (CAP or CAPP), computer-assisted part programming (CAP or CAPP), computer-aided process planning (CAPP) and computer-aided publishing (CAP)* further complicate the issue!

The four discrete islands which make up the CAD/CAM whole are:

CAD: Defining what the product is;
CAM: Defining how to make the product;

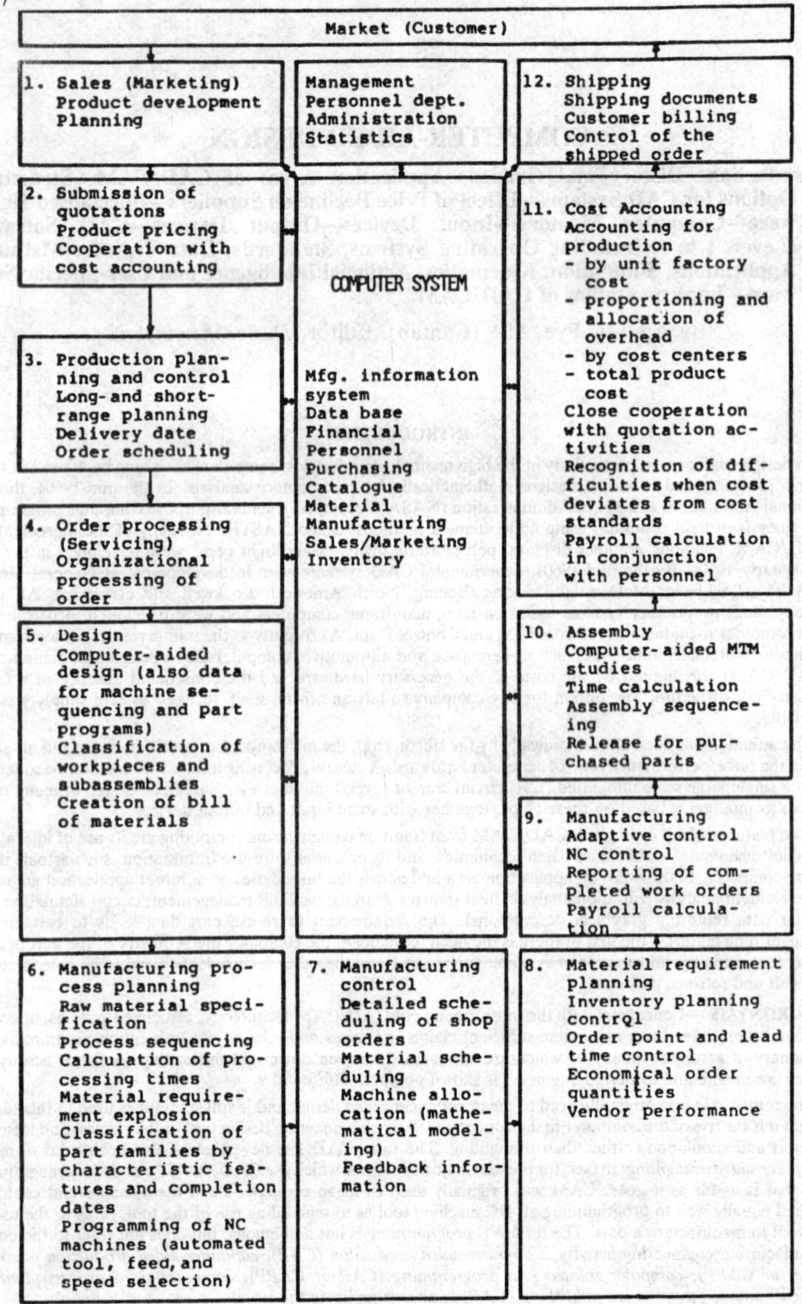

FIG. 1.—Functions of the computer in a manufacturing organisation. Source: Electronic Data Processing for Production Planning and Control, VDI Taschenbücher, VDI-Verlag, Düsseldorf, West Germany.

MRP/MRP II: Materials Requirements Planning/Manufacturing Resource Planning: defining when to make the product;
FA (Factory Automation): Making the product.

The overall drive is towards a totally integrated set of systems, drawing together the so-called *islands of automation*. The intervention of major users, such as General Motors, with its Manufacturing Automation Protocol (MAP), described in Computer-Aided Manufacture (H7), should force the pace, but there is still a long way to go. Two further acronyms which describe pertinent concepts but which do not have currently agreed meanings are:

CAE Computer-based Engineering: all computer-based techniques used in the design engineering and manufacturing engineering areas—*ie* CAD/CAM plus analysis and simulation;

CIM Computer-Integrated Manufacturing: integration of all computer-based techniques applied to all functions throughout a manufacturing company. The extent of potential functions of the computer in a manufacturing organisation is illustrated in Fig. 1. The integration in CIM implies that all decisions command and information flows in the company are computer-assisted. The concept of CIM and its relationship to CAD/CAM form the basis of the later sections in this chapter.

The CAD/CAM industry is now mature enough to recognise its objectives and is beginning to understand the real needs of the end-users to whom it must address its products. Thankfully there are now discernible directions which may be resolved out of the confusion which preceded them. It is the objective of this chapter to explain to potential end-users: the technology of CAD/CAM; the components which make it up; how the systems can—and will in the future—link together with each other and other industrial and business computers; and how to select and benchmark CAD/CAM systems.

Information is given on the current state of the market, but wherever possible, reference to proprietary materials has been avoided. The reader will appreciate, however, that it is impossible to describe some aspects of CAD/CAM technology without reference to individual companies and proprietary items of equipment.

The chapter is concluded with a glossary of terms which it is hoped will help to reduce some of the headaches caused by the 'jargonese' which, as described above, is so endemic to the computing population.

Finally, an extensive set of references used in the preparation of this chapter and the next (H7) are given at the end of chapter H7. I am grateful to all those authors who will find their influence reflected in these pages and trust that I have correctly interpreted their work in this field. All of these references are to be recommended for acquiring a deeper understanding of this subject.

HISTORY AND ORIGINS OF CAD

Computer-aided design can be traced back to the computerisation of three distinct areas of the design process—graphics, design analysis and numerical control (NC) technology. Many current CAD systems have been derived from one or other of these sources. The latter is the bridge which links CAD to CAM. It will be dealt with extensively later on and, in contrast to CAD, had been widely adopted by the 1960s.

GRAPHICS.—The earliest forms of computer graphics were *passive graphics*, batch orientated and usually mainframe-based. Graphics programs were used in which the problem is described and input (usually in alphanumeric terms); the computer crunches the problem, and produces the plotted output. Hours or days may pass between input and output, depending upon the system turn-around time and the system queue. Several repeat loops may be necessary. *Conversational graphics* is a form of passive graphics in which a dedicated stand-alone computer is available.

[1] *Interactive graphics* uses the same basic configuration as for conversational graphics but more computer power and more sophisticated software are employed. The input terminal, as well as the interactive terminal, usually the same device, is always a graphics terminal, rather than an alphanumeric terminal. If the display is incorrect, it can be edited there and then, at the terminal. This mode of computer graphics provided the impetus for developing CAD/CAM systems. Engineering drawings have always been the means of communicating complex engineering information: the paper output requirement may conceivably disappear and the graphical method of communicating engineering information is expected to prevail.

Much of the research that led to current graphics programs (many of which are in reality different versions of the same thing) was carried out in the early 1960s, notably by Dr Patrick Hanratty, then working for General Motors Research Laboratories and currently still active in the industry. Because CAD makes great demands on computer processing time and memory capacity, as a technique it was not completely compatible with the concept of traditional mainframe computing, where the emphasis is on multi-tasking and the simultaneous servicing of hundreds of users. Capital-intensive mainframe machines either had to be shared with non-

---

[1] *Design graphics* is a more sophisticated version of an interactive graphics system: usually, libraries of stored menus are available from which a designer can select and produce new designs. CAD/CAM systems employ both design graphics and interactive graphics.

Data representation graphics displays the results of analytical programs: in all cases, alphanumerical printouts have been replaced with charts or drawings. The systems can be passive or interactive and most are batch orientated.

engineering functions (which always seemed to have a higher priority) or bureau facilities were used. So, it was the arrival of the minicomputer and, subsequently, the microcomputer, of which more concise definitions are given below, which made it possible to dedicate a single computer to CAD functions only, servicing first a limited number of users and, ultimately, just one.

ANALYTICAL TECHNIQUES.—Evidently, techniques such as finite element analysis and circuit simulation have their roots in high technology industries where the cost of computing resources required in the 1950s and 1960s to cope with the necessary number-crunching was a secondary consideration to the feasibility of using the technique. Many of the early analytical programs were developed in-house and some survive today with their origins largely intact.

NC PROGRAMMING.—NC technology had, in contrast, been widely adopted by the mid-1960s. Some CAD programs arose from the effort to improve the flow of information from design office to factory floor by building upon this technology.

CATEGORIES OF COMPUTER.—Although the architecture of different types of computer is roughly the same, the classical distinction was made according to their word length, which represents the width of the internal data transfer paths of the computer.

In general, the mainframe has a word length of 32 bits or more and is the most powerful of the three categories in many ways. The minicomputer originally had a word length of 16 bits, whereas the microcomputer, which is the smallest of the three categories, had a word length of 8 bits.

However, this classification of computers has gradually become more difficult: the 16-bit microcomputer, often called the *supermicro*, has already been in existence for some time and the launch of the 32-bit microcomputer, sometimes referred to as the *megamicro*, has been announced by some computer manufacturers. Further, 32-bit minicomputer machines, known as *superminis* or *midis* have been in production for several years.

The 32-bit microprocessor market is distinguished from the earlier microprocessor market in the same way that mainframe applications are distinguished from minicomputer applications. As such, 32-bit microprocessors can be viewed as a new market with mainframe-style requirements. Mainframe computers address multiuser/multiprogramming needs, while microprocessors are focused primarily on the reprogrammable market. Mainframes incorporate scientific functions such as high-performance floating point arithmetic, process high-speed interrupts and perform elegant virtual memory operations. These features were not available with early generation microprocessors.

State-of-the-art 8- and 16-bit microprocessors, on the other hand, are typically targeted to replace minicomputer systems dedicated to performing a single application efficiently.

RANGE OF SYSTEMS.—The introduction of the first minicomputer in the early 1970s was the first signal of the steady shrinkage in size and cost of computer hardware which still continues apace today, Fig. 2.

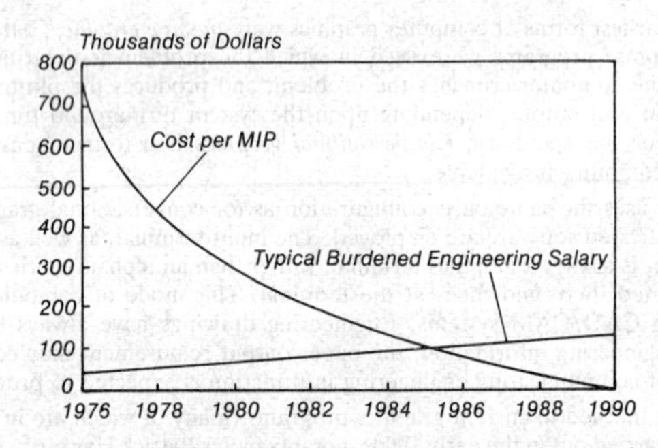

FIG. 2.—The cost of compensating a design engineer in the USA frequently exceeds the cost of today's CAE workstations; engineering productivity improvements resulting from their use can often pay for the equipment in less than a year. Source: Dataquest.

Minicomputers, though, only made slow inroads into engineering and they first followed the path of the mainframe into commercial applications. The real significance of the minicomputer to CAD was the ability to design machines which could be dedicated to the exclusive use of CAD; the development of graphics display terminals, coupled to menu command systems and minicomputers with power levels comparable to that of early mainframes, brought computing to the engineering fraternity. Furthermore, because the computer operating experience was slowly being built into the system, the requirement for users to be computing professionals was reduced.

Hanratty's Adam, which was launched in 1972, was the world's first commercially available machine-independent CAD package. It was licensed to companies developing and selling their own systems. Altogether a dozen turnkey companies took up licences for Adam. Many of the first turnkey CAD companies which sprang into existence at that time are still dominant in the CAD industry; this is despite an acceleration in hardware trends away from the dedicated centralised processor concept which formed the basis for the early turnkey systems. Partly because development timescales are so short in relation to the investment needed to purchase CAD systems, a full range of system types is to be found in use in industry and manufacturers are selling systems based on all types of hardware, from mainframes to 8-bit personal computers.

APPLICATION AREAS OF CAD/CAM

Sales of CAD/CAM/CAE equipment in general reached an estimated $3·6 × 10^9$ in 1985, representing an annual growth rate of 25%. This followed two years of growth exceeding 50%. Predictions are for the slower growth trend to continue (Ref 2). Table 1 lists some of the application areas of CAD/CAM, whilst it can be seen from Table 2 that a wide range of benefits can stem from its use.

TABLE 1.—SOME APPLICATION AREAS OF CAD/CAM

Sector	Applications
Design	Conceptual design Styling Detailed design Draughting Quality assurance Parts Lists
Mechanical Engineering	Finite element stress and vibration analysis Kinematic analysis of mechanisms Simulation
Electronics	Logic design, simulation and analysis Design and layout of Large Scale and Very Large Scale Integrated (VLSI) circuits Wiring diagrams Electromechanical packaging
(CAM)	Electron beam machining of masks Computer-controlled systems for automatic insertion of components on PCBs NC drilling and shape profiling of printed circuit boards (PCBs) Computer-aided testing of VSLI chips Computer-aided testing of PCBs
Electrical	Electrical circuit analysis Schematics and wiring diagrams
Manufacturing	Tool and fixture design NC machine tool programming Sheet metal forming Robot programming Quality control machine programming Process planning Preparation for automated testing Plant layout Material handling simulation PLC programming
Process Engineering	Pressure vessel design and analysis Process plant design and analysis Heat exchanger design and analysis Piping layout and interface checking

Table 1 cont. on H6/6

TABLE 1.—(*continued*)

Sector	Applications
Architecture	Conceptual design Floor plan layout Structural design and analysis 3D layouts, including interference checking of: HVAC, electrical, plumbing and communications lines Interior design of walls and ceilings Site planning Mapping Determination of cut and fill volumes for landscaping Building facilities management
Cartography	Utility mapping Digital terrain modelling Interpretation of satellite images
Simulation	Creation and analysis of scenarios: eg flight simulation, nuclear power plant training
Garments and Textiles	Patternmaking (nesting)
Sales and Marketing	Technical publications Business graphics
Construction	Reinforced concrete design and analysis

There is a large choice (1000+) of both generalised and specific application software covering a broad range of functions from draughting to molecular modelling and simulation. The major markets are in mechanical, electronic and civil engineering. UK companies and universities have played an important role in the devel-

TABLE 2.—BENEFITS OF USING CAD/CAM

Better, faster and more accurate quotations
Increased product design quality
Wider use of analysis and simulation techniques
Possibility to study more design alternatives
Design of more complex and/or more precise parts
Reduced design and draughting cycle time
Investigating interference between parts
Easier updating of designs
Reduced requirements for prototypes
Improved techniques for checking assemblies
Improved visual understanding of part
Easier calculations of geometric properties
Reduced scrap resulting from improved nesting
Production of parts lists
Improved quality of documentation
Improved drawing quality
Facilitated production of isometric, perspective and exploded views
Improved documentation for after-sales service
Reduced NC part-programming time
Facilitated part-programming of complex parts
Improvement in potential for re-using existing parts and tools
Reduced requirement for subcontracting
Improved receptivity to modifications requested by customers
Reduced materials cost resulting from design optimisation
Reduced energy cost resulting from design and manufacturing optimisation
Reductions in problems associated with using paper as information medium
Increased usage of standard parts
Reduced transcription errors due to use of same data
Possibility to increase enforcement of standardisation procedures

Based on: Stark J. Practical CAD/CAM Applications, p. 16 (see Ref. 42).

opment of CAD and analytical software. With a few exceptions, however, little has been made of the early participation and many of the larger software houses have been acquired by US corporations.

MECHANICAL DESIGN.—The distribution of design activities in mechanical engineering is shown in Fig. 3. Draughting and the processing of the bill of materials are most easily automated with the aid of the computer, whereas product engineering has many creative activities that require a greater degree of human input.

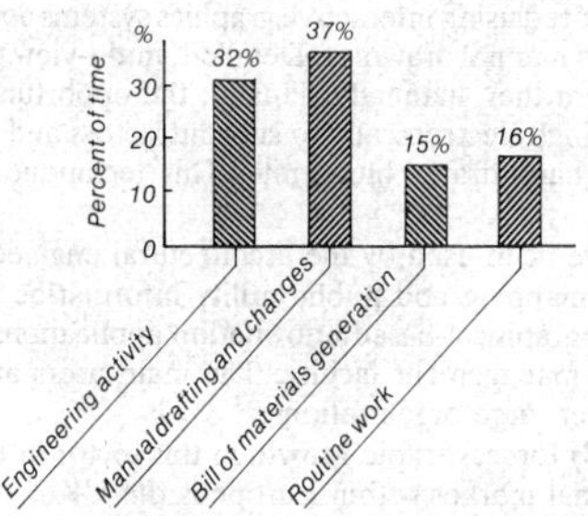

FIG. 3.—Distribution of design activities. Source: Opitz, H. Trends in Manufacturing Technology, VDI-Zeitschrift, 7, May 1972.

The mechanical engineering segment of the CAD/CAM/CAE market has grown at annual rates of up to 35% and represents about 60% of the total. Software accounts for about 29% of mechanical engineering revenues and information in Fig. 4, compiled by Hewlett-Packard (Ref 3) from a consolidation of reports, shows two major trends: first, the market for 2D systems will continue to be a major part of the overall market; secondly and most importantly, the major growth area will be the solid modelling area, which is expected to

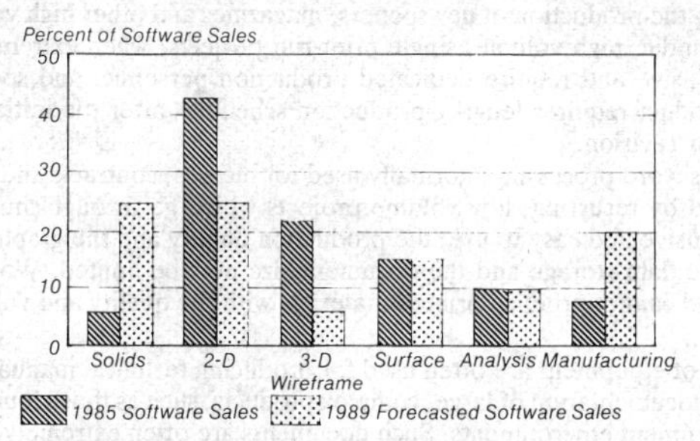

FIG. 4.—Forecast software sales for mechanical engineering sector. Source: Hewlett-Packard, consolidated from reports by Dataquest, Daratech and Strategic Inc.

average more than 100% growth in software revenue. In spite of this rapid growth, other sources suggest (Ref 2) that only 22% of all engineering plants in the UK run draughting modules and as few as 5% have solid modelling installed. Over two dozen vendors participate in the solid modelling market, although in 1985 three-quarters of current solid modelling software was shared by just six vendors (Ref 4). It is interesting to note that the software products of the top three vendors (Matra Datavision—Euclid; IBM—Catia; SDRC—Geomod) were developed in Europe. The number one supplier is a French company, Matra Datavision, with a 27·1% share of the solid modelling software market, 80% of which sales are in Europe.

ELECTRONICS.—In the electronics industry, the financial strength of the companies involved and the complexity of the problems with which they had to deal led to the early development of computer aids beyond traditional mathematical modelling and circuit analysis. The electronics industry was the first sector to use commercially available CAD/CAM systems. By the end of the 1960s, the number and complexity of printed circuit boards had become so great that further development and exploitation of electronics technology was being held back by the limitations of manual draughting and design methods. These systems have been so successful that it is no longer economically justifiable to design integrated circuits and printed circuit boards manually.

Whilst the electronics industry has been the most enthusiastic adopter of engineering workstations to date, mechanical and architectural applications have yet to take off in the same way. The application of computers to help engineer new electronic devices is snowballing in the US at a rate of nearly 30%/annum (Ref 5)—from an estimated 50,000 seats in 1986 to about 151,000 by 1990. Industry consultants estimate (Ref 6), that the electrical CAD market will represent around 25% of a 1990 total CAD/CAM market of $12 × 10^9$. It is clear therefore, that a great deal of growth is also implied in the mechanical and AEC (architectural/engineering/construction) sectors, which, according to Dataquest, accounted for 71% of total CAD/CAM industry revenue in 1984.

ARCHITECTURE, ENGINEERING & CONSTRUCTION (AEC).—Applications in this area are typically specialised cases of two- and three-dimensional draughting whose end-product is typically the drawing itself. High quality renderings can be prepared using interactive graphics systems and can be customised and artistically embellished far more easily than can manual drawings. Detailed, multi-view plans can be produced and updated far more easily on a graphics system than manually. Finally, the opportunity exists, although it is still not a common practice, to transfer drawings electronically to subcontractors and design firms using discs and tapes, instead of the traditional rolls of hand-drawn blueprints. This technique is not only easier, but it assures absolute accuracy of information.

Structural analysis programs have been used by the architectural engineering industry for many years.

In growth terms, however, the mapping and public utility information systems is the sector showing the greatest promise. Mapping and geographical-based information applications usually involve linking a graphics capability to an external database management facility. The main users are government, regional and local authorities, public utilities and other large organisations.

A market research survey (Ref 7) forecast rapid growth in this sector in Europe of 26% per annum slowing to 18% by 1990. The largest national market within Europe is the UK.

PROCESS ENGINEERING.—3D piping layouts have been developed by and for the petrochemical construction industry. Earlier programs were similar to 3D wireframe models: before the emergence of solid modelling, true dimensions of pipes and fittings were not included in the solutions, nor were the dimensions included in any automatic interference checking program. From the early 3D piping design programs, the application to *Heating, Ventilation and Air Conditioning (HVAC)* and utility layout programs has evolved.

TECHNICAL PUBLICATIONS SOFTWARE.—In the past 10 years, computers have revolutionised the publishing industry. Automation of the production of printed materials, known as *Electronic Technical Publishing (ETP)* or *Computer-Aided Publishing (CAP)*, extends into several market segments. At one extreme is commercial publishing, the production of newspapers, magazines and other high volume publications. These systems are used for periodic, high volume, single print-run projects, when extremely high quality output is required. They are expensive and require dedicated production personnel and specialised maintenance. In addition, this type of product requires lengthy production schedules after the initial writing is complete and provides little support for revision.

At the other extreme is word processing, normally used for memos, contracts and reports. Word processing systems are characterised by recurring, low volume projects which go through multiple printings. Although these systems are inexpensive and easy to use, the production quality and the graphic content and quality are low, there is little on-line data storage and the document size may be limited. Word processing systems are internal to a company and cannot produce printed materials with the quality and volume levels of commercial printing systems.

Although both groups of equipment are often used for producing technical manuals, neither offers products specifically aimed at the documentation of large, complex products, such as those found in aerospace, computer manufacturing and government environments. Such documents are often extremely large, multi-authored and go through numerous revisions. Until very recently, it has been impossible to intermix text and graphics in a document without resorting to customised programming or manual cut-and-paste methods. New generation ETP systems are more suited for recurring medium volume, multiple print-run documents with high quality text and graphics production. This market segment is also increasing its use of CAD/CAE systems and is looking for ways to reduce the labour-intensive steps in the documentation of products designed with these systems.

Products are offered both by start-up CAP vendors and by vendors of CAD-based systems. The first group of systems offer integrated text and graphics and WYSIWYG display, but are relatively expensive, frequently require dedicated personnel and often have difficulty integrating CAD graphics and data. Their focus is largely on improving the final production process and their applications are necessarily general-purpose. Some start-up systems are based on proprietary hardware.

Industry analysts (Ref 8) predict major market share gains in ETP by vendors of CAD-based systems, because the bulk of technical publishing is closely related to the graphics-orientated design data created by automated design tools. Engineering workstations have made possible the development of specialised software for the creation of technical publications, manuals and data sheets.

COMMON CAE ACRONYMS

AFEM	Adaptive Finite Element Modelling
AIX	Advanced Interactive Executive (version of UNIX)
ANSI	American National Standards Institute
ATE	Automatic Test Equipment
BEM	Boundary Element Modelling

CAD(CADD)	Computer-Aided Design
	Computer-Aided Draughting
CADMAT	Computer-Aided Design, Manufacture and Test
CAE	Computer-Aided Engineering
	Computer-Aided Electronic Engineering
CAEE	Computer-Aided Electronic Engineering
CAM	Computer-Aided Manufacture
CAP	Computer-Aided Production
	Computer-Aided Publishing
	Computer-Aided Production Planning
	Computer-Assisted Part Programming
CAPM	Computer-Aided Production Management
CAPP	Computer-Aided Process Planning
	Computer-Aided Production Planning
	Computer-Assisted Part Programming
CASE	Computer-Aided Software Engineering
CAT	Computer-Aided Test
CEP	Corporate Electronic Publishing
CGI	Computer Graphic Interface*
CIEE	Computer-Integrated Electronic Engineering
CIM	Computer Integrated Manufacturing
CNC	Computer Numerical Control
CORE	ANSI-backed graphics sub-routine requirements*
CPU	Central Processor Unit
	(Computer Processor Unit)
CSMA/CD	Carrier Sense Multiple Access with Collision Detection
ECAD	Electronic CAD
EDIF	Electronic Design Interchange Format*
EL	Electroluminescent (display)
ESP	Experimental Solids Proposal (IGES)*
ETP	Electronic Technical Publishing
FA	Factory Automation
FE/FEA/FEM	Finite Element (Analysis)
FMS	Flexible Manufacturing System
GKS	Graphics Kernel System*
IGES	Initial Graphics Exchange Standard*
ISO	International Standards Organisation
JIT	Just In Time
LAN	Local Area Network
LC	Liquid Crystal
LCD	Liquid Crystal Display
MAP	Manufacturing Automation Protocol
MCAD	Mechanical CAD
MIPS	Millions of Instructions per Second
MPS	Master Production Schedule
MRP	Materials Requirements Planning
MRP II/MRP 2	Manufacturing Resource Planning
NFS	Network File System
NURBS	Non-Uniform Rational B-Spline
OSI	Open Systems Interconnect
PBX	Private Branch Exchange
PCB	Printed Circuit Board
PDDI	Product Definition Data Interface*
	US Airforce ICAM Project
PDES	Product Definition Exchange Standard*
PHIGS	Programmers Hierarchical Interactive Graphics System*
RISC	Reduced Instruction Set Computing
SET	Standard d'Echange et Transfert*
STEP	Standard for The Exchange of Product data*
TFT	Thin Film Transistor
TIM	Token Interface Module
TOP	Technical and Office Protocol
VDA-FS	West German national standard for the exchange of complex surface data
WYSIWYG	What You See Is What You Get

* Standard

STRUCTURAL OPTIONS FOR CAD SYSTEMS

SERVICE BUREAU.—This is a relatively uncommon option nowadays, but describes a situation where users with terminals on their own sites can run CAD/CAM packages on remote computers belonging to service bureaux.

CENTRALISED MAINFRAME.—Here a company runs a large number of terminals, up to about 30, off a mainframe computer.

HOST-TERMINAL.—As suggested above, the first turnkey CAD systems relied upon a central processor, usually a minicomputer, which served a number of dumb satellite terminals, or consoles through which a designer and the central computer could communicate with one another. In networking terminology, this type of configuration is known as a *Hierarchical* or *Star Network*. When raster display terminals were used (see the section on graphics), the terminal might contain the minimal amount of computer hardware needed to control the display screen. This produced a typical layout of the type shown in Fig. 5.

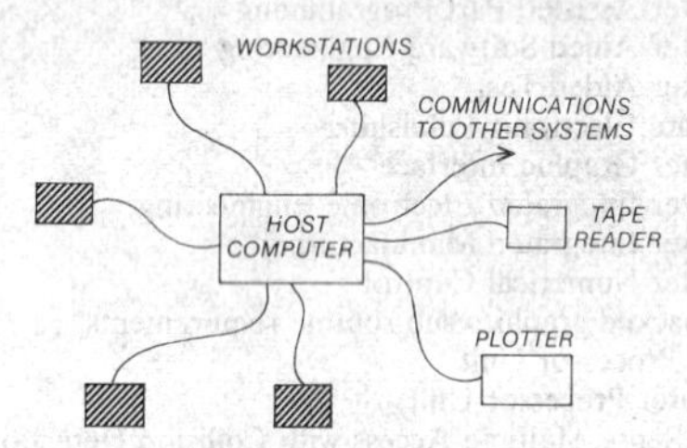

FIG. 5.—Host-based CAD system, centred on a minicomputer. Source: Medland and Piers-Burnett. CAD/CAM in Practice; Fig. 33, p. 57.

However, as CAD programming became more elaborate, the practice of channelling all information processing through the minicomputer's CPU was beginning to produce a bottleneck and this manifested itself in a limit to the number of terminals which could be serviced. This itself was a function of the nature of the work being carried out, whilst the vendor's assessment of acceptable waiting time did not always accord with the user's! As a result, figures given for the maximum number of terminals which could be run from one host tended to be within a wide range. In any event, once the performance is degraded beyond whatever the end user decides is the lower limit of acceptability, the only way out is to buy another system, with an attendant quantum leap in total system cost and aggregated cost-per-seat.

LOCALLY INTELLIGENT TERMINALS.—The first response to this problem was to increase the amount of intelligence available at the terminal by building in one or more microprocessors and some memory capacity. The sort of tasks which were carried out locally, in addition to screen control, were routine graphics functions, such as those involved in zooming or panning across a given view of a model. The model itself was still stored in the central computer and the power of the host was invoked for computationally-intensive tasks.

NETWORKED (DISTRIBUTED) HARDWARE.—As local intelligence increases further, a point is reached where the effectiveness of the central processor is reduced and the 2 individual terminals are linked together to form a distributed-resource, non-hierarchical chain or ring network. Every engineer can then be provided with an individual computing facility. Figure 6 shows how a number of computer complexes may be connected

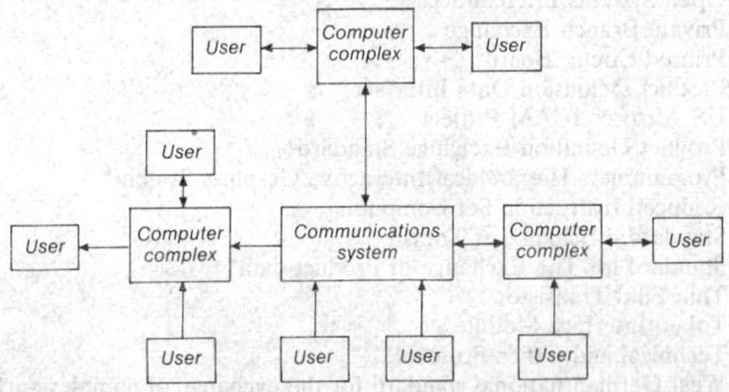

FIG. 6.—Distributed computer network—general case. Source: Besant and Lui. Computer-Aided Design & Manufacturer; Fig. 2.9, p. 52.

via a communications system. Networks may either be in the form of a continuous or non-continuous loop, according to the networking system used; the relative merits of each type are discussed in the section on Networking. Figure 7 shows conceptually how a series of workstations may be linked into a ring, which is a special case of a distributed network, thus offering the possibility of building up the system in stages. Each activity centre on the ring is described as a *node*. When any node requires additional computational power, it

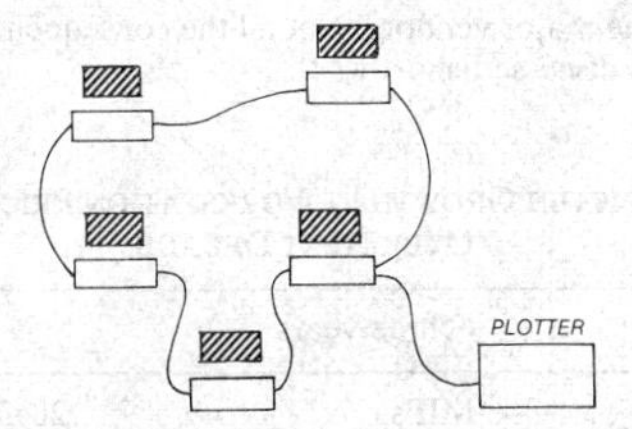

FIG. 7.—Series of self-contained, stand-alone workstations linked together to form a ring. Source: Medland and Piers-Burnett. CAD/CAM in Practice; Fig. 34, p. 59.

is 'borrowed' from other workstations in the network: many different configurations of node are now possible, Fig. 8, some of which are not graphics workstations, but server systems designed to assist all users with certain utility activities and off-load unproductive functions from the interactive graphics workstations.

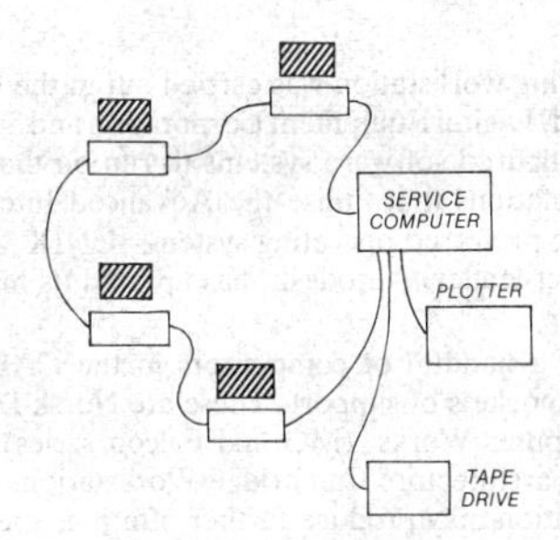

FIG. 8.—Networked CAD system containing a service computer. Source: Medland and Piers-Burnett. CAD/CAM in Practice; Fig. 35, p. 60.

One of the disadvantages of a networked system, as opposed to a system under the control of a central host, is the question of control over all the information in the system. Once the host computer loses control, there are questions to be answered concerning authorising changes to and access to data within the system. As networks grow larger, the data management considerations become more pressing still. The relationship between the systems comprising the network and the precise nature of the data flow that can occur between them are governed by the network configuration employed. This aspect is considered further in the sections on Networking and on Databases[2].

THE ENGINEERING WORKSTATION.—The current norm in the CAD industry is therefore the engineering workstation. The engineer's new workplace is a self-contained and purpose-built unit containing all the intelligence necessary to perform its intended function, whilst being networkable to other engineering workstations, enabling data to be shared between complementary users. The industry-standard engineering workstation is based upon 32-bit computer engines, being essentially tuned, dedicated minicomputers.

Because the workstation is the focal point for man–machine interaction, its utility and appearance contribute

[2] Although the trend is to eliminate the central processor altogether, where it is wished to preserve the benefits of a centralised information system or even greater computational resources are required, hybrid structures may be seen where a network of workstations is also connected to a large minicomputer or mainframe. As the era of mainframes in the traditional 1960s sense comes to an end, mainframes as centralised servers are just beginning. This will almost certainly be the case in organisations which opt for full Computer Integrated Manufacture (CIM).

Centralised support will be structured as several coordinated server machines, all tied into the multi-work-group network and each optimised for a particular server function. Possible server functions include: technical computer server (eg a Cray number cruncher); business computer server (eg an IBM 'text cruncher'); database server (eg a Britton-Lee, as briefly described in the section on databases); file machine (back-up for workstations); a communication server to the outside world (eg a PBX).

much to a system's 'personality'. Suppliers are well aware of this and have devoted a great deal of attention to workstation ergonomics.

The available range of 32-bit engineering computer workstations offer high resolution graphics and many features of the minicomputer in a price range approaching, at the lower end, that of the desk-top computer. In terms of power and memory, the workstation will ultimately be a desktop mainframe, Table 3. The price/performance ratio of engineering workstations is currently in steep decline and a battle for market share is very much in evidence amongst the major vendors. Not all the consequences of this competition are beneficial to the end-user, a factor which is discussed shortly.

TABLE 3.—PREDICTED GROWTH IN WORKSTATION PRICE/PERFORMANCE OVER NEXT DECADE

Workstation	Three years	Eight years
Power	3–6 MIPs	20–30 MIPs
Memory	8–10 MBs	50–90 MBs
Screen	1,000 × 1,000 pixels	3,000 × 3,000 pixels
Voice input	2,000 words	6,000 words
AI	'limited'	'yes'
Interface	'user-friendly'	'virtual co-worker'
Cost	$10,000–20,000	$4,000–8,000

Source: Seybold Report on Professional Computing (see Ref 12).

The development of the engineering workstation was carried out in the United States by such companies as Apollo, Tektronix, Hewlett-Packard, Digital Equipment Corporation and Sun Microsystems—many established vendors of CAD/CAM have reconfigured software systems to run on these workstations. IBM (Ref 13) has recently launched two 32-bit workstations that utilise the Advanced Interactive Executive (AIX) operating systems, an enhanced version of the preferred operating system—UNIX V Release 1 with selected Release 2 enhancements. The PC CAD market-leader, Autodesk, has uprated its highly successful AutoCAD software for use on this new equipment.

By contrast, Europe offers only a handful of competitors in the CAD processor market, which appear unlikely to gain more than isolated pockets of support. These are Norsk Data, with its ND500-based Techno-vision products, Whitechapel Computer Works, (MG and Falcon series), Torch/Primagraphics (Topaz and Triple X) and Acorn with its RISC architecture Cambridge Workstation. Some sources predict (Ref 14) that the Olivetti/AT&T/Acorn combination may produce further offerings specifically for the CAD/CAM arena. ICL's Perq workstation has now been gracefully retired and future ICL activities will be based on Sun hardware.

MICROCOMPUTER-BASED SYSTEMS.—At the bottom end of the hardware scale, the capabilities of the microcomputer have increased to the point where a viable stand-alone personal computer (PC) could run CAD graphics software. Inevitably, low-cost hardware is accompanied by relatively low-cost software. Most engineering companies in the UK are using packages which cost less than £12,000. Systems based on PCs have pushed CAD costs below the $10,000 level: in fact, CAD can be implemented on an in-place PC for as little as $1,000. In the late 1970s, only a handful of vendors offered PC CAD products and few realised the potential size of the PC CAD market: microcomputer-based workstations have now soared in popularity (Ref 15) and now account for 54% of all design installations. The rapid success of AutoCAD and other PC CAD products in the early 1980s prompted many other companies (mostly start-ups) to enter the market in 1983 and 1984: the number of PC CAD vendors is now in excess of 150.

Electrical/electronics design accounts for a quarter of the PC CAD market. This segment is the largest because there are proportionately more designers in this area than in any other, and because circuit design effectively uses the 2D features, especially the standard component symbols. By 1990, a proportionately higher percentage of mechanical designers can be expected to be using PC CAD.

There are, unfortunately, penalties associated with the use of these low-cost systems.[4] The most serious

[3] The reader will note the analogy between CAD/CAM system structure options and the database options for manufacturing information systems referred to in the later section on databases. In the context of databases, networked systems with a central master are referred to as *distributed* and those without as *interfaced*. This terminology does not seem to be explicitly emulated for CAD, which is just one 'island' within the overall concept of an integrated manufacturing system. Nevertheless, the same general advantages and limitations still apply, albeit on a microcosmic scale.

[4] With today's simpler computing architectures employing microprocessor technologies and RISC architectures, the types of instructions that these computers are processing are very different from their mainframe ancestors. For example, a RISC computer that boasts two MIPS in computing performance may only produce a fraction of that speed when running a particular application, due to the complexity of the operating software. Vendors are also guilty of quoting MIPS ratings on instructions that operate the quickest, such as an integer add, instead of advertising ratings that indicate performance over an average range of instructions.

limitation of PC-based CAD systems at present appears to be the insufficient main memory. Other problems are slower processing speed, a narrow range of applications and minimal support from vendors.

Because of their relatively low speed, PC-based systems take longer to do a task than do their larger counterparts. Speed limitations result from the fact that PCs process information in small units (words): as previously explained, the largest word a PC can fetch at one time from its memory measures 16 bits. By comparison, recent minicomputers process 32-bit words. The addition of a specialised device, called a *Floating Point Processor*, can boost the top speed of a PC to one million instructions per second (MIPS). This compares to the use of *Reduced Instruction Set Computing (RISC)* architecture, which can boost the performance of 32-bit machines up to five MIPS (Ref 16) and mainframes can perform at nearly 100 MIPS by performing operations in parallel.

PC memory capacity is similarly limited: most PCs can accommodate at most 1 Mbyte of main memory, compared to the 16 Mbytes which would be common for mainframes. Moreover, PCs typically have only one hard disc drive, providing only a few Mbytes of storage. In contrast, system disc storage can accommodate several Gbytes and can transfer data at a much faster rate. A moderately complex drawing comprising 500–1,000 lines can consume as much as 50 kbytes of memory. Serious professional applications usually require at least 128 kbytes of memory and applications specifying a minimum of 256 kbytes of memory and applications specifying a minimum of 256 kbytes are not uncommon. As a result, memory-expansion boards are often inserted into low-end systems to boost memory capacity. To keep program size within memory limits, PC CAD software vendors may omit help functions found on large systems. Most PC systems have fewer menus, so additional keystroking may also be needed to enter data and commands.

These radical differences in performance have narrowed the range of applications that a PC could handle: initially, PC-based systems supported only 2D draughting but software is now becoming available for 3D design, solid modelling, finite element modelling and kinematics. For example, a typical PC-based system can only conveniently handle a drawing with 2,000 elements (an element is a line, symbol, dimension, string of text, etc.), compared to the 10,000 elements easily handled by larger systems. A complex design analysis that might tie up a PC for hours could be polished off by a mainframe in only a few minutes. Mainframes can produce images comprising several dozen colours selected from a palette of millions. A PC typically can produce only 16 colours selected from a palette of a few hundred colours. PCs generally cannot do animations, an application readily handled by large systems.

Because of the low prices, PC CAD systems vendors cannot afford to devote as much individual attention to customers. In fact, sales people in most PC product centres are not knowledgeable of the machine's use in engineering. So users may have to navigate a greater part of the learning curve on their own, or pay extra for training.

Although there are few interfaces available to interconnect PCs into networks, the ability to network micro-based systems (see section on Networking for an assessment of the possibilities and problems) makes it possible to start with the minimum commitment and purchase additional workstations at a constant incremental cost. Vendors are moving rapidly to close this gap and several hundred systems for linking PCs by Local Area Networks (LANs) are now commercially available: however, most of these systems merely transmit signals along a cable between the computers and have no data-flow management capabilities, nor can they provide for device sharing, common files or electronic mail. Moreover, the time required to read and write data over one of these networks may vary from vendor to vendor by a factor of 10, demonstrating the inconsistency of LAN technology for PCs. IBM's PC NET network uses coaxial cable to link PCs to a central translator unit: this transmits data at the (currently relatively low) speed of 2 Mbits/s. An SNA 3270 Emulation Program enables a PC network to communicate with IBM mainframes via the SNA communications protocol. It is expected to be phased out and replaced by a token-based network.

Thus, PC CAD systems are destined to operate primarily as stand-alone units and will not benefit from the shared database concept. In contrast, IGES data exchange is becoming part of a growing number of mainframe and minicomputer-based systems. PC-based systems are also often not upwardly compatible with larger systems (minicomputers or mainframes). A network of interlinked micros cannot match the power of a minicomputer, nor handle the equivalent amount of back-up memory without incorporating a node in the network dedicated to storage.

THE IBM PC, CLONES AND UPGRADES.—Microcomputers appeared first as 8-bit, then as 16-bit machines, followed more recently by 32-bit machines as the concepts of the minicomputer and the microcomputer have merged. Early developments based on the Apple series {the Apple is still the second most popular machine for PC CAD in the USA and the concept of Apple-power is still used widely in the USA to assess comparatively microcomputer performance! (Ref 16)}, the ACT Sirius (now the Victor 9000) and the ubiquitous 8-bit BBC B have progressively given way in the business environment to the IBM PC, since its entry into the field in 1981. The IBM PC is not considered the most technically sophisticated PC available, but this competitively priced machine has grown steadily in acceptability and it is now a *de facto* standard. The operating system has, notwithstanding certain inherent limitations, a large amount of business, office automation and, increasingly, engineering software available. The open nature of the system has encouraged production of look-alikes, or *clones* (the most expensive of the Amstrad range costs £1,000) to such an extent that IBM itself will probably stop making the lower model ranges and concentrate on up-market 16-bit and 32-bit models. The introduction of more powerful IBM PC upgrades—the XT and particularly the AT—has itself promoted the rapid appearance of sophisticated yet economical software for draughting and training. It would appear to be a particularly suitable candidate for the engineering workstation concept, given a screen of suitable resolution. The AT derives its power from the use of a 16-bit 80286 microprocessor that handles information more quickly than the 8088 in the standard PC. As a result, the AT responds much more quickly to user commands and it can handle computationally-intensive tasks such as animation or shaded-surface generation. Probably the most impressive feature of the AT, however, is its main memory capacity—3 Mbytes. This capability should allow the AT to handle simulation and analysis problems that are beyond the capacity of other PCs.

The AT also has a new type of floppy disc drive that stores 1·2 Mbytes/disc (360–720 kbyte is conventional). In addition, the AT can incorporate an optional hard disc drive that not only holds more data (20 Mbytes), but is about three times as fast as 10 Mbyte drives employed on other machines. These high capacity drives open up PC/CAD to applications that require manipulation of large databases such as those found in finite element analysis and logic simulation.

Note that micros such as the IBM-XT may differ from purpose-built CAD workstations based upon the same hardware: the latter can incorporate extra facilities designed for the CAD role and will offer consequent advantages over the standard machine. As personal computers become more powerful, it is likely that by the end of the decade they will be able to offer the same applications as engineering workstations and the distinction being made between the two will no longer be valid.

Impressive though the AT is, the subsequent RT has not attracted so much enthusiasm (Ref 17). This is interpreted to be consistent with the expectation that the main thrust of IBM is to be directed towards the 32-bit engineering workstation market. Either way, the security afforded by the IBM product line will ensure that IBM will remain the major force in the industry.

The relatively fast graphics processing of IBM PCs and look-alikes can be speeded with an Intel 8087 co-processor chip which performs arithmetic operations much faster than the PC's standard 8088 processor. For example, it multiplies two numbers in 30 μs, whereas the 8088 processor takes 900 μs to do the same job. For the user, this speed translates into faster generation of screen display images: an image that takes five seconds to generate on a bare IBM PC, for example, requires only one second to be produced on one having a co-processor chip.

SOFTWARE PACKAGE.—Here, the vendor sells only the CAD/CAM software and not the hardware. Vendors in this category often supply the software to run on several types of computer system. Although a user may appreciate the potential of running the software on various computer systems, the software vendor has less freedom to optimise the software on particular devices.

CONVERGENT TECHNOLOGIES.—Although growth of sales prevails in all three hardware areas—micro, mini and mainframe, the mini market is beginning to suffer from sales won by high performance micros and the workstations now available at a fraction of their old price. Similarly, many authorities anticipate that the personal computer era in CAD/CAM will level off dramatically and eventually give way to this powerful and low-cost generation of engineering workstations. Workstation prices are now moving closer to those of good micros, and workstation suppliers have also introduced models that can run most personal computer software. The traditional CAE vendors are also adapting versions of engineering software to run on the forthcoming 32-bit business microcomputers. $20,000 was considered by many to be an important economic target and the new breed of workstations has now crossed this critical price/performance barrier.

One effect of this is to blur the traditional distinctions between the types of computers: the top end and

TABLE 4.—TYPICAL COST PER SEAT FOR DIFFERENT CAD SYSTEMS

Type	Configuration	Price/seat £000	Remarks
Mainframe	4 seats + plotter	70–90	Depends on s/w
Mini-computer			
Turnkey	4 seats + plotter	55–70	Depends on s/w
Independent	4 seats + plotter	25–40	Depends on s/w
Workstation	1 seat + plotter	20–65	Depends on performance and s/w
	4 seats + plotter	15–60	Depends on performance and s/w
PC Based	1 seat + plotter	7·5	14″ b&w, A4 plotter
	1 seat + plotter	14	19″ b&w, A1 plotter
	1 seat + plotter	22	19″ col., A0 plotter

Note: The volatile nature of the prices quoted means that the figures have only short-term validity.
Definition: s/w = seats per workstation.
Source: Smith, J. Does CAD for the Smaller Enterprise Really Mean Small CAD for the Enterprise? (see Ref 17).

bottom end of the CAD hardware market are converging to a common format, that of the networked, locally-intelligent workstation. The main distribution channel for CAD systems remains the turnkey system vendor, due to the industry's technical nature, high unit price and historic roots in minicomputers. Although system prices are falling with the introduction of the 32-bit microcomputer-based workstations, the requirement to integrate design, production and administration systems will reinforce the need for a close supplier/customer relationship.

However, the entry-level enhanced business PC products lend themselves to distribution through the existing full-service PC dealer channel, as both the application software and add-on graphics controller boards are packaged products.

For the smaller enterprise, it is clear that cost is of paramount importance, leading to considerations of the merits of workstations versus PC-based systems. It is vital, however, to have a formulated strategy and to consider properly longer term ambitions and upgrade options. Examples of all systems are currently available, and using the criterion of cost per seat, with all its inherent drawbacks and inconsistencies, the price range is something like that shown in Table 4.

EFFECT OF PRICE DECLINE ON SUPPLIERS

Vendors are facing the enormous hurdle of maintaining their average revenue per installation and their profitability in a world of open architecture, third-party software and increasing end-user demands. We have seen that growth in the CAD/CAM industry has slowed significantly and is now running at about 25% per annum, about half of what has been the norm in recent years. This is due to a combination of factors: some of the end-user industries, particularly in electronics and heavy engineering, have been through difficult times; more importantly, the entire price/performance curve is shifting downwards as distributed systems replace host-based ones, with the average price per seat coming down rapidly. The number of industry installations may be up sharply, but the average revenue per installation may still be lower. This trend is probably unstoppable. Major consequences have resulted: turmoil amongst vendors, who have been frantically scrambling to re-direct the mainstream of their product line. While marketing and sales divisions are trying to keep sales levels up by cutting prices, holding hands and laying out their company's future plans, the technical people are working hard to get software into these new, lower-end platforms and trying to get some integration between their old and new systems, in order not to thoroughly enrage their current and future customers. The result has been some incomplete, patched-up products, sold as integrated, user-friendly solutions. Exaggerated performance claims have returned to the CAD/CAM market. If the profits are too low, then company financial models built on high R&D spending, direct distribution and direct sales, traditionally the scenario of CAD/CAM companies, will have to change.

SPECIALISED HARDWARE

The hardware for a CAD/CAM system will be made up of a central processing unit (CPU) and peripheral devices for data storage, data input and data output. The different CPU options have already been discussed, whilst input and output devices are covered in later sections. This section deals with specialised hardware which may be encountered.

Table 5 shows the various hardware configurations and lists their advantages and limitations.

Several prominent vendors have adopted a strategy of building specific hardware for their workstations, in addition to writing software. In this event, such suppliers understandably take full advantage of the facilities provided by that particular computer. For example, some assembly language routines may be used to achieve faster response times than are possible using the standard high level languages such as Fortran or 'C'. On the other hand, these suppliers find it much more expensive and time-consuming to develop new products as more powerful computing hardware becomes available. Given the performance of many standard, general-purpose computers, vendors now have a very safe and flexible option which gives insurance against hardware obsolescence and benefits from the availability of third-party software packages. A summary of the strengths and weaknesses of adopting these approaches are discussed in Table 6. Some specialist hardware implementations are mentioned briefly below.

In some cases, such as Intergraph's use of Digital Equipment's VAX hardware, supplementary processing is added at key points in standard system architecture, to enhance performance, or where applicable, to relieve the central host from routine time-consuming tasks. This approach offers many of the advantages of specialised hardware, without all of the inherent limitations.

Microprograms.—A microprogrammed processor is one that is itself implemented as a small, special-purpose computer: it consists of a limited function processor and a control store containing a microprogram for fetching, decoding and executing the program instruction set of the main processor. Because new instructions can be added by adding microcode to the microprogram in the control store, the computer may be tailored to a particular application.

Floating-Point Hardware.—This is special-purpose, plug-in hardware that performs floating-point arithmetic at a much higher speed than is possible with software. There is a large volume of floating-point arithmetic associated with the manipulation of graphics models. It may either comprise an extended microprogram or an entirely separate processor.

TABLE 5.—CHARACTERISTICS OF AVAILABLE HARDWARE CONFIGURATIONS

Configuration	Description	Advantages	Limitations
Service Bureau	Users with terminals on their own sites can run CAD/CAM packages on remote computers	Useful for expensive, specialist software Means of evaluating unknown software packages	Hard to justify for most CAD/CAM Many bureaux now operate as engineering consultants
Centralised Mainframe	Large number of terminals operated off mainframe computer	Low incremental cost for addition users *See also Central Host (mini)*	Computing resource unlikely to be dedicated *See also Central Host (mini)*
Central Host	Number of graphics display terminals connected to single host minicomputer or mainframe	Large computer available for analysis New workstations cheap to add Single computer to maintain Easy to optimise environment	High capital outlay Response rate depends on heaviest job Breakdown removes entire facility Fewer terminals can be added than with mainframe
Multiple Host	Small number of terminals connected to each of several minicomputers, which are networked, so that the system appears to be central host	Advantages as above, plus: Breadown not catastrophic Intensive tasks lock up only 1 mini Computers are cheaper, so outlay for pilot system is less	*Limitations as above, plus:* Higher cost for similar size Higher maintenance costs More floor space needed More air conditioning needed
Distributed Systems	Each graphics terminal is associated with its own computer, and these are networked together to provide an integrated system	Response unaffected by other users Minimum failure implications Low incremental cost Multi-tasking via windows	Cost per seat remains constant, irrespective of network size Many processors to maintain
Stand-alone	Single user having small computer dedicated to single workstation driving single graphics display terminal	Low cost Easy to learn Systems based on 32-bit technology have more potential and can be upgraded more readily Suited to small enterprises Convenient to buy	Productivity increases limited by absence of database * Narrow applications range. * Slow Low resolution. * Small memory Limited networking * Limited range of colours Limited training offered * Programs can have fewer features (to save memory)
Software Package	Vendor sells software only	Usually hardware-independent software More freedom to build custom system	Software may not be optimised for hardware Need to arrange hardware support

Note: * With recent technology (eg IBM PC AT) these are minor limitations

TABLE 6.—THE CASE FOR AND AGAINST SPECIALISED HARDWARE

Hardware option	Advantages	Limitations
Specialised hardware	Can increase the efficiency of specialist software such as graphics, FEA and analog circuit simulation Hardware solutions can be fully integrated and compatible with proprietary software Servicing advantages, since whole system derives from one source	Later integration of special hardware into system can introduce compatibility problems No great advantage for standard tasks like word processing Limited range of processors likely
General purpose hardware	Vendor released from investment in hardware development and support Third party suppliers of hardware generally offer range of products at various points on the price/performance curve Third party software can be employed for other application areas Ability to cooperate with systems for other (eg office) functions	Hardware performance not optimised for specific application software

Parallel Processing.—Academic researchers have for many years been working on the concept of parallel processing—a system whereby multiple processors are employed to co-operate simultaneously to handle different parts of a single problem.

Parallel processing is used to describe many different computer architectures and all parallel processing design may be divided into three, not totally exclusive classes.

The first is *multiprocessing*, whereby multiple jobs are executed on multiple processors. Here, system throughput is increased, but the time-to-solution for a single task is not decreased.

The second group is *instruction level parallelism*, the system used by supercomputers. The performance of a single CPU is enhanced by carrying out a single instruction on groups of data (or vectors) simultaneously. This method of parallelism is limited, however, as very few real applications can be entirely vectorised. Thus, only a small percentage of the peak performance of a supercomputer would be used in these applications.

The third method of parallel processing overcomes many of the limitations of instruction level parallelism by speeding up the areas of program which cannot be run in vector mode. *Concurrency* executes operations by allowing existing applications programs to be run through a special compiler without modifying the source code. The compiler picks out simple and complex program loops, which on a single CPU system would have each iteration processed serially, and identifies them for allocation to available computational elements that can process them in parallel. Having automatically identified those sections of code that can be executed concurrently, appropriate control instructions are inserted into the object code stream.

REDUCED INSTRUCTION SET COMPUTERS.—Customer requirements to add specialised functions are driving the 32-bit processor market towards niches: these include image processing, speech processing, artificial intelligence, programmable control, avionics, high-speed data acquisition, data compression and communication network management. Whereas mainframes can operate at nearly 100 million instructions/s (MIPS) by performing operations in parallel, conventional microprocessor architectures are inherently capable of performance beyond two MIPS. However, using versions of the Reduced Instruction Set Computer (RISC) explored and developed at IBM, Stanford University and the University of California, Berkeley, microprocessor architectures capable of five MIPS are employed in the IBM PC-RT, the Hewlett-Packard Spectrum and the Fairchild Clipper. Whereas the performance limitations of earlier microprocessors led to the design of several CPU boards to perform separate functions within a single system—graphics processors, arithmetic units, pre- and post-processors, etc—these advanced 32-bit microprocessors have the processing power to perform many of these tasks on-chip. Clipper is a three-chip module incorporating a CPU with on-chip floating-point execution unit and two combination cache memory management chips (one each for instructions and data). The three chips are mounted on a small six-layer printed circuit board that can be assembled 'piggy-back' on a larger circuit board.

RISC architecture extensions incorporate three architectural features essential to a successful commercial design:

(1) Multiple buses to provide the memory bandwidth necessary to match high execution speeds;
(2) Set-associative cache memory organisation to eliminate the performance-draining data overlap and 'cache-thrashing' associated with direct memory mapping;
(3) Pipeline interlocking to ensure that the machine will never crash, even when using debuggers.

Further enhancements of these high-performance microprocessors are expected to lead to 20 MIPS versions by the end of this decade.

HARDWARE FOR ELECTRONIC DESIGN.—Specialised hardware targeted at electronic design applications represents some of the most advanced and widely available technology. Similar developments can be expected to influence other disciplines, notably for upgrading graphics performance for three-dimensional image generation and for performing finite element analysis.

Simulation Accelerators.—Accelerators are special purpose computers which perform a particular computational process much faster than a software solution. Logic accelerators potentially solve the problem of throughput for large simulations, but depend for their success on hardware models that accurately represent the logic primitives used by electronic designers. In practice, accurate representation of designer's logic often requires a compiler to translate it into the appropriate models for simulation. This raises the question of whether or not the translation introduces a level of abstraction which makes accurate simulation impossible.

Logic Analysers.—Logic analysers are a specialised type of digital oscilloscope for debugging, some of which are specifically designed for use with electronic CAD systems.

Physical Modelling Systems.—Physical modelling systems are an innovative class of specialised hardware aimed specifically at designers of electronic systems. This technology is in a formative stage and a number of problems have been experienced in the systems available (Ref 19). They consist of a set of reference elements, each comprising a physical component (eg a microprocessor), an outline drawing and a device definition text file. This 'hardware model' may then be treated exactly as if it were a conventional logic primitive, using it in multiple instances throughout a design if required. The great advantage is to free the user from developing complex software models of standard microprocessors and the like, merely to design systems around such components. The workstation's software tools operate in an identical fashion, whether dealing with physical components, software models or a combination. A further advantage is the ability to simulate a custom component, such as a gate array, prior to building the component and later to substitute the real thing into a system design and validate its performance. Furthermore, the speed of the physical component is claimed to be independent of its simulated speed: this means that a low performance, pre-production version of a chip may be used with a device definition which declares it to be a full-speed component. Thus, designers may cut development times by designing new systems before full performance chips are available.

COMPUTER MEMORY

MAIN MEMORY.—In the late seventies, a typical 2D draughting system may have comprised 30,000 lines of Fortran code, occupying 30–50 kbytes of memory and addressing 30–50 kbytes of data. If greater functionality resulted in larger software, then special techniques were used to organise the code for the available space. The more general introduction of *virtual memory operating systems* (defined below) meant that, by 1981/82, a typical system might comprise 1 Mbyte of code and data for a single user. Re-entrant compilers meant that only one code set was needed for many users on multi-user systems. However, data sets were also growing in size.

By 1986/87, a typical full function system may contain 1 Mbyte of code only, say about 400,000–500,000 equivalent lines of Fortran and data sets alone can be up to 1 Mbyte. Coupled with operating system kernel and window management requirements, for good performance a 2–3 Mbyte/user machine is needed. It is no surprise that this is typically the machine that has evolved to be today's engineering workstation.

In contrast, the basic PC architecture and operating system software limit the code-plus-data space to 640 kbytes, rather less than the 1981/82 standard mentioned above. Recent developments of add-on boards, in particular for running spreadsheet software, have raised this limit, but it should not be thought that this solution will necessarily be ideal for the CAD/CAM user.

Memory size and speed have a major influence on computer price and throughput, so CAD/CAM system suppliers offer systems with varying amounts and types of main memory. Most computers with 16-bit word length are limited to a memory size of 64 k words, but with *memory mapping* this is often extended to as much as 10^6 words of memory. Larger, 32-bit computers and microprocessors are designed to support as much as 8×10^6 bytes of main storage.

Most modern computers use solid-state memory, replacing the relatively slow magnetic core memory which was popular in the past. One advantage of magnetic core memory is its ability to retain data stored in it for many weeks without electric power. Two kinds of solid-state technologies are generally used for main memory: MOS and bipolar. MOS memory is about 40% faster than core; bipolar storage is a premium, expensive, high-performance memory that operates at more than three times the speed of core.

MEMORY MAPPING.—Memory mapping is a scheme that enables a computer to access additional amounts of main memory; it is also used to limit the memory access of a program to designated areas and provides protection to data stored in memory outside this area.

VIRTUAL MEMORY.—Virtual memory is a technique that simplifies the writing of large programs by making it appear to the programmer that the computer has a large main memory when in fact it does not. It is implemented using enhanced memory-mapping hardware and on-line disc storage. When dealing with long programs, virtual memory allows a sector of the main memory to be designated as the sector to accept the program: the program is then broken up into sections that will fit within the designated sector of memory. The remainder of the program is then stored on a secondary storage device, usually a disc. Each time a successive piece of the program has been used and the next section is required, it is transferred from the disc and overlaid on the designated sector of main memory. The new section actually replaces the old section in memory. This process is repeated until the entire program is run.

CACHE MEMORY.—Cache memory is a technique used to improve processor throughput: it is a small, high-speed memory used to store frequently accessed portions of main memory. The contents of cache are continually replaced with more frequently referenced data in order that the probability remains that future memory references can be satisfied from the cache, in preference to the slower main memory.

MASS STORAGE MEMORY DEVICES.—No matter how large the main memory in the CPU, it is still finite and very limited in comparison to the vast quantity of data that it has to process. The purpose of the main memory is essentially to provide a working area for the current program and it only retains information on a temporary basis until the termination of the program or program segment. Backing memory stores are therefore universally used to supplement the main memory and to save the data on a permanent basis. The various options of back-up memory, or mass storage are described in Table 7. These options fall into two camps: *on-line storage* and *off-line storage.* On-line storage is for data which is needed for immediate access and interactive operation of a computer system and will include the database plus all the software needed by the system. Virtually all on-line memory is disc storage, although technically it includes the computer control store, the main memory and the cache memory, if fitted. To qualify as on-line, data must be accessible in less than a second: accordingly, on-line storage capacity does not include data stored on magnetic tape and on disc packs not mounted on a drive, nor does it include high-speed tape drives, because, relying as it does on sequential access, some data may take minutes to find. Off-line storage provides an inexpensive method of

TABLE 7.—CHARACTERISTICS OF MASS STORAGE DEVICES

Type	Description	Advantages	Limitations
1. **Sequential access storage (serial access storage)**	**Used for rarely accessed archival storage**	**Low cost per bit**	**Information can only be accessed in the same order that it is stored originally.** **To read data, all preceding items must be read.** **Data must be written at end of file**
Magnetic tape	Similar to tape recorder tape but higher quality and more durable Also used for input/output, back-up crash protection and data transfer between unlinked systems	Cheap Large amount of data for given size Data may be re-read or overwritten Wide range of storage densities Wide range of operating speeds	Slow
2. **Direct access storage (random access storage)**	**Used for storing files requiring frequent access**	**Individual items can be located immediately for read and write**	**More expensive (cost per bit)**
(*a*) Magnetic disc (hard disc)	Magnetic metal stack of platters with concentric tracks. Data read as platters rotate Stack of platters (disc volume) may be permanently fixed or removable (disc pack) **See text for details of read/write heads**	Very high storage density Very high data transfer rate Can also be used for sequential access Data may be re-read or overwritten With disc packs, incremental cost of adding memory is lower	More expensive than floppy discs
(*b*) Winchester disc	Sealed unit Low cost, fixed media drive Read/write heads make contact with platter Used with powerful micros and minis	Minimum contamination and low preventative maintenance High precision, leading to high storage density Cheaper than hard disc drive, yet offers similar high data access rate	More expensive than floppy discs Platters not removable
(*c*) Floppy disc (flexible disc)	Similar to above, but disc made of flexible plastic Combination of speed, capacity and cost make it suited to small microcomputer systems	Compact Can be used for input and output (as hard disc) Removable from disc drive Low cost	Prone to physical damage Holds fewer data than hard disc Slower than hard disc
(*d*) Magnetic drum	Old form of mass storage Uses metal cylinder with data stored in circular tracks on drum surface	Higher data transfer rates than discs Fast access times Storage capacity similar to discs, but multiple drums possible	Multiple read/write heads needed Extensive control electronics More expensive than disc storage Drum not removable

(*e*) Optical memory		Storage costs/byte comparable to microfilm and much faster access Very compact space needed Enormous capacity (eg 8×10^{11} bytes) Erasable or non-erasable	Limited commercial availability High one-off cost Life span limited (10–15 years)
(*f*) Laser beam			
(*g*) Videodisc			
(*h*) Bubble memory			
(*j*) Electron beam			

TABLE 8.—CHARACTERISTICS OF INPUT DEVICES

Device	Description	Advantages	Limitations
1. **Light Pen**	Electronic pointing device connected by cable to computer which detects electron beam and signals its position to the computer	Easy-to-use Analogous to pen and paper Adequate precision for point-select use	Imprecise for drawing User leans forward Not suitable for storage tubes Requires specialised display hardware
2. **Hand cursors**	Methods of steering and tagging cross-hairs on display	More accurate and reliable than light pen Comfortable for operator	Require high processing power for real-time operation
(*a*) Joystick		Easy to control Fast and/or controllably rate-sensitive Precise	Self-centering, hence must hold on continuously
(*b*) Tracker Ball (Rollerball)	Mounted rotatable ball	Very high accuracy	Slow for large-scale movements
(*c*) Dial (Thumbwheel)	One-axis device which may be a lever or rotating knob Distance and direction of motion varies with angle of rotation	Fast for straight line movement	Poor for diagonals or curved motion One devide may be needed for each axis Relies on operator's sense of touch to manipulate properly
(*d*) Rockerpanels			
(*e*) Touch-sensitive panels	Special display screen which functions as a tablet. Touch-sensitivity obtained by:		
	Infra-red:	High resolution Reliable	

Table 8 cont. on H6/22

TABLE 8.—(*continued*)

Device	Description	Advantages	Limitations
	Capacitance:	Depends on coating for glass which can be retrofitted Reliable	Low resolution Environmentally sensitive
	Mechanical: (analog voltage)	High resolution	Complex to integrate into computer systems
(*f*) Mouse	Hand-held device moved over flat surface related to screen position	Combines speed of joystick with tracker ball precision	Needs consistent orientation relative to screen
3. **Menu**	Used in conjuction with cursor to select choices May be on-screen or on a separate screen or used with digitiser/tablet	Facilities may be provided to enable users to create their own function menus	On-screen not suited to storage tubes Separate screens may require input from keyboard or array of push-buttons
4. **Digitiser**	Table/board similar to drawing board used to take coordinates off an existing drawing. Detection by means of pointer devices (see below) which react to: electric fields from wire grid; acoustic signals from sonic source; pressure; light; distance-increment count generated by rotary or linear encoders using optical, magnetic, mechanical or brush contact		
5. **Graphics tablet**	Low-resolution digitiser Desk-top representation of screen display Used with pointer systems (below)	Includes menu and blank screen area Menus can be easily changed No second screen required Fast to use (no hierarchical data structure) Economical (standard display equipment and simple software)	
6. **Pointer devices**	Device incorporating cross-hair gunsight Puck/Digitizer Pencil-stylus	Good for transferring graphical information from existing drawings	

7. **Optical Scanning Systems**	Employed to capture large database: municipal mapping projects are prime targets	For many applications Better approaches use teach mode	Insufficient database intelligence Inability to scan and utilise commonly available documents Quality of documents critical Problems with character recognition
8. **Keyboard**	Standard alphanumeric input	Useful as secondary input method for data entry Good for text entry	Not suited to interactive graphics Necessary if menu appears on second screen
9. **Keypad**	Part of digitiser which allows rapid signalling of numerical data		
10. **Voice data entry**	Graphics information entered using speech commands	Potential to replace keyboards, function keys and tablet menus Easy for operator to learn Freedom of operator movement Potentially high accuracy Promising for handicapped users	Predefined vocabulary needed for each user Technology in early stages of development Cannot recognise operators with laryngitis or colds Not suited to occasional users
11. **Card reader**	Device for transferring data from punched cards to computer Virtually obsolete		Cumbersome to handle Bulky to keep Difficult for humans to interpret Errors difficult to correct Slow
12. **Paper tape reader**	Similar to card reader Virtually obsolete, but may be found in a few NC applications		Superior media available Slow Errors difficult to correct
13. **Magnetic ink and readers**	Data stored by printing with ferromagnetic ink	Readable by people and computers Commonly used for bank cheques	Not used in CAD/CAM
14. **Optical characters and reader**	Scanner reads document and compares with pre-defined patterns		Some problems with unrecognised characters Little CAD/CAM use
15. **Bar codes and readers**	Patterns of contrasting optical density scanned by light pen or other scanner	Good for stock control	

both long-term and short-term retention of a virtually unlimited amount of data and is invaluable as a back-up to more volatile data held in the on-line storage system. Off-line data storage should include copies of vital on-line data to insulate it from operator, hardware and software failures. Established archiving techniques ensure that appropriate numbers of backup copies are maintained to cater for all eventualities. Typical examples are reels of magnetic tape and removable disc-packs.

Read/Write Heads for Magnetic Discs.—Two kinds of read/write head units for magnetic disc devices are in general use: the moving head unit and the fixed head unit. Moving head units contain a certain number of access arms, depending upon the number of platters in the pack. For each platter, there is an access arm to control two read/write heads, one for the upper surface and one for the lower surface of the platter. The access arms form a single assembly and move in and out together across the surface of the disc, so that it is possible to access each track individually. In the case of fixed-head units, one read/write head is used for each track. Because there is no head movement, data are stored or retrieved more rapidly.

For moving-head types, two kinds of head-positioning methods are in use: open-loop, stepper-motor positioners and the more expensive, closed-loop, servo-motor positioners. Open-loop systems are slower and more prone to positioning errors. Removable disc packs are usually associated only with moving-head units having closed-loop head positioning; this is because this system can adapt itself to each disc pack individually, without special adjustments being necessary to correct for slight mechanical head misalignments. The greater accuracy of closed-loop positioning also allows higher track densities to be achieved.

Most Winchester drives are moving-head types, but open-loop or closed-loop positioning systems may be used. Storage densities range from 30–300 Mbytes. In addition to improving head positioning technology, greater storage densities on smaller Winchester discs have been provided by thin-film recording heads and different data encoding methods.

INPUT DEVICES

In CAD/CAM, some special input/output devices are needed for the performance of required functions. These mainly consist of graphics devices which enable coordinate data to be input and allow graphical information to be displayed on a screen. There are essentially two modes in which these interactive devices may be used: *picking* and *locating*. Picking is the selection of some part of the picture on the screen, by choosing from among existing parts of a picture; the most common example is the *menu*, which is simply a list of commands. Locating is the specification of a new coordinate position, at which something is to be drawn: this is the way in which graphics cursors naturally operate.

Many of these graphics input devices are analogue-to-digital (A/D) converters, which are essentially devices that detect some physical quantity, such as speed, acceleration, force, position, direction, rotation, distance, etc. and then translate it into a numerical quantity, such as a binary value, that the computer can understand. Some examples of these analogue devices are the digitiser, tablet, joystick, tracker ball and dial. These, together with other graphics input devices, such as light pens and keyboard devices, are considered in more detail in Table 8.

For a light pen to act as a locating device, it is necessary to introduce a dummy symbol on the screen, usually a *tracking cross*. The computer is able to use this to follow the light pen across the screen.

TERMINALS

The earliest types of terminals were teleprinters (teletypewriters), which resembled typewriters, but were connected directly to the computer via data communication lines. Relative to the visual display units (VDUs) which have largely replaced them teleprinters are noisy, slow and wasteful of paper. The rate of communication of a teleprinter is often in the range 110–300 baud (bits/s), whilst VDUs operate between 110 and 19,200, with 9,600 the most common. Teleprinters are still used as console terminals when an operating log is required of the status of all programs or data which have been processed by a computer.

GRAPHICS DISPLAYS.—Graphics displays are currently all based on cathode ray tubes (CRTs) and are likely to stay that way for the immediate future. Much work has been done on solid state (ie plasma discharge, cathodoluminescence, electroluminescence and liquid-crystal) flat-panel picture displays, but they have still

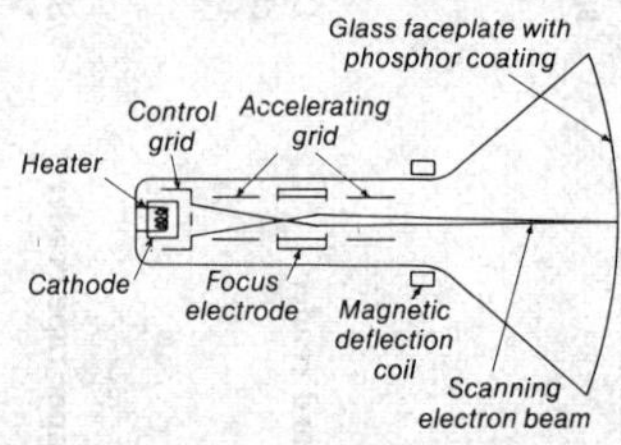

FIG. 9.—Cathode ray tube (CRT). Source: Besant and Lui. Computer-Aided Design and Manufacture; Fig. 3.2, p. 60.

not progressed beyond the introductory stage: panel costs, picture quality and power consumption will all have to be improved before flat-panel displays can rival CRTs for displaying graphics.

In a CRT display (Fig. 9), a heated cathode emits a continuous, high-speed stream of electrons, which is formed into a beam by an aperture in a control grid surrounding the cathode. The electrons are then accelerated and focussed to a point on the display surface. The electron beam is swept rapidly across the phosphor-coated face of the tube line-by-line. The beam current is regulated to increase or decrease its intensity in order that brighter or darker points are created along each swept line.

The two major techniques of generating an image are *stroke-writing* and *raster scan*. A stroke-writing device draws vectors or lines to create an image, whereas a raster scan device uses a matrix of closely-spaced dots to form a picture. Regardless of whether the stroke-writing or raster scan method was used to create the picture on the screen in the first place, it has to be maintained by some means, as the *persistence* of the screen's phosphor coating is short and finite. Persistence is defined as the length of time that a phosphor continues to glow after it is excited by the CRT electron beam. The screen has a certain amount of persistence: it can sustain the image for about 1 ms when white or green phosphorus is used and up to 1 s with orange phosphorus; for interactive work using a light pen, the shorter times are preferred. The two primary methods of maintaining an image on a screen are *refreshment*, where the image is continuously regenerated, or *storage*, where the tube retains the picture until it is erased.

The three main categories of CRT graphics displays commonly used in CAD systems are the *direct-view storage tube (DVST)*, the *directed-beam refresh tube (DBRT)* and the *refreshed raster scan display*. The various options are compared and contrasted in Tables 9, 10 and 11 and illustrated in Figs 10 and 11.

TABLE 9.—CRT IMAGE GENERATION AND IMAGE MAINTENANCE METHODS

Image maintenance method	Image generation method	
	Stroke writing	Raster scan
Storage	Storage tube (DVST)	—
Refreshed	Vector (DBRT)	Refreshed raster scan
		Plasma panel

Source: Besant and Lui. Computer-Aided Design and Manufacture; p. 61 (see Ref. 25).

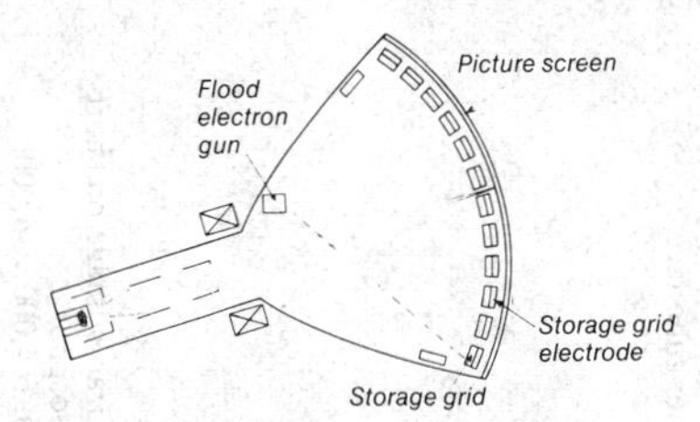

FIG. 10.—Storage tube. Source: Turner, L. Electronics, 17 February 1977.

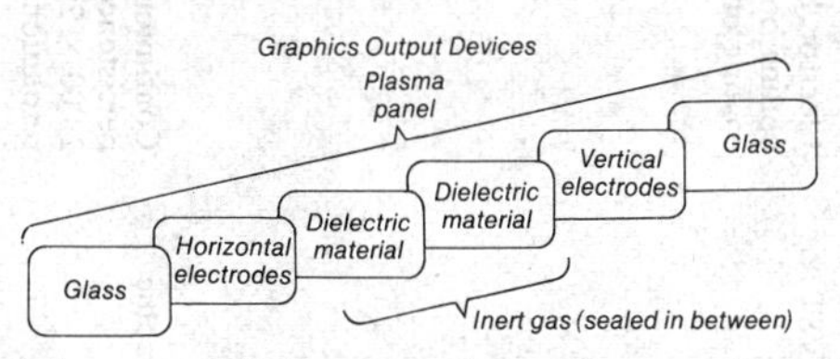

FIG. 11.—Exploded view of plasma panel display screen. Source: Besant and Lui. Computer-Aided Design & Manufacture; Fig. 3.6, p. 67.

The Raster Scan Display

In a raster scan display, the viewing screen is divided into a large number of tiny phosphor picture elements, known as *pixels* (or pels—short for picture elements). These are arranged into a matrix, which defines both the display area and the resolution of the screen. A raster scan display is typically 1,024 × 1,024 pixels, although it can be less, and high resolution screens go up to 2,048 × 1,568; this represents a total of over 3×10^6 pixels.

TABLE 10.—CHARACTERISTICS OF GRAPHICS DISPLAY TYPES

A—**Established Technologies**

Type	Description	Advantages	Limitations
1. **Cathode Ray Tubes**			
(*a*) Storage tube (DVST)	Electron beam traces an image or outline on a long memory phosphor coating on inner tube face	High resolution graphics Good for high density line detail *De facto* standard for graphics displays, against which other display devices are judged No staircasing effect Random deflection Almost unlimited storage capacity: (no flicker, light spot jitter, refreshing or dynamic limitations) Well suited to mapping work Relatively high writing rate Can overlay refreshed image with stored image without dstroying stored image No computing resources needed for keeping image on screen	Image fades and needs refreshing Poor contrast, low brightness: darkened viewing room necessary Tubes have limited life: images tend to fade at edges and corners High cost Selective erasure, grey-scale and colour only with recent types Limited brightness and contrast Use with light pen impossible Unsuitable with on-screen menus Intense erase flash
(*b*) Vector or calligraphic (DBRT)	Continuously traces image on short persistence phosphor 2,000 × 2,000 to 4,000 × 4,000 resolutions available	High resolution Continuous refresh/update Sharp, bright image: only lines of interest emit light Low memory requirement Colour versions available Selective erasure easy Can use interactively with light pen Can manipulate picture without loading main graphics processor Can show moving images	Most expensive Limited number of vectors/lines can be displayed at once without flicker (about 170 in.) Expensive and sophisticated circuitry to maintain refresh time Positioning vectors time-consuming No shaded images or colour RAM needed to store image

(*c*) Raster	High resolution version of domestic television Typical resolution 1,024 × 1,024 up to 2,048 × 1,568 Anti-aliasing (blurring) technique used to avoid 'staircase' effect on diagnosis Now most common display type	Easily controlled grey-scales Colour available Limited flicker No limit to displayable vectors Viewable in normal lighting levels Relevance of mass-produced TV tube technology keeps costs low and technology at frontier Picture updated at refresh rate Can show moving images	Some limit on resolution, but satisfies most engineering requirements Memory intensive because image must be stored for refresh function ('metafiles') Manipulating pictures difficult
(*d*) Flat-screen raster	Slim-line version which incorporates a 'mirror' electrode to turn the electron beam back on itself	Full colour possible	Currently monochrome Expensive because of low current production numbers
(*e*) Electrostatic CRT	Current resolution 720 × 540 pixels Work processing on 1,000 line unit	Well-established technology Rugged and compact	Expensive Aimed at miliary market
	B—Newer Technologies		
2. **Solid State**			All at introductory stage High panel costs Poor picture quality High power consumption
(*a*) Plasma panel	Inert gas sandwiched between glass panels; light produced by single intensity electrical excitation of gas	Light, compact Low power consumption Very flat screen Selective reading and writing possible Transparent screen allows related information to be superimposed from the rear of the displayed image Picture has high dimensional accuracy	Unconventional technology Rather low resolution Additional control hardware needed Currently only light and dark picture: no grey-scale
(*b*) Cathodoluminescence			

Table 10 cont. on H6/28

TABLE 10.—(*continued*)

B—Newer Technologies

Type	Description	Advantages	Limitations
(*c*) Electroluminescence	Based on a sheet coated with a conductive, transparent oxide film, which forms the positive electrode. A layer of powder phosphor is deposited onto the oxide and covered by a vacuum evaporated aluminium layer Refresh rate adequate at 50–60 Hz	Use of powder phosphor and dc supply ensures that minor imperfections in manufacture do not lead to catastrophic failure of picture elements Full colour technically feasible by using 3 primary phosphors	Considered by some to be of limited use Thin film types can suffer irreparable damage to individual picture elements
(*d*) Liquid crystal	Orientation of crystals, combined with a twist in molecular alignment, gives the difference between the ON and OFF states		
	Conventional LC displays use twisted nematic (TN) crystals, with a twist of 90° Colour is achieved by using LCs in reverse video mode with back illumination and series fine filters	Good contrast if not multiplexed above 100:1	Do not offer switching speeds compatible with TV line scans Only 7 colours possible
	Challenge to produce alternative to support 500–1,050 line displays had identified three approaches: (1) Increased twist angle	Improves contrast and the effective level of multiplexing	Expensive to product
	(2) Active matrix: switch for each pixel in display, usually effected with thin film transistors (TFT)	Commercialisation expected 1987	Quality control difficulties
	(3) Smectic LCs will remember the information carried on the last pulse indefinitely and only require a pulse to change state. This removes the multiplexing problem	May offer better viewing characteristics than some CRTs Smectic C has high switching speed	Smectic A has slow refresh rate but is in early stages of development

TABLE 11.—CAPABILITIES OF VARIOUS DISPLAY TECHNOLOGIES

Capability	Type			
	Raster	Vector	Storage	Plasma
Resolution	2,048 × 2,048	4,096 × 4,096	4,096 × 4,096	512 × 512
Gray-scale display	Yes	Limited	No	No
Colour	Yes	No	No	No
Contrast	100 ft-lamberts		8 ft-lamberts	
Price	Inexpensive	High	Fair	
Refresh	30–100 times/s	30–100 times/s	Approx. once/h	
Flicker	Possible	Possible	Not possible	Not possible
Dimensional accuracy	Poor	Fair	Fair	Good
Interactive operation	Yes	Yes	No	Yes
Refresh memory	Yes	Yes	Not needed	Not needed
Memory size	Large	Medium	None	None
Smearing effect	Possible	Possible		
Graphics				
Number of vectors		Limited	Unlimited	
Line straightness	Poor	Excellent	Excellent	Poor
Shading	Good	No	No	No
Re-reading of display	Yes	No	No	Yes
Areas	Yes	No	No	Yes

Source: Rembold *et al.* Computer-Integrated Manufacturing Technology and Systems, Fig. 5.1, p. 170 (see Ref. 58).

During redrawing, or *refreshing*, one or more bits of digital information are read to determine the state of each pixel each time it is drawn. If there is only one bit of memory per pixel, then that dot is either black or white. A single bit per pixel constitutes a *pixel plane* of memory. Raster-scan displays have a number of pixel planes, which can be used to store more than one picture. Alternatively, the bits corresponding to each pixel may be considered together as a single binary number, which allows each pixel to exhibit a range of different intensities or colours. Originally, multi-plane raster scan displays were extremely expensive, because of the huge amount of memory required to store a high-resolution display with many colours. As computer memory has become very much cheaper, this cost has become minimal relative to the cost of electronics and the tube and raster-scan displays have the enormous advantage of using television tube technology, for which a vast market and mass-produced components already exist.

Anti-Aliasing.—One reason for the lack of popularity of raster scan displays among engineers is their perceived poor line quality. Lines which are not horizontal, vertical or at 45° appear to be jagged, or 'staircased'. Staircasing can be countered by higher resolution or by anti-aliasing. This involves using colours which are a mixture of the colour of a line and of the background. Pixels are coloured with denser shades if they lie right on the middle of the line and less dense shades if they are further away. The eye is fooled into seeing a smooth line or curve. A prerequisite for anti-aliasing is a display that has many pixel planes.

Interlacing.—There are two common methods of refreshing a raster display: sequential, or non-interlaced, scanning and interlaced scanning.

Sequential scanning (Fig. 12) involves sweeping each horizontal line starting from the top to the bottom. The problem is that if the refresh rate is not high enough, the top part of the display appears to fade while the bottom part is still being scanned.

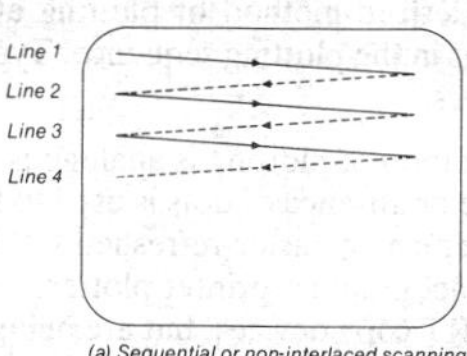

(a) Sequential or non-interlaced scanning

FIG. 12.—Sequential or non-interlaced scanning. Source: Besant and Lui. Computer-Aided Design and Manufacture; Fig. 3.5a, p. 65.

Interlaced scanning, Fig. 13, involves sweeping alternate lines and sweeping the screen twice in each refresh cycle. The problem of flicker is overcome by refreshing at a fixed rate of between 30 and 100 Hz, slightly faster than a domestic television set in which the picture is redrawn at 25 Hz; the rate is determined by the persistence of the phosphor of the CRT.

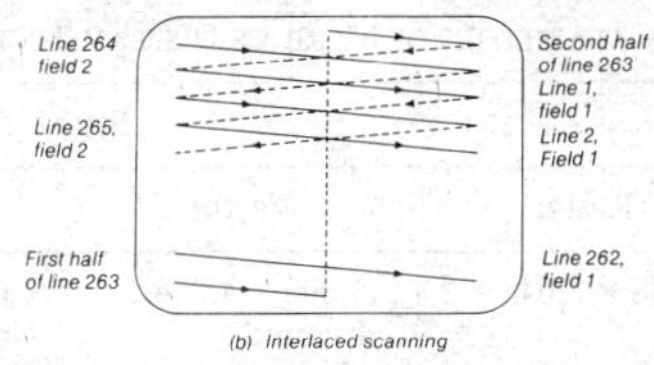

FIG. 13.—Interlaced scanning. Source: Besant and Lui. Computer-Aided Design & Manufacture; Fig. 3.5b, p. 65.

TEXT DISPLAY UNITS

A text display unit, dedicated to alphanumerics only, is a feature of many workstation designs. In addition to displaying text whilst it is being typed in by the operator, this display is used by the system to prompt for input, it will complain if mistakes are detected and it keeps the operator informed of the system's status. Most systems employ an alphanumeric CRT for this purpose, though some employ a single-line (or more recently multi-line) flat-panel display. In the CRT case, features such as scrolling, reverse contrast, blinking fields or an alternate large-character display mode are sometimes available.

Windows.—However, the use of screens in the so-called multi-window style (which simulates multiple pieces of paper arranged on a desk) seems certain to continue to be a target system builders will aim for. Commands are selected from *icons* (tiny pictures) and menus that pop up all over the screen. Improved speed of interaction, achieved both via higher performance hardware and improved command facilities such as screen menu handling, allow much more to be achieved through a single screen. Since this reduces cost, there will be considerable pressure to reduce twin screen systems to one.

Generally, window-managed software displays have been tightly coupled with workstations or micro-computers and not available with larger computers. Frequently, each workstation has supported only a single 'integrated' window-managed display. As a result, fitting out a department with window-managed systems has meant buying an entire workstation-and-display system for each user. Then, because graphics software must be developed for the new bit-mapped display, engineering management has had to choose from the following alternatives: discard terminals and host-based software; run existing software under an emulator, with possible reduced performance; or maintain a dual-format environment, using one terminal for previously developed software, while current software is ported or new software is developed for the window-managed graphics displays. In addition, the lack of standards for window-managed graphics has meant that software developers have had to re-do their code for each new host or display they want to support. Window-management software packages are now becoming available (Ref 30) to support multiple, host-based window-managed terminals.

OUTPUT DEVICES

OUTPUT PLOTTING METHODS.—For communication from a computer to people, output devices are needed. Hardcopy devices are used for: creating checkplots for off-line editing purposes; making permanent and semi-permanent copies of CRT displays; producing final drawings and documentation on paper, film or microfilm. Printers are output devices used mainly for text, while plotters are used for graphics output.

Vector Plotting.—Vector plotting is analogous to the method of displaying vectors or strokes on a vector refreshed CRT. Vector plotting can employ either incremental plotting or absolute plotting. Incremental plotting uses only updated information, which in effect drives the writing device from its last point of origin or move to the next incremental point. Absolute vector plotters work with base coordinate information, so that each point of plotting is an absolute coordinate point, which may or may not be related to the last point of plotting. Absolute vector plotting is a desired method of plotting at any remote installation that could be subject to line noise or other interruptions in the plotting sequence. Typical vector plotters include pen plotters, photoplotters and some microfilm plotters.

Dot Matrix (Raster) Plotting.—This method of plotting is analogous to the method of displaying information on a raster refreshed CRT. The presence or absence of dots is used to formulate the information. Such devices can be subject to the same staircasing effect of raster-refreshed CRTs. Raster plotters include electrostatic plotters, ink-jet plotters, dot matrix impact graphics printer plotters and some microfilm plotters. In addition, thermal plotters are still used as quick CRT copy devices, but are being replaced by dot matrix impact graphics printer plotters, in-jet plotters and electrostatic plotters. All of these can produce colour and multi-tonal images.

Vector-to-Raster Conversion.—Since all CAD/CAM databases are in a vector format, it is necessary to convert the vector information into equivalent raster information acceptable to a raster plotter. Substantial amounts of computer memory and software processing are necessary to make this conversion and this can slow down interactive activity at workstations, making on-line use of raster plotters undesirable. However, microprocessor-based dedicated converters are now available to support the conversion for the electrostatic plotter and off-load the graphics processor. From the telecommunications standpoint, raster transmission is more costly and slower.

CAD SOFTWARE

CAD software is built up from six levels, as shown in Table 12. Level 1 is the basic software which makes the computer and its peripherals work. The second level drives the graphics. The third level, the kernel of the CAD/CAM software, includes the user interface, data management and data exchange software. The fourth level and the main subject of this section, is the geometry modelling software. The fifth level, applications software, links the lower levels to the various application areas such as draughting, analysis, part programming. The first five levels are usually bought from a vendor. The sixth level, and the subject of its own section, is made up of user-written, company-specific software.

TABLE 12.—SIX LEVELS OF CAD/CAM SOFTWARE

Developed in-house:	Level 6	User-developed software
Supplied by vendor:	Level 5	Applications software (eg draughting, NC programming, kinematics)
	Level 4	Product modelling software (eg wireframe modeller, surface modeller)
	Level 3	CAD/CAM systems software (eg user interface, data management)
	Level 2	Graphics software
	Level 1	Computer systems software (eg operating system, compilers)

Source: Stark, J. Practical CAD/CAM Applications, p. 21 (see Ref. 42).

It is not really valid to compare the performance of CAD/CAM hardware without taking into account the effects of software: how well the graphics software exploits the operating system and how well the operating system exploits the computer hardware have a major bearing on useful processor throughput: it is not unusual to find that poor software designs reduce throughput by a factor of 10 or more!

SOFTWARE STANDARDISATION

The speed with which the CAD industry has developed, together with its decentralised strcture, has left little time for standardisation issues to be resolved. In fact, the early intentions were to avoid standardisation, in order that a customer became locked into one manufacturer's equipment. This is a most undesirable situation for a buyer, particularly if the vendor is a very immature company which is growing at an astonishing rate; less common, but even more serious, is the prospect of the vendor disappearing altogether.

Standards can also help applications programmers in the understanding and use of certain techniques, such as the exploitation of graphics routines. *Programmer portability* enables a programmer to leave one project for another without the need to learn a new set of commands, whilst manufacturers of hardware can use standards as a guideline for providing useful combinations of capabilities, thereby obviating the need for writing commands and interpreters. All of these factors serve to speed up project development, to the ultimate further benefit of the user.

There are few standards for databases in the CAD/CAM industry and none of them are yet sufficiently comprehensive to guarantee in all cases that a design can be transferred intact from one type of system to another. Many large end-users have opted, quite deliberately, for incompatible CAD software systems, on their individual merits for different sectors of their business; thereafter they have had accept that the transfer of data from one division to another is difficult, if not impossible.

One negative side to standardisation is that a desire to standardise could lead to a set of standards based upon the lowest common denominator of existing technology: standards must represent a compromise between many companies and approaches. Since future developments have to be able to be incorporated into a carefully-defined framework, moves towards vendor-independent communication between computer systems are taking much time, committee work and effort to get off the ground. For example, from the time a need is recognised for a few feature in the IGES Level 4 database format standard (described below) until the time it actually becomes part of that standard, two years may elapse.

LEVEL 1—OPERATING SYSTEM SOFTWARE AND STANDARDS

This level of software includes operating systems (see later section) and compilers and these operate in conjunction with programming languages, such as Fortran, Cobol and C (see Chapter H2 for details).

An operating system is the software that looks after the running of all the *boot-up* (or start-up) functions, file handling, maintenance of disc and tape directories, the actual operation of the disc drive and magnetic tape storage devices, all the input/output routines for line printers and other 'housekeeping' duties.

In spite of these common functions, there are differences between operating systems: the features that help the user, such as editing facilities, data security and the support of particular languages all influence the choice of operating system. Because operating systems have traditionally been indigenous to a manufacturer, they may have also influenced the choice of computer. Some CAD vendors have developed their own operating systems that are specifically tailored to the needs of their systems. While this approach is inherently superior (more efficient, better response times and occupying less memory), it does limit the amount of third party software that can be run on a system and makes in-house development of software by users (Level 6) more difficult.

The problems inherent in the existence of a wide variety of operating systems appear to be on the way to resolution with the spread in popularity of the UNIX operating system, which is now available on many different computer systems. It should be possible to get an application program running under UNIX and then move it to other machines running the UNIX operating system.

UNIX.—UNIX has become the effective operating system standard, directly supported by its developer, AT&T. Although UNIX was developed at AT&T's Bell Laboratories, major enhancements were added to it at the University of California, Berkeley. These differences created two camps in the UNIX community: System V (AT&T) and 4.2BSD. While this sometimes make portability difficult to implement, AT&T support and industry acceptance of the emerging UNIX V promises to correct this situation. UNIX System V Release 2 incorporates elements of the UNIX System 4.2 (4.2BSD) and in Europe, the X/OPEN group is further refining the UNIX System V environment definition.

Currently, not too many public domain or common engineering programs or business software are running under UNIX, but this is merely a transition phase. Many recent CAD workstations cope with this current limitation by offering dual operating systems, the second being PC-DOS, the operating system of the IBM PC series. The long-term problems are minimal, because a number of computer languages are available which run under UNIX, including Pascal, Fortran, Cobol, Basic and C; engineering software is predominantly written in Fortran—or latterly in 'C', the language best suited to UNIX and the obvious choice for development of CAD/CAM extensions to UNIX facilities.

Some industry sources believe that UNIX is in itself a transitional phase and later versions of PC-DOS may ultimately, however, become the standard operating system.

LEVEL 2—GRAPHICS SOFTWARE AND STANDARDS

The second level of software within the CAD/CAM system is the graphics software that controls the graphics terminal. Amongst the tasks of the graphics software are to communicate with the main computer, manage the input/output devices, such as the keyboard and the puck that are associated with the screen, and to draw the image on the screen.

Graphics software, like programming languages, comes with different degrees of sophistication. The least sophisticated understand little more than commands to move the beam from one point to another, or to switch the beam on and off. The programming instructions in such languages are very specific to the particular screen, thus a program written to run on one screen would not be usable on another screen. In the more sophisticated graphics languages, an attempt is made to ease the difficulty of preparing programs by offering the programmer a library of routines, capable of carrying out higher level functions such as drawing a line with a given width and style, using colours, generating polygons, erasing and recalling lines, reading a value input at the keyboard, etc. These routines can be called by the programmer from a program written in a high-level programming language such as Fortran. Unfortunately, the majority of these sophisticated graphics languages are *screen-dependent:* thus a program written for one screen will not run on another.

GKS AND CORE.—As an attempt to provide functional international standards for device-independent software and firmware and implementations of computer graphics utilities, standards such as GKS and CORE exist: neither is currently suitable for all applications. These standards act as a software interface between the application program and the graphics functions and will typically provide a library of subroutines or procedures which can be called from an application program.

When the need for graphics standards was first recognised in 1974, the Graphics Standards Planning Committee (GSPC) was formed by SIGGRAPH, a special-interest group of the US Association for Computing Machinery (ACM). In 1977, the GSPC published the CORE specification, but it assumed that vector graphics was the dominant display technology and it did not support raster graphics. Subsequent CORE specifications included raster graphics, machine/device interfaces and the need for metafiles (see Table 15) to store images before displaying them.

Meanwhile, the West German body responsible for standards, Deutsche Institut für Normung (DIN) came up with the Graphics Kernal System (GKS) (Refs 34 and 35). This kernel system is independent of the programming language, the computer and the application program: thus it is only necessary to describe its function and structure. Subsequently, the International Standards Organisation (ISO) and the American

National Standards Institute (ANSI) have cooperated to refine GKS further. Because it is a standard now approved internationally, software written to utilise this standard has the widest possible transportability among various computer and graphics hardware devices.

GKS has to acknowledge the whole range of graphics, from simple passive output to highly interactive applications and all types of graphics displays must be controllable in a consistent way. It contains the following: methods for the abstract definition of peripherals; definitions for basic graphic elements; definitions for graphic operations; methods for abstraction of graphic applications; a definition of a user model.

Figure 14 shows the layer model of this approach. The GKS software is located between the operating system and the user program. The design of the interface between the operating system and the GKS kernel is the task of the system supplier.

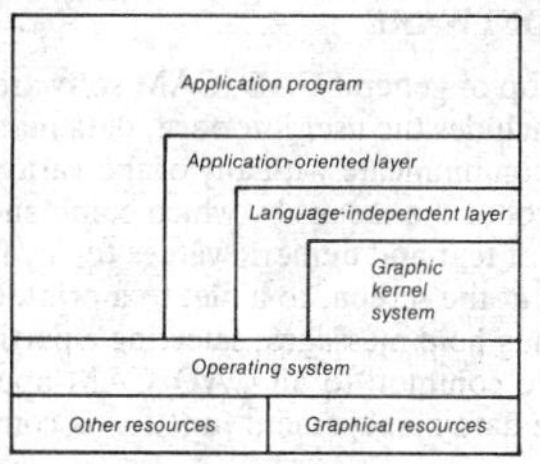

FIG. 14.—The layer model of GKS. Source: Encarnacao, J. Computer-Aided Design, Modeling, and Systems Engineering. 1980.

A variety of GKS functions is available to the programmer: they may consist of a simple instruction to a plotter or may be very complex, as when a picture is manipulated interactively. Typical functions include the following:

(*a*) **Output primitives.**—These allow graphic output of drawings or images on a graphic display or plotter.
(*b*) **Input primitives.**—These allow input of graphic information to a graphic display.
(*c*) **Picture manipulation and transformation.**—For design or draughting operations, it is necessary to perform manipulations, transformations and editing with pictures.
(*d*) **Picture structure.**—When pictures are created on a screen, they may have to be superimposed or changed or gradually built-up. For this reason, it is necessary to identify sub-pictures. It is the task of GKS to provide the tools for identifying such partial pictures, or segments.
(*e*) **Peripheral allocation.**—A graphic system usually has numerous peripherals: these must be allocated to the individual user or process. The GKS system has to schedule the peripherals, though the operation of the peripherals is done by dedicated drivers.
(*f*) **Storage.**—The storage provision allows users to save graphic information temporarily over a lengthy period.

GKS benefits from a controlled sub-set structure, which allows specific, rather than arbitrary, sub-sets of the specification to be implemented. This allows vendors to avoid redundancy without the anarchic sub-set system which will be described in connection with the IGES model data transfer standard. GKS sets down two axes of functionality—input and output—with three dimensions of each. Implementations of GKS thus quote the level of implementation, which specifies exactly what functionality is supported in each instance.

GKS-3D AND PHIGS.—One of the differences between CORE and GKS is that CORE allows coordinate data to be specified in either two-dimensional or three-dimensional form, whereas GKS accepts only two-dimensional data. Work is now being carried out in two directions to extend GKS into a full 3D standard: GKS-3D and PHIGS are both in the early stages of development and are considered to be complementary, rather than competitive.

GKS-3D, whilst attempting to retain compatibility with GKS (2D), deals with the definition and display of 3D graphical primitives; mechanisms to control viewing transformations and associated parameters; control of the appearance of primitives, including hidden line considerations, but not light source and shading and shadow computation; and the input of 3D information.

PHIGS deals with the definition, display and modification of either 2D or 3D graphical data; definition, display and manipulation of geometrically related objects; and the rapid dynamic articulation of graphical entities. PHIGS extends beyond the scope of GKS/GKS-3D in recognising the need for displaying an object more than once with different attributes: whereas GKS binds primitives and attributes together in a permanent manner, PHIGS supports a multi-level hierarchical data structure which allows the values of attributes to be inherited from the context of the object.

FORMAT STANDARDS (VDI/CGI AND VDM/CGM).—The aim of standards which describe the format for transferring graphics data between the application programs and different graphics devices is primarily to overcome the problem of graphics device dependence. Many devices for graphics output and input use different protocols for the production of graphics. Virtual Interface Device (VDI), renamed Computer Graphics

Interface (CGI), is a set of commands for creating picture primitives such as lines and circles and for reading from graphics devices that an application program requests; using VDI/CGI, it is not necessary to modify an application program as new graphics devices are added to a system—all that is required is to write a device driver for the new unit. Virtual Device Metafile (VDM), renamed Computer Graphics Metafile (CGM), is a definition for storing graphics images in computer memory, in order to transfer images from one system to another.

COMMUNICATIONS STANDARD (NAPLPS).—A videotex standard called NAPLPS, in covering the presentation of graphical information via Prestel-type communications, provides for low cost but relatively rapid transmission of graphics images over a communications link.

LEVEL 3—CAD/CAM SYSTEMS SOFTWARE

The third level of software is made up of general CAD/CAM software that will be used by all the individual CAD/CAM applications. This level includes the user interface, data management and data exchange software. The user interface allows the user to communicate with any of the various CAD/CAM applications programs. It contains functions such as the control of the means by which commands are entered (eg by screen menu, by tablet menu, by keyboard), the input of text and numeric values (eg by function keys, from the tablet) and the output of text and numeric values (eg at the screen, to a file, to a printer). It is also the part of the system that is used in prompting the user, displaying help messages, selecting a particular entity among all those available, digitising a point. These functions are common to all CAD/CAM applications. Similarly, since the various applications access the same data, the data management function is common to the system, rather than to the specific application.

The role of different standards, within the three levels of software so far discussed, for a conceptional graphics system is shown in Fig. 15.

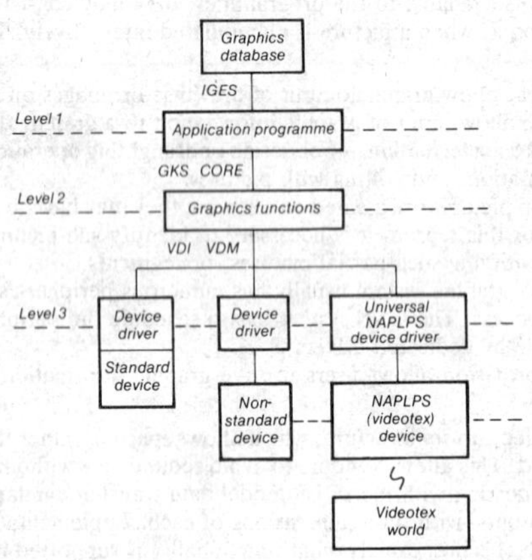

FIG. 15.—The role of different standards within a conceptual graphics system. Electronic Design, 12 July 1984.

LEVEL 4—CAD SOFTWARE

The fourth level, containing the geometric modelling software, is one of the most important. CAD systems share a common reliance upon the ability of the computer to construct and store representations of geometrical models.

The model is, loosely, the equivalent of the traditional, plans-on-paper description which a designer produces with the aid of pencil, paper and drawing boards. The existence of the geometric model is fundamental to all aspects of CAD/CAM and, more than any other factor, is responsible for its advantages over traditional methods. It is the geometrical model of an object, contained in mathematical form in computer memory, which an analytical program operates on. The programs which generate NC data, specifying the path to be followed by a tool, are designed to reproduce the geometric forms represented by the computer's model.

Nevertheless, there are fundamental differences in the ways in which models are developed and these strongly influence the ways in which they may be used. This section looks at the different modelling techniques and applications.

2, 2½ OR 3 DIMENSIONS?.—Most draughting/design software used on traditional CAD/CAM systems deals with portrayals of three-dimensional objects. This means that these software packages must deal with much more complex mathematics than two-dimensional packages and thus require substantially more computing resources.

However, many draughting systems on small machines, such as personal computers, are simple two-dimensional packages. These systems lack the concept of an underlying model and are only capable of creating lines, arcs and text on a flat drawing. This is the fundamental difference between a design system and a draughting system. Nevertheless, the most popular and widespread CAD package available today, until most recently, was capable only of two-dimensional draughing functions. Some three-dimensional draughting packages are available on personal computers and recently a few full solid modellers have appeared which can run on the IBM PC series.

It is easy to visualise that a 2D model represents a flat part and a 3D model provides representation of a generalised part shape. A 2½D model can be used to represent a part of constant section with no side-wall details—ie a constant z-axis dimension can be applied to the 2D database. The major advantage of a 2½D model is that it gives a certain amount of 3D information about a part without the need to create a database of a full 3D model. Illustrations of isometric and perspective views can be performed on some of the 2½D systems. The main reason for its popularity is related to the geometry of machining carried out on a milling machine and the existence of a large number of NC machine tools of this type. When a cylindrical milling cutter moves either in the direction of its axis or perpendicular to it, it creates a cavity with a flat bottom and sides composed of straight line segments and arcs: in fact a 2½D shape. Very often, components can be milled in a 2½D way; more than one face can be machined by using either rotary axes on the machine or multiple set-ups and in such cases each such face can be considered a separate 2½D shape.

THREE-DIMENSIONAL MODELS.—Most designers of complex parts and assemblies have to think extensively in three dimensions, a fact borne out by the paper, wood and clay models which are extensively employed in many design offices.

In general, there are three types of model in common use to represent a physical object in CAD/CAM systems: wireframe, surface and solid models.

Display List.—In conventional 3D systems, the displayed view is derived from the geometric 3D data. This is accomplished using a mathematical transformation to compute the projection of the model geometry onto the view plane at the desired scale. In some systems, the transformed data are retained in a display list, which is used to drive the display. In others, the transformed data are computed during the repaint (display generation) cycle and are not retained. Systems that retain display lists and update them as the model is updated have faster repaint cycles than systems that must re-compute the display list vectors whilst repainting the display. Also, their repaint times are substantially independent of computational load. On the other hand, systems with display lists require more memory to store the display lists and additional software to keep the display lists current. In three-dimensional work, the additional costs are usually justified by the time saved.

Wireframe Models.—These models, also called *edge-vertex* or *stick-figure* models, are the simplest form of three-dimensional modelling and are commonly used to define computer models of parts in draughting systems. They are simple and easy to create and demand limited computer time and memory.

Unfortunately, they do not offer a complete description of the part: they contain little information about the surfaces of the part and cannot distinguish the inside from the outside of part surfaces. This leads to ambiguity in representing three-dimensional parts (Fig. 16) and this increases with component complexity; another

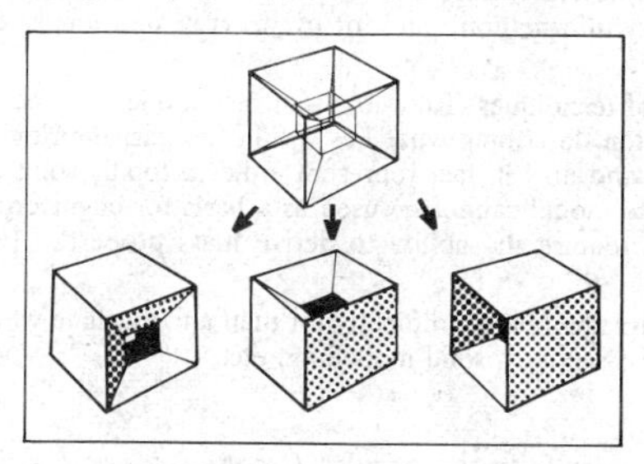

FIG. 16.—The Ambiguity of Wireframe Models. Source: Nicols, K. W. The Wider Benefits of Solid Modelling. p. 3–9.

deficiency is the tolerance of 'nonsense' objects (Fig. 17); in each case, these meaningless representations would have to be detected and removed by the operator. As a consequence, wireframe modellers cannot be used to generate NC machining instructions automatically.

SURFACE MODELLERS.—A surface model is built by defining the surfaces on the wireframe model by a process analogous to stretching a thin sheet of material over a framework. Thus, whereas the wireframe modeller would represent a cube as twelve lines, the surface modeller would represent it as six surfaces, Fig. 18. A variety of construction features is provided on CAD/CAM systems for this purpose. Surface models

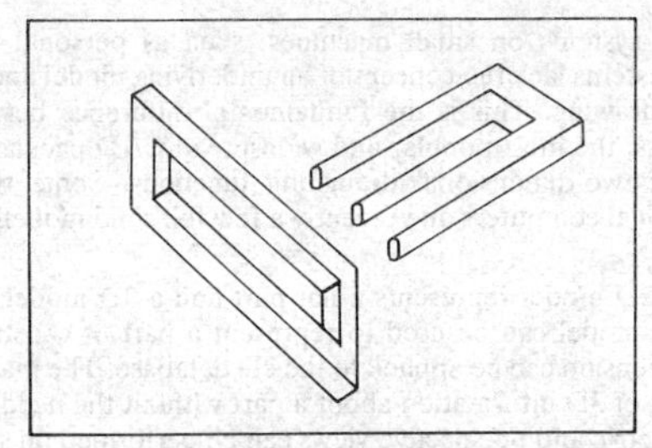

FIG. 17.—The Tolerance of Wireframe Models to Nonsense Objects. Source: Nichols, K. W. The Wider Benefits of Solid Modelling. pp. 3–9.

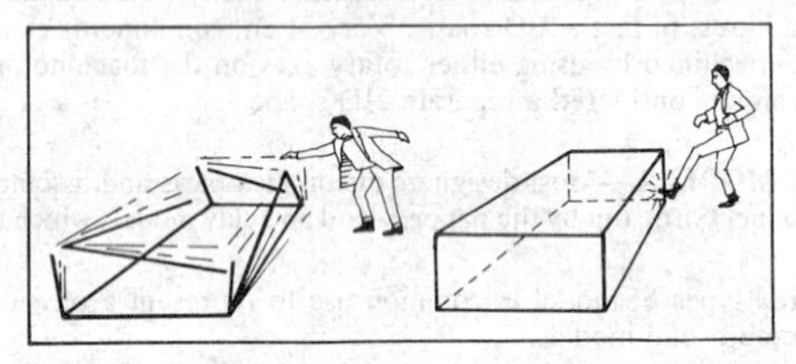

FIG. 18.—One view of the difference between wireframe and solid models. Source: Fegs Ltd and reprinted in Design Engineering, July 1983.

define precisely part geometry, such as surfaces and structure boundaries and can therefore produce NC machining instructions automatically.

The plane is the most basic feature to represent a surface element; more complex shapes can be defined by tabulated cylinders, ruled surfaces of revolution, sweep surfaces and fillet surfaces: many manufactured shapes have surfaces which are more complex than these and can readily be produced on conventional machine tools. It is difficult to draw them and impossible using straight lines and circular arcs alone.

One of the great advantages of surface modelling is in modelling sculptured (or doubly curved) surfaces; these are general and complex surface representations, also known as *curve-mesh surfaces*, *B-surfaces* and *cubic-patch surfaces*. A sculptured surface may be considered as a surface produced from combining two families of curves that intersect in a criss-cross manner, creating a network of interconnected patches. A later section will deal with the mathematical representation of surface geometry. Typical uses are in modelling car bodies, helicopter rotor blades, aircraft wings and turbine blades. Conversely, for simple shapes, a surface model may contain unnecessary information, paid for by the user in a longer data entry time and a slower response time.

By using hidden-line removal techniques (Ref. 40), a surface model may be made to appear solid, but in reality it contains no information describing what lies within the part interior. For this reason, the surface model can also be ambiguous and may in fact represent either a totally solid object or a thin-walled sheet structure. As a result, a surface model cannot be used as a basis for engineering analysis programs such as finite element analysis, which require the ability to derive mass properties (weight, volume, moments of inertia).

Figure 19 puts into perspective the relative difficulty for man and machine when performing different types of CAD, such as 2D, 2½D, cross-sections, solid modelling, etc.

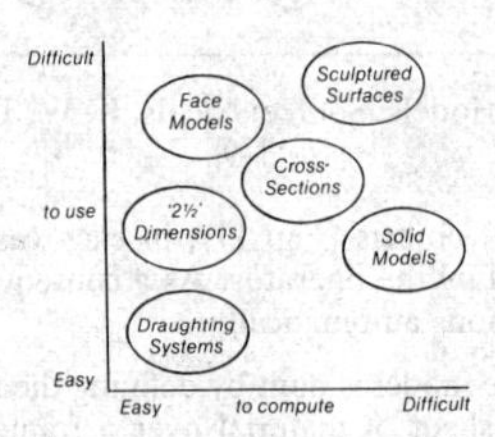

FIG. 19.—Categorisation of shape description techniques. Source: Woodwark, J. Computing Shape; Fig. 3.1, pp. 22.

Mathematics of Curves and Curved Surfaces.—It is not easy to construct shape elements that can be used by a designer which not only behave well in the mathematical sense, but which also behave predictably in response to actions by the user.

It is possible to create complex curves from multiple segments of the classical curves, usually circular or parabolic arcs. However, these can only give limited continuity (differentiability) and the large numbers of segments required are not easy to organise and control. In general, it is more satisfactory to use fewer segments of more complex form.

Because it is necessary to determine tangents, normals, curvatures, etc., a parameterisation needs to be chosen which will make differentiation easy. Polynomial functions are an obvious choice, especially because the evaluation of all functions in the computer eventually reduces anyway to the computation of polynomials—expressions of the form shown in equation (1):

$$a + bx + cx^2 + dx^3 + \dots \quad (1)$$

and rational polynomials equation (2):

$$\frac{a + bx + cx^2 + dx^3 + \dots}{a + ex + fx^2 + gx^3 + \dots} \quad (2)$$

Writing separate equations in each of the two coordinates is rather repetitive and so the form of equation (3)

$$\boldsymbol{Q}(t) = \boldsymbol{A} + \boldsymbol{B}t + \boldsymbol{C}t^2 + \boldsymbol{D}t^3 + \dots \quad (3)$$

is often used, where $\boldsymbol{Q}$, $\boldsymbol{A}$, $\boldsymbol{B}$, $\boldsymbol{C}$ and $\boldsymbol{D}$ are vectors.

Interpolation.—Using parametric polynomial equations does not lead directly to curves which are controllable, or in which the effects of changing the coefficients are easy to visualise. One of the simplest ways to control a parametric polynomial curve is to constrain it to pass, or interpolate, through a number of points. This form of interpolation is called *Lagrangian interpolation.* In most cases, however, a curve segment must have given slopes, as well as positions at its ends or elsewhere, to allow it to mate with adjoining curves. Interpolation to both position and slope constraints is known as *Hermite interpolation.* Satisfying each slope constraint requires one more term to be added to the equations in each of x and y: since the lowest order polynomial which can describe any curve more complex than a straight line is a quadratic, this means that the lowest order parametric polynomial which can satisfy both position and slope constraints is the cubic, which has four terms, as in equation (4):

$$\boldsymbol{Q}(t) = \boldsymbol{A} + \boldsymbol{B}t + \boldsymbol{C}t^2 + \boldsymbol{D}t^3 \quad (4)$$

There is often a requirement for curves with more flexibility than parametric cubic permits. However, if such curves are generated by specifying many intermediate data points, then the problem of choosing appropriate parameter values becomes acute: wrong choices lead to 'wiggles' between data points, which can be very difficult to eliminate.

One well-known alternative approach to interpolation is the Bézier curve. This is a method of formulating a parametric polynomial to meet the constraints of a designer's conceptions, rather than the rigid specification of interpolation. The technique is based upon the input of a series of points, which may be joined together to form a track. The resulting curve starts at the first point of the track and finishes at the last. Additionally, the curve starts and finishes with the gradients of the first and last track lines respectively. Otherwise, the intermediate points only influence the curve: it does not have to pass through them. The resulting curve is guaranteed to be smoother than its track (it is said to have a *variation diminishing* property). The Bézier curve for a track of $(m + 1)$ points is actually given by equation (5):

$$Q(t) = \sum_{g=0}^{g=m} \frac{m!}{(m-g)!} t^g (1-t)^{m-g} P_g \quad (5)$$

Composite Curves (Splines).—If a long curve is to be designed, it is common practice to join together more than one curve segment: such composite curves are called *splines* and are analogous to the physical device of the same shape used for drawing smooth curves. The properties of the physical spline which must be emulated are that both the slope and the derivative of the slope must be continuous. The simplest curve which has this property is the cubic parametric polynomial.

The B-spline is a relatively recent generalisation of the Bézier curve which is making a considerable contribution to CAE systems. It combines the controllability of the Bézier curve with the stability over long spans exhibited by the composite curves. The B-spline is based on the same kind of track as the Bézier curve, but the effect of each track point is limited to a proportion of the span. B-spline polynomials are mathematical expressions that can be defined recursively (in terms of themselves): this makes the mathematical concepts hard to understand, but easy to program, especially in a computer language which permits sub-programs to call themselves.

The equation of a B-spline is given by equations (6) and (7):

$$Q(t) = \sum_{g=0}^{g=m} B_{g,k}(t) P_g \tag{6}$$

where $B_{g,k}(t)$ is given by the recursive formula:

$$B_{g,k}(t) = \frac{t - T_g}{T_{g+k-1} - T_g} B_{g,k-1}(t) + \frac{T_{g+k} - t}{T_{g+k} - T_{g+1}} B_{g+1,k-1}(t) \tag{7}$$

(In other words, it is defined in terms of two further B-spline polynomials of order $k - 1$. The process comes to a halt when discontinuities arise, such as when $B_{g,1}(t)$ is equated to 1 or 0.)

Patches for Surface Construction.—Just as long curves must be broken down into segments, so large surfaces can be constructed from a number of pieces, called *patches*. Taking the analogy further, patches must be capable of being joined together without discontinuities. By far the most common type of sculptured surface element is the *bi-parametric patch*: this has one equation for each of x, y and z, like a space curve, but each equation is in terms of not one, but two parameters, say t and u. A patch, like a curve, is defined over a certain range of parameter values: if this range takes in values of t and u between 0 and 1, the patch is said to be *parametrically square*.

The detailed discussion of patch mathematics is beyond the scope of this chapter; for a more detailed treatment, the reader is referred to Refs. 37 and 38. Nevertheless, it is worth noting that, just as the Bézier formulation is able to overcome some of the difficulties in specifying parametric curves, so it comes to the rescue of the parametric patch. The Bézier patch has the equation (8):

$$Q(t, u) = \sum_{g=0}^{g=m} \sum_{h=0}^{h=n} \frac{m!}{(m-g)!g!} \frac{n!}{(n-h)!h!} t^g (1-t)^{(m-g)} u^h (1-u)^{(n-h)} p_{g,h} \tag{8}$$

Completing the analogy, large patches can be treated by using B-splines, rather than Bézier curves as a basis. The B-spline patch definition is given in equation (9).

$$Q(t, u) = \sum_{g=0}^{g=m} \sum_{h=0}^{h=n} B_{g,k}(t) B_{h,k}(u) P_{g,h} \tag{9}$$

This equation uses the polynomials defined in equation (7), but it is assumed that the order of the patch (k) is the same in each direction, which usually simplifies things. The grid can, however, be made rectangular rather than square by choosing different values for m and n, which is a useful improvement on the Bézier form. Large patches also make more sense using B-splines, because the localisation of the control of the track points that applies with B-spline curves applies also to patches: large B-spline patches can provide the same degree of control as a number of Bézier patches, while avoiding the need for so many joints.

SOLID MODELLING TECHNIQUES.—To allow a computer model to understand the concept of a solid, it must be able to distinguish the inside of a surface from the outside. Solid models, the highest level of sophistication in geometric modelling, are recorded mathematically as volumes bounded by surfaces, rather than as stick-figure structures. Accordingly, the mass properties required for finite element analysis, kinematics and interference checking can be calculated; the presence of a full geometric description provided by solid modelling has prompted development of a number of facilities to help the NC part programmer. These advantages are offset by the need to use much more memory to represent a model than do wireframes or surface models, and a requirement for extensive processing for manipulation, owing to the more complicated data structure and associated mathematics. These disadvantages have become relatively less significant as the cost of memory has fallen and the processing power of hardware has increased.

Three-dimensional modellers normally allow for generating cross-sections or cutaway views. Whilst a wireframe modeller can only join the exposed 'wire ends' with straight lines, surface or solid modeller should be able to eliminate the hidden parts and generate cross-hatching or solid colour to clarify the image further.

Solid Model Construction.—The many experimental solid models of the early seventies have spawned a family of commercially available solid modelling systems[5] most have used one of two common approaches to construct solid models: Boundary Representation (B-rep), in which elastic lines are stretched to form the outlines to define the boundary of the part to be modelled, or Primitive Modelling (Constructive Solid Geometry, CSG, Set-Theoretic or Boolean), in which building blocks are combined together to build up the solid model. Both representations are implemented in some systems and a pure CSG modeller is a rarity. In fact, the creation of models of both types may use the Boolean operators, so it is not always obvious to the user which sort of modelling system he is using (Ref. 42). The type of model is determined not by the methods employed to create the model, but by the mathematical way (the command file) in which the model is actually stored in the computer. The data structure of a CSG model is referred to as unevaluated, because it is held in

[5] A recent trend adopted by a few major manufacturers is to simplify the user interface of the system so that the solid model is constructed using concepts which are more familiar to design engineers. Instructions such as MILL, BORE, STAMP, EXTRUDE may be issued to the system and a 2D profile will be operated on to produce the desired 3D shape. The solid model creation processes remain the same, but an additional interface is imposed between the model-building software and the model builder.

the computer as a collection of primitives, together with their relative positions in the structure. This has the advantage of providing a compact model description, but does require extensive computer processing to evaluate the faces and edges prior to displaying or calculating properties. Deriving a B-rep model from a CSG model is feasible (most CSG modellers have a B-rep file model as well, but it may only function as a graphical file), yet converting a B-rep model into a CSG model is, owing to the ambiguities encountered, extremely difficult and, as far as is known, no program to do it has yet been written. Some of the relative merits of solid modelling types are considered in Table 13.

Boundary Modelling.—The principle behind boundary modelling is that part geometry is different from part topology and that they can be defined separately. The topology of an object is the property that describes how its vertices, edges and faces are connected, whilst the geometry subsequently defines the actual dimensions and positions of those vertices, edges and faces. Combining geometry with topology then, and only then, uniquely defines an object. Treating topology and geometry separately, therefore, makes it much simpler to adjust geometry without changing basic topology: in practice this means that making changes to the model does not require the model to be recalculated from scratch.

In boundary modelling, the shapes defined have to follow Euler's Rule, which, in its familiar form, states:

$$\text{Vertices} + \text{Faces} = \text{Edges} + 2 \qquad (10)$$

or:

$$V + F = E + 2. \qquad (11)$$

When the bodies contain holes and passages, the relationship becomes:

$$\text{Vertices} + \text{Faces} - \text{Edges} - \text{Holes} - (2 \times \text{Bodies}) + (2 \times \text{Passages}) = 0$$

In truth, even if topological consistency is ensured, sets of faces may still not be geometrically consistent: in particular, a concavity in the object could protrude through the opposite side of the polyhedron. Ensuring that complex B-rep models are geometrically consistent representations of solids is a matter of ensuring that the input processes are incapable of producing geometric anomalies. The *Build system* (Ref. 39), of which the well-respected Romulus solid modeller is a descendant, was an early B-rep modeller capable of representing moderately complex component geometries, with input and data structure both efficiently controlled to give some confidence in the solidity of the resulting model.

Boundary representation starts with a two-dimensional outline drawing of a part, similar to an orthographic view, and produces the three-dimensional entity by 'sweeping' ('lifting') that boundary to produce a part with thickness, or by 'spinning' to generate contours about an axis. Various degrees of linear sweep or spin may be performed on different parts of the model.

The main advantage of B-rep is that it is essentially a further continuation of the process which generates first a wireframe and then its surface cladding; this means that a B-rep system can be used in a wide variety of ways. If a simple 2D model will be adequate for a particular purpose, or there is no need to go beyond the surface modelling stage, then a system using B-rep can still handle the job. It is also relatively easy, unlike systems using constructive solid geometry (CSG), to derive one sort of model from another—for example, to reconvert a solid model into a wireframe.

Primitive Modelling.—With CSG techniques, primitive solid forms, such as cubes, cones and cylinders, are combined together to produce more complex shapes. The so-called *Boolean* addition (intersection), subtraction (difference) and union (unification) mathematical operations (Fig. 20) used in the CSG approach are based upon the algebra developed by the nineteenth-century mathematician George Boole. They derive from the same root as the algebra which forms the basis of computer logic circuitry.

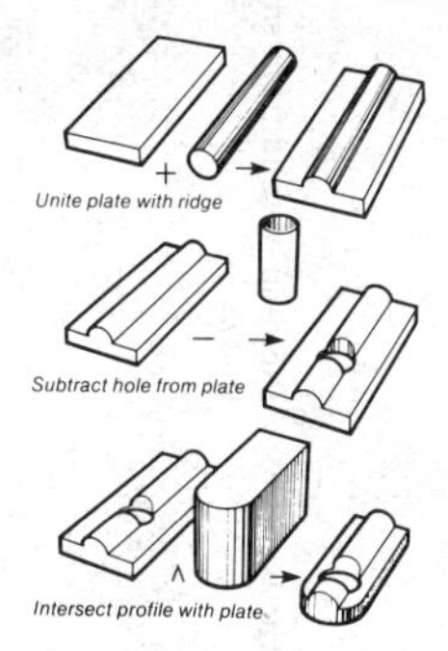

FIG. 20.—The three basic Boolean operations: union (A ∪ B); subtraction (A − B); intersection (A ∩ B). Source: Pye, A. M. 3D Solid Modelling Applications and Options. Design Engineering, July 1983, pp. 29–37.

TABLE 13.—CHARACTERISTICS OF SOLID MODELLING METHODS

Method	Description	Advantages	Limitations
Boundary Representation (B-rep)	Sweeping or extruding lines or surfaces In the model, topology and geometry are held separately	Natural extension of 2D construction method Easily derive lower 2D/3D models Modifying geometry does not require full recalculation of model Easy to operate simple analysis programs because information about each face is localised: eg easy to calculate surface area Local model changes easier	Difficult to represent curved edges Not always easy to determine if a point lies inside or outside model (membership test—fundamental to solid modelling) Limited danger of geometric inconsistency
Constructive Solid Geometry (CSG)	Build-up of solid from simple primitive shapes	Easy to calculate solid properties Easy to display sections Hidden line removal easy Analogy between method of construction and manufacturing processes Works best on parts without complex surfaces Numerically stable and consistent: easy to perform membership test	Deviates from standard drawing construction methods Generation of wireframe model difficult Model is unevaluated: difficult to display/compute faces/edges; local changes difficult or impossible Weak for pcb design Poor for parts with complex surfaces Slow to build complex models
Facetted Model	Curved surface represented by approximation to many flat facets	Fast, computation reduced Useful as alternative option for rough calculations or fast picture generation Well-established algorithms 2½D machining with some types	Inaccurate with few facets With many facets, speed benefits lost Does not provide for analysis of non-planar surfaces Does not support adjacency relationships: changing features means remodelling

In principle any part, no matter how complex, can be constructed in this way. However, to create a simple plate with rounded corners would require the combination of seven primitives: for more representative engineering parts, some hundreds of such primitives may be involved, making the input process unavoidably lengthy.

Most modelling systems usually provide about a dozen building-blocks, although only four of them (plane, cylinder, cone and sphere) are really necessary to describe the majority of engineering parts. These four primitives are sometimes called *natural quadrics*. In addition to the natural quadrics, the torus is quite commonly used as a primitive. The implications of these shapes to the generation of curved surfaces in solid modellers is discussed below.

Primitive modelling systems work best on parts that do not have complex surfaces. Although primitive modelling can be used to synthesise complex sculptured surfaces, it may be achieved only with some assistance from the user. The main problem is that if sculptured surfaces are to be modelled using primitives, the computer will have difficulty in finding the points where primitives intersect to generate these surfaces because the number of possible intersection points is very large. Thus, a great deal of computer time is needed to produce the required surface model.

Whilst 2-D drawing, 2½D, wireframe modelling, surface modelling and B-rep solid modellers provide a logical upgrade path from traditional draughting to a full three-dimensional electronic design system, CSG modellers require users to change their work practices and are incompatible with other systems. How desirable and easy-to-use the CSG approach is in practice depends as much upon the nature of the work and the thought processes of the user as it does on the features of the software itself. Much work has been carried out to develop a modelling system that combines both primitive and B-rep modelling techniques. With these systems, solid models may be created using either approach, whichever is more appropriate to the complexity of the model under consideration.

Curved Surfaces and Facetted Models.—Some solid models allow only planar surfaces and represent curved surfaces inexactly as a number of flat facets. Using facets vastly reduces the amount of algebra that must be incorporated into a program and there is usually a substantial improvement in program speed: the algorithms for facetted modellers are now well established and require proportionately less development effort to produce, a feature which has appealed to a number of CAD/CAM vendors. On the other hand, the approach is quite inadequate in some applications, especially those where analytical knowledge of the non-planar surfaces is essential. Some vendors have been able to make use of the stored input description to recover a limited degree of 2½D axis NC machining capability. Solid modellers often have a facetted model as an option, for rough calculations and fast picture generation: approximating a cylinder by 16 facets is accurate to $\pm 3\%$ and by 32 facets to $\pm 1{\cdot}5\%$.

Exactness is not quite the same thing as accuracy, however; different levels of accuracy can be specified with a facetted modeller—the more facets, the higher the accuracy and the slower the model construction: it is up to the user to find a compromise. Computation of a very large number of small faces will make picture generation extremely slow and for this reason a few vendors have built into their programs an upper limit on the number of faces which can be processed, but this limits the usefulness of the modeller to simple tasks.

In contrast to the B-rep scheme, the facetted model generally does not support adjacency relationships between vertices, edges and the approximate planar faces. As a consequence, adjusting individual features, or changing a face size to obtain greater accuracy generally requires full re-modelling.

Without facets and other than by interfacing with a surface modeller, most solid modellers cannot yet handle double-curved surfaces: before 3 and 5-axis problems can be universally tackled, improvements in geometric coverage to include sculptured surfaces will have to be achieved. However, the most generally useful non-planar surfaces in the engineering world are the cylinder, cone, sphere and torus. The first three of these are examples of a set of surfaces called *quadrics*, which have the general equation set out in equation (12):

$$ax^2 + by^2 + cz^2 + dxy + exz + fyz + gx + hy + jz + k = 0 \tag{12}$$

The torus, which is significant because it is generated by radiused cutters on a lathe, and is commonly encountered in surfaces around the edge of a cylindrical hole or boss, has a quartic equation.

Having allowed solids with curved faces, it becomes necessary to represent curved edges and this represents a problem, particularly for B-rep modellers. The problem of two cylindrical surfaces meeting is particularly problematical (Ref. 45). In general, obtaining the intersections between curved surfaces involves both algebraic and numerical difficulties and an alternative which is often taken is to represent edges approximately, for example by a number of straight line segments; as a result, there is a compromise on accuracy.

The long-term solution to the problem of curves in solid models may be to store, along with the operational sequence used to form them, the edges and faces of the solid model as a fundamental geometric element called a non-uniform rational B-spline (NURBS) (Ref. 41); this mathematical entity can be used to represent any geometric data, from a point to a sculptured surface to a solid. Combined with a hierarchical data structure, a single data selection can then be used to access a complete solid model, or a specific 3D coordinate, edge or face of the model: thus modifications can either be made on a local level (moving edges, vertices or faces) or at a global level (moving one solid entity relative to another).

Extended Solid Modelling Features.—In the future, better facilities for graphics manipulation and new designs for user interfaces will enable definition of solids by more natural means—for example, accurate definition can include glueing faces to each other, or positioning to make edges colinear or parallel.

It is often useful to be able to attach additional information to faces or edges using a method commonly known as *tweaking*.

Unfortunately, many of the potential benefits of this process are lost with CSG modellers: firstly, the behaviour of the part being tweaked will depend upon how it was constructed; secondly, the scheme precludes many direct operations on its edges because it would require a change in shape to the affected primitives—for example, the more desirable modifications, such as adding draft anoles, fillets or chamfers would not be possible.

Conversely, the B-rep model is very versatile should a designer wish to manipulate local features, such as chamfering or deburring an edge, or adding draft angles, provided that the radiusing of the edge does not alter the essential topology of the model.

Tolerances are vital to production engineering and have crucial implications on manufacture—for example, a 0·02 mm tolerance on a 100 mm dimension is 20 times more difficult to comply with on a horizontal borer than on a lathe. Solid models should ideally be capable of accepting tolerances—that is, a margin of acceptability on dimensions and/or form—using simple cursor or joystick controls. For dimensional tolerances, this has only been achieved on a very limited range of geometries, partly because existing standards are vague and difficult to quantify and partly because engineers tend to adopt an intuitive approach; frequently, dimensions and tolerances are added as an afterthought, often through a draughting process. To be the basis of improved simulation facilities, however, more emphasis has to be placed on the non-ideal nature of real geometry. The type of tolerancing that seems to fit solid modelling technology most closely is geometric tolerancing—tolerances of form rather than dimension—which is still largely a matter for research.

Currently, it is necessary to define all of the solid precisely, whereas in reality, there are parts that may not be relevant to the job.

STANDARDS FOR MODEL DATA TRANSFER.—Some of the major differences between CAD/CAM systems derive from the differences in their geometric modelling capability. Not only do wireframe, surface and solid modellers work with different descriptions of the same part, but often modellers of the same type, available in different commercial CAD/CAM systems, create and store their models differently.

Direct Transfer.—To transfer data from one system to another, it is possible, at least in principle, to write a software package that translates each item of data from the format of System A directly to the format of System B.

This process requires an understanding of the exact, detailed representation of data used by each vendor. Unfortunately, these data are usually not published and are considered to be confidential by many vendors. Thus, it is usually very difficult to write a good translator between any two given systems. Some translators are bespoke, to suit one user's specific requirements, others are more generalised for common system pairs. Where good translators do exist, they offer better functionality and reliability than the generalised translators such as IGES described below. Typically, translators cost about £5,000 each. However, vendors may frequently change the format of their internal data without notice to customers and if this happens, the translator in use will no longer work. Finally to interchange between two systems requires at least two programs. But if there are more than two systems, say N systems, then $N(N-1)$ translators will be required; therefore where more than about three different CAD systems are involved, direct translation becomes unmanageable: to overcome this problem, the concept of indirect transfer, allied to a standard, such as IGES, VDA or SET, has been proposed.[6]

Indirect Transfer.—Indirect transfer to a neutral file format solves many of these problems. In this scenario a pre-processor program reads the format of System A and writes the intermediate format; a second post-processor program reads the intermediate format, writing it out to System B. Each program only requires intimate knowledge of one system's data format and thus it is practical for system vendors, as opposed to users, to write and support such programs and to incorporate changes in software releases to customers. Secondly, only two programs, a writer and a reader, are required for each manufacturer's products. How this operates in the specific example of the graphics interchange standard IGES (discussed below) is illustrated in Fig. 21. Graphics standards operate at several different levels, as was shown in Fig. 14; the different standards which apply and the significance of the levels to which they apply are dealt with in the next section.

GRAPHICS DATABASE FORMAT STANDARDS

IGES.—The Intitial Graphics Exchange Specification (IGES) was originally developed under the United

[6] Autodesk, for example, has developed a series of translators that permit two-way data transfer between its PC-based CAD product, AutoCAD, and CAD systems running on mainframes, minis and workstations. The first one available was the AutoCAD-Intergraph translator. This translator converts the AutoCAD system from a stand-alone package into an inexpensive remote terminal that can create drawing for eventual entry into an overall Intergraph database. The translator also enables a PC to be used to modify drawings already stored there.

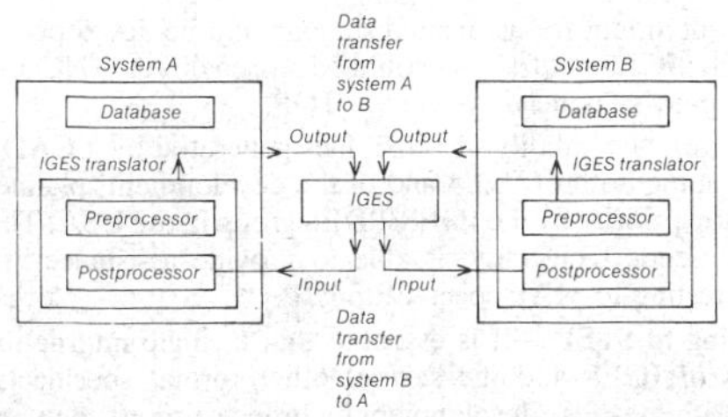

FIG. 21.—Data transfer between CAD/CAM systems using IGES. Source: Besant and Lui. Computer-aided Design and Manufacture; Fig. 4.12, pp. 120.

States Air Force's ICAM (Integrated Computer-Aided Manufacturing) program with coordination by the National Bureau of Standards (NBS). The initial specification was published in 1980 and has since been augmented several times through a committee of the American National Standards Institute (ANSI). IGES has recently been given a further push in the UK by support from NEDO and the DTI. It is currently supported extensively by vendors of CAD/CAM systems and is also being considered as the basis for converting CAD descriptions into a form for NC programming systems.

IGES format can be used to describe draughting and geometric entities such as point, line, arc, spline, dimensions, drawing notes, properties, associations, groups, etc. The IGES Version 1.0 specification supports only basic three-dimensional wireframe geometry, text and dimensional data: it is at best a means for archiving and transferring drawings. Version 2.0 contains definitions for finite element modelling entities, node, ruled surface (parameterisation), tabulated cylinder (more general form), surface of revolution (related to spheres and cones), rational B-spline surface, rational B-spline curve and some electrical product data.

Eventually, the idea is to create a standard which enable the true interchange of designs, not just drawings; this would have to include the ability to transfer the meaning of non-graphical information, such as properties, which mechanical design systems allow to be attached to objects in the model.

Most of the neutral format is generated automatically by the pre-processor, although there is a human-readable Start Section, into which messages can be inserted for the recipient of the data. It is assumed that the CAE data file is structured to reflect higher level entities than, for example, lines, points, arcs and text. Higher level entities are structured combinations of simpler ones. The IGES specification attempts to cater for these structured combinations because they reflect the design intent in the product development. Without this facility, intelligence in a drawing would be largely lost. Presently, most pre-processors do not support the IGES structure entities which are the mechanisms for symbols, groups, properties, views and drawings; in this event, the drawing appearance and scale would be adequate, but symbol structure, parts listing and wiring connectivity are typical areas where functionality would be adversely affected. Other problem areas include cross-hatching and arrow-heads. Today, as solid modelling is becoming widespread, there is no IGES standard for transporting solids data from one system to another (Refs. 46 and 51). However, later versions of the specification will include specific data for a number of specialised fields, such as piping, solid models and mapping.

The Prism solids modeller from Calma (Ref. 47) is the first commercial implementation of the IGES Experimental Solids Proposal (ESP). In this case, it provides a link to the SDRC I-DEAS software for conceptualisation and analysis.

A post-processor reads an assumed neutral format file and should interpret all entities as best it can into the receiving CAE system. It should detect and report errors in the file and also report entities which the CAE system cannot interpret exactly and what it is doing to send them in some form to the receiving system. For example, it may need to discard information if it receives a conic arc, but can only support lines and circular arcs. On occasions, the received data can be used to generate a drawing which mirrors the one sent, but the CAE file does not retain the structure that was despatched. Constant iterations can lead to degeneration to graphics form: this even happens, where the processors are not symmetric, with reflection tests, in which an IGES file is re-input into the sending CAE system. A common post-processing problem concerns scaling and positioning: most CAE data are viewed on a VDU, for which scaling should not be important, as long as aspect ratios are maintained. But pre-processors may not send the correct maximum coordinate size and post-preocessors may not provide the CAE system with enough information to display the picture. These problems are the main reasons for neutral formats falling into disrepute.

IGES requires an extensive amount of computer overhead in the form of vendor post-processors and pre-processors to make the exchange. File sizes are large, sometimes an order of magnitude larger than the native drawing file on the originating CAD system. This probably means that data should not be exchanged between systems on a daily basis, but as far as possible on a once-only basis.

In chapter H7 Computer Aided Manufacture, the question of vendor-independent networking via the Manufacturing Automation Protocol (MAP) and Technical and Office Protocol (TOP) is discussed in depth. Note that, once a MAP or TOP highway is built, data format differences will remain. As MAP and TOP gain more acceptance, pressure will mount for associated standards to be developed to match. The need for IGES may be increased substantially: IGES neutral files could be passed direct to NC machines via the MAP network, or text data sent to the company's financial system via TOP.

Programs are available to test the validity of IGES files generated by a CAD system. Validation has been identified as a major shortcoming both of IGES and of the developments planned by the IGES committee; it has recently been voted the top priority by the IGES/PDES group in the USA. The CAD-CAM Data Exchange Technical Centre, based at Leeds University, is able to provide assistance in this area, as well as having experience in conformance testing to MAP specifications.

Extensions to IGES Leading to STEP.—It is essential that a single internationally used standard emerges from the different versions of IGES and the several other format specifications. Standard d'Échange et Transfert, SET, is a French format whose development by French aircraft company Aérospatiale was provoked by perceived inadequacies in IGES; VDA-FS, widely used by the German motor industry, tackles the problem of surfaces, an area not adequately covered by earlier versions, as described above; Product Definition Data Interface, PDDI, was a research contract executed for USAF by McDonnell Douglas, the findings of which are being incorporated in Product Data Exchange Standard, PDES. PDES is the US successor to IGES which will converge in the 1990s, if all goes well, with the proposed standard neutral format, Standard for the Exchange of Product Data, STEP. Interested groups from all over the world are contributing to STEP under the aegis of the International Standards Organisation (ISO).

Many vendors provide IGES pre-processors and post-processors for their CAD products. IGES processors for certain CAD systems can also be purchased from third party software houses. A major difficulty with IGES has been the ambiguities which face processor writers when interpreting the specification. The STEP Working Group is developing a formal data definition language, Express, in which the entities will be presented, thereby eliminating these problems.

STEP is divided into three layers: application, logical and physical. Thus the physical file format is not mixed and confused with other issues.

In addition to the STEP standard document itself, there will be several other documents written both in parallel and in advance of it. These are designed to help both users and implentors of the standard, by explaining the fundamental concepts on which the standard is based and providing explicit guidelines. For the implementor, the guidelines will probably include software to read or write a STEP file, thereby providing a common interface for all processors and saving vendors a considerable amount of repetitive work.

Data Exchange Sub-sets.—Existing sub-sets for the exchange of product data (IGES, SET, VDA-FS) define entities for such exchange, but do not define a sub-set structure. Vendors of pre- and post-processors can either implement the complete set of entities or—as they invariably do—make an arbitrary decision on which entities they do support. This results in uncontrolled incompatibility between systems: communication between two systems is only possible for the entities included in both *ad-hoc* sub-sets involved in the exchange. In this way, only a minimal amount of a drawing may be transferred, even though the two systems may each support a significant number of IGES entities (for example, if the receiving system does not recognise cubic splines, the only alternative may be for the sending systems to substitute an alternative acceptable curve). A controlled sub-set structure has been proposed for IGES, similar in principle to that which exists for GKS, Fig. 14, for which the need was perceived much earlier than it was in the case of IGES. Adherence to this would alleviate many of the problems prevalent in IGES exchanges caused by mis-matching processor coverage.

STEP is intended to be more comprehensive than existing product data exchange standards, because it covers a wide range of applications and more stages of the product life cycle. Hence, it would be uneconomical, if not impossible, for all STEP processors to be mandated to implement all STEP entities. In order to achieve a reliable communication between systems within a given application area, there is a proposal (Ref. 51) that the entities in the logical layer of STEP be ordered into functional sub-sets, according to application area, product definition stage and geometric functionality, Fig. 22. This would enable STEP processors to be developed in accordance with the needs of established user constituencies in different areas of product data definition. If such a sub-set structure were introduced, the following advantages would result:

(1) The development effort for STEP processors for any given application area will be limited to the essential needs of that area;
(2) Any STEP processor can be required to support the full sub-set of its application area, leaving no room for ambiguities;
(3) Processor testing can be internationally standardised, helping to ensure uniform processor quality;
(4) The sub-set designation will clearly define which product definition systems can or cannot communicate with each other.

Electronics Industry Standards.—In the electronics industry, there is as yet no accepted standard for interchanging data between different vendors. In many cases, it is even impossible to protect against changes in a vendor's own database. In certain cases, *de facto* standards (ie vendor formats adopted by other vendors out of competitive necessity) have been adopted. The limiting factor with *de facto* standards is that, should the originating vendor choose to change or augment the format, and there are no guarantees in most cases, other vendors are forced to follow. Frequently, the process of following is a matter of trial and error, depending upon the original vendors willingness to share format details with competitors and users.

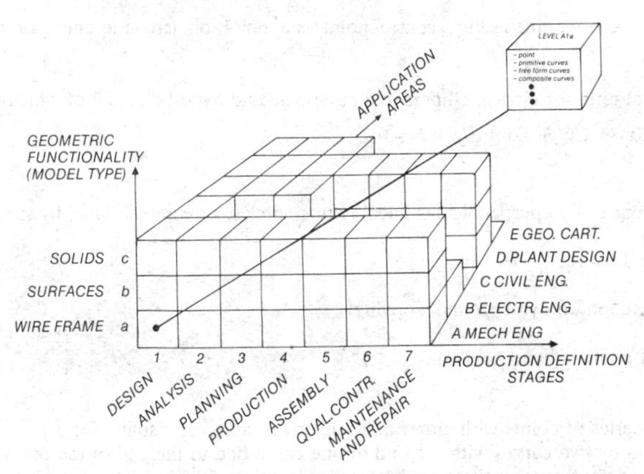

FIG. 22.—Proposed sub-set structure for STEP. Source: Position paper by DIN NAM 96.4.1 as a contribution to the Zurich meeting of ISO TC184/SC4/WG1, March 1986.

Electronic Design Interchange Format (EDIF).—The EDIF committee was formed in early 1984 in an attempt to create a standard for workstation users in the electronics design sector, before the industry settled on the sort of pseudo-standards used by the electronics CAD/CAM industry. EDIF would not only provide for interchange between systems, but would also provide a means for vendors of semiconductor devices to support libraries of their products on the dozens of different workstations being used by their customers. The committee is not sponsored by any government or traditional standards organisation, but is a cooperative effort between a group of electronics companies (Motorola, National Semiconductor, Texas Instruments and Tektronix), two workstation vendors (Mentor Graphics and Daisy Systems) and the University of California at Berkeley. The initial release of the specification was released in November 1984. It is intended that the standard will be transferred to ANSI or IEEE as soon as its major features have been defined and accepted by users.

The EDIF specification provides a comprehensive framework for all the types of information present in a complete electronic system design. The format is open-ended, in that it provides a standardised way to represent new data types as they are devised, together with a means for users and programs to omit data that are not understood or not needed for any particular application. However, its functionality is presently not in advance of that of the electronic extensions to IGES.

LEVEL 5—APPLICATIONS SOFTWARE

The CAD/CAM applications software makes use of all the underlying levels. This section discusses some CAD/CAM applications, whilst others, such as the programming of NC tools and robots, will be covered in later sections. In addition, there are many other CAD/CAM applications: wiring diagrams, piping design/ manufacture and plant layout, being some of those not discussed in detail.

DRAUGHTING.—Draughting is the most widely used applications software and a wide range of products is available. Draughting productivity is still probably the main reason for a user to buy a CAD system: in mechanical CAD, the productivity improvement is typically 3:1 to 4:1, whilst for electrical circuits the improvement is typically somewhat higher at 6:1 to 10:1. This is primarily because in the latter case operators can use standard symbols and circuit configurations to a higher degree: the whole point about computer-aided draughting is not to re-invent the wheel. Such capabilities are used to an even greater extent in designing printed circuits boards and ICs, in which productivity improvements may range from 10:1 to more than 60:1. Some systems do little more than replace the drawing board surface by the screen surface, leaving all but line and character drawing to be carried out by the user. At the other end of the range, are systems with functions such as automatic cross-hatching and dimensioning. Some of the more significant features of draughting systems are described below.

Mechanical Layout.—Mechanical layout of mechanical assemblies made up of many individual parts usually precedes detail draughting of the individual parts. It requires close dimensioning and accumulating tolerances—many systems do not automatically accumulate tolerances.

Detailing.—The process of draughting all of the component details which make up an assembly.

Drawing Features.—Typical drawing features include:

Arcs: two end points and radius of curvature;
Chamfers: (outside radius fillet);

Circles: specified by centre point/radius, centre point/one point on circumference, or three points on circumference;
Circles, concentric;
Conic sections: general term for circles, ellipses and parabolae and hyperbolae, all of which fulfil the locus:

$$Ax^2 + Bxy + Cy^2 + Dx + Ey + F = 0;$$

Ellipses;
Exploded views;
Fillet: automatic tangent to two perpendicular lines, points, circles, or combinations, by specifying radius of fillet;
Hyperbolae: very rare feature;
Lines;
Mirror imaging: see section on Symbols and Copying;
Parabolae;
Perpendicularity from point to line;
Planes;
Points;
Profiling: outlining a series of points with either a radius or curvature or a spline fit;
Ruled surfaces: defined by two curves with the end of one curve tied to the end of the other curve;
Spline fitting—drawing smooth curves through three or more points. See previous section on Mathematics of Curves and Surfaces;
Surfaces of revolution;
Tabulated cylinders: translates a curve along a direction line with limits on distance of translation.

Layers.—One feature of CAD/CAM systems is the ability to overlay many layers of information within the same reference coordinate points. These overlays are referred to as *layers*.

Dimensioning.—Most systems provide the user with a complete range of dimensioning conventions, which cover British, American and German standards. Usually, a user specifies the positions of each of the witness lines and that of the text or dimension, using the cursor; the system then produces the witness lines to the correct length for the required dimension position, draws the dimension lines and inserts the appropriate dimension. Also, the system will automatically check whether or not there is space to place the dimension between the witness lines and, if not, it is put externally with a split dimension line.

Very few systems provide fully automatic dimensioning: most provide semi-automatic dimensioning. Automatic dimensioning systems are capable of automatically aligning text, accepting text from keyboard or other input device, making use of standard symbols where appropriate; they are thus used to take much of the hard slog out of the presentation effort which goes into a traditional engineering drawing. However, at the same time, ambiguity and omission can result from the tendency to expect the automatic dimensioning system to interpret the drawing as well, which, of course, it is unable to do. It remains the responsibility of the designer to decide which dimensions should be included, what the tolerances should be and which may be safely omitted.

Some systems provide baseline dimensioning, desirable for stepping off the dimensions of a part on a machine tool and for interfacing with an NC program.

Symbols and Copying.—One of the most important parts of a draughting system is the ability to copy repeated parts of a drawing. If a drawing contains a major portion that is symmetrical about a centre line, for instance, then making a mirror image can halve the work involved. The part of the drawing to be mirrored may be determined by placing it alone on a layer, or by some other method such as drawing a rectangle around the elements to be replicated. This facility can be extended by allowing elements which originate outside the current drawing to be copied onto it, either from another drawing or from a library of symbols; symbols are frequently used pieces of drawing and may be created by a draughtsman for his own convenience or be held centrally for a whole department/company. The creation of user-developed symbols and software is considered further in the Level 6 Software section.

Various transformations are required when positioning symbols or when copying within a drawing: shift, rotate, reflect/mirror and scaling are examples. Uniform scaling just makes a symbol larger or smaller, while unidirectional scaling can be used to stretch or squash it.

A major consideration when using symbols is how the symbol data are incorporated onto the drawing. Every piece of geometry in the symbol can be copied into the data structure of the drawing: this procedure is essential if a symbol is subsequently to be modified, but it prohibits the symbol from being moved or deleted as a whole once it is in position. Alternatively, a reference to the symbol and the position in which it has been placed may be recorded: this is more flexible, although a time penalty will be incurred because the symbol must be retrieved every time it is required. However, with the second approach, a company standard may be changed centrally and this effectively changes every drawing which contains it. Many systems allow, in addition, that symbols may be constructed from other symbols: in this case the way in which symbols are stored requires careful consideration.

Cross-Hatching.—It is often necessary to produce cross-sections in an engineering drawing to reveal the interior details of a certain component. Cross-sections are commonly indicated in a drawing by cross-hatching, which is a time-consuming and tedious process if performed by hand. Most CAD/CAM systems can do this task automatically through menu commands. The appearance of cross-hatching varies, depending on the hatch angle and the spacing between successive hatch lines. These parameters can be specified and changed by the user.

Rubber Banding.—This is a technique where one end of a geometric entity, usually a line or curve is fixed in position and the other remains attached to the cursor, so that the line itself swivels and stretches like a rubber band, until the cursor has been satisfactorily positioned and the other end of the line can be tagged. Very recently, the technique has also been applied to surfaces (Ref. 41), so that an irregular curved three-dimensional surface can be fixed at its perimeter and stretched to a suitable contour.

Zoom and Pan.—Zoom may be very limited or very extensive. Some vendors provide one or two degrees of zoom using hardware methods with very fast response. Additional degrees of zoom may require software calculation of the data points, as well as data access to disc. This method of zooming may be relatively slow in response.

Very few systems provide true panning, which is the ability to scan an entire drawing at close range dynamically. It can only be done if most of the drawing is stored near the workstation: data access will tend to slow the response of panning.

Windowing and Clipping.—When it is necessary to examine in detail a part of a picture being displayed, a window may be placed around the desired part and the windowed area magnified to fill the whole screen. This involves scaling the data which lies within the window, so that the window fills the entire screen. Data lying outside the window must be eliminated, so that only the data required for display are processed. This process is known as clipping. Some hardware devices have automatic scissoring, in which the window and the display vectors may be larger than the display raster. For some systems, hardware clipping is not available and so software clipping is employed.

SIMULATION CAPABILITIES

These include finite element modelling/analysis, structural analysis, thermal analysis and other programs for static and dynamic (kinematic) testing. Solid modelling can also be a simulation process, particularly for those systems that provide shaded solid images.

FINITE ELEMENT ANALYSIS.—The analytical software in most general and widespread use is that of finite element techniques. In fact there are four techniques which generally fall into this broad category of analysis: finite difference, finite element, boundary element and adaptive element analyses. The basic technique involves breaking down complex structures into small, simple, manageable elements, such as triangular and quadrilateral plane elements, or tetrahedral and hexahedral solid elements (the process known as *mesh generation*), and using computational methods to solve the multiple simultaneous equations which accrue.

Finite Differences.—This technique was used when computers made their first impact in structural analysis but it has not been used since in this area. The finite difference method has been most successfully developed for fluid mechanics.

Finite Elements.—In the most common technique, finite element analysis, the number and size of the elements will depend upon the nature of the design and will determine the degree of accuracy obtained in the answer. It is observed that if the stresses predicted in adjacent elements are rather dissimilar then the whole solution is in some doubt. If a solution is inaccurate in some way, it may need to be repeated. This difficulty is overcome by the use of adaptive finite elements (see below).

Finite element analysts try to keep computational overheads to a minimum by searching for symmetry in the structures under investigation. The software used for the analysis will define relationships between properties of the structure, such as between strength and stiffness via Young's Modulus, and will then be able to generate contours of, for example, stress as a function of displacement. The technique is not purely limited to statics (elasticity, plasticity, creep, swelling, large deflections), but also may be applied to vibration analysis (to find resonant frequency, mode shapes, spectral analysis), linear and non-linear transient dynamics (with transient force functions, friction, plasticity and large deflections), heat transfer (with steady-state and transient temperature distributions, conduction, convection, radiation and internal heat generation), electrical potentials and magnetic fields; even the performance of materials and structures on a microscopic level may be simulated by this method. One specialised example of a finite element program is one which has been developed to predict the flow of molten polymer in injection moulding machines, as a function of key processing parameters; it is used interactively to determine optimum processing conditions and gating arrangements for plastic moulded parts.

One of the difficulties of implementing finite element analysis remains its appetite for computer power. The analysis programs used in finite element analysis are very large and require huge amounts of file space. It is common for runs to last for hours on large mainframes. The systems that perform finite element analysis on personal computers and small workstations can perform useful analyses only on very restricted problems: memory restrictions often limit problem size. In these cases, a finite element problem that might be executed in only a few minutes on a mini might take an hour or two on a microcomputer. However, the time saved in using the mini or mainframe could be offset by increased time spent on overhead tasks such as waiting in-line to use a terminal and completing forms to run the program: because most finite element problems require large amounts of computer resources, they are typically run only during off-peak hours, creating further delays.

Boundary Elements.—It is sometimes quite difficult to mesh complicated regions properly. This occurs particularly when three dimensional intersection problems are being tackled. This difficulty may be overcome by using boundary element modelling (BEM) and, perhaps, to a lesser extent, by the use of adaptive elements. With the finite element method, the whole of the region to be analysed is meshed. This always implies a large number of elements, nodes and unknowns on the boundary of a structure, but also it means an even larger number of unknowns in the interior. With the boundary element method, an exact solution of the interior is used and only unknowns on the boundary are needed. This gives a dramatic reduction in the total number of unknowns. The difficulty is that the coupling between the unknowns becomes far more complex and the question of whether boundary elements are more efficient than finite elements depends upon the application. For example, since an exact solution is used inside a region, it is difficult to accommodate non-linearity without an interior mesh. Boundary elements are most useful when a number of the following conditions apply: the problem is linear and static; the material is isotropic; the structure has a large volume/surface area ratio; there are boundaries at infinity; there are cracks; the mesh generation inside the region is awkward (not just tedious—that problem can be overcome by mesh generators!).

A unique feature of BEM is the ability to model problems with infinite boundaries. This enables problems to be modelled without the need to introduce artificial boundaries, which significantly increase the size of the problem and are sources of error.

Adaptive Finite Elements.—Finite elements are only approximate: better accuracy is obtained by using more of them. Alternatively accuracy can be improved by improving the finite elements—in practice, this means making them more complex. The very simplest elements use constant stress and just by changing to linear stress gives enormous improvement. Generally, it is more efficient to keep the number of elements small and to allow the complexity of each element to grow. In some simple cases, it can be proven mathematically that increasing the element order is better. Adaptive elements are based upon this principle: first, a very crude mesh is used and the adaptive finite element method (AFEM) is used to sort out just how bad each element is and to improve each of them in a series of steps, so that a thoroughly good set of answers is obtained.

With AFEM, generation of meshes is very easy and efficiencies are usually better than with FEM or BEM. But AFEM is new and not exhaustively tested. The method has not been developed to cover a wide range of types of applications.

Mesh Generation.—One of the uses for CAD/CAM at the analysis stage is in preparation of the finite element mesh. Mesh generation requires a skilled analyst who will nevertheless benefit from the interactive graphics capabilities of a CAD system.

Deriving the meshes from solid models is possible and the existence of such a model is a great help in ensuring that the mesh is self-consistent. The powerful tweaking (local feature modification) capabilities of B-rep modellers make them well suited for supporting this operation. Some CSG modellers have the option to convert the data structure to a temporary evaluated B-rep form to enable this application to be addressed; however, any simplification of the geometry has still to be done prior to conversion with the more restrictive tweaking capability offered by CSGs.

Fully automatic mesh generation has been attempted with some success, but so far programs written have produced large numbers of simple mesh elements, whereas the trend in finite element analysis in general is towards smaller numbers of more complex elements, as in the adaptive elements technique mentioned above (Ref. 54). There are several software programs that can generate meshes semi-automatically, given some guidance; such guidance would typically comprise resolving ambiguities in the model, supplying suggested location and density of node points and manually correcting mistakes made by the software.

Personal computers, when used with a larger system, can lower the cost of performing finite element analysis. Some proprietary FE program vendors offer programs which can be run on a PC to generate a so-called *neutral file*: this enables models to be constructed on the PC—a process that sometimes can take days—instead of tying up an expensive minicomputer-based workstation. These models can then be analysed on larger computers running the full FE software.

There is a high degree of compatibility in the type of information required by BEM and FE: consequently many of the graphics-based pre- and post-processors can be used to generate FE and BEM models.

KINEMATICS

Using CAD, the designer cannot only check that all the parts fit together correctly, but, given the correct software, can simulate the actual operation of a mechanism. Kinematics programs range from the capability to simulate basic mechanisms to the real-time animation of the type which would be found in flight simulators.

EXPERT SYSTEMS AND ARTIFICIAL INTELLIGENCE

Sophisticated though the present generation of CAD systems are, many aspects of the design process remain dependent on the individual user: modelling and analysis software may present the designer with data on a proposed design, but the process of refinement and optimisation still relies on the user's experience and intuition. Constant reiterations of modification, modelling and analysis, even with the aid of the computer, are time-consuming and costly and by no means free from human errors.

The term *expert system* describes a computer programmed with knowledge acquired from human experts, together with a set of rules and specifications for the use of this knowledge. Pioneering areas for this work are in finance, actuarial functions and medical diagnostics. Design engineering has many aspects which make it suited to the application of expert systems: it is subject to restraints which reduce it to the level at which an engineer applies a set of design rules and specifications to a defined problem: in this way, the CAD system itself is allowed scope to modify elements of the design. In one such program (Ref. 56), the program uses overall mass of the design for the basis of its operation: at the outset, the user defines minimum acceptable thicknesses for the standard sections and shells used in the structure. Working from these, the computer examines the effect of varying dimensions within the design, keeping the performance of the overall structure within the preset limits of performance.

Many engineers are employed by companies specialising in a particular product or systems area, which is subject to company design standards and procedures, industry, national or international design standards for safety, environmental requirements and accepted design practices based on experience. Electrical transformer design, electric motor and generator design and reinforced concrete design are three areas where the concept has been provisionally applied.

Artificial intelligence takes the concept a stage further and postulates the ability of the machine to learn vast amounts of knowledge and interrelationships in its own right. This is an area targetted for future research and at some stage in the future may be applied to problems such as parts nesting, where the objective is to cut metal in such a way to maximise raw material utilisation and minimise scrap.

LEVEL 6—USER-SPECIFIC SOFTWARE

The CAD/CAM applications software described under Level 5 is made available by the CAD/CAM system vendor. However, there are generally some industry-specific or company-specific application functions not supplied: these will have to be written, or at least specified, by the user. Generally, the vendor makes available access points in the CAD/CAM system at which user-developed software can be added.

UNBUNDLING.—By unbundling, software vendors can tailor systems for specific applications. In some situations, this can save significant amounts of on-line and off-line storage which would otherwise be occupied by unused software. Unbundling can also reduce the initial purchase price and maintenance fees.

SOFTWARE ENHANCEMENTS.—System software enhancements are user-specific extensions of the general-purpose capabilities of standard graphics software: these may include, if not provided as standard with the base system, additional graphics functions (eg building blocks to create certain geometric entities, such as curves, trim and stretch functions), graphics analysis, semi-graphics and non-graphics processing (eg for engineering documentation), user programming support (rarely provided as standard), system management support (eg passwords, data protection systems, drawing control systems, system resource usage accounting, operator activity accounting), interface software.

USER PROGRAMMING.—Some buyers of CAD/CAM systems plan to avoid programming and are often assured by vendors that none is necessary. Nevertheless, about two-thirds of CAD/CAM users do undertake software development projects within two years of purchasing a system. The results of their efforts, in terms of results achieved for effort expended, appear to be very mixed. The fact is, however, that users of any even semi-serious computer software cannot expect to get the best out of their systems unless they take the time to program them to some degree[7]. A little customised software to fine-tune a system can often substantially improve the functionality of the system. Looked at another way, any software which does not offer the capability of being user-programmed must be penalised for this in any benchmarking or system assessment exercise. Programmability and user-friendliness are not conflicting requirements, even though the programming involves a lot of learning effort, since programming and operation are two distinct disciplines. Since user programming does not demand the esoteric, hard-to-grasp skills which many computer programmers and software consultancies like to persuade us are needed, there is no reason for not considering this method of enhancing immeasurably the power of a CAD/CAM system.

Specifically, programming a CAD/CAM system allows the user to create his own special-purpose problem-solving tools. At the most elementary level, this may involve capturing a series of often-used operator commands and turning them into a single command—the equivalent of programming a function key on a personal

[7] This comment applies equally to database systems and word processors as it does to CAD/CAM systems. This chapter is prepared using a programmable word processor (Wordwise-Plus on an Acorn BBC B computer) and the programming language is used by the author and others to generate several hundred routines which improve personal productivity, yet which would not be cost-effective or even desirable to include as part of the system's general purpose capabilities. Similarly, the glossary of terms and the *Design Engineering* CAD/CAM Locator are produced using a programmable database, DBase III on IBM PC compatible hardware. Note also that the advice given elsewhere in this chapter to select software required ahead of hardware which can run it has been self-heeded!

computer. At the other end of the scale, a user-written applications program can harness the full resources of the computer to process a system's database to achieve such ends as design rule checks, cost analyses, machine tool manufacturing schedules, materials utilisation reports. This full spectrum of possible applications can be divided up into four kinds of programming:

(1) Function menus;
(2) Macros;
(3) Special-purpose graphics or design language programming—these dedicated languages are sometimes referred to as 3½GLs (GL = generation language)[8];
(4) Conventional computer programming using general-purpose, third generation (3GL) computer programming languages.

Software supplied to support programming by the user ranges from the macro-command facilities used in family-of-parts applications to special purpose language compilers or interpreters, general purpose language compilers, user programming interfaces, additional database management software and the associated debugging, linking and system-building.

Function Menus.—Most CAD systems are sold with a basic set of function menus, each having general applicability to one specific area of engineering or input mode, to facilitate data entry and to control workstations. Since these are too broad and inefficient for many users, particularly those having proprietary symbols and unique or unusual products, most vendors provide users with the tools to modify standard menus, or to design and install specialised menus tailored to individual needs. Although the process by which this is achieved varies from system to system, menu-building requires only a very rudimentary level of programming skill. Where new menu items are sub-models, created from combinations of existing items, yet treated by the computer as a single entity, they are called *macros*.

Graphics Language Programming—Parametrics.—With many repetitive workstation activities, progress is determined by intermediate decisions based on calculations and references to the system's database. The need to create procedures of this type has led to the extension of the simple macro capability into graphics languages which include provisions for expressing conditional branching, arithmetic and logical calculations, database references and procedures for the analysis of graphical data. Examples of such languages are GRIP with Unigraphics (McDonnell Douglas), NEWVAR with CADDS4 (Computervision), AutoLISP with AutoCAD (Autodesk). For example, when a component from a family of parts is required, a small program is run, which determines all its dimensions from a number of key sizes.

The distinction between a macro facility and a language has become quite blurred as the capabilities of macro facilities have grown and the term *macro language* has evolved as a result. One distinction between macros and graphics languages is that more sophisticated programming skills are required to take advantage of the latter, and additional training may be needed.

Parametrics relies upon the recognition of exact or partial similarities in geometric entities to improve productivity. Use of parametrics ranges from simple copying or mirroring to the definition of algebraic relationships between the dimensions of objects. Thus by stretching or squeezing one object, it may be possible to generate another useful object with the minimum of effort. The value of this technique is best seen in the context of a range of products produced by one manufacturer: frequently, all the products in the range can be generated from a single master simply by altering the dimensional relationship between certain key parameters.

Such parameterised symbols are relatively difficult to create, as some programming is needed, but easily justified for features common to many drawings. Draughting systems for producing electrical and electronic schematic drawings would be almost useless without a huge number of parameterised symbols for common components. Specialised symbol libraries can be built up by users, or in some cases even purchased as off-the-shelf add-on items.

One approach to language design for CAD systems is to borrow well-understood elements from existing computer languages (eg APT, Fortran) with which engineers may be expected to be familiar and combine these with other elements to create the new language.

General-purpose Programming Languages.—As an alternative, using a programming interface, users can write application programs in many of the established, high-level general-purpose programming languages, but progressively more extensive programming skills are required. An alternative solution is to hire professional programmers, but this has the problem that engineers must then communicate their needs to programmers. Programming interfaces normally consist of a library of subroutines that do such things as access the system's database, perform graphical transformations or perform calculations. The subroutines obviate the need for the

[8] Basic, Cobol, Fortran and 'C' are examples of what are commonly known as third generation languages (the first generation being machine code, the second generation being assembler). A great advance has been the evolution of fourth generation languages (abbreviated to '4GL's, while third generation languages are '3GL'): 4GLs use a comparatively small range of commands and statements, with a syntax which is very close to written or spoken English, to achieve in a few lines what may take pages and pages of third generation code. The importance of the distinction between 3GL and 4GL is important in that a fairly capable business user, with no programming skills, can, in a few hours, learn to use a 4GL, whereas to use a 3GL you need to be a programmer of some experience. A well-known example of a 4GL is SQL, a sequential query language developed by IBM for manipulating databases and widely available on powerful databases such as Informix and Unify. The programming languages used for special-purpose graphics programming, in common with DBase III and Wordwise-Plus, lie somewhere in between, hence the label of 3½GL. Progressively, the trend is towards 4GL status for obvious reasons.

programmer to be concerned with the physical structure of the data and eliminate the specialised application programming required to manipulate and analyse graphical structures, except at the highest level. In addition, the applications programs have immunity to changes in the database format, provided that these changes are reflected in corresponding changes in the interface subroutines.

For major customising work or for linking with other systems, sound CAD system interfaces are required: it is not unusual to encounter poor, inaccurate or non-existent system documentation, or software bugs which cause system crashes, data corruption or which simply produce different results to those which may be inferred from the documentation provided.

IMPLEMENTATION OF CAD/CAM

In its present state, a CAD/CAM system can neither design a new part, nor make a decision as to which of two designs is the better. The designer uses the system as a tool to design a new part and it remains the designer who makes the decisions. The choice and management of CAD/CAM systems are both critical issues.

Many attempts to implement CAD/CAM in industry have not led to the results hoped for (Refs 76 and 77), even though no-one is keen to admit to failure after a wrong decision: after recommending that a company spend up to £250,000 or so on a CAD system, the managers responsible will make sure that it at least appears to work. The Kearney Report, sponsored by the DTI, suggested that UK buyers of information technology waste around £700–800M each through poorly specified, under-utilised computing system investments. It is logical that less experienced users must make proportionately more mistakes: technical computing, being one of the newest markets and attracting many first-time buyers, is naturally high up the league for such wastage. Bryar & Gaskell has been researching the subject over the past five years: according to its findings, most firms stand a three in four chance of getting their first investment wrong, to the level of getting about half the performance improvement they might reasonably expect. The company further estimates that very soon, probably well within the next five years, virtually any engineering organisation that has not adopted a quite comprehensive and effective technical computing strategy, will be near or at closure.

The much-vaunted claims of massive productivity increases within the drawing office are now being seen as early optimism. It is true that, especially for symbolic draughting such as electrical circuits, gains have been achieved; but for other applications such as mechanical parts, the time taken to produce a new drawing is about the same as by manual methods. Salesmen are nowadays more likely to stress the wider benefits of CAD/CAM, such as reduced lead times, data links with manufacture and increased sales though improved customer relations. Currently, however, most CAD systems are, at best, an indispensible tool for draughting after the design has been agreed.

One mistake was to see the potential for productivity increase as a property of the computer. In fact, the user is largely responsible for the efficiency of the system. Some companies have bought a CAD/CAM system and then found that they did not know how to use it, or that it was not suitable for their particular type of product. Others have bought a system and then found it necessary to buy a replacement or complementary system. Even amongst companies that claim to have successfully introduced CAD/CAM, some say that, although they could not go back to manual methods, there is no directly measurable productive gain. Almost all companies find that the productivity gain varies significantly from one application to another; there are some applications for which a loss in productivity may ensue.

Many users would say that CAD/CAM has not been successful because CAD/CAM systems are not all that they claim to be. There is a certain amount of truth in this, since many systems, in reality mechanised draughting systems, do not really aid the design process. Dissatisfaction with CAD/CAM occurs in many mechanical engineering companies where CAD/CAM has been equated to computer-aided draughting: although computer-aided draughting can rapidly give productivity gains, these gains are limited.

When CAD/CAM is used in the true sense, it represents an entry point into a sophisticated information system. As CAD/CAM systems are improved, it becomes possible to use them in the complete design engineering and manufacturing engineering cycle and increased productivity gains result. Unfortunately, from a cost-justification point of view, many of these benefits may be difficult to quantity (eg reduced scrap, reduced product development time, more responsive tendering, better communication between design and production). If investing in CAD/CAM requires faith and vision without a watertight case, the accountant may be as much of a problem as selecting the right system.

Management of CAD/CAM.—However, even the best CAD/CAM systems will not flourish under poor management. Even with sound management practice of the type recommended below, a chaotic six month spell can be anticipated before procedures are in place and operating. Due to rapid technological advances, managers today have less understanding of the processes they try to manage than at any time in history. Many of them received their formal education before the computer was invented and very few have been trained to manage computer-assisted techniques. There is a tremendous need for both managers and users to learn what CAD/CAM really is and how it can be successfully implemented. As CAD/CAM progresses into CIM, companies, through their management, will need to have an overall implementation policy, under which individual functions can be assessed for potential benefits of introducing computing techniques and can then be computerised as efficiently as possible.

With the amount of investment needed, there is a temptation, when considering the introduction of new technology into an area of work, to see the issues only from an accounting angle. These feelings naturally elicit a response from the workforce in the same terms: will they get more money or will they be made redundant? One method of producing a good payback time on paper for the money spent on CAD is to introduce shifts into the design office, a strange concept to designers and draughtsmen. Some of the most bitter disputes over CAD have been in this area. The same rules are not applied to investment in company cars—or even delivery vehicles! However, the unions are not against the introduction of CAD and TASS has called for more investment in CAD to improve the competitiveness of companies.

CAD should not be regarded as a one-off purchase. As the system grows and the company adopts the tool more widely, extra hardware, software and personnel may be required. It is therefore very important that support at Board level is forthcoming. In many instances, such purchases may defy financial justification but are nevertheless worthwhile investments. Without an educated top management team, such purchases are unlikely to be sanctioned.

For most engineering companies, the overall aim for CAD is as part of a CIM concept. While this may be five years away, CAD and other elements must be developed with this in mind. Depending upon the size of the company, this may require an individual who will plan the strategy and sanction software and hardware purchases that will ultimately be compatible.

A CAD Manager must be appointed who will be responsible for the day-to-day running of CAD and its development as a tool for the drawing office. His tasks will include: training of new users; demonstrations; formulation of future CAD strategy, budgets, etc; liaison with other computer management; planning installation and standards; managing maintenance and enhancement; software development. The CAD Manager will need training and arguably his performance will be more important to the future of the user than that of the user. The CAD Manager must be one of the first for CAD training and there are system administrator courses available for most computers.

A computer applications engineer/programmer may be needed to develop specific application programs. A computer operator, possibly part-time, might be needed for housekeeping tasks (regular tape archiving, changing or renewing plotter paper and pens, realignment of menus, cleaning equipment, database housekeeping).

Table 14 lists some of the problems that can arise from implementation of CAD/CAM.

TABLE 14. PROBLEMS ARISING FROM USING CAD/CAM

High cost of initial outlay may increase overhead charges.
Pressure to maximise use of system may lead to shift-working.
Since one possible benefit is reduction in direct labour costs, installation may be opposed by unions and staff.
Wrong system selection can decrease productivity.
Draughting system may not give maximum productivity gains.
Some systems can be difficult to work with, boring or frustrating.
Unreliable system may decrease productivity and credibility of technology.
Vendor may not develop system properly, or go out of business.
Large volumes of data have to be efficiently managed.
Computer literacy amongst managers can be very low.
Aptitude to CAD/CAM seems to vary.
Insufficient training of operators and managers.
Improper installation procedures by vendor.
Improper installation procedures by user.

Based on: Stark, J., Practical CAD/CAM Applications, pp. 15–16.

TRAINING.—In the design office, the need has never been greater for an updating of skills and knowledge. Most CAD vendors offer some free training with the purchase which usually takes place at the vendor's premises. The CAD manager should use this as a model for an internal training course tailored to the particular needs of the company. It may also be necessary to give periodic re-training after major software upgrades or additions to maintain progress and individual competence.

There are two schools of thought regarding who should be trained to use a new CAD facility. The first advocates an elitist group, while the second would train all potential users. The advantage of the first approach is that CAD users become adept in all aspects of the system in a relatively short time, whilst the second tends to throw up users of varying degrees of skill. Some will improve in due course, whilst others will not and may actually become less skilled. This makes the identification of skills at an early stage very difficult: a process of natural selection seems to be the best compromise between the two. Hence all potential users should be trained in the first place: any training course can only provide a basic understanding of the tool and most users can be trained in a few weeks to a moderate level of competence. Comprehensive and continuing training of all prospective users will also ensure that nobody's job prospects are affected. A period of up to a year will then be needed to allow the user to build up his initial knowledge; it is during this time that extra resources may have to be found to allow the trainee to practise.

INSTALLATION OF CAD SYSTEMS.—A separately partitioned area in the DO gives the user the benefit of a quiet area to work in, with a minimum of interruptions, but it can create an elitist department within a department, which may inhibit reticent CAD users. It also means that designers have to make a conscious effort to use CAD—they have to book time, collect their things together and walk the length of the office to draw even the smallest component.

The alternative is to position workstations in each design area, say one per project group of 2–3 designers. The latest screens should not require a low-light environment, making this installation more like the drawing board it aims to replace. However, the user will be prone to interruptions and will also be separated from other CAD users who can provide cross-fertilisation of ideas and methods. It might allow more *ad hoc* usage: this could encourage the use of CAD for tasks which might otherwise be done on the board. Separate locations can also give management problems: in times of overload it might be difficult to commandeer another terminal and it is also difficult for the manager to keep in touch and assist remote users.

3D COST JUSTIFICATION.—In some applications, 3D design is mandatory and in these cases, provided there is sufficient value of work, then the cost justification is obvious. Where it can only be rated desirable, the first consideration is that the cost will be about double that of a 2D system. A much bigger hidden cost is the extension of the learning curve. With a 2D draughting system, a well-motivated user can achieve high productivity within 6–12 weeks of starting. Because of the greater sophistication of 3D systems, which are also generally much less user-friendly, the corresponding period is normally 6–18 months. The implications of not having a 3D model to work with, however, may be felt beyond the design office, as previously discussed.

DESIRABLE FEATURES OF SOFTWARE.—The CAD industry has traditionally promised wonderful future developments: many have not materialised and those that have have usually been later than predicted or substantially different. New developments in CAD have often proved expensive for the early users. The alternative is to give up some of the state-of-the-art features in favour of the safe harbour of a well-proven option. But it is possible to minimise the negative effects of this by ensuring that the safe option also offers the maximum flexibility and options for future upgrades. There are a number of general features that should be considered in the purchase or lease of any software package:

(a) PORTABILITY: The ease of transferring a vendor's software from one computer to another—may need to compromise portability with the efficiency with which a software program uses the computer hardware for which it was written; provides communications facilities, such as IGES;

(b) ADAPTABILITY: the ease with which a program can be modified for different user applications; user friendliness; provides facilities for customising to enhance functionality;

(c) DOCUMENTATION: if possible, this should include source code, in the event that a vendor should discontinue support—this may demand a contingency clause in a licencing agreement; error reporting and/or on-line documentation;

(d) MAINTENANCE: updates and new releases;

(e) TECHNICAL CAPABILITY: additional consulting services for tailoring software packages and making them more productive;

(f) FINANCIAL SOUNDNESS: financial soundness must provide the resources necessary to fund the substantial R & D and marketing effort required to maintain a presence in the competitive CAD market; substantial financial backing by a parent company will reduce the risk of the vendor being taken over, but subsidiaries are sometimes divested, with the effect of slowing the rate of system development;

(g) INSTALLATIONS: the accepted minimum number of installations for any given text and financial processing software package is 400; for graphics software installations it is 200. For an operating system, several thousand installations is a desirable number. Only with these numbers of installations can it be expected that the software will be adequately debugged and ready for productive use;

(h) TRAINING: a number of training media are available, including training films, video tapes, audio cassettes and live training sessions; user groups.

SELECTING AND BENCHMARKING CAD/CAM SYSTEMS.—To evaluate a given software package alone, one can best compare it to another competitive software package, both of which are benchmarked on the same computer system.

No single system is the best for all application areas and all types of product. The first stage in selecting a system is for each viable supplier (say 8–10) to submit a full system proposal with pricing, matching as closely as possible a list of stated requirements. This technical specification should be an application specification and not a statement of the technologies which must be used to achieve it. Note, however, that there can be a considerable gap between the claimed facilities and those which are released and supported for customer use. For many companies, the act of buying a CAD/CAM system rests largely on faith: that the supplier will actually do what he says he will do and that the hardware and software will be up to the job. Suppliers are adept at presenting their products in the most favourable light and, through a sequence of carefully designed demonstrations, are usually able to avoid revealing their deficiencies. Furthermore, each supplier shows different work samples in its demonstrations, none of which may resemble the buyer's requirements, so direct comparisons of suitability between systems are virtually impossible.

All buyers of CAD/CAM systems should accordingly perform a benchmark test of some description on short-listed suppliers (no more than three or four companies in total) and the benchmark should be viewed as having the objective of confirming claimed facilities, rather than as an attempt to prove what the system cannot do.

The term *benchmark* was first used in surveying, for the measurement of points of unknown height against a known datum. Benchmarking has been carried out on scientific and data processing computers for many years, usually to assess relative processing power and program execution speed and *de facto* standards for such testing have evolved. CAD/CAM systems are very different, because the factor of greatest importance to the buyer is the functional ability of the software.

Benchmarking is not an optional item, no matter how reluctant the supplier may be to undertake it. Assuming the facilities of the system have been shortlisted because they are appropriate to the activities of the buyer, it is obvious that the benchmark test should comprise elements of the buyer's actual work and not hypothetical examples; since the same work is performed on all the systems, comparison will be far easier. The benchmark test should also concentrate on those aspects of the system which cannot be confirmed by other more efficient means, such as by visiting existing users. It should be created and executed by the staff who will use the system, not by a separate group such as computer department. No more than four representatives of the buying company should be involved with the test and all should have seen previously the general demonstration of system capabilities.

On the test day, the supplier should be shown the test program and told exactly what is required. The supplier's operator should drive the system, in order that an assessment may be made of how the system performed when handled by a fully trained operator, as ultimately, the buyer's staff will become.

The areas which it should be possible to measure include system accuracy, range and flexibility of commands appropriate to the buyer's applications and the scope and structure of the database supported by the system. Using existing drawings, particularly complex ones containing much repetition, even if the security risk is acceptable, may not be the best way to extract the maximum from a benchmark test; the option of concocting a special set of drawings just for the benchmark should be considered. A compromise also has to be struck between providing no data to the supplier in advance of the test and providing everything: whilst not revealing until the day the actual steps which the suppliers will be required to accomplish with the material they have prepared, it is best to provide in advance (say, 4–6 weeks in advance) most of the drawings and other data, such as dimensions and standard library parts. However, a few items should be withheld, to be created live on the day. Printouts and plotted drawings should be requested at the same points in the test for every supplier conducting the test.

The only comprehensive guide of which the author is aware to assist companies with the task of benchmarking CAD systems has recently been released by CAD Source (Ref 87). It is the seventh in a series of Technology Brief produced for the Department of Trade & Industry Advanced Manufacturing Technology Awareness Programme. The guide comprises an audio cassette, a video cassette and an 80-page background book.

This package is about how the most can be obtained from a benchmarking without demanding unreasonable time and effort from all concerned.

REFERENCES AND BIBLIOGRAPHY

Note that all References and Bibliography for this Chapter and also Chapter H7 (Computer-aided Manufacture) are listed at the end of Chapter H7 on pages H7/33/34/35.

COMPUTER-AIDED MANUFACTURE

Linking Design to Manufacture—Computer Integrated Manufacture—Factory Management and Control—Databases—Networking of Computer Systems—Standards for Integrated Manufacturing Systems—MAP and TOP—Construction of MAP Networks—Seven Layers of OSI Model—Implementation of CAD/CAM—Bibliography and References.

By Andrew Pye, MA (Cantab), Editor, *Design Engineering*

LINKING DESIGN TO MANUFACTURE

An attractive and orderly way of looking at the relationship between design and production, which unfortunately bears no relationship to reality, is that they are totally distinct and separate functions: in this representation, the designer would simply hand over his work to someone who would use that information as a guide to make the object.

In reality, of course, designs consist not merely of descriptions of what is to be made, but also of instructions as to how it is to be made. Even if the designer does not tell the manufacturer how he should set about his work, or what equipment he should use, it is still likely that the choice of techniques at the manufacturing stage will be—or should have been—a major factor in the designer's thinking.

A more realistic approach, therefore, is to view design and manufacture as two aspects of a single continuum. Figure 1 illustrates a constant flow of information in both directions: from the design sector, descriptions and

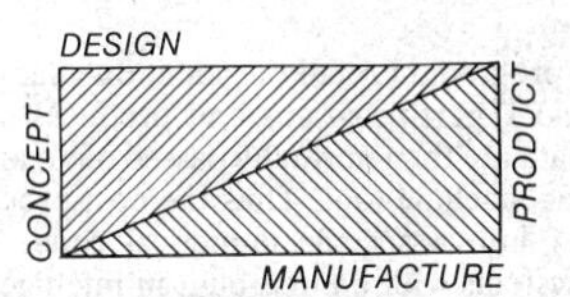

FIG. 1 Design-manufacturing Continuum. Source: Medland & Piers-Burnett. CAD/CAM in Practice: Fig. 21, Page 33.

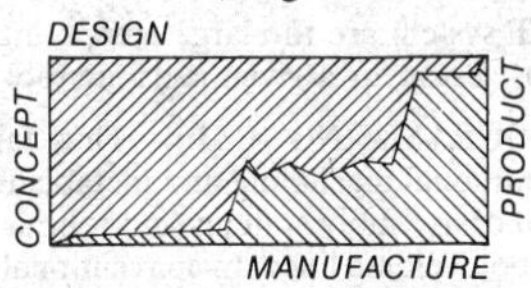

FIG. 2.—Use of Techniques, such as Numerical Control Allows a Designer to Exercise Extensive Control Over the Manufacturing Process. Source: Medland & Piers-Burnett. CAD/CAM in Practice; Fig. 23, Page 35.

instructions are passed to the production sector; in return, information about the availability of tools and materials and the relative economics of different processes flows in the opposite direction. In cases where the designer, by virtue of supplying detailed instructions about how a part is to be made, has excluded the opportunity for those involved in manufacturing to exercise any discretion, the design-manufacture continuum is more typically as shown in Fig. 2. Although there are cases where the opposite situation applies, Fig. 2 is a more typical representation of what is likely to become the norm for systems where CAD is linked to a manufacturing process. CAD allows a designer to create simulated objects and simulate their behaviour in order to analyse it; similarly, the processes involved in manufacture may also be simulated. As a result, the designer will have been obliged to foresee, and provide the instructions required at, every stage in the manufacturing process. The designer can no longer work in isolation and leave manufacture to another group—he must be well versed in manufacturing activities and be fully aware of the possibilities; mass production is becoming manufacture controlled by playing back preprogrammed instructions from the design department[1].

[1] Lest it should be thought, however, that the design engineer will ultimately exercise absolute control over the entire manufacturing operation, the reader is referred to the section on Computer Integrated Manufacture (CIM), where it is shown that the engineering department will remain an autonomous cell under the control of a management hierarchy which itself will be computerised.

NUMERICAL CONTROL.—The term CAM is applied to manufacturing processes where the basic control data are geometrical. Computerised control of the machine parameters themselves is not conventionally categorised as CAM.

By the early 1950s, control units had been designed which provided automatic control of repetitive metal-cutting operations—drilling, milling and turning. Specialised languages encoded on punched paper tape was the recognised method, but it was a long exercise, and the tapes were prone to damage and wear. A specialised part programmer was required whose job was to take a designer's drawing and translate all the geometrical forms into one of the NC languages which described the necessary movements of the tool, while hopefully taking account of tool offsets, jigging, cutting speeds and feed rates; the resulting program then had to be converted into a punched tape. The lack of interactivity or visual aids of any kind made this an error-prone method which might have to be repeated many times. Accordingly, it could only be justified for long production runs.

The APT System—Automatically Programmed Tools (APT) is a programming language which allows complex three-dimensional geometrical data to be specified, together with tool motion statements in order for any NC material processing machine to produce complex shapes. It is suitable for positioning and continuous-path programming in five axes. It was developed by the Electronics Systems Laboratory of Massachusetts Institute of Technology, in collaboration with the United States' aircraft industry, and was the first of a number of computer programs produced for manufacturing departments to prepare control tapes for NC machine tools. One of APT's biggest advantages is that it has become a world-wide standard for NC machines, although many dialects exist, some having special features not found in APT. The user of APT defines the geometry of the workpiece and the requisite tool motions using English-like statements. Its objective is to relieve the numerical control part-programmer from the time-consuming task of calculating relative motions between the tool and workpiece to produce a certain shape.

The APT system consists of three parts: the APT part-program, the APT program processor and the APT program post-processor. The APT program is first written in APT language to specify the geometry of a component or workpiece together with a certain tool and the direction of relative motion between the two. There are provisions within the language to allow for the specification of machine tool dependent data such as feed-rates and spindle speeds. This information is not processed by the APT processor but is used later by the APT post-processor.

The APT processor is a very large program normally resident on a large storage unit which is run mostly on a mainframe computer. It accepts APT part-programs and produces an output which is called the Cutter Location Data (CL DATA). These data are then normally passed on to an APT post-processor which produces a numerical control tape for a specific machine tool. Thus the post-processor is machine-tool-dependent and converts the generalised CL DATA into a specific numerical code. The post-processing activity can be considerable for older types of NC systems with limited built-in intelligence, since it has to deal with specific tool motion parameters. With modern systems, machine control parameters and characteristics are built into a minicomputer or microcomputer controller attached to the machine tool.

Disadvantages in the use of the APT system are the large computing overhead even for relatively simple components and the need for a post-processor for a given machine tool to be available.

COMPUTER-ASSISTED PART PROGRAMMING (CAP).—Thus far, NC is applied to a rather limited range of processes, most commonly traditional machining and metal-cutting operations. Also, NC techniques are already being applied to the control of assembly systems and robotic devices; here, CAD is being used to design and simulate the operation of robot welding lines. In conventional NC programming, even if interactive graphics *are* used, this would not be considered to be part of CAD/CAM. An integrated CAD/CAM system can be defined as a system where the link between design and manufacture is accomplished by the use of a computer: the block diagram in Fig. 3 shows an idealised structure. Specialised industries, such as the aircraft industry, where the use of computers is well suited to the design and manufactuer of complex parts, such as wing sections, are using integrated CAD/CAM techniques.

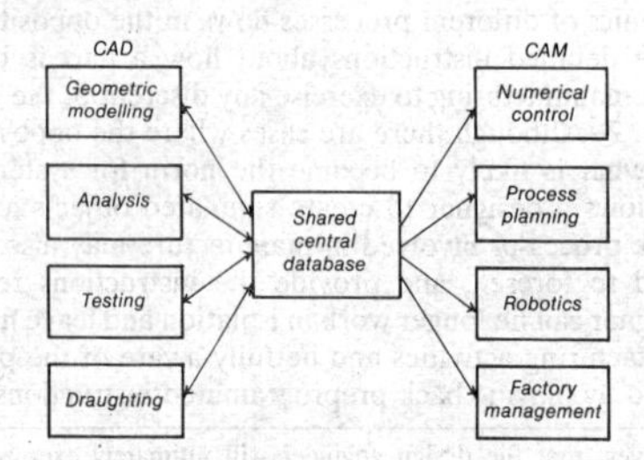

FIG. 3.—The Concept of Integrated Computer-aided Design and Manufactuer (CAD/CAM). Source: Besant & Lui. Computer-aided Design and Manufacture; Fig. 1.3, page 21.

Some commercially available CAD/CAM systems have all the CAD functions integrated, although many are restricted to the use of the geometric data which can be extracted from the model and know little of the manufacturing properties (hardness, temperature, weight, strength, toughness); some even have full NC capabilities. However, the other CAM functions are still in different stages of development and are usually performed independently of the CAD/CAM system.

Computer-assisted part programming is the utilisation by a CAD system of the information contained within the geometric model to produce a program for NC applications (Fig. 4). The output from CAD systems offering

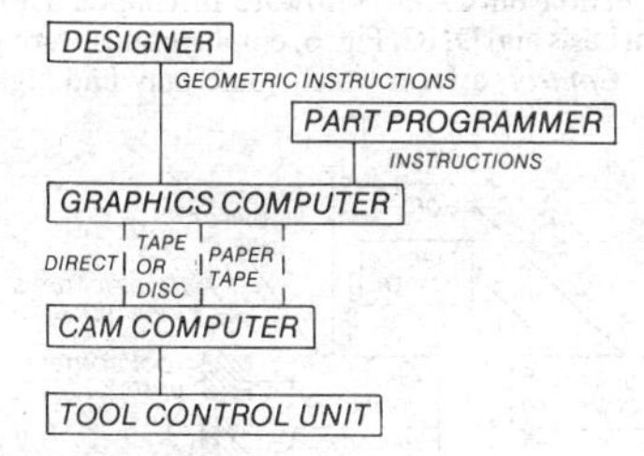

FIG. 4.—Computer-assisted Part Programming. Source: Medland & Piers-Burnett. CAD/CAM in Practice; Fig. 25, Page 40.

this capability will be based on a set of geometrical elements similar in format to the APT language and will be compatible with APT CL DATA. The bridge provided between CAD and CAM by computer-aided part programming is as important a development as the two alternative systems for computer-controlling machine tools, CNC and DNC, since it eliminates the need for regeneration of graphical data for manufacturing programs, with consequent reduction in data redundancy, the elimination of errors in interpretation and a reduction in cycle time. In order to achieve this, the CAD system requires additional basic information about the parameters of the tools which will be used.

Although these can be automatically acquired by the system from look-up tables, it is not yet possible to automate the part-programming task. Decision-making based on the interpretation of this information is one of the reasons why it is still necessary for the computer's part-programming work to be supervised by a skilled human part programmer. His efforts are made easier by the ability of the computer to show a tool path, or even simulate its movement, perhaps in real time and/or in up to three dimension.

In some cases, the CAD computer will also have to cope with post-processing, which is the translation of the program into a form intelligible to the control unit of the machine tool concerned: with direct numerically-controlled (DNC) manufacturing systems, the DNC computer will perform the post-processing function. In either case, post-processing is hindered by the existence of dialects of the small number of NC part-programming languages of which APT is the commonest. Many CAD/CAM vendors also provide post-processors for COMPACT II. Dialects are in fact a necessary evil, due to the diversity of capabilities of machine tools and the need to optimise the performance of each. Post-processing also has a healthy appetite for processing time. This is one advantage of having the DNC system perform the post-processing task, the second being that the program may be stored in a general form prior to customising it for a particular machine tool.

The final post-processed part program may then be output via a tape punch, still the most common method of communicating it to the machine tools. This method is losing ground to magnetic tape or floppy discs which can be loaded into another computer. In other instances, the part program may be transferred directly from the graphics computer of the CAD system to its counterpart in the CAM system; in some cases, the graphics computer may run the program and exercise direct control over the tool.

Graphical Numerical Control (GNC).—It is possible to automate many parts of 2½D cutter path generation with some success, though it is difficult for automatic systems to take account of all machining systems and many commercial systems, such as the GNC (Graphical Numerical Control) system developed in the early 70s, prefer the interactive approach. A user of GNC starts by creating profiles with a language which has two parts: the first part is used to create the unbounded geometry required (points, infinite straight lines and circles); the unbounded geometry is then used as the basis for defining profiles, called 'K-curves' in GNC. When the K-curves have been defined, the programmer uses the graphics cursor to specify tool movements. GNC will produce offsets from the K-curves, which form the basis of the profiling cutter path. The area clearance cutter path, on the other hand, is input entirely freehand using the cursor. Cutter descents can be positioned where the program knows they will give no trouble.

Whatever the cutting strategy employed, care must be taken that the cutter does not collide with other parts of the workpiece. Some languages, among them APT and NMG (Numerical Master Geometry), provide for the definition of *check surfaces*, which are surfaces beyond which cutting must not proceed. This effectively provides a blending facility: because a ball-nosed cutter cannot get into the corner between the surface being cut and the check surface, a radius will be implemented. It is considerably simpler to implement the check surface facility than to define the blend explicity.

DIRECT AND COMPUTER NUMERICAL CONTROL (CNC & DNC).—Just as every item of equipment must be fitted with a numerical controller if it is to form part of a CAD/CAM environment, so must every NC system link up to a supervisory computer. This communications strategy is often referred to as *Direct Numerical Control* (*DNC*) or *Computer Numerical Control* (*CNC*).

The difference between DNC and CNC is similar to the differences between a host-terminal CAD system and a standalone CAD system (see section on CAD Hardware in chapter H6). CNC, Fig. 5, employes micro-computers on a one-micro-per-tool basis and DNC, Fig. 6, employes host-terminal structures. DNC is sometimes defined as *Distributive Numerical Control*, a term which some may find highly misleading.

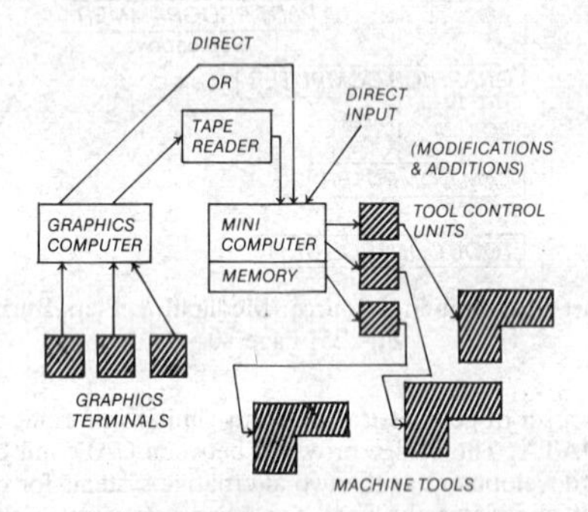

FIG. 5.—CAD-DNC Relationship and Information Flow. Source: Medland & Piers-Burnett. CAD/CAM in Practice; Fig. 27, Page 43.

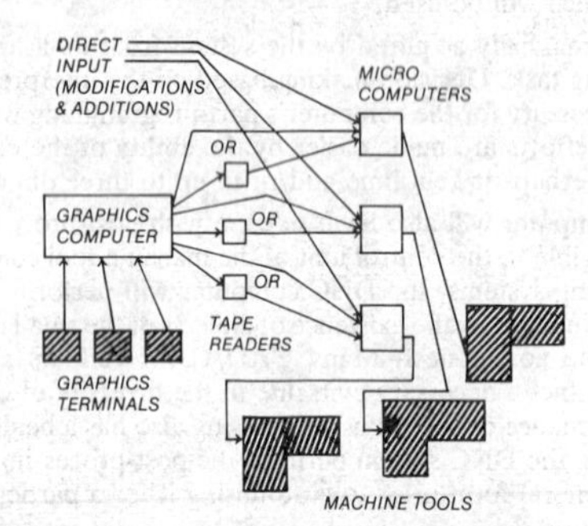

FIG. 6.—CAD-CNC Relationship and Information Flow. Source: Medland & Piers-Burnett. CAD/CAM in Practice; Fig. 28, Page 44.

Like the CAD analogy, DNC was the first to appear on the scene. DNC was originally introduced to eliminate paper-tape programs and to enable data collection from the machine tool. With both DNC and CNC, programs may be modified while in computer memory, should problems appear which were not identified during computer-assisted part programming on the CAD system. The main advantage of DNC is that an extensive library of programs can be stored in instantly accessible form and the system can easily switch any of the machine tools under its command from one program to another. DNC is thus still the favoured option for *Flexible Manufacturing Systems* (*FMS*), in which a number of tools must work together and adapt rapidly from one sequence of operations to another.

With DNC, a central computer can coordinate the operation of up to 100 machines. It stores a considerable number of programs, all of which are ready for loading on the machines. Programs are sent to the machines as they are needed, which involves real-time two-way communications between the central computer and the machine-tool controllers. The DNC system should be linked with the part programming systems, so that direct transfer of part programs can be effected.

In any one plant, several DNC computers are likely to be needed, each responsible for a group of machines, either similar or dissimilar, depending on its application. If dissimilar, the machines would be grouped into those which process the same part family.

As with CAD systems, a frequently proposed advantage of CNC, the standalone option, is that systems can be introduced piecemeal and progressively at a constant incremental cost. Against this, CNC systems can store only one part program at a time, so a new program must be loaded every time a tool is switched from one task to another.

In reality, hybridisation between these two concepts has occurred, as it has with the analogous CAD systems: DNC systems using the inherently more flexible micro-based control units rather than the old-fashioned hard-wired type; CNC systems which can be used as either standalone units or as parts of a larger system, when operating under the supervision of a larger host computer make fewer demands on the host machine because an entire program can be loaded into memory. It is vitally important that the continued operation of a group of machines is not wholly dependent upon the DNC computer, so that production can continue should the computer fail. Some DNC systems incorporate an intermediate level of control with a number of super-micros each controlling a few tools under the overall supervision of a microcomputer. Another possibility is to keep all part programs not only with the DNC computer, but also separately, so that, in the event of a failure, the machines can be run on a standalone, CNC basis (assuming their NC systems have the facility to accept part programs from an external source). A third alternative is to install a standby DNC computer, which, to help justify the expense, can also be used for software development.

ROBOT PROGRAMMING.—Numerically controlled programming is generally taken to mean the programming of numerically-controlled machine tools. The programming of robots is considered a separate problem and is often carried out in a teach mode, during which the user physically moves the robot through the steps of an operation. An alternative is to define the robot path in a CAD/CAM robot programming application package and to carry out the teaching process on an interactive graphics terminal. This would take part geometry coming directly from the CAD/CAM database; solid modelling has recently been connected with robotics in this respect, but it is in the early stages of investigation.

The Japanese Industrial Robot Association has classified the types of robots as shown in Table 1. Classes 3 to 6 are capable of being controlled by a CAD/CAM system, though classes 3 and 5 are most likely to be. Class 4 robots are normally programmed as standalone systems left to do repetitive tasks, whilst class 6 robots are intended to be used with limited decision-making capabilities, such as inspection and rejection of parts.

TABLE 1.—SIX CLASSICS OF ROBOT

Class	Definition
1	Manual Manipulator.
2	Fixed Sequenced Robot-Sequence Not Easily Changed.
3	Variable Sequence Robot-Sequence Easily Changed.
4	Playback Robot-Teach with Memory.
5	NC Robot-Program with Memory.
6	Intelligent Robot-Vision and Touch Feedback, Limited Decision-Making Ability.

Source: Japanese Industrial Robot Association (JIRA).

PARTS NESTING.—Automatic nesting programs are available and are in use by a number of companies. A program capable of yielding the optimum percentage of plate usage is relatively slow; consequently programs are often run overnight, allowing the programs to run for the maximum number of attempts. If complicated shapes are involved, the usage achieved also does not necessarily match that which could be achieved by manual methods. Faster and more efficient are interactive methods of computer-aided parts nesting, where the computer is used as an aid to layout, visualisation and calculation.

GROUP TECHNOLOGY.—Logically, a manufacturer should attach more importance to the processes that comprise the manufacture of an object than to its ultimate function. The purpose of group technology, which can be used with or without computer assistance, is to classify objects in a fashion which reflects their true relationship to each other, so that things which are related by similarities in shape, size, ratio of width to length, or manufacturing technology are classified into families. The significance of group technology in the context of CAD is that the designer dictates manufacturing methods to an increasing extent and is also in possession of an electronic catalogue of geometric models which could provide the foundation for a group technology database. If a new part already exists in a family, there is no need to redesign it, or it may be possible to create a slightly modified version of an existing family member, thus reducing design time. Similarly, it may be possible to use the process plan of an existing part, or to make minor modifications to an existing process plan. Therefore, information generated by group technology techniques is expected to become indispensable in enabling a computer to organise the proper utilisation of CIM and FMS installations. *Parametrics* is the concept of group technology applied to the drawing board.

COMPUTER INTEGRATED MANUFACTURE

During the 70s, the driving force behind the installation of computer systems in manufacturing industry was technology (promoted by vendors), aided and abetted by an end user demand for information, control of that information and relatively localised productivity improvements. As we have already seen, CAD/CAM is just one of many computer-based tools used throughout a manufacturing company, so the result was a large number of incompatible computer systems, which were potentially successful only in achieving local improvements in quality of information, productivity and control of manufacturing facilities. These local areas are often referred to as *islands of autmation*. Examples of islands are CAD/CAM, MRP (Manufacturing Resource Planning), SFC (Shop Floor Control), Factory Automation (eg Numerically Controlled Machine Tools) and Office Automation (including Word Processing).

During the 80s, there has been increasing awareness that this approach only achieves some of the benefits that computers have to offer manufacturing industry. The key is that, even though the different computer systems are dealing with what human beings recognise as the same information, it is usually necessary to manually interpret the output from one system as input to another. Thus a lot of time is wasted re-inputting information and it is not possible to achieve the sorts of improvements on paper-based information systems that should be possible using computers.

This means that buyers are increasingly approaching a CAD/CAM system purchase decision with a strategic company plan in mind. This plan will include communications standards and some control system to administer data with the objective of all users having access to consistent and up-to-date information. Ultimately, the idealistic aim is a totally automated factory with many different levels of computer control existing between the input of a part/product description and the output of a finished part/product at the other end. It will be necessary to ensure that information and commands can flow smoothly between the islands of automation: for example, information in a parts list generated by a CAD/CAM system will be needed by MRP to calculate material requirements and to schedule machine loadings; a machine tool control program generated in the CAD/CAM system will have to be transferred to the shop floor to control the machine, but if the machine breaks down then that information will have to be transferred back to MRP so that machines can be rescheduled. Through the DNC links, data collection can be carried out and factory production monitored. The DNC computer has the task of sorting the data and producing reports for management personnel: thus production problems may be spotted before any bottlenecks occur. Consequently, in a CIM system, it should also connect with the main plant control network in order to participate in the management information function.

The term *Computer-Integrated Manufacturing* (*CIM*) is now used to describe such a manufacturing entity in which all decision, commands and information flows rely on assistance from computer systems. In CIM, the various business functions, whether they be engineering, production, sales or finance, will all be computer-aided and the flow of information between them will be computer-based. Figure 7 depicts a model of a CIM system. Implementation of CIM will lead to a global increase in productivity, not merely the local improvements associated with the computerisation of the individual areas. CIM eliminates the sequential processing which takes place in most manual operations.

A CIM system might be based on a mainframe (certainly nothing less than a powerful minicomputer), which exercises total authority via a network of satellite computers, which in turn are linked to individual control units. The reason is robustness—the redundancy implied by having three copies of an NC program in this set-

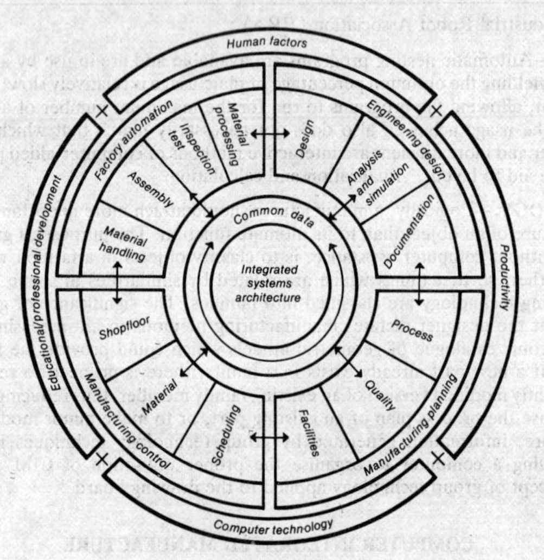

FIG. 7.—Model of CIM System (Courtesy SME).

up is deliberate and improves the overall reliability of the system. This hardware architecture also includes a management computer and it is interesting to observe how this proposed computer hierarchy mirrors the traditional company infrastructure which evolved in manually-controlled organisations before the concept of CIM was born: the application of computers in these areas is emulating the engineering processes that have been with us for many years. The management computer is likely to have the hardware facilities and company-wide procedures associated with it that will provide effective archiving, indexing, distribution and access control of the information output by the engineering department.

It seems unlikely that personal computers will figure in plans on this scale, except as workstations or terminals to the engineering computer. An important point is that data held on the PCs would be peripheral to the company's main engineering database. A possible Achilles heel of shared resource (distributed) computer systems in the context of full CIM systems is in database handling.

In general, CIM is not financially feasible yet, because of the high capital cost of pioneer systems, which have fundamental compatibility problems to overcome. Outside the Shangri-La world of showpiece installations, industrialists are currently happier replacing and modernising existing plants piecemeal rather than constructing expensive futuristic factories. However, as a result of increasing power and falling cost of computer hardware and software, it is now apparent that before long all operations within a manufacturing company will become computer-assisted. This will become a factor when the first generation of CAD/CAM systems come up for replacement.

MANUFACTURE WITHIN CIM.—Within a CIM system, tools are assembled in much larger combinations and linked by means of hard automation (transfer lines, pallet conveyors, automatic trolley systems, etc). Rather than being semi-autonomous and separately programmed, all the elements in the system are integrated under a centralised and hierarchical control system. A CIM system is also likely to be tied into databases and information systems concerned with functions such as inventory control and production planning. Conversely, an FMS cell will have access only to geometric information.

The technologies of CAD, CAM and CIM, together with all the other acronyms, offer no panacea to the engineering team faced with the tasks of designing, testing, tooling-up, prototyping and manufacturing a new product. The basic engineering thought process and logical progression of actions do not change—the new technology has emulated the manual procedures on which it is based. When the CAD system is in place, with the communications links to an FE bureau, the CAM NC tape terminal next door and the MRP system on the central computer, there still remains the design engineering department, little changed, facing the same problems of how to attach a component, the estimating department allowing for scrap, the process planner searching for the similar product made before and the production controller not having the appropriate forming machines. In some ways, the introduction of FMS and robots actually makes the job more difficult because of the more complex planning involved to use them efficiently.

CIM Strategies must be supported and promoted at the highest company level. CIM is sometimes described as being developed with a top-down approach and implemented from the bottom up. Several management aids have been created: one is a methodology known as *IDEF.*

IDEF is a tool developed by the US Air Force to assist companies to analyse and evaluate an organisation and to plan and implement its improvement. It consists of two parts: IDEF 0 and IDEF 1. IDEF 0 is a function modelling tool which analyses the organisation by function using an hierarchical top-down approach. IDEF 1 is an information modelling tool which is complementary to IDEF 0 and analyses, from the bottom up, data sources, uses and inter-relationships to determine the documentation required and to define file and database structures which generate minimum duplication.

Using these two IDEF tools, a thorough understanding of how an organisation works can be gained. At this stage, a company is likely to be able to identify anomalies, duplication and inefficiencies that have crept into the operation over a period of time.

Flexible Manufacturing Systems (FMS).—Between the large-scale industries which can afford and make use of fully automated systems, such as those conceived as CIM, and on the other hand small machine shops containing a few NC or CNC tools where further automation would be inappropriate, lie the medium-sized majority of companies which operate batch production processes because, although manufacturing operations are large and complex enough for automation to be cost-effective, the production runs are individually too short to justify the installation of special purpose equipment.

To solve this problem, the requirement is for an integrated system which provides for the automatic transfer of workpieces from one machine station to another, but is also flexible in the sense that it can be switched from one task to another. FMS aims to produce small batches of components (even single components) in a fully automatic mode on a single production line. Every part of the line is computer-controlled and can be programmed to produce first one type of component, followed by another without manual intervention. A central computer coordinates the operations of all the different elements and links up to the plant's main data-processing computer to provide reports.

In Japan, where many FMS systems are employed, operation is particularly intended for second and third shifts (night shifts), when workers are less interested in working. A typical plant may use an FMS system with supplementary workers to do assembly operations. During the third shift, the assembly operations may completely cease and the production of parts will continue with only one or two workers monitoring the entire operation.

Some combination of CNC and DNC can be used to provide individual tools with suitable repertoires of programs which may be widened as the need arises. Different tasks may require different tools to be used in different combinations or sequences, with different checks being applied at different stages. The industrial robot provides a partial answer to this problem: robots are relatively easily equipped with grippers for loading/unloading machine tools; being themselves computer controlled, they can readily be interfaced with machine tool control units to coordinate their movements and a modern robot can store a variety of different programs.

An FMS is therefore a cell made up of two or more machine tools, plus, perhaps, testing and calibration devices, grouped around a robot which services the tools. At present, the self-sufficiency of such a cell is limited by the extremely rudimentary robot senses (Refs 60 and 61); it will therefore be reliant on a human operative, or on hard automation, such as conveyors and indexing machines, to deliver workpieces in predetermined and consistent positions and orientations. Manual help and intervention also become necessary if the manufacturing process requires work to be transferred between cells.

Within an FMS cell, the individual units retain a high degree of autonomy. Essentially, each is separately programmed and communication between them is limited to ensuring that their actions are coordinated. Because the system is subject to no overall supervisory control, the task of reorganising it for a novel sequence of processes can be a lengthy one. Although, in theory, the information required to accomplish it may be generated by CAD techniques, there is a long way to go before it can be conveyed directly to the machine's own control units without the need for the services of human programmers.

Whilst a CIM system is likely to be tied into databases and information systems concerned with functions such as inventory control and production planning, an FMS cell will have access only to geometric information. However, as the concepts of CIM come to be progressively applied, as hard automation becomes more flexible and robots become more skilled, the theoretical distinctions between CIM and FMS will blur and the technologies will merge on the factory floor.

SUB-CONTRACTORS.—The sub-contractors who are not already conversant with the new technologies are at an immediate disadvantage. These companies will have to install a computer, together with CAD and commercial software, undertake training and have access to the expertise needed to adapt the system to the requirements of their customers. Sub-contractors which anticipated this development a few years ago will now be in a position of strength.

FACTORY MANAGEMENT AND CONTROL.—The most important asset a firm possesses is manufacturing know-how. As well as resources to convert the knowledge into a product, it requires planning, scheduling, controlling, machining and material movement operations. Although at the present time most controlling functions are done by human beings, production control packages have existed much longer than CAD/CAM, having been developed to meet commercial and administrative objectives. Early packages have a financial bias and some are weak on shop floor matters.

Some small production control packages, designed to control a specific operation, such as *job costing*, may form part of a CAD/CAM system; others are independent packages which have to be individually integrated into a system. These packages vary in capability from simple parts costing, some relating to a particular operation where a lot of information may be extracted from an NC program to the costing of large projects. Packages for *bill-of-material*, *shop-floor documentation* and *work schedule/work-in-progress* are also available, often aimed at the small production unit, without any intention of the package being incorporated into an integrated manufacturing system.

In tandem with the concepts of Flexible Manufacturing Systems (FMS) and Computer Integrated Manufacturing (CIM), of which more later, are being developed a new generation of production control systems. Computer-aided factory management, or computer-aided process planning (CAPP), are usually organised into modules, each of which performs a specific factory management function, as shown in Fig. 8. In the factory of the future, these modules will be controlled by a complex feedback system that will have many interconnected loops: beginning with planning, a typical system draws its input from the human knowledge database of manufacturing resources, manufacturing methods and planning algorithms. Usually, this knowledge database remains stable over a long time period; changes are introduced by technological innovations or changes in the resource supply. The product description will change much more dynamically: it needs data from the market, the customer, competing products and new inventions. The output of planning is input scheduling: input data are combined with knowledge of factory resources and customer orders to produce factory schedules. The factory orders activate manufacturing control: the manufacturing process is supervised with the help of control algorithms, control parameters and feedback knowledge of the quality produced. Control has two outputs: equipment performance and the product quality parameter, which, together with performance standards and customer quality data, are the input for verification. The output of this function is the product quality, brought to control, and manufacturing resource utilisation, brought to planning, scheduling and order release. This closes the control loop.

Materials Requirements Planning (MRP).—This is the modern descendant of the stock control system and performs similar functions. Materials Requirements Planning has changed significantly over the years, from

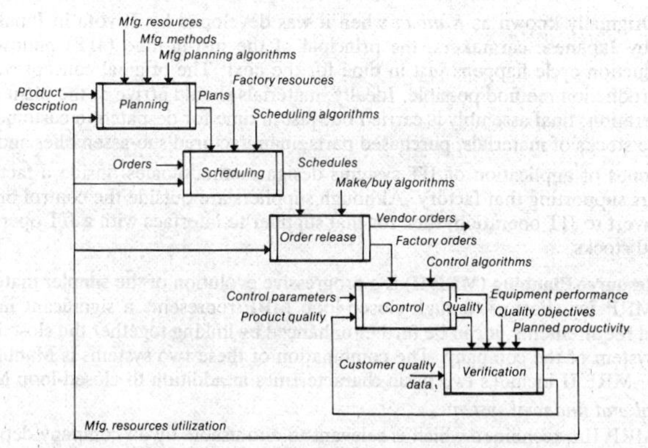

FIG. 8.—Control Loop of a Manufacturing System. Source: Rembold et al. Computer-integrated Manufacturing Technology and Systems, Fig. 1.2, Page 5.

being merely an improved ordering method to a system incorporating priority planning to produce production schedules which take account of the limitations imposed by plant capacity and other constraints.

MRP with priority planning is still not complete without some feedback information about the execution of the priority plan. By integrating the various functions in production planning and control, such as inventory management, capacity planning, shop-floor control, etc into a unified system, this closed-loop MRP represents a major advance. Closed-loop MRP also means that feedback data from suppliers of raw materials and components, the production shop, etc. allow potential problems to be detected and then corrected during the implementation of the production plan.

An MRP package is designed to:

(1) Forecast materials and dates by which they will be required;

(2) Take into account supplier delivery capabilities, optimum ordering quantities, carrying costs and shop floor scheduling;

(3) Control material orders, monitor deliveries, supply updated information for shop floor production schedule modifications, and monitor work-in-progress.

Figure 9 shows schematically the structure of a typical requirements planning system, which usually contains four basic sub-systems: the master production schedule (MPS); the bill of materials (BOM) file; the inventory status file; the materials requirements planning software package.

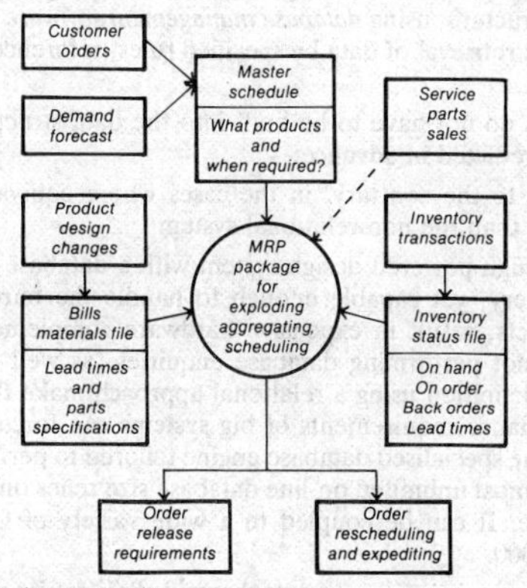

FIG. 9.—Structure of an MRP (Material Requirements Planning) System. Source: Besant & Lui. Computer-Aided Design & Manufacture; Fig. 18.2, Page 369.

Accordingly, MRP packages tend to be fairly large, are normally implemented on mainframe computers or large minicomputers and will probably be part of a large, integrated CAM system, because this function is heavily dependent upon information which has to be current.

Just-in-Time.—Originally known as *Kanban* when it was developed by Toyota in Japan and applied with legendary success by Japanese carmakers, the principal of the just-in-time (JIT) philosophy is that every process in the production cycle happens just in time for the next. The original concept was simply to create the most rational production method possible. Ideally, materials should arrive at the plant just in time for the first production operation; final assembly is carried out just in time for despatch to customers, etc. The whole purpose is to reduce stocks of materials, purchased parts, manufactured sub-assemblies and work-in-progress.

There are two zones of application of JIT systems design methodologies: inside a factory and inside the factories of suppliers supporting that factory. Although suppliers are outside the control of the factory, if any supplier fails to convert to JIT operation, then for that supplier to interface with a JIT operation will carry the penalty of increased stocks.

Manufacturing Resource Planning (MRP II) is a progressive evolution of the simpler materials requirements planning, or just MRP for short. Although closed-loop MRP represents a significant improvement in the planning of material requirements, it can be further enhanced by linking together the closed-loop MRP system with the financial system of the company. The combination of these two systems is Manufacturing Resource Planning (MRP II). MRP II includes two basic characteristics in addition to closed-loop MRP:

(a) *an operational and financial system*
This makes MRP II a technique which is relevant to and usable by all company departments; it covers all aspects of the business (sales, production, engineering, inventories and accounting). MRP II uses financial data as the common medium for the operations of each independent department and between separate departments. The common medium allows operating data to be converted into monetary terms so that a better picture of the company's financial performance can be obtained. The objective is for departments to work more closely together through this common medium, and for management to obtain the information it requires.

(b) *a simulator*
MRP II can be used as a simulator to answer 'what if' questions; alternative production plans and possible management decisions can be simulated, prior to full commitment.

Critical Path Project Analysis.—Critical path analysis methods, such as PERT or RPD, may be used to control all the steps in a specific project, but the approach is equally useful for processing a particular product or works order through the manufacturing process for MRP. PERT is now available on computers ranging in size from micros to mainframes.

DATABASES

CAD/CAM DATABASES.—All CAD/CAM systems require databases of current and archival information from which the user can produce new designs and drawings and support CAM operations. In principle, a computer database is no different from a database held in paper drawings, manuals or record cards. The difference is that when the information is loaded into a computer database, relationships may be established between previously unrelated data. A *relational database* is a software program which allows users to obtain information drawn from two or more databases that are made up of two-dimensional arrays of data. The term is something of a misnomer in that a relational database only fixes relationships between data items into the data structure at the lowest level. Higher level, more general (and meaningful) relationships have to be inferred by software searching the data structure, using *database management software* (*DBMS*), a software system that manages the database and allows retrieval of data by specified rules, references and cross-references. This has two effects:

(1) Because data relationships do not have to be built into the data structure, relationships between data items do not have to be predicted in advance;

(2) Despite theoretical claims to the contrary, in the cases where equivalent implementations exist, the relational system is slower than the non-relational system.

Many attempts to combine a high-powered design system with a database tool powerful enough to run on conventional computing machinery, yet capable enough to handle the burden of the enormous databases required for large capital projects, result in expensive hardware complement requirements or impractical response times for those users not performing database enquiries (as well as those who are). As a result, although the simplicity of data definition using a relational approach make this form common, especially for single user systems, the performance requirements of big systems can force the use of some non-relational techniques. As an alternative, one specialised database engine tailored to perform relational database manipulation at ultra-high speed with almost unlimited on-line database size relies on a technology introduced in 1979 by a firm known as Britton-Lee. It can be coupled to a wide variety of CAD systems and, in its largest configuration, costs around $75000.

CAD/CAM databases should contain intelligent data that will allow retrieval of usable pieces of information. This intelligence should fit the requirements of database management, which are two fundamental properties of the data: *connectivity* and *associativity*. These intelligent properties also enable a CAD/CAM system to update corresponding text and graphics files to reflect revisions made to either. If an associative database is not used, the system should provide some minimal method of extracting a parts list or bill of materials from the drawing.

In some networks, all the systems share a single database; in others, each system has a local, private database, as well as access to a common database that may be centrally located or distributed among the various systems. In each case, the relationship between the systems comprising the network and the precise nature of the data flow that can occur between them are governed by the network configuration employed. A database can be as simple as standard notes and text for placing on mechanical drawings to a complete set of maps for a municipality, or a complete manufacturing system. Consideration of the selection of databases is given below. Between these extremes lie those applications that require libraries of symbols, such as electronic (ICs, PCs), mechanical (gears, valves, screws) and architectural (fixtures, furnishes, standard room layouts). In addition, archival information can be used as a base for new designs and drawings. In manufacturing operations, Group Technology, the function that provides grouping of designs, parts, components, sub-assemblies that are similar in design and manufacturing methods, needs the database of all previously designed and manufactured parts.

Associativity is the ability to permanently link non-graphical text or *attribute data* (descriptive information) with specific graphical items. In this event, minor changes in the model are automatically reflected in derivative drawings (but not vice-versa—model/draw operation): this linkage is permanently maintained because the drawing data contain, rather than absolute values, parameters which must be extracted from the associated model. Associativity should also allow the selection of drawings according to groups (those combinations of lines and symbols that make up a specific component), level and drawing family (a drawing family could relate to an assembly, sub-assembly or even a product line). The non-graphical information can be visible and shown on a drawing or invisible and stored in a separate file. If the attribute data are stored separately, pointers must be provided back to the specific graphical items. Associativity permits the receipt of all related information from the selection of a symbol. Thus, it is possible to store all cost and ordering information with a specific component, if so desired.

Connectivity.—This is the ability to distinguish which graphical items are linked to each other simply by selecting a specific item.

MANUFACTURING DATABASES.—The amount of data to be stored in a manufacturing information system makes it necessary to give careful attention to the design of the database. Information concerning the product, process capability, manufacturing operations and manufacturing machines is relatively permanent in nature and will be changed only if a product is added or removed from a production plan, or if production equipment is updated. Conversely, order processing information is assembled to perform processing of the part and will be deleted, or at least archived, upon completion of the operation.

In order to handle this information flow, five types of database can be proposed:

(*a*) A collection of independent databases (Fig. 10(a));

(*b*) A centralised or solitary database (Fig. 10(b));

(*c*) An interfaced database (Fig. 10(c));

(*d*) A distributed database (Fig. 10(d));

(*e*) A distributed database without central file;

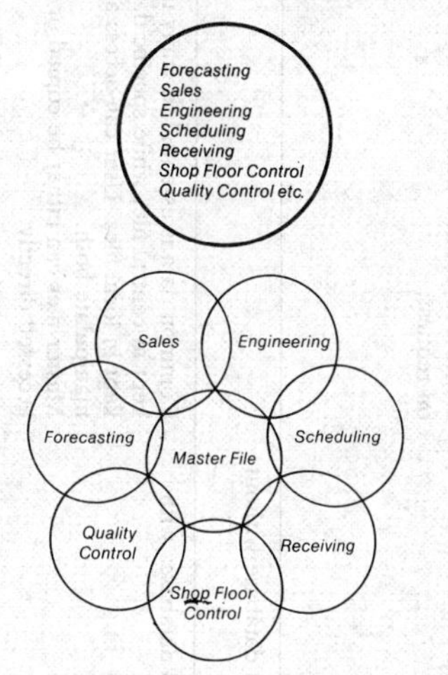

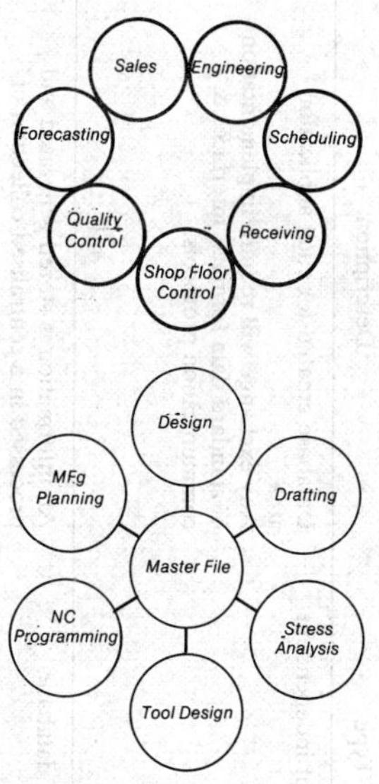

FIG. 10.—Different Types of Database: a) Independent; b) Centralised; c) Interfaced; d) Distributed. Source: Rembold et al. Computer-Integrated Manufacturing Technology and Systems, Fig. 2.4–2.7, pp. 15–19.

TABLE 2.—CHARACTERISTICS OF DATABASE TYPES

Type	Description	Advantages	Limitations
Collection of independent databases	Database created for each application area. Any exchange will require implementation of standard data formats, interfaces & communication protocols.	Useful for standalone applications where access limited to one user (eg stress analysis).	Difficult to combine databases into single systems. Change in database organisation demands changing all programs for which file is used. Redundant data files required. Maintenance expensive. Data exchange between files hard.
Centralised database	All information is stored generated and processed in a centralised collection of files.	All information is stored in one place Valuable in forecasting, payroll and financial activities.	Unwieldy administration. Long access times. Programming and maintenance difficult. Much information is relevant to small number of users and need not be on large file.
Interfaced database	Information is entered once and distributed automatically to different users on request.	Useful where large amounts of common data exist (eg bill of materials) Hence fast and accurate.	System structure complex. Difficult to control and maintain files in diverse locations. System programs to provide each user with information requirements. Needs common data formats, interfaces and communication protocols.
Distributed database without central file			Vast amounts of research effort have yielded limited progress.
Distributed databases with central file	Common data is essential to many users kept in central file, while specific data are kept in local files. User can access and manipulate both. Master files can either be copied or accessed directly.	Modular structure. Easier to implement and maintain.	One section may operate whilst being insensitive to failure of central computer. Compromise approach: complicates sharing of company standard data. Provision must be made to protect master file from unauthorised changes.

Each of these database types has advantages and limitations, which are summarised in Table 2, and it is often necessary to use a combination of them in a comprehensive manufacturing database. In particular, the true distributed database, without a central file, has had considerable amounts of research effort expended on it without much hope of commercial results within reasonable timescales: accordingly, the distributed database (Fig. 10(d)) with a central file, the compromise approach where enough data is transferred to do a job and then sent back, will remain the optimum approach for a while. Unfortunately, this complicates sharing of information, which, in a CIM environment, is a strategic objective.

When selecting the database, the following criteria should be considered: type of data; quantity of data; number of data files; access speed; user of data; ease of file updating/changing; file flexibility; redundancy of storage; access control and security; and maintainability of the file.

NETWORKING OF COMPUTER SYSTEMS

Most computer systems used in manufacturing, including engineering CAD workstations, employ some sort of interconnection method which allows engineers at different stations to communicate and share data. A *Local Area Network* (*LAN*) is the most commonly used term: the LAN is merely a high speed, short haul, multi-dropped party-line link to which all kinds of electronic machinery can be attached. LANs start to be necessary when a number of different machines or devices need to communicate with each other. With a LAN, a maximum of two connections have to be made at each node.

Any implementation of a LAN has many different solutions and there is a variety of performance and operational differences between them: therefore the design of a LAN must be given careful consideration. Depending upon the application, speed of communication, for example, may be of higher priority than reliability. Whatever the application, the following features should be considered: compatibility of devices; expandability of the network; reliability of the network.

LANs are defined by specifying:

(1) Topology, such as ring, star or bus;

(2) Method of control, such as polling or contention;

(3) The access method, such as direct connection or via modem;

(4) The multiplexing or switching technique, such as time division multiplexing or frequency division multiplexing;

(5) The transmission medium, such as fibre optics or coaxial cable.

Based on these characteristics, LANs fall into three general categories: *Private Branch Exchange* (*PBE*), *Baseband* and *Broadband.*

Like the operating system of a computer, a network architecture takes the form of a seven-layer model, from the physical characteristics of cables and connectors to communication between applications programs. This structure, known as the *OSI* (*Open Systems Interconnection*) *Model*,[2] was defined by the International Standards Organisation in 1978 and has now been widely accepted. Further reference to this model will be made in a later section dealing with the implementation of vendor-independent computer networks. Before this, a number of common network designs will be described, most of which conform to the OSI model.

Standards (*ie* written rules of uniform practice) also exist to facilitate interconnection in the physical sense between various machines. Several organisations generate and publish these standards, including the National Bureau of Standards (NBS) and the Electronic Industry Association (EIA). One of the most popular EIA standards is called RS232-C (RS stands for Recommended Standard). The *RS-232 standard* incorporates rules of operation which are categorised in the Data Link (Layer 2) level of the OSI model, as well as definitions and specifications which belong to the physical level (Layer 1). The standard is intended to make possible the interconnection or interface between terminal equipment and communicating equipment. Serial data interchange could take place on a single wire or circuit, but other wires or circuits are included to envelope all the options which might be offered by various manufacturers.

NETWORKING OPTIONS.—In host-terminal CAD systems, or when PC-based systems are connected to a shared host for simple communications, a low speed serial line point-to-point (Fig. 11(a)) connection is used. This type of network grew up out of the telephone industries' interconnection of individual subscribers. In these systems there is no convenient way for users to share resources or design data, other than by file transfers through the central computer. But as the number of devices to be connected increases, the problems of point-to-point wiring multiply with the number of individual connections which have to be made: the wiring is expensive, prone to failures and is (conceptually rather than physically!) inflexible.

Early communication networks are implemented with an hierarchical, *star* (Fig. 11(b)) configuration, or *topology* (the topology of a network is its physical arrangement and the number of interconnects between different nodes on the network), whilst modern networks may also be configured as *ring bus*, Figs. 11(c) and

---

[2] Note that the OSI model provides a broad framework within which a number of different standards can exist side-by-side to satisfy the great variety of different networking standards, so conformance to standards within the OSI model does not guarantee that items of equipment can communicate with each other.

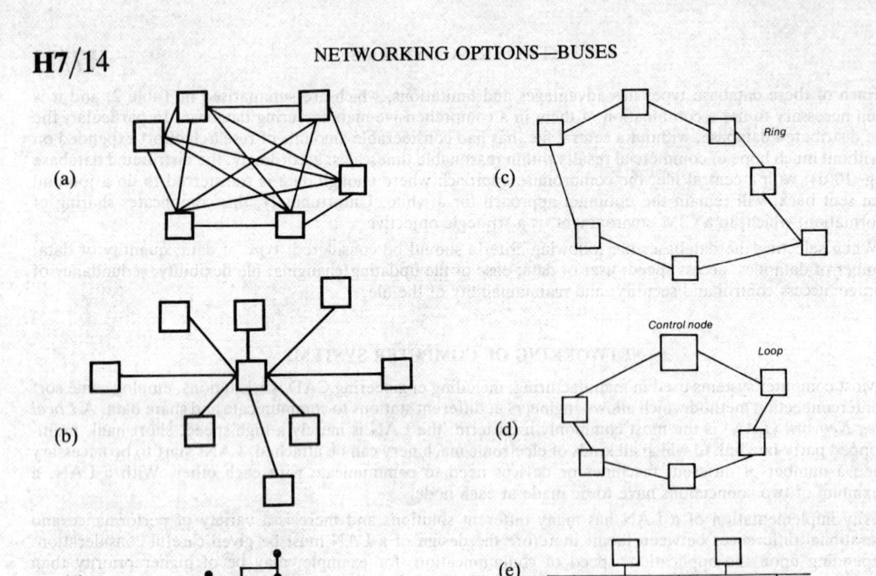

FIG. 11.—Available Networking Options—a): Point-to-Point Connection; b): Star Network; c) Closed ring; d) Closed Ring Containing Master Node; e) Open Bus Network; f) Tree. Sources: Hollinghum, J. The MAP Report; pp. 32–35; Clifton, C S. Data Communications, Page 59.

11(d), or *open bus*, Fig. 11(e), systems[3]. There appears to be much confusion existing between the general or possible capabilities of each type and the properties of certain proprietary examples. In general, communication is either bit parallel or bit serial; several buses may be connected to hierarchies with interface and control elements; the nodes in the network can be active or passive or both (sender, receiver of data). Most networks operate in a single master mode: this means that only one node has control of the network at any one time. In non-hierarchical networks, this master function can in some cases be shifted from one node to another.

The *star system* is hierarchical, with the same system always acting as master and the others as subordinates or slaves: this type of system is most efficient when most of the communications are between the centre and outlying nodes. However, if anything goes wrong at the central node, the whole network goes out of action. An everyday example of a star network is a PBX telephone exchange.

An *open bus system* employs a single cable with taps at each station (this can create difficulties for fibre-optic cables). The bus topology is very flexible: the network is easy to extend—nodes can be added or removed without difficulty. Open bus networks can be controlled by a master node, or control can be distributed. In the currently most common form, the *Ethernet*, each node has equal rights and privileges, there is no master and each station must compete with all others for access by a collision detection method (described below). Whilst currently the most familiar form of open bus network, the Ethernet is specified by the Technical and Office Protocol (TOP) to IEEE 802.3, while the Manufacturing Automation Protocol (MAP) specification (described later) opts for a token passing method, similar to that described below for Apollo Computer's Domain Ring system, but on an open bus network; IEEE specifies this in 802.4.

A *ring bus system* is one in which each node is connected to just two others to form a ring. Either a control node is adopted to synchronise the other nodes (*ie* tell them when they can send messages), or control is distributed among the nodes by only allowing them to transmit when they possess a token, which is passed around the ring—analogous to the system used on single track railways. This method is based on research done by IBM and is covered by IEEE 802.5.

Most microcomputer manufacturers supply their systems with communication chips that control access to the bus. These chips also generate protocols for different link levels, encode and decode signals and perform master or slave functions.

The efficiency of a bus system depends upon the following parameters: data rate; maximum transmission distance; delay in responding to interrupts and data requests; additional hardware and software needed for

[3] A further topology, known as a *tree*, Fig. 11(f), has roots from which information flows towards branches where individual stations are connected. The best example of this kind of network is a CATV (community antenna television) system which brings programming to individual homes throughout a city.

TABLE 3.—CHARACTERISTICS OF BUS AND RING NETWORK SYSTEMS

Network system	Description	Advantages	Limitations
1. Point-to-point connections	Every station connected to every other station with which it has to communicate.	Adequate for standalone system with a few peripherals.	N stations need N(N – 1)/2 connections. Wiring becomes expensive & unreliable Inflexible system.
2. Star networks	Connect each node to one central node, which routes all messages.	Efficient if most communications occur between central host and satellite.	Failure of central node is total failure of system.
3. Bus networks	Connect every node to single cable. Control by collision detection, token passing or master node.	Only one connection needed at each node.	Cable must be tapped into bus.
(a) Ethernet	Collision detection: Analogous to traffic roundabout.		Poorest performance when traffic saturated. Complicated restrictions on total bus length, bus segment length, number of nodes, relationship of branches, repeaters and links.
(b) (IEEE 802.3) (CSMA/ID) TCP/IP	Single cable. Multiple access.	Cable need not form continuous loop hence more flexible routing than ring. Multiple vendor systems easier. Easy to add nodes without stopping the network.	Not originally designed for real-time computing.
XNS	No master node. Up to 1024 stations. Typical data transmission rate: 200–400kbyte/s.	Performance relative to ring improves for bulk (eg graphics) data transmission because single node can dominate network. Ethernet networks can themselves be joined together.	Message passing time depends on loading of network. Maximum length 2.5 km.
(c) IEEE 488	Connection system for local acquisition of process and quality control data. Typical data transmission rate: 200–400kbyte/s.	Supported by most makers of test and measurement equipment.	Second bus needed for distances over 20m.

TABLE 3.—*continued*

Network system	Description	Advantages	Limitations
(d) MAP specification (IEEE 802.41)	Bus network which operates by token ring passing.		
4. Ring Networks	Each node connected to two others to form closed ring.	No need to tap cable.	Two connections per node. Cable must be continuous ring. Most ring systems proprietary, hence multiple vendor systems harder. Continous ring compulsory.
(a) IEEE 802.5 covers token ring types	Work by token passing or control (master) node. Analogous to traffic lights:	Poorest performance when minimum traffic on network.	
(b) Domain	Token passing.	Single node cannot dominate network. Consistent message passing time especially for small data transfers. File storage invisible to user.	Failsafe mechanism necessary to prevent disruption of network by node failure.
(c) PDV Bus	System for interconnection of control computers in hierarchical manufacturing control environment. Typical data transmission rate: 100–500kbyte/s.	Up to 3km. Similar speed range to IEEE 488. Fast and slow versions available. Can use electric or fibre-optic cable.	

expansion; reliability and fault tolerance; unique logic structure; standard plug-in capability; possible geographic distribution of communication process; cost of system components; availability.

Common communication networks are now described and Table 3 considers the advantages and limitations of each system.

While most links between CAD/CAM system components work best when they are local (less than 1000 ft), remote linking is frequently possible. Workstations may be located off-site and linked via phone lines or private microwave links. Plotters, microfile systems and perforated tape units may also be remotely located: however, when an output-only unit such as a plotter is remotely located, a computer terminal is usually installed with it to help operate the link. Local interface hardware may be a parallel, computer-to-computer bus with transfer rates measured in millions of bits/s, or a single high-speed (19.2–64 kilobit/s) synchronous or asynchronous serial link. Conversely, remote interfaces are generally made to conform to the data rate capacity of a voice-grade telephone line (about 9.6 kilobit/s): this makes remote workstations slower than local stations.

IEEE 488 Bus is a bit parallel/byte serial data transmission system. The transmission speed is about 200–400 kbyte/s. The area of application for this bus is local acquisition of process and quality control data. Most instrument manufacturers support their instruments with standard IEEE 488 interfaces (25 pins, 8 data lines, 5 control lines, 3 lines for acknowledge signals, 8 twisted pair lines). The nodes may have master functions and can be listeners or talkers or both. The system master controls data transfer between talkers and listeners. An unique programming language is not defined: software is usually written in Basic, Fortran, Pearl or Pascal; for data communication, ASCII code is used.

If communication over distances exceeding 20 m is necessary, a second bus system has to be used. A typical bus system for local distributed processes is the PDV bus, see below. The second bus system connects multiple distributed clusters of IEEE 488 bus-controlled devices.

The Ethernet Bus.—Many engineering workstations use the Ethernet (origin Xerox Corporation and supported by Intel, Digital Equipment and Xerox) to interconnect workstations. Integrated circuits or transceivers interface computers and peripherals with the bus. Ethernet systems (Fig. 12) are characterised by a

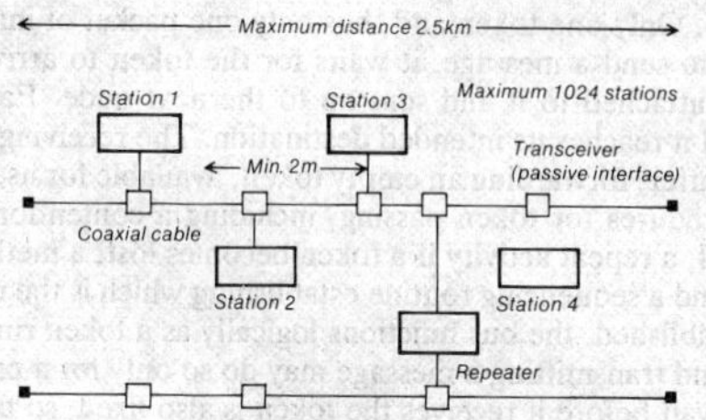

FIG. 12.—Principle of the Ethernet Bus. Source: Rembold et al. Computer-integrated Manufacturing Technology and Systems, Fig. 4.3, Page 118.

single 50 ohm, 10 mm coaxial cable connecting each station for bit-serial data transfer, with standardised interfaces and the lack of a master node. A physical layer is standardised: this includes cable diameter and impedance, pin arrangement and plug dimension, the coding method, the voltage level and the noise margin. The next layer is the data-link layer: here, the frames, the protocol, address coding and decoding and error detection are subject to this standard. All following layers are to be specified by the user: with the Ethernet it is possible to interconnect existing network architecture and communication systems, whilst with the aid of a transceiver, the user can connect different Ethernet modules.

The Ethernet allows a transmission rate of 10 Mbits/s. The maximum length is about 2.5 km and it is possible to interconnect 1024 participants. This network was intended primarily for use in automation, distributed data processing, terminal access and other situations requiring an economical connection to a local communication medium. Originally, the Ethernet was not designed for real-time computer systems, although this application was not specifically excluded. The lack of an interrupt possibility limits the bus to the control of slow or non-critical processes.

The Ethernet is a 'Carrier-Sense, Multiple Access with Collision Detection' (CSMA/CD) system (otherwise known as contention-type access): a station which has a message to send builds a packet of information which contains the address of the intended receiver, the data to be sent and the appropriate error-correction codes. The sending node listens to the bus (carrier sense) and waits for a time when there are no data being sent by another node (multiple access). When it detects a quiet period, the sender broadcasts its packet of data onto the network.

As it sends its data, the sender continues to listen; in the (unlikely) event that another node begins broadcasting simultaneously, the node in question will sense the collision between its data and that of the other node by comparing the data it sent to the data it 'hears' on the network. If the two (or more) senders hear the collision, both will enter a state called 'backoff'. In this state, each sender waits for a randomly determined time interval and then re-initiates the send sequence.

Assuming the network is not heavily loaded, the random occurrence of a collision is quickly corrected by the random backoff and retransmission. Problems only occur on such a network when the amount of traffic increases to about 50% of the therоretical capacity of the cable: the number of collisions will increase and this increases the load further by blocking the line with frustrated messages. The efficiency of CSMA/CD depends on the ratio of the slot time—the minimum allowed length for an individual message packet—and the average length of packets; it is highest with relatively long packets which are heard by the other nodes and which 'fend off' collisions. Beyond this level, there may be a marked degradation of the throughput of the network.

The above description is a general explanation of the physical transmission procedure, as defined by the IEEE 802.3 standard. Manufacturers of systems define their own standards for the arrangement and formatting of data packets, the type of data which can be communicated, the means by which the network is used to implement file transfers, etc. Many developers support higher level *de facto* standards, such as TCP/IP, the scheme developed by the US Department of Defense for interconnecting the systems of many vendors, and XNS, the simpler protocol defined by Xerox Corporation for communicating between office systems. Systems which support these standards can at least communicate with each other, although such communications may be limited to simple messages and perhaps file transfers.

Although adopted in the Technical and Office Protocol (TOP), because the greater flexibility of message length is more appropriate to the free-format messages of the engineering and design office functions, CSMA/CD data transmission is unacceptable to the Manufacturing Automation Protocol (MAP) Steering Committee, due to the probabilistic nature of the the time for data transmission by the CSMA/CD method. In a factory environment, there must be certainty about the time taken for a message to be successfully transmitted. This has important implications within the specification and for the vendors of Ethernet-based products. MAP, which is the subject of the next section, has adopted an alternative communication protocol, based on token passing, that specified in IEEE 802.4, for a factory bus.

IEEE 802.4: Token-passing Bus.—In token-passing networks, technically known as *Newall Loops*, a token, or small packet of information, to which messages are attached by the computers in the ring, is passed from node to node around the loop. Only one token and thus only one packet of information can be circulating at a time. When a node wishes to send a message, it waits for the token to arrive at its network input; as the token passes, the message is attached to it and sent on to the next node. Each node in turn examines the message and passes it on, until it reaches its intended destination. The receiving node passes on the token, but absorbs the message into its buffer, forwarding an empty token, available for use by another node. IEEE 802.4 lays down the automatic procedures for token passing, including a contention procedure to start operation when the network is initialised, a repeat activity if a token becomes lost, a method for adding and subtracting active nodes on the network and a sequencing routine establishing which is the next node to receive the token. Once the active nodes are established, the bus functions logically as a token ring connecting the active nodes. The node holding the token and transmitting a message may do so only for a preset time. The maximum time that any network node must wait before it receives the token is also fixed, so that within a given time, arrival of a message is guaranteed. This is one of the basic reasons why GM originally opted for token passing and it is very important for network handling a large number of messages in real time (Fig. 13).

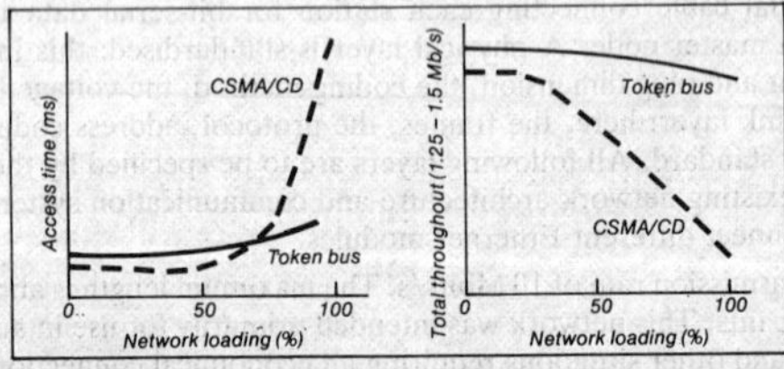

FIG. 13.—How Access Time and Message Throughput Time Remain at a Predetermined Constant Level for Token Bus Media Access Method and the Degeneration in Performance Experienced with CSMA/CD Systems. Source: US National Bureau of Standards Network Study.

RING NETWORK SYSTEMS.—Ring bus networks, like open bus networks, use a single cable between nodes and have no master node. However, whereas an Ethernet system is open, with terminators at each end to absorb the message, the ring network consists of a cable that circulates through all nodes and returns to the beginning.

There are several ring bus networks in use; the trend is for each manufacturer to implement a proprietary network strategy.

The first and most well-known ring network used extensively in CAD applications is the *Apollo Computer Domain* network, which is a token-passing network.

PDV BUS.—This is a ring bus for long distances (1–3 km), with standardised interfaces and bit-serial data transfer. Its transmission rate over these distances is 100–500 kbytes/s. The bus is capable of hosting 252 stations and is qualified to connect hierarchical computer systems. The system has been developed for the industrial environment and was sponsored by the West German Ministry of Research and Technology. Typical applications are the interconnection of control computers of a hierarchical control system for manufacturing equipment. Real-time and high safety requirements were an important criterion for the design of this bus. Presently, this bus is offered for industrial use by several manufacturers in fast and slow versions: the fast version is used for direct process communication with process peripherals and the slower version interconnects computers at a higher hierarchical level.

CAD System-Mainframe Interfacing.—A popular CAD system to mainframe interace is IBM's *bisynchronous communications protocol BSC* or *BISYNC*. IBM's *SDLC* and DEC's *DDCMP* are also used. Each of these protocols has a different hardware and software interface specification, data-rate range and network configuration specifications. BISYNC itself has many dialects and small software adjustments are often necessary to accommodate minor incompatibilities: common ones are the 2780 or 3270 interfaces, which make the CAD system appear to the mainframe to be an RJE terminal.

Network File System.—The Network File System, designed by *Sun* (Ref 69), provides transparent access to files in a heterogeneous network. Machine and operating system independence, crash recoverability, transparent access and performance were the design objectives, so the protocols were designed independently of the operating system and transport network. Importantly, NFS is not a network operating system, but an independent network service. The implementation of NFS is encouraged on non-Sun machines and the protocols are distributed freely without licensing fees. Many companies have adopted these protocols and services on various architectures for numerous applications.

STANDARDS FOR INTEGRATED MANUFACTURING SYSTEMS

ISLANDS OF AUTOMATION.—We have seen in previous sections of this chapter the justification for the ambitions of Computer Integrated Manufacture (CIM). Currently, throughout a manufacturing company, one is likely to find a large number of incompatible computer systems, potentially successful only in achieving local improvements in quality of information, producitivity and control of manufacturing facilities. These local areas are often referred to as *islands of automation*. Examples of islands are CAD/CAM, MRP (Manufacturing Resource Planning), SFC (Shop Floor Control), Factory Automation (eg Numerically Controlled Machine Tools) and Office Automation (including Word Processing). In a large manufacturing plant, there can be tens of thousands of computer systems, PLCs and robots, of which, perhaps, only about 15% communicate outside their own process; thus the number of islands of automation can run into thousands. Because agreed standards and protocols for communications between intelligent devices are lacking, the only way that a high degree of automation can currently be achieved is to start with a greenfield site and to give the contract for the entire automation system to a single manufacturer: the user is then held hostage to one vendor's development programme. Examples of networks which are used for this single-source compatibility approach are the US Department of Defense' Arpanet, IBM's System Network Architecture (SNA), Apollo Computer's Domain, Prime's Primenet and Digital Equipment Corporation's Decnet; fundamentally, however, this is an unsatisfactory approach because no one vendor can offer a broad enough range of products. The absence of such standards and protocols has arisen because individual companies have put extensive R & D and marketing efforts into proprietary systems at the same time as the rate of change of technology has been too great for standards organisations to be able to keep pace with developments.

OPEN SYSTEMS INTERCONNECTIVITY.—An early step in recognising these difficulties was taken as early (in the context of CIM and CAD/CAM) as 1978 when the International Organisation for Standardisation (ISO) and the Comité Consultatif International de Télégraphie et Telephonie (CCITT[4]) jointly addressed the problem of producing a framework within which standards could be progressively built up to cover the many complicated aspects of computer communications.

The so-called *Open Systems Interconnectivity* (*OSI*) framework is a very broad one embracing all kinds of communications, covering not only physical standards for things like plugs and cables but also protocols. An open system means one with publicly standardised architectures, so that any supplier of computer-related equipment can build into it in such a way that it will conform to the requirements of the system. Agreement on international standards is a very slow process, partly because suppliers of computing and networking equipment are often strongly represented on the standards committees and each will have good technical reasons—as well as a vested interest—for the standard to go into a particular direction. In fact, major computer vendors first resisted the idea of standards for local area networks, preferring to differentiate their systems and attempt to tie users to proprietary products.

[4] One of the most utilised protocols from CCITT is the X.25 protocol implementation: this contains software rules for information interchange, as well as specifying the lower layers of the OSI model which includes data link and physical layers. The X.25 protocol is used on public packet switched networks to provide flow control for information, and commands and responses between two communicating devices.

Accordingly, it has been left to the major users of computing and control equipment, like the automotive and aerospace manufacturers[5], to exert the main pressure for the adoption of standards.

MAP—Manufacturing Automation Protocol.—The decisive event which started a rapid acceleration of standards activity occurred in 1980 when General Motors set up a study group. The company then declared its intention to press ahead with the establishment of its own rules for communications, insisting that adherence to these rules, when established, would be mandatory for all suppliers of equipment to General Motors. Thus General Motors, and in particular Michael A Kaminski Jr. and the MAP Task Force, became the driving force behind the *Manufacturing Automation Protocol* (*MAP*) from its inception.

MAP is significant because, together with TOP (Technical and Office Protocol), it is an essential step in the achievement of CIM. What sets MAP and TOP apart from other networking protocols is that these standards are being adopted by a large number of computer, CAD and systems vendors. Once the standard is finalised, (which is by no means a trivial matter, as this section will proceed to explain), and conformance testing is completed, manufacturers will have a wide choice of hardware and software systems which will communicate together without a bespoke interface. In each area of operation, the appropriate automation system can be selected for the job, in the security of knowing that it will not be isolated from other computer systems in the factory. So MAP and TOP are the communications specifications that look certain to form the basis for computer-based automation well into the 21st century.

Together with aerospace manufacturer McDonnell Douglas, GM initiated the formation of the MAP Users' Group. Currently, over 400 companies in 15 countries have joined MAP/TOP user groups in North America, Europe, Asia and Australia to accelerate the development of standards, the introduction of viable products and to share implementation experiences. Even though it was thought, at one time, that MAP products would be supplied, at a price, to General Motors and the few others who might insist on them, while proprietary products would continue to be the main selling items, the rapidly growing strength of the MAP user groups has led to all the major suppliers of computing, control and networking equipment now committing themselves to supporting MAP.

TOP—Technical and Office Protocol.—More recently, a parallel pressure group for standardising networks used in the engineering and office areas has been founded. In this case, the catalyst was the Boeing Company, producing the first version, 1.0, of the Technical and Office Protocol (TOP) specification in November 1985. This led to the formation of a TOP Users' Group in December 1985 and the setting up of a joint steering committee for the two activities. In most respects, the MAP and TOP specifications are—and will remain—identical. They differ only in that they are designed to interface with different kinds of application software and in the way messages are sent round the network. (TOP has chosen the IEEE 802.3 standard Ethernet-type CSMA/CD local area network which has been implemented by many manufacturers of office systems.)

TOP is more relevant than MAP in the design office, where data transfer time is less relevant and the electromagnetic environment less hostile. Since the Ethernet network costs about one fifth of the equivalent MAP network, it will be the preferred choice: even with the predicted fall in price, MAP is unlikely to become cheaper than Ethernet. On the other hand, a substantial manufacturing operation may require a MAP broadband network, which could be extended to the design office, in which case the CAD/CAM system would reside on MAP. As a third option, a CAD/CAM system residing on TOP could be linked to MAP, inexpensively and transparently, via a bridge. A company with a bent towards design and prototyping would probably restrict itself to a TOP installation and extend its TOP network from the design office to prototyping operations. There are no firm rules. Theories of optimum configuration are likely to change as MAP and TOP networks begin to be implemented; a major factor in the short term is whether the vendor concerned has actually developed a MAP or TOP interface for its equipment.

In addition, high level computer systems, such as mainframes and minicomputers, serving lower order computers in individual disciplines, will best be served by TOP networks: the TOP specification, as it evolves, will provide for a hierarchy of local area networks and their connection through metropolitan and wide area networks.

Introduction to the OSI Model.—Out of the 1978 Open Systems Interconnection committee came the establishment of a reference model, Table 4, for a communications network to which all subsequent communications standards and protocols should conform. The idea of models is central to this whole area of standards activity, because a model can describe an idealised set of relationships within which an evolving programme of creating new standards can develop. The architecture of the OSI model defines two kinds of relationships between functional models in a network:

INTERFACES — Relationships between different modules that are usually operating within a single mode in a network; typically, a module in one layer will interface with a module in the layer below it to receive a service;

PROTOCOLS — Relationships between equivalent modules, usually in different nodes; protocols define message formats and the rules for message exchange.

---

[5] In a sense, the wheel has turned full circle and it is also somewhat ironic that the very companies who first stimulated the development of the CAD industry, with a diverse collection of proprietary and mainframe-based systems, are now the major driving force behind a move towards standardisation!

The OSI model is intended to embrace all types of computer communications, from the automated machining cell in a factory to the complex data networks of multinational corporations and the public service networks. The OSI model provides a broad framework within which a number of different standards can exist side-by-side to satisfy the great variety of different networking standards, so conformance to standards within the OSI model does not guarantee that items of equipment can communicate with each other: agreement between implementors is also required to ensure both conform to the standard, and more importantly, inter-operability. A number of different, and in some cases only partly compatible, standards at present come within its scope, though the whole situation is fluid and the intention is that computer communications will grow into harmony. The OSI model has seven different categories, or layers, of well-defined functions, in order that manufacturers may write protocols which apply directly to the machinery that will implement these protocols. For example, a terminal only needs to implement protocols in the first two layers—the physical layer and the data link layer; modems would implement protocols in the first three layers—network, data link and physical; a mainframe computer would implement protocols in all seven layers. Each of the seven layers is dealt with explicitly in a later section.

Construction of MAP Networks.—MAP networks are concerned with communication between computer systems, cell controllers and other devices controlling and dealing with factory processes, design, process planning, scheduling, quality control testing and maintenance. The MAP specification envisages a backbone network of coaxial cables of the same type as are used for cable TV. This network will serve the entire network and provide a bus—in the same way as the factory electricity supply: equipment can be plugged in or removed from the bus just as it would be connected/disconnected from the electricity supply.

Building the MAP Specification.—MAP and TOP are not themselves standards: wherever international standards exist, elements within those broad standards are specified. Primarily, the GM Task Force very quickly identified the OSI model as the most widely accepted and useful basis for standardised networks and proceeded to decide upon a mutually-compatible set of existing and proposed standards appropriate to the manufacturing area which are in harmony with OSI and which appeared to be destined to become international standards. However, although MAP identifies particular elements of the OSI standards, it also includes non-OSI protocols for messaging, network management and directory services.

The MAP Task Force has concentrated primarily on evaluation of IEEE Project 802 and emerging ISO/NBS (National Bureau of Standards) specifications. Where international standards are not yet finalised, MAP and TOP have to make a best estimate of the likely structure of these standards, yet retain the ability to modify the specifications as standards do become established. The state of the international standards associated with MAP Version 2.1 is shown in Table 4; at that time, layers 1 and 2 of the OSI model were becoming the subject of international standards based on the IEE 802 series of standards, so the decision became one of selecting from amongst the possible alternatives: references in the specifications are to the IEEE 802 standard numbers. The other hardware layers, 3 and 4, were in the process of being finalised and the higher layers were in various draft stages. A compromise has to be struck between the urgent need to get standardised networks established in factories and the concern that networks will not be rendered obsolete and useless by newly agreed standards in the near future.

GM is now reported to have MAP up and running for control systems in its body, paint, trim, guided vehicle and test areas, and is now in the process of building a MAP-based factory for steering gear. Otherwise, there are no full implementations in industry of the entire MAP specification: even local area networks (LANs) are not yet very widely used in industry. There are, though, already some places where the foundations have been laid on which a fully MAP-networked CIM system will be operating in the near future. In the UK, some companies have been installing broadband cable in anticipation of moving into MAP as it becomes available. ICL proposes to open a MAP implementation at its printed circuit board factory in Staffordshire in 1987: based at Kidsgrove—and as a result named Kidmap—the project will initially use MAP for stores management and parts kitting. Ultimately, it is anticipated that all the design and production control procedures will be interlinked on a single open systems network. ICL's project is receiving DTI backing through a 25% grant towards the cost, which is estimated at approximately £0.5 M. Jaguar Cars, also, has broadband on all its three sites and as part of its current CIM programme, the company is working on the specification for an hierarchy of MAP networks to be used in a pilot manufacturing project.

Although a survey by Frost & Sullivan estimates that in the USA there were fewer than 1600 factory-based LANs in use in 1984, by 1989 the number is expected to have increased to about 40,000. Within its limited aims, MAP is a very important enabling technology: a study undertaken by the UK National Computing Centre (NCC) argues that, while it would be cheaper to stay with proprietary networks (which are mainly baseband), companies must be prepared to pay for the privilege of gaining hands-on experience with MAP. They must abandon the idea of three-year payback periods for their investment and count the experience won as sufficient reward for their efforts. This implies strongly that it will be the largest companies which will continue to be involved with the initial development of MAP.

CIMAP Demonstration.—An ambitious MAP demonstration, CIMAP, took place at the NEC in Birmingham on December 2–4, 1986. This demonstration was sponsored by the Department of Trade & Industry (DTI), following a DTI assessment which revealed a relatively low awareness in the UK of MAP and a general underestimation or misunderstanding of communication techniques in automation. It was felt that this might

TABLE 4.—THE OSI MODEL AND CURRENT MAP/TOP SPECIFICATIONS

Layers	TOP Version 1.0 Protocols	OSI Reference Model Defined Function	MAP Version 2.1 Protocols	Layers
Layer 7 Application	Network Management Directory Service ISO FTAM (DP) 8571 File transfer. Limited file management. ASCII and binary data only.	Provides all services directly comprehensible to application programs	Network Management Directory Service ISO FTAM 8571 File Transfer Protocol Manuf. Mess. Std. MMFS/EIA 1393A*. Common Application Service Elements (CASE) (eg Association Control). Special Application Service Elements (SASE) (eg FTAM).	Layer 7 Application
Layer 6 Presentation	Null† ASCII & binary encoding.	Transforms data to/from negotiated standardised formats	Null† ASCII and binary encoding	Layer 6 Presentation
Layer 5 Session	ISO Session (IS) 8327. Session kernel. Full duplex.	Synchronise and manage dialogues	ISO Session (IS) 8327. Session kernel. Full duplex.	Layer 5 Session

TABLE 4.—*continued*

Layers	TOP Version 1.0 Protocols	OSI Reference Model Defined Function	MAP Version 2.1 Protocols	Layers
Layer 4 Transport	ISO Transport (IS) 8073, Class 4.	Provides transparent, reliable data transfer from end-node to end-node	ISO Transport (IS) 8073, Class 4	Layer 4 Transport
Layer 3 Network	ISO Internet (DIS) 8473. Connectionless and for X-25. Subnetwork-dependent, convergence protocol (SNDCP).	Performs message routing for data transfer between nodes	ISO Internet (DIS) 8473. Connectionless and for X.25. Subnetwork-dependent convergence protocol (SNDCP).	Layer 3 Network
Layer 2 (upper) Data Link: Logical	ISO Logical. Link Control. (DIS) 2/3. (IEEE 802.2) Type 1, Class 1.	Error detection for messages moved between nodes	ISO Logical. Link Control. (DIS) 2/3. (IEEE 802.2) Type 1, Class 1.	Layer 2 (upper) Data Link: Logical
Layer 2 (lower) Data Link: Media Access‡	ISO CSMA/CD. (DIS) 8802/3. (IEEE 802.3)	Type of data transfer	ISO token-passing bus. (DIS) 8802/4. (IEEE 802.4).	Layer 2 (lower) Data Link: Media Access
Layer 1 Physical	CSMA/CD media access. Control 10 Base 5. 10–12Mbit/s baseband cable	Electrically encodes and physically transfers messages between nodes	Token-passing-bus media access control. 10Mbit/s broadband cable. Transmission medium (LAN cable)	Layer 1 Physical

* Full revision to MFS expected in MAP Version 3.0.
† A null layer provides no additional services, but exists only to provide a logical path for the flow of network data and control.
‡ ISO is considering moving the IEEE-defined media access control (MAC) sub-layer of the Data Link Layer (Layer 2) to the Physical Layer (Layer 1).

not only lead to a damaging effect on Britain's relative industrial performance in the long term, but also result in a loss of significant opportunities as suppliers of MAP-compatible equipment.

CIMAP was coordinated by Coopers & Lybrand, the results of whose analysis, shown in Table 5, show a cost comparison of installing a factory network for CIM using MAP, as against an equivalent installation using proprietary networks. Clearly, the greatest discrepancy is in interfacing the application areas—the islands of automation—as would be expected: it is worth noting that in subsequent years, as further systems are added to the network, this discrepancy would tend to increase.

TABLE 5.—MAP INSTALLATION COST COMPARISONS

Activity	MAP		Other	
	1st year cost (£K)	Percentage of 1st year spent (%)	1st year cost (£K)	Percentage of 1st year spent
Network design and installation	4	1	8	1
Network interface devices	100	25	100	12.5
Applications interface	196	49	412	64
Staff	20	5	20	2.5
Project management and training	40	10	80	10
Maintenance	40	10	80	10
Totals	400	100	800	100

Cost figures are based on a medium-sized manufacturing unit with £10 M annual sales, 200 employees, 2,500yd^2 of manufacturing facility, and 150 programmable devices of which, in the MAP network, 40 are linked using broadband and the remainder with carrierband. Source: Coopers & Lybrand.

Currently (and unfortunately), there are two versions of the networking systems used with MAP: *Industrial Networking Incorporation* (*INI*) and *Concord Data Systems* (*CDS*). Both were demonstrated at CIMAP (Fig. 14) and both make interfaces to MAP, but are different interpretations of the specification. The demonstration itself comprised two MAP networks (ie one built by INI and one by CDS), plus a TOP network built by BICC. All three were connected by intermediate systems called routers. Gateways linked the INI MAP network to a remote MAP network at GM's Technical Center in the USA and the BICC TOP network to British Aerospace. The configuration provided authentic MAP features, including Network Management and Directory Services.

The CIMAP demonstration was designed for European production conditions—mostly smaller automation groupings which form a computer integrated plant, as opposed to US conditions where the plants are larger. The network therefore reflected a multiplicity of application partnerships—in fact 15 separate cells each concentrating on a particular aspect of manufacturing activity—as opposed to previous MAP demonstrations which had a large number of vendors on a single application.

One of the cells, however, was based on an actual factory which is already operational in the UK. This is a just-in-time diesel engine assembly operation established by Honeywell and Cummins. Currently though, manual involvement is necessary, but many assembly operations, including torquing nuts, are fully automatic.

MAP Versions and Amendments.—Within the section on the IGES standard for product model data transfer (see Chapter H6), we have already seen the difficulties which have been encountered in the implementation of just one standard (IGES has aided in file storage standardisation, but not in the communications area: it was developed by the NBS and has been made the cornerstone of GM's integrated CAD/CAM plan). Against this background, it would be foolish to suggest MAP and TOP will be the answer to all problems in standardising computer integrated manufacturing systems, or that MAP and TOP compatibility is something which is about to happen overnight, even with such intensive commercial pressure behind it.

As we shall shortly see, short cuts have been necessary in drawing up the early versions of the MAP specifications. Some layer services have only been defined for restricted applications. The Presentation Layer (Layer 6) services have been omitted altogether. It has been necessary to anticipate the finalising of International Standards and to specify interim protocols which may ultimately have to be modified considerably to conform with International Standards.

Partly as a result of these short cuts, and partly despite them, a number of inaccuracies or incompletely defined interpretations of the specification found their way into MAP Version 2.1, with the result that an almost equal thickness of published errata and amplifications has had to be appended to the already bulky specification, for those concerned with implementing it. These additions do not alter the specification, except in making it more precise. The CIMAP demonstration described above was based on this tidied-up version 2.1.

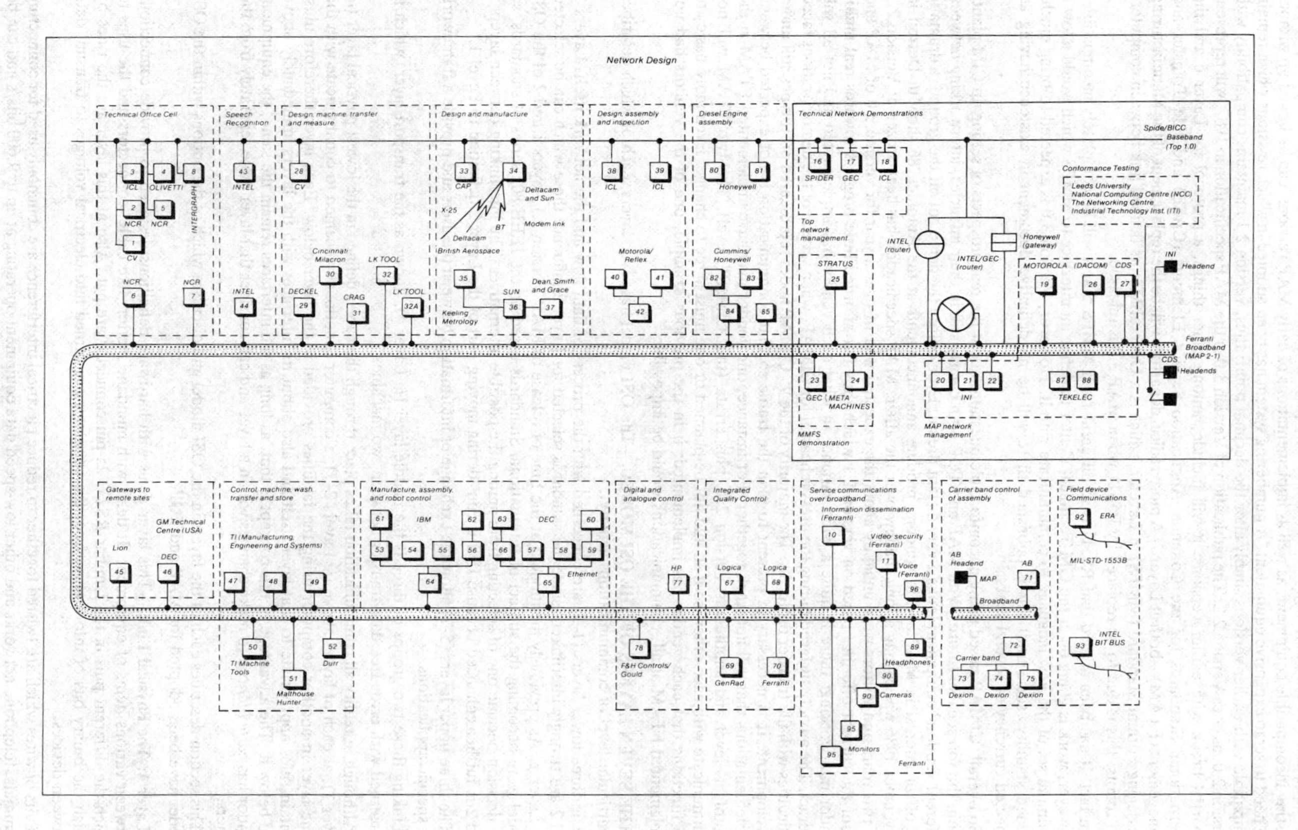

FIG. 14.—CIMAP Network Illustration.

But a specification developing as quickly as this could also present an obstacle to potential buyers of MAP-compatible equipment, who might fear premature obsolecence. Therefore the GM Task Force has stipulated that equipment at all these stages should remain compatible: a migration path has been defined, by which existing incompatible equipment, as well as implementations of early MAP versions, can be linked up without the need to scrap expensive equipment. A numbering system has been adopted in which revisions which remain compatible with earlier versions simply alter the decimal point: thus, version 2.1 maintains compatibility with Version 2.0, as does Version 2.2. The publication of Version 3.0 of the MAP specification in 1987, will represent a partial break with earlier versions: it will include, among other things, a protocol for Layer 6 and the International Standards for the Common Application Service Elements (CASE) and File Transfer and Management (FTAM)—both at Layer 7. A more radical departure will be the replacement of the Manufacturing Messaging Format Standard (MMFS) at Layer 7, which is a General Motors defined link between computers and robots: this is due to be replaced by RS511 when MAP 3.0 is released.

In fact, it has been argued that RS511 is so different from MMFS that it will be completely incompatible. However, work is going on at the GM Technical Center to define an interface to MMFS which would allow a minimum set of the new language to communicate with it. However, Version 3.0 is expected to bring much-needed stability, since until this is published there will be no definitive document in existence having an expected currency of several years.

So overall, CIMAP raised many uncomfortable questions about the real prospects of setting up CIM plants within the foreseeable future. With MAP and TOP both clearly still in their infancies, interworking between different vendors' equipment looks a very distant dream. Even before the demo got off the ground, a dramatic fall-off of interest in MAP and in vendors' product announcements at the Autofact '86 show in Detroit in November 1986 was casting a long shadow over the affair. MAP specification has been frozen at Version 2.1 for two years and visitors were unhappy about the expected wait of over a year for version 3.0 of MAP and about the current offerings based on version 2.1 which they felt afforded little progress towards real multi-vendor interworking: there is quite a wide variance in what each vendor has implemented and not all will interact. The anxiety surfaced during the dress rehearsal for CIMAP, when several of the demonstrations faced difficulties with file transfer protocols. The majority of the 95 CIMAP nodes represented prototypes still under development. It is necessary at present to plan the traffic so that communication is not expected between implementations that will not work together. For instance, one vendor may have implemented FTAM at the 'Autofact' level and another at Version 2.1, plus errata (the 'CIMAP' level). The two FTAM will not communicate with each other, so it should not be planned or one must agree to change. Even more basic are the functions that each vendor has implemented: if in the previous example, one of the vendors had not implemented FTAM at all, communications would be impossible.

THE SEVEN LAYERS OF THE OSI MODEL.—The OSI model has seven layers, each of which describes a particular level of communications activity.

The three lower layers (1–3) are concerned with the process of data flow and the network itself. Layers 1 and 2 are strongly interlinked, since the standards selected for Layer 2 influence those which can be selected for Layer 1. As previously mentioned, at the time of release of MAP Version 2.1, layers 1 and 2 of the OSI model were becoming the subject of International Standards based on the IEEE 802 series of standards, so the decision became one of selecting from among the possible alternatives. The interlinking between layers 1 and 2 is further enhanced because ISO is considering moving part of the Layer 2 definition to Level 1.

The three upper layers (5–7) allow the exchange of information between the users and provide a framework for specific applications.

Linking these two groups of three is the middle layer (*ie* Layer 4), known as the transport layer, which is concerned with error-free data transfer between two machines.

Although in reality all communication takes place through the cables defined in the lowest physical layer (*ie* Layer 1), at each of layers above (*ie* Layers 2–7), a computer is notionally deemed to communicate with the same layer in another computer using the facilities provided in the layer below. Each layer therefore must contain rules appropriate to that layer itself and also about its interfaces with the layers immediately above and below it. The advantage of this concept is that, as long as the interfaces remain the same, the equipment vendor has *carte blanche* to make changes within a layer and can consider that layer quite separately from the others.

This section describes each of the layers in the OSI model and discusses which of the options within the OSI model have been adopted for MAP and TOP.

Layer 1: The Physical Link.—This layer deals with hardware definitions designed to provide connections between various items of equipment. It deals with mundane matters like cable, connectors and the uses to which the different pins in the familiar RS232 25-pin connector are put. Also at this layer are the rules by which the binary bits of information from the computer are turned into electrical voltages to transmit data between devices.

Pairs of wires which are twisted together to reduce electrical interference are commonly used for connecting terminals, telephone networks and other low-speed data equipment operating at up to 9,600 bits/s and can be used at higher data rates. They are inexpensive and adequate, but have to be enclosed in metal conduit in high electrical interference (EMI/FRI) régimes. Coaxial cable, which is more commonly used for high-speed data communications, has a much higher immunity and generally only needs to be shielded where it passes close to electrical machinery; its cost, like the cathode ray tube, has been brought down by its extensive use in the television industry, this time for cable TV. The MAP 2.1 specification calls for ½ in coaxial cable (we may have standardised communications protocols for computer systems, but good old Imperial units will prevail), sometimes described as broadband cable[6], capable of transmitting data at 10 Mb/s (although early versions allowed a 5 Mb/s data rate). Cable is also specified in terms of its resistance—the MAP cable is 75 ohms.

The amount of information a cable can carry is determined by its bandwidth, which is the range of electrical frequencies which it can transmit with not more than a specified error fraction. But since data transmitted by computers consists of a series of electrical pulses corresponding to the bits of information transmitted, bandwidth also gives an indication of the speed at which data can be transmitted. Broadband cable is intended to carry a wide range of frequencies up to 300 MHz or more. This wide bandwidth can be divided up into a number of different channels for different frequency ranges and different types of signals—*eg* MAP, Ethernet-type, voice and video communications (*eg* cable TV surveillance), fire detection systems—and can be doctored by a process called *frequency division multiplexing*, so that they can all use the same cable simultaneously without becoming confused with each other.

The token-passing broadband network specified in MAP is rather more complicated than the network needed for the CSMA/CD data transmission system favoured by Ethernet and TOP. Besides the heavier-duty cable and more complicated cable taps employed, the system utilises dual frequencies: messages are transmitted at one frequency and received at another, so two adjacent 6 MHz frequencies on the broadband network are allocated to a MAP network. At one end of the bus system is a piece of equipment called a *head end remodulator*: this picks up all outgoing signals, checks them for accuracy, amplifies them and sends them out again on a different carrier frequency. If the network is large, it may need two or more amplifiers, but only one remodulator is employed in each network.

In future, an increasing usage of fibre-optic cable can be expected. Fibre-optic cables have bandwidths and data rates about two orders of magnitude higher than coaxial cables. However, the problems of tapping into such cables make them less attractive for use in LANs in the immediate future.

Layer 2: Data Link.—The standard protocol used in OSI is called *High-Level Data Link* (HDLC), but this itself includes a number of variations covering different types of applications, so that even at this level it is not possible simply to plug two OSI-compatible computers into a network and expect them to communicate. If the data were simply sent as a continuous stream, there would be no guarantee that the receiving device would be able to receive it at the same speed, or that no errors had crept into the transmission. So on top of the Physical Layer is superimposed a Data Link Layer, the chief purpose of which is to ensure that a message gets from one device to another without mishap.

Previous sections have discussed in some depth the several different technologies (Media Access Controls) being used in local area networks. The Project 802 group was faced with the choice of adopting one of them as its standard or accepting several different standards and trying to find some way of accommodating them. It opted for the latter approach: CSMA/CD is specified in IEEE 802.3 and is adopted in the TOP specification; token bus, specified in IEEE 802.4, is adopted in the MAP specification; token ring is covered by the IEEE 802.5. As a result of its attempt at accommodation, two sub-layers, Media Access Control and Logical Link Control are defined by IEEE within Layer 2.

This leads to untidiness in that the IEEE terminology is a little different from that of OSI: although it conforms to the OSI model in distinguishing Layers 1 and 2, it also divides Layer 2 into lower and upper sub-layers, that is, the Media Access Control sub-layer an the Logical Link Sub-Layer, ISO is now considering moving the IEEE-defined Media Access Control (MAC) sub-layer of the Data Link Layer (Layer 2) to the Physical Layer (Layer 1).

A particularly important function of Layer 2 is the process, known as *framing*, which involves dividing up the stream of bits into small packets, or frames, separating them by a special sequence of bits defined so that they cannot be confused with the data themselves. Since GM had decided on the token bus network method, the appropriate framing procedure was that defined in IEEE 802.4. for Media Access Control.

Logical Link Control, as defined by the IEEE, deals with error-checking and other functions, so a local area network can be connected into a wider OSI network at the Data Link Layer. A number of different variations

---

[6] As opposed to baseband cable, which is ⅜ in—a broadband network is quite capable of carrying baseband signals!!

Broadband cable is more expensive than baseband cable and a little less tolerant of reorganisations when installed. The coaxial cable is not strictly flexible, though it can be bent by hand: it comprises a copper-clad aluminium core surrounded by a thick plastic dielectric layer contained in a thin aluminium extruded tubular sleeve, which is in turn protected and insulated by a plastic cover. The cable has to be cut to be tapped and the inner and outer insulators stripped back to allow the joints to be made. The splitter box, within which the connection is made, contains provision for a small inductance to be inserted between the backbone network and the cables leading to the various devices. When the network is installed, it is tuned by adjusting these inductances to obtain approximately the same signal strength at every node throughout the network. Up to four cables can be tapped into the network at a splitter box and further subdivision is possible at the end of each cable.

Baseband cable is used to transmit one signal at a time at high speeds (10–12 Mbit/s). This is the type of cable normally used in networks conforming to the Ethernet specification and is also included in the TOP specification. The cable itself is flexible, so similar cables leading from computers and other devices can easily be 'tapped' into it without cutting the cable, using a connector called a *cable tap*.

are provided within OSI and IEEE standards, providing for different services to connection-orientated and connectionless networks (see Layer 3); a third type, the acknowledged connectionless service is being added. MAP calls for the IEEE 802.2 Type 1 Logical Link Control: this is the connectionless service which ties in with the connectionless protocol called for in Layer 3. Activity in Layer 2 is simplified because tasks such as acknowledging the sequence of messages, controlling the flow of messages and arranging selective re-transmission of messages which contain errors or are lost are made the responsibility of higher layers.

One task of layer 2 is to pin an address on the front of each message: MAP 2.1 specifies the high option of a uniform 48-bit addressing scheme on all types of LAN: this allows space for a unique identifier for each local area network, followed by an identifier for each station and entity within the network.

Adding to the complications at these layers of model is the fact that for local area networks, ISO is in the process of adopting, more or less in their original form, the set of standards developed by the IEEE's Project 802 committees; at present it is the IEEE standards, rather than international standards, which are usually quoted in references to Layers 1 and 2. However, the ISO standard will simply have an '8' prefixed, so that for example, IEEE 802.4 will become ISO 8802/4.

The first two layers of the OSI model are thus sufficient to establish and maintain data communications between two computers: many microcomputer users are frequent beneficiaries of the standards and protocols included in these layers of the model when they communicate with bulletin boards or electronic mail services.

Layer 3: Network Layer.—This layer provides the routing of messages from one station to another and it extends the scope of the model to include the interconnection of various sub-networks: it becomes important when messages have to be sent between different sub-networks, such as a MAP and a TOP network. It concerns not only connections between local area networks, but also the linking of remote LANs through, for example, the public service networks. One major difficulty which has arisen at this level is that there are two fundamentally different ways of providing a service from one end of a network to the other: connection-orientated and connectionless network services.

Connection-orientated networks are, to a limited extent, analogous to a telephone call, in which all subsequent activities stem from the physical process of making a connection between two parties. Two separate data connections between two parties may take two different routes, but the link is set up and maintained as long as the communication persists. The telephone call analogy ends, however, because while vocal communications need to be continuous as long as the conversation lasts, computers communicate most efficiently in small bursts of very rapid transfer, occupying a very large bandwidth. Packet switching techniques divide up the complete message into short packets which themselves can choose alternative routes through the network, as appropriate to minimise travelling time. Despite the variations, a connection is established between the two ends.

The connectionless network system (CLNS) is analogous to the postal service: the network service attempts to deliver one or more addressed information packages by what it considers to be the most convenient route(s). There is no guarantee that the messages will arrive in the same sequence in which they were despatched, nor that the recipient will be in a position to accept them. It is the task of protocols in the next layer (Layer 4) to sort out these matters.

MAP has adopted the connectionless network service for communication between stations across a network, though it also provides for an X.25 link to wide area networks. One protocol has been defined by ISO for providing the connectionless service, known as the *Internet Protocol*, which has become Draft International Standard 8473. This is quite complex, because it has to spell out everything that must go on the 'envelope' for each message to ensure that it arrives safely at its destination. Besides the destination, there is provision in the *datagram* for the address of the sender, some information about the route to the destination and a check that the datagram itself has not become corrupted during transit. Its layout is a little like an international telephone number and it can run to 40 decimal digits. However, if the source and destination are both within the same sub-network, the MAP specification permits the use of a truncated header, which reduces the amount of information which has to be sent with each message and makes for faster communication.

Because public service networks are generally connection-orientated, while LANs are frequently connectionless, ISO has had to provide a standard in the Network Layer to allow communication across networks involving both types of service. This has resulted in quite a complicated structure for the internal architecture of the Network Layer, which has to specify relays between sub-networks, which will employ one protocol to talk to one network and another protocol to talk to another. Where connection-orientated services are involved, the relay also has to concern itself with the route to be taken through the network towards the destination of the message.

Bridges, Routers and Gateways.—Companies which already make extensive use of networking in their manufacturing operations will probably want to evolve into MAP, starting by connecting their existing networks into a linking MAP network. There are varying degrees of difficulty and cost in this operation, depending upon the degree of compatibility between the two networks. At the physical level, the transmission media may be different, with twisted-pair wires or a lower rating of coaxial cable. The network topology may be different, with a star or ring configuration instead of the bus topology used in MAP.

The majority of present-day networks in the manufacturing environment are of the collision-detecting Ethernet type, quite different from the token-passing method used in MAP.

Three types of devices can be used to connect different networks, depending on the degree of compatibility between them. They are called *bridges*, *routers* and *gateways*. A gateway is very much more complicated and expensive than the other two devices.

If it becomes necessary to extend an existing network, or where, say, a carrierband MAP network has to be connected to a broadband MAP network, or even to connect a TOP network to a MAP network, the bridge can be used. The MAP specification defines a bridge as a transparent device used to connect segments of a single LAN with a common network address. It treats the two networks as one and it therefore does not need an address of its own for transmission of messages, though it has one for use by the network manager software. The networks on either side of a bridge may differ only in the Physical Layer (Layer 1) and/or in the Media Access Control sub-layer of the Data Link Layer (Layer 2). A bridge can link a MAP network with a TOP network, because the two systems have adopted the same protocols, except that TOP uses the contention CSMA/CD media access method at Layers 1 and 2. Within a TOP network, such a connection can be made at Level 1 with a device called a *repeater*, but the token-passing system used in MAP calls for a rather more complex interface.

A router is similar to a bridge, but is able to connect several LANs together (different MAP networks and CSMA/CD networks and also, through an X.25 link and a wide area network, to a remote host computer), with a common address on all networks, so it also involves the Network Layer, Layer 3. A router can also be used if it is necessary or desirable to separate two MAP networks, while allowing them to communicate. Where all the layers above Layer 3 conform to the OSI model and are compatible, the router performs the translation at Layer 3, allowing the different networks to communicate with each other. The router functions as a node on each of the networks connected to it, with a common address on all of them. It provides path selection and alternative routing based on the destination network layer addresses and status of connected networks. The MAP specification describes an interconnecting set of networks with links at Layers 2 and 3 as a *catanet*.

Any differences at higher layers require the use of a *gateway*. This is a device to connect different network architectures by performing protocol translation, invoking all seven OSI layers. Many connections to existing LANs will require a gateway, though it can be expected that many vendors of proprietary systems will gradually migrate their systems to connect more easily with MAP: gateways are not a long-term solution to interconnection problems because they are relatively expensive, slow and restrictive in operation. A gateway is not a transparent interface, so it must have a separate network address on each of the networks connected.

Layer 4: Transport Layer.—This layer is the one which exists between three layers of communications and three layers of user information exchange. This is the lowest layer which exists *only in the equipment* at the two ends of the communications link and it provides the basic facilities to allow the exchange of data (higher layers are concerned with managing the sending of messages, the format in which they are to be sent and providing services for particular applications). The transport layer takes away from the users at each end the need to know anything about the network through which the information is flowing: it provides control of the flow of data, ensuring that messages arrive at the receivers' end free of errors, checking for errors, duplications and missing packets of information. All this is necessary, as indicated under Layer 3, when packets may travel by different routes, may be subject to congestion and may not arrive in the correct sequence.

The user does, however, have to opt for one of five classes of transport service and this will probably relate to the type of network and communication involved. The lowest is Class 0, which is used for teletext services. Some of the tasks which could be carried out at lower layers are passed up to this layer, which uses the most comprehensive of the options provided in the OSI model, Class 4. MAP 2.1 calls for the version of Class 4 defined by the National Bureau of Standards, which has now been incorporated into ISO IS 8073.

There are two main services provided at the transport layer—connection management and data transfer. Connection management allows the user to set up and maintain a path through the network to another user. It has four parts: establishing a connection; terminating a connection gracefully; an abort termination, or disconnect, which may result in loss of data; telling the user about the status of the connection. Data transfer provides three services: transferring data; expedited data—an urgent service for sending a limited amount of data outside the normal data stream; and unit data—a service allowing the transferring of data without previously establishing (and later terminating) a transport connection.

Layer 5: Sesssion Layer.—This layer provides mechanisms for managing and structuring data transfer being carried out by the transport layer (Layer 4). It includes the establishment and release of connections, some refinements in synchronisation to keep the two end devices in step with each other and selection of the type of dialogue which is to take place (ie whether it is to be simultaneous in both directions, known as *full duplex*, or to flow alternately one way and then the other, called *half duplex*). These and other functional units are included as options in the international standard for the Session Layer, IS 8327, together with a kernel unit (which must be provided and tells the transport layer to start and stop a connection). The MAP specification calls at present only for some of the facilities provided by IS 8327: the essential kernel and a full duplex facility.

Layer 6: Presentation Layer.— This layer deals with the different ways in which numbers, alphabetical characters and so on are represented by different types of equipment. If they are to communicate, they must speak the same language! A set of rules has been adopted for converting what is called *abstract syntax—eg* the letter 'A'—being presented from Layer 7 into a standard code for transmission. This encoding process extends beyond alphanumeric characters into image data and is intended ultimately to include digitally encoded voice signals.

MAP 2.1 treats this layer as null and bypasses it. It is therefore necessary for all equipment using a Version 2.1 network to employ either binary data or ASCII syntax, which is the standard adopted by most computer manufacturers.

Layer 7: Application Layer.—At the top of the OSI tree is Layer 7, the Application Layer and this is the only part of the whole structure (apart from the cables from Layer 1) which is directly encountered by the user—or the user's software. Although a little standards development is still in progress in Layers 1–6, Layer 7 is still the subject of considerable work; however, the elements of greatest interest to MAP are now largely defined.

At this level, the system has to cater for the many different types of information that will be sent through the networks—text files, databases, videotex, fascimile images, voice messaging, etc. To deal with a variety of needs, Layer 7 offers a Common Application Service Element (CASE) which provides a toolkit of useful functions which are common to many individual functions, plus a number of Specific Application Service Elements (SASE) for different types of applications. Some of the SASEs are, or will be, the subject of international standards, while others will be proprietary elements for specific applications, such as banking or airlines.

Thus far, three functions in the CASE are defined in the OSI model and are now partly covered by International Standards, covering:

(1) Association Control allows applications to establish associations among themselves, transfer messages over those associated connections and either gracefully terminate or abort the associations;

(2) Context Control allows application processes to define and manipulate the meaning of the information they wish to exchange;

(3) Commitment Concurrency and Recovery (CCR) allows application processes to coordinate the activities of separate associations.

MAP 2.1 calls tentatively for CASE and this facility will inevitably be included in the next MAP specification, 3.0. Only one CASE, Association Control, is called for in MAP 2.1. In consequence, the meaning of transferred messages and the coordination of associations must be defined by the programmers of the distributed applications. This is a restriction which applies to all demonstrations of MAP so far.

One important SASE, which is called for in the MAP 2.1 specification is File Transfer, Access and Management (FTAM). This is designed to allow files to be transferred in binary or ASCII text format between different types of systems and also to allow some degree of manipulation of files or parts of files: they may be created or deleted remotely or read. The MAP 2.1 version provides its own association and connection services, which are not available in the truncated version of the CASE. In order to gain access to files of unknown structure in other computer systems, there must be some intermediate facility in the software of each computer which allows its files to be treated as though they have some universally agreed properties. In order to achieve this, the drafters of the international standard have adopted a model called the *Virtual Filestore*. This describes three characteristics of any file:

(1) Attributes: name, size, when created, who owns it, type of access (serial or random) and who is allowed to access it;

(2) Structure;

(3) Actions which may be performed, such as changing attributes, reading, extending, etc.

By means of the virtual filestore, FTAM provides for: bulk transfer of files between nodes; reading from and writing to the files; adding and erasing records; various file management functions.

Another SASE under development as an international standard is a Virtual Terminal service, which will allow any terminal to work with any host computer.

Besides these and other SASEs of wide interest, which will be covered by international standards, there will be others of more limited scope, which may or may not come within the purview of the ISO. Within the MAP specification, there is a *Manufacturing Messaging Service* at Layer 7 for achieving communication with different types of programmable logic controllers and other intelligent devices. The TOP specification, as it develops, is expected to lead to SASEs covering document revision and exchange, directory services, graphics and database management.

Intra-cell MAP Architectures.—Within cells, there is not the same need for all the non-MAP supplementary services which can be superimposed on the broadband cable. MAP is also not as fast as is often necessary for real-time control, monitoring and maintenance of machines, handling equipment, etc, which are the main requirements of networking between cells. An important development for intra-cell operations is the extension of MAP to include carrierband networks at the Physical Layer (Layer 1).

Carrierband MAP combines some of the advantages of baseband and broadband systems: one of the disadvantages with MAP is that it is expensive and complicated, compared with many existing proprietary cell networks.

A carrierband signal is similar to a baseband signal, but the bits of data are superimposed on a continuous carrier electrical frequency. In the MAP version, the same broadband cable is used, but the whole bandwidth is reserved for the MAP network. All the stations in the network transmit and receive on the same carrier frequency, so there is no need for frequency translation via a head end remodulator. Within carrierband technology there are some options, and as a result of testing, it has been decided to opt for what is called *phase coherent signalling* at 5 Mb/s (the same cable and taps are used as in the broadband network).

It has been suggested that some companies may be able to dispense with the broadband backbone network altogether and use carrierband for all their factory communications. The feeling within General Motors is now that with this one change, leaving the other six layers intact, the MAP specifications will be adequate to deal with the vast majority of network requirements within cells. Simulation studies suggest that response time as short as 20–30ms can be expected in the absence of errors and perhaps double that where errors occur. Response time is limited by the efficiency with which the network can be tuned and is related to the number of nodes and the applications which they are supporting, but GM is quite happy to live with a response time of 50ms with full MAP and OSI capability.

Still faster communications may be obtained with two further MAP modifications, intended for robotics and sensing devices: mini-MAP and Enhanced Performance Architecture (EPA). Mini-MAP is so scaled down a version of MAP that it cannot function properly as a MAP node; it is being developed particularly at the request of the process industries for very fast real-time communications. It differs from MAP in the Logical Link Control sub-layer of the Data Link Layer (Layer 2), in adopting part of the newly specified Type 3 acknowledged connectionless LLC service of IEEE 802.2 (LLC3). All layers above Layer 2 are bypassed. Mini-MAP nodes sacrifice the ability to communicate as peer nodes outside the mini-MAP network for the sake of guaranteed rapid sending and acknowledgement of messages: a response time of less than 20ms can, however, be guaranteed. Enhanced Performance Architecture (EPA) consists of mini-MAP with the addition of the five upper layers of MAP; it has a dual role: it can communicate as a full node in the MAP network, but it can also take a shortcut route to a subsidiary device.

Applications envisaged for mini-MAP and EPA include intelligent sensors, such as vision systems, and devices such as barcode readers.

Manufacturing Messaging.—What has been described so far is a pipeline, down which messages and instructions can be sent and a procedure to ensure that communication can take place reliably, accurately and with minimum delay. The protocols at each layer have been selected from the range available within the OSI model to be particularly suitable to the manufacturing environment, but they do not deal specifically with the problems of communication within manufacturing with devices like PLCs and robot controllers. Cell controllers need to have two-way communications with the individual devices controlling the equipment in the cells: for reasons of efficiency, the *Manufacturing Messaging Special Application Service Element* is being developed which, while maintaining full compatibility with the backbone network, will allow faster communications at substantially less cost per station added to the network.

It is a long-term goal of the MAP specification that all of these devices should be able to participate fully in a MAP network by direct connection as *peer nodes*. It is not enough that a company supplying a DNC machining cell should provide a gateway linking its control computer to the MAP network; all the key internal cell connections linking computer, programmable controllers, machine tool controllers, etc, should also conform to the MAP specification.

If this is to be achieved, two requirements must be satisfied. One is that a streamlined communications specification must be developed to cope with situations where very fast real-time controls are essential. Work is going ahead on three such specifications. The other requirement is for a common language which is understood by all the programmable devices, allowing them to send and receive messages within the network. The FTAM service can be used for transmission of files like CNC programs, but there remains a larger number of instructions and messages which need to be coded in a manner which can be understood by the various devices involved.

The GM MAP Task Force set up a Programmable Devices Committee to develop a suitable protocol and this led to the creation of the Standard Message Format, which included facilities for reading, writing, uploading and downloading of programmable controller memory. The work was then extended to bring in contributions from control system companies and the result of this effort was the 1984 Manufacturing Message Format Standard (MMFS—pronounced 'Memphis'). This was published in the MAP 2.0 and 2.1 specifications; it defines a syntax, or standard format, for messages and a semantics—a set of standard meanings—for the components of a message. The minimum set of functions called for in the specification required that program memory—meaning an entire program or selected sub-set, such as a parameter table—should upload to a central computer system and down to a shop-floor device. It should be possible to retrieve the status, diagnostics or identification of a device. Static and dynamic programming functions should be carried out via the network, which should carry error condition reports and reports of diagnostic test results. Highly desirable additional tests proposed were remote programming of a device over a network by attaching or emulating a programming panel on the network and mimic facilities on device front panels supported on the network, either by remote panel connection or emulation on the network.

The MAP Version 2.1 specification gives in detail the syntax or message format to be used for messages between devices and the semantics or vocabulary contents of the message. The messages are expressed in a shorthand form of mnemonics and cover all the instructions and data likely to be required, not only by programmable controllers, but also by numerically controlled machines and robots. In the version 2.1 specification, it was also pointed out that the US Electronic Industry Association was working on a changed and enhanced version to be re-issued as a draft standard RS-511.

A new Manufacturing Service (MMS) is scheduled for inclusion as a SASE in Version 3.0, which is to take the place of MMFS. It has been argued that it will be so different as to be completely incompatible. Work is going on at the GM Technical Center to define an interface to MMFS which would allow a minimum set of the MMS language to communicate with it. MMS will specify the draft standard RS-511, which is more reliable and brings the protocol into line with other standards at Layer 7.

Network Support and Management Services.—An important part of the MAP specification deals with network management: this is a range of functions covering, in the MAP specification, four applications, though work at ISO level embraces a wider view of communications management. The four applications considered are configuration management (determining and controlling the state of the system); performance management (controlling and assessing the performance of the nodes and of network operation); event processing (looking for changes in the state of the system); fault management (fault diagnosis using tests automatically initiated by the network manager). Each application embraces four activities—collecting, controlling, storing and presenting information appropriate to the particular application. The specification envisages a network manager as a separate node on the network, holding the management application software and manager-agent protocol carrying out communication between them at the level of the Application Layer.

Closely associated with network management, but treated separately in the 2.1 specification, is the provision for keeping a directory of all the programs accessible to network users and the addresses needed for calling them up, held as an ASCII format database on the network. At this stage, the directory is envisaged as offering read-only access to the nodes. Keeping the directory up-to-date would be the responsibility of a knowledgeable network administrator.

MAP Products have started to come onto the market and conformance testing facilities are being set up to guarantee their adherence to the MAP specification. These are largely concerned with links between proprietary networks and are intended to avoid companies having to discard existing LANs. They do not form the basis of vendors' proprietary products, which would lead to the much more remote target of the guaranteed interworking of different vendors' products, except in a few very highly specialised application areas.

DECnet.—Digital Equipment Corporation has a networking product, DECnet, based on the Ethernet specification. This is being migrated to conform completely with the OSI standards of which MAP is a sub-set, in such a way that existing DEC networks will remain compatible. DECnet itself does not conform to the MAP specification, but DEC is planning to offer MAP products at exactly the same price as corresponding DECnet products, so that users can make their choice purely on the basis of technical merit.

MAP Conformance Testing.—With such a complex specification, it is not sufficient for a supplier to design, build and test a product and then market it as MAP-compatible. There are products already so-labelled on the market, but at present, to achieve interworking between vendors requires a high level of expertise.

Before products can be labelled as conforming to MAP, it is essential that they should not only go through the usual test and quality assurance procedures of the manufacturer, but should also be tested by an independent organisation. Besides testing products for conformance to the MAP specification, it would also be desirable to automatically guarantee interworking with other manufacturers, products—at the moment this is not at all the same thing. Because MAP is about the inter-connection of different suppliers' products, there is also a strong case for independent testing of the performance of MAP products: systems integration testing takes up where conformance testing ends. Whereas conformance testing tests the protocol implementation of one vendor's product independently, systems integration testing tests the network, all the devices interconnected across the network and the applications to ensure communication functionally and inter-operability between all the devices.

At present, another important role for conformance testing is in verifying and refining the MAP specification itself. International Standards, once finalised and published, remain fixed, but questions of interpretation remain: these it is the responsibility of organisations like the NBS implementation workshops for OSI and the MAP/TOP committees to resolve—the MAP specifications, besides indicating which parts of which standards are to be followed, contain some amplifications and interpretations which help to define the requirements more precisely.

To date, the Industrial Technology Institute (ITI), an independent US research and development organisation, is alone in having developed MAP conformance test procedures and even these are by no means complete. In West Germany, the Fraunhofer-Institut für Informations-und Datenvararbeitung (IITB) in Karlsruhe is providing the test facilities for the European Esprit CNMA project and has obtained software from ITI. It is believed that France is making similar plans. The subsequent problem which arises is that of uniformity of testing.

During the dress rehearsal for CIMAP, several of the demonstrations faced difficulties with file transfer protocols which had not been updated since Autofact 85. These protocols failed to meet the required standards of the specially set-up MAP conformance committee, which included Leeds University, the National Computing Centre and the Networking Centre—all of whom reported to EDS (the DTI is also planning to support the establishment by January of a UK conformance test centre for MAP for use by vendors and users in UK industry). One representative from the Networking Centre said that all the implementations that were on show at CIMAP had required work to get them up to the required level; of the 95 nodes connecting into the CIMAP network, less than half had been through the conformance testing suites developed by ITI.

There are signs of a move to combine testing activities for MAP and TOP, but it must be remembered that both are individual protocols within the much larger framework of OSI.

REFERENCES TO CHAPTERS H6 AND H7

(1) WARHURST, J. and VINCENT (Affiliation: Henry Cooke, Lumsden Ltd.). Communications and Information Technology Review—Computer-aided Engineering. September 1986.
(2) 1986 Software Applications Survey. Benchmark Research Ltd.
(3) Hewlett-Packard (UK) Ltd. Backgrounder: *HP's view of the ME-CAD Marketplace.*
(4) *Solid Modelling: an Emerging Technology*. Solid Modelling Today, Vol 1, No 1. May 1986. The Merritt Company (with thanks to Lucien C. Coenen Jr., Managing Director, Matra Datavision UK).
(5) FROST & SULLIVAN INC. Computer-Aided Electronics (CAEE) in the US. Report 1632.
(6) Scientific Calculation/Harris. Backgrounder: *Acquisition of Scientific Calculations Strengthens Harris' Position in CAD/CAM Market.* Autumn 1986.
(7) FROST & SULLIVAN LTD. *European CAD and Computer Graphics Systems Market in AEC (architecture, engineering, construction) and Mapping*. Report E853. Publication scheduled December 1986.
(8) CONTEXT CORPORATION. Backgrounder: *Market Trends: Electronic Technical Publishing*. September 1986.
(9) OPITZ, H. *Trends in Manufacturing Technology*, VDI-Zeitschrift, 7, May 1972.
(10) FELLOWS, J. W. (Affiliation: Cybergraph). *All about Computer-aided Design and Manufacture.* Sigma Technical Press. 1983. ISBN 0 905104 61 7.
(11) FOCUS CONFERENCE, DATAQUEST INC. *Workstations: the Evolution of an Industry*, 21 September 1984, Boston, MA, USA.
(12) DRESSLER, F. R. S. *Workstations: the Third Wave of Computing Technology*. Seybold Report on Professional Computing. Vol. 4, No. 5, 20 January 1986.
(13) IBM. IBM 6150 Micro Computer Hardware and Software Technical Literature.
(14) BURDICK, D. B. Dataquest Inc. Research Newsletter, March 1986.
(15) KROUSE ASSOCIATES. *Doing CAD on a Personal Computer/Doing CAD on a Personal Computer: A Market Study*. Technology & Business Communications. 1985. Two-volume report published in conjunction with the S Klein Newsletter on Computer Graphics. ISBN 0-914849-03-4.
(16) LAZEAR T. (Affiliation: Versacad, formerly T. & W. Systems). Private communication.
(17) SMITH, J. P. (Affiliation: ASA). *Does CAD for the Smaller Enterprise Really Mean Small CAD for the Enterprise?* Proc. Design Engineering Conference, Institution of Mechanical Engineers. September 1986, NEC, Birmingham.
(18) CONIGLIARO, L. (Affiliation: Prudential-Bache Securities Inc.). *CAD/CAM: Challenges, Hurdles and Pitfalls.* Paper of unknown origin.
(19) HARLOW, JUSTIN E. III (Affiliation: Fairchild Camera & Instrument Corporation). *What Every Engineer Should Know About Engineering Workstations*; Dekker. 1986. ISBN 0-8247-7509-0.
(20) FAIRCHILD EUROPE SEMICONDUCTOR. Backgrounder: *Clipper and the Market for the 32-bit Microprocessor.*
(21) APOLLO COMPUTER. Backgrounder: *Parallel Processing*. 30 September 1986.
(22) PRICE, R. F. *Applying Optical Mass Memory to CAD Storage.* Computer Graphics World, January 1983, pp. 79–80.
(23) FOUNDYLLER, C. M. (Affiliation: Daratech Associates). *CAD/CAM CAE: the Contemporary Technology;* Daratech/North Holland. 1984. Part 1: *The Contemporary Technology*. ISBN 0-444-86861-5. Part 2: *Evaluating Today's Systems*. ISBN 0-444-86862-3. Part 3: *Survey, Review and Buyers' Guide.* ISBN 0-444-86863-1.
(24) MEDLAND, A. J. and PIERS BURNETT (Affiliation: Brunel University). *CADCAM in Practice*; Kogan Page. 1986. ISBN 0-85038-817-1.
(25) BESANT, C. B. and LUI (Affiliation: Imperial College, University of London). *Computer-aided Design and Manufacture* (3rd edition). ISBN 0-85312-909-6.
(26) BILLET, A. (Affiliation: Radan Computational). *Cost-Effective Computerised Design and Draughting.* Proc. New Horizons in Design Office Practice. Mechanical Engineering Publications. 1986.
(27) TURNER, L. *Which Data Terminal Display?* Electronics, 17 February 1977.
(28) SHAW, D. *Towards the Flatter, Brighter Tube*. Eng. Mat. Des. September 1986, pp. 61–64.
(29) GOETSCH, D. L. *Computer-aided Drafting*. Prentice-Hall. March 1985. ISBN 13-163957-9.
(30) TEKTRONIX INFORMATION DISPLAY GROUP. Backgrounder IDG/030: *Workstation Overview and Host-based Window Management.*
(31) *Single Pass Electrostatic Colour Plotter*. Design Engineering, November 1986, p. 31.

(32) BENSON ELECTRONICS. Backgrounder: *Electrostatic vs Thermal Transfer Plotting.* 1986.
(33) TEKTRONIX INFORMATION DISPLAY GROUP. Backgrounder: *Ink-Jet Technology.* 1986.
(34) ENCARNACAO, J. *Computer-Aided Design, Modeling, and System Engineering.* Springer-Verlag, West Berlin. 1980.
(35) *BS 6390: 1983, A Set of Functions for Computer Graphics Programming, the Graphics Kernal System.* British Standards Institution, 1983.
(36) HOPGOOD, F. R. A., DUCE and GALLOP. *Introduction to the GKS.* Academic Press, New York, 1983.
(37) WOODWARK, J. (Affiliation: IBM UK Scientific Centre). *Computing Shape.* Butterworths. 1986. ISBN 0-408-01402-4.
(38) FAUX, I. D. & PRATT (Affiliation: Cranfield Institute of Technology). *Computational Geometry for Design and Manufacture.* Ellis Horwood.
(39) NICHOLS, K. W. (Affiliation: Ferranti Inforgraphics). *The Wider Benefits of Solid Modelling.* Proc. New Horizons in Design Office Practice. Mechanical Engineering Publications. 1986.
(40) SUTHERLAND, I. F., SPROULL and SCHUMACKER. *A Characterisation of Ten Hidden-Surface Algorithms.* ACM Computing Surveys, 1974, Vol 6, 1, pp. 1–55.
(41) INTERGRAPH CORPORATION: Demonstration of Interact/Interpro 32C system using NURBS.
(42) STARK, J. *What Every Engineer Should Know About Practical CAD/CAM Applications.* Dekker. 1986. ISBN 0-8247-7593-7.
(43) PYE, A. M. *3D Solid Modelling Applications and Options.* Design Engineering, July 1983, pp. 29–37.
(44) BRAID, I. C. *The Synthesis of Solids Bounded by Many Faces.* Communications of the ACM, 1975, Vol. 18, No. 4, pp. 209–16.
(45) *The Hanover Challenge.* Design Engineering, October 1983, pp. 102–105, from an original report in Finite Element News, June 1982.
(46) PARKS and CURTIS, H. *IGES Assessment; Present and Future.* CAD/CAM Management Strategies. Auerbach Publishers Inc., 1984.
(47) GE CALMA. Backgrounder: *Prism/DDM System Features Production-oriented Solids Modelling.* 23rd September 1986.
(48) LAMBOURNE, E. B. (Affiliation: Deltacam Systems). *Data Exchange in the Design and Manufacture of Automotive Components.* Design Engineering, September 1986.
(49) BRYCE, A. G. (Affiliation: Inbucon Management Consultants). *CADCAM Integration.* CME, January 1985.
(50) BLOOR, S. M. & OWEN (Affiliation: Department of Mechanical Engineering, University of Leeds). Requirements Extra to the Standard. Proc. Design Engineering Conference, Institution of Mechanical Engineers. September 1986, NEC, Birmingham.
(51) Position paper by DIN NAM 96.4.1 as a contribution to the Zurich meeting of ISO TC184/SC4/WG1, March 1986.
(52) Preliminary EDIF report, version 1.0.0. The EDIF User's Group, Design Automation Dept, Texas Instruments, PO Box 225474, MS3668, Dallas TX 75265, USA.
(53) LAZEAR, T. (Affiliation: Versacad, formerly T. & W. Systems). *Drafting by Microcomputer.* Proc. CADCON '83, January 83.
(54) HENSHELL, R. D. (Affiliation: Pafec Ltd.). *Adaptive and Boundary Techniques—the Challenges to Finite Elements.* Design Engineering, May 1986, pp. 47–52.
(55) ADEY, R. A. (Affiliation: Computational Mechanics). *Boundary or Finite? Elementary, my dear . . . .* CME, September 1985, pp. 62–64.
(56) HANIFAN, P. V. A. *Optimisation Software Speeds Design Refinements of Complex Structures.* Design Engineering, June 1986, p. 18.
(57) STOVER, R., *An Analysis of CAD/CAM Applications (with an introduction to CIM)*, Prentice-Hall, 1984 (ISBN 0-13-032871-5).
(58) REMBOLD, U., BLUME & DILLMAN (Affiliation: University of Karlsruhe), *Computer-Integrated Manufacturing Technology and Systems*, Dekker, 1985 (ISBN 0-8247-7403-5).
(59) *Electronic Data Processing for Production Planning and Control*, VDI Taschenbücher, VDI-Verlag, Düsseldorf, West Germany.
(60) SHARPE, C., *Elements for Robotic Systems*, Design Engineering May 1986, pp. 111.
(61) WARWICK UNIVERSITY ROBOT LABORATORY. *Robots in Hazardous Environments*, EEC Report and Design Engineering, March 1986, pp. 80–84.
(62) VOELLER, J. (Affiliation: Black & Veatch), *A New Approach to Computer-Aided Engineering*, from SMITH, A. (ed), *Knowledge Engineering and Computer Modelling in CAD.* Proceedings CAD 86, pp. 170–193, Butterworths, Sept 1986 (ISBN 0-408-008-245).
(63) KOCHAN, A. & COWAN, (Affiliation: (IFS Publications)), *Implementing CIM,* IFS (Publications) 1986, (ISBN 0-948507-20-9).
(64) MORTIMER, J. (ed) Affiliation: IFS (Publications)), *Just-in-Time: An Executive Briefing*, IFS (Publications), 1986 (ISBN 0-948507-38-1).
(65) TROPPER, CARL, *Local Computer Network Technologies*, Academic Press, New York, NY, 1981.
(66) FLINT, DAVID C., *The Data Ring Main: an Introduction to Local Area Networks*, Wiley, Hayden & Sons, Chichester, UK, 1983.

(67) CLIFTON, C. S. (Affiliation: Copestone), *What Every Engineer Should Know About Data Communications*, Marcel Dekker, 1987 (ISBN 0-8247-7534-1).
(68) MAINE, A. C. (Affiliation: Portsmouth Polytechnic), *Interfacing Standards for Computers* (an IEEIE Monograph), IEEIE 1986 (ISBN 0-904239-08-X).
(69) Sun Microsystems Technical Literature: *Sun-3 Architecture*, FF121/20K, Jan 1986.
(70) HOLLINGUM, J. (Affiliation: (IFS Publications)), *The MAP Report*, IFS (Publications), 1986 (ISBN 0-948507-26-8).
(71) *CIMAP: The Way Ahead*, Computer-Aided Design and Manufacture, Vol V No 4, Dec 1986, IBC Technical Services (ISSN 0263-1903).
(72) EDWARDS, G. (Affiliation: Electronic Data Systems), Backgrounder: *MAP—The First OSI Implementation*, Dec 1986.
(73) DOMENICO, A. (Affiliation: Electronic Data Systems), Backgrounder: *MAP—Guidelines for Management and Implementation*. Dec 1986.
(74) DOMENICO, A. (Affiliation: Electronic Data Systems), *Design, and the Manufacturing Automation Protocol*, Proceedings, Design Engineering Conference, Institution of Mechanical Engineers, September 1986, NEC, Birmingham.
(75) TEMPEST, R. (Affiliation: Coopers & Lybrand), *Putting CADCAM on the MAP*, CADCAM International, Oct 1986.
(76) Morgan-Grampian Corporate Marketing Department, *The Design Engineer in Britain Today*, 1983.
(77) BILLISDON, R. (Affiliation: Analysis and Design Engineering (ADE)), *Five Ways to Minimise the Risk of Buying the Wrong CAD System*, Proceedings, Design Engineering Conference, Institution of Mechanical Engineers, September 1986, NEC, Birmingham.
(78) THORNE, P. (Affiliation: CADCentre), *Hardware and Software Futures*, Proceedings, Design Engineering Conference, Institution of Mechanical Engineers, September 1986, NEC, Birmingham.
(79) WATT, J. M. (Affiliation: CADCentre), *The Design Engineering Environment in the 1990s*. Proceedings, Design Engineering Conference, Institution of Mechanical Engineers. September 1986, NEC, Birmingham.
(80) THORNTON-BRYAR, I.C.M. (Affiliation: Bryar & Gaskell Ltd), *CAD Cost Justification*, Proceedings, CADCAM First Time Seminars, EMAP Ltd, January 1985.
(81) THORNTON-BRYAR, I. C. M. (Affiliation: Bryar & Gaskell Ltd), *CAD—First Design Your Strategy*. Proceedings, Design Engineering Conference, Institute of Mechanical Engineers, September 1986, NEC, Birmingham.
(82) CREAMER, G. & OGDEN (Affiliation: Edbro Ltd), *Preparing the Ground*, CADCAM First Time Seminars, EMAP Ltd, January 1985.
(83) SIMON, M., DOWNS & LEACH (Affiliation: Manchester Polytechnic), *The Human Element in the Design Office*, Proceedings, New Horizons in Design Office Practice, Mechanical Engineering Publications, 1986.
(84) THORNTON-BRYAR, I. C. M. (Affiliation: Bryar & Gaskell Ltd), *Industrial Relations—Strategy for Success*, CAD/CAM International, Vol 4, No 2, Feb 1985.
(85) NEILL, T. (Affiliation: CAD Source Ltd), *Creating, Performing and Analysing a Benchmark Test*, Proceedings, Computer Graphics User 85, Feb 19–21, 1985.
(86) NEILL, T. (Affiliation: CAD Source Ltd), *The Complete CAD/CAM Buyers Guide*, Vol 2—Selection, CAD Source Ltd, October 1984 (ISBN 0-946740-01-1).
(87) NEILL, T. (Affilitation: CAD Source Ltd), *Benchmarking CADCAM: a Practical Guide to Testing Systems Before Purchase*. Department of Trade & Industry, 1986 (Includes video and audio cassettes).
(88) SMITH, ALISON (ed), *CAD International Directory 1986*, Butterworths, 1985 (ISSN 0010-4485/ISBN 0408 255 552/CADA5 17 (6) 256–298).
(89) PRESTON, E. J., CRAWFORD & COTICCHIA (Affiliation: Computervision, Westinghouse & Westinghouse), *CAD/CAM Dictionary*, Marcel Dekker, 1986 (ISBN 0-8247-7524-4).

SURVEYING

Chaining—Ranging—Field Book—Determination of Areas—Levelling—Instruments—Contours—Theodolite—Traverse Surveys—Triangulation—Ordnance Survey—Electromagnetic Distance Measurement—Tacheometry—Plane Table—Photographic and Aerial Survey—Curve Ranging—Earthworks—Hydrographic Survey—Field Astronomy—Latitude, Azimuth and Time Determinations—Geodesy—Bibliography.

By Professor L. A. Beaufoy, MSc(Eng), PhD, AKC, CEng, FIStructE, FRSA

Land surveying is the art of land measurement, with the object of determining its dimensions, shape and area, or finding the relative positions of distinctive features. The term usually includes levelling, ie the determination of heights of points on the earth's surface. In most cases the measurements are used to prepare a 'true-to-scale' plan or map, ie one in which every dimension on the plan is the same proportion of the corresponding dimension on the land, so that shape is preserved. Whereas a plan is a representation of a comparatively small area or strip of land to a scale large enough to show all the details required for the particular purpose of the survey, a map is a representation of a comparatively large area to a smaller scale, so that much of the details such as boundaries of individual buildings are omitted or indicated by symbols. A further distinction is that whereas a plan is normally, in all respects and in all its details, true to scale, it is usually the case that certain features in a map are enlarged for the purpose of emphasis; for instance, the widths of roads, rivers, canals, railways, etc, are often exaggerated on maps so that these important features can be more readily observed; had they been drawn to scale they would probably be hardly visible.

TYPES OF SURVEYS.—One method of classifying surveys is by the use or purpose of the resulting plan or map.

A *topographical* survey is made to determine such natural features as coastline, rivers and streams, lakes, woods, hills and valleys, etc; artificial features such as railways, roads, canals, towns and villages.

A *cadastral* or property survey determines additional details such as boundaries of fields, houses and buildings generally. *Geographical* surveys, *railway* surveys, *engineering* surveys are other types whose description defines the purpose of the survey.

ORDNANCE SURVEY SCALES AND MAPS.—These are produced to one scale or another for the whole of Great Britain. Those most commonly used are:

(*a*) *6-inch maps*. These are produced to a scale of 6 inches to 1 mile, ie 1/10,560. They exist for the whole of Great Britain and show natural and artificial features, built-up areas, but not individual buildings or property boundaries.

(*b*) 25-*inch maps*. These are shown to a scale of 1/2,500, which corresponds to a scale of 25·344 inches to 1 mile. They exist for the whole country except some waste and mountainous regions, and show the detail of ground features, including hedge and fence boundaries.

(*c*) 50-*inch maps*. These are produced to a scale of 1/1,250, ie 50·688 inches to a mile.

The above are known as 'Large-scale' Ordnance Maps. The first two are the chief national maps and are revised periodically. Other larger scale maps exist, particularly of provincial towns, but these are now obsolete.

The 'Small-scale' Ordnance Maps most frequently used are to scales of 2½″, 1″, ½″, ¼″ to 1 mile and 10 miles to an inch. They are mainly for route and location purposes.

A new metric series, at the scale 1/10,000, replaces the sheets at the six-inch scale. The 1/1,250 and 1/2,500 scales are retained, but on metric sheets.

CHAIN SURVEYING

The chain survey is suitable only for moderately small areas. The chief appliances required are the chain, ranging rods, arrows, tape, offset staff, and optical square.

(*a*) There are two principal types of chain in the British system: (i) THE 100-FOOT CHAIN, usually called the engineer's chain, because it is mainly used for engineering and municipal surveys. It consists of 100 steel links, connected at their extremities by three small oval rings, except at the centre of the chain and 25 links from each end where swivel joints are usually provided. At every 10th link is a brass tab or 'tally'; the tally which has only one prong indicates 10 links from either end of the chain, ie the 10th or 90th link; that with two prongs marks the 20th or 80th link; three prongs the 30th or 70th link; four prongs the 40th or 60th link; and a circular tab the centre of the chain, ie the 50th link. At each end of the chain is a brass handle, the overall length of 100 ft measuring from the outside of one handle to the outside of the other. As the chain is 100 ft long and there are 100 links, each link is 1 ft long. (ii) THE GUNTER'S CHAIN is similar to the 100-ft chain in construction, consisting also of 100 links, but the overall length is 66 ft, this being the statutory chain in lineal measurement. It follows that as there are 100 links in the chain of 66 ft, each link is 7·92 inches long.

METRIC CHAINS are 20 m long, and are formed of links measuring 200 mm from centre to centre of each middle connecting ring, while the first and last links are such that the linear dimension from the extremity of the handle to the centre of the middle connecting rings is also 200 mm. Tally markers of a synthetic material are attached to the middle connecting ring at every whole-metre position, those marking each 5-m position being red with raised numerals, the remainder being yellow, of a different shape, and not marked.

The two principal types of chain, in the British system, represent the standard units of measurement in survey work in that system, distances being expressed according to the nature of the survey either in chains or feet, unless these distances are exceptionally long (as in railway work) when they may be expressed in miles, furlongs and chains. It should be noted that one link of a chain is the 'statutory link' only when a Gunter's chain is being used.

To bring feet into links add one-half more; to bring links into feet take one-third less.

Areas are usually expressed in acres and decimals of an acre, or in acres and square yards, though small areas may be expressed in square feet or square yards, and exceptionally large areas in square miles. In the metric system, areas are usually expressed in hectares (1 ha = 2·47105 acres), small areas are expressed in square metres, and large areas in square kilometres.

(*b*) RANGING RODS are wooden poles 6, 8 or 10 feet long with pointed steel ends, so that they can be pushed into the ground; they have bands of colour, usually black, white and red alternately, so that they can be seen at a distance against any background, and it is an advantage to have small red or white flags attached to the tops, as anything fluttering can more easily be seen at a distance.

(*c*) STEEL ARROWS, usually in sets of ten, for marking the ends of each chain length.

(*d*) TAPES are of steel or synthetic material, generally 33, 50, 66 or 100 feet in length, graduated in feet and inches on one side and links on the reverse. Metric tapes are 10, 25, or 30 m in length, with sub-divisions at 10 mm intervals.

(*e*) OFFSET STAFF, used in conjunction with a Gunter's chain only, is similar to a ranging rod, the bands of alternate colours being in lengths of 1 link. The offset staff is an alternative to the use of a tape.

(*f*) OPTICAL SQUARE.—This is a small instrument varying in construction according to the maker. A normal type consists of a cylindrical box about two inches in diameter, fitted with two mirrors at right angles to the plane of the instrument, so arranged that the apparent view of a ranging rod or other object at right angles to a chain line at a particular point coincides with the view of one of the ranging rods marking the chain line. This enables points and features at right angles to a chain line to be located. A pentagonal prism is increasingly used today in place of the mirror-type instrument.

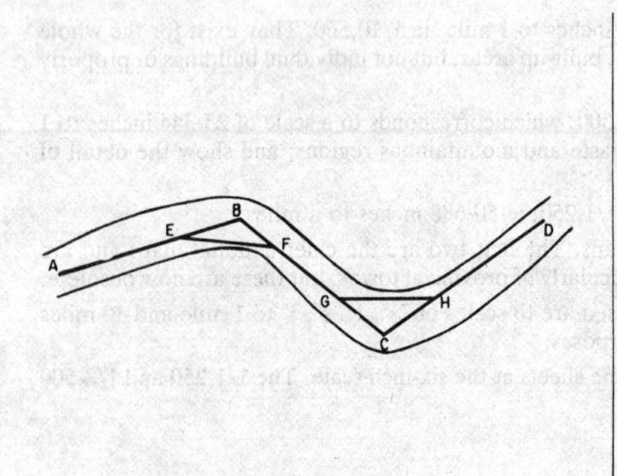

FIG. 1.

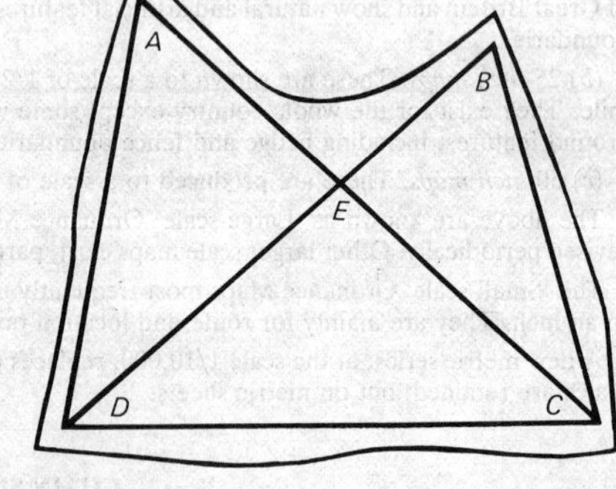

FIG. 2.

PRINCIPLES OF CHAIN SURVEYING.—The basis of a chain survey is the provision of a skeleton framework of straight lines covering the area or strip of ground to be surveyed. The lines must be capable of being measured and subsequently drawn to scale. The ends of the survey lines or chain lines, ie the points of the framework, are known as 'stations', and although the selection of positions for these must necessarily be governed by the nature of the particular ground being surveyed, the following broad principles apply:

(*a*) The stations should be clearly visible from each other and should not be located in marshy ground, in hollows, or surrounded by trees or shrubs.

(*b*) The framework joining the stations should be capable of being 'plotted', ie drawn to scale, from the measurements taken in the field. A sufficient number of measurements must therefore be taken to ensure that this can be done. For example, in a quadrilateral the measurement of the four sides only would not be sufficient and the measurement of at least one of the diagonals would be necessary.

(*c*) From (*b*) it will be seen that the framework of chain lines for the survey of an area of ground should be composed of a series of triangles. These triangles should be 'well-proportioned', ie approaching an equilateral triangle as nearly as possible. A simple rule is that no angle should be less than 30°.

(*d*) The framework should if possible contain at least one long chain line as a base on which the remainder can be constructed.

(*e*) A few extra lines should be measured to act as a check on the main measurements.

(*f*) The survey lines should preferably run close to the boundaries and hedges of the area to be surveyed, to minimise the work involved in taking offsets.

Where a strip of country is being surveyed, a single chain line or a series of lines as in Fig. 1 would be all that is necessary. Figures 2 and 3 show typical frameworks composed of well-proportioned triangles to suit the particular areas being surveyed.

RANGING A LINE OVER A HILL.—Sometimes it is necessary to range a line between two stations hidden from each other by an intervening hillock. Suppose *A* and *B* (Fig. 4) represent two such stations and it is required to range and chain the line *AB*. Two persons, each with a ranging rod, take up intermediate positions at *C* and *D*, selected so that *A* can be seen from *D* and *B* from *C*. The points *C* and *D* should be roughly on the line *AB* as nearly as can be judged. The rod at *C* is then directed into the line *AD* by the person at *D*, and the rod at *D* into the line *CB* by the person at *C* to give new positions C_1 and D_1. These will be nearer to the line *AB* but not exactly on it. The process is repeated to fix new positions C_2 and D_2 and after two or three trials the rods at *C* and *D* are in the same straight line *AB* which can then be chained.

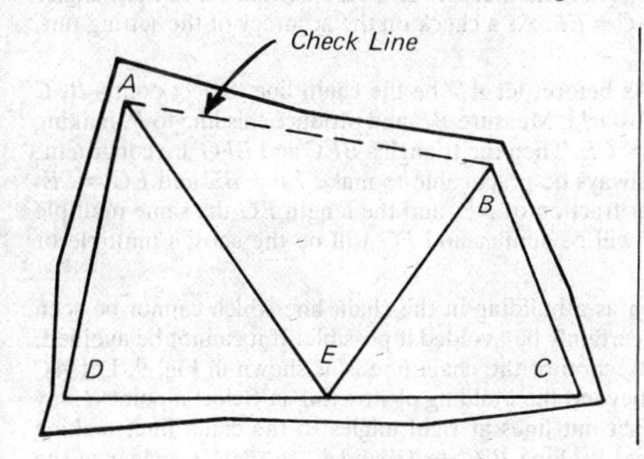

FIG. 3.

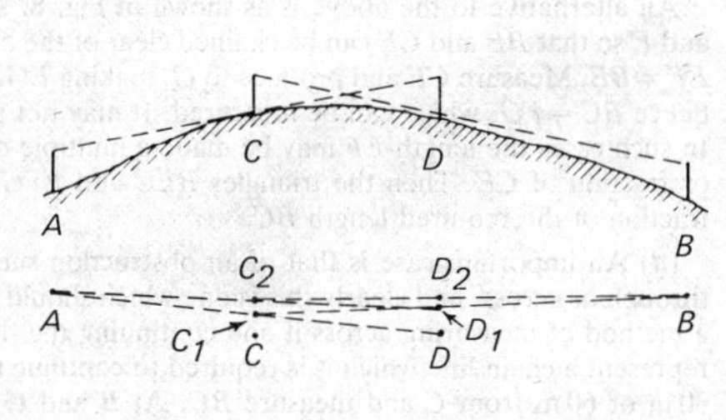

FIG. 4.

Obstructions.—(*a*) Let *DA* (Fig. 5) be the direction of a line which has been measured up to the river. It is required to ascertain the distance *BA*, so as to continue the measurement of the line. On the line *DA* take any point, *B*, whence a perpendicular, *BC*, can be set out, which will be free from obstruction, so that *BC* can be accurately measured; carry the range on across the river, and at *A* set up a flag; on *BC* take any point, *C*, whence *A* can be seen; and at *C* set out perpendicular to *AC*, intersecting the line *AD* at *D*. Measure *DB*; then:

$$AB = (BC)^2/BD.$$

The angles can either be set out by a cross-staff or by the chain, with the distances of 3 m, 4 m, and 5 m; 5 being the hypotenuse of a right-angled triangle when the base and perpendicular are respectively 3 and 4.

(*b*) Let *AO* (Fig. 6) be the distance required. From *A* set out *AB* at any angle to *AO*. Produce *OA* to *C*, making *AC* about one-third length of *AB*; from *C* set out *CD*, parallel to *AB*, *OBD* being in one straight line. To make *CD* parallel to *AB*, at *A* and *B* erect equal perpendiculars, which can be done either by a cross-staff or by means of the 3–4–5 triangle. Then:

$$AO = (AB.CA)/(CD - AB).$$

If the perpendicular distance *OF* be required, then this can be obtained from:

$$OF = FE\ (OA/AC).$$

(*c*) Let *AD* (Fig. 7) be the chain line. At any point *B* near the edge of the pond set out *BE* at right angles to *AD*, making *BE* of sufficient length to clear the obstacle. At *E* set out another line *EF* at right angles to

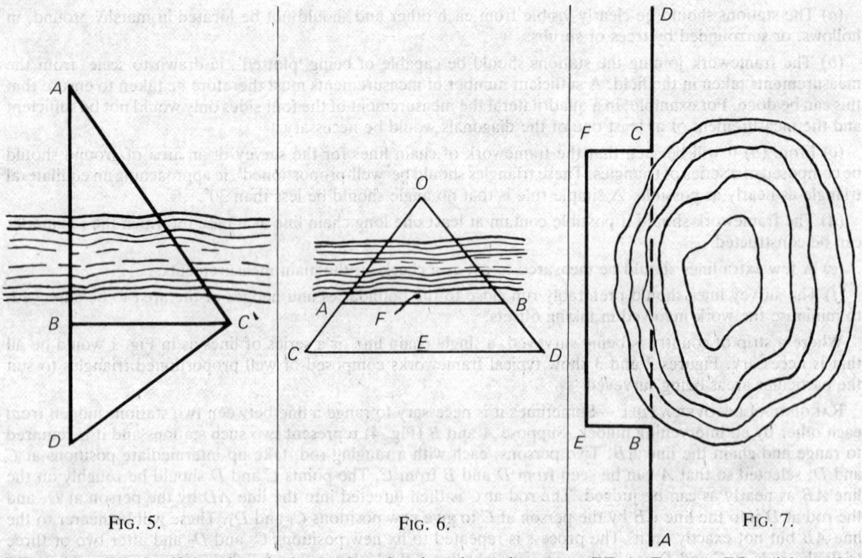

FIG. 5. FIG. 6. FIG. 7.

BE, making EF of sufficient length also to clear the obstacle, and measure EF. At F set out FC at right angles to EF, making $FC = BE$. Then the required distance $BC = EF$. As a check on the accuracy of the setting-out, A and B, C and D should be in line.

An alternative to the above is as shown in Fig. 8. As before, let AD be the chain line. Select points B, C and E so that BE and CE can be chained clear of the obstacle. Measure BE and produce this line to F, making $EF = BE$. Measure CE and produce to G, making $EG = CE$. Then the triangles BEC and EFG are congruent; hence $BC = FG$, which can be measured. It may not always be practicable to make $EF = BE$ and $EG = CE$. In such cases the length EF may be made a multiple or fraction of BE, and the length EG the same multiple or fraction of CE. Then the triangles BEC and EFG will be similar and FG will be the chosen multiple or fraction of the required length BC.

(*d*) An important case is that of an obstruction such as a building in the chain line which cannot be seen through or across, and clearly this is one which should certainly be avoided if possible. If it cannot be avoided, a method of measuring across it and continuing the direction of the chain line is as shown in Fig. 9. Let AC represent a chain line which it is required to continue beyond the building obstructing it. Select a point B, say 30 m or 60 m from C and measure BC. At B and C set out lines at right angles to the chain line, making $BB' = CC'$ and of sufficient length to clear the building. Prolong $B'C'$ to D' and E' so that D is clear of the building and $D'E'$ is a convenient length as before. At D' and E' set out lines $D'D$ and $E'E$ at right angles to $D'E'$ making $D'D = E'E$ and equal to BB' and CC'. Then the required length CD equals the measured length $C'D'$ and DE gives the direction in which the chain line AC should continue.

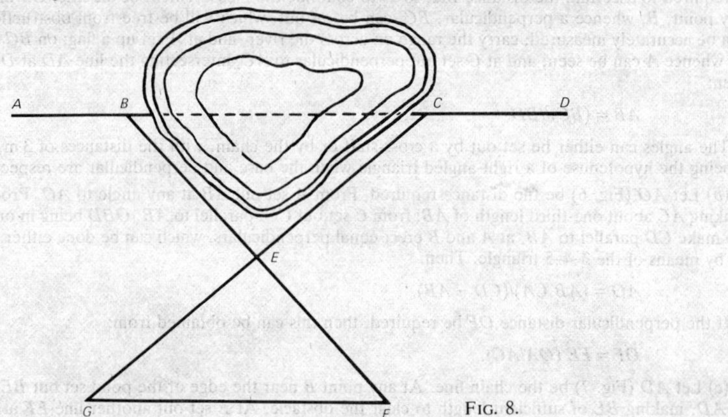

FIG. 8.

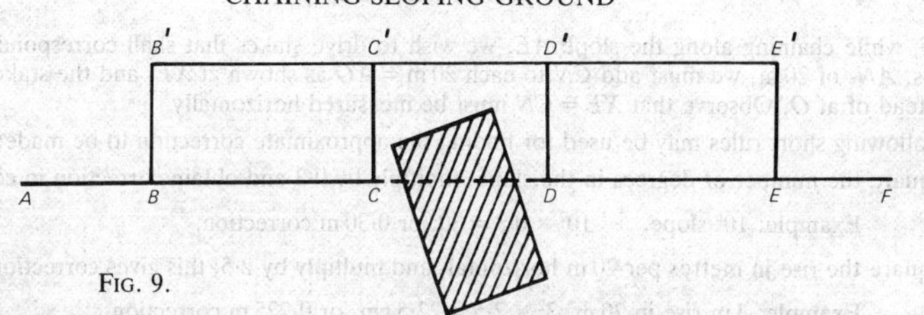

FIG. 9.

Sloping Ground.—All measurements must be taken in a horizontal plane, or reduced to their horizontal equivalent. Where the ground has a considerable slope in the direction of measurement, distances measured directly on the slope would obviously be too long. The following two alternative methods of correction may therefore be employed:

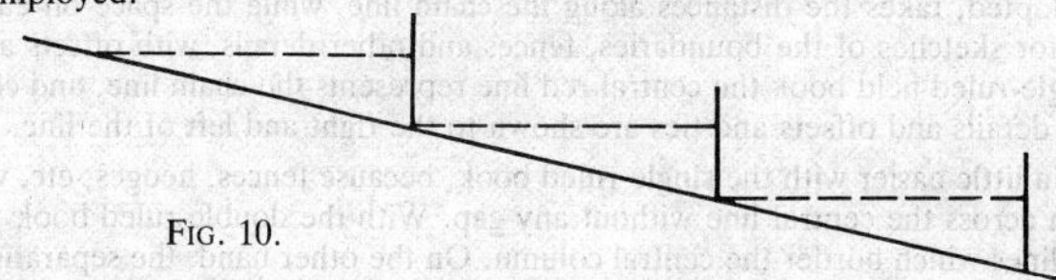

FIG. 10.

(1) By 'stepping' the chain (Fig. 10). Depending on the slope of the ground, a suitable length of 'step' is selected, say ½-chain, and each ½-chain length is measured horizontally holding a plumb bob to mark the end of each 'step'.

(2) By measuring along the surface in the ordinary way, obtaining the angle of slope by an clinometer, and making a correction for the difference between sloping and horizontal measurements by the use of trigonometrical ratios or a table of allowances composed for the purpose (Table 1). This method is useful when the slope is uniform for a long distance. In Fig. 11 each 20 m AO measured up or down the slope AE corresponds to the shorter horizontal distance, AC, which is AO multiplied by the cosine of the angle of slope. This distance, AC, taken from AO, gives the deduction CN of Table 1.

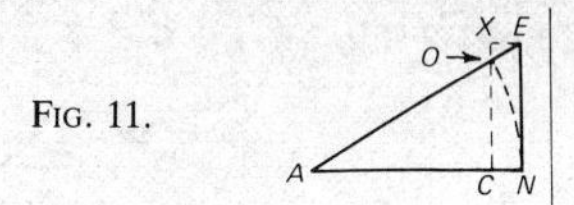

FIG. 11.

TABLE 1.—DEDUCTIONS OR ADDITIONS TO BE MADE PER 20 METRES IN CHAINING OVER SLOPING GROUND.

Slope in Deg	Deduct or add m	Rise in 20 m Hor	Slope in Deg	Deduct or add m	Rise in 20 m Hor	Slope in Deg	Deduct or add m	Rise in 20 m Hor	Slope in Deg	Deduct or add m	Rise in 20 m Hor
¼	0·00	0·087	5¼	0·08	1·838	10¼	0·32	3·616	15¼	0·70	5·452
½	0·00	0·175	½	0·09	1·926	½	0·34	3·706	½	0·73	5·546
¾	0·00	0·262	¾	0·10	2·014	¾	0·35	3·798	¾	0·75	5·640
1	0·00	0·349	6	0·11	2·102	11	0·37	3·888	16	0·77	5·734
¼	0·00	0·438	¼	0·12	2·190	¼	0·38	3·978	¼	0·80	5·830
½	0·01	0·524	½	0·13	2·278	½	0·40	4·070	½	0·82	5·924
¾	0·01	0·611	¾	0·14	2·368	¾	0·42	4·160	¾	0·85	6·020
2	0·01	0·698	7	0·15	2·456	12	0·44	4·252	17	0·87	6·114
¼	0·02	0·786	¼	0·16	2·544	¼	0·46	4·342	¼	0·90	6·210
½	0·02	0·873	½	0·17	2·634	½	0·47	4·434	½	0·93	6·306
¾	0·02	0·961	¾	0·18	2·722	¾	0·49	4·526	¾	0·95	6·402
3	0·03	1·048	8	0·19	2·810	13	0·51	4·618	18	0·98	6·498
¼	0·03	1·136	¼	0·21	2·900	¼	0·53	4·710	¼	1·01	6·596
½	0·04	1·223	½	0·22	2·990	½	0·55	4·802	½	1·03	6·692
¾	0·04	1·311	¾	0·23	3·078	¾	0·57	4·894	¾	1·06	6·790
4	0·05	1·399	9	0·25	3·168	14	0·59	4·986	19	1·09	6·886
¼	0·05	1·486	¼	0·26	3·258	¼	0·62	5·080	¼	1·12	6·984
½	0·06	1·574	½	0·27	3·346	½	0·64	5·172	½	1·15	7·082
¾	0·07	1·662	¾	0·29	3·436	¾	0·66	5·266	¾	1·18	7·180
5	0·08	1·750	10	0·30	3·526	15	0·68	5·358	20	1·21	7·280

But if, while chaining along the slope AE, we wish to drive stakes that shall correspond with horizontal distances, AN, of 20 m, we must add CN to each 20 m = AO as shown at XE, and the stake must be driven at E instead of at O. Observe that $XE = CN$ must be measured horizontally.

The following short rules may be used for finding the approximate correction to be made:

(*a*) Square the number of degrees in the slope, multiply by 0·3 and obtain correction in centimetres.

Example: 10° slope. $10^2 \times 0{\cdot}3 = 30$, or 0·30 m correction.

(*b*) Square the rise in metres per 20 m horizontal, and multiply by 2·5; this gives correction in centimetres.

Example: 3 m rise in 20 m. $3^2 \times 2{\cdot}5 = 22{\cdot}5$ cm, or 0·225 m correction.

The Field Book.—The field book generally used for chain surveying opens endwise, like a reporters notebook, and has pages about 18 cm long and 12 cm wide. Usually there is a column 2 cm wide, ruled in red, down the centre of the page, though in some books this column is replaced by a single red line. The central column, when this method is adopted, takes the distances along the chain line, while the space on each side (about 5 cm wide) is reserved for sketches of the boundaries, fences and other details, with offsets and ties figured beside them. In the single-ruled field book the central red line represents the chain line, and chainage figures are written on it, while details and offsets and ties are shown to the right and left of the line.

Sketching of detail is a little easier with the single-ruled book, because fences, hedges, etc, which cross the chain line can be drawn across the central line without any gap. With the double-ruled book they should be brought only up to the lines which border the central column. On the other hand, the separation of distances on the chain line from other dimensions, by placing them in a central column, makes the double-ruled book easier to follow.

In Fig. 12 are shown entries in the field book for three lines of a survey. For two of these lines double-ruling is used and for the other line single-ruling. The figure relates to a survey made in metres.

The following notes explain how the field book should be used:

(1) Open the book to what in other books would be regarded as the last page, begin at the bottom of the page and work upwards. The reason for this procedure is that, when the surveyor is facing in the direction in which he is chaining, details which are on the left of the chain can be sketched on the left side in his book and those which are on the right side of the chain can be shown on the right. The first entry will be the title of the estate, or description of the land, and the date. A line is drawn across the page above this description.

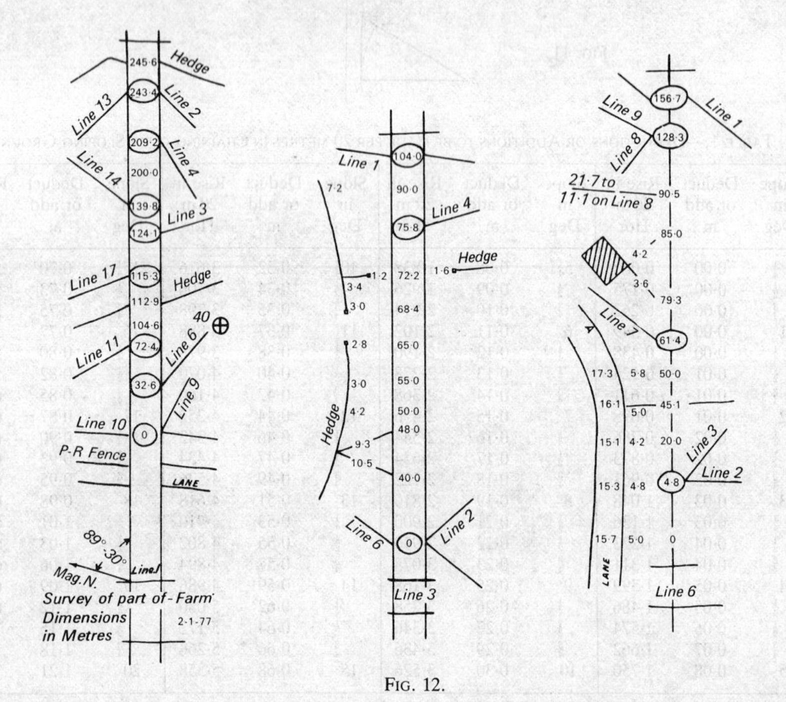

FIG. 12.

(2) The next entry will be a sketch plan, to form a 'key' to the survey, and on which the order of chaining the lines will be shown.

(3) State whether dimensions are in feet, links or metres.

(4) Having decided which line is to be chained first, enter in the central column 'Line 1', and show the direction of 'bearing' of the line; ie the angle which it makes with magnetic north. This angle is usually taken with a prismatic compass.

(5) The booking of the measurements along Line 1 and the offsets and ties from it can now commence. If a Gunter's chain is employed it is usual to record (say) 137, the distance in links, rather than 1·37, the distance in chains; similarly with an engineer's chain, distances are recorded in feet. With a metric chain, chainages are noted in metres and decimals of a metre. The various features, such as fences, hedges and buildings, will be sketched as they occur. Only chain readings will be entered in the central column, offset distances being figured close beside the objects to which they are taken. The starting point of the chain line is marked 00, or simply 0.

(6) Wherever a station point is reached, a ring should be drawn around the distance figure in the central column to indicate that it is such. From this ring the approximate direction of any other survey line which runs to or from this station should be shown by a short line, and the number or letters written against it.

(7) Having reached the end of a survey line, draw a single line over the last figures in the central column and then after a short gap commence the next line; there is no need to begin this on a new page. Proceed with all the survey lines in the same way, and at the end of the last line draw a double line across the column.

Magnetic Declination of the Compass.—The longitudinal axis of a compass needle points towards magnetic north along the magnetic meridian. In surveying, however, maps and plans are oriented in relation to the geographical north, ie the north pole, and it is the direction of 'true north' which should be shown on the plan as a 'north point'.

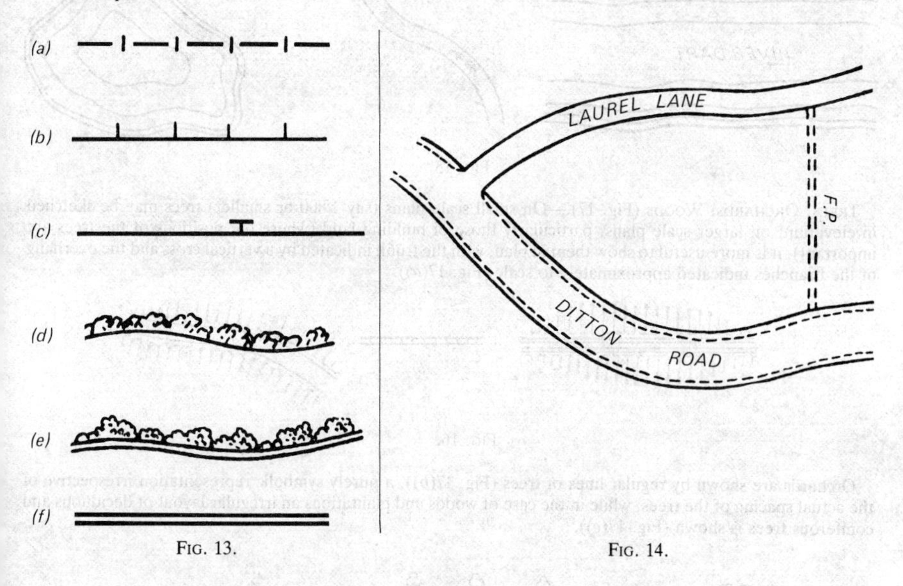

FIG. 13. FIG. 14.

At the present time (1977) the needle at Greenwich points about 6° 30′ to the west of true north, but this angle is decreasing at the rate of 6′·5 per annum. This angle between true and magnetic north at any time and place is known as the 'magnetic declination'. Its amount differs not only from time to time, but also (to a much greater extent) from place to place. In this country it increases as one travels west or north; very rough values may be found by increasing 28′ for each degree of longitude, W, and increasing 18′ for each degree of latitude, N.; but local variations are considerable. Thus, on a line passing through Scilly Isles, Anglesey and Edinburgh magnetic declination is about 3° more than at Greenwich.

In taking the direction of a line in the field it is the magnetic bearing which is booked; the allowance for declination is made when plotting the north point.

Conventional Signs on Plans and Maps.—Certain recognised methods of showing natural and artificial features on plans and maps are adopted, some of the more important being the following:

BOUNDARIES.—Boundaries of every sort are shown by single firm lines, if they are well defined, or by dotted lines if there is no definite line of demarcation on the site. Where, however, it is necessary to specify a particular type of fence, special symbols are employed, as shown in Fig. 13 which illustrates the following:

(*a*) Post and rail fence; (*b*) Close-paled fence. In such fences the posts are placed on the land of the owner of the fence and are shown on that side of the plan; (*c*) Fence of unspecified type. The small 'T' is placed at intervals on the side which belongs to the owner of the fence; (*d*) Quick set hedge; (*e*) Hedge and ditch; (*f*) Brick walls, but these should be shown by a single line if the scale of the plan is small.

ROADS, LANES, FOOTPATHS (Fig. 14).—Roads generally are shown by two full lines plotted to the overall width of the road. Main roads with kerbs and footways would be shown on large scale plans as illustrated. Footpaths are as shown, with the letters FP. Unmade roads and bridle paths are indicated by dotted lines. In all cases where dotted lines are shown on plans, the strokes should be of equal length as nearly as practicable, with equal spaces between.

RIVERS, STREAMS AND PONDS (Fig. 15).—Lines are drawn parallel to the banks of the river or pond, the spacing between the lines increasing with distance from the bank. In rivers and streams, the direction of flow is shown.

RAILWAYS, CANALS, CUTTINGS AND EMBANKMENTS (Fig. 16).—Railways are drawn to scale on large scale plans as in (*a*) which shows a railway in cutting. The symbol (*b*) would be shown on small scale plans and maps, and if the scale is very small a single black or blue line would be used. The thick part of the wavy lines in cuttings and embankments is always at the top of the slope, eg a road on embankment would have the thick part close to the road edge whereas in a cutting it would be remote from the road. Figure 16(*c*) shows a canal or embankment.

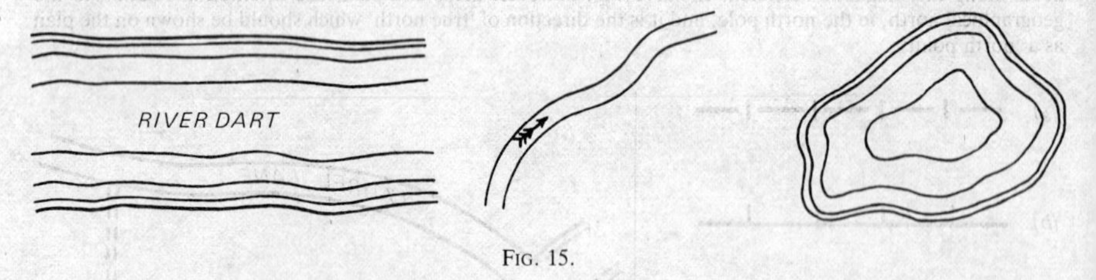

FIG. 15.

TREES, ORCHARDS, WOODS (Fig. 17).—On small scale plans (say 1/800 or smaller) trees may be sketched in elevation; on larger scale plans, particularly those of building land (where the positions of the trees are important), it is more useful to show them in plan, with the trunk indicated by a vertical cross and the overhang of the branches indicated approximately to scale (Fig. 17(*a*)).

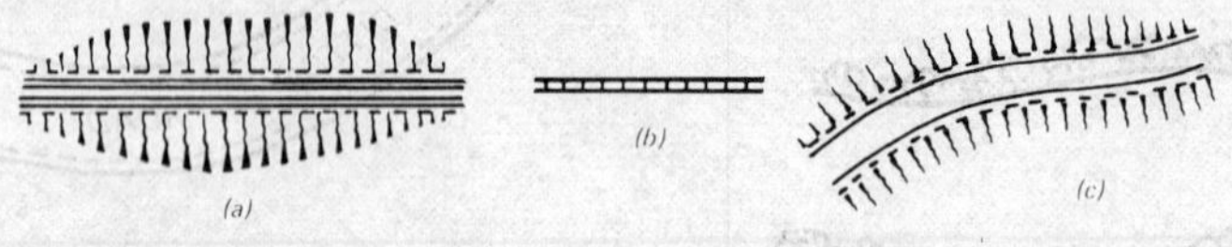

FIG. 16.

Orchards are shown by regular lines of trees (Fig. 17(*b*)), a purely symbolic representation irrespective of the actual spacing of the trees, while in the case of woods and plantations an irregular layout of deciduous and coniferous trees is shown (Fig. 17(*c*)).

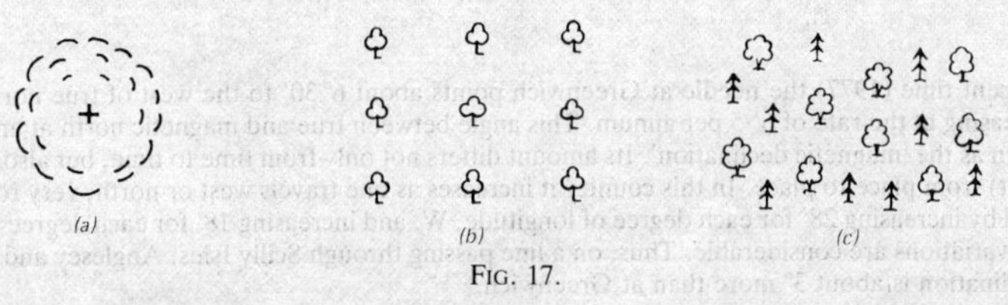

FIG. 17.

MARSHY GROUND (*a*); REEDS (*b*); OSIERS (*c*); AND ROUGH PASTURE (*d*); (Fig. 18).—An irregular spacing of the particular symbols is shown over the whole area.

GATES (*a*); AND STILES (*b*); (Fig. 19).—On large-scale plans the posts and gate width would be drawn to scale.

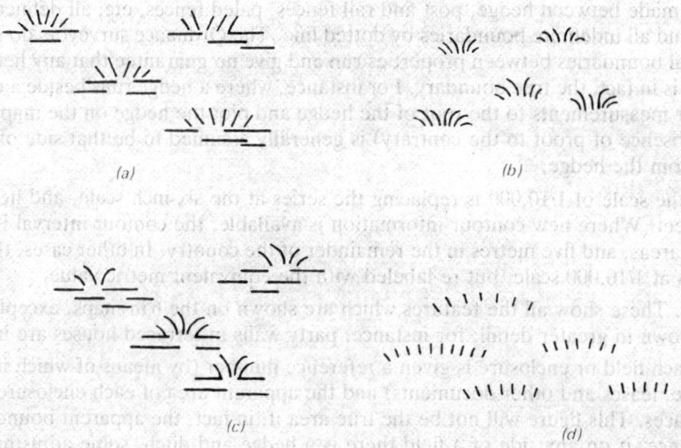

(a) (b)

(c) (d)

FIG. 18.

QUARRIES AND PITS (Fig. 20).—Although a symbolic representation is shown, the area covered on plan should conform closely to the outline and extent of the quarry or pit surveyed.

BRIDGES AND LOCKS (Fig. 21).—The same remarks apply as for quarries and pits. Figure 21(*a*) shows a bridge over a river and Fig. 21(*b*) a lock.

BUILDINGS are shown with a heavy outline, or cross-hatched. Telegraph poles, electric pylons, signposts, letter boxes, are all represented by a small circle with the letters TP, EP, SP, LB respectively, against them.

Fire hydrants, stop valves, manholes, are represented by small squares or rectangles, with the letters FH, SV, MH against them, although round cover manholes would be shown by a small circle.

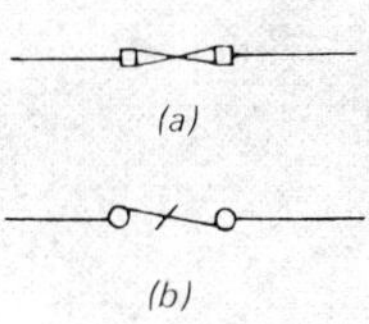

(a) (b)

FIG. 19.

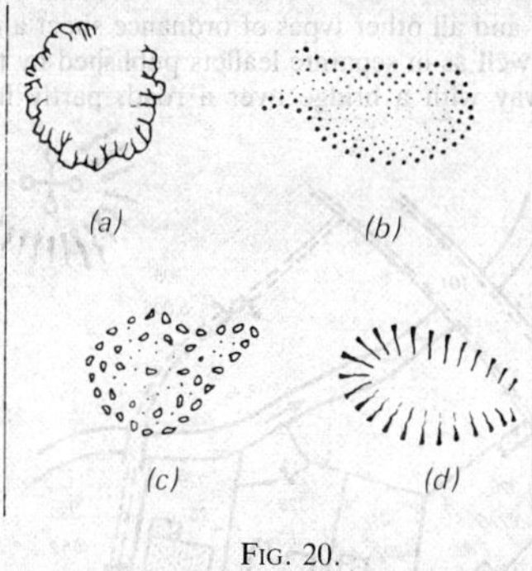

(a) (b) (c) (d)

FIG. 20.

(a) (b)

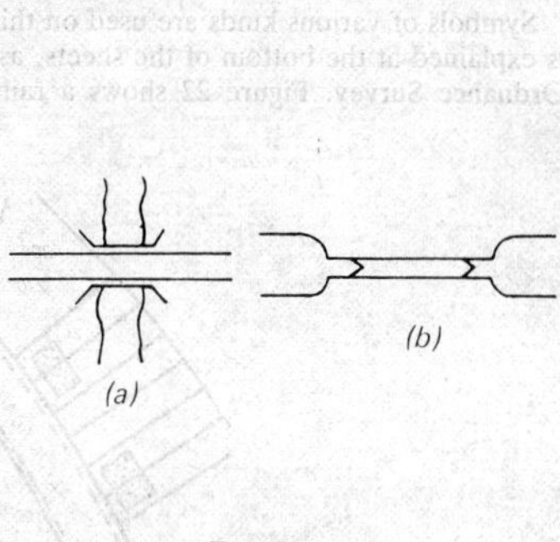

FIG. 21.

The above is not exhaustive, but covers the more common features on plans and maps and gives an indication of how similar items should be dealt with. The conventional signs and details shown on the two principal series of Ordnance Maps are as follows:

(*a*) Six inches to a mile. All buildings, roads, footpaths, enclosures, fences, field boundaries and waterways are shown, except in the close detail of towns, where they would be illegible. Minor details of individual buildings are necessarily omitted, and the divisions between houses are not shown where these are built in continuous terraces. Features such as woods, rough pasture, rocks, cliffs, and foreshore are shown by symbols. The direction of flow of streams is shown by arrows. Street names in towns are printed. Everything is as far as possible true to scale, except that in towns street widths are often increased to give room for the street names.

Contour lines are drawn in red at heights of 50 ft, 100 ft, 200 ft, and every succeeding 100 ft up to 1,000 ft above sea level. 'Spot levels', ie heights above sea level, are figured at intervals along the roads, the spot at which the level was taken being marked by a small cross; they occur chiefly at the tops and bottoms of hills and at road intersections. There is nothing on the site to mark the position of these spots, and they can therefore be located only approximately. At places on each sheet there will be found figures such as 'BM 113·1,' with an arrowhead close by. This indicates that the ordnance surveyors have cut marks (called 'bench marks') on some permanent structure at the place where the arrow is situated, at a level above sea of 113·1 ft or whatever the printed figure may be; these marks can be found on the structure and are useful as a starting point for levelling operations.

No distinction is made between hedge, post and rail fences, paled fences, etc, all defined boundaries being shown by full line and all indefinite boundaries by dotted line. The Ordnance surveyors do not make enquiries as to where the legal boundaries between properties run and give no guarantee that any hedge, fence or other apparent boundary is in fact, the true boundary. For instance, where a hedge runs beside a ditch the Ordnance surveyors take their measurements to the root of the hedge and plot the hedge on the map, although the true boundary (in the absence of proof to the contrary) is generally assumed to be that side of the ditch which is the more remote from the hedge.

A new series at the scale of 1/10,000 is replacing the series at the six-inch scale, and heights are shown in metres instead of feet. Where new contour information is available, the contour interval is ten metres in the more mountainous areas, and five metres in the remainder of the country. In other cases, the existing interval is retained on maps at 1/10,000 scale, but re-labeled with the equivalent metric value.

(*b*) 1/2,500 Maps. These show all the features which are shown on the 6 in maps, except the contour lines. The features are shown in greater detail; for instance, party walls in terraced houses are indicated.

On these plans each field or enclosure is given a reference number (by means of which it may be described in particulars of sale, leases and other documents) and the apparent area of each enclosure is figured in acres to three decimal places. This figure will not be the true area if, in fact, the apparent boundary is not the true boundary; for instance, if on any side of a field there is a hedge and ditch, some adjustment must be made to the area given on the map, because this will have been taken to the root of the hedge, whereas the real boundary is usually at the other side of the ditch.

Roads, railways, rivers, etc, as well as fields, are given numbers and the area occupied by each within the sheet is figured. Heights are shown in metres instead of feet on new revised maps at this scale. It is also proposed to show areas of parcels of land in hectares to the nearest 0·001 hectare: also, for an interim period, to retain the value in acres, to the nearest 0·01 acre.

Where an enclosure is very small, and in particular where it has resulted from the subdivision of a field by the erection of a fence, it is common for two or more enclosures to be included in one reference number and area. In this case they are bracketed together on the map by links; examples of this will be seen in Enclosures Nos. 305, 326 and 328 in Fig. 22 which depicts a typical piece of land on a 1/2,500 Ordnance sheet.

Symbols of various kinds are used on this and all other types of ordnance sheet and the meaning of these is explained at the bottom of the sheets, as well as in separate leaflets published by the Director-General of Ordnance Survey. Figure 22 shows a railway with a bridge over a road, partly in cutting and partly in

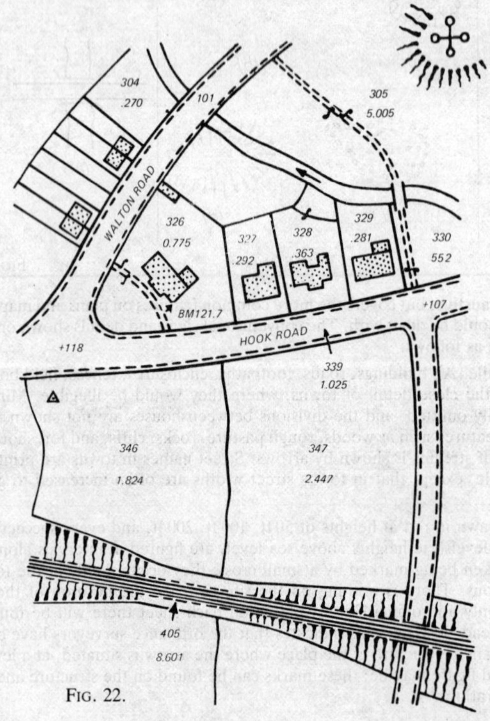

FIG. 22.

embankment; a stream with a footpath crossing over it; a site of antiquarian interest on a mound in Field 305; a trigonometrical station of the Ordnance Survey, marked by a triangle, in field 346.

Colouring of Plans.—It is often desired, for display to a client for example, that plans of estates of proposed development areas should be coloured. An important principle is that any colouring shall be in a very pale wash only; a well-executed survey and plan can be gravely spoiled by heavy and uneven colouring. There is no precise scheme to be followed, but certain conventions are usual. Grassland and arable land generally are coloured with a pale wash of Hooker's green, with a slightly darker shade on trees, hedges and bushes. Roads and footpaths are in burnt sienna; rivers, streams, ponds, etc, in pale blue; buildings in slate. If a plan is to be coloured, the wash should be laid over the whole extent of the area, though it is sometimes suggested that a border of colour around a particular area is sufficient.

DETERMINATION OF AREAS OF LAND.—The calculation of the areas of common figures is the subject of mensuration, but there are some special considerations which apply in the determination of areas of land. In many cases the method which can most conveniently be adopted will depend upon whether the measurements are to be taken from dimensions scaled off a plan or obtained by means of a chain or tape on the site. Where it is convenient, there are advantages in calculating the area from the site measurements, for the inaccuracies which may occur in plotting a plan and the further inaccuracies which may occur in scaling dimensions from the plan are eliminated.

In some cases the method will be to calculate part of the area from the site dimensions and the remainder from scaled dimensions. Where the area required is bounded by straight lines, such as would be enclosed by the main framework of survey lines in a chain survey, the area may be divided into a number of triangles and the area of each found as follows:

(1) AREA OF A TRIANGLE. If the dimensions are to be taken from a plan, draw a perpendicular from one of the angles to the opposite side (called the 'base'). Then the area is obtained by multiplying the base by the perpendicular and dividing by two. This would not be a convenient method if the measurements are to be obtained from the site, or if site measurements are used so as to avoid errors of plotting and scaling, because it is not easy to set out a long perpendicular from a given point to a given line accurately on the site. In this case, measure the three sides of the triangle and use the formula:

$$\text{Area} = \sqrt{[s(s-a)(s-b)(s-c)]}$$

where a, b and c are the lengths of the three sides and s is half their sum.

(2) AREA OF TRAPEZOID (ie a four-sided figure having two of its sides parallel). Multiply the sum of the two parallel sides by the perpendicular distance between them and divide by two.

Thus in Fig. 23, area $= \frac{1}{2}(BC + AD) \times EF$.

Building plots are often trapezoidal, but the chief application of this rule is in the determination of the area of a strip of land between a chain line and a boundary fence.

(3) AREA OF A QUADRILATERAL (Fig. 24). If the area of $ABCD$ is to be obtained from a plan, join two opposite corners and draw from the other two corners perpendiculars to the line so formed. Thus, for example, join AC and draw perpendiculars DF and BE to it.

Then since area $ACD = AC \times \frac{1}{2}DF$, and area $ABC = AC \times \frac{1}{2}BE$, area $ABCD = AC \times \frac{1}{2}(BE + DF)$.

This would not be a convenient method if the measurements are to be obtained on the site, because of the difficulty of setting out the perpendiculars from B and D. In this case measure the four sides of the quadrilateral and the diagonal AC; the areas of the two triangles can then be found separately (as in (1) above), as the lengths of the three sides of each of them are known.

(4) AREA OF ANY POLYGON. Divide the polygon up into triangles by joining one of its corners to all the other corners (Fig. 25, in which C is joined to A and E).

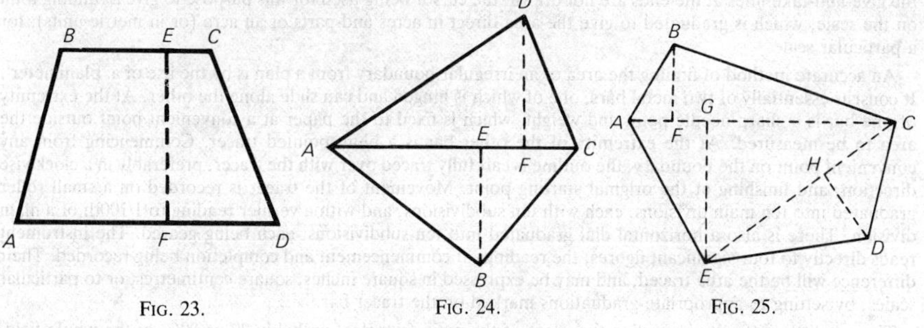

FIG. 23. FIG. 24. FIG. 25.

If working from a plan, draw BF and EG perpendicular to AC, and DH perpendicular to CE. Then area $ABCE = AC \times \frac{1}{2}(BF + GE)$ and area $ECD = EC \times \frac{1}{2}DH$. The sum of these two areas gives the whole area.

If working from field measurements, measure the lengths of all the sides and the diagonals *CA* and *CE* and calculate the area of each of the triangles *ABC*, *ACE*, *ECD* from the formula

$$\text{Area} = \sqrt{[s(s-a)(s-b)(s-c)]}.$$

Areas of Figures with Irregular Boundaries.—It will be seen from the above that any area bounded by straight lines can be found by dividing it into triangles, and this is the method used to find the area enclosed by a framework of survey lines in a chain survey. This area, however, will not be the total area contained within the irregular boundaries such as fences, hedges, etc, and several methods are available where the total area is to be obtained: (*a*) from a plan; (*b*) from site measurements; (*c*) partly from site measurements and partly from a plan.

When areas are to be taken from a plan, 'give-and-take' lines may be used. These are straight lines which follow the boundaries very closely, such that an irregular polygon of straight lines is formed having an area equal to that bounded by the true boundaries. Figure 26 shows give-and-take lines (in broken lines) for the field shown by full lines. By their use, the figure of irregular outline has been replaced by one bounded by five straight lines (which can be dealt with as in Fig. 25). Care must be taken in using this method which, however, is quick and reasonably accurate.

A rough method of finding the area bounded by an irregular boundary, which has been plotted, is by the 'method of squares'. The area is divided up into squares of equal size (Fig. 27), the length of side of each square being chosen according to the scale of the plan, eg if the scale is 1/800, squares with sides of 25 mm would be convenient as each would represent an area of 1 square chain, ie 400 m². The squares are then counted, portions of whole squares being aggregated as closely as practicable. Ths smaller the size of square, the greater is the accuracy likely to be achieved, but in any event the method is only used to give approximate results or as a check on other methods.

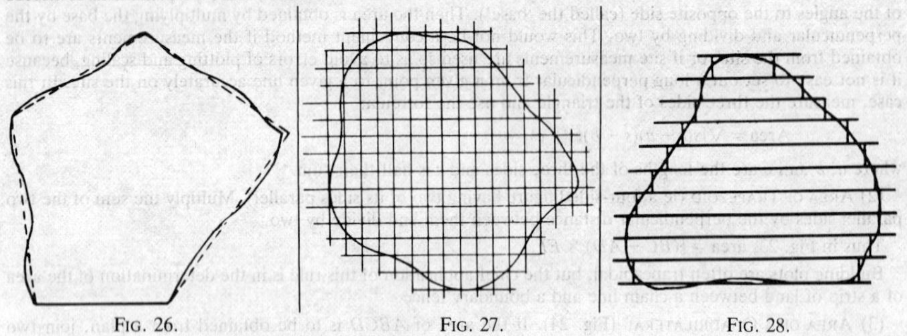

FIG. 26. FIG. 27. FIG. 28.

A method sometimes employed to find areas with irregular boundaries is to divide the area into parallel strips of equal width, the width being chosen according to the scale (Fig. 28). Perpendicular give-and-take lines are then set out at the ends of each strip and the new mean length scaled off. The sum of all the mean lengths multiplied by the distance between the strip lines will give the total area. There is no need to write down the lengths of each strip separately, as a 'running total' may be kept on the scale by setting the measurement at the end of a strip to the commencement point of the next strip, and so on. The 'computing scale' is a means of still further simplifying the above process. The instrument is similar to an ordinary graduated scale except that it has a sliding cursor at right angles to it. Parallel strips are set out as before, but the give-and-take lines at the ends are not drawn, the cursor being used for this purpose to give a running total on the scale, which is graduated to give the area direct in acres and parts of an acre (or in metric units), for a particular scale.

An accurate method of finding the area of an irregular boundary from a plan is by the use of a 'planimeter'. It consists essentially of two metal bars, one of which is hinged and can slide along the other. At the extremity of one bar is a sharp needle point and weight, which is fixed to the paper at a convenient point outside the area to be measured. At the extremity of the other bar is a blunt-pointed tracer. Commencing from any convenient point on the boundary, the outline is carefully traced over with the tracer, preferably in a clockwise direction, and finishing at the original starting point. Movement of the tracer is recorded on a small roller graduated into ten main divisions, each with ten subdivisions, and with a vernier reading to 1/100th of a main division. There is also a horizontal dial graduated into ten subdivisions, each being geared. The instrument reads directly to four significant figures, the readings at commencement and completion being recorded. Their difference will be the area traced, and may be expressed in square inches, square centimetres, or to particular scales, by setting to appropriate graduations marked on the tracer bar.

There is little difficulty in finding the areas of the main triangles, probably 80 or 90% of the whole field, but if offsets are numerous, there will be much tedious work in determining the area of the relatively small parts which lie outside the main survey lines. It is therefore usual to calculate the areas of the main triangles from the field measurements and to find the areas of the strips from the plan. For the latter there are several recognised methods, the following being the most important.

AVERAGE ORDINATE RULE (Fig. 29).—Suppose AB is a chain line and CD an irregular boundary. Divide AB into a number of equal parts, say n, either odd or even. At each division point, scale the ordinates (ie offsets) from the chain line to the boundary: 0_1, 0_2, 0_3, 0_4, etc. If AB has been divided into n parts there will be $(n + 1)$ ordinates, ie one more than the number of equal parts. Then the area is equal to the average of these ordinates multiplied by the length AB.

$$\text{Area} = AB(0_1 + 0_2 + 0_3 + 0_4 \ldots + 0_{n+1}) \div (n + 1).$$

The method is approximate and can also be used to find an area direct from field measurements, where offsets have been taken at equal intervals along a chain line.

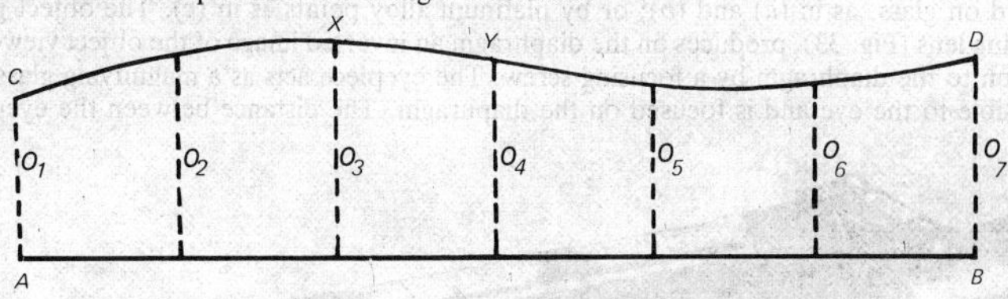

FIG. 29.

TRAPEZOIDAL RULE.—This assumes that the portions of the boundary between adjacent ordinates, such as XY in Fig. 29, are straight lines. Let d be the distance between ordinates.

$$\text{Area} = \frac{d}{2}[0_1 + 2(0_2 + 0_3 + 0_4 + \ldots + 0_n) + 0_{n+1}]$$

SIMPSON'S RULE.—This assumes that the boundary between adjacent ordinates approximates more closely to a parabolic arc than to a straight line. In this case, n must be *even*, and the number of ordinates $(n + 1)$ will therefore be *odd*. The rule states that the area is equal to the sum of the first and last ordinates plus twice the sum of the remaining odd ordinates plus four times the sum of the even ordinates, the whole being multiplied by one-third the distance between the ordinates.

$$\text{Area} = \frac{d}{3}[0_1 + 2(0_3 + 0_5 + 0_7 + \ldots) + 4(0_2 + 0_4 + 0_6 + \ldots) + 0_{n+1}]$$

If there happen to be an even number of ordinates along a particular line, ie n is odd and $(n + 1)$ is even, the area must be found by applying the rule to all ordinates except the last, then adding the separate area of the last section which could conveniently be found by the trapezoidal rule.

LEVELLING

Levelling is the process of determining the relative heights of points on the earth's surface. As the shape of the earth is approximately spherical the height of a point A (Fig. 30) above the earth's surface BD is represented by AB and the height of C by CD. The difference of height between A and C is represented by EC. Contrary to the common use of the word 'level', the line AE, concentric with BD, is a 'level' line, so that a truly 'level' line is curved and not straight. The effect of curvature of the earth in levelling operations will be dealt with later. For short distances however (say up to 180 m), a level line approximates very closely to a horizontal line.

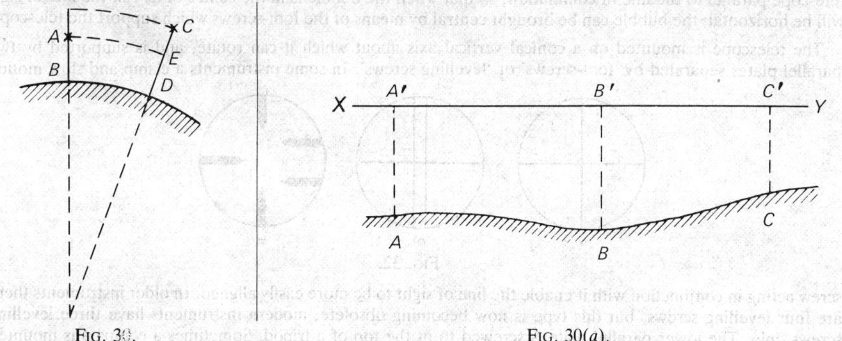

FIG. 30. FIG. 30(a).

In Fig. 30(a) suppose XY is an imaginary wire stretched taut and horizontal above the ground, whose surface is represented by ABC. The height of A below XY is AA'; the height of B below XY is BB'. The difference in level between A and B is $(BB' - AA')$, and if BB' is greater than AA', B is clearly lower than A. Similarly if CC' is less than BB', the difference in level between B and C is $(BB' - CC')$, and C is higher than B. This is the basic principle of levelling. Instead of the imaginary fine wire XY, the horizontal plane is provided in practice by the line of sight of the telescope of the level, known as the 'line of collimation'.

The instrument used in levelling is the level, the main types of which will now be described.

DUMPY LEVEL.—This is a basic type of level (Fig. 31). It includes a telescope containing an object glass, a diaphragm and an eyepiece. There are several types of diaphragm used in levels, some of which are illustrated in Fig. 32. The lines on the diaphragm are known as 'webs', 'cross-hairs' or 'cross-wires' and are formed by fine lines etched on glass, as in (a) and (b); or by platinum alloy points as in (c). The object glass, being a simple converging lens (Fig. 33), produces on the diaphragm an inverted image of the object viewed, the image being brought on to the diaphragm by a focusing screw. The eyepiece acts as a magnifying glass to make the image more visible to the eye and is focused on the diaphragm. The distance between the eyepiece and the

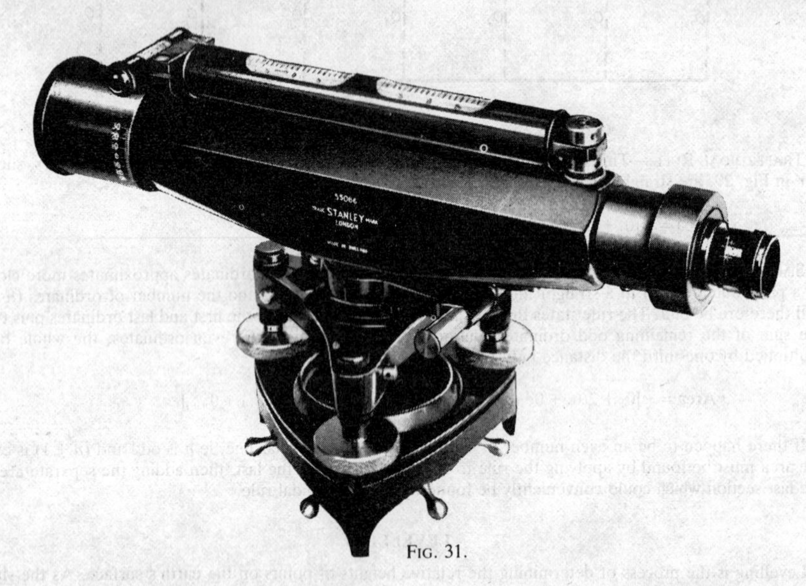

FIG. 31.

object glass is constant, focusing being achieved by the movement of a subsidiary lens between them. In a properly adjusted level, the centre of the eyepiece, the intersection of the cross-wires of the diaphragm and the centre of the object glass will be in a straight line. The line joining the intersection of cross-hairs and the optical centre of the object glass, and its extension in both directions, is called the 'line of collimation' and the horizontal plane through which it rotates is the 'plane of collimation'. A bubble tube is fixed on top of the telescope parallel to the line of collimation, so that when the bubble is in the centre of its run the line of sight will be horizontal; the bubble can be brought central by means of the foot-screws which support the telescope.

The telescope is mounted on a conical vertical axis about which it can rotate, and is supported by two parallel plates separated by 'foot-screws' or 'levelling screws'. In some instruments a clamp and slow motion

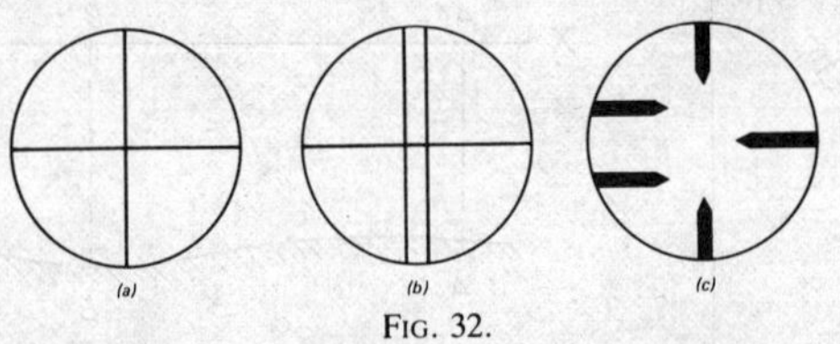

FIG. 32.

screw acting in conjunction with it enable the line of sight to be more easily aligned. In older instruments there are four levelling screws, but this type is now becoming obsolete; modern instruments have three levelling screws only. The lower parallel plate is screwed to fit the top of a tripod. Sometimes a compass is mounted

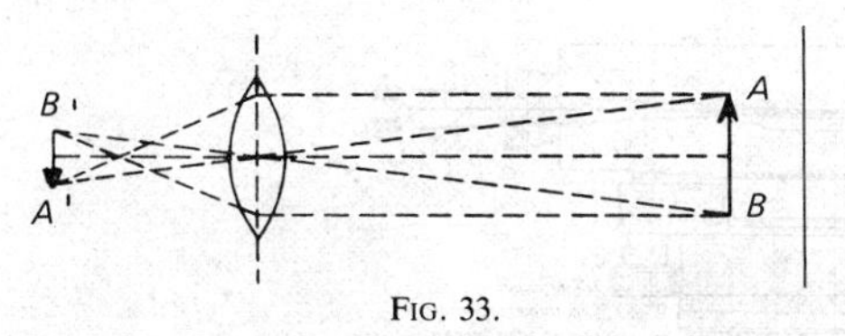

Fig. 33.

below the telescope.

In setting up the level, the instrument is first set, by appropriate movement of the tripod legs, so that the telescope is approximately level in any position. The bubble is then brought to the centre of its run with the levelling screws by the following procedure. The telescope is set parallel to two of the screws and the bubble brought to the centre by moving both screws simultaneously in the direction of the arrows (Fig. 34). After

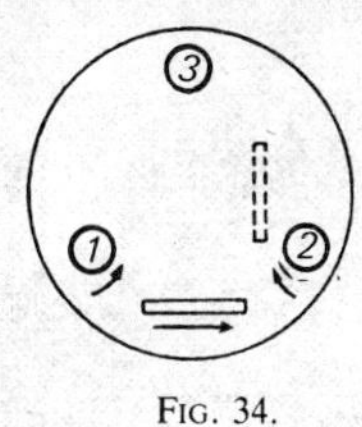

Fig. 34.

turning the telescope through a right angle, the bubble is again brought central by the third screw alone. The process is repeated until the bubble remains central.

The essential requirement of any level is that its line of collimation shall be horizontal at the time a reading is taken. The disadvantage of the dumpy level is that even after careful levelling up initially in two directions at right angles, the bubble seldom remains central in all positions of the telescope and frequent adjustment of the relative positions of the telescope and vertical axis become necessary.

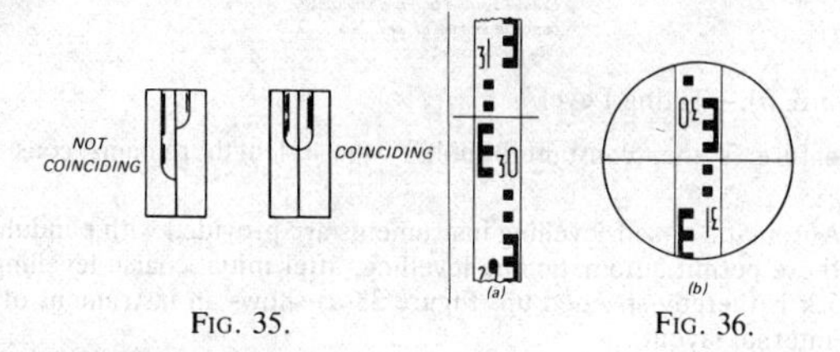

Fig. 35. Fig. 36.

TILTING LEVEL.—Sometimes known as the quickset level, this type differs essentially from the dumpy in that the telescope is not attached rigidly to the vertical axis but is pivoted at the top so that it can be tilted in a vertical plane. The instrument is constructed so that the telescope may be levelled for each sight by manipulating a micrometer screw situated under the eyepiece. A small circular spirit-level known as a 'quickset' bubble is mounted either in the upper parallel plate or on top of the micrometer screw and enables rapid setting up initially. There is an adjustable ball-and-socket arrangement instead of (or as well as) footscrews. The tripod can be set up at any angle, the rough levelling up being made with the ball-and-socket joint and its accompanying clamp; the spirit level is brought exactly horizontal for each reading by the micrometer screw.

The tilting level shown in Fig. 37(*a*) is convenient for use in construction, highway, bridge, and tunnel engineering work. A design feature allows the coincidence reading to be viewed while sighting through the telescope. A domed tripod head facilitates rapid setting-up. This level is shown diagrammatically in Fig. 37(*b*).

REVERSIBLE LEVEL.—In the reversible type, the main bubble tube, which has both upper and lower surfaces visible, is attached to the side of the telescope and is so constructed that the telescope can be turned through 180° about the axis of collimation so that the position of the bubble is reversed. The bubble can be viewed by the observer from the sighting position at the eyepiece by reflection from an inclined mirror. In other types the bubble tube is enclosed and the two ends are reflected through prisms so that the ends of the bubble appear together when the bubble is central (Fig. 35). The chief feature of these levels is that if readings are taken with the bubble tube first on the left of the telescope and then on the right, the mean reading will give 'true level' even if the instrument is out of adjustment.

Precise Level.—There are several types of precise level, most of which embody the features of reversible levels and observation of the bubble ends through prisms. To ensure accuracy of the line of collimation, the parts immediately affecting it are made out of Invar, of which the coefficient of expansion is extremely low.

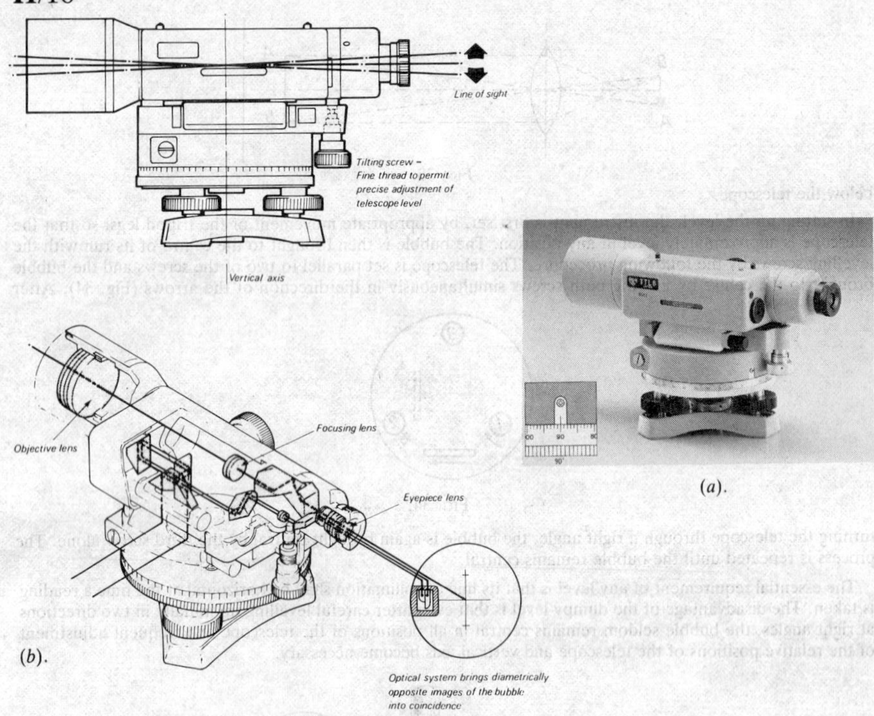

FIG. 37(*a* & *b*).—Tilting Level.

Another distinguishing feature is the 'constant bubble', whose length remains constant under varying temperatures.

AUTOMATIC LEVEL.—Automatic or self-levelling instruments are provided with pendulum prisms mounted within the telescope and these permit automatic fine levelling, after initial coarse levelling by footscrews has been carried out. Fieldwork is thereby speeded up. Figure 38(*a*) shows an instrument of this type, and Fig. 38(*b*) is a diagram of the internal layout.

FIG. 38(*a*).—Engineers Level, Automatic Type, with Adapter Plate for Tripod (*Kern*).

FIG. 38(*b*).—Engineers Level; Automatic Type; Internal Layout (*Kern*).

The Staff.—The most usual type is made of seasoned hardwood, or of aluminium alloy, and graduated on its face in feet and decimals of a foot, or in metres, cm and mm. As the base of the staff is subject to considerable wear it carries a brass plate. Usual lengths are 14, 16 or 18 ft (or 3, 4 or 5 m) in three telescopic sections. For precise work a single-length staff is generally adopted, the graduations being on Invar to reduce the effects of temperature changes. Staffs produced by different makers vary little in pattern, but occasionally the figures are printed upside down on the staff so that they appear erect when viewed through the telescope. This may seem at first an improvement, for presumably figures can be read more easily when seen the right way up than when inverted; in fact there is no difficulty in reading the figures in either case; the early difficulty is in understanding to what precise point on the staff the figures refer and the inverting of the figures does little to help in this. The staff reading is given by the position on the staff of the central horizontal line of the diaphragm. A typical reading 3·055 is as illustrated in Fig. 36. where (*a*) represents a portion of the staff viewed normally and (*b*) the reading as observed through the telescope.

On the metric staff all graduation marks and the spaces between graduation marks have a vertical dimension of 10 mm, so that by estimation, readings can be obtained to the nearest mm (ie 0·001 m).

It is usual to express levels as heights above some 'datum' or base line. This datum may be either: (1) the Ordnance datum, as determined by the Surveyors of the Ordnance Survey, or (2) some arbitrary datum, such as (say) 50 m below some permanent object on or near the site, such as the plinth of a building or a gatestop.

Ordnance Datum.—The datum or base to which heights are related in the Ordnance Survey is known as Ordnance datum. The original OD was the mean sea-level, as determined by gauging of the tides at Liverpool in 1844. It was later found, by means of self-registering tide gauges, that mean sea-level at Liverpool was 0·018 m lower than was supposed, whilst the mean sea-level for the whole of the United Kingdom was 0·198 m higher. The old Liverpool Ordnance datum was used for all Ordnance plans printed up to April, 1929. Levels on Ordnance sheets revised since 1929 are, generally, referred to the Newlyn datum and in some parts of the country there is quite a difference between the old and new levels. Near Liverpool the difference is small but in the Eastern Counties it may be as much as 0·533 m, chiefly due to a slow tilting of the country which has occurred in the last hundred years. Care should therefore be taken, when using heights figured on Ordnance sheets, to see to which datum they are related, particularly if a comparison has to be made with levels on an old plan or section. As a rule the difference on any particular Ordnance sheet will be practically constant throughout that sheet, and the Ordnance Survey Office therefore prints, on each sheet revised since 1929, the difference between the Liverpool and Newlyn datums for that sheet. If, therefore, an Ordnance sheet has no note on the point, it can be assumed that the levels are referred to Liverpool datum. If they are referred to the Newlyn datum the fact will be stated and the difference between the two will be given as a plus or minus figure.

A datum sometimes used in the Thames Valley, particularly in relation to flood-prevention works, is the Trinity High-Water Mark, which is 3·804 m above the Liverpool OD. It is the level of the lower edge of a stone fixed in the river wall on the east side of the Hermitage entrance to the London docks.

Bench Marks.—A 'bench mark' is a clearly-defined point or mark of fixed height in a stable position, which can be used as a point of reference to check levelling operations or to connect these operations with past or future work. An 'Ordnance bench mark' (OBM) is one fixed by the Ordnance Survey of known height above Ordnance datum. A 'private' BM is one fixed other than by the Ordnance Survey. It may be of known height above OD or not. For instance, if an area is situated at a considerable distance from the nearest OBM and levelling operations may be needed on the area from time to time, the surveyor may 'establish' his own BM or BMs on the area by taking levels from the nearest OBM. He will then know the height of his own BM above OD and thereafter will always start his levelling from this. If, however, levelling has to be done at a distance from any OBM and there is no need to refer the levels to Ordnance datum, any clearly defined mark can be chosen as a BM and datum taken as (say) 50 or other convenient number of metres below it, ie the BM will have a value of 50·000 (above datum).

If a bench mark is needed only for particular levelling operations no mark need be made (except perhaps with chalk), provided its position is clearly described in the level book. This is sometimes known as a 'temporary bench mark' (TBM). If, however, it is intended to be a permanent point of reference a permanent mark must be made and its position should be shown on any plan or other drawing. The reference to it should be such that it is not mistaken for an OBM.

The commonest form of OBM is the 'crow's foot' or broad arrow with horizontal line at the top. It is cut into any suitably placed permanent erection, such as a milestone, bridge abutment, gate pillar or wall of a building. The arrow shows the level at which the base of the staff should be held, ie the centre of the horizontal incision. This type of mark is not very convenient because it is not easy for the staff-holder to hold the staff upright with its base exactly at the mark, especially if the telescopic lengths have to be fully extended, for it is then difficult to ensure that the base of the staff is at its right height and at the same time steady. There is an improved type of bracket bench mark, consisting of a metal plate, let into the face of a wall or similar surface and carrying slots into which a specially designed bracket may be fitted by the staff holder; this bracket forms a solid support for the base of the staff.

PROCEDURE IN LEVELLING.—The first reading from any one position of the level is called a *backsight*; the last reading is called a *foresight*; readings to points in between are called *intermediate sights*. These descriptions apply to whatever method of booking is used. It is seldom possible to take all the readings in a particular levelling operation from one position of the level, for the following reasons:

(*a*) When the distance from the staff position to the level is considerable, the graduations of the staff cannot be clearly distinguished. Although the distance depends on the magnifying factor of the telescope, according to the type of instrument, a maximum length of sight of 90–120 m, is generally adequate for most purposes.

(*b*) When the ground level at the staff position is above the plane of collimation the staff cannot be read; nor can a reading be taken if the ground level at the staff position is below the plane of collimation by an amount greater than the overall length of the staff, ie when the plane of collimation is above the top of the staff when fully extended.

(*c*) When there is an obstruction between the level and the staff position it is not possible to read the staff; the obstruction may be due to a natural feature such as a wood, hedge, trees, etc, or to artificial features such as a wall, fence, building, etc. Often when levelling along roads an obstruction is caused by vehicles temporarily parked in the line of sight.

In all the above circumstances the position of the level must be changed and the procedure for this is as follows. The last point at which the staff can be observed conveniently before a change is necessary is known as a 'change point' or 'turning point' and is selected preferably on firm ground, a projecting piece of rock or similar feature, or alternatively marked with chalk on a road or paved surface. The staff reading is observed at the point and will be a foresight because it is the last reading taken with the level from that position. The instrument is then moved to a new position convenient for proceeding with the next levels to be taken and so situated that a reading back on to the change point can be taken. This latter reading, with the staff still at the change point, will be a backsight because it is the first of the readings taken with the level in its new position. Thus at every change point, two readings are taken; first a foresight, then a backsight, with the staff held on the *same* point. Note that it is the staff position which is the change point, not the position of the level.

The use of change points is illustrated by Fig. 39(*a*). Levels are required at points numbered 1 to 6. The level is first set up at *A* and a backsight reading taken on an OBM at 0. Intermediate sights are then taken at points 1 and 2. Because the level of the ground at point 4 is such that the top of the staff would be below

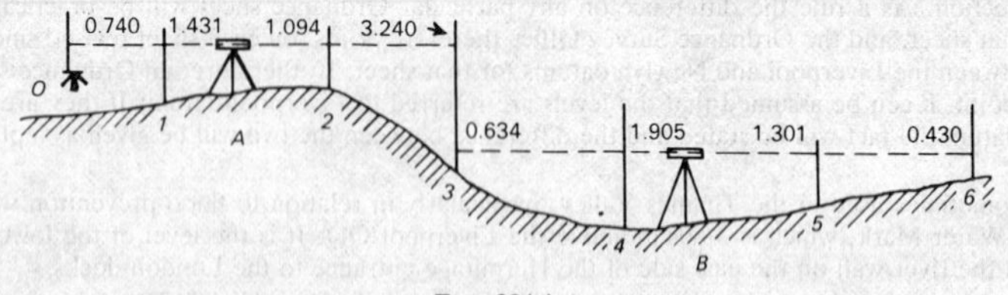

FIG. 39(*a*).

the plane of collimation of the level at *A*, the instrument would need to be moved before a reading at 4 could be taken; point 3 is therefore made a change point and a foresight reading taken. The level is then moved to a convenient position *B* and a backsight reading taken to point 3; intermediate sights to points 4 and 5, with a final foresight reading to point 6.

The following summarises the important features of booking readings:

(*a*) The reading entered in the backsight column is always the first reading taken when the instrument is set up in any position. The reading entered in the foresight column is always the last reading taken with the instrument in any particular position. Any reading which is neither the first nor the last taken from any position of the level is entered as an intermediate.

(*b*) Each horizontal line in the book indicates a particular position of the staff and generally needs a description in the Remarks column (or in a column of distances) so that its ground position may be defined and plotted on a plan if required.

(*c*) At each horizontal line relating to a change point there will be two readings, one in the foresight column and one in the backsight column.

REDUCING LEVELS.—The process of determining the heights, above (or sometimes below) a selected datum, of the points at which staff readings have been taken is known as 'reducing' the levels; the heights related to the particular datum are known as 'reduced levels'. There are two recognised methods of reducing levels.

(1) RISE-AND-FALL METHOD.—Referring to Fig. 39(*a*) suppose the reduced level of the OBM at 0, ie the height above Ordnance datum as found from an Ordnance sheet, is 21·711. The rises and falls of the ground between successive staff readings are calculated. The reduced levels and the method of setting out the rise and fall columns are as shown in Table 2. The check shown in this table is purely arithmetical and is *not* a check on the accuracy of the field-work.

(2) COLLIMATION METHOD.—In the second method, reduced levels are found by simply subtracting the staff readings in turn from the height of the plane of collimation (HPC) which has been first determined. The method is set out in Table 3. The column for height of collimation may be headed 'Coll Ht', 'Height of Coll', 'Inst Height' or 'HPC'.

TABLE 2.

BS	Inter	FS	Rise	Fall	RL	Distance	Remarks
0·740					21·711		OBM on stone wall at 0
	1·431			0·691	21·020		Point 1
	1·094		0·337		21·357		Point 2
0·634		3·240		2·146	19·211		Point 3 (Change point)
	1·905			1·271	17·940		Point 4
	1·301		0·604		18·544		Point 5
		0·430	0·871		19·415		Point 6
1·374		3·670	1·812	4·108	21·711		
		1·374		1·812	19·415		
	Checks:	2·296		2·296	2·296		

TABLE 3.

BS	Inter	FS	HPC	RL	Distance	Remarks
0·740			22·451	21·711		OBM on stone wall at 0
	1·431			21·020		Point 1
	1·094			21·357		Point 2
0·634		3·240	19·845	19·211		Point 3 (Change point)
	1·905			17·940		Point 4
	1·301			18·544		Point 5
		0·430		19·415		Point 6
1·374		3·670		21·711		
		1·374		19·415		
	Checks:	2·296		2·296		

The reduction can largely be checked by finding whether the difference between the first and last reduced levels is the same as the difference between the sum of the backsights and the sum of the foresights. This is not a complete check, however; it is a check upon the entries in the HPC column and on the calculations of the reduced levels of the change points, but it is not a check on the reduced levels of intermediates. For instance, if on subtracting 1·431 from the first collimation height the reduced level of point 1 is made 21·030 instead of 21·020 this mistake might remain undetected, for it would not affect the level of any subsequent points and it would not affect the totals of backsights and foresights. In this respect the method is inferior to the rise-and-fall method which provides a complete check. The amount of arithmetic involved is, however, less with the HPC method and for this reason it is usually preferred. For setting out work such as the levels for drains and sewers, foundations, contour lines, etc, the collimation method is invariably adopted, for in these cases it is essential that the reduction shall be done in the field. When, as in Tables 2 and 3, work is done in metres readings are taken to the nearest millimetre and values are shown to three decimal places.

PAGE-BY-PAGE CHECKING OF LEVELS.—When the entries in the level book extend to two or more pages it is important to provide a check upon the reduction of levels on each page rather than to check the whole of the reduction in one operation. The reduction on each page should be checked before beginning to reduce the levels on the next page; this will avoid mistakes being carried forward from page to page. To enable each page to be checked separately, each page must begin with a backsight and end with a foresight; there will thus be an equal number of backsights and foresights on each page.

Checking the Field Work.—The checks which have been described are checks only on the reduction of the levels and do not check the accuracy of the staff readings, ie they check the office work but not the field work. As the value of levels taken is dependent on their field accuracy it is clearly desirable to apply a field check. This may be done by one of the following methods: (1) If the levelling has commenced at an OBM, continue taking levels to another OBM, or to some other mark whose level has been determined by previous levelling operations, or (2) level back to the BM from which the levelling commenced. If levelling was begun from a private BM whose height above OD is not known, only method (2) is possible. In either method, when proceeding to another OBM or back to the original BM there is no need to take intermediates, the object being to check on to a known level as expeditiously as possible; this process in levelling is known as taking 'flying levels'.

ACCURACY OF LEVELLING AND PERMISSIBLE ERRORS.—For general work using a metric telescopic staff graduated to 10 mm, staff readings may be read by estimation to 1 mm. In a levelling operation, the error which is likely to arise will depend on the number and length of the sights, number of change points, etc. Taking a length of sight of (say) 100 m at change points, a length of 200 m would be covered by each position of the level and there would therefore be about 5 changes per kilometre in average country, ie 10 readings (neglecting intermediates, which do not affect the accuracy of change points). For each position of the level, the foresight and backsight readings might each be read to an accuracy of 0·002 m and as there is an equal likelihood of a reading being either too high or too low the error may be taken as 0·004 m per change point. If n is the number of positions of the level, by the 'mean square rule' the error will be $0{\cdot}004\sqrt{n}$ m, ie $0{\cdot}004\sqrt{5} = 0{\cdot}009$ m per kilometre in the above case. This would be a permissible error for general work, but for precise levelling as on the Ordnance Survey for instance, errors would be less than 0·002 metre per kilometre.

ADJUSTMENTS OF THE DUMPY LEVEL.—Accurate levelling is not possible unless the instrument is in good order and is properly handled. The operations performed to secure the best use of the instrument are known as the 'adjustments', divided into 'temporary' adjustments, which have to be made each time the level is set up, and 'permanent' adjustments, which need to be made only occasionally.

The temporary adjustments consist of (1) setting up the tripod with the legs firm and the lower plate approximately horizontal, (2) accurately levelling the instrument with the foot-screws, and (3) focusing the telescope and eliminating parallax. With a three-screw instrument the levelling is carried out as follows. Turn the telescope so that it is parallel to two foot-screws, centre the bubble by turning these foot-screws equally in opposite directions; the bubble follows the left thumb. Turn the instrument through 90° and centre the bubble again by turning the third foot-screw only. Repeat these operations until the bubble is central in both positions. If the permanent adjustments of the instrument are good, the bubble will remain central for any other position of the telescope. If, however, the bubble moves from the central position when the telescope points in another direction the above procedure should be repeated to find a position of the bubble such that on turning the instrument slowly through 360° the bubble remains stationary.

When focusing the instrument first point the telescope at the sky or at a piece of blank paper and adjust the eyepiece so that the cross-hairs are clearly seen. This adjustment depends only on the observer's eyesight and not on the distance to the object viewed. Then, for any staff reading, focus the telescope so that the image of the staff is in the plane of the cross-hairs. Test for this by nodding the head while looking through the eyepiece; there should be no apparent relative movement of the staff and crosshairs. There will then be no parallax.

The permanent adjustments are needed to correct faults which have developed in the instrument itself. Major faults such as breakage of parts, will necessitate the instrument being sent to the makers, but there are certain faults which should be corrected by the surveyor. The two most common are (*a*) the telescope bubble not being at right angles to the vertical axis of the instrument, (*b*) the line of collimation not being parallel to the telescope bubble. These can be tested and adjusted as follows:

(*a*) Adjustment of Telescopic Bubble at Right Angles to the Vertical Axis.—Having set up the level the telescope bubble is brought parallel to any two foot-screws and centred with the foot screws. The telescope is then reversed (ie turned through 180° horizontally). If the bubble runs out of centre, half the error should be corrected by the foot-screws and the remaining half with the capstan screw at one end of the spirit level, the other end usually being hinged. The telescope is then turned through 90° horizontally and the process repeated using the third screw. The whole process is repeated until the bubble reverses properly in both positions; the vertical axis is then truly vertical when the bubble is central.

(*b*) Adjustment of Line of Collimation Parallel to the Telescope Bubble.—Levelling depends for its accuracy on the line of collimation being horizontal; this adjustment is to make the line of collimation parallel to the telescope bubble so that it shall be horizontal when the bubble is in the centre of its run. Adjustment (*a*) must first be completed. The level is set up at C midway between two pegs or marks A and B about 100 metres apart on fairly level ground (Fig. 39(*b*)). Having made the temporary adjustments, readings are taken on a staff held first at A and then at B; the difference between the two readings is the true rise or fall even if the line of collimation is not parallel to the bubble tube. The level is next set up at D, fairly close to B; the temporary adjustments are made, and readings taken on the staff at A and B as before. If the rise or fall obtained is the same as previously, no adjustment is needed; if not, the line of collimation is not parallel to the bubble tube. As the distance to B is very small there should be no appreciable error in this reading. The corrected staff reading at A can therefore be calculated from the true difference of level already found by adding it to the reading at B if there is a fall from B to A, or subtracting if there is a rise. Raise or lower the diaphragm cell by means of the screws holding it in the telescope tube so as to make the cross-hair give the corrected staff reading on A.

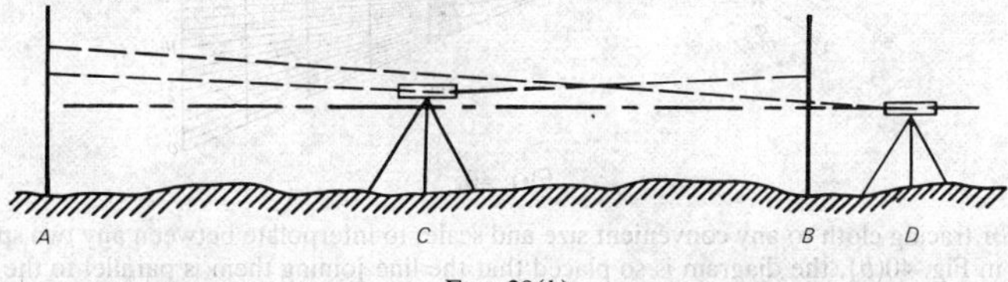

FIG. 39(*b*).

EQUALISING BACKSIGHTS AND FORESIGHTS.—Figure 38(*b*) shows that even if the level is not in adjustment the difference between two staff readings will give the true rise or fall if the lengths of sights are equal. It is clearly not practicable to make the length of sight to every intermediate reading the same, but it is important that where possible the length of backsight should be the same (or nearly the same) as the length of foresight for every position of the level, so that a true difference of level between change points will be obtained. This is known as 'equalising backsights and foresights'. The term is inclined to be misleading since it is not the actual backsight and foresight readings which are to be made equal, but the distances from the level to the staff positions.

CONTOURS.—A contour is a line connecting points which are at the same level on the ground. Its height above some datum (usually Ordnance datum) is figured on the plan beside the line. The line is generally shown in a distinctive colour, such as red, or as a dotted or dot-and-dash line. Contoured plans are of particular value in planning routes for railways, canals and roads and are indispensible in preparing a town planning project. The distance apart (vertically) of the contour lines selected for a particular plan will depend mainly on the purpose for which the plan is prepared and on the amount of time and labour which is thought to be justified in the necessary work of surveying and levelling; but where the ground is rather flat it is usual to draw contour lines at closer vertical intervals than on hilly ground. The vertical distance between contours is known as the *contour interval*. Reasonable intervals are as follows:

For mapping a country	25 m
For railways, town planning and building estates	1 to 5 m
For building sites	0·5 m

The 6-inch to one mile Ordnance maps show (in fine red lines) contours at 100 ft vertical intervals, determined instrumentally by exact methods; but in some parts of the country intermediate contours at 25 ft intervals are also shown, these having been determined by less precise methods, such as sketching in by judgment.

On the new series at 1/10,000 scale, contours are shown at 10-metre vertical intervals in areas of high elevation and at 5-metre vertical intervals elsewhere.

Methods of Contouring.—These are classified as either 'direct' or 'indirect'. The choice between them will vary with the nature of the ground and the purpose of the survey.

DIRECT METHOD.—The positions on the site of numerous points on each of the various contour lines are located by levelling and are marked by laths. These are then surveyed and plotted on the plan. For the survey of the laths, traversing is probably the most convenient method. In rather flat land it may be necessary to have a separate traverse for each contour line, but if the contours are close together two or three of them may be surveyed together, offsets being taken to all laths. The direct method is the most accurate but, if there are many contour lines to be set out, it is laborious because of the extensive time required for fixing and surveying the laths. It is particularly applicable where only a single contour has to be set out, such as the top water line of a proposed reservoir.

INDIRECT METHODS.—(*a*) A large number of points is chosen on the site and marked by laths. Their positions are surveyed by any of the ordinary methods and their ground heights found by levelling. This will give a large number of 'spot levels' whose positions can be plotted on the plan. It is important that the points chosen for the laths shall be points at which the land shows a distinct change in slope. If this is done carefully it will be justifiable to assume that the ground slopes in a straight line from one point to the next so that the position of any intervening contour can be found by proportion. This is known as 'interpolation'. Thus, suppose that at one lath the level is 27·2 and at the next 16·4 (Fig. 40(*a*)). The difference between 27·2 and the 20 contour is 7·2 and between 16·4 and the 20 contour, 3·6. If at point 27·2 an offset, to any convenient scale, of 7·2 is made at right angles to the line joining the lath-points, and at 16·4 an offset of 3·6 on the opposite side, the line joining these points will show the position of the 20 m contour between the lath points. Similarly a line joining offsets of 2·2 and 8·6 respectively will indicate the position of the 25 m contour. An alternative method, where many contours are to be interpolated, is the use of an 'interpolation diagram' (Fig. 40(*b*)). This is drawn on

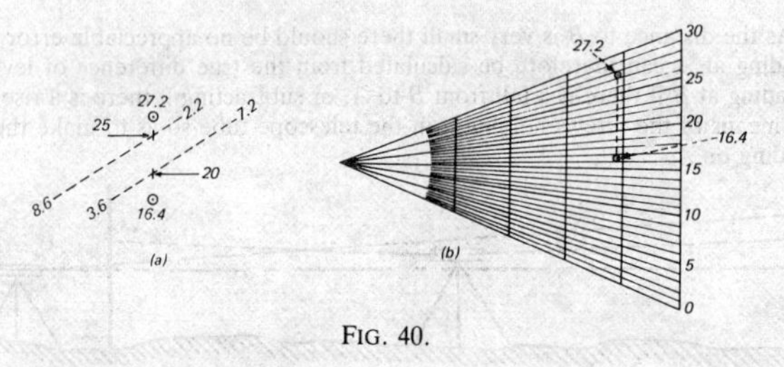

FIG. 40.

tracing paper or tracing cloth to any convenient size and scale; to interpolate between any two spot levels, say 16·4 and 27·2 in Fig. 40(*b*), the diagram is so placed that the line joining them is parallel to the vertical lines and the spot levels fit the appropriate positions on the diagram. The intermediate thick lines will then represent 5 m contour intervals and the 20 and 25 m contours can be pricked through accordingly.

(*b*) Several 'sections', parallel to one another at short intervals, are chained and levelled. Horizontal lines are drawn on the plotted sections at the levels of the required contours. The positions of the points where these horizontal lines cut the ground surface on the sections can be scaled and transferred to the plan and the contours can then be sketched in. The amount of levelling required in this method generally is greater than in either of the earlier methods, because the sections will normally be taken roughly in the direction of greatest slope, involving many 'changes'. It should give accurate results unless there are abrupt changes of slope between the sections.

(*c*) This is similar to (*b*) except that instead of the sections being made parallel to one another, they radiate from one central station, or from two or more stations, the angles between the radiating lines being measured. The method is frequently used for contouring a hillside, where the radiating lines can be set out conveniently with a theodolite at the summit. The levelling of the sections can be done in the normal way but much time will be saved if tacheometry is employed.

A modification of the contoured map is the 'layered map', in which the areas between selected pairs of contour lines are coloured with distinctive tints. For instance, in the Half-Inch OS Layered Maps the area between sea-level and the 100 ft contour line is coloured green, that between 100 and 200 ft is coloured very pale green; land between 200 and 400 ft above sea-level is tinted very light brown, that between 400 and 600 ft a shade darker, and so on until the highest altitudes have a very dark shade of brown.

PRECISE LEVELLING.—When levels are taken for the purpose of establishing a chain of permanent bench marks, or for tunnels, bridges and other important engineering work in which great precision in needed, every precaution should be taken, and only high-grade instruments should be used. If there is only one pair of intervisible stations, whose relative levels have to be determined, these may be found by trigonometrical levelling with the theodolite, otherwise a level will be used. Apart from the use of the precise level, special levelling staffs are used.

The ordinary telescopic staff has the defect that the clamps become worn with use so that a small error occurs in the transition from one telescopic length to the next. This in not permissible in precise levelling, so that 'one-piece' staffs are generally used for such work. Such a staff is marked with scales both on the front and on the back, these being marked *A* and *B* respectively, the figures and divisions on the one side being in black and those on the other in red to avoid confusion. The *B* scale does not start at the bottom of the staff, but a few centimetres higher up, so that the readings shall not be the same on both sides. No error is introduced thereby because in the reduction of levels one reading is subtracted from another and the zero error of the *B* scale will be cancelled out in the subtraction. In addition, the staff is provided with a gunmetal boss at each end, so that additional readings (*C* and *D*) can be taken on each side with the staff inverted. A specially-ruled level book is used, enabling the *A*, *B*, *C* and *D* readings for each staff position to be recorded in separate columns. Each column is separately reduced so that four reduced levels will be obtained for each staff position and in the event of any slight disagreement the mean is taken.

Sometimes the staff is marked in different units on front and back: for example, in feet on one side and decimetres on the other. This gives a still better check, for there will be no likelihood of the readings on one side being influenced by those already obtained on the other, the results not being compared until the reduced levels obtained in the one unit are converted into the other. Where precise levelling involves very long sights a 'target' staff is used. This has a movable cross-piece which is adjusted by the staffman until signalled by the instrument man that the central web of the diaphragm coincides with the central mark on the cross-piece. The staffholder then records the reading.

In precise levelling it is not usually accurate enough to read the staff to the nearest centimetre, and the nearest millimetre is estimated; for this purpose a 'parallel plate glass micrometer' may be used.

PARALLEL PLATE GLASS MICROMETER (Fig. 41).—This attachment enables the interval between the diaphragm line and the nearest division on the staff to be measured directly to the nearest 0·001 m. It consists of a parallel glass plate, placed in front of the object glass of the telescope and mounted so that it may be tilted

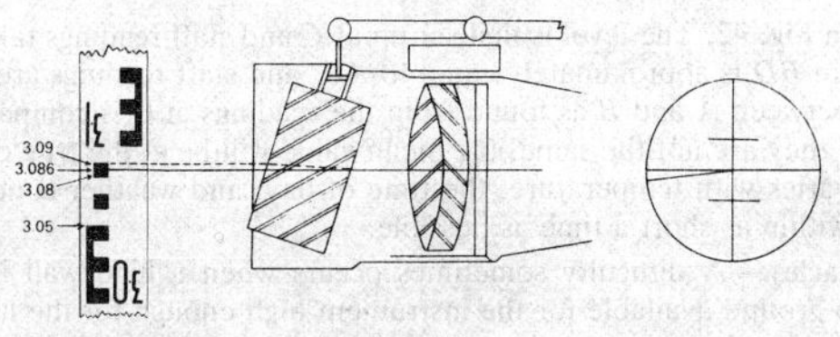

FIG. 41.

by movement of a micrometer head, this being divided into 20 divisions and situated at the eye-end of the telescope. When the plate is vertical, the direction of the line of collimation is not affected, and the horizontal cross-line of the diaphragm intersects the same reading on the staff as when the attachment is not in use. If the glass plate be inclined to the vertical, the direction of the line of collimation is slightly displaced by double refraction with the result that the horizontal cross-line may be brought to coincide with the nearest staff division. The amount of the displacement is read from the graduated screw, which carries 20 divisions corresponding to a total displacement of 0·02 m. Hence one division on the micrometer head represents a vertical interval on the staff of 0·001 m, irrespective of distance.

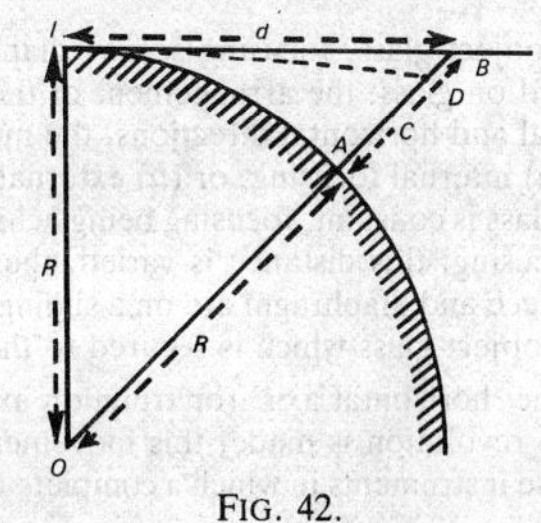

FIG. 42.

CURVATURE AND REFRACTION.—Referring to Fig. 42, if I is the position at which a level is set up, IA is a level line and IB a horizontal line, tangential to the earth's surface at I, which represents the line of collimation when the bubble is central, and AB is a portion of a staff held vertically at A, then AB is the amount cm. of curvature at a distance d kilometres, from the instrument, and is the amount by which the line of collimation IB differs from the level line IA. Then it can be shown that approximately

$$c = 0{\cdot}08\, d^2.$$

In a distance of 1 kilometre, therefore, the amount of curvature is about 80 mm. In 1/5 km, which is about the limit of sight with an ordinary level, the amount would be $(1/5)^2 = 1/25$ of this, ie 3 mm and is therefore negligible for general purposes.

The error due to curvature is partly offset by that due to atmospheric refraction. Owing to the varying density of the atmosphere and to irregularities in temperature, a line of sight is not a perfectly straight linc, but is bent downwards in a curved line towards the surface of the earth. Thus in Fig. 42 the line of sight would not cut the staff at 'B' but at 'D', lower down. It is difficult to make a precise allowance for this error BD because it varies with the time of day and with temperature. The usual allowance adopted is one-seventh of the allowance for curvature. Therefore, the combined allowance for curvature and refraction $(=DA)$ is $(6/7) \times 0{\cdot}08\, d^2 = 0{\cdot}067\, d^2$ m.

The correction for curvature and refraction may be ignored (*a*) if the distance is less than 200 m; (*b*) if backsights and foresights are equalised; (*c*) if reciprocal levels are taken.

Reciprocal Levelling.—It may sometimes be necessary to take a very long sight, say from one bank of a wide river or ravine to another. In such a case it may not be possible to take a backsight on the near bank of the river at anything like the same distance as the foresight on the far bank. Thus, errors may arise in such a reading: (*a*) because the plane of collimation may not be parallel to the telescope bubble; (*b*) because of curvature and refraction. Errors due to both these causes may be eliminated by 'reciprocal levelling'. The

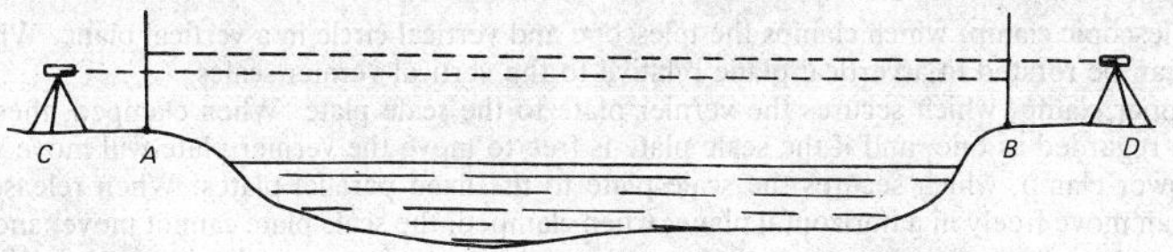

FIG. 43.

procedure is illustrated in Fig. 42. The level is first set up at *C* and staff readings taken at *A* and *B*. The level is then set up at *D*, where *BD* is approximately equal to *AC*, and staff readings are again taken at *A* and *B*. The difference of level between *A* and *B* as found from the readings at *C* is compared with that found from the readings at *D* and, if they are not the same, the mean value will be at the true difference of level. As the error due to refraction varies with temperature, the time of day, and weather conditions, the readings at *C* and *D* should be taken within as short a time as possible.

Levelling Across Obstacles.—A difficulty sometimes occurs when a high wall intervenes on the line of levelling, and there is no ground available for the instrument high enough for the line of collimation to clear the top of the wall. To avoid a long detour, the top of the wall is made a change point but, since it is above the line of collimation, the staff is turned upsidedown with its base level with the top of the wall. This is done on both sides of the wall, the staff being moved from the one face of the wall to the other. These readings, taken with the staff inverted, are negative quantities because they are heights above the line of collimation instead of below; they must therefore be given a minus sign in the level book. When subtracting a negative reading from a positive reading to obtain a rise or fall, the numerical values must be added together instead of subtracting the one from the other.

THE THEODOLITE

This is the principal instrument used in surveying for measuring horizontal and vertical angles. The essential parts of a theodolite (Fig. 44(*a*)) are:

(1) The telescope, comprising an object glass, focusing screw, diaphragm and adjustable eyepiece. The diaphragm consists of fine lines etched on glass; the arrangement of the webs is such that it can be used for intersecting objects both in the vertical and horizontal directions, the most common types being as illustrated in Fig. 44(*b*). Telescopes are either (*a*) internal focusing, or (*b*) external focusing. In the former, the distance between the eyepiece and the object glass is constant, focusing being achieved by the movement of a subsidiary lens between them; with external focusing, this distance is varied, the object glass being fixed to the main barrel of the telescope while the eyepiece and diaphragm are on a sliding inner tube controlled by the focusing screw. (In some instruments it is the object glass which is secured to the sliding tube.)

(2) The telescope is mounted on the 'horizontal axis' (or trunnion axis), about which it is free to revolve in a vertical plane. When a complete revolution is made, this movement is known as 'transitting', the term transit theodolite being applied to those instruments in which a complete revolution of the telescope is possible.

(3) The horizontal axis is supported by two upright 'A' frames, the lower ends of which are rigidly fixed to the circular 'upper plate', or what is more usually known as the 'vernier plate'; this carries two diametrically opposite vernier scales, each having an index arrow. The vernier plate can rotate in a horizontal plane about the vertical axis of the instrument and its movement is therefore a measure of the rotation of the telescope horizontally, for the telescope cannot move in a horizontal direction except in unison with the vernier plate.

(4) Attached to the telescope is a vertical circle graduated in degrees and parts of a degree, for reading vertical angles. In conjunction with this scale, vernier scales are provided on the horizontal arms of a T-frame, the leg of which is secured by 'clip screws' to the A frames.

(5) Immediately below the vernier plate and mounted concentrically with it is another circular plate known as the 'lower horizontal plate', or more generally as the 'scale plate', its circumference being graduated in degrees and parts of a degree, the usual subdivisions being 1/2-degree, 1/3-degree, or 1/6-degree. It is the diameter of the scale plate which defines the size of the instrument, eg a 5-inch theodolite has a scale plate of diameter 5 inches. The scale plate and the vernier plate can normally be rotated independently in a horizontal plane, but can be clamped together when required.

(6) The instrument is supported by a tribrach similar to the three-screw base of a dumpy level and levelling screws (or foot-screws), provided for the purpose of bringing the vertical axis truly vertical.

(7) The lower ends of the foot screws are carried in a 'wall plate' which is screwed to fit the head of the instrument tripod about 4½ or 5 ft high, and carries a hook to which a plumb-bob can be attached for centering the theodolite exactly over a station point. Modern instruments have a 'shifting base' to facilitate the process of centering.

(8) A plate bubble is mounted on the vernier plate for use in levelling up, in conjunction with the levelling screws. A second spirit level is either mounted on the telescope (the 'telescope bubble') or attached to the vernier arm associated with the vertical circle, and is used normally when vertical angles are being taken.

(9) All movements of the instrument parts are controlled by clamps and 'slow motion screws' (or tangent screws), acting in conjunction with them. These are:

(*a*) The telescopic clamp, which clamps the telescope and vertical circle in a vertical plane. When released, these can be rotated in a vertical plane relative to the vertical vernier scales.

(*b*) The upper clamp, which secures the vernier plate to the scale plate. When clamped, these two plates can be regarded as one, and if the scale plate is free to move the vernier plate will move with it.

(*c*) The lower clamp, which secures the scale plate to the fixed parallel plates. When released, the scale plate can move freely in a horizontal plane; when clamped, the scale plate cannot move, and if the upper clamp too is clamped, movement of the vernier plate, 'A' frames and telescopes is also restrained horizontally.

Separate slow motion screws act in conjunction with each of the above clamps for fine adjustment and are only effective after the particular clamp has been tightened.

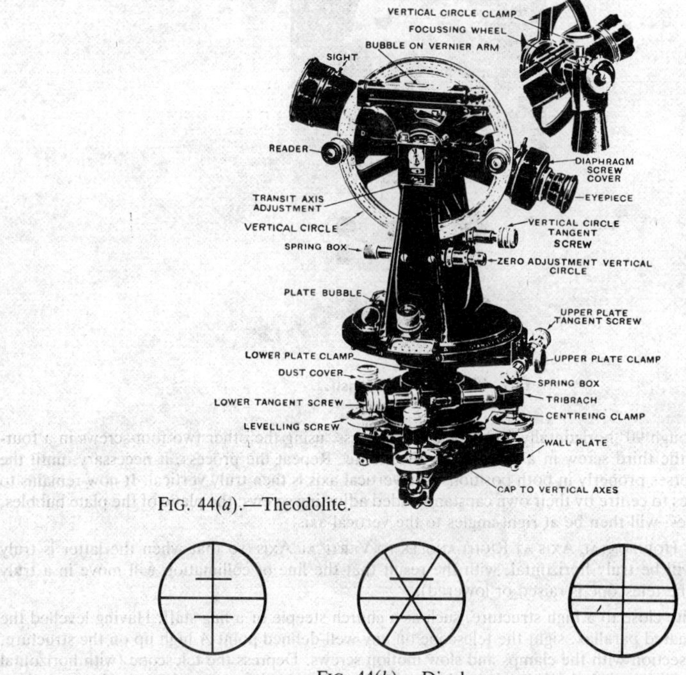

FIG. 44(*a*).—Theodolite.

FIG. 44(*b*).—Diaphragms.

There are thus three clamps and three slow motion screws, and the following is a summary of their main uses: (1) *All clamps free.* Vernier plate and scale plate can rotate independently. Telescope free horizontally and vertically. (2) *Upper clamp tight, other two free.* Vernier plate and scale plate secured together but can rotate in unison. Telescope free horizontally and vertically. (3) *Upper and lower clamps tight, telescope clamp free.* Scale plate fixed. Vernier plate fixed. Telescope free vertically only. (4) *All clamps tight.* Scale plate, vernier plate, telescope all fixed.

The above is a description of a standard type of transit theodolite. Various refinements and modifications have been introduced by different makers, but the broad principles are the same. The theodolite shown in Fig. 44(*a*) has been chosen for the present purpose as the representative instrument because the working parts and their relationships to one another can be clearly seen in the figure. The tendency with contemporary glass-arc instruments is that the working parts are totally enclosed, so that the relationships between them are not so readily visible, and an illustration is not therefore at once so meaningful (See Fig. 45).

ADJUSTMENTS OF THE THEODOLITE.—As with the level, these can be divided into temporary and permanent adjustments.

The temporary adjustments consist of (1) setting up over a station, using the plumb-bob for centering the instrument, (2) levelling the horizontal plates, using the plate bubbles and levelling screws, and (3) focusing the telescope and eliminating parallax, which is just as important as in levelling. The eyepiece normally needs but one adjustment on webs for the day's work, but the object glass must be focused afresh by means of the focusing screw for every sight if the length of sight is appreciably changed.

There are four permanent adjustments, as follows:

(1) ADJUSTMENT OF PLATE BUBBLES AT RIGHT-ANGLES TO VERTICAL AXIS.—The plate bubbles are very short and the telescope bubble is therefore more reliable for making the vertical axis truly vertical. The procedure is:

Set up the instrument approximately level by the foot-screws. Bring the telescope bubble to the centre by the vertical clamp and slow-motion screw over any diagonally opposite foot-screws (in a four-screw instrument) or parallel to any two screws (in a three-screw instrument). Reverse (ie turn through 180° horizontally); if the bubble has run out of centre bring it halfway back by the vertical tangent screw and the other half by the

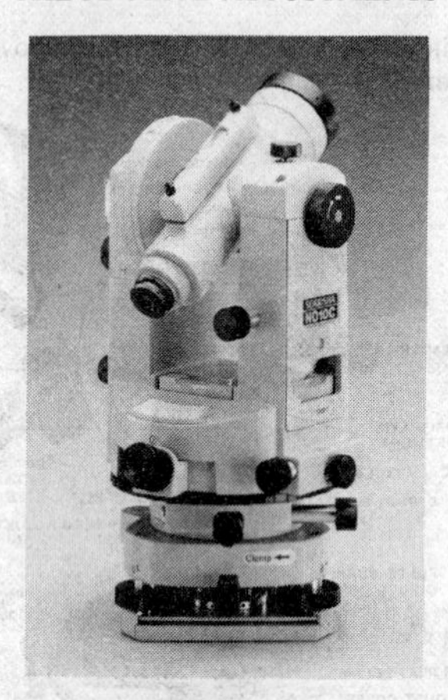

FIG. 45.—Optical Transit.

footscrews. Turn through 90° horizontally and repeat the process, using the other two foot-screws in a four-screw instrument or the third screw in a three-screw theodolite. Repeat the process, if necessary, until the telescope bubble reverses properly in both positions; the vertical axis is then truly vertical. It now remains to bring the plate bubbles to centre by their own capstan-headed adjusting screws; the plane of the plate bubbles, ie the horizontal plates, will then be at right-angles to the vertical axis.

(2) ADJUSTMENT OF HORIZONTAL AXIS AT RIGHT-ANGLES TO VERTICAL AXIS (so that when the latter is truly vertical the former will be truly horizontal, with the result that the line of collimation will move in a truly vertical plane when the telescope is raised or lowered).

Set up the theodolite close to a high structure, such as a church steeple or a flag staff. Having levelled the instrument and eliminated parallax, sight the telescope on any well-defined point A high up on the structure, obtaining accurate bisection with the clamps and slow motion screws. Depress the telescope (with horizontal clamps tight) to an approximately horizontal position and make a mark (eg on a card fastened to a wall) at a point B intersected by the cross wires. Change face and again sight the telescope on A. Once more depress the telescope and, if it does not coincide with B, make a fresh mark D beside B. The point C, midway between B and D, will be in the same vertical plane as A, for in the operation of changing face the two ends of the horizontal axis have been interchanged.

On one side of the horizontal axis there is usually an adjusting screw by which the axis can be raised or lowered until, on sighting to A and depressing the telescope the cross wires intersect C. This operation will need a few trial adjustments.

(3) ADJUSTMENT OF LINE OF COLLIMATION AT RIGHT-ANGLES TO HORIZONTAL AXIS.—If the line of collimation is not perpendicular to the horizontal axis it will describe a flat cone instead of a vertical plane when the telescope is raised or lowered or during 'transiting'. The procedure in making the adjustment is as follows: Set up a A (Fig. 46(a)) and sight to a distant ranging rod or peg in the ground at B, roughly at the same level as the instrument, obtaining accurate bisection of B with both horizontal clamps tightened and using one of the slow motion screws. There is no need in this adjustment to set to zero. Transit the telescope and set a peg C_1 on the line of sight. Release the upper clamp, turn the telescope through 180° in a horizontal plane, re-clamp and again obtain bisection of B, using the upper slow motion screw. Transit the telescope once more and set a peg C_2 at the same distance from A as C_1. If C_1 and C_2 coincide, there is no need for adjustment; if they do not coincide, set a peg D such that $C_2D = \frac{1}{4}C_1C_2$ and adjust the diaphragm screws laterally until the line of sight moves from C_2 to D. After one or two trial adjustments it will be found that C_1 and C_2 will coincide. The reason for making the adjustment an amount $\frac{1}{4}C_1C_2$ will be seen by reference to Fig. 46(a), in which 1–1 and 2–2 are the positions of the trunnion axis and true perpendiculars in the two instrument positions.

(4) ADJUSTMENT OF TELESCOPE BUBBLE TO LINE OF COLLIMATION.—The theodolite is set up at C midway between two pegs or marks, A and B (Fig. 46(b)). After temporary adjustments have been made, the telescope bubble is brought central with the vertical clamp and slow-motion screw, so that the instrument can be used as if it were a level. Readings are taken on a staff held first at A and then at B, the difference between the two readings being the true rise or fall from A to B, whether the instrument is in adjustment or not. Next set up the theodolite at D fairly close to B, bring the telescope bubble central with the vertical slow-motion screw as before, and read the staff held at B. As the distance to B is very small there should be no appreciable error in this reading. The correct reading to a staff held at A can now be calculated from the true difference in level between A and B already found. This difference will be added to the reading at B if there is a fall from B to

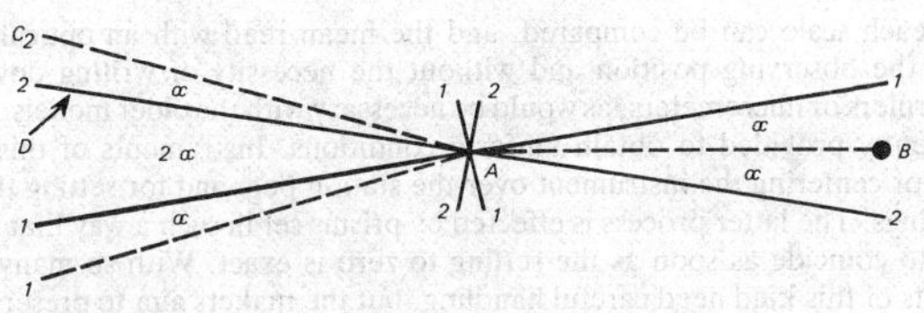

FIG. 46(*a*).

A or subtracted if a rise. The vertical slow-motion screw is turned (if necessary) until this reading is obtained on the staff when held at *B*. The line of collimation will now be horizontal and all that is then needed is to bring the bubble central by means of its own capstan screws.

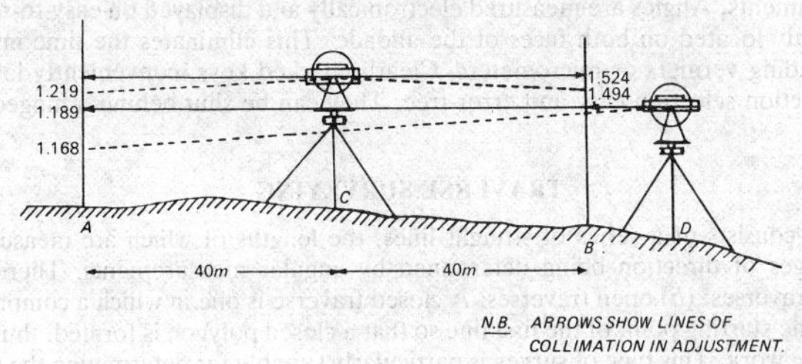

FIG. 46(*b*).

MICROMETER MICROSCOPE.—Large theodolites, and those used for work where great precision in reading is called for, are sometimes provided with micrometer microscopes instead of verniers, because they can be read to a greater degree of accuracy than a vernier and with less eye strain. The mechanism is that of a precision-cut screw thread, having an enlarged micrometer head. The pitch of the threads is chosen to correspond to a definite number of minutes on the main scale, and any fraction of a turn of the screw can be read off a scale engraved on the micrometer head of the screw. Thus, a main scale marked in sixths of a degree (ie 10-minute intervals) would have a micrometer screw with a pitch equal to the length of a 10-minute interval on the main scale, and the micrometer head would be divided into 60 divisions, each representing 10 seconds, thus giving direct reading to the nearest 10 seconds and by estimation to the nearest second. As in the case of verniers, there are two micrometers for the horizontal scale and two for the vertical scale.

'UNIVERSAL' OR 'MEAN READING MICROMETER'.—Modern surveying instruments include transit theodolites in which the engraved silver edges of the horizontal and vertical circles are replaced by annealed optical glass engraved with the scale of degrees, etc, in such a way that a reflector can pass light through the scale on to a chain of prisms, situated in tubular telescopic supports (which replace the A frames) and in the hollow 'trunnion' (or horizontal) axis. The effect of this arrangement is to transfer the images of opposite sides of both vertical and horizontal circles to a single microscope or eyepiece close beside the telescope eyepiece,

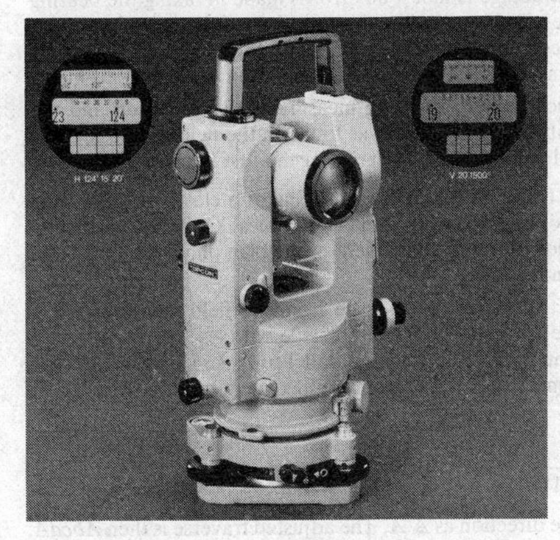

FIG. 47(*a*).

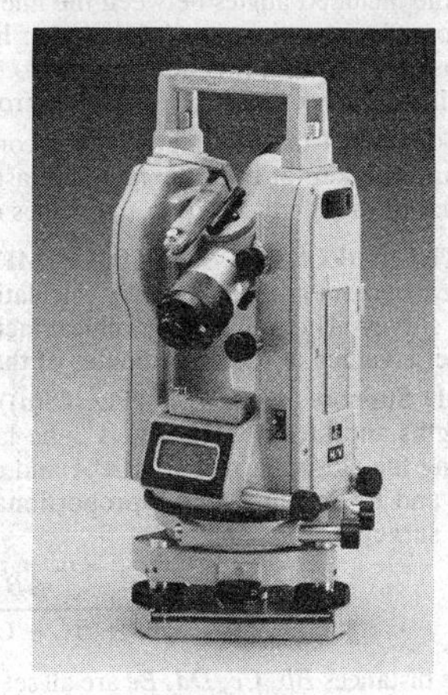

FIG. 47(*b*).

so that both sides of each scale can be compared, and the mean read with an optical micrometer, without moving the eye from the observing position and without the necessity of writing down and averaging the readings of A and B verniers or micrometers, as would be necessary with the older models. Artificial illumination of the circles is frequently provided to obtain uniform conditions. Instruments of this type usually employ reflecting prisms also for centering the instrument over the station peg, and for setting the magnetic needle to zero when taking bearings. The latter process is effected by prisms set in such a way that the two opposite ends of the needle appear to coincide as soon as the setting to zero is exact. With so many adjustable parts and accessories, instruments of this kind need careful handling, but the makers aim to preserve the adjustments by putting as many such parts as possible inside the instrument. The telescope is invariably of the internal focusing variety so that it can be made practically dust- and damp-proof. Figure 47(*a*) illustrates an instrument of this type and shows an example of a horizontal reading with this instrument.

ELECTRONIC DIGITAL THEODOLITE.—The electronic digital theodolite (Fig. 47(*b*)) is a recent addition to the range of instruments. Angles are measured electronically and displayed on easy-to-read eight-digit LCD read-outs conveniently located on both faces of the alidade. This eliminates the time involved and possible errors caused by reading verniers or micrometers. Clearly-marked keys, conveniently located on one of the standards, make function selection easy and error-free. They can be shut behind a hinged cover fitted with a magnetic catch.

TRAVERSE SURVEYING

A traverse survey consists of a series of straight lines, the lengths of which are measured by chaining or otherwise, the changes of direction being determined by angular measurements. There are two types of traverse: (*a*) closed traverses; (*b*) open traverses. A closed traverse is one in which a complete circuit is made; the last line ends at the starting point of the first line so that a closed polygon is formed, thus providing a check on the accuracy of the work. This type of survey is particularly suitable for determining the boundaries of large areas, woods, lakes, etc, where interior detail is not required. If the last line FA in a closed traverse $ABCDEFA$ does not return to the starting point A (this being shown either by calculation or by plotting), but finishes at a point A', the distance AA' is known as the 'closing error' and must be 'adjusted' or 'balanced'. An open traverse is one in which a complete circuit is not made, and it cannot therefore be adjusted with the same accuracy as a closed traverse unless it is made between two points whose positions are accurately known. It is suitable for the survey of long narrow strips of land, roads, railways, rivers, etc.

There are two principal methods of traversing: (1) by measuring the angles included between adjacent survey lines; a theodolite is almost invariably used for this purpose, but for approximate surveys a box sextant could be substituted; (2) by taking the magnetic bearing of each line; as in the previous case, a theodolite would generally be used, though for approximate surveys it could be done with a prismatic compass.

METHOD OF INCLUDED ANGLES.—The angles between successive lines of a closed traverse may be either the interior angles of the polygon or the exterior angles, depending on the direction in which the traverse is made. Since theodolites are graduated in a clockwise direction, exterior angles are measured in a clockwise traverse and interior angles in an anti-clockwise traverse.

The sum of the angles in a traverse should equal $(2n \pm 4)$ right angles, where the plus sign is used for a clockwise traverse and the minus sign for an anti-clockwise traverse and n is the number of legs in the traverse.

METHOD OF BEARINGS.—In this method, the magnetic bearing of each line is measured independently, instead of the included angles between the lines. The main advantage is that if an error is made in taking the bearing of one line the directions of the other lines will not be affected. Against this must be put the more important consideration that it is not possible to check the correctness of the observations while in the field, except by taking the back bearing of each line from its far end, as well as the forward bearing from its commencement.

Sometimes the two methods are combined, the included angles being measured at each station and the bearings taken of both the first and last lines; the bearing of the last line as found in the field should then be equal to that deduced from the values of the included angles and the bearing of the first line.

THE CHECKING AND ADJUSTMENT OF TRAVERSE SURVEYS.—Checking of a closed traverse may be carried out graphically or by calculation, and any closing error distributed by a process known as 'balancing' the survey. The following graphical methods are employed where adjustment of the plan only is required and precise values of the co-ordinates of the stations are not needed.

(1) Suppose $ABCDEA'$ (Fig. 48(*a*)) is a closed traverse plotted to scale from the field measurement of lengths and included angles. A', the last point of the traverse, does not coincide with A, the distance $A'A$ being the closing error. Join $A'A$ and draw lines through B, C, D and E parallel to $A'A$. Distances Bb, Cc, Dd and Ee are then set out proportionate to the distances of B, C, D and E respectively from the origin A of the survey; for instance,

$$Cc = A'A\left(\frac{AB + BC}{AB + BC + CD + DE + EA'}\right)$$

The distances Bb, Cc, Dd, Ee are all set out in the same direction as $A'A$. The adjusted traverse is then $AbcdA$. Instead of calculating the proportionate distances as above, the process may be done graphically (Fig. 48(*b*)).

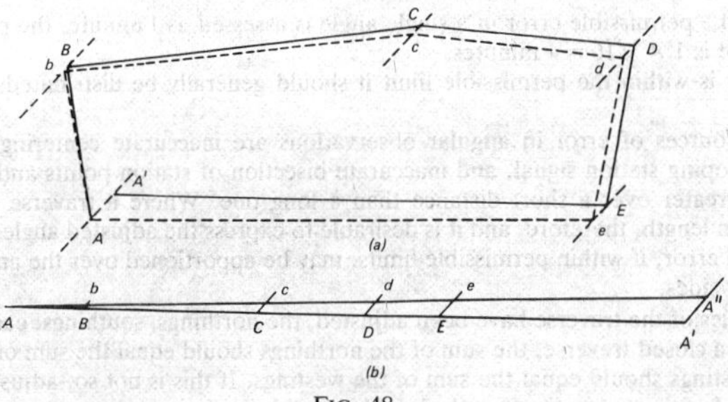

FIG. 48.

Set out, to any convenient scale, a straight line $ABCDEA'$ such that AB, BC, CD, DE, EA' represent the respective lengths of the sides of the traverse. From A' draw $A'A''$ parallel and equal to the closing error, and join AA''. Through B, C, D and E draw lines parallel to $A'A''$ to meet AA'' in b, c, d and e respectively. Then Bb, Cc, Dd, Ee are the required distances.

(2) An alternative graphical method of adjustment is illustrated in Fig. 48. $ABCDEA'$ is a closed traverse, with a closing error AA'. Join AA' and produce it to cut the perimeter of the traverse at Y such that AY divides the figure roughly in half. If AY does not produce this condition, the closing error is transferred to another station by drawing lines parallel and equal to the sides of the traverse from each station in turn until

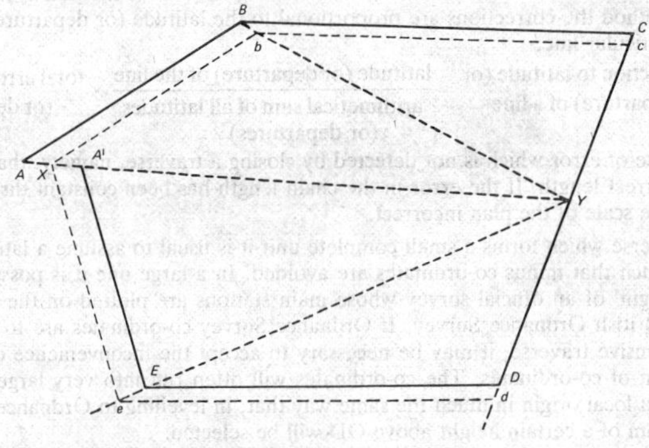

FIG. 49.

the new position of the closing error gives a line which will roughly bisect the figure. Divide the closing error AA' at a point X such that $[AX/A'X]$ = (perimeter $ABCY$/perimeter $YDEA'$). Join Y to the remaining stations B and E. Through X draw a line parallel to AB to cut BY in b. Through b draw a line parallel to BC to cut CY in c. Through X draw a line parallel to $A'E$ to cut YE produced in e. Through e draw a line parallel to ED to meet YD produced in d. Then $XbcdeX$ is the adjusted traverse.

It will be noted that in Method (1) both the lengths of the sides and the values of the angles are altered by adjustment, whereas in Method (2) it is only the lengths of the sides which are adjusted, the final figure having the same angles as the original.

Graphical methods of adjustment would seldom be adopted if the co-ordinates of the stations are to be calculated or the closing error eliminated with greater precision. The method to be used for such traverses is as follows:

(3) (*a*) First check and if necessary adjust the angles. (*b*) Calculate the northings, southings, eastings and westings, using these adjusted angles. (*c*) Check and adjust the values in (*b*), as will be described below, and deduce the latitudes and departures of the stations. Each of these will now be described in detail:

(*a*) The angles of a closed traverse should total $(2n \pm 4)$ right angles, where n is the number of sides, the plus sign being used where exterior angles are measured and the minus sign when the angles are interior ones.

If the angles do not add up to the required figure the question then arises as to what amount of error is permissible. By the 'Rule of Least Squares', if the error in a single angle of a traverse is 1 minute, then the total error in the whole traverse will amount to 1 minute multiplied by $\sqrt{n}$, where n is the number of sides in the traverse and hence the number of angles. Thus, if there are 16 sides in a particular traverse and the permissible error in a single angle is assessed as 1 minute, the permissible error in the whole traverse is $1 \times \sqrt{16} = 4$ minutes.

If the error is within the permissible limit it should generally be distributed equally among all the angles.

The chief sources of error in angular observations are inaccurate centering over a station point, observing a sloping station signal, and inaccurate bisection of station points and any of these errors is likely to be greater over a short distance than a long one. Where a traverse has sides which differ considerably in length, therefore, and it is desirable to express the adjusted angles to the nearest minute only, the total error, if within permissible limits, may be apportioned over the angles which are formed by the shorter sides.

(*b*) When the angles of the traverse have been adjusted, the northings, southings, eastings and westings are calculated. In a closed traverse, the sum of the northings should equal the sum of the southings and the sum of the eastings should equal the sum of the westings. If this is not so, adjustments will need to be made in these before proceeding to calculate the total latitudes and departures of the stations.

(*c*) Two methods of making these adjustments are as follows:

(1) *Bowditch's Method.* Corrections are found from the following expression:

$$\text{Correction to latitude (or departure) of a line} = \frac{\text{length of the line}}{\text{perimeter of the traverse}} \times \text{total error in latitude (or departure)}$$

This method may be carried out graphically as described in Method (1) of the graphical adjustments. It was explained that by this method, both the lengths of the sides and the values of the angles are altered by adjustment. As, however, the measurement of the angles in a traverse is much more precise than the chaining of the lines, the following alternative method is often used.

(2) In this method the corrections are proportional to the latitude (or departure) and not to the length of the particular line.

$$\text{Correction to latitude (or departure) of a line} = \frac{\text{latitude (or departure) of the line}}{\text{arithmetical sum of all latitudes (or departures)}} \times \text{total error in latitude (or departure)}$$

There is one cause of error which is not detected by closing a traverse, namely, that due to the measuring chain being of incorrect length. If the error in the chain length has been constant throughout the survey the effect is to make the scale of the plan incorrect.

In plotting a traverse which forms a small complete unit it is usual to assume a latitude and departure for the starting point such that minus co-ordinates are avoided. In a large one it is possible that it will have to conform to the 'origin' of an official survey whose main stations are plotted on the co-ordinate system; an example is in the British Ordnance Survey. If Ordnance Survey co-ordinates are to be used to help in the checking of an extensive traverse, it may be necessary to accept the inconvenience of having minus figures related to the origin of co-ordinates. The co-ordinates will often run into very large figures and it may be necessary to adopt a local origin in much the same way that, in levelling to Ordnance Datum in an elevated district, a local datum of a certain height above OD will be selected.

Areas Included in Traverse Surveys.—For a closed traverse in which the co-ordinates of the stations are known, the following method may be used for calculating the area enclosed by the traverse lines. Consider a reference meridian through the most westerly station. Departure distances measured from this reference meridian to the mid points of the sides of the traverse are known as the *longitudes* of those sides. Then the area enclosed by the traverse is the algebraic sum of the products (latitude × longitude) for all lines. Note that latitudes may be plus or minus; longitudes are always positive. In practice, it is more convenient to use double longitudes and to halve the resultant area. The double longitude of a given line is the algebraic sum of the double longitude of the preceding line, the departure of the preceding line, and the departure of the given line.

TRIANGULATION

Triangulation surveys are a means of determining the positions of particular points on land surfaces by the use of triangles, in which the length of one side is known either by direct measurement or calculation from other known positions, and the three angles are measured with a theodolite. The object of these surveys is to form a skeleton framework of triangles, usually over a very large area of land or a complete country; they do not in themselves show natural or artificial features but merely fix the positions of isolated stations which can be subsequently used for smaller and detailed surveys.

Selection of Stations.—The following general rules govern the choice of suitable positions for triangulation stations; (1) the triangles should be 'well conditioned', ie as nearly equilateral as possible and no angle should perferably be less than 30°; (2) each station should be clearly visible from adjoining stations to enable direct sights to be taken; positions on high ground with an all round view are therefore very suitable; (3) the distances between stations should not be so great that there is difficulty in sighting accurately with a theodolite nor so small that any errors in centering the instrument or bisecting the station point will seriously affect the angle. The type of country is frequently the deciding factor in determining the distance between stations. In flat country for example the effect of curvature of the earth becomes apparent at great distances and tall beacons have to be erected in order to make stations visible.

Arrangement of Triangles.—A basic principle in triangulation is to work 'from the whole to the part' and not conversely, ie firstly to form a main framework of large triangles from which smaller triangles can be established. The most satisfactory framework is obtained by starting from one very carefully measured base line, the length of which varies in accordance with the size and nature of the land to be surveyed, and selecting prominent landmarks on either side of this base to give well-conditioned triangles. Each angle of the triangle is measured with the theodolite and the sides are calculated by trigonometry. These calculated sides then form the bases from which other triangles can be set out, angles being measured and sides calculated as before. The calculated side of one triangle continues to be used as the base of another until eventually the whole area is covered. Thus, the whole framework is established from one measured line and many measured angles; since it is always easier to measure an angle with greater precision than a line, the accuracy of the framework is of a high order. This main framework of *primary* triangles is then split up into smaller or *secondary* triangles, and these in turn are sub-divided into *tertiary* triangles having sides of shorter length. The detail surveys can then be carried out using the tertiary sides as the base lines. In most cases the methods of chain survey or traversing are suitable for the detail work, but tacheometry, plane tabling and photographic surveying are also widely used.

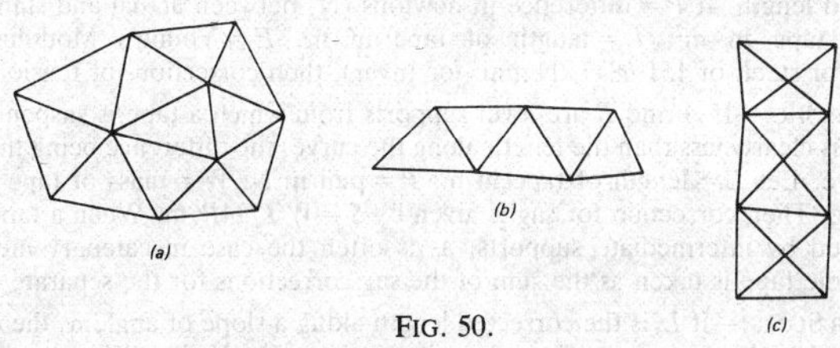

FIG. 50.

The best arrangement is to cover the whole area with triangles formed by a network of intersecting polygons (Fig. 50(*a*)). but where this would be too lengthy or costly simplified arrangements such as simple chains of triangles (Fig. 50(*b*)) or interlacing triangles (Fig. 50(*c*)) are adopted.

BASE LINE MEASUREMENT.—Upon the accuracy of measurement of the base line depends the accuracy of the whole of the triangulation; an error in the base measurement will be reflected proportionately in all lengths in the survey and is equivalent to an error in the scale of plotting. Great care is therefore necessary in base measurement. The 'catenary' method is commonly employed, in which a steel band or tape is suspended above the ground so as to be clear of low obstructions. When a tape or wire of uniform cross section and weight per unit length throughout is suspended at its ends, it assumes the natural curve known as the *catenary*; it is from the properties of this curve that the lineal distances are calculated. For precise work the tapes or wires are made of a nickel steel alloy known as *Invar*, which has a very low coefficient of expansion (about 0·00000055 per degree C, compared with 0·0000117 for steel). The tapes are not graduated for their full length, but only for a short distance on either side of the terminal marks.

Field Procedure.—For precise work, Invar tapes or wires 25–100m long are used, the length selected being governed by the nature and undulations of the ground. Commencing at the beginning of the line to be measured, the tape is suspended on special tripod supports so as to hang freely between them. These supports have a metal plate on top, with an engraved mark against which the tape reading is indicated. A tension is applied to the tape by suspended weights (usually not less than about 20 × weight of tape) or by spring balance, the tape being supported on trestles during the straining process to avoid displacement of the tripod supports. Figure 51 illustrates the arrangement, *A* being the straining trestle at which the tension is applied and *B* the

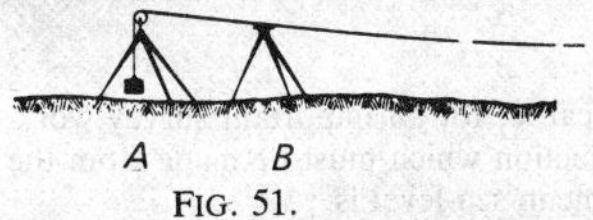

FIG. 51.

measuring tripod. To ensure that the supports are in a straight line, a theodolite set up at one end of the line is used for alignment. When the required tension is obtained, the tape is read through a magnifying lens against the indicator marks on the measuring tripods at each end of the tape, several pairs of readings being taken. The tension is recorded, also the temperature of the tape (obtained by reading the thermometer while it is in contact with the tape, but shaded from the sun at the time of measurement), and the levels of the supports are found by normal precise levelling. The process is repeated for succeeding tape lengths until the end of the base line is reached, the last length being generally an odd amount. When a tape more than 25 m long is employed, it is usual to support it by intermediate supports over a number of equal spans; a 100 m tape in four spans of 25 m each, for instance. The slope is usually deduced from the length of each span and the difference of level between its ends, but sometimes it is measured direct by the theodolite used for alignment.

Corrections.—The corrections to be applied to the observed lengths to ascertain true horizontal distances are: (1) to standard length; (2) for temperature; (3) for tension; (4) for sag; (5) for slope; (6) to mean sea-level.

(1) CORRECTION TO STANDARD LENGTH.—In order to have a ready check on the accuracy of tapes used in the field and to guard against permanent variations in length which may arise, it is usual to have a reference tape which has been tested against a standard length at the National Physical Laboratory, Teddington, or the Ordnance Survey Office, Chessington. Comparison of the field tape with the reference tape, under the same conditions of tension and temperature, will give the necessary correction to be applied. If the field tape is too long, measurements taken with it are too small and the correction must be added; if the field tape is too short, observed measurements are too great and the correction must be deducted.

(2) CORRECTION FOR TEMPERATURE.—Tapes for precision work are generally calibrated and standardised at a stated temperature. If L_s is the length of tape at the standard temperature T_s, and c is the coefficient of expansion, then at a temperature T, the correction to be applied is $L_s \times (T - T_s)c$; if T is greater than T_s, the correction is deducted.

(3) CORRECTION FOR TENSION.—When a pull is applied at the straining trestles, the tape is in tension and is stretched a small amount, thereby making the observed length too small; the correction therefore has to be added to the observed length. If P = difference in newtons (N) between actual and standard pull, A = area of cross section of tape in m², L = length of tape in m, E = Young's Modulus for the material (=206·8428 kN/mm² for steel, or 151·6847 kN/mm² for Invar), then correction for tension = PL/AE (in m).

(4) CORRECTION FOR SAG.—If A and B are level supports from which a tape is suspended in catenary, the horizontal length AB is clearly less than the length along the curve, the difference being the correction for sag, which will be negative. Let L = length of tape in m; P = pull in N; W = mass of tape suspended between indicator marks, in kg. Then correction for sag is given by $S = W^2L/24P^2$ m. When a tape is suspended from its ends and supported by intermediate supports, as is often the case in catenary measurement, the sag correction for the whole tape is taken as the sum of the sag corrections for the separate spans.

(5) CORRECTION FOR SLOPE.—If L_s is the corrected length along a slope of angle α, the corrected horizontal length L_H is given by $L_H = L_S \cos \alpha$ and the correction is $L_S - L_H$. If the difference in level between the supports is found by levelling to be h, the angle of slope can be found from $\sin \alpha = h/L_s$, or alternatively the correction is given by $-(h^2/2L_s)$.

(6) CORRECTION TO MEAN SEA-LEVEL.—When corrections have been made for temperature, slope, tension, sag, and correction to standard, there remains a further correction for elevation, because the distance between the vertical lines at two points on the earth's surface will vary directly as the distance from the earth's centre. Thus, in Fig. 52, the circle passing through A and B represents the spherical surface of the earth at mean sea-level while the points C and D are points some hundreds of metres above A and B respectively, C being vertically over A, and D vertically over B. It is not practicable to measure lines at sea-level; measurements must be made at the level of the land in question. If, then, the length at CD is measured, a deduction to arrive

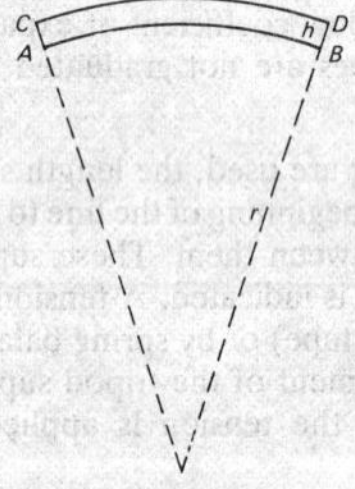

FIG. 52. FIG. 53.

at the length AB must be made because, for all important survey work, distances are reduced to mean sea-level. It can be shown that the deduction which must be made from the measured length of the base line in order to reduce it to a distance at mean sea-level is:

$$CD - AB = CD\{h/(r + h)\},$$

which is practically equivalent to $CD \times h/r$ because h is so small in comparison with r that the denominator $(r + h)$ will not differ appreciably from r. An average value of r is 6·367 km.

Extension of Base Line.—The measured base line is seldom long enough to form one of the sides of the triangles which comprise the triangulation and it is therefore necessary to extend the base line. The method is indicated in Fig. 53. AB is the directly-measured base. Two points E and F on opposite sides of AB are selected so as to form well-conditioned triangles. At each of the stations A, B, and F the angles subtended at the remaining three stations are observed. The length EF is then calculated from each triangle and the mean result determined. A further extension to the base may be made by selecting two more distant points G and H, the line GH acting as the new base line, its length being calculated as before.

PROCEDURE IN TRIANGULATION.—Having selected and measured a suitable base line such as *AB* in Fig. 53, we may use this as the foundation for the system of primary triangulation which will cover the whole of the area or country to be surveyed. The base *AB* will first be extended to a length *GH* as indicated above. If required, the process is continued by observations from *G* and *H* to another point *K* to find the length of *KF*, which is far longer than the original base *AB* and may be near the limit of visibility. The line *KF* will now be made to form the base of at least two more triangles, extending further afield and the sides of those triangles will in their turn form bases of still more triangles, as shown (on a much smaller scale) in Fig. 53. In this way the whole area is covered by a network of triangles, with sides which may be 50 or 60 km long. These are the *primary* triangles, which serve as the foundation for the *secondary* triangles and these in turn for the *tertiary* triangles. Sometimes the triangulation is made up of two groups of triangles, *major* triangles approximating closely to primary triangles and *minor* triangles to secondary or tertiary triangles.

Measurement and Adjustment of Angles.—In conducting a triangulation, the three angles of each triangle should be observed, for in this way a ready check is obtained and any slight error may be apportioned. The extent to which repetition, reiteration and changing swing are adopted will depend upon the degree of accuracy required, but in all cases it will be advisible to change face, and generally the other precautionary measures are also adopted. In practice the work of checking and adjusting the angles of a large trigonometrical survey

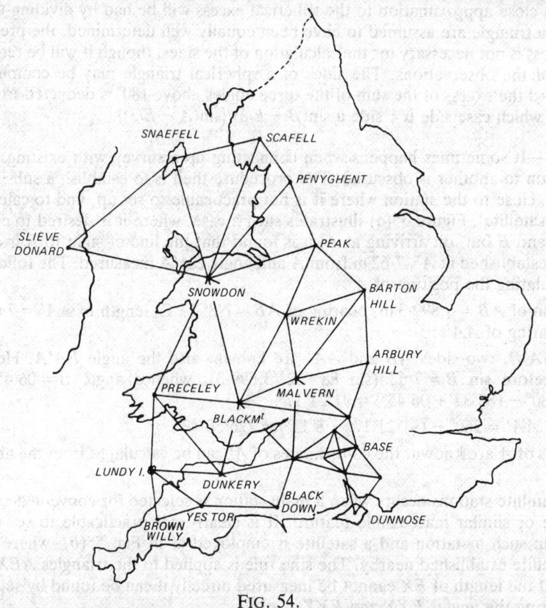

FIG. 54.

is an arduous task involving considerable calculation. Briefly, the angles should comply with the following equations of condition: (1) the three angles of each triangle should total 180°; (2) all the angles meeting at a given station (say at Snowdon in Fig. 54) should total 360°; (3) all the angles at the corners of every polygon formed (such as those encircling Snowdon and Scafell, Penyghent, The Peak, Wrekin, Black Mountain, etc) should total twice as many right angles as the figure has sides plus (or minus) four right-angles.

Any adjustment of angles to comply with equation (1) must be carried out in such a manner as to leave equations (2) and (3) satisfied, and also so as not to upset the adjustments of adjoining triangles and polygons, many of which overlap. Owing to the curvature of the earth the triangles formed at sea-level are not plane triangles, but spherical triangles. The three angles of a spherical triangle do not add up exactly to 180°, but to a little more, the difference being called the *spherical excess*; the amount of this is, however, negligible except in very large triangles. The test of the correctness of the angular observations taken in any one triangle is therefore to see whether the three angles of each triangle add up exactly to 180° plus (in the larger triangles) the spherical excess; and, if not, to distribute the error among the angles, unless it is so great to necessitate the work being done again.

The observation of the angles should not be made in strong sunshine. It may be done on any cloudy but clear day, or during the evening, but the best conditions are obtained at night, the stations being illuminated. Some of the sights may be so long that they are possible only in exceptional weather, in which case these particular observations must be postponed until the necessary conditions occur. An example of this was the triangle on the Ordnance Survey, connecting Snowdon, Snaefell and Slieve Donard in Northern Ireland, the sides of which were well over 160 km in length.

The error (ie discrepancy from 180°) should be divided equally amongst the three angles only if the angles have been measured with equal accuracy and under similar conditions. It may be, however, that the weather during the observation of one angle was not entirely favourable, or perhaps the number of observations differed for each angle. In such cases it is usual to give *weights* to each angle, judged as a measure of their relative dependability; the error is then apportioned amongst the angles in the ratio of the reciprocals of the weights. Thus, if W_1, W_2, W_3 are the weights given to angles 1, 2 and 3 respectively of a particular triangle, and if E is the error, then the correction to any angle is equal to the reciprocal of the weight given to the angle, divided by the addition of the reciprocals of each of the three weights given to the three angles of the triangle. For example, the correction to angle 1 = Excess $\{(1/W_1)/(1/W_1 + 1/W_2 + 1/W_3)\}$

Spherical Excess.—E, in sec $= S/(r^2 \sin 1'') = ab \sin C/(2r^2 \sin 1'')$ where S = area of the triangle, r = radius of the earth.

$$S = (ab \sin C)/2 = \sqrt{\{s(s-a)(s-b)(s-c)\}},\ s \text{ being } (a+b+c)/2.$$

Between latitudes 45° and 25° the spherical excess amounts to about 1′ for an area of 195·5 km². If the area in km² be known, a close approximation to the spherical excess will be had by dividing the area by 195·5. If the three angles of a triangle are assumed to have been equally well determined, the previous determination of the spherical excess is not necessary for the calculation of the sides, though it will be required for estimating the relative value of the observations. The sides of a spherical triangle may be computed as if they were rectilineal if one-third the excess of the sum of the three angles above 180° is deducted from each of the three observed angles, in which case side b = side $a \sin(B - E/3)/\{\sin(A - E/3)\}$.

Satellite Stations.—It sometimes happens when connecting up a survey with existing trig stations that the view from one station to another is obscured. The procedure then is to establish a subsidiary station, known as a *satellite* station, close to the station where it is not practicable to set up, and to calculate the position or coordinates of the 'satellite'. Figure 55(a) illustrates such a case, where it is desired to connect a survey with two trig stations A and B but, on arriving at A, it is found that the line of sight to B is obscured. A satellite station is therefore established at A', 7·62 m from A and angle $BA'A$ measured. The following example shows the method of calculating the position of A'.

Example.—Length of AB = 3,899·3 m, bearing of AB = N8° 12′E, length of AA' = 7·62 m, angle $BA'A$ = 88°32′. Find the bearing of AA'.

In the triangle $AA'B$, two sides AB and AA' are known, also the angle $BA'A$. Hence, $\sin B/(A'A) = \sin A'/(AB)$. Therefore $\sin B = 7{\cdot}62\ (\sin 88°\ 32'/3{,}899{\cdot}3)$; whence angle B = 06′43″, Now angle A = 180° − (A'+B) = 180° − (88°32′ + 06′43″) = 91°21′17″.

Hence bearing of AA' = 360° − (91°21′17″ − 8°12′) = 276°50′43″.

If the co-ordinates of A are known, the co-ordinates of A' can be calculated from the above bearing and the length of AA'.

Another use of satellite stations occurs when a main station is selected for convenience and ease of sighting on say a lofty spire or similar inaccessible feature. It is clearly not practicable to set up the theodolite to measure angles from such a station and a satellite is employed as in Fig. 55(b), where E is an inaccessible station and X a satellite established nearby. The sine rule is applied to the triangles AEX, BEX, CEX, DEX as in the example. If the length of EX cannot be measured directly it can be found by setting out a short base line XY and measuring the angles EXY and EYX.

ORDNANCE SURVEY.—In illustration of the method of triangulation on a large scale, the following is a brief description of the British Ordnance Survey. A new triangulation was commenced in 1936, but the original survey will first be described, then some of the improvements introduced in the new one. Figure 54 shows a portion of the main triangulation of the United Kingdom made between 1783 and 1853. The base line originally intended to be used was measured in 1983 on Hounslow Heath, a few kilometres out of London, but it was found to be too short and a new one, just over 11 km in length, was set up on Salisbury Plain. Colby's 'compensation rods' were used in the measurement, and the remarkable degree of precision of 1/93,000 was attained.

A theodolite, made by Ramsden, having a 36 in primary plate was erected in the highest points up and down the country, and a system of primary triangles, the sides of which were capable of being calculated to within one inch, was established. Certain of the sides were used to connect up with the survey of Ireland and of the numerous small islands around the coast thus making one complete survey instead of a number of small independent ones. So accurate was primary triangulation that a 'base of verification' measured by Lough Foyle in Northern Ireland was found to differ less than five inches from its length as calculated through the network of triangles from the base at Salisbury, some 360 miles away. The position of suitable hills naturally influenced the size and shape of the primary triangles very largely, and those along the East coast were very much smaller than those in the West because the East Counties are very flat. Nevertheless all triangles were well-conditioned.

The main triangulation was split up with the aid of 24 in and 18 in and smaller theodolites, into secondary and tertiary triangulations before any attempt was made to survey the detail of physical features of the country. The average length of side in the primary triangulation was 35 miles, and in secondary and tertiary triangles it was 11 and 2 miles respectively. The primary and secondary triangulation stations (usually called *trig stations*) were made permanent and were buried at varying distances below ground surface according to the nature of the subsoil. Their exact location was not disclosed to public view. Tertiary stations were made semi-permanent and consisted of a heavy tile with the station mark in the centre buried 20 in below the surface with a wooden erection above ground while the survey work work was in progress. In towns, the tertiary stations took the form of a brass plug set in a block of concrete or cemented into a hole in the paving or kerb.

The detail work was performed by independent parties of surveyors each responsible for a certain number of tertiary triangles, and the method used was principally chain and offset.

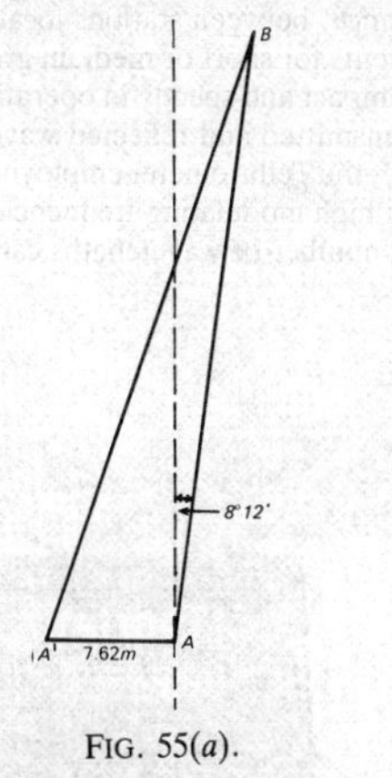

FIG. 55(*a*).

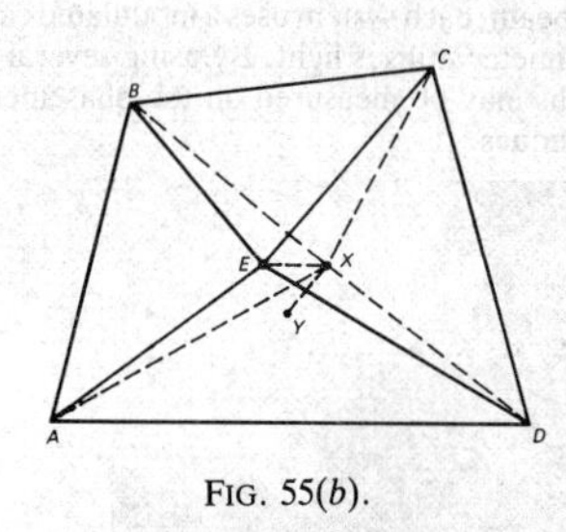

FIG. 55(*b*).

Notes on the Re-Triangulation.—The re-triangulation (begun in 1935) was considered necessary for the following reasons: (1) considerable changes had taken place in the nature of the countryside; (2) it is important to have accurate maps and accurate station points and levels for military and civil purposes; (3) mine surveyors require accurate maps in order to determine the exact extent of their workings; (4) many of the original secondary and tertiary triangulation stations had been lost; satisfactory records had not been kept of their positions and in many cases they had been removed or built over.

For various reasons it was decided not to use the old Salisbury Plain base, and a new one was accordingly chosen on a site farther north, in Berkshire. It was about eleven km long and was measured at the surprising speed of 2·4 km per day to an even greater degree of precision than its predecessor. Three Invar tapes and a series of tripods with weights and pulleys were used in the measurement, and two more Invar tapes were kept solely for the purpose of constantly checking the accuracy of those actually in use. The tapes were tested at the National Physical Laboratory to a degree of 1/1,000,000. A check base measured at Lossiemouth gave a very satisfactory proof of the accuracy of the work. The theodolites used were of the 'Tavistock' class made by Cooke, Troughton and Simms. Their principal advantage is that a single observation gives the mean of the readings on opposite sides of the scale, thus greatly reducing errors of graduation. The angle can be read direct to the nearest half-second, and by estimation to the nearest tenth of a second. The horizontal circle is 133 mm dia and the instrument is easily portable, a great improvement on the Ramsden theodolite used in the first triangulation which had a 914 mm circle and required several men to carry it about. Angles were observed eight times on each face.

The primary and secondary triangles had sides of average lengths of 40 and 13 km respectively, and the shortness of the secondary sides rendered a complete tertiary triangulation unnecessary. To secure longer sides and better-conditioned triangles in the flat Eastern Counties, portable steel towers 34 m high were used. The average angular error in primary triangulation was just about one second per triangle. Care was taken to give permanency to the position of primary and secondary trig stations, not only for the OS records but also so that they could be used by surveyors and engineers. A concrete pillar 1·06 m high above ground surface was erected over each station, a special device being provided to take three-screw theodolites, heliographs and beacon reflectors. A bench mark of the bracket type was let into the side. Much of the detail was measured with chain and offset staff, but several hundred square kilometers of country in the Midlands were surveyed by air photography. It remains to be seen whether this method of detail survey is entirely satisfactory, but great strides have been made in recent years and especially during the war.

The National Grid.—The National Grid is the system of co-ordinates adopted to define the position of any point in the United Kingdom. The grid comprises a rectangle 1,000 kilometres (km) by 700 km containing the whole of Great Britain with the exception of the Orkney and Shetland Islands, which have special grid references prefixed by the letter N. The grid is divided into squares having sides of 10 km, 1 km, or 100 metres long according to the scale of the Ordnance Map used. The 'origin' of the grid is a point a little to the south-west of Land's End so that all points within the grid have positive Easting and Northing distances. The position of any point is defined by its easting and northing, in that order (the letters E and N do not appear, as the convention is sufficiently well recognised).

The sizes of grid squares adopted for various scales of Ordnance maps and plans enable a point to be defined with an accuracy appropriate to the scale of the map. They are as follows: ten mile and $\frac{1}{4}$ in maps, 10 km; one inch, six inch and 1/25,000 maps, 1 km; 1/2,500 and 1/1,250 maps, 100 metres.

ELECTRONIC INSTRUMENTS FOR DISTANCE MEASUREMENT.—A number of techniques have been developed for the measurement of distances, or differences of distance, between stations located from air to land, sea to land, or land to land. Among the high precision instruments for short or medium ground distances are the Tellurometer and the Geodimeter, which are lightweight, compact and speedy in operation. They each measure the distance between stations in terms of the phases of transmitted and reflected waves. In order to concentrate the beam, each system uses a modulated carrier technique, the Tellurometer employing microwaves, whilst the Geodimeter utilises light. By using several closely spaced high modulating frequencies, fractions of short wavelengths may be measured on the phasemeter, whilst the number of wavelengths can be calculated by vernier techniques.

FIG. 56.—Tellumat. (*Tellumat Ltd*)

FIG. 57.—Geodimeter 210 (*Geotronics Ltd*).

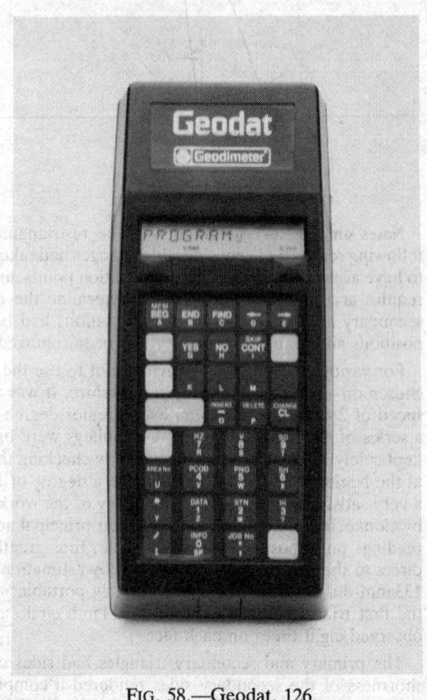

FIG. 58.—Geodat. 126.

Tellurometer.—Measurements are made between two instruments known as the master and remote stations which are mounted on tripods plumbed over the stations. Observations are taken at the master station while another operator manipulates the remote station on telephone instructions from the master operator. This duplex telephone is part of the instrument. A modulated wave is emitted from the master, received at the remote and re-radiated back to the master in a different form. The return wave is electronically compared with the transmitted wave, the phase shift being measured. The phase is indicated on a cathode ray tube. The patterns shown by various frequencies are compared and the resulting calculations corrected by various factors proportional to atmospheric temperature, pressure and vapour pressure.

Master and remote stations are illustrated, in Fig. 56, of the Tellumat CMW 20, a recent development. The figure shows the hand-held unit with touch-key pad and large LCD display which allows measurements to be made remotely from the instrument, thereby avoiding the possibility of misalignment due to accidental bumping. The unit incorporates a duplex speech link and audible alignment facility, and provides access for retrieval of survey data, stored in the internal system memory.

Geodimeter.—Measurements between two ground stations involve the use of a manned instrument at one station and a passive unmanned reflector at the other. Both are set up on tripods and plumbed over the survey points in the same manner as a theodolite. The instrument transmits modulated light to the reflector. A short interval elapses before the light returns and the phase of the modulation is therefore retarded. The phases of the outgoing and returned signal are then measured. (The frequency of the modulation is determined by a crystal oscillator which is coupled to an electronic shutter known as a Kerr cell.) As the modulation wavelength is accurately known, the readings obtained are a function of the distance and are afterwards computed taking into account the atmospheric conditions of temperature and air pressure only.

The passive reflectors used do not require accurate pointing at the instrument, as being retrodirective prisms each made in the form of three planes mutually perpendicular to each other, the tolerance of pointing is some ±20°. The accuracy of the Geodimeter is a standard deviation of less than 10 mm plus 2 ($10^{-6} \times$ distance), and the Geodimeter light wave is unaffected by external influences such as spurious reflection, etc. The instrument is ideal for taking accurate measurements along busy roads, in tunnels and mine shafts, etc, in a fraction of the time taken by conventional methods.

Fig. 57 shows the Geodimeter 210, in conjunction with which one can use the Geodat 126 (Fig. 58) for data-recording and field calculations.

TACHEOMETRY

The name is derived from Greek words meaning 'quick measurement'. In this method distances and heights may be computed by observations from a tacheometer to a levelling staff and the application of trigonometry; no direct measurement such as chaining or taping is required. Tacheometry is based on the geometrical principle of similar triangles. Most present-day theodolites may be used as tacheometers provided they are fitted with a diaphragm having, in addition to the central horizontal web, two other webs equidistant from and parallel to the central web; these additional webs are known as stadia lines or hairs. Figure 59 illustrates the arrangement in a theodolite fitted with such a diaphragm. Here a, b and c represent the stadia lines and O the object glass. Rays of light from the staff at A and C will be inverted at a and c respectively, while ray B passes through the optical centre of the object glass and is the line of collimation. Triangles FAC and FKL are similar, therefore $FB/AC = FO/KL = FO/ac$, ie $FB = AC.FO/ac$.

If $FB = d$, AC = staff intercept s, FO = focal length f of object glass, ac = distance i between outer stadia lines, then $d = s\,(f/i)$. Now, if X is the trunnion axis of the instrument and D its distance from the staff, then $D = d + FX$. But FX is the focal length f plus the distance of the object glass from the trunnion axis; it is generally constant for a particular instrument and is known as the additive constant, denoted by k. Hence $D = s(f/i) + k$. The quantity f/i is usually made exactly 100 and is known as the multiplying constant, denoted by m. Thus $D = ms + k$.

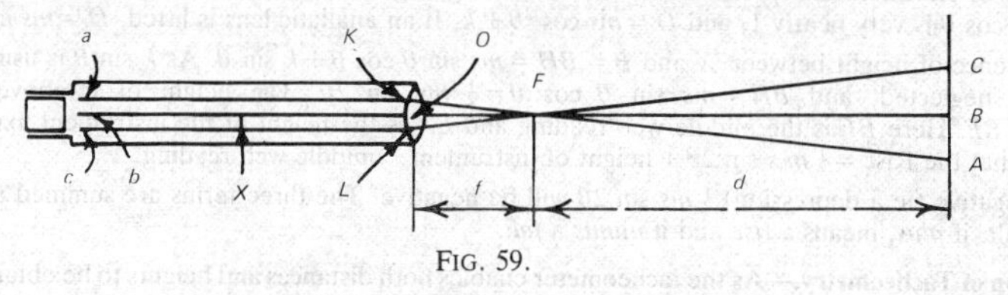

FIG. 59.

To Find the Tacheometric Constants.—Although it is usual for the values of the constants m and k for a particular instrument to be labelled inside the instrument box, it is desirable to check them periodically. The procedure is as follows: A line AB say 30 m long is set out on fairly level ground. The theodolite is set up at A and levelled, and readings of the stadia lines observed on a staff at B with the telescope horizontal. Similar readings are taken to the staff held at a point C, say 60 m from A. Then, if D_1 is the distance to the first staff position, intercept s_1, and if D_2 is the distance to the second staff position, intercept s_2, and if m and k are the required constants, then $D_1 = ms_1 + k$, and $D_2 = ms_2 + k$, from which values of m and k can be found.

Anallatic Lens.—To avoid the necessity of adding a constant k for every reading, an extra lens, the anallatic lens, may be inserted in the telescope. Figure 57 illustrates its effect. The rays from a and c backwards must pass through the focus F of the anallatic lens K at a constant angle. Hence as K and O are fixed with respect to one another, these rays will strike the object glass O at fixed points G and H, and in fixed directions (GC and HA). Consequently their paths GC and HA *outside* the object glass will be fixed also; if produced backwards they will meet at the axis of the telescope in a fixed point X at a fixed angle CXA. These both depend upon four quantities: distance ac; focal length of anallatic lens; focal length of object glass; distance between these lenses. The makers adjust these quantities so that X coincides with the trunnion axis of the instrument and the constant angle BXC is such that its cotangent is some round number, usually 200. Then $XB/BC = 200$; or $XB/AC = 100$; or $XB = 100\ AC$. The multiplying constant is no longer represented by f/i but by $\frac{1}{2}$ cot BXC, and there is no additive constant, all distances being obtained directly from X. The value of the multiplying constant may be found by test as before, but omitting k.

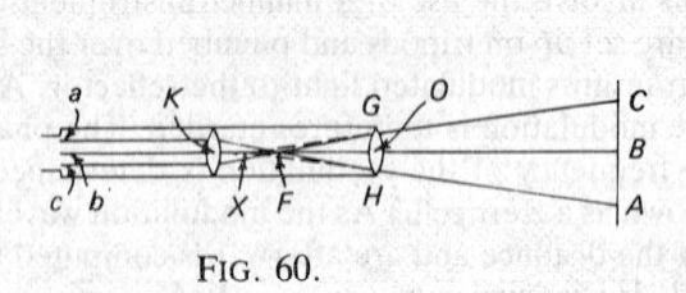

FIG. 60.

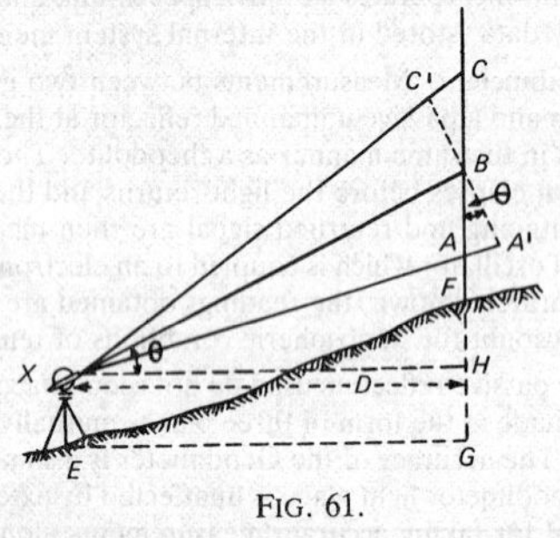

FIG. 61.

Although the anallatic lens is primarily used to eliminate the additive constant, this is by no means its chief advantage. If the stadia lines are spider's webs, it is impossible to adjust them with such accuracy that the multiplying constant shall be exactly 100. With an anallatic lens the multiplying constant depends upon the distance between the lenses as well as the spacing of the hairs. Hence the anallatic lens is sometimes mounted on a special rack, and after proportioning the remaining parts as closely as possible, the distance between the lenses is finally adjusted by direct experiment so as to make the multiplying constant the required value. Some instruments are supplied with a special key so that the adjustment can be tested and corrected if necessary. The staff AC must be vertical during tests so that it is at right angles to the line of collimation XB.

Measurement of Distances and Heights.—On level ground, with the telescope horizontal, it has been shown that the distance from the instrument to the staff position is given by $D = ms + k$, where s is the staff intercept. If, in addition to the outer stadia readings, the middle web reading is also observed, the latter will be the height of the line of collimation above the ground at the staff position: if the height of collimation of the instrument is found by levelling from a BM (using the theodolite or tacheometer as a level), the level of the ground at the staff position may be ascertained. Generally, however, the point at which levels and distances are required in tacheometry involve inclined sights and the telescope is not horizontal but has an angle of elevation or depression. Referring to Fig. 61, suppose the angle of elevation is θ when observing a staff held vertically at F. A, B and C are the lower, middle and upper stadia readings respectively, and AC = staff intercept s. Consider the projection of AC into a position $A'C'$ at right angles to the line of collimation XB. Then $A'C' = AC \cos \theta = s \cos \theta$, and distance XB along the line of collimation $= ms \cos \theta + k$. Hence horizontal distance $D = ms \cos^2\theta + k \cos \theta$.

For angles of elevation or depression less than 5°, ie angles generally met with in practice in tacheometry, the value of $\cos \theta$ is very nearly 1, and $D = ms \cos^2\theta + k$. If an anallatic lens is fitted, $D = ms \cos^2\theta$.

The difference of height between X and $B = BH = ms \sin \theta \cos \theta + k \sin \theta$. As $k \sin \theta$ is usually small it is generally neglected, and $BH = ms \sin \theta \cos \theta = \frac{1}{2} ms \sin 2\theta$. The height of F above $E = FG = BH + EX - BF$. Here BF is the middle web reading and EX is the height of the instrument axis above the ground, so that the Rise $= \frac{1}{2} m,s \sin 2\theta$ + height of instrument − middle web reading.

If θ be negative (ie a depression) $\frac{1}{2} ms \sin 2\theta$ will be negative. The three terms are summed algebraically and the result, if *plus*, means a *rise* and if *minus* a *fall*.

Application of Tacheometry.—As the tacheometer enables both distances and heights to be obtained without chaining, it is possible to make a complete tacheometric survey, including the fixing of a framework of stations, the measurement of detail from these stations and the determination of the heights of sufficient points to enable contour lines to be sketched. It is usual, however, to fix the stations by more accurate methods with a theodolite (ie by triangulation from an accurately measured base or by traversing) and to reserve the tacheometer for the measurement of subsidiary detail and the determination of heights.

Tacheometric levelling or contouring is performed by taking a series of *spot-levels* along lines radiating from the principal tacheometric stations, the points chosen for the staff being points where there are pronounced changes of slope. When the heights of all the spot levels have been calculated, the points are plotted on the plan with reduced levels alongside and contours are interpolated between them.

Fieldwork.—The following observations must be made to any point to fix it in relation to the rest of the survey: (1) horizontal angle or bearing; (2) angle of elevation or depression; (3) staff reading at each diaphragm line. In addition, the height of instrument must be measured.

Where observations are made to a vertical staff, the latter should not be waved. The staff used in tacheometry is usually a one-piece staff and is sometimes fitted with a spirit level or plumb-bob to ensure its being held vertical. An alternative procedure in the field is to observe on a staff held at right-angles to the line of collimation. This slightly modifies the formulae required for the different cases.

Direct Reading Tacheometers.—The application of the tacheometric principles so far described involves extensive calculations to obtain horizontal distances and differences in height from the stadia readings. There are, however, a number of instruments, called *direct-reading* or *self-reducing* tacheometers, which enable readings of horizontal distance and vertical height to be made direct.

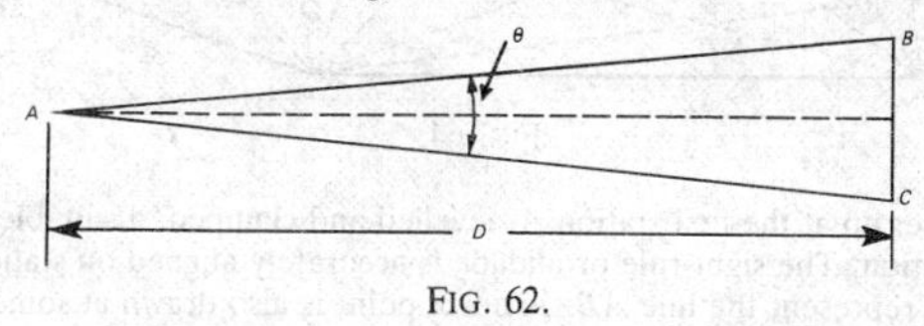

FIG. 62.

Some of these consist in an electronic distance meter and an electronic digital theodolite combined in one compact instrument. Through a single objective lens, one target sighting is enough for both angle and distance measurement. A built-in calculator provides a range of measuring functions such as: slope, horizontal, and vertical distance measurements, N, E co-ordinate measurements, and setting-out measurements. Such an instrument is illustrated in Fig. 63.

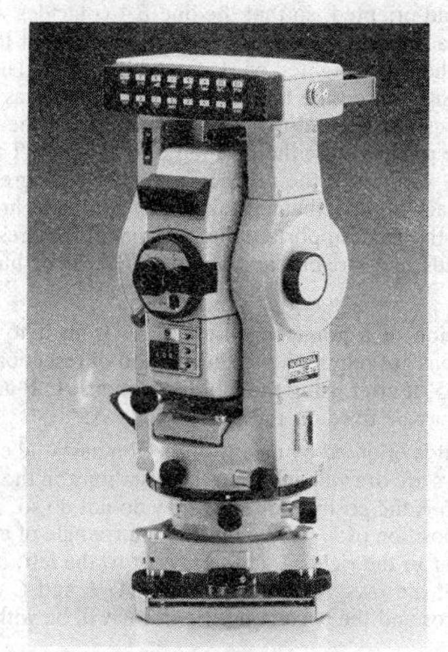

FIG. 63.—Electronic Tachometer.

Subtense Measurements.—Where the distances are too great to be observed by stadia readings or where marshy ground does not permit chaining to be conveniently employed, distances can be obtained by *subtense* measurement. The principle is illustrated in Fig. 62. A theodolite is set up at *A*, and *BC* represents a horizontal staff of fixed length, say 3 m. The horizontal angle *BAC* is read in the normal way. Then, horizontal distance *D* from the instrument to the staff = $\frac{1}{2}(BC)\cot(\theta/2)$. The angle θ is measured accurately by the method of repetitions.

PLANE TABLE SURVEYING

A plane table is essentially a small drawing board mounted on a light tripod (to which it can be clamped), used in conjunction with a sight-rule of alidade to survey the detail for a map of comparatively small scale, in which precision of details is not needed. A sheet of drawing paper is secured to the table. A spirit level and magnetic compass are often provided on the surface of the table, or are carried as accessories; if the table is to be used for contouring, a clinometer such as the *Indian clinometer* is sometimes carried in addition. Although the method is normally used to measure the detail of a survey whose station points have been fixed by more precise methods, eg triangulation, it is possible to make a complete traverse by plane table. Figure 64 illustrates a survey of the latter type, in which the course of a winding river is to be surveyed and plotted to a given scale. Station points A, B, C, etc, are selected at the principal bends of the stream and marked by pegs or ranging rods and the table set up at each of these in turn, the procedure being as follows:

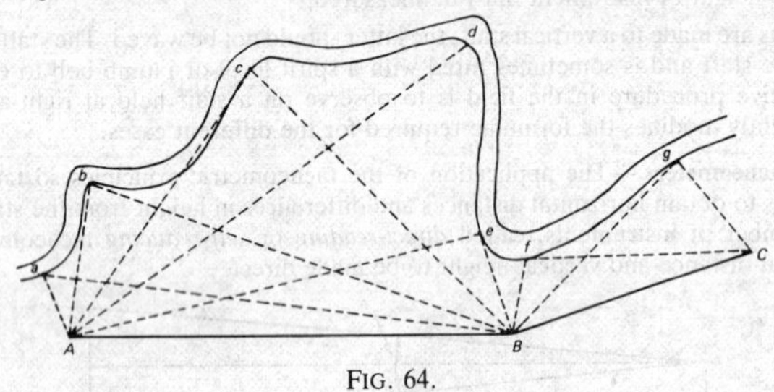

FIG. 64.

The table having been set up at the first station A, levelled and clamped, a suitable point is marked on the paper to represent this station. The sight-rule or alidade is accurately aligned on station B and a straight line ruled along the alidade to represent the line AB. A north point is also drawn at some convenient part of the paper, by ruling it along the edge of the rectangular compass box, first ensuring that the magnetic needle in the box is set at zero on its scale. Sights are also taken with the alidade (which must be set to pass through point A on the plan) to a number of points of detail such as a, b, c, d and e, and lines drawn along the rule, as shown by Aa, Ab, etc. These points must be marked on the ground by pegs or rods, or in some other way for subsequent identification.

Having completed the observation from A, the length of AB is chained and set out to scale on the paper. The table is moved to station B, set up, levelled and oriented, so that the line BA coincides with the line of sight of the alidade when directed towards A. To achieve this, the rule is placed exactly on the line already drawn to represent BA and the table rotated until the rule is sighted on A; the table is then clamped. The line BC is drawn against the rule when sighted on C. Sights are then taken to the same details as before, viz, a, b, c, d and e, and to other points f, g, etc, which can be seen also from station C. Then the intersection of the two radiating lines (such as Ac and Bc) to any point will fix the position of that point. There is no limit to the number of points which can be fixed in this way, but if the number is excessive progress will be slow and there will be so many radiating lines from each station that mistakes may be made in marking their intersections. It is therefore usual to observe only the most important and prominent features and to sketch in the less important by judgment; widths of roads and streams and lengths of walls of buildings can be measured with a tape.

Resection.—Resection is the fixing of the position of a point by observations from it to stations whose positions are known. Generally, three known stations are required and the method of resection is then known as the *Three-point-problem.* For instance, in Fig. 65, if after using the table at stations A, B and C it is found necessary to set it up at any other station K this may be fixed on the plan as follows:

(a) Having set up the table at K and levelled it, it is oriented by means of the compass and clamped. Then, sighting the alidade successively on A, B and C, rays are drawn back from these stations on the plan until they intersect. They should intersect in one point, which is the position of K. If they do not do so, a small *triangle of error* will be formed, as in the figure. The true position of K will be outside the triangle of error and it will be such that when facing the three points it is either to the right of all the rays or to the left, and its distance from each ray will be proportional to the length of the rays. When the stations A, B and C form a triangle around K, the three rays will form a triangle of error and the correct position of K will be within the triangle

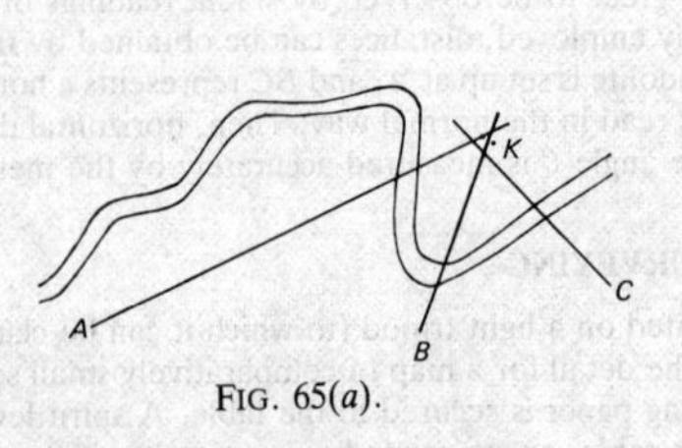

FIG. 65(a).

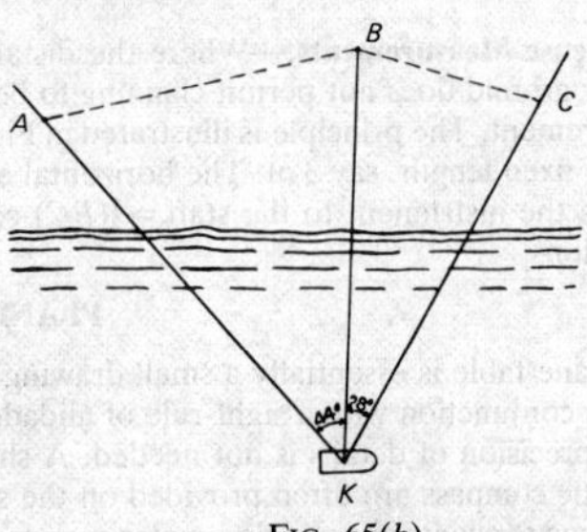

FIG. 65(b).

at a point whose distance from each ray is proportional to the length of the ray. The exact position will be found by a process of trial and error, the triangle of error diminishing in size each time. Alternatively: (*b*) judge the approximate position of *K* on the plan by inspection and test its accuracy. For this purpose, having set up the table at *K*, orient it so that the line of sight to one of the stations (say *A*) coincides with *KA* on plan. Then draw from *B* and *C* the lines of sight to those stations. If these pass through *K* on the plan the position of *K* has been accurately judged, but if not, a triangle of error will be formed and must be eliminated as above.

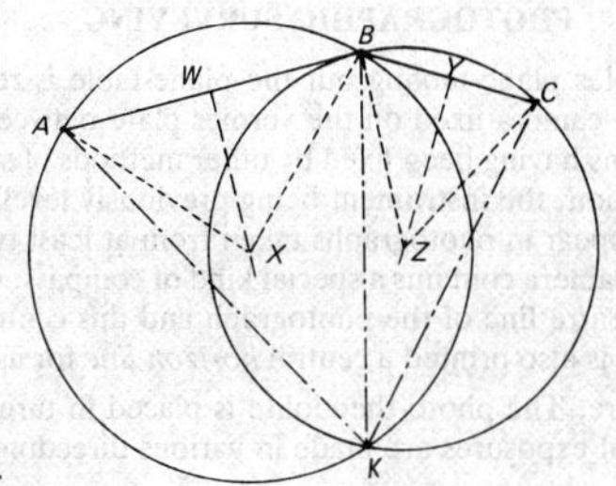

FIG. 65(*c*).

Other methods of resection available involve the measurement of the angles subtended by *AB* and *BC* at the point *K*, but are seldom used except when it is impossible to set up the plane table at the point whose position has to be located. The problem is common in coast and harbour surveying, when soundings are being taken from a boat and it is required to plot on a plan the positions from which the sounding were taken. Provided three stations are visible from the boat, or three clearly defined objects (such as flagstaffs, spires, etc) whose positions are known on the plan, and the subtended angles are measured, the position of the boat can be located in any of the following ways:

(*a*) By means of a *station pointer*, which is a form of protractor having one fixed projecting arm and two movable ones capable of being clamped. The fixed arm is at zero on the circular arc and the arc is graduated from zero up to 180° in both directions. Suppose the observed angles are $AKB = 44°$ and $BKC = 28°$ (Fig. 65(*b*)). To find the position of *K* on the map, clamp the left hand movable pointer at 44° and the right hand one at 28°, and adjust the instrument on the plan until the arms pass through *A*, *B*, and *C* respectively. The centre of the protractor will then be at *K* which can be marked accordingly.

(*b*) Set out the radiating lines *KA*, *KB* and *KC* on a sheet of tracing paper, at the required angles, using a protractor. Slide the tracing paper over the plan until these lines pass through *A*, *B* and *C* respectively. The point *K* can then be pricked through.

(*c*) This method is by a geometrical construction shown in Fig. 65(*c*). *AB* and *BC* are joined on the plan and bisected at *W* and *Y* respectively; perpendiculars *WZ* and *YZ* are drawn. *AX* and *BX* are drawn at angles of $90° - 44°$ ($=46°$) with *AB*, meeting at *X* on *WX*, and similarly *BZ* and *CZ* are drawn at angles of $90° - 28°$ ($=62°$) with *BC*, meeting at *Z* on *YZ*. A circle is drawn with *X* as centre and *XA* as radius, and another circle with *Z* as centre and *ZC* as radius. Both these circles will pass through *B* and will also intersect at another point *K*, which will be the required point at which the angles were taken.

Contouring with the Plane Table.—If a plane table survey is to include contour lines it is usual to observe vertical angles with an *Indian clinometer*. This instrument (Fig. 66), has a baseplate *A*, supported by three knobs or feet, and above this a second plate *B*, hinged at one end and adjusted at the other end by an elevating screw so that a spirit level *L*, fixed to it, may be brought level. At either end of this second plate are sights, a pinhole sight *C* being near the adjustable end and a long hinged sight *D* with a graduated vertical slit at the other end. At each station, after sights have been taken for locating positions of detail points, the clinometer is set up on the table and levelled after directing it on some feature which has been plotted. By placing the eye to the pinhole eyepiece and sighting to the ground at the feature, the angle of rise or fall in degrees can be read on the left side of the sight-vane, whilst on the right the tangent of the angle can be read. By scaling the distance from the plan and multiplying this by the tangent of the angle, the rise or fall from the level of the table to the ground at the particular feature can be ascertained. The reduced level of the plane table is found

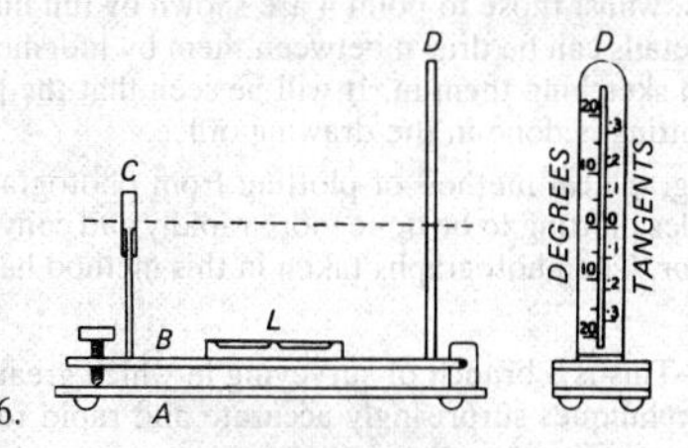

FIG. 66.

by adding the height of the table to the RL of the point over which it is set up. By applying to the RL of the table the rise or fall to the feature the RL of the latter is obtained.

A number of spot levels is obtained in this way from each plane table station. Their RL's are figured on the plan and the contour lines can be sketched in by interpolation. The resulting contour lines are generally only approximate, but their accuracy will depend upon how many spot levels are taken and the care taken in choosing their positions.

PHOTOGRAPHIC SURVEYING

In principle this method resembles plane-tabling but the plane-table is replaced by a *photo-theodolite*, a special form of theodolite having a camera fixed on the vernier plate between the supports of the telescope. The positions of a number of stations having been fixed by other methods of surveying, photographs are taken in various directions from each station, the instrument being previously levelled. The views should be chosen so that given prominent features appear in photographs taken from at least two stations, and preferably from three, so as to secure a check. The camera contains a special kind of compass, which prints on the photographic plate the compass bearing of the centre line of the photograph and this centre line is printed on the plate by a vertical hair in the camera. There is also printed a central *horizon line* for use if elevations have to be found.

Figure 65 illustrates the procedure. The photo-theodolite is placed in turn at the known stations A and B and at each of these stations several exposures are made in various directions, so as to get good views of the

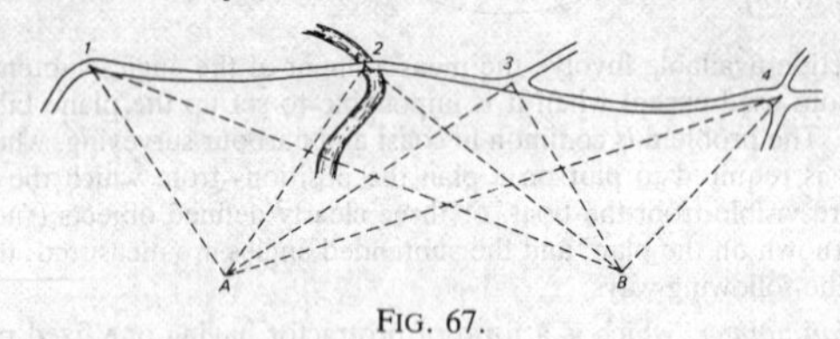

FIG. 67.

area to be surveyed, the bearings of the centre line of each picture being printed automatically on the negative. The figure shows only the field of view of one picture from each station, the camera being oriented at A on a bearing of 25° and at B of 345°.

To plot the work, lines are drawn from each station in the directions of the centre lines of the various photographs, using the bearings recorded thereon as in Fig. 66. At right angles to each centre line is drawn a cross line, of width not less than the width of the photograph, at a distance from the station equal to the

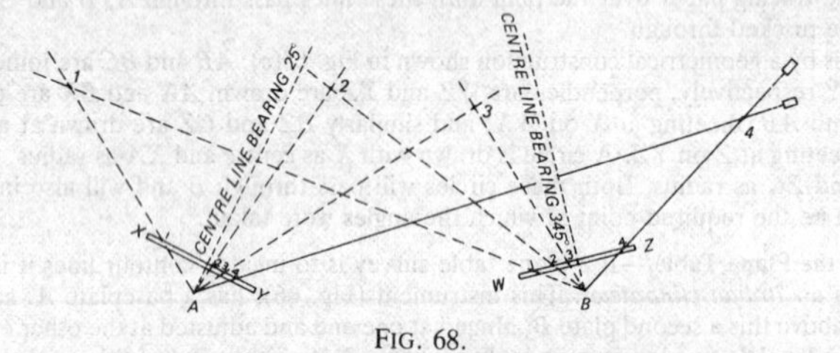

FIG. 68.

focal length of the lens of the camera. The distances of the points of detail from the centre line of each photograph (either to the right or left as the case may be) are marked on a narrow strip of paper, which is applied to the cross line of that view, as shown by XY and WZ in the figure. For convenience of reference and to avoid mistakes, the detail points are numbered and these numbers are marked on the narrow strips of paper. Radiating lines are then drawn from the station through the points on the cross line as shown. The intersection of two such radiating lines from different stations to the same detail will give its position, while another radial from a third station will act as a check. In the figure the converging lines to detail points 1 to 3 are shown by broken lines, whilst those to point 4 are shown by full lines. When sufficient points have been located in this way, minor details can be drawn between them by judgment, with the help of the photographs, or by re-visiting the site and sketching them in. It will be seen that the procedure is very similar to that used in plane-tabling, but the plotting is done in the drawing office.

The above is the simple graphical method of plotting from photographs. An improved method based on stereoscopic principles enables plotting to be done more rapidly and conveniently by using a special instrument known as a *stereo-comparator*. The photographs taken in this method have to be exactly at right angles to the base line.

AERIAL SURVEYING.—This is a branch of surveying in which great advances have been made in the last decade, and with modern techniques surprisingly accurate and rapid results are obtainable. The area is first covered with a network of triangles, fixed by triangulation, and the stations are made clearly visible from the air. Aircraft then fly over the area, maintaining as constant a course and height as possible and making exposures at regular intervals so as completely to cover the ground, with a certain amount of overlapping of views. Instruments recording the bearing, height and angle of tilt of the camera are read by an observer, so that irregularities in course and elevation may be adjusted when developing and printing the photographs. The photographs may be either (*a*) vertical or (*b*) oblique, their difference being illustrated in Fig. 69. Vertical photographs are those most generally used, although they present a somewhat abnormal view and are rather more difficult to interpret than obliques. For small scale work, high obliques are often used.

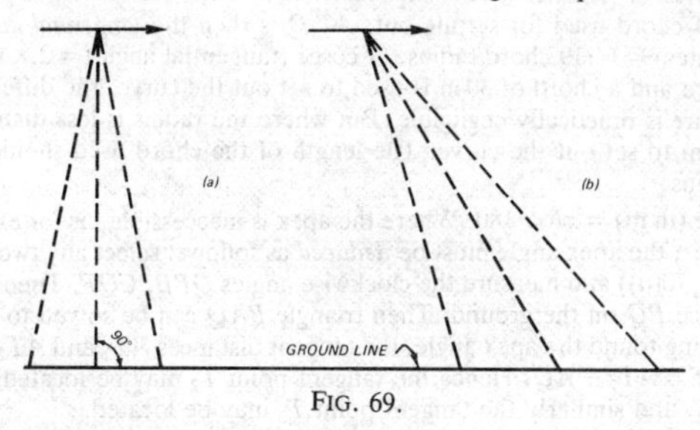

FIG. 69.

By means of the overlapping exposures in vertical photography, every ground feature is photographed at least twice, with an overlap of about 60% in the direction of flight. Examination of two adjacent photographs with a stereoscope reveals the ground features in exaggerated relief. The heights of buildings, trees, etc, appear doubled or trebled and this stereoscopic effect is the whole basis of modern aerial surveying.

The prints of overlapping photographs are joined together into a patchwork picture large enough to include at least three ground stations. These are carefully marked and the patchwork is re-photographed and converted into a transparency or lantern slide, ready to be placed in the adjustable carrier of a special form of vertical enlarging lantern. A skeleton map showing that portion of the triangulation survey is now placed on the horizontal screen and the transparency is tilted and adjusted until the three stations on the photographic patchwork coincide with the corresponding stations on the screen below. Alternatively, the screen, instead of the transparency, can be tilted and adjusted. The skeleton map is then replaced by a sheet of sensitised paper and a positive print or enlargement is made. The next stage is to ink in such detail as is needed in the finished map and to eliminate the photographic image in a chemical bath. The result is a portion of the finished map, fitting exactly into the ground framework and giving as much detail as is desired within the scope of the scale adopted. This is known as a *mosaic*. Although mosaics have not generally the accuracy of a normal map they have other advantages in that details of vegetation, woodland, purpose for which the land is being used, etc, are revealed and at the same time distances obtained by scaling from them are substantially correct. No system of aerial surveying is yet able to be entirely independent of at least some ground work in establishing a framework of *control points*, the extent of which will vary according to the scale and accuracy of the maps and the methods used for plotting.

Aerial surveying is a valuable method of producing military maps and reconnaissance or preliminary maps of large areas, but its use is not confined to such purposes. The Ordnance Survey use it for the temporary revision of parts of the country, clearly marked buildings on the existing maps being used as control points instead of trigonometrical stations. Such a method of revision is not considered to be sufficiently accurate for the permanent record on the large scale Ordnance sheets, but the ordinary user can find very little fault with the revised sheets published and it is a useful method for the rapid revision of a developing neighbourhood.

Aerial surveying is most useful for large newly-developing or underdeveloped countries. In such cases it may be found difficult to place the trigonometrical stations in such a way that they will show clearly in the photographs, particularly if much of the area is covered by forest or jungle. In some recent surveys the photographs were taken first; points which were clearly visible in the photographs were then located and the triangulation survey used to establish their relative positions.

CURVE RANGING

Circular curves may be defined by either of the following systems: (*a*) *Radius* system, in which curves are defined by their radius. This is the system adopted in Great Britain where it is usual to select curves according to their radius in metres. By using a radius of some round figure, the angles used in setting out the curve will be an odd number of degrees and minutes, thus causing inconvenience in setting out. (*b*) *Degree* system, used largely in Canada and the United States. The curve is defined by its *degree of curve*, which is the number of degrees subtended at the centre of the curve by a chord of 30 m. Some engineers use an *arc* of 30 m to define the degree of curve. The advantage of the degree system is that the angle used for setting out is exactly one-half the degree of curve; the radius, however, will be an odd length.

Figure 68 shows two lines AB and AC which are to be joined by a circular curve. AB and AC are the *straights*. The point A, the intersection of the two straights, is the *apex* of the curve, and the angle CAB is the *apex* or *intersection angle*, ie the *interior* angle measured clockwise between the straights; the exterior clockwise angle BAC is not generally referred to as the apex angle. The points T_1 and T_2 where the curve meets the straights are called *tangent points*, and the distances AT_1 and AT_2 *tangent distances*, which each equal R. tan ø/2. The angle ZAC is the *deflection angle*, denoted by ϕ (equal to the angle T_1OT_2 at the centre of curvature). The chord T_1T_2 is called the *long chord*, and the angle AT_1T_2 between tangent AT_1 and chord T_1T_2 the *total tangential angle*. The total tangential angle equals half the deflection angle.

If T_1D is the length of chord used for setting out, AT_1D is then the *tangential angle* for that chord. The tangential angle (in minutes) = 1,719 chord/radius, or cosec (tangential angle) = 2 × radius/chord. Where the radius is of 600 m or more and a chord of 30 m is used to set out the curve, the difference in length between a chord of 30 m and its arc is practically negligible. But where the radius is less than 300 m it is desirable to use a chord of 10 or 15 m to set out the curve. The length of the chord used should not in general exceed one-twentieth of the radius.

The length of the curve (in m) = $\pi R\phi/180$. Where the apex is inaccessible, as for example where it is on the site of a building or a river, the apex angle must be *deduced* as follows: select any two accessible points on the straights (P and Q in Fig. 70(a)) and measure the clockwise angles QPB, CQP. Then $PAQ = QPB + CQP -$ 180°. Measure the distance PQ on the ground. Then triangle PAQ can be solved to find angle PAQ and the lengths AP and AQ. Having found the apex angle, the tangent distances AT_1 and AT_2 can be calculated. Then $PT_1 = AT_1 - AP$ and $QT = AT_2 - AQ$. Hence the tangent point T_2 may be located by measuring PT_1 back from P along the straight, and similarly the tangent point T_2 may be located.

Setting out Circular Curves.

(a) Offsets from the Long Chord.—It often happens that where it is intended, from a previous study of a plan, to set out a curve of reasonably small radius (say 15 or 30 m) by taping from the centre, that this procedure is found on the site to be impracticable, if for instance the centre is inaccessible because of obstruction by buildings or marshy ground. In such cases the curve may be set out by offsets from the long chord by calculating a number of offsets as follows: in Fig. 70(b), suppose T_1 and T_2 are the known positions of the tangent points which are to be joined by a curve of radius R. The long chord T_1T_2 is first measured, say length $2L$. Then if S is the mid-point of the long chord, it can be shown that $y = \sqrt{(R^2 - x^2)} - \sqrt{(R^2 - L^2)}$.

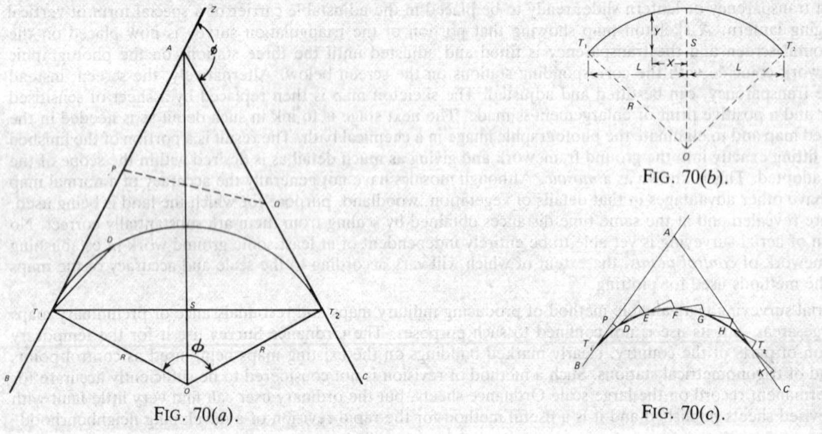

Fig. 70(a). Fig. 70(b). Fig. 70(c).

(b) Method of Chords.—This is a method applicable to curves of any radius and although not as precise as theodolite methods it gives reasonably accurate results on flat and unobstructed ground.

Suppose two straights AB and AC (Fig. 70(c)) are to be connected by a curve of radius R and that the curve is to be set out between the tangent points T_1 and T_2 in equal chords, of length, say, one chain. One chain length is measured from T_1 towards A and at the end of the chain is set off an offset of length chord^2/(2 × radius). This gives the first point D on the curve. The offset should not be set off perpendicular to the chain, the method being to swing the chain into the line T_1D through the required offset measured by tape. The chain is now laid in the line T_1D produced with the back handle at D and an offset is set off at the forward end of (chord^2/radius), ie twice as much as before. This gives point E. Next, the chain is laid in the line DE produced with the back handle at E, and at the forward end another offset of (chord^2/radius) is set out. The work is thus continued.

If the length of the curve is an exact number of chord lengths, the same offset from the continuation of line

GH should fall exactly on the tangent point T_2, whilst an offset of chord^2/(2 × radius) from the continuation of the line HT_2 should fall on the line KC. These last two offsets should therefore act as a check upon the accuracy of the work; a large accumulation of error is likely to be avoided however by setting out half the curve from T_1 and half from T_2, and checking on a central peg. The method is not precise, and is not suitable for work requiring a high degree of accuracy. In practice it is unlikely that the length of curve will be an exact number of chains or half-chains; it is desirable, however, that the *through* chainage on the centre line of the road, railway, etc, that is being set out should be maintained, eg that pegs at every chain length commencing from zero should be set out. For this reason it is usual to introduce a shorter length of chord, known as a *sub-chord*, at each end of the curve.

The formulae chord^2/(2 × radius) or chord^2/radius need to be modified if there are sub-chords, as follows: if C_1 is the first sub-chord, C the 'standard' chord, and C_2 the last sub-chord; then 1st offset (for 1st sub-chord) = $C_1^2/2R$; 2nd offset (for standard chord) = $C(C_1 + C)/2R$; 3rd offset and all succeeding offsets for standard chords = C^2/R; last offset (for last sub-chord) = $C_2(C + C_2)/2R$.

(*c*) METHOD OF TANGENTIAL ANGLES.—This is the most usual method where a theodolite is available. The procedure in the field is as follows. The theodolite is set up at A (Fig. 68), the apex angle is measured and the tangent distance calculated. The tangent distances are then chained back along the straights to fix the positions of the tangent points. If the chainage of the apex is known, then the chainage of T_1 can be found by subtraction. The length of the curve is next found and hence the chainage at T_2, the end of the curve, can be found by addition. A standard chord length is then selected, depending on the radius of the curve, and the first and last sub-chords deduced. If θ is the tangential angle for a standard chord, then tangential angle for sub-chord = θ × sub-chord/standard chord.

The theodolite is next set up at T_1 and the apex sighted, the vernier reading zero and both plates clamped. The upper clamp is then released and the telescope turned through the first tangential angle (ie for the first sub-chord), the sub-chord length being chained from T_1 and the end of the chord pegged where it intersects the line of sight. The second tangential angle is then set on the vernier (ie first tangential angle plus tangential angle for standard chord) and the second chord point pegged similarly, the chord length in this case commencing from chord point 1. The remaining chord points are similarly set out, the final angle to be set on the theodolite being the total tangential angle, which should exactly equal half the deflection angle, thus providing a check on the accuracy of the work. The second tangent point should be on the line of the second straight.

The tangential angles should be computed preferably to the nearest second, to minimise cumulative errors which may arise in the addition of the tangential angles.

Obstructions in Setting-out.—It is seldom possible to see all points on a long curve from one position of the theodolite. Obstructions in sighting are frequently encountered; in any case, as errors of sighting and chaining are cumulative, it is generally advisable to move the instrument after every four or five pegs are set out whether or no the next alignment is obstructed. The procedure is as follows (Fig. 71): move the theodolite to the last point of the curve which has been set out. Set vernier or micro 'A' to read 0°00′ and direct the telescope to the tangent point or the point where the theodolite was last set up. Transit the telescope and set the vernier (still keeping the lower clamp fixed) to read the next tangential angle in the table; the telescope will then be in the required line for setting the next peg.

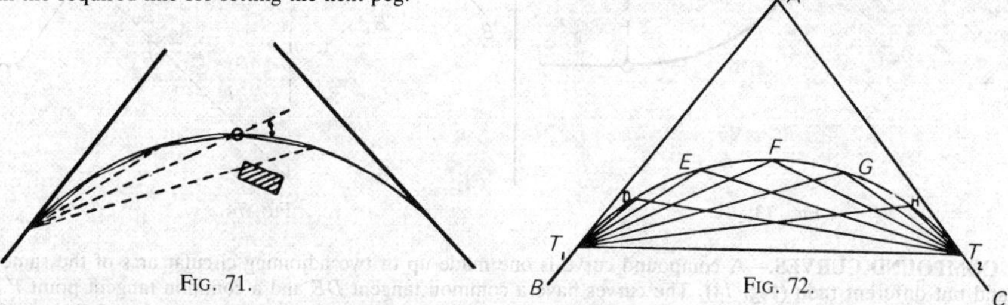

FIG. 71. FIG. 72.

Two-theodolite Method.—A method sometimes used in open country where the curve lies across rough or marshy ground is to set out with two theodolites thereby avoiding the use of the chain. In such circumstances the method has much to recommend it but it has the disadvantage that two surveyors and two theodolites are required, in addition to the chainman, and these may not always be available. Referring to Fig. 72, one theodolite is set up at T_1 and the other at T_2. The table of tangential angles is prepared in the normal way as if setting out from T_1, ie, the first tangential angle for setting chord point D will be angle AT_1D, and this angle is by geometry equal to the angle in the alternate segment, angle T_1T_2D. The procedure in setting out is as follows: the theodolite at T_1 is sighted to A with the vernier at zero; the telescope is then turned through the first tangential angle AT_1D so that it points along the line T_1D. The theodolite at T_2 is sighted to T_1 with the vernier at zero and the telescope also turned through the same tangential angle (T_1T_2D) so that it points along the line T_2D. A chainman holding an arrow at D is then directed into position until the arrow is bisected by the line of collimation of both theodolites. The remaining chord points E, F, G, H, etc are set out similarly, using their respective tangential angles.

SOURCES OF ERROR AND CHECKING CURVES.—The errors which arise in setting out curves by theodolite may be summarised as follows:

(*a*) Inequality of chord and arc. As curves are set out by a series of chords instead of arcs there will be a difference between the total length of the chords set out and the overall length of curve as calculated; provided the chord length selected does not exceed one-twentieth of the radius there will however be no appreciable error.

(*b*) The accuracy of setting out a particular curve depends largely on the precision with which the apex angle (or the deflection angle) is measured. Since the length of curve is calculated from this angle, any appreciable error will be revealed when the curve fails to close on the second tangent point.

(*c*) In using the method of tangential angles, each chord point is set out from the preceding chord point, so that any error in a particular chord point will be carried through to the end of the curve. To minimise such cumulative effects, long curves are sometimes set out in two halves, working from each tangent point, so that any error of closure appears at the centre of the curve. It is important that the tangential angles shall be calculated with precision and the table of angles prepared by the addition of these precise values, any approximation to within the least count of the particular instrument being made subsequently.

(*d*) The total tangential angle as derived from the summation of the separate tangential angles for each chord point should equal exactly half the deflection angle. If there is any appreciable discrepancy the calculation should be checked.

(*e*) The final chord point as set out by the theodolite should coincide with the second tangent point, previously located by chaining from the apex the calculated tangent distance.

REVERSE CURVES.—A reverse curve is one in which a right-hand curve is followed immediately by a left-hand curve, or vice versa (Fig. 73). In railway and highway work it is usual to avoid having a common tangent point and it is good practice to insert a length of straight between the curves. The radii of the two curves are not necessarily the same. Each curve may be treated separately for the purpose of setting out; each apex angle must be measured and separate tables prepared for tangential angles or to provide the data for the particular method of setting out selected.

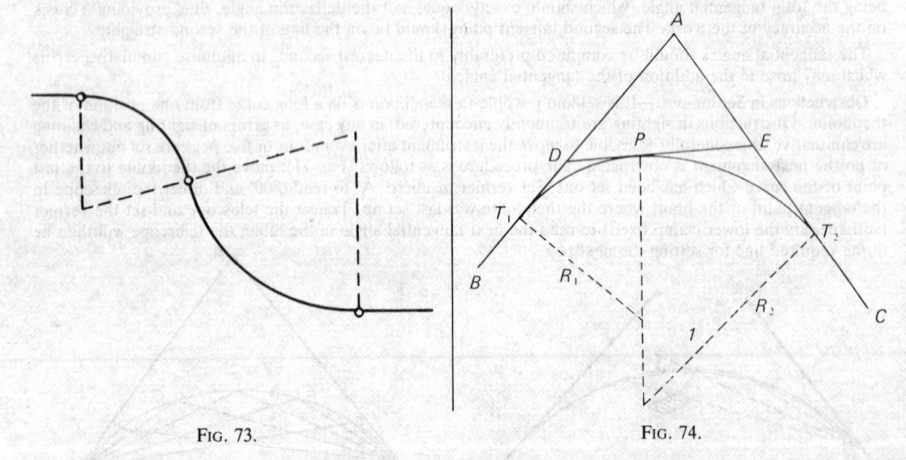

FIG. 73. FIG. 74.

COMPOUND CURVES.—A compound curve is one made up of two adjoining circular arcs of the same hand but different radii (Fig. 74). The curves have a common tangent *DE* and a common tangent point *P*. Then tangent distance *DP* (for curve T_1P) plus tangent distance *EP* (for curve PT_2) is equal to *DE*, and, if the position of *P* along *DE* is known, the respective radii of the curves can be found as follows: the angles *EDB* and *CED* are measured, ie the apex angles of the separate curves; then if R_1 and R_2 are the respective radii and a_1 and a_2 the apex angles, $R_1 = DP/\tan(a_1/2)$ and $R_2 = EP/\tan(a_2/2)$.

VERTICAL CURVES.—On highways and railways it is clearly not acceptable from a traffic viewpoint for longitudinal gradients to meet at a sharp apex and vertical curves are therefore inserted to ease the change from one gradient to another. Not only are these required to avoid inconvenience to traffic but also to provide adequate sighting on summits. The most usual form of vertical curve is the simple parabola, which joins the two gradients tangentially. The length of the curve is governed by (*a*) the sight distance required, (*b*) the slopes of the intersecting gradients, and (*c*) the rate of *change* of gradient in passing from one slope to the other.

Definitions.—Gradients are expressed in either of two ways: (*a*) as 1 in *x*, meaning 1 vertical in *x* horizontal, or (*b*) as a percentage grade, eg 1 in 100 is a 1% grade. *Grade angle* is the algebraic difference of grades expressed in percentages, ie if an uphill gradient of 1 in 20 (+5%) meets a downhill gradient of 1 in 50 (−2%), the grade-angle is 5 − (−2) = 7%. The grade angle is therefore the *sum* of the numerical values of the grades in this case, which is that of a *summit* curve (top of a hill).

Length of Curve.—If L is the length of the vertical curve (measured as a *horizontal* distance) as shown in Fig. 75; r = permissible rate of change of gradient; a and b = percentage gradients, then $L = 100(a + b)/r$.

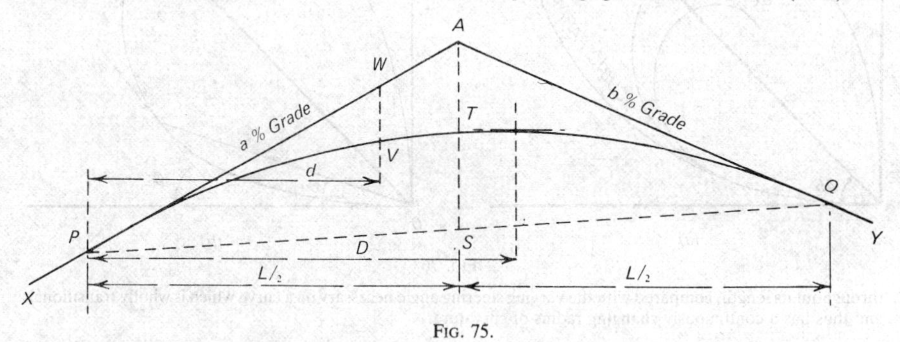

FIG. 75.

Levels on Vertical Curves.—Referring to Fig. 75, two gradients AX and AY, intersecting at A, are to be joined by a vertical curve of length L. Generally the reduced level of A will be known or can be ascertained from a knowledge of the gradients and the known level at the beginning or end of the curve. Suppose the curve meets the gradients at P and Q. The curve will generally be symmetrical about A, ie there will be a length of $L/2$ (horizontal) on either side of A. The properties of the simple parabola are such that the mid-point T of the curve bisects AS. The mid-ordinate AT is given by: grade angle × ½ length of curve/400; and since the level of A is known, the level of T can be found by subtraction. Intermediate ordinates between P and A will be proportional to the square of the distance from P.

For instance, ordinate $WV = AT(2d/L)^2$.

The level of W can be deduced from the gradient and the distance d; hence the level of V can be found by subtracting WV. Similarly, the levels of other points on the curve can be found. It is usual to ascertain the levels on vertical curves at 15 or 30 m intervals.

It will be noted that the highest point of the curve in the above example is not at the mid-point of the curve. For drainage purposes it is necessary to find the position of the highest point of a summit curve and the lowest point of a valley curve. The highest point of the curve (Fig. 75) is that at which the curve is tangential to a horizontal line. The distance D from the commencement of the curve to this point is given by $D = aL/(a + b)$.

TRANSITION CURVES.—The purpose of a transition curve is to achieve a gradual change of direction from the straight (of radius infinity) to the minimum radius of the curve in order to eliminate the sudden shock caused by the introduction of the centrifugal force $P = WV^2/gR$, where W = weight of vehicle, V = velocity round the curve; R = radius of curvature on the curved path; g = acceleration due to gravity.

For any constant speed V, the value of the centrifugal ratio P/W is proportional to the radial acceleration V^2/R. A basic requirement in transition curve design is that the rate of change of radial acceleration shall be constant throughout the curve and of such value that there is no discomfort to passengers travelling on the curve. If the speed V is constant (transition curves are normally designed for a particular speed dependent on the class of route, eg main line, trunk road, secondary road, etc), the radial acceleration will be inversely proportional to the radius of curvature R, and consequently if the rate of change of radial acceleration is to be constant, the radius of curvature at any point on the curve will be inversely proportional to the distance of that point from the start of the curve. The *rate* of change of radial acceleration $c = V^3/RL$. The maximum value of c to provide conditions without noticeable discomfort has been assessed at 0·3 m/sec^3 for main routes but higher values of 0·6 or 0·9 m/sec^3 are acceptable for lesser routes.

The maximum value of the centrifugal ratio for highway work is generally taken as 0·25 and for railway work 0·125. Having regard to the purpose of a transition curve, ie the avoidance of a suddenly applied centrifugal force, transitions are not required when two straights are joined by curves of large radius; thus, curves of 1,500 m radius or above are not normally made transitional and are formed by simple circular curves.

Forms of Transition Curve.—The several forms of transition curve generally employed for railway and highway design are shown in Fig. 76(*a*). These are (i) cubic parabola; (ii) spiral; (iii) lemniscate. The first two are generally used in conjunction with a circular arc of radius equal to the minimum radius of the curve to be adopted, as indicated in Fig. 77. The lemniscate may be similarly used but is generally transitional throughout. The advantage of an intermediate circular arc is that a constant steering angle may be maintained

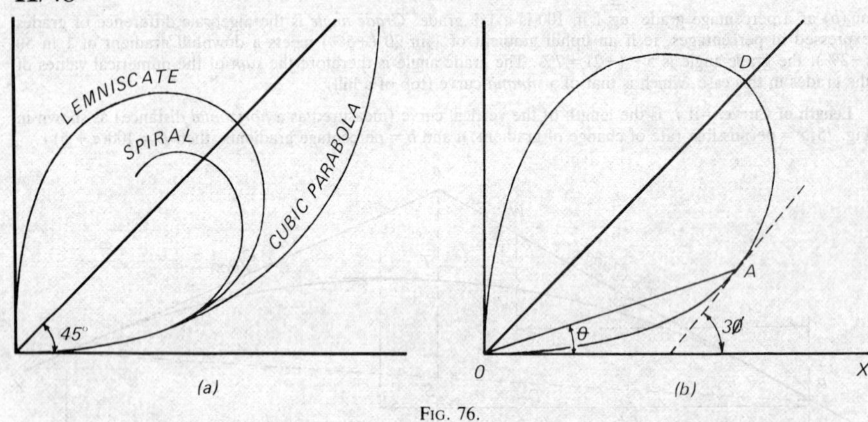

FIG. 76.

throughout its length, compared with the varying steering angle necessary on a curve which is wholly transitional and thus has a continuously changing radius of curvature.

(i) **Cubic Parabola.**—This curve commences, at a point on the straight, with a radius of infinity, which reduces to the minimum radius of the curve at a gradually reducing rate. The use of the curve is generally restricted to layouts with small deflections, as in railway work or in highways through open country. The equation of the cubic parabola used for transitions (Fig. 78) is $y = x^3/6RL$, where R = radius of circular curve (ie minimum radius); L = length of transition curve; y = offset to the curve from a point on the tangent straight, distant x from the start of the curve.

Suppose two straights (Fig. 77) are joined by a circular curve of radius R and it is desired to provide transition curves of this form at each end. In order to accommodate the transitions, which will start at radius infinity and end at radius R, it is necessary either (*a*) to move the circular curve inwards, or (*b*) to move the straights outwards; it is usual to adopt method (*a*). The amount by which it is necessary to move the circular curve inwards is known as the 'shift', and the shift $AC = L^2/24R$. The offset to the transition curve at A is half the shift and offsets to the curve from other points between F and X are obtained from $y = x^3/6RL$.

Within the limiting deflection angles for which the cubic parabola is used in practice, the angle between the straight and the tangent at any point on the curve = length of curve from the origin to that point ÷ $2R$ (Fig. 78). At the end of the transition, $\phi = L/2R$ (radians). From the origin of the curve, the tangential angle θ to any point on the curve is given by $\theta = \phi/3$ very nearly.

In Fig. 77, the deflection angle between the straights is Δ, and the amount of deflection accounted for by each transition is ϕ. Hence the angle subtended by the circular arc is $(\Delta - 2\phi)$. The transitions may be set out by polar deflection angles θ, using a theodolite at the tangent point, the chord distance L being measured from the tangent point.

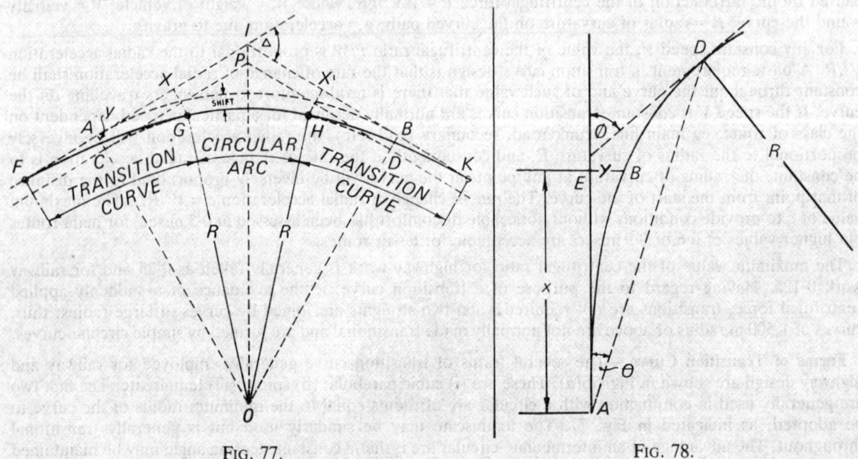

FIG. 77. FIG. 78.

Locating the Common Tangent at Junction of Transition and Circular Arc.—The transitions AC and GD (Fig. 79) may be set out either by offsets from the straights or polar deflection angles as explained above. There remains to be set out the circular arc CD for which the method of tangential angles is preferred. In order that setting out may proceed, it is first necessary to locate the direction of the common tangent FE at C, as follows: for triangle AFC, the external angle $BFC = \phi$, and angle $FAC = \phi/3$, so that angle $FCA = \phi - \theta = (\frac{2}{3})\phi$. The procedure is to set up the theodolite at C and sight to A with the vernier reading $(360° - (\frac{2}{3})\phi)$. With the lower plate clamped, the upper plate is then set to zero on the vernier and the telescope transitted. The telescope will now be pointing in the direction of the tangent CE, ready for setting out the circular arc CD. In the case of a left-hand curve, such as in setting out from G to A, the theodolite would be set up at D and sighted to G with the vernier reading $(\frac{2}{3})\phi$; after setting to zero and transitting as before, the telescope will be pointing in the direction of the tangent DE.

(ii) **The Spiral.**—In this curve, the radius R is inversely proportional to the length L, ie RL is a constant, thus satisfying completely the basic requirements of a transition curve stated earlier. If L is the length to any point, measured along the curve from its start, and ϕ is the angle which the tangent at that point makes with the straight produced (Fig. 79), then $L = m\sqrt{\phi}$, where $m = \sqrt{(2RL)}$ = a constant.

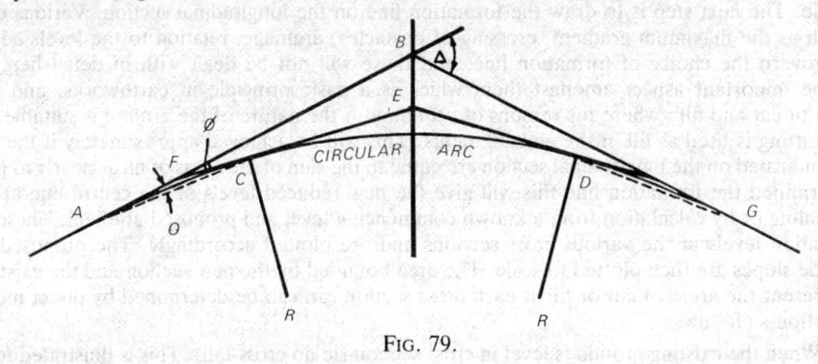

Fig. 79.

The deflection angle ϕ between the tangents plays an important part in the calculation and setting out of the curve, for the points on the curve are expressed in terms of the deflection angle and length along the curve, ie by polar co-ordinates, instead of the more usual Cartesian co-ordinates x and y. Substituting for m in the above equation: $L = \sqrt{(2RL)}\sqrt{\phi}$, whence $\phi = L/2R$ (in radians). This is an exact relationship for any value of deflection angle, not merely a limiting value as in the case of the cubic parabola. In Fig. 78, for the point D, the polar deflection is θ and the deflection angle between tangents is ϕ. It can be shown that

$$\tan\theta = \left[\frac{\phi}{3} + \frac{\phi^2}{105} + \frac{\phi^3}{5997}\right] \text{ approx.}$$

The third order term can be neglected in all practical cases, and in fact for the comparatively large value of 25° for ϕ, the error introduced by assuming that $\theta = \phi/3$ is only 40 seconds.

Spirals of Small Deflection.—Here, $\theta = \phi/3$ without appreciable error up to $\phi = 15°$. As $\phi = L/2R$, and RL = a constant, say k, therefore $\theta = L^2/6k$. Hence, up to the limiting value, the polar deflection angle is proportional to the square of the distance along the curve.

If it is desired to set out by offsets, rather than by polar deflection angles, then, provided ϕ does not exceed 9°, $x = L$ nearly enough. The length of offset y is obtained from $y = x^3/6RL$. As RL is a constant for a spiral this last equation is that of a cubic parabola, so that up to $\phi = 9°$ the cubic parabola and spiral are practically identical.

(iii) **The Lemniscate.** This curve approximates to the transition spiral over the working range, and differs from it principally because there is a slight falling-off of the rate of increase of radial acceleration as the distance from the starting point increases. It can be argued that this falling off corresponds to the natural reaction of a driver when he approaches the mid-point of a curve at the instant before he has to consider turning in the reverse direction. There is some justification for this, but in practice, as each driver tends to travel his own path, the choice of curve is not vitally important.

In Fig. 76(*b*) is shown a diagram of the complete lemniscate. Let A be a point in the curve, at which the *chord length* from the origin O is $OA = l$. The polar deflection angle $AOX = \theta$, while the deflection angle between the tangent at O and that at A is 3θ. The essential difference between the lemniscate and the spiral is that, whereas in the spiral $\phi = 3\theta$ approximately, in the lemniscate $\phi = 3\theta$ exactly.

Equations of the curve are $l = 3R\sin 2\theta = C\sqrt{\sin 2\theta}$, where C is the major axis OD, and is equal to $\sqrt{(3lR)}$ and R is the radius of the circular curve at the point A. Hence Rl is constant and the radius of curvature R at any point is inversely proportional to the chord length l from the origin O. The cartesian co-ordinates of the point A for a particular value of θ are given by $x E = l\cos\theta$ and $y = l\sin\theta$. For small polar deflection angles, θ is proportional to the square of the distance along the curve, as in the case of the spiral.

The assumption applies for values of θ up to about 6°. Since for small angles $y = L\theta$ and $x = L$, it follows that $y = L^3/6RL = x^3/6RL$, which is the equation of a cubic parabola exactly, as in the case of a spiral for small deflections.

EARTHWORKS

Most engineering projects involve earthworks in some form or other, ie there is either excavation (*cut*) to reduce the existing level of the ground to the new level, or embankment (*fill*) to make up to the new level. Surveys carried out for such projects must provide sufficient data to enable the proposed new levels to be determined, the volumes of earthwork computed, and the information required for setting out to be prepared. The volumes of earthworks are usually determined by one of the following methods:

(1) **Computing Earthworks from Sections.**—The survey in this case includes a longitudinal section of levels along the centre line of the road, railway, culvert, etc (to which projects the method is particularly applicable) and cross sections at suitable intervals along the centre line, preferably at equal intervals. The longitudinal and cross sections are then plotted, the former to an 'exaggerated' vertical scale and the cross sections to a 'natural' scale. The next step is to draw the formation line on the longitudinal section. Various engineering reasons, such as the maximum gradient, crossing of obstacles, drainage, relation to the levels adjoining the route, will govern the choice of formation line, and these will not be dealt with in detail here. There is, however, one important aspect amongst them which is a basic principle in earthworks, and that is the 'equalisation of cut and fill'; where for reasons of economy, if the nature of the ground is suitable, excavated material in cutting is used as fill in the embankments. This will be achieved approximately if the sum of the areas of cut indicated on the longitudinal section are equal to the sum of the areas of fill as nearly as practicable. Having determined the formation line this will give the new reduced levels of the centre line at each cross section by scaling or by calculation from a known commencing level and proposed gradient. These levels will be the formation levels at the various cross sections and are plotted accordingly. The proposed formation width and side slopes are then plotted to scale. The area bounded by the new section and the existing ground line will represent the areas of cut or fill at each cross section can can be determined by direct measurement or by calculation as follows:

Case (*a*). When the existing ground is level in cross section (ie no cross-fall). This is illustrated for a cutting in Fig. 80, where $2b$ is the width of formation, h is the depth of cut, s to 1 are the side slopes. Then area of cut = $2bh + sh^2$.

Case (*b*). When the existing ground has a cross-fall as in Fig. 81, where w_1 and w_2 are the side-widths. Then area of cut = $(w_1w_2 - b^2)/s$. If the side widths are not known, these may be calculated from a knowledge of the cross-fall, formation width, depth of cut (or fill) and the side-slopes as follows:

$$w_1 = x(b + sh)/(x + s);\ w_2 = x(b + sh)/(x - s).$$

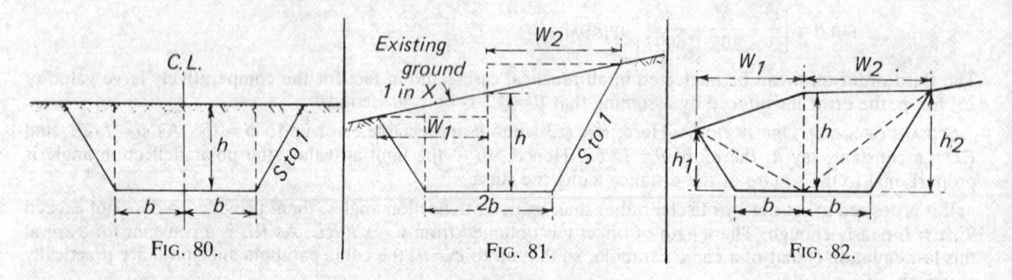

FIG. 80. FIG. 81. FIG. 82.

Case (*c*). Where the existing ground is not flat, as in Fig. 82, where h_1 and h_2 are the heights above formation at the top of each slope.

Then area of cut = $\frac{1}{2}b(h_1 + h_2) + \frac{1}{2}h(w_1 + w_2)$.

Also area of cut = $\frac{1}{2}(w_1 + w_2)\{h + (b/s)\} - (b^2/s)$.

Case (*d*). When the existing ground has a cross-fall, with one portion of the formation width in cutting and the other portion in fill (Fig. 83). Formulae may be derived for the area of cut and fill as in the previous cases, but as the side slopes of cuttings and embankments are seldom the same in practice it is preferable to deal with such sections by plotting to scale and finding the area by direct measurement. This would in any event be necessary where the existing ground line has not a uniform slope; even small changes in the cross-fall would substantially affect the areas of cross sections calculated from formulae based on straight line assumptions and the volumes derived in this way would thus be inaccurate.

Calculation of Volumes from Areas of Cross Section.—Having found the areas of cut or fill at each cross section, the volumes of cut or fill between particular sections are found by applying one of the following formulae:

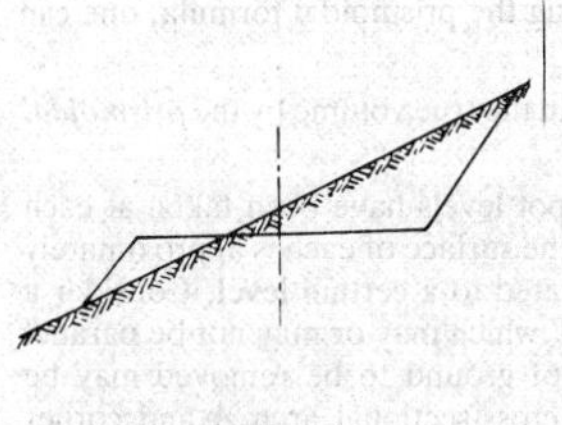

FIG. 83.

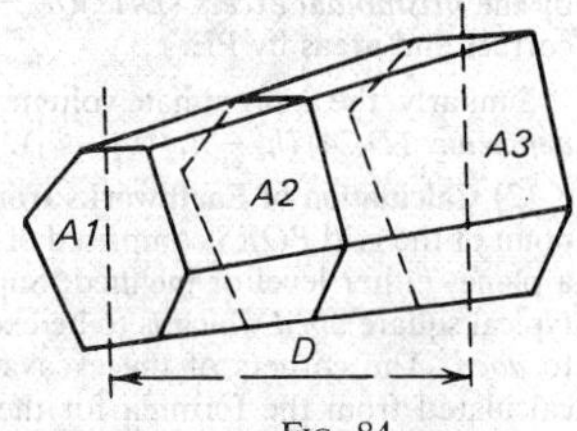

FIG. 84.

(i) *Prismoidal Formula.* A 'prismoid' is a solid having for its ends any two parallel plane figures with the same number of sides, the ends being joined by straight lines between the perimeters. Referring to Fig. 84, D is the distance between the end sections, A_1 and A_3 the areas of the end sections, and A_2 the area of the middle section.

Then, volume between A_1 and $A_3 = (D/6)(A_1 + 4A_2 + A_3)$.

If sufficient sections are taken along a cutting or embankment to ensure that the solids formed between alternate sections, ie A_1 to A_3, A_2 to A_4, etc, are approximate prismoids, the above formula then becomes a particular statement of Simpson's Rule.

$$\text{Volume} = (D/3)\,[A_1 + 2(A_3 + A_5 + -) + 4(A_2 + A_4 + A_6 + -) - + A_x]$$

where the sections are equidistant at a distance D apart, and there is an *odd* number of sections x. Expressed in general form, the volume is equal to the sum of the end areas plus twice the sum of the odd areas plus four times the sum of the even areas, the whole multiplied by one-third the distance between the sections.

Where there is an even number of cross-sections, the prismoidal formula is applied to all sections except one end section, which is treated separately by the *end area* formula below.

If for certain reasons at site or the nature of the ground the distance between sections cannot be constant, the formula must be applied separately to each group of sections which are equidistant, and the separate results added together to give the total volume.

(ii) *Trapezoidal Formula.*—This more simple but less accurate formula has the advantage that it can be applied direct to any number of sections, either odd or even. The volume is given by: Volume = $(D/2)[A_1 + 2(A_2 + A_3 + A_4 + -----) + A_x]$ where D is the distance between adjacent sections.

(iii) *End Area Formula.*—The average of the areas of two end sections is found and multiplied by the distance between them. If A_1 and A_2 are parallel end sections and D the distance between them, then approximately, Volume = $D(A_1 + A_2)/2$. This is the formula often applied to the end section of an even series of sections which have been dealt with by the prismoidal formula except for an end section. The average of the areas of the end section and the preceding one are found and the above formula used to find the separate end volume to be added to the remainder.

TRIANGULAR PRISMOID.—If the prismoid has triangular ends of base lengths b_1 and b_2 and perpendicular heights h_1 and h_2, the approximate volume obtained by averaging end areas is greater than the true volume

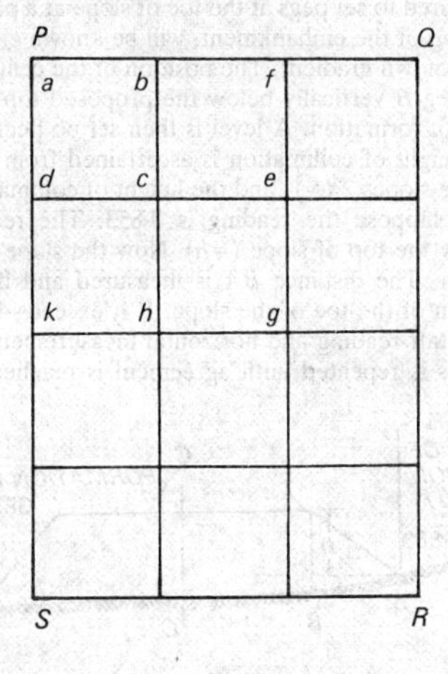

FIG. 85.

by the *prismoidal excess* $(D/12)(h_2 - h_1)(b_2 - b_1)$ so that, instead of applying the prismoidal formula, one can correct end areas by PE.

Similarly, the approximate volume obtained by writing $V = DA_2$ is less than the true volume by the *prismoidal deficiency* $(D/24)(h_2 - h_1)(b_2 - b_1)$. Here A_2 is the mid-area in length D.

(2) **Calculation of Earthworks from Spot Levels.**—In Fig. 85, suppose spot levels have been taken at each point of the grid *PQRS* comprised of squares or rectangles of such size that the surface of each is approximately a plane, either level or inclined. Suppose also that the grid is to be excavated to a certain level. Consider a typical square *abcd* which is to be excavated down to another plane *a'b'c'd'* which may or may not be parallel to *abcd*. The corners of the excavation will be vertical and the portion of ground to be removed may be calculated from the formula for the volume of a triangular prismoid of cross-sectional area A and corner heights h_1, h_2 and h_3. This is: volume $= A\{(h_1 + h_2 + h_3)/3\}$. In this way, the volume for the whole excavation may be taken out.

VOLUMES OF EARTHWORK ON CURVES.—In road, railway, canal projects, etc, the centre line frequently lies on a curve and the formulae for volumes derived from the areas of cross section do not apply in direct form. If the cross sections are of equal A, the volume will be the product of A and the length of the path of the centroid of section measured along the curve. In practice, however, the areas of cross section are seldom equal and the positions of their centroids vary, being sometimes outside the radius of curvature of the centre line and sometimes inside. A correction is therefore applied separately to each cross-section, as follows:

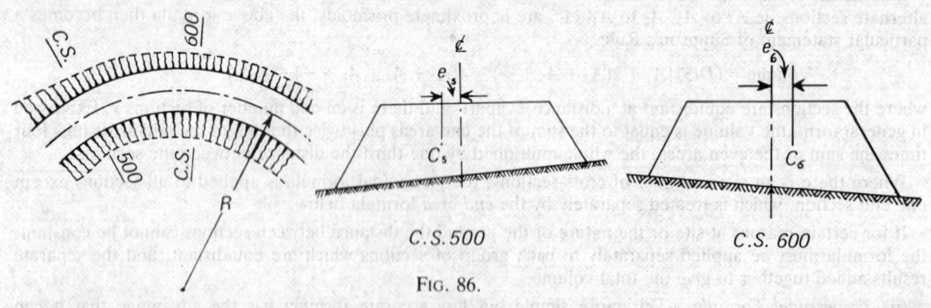

Fig. 86.

Figure 86 illustrates an embankment on a curve of radius R, and typical cross sections at chainage 500 and 600 are shown. The centres of gravity, ie centres of area, c_5 and c_6, are found and their eccentricity e measured horizontally from the centre line. Assume that c_5 lies outside and c_6 inside the centre line. The areas of cross section are A_5 and A_6 respectively. Then, corrections to areas A_5 and A_6 are $+(A_5e_5)/R$ and $-(A_6e_6)/R$ respectively. Having applied these corrections, standard formulae for volumes may be used, the distances between sections being the distances along the curve.

SETTING OUT SIDE SLOPES.—The setting out of earthworks includes generally the setting of pegs at the positions proposed for top of cutting and toe of bank to mark the limits of construction work or to indicate boundaries of land to be acquired. (The boundary will not necessarily be at the exact position of the top or toe of slope and is usually several feet away). Slope pegs are set by trial and error. Figure 87 illustrates a proposed embankment; it is required to set pegs at the toe of slope at a particular cross section. The proposed formation level, ie the level on top of the embankment, will be known either by scaling from the longitudinal section or by calculating from a known gradient. The position of the centre line will be known and can be set out by a peg C, from which a peg B vertically below the proposed top of slope can be set by measuring a distance equal to the half-width of formation. A level is then set up near A, assumed to be the approximate position of the toe slope. The height of collimation is ascertained from a nearby bench mark. Suppose the formation level is 38·862, the side slopes 2 to 1, and the height of collimation 37·277. A staff reading is taken at the assumed position of A; suppose the reading is 0·853. The reduced level at A is then 37·277 − 0·853 = 36·424, ie 2·438 m below the top of slope $(=h)$. Now the slope is 2 to 1, so the distance of A from B should be $2 \times 2{\cdot}438 = 4{\cdot}876$ m. The distance BA is measured and if it then agrees with the calculated distance, A is the correct position of the toe of the slope. If it exceeds 4·876 m, the trial position of A must be moved inwards and another staff reading and horizontal measurement taken; if less than 4·876 m it must be moved outwards. The process is repeated until agreement is reached between the measured and calculated horizontal distance BA.

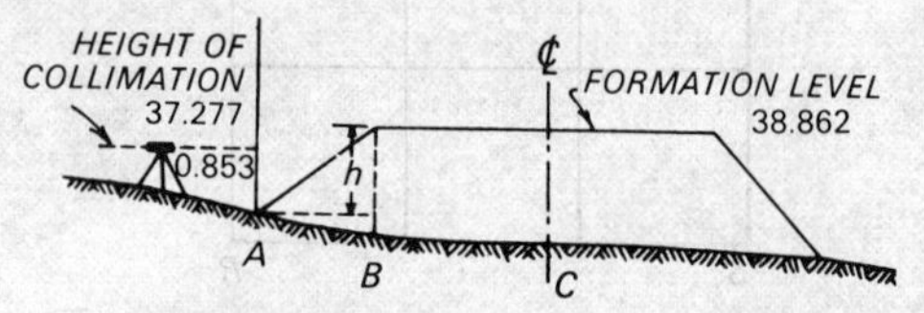

Fig. 87.

HYDROGRAPHIC SURVEYING

This branch of surveying embraces both tidal and non-tidal waters, ponds, lakes, rivers and streams; the undulations of the bottom, the rate of flow of rivers and streams, the determination of volumes and areas of water, and the phenomena of tides and currents.

SOUNDINGS.—For many purposes connected with river surveys, the location of dams and bridges, harbour and marine works generally, it is necessary to ascertain the levels of the river or sea bed. The taking of levels below water is known as *sounding*. The work may be considered under two headings: (*a*) in non-tidal waters such as ponds, lakes, and rivers above the tide, and (*b*) in tidal waters.

(*a*) **Non-tidal Waters.**—If the water is very shallow, levels on the bottom can be taken in the normal way with a level and staff by wading to the points where levels are required, eg along a particular cross section. The method is precisely the same as in levelling, and can be extended to under-water contours. The occasions on which the water is shallow enough to enable this procedure to be used are limited. Where the water is deeper, soundings are taken from the surface of the water by measuring to the bottom with a rod similar to a levelling staff (up to 4 or 5 m) or by dropping a sounding line or chain. The level of the surface of the water is found by the usual levelling methods and the values of the soundings deducted to give the under water levels. Either a steel chain is used, weighted at the bottom with a lead sinker, and graduated by tellers every whole metre, or a hemp sounding line similarly weighted and tagged. The chain is generally preferable in that it is less liable to changes in length. Methods of taking soundings in non-tidal water are as follows:

(i) Where a line of soundings is required across a narrow stream or river, a rope or tape may be stretched from bank to bank along the required line, and the soundings taken at specified intervals across. It is not possible to lay down a firm interval for universal adoption, the spacing being dependent on the nature of the survey and the site, but usual distances for soundings are 2, 5, 10 or 20 m apart along a definite line; the lines being similarly spaced. Soundings are taken from a boat, care being taken that the boat is kept along the specified line. To assist in this, shore markers are frequently provided, in the form of ordinary ranging rods marking the ends of the line, or poles with diamond-shaped or triangular top marks where longer distances are involved.

(ii) Where the width is too great for a rope or tape to be stretched across, a method such as the following may be used. Referring to Fig. 88, suppose it is desired to take soundings along the line *XY* produced. A point *Z* is first located with reference to *X* and *Y* by measuring *XY* and the angles *X* and *Y* or by setting out a right-angle at *Y* and measuring along *YZ*. Ranging rods or markers are set up at *X* and *Y* and a theodolite at *Z*. The sounding boat proceeds along the line *XY* produced, with the aid of the markers, and at a given signal from the boat, when a sounding is taken, the instrument man at *Z* records the angle θ to the sounding position *P*. The boat continues along its line, and succeeding positions of soundings are recorded by the angle θ. The positions can be located either by plotting or by calculation from the known length of *YZ* and angle θ. The disadvantage of the method is chiefly that a surveyor is required at *Z* in addition to the sounding party in the boat.

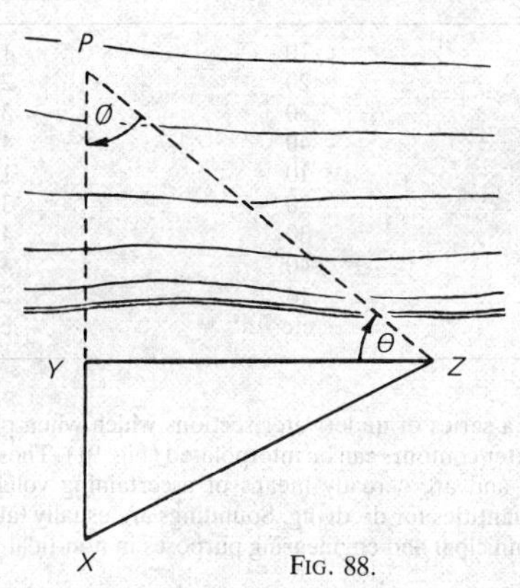

FIG. 88.

(iii) An alternative to method (ii) is to measure from the sounding boat with a sextant the angle ϕ subtended by *YZ* (Fig. 88). This is a common method of locating soundings, prominent features such as tall buildings, church spires, etc, being used in practice instead of ranging rods at *Y* and *Z*, although rods or markers are used where no suitable features exist and where the distances from the shore are great.

(iv) The two-theodolite method is a precise means of locating sounding poisitions. A base line *XY* (Fig. 89) is set out close to the shore and measured. *X* and *Y* are then used as instrument stations for angular observations by theodolite or sextant to the position of the sounding boat. The position *P* of the boat is fixed by reading

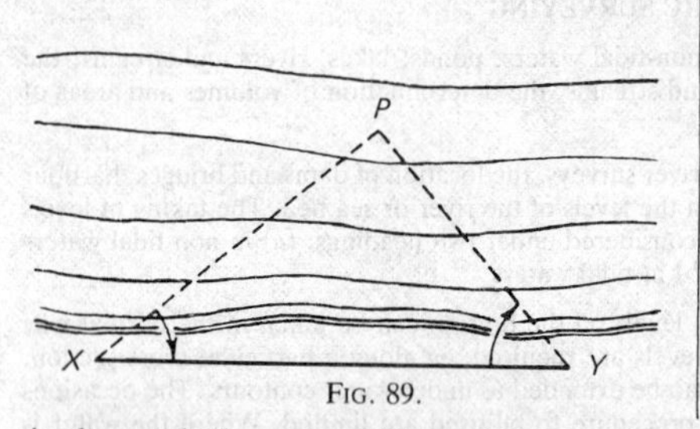

FIG. 89.

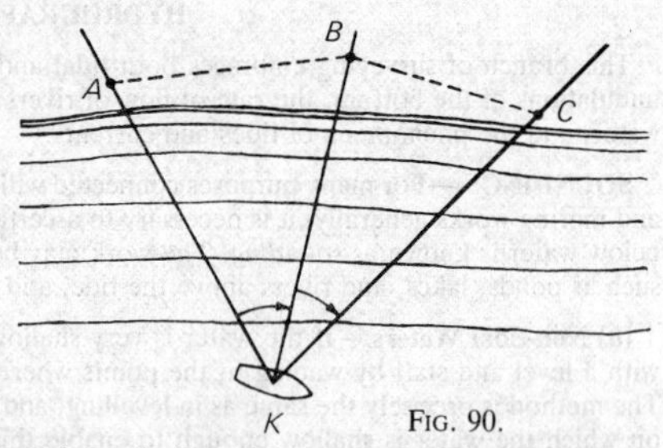

FIG. 90.

simultaneously the angles PXY and XYP on a given signal from the boat. The method, although accurate, has the disadvantage that two instruments and two surveyors are required ashore in addition to the sounding party.

(v) The method of resection is commonly used for the location of soundings and consists of observing from the sounding boat the angles subtended by three stations or prominent features ashore whose positions are known (Fig. 90). The method and solution of the 'three-point problem' were dealt with previously for the plane table. It has the particular advantage that the whole of the work can be done from the boat without assistance from shore observers and a high standard of accuracy can be obtained. The angles are observed by sextant and it is important that there should be as little time lag as possible between the observations of the separate angles.

In the preceding paragraphs, describing the methods of taking and locating soundings in non-tidal waters, it has been assumed that the level of the surface of the water remains constant during the whole of the operation. Having found the level of the surface by ordinary levelling, the levels of the bed can be found by subtracting the soundings from the surface level. Generally, however, the soundings are shown on plan as depths below the surface. It is usual to take soundings in straight lines rather than at random, the lines being equidistant at distances of 5, 10 or 20 m. In plotting the soundings, these lines are first set out on plan, the distances at which soundings were taken are then marked along the lines and the soundings recorded against these points (Fig. 91). The soundings would be booked as follows:

SURVEY OF WELBY LAKE. DATE: 1.8.1977. Soundings in metres below surface.
Level of surface 34·235.

Line	Distance (m)	Soundings (m)
1	10	1·6
	20	2·4
	30	3·3
	40	4·0
2	10	1·8
	20	3·2
	30	4·0
	40	4·6
3	10	2·0
	etc	etc

The process really provides a series of underwater sections which when plotted produce a number of spot soundings from which underwater contours can be interpolated (Fig. 91). These contours are useful in providing data for engineering projects and are a ready means of ascertaining volumes of water in natural storage reservoirs or in determining quantities for dredging. Soundings are usually taken in metres to the nearest tenth of a metre and contours for municipal and engineering purposes in non-tidal waters drawn at vertical intervals of 0·5, 1·0, 2·5, or 5 metres.

(*b*) **Tidal Waters.**—Although the general principles described above apply equally to tidal waters, there is one fundamental difference. Whereas in non-tidal waters the surface remains at a constant level, in tidal waters the surface rises and falls with the tide; the surface cannot therefore be used as a datum.

TIDES.—Tides are the periodical changes in level of the surface of the ocean and of tidal rivers and estuaries. The height from low water level to the next high water level is known as the *range of tide*. The greatest ranges occur at *spring tides* and the smallest at *neap tides*, these series of tides alternating and each occurring twice in a lunar month. The rising tide is the *flood* and the falling tide, the *ebb*.

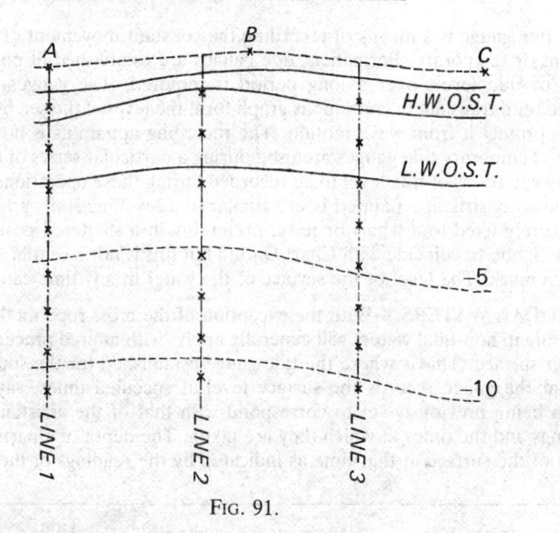

FIG. 91.

The following are standard abbreviations used on plans and charts: LWOST—Low water ordinary spring tides; LWONT—Low water ordinary neap tides; HWOST—High water ordinary spring tides; HWONT—High water ordinary neap tides.

The letter M appearing as a prefix to the above refers to 'mean' value. The time and height of tides may be predicted astronomically for long periods ahead, and these predictions for various ports are published for each year in Tide Tables. Although the predictions are reliable, wind and weather may cause the actual tide levels to be 'extraordinary', ie very high or abnormally low.

When discussing Ordnance Datum earlier, it was explained that this is the mean sea level at Newlyn. This mean sea level is the mean level of the tide recorded over a long period. Although it is the datum for levelling throughout Great Britain it is not usually the datum for hydrographic surveying in tidal waters, in which low water springs (Chart Datum) is generally adopted. The level of Chart Datum related to Ordnance Datum is given in Tide Tables for various 'standard' ports around the coast.

Example.—A sounding taken at HWOST shows a depth of 6·4 m at a certain distance from the shore (Fig. 92). If the range of that particular tide was 2·9 m, and chart datum is −2·57 OD, find the level of the sea bed where the sounding was taken, reduced to Ordnance Datum.

Chart Datum = LOWST = −2·57 OD
HWOST = LWOST + range = −2·57 + 2·9 = 0·33
Sea Bed = HWOST − 6·4 = 0·33 − 6·4 = −6·07 OD

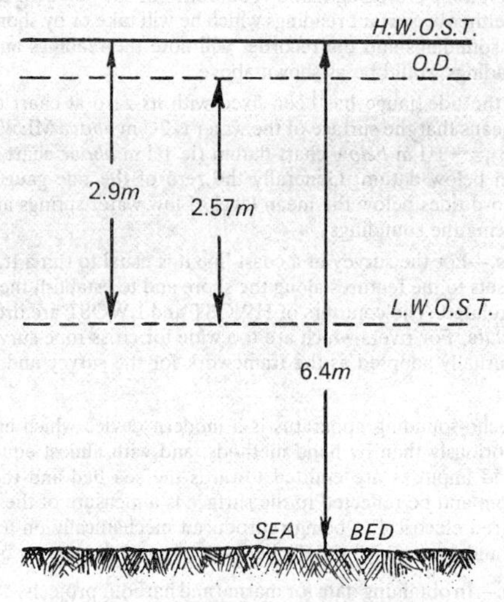

FIG. 92.

Tide Gauge.—A tide gauge is a means of recording the constant movement of tide level. Tide gauges may be either permanent or temporary. Permanent tide gauges are established at ports and in localities where a continuous record of tide levels over a long period is required. The gauges are usually self-registering, electrically operated, and translate in continuous graph form the level of the sea by means of a float suspended inside a cylinder to protect it from wave motion. The recording apparatus is housed under cover to protect it from the weather. Temporary tide gauges are used during a particular series of soundings or a hydrographic survey to enable the variations of tide level to be recorded during these operations. In its simplest form, a tide gauge for this purpose consists of a painted board similar to a levelling staff, graduated in metres and tenths of a metre, and securely fixed to a wharf or jetty, preferably in a sheltered position. The zero of the gauge should if possible be made to coincide with Chart Datum but this is not essential and it may be related merely to the nearest bench mark. The level of the surface of the water at any time can be read against the gauge.

SOUNDING IN TIDAL WATERS.—With the exception of the cross rope method, the methods previously described for sounding in non-tidal waters will generally apply, with altered procedure arising from the change in level of the water surface. This is where the tide gauge established for the sounding operation comes into use. An observer at the gauge records the surface level at specified times, say at quarter-hour or 10 min intervals, his watch being previously set to correspond with that of the assistant in the sounding boat who records the soundings and the times at which they are taken. The depth of a particular sounding may then be related to the level of the surface at that time as indicated by the readings of the tide gauge.

Line	Distance (m)	Sounding (m)	Time (h min)	Tide Gauge (m)	Reduced Sounding (m)
1	10	1·2	11 15	2·3	−1·1
	20	2·2			−0·1
	30	3·0			0·7
	40	3·8	11 20		1·5
	50	4·6			2·3
	60	5·4			3·1
	70	6·4			4·1
	80	7·3	11 25	2·4	4·9
	90	8·1			5·7
	100	8·8			6·4
	110	9·5			7·1
	120	10·1	11 30		7·7

The sounding party will generally consist of the boatmen or crew (of a motor boat), the surveyor, the leadsman (or chainman), and the recorder. In addition there will be the tide gauge recorder and instrument men ashore if shore observations are being made. The duties of the surveyor are to ensure that the location of each sounding is fixed, either by sextant readings which he will take or by shore observations. The leadsman will take and call out the soundings and the recorder will note the readings and the times at which they are taken. A typical set of readings would be as shown above.

In the above example, the tide gauge has been fixed with its zero at chart datum (MLWOST). A gauge reading of 2·3 therefore means that the surface of the water is 2·3 m *above* MLWOST (Fig. 93) and a sounding of 1·2 m will be (1·2 − 2·3) = −1·1 m *below* chart datum (ie 1·1 m *above* chart datum). A sounding of 3·8 m will be (3·8 − 2·3) = 1·5 m below datum. Generally the zero of the tide gauge is set several metres below MLWOST in order to record tides below the mean level of low water springs and the gauge reading must be duly corrected when reducing the soundings.

Coast and River Surveys.—For the survey of a coast line it is usual to run a traverse along the shore for the dual purpose of taking offsets to the features along the shore and to establish the positions of stations to which lines of soundings can be related. The contours of HWOST and LWOST are drawn by interpolation from the soundings and local tidal data. For rivers which are too wide for cross-rope surveying and sounding, a system of interlacing triangles is usually adopted as the framework for the survey and as a basis for soundings (Fig. 94).

Echo Sounding.—The echo-sounding apparatus is a modern device which enables soundings to be taken more rapidly and less laboriously than by hand methods, and with almost equal precision. The principle of the apparatus is that sound impulses are emitted towards the sea bed and the time taken for a particular impulse to strike the bottom and be reflected to the surface is a measure of the depth. The time intervals are very small and are measured electrically, being reproduced mechanically on a recording sheet which shows the profile of the sea bed and from which depths below a selected datum can be deduced.

Observation of Currents.—In obtaining data for marine and harbour projects, coastal protection, breakwaters and sea walls, dredging, sewerage outfall schemes, etc, it is often essential to ascertain the direction and the

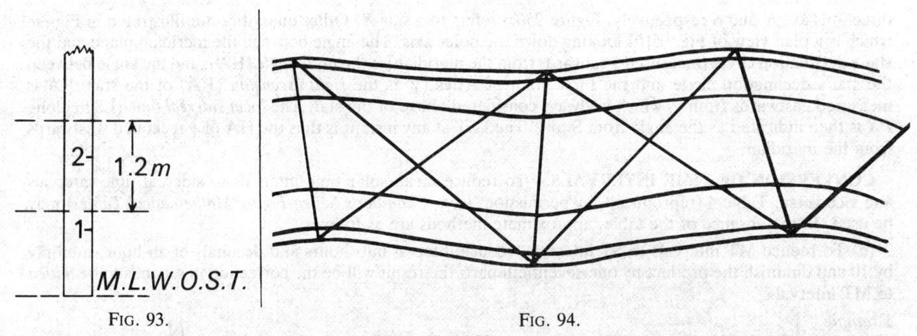

FIG. 93. FIG. 94.

speed of the current. Observations are generally necessary over a complete range of tides covering a period. A common method of finding the direction and speed of currents is by observing the time taken for an immersed float to pass from one located position to another. The calculated distance between the two observed points divided by the time will be the speed of the current. The speed of current is generally expressed in kilometres per hour.

The floats used for observing currents must be such as to indicate the true motion of the current and not be affected by wind or surface turbulence. There are several types of floats: (*a*) surface floats, made of wood or cork, which project above the surface; although they float easily, they are affected to a great extent by wind and turbulence and are therefore suitable only in very calm conditions; (*b*) sub-surface floats, in which the main float is submerged below the surface and connected to a small surface float carrying a pennant which acts as a marker for observations; (*c*) rod floats are wooden rods, about 1 m in length, suitably weighted at the bottom so that most of the rod is below the surface and a small portion projects for observation purposes. The positions of the float are located from time to time by the two-theodolite method from shore stations, or by sextant observations from a boat alongside the float. Whereas the former method is slow and needs careful synchronisation between the instrument men, the latter must be performed with care to ensure that the direction of the float is not influenced by the movement of the boat. The speed of currents may also be ascertained with the aid of a *current meter*. This instrument is a mechanical contrivance which is lowered into the water by a chain at the point where the observation is to be made. The current rotates projecting blades on the meter, the rate of revolution of the blades being a measure of the speed, which is recorded through suitable gearing by meter readings over a specified interval of time.

FIELD ASTRONOMY

Definitions of some basic quantities used in field astronomy are indicated in Fig. 95, which has been drawn to represent the case of a station in latitude N50°, approximately. The observer is at O and his north and south

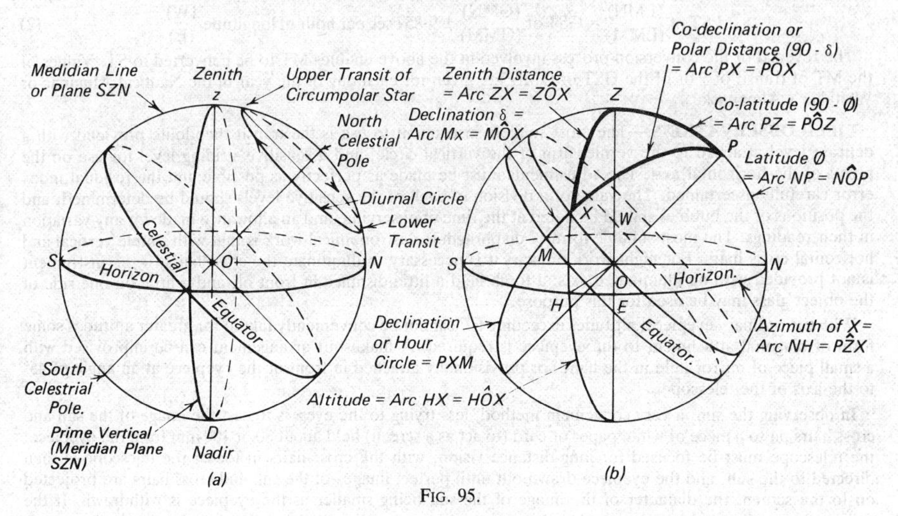

FIG. 95.

directions are N and S respectively. Figure 95(b) refers to a star X. Other quantities are illustrated in Fig. 96 which is a plan view of Fig. 95(b) looking down the polar axis. The angle between the meridian plane and the star's declination circle (measured westwards from the meridian) is the *hour angle* (HA), and the angle between the star's declination circle and the First Point of Aries (γ) is the *right ascension* (RA) of the star. RA is measured eastwards from γ, which is always considered ahead of the star. The *local sidereal time* (LST) along PX is then indicated as the angle from S to γ. The LST at any instant is thus the HA of γ reckoned westwards from the meridian.

CONVERSION OF TIME INTERVALS.—To reduce mean solar time intervals to sidereal time intervals and vice versa, Table 4 (reproduced, by permission, from *Chamber's Seven-Figure Mathematical Tables*) may be used. In the absence of the table, approximate methods are as follows:

(a) To reduce MT intervals to ST intervals, reduce interval into hours and decimals of an hour, multiply by 10 and diminish the product by one-seventieth part; the result will be the correction in seconds to be *added* to MT interval.

Example

16 h 30 m 18s MT ⟶ 16·505 × 10 = 165·05
less one-seventieth part = 2·36

Corr^n + 2 m 42·7 s ⟵ 162·69

16 h 33 m 00·7 s ST

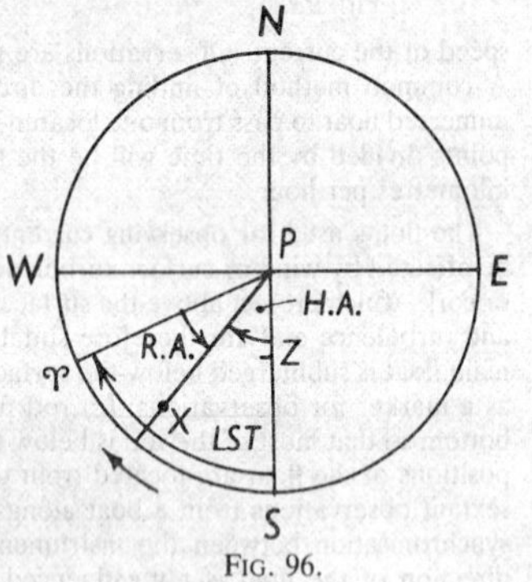

(b) To reduce ST intervals to MT intervals, reduce interval into hours and decimals of an hour, multiply by 10 and diminish the product by one-sixtieth part; the result will be the correction in seconds to be *subtracted* from ST interval.

Example

16 h 33 m 00·7 s ST ⟶ 16·550 × 10 = 165·50
less one-sixtieth part = 2·76

Corr^n −2 m 42·7 s ⟵ 162·74

16 h 30 m 18 s MT

FIG. 96.

The error in using these approximations is less than one-tenth sec in a 24-hour interval.

EQUATION OF TIME (E) is defined by LAT + E = LMT. The approximate variation of E during the year is indicated in Table 5.

CONVERSION OF TIME.—Two relations of value in the conversion of sidereal time (as distinct from ST intervals) into mean time are:

$$\text{LMT of transit of } \gamma = \text{MT of transit of } \gamma \text{ at Greenwich } \pm 9{\cdot}83 \text{ sec per hour of longitude } \begin{matrix}(E)\\(W)\end{matrix} \quad (1)$$

$$\text{LST of } \begin{matrix}(\text{LMN})\\(\text{LMM})\end{matrix} = \text{GST of } \begin{matrix}(\text{GMN})\\(\text{GMM})\end{matrix} \pm 9{\cdot}857 \text{ sec per hour of longitude } \begin{matrix}(W)\\(E)\end{matrix} \quad (2)$$

The reversal of the conversion process involved in the above enables MT to be converted to ST. Values of the MT of transit of γ or of the GST of GMN are given for each day of the year in the Nautical Almanac or Whitaker's Almanack.

FIELD OBSERVATIONS.—The most suitable instrument to use is the transit theodolite provided with a delicate level attached to the vernier arm of the vertical circle, and a sensitive striding level for use on the pivots of the horizontal axis. The adjustments must be made as perfectly as possible and the residual index error carefully ascertained. The value of a division of each of the sensitive levels should be determined, and the positions of the bubbles should be noted at the time of observing, and an allowance made for any variation in their readings. The most suitable form of diaphragm for astronomical work is that with simple vertical and horizontal cross hairs. For night work on stars it is necessary to illuminate the cross hairs, if the instrument is not provided with an illuminated axis; a torch held a little distance in front of, and a little on one side of the object glass may be used for this purpose.

With the ordinary eyepiece, altitudes exceeding 60° cannot be conveniently taken; for greater altitudes some form of diagonal attachment to the eyepiece is required. A makeshift arrangement can be improvised with a small piece of mirror held in the hand, or provisionally attached in front of the eyepiece at an angle of 45° to the axis of the telescope.

In observing the sun, a very convenient method, less trying to the eyes, is to cast the image of the sun and cross hairs on to a piece of white paper or card (to act as a screen) held about 80 or 100 mm from the eyepiece; the telescope must be focused for long-distance vision, with the cross hairs in focus; the telescope is then directed to the sun, and the eyepiece drawn out until perfect images of the sun and cross hairs are projected on to the screen, the diameter of the image of the sun being smaller as the eyepiece is withdrawn. If the

TABLE 4.—MUTUAL CONVERSION OF SIDEREAL AND MEAN TIME INTERVALS.

To Reduce Mean to Sidereal Time Intervals

Solar hrs	Add Min	Add Sec	Solar Min	Add Sec	Solar Min	Add Sec	Solar Sec	Add Sec	Solar Sec	Add Sec
1	0	9·86	1	0·16	31	5·09	1	0·00	31	0·08
2	0	19·71	2	0·33	32	5·26	2	0·01	32	0·09
3	0	29·57	3	0·49	33	5·42	3	0·01	33	0·09
4	0	39·43	4	0·66	34	5·59	4	0·01	34	0·09
5	0	49·28	5	0·82	35	5·75	5	0·01	35	0·10
6	0	59·14	6	0·99	36	5·92	6	0·02	36	0·10
7	1	9·00	7	1·15	37	6·08	7	0·02	37	0·10
8	1	18·85	8	1·31	38	6·24	8	0·02	38	0·10
9	1	28·71	9	1·48	39	6·41	9	0·03	39	0·11
10	1	38·56	10	1·64	40	6·57	10	0·03	40	0·11
11	1	48·42	11	1·81	41	6·74	11	0·03	41	0·11
12	1	58·28	12	1·97	42	6·90	12	0·03	42	0·12
13	2	8·13	13	2·14	43	7·07	13	0·04	43	0·12
14	2	17·99	14	2·30	44	7·23	14	0·04	44	0·12
15	2	27·85	15	2·46	45	7·39	15	0·04	45	0·12
16	2	37·70	16	2·63	46	7·56	16	0·04	46	0·13
17	2	47·56	17	2·79	47	7·72	17	0·05	47	0·13
18	2	57·42	18	2·96	48	7·89	18	0·05	48	0·13
19	3	7·27	19	3·12	49	8·05	19	0·05	49	0·13
20	3	17·13	20	3·29	50	8·22	20	0·06	50	0·14
21	3	26·99	21	3·45	51	8·38	21	0·06	51	0·14
22	3	36·84	22	3·61	52	8·54	22	0·06	52	0·14
23	3	46·70	23	3·78	53	8·71	23	0·06	53	0·15
24	3	56·56	24	3·94	54	8·87	24	0·07	54	0·15
25	4	6·41	25	4·11	55	9·04	25	0·07	55	0·15
26	4	16·27	26	4·27	56	9·20	26	0·07	56	0·15
27	4	26·12	27	4·44	57	9·37	27	0·08	57	0·16
28	4	35·98	28	4·60	58	9·53	28	0·08	58	0·16
29	4	45·84	29	4·76	59	9·69	29	0·08	59	0·16
30	4	55·69	30	4·93	60	9·86	30	0·08	60	0·16

To Reduce Sidereal to Mean Time Intervals

Sid hrs	Subtract Min	Subtract Sec	Sid Min	Subtract Sec	Sid Min	Subtract Sec	Sid Sec	Subtract Sec	Sid Sec	Subtract Sec
1	0	9·83	1	0·16	31	5·08	1	0·00	31	0·08
2	0	19·66	2	0·33	32	5·24	2	0·01	32	0·09
3	0	29·49	3	0·49	33	5·41	3	0·01	33	0·09
4	0	39·32	4	0·66	34	5·57	4	0·01	34	0·09
5	0	49·15	5	0·82	35	5·73	5	0·01	35	0·10
6	0	58·98	6	0·98	36	5·90	6	0·02	36	0·10
7	1	8·81	7	1·15	37	6·06	7	0·02	37	0·10
8	1	18·64	8	1·31	38	6·23	8	0·02	38	0·10
9	1	28·47	9	1·47	39	6·39	9	0·02	39	0·11
10	1	38·30	10	1·64	40	6·55	10	0·03	40	0·11
11	1	48·13	11	1·80	41	6·72	11	0·03	41	0·11
12	1	57·95	12	1·97	42	6·88	12	0·03	42	0·11
13	2	7·78	13	2·13	43	7·04	13	0·04	43	0·12
14	2	17·61	14	2·29	44	7·21	14	0·04	44	0·12
15	2	27·44	15	2·46	45	7·37	15	0·04	45	0·12
16	2	37·27	16	2·62	46	7·54	16	0·04	46	0·13
17	2	47·10	17	2·79	47	7·70	17	0·05	47	0·13
18	2	56·93	18	2·95	48	7·86	18	0·05	48	0·13
19	3	6·76	19	3·11	49	8·03	19	0·05	49	0·13
20	3	16·59	20	3·28	50	8·19	20	0·06	50	0·14
21	3	26·42	21	3·44	51	8·36	21	0·06	51	0·14

(continued)

TABLE 4.—(*Continued*)

Sid hrs	Subtract Min	Sec	Sid Min	Sub-tract Sec	Sid Min	Sub-tract Sec	Sid Sec	Sub-tract Sec	Sid Sec	Sub-tract Sec
22	3	36·25	22	3·60	52	8·52	22	0·06	52	0·14
23	3	46·08	23	3·77	53	8·68	23	0·06	53	0·14
24	3	55·91	24	3·93	54	8·85	24	0·07	54	0·15
25	4	5·74	25	4·10	55	9·01	25	0·07	55	0·15
26	4	15·57	26	4·26	56	9·17	26	0·07	56	0·15
27	4	25·40	27	4·42	57	9·34	27	0·07	57	0·16
28	4	35·23	28	4·59	58	9·50	28	0·08	58	0·16
29	4	45·06	29	4·75	59	9·67	29	0·08	59	0·16
30	4	54·89	30	4·92	60	9·83	30	0·08	60	0·16

TABLE 5.—EQUATION OF TIME.
SHOWING TIME TO BE ADDED TO OR SUBTRACTED FROM LOCAL APPARENT TIME IN ORDER TO OBTAIN LOCAL MEAN TIME.

Date	Minutes (approximate)	Date	Minutes (approximate)	Date	Minutes (approximate)	Date	Minutes (approximate)
Jan 2	+ 4	Apr 1	+4	Aug 18	+ 4	Nov 11	−16
Jan 4	+ 5	Apr 5	+3	Aug 22	+ 3	Nov 17	−15
Jan 7	+ 6	Apr 8	+2	Aug 26	+ 2	Nov 22	−14
Jan 9	+ 7	Apr 12	+1	Aug 29	+ 1	Nov 25	−13
Jan 12	+ 8	Apr 16	0	Sept 1	0	Nov 29	−12
Jan 14	+ 9	Apr 20	−1	Sept 5	− 1	Dec 1	−11
Jan 17	+10	Apr 25	−2	Sept 8	− 2	Dec 4	−10
Jan 20	+11	May 2	−3	Sept 10	− 3	Dec 6	− 9
Jan 24	+12	May 15	−4	Sept 13	− 4	Dec 9	− 8
Jan 28	+13	May 27	−3	Sept 16	− 5	Dec 11	− 7
Feb 5	+14	June 3	−2	Sept 19	− 6	Dec 13	− 6
Feb 19	+14	June 9	−1	Sept 22	− 7	Dec 15	− 5
Feb 26	+13	June 14	0	Sept 25	− 8	Dec 17	− 4
Mar 4	+12	June 19	+1	Sept 28	− 9	Dec 19	− 3
Mar 8	+11	June 23	+2	Oct 1	−10	Dec 21	− 2
Mar 12	+10	June 28	+3	Oct 4	−11	Dec 23	− 1
Mar 15	+ 9	July 3	+4	Oct 7	−12	Dec 25	0
Mar 19	+ 8	July 9	+5	Oct 11	−13	Dec 27	+ 1
Mar 22	+ 7	July 17	+6	Oct 15	−14	Dec 29	+ 2
Mar 26	+ 6	Aug 5	+6	Oct 20	−15	Dec 31	+ 3
Mar 29	+ 5	Aug 12	+5	Oct 27	−16		

telescope inverts with direct vision, the image on the screen will be erect. The limbs of the sun are observed when tangential to the respective cross hairs; one cross hair is clamped a little in advance of the movement of the image of the sun which is followed with the other cross hair, using the tangent motion, so that the moving hair is brought tangential to the other limb as the first limb is just leaving the fixed hair; in this way only one hand is occupied with the tangent motion (Fig. 97).

CORRECTIONS OF ALTITUDE.—Observed altitudes in astronomical work have to be corrected due to the following causes;

(*a*) **Atmospheric Refraction.**—An approximate correction for ordinary temperatures and pressures is $r'' = -58''$. cot α where r = refraction correction; α = observed altitude. This should not be used when α is less than 20°.

For greater accuracy, Table 6 may be used to give values of mean refraction to be subtracted from observed altitude to give true altitude. The mean refraction values are near enough for ordinary purposes when the altitude observed is over 20°, but for lower altitudes a correction may be necessary, corresponding to the altitude, temperature, and barometric pressure; refraction decreasing with higher temperature and increasing with higher barometric pressure.

(*b*) **Geocentric Parallax.**—The horizontal parallax of the sun (always +) is approximately 8·8″, and for any given altitude = 8·8″ × cosine of altitude, in seconds. Table 7 gives values of the sun's parallax in altitude.

TABLE 6.—MEAN REFRACTIONS. Corresponding to altitudes α (at 10°C and Barometer 750 mm).

α	0′	5′	10′	15′	20′	25′	30′	35′	40′	45′	50′	55′
°	′ ″	′ ″	′ ″	′ ″	′ ″	′ ″	′ ″	′ ″	′ ″	′ ″	′ ″	′ ″
0	34 54	33 15	32 49	31 50	30 52	29 57	29 3	28 12	27 23	26 35	25 50	25 6
1	24 25	23 45	23 7	22 30	21 56	21 23	20 51	20 21	19 52	19 24	18 58	18 33
2	18 7	17 45	17 23	17 1	16 41	16 20	16 1	15 42	15 23	15 5	14 48	14 31
3	14 15	13 59	13 44	13 29	13 15	13 1	12 48	12 36	12 24	12 12	12 1	11 50
4	11 39	11 28	11 18	11 8	10 59	10 49	10 40	10 30	10 21	10 12	10 3	9 55
5	9 47	9 39	9 31	9 23	9 16	9 9	9 2	8 55	8 48	8 54	8 36	8 29
6	8 23	8 17	8 12	8 6	8 0	7 55	7 49	7 44	7 39	7 34	7 29	7 24
7	7 20	7 15	7 11	7 6	7 2	6 57	6 53	6 49	6 45	6 42	6 37	6 33
8	6 30	6 26	6 22	6 18	6 15	6 12	6 8	6 5	6 2	5 59	5 55	5 52
9	5 49	5 46	5 43	5 40	5 38	5 35	5 32	5 29	5 26	5 24	5 21	5 19
10	5 16	5 14	5 11	5 9	5 6	5 4	5 2	4 59	4 57	4 55	4 53	4 51
11	4 49	4 46	4 44	4 42	4 40	4 38	4 36	4 34	4 32	4 30	4 29	4 27
12	4 25	4 23	4 21	4 20	4 18	4 16	4 15	4 13	4 11	4 10	4 8	4 7
13	4 5	4 3	4 2	4 0	3 59	3 57	3 56	3 54	3 53	3 52	3 50	3 49
14	3 47	3 46	3 45	3 43	3 42	3 41	3 39	3 38	3 37	3 36	3 35	3 33
15	3 32	3 31	3 30	3 29	3 27	3 26	3 25	3 24	3 23	3 22	3 21	3 20
16	3 19	3 18	3 16	3 15	3 14	3 13	3 12	3 11	3 10	3 9	3 8	3 7
17	3 7	3 6	3 5	3 4	3 3	3 2	3 1	3 0	2 59	2 58	2 57	2 57
18	2 56	2 55	2 54	2 53	2 52	2 52	2 51	2 50	2 49	2 48	2 48	2 47
19	2 46	2 45	2 45	2 44	2 43	2 42	2 42	2 41	2 40	2 39	2 39	2 38
20	2 37	2 37	2 36	2 35	2 35	2 34	2 33	2 33	2 32	2 31	2 31	2 30
21	2 29	2 29	2 28	2 27	2 27	2 26	2 26	2 25	2 24	2 24	2 23	2 22
22	2 22	2 21	2 21	2 20	2 20	2 19	2 18	2 18	2 17	2 17	2 16	2 16
23	2 15	2 15	2 14	2 14	2 13	2 13	2 12	2 11	2 11	2 10	2 10	2 9
24	2 9	2 8	2 8	2 7	2 7	2 7	2 6	2 6	2 5	2 5	2 4	2 4

α	0′	10′	20′	30′	40′	50′	α	0′	10′	20′	30′	40′	50′
°	′ ″	′ ″	′ ″	′ ″	′ ″	′ ″	°	′ ″	′ ″	′ ″	′ ″	′ ″	′ ″
25	2 3	2 2	2 1	2 0	2 0	1 59	40	1 9	1 8	1 8	1 8	1 7	1 7
26	1 58	1 57	1 56	1 55	1 54	1 54	41	1 6	1 6	1 6	1 5	1 5	1 4
27	1 53	1 52	1 51	1 50	1 50	1 49	42	1 4	1 4	1 3	1 3	1 3	1 2
28	1 48	1 47	1 47	1 46	1 45	1 45	43	1 2	1 1	1 1	1 1	1 1	1 0
29	1 44	1 43	1 42	1 42	1 41	1 40	44	1 0	59	59	59	58	58
30	1 40	1 39	1 38	1 38	1 37	1 36	45	58	57	57	57	56	56
31	1 36	1 35	1 35	1 34	1 33	1 33	46	56	55	55	55	54	54
32	1 32	1 32	1 31	1 30	1 30	1 29	47	54	54	54	53	53	52
33	1 29	1 28	1 27	1 27	1 26	1 26	48	52	52	51	51	51	50
34	1 25	1 25	1 24	1 24	1 23	1 23	49	50	50	50	49	49	49
35	1 22	1 22	1 21	1 21	1 20	1 20	50	48	48	48	48	47	47
36	1 19	1 19	1 18	1 18	1 17	1 17	51	47	46	46	46	46	45
37	1 16	1 16	1 16	1 15	1 15	1 14	52	45	45	45	45	44	44
38	1 14	1 13	1 13	1 12	1 12	1 12	53	43	43	43	43	42	42
39	1 11	1 11	1 10	1 10	1 10	1 9	54	42	42	41	41	41	41

α	0°	1°	2°	3°	4°	5°	6°	7°	8°	9°
°	″	″	″	″	″	″	″	″	″	″
50	48	47	45	43	42	40	39	37	36	35
60	33	32	31	29	28	27	26	25	23	22
70	21	20	19	18	17	15	14	13	12	11
80	10	9	8	7	6	5	4	3	2	1

TABLE 7.—SUN'S PARALLAX IN ALTITUDE.

Altitude	0°	10°	20°	30°	40°	50°	60°	70°	80°	90°
Parallax	9″	9″	8″	8″	7″	6″	5″	3″	2″	0″

(*c*) **Sun's Semi-diameter.**—The corrections for semi-diameter must be applied to the readings in altitude and azimuth. In the case of the altitudes, the correction for semi-diameter is applied as taken from the Almanac; in that of the aximuths, the correction to be applied to the horizontal circle reading is approximately the semi-diameter, taken from the Almanac, multiplied by the secant of the angle of altitude. These corrections apply to observations taken on any one limb of the sun to reduce the reading to the centre of the sun; but by taking the means of pairs of observations, on the upper and lower limbs for altitude, and on the right and left limbs for azimuth, the necessity for correction for semi-diameter is eliminated.

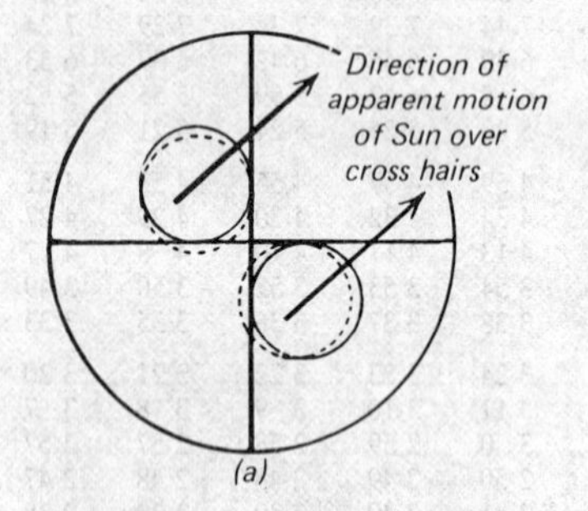

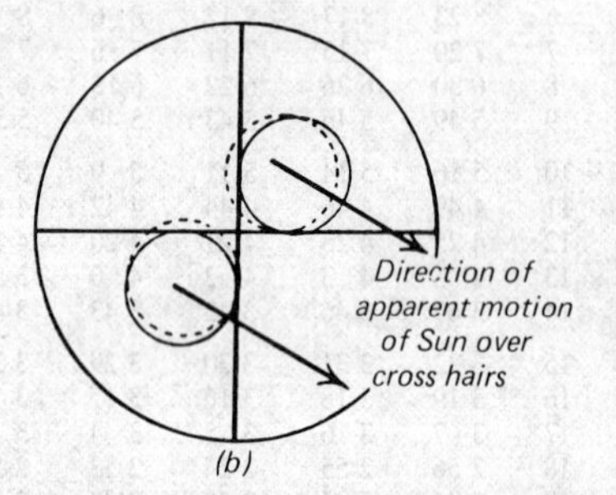

FIG. 97.

In a double observation on upper and lower and right and left limbs, two observations are made, one in which the horizontal hair is fixed in advance, the vertical hair being moved by the tangent motion of the horizontal circle; the other observation is then made with the vertical hair fixed in advance, the tangent motion of the vertical circle being then used to follow the lower or upper limb with the horizontal cross hair, up to the time when the right or left limb which is being observed is just leaving the fixed hair (Fig. 97). The crosshair which is being moved should always be kept slightly on the disc of the sun, up to the time of contact with the other hair, as it becomes indistinct when off the disc. The means of the circle readings of the altitudes and azimuths taken in this way will be thus reduced to the centre, and will correspond to the mean of the times of observations, and no correction for semi-diameter is required.

(*d*) **Dip or Apparent Depression of Horizon.**—At sea, altitude is measured from a visible horizon. From this observed altitude must be subtracted the dip d from true horizon to visible horizon, which depends on the observer's height h m above the sea ($d'' = 105{\cdot}2\sqrt{h}$ approximately, varying with temperature). Table 8 refers and also gives the distance of the horizon at various lengths. Distance l, is in kilometres; and n in UK nautical miles (6,080 ft). Values have been corrected for refraction. ($h = 0{\cdot}0673\, l^2 = 0{\cdot}231\, n^2$).

TABLE 8.—DIP AND DISTANCE OF HORIZON AT VARIOUS HEIGHTS.

h (m)	*l* (km)	*n* (miles UK naut)	*d* (′ ″)	*h* (m)	*l* (km)	*n* (miles UK naut)	*d* (′ ″)
2	5·45	2·94	2 29	50	27·25	14·71	12 24
4	7·71	4·16	3 30	75	33·38	18·01	15 11
6	9·44	5·09	4 18	100	38·54	20·80	17 32
8	10·90	5·88	4 58	200	54·50	29·41	24 48
10	12·19	6·58	5 33	300	66·75	36·03	30 22
15	14·93	8·06	6 47	400	77·08	41·60	35 04
20	17·24	9·30	7 50	500	86·18	46·51	39 12
25	19·27	10·40	8 46	600	94·38	50·94	42 56
30	21·11	11·39	9 36	700	101·98	55·04	46 24
35	22·80	12·31	10 22	800	108·99	58·82	49 35
40	24·38	13·16	11 05	900	115·62	62·40	52 36
45	25·85	13·95	11 46	1000	121·86	65·77	55 26

LATITUDE DETERMINATIONS.—(1) Latitude may be deduced from a single altitude of a star, or the upper or lower limb of the sun, when crossing the meridian. This altitude is corrected for index error and refraction in the case of a star; in that of the sun, further corrections are required for parallax and semi-diameter to reduce the altitude to the sun's centre. The declination is corrected to the time of observation.

In the case of the sun, and of stars with declination less than the latitude if of the same name:

Latitude = (90° − altitude − declination), if declination is of the opposite name to latitude.
Latitude = (90° − altitude + declination), if declination is of the same name as latitude.

In the case of stars with declination of the same name, but greater than latitude:

Latitude = (altitude + declination − 90°) at upper transit.
Latitude = (altitude + 90° − declination) at lower transit of circumpolar stars.

(2) More exact determination of the meridian altitude can be obtained from a circum-meridian observation, ie a series of ex-meridian altitudes taken about the time of the star's (or sun's) meridian passage, provided they do not extend more than about ten minutes on either side of the meridian passage. The corrected altitude at the meridian may be obtained by the following reduction:

$$\text{Maximum altitude} = \text{average of observed altitudes} + \frac{\cos\delta\cos\phi}{\cos A}\cdot\frac{(t)^2}{1{,}833\cdot 5}$$

where δ = declination of sun or star; ϕ = aproximate latitude of station; A = approximate value of meridian altitude from two highest observed altitudes, corrected for level, refraction and (where necessary) parallax; $(t)^2$ = average value of the squares of the number of sidereal seconds, t, to or from transit.

AZIMUTH DETERMINATIONS

(1) **By a Circumpolar Star at Elongation.**—At the instant of greatest elongation: sin (azimuth) = $\cos\delta/\cos\phi$; cos (hour angle) = $\tan\delta/\tan\phi$; sin (altitude) = $\sin\delta/\sin\phi$; where δ is the declination of the star, ϕ is the latitude of the station.

The hour angle, reduced to time, is added to the right ascension of the star if the elongation is to the west of the meridian, or subtracted if to the east; this will give the sidereal time of elongation. The sidereal time of the mean sun's passage of meridian for the succeeding noon subtracted from this will give the sidereal interval of time from noon, which, reduced to mean time, will give the mean time of elongation. The altitude at elongation is useful in setting the instrument for the observation. Without knowledge of the latitude, the azimuth may be obtained from two observations on stars, one to the east, the other to the west of the meridian, and from the horizontal angle between them, which will be the sum of their azimuths. Let this angle be denoted by $(Z_1 + Z_2)$, and let δ_1 and δ_2 be the respective declinations of the stars used, then,

$$\tan\frac{Z_1 - Z_2}{2} = \tan\frac{\delta_1 + \delta_2}{2} \times \tan\frac{\delta_1 - \delta_2}{2} \times \tan\frac{Z_1 + Z_2}{2}$$

giving the half difference of azimuths, which, added to and subtracted from the half sum of azimuths will give Z_1 and Z_2 respectively. The latitude can then be computed from one of the aximuths and found by the formula $\cos\phi = \cos\delta/\sin Z$.

Example. Taking stars β Crucis (δ_2 = 59° 06′ 30″ S); γ Hydri (δ_1 = 74° 33′ 59″S); angle between their elongations 57° 33′ 33″ (=$Z_1 + Z_2$).

$(\delta_1 + \delta_2)/2$ =	66	50	14½	log tan 0·36874
$(\delta_1 - \delta_2)/2$ =	7	43	44½	log tan 9·13264
$(Z_1 + Z_2)/2$ =	28	46	46½	log tan 9·73980
$(Z_1 - Z_2)/2$ =	9	53	05	log tan 9·24118
	± 28	46	46½	

Elongation

γ Hydri	18	53	41½
β Crucis	38	39	51

The latitude may then be calculated as follows, from γ Hydri:

Azimuth	18	53	41½	log cosec 0·48968
Declination	74	33	59	log cos 9·42508
				log cos 9·91476 latitude = 34° 43′ 55″ S

(2) **By Extra-meridian Observations of Star or Sun** (Fig. 98). Best made when star is on or near prime vertical. Readings of vertical and horizontal circles taken on changed faces, at moments when star is at intersection of cross hairs (or sun in diagonally opposite quadrants). Azimuth Z calculated from

$$\tan\frac{Z}{2} = \sqrt{\left(\frac{\sin(s - ZX)\sin(s - ZP)}{\sin s.\ \sin(s - PX)}\right)}$$

where $s = \frac{1}{2}(ZX + ZP + PX)$.

Times should be noted so that declination at average time can be found.

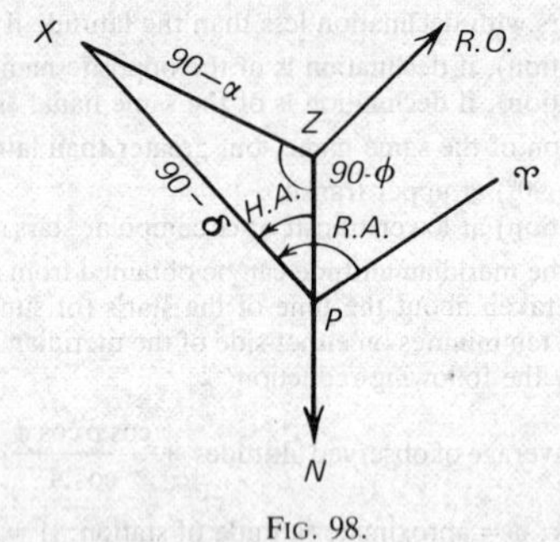

FIG. 98.

Time Determination.—This may also be made by an extra-meridian observation (Fig. 98), the times of passage of sun or star over the horizontal hair being noted on two faces, and the hour angle P being calculated from

$$\tan\frac{P}{2} = \sqrt{\left(\frac{\sin(s-ZP)\sin(s-PX)}{\sin s.\ \sin(s-ZX)}\right)}.$$

Then, for a star, $RA \pm P = LST$ (+ for west HA, − for east HA); for the sun, $P \pm E =$ LMT.

TO FIND TIME AND AZIMUTH FROM SUN OR STAR ALTITUDES.—Let $\alpha =$ observed altitude (corrected for atmospheric refraction in case of star, as well as for parallax and semi-diameter in case of sun); $\phi =$ latitude; $p =$ polar distance = (90° − declination) if latitude and declination are of the same name, or (90° + declination) if latitude and declination are of different names;

$s = \dfrac{\alpha + \phi + p}{2}$. Then

$$\log\sin(\tfrac{1}{2}\text{ hour angle}) = \frac{\log\sec\phi + \log\text{cosec}\,p + \log\cos s + \log\sin(s-\alpha)}{2}$$

$$\log\cos(\tfrac{1}{2}\text{ azimuth}) = \frac{\log\sec\alpha + \log\sec\phi + \log\cos s + \log\cos(p-s)}{2}$$

The hour angle in arc is reduced to time; if from a pm observation of the sun this will be apparent time pm, but if from an am observation this hour angle in time should be deducted from 12, the result being apparent time am. To arrive at mean time, the equation of time must be added or subtracted as directed in the Almanac, this equation of time being first corrected to correspond to the approximate time of the observation at the principal meridian to which the Almanac refers.

In star observations for time, the hour angle found and reduced to time is deducted from or added to the right ascension of the star (deducted from if before the meridian transit, but added to if after); this gives the sidereal time of observation. Take the right ascension of the mean sun for the previous noon from the Almanac, and correct this to the meridian of the place of observation; this, deducted from the sidereal time of observation, and the difference reduced to solar time, will give the mean time of the observation.

Example			h m s
	Suppose hour angle found after transit of meridian		4 30 24
	Right ascension of star		8 10 43
	Sidereal time at observation		12 41 07
	RA mean sun	1 35 28	
	Correction for longitude West 3 h 54 m	+38	
			1 36 06
	Interval in sidereal time from mean noon		11 05 01
	Correction of interval, sidereal to mean time		−1 49
	Mean time of observation		11 03 12

The horizontal circle reading corresponding to the azimuth found as above should be corrected for the inclination of the horizontal axis of the vertical circle as denoted by the reading of the striding level; the difference of level in seconds of arc multiplied by the tangent of the altitude taken will give the correction to the horizontal circle reading, this being added if the left-hand pivot is higher, and subtracted if the right-hand pivot is higher. The circle reading of some distant well-defined object should be used as a reference object to which the azimuth observed will then be connected. In a series of observations where the sun has been utilised in the daytime and it is desired to connect up a series of observations on stars, the adjustment of the instrument should be carefully gone over after sundown, and, when the instrument has attained an even temperature, the reference object should be utilised to check the results of the day observations with those of the night.

The degree of accuracy of the results will depend upon the care taken to eliminate slight errors in the data assumed or instrumental defects. In the case of observations for time, the taking of the mean of a combination of am and pm observations will to a great extent eliminate the slight errors that may be due to instrumental defects, incorrect latitude assumed, or Almanac corrections to date. The same remarks apply also to azimuth except that the cross level error can only be eliminated by observations taken with reversed positions of vertical axis. (In observations for latitude the errors of the instrument can be to a great extent corrected by taking the mean of meridian observations on stars to the north and to the south of the zenith.)

Example (in time and azimuth; pm observation). Data: latitude (ϕ) 53° 29′ 50″ N; corrected declination (δ) 0° 35′ 13″ S; corrected altitude of the sun's centre (α) 20° 37′ 18″; polar distance (p) 90° + 0° 35′ 13″ = 90° 35′ 13″.

Time

	°	′	″		
$\alpha =$	20	37	18		
$\phi =$	53	29	05	log sec	0·22546
$p =$	90	35	13	log cosec	0·00002
2)	164	41	36		
$s =$	82	20	48	log cos	9·12444
$s - \alpha =$	61	43	30	log sin	9·94482
				2)	19·29474
½ hour angle	26	21	30	log sin	9·64787
			2		
hour angle	52	43	00	in arc	
			4		
hour angle	3	30	52	in time	

Azimuth

	°	′	″	
$\alpha =$	20	37	18	log sec 0·02876
$\phi =$	53	29	05	log sec 0·22546
$p =$	90	35	13	
2)	164	41	36	
$s =$	82	20	48	log cos 9·12444
$(p - s) =$	8	14	25	log cos 9·99549
				2) 19·37415
½ azimuth	60	53	30	log cos 9·68707
			2	
Azimuth N	121	47	00	W

TIMING OBSERVATIONS.—When working with an assistant, the time may be noted at the instant a signal is given by the observer, but when observing alone it is difficult to note the exact time of contact or transit on watch or chronometer, when the hands are employed in manipulating the instrument and the eye engaged in taking the sight. In this case, a convenient method is to use a watch whose time of beat is known (in modern watches usually one-fifth second); this watch should be in such a position that the beats are distinctly heard, for example, suspended over the ear from the hat, in a small bag or watch pocket. The beats are then counted from the instant of contact or transit and continued until the seconds hand of the standard timepiece can be noted on some convenient second; this time noted, less the number of beats of the auxiliary watch, reduced to seconds and fractions, will be the actual time of the observation.

As probably some little time may elapse after the observation before the standard timepiece can be read, especially at night where a lamp has to be used, this extended counting of beats of say one-fifth second becomes difficult when arriving at the double syllable numbers; but, by adding a 'dummy' syllable to the first twelve counted, and then continuing with 'thir-teen, four-teen', and so on, giving one syllable to each beat, the counting of one-fifth seconds becomes quite easy, even if carried to 100 beats and over, eg taking the dummy syllable as 'and' and starting the instant of observation with 'nought', the counting would continue: 'nought-and', 'one-and', 'two-and', 'three-and',... ''leven-and', 'twelve-and', 'thir-teen', 'four-teen',... 'twen-ty', 'twent'-one', and so on. Then, taking the first syllable as units and the second syllable as half, the counted beats multiplied by 4 and divided by 10 will give the required intervals in seconds and tenths, in the case of the auxiliary watch beating fifths of seconds.

Taking examples, say the beats counted between the instant of observation and the time noted on the timepiece was on the first syllable to thirty-seven, the time at that beat being 3 h 47 m 15 s; then the interval to be deducted would be (37 × 4)/10 = 14·8 seconds and the corrected time of the observation would be 3 h 47 m 15 s − 14·8 s = 3 h 47 m 0·2 s. In another case, say the second syllable of 'nine-and' corresponded to 6 h 22 m 55 s on the timepiece; the correction would then be (9½ × 4)/10 = 3·8 seconds, and the corrected time of observation 6 h 23 m 55 s − 3·8 s = 6 h 23 m 51·2 s.

This method of measuring short intervals of time is useful in other instances; for example, in estimating distances by the velocity of sound, etc.

GRAPHICAL METHOD OF FINDING TIME AND AZIMUTH FROM ALTITUDE OF SUN OR STAR.—Describe a circle (Fig. 99) of any convenient radius; through the centre O draw diameter MOM_1. From O draw OP making angle POM_1 equal to the latitude; draw OQ at right angles to PO. Through O draw OA, making AOM equal to the correct altitude, and OD, making DOQ equal to the corrected declination, and on the side of OQ towards P if the declination and latitude are of the same name, or on the opposite side if of different names. Through A draw AA_1 parallel to MM_1 and through D draw DD_1 parallel to QO, intersecting AA_1 in s.

To find the azimuth, drop a perpendicular from A to OM, intersecting this latter in a; with centre O and radius Oa draw arc az, and from s draw sz perpendicular to MOM_1, intersecting arc az in z; through z draw Oz. Then the angle M_1Oz will represent the azimuth from the elevated pole east or west of the meridian according as the time (am or pm) at which the observation was made. To find the hour angle, draw Dd at right angles to QO, and with centre O and radius Od draw arc dh; from s draw line sh perpendicular to QO, intersecting arc dh in h; draw line Oh. Then QOh will be the hour angle at the time of observation before or after apparent noon. This diagrammatic method may be utilised for approximate determination of other problems, such as azimuth and time of sun or stars at instant of rising or setting; altitude and azimuth at a given time; or for altitude and time of passing prime vertical.

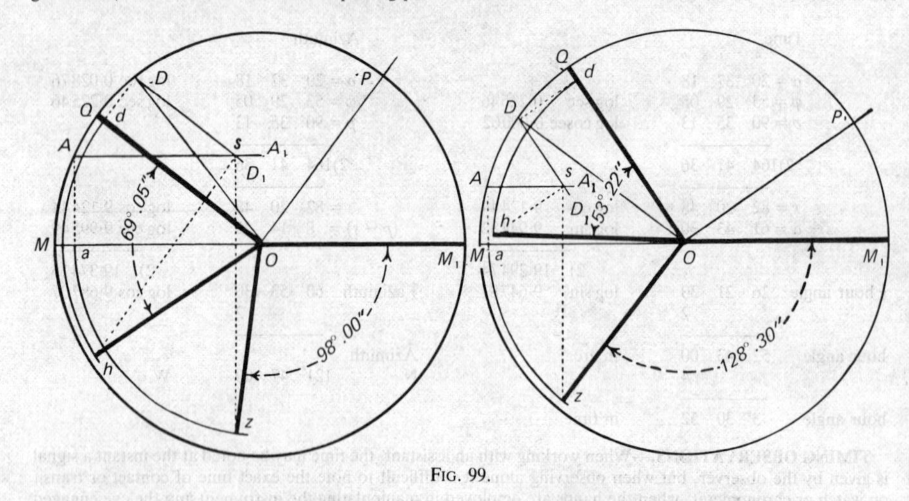

FIG. 99.

	Data	Result			Data	Result	
Lat	53° 30′ N	Azimuth N	98° 00′ W	Lat	34· 30′ S	Azimuth S	128° 30′ W.
Dec	14° 50′ N	Hour Angle	69° 05′	Dec	19° 50′ N	Hour Angle	53° 22′
Alt	24° 20′ pm			Alt	15° 40′ pm		

GEODESY

From measurements made of various meridians and parallels it has been found that the earth has the form of an ellipsoid of revolution with its greatest diameter at the equator and its least between the poles, and that the radius of curvature of the meridian varies with the latitude, being least at the equator and greatest at the poles, so that the length of a degree of latitude is more at the poles than at the equator. The length of a degree of longitude varies also with the latitude, being greatest at the equator and zero at the poles.

In treating with measurements of an extensive character over the surface of the earth, it is necessary to take into account its ellipsoidal shape, and it is convenient to employ certain approximations so that spherical trigonometry may be used in the solution of the problems involved. The following formulae enable the radius of a spherical surface to be found that approximates most nearly to the ellipsoidal surface embracing the area under consideration. In these formulae a = the equatorial radius of the earth; e = the eccentricity; ϕ = the mean latitude; A = the azimuth. Radius of curvature of meridian = $Q = a(1 - e^2)/\sqrt{(1 - e^2 \sin^2 \phi)^3}$; Radius of curvature of normal section perpendicular to meridian = $N = a/\sqrt{(1 - e^2 \sin^2 \phi)}$; Radius of curvature of a normal section which cuts meridian at an angle $A = QN/(Q \sin^2 A + N \cos^2 A)$; Radius of curvature of an area of the earth's surface, or mean curvature = $\sqrt{QN}$; Radius of a parallel of latitude = $N \cos \phi = a \cos \phi \sqrt{(1 - e^2 \sin^2 \phi)}$.

The logarithms of the most probable values of the constants used above are as follows (taking a in kilometres): $\log a = 3{\cdot}80471$; $\log e^2 = 7{\cdot}83047$; $\log (1 - e^2) = 9{\cdot}99853$.

TABLE 9.—LENGTH OF A DEGREE OF LONGITUDE AND LATITUDE.

Latitude	Degree of Longitude		Degree of Latitude		Latitude	Degree of Longitude		Degree of Latitude	
ϕ	km	n mile	km	n mile	ϕ	km	n mile	km	n mile
0	111·324	60·000	110·579	59·598	45	78·851	42·503	111·146	59·905
1	111·305	59·991	110·579	59·598	46	77·467	41·752	111·168	59·916
2	111·257	59·964	110·581	59·599	47	76·059	40·993	111·188	59·926
3	111·173	59·918	110·583	59·600	48	74·628	40·222	111·207	59·937
4	111·054	59·854	110·586	59·602	49	73·175	39·439	111·226	59·947
5	110·901	59·774	110·591	59·604	50	71·699	38·643	111·246	59·958
6	110·719	59·674	110·594	59·606	51	70·201	37·836	111·265	59·968
7	110·499	59·557	110·599	59·609	52	68·682	37·017	111·284	59·978
8	110·248	59·420	110·602	59·611	53	67·140	36·186	111·302	59·988
9	109·961	59·265	110·610	59·615	54	65·579	35·345	111·321	59·998
10	109·644	59·094	110·616	59·618	55	63·997	34·492	111·339	60·008
11	109·293	58·905	110·624	59·622	56	62·396	33·629	111·358	60·018
12	108·909	58·698	110·632	59·627	57	60·777	32·777	111·376	60·028
13	108·490	58·473	110·641	59·631	58	59·137	31·896	111·392	60·037
14	108·040	58·230	110·650	59·637	59	57·479	30·979	111·410	60·046
15	107·555	57·969	110·660	59·642	60	55·804	30·076	111·427	60·056
16	107·039	57·690	110·669	59·647	61	54·111	29·163	111·444	60·064
17	106·493	57·396	110·681	59·653	62	52·402	28·242	111·460	60·073
18	105·911	57·080	110·690	59·658	63	50·675	27·312	111·476	60·082
19	105·296	56·751	110·705	59·666	64	48·934	26·374	111·490	60·089
20	104·652	56·404		59·672	65	47·148	25·427	111·506	60·098
21	103·976	56·040		59·679	66	45·408	24·479	111·521	60·106
22	103·267	55·654	110·744	59·687	67	43·623	23·511	111·532	60·112
23	102·529	55·260	110·758	59·695	68	41·824	22·594	111·548	60·121
24	101·755	54·843	110·771	59·702	69	40·011	21·565	111·561	60·128
25	100·956	54·411	110·787	59·710	70	38·188	20·582	111·574	60·135
26	100·120	53·961	110·801	59·718	71	36·353	19·598	111·585	60·140
27	99·258	53·496	110·818	59·727	72	34·506	18·597	111·596	60·147
28	98·361	53·013	110·834	59·736	73	32·649	17·596	111·608	60·153
29	97·446	52·520	110·850	59·744	74	30·780	16·590	111·619	60·158
30	96·491	52·005	110·867	59·754	75	28·904	15·562	111·629	60·164
31	95·510	51·476	110·885	59·763	76	27·018	14·561	111·637	60·168
32	94·497	50·933	110·901	59·772	77	25·123	13·540	111·646	60·174
33	93·456	50·372	110·921	59·782	78	23·221	12·515	111·654	60·177
34	92·391	49·795	110·940	59·792	79	21·311	11·486	111·661	60·181
35	91·291	49·203	110·958	59·802	80	19·394	10·453	111·667	60·185
36	90·166	48·597	110·975	59·812	81	17·038	9·417	111·674	60·188
37	89·016	47·976	110·993	59·822	82	15·545	8·378	111·679	60·191
38	87·836	47·232	111·012	59·832	83	13·612	7·336	111·683	60·193
39	86·629	46·583	111·032	59·842	84	11·674	6·292	111·688	60·196
40	85·398	46·027	111·051	59·853	85	9·735	5·247	111·691	60·198
41	84·140	45·348	111·070	59·863	86	7·792	4·199	111·695	60·200
42	82·854	44·655	111·090	59·874	87	5·845	3·151	111·696	60·200
43	81·545	43·950	111·110	59·885	88	3·898	2·102	111·698	60·201
44	80·210	43·230	111·130	59·895	89	1·949	1·051	111·698	60·201
45	78·851	42·503			90	0·000	0·000		

Adopting the radius which most nearly corresponds to the surface considered at the mean latitude ϕ, any measured length l on this surface may be reduced to arc by one of the following formulae, ρ being the radius adopted reduced to the same unit as l: $l \times 57{\cdot}2958\ \rho$ in degrees of arc; $l \times 3{,}437{\cdot}747/\rho$ in minutes of arc; $l \times 206265/\rho$ in seconds of arc.

Table 9 is calculated from the accepted dimensions of the earth. Values for intermediate latitudes may be obtained from this table by interpolating, with sufficient exactitude for most purposes. The length of a degree on a great circle at right angles to the meridian at a given latitude may be obtained by multiplying the length of a degree of longitude (as taken from the table) by the secant of the latitude. The following illustrations of Table 9 are given:

(*a*) Length of a degree of longitude at $\phi°$ latitude $= \cos \phi_1° \times 111{\cdot}324$ km, where $\tan \phi_1° = (b/a) \tan \phi°$; a = equatorial radius (6,378·39 km); b = polar radius (6,356·96 km); $b/a = 0{\cdot}99664$.

Example.—What is the length of a degree of longitude at 50° latitude?

Tan 50° = 1·1917536, therefore, tan $\phi°$ = 0·99664 × 1·1917536 = 1·1877493 = tan 49° 54′ 18″; cos 49° 54′ 18″ = 0·6440569, therefore length of degree = 0·6440569 × 111·324 = 71·699 km.

(*b*) Length of a degree of latitude at $\phi°$ latitude ($\phi°$ being at the middle of the arc) = 111·324 × (0·99330 + 0·01005 $\sin^2 \phi°$) = (110·578 + 1·1188 $\sin^2 \phi°$) km.

Example.—What is the length of a degree of latitude between 30° and 31°?

ϕ = 30° 30′; sin 30° 30′ = 0·5075384, therefore length of degree = 110·578 + 1·1188 $(0{\cdot}5075384)^2$ = 110·866 km.

Convergence of Meridians.—In transverse and route surveys, a survey line is referred to a meridian at a certain point and crosses the meridian with an azimuth Z; this line, if continued in the same direction, will have increased or diminished azimuths. The difference of azimuth can be approximately determined by calculating the convergence of the meridian corresponding to a given unit departure at the mean of the latitudes, and multiplying this by the departure as calculated from the traverse. To obtain the azimuth on crossing the second meridian, the convergence obtained in the manner just explained is added to or subtracted from the azimuth crossing the first meridian, being added where the longitude is increased and subtracted where the longitude is diminished. The convergence may be calculated by the following formula, with sufficient approximation for use in ordinary traverse surveying. The length of a degree of longitude corresponding to the mean latitude is taken in km from Table 9, interpolating if necessary; then:

Log (convergence in seconds per kilometre of departure) = log sin ϕ + 3·55630 − log (km per 1° longitude).

To range a parallel of latitude by setting out chords of a given length: the chords are ranged making an angle to the meridian of (90° − half the angle of convergence corresponding to the length of the chord at the proposed latitude). The succeeding chords will have an angle of deflection, from the preceding chord produced, equal to the convergence corresponding to the length of chord used.

To range a parallel of latitude by means of offsets: a line is run, perpendicular to the meridian; then the lengths of offsets are equal to the distances along this perpendicular line multiplied by the sine of half the angle of convergence corresponding to the lengths. If the offsets are equidistant, the length of the second offset will be four times the length of the first; the third, nine times the first, and so on; the nth offset will be n^2 times the length of the first.

BIBLIOGRAPHY

CLARK, *Plane and Geodetic Surveying*, Vols I and II Constable.
THOMAS, *Surveying* Arnold.
SKELTON, *Route Surveys* McGraw-Hill.
HIGGINS, *Higher Surveying* Macmillan.
REDMOND, *Tacheometry* Technical Press.
HART, *Air Photography Applied to Surveying* Longmans.
JAMESON, *Contour Geometry* Pitman.
HOSMER AND ROBBINS, *Practical Astronomy* Chapman and Hall.
RAPPLEYE, *Manual of Levelling Computation and Adjustment* US Government Printing Office.
COMRIE. *Chambers's Shorter Six-Figure Mathematical Tables* Chambers.
LOUIS AND CAUNT. *Traverse Tables* Arnold.
REDMOND, *Tacheometric Tables* Technical Press.
WHYTE and PAUL, *Basic Metric Surveying* Butterworths.
UREN and PRICE, *Calculations for Engineering Surveys* Van Nostrand Reinhold (UK).
HEWITT (ed.), *Guide to Site Surveying* Architectural Press.
SIEGLE, *Basic Plane Surveying* Van Nostrand Reinhold.
ALLAN, HOLLWEY and MAYNES, *Practical Field Surveying and Computations* Heinemann.
SCHWIDEFSKY, *An Outline of Photogrammetry* Pitman.
HAMMOND, *Air Survey in Economic Development* Muller.
COOPER, *Modern Theodolites and Levels* Crosby Lockwood.
LUEDER, *Aerial Photographic Interpretation* McGraw-Hill.
MUNSEY, *Tacheometric Tables for the Metric User* Technical Press.
KILFORD, *Elementary Air Survey* Pitman.
MILNE, *Underwater Engineering Surveys* Spon.
HODGES and GREENWOOD, *Optical Distance Measurement* Butterworths.
SAASTAMOINEN (ed.), *Surveyor's Guide to Electromagnetic Distance Measurement* Adam Hilger.
BANNISTER and RAYMOND, *Surveying* Pitman.
SCHMIDT and RAYNER, *Fundamentals of Surveying* Van Nostrand.
KISSAM, *Surveying for Civil Engineers* McGraw-Hill.
The Nautical Almanac HMSO.
The Star Almanac HMSO.
Whitaker's Almanac.

FOUNDATIONS AND EARTHWORK

Properties of Soils—Foundations—Earth-Retaining Structures—Earthwork—Bibliography

by E. N. Bromhead, PhD, MSc, DIC, MICE, FGS

PROPERTIES OF SOILS

The safe and efficient design and construction of foundations, earth-retaining structures, and earthworks requires accurate data on the physical properties of the ground. These physical properties are the shear strength of the soil, which governs all problems of stability and bearing capacity (including loads on soil retaining structures), and the deformation parameters which govern settlement.

The term 'Soils' is generally considered to include all materials from soft earth to rock, and the study of the physical properties of these materials is called Soil Mechanics. It is today a combination of knowledge gained from theoretical analyses, laboratory tests, and particularly practical experience. Problems regarding soils in relation to Earth Embankments and Dams are dealt with in chapter 'Water Engineering'.

TYPES OF SOILS.—The geological classification of various types of soil is not directly applicable to problems of foundations and earthworks, and a classification based on certain physical characteristics is adopted. Broadly, there are three distinct types of ground: (i) Cohesionless or Granular Soils (such as sands, gravels, etc);

TABLE 1.—CLASSIFICATION OF SOILS.

		Simple Types			Important Composite Types
		Name	Field Identification		
Particle size increasing	Non-cohesive	Gravels	Most particles above No 7 BS Sieve (1·6 mm)		Boulder Gravels Sand Gravels Hoggin
		Coarse Sands	Most particles lie between Nos 7 and 25 BS Sieves	Particles visible to naked eye. No cohesion when dry	Well Graded Sands Silty Sands Clayey Sands Shelly Sands
		Medium Sands	Most particles lie between Nos 25 and 72 BS Sieves		
		Fine Sands	Most particles lie between Nos 72 and 200 BS Sieves Exhibit dilatancy*		
	Cohesive	Silts	Most particles will pass No 200 BS Sieve. Particles invisible or barely visible to the naked eye. Gritty touch. Exhibit dilatancy. May show slight cohesion		Organic Silt Micaceous Silt
		Clays	Predominant influence of particles under 0·002 mm diameter. Smooth touch. Plastic. No dilatancy. Considerable cohesion		Boulder Clay Sandy Clay Silty Clay Marls, (calcareous clays) Organic Clay
		Peats	Identified by visual examination. High compressibility. Fibrous. Brown or black colour. May have odour of decomposing vegetation.		Sandy, Silty or clayey Peats

* Dilatancy is the property of a soil whereby if lightly shaken or tapped it exudes its own water, but if then pinched or compressed, will reabsorb it.

TABLE 2.—A GUIDE TO THE PHYSICAL PROPERTIES OF SOILS.

Type of soil		Density in bulk (w): General (before excavation)		Density in bulk (w): Moist (drained)		Angle of internal friction θ_1		Apparent cohesion (undrained condition) kN/m²	Safe bearing pressure (very approximate—check by test.)	
			kg/m³		kg/m³		deg			k N/m²
Cohesionless	Sand (1)	Dry	1,450	Loose:		Compact:		Not applicable	Compact:	
		Dry fine	1,600	Fine or silty	1,600–1,775	Well-graded	40–50		Well-graded	400–600
		Wet	1,850	Coarse or medium	1,675–1,925	Uniform, coarse, medium, fine or silty	35–40		Uniform	200–400
		Very wet	1,925	Compact:		Loose:			Loose:	
				Fine or silty	1,750–2,175	Well-graded	35–40		Well-graded	200–400
				Coarse or medium	1,900–2,100	Uniform, coarse, medium, fine or silty	30–35		Uniform	100–200
						Fine, dry	30–35			
						Wet	Below 30			
	Gravel (1)	Very loose	1,775		1,600–2,000	Common	35–45	Not applicable	Compact	400–700
		River gravel	2,250			Shingle	40		Loose	200–400
		Loose shingle	1,850			Sandy: compact	40–45		Sandy: compact	400–600
		Sandy	1,925			loose	35–40		loose	200–400
	Rock† (2)	Grey chalk	2,400						Chalk: soft	200–400
		Sandstone	2,475						hard	400–800
		Limestone (hard)	3,200						Rock: very soft	200–500
		Shale	2,575						moderately hard	500–1,000
									hard	< 1,000
	Filling	Crushed rock:				Crushed rock:	35–45	Not applicable	Bearing pressures on filling depend on degree of compaction and must be determined by test.	
		Granite	1,600–2,100							
		Basalts, dolerites	1,775–2,250							
		Limestone, sandstone	1,275–1,925							
		Broken chalk	950–1,300				35–45			
		Broken shale	1,600–2,100				30–35			
		Broken brick	1,125–1,775				35–45			
		Ashes	640–975				35–45			

Cohesive	Clay (3)	Dry*	1,775	Saturated Density		Generally low or zero in undrained condition.		Hard	250	Hard	550
		Damp	1,850	Very stiff (boulder),		When expressed in effective stress		V. Stiff	150–250	V. Stiff	330–550
		Wet	1,975	Hard shaley clay,		terms may vary widely depending		Stiff	15–150	Stiff	170–330
				Stiff	1,925–2,250	on minerals present and stress his-		Firm	37–75	Firm	85–170
				Firm	1,750–2,100	tory; Determine by test		Soft	18–37	Soft	40–85
		Sandy loam	1,600	Soft,				V. Soft	< 18	V. Soft	< 40
		Marl	1,775	Very soft	1,600–1,925						
		Gravelly clay	2,000								
	Earth‡	Top soil	1,375			Dry	30	Properties not tabulated should be determined by test as average values are much more variable.			
		Common	1,600			Moist	45–50				
		Dry	1,450			Very wet	17				
		Moist	1,600			Punned	65–75				
		Very wet	1,525								
		Punned	1,600								
	Peat	Dry	500				15–45				
		Wet	1,000								

* eg dry to touch etc. † solid. ‡ wide range of particle sizes.

Notes: (1) Bearing pressures quoted are for dry sands, gravel etc:—take 50% of tabulated values if waterlogged. See also Table 3.
(2) Bearing pressure on rock should not exceed $\frac{1}{8}$ × crushing strength of the rock, nor $\frac{1}{3}$ × crushing strength of the concrete base.
(3) Bearing pressures relate to strength whereas settlement may be design criterion.
(4) All figures given as guides for initial estimates, but should be verified in each case by individual site testing.
(5) Descriptive terms include loose phrasing in common use not coincident with preferred usage of BS 5930.

Clay.—Properties depend mainly on the consistency, the moisture being most important. Highly cohesive and has a definite mobility, and yields under pressure when the moisture content exceeds 20%. Yielding takes place by expulsion of the water in the pores, hence the rate at which compression occurs is slow owing to the low permeability. Often mixed or stratified with sands. Clays and silts, or soils which are largely clay, may have a small or zero angle of shearing resistance in the undrained state.

Silt.—Similar to coarse clay, fine-grained micaceous silts can be mistaken for clay, although unsatisfactory for load-bearing because disturbance of the ground water may completely alter the nature of the material. Organic silts containing vegetable matter or shells are highly compressible and not suitable for bearing.

Peat.—Partially-carbonised vegetable material; extremely compressible; little or no bearing value.

Shale.—Laminated but otherwise similar to clay. If not exposed to the air, it maintains a soft-rock like compactness, but disintegrates when exposed.

Sand.—Cohesionless granular materials formed generally of hard particles, but in bulk are very permeable owing to the voids. Primary characteristic is frictional resistance to shearing forces. Often found mixed with gravels.

Gravels.—Comprises larger particles than sand.

(ii) Cohesive Soils (clay, silts, and some organic soils); and (iii) Rock. In few cases can actual types be so sharply defined, as they are intermediate between (i) and (ii). Rocks can vary considerably from those with weak strata interposed to solid hard rocks; filling below foundations and behind walls may be of broken or crushed rock or artificial materials.

Most soils can behave in both cohesive and cohesionless ways. This is due to the response of the water in the pores of the soil to the applied loads. If the flow of water into or out of the soil is prevented (in a test by deliberate means; or in the field either due to the relative impermeability of the soil or the distance which the water may have to flow) then *cohesive* strength behaviour is generally found—but if this drainage is allowed, the soil may be found to be cohesionless. In practice, soils coarser than fine sands will allow any excess water pressures in the soil voids to dissipate rapidly and to all intents and purposes may be considered to be *cohesionless*. However, clays and silts will behave as cohesive soils in the *short term* and as frictional soils in the *long term* (which may be from months to years after the end of construction). In some cases, such as foundations and embankments, it is the *short term* case that is critical, because the loading increases the water pressure in the pores, and as this excess pore water pressure dissipates, the strength of the soil increases. The opposite situation occurs when the soil is unloaded, for example, in retaining walls, cuttings and other permanent excavations. Here the *long-term* case is critical. It is important to identify which case is critical so that the appropriate soil strength parameters are obtained.

A commonly-adopted classification of soils (excluding rock) is given in Table 1 and is based mainly on the fineness of the particles which is one distinguishing feature of cohesionless and cohesive soils, due to the corresponding changes in the soils permeability which is entailed. The granulometry of a soil (that is, the sizes and grading of particles of solid matter) is needed, not only to enable the soil to be properly classified, but also to determine its suitability for treatment such as grouting, ground-water lowering and chemical consolidation. Tests for particle size distribution are given in BS 1377. Characteristics of certain common soils are given after the footnotes for Table 2, and for a wide variety of soils and rocks by Bell.

The physical properties of soils are considered in the following pages and particulars are given of tests to determine such properties. Some soils, however, contain chemical constituents which may be harmful to concrete or other materials, and chemical analysis is necessary to determine whether such constituents, especially sulphates and acids, are present in harmful quantity (BRS Digest 90; CP 2004).

BULKING, SETTLEMENT, COMPACTION AND CONSOLIDATION.—The normal *weights* of soils in their undisturbed state in the ground are given in Table 2. The weight may vary considerably depending on the moisture content, and therefore there is also tabulated the *Moist Density* of cohesionless soils, and the *Saturated Density* of cohesive soils. These densities take account of natural voids in the soils and, except in the case of solid rock, are therefore lower than the densities of the solid particles forming the soil. When excavated, all soils, including rocks, loosen and occupy a greater volume than before being disturbed. This *bulking* determines the required capacity of the means of transport of excavated soil. Some typical increases in volume are 10% for gravel, 12½% for sand, 20% and upwards for clay, 25% for well graded soil, 33⅓% for chalk, and up to 50% for rock.

When excavated material is refilled or built-up in the form of embankments, it compacts and settles. The probable degree of this *natural settlement* expressed as a percentage reduction of the excavated loose volume is up to 25% for well graded soil, up to 35% for clay and about 15% for sand. The settlement can, however, vary considerably as it depends on the depth of the filling, the wetness of the material, the amount of tamping, rolling, or other artificial means of compaction, the rate of depositing, and the age of the filling. Reliable ratios to take account of any of these factors are not readily obtainable and generally are only determinable from testing or experience with particular soils and conditions. Natural settlement can be accelerated, and augmented if necessary, by artificial compaction.

It is necessary to differentiate between artificial compaction and consolidation. *Compaction* is the packing together of the particles of a non-cohesive soil by the expulsion of air in the interstices; whereas *consolidation* is the gradual expulsion of water from the voids of a saturated cohesive soil. Natural settlement and artificial compaction and consolidation are additional to the phenomena of compression and *foundation settlement*, which is produced by the load imposed on the ground by a structure (see 'Compressibility and Foundation Settlement').

ANGLES OF REPOSE AND INTERNAL FRICTION AND COHESION.—The pressures on earth-retaining works, and the slopes at which the sides of cuttings and embankments will stand depend on a variety of factors including the shear strength parameters and the behaviour of the pore water pressure in the slope or behind the wall. In the simple case of a dry cohesionless soil, this will stand in a slope at an angle (the angle of repose), equal to the angle of shearing resistance of the soil.

When a soil is subjected to stresses (either shear or direct stresses), this results in a change in the pressure in the water in the pores of the soil. These changes in pore water pressure have an important role in the shear strength behaviour of the soil—if they are not allowed to dissipate (the *undrained* condition), then the strength will be different from that if they do (the *drained* state).

The behaviour of natural clays and silts in the undrained condition is simple *cohesion* (ie shear strength independent of the level of direct stress in the soil), but in other soils such as sands and gravels the undrained state is unlikely to exist in the field. Partly saturated soils sometimes exhibit some friction when in the undrained state. In the *drained* state, the shear strength on any plane on the soil depends in part on cohesion and in part on friction, and the shear strength(s) may be expressed as:

$$s = c_1 + p' \tan \theta_1$$

in which p' is the *effective stress*—the numerical difference between the direct stress on the plane in question and the pore water pressure. It is usually found that the cohesion (or intercept of the strength envelope, see Fig. 1, when expressed in terms of effective stress on the horizontal axis), may be quite small, or zero in the case of gravels, sand and normally consolidated clays and silts, but that it may be much larger in over-consolidated soils such as stiff fissured clays commonly found in Southern England.

It is important that values for the shear strength parameters c, and θ, are measured in every case under the appropriate conditions. In problems of *increased loading* such as the bearing capacity of foundations, stability of embankments etc, the most critical condition is the *short term* one for which *undrained* strength parameters are appropriate since with the passage of time, the disturbing influence of pressures in the soil pore water will lessen, and the soil gain strength by the process of *consolidation*. On the other hand, in problems where the loads on the soil are decreased, say by removal of lateral pressures in the case of the excavation in a cutting, there will be a decrease in the pore water pressures at first, followed by a gradual increase as the ground water table returns to its equilibrium position. In this case (the *long term* situation), it is appropriate to use the *drained* shear strength parameters together with a reasonable estimate of the long term ground water level, to obtain the shear strength.

Triaxial Compression Test.—The great advantage of this test is the ease with which the drainage of water into or out of the sample can be controlled. Tests may be *undrained*, simulating short term behaviour of silts and clays (not normally carried out on coarser soils which will be effectively drained at all times in the field), or *drained* where full dissipation of excess pore water pressures is allowed. An alternative form of undrained tests involves the measurement of the response of the pore water pressures to load—in this and drained tests it is conventional to allow some drainage at first to initialise the state of stress and pore water pressure in the sample, a process termed consolidation. Results of tests where pore water pressures are measured (or zero) are generally expressed in terms of *effective stress* which is the difference between the normal stress on a plane in the soil and the pore water pressure.

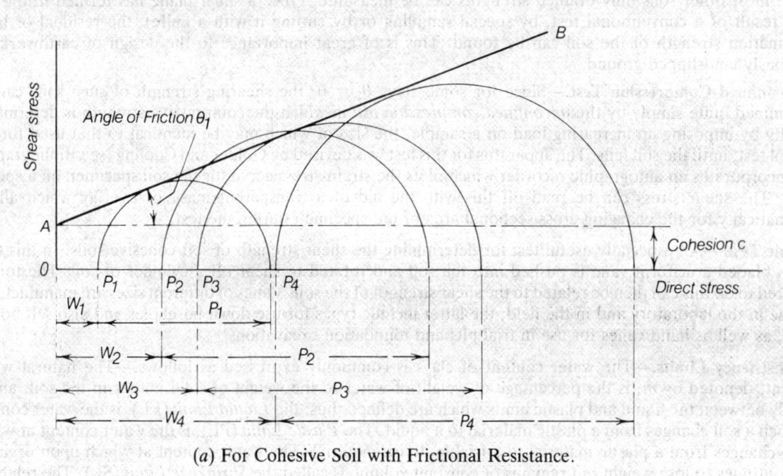

(*a*) For Cohesive Soil with Frictional Resistance.

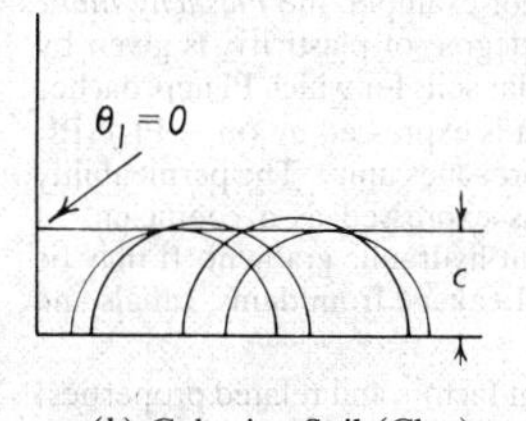

(*b*) Cohesive Soil (Clay). No Friction

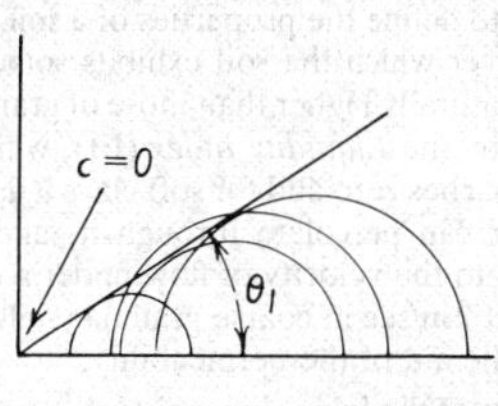

(*c*) Cohesionless Soil (Sand).

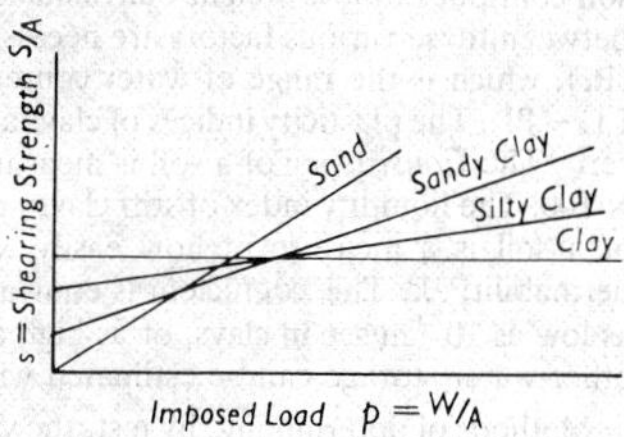

(*d*) Shear-box Tests. Typical Results.

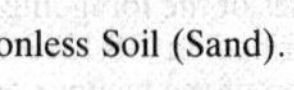

FIG. 1.—Mohr Diagrams.

Primarily, the triaxial compression test enables the relation between the cohesion, shearing strength, angle of internal friction, and compressive resistance to be determined. A cylindrical sample of soil with metal or perspex ends, generally twice as high as wide, is sealed within an air and watertight rubber sleeve. The sample is then placed in a pressure cell and surrounded by water under pressure; this gives the soil specimen a lateral restraint simulating that which would be experienced by the soil at depth in the ground. A piston bears on the top of the sample and the load required to compress the sample at a constant rate of strain is measured until shearing failure occurs. Failure takes place at an angle depending on the angle of internal friction. If three or more samples are tested in this manner but with different cell pressures w_1, w_2, etc, and the intensities of loading to cause failure are p_1, p_2, etc, a series of Mohr's diagrams can be drawn as in Fig. 1(*a*). The distances from the origin O, to points p_1, p_2, etc, where the semi-circles of diameter p_1, p_2, etc, cut the horizontal base of the diagram are equal to the respective pressure intensities w_1, w_2, etc. The nearest common tangent AB to the four semi-circles is drawn. The distance AO (to the same scale as p and w) represents the cohesion c, and θ_1 is the angle of internal friction. The relationship between these factors and the shearing stress is: $s = c + p \tan \theta_1$. Figure 1(*b*) and 1(*c*) show the types of diagram obtained respectively for clays having no angle of internal friction and for cohesionless or granular soils such as sand for which $c = 0$, and $s = p' \tan \theta_1$. In the case of clay, $\theta_u = 0$, and $s = c =$ radius of semi-circle $\pm 0{\cdot}5 p_u$; that is, the shearing strength is half the compressive strength. Full details of testing equipment and procedure, and the interpretation of the results of the many variations on this test, can be found in Bishop and Henkel, *The Triaxial Test* (see bibliography).

Shear-box Test.—The shearing strength and angle of friction can also be determined from the *shear-box test*, the apparatus for which comprises a box, split horizontally, containing the sample of soil. A vertical load W is applied uniformly to the top surface of the sample and the horizontal force S required to slide the top part of the box over the lowest part, and thereby shear the sample, is measured. If the cross-sectional area of the box (in plan) is A, the imposed intensity of pressure p is W/A and the intensity of shearing resistance s is S/A. A series of tests are made with different values of W and the results are plotted to give an inclined line as in Fig. 1(*d*), which cuts the vertical through $p = 0$, at $s = c$. The slope of the line depends on the magnitude of the cohesion and angle of friction; lines for some typical materials are shown. As before, in general, $s = c + p_u \tan \theta_1$. It is difficult to control the drainage in this form of test; clays can just about be tested undrained but in most other soils only drained strengths can be measured. Once a shear plane has formed in the soil (as a result of a conventional test, by special sampling or by cutting it with a knife), the residual or large deformation strength of the soil can be found. This is of great importance to the design of earthworks in previously landslipped ground.

Unconfined Compression Test.—Since for some clays $\theta_1 = 0$, the shearing strength of such soils can be determined quite simply by the *unconfined compression test* in which the compressive strength is determined directly by imposing an increasing load on a sample, the size of which may be identical to that used for the triaxial test, until the soil fails. The apparatus for this test was devised by Golder and Cooling (see Bibliography) and incorporates an autographic recorder which plots the strain-stress curve for the soil specimen on a special chart. The shear stress can be read off this with the aid of a transparent mask or overlay which allows automatically for the changing cross-sectional area of the specimen during the test.

Vane Test.—An especially useful test for determining the shear strength of soft cohesive soils. In this test, a thin bladed cruciform vane is pushed into the soil and rotated to shear off a cylinder of soil. The torque required to do this can then be related to the shear strength of the soil. Vanes of different sizes are manufactured for use in the laboratory and in the field; the latter include types for use down boreholes and also self boring types, as well as hand vanes for use in trial pits and foundation excavations.

Consistency Limits.—The water content of clays is commonly expressed as follows.—The natural water content, denoted by m, is the percentage of weight of water to the weight of solid matter in the soil, and is usually between the liquid and plastic limits which are defined thus: the *Liquid Limit* (LL), is the water content at which a soil changes from a plastic material to a liquid. The *Plastic Limit* (PL), is the water content at which a soil changes from a plastic material to a friable dryish material. The water content at which upon drying a soil continues to lose weight but remains of constant volume is called the *Shrinkage Limit* (SL). The relations between these various factors are necessary to define the properties of a soil. For example, the *Plasticity Index* (PI), which is the range of water content over which the soil exhibits some degree of plasticity, is given by LL − PL. The plasticity indices of clays are naturally higher than those of granular soils for which PI approaches zero. The *Consistency* of a soil is measured by the *Liquidity Index* (LI), which is expressed by $(m - \text{PL})/(\text{PI}) \times 100$. The liquidity index of stiff clays approaches zero and for soft clays it approaches unity. The permeability of a soil is a measure of how easily water can percolate through it, and is expressed as a coefficient of permability, k. This coefficient is equivalent to the velocity of flow under a unit hydraulic gradient. It may be as low as 10^{-1} m/sec in clays, or as high as 10^{-3} m/sec in coarse granular soils. Leakage from dams, canals and other water storage can be estimated with the aid of the permeability.

Methods of determining, by test, the values of the foregoing moisture-content factors and related properties, are given by the *Classification Tests* described in BS 1377 'Method of Testing Soils for Civil Engineering Purposes' in which is also given a description of the manner of preparing disturbed samples of soil for testing. The tests include field and laboratory methods of determining the moisture content of a soil, the specific gravity of particles of soil, and particle-size distribution in a soil. Tests for the determination of the liquid and plastic limits and methods of calculating plasticity and liquidity are also given. BS 1377 also gives particulars of *Soil Compaction Tests* which include methods of determining the density-moisture ratio and the dry density of soil, the latter applying to most types of soils, soil containing stones and fine-grained soils and chalk soils free from stones. The terms used in compaction tests are: *Bulk Density* is the mass of unit volume of the soil including the mass of solid matter and the moisture in the voids, and is the mass in kg/m³ given in Table 2. *Dry density* is the mass of the dry material contained in unit volume of the soil when dried to constant weight. The *Density Moisture Relation* is the relation between dry density and moisture content of a soil when a given amount of compaction is applied. The *Optimum Moisture Content* is the moisture at which a specified amount of compaction produces the *Maximum Dry Density*. The percentage ratio of the dry density of the soil as occurring naturally to the maximum dry density of the soil as determined by the standard test is the *Relative Compaction*.

BEARING RESISTANCES.—The size of a foundation depends on the bearing resistance of the soil. A guide to the *safe bearing pressure* that can usually be applied to common types of soil is given in Table 2, and is applicable if the foundation stratum is homogeneous for some depth below the foundation and if local experience of building on such soil is extensive. The safe bearing resistance for strip foundations is given in chapter 'Building', Table 1. Use caution in accepting tabulated bearing pressures in design. This is particularly so in areas known to be liable to the collapse of sinkholes, abandoned mineworkings and shafts, on filled ground (especially on combustible fills), or on sloping ground where there is a possibility of slips. Where the tabulated values are not applicable, care must be exercised in assessing the safe bearing resistance, which is the ultimate bearing resistance divided by a factor of safety. This factor may vary from 3 to 5 inversely as the accuracy of the value for the ultimate bearing resistance, which is determined either (i) by actual loading tests (as described later) or (ii) by computative rules embodying the strength of the soil as determined by the laboratory tests already described. Some rules which are fairly widely accepted are given in the following.

The ultimate bearing resistance, p_u, depends on the size of the foundation (A = width of strip footing) and the depth, h, of the foundation below the surface, and on the cohesion, c, the bulk density, w, and the angle of friction, θ_1 of the soil. Terzaghi's general formula for homogeneous soils is:

$$p_u = N_c c + N_w wh + 0{\cdot}5 N_a wA$$

where N_c, N_w, and N_a, are functions of the angle of friction. For *cohesive soils* (eg clays), $\theta_1 = 0$, $N_w = 1$, $N_a = 0$, and $p_u = N_c c + wh$. A theoretical value of N_c for a strip footing is 5·51, and is calculated by equating the moment WxA of the imposed load W (Fig. 2) about the centre of the slip circle (radius R) to the moment of the resisting cohesion (intensity c) along the length of the arc of the shearing failure, allowance being made for the weight of earth due to the depth h of the foundation. The arc is that for which the least value of W produces equilibrium. Therefore theoretically, $p\dagger = W/A = 5{\cdot}51c + wh$. Approximate values of the coordinates xA and yA defining the centre of the slip circle for various ratios of depth h to width A of the footing on cohesive soil are:

h/A	0	1·0	2·0	2·5	3·0
x	2·0	2·2	2·3	2·4	2·7
v	0·9	0·8	0·85	0·95	1·05

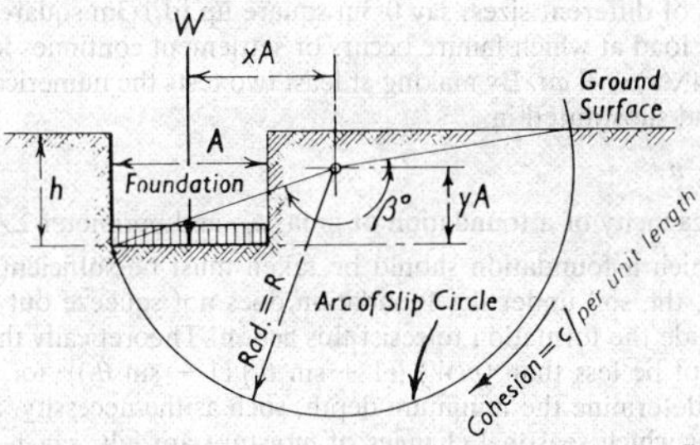

FIG. 2.—Equilibrium of Strip Footing in Cohesive Soils.

† Alternatively, practical values of N_c for substitution in $p_u = N_c c + wh$ for cohesive soil and based on recommendations by Skempton are:

Ratio of depth of foundation to width = h/A	Strip footing width = A	Square or circular base width = A	Rectangular base $A \times L$
$\not> 2\frac{1}{2}$	$5 + h/A$	$6 + 1{\cdot}2h/A$	$(1 + A/5L) + (5 + h/A)$
$> 2\frac{1}{2}$	7·5	9	$(1 + A/5L) + 7{\cdot}5$

For *granular cohesionless soils* ($c = 0$), the ultimate bearing resistance of a strip footing is given by Terzaghi's formula $p_u = (N_w h + 0{\cdot}5 N_a A)w$ where the coefficients N_w and N_a have the following values:

Angle of Internal Friction θ_1	0°	10°	20°	30°	40°
N_w	1·0	3·0	7·5	22	75
N_a	—	1·0	4·5	20	—

Alternatively, for a rectangular foundation on dry granular soil, $p_u = wN(h + 0{\cdot}5A)$, where N is about 25 for $\theta_1 = 30°$., 45 for 35°, and 125 for 40°, but if such soil becomes saturated, p_u may be reduced to half the value calculated for a dry soil. The foregoing data are applicable whether imperial or metric units are used, so long as the units are consistent. The factors N, x and y are non-dimensional.

In Table 3, some acceptable safe bearing pressures on dry compact sands and gravels at various depths below the surface and under foundations of different widths are given. These safe pressures must be reduced to about half of the amount given in the Table, if the sand or gravel is waterlogged, and are based on Terzaghi's suggestions for pressures which limit settlement to 25 mm, rather than on a criterion of shear failure in the soil.

TABLE 3.—SAFE BEARING PRESSURES kN/m².

Soil		Fine to Medium Sand				Coarse Sand to Gravel			
Width of Foundation		1 m	3 m	6 m	9 m	1 m	3 m	6 m	9 m
Depth of Foundation (m)	0·6	210	270	310	340	290	360	440	500
	0·9	280	320	390	460	310	410	500	560
	1·3	300	390	460	520	350	460	570	660
	1·8	320	410	500	590	400	510	610	710

Bearing capacity may not be the sole or even main criterion for selecting an allowable bearing pressure. Settlements, or differential settlements may well be more important (see below).

A direct method of determining the ultimate bearing resistance of the ground under a proposed foundation is to carry out a *loading test* in which a load is applied to a plate on the ground at the foundation level. The load is applied in increments with an interval of an hour or so between each and a record is made of the settlement of the plate immediately before and after each increment of load. If readings are also taken at intervals during the period between loadings, the load can be established at which settlement becomes continuous, and this load is a measure of the ultimate bearing capacity. In some soils it is only necessary to take and plot readings before and after each increment of load, as it is obvious by a break in the curve where failure occurs. As the load in this test is only applied to a limited area compared with the area of the foundation, conditions are not quite comparable. To overcome this, a method sometimes adopted is to carry out successive tests with two or more plates of different sizes, say 0·3m square up to 1·3m square. If the area of the square plate in one is a sq ft and the load at which failure occurs or settlement continues indefinitely is W, a relation proposed by Housel is $W = (4\sqrt{a})m + an$. By making at least two tests the numerical values of the parameters m and n can be calculated and substituted in

$$p_u = m\Sigma A/a_F + n$$

to give the ultimate bearing capacity of a foundation of area, a_F, and perimeter ΣA.

The *minimum depth* to which a foundation should be taken must be sufficient to ensure that under the imposed bearing pressure, p, the soil under the foundation does not squeeze out and that, therefore, there is sufficient depth of soil outside the formation to resist this action. Theoretically the depth below the general level of the ground should not be less than $(p/W)\,\{(1 + \sin\theta_1)/(1 - \sin\theta_2)\}^2$ for a cohesionless soil. Other practical considerations also determine the minimum depth, such as the necessity, in clay, for the foundation level to be below the level at which seasonal changes of moisture are felt, say 1–1·3 m. It is also necessary to ensure that the foundation is below the probable frost line, which, in most parts of the UK, is provided for if the foundation is not less than 1 m deep.

The bearing resistance of a soil can be increased by one of the following means. The soil, whether it be a natural deposit or a filling, can be subjected to *artificial compaction* or *consolidation* by tamping by hand or machine, or by rolling with either an ordinary smooth roller or by a spiked sheepsfoot roller. In the case of natural deposits this effect is only superficial, but consolidation in depth can be effected in the case of filling, by depositing the filling in layers from 0·15 to 0·3m deep and rolling or tamping each layer before depositing the succeeding layer; as already stated this process also reduces the tendency for filling to consolidate or compact naturally over a period of time. Vibratory methods are also used to consolidate granular soils or to form columns of compacted stone or slag within cohesive soils. In the *Vibroflotation* process, à vibrator is suspended from a crane. Water is jetted from openings at the foot of the vibrator to saturate the ground prior to insertion. While jetting continues, the vibrator is allowed to sink into the ground under its own weight. The combination of vibration with an upward flow of water creates quicksand conditions as the vibrator descends rapidly into the soil. When the required depth is reached, jetting is transferred to openings near the top of the machine. The downward flow of water combined with the vibration further compacts the soil and the treatment continues as the machine is raised in stages to the surface. The equipment may also be used to form cylindrical holes in cohesive soils, which are filled with compacted stone or slag, the columns so formed substantially strenghening clay soils and accelerating consolidation of the soil under later loading.

Other methods of obtaining a firm superficial layer of soil, as is required for secondary roads and for the subgrades of concrete roads and runways, include rolling in *hardcore* or by *cement-soil* processes in which cement is mixed with the top soil. *Cementation* processes are also suitable for increasing the strength of normal soils *in situ* at considerable depth below the surface. The ordinary process comprises injecting cement grout into the soil through pipes penetrating into the stratum to be consolidated. This process is suitable for loose sands and gravels, the voids between the particles being filled with the grout which upon setting solidifies the material. Other materials sometimes used in place of cement grout are mixtures of cement and clay, or bituminous emulsions. *Chemical consolidation* comprises the injection of silica into the soil. In the single-fluid process, the soil is injected with a mixture the essential constituent of which is sodium silicate. In the two-fluid process, the silica and the solution (usually strong brine), required to bring about the precipitation of the silica, are injected separately.

PRESSURES ON SOILS.—The two primary aspects of the pressure distribution on and in soils under foundations are (i) the distribution of the pressure imposed by the foundation at the level of the bottom of the foundation, and (ii) the variation of intensity of pressure as the imposed pressure is dispersed through the mass of soil below the foundation.

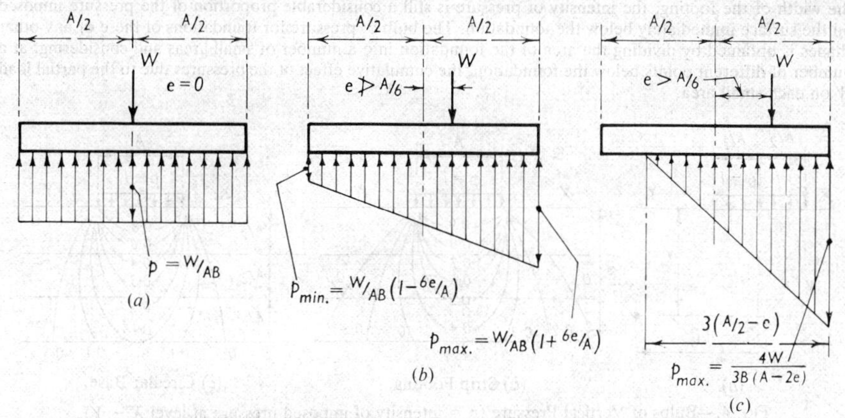

FIG. 3.—Theoretical Pressure Distribution under Rectangular Foundations. (Bases: $A \times B$).

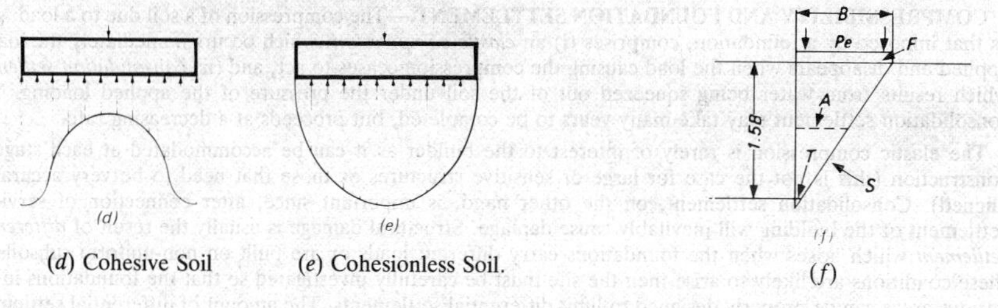

(*d*) Cohesive Soil (*e*) Cohesionless Soil. (*f*)

FIG. 3.—Distribution of Pressures under Foundations.

The average intensity of the pressure imposed by a *concentrically-loaded foundation* is the total load (including the weight of the foundation), divided by the area of the foundation, as in Fig. 3(*a*). It is likely that the pressure may not be quite uniformly distributed as shown and the distribution may vary as to whether the soil is cohesive or granular, but for practical purposes a uniform intensity is generally assumed. For an *eccentrically-loaded foundation* (or, a foundation subjected to a moment, *We*), the intensity of pressure varies from a maximum at one edge of the footing to a minimum (or zero) at or near the opposite edge depending on the relative eccentricity e/A. Assuming a straight-line variation, the pressures under a rectangular foundation of length B are as given in Fig. 3(*b*) and (*c*) for the cases when the eccentricity e does not exceed one-sixth of the width A and when e exceeds $A/6$ respectively. The limiting case when $e = A/6$ produces a triangular pressure diagram with $p_{min} = 0$ and $p_{max} = 2W/AB$. The condition in Fig. 3(*c*) should be avoided if practicable, although this is not always possible especially for foundations (say, of trestles) where moments may be reversible.

The distribution of pressures in Fig. 3(*a*), (*b*) and (*c*) are theoretical. In actuality, the distribution of pressure immediately below a concentrically loaded foundation depends on the type of soil. For a cohesive soil, the actual distribution is as shown in Fig. 3(*d*), and for a fully cohesionless soil, the distribution is as in Fig. 3(*e*). For soils of intermediate types, say a sandy clay, the distribution would be between these two extremes, that is, it might approximate to the uniform distribution shown in Fig. 3(*a*).

Figure 3(*f*) shows an approximate method of calculating the pressure distribution, for use where foundations are fairly small, and where they are to be constructed on uniform stiff and relatively incompressible clays. In Fig. 3(*f*), F = foundation with load, P_e, and B = length of span. A = average pressure in centre of layer = $0{\cdot}55\, P_e$, T = pressure of foundation at depth of $1{\cdot}5B = 0{\cdot}1P_e$.

The basic theoretical formula (due to Boussinesq) for the intensity of vertical pressure p_v at any point in an elastic mass enables the *distribution of pressure in the ground below a foundation* to be studied. If the co-ordinates of any point are u and v (Fig. 4(*a*)), in relation to the point of application of a concentrated load W at the surface, the formula is:

$$p_v = 0{\cdot}48W/v^2\{\sqrt{[1 + (u/v)^2]}\}^5$$

Application of this formula to the ground under a strip footing, and under a circular base results in the *bulb of pressure* given in Fig. 4(*b*) and (*c*) respectively, from which it is seen that even at a depth equal to 1½ times the width of the footing, the intensity of pressure is still a considerable proportion of the pressure imposed on the surface immediately below the foundation. The bulb of pressure for foundations of these or any other shapes is obtained by dividing the area of the foundation into a number of small areas and considering, at a number of different points below the foundation, the cumulative effect of the pressures due to the partial load W on each small area.

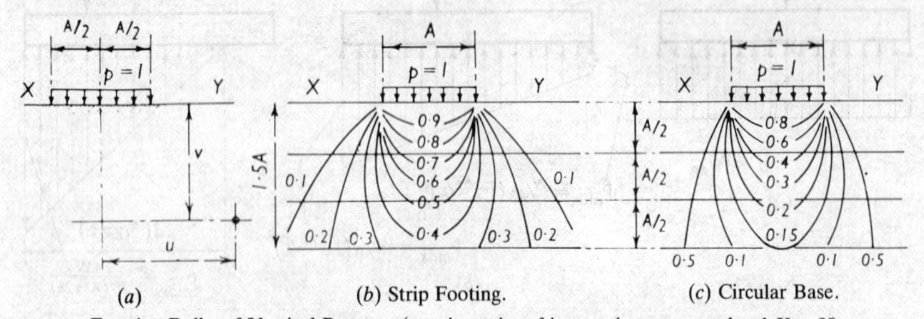

(*a*) (*b*) Strip Footing. (*c*) Circular Base.

FIG. 4.—Bulbs of Vertical Pressure (p = intensity of imposed pressure at level $X - Y$).

COMPRESSIBILITY AND FOUNDATION SETTLEMENT.—The compression of a soil due to a load, such as that imposed by a foundation, comprises (i) an *elastic compression*, which occurs immediately the load is applied and disappears when the load causing the compression ceases to act, and (ii) *consolidation settlement* which results from water being squeezed out of the soil under the pressure of the applied loading. This consolidation settlement may take many years to be completed, but proceeds at a decreasing rate.

The elastic compression is rarely of interest to the builder as it can be accommodated at each stage in construction (this is not the case for large or sensitive structures or those that need to be very accurately aligned). Consolidation settlement, on the other hand, is important since, after connection of services, settlement of the building will inevitably cause damage. Structural damage is usually the result of *differential settlement* which arises when the foundations carry different loads or are built on non-uniform subsoils. If these conditions are likely to arise then the site must be carefully investigated so that the foundations in the various areas can be properly designed to limit differential settlements. The amount of differential settlement which can be accommodated is highly dependent on the structural details of the superstructure.

Consolidation settlements will also occur if the ground is dewatered by evaporation (protracted dry weather), transpiration (trees mainly) or artificial ground water lowering. They are usually important only in soils with an appreciable clay fraction, since granular soils rarely exhibit settlement after the initial elastic compression. Organic soils are particularly susceptible to consolidation.

In the tropics, building construction may impede natural evaporation, leading to an increase in moisture content and heaving of the ground surface. In temperate regions similar heaving of the ground may result from moisture content increases in the soil after tree clearance or freezing of ground water under refrigeration plants.

THE OEDOMETER TEST.—The amount of consolidation of a soil specimen under load and the rate at which this takes place are measured in the oedometer. This is basically a lever loading system which applies vertical loads to a disc-shaped and laterally-confined soil specimen with special provision for the drainage of water and for the measurement of the changes in its thickness. In most cases the results of this test are expressed as a graph of voids ratio versus effective stress (see Fig. 5(*b*)) together with data on the time taken for the consolidation process.

Settlement of foundations, due to compression, may be the criterion of the load-carrying capacity of some soils (mainly clays), rather than the ultimate bearing resistance of the soil. The squeezing out of the water from clays due to the pressure imposed by the foundations may cause settlement at a decreasing rate to continue for many years. The probable amount of settlement can be estimated as follows.

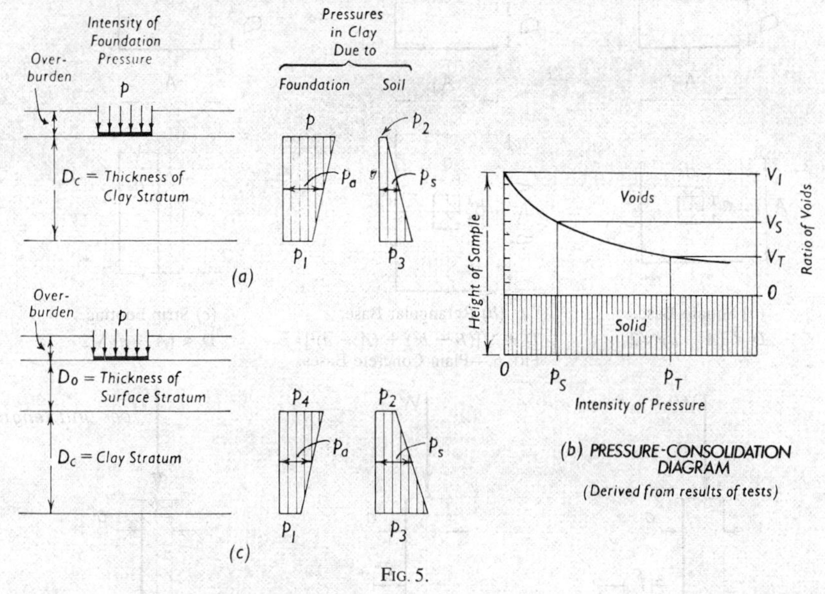

FIG. 5.

If a load imposes a pressure of intensity, p, on the surface of a clay stratum of thickness, D_c (Fig. 5(*a*)), the pressure, p_1, at the bottom of the stratum, can be calculated from Boussinesq's formula, given in the foregoing. The average pressure, p_a, in the clay is $0{\cdot}5\ (p + p_1)$, due to p only. It is established by tests on samples of the clay that the relation between loading and consolidation is given by a curve such as that in Fig. 5(*b*), in which V_1, is the ratio of voids in the soil in its natural condition, that is before p operates. Due to the weight of the soil itself and any overburden thereon, the average pressure p_s in the clay is $0{\cdot}5\ (p_2 + p_3)$; p_T, the average intensity of total pressure due to the weight of the soil, overburden, and imposed load is $p_a + p_s$. From the curve in (*b*), the voids ratios, V_T and V_S, corresponding to p_T and p_S, respectively, can be determined and the probable compression d_c, of the clay stratum (and therefore the settlement of the foundation) is given by $d_c = D_c\{(V_S - V_V)/(1 + V_S)\}$.

If the foundation is on a layer of thickness D_0 of non-compressible soil overlying the clay (Fig. 5(*c*)), p in the foregoing calculation is replaced by p_4, which is the intensity of pressure due to p at depth D_1 below the surface, as calculated by Boussinesq's formula.

To estimate the *time of settlement* or the amount of settlement after a given period of time, a test is made on a sample of thickness d_c, subjected to the same average total pressure p_T, as in the clay stratum, and the time, T, for the sample to become almost stable (that is until consolidation almost ceases) is determined. Then, the time during which the settlement will continue, is $T(D_c/d_c)^2$, or, $4T(D_c/d_c)^2$. The former expression applies if the stratum immediately below the clay is pervious so that water can escape from the clay, both upwards and downwards. If the underlying stratum is impervious, the second expression applies, since the water can only escape upwards and the settlement takes longer. From the foregoing considerations it is possible to estimate the probable settlement of foundations on stratified ground of variable characteristics, by considering the pressures on, and consequent compaction of each stratum separately, so long as the results of compaction tests on each of the types of soils are available.

Although total settlements can be calculated with reasonable accuracy from laboratory tests, the estimation of the time for settlement often produces answers which are grossly inaccurate. This normally arises from incorrect assessment of the drainage path, particularly in laminated or layered strata. For this reason it is often necessary to obtain a continuous vertical profile of the ground in order to estimate more realistically the length of the drainage path.

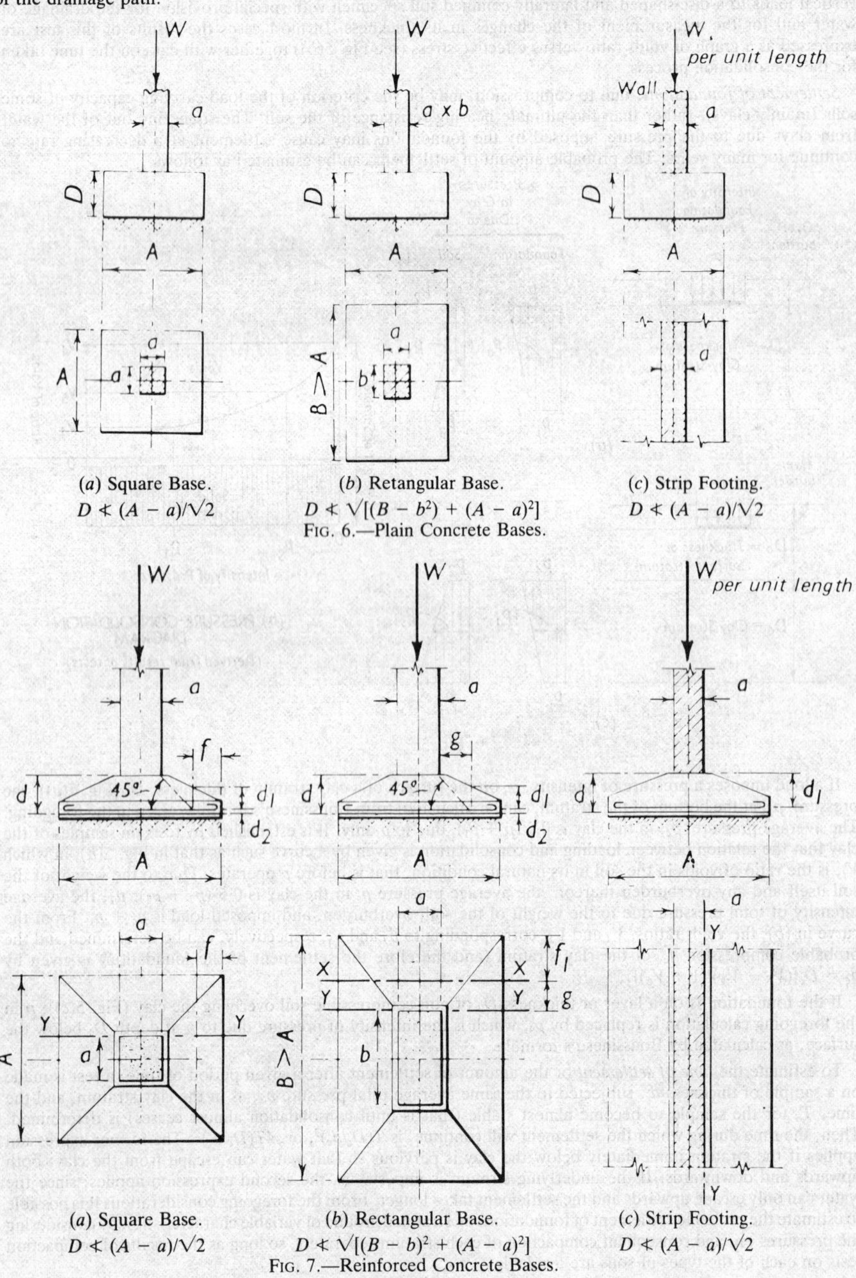

(*a*) Square Base. $D \nless (A - a)/\sqrt{2}$

(*b*) Retangular Base. $D \nless \sqrt{[(B - b^2) + (A - a)^2]}$

(*c*) Strip Footing. $D \nless (A - a)/\sqrt{2}$

FIG. 6.—Plain Concrete Bases.

(*a*) Square Base. $D \nless (A - a)/\sqrt{2}$

(*b*) Rectangular Base. $D \nless \sqrt{[(B - b)^2 + (A - a)^2]}$

(*c*) Strip Footing. $D \nless (A - a)/\sqrt{2}$

FIG. 7.—Reinforced Concrete Bases.

FOUNDATIONS

A *foundation* is the term normally applied in civil and structural engineering, to describe the part of a structure that transmits the weight and other forces and moments from the structure to the ground, and distributes this loading in such a way that the safe bearing capacity of the ground is not exceeded under the most adverse conditions. (In some quarters, the term foundation implies the excavated or otherwise prepared ground on which the base of the structure bears). The type and design of a foundation, therefore, depends primarily on the magnitude and distribution of the load and the nature of the ground.

SITE INVESTIGATION.—The obvious preliminary to the design of a foundation is to determine the character of the ground at the site of the structure. Such an investigation may vary from a superficial inspection, allied with experience of similar or neighbouring sites, to an elaborate examination involving the testing of samples of the ground as described in the previous section on soil mechanics. All forms of such inspections are dealt with in detail in BS Code of Practice, BS 5930:1981 'Site Investigations' and by Simons Clayton and Matthews. The primary object of the inspection is to determine the depth at which a satisfactory bearing stratum occurs, and the safe bearing capacity of this stratum. Other important factors usually determined at the same time are the level of the ground water and the necessity or otherwise to provide timbering for the excavations.

If the bearing stratum is within a few feet of the surface, it is possible to expose it at selected places by *trial pits* in which the actual ground can be studied and, if necessary, can be loaded to determine the safe bearing resistance. Great care must be taken if trial pits in soft soils, loose fill, or cohesionless soils near the water table are employed, since these can be dangerous without adequate timbering. If the bearing stratum is at great depth, *bore holes* are usually sunk and samples of the various strata encountered are brought up for examination and assessment. The drawback of trial pits and bore holes is that inspection by these means is only local, and unless there is reason to believe that the underground conditions are fairly uniform a large number of fairly expensive trials has to be made to obtain a true picture of the subsoil over a large area. If the bearing stratum lies at such a depth that a piled foundation may have to provided, examination by *test piles* is often made. Another method involves driving a sounding device into the ground which measures separately the frictional resistance of the ground and the bearing resistance under the toe of the pile. This apparatus can also be used for determining the resistance of the surface strata if deep foundations are not necessary.

TYPES OF FOUNDATIONS.—The common types of foundation include in order of complexity: blocks of plain concrete for stanchion bases, strip footings for brick walls, reinforced concrete bases for single or multiple loads, rafts, piles, cylinders and caissons, the type chosen for a given structure depending on the bearing capacity of the bearing stratum selected, the depth at which this stratum occurs, and the magnitude and distribution of the loads from the structure. Some special types of foundations are dealt with elsewhere in this year-book, namely, foundations for bridges (chapter, 'Bridges and Bridgework'); foundations for buildings (chapter, 'Building'); bases for drop-hammers (chapter, 'Forging Hammers, etc') and engine bases (chapter, 'Internal Combustion Engine').

SINGLE BASES.—For the support of a concrete column, brick pier or steel stanchion, a *concentrically loaded* single base is usually sufficient if the load is not large or the permissible ground pressure is high. In its simplest form the base may be a *plain concrete block* (Fig. 6(*a*)) which is assumed to spread the load to the ground by dispersion at an angle not less than 45° to the horizontal. A *square base* of side A is the most economical in which $A = \surd(W_T/p)$, where W_T is the load imposed on the base plus the weight of the base and any earth carried by the base; and p is the safe bearing pressure to which the ground can be subjected at the level of the bottom of the base as determined in the previous section, 'Bearing Resistances'. The thickness D, of the base must not be less than $(A - a)/\surd 2$. If a square base is not convenient, a rectangular base of width A, and length B, will be necessary, the proportions of which must be such that ABp is not less than W_T. If B is greater than A (Fig. 6(*b*)), D must not be less than $\surd[(B - b)^2 + (A - a)^2]/2$. A *strip footing* (Fig. 6(*c*)), for a 'line-load' such as a wall may also be of plain concrete, in which case, if W_T is the load per unit length of wall plus the weight of the footing of wall, the breadth A must not be less than W_T/p, and the thickness D, not less than $(A - a)/2$. In all the foregoing bases the stresses due to bending and shearing force are generally so small that they are ignored.

If the dimensions A or B are large in relation to a and b respectively, it may probably be more economical to provide a *reinforced concrete base*, but the more economical design can only be determined by comparison of the alternatives. In Fig. 7 are given typical forms of (*a*) a square base, (*b*) a rectangular base, and (*c*) strip footing in reinforced concrete. Each must be designed so that the safe shearing stress is not exceeded, and that there is adequate resistance to the maximum total bending moments M (see chapter, 'Concrete: Reinforced and Prestressed'). Appropriate formulae are given in the following, in which q is the permissible shearing stress.

Square Base.—$A \nless W_T/p$; $p_1 = W/A^2$; $M_{YY} = p_1 (A/8)(A - a)^2$; $p_1 f/\frac{7}{8}d \ngtr q$.

Rectangular Base.—$AB \nless W_T/p$; $p_1 = W/AB$; $M_{YY} = (p_1 A/8)(B - b)^2$; $p_1 f/\frac{7}{8}d \ngtr q$.

Strip Footing.—$A \nless W_T/p$; $p_1 = W/A$.

With concrete wall monolithic with footing: $M_{YY} = (p_1/8)(A - a)^2$

With brick wall (or similar): $M_{YY} = (p_1 A/8)(A = a)$

If a single base is *eccentrically loaded*, that is the centre of action of the applied load does not coincide with the centroid of the base, or if the base is subjected to an external moment in addition to a concentric or eccentric applied load, the ground pressure will not be uniform under the base, but will vary as shown in Fig. 3(*b*) or 3(*c*) (section, 'Pressures on Soils'). Square or rectangular bases are designed for this condition in a similar manner to those with concentric load, allowance being made, however, for the variable ground pressure when computing the bending moments and shearing forces. If the base is not square or rectangular, for example, octagonal bases which are common under chimneys, the maximum and minimum ground pressures due to the applied load. W, and the external bending moment, M, are calculated from

$$\frac{p_{max}}{p_{min}} > \frac{W}{\text{area}} \pm \frac{M}{Z}$$

where Z is the modulus of the area of the base. This formula applies if p_{min} is not negative.

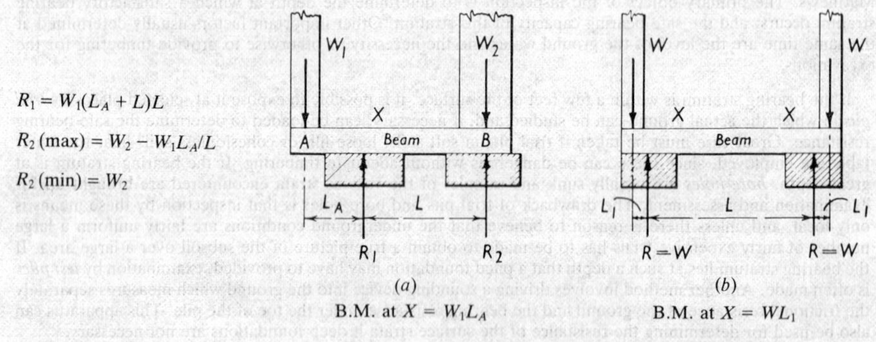

(*a*) B.M. at $X = W_1L_A$

(*b*) B.M. at $X = WL_1$

FIG. 8.—Balanced Foundations.

COMBINED BASES.—Eccentrically loaded bases can be avoided if a *balanced foundation* can be provided. This type of base is common where one load is so near the the boundary of the site that there is insufficient space for a concentric base. Figure 8(*a*) illustrates a balanced foundation where the counterbalance to the overhanging effect of the column load W_1, at A, is provided at B by part of the load W_2 from another column or part of the structure. The reactions, R_1 and R_2 on the concentrically loaded bases, and the bending moments and shearing forces on the beam, are calculated from the appropriate formulae, given in Fig. 8(*a*). An example where two equal loads are carried on a beam supported on two symmetrically opposed bases is shown in Fig. 8(*b*). The bases are designed as concentrically-loaded foundations, each subjected to a load W. In these examples, the weights of the bases and beams must be added to the effects of the applied loads W, etc.

If two or more loads in line are so close that individual bases would practically overlap, a *combined base* is more suitable than separate bases. Where possible the centre of gravity of the load should coincide with the centroid of the base and to obtain this coincidence it may require a trapezoidal base as in Fig. 9(*a*), in which case the ground pressure is uniform. If a base of such shape is inconvenient because of site or other restrictive conditions, a rectangular base as in Fig. 9(*b*) would be provided, but in this case coincidence of centre of gravity and centroid might not be possible and the ground pressure would vary. The eccentricity, e, in the pressure formulae (see Fig. 3(*b*)), is the distance between the centre of gravity and the centroid. The longitudinal bending moment at any section is the algebraic sum of the moments of the downward loads and the moments of the upward ground pressures on one side of the section. Likewise the shearing force at any section is the algebraic sum of the downward loads and upward ground pressures on one side of the section. The transverse moments, that is, the cantilever effect of the upward ground pressures, must also be taken into account.

When a number of closely-spaced loads are disposed over an area, such as the site of a building, instead of in a single line, a *raft foundation* is provided if the safe ground pressure is such that individual bases would almost touch or overlap each other. A raft is designed, more or less, as an inverted floor with the ground pressure taking the place of the floor loading and may be merely a slab of uniform thickness, or a slab stiffened with ribs (or beams); or, in large rafts (exceeding 1 m deep), of cellular construction. Some designs of combined foundations including rafts are given in text books on the subject of reinforced concrete foundations. It is important in the design of combined foundations that the ground pressures, bending moments, and shearing forces should be considered also for the maximum loads being imposed at some points and dead loads only at others, since the eccentricities arising from such conditions may cause greater maximum ground pressures than when all loads are maxima.

CYLINDERS AND CAISSONS.—When the bearing stratum lies at some depth below the ground surface or below water and the loads are heavy, cylinder and caisson foundations are often provided. *Cylinders* are

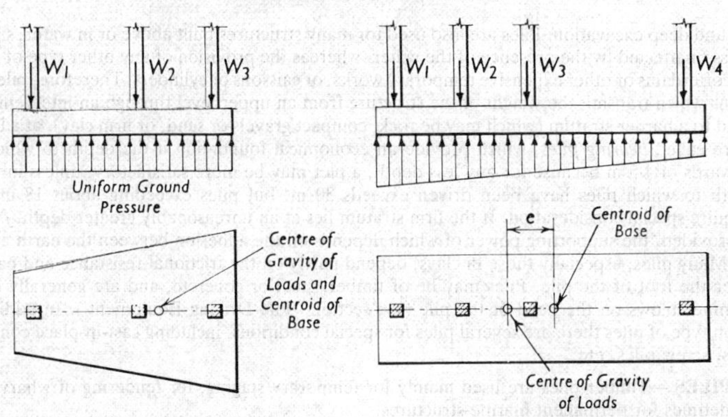

(*a*) Concentrically Loaded Base. (*b*) Eccentrically Loaded Base.

FIG. 9.—Combined Bases.

suitable under such conditions if the presence of boulders, or the like, makes the driving of ordinary piles impracticable, and where a temporary cofferdam (see section, 'Earthworks') would be uneconomical because of the small area to be enclosed at each foundation point. The cylinders usually comprise a number of rings which are lowered to the foundation level by excavating inside them and letting them sink by their own weight, rings being added successively as sinking proceeds. If their own weight is insufficient, additional load, called kentledge, is imposed. The rings may be of steel, cast-iron or, more frequently, of precast reinforced concrete and may be several metres in diameter. If in the dry, excavation inside the cylinder is carried out by hand and the spoil is loaded into crane skips. If in water, and the cylinder cannot be kept clear by pumping, excavation would be by grab, or if the nature of the ground permits, by water jet and pumping. The cylinder becomes part of the permanent foundation when sunk to the required depth and filled with concrete, and as such is particularly suitable for bridge piers and the support of heavy wharves. Steel cylinders of, say, less than 1 m diameter are sometimes impact-driven (see section, 'Cast-in-Place Piles'). In sinking cylinders by impact and in excavation within cylinders by grab or pumping, difficulties arise if boulders or other obstructions are encountered.

Caissons are used for bridge piers and similar major structures founded below water, in cases where cylinders are not suitable. They are generally of much larger dimensions than cylinders, and different types are adapted to different site conditions. If a level bearing can be prepared at foundation level to receive the caisson, a *box caisson* is suitable. This comprises a reinforced concrete open box with a bottom, and stiffened if necessary with cross walls. The box is cast on-shore and floated out to the site where it is sunk by flooding on to the prepared bed. An *open caisson*, that is a reinforced concrete bottomless box, is used where no level bed can be prepared. In this case, the caisson may be made in precast horizontal sections and sunk by excavating within as for cylinders, adding successive sections as sinking proceeds. The sections are usually precast on-shore and floated out to the site on barges, from which they are lowered into position by cranes. The lower section has a cutting edge, generally of steel, to facilitate sinking under the weight of the caisson as excavation proceeds by grab (or by hand if in the dry), within the cells formed by the cross walls. If the site is above water level, an open caisson can be constructed completely on the site where it has to be sunk, and then sunk as a whole. An open caisson, to be sunk through water, can be constructed completely in the dry and provided with a false bottom to enable it to be floated out to the site. When an open caisson has been sunk to the required depth, a concrete seal is laid across the bottom. If in the dry, the concrete can be levelled and rammed by hand, but if under water, the concrete is placed through a tremie. If a caisson has to be sunk in permeable soil, to a depth below water, so great, that pumping can not deal with the inflow of water and grabs are impracticable because of boulders or other obstructions, a *pneumatic caisson* is used. This is similar to an open caisson except that the lower section is roofed over and the working chamber thus formed is charged with compressed air which prevents the inflow of water and permits excavation to proceed by hand in the dry in this chamber. Entrance and exit for workmen, equipment, and excavated material is through an airlock in the roof of the working chamber. The depth to which pneumatic caissons can be sunk is limited by working conditions in compressed air, and the greatest depth is about 35 m below water level, but working hours at this depth are limited. The air pressure required for depths up to 15 m enables work to proceed for a normal day. When sunk to the required depth, the working chamber is completely filled with concrete, placed by hand until the space is too restricted for working in; the space is then filled with grout under pressure. An example of a caisson foundation for bridge piers is illustrated in chapter, 'Bridges and Bridgework'.

PILES.—If the bearing stratum is some distance below level of ground, or below the bottom of the excavation for the structure to be supported, piles are driven down to and into the bearing stratum instead of taking out an extensive and deep excavation. Piles are also used for many structures built above or in water, since driving is more or less unaffected by the presence of the water, whereas the provision of any other type of foundation necessitates cofferdams or other expensive temporary works, or caissons or cylinders. Therefore, piles generally act as columns which transmit the weight of the structure from an upper level through an intervening stratum of soft ground to a harder stratum (which may be rock, compact gravels or sand, or firm clay), at a lower level. Such piles are called *bearing piles*, which provide an economical foundation if the depth to which they are driven is upwards of 4·5 m because for any less depth, a pier may be more satisfactory, unless in water. The greatest depth to which piles have been driven exceeds 30 m, but piles exceeding about 18 m in length, generally require special consideration. If the firm stratum lies at an unreasonably greater depth, *friction piles* are usually provided, the supporting power of which depends on the adhesion between the earth and the side of the piles. Many piles, especially those in clays, depend partly on the frictional resistance and partly on the bearing under the foot of the pile. Piles may be of timber, steel or concrete, and are generally driven into place by hammer blows on the head of the pile (see section, 'Pile-Driving Equipment'). In addition to the more common type of piles there are several piles for special conditions, including cast-in-place concrete piles, cylinder piles, screw piles, etc.

TIMBER PILES.—Timber piles are used mainly for temporary staging, for fendering of wharves and the like, and sometimes for permanent marine structures.

The head of a timber pile (Fig. 10(*a*)) is protected by a mild steel hoop to prevent the pile being split during driving. The lower end of the pile is tapered, the length of the tapered part being about 1½ to twice the width of the pile. A cast iron show is fixed to the end and secured to the sides of the pile by bolts or screws passing through wrought-iron straps. There is generally no need for a metal shoe if the pile is a friction pile in soft or fairly firm ground throughout.

TABLE 4.—STEEL BOX-PILES (*LARSSEN*): Some Typical Values.

H mm	B mm	d mm	Weight kg/m	Modulus About XX cm²	Modulus About YY cm²	Sectional area cm²
165	432	9·4	84·8	533	1,087	10·8
240	438	10·2	97·6	850	1,177	12·4
289	438	14·2	124	1,132	1,338	15·8
394	467	22·1	200	2,973	2,973	25·5

STEEL BOX-PILES.—Steel box-piles (Fig. 10(*b*)) are generally made up by welding together two steel sheet-piles, such as those given in Table 7. The sizes, weights and strength properties of some sections of one form of proprietary steel box-piles, are given in Table 4, the dimensions B, H, etc, referring to Fig. 10(*b*) (Larssen type). The values in Table 4 are typical only; many other sizes and types are available.

Other forms of steel box-piles comprise rolled steel channels with plates welded across the flanges as also shown in Fig. 10(*b*). Allowance can be made for the loss of strength of steel piles due to corrosion during several decades of useful life by assuming that the thickness of the metal is ultimately reduced by about 50%, that is the cross-section areas and moduli are approximately half the values given above. This allowance may be excessive in the case of the larger sections and reference should be made to makers' handbooks for more accurate values. Steel box-piles have been driven up to 45 m long but in such cases, the pile is supplied in three or more lengths which are successively connected by welding or other means after each preceding section has been driven. The piles are sometimes driven with an open end at the bottom, which means that the cavity becomes practically filled with earth. If the load-carrying capacity required exceeds that of an open-ended pile, a steel shoe is provided, and the pile can be filled with concrete.

PRECAST CONCRETE PILES.—See Fig. 10(*c*). *Precast Reinforced Concrete Piles* are generally from 250 to 400 mm square, and up to 18 m long; large and longer piles are usually of octagonal section, or may be hollow. They are more durable than steel or timber piles. The lower end of the pile is generally pointed, unless entirely in soft ground, and is fitted with a tapered cast iron shoe weighing 12–50 kg, or up to 150 kg (with a hard steel rod projecting from the point) if driven down to rock. The taper on each side of the point is about 1:2 for clay, 1:3 for gravel, and 1:4 for sand. To ease driving of piles in compact sand, a water jet is used; water under pressure is pumped down a pipe embedded down the centre of the pile (or in grooves in the face of a timber pile) and emitted at the shoe or at intermediate points causing the sand to be disturbed thereby facilitating downward movement. The reinforcement provides resistance to carry the load on the pile and to resist stresses during handling and driving. The main bars are extended from the point to the head and are kept in position by cast-iron or pressed-steel forks, and are bound by links which are closely spaced at the head where driving stresses are severe. To increase the strength of the head additional bars with helical binding are provided.

A concrete pile must be handled in such a way that it is not unduly stressed; tubes cast in the pile enable lifting tackle to be attached at predetermined points which, to ensure that the bending movements are minimal, should be at the following distances from the head: 0·3L for single-point lifting; 0·2L and 0·8L for two-point lifting; where L is the length of the pile. The toggle-hole provided near the head for attachment to the driving frame, may be in a suitable position for lifting short piles. The concrete in a pile is generally mixed in the porportions of $1:1\frac{2}{3}:3\frac{1}{3}$. Piles up to 90 m long are sometimes provided by driving a steel pile followed by a reinforced or prestressed concrete pile, the connection being made by welding *in situ* to the head of the steel pile a length of steel (of the same section) projecting from the lower end of the concrete pile.

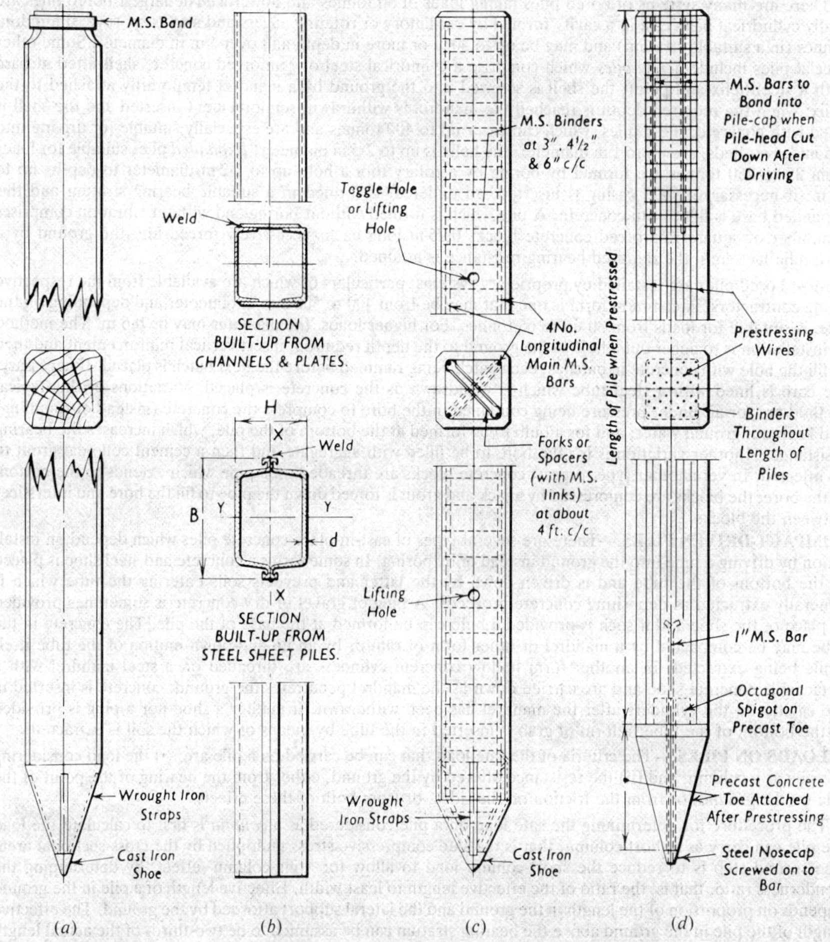

FIG. 10.—Bearing Piles. (*a*) Timber. (*b*) Steel Box-Pile (Alternative sections). (*c*) Reinforced Concrete (precast). (*d*) Prestressed Concrete.

Prestressed Concrete Piles. See Fig. 10(*d*). These are precast piles in which the concrete is compressed during the manufacture of the pile, by a number of stretched high-tensile steel wires extending the entire length of the pile (see chapter 'Concrete: Reinforced and Prestressed', section 'Prestressed Concrete'). The pre-compression ensures that the pile has no open cracks when in service, and therefore is likely to be more durable than a reinforced concrete pile. A square prestressed concrete pile is smaller than a precast reinforced concrete pile of the same load-bearing capacity and length. Less concrete is required and there is much less steel, although the cost of the high-tensile wires or bars may be as much as the cost of the reinforcement in the unstressed pile.

CAST-IN-PLACE CONCRETE PILES.—Concrete piles are formed *in situ*, either by boring or driving; an advantage is that only the required length is formed, whatever variations there may be in the level of the bearing stratum.

BORED PILES.—These are formed with little or no vibration and, the equipment in some systems being approx 2 m high, they are suitable in positions of limited headroom. The most simple bored pile is the *auger pile* which can be formed in clayey soils by augering out by hand a cavity 120–200 mm in diameter, and 1·5–3 m deep and filling this with concrete; greater depths can be reached by a mechanical auger. Such piles only carry small loads but are suitable for light buildings where a bearing stratum occurs only a few feet below the surface.

There are many systems of bored piles taking loads of 50 tonnes and upwards. The largest bored piles are really cylindrical piers cast in a cavity formed by oscillatory or rotating augers and may carry several hundred tonnes (in a suitable stratum) and may be up to 30 m or more in depth and over 1 m in diameter. Some other special piles include *Screw-piles* which comprise a cylindrical steel or reinforced concrete shell fitted at base with a steel helix and point; the shell is screwed into the ground by a mandrel temporarily attached to the helix; when the required depth is reached the mandrel is withdrawn, reinforcement inserted and the shell is filled with concrete; these piles, which can carry up to 400 tonnes and are especially suitable for driving into sea and river beds, are up to 1 m diameter; the helix is up to 2·5 m diameter. *Expanded* piles suitable for loads from 25 to 250 tonnes are formed by boring by a rotary tool a hole up to 1·2 m diameter to depths up to 60 m; if necessary a steel casing is inserted; an undercut is formed in a suitable bearing stratum and this expanded base is filled with concrete. A pile which is formed without boring and without vibration comprises a number of square reinforced concrete blocks 0·75 m long each successively forced into the ground by a hydraulic jack until the required bearing resistance is attained.

Most bored piles are installed by proprietary systems, particulars of which are available from the respective piling contractors. A common form is one that may be from 400 to 500 mm in diameter and depending on the size, is suitable for loads from 30 up to 65 tonnes. For higher loads, the diameter may be 0·6 m. The method of installation is to auger out a hole in the ground to the depth required, insert vertical reinforcement and then to fill the hole with concrete in batches, each batch being rammed before the next batch is placed. If necessary, the core is lined with a steel tube which is withdrawn as the concrete is placed. Variations of this typical method are for air under pressure being contained in the bore to compress the concrete (instead of ramming) and keep out ground water; and for a bulb to be formed at the bottom of the pile, which increases the bearing resistance. Another variation is for the bore to be filled with aggregate and then a cement colloidal grout to be injected. In yet another type, precast concrete blocks are threaded on a pipe which extends to the bottom of the bore; the blocks are compressed by a jack and grout is forced down the pipe to fill the bore and interstices between the blocks.

IMPACT-DRIVEN PILES.—There are several types of cast-in-place concrete piles which depend on installation by driving a tube into the ground instead of by boring. In some forms a concrete and steel shoe is placed at the bottom of the tube and is driven down by the latter and prevents soils entering the tube which is generally extracted as depositing concrete proceeds. A plug of gravel or dry concrete is sometimes provided in place of the shoe and if such is provided a bulb can be formed at the base of the pile. The concrete in the tube may be compacted by a mandrel or other form of ram or by an up-and-down motion of the tube itself while being extracted. In another form hollow concrete cylinders are threaded on a steel mandrel with a detachable concrete shoe and are carried down as the mandrel penetrates the ground; concrete is inserted in the cavities in the cylinders after the mandrel has been withdrawn. If neither a shoe nor a plug is provided at the bottom of the tube, a form of grab is inserted in the tube by means of which the soil is extracted.

LOADS ON PILES.—The criteria of the safe load that can be carried on a pile are: (i) the load considering the pile as a column, and (ii) the resistance offered by the ground, either from the bearing of the point of the pile on the ground, or from the friction on the sides, or from both of these effects.

The procedure for determining the safe load on a pile considered as a *column* is first to calculate the load the pile can carry as a short column, that is the safe compressive stress multiplied by the cross-sectional area. The second step is to reduce the short-column load to allow for 'long-column' effect, by determining the slenderness ratio, that is, the ratio of the effective length to least width. Effective length of a pile in the ground depends on proportion of the length in the ground and the lateral support afforded by the ground. The effective length of the pile in the ground above the bearing stratum can be assumed to be two-thirds of the actual length in the ground for firm soils, but for piles driven through silt or other very soft ground, no reduction should be made. The length of pile penetrating the bearing stratum can generally be neglected. The effective length of the part of a friction pile embedded in the ground can be taken as half the actual embedded length. To the effective length in the ground must be added the actual length of the part of the pile above the ground, to give the overall effective length for the purpose of determining the slenderness ratio.

For a *timber pile* the safe stress can vary considerably depending on the nature and quality of the wood; some safe stresses on struts are given in Table 8. For temporary piling, the safe direct compressive stress acting along the grain, can be taken as 6 N/mm^2 for pitch-pine, spruce, larch, elm and beech. Stresses of 8 N/mm^2 can be used for ash, teak and oak, but only 4 N/mm^2 for yellow or red pine. Half these stresses should be assumed if the piles are permanently in water and three-quarters, if green timber is used. The cross-section considered must be the minimum section allowing for any reduction due to jointing, connections, bolts and other cutting. No reduction for the long-column effect of timber piles is necessary if the slenderness ratio is not greater than 15, but a reduction factor of 5/6 should be applied if the ratio is 20, and 2/3 if 25; intermediate values can be interpolated.

The working stresses and reduction factors for slenderness for the calculation of the safe load on *steel piles* acting as columns should be calculated in accordance with the rules given in BS 449. (See chapter, 'Design of Steel Structures' section, 'Stanchions and Struts'.) Cross-sectional areas of some types of steel-box piles are given in a preceding paragraph. Allowance must be made, as described, for probable corrosion of steel piles in permanent work.

The safe column-load on *concrete piles* is calculated, in the case of ordinary precast reinforced concrete piles, as reinforced concrete columns (see section 'Columns' in chapter, 'Concrete: Reinforced and Prestressed'), taking into account the effective length of the part of the pile in the ground when assessing the overall effective length. No approximate rules can be given for the safe load on a prestressed concrete pile considered as a column as so much depends on the margin between the amount of precompression and safe compressive stress of the concrete. It is generally true that the safe load will exceed that of a reinforced concrete pile of the same cross-sectional area, and the reducing effect of the slenderness is negligible over a very wide range. The safe-load as a column of a cast-in-place concrete pile depends on the type of pile, and reference should be made to the literature published by the respective suppliers.

The safe-load on an *impact-driven pile*, due to resistance of the ground, is not readily assessed, as so many factors enter into the problem. The most satisfactory method is to subject a pile to test load, either until the ground fails, or up to a load at least 50% greater than the working load. The results of the test should be allied to the driving data. It is, however, important to note that the safe load on a group of piles is less than the safe load on one pile multiplied by the number of piles in the group, and is the safe bearing resistance of the area of the bearing stratum covered by the group. The safe load is often calculated by *piling formulae*, which can be a reliable method if combined with the results of test loads, or if considerable experience has been had of piling in identical ground conditions, or if a large factor of safety is included in the calculation. Many piling formulae have been published from time to time, generally for use under specific conditions, and such may be valuable if used only within the limitations stated by their authors. A formula, that has wide acceptance because it takes into account most of the principal variable factors encountered in driving piles, is the *Hiley formula*, which is most suitable for piles driven through fairly *cohesionless soil down to a hard stratum.* In a modified working form this formula can be expressed to give the safe load, P tons, on an impact driven pile as $P = p_1A/F$; where p_1 (= PF/A), the driving pressure (tons per in^2), A, is the cross-sectional area (in^2) of the pile, and F is a factor of safety, varying from 1·5 for very hard driving ($p_1 = 1$), to 3 for easy driving ($p_1 = \frac{1}{4}$), and,

$$p_1A = W\{[(eh_1)/(s + c_0)] + 1 + R\}$$

in which $R = W_p/W$; W = the weight in tons, of a drop hammer or falling weight of powerhammer; W_p = weight, in tons, of pile, helmet, dolly (if any) and parts of power-hammer resting on the head of the pile; h_1 = effective fall in inches of the hammer, assumed to be 0·8 of the free fall of a winch operated hammer, and 0·9 of the stroke of a power hammer; s = penetration in inches of pile for one blow (= $1/n$, if n is the number of blows per final inch of penetration); c_0 = a temporary compression factor (see below); and e = efficiency of the hammer blow, depending on the ratio R, of the weight of the pile etc, to the weight of the hammer, and the material and condition of the head of the pile; e, has the following values:

$R = \dfrac{W_p}{W}$	$\frac{1}{2}$	1	$1\frac{1}{2}$	2	3	4	r
Case 1	0·75	0·63	0·55	0·50	0·42	0·36	$\frac{1}{2}$
Case 2	0·70	0·55	0·46	0·40	0·33	0·28	$\frac{1}{3}$
Case 3	0·69	0·53	0·44	0·37	0·30	0·25	$\frac{1}{4}$
Case 4	0·67	0·50	0·40	0·33	0·25	0·20	0

The references in the foregoing are as follows; Case 1: Double-acting hammer driving a steel pile without a helmet. Case 2: Single-acting or drop hammer driving steel box-pile with helmet and short dolly. Case 3: Hammer as in Case 2, driving a timber pile or a concrete pile, with helmet and packing and with a dolly in good condition. Case 4: As Case 3, but with pile head or dolly in poor condition. The term r, is the coefficient of restitution. If the pile is driven down to impenetrable rock, e should be calculated from $e = (2 + Rr^2)/(2 + R)$. Preferably the ratio, R, should be about unity, but for heavy concrete piles this is not usually practicable. A heavy hammer with a small drop is preferable to a lighter hammer with a greater drop, although the value of Wh_1 may be the same in each case. The temporary compression factor is $c_0 = 0{\cdot}5\ (c_1 + c_2)$, in which c_1 is the temporary elastic compression of the pile and the quake of the ground, and c_2 is the elastic compression of the helmet, dolly, etc. Some values of c_2, for p_1 = 0·5 t/in^2 (and pro-rata for other driving pressures), are:

Hammer blow taken by timber dolly in helmet (or directly on a timber pile)	0·10 in
With 3 in packing under helmet	0·15 in
With 1 in pad on head of concrete pile	0·05 in

For steel piles driven by a double-acting hammer without a helmet, $c_2 \pm 0$. The value of c_1 should, if possible, be determined by actual measurement while the pile is being driven. It can be recorded on a card, attached near the head of the pile, by slowly drawing a pencil across a straight edge held close to the pile (Fig. 11). If such measurement cannot be made, the following approximate values of c_1 can be assumed; for other values of p_1, between 0·25 and 1 ton per t/in², values of c_1 can be interpolated.

Length of Pile (ft)	Timber Piles $p_1 = \frac{1}{2}$	Timber Piles $p_1 = 1$	Concrete and Steel Piles $p_1 = \frac{1}{2}$	Concrete and Steel Piles $p_1 = 1$
30	0·34	0·53	0·28	0·41
40	0·42	0·69	0·34	0·53
50	0·50	0·85	0·40	0·65
60	0·58	1·00	0·46	0·77

For piles driven to rock or other relatively incompressible ground, the allowance for quake should be deducted from the foregoing values, the amounts being 0·1 in for p_1 = 0·5 t/in², and 0·05 in for p_1 = 1 t/in².

The procedure for applying the Hiley formulae is to assume a value for p_1, and then substitute appropriate values in the right-hand side of the formula for p_1A, and compare the result with the assumed value of p_1 multiplied by A; if there is much difference, another trial value of p_1 should be made. If piles are driven to a batter (or rake), the calculated value of p_1A must be reduced by 2% if the slope is 1 in 8; 4% if 1 in 5; 5½% if 1 in 4; 8% if 1 in 3; and 14% if 1 in 2.

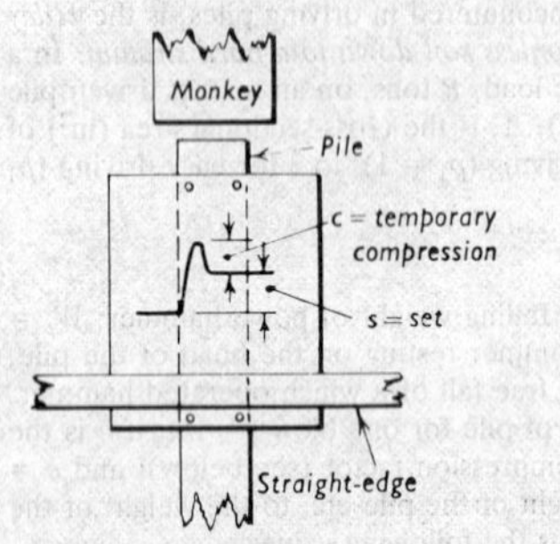

FIG. 11.—Measurement of Temporary Compression of Pile.

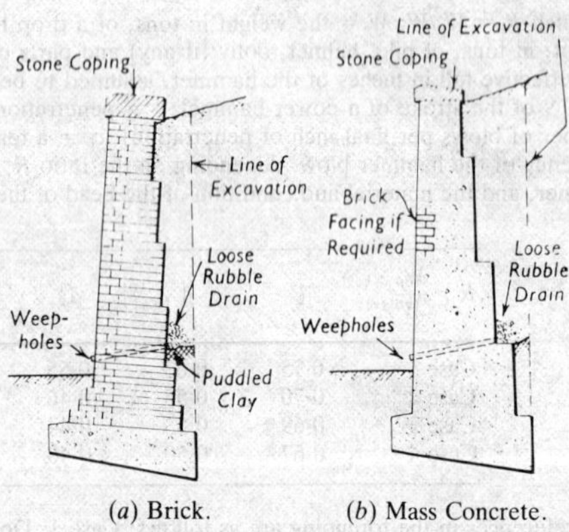

(*a*) Brick. (*b*) Mass Concrete.

FIG. 12.—Gravity Retaining Walls.

The *stress-wave theory* for calculating the resistance of the ground to penetration of an impact-driven pile has gained acceptance in place of the ordinary impact formulae.

It is also possible to calculate the probable load carrying capacity of a pile, particularly a *friction pile*, from consideration of soil mechanics, and the following formula is put forward by Mr. Button (*Journal Jun Inst of Engrs*, March, 1952). For a pile in clay having a cohesion or shearing strength of c lb/ft², the safe load, in lb is given by

$$P = 1/F[0{\cdot}5A_sc + A_1(7{\cdot}5c + wL)]$$

where the notation is the same as in the Hiley and Faber formulae with the additional symbols: L = embedded length (ft), of pile; w = density of the soil (lb/ft³) through which the pile is driven; A_1 = cross-sectional area of pile (ft²). All factors in the above formulae are in imperial units.

EARTH-RETAINING STRUCTURES

TYPES OF RETAINING WALLS.—Structures holding up banks of earth are called *retaining walls*, which are designed primarily to withstand the forward pressure of the retained earth. Various types of walls are shown in Figs. 12, 13 and 14. The stability of walls of brick, masonry, or plain concrete (with or without a facing of brick), depends principally on the weight of the wall, and such walls are generally termed *gravity walls*. The stability of most types of *reinforced concrete walls*, however, depends largely on the counterbalancing effect of the weight of the earth on an integral base extending backward under the bank of earth, as in Fig. 13(*b*). If site conditions do not permit the base to extend far enough behind the wall to obtain sufficient counterweight, the base is projected forward as well as backward, and in the extreme condition in (*a*), the base may extend wholly forward, in which case the stability is due primarily to the weight of the wall alone. In designs Fig. 13(*a*) and (*b*), the wall itself is a simple vertical cantilever. If the wall exceeds 3·5 m in height, it may be more economical to provide vertical counterforts and to span the intermediate panels of wall horizontally between them. For very high walls, the panel may be stiffened by horizontal beams which transfer, to the counterforts, the horizontal forces due to the earth pressures on the vertically-spanning slabs. Whatever design is adopted, the underlying principle is that the wall as a whole acts as a vertical cantilever.

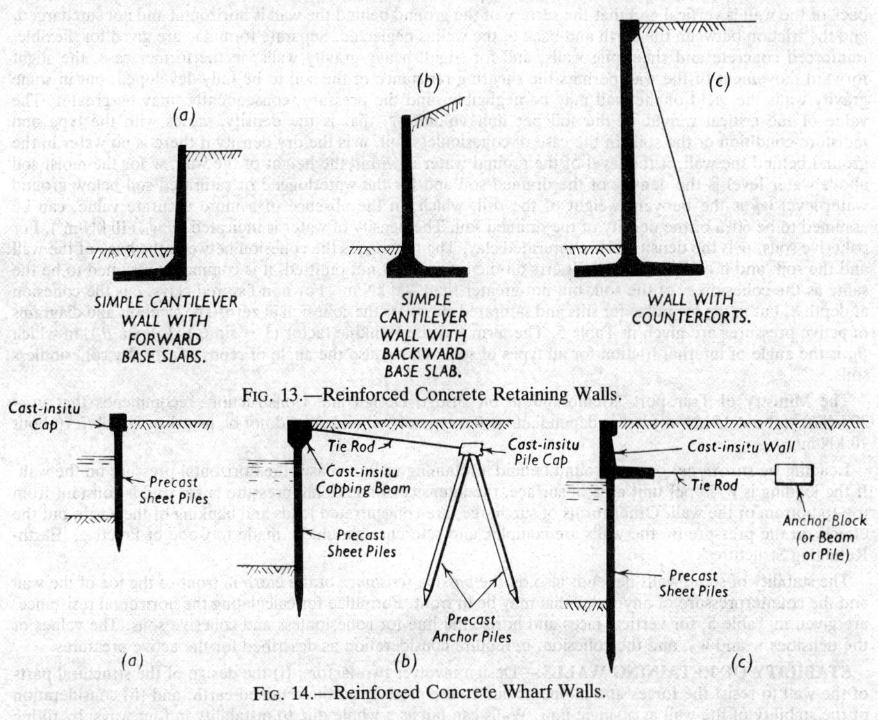

FIG. 13.—Reinforced Concrete Retaining Walls.

FIG. 14.—Reinforced Concrete Wharf Walls.

Sheet-pile walls comprise close-fitting sheeting driven into the ground in front of the retained bank to a depth sufficient to ensure that the sheeting will not move forward and to develop sufficient restraint to the vertical cantilever effect. The sheeting may be reinforced concrete piles or steel piles; in some cases of low walls, timber sheeting may be suitable. Sheet-pile walls are generally suitable for cases where the foot of the retained bank is in water, under which conditions excavation for the foundations of other types of walls would be difficult. Many marine and riverside structures such as wharves, dockwalls, and the like, are primarily retaining walls. Simple types of sheet-pile walls with precast reinforced concrete sheet piles are illustrated in Fig. 14. The heads of the sheet piles are embedded in a simple capping beam. The sheet piles may cantilever directly from the ground as in Fig. 14(*a*), or may be tied back at the top as in Fig. 14(*b*). The tie-rod is anchored to a block of concrete, or to precast anchor piles, as in Fig. 14(*b*). For higher walls it is more economical to place the tie-rod some distance below the top of the wall, and to construct a cantilever cast-in-place wall over the sheet piles, as in Fig. 14(*c*). In all cases it is most important that the sheet piles are driven sufficiently far below the bed of the waterway to ensure freedom from forward movement, spewing, and overturning. Timber and steel-sheet piles are also used for the temporary retention of earth during excavation; these aspects are dealt with in the following section, 'Earthwork'.

A more recent development is the so-called 'reinforced earth' wall in which the concrete (or other) facade is restrained by straps embedded in the earth behind the wall.

Much theoretical and practical data relating to the design of retaining walls is given in 'Earth Retaining Structures' (Civil Engineering Code of Practice No 2; *Inst of Structural Engineers*). The basic principles only are given in the following.

PRESSURES ON RETAINING WALLS.—The *active pressure* on the back of a retaining wall depends on the height of the wall and the nature and moisture content of the retained soils; the slope of the top of the retained bank; the loading (surcharge) on the bank, and to some extent on the type of the wall. Several earth pressure theories have been put forward, some of which are supported by test results. The probable pressures can be calculated from the formulae in Table 5 (which are based on those in Code of Practice No 2, *ante*, although not identical in all cases). It is important to differentiate between cohesive and cohesionless soils. Some values of the angle of internal friction θ_1, cohesion c, and the weight per unit volume of common types of soil, on which factors depend the intensity of horizontal pressure p_h, at any depth h, below the surface of the retained bank, are given in Table 2. When values of these factors can be obtained from tests on the actual soils to be retained, such values should be given preference. In the formulae in Table 5, it is assumed that the back of the wall is vertical and that the surface of the ground behind the wall is horizontal and not surcharged, and the friction between the earth and back of the wall is neglected. Separate formulae are given for 'flexible' reinforced concrete and sheet-pile walls, and for 'rigid' heavy gravity walls; in the former case, the slight forward movement of the wall permits the shearing resistance of the soil to be fully developed, but in some gravity walls the yield of the wall may be negligible, and the pressure, consequently, may be greater. The value of the critical weight of the soil per unit volume w, that is the density, varies with the type and moisture-condition of the soil. In the case of cohesionless soil, w is the dry density if there is no water in the ground behind the wall; if the level of the ground water is within the height of the wall, w for the moist soil above water level is the density of the drained soil and for the waterlogged or saturated soil below ground water-level w_B is the buoyant weight of the soil, which, in the absence of a more accurate value, can be assumed to be 60% of the density of the drained soil. The density of water is indicated by w_W (10 kN/m^2). For cohesive soils, w is the density of the saturated clay. The term c_w, is the cohesion between the back of the wall and the soil, and if omitted, the result errs on the safe side; if not omitted, it is commonly assumed to be the same as the cohesion c, of the soil, but not greater than 400 kN/m^2. For non-fissured clays, c is the cohesion at depth h, but in the formulae for silts and saturated clays, c is the cohesion at zero. The symbols and diagrams of active pressures are given in Table 5. The term k is the Rankine factor $(1 - \sin\theta_1)/(1 + \sin\theta_1)$, in which θ_1, is the angle of internal friction for all types of soils, and is also the angle of repose θ, for dry cohesionless soils.

The Ministry of Transport 'Memorandum on Bridge Design and Construction' recommends that $p_h = 30\,h$ lb/ft^2 (about 15 kN/m^2) but is dependent on the type of soil and should not be less than $20\,h$ lb/ft^2 (about 10 kN/m^2).

Loading (ie *surcharge*) on the ground behind a retaining wall increases the horizontal pressure on the wall. If the loading is w_s lb per unit area of surface, the intensity of additional pressure is kw_s and is constant from top to bottom of the wall. Other forms of surcharge, are concentrated loads and banking of the earth, but the effects on the pressure on the walls are complex and reference should be made to Code of Practice, 'Earth-Retaining Structures'.

The stability of some walls depends also on the *passive resistance* of the earth in front of the toe of the wall and the counterpressure of any water that may be in front. Formulae for calculating the horizontal resistance, are given in Table 5, for vertical faces and horizontal line for cohesionless and cohesive soils. The values of the densities w and w_B, and the cohesion, c, require consideration as described for the active pressures.

STABILITY OF RETAINING WALLS.—Design involves two factors: (i) the design of the structural parts of the wall to resist the forces and moments due to the pressure of the retained earth; and (ii) consideration of the stability of the wall as a single unit. Walls can fail as a whole due to instability in four ways; by tilting and overturning; by sliding forward; by slipping of the mass of earth behind the wall and on which the wall is founded; and by settlement of the ground under the foundation due to excessive bearing pressure.

Resistance to *tilting* or *overturning* is provided simply by providing sufficient weight to counteract the overturning effects. The total active pressure, P, behind the wall (Fig. 15(*a*)), is calculated from the area of the pressure diagram (as in Table 5), which in most cases is a triangle, although part of the diagram may be rectangular due to pressure due to surcharge. The height H_p, at which P acts is the distance from the foundation level to the centroid of the pressure diagram, that is, in the simple case of a wall retaining a granular material with a non-surcharged level filling, $h_p = H/3$ and $P = p_{max}\,H/2$ per unit length of wall. The wall tends to overturn about the front of the toe A, and the overturning moment about this point is Ph_p. The resistance to overturning is provided primarily by the total weight W, of the wall and its base and any earth superimposed on the base, and corresponds to the shaded-area in Fig. 15(*a*). Since the earth, generally, has a lower density than that of the material of which the wall is constructed, the difference must be taken into account when calculating W and the centre of gravity of the shaded-area. If X is the distance from A to the vertical line of action of W, the moment of the forces resisting overturning, is WX. There is, in addition to W, the stabilising effect of the pressure of the earth in front of the toe of the wall, but, whether the active or passive pressure

TABLE 5.—EARTH PRESSURES ON RETAINING WALLS.
Vertical Wall. Level fill. Friction on back of wall neglected. $k = (1 - \sin\theta_1)/(1 + \sin\theta_1)$. θ_1 = Angle of Internal Friction.

	Type of soil	Conditions		Expressions for Intensity of Horizontal Pressures: Reinforced Concrete Walls, Sheet-pile Walls, Etc.	Expressions for Intensity of Horizontal Pressures: Heavy Gravity Walls	Pressure Diagrams
Active Pressures (p_h)	Cohesionless ($c = 0$)	Dry soil and drained soil above ground water level ($h < h_w$)		$[kwh]$ (1)	$[k'wh]$ (1a) k' for sands $= 0{\cdot}4$ to $0{\cdot}6$	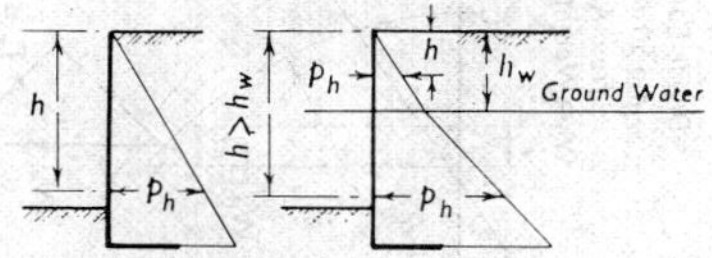
		Saturated soil below ground level level ($h > h_w$)		$[kwh_w + (kw_B + w_w)(h - h_w)]$ (2)	$[k'wh + w_w(h - h_w)]$ (2a)	
	Cohesive	Non-fissured clays ($\theta_1 = 0$) (c at depth h) and Fissured clays (c for softened clay)		$h > h_0$ $[wh - 2c\sqrt{(1 + c_w/c)}]$ (3)	As formulae (1a) and (2a)	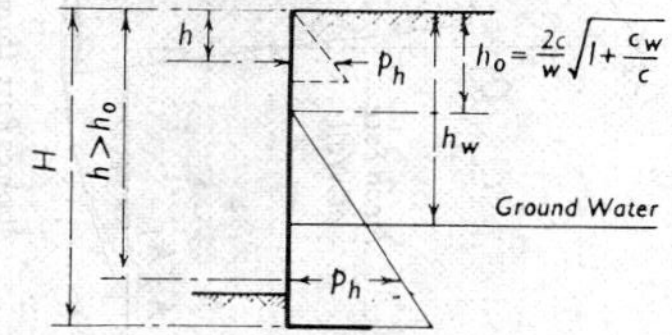
				$h < h_0 \ngtr 5$ ft $\ngtr 0{\cdot}5$H $[w_w h]$ (4)		
		Silts and partially-saturated clays ($\theta_1 > 0$)	Above ground water level $h < h_w$	$[kwh - 2c\sqrt{k}]$ (Bell's formula) (5)	Ordinary clay: $k' = \frac{1}{2}$ to $\frac{3}{4}$	
			Below ground water level $h > h_w$	$[kwh_w + (kw_B + w_w)(h - h_w) - 2c\sqrt{k}]$ (6)	Highly compressed clays: $k = 1$	
Passive Pressures (p_p)	Cohesionless ($c = 0$)	Dry soil and drained soil above ground water level		$h < h_w$	$[wh/k]$	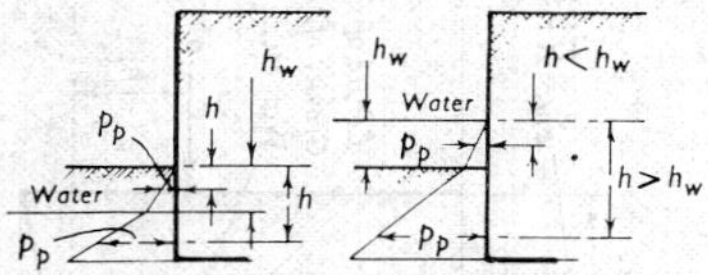
		Saturated soils below ground water level		Water level below ground: $h > h_w$ $[wh_w/k + (w_B/k + w_w)(h - h_w)]$	Water level above ground: $h < h_w$ $[w_w h]$ $h > h_w [(w_B/k)(h - h_w) + w_w h]$	
	Cohesive	Non-fissured clays ($\theta_1 = 0$)		$wh + 2c/\sqrt{k}]$		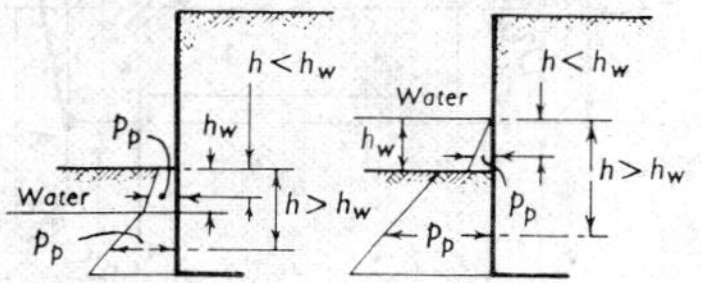
		Silts and partially-saturated clays ($\theta_1 > 0$)	$h < h_w$	Water level below ground: $[wh/k + 2c/\sqrt{k}]$	Water level above ground: $[w_w h]$	
			$h > h_w$	$\left[wh_w/k + \left(\frac{w_B}{k} kw_w\right)(h - h_w) + \frac{2c}{\sqrt{k}}\right]$	$\left[\frac{w_B}{k}(h - h_w) + w_w h + \frac{2c}{\sqrt{k}}\right]$	

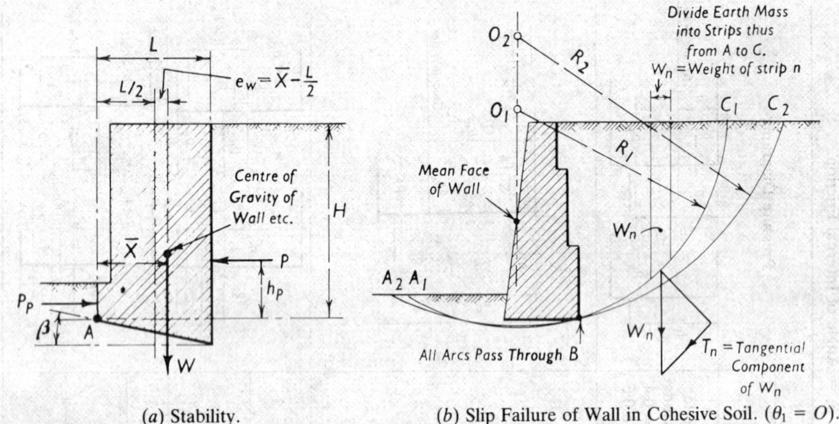

(*a*) Stability.

(*b*) Slip Failure of Wall in Cohesive Soil. ($\theta_1 = O$).

Shaded area represents cross-sectional area of wall and any earth carried on base.

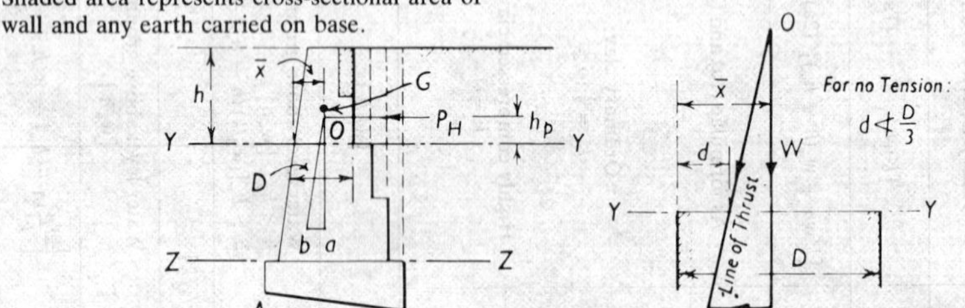

(*c*) Line of Thrust

FIG. 15.—Design of Retaining Walls.

of this earth is considered, the resulting counter-moment is generally so small that, except in the case of sheet-pile walls, it should be neglected and considered as additional factor of safety. For stability to be established, WX must not be less than Ph_p, and since a factor of safety F_T, of about 1·5 or more, is desirable, the design condition is $WX = F_T P h_p$.

Resistance to *sliding*, that is, to the tendency of the entire wall to slide foward on its foundation, due to the horizontal pressure of the retained earth, is provided by the frictional resistance between the ground and the bottom of the foundation. If the coefficient of friction is μ, the frictional resistance is $W\mu$, which must equal, or exceed, the force P, tending to cause sliding. With a factor of safety F_s (not less than 1·5), the design condition is $W\mu = F_s P$, or if the bottom of the foundation is inclined upwards towards A, $W(\mu + \sin\beta) = F_s P$. It is important that a rational value should be attributed to μ, which for gravel and the like may be about one-third, but on wet clays it may approach zero. (See 'Friction', in chapter, 'Mechanics'.) In such cases, resistance to sliding must be provided by the passive pressure in front of the toe of the wall, and if this is insufficient, a heel must be provided extending downwards at the back of the wall to increase the passive resistance to a total of P_p. Since the calculation of the passive resistance by the method described previously may err on the high side, it is necessary to allow for a higher factor of safety than 1·5, or, to assume that the probable value of this resistance is half the calculated value, in which case the design condition is $P_p = F_s P$. In the general case when $\mu > O$, and part of the passive resistance is allowed for, $W(\mu + \sin\beta) + p_p = F_s P$. It is important to remember that the passive resistance can only be mobilised by means of movement of the wall; if such movement is unacceptable, the resistance to sliding must be provided by friction and active resistance alone.

The tendency for the retained bank of earth to slip as a whole and carry the retaining wall with it (Fig. 15(*b*)), is a similar problem to the slipping of the sides of cuttings and should be dealt with as described in the succeeding section, 'Earthwork'. This form of failure is only likely in the case of walls retaining banks of clay. Referring to Fig. 15(*b*), the stability against slipping is determined as follows. The length of the arc of the slip circle from A_1 to $C_1 = L_1$. If the cohesion of the soil is C, the resistance to slipping is $L_1 C$, which must not be less than $F\Sigma T_n$, where T_n is the tangential component of W_n, the weight of an elemental slip of soil; and F is a factor of safety. It is necessary to draw a number of arcs or radius, R_1, R_2, etc, to determine which gives the minimum factor of safety, which should not be less than 2.

Consideration of the *foundation* of a retaining wall is similar to that for any other foundation subjected to an eccentric load. In the case of a wall foundation, the vertical load is W. The effect of the eccentricity e_w, of W, and the moment Ph_p, due to P, is to impose a resultant moment of $Ph_p - We_w$ on the ground. The pressures on the ground are then calculated, from the formulae given in section, 'Properties of Soils', with $e = Ph_p/(W - e_w)$, and obviously, the maximum pressure must not exceed the safe bearing resistance of the ground (Table 2). In this expression it is assumed that $e_w = \overline{X} - L/2$, that is, that the line of action of W, falls to the right of the centre of the base; if it falls to the left (which is not desirable), $e_w = (L/2) - X$.

TABLE 6.—PERMISSIBLE COMPRESSIVE STRESSES IN GRAVITY RETAINING WALLS.

Brickwork*		Masonry		Portland Cement Concrete (Non-reinforced)	
Type	Tonnes per m²	Type	Tonnes per m²	Mix	Tonnes per m²
Common Bricks		Rubble in Portland			
In Lime Mortar	40–50	Cement Mortar	45	1:4:8	90
In Portland		Limestone	100	1:3:6	110
Cement Mortar	55	Sandstone	130	1:2:4	165
Stock Bricks	90	Granite	130		
Blue (Eng'g)	130				
Bricks in PC Mortar					

* See also 'Brickwork' (chapter 'Building') and 'Bricks' (chapter 'Cements, Mortars, etc')

DESIGN OF RETAINING WALLS.—The design of the structural parts of a retaining wall depends on the type of wall. A primary factor in a *gravity wall* (Fig. 12), is to provide enough weight to result in sufficient resistance to overturning and sliding in accordance with the design conditions established in the preceding paragraphs, and yet not to exceed the safe bearing capacity of the ground. 'Rules for Retaining Walls', giving the thicknesses of walls of concrete and brickwork in proportion to their height, are often quoted, but should be used with caution since the pressures from different types of soil vary so considerably that no single set of rules can apply to all cases. Since the design of retaining walls is a matter of trial and error, such rules may be useful in giving a first trial section, which must be checked against actual conditions and modified accordingly. With this proviso, some rules are given as follows: plain mass concrete walls should have a mean thickness of $H/4$ with a back batter of 1 to 5 built in steps, giving a thickness at the top of about $H/7$ and at the bottom $H/3$; the foundation slab may have to be wider than this to restrict the pressure on the ground. Brick walls should have a thickness at the top of about 0·6 m, a batter on the front face not exceeding 1–6 (otherwise moisture may penetrate and vegetable growth occur in the joints); at the back, an offset of half a brick for every five courses from the top should be provided. The concrete base should be proportioned to suit the permissible ground pressure. Long brick walls should have counterforts at the back.

In walls of plain concrete, brick, or masonry, no tensile stress must be developed, and therefore, throughout the height of the wall the line of thrust must not be outside the middle-third of the section. The analysis of conditions at any plane YY, at depth h, from the top, is shown in Fig. 15(c). First calculate the weight W, of the part of the wall and any earth carried by the wall above YY; determine $\overline{X}$, the position of the centre of gravity of this part of the wall and earth. Also determine the magnitude P_h, and position h_p, of the total horizontal pressure on the back of the wall for the height, h. To some convenient force scale set out Oa equal to W, and ab equal to P. Join Ob, and where this line cuts YY, measure the distance, d, which should be no greater than $D/3$. An important plane to be investigated on these lines is ZZ, at the top of the foundation, as this may generally be the critical position as regards stresses in the material of which the wall is constructed. The maximum compressive stress, c_{max}, in the material, can be calculated from

$$c_{max} = W/D + (6/D^2)[P_h h_p - W(\overline{X} - D/2)].$$

If all dimensions are in metres and P and W are in tonnes/m of wall, the stress c_{max}, is in tonnes/m². This formula assumes that $\overline{X} > 0{\cdot}5\ D$; if otherwise, the expression involving W should be $\approx W(0{\cdot}5D - X)$. Some permissible values of c_{max}, for walls, are given in Table 6.

Some types of *reinforced concrete retaining walls* are illustrated in Fig. 13. The first step in the detail design of walls of the types shown in Fig. 13(a) and 13(b) is to determine the bending moment at the bottom of the stem of the wall due to cantilever action resisting the horizontal pressure. Then, from the formulae and stresses given in chapter, 'Concrete: Reinforced and Prestressed', the thickness and reinforcement are determined. The principal reinforcement is placed near the back face of the wall, the thickness of which and the reinforcement in which can be reduced towards the top, as the bending moment falls off rapidly to zero at the top. A minimum thickness of 125 mm is advisable to facilitate placing of the concrete. The width of the base slab is determined so as to give the required stability against tilting, and the thickness and reinforcement at the junction with the wall is made the same as that at the bottom of the wall. The reinforcement is placed near the top face of the base slab behind the wall, which slab is sloped, downwards, away from the wall to facilitate drainage. In the type in Fig. 13(*c*) the wall slab spans horizontally, and it is sufficient if the maximum bending moments per strip of unit width at depth h, are calculated from $p_h L^2/12$, if L is the distance between centres of counterforts. This bending moment determines the thickness of the slab and the amount of principal reinforcement at various heights. The principal reinforcement in the wall slab spans horizontally and is on the back face at the counterforts, and on the front face for a length of the panel midway between the counterforts. The counterforts are designed as vertical cantilevers resisting the whole of the pressure P_T, on the back of the wall for the length L, that is, the bending moment is $P_T h_p$, where h_p is the height above the base of the line of action of P_T. The principal reinforcement resisting this bending moment is at the back sloping edge of the counterfort. The resistance of the counterfort to the shearing force P_T, must be provided for, as described in chapter, 'Concrete: Reinforced and Prestressed'. The base slab is designed more or less in the same manner as the base slab of the wall in Fig. 13(*b*), but provision must be made for the bending moment due to spanning longitudinally between the counterforts.

Sheet pile Walls with concrete sheet-piles, as in Fig. 14, or similar walls with steel sheet-piles are designed more or less in the same way, and some data is given in Code of Practice, 'Earth Retaining Structures'. A steel-pile wall may be a simple cantilever, similar to the concrete pile wall in Fig. 14(*a*), or, the cantilevering

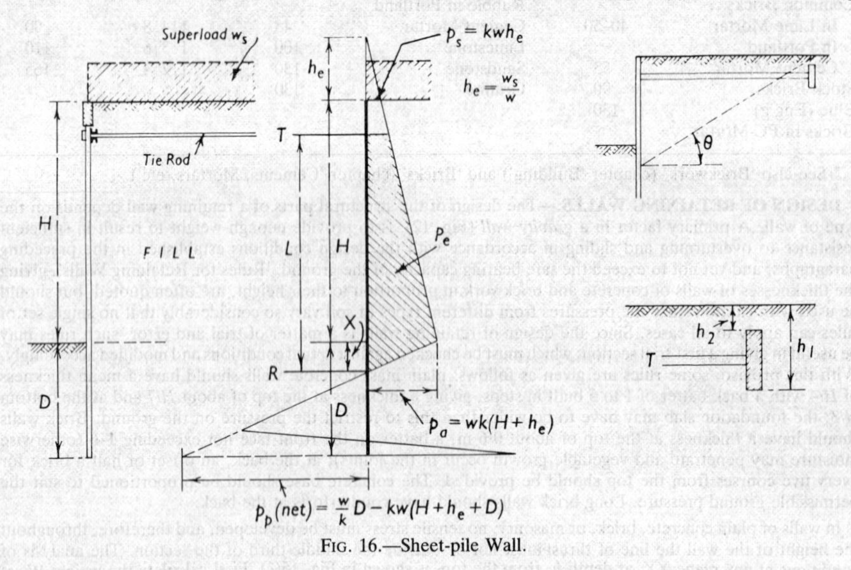

FIG. 16.—Sheet-pile Wall.

piling may be backed with cast-in-place concrete, for which it forms permanent formwork. A steel sheet-pile wall, similar to the concrete walls in Fig. 14(*b*) or 14(*c*), comprises a waling fixed in front of the piles and anchored by tie-rods to a concrete block, or other anchorage, buried in the ground some distance behind the wall. In this type of construction the piles are designed to span vertically and are generally considered to act as a simply-supported beam between the waling and a 'fulcrum', point, that is, some point between the river-bed and the toes of the piles. Another form of steel sheet-pile wall is for ordinary square steel or concrete piles (king piles), to be driven at regular intervals along the front of the structure; walings are fixed to the back of these piles; steel sheet-piles, penetrating only a small distance into the river-bed, are driven behind the walings. The king piles are anchored to concrete blocks with tie-rods. A common method of designing a sheet-pile wall retaining cohesionless soil is shown in Fig. 16. Let H be the height of the wall, and D represent the distance the piles are driven below the river-bed. The maximum intensity of active pressure p_a, behind the wall at depth H, and of the net passive pressure p_p, in front of the wall are calculated from Table 4, and result in the pressure diagram, as illustrated. The lower point from which the piles are assumed to span, the 'fulcrum' point, is at a distance $\bar{X}$, below the river bed, some values of which are as follows:

Angle of repose of filling θ =	20°	25°	30°	35°
$\bar{X}$ =	0·25h	0·15h	0·08h	0·03h

The span of the sheet-piling is L ft, the distance from the point of contraflexure to the position of the waling and tie-rod. If P_e lb is the total active earth pressure per horizontal unit length on the span (that is, the area of the shaded diagram in Fig. 16), the bending movement to be resisted per unit width of the sheet-piling is

$P_e L/8$ft-lb per ft. The force R, is the reaction on the lower support of a beam of span L, that is, the shearing force at the 'fulcrum' point. The minimum depth of penetration to give a reasonable factor of safety is given by:

$$D = \bar{X} + 1{\cdot}2\sqrt{\{(6Rk)/[w(1 - k^2)]\}}$$

The force T per unit length of wall is the top reaction from the beam of span L, plus the pressure on the piling on the part of the wall above the waling. The waling is designed as a beam bending in a horizontal plane of span equal to the distance between the tie-rod, and subjected to a uniformly-distributed load of T per unit length. The tie-rods are each designed to take a minimum tensile force of T lb, multiplied by the distance between the tie-rods, plus about 20%, to allow for redistribution of the pressures. The effective cross-sectional area of the tie-rod is the area at the bottom of the threads. The concrete anchor blocks or wall must resist, by passive resistance of the earth in front of the block, the pull in the tie-rod multiplied by an adequate factor of safety of 1·5–2. The passive resistance is calculated from Table 5, and is: $(w/2k)(h_1^2 - h_2^2)$; the depths h_1 and h_2 are denoted on Fig. 16. The anchorage should be placed well behind the wall, and at least behind the line drawn from the 'fulcrum' point at the angle of repose θ (Fig. 16).

EARTHWORK

Earthwork comprises the operation of excavating and levelling for foundations and the like, tunnelling, forming cuttings, and building embankments and earth dams. Complementary to these operations are such temporary works as timbering, cofferdams, etc.

EXCAVATION.—The operation of excavation is done either by hand or machines, or by these two methods in combination. If the material to be excavated is entirely below water, dredging or a similar method is used. For details of the machines and equipment for excavating and handling earth see section, 'Earthwork Plant'. In *dry soil*, excavation to a moderate depth does not generally present any difficulty, although temporary timbering or the like is usually required if the depth exceeds 1 m. In *waterlogged ground*, it is generally necessary to keep the excavation dry by one of the following means. If the inflow of water is not excessive, it can be allowed to flow to sumps in the bottom of the excavation and is removed therefrom by pumps. If the water cannot be dealt with by pumping, it is necessary to isolate the site of the excavation by surrounding it by a cofferdam, or to sink cylinders or caissons, with or without use of compressed air. In some cases, the level of the ground water can be lowered by wells from which the water is pumped. Alternatively, if the nature of the ground permits, chemical-consolidation and electro-osmosis methods may be used. Some of these are described later.

TIMBERING.—Excavations must be timbered (or sheeted with timber or steel sheet-piles), if the ground cannot stand without support to make possible the construction of the work, to ensure the safety of the men engaged upon it, and to prevent settlement which may result in damage to adjacent buildings or other structures, mains and roads. Settlement may result in movement of the timbering, because disturbance of loose ground may exert a pressure on the timbering greater than that exerted by the undisturbed ground. The amount of timbering required depends on the nature of the ground and the length of time during which the excavation is to remain open, and may range from an occasional support, to covering completely the excavated faces. In extreme cases it may be necessary to timber the bottom of the excavation to prevent the ground from being squeezed upwards by the pressure at the sides. It is important that the area of ground temporarily unsupported during the fixing of timber should be restricted to safe limits. In many cases the ground will stand with little or no support for a short time, but heavy timbering may be required if the excavation is to remain open for a long period. In view of the difficulty of fixing timbering perfectly plumb, and of the possible reduction in the size of the excavation due to distortion under pressure, and, in some cases, due to the swelling of the ground, it is desirable to take out the excavation in excess of the space actually required for the foundation or other work to be constructed.

The timber in contact with the ground comprises poling boards or long timbers (called runners), which are driven down as excavation proceeds. Cavities in the ground behind the timbering should be filled, either with rammed material, bricks, wood or other suitable packing. In loose sand, especially if water be present, the leakage of particles through gaps between the timbers is prevented by stemming, ie packing with hay, straw or similar material, which, although not preventing the flow of water, stops much of the sand. Poling boards and runners are generally of spruce, although pitch pine is preferable and possibly more economical because of its greater durability. Large squared timber is usually of pitch pine. Round struts are often of larch. Wedges may be of beech or other hard wood, although pitch pine is frequently used.

TRENCHES.—Timbering trenches (Fig. 17) comprises the following items and procedure. *Poling boards* are generally from 1 to 1·4 m long and 25–40 mm thick and are held against the ground by longitudinal timbers called *walings*, between which and the boards *pages* (small wedges) are driven. Walings vary from 100 by 50 mm to 360 by 300 mm. If rectangular in cross-section, they are fixed with the longer dimension vertical for convenience, although this is not the most economical way of resisting lateral bending.

The walings are held apart by *struts*, which are preferably square, although round and rectangular timbers are frequently used. In most cases strips of wood called *lips* are nailed to the tops of the struts at the ends to

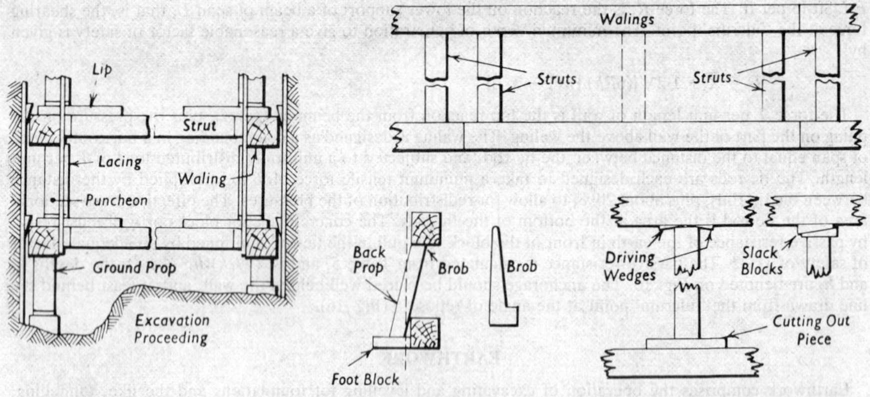

FIG. 17.—Timbering Trenches.

hold them level with the walings while being driven into position. Large wedges, called *driving wedges*, are generally used to tighten up the struts, but in some cases *slack blocks* are provided, as shown in Fig. 17. Steel struts for trenches are now in common use.

When it is anticipated that the pressure on the timbering will force the ends of the struts into the walings, and thereby, making removal of the struts difficult, *cutting-out pieces* are inserted between the struts and the walings when these timbers are fixed, and are removed by cutting away. Struts are fixed at both ends of walings and intermediate struts are added as necessary; the distance apart of the struts depending on the nature of the ground, the size of the walings and the working room required between the struts. Two opposite walings with the struts between them, form a complete frame as shown in Fig. 17. In order to prevent the walings dropping, vertical props, called *puncheons*, are wedged between them, the feet of the puncheons resting on the lips of the struts. *Lacing boards* are also nailed vertically to the face of the walings near their ends. As the excavation proceeds, the lowest waling should be securely propped from the bottom of the excavation. If the bottom of the trench is very soft, it is necessary to prevent settlement of the timbering by

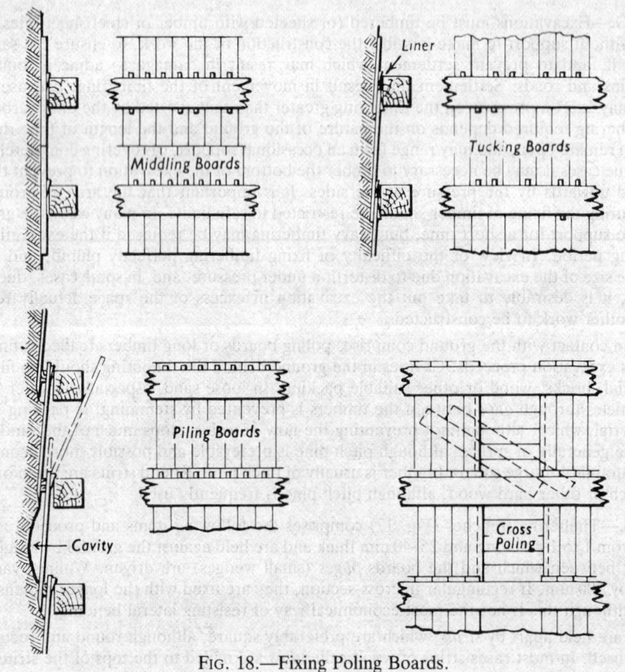

FIG. 18.—Fixing Poling Boards.

slinging it from timbers laid transversely across the top of the trench. To prevent settlement of timbering deep trenches, raking *back props* are inserted under every third or fourth frame, midway between the struts. These props are fixed as excavation proceeds, resting on *foot blocks*.

There are three methods of fixing poling boards, namely the middling-board, tucking board and piling-board methods, which are illustrated in Fig. 18. In the *middling-board* method, each setting of boards is held in position by one waling. It is used in fairly good ground but has the disadvantage that it cannot readily be modified to the piling-board method if bad ground is met below. To fix first setting, the trench is excavated to the requisite depth and the walings are placed in position opposite the points at which the struts are to be fixed. The walings with poling boards behind them rest on temporary supports. Packing pieces, called *chogs*, are put in between the boards and the walings to form a gap, for the pages in front of the boards to be inserted subsequently. The struts are then fixed. The remaining boards are finally placed behind the walings and held against the ground by means of pages driven in behind the walings, usually at the top only, but sometimes also at the bottom. If the ground is firm, the boards are inserted with spaces between them. In the second and lower settings all the boards may be placed in position before the walings are fixed, the lower ends being toed into the ground, or kept in position by pegs or pages driven into the ground, and the tops held by nails driven obliquely into the boards above.

The *tucking-board* method is used if the ground is not good enough for middling-boards, or if bad ground is expected to be met with below. The poling boards are held at both ends. The walings, with the exception of the top setting, have liners of the same thickness as the boards nailed to them. The poling boards above the walings pass behind the liners, and their lower ends are level with or slightly below the bottom of the walings. The boards of the setting below are subsequently tucked into the space below the liners. The fixing of the frames is as described for middling-boards except that the temporary support of the top walings while the struts are inserted, is usually afforded by raking ground props which do not intefere with the fixing of the frame below.

The *piling-board* method is used in bad ground. The boards are usually bevelled at the lower ends and are driven as indicated by the broken lines in Fig. 18. Chogs are first inserted between the liners and the walings and are removed as the driving proceeds. This method has the advantage that the sides of the trench are supported the whole of the time excavation is proceeding, the toes of the boards being kept slightly below the level to which the bottom has been excavated. Although driving commences at a considerable angle from the vertical, the boards assume the right batter as they are driven. To prevent them becoming too vertical, chogs are placed between them and the boards above. A small cavity occurs behind the boards in this method, but can be avoided if the boards are driven slantwise and are gradually righted. When only a small gap is left between boards driven in opposite directions towards each other, the gap is filled with cross poling as shown

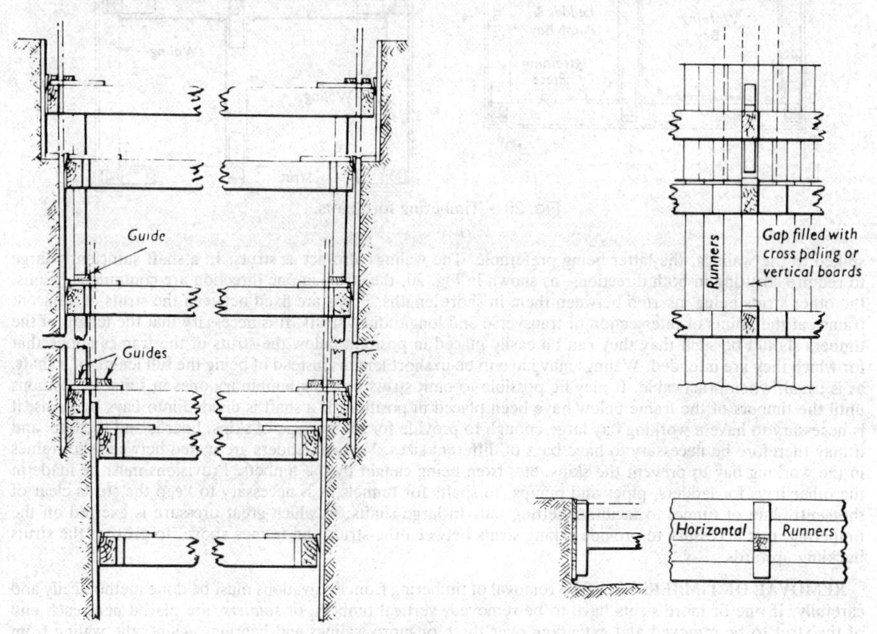

FIG. 19.—Timbering with Runners.

in Fig. 18. If it is necessary to use piling boards below tucking boards, the liners from the walings of the lowest tucking frame are removed.

Runners (Fig. 19), which are used in bad ground instead of poling boards, are timbers 5 m long or more, 50–75 mm thick, and 150–175 mm wide. The lower ends are bevelled and the heads are bound with hoop iron. The runners are driven down behind the frames which are from 1 to 1·5 m apart, the pages being loosened to enable this to be done. The toes of the runners are kept slightly below the bottom of the trench, the sides of which, therefore, are never unsupported. If runners extend the full depth of the trench, the top frame may be at the surface and a guide fixed at a higher level to ensure the runners being driven vertically. A scaffold from which the runners are driven is required. It is sometimes possible to avoid driving until the runners are some distance to the ground. A setting of poling boards is often used at the surface, as shown in Fig. 19, to avoid the use of the guide and reduce the height of the scaffolding, or if the trench is deeper than can be covered by one or more sets of runners. If runners are used below poling boards or runners, an internal frame is needed to enable the runners to be driven in front of the frames above. This necessitates the upper part of the trench being wider. The gaps which occur between the runners, below the struts, are left until the fixing of the frames below enables boards to be inserted, but cross poling is inserted behind the runners as excavation proceeds if the ground is bad. Horizontal runners are used in small trenches (Fig. 19). Sufficient ground is excavated to enable a pair of runners on opposite sides to be placed on edge and temporarily strutted. When several runners are in position, vertical timbers, called *soldiers* are placed and strutted with one or more struts for each pair.

SHAFTS.—The methods of timbering trenches are generally applicable to timbering shafts (Fig. 20) although shafts are generally sunk to greater depths and remain open longer than trenches. It is necessary, therefore, that great care should be taken in timbering. In deep shafts the provision of back props, as previously described, is important. The struts are fixed across the smaller width of a small rectangular shaft. The struts at the end, sometimes called *stretchers*, also act as walings. Lateral movement is prevented by cleats or straining pieces

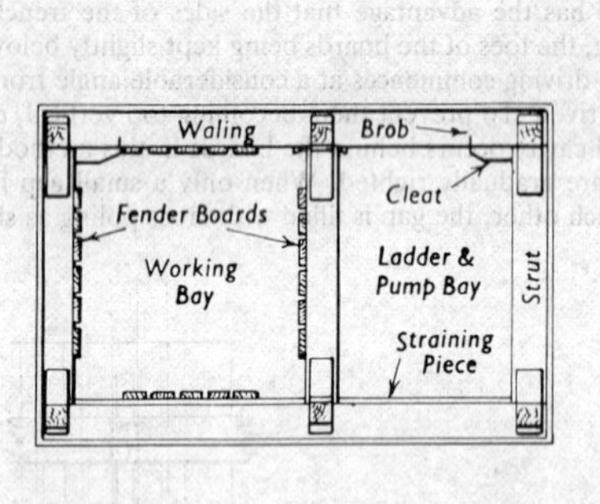

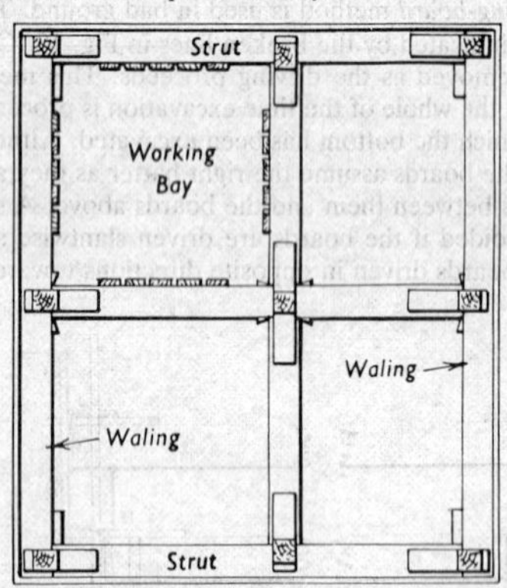

FIG. 20.—Timbering for Shafts.

spiked to the walings, the latter being preferable. The walings also act as struts. In a shaft sufficiently large to require strutting in both directions, as shown in Fig. 20, the struts in one direction are continuous beams, the other struts being inserted between them in short lengths. Props are fixed between the struts of adjacent frames at the points of intersection of transverse and longitudinal struts. It is necessary that the length of the timbers should be such thay they can be easily placed in position below the struts of the frames above that for which they are intended. Walings may have to be in short lengths instead of being the full length of a shaft, as is usual, when practicable. It may be possible to omit struts or to fix temporary ones in suitable positions until the timbers of the frame below have been placed in position. If a shaft is divided into bays by struts, it is necessary to have a working bay large enough to provide for the passage of skips, boards and the like, and it may therefore be necessary to have bays of different sizes. Vertical fenders are nailed between the frames in the working bay to prevent the skips, etc, from being caught by the timbers. Provisions must be made in the other bays for ladders, pipes and pumps. In shafts for tunnels, it is necessary to keep the struts clear of the centre-line of tunnel to facilitate setting out. In large shafts, in which great pressure is exerted on the timbering, it is necessary to provide raking struts between the struts and frames above, to prevent the struts buckling upwards.

REMOVAL OF TIMBERING.—The removal of timbering from excavations must be done methodically and carefully. If one or more struts have to be removed, vertical timbers, or *soldiers*, are placed near each end of the strut to be removed and extending over three or more walings and bearings against the waling from which the strut is to be removed (Fig. 21). The soldiers are held against the walings by means of soldier struts.

Wedges and packings are used to hold the walings securely. When *refilling excavations*, only as much timbering is removed as can be done with safety, and unless the work is so situated that settlement is of no importance, it is essential that the ground should be well supported during refilling. Thorough punning of the refilled material is very important. In some cases all timber is left in; in others the frames are removed, boards or runners being buried. Generally, all timber can be taken out. Frames are removed just in advance of the refilling or construction of the permanent work. If boards only are left in, the securing of a setting of piling or tucking boards by filled-in material or permanent work holds the toe of the setting above, due to overlapping of the settings. Middling boards used in good ground, do not have to be left in. In removing middling boards or tucking boards the ground is unsupported between the removal of a setting of boards and refilling, but piling boards and runners can be gradually withdrawn as the filling proceeds.

SHEET-PILING.—In bad ground and especially in waterlogged ground, timber *sheet-piling* is used in place of runners in the timbering of trenches and shafts. If *timber sheet piles* are used, the toes of the sheet-piles are shod with iron and cut obliquely so that during driving the pile is forced against the adjacent pile. The joints between the piles are caulked with yarn, clay, or other suitable material.

Interlocking *steel sheet-piles* are now used more commonly than timber piles. The cross-section of the pipe is such that for the minimum amount of metal, a pile of great strength in bending or direct load is obtained, thus permitting driving and extraction without distortion. Details of two proprietary steel sheet-piles available in the UK are given in Table 7. Steel sheet-piles are used not only for holding up the faces of excavations, cofferdams and similar temporary work, but for permanent structures such as quay or wharf walls, river-bank retaining walls, and the like.

COFFERDAMS.—Cofferdams are temporary structures to exclude water either from waterlogged ground, a river, or the sea, to enable construction to be carried out in the dry. The most common type is the box type used for bridge piers and the like, such as the *single-wall cofferdam* illustrated in Fig. 22. Steel sheet-piles are driven down into an impermeable stratum. The sheet piling is supported by several settings of bracing with the top waling at water level and the lower walings spaced so that the loads on each are approximately equal. The maximum bending moment on the piling, which occurs between the top and second walings is $w_w h^3/16$ per unit width of filing, where w_w is the density of water (fresh water, 1,000 kg/m^3; sea water, 1,025 kg/m^3), and h is the depth from the top waling (at water level) to the second waling. The section modulus Z of the sheet piling to be used being known (see Table 7), and assuming a safe working stress of f_s, the distance h, is $\sqrt[4]{(f_s Z/w_w)}$. The spacing of lower walings to give approximately equal loads on each, can be expressed as a function of h, and are, successively from the second waling downwards, $0{\cdot}6h$, $0{\cdot}43h$, $0{\cdot}35h$, $0{\cdot}21h$, etc.

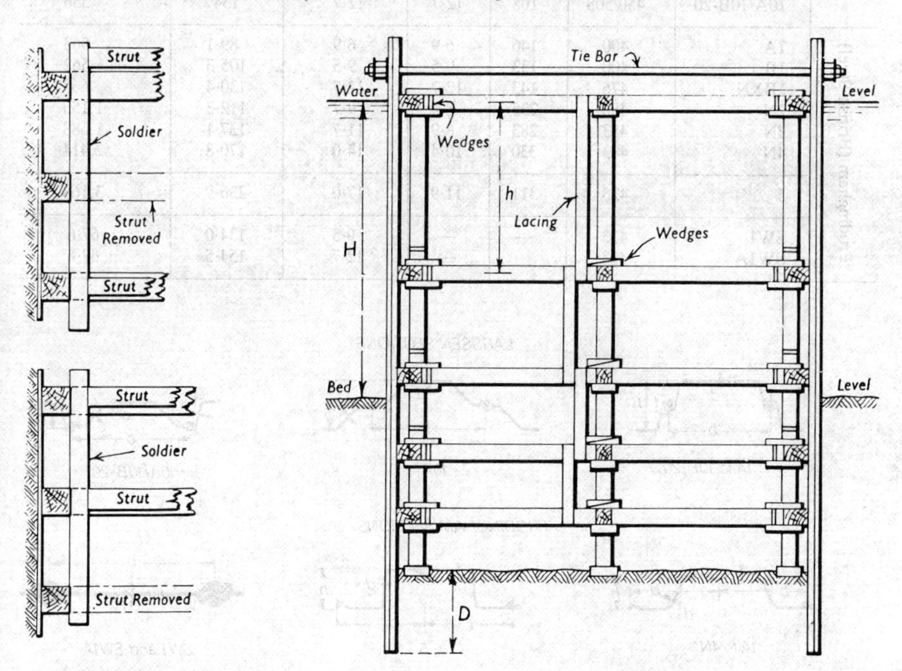

FIG. 21.—Removing Struts.

FIG. 22.—Cofferdam.

The walings are subjected simultaneously to axial thrust and bending, and are generally considered to be freely supported beams unless they are continuous over not less than three spans. The bending movement in most cases, therefore, is $TL^2/8$, where L = distance between strut centres; T = load per unit length of walings; the top waling is subject to about 15% of this load. Struts can be of timber or steel but the end struts will normally act as walings and the direct compressive stress added to the bending stress must not exceed the safe stress. The load on a strut is equal to TL, and half of this on an end strut.

TABLE 7.—STEEL SHEET PILING (See Figures for Profiles).

Type	Section	b mm	h mm	d mm	t (Nominal) mm	Weight kg/m² of wall	Section Modulus mm³ per metre of wall × 10³
Larssen (British Steel Corporation)	1A	400	130	7·2	5·8	84	384
	1B	400	178	7·1	6·4	89	562
	1GB	400	130	8·1	5·8	90	419
	1U	400	130	9·4	9·4	106	489
	2	400	200	10·2	7·8	122	850
	2B	400	270	8·6	7·1	117	1,013
	2N	400	270	9·4	7·1	122	1,101
	3	400	247	14·0	8·9	155	1,360
	3B	400	298	13·5	8·9	155	1,602
	3/20	508	343	11·7	8·4	137	1,665
	4A	400	381	15·7	9·4	184	2,371
	4B	420	343	15·5	10·9	201	2,285
	4/20	508	381	15·7	9·4	171	2,414
	5	420	343	22·1	11·9	238	2,962
	6	420	440	28·6	14·0	330	5,000
	10B/20	508	171	12·7	12·7	131	706
	10A	450	171	12·7	12·7	138	486
	10A/10B-20	450/508	108	12·7	12·7	134	356
Frodingham (British Steel)	1A	400	146	6·9	6·9	89·1	563
	1B	400	133	9·5	9·5	105·3	562
	1BXN	476	143	12·7	12·7	130·4	668
	2N	483	235	8·4	9·7	112·3	1,150
	3N	483	283	8·9	11·7	137·1	1,688
	4N	483	330	10·4	14·0	170·8	2,414
	5	425	311	11·9	17·0	236·9	3,168
	SW1	413	—	—	9·5	134·0	67·6
	SW1A	413	—	—	12·7	154·5	67·6

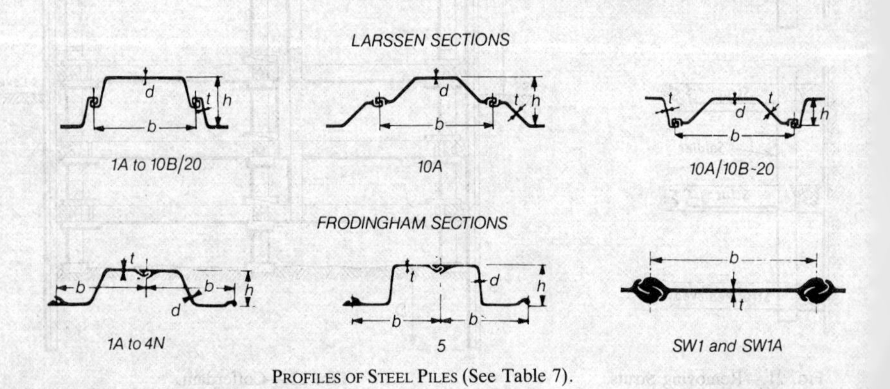

PROFILES OF STEEL PILES (See Table 7).

The stresses to be used for the design of timber walings and struts should be based on the recommendations of BS Code of Practice 112, an extract of which is given in Table 8. The strength of timber depends upon its quality and the stresses (in N/mm^2) given in the Table are for material conforming to the requirements of BS 4978 as regards the size and location of any knots, shakes, splits and wane that are present.

Walings and struts should be securely cleated and preferably bolted together. The first setting is usually suspended from the top of the sheet piling. When the second setting has been installed, it should be supported on puncheons from the ground inside the dam. Puncheons between the first and second settings, and diagonal or vertical lacings should also be provided. The depth D to which the sheet piling is driven must be sufficient to develop sufficient passive resistance to prevent forward movement of the toe of the piling and to provide a seal against percolation of water into the dam. In permeable ground, a complete seal is impracticable and the depth should restrict seepage sufficiently to reduce pumping to a reasonable degree and to prevent the soil being forced up into the dam. Where practicable, the sheeting should be driven through the permeable stratum into an impermeable stratum.

TABLE 8.—STRESSES IN TIMBER USED FOR WALINGS AND STRUTS. (N/mm^2).
BS Code of Practice 112. Timber conforming to BS 4978.

Species	Bending	Compression		Shear Parallel to Grain	Modulus of Elasticity	
		Parallel to Grain	Perpendicular to Grain		Mean*	Minimum
Douglas Fir Longleaf Pitch Pine Shortleaf Pitch Pine	7	7	2·5	0·7	11,250	7,000
Canadian Spruce European Larch Redwood Whitewood Western Hemlock	5·6	5·6	1·8	0·7	8,500	5,300

* *Note.*—The mean value for modulus of elasticity may be used when more than one member supports the load.

Clay-puddle cofferdams generally comprise two parallel rows of sheet piling, the space between being filled with puddled clay. Sometimes three or four rows, with clay puddle filling between each, are necessary to provide sufficient stability and water-tightness. The puddle wall should be as narrow as possible, and is seldom more than 1·5 m thick. Bolts through cofferdams should be avoided since as the puddle settles, cavities formed below the bolts may cause leaks. If bolts are used, a puddle flange should be provided in the middle of the wall. Through bolts are unnecessary if piles are driven outside the dam to resist the pressure from the puddle.

Clay-puddle is a highly plastic paste made by mixing clay with about one-fifth of its weight of water, the precise amount depending on the plasticity and dryness of the clay. A perfectly pure clay does not usually produce good puddle, as it is either deficient in plasticity (like china clay), or it shrinks excessively. The former defect cannot be remedied and a more highly plastic material should be used. Excessive shrinkage may be prevented by mixing sand with the clay. For best results, when dried the linear shrinkage of the puddle should be not more than 12½% nor less than 6¼% or it will probably not be sufficiently impermeable. The materials must be carefully selected and thoroughly mixed. The correct consistency for good puddle is that at which the paste can be squeezed easily in the hand without an appreciable amount adhering. Puddle of the consistency of porridge is much too soft, but it is better than an over-dry or badly mixed stiff paste. A softer mixture of the consistency of mortar is sometimes preferred, but if it is to be tamped it would be too soft. The worst puddle is formed by allowing a slurry of clay to settle. Sand and other non-plastic material segregates and the puddle has too great a shrinkage. If possible, the materials should, before being mixed with water, be passed between a pair of rollers not more than 3 mm apart to crush any stones. Roots and large stones should be picked out before mixing the clay. The usual method of preparing puddle is to mix the available clay in a pugmill, with sufficient water to form a soft paste. The available clay may contain a large proportion of sand and therefore be unable to produce a puddle impermeable to water except within narrow limits of consistency, which are seldom determined. It may, however, be so rich in colloidal matter as to shrink abnormally on drying, thereby causing detrimental cracks, which may be prevented by using a plastic mixture of the clay and very fine sand. The sand and clay must be thoroughly mixed to a uniform consistency by first mixing the clay, sand and water in a pan-mill (mortar mill), and then in a pugmill to consolidate it.

EXCAVATION IN WATERLOGGED GROUND.—In the following some methods for excavating in wet ground are described. Chemical consolidation as described previously (see 'Bearing Resistances'), is also useful.

Dewatering by Well Points is effected by sinking vertical steel pipes, or wells, around the site. The wells are connected to a common suction main or header leading to a central pump. The pipes are from 35–50 mm diameter, 7–10 m long and have at the lower end perforations, corrugations, or flutes to allow the entry of water. Spacing of the pipes is dependent upon the permeability of the ground and depth of excavation below the water-table. A *freezing process* is used if large foundations are to be constructed in waterlogged soft ground, such as quicksand. Pipes 25 cm diameter, open at the bottom, are sunk vertically about 1 m apart around the site to be excavated. Within these pipes are lowered 20 cm diameter pipes, closed at the bottom, and within the latter smaller pipes are inserted. The freezing liquid is pumped into the smaller pipes and returns to the cooling tank through the larger ones. A solid cylinder of frozen ground is gradually formed round the pipes and when these frozen cylinders unite they form a solid ring around the ground to be excavated. Some of the material to be excavated will be frozen and, therefore, more difficult to excavate.

Electro-Osmosis is a process that has been developed for the drainage of fine-grained soil for the stabilisation of excavations. When a current is passed through moist soil, the water travels to the negative electrode which is designed to be a drainage well from which the water can be removed. The application of electro-osmosis is limited because of the high consumption of electricity. (See Building Research Technical Paper No. 30.)

Bentonite Processes.—A number of proprietary systems are available which employ bentonite slurry to retain the sides of trenches in poor ground during excavation and subsequent concreting. The slurry, which is a suspension of clay in water, has thixotropic properties and exerts lateral pressure sufficient to retain the sides of an excavation. In the *ICOS-Veder* and *Terrephragm* systems, dwarf concrete walls are constructed on both sides of the line of the diaphragm wall to ensure correct alignment, to prevent the sides of the trench slipping at ground level, and to act as a reservoir for the bentonite slurry. The trenches are then excavated by special machines, the slurry displacing the material removed. Concrete is then placed by means of a tremie. In the *ETFE Membrane Grouting* system watertight cut-off walls are formed by driving a series of seven special H-section steel piles flange to flange. The rear pile is then withdrawn and the void filled with a slurry of clay, cement, bentonite and water, injected through a pipe welded to one of the piles. The extracted pile is then re-driven as the leading pile and the process repeated.

TUNNELLING.—The excavation of tunnels is a highly-specialised operation, details of which are given in text books on the subject; reference should also be made to technical journals and the proceedings of civil engineering societies which describe the methods adopted to suit the practical conditions encountered in specific works. Recent large-scale tunnelling works in Britain, are the London underground railway extensions; hydroelectric works in Scotland and elsewhere; various sewer installations; and railway tunnels. A feature of recent works is the wider use of mechanical aids to excavation and disposal of spoil. The miner's hand pick is superseded by the pneumatic spader for excavation in *soft ground* such as clays, and in tunnels of small diameter, the resulting speed of construction has been such that no advantage would be derived by the use of a tunnelling shield. In tunnels of larger diameter where a tunnelling shield is employed and the pneumatic spader used, progress has been much quicker, with a smaller number of miners at the tunnel face. Another method of excavation is by the use of a rotary digger shield which is a combination of the ordinary tunnelling shields with six arms to which cutting knives are fixed, rotating about the central axis of the shield. In wet silt and sand and waterlogged ballast, excavation in free air is generally extremely slow, owing to the amount of timbering required and in such cases compressed air is used to hold back the water. Excavation in *rock* such as soft sandstone or chalk, is carried out by pneumatic picks if the use of explosives is forbidden. Generally, excavation in all rocks is expedited by blasting (see chapter, 'Explosives'). In blasting, for efficient working it is necessary to remove the spoil quickly, by installing such equipment as scraper loaders.

A method of contructing comparatively short tunnels of diameters up to about 2·5 m is the *thrust-bore* method, whereby steel or concrete pipes are forced through an embankment or similar ground by jacks, the earth within the pipe being excavated as thrusting proceeds. This method has been used successfully for pipe-ducts, pedestrian subways, and the like, which may be of either circular or rectangular cross-section. The method has also been applied to the construction of abutments for railway bridges.

CUTTINGS.—The stability of the sideslopes of cuttings depends on their slope, height, make-up of different soil types, and most important of all, the ground-water pressure distribution. This latter factor is often neglected by designers, and the use of arbitrary slope angles for different soil types without due regard to their precise soil properties and ground water conditions is inadvisable. In dry non-cohesive soils, however, side slopes equivalent to the angle of shearing resistance may be used, with angles of approximately half of this if the ground water table is high. Attempts should be made to provide drainage in the latter case.

In cohesive soils, *slip circle* methods should be used to assess the stability of side slopes, with a sensible prediction of the long term ground water pressure distribution (say from a flow net) and with the use of effective stress related shear strength parameters. It is *unsafe* to use undrained shear strengths in the analysis of long term cutting side slope stability.

EMBANKMENTS.—In contrast to cuttings, short term (i.e. end of construction) conditions are usually critical for embankment stability. This gives the choice of either the use of undrained shear strengths (simple and cheap) or the use of effective stress shear strengths in combination with assessed pore water pressure build-up in the foundation (more exprensive to do the tests, more complex analysis, but the chance to incorporate strength gains in both fills and the foundation due to consolidation).

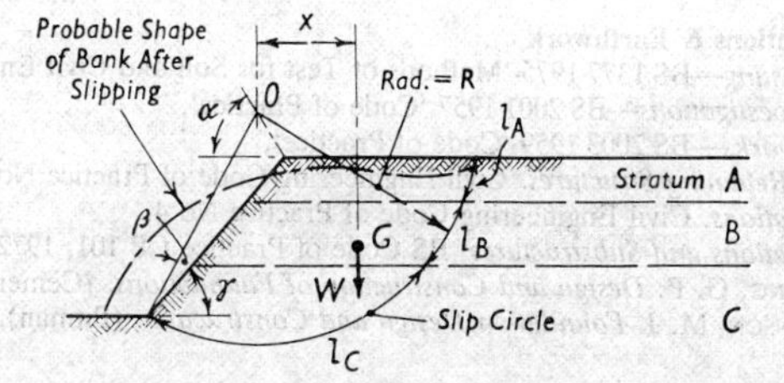

FIG. 23.—Slip Failure of Cutting.

SLIP CIRCLE METHODS.—The stabilility of soil slopes is assessed by investigating the possibility of failure around 'slip circles' drawn on to the slope cross section. Causing destabilisation, there is the moment of the weight of soil bounded by the slope face and the slip surface. This can most easily be estimated by dividing the soil mass into slices, and taking the moment of each about the centre of rotation. Resisting destabilisation is the sum of the moments of the shear resistance from the many segments of slip surface at the base of each slice. In purely cohesive soils this is the strength times the segment length. In frictional soils, the internal forces must be evaluated more rigorously. An account of this is given by Bromhead (1984). A factor of safety can be obtained as the ratio of stabilising to destabilising forces, and the factor of safety for the whole slope is that found for the worst slip circle. Many simple cases have been investigated already, and charts for the evaluation of factors of safety are given by Spencer (1967).

EARTHWORKS MEASUREMENT.—See the chapter 'Surveying' for the measurement of embankment and cutting quantities. Remember that materials will bulk following excavation, and compaction will mean that larger volumes need to be transported than the finished volume of embankment.

SLIPS.—If slips occur, then the strength of soil along the sliding surface may be permanently reduced to a lower bound value termed the 'residual strength'. Remedial measures must be designed on the basis of this reduced strength. Further, when dealing with the previously-landslipped ground (and this may not be obvious if the slips are of great age), the presence of, and the strength along, the major pre-existing sliding surfaces must be investigated. Specialist geotechnical advice should be sought in all but clear cut cases.

DAMS AND WATER RETAINING EMBANKMENTS.—These are dealt with in detail in the chapter, 'Water Engineering'.

BIBLIOGRAPHY

Soil Mechanics

BS 6031:1981 *Code of Practice for Earthworks*

CRAIG, R. F., *Soil Mechanics,* Van Nostrand Reinhold.

SCOTT, C. R., *An Introduction to Soil Mechanics and Foundations,* Applied Science Publications.

KING, H. G. and CRESSWELL, D. A., *Soil Mechanics Related to Building.*

LAMBE, T. W. and WHITMAN, R. V., *Soil Mechanics,* John Wiley.

Soil Testing

BS 1377:1975 *Methods of test for soil for civil engineering purposes.*

BRS Digest 90, *Concrete in sulphate bearing soils and groundwaters.*

BISHOP, A. W. and HENKEL, D. J., *The Measurement of Soil Properties in the Triaxial Test,* Arnold.

HEAD, K. *Manual of Soil Laboratory Testing,* Pentech Press.

VICKERS, *Laboratory Testing in Soil Mechanics,* Crosby, Lockwood and Staples.

BELL, F. G. *Engineering Properties of Soils and Rocks,* Butterworth.

Foundation Design

TOMLINSON, M. J. *Foundation Design and Construction,* Pitman.

TOMLINSON, M. J. *Pile Design and Construction Practice,* Cement and Concrete Association.

BSCP 2004 *Code of Practice for Foundations.*

MANNING, C. P. *Design and Construction of Foundations.* Cement and Concrete Association.

SIMONS, N. E. and MENZIES, B. K. *A Short Course in Foundation Engineering,* I.P.C. Science & Technology.

BSCP 101:1972 *Foundations and superstructures for non-industrial buildings of not more than four storeys.*

Slope Stability

BROMHEAD, E. N. *Slopes and Embankments; Chapter 3 of Ground Movements* (Eds ATTEWELL & TAYLOR) Blackie.

SPENCER, E. E. *A Method of the Analysis of the Stability of Embankments Assuming Interslice Forces,* Geotechnique 17 (1967).

Site Investigations

BS 5930 *Code of Practice for Site Investigations.*

SIMONS, N. E., CLAYTON, C. R. I., and MATTHEWS, M. *Site Investigation,* Granada.

Foundations & Earthwork

Soil Testing—BS 1377 1975 'Methods of Test for Soil and Civil Engineering Purposes'.
Site Investigations—BS 2001 1957 'Code of Practice'.
Earthworks—BS 2003 1959 'Code of Practice'.
Earth Retaining Structures. Civil Engineering Code of Practice No 2.
Foundations. Civil Engineering Code of Practice No 4.
Foundations and Substructures. BS Code of Practice CP 101, 1972.
MANNING, G. P. *Design and Construction of Foundations*. (Cement and Concrete Association).
TOMLINSON, M. J. *Foundation Design and Construction*. (Pitman).

STRUCTURAL CONCRETE

Introduction—Materials for Concrete—Properties of Concrete—Mix Design and Specification—Testing and Quality Control—Site Practice—References—British Standards.

By Dennis Palmer, BSc(Eng), DIC, CEng, MICE.

INTRODUCTION

Concrete is probably the world's most widely used and most versatile construction material. Even when other materials are used—steel, brick, timber—almost every building or civil engineering structure contains concrete somewhere in its construction. In addition, there are few countries in the world where the raw materials for making concrete cannot be found.

Although the development of modern Portland cement, the essential ingredient for most concrete, dates from the first half of the nineteenth century, similar cements and concrete made with them have a far longer history. The earliest known concrete probably is that discovered at Lepenski Vir in Yugoslavia which dates from about 5600 BC. The Romans used concrete extensively and many of their structures, such as the Pantheon in Rome, are still well-known landmarks and tourist attractions. A longer introduction to the history of concrete will be found in reference (1).

This section deals only with structural concrete used as the main load-bearing components of a structure. Other uses of cement and concrete, such as in floor toppings, concrete blocks and blockwork and other precast concrete elements, are covered elsewhere.

The design and construction of structural concrete in Britain is covered by a number of British Standards, Codes of Practice and other Regulations. Some particular types of structure have their own British Standards and Codes, e.g. BS 5337:1976, 'Code of practice for the structural use of concrete for retaining acqueous liquids' and BS 5400: Pt. 4: 1984, 'Code of practice for the design of concrete bridges', but the majority of structural concrete will be covered by BS 8110:1985, 'Structural use of concrete', which is in two parts, and BS 5328:1981, 'Methods for specifying concrete, including ready-mixed concrete'. This section will, in general, refer to the requirements of these latter two British Standards.

MATERIALS FOR CONCRETE

Structural Concrete contains three essential ingredients:

Aggregate
Cement
Water

The most common aggregates are natural gravels or crushed rock particles, but manufactured aggregates are often used for applications such as reducing or increasing the density of the concrete.

The cement most commonly used is a 'Portland' cement or similar material which reacts with the water to form a paste which surrounds the aggregates. When freshly mixed, concrete is a semi-liquid or plastic material which can be placed and compacted into forms or moulds of almost any shape. It subsequently hardens to form a solid mass with useful structural properties.

In addition to the three essential ingredients, other materials may be used in the mix:

(i) admixtures, which are chemicals used in small amounts to change some property of the fresh or hardened concrete.
(ii) pozzolanas or latent cementitious materials, which can be used in addition to, or in place of, some of the Portland cement, again changing some properties of the fresh or hardened concrete.

All these materials are covered in more detail below.

CEMENT

PORTLAND CEMENT.—Nearly all structural concrete is made using Portland cements or cementitious materials based on Portland cement.

Portland cements are manufactured from natural raw materials. Most commonly a source of calcareous minerals, such as chalk or limestone, is ground together with a source of silica and alumina, such as clay or shale, and the mixture fed into à rotary kiln where it is heated to a temperature of about 1450°C. The raw 'meal' may be fed into the kiln as a slurry (the wet process) or it may be semi-dry or dry.

After firing in the kiln, the material cools, forming a clinker which is ground in a ball mill to produce a fine powder. At the grinding stage a small percentage of gypsum, about 5%, is added to help control the rate of setting when water is added.

The proportions of the different raw materials, the rate and temperature of firing in the kiln and the fineness to which the clinker is ground, can be adjusted to produce a number of types of Portland cement, each having different properties. These are then sometimes blended with other materials to produce an even wider range of cements.

In addition to the essential ingredients of calcium and silica, a number of other minerals, notably alumina and iron compounds, are normally present in trace or larger amounts and firing in the kiln produces a number of complex compounds with long formulae. For convenience, the cement chemist refers to these in a short-hand form. These compounds, with their composition and short formulae, are listed in Table 1. This Table also gives the typical percentages of these components contained in the various types of Portland cement described in the next section.

TABLE 1. TYPICAL MINERAL COMPOSITIONS OF PORTLAND CEMENTS AND CHARACTERISTICS OF EACH MINERAL

Mineral	Heat of hydration cal/g	Typical percentage compositions of British Portland cements					Characteristics of the minerals (in concrete)
		OPC	RHPC	SRPC	LHC	White	
Tricalcium silicate $3CaO.SiO_2$ (C_3S)	120	53	53	49	25	5	Hardens quickly. Evolves heat in the process. White in colour.
Dicalcium silicate $2CaO.SiO_2$ (C_2S)	60	20	20	25	50	22	Hardens slowly with slow evolution of heat. White in colour.
Tricalcium aluminate $3CaO.Al_2O_3$ (C_3A)	207	10	10	2	7	15	Stiffens very quickly on hydration with evolution of much heat. Contributes only little to strength. White in colour.
Tetracalcium alumino-ferrite $4CaO.Al_2O_3.Fe_2O_3$ (C_4AF)	80	7	7	14	8	1	Dark coloured compound of little cementing value.
Calcium sulphate $CaSO_4.2H_2O$	—	6	6	5	6	6	Controls reaction of C_3S and C_3A with water.
Uncombined lime, CaO, magnesia. MgO, alkalis, etc.		4	4	5	4	4	Generally of no significance.
Fineness (m^2/kg)		330	420	380	320	330	

These compounds vary in the rate at which they react with water, a process known as hydration, and in the rate at which they produce heat during hydration. An indication of these differences is also given in Table 1.

The tricalcium aluminate, C_3A, reacts first and would cause very rapid stiffening of the cement/water paste if the reaction were not reduced to a manageable rate by the gypsum added during grinding.

C_3A is also able to react with other sulphate compounds, apart from gypsum, once the concrete has hardened. This can cause expansion and cracking of the concrete, so only a very small percentage of C_3A is permitted in sulphate-resisting Portland cement, see below.

The tricalcium and dicalcium silicates, C_3S and C_2S, react more slowly and it is the gel-like calcium silicate hydrate formed by their hydration which provides the main long-term strength in the concrete.

The tetracalcium aluminoferrite, C_4AF, reacts very slowly and has very little cementing effect. It is a dark coloured compound and is the main reason for most Portland cements having their distinctive grey colour.

Provided that the cement remains in contact with water, hydration will continue almost indefinitely with a continuing gain in strength, rapid at first then decreasing in rate with time.

The reactions are exothermic, i.e. they evolve heat, known as the heat of hydration. This can be useful at times in assisting the concrete to gain strength and resist the effects of low ambient temperatures. At other times the heat of hydration may be a disadvantage by causing thermal stress and possible cracking of the concrete. This is of particular concern in large masses of concrete, where the heat evolved cannot dissipate quickly and so produces high internal temperatures.

During these chemical reactions, calcium hydroxide, $Ca(OH)_2$, is released. This is often referred to as the "free lime". The free lime is taken up by the water within the concrete to become a saturated solution of calcium hydroxide with a pH of between 12 and 13. A highly alkaline environment thus exists within the concrete which protects most embedded metal, such as steel reinforcement from corrosion, see 'Durability, protection of reinforcement'.

From the above it is obvious that the cementing properties of Portland cement depend on its chemical reactions with water. It does not gain strength by drying out. If the cement is to continue to gain strength, the presence of moisture must be maintained.

The need for water also means that Portland cements will set and harden under water, so they are sometimes referred to as 'hydraulic' cements.

Nearly all Portland and other cements used in structural concrete are covered by British Standards which specify limits for the chemical and physical properties of the materials. Tests for these properties are described in the various parts of BS 4550. For the most part, the detailed requirements of these British Standards will not be described here. The reader should consult the individual Standards for more information.

All Portland cements produced by British manufacturers is Quality Assured under a scheme monitored by the British Standards Institution and controlled by an independent reference testing Laboratory.

TYPES OF PORTLAND CEMENT.—Ordinary Portland cement (BS 12:1978).—About 80% of all Portland cement manufactured in the UK is ordinary Portland cement, OPC, making it the most common type of cement. It has a moderate rate of hardening and is suitable for most structural concrete.

Rapid-hardening Portland cement (BS 12:1978).—Rapid-hardening Portland cement, RHPC, is chemically the same, or very similar to OPC, but normally it is ground more finely which increases the rate at which the cement gains strength following the initial stiffening. This is a useful property when it is necessary or more economical to remove concrete elements from their moulds at early ages.

With the greater rate of strength development, there is also a greater rate of heat evolution which makes this cement unsuitable for thick sections, or for concrete with a high cement content, but it can be useful in cold weather when the faster rate of hydration reduces the time during which the newly cast concrete is susceptible to damage by frost.

Sulphate-resisting Portland Cement (BS 4027:1980).—Some soils, soil water and other water, such as sea water, contain sulphates. These can attack concrete in more than one way, but a major form of attack is a reaction between sulphates and the hydrated calcium aluminate, C_3A, in the concrete. Sulphate attack can be reduced by using sulphate-resisting Portland cement, SRPC, in which the C_3A content has been reduced. BS 4027 limits the C_3A content to a maximum of 3.5%. SRPC normally is darker in colour than OPC.

The design of concrete to resist sulphate attack is dealt with under 'Sulphate attack'.

Like other Portland cements, SRPC is not resistant to attack by acids.

Low heat Portland cement (BS 1370:1979).—As its name suggests, low heat Portland cement, LHPC, evolves less heat than ordinary Portland cement. This is achieved by reducing the proportions of tricalcium silicate, C_3S, and tricalcium aluminate, C_3A, in the cement. It is intended for use in large concrete sections or for applications where it is necessary or useful to reduce the temperature rise in the concrete.

The rate of gain of strength at early ages may be less than with OPC, but the ultimate strength will be similar. LHPC is made only to special order.

White Portland cement.—White Portland cement is used when the concrete surface is required to be white rather than the normal grey of other Portland cements. There is no separate British Standard for white Portland cement, but consignments from British manufacturers will comply with BS 12. The whiteness is achieved by careful selection of the raw materials, usually white china clay and limestone, and making sure that no contamination from coloured materials occurs at any stage in the manufacturing process.

OTHER CEMENTS BASED ON PORTLAND CEMENT CLINKER.—For some special uses, cements based on Portland cement clinker have been evolved.

Waterproof and water-repellent cements.—Both grey and white Portland cement concretes can have their water resisting properties enhanced by the use of waterproof or water-repellent cements, in which a small amount of metallic soap, such as calcium stearate, is mixed in or interground with the clinker. They are often used in decorative finishes where the water repellent properties help the surface to weather more uniformly.

Concrete made with normal types of Portland cement can be made sufficiently waterproof for all but very stringent engineering applications and waterproof Portland cement should not be relied upon alone to produce the necessary watertight performance.

Masonry cement (BS 5224: 1976).—This cement is a blend of Portland cement, an inert filler and other admixtures. It is specially designed for use in mortars and renderings and should never be used in structural concrete.

Hydrophobic cement.—In this cement the particles of a Portland cement are coated with a waterproof skin of oleic acid or similar material. This increases the storage life of the cement by resisting the penetration of water vapour.

The coating is rubbed off by friction in the concrete mixer, leaving the cement particles exposed to hydration in the normal manner. When mixing hydrophobic cement concrete it is normal to increase the mixing time to ensure that all the coating is removed. Hydrophobic cements should not be used when mixing by hand, which cannot supply sufficient friction.

BLENDS OF PORTLAND CEMENT AND OTHER MATERIALS.—Certain materials have cementitious properties when combined with Portland cement, or have latent cementitious properties of their own. These are described under 'Latent by hydraulic binders' below. They may also be sold by the cement manufacturer already blended with Portland cement. A number of these blends of materials are covered by British Standards.

Portland-blastfurnace cement (BS 146: 1980).—Portland-blastfurnace cement, PBFC, is a mixture of ordinary Portland cement and granulated blastfurnace slag. The slag may be interground with the Portland cement clinker, or the two materials ground separately and blended afterwards. BS 146 allows the blend to contain up to 65% slag and lays down the chemical and physical properties of the resulting cement. In practice, commercially available PBFC rarely contains more than about 50% slag.

Low heat Portland-blastfurnace cement (BS 4246: 1974).— This cement, LHPBFC, is a special grade of PBFC in which the heat of hydration is reduced by allowing the proportion of slag in the blend to increase to between 50 and 90%. BS 4246 lays down limits for the heat of hydration.

Portland pulverised-fuel ash cement (BS 6588: 1985).—This cement contains between 15 and 35% by mass of pulverised fuel ash, pfa. Where pfa is used in structural concrete, the percentage of pfa in the total cementitious material normally falls within this range.

Pozzolanic cement with pulverised-fuel ash as pozzalana (BS 6610: 1985).—This cement contains between 35 and 50% by mass of pulverised fuel ash, pfa. Proportions of pfa in the cement higher than 35% are not often used in structural concrete, but they may be useful when a lower heat of hydration or a degree of chemical resistance is required.

Both BS 6588 and 6610 cements have only recently been introduced and as yet there is little experience of their use in the UK.

OTHER HYDRAULIC CEMENTS.—Supersulphated cement (BS 4248: 1974).—This cement consists of granulated blastfurnace slag, gypsum and ordinary Portland cement in the approximate proportion 85:12:3 respectively. The Portland cement merely serves to activate the reaction between the other two components.

This cement is off-white in colour, slow to harden, especially at low temperatures, and deteriorates more rapidly than OPC in storage. It is, however, particularly resistant to sulphate attack.

Supersulphated cement is not generally available in Britain at present.

High alumina cement (BS 915: 1972).—High alumina or aluminous cement is different from Portland cement both in composition and properties; it is very dark grey in colour. It is made by fusing a mixture of bauxite with chalk or limestone and grinding the resulting clinker. Upon the addition of water it sets comparatively slowly in from 2 to 6 hours, but thereafter gains strength very rapidly, attaining a high strength at 12 hours and a large proportion of its final strength at 24 hours. As a considerable amount of heat is generated, this needs to be considered when concreting large masses, and it is essential that it should be kept continuously wet for the first 24 hours.

Recent research, following structural collapses in 1973 and 1974, has considerably altered the understanding of the behaviour and sensitivity of high alumina cement concrete. As a result of both the research and the events themselves there is not, at this time, the consensus of opinion necessary for agreement on recommendations for the structural use of this material. Consequently, the sections of the British Standards and Codes of Practice which refer to high alumina cement concrete have been withdrawn or modified, and the latest amendments to the Standards and Codes of Practice should be consulted. Until new recommendations are issued, an engineer wishing to specify concrete made with high alumina cement must rely entirely on his own engineering judgement without guidance from the BS Codes and Specifications.

High alumina cement requires rather different treatment from Portland cements and the manufacturer should preferably be consulted before use. Depending on temperature and humidity, the calcium aluminates in the cement undergo 'conversion' leading to a reduction in compressive strength down to a minimum value on which structural design should be based. Currently in the UK, special consent of the local Authority is required before high alumina cement is used for structural applications.

Accidental contamination with lime, plaster, Portland cement etc. should be avoided and all utensils and containers used with it must be clean. Alkaline materials, such as lime and Portland cement, accelerate the setting time of high alumina cement and may even produce a flash set. Mixes of Portland and high alumina cements made under controlled conditions are therefore used when a very rapid-setting cement is required, eg for emergency sealing of water leaks. Such mixes should never be used for structural reinforced concrete.

In a different application, high alumina cement is used with special aggregates to make refractory concretes for service up to 1,350°C. On heating, the strong hydraulic bond is lost and a weaker but very useful ceramic bond develops. This is the major use of high alumina cement in the U.K.

LATENT HYDRAULIC BINDERS.—Some materials can react with the free lime evolved during the hydration of Portland cement, forming further cementing compounds. These are known as pozzolanas. Other materials are latent hydraulic cements, needing only the presence of small amounts of lime or Portland cement to enable reaction with water to commence. All these materials are now referred to as 'latent hydraulic binders'.

A number of natural materials, notably volcanic ashes, have pozzolanic properties, but the only pozzolanic material generally available in quantity in Britain is pulverised fuel ash, pfa. This is the ash removed from the electrostatic precipitators in the flues of electricity generating power-stations which burn pulverised coal. When used as a hydraulic binder, pfa should comply with BS 3892: Part 1: 1982. The most common proportion are about 70% OPC and 30% pfa.

Ground granulated blastfurnace slag, ggbfs, is a by-product of the iron producing industry. Hot slag from blasfurnaces is 'granulated' by quenching it with cold water, after which it is ground to a powder with a fineness similar to that of Portland cement. Ggbfs acts as a latent hydraulic cement. Concrete made with a mixture of OPC and ggbfs will have properties generally similar to those containing pfa, although the proportions of ggbfs is normally higher, commonly 50 to 70% of the OPC/ggbfs blend.

Ggbfs for use with Portland cement should comply with BS 6699:1986.

Ggbfs and pfa can either be blended with OPC at the cement works to produce PBFC, LHPBFC, Portland pulverised fuel ash cement etc. as already described, or they may be combined with the OPC and other materials in the concrete mixer. In either case, the properties of the resulting concrete will be very similar if the proportions of the cement and pfa or ggbfs are the same.

Within certain limitations, concrete containing pfa can be designed to have most required properties, but as a broad generalisation, when compared with all OPC mixes, concrete containing pfa will have lower early strengths and heats of hydration, although later age strengths may be higher. The workability of the fresh concrete may be higher and the sulphate resistance of the hardened concrete improved.

The low early strengths and hydration rates can increase the striking times for formwork, particularly in cold weather, and extra care must be taken in curing the concrete if adequate hydration is to be achieved.

Another pozzolanic material has recently been introduced into Britain. This is microsilica or silica fume, which is an extremely fine powder produced as a by-product of the silicon alloy industry. Its use in Britain so far is limited, so no British Standards or general recommendations have yet been produced, but there is a growing literature on this material (2).

AGGREGATES

Aggregates are the particles of stone or similar materials which are mixed with the cementitious material and water to produce concrete.

BS 8110 divides aggregates into three types depending on their density.

(*a*) Normal weight—having a particle density between 2000 kg/m^3 and 3000 kg/m^3.
(*b*) Lightweight—having a particle density less than 2000 kg/m^3.
(*c*) Heavyweight—having a particle density greater than 3000 kg/m^3.

Most structural concrete is made with normal weight aggregate so this will be dealt with in more detail than the others.

NORMAL WEIGHT NATURAL AGGREGATE.—Normal weight aggregates almost always consist of naturally occurring materials such as gravels or crushed rock. Natural aggregates for concrete are covered by the various parts of BS 812 which lay down methods of sampling and testing, and BS 882: 1983 which gives the requirements for aggregates for concrete.

Natural aggregates are also defined by their maximum size and grading.

Coarse aggregates are those where nearly all the material would be retained on a 5 mm sieve. The maximum sizes are normally 40, 20 or 14 mm. BS 882 requirements for the gradings of various sizes of 'graded' and 'single-sized' coarse aggregates are given in Table 2. The most common size of coarse aggregate is 20 mm graded. 14 mm maximum size aggregate is sometimes used where the concrete section is small or the reinforcement congested. Where there is little or no reinforcement and the concrete section is large, there are advantages in using 40 mm, or even larger sized aggregate, if possible.

For most concrete a graded aggregate will be purchased and used. When greater accuracy and uniformity of grading is required, single sized aggregates are bought and stored separately, then combined at the concrete mixer to give the required grading.

TABLE 2. GRADING LIMITS FOR COARSE AGGREGATE.
[From BS 882, Table 4]

Sieve size	Percentage by mass passing BS sieves for nominal sizes						
	Graded aggregate			Single-sized aggregate			
	40 mm to 5 mm	20 mm to 5 mm	14 mm to 5 mm	40 mm	20 mm	14 mm	10 mm
mm							
50.0	100	—	—	100	—	—	—
37.5	90–100	100	—	85–100	100	—	—
20.0	37–70	90–100	100	0–25	85–100	100	—
14.0	—	—	90–100	—	—	85–100	100
10.0	10–40	30–60	50–85	0–5	0–25	0–50	85–100
5.0	0–5	0–10	0–10	—	0–5	0–10	0–25
2.36	—	—	—	—	—	—	0–5

Fine aggregates are those where nearly all the particles pass a 5 mm sieve and BS 882 specifies three gradings, coarse (C), medium (M) and fine (F). The BS requirements for these grades are given in Table 3.

TABLE 3. GRADING LIMITS FOR FINE AGGREGATE
[From BS 882, Table 5]

Sieve size	Percentages by mass passing BS sieve			
	Overall limits	Additional limits for grading		
		C	M	F
10.00 mm	100	—	—	—
5.00 mm	89–100	—	—	—
2.36 mm	60–100	60–100	65–100	80–100
1.18 mm	30–100	30–90	45–100	70–100
600 μm	15–100	15–54	25–80	55–100
300 μm	5–70	5–40	5–48	5–70
150 μm	0–15*	—	—	—

* Increased to 20% for crushed rock fines, except when they are used for heavy duty floors.

NOTE. Fine aggregate not complying with table 5 may also be used provided that the supplier can satisfy the purchaser that such materials can produce concrete of the required quality.

Both coarse and fine aggregates can be natural gravels which are washed and graded, natural gravels where some of the material is crushed to produce the required grading, or crushed rock of a variety of geological types. However, crushed rock fine aggregate tends to produce concrete which is 'harsh' and more difficult to work in its fresh state, so most concrete is made with natural sand fine aggregate, even where crushed rock coarse aggregate is used.

Nevertheless, almost any combination of natural aggregates complying with BS 882 can be used to produce satisfactory structural concrete except for the most stringent requirements, so most concrete is made with aggregate from the nearest and most economical source.

In addition to land-based pit and quarried natural aggregates, a significant percentage of aggregate used in the UK and some other countries is dredged from the sea. Sea dredged aggregates need to satisfy the same requirements as land-based materials, but they may have some extra difficulties in doing so, in particular:

(*a*) grading—some sources of sea dredged aggregates tend to be extra fine or single sized, but these can still be used successfully with careful mix design, or by combining them with other materials.

(*b*) shell content—some land-based aggregates contain shell, but obviously it is of greater concern with sea dredged material. BS 882 limits the amount of shell in coarse aggregate, see Table 4.

(*c*) salt—if sea dredged aggregates are not washed efficiently in fresh water, some salt (sodium chloride) will be retained in the aggregate. Chlorides present in the concrete can lead to corrosion of the reinforcement or other embedded metal. This is dealt with under 'Durability'.

TABLE 4. LIMITS ON SHELL CONTENT OF AGGREGATE
[From BS 882, Table 2].

Size	Limits on shell content (%)
Fractions of 10 mm single size, or of graded or all-in aggregate that are finer than 10 mm and coarser than 5 mm	20
Fractions of single sizes or of graded or all-in aggregate that are coarser than 10 mm	8
Aggregates finer than 5 mm	No requirement

Certain aggregates, such as some dolerites and whinstones found in Scotland, are known to have a high moisture movement which can cause a high initial shrinkage in the concrete. Further information can be found in BRE Digest 35 (3).

With some siliceous aggregates, care may need to be taken to ensure that the concrete does not suffer damage due to alkali-silica reaction. This is dealth with more fully under 'Durability'.

LIGHTWEIGHT AGGREGATES.—A number of lightweight aggregates are available. Most of these are manufactured materials such as expanded shale or clay, or pelletised pulverised fuel ash. Some natural materials such as pumice are also used as aggregate but these tend to be very light and unsuitable for structural concrete. Lightweight aggregates have been used successfully in many structures, such as buildings and bridge decks, where the saving in dead weight is an obvious advantage. For these applications a lightweight coarse aggregate usually is combined with a natural fine aggregate to produce the required strength.

BS 8110: Part 2 contains special considerations for the use of lightweight aggregate concrete.

HEAVYWEIGHT AGGREGATES.—For some applications, such as for screening radio-active sources, or just to produce additional dead-weight, concrete with a density higher than normal is required. This can be produced using heavyweight aggregate. Barytes (barium sulphate), ferrous metal shot and punchings, and ores such as magnetite, limonite and haematite are used. Concrete with densities up to about 4800 kg/m^3 can be obtained with careful choice of materials and mix design.

More details of the design and use of heavyweight aggregate concrete will be found elsewhere (4).

WATER

In the UK and most other parts of the world, it can be assumed that mains water, suitable for drinking, will be suitable for use in mixing concrete.

Where water other than mains water must be used, BS 3148: 1980 gives guidance, but does not give limits for impurities. Suitability of the water may be determined by conducting setting time and concrete cube strength tests, as described in BS 3148 and BS 4550: Part 3, comparing concretes made with the water under test with concrete made with distilled water.

ADMIXTURES

These materials are added in small quantities to the concrete mix in order to modify the properties of the concrete in the fresh or hardened state. They are sometimes referred to as 'additives', but this term should be used only for materials added to cement during its manufacture.

Admixtures are referred to by the effect they have on the properties of the concrete. Brief details are given below and more information is given elsewhere (5) (6).

Accelerators (BS 5075: Part 1: 1982).—A number of chemical compounds increase the rate of hydration of the cement. They will, therefore, increase the rate of setting and hardening of the concrete and also increase the rate of heat evolution of the cement.

The use of an accelerator can be useful when it is required to strike formwork early, or where a more rapid strength development and heat evolution will help to protect the fresh concrete from freezing temperatures.

Most accelerators used to be based on calcium chloride, but the presence of chloride greatly increases the risk of corrosion of reinforcement, so BS 8110 effectively prevents the use of such admixtures in reinforced and prestressed concrete. Accelerators based on non-chloride-containing compounds are now available.

Retarders (BS 5075: Part 1: 1982).—These admixtures, usually based on sugar-type compounds, reduce the rate of cement hydration, thus extending the time of setting and hardening. This property is often useful to counteract the accelerating effects of hot weather. Retarders are also useful when the concrete pour is large and will take a long time to place, or where there will be an extended time between mixing and placing the concrete.

Water reducers (BS 5075: Part 1: 1982).—Also known as 'plasticizers' or 'workability-aids', these admixtures reduce the amount of water needed to produce the required workability in the concrete. This can be useful to reduce the water/cement ratio and improve the strength and durability of the cement. They can also be used to increase the workability of the fresh concrete without increasing the water content. They are not known to have any significant effect on the hardened concrete except indirectly by permitting a change in water content.

Superplasticizers (BS 5057: Part 3: 1985).—As the name suggests, superplasticisers have an effect similar to water reducers but to a much greater degree. They are based on different chemical compounds and are added in larger quantities, typically 1 to 6 litres of admixture per cubic metre of concrete.

Superplasticizers can be used as extremely effective water reducers, but more commonly they are used to produce very workable or 'flowing' concrete which can be placed with little or no compaction. This can be useful when the reinforcement is very congested, making it difficult to use internal vibrators efficiently.

Superplastizers may also help to lower construction costs by reducing the manpower needed for placing and compaction.

Further information on superplasticisers is given in reference (7).

Air-entraining agents (BS 5075: Part 2: 1982).—Hardened concrete can be damaged if it freezes whilst saturated or nearly saturated, particularly when de-icing salts such as those used on roads are present. This damage can be virtually eliminated by the use of an air-entraining agent.

These admixtures produce a large number of very small, discrete air bubbles in the fresh concrete which get trapped or 'entrained' as the concrete hardens. Entrained air is quite distinct from 'entrapped' air, which is air that has not been removed during compaction of the fresh concrete and remains as larger air-voids within the mass.

BS 8110 and other specifications, such as that issued by the Department of Transport, lay down the amount of air to be entrained and its method of measurement, see under 'Durability—frost attack'.

Entraining air reduces the compressive strength of the concrete, but the effect of the air bubbles is to improve workability and enable the water content to be reduced. This compensates to some extent for the loss of strength due to the presence of air.

Pigments (BS 1014: 1975).—Pigments have little or no effect on the structural properties of concrete, but are used to alter its colour. Pigments for concrete generally should comply with BS 1014, although some materials used as pigments are not covered by this standard. Normally about 5% pigment by weight of the cement is added to white or ordinary Portland cement. Great care is needed when batching and mixing the concrete to obtain an even colour.

Water-repelling admixtures.—Good quality structural concrete is sufficiently impermeable for almost all purposes and no normal admixture will make a significant improvement in the impermeability. However, using a water-repelling admixture can reduce the surface absorbancy of concrete and so improve its appearance by decreasing the absorption of dirt.

These admixtures are normally based on calcium stearate, a metallic soap.

PROPERTIES OF CONCRETE

Concrete needs to have a number of properties in order to produce the required performance at various stages in its life. The most important of these properties and those which can be altered substantially by the choice of materials and mix proportions are described here.

WORKABILITY.—Fresh concrete has to be transported to its place of casting, poured into the mould or form and compacted to remove all the entrapped air—or as much of it as possible. Full compaction is one of the most important factors in ensuring a sound, durable concrete. 'Workability' is an indication of the ease with which the concrete can be compacted and is thus the most important property of fresh concrete.

There are a number of standard and non-standard tests for workability but the most commonly used, by far, is the slump test. Full details of the slump test are given in BS 1881: Part 102 and this procedure should be followed meticulously, but a simplified description of the test is:

(i) a 'slump cone' consisting of a sheet-steel mould in the form of a truncated cone of standard dimensions is placed on a sheet-steel base plate with its small end uppermost.
(ii) the cone is filled with concrete and compacted by hand in a standardised method using a standard tamping rod.
(iii) the cone is gently lifted off the concrete which then 'slumps' down under its own weight.
(iv) the vertical distance between the highest point of the slumped concrete and its original height, ie the height of the cone, is measured. This is the 'slump'.

Obviously, the greater the slump, the greater the workability. The slump test is not very sensitive in some cases of very high or low workability and the relationship between the slump and the ability of the concrete to be fully compacted varies with different concreting materials. The test is, however, easy and quick to conduct and the apparatus is simple, so it has become the almost universal test for workability.

Workability can be affected by the aggregate, especially by its maximum size and particle shape. The particular supply of Portland cement can have a similar but smaller effect, but with given sources of dry materials, the workability is almost solely governed by the amount of water in the mix, with the workability increasing with the water content.

Apart from workability, almost every other desirable property of concrete is adversely affected by an increase in the water content, so concrete mixes should be designed to have a workability high enough to ensure that the concrete can be fully compacted, but no higher.

COHESION.—Cohesion is a vague property with no precise definition or method of measurement. It is the ability of the concrete to be transported, placed, compacted and harden with the minimum amount of segregation and bleeding.

Concrete mixes are designed to have a certain proportion of coarse and fine aggregate, cement and water. Ideally samples of concrete taken from different points in the hardened mass should have the same proportions. Some degree of segregation of materials, for example coarse, heavy aggregate sinking to the bottom and finer materials rising to the top, almost inevitably occurs, but proper mix design and construction methods should reduce this to a minimum.

Bleeding is a form of segregation in which the water in the mix rises to the top of the pour, allowing the solid material to settle. A very small amount of bleeding can be useful to keep the top surface moist in hot weather but, in general, bleeding should be prevented by keeping down the water content and choosing the type and proportions of the solid materials to minimise the ability of the water to migrate upwards. Where necessary, the use of air entrainment greatly reduces bleeding.

DRYING SHRINKAGE.—In common with most materials, concrete shrinks as it dries out. The amount of drying shrinkage will be affected by the properties of the solid materials, particularly the aggregates, but the overriding factor controlling shrinkage is the water content of the original mix. This is a further reason for keeping the water content to the minimum consistent with obtaining adequate workability.

STRENGTH.—Structural concrete must have sufficient strength to resist the stresses imposed on it. Sometimes concrete is required to have a certain tensile or flexural strength, but usually it is the compressive strength which is required and specified.

BS 1881: Parts 101, 108, 111 and 116, give full details of sampling the mix and of making, storing and crushing test specimens to produce a measure of the compressive strength of the concrete. The standard specimen is a 150 mm or 100 mm cube and the most usual age at which the cube is crushed is 28 days. The accuracy of the cube moulds, method of compaction of the concrete, storage conditions, the testing machine, and method of crushing the cubes can all affect the final result, so it is essential for the standard to be followed meticulously, otherwise the result will be invalid.

In other countries the size or shape of the test specimens, and other details of the testing may be different, so that it is often not easy or possible to compare concretes tested to different national standards.

It is also essential to remember that the result will only be the compressive strength of the concrete in the sample as indicated by that particular method of test. It will only serve as a guide to the strength of the concrete in the structure, which will have experienced a different form of casting and compaction and a different temperature and humidity regime following casting.

The strength of concrete in the structure will be lower than that indicated by the test cubes and will also vary from place to place in the structure. Codes of practice for the design of concrete structures, such as BS 8110, introduce factors to allow for these differences.

Mix design for strength and methods for specifying strength and assessing compliance with the specification are dealt with under 'Concrete mix design and specification'.

DURABILITY.—This is the ability of the concrete to continue to perform its required function for its design life with the minimum of repair and maintenance. The great majority of concrete structures perform with excellent durability, but concrete can be attacked by external chemical agents, such as sulphates and acids, and by physical effects such as frost action and abrasion. It may also be damaged by internal reactions such as alkali-aggregate reaction, but the most common cause of deterioration of concrete structures is corrosion of the steel reinforcement.

The major defence against all these forms of deterioration, except alkali-aggregate reaction, is to produce concrete with a low permeability so that the agents attacking the concrete or reinforcement have difficulty in penetrating the body of the concrete.

It is generally accepted that the permeability of concrete will be reduced as the cement content is increased and the water/cement ratio is reduced. The major defence against concrete deterioration is, therefore, to ensure an adequately high cement content and a low water/cement ratio. The effect of the water/cement ratio is the predominant factor.

Equally important is to ensure good workmanship. The concrete must be fully compacted and the correct depth of cover to the reinforcement obtained, otherwise all the advantages of care taken in specifying, designing and mixing the concrete will be lost. Proper curing also is very important if a durable concrete is to be obtained.

Protection of reinforcement.—It has already been stated that the major cause of deterioration of concrete structures is corrosion of reinforcement.

As mentioned under 'Portland cement', the interior of Portland cement concrete normally is highly alkaline. In this environment steel is 'passivated' and will not rust or corrode. However, carbon dioxide in the air will cause 'carbonation' of the concrete, reducing the alkalinity and de-passivating the steel. In the presence of water and oxygen the steel will then corrode. The corrosion product, or rust, occupies a volume much greater than the original steel so, in rusting, the steel expands and pushes off its concrete cover. This is known as spalling. Carbonation of concrete is explained more fully elsewhere (8).

To produce carbonation, the carbon dioxide from the air has to diffuse into the concrete from the surface. If the steel reinforcement is protected by an adequate cover of good quality concrete, this diffusion will be very slow and it will take a long time for the carbonation front to reach the steel and corrosion to commence.

TABLE 5. EXPOSURE CONDITIONS FOR CONCRETE
[From BS 8110: Part 1, Table 3.2]

Environment	Exposure conditions
Mild	Concrete surfaces protected against weather or aggressive conditions.
Moderate	Concrete surfaces sheltered from severe rain or freezing whilst wet Concrete subject to condensation Concrete surfaces continuously under water Concrete in contact with non-aggressive soil (see class 1 of Table 10)
Severe	Concrete surfaces exposed to severe rain, alternate wetting and drying or occasional freezing or severe condensation
Very severe	Concrete surfaces exposed to sea water spray, de-icing salts (directly or indirectly), corrosive fumes or severe freezing conditions whilst wet
Extreme	Concrete surfaces exposed to abrasive action, e.g. sea water carrying solid or flowing water with pH $\leqslant 4.5$ or machinery or vehicles

Specification for durable concrete.—BS 8110 lists a number of exposure conditions, Table 5, and specifies minimum depths of cover, and qualities of concrete in terms of minimum cement contents, maximum water/cement ratios and concrete strengths, for each condition and for reinforced and unreinforced concrete, Tables 6 and 7. These recommendations are for concrete with 20 mm aggregate. Adjustments for other sizes of aggregate are given in Table 8. With concrete complying with these requirements, and given good workmanship, the reinforcement should remain adequately protected for the lifetime normally expected of a structure.

Effect of chlorides on concrete and reinforcement.—The presence of chlorides in the concrete will increase the risk of steel corrosion. The use of calcium chloride as an accelerating admixture in the past has led to a great deal of damage due to reinforcement corrosion and spalling concrete. Chloride, as sodium chloride, can be incorporated into the mix if sea water is used for mixing, or if the aggregate contains chlorides. This is particularly so if sea-dredged aggregates are used.

The effect of chlorides in the mix in causing corrosion of the reinforcement is increased with higher curing temperatures. Chlorides may also reduce the sulphate resistance of concrete.

TABLE 6. REQUIREMENTS FOR CONCRETE AND COVER TO REINFORCEMENT TO MEET DURABILITY REQUIREMENTS
[From BS 8110: Part 1, Table 3.4]

Conditions of exposure see Table 5	Nominal cover				
	mm	mm	mm	mm	mm
Mild	25	20	20*	20*	20*
Moderate	—	35	30	25	20
Severe	—	—	40	30	25
Very severe	—	—	50†	40†	30
Extreme	—	—	—	60†	50
Maximum free water/cement ratio	0.65	0.60	0.55	0.50	0.45
Minimum cement content (kg/m³)	275	300	325	350	400
Lowest grade of concrete	C30	C35	C40	C45	C50

* These covers may be reduced to 15 mm provided that the nominal maximum size of aggregate does not exceed 15 mm.

† Where concrete is subject to freezing whilst wet, air-entrainment should be used.

NOTE. This table relates to normal-weight aggregate of 20 mm nominal maximum size.

BS 8110 places limits on the total chloride content of concrete containing embedded metal or made with sulphate-resisting Portland cement, see Table 9.

In order to comply with these requirements, chlorides from all sources—cement, water, aggregates, admixtures etc., must be taken into account.

Chlorides can also penetrate the concrete from outside. Obvious cases are concrete structures exposed to sea water or sea spray and structures, such as highway bridges, exposed to de-icing salts used on roads in winter. The deterioration of highway bridge decks due to the use of de-icing salts is a major concern in many countries, including Britain.

BS 8110 includes exposure to sea water, sea spray and de-icing salts in its 'very severe' exposure category and recommends the concrete quality and cover to reinforcement to obtain durability in these conditions, see Tables 5 to 8.

TABLE 7. REQUIREMENTS FOR UNREINFORCED CONCRETE WITH 20 MM AGGREGATES

Conditions of exposure see Table 6	Concrete not containing embedded material		
	Maximum free water/cement ratio	Minimum cement* content	Lowest grade of concrete
		kg/m³	
Mild	0.80	180	C20
Moderate	0.65	275	C30
Severe	0.60	300	C35
Very severe	0.55	325	C35†
Extreme	0.50	350	C45

* Inclusive of ggbfs or pfa content.

† Applicable only to air-entrained concrete.

NOTE. The lowest grades of concrete may be reduced by not more than 5 N/mm², provided there is evidence showing that with the materials to be used, this lower grade will ensure compliance with the required minimum cement content and maximum free water/cement ratio.

TABLE 8. ADJUSTMENTS TO MINIMUM CEMENT CONTENTS IN TABLES 6, 7 AND 10 FOR AGGREGATES OTHER THAN 20 MM. [BS 8110: Part 1, Table 6.3]

Nominal maximum aggregate size	Adjustments to minimum cement contents in Table 6
mm	kg/m³
10	+40
14	+20
20	0
40	−30

NOTE. In no case should the cement content be less than 240 kg/m³ for reinforced concrete or 300 kg/m³ for prestressed concrete.

TABLE 9. LIMITS ON CHLORIDE CONTENT OF CONCRETE [BS 8110: Part 1, Table 6.4]

Types or use of concrete	Maximum total chloride content expressed as a percentage of chloride ion by mass of cement (inclusive of pfa or ggbfs when used)
Prestressed concrete Heat-cured concrete containing embedded metal	0.1
Concrete made with cement complying with BS 4027 or BS 4248	0.2
Concrete containing embedded metal and made with cement complying with BS 12, BS 146, BS 1370, BS 4246 or combinations with ggbfs or pfa	0.4

Sulphate attack.—Sulphates can attack the hydrated Portland cement in the concrete causing expansion and cracking and, in extreme cases, complete break-down of the concrete. Portland cement itself contains a small amount of sulphate, mainly from the gypsum which is interground with the cement clinker to control the rate of setting. Some aggregates also may contain some sulphates.

BS 8110 limits the total amount of sulphate in the concrete mix, expressed as SO_3, to 4% by weight of the cement in the mix.

Sulphates are also present in some soils and ground-water. If these penetrate the concrete sulphate attack can occur, as described above. The best protection against sulphate attack is to reduce penetration by producing concrete with a low permeability and to use materials more resistant to sulphate attack, such as sulphate-resisting Portland cement or combinations of ordinary Portland cement and pfa or ggbfs.

More information on sulphate attack is given in BRE Digest 250 (9) and BS 8110. Table 10 gives the BS 8110 requirements for concrete to resist sulphate attack from soil and ground-water.

Other chemical attack.—All acids will attack concrete to some extent, but with good quality concrete in mild natural acid conditions this attack normally may be ignored. BS 8110 recommends that Portland cement concrete should not be used in persistently acid conditions, i.e. where the pH is 5.5 or less, although concrete can perform well in some ground waters with a lower pH, such as peaty water.

Care should be taken where concrete will be subject to acidic or other industrial wastes and products. In some instances the concrete will need protection by surface coatings, acid resisting tiles etc. Guidance will be found in specialist publications (10).

TABLE 10. REQUIREMENTS FOR CONCRETE EXPOSED TO SULPHATE ATTACK
[From BS 8110: Part 1, Table 6.1]

Class	Concentration of sulphates expressed as SO_3			Type of cement	Dense, fully compacted concrete made with 20 mm nominal maximum size aggregates complying with BS 882 or BS 1047	
	In soil		In groundwater		Cement* content not less than	Free water/cement* ratio not more than
	Total SO_3	SO_3 in 2:1 water:soil extract				
	%	g/L	g/L		kg/m³	
1	Less than 0.2	Less than 1.0	Less than 0.3	Cements to BS12, 1370, 4027, 146, 4246 or 6588 BS 12 cements combined with pfa† BS 12 cements combined with ggbfs†	—	—
2	0.2 to 0.5	1.0 to 1.9	0.3 to 1.2	Cements to BS12, 1370, 4027, 146, 4246 or 6588 BS 12 cements combined with pfa BS 12 cements combined with ggbfs	330	0.50
				BS 12 cements combined with minimum 25% or maximum 40% pfa‡ BS 12 cements combined with minimum 70% or maximum 90% ggbfs	310	0.55
				BS 4027 cements (SRPC) BS 4248 cements (SSC)	280	0.55

(continued)

TABLE 10.—(*Continued*)

Class	Concentration of sulphates expressed as SO_3			Type of cement	Dense, fully compacted concrete made with 20 mm nominal maximum size aggregates complying with BS 882 or BS 1047	
	In soil					
	Total SO_3	SO_3 in 2:1 water:soil extract	In groundwater		Cement* content not less than	Free water/cement* ratio not more than
3	0.5 to 1.0	1.9 to 3.1	1.2 to 2.5	BS 12 cements combined with minimum 25% or maximum 40% pfa† BS 12 cements combined with minimum 70% or maximum 90% ggbfs	380	0.45
				BS 4027 cements (SRPC) BS 4248 cements (SSC)	330	0.50
4	1.0 to 2.0	3.1 to 5.6	2.5 to 5.0	BS 4027 cements (SRPC) BS 4248 cements (SSC)	370	0.45
5	Over 2	Over 5.6	Over 5.0	BS 4027 cements (SRPC) and BS 4248 cements (SSC) with adequate protective coating	370	0.45

* Inclusive of pfa and ggbfs content.

† Values expressed as percentages by mass of total content of cement, pfa and ggbfs

NOTE 1. See Table 8 for adjustments to the mix proportions.

NOTE 2. Within the limits given in this table, the use of pfa or ggbfs in combination with sulphate-resisting Portland cement (SRPC) will not give lower sulphate resistance than combinations with cements to BS 12.

NOTE 3. If much of the sulphate is present as low solubility calcium sulphate, analysis on the basis of a 2:1 water extract may permit a lower site classification than that obtained from the extraction of total SO_3. Reference should be made to BRE Current Paper 2/79 for methods of analysis, and to BRE Digests 250 and 222 for interpretation in relation to natural soils and fills, respectively.

Frost attack.—Both fresh and hardened concrete can be damaged by frost. The prevention of damage to fresh concrete is dealt with under 'Cold-weather concreting'.

Hardened concrete can be damaged by freezing temperatures if these occur when the concrete is saturated, or nearly so. This is most commonly a surface effect, especially on horizontal surfaces, where flakes of concrete spall off due to ice forming just below the surface.

In more severe cases, cracking or even complete disintegration of the concrete can occur.

The presence of de-icing salt can greatly aggravate the problem.

Once more, the primary defence against deterioration is a good quality impermeable concrete so that absorption of water will be reduced. However, with concrete which is likely to be frequently frozen whilst saturated, such as horizontal slabs exposed to the weather, the only satisfactory defence is to use air-entrained concrete. If the concrete is to be exposed to de-icing salts then air-entrainment is essential.

BS 8110 recommends that all concrete lower than grade C50 and exposed to de-icing salts should have an air-entraining agent incorporated to produce an amount of entrained air, by volume of fresh concrete, which varies with the maximum size of aggregate as follows:

for 10 mm maximum size aggregate — 7%
for 14 mm maximum size aggregate — 6%
for 20 mm maximum size aggregate — 5%
for 40 mm maximum size aggregate — 4%

The standard method of measuring air content is given in BS 1881: Part 106. The design and detailing of the structure can help by reducing areas which will be subjected to prolonged contact with moisture and salt-laden water. Leaking expansion joints are a major cause of trouble.

Alkali-silica reaction.—As has already been described, the interior of Portland cement concrete is a highly alkaline environment due to the concentration of calcium hydroxide, $Ca(OH)_2$, ions in the pore water. This concentration can be increased by the presence of alkali metals, notably sodium and potassium which are contained in nearly all Portland cements. The amounts of sodium and potassium in Portland cements normally are combined and expressed as 'equivalent sodium oxide'. This is usually referred to as the 'alkali content'.

The alkali content of concrete may also be increased if alkali metals are incorporated into the mix from sources other than the Portland cement or penetrate the hardened concrete. The penetration of de-icing salt, sodium chloride, is one such case.

Certain constituents of aggregates can react with the highly alkaline pore water. More than one form of alkali-aggregate reaction, AAR, is known, but only alkali-silica reaction, ASR, has been identified in Great Britain. It is also by far the most common type of AAR throughout the world.

The reaction will occur whenever a reactive form of silica (not all forms are reactive), comes in contact with a highly alkaline environment. The reaction product is an alkali-silica gel. A high proportion of natural aggregate in Great Britain contains some proportion of reactive silica, so a lot of concrete would, if examined under a microscope, be seen to contain some evidence of reaction. This usually does no harm and may be ignored.

The alkali-silica gel is hygroscopic so it can absorb more of the pore-water and swell. In certain circumstances the pressures exerted by this swelling can be sufficient to crack the concrete.

Although a number of cases of damage due to ASR have been reported in Great Britain, its incidence is extremely low when compared with the vast amount of concrete which has been cast.

For damage due to ASR to occur all three of the following factors must be present:

(a) sufficient moisture
and (b) sufficient alkali
and (c) a critical amount of reactive silica

The risk of damage due to ASR may be minimised by designing the structure or the concrete mix to reduce one of these three factors.

A description of the methods for doing this are too lengthy to include here, but guidance on this and on the assessment of concrete structures thought to be damaged due to ASR may be obtained elsewhere (11) (12).

CONCRETE MIX DESIGN AND SPECIFICATION

MIX DESIGN.—Concrete mix design is the determination of the proportions and types of the mix constituents—cement or cementitious material, coarse and fine aggregates, water and admixtures (if used), to produce concrete with the required workability, strength and durability.

Given the particular sources of materials, strength and general durability are dependent almost completely on the water/cement ratio, both increasing as the water/cement ratio is reduced. On the other hand, workability, which is essential to ensure full compaction, depends almost solely on the water content and will increase as the water content increases.

To produce a mix satisfying these conflicting requirements is often a major problem in concrete mix design. Many papers and other publications have proposed theoretical methods for designing concrete mixes to give the required strength and workability, but the only reliable procedure is to make and test trial mixes. Methods for choosing proportions for the first trial mixes and adjusting these when the results of tests have been obtained are given elsewhere (13) (14).

The maximum water/cement ratios and minimum cement contents required for durability, see Table 6, should always be included in the mix design and no compromise should be permitted on these. This may lead to the concrete having a strength higher than that required solely for structural purposes. If this is the case, the higher strength must be accepted. If the higher strength is known in time, it may be possible to re-design the structure to take advantage of it.

TYPES OF SPECIFICATION.—When dealing with methods for specifying concrete, BS 8110 refers to BS 5328.

BS 5328 contains three types of concrete mix specification:

(*a*) Designed mixes, for which the purchaser specifies the type of materials and the concrete strength required; acceptance of the concrete is based solely on whether the materials meet the specification and on whether the specified strength is obtained.

(*b*) Special prescribed mixes, for which the purchaser specifies the materials and their proportions in the mix; the concrete's strength plays no part in the specification or its acceptance.

(*c*) Ordinary prescribed mixes, are mixes for which proportions are given in a table in BS 5328; although these mixes may be expected to have certain strengths, the strength is not included in the acceptance criteria for the concrete.
NOTE: BS 8110 refers to these mixes as 'Ordinary standard mixes',

Concrete strength or grade.—As described in 'Properties of concrete—strength', concrete strength is usually regarded and specified as the compressive strength reached by concrete specimens mixed, cast, stored and tested in a standard manner. In British practice the standard test specimen is a concrete cube made and tested in accordance with BS 1881.

All concreting materials are variable and further variations will be introduced during all stages of producing and testing the concrete specimens. The compressive test results will, therefore, show a variation which approximates to the 'normal distribution' used by statisticians. In modern practice, the specification, control and acceptance of concrete strength is an exercise in applied statistics, based on this assumption of the normal distribution of concrete compressive test results.

The strength of concrete is given in terms of its 'characteristic strength'. BS 8110 defines this as 'that value of cube strength of concrete below which 5% of all possible test results would be expected to fall'.

The 'Grade' of concrete is its characteristic strength at an age of 28 days.

These are precise methods of defining concrete strength, but they are unsuitable as practical methods for accepting concrete specified by strength. BS 5328 gives rules by which concrete may be deemed to have reached the specified grade. These rules are based on taking the means of successive groups for four test results.

BS 5328 should be consulted for full details of these procedures. Further information on the use of statistics for the quality control of concrete is given in reference (15).

TESTING AND QUALITY CONTROL

Where the concrete has to meet particular requirements, such as very high strength concrete, or special surface finishes, materials may have to be tested and trials made in sufficient time to prove their ability to satisfy these requirements before work starts. This will also be necessary where the materials have not previously been used, such as those from a quarry opened up to produce aggregate for a concrete dam in a remote location.

For most work it will be sufficient to show that the materials comply with the relevant British Standards or other specified documents. On large contracts a site laboratory may be set up to do this work, otherwise materials will be sampled on the site after delivery, or sometimes on the suppliers premises before delivery, then transported to a central or commercial laboratory for testing.

There are a large number of tests which may be required for general or more particular uses. Nearly all are described in detail in the relevant British Standards and these details will not be repeated here, but mention should be made of the tests more commonly required.

Cement and cement replacement materials.—Most tests on these materials require a well-equipped laboratory, which is rarely available on site. If test results are required in addition to those supplied by the manufacturer, these should be produced by a specialist laboratory.

Aggregates.—The day-to-day control of aggregate quality should be within the capability of a site laboratory equipped to conduct some of the simpler tests described in BS 812. These would include cleanness using the field settling test for natural sand, (although cleanness can be reasonably assessed visually), sieve analysis and moisture content, for which there is more than one method.

Other and more sophisticated tests may be needed for special requirements such as mechanical properties, or where site inspection and tests have given rise to doubts about the material delivered.

Where sea-dredged aggregate is being used, it may be necessary to keep a check on the chloride content. Methods of checking and testing for chlorides on site are given in reference (16).

Water.—It is not usual to test water for mixing concrete if it comes from drinking water mains supply. If other sources of supply have to be used, refer to 'Materials for Concrete: Water'.

Concrete.—On most sites, two tests will be undertaken regularly. These are the slump test for workability, which is also a good indicator of inadequacy or undue variability in the mix, and the concrete cube test for measuring the concrete strength, usually at 7 and 28 days.

Where concrete is being air-entrained, there will need to be a constant check on the concrete's air content, using an air meter.

Additional or alternative tests may be used, such as measurement of the density of fresh concrete, the cement content of fresh concrete using apparatus such as the Rapid Analysis Machine, RAM (17), or accelerated curing and testing of cubes.

Tests on hardened concrete in situ are not often carried out regularly, but may be called for when there is some doubt about the acceptability of the structure. This may be caused by failure of cube-test results, or suspect workmanship such as leaking or moving formwork or displaced reinforcement.

In these circumstances concrete cores are often taken and tested, but a number of non-destructive tests are available including ultrasonic pulse velocity, rebound hammers, covermeters and gamma radiography.

Most of the tests for concrete mentioned above are described in the various parts of BS 1881. Non-destructive tests are covered by BS 4408.

TEST METHODS AND PHILOSOPHY.—The testing strategy and programme should be designed and conducted so as to ensure that the structure complies with the design and specification, and that it will perform as required in terms of both structural performance and durability.

No test should be specified or undertaken unless there is a clear understanding of why it is needed and what action will be taken if the compliance criteria are not met.

To ensure the results give a reliable indication of the properties of the material tested, tests are designed to minimise errors, bias or variability introduced by the test methods themselves. It follows that the tests must be conducted consistently and strictly in accordance with the specified procedures, by trained and capable personnel.

This includes sampling. Most tests are carried out on small samples which are deemed to be representative of the delivery or batch of material as a whole. Most British Standards specify sampling methods and these should be followed meticulously. Modern statistical methods of quality control, such as those in BS 5328 for concrete cube strength, rely on random sampling of the material produced. Any deliberate choice of material to sample could bias the result.

If sampling and testing are not done properly then the results will have no value, control of the quality of the structure will be lost and contractual disputes over compliance will inevitably follow.

ASSESSMENT OF RESULTS.—The results of tests on individual materials such as cement and aggregates are assumed to represent the materials used in the concrete. With concrete cube tests, however, it must be remembered that the method of compaction and the curing regime of the concrete in the cube will be different from that of the concrete in the structure. This means that the cube strength will only indicate the 'potential' strength of the site concrete which normally will be lower and more variable. In design this difference is allowed for by the use of load factors in BS 8110 and it should also be allowed for when assessing the results of any tests made on hardened site concrete. This is particularly so when core testing is used to obtain an 'equivalent cube strength'. Recommendations for the interpretation of the results of strength tests on concrete cores are given in reference (18).

SITE PRACTICE

CONCRETE.—These days it is only on the largest or more remote sites that one finds concrete being mixed on site. Most structural concrete to be cast in situ is purchased ready-mixed.

STORAGE OF MATERIALS, BATCHING, MIXING.—The general principles given here will apply to both site-mixed and ready-mixed concrete.

Materials for concreting should be stored separately so that they:

(*a*) do not become contaminated by harmful substances
(*b*) do not get mixed with other materials before use
(*c*) do not deteriorate before use.

Different sizes of aggregates should be stored in separate heaps or hoppers. Heaps should be separated by dividing walls so that sizes do not get mixed, and stored on a concrete slab laid to falls so that water drains away.

Cement and cement replacement materials almost always are purchased in bulk, when they are delivered by tankers and stored in silos (19). Separate silos should be provided for each type of cement and cement replacement material being used, and care taken that the material is not delivered into the wrong hopper.

If bagged cement is used, it should be stored on a raised floor in a damp-proof shed. The stacks should not be higher than about 1½m and the bags should be used in the order they were delivered.

Admixtures should be stored as recommended by the manufacturer. This usually means storing in a shed and protecting them from frost and high temperatures.

All solid materials should be batched by weight. Volume batching is no longer considered suitable for structural concrete. Water and admixtures may be batched by weight or volume.

Batching and mixing plants are commonly supplied as a package from the manufacturer where each separate item is chosen and matched to give the output volume and mixing efficiency required. BS 5328 requires that the accuracy of measuring equipment shall be within ± 3% of the quantity of the cement, water and total aggregates being measured.

Batching and mixing plants should be set up on firm, level foundations and regularly cleaned, serviced and calibrated to maintain their accuracy.

Where materials are batched in weigh-hoppers, these must be emptied completely into the mixer before being re-charged.

The most common types of mixers are tilting-drum, reversing drum, non-tilting drum, and pan type, which are covered by BS 1305:1974, although other types are available. All types are made in various sizes to suit the maximum capacity required. Truck mixers used for ready-mixed concrete are covered by BS 4251:1974.

Mixing times will vary with the mixer, the mix design and whether the mixer is fully charged or not. The manufacturer's mixing time will not necessarily apply in all conditions. The best guide is the uniformity of colour throughout the mix. Prolonged mixing will not normally harm the concrete except to reduce the workability which could be detrimental if it is reduced below the minimum required to compact the concrete fully.

READY-MIXED CONCRETE.—For the efficient use of ready-mixed concrete the following general principles should be applied.

(*a*) the supplier should be given a full specification for the mix, preferably by providing a copy of the relevant section of the client's general specification

(*b*) the supplier should be told, with as much notice as possible, of the mix required, its total volume, time of delivery and delivery rate

(*c*) the delivery truck should be able to deliver the concrete as close as possible to the point of placing and firm access roads should be provided

(*d*) where delivery will be into hoppers for temporary storage, these should be at a height to suit the discharge of the delivery vehicle

(*e*) sufficient space should be provided for delivery vehicles to reverse or turn as necessary when leaving the site, and also for further vehicles to wait if required.

Most ready-mixed concrete suppliers are members either of the British Ready-Mixed Concrete Association (BRMCA), or the British Aggregate Construction Materials Industries (BACMI). A quality assurance scheme for ready-mixed concrete is operated by the Quality Scheme for Ready Mixed Concrete, which is independent of BRMCA and BACMI.

These organisations will supply further details of the supply and control of ready-mixed concrete.

TRANSPORTING AND PLACING CONCRETE ON SITE.—Most concrete has to be transported from the mixer or ready-mixed truck to its final place in the formwork. A number of methods of transport is available, including dumpers, crane and skip, monorails and conveyers. The chosen method will depend on the site conditions, including distance, both horizontal and vertical, ground and other support conditions, and volumes to be placed (20).

Concrete pumping is a common method of transporting concrete on a modern site. There are few sites where the transporting requirements cannot be met by a modern mobile pump. The pump, however, produces its own demands on the concrete mix and supply. Although the modern pump can handle a range of mixes satisfactorily, the concrete has to have a workability and cohesion which enable it to be pumped over the distance and height required. The concrete also has to be consistent in mix, and the delivery to the pump must avoid delays otherwise expensive pump and pipe blockages can occur.

Large concrete pours placed by pump need careful planning and collaboration between concrete supplier, pumping contractor and placing gang if all is to proceed smoothly.

A handbook on concrete pumping (21) is produced by the British Concrete Pumping Association, (BCPA) who will also supply further information if required.

Whichever method of transport is used, the concrete should be delivered as closely as possible to its final required position. If the pour is deep, a good cohesive mix may be dropped freely into place without harm, but if there is a danger that concrete will strike and be left on formwork or reinforcement during its fall, this should be prevented by using elephant trunking, or some other form of chute.

Immediately after placing, the concrete should be compacted as fully as possible. It must be emphasised that, however carefully the materials have been chosen and the concrete mixed and transported, the concrete's strength and durability will be severely reduced if it is not fully compacted. In particular the reinforcement must be completely surrounded by dense, fully compacted concrete.

The best compaction is produced by using poker vibrators, which are inserted through the top layer of concrete into the layer below and left until air bubbles cease to appear on the surface. They should then be withdrawn slowly and replaced in the concrete about half a meter away and the process repeated.

Where reinforcement is heavily congested, leaving no room for poker vibrators, then external vibrators, clamped onto the framework may have to be used. These are not so efficient and the formwork has to be specially designed to withstand the forces produced. Alternatively, the use of a superplasticizer may be useful, enabling full compaction to be obtained with the minimum of applied vibration.

CURING.—Placing and compacting must be followed by curing. The objects of curing are to prevent the concrete drying out before sufficient hydration of the cement has taken place to ensure the required strength and durability of the concrete and, in cold weather, to maintain an adequately high temperature to ensure hydration and prevent frost damage to the new concrete—see 'Cold weather Concreting', below.

Curing to maintain moisture content is normally achieved by:

(*a*) leaving the formwork in place

or (*b*) covering the concrete surface with an impermeable material such as polyethylene sheeting (polythene) which, if used, should be well sealed at all edges to prevent drafts and evaporation

or (*c*) use of a spray-on curing membrane.

Other materials, such as the use of damp hessian or similar material, or spraying with water are sometimes used, but they pose many practical difficulties on site and are seldom very effective.

Curing should be maintained for a minimum period after casting. BS 8110 gives recommendations on minimum curing periods which are reproduced in Table 11.

TABLE 11. MINIMUM PERIODS FOR CURING AND PROTECTION
[BS 8110: Part 1, Table 6.5]

Type of cement	Ambient conditions after casting	Average surface temperature of concrete		
		5°C to 10°C	Above 10°C	t (any temperature between 5°C and 25°C)
		Days	Days	Days
OPC, RHPC, SRPC	Average	4	3	$\frac{60}{t+10}$
	Poor	6	4	$\frac{80}{t+10}$
All except RHPC, OPC and SRPC and all with ggbfs or pfa	Average	6	4	$\frac{80}{t+10}$
	Poor	10	7	$\frac{140}{t+10}$
All	Good	No special requirements		

NOTE 1. Abbreviations for the type of cement used are as follows:
OPC: ordinary Portland cement (see BS 12);
RHPC: rapid-hardening Portland cement (see BS 12);
SRPC: sulphate-resisting Portland cement (see BS 4027).

NOTE 2. Ambient conditions after casting are as follows:
good: damp and protected (relative humidity greater than 80%; protected from sun and wind);
average: intermediate between good and poor;
poor: dry or unprotected (relative humidity less than 50%; not protected from sun and wind).

When pfa or ggbfs are used in the mix, either incorporated in the cement as purchased, or incorporated at the concrete mixer, adequate curing becomes even more important.

REINFORCEMENT AND COVER.—Most reinforcement on a modern site will be ordered and delivered ready cut and bent to the dimensions detailed in the contract documents. Whether cut and bent on or off site, it should be stored off the ground so that it is not contaminated by mud and soil.

Care should also be taken that at no time is reinforcement contaminated with formwork release agents or any other material likely to affect the hydration of the cement or the bond between reinforcement and concrete.

Some degree of surface rust does no harm and may even increase bond, but all loose rust and mill scale should be removed before the reinforcement is placed.

It is obvious that care should be taken to ensure that the bars are the right size and shape and positioned in accordance with the reinforcement drawings and schedules.

It is also essential to ensure that the correct type of bar is used and especially that mild steel is not used when high-yield steel bars have been specified. High-yield bars usually have ribs and are easily distinguishable from plain, round, mild steel bars.

It is extremely important that the reinforcement is protected by the correct amount of concrete cover. All reinforcement should be provided with sufficient spacer blocks of the correct size to maintain the cover during all site operations. If insufficient spacers are provided, loads from plant and workmen, and from concrete placing and compaction operations, can crush the spacers or cause them to punch into the form surface (22).

No steel or other metal should encroach into the cover concrete. This obviously includes all reinforcing bars, but it also includes any tying wire or clips used to fix the reinforcement.

FORMWORK AND FALSEWORK.—Formwork may be purpose made or assembled from proprietory formwork components. In either case, it will need to satisfy a number of requirements.

(*a*) it should be of the correct size and shape, and be in the correct position to produce the specified concrete structure.
(*b*) it should be strong and rigid enough not to move or distort under the loads of site plant, workmen, and the placing and compaction of concrete
(*c*) it should be sufficiently watertight to prevent grout loss from the concrete
(*d*) it should produce the required surface finish to the concrete
(*e*) it should be capable of being removed without damage to itself or the concrete
(*f*) it should continue to perform as above for the number of uses required of it.

A number of materials are used for formwork including sawn timber, plywood and other boards, steel, aluminium and glass reinforced and other plastics.

Where formwork needs to be supported on scaffolding or other falsework, this needs careful design to ensure its structural stability during all phases of the concrete construction. Heavy loads, including horizontal and inclined loads, can be applied by plant and fresh concrete.

Many accidents have occurred due to failure of falsework. Falsework should be subjected to the same care in design and construction as that given to the permanent work.

The design and construction of falsework is covered by BS 5975:1982. Other references give methods for calculating the pressures on formwork and help in formwork design and detailing (23) (24).

COLD WEATHER CONCRETING.—Low temperatures reduce the rate of hydration of cement and, if the temperatures are low enough, frost attack can affect the freshly placed concrete, see 'Durability—frost attack'. Concreting during cold weather, or when cold weather is expected, needs special precautions to be taken:

(*a*) aggregate stock piles and water should be protected from frost
(*b*) frozen materials should not be used in the mix
(*c*) concrete should not be cast against frozen ground or formwork surfaces
(*d*) surfaces of freshly placed concrete should be maintained at a temperature sufficiently high to prevent damage from frost.

BS 8110 requires that fresh concrete, at the time of placing, should have a temperature of at least 5°C, preferably 10°C, and that the temperature of the concrete should not fall below 5°C until its cube strength has reached 5N/mm^2.

More detailed guidance on methods for achieving compliance with these requirements is given in references (25) and (26).

HOT WEATHER CONCRETING.—At higher temperatures the rate of hydration of cement increases significantly. The effects of this on site during hot weather include more rapid stiffening and loss of workability between mixing and placing, greater temperature rises within the concrete mass, leading to higher thermal gradients and greater risk of early thermal cracking, and greater loss of moisture with more risk of plastic shrinkage cracking.

BS 8110 requires the concrete temperature to be below 30°C at the time of placing. Lower temperatures than this would be preferable in large pours. The temperature of the fresh concrete may be lowered by cooling the mixing water and the aggregate.

Workability may be increased, if necessary, by using a water reducing or plasticizing admixture, and the heat of hydration may be decreased by replacing some of the Portland cement by pfa or ggbfs.

Curing to prevent loss of water is even more important in hot weather than at other times if premature drying out, leading to loss of strength and surface drying shrinkage cracking, is to be avoided.

More information on hot weather concreting is given in reference (27).

SURFACE FINISH.—The requirements for the surface finish of structural concrete can vary widely. If the concrete is to be hidden from view, such as in a foundation, then a sound, dense durable surface is all that is required. Its visual appearance does not matter.

In contrast, the surface finish to concrete often is an essential element in the architect's or designer's concept, and the success of the project may rely heavily on producing the required finish.

Colour can be created by using pigments in the mix, or by exposing the aggregate by tooling or abrasive blasting to remove the surface layer. Profiled and textured surfaces can be produced by the formwork.

There are so many possibilities to choose from when deciding on the finish to be used, that it is impossible to cover the subject here, but some general principles can be stated:

(*a*) Contrary to some expectations, many examples have shown that it is impossible to produce a large plane, smooth, uniform surface. There always will be some colour variation and joints in the formwork will always show on the concrete surface.

(*b*) The formwork has to be of the highest standard, any slight lack of workmanship, allowing grout to escape, will show in the concrete surface produced even when the outer surface is removed to expose the aggregate.

(*c*) The choice of finish may often dictate the choice of cement and aggregate, and the mix design. These requirements often are more critical than those for structural performance.

(*d*) To attain a high quality surface may add considerably to the cost of the concrete work. This must be recognised early in the design process.

The general requirements for the production of high quality concrete finishes are given in references (28) and (29). The Cement and Concrete Association also publishes more detailed recommendations on methods for producing various types of surface finish.

REFERENCES

(1) STANLEY, C.C. *Highlights in the history of concrete.* Slough, Cement and Concrete Association, 1979. pp. 44 (97.408)

(2) PARKER, D. G. *Microsilica concrete. Part 1: The material.* Concrete, Vol. 19, No. 10, October 1985. pp. 21–22 (Concrete Society Current Practice Sheet No. 104)

(3) BUILDING RESEARCH ESTABLISHMENT. *Shrinkage of natural aggregates in concrete.* Garston, The Establishment, 1968, reprinted 1980. pp. 7 (Digest 35)

(4) ACI COMMITTEE 304. *High density concrete: measuring, mixing, transporting and placing.* Detroit, American Concrete Institute, 1975 (Reaffirmed 1980) pp. 8. (In ACI Manual of Concrete Practice, Part 2)

(5) HIGGINS, D. D. *Admixtures for concrete.* Slough, Cement and Concrete Association, 1984, reprinted 1985. pp. 8 (45.041)

(6) RIXOM, M. R. and MAILVAGANAM, N. P. *Chemical admixtures for concrete.* London, E. & F. N. Spon Ltd, 2nd edition 1986. pp. 306

(7) JOINT WORKING PARTY OF THE CEMENT ADMIXTURES ASSOCIATION & CEMENT AND CONCRETE ASSOCIATION. *Superplasticizing admixtures in concrete.* Slough, Cement & Concrete Association 1976, reprinted with amendments 1978. pp. 32 (45.030)

(8) ROBERTS, M. H. *Carbonation of concrete made with dense natural aggregates.* Garston, Building Research Establishment, 1981. pp. 4 (IP6/81)

(9) BUILDING RESEARCH ESTABLISHMENT. *Concrete in sulphate-bearing soils and ground waters.* Garston, The Establishment, 1981. Reprinted with minor revisions 1984. pp. 4 (Digest 250)

(10) ACI COMMITTEE 515. *A guide to the use of waterproofing, damp-proofing, protective and decorative barrier systems for concrete.* Detroit, American Concrete Institute, 1979. pp. 41 (In ACI Manual of Concrete Practice, Part 5)

(11) HAWKINS, M. R. Chairman. *Minimising the risk of alkali-silica reaction. Guidance Notes.* Report of a Working Party. Slough, Cement and Concrete Association, 1983. pp. 8 (97.304)

(12) HOBBS, D. W. *Alkali-silica reaction in Concrete.* The Structural Engineer, Vol 69A, No 12, Dec. 1986, pp. 381–383

(13) TEYCHENNE, D. C. FRANKLIN, R. E. AND ERNTROY, H. C. *Design of normal concrete mixes.* London, H.M.S.O., 1975. pp. 31

(14) OWENS, P. L. *Basic mix method and selection of proportions for medium strength concretes.* Slough, Cement and Concrete Association, 1973. pp. 19 (11.005)

(15) HARRIS, C. A. R. *Statistics for concrete—Part 1.* London, Concrete Society, 1984. pp. 7 (Concrete Society Digest No. 5) (53.049)

(16) LEES, T. P. *Field tests for chlorides in concreting aggregates.* Slough, Cement and Concrete Association, 1982. pp. 5 (45.039)
(17) DHIR, R. K. *Analysis of fresh concrete: determinations of cement content by the rapid analysis machine.* Magazine of Concrete Research, Vol. 34, No. 119, June 1982, pp 59–73
(18) CONCRETE SOCIETY WORKING PARTY. *Concrete core testing for strength.* London, Concrete Society, 1976. pp. 44 (Concrete Society Technical Report No. 11) (51.071)
(19) WATSON, R. V. *Storing cement in silos on site.* Slough, Cement and Concrete Association, 1975. 2nd edition 1979. pp. 3 (45.029)
(20) ILLINGWORTH, J. R. *Movement and distribution of concrete.* London, McGraw-Hill Book Company (UK) Ltd, 1972. pp. 239
(21) BRITISH CONCRETE PUMPING ASSOCIATION. *Concrete Pumping Handbook.* London, The Association, 1974. pp. 50
(22) ROBERTS, R. F. *Spacers for reinforcement.* Slough, Cement and Concrete Association, 1969, Third edition 1981. pp. 8 (47.007)
(23) CLEAR, C. A. & HARRISON, T. A. *Concrete pressure on formwork.* London, Construction Industry Research and Information Association, 1985. pp. 31 (Report 108)
(24) RICHARDSON, J. G. *Formwork construction and practice.* London, Palladian Publications Ltd., 1977. pp. 275
(25) HARRISON, T. A. *Tables of minimum striking times for soffit and vertical formwork.* London, Construction Industry Research and Information Association, 1977, reprinted 1979. pp. 24 (Report 67)
(26) PINK, A. *Winter concreting.* Slough, Cement and Concrete Association, 1976, Third edition 1978, reprinted 1985. pp. 19 (45.007)
(27) SHIRLEY, D. E. *Concreting in hot weather.* Slough, Cement and Concrete Association, 1966, Fourth edition 1980, reprinted 1985. pp. 7 (45.013)
(28) MONKS, W. *Visual concrete: Design and production.* Slough, Cement and Concrete Association, 1980, reprinted with minor amendments, 1981. pp. 28 (Appearance Matters—1) (47.101)
(29) MONKS, W. *The control of blemishes in concrete.* Slough, Cement and Concrete Association, 1981. pp. 20 (Appearance Matters—3) (47.103)

BRITISH STANDARDS

(The following Standards, referred to in the text and listed here in numerical order, are published by the British Standards Institution, London).

BS 12:1978. Specification for ordinary and rapid-hardening Portland cement. 1978. pp. 4.
BS 146. Portland-blastfurnace cement.
BS 146 Pt.2:1973. Metric Units. 1973. pp. 8.

BS 812 Testing Aggregates.
BS 812 Pt.1:1975. Methods for determination of particle size and shape. 1975. pp. 24.
BS 812 Pt.2:1975. Methods for determination of physical properties. 1975. pp. 20.
BS 812 Pt.3:1975. Mechanical properties. 1975. pp. 20.
BS 812 Pt.4:1976. Methods for determination of chemical properties. 1976. pp. 4.
BS 812 Pt.101:1984. Guide to sampling and testing aggregates. 1984. pp. 4.
BS 812 Pt.102:1984. Methods for sampling. 1984. pp. 8.
BS 812 Pt.103:1985. Method for determination of particle size distribution. 1985. pp. 8.
BS 812 Pt.105:Section 105-1:1985. Flakiness index. 1985. pp.4.
BS 812 Pt.106:1985. Method for determination of shell content in coarse aggregate. 1985. pp. 4.
BS 812 Pt.119:1985. Method for determination of acid-soluble material in fine aggregate. 1985. pp. 4.

BS 882:1983. Specification for aggregates from natural sources for concrete. 1983. pp. 8.
BS 915 High alumina cement.
BS 915 Pt.2:1972 (1984). Metric Units. 1972. pp. 4.

BS 1014:1975. Pigments for Portland cement and Portland cement products. 1975. pp. 12.
BS 1305:1974. Batch type concrete mixers. 1974. pp. 12.
BS 1370:1979. Specification for low heat Portland cement. 1979. pp. 4.
BS 1881. Methods of testing concrete: Parts 1 + 5 + 6 + 101-122. Separately paginated.
BS 3148:1980. Methods of test for water for making concrete (including notes on the suitability of the water). 1980. pp. 4.

BS 3797 Specification for lighweight aggregates for concrete.
BS 3797:Pt.2:1976. Metric Units. 1976. pp. 4.

BS 3892 Pulverised fuel ash.
BS 3892 Pt.1:1982. Specification for pulverised fuel ash for use as a cementitious component in structural concrete. 1982. pp. 12.
BS 4027:1980. Specification for sulphate-resisting Portland cement. 1980. pp. 4.

BS 4246. Low heat Portland-blastfurnace cement.
BS 4246 Pt.2:1974. Metric Units. 1974. pp. 12.

BS 4248:1974. Specification for supersulphated cement. 1974. pp. 24.
BS 4251:1974 (1980). Truck type concrete mixers. 1974. pp. 8.
BS 4408. Recommendations for non-destructive methods of test for concrete. Parts 1-5. Separately paginated.
BS 4550. Methods of testing cement. Parts 0-6. Separately paginated.

BS 5075. Concrete admixtures.
BS 5075 Pt.1:1982. Specification for accelerating admixtures, retarding admixtures and water-reducing admixtures. 1982. pp. 16.
BS 5075 Pt.2:1982. Specification for air-entraining admixtures. 1982. pp. 8.
BS 5075 Pt.3:1985. Specification for superplasticizing admixtures. 1985. pp. 8.

BS 5224:1976. Specification for masonry cement. 1976. pp. 8.
BS 5328;1981. Methods for specifying concrete, including ready-mixed concrete. 1981. pp. 16.
BS 5337:1976. Code of practice for the structural use of concrete for retaining aqueous liquids. 1976. pp. 16.

BS 5400. Steel, concrete and composite bridges.
BS 5400:Pt.4:1984. Code of practice for design of concrete bridges. 1984. pp. 64.
BS 5975:1982. Code of practice for falsework. 1982. pp. 80.
BS 6588:1985. Specification for Portland pulverised fuel ash cement. 1985. pp. 4.
BS 6610:1985. Specification for pozzolanic cement with pulverised fuel ash as pozzolana. 1985. pp. 4.
BS 6699:1986. Specification for ground granulated blastfurnace slag for use with Portland cement 1986. pp. 16.

BS 8110. Structural use of concrete.
BS 8110:Pt.1:1985. Code of practice for design and construction. 1985. pp. 124.
BS 8110:Pt.2:1985. Code of practice for special circumstances. 1984. pp. 52.

DESIGN OF STEEL STRUCTURES

Materials—Design Strengths—Section Classification—Bolted and Welded Connections—Tension Members—Beams—Unsymmetrical Sections—Shear Capacity of Beams—Beam Web Bearing and Buckling—Plate Girders—Stanchions and Struts—Eccentrically Loaded Members—Angle Struts—Types of Stanchions—Stanchion Bases—Roof Trusses—Stability—Tables of British Standard Sections.

By P. J. Loveridge, C.Eng., M.I.Struct.E.

INTRODUCTION.—Part 1 of BS 5950 'Structural use of steelwork in building' was issued in 1985 and will eventually replace its predecessor BS 449 as the code of practice for the design of structures constructed using hot rolled and fabricated steel sections. We are, at the time of writing, in an overlap period in which both documents have 'Deemed-to-satisfy' status under the Building Regulations. It was the original intention of the Building Regulations Division of the Department of the Environment to withdraw this status for BS 449 by the end of 1987. However after consultation with the various organisations whose members use these documents this intention has been modified to the extent that a revised and up dated version of BS 449 is to be issued to co-exist for the time being with BS 5950. Thus the overlap period will now extend into the foreseeable future. This chapter will deal solely with the new code, as the rules laid down in the existing BS 449 are generally well known and its revised version is still in the course of preparation.

Part 2 of BS 5950 deals with materials, fabrication and erection, Parts 3 to 9, which are yet to be issued, will deal with design of specialised structural elements such as profiled sheeting, cold formed sections, fire protection for steelwork etc. which are outside the scope of this chapter. Part 1 of BS 5950 differs from BS 449 in two major respects. Firstly it contains a number of new design rules and concepts and secondly it is written in terms of limit state design.

Hitherto an acceptable factor of safety has been imparted to steel structures by limiting stresses under working loads to some proportion of the material strength. In BS 449 this proportion has been taken to be approximately two thirds of the yield strength. With limit state design the designer must ensure that there is an acceptable probability that the structure will not become unfit for its intended use. Or, to put this situation in other words, he must ensure that the structure will not reach a limit state. In BS 5950 limit states are grouped together in two categories:

(1) Ultimate limit states such as Strength, Stability against overturning and sway, Fracture due to fatigue, and Brittle fracture.

(2) Serviceability limit states such as Deflection, Vibration, Repairable damage due to fatigue, Corrosion and Durability.

Partial safety factors are used, γ_m to allow for variations of material strength, γ_l to allow for variations of applied loading and γ_p the structural performance factor. Thus the overall safety factor becomes the product of γ_m, γ_l and γ_p and has a value which varies according to the circumstances; this is further explained by the following. In BS 5950 γ_m to be applied to the design strength is taken as 1·0, the product of γ_l and γ_p is

TABLE 1.—LOAD FACTORS AND COMBINATIONS

Loading	Factor γ_f
Dead load	1·4
Dead load restraining uplift or overturning	1·0
Dead load acting with wind and imposed load combined	1·2
Imposed load	1·6
Imposed load acting with wind load	1·2
Wind load	1·4
Wind load acting with imposed load or crane load	1·2
Forces due to temperature effects	1·2
Crane loading effects:	
Vertical load	1·6
Vertical load acting with horizontal loads (crabbing or surge)	1·4
Horizontal load	1·6
Horizontal load acting with vertical load	1·4
Crane load acting with wind load*	1·2

* When considering wind or imposed load and crane loading acting together the value of γ_f for the dead load may be taken as 1·2.

designated as γ_f and applied to the specified loading on the structure. The values assigned to γ_f for various ultimate limit state loading conditions are set out in Table 1. γ_f for the serviceability limit state is taken as 1·0.

Note this chapter is intended as an introduction to its subject title. As such it deals with basic structural elements and considers only the ultimate limit states of strength and stability and serviceability limit state of deflection as applicable. For basic structural design practice this is all that is required except in specific circumstances. The reader is referred to Section two of BS 5950 Part 1 for further details of general principles and design methods.

MATERIALS.—Parts 1 and 2 of BS 5950 make reference to BS 4360 'Weldable structural steels' a new revision of which was issued in 1986. BS 5950 states that it covers the design of structures fabricated from steel supplied to this standard. It also states that other steels may be used provided due allowance is made for variation in properties including ductility. Steel to BS 4360 is supplied in four main grades designated 40, 43, 50 and 55 with each grade divided into subgrades A to D, DD, EE and F. Steel to grade 43A is that most widely used for general structural purposes. This has a minimum yield strength which varies from 225 N/mm^2 to 275 N/mm^2 depending upon thickness and a minimum elongation of 20% on a gauge length of 200 mm. When higher strength is required steel to grade 50B may be used. This has a minimum yield strength which varies from 305 N/mm^2 to 355 N/mm^2 depending upon thickness. Still higher strength is obtained by using grade 55 steel which has a yield strength which varies from 400 N/mm^2 to 450 N/mm^2 depending upon thickness. These higher strength steels are somewhat less ductile than grade 43 steel having a minimum elongation of 18% and 17% respectively on a gauge length of 200 mm.

Although all steels specified in BS 4360 are weldable, the proper procedures must always be followed; these are laid down in BS 5135 'Process of Arc Welding of Carbon and Carbon Manganese Steels'.

For bolts the strength designations of ISO/DR 911 have been adopted in BS 4190 for Black Bolts (Strength grade 4·6) and BS 3692 for Precision Bolts (Strength grade 8·8).

Steel is prepared for the use of the Structural Engineer in the form of hot-rolled sections most of which are to dimensions laid down in BS 4: Part 1 'Structural Steel Sections'. Steel angles are covered by BS 4848, Part 4. The most common cross-sectional forms are shown in Fig. 1 and a selection of these sections with their

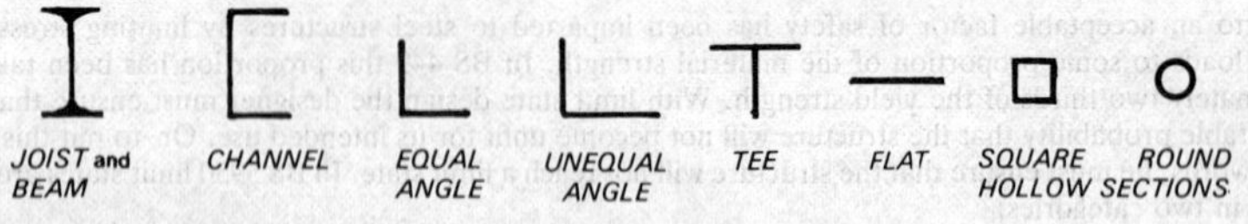

FIG. 1.—Common Rolled Steel Sections.

dimensions and properties are given in Tables 10 to 17 inclusive. Sections are generally rolled in lengths of from 12 m to 18 m. Longer lengths may be obtained by special arrangement. For structures in the form of beam and column frameworks the most useful components are the Universal beam and Universal column sections; see Tables 11 and 12. BS 4: Part 1, also specifies joists, channels, bulb angles, bulb flats, short stalk and long stalk tees. Large tee sections made by cutting in half Universal beams and columns are also listed as standards in BS 4. Castellated beams made by cutting and welding standard sections are useful when deep but lightweight sections are appropriate. Castellated Universal beams are available in sizes up to 1371 mm × 419 mm, and castellated Universal columns, joists and Z-beams are also available.

BS 4848: Part 2, covers hot-rolled hollow sections of circular, rectangular and square form which are finding increasing application in building and other structures. The range of overall dimensions for standard sections are: Circular sections, 21·3 mm to 457 mm outside diameter; rectangular sections 50 mm × 30 mm to 450 mm × 250 mm; square sections 20 mm × 20 mm to 400 mm × 400 mm.

Steel plates are used either separately as 'flats', to augment other sections or built up into sections by welding. Two types of plate in thicknesses up to 150 mm are available: viz. Universal plates with both edges rolled, in widths up to 1150 mm, and ordinary plate, the edges of which are not rolled, in widths up to 2000 mm. Slabs are sometimes required for stanchion bases, etc. and are obtainable in thicknesses up to about 400 mm. Bars of circular section up to 40 mm in diameter are rolled principally for use in reinforced concrete construction, but are sometimes required in steel structures. Other sections which are sometimes useful are shown in Fig. 2. Special sections such as these are not generally available from stock and may have to be specially rolled.

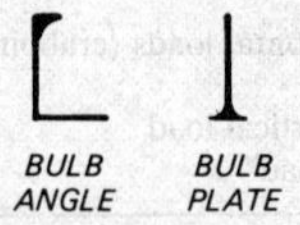

FIG. 2.—R.S. Sections for Special Purposes.

DESIGN STRENGTHS.—These should be taken as γ_m times the minimum yield strength (Y_s), and γ_m is taken as 1·0 (see Introduction). It follows that the design strength ρ_y should be 1·0 Y_s. This is stated in Section three of BS 5950 which adds that design strength should not exceed 0·84 of the minimum ultimate tensile strength. Design strengths taken from BS 5950 for the more commonly used steel grades are given in Table 2:

TABLE 2.—DESIGN STRENGTHS FOR STEEL TO BS 4360

BS 4360 Grade	Thickness less than or equal to mm	Sections, plates and hollow sections ρ_y N/mm^2
43 A, B and C	16	275
	40	265
	100	245
50 B and C	16	355
	63	340
	100	325
55 C	16	450
	25	430
	40	415

Section three of BS 5950 lists elastic properties to be used, which do not appear in BS 4360. These are:

Modulus of Elasticity, E = 205 kN/mm^2

Poisson's ratio = 0·3

Coefficient of linear expansion = 12×10^{-6} per °C.

The underlying assumption in the design of steel structures is that the tensile stress/strain curve follows that usually associated with steel. That is that there is a linear relationship up to the point of yield, a plateau of ductility, followed by strain hardening and ultimate failure after further substantial strain. Examples of stress/strain curves for steels of grades 43, 50 and 55 are given in Fig. 3.

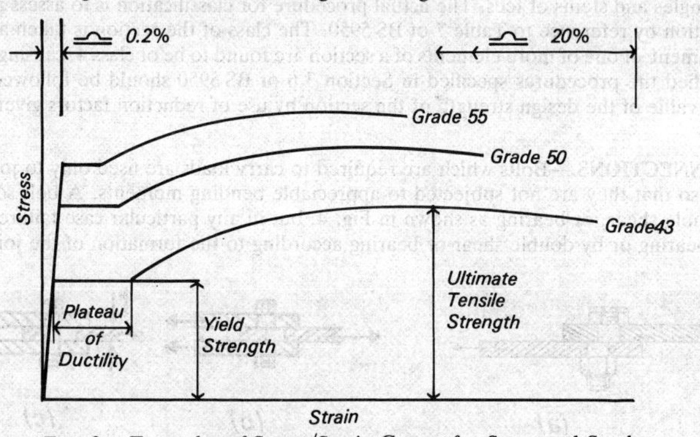

FIG. 3.—Examples of Stress/Strain Curves for Structural Steels

SECTION CLASSIFICATION.—Local buckling can be avoided by limiting the width to thickness ratios of each element of the cross section subject to compression due to bending or axial load. BS 5950 introduces rules from which sections can be classified as plastic, compact, semi-compact or slender and states that cross sections may be composed of elements of different classes. Beams may fall into any one of the four classes mentioned above depending on their local buckling performance.

Class 1. Plastic section. Full plastic moment can be developed with adequate rotation capacity to allow plastic design. Local buckling can be ignored.

Class 2. Compact section. The full plastic moment can be developed but local buckling may prevent the development of a plastic hinge.

Class 3. Semi-compact section. The member can attain the design strength at the extreme fibres but local buckling may prevent the development of a plastic hinge.

Class 4. Slender section. Local buckling may prevent the member attaining the full design strength.

For struts loaded in axial compression classes 1, 2 and 3 coalesce into one:

Classes 1, 2 and 3; now referred to as compact. The member is able to develop the full design strength without local buckling.

Class 4. Slender section. The member may fail to attain the full design strength due to local buckling.

Table 7 of BS 5950 gives limiting width/thickness ratios for elements of sections of classes 1, 2 and 3. When these limits are exceeded the element is taken as class 4. For elements under uniform compression (excluding angles and tees) these limits are summarized in Table 3:

TABLE 3.—LIMITING WIDTH/THICKNESS RATIOS FOR ELEMENTS UNDER UNIFORM COMPRESSION

Class	Limiting ratio $b/T\varepsilon$					
	Internal			Outstand		
	1	2	3	1	2	3
Rolled sections	26	32	39	8·5	9·5	15
Welded sections	23	25	28	7·5	8·5	13

Note $\varepsilon = \left(\frac{275}{p_y}\right)^{\frac{1}{2}}$

A web element, being only partly in compression, is more resistant to local buckling than an equivalent element under uniform compression. Table 7 of BS 5950 gives limiting width thickness ratios for webs as follows.

Neutral axis at mid depth: Class 1 limit $d/t = 79$

Class 2 limit $d/t = 98$

Class 3 limit $d/t = 120$

Table 7 of BS 5950 also gives limits for the situation when the neutral axis of the web is not at mid depth and for legs of angles and stems of tees. The actual procedure for classification is to assess all elements which make up the section by reference to Table 7 of BS 5950. The class of the section is taken as that of the most unfavourable element. If one of more elements of a section are found to be of class 4, causing the whole section to be thus classified the procedures specified in Section 3.6 of BS 5950 should be followed. This involves a reduction in the value of the design strength of the section by use of reduction factors given in Table 8 of BS 5950.

BOLTED CONNECTIONS.—Bolts which are required to carry loads are used only to join parts which are in close contact so that they are not subjected to appreciable bending moments. A bolt so used may fail by single shear, double shear, or bearing as shown in Fig. 4, but in any particular case failure may be either by single shear or bearing or by double shear or bearing according to the formation of the joint.

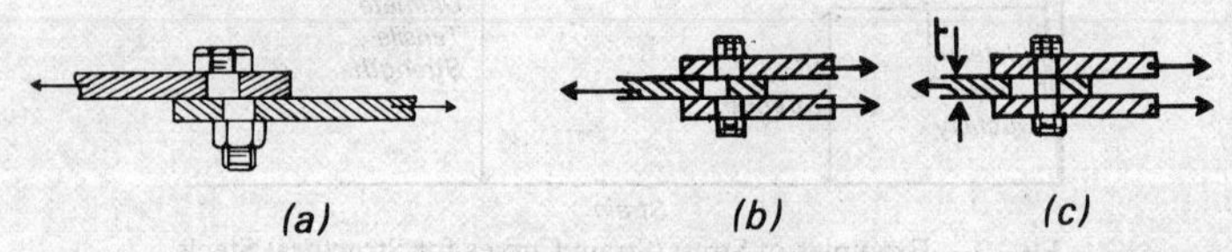

FIG. 4.—Modes of Failure of Bolts: (*a*) Single Shear Failure. (*b*) Double Shear Failure. (*c*) Bearing Failure.

In a given case the permissible load is the lesser of the shear and bearing capacities which are given in BS 5950 by:

Shear capacity $p_s = p_s A_s$

Bearing capacity of bolt $p_{bb} = dtp_{bb}$

Bearing capacity of connected ply $p_{bs} = dtp_{bs} \leq \frac{1}{2}etp_{bs}$

where p_s is the shear strength from Table 4; A_s is the shear area taken as the tensile stress area at the bottom of threads or the shank area as considered appropriate; d is the nominal diameter; t is the thickness of the connected ply; p_{bb} is the bearing strength of the bolt from Table 4; p_{bs} is the bearing strength of the connected parts from Table 5; e is the end distance i.e. the distance from the centre of the hole to the adjacent edge in the direction in which the fastener bears.

The strengths of bolts according to BS 5950 are given in Table 4.

TABLE 4. STRENGTH OF BOLTS IN CLEARANCE HOLES

	Bolt grade		Other grades of fasteners
	4·6	8·8	
	N/mm²	N/mm²	N/mm²
Shear strength p_s	160	375	$0{\cdot}48\ U_f$ but $\leqslant 0{\cdot}69\ Y_f$
Bearing strength p_{bb}	435	970	$0{\cdot}64\ (U_f + Y_f)$
Tension strength p_t	195	450	$0{\cdot}58\ U_f$ but $\leqslant 0{\cdot}83\ Y_f$

Y_f is the specified minimum yield strength of the fastener.
U_f is the specified minimum ultimate tensile strength of the fastener.

The bearing strengths of connected parts according to BS 5950 are given in Table 5.

TABLE 5.—BEARING STRENGTH OF CONNECTED PARTS FOR ORDINARY BOLTS IN CLEARANCE HOLES, p_{bs}

Steel grade to BS 4360			Other grade of steel
43	50	55	
N/mm²	N/mm²	N/mm²	N/mm²
460	550	650	$0{\cdot}65\ (U_s + Y_s)$

Y_s is the specified minimum yield strength of the steel.
U_s is the specified minimum ultimate tensile strength of the steel.

BS 5950 has rules for long joints and large grip lengths, these are:

Long joints.—When the joint length of a splice or end connection in a compression or tension element containing more than two bolts (i.e. the distance between the first and last rows of bolts measured in the direction of load transfer) exceeds 500 mm, the shear capacity should be taken as:

$$P_s = p_s A_s \left(\frac{5500 - L_j}{5000}\right), \text{ but not more than given for large grips, if applicable}$$

where L_j is the joint length in mm.

Large grips.—When the grip length (i.e. the total thickness of the connected plies) exceeds five times the nominal diameter of the bolts the shear capacity should be taken as:

$$P_s = p_s A_s \left(\frac{8d}{3d + T_g}\right), \text{ but not more than given for long joints, if applicable}$$

where T_g is the grip length in mm.

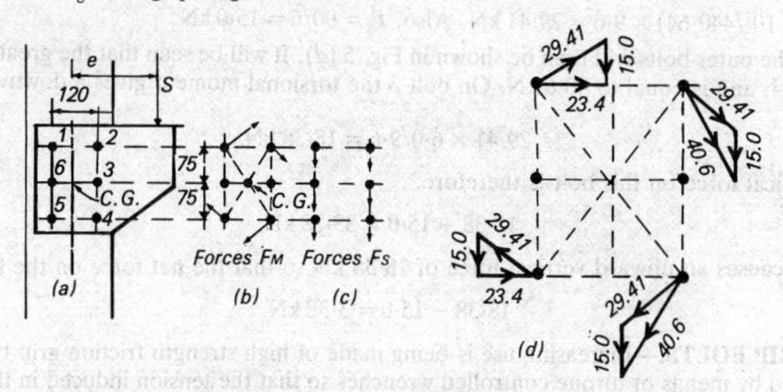

FIG. 5.—Eccentric Bolted Connection.

BOLTS IN TENSION.—The tension capacity of a bolt is given in BS 5950 by:

Tension capacity $P_t = p_t A_t$

where p_t is the tension strength from Table 3; A_t is the specified tensile stress area which, where not defined, should be taken as the area at the bottom of the threads.

BOLTS IN SHEAR AND TENSION.—When bolts are subject to both shear and tension in addition to the foregoing capacities being adequate the following relationship should be satisfied:

$$\frac{F_s}{P_s} + \frac{F_t}{P_t} \leqslant 1{\cdot}4$$

where F_s is the applied shear; F_t is the applied tension; P_s and P_t are the shear and tension capacities respectively.

BOLT SPACING AND EDGE DISTANCES.—The minimum distance between centres of bolts should not be less than 2·5 times the nominal diameter. The maximum distance between centres of bolts in the direction of load should not exceed 14 times the thickness of the thinner ply and, in any case, 16 times the thickness of the thinner outside ply or 200 mm in corrosive conditions.

The minimum distance from the centre of a bolt to the edge or end of any part should not be less than 1·25 times the bolt hole diameter for rolled, machine flame cut, sawn or planed edges and 1·4 times the bolt hole diameter for sheared or hand flame cut edges. The maximum edge or end distance should not exceed 40 mm plus 4 times the thickness of the thinner outside ply in corrosive conditions.

ECCENTRIC BOLTED CONNECTIONS.—In Fig. 5 (*a*) the group of six bolts connecting the bracket to the stanchion is subjected to a torsional moment in addition to the vertical force. The shear stresses in the bolts due to the torsional moment are obtained on the assumption that the group tends to rotate about its centre of gravity and has a polar moment of inertia of:

$$\mathrm{I} = a\Sigma d^2$$

where a is the cross-sectional area of one bolt and d is the distance of any bolt from the centre of gravity. The stress in each bolt is proportional to its distance from the centre of gravity so that the mean stress in the most remote bolt (distance d_{max}) will be:

$$f_m = (M_T/a\Sigma d^2)\,.\,d_{max}$$

where M_T is the torsional moment. The force on this bolt due to M_T will be:

$$F_M = (M_T/\Sigma d^2)\,.\,d_{max}$$

This force acts in a direction at right angles to the arm of the bolt as shown in Fig. 5 (*b*).

Due to the vertical shear force S the force on each bolt will be the same and given by:

$$F_s = \mathrm{S/N}$$

where N is the number of bolts in the group acting as shown in Fig. 5 (*c*).

The resultant force on the bolt or bolts most remote from the centre-of-gravity is then obtained by vectorial combination of F_M and F_s as shown in the following example.

If in Fig. 5(*a*), S = 90 kN factored load and e = 150 mm, then $M_T = \mathrm{S} \times e = 90 \times 0{\cdot}15 = 13{\cdot}5$ kNm.

For the dimensions given, the four outer bolts 1, 2, 4 and 5 are distant: $\sqrt{(7{\cdot}5^2 + 6{\cdot}0^2)} = 9{\cdot}6$ cm from the centre of gravity.

Then $\Sigma d^2 = 4 \times 9{\cdot}6^2 + 2 \times 6{\cdot}0^2 = 368{\cdot}64 + 72{\cdot}0 = 440{\cdot}64\ \mathrm{cm}^2$.

For the outer bolts, $d_{max} = 9{\cdot}6$ cm.

and $F_M = (13{\cdot}5 \times 10^2/440{\cdot}64) \times 9{\cdot}6 = 29{\cdot}41$ kN. Also, $F_s = 90/6 = 15{\cdot}0$ kN.

The forces on the outer bolts will then be shown in Fig. 5 (*d*). It will be seen that the greatest resultant force is on bolts 2 and 4, and is equal to 40·6 kN. On bolt 3 the torsional moment gives a downward vertical force of:

$$29{\cdot}41 \times 6{\cdot}0/9{\cdot}6 = 18{\cdot}38\ \mathrm{kN}$$

and the total vertical force on this bolt is therefore:

$$18{\cdot}38 + 15{\cdot}0 = 33{\cdot}38\ \mathrm{kN}.$$

On bolt 6, M_T causes an upward vertical force of 18·38 kN so that the net force on the bolt is:

$$18{\cdot}38 - 15{\cdot}0 = 3{\cdot}38\ \mathrm{kN}.$$

FRICTION GRIP BOLTS.—Increasing use is being made of high strength friction grip bolts. Friction grip bolts are tightened by means of torque controlled wrenches so that the tension induced in the bolts is not less than the proof load. In a connection made with these bolts load transfer is affected entirely by friction. Advantages are that the bolts are pretested in the tightening process and no slip occurs in the connections. These bolts and their use are covered by BS 4395 and BS 4604. Design rules for friction grip bolts are given in Section 6·4 of BS 5950.

WELDED CONNECTIONS.—Two types of weld are used, these are butt welds and fillet welds as shown in Fig. 6. Fillet welds are classified as side fillet welds, parallel to the direction of force transmission, and end fillet welds, perpendicular to the direction of force transmission. Butt welds are specified according to the manner in which the joint faces are prepared for welding. The type shown in Fig. 6 is a 'single vee' butt weld. There are many types of butt weld which are fully described in BS 5135 Process of Arc Welding of Carbon and Carbon Manganese Steels. Fillet welds are specified by the leg length (see Fig. 7) which is loosely termed the 'size' of the weld.

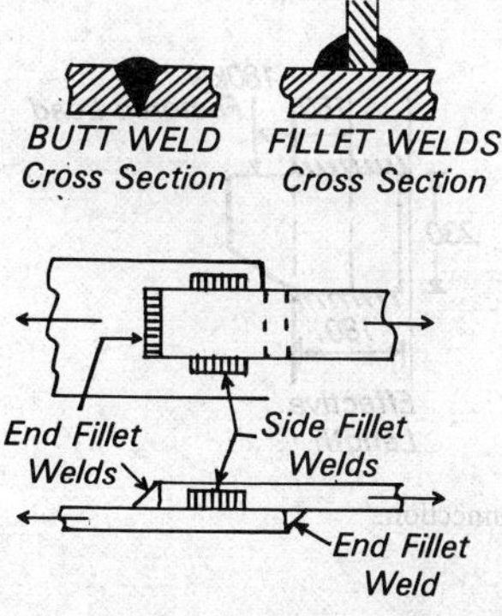

FIG. 6.—Types of Weld.

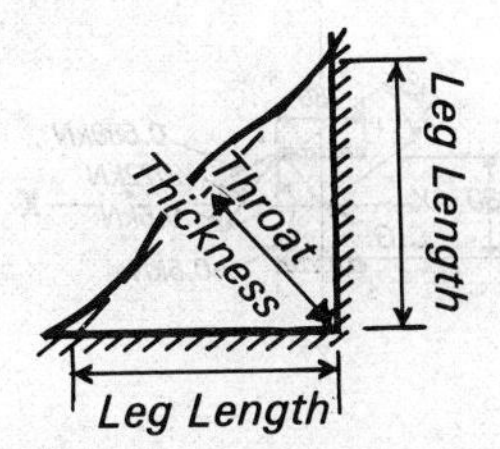

FIG. 7.—Cross-sectional Dimensions of a Fillet Weld.

THE STRENGTH OF WELDS.—Properly formed full-depth butt welds in mild steel can be assumed to have the same strength as the metal joined in tension, compression and shear. The strength of both side and end fillet welds is governed by the throat thickness and the shear strength of the metal. In a properly formed weld the actual throat thickness is slightly greater than the nominal thickness (see Fig. 7) which for the purpose of calculation is taken as 0·7 of the nominal leg length. The permissible stress on the cross-sectional area of the throat is specified in BS 5950 as 215 N/mm^2 for steel to grade 43 of BS 4360. Fillet welds are designed on the basis of the permissible load per mm run. For example a 6 mm fillet weld has a nominal leg length of 6 mm and a nominal throat thickness of $6 \times 0{\cdot}7 = 4{\cdot}2$ mm. Then the cross-sectional area at the throat for a length of weld of 1 mm is 4·2 mm^2 and the permissible load per mm run of weld is $4{\cdot}2 \times 215 = 903$ N $= 0{\cdot}903$ kN. The permissible loads for fillet welds of various sizes are given in Table 6.

ECCENTRIC WELDED CONNECTIONS.—The treatment of welded eccentric connections is basically similar to that for eccentric bolted connections. Providing all the fillet welds in the connection are the same size, they can be assumed of unit area per mm run for the purpose of finding the polar moment of inertia. I_p. Then the force per mm run of weld at a point distance r from the centre of gravity due to a torsional moment M_T will be:

$$F_M = (M_T/I_p)r$$

This force is then combined vectorially with the direct shear force which is assumed to be constant for all points, ie:

$F_s = S/\Sigma l$, where Σl is the total effective length of weld.

TABLE 6.—STRENGTH OF FILLET WELDS FOR GRADE 43 STEEL

Fillet size (leg length) mm	Throat thickness mm	Permissible load per mm run at 215 N/mm^2 kN
4	2·8	0·602
6	4·2	0·903
8	5·6	1·20
10	7·0	1·51
12	8·4	1·81
15	10·5	2·26
20	14·0	3·01

Fig. 8 shows a welded alternative to the bolted connection in Fig. 5 (*a*). Taking the effective length of each weld as 180 mm we have $I_p = I_x + I_y$

$$= 2 \times 18{\cdot}0 \times 11{\cdot}5^2 + 2 \times 18{\cdot}0^3/12$$

$$= 4761{\cdot}0 + 972{\cdot}0 = 5733{\cdot}0 \text{ cm}^4$$

and

$$\Sigma l = 2 \times 18{\cdot}0 = 36{\cdot}0 \text{ cm.}$$

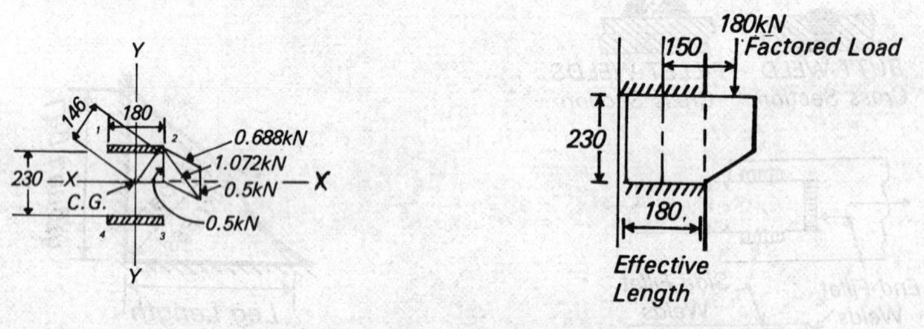

FIG. 8.—Eccentric Welded Connection.

Then for points 1, 2, 3 and 4, $r = 14{\cdot}6$ cm and

$$F_M = 180{\cdot}0 \times 15{\cdot}0 \times 14{\cdot}6/5733{\cdot}0 \times 10{\cdot}0 = 0{\cdot}688 \text{ kN/mm}$$

and

$$F_s = 180{\cdot}0/36{\cdot}0 \times 10{\cdot}0 = 0{\cdot}5 \text{ kN/mm.}$$

The maximum resultant force will be at points 2 and 3 and has a value of 1·072 kN/mm. By reference to Table 6 it will be seen that an 8 mm fillet is required.

CONTINUITY IN WELDED STEEL STRUCTURES.—There is a general tendency for welded connections to confer a greater degree of rigidity on a steel structure than the conventional types of bolted connections. This is sometimes an advantage both in the detail design and for the general stability and efficiency of the structure, but if the use of welding creates continuity of the members at the joints allowance should always be made for this both in the design of the members and the welded connections.

TENSION MEMBERS

Axially loaded tension members are dealt with in Section 4.6 of BS 5950.

The load capacity of an axially loaded tension member is given by:

$$\text{Tension capacity } P_t = A_e p_y$$

where A_e is the effective area of the section; p_y is the appropriate design strength of the steel.

When a tension member is subject to eccentric loading due allowance should be made for the resulting bending moment. The following relationship should be satisfied:

$$\frac{F}{A_e p_y} + \frac{M_x}{M_{cx}} + \frac{M_y}{M_{cy}} \leqslant 1$$

where F is the applied axial load; M_x and M_y are the moments applied at the critical regions about the major and minor axes respectively; M_{cx} and M_{cy} are the moment capacities in the absence of axial load about the major and minor axes respectively (for moment capacities see section on beams which follows); A_e and p_y are as defined above for axially loaded members.

ROOF TRUSS TIES.—When single ties are used eccentricity occurs at the connections to the gusset plates. Load concentrates in the connected leg and there may be a considerable reduction of stress at the tip of the outstanding leg. The outstanding leg is thus relatively inefficient in carrying the load and approximate allowance for the effect of the eccentricity is generally made as follows:

The load is assumed to be axially applied to a member having an effective area equal to that of the connected leg less holes plus part of the area of the outstanding leg. This will be made clear by reference to Fig. 9, where the effective area for axial loading is shown shaded and X is equal to $(3a_1/3a_1 + a_2)$; a_1 and a_2 being the effective area as shown. Double angle ties connected on both sides of the gussets are treated as axially loaded with no reduction in cross section other than for the holes.

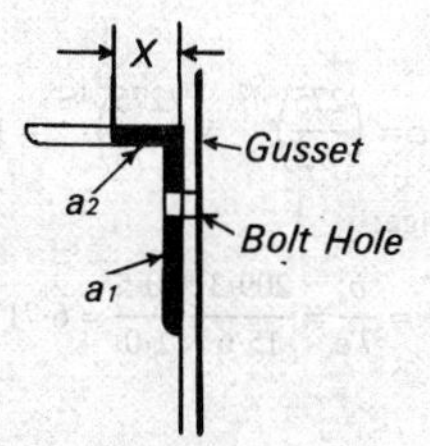

FIG. 9.—Single Angle Ties.

BEAMS

The first stage in design is to calculate the bending moments and shear forces using factored loads. BS 5950 gives the following expressions for moment capacity M_c:

Where average shear force $F_v \leqslant 0{\cdot}6\ P_v$
For plastic compact sections (classes 1 and 2):

$$M_c = p_y S \text{ but } \leqslant 1{\cdot}2\, p_y Z$$

For semi-compact sections (class 3):

$$M_c = p_y Z$$

For slender sections (class 4):

$$M_c = p_y Z$$

where P_v is the shear capacity of the section $= 0{\cdot}6\ p_y A_v$ where A_v is the shear area; p_y is the design strength (reduced for slender sections in accordance with section 3.6 of BS 5950); S is the plastic modulus of the section about the relevant axis; Z is the elastic modulus of the section about the relevant axis.

Where average shear force $F_v > 0{\cdot}6\ P_v$.
For plastic or compact sections (classes 1 and 2):

$$M_c = p_y(S - S_v p_1) \text{ but } \leqslant 1{\cdot}2\, p_y Z$$

where

$$p_1 = \frac{2{\cdot}5\ F_v}{P_v} - 1{\cdot}5$$

S_v is the plastic modulus of the shear area A_v for sections with equal flanges and the plastic modulus of the gross section less the plastic modulus of the section remaining after deduction of the shear area for sections with unequal flanges.

For semi-compact and slender sections (classes 3 and 4) M_c is as given before.

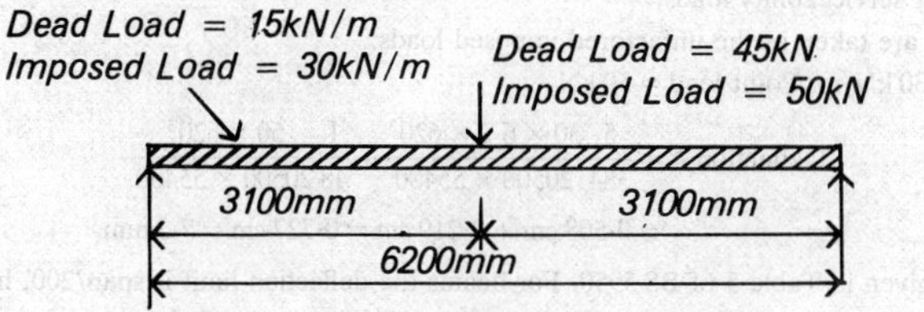

FIG. 10.—Beam Loading Diagram (Example 1).

EXAMPLE 1.—The beam shown in Figure 10 is fully restrained along its length. For the loading shown design a suitable section using grade 43 steel.

$$\text{Factored loads} = (15 \times 1{\cdot}4) + (30 \times 1{\cdot}6) = 69 \text{ kN/m.}$$

$$= (45 \times 1{\cdot}4) + (50 \times 1{\cdot}6) = 143 \text{ kN}$$

$$\text{Design moment} = \frac{69 \times 6{\cdot}2^2}{8} + \frac{143 \times 6{\cdot}2}{4} = 554 \text{ kN m.}$$

$$\text{Design shear force at ends} = \frac{69 \times 6{\cdot}2}{2} + \frac{143}{2} = 285{\cdot}4 \text{ kN}$$

$$\text{at centre} = 285{\cdot}4 - \frac{69 \times 6{\cdot}2}{2} = 71{\cdot}5 \text{ kN}$$

Try 533 × 210×92 UB

$$\varepsilon = \left(\frac{275}{p_y}\right)^{1/2} = \left(\frac{275}{275}\right)^{1/2} = 1$$

width/thickness ratio of compression flange:

$$= \frac{b}{T\varepsilon} = \frac{209{\cdot}3 \times 0{\cdot}5}{15{\cdot}6 \times 1{\cdot}0} = 6{\cdot}71$$

depth/thickness ratio of web:

$$= \frac{d}{t\varepsilon} = \frac{476{\cdot}5}{10{\cdot}2 \times 1{\cdot}0} = 46{\cdot}7$$

Therefore the section is plastic (class 1). Note since a simply supported beam is not required to have any plastic rotation capacity it is sufficient to ensure that the section is compact.

Check section at mid span:

$$\text{Shear capacity } P_v = 0{\cdot}6\,p_y A_v = \frac{0{\cdot}6 \times 275 \times 533{\cdot}1 \times 10{\cdot}2}{10^3} = 897{\cdot}2 \text{ kN}$$

Therefore $0{\cdot}6\,P_v = 0{\cdot}6 \times 897{\cdot}2 = 538{\cdot}3$ kN.

Shear force at centre $F_v = 71{\cdot}5$ kN.

Since $F_v < 0{\cdot}6\,P_v$, $M_c = p_y S \leqslant 1{\cdot}2\,p_y Z$

$$M_c = \frac{275 \times 2370 \times 10^3}{10^6} = 651{\cdot}7 \text{ kN m.}$$

$$1{\cdot}2\,p_y Z = \frac{1{\cdot}2 \times 275 \times 2080 \times 10^3}{10^6} = 686{\cdot}4 \text{ kN m.}$$

$\therefore M_c = 651{\cdot}7$ kN m.

Design moment = 554 kNm.

Therefore as M_c exceeds design moment, section is adequate.

Check shear force on section:

Shear capacity $P_v = 897{\cdot}2$ kN

Design shear force at ends = 285·4 kN

Therefore, as P_v exceeds design shear force, section is adequate.

Check deflection for serviceability loads.

Serviceability loads are taken as the unfactored imposed loads:

Distributed load = 30 kN/m, Point load = 50 kN.

$$\text{Deflection } \delta = \frac{5}{384}\,\frac{30 \times 6{\cdot}2 \times 620^3}{20500 \times 55400} + \frac{1}{48}\,\frac{50 \times 620^3}{20500 \times 55400}$$

$$= 0{\cdot}508 \text{ cm} + 0{\cdot}219 \text{ cm} = 0{\cdot}727 \text{ cm} = 7{\cdot}3 \text{ mm}$$

Deflection limits are given in Table 5 of BS 5950. For beams the deflection limit is span/200, hence

$$\delta \text{ limit} = \frac{6200}{200} = 31{\cdot}0 \text{ mm}$$

Therefore, as δ limit exceeds actual deflection, section is adequate.

USE 533 × 210 × 92 UB GRADE 43.

Note. If the beam supports construction having a brittle finish, such as plaster Table 5 of BS 5950 sets a deflection limit of Span/360. Refer to section entitled 'Section Classification' or to Table 7 of BS 5950 for limiting width/thickness ratios.

LATERALLY UNRESTRAINED BEAMS.—In example 1 the beam is fully restrained along its length. In beams without continuous restraint there is a tendency for the compression flange to buckle at right angles to the plane of bending as in Fig. 11 which shows the displacement of the mid-span section of a beam relative to the ends which are supported laterally and vertically. Fig. 12 shows (a) acceptable and (b) unacceptable forms of lateral support, BS 5950 states that when a member is not provided with full lateral restraint the resistance of the member to lateral torsional buckling should be checked. Section 4.3 of BS 5950 gives rules for the

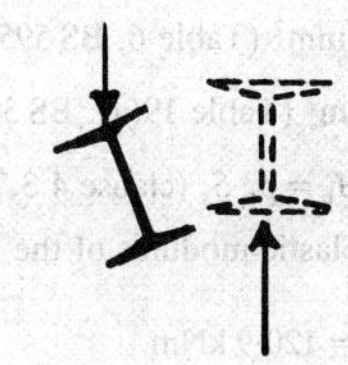

FIG.—11. Lateral Displacement of Beam.

assessment of this resistance. A conservative approach is given for rolled sections with equal flanges where the buckling resistance moment M_b is calculated and the maximum moment between lateral restraints is checked to ensure this value is not exceeded. It should be noted that if a more rigorous analysis is required or the member is not a rolled section having equal flanges the more detailed procedures in Section 4.3 of BS 5950 must be used. Example 2, which follows, illustrates the conservative approach.

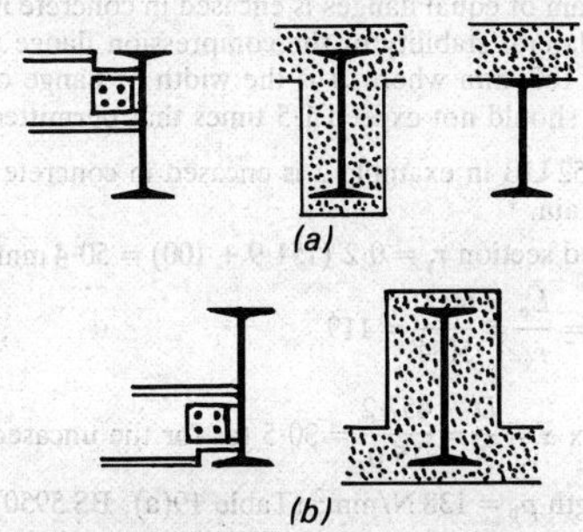

FIG. 12. (a)—Laterally Supported I-Beams.
(b)—Laterally Unsupported I-Beams.

EXAMPLE 2.—Design a suitable section for a beam spanning 6·0 m and supporting uniform imposed and dead loads of 10 kN/m and 5 kN/m respectively. The beam is restrained against lateral deflection and torsion at its supports and is unrestrained throughout its length.

$$\text{Factored load} = (5 \times 1{\cdot}4) + (10 \times 1{\cdot}6) = 23 \text{ kN/m}$$

$$\text{Design moment} = \frac{23 \times 6{\cdot}0^2}{8} = 103{\cdot}5 \text{ kNm.}$$

$$\text{Design shear force at ends} = \frac{23 \times 6{\cdot}0}{2} = 69{\cdot}0 \text{ kN.}$$

Try 457 × 152 × 67 UB

$$\varepsilon = \left(\frac{275}{p_y}\right)^{1/2} = \left(\frac{275}{275}\right)^{1/2} = 1$$

Width/thickness ratio of compression flange:

$$= \frac{b}{T\varepsilon} = \frac{151{\cdot}9 \times 0{\cdot}5}{15{\cdot}0 \times 1{\cdot}0} = 5{\cdot}06$$

Depth/thickness ratio of web:

$$= \frac{d}{t\varepsilon} = \frac{407{\cdot}0}{9{\cdot}1 \times 1{\cdot}0} = 44{\cdot}7$$

Therefore the section is plastic (class 1). Note: since a simply supported beam is not required to have any plastic rotation capacity it is sufficient to ensure that the section is compact.

Effective length $L_e = 1{\cdot}0L = 6000$ mm (Table 9, BS 5950).

$$\text{Slenderness } \lambda = \frac{Le}{r} = \frac{6000}{32{\cdot}1} = 187 \text{ (clause 4.3.7.7., BS 5950)}$$

$$\text{Torsional index } x = \frac{D}{T} = \frac{457{\cdot}2}{15{\cdot}0} = 30{\cdot}5 \text{ (clause 4.3.7.7, BS 5950).}$$

For grade 43 steel $p_y = 275$ N/mm^2 (Table 6, BS 5950).

Bending strength $p_b = 84$ N/mm^2 (Table 19(a), BS 5950).

Buckling resistance moment $M_b = p_b\, S_x$ (clause 4.3.7.7., BS 5950), where

p_b is the bending strength; S_x is the plastic modulus of the section about the $x - x$ axis.

$$M_b = \frac{84 \times 1440 \times 10^3}{10^6} = 120{\cdot}9 \text{ kNm}.$$

Therefore, as M_b exceeds the design moment, the section is adequate

USE 457 × 152 × 67UB GRADE 43

Note: if considered appropriate shear capacity and deflection should also be checked as outlined in example 1. Refer to section entitled 'Section Classification' or to Table 7 of BS 5950 for limiting width/thickness ratios.

CASED BEAMS.—When a beam of equal flanges is encased in concrete in accordance with clause 4.14.1 of BS 5950 the resulting increased lateral stability of the compression flange may be allowed for by taking the radius-of-gyration r_y as $0{\cdot}2\,(B + 100)$ mm where B is the width of flange of the steel section. The increased buckling resistance moment M_b, should not exceed 1·5 times that permitted for the uncased section.

EXAMPLE 3.—If the 457 × 152 UB in example 2 is encased in concrete in accordance with BS 5950 what bending moment can it then sustain.

For the encased section $r_y = 0{\cdot}2\,(151{\cdot}9 + 100) = 50{\cdot}4$ mm.

$$\text{Slenderness } \lambda = \frac{L_e}{r_y} = \frac{6000}{50{\cdot}4} = 119$$

$$\text{Torsional index } x = \frac{D}{T} = \frac{457{\cdot}2}{15{\cdot}0} = 30{\cdot}5 \text{ (as for the uncased section).}$$

Bending strength $p_b = 138$ N/mm^2 (Table 19(a), BS 5950).

From example 2 for uncased section $p_b = 84$ N/mm^2.

Therefore maximum allowable p_b for cased section $= 84 \times 1{\cdot}5 = 126$ N/mm.

$$\text{Buckling resistance moment } M_b = \frac{126 \times 1440 \times 10^3}{10^6} = 181{\cdot}4 \text{ kN m}.$$

Therefore the buckling resistance moment for the section is increased by 50%.

LIGHT WEIGHT BEAM CASINGS.—Byelaws and other regulations usually require that a steel framed structure of more than one storey must be cased for fire protection. It may be economical to encase stanchions with high quality concrete in accordance with BS 5950 so as to take advantage of the much increased load capacity, but in many instances the casing of beams involves increased cost without any structural benefit. Consideration should therefore be given to encasing steel beams with light weight material such as vermiculite-gypsum plaster. This technique confers the necessary fire resistance but involves materials of very much less weight and less cost than *in situ* concrete. Frequently the fire protection specified is for a two hour period and the Fire Research Station have shown that a 12·5 mm thickness of vermiculite-gypsum plaster suitably supported is adequate.

UNSYMMETRICAL SECTIONS.—Bending should always be related to the principal axes of the beam section, and if neither axis lies in the plane of loading as is generally the case when the section is unsymmetrical about both principal axes, the loading must be resolved into components parallel thereto. Thus in the case of the angle section shown in Fig. 13, the load W is resolved into components parallel to the principal axes UU

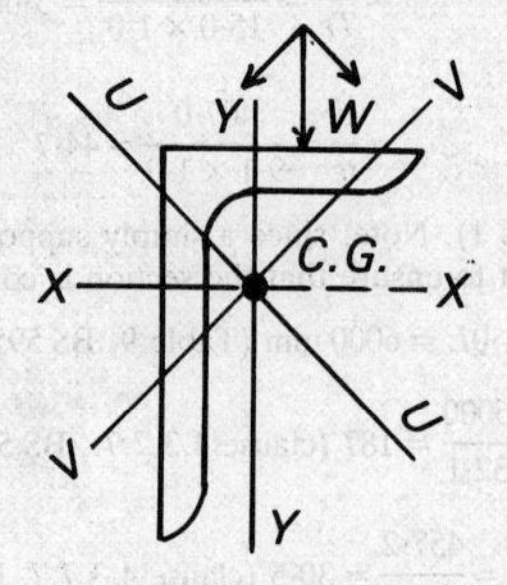

FIG. 13.—Resolved Components of Load W.

and VV. Then each component will cause bending in the plane of a principal axis and the total stress at a given point on the cross-section is the sum of the stresses due to the load components considered separately. Note that it is incorrect to work to the axes XX and YY which are not principal axes, but for subsidiary members such as purlins and bracing angles this is often done as a matter of convenience, and because sheeting, etc., fixed to the member tends to restrict bending so that it is primarily in the plane of the YY or XX axis.

SHEAR CENTRE.—When dealing with unsymmetrical sections it is particularly important to recall that the beam will be subjected to torsion if the plane of loading does not contain the shear centre. The location of the shear centre of some typical rolled steel sections is shown in Fig. 14. Note that the shear centre of a channel

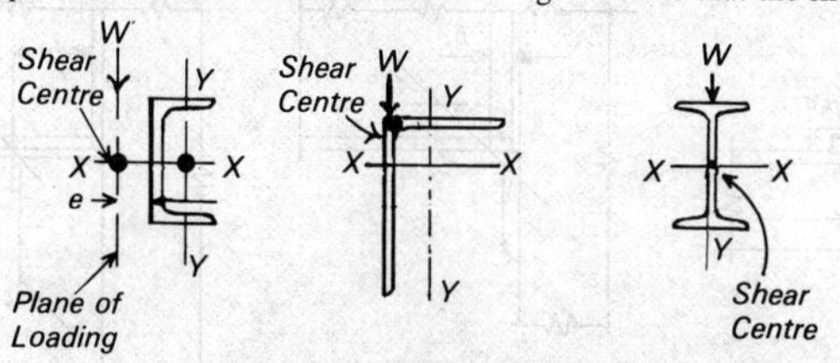

FIG. 14.—Shear Centres for Rolled Steel Sections.

section is outside the section and such members should be loaded as shown if torsion is to be avoided. In practice channel beams are generally loaded by attachment to the back of the web which results in a small amount of torsion.

SHEAR CAPACITY OF BEAMS.—The shear force F_v applied to any section shall not be greater than its shear capacity. BS 5950 clause 4.2.3 gives the following general expression for shear capacity:

$$\text{Shear capacity } P_v = 0{\cdot}6\, p_y\, A_v$$

where p_y is the design strength; A_v is the shear area.

The shear area to be considered varies according to the shape of the section, some examples are as follows:

Rolled UB, UC, joist and channel sections (load parallel to web), shear area is overall depth multiplied by web thickness. Plate girders and fabricated box sections (load parallel to web or webs), shear area is web depth multiplied by web thickness or total thickness of webs. Solid bars and plates, shear area is 0·9 times total area of the section. Circular hollow sections, shear area is 0·6 times total area of the section. Fig. 15 illustrates shear areas of some sections.

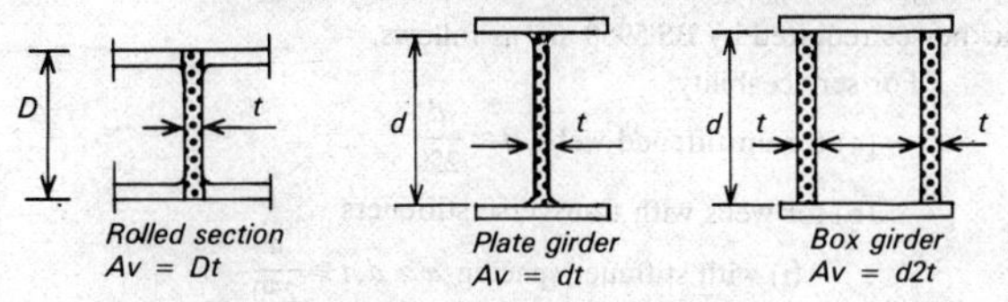

FIG. 15.—Shear Areas of Steel Sections.

When the depth/thickness ratio d/t of a web exceeds 63ε it should be checked for shear buckling in accordance with clause 4.4.5 of BS 5950. Further details of this are given later in the section on plate girders.

BEAM WEB BEARING AND BUCKLING.—BS 5950 requires that consideration shall be given to the local effects of concentrated loads and reactions on beam webs.

Bearing stiffeners should be provided for webs where forces applied through a flange by loads or reactions exceed the capacity of the web at its connection to the flange. Bearing capacity is given by:

$$(b_1 + n_2)tp_{yw}$$

where b_1 is the stiff bearing length; n_2 is the length obtained by dispersion through the flange to the flange to web connection at a slope of 1:2·5 to the plane of the flange; t is the web thickness; p_{yw} is the design strength of the web.

Load carrying web stiffeners should be provided where forces applied through a flange by loads or reactions exceed the buckling resistance which is given by:

$$(b_1 + n_1)tp_c$$

where b_1 is the stiff bearing length; n_1 is the length obtained by dispersion at 45° through half the depth of the section; t is the web thickness; p_c is the compressive strength from Table 27(c) of BS 5950, using a slenderness λ of $2{\cdot}5\, d/t$ (d/t being the depth/thickness of the web).

Note: if the loaded flange is not restrained against rotation relative to the web, or lateral movement relative to the other flange, the slenderness of the web λ should be determined in accordance with clause 4.5.1.5 of BS 5950.

Stiff bearing length b_1 is defined as that length which cannot deform appreciably in bending. Examples illustrating stiff bearing lengths are given in Fig. 16. The angle of dispersion through solid steel should be taken as 45°.

Details of the design procedure for web stiffeners are given later in the section on plate girders.

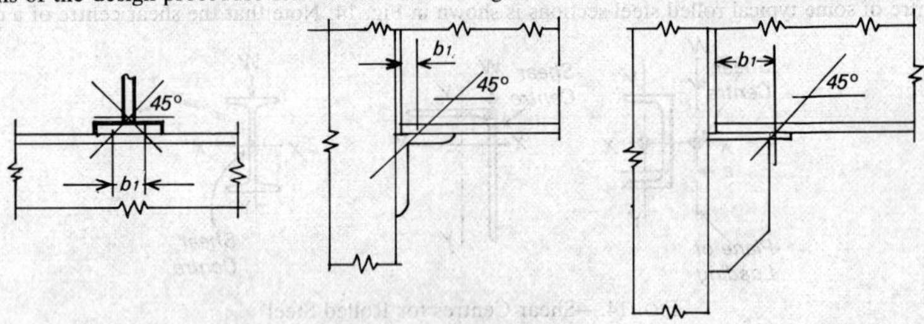

FIG.—16. Stiff Bearing Lengths.

PLATE GIRDERS

Plate girders are used in situations where large spans and the consequent increased loads produce bending moments and shear forces which exceed the capacity of rolled universal sections. Rules for plate girders are given in section 4.4 of BS 5950.

When no restrictions are placed on the girder depth the dimension should be chosen in relation to the span and to keep the flange size in reasonable proportions. The relatively large depth produces a slender web which is susceptible to shear buckling. The slenderness (depth/thickness ratio) at which web plates become liable to shear buckling is defined in BS 5950 as 63ε. Buckling capacity is increased by the provision of web stiffeners. In general plate girder webs may be unstiffened, with transverse stiffeners only or with transverse and longitudinal stiffeners. This last alternative is unusual in building structures and BS 5950 refers the designer to BS 5400, *Steel,* 'Concrete and Composite Bridges'. Considerations of section classification and lateral restraint, outlined in the foregoing text of this chapter, apply also to plate girders. It is obviously good practice to ensure that adequate lateral restraints are provided and that the flanges are kept to the proportions to permit the use of maximum design strengths.

Minimum web thicknesses required by BS 5950 are as follows.

For serviceability:

(a) for unstiffened webs, $t \geqslant \dfrac{d}{250}$

(b) for webs with transverse stiffeners

(i) with stiffener spacing $a > d,\ t \geqslant \dfrac{d}{250}$

(ii) with stiffener spacing $a \leqslant d,\ t \geqslant \dfrac{d}{250}\left(\dfrac{a}{d}\right)^{1/2}$.

To prevent the flange buckling into the web:

(a) for unstiffened webs $t \geqslant \dfrac{d}{250}\left(\dfrac{p_{yf}}{345}\right)$

(b) for webs with transverse stiffeners

(i) with stiffener spacing $a > 1{\cdot}5d,\ t \geqslant \dfrac{d}{250}\left(\dfrac{p_{yf}}{345}\right)$

(ii) with stiffener spacing $a \leqslant 1{\cdot}5d,\ t \geqslant \dfrac{d}{250}\left(\dfrac{p_{yf}}{455}\right)^{1/2}$

where p_{yf} is the design strength of the compression flange; a is the stiffener spacing, d is the web depth, and t the thickness of the web.

For sections with plastic, compact or semi-compact flanges and slender webs (i.e. $d/t \geqslant 63\varepsilon$), BS 5950 gives three alternative methods for use in determining the moment capacity:

(a) The moment may be assumed to be resisted by the flanges alone and the web designed for shear only.
(b) The moment may be assumed to be resisted by the whole section, the web being designed for combined shear and longitudinal stresses.

(c) A proportion of the load may be assumed to be resisted by method (b), the remainder being resisted by method (a) and the web designed accordingly.

From these methods (a) is the most straightforward and will probably be the one used by practical designers. This leads to an expression for the overall moment capacity as follows.

$$M_c = p_{yf} S_{xf}$$

where p_{yf} is the design strength of the flanges; S_{xf} is the plastic modulus of the flanges only about the section axis.

For unstiffened webs the shear capacity is given by the following expression:

$$V_{cr} = q_{cr} dt$$

where q_{cr} is the critical shear strength obtained from Tables 21(a) to (d) of BS 5950 (for webs without stiffeners the spacing should be taken as infinity); d is the web depth; t is the web thickness.

Webs with transverse stiffeners may be assessed using the foregoing expression for unstiffened webs, or by using the following expressions for shear capacity which allow for tension field action:

$$V_b = q_b dt$$

and if the flanges in the panel are not fully stressed

$$V_b = (q_b + q_f \sqrt{K_f}) dt \quad \text{but} \leqslant 0{\cdot}6\, p_y\, dt$$

where q_b is the basic shear strength obtained from Tables 22(a) to (d) of BS 5950 as appropriate; q_f is the flange dependent shear strength factor obtained from Tables 23(a) to (d) of BS 5950 as appropriate; d and t are the web depth and thickness as before

$$K_f = \frac{M_{pf}}{4M_{pw}}\left(1 - \frac{f}{p_{yf}}\right)$$

M_{pf} is the plastic moment capacity of the smaller flange about its own equal area axis parallel to the flange; f is the mean longitudinal stress in the smaller flange; p_{yf} is the design strength of the flange; M_{pw} is the plastic moment capacity of the web about its own equal area axis perpendicular to the web.

Tension field action is the situation where the web of the girder forms diagonal tension bands or fields which act with the flanges and intermediate stiffeners to produce a load supporting action similar to that of an 'N' truss, see Fig. 17.

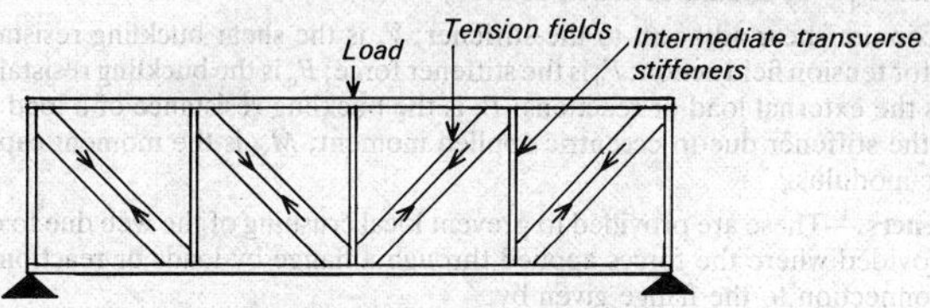

FIG. 17.—Tension Field Action.

There are requirements in BS 5950 for the design of end panels of girders where allowance is made for tension field action. These are intended to ensure that adequate anchorage is provided to allow tension field forces to develop. It is stated that the end panel may be designed without tension field action and additionally should be checked as a beam spanning between the girder flanges and be capable of resisting a shear force R_{tf} and a moment M_{tf}.

Alternatively the end panel may be designed using tension field action and additionally be provided with an end post formed by a single or a double stiffener. The single stiffener end post should be capable of resisting the reaction from the girder plus a moment of 2/3 M_{tf}, should be rigidly connected to the flanges with full strength welds and should not exceed the width and thickness of the flanges. The double stiffener end post should be checked as a beam spanning between the girder flanges and be capable of resisting a shear force R_{tf} and a moment M_{tf}.

$$R_{tf} = H_q/2 \quad \text{and} \quad M_{tf} = H_q d/10$$

where

$$H_q = 0{\cdot}75\, dt p_y \left(1 - \frac{q_{cr}}{0{\cdot}6\, p_y}\right)^{1/2}$$

and if $f_v < q_b$, H_q may be reduced by the ratio $\dfrac{f_v - q_{cr}}{q_b - q_{cr}}$ where f_v is the applied shear stress in the panel utilizing tension field action; q_b is the basic shear strength of the panel utilizing tension field action; q_{cr} is the critical shear strength for the panel utilizing tension field action; d and t are the web depth and thickness as before.

PLATE GIRDER STIFFENERS.—These are divided into three main categories. Rules for the design of web stiffeners are given in section 4.5 of BS 5950, the main points of which, as applicable to plate girders, are given in the following:

(a) **Intermediate transverse stiffeners.**—The shear capacity of the girder is governed by the intermediate transverse stiffener spacing as described in the foregoing text. It is a requirement of BS 5950 that transverse stiffeners should have a second moment of area I_s about the centre line of the web such that:

$$I_s \geqslant 0{\cdot}75\, dt^3 \quad \text{for} \quad a \geqslant \sqrt{2}d$$

and

$$I_s \geqslant \frac{1{\cdot}5\, d^3 t^3}{a^2} \quad \text{for } a < \sqrt{2}d$$

where d and t are the web depth and thickness as before; a is the stiffener spacing.

When transverse stiffeners are subject to lateral forces or the moments due to eccentricity of transverse loading relative to the web, I_s as calculated above should be increased:

$$\text{for lateral forces by } 2FD^3/Et$$

$$\text{for moments by } M_s D^2/Et$$

where D is the overall depth of the section; E is the modulus of elasticity; F is the factored lateral force on the stiffener deemed to be applied at the compression flange; M_s is the moment on the stiffener due to eccentric loading.

Stiffeners not subject to external loads or moments should be checked for a stiffener force:

$$F_q = V - V_s \leqslant P_q$$

Stiffeners subject to external loads and moments should meet the conditions for load carrying stiffeners and in addition should satisfy the following expression:

$$\frac{F_q - F_x}{P_q} + \frac{F_x}{P_x} + \frac{M_s}{M_{ys}} \leqslant 1$$

(note if $F_q < F_x$, then $F_q - F_x$ should be taken as zero)

where V is the maximum shear adjacent to the stiffener; V_s is the shear buckling resistance of the web panel without allowance for tension field action; F_q is the stiffener force; P_q is the buckling resistance of an intermediate web stiffener; F_x is the external load or reactions; P_x is the buckling resistance of a load carrying stiffener; M_s is the moment on the stiffener due to eccentric applied moment; M_{ys} is the moment capacity of the stiffeners based on its elastic modulus.

(b) **Bearing stiffeners.**—These are provided to prevent local crushing of the web due to concentrated loading. They should be provided where the forces applied through a flange by loads or reactions exceed the capacity of the web at its connection to the flange given by.

$$(b_1 + n_2)tp_{yw}$$

where b_1 is the stiff bearing length; n_2 is the length obtained by dispersion through the flange to web connection at a slope of 1:2·5 to the plane of the flange; t is the web thickness; p_{yw} is the design strength of the web.

(c) **Load carrying stiffeners.**—These are provided to prevent local buckling of the web due to concentrated loading. They should be provided where forces applied through a flange by loads or reactions exceed the buckling resistance given by

$$(b_1 + n_1)tp_c$$

where b_1 is the stiff bearing length; n_1 is the length obtained by dispersion at 45° through half the depth of the section; t is the web thickness; p_c is the compressive strength from Table 27(c) of BS 5950 using a slenderness λ of 2·5 d/t (d/t being the depth/thickness of the web).

Note that if the loaded flange is not restrained against rotation relative to the web, or torsional lateral movement relative to the other flange the slenderness of the web λ should be determined in accordance with Clause 4.5.1.5 of BS 5950. Examples illustrating stiff bearing length b_1 are shown in Fig. 16 in the section dealing with beam web bearing and buckling.

The buckling resistance of stiffeners should be based on a compressive strength p_c of a strut using Table 27(c) of BS 5950. The effective section should be the area of the stiffener plus an effective web length on each side of the centre line of the stiffener of 20 times the web thickness. The effective length used in calculating the buckling resistance should be 0·7 times the length for intermediate stiffeners. For load carrying stiffeners the effective length should also be 0·7 times the length if the girder flange is restrained against rotation in the plane of the stiffener and should be taken as the full length of the stiffener if not so restrained. If the stiffener is attached to a welded section the design strength used should be reduced by 20 N/mm². A check for bearing should also be carried out such that the following expression is satisfied.

$$A > \frac{0{\cdot}8\,F_x}{p_{ys}}$$

where F_x is the external load or reaction; A is the area of the stiffener in contact with the girder flange; p_{ys} is the design strength of the stiffener.

Unless the outer edge of a web stiffener is continuously stiffened the outstand from the web face should not exceed 19 $t_s\varepsilon$. When the outstand is between 13 $t_s\varepsilon$ and 19 $t_s\varepsilon$ the stiffener design should be based on a core area whose outstand is 13 $t_s\varepsilon$. In the foregoing t_s is the stiffener thickness and ε is as defined previously at the end of Table 3.

Where load is applied between web stiffeners an additional check should be made to ensure that the compressive stress f_{ed} on the compression edge of the web does not exceed the compressive strength for edge loading p_{ed}. Compressive stress f_{ed} should be obtained as follows:

(a) Divide point loads and distributed load shorter than the smaller panel dimension by the smaller panel dimension a or d
(b) Add the intensity (force per unit length) of any other distributed loads.
(c) Divide by the web thickness t.

Compressive strength for edge loading p_{ed} is given as follows:

When the compression flange is restrained against rotation relative to the web:

$$p_{ed} = \left[2{\cdot}75 + \frac{2}{(a/d)^2}\right]\frac{E}{(d/t)^2}$$

and when the compression flange is not so restrained:

$$p_{ed} = \left[1{\cdot}0 + \frac{2}{(a/d)^2}\right]\frac{E}{(d/t)^2}$$

where a is the distance between transverse web stiffeners.

EXAMPLE 4.—The girder shown in Fig. 18 is fully restrained along its length. For the loading shown design a stiffened plate girder using grade 43 steel.

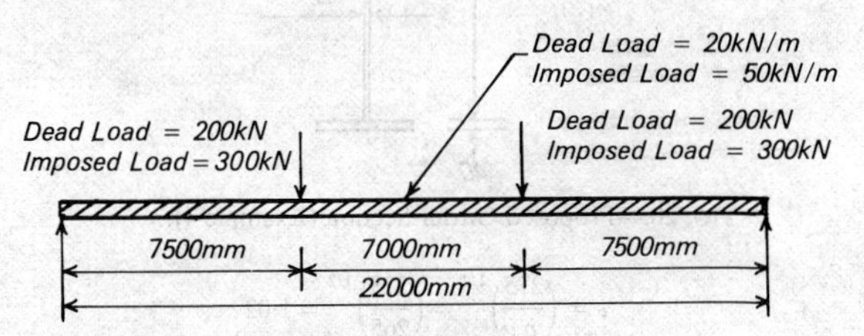

FIG.—18 Girder Loading Diagram (Example 4).

Factored loads = (20 × 1·4) + (50 × 1·6) = 108 kN/m

= (200 × 1·4) + (300 × 1·6) = 760 kN.

Shear force and bending moment diagrams are shown in Fig. 19.

It is usual to choose a girder depth of 1/10 to 1/12 of the span.

$$\text{Depth} = \frac{22000}{12} = 1833 \text{ mm, say } 1950 \text{ mm approx.}$$

Design strength for grade 43 steel = 265 N/mm².

$$\text{Approx flange area} = \frac{\text{Bending moment}}{\text{Depth} \times \text{Design strength}} = \frac{12234 \times 10^6}{1950 \times 265} = 23675 \text{ mm}^2.$$

$$\text{Approx web thickness, say} = \frac{\text{Depth}}{150} = \frac{1950}{150} = \text{say } 12 \text{ mm.}$$

Try girder with 700 mm × 40 mm flanges and 12 mm web as shown in figure 20.

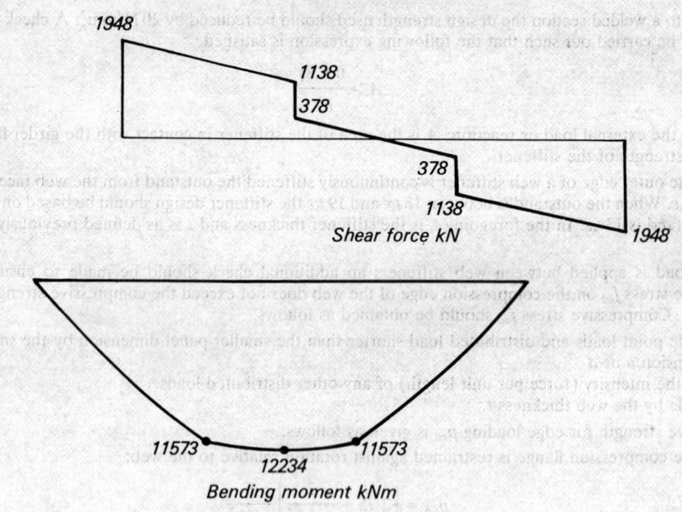

FIG. 19.—Shear Force and Bending diagrams.

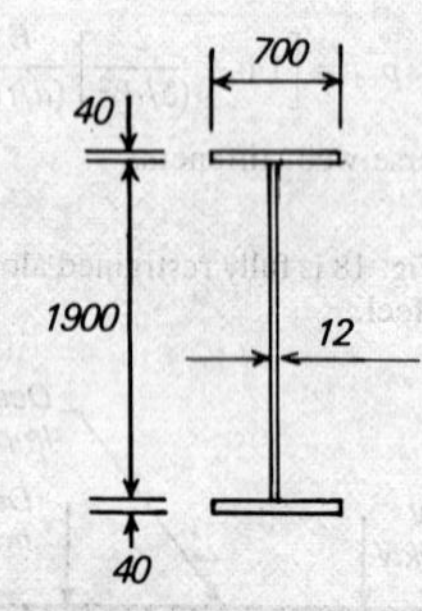

FIG. 20.—Proposed Girder Section (Example 4).

$$\varepsilon = \left(\frac{275}{p_y}\right)^{1/2} = \left(\frac{275}{265}\right)^{1/2} = 1{\cdot}02$$

$$b = \frac{700 - 12}{2} = 344$$

width/thickness ratio of compression flange:

$$= \frac{b}{T\varepsilon} = \frac{344}{40 \times 1{\cdot}02} = 8{\cdot}43$$

depth/thickness ratio of web:

$$= \frac{d}{t\varepsilon} = \frac{1900}{12 \times 1{\cdot}02} = 155.$$

Flange is compact and the web is slender.

Minimum web thickness for serviceability:

$$\text{assuming } a > d,\ t \geqslant \frac{d}{250} = \frac{1900}{250} = 7{\cdot}6\ \text{mm}.$$

Minimum web thickness for flange buckling into web:

$$\text{assuming } a > 1{\cdot}5d,\ t \geqslant \frac{d}{250}\left(\frac{p_{yf}}{345}\right) = \frac{1900}{250} \times \frac{265}{345} = 5{\cdot}9\ \text{mm}.$$

Web thickness of 12 mm satisfies the above requirements.

As stated previously, moment capacity $M_c = p_{yf} S_{xf}$.

Area of flanges = 700 × 40 = 28000 mm².

Distance from centroid of flange to neutral axis of girder = 970 mm, $p_{yf} = 265\ \text{N/mm}^2$, hence:

$$M_c = \frac{265 \times 2 \times 28000 \times 970}{10^6} = 14394\ \text{kNm}.$$

This exceeds the maximum design moment of 12234 kNm and is therefore satisfactory.

Web shear capacity will be assessed allowing for tension field action. An elevation showing stiffener positions is shown in Fig. 21.

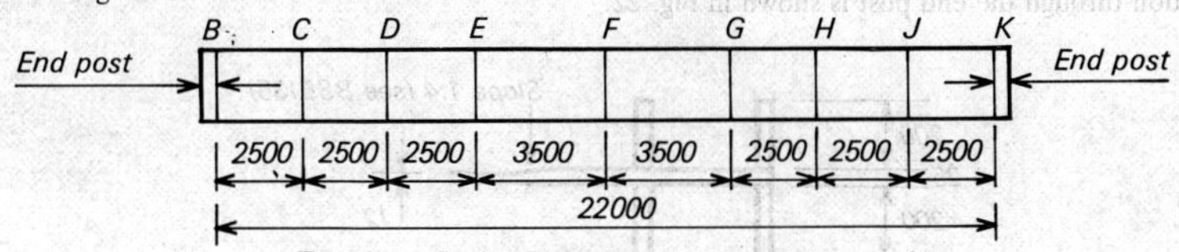

FIG. 21.—Girder Elevation showing Positions of Stiffeners.

Consider end panel B–C:

$$\frac{a}{d} = \frac{2500}{1900} = 1{\cdot}32 \qquad \frac{d}{t} = \frac{1900}{12} = 158$$

$q_b = 92\ \text{N/mm}^2$ from Table 22(b) of BS 5950 ($p_y = 275\ \text{N/mm}^2$ for web)

$$V_b = \frac{92 \times 1900 \times 12}{10^3} = 2097\ \text{kN}.$$

This exceeds the maximum shear force of 1948 kN and is therefore satisfactory.

As tension field action has been taken into account in the design of end panel B–C an end post must be provided. In this case the end post is formed by a double stiffener. The end post should be checked as a beam spanning between the girder flanges and be capable of resisting a shear force R_{tf} and a moment M_{tf}.

$q_{cr} = 57\ \text{N/mm}^2$ for panel B–C from Table 21(b) of BS 5950

$$H_q = 0{\cdot}75 \times 1900 \times 12 \times 275 \left(1 - \frac{57}{0{\cdot}6 \times 275}\right)^{1/2} \times \frac{1}{10^3} = 3804\ \text{kN}.$$

$$\text{Now } f_v = \frac{1948 \times 10^3}{1900 \times 12} = 85{\cdot}5\ \text{N/mm}^2 \text{ for panel B–C}$$

$$H_q \text{ may be reduced by the ratio } \frac{f_v - q_{cr}}{q_b - q_{cr}} = \frac{85{\cdot}5 - 57{\cdot}0}{92{\cdot}0 - 57{\cdot}0} = 0{\cdot}81$$

thus, reduced $H_q = 0{\cdot}81 \times 3804 = 3081$ kN.

$$R_{tf} = \frac{3081}{2} = 1541\ \text{kN},\ M_{tf} = \frac{3081 \times 1900}{10 \times 10^3} = 586\ \text{kNm}.$$

Web area A_v required to resist a shear force of 1541 kN:

$$A_v = \frac{1541 \times 10^3}{0{\cdot}6 \times 275} = 9340\ \text{mm}^2$$

Therefore, with a 12 mm web thickness, the depth of end post $= \frac{9340}{12} = 778$ mm, say 800 mm.

In many situations it would be desirable to reduce this depth, this can be achieved by increasing the end post web thickness. Alternatively the end post could be eliminated and the end panel B–C designed without allowing for tension field action which would lead to an increase in the web thickness of this panel. In this case the end post web will be increased to 25 mm thick to provide a design strength of 265 N/mm², therefore:

$$A_v = \frac{1541 \times 10^3}{0{\cdot}6 \times 265} = 9692\ \text{mm}^2.$$

$$\text{Depth of end post} = \frac{9692}{25} = 388\ \text{mm, say 400 mm.}$$

Furthermore, the end post stiffener at B must be checked in bearing for the girder end reaction. To satisfy this requirement:

$$\text{Area of stiffener in contact with flange } A > \frac{0{\cdot}8\,F_x}{p_{ys}}$$

$$A > \frac{0{\cdot}8 \times 1948 \times 10^3}{265} = 5880\ \text{mm}^2.$$

Try two 200 mm × 20 mm stiffeners and allow a 12 mm cope for the web to flange weld.

$$A = 2 \times 20 \times (200 - 12) = 7520\ \text{mm}^2$$

A section through the end post is shown in Fig. 22.

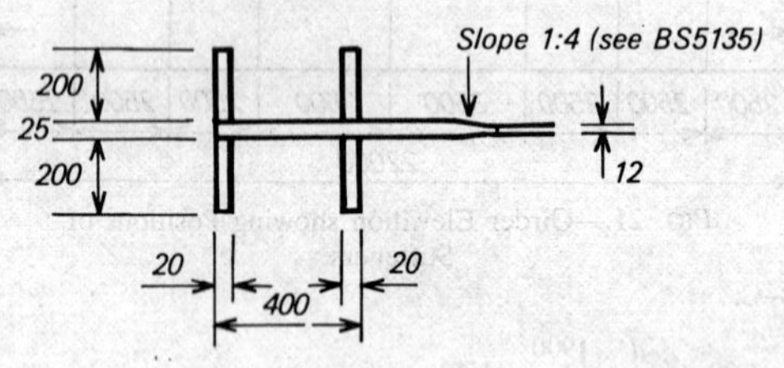

FIG. 22.—Section through End Post.

Maximum effective outstand of end post stiffeners = $13\,t_s\varepsilon = 13 \times 20 \times 1{\cdot}02 = 265$ mm, therefore use actual dimension = 200 mm.

Check end post stiffener at B for buckling:

The effective section of the stiffener plus girder web is shown in Fig. 23, the maximum effective web length on each side of the stiffener centre line is 20 times the thickness = 20 × 25 = 500 mm. The actual dimension is 390 mm and will therefore be used.

$$\text{For stiffener } I = \frac{2{\cdot}0 \times 42{\cdot}5^3}{12} + \frac{78{\cdot}0 \times 2{\cdot}5^3}{12} = 12895\ \text{cm}^4$$

$$\text{Effective area} = (40 \times 2{\cdot}0) + (78 \times 2{\cdot}5) = 275\ \text{cm}^2$$

$$\text{Radius of gyration} = \sqrt{\frac{12895}{275}} = 6{\cdot}84\ \text{cm}.$$

Flange is restrained against rotation in the plane of the stiffener, therefore effective length is 0·7 times the stiffener length.

$$\text{Slenderness } \lambda = \frac{0{\cdot}7 \times 1900}{68{\cdot}4} = 19{\cdot}4$$

The stiffeners are attached to a welded section therefore the design strength should be reduced by 20 N/mm² to 245 N/mm² when using Table 27(c) of BS 5950.

$$p_c = 242\ \text{N/mm}^2.$$

$$\text{Buckling resistance of stiffener} = \frac{242 \times 275 \times 10^2}{10^3} = 6655\ \text{kN}$$

Check end post stiffener at B for bearing:

$$\text{Assume } b_1 = 30\ \text{mm}$$

$$n_2 = 2 \times 40 \times 2{\cdot}5 = 200\ \text{mm}$$

$$\text{Bearing capacity of the web} = \frac{(30 + 200) \times 25 \times 265}{10^3} = 1524\ \text{kN}$$

Bearing area of stiffeners calculated previously = 7520 mm²

$$\text{Bearing capacity of stiffeners} = \frac{7520 \times 265}{10^3} = 1993\ \text{kN}$$

Total bearing capacity = 1524 + 1993 = 3517 kN

Actual load on end post stiffener at B:

$$\text{From tension field action} = \frac{M_{tf}}{\text{centres of stiffeners}} = \frac{586 \times 10^3}{380} = 1542 \text{ kN}$$

From girder reaction = 1948 kN.

Total load = 1542 + 1948 = 3490 kN which is less than the buckling resistance and the total bearing capacity.

The outer end post stiffener is required to resist the load from tension field action only. Its size could be reduced but, in this case the end post, will have equal size stiffeners.

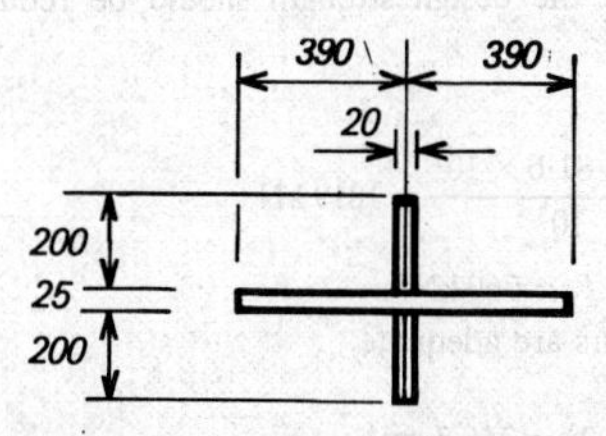

FIG. 23.—Effective Section of End Post Stiffener.

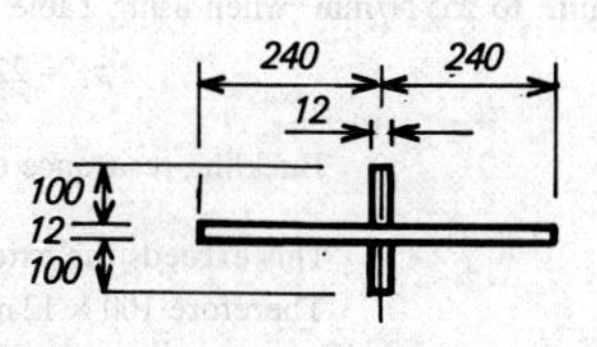

FIG. 24.—Effective Section of Load Bearing and Intermediate Stiffener

Therefore the end post will have a 25 mm web and 200 × 20 mm stiffeners as shown in Fig. 22.

For intermediate stiffeners E and G (See Fig. 21) subject to an external factored load of 760 kN, the following expression must be satisfied:

$$\frac{F_q - F_x}{P_q} + \frac{F_x}{P_x} + \frac{M_s}{M_{ys}} \leqslant 1$$

$F_q = V - V_s$ and $V = 1138$ kN from shear force diagram, Fig. 19

$V_s = V_{cr}$ for panel D–E and $V_{cr} = q_{cr}dt$

$$\text{For panel D–E, } \frac{a}{d} = \frac{2500}{1900} = 1{\cdot}32$$

$$\frac{d}{t} = \frac{1900}{12} = 159$$

Assuming 12 mm stiffeners are used, $p_y = 275$ N/mm²

$q_{cr} = 56$ N/mm² from Table 21(b) of BS 5950

$$V_{cr} = \frac{56 \times 1900 \times 12}{10^3} = 1277 \text{ kN}$$

$F_q = 1138 - 1277$, F_q is negative i.e. no tension field action. Therefore:

$$F_q - F_x = 0$$

$$M_s = 0$$

$$F_x = 760 \text{ kN}$$

To determine buckling resistance P_x of stiffeners:

Try two 100 mm × 12 mm stiffeners the effective section with girder web is shown in Fig. 24, the maximum effective web length on each side of the stiffener centre line is 20 times the thickness = 20 × 12 = 240 mm.

Maximum effective outstand of stiffener = $13\, t_s \varepsilon$, where

$$\varepsilon = \left(\frac{275}{275}\right)^{1/2} = 1{\cdot}0 \text{ and } 13\, t_s \varepsilon = 13 \times 12 \times 1{\cdot}0 = 156 \text{ mm.}$$

Actual outstand is 100 mm therefore this dimension will be used.

$$\text{For stiffener } I = \frac{1{\cdot}2 \times 21{\cdot}2^3}{12} + \frac{48{\cdot}0 \times 1{\cdot}2^3}{12} = 960 \text{ cm}^4.$$

$$\text{Effective area} = (20 \times 1{\cdot}2) + (48 \times 1{\cdot}2) = 81{\cdot}6\ \text{cm}^2.$$

$$\text{Radius-of-gyration} = \sqrt{\frac{960}{81{\cdot}6}} = 3{\cdot}43\ \text{cm}.$$

Flange is restrained against rotation in the plane of the stiffener, therefore effective length is 0·7 times the stiffener length.

$$\text{Slenderness } \lambda = \frac{0{\cdot}7 \times 1900}{34{\cdot}3} = 38{\cdot}8.$$

The stiffeners are attached to a welded section therefore the design strength should be reduced by 20 N/mm² to 255 N/mm² when using Table 27(c) of BS 5950.

$$p_c = 223\ \text{N/mm}^2.$$

$$\text{Buckling resistance of stiffener} = \frac{223 \times 81{\cdot}6 \times 10^2}{10^3} = 1819\ \text{kN}.$$

This exceeds the external factored load $F_x = 760$ kN.

Therefore 100 × 12 mm stiffeners in pairs are adequate.

For intermediate stiffeners:

$$\text{Minimum stiffness } I_s = 0{\cdot}75 \times 190{\cdot}0 \times 1{\cdot}2^3 = 246{\cdot}3\ \text{cm}^4$$

for stiffener spacing $a \geqslant \sqrt{2} \times 1900 = 2687$ mm.

$$\text{Minimum stiffness } I_s = \frac{1{\cdot}5 \times 190{\cdot}0^3 \times 1{\cdot}2^3}{250{\cdot}0^2} = 284{\cdot}5\ \text{cm}^4$$

for stiffener spacing $a < \sqrt{2} \times 1900 = 2687$ mm.

In this case we have stiffeners spaced at 2500 mm and at 3500 mm therefore both the above requirements must be satisfied. Furthermore stiffeners not subject to external loads or moments should be checked for a force of $F_q = V - V_s$.

Try two 100 mm × 12 mm stiffeners as used at E and G (Fig. 21):

As calculated previously for a 2500 mm wide panel $V_{cr} = 1277$ kN and $V_s = V_{cr}$;

V is the maximum shear adjacent to a stiffener which in this case is at stiffener C.

From shear force diagram, Fig. 19, $V = 1948 - (2{\cdot}5 \times 108) = 1678$ kN.

$$\therefore F_q = 1678 - 1277 = 401\ \text{kN}.$$

As calculated previously for two 100 × 12 mm stiffeners:

Stiffness $I = 960\ \text{cm}^4$ which exceeds minimum requirement above.

Buckling resistance = 1819 kN which exceeds 401 kN.

Therefore 100 × 12 mm stiffeners in pairs are adequate.

Web check between stiffeners:

Where load is applied between stiffeners a check should be made to ensure that compressive stress f_{ed} on the compression edge does not exceed compressive strength for edge loading p_{ed}.

$$f_{ed} = \frac{108}{12} = 9{\cdot}0\ \text{N/mm}^2.$$

When the compression flange is restrained against rotation relative to web:

$$p_{ed} = \left[2{\cdot}75 + \frac{2}{\left(\dfrac{3500}{1900}\right)^2}\right]\frac{205000}{\left(\dfrac{1900}{12}\right)^2} = 27{\cdot}3\ \text{N/mm}^2.$$

Therefore the web satisfies this requirement. The final design is shown in Fig. 25.

STANCHIONS AND STRUTS

AXIALLY LOADED MEMBERS.—Compression members are dealt with in Section 4.7 of BS 5950. The load capacity of an axially loaded compression member is given by:

$$\text{Compression resistance } P_c = A_g p_c$$

where A_g is the gross sectional area; p_c is the compressive strength.

The compressive strength for use in the foregoing expression is obtained from BS 5950 as follows:

First reference is made to Tables 25 and 26. These indicate, for any shape, thickness of material and axis of buckling, which of the four strut Tables 27(a) to (d) is relevant to the member under consideration. The slenderness of the member for the axes of buckling are then calculated and used to read off the value of compressive strength from Table 27(a) to (d) as appropriate to the design strength. Note for welded fabricated sections BS 5950 requires that the value of the design strength be reduced by 20 N/mm^2 to make allowance for residual stresses.

It is recognised in BS 5950 that the strength of compression members is influenced, not only by slenderness, but also by the geometry of their cross section and the method of fabrication. Allowance is made for these factors by the provision of the four Tables 27(a) to (d) which give different ranges of values for compressive strength according to the member type as categorised in Tables 25 and 26.

The effective length depends upon conditions of positional and directional restraint at the ends of the member or portion thereof which is being considered. The recommendations of BS 5950 are given in Table 7. The main difficulty is in deciding upon the degree of directional restraint, which may be due to continuity over the points of positional support, the stiffness of beams and other members connecting into the stanchion, fixing to foundations etc. Advice on the assessment of effective lengths is given for simple construction in Appendix D of BS 5950 and Appendix E gives rules for situations where the stanchion forms part of a rigid frame.

Maximum limits are given in BS 5950 for slenderness as follows.

(a) for members resisting load other than wind loads 180
(b) for members resisting self weight and wind loads only 250
(c) for members normally acting as a tie but subject to reversal of stress due to wind action 350

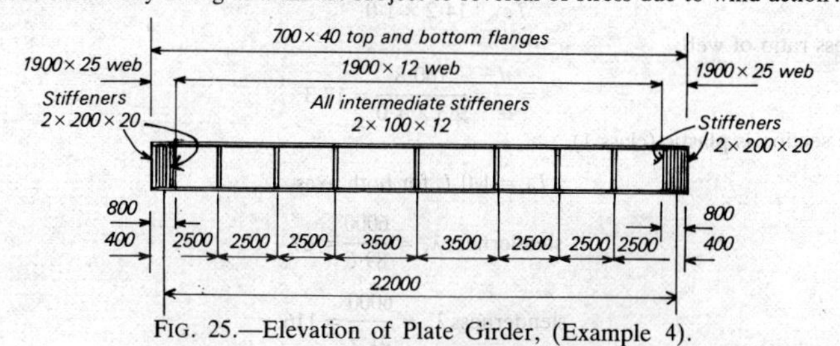

FIG. 25.—Elevation of Plate Girder, (Example 4).

TABLE 7.—EFFECTIVE LENGTH (L_E) OF STRUTS.
(L = Actual distance between the positions of effective restraint).

Type	Effective length
Effectively held in position and restrained in direction at both ends	0·7 L
Effectively held in position at both ends and restrained in direction at one end	0·85 L
Effectively held in position at both ends and partially restrained in direction at both ends	0·85 L
Effectively held in position at both ends but not restrained in direction	L
Effectively held in position and restrained in direction at one end and at the other end effectively restrained in direction but not held in position	1·2 L
Effectively held in position and restrained in direction at one end and at the other end partially restrained in direction but not held in position	1·5 L
Effectively held in position and restrained in direction at one end but not held in position or restrained in direction at the other end	2·0 L

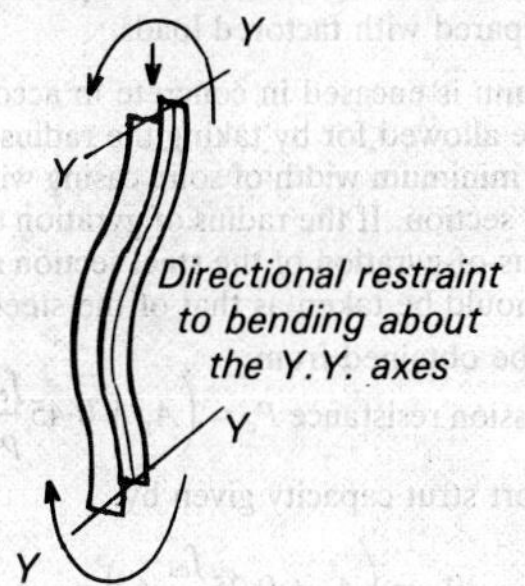

FIG. 26.—Directional Restraint of Stanchion.

It is often necessary to consider two values of slenderness when designing a stanchion since generally the radii of gyration of the section about its principal axes will not be equal. When assessing the effective length of the stanchion it must be assumed that the member will tend to bend (i.e., buckle) about the principal axis to which the radius of gyration is related, and the relevant directional restraints are those which will reduce this bending by developing end moments in the stanchion, as shown in Fig. 26.

In the case of 'I' sections the radius-of-gyration r_y is smaller than r_x, consequently the slenderness with respect to the Y–Y axis governs the design of the stanchion. Often the slenderness with respect to the Y–Y axis is so much greater than that with respect to the X–X axis that it is economical to provide tie beams to reduce the effective length and thus the slenderness with respect to Y–Y. This is illustrated by the following example.

EXAMPLE 5.—A stanchion 6 m long consisting of a 203 × 203 × 60 kg/m UC in grade 43 steel is effectively held at the ends in position only. Determine the compression resistance of this stanchion and also the increase in compression resistance if the stanchion is provided with ties at mid height running in a direction at right angles to the Y–Y axis.

$$\varepsilon = \left(\frac{275}{p_y}\right)^{1/2} = \left(\frac{275}{275}\right)^{1/2} = 1$$

width/thickness ratio of compression flange:

$$\frac{b}{T\varepsilon} = \frac{205{\cdot}2 \times 0{\cdot}5}{14{\cdot}2 \times 1{\cdot}0} = 7{\cdot}22$$

depth/thickness ratio of web:

$$= \frac{d}{t\varepsilon} = \frac{160{\cdot}8}{9{\cdot}3 \times 1{\cdot}0} = 17{\cdot}3$$

Therefore the section is plastic (class 1).

$$L_E = 1{\cdot}0\ L \text{ for both axes}$$

$$\text{slenderness } \lambda_x = \frac{6000}{89{\cdot}6} = 67$$

$$\text{slenderness } \lambda_y = \frac{6000}{51{\cdot}9} = 116.$$

For buckling about X–X axis, use Table 27(b), $p_{cx} = 208$ N/mm².
For buckling about Y–Y axis, use Table 27(c), $p_{cy} = 102$ N/mm².

$$\text{Compression resistance } P_c = \frac{75{\cdot}8 \times 10^2 \times 102}{10^3} = 773{\cdot}2 \text{ kN}.$$

If ties are provided at mid height at right angles to the Y–Y axis, slenderness is reduced:

$$\text{slenderness } \lambda = \frac{3000}{51{\cdot}9} = 58$$

From Table 27(c), $p_{cy} = 205$ N/mm².
The value of p_{cx} remains as before = 208 N/mm².

$$\text{Compression resistance } P_c = \frac{75{\cdot}8 \times 10^2 \times 205}{10^3} = 1553{\cdot}9 \text{ kN}.$$

Therefore the provision of ties has more than doubled the compression resistance. Note that the values of compression resistance should be compared with factored loads.

CASED COLUMNS.—When a column is encased in concrete in accordance with clause 4.14.1 of BS 5950 the resulting increased stability may be allowed for by taking the radius-of-gyration r_y as $0{\cdot}2\, b_c$, but not more than $0{\cdot}2\,(B + 150)$ mm where b_c is the minimum width of solid casing within the depth of the steel section and B is the width of the flange of the steel section. If the radius of gyration of the steel section is greater than that of the composite section then the radius-of-gyration of the steel section may be used for design purposes. The radius-of-gyration r_x of the member should be taken as that of the steel section alone.

The compression resistance should be obtained from:

$$\text{Compression resistance } P_c = \left(A_g + 0{\cdot}45\frac{f_{cu}}{p_y}A_c\right)p_c$$

but should be not greater than the short strut capacity given by:

$$P_{cs} = \left(A_g + 0{\cdot}25\frac{f_{cu}}{p_y}A_c\right)p_y$$

where A_g is the gross sectional area of the steel section; A_c is the gross sectional area of the concrete ignoring any casing in excess of 75 mm of the overall dimensions of the steel section; f_{cu} is the characteristic cube strength of the concrete encasement at 28 days but not more than 40 N/mm²; p_c is the compressive strength of the steel section determined from Tables 25, 26 and 27 of BS 5950 using the enhanced value of r_y and taking p_y as not more than 355 N/mm²; p_y is the design strength of the steel taken as not more than 355 N/mm².

ECCENTRICALLY LOADED MEMBERS.—When a stanchion is loaded eccentrically it will be subjected to a bending moment in addition to direct compression. It is a requirement of BS 5950 that compression members should be checked for local capacity at the points of greatest bending moment and axial load which is usually at the ends. For the local capacity check, the appropriate relationship given below should be satisfied:

$$\frac{F}{A_g p_y} + \frac{M_x}{M_{cx}} + \frac{M_y}{M_{cy}} \leqslant 1$$

where F is the applied load; M_x and M_y are the moments applied at the critical regions about the major and minor axes respectively; M_{cx} and M_{cy} are the moment capacities in the absence of axial load about the major and minor axes respectively; A_g is the gross cross sectional area; p_y is the appropriate design strength of the steel.

It is also required that members should be checked for overall buckling and, for the simplified approach in BS 5950, the following relationship should be satisfied:

$$\frac{F}{A_g p_c} + \frac{mM_x}{M_b} + \frac{mM_y}{p_y Z_y} \leqslant 1$$

where p_c is the compressive strength; m is the equivalent uniform moment factor obtained from Table 18 of BS 5950; Z_y is the elastic modulus of the section about the minor axis; M_b is the buckling resistance moment capacity about the major axis = $S_x p_b$ where S_x is the plastic modulus and p_b is the bending strength from Table 11 or 12 of BS 5950; other terms are as defined above.

The example which follows illustrates the overall buckling check.

EXAMPLE 6.—A stanchion 4·2 m long consisting of a 254 × 254 × 107 kg/m UC in grade 43 steel is effectively held at the ends in position only. Carry out an overall buckling check on the stanchion for the following factored axial loads and moments assuming the moments to be applied at one end of the member.

Factored axial load = 900 kN.

Factored moment X–X axis = 150 kNm.

Factored moment Y–Y axis = 30 kNm.

$$\varepsilon = \left(\frac{275}{p_y}\right)^{1/2} = \left(\frac{275}{265}\right)^{1/2} = 1{\cdot}02.$$

width/thickness ratio of compression flange:

$$= \frac{b}{T\varepsilon} = \frac{258{\cdot}3 \times 0{\cdot}5}{20{\cdot}5 \times 1{\cdot}02} = 6{\cdot}18$$

depth/thickness ratio of web:

$$= \frac{d}{t\varepsilon} = \frac{200{\cdot}2}{13{\cdot}0 \times 1{\cdot}02} = 15{\cdot}1.$$

Therefore the section is plastic (class 1).

$L_E = 1{\cdot}0\,L$ for both axes,

$$\text{slenderness } \lambda_x = \frac{4200}{113{\cdot}0} = 37{\cdot}2,$$

$$\text{slenderness } \lambda_y = \frac{4200}{65{\cdot}7} = 64{\cdot}0.$$

For buckling about X–X axis, use Table 27(b), $p_{cx} = 243$ N/mm².
For buckling about Y–Y axis, use Table 27(c), $p_{cy} = 188$ N/mm².

$$\text{Using the minimum value } A_g p_c = \frac{136{\cdot}6 \times 10^2 \times 188}{10^3} = 2568 \text{ kN}$$

to calculate M_b, λ_{LT} may be taken as $0{\cdot}5(L/r_y)$, clause 4.7.7. of BS 5950:

$$\lambda_{LT} = 0{\cdot}5 \times 64{\cdot}0 = 32{\cdot}0$$

From Table 11 of BS 5950, $p_b = 265\ \text{N/mm}^2$, therefore:

$$M_b = S_x p_b = \frac{1490 \times 10^3 \times 265}{10^6} = 394{\cdot}8\ \text{kNm}.$$

For overall buckling check:

$$\frac{F}{A_g p_c} + \frac{mM_x}{M_b} + \frac{mM_y}{p_y Z_y} \leqslant 1$$

m may be taken as 1·0, clause 4.7.7. of BS 5950, therefore:

$$\frac{900}{2568} + \frac{1{\cdot}0 \times 150}{394{\cdot}8} + \frac{1{\cdot}0 \times 30}{265 \times 457 \times 10^3/10^6} = 0{\cdot}351 + 0{\cdot}380 + 0{\cdot}248 = 0{\cdot}979 < 1$$

Hence, the section satisfies the overall buckling check.

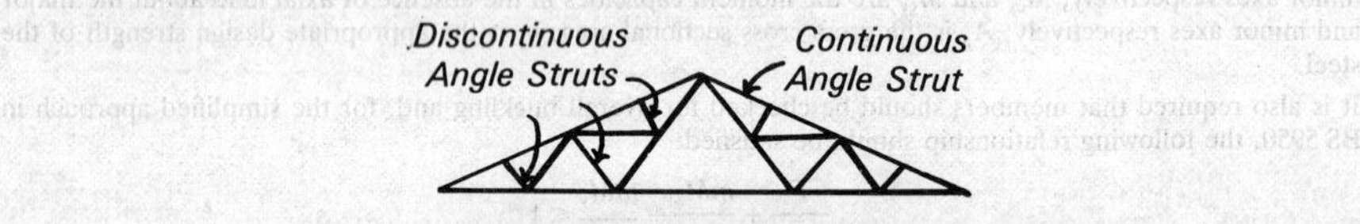

FIG. 27.—Angle Struts.

ANGLE STRUTS.—Single and double angle struts are the types of compression member most widely used in roof trusses and lattice girders. Figure 27 gives a diagramatic illustration of continuous and discontinuous angle struts. The various types of discontinuous angle strut are dealt with as follows:

(a) Providing the connections at each end are made with at least two bolts in line, or the equivalent in welding, BS 5950 permits a single angle discontinuous strut to be treated as an axially loaded member. The slenderness should be taken as not less than $0{\cdot}85\ L/r_{vv}$ or $0{\cdot}7\ L/r_{aa} + 30$ as shown in Table 8.

(b) Single angle discontinuous struts connected with only single bolts should be treated similarly but the slenderness should be taken as not less than $1{\cdot}0\ L/r_{vv}$ or $0{\cdot}7\ L/r_{aa} + 30$ as shown in Table 8 and the compression resistance taken as 80% of the compression resistance when treated as an axially loaded strut.

(c) Double angle discontinuous struts connected to one side of a gusset by one or more bolts in each angle or the equivalent in welding, are designed in the manner described in (a) for single angles. The slenderness should be taken as not less than $0{\cdot}85\ L/r$ about the weakest axis or $0{\cdot}7\ L/r_{xx} + 30$ as shown in Table 8.

(d) Double angle discontinuous struts connected to both sides of a gusset with not less than two bolts in line in each angle or the equivalent in welding may be designed in the manner described in (a) for single angles. The slenderness should be taken as not less than $0{\cdot}85\ L/r$ about the weakest axis or $0{\cdot}7\ L/r_{xx} + 30$ as shown in Table 8.

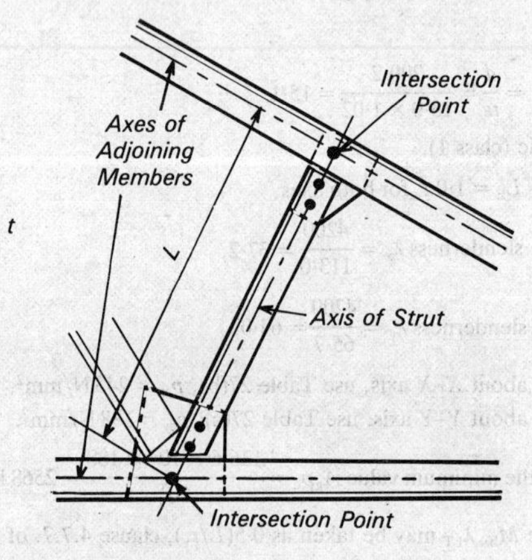

FIG. 28.—Length of Struts.

(e) Double angle discontinuous struts connected directly to one or both sides of another member may be designed in the manner described in (a) for single angles. The slenderness should be taken as not less than $1{\cdot}0\,L/r$ about the weakest axis or $0{\cdot}7\,L/r_{xx}+30$, as shown in Table 8.

Figure 28 illustrates the dimension *L,* the distance between intersection points, to be used when calculating *L*/*r* values.

TABLE 8. SLENDERNESS VALUES FOR DISCONTINUOUS ANGLE STRUTS

Condition		Slenderness
Single angles		0.85L/rvv or 0.7L/raa + 30
		1.0L/rvv or 0.7L/raa + 30
Double angles		0.85L/ryy or 0.85L/rxx or 0.7L/rxx + 30
		0.85L/ryy or 0.85L/rxx or 0.7L/rxx + 30
		1.0L/ryy or 1.0L/rxx or 0.7L/rxx + 30

Continuous angle struts do not receive detailed consideration in BS 5950. The usual practice with such members is to ignore eccentricity at the connections since its effects are considerably reduced by continuity and the restraint of the connections. The design procedure as described in the foregoing text for stanchions should be followed. Often continuous angle struts such as roof truss principals and lattice girder booms are subjected to bending by transverse loads, and the combined bending and direct stresses are then dealt with as in the case of eccentrically loaded stanchions as described previously.

When a compression member consists of two angles, the efficiency of the member depends upon the two angles being so connected that they function as a unit. This is usually done by bolting or welding the angles together at intervals, distance pieces or packs being used to maintain the angles at the correct distance apart if they are not in contact. The connections are so spaced that the slenderness of each angle should not exceed 50.

WELDED STANCHIONS.—Welding permits the fabrication of stanchions of special section such as those shown in Fig. 29 (a) and (b). In other cases, such as those shown in Fig. 29 (c) and (d) welding provides a neat

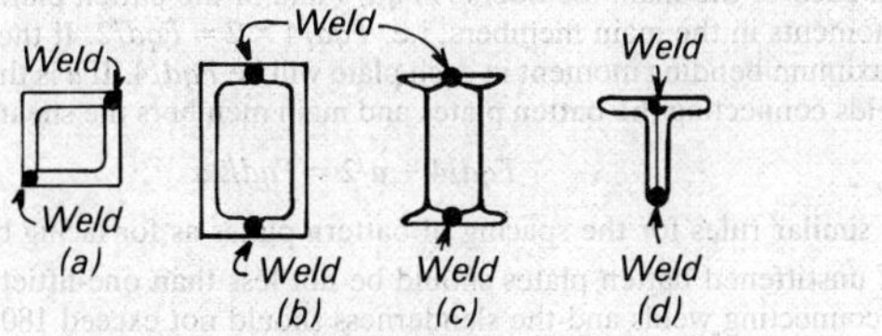

FIG. 29.—Welded Stanchions.

alternative to batten plates and connecting bolts. Welding is also used to fabricate special I sections. In the sections shown in Fig. 29 and in other cases where longitudinal welds occur it is often desirable to use intermittent welds. However intermittent welds should not be used in fatigue situations or where capillary action could lead to the formation of corrosion pockets. Each effective weld length should be not less than four times the weld size, and the distance between each length is limited to 300 mm or 16 times the thickness of the thinner part joined for compression members and 24 times this thickness for tension members.

LACED COMPOUND STANCHIONS.—Stanchions comprising two main components laced together as shown in Fig. 30 (a) are sometimes more convenient and economical than members of solid construction.

For the design of the lacing the stanchion is treated as a vertical lattice girder subjected to a shear force equal to 1% of the maximum factored axial load plus the shear due to eccentric loads, end moments or lateral forces. Except at the ends of the stanchions, ties at right angles to the main members should not be used in conjunction with lacing since they modify the action of the member so that the lacing carries part of the axial load and will be subjected to much higher stresses than would otherwise be the case: see Fig. 30 (b).

The inclination of lacing bars should be set between 40° and 70° to the axis of the stanchion and their spacing should be such that the slenderness λ_c of either main component on the length l as shown in Fig. 30 (a) is not greater than 50. The maximum slenderness of the strut as a whole should not be taken as less than $1{\cdot}4\,\lambda_c$. Usually the main members of a laced stanchion are of substantial section, and since the forces in the lacing members are generally small, there is no need to insist on the axes of lacing bars intersecting on the axes of the main members: the detail shown in Fig. 31 is quite satisfactory. The effective length of a lacing should be taken as the distance between the inner welds or fasteners. The slenderness should not exceed 180.

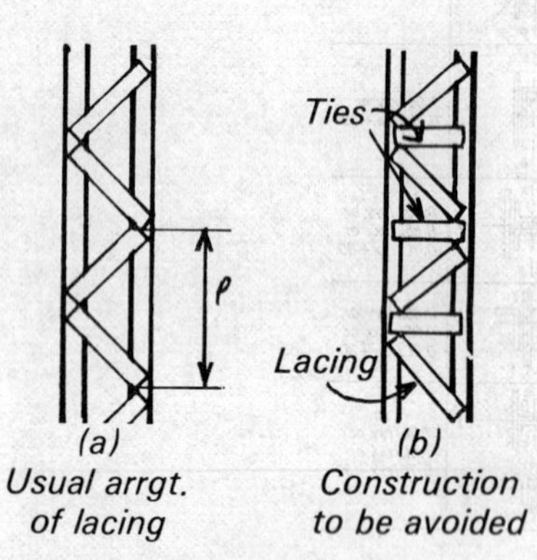

FIG. 30.—Laced Compound Stanchions.

FIG. 31.—Lacing detail: Compound Stanchions.

BATTENED STANCHIONS.—It is sometimes preferable to connect two members to form one stanchion by means of battens instead of lacing. Battened stanchions are of neater appearance than laced stanchions, require less fabrication and offer fewer obstructions to the connection of other members and equipment to the stanchion. Battened stanchions are designed to resist the total transverse shear assessed in the manner described above for laced stanchions, but the design of the batten plates is quite different from that of lacing bars. A battened stanchion behaves under transverse forces as a Vierendeel girder and the batten plates and their connections to the main members are subjected to bending moment and shear force. Thus if in Fig. 32 (a), the shear force on the column is Fq, then if we assume that points of contraflexure occur at the centres of the batten plates and midway between them, the bending moments will be as shown in Fig. 32 (b). The maximum bending moment in each of the main members is $Fqd/4$ and in the batten plates the total maximum moment is the sum of the moments in the main members, i.e. $Fqd/4 \times 2 = Fqd/2$. If the batten plates are in pairs one on each side the maximum bending moment in each plate will be $Fqd/4$. If a is the distance between the centres of the groups of welds connecting the batten plates and main members the shear force in each batten plate will be:

$$Fqd/4 \div a/2 = Fqd/2a$$

BS 5950 lays down similar rules for the spacing of battern plates as for lacing bars.

The thickness of unstiffened batten plates should be not less than one-fiftieth of the distance between the innermost lines of connecting welds and the slenderness should not exceed 180. Thus for the example shown in Fig. 33 the thickness should be at least $(250 + 2 \times 55)/50 = 7{\cdot}2$ mm. An 8 mm plate is therefore proposed. The radius of gyration is $8/\sqrt{12} = 2{\cdot}31$ mm and therefore the slenderness is $360/2{\cdot}31 = 156$. The 8 mm plate is therefore suitable.

EXAMPLE 7.—Fig. 33 shows part of a battened stanchion comprising two 305 × 102 × 46·18 kg/m channels with 8 mm thick batten plates at 900 mm centres welded to each of the channels. It is required to ascertain if this assembly is suitable for a factored transverse shear force of 20 kN.

$Fq = 20$ kN, and $d = 900$ mm, and therefore the maximum bending moment in batten plate and connecting welds is:

$$Fqd/4 = 20 \times 900/4 \times 10^3 = 4{\cdot}5 \text{ kNm}$$

$a = 250 + 55 + 55 = 360$ mm; therefore the vertical shear on plate and welds is:

$$Fqd/2a = (20 \times 900)/(2 \times 360) = 25{\cdot}0 \text{ kN.}$$

To find the weld size required between batten plates and channels, consider only the outside vertical welds. In practise the welds would be returned horizontally and at least a sealing run provided between the toes of the channels and the inside face of the batten plates.

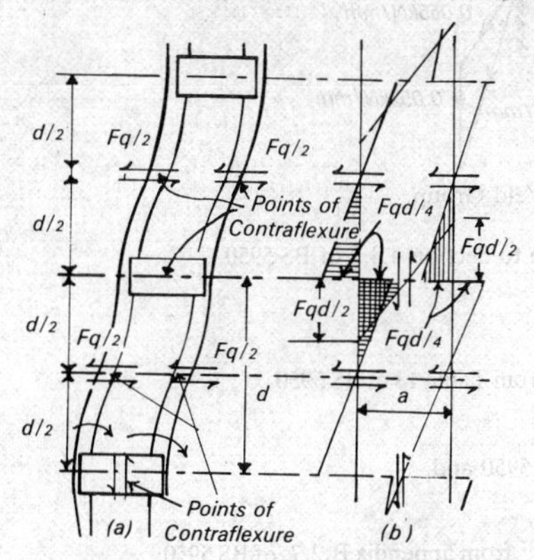

FIG. 32.—Battened Stanchions.
(a) Deflected form of stanchion due to transverse shear Fq.
(b) Bending moments in stanchion due to transverse shear Fq.

For weld group:

$$I_p = I_x + I_y = 2 \times 24{\cdot}0^3/12 + 2 \times 24{\cdot}0 \times 18{\cdot}0^2 = 2304 + 15552 = 17856 \text{ cm}^4$$

$$\Sigma L = 2 \times 24{\cdot}0 = 48{\cdot}0 \text{ cm}$$

$$r = \sqrt{18{\cdot}0^2 + 12{\cdot}0^2} = 21{\cdot}6 \text{ cm.}$$

$$F_M = 4{\cdot}5 \times 10^2 \times 21{\cdot}6/17856 \times 10 = 0{\cdot}055 \text{ kN/mm}$$

$$F_S = 25{\cdot}0/48{\cdot}0 \times 10 = 0{\cdot}052 \text{ kN/mm}$$

Resultant force $F_R = 0{\cdot}105$ kN/mm (see Fig. 34).

From Table 6 a 4 mm fillet weld is adequate but in many projects 6 mm fillet welds are used as a minimum.
To check the section of the batten plates:
Shear capacity $P_v = 0{\cdot}6\,p_y A_v$ and for solid plates A_v is 0·9 times the area of the section

$$P_v = \frac{0{\cdot}6 \times 275 \times 0{\cdot}9 \times 240 \times 8}{10^3} = 285{\cdot}1 \text{ kN} > F_v = 25{\cdot}0 \text{ kN.}$$

As $F_v < 0{\cdot}6\,P_v$, $M_c = p_y S \leqslant 1{\cdot}2 p_y Z$

$$S = 0{\cdot}8 \times 24{\cdot}0^2/4 = 115{\cdot}2 \text{ cm}^3, \quad \therefore M_c = \frac{275 \times 115{\cdot}2 \times 10^3}{10^6} = 31{\cdot}68 \text{ kNm}$$

$$Z = 0{\cdot}8 \times 24{\cdot}0^2/6 = 76{\cdot}8 \text{ cm}^3, \quad \therefore M_c = \frac{1{\cdot}2 \times 275 \times 76{\cdot}8 \times 10^3}{10^6} = 25{\cdot}34 \text{ kNm}$$

$M_c = 1{\cdot}2 p_y Z$ governs $> 4{\cdot}5$ kNm.

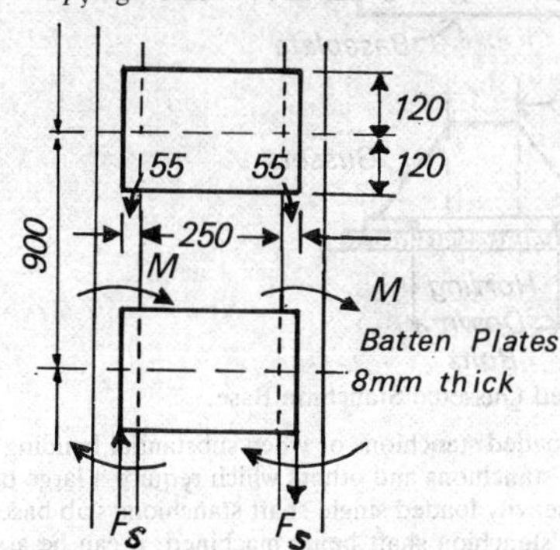

FIG. 33.—Batten Plates 8 mm.

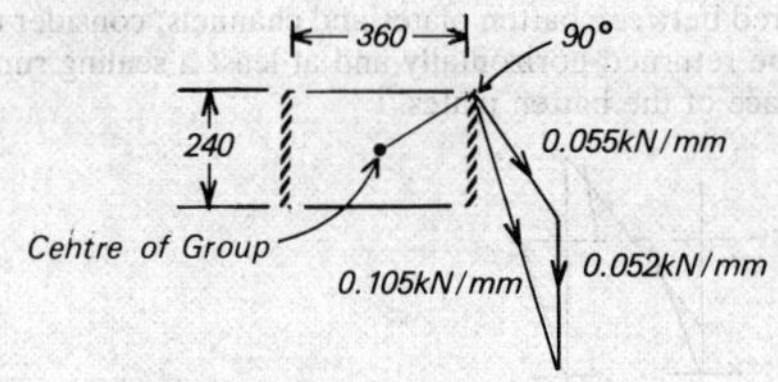

FIG. 34.—Forces on Weld Group.

The section should be checked for buckling by reference to Section 4.3.7 of BS 5950.
To satisfy this requirement:

$\bar{M} \leq M_b$ where $\bar{M} = mM_A$ and $M_A = M$.

$\bar{M} = m \times 4{\cdot}5$ kNm and for $\beta = -1$, $m = 0{\cdot}43$ from Table 18 of BS 5950

$\therefore \bar{M} = 0{\cdot}43 \times 4{\cdot}5 = 1{\cdot}935$ kNm.

Buckling resistance $M_b = S_x p_b$ from clause 4.3.7.3 of BS 5950 and

$S_x = 115{\cdot}2\ \text{cm}^3$ as calculated before.

For an individual plate, $\lambda_{LT} = n \times 2{\cdot}8\left(\frac{L_E d}{t^2}\right)^{1/2}$ from appendix B.2.7. of BS 5950:

take $L_E = 0{\cdot}85 \times 360 = 306$ mm,

$n = 1{\cdot}0$ from Table 13 of BS 5950,

$$\lambda_{LT} = 1{\cdot}0 \times 2{\cdot}8\left(\frac{306 \times 240}{8^2}\right)^{1/2} = 94{\cdot}8,$$

and $p_b = 134\ \text{N/mm}^2$ from Table 11 of BS 5950,

$$\therefore M_b = \frac{115{\cdot}2 \times 10^3 \times 134}{10^6} = 15{\cdot}4\ \text{kNm}.$$

$\bar{M} < M_b$ and therefore the requirement is satisfied.

240 mm × 8 mm thick batten plates are satisfactory, indeed from the above calculations the section could be reduced. The thickness must remain at 8 mm to satisfy the minimum requirement but the 240 mm dimension could be reduced.

STANCHION BASES.—A stanchion base is required to distribute the load from the stanchion to the foundation, to provide positional fixity to the lower end of the stanchion and to develop bending moment if required. Stanchion bases are of two types, gusseted bases and slab bases. A typical gusseted base for a UC stanchion is shown in Fig. 35.

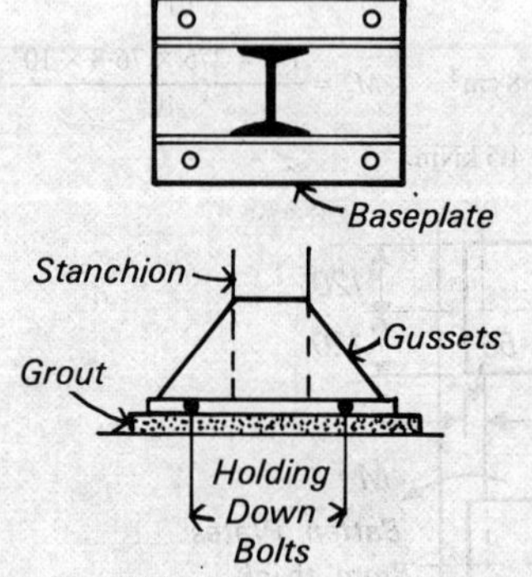

FIG. 35.—Welded Gusseted Stanchion Base.

Gusseted bases are normally used for lightly loaded stanchions or when substantial bending moments have to be transmitted. They are also used for gantry stanchions and others which require a large base for reasons other than the load transmitted. For the more heavily loaded single shaft stanchions slab bases are generally used: see Fig. 36. Subject to the bottom of the stanchion shaft being machined, it can be assumed that the

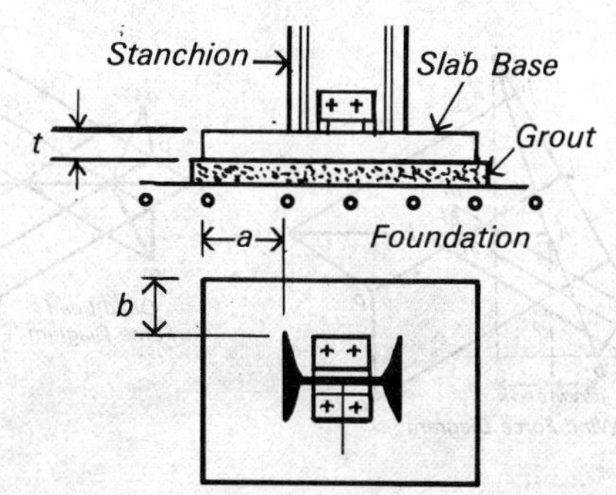

FIG. 36.—Slab Base to Stanchion.

entire load is transmitted by dead bearing to the base, only sufficient fastenings being provided to locate the stanchion on the base and ensure that the base is not detached from the stanchion during handling, transport and erection. For slab bases of steel to BS 4360 the required thickness is given by the expression:

$$t = [2{\cdot}5w/p_{yp}(a^2 - 0{\cdot}3b^2)]^{1/2}$$

where a is the greater projection of the baseplate beyond the stanchion; b is the lesser projection of the baseplate beyond the stanchion; w is the pressure on the underside of the baseplate assuming a uniform distribution; p_{yp} is the design strength of the plate as given in Table 2, but should not be taken as greater than 270 N/mm².

If gussets are provided to the baseplate the projections a and b may be measured from the extremities of the gussets, provided that the gussets are designed for the resulting forces.

Slab bases are usually specified in thicknesses which are multiples of 10 mm.

ROOF TRUSSES

A truss is a convenient and efficient means of providing a pitched roof over spans up to 30 m or more. The internal members are so arranged that the rafters are supported at suitable intervals—generally between 1·5 and 2·0 m. Types of truss suitable for various spans are shown in Fig. 37.

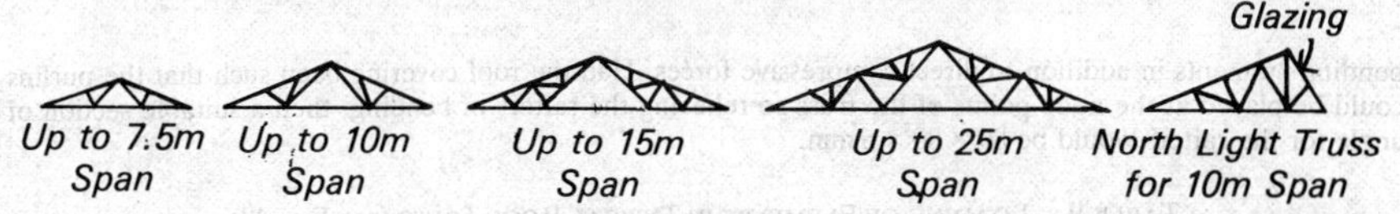

FIG. 37.—Types of Roof Truss for Various Spans.

When it is important to provide roof lighting without direct sunlight the 'North Light' type of truss is suitable. These trusses are seldom used on spans exceeding 12 m; for larger spans a composite form of construction comprising lattice girders and North Light trusses is used. A suitable arrangement is shown in Fig. 38.

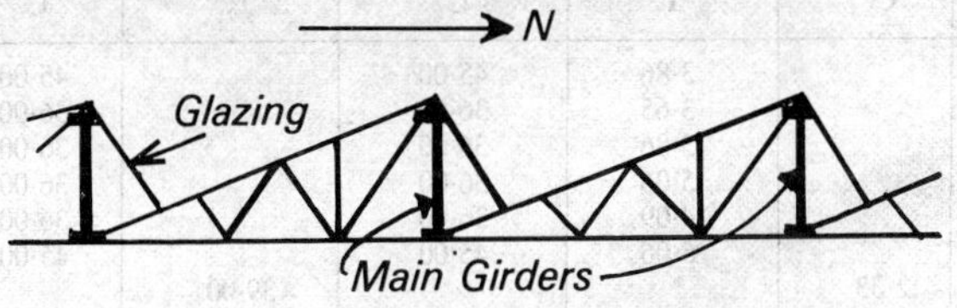

FIG. 38.—System of Main Lattice Girders and North Light Trusses.

The design of roof truss members can be carried out by using the well established method of force diagrams to obtain the loads in the members. Fig. 39 shows the details of a typical roof truss and the relevant force diagrams. Fig. 40 shows the applied loading and Table 9 gives a member load table. It should be noted that these are actual loads and must therefore be multiplied by the relevant load factor before use in design to BS 5950.

It should be noted that the rafter members for this truss are of much heavier section than the remaining members. This is due to the fact that the purlins do not occur at the node points of the truss because provision had to be made to allow for the maximum span of the roof sheeting. The rafters are therefore subjected to

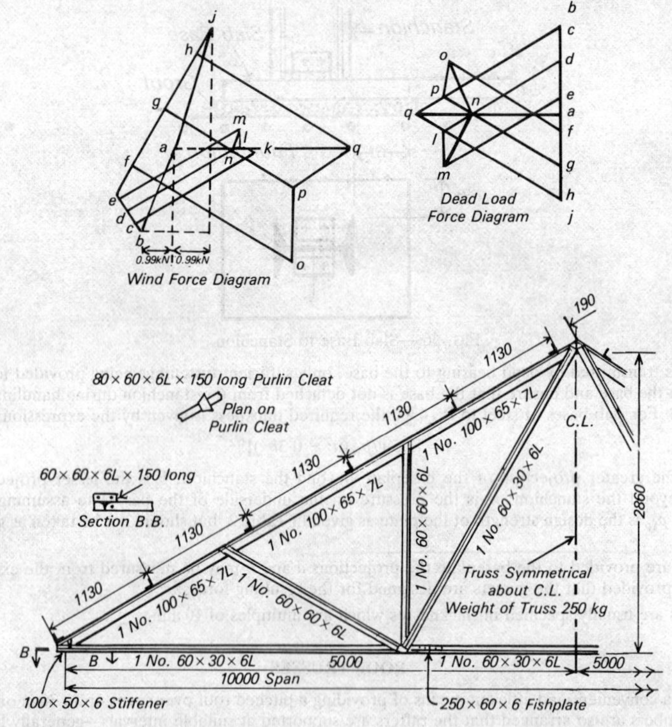

FIG. 39.—Details of Welded Truss for 10 m Span Roof Structure. For Loads see Fig. 40.

bending moments in addition to direct compressive forces. Had the roof covering been such that the purlins could be placed at the node points of the truss so relieving the rafters of bending, then a suitable section of angle for the rafters would be 80 × 80 × 6 mm.

TABLE 9.—LOADING OF ELEMENTS IN TYPICAL ROOF TRUSS (see Fig. 40)

C = compression (kN) T = tension (kN)

MEMBER	WIND		DEAD		MAXIMUM	
	C.	T.	C.	T.	C.	T.
C. K.		3·86	45·00		45·00	
D. L.		3·65	36·00		36·00	
E. M.		3·86	36·00		36·00	
F. O.		5·06	36·00		36·00	
G. P.		4·09	36·00		36·00	
H. Q.		5·06	45·00		45·00	
K. A.	2·33			39·00		39·00
N. A.	1·51			23·40		23·40
Q. A.	4·96			39·00		39·00
K. L.		0·43	9·00		9.00	
L. M.		0·43	9·00		9.00	
M. N.	0·72			15·50		15·50
N. O.	3·40			15·50		15·50
O. P.		1·94	9·00		9.00	
P. Q.		1·94	9·00		9.00	

It is in truss and lattice girder work that the greatest economy in materal by the use of welding can be obtained. This is due to the following: (a) no loss of section due to bolt holes; (b) no limitation on size of members due to the need for accommodating bolts; (c) most gussets can be eliminated; (d) Simpler and lighter sections can be used for cleats and other details.

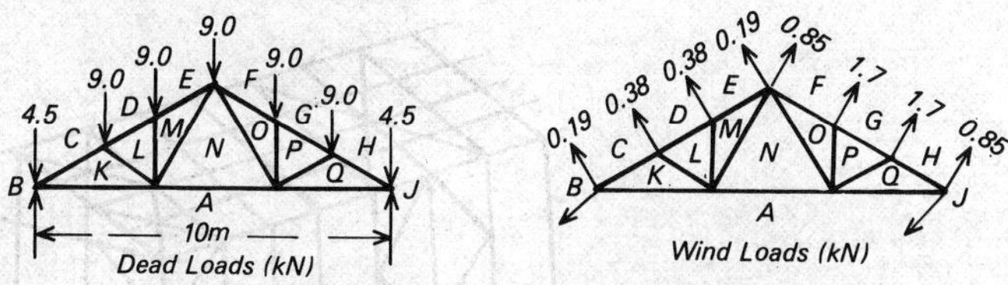

FIG. 40.—Applied Loading for 10 m Span Roof Truss.

THE STABILITY OF STEEL FRAMED STRUCTURES

A structure is said to be 'steel framed' when its stability under load depends solely upon the steel members and the foundations thereto. Thus the building shown in Fig. 41(a) is not steel framed because the roof trusses are carried on load-bearing walls which must themselves be stable. If the trusses are carried on stanchions as shown in Fig. 41(b) the building becomes steel framed and the walls need not be of load-bearing construction.

In practice the stability of many steel framed structures is much enhanced by the walls, floors, roof, encasing, etc., and the designer can sometimes take advantage of this when dealing with wind forces. There are however, exceptions which require the special treatment outlined below.

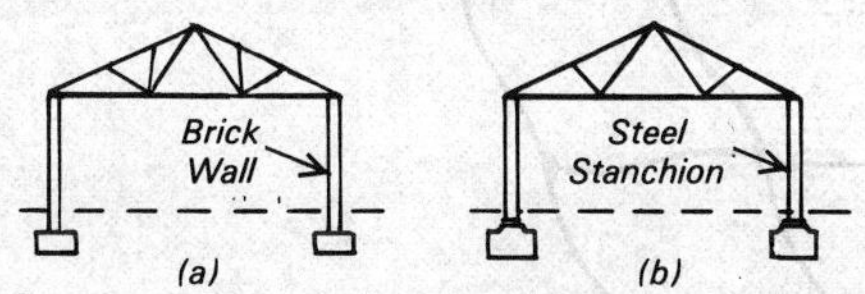

FIG. 41.—Alternative Structures. (a) Non Steel Framed (b) Steel Framed.

SINGLE STOREY STRUCTURES.—In the case of single storey buildings, particularly, those with light wall and roof cladding such as steel profiled sheeting the entire stability of the structure under all conditions of loading must be provided by the steel frame and its foundations.

There are various methods by which stability may be ensured and the most suitable treatment of a given case must be decided by considerations of economy, soil conditions, window and door openings, headroom, etc. For example, the stability of the frame shown in Fig. 42(a) under the action of wind and other lateral forces depends primarily on the cantilever action of the stanchions about their bases. This arrangement generally requires larger foundations and stanchion bases than would otherwise be necessary and is not usually

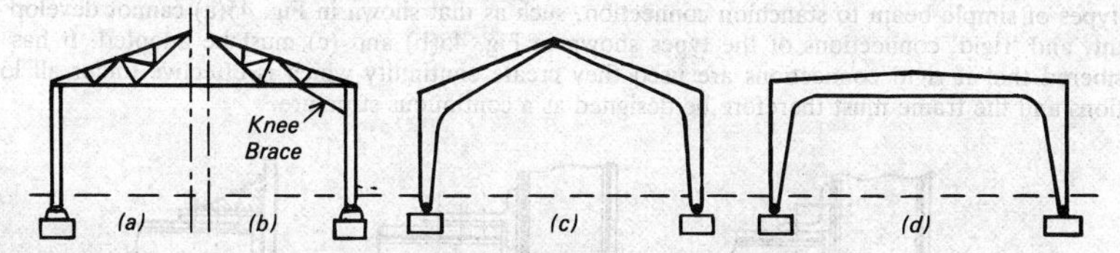

FIG. 42.—Methods of Ensuring Stability in Single Storey Structures.

considered satisfactory for tall or large-span structures. The alternative, shown in Fig. 42(b) is to provide knee braces to the trusses so that they become continuous with the stanchions. This is preferable structurally but has the disadvantage that there is a loss of headroom where the knee braces occur, which is particularly embarrassing when the stanchions carry a travelling crane, and it may be necessary to increase the height of the building to allow for loss of head-room due to the knee braces.

Other forms of construction which are stable in themselves and require no assistance from the foundations are shown in Fig. 42(c) and (d).

In addition to ensuring stability in a transverse direction provision must also be made for stability in the length of the building. This is generally done by the use of angle section bracing in the walls and the plane of the roof truss rafters as shown in Fig. 43. It will be seen that the bracing in the plane of the rafters at the ends of the building serves to support the upper ends of the gable stanchions, but in some cases this results in the stanchions having too long an unsupported length and it is necessary to provide a 'wind girder' in the plane of the truss ties to support the gable stanchions at eaves level.

The forces in bracing members are usually small and the sizes of the angles are governed by the minima specified in BS 5950 and noted in previous text. The judicious use of hangers to purlins, etc., will do much to reduce bending stresses in long bracing members due to their own weight and enable the minimum sections to be used.

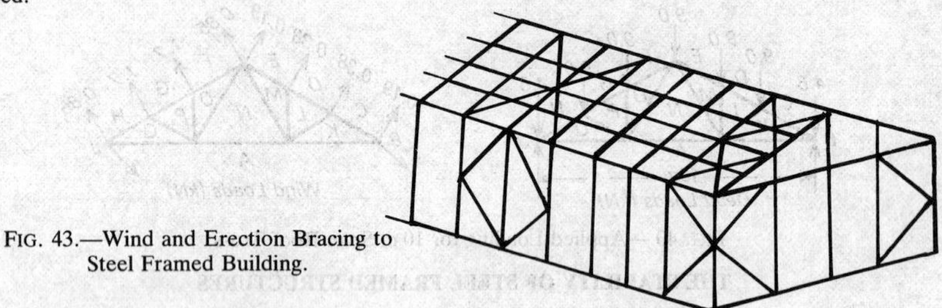

FIG. 43.—Wind and Erection Bracing to Steel Framed Building.

MULTI-STOREY STRUCTURES.—Some multi-storey steel framed buildings are so constructed that it is unnecessary to consider wind forces when designing the frame. In these cases the wind is considered as being resisted by gable end walls and lift cores acting as shear walls, and the steelwork designed for dead and super loads only. In situations where shear walls are not available the wind forces must be sustained by the steel frame.

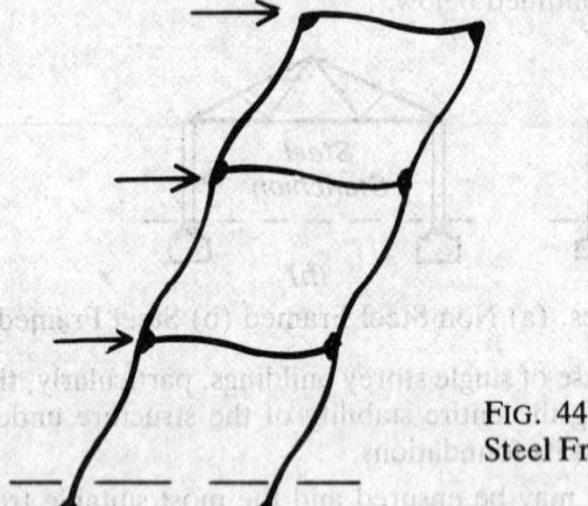

FIG. 44.—Deflection of Multi-storey Steel Frame under the action of Wind Forces.

Fig. 44 shows how a simple three-storey building frame deflects under the action of horizontal wind forces. It will be seen that bending moments are developed at the junctions of beams and stanchions and that the general transverse stability of the frame depends on the connections being able to resist these moments. The usual types of simple beam to stanchion connection, such as that shown in Fig. 45(a) cannot develop much moment, and 'rigid' connections of the types shown in Fig. 45(b) and (c) must be adopted. It has to be remembered that if rigid connections are used they create continuity which is effective under all loading conditions and the frame must therefore be designed as a continuous structure.

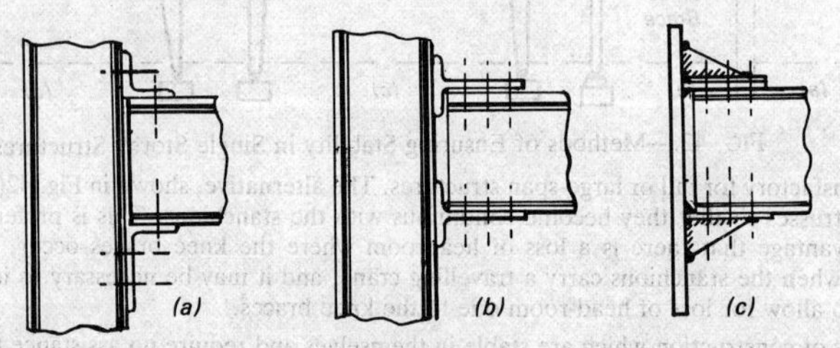

FIG. 45.—Beam to Stanchion Connections.

In some countries it is necessary to design structures to resist the effects of earthquakes. It is customary in such cases to assume that the earth tremors impart a horizontal acceleration of one-tenth that of gravity to the structure which means, in effect, that the structural frame must be designed to resist horizontal forces equivalent to one-tenth of its weight and superimposed loads.

BRITISH STANDARD SECTIONS.—The following Tables 10 to 17 inclusive are extracts from BS 4, Part 1 'Structural Steel Sections'.

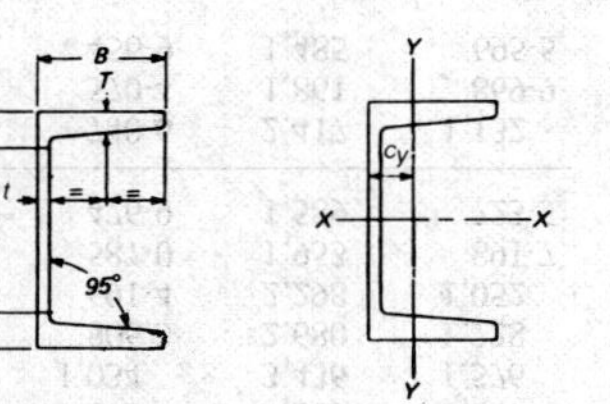

TABLE 10.—CHANNELS.

DESIGNATION		Depth of section	With of section	Thickness		Area of section	Distance of centre of gravity	Second Moment of Area		Radius of gyration		Elastic modulus		Plastic modulus	
Nominal size	Mass/unit length	D	B	Web t	Flange T		c_y	About X–X	About Y–Y	About X–X	About Y–Y	About X–X	About Y–Y	About X–X	About Y–Y
mm	kg/m	mm	mm	mm	mm	cm²	cm	cm⁴	cm⁴	cm²	cm²	cm³	cm³	cm³	cm³
432 × 102	65·54	431·8	101·6	12·2	16·8	83·49	2·32	21,399	628·6	16·0	2·74	991·1	80·15	1,210	153
381 × 102	55·10	381·0	101·6	10·4	16·3	70·19	2·52	14,894	579·8	14·6	2·87	781·8	75·87	933	144
305 × 102	46·18	304·8	101·6	10·2	14·8	58·83	2·66	8,214	499·5	11·8	2·91	539·0	66·60	638	128
305 × 89	41·69	304·8	88·9	10·2	13·7	53·11	2·18	7,061	325·4	11·5	2·47	463·3	48·49	557	92·6
254 × 89	35·74	254·0	88·9	9·1	13·6	45·52	2·42	4,448	302·4	9·88	2·58	350·2	46·71	414	89·6
254 × 76	28·29	254·0	76·2	8·1	10·9	36·03	1·86	3,367	162·6	9·67	2·12	265·1	28·22	317	54·1
229 × 89	32·76	228·6	88·9	8·6	13·3	41·73	2·53	3,387	285·0	9·01	2·61	296·4	44·82	348	86·4
229 × 76	26·06	228·6	76·2	7·6	11·2	33·20	2·00	2,610	158·7	8·87	2·19	228·3	28·22	270	54·2
203 × 89	29·78	203·2	88·9	8·1	12·9	37·94	2·65	2,491	264·4	8·10	2·64	245·2	42·34	287	81·6
203 × 76	23·82	203·2	76·2	7·1	11·2	30·34	2·13	1,950	151·4	8·02	2·23	192·0	27·59	225	53·3
178 × 89	26·81	177·8	88·9	7·6	12·3	34·15	2·76	1,753	241·0	7·16	2·66	197·2	39·29	230	75·4
178 × 76	20·84	177·8	76·2	6·6	10·3	26·54	2·20	1,337	134·0	7·10	2·25	150·4	24·73	175	48·1
152 × 89	23·84	152·4	88·9	7·1	11·6	30·36	2·86	1,166	215·1	6·20	2·66	153·0	35·70	178	68·1
152 × 76	17·88	152·4	76·2	6·4	9·0	22·77	2·21	851·6	113·8	6·11	2·24	111·8	21·05	130	41·3
127 × 64	14·90	127·0	63·5	6·4	9·2	18·98	1·94	482·6	67·24	5·04	1·88	75·99	15·25	89·4	29·3
102 × 51	10·42	101·6	50·8	6·1	7·6	13·28	1·51	207·7	29·10	3·96	1·48	40·89	8·16	48·8	15·7
76 × 38	6·70	76·2	38·1	5·1	6·8	8·53	1·19	74·14	10·66	2·95	1·12	19·46	4·07	23·4	7·76

NOTE. Channels ordered to the standard thickness shall be practically accurate in profile. If the web thickness ordered is greater than the standard the width of the flanges will be increased by the same amount as the increase in web thickness.

TABLE 11.—UNIVERSAL COLUMNS.

DESIGNATION		Depth of section D	Width of section B	Thickness		Area of section	Second Moment of Area		Radius of gyration		Elastic modulus		Plastic modulus	
Serial size	Mass/unit length			Web t	Flange T		About X–X	About Y–Y	About X–X	About Y–Y	About X–X	About Y–Y	About X–X	About Y–Y
mm	kg/m	mm	mm	mm	mm	cm^2	cm^4	cm^4	cm	cm	cm^3	cm^3	cm^3	cm^3
	634	474·7	424·1	47·6	77·0	808·1	275,140	98,211	18·5	11·0	11,592	4,632	14,247	7,114
	551	455·7	418·5	42·0	67·5	701·8	227,023	82,665	18·0	10·9	9,964	3,951	12,078	6,058
	467	436·6	412·4	35·9	58·0	595·5	183,118	67,905	17·5	10·7	8,388	3,293	10,009	5,038
356 × 406	393	419·1	407·0	30·6	49·2	500·9	146,765	55,410	17·1	10·5	7,004	2,723	8,229	4,157
	340	406·4	403·0	26·5	42·9	432·7	122,474	46,816	16·8	10·4	6,027	2,324	6,994	3,541
	287	393·7	399·0	22·6	36·5	366·0	99,994	38,714	16·5	10·3	5,080	1,940	5,818	2,952
	235	381·0	395·0	18·5	30·2	299·8	79,110	31,008	16·2	10·2	4,153	1,570	4,689	2,384
Column core	477	427·0	424·4	48·0	53·2	607·2	172,391	68,057	16·8	10·6	8,075	3,207	9,700	4,979
	202	374·7	374·4	16·8	27·0	257·9	66,307	23,632	16·0	9·57	3,540	1,262	3,976	1,917
356 × 368	177	368·3	372·1	14·5	23·8	225·7	57,153	20,470	15·9	9·52	2,104	1,100	3,457	1,668
	153	362·0	370·2	12·6	20·7	195·2	48,525	17,470	15·8	9·46	2,681	943.8	2,964	1,430
	129	355·6	368·3	10·7	17·5	164·9	40,246	14,555	15·6	9·39	2,264	790·4	2,482	1,196
	283	365·3	321·8	26·9	44·1	360·4	78,777	24,545	14·8	8·25	4,314	1,525	5,101	2,337
	240	352·6	317·9	23·0	37·7	305·6	64,177	20,239	14·5	8·14	3,641	1,273	4,245	1,947
	198	339·9	314·1	19·2	31·4	252·3	50,832	16,230	14·2	8·02	2,991	1,034	3,436	1,576
305 × 305	158	327·2	310·6	15·7	25·0	201·2	38,740	12,524	13·9	7·89	2,368	806.3	2,680	1,228
	137	320·5	308·7	13·8	21·7	174·6	32,838	10,672	13·7	7·82	2,049	691·4	2,298	1,052
	118	314·5	306·8	11·9	18·7	149·8	27,601	9,006	13·6	7·75	1,755	587·0	1,953	891·7
	97	307·8	304·8	9·9	15·4	123·3	22,202	7,268	13·4	7·68	1,442	476·9	1,589	723·5
	167	289·1	264·5	19·2	31·7	212·4	29,914	9,796	11·9	6.79	2,070	740·6	2,417	1,132
	132	276·4	261·0	15·6	25·1	167·7	22,416	7,444	11·6	6·66	1,622	570·4	1,861	869·9
254 × 254	107	266·7	258·3	13·0	20·5	136·6	17,510	5,901	11·3	6.57	1,313	456·9	1,485	695·5

(Continuation of Table 11)—Universal Columns

	89	260·4	255·9	10·5	17·3	114·0	14,307	4,849	11·2	6·52	1,099	378·9	1,228	575·4
	73	254·0	254·0	8·6	14·2	92·9	11,360	3,873	11·1	6·46	894·5	305·0	988·5	462·4
	86	222·3	208·8	13·0	20·5	110·1	9,462	3,119	9·27	5·32	851·5	298·7	978·8	455·9
	71	215·9	206·2	10·3	17·3	91·1	7,647	2,536	9·16	5·28	708·4	246·0	802·4	374·2
203 × 203	60	209·6	205·2	9·3	14·2	75·6	6,088	2,041	8·96	5·19	581·1	199·0	652·0	302·8
	52	206·2	203·9	8·0	12·5	66·4	5,263	1,770	8·90	5·16	510·4	173·6	568·1	263·7
	46	203·2	203·2	7·3	11·0	58·8	4,564	1,539	8·81	5·11	449·2	151·5	497·4	230·0
	37	161·8	154·4	8·1	11·5	47·4	2,218	709	6·84	3·87	274·2	91·78	310·1	140·1
152 × 152	30	157·5	152·9	6·6	9·4	38·2	1,742	558	6·75	3·82	221·2	73·06	247·1	111·2
	23	152·4	152·4	6·1	6·8	29·8	1,263	403	6·51	3·68	165·7	52·95	184·3	80·87

Table 12.—Universal Beams.

DESIGNATION		Depth of section D	Width of section B	Thickness		Area of section	Second Moment of Area		Radius of gyration		Elastic modulus		Plastic modulus	
Serial size	Mass/unit length			Web t	Flange T		About X–X	About Y–Y	About X–X	About Y–Y	About X–X	About Y–Y	About X–X	About Y–Y
mm	kg/m	mm	mm	mm	mm	cm²	cm⁴	cm⁴	cm	cm	cm³	cm³	cm³	cm³
914 × 419	388	920·5	420·5	21·5	36·6	494·5	718,742	45,407	38·13	9·58	15,616	2,160	17,657	3,339
	343	911·4	418·5	19·4	32·0	437·5	625,282	39,150	37·81	9·46	13,722	1,871	15,474	2,890
914 × 305	289	926·6	307·8	19·6	32·0	368·8	504,594	15,610	36·99	6·51	10,891	1,014	12,583	1,603
	253	918·5	305·5	17·3	27·9	322·8	436,610	13,318	36·78	6·42	9,507	871·9	10,947	1,372
	224	910·3	304·1	15·9	23·9	285·3	375,924	11,223	36·30	6·27	8,259	738·1	9,522	1,162
	201	903·0	303·4	15·2	20·2	256·4	325,529	9,427	35·63	6·06	7,210	621·4	8,362	982·5

(CONTINUATION OF TABLE 12)—UNIVERSAL BEAMS

838 × 292	226	850·9	293·8	16·1	26·8	288·7	339,747	11,353	34·30	6·27	7,986	772·9	9,157	1,211
	194	840·7	292·4	14·7	21·7	247·2	279,450	9,069	33·63	6·06	6,648	620·4	7,648	974·4
	176	834·9	291·6	14·0	18·8	224·1	246,029	7,792	33·13	5·90	5,894	534·4	6,809	841·5
762 × 267	197	769·6	268·0	15·6	25·4	250·8	239,894	8,174	30·93	5·71	6,234	610·0	7,167	958·7
	173	762·0	266·7	14·3	21·6	220·5	205,177	6,846	30·51	5·57	5,385	513·4	6,197	807·3
	147	753·9	265·3	12·9	17·5	188·1	168,966	5,468	29·97	5·39	4,483	412·3	5,174	649·0
686 × 254	170	692·9	255·8	14·5	23·7	216·6	170,147	6,621	28·03	5·53	4,911	517·7	5,624	810·3
	152	687·6	254·5	13·2	21·0	193·8	150,319	5,782	27·85	5·46	4,372	454·5	4,997	710·0
	140	683·5	253·7	12·4	19·0	178·6	136,276	5,179	27·62	5·38	3,988	408·2	4,560	637·8
	125	677·9	253·0	11·7	16·2	159·6	118,003	4,379	27·19	5·24	3,481	346·1	3,996	542·0
610 × 305	238	633·0	311·5	18·6	31·4	303·8	207,571	15,838	26·14	7·22	6,559	1,017	7,456	1,574
	179	617·5	307·0	14·1	23·6	227·9	151,631	11,412	25·79	7·08	4,911	743·3	5,521	1,144
	149	609·6	304·8	11·9	19·7	190·1	124,660	9,300	25·61	6·99	4,090	610·3	4,572	936·8
610 × 229	140	617·0	230·1	13·1	22·1	178·4	111,844	4,512	25·04	5·03	3,626	392·1	4,146	612·5
	125	611·9	229·0	11·9	19·6	159·6	98,579	3,933	24·86	4·96	3,222	343·5	3,677	535·7
	113	607·3	228·2	11·2	17·3	144·5	87,431	3,439	24·60	4·88	2,879	301·4	3,288	470·2
	101	602·2	227·6	10·6	14·8	129·2	75,720	2,912	24·21	4·75	2,515	255·9	2,882	400·0
533 × 210	122	544·6	211·9	12·8	21·3	155·8	76,207	3,393	22·12	4·67	2,799	320·2	3,203	500·6
	109	539·5	210·7	11·6	18·8	138·6	66,739	2,937	21·94	4·60	2,474	278·8	2,824	435·1
	101	536·7	210·1	10·9	17·4	129·3	61,659	2,694	21·84	4·56	2,298	256·5	2,620	400·0
	92	533·1	209·3	10·2	15·6	117·8	55,353	2,392	21·68	4·51	2,076	228·6	2,366	356·2
	82	528·3	208·7	9·6	13·2	104·4	47,491	2,005	21·32	4·38	1,798	192·2	2,056	300·1
457 × 191	98	467·4	192·8	11·4	19·6	125·3	45,717	2,343	19·10	4·33	1,956	243·0	2,232	378·3
	89	463·6	192·0	10·6	17·7	113·9	41,021	2,086	18·98	4·28	1,770	217·4	2,014	337·9
	82	460·2	191·3	9·9	16·0	104·5	37,103	1,871	18·84	4·23	1,612	195·6	1,833	304·0
	74	457·2	190·5	9·1	14·5	95·0	33,388	1,671	18·75	4·19	1,461	175·5	1,657	272·2
	67	453·6	189·9	8·5	12·7	85·4	29,401	1,452	18·55	4·12	1,296	152·9	1,471	237·3
457 × 152	82	465·1	153·5	10·7	18·9	104·5	36,215	1,143	18·62	3·31	1,557	149·0	1,800	235·4
	74	461·3	152·7	9·9	17·0	95·0	32,435	1,012	18·48	3·26	1,406	132·5	1,622	209·1
	67	457·2	151·9	9·1	15·0	85·4	28,577	878	18·29	3·21	1,250	115·5	1,441	182·2
	60*	454·7	152·9	8·0	13·3	75·9	25,464	794	18·31	3·23	1,120	103·9	1,284	162·9
	52*	449·8	152·4	7·6	10·9	66·5	21,345	645	17·92	3·11	949·0	84·6	1,094	133·2

(Continuation of Table 12)—Universal Beams

406 × 178	74	412·8	179·7	9·7	16·0	95·0	27,329	1,545	16·96	4·03	1,324	172·0	1,504	266·9
	67	409·4	178·8	8·8	14·3	85·5	24,329	1,365	16·87	4·00	1,188	152·7	1,346	236·5
	60	406·4	177·8	7·8	12·8	76·0	21,508	1,199	16·82	3·97	1,058	134·8	1,194	208·3
	54	402·6	177·6	7·6	10·9	68·4	18,626	1,017	16·50	3·85	925·3	114·5	1,048	177·5
406 × 140	46	402·3	142·4	6·9	11·2	59·0	15,647	539	16·29	3·02	777·8	75·7	888·4	118·3
	39	397·3	141·8	6·3	8·6	49·4	12,452	411	15·88	2·89	626·9	58·0	720·8	91·08
356 × 171	67	364·0	173·2	9·1	15·7	85·4	19,522	1,362	15·12	3·99	1,073	157·3	1,212	243·0
	57	358·6	172·1	8·0	13·0	72·2	16,077	1,109	14·92	3·92	896·5	128·9	1,009	198·8
	51	355·6	171·5	7·3	11·5	64·6	14,156	968	14·80	3·87	796·2	112·9	894·9	174·1
	45	352·0	171·0	6·9	9·7	57·0	12,091	812	14·57	3·78	686·9	95·0	773·7	146·7
356 × 127	39	352·8	126·0	6·5	10·7	49·4	10,087	357	14·29	2·69	571·8	56·6	653·6	88·68
	33	348·5	125·4	5·9	8·5	41·8	8,200	280	14·00	2·59	470·6	44·7	539·8	70·24
305 × 165	54	310·9	166·8	7·7	13·7	68·4	11,710	1,061	13·09	3·94	753·3	127·3	844·8	195·3
	46	307·1	165·7	6·7	11·8	58·9	9,948	897	13·00	3·90	647·9	108·3	722·7	165·8
	40	303·8	165·1	6·1	10·2	51·5	8,523	763	12·86	3·85	561·2	92·4	624·5	141·5
305 × 127	48	310·4	125·2	8·9	14·0	60·8	9,504	460	12·50	2·75	612·4	73·5	706·1	115·7
	42	306·6	124·3	8·0	12·1	53·2	8,143	388	12·37	2·70	531·2	62·5	610·5	98·24
	37	303·8	123·5	7·2	10·7	47·5	7,162	337	12·28	2·67	471·5	54·6	540·5	85·66
305 × 102	33	312·7	102·4	6·6	10·8	41·8	6,487	193	12·46	2·15	415·0	37·8	479·9	59·85
	28	308·9	101·9	6·1	8·9	36·3	5,421	157	12·22	2·08	351·0	30·8	407·2	48·92
	25	304·8	101·6	5·8	6·8	31·4	4,387	120	11·82	1·96	287·9	23·6	337·8	37·98
254 × 146	43	259·6	147·3	7·3	12·7	55·1	6,558	677	10·91	3·51	505·3	92·0	568·2	141·2
	37	256·0	146·4	6·4	10·9	47·5	5,556	571	10·82	3·47	434·0	78·1	485·3	119·6
	31	251·5	146·1	6·1	8·6	40·0	4,439	449	10·53	3·35	353·1	61·5	395·6	94·52
254 × 102	28	260·4	102·1	6·4	10·0	36·2	4,008	178	10·52	2·22	307·9	34·9	353·4	54.84
	25	257·0	101·9	6·1	8·4	32·2	3,408	148	10·29	2·14	265·2	29·0	305·4	45.82
	22	254·0	101·6	5·8	6·8	28·4	2,867	120	10·04	2·05	225·7	23·6	261·9	37.55
203 × 133	30	206·8	133·8	6·3	9·6	38·0	2,887	384	8·72	3·18	279·3	57·4	313·3	88·05
	25	203·2	133·4	5·8	7·8	32·3	2,356	310	8·54	3·10	231·9	46·4	259·8	71·39

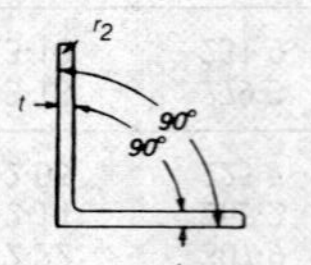

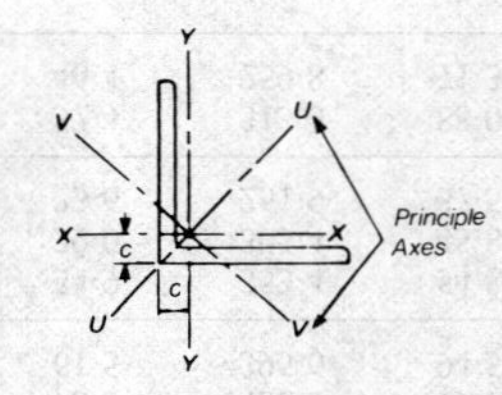

TABLE 13.—EQUAL ANGLES.

Size	Thickness t	Mass/unit length	Area of section	Distance of centre of gravity c	Second Moment of Area			Radius of gyration			Elastic modulus
					About X–X, Y–Y	About U–U	About V–V	About X–X, Y–Y	About U–U	About V–V	About X–X, Y–Y
mm	mm	kg/m	cm²	cm	cm⁴	cm⁴	cm⁴	cm	cm	cm	cm³
25 × 25	3	1·11	1.42	0·72	0·80	1·26	0·33	0·75	0·94	0·48	0·45
25 × 25	4	1·45	1·85	0·76	1·01	1·60	0·43	0·74	0·93	0·48	0·58
25 × 25	5	1·77	2·26	0·80	1·20	1·89	0·52	0·73	0·91	0·48	0·71
30 × 30	3	1·36	1·74	0·84	1·40	2·23	0·58	0·90	1·13	0·58	0·65
30 × 30	4	1·78	2·27	0·88	1·80	2·85	0·75	0·89	1·12	0·58	0·85
30 × 30	5	2·18	2·78	0·92	2·16	3·41	0·92	0·88	1·11	0·57	1·04
40 × 40	4	2·42	3·08	1·12	4·47	7·09	1·85	1·21	1·52	0·78	1·55
40 × 40	5	2·97	3·79	1·16	5·43	8·60	2·26	1·20	1·51	0·77	1·91
40 × 40	6	3·52	4·48	1·20	6·31	9·98	2·65	1·19	1·49	0·77	2·26
45 × 45	4	2·74	3·49	1·23	6·43	10·2	2·67	1·36	1·71	0·87	1·97
45 × 45	5	3·38	4·30	1·28	7·84	12·4	3·25	1·35	1·70	0·87	2·43
45 × 45	6	4·00	5·09	1·32	9·16	14·5	3·82	1·34	1·69	0·87	2·88
50 × 50	5	3·77	4·80	1·40	11·0	17·4	4·54	1·51	1·90	0·97	3·05
50 × 50	6	4·47	5·69	1·45	12·8	20·4	5·33	1·50	1·89	0·97	3·61
50 × 50	8	5·82	7·41	1·52	16·3	25·7	6·87	1·48	1·86	0·96	4·68
60 × 60	5	4·57	5·82	1·64	19·4	30·7	8·02	1·82	2·30	1·17	4·45
60 × 60	6	5·42	6·91	1·69	22·8	36·2	9·43	1·82	2·29	1·17	5·29
60 × 60	8	7·09	9·03	1·77	29·2	46·2	12·1	1·80	2·26	1·16	6·89
60 × 60	10	8·69	11·1	1·85	34·9	55·1	14·8	1·78	2·23	1·16	8·41

(CONTINUATION OF TABLE 13)—EQUAL ANGLES.

70 × 70	6	6·38	8·13	1·93	36·9	58·5	15·2	2·13	2·68	1·37	7·27
70 × 70	8	8·36	10·6	2·01	47·5	75·3	19·7	2·11	2·66	1·36	9·52
70 × 70	10	10·3	13·1	2·09	57·2	90·5	23·9	2·09	2·63	1·35	11·7
80 × 80	6	7·34	9·35	2·17	55·8	88·5	23·1	2·44	3·08	1·57	9·57
80 × 80	8	9·63	12·3	2·26	72·2	115	29·8	2·43	3·06	1·56	12·6
80 × 80	10	11·9	15·1	2·34	87·5	139	36·3	2·41	3·03	1·55	15·4
90 × 90	6	8·30	10·6	2·41	80·3	127	33·3	2·76	3·47	1·78	12·2
90 × 90	8	10·9	13·9	2·50	104	166	43·1	2·74	3·45	1·76	16·1
90 × 90	10	13·4	17·1	2·58	127	201	52·6	2·72	3·42	1·76	19·8
90 × 90	12	15·9	20·3	2·66	148	234	61·7	2·70	3·40	1·75	23·3
100 × 100	8	12·2	15·5	2·74	145	230	59·8	3·06	3·85	1·96	19·9
100 × 100	12	17·8	22·7	2·90	207	328	85·7	3·02	3·80	1·94	29·1
100 × 100	15	21·9	27·9	3·02	249	393	104	2·98	3·75	1·93	35·6
120 × 120	8	14·7	18·7	3·23	255	405	105	3·69	4·65	2·37	29·1
120 × 120	10	18·2	23·2	3·31	313	497	129	3·67	4·63	2·36	36·0
120 × 120	12	21·6	27·5	3·40	368	584	151	3·65	4·60	2·35	42·7
120 × 120	15	26·6	33·9	3·51	445	705	185	3·62	4·56	2·33	52·4
150 × 150	10	23·0	29·3	4·03	624	991	258	4·62	5·82	2·97	56·9
150 × 150	12	27·3	34·8	4·12	737	1,170	303	4·60	5·80	2·95	67·7
150 × 150	15	33·8	43·0	4·25	898	1,430	370	4·57	5·76	2·93	83·5
150 × 150	18	40·1	51·0	4·37	1,050	1,670	435	4·54	5·71	2·92	98·7
200 × 200	16	48·5	61·8	5·52	2,340	3,720	959	6·16	7·76	3·94	162
200 × 200	18	54·2	69·1	5·60	2,600	4,130	1,070	6·13	7·73	3·93	181
200 × 200	20	59·9	76·3	5·68	2,850	4,530	1,170	6·11	7·70	3·92	199
200 × 200	24	71·1	90·6	5·84	3,330	5,280	1,380	6·06	7·64	3·90	235

NOTE 1. Some of the thicknesses given in this table are obtained by raising the rolls. (Practice in this respect is not uniform throughout the industry.) In such cases the legs will be slightly longer and the backs of the toes will be slightly rounded.
NOTE 2. Angles should be ordered by the flange length and thickness.
NOTE 3. Finished sections in which the angle between the legs is not less than 89° and not more than 91° shall be deemed to comply with the requirements of this British Standard.

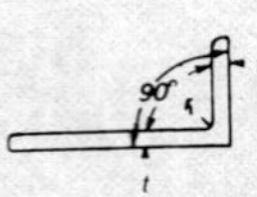

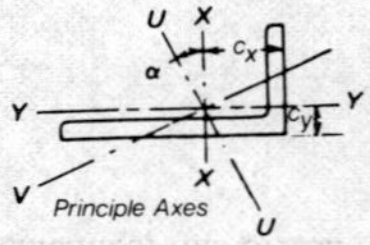

TABLE 14.—UNEQUAL ANGLES.

Size	Thickness t	Mass/unit length	Area of section	Distance of centre of gravity c_x	c_y	Second Moment of Area About X–X	About Y–Y	About U–U	About V–V	Radius of gyration About X–X	About Y–Y	About U–U	About V–V	Angle α
mm	mm	kg/m	cm^2	cm	cm	cm^4	cm^4	cm^4	cm^4	cm	cm	cm	cm	tan α
40 × 25	4	1·93	2·46	1·36	0·62	3·89	1·16	4·35	0·70	1·26	0·69	1·33	0·53	0·380
60 × 30	5	3·37	4·29	2·15	0·68	15·6	2·60	16·5	1·69	1·90	0·78	1·96	0·63	0·256
60 × 30	6	3·99	5·08	2·20	0·72	18·2	3·02	19·2	1·99	1·89	0·77	1·95	0·63	0·252
65 × 50	5	4·35	5·54	1·99	1·25	23·2	11·9	28·8	6·32	2·05	1·47	2·28	1·07	0·577
65 × 50	6	5·16	6·58	2·04	1·29	27·2	14·0	33·8	7·43	2·03	1·46	2·27	1·06	0·575
65 × 50	8	6·75	8·60	2·11	1·37	34·8	17·7	43·0	9·57	2·01	1·44	2·23	1·05	0·569
75 × 50	6	5·65	7·19	2·44	1·21	40·5	14·4	46·6	8·36	2·37	1·42	2·55	1·08	0·435
75 × 50	8	7·39	9·41	2·52	1·29	52·0	18·4	59·6	10·8	2·35	1·40	2·52	1·07	0·430
80 × 60	6	6·37	8·11	2·47	1·48	51·4	24·8	62·8	13·4	2·52	1·75	2·78	1·29	0·547
80 × 60	7	7·36	9·38	2·51	1·52	59·0	28·4	72·0	15·4	2·51	1·74	2·77	1·28	0·546
80 × 60	8	8·34	10·6	2·55	1·56	66·3	31·8	80·8	17·3	2·50	1·73	2·76	1·28	0·544
100 × 65	7	8·77	11·2	3·23	1·51	113	37·6	128	22·0	3·17	1·83	3·39	1·40	0·415
100 × 65	8	9·94	12·7	3·27	1·55	127	42·2	144	24·8	3·16	1·83	3·37	1·40	0·414
100 × 65	10	12·3	15·6	3·36	1·63	154	51·0	175	30·1	3·14	1·81	3·35	1·39	0·410
100 × 75	8	10·6	13·5	3·10	1·87	133	64·1	163	34·6	3·14	2·18	3·47	1·60	0·547
100 × 75	10	13·0	16·6	3·19	1·95	162	77·6	197	42·1	3·12	2·16	3·45	1·59	0·544
100 × 75	12	15·4	19·7	3·27	2·03	189	90·2	230	49·5	3·10	2·14	3·42	1·59	0·540
125 × 75	8	12·2	15·5	4·14	1·68	247	67·6	274	40·9	4·00	2·09	4·20	1·63	0·359
125 × 75	10	15·0	19·1	4·23	1·76	302	82·1	334	50·0	3·97	2·07	4·18	1·62	0·356
125 × 75	12	17·8	22·7	4·31	1·84	354	95·5	391	58·5	3·95	2·05	4·15	1·61	0·353
150 × 75	10	17·0	21·6	5·32	1·61	501	85·8	532	55·3	4·81	1·99	4·96	1·60	0·261
150 × 75	12	20·2	25·7	5·41	1·69	589	99·9	624	64·9	4·79	1·97	4·93	1·59	0·259
150 × 75	15	24·8	31·6	5·53	1·81	713	120	754	78·8	4·75	1·94	4·88	1·58	0·254

(CONTINUATION OF TABLE 14)—UNEQUAL ANGLES

mm	mm	kg/m	cm²	cm	cm	cm⁴	cm⁴	cm⁴	cm⁴	cm	cm	cm	cm	tan α
150 × 90	10	18·2	23·2	5·00	2·04	533	146	591	88·3	4·80	2·51	5·05	1·95	0·360
150 × 90	12	21·6	27·5	5·08	2·12	627	171	694	104	4·77	2·49	5·02	1·94	0·358
150 × 90	15	26·6	33·9	5·21	2·23	761	205	841	126	4·74	2·46	4·98	1·93	0·354
200 × 100	10	23·0	29·2	6·93	2·01	1,220	210	1,290	135	6·46	2·68	6·65	2·15	0·263
200 × 100	12	27·3	34·8	7·03	2·10	1,440	247	1,530	159	6·43	2·67	6·63	2·14	0·262
200 × 100	15	33·7	43·0	7·16	2·22	1,758	299	1,863	194	6·40	2·64	6·58	2·13	0·259
200 × 150	12	32·0	40·8	6·08	3·61	1,652	803	2,024	431	6·36	4·44	7·04	3·25	0·552
200 × 150	15	39·6	50·5	6·21	3·73	2,022	979	2,475	527	6·33	4·40	7·00	3·23	0·550
200 × 150	18	47·1	60·0	6·33	3·85	2,376	1,146	2,902	618	6·29	4·37	6·95	3·21	0·548

NOTE 1. Some of the thicknesses given in this table are obtained by raising the rolls. (Practice in this respect is not uniform throughout the industry.) In such cases the legs will be slightly longer and the backs of the toes will be slightly rounded.
NOTE 2. Angles should be ordered by the flange length and thickness.
NOTE 3. Finished sections in which the angle between the legs is not less than 89° and not more than 91° shall be deemed to comply with the requirements of this British Standard.

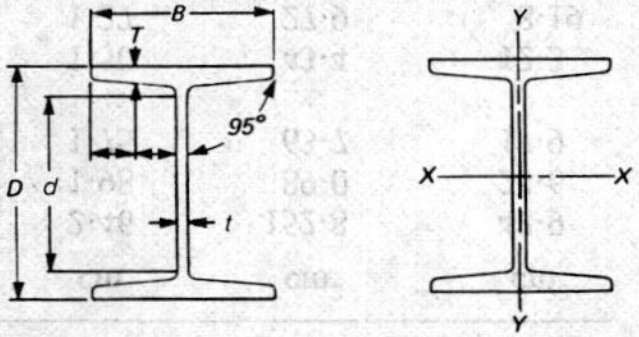

TABLE 15.—JOISTS.

DESIGNATION		Depth of section	Width of section	Thickness		Area of section	Second Moment of Area		Radius of gyration		Elstic modulus		Plastic modulus	
Nominal size	Mass/unit length	D	B	Web t	Flange T		About X–X	About Y–Y	About X–X	About Y–Y	About X–X	About Y–Y	About X–X	About Y–Y
mm	kg/m	mm	mm	mm	mm	cm²	cm⁴	cm⁴	cm	cm	cm³	cm³	cm³	cm³
203 × 102	25·33	203·2	101·6	5·8	10·4	32·26	2,294	162·6	8·43	2·25	225·8	32·02	256·3	51·79
178 × 102	21·54	177·8	101·6	5·3	9·0	27·44	1,519	139·2	7·44	2·25	170·9	27·41	193·0	44·48
152 × 89	17·09	152·4	88·9	4·9	8·3	21·77	881·1	85·98	6·36	1·99	115·6	19·34	131·0	31·29
127 × 76	13·36	127·0	76·2	4·5	7·6	17·02	475·9	50·18	5·29	1·72	74·94	13·17	85·23	21·29
102 × 64	9·65	101·6	63·5	4·1	6·6	12·29	217·6	25·30	4·21	1·43	42·84	7·97	48·98	12·91
76 × 51	6·67	76·2	50·8	3·8	5·6	8·49	82·58	11·11	3·12	1·14	21·67	4·37	25·07	7·14

TABLE 16.—LONG STALK TEES.

DESIGNATION		Thickness			Area of section	Distance of centre of gravity c_x	Second Moment of Area		Radius of gyration		Elastic modulus	
Nominal size	Mass/unit length	T	t_1	t_2			About X–X	About Y–Y	About X–X	About Y–Y	About X–X	About Y–Y
mm	kg/m	mm	mm	mm	cm^2	cm	cm^4	cm^4	cm	cm	cm^3	cm^3
127 × 254	35·60	18·3	9·4	8·9	45·35	6·93	2,811	273·0	7·85	2·46	152·8	42·9
102 × 203	25·07	16·3	8·4	7·9	31·94	5·84	1,289	124·9	6·38	1·98	89·0	24·6
89 × 178	20·46	15·2	7·9	7·4	26·06	5·18	804·9	79·49	5·56	1·75	63·7	17·9
76 × 152	16·41	14·2	7·4	6·9	20·90	4·44	468·2	46·61	4·72	1·50	43·4	12·3
64 × 127	12·66	13·4	6·9	6·4	16·13	3·76	248·5	25·80	3·94	1·27	27·9	8·19
44 × 114	7·44	9·5	5·1	5·1	9·48	3·66	126·1	7·08	3·63	0·86	16·2	3·11
25 × 76	3·65	6·4	4·4	4·4	4·64	2·82	27·89	0·83	2·44	0·43	5·74	0·66

TABLE 17.—SHORT STALK TEES.

DESIGNATION		Thickness t	Area of section	Distance of centre of gravity c_x	Second Moment of Area		Radius of gyration		Elastic modulus	
Nominal size	Mass/unit length				About X–X	About Y–Y	About X–X	About Y–Y	About X–X	About Y–Y
mm	kg/m	mm	cm^2	cm	cm^4	cm^4	cm	cm	cm^3	cm^3
152 × 152	36·09	15·9	45·97	4·29	970·2	452·4	4·57	3·12	88·49	59·32
	29·23	12·7	37·23	4·14	792·5	356·3	4·62	3·10	71·45	46·70
152 × 102	29·78	15·9	37·94	2·59	304·7	454·9	2·84	3·45	40·31	59·65
	24·16	12·7	30·78	2·46	252·7	359·6	2·87	3·53	32·77	47·19
152 × 76	21·63	12·7	27·55	1·73	109·5	360·9	1·98	3·61	18·68	47·36
	16·50	9·5	21·02	1·60	85·74	266·4	2·03	3·56	14·26	34·90
127 × 102	21·63	12·7	27·55	2·67	240·2	209·0	2·95	2·77	32·12	32·94
	16·45	9·5	20·96	2·54	186·1	154·0	2·97	2·72	24·42	24·25
127 × 76	19·09	12·7	24·32	1·88	104·5	209·8	2·08	2·95	18·19	32·94
	14·59	9·5	18·58	1·75	82·00	154·8	2·18	2·90	13·93	24·42
102 × 102	19·04	12·7	24·25	2·95	224·8	107·8	3·05	2·11	31·14	21·30
	14·53	9·5	18·51	2·79	174·4	79·08	3·07	2·06	23·76	15·57
102 × 76	16·50	12·7	21·02	2·08	98·65	108·2	2·16	2·26	17·70	21·30
	12·66	9·5	16·13	1·96	77·42	79·50	2·18	2·21	13·60	15·73
76 × 76	10·73	9·5	13·67	2·21	71·18	33·71	2·29	1·57	13·11	8·85
64 × 64	8·81	9·5	11·22	1·90	39·96	19·56	1·88	1·32	9·01	6·23
	6·08	6·4	7·74	1·78	28·30	12·49	1·90	1·27	6·23	3·93
51 × 51	4·76	6·4	6·06	1·47	14·15	6·66	1·52	1·04	3·93	2·62
38 × 38	3·49	6·4	4·45	1·17	5·83	2·91	1·12	0·79	2·14	1·47

EARTHQUAKE SHOCK RESISTANCE; DESIGN CALCULATION AND TESTING

Earthquakes; Causes and Facts—Forcing Function—Intensity Scales and Measurement—Design Calculation—Siesmic Design Criteria—Modal Spectrum Analysis—Simplified Earthquake Calculations—Computer Software—Liquid Filled Tanks—Siesmic Testing Methods—Earthquake Simulation Tests—Large Structures—Complex Multi-component Assemblies—Scale Model Testing—Testing Techniques and Processes—Finite Element Calculations—Damping Evaluation—Mathematical Models—Practical Details in Siesmic Design.

By L. Yeh, PhD, CEng, MIMechE, AMIMarineE, SEEE

Earthquakes—Earthquakes are responsible for the destruction of life and property on a very large scale. To limit the devastation caused by earthquakes it is vital that engineers should have a knowledge of those measures which can be taken to design structures to withstand earthquake shock.

Electrical and electronic engineers also need to know how to carry out an earthquake qualification test and how to safeguard against functional failure during earthquakes. The purpose of this chapter is to review present methods and degrees of sophistication necessary to do calculations and testing and to introduce methods of shock isolation in order to prevent earthquake disasters. The seismic design is especially important when applied to equipment involved in the safe operation of public utility services, communications and transport, electrical supply distribution industries and telephone systems.

The principle of failure design criteria from over-stressing, or cumulative damage from metal fatigue generally applicable to mechanical engineering design, cannot readily be applied to the failure of computer components, circuit breakers, relays, solenoids and other electrically or pneumatically operated control systems. For this reason seismic qualification by simulated earthquake testing has become an important technique to ensure that electrical and electronic systems, including computers, survive earthquakes.

Causes and Facts.—The cause of most earthquakes is believed to be the result of linear movements in the earth's crust. Modern seismology views the crust of the earth as a series of large blocks (plates), which are continually in motion relative to one another on the semi-liquid magma underneath. At points of interface, interaction and collision between these blocks, faults or cracks in the crust occur. Seismically active zones are found in a belt running in a line from Japan through China and the Himalayan Mountains into Iran and Turkey, to Italy and the Mediterranean, across the Atlantic to Mexico, then to California; this is known as a fault line. The origin of the earthquake shock varies in depth from seven to four hundred miles below the earth's surface. The point on the earth's surface directly above the origin is called the epicenter. The origin of the shock in the earth is called the hypocenter.

In Japan and China the hypocenter is rather deep and the motion is more predominant in the vertical direction whilst, in California, the crust is shallow and earthquakes tend to be more localised and intense with a relatively higher frequency content, the motion being predominantly in the horizontal direction.

It should be pointed out that earthquake motions are random in X, Y and Z directions, and are not rectilinear but are of complex 'ellipsoidal' form in horizontal and vertical planes, Fig. 1, (Refs 1 and 2). The local response is modified by the strata or layered geological structure, which has the effect of amplifying the shock waves in certain frequencies and is equivalent to introducing further reverberatory phases into the time history of ground motion. This phenomenon is similar to reverberations of shock waves observed in reflection during surveying, which makes the intensity and location unpredictable.

It is of particular importance to note that five per cent of all earthquakes occur in regions where there is little or no known seismic activity. In the USA during the last 250 years at least three major earthquakes have followed this pattern, e.g. Boston, Massachusetts in 1955: New Madrid, Missouri in 1812: and Charleston, South Carolina in 1876. The latter affected an area of 2,000,000 square miles. It is the existence of the unexpected and unexplained five per cent which gives greater importance to the design and testing of earthquake resistance equipment.

With the advent of nuclear power and computers, it is clear that seismic qualification of equipment used in nuclear power stations is necessary in order to provide for the safe operation of the electricity supply, especially in the case of emergency shut-down equipment (to prevent radiation hazard). Both CEGB (Central Electricity Generating Board) and SSEB (South Scottish Electricity Board) in Great Britain accept that seismic activity can occur in the most unexpected zones, including Britain, and have made seismic qualification compulsory.

Finally, it should be mentioned that future research directed towards the prediction of earthquakes on a global scale, may be able to make use of satellite observation and warning systems to determine areas of magnetic disturbance. Recently, high frequency radio probes have been developed to determine the thickness of coal seams, using the shock principle; this might be further developed into an earthquake warning system.

Problems involved in protection from earthquake shock.—Figure 2 gives an outline diagram to show the technology involved in solving the problem. The seismic dynamic loading study is fully described to enable seismic scientists and engineers to reproduce it in practice. As a result various interested organisations may be

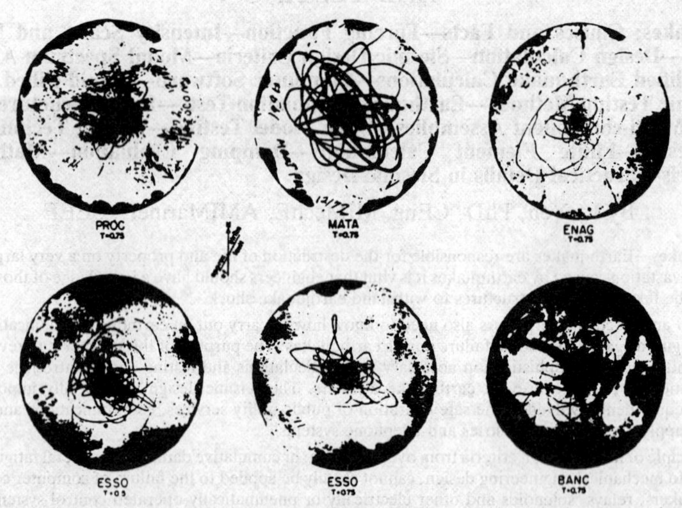

FIG. 1.—Seismic Motion in a Horizontal Plane as Recorded by a Seismoscope. Particle Motions of the Managua Earthquake of December 1972 (Names refer to Stations; T is the Natural Period of the Device).

GLOSSARY OF TERMS

These definitions establish the meaning of words in the context of their use in this chapter.

Artificially Synthesized time History.—[*An*] artificially produced accelerogram from a particular response spectrum.

Broadband Response Spectrum.—A response spectrum that describes the motion indicating that multiple frequency excitation predominates.

Broadening of Response Spectrum.—The technique of increasing the width of floor response spectrum peaks, to account for uncertainties considered to exist in the structure response.

Critical Frequencies.—The natural frequencies and/or those for which malfunction of the specimen may be expected.

Design Floor Response Spectrum.—The response spectrum issued by the Contractor of Utility as part of the seismic analysis and which may form the basis for the Required Response Spectrum (RRS).

Finite Element Model.—An analytical model in which the system to be analysed is represented or idealised as an assemblage of simple components called finite elements. The elements may be considered to be connected together at a finite number of discrete nodes at which the displacements or their derivatives completely define the behaviour of the system. Such elements vary in complexity from simple one-dimensional springs and lumped masses to three-dimensional deformable solids.

Floor Acceleration.—The acceleration of a particular building floor (or equipment mounting) resulting from a given earthquake's motion. The maximum floor acceleration can be obtained from the required response spectrum. The acceleration at high frequencies (in excess of 35 Hz) is sometimes referred to as the ZPA (Zero Period Acceleration) (see Fig. 7).

Fragility.—The susceptibility of equipment to malfunction as the result of structural or operational limitations or both.

Fragility Level.—The highest level of input excitation, expressed as a function of input frequency, that an equipment can withstand and still perform the required functions.

Ground Acceleration.—The acceleration of the ground resulting from a given earthquake's motion. The

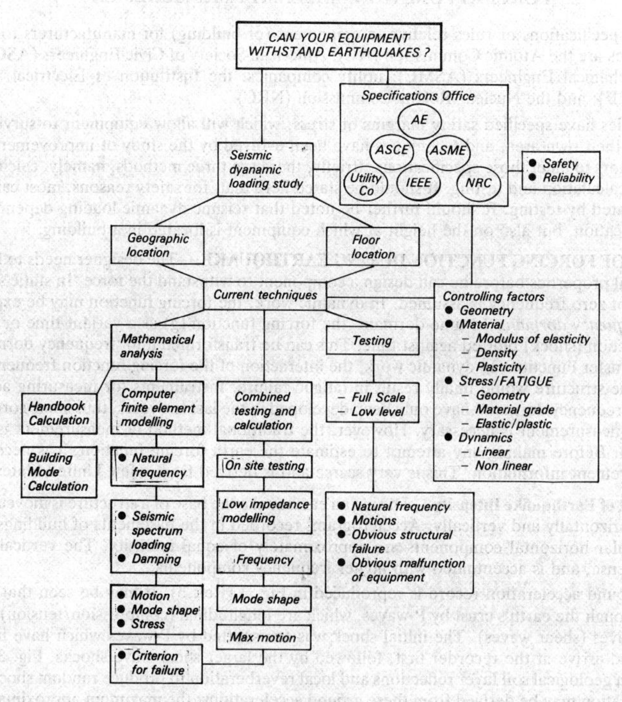

FIG. 2.—An Approach to Solving the Problems Encountered when Designing to Protect a Structure against Earthquake Shock.

---

maximum ground acceleration can be obtained from the ground response spectrum as the acceleration at high frequencies (in excess of 35 Hz).

Narrow Band Response Spectrum.—A response spectrum where a single frequency excitation predominates.

Octave.—The interval between two frequencies which have a frequency ratio of 2.

Pass-Band at 3 dB.—A test to qualify a device or assembly for a particular requirement or application.

Random Motion.—Test motion emanating from a white noise source controlled in defined bandwidths to a particular power spectral density, used in the context of this chapter to produce an acceptable level of TRS (Test Response Spectrum).

Required Response Spectrum (RRS).—The response spectrum issued by the Contractor or Utility as part of his specifications for proof testing, or artificially created to cover future applications.

Response Spectrum.—A plot of the maximum response of an infinite number of single-degree-of-freedom bodies of differing natural frequencies, at a damping value expressed as a percentage of critical damping, when these bodies are rigidly mounted on the surface of interest (that is, on the ground for the ground response spectrum or on the floor for the floor response spectrum), and when that surface is subjected to a given earthquake's motion as modified by any intervening structures.

Sine Beat.—A continuous sinusoid of one frequency, its amplitude modulated by a sinusoid of a lower frequency. Beats are usually considered to be the result of the summation of two sinusoids of slightly different frequencies with the frequencies within the beats as the average of the two and the beat frequency as one half the difference between the two. As used in this chapter the amplitudes of the sinusoids represent acceleration and the modulated frequency represents the frequency of the applied seismic stimulus. The sine beats may be an amplitude-modulated sinusoid with pauses between the beats.

Strong Motion Portion of Time History.—The time interval during which the signal reaches levels larger than or equal to 25% of the maximum value generally used in conjunction with distances to predict events and time histories.

Test Response Spectrum (TRS).—The response spectrum that is constructed using analysis or derived using spectrum analysis equipment based on the actual motion of the shake table.

able to set up specifications or rules relative to equipment (or building) for manufacturers to follow. In the USA such bodies are the Atomic Commission (AC); American Society of Civic Engineers (ASCE); American Society of Mechanical Engineers (ASME); utility companies; the Institution of Electrical and Electronic Engineers (IEEE); and the Nuclear Rector Commission (NRC).

Many countries have specified safety margins of stress, which will allow equipment to survive earthquake damage within their own area, and techniques have been evolved by the study of improvements in materials and control factors to meet those specifications. Briefly, there are three methods, namely, calculation, testing, and combined calculation and testing. It should be stated here that, for safety reasons, most calculations have to be substantiated by testing. It should further be noted that seismic dynamic loading depends, not only on geographical location, but also on the height at which equipment is located in a building.

ESTIMATE OF FORCING FUNCTION DURING EARTHQUAKE.—The designer needs to know the force and the material properties before he can design a component to withstand the force. In static structure work, a steady force of zero frequency is assumed. In dynamic work, the forcing function may be expressed in *time dormant* or *frequency dormant.* In time dormant, the forcing function (g) as a variant time or time history is the forcing function (shock) plotted against time. This can be transformed into 'frequency dormant' by use of the Fourier Transfer Function. In dynamic work, the interaction of the forcing function frequency and natural frequency of the structure would finally result in fatigue failure. Instruments for measuring accurately 'time dormant' and 'frequency dormant' have only been developed in the last ten years, thus some sort of re-thinking of earthquake measurement is necessary. However, the traditional method of measurement is outlined here for information. Before making any attempt to estimate the earth forcing function, it is necessary to study existing measurement information. This is very scarce and is derived from a few United States' recordings.

Measurement of Earthquake Intensity.—During an earthquake the base of a structure is moved by the ground motion both horizontally and vertically. Accelerograms recorded in the basements of buildings show that the two perpendicular horizontal components are approximately of equal intensity. The vertical component is usually less intense, and is accentuated with higher frequency components.

A typical ground acceleration record is reproduced in Fig. 3 (Ref. 3). It may be seen that the shock was transmitted through the earth's crust by P-waves, which are longitudinal (compression/tension) waves and the transverse S-waves (shear waves). The initial shock was transmitted by P-waves which have higher velocity, travel faster and arrive at the recorder first, followed by the larger shear-wave shocks, Fig. 3. These waves then mixed with geological soil layer reflections and local reverberation to produce random shock waves. More detailed information may be derived from these ground accelerations: the maximum approximately 0·33 g and the duration approximately 30 seconds. At El Centro, California 1940 (Fig. 3) the magnitude of shock, according to the Richter scale, was 7·0.

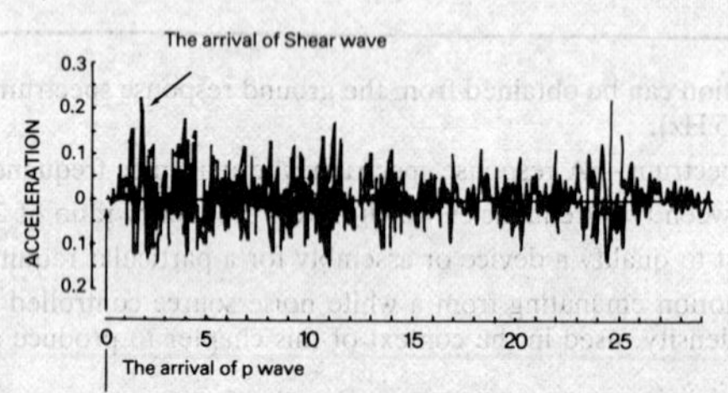

FIG. 3.—Record of Ground Motion in the East-West Horizontal Direction at El Centro, Calif., 18th May 1940. Disturbance was Centred Approximately 30 Miles Away Horizontally, 15 Miles Beneath the Surface of the Ground with Max. Acceleration of 0·33 g. The Vertical Component has 60% the Max. 'g' Level, but with Higher Frequency.

On firm ground, where there was negligible interplay between the ground and the building, the accelerations were similar. With very soft soil, it has been observed that the vibrations of the building influence the recorded motion of the basement floor. This indicates that soil conditions could affect the intensity of an earthquake.

An average acceleration spectrum (Fig. 4) is derived from earthquake records of El Centro, Olympia and Taft, USA. The ordinates of the average spectrum should be multiplied by the factors (see Fig. 4) to obtain the respective ground motions. It is given for a different percentage damping factor.

The average acceleration spectra, S_a, were computed for a single degree of freedom system:

$$S_a = (\ddot{y} + \ddot{z})_{\text{maximum}} \tag{1}$$

Where $\ddot{y}$ = mass acceleration relative to ground
$\ddot{z}$ = ground acceleration

A record of spectrum intensities of recorded ground motion (Ref. 3) taken between 1945 and 1957 in the USA is given in Table 1. It should be noted that for general design and testing guidance, the maximum ground

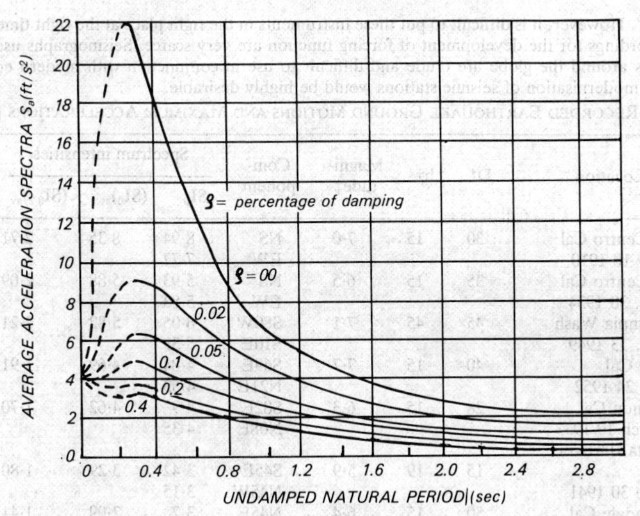

FIG. 4.—Average Acceleration Spectrum Derived from Records of Horizontal Ground Motions. To get maximum, multiply the following factors: 1. El Centro, May 18th 1940 by 2·7; 2. El Centro, Dec. 30th 1934 by 1·9; 3. Olympia, April 13th 1949 by 1·9; 4. Taft, July 21st 1952 by 1·6.

acceleration recorded was 0·33 g with a duration of 30 seconds at El Centro and a Richter scale of 7·0. However, Taft, California, has a record of a maximum Richter reading of 7·7. It should be pointed out that guidance values should be changed according to their locations. For example, the 1977 earthquake at Tangshan, China, registered 7·8 on the Richter scale with a duration of 30 seconds, while the earthquake at Hawaii in 1977 reached 7·2 with a duration of 40 seconds. Recently at Mexico City in 1985, the severe earthquake reached 6·5 on the Richter scale for 3 minutes 17 seconds and this damaged a number of tall buildings, bridges and the whole of the telephone exchange system and killed about 20,000 people.

Richter Scale.—The magnitude scale commonly used was developed by the French Scientist, Charles F. Richter in 1935, and is defined by the maximum amplitude of the record of a standard seismograph (e.g. Wood-Anderson seismometer) at a distance of 100 km from the epicenter. The energy released as a function of magnitude M is roughly approximated (Ref. 5):

$$\text{Log}\, E = 9{\cdot}4 + 2{\cdot}14M - 0{\cdot}054\, M^2 \qquad (2)$$

Where E is the energy released in ergs. The value of M is usually arrived at by averaging the extrapolation, by means of inverse square law, using the distance from the hypocenter. The magnitude of the earthquake varies as the logarithm of the energy released. A Richter scale of 6 indicates a powerful earthquake. The upper limit is suggested as 8·7.

Modified Mercelli Intensity Scale.—In the absence of precise instruments for measuring the severity of the ground motion, it is the usual practice to assess the intensity of ground motion on the basis of human reactions and observed damage. In 1883, Rossi-Forel defined 10 categories as shown in column 1 Table 2. Later the modified G. Mercelli Intensity Scale was introduced and this is most commonly used. The scale has twelve categories, which are specified by Roman numerals; these are defined by the extent of the damage and condensed in column 2 of Table 2. Correlation between intensity and ground accelerations are given in column 3. Column 4 gives the approximate Richter scale measurement although this is difficult to correlate exactly, because the Richter scale attempts to correlate the energy at the source or hypocenter, whereas the Mercelli intensity Scale tries to describe the damage of the earthquake at an unknown distance away; therefore correlation between the two scales cannot be exact. Figure 5 (page I5/8) shows some correlation between the measured ground acceleration and the Mercelli intensity scale as demonstrated by various authors (Data from G. A. Eiby (1965)). The classification A, B, C, D and E, referred to by the U.S. IEEE standard 344 1975 is also included (Ref. 4).

Recent instrumentation for the recording of Ground Motion.—On examining early records of earthquakes, it can be seen that the natural period of the instrument and damping in some way affects the reading. For engineering design purposes, one requires the earthquake spectra, i.e. both frequency and intensity of shock, and therefore, records should be made as near to the epicenter as possible, so that the maximum value is recorded. Special electronic instruments are now available, such as low frequency accelerometers and the FFT (Fast Fourier Transfer Function Analyser) suitable for analysing earthquake shocks, both in frequency and amplitude in 'g'. However, it is difficult to put these instruments in the right place at the right time; as a result, the usable recordings for the development of forcing function are very scarce. Seismographs used in various seismic stations around the globe are crude and difficult to use in conjunction with modern equipment. A programme of modernisation of seismic stations would be highly desirable.

TABLE 1.—RECORDED EARTHQUAKE GROUND MOTIONS AND MAXIMUM ACCELERATIONS (IN USA)

No.	Location	D*	h†	Magnitude‡	Component	Spectrum intensities			Max accel. g⁑
						SI_0	$(SI_0)_{av}$	$(SI_{0\cdot2})_{av}$	
1a	El Centro Cal	30	15	7·0	NS	8·94	8·35	2·71	0·33**
1b	May 18 1910				EW	7·77			0·23
2a	El Centro Cal	35	15	6·5	NS	5·93	5·88	2·09	0·26
2b	Dec. 30 1934				EW	5·83			0·20
3a	Olympia Wash	45	45	7·1	S80W	6·05	5·82	2·21	0·31
3b	Apr. 13 1949				S10E	5·39			0·18
4a	Toft Cal	40	15	7·7	S69E	4·84	4·69	1·91	0·13
4b	July 24 1952				N21E	4·53			0·17
5a	Vernon Cal	28	15	6·3	S82E	4·9	4·62	1·70	0·19
5b	March 10 1933				N08E	4·35			0·13
6a	Santa Barbara Cal	15	19	5·9	S45E	3·42	3·29	1·80	0·24
6b	June 30 1941				N45W	3·15			0·23
7a	Ferndale Cal	50	15	6·4	N45E	3·2	2·09	1·41	0·13
7b	Oct 3 1941				S45E	2·78			0·12
8a	Los Angeles Subway Terminal	33	15	6·3	N61W	3·21	2·04	0·82	0·065
8b	Mar 10 1933				N39E	2·67			0·04
9a	Seattle Wash	65	45	7·1	N8SW	2·81	2·63	1·10	0·076
9b	Apr 13 1949				S02W	2·16			0·058
10a	Hollister Cal	10	15	5·3	S01W	2·11	2·36	1·27	0·23
10b	Mar 9 1949				N89W	2·29			0·11
11a	Helena Mont	15	25	6·0	EW	2·49	1·82	1·02	0·16
11b	Oct 31 1945				NS	1·16			0·14
12a	Ferndale Cal	35	10	5·5	N45E	1·64	1·45	0·64	0·082
12b	Sept 11 1938				S45E	1·27			0·16
13a	Vernca Cal	17	15	5·3	S82E	1·65	1·32	0·69	0·12
13b	Oct 2 1933				N08E	0·09			0·085
14a	Ferndale Cal	75	15	6·6	N45E	1·31	1·10	0·40	0·075
14b	Feb 9 1941				S45E	0·88			0·04
15a	LA Subway Term	22	15	5·3	N39E	1·14	0·90	0·45	0·065
15b	Oct 2 1933				N51W	0·78			0·050
16a	Golden Gate Park	7·8	7	5·3	S80E	1·04	0·84	0·49	0·13
16b	San Francisco March 22 1957				N10E	0·64			0·095
17a	San Francisco State Bldg	9·8	7	5·3	S0E	1·29	1·12	0·58	0·40§
17b	Mar 22 1957				S81W	0·95			0·06
18a	San Francisco Alexander Bldg	10·8	7	5·3	N81E	0·50	0·48	0·28	0·05
18b	Mar 22 1957				N9W	0·45			0·05
19a	Southern Pac Building	11·4	7	5·3	N45E	1·32	1·22	0·43	0·05
19b	San Francisco Mar 22 1957				N45W	1·12			0·046
20a	Oakland Cal	17·2	7	5·3	N26E	0·46	0·38	0·2	0·05
20b	Mar 22 1957				S61E	0·29			0·04

* D = Estimated true epicentral distance in miles.
† h = Estimated depth of centre of fault in miles.
‡ = Magnitude is that reported by the Seismological Laboratory of the California Institute of Technology.
⁑ g = Acceleration of gravity.
** Maximum 'g' recorded ground acceleration 0·33 g at El Centro, California 1910.
§ Locally on building: 0·4 g at San Francisco.
Richter scale $\text{Log } E = 9{\cdot}4 + 2{\cdot}14\,m - 0{\cdot}054\,m^2$ where m = amplitude in mm/1000 at 100 km from epicentre

TABLE 2.—CORRELATION BETWEEN MAGNITUDE, INTENSITY AND ZERO RATED GROUND ACCELERATION

Col. 1 — Ross-Force Intensity Scale 1983

	Ross-Force Intensity Scale 1983
I	The shock felt only by experienced observer under very favourable conditions.
II	Felt by a few people at rest, recorded by several seismographs.
III	Felt by several people at rest; strong enough for the duration or direction to be appreciable.
IV	Felt by several people in motion; disturbance of movable objects. cracking of floors.
V	Felt generally by everyone; disturbances of furniture, ringing of some bells.
VI	General awakening of those asleep, ringing of bells, swinging chandeliers, startled people ran outdoors.
VII	Overthrow of movable objects, fall of plaster, ringing of bells, panic with great damage to buildings.
VIII	Fall of chimneys; cracks in walls of buildings.
IX	Partial or total destruction of some buildings.
X	Great disasters; ruins; disturbance of strata, fissures, rockfalls, landslides etc.

Col. 2 — Modified-Merculli-Intensity Scale (1930) Wood & Newman

I	Modified-Merculli-Intensity Scale (1930) Wood & Newman
I	Detected only by sensitive instruments.
II	Felt by a few persons at rest, especially on upper floors; delicate suspended objects may swing.
III	Felt noticeably indoors, but not always recognized as a quake; standing autos rock slightly, vibration like passing truck.
IV	Felt indoors by many, outdoors by a few; at night some awoken; dishes, windows, doors disturbed; motor cars rock noticeably.
V	Felt by most people; some breakage of dishes, windows and plaster; disturbance of tall objects.
VI	Felt by all; many frightened and run outdoors; falling plaster and chimneys; damage small.
VII	Everyone runs outdoors; damage to buildings varies, depending on quality of construction, noticed by drivers of autos.
VIII	Panel walls thrown out of frames; fall of walls, monuments, chimneys; sand and mud ejected; drivers of autos disturbed.
IX	Buildings shifted off foundations, cracked, thrown out of plumb; ground cracked; underground pipes broken.
X	Most masonry and frame structures destroyed; ground cracked, rails bent, landslides.
XI	Few structures remain standing; bridges destroyed, fissures in ground; pipes broken, landslide, rails bent.
XII	Damage total; waves seen on ground surface; lines of sight and level distorted; objects thrown up into air.

Col. 3 — Ground Acceleration a ($\frac{cm}{sec^2}$, $\frac{a}{g}$): scale 2, 3, 4, 5, 6, 7, 8, 9, 10, 20, 30, 40, 50, 60, 70, 80, 90, 100, 200, 300, 400, 500, 600, 700, 800, 900, 1000, 2000, 3000, 4000, 5000, 6000; 0·005g, 0·01g, 0·05g, 0·1g, 0·5g, 1·0g, 5·0g

Col. 4 — Approx. Richter Scale (No.): 3, 4, 5, 6, 7, 8; CLASS E, CLASS D, CLASS E, CLASS B, CLASS A

Col. 5 — Energy (Erg): 10^{14}, 10^{15}, 10^{16}, 10^{17}, 10^{18}, 10^{19}, 10^{20}, 10^{21}, 10^{22}, 10^{23}, 10^{24}

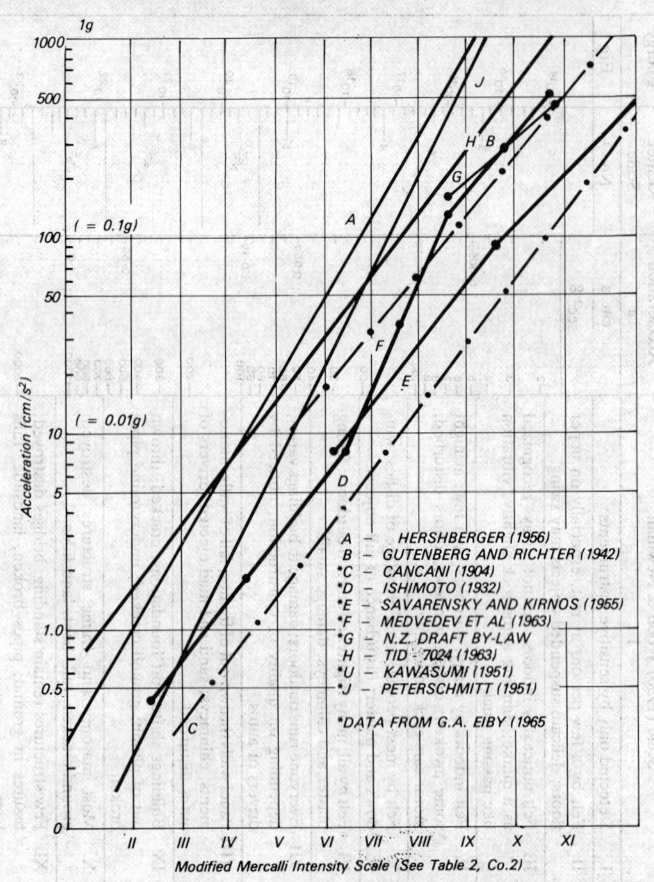

FIG. 5.—Various Ground Acceleration-Intensity Correlation Curves.

DESIGN CALCULATION METHODS AND CRITERIA

HISTORY AND DEVELOPMENT: SEISMIC DESIGN CRITERIA

In the early 1900s empirical rules were developed for buildings and were used as a rough guide in handbooks or building codes. Recently with the advent of computers more sophisticated mathematical analysis has become possible. Improvements in instrumentation for the measurement of vibration and shock, and the development of hydraulic forcing control systems enable earthquake simulation tests to be carried out.

Static Design Technique; Building Design Code.—At the beginning of the twentieth century there were no specific design requirements. In general, buildings in seismically active areas were constructed with lightweight material, such as timber, and with sufficient space so that failure of one structure would not cause the failure of any adjacent structures; the traditional one-storey Japanese architecture fulfils such requirements.

With the emergence of modern industrial society densely populated cities, earthquake-resistant structural designs became a necessity. The adoption of an earthquake-resistant design code was prompted in the USA by the Santa Barbara earthquake of 1925. The Japanese building code was first developed as a consequence of the 1923 Kanto earthquake, which did much damage to Tokyo and Yokohama.

In the early US building code, seismic shear loads 'V' were based on a four factor equation:

$$V = ZKCW \qquad (3)$$

Where Z is a zone coefficient varying from 0·25 to 1·0 depending on the seismic probability of the earthquake. The US divides into four zones:

Zone 0, $Z = 0{\cdot}00$; Zone 1, $Z = 0{\cdot}25$; Zone 2, $Z = 0{\cdot}50$; and Zone 3, $Z = 1{\cdot}00$.

K = coefficient depending on the type of building structure
C = coefficient of natural period of the structure not greater than 0·10
W = dead weight of the structure V = total lateral shear on the base

Typically, the lateral design load coefficient has an upper limit of about 0·1 g, where 'g' = acceleration due to gravity. It is interesting to note that the United States Uniform Building Code is one of the least conservative of the general Seismic Design Codes in use in the world today. Wiggins and Moran developed a comparison, shown in Table 3, which identifies the US as having the least conservative requirements in six out of eight categories evaluated for fourteen countries.

Recent US codes (Ref. 7) further identify nine factors, which should be recognised as important in the development of a base shear coefficient, i.e:

$$V = (ZLI)\ (KCRSFW) \tag{4}$$

The additional factors are:

L = structural life expectation factor
I = structural importance factor dependent upon:
(a) cost: (b) occupancy: (c) function.
K = ductility factor
C = resonance effect
R = mode participation factor
S = soil or site factor
F = foundation design factor
W = dead load plus some percentage of live load.

Comparisons of Worldwide Seismic Design Criteria.—The comparisons shown in Table 3 reflect the differences in the base shear coefficient applied to various heights of buildings (N refers to number of storeys) in various seismic zones and soils.

Assumptions:
1. Two buildings: $N = 1$, $T = 0{\cdot}1$ sec, $N = 15$, $T = 1{\cdot}5$ sec.
2. Two soils: best and worst.
3. Two seismic zones: highest and lowest which has activity other than zero.
4. Ductile frame and important structure with good foundation.

A worldwide Seismic Design Criterion for a base shear coefficient is given in Table 3 (Refs. 8 and 9). It may be seen that these coefficients can vary from country to country. For a one-storey building in a high seismic

TABLE 3.—COMPARISON OF WORLDWIDE SEISMIC DESIGN CRITERIA

Bldg. Type:	N = 1				N = 15			
Soil Type:	BEST		WORST		BEST		WORST	
Seismic Zone:	High	Low	High	Low	High	Low	High	Low
Country								
Argentina	0·075	0·075	0·150	0·150	0·075	0·075	0·150	0·150
Canada	0·098	0·024	0·147	0·037	0·041	0·010	0·061	0·015
Chile	0·080	0·080	0·100	0·100	0·050	0·050	0·120	0·120
France	0·448	0·057	0·728	0·092	0·182	0·023	0·296	0·038
Greece	0·080	0·040	0·160	0·080	0·080	0·040	0·160	0·080
India	0·120	0·030	0·180	0·060	0·036	0·009	0·054	0·018
Italy	0·100	0·050	0·100	0·050	0·100	0·050	0·100	0·050
Japan	0·120	0·096	0·200	0·160	0·186	0·149	0·310	0·248
Mexico	0·052	0·052	0·078	0·078	0·052	0·052	0·078	0·078
Rumania	0·300	0·075	0·300	0·075	0·060	0·015	0·090	0·023
Russia	0·300	0·075	?	?	0·060	0·015	?	?
Turkey	0·036	0·022	0·060	0·036	0·056	0·034	0·095	0·056
United States	0·067	0·017	0·067	0·017	0·029	0·007	0·029	0·007
West Germany	0·050	0·050	0·100	0·050	0·050	0·050	0·100	0·050
Mean	0·138	0·053	0·182	0·076	0·076	0·041	0·126	0·072
Hi	*0·448	*0·096	*0·728	*0·160	*0·186	*0·149	*0·310	*0·248
Lo	†0·036	†0·017	†0·060	†0·017	†0·029	†0·007	†0·029	†0·007
	*France †Turkey	*Japan ‡U.S.	*France ‡Turkey	*Japan ‡U.S.	*Japan ‡U.S.	*Japan †U.S.	*Japan †U.S.	*Japan †U.S.

zone, the coefficient varied from 0·728 in France to 0·067 in USA, a factor of about ten. This variation is dependent upon the type of building, the type of soil and the seismic zone concerned. These large variations in seismic design criteria, indicate that further research is necessary.

Development of Dynamic Design Criteria. (Refs. 11 to 15)—In earlier days only the static design code was used and there was no separate seismic design requirement for equipment contained in buildings. This fact was clearly demonstrated by an event during a Los Angeles earthquake; the building survived the earthquake without structural damage, but the elevator motor had jumped ten feet. The motor was spring-mounted to reduce vibration and had not been secured to the foundation. As a result, separate seismic design of equipment and buildings is considered to be desirable.

Until about 1964, the design of nuclear power plant facilities with respect to seismic requirements was generally parallel to that of conventional civil structures. The seismic design was usually accomplished by applying a static horizontal load at the equipment's centre of gravity without due regard to its location in the plant, or indeed, the location of the plant in the building.

Beginning in 1967, the potential for resonance between the building and the equipment contained therein was considered during the equipment design process. This resulted in the generation of specific floor or 'amplified' response spectra to be used in the design of equipment located at a specific point in the building. Thus the floor level is normally specified for the equipment under consideration.

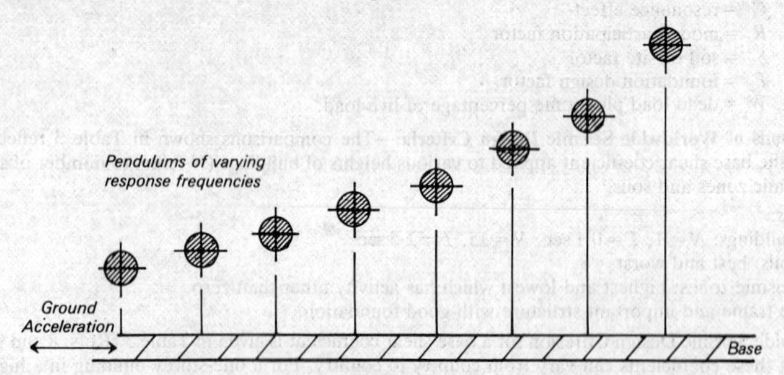

FIG. 6.—Simulated Cantilever Beams of Varying Response Frequencies.

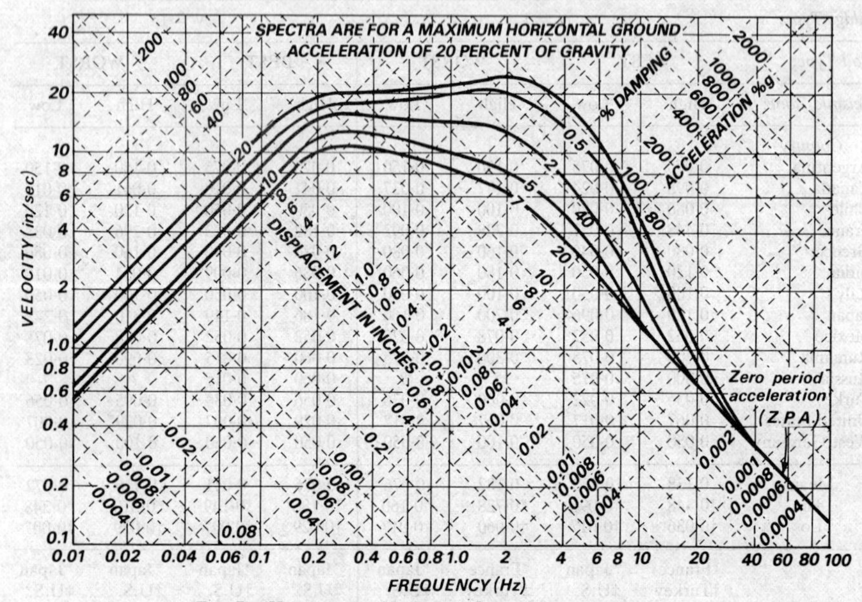

FIG. 7.—Housner-type Horizontal Ground Response Spectra.

The response spectrum can be visualised by using a movable base as shown at the bottom of Fig. 6. Fixed on to it are a series of cantilever pendulums representing the structure with varying fundamental frequencies. If the base is moved during the earthquake, the peak motion of the mass represents maximum response (generally in acceleration) during the earthquake. The maximum acceleration response is plotted against the frequency of each pendulum; a curve can be developed, which represents the response spectrum of the structure, due to earthquakes.

Since 1967, developments have been mainly centred around the production of more conservative response spectra. In this respect, there has been a steady movement away from the Housner type response spectra (Ref. 19) Fig. 7. This was based on averaging individual response spectra towards the more conservative type response spectra (Ref. 7). The latter was based on enveloping individual response spectra. The net result is the reduction of maximum acceleration amplification from 4·3 to 3·5 giving a damping factor of two per cent. Finally the Newmark, Blume and Kapur (NBK, Refs. 19 and 21) type response spectrum was used. The spectrum now used in the USA is the AEC (Atomic Energy Commission) basis for licensing, which is based on one standard deviation from the mean value of the spectra used to develop the standard (Refs. 21 and 22) Fig. 3. This is given in the US Atomic Energy Commission Regulatory Guides (Ref. 23). Figure 8 gives the Design Response Spectra (DRS) in the horizontal direction, and Fig. 9 shows the DRS in the vertical direction.

CATEGORIES FOR DESIGN AND TESTING.—Before proceeding with detailed design calculations, one must realise the importance of the functional failure of the equipment. Nuclear plant equipment typically falls into two basic seismic design categories, based on design function:

CATEGORY I.—Those structures and components necessary to assure:

(1) The integrity of the reactor coolant pressure boundary.

(2) The capability to shut down the reactor and maintain it in a safe shut down condition.

(3) The capability to prevent or mitigate the consequences of accidents, which could result in potential off-site exposures comparable to the guide-line exposures of 10 CFR in part 10 of the Federal Regulations (Refs. 22 and 23).

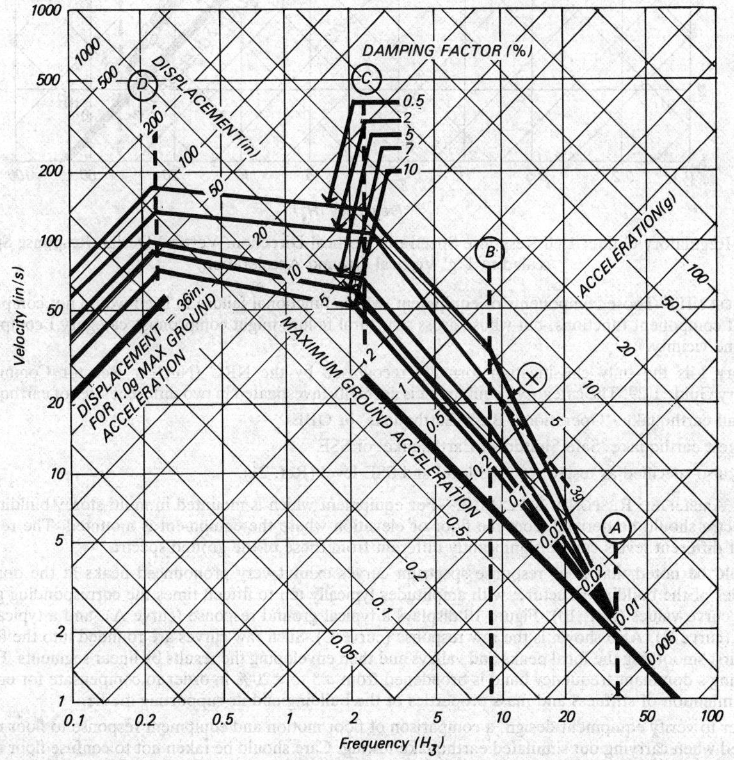

FIG. 8.—Regulatory Guide: 1·60 Response Spectra in Horizontal Direction. Horizontal Design Response Spectra-scaled 1 'g' Horizontal Ground Acceleration; ISO shows Point 'X', as described on Page I5/16 at 10 Hz.

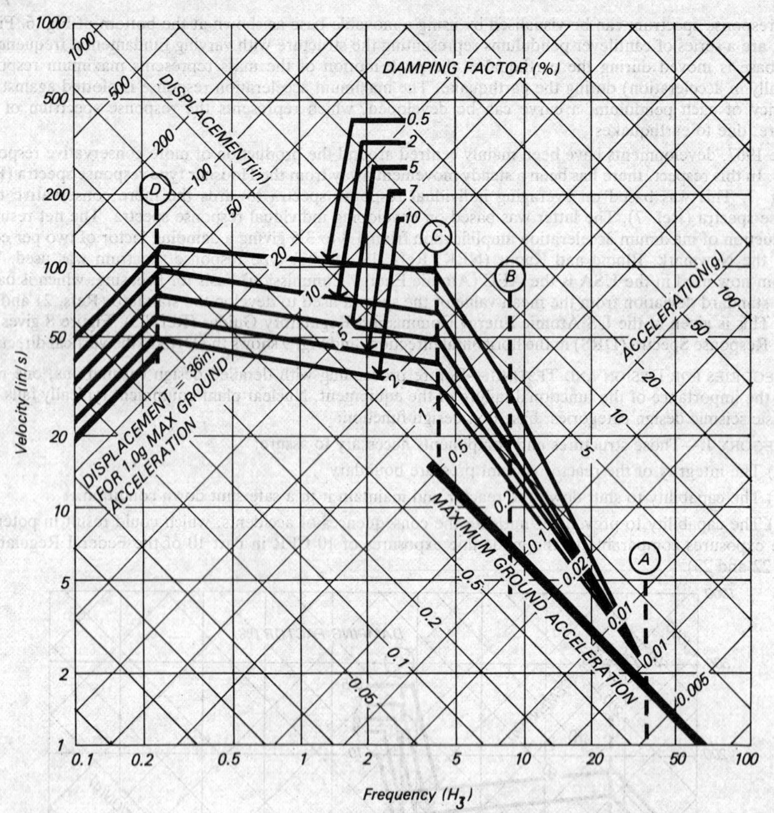

FIG. 9.—Regulatory Guide: 1·60 Response Spectra in Vertical Direction. Vertical Design Response Spectra-scaled to 1 'g' Vertical Ground Acceleration.

CATEGORY II.—Those components or equipment, whose functional failure in itself would not compromise category I component functions, but whose gross structural failure might compromise category I components in the same vicinity.

Category I is the only classification formally recognised by the NRC (Nuclear Reactor Commission) Regulatory Guide 1.29. The category I equipment is normally investigated in two different sizes of earthquakes:

(a) small earthquake, 'Operational Basis Earthquake' or OBE

(b) largest earthquake 'Safe Shutdown Earthquake' or SSE

Tests are also specified as tested to OBE level and SSE level (Ref. 21).

FLOOR AMPLIFIED RESPONSE SPECTRUM.—For equipment which is mounted in multi-storey buildings the input spectra should be derived from the floor or elevation where the equipment is mounted. The response spectra at different levels can be significantly different from those of the ground spectra.

It should be noted that floor response spectrum curves exhibit very pronounced peaks at the dominant frequencies of the building structure, with amplitudes typically ten to fifteen times the corresponding ground response curve values (Ref. 10). Figure 10 displays a typical ground response (curve A), and a typical floor response (curve B). Also shown is the raw response (curve C). Such raw curves are rounded into the form of curve B first smoothing the local peaks and valleys and then enveloping the results by linear segments. Finally, the building's dominant frequency band is broadened from ±5 to ±20% in order to compensate for errors in the determination of stiffness and mass properties of the building and its supporting media.

In order to verify equipment design, a comparison of floor motion and equipment response to floor motion is required when carrying out simulated earthquake testing. Care should be taken not to confuse floor motion acceleration with floor response acceleration. The former is the motion of the floor, the latter represents the motion of a one degree of freedom system attached to the floor.

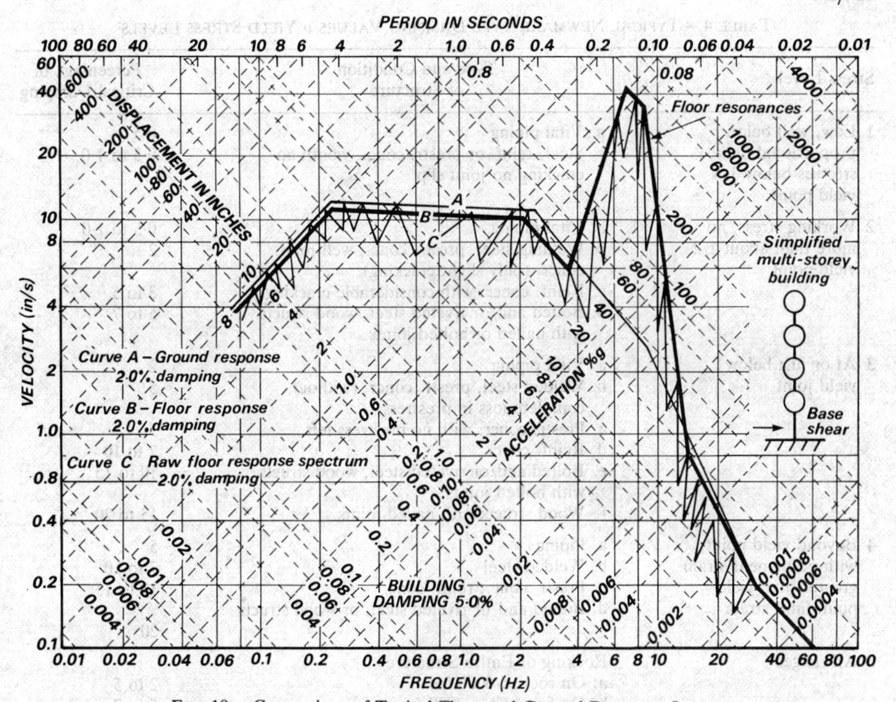

FIG. 10.—Comparison of Typical Floor and Ground Response Spectra.

In the USA, the vertical response generally has a resultant input equal to 0·67 of the horizontal zero period ground acceleration response. The zero period acceleration is defined as the acceleration at very small periods, i.e. above 30 Hz in frequency (Figs. 8, 9 and 10).

DAMPING FACTOR.—Damping, as it is normally defined, is the amount by which the response motion of a structural system is reduced as a result of energy losses from friction, impact and joint slippage, etc. In the context of nuclear plant design, the effect of changes in structural stiffness, geometry, support configuration and modulus of elasticity are also often grouped together under the general heading of damping.

Firstly, material damping or hysteresis loss in material is extremely small, typically 0·1% to 0·2% of the critical damping ratio, i.e. C/C_c, where C is the damping coefficient referred to velocity and C_c is the critical damping.

The second form of damping is structural damping. This form of damping is generally caused by friction and joint slippage plus non-linear or detuning effects, such as changes in boundary conditions and changes in modulus of elasticity. For steel piping this form of equivalent damping typically ranges between 1% to 14% of the critical damping ratio at, or near, the resonance.

Lastly, there is impact damping, which includes impact, or banging, resulting from the closing of gaps in supports and changes in structural geometry.

Recent measurements on structures under seismic test in the GEC Mechanical Engineering Laboratory at Whetstone, Leicester, showed the damping varied with frequency, mode of vibration, location and ageing (time). A figure of 25% was measured at a frequency of 6 Hz for this type of damping, in the cantilever mode. Other modes varied from 2% to 12% with an arithmetical average of 10%. These results were taken from forty records of the structure's vibration recorded during exploratory testing.

Some recommended damping factors may be seen in Table 4 for Newmark type design criteria, related to yield stress, and Table 5 for Regulatory Guide damping values of OBE (Operational Basis Earthquake) and SSE (Safe Shutdown Earthquake).

Finally, it should be mentioned that the accuracy of the finite element calculated results depends upon the art of choosing the damping factor, this being largely reliant on the experience of the designer. A design criterion is shown later that has been expressly developed to overcome the stress/damping dependence effects.

TABLE 4.—TYPICAL NEWMARK TYPE DAMPING VALUES v YIELD STRESS LEVELS

Stress Level	Type and Condition of Structure	Percentage of Critical Damping
1 Low, well below proportional limit, stresses below 1/4 yield point	a. Vital piping	0·5
	b. Steel, reinf. or prestr. conc., wood; no cracking no joint slip	0·5 to 1·0
2 Working stress, no more than about 1/2 yield point	a. Vital piping	0·5 to 1·0
	b. Welding steel, prestr. conc., well reinf. concr. (only slight cracking)	2
	c. Reinf. concr. with considerable cracking.	3 to 5
	d. Bolted and/or riveted steel, wood structs with nailed or bolted joints.	5 to 7
3 At or just below yield joint	a. Vital piping	2
	b. Welded steel, prestr. concr. (without complete loss in prestress)	5
	c. Prestr. concr. with no prestress left.	7
	d. Reinf. concr.	7 to 10
	e. Bolted and/or riveted steel, wood structs, with bolted joints.	10 to 15
	f. Wood structs with nailed joints.	15 to 20
4 Beyond yield point, with permanent strain greater than yield point limit strain	a. Piping	5
	b. Welded steel	7 to 10
	c. Prestr. conc., reinf. conc.	10 to 15
	d. Bolted and/or riveted steel, or wood structs	20
5 All ranges	Rocking of Entire Structure*	
	a. On rock, c 6000 fps	2 to 5
	b. On firm soil, c 2000 fps	5 to 7
	c. On soft soil, c 2000 fps	7 to 10

* Higher damping values for lower values of seismic velocity, c.

TABLE 5.—TYPICAL REGULATORY GUIDE DAMPING VALUES v INTENSITY OF EARTHQUAKES
Percent of Critical Damping

Structure of Component	Operating Basis Earthquake or ½ Safe Shutdown Earthquake[20]	Safe Shutdown Earthquake
	OBE	SSE
Equipment and large diameter piping systems, with diameter greater than 12 in	2	3
Small diameter piping systems, diameter equal to or less than 12 in	1	2
Welded steel structures	2	4
Bolted steel structures	4	7
Unstressed concrete structures	2	5
Reinforced concrete structures	4	7

The Table is derived from the recommendations given in Ref. 20.
For the dynamic analysis of active components as defined in Regulatory Guide 1.48. These values should also be used for SSE. (Ref. 22).
This includes both material and structural damping. If the pipe system consists of only one or two spans with little structural restraint use values for small diameter piping.

RESONANCES.—With small periodic force, when the frequency reaches the natural frequency of the structure, the amplitude increases alarmingly; this is termed resonance effect. In practice resonant conditions seldom occur in response to major seismic motions. This is because the forcing is so large that the resonating equipment, in attempting to respond to the much increased seismic load, tends to change stiffness and thus shifts its dominant frequency due to joint slippage, change in modulus of elasticity, etc. and automatically detunes itself until it falls out of resonance. Unfortunately, the methods of linear-elastic analysis commonly used today are not capable of introducing changes in stiffness, damping and other non-linear effects. Thus the calculated results tend to give higher stress values than occur in reality.

NOTATION

A	Acceleration in general or acceleration required to make the structure yield in rigid-plastic systems.
A_m	Maximum modal accelerations.
$A_n(t)$	Maximum modal response amplitude at 'n' th mass.
A_rZ	Force due to foundation acceleration Z in the appropriate direction for the 'r th' mode linked with mass M_r.
a	Horizontal ground acceleration on the tank calculation.
C	Seismic coefficient of natural period.
c	Velocity damping coefficient.
C_1, C_2	Constants in the multi-degree freedom equation.
C_r	Damping of the 'r th' mode.
$d_{\max}$	Maximum displacement of water level due to the sloshing in the tank.
D	Maximum deformation in non-elastic system.
EBP	Excluding Base Pressure, in the tank calculation.
F_r	Maximum inertia force on 'r th' mass of a lumped mass system.
F	Non-linear spring force $F = (1 + K^2y^2)K_0y$, K_0 = stiffness for small deflection, y = deflection, $K^2 = 3{\cdot}3$ for typical system.
$f(t)$	Arbitrary force input to the single-degree-of-freedom system to time (t_2).
$f(i)$	Frequency of 'ith' mode.
$h(t)$	System inpulse response function.
h_r	Height above ground of the 'r th' mass.
h	Height of water in the tank calculation.
h_0	Height of horizontal impulsive force of a tank partially filled with water or liquid excluding base pressure (EBP).
h_0'	h_0 including base tank pressure (IBP).
h_1	Height of convective force of a tank partially filled with water or liquid.
i-i	Total height of the building.
IBP	Including base pressure in the tank calculation.
k	Stiffness of a single-degree-of-fredom system.
k'	Coefficient intended to extend the ability of structure into the plastic range.
M_c	Overturning moments due to convective force (EBP).
M_c'	Overturning moments due to convective force (IBP).
M_0	Equivalent mass to produce impulsive force in a tank filled with water or liquid, attached rigidly to the tank at a height 'h_0'.
M_1	Equivalent mass to produce convective force in a tank filled with water or liquid, attached rigidly to the tank at a height 'h_1'.
M_i	Overturning moments due to impulsive force in a tank (IBP).
M_i'	Overturning moments due to impulsive force in a tank (EBP).
M_r	The 'r th' mass in a lumped mass system.
m	Equivalent mass of a single-degree-of-freedom system.
N	Total number of SSE stress cycles allowable in design, to be demonstrated or supported by high strain fatigue testing data.
n	Frequency of mode 1 to n in two-dimensional multi-degree system.
$P(t)$	Forcing function.
P_0	Equivalent impulsive force due to water sloshing in a tank at height 'h_0'.
P_1	Equivalent impulsive force due to water sloshing in a tank at height 'h_1'.
$S_{in,y}$	Response spectra 'i th' mode 'n th' position at frequency 'f_i' in the 'y' direction.
$S_{in,x}$	Response spectra 'i th' mode 'n th' position at frequency 'f_i' in the 'x' direction.
$S_{\max}$	Maximum values of integral in Equation (4.1).
$[S]$	Function linked displacement $\{q\}$ to stress $\{\sigma\}$, where $\{\sigma\} = [S]\{q\}$.
t	Time, t_1 and t_2 two different times.
T_i	Natural period of the 1st mode.
$\{q\}$	Displacement matrix of a multiple degree of freedom system.
$\{\dot{q}\}$	Velocity matrix of a multiple degree of freedom system.

Seismic Analysis Methods

METHOD A (One degree of freedom).—If the equipment is structurally simple, so that it can be defined as a one-degree-of-freedom system, the dynamic model may consist of one mass and one equivalent spring. Using the values of the mass and the spring constant, the natural frequency of the equipment can be determined. Table 6 (Ref. 7) gives a list of measured natural frequencies of various types of buildings, which are up to 19 storeys high. Using the damping value for SSE and OBE (Table 5) and the natural frequency of the building. The response spectra may be read off from Figs 8 and 9. Note for a horizontal and vertical acceleration of 1 g, if horizontal ground acceleration is 0·3 g and vertical acceleration is 0·15 g, these factors should be multiplied together, giving the acceleration in 'g' at the appropriate frequency. The inertia force is then obtained by multiplying the distributed mass of the equipment and the acceleration. For example, if the horizontal resonance frequency of a structure is 10 Hz, and damping is 2%, draw a vertical line from 10 Hz to intersect 2% damping at 'X', which gives an acceleration of 3 g. (Fig. 8). As the horizontal ground acceleration is only 0·3 g, the final acceleration is $0{\cdot}3 \times 3 = 0{\cdot}9$ g, which should be used in the calculation of the response of the structure.

NOTATION (*continued*)

$\{\ddot{q}\}$	Acceleration matrix of a multiple degree of freedom system.
q_{di}	$q_{di} = \sqrt{\Sigma_{r=1}^{n} \phi_{r1}^2 \gamma_{rd}^2}$ Root sum squares of different modes, combined response of co-ordinate 'q_i'.
Q	Resistance function = non-linear function.
R	Radius of tank.
W	Total weight of water within the tank.
W_0	Weight corresponding to equivalent impulsive mass 'M_0'.
W_0'	Weight corresponding to equivalent impulsive mass 'M_0'.
W_1	Weight corresponding to equivalent corrective mass 'M_1'.
u_0	Ground acceleration values obtained in Response Spectrum DBE at different periods.
$U_{n\max}^0$	Relative displacement response spectrum at natural frequency 'f' (see Fig. 9).
$U_{\max}$	Maximum displacement of a building, single degree system.
U_i	Combined vertical and horizontal earthquake acceleration $=\sqrt{\ddot{y}_{im}{}^2 + \ddot{x}_{im}{}^2}$ at 'i th' mode.
V	Total dynamic base shear.
W	Total weight of a building or total weight of water in a tank.
x_i	'i th' mode modal acceleration in 'x' direction due to all mass position.
x_{ij}	'x' acceleration 'i th' mode 'j th' position.
y_i	'i th' modal acceleration in y direction due to all mass positions.
y_{ij}	'y' acceleration 'i th' mode 'j th' position.
y	Motion of single degree system mass relative to its base.
y_d	Displacement response taken from the spectrum curve.
$\dot{y}$	dy/dt. Velocity of 'y'.
$\ddot{y}$	d^2y/dt^2. Acceleration of 'y'.
y_y	Deformation at yielding point.
Z	Motion of the base relative to a fixed co-ordinate system.
$\dot{Z}$	Velocity of the base.
$\ddot{Z}$	Acceleration of the base.
α_1, α_2	Roots of equations with $[\phi]$ in the modal matrix.
ζ	% damping.
ζ_0	% damping in linear range.
ζ'	% damping in non-linear range.
$[\phi]$	Modal matrix, $[\phi_r]$ the 'r th' modes.
ϕ_{ij}	Modal deflection 'i th' mode, 'f th' position.
ϕ_r	Co-ordinate of the characteristic mode shape at mass 'r'.
$\{\sigma\}$	Modal stress linked with displacement $\{q\}$ by $[S]$; $\{\sigma\} = [S]\{q\}$.
Γ_{ja}	Modal participation factor.
Γ_n	Modal participation factor of 'n th' mode.
μ	Ductility factor D/y_y.
ν	Local ductility factor Y/y_y.
γ	Normal uncoupled co-ordinate, link with the original co-ordinate 'g' by the transformation. $\{q\} = [\phi]\{\gamma\}$.
$\dot{\gamma}\,\ddot{\gamma}$	Derivatives of γ.
$r\,\dot{r}\,\ddot{r}$	Co-ordinates and derivatives of the 'r th' mode.
ω	Angular frequency, ω_0, at a particular angular frequency.

TABLE 6.—TYPICAL MEASURED NATURAL PERIOD OF TALL BUILDINGS

No.	Height		Length, ft	Width, ft	Period, sec*	
	Stories	Feet			*l*	*w*
1	2	33	209	42	0·13	0·14
2	3	40	120	108	0·27	0·27
3	4	35	100	100	0·30	0·31
4	4	74	113	100	0·37	0·43
5	4	62	150	150	0·43	0·45
6	6	85	76	40	0·45	0·50
7	7	71	106	60	0·32	0·34
8	7	108	75	58	0·79	0·90
9	7	96	74	50	0·85	0·95
10	7	100	100	53	0·62	0·82
11	7	110	329	213	0·80	0·60
12	8	99	137	90	0·7	0·74
13	8	102	70	61	0·50	0·61
14	8	135	100	50	0·93	1·16
15	8	100	102	60	0·72	0·79
16	8	90	100	50	0·41	0·50
17	8	110	160	95	0·70	0·58
18	9	130	355	322	1·80	2·08
19	9	112	179	135	0·70	0·74
20	9	130	100	58	0·74	0·86
21	10	136	100	54	0·87	1.00
22	10	124	148	54	1·00	1.00
23	10	130	100	60	0·77	0·81
24	10	141	217	51	0·49	1·20
25	10	126	57	46	1·00	1·00
26	11	160	105	52	1·18	1·67
27	11	150	150	150	0·78	0·96
28	11	140	60	35	0·88	1·16
29	11	150	318	108	1·23	1·85
30	11	165	155	64	0·95	1·44
31	12	150	95	70	0·81	0·98
32	12	175	157	41	1·15	1·20
33	12	145	90	81	0·50	0·93
34	12	150	150	100	0·75	0·94
35	12	150	156	86	1·06	1·25
36	12	150	150	53	1·20	1·20
37	12	150	160	138	0·85	0·92
38	12	150	124	55	0·84	1·24
39	12	163	65	65	1·05	1·25
40	13	175	125	54	1·20	1·31
41	13	150	99	60	0·88	0·98
42	13	156	100	60	1·06	1·22
43	14	175	92	55	1·30	1·53
44	15	196	68	60	1·25	1·33
45	15	178	85	45	1·10	1·45
46	19	266	75	75	1·95	2·20

* The period *l* is for vibration in a direction parallel with the length dimension; period *w* is for direction parallel with the width dimension.

METHOD B. (Multi-degrees-of-freedom).—If the equipment is structurally complex, such that it cannot be modelled as a single-degree-of-freedom system, the following method of analysis should be used.—

1. Model the equipment using a multi-degree-of-freedom representation. The lumped mass technique can be used, also using the transient vibration or the modal participation factor methods (Ref. 7).
2. Determine the natural frequencies and mode shapes for the equipment, by using the matrix equations.

3. Determine the damping factors for the equipment by experiments.
4. For each significant mode, determine the motion spectra from the response spectra as a function of frequency and damping value.
5. Determine the resultant design motion of a point by equivalent mass technique.
6. Determine the resultant motion by combining the motion of the individual modes on a square root sum of squares basis. Both horizontal motion as well as the simultaneous vertical mode should be considered.
7. If motions are used to determine resultant deflection, moments, shears, stresses, etc., these quantities should be determined on a per mode basis and then combined on the basis of a square root of sum of squares.

For most complex equipment, such as electrical cubicles, seismic testing is recommended. Finite element methods of calculation may also be used for qualification, but this is very costly if no in-house computer and software are available.

Seismic Design Conditions.—Before starting to design it is necessary to define two conditions of earthquake—the small earthquake, the Operational Basis Earthquake (OBE), and the large earthquake, the Safe Shutdown Earthquake (SSE), and the number of OBE and SSE stress cycles anticipated for the design.

(a) OPERATIONAL BASIS EARTHQUAKE CONDITION (OBE).—The load combinations shall include gravity loads, operating loads, applicable operating temperatures and pressures combined with the simultaneously applied horizontal and vertical OBE inertia force or stresses.

The horizontal and vertical inertia force shall be obtained by using Response Spectra (see Figs 8 and 9) and OBE damping (see Table 5) (U.S. Regulatory Guide) (Refs. 22, 23).

Resultant stresses in the structure shall not exceed the allowable working stress limits accepted as good practice, as set forth in the appropriate design standards, AISC Manual of Steel Construction; ASME Vessel Code; British Standards; or other applicable codes or specifications. As a rough guide, 50% to 90% of the yielding stress is acceptable, depending on the method of calculation and the design code used by the calculation; the percentage of damping used; and the material properties and non-linearity of the structure (Refs. 24 to 37).

The resulting deflections shall not impair normal operation of the equipment.

The total number of maximum stress cycles to be considered in OBE design shall be determined and supported by high strain fatigue testing data.

(b) SAFE SHUTDOWN EARTHQUAKE CONDITIONS (SSE).—The load combination shall include the resultant stresses, deformations, etc., from gravity loads, operating loads, and applicable temperatures and pressures combined with the simultaneously applied horizontal and vertical maximum earthquake inertia stresses, deformations, etc. The horizontal and vertical inertia effects shall be obtained by using the SSE damping, (Table 5) and Response Spectra (Figs 8 and 9).

Allowable stresses shall be within code provisions. The resulting deflections shall not prevent operation of the equipment during the seismic disturbance, if necessary, or distort the equipment so as to prevent its subsequent required operation to maintain the plant in a safe condition.

The total number of SSE stress cycles to be considered in design as applicable is 'N', which should be demonstrated or supported by test data, as these are important with respect to high strain fatigue properties of the materials.

Modal Analysis Method (using transient vibration analysis)

(a) SINGLE DIRECTION MULTI-DEGREE-OF-FREEDOM SYSTEM

Idealize the system into a number of lumped masses and springs, then apply the modal analysis technique developed for seismic calculation, which uses: *the modal participation factor* and *the response spectrum.* The modal participation factor is a function of the dynamic property of the structure in terms of mode shape (or eigen vector) and the directionality of the earthquake at various nodal points or mass centre of gravity. The forces applied at each node are, in fact, the inertial loads i.e. the nodal mass multiplied by accelerations at a particular frequency from the *response spectrum* for Design Basis Earthquake (DBE), the response spectrum is derived from the location of the earthquake involved and specified by the customer, (e.g. CEGB).

It should be noted that modal analysis is limited to a simple forcing function and direction, and the assumption of equal damping of all mass points. This can be a severe limitation to mixed material or soil structure interaction, but works well with conventional mechanical structures.

The modal participation factor can be defined in general terms:

$$\Gamma_j = \sum_{i=1}^{n} \phi_{ij} \bar{f}_i \tag{5}$$

where Γ_j = participation factor in the jth mode.
$\bar{f}_i$ = the generalized force acting on the system.
ϕ_{ij} = the ith relative displacement in the jth mode.

In seismic analysis the forces on the system are a function of the product of inertial mass and the acceleration. It is convenient to define the modal participation factor in terms of mass and relative displacement:

$$\Gamma_j = \frac{\Sigma_{i=1}^{n} M_i \phi'_{ij}}{\Sigma_{i=1}^{n} M_i \phi_{ij}^2} \tag{6}$$

where M_i = the ith mass.

ϕ'_{ij} = the ith relative displacement in the jth mode excited by the earthquake in one direction only from DBE.

ϕ_{ij} = the ith relative displacement in the jth mode, is the mode shape produced by eigen vector.

The modal participation factor may be considered as a measure of the extent to which any given mode participates in determining the total load on the structure.

(b) Two-Dimensional Multi-Degree System (Ref. 17).

Figure 11 shows a three mass system, simply supported at each end, and capable of moving in 'x' and 'y' directions. The modal deflection of m_1 for the first mode is ϕ_{11y} in Y direction and is ϕ_{11x} in the X direction. Similarly, for the 2nd mode, is ϕ_{21y} and ϕ_{21x} and for the 3rd mode is ϕ_{31y} and ϕ_{31x}, where the modal participation factor for each direction is:

$$\Gamma_{ja} = \frac{\Sigma_{i=1}^{n} M_i \phi_{ij}^1}{\Sigma_{i=1}^{n} M_i \phi_{ij}^2} \tag{7}$$

where ϕ'_{ij} = modal deflection ith mode, jth position.

Y_{ij} = modal deflection due to earthquake loading in 'y' direction.

Inertia acceleration at positions 'j' in 'y' direction is:

$$\ddot{y}_{ij} = S_{ijy} \Gamma_{ja} \phi_{ijy} \tag{8}$$

where S_{ijy} = response spectra 'ith' mode at frequency (f_i) in vertical or 'y' direction (see Fig. 9); and S_{ijy} is derived from response spectrum due to earthquake at the frequency of the mode.

In like manner; inertial load or acceleration at positions 'j' in 'x' direction is:

$$\ddot{X}_{ij} = S_{ijx} \Gamma_{ji} \phi_{ijx} \tag{9}$$

where S_{ijx} = response spectra 'ith' mode at frequency (f_i) in horizontal or 'x' direction (Fig. 8).

Determine 'ith' modal acceleration of all mass points due to a vertical earthquake (in 'y' direction)

$$\ddot{y}_{im} = \sqrt{\ddot{y}_{i1}^2 + \ddot{y}_{i2}^2 + \ddot{y}_{i3}^2 + \cdots \ddot{y}_{ij}^2} \tag{10}$$

Similarly due to a horizontal earthquake

$$\ddot{x}_{im} = \sqrt{\ddot{x}_{i1}^2 + \ddot{x}_{i2}^2 + \ddot{x}_{i3}^2 + \cdots x_{ij}^2} \tag{11}$$

Finally, the accelerations of combined vertical and horizontal earthquakes in the 'ith' mode, are:

$$\ddot{U}_i = \sqrt{\ddot{y}_{im}^2 + \ddot{x}_{im}^2} \tag{12}$$

So far, only linear elastic systems have been discussed. Other systems, such as linear system with uniform and non-uniform stiffness, non-linear systems, bi-linear elastic systems, elasto-plastic systems and rigid-plastic systems, etc. are subjects of different mathematical treatment.

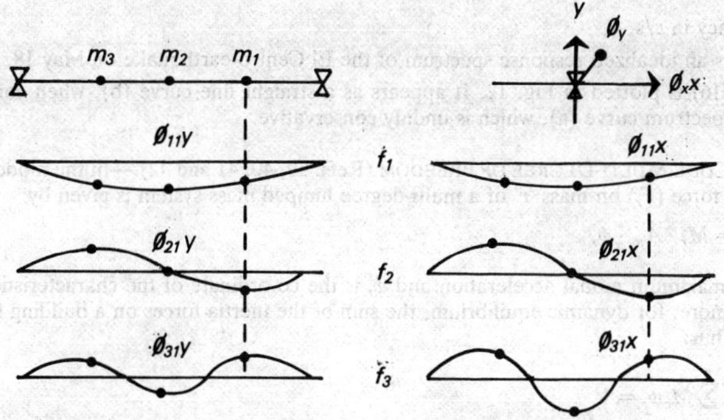

Fig. 11.—Two-dimensional, Multi-degree of Freedom System with Stiffness Different in Two Directions.

Examples of Simplified Earthquake Calculations.—An attempt to present some examples of simple and practical design calculations derived from a number of references (Refs. 38, 43 and 44). These methods demonstrate that large discrepancies do exist between theory and empirical rules.

US BUILDING CODE DESIGN (REF. 38) (SINGLE DEGREE OF FREEDOM). US Building Code (1964). (Essentially; SEADC Structural Engineering Association of California) recommend the following two formulae:

$$V = ZK'CW \tag{13}$$

and $$C = \frac{0{\cdot}05}{T^{1/3}}$$

where C = coefficient of natural period
V = total dynamic base shear
W = total weight of building = mg
T = natural period of the first mode (see Table 6)
K' = coefficient varying between 0·67 and 1·50
Z = the seismic coefficient depending on US seismic zones
$\ddot{y}$ = maximum acceleration in fraction of 'g'
$M\ddot{y}_m$ = maximum horizontal inertia force = Kcw.

The lateral design load (base shear) coefficient typically has an upper limit of 0·1 g (See Table 3). The value could vary from 0·067 to 0·728, a factor of ten.

Assume a single degree-of-freedom system:

$$M\ddot{y} = K'cw \text{ (with } Z = 1) = K'cgm \tag{14}$$

Base Shear $V = K'cw$ (with $Z = 1$).

The coefficient K' is intended to reflect the ability of the structure to extend into the plastic range.

$K' = 0{\cdot}67$ for moment resisting frames and relative ductile materials.
$K' = 1{\cdot}33$ for concrete shear walls.
$K' = 1$ for elastic spring mass system.

The spring displacement for single degree free system related to seismic coefficient is as follows: the base shear V is equal to maximum displacement U_{max} multiplied by spring stiffness, or:

$$V = KU_{max} = Cgm$$

Therefore:

$$U_{max} = Cg\,.\,\frac{m}{K} = \frac{Cg}{\omega^2} \text{ where } \omega = \sqrt{\frac{K}{m}} = \text{system frequency} \tag{15}$$

Substitute: $\omega^2 = (2\pi f)^2 = 4\pi^2\left(\frac{1}{T}\right)^2$

where $z = 1$, $1/f = T$ and $2\pi f = \omega$, and $C = \frac{0{\cdot}05}{T^{1/3}}$

$$U_{max} = \frac{0{\cdot}05}{T^{1/3}} \times \frac{gT^2}{4\pi^2} = \left(\frac{0{\cdot}05g}{4\pi^2}\right)\frac{1}{f^{5/3}} = \frac{0{\cdot}49}{f^{5/3}} \tag{16}$$

where f = frequency in c/s.

Figure 12 shows an idealized response spectrum of the El Centro earthquake on May 18, 1940.

The equation (16) is plotted in Fig. 12. It appears as a straight line curve (b), when compared with the idealized elastic spectrum curve (a), which is unduly conservative.

US BUILDING CODE MULTI-DEGREE OF FREEDOM (Refs. 39, 40, 41 and 42).—In the mode considered, the maximum inertia force (F_r) on mass 'r' of a multi-degree lumped mass system is given by:

$$F_r = M_r \cdot \ddot{A}_m \cdot \phi_r \tag{17}$$

where $\ddot{A}_m$ is the maximum modal acceleration and ϕ_r is the co-ordinate of the characteristic mode shape at mass 'r'. Furthermore, for dynamic equilibrium, the sum of the inertia forces on a building must be equal to the base shear. Thus:

$$\ddot{A}_m \sum^{r} M_r\phi_r = V \tag{18}$$

Eliminating $\ddot{A}_m$ from equations (17) and (18) we have

$$F_r = \frac{M_r\phi_r}{\sum^{r} M_r\phi_r} \cdot V \tag{19}$$

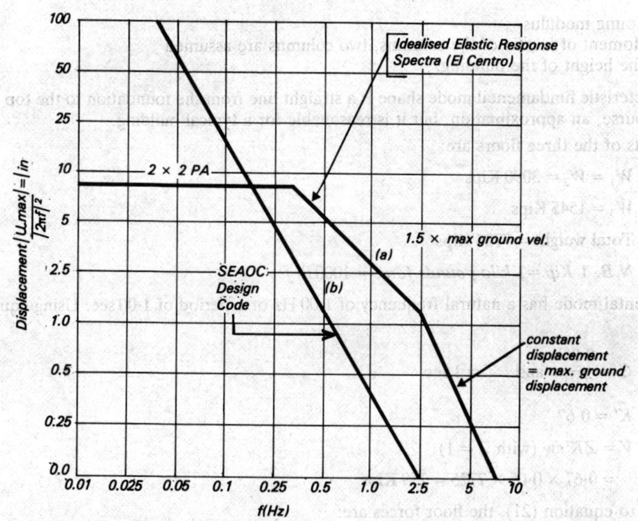

FIG. 12.—Idealised Response Spectra for El Centro Earthquake, May 18th 1940, N–S Component and SEAOC Design Recommendation.

The SEAOC recommendation implies that $\phi_r = h_r/H$, where h_r is the height above ground of the rth mass and H is the total height of the structure. By this assumption

$$F_r = \frac{M_r(h_r/H)}{\sum_r M_r(h_r/H)} \cdot V \tag{20}$$

$$F_r = \frac{W_r h_r}{\sum_r W_r h_r} \cdot V \tag{21}$$

which is the SEAOC recommendation for the distribution of lateral force.

The resulting set of forces of dynamic equilibrium is shown in Fig. 13.

To illustrate the application of the SEAOC code, we consider a three-storey building frame Fig. 13a from which

$$K = \frac{12E\,(2I)}{h^3}$$

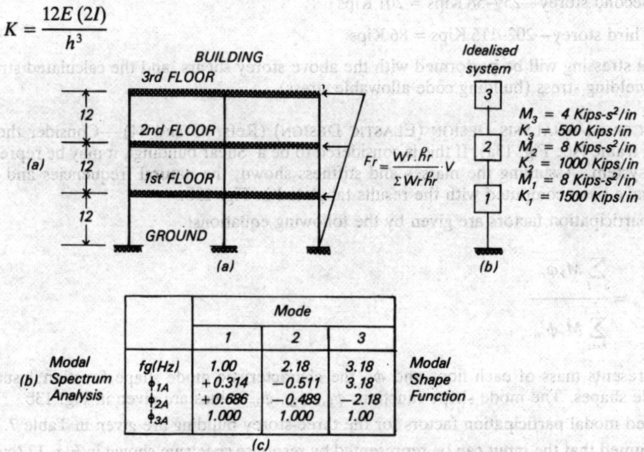

	Mode 1	Mode 2	Mode 3
fg(Hz)	1.00	2.18	3.18
ϕ_{1A}	+0.314	−0.511	3.18
ϕ_{2A}	+0.686	−0.489	−2.18
ϕ_{3A}	1.000	1.000	1.00

Note: Force in Kips = 1,000 lbf K_1' = 1500 Kips/in ≡ 1,500,000 lbf/in
M_1 = 8 Kips–s²/in = 8,000 lb – s²/in

FIG. 13.—Three-storey Shear Building.

where E = Young modulus
I = Moment of inertia of the columns, two columns are assumed
h = The height of the building.

The characteristic fundamental mode shape is a straight line from the foundation to the top of the building. This is, of course, an approximation, but it is reasonable for a typical building.

The weights of the three floors are:

$W_1 = W_2 = 3090$ Kips

$W_3 = 1545$ Kips

Total weight = 7725 Kips

N.B. 1 *Kip* =1 *kilo pounds force* = 1000 *lb f*

The fundamental mode has a natural frequency of 1·00 Hz or a period of 1·00 sec. Using equations (16) and (13):

$$C = \frac{0{\cdot}05}{T^{1/3}} \quad \text{and} \quad T = 1 \text{ sec}$$

$$K' = 0{\cdot}67$$

$$V = ZK'cw \text{ (with } Z = 1)$$

$$= 0{\cdot}67 \times 0{\cdot}05 \times 7725 = 259 \text{ Kips}$$

According to equation (21), the floor forces are:

$$F_r = \frac{Wr\,hr}{\sum\limits_{r} Wr\,hr} \cdot V$$

$$F_1 = \frac{3090 \times 12}{3090 \times (12 + 3090) \times (24 + 1545) \times 36} \times 259 = 58 \text{ Kips}$$

$$F_2 = \frac{3090 \times 24}{166{,}700} \times 259 = 115 \text{ Kips}$$

$$F_3 = \frac{1545 \times 36}{166{,}700} \times 259 = 86 \text{ Kips.}$$

Thus, the design values of the storey shears during earthquake are:

First storey—259 Kips

Second storey—259–58 Kips = 201 Kips

Third storey—202–115 Kips = 86 Kips.

A static local stressing will be performed with the above storey shears, and the calculated stress should be less than half yielding stress (building code allowable stress).

MODAL SPECTRUM ANALYSIS DESIGN (ELASTIC DESIGN) (Refs. 43 and 44).—Consider the same three-storey building frame (see Fig. 13a). If this is considered to be a 'Shear building', it may be represented by the close-coupled system. Assuming the masses and stiffness shown, the natural frequencies and characteristic mode shapes have been computed with the results tabulated in Fig. 13b.

The modal participation factors are given by the following equations:

$$\Gamma_n = \frac{\sum\limits_{r=i}^{j} M_r \phi_{rn}}{\sum\limits_{r=i}^{j} M_r \phi_{rn}^2} \tag{22}$$

Where M_r represents mass of each floor and ϕ_{rn} the characteristic mode shape function, usually assuming cantilever mode shapes. The mode shape function, ϕ_{1n}, ϕ_{2n}, ϕ_{3n} values are given in Fig. 13b.

The calculated modal participation factors for the three-storey building are given in Table 7.

It will be assumed that the input can be represented by response spectrum shown in Fig. 12 (curve a), which is an empirical representation of a particular earthquake and assumes a 3% damping in the system. The response to one-degree systems in terms of relative displacement U^0n max are read directly from Fig. 12 and depend only on natural frequency. The modal responses' amplitude $An(t)$ are simply:

$$An(t) = \Gamma n U n^0(t) \quad (23)$$

This is given in Table 8.

Having the maximum modal amplitudes $An(t)$ the displacement may be computed by the following equation in which the modal displacement at mass rn is:

$$\Delta_{rn} = Urn(t) = \Gamma_n Un^0(t)\,\phi_{rn} = An(t)\,\phi_{rn} \quad (24)$$

Of primary interest in earthquake design are the maximum values of the storey shears. To obtain these, we first multiply the max in modal amplitudes $An(t)$ by ϕ_{rn}, which is the displacement of that floor, Δ_{rn}, then multiply by the spring constant to give the storey shear. Negative signs are ignored to get a maximum positive value in modal function only.

TABLE 7.—MODAL PARTICIPATION FACTORS FOR A THREE-STOREY BUILDING

Mass	Mr	First Mode		Second Mode		Third Mode	
		$Mr\phi r1$	$Mr\phi r1^2$	$Mr\phi r2$	$Mr\phi r2^2$	$Mr\phi r3$	$Mr\phi r3^2$
1	8	2·51	0·79	−4·09	2·09	25·40	80·90
2	8	5·49	3·77	−3·91	1·91	−17·40	38·00
3	4	4·00	4·00	4·00	4·00	4·00	4·00
	Σ	12·00	8·56	−4·00	8·00	12·00	122·90
$\Gamma_n = \dfrac{\Sigma Mr\phi rn}{\Sigma Mr\phi rn^2}$		$\Gamma_1 = +1·40$		$\Gamma_2 = -0·50$		$\Gamma_3 = +0·098$	

TABLE 8.—MODAL RESPONSE AMPLITUDE

Mode	f	Un^0 max	$A_n(t) = \Gamma_n Un^0$ max
1	1·00 Hz	3·3 in	4·6 in
2	2·18 Hz	1·4 in	0·70 in
3	3·18 Hz	0·66 in	0·065 in

The computation leads to the values given in Table 9.

Comparison of these values with the building code calculation, Table 10, reveals that they are approximately in the same proportion, but the building code shears are roughly one-tenth of those given by the elastic calculation using modal spectrum analysis.

The reasons for the large differences are—

(1) A factor of ten in the calculated results between the building code design against modal spectrum design. This is because the building code design depends on selected base shear, which amounts to fixing an empirical constant of the base shear coefficients from experience. For design guidance see Table 3. A difference of a factor of ten exists between various countries. Also the response spectrum is different, Figs. 12(a) and (b). The SEAOC allows considerably higher response spectra at low frequency. The calculated shear results would depend on the damping assumed. The design code uses $C = 0·05$, equivalent to a heavily damped structure. The elastic design assumes a damping factor of 2·5%. The real truth is, that once a damping factor is arbitrarily selected, calculation results will be fixed. This is one of the reasons why testing is more favourable, because the structure damping is automatically and naturally included during testing. There is no arbitrary selection of damping of structures required; in any case, the damping varies from component to component, location to location; and is also affected by forcing level, friction resistance, temperature, etc. The author has recently found experimentally that the real structure damping of a wall-mounted starter, which has a number of resonances with a first resonance of 6 Hz, has a damping factor of 25·9% on some occasions and the damping factors are different for all other resonances at higher frequencies by an overall value of 10%.

(2) Elastic analysis is known to be excessively conservative and ignores plastic deformation; stress–strain relationship is held to be linear, which ignores yielding or non-linear effects. If the displacement is large and stress is greater than yield however, elastic design would give higher results.

(3) The code allowable design stress values are smaller, i.e. half yield and not the yield stress, which is allowable for the modal spectrum elastic design.

(4) The modes considered in the building design code probably covered only the fundamental mode, while the modal spectrum analysis considered three modes in this example. The other major factor giving rise to

difference appeared to be the use of the 'Sum of root mean square stress' which assumes that all modes are in phase and occur simultaneously. This gives a safe design, but tends to give higher shear stresses.

(5) Much research work is needed in the field of damping and also the fatigue damage due to this in multi-modal response system (Ref. 16).

From the results of the comparison, it can be seen that the calculation results depend on assumptions made, and the validity of these assumptions. Thus it must be stressed, all calculations should be supported by testing results, as suggested by the IEEE specification. This leads to the development of sophisticated larger testing rigs and complicated testing techniques and instrumentations. However, recent development of finite element calculation and mathematical modelling techniques enable the calculation and testing to be co-ordinated by repeated computer runs. Trustworthy results have been achieved by finite element computer calculations.

TABLE 9.—MAXIMUM STOREY SHEARS BY MODAL SPECTRUM ANALYSIS

Mode	First Storey		Second Storey		Third Storey	
	$\phi_{\Delta 1} = \phi_{1n}$	$\Delta_{1n} = A_n\phi_{\Delta 1}$	$\phi_{\Delta 2} = \phi_{2n} - \phi_{1n}$	$\Delta_{2n} = A_n\phi_{\Delta 2}$	$\phi_{\Delta 3} = \phi_{2n} - \phi_{3n}$	$\Delta_{3n} = A_n\phi_{\Delta 3}$
1	0·314	1·44	0·372	1·71	0·314	1·44
2	0·511	0·36	0·022	0·02	1·489	1·04
3	3·18C	0·21	5·36	0·35	3·18	0·21
Ref.	Fig. 13b	Table 8	Fig. 13b	Table 8	Fig. 13b	Table 8
Max. Storey Disp.	$\Sigma\Delta_{1n}$	2·0 in	$\Sigma\Delta_{2n}$	2·08 in	$\Sigma\Delta_{3n}$	2·69 in
Prob. max.	Sum of Root mean sq. SRMS	1·5 in	SRMS	1·74 in	SRMS	1·79 in
Abso. max. shear	$\Sigma\Delta_{1nx}$ $K_1 = 1500$	3020 kips	$\Sigma\Delta_{2nx}$ $K_2 = 1000$	2080 kips	$\Sigma\Delta_{3\phi x}$ $K_3 = 500$	1345 kips
Prob. max. shear	SRMSΔ_{1n} $\times K_1$	2250 kips	SRMSΔ_{2n} $\times K_2$	1740 kips	SRMSΔ_{3n} $\times K_3$	995 kips

TABLE 10.—COMPARISON OF BUILDING CODE CALCULATION WITH MODAL SPECTRUM CALCULATION ON BASE SHEARS

	First Storey	Second Storey	Third Storey
US Building Code Design	259 kips	201 kips	86 kips
Ratio	1	0·77	0·33
Modal Spectrum Analysis SRMS	2250 kips	1740 kips	895 kips
Ratio	1	0·77	0·39

NUMERICAL SOLUTION AND COMPUTER SOFTWARE FOR SIMPLE SYSTEMS

Considerable progress is being made on the design of structures to withstand earthquakes, especially in the field of computer calculations using finite element and shock spectrum and transient vibration analysis, but in spite of this fact, a really satisfactory method of calculation to predict real earthquake magnitude is still elusive.

The major difficulty lies in the prediction of the intensity of the earthquakes to which a structure might be subjected during its life. The creation of a Design Basis Earthquake (DBE) spectrum based on a rather crude estimate of the expected ground motion must be an art of statistics, Fig. 14. Strong motion earthquake records especially are very scarce. Estimates must be made to change the ground floor vibrations on each individual floor of a building where the equipment stands, Fig. 15.

Another difficulty lies in the fact that a realistic calculation for earthquake should take into account the

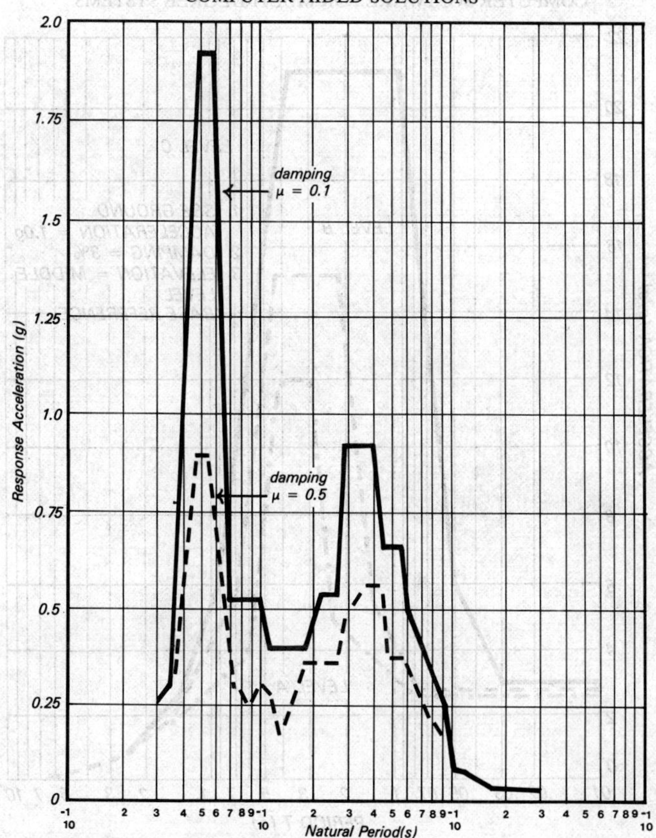

FIG. 14.—Horizontal DBE (Design Basis Earthquake) of a Building at Ground Level.

inelastic behaviour of the structure. Very few structures could withstand a strong earthquake without some plastic deformation.

The inherent difficulty of inelastic analysis of multi-degree systems, coupled with the irregular and uncertain nature of the ground motion, make a rigorous solution to the problem impractical. Essentially, it is a transient vibration problem, as input time history (Fig. 3) and spectra of previous earthquake records (Fig. 4).

Digital computers enable the calculation of dynamic response of structures to be performed in a more sophisticated manner, including non-linear and elastic-plastic elements. Also for a large number of modes of vibration, the deflection and stresses may be shown as a print-out by computer at all the nodal points.

Many finite element programs are available such as ASAS, ANSYS, NASTRAN, BIRDYE, PAREC, SUPERB and GEC's MELDAP, etc. The degree of sophistication depends on the elements chosen and the idealization of the structures, and the impact time history or response spectra, etc. Later in the Chapter some examples are given which show how the ANSYS calculation is used for a wall mounted starter of a control system installed in a nuclear power station.

However, these are large programs which consist of a great many simple computer programs. Several useful computer programs are listed below, all of which are coded in the time-sharing language, BASIC.

Five classical numerical solution and computer programs are given in Ref. 45:

(1) Numerical Solutions for Linear Systems (PRM 411)
(2) Numerical Solutions for Nonlinear Systems (PRM 421)
(3) Cubic Hardening Spring (PRM 422)
(4) Iteration of Eigenvalues and Eigenvectors (PRM 431)
(5) Numerical Solution for Multi-Degree Systems. (PRM 441)

Note.—the software of multi-degree systems is given here so that the reader may be able to use a desk-top or personal computer to make a preliminary survey of the problem.

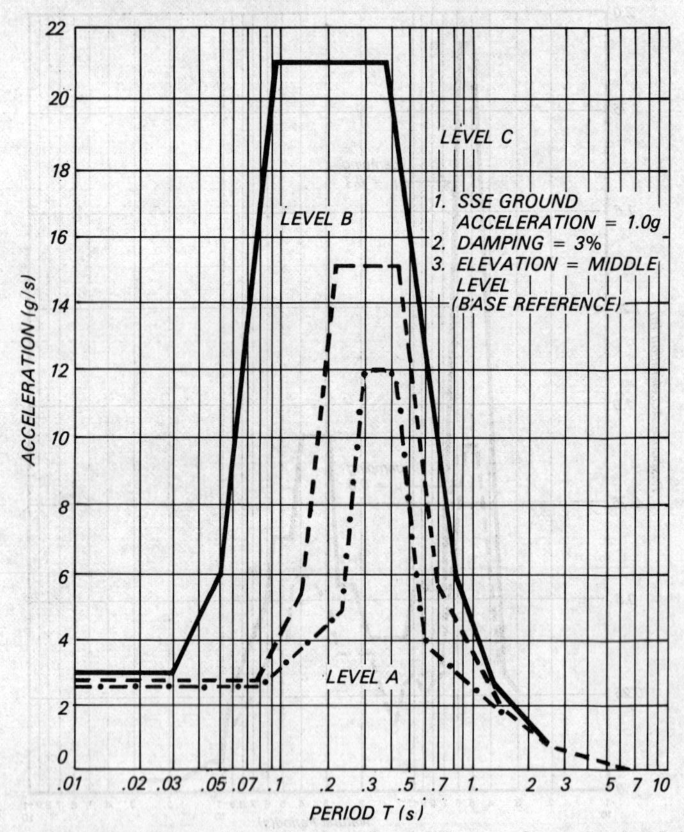

FIG. 15.—Example of Relationships of Levels A, B and C Response Spectra in a Tall Building.

COMPUTER SOFTWARE FOR MULTI-DEGREE DESIGN CALCULATIONS

PRM 441 NUMERICAL SOLUTION FOR MULTI-DEGREE SYSTEMS (see Appendix I, page I5/68).—The normal-mode method is applied to the task of calculating the transient response of damped, linear multi-degree systems subjected to piecewise–constant function. The software implements the following equations for the first three modes of a system with piecewise constant forcing functions (Ref. 27). The damped response of the ith mode at time station t_j is:

$$x_{pi,j} = \mathrm{e}^{-n_i\Delta t_j}\left[x_{pi,j-1}\cos P_{di}\Delta t_j + \frac{\dot{x}_{pi,j-1} + n_i x_{pi,j-1}}{p_{di}}\sin P_{di}\Delta t_j\right] + \frac{q_{pi,j}}{p_i^2}\left[1 - \mathrm{e}^{ni\Delta f_j}\left(\cos P_{di}\Delta_{tj} + \frac{n_i}{Pd_i}\sin P_{di}\Delta_{ti}\right)\right] \quad (25)$$

By differentiating this expression with respect to time and dividing the result by P_{di}, we also obtain

$$\frac{\dot{x}p_{i,j}}{P_{di}} = \mathrm{e}^{-n_i\Delta t_j}\left[-x_{pi,j-1}\sin P_{di}\Delta_{tj} + \frac{\dot{x}_{pi,j-1} + n_i x_{pi,j-1}}{P_{di}}\cos P_{di}\Delta_{ti} - \frac{n_i}{P_{di}}\left(x_{pi,j-1}\cos P_{di}\Delta_{tj} + \frac{\dot{x}_{pi,j-1} + n_i x_{pi,j-1}}{P_{di}}\sin P_{di}\Delta_{tj}\right)\right] + \frac{q_{pi,j}}{p_i^2}\mathrm{e}^{-n_i\Delta_{tj}}\left(1 + \frac{n_i^2}{P_{di}^2}\right)\sin P_{di}\Delta_{tj} \quad (26)$$

These two equations represent recurrence formulae for calculating the damped response of each normal mode at the end of the *j*th time step. They also provide the initial conditions of displacement and velocity at the beginning of step *j*th. These formulae may be applied repetitively to produce the time history of response for each of the normal modes.

DEBUGGING THE PROGRAM.—Using Fig 16 three mass-three spring system, we have the damping $C_1 = C_2 = C_3 = 0{\cdot}05$, $k_1 = k_2 = k_3 = 1$ lb/in, and $m_1 = m_2 = m_3 = 1$ lb-sec²/in. The initial displacements and velocities are all zero and a unit step function Fig. 17a is applied to the third mass. The response is calculated for 15 seconds, with a uniform time step of $t = 1$ sec. Following the program is a plot of the output for this data, and we have the eigenvalues, eigenvectors and responses for the first three modes of the system. The results may be checked with Table 11 and Fig. 17b.

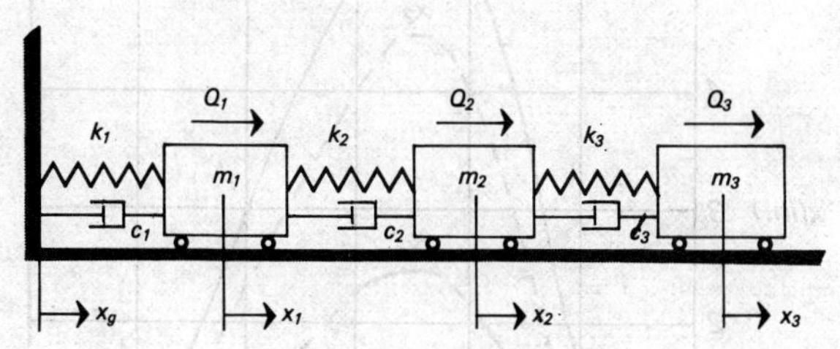

FIG. 16.—Three-mass Spring System.

TABLE 11.—RESULTS FROM PROGRAM PRM 441

j	t_j (sec)	Δ_{tj} (sec)	f_{cj} (lb)	x_{1j} (in)	x_{2j} (in)	x_{3j} (in)
0	0	—	—	0	0	0
1	0·5	0·5	1·0	0·025	0·038	0·074
2	1·0	0·5	1·0	0·095	0·156	0·283
3	1·5	0·5	1·0	0·205	0·363	0·603
4	2·0	0·5	1·0	0·352	0·660	1·004
5	2·5	0·5	1·8	0·555	1·062	1·518
6	3·0	0·5	1·8	0·830	1·576	2·175
7	3·5	0·5	1·8	1·167	2·176	2·935
8	4·0	0·5	1·8	1·545	2·834	3·757
9	4·5	0·5	0·4	1·906	3·468	4·498
10	5·0	0·5	0·4	2·193	3·983	5·030
11	5·5	0·5	0·4	2·394	4·330	5·355
12	6·0	0·5	0·4	2·495	4·475	5·480
13	6·5	0·5	1·2	2·506	4·438	5·472
14	7·0	0·5	1·2	2·433	4·273	5·384
15	7·5	0·5	1·2	2·277	4·024	5·199
16	8·0	0·5	1·2	2·057	3·728	4·904
17	8·5	0·5	1·2	1·809	3·403	4·504
18	9·0	0·5	1·2	1·574	3·050	4·020
19	9·5	0·5	1·7	1·390	2·688	3·523
20	10·0	0·5	1·7	1·267	2·346	3·082
21	10·5	0·5	0·6	1·153	2·014	2·641
22	11·0	0·5	0·6	0·998	1·673	2·146
23	11·5	0·5	0·6	0·798	1·332	1·636
24	12·0	0·5	0·6	0·568	0·984	1·151
25	12·5	0·5	1·0	0·347	0·642	0·754
26	13·0	0·5	1·0	0·167	0·340	0·482
27	13·5	0·5	1·5	0·055	0·133	0·363
28	14·0	0·5	1·5	0·025	0·082	0·409
29	14·5	0·5	1·5	0·079	0·208	0·595
30	15·0	0·5	1·5	0·219	0·503	0·905

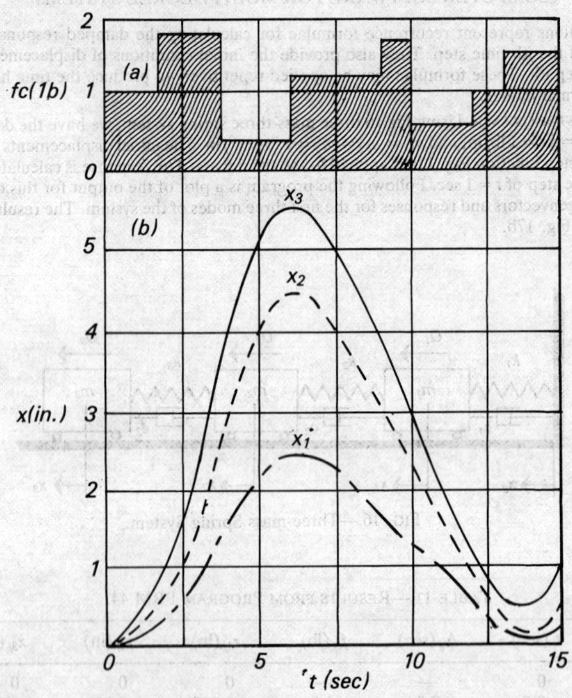

FIG. 17.—Time History Responses: (*a*) Input Forcing; (*b*) Output Displacement.

SEISMIC CALCULATION OF LIQUID FILLED TANKS AND EFFECT OF SLOSHING (Refs. 46 and 47)

Seismic qualification testing for large structures, which are impossible to divide into small components, is limited by seismic table size and hydraulic force installed; as a result, qualification by testing becomes very difficult.

Scale model testing may be possible, but modelling a joint under dynamic conditions, taking into account all the damping and non-linear effects, makes the results of testing difficult to interpret. In addition, the forcing function is inversely proportional to model scale effect, therefore the 'g' value required should be multiplied by the scale effect in order to produce the same damage; the forcing function frequency and amplitude may be difficult to achieve. An unequal X, Y, Z, scale model may be possible, but subject to further research.

For liquid filled tanks, Jacobson (Ref. 46) and Housner (Ref. 47) derived a simplified mathematical model and calculated results, which were checked with seismic damage in the past for a number of cases. A typical

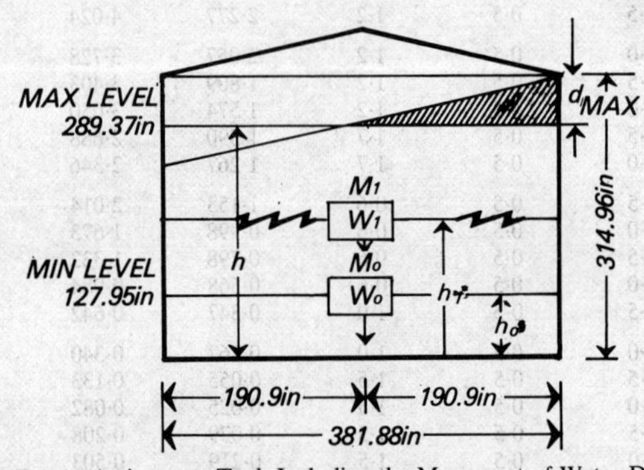

FIG. 18.—Dynamic Forces Acting on a Tank Including the Movement of Water During an Earthquake.

example of the calculation of seismic effects on liquid filled tanks, or water towers is given here, also including the effect of sloshing during the earthquake.

If a tank with a free water surface (Fig. 18) is subjected to horizontal ground acceleration 'a', the forces exerted on the tank by the water are of two kinds:

(a) IMPULSIVE FORCE DUE TO EQUIVALENT MASS 'MO'
The walls of the tank accelerate back and forth; a certain fraction of the water is forced to participate in this motion, which exerts a reactive force on the tank equivalent to a mass 'Mo', attached rigidly to the tank at a height 'ho'.

(b) CONVECTIVE FORCE DUE TO SLOSHING OF WATER IN TANK
The motion of the tank walls excites the water into oscillations, which, in turn, exert an oscillating force on the tank. This oscillating force is the same as would be exerted by a mass M_1 that can oscillate horizontally against a restraining spring, as shown in Fig. 18, at a height of h_1.

The formulae shown in Table 12 was obtained by Jacobson (Ref. 46) and Housner (Ref. 47) for the equivalent mass and spring and heights, etc. Finally, the frequency of oscillation and amplitude of sloshing may be worked out, together with overturning moments for both cylindrical and rectangular tanks. The following is an example of the calculation involved.

EXAMPLE OF CALCULATION: WATER SLOSHING IN RESERVE FEED TANKS USING FORMULAE FROM DYNAMIC PRESSURE ON FLUID CONTAINER (Ref. 46).
The circular tank is mounted at a floor level of (26.31m) with:

$$h = 289.3 \text{ in} \quad \text{(height of tank)}$$

$$R = 190.9 \text{ in} \quad \text{(radius of tank)}$$

$$\frac{h}{R} = \frac{289{\cdot}3}{190{\cdot}0} = 1{\cdot}515.$$

From equation 7.12 (Table 12) substitute $\frac{R}{h} = 0{\cdot}66$

then $$\frac{W_0}{W} = \frac{\tan h\left(\sqrt{3} \times \frac{R}{h}\right)}{\sqrt{3} \times \frac{R}{h}} = \frac{\tan h(\sqrt{3} \times 0{\cdot}66)}{1{\cdot}143} = \frac{0{\cdot}8152}{1{\cdot}143} = 0{\cdot}7132$$

The total weight of the water is:

$$W = \frac{\frac{\pi}{4} \times 190{\cdot}9^2 \times 289{\cdot}37 \times 62{\cdot}4 \text{ lb/ft}^3}{1728 \frac{\text{in}^3}{\text{ft}} \times 1000} = 1196.34 \text{ kips}$$

IMPULSIVE FORCE

$$W_0 = 0{\cdot}7132 \times (1196{\cdot}34) = 853{\cdot}23 \text{ kips}$$

For simplicity, assume the weight of tank 20 × 2200 = 44000 lbs or 44 kips acting at the centre of gravity of W_0. The gross value of $W_0 = 853{\cdot}22 + 44 = 897{\cdot}23$ kips.

Using Eq. 7.13 (Table 12):

$$h_0 = \frac{3}{8} \cdot h = \frac{3}{8} \times 289{\cdot}37 = 108{\cdot}51 \text{ in (EBP) (excluding base pressure)}$$

$$= 9{\cdot}0425\, ft$$

From Eq. 7.14 (Table 12):

$$h_0' = \frac{h}{8}\left[\frac{4}{\frac{\tanh 1{\cdot}143}{1{\cdot}143}} - 1\right] = 0{\cdot}569\, h$$

$$= 164{\cdot}7 = 13{\cdot}728 \text{ ft (IBP) (including tank pressure).}$$

$u_0 = 0{\cdot}344$ g (from Fig. 9 horizontal design spectrum) = 10·6 ft/sec², at period $t = 0{\cdot}02$ sec i.e. zero period acceleration. Later, a floor level factor of 0·907 was introduced. Period results with level factor at 26·3 metres. The acceleration excitation level was 0·334 × 0·907 = 0·304 g. The safe factor of 0·907 for this calculation is given by the vendor, the SSEB (South Scottish Electricity Board).

From Eq. 7.15 (Table 12) substitute $\dot{u}_0$ and w_0, hence:

$$P_0 = \dot{u}_0 \cdot \frac{w_0}{g} = 0{\cdot}304\ (897{\cdot}23)\ \text{kips} = 272{\cdot}758\ \text{kips}$$

$$M_i = P_0(h_0)$$

where

M_i = overturning moment due to impulsive force, Including Base Pressure (IBP)

$$M_i = 272{\cdot}758 \times 13{\cdot}89$$

$$= 3788{\cdot}6\ \text{(IBP)}$$

$$M_i = P_0(h_0)$$

where

M_i = overturning moment due to impulsive force, Excluding Base Pressure (EBP)

$$= 272{\cdot}758 \times 9{\cdot}0425\ \text{(EBP)}$$

$$= 2466{\cdot}414\ \text{(EBP)}.$$

Convective Force

From Eq. 7.16 (Table 12)

$$W_1 = W \times 0{\cdot}318 \times \frac{R}{h} \times \tanh\left(1{\cdot}84 \times \frac{h}{R}\right)$$

$$= 1196{\cdot}34 \times 0{\cdot}318 \times \frac{190{\cdot}9}{289{\cdot}37} \times \tanh\left(1{\cdot}84 \times \frac{289{\cdot}37}{190{\cdot}9}\right)$$

$$= 250{\cdot}977 \times \tanh 2{\cdot}789 = 249{\cdot}0695\ \text{kips}$$

From Eq. 7.17 (Table 12)

$$\frac{h_1}{h} = 1 - \frac{\cosh 2{\cdot}789 - 1}{2{\cdot}789 \sinh 2{\cdot}789} = 1 - 0{\cdot}317 = 0{\cdot}6829$$

$$h_1 = 0{\cdot}6829\ (289{\cdot}3) = 197{\cdot}58 = 16{\cdot}465\ \text{ft (EBP) (excluding base pressure)}$$

Using Eq. 7.18 (Table 12)

$$\frac{h_1}{h} = 1 - \frac{\cosh\left(1{\cdot}84\frac{h}{R}\right) - 2{\cdot}01}{1{\cdot}84 \times \frac{h}{R} \times \sinh\left(1{\cdot}84\frac{h}{R}\right)} = 1 - \frac{6{\cdot}161}{22{\cdot}6187} = 0{\cdot}7276$$

$$h_1 = 0{\cdot}7276 \times 289{\cdot}3 = 210{\cdot}498\ \text{in} = 17{\cdot}541\ \text{ft (IBP) (including base pressure)}$$

Using Eq. 7.19 (Table 12)

$$\omega^2 = \frac{1{\cdot}84g}{R} \times \tanh\left(1{\cdot}84\frac{h}{R}\right)$$

$$= \frac{1{\cdot}84 \times 32{\cdot}2}{190{\cdot}9/T2} \times \tanh\left(1{\cdot}84\frac{h}{R}\right)$$

$$= \frac{1{\cdot}84 \times 32{\cdot}2}{190{\cdot}9/T2} \times \tanh 2{\cdot}789$$

$$\omega = 1{\cdot}922\ \text{rad/sec}\quad f = 0{\cdot}305\ \text{Hz}$$

$$T = 3{\cdot}269\ \text{sec}$$

For $T = 3{\cdot}269$ sec, 1% damping (see Fig. 9 horizontal Design Basis Earthquake (DBE))

Spectrum 'S' = $0{\cdot}02\ g/\omega$

$$= 0{\cdot}02 \times 32{\cdot}2/1{\cdot}922\ \text{ft/sec}$$

$$= 0{\cdot}335\ \text{ft/sec}$$

cont. on I5/32

TABLE 12.—FORMULAE FOR CALCULATING SEISMIC FORCES ON WATER TANKS

Rectangular tank

$$\frac{W_0}{W} = \frac{\tan\left(\sqrt{3}\,\frac{l}{h}\right)}{\sqrt{3}\,\frac{l}{h}} \qquad (7.1)$$

$$h_0 = \frac{3}{8}h \text{ (EBP)} \qquad (7.2)$$

$$\frac{h_0'}{h} = \frac{1}{8}\left[\frac{\dfrac{4}{\tanh\left(\sqrt{3}\,\frac{l}{h}\right)^{-1}}}{\sqrt{3}\,\frac{l}{h}}\right] \text{(IBP)} \qquad (7.3)$$

$$P_0 = \dot{u}_0 \frac{W}{g}\,\frac{\tan\left(\sqrt{3}\,\frac{l}{h}\right)}{\sqrt{3}\,\frac{l}{h}} = \frac{\dot{u}_0 W_0}{g} \qquad (7.4)$$

$$\frac{W_1}{W} = 0{\cdot}527\,\frac{l}{h}\tanh\left(1{\cdot}58\,\frac{h}{l}\right) \qquad (7.5)$$

$$\frac{h_1}{h} = 1 - \frac{\cosh\left(1{\cdot}58\,\frac{h}{l}\right) - 1}{1{\cdot}58\,\frac{h}{l}\sinh\left(1{\cdot}58\,\frac{h}{l}\right)} \text{(EBP)} \qquad (7.6)$$

$$\frac{h_1'}{h} = 1 - \frac{\cosh\left(1{\cdot}58\,\frac{h}{l}\right) - 2}{1{\cdot}58\,\frac{h}{l}\sinh\left(1{\cdot}58\,\frac{h}{l}\right)} \text{(IBP)} \qquad (7.7)$$

$$\omega^2 = \frac{1{\cdot}58g}{l}\tanh\left(1{\cdot}58\,\frac{h}{l}\right) \qquad (7.8)$$

$$\theta_h = 1{\cdot}58\,\frac{A_1}{l}\tanh\left(1{\cdot}58\,\frac{h}{l}\right) \qquad (7.9)$$

$$P_1 = W_1\theta_h \sin\omega t \qquad (7.10)$$

$$d_{\max} = \frac{0{\cdot}527\,l\coth\left(1{\cdot}58\,\frac{h}{l}\right)}{\dfrac{g}{\omega^2\theta_h l} - 1} \qquad (7.11)$$

Cylindrical tank

$$\frac{W_0}{W} = \frac{\tanh\left(\sqrt{3}\,\frac{R}{h}\right)}{\sqrt{3}\,\frac{R}{h}} \qquad (7.12)$$

$$h_0 = \frac{3}{8}h \text{ (EBP)} \qquad (7.13)$$

$$\frac{h_0'}{h} = \frac{1}{8}\left[\frac{4}{\dfrac{\tan\left(\sqrt{3}\,\frac{R}{h}\right)}{\sqrt{3}\,\frac{R}{h}}} - 1\right] \text{(IBP)} \qquad (7.14)$$

$$P_0 = \dot{u}_0 \frac{W}{g}\,\frac{\tanh\left(\sqrt{3}\,\frac{R}{h}\right)}{\sqrt{3}\,\frac{R}{h}} = \dot{u}_0\frac{W_0}{g} \qquad (7.15)$$

$$\frac{W_1}{W} = 0{\cdot}318\,\frac{R}{h}\tanh\left(1{\cdot}84\,\frac{h}{R}\right) \qquad (7.16)$$

$$\frac{h_1}{h} = 1 - \frac{\cosh\left(1{\cdot}84\,\frac{h}{R}\right) - 1}{1{\cdot}84\,\frac{h}{R}\sinh\left(1{\cdot}84\,\frac{h}{R}\right)} \text{(EBP)} \qquad (7.17)$$

$$\frac{h_1'}{h} = 1 - \frac{\cosh\left(1{\cdot}84\,\frac{h}{R}\right) - 2{\cdot}01}{1{\cdot}84\,\frac{h}{R}\sinh\left(1{\cdot}84\,\frac{h}{R}\right)} \text{(IBP)} \qquad (7.18)$$

$$\omega^2 = \frac{1{\cdot}84g}{R}\tanh\left(1{\cdot}84\,\frac{h}{R}\right) \qquad (7.19)$$

$$\theta_h = 1{\cdot}534\,\frac{A_1}{R}\tanh\left(1{\cdot}84\,\frac{h}{R}\right) \qquad (7.20)$$

$$P_1 = 1{\cdot}2\,W_1\theta_h \sin\omega t \qquad (7.21)$$

$$d_{\max} = \frac{0{\cdot}408R\coth\left(1{\cdot}84\,\frac{h}{R}\right)}{\dfrac{g}{\omega^2\theta_h R} - 1} \qquad (7.22)$$

W = Total Weight of Water up to Maximum Height h
h = Maximum Height of Water (for Design Purposes)
W_0 = Equivalent Weight due to Impulsive Force
h_0 = Height of Equivalent Reactive Force Exerted on the Tank by Equivalent Mass during Earthquake
l = Width of Tank Associated with the Direction of Motion during Earthquake
R = Radius of Circular Tank
P_u = Impulsive Force due to Earthquake on the Tank
h_0' = Equivalent Impulsive Force Height Including Base Tank Pressure (IBP)
IBP = Including Base Tank Pressure
$\dot{u}_0$ = Acceleration Obtained from Horizontal Design Spectra
EBP = Excluding Base Tank Pressure
ω = Circular Frequency during Earthquake
θ_h = Amplitude of Vibration during Earthquake
$d_{\max}$ = Maximum Shock Amplitude.

$$Y\max = A_1 = \frac{S}{\omega} = \frac{0{\cdot}335}{1{\cdot}922} = 0{\cdot}1742 \text{ ft}$$

From Eq. 7.20 (Table 12)

$$\theta_h = 1{\cdot}534 \times \frac{Al}{R} \times \tanh\left(1{\cdot}84\frac{h}{R}\right)$$

$$= 1{\cdot}534 \times \frac{0{\cdot}1742 \times 12}{190{\cdot}9} \times 0{\cdot}9925$$

$$= 0{\cdot}0166$$

From Eq. 7.21 where P_1 = convective force

$$P_1 = 1{\cdot}2\, W_1 \theta_h \sin \omega t \text{ let } \sin \omega t = 1$$
$$= 1{\cdot}2 \times 249{\cdot}0615 \times 0{\cdot}0166 = 4{\cdot}9827 \text{ kips}$$

$$M_c = 4{\cdot}9827\, \underline{h_{1\,(EBP)}} = 82{\cdot}040 \text{ kip ft (EBP)}$$

$$M'_c = 4.9827\, \underline{h'_{1\,(IBP)}} = 87{\cdot}40 \text{ kip ft (IBP)}$$

M_c = overturning moment due to convective force (DBE)
M'_c = overturning moment due to convective force (IBP)

DISPLACEMENT OF WATER SURFACE
Using Eq. 7.22

$$d_{max} = \frac{0{\cdot}408R \times \coth\left(1{\cdot}84\frac{h}{R}\right)}{\dfrac{q}{\omega^2\theta_h R} - 1}$$

$$= \frac{0{\cdot}408 \times \dfrac{190{\cdot}9}{12} \times 1{\cdot}0076}{\dfrac{32{\cdot}2}{1{\cdot}922^2 \times 0{\cdot}0166 \times 15{\cdot}9} - 1}$$

$$= 0{\cdot}2041 \text{ ft} = 2{\cdot}449 \text{ inches}$$

Maximum Bending Moment on the tank at a section first above the bottom

$$\underbrace{M_1 + M_c}_{EBP} = 3148{\cdot}56 + 82{\cdot}040 = 2548{\cdot}45 \text{ kip ft (EBP)}$$
$$= 30{,}581{,}450 \text{ in lb (EBP)}$$

Maximum Overturning Moment

$$\underbrace{M'_i + M'_c}_{IBP} = 3788{\cdot}6 + 87{\cdot}4 = 3876 \text{ kip ft (IBP)}$$
$$= 46{,}512{,}000 \text{ in lb (IBP)}$$

Maximum Shear at Base

= Impulsive force + Convective force

$= P_0 + P_1 = 272{\cdot}758 + 4{\cdot}9827 = 277{\cdot}74$ kips = 277,740 lbf

Max allowable overturning moment given by SSEB (South of Scotland Electricity Board) = 93,102,400 in lbs, therefore, this design with a calculated value of 46,512,000 in/lbs (IBP) is acceptable. The author used this simplified method to check a sophisticated finite element calculation on a reserve feed tank of about 62 ft diameter and 27 ft high (Ref. 48). Good agreements on slosh frequencies were obtained.

SEISMIC TESTING METHODS

FULL SCALE, FULL INTENSITY EARTHQUAKE SIMULATING TEST.—From the previous section it may be seen that although a mathematical model can be made, the accuracy of the results may be questionable, due to uncertainty of damping of structures, resonance effects, non-linearities, plastic ductility effects of material, etc. All need to be determined correctly. For the USA, the IEEE Standard 344—1975 (Ref. 4) demands that the adequacy of the design calculation be demonstrated by testing.

With some electrical equipment, e.g. circuit breakers, consisting of thousands of ccomplex electrical and electronic components, stress/strain and metal fatigue criteria used in the mathematical model are not applicable. Moreover the intricacy of the equipment makes a mathematical model too complex, and the expense of computer calculation uneconomic. Testing by simulating the earthquake on a seismic table in bi-axial directions with random input according to the floor vibrations during earthquake, i.e. with the defined Required Response Spectrum (RRS) in horizontal and vertical directions is more satisfactory for a wide range of diverse equipment.

Initially, IEEE 1971, postulated tests to be carried out in vertical, horizontal/fore and aft, and horizontal/side to side directions. Simple sine waves and sine sweeps to determine resonance and sine tests or sine beat tests were acceptable. Later more sophisticated testing techniques were developed. IEEE 1975 (Ref. 4) suggesting more complex testing. For some authorities, e.g. Great Britain (Refs 49 and 50), only independent bi-axial table (i.e. testing with two independent phase random signals in two axes) and indirect plane bi-axial table or bi-axial linked table (i.e. in phase random two-axis testing) are acceptable.

The emergency power supplies and ventilation and cooling plants for electric power stations, emergency gas and water supplies, emergency ventilation plants for underground railway systems, emergency power/ventilation plants for hospitals and large public buildings in a city, etc, should all be designed in such a way that in the event of an earthquake they would be able to operate normally without any malfunctioning. Special attention should be paid to control panels and supply lines etc. For safety reasons, equipment belonging to the emergency power supply in a nuclear power station is the object of compulsory seismic qualification testing.

This applies to British nuclear plants although the chance of a seismic event is quite remote in the British Isles. However, for safety reasons it is considered to be within the 5% of unexpected and unexplained earthquakes.

The seismic qualification methods and guidance issued by the UK Electricity Authority, CEGB, SSEB are described in NNC C92/SDS/151/012 and GDCN/NP333 (Ref. 49). Technical specification and schedules for seismic qualification of electrical plant are set out in Ref. 50. International Electro Technical Commission: Guide for Seismic testing procedures for equipment issued by sub-committee (50A) is given in Ref. 51.

The purpose of testing is to simulate a real seismic condition and to demonstrate that the equipment is capable of withstanding earthquakes without failure or malfunction. It is important to look at two aspects of the testing:

(i) How to simulate the real time ground motion of an earthquake which depends on different earthquake zones and the location of the equipment on different floor levels and in different types of building structures.
(ii) How to simulate the real structure fixing, including the coupling effect of soil structures, etc.

EARTHQUAKE TESTING INPUTS—FREQUENCY AND INTENSITY.—From earthquake records (Fig. 3), one would conclude the ground motion to be of broad band random nature, therefore for structures mounted at soil level, random testing would be more suitable. However after the shock passes through the soil structure, building floors, etc., the final waves reach the equipment mounted in buildings perhaps in the form of a series of narrow band spectra not unlike sine beats. These floor response spectra are to be specified in terms of Required Response Spectrum (RRS). The testing house is required to produce testing response spectrum to develop the RRS in both horizontal and vertical directions.

Qualification Test Motion Selection.—Test motions to qualify equipment may be selected from:

(i) Artificial time history or modified time histories.
(ii) Random input test motion.
(iii) Complex input test motion.
(iv) Sine input test motion. Continuous sine or sine beat.

It should be stated that multi-frequency derived from time history would give the best simulated earthquakes.

Figure 19 shows the derivation and inter-relationship of the above test methods. The flow chart starts from the local district Power Station seismic history analysis or survey, which eventually produced a ground acceleration time history at the equipment location. Generally, the worst earthquake in the district is used as a guide. From the ground acceleration time history, with the knowledge of the building structure, the design floor response spectrum could be computed. Further calculations assume a single degree of freedom system and damping value of 1% or 5%. The RRS may be computed at the floor level, or at the location where the equipment will be fixed. On the other hand, if the purchaser lacks information on the final building, he could include response uncertainties and compute a new time history and produce Fourier spectra and then the RRS.

From the RRS, through analysis, an artificial time history is produced. For hydraulic actuators, a displacement time history is required, which causes the seismic testing table to move. This movement is detected by accelerometer mounted on the table. The acceleration of the table motion is then converted into Test Response Spectrum (TRS) using Duhammel Integral and computer programs (See Appendix II: Computer Program PRM 421). The TRS derived must envelope the RRS.

LARGE STRUCTURE EARTHQUAKE TESTING.—To simulate earthquake shock for large structures, one may use a blast test by the use of explosive or 'snap back' test in order to see non-linear responses of the structure.

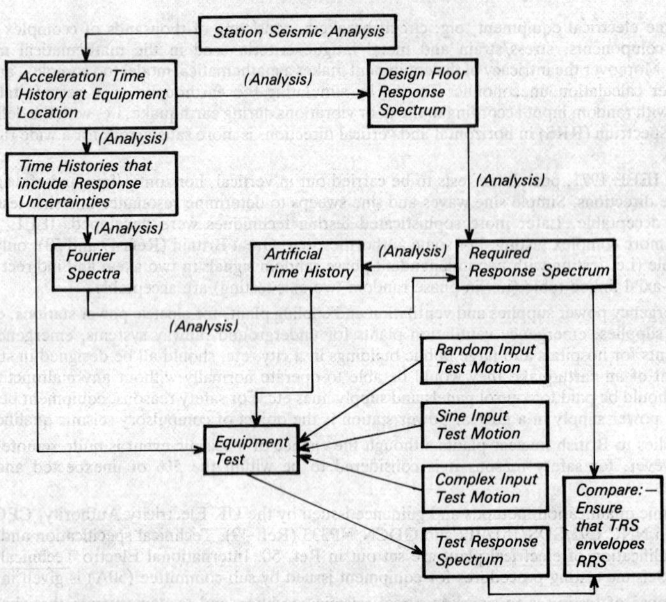

FIG. 19.—Test Motion Derivation.

Figure 20 shows a typical 'snap back' test by the GEC Mechanical Engineering Laboratory, on a Birlec 140 ton steel-making electric furnace. Here a Tinsley steel-works crane was used and a ½ in rope, which snaps when a 2 ton force is reached. The purpose of the work was to determine the natural frequency and damping of the large electrode for electrode feeding control purposes. The test results, in the form of transfer function, may be used in conjunction with natural frequency and damping to produce a horizontal and vertical required response spectrum (Figs 8 and 9), which provides the forcing function. The stress on the essential parts by the graphite electrode may be estimated by multiplying the forcing function by transfer function and obtained stresses or acceleration during an earthquake event. Thus the suitability of the electronic control circuit of the furnace may be assessed.

C. B. Smith (Ref. 52) has carried out 'snap back' testing on an EGCR steam generator of a nuclear power station, using a 100 ton hydraulic ram with a specially designed valve system. The test involved giving 0·7 in deflection on the top of the steam generator and recording the response by the use of accelerometers.

He also carried out forcing vibration testing using an hydraulic vibrator, and blast tests using explosives. Figure 21a shows results of blasting, snap back and forced vibration, with a smaller force appearing to produce higher frequencies than those produced by a larger force. Figure 21b provides clear evidence that the steam generator behaves as a softening system i.e. the structure is non-linear and the stiffness becomes softer under large forces. These results indicate that during the test it is necessary to reproduce, not only the correct frequency but also the level of force required to produce reliable results.

COMPLEX EQUIPMENT EARTHQUAKE TESTING.—Most electrical equipment falls into this range of complex equipment. The Institute of Electrical and Electronic Engineers (USA) the IEEE (generally known as I triple E) gives the guidance for Class I electrical equipment testing (Ref. 4). In 1979 IEC (International Electrotechnical Commission), the IEC, also issued a guide for seismic qualification of electrical and electronic equipment in Europe (Ref. 51).

In order to test this equipment a test facility is required, and typical earthquake testing equipment at the Mechanical Engineering Laboratory, GEC Engineering Research Centre, is shown Fig. 22(*a*). Larger seismic tables capable of carrying weights up to 100 tons are also available.

The structure under test is mounted on a platform supported by hoverpads. The exciting force is generated by a hydraulic/electronic system (Fig. 22(*a*), foreground), which drives the floating table directly in any of three mutually perpendicular directions individually or simultaneously.

The platform consists of a cast iron T-slot table weighing about 3 tons with dimensions 5 ft × 10 ft, which is floating on four hoverpads and is capable of supporting equipment of up to 10 tons in weight. The air bearing thus formed (by the hoverpads) provides the de-coupling of the resonance of the testing equipment from the supporting structure of the rig.

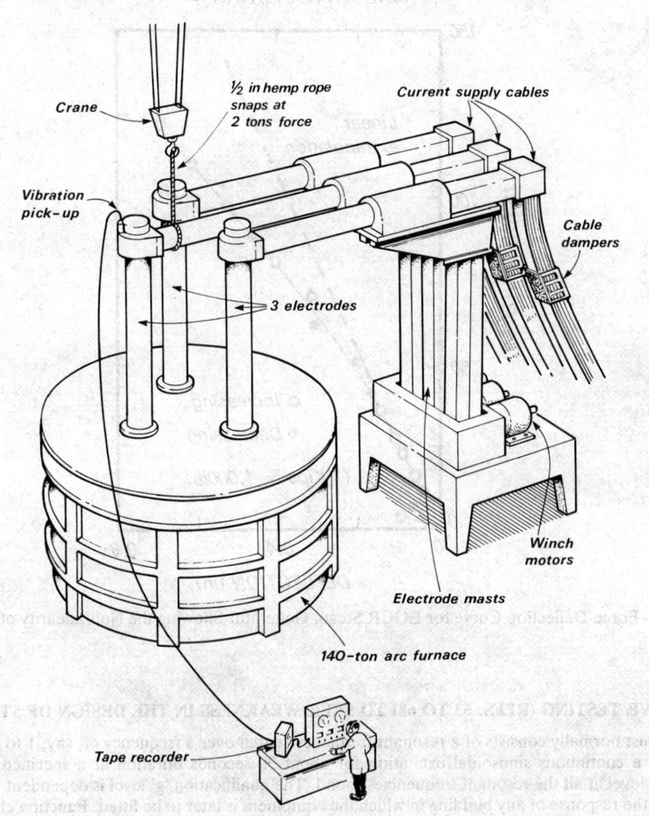

FIG. 20.—Impulse Test of Birlec 140-ton Electric Arc Furnace to Determine Mast and Electrode Resonant Frequencies.

The lower part of the structure, which carries the floating platform, consists of two lifting beams, similar to a heavy vehicle lift, driven by 4 vertical screw-threaded shafts chain-linked together and rotated by a control motor. This enables the hydraulic ram to be easily aligned to the testing platform.

For multi-axis testing, three mutually perpendicular hydraulic rams may be installed, three different control signals may be fed through three separate systems to produce phase independent earthquake movements, Fig. 22(*a*).

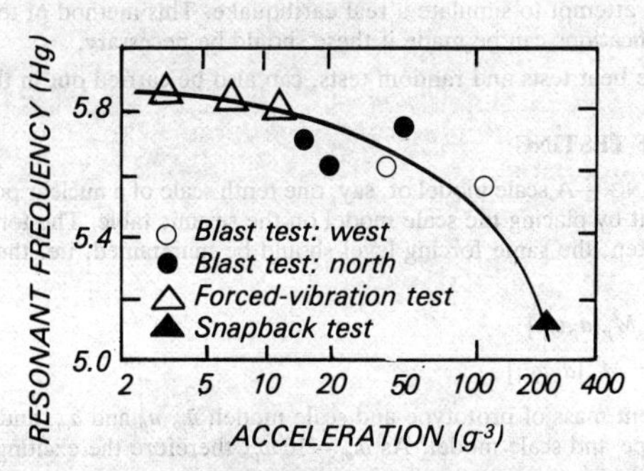

FIG. 21(*a*).—Frequency-Acceleration Relationship Plotted from N–S Response of an Emergency Gas-cooled Reactor Steam Generator. Blast Test arranged using Explosives.

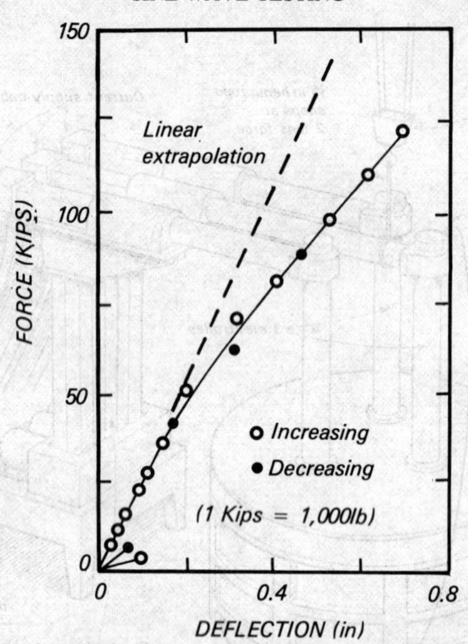

FIG. 21(*b*).—Force-Deflection Curve for EGCR Steam Generator Showing the Non-linearity of the Structure.

SINE WAVE TESTING (REFS. 53 TO 68) TO SEEK WEAKNESS IN THE DESIGN OF STRUCTURES

The sine test normally consists of a resonant frequency search over a frequency of, say, 1 to 35 Hz at 0·1 g, followed by a continuous sinusoidal excitation for about 30 seconds duration at a specified 'qualification' acceleration level at all the resonant frequencies found. The qualification 'g' level is dependent on earthquake data and on the response of any building in which the equipment is later to be fitted. Function electrical testing will then be carried out to see if the structure would remain intact and whether the equipment would operate normally. The tests are carried out in vertical, side-to-side and fore-aft directions.

For equipment mounted on the ground floor, the testing level should be equivalent to the earthquake force level, i.e. at zero period acceleration (accelerations above 33 Hz). For US, California earthquake, the testing level should be 0·3 g in the horizontal direction. For vertical earthquake, the testing level should be 0·67 the zero period horizontal ground acceleration, i.e. $0{\cdot}67 \times 0{\cdot}3\ g = 0{\cdot}21\ g$.

For equipment mounted on higher floors, the shaker table motion should be made to be equivalent to the floor motion at that level combined with a single-degree of freedom system, representing the equipment attached to that floor in the frequency range of 0 to 33 Hz. The sine test is the simplest testing method, easy to carry out, but does not attempt to simulate a real earthquake. This method of testing is to seek weakness in structures so that modifications can be made if these should be necessary.

Other tests, such as sine beat tests and random tests, can also be carried out in the single direction.

OTHER METHODS OF TESTING

(i) SCALE MODEL TESTING.—A scale model of, say, one tenth scale of a nuclear power station may be built. A test could be carried out by placing the scale model on the seismic table. The forcing frequency should be multiplied by a factor of ten; the same forcing level should be maintained, i.e. the force applied should be equal:

$$F = M_p \ddot{a}_p = M_p[a_p \omega_p^2]$$

$$= M_m \ddot{a}_m = M_m[a_p \omega_m^2] \tag{27}$$

where M_p and M_m represent mass of prototype and scale model; $\ddot{a}_p$, a_p and $\ddot{a}_m$, and a_m are accelerations and amplitudes of the prototype and scale model. As $\omega_m = 10\,\omega_p$, therefore the exciting frequency and response frequencies are 10 times higher.

$$\omega_m^2 = 100\,\omega_p^2$$

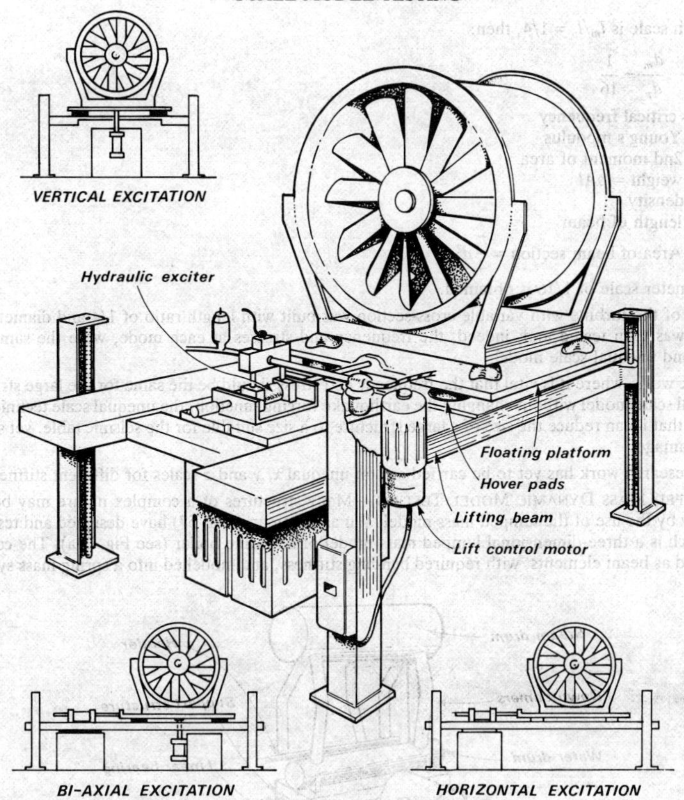

FIG. 22(*a*).—Earthquake Testing Equipment at GEC, Whetstone.

Thus the acceleration required to produce the same damage is 100 times higher. For example, if 0·3 g is used for full size prototype testing at 10 Hz, 30 'g' is required for a 1/10th scale model at 100 Hz. This may not be possible to achieve in practice.

(ii) UNEQUAL SCALE MODEL.—Reference 9 shows how to design an unequal scale model to provide a beam of the same bending stiffness as the prototype and at the same vibration frequency. This is based upon the bending stiffness $Kb = \text{Constant} \times [E_p I_p/\rho_p A_p A_p l^4]$. If E_p/ρ_p is constant, i.e. if the prototype and model are made of the same material, then for a circular beam:

$$I_p = \frac{\pi d^4}{64}; A_p = \frac{\pi d^2}{4}; I_p/A_p = \frac{d^2}{16};$$

then

$$K_b = \text{const.} \times \left[\frac{d_p^2}{l_p^4}\right]$$

If the same frequency is desired, i.e.:

$$1 = \frac{f_p}{f_m} = \sqrt{\frac{\dfrac{E_m I_m}{W_m L_m^3}}{\dfrac{E_p I_p}{W_p l_p}}} \tag{28}$$

and

$$\frac{d_m}{d_p} = \left(\frac{l_m}{l_p}\right)^2 \quad \text{and} \quad \frac{W_m}{W_p} = \left(\frac{l_m}{l_p}\right)^5 \tag{29}$$

If the length scale is $l_m/l_p = 1/4$, then:

$$\frac{d_m}{d_p} = \frac{1}{16}$$

where f = critical frequency
E = Young's modulus
I = 2nd moment of area
W = weight = ρAl
ρ = density
l = length of beam
A = Area of beam section = $\frac{\pi}{4}d^2$

Thus a diameter scale of 1/16 is obtained.

A model of the turbine with variable cross-section was built with length ratio of 1/4 and diameter ratio of 1/16. This was then tested and, indeed, the frequency and stresses at each mode, were the same for both prototype and unequal scale model.

In seismic work, where it is vital that the frequency and stress should be the same for the large structure and for the small scale model without changing the earthquake forcing function, the unequal scale technique is very suitable, in that it can reduce the size of a large structure to a size suitable for the seismic table, yet suffer from the same damage.

Further research work has yet to be carried out on unequal x, y and z scales for different stiffness criteria.

(iii) LUMPED MASS DYNAMIC MODEL TESTING.—Many structures of a complex nature may be analysed dynamically by the use of the lumped mass model. Wu and Roman (Ref. 57) have designed and tested such a model, which is a three-dimensional lumped mass model of a Marine boiler (see Fig. 23a). The components are idealized as beam elements, with required bending stiffness, and modelled into a spring-mass system (Fig. 23b).

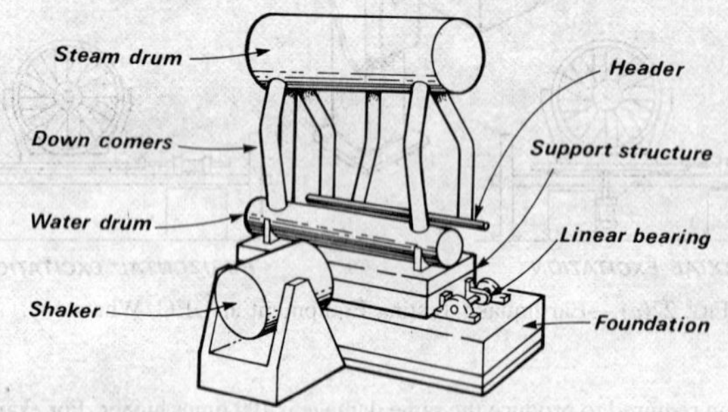

FIG. 23(a).—Shaker Test of Marine Boiler.

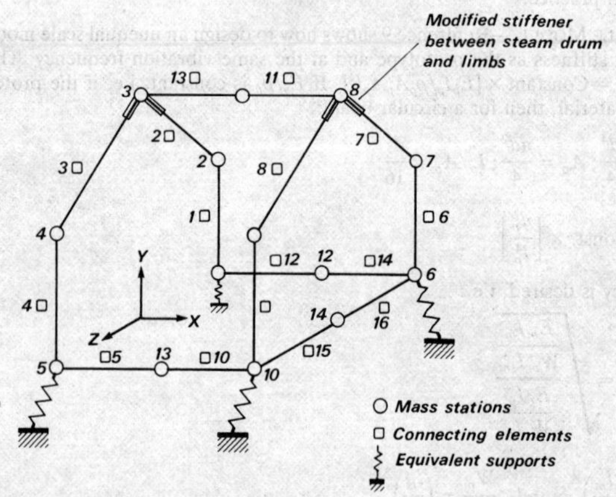

FIG. 23(b).—Lumped Mass Model of a Marine Boiler.

The test consists of first performing a shaker test on the boiler to determine natural frequencies. Then, using a computer program and the lumped mass system the natural frequencies are calculated. After this a pendulum impacter is used and reed shock analysis to perform the earthquake shock testing.

The results of the calculation indicate that the first 5 modes of vibration for the modified lump system are within 15% of deviation from the experimental value. The first 10 modes are within 36%. These discrepancies may be due to inaccuracy in damping and stiffness of the model.

MODERN TESTING TECHNIQUES

The progress of recent technology has made sine testing earthquake simulation a technique of the past. Advancements in testing are briefly as follows.

(1) The development of magnetic tape recording and reproduction of electronic signals. Good instrumentation tape recorders are available with greatly improved accuracy in amplitude and frequency recording and reproduction.

(2) The conversion of an analogue signal into a digital signal (A to D converter) introduced the 'hanging' technique to remove errors due to 'windowing'. (Ref. 69). D to A, (digital to analogue) Converters are also available. These converters have facilitated the use of computers.

(3) The introduction of the mini-computer, and micro-computer has enabled mathematical calculations to be made in milli-seconds with digitized information. The development of software packages such as *Fast Fourier Transfer* (FFT) (Ref. 69), has enabled vibration signals to be transformed from *Time* domain to *Frequency* domain simply and quickly. It has made the synthesising of electric signals possible, by first analysing the signal from a sensor or an accelerometer in time domain, transforming it into frequency domain and re-constructing it at all frequency ranges.

(4) Microprocessor and feedback control technology in hydraulic ram systems has enabled the earthquake signals to be reproduced accurately in different directions simultaneously. Thus the equipment undergoing test on the table experiences a true-time earthquake exactly similar to a real earthquake for 10 to 30 seconds.

These advances make earthquake testing very sophisticated and complicated, but simulation is much improved. The Required Test Response Spectrum (TRS) could be made to envelope the Required Response Spectrum (RRS) accurately using computer controls. The following paragraphs describe one of the tables and control systems at the GEC Research Centre.

20-TON BI-AXIAL SEISMIC TESTING TABLE FOR THREE-AXIS SEISMIC QUALIFICATION TEST.— Figure 24 shows the general view of the rig. The table consists of a 'T' slot table 5 ft × 10 ft, weighing about 3 tons, to simulate the foundation or earth carried during the quake. It also provides a facility to enable the equipment under test to be secured to the table.

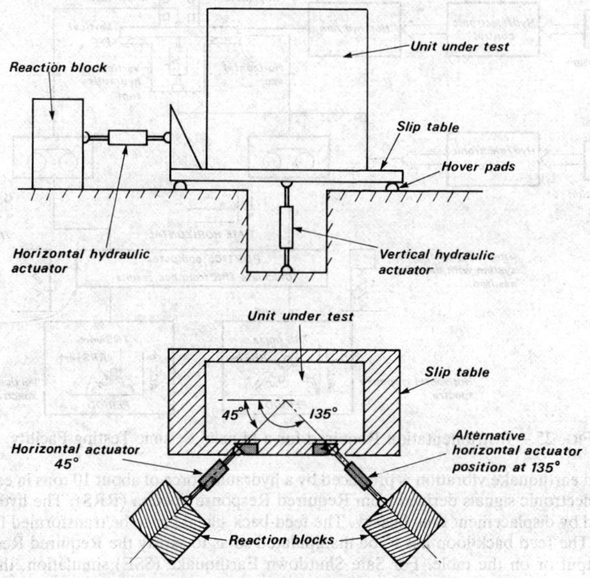

FIG. 24.—Principle of Operation of Bi-axial Seismic Test Rig.

Four air inflated hover pads, designed to carry 2½ tons each, provide foundation stiffness and ground resonance if required, and also provide a de-coupling effect to prevent the force applied to the table from being transmitted to the supporting structure. Four linear bearings, vertical and horizontal guide bearings, are provided to prevent the table wandering out of place.

The earthquake forcing function is provided in two directions by two 10-ton hydraulic actuators. Each may be controlled separately by two electronic systems to provide static and dynamic force of 10 tons, controlled by electronic control equipment. Two ranges of frequencies are provided by two sets of actuators. 1 to 5 Hz frequency range has a maximum of ±3 inch stroke, 1 to 100 Hz frequency range has a maximum of ±1 inch stroke.

Normally force is applied in two horizontal directions and one vertical direction for seismic testing by mounting the equipment at an angle of 45° to the axis of horizontal force, which is equivalent to resolving vectorily two horizontal directions into one force. A second test is carried out with the equipment turned to 90° from the original setting. Thus a three-axis seismic test can be carried out on a bi-axial table.

INSTRUMENTATION TO SIMULATE EARTHQUAKE.—There are many ways in which an input to the hydraulic actuator can be provided. The output will be modified by the system resonances, and phase lag which are invariably different from the input.

A technique, developed for the high intensity acoustic test facility (spectrum shaping technique Fig. 25) is used. Two random noise generators and a 1/3 octave band variable gain filter are used for horizontal and vertical directions independently. Most of these instruments will not give reliable results below a frequency of 3 Hz. To overcome this problem, a tape recorder is used to record the synthesized signal at high frequency and using the speed change mechanism to slow it down by 32 times to provide a signal proportional to displacement time history of an earthquake in the low frequency range, of say, 1–35 Hz (Fig. 25). The variable gain 1/3 O.B. filter allows the forces in a certain frequency range to be increased or decreased if the output is low or high in these frequencies, as measured by an accelerometer on the table.

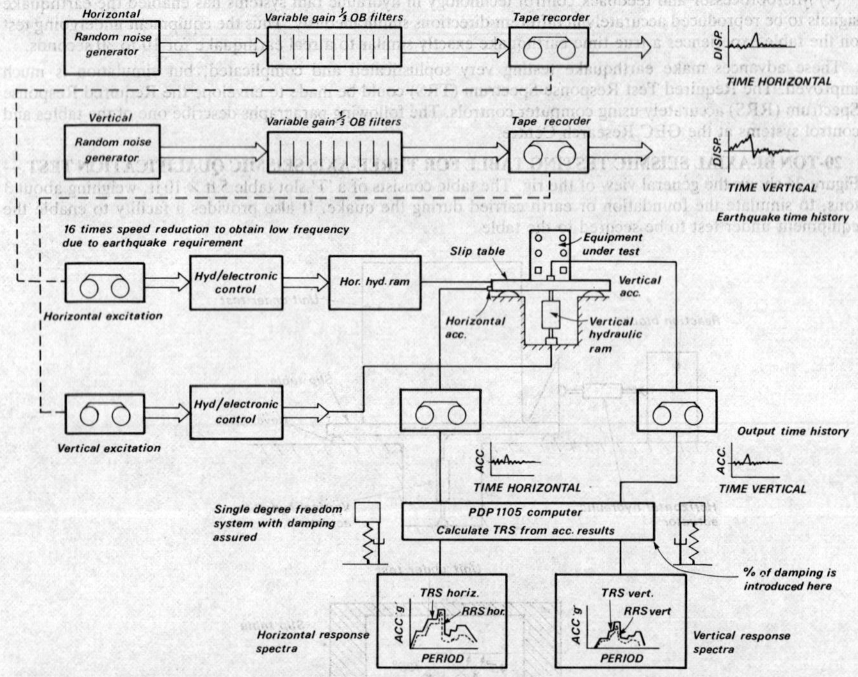

FIG. 25.—Instrumentation Required for a bi-axial Seismic Testing Facility.

The synthesised earthquake vibration is produced by a hydraulic force of about 10 tons in each direction and is controlled by electronic signals derived from Required Response Spectra (RRS). The hydraulic piston can only be controlled by displacement time history. The feed-back signal has to be transformed from acceleration to displacement. The feed-back loop has to be manipulated so as to satisfy the Required Response Spectrum (RRS) at the output or on the table. For Safe Shutdown Earthquake (SSE) simulation, the acceleration is about twice that of Design Basis Earthquake (DBE). The output is measured by accelerometers in horizontal and vertical planes. The results in acceleration v time are recorded in both directions and are fed back to a computer, where they are digitized, a Duhamel integration (Ref. 3) of the time history of acceleration is performed and the damping values introduced. A method of deriving the Test Response Spectra, TRS from the tape recording of table acceleration is given in Appendix II.

The results are then presented as test response spectra in acceleration 'g' plotted against frequency (or period) for 1% or 5% damping, which may be compared with the RRS. A typical computer printout is shown in Fig. 28, which shows that the TRS completely envelopes the RRS.

DERIVATION OF RRS TESTING LEVELS FROM DRS.—A typical Design Response Spectrum (DRS) for horizontal and vertical directions at all levels in the Reactor Island is given, Figs. 26 and 27. These represent the Design Basis Earthquake (DBE) values. The testing levels (RRS) are derived as follows:

Horizontal Safe Shutdown Earthquake RRS = 2 × 1·2 × DBE for 45° bi-axial tests = 2·4 DBE.

The value of 2 is required to obtain the SSE levels from DBE values.

The value of 1·2 is derived by increasing the random response acceleration in Fig. 26 by a factor of 20%. This represents the statistical mean value between—

(i) The vectorical addition of the RRS for the horizontal direction shown in Fig. 26, to the same RRS applied to the mutually perpendicular horizontal direction.

(ii) The RRS for any (one) horizontal direction shown Fig. 26 (Ref. 70).

$$\text{i.e. Factor} = \frac{(\sqrt{x^2 + x^2} + x}{2} = 1{\cdot}2x \qquad (30)$$

The vertical RRS for bi-axial testing adjusted to the SSE levels are given by the equation:

Vertical Safe Shutdown Earthquake = RRS = 2 × DBE for bi-axial tests.

The synthesised earthquake vibration has to satisfy the required response spectrum RRS at the output or on the table. This may include the floor response of the building. For SSE simulation, the acceleration is about twice that of a design basis earthquake (DBE) (Ref. 4). The output is measured by accelerometers on the table in horizontal and vertical planes. The results in Acceleration v Time is again recorded on tape in both directions. These are then fed back to a computer, where the information is digitized, a Duhamel integration of the time history of acceleration is performed and the damping values are introduced. Computer Program PRM 421, Appendix II.

The results are then presented as test response spectra (TRS) in acceleration 'g' plotted against frequency or period for 1% or 5% damping, which may be compared with the RRS. A typical computer print-out is shown Fig. 28 and Table 13, which shows that the TRS (top curve) completely envelops the RRS (lower curve).

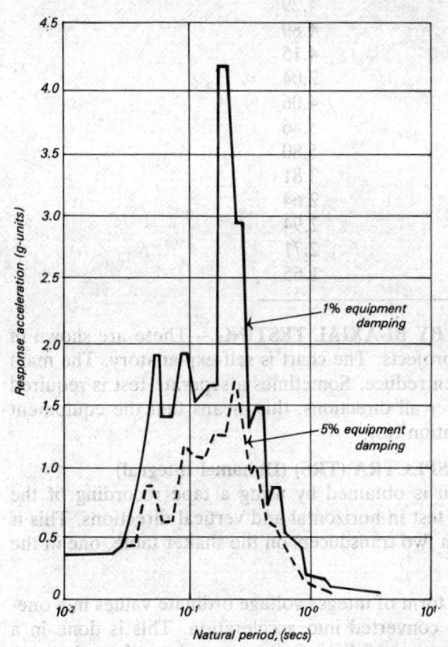

FIG. 26.—Horizontal Design Response Spectra for Control and Instrumentation Equipment at all Levels in the Reactor Island. Ground Acceleration = 0·125 g.

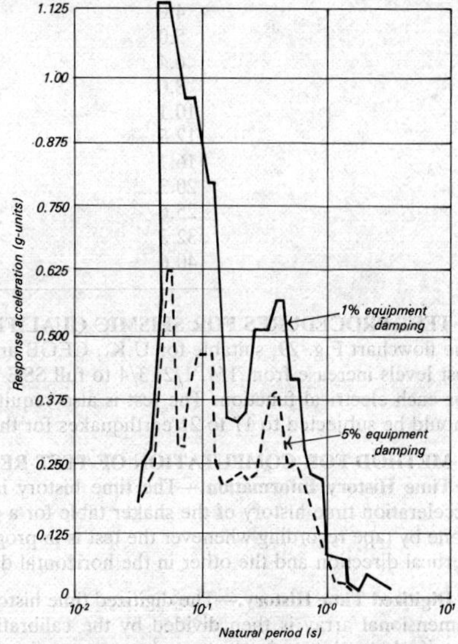

FIG. 27.—Vertical Design Response Spectra for Control and Instrumentation Equipment at all Levels in the Reactor Island. Ground Acceleration = 0·0833 g.

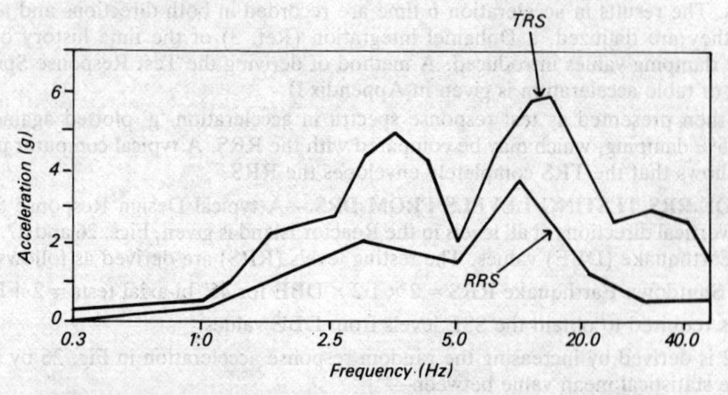

FIG. 28.—Results of Simulated Earthquake, with Recording Instrument Supported on Seismic Table, for Essential Supplies Building at 9m Level. Curves show Seismic Test Response Spectrum with 1% Damping; note TRS Curve Envelopes the RRS.

TABLE 13.—TYPICAL COMPUTER PRINT-OUT OF RRS AND TRS FOR SIMULATED EARTHQUAKE VIBRATION (SEE FIG. 28 FOR CURVES)

FREO	RRS	TRS
0.3	0.05	0.22
0.5	0.08	0.27
0.6	0.08	0.31
0.8	0.20	0.34
1.0	0.31	0.54
1.2	0.75	1.16
1.6	1.13	2.22
2.0	1.5	2.53
2.5	1.76	2.64
3.2	2.06	4.29
4.0	1.89	4.89
5.0	1.62	4.15
6.4	1.64	2.04
8.0	2.83	4.06
10.1	3.78	5.46
12.8	2.63	5.80
16.1	1.38	3.81
20.3	1.00	2.64
25.6	0.63	2.94
32.2	0.52	2.71
40.6	0.52	1.65

TEST PROCEDURES FOR SEISMIC QUALIFICATION BY BI-AXIAL TESTING.—These are shown in the flowchart Fig. 29, suitable for U.K., CEGB and SSEB projects. The chart is self-explanatory. The main test levels increase from 1/4, 1/2, 3/4 to full SSE levels, then reduce. Sometimes a separate test is required for each electrical function. The test is also required to cover all directions; this means that the equipment should be subjected to 17 to 21 earthquakes for the qualification test.

METHOD FOR COMPUTATION OF TEST RESPONSE SPECTRA (TRS) (Duhamel Integral)

Time History Information.—The time history information is obtained by using a tape recording of the acceleration time history of the shaker table for a particular test in horizontal and vertical directions. This is done by tape recording whenever the test is in progress, from two transducers on the shaker table, one in the vertical direction and the other in the horizontal direction.

Digitized Time History.—The digitized time history, in the form of integer voltage ordinate values in a one-dimensional array is then divided by the calibration factor converted into acceleration. This is done in a specified time interval, which produces a one-dimensional array, consisting of alternate values of acceleration and time. This is used as input of the forcing function for Duhamel integral, Fig. 30.

Numerical Solution of Single Degree Damped System.—A numerical solution for response was used (Ref. 27), pp 129–143 *Vibration Problems in Engineering*, 4th edition, by S. P. Timoshenko, P. H. Young and

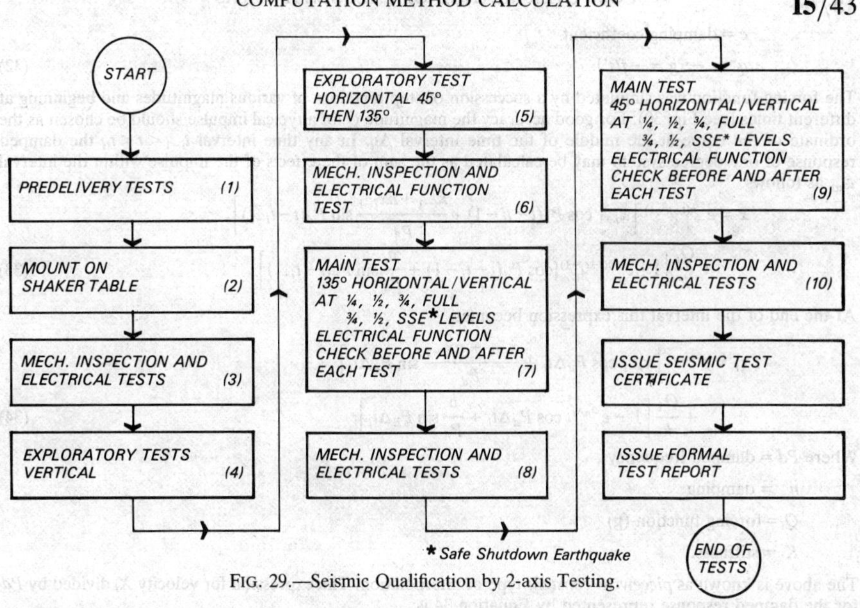

FIG. 29.—Seismic Qualification by 2-axis Testing.

W. Weaver Junior. The method assumes the system is a single degree damping spring and mass system with forcing function proportional to acceleration time history Fig. 30 (Ref. 27).

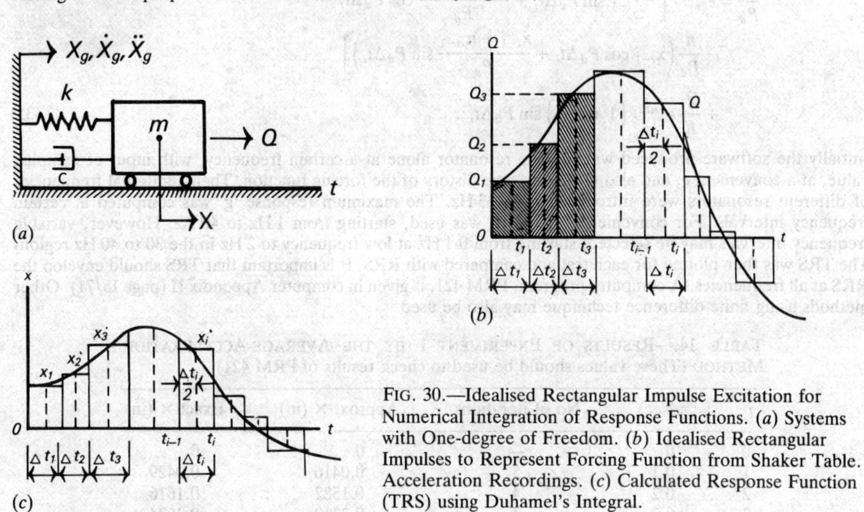

FIG. 30.—Idealised Rectangular Impulse Excitation for Numerical Integration of Response Functions. (*a*) Systems with One-degree of Freedom. (*b*) Idealised Rectangular Impulses to Represent Forcing Function from Shaker Table. Acceleration Recordings. (*c*) Calculated Response Function (TRS) using Duhamel's Integral.

Damped response of mass relative to ground is:

$$x^* = \frac{e^{-nt}}{P_d}\int_0^t ent' \times q_q \sin P_d(t - t')\, dt' \tag{31}$$

x^* = relative displacement of mass, ω = natural frequency

$$\eta = \frac{c}{2m} = \frac{\gamma m\omega}{2m} = \frac{\gamma\omega}{2}. \text{ Where } m = \text{critical damping ratio}$$

$$\gamma = 2\eta;\ \eta = \text{loss factor} = \frac{c}{\sqrt{mk}}$$

c = damping coefficient

$$q^* = -\ddot{x}g = -f(t') \tag{32}$$

The forcing function was simulated by a succession of step functions of various magnitudes and beginning at different times (see Fig. 30). For good accuracy the magnitude Q_i of a typical impulse should be chosen as the ordinate of the curve at the middle of the time interval Δt_i. In any time interval $t_{i-1} < t < t_i$, the damped response of one degree system may be calculated as the sum of the effects of the impulse within the interval Δ_{ti}, as follows:

$$x = e^{-n(t-ti-1)}\left[x_{i-1}\cos P_d(t-ti-1) + \frac{\dot{x}_{i-1}+nx_{i-1}}{p_d}\sin P_d(t-t_{i-1})\right]$$
$$+\frac{Q_i}{k}\left\{1-e^{-n(t-t_i-1)}[\cos P_d(t-t_i-1)+\frac{n}{P_d}\sin P_d(t-t_{i-1})\right] \tag{33}$$

At the end of the interval this expression becomes:

$$x_i = e^{-n\Delta t_i}\left[x_{i-1}\cos P_d\Delta t_i + \frac{\dot{x}_{i-1}+nx_{i-1}}{P_d}\sin P_d\Delta t_i\right]$$
$$+\frac{Q_1}{k}\left[1-e^{-n\Delta t_i}\cos P_d\Delta t_i + \frac{n}{P_d}\sin P_d\Delta t_i\right] \tag{34}$$

Where Pd = damped frequency

n = damping

Q_i = forcing function (g)

K = stiffness.

The above is known as *piecewise–constant* type of interpolation. The expression for velocity X_i divided by Pd for the damped response represented by Equation 34 is:

$$\frac{\dot{x}_i}{P_d} = e^{-n\Delta t_i}\left[-x_{i-1}\sin P_d\Delta t_i + \frac{\dot{x}_{i-1}+n_{xi-1}}{P_d}\cos P_d\Delta t_i\right.$$
$$\left.-\frac{n}{P_d}\left(x_{i-1}\cos P_d\Delta t_i + \frac{\dot{x}_{i-1}+n_{xi-1}}{P_d}\sin P_d\Delta t_i\right)\right]$$
$$+\frac{Q_i}{K}e^{-n\Delta t_i}\left(1+\frac{n^2}{P_d{}^2}\right)\sin P_d\Delta t_i \tag{35}$$

Initially the software produced was for one resonator alone at a certain frequency, with input of damping value, at a convenient t_i, and also Q_i/K, the time history of the forcing function. Then additional frequencies of different resonators were introduced by 1–33 Hz. The maximum response 'g' was computed at certain frequency intervals. For convenience 1/3 O.B. was used, starting from 1 Hz to 40 Hz. However, variable frequency intervals may be selected, starting from 0·1 Hz at low frequency to 2 Hz in the 30 to 40 Hz region. The TRS was then plotted for each test and compared with RRS. It is important that TRS should envelop the RRS at all frequencies. A computer program, PRM 421, is given in computer Appendix II (page I5/71). Other methods using finite difference technique may also be used.

TABLE 14.—RESULTS OF EXPERIMENT 1 BY THE AVERAGE-ACCELERATION METHOD (These values should be used to check results of PRM 421)

i	t_i (sec)	No of iterations	Approx. × (in)	Exact × (in)
0	0	—	0	0
1	0.1	5	0.0416	0.0429
2	0.2	4	0.1582	0.1616
3	0.3	4	0.3319	0.3374
4	0.4	3	0.5419	0.5491
5	0.5	3	0.7667	0.7748
6	0.6	3	0.9860	0.9939
7	0.7	3	1.1821	1.1888
8	0.8	3	1.3413	1.3458
9	0.9	3	1.4545	1.4559
10	1.0	3	1.5173	1.5151
11	1.1	3	1.5302	1.5243
12	1.2	3	1.4975	1.4884
13	1.3	3	1.4271	1.4154

TABLE 14.—(*Continued*)

i	t_i (sec)	No of iterations	Approx. × (in)	Exact × (in)
14	1.4	3	1.3289	1.3156
15	1.5	2	1.2143	1.2006
16	1.6	3	1.0946	1.0817
17	1.7	3	0.9803	0.9694
18	1.8	3	0.8803	0.8724
19	1.9	3	0.8014	0.7970
20	2.0	3	0.7477	0.7473

NEW APPROACHES TO THE SEISMIC QUALIFICATION OF CLASS I.E.1 EQUIPMENT USING LOW LEVEL IMPEDANCE TESTING.—A Mechanical Impedance Model may be derived from low level impedance testing of full scale equipment on site, when the equipment is too large for full scale tests on the seismic table.

An advanced approach using test data at low level impedance tests to develop a mathematical model called, *Mechanical Impedance Modelling,* has been developed (Refs 71–76) to represent the full equation of motion of a real system. This approach has been used successfully in the aerospace and automobile industries, where complex structures would be costly to calculate by finite element modelling. Briefly, the system is represented by a series of single-degree of freedom damped equations. These single-degree damped systems are derived from the response curve of the full scale response testing by a technique of curve fitting of the frequency response curve. This eventually provides a small number of single-degree damped equations for a complex system in the seismic frequency range (1–33 Hz).

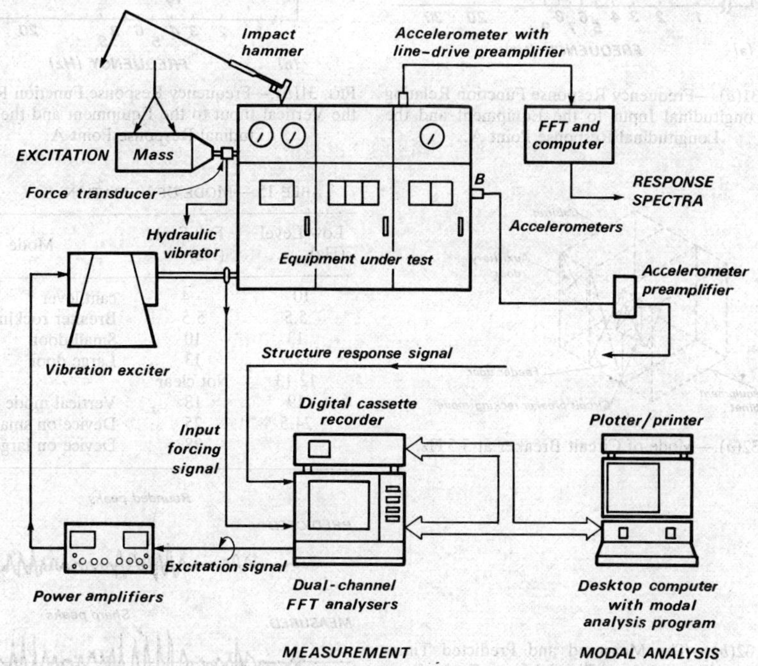

FIG. 31.—General Set-up for Low Level Impedance Test.

In mechanical impedance testing, an input force is applied at one point of the structure, and a response is measured by an accelerometer at another location. Sine sweep or random excitation is used. The results are recorded on a tape recorder; a typical test configuration is shown in Fig. 31.

A hydraulic force exciter, electro-mechanical exciter, or impedance hammer may be used to provide the excitation force. A load cell on the exciter is used to measure the applied force and an accelerometer will give the response at 30 to 40 key points. A digital Fourier analyser is used to analyse the input/output signals; the ratio of these transformed signals being the frequency response of the system (see Figs 31a and b). The frequency responses at all 40 points are plotted in curves similar to those in Figure 31a, with longitudinal input to the equipment and longitudinal response at point A. Figure 31b shows vertical input to the equipment and the longitudinal response at a point A. In addition, the phase relationship between the input and the response motions are plotted. The natural frequencies of the equipment are indicated by peaks in the frequency responses. Corresponding with each natural frequency, there is a mode of vibration in which all points of a structure vibrate at the same frequency. Modes of vibration of the equipment may be obtained for any frequency by comparing the amplitude and phase relationship of motion at the selected points. Figure 32 shows a mode of vibration of the equipment at frequency of 5·5 Hz (Ref. 73). Figure 32a shows the measured and predicted time history at point A. Good agreements can be seen.

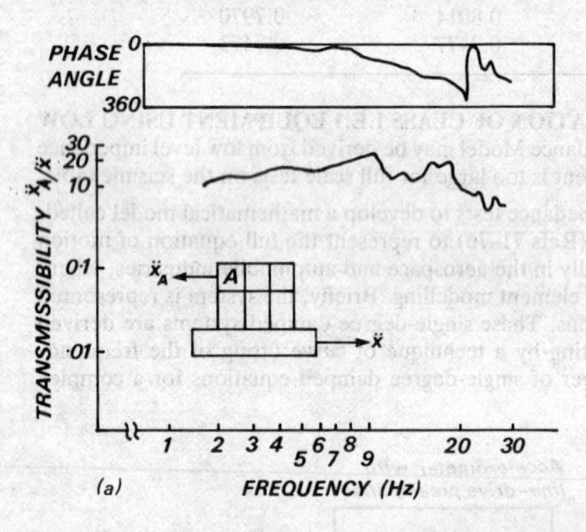

FIG. 31(*a*).—Frequency Response Function Relating the Longitudinal Input to the Equipment and the Longitudinal Response Point A.

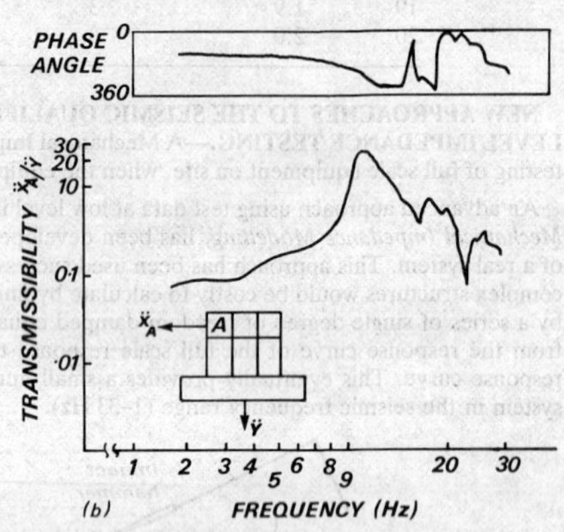

FIG. 31(*b*).—Frequency Response Function Relating the Vertical Input to the Equipment and the Longitudinal Response Point A.

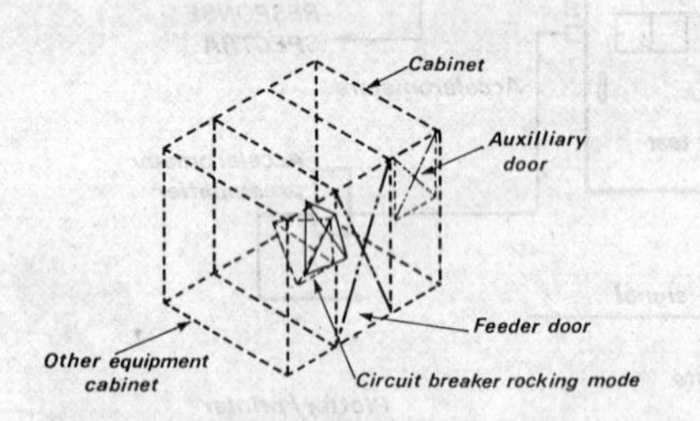

FIG. 32(*a*).—Mode of Circuit Breaker at 5.5 Hz.

TABLE 15.—MODE OF VIBRATION

Low Level (Hz)	Full Scale (Hz)	Mode
10	4	cantilever
5.5	5.5	Breaker rocking
13	10	Small door
12.7	13	Large door
12.13	Not clear	
19	18	Vertical mode
24.5	25	Device on small door
	28	Device on large door

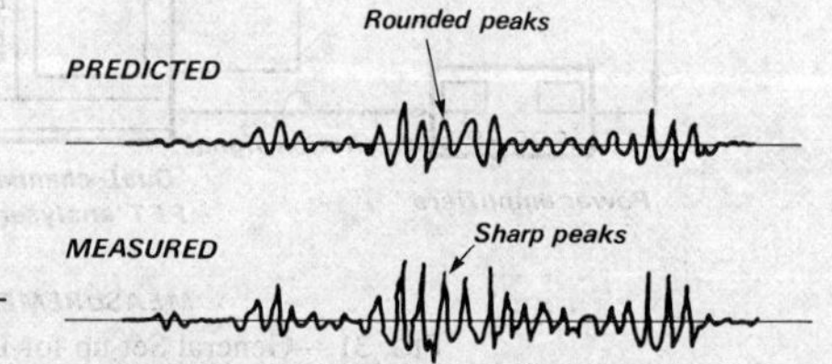

FIG. 32(*b*).—The Measured and Predicted Time-history at Point A for a Bi-axial Input Excitation.

Modal Analysis of a Low Impedance Model (Ref. 77 to 79).—In modal analysis, the measured data is further processed to extract the *Modal Parameters* of the structure under test. The parameters are—

(1) The *Modal Frequencies*, that is the resonant or natural frequency of the structure.

(2) The *Modal Damping*, which is a measure of the sharpness of the resonance at various modal frequencies.

(3) The *Mode Shapes*, that is, the relative deflection shapes that the structure will assume at its various natural frequencies assuming free vibration.

Using these Modal Parameters, the *low impedance model* of the structure under test is constructed and a computer model may be established. Modal analysis is performed by a curve fitting technique using a desk-top computer equipped with an appropriate software program.

Mechanical impedance data can be thought of as a graphical representation of the differential equations of motion of the structure and, as such, it contains mass, stiffness and damping associated with each mode of vibration.

Seismic Qualification using Mechanical Impedance Modelling.—After the modal parameter has been obtained from the real system, it is necessary to apply the seismic forcing function, in the form of time history or response spectrum, to the computer model and check with full-scale stresses at all locations (Figs 31a and 31b), in order to qualify the structure for seismic acceptance (Ref. 73). Having proved that the low impedance tests would predict the full scale testing time history, with acceleration within about 15% for 30 seconds at the mounting location 'A'; this can be used as input RRS to qualify appendages, such as relays, mounted at that location, by separate figure testing, or may be used to identify appendage resonances on large structures (Ref. 73).

COMBINING AMPLITUDE OF RESPONSES OF VARIOUS MODES FOR CALCULATION AND TESTING.—So far we have postulated that a number of modes at various different frequencies could exist simultaneously at any location. Methods are presented here, which are commonly used with a view to combining these, so that a maximum value can be obtained during vibration (Refs 80 and 81):

(1) Combining the values of the response of individual modes in a response spectrum modal dynamic analysis to find the representative maximum value of a particular response of interest, for the design of a given element of a nuclear power plant structure, system, or component.

(2) Combining the maximum values (in the case of time-history dynamic analysis) or the representative maximum values (in the case of spectrum dynamic analysis) of the response of a given element of a structure, system, or component, when such values are calculated independently for each of the three orthogonal spatial components (two horizontal and one vertical) of an earthquake. The combined value will be the representative maximum value of the combined response of that element of the structure, system, or component, to simultaneous action of the three spatials.

Combination of Modal Responses

(1) WITH NO CLOSELY SPACED MODES.—In a response spectrum modal dynamic analysis, if the modes are not closely spaced (two consecutive modes are defined as closely spaced if their frequencies differ from each other by 10 per cent or less of the lower frequency), the representative maximum value of a particular response of interest for design (e.g. components of stress, strain, moment, shear, or displacement) of a given element of a nuclear power plant structure, system, or component subjected to a single independent spatial component (response spectrum) of a three-component earthquake should be obtained by taking the square root of the sum of the squares (SRSS) of corresponding maximum values of the response of the element attributed to individual significant modes of the structure, system, or component. Mathematically, this can be expressed as follows:

$$R = \left[\sum_{k=1}^{N} R_k^2 \right]^{1/2} \tag{40}$$

where R is the representative maximum value of a particular response of a given element to a given component of an earthquake, R_k is the peak value of the response of the element due to the kth mode, and N is the number of significant modes considered in the modal response combination.

(2) WITH CLOSELY SPACED MODES.—In a response spectrum modal dynamic analysis, if some or all of the modes are closely spaced, any of the following methods may be used to combine the modal responses.

(3) GROUPING METHOD.—Closely spaced modes should be divided into groups that include all modes having frequencies lying between the lowest frequency in the group and a frequency 10 percent higher. (Groups should be formed starting from the lowest frequency and working towards successively higher frequencies. No one frequency is to be in more than one group). (Refs 80 and 81). The representative maximum value of a particular response of interest for the design of a given element of a nuclear power plant structure, system or component attributed to each such group of modes should first be obtained by taking the sum of the absolute values of the corresponding peak values of the response of the element attributed to individual modes in that group. The representative maximum value of this particular response, attributed to all the significant modes of the structure, system or component, should then be obtained by taking the square root of the sum of the squares of corresponding representative maximum values of the response of the element attributed to each closely spaced group of modes and the remaining modal response for the modes that are not closely spaced.

Mathematically, this can be expressed as follows:

$$R = \left[\sum_{k=1}^{N} R_k^2 + \sum_{q=1}^{P} \sum_{l=i}^{j} \sum_{m=i}^{j} |R_{lq} \cdot R_{mq}| \right]^{1/2} \quad l \neq m \tag{41}$$

where R_{lq} and R_{mq} are modal responses, R_l and R_m within the qth group, respectively; 'i' is the number of the mode where a group starts; 'j' is the number of the mode where a group ends; and 'P' is the number of groups of closely spaced modes, excluding individual separated modes. Other methods, such as the ten per cent method (Refs 80 and 81) and the double sum method may also be used.

Combination of Effects Due to Three Spatial Components of an Earthquake.—Depending on which basic method is used in the seismic analysis, i.e. response spectra or time-history method, the following two approaches are considered acceptable for the combination of three-dimensional earthquake effects.

(1) RESPONSE SPECTRA METHOD.—When the response spectra method is adopted for seismic analysis, the representative maximum values of the structural responses to each of the three components of earthquake motion should be combined by taking the square root of the sum of the squares of the maximum representative values of the co-directional responses caused by each of the three components of earthquake motion at a particular point of the structure or of the mathematical model.

(2) TIME-HISTORY ANALYSIS METHOD.—When the time-history analysis method is employed for seismic analysis, two types of analysis are generally performed depending on the complexity of the problem:

(a) When the maximum responses due to each of the three components of the earthquake motion are calculated separately, the method for combining the three-dimensional effects is identical to that described in (1) except that the maximum responses are calculated using the time-history method instead of the spectrum method.

(b) When the time-history responses from each of the three components of the earthquake motion are calculated by the step-by-step method and combined algebraically at each time step, the maximum response can be obtained from the combined time solution. When this method is used, the earthquake motions specified in the three different directions should be statistically independent. The methods described so far are safe methods for design purposes. In practice, during the testing, the effect of phase of the vibration is automatically taken into account. Thus test vibration amplitude is always less than that given by the methods of combination of modes and directions described in this chapter.

MODERN FINITE ELEMENT CALCULATION (Ref. 86)

A number of well-tried computer software packages dealing with finite element calculations are available to the designer. As many man years of research and editing are involved they are very expensive. They may be obtained from computer bureaux or from the computer centres of companies, such as ANSYS†, MARC-CDC, NASTRAN, SAP, STARDYNE, etc. A brief outline of these programs is given in Table 16. A number of them are suitable for seismic analysis. For some examples of this type of calculation see Refs 48 and 82.

To confirm the credibility of these calculations IEEE regulations require all calculations to be supported by tests to demonstrate suitability for seismic qualification†. The following examples demonstrates that the computed frequency can be tuned to agree with experimental values by repeated changes of boundary conditions of the structure in the computer programming until the modal frequencies are agreed. The computer model then agrees with the real structure. Once credibility is established, the calculation can be used to qualify the structure seismically to an established criterion of acceptance. These tasks can be carried out on site or with unequal scale models. Sine sweep or random or impact tests can be used.

EXAMPLE.—A piece of electrical equipment has been tested for seismic qualification, Fig. 33. It is a wall mounted starter, consisting of a cubicle mounted on a channel and angle section frame which is fixed to the ground. The cubicle contains a transformer, a relay box, an isolator, an overload trip, electro-magnetic controllers and fuse boxes (see Figs 33 and 33a).

The calculations should also yield answers to the following questions—

(1) With the known input spectra, i.e. TRS measured on a table as computer input spectra for a three dimensional seismic calculation, what frequency agreement can be obtained in the locations of 10 accelerometers during the exploratory tests (Fig. 36).

(2) What agreement can be obtained in acceleration in 'g' value on the instruments mounted inside the

† ANSYS.—This programme was judged to be the most suitable for the finite element exploration reported in this chapter (Ref. 83). The brief details are—

Capability.—Static and dynamic linear and nonlinear structural analysis and heat transfer analysis. Program has plasticity, creep, and large displacement and rotation capability.

Method.—Finite element displacement method. Program uses the incremental method of solution accounting for plasticity with isotropic and kinematic hardening. Program uses the wave-front method coupled with an explicit time integration scheme for the solution of the nonlinear equations of motion. Eigenvalues are extracted via Jacobi iteration with Guyan reduction.

Language.—FORTRAN. Hardware.—Program runs on CDC, IBM, and UNIVAC machines. Usage.—Program has been used in the nuclear industry and indications of its reliability are available. Developed by.—Swanson Analysis Systems, Inc., 870 Pine View Drive, Elizabeth, PA 15037.

TABLE 16.—GENERAL INFORMATION ON FINITE ELEMENT COMPUTER SOFTWARE

Features	Program*				
	ANSYS	MARC	NASTRAN	SAP	STARDYNE
Straight beam, straight pipe, solid and flat plate elements	X	X	X	X	X
Axisymmetric elements	X	X	X	X	O
Curved beam/curved pipe elements	O/X	X/X	O/O	O/X	O/X
Curved shell elements	O	X	O	O	O
Inviscid fluid element	O	O	X	O	O
Bucking analysis	O	X	X	O	O
Shock spectra	X	O	O	X	X
Mesh generation	Yes	Yes	Yes	Some	Some
Nonlinear analysis	Extensive	Extensive	Limited	Limited†	None
Pages in manual describing elements, input and output (approximate)	830	820	980	130	560
Proprietary/public	Prop.	Prop.	Public	Public	Prop.
Availability‡	CDC, W, D	CDC, D	CDC, W	CDC, D	CDC

* X = program has this capability; O = program lacks this capability.

† Nonlinear capability in MODSAP version.

‡ CDC = Control Data Corporation Cybernet; W = Westinghouse Telecomputer Center, Pittsburgh, PA: D = developer (see text).

cubicle, at the accelerometer locations between the calculated and tested values and how close are the corresponding frequencies?

(3) What maximum stresses will be given by the calculation, and what percentage of damping should be used to simulate real-life conditions, so that a realistic computer qualification based on actual material strength is obtained?

(4) What will be the effect on mode of vibration frequencies, amplitude and stress by joining together two or three cubicles?

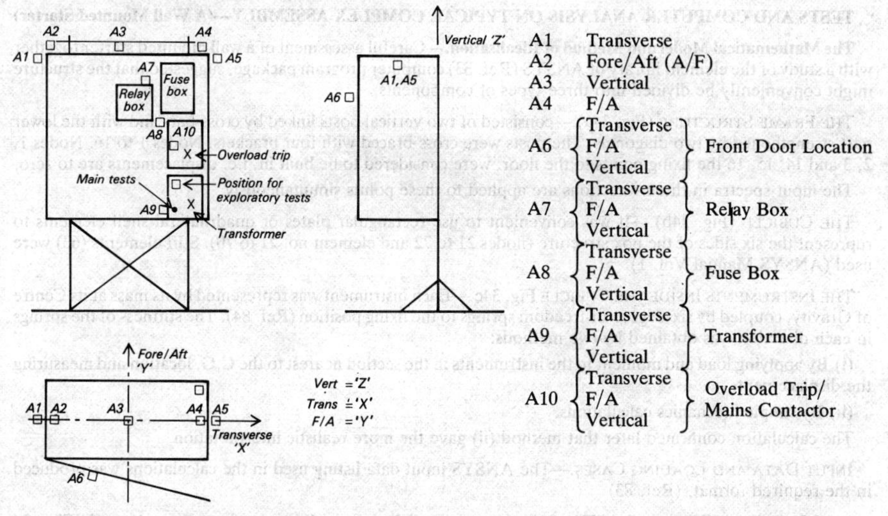

FIG. 33.—Location of Accelerometers (A1 to A10) for a Wall-mounted Electrical Starter Equipment During Seismic Tests.

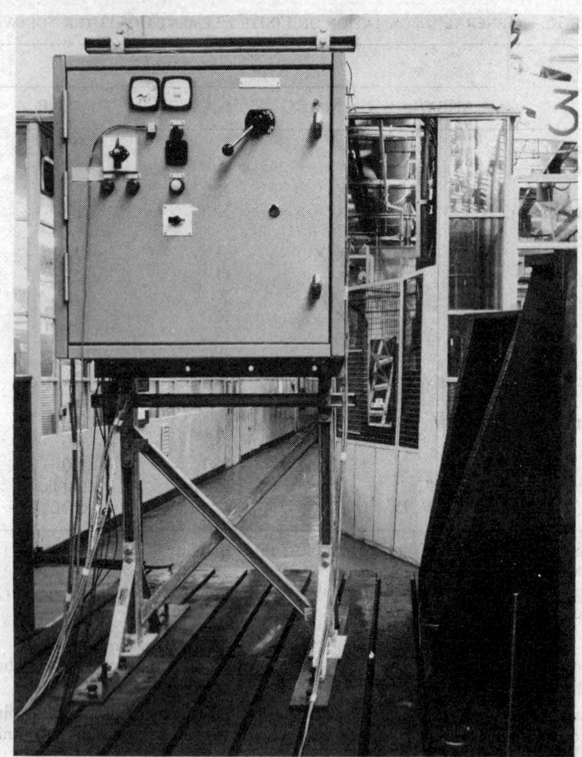

FIG. 33(*a*).—Wall-mounted Starter on Seismic Table in Readiness for Seismic Qualification Test for CEGB Heysham Nuclear Power Station.

TESTS AND COMPUTER ANALYSIS ON TYPICAL COMPLEX ASSEMBLY—(A Wall Mounted Starter)

The Mathematical Model and Method of Idealisation.—Careful assessment of a wall mounted starter together with a study of the element library of ANSYS (Ref. 83) computer program package, suggested that the structure might conveniently be divided into three types of components.

THE FRAME STRUCTURE (Fig. 34a).—consisted of two vertical posts linked by cross-bars and with the lower part strengthened by two diagonals. The posts were cross-braced with four brackets. Nodes 1 to 16. Nodes 1, 2, 3 and 14, 15, 16 the fixing points to the floor, were considered to be built in, i.e. displacements are to zero.

The input spectra in three directions are applied to these points simultaneously.

THE CUBICLE (Fig. 34b).—It was convenient to use rectangular plates or quadrilateral shell elements to represent the six sides of the box structure (nodes 21 to 72 and element no. 21 to 70). Stiff elements (63) were used (ANSYS Manual Vol. 1).

THE INSTRUMENTS INSIDE THE CUBICLE Fig. 34c.—Each instrument was represented by its mass at its Centre of Gravity, coupled by six-degree-of-freedom springs to the fixing position (Ref. 84). The stiffness of the springs in each direction was obtained by two methods:

(i) By applying load and moment to the instruments in the section nearest to the C.G. location and measuring the displacement.

(ii) By simple mechanics calculations.

The calculation confirmed later that method (ii) gave the more realistic interpretation.

INPUT DATA AND LOADING CASES.—The ANSYS input data listing used in the calculations was produced in the required format. (Ref. 83)

(A) METHOD OF COMPUTING.—The finite element model of the wall-mounted starter is shown in Figs. 34 and 35. The node numbers are shown in Fig. 34 (a, b and c).

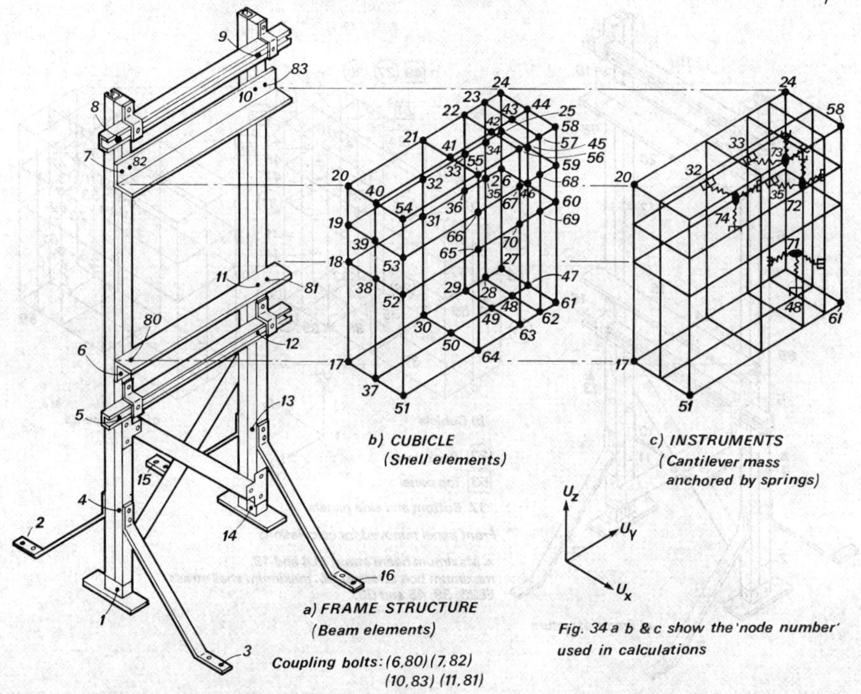

FIG. 34.—Finite Element Model of Wall-mounted Starter Showing the Various Node Numbers Used in Computer Calculations whilst Determining Cubicle Stiffness Values.

The seismic input was applied through the nodes at the base and end of the braces, nodes 1, 2, 3 and 14, 15 and 16.

The vertical and horizontal design input spectra were TRS computed from vertical to horizontal accelerometers on the seismic table during the test in conjunction with Duhamel integral computer software, Fig. 36. These were real input response spectra to the seismic table. The loading spectra at 1% damping, 10% damping and 25% damping, were computed from bi-axial testing of the table, (Ref. 85).

The program calculated natural frequencies, eigenvectors, modal participation factors, modal coefficients, displacement, stress and reaction forces and moments.

(B) LOADING CASES AND INPUT SPECTRA AND METHOD OF ANALYSIS.—The loading steps were carried out in three directions separately, two horizontal and one vertical and input spectra used are given in Fig. 36.

A typical example of participation factors, mode coefficient and mode coefficient ratio are given in the three directions, i.e. 'X' fore-aft direction, 'Y' side-to-side and 'Z' vertical direction. The participation factor (PF) is a measure of how readily a particular mode is excited for a particular direction of disturbance. A typical PF is 1·33 and is related to the modal coefficient by the expression:

$$MC = PF \times \frac{\ddot{a}}{\omega^2} \tag{38}$$

where PF = participation factor

$\ddot{a}$ = acceleration from response spectrum

ω = frequency in rads/sec.

Mode 1 at 5·866 Hz,

PF = 1·133 Mode Coeff. = 2·16 MC Ratio = 1·0

To obtain actual displacements, the eigenvectors were calculated in the frequency analysis and multiplied by the modal coefficient for the appropriate load case and direction (i.e. direction and frequency).

The modal coefficient ratio (MCR) is a ratio obtained by dividing the modal coefficients by the largest MC value. This value provides within ANSYS a means of selecting significant modes of interest for full calculation of results. Typical examples of computer plots are of elements of the wall-mounted starter, Fig. 37 (page I5/52) and vibration modes, Figs. 38(a), (b), (c) and (d).

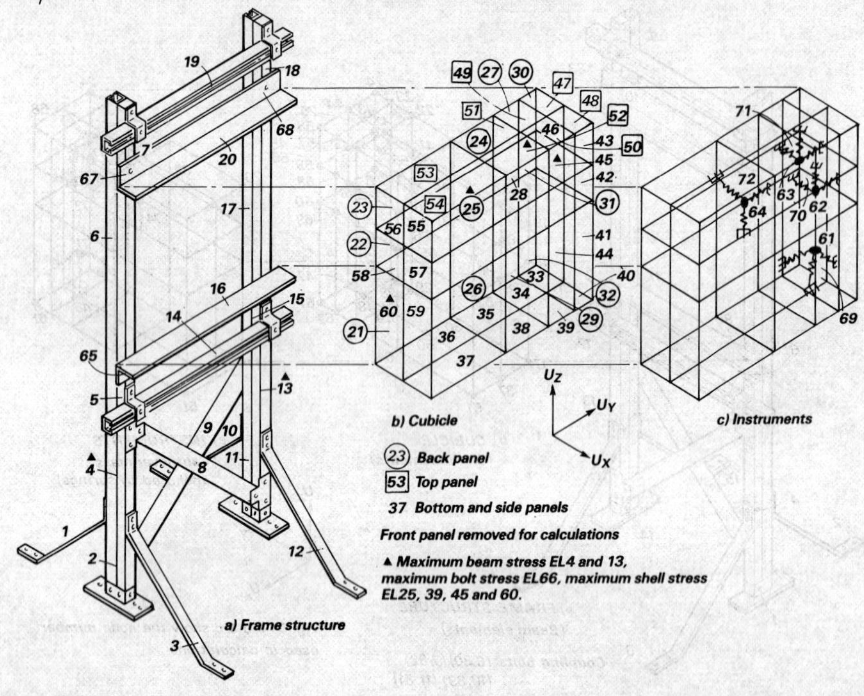

FIG. 35.—For Computer Modelling, the Frame Structure, Starter Cubicle, and the Spring-mass System, Representing the Recording Instruments, are Allocated with Element Numbers.

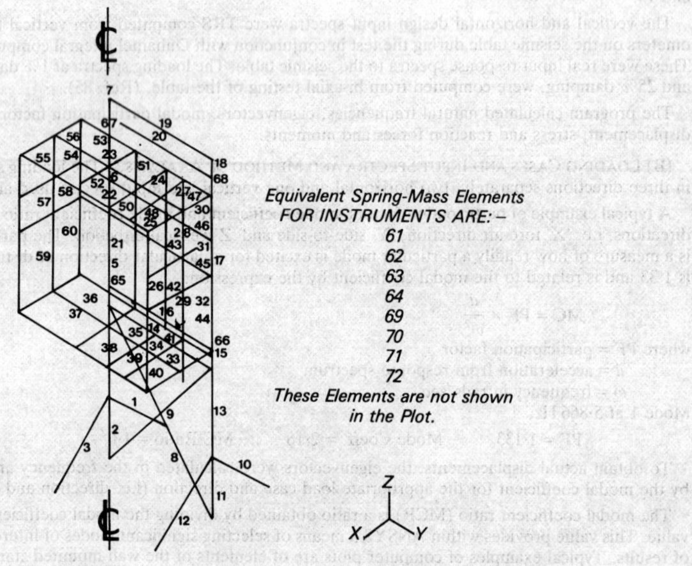

FIG. 37.—Computer Plot of Elements of a Single Wall-mounted Starter.

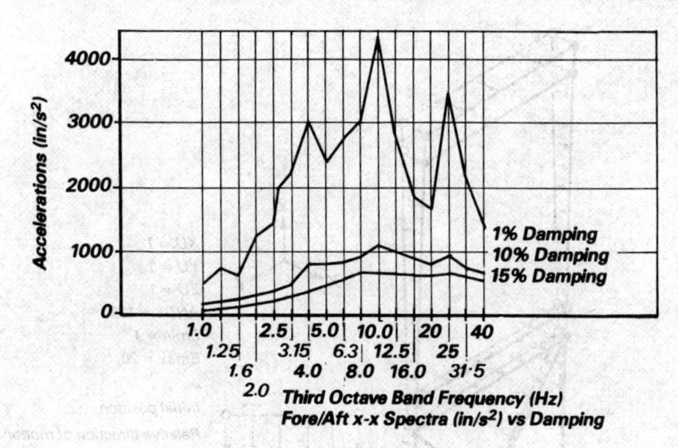

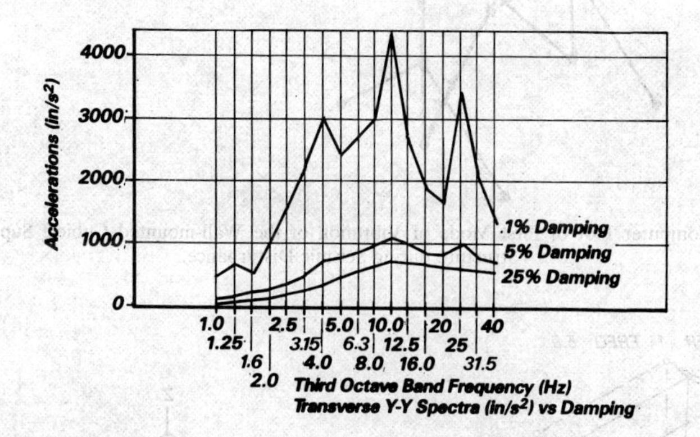

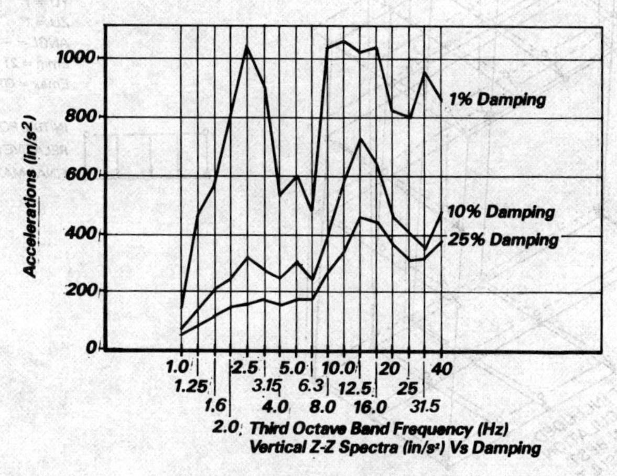

FIG. 36.—Computer Input Response Spectra for 3 Values of Damping Derived from TRS, Measured by Table Accelerometers.

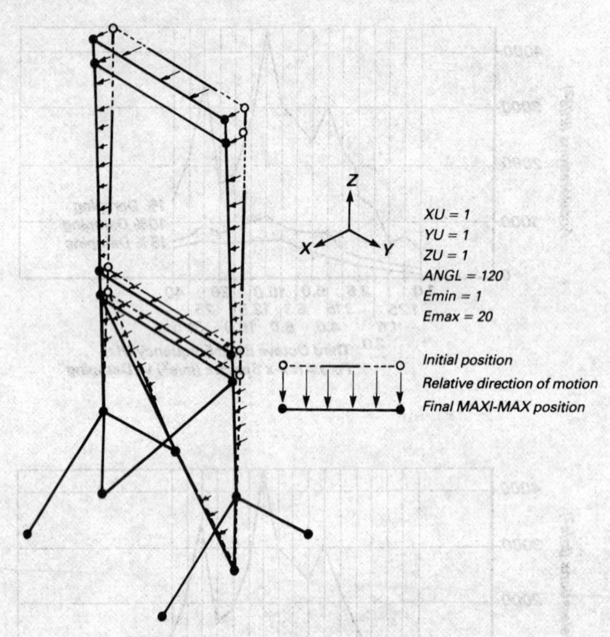

FIG. 38(*a*).—Computer Plot of First Mode of Vibration of the Wall-mounted Cubicle Supporting Frame Structure during Seismic Disturbance.

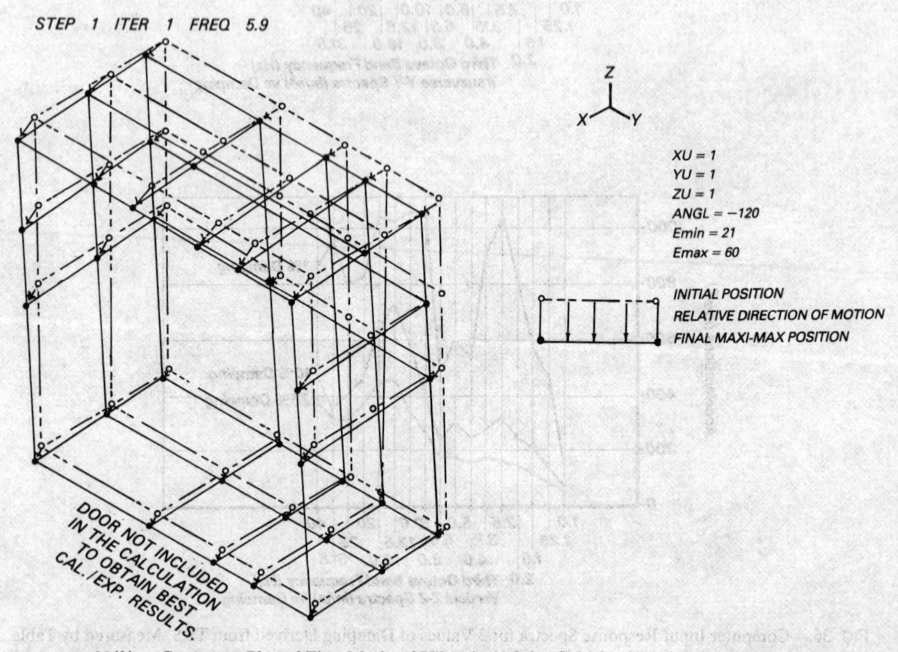

FIG. 38(*b*).—Computer Plot of First Mode of Vibration of the Cubicle, Showing Seismic Response.

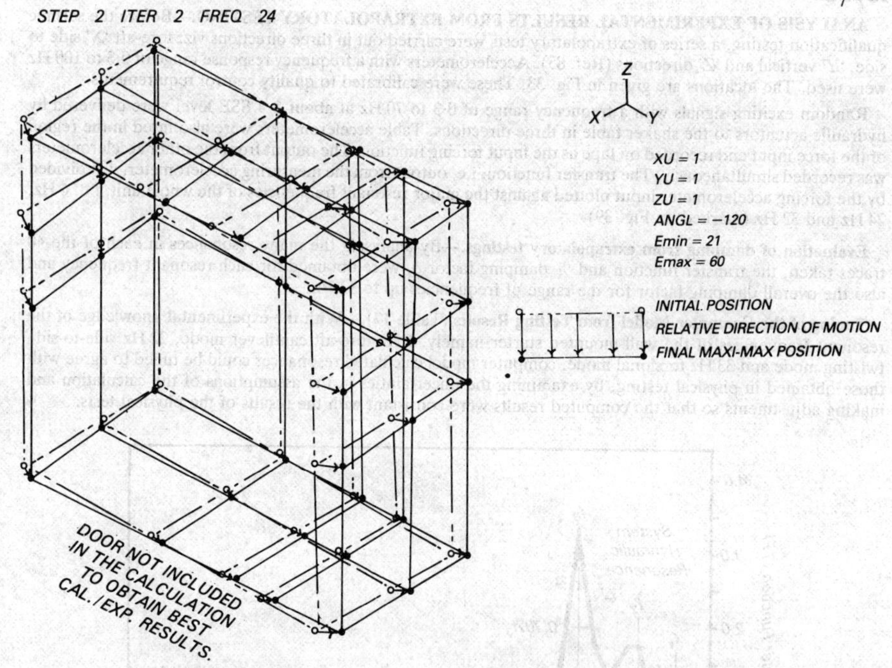

FIG. 38(*c*).—Mode of Vibration of Cubicle at 24 Hz Showing Sideways and Twisting Effects.

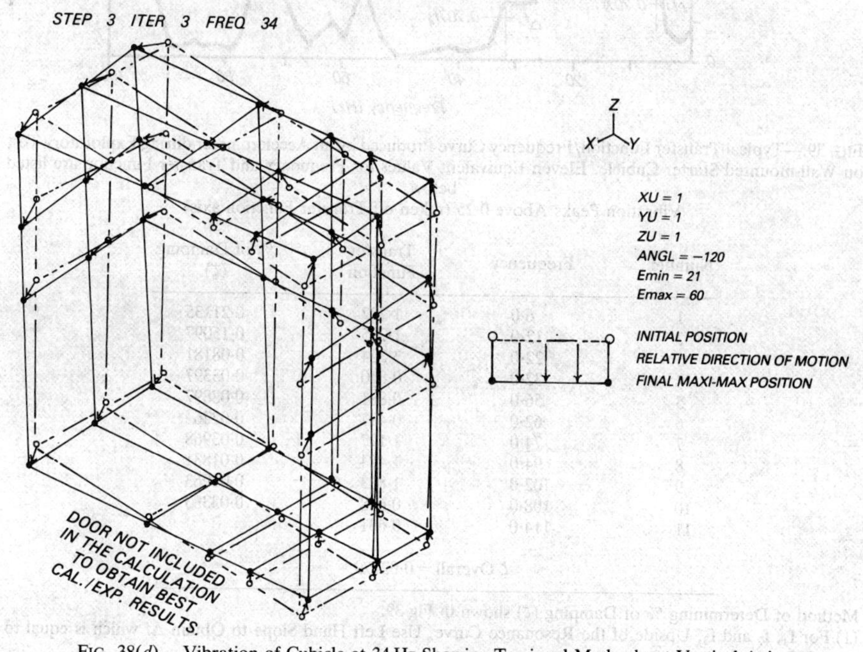

FIG. 38(*d*).—Vibration of Cubicle at 34 Hz Showing Torsional Mode about Vertical Axis.

ANALYSIS OF EXPERIMENTAL RESULTS FROM EXTRAPOLATORY TESTING.—Before the seismic qualification testing, a series of extrapolatory tests were carried out in three directions viz: fore-aft 'X' side to side, 'Y' vertical and 'Z' directions (Ref. 85). Accelerometers with a frequency response range of 0·3 to 100 Hz were used. The locations are given in Fig. 33. These were calibrated to quality control requirements.

Random exciting signals with a frequency range of 0·3 to 70 Hz at about 1/4 SSE level were delivered by hydraulic actuators to the shaker table in three directions. Table accelerometers were also fitted in the region of the force input and recorded on tape as the input forcing function. The output from the other accelerometers was recorded simultaneously. The transfer function, i.e. output from the measuring accelerometer, was divided by the forcing accelerometer input plotted against the major resonant frequencies of the whole unit, i.e. 6 Hz, 24 Hz and 32 Hz (marked on Fig. 39).

Evaluation of damping from extrapolatory testings.—By analysing the many resonances in each of the 40 traces taken, the transfer function and % damping factor δ, were obtained for each resonant frequency and also the overall damping factor for the range of frequencies up to 32 Hz.

Tuning of the Computer Model from Testing Results (Table 17).—With the experimental knowledge of the resonant frequencies of the wall-mounted starter namely, 6 Hz fore-aft cantilever mode, 22 Hz side-to-side twisting mode and 33 Hz torsional mode, computer model calculated resonances could be tuned to agree with those obtained in physical testing, by examining the uncertainties in the assumptions of the calculation and making adjustments so that the computed results were consistant with the results of the physical tests.

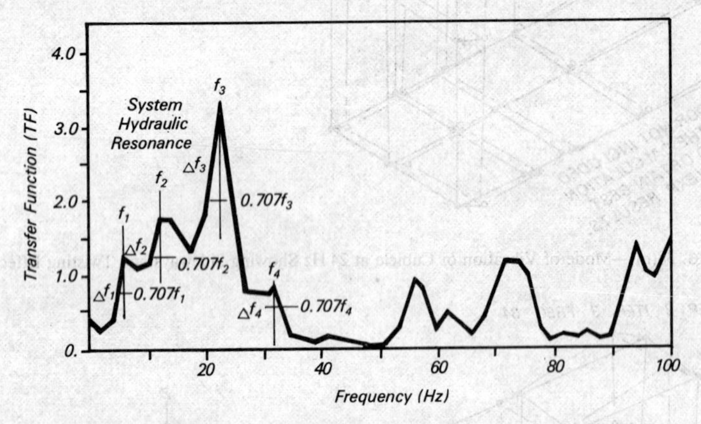

FIG. 39.—Typical Transfer Function/Frequency Curve Produced by an Accelerometer during Exploratory Test on Wall-mounted Starter Cubicle. Eleven Equivalent Values for Frequency and Transfer Function are listed below.

Vibration Peaks Above 0·25 (taken off Transfer Function axis)

Number	Frequency	Transfer Function	% of Damping (ζ)
1	6·0	1·232	0·21135
2	12·0	1·735	0·15097
3	22·0	3·324	0·08181
4	32·0	0·810	0·03397
5	56·0	0·881	0·08897
6	62·0	0·497	0·0226
7	74·0	1·197	0·03968
8	94·0	1·424	0·01831
9	102·0	1·833	0·01963
10	108·0	0·658	0·03383
11	114·0	0·631	

ζ Overall = 0·02479

Method of Determining % of Damping (ζ) shown in Fig 39:

(1) For f_1, f_2 and f_3, Upside of the Resonance Curve, Use Left Hand Slope to Obtain Δf which is equal to $0{\cdot}707 \times f_{peak}$.

(2) For f_4 on Downside of Resonance Curve, Use Right Hand Slope to Obtain Δf which is Equal to $0{\cdot}707 \times f_{peak}$ (as Shown at f_4) and this gives lowest damping value.

(3) % of Damping $= \dfrac{\Delta f}{2f} \times 100$

$$\text{TF} = \text{Transfer Function} = \frac{\text{Acceleration at Output}}{\text{Acceleration at Input}}.$$

TABLE 17.—TUNING OF THE MATHEMATICAL MODEL WALL-MOUNTED STARTER

Key for *Results*: ···· (underlined) main modes, (····) local effects

Run No	*Data*	*Results*
4	Coupled Mass Nodes with stress stiffening	Freq: 6.4, 33.8, (35.9), 47.8
6	STIF27 (high K)	Freq: 6.4, 33.6, (36.4), 49.4, 52
7	STIF27 (low K) UZ removed @ Node 1	Freq: 5.7, 7.5, (18.8), (19.1), (20.8), (28.4), (31.7), (32.9)
8	STIF27 (Low K) Cross beams as spars	Freq: 5.4, (18.0), (19.1), (20.4), (28.3), (28.6), (32.9), (34.2)
9	STIF27 (Low K) Cabinet door removed Cross beams as spars	Freq: 5.5, (18.0), (19.1), (20.4), 25.8, (28.4), (32.9), (34.2)
10	STIF27 (Low K) Cabinet door removed Cross beams as spars Masters at all nodes	Freq: 5.5, (22.1—top of cabinet), 25.5, 40.0
11	STIF27 (High K) Cubicle door removed All cross beams as spars Additional 4 bolts included for cubicle connections	Freq: X–X 5.4, X–Y 16.9, Y–Y 24.2, 35.3 max. displacement at elements 9 and 7 X_9 = 3.1 in at 5.4 Hz Y_9 = 0.15 in at 24.2 Hz
12	STIF27 (High K) No door, all cross beam as beam. Additional 4 bolts	Freq: X–X 5.9, X–Y 23.5, Y–Y 33.6 35.7 max. displ. at elements 9 and 55 X_9 = 2.8 in at (5.9 Hz) X_{55} = 0.14 in at (23.5 Hz)

RESULTS OF COMPUTER CALCULATION‡

Vibration modes.—The natural frequencies of seismic interest include only those below 35 Hz, thus eigenvalue solution of a limited number of modes were determined.

The modal participation factors, modal coefficient (MC) and the MCR, modal coefficient ratios, were printed. If the MC ratio is less than 0·01, the contribution of the mode has no drastic effect on the vibration of the whole system is not printed.

The mode shapes for each frequency and loading cases were printed, as were the displacements at each node and stresses for each element.

‡ Basic information required for computer calculation to meet Earthquake Criterion:

1. Seismic shock input to structure at its foundation is obtained from time-history in the past seismic motion, locally recorded by sensors and tape recorded, and then extrapolated as necessary.
2. All seismic motion in the time domain is broken down into individual frequency components by FFT (Fast Fourier Transfer function) analyser, with computer assistance to obtain resonant frequency and amplitude in the frequency domain.
3. The structural resonances amplify some frequencies and structural damping reduces some frequency components. Resonances and damping are obtained by vibration testing, or computer calculation with assumed damping factors.
4. The computer calculation assumes each frequency component as a single-degree-of-freedom system with damping factors.
5. The results of each frequency component, in the frequency domain, is then summed to give the overall effects in the time domain.

Displacements.—Table 18 shows a typical example of the summary of computed maximum displacements and stresses for single cubicle conditions and 1% damping. Similar tables were produced for 10% and 25% damping.

The SRSS sum of root of squares method is used to sum the displacement and stress to give an overall value. The maxi-max value is the maximum of the maximum SRSS values.

Stresses and Damping.—The maxi-max displacement v % damping of input response spectra and maxi-max stress‡ (highest stress produced by max. stress at peaks of random vibration) v % damping of input response spectra are plotted (Figs. 40 and 41) that the computed displacement and stresses vary with the % damping and underlines the importance of the level of damping chosen for use in the calculations.

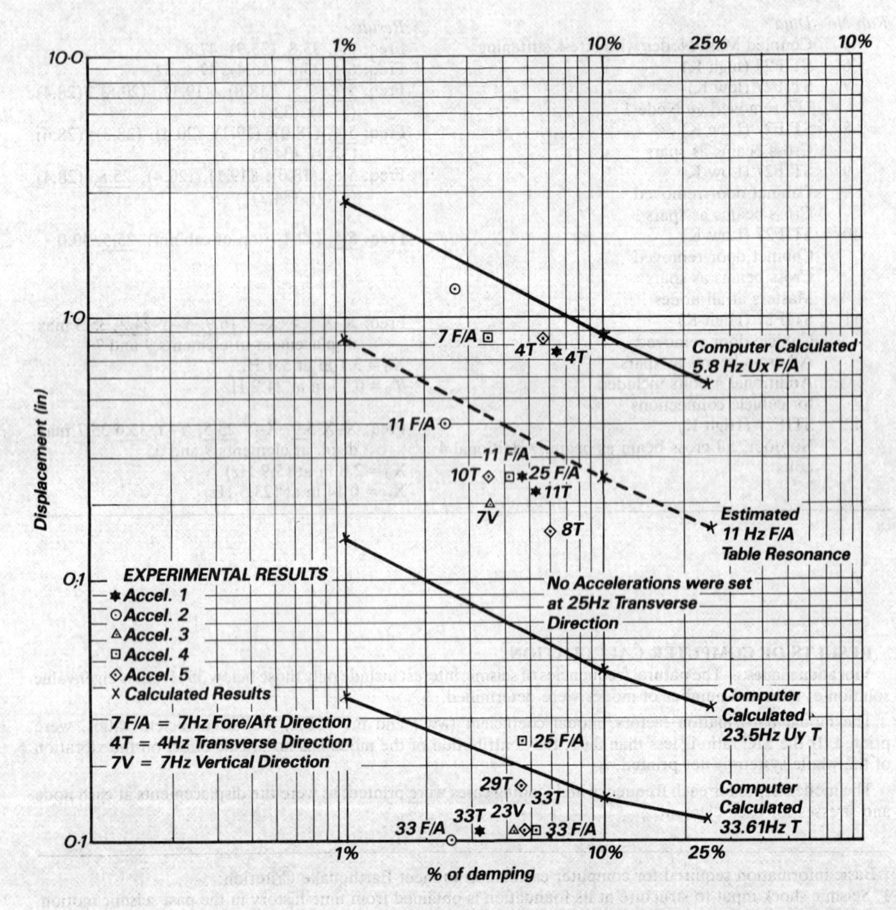

FIG. 40.—Comparison of Calculated Displacement vs Damping against Experimental Results at Different Frequencies. Note, to Achieve Good Comparison, the Accelerometers should give Good Agreement on Displacement, Frequency, and in the Same Direction as the Calculated Value.

‡ The Maxi-max amplitude or stress refers to the maximum of all maximum cyclic amplitude or stress peaks that occur during an earthquake, typically over the period of 10 to 40 seconds.
A comparison is then made with the acceptance criterion for the structure, using a finite element computer program and different percentage damping ratings applied to the Maxi-max amplitude of the earthquake shock.

TABLE 18.—SUMMARY OF COMPUTED MAXIMUM DISPLACEMENT AND STRESS (SINGLE CUBICLE, 1% DAMPING)

Load Step Direction	Mode/ Frequency Hz	DISPLACEMENT IN INCHES/RADIANS						MAXIMUM STRESS lbs/in²		
		Uxmax	Uymax	Uzmax	Rotz	Roty	Rotz	Frame	Cubicle	Bolts
	Undamped	N9	N52	N63	N64	N10	N5	EL13 SIG3/I	EL25 SIG3/TOP	EL66 SIG1/I
1/X-X (1)	5·866	2·7989	−0·00477	−1·076	0·000561	0·0626	0·00472	−100,510	704·65	31,736
		N9	N52	N63	N64	N10	N5	EL13 SIG1/I	EL25 SIG1/TOP	EL66 SIG3/I
2/Y-Y (1)	5·866	−0·179E-2	0·298E-5	0·673E-3	0·351E-6	−0·391E-5	0·258E-6	69·13	0·4408	−19·853
		N9	N52	N63	N64	N10	N5	EL13 SIG/I	EL25 SIG1/TOP	EL66 SIG3/I
3/Z-Z (1)	5·866	−0·152517	0·260E-3	0·586E-1	0·305E-4	−0·341E-2	0·258E-4	6021.8	38·396*	−1729·3
	SRSS	2·80314*	0·004777	1·0776	0·000561	0·06263	0·00472	100,674*	705.7	31,783·1
1/X-X (2)	23·51	Modal coefficients less than 0·01, displacement and stress are negligible								
		N8	N55	N26	N64	N81	N8	EL13 SIG3/I	EL57 SIG1/TOP	EL66 SIG3/I
2/Y-Y (2)	23·51	0·100239	0·142241	−0·164E-1	0·229E-2	0·735E-2	0·742E-2	−21871	987·86	−19965
		N8	N55	N26	N64	N81	N8	EL13 SIG1/I	EL57 SIG3/TOP	EL66 SIG1/I
3/Z-Z (2)	23·51	−0·147E-2	−0·209E-2	0·241E-3	−0·336E-4	−0·108E-3	−0·109E-3	321·44	−14·52	293·44
	SRSS	0·100249	0·142256*	0·01640	0·00229	0·00735	0·00742	21,873	988*	19,967·15
1/X-X (3)	33·61									
		N8	N9	N61	N64	N81	N9	EL4 SIG1/I	EL34 SIG3/BOT	EL66 SIG1/I
2/Y-Y (3)	33·61	−0·245E-1	0·3543E-1	−0·1959E-1	−0·1895E-2	0·5724E-2	−0·1826E.2	4,381·2	−500·82	10407
		N8	N9	N61	N64	N81	N9	EL4 SIG3/I	EL34 SIG3/TOP	EL66 SIG3/I
3/Z-Z (3)	33·61	0·2775E-2	−0·4013E-2	0·2219E-2	0·2146E-3	−0·6483E-3	0·2068E-3	496·2	−58·31	−1178·7
	SRSS	0·02465	0·03565*	0·00222	0·001907	0·00576	0·001837	4,409	504	10,473

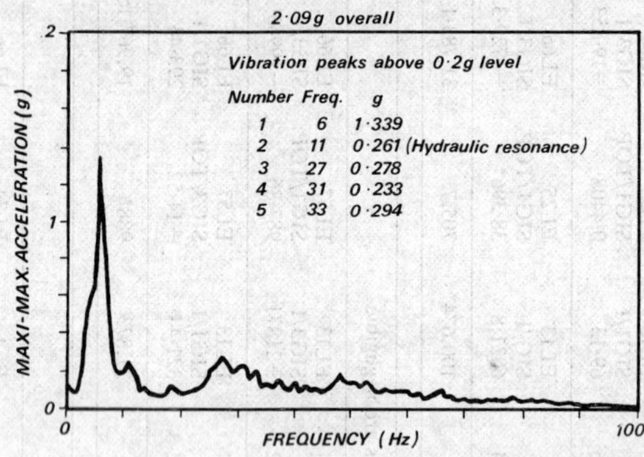

FIG. 41(*a*).—Vibration Analysis Results, using the Fast Fourier Transfer (FFT) Method, for Safe Shutdown Earthquake Test (SSE) on a Single Cubicle. At 6 Hz Amplitude, Maxi-max Value is 1·339 g RMS.

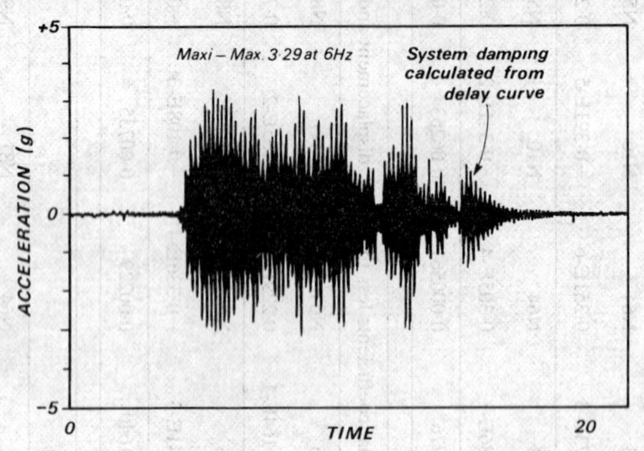

FIG. 41(*b*).—Maxi-max Amplitude during SSE Test is 3·29 g (Zero to Peak).

ANALYSIS OF EXPERIMENTAL RESULTS

During the full SSE testing, with the input as in Fig. 36 and accelerometers as in Fig. 33, all accelerations were recorded simultaneously on tape.

Maxi-max displacement and stresses.—To obtain the testing maxi-max displacement and stress, the recordings were analysed by FFT analyser. All accelerometer recordings for the whole series of tests were analysed; the results are listed in Table 19, and Fig. 41(*a*) shows examples of a frequency trace. Figure 41(*b*) shows time history at 6 Hz, and Maxi-max amplitude of 3·29 g. The system damping was calculated from the system decay curve at the end of the test.

TABLE 19.—RESULTS OF SSE (SAFE SHUTDOWN EARTHQUAKE) TEST: 45° VERTICAL EXCITATION

Accelerations		Freq. (Hz)	Maxi-Max 'g' 0–peak See note (1)	Maximum Displacement (in)	% of damping ζ See note (2)
No	Direction				
1	Tran.	4	1·27	0·776	6·38%
1	Tran.	11	2·63	0·212	4·03%
1	Tran.	33	1·27	0·011	3·15%
2	F/A	7	6·20	1·357	2·63%
2	F/A	11	5·0	0·404	2·40%
2	F/A	33	1·14	0·010	2·65%
3	Vert.	7	1·00	0·199	3·50%
3	Vert.	23	0·614	0·011	4·25%
3	Vert.	31	0·70	0·007	3·30%

TABLE 19.—(*Continued*)

Accelerations No	Direction	Freq. (Hz)	Maxi-Max 'g' 0–peak See note (1)	Maximum Displacement (in)	% of damping ζ See note (2)
4	F/A	7	4·32	0·862	3·39%
4	F/A	11	2·95	0·238	4·15%
4	F/A	25	1·60	0·025	4·70%
4	F/A	33	1·23	0·011	5·25%
5	Tran.	4	1·32	0·806	5·62%
5	Tran.	8	1·00	0·153	5·00%
5	Tran.	10	2·38	0·233	3·67%
5	Tran.	29	1·45	0·017	4·65%
5	Tran.	33	1·23	0·011	4·65%

Results shown in Table 19 are plotted in Fig. 42.

(1) Tape recording was first analysed using a Gen Rad TDA FFT instrument. Resonance frequencies were obtained, then a 1 Hz band width filter was selected and the maxi-max peak 'g' obtained from the time history for the full time of the test.

(2) The % of damping (ζ) was obtained during the decay of the vibration over the period of the test.

For method of determination of percentage of damping refer to Fig. 39 (pages I5/56 and 57).

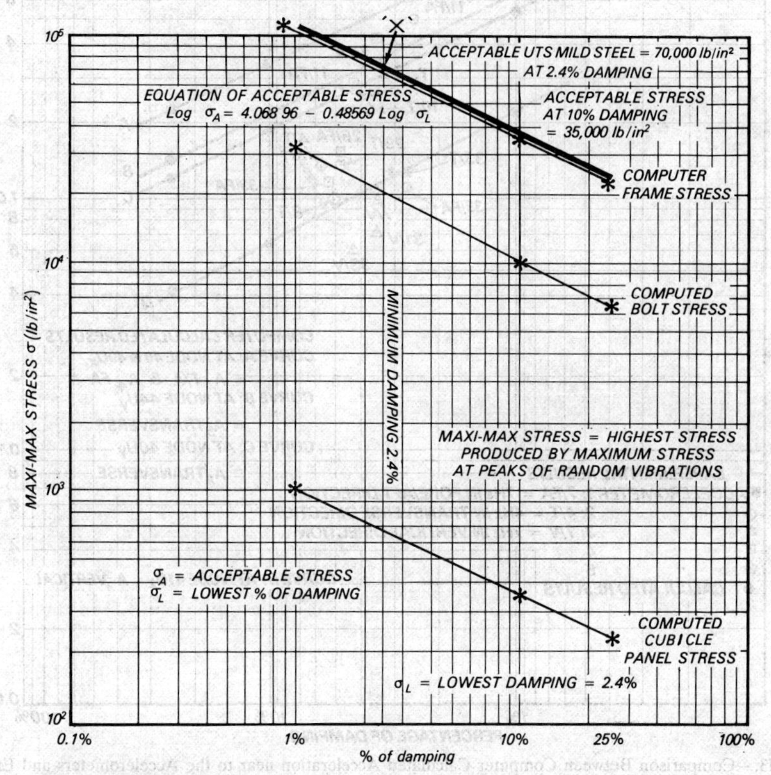

FIG. 42.—Computed Maxi-max Stresses on Frame, Bolts and Cubicle vs % of Damping on the Response Spectra Input (UTS = 70,000 lb/in²). Also Shown is Equation of Acceptance Criterion.

COMPARISON OF COMPUTER AND EXPERIMENTAL RESULTS.—The results of calculation showed that for the single switch cubicle a 10 fold change of damping (1% to 10%), changed the displacement from 3·5 in to 2·5 in and, similarly, stress ratio for 5·9 Hz mode is 3·14, for 23·51 Hz mode is 3·03, and for 33·61 Hz mode is 2·57 for similar changes in damping.

The important fact to note was that by fixing the value of damping the stress level was fixed accordingly. Since there is no way of calculating damping, engineers must make an arbitrary choice thus arbitrarily fixing the stress. Only testing the real structure at the appropriate earthquake level can give the true damping. Seismic testing therefore is the only acceptable qualification technique. As suggested by IEEE 344 standards, all calculations should be supported by testing.

However, in general the calculated displacement and stresses are in the correct range; the experimental values for SSE fall within 2·4% damping minimum and 6·38% damping maximum (Table 19). Therefore, for safety calculations, 2·4% damping appears to be a good general guide.

Assuming that failure occurs when the shock stress exceeds U.T.S., then the calculated maximum value of maxi-max stress should be below U.T.S., that is 70,000 lb/in^2 for mild steel. An inclined line can be drawn on the plot, through 2·4% damping as a vertical and 70,000 lb/in^2 as a horizontal, shown 'X' on Fig. 42 (page I5/61).

Thus, if a safety design is once established and proved by testing, as in the foregoing example, an appropriate criterion for acceptance can be developed and there is no reason why calculation should not be used for seismic qualification. Figure 43 shows results of experimental testing using accelerometers and those derived by using computer-based calculations. It can be seen that there is good agreement between the methods, but values from the tests were scattered because of difficulty in obtaining damping values.

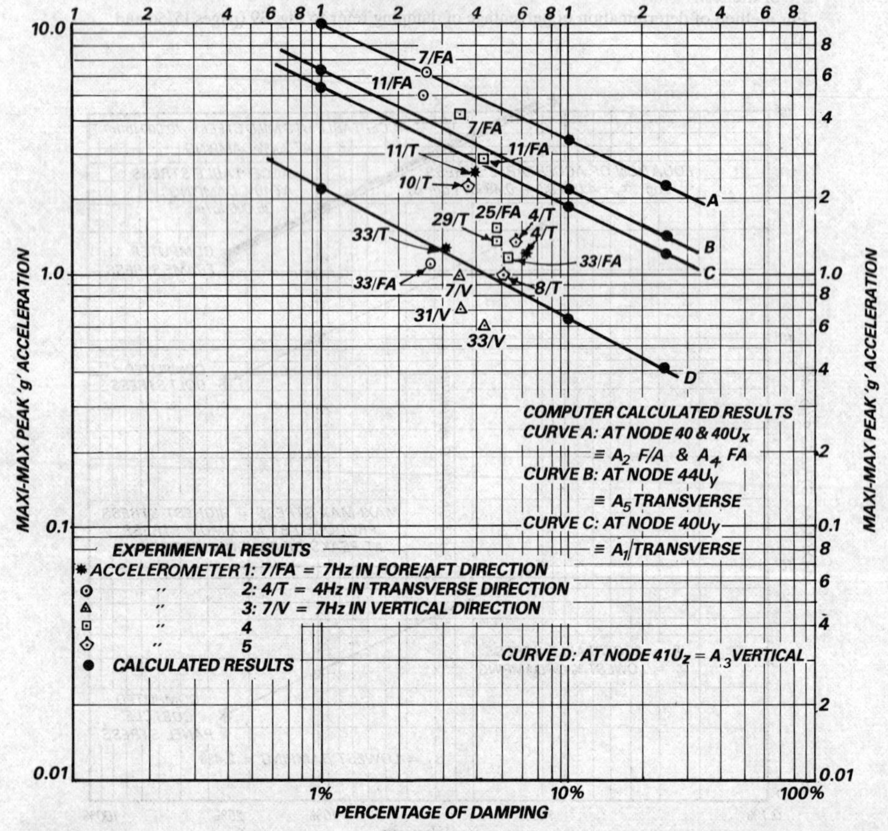

FIG. 43.—Comparison Between Computer Calculated Acceleration near to the Accelerometers and Experimental Results during 45°/Vertical SSE Test. Good Agreement can be Seen. Note that High Frequency Mode Tends to get Lower 'g' Value.

METHOD OF DETERMINING ACCEPTABLE STRESS LEVELS FOR DIFFERENT DAMPING INPUT.—It has been demonstrated that the finite element technique, using well-tried methods of modelling, can produce correct frequency, modes, displacement and stresses. If the damping is assumed as 2·4%, U.T.S. of 70,000 lb/in^2 may be used as a guide for acceptable stress calculation. This is shown by the inclined heavy line Fig. 42 for which a simplified equation relating stress and damping is:

$$\sigma_A = 0{\cdot}1674\ \text{U.T.S.}/(\delta_L)\ 0{\cdot}4857 \qquad \text{(Eq. 42)}$$

where σ_A = acceptable stress of the materials (UTS) and δ_L is the lowest damping of the structure, i.e. 2·4%, in this case. All calculated stress should be below the line represented by this equation. From this equation it may be calculated that acceptance level of 35,000 lb/in^2 should be allowed at 10% damping.

MULTI-CUBICLE COMPUTER CALCULATIONS.—Based on the close comparison between the results of physical testing and the computer finite element calculations following adjustments to the input assumptions, two and three cubicle switchgear units were examined using the established finite element techniques. As anticipated the results were comparable with those tested and proved for the single unit.

(A) Two Cubicle Unit

The mode of vibration at 5·9 Hz was similar to the single cubicle unit, in fore/aft direction and cantilevered at the base. The side to side and twisting mode was lower from 22 to 17 Hz. The whole structure acting as a unit, the two cubicles were moving out of phase. The torsional mode at 32 Hz, remained the same, each performing a torsional mode about its own vertical axis. The frequency had not changed from the single cubicle unit.

(B) Three Cubicle Unit

The computer calculation of the triple cubicle unit gave the result seen in Fig. 44, which shows the cubicle unit in phase cantilever mode at 5·9 Hz; Fig. 45 shows the side-to-side twisting mode acting on the whole unit. With the frequency lowered to 14 Hz, the individual torsional mode about the vertical axis the cubicle was at the same frequency i.e. 32 Hz.

It was clear that the computed maxi-max stresses were of a similar order to those of the single unit, the triple unit being only marginally higher, and the stresses are below 35,000 lb/in^2, i.e. within the acceptable level. Therefore, the structure was considered to have been qualified by earthquake test and no failure would occur during earthquake.

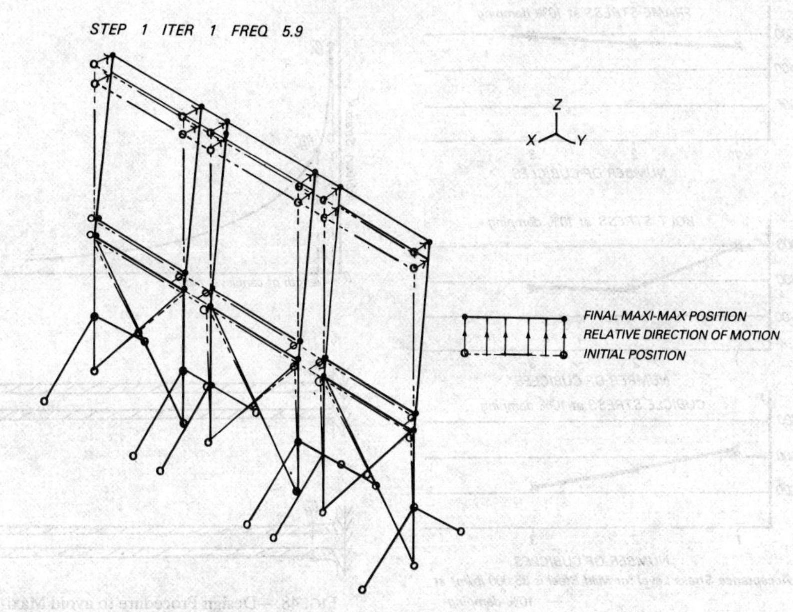

Fig. 44.—Seismic Response of Wall-mounted Triple Cubicle Unit Showing the Computer Plot of the First Mode of Vibration. The Cubicles are Moving in Phase at 5·9 Hz.

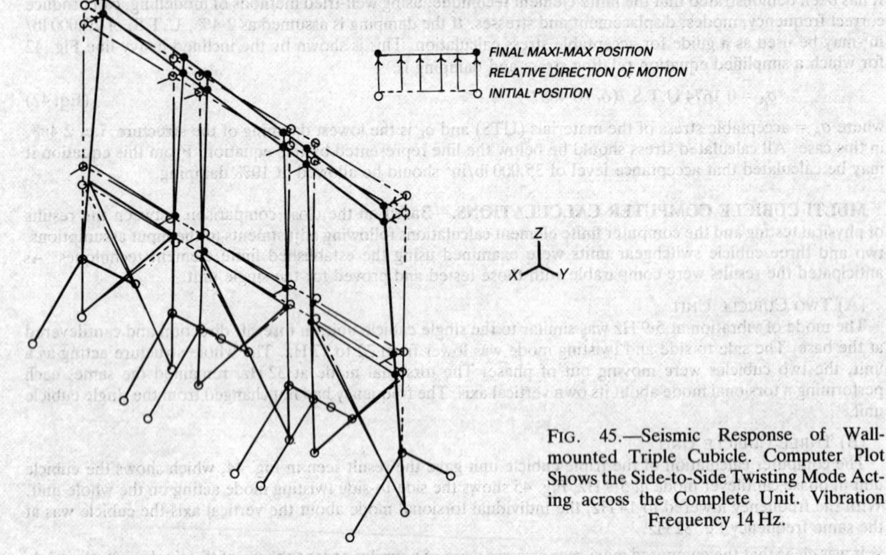

FIG. 45.—Seismic Response of Wall-mounted Triple Cubicle. Computer Plot Shows the Side-to-Side Twisting Mode Acting across the Complete Unit. Vibration Frequency 14 Hz.

EFFECT OF A NUMBER OF CUBICLES BOLTED TOGETHER.—A comparison was made by computing maxi-max frame stress, bolt stress and cubicle stress (plate) for 10% damping plotted against the number of cubicles (Fig. 46). It can be seen that the maximum stress occurs in the frame of the structure and an increase in the number of cubicles only marginally increases frame stress. This is probably due to the fact that the cantilever mode of vibration is of similar displacement and frequencies.

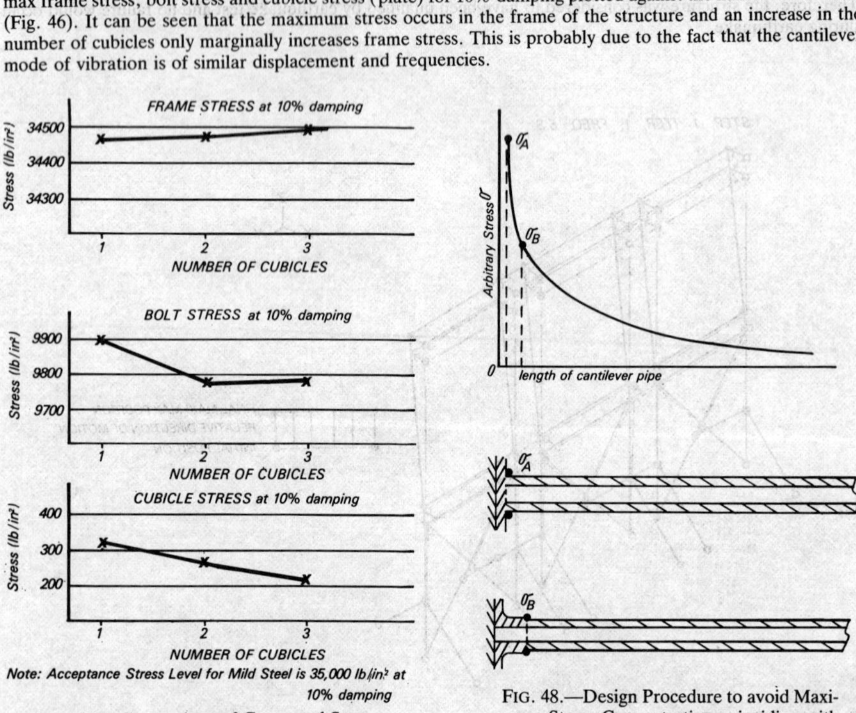

FIG. 46.—Comparison of Computed Stress for a Number of Cubicles Bolted Together.

FIG. 48.—Design Procedure to avoid Maximum Stress Concentration coinciding with Maximum Stress Location.

CONCLUSION ON FINITE ELEMENT COMPUTATION

(1) The finite element calculation produced fairly good results, which agreed well with results from experiments. More detailed stresses and displacements could easily be obtained from the computer printout.

(2) Some method of tuning the frequency of the computer model with various boundary conditions to agree with some test results would be advantageous and would increase the credibility of the computed results.

(3) The development of the correlation between acceptable stress level and percentage of damping clarifies the conditions of acceptance of the computed stresses and their relationship with allowable stresses.

EARTHQUAKE RESISTANT DESIGN (PRACTICAL ADVICE). (Refs 30 to 34)

(1) **Rigidity.**—Design for a fundamental frequency exceeding 25 Hz. When such equipment is adequately supported and anchored it can withstand severe tremors without structural or operational failure. This is particularly true of pumps, motors, generators, electrical control panels, elevator hoisting equipment, and some types of heavy industrial equipment.

(2) **Location of heavy equipment.**—Where possible heavy components should be located at low levels. Eccentric loading of the mass relative to the supporting frame, should be avoided, as this produces torsional modes of vibration which in turn produces uneven loading of the supporting structure.

(3) **Mass.**—Select the lightest equipment assembly, particularly where resiliently mounted.

(4) **Materials.**—Select materials with high ductility and damping when the natural frequency is between 2 and 20 Hz. Avoid brittle material where possible, e.g., refractory lined chimneys.

(5) **Stiffness.**—Select stiff moments, with a natural frequency of above 20 Hz. Use thicker material, and brace legs. Increase the stiffness in order to bring it outside the region of dynamic amplification.

(6) **Configuration.**—Select wide bases, symmetrical mass and stiffness distributions and a low centre of gravity. Avoid low frequency mounts by using dynamic balance. Provide flexibility in pipe and duct systems.

(7) **Supports.**—Provide lateral and vertical restraints on flexibly mounted machines, anchor rigid machines, cross brace stands. Provide sway bracing on pipes and ducts. Reduce shock loads by means of resilient surfaces. Use material ductility to provide stress damping. Cantilever type support should be avoided.

(8) **Fixing.**—(Fig. 47 (*a*)) Vertical components of earthquake motion and rocking action require the equipment to be fixed in place. Base friction alone can be unreliable. Using the 'fail safe' idea provides a secondary local path when first fixing fails. Yielding of anchor bolts will result in a loose attachment which can cause shock loading on equipment. Brackets can be designed to yield and reduce loading on equipment.

(9) **During construction.**—Consider malfunction of earthquake sensitive controls and devices such as relays and mercury switches. Check for internal parts which may break loose or be driven out of alignment.

(10) **Anchors into concrete.**—Anchors that are cast into concrete using inserts attached to the reinforcement or those welded to cast-in steel plates are the most satisfactory. Where adjustable fixings using slotted or oversize holes are provided, the use of close fitting 'workers' welded in place after positioning is recommended. Post drilled anchors should be of a type which expand with the tightening of the bolts, in order to inhibit loosening under the strain of shock loading.

Tall narrow equipment is likely to yield at the base unless it is stiffened locally and should be supported by high level stints or tie braces.

(11) **Anchorage of flexible mounted equipment.**—(Fig. 47(*b*)). Flexible mounts should be of the captive type. To prevent pulling apart some sort of limit stop or 'snubber' should be fitted. Sway bracing should be provided. Pipes and services should have flexible connections when joined to the flexible mounted equipment (for freely suspended equipment). Precautions should be taken for crashing into the adjacent structure. Clearance of at least 45° (0·5 g) should be allowed for its movement.

(12) **Pipework and ductwork.**—Failure of a pipe will often result in secondary damage far in excess of the cost of repair to the pipe.

Cold pipework can be fixed to the structure with short brackets but hot pipes must be flexibly supported to provide for thermal movement. Suspended pipes with long hangers should be braced to move with the supporting structure. Pitch filled liquid dampers should be provided at free ends or bends of pipes.

For light ductwork, bracing similar to that used for pipes should be specified. Adequate clearance should be allowed to prevent damage to the ceiling suspension system.

(13) **Stress Concentrations.**—Avoid putting a stress concentration at a maximum stress location, e.g. a hole or saw cuts at the centre of a bracing bar, or a sharp cornered bend at the root of a cantilever. This would considerably weaken the structure at that location. The point is illustrated in Fig. 48 for a welded cantilever tube. Avoid dynamic stress concentration, due to the fillet weld, coinciding with the maximum stress location (central diagram). A better design (lower diagram) shows maximum stress located in the solid part of the flange so that the maximum dynamic stress caused by the weld is at a lower stress region, at least 50 mm away.

(14) **Fillet Welds.**—A fillet weld has a dynamic stress concentration factor of ten. This reduces the design fatigue strength of black mild steel plate from 10 to 12 ton/in^2 and 1·2 ton/in^2 when a raw fillet weld is introduced.

A large number of the failures which have occurred in service are of cantilever type structures with fillet weld at the root. These can be improved by adding a small length of angle iron at the root, with butt welds between the bar and the angle. The butt weld normally has a dynamic stress concentration factor of 2–5. As the joint is no longer at a maximum stress location, the stress can be lowered to 50 to 70% of the root stress, thereby creating a better design.

(15) **Isolation of Equipment.**—Isolation of an earthquake shock has long been a designer's dream for solving earthquake problems. (Refs. 7, 88 to 92). Many interesting devices have been incorporated into designs but the success of these devices, in surviving real earthquakes however, has yet to be proved.

The difficulty is that the major earthquake frequencies are between 1 and 3 Hz. To isolate these frequencies, the suspension system resonance should be designed lower than 0·5 Hz.

EXAMPLE 1: SEISMIC FIXING

Design a holding down bracket for a packaged boiler having 3500 kg mass which is mounted on top of a multi-storey building (Class 2) Seismic Zone B.

Seismic force:

$$Cp = 1{\cdot}3$$

$$Fs = \frac{5}{6} \times 1{\cdot}3 \times 1{\cdot}3 \times 3{\cdot}5 \times 9{\cdot}81$$

$$= 48{\cdot}35 \text{ kN}$$

Holding down bolt size:

$$\text{Shear force/bolt} = \frac{48{\cdot}35}{2} \times \frac{1}{1{\cdot}1}$$

$$= 22 \text{ kN}$$

For combined tensile/shear select M20 bolt. Tensile stress = 90 MPa

$$\text{Yield load for bolt} = 144 \times 245$$

$$= 35280 \text{ N}$$

Angle bracket design

Size is selected to suit fan base dimensions.

Minimum length determined by max. allowable stress

$$= 0{\cdot}75 \text{ Yield stress}$$

$$= 108 \text{ MPa}$$

Bending about $x - x$

$$b_{\min} = \frac{6 \times 22 \times 30}{108 \times (10)^2}$$

$$= 366 \text{ mm}$$

Bracket must yield before bolt. Max. length

$$b_{\max} = \frac{6 \times a \times A}{d^2}$$

$$= \frac{6 \times 30 \times 245}{(10)^2}$$

$$= 441 \text{ mm}$$

(where A = effective area of bolt).

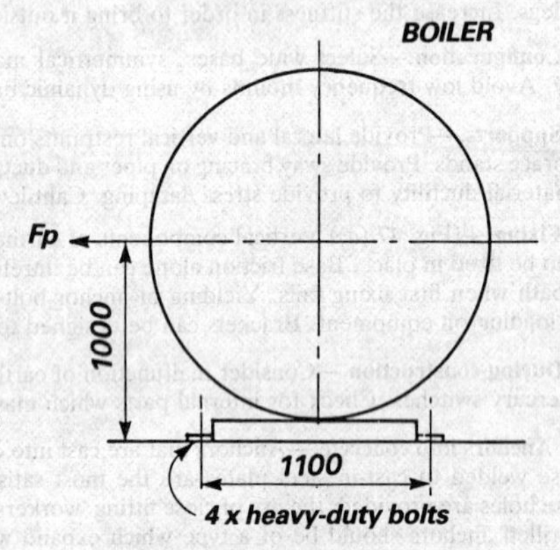

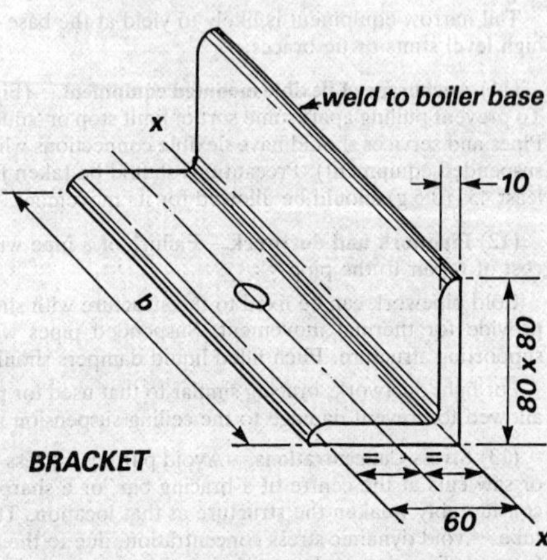

FIG. 47 (*a*) (above) and 47(*b*) (right): show examples of seismic fixing designs.

A suspension system which met this specification satisfactorily and for which the author was responsible involved the isolation of the 60 ton hydraulic force of a Losenhausen Fatigue Machine about 20 ft in height.

The machine was rigidly mounted on a 20 ton concrete block. The whole system was suspended by four torsion bars, with one end of the bars fixed and the free end supported by the bearings, with a cantilever end connected to four suspension points via a pendulum chain, Fig. 49. The vertical deflection at the end of the cantilever was about six inches, which gave an isolator/body resonance of 0·5 Hz. The horizontal resonance was adjustable by varying the length of the pendulum, to 0·5 Hz or less by means of multi-piston viscous dampers.

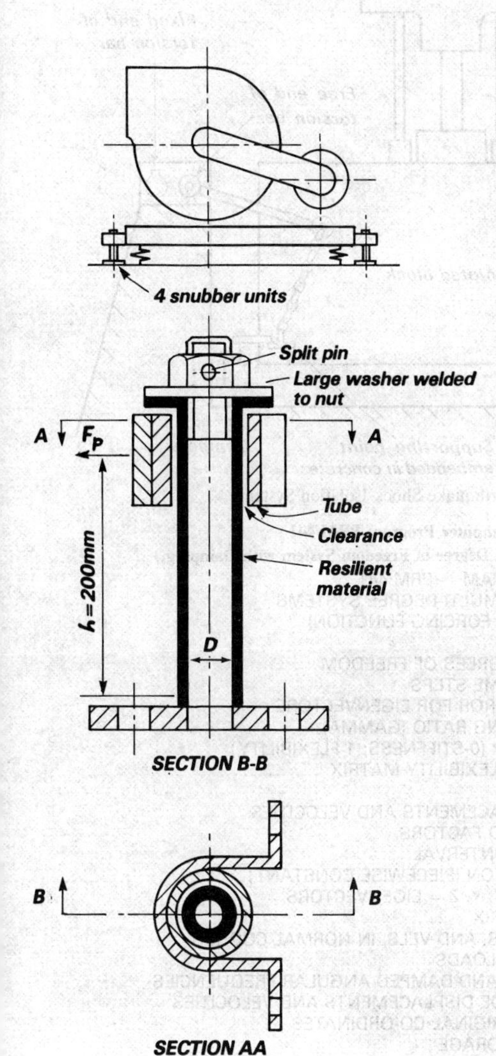

EXAMPLE 2: DESIGN OF FLEXIBLE EQUIPMENT RESTRAINT

Fan with motor and base on ground; mass 500 kg; speed 1400 rev/min (23 Hz); mounts selected for 90% efficiency, 7 Hz natural frequency.

Design Basis:
Mounts will have low damping, high accelerations could result. Design bolts to yield at about 0·6 g; system will then lock and be subjected to ground acceleration only.

Seismic Force (F_p)

$$F_p = \frac{0{\cdot}6 \times 500 \times 9{\cdot}81}{1000}$$

$$= 2{\cdot}94 \text{ kN}$$

$$= 0{\cdot}73 \text{ kN/snubber}$$

Bolt diameter (D)

Yield stress (f_y) = 144 NPa

$$Z = \frac{M}{f_y}$$

$$\frac{\pi D^3}{32} = \frac{F_p \times h}{f_y}$$

$$D = \sqrt[3]{\frac{32 \times 730 \times 200}{\pi \times 144}}$$

$$= 21{\cdot}7 \text{ mm}$$

Select 24 mm diameter bolt

F_p max. = 997 N

Fp now becomes 0·79 kN/snubber

(If this is not satisfactory a smaller bolt would be selected).

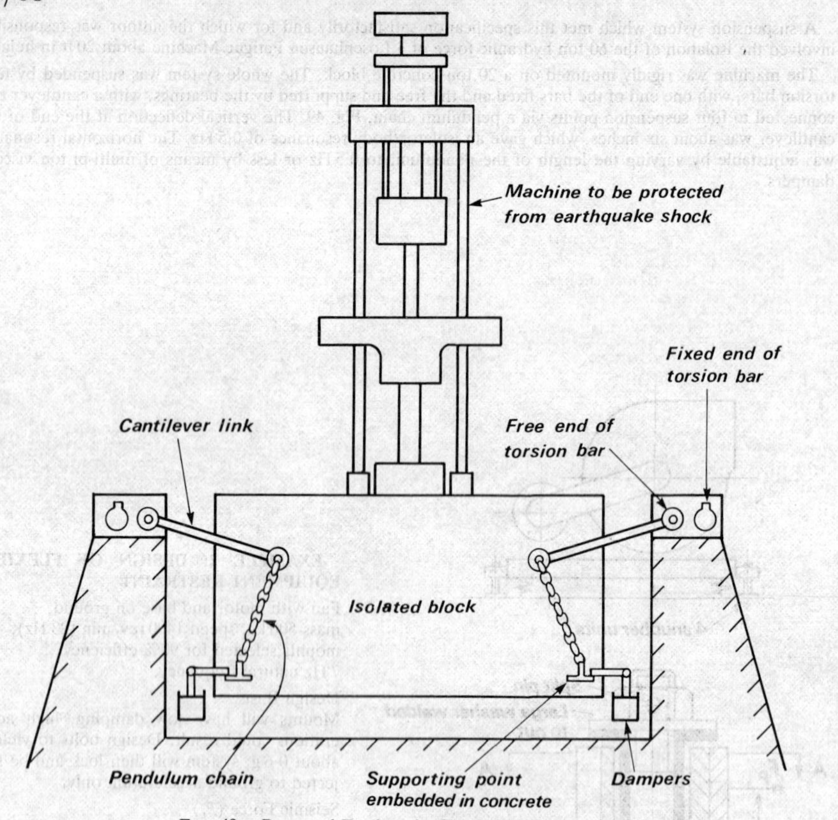

FIG. 49.—Proposed Earthquake Shock Isolation System.

APPENDIX I.—Computer Program PRM 441

Computer Software for a Forced Transient Multi Degree of Freedom System with Damping.

```
1.    REM - - - - - VIBRATIONS PROGRAM - - PRM 441
2.    REM (DYNAMIC RESPONSE OF MULTI-DEGREE SYSTEMS
3.    REM TO PIECEWISE-CONSTANT FORCING FUNCTION)
4.    REM - - - - - NOTATION
5.    REM    N = NUMBER OF DEGREES OF FREEDOM
6.    REM    N1 = NUMBER OF TIME STEPS
7.    REM    E1 = ALLOWABLE ERROR FOR EIGENVECTORS
8.    REM    G1 = MODAL DAMPING RATIO (GAMMA)
9.    REM    I1 = TYPE INDICATOR (0-STIFFNESS; 1-FLEXIBILITY)
10.   REM    A = STIFFNESS OR FLEXIBILITY MATRIX
11.   REM    M = MASS VECTOR
12.   REM    B, C = INITIAL DISPLACEMENTS AND VELOCITIES
13.   REM    P = VECTOR OF LOAD FACTORS
14.   REM    T = TIME; D = TIME INTERVAL
15.   REM    F = FORCING FUNCTION (PIECEWISE-CONSTANT)
16.   REM    E = EIGENVALUES: X, Y, Z = EIGENVECTORS
17.   REM    S = SWEEPING MATRIX
18.   REM    G, H = INITIAL DISPLS. AND VELS. IN NORMAL COORDS.
19.   REM    Q = NORMAL-MODE LOADS
20.   REM    P1,P2 = UNDAMPED AND DAMPED ANGULAR FREQUENCIES
21.   REM    U, V = NORMAL-MODE DISPLACEMENTS AND VELOCITIES
22.   REM    R = RESPONSE IN ORIGINAL CO-ORDINATES
23.   REM    W, L = WORKING STORAGE
```

```
24.   DIM A(10,10),M(10),B(10),C(10),P(10),T(100),D(100),F(100),E(3),X(10)
25.   DIM Y(10),Z(10,3),Q(3,100),U(3,100),V(3,100),R(1,10),W(10,10),L(10)
26.   READ N,N1,E1,G1,I1
27.   MAT READ A(N,N),M(N), B(N),C(N),P(N),T(N1),F(N1)
28.   IF I1 = 0 THEN MAT A = INV(A)
29.   FOR K = 1 TO N
30.       FOR J = 1 TO N
31.           A(J,K) = A(J,K)*M(K)
32.       NEXT J
33.   NEXT K
34.   D(1) = T(1)
35.   FOR J = 2 to N1
36.       D(J) = T(J) - T(J - 1)
37.   NEXT J
38.   PRINT 'PRM 4.41 - - DYNAMIC RESPONSE OF FIRST THREE MODES OF DAMPED'
39.   PRINT 'MULTI-DEGREE SYSTEM TO PIECEWISE-CONSTANT FORCING FUNCTION'
40.   PRINT
41.   PRINT
42.   PRINT 'THREE EIGENVALUES AND VECTORS BY ITERATION'
43.   MAT Z = ZER(N,3)
44.   I = 0
45.   REM - - - - - ITERATE AND PRINT EIGENVALUE AND ANGULAR FREQUENCY
46.   I = I + 1
47.   MAT X = CON(N)
48.   FOR K = 1 TO 20
49.       MAT Y = A*X
50.       E(I) = Y(N)/X(N)
51.       J1 = 0
52.       FOR J = 1 TO N
53.           Y(J) = Y(J)/Y(N)
54.           IF ABS(Y(J) - X(J)) < E1, THEN J1 = J1 + 1
55.       X(J) = Y(J)
56.       NEXT J
57.       IF J1 = N THEN GO TO 59
58.   NEXT K
59.   FOR J = 1 TO N
60.       Z(J, I) = X(J)
61.   NEXT J
62.   P1 = 1/SQR(E(I))
63.   PRINT
64.   PRINT 'MODE'; I; 'E-VAL. = '; E(I); 'ANG. FREQ. = '; P1; 'ITERS. = '; K
65.   IF I = 3 THEN GO TO 84
66.   REM - - - - - SET UP AND APPLY SWEEPING MATRIX
67.   MAT S = IDN(N, N)
68.   IF I = 2 THEN GO TO 75
69.   S(1, 1) = 0
70.   C1 = M(1)*X(1)
71.   FOR J = 2 TO N
72.       S(1, J) = - M(J)*X(J)/C1
73.   NEXT J
74.   GO TO 81
75.   IF N = 2 THEN GO TO 84
76.   S(2,2) = 0
77.   C2 = M(2)*(Z(1,1)*Z(2,2) - Z(1,2)*Z(2,1))
78.   FOR J = 3 TO N
79.       S(2, J) = - M(J)*(Z(1,1)*Z(J,2) - Z(1,2)*Z(J,1))/C2
80.   NEXT J
81.   MAT W = A*S
82.   MAT A = W
83.   GO TO 46
84.   PRINT
85.   PRINT 'MODAL MATRIX'
86.   PRINT
87.   MAT PRINT Z
88.   REM - - - - - NORMALIZE MODAL MATRIX WITH RESPECT TO M
```

```
89.   FOR I = 1 TO 3
90.       C1 = 0
91.       FOR J = 1 TO N
92.           C1 = C1 + M(J)*Z(J, I)*(J, I)
93.       NEXT J
94.       IF C1 = 0 THEN GO TO 100
95.       C1 = SQR(C1)
96.       FOR J = 1 TO N
97.           Z(J, I) = Z(J, I)/C1
98.       NEXT J
99.   NEXT I
100.  REM - - - - - TRANSFORM INFORMATION TO NORMAL CO-ORDINATES
101.  FOR I = 1 TO 3
102.      G(I) = H(I) = L(I) = 0
103.      FOR K = 1 TO N
104.          G(I) = G(I) + Z(K, I)*M(K)*B(K)
105.          H(I) = H(I) + Z(K, I)*M(K)*C(K)
106.          L(I) = L(I) + Z(K, I)*P(K)
107.      NEXT K
108.      FOR J = 1 TO N1
109.          Q(I, J) = L(I)*F(J)
110.  NEXT J
111.  NEXT I
112.  REM - - - - - COMPUTE RESPONSE IN NORMAL CO-ORDINATES
113.  FOR I = 1 TO 3
114.      U1 = G(I)
115.      V1 = H(I)
116.      IF E(I) = 0 THEN GO TO 134
117.      P1 = 1/SQR(E(I))
118.      P2 = P1*SQR(1 - G1*G1)
119.      FOR J = 1 TO N1
120.          IF J = 1 THEN GO TO 123
121.          U1 = U(I, J - 1)
122.          V1 = V(I, J - 1)
123.          C1 = EXP( - P1*G1*D(J))
124.          C2 = COS(P2*D(J))
125.          C3 = SIN(P2*D(J))
126.          C4 = (V1 + P1*G1*U1)/P2
127.          G5 = P1*G1/P2
128.          C6 = Q(I, J)/(P1*P1)
129.          U(I, J) = C1*(U1*C2 + C4*C3) + C6*(1 - C1*(C2 + C5*C3))
130.          V(I, J) = C1*( - U1*C3 + C4*C2 - C5*(U1*C2 + C4*C3))*P2
131.          V(I, J) = V(I, J) + C6*C1*(1 + C5*C5)*C3*P2
132.      NEXT J
133.  NEXT I
134.  REM - - - - - TRANSFORM AND PRINT RESPONSE
135.  PRINT
136.  PRINT 'RESPONSE IN ORIGINAL CO-ORDINATES (PRINTED COLUMN-WISE)'
137.  PRINT
138.  FOR J = 1 TO N1
139.      MAT R = ZER (1, N)
140.      FOR K = 1 TO N
141.          FOR I = 1 TO 3
142.              R(1, K) = R(1, K) + Z(K, I)*U(I, J)
143.          NEXT I
144.      NEXT K
145.      MAT PRINT R
146.  NEXT J
147.  PRINT
148.  STOP
149.  DATA 3,10,0.00001,0.05,0
150.  DATA 2,-1,0,-1,2,-1,0,-1,1
151.  DATA 1,1,1, 0,0,0, 0,0,0, 0,0,1
152.  DATA 1,2,3,4,5,6,7,8,9,10
153.  DATA 1,1,1,1,1,1,1,1,1,1
154.  END
```

```
COMMAND ? go
PROGRAM 4.41.—DYNAMIC RESPONSE OF FIRST THREE MODES OF DAMPED
MULTI-DEGREE SYSTEM TO PIECEWISE-CONSTANT FORCING FUNCTION
THREE EIGEN-VALUES AND VECTORS BY ITERATION
MODE 1  E-VAL. = 5.048018   ANG. FREQ. = 0.445042   ITERATION = 7
MODE 2  E-VAL. = 0.6431057   ANG. FREQ. = 1.246973   ITERATION = 17
MODE 3  E-VAL. = 0.3079775   ANG. FREQ. = 1.801941   ITERATION = 2
MODAL MATRIX
0.445042      -1.246984      1.801909
0.8019375     -0.5549535   -2.246933
 1              1              1
RESPONSE IN ORIGINAL CO-ORDINATES (PRINTED COLUMN-WISE)
3.058553E - 03   4.285055E - 02   0.4488853
7.557404E - 02   0.4513053        1.422269
0.4499555        1.361509         2.416564
1.195432         2.370045         3.339921
1.856796         3.163614         4.245371
2.014587         3.692737         5.019314
1.878725         3.859205         5.430094
1.811241         3.647371         5.271109
1.74055          3.225843         4.54407
1.438758         2.635145         3.558956
```

APPENDIX II.—Computer Software for Evaluating TRS Program (PRM 421)

Debugging of PRM 421 and Example of Calculation.

PRM 421 is for a forced vibration of a one degree damped system. It can be used to calculate TRS of seismic testing from time history results of accelerations measured on the vibration table. The equation of motion is:

$$m\ddot{x} + c\dot{x} + Kn = Q(t) \qquad \text{(Eq. 36)}$$

Let $m = 1$ lb-sec^2/in; $c = 1.2$ lb sec/in, $k = 9$ lb/in; and $Q(t) = Q_1 = 9$ lb (step function). Then $p = \sqrt{k/m} = 3\ \text{sec}^{-1}$; $n = C/2m = 0.6\ \text{sec}^{-1}$; $\gamma = n/p = 0.2$.

Equation (35) becomes

$$\ddot{x} + 1.2\dot{x} + 9x = 9 \qquad \text{(Eq. 37)}$$

The exact expression for the damped response to a step function of magnitude Q_1 is

$$x = \frac{Q_1}{k}\left[1 - e^{-nt}\left(\cos P_d t + \frac{n}{P_d}\sin P_d t\right)\right]$$

$$= \frac{Q_1}{k}[1 - A\, e^{-nt}\cos(P_d t - \alpha d)] \qquad \text{(Eq. 38)}$$

where

$$P_d = P\sqrt{1-\gamma^2} = 3\sqrt{0.96}\ \text{sec}^{-1},\ A = \sqrt{1 + (n/P_d)^2} \qquad \text{(Eq. 39)}$$

$$= 3\sqrt{2}/4; \text{ and } \alpha_d = \tan^{-1}(n/P_d) = \tan^{-1}(0.2/\sqrt{0.96})$$

For numerical solution put Eq. (37) as $\ddot{x} = f(t, x, \dot{x})$ we have

$$\ddot{x} = 9 - 9x - 1.2\dot{x}$$

for initial conditions we have $x_0 = 0$ and $\dot{x}_0 = 0$, the initial acceleration becomes

$$\ddot{x}_0 = 9.$$

Also take a uniform duration $\Delta t = 0.1$ sec and work to an accuracy of four significant figures for displacement and $\varepsilon_x = 0.0001$.

COMPUTER PROGRAM PRM 421

Forced vibration with damped linear one-degree system

```
1.      REM - - - - - VIBRATIONS PROGRAM - - PRM 4.2.1.
2.      REM        (AVERAGE-ACCELERATION METHOD)
3.      REM - - - - - NOTATION
```

```
4.    REM    T = TIME: D = TIME INTERVAL
5.    REM    X, Y, Z = DISPLACEMENT, VELOCITY, AND ACCELERATION
6.    REM    M, C, K = MASS, DAMPING, AND SPRING CONSTANTS
7.    REM    X0, Y0 = INITIAL VALUES OF X AND Y AT TIME T = 0
8.    REM    T1 = TIME RANGE OF INTEREST
9.    REM    N1 = NUMBER OF TIME INTERVALS
10.   REM    E1 = ALLOWABLE ERROR RATIO
11.   REM    Q1 = MAGNITUDE OF STEP FUNCTION
12.   DIM T(100), X(100), Y(100), Z(100)
13.   READ M, C, K, X0, Y0, T1, N1, E1, Q1
14.   N = C/(2*M)
15.   P = SQR(K/M - N*N)
16.   D = T1/N1
17.   PRINT 'PRM 4.21 - - - - - TIME INTERVAL = ',D
18.   PRINT
19.   PRINT
20.   PRINT 'TIME ITERATIONS APPROX. X EXACT X'
21.   PRINT
22.   PRINT' 0          ', X0, X0
101.  REM - - - - - INITIAL Z0 AND ITERATE Y(I), X(I), Z(I)
102.  Z0 = (O1 - C*Y0 - K*X0)/M
103.  FOR I = 1 TO N1
104.      T(I) = 1*D
105.      IF I = 1 THEN GO TO 111
106.      IF I = 2 THEN GO TO 115
107.      A = Y(I - 1) + Z(I - 1)*D/2
108.      B = X(I - 1) + Y(I - 1)*D/2
109.      Y1 = Y(I - 2) + 2*Z(I - 1)*D
110.      GO TO 118
111.      A = Y0 + Z0*D/2
112.      B = X0 + Y0*D/2
113.      Y1 = Y0 + Z0*D
114.      GO TO 113
115.      A = Y(1) + Z(1)*D/2
116.      B = X(1) + Y(1)*D/2
117.      Y1 = Y0 + 2*Z(1)*D
118.      J = 1
119.      GO TO 123
120.      J = J + 1
121.      X(I) = X1
122.      Y1 = A + Z1*D/2
123.      X1 = B + Y1*D/2
124.      Z1 = (Q1 - C*Y1 - K*X1)/M
125.      IF J = 10 THEN GO TO 127
126.      IF ABS (X1 - X(I)) > = E1*ABS(X1) THEN GO TO 120
127.      X(I) = X1
128.      Y(I) = Y1
129.      Z(I) = Z1
130.      E = EXP(-N*T(I))*(XO*COS(P*T(I)) + (YO + N*XO)*SIN(P*T(I))/P)
131.      E = EXP(-N*T(I))*(COS(P*T(I)) + N*SIN(P*T(I))/P)
132.      E = E + (O1/K)*(1 - F)
133.      PRINT T(I), J, X(I), E
134.  NEXT I
135.  PRINT
136.  STOP
137.  DATA 1,1.2,9,0,0,2,20,0.0001,9
138.  END
COMMAND?
```

Check the PRM 421 to see if it produces the values shown in Table 14 (page I5/44) before applying it to individual problems.

(1) LONG, R. E., Paper C176178 *The Problem of Estimating Seismic Motions* Engineering Design for Earthquake Environments. Sponsored by IMechE 1978 Applied Mechanics Group, the Japan Society of MechE, and the Society for Earthquake and Civil Engineering and Dynamics.

(2) KNUDSON, C. F., PEREZ, V., MATTHUSIN, R. B. *Strong Motion Instrumental Records and the Monagua Earthquake of December 2 and 3 1972*. Bull. Seism. Soc. Am., 1974, 64, 1049–1067.

(3) HARRIS, CYRIL M., and CREDE, CHARLES E. *Shock and Vibration Handbook*. p. 50.5, p. 50.7 and p. 50.9. McGraw-Hill Book Co., New York and London (1961).

(4) IEEE, STD 344.75. *IEEE Recommended Practices for Seismic Qualification of Class 1 Equipment for Nuclear Power Generation Stations*, 1975.

(5) *U.S. Atomic Energy Commission*, TID/7024, 1963. *Nuclear Reactors and Earthquakes*.

(6) TRIFIMAE, M. D. and BRADY, A. G. *On Correlation of Seismic Intensity Scales with the Peaks of Recorded Strong Ground Motion*. Bull of Seismological Society of America, Vol. 65 No. 1, pp 137–162, Feb. 1975.

(7) STEINBRUGGE, K. V. and MORAN, D. F. *An Engineering Study of the Southern California Earthquake of July 21, 1952 and its Aftershocks*. Bull. Seism. Soc. Am. 442B, April 1954.

(8) STEINBRUGGE, K. V. and MORAN, D. F. *Structural Damage to Buildings due to the Earthquake in Kern County, California, during 1952*, USA, Bull. 171. California Div. Mines 1955.

(9) STEINBRUGGE, K. V., BUSH, V. R. and ZACHER, E. G. *Damage to Building and other Structures by the San Francisco Earthquake of March 22, 1957*, San Francisco Earthquake of March 1957, Special Report 57. California Div. Mines, 1959.

(10) AYRES, J. M., SUN, T. Y., and BROWN, F. R. *Nonstructural Damage to Buildings in Report from the Great Alaska Earthquake of 1964*. Engineering, 6. National Acad. Scie. Washington D.C. 1964 346–456.

(11) JOHN A. BLUME and ASSOCIATES. RESEARCH DIVISION, *1967 Columbian Earthquakes* Report NVO-99-25 to the Nevada Operations Office, UAAEC, San Francisco, California, May 1968.

(12) AYRES, J. M. *Damage to Building, Equipment and Contents The San Fernando California Earthquake of 9th February 1971*. Geol. Survey Prof. Paper 733, 1971.

(13) FRAZIER. G. A., WOOD, J. H. and HOUSNER, G. W. *Earthquake Damage to Buildings. Engineering Features of the San Fernando Earthquake, 9th February 1971*. Earthquake Eng. Res. Lab. Calif. Inst. Tech. EER1 71-02.

(14) AYRES, J. M. and SUN, T. Y. *Nonstructural Damage. San Fernando California Earthquake of 9th February 1971*. IBUS Dept. Comm. 1973.

(15) WRIGHT, R. N. and KRAMER, S. *Building Performance in the 1972 Managua Earthquake*. National Bureau Standards, Tech. Note 807, November 1973.

(16) YANEV, P. I. *Industrial Damage—Managua, Nicaragua, Earthquake of 1972*. Proc. Earthquake Eng. Res. Inst. Cont. on Managua Earthquake, San Francisco, California, 1973.

(17) STEVENSON, J. D. *Seismic Design of Industrial Plant Equipment and Structures*. EDAC Inc. 21275 Fairmount Blvd., Cleveland, OHIO 44118. p. 105. 28.8.75. Also p. 107.

(18) WIGGIN, J. H. and MORAN, D. F. *Earthquake Safety in the City of Long Beach Based on the Concept of Balanced Risk*. J. H. Wiggins Company, Los Angeles, California, September 1971.

(19) HOUSNER, G. W., MARTEL, R. R. and ALFORD, J. L. *Spectrum Analysis of Strong Motion Earthquakes*. Bull. Seismol. Soc. Am. 43: 1953.

(20) NEWMARK, N. M. *Design Criteria for Nuclear Reactors subjected to Earthquake Hazards*. Proceedings of the IAEA Panel on a Seismic Design and Testing of Nuclear Facilities, Tokyo, Japan, June 1967.

(21) NEWMARK, N. M., BLUME, J. A. and KAPUR, K. K. *Design Response Spectra for Nuclear Power Plants*. Presented at the ASCE National Structural Engineering Meeting, 9–13 April 1973, San Francisco, California.

(22) Regulatory Guide 1.60. *Design Response Spectra for Seismic Design of Nuclear Power Plants*. Revision 1, U.S. Atomic Energy Commission, Directorate of Regulatory Standards, Dec. 1973.

(23) Regulatory Guide 1.12. *Instrumentation for Earthquakes, U.S. Atomic Energy Commission*. Directorate of Regulatory Standards, Dec. 1971.

(24) HUDSON, D. E. Proceedings of World Conference on Earthquake Engineering, Berkeley, 1956.

(25) HALFMAN, R. L., *Dynamics,* Vol. II, Section 9.2. Addison-Wesley, 1972.

(26) PIPES, L. A. *Matrix Methods for Engineering*. Prentice-Hall, 1963.

(27) TIMOSHENKO, S. P., YOUNG, D. H., WEAVER, W. JNR. *Vibration Problems in Engineering*. 4th Edition. p. 129–143. John Wiley & Sons, New York, London, Sydney, Toronto.

(28) N254203: 1976 *Code of Practice for General Structural Design and Design Loadings for Buildings*. New Zealand Standard Institute.

(29) VELETSOS, A. S. and NEWMARK, N. N. (1957) *Natural Frequencies of Continuous Flexural Members*. Trans ASCE 122, p. 249–285.

(30) NEWMARK, N. N., *Matrix Methods for Engineering. Fundamentals of Earthquake Engineering*. Civil Engineering and Engineering Mechanics Series. Prentice-Hall International Inc., London.

(31) UPRITCHARD, G. J. and MENZIE, B. E. *The Effect of Earthquakes on Services and Equipment in Buildings and a proposed Code of Practice*. Paper C179/78 I. Mech. E. Conference Publications 1978-12, *Engineering Design for Earthquake Environments*.

(32) SIMONSON, G. M. and T. R. Engineering Decision Analysis Co. Inc. *Basis for Seismic Resistant Design of Mechanical and Electrical Service Systems*. May 1976, National Science Foundation RANN. Washington D.C.

(33) UPRITCHARD, G. J. *Earthquakes and the Building Services Engineers*. Paper presented to NZIE Annual Conference 1977, Christchurch, New Zealand.

(34) MERZ, K. L. *The Problem of Damage to Non-structural Components and Equipment*. Workshop on Earthquake-Resistant Reinforced Building Construction, University of California, Berkeley, June 1977.

(35) Ministry of Works and Development, New Zealand. *A Guide to the Design of Earthquake Resistant Engineering Installations in Buildings*. May 1977.

(36) CAME, R. J. *The Effects of Earthquake Loads on the Design of Pressure Vessel Shells*. Paper C169/78 I Mech E. Conference Publication 1978-12, *Engineering design for earthquake environments*.

(37) CARR, A. J. and MOSS, P. J. *The Analysis of Cylindrical Shells under Local Loadings*. University of Canterbury, N.Z. Research Report 77/6 March 1977.

(38) Uniform Building Code, Vol. 1. 1973 Edition, International Conference of Building Officials.

(39) WYLLIE, L. A. ET AL. *Effects on Structure of the Managua Earthquake of December 23rd, 1972*. Bull. Seism. Soc. Am. 674. August 1974.

(40) Uniform Building Code. 1976 Ed. International Conference of Building Officials, Whltier, California.

(41) *Seismic Design for Buildings*. Tech, Man. 5-809-10, U.S. Dept. Army, Navy, Air Force. April 1973 (U.S. Government Printing Office, Washington D.C. 20402).

(42) *Earthquake Resistance Design Requirement for VA Hospital Facilities Handbook* 4-08-8, Office Constitution, Veterans Admin., 1973 revised 1974, Veterans Administration, Washington, D.C. 20420.

(43) BIGGS, J. M. *Introduction to Structural Dynamics*. Chapter 6. McGraw Hill, London, Oxford and New York, 1964.

(44) YEH, L. 12(1) pp. 107–116. *A Broad Band Acoustic Fatigue Theory as Applied to Multi-Modal Structural Vibration*. The Journal of the British Nuclear Energy Society, 1973.

(45) HADJIAN, A. H. ET AL. *The Seismic Environment for Nuclear Power Plant Components—an Interface Problem*. ASME pre 75-DE-53, Design Eng. Tech. Conf. Washington D.C. September 1975.

(46) JACOBSON, L. S. *Impulsive Hydrodynamics of Flud inside a Cylindrical Tank*. Bull. Seism. Soc. Am. Vol. 39. 1949.

(47) HOUSNER, G. W. *Dynamic Pressure on Accelerated Fluid Containers*. Bull. Seism. Soc. Am. Vol. 47. 1957.

(48) VESTY, I., YEH, L., MILES, G. A. *Seismic Response Calculations for Reserve Feedwater Tank at Torness Nuclear Power Station*. GEC MEL Report MEL 130132 May 1982.

(49) *Seismic Qualification Methods for Mechanical and Electrical Plant for Nuclear Power Stations*. Ref. C92/SDS/151/012 and GDCD/NP333. CEGB, SSEB and NNC. (UK).

(50) *Technical Specification and Schedules for Seismic Qualification of Electrical Plant*. Ref. E/TSS/Seismic. CEGB (UK).

(51) *Guide for Seismic Testing of Equipment*. (Draft) Issued by Sub-Committee 50A. IEC International Commission on Seismic Testing.

(52) SMITH, C. B. and MATHIESON, R. B. *Stimulating Strong-Motion Earthquake Effects on Nuclear Power Plants* (pp. 114–121). Nuclear Safety, Vol. 13, No. 2, March–April 1972.

(53) *Guide for Seismic Qualification of Equipment*, IEC-50A-GT8 (Fabries/Cotel) 4th October 1977. Issued IEC. 1979.

(54) VON DAWN, C. A. *Seismic Testing for Reliable Instrumentation and Control System Transactions*. IEEE Paper No. T92, p. 230–6, 345 East 47th Street, NY 10017, USA, 18th February 1972.

(55) FERGUSON, W. H. *Test Method to Demonstrate the Seismic Capabilities of Equipment Transactions*. IEEE Paper T72-052-4, USA.

(56) ALBERT, W. S. *Seismic Testing of Metal Clad and Metal Enclosed Switchgear using Sine Beat Vibration*. IEEE Transactions paper T72-050-8, USA.

(57) WU, J. N. C. and ROMAN, G. W. *Dynamic Modelling of Marine Boilers Experimental Verification of a Simplified Shock Analysis on a Boiler Model*. Experimental Mechanics. April 1976.

(58) YEH, L. *Critical Speed Investigations of Turbo-machines*. Applied Mechanics Convention, 1966. Proceedings I. Mech. E. 1965–66, Vol. 180, Part 31.

(59*) LYON, D. and YEH, L. *Seismic Response Calculation for Nuclear Reactor at Brasimore, Italy*. GEC (UK) Report W/M (1C)u.9236.

(60*) SMITH, C. P. and YEH, L. *Seismic Tests on GEC Type F8 Switchgear*. GEC (UK) Report W/M(1.3)u.9441.

(61*) SMITH, C. P. and YEH, L. *Seismic Tests on Whipp and Bourne Switchgear*. GEC (UK) Report W/M(1.3)u.9448.

(62*) ENDERBY, L. R. and YEH, L. *Seismic Test on a VAJX12 Relay for a Steam Turbine Control*. GEC (UK) Report W/M(1.3)u.9472.

(63*) MEADS, F. S. and YEH, L. *Seismic Test on a VAJX12 Relay for a Steam Turbine Control after Modification*. GEC Report W/M (1.3)u.9484.

Note: Copies of the Reports (Refs 59 to 68) may be available from GEC, but a small service charge may be required, according to Dr. R. D. Tyler, Research Director. For copies, please contact Mr. N. Otter, Director, GEC Research Centre, Whetstone, Leicester LE8 3LH.

(64*) EVANS, T. C. and YEH, L. *GEC Rack Mounted Governor for Gas Turbine*. GEC (UK) Report W/M(1.3).u.9495.
(65*) SMITH, C. P. and YEH, L. *Seismic Tests on a Woods Axial Flow Fan*. GEC (UK) Report W/M(1.3)u.9510.
(66*) SMITH, C. P. and YEH, L. *Axial Flow Fan Seismic Testing*. GEC (UK) Report W/M(1.3)u.9511.
(67*) SMITH, C. P. and YEH, L. *Seismic Simulation Test on a Steam Control valve with Hydraulic Actuators*. GEC (UK) Report W/M(1.3)u.9517.
(68*) SMITH, C. P. and YEH, L. *Seismic Tests on an EWP Control Valve Body Complete with Type 667 size 70 Actuator*. GEC (UK) Report W/M(1.3)u.9524.
(69) BRIGHAM, D. O. *The Fast Fourier Transform*. Prentice Hall, New Jersey, USA, 1974.
(70) *Technical Particulars of Definite Work. (Required Seismic Response)*. Schedule F2.5 CEGB.
(71) PETERSON, E. L., KLOSTERMAN, A. L. *Obtaining Good Results from an Experimental Modal Survey*. Society of Environmental Engineers Symposium Imperial College, London, UK. 1977.
(72) SKRELNER, K. M., FITZGERALD, E. M. *Seismic Certification of Metalclad Switchgear by Combined Methods of Testing and Analysis*. Paper C74 197-G, IEEE Winter Power Meeting, New York. Jan 27–Feb 1 1974.
(73) SKRELNER, K. M., FITZGERALD, E. M., MARTZ, J. W., SHERLOCK, J. E. *New Seismic Qualification Methods for Class IE Switchgear and Equipment*. IEEE Transactions; Power Apparatus and Systems Vol. PAS-95 No. 1. Jan/Feb 1976.
(74) SISSON, T., ZIMMERMAN, R. and MARTZ, J. *Determination of Modal Properties of Automative Bodies and Frames using Transient Testing Techniques*. S.A.E. Paper 730502 May 1973.
(75) *Dynamic Simulation of Complex Systems*. SPRC Manual 9. Structural Dynamics Research Center Corp. Cincinnati, Ohio, 1974.
(76) KLOSTERMAN, A. L., MCCELLAND, W. A. *Combining Experimental and Analytical Techniques for Dynamic System Analysis*. Seminar on Finite Element Analysis, Tokyo, Soc. Steel Construction of Japan Nov. 5–10 1973.
(77) VESTY, I., *Determination of T.R.S. from Table Acceleration Measurement by the use of Computer Software*. GEC Mechanical Engineering Laboratory. Internal Memo, (see Note applicable to References 59 to 68).
(78) LEVY, S., *Calculation of Response Spectrum from an Acceleration Time History*. S.D.R.C. Program Spectrum, Structural Dynamics Research Corporation, UK Branch, York House, Stevenage Rd, Hitchin, Herts S64 9DY.
(79) YANG, R. T. M. *Determination of the Dynamic Structural Response Characteristics of a large Diesel Engine by means of Low Level Impedance Method*. Diesel and Gas Engine Power Conference and Exhibition, Chicago, USA. April 4th–8th 1976. Published by ASME, United Engineering Centre, 345 East 47th Street, NY 10017, USA.
(80) DAY, J., FULLER, I., PARKER, J., TO, K., ALLEN, C. F. *A Seismic Qualification Method for Mechanical and Electrical Plant for Nuclear Power Stations*. GDCD/NP333 Issue, Dec. 1980, by General Design and Construction Dept., CEGB, Cheltenham, UK.
(81) CHEN, C. *Definition of Statistically Independent Time Histories*. Journal of the Structural Division A.S.C.E. February 1975.
(82) VESTY, I., YEH, L. and MILES, G. A. *Seismic Response Calculations for the Deaerator, Storage Tank and Vent Condenser at Torness Nuclear Power Station*. Mechanical Engineering Laboratory Report 130131, May 1982. GEC UK, Whetstone, Leicester LE8 3LH.
(83) ANSYS *Computer Program Technical Manual 1982,* Vol. I and Vol. II. Element Library. ANSYS Swanson Analysis System Inc., PO Box 65, Houston, Pennsylvania, USA 15342.
(84) SKRESSIES, K. M. and FITZGERALD, F. M. *Seismic Certification of Metalclad Switchgear and Combination Method of Testing and Analysis*. IEEE PFS Winter Meeting. IEEE (see Ref. 54), New York, Jan 27–Feb 1974.
(85) VESTY, I. and YEH, L. *Seismic Test on Type W1 Wall Mounted Starter:* GEC Industrial Controls Ltd., Test Results Fig. 59–98. GEC MEL UK W/M(913)0006 July 1983 (See Note applicable to Refs 59 to 68).
(86) ZIENKIEWICZ, O. C. and CHEUNG, Y. K. *The Finite Element Method in Structural and Continuum Mechanics*. McGraw-Hill, New York, 1967.
(87) PILKEY, W. and PILKEY, B. (Eds.) *Shock and Vibration Computer Programs, Reviews and Summaries*. The Shock and Vibration Information Center, Naval Research Laboratory, Washington D.C. 1975.
(88) ROSENBLUETH, PROFESSOR E. Universidad Nacional Autonomade, Mexico. Earthquake Engineering. Earthquake—Resistant Design of Building. Chapter 15, p. 477 to 530 Computational Mechanics. 18 Spring Crescent, Southampton SO2 1GA.
(89) Bivot 1943. Flexible First Storey Earthquake-resistant Building Design. See Ref. 88, p. 528.
(90) Joshi 1960. The Use of Soft Pads Under Basement or Ground-storey Column as Earthquake Resistance Design of Buildings. See Ref. 88, p. 529.
(91) Gonzalez-Flores 1964. The Use of Rollers Between Building Beams and Foundation for Isolation from Earthquake Motions. See Ref. 88, p. 530.
(92) Garza-Tamez 1964. The Adoption of Suspended Supports as Earthquake Isolation. See Ref. 88, p. 531.

BUILDING

Planning Permission—Other Development Controls—Building Control—Fire Resistance—Thermal Insulation Requirements—Acoustic Requirements and Characteristics of Buildings—Design of Structures—Load-bearing Masonry—Reinforced and Prestressed Masonry—Building Construction—Foundations—Concrete Work—Brickwork and Blockwork—Rubble Walling and Stone Masonry—Asphalt Work—Roofing—Carpentry and Joinery—Metal Work—Drainage—Plumbing and Engineering Installations—Building Services—Plasterwork and Floor Finishings—Glazing—Painting and Decorating—Fencing—Bibliography.

By H. W. H. West, BSc, FGS, FICeram, FBIM, FInstE, FIQA, and W. A. Durose, Dip Arch (Birmingham)

This chapter relates both to wholly new construction and to modifications, extensions, repairs and renovations to existing buildings. Planning permission is required for the appearance and siting of new buildings and for the change of use of existing ones. Building Regulations approval is normally needed to ensure that the constructional, equipment and safety of the occupants' aspects of the finished building meet the requirements of various regulations brought together by Act of Parliament. New Building Regulations came into force on 11th November, 1985.

It is not possible, nor indeed desirable, to cover all aspects of building in a year book and this Chapter merely seeks to record the latest requirements of Statutory regulations, codes of practice, British Standards and, where appropriate, European or International Standards and to record some general principles to be observed. European Norms (EN) are exactly equivalent. For ISO Standards the BSI convention is used: ≡ identical; = technically equivalent but the wording may differ substantially; ≠ related standard covering similar subject matter but in a different way. The main usefulness of the chapter will be for low-rise, ie up to four storeys, constructions but even these require professional assistance in design. The design codes presume that the designer and supervisor during construction are appropriately qualified. Although the detailed procedures of limit state design have been introduced to masonry they essentially apply to individual elements and the Code (BS 5628 Part 1) therefore rightly draws attention to the need to consider the overall behaviour of the whole structure and its stability both during construction and afterwards.

PLANNING PERMISSION

PLANNING.—Planning Control is concerned with the appearance, siting and use of buildings.

While Building Control problems are ultimately capable of solution because of their generally technical nature, the control of the shape, position and function of buildings is largely subjective and differences of opinion may cause difficulty.

The Town and Country Planning Act 1971 consolidated earlier Acts. Generally any development requires prior permission from the Local Planning Authority. Development is the carrying out of building, engineering, mining or other operations or material change of use. Operations not deemed to be development include, maintaining, improving or altering the interior of a building providing there is no material change to the exterior, though any expansion of a building below ground level constitutes development, change of use within the curtilage of a dwellinghouse for a purpose incidental to its use as a dwelling.

Planning permission is needed for a wide range of activities from formation of a vehicular access to open cast mining, but the Secretary of State may make Development Orders giving general permission for a particular type of development, eg the enlargement of a dwelling up to 50 cubic metres or one tenth the volume of the house up to a maximum of 115 cubic metres.

Application for planning permission is made to the local planning authority. Each planning authority has to produce a Town Plan to indicate the proposed and actual disposition of various uses throughout its area available for inspection at the planning office.

The submission of an application where the proposed use does not conform with the Town Plan use will be at an automatic disadvantage and may take much longer to be decided. Noisy, smelly or dust producing operations are also inherently at a disadvantage and are virtually banned in residential areas. The political or economic objectives of the Government often dictate planning decisions where employment may be affected. Thus in Part 3 of the application the applicant has to indicate the pattern of employment and, in Greater London, has to state why he proposes that his development should be in London as well as what his import/export pattern is likely to be.

Trunk Roads.—Application for sites on or near a trunk road are referred to the Ministry of Transport and proposed vehicle accesses, if permitted, must be of approved types according to the maximum speed limit applying to the road. Accesses near junctions, bends or other hazards may not be permitted at all.

Overhead Electricity Lines.—Sites adjacent to or beneath main Grid Lines have to be referred to the CEGB for comment and approval, on account of sway in the cables and other risks.

Statutory Undertakings.—Four principal types of undertakings exist in the UK. They are:

Water Authorities (including main sewerage)
Gas Boards
Electricity Boards
British Telecom

All four types have the duty of giving supplies to applicants and have the right to pass their service under, through or over property subject to certain limitations. The capacity of the supply is theoretically unlimited but failures of forward planning or sudden changes in demand can, of course, bring about restrictions.

Any project depending upon very large services should be discussed at the earliest possible stage with the supply authority concerned, as the cost of bringing large capacity services from a suitable source which may be remote from the intended site may affect the viability of the proposal.

Outline Applications.—Outline applications can be made to establish whether a particular use, or change of use, will be permitted. Theoretically all the applicant needs to send with the forms is a site plan coloured or outlined in red, with any adjacent land also owned by the applicant coloured or outlined in blue but frequently the planners require a sketch or details of the form and appearance of the proposal.

Outline applications can take just as long to determine as full applications, and since a full application has to be made even when the outline application is approved, it is questionable whether much advantage lies in what was intended to be a quick procedure for guidance of the applicant.

Full Applications.—A full application comprises the forms plus triplicate copies of plans of every floor level, elevations of every exposed wall and roof, site plan showing the precise positioning of the project on the site plus a location plan showing the situation of the site in the surrounding area. All types and colours of materials must be indicated, either in the appropriate box on the application forms or on the drawings. This requirement is always taken to refer to bricks, stone, tiles, and glass or metals where tinted, and not to surfaces usually repainted like window frames and doors.

If the project is in the centre of an historic town, or in an area of outstanding natural beauty it is also desirable, if not essential, to attach a perspective view of the proposal in its surroundings.

Aesthetic Controls.—These probably give rise to more acrimony or irritation for the applicant than any of the other controls, in which a basis of common-sense is visible. On the other hand, a total lack of control has, in other countries, led to unsightly, sprawling development which has ruined many otherwise attractive areas.

One of the most used reasons for refusal is "detrimental to the amenities of the neighbourhood" but the planners have to be specific in explaining which amenities and in what way the scheme is detrimental.

Landscaping is an aspect where the planners may apply a condition of permission and although a complex scheme can be expensive, often the provision of grassed areas with shrubs and trees where no traffic hazards would arise will suffice. Adequate off-street parking is now an almost inescapable requirement.

Certain areas where there is a strong local traditional use of a particular material require the use of these materials and will not approve schemes which do not conform. For example areas of the Cotswolds require local stone, or stone derivatives.

Use Classes.—In order to identify differing types of use of buildings a list of Use Classes is promulgated as an Order under the Planning Acts. In general terms there are four principal types of use:

Buildings for living in
Buildings for entertainment or communal activity
Buildings for working in
Buildings for storage

but these are subdivided for reasons of traffic generation and nuisance creation, thus industry is divided into heavy and light, while living uses are divided into small dwellings, multiple dwellings, and institutional and hotel-type accommodation.

OTHER DEVELOPMENT CONTROLS

Development Land Tax.—This tax, the latest in a line starting with 'Land Charges' in the late 1940's and 'Betterment Levy' in the 1960's, is, like its predecessors, based on the theory that ultimate ownership of all land is vested in the people and therefore when the State enhances the value by permitting development it is entitled to some payment in return. From time to time the future of DLT is in doubt, because some governments believe that ownership of land carries with it the right to development provided no nuisance is caused and no other person's rights be diminished. Thus it is likely that if DLT is abolished a change of government will bring it back in another guise.

Listed Buildings Control.—Under legislation concerning Historic Buildings, all buildings over a certain age are listed while others, selected on merit, as judged by an appropriately qualified panel, may also be listed. Appeals may be made against a proposed listing, but once listed additional permissions are required for any proposal to alter, enlarge or demolish the building. While demolition of ordinary buildings is not controlled by Planning Acts the demolition of listed buildings is controlled and substantial penalties now apply to those responsible for unauthorised demolition.

Mineral Workings.—There are powers to control mineral extraction and to require restoration of the land after extraction is complete. Opencast extraction of minerals, inevitably leads to pollution by dust, noise and traffic, and proposals of any magnitude are the subject of public hearings on appeal.

Appeals.—Unless an extension of time is granted by the applicant, a Local Authority has to give a decision on a planning application within two months of its registration on receipt at the Council Offices. Should the LA fail to give a decision the applicant has a right to appeal to the Secretary of State for the Environment, within six months of the due date of decision.

Similarly, if a refusal to approve an application is decided by the Council, or if an approval is subject to conditions which the applicant is aggrieved about, he may also appeal within six months.

BUILDING CONTROL

GENERALLY.—Building control is concerned with the constructional and equipment aspects of building. Because of the increasingly technological nature of building construction, the codification of methods and the supervision of proposals and site works has become more and more intensive. The new 1985 Building Regulations replaced the old Building Regulations on 11th November, 1985 but for three years, buildings approved to the latter may be commenced. British Standards including BS Codes of Practice, were recognised by the old Building Regulations as providing acceptable standards for components and methods. Thus design of the structure according to the appropriate code was 'deemed to satisfy'.

Changes to the building regulations required a separate Act of Parliament but the whole concept has now been changed to a much simpler form with the detailed requirements appearing in 'approved documents' which may thus be changed without an Act of Parliament although such change will still require sanction by the Building Regulations branch of the Department of the Environment.

BUILDINGS FREE OF CONTROL.—Government Buildings and buildings erected for the specialised purposes of many statutory authorities (eg mine buildings for NCB) do not have to conform with Building Regulations. In theory neither do buildings for Local Authorities, but since much of their building programme consists of housing and other non-specialised functions it is unusual to find any major departures. Changes in these provisions are under consideration.

BUILDING REGULATIONS IN ENGLAND AND WALES.—The old Building Regulations were made under the Public Health Acts and laid before Parliament. Relevant sections were amended as necessary when some disaster, whether economic (eg the oil crisis precipitating the intensification of thermal insulation rules) or structural (eg the High Alumina Cement scare), occurred.

As a result of this method of production and the frequency of change there were doubts as to the precise meaning of many regulations even among the Building Control Officers of the Local Authorities. The new Regulations are shorter and in principle changes to meet changing circumstances can be made in ancillary documents without the need to lay an amendment before Parliament. Certainly in the early stages of use of the new Regulations confusion will exist. Thus both under the old and the new Regulations it is advisable to discuss any dubious or contentious points at an early stage with the relevant officer, and essential to work to the latest issue and amendments available.

THE REGULATIONS.—The 1976 Building Regulations, as amended by the Building (Fourth Amendment) Regulations 1985, have been superseded by the 1985 Building Regulations. However, the revocation of the earlier Regulations is subject to transitional provisions such that they remain applicable to plans deposited before 11th November 1985. Once such plans have been passed they will only lapse if the work has not been commenced within three years and the local authority has served notice that the deposit of the plans is of no effect. Information about the old Building Regulations is given in the Kempe Editions of 1986 and earlier.

The new Regulations comprise 25 pages instead of some 300 and are intended to be simpler to interpret and apply. They are well described and explained in the 'Manual to the Building Regulations 1985' which is accompanied by the Approved Documents, all published by HMSO.

The Building Regulations apply to building work and certain changes of use of an existing building.

'Building work' is defined as erection or extension or material alteration of a building, provision, extension or material alteration of a controlled service or fitting and work required for a material change of use.

An alteration is material if, carried out by itself it would, at any stage, adversely affect the existing building in regard to the requirements of Structure and Fire; or it involves the insertion of cavity insulation; or it involves under-pinning.

A controlled service or fitting is one for which there is a requirement under Parts G, H, J or L (vide infra).

A material change of use is where a building was not one of the following and is changed to become so—a dwelling, a flat, a hotel or institution, a public building—or it was an exempt building under Schedule 3 and ceases to be.

If the Regulations apply to a project the local authority must be notified. There are now two systems of building control, and you may choose to have the local authority responsible for supervising the work or to employ a private approved inspector. The inspector must be independent of the designer or builder except for alteration or extension of one and two storey houses. The means for approval of inspectors and details of the way they are to operate in certifying plans and supervising the work are laid down in The Building (Approved Inspectors etc.) Regulations 1985.

The Regulations were made by the Secretary of State for the Environment through Statutory Instrument 1985 No. 1065 by virtue of the powers conferred on him by the Building Act 1984. They consist of five parts covering broadly definitions, control of building work, relaxations, notices and plans and miscellaneous, followed by three Schedules:

Schedule 1 Requirements, is the most important part. Under the Regulations it is not essential to build exactly in conformity with the plans deposited. The obligation is to comply with the Regulations by compliance, in whatever way, with the Requirements. The general pattern is as follows:—

Part A – Structure
Part B — Fire
Part C — Site Preparation and Resistance to Moisture
Part D — Toxic Substances
Part E — Resistance to the Passage of Sound
Part F — Ventilation
Part G — Hygiene
Part H — Drainage and Waste Disposal
Part J — Heat Producing Appliances
Part K — Stairways, Ramps and Guards
Part L — Conservation of Fuel and Power

Schedule 2—Facilities for Disabled People gives requirements and deemed to satisfy provisions which for schools etc., are in Department of Education and Science Design Note 18 (1984)—'Access for Disabled People to Educational Buildings', and for other buildings the design recommendations in BS 5810:1979 'Code of Practice for Access for the Disabled to Buildings'.

Schedule 3—Exempt Buildings and Work lists the classes of buildings which are exempt as follows:—

Class I. Buildings controlled under other legislation including the Explosives Acts 1875 and 1923, the Nuclear Installations Act 1965 or the Ancient Monuments and Archaeological Areas Act 1979.

Class II. Buildings not frequented by people.

Class III. Greenhouses and agricultural buildings, unless the main purpose of the building is retailing, packing or exhibiting. The structural design of agricultural buildings for equipment or fodder storage is the subject of a less onerous code (BS 5502:Part 1:1978, 7 sections, Part 2:1981, 5 sections, Part 3:1978, 8 sections) in respect of wind loading and fire resistance on the grounds that the 'dutch barn' with open sides does not attract the same wind forces as a clad building and is usually remote from other buildings so that collapse in fire does not carry the same risks as urban storage buildings. However, if these buildings are clad with sheeting the structural safety factor is inadequate and therefore structures designed to the agricultural code should not be considered as a suitable framework for later enclosure for other uses.

Class IV. Temporary buildings and mobile homes.

Class V. Ancillary buildings.

Class VI. Small detached buildings. This includes small detached buildings less than 30m^2 floor area containing no sleeping accommodation and either more than one metre from the boundary of the curtilage or a single storey building constructed wholly of non-combustible material and also detached fall-out shelters.

Class VII. Extensions by less than 30m^2 of a building at ground level by the addition of a greenhouse, conservatory, porch, covered yard or covered way; or a carport open on at least two sides.

APPROVED DOCUMENTS.—Approved Documents are issued by the Secretary of State to give practical guidance on some of the ways of meeting each of the requirements of Schedule 1 to the Regulations and are for Regulation 7 Materials and Workmanship.

Approved Documents are not the same as the old 'deemed to satisfy' clauses. The Approved Documents may be followed in whole or in part or not at all. The obligation is only to meet the Requirements. There is an exception in the case of Requirement B1 when the document 'Mandatory rules for means of escape in case of fire' must be used, though the local authority may agree to relaxation in some circumstances.

If the guidance in Approved Documents is followed it is evidence tending to show that any allegation that the Regulations have been contravened is not well founded. If the guidance is not followed it could be used as evidence tending to show non-compliance.

Approved Documents may give guidance in more than one form:

Technical Solutions give details of some of the more widely used forms of construction which achieve an Acceptable Level of Performance.

Alternative Approaches give references to other publications if none of the Technical Solutions seems appropriate. They are usually based on BS and enable more complex procedures to be used which may be actually more relevant and economic.

An Acceptable Level of Performance is given in some Approved documents. It is not a minimum standard and something less may satisfy the Requirements in a particular case.

The very important Approved Document on Materials and Workmanship notes that materials covered by BS or Agrément Certificates are likely to be suitable but other materials or products may be suitable in particular circumstances. The Document also refers to Independent Certification Schemes for product quality and quality management systems in accordance with BS 5750 Quality Systems. It is, however, unfortunate that a Government publication should note only BSI as a Certifying Body when there are many long standing sector schemes such as ASTA, the Association of Short Circuit Testing Authorities or PVQAB, the Pressure Vessels Quality Assurance Board and newer ones such as CARES, the Certification Authority for Reinforcing Steels and CICS, the Ceramic Industry Certification Scheme, which are more expert in their sector and hence equally, if not more, appropriate.

RELAXATIONS AND DISPENSATIONS.—If a local authority accepts that all the terms of a requirement need not be met because of special circumstances, they may issue a relaxation. Dispensation is an agreement by the local authority that the requirement need not be complied with at all. One or the other may be applied for if in the circumstances of the particular proposal a requirement is considered unreasonable. Prior application must be made since the Approved Inspector has no power to relax or dispense with any requirement.

Most of the requirements in Schedule 1 are functional in the sense that compliance requires 'adequate' provision. They cannot therefore be relaxed because then the provision would be less than adequate. It might, however, be reasonable to dispense with the requirement. Where requirements are specific—B1, means of escape in fire, L2 and L3, resistance to the passage of heat and Schedule 2, access for disabled people—relaxation can be considered.

A relaxation or dispensation cannot be given if the local authority has already given notice under Section 36 of the Building Act requiring the demolition of unsuitable work and this has not been done. Equally they cannot issue a Section 36 notice if an application for relaxation is still extant.

If an application for relaxation or dispensation is refused an appeal can be lodged with the Secretary of State for the Environment within one month of the date of the refusal. An appeal may also be lodged if the local authority fail to notify their decision within two months.

DETERMINATIONS.—If the local authority rejects plans or the approved inspector refuses to give a plans certificate on the grounds that the Regulations are contravened, the applicant may ask the Secretary of State to determine the issue. The plans, precise grounds for rejection and a statement of the applicant's case should be sent to DoE. The agreement of the local authority or approved inspector is not necessary.

BUILDING CONTROL IN SCOTLAND.—The Building Regulations referred to above apply to England and Wales. Scotland has its own system, the Building (Scotland) Regulations, which differs in that some more onerous requirements apply to combat the more severe weather conditions, and in many other minor matters, including terminology. The mode of making application is also somewhat different.

BUILDING CONTROL IN INNER LONDON.—Inner London comprises the area previous covered by Metropolitan London before the London Government Act. (The LCC area). Its boundaries do not always conform with the boundaries of the new London Boroughs and thus many Boroughs cover areas in which the jurisdiction over building was split between the Borough Council operating the Building Regulations, and the Greater London Council operating the London Constructional By-Laws. With effect from the 1st April 1986 the new Building Regulations apply in London also.

OTHER CONTROLS RELATED TO BUILDINGS.—There is a plethora of Acts controlling special aspects of buildings and certain types of use of buildings. Many of these specialised requirements are enforced or supervised by Factory Inspectors, Public Health Inspectors, or Petroleum Acts personnel and they relate to such matters as the storage of low-flashpoint materials or the provision of adequate ventilation where dusts of organic components may be produced or used. Pest control is a matter for Public Health, as is the provision of washing facilities in food preparation areas.

A major area of control is vested in the Offices, Shops and Railway Premises Act which is administered by Building Control while the Fire Precautions Act is dealt with on a joint basis by Building Control and the Fire Brigade. Means of Escape other than that imposed by the Fire Precautions Act (which has particular reference to Hotels, Hostels and similar multiple occupancy uses) is largely an advisory function of the Fire Brigade operating through the Building Control System.

FIRE RESISTANCE

PASSIVE FIRE RESISTANCE.—Passive resistance to the action of fire on buildings has three objects—to prevent or delay the collapse of the structure, to prevent the spread of fire to other buildings and to allow time for escape and for the setting in motion of inbuilt or external active fire-fighting measures. The behaviour of some classes of materials is dealt with below:

Metals.—Although metals in common building use will not burn or melt at normal building fire temperatures (approx. 1,000°C) they all lose strength and may buckle or bend and thus lead to collapse of other elements. Ordinary mild steel begins seriously to lose structural integrity at about 600°C and thus can contribute to the spread of a local fire by local failure. Aluminum fails earlier than this but cast iron, depending upon its quality, usually survives steel.

Plastics.—No plastics provide fire resistance. They produce quantities of gases, many toxic, when burning and therefore add a further hazard. Glass-reinforced polyesters can provide a limited degree of protection in maintaining the integrity of lightweight roofings used in industrial building, and certain wire-reinforced translucent pvc sheets are also acceptable in limited areas. Thermosetting plastics such as bakelite and ebonite do not soften or melt like the thermoplastics, but fuse and carbonise giving off fumes. Any description as fire resistant and the claimed performance should be supported by independent tests to BS 476.

Masonry, Bricks etc.—Clay blocks and bricks are made by firing at temperatures of 1,000°C or more and thus are reliable in fires but the rapid build-up of a building fire and its subsequent quenching by water may lead to cracking. Concrete blocks similarly may crack due to thermal stress. Special blocks of vermiculite aggregate, expanded clay pellets or diatomaceous earths provide a very high resistance to fire. Stones vary widely and suffer in the same way as bricks, however most common limestones are as good. Stones containing mica and similar inclusions including granites are relatively poor as the expansion of mica flakes causes spalling. When used in thin cladding sheets they may fracture and fall.

Timber.—All timbers burn to a greater or lesser degree but the softwoods commonly used for structural systems are among the more easily ignited woods. The build-up of carbonised material forms a protective layer, so that if the overall section is large enough to tolerate the loss of about 15 mm all round and yet support the load collapse need not result. However overdesign of this magnitude cannot usually be justified. Thin sections such as floor boards, or match-boarding, burn very rapidly especially when in a vertical plane and provide no protection against fire. Modern trussed timber frames, such as trussed purlins or pitched roof trusses are rapidly consumed and collapse, whereas the old-style king-post trusses could survive quite fierce fires. Chipboard and plywood burn more slowly than natural wood but chipboard loses its structural strength more rapidly than natural floorboards.

Glass.—Glass cracks and may fall from frames thus allowing more oxygen to enter and stimulate the fire, but of itself it requires very high temperatures to melt. Wired glasses last longer but must be fairly small panes to avoid failure of the wires due to excessive expansion. Toughened glasses perform well unless the fire is really intense, when the release of stress on one side leads to failure on the other. Double glazing delays overall failure but if the fire-exposed pane collapses the protected pane rapidly follows. Despite cracking the integrity of laminated glasses is retained for a longer period but when the interlayer becomes embrittled no further advantage remains.

Because of the dangers of asbestosis replacements for asbestos are now readily available and are claimed to perform just as well for internal purposes as the high-fibre-content boards.

Renderings etc.—Renderings of cement-sand mixes possess the same qualities as concretes. The mix used determines the adhesion to the substrate, to prevent the rendering falling off due to differential expansion, while the thickness affects the time for which adhesion can be expected to persist. Plasters too, provide fire resistance, particularly those lightweight plasters using exfoliated vermiculite granules as the aggregate. All gypsum-based plasters however, suffer irreversible chemical changes when subjected to fire and have to be renewed afterwards.

Measurement of Fire Resistance.—The fire-resistance of structures is measured in terms of time with the essential purpose of permitting occupants to escape. Limitation of damage is secondary. The fire resistance of materials and elements of structure is determined according to tests given in BS 476 'Fire tests on building materials and structures'.

Scottish Building Standards and the Building Regulations 1985 Approved Document B2/3/4, "Fire Spread" set down the various periods of fire resistance required of buildings. They vary according to the type of occupancy, size of building and the proximity of a site boundary.

Extrinsic Fire Resistance.—Where structural materials do not possess inherent fire resistance applied protection is permitted. Thus in reinforced concrete the cover to the reinforcement may be increased, while with structural steel a number of materials may be used. Hollow protection includes the various special boards, such as vermiculite, mineral fibre and plasterboard. Similarly, suspended floors can be made to comply by the use of fire resistant boards and renderings giving resistance to the highest levels required by regulation. Examples are given in Appendix A of Approved Document B2/3/4 taken from the BRE report 'Guidelines for the Construction of Fire Resisting Structural Elements' (HMSO 1982).

Fire Resisting Doors etc.—In order to localise fire in commercial or industrial buildings they must be subdivided into smaller units by fire resisting walls, usually of 4 h resistance eg one-brick thick walls (215 mm) or 150 mm thick autoclaved aerated concrete blocks. Access from one division of the building to another is by fire resisting doors or shutters. Steel doors of 6 mm plate, with similar styles and rails, hung in 6 mm steel frames or sliding satisfy this requirement, but combinations of metal and inert minerals provide a better appearance and reduced weight. Rolling shutters cannot meet a 4 h requirement unless used in pairs, one to each face of the wall, with a minimum space of 340 mm between the shutters.

In all these applications the doors or shutters have to be made self-closing or automatic in the event of fire, and no obstructions which would impede their effective closure are permitted in the openings. Where large ducts pass through fire-resisting walls or floors similar mechanisms operate shutters, usually multi-bladed 6 mm plate steel louvre-type systems, to close off the passage of fire through the duct.

BSI's Published Documents series PD 6512 is entitled 'Use of elements of structural fire protection with particular reference to the recommendations given in BS 5588 'Fire precautions in the design and construction of buildings''. Only PD 6512: Pt. 1: 1985 'Guide to fire doors' has been published. This gives performance criteria and explains the logic of the provision of fire doors.

Smoke-Check Doors.—Where the object of fire-resistance in doors is to provide time for escape, as opposed to confining the fire to one section of a building, the periods of resistance are in general ½ h or 1 h but it should be noted that the doors described in BS 459 Part 3 'Fire-check flush doors and wood and metal frames (½ h and 1 h types)' did not comply for the appropriate periods with all the requirements of BS 476 Pt. 8 and BS 459 has been withdrawn. The permitted areas of wired glazing in certain doors may show unacceptable levels of transmission of radiant heat thus effectively closing an escape route.

The prime objective of these doors is, however, the prevention of smoke-clogging of escape routes. All such doors are necessarily self-closing. Better safety is achieved if the closing mechanism applies a firm pressure to the door in the closed position so as to combat draught pressures which may nullify the smoke checking. BS 476: Pt. 31: 'Methods for measuring smoke penetration through door sets and shutter assemblies' has only one section BS 476: Pt. 31: Section 31.1: 1983 'Method of measurement under ambient temperature conditions' (≠ISO 5925/1). This enables air in-leakage of door and shutter assemblies to be measured at ambient temperature as representing smoke penetration in the early stages of a fire or at a remote position in the building.

The rapid distribution of smoke by means of ventilation ducts cannot be dealt with by passive means.

ACTIVE FIRE PROTECTION.—Automatic shutters and doors rely upon mechanisms of a simple direct-acting type and have little to go wrong. In London regular inspections and tests of such equipment by the London Fire Brigade are required, but elsewhere the system is less well-established and routine maintenance should be carried out by the building owner. BS 5306 is the 'Code of Practice for fire extinguishing installations and equipment on premises'. Part 1: 1976 (1983) is Hydrant systems, hose reels and foam inlets; Part 2: 1979, sprinkler systems; Part 3: 1985 'Code of Practice for selection, installation and maintenance of portable fire extinguishers, Part 4: 1986 'Carbon dioxide systems', Part 5: Section 5.1: 1982 'Halon 1301 total flooding systems'; and Section 5.2: 1984 'Halon 1211 total flooding systems'. In addition BS 5041 'Fire hydrant system equipments' in five parts covers risers.

Sprinkler Systems.—A sprinkler system is a network of pipes fitted with special sprinkler heads supplied with water from a storage tank. The nozzles have a gelatinous plug which melts at a predetermined temperature thus allowing the water to spray out. Only those sprinklers affected by the fire are actuated, minimising water damage to stock or equipment, but the operation of even one causes a pressure change in the supply system which operates an alarm bell. The alarms can be identified with defined areas. Usually the sprinkler heads are at about 3 m centres in both directions but recesses and stairs have individual heads, often placed to spray the stair itself to protect the escape route. Sprinkler systems are usually tested at weekly intervals by opening valves to run water to waste thus triggering the alarm bells.

Drenchers.—Drenchers apply a concentrated spray of water on to a particular element of a structure so as to further ensure that a fire cannot pass through that element. They have also been used to provide a higher standard of fire resistance to walls (particularly when formed of sheeting materials) when close to a boundary where Regulations would otherwise require higher standards of construction.

Wet Risers.—It used to be common, in multi-storey buildings, to install vertical runs of large-bore pipe provided with standard valved hose-coupling branches at each floor so that the Fire Brigade could connect their hoses direct to a supply at the threatened level. These were maintained full of water from the mains supply.

Dry Risers.—In very tall buildings where ordinary mains water pressure cannot provide a supply to upper floors dry risers enable the Fire Brigade to connect powerful pumps at the base and pump water to the height required.

Hose Reels.—For 'first-aid' action against fire, hose reels of 25 mm bore flexible hose, 15 or 30 m in length, are frequently required by fire-control officers. They are mounted on walls and permanently connected to mains supply. The radius of action of hoses is set out to give virtually complete coverage.

Foam Units.—For high-risk areas where oils are present, such as boiler houses and stores, a foam unit can be installed. Usually operated by thermal devices, it produces a dense foam smothering the fire.

Carbon Dioxide Units.—Where electrical risks exist cylinders of compressed CO_2 are connected to thermal sensors and, on activation, release the gas thus driving out oxygen and smothering the fire.

Fuel Cut-Offs.—In boiler houses a fusible link is connected to a spring-loaded valve on the gas or oil supply line, and to fuel pump switches so that in the event of fire no further fuel will be fed into the system. For mechanical stoking of solid fuels the fusible link or other sensor trips the electrical supply to the stoker.

Fire Venting.—Large industrial workshops are difficult to protect by active measures and yet the accumulation of dense smoke hampers the fire-fighting and the build-up of temperature from an initially localised fire causes rapid spread. While the provision of air supply to a fire will cause intensification of the blaze, the creation of an exit for smoke and the channelling of the blaze towards the exit helps clear the space and enables the Brigade to tackle the fire without resort to breathing apparatus.

Several types of automatic vents are available for industrial roofs. Similarly stairs in multistorey buildings are frequently provided with automatic smoke vents. Sometimes the vents are released by a switch at ground floor. Lift shafts are also provided with permanent vents immediately beneath the lift motor room floor, which also allow air to be induced or extracted by the piston action of the lift car.

Fire Brigade Access.—The positioning of buildings, especially those with high fire-loading (eg buildings for storage or manufacture of oils, paints, rubber, cellulose etc) must take account of the need for adequate access to all parts for Fire Brigade vehicles. The provision of fire mains throughout large sites is frequently obligatory. Pedestrianised areas of towns or large shopping precincts must incorporate routes of suitable width and height for fire engines and any bollards must be of the removable or hinged type.

FIRE WARNING SYSTEMS.—Fire detection and alarm systems in buildings are covered by BS 5839 of that title. Part 1 1980 is the 'Code of Practice for installation and servicing' (formerly CP 1019) and Part 2 1983 is the 'Specification for manual call points'. The sprinkler system alarm is sounded only when the fire reaches an intensity, at ceiling level, sufficient to set the process in action, and this may be after a blaze has spread widely, rather than intensely. Manual fire alarm call points, usually a push button in a glass-fronted case, operate only when personnel are present. They are obligatory in most office and commercial buildings. Backed up by staff with some training in the use of extinguishers to deal with the early onset, if within their capacity, they can assist to delay or confine matters until the arrival of the Brigade.

However, the most effective warning systems are those designed to sense the earliest stages of a fire by detection of smoke. These use light or ionized beams and are covered by BS 5445 Part 7 1984, (EN 54 Part 7 1982) 'Point-type smoke detectors using scattered light, transmitted light or ionization'. There is a separate standard for residential applications where people sleep, BS 5446 Part 1 1977 'Point-type smoke detectors'. The equipment is set so that dust motes or tobacco smoke do not operate the system.

In air conditioning and ventilating systems, smoke detectors are essential if the system is not to spread smoke into all areas from what may be a small localised source. The detectors frequently switch off the fan system as well as sounding an alarm.

Thermal detectors capable of sensing undue levels of heat are particularly useful for dealing with enclosed plant where the first indication may be by heat rather than smoke. There are two temperature levels covered by BS 5445 Part 5 1977 (EN 54 Pt. 5), 'Heat sensitive detectors—point detectors containing a static element' and Part 8 1984 (EN 54 Pt. 8, 1982) 'High temperature heat detectors'.

A centralised panel, with test rigs incorporated, receives the information from the detectors and registers any alarm visually. Such panels also incorporate a telephone device to transmit a pre-recorded message to the Brigade, and an alarm repeater panel is sited near the main entrance so that the location of the incident is immediately apparent. Regular and rigorous maintenance of such systems is necessary so as to prevent false alarms being given.

FIRE PRECAUTIONS.—BS 5588 'Fire precautions in the design and construction of buildings' gives guidance on various aspects both mandatory and advisable. It supersedes CP3: chapter IV: 1948. Part 1 'Residential buildings' has Section 1.1 1984 as a 'Code of Practice for single-family dwellinghouses'. It gives guidance on structural fire precautions and the provision of means of escape in houses. Part 2: 1985 'Code of Practice for shops' is applicable to premises used for retail services and trades and places of refreshment as well as shops of all sizes. It covers similar areas of protection etc as Part 3. Part 3 1983 is the 'Code of Practice for office buildings' and gives recommendations for planning, construction and protection of escape routes, fire precautions in engineering services, fire alarms and procedures, extinguishing and fire fighting equipment water supplies, access for fire fighting and smoke control. Part 4 1978 is 'Smoke control in protected escape routes using pressurization.' This is an alternative to the natural ventilation required by certain regulations. BS 5908 1980 'Code of Practice for fire precautions in chemical plant' gives recommendations governing hazards in operating chemical plant, and precautions to be taken in design and layout and advice on fire protection. Computer installations have a special code BS 6266 1982 'Code of Practice for fire protection for electronic data processing installations'.

THERMAL INSULATION REQUIREMENTS

The requirements of the Building regulations 1985 are given in Part L "Conservation of Fuel and Power". Compliance is based on the windows and rooflights having a U value of 5.7 when the areas should be no more than those given in Table 1 reproduced from the Approved Document L2/3 as are Tables 2 and 3.

TABLE 1.—MAXIMUM AREA OF WINDOWS (SINGLE GLAZED)

Building type	Windows	Rooflights
dwellings	windows and rooflights together 12 per cent of perimeter wall area	
other residential (including hotels and institutional)	25 per cent exposed wall area	20 per cent of roof area
places of assembly offices shops	35 per cent of exposed wall area	20 per cent of roof area
industrial and storage	15 per cent of exposed wall area	20 per cent of roof area

Double glazing permits twice the areas to be used and triple glazing or low emissivity coatings three times.

There are two approved procedures. Procedure 1 uses tables of specified insulation thickness and Procedure 2 uses Specified U values. The second method enables full account to be taken of the insulating properties of the construction. In either case the areas of windows and rooflights must comply with Table 1 above and the U values of the construction must be not more than those given in Table 2.

TABLE 2.—MAXIMUM U VALUES (W/m^2K)

Building type	Exposed walls	Roofs	Exposed floors
dwellings	0·6	0·35	0·6
other residential (including hotels and institutional)	0·6	0·6	0·6
places of assembly offices, shops'	0·6	0·6	0·6
industrial and storage	0·7	0·7	0·7

For a typical wall construction of clay facing brick, cavity, autoclaved aerated concrete block, insulating plaster and insulation in the cavity, the Approved Document shows how the U value is calculated as shown in table 3 below.

TABLE 3.—CALCULATION OF U VALUE OF TYPICAL WALL CONSTRUCTION TO MEET 0·6 W/m^2K

Construction	Thickness m	Thermal Conductivity W/mK	Thermal Resistance $m^2/K/W$
outside wall surface	—	—	0·06
brick outer leaf	0·1	0·84	0·12

TABLE 3 (*continued*).—CALCULATION OF U VALUE OF TYPICAL WALL CONSTRUCTION TO MEET 0·6 W/m²K

Construction	Thickness m	Thermal Conductivity W/mK	Thermal Resistance m²/K/W
air space	—	—	0·18
thermal insulation	0·025	0·035	0·71
block inner leaf	0·1	0·23	0·43
plaster	0·015	0·17	0·09
inside wall surface	—	—	0·12
		total thermal resistance	1·71

$$\text{U value} = \frac{1}{\text{total thermal resistance}} = \frac{1}{1{\cdot}71} = 0{\cdot}58\ \text{W/m}^2\text{K}$$

Thus the wall meets the requirement.

The Regulations also require that space heating or hot water systems have automatic controls and that hot water pipes, with certain exceptions, and hot water storage vessels shall have adequate thermal insulation.

Heat Loss and Conservation.—The process of heat exchange depends upon the area, thickness and type of materials through which heat has to pass. In buildings the usual principal concern is the loss of internal heat to the external air via the enclosing skin of the structure (fabric loss), but the direct loss of warmed internal air to the exterior (ventilation loss) is always a significant proportion of total heat loss and sometimes can be the major factor, particularly in industrial buildings with large loading doors. Similarly, many industrial processes require large quantities of air, either for cooling or to provide suitable working conditions for operatives, and where those requirements are unavoidable a great deal of energy is wasted in warming air which is then discharged to the exterior.

The measurement of heat loss and methods of heating and ventilating are dealt with in the Heating, Ventilation and Air Conditioning chapter (J1).

The design of a building to produce optimum thermal performance has more influence upon the costs of installation and running than the selection of heating methods and controls. The materials used in the enclosure can be selected to provide high thermal insulation, reducing energy loss, but the provision of daylighting for functional or psychological purposes brings the problem of increased losses. Double glazing reduces conduction losses but has only a marginal effect on radiation losses. Insulation should be provided to prevent loss through the ground floor.

Ventilation losses occur by the infiltration and exfiltration of air through the fabric particularly in sheeted construction of roofs and walls, and ventilation by open windows and doors or by fan systems. A closely-fitting system of sheeting and lining must be selected and all cracks and unsealed junctions (eg where walls meet roof) should be sealed up. The reduction of the second type of loss can only be by good discipline in controlling casual opening of windows and doors (and by efficient door closers) and by flexible control systems on fan installations so that modulation to suit varying conditions is available or automatic. The provision of air locks to large door openings and the use of 'crash doors' of rubber or plastics provide useful control of air movements at busy entrances, as do automatically opening doors. The effect of high ventilation rates demanded by certain processes is less easy to deal with but if all fume-entrainment systems are designed with the supply air discharge as close to the fume production point as possible so as not to draw air from the working area, the conditions in the remainder of the workshop will be more controllable. This principle applies equally to chemical processes such as plating and dipping, paint spraying, and to deep fat frying in commercial kitchens. Even where the entrainment process requires that the entraining air be heated it is better that a controlled supply be made to the plant than to accept the vagaries of temperature otherwise applicable to workshop air.

By contrast, there are many industrial processes which produce waste heat in such quantity that the main problem is the disposal of unwanted energy. Many heat-recovery systems have been designed and can convert low-grade waste-heat into high-grade primary heat to provide hot water and space heating, eg heat pumps.

Performance of Materials.—The thermal insulation performance of building materials is closely inversely related to their density; thus, for a given thickness, lightweight plastic foams provide greater insulation than concrete. But the capacity of materials to store heat energy is closely directly related to their density and thus heavy materials, once heated, will release heat for a longer period of time than lightweight materials. Striking a balance between the use of dense and light materials depends upon the response characteristics required of the building. A building in constant use may be constructed so that dense materials are contained within an insulating layer, permitting a relatively unsophisticated control system for the heating plant because the heavy mass of materials provides a 'fly-wheel' of heat energy, while a building of intermittent use may be designed with the insulation internally so as to provide a quick warm-up, accompanied by an equally quick cool-down. The control system for the second type of construction must include sensitive detectors if a reasonable consistency of heating levels is to be achieved. (For thermal performance values see chapter J1).

ACOUSTIC REQUIREMENTS AND CHARACTERISTICS OF BUILDINGS

The Airborne sound insulation requirements between adjacent dwellings are specified by Part E "Resistance to the Passage of Sound" of the Building Regulations 1985. The Regulations do not deal with noise from outside the dwelling as this is regarded primarily as a matter of planning rather than structural control.

The requirement now is, quite simply, that floors and walls shall have a reasonable resistance to sound. Floors must meet the requirements for both Airborne and Impact sound transmission while separating walls are only required to meet the requirement in respect of Airborne sound transmission.

The Approved Document E1/2/3 gives examples of types of construction giving suitable insulation against direct sound transmission. Broadly the weight of a brick wall including plaster should be at least 375 kg/m^2 and the masonry alone 355 kg/m^2 with bricks laid frog up. The weight of a concrete wall, blocks or insitu or precast concrete should be 415 kg/m^2 including plaster.

Attention is drawn to key junctions to minimize flanking transmission, the indirect transmission of sound from one side of a floor or wall to the other. This includes floor junctions and the minimum distance of windows on each side of a separating wall.

BS 4142 1967 'Method of rating industrial noise affecting mixed residential and industrial areas' (≠ ISO/R1996) gives measurement procedures and criteria for mixed development.

The exposure of operators to noise is covered in the main by a 'Code of Practice for reducing the exposure of employed persons to noise' published by the Health and Safety Executive and the Woodworking Machines Regulations 1974 which set down a maximum of 90dB over an eight hour average.

Room Acoustics and Noise.—These two aspects of acoustic engineering in buildings are quite distinct, and each has only a marginal effect upon the other. Room acoustics are concerned with the propagation and reverberation of sound within a space, while noise which can be described as intrusive noise concerns the transmission of sound from one space to another. CP3 Chapter III 1972. 'Sound insulation and noise reduction' gives guidance as to the design, siting and construction of buildings to ensure adequate sound insulation and noise reduction. It includes a section on the legal aspects of noise nuisance. BS 2750: 1980. 'Methods of measurement of sound insulation in buildings and of building elements.' (≡ ISO 140/1–8) is in eight parts.

Room Acoustics.—The control of the quality of a sound generated in a room is achieved by the provision of surfaces whose reflective and absorptive qualities differ. In general terms sound is reflected by smooth dense surfaces, diffused by rough-textured surfaces and absorbed by pocketed surfaces. Thus for an auditorium it is usual to provide a smooth hard reflector around the sound source, the stage, diffusing surfaces to side walls and absorbent surfaces to the rear in order to prevent the creation of echoes. The audience and seating provide absorbent surfaces, the seats being designed to afford much the same values when empty as do seated persons. Finally the air itself provides absorption of sound, particularly at higher frequencies.

The shape of the room also affects sound quality, and it is important to avoid concave surfaces which act as focussing agents creating intensive sound in one area while starving adjacent areas. Furthermore, in industrial applications where the generated sound may be of a limited range of frequencies, it is important to ensure that the lengths of the principal axes of the room do not coincide with a near harmonic of any of the principal frequencies as a magnification of that frequency will occur.

Noise.—Noise is unwanted sound and its control depends upon the mode of transmission from the source to the affected area. In general terms the provision of dense or massive barriers is the method most used in buildings, the sound energy being absorbed as heat or mechanical energy. Such conducted energy can travel from room to room via external walls and a structural discontinuity at junctions is desirable. Similarly continuous floors can transmit sound to adjacent areas.

An alternative to absorption by mass of material is the provision of multiple but disconnected barriers with absorptive mats in the cavities, while in double glazing the absorptive material is placed around the sides of the interspace, which must be at least 125 mm wide.

Sympathetic vibration of flexible barriers can reproduce a noise in an adjacent room, even in double-skin construction unless the leaves are constructed of different thicknesses or materials. Similar precautions should be taken with double glazing.

Impact Noise.—With impact noise, whether by footsteps or mechanical plant the energy is transmitted direct to the structure and passes rapidly to all connected elements. In principle, the more dense the connecting medium the more rapid and complete the transmission. Thus discontinuity and the interposition of 'floppy' materials is the only defence against such intrusive noise. Traffic surfaces should be separated from the structural floor by fibrous interlayers or mounted on acoustically-designed clips, and plant should be mounted on bases separated from the remainder of the structure by compressible membranes.

Vibration.—Vibration is a frequent accompaniment of impact noise and may be contained by similar discontinuity, but where the vibration is due to rotatory plant, including reciprocating engines, the effects can be even more severe as the structure is subjected to a patterned series of pulses of energy which can give rise to harmonic vibration of the structure. Large span structures can in this way be induced to deflect and develop increasingly large reversals of stress, even to the point of collapse. Structural stiffness which raises the harmonic frequency to safe levels, allied with primary isolation of the vibration source, should be adopted.

Vibratory Noise.—External wind forces applied to buildings increase in magnitude with height and can give rise to vibrations of such elements as windows, louvres and roof-mounted plant and pipework. Robust construction and positive fixings against multi-directional application of such forces are essential if vibration and vibration-induced noise are to be controlled. Similarly, louvres to extract and intake ducts of ventilation systems can, if too light and flexible, vibrate to produce 'reed' conditions and give rise to loud musical notes. Additional strutting or the removal of alternate blades may have to be resorted to.

Automatic Noise Control Devices.— For locations close to aircraft take-off and landing flight paths, where ambient noise levels can rise to 100 decibels, the construction of buildings must be generally of massive materials and roofs must be constructed much more carefully than is normal. Solid reinforced concrete slabs with high stiffness, to reduce vibration from the sound pressure applied, are virtually obligatory if tolerable conditions are to be achieved internally. Treatment of glazed areas in walls and roofs is usually by multiple glazing, but where openable ventilators are required several types of automatic devices are available. All are operated by a sound-level metering sensor which in sophisticated versions senses the rate of rise of sound pressure and energises the motorised closing mechanisms according to the extrapolated configuration of the rise thus achieving closure in advance of peak pressure. Less complex systems operate on achievement of a selected sound pressure and may close the windows when a particular aircraft movement does not actually achieve nuisance levels.

DESIGN OF STRUCTURES

The structure of a building may be load-bearing masonry or a frame. The design and construction of concrete structures is described in Chapter I3, steel structures in Chapter I4 and general information about timber is given in Chapter C1. The relevant design code for concrete is BS 8110: 'Structural Use of Concrete', Part 1: 1985 'Code of Practice for Design and Construction' Part 2: 1985 'Code of Practice for Special Circumstances'. For steel and timber the codes are, BS 5950, 'The Structural Use of Steelwork in Building'; and BS 5268, 'The Structural Use of Timber'. CP 112 Part 3 1973 'Trussed Rafters for Roofs of Dwellings' give details of materials, functional requirements, permissible spans and handling and erection of Fink and Fan type trussed rafters. This Chapter is generally confined to traditional building methods, typified in domestic construction by the cavity wall with a facing brick outer leaf and concrete block inner leaf.

This form of construction, which is the most frequent in single to four storey construction, has been used for load-bearing or reinforced or prestressed structures more than 20 storeys high. The design of masonry is codified in BS 5628 'The Structural Use of Masonry'. Part 1 1978 covers unreinforced masonry and Part 2 1985 reinforced and prestressed masonry. The constructional and other aspects are dealt with in Part 3 : 1985 'Materials and components, design and workmanship'. This supersedes CP 121 Part 1 1973 'Brick and Block Masonry'. In general most structural Codes and Standards are quoted in Approved Documents as meeting the requirements of the Building Regulations 1985. The loading requirements for masonry are given in BS 6399 : Part 1 : 1984 'Code of Practice for Dead and Imposed Loads' and the lateral wind pressures to be allowed for in design in CP 3 : Chapter V : Part 2 : 1972 'Wind Loads'. It is also necessary to allow for additional loads, for example, if materials are stacked against walls, and for reduced resistance as in gable walls upstanding before the roof is emplaced.

LOAD-BEARING MASONRY.—Simple structures, including two-storey domestic housing, can be, and frequently are, designed by what are essentially rule-of-thumb methods, the more important requirements for which were incorporated in Schedule 7 of the old Building Regulations. Such methods have the disadvantage that seemingly small, indeed insignificant, changes in materials or methods of construction may lead to significant redistribution of loads. As an example, the use of trussed rafters has transferred the roof load from purlins set in entire cavity wall gables to the inner leaf of low strength lightweight autoclaved aerated concrete blocks often containing large window and door openings. With the end of the old Regulations a BS is being drafted to codify the design of small dwellings with the intention that it should be cited in Approved Documents.

Masonry is a remarkably resilient material with traditionally large inherent factors of safety, but in large or more complex structures not only is engineering design required for safety it is also necessary to achieve the most efficient and economical use of the material. Post war design of loadbearing walls was formalized in CP 111, starting in 1948 and revised significantly to take account of modern research in 1964, and finally in 1970. These 'Structural recommendations for loadbearing walls' were based on permissible stress. In this method of design the ultimate stress at which the various materials fail are determined and divided by a single factor of safety to arrive at the permissible or working stress. In other countries a load-factor approach is used in which the working loads are multiplied by a factor of safety and the ultimate stresses of the materials are used to compute a safe combination in the structure.

CP 111 1970 has been withdrawn and superseded by the new limit state code BS 5628 Part 1 1978 'Unreinforced masonry' and Part 2 : 1985 'Structural use of reinforced and prestressed masonry'.

The basis of limit state design is that consideration should be given to all the likely ways in which an element or structure might fail to carry out its design function, and that the designer then ensures that there is an acceptable probability that failure will not take place. Limit state design recognizes the inherent variability of applied loads, the materials used and the process of construction.

The modes of failure (limit states) are:

Ultimate limit states—failure in compression, tension, flexure or shear.

Serviceability limit states—cracking, deflection, displacement.

In masonry permissible stresses have usually been related to ultimate stresses so the limit state method is a more refined approach. The serviceability limit state is governed more by general layout and detailing covered in BS 5628 : Part 3 : 1985. BS 5628 Parts 1 and 3 are quoted in Approved Document A1/2 as able to be used to meet the requirements of the Building Regulations 1985.

Despite very considerable research there is still inadequate statistical knowledge of the parameters involved in structural design, and, in consequence, a simplified approach has been used in BS 5628 Part 1 based on partial safety factors and using characteristic values of the various parameters, eg compressive strength, flexural strength, required.

It should be noted that quite apart from the new limit state approach BS 5628 Part 1 provides for the first time a design method for the lateral resistance of non-loadbearing walls subjected to a uniformly distributed wind load and a whole section on design against accidental damage which is mandatory for all buildings of 5-storeys and above.

Not only must buildings be designed properly, they must also be properly constructed and the standard of workmanship must be ensured. BS 5628 : Part 3 : 1985 deals with the design and erection of brick and block walls including recommendations regarding the type and quality of materials to be used. In general reference is made to BS 5628 : Part 1 for design methods, but certain rules of thumb are given, including design of free-standing single leaf walls without piers subject to windloads only, by reference to maximum permitted height to thickness ratios related to wind zones, and the maximum sizes of rectangular walls and gables up to four storeys in relation to wind zone, height and edge conditions. Some guidance is also given on the effect of openings on the lateral load resistance to be allowed. An important section concerns structural detailing for stability including floors, roofs, supports over openings, anchorages, dowels and fixings, the requirements for the spacing of wall ties, cautionary notes on fixings, chases and holes for services and limitations on the height of the chimney upstand above the highest point of the roof in relation to its width.

It also gives design recommendations for movements in masonry, exclusion of moisture and durability which are referred to further in the section 'Brickwork and Blockwork' below. Tables of notional fire resistance enable different types and thicknesses of masonry to be related to the period of fire resistance in hours. Some guidance is given on design to comply with thermal insulation and sound absorption requirements. The design section includes information on masonry bonds, brick arches and the limitation on corbelling on one third of the thickness of the wall.

A useful additional document for engineers and architects which has run through several editions and revisions since it was first published in 1967 is the Model Specification for Clay and Calcium Silicate Structural Brickwork published by the British Ceramic Research Association as Special Publication 56 : 1980. This gives model clauses to be written into the designer's own specification the better to ensure the quality of the workmanship and the most advantageous use of the materials.

REINFORCED AND PRE-STRESSED MASONRY.—Brief and inadequate guidance on reinforcement was given in CP 111 1970 but has been superseded by a completely new code of practice BS 5628 Part 2 1985 'Reinforced and Prestressed Masonry'. As in the case of Part 1, this is written in limit state terms and contains recommendations based on the latest research results available. It deals with design principles, including loads and partial safety factors, and gives data on the properties of materials including the characteristic strengths of brickwork and blockwork in compression and shear, the characteristic tensile strength of reinforcement and the anchorage bond strength. Separate sections cover the design of masonry walls and columns under vertical axial loading; design to resist lateral loads including masonry retaining walls and pocket type retaining walls; design of walls and columns subjected to simultaneous vertical loads and moments or horizontal loads; reinforced masonry beams; prestressed masonry; detailing of reinforced and prestressed masonry; and work on site. It is the first attempt at a unified limit state code for reinforced and prestressed masonry and although much of the background to the thinking inevitably derives from data on reinforced concrete, there is now a good deal of experimental data on masonry and the continuing research and experience of engineers in use is expected to lead to revisions, as more information becomes available.

BUILDING CONSTRUCTION

GENERALLY.—Buildings are designed to enclose space and keep out the elements. They must therefore be founded on suitable subsoil in an adequate manner, must resist the forces of the wind, the penetration of water (whether from the ground or by rain) and the ingress of intruders. These are the basic performance requirements, but they are supplemented by many secondary factors concerned with heating, lighting, noise and finishings for durability and appearance.

In the following text, subjects are dealt with in the conventional order of construction. Often the design process works in a reverse direction.

DEMOLITION AND SITE CLEARANCE.—The Code of Practice for demolition is BS 6187 : 1982 which superseded CP 94. It deals with the preliminary procedures for demolition work, the methods of demolition and their suitability for various types and elements of structure and the protective precautions to be taken.

The necessity to demolish relatively recent structures built in the industrialized building boom of the Sixties has focussed attention on the problems of dealing with reinforced and particularly prestressed concrete. Any complex case or one on a site with restricted access will usually be best dealt with by employing a specialist demolition contractor who has the necessary equipment, transport and a market for the recovered material. On some jobs taking down by hand and clearing the site as the work proceeds makes for safe working conditions and best salvage value, but the use of explosives and/or machines may enable an earlier start to be made on redevelopment thus far outweighing the credit on old materials.

To ensure that the site has been thoroughly cleared and made safe with no hidden hazards, it may be necessary to search historical records, particularly on city centre sites where buildings have existed for centuries. Old Ordnance Survey maps and Goad's Insurance maps often provide information on the location of forgotten vaults, basements or wells and may pinpoint buried foundations.

SITE INVESTIGATIONS.—BS 5930 : 1981 'Code of practice for site investigations' covers the investigations of sites to assess their suitability for building works and the acquisition of knowledge concerning the characteristics of the site that affect the design and construction and the security of neighbouring land and property. Information on the properties of soil is given in Chapter I2 'Foundation and Earthwork'.

LEVELLING AND SETTING OUT

LEVELLING FOR EXCAVATION.—Levelling of a site to establish its topography is carried out by the engineer or land surveyor using various optical and electronic instruments. Each survey is normally referred back to Ordance Datum, the mean sea level datum, at Newlyn in Cornwall, but can be referred to a local datum, normally some relatively permanent surfące which will not be affected by the development proposed. When reference is made to Ordnance Datum a local 'bench-mark' is used and all levels are recorded as AOD (Above Ordance Datum).

Maintaining levels throughout the progress of building works is frequently carried out by means of rods and other vertical measures, though the bottoms of foundation and drain trenches are controlled by the use of 'boning'. In this system a number of pegs (and cross-bars) are levelled to a convenient height above the excavated level required and it is simple for the site supervisors, using a T-shaped rod, to sight along the levelled marks as the excavation proceeds until the top of the rod, held upright on the trench bottom, is in line with the templates originally set up.

Water levels, first used by the Egyptians, are still conveniently used on building sites where their capacity for use around blind corners saves much time.

A simple and reliable short-range optical level devised for builders uses a split image where on half of the staff image seen through the eyepiece is an erect visual image, the other half being an inverted visual image of the same area. A sliding cross-bar on the staff is moved up or down until the two images coincide and the level is read off from the back of the staff. The level instrument can be mounted on a tripod for general surveying, or upon a special short base-plate for levelling of brickwork. Its maximum range is about 30 m and its accuracy ± 2 mm at that range.

A 'storey-rod' is used for small works. It consists of a length of timber marked with saw cuts at various points to denote cill heights, door heights, lintols, ceilings and floor levels. This, if accurately done, is the most convenient template for practical use on site, but it depends upon the base level on which it is stood being accurately levelled in the first place. Accuracy of levelling in industrialised constructions where large units are assembled can be much higher than in traditional buildings but surveys by BRE have shown a wide range of deviation from the planned levels. In the end the accuracy of working depends upon the quality of the site supervision. (See also chapter I1, Surveying.)

EXCAVATION

EXCAVATION FOR FOUNDATIONS.—Hand digging of foundations is only resorted to for very small projects, but where it arises it should be borne in mind that 1.8 m is regarded as the maximum height that a man can conveniently throw out soil and that he requires a space about 1.5 m long in at least one dimension to do this. A very deep localised excavation will require intermediate stagings at 1.5 m intervals for successive lifts to be made.

Hand digging should also be employed where underground services may be encountered and in such cases a thorough search for record drawings should be made, including by enquiry at the offices of the Local Authority and the various statutory undertakers.

Mechanical digging by hydraulic shovels is otherwise almost always used for excavation whether of trenches or local pits and can be very accurately performed by skilled operators. Trenches as narrow as 450 mm wide may be dug to a depth of 2.4 m with appropriate equipment, the spoil being either deposited beside the trench or loaded direct to lorries. In soils with adequate bearing capacity and where the loads are domestic it is common in such narrow trenches to pour concrete direct to within about 150 mm of the ground surface and then commence brickwork, rather than have to dig a wider trench to enable the bricklayers to work at the lower levels on a shallow strip foundation. With this method of 'trench fill' it is important to locate all the service holes for drains, pipes or cables before filling, in order to avoid wasteful cutting.

When excavating in clay the last 100 mm of clay should only be removed immediately prior to concreting as exposure to weather for long periods leads to excessive drying of the trench bottom and subsequent cracking of the foundation strip as rehumidification takes place.

Occasionally an inclusion or 'lens' of different soil occurs in a run of excavation. These 'soft spots' can be bridged by the reinforcement of the strip but if the span exceeds 2 m, or the soft spot occurs at the corner or end of a trench, further excavation should be carried out and the foundations revised or redesigned to cope with the problem.

SUPPORTING EXCAVATIONS.—Rock and chalk can be dug and cut to vertical faces without difficulty, as can peat, but granular soils and vegetable soils with high humus content tend to crumble away. Stiff clays can be cut vertically but can be unreliable in wet weather. All soils which are liable to slump should be restrained by timbering. (See chapter, I2 'Foundations and Earthwork'.)

Very wet and waterlogged sites present difficulties for excavation. Pumping of excavations can be satisfactory if flow is moderate and if a suitable discharge is available. An extension of the idea is to 'de-water' the ground by inserting a large number of small boreholes about the site and extracting the water from them all, so that the water table is locally dropped and excavation can proceed in relatively dry soil. Another method of dealing with waterlogging is to fill the excavation with a suitable foundation material as digging proceeds.

Made ground is one of the most difficult soils to deal with as its variability necessitates different treatment for each filling type encountered. Where the filling is of rubbish the work must be carried out largely by hand and precautions taken for the safety of the workmen. As a general rule it should be ensured that no workman is alone in any trench more than 1.5 m deep and close supervision should be given from above so that accidental falls of soil are immediately dealt with.

FOUNDATIONS

Ultimately all building forces find their way to the ground and thus the design of the foundations can only be commenced when all the known and anticipated loads and the weight of the structure are calculated and positioned. The size and type of foundation vary according to the capacity of the subsoil to carry load without undue compression or movements, and according to adjacent conditions of loading from other buildings or plant. Some types of soil vary in their load capacity according to their moisture content which may vary seasonally. BS 8004:1986 'Foundations' is the Code of Practice for the design and construction of all types of foundations for the normal range of buildings; CP 101 : 1972, 'Foundations and Substructures for Non-Industrial Buildings of not more than Four Stories' relates only to buildings of such a type that the foundation loads are evenly dispersed. In addition the first part of the small buildings code, BS 8103 'Structural Design of Low-rise Buildings', contains recommendations in Part 1:1986 'Code of Practice for Stability, Site Investigation, Foundations and Ground Floor Slabs for Housing' for detached, semi-detached and terraced houses of not more than three storeys above ground for single family occupancy and of traditional masonry construction. (See also, Chapter 'Foundations and Earthworks').

SPECIAL CIRCUMSTANCES.—Foundations may have to be specially designed to cope with external problems imposed by nature or human activities which can cause movement of the subsoil itself. Such causes are:

Subsidence.—This can occur where mining or brine pumping takes place. Foundations in such areas require careful engineering design. Large continuous foundations should be avoided and flexible building structures are necessary. Many systems of design for use in mining areas have been devised, most of them using 'three point' or 'tripod' base patterns. The tripod base system is applied to each of a series of building cells which make up the whole development, its virtue being that settlement of one or even two 'legs' still leaves the base resting fully on the ground. The building cell is jacked on the base to maintain levels. In general consultation with the mining undertaking concerned is advisable in order that directions and anticipated rates of subsidence can be established in advance.

Landslip.—Geological investigation can establish the probable 'slip circles' of a given site with a moderate degree of accuracy, but the restraint of the unstable section and the design of foundations are matters for an experienced engineer. These areas should be avoided if possible.

Settlement.—This the vertical movement of a building into the soil under the influence of its own weight. Short-term settlement arising from compaction of the soil beneath the foundations can usually be accommodated by structures without difficulty unless a subsoil fault or weakness exists which imposes high stresses at local points. Long-term settlement of heavy structures can be serious, and the juxtaposition of diverse structural types can raise problems.

For short-term differential settlement in extensive buildings the following measures can be adopted:—(*a*) Ensuring uniform foundation pressures. (*b*) Reinforcement of foundations. (*c*) Piling to a suitable bottom or set. (*d*) Forming constructional breaks in the building structure to allow separate parts to settle independently. This is essential where ground pressures can not be made uniform, and where long-term settlement of a section of the building can be anticipated.

Earthquakes.—These are rare in Britain, but earth tremors do occur, usually of such a low magnitude that normal building is well able to withstand them. Other areas of the world are, however, subject to frequent tremors and buildings have to be designed with this in mind. The foundations for such buildings can be of the subsidence type, (ie the tripod base system) for low-rise or large spreading plans, but high buildings are sometimes constructed on the 'tree-trunk' principle of a single massive support system resting on a very deep and rigid base block. For further general guidance see BRE Digests Nos. 63, 64, 67, 75, 92 and 95.

FOUNDATION WIDTHS AND THICKNESSES.—Mass concrete foundations must be spread sufficiently to reduce the pressure on the supporting stratum to a safe intensity. They must also be sufficiently thick to resist shear failure and uneven settlement. While framed buildings commonly rest upon pad foundations (ie local blocks of in-situ concrete under the frame legs) conventional walls are set on strip foundations of concrete centrally located under the wall. Excluding foundations direct on firm rock, it is usual to project the strip footing about 150 mm from the wall face each side, even if loading does not warrant this, as the smallest convenient width for excavation by hand is about 600 mm. The thickness should also be a minimum of 150 mm, or, where the width is calculated, equal to the projection of the footing beyond the wall face. For more heavily loaded walls on soils other than rock, the minimum thickness should be half the width.

Table 4 shows some general guidance figures for the width of strip foundations in various types of soil according to a number of different loadings. In doubtful circumstances the soil should be tested by a qualified engineer to establish its probable capacity, but the tabulated figures will permit a preliminary design to be arrived at. It should be noted that where the soil is weak and the loads are excessive strip foundations are not a suitable solution. Bearing pressures are limited by the type of soil and CP 101 : 1972 gives guidance on this.

TABLE 4.—MINIMUM WIDTHS OF STRIP FOUNDATIONS (mm)

	Type of Subsoil	Condition of subsoil	Total load in kN/lineal metre of not more than 20	30	40	50	60	70
I	Rock	*	Equal to width of wall					
II III	Gravel Sand Clay Sandy Clay	Compact Stiff	250	300	400	500	600	650
IV	Clay Sandy Clay	Firm	300	350	450	600	750	850
V	Sand Silty Sand Clayey Sand	Loose	400	600				
VI	Silt Clay Sandy Clay Silty Sand	Soft	450	650	Foundations do not fall within this section of Building Regulations at loads >30 kN/m.			
VII	Silt Clay Sandy Clay Silty Clay	Very soft	600	850				

* Not inferior to sandstone, limestone or firm chalk.

FOUNDATION DEPTH.—The depth of foundations depends upon various factors:
(*a*) Thickness of vegetable soil and root conditions.
(*b*) Thickness of any filling over the site.
(*c*) Level at which a suitable bearing soil (of adequate thickness) can be found.
(*d*) Effects of frost.

(*e*) Nature of soil.
(*f*) Underground rooms etc.

(*a*) Vegetable soil thickness varies widely but for costing purposes is commonly taken at 150 mm, however if substantial roots of live trees and large shrubs are encountered (say 5 mm diameter) the foundation excavation must be carried down clear of these. Dead roots from trees taken down more than two years previously may be ignored as any readjustment of the subsoil to an equilibrium moisture content should have been completed in two annual cycles in most soils.

Excavations near live trees, that is, within a distance equal to the height of the tree, involves problems of root growth and desiccation of the soil and can result in a 'drag' of the building by the shrinkage of the soil, causing severe cracking and ultimate instability of the building. The construction of a root barrier clear of the building is a possible solution, but in the case of potential forest trees this can be an extensive and costly operation.

Equally, the removal of large trees from the site and immediate environs of a building just prior to construction can lead to a 'thrust' on the building by the expansion of the soil previously being drained by the root system.

Finally, when building in woodland a combination of both drag and thrust can be exerted on a building by the powerful forces of expansion and contraction of the soil and the continuing, or accelerated, growth of the peripheral trees at the edge of the felled area. Little definitive information is available on the subject and the services of an experienced engineer who has met the problems before will be essential as the rates of movement and their magnitude vary according to the type of soil.

(*b*) Filled sites are always difficult and more costly to build on than equivalent unfilled sites. In principle all foundations should be carried down to virgin subsoil, but provided that the fill is fully compacted and is of hard material (ie not organic rubbish or hollow objects such as oil drums), and the requisite reinforcement is provided in the floor slab, non-load-bearing partitions may be built off the slab. Strip foundations should be rejected where the fill is very thick (say more than 900 mm thick) and a combination of pads and beams used.

Never found a building on fill.

(*c*) The subsoil under a building is frequently found to be in strata of varying compositions. The strata can be immensely thick or as thin as 300 mm thus if excavation reveals a good bearing stratum at an appropriate depth it is wise to establish the thickness of that material in case there may be a weak underlying material. It should be borne in mind that the stratum revealed by excavation has been carrying the weight of the material excavated and that the building loads imposed on the stratum can be regarded as reduced by that weight: however, there is always a massive increase in loading for conventional buildings and the failure to establish the thickness of the proposed bearing stratum can be disastrous. Clearly all such investigations can only be a sampling of the conditions but if one trial hole in a group reveals a disquieting lack of thickness the design of the foundations should be reconsidered so as to reduce the intensity of the bearing pressure.

Subsoils in which a more intensive investigation may be justified are limestones and particularly, chalks in certain localities. Limestone has its 'pot-holes' which are usually known about in the district, but the propensity of chalk to be eroded underground by natural water movements can lead to 'swallow-holes' of quite alarming proportions. Their formation takes years to accomplish and thus it is possible, although expensive, to carry out a series of drillings to ensure that none exist beneath the proposed building. This work should be undertaken by a specialist.

(*d*) In most parts of the UK the ground is affected by frost to a depth not exceeding about 600 mm. The expansion caused by the freezing of water will lift a building which is inadequately founded, thus foundations should always be taken down a minimum of 600 mm. In fact, for various reasons the conventional minimum is now 1 m. Cold storage buildings can give rise to 'frost heave' if the insulation of the floor structure is inadequate.

(*e*) Some of the characteristics of different soils have already been referred to, but one particular group which poses problems is the clays. Some clays respond to humidification by large expansion, balanced by equivalent shrinkage on drying out, so that seasonal variations can cause these soils to move dramatically, and with them the building. In general 'shrinkable clays', as they are known, are vulnerable to seasonal change to a depth of about 1 metre, after a long dry summer, and therefore in these soils foundations must always be taken down at least that amount, and preferably 1200 mm. The Local Authority building control staff are always conversant with any local incidence of shrinkable clays and the Building Research Establishment has published a Digest giving the broad geographical distribution of such soils. A combination of shrinkable clays and the felling of trees on a site should be dealt with by extra care in preventing soil movements.

(*f*) Undergound rooms are frequently constructed for the siting of machinery or other plant in connection with the servicing of the building or for storage, filing, or strong rooms. The depths involved therefore supervene over the other parameters and demand that the investigation of bearing strata be carried out to appropriately greater depths. (In large conurbations the presence of underground railways must be investigated as any foundations near to the tunnels must be approved by the railway authority). Similarly, a check should be made with the Local Authority for the presence of any culverted streams, some of which, due to the gradual rising of building levels over centuries, may be well down in the ground and thus not obvious to view.

Sometimes the investigation of a site may show that a suitable bearing level is at a depth which makes it more economic to form a basement than to dig deep foundations for strip walls. Equally, a sloping site may direct the designer towards a part-basement with the foundations stepping downwards in conformity with the surface.

In all these cases the foundations effectively become part of the enclosure and will have to be specially constructed to ensure that ground moisture does not penetrate the elements involved.

PILED FOUNDATIONS.—Piling will normally be undertaken on the advice of a qualified engineer, but some generalities can be useful in assessing the requirement for such work, and the implications of its performance. (*a*) When the loads transmitted to the ground by the walls or columns of a building or other structure are of such a magnitude that the use of conventional foundations would result in uneconomically large bases, the use of piling may be justified. (*b*) When the loads cannot be taken on shallow foundations even if the bases occupy the whole of the building area, piling may be essential. (*c*) When the upper strata are very weak or include unstable soils, such as peat or unconfined sand, piling may enable the loads to be carried through the faulty strata to a firm subsoil capable of supporting the loads. (*d*) When the upper strata are subject to large moisture movements piling may be desirable to ensure foundation at a stable level.

Two basic types of piling design are used. The first is, in effect, a column sunk into the ground whose base rests upon a suitable bearing such as rock. Some of this type have 'belled' bottoms to increase the bearing surface. The second type of pile is the friction pile which derives its support from the friction of the surface of the pile against the surrounding soil. Obviously such piles also tend to gain support at the bottom bearing too, but their principal design thesis is frictional resistance to movement. The physical form of a particular pile depends upon the method of its sinking. Piles can be preformed and driven into the ground, or they may be cast in a hole formed in the ground.

Driven Piles.—(i) Steel Piling—either as columns or in sheet form (ii) Concrete Piling—usually precast with a steel tip to aid driving.

Bored Piles.—(i) A steel tube is dropped into the soil and then withdrawn and the soil retained in the bore removed. An outer steel shell is driven down the bore as the work proceeds to prevent collapse of the sides. When concrete casting takes place the shell is withdrawn by stages as the work proceeds. (ii) A rotating drill with shell casing cuts into the soil. (iii) A large diameter auger cuts broad and short piles.

The sinking of driven piles or sheet piling can be by the traditional pile-driver or in some cases by highspeed vibration. The latter is much preferred in towns. Shells for bored piles can also be sunk by similar methods. Boulders in clay can cause the pile to be diverted seriously from its planned path. Similarly, old wharfs where timber piling has been used can be difficult sites as any driven pile meeting a long-buried timber in river bottoms simply tends to bounce off and clearance of the obstruction may have to be manual.

The short-bored piles may be up to 1·05 m in diameter but are rarely more than 3·0 m deep, usually rather less. They have advantages for low rise work in shrinkable clays or where a thick stratum of peat overlays a good bearing soil. Driven and long-bored piles are usually around 450 mm in diameter, and are rarely used less than 7·5 m long.

When a load from the building requires more than one pile to give adequate support, a number of piles is grouped in a 'cluster' under a common pile cap to deal with the load. The distance between the piles in a cluster depends upon soil conditions. The minimum headroom required for driving conventional piles is 6 m and can go up to 15 m. Short-bored piles require about 3 m headroom. See BRE Digest Nos. 63, 67 and 95.

UNDERPINNING.—When the foundations of a structure must be modified so as to alter the method of support the process of underpinning is carried out. The need to underpin may arise from a number of causes.—(*a*) Settlement of foundations due to inadequacy of the soil or the design of foundations. (*b*) Deterioration of foundation materials. (*c*) Change in conditions of support as a result of other building works, or natural phenomena. (*d*) Change in conditions of loading of the building.

Settlement.—The settlement of buildings occurs due to the inadequacy of the soil to support the loads imposed without a certain amount of compaction taking place. Uneven settlement may cause tilting of a rigid building or cracking of walls, both of which involve an element of danger to the structure and the occupants, and it is necessary to halt the trend before serious damage results. Similarly, if foundations inadequate in width have been used, the high ground pressures compact the soil and in certain conditions force the soil aside, causing severe settlement.

Deterioration of Foundations.—Foundation materials, such as concrete and brickwork can deteriorate after laying from a number of causes. (i) Bad design of concrete mix or inferior materials. (ii) Use of bricks not suited to underground conditions. (iii) Sulphate or other chemical attack. (iv) Attack by roots of trees.

Change in Conditions of Support.—Shrinkable clays give rise to seasonal variations in support conditions.

Running sand subsoils and some types of chalk and limestone can be eroded by underground water movements leading to unpredictable collapse beneath buildings leaving the foundations spanning the hole.

Other building works can also necessitate working under existing foundations in a manner which modifies the support pattern. Excavations for services or ducts normally pose only small problems, but larger works, as for pedestrian underpasses and underground railways involve complex engineering problems. One common problem is that of siting a new building requiring basements of special foundations adjacent to an existing building with shallow traditional foundations.

Change in Conditions of Loading.—A building designed for relatively light loadings may be required to house a new function with more intense loadings. Similarly the installation of new plant in one section of a building may create unbalanced conditions which necessitate revision of the foundations.

Methods.—Underpinning of foundations can be carried out in several ways. The traditional method is the excavation of short sections of the work to a firm new bottom and the building up of a new foundation in that section, pinning up to the underside of the old work using slates and hard-rammed mortar at the meeting level. This work is backfilled with material from the excavation of the alternate short sections which are then underpinned in the same way. This method is only suitable for relatively lightly loaded traditional walls, though a modified method uses precast concrete sections capable of easier insertion and high early strength to speed up the operation. Alternatively, it is possible to cast concrete sections under the old work and here greater continuity is available by the formation of beams to span weak spots. High pressure grouting is also useful in these static methods to ensure good support. All these methods are designed to maintain the existing situation and prevent further movement, but they have no corrective capability.

Corrective underpinning is a difficult and dangerous operation requiring skilled design, operation and control. The object is to move the settled part of the building back to its original position, an operation which must be carried out slowly and smoothly. Normally hydraulic jacks are used for this purpose. First a new and adequate foundation is formed at a suitable level to provide a base for the jacks at both sides of the wall at a number of points. 'Needles' are inserted through the wall resting on the jacks which are then slowly raised to reposition the wall. On reaching the correct position the wall is re-founded by underpinning methods and, after a suitable curing period, the jacks and needles are removed and the holes made good. Jacking is carried out by stages to ensure progressive lifting of the structure without causing further cracking. Often shoring and bracing of the structure is carried out before jacking.

Underpinning can only be carried out to sound work. Where foundations have been chemically attacked all the damaged work must be removed and the new materials must possess adequate resistance to the form of attack concerned.

CONCRETE FOUNDATIONS.—The mix for mass concrete foundations should be designed by the engineer. In domestic and other low rise construction it is usually 1:3:6 (1 part Portland cement: 3 parts fine aggregate: 6 parts coarse aggregate by volume) the coarse aggregate being no larger than 30 mm. This is 50 kg cement : 0·1 m^3 sand : 0·2 m^3 aggregate or Grade C15P concrete to BS 5328 : 1981 'Methods for Specifying Concrete including Ready-Mixed Concrete'. Floor slabs should be 1:2:4. Where soft places are encountered or voids have to be bridged, reinforcement must be used in the lower part of the foundation strip. If, among relatively soft ground, such as clays, small unyielding areas exist they should be cut away to well below the foundation bottom level, the level made up to normal formation with compressible material and the 'soft spot' bridged by reinforced concrete. If the unyielding area is large, it is better to form constructional breaks in the building. Where the ground is variable and the probability of settlement exists but cannot be pinpointed, the foundation concrete should be reinforced at both top and bottom of the section. A notional span of 3·0 m may be taken for design purposes using the full wall load and a fixed-end condition.

In large mass foundations and where large volumes of concrete filling are required, 'plums' of hard and clean rock, concrete or hard brick may be used to fill out the mix, provided the plums are as hard as the finished concrete and no larger than one-third of the cross-section of the foundation concrete. Plaster and other foreign adhesions must not be allowed to contaminate the concrete.

Sulphate Attack.—Certain soils contain quantities of sulphates (usually calcium sulphate, magnesium sulphate or sodium sulphate). They also occur in acid solutions in marshy country, near colliery tips and where pyrites in the soil is oxidised. Sulphates attack the cement in concrete and cause the matrix to disintegrate. Where attack is likely, chemical analysis of the soil should be undertaken to ascertain the type of sulphate and a suitable cement should be used. 'Sulphate-resisting cement' appears to resist magnesium sulphate attack better than calcium sulphate.

Soils are classified into five types representing different concentrations of sulphates and have different requirements for the use of the various types of cement.

OVERSITE CONCRETE.—The Building Regulations 1985 under C4 Site Preparation and Resistance to Moisture require that the walls, floors and roof shall adequately resist the passage of water to the inside of the building. The Approved Document states that any ground supported floor will meet it if dense concrete is laid on a hard-core bed and a damp-proof membrane is provided. A Technical Solution is concrete at least 100 mm thick composed of 50 kg : 0·11 m^3 : 0·16 m^3, cement : fine : coarse aggregates, or BS 5328 mix C 10P. If it is reinforced the concrete should be 50 kg : 0·08 m^3 : 0·13 m^3 or BS 5328 mix C 20P. Technical Solutions are also given for suspended timber ground floors requiring oversite concrete as ground cover and suspended concrete ground floors.

One common method of providing a damp-proof membrane to oversite concrete is to lay a concrete or sand blinding on the hardcore, the blinding being not less than 50 mm thick, and covered with an imperforate sheet of polyethylene of not less than 1000 gauge (1·0 mm) preferably black and with welded seams. This sheet is then covered by the oversite concrete. The edges of the sheet must be turned up and carried into the walls at dpc level. If welding of joints for large areas is not available it is possible to lap the sheets and use a solvent adhesive. This should be in two bands of adhesive at least 25 mm wide in a lap of 150 mm. Great care must be taken to ensure that any membrane is not punctured by grit under foot or barrow traffic, and if the overlying slab is to be reinforced it is essential to use properly fabricated stools and spacers to ensure that tying wire ends are not allowed to damage the membrane.

Integral waterproofers may be in powder or liquid form, and their use involves consideration of the water-cement ratio to be adopted and the workability desired. Their advantage may lie mainly in the extra care which their use demands. In general, a vibrator compacted (power floated) slab will be more dense and water resistant than a hand-compacted slab and the waterproofer is more likely to succeed in a closely-knit matrix than in an open-textured and porous matrix. Surface applications of waterproofers are not to be recommended especially if the finished surface is to be the wearing surface.

GROUND FLOOR SLABS.—For domestic loading a 100 mm slab is normally adequate. For light factory or commercial loadings a similar mix (1:2:4) may be used but a minimum thickness of 150 mm is desirable. Where heavy loadings are to be applied it may be necessary to use thicker slabs and reinforcement. If a considerable depth of filling has been needed under a slab or portion of a slab, or if there are prospects of settlement from other causes the area affected should be designed accordingly as a reinforced slab. In areas where very large or heavy machines are to be sited it is desirable to take the machine loads as a distinct problem and design the slabs thereunder for that particular purpose. Where the machine may impose dynamic or vibration loads, separation of the slabs from the remainder of the floor is essential. Certain machines impose such loads, both static and dynamic, that they require purpose-designed bases whose top surface is usually at slab level though the hidden mass of concrete is of special design by an engineer. Certain machines require pits for their operation. These again must be the subject of detailed engineering design and their divorce from the rest of the slab must be correctly arranged.

The laying of the slab of a large area is spread over a long period of time and hence shrinkage of the areas laid can be minimised by laying the floor in a series of panels, usually rectangular, in such a way as to permit the shrinkage of earlier bays to have taken place before adjoining bays are laid. The usual pattern takes the form of a chequer board where 'white' squares are laid first and the 'black' squares later. The recommended size of bay is a maximum area of 10 m^2, the proportion of lengths of side of any such rectangle being not more than 1·5 to 1·0.

The slabs must be cured correctly by keeping them damp for at least seven (preferably 10) days. Failure to do this can result in curling of the slab, particularly at the edges which are then not properly supported on the hardcore and fail when heavy load is applied. Efforts have been made to restrain edges of bays by the insertion of dowel rods of steel from bay to bay but corrosion of the steel is rapid owing to the joint in the concrete. Carrying the reinforcement of an r.c. slab through the joint has similar problems. Another reason for dowels or other connectors is to reduce the 'lipping' of slabs when heavy vehicle loads pass over the joint. The floor slab bays may be laid in a pattern diagonal to traffic flow so that only one wheel at a time is applied to the joint, thus lessening the impact and reducing the risk of damaging the floor.

Floor hardeners and treatments to the surface of concrete floors have a limited life. They are dealt with under section 'Plasterwork and Floor Finishings'.

SUSPENDED SLABS.—Concrete suspended slabs are capable of supporting heavy loads and have the merit of providing inherent fire resistance. They also need sufficient mass for resistance to transmitted sound. For impact sound insulation resilient cushioning of the wearing surface is necessary.

Suspended slabs can be of solid reinforced concrete, or of a large number of 'patent' types. The 'hollow pot' floors are frequently capable of two-way reinforcement which increases their capacity to distribute point loads and reduces or eliminates the cracking between units which is associated with precast beam floors. On the other hand the quality of soffit finish achieved with beam floors can be high where that of most 'pot' floors is poor and requires full plaster finishing.

Some types of wide beam floors are available. These require the use of medium-duty cranes for lifting whereas narrow beams can be hauled up by small hoists. The wide-beam floors reduce the frequency of cracking but, unless thoroughly cured before delivery, can increase the magnitude of the crack width as against narrow beams. They are usually cast with purpose-designed inserts, conduits and lighting boxes already in place.

Precast floors are rarely capable of continuous structural design. In the main they span simply from wall to wall or beam to beam. Hollow-pot floors are frequently incorporated into a continuous span system where the beams are T or L-beams. This gives an economical structure of small depth and high structural integrity, but obviously takes rather longer to erect than the fully precast floor.

Prestressed precast floors often utilise a system of precast soffits, little more than planks upon which is cast the main slab concrete. High continuity can be achieved in this way, and, for appropriate buildings, the soffit can be left unfinished. Other types of prestressed precast floors use a hollow beam or wide beam. These compare with ordinary reinforced concrete but can be thinner. All types of patent floor depend upon the laying of a suitable topping of fine-aggregate concrete, usually 50 mm thick, over the pots or beams. This binds the units together and may in itself be reinforced. The surface of the topping is not used as the wearing surface.

Concrete Roofs.—These follow the same pattern as suspended floors if flat, but a great many complex shapes have been used in roof construction, some as vaults or domes, others as 'folded plates'. In general, such designs are highly specialised, not without problems, and therefore necessitate the services of an experienced engineer.

TYPES OF CONCRETE.—See chapter I3.

BRICKWORK AND BLOCKWORK

The characteristics of the materials, bricks, blocks and mortars are described in Chapter C8. The combination to form brick or block masonry has distinctive characteristics which nevertheless derive from the properties of the materials. Thus the compressive strength depends upon the mean compressive strength of the individual bricks and mortar and the eccentricity of loading. The flexural strength of masonry depends upon the water absorption of the bricks or the strength class of blocks.

Bricklaying.—The trade of bricklaying is one demanding care in levelling and maintaining a regular coursing so that when openings are formed the bed joints line up where they meet above the opening. The bricklayer requires a reasonably level base from which to work, though the skilled tradesman can, by cropping bricks, level up a bad base. The corners of a building are set up first, plumbed and checked for wall length and from these points a taut line is strung along the wall face to act as a guide for laying of each course. Lines should be supported by tingles at not more than 6 m intervals to avoid excessive deflection. Corners should be racked back not more than 1·2 m in one lift.

The bricks must be at the right moisture content for ease of laying and in warm weather are often wetted by hose spray in the stack. For calculated loadbearing brickwork the specification may require that the suction rate of the bricks be adjusted. For clay bricks this is done by docking them in water for up to 2 min just before laying. Overwetting causes the bricks to skate on the mortar, while dry bricks suck water from the mortar making it stiff and unworkable for bedding and levelling on each brick. In such cases the adhesion of the mortar to the brick may be greatly reduced as is the case when masonry dries out rapidly in warm weather. To avoid this the mortar beds should be laid in shorter lengths. Adhesion may also be improved by adjusting the consistence of the mortar and this, rather than wetting, should be done with calcium silicate and concrete units.

The traditional brick is of a size and weight which is convenient to the human hand. A good bricklayer on straight work (ie without complex bonding or many reveals to plumb) and served by good labourers can lay up to 800 bricks a day but output rarely reaches this level because of such interruptions as moving scaffolds, re-stocking the work area and work by other trades, and 400–500/day is more typical.

Bricks and solid or cellular blocks should be laid on a full bed of mortar with perpends and collar joints filled. Shell bedding affects the strength of the wall and may only be used with the permission of the designer. Frogged bricks should be laid with the larger or only frog up and the frogs completely filled with mortar. Cellular bricks and blocks should be laid with the openings downward and not filled. Hollow blocks should be shell bedded and may have mortar strips under the cross webs or not. Similarly the perpends may be filled or shell bedded. Grout used to fill collar joints or voids in the thickness of a wall should have the minimum amount of water to enable it to be poured in order to minimize segregation and shrinkage.

Jointing and pointing.—The average thickness of vertical and horizontal joints is taken as 10 mm and this is the difference between the work size and the coordinating size of the units. The joint size may be varied to accommodate the tolerances of units but for appearance sake they should be kept as evenly spaced as possible. It is preferable to compact the joint to the required profile (Figure 3) as the work proceeds rather than pointing afterwards. Flush joints are formed using the bedding mortar as the work goes on; struck or recessed joints formed with a tool when the mortar is partly set; joints raked out while the mortar is still soft and pointed subsequently or left open as a key for plaster or rendering.

Masonry bonds.—Masonry units are arranged in a wall so that the vertical joints (perpends) of one course are not less than one quarter brick from the perpends of the courses above and below and in no case less than 50 mm for bricks or 75 mm for blocks. This distribution of units is called bond. Bricks and blocks in cavity construction or in half brick walls (102·5 mm thick) are laid in stretcher bond so that each unit is placed in the same orientation. Facing brickwork may employ more decorative bonds, both to present a pleasing appearance and to distribute the stresses and tie the work together when it is more than half a brick thick. (Figure 1). Such bonds should not be used for cavity walls unless purpose made bats are available. Sleeper walls and non-loadbearing partitions may be laid in honeycomb construction. Various special bonds or even special shaped bricks are used to enable vertical reinforcement to be incorporated and Figure 1 also shows Quetta Bond and Rat-trap Bond. In the latter edge bedding makes the wall economical in material for garden walls for example, but they are less strong than a single-leaf wall of the same overall thickness. Bed joint reinforcement may be incorporated in conventional bonds.

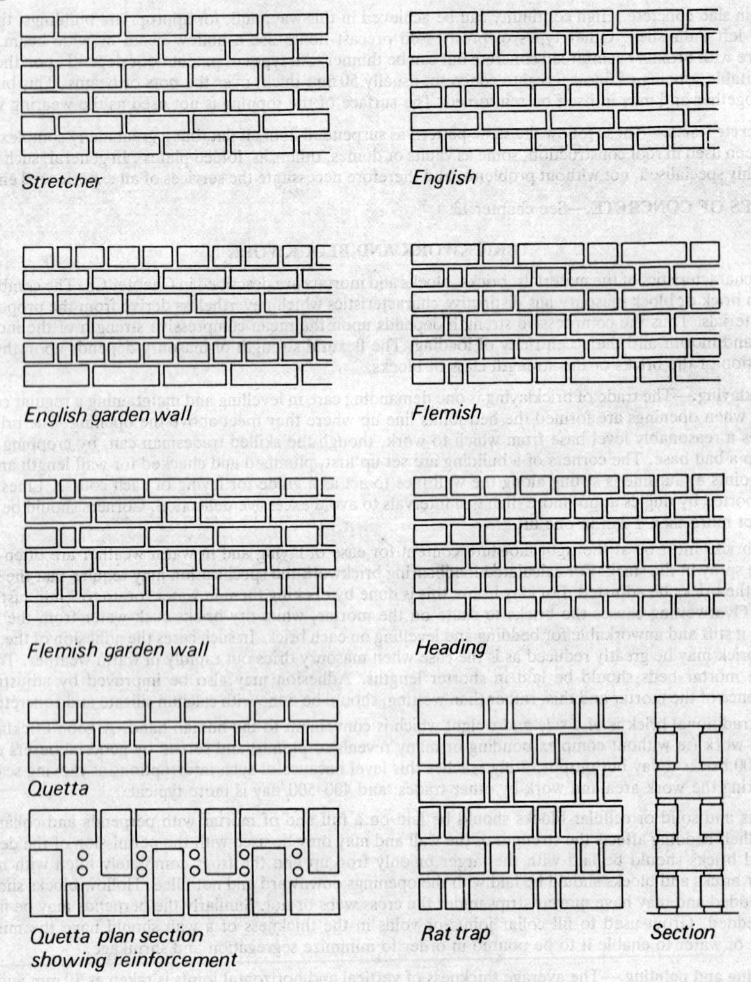

FIG. 1.—Brickwork Bonds.

There is a wide range of shapes and sizes of blocks so many facing patterns are possible. Some common ones are shown in Figure 2. Hollow blockwork may have vertical reinforcement inserted in the holes which are then filled with concrete in lift heights designed to ensure proper compaction. At quoins and reveals the bond should be maintained by the use of alternate long and short blocks.

Ordering materials.—Although there is only one standard size (215 × 102·5 × 65 mm), bricks may be solid, perforated or have hollows (frogs). There is a great variety of colours and textures and the different methods of making give quite different characteristics in the performance of the bricks. Combined with the different classes of mortar, brickwork to meet almost any need may be specified. It is therefore important to understand these differences when ordering and to explain the requirements to the supplier so that, for example, facings for a large job are ordered in the full amount and well in advance so that consistent colour and texture are supplied. It is even more important to give maximum notice for the provision of specials. Even standard specials to BS 4729 : 1971 may not always be available from stock. Engineering bricks are clay bricks with defined strength and water absorption and are used where these properties, or acid resistance or improved durability are required. Class B Engineering clay bricks are especially suitable for work below dpc and for manholes, etc.

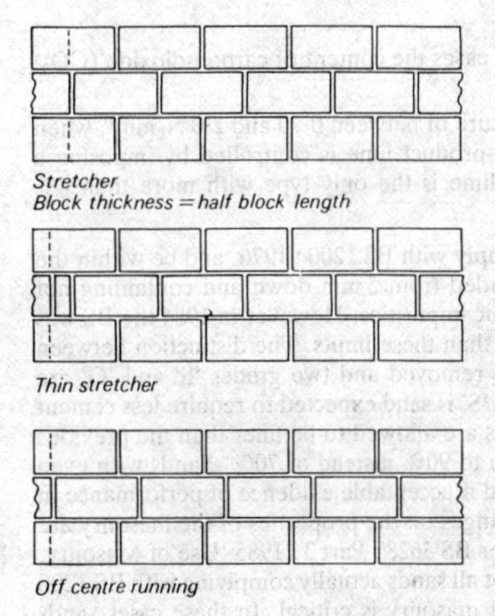

FIG. 2.—Blockwork Bonds.

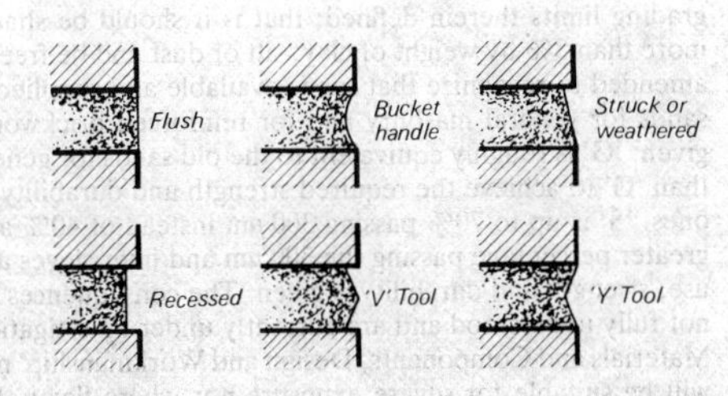

FIG. 3.—Joint Profiles.

Bricklayer sundries.—The bricklayer is also involved in the placing and fixing of other items allied to his work. Frequently he sets the door frames in position in conjunction with the carpenter and builds his work up to them, incorporating ties into his bed joints, he also usually sets tile and stone or concrete cills and sets up the windows as plumbs for his reveals. Padstones for trusses and beams, whether in stone or concrete are laid by the bricklayer. Flues are parged by the bricklayer as his work proceeds, and where flue linings are used he is responsible for plumbing, jointing and back filling and also for the fixing, setting and flaunching of chimney pots.

BEDDING MORTAR

Mortar is a mixture of a cementing agent, such as lime, Portland cement, or a mixture of the two, with water and fine aggregate, generally sand; masonry cement or an ordinary cement with a mortar plasticiser may be use in place of a mixture of cement and lime as the binding agent. Ready mixed mortars, both sand/lime to be gauged with cement on site and retarded mixes containing cement are available. If coloured pigments are to be added to the mortar, greater consistancy is achieved with ready mix. It is used for bedding masonry, brickwork and blockwork, for rendering and plastering and for laying screeds.

The qualities required in bedding mortar for masonry and brickwork are that it should be workable, retain its water content, stiffen quickly enough, develop sufficient but not too much strength, bond well and be durable. Lime mortar works easily and holds water well, but if non-hydraulic is neither durable nor strong Portland cement mortar stiffens quickly and is durable, but if gauged richly enough to be readily workable is too strong to be used with any but the strongest bricks. In shrinking, while drying out, it sets up stresses which may cause cracks in a structure whilst it is too rigid to yield to slight settlement movement. As an alternative to hydraulic lime, therefore, a blend of lime and Portland cement is generally used, combining the good qualities of both materials. Masonry cement, however, which is specially made for this purpose and contains a plasticiser, may be used instead. Finally, as an alternative to lime, surfactants which entrain air are widely used nowadays as plasticisers for Portland cement in mortar.

Mortar Materials.—Details of cements are given in Chapter I3. Other materials are.–

Building Limes.—(BS 890 : 1972).—Lime is made by heating calcium carbonate (chalk or limestone) so as to form calcium oxide or quicklime, which is slaked with water to form calcium hydroxide, slaked or hydrated lime. Near pure lime can be readily slaked and makes workable mortars, but gains strength very slowly. The composition of the raw material, is, however, seldom pure and varies in different deposits. Some contain a large proportion of magnesium oxide and produce magnesian lime which requires special care in slaking. Some contain aluminous or siliceous material and produce a hydraulic lime having some of the hardening properties of Portland cement. Lime is further made as a by-product of certain industrial processes, for instance, bleaching and the manufacture of acetylene gas. Lime is seldom used by itself as a building material but is blended with sand and also often with gypsum plaster or Portland cement to form mortar (see below).

The BS specification for building limes (BS 890), deals with hydrated lime (powder), quicklime and lime putty made from hydrated lime. Four types of lime are distinguished in the standard: high-calcium; high-calcium by-product; semi-hydraulic (grey) and magnesian. When testing hydrated lime or lime putty, the minimum lime plus magnesia (CaO + MgO) content is 60% for semi-hydraulic lime and 65% for the other types. Corresponding limits for quicklime are 70% and 85%. In all cases the content of carbon-dioxide (CO_2) must not be more than 6%.

Semi-hydraulic lime mortar is required to have a modulus of rupture of between 0·70 and 2·0 N/mm², when tested by the procedure given in the standard. The quality of by-product lime is controlled by imposing a maximum limit of 0·5% on the soluble salt content. Magnesian lime is the only type with more than 4% magnesia (MgO) present.

Sands for Mortars and Renderings.—Sand for mortar should comply with BS 1200 : 1976, and be within the grading limits therein defined; that is it should be sharp sand, graded from 5 mm down and containing not more than 3% by weight of clay, silt or dust and be free from organic impurities. However in 1984 the BS was amended to recognize that sands available and supplied were finer than these limits. The distinction between sands for general masonry and for reinforced brickwork has been removed and two grades 'S' and 'G' are given. 'G' is roughly equivalent to the old sands for general use and 'S' is sand expected to require less cement than 'G' to achieve the required strength and durability. Both sands are allowed to be finer than the previous ones. 'S' is up to 70% passing 300 μm instead of 40% and 'G' is up to 90% instead of 70%. Sands with even greater percentage passing the 300 μm and finer sieves are permitted if acceptable evidence of performance in use, strength and durability is given. The consequences of these changes on the properties of the masonry are not fully understood and are currently under investigation. However BS 5628 : Part 3 : 1985 'Use of Masonry, Materials and Components, Design and Workmanship' notes that not all sands actually complying with BS 1200 will be suitable for severe exposure nor where flexural strength of masonry is critical. In these cases sands towards the coarse end of the BS 1200 size distribution should be selected or those complying with grade M of BS 882 : 1983 'Aggregates from Natural Sources for Concrete'.

The standard is numbered BS 1199 and 1200:1976 'Building sands from natural sources' to include also BS 1199 for sands for external renderings, internal plastering with lime and Portland cement and floor screeds.

Mortar mixes.—BS 5628 : Part 3 : 1985 includes details of mortar mixes of five different designations, tabulated with reference to strength and ability to accommodate settlement, temperature and moisture changes, etc. Tables 5 and 6 are taken from BRE Digest No. 160 as a guide to the use of mortar for jointing.

In winter, the richer mortars are preferred because they quickly develop strength enough to resist the effects of frost. Richer mortars may also be desirable for exposed work with bricks that contain appreciable quantities of soluble sulphates (see BRE Digest No. 89).

An unnecessarily strong mortar concentrates the effects of any differential movement in fewer and wider cracks; a weaker mortar will accommodate small movements and any cracking will be distributed as hair cracks in the joints, where they are less noticeable. The stresses resulting from restraint of any expansion of bricks

TABLE 5.—SELECTION OF MORTAR DESIGNATIONS. (Mortars are designated (1) to (5) according to the type of construction for which they are suitable.)

Type of Brick	Clay		Concrete and calcium silicate	
Early Frost Hazard (*a*)	NO	YES	NO	YES
Internal walls	(5)	(3) or (4) (*b*)	5 (*c*)	(3) or plast (4) (*b*)
Inner leaf of cavity walls	(5)	(3) or (4) (*b*)	5 (c)	(3) or plast (4) (*b*)
Backing to external solid walls	(4)	(3) or (4) (*b*)	(4)	(3) or plast (4) (*b*)
External walls; outer leaf of cavity walls:				
above damp-proof course	(4) (*d*)	(3) (*d*)	(4)	(3)
below damp-proof course	(4) (*e*)	3 (*b*) (*e*)	(3) (*e*)	(3) (*e*)
Parapet walls; domestic chimneys:				
rendered	(3) (*f*) (*g*)	(3) (*f*) (*g*)	(4)	(3)
not rendered	(2) (*h*) or (3)	(1)	(3)	(3)
External free-standing walls	(3)	(3) (*b*).	(3)	(3)
Sills; copings	(1)	(1)	(2)	(2)
Earth-retaining walls (back-filled with free-draining material)	(1)	(1)	(2) (*e*)	(2) (*e*)

NOTES.—(*a*) During construction, before mortar has hardened (say 7 days after laying), or before the wall is completed and protected against the entry of rain at the top. (*b*) If bricks are to be laid wet, see *Winter Building*, HMSO. (*c*) If not plastered, use group (4). (*d*) If to be rendered, use group (3) mortar made with sulphate-resisting cement. (*e*) If sulphates are present in the ground-water, use sulphate-resisting cement. (*f*) Parapet walls of clay units should not be rendered on both sides; if this is unavoidable, select mortar as though *not* rendered. (*g*) Use sulphate-resisting cement. (*h*) With 'special' quality bricks, or with bricks that contain appreciable quantities of soluble sulphates.

are reduced if a relatively weak mortar is used. The choice may entail risk of frost damage and precautions should be taken to protect work in cold weather.

Lime putty made by slaking quicklime is more workable than dry hydrated lime and it is preferable to soak the latter for a period before use. Cement, on the other hand, should normally be mixed with sand dry and the water added later. Mortar containing cement should be used within two hours of mixing.

In the above range of mixes the cementing medium fills up the voids present in the sand so that the volume yield of the mix can be taken as approximately equal to the volume of sand. Sand itself, however, is very variable in volume depending on its water content. Dry sand and inundated sand occupy the same minimum volume for a given weight, but damp sand containing, say, 5% of its weight of water will 'bulk' or occupy 25 to 30% more space.

Mortar may be mixed either by hand or, preferably, by machine; the most effective type being a pan mill in which mixing continues for 20 to 30 minutes. A mortar that has been thoroughly mixed by pan mill is more workable and economical in use than a hand-mixed mortar. The water should be potable or analysed to ensure that it is free from harmful impurities.

Where a range of sand contents is given, the larger quantity should be used for sand that is well graded and the smaller for coarse or uniformly fine sand. Because damp sands bulk, the volume of damp sand used may need to be increased. For cement : lime : sand mixes, the error due to bulking is reduced if the mortar is prepared from lime : sand coarse stuff and cement in appropriate proportions; in these mixes 'lime' refers to non-hydraulic or semi-hydraulic lime and the proportions given are for lime putty. If hydrated lime is batched dry, the volume may be increased by up to 50% to get adequate workability.

TABLE 6.—MORTAR MIXES (PROPORTIONS BY VOLUME)

	Mortar Designation No.	Cement lime : sand	Masonry-cement : sand	Cement : sand, with plasticiser
↑ Increasing strength but decreasing ability to accommodate movements caused by settlement, shrinkage, etc.	(1)	1 : 0–¼ : 3	—	—
	(2)	1 : ½ : 4–4½	1 : 2½–3½	1 : 3–4
	(3)	1 : 1 : 5–6	1 : 4–5	1 : 5–6
	(4)	1 : 2 : 8–9	1 : 5½–6½	1 : 7–8
	(5)	1 : 3 : 10–12	1 : 6½–7	1 : 8
Direction of changes in properties		equivalent strengths ⟷ within each group		
		increasing frost resistance ⟶		
		improving bond and resistance ⟵ to rain penetration		

Exclusion of rain.—After its structural performance, the most important property of a wall is its ability to exclude rain. CP 121 : Part 1 : 1973 'Brick and Block Masonry' divided the environmental conditions into three categories based upon the 'Driving rain index' described in BRE Digest No. 127 'An index of exposure to driving rain'. The categories were Sheltered, Moderate, Severe. CP 121 has now been withdrawn and replaced by BS 5628 : Part 3 : 1985 'Use of Masonry: Materials and Components, Design and Workmanship'. In this the three exposure categories have been replaced by six and the Annual Mean Driving Rain Index of $>7\ m^2/s$, $3\ m^2/s$ to $7\ m^2/s$ and $<3\ m^2/s$ replaced by a Local Spell Index calculated according to DD 93 : 1984, 'Methods for Assessing Exposure to Wind Driven Rain'. Unrendered solid masonry is not now recommended in areas more exposed than Sheltered/Moderate, but a properly constructed cavity wall with a cavity at least 50 mm wide is an effective barrier to rain penetration under all conditions of exposure. The code gives a table of the anticipated performance of different wall constructions under the six exposure conditions and tabulates the factors which affect rain penetration of cavity walls. The new code reflects less the properties of well constructed masonry than the quality of current workmanship and supervision.

Damp-proof courses.—An important element in the exclusion of rain from the inside of the building is the provision of proper damp-proof courses and flashing details. The critical nature of these details both in design and in workmanship cannot be overstressed. BS 5628 : Part 3 gives some excellent illustrations of satisfactory details. In fact the largest single section in the new code is that concerned with exclusion of moisture. It gives detailed guidance on the material properties needed to ensure adequate performance in dpc's and cavity trays. It tabulates the physical properties and performance of various dpc materials showing the joint treatment needed to prevent water moving up or down, the liability to extrusion, durability and other considerations. It describes and illustrates the positioning of dpc's at various places and stresses that many common details cannot be formed satisfactorily on site except in lead so pre-formed cloaks will often need to be specified.

CP 102 : 1973 'Protection of Buildings Against Water from the Ground' gives methods of preventing ground and surface water entering the building. BS 743: 1970 'Materials for Damp-Proof Courses' gives guidance on selection and laying. Other specifications are: BS 6398 : 1983 'Bitumen Damp-Proof Courses for Masonry'; BS 2870: 1980 'Rolled Copper and Copper Alloys: Sheet Strip and Foil'; BS 1178 : 1982 'Milled Lead Sheet for Building Purposes'; BS 6515 : 1984 'Polythene Damp-Proof Courses for Masonry'. All these sheet materials are supplied in rolls of the usual wall width.

Sheet materials and mastic asphalt to BS 988, 1076, 1097, 1451 : 1973, 'Mastic Asphalt for Building (Limestone Aggregate)' or BS 6577 : 1985, 'Mastic Asphalt for Building (Natural Rock Asphalt Aggregate)' are used for dpc's in parapets where protection against downward movement of water is required and a continuous flexible membrane is needed. Rigid dpc's, engineering bricks or slates laid in at least two courses to break joint and in cement mortar may be used to prevent the rise of moisture from the ground.

Flashings.—Flashings and other weatherings may be metal, bituminous materials or plastics. They should be malleable enough to be able to be dressed into shape but nevertheless stiff enough to prevent uplift by wind. Where flues pass through the roof, flashings of metal able to resist the heat of the flue are built into the brickwork. Corner, etc. flashings in plastic materials and metals other than lead should be preformed to size and shape. All flashings should be bedded into the work a minimum of 25 mm and joints sealed or adequate overlap provided. Metal flashings should be wedged with the same material.

Wall ties.—Wall ties should comply with BS 1243 1978 'Metal ties for cavity wall construction'. In standard cavity construction they are spaced at 900 mm intervals horizontally and 450 mm vertically in accordance with BS 5628 Part 3:1985.

DURABILITY OF BRICKWORK.—All exposed facing materials are subject to attack by weather and guidance and assurances on the performance in use should be sought from the manufacturer in the case of non-traditional materials. The most common problems in cementitious facings—high density concrete blocks and renderings—relate to shrinkage cracking which may subsequently allow rain penetration and ultimately frost attack. The most common facing material, however is clay brickwork and some consideration of its performance in use is appropriate.

All materials have properties which may be advantageous or disadvantageous but which have to be taken into account by the designer and builder if a durable structure is to result.

Dimensional changes.—All buildings are subject to thermal expansion and contraction due to diurnal variations in temperature. A more important factor, needing considerable care in design, however, is the differential thermal movement between exposed areas in full direct sunlight and recessed areas in shade. Particular care is therefore needed in designing movement joints in, for example, screen wall or deep fin constructions, especially if they are clad in a material such as glazed tiles which relies on adhesion to the backing being maintained.

In addition all porous building materials expand and contract under the influence of adsorbed moisture. Wetting is associated with expansion of the materials and drying with shrinkage. Cement products show, in general, an initial contraction during setting followed by expansion and further contraction on subsequent wetting and drying, but some proportion of the initial shrinkage is irreversible. Calcium silicate products similarly show a residual irreversible shrinkage which increases slowly with time and repeated wetting and drying. Fired clay products also show expansion on wetting and contraction on drying, the expansion being quite rapid at first and continuing at a much lower rate over very long periods. The expansion is not wholly reversible on drying and this is referred to as the irreversible moisture expansion. The net effect in conditions of varying humidity, once the initial rapid expansion is completed, is a very gradual continuing expansion.

The magnitude of these movements varies with the material and is greater when determined in tests on individual pieces than will be the case in the wall where much of the movement is restrained. Nevertheless properly designed movement joints to accommodate the drying shrinkage of cementitious and calcium silicate products and the moisture expansion of fired clay must be installed appropriately in accordance with the recommendations of BS 5628 Part 3 1985.

Rain penetration.—A properly constructed cavity wall is an absolute barrier to rain penetration. When water does penetrate to the inner leaf it is the result of bad workmanship and inadequate supervision or bad design detailing. Dirty wall ties, ties sloping towards instead of away from the inner leaf, the bottom of the cavity full of mortar droppings, incompletely filled perpend joints allowing rain to be blown through onto the inner leaf. These are some of the common faults which lead to dampness inside the building.

The installation of cavity insulation need not make matters worse but sometimes seems to. Cavities filled with foam or blown fills seem intuitively undesirable, but if the filling is properly carried out and the cavity was originally properly constructed, rain penetration should not occur. Slab insulation fixed to the inner leaf which leaves a gap to the outer leaf should be completely satisfactory, but layers of mortar dropping between one row of slabs and the superimposed one may allow the cavity to be bridged, particularly at tie positions.

Frost.—Frost damage is normally restricted to brickwork which is frozen while saturated with water, that is parapets and copings, some chimneys, retaining walls and bricks between dpc and finished ground level. Brickwork between dpc and eaves may be affected in very exposed situations and gable walls which have no eaves to protect them are thus more exposed than other elevations.

The selection of bricks known to be frost resistant in similar situations and the provision of correct damp proofing and sensible details at cills and copings to shed water clear of the brickwork beneath are important. Most brick companies will now provide information on the performance of their bricks. The BCRA panel freezing test has been designated in the revised brick standard, BS 3921 1985, as an acceptable test of frost resistance. Bricks which withstand 100 cycles are likely to be frost resistant under saturated conditions in work. The recommendations of the earlier versions of BS 3921 may still be used, ie bricks which are known to have performed well over the years in similar exposure situations may be expected to be frost resistant as may also a brick with a water absorption of less than 7% or a compressive strength greater than 49 N/mm^2.

Soluble salts and efflorescence.—Efflorescence is the visible effect of crystallization at the surface of salts which have percolated in solution through the brickwork. On external brickwork it may be unsightly but harmless or it may be destructive of the facing bricks themselves. On internal walls efflorescence from bricks, blocks or plaster may cause decoration to be delayed or cause damage to decoration already applied. The amount seen depends upon the quantity and availability of soluble material and water and the damage it causes depends upon the chemical nature of the salts. Thus magnesium sulphate, which crystallizes just behind the face of the brickwork causes spalling, potassium sulphate may cause pitting, while other salts, apart from lifting the decoration, are merely unsightly.

The salts may be derived from the walling units, the mortar and plaster, or from contamination from some sources other than the wall (Fig. 4). Most clay building materials contain a small percentage of salts soluble in water, commonly the sulphates of calcium, magnesium, sodium and potassium. BS 3921 1985 Clay Bricks lays down limits for bricks of low soluble salt content (see Chapter C8). Low and normal salt contents are combined with resistance to frost to form a table of categories of durability.

The presence of soluble salts in a brick does not necessarily mean that efflorescence will ensue. This depends, among other things, upon the solubilities of the salts concerned. For example, calcium sulphate, which makes up the greater part of the soluble salts in many materials, has a relatively low solubility. This apart, however, some bricks with a high content of soluble salts show no efflorescence.

Even if facing-bricks of low soluble-salt content are used, salts in backing bricks, or breeze or concrete blocks, may be taken into solution and migrate through the wall to appear as efflorescence at the drying surface.

Portland cement and hydraulic lime mortars may provide soluble salts, usually the sulphates and carbonates of sodium and potassium.

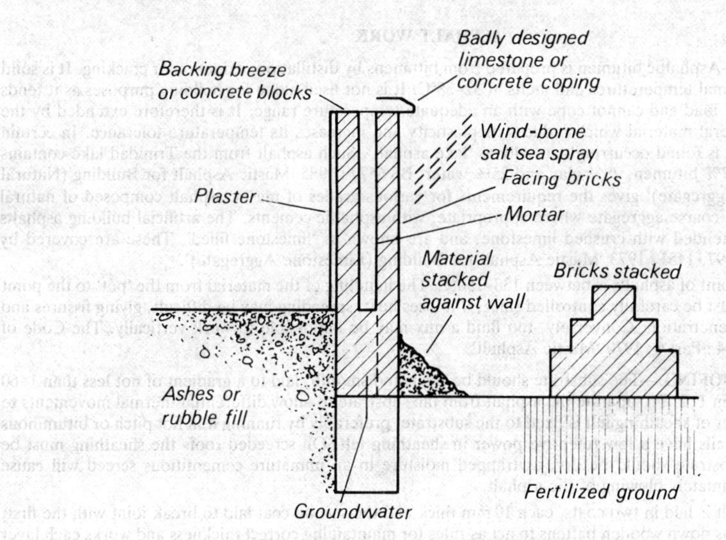

FIG. 4.—Some Sources of Soluble Salts.

Contamination may occur from outside—from ground water, from substances stacked against the wall, or even from spray borne inland from the sea. Materials may pick up salts before use if stacked on ground contaminated by, for example, fertilizers. The presence of nitrates or chlorides in the efflorescence is usually an indication of this sort of external contamination. In one case of recurring potassium nitrate efflorescence in floor quarries, it was found that the tiles were laid on concrete which had been placed on prepared ground containing material from a demolished larder in which pigs had been cured with saltpetre.

Soil, and particularly ashes and rubble filling, behind retaining walls may contain high proportions of soluble salts which appear on the brickwork and perhaps destroy it.

Rainwater will take calcium carbonate or calcium sulphate into solution from limestone or concrete copings, etc., and if this solution does not fall clear of the building it may be taken up by the brickwork to give rise to efflorescence on subsequent drying out.

The salt solutions may migrate some distance in the wall and their appearance on a particular material merely indicates that it provides a convenient drying surface. Very dense mortar used with a more permeable brick will allow water to flow into the wall mainly through the brick and dry out the same way, so efflorescence will appear on the brick, though the salts may have come from the brick or mortar or even elsewhere.

For efflorescence to occur salts must be present, water available to take them into solution and a drying surface must exist. If no water were present efflorescence would not occur, but of course quantities of water are used in the building process and rain may saturate the rising work, so brickwork erected in the winter often shows efflorescence when it dries out in spring. The work should be covered at night and the stacks of material kept dry. This will minimize efflorescence and if it does appear the best treatment is to brush it off. Washing dissolves the salts but they are absorbed by the brickwork lower down. If efflorescence continues to recur in dry periods following rain this usually means that excessive water is entering the wall through faulty detailing, eg parapet walls with no dpc or a wrongly placed one.

Sulphate attack.—This is a fault of the mortar not the bricks and is more properly called mortar decay due to the formation of calcium sulpho-aluminate. Portland cement containing tricalcium aluminate reacts with sulphates in solution to form calcium sulpho-aluminate which causes expansion and loss of stength in the mortar. Persistently damp conditions are necessary for this to occur, so mortar between dpc and eaves does not often suffer from this defect. Dense renderings, however, may crack and allow water to penetrate behind them, producing conditions in which decay can occur. The defect can be avoided by the use of sulphate-resistant cement. Other guidance is given in Building Research Establishment Digest 89 'Sulphate attack on brickwork'.

RUBBLE WALLING AND STONE MASONRY.—Stone masonry, whether rubble walling, block in course masonry or ashlar masonry is now so rare and labour intensive that it should be regarded as a specialist technique. However, earlier editions of Kempe may be consulted for details. Stone and artificial stone facings are similarly omitted from this edition. There is, however, a separate code BS 5390 1976 (1984) 'Code of Practice for Stone Masonry' which deals with design, construction and the selection of materials.

ASPHALT WORK

ASPHALTS.—Asphaltic bitumen is prepared from bitumens by distillation, oxidation or cracking. It is solid or viscous at normal temperatures and melts at 32–38°C. It is not used alone for building purposes as it tends to extrude under load and cannot cope with an adequate temperature range. It is therefore extended by the use of inert mineral material which reduces its plasticity and increases its temperature tolerance. In certain areas such a mix is found occurring naturally as 'lake asphalt'. Such asphalt from the Trinidad lake contains approximately 47% bitumen, 28% clay and 25% water. BS 6577 : 1985 'Mastic Asphalt for Building (Natural Rock Asphalt Aggregate)' gives the requirements for various grades of mastic asphalt composed of natural rock asphalt and coarse aggregate where appropriate, with asphaltic cements. The artificial building asphalts are bitumens extended with crushed limestone, and are known as 'limestone filled'. These are covered by BS 988, 1076, 1097, 1451 : 1973 'Mastic Asphalt for Building (Limestone Aggregate)'.

The melting point of asphalts is between 138–150°C. The handling of the material from the 'pot' to the point of application must be carefully controlled since, if it loses heat, spreading may be difficult, giving fissures and possible water penetration. Conversely, too fluid a mix may be impossible to work vertically. The Code of Practice is CP 144 : Part 4 : 1970 'Mastic Asphalt'.

ASPHALT ROOFING.—The substrate should be clean and smooth, laid to a gradient of not less than 1:60 and not more than 1:2. To separate the asphalt from the substrate to allow differential thermal movements to take place, a layer of sheathing felt is fixed to the substrate, preferably by running it in hot pitch or bituminous emulsion since nails have a low retentive power in sheathing felt. On screeded roofs the sheathing must be hot-run. The substrate should be dry, as trapped moisture in an immature cementitious screed will cause bubbling and ultimately blowing of the asphalt.

Roofing asphalt is laid in two coats, each 10 mm thick and the second coat laid to break joint with the first. The asphalter lays down wooden battens to act as rules for maintaining correct thickness and works each layer thoroughly by heavy trowelling to produce a dense lamination. The top surface of the finished roofing is sanded and the sand trowelled in as the work proceeds to improve wear resistance and eliminate any bituminous bleeds.

Where exposed asphalt is to be carried up gradients steeper than 1:2 it is necessary to reinforce them with either expanded metal or woven fibreglass fabric. When the gradient exceeds 1:1 the reinforcement must be fixed to the substrate, the mesh being secured by stapling to a timber substrate, or by twisted wire ties left protruding from cementitious screeds. Exposed asphalt should not be carried vertically for more than about 0·5 m whether reinforced or not, as the high thermal absorption of the material causes considerable temperature rise and consequent softening of the material which ripples and slumps causing fracture and leakage. Protection of the asphalt by means of reflective coatings is useful where greater heights are essential.

Asphalt tanking.—Tanking is the formation of an impermeable skin to a construction subject to external water pressure from the ground. It should always be carried out on the outside of the structural wall so that water pressure cannot force the tanking off the wall. This also ensures that the wall itself is dry. Similarly, the horizontal tankings to the basement floor must be held down by a sufficient weight of material, and these requirements imply that the great mass of the basement structure is floating within the tanking skin. Vertical tanking is carried out in two or three coats and horizontal tanking in three coats.

ROOFING

Slating and tiling.—BS 5534 'Code of Practice for slating and tiling' Part 1 1978 (1985) 'Design' gives the requirements to ensure compliance with CP 3 Chapter 5 Part 2 1972 'Wind loads'.

Clay and concrete roofing tiles are the most frequently used finish for pitched roofs. The materials are described in Chapter C8. Slating is of historical significance and in renovation. It and other now less frequently used forms of roofing are described in earlier editions of Kempe. BS 680 'Roofing slates' is in two parts, Part 1 : 1944 'Imperial units' and Part 2 : 1971 'Metric units'. It gives the characteristics, standard designations, thickness gradings, lengths and widths and testing for atmospheric conditions. Part 2 in addition gives work sizes and tolerances.

Asbestos-cement slates used for roofing and cladding are described in BS 690 'Asbestos-cement slates and sheets' Part 4 1974 'Slates'.

Bituminous felt tiles are made in strips six or eight tiles wide. The tail of the strip is notched so that when the next strip above is laid bonded, the appearance is of separate tiles. Felt tiles are finished in red, brown or green mineral granules and are light but not as durable as other tiles. Fixing is by means of broad headed nails to a solid boarded roof and in high winds the material can be stripped off.

ROOF SHEETING.—A wide range of materials is available for roofing direct to purlins, including galvanised steel, bitumen-coated steel, plastic-coated steel, aluminum (plain or anodised), asbestos-cement and plastics. Most sheets are made in various corrugated sections.

Relevant standards are:

CP 143 'Sheet roof and wall coverings' (in seven remaining parts for different materials)

CP 144 'Roof coverings' Pt 3 1970 'Built up bitumen felt' Pt 4 1970 'Mastic asphalt'.

BS 849 1939 'Plain zinc sheet roofing'. BS 1178 1982 'Milled lead sheet for building purposes'. BS 2870 1980 'Rolled copper and copper alloys: sheet, strip and foil'. BS 5247 'Code of Practice for sheet, roof and wall coverings' Part 14 1975 'Corrugated asbestos cement'.

Galvanised steel has a limited life and is declining in building use, but patent bitumen-coated sheets, some with colour finishes, are widely used. Plastic-coated steels are light and externally durable but corrosion at cut edges must be guarded against. Plastic-coated aluminum is not so subject to corrosion and can be obtained in a wide range of colours, while anodised aluminum can be found in the blue, green or gold range.

Asbestos-cement sheets are made in a very wide range of sections including composite 'sandwich' forms interlaid with fibreglass insulation. Asbestos-cement tends to harden and embrittle with age in normal atmospheres and care must be taken to use crawling boards when working over asbestos roofing. In certain circumstances it can soften or grow mould.

Plastic roofing sheets are available in various PVC formulations, both opaque and transparent, and in acrylic sheets ('Perspex') in a wide range of colours. Fibreglass reinforced polyester sheets are also available. Certain transparent PVC's are reinforced with fine wire mesh for added strength.

PURLIN ROOFING.—Slates and tiles depend upon the construction of a fine grid of rafters and battens (or boarding) but purling roofing requires only trusses and purlins. Hence the various sheets referred to above must be capable of spanning between purlins to eliminate the complicated work involved in traditional roofing. For most materials purlin spacings range from 900 mm to 1·8 m according to the type of sheet used and its section. Most patterns of asbestos sheeting are designed for use on slopes of 15° and upward. For very low pitches down to 5° various forms of troughing are used. Ordinary corrugated sheets can be used at low pitches but only by double lapping and double sealing, which raises problems of cutting the corners at sheet junctions.

Long-strip anodised aluminum sheets are made up to 6·1 m long and incorporate three rolls, the outer ones being alternately an overcapping and an undercloak each with a snap-fixing rib. These sheets can therefore be fixed at the undercloak edge only, the overlapping being snapped over the previous sheet.

ROOF LIGHTING.—Roof lighting to purlin roofs can be obtained by the use of patent glazing or of transparent or translucent sheets of 6 mm wired glass or plastic which match and mate with the opaque sheets of the roof. Glass sections are too thick to mix with thin metallic roofings. The flammability and spread of flame characteristics of plastic sheets may require their restricted use in panels of limited size.

ROOF DECKING.—Roofs both flat and pitched may be covered with patent deckings which produce complete roofings in large units for greater spans than those available with single sheet or thin sandwich sheets. They are made in a wide range of single materials, and multiple constructions. Wood-wool slabs are normally 51 mm thick but can be obtained in 76 mm thickness for heavy duty use. It is also made with channel reinforcement to the long edges. Straw board slabs are 51 mm thick and unlike wood-wool, stronger in one direction than the other. Strawboard is seriously affected by moisture which causes loss of strength as well as giving rise to mould growth.

WEATHER SKIN ON DECKS.—The normal weatherproofing of decking is bituminous felt roofing. CP 144 covers aspects of choice and laying of bituminous felts and asphalts for such purposes, and the Building Regulations, B2/3/4 for the various purpose groups indicate the acceptability of various types under fire requirements. The proper placing of thermal insulation and vapour barriers is essential to prevent condensation on the underside of the roofing and particularly on light metal skins.

There is also the single skin plastic roofing membrane. Neoprenes and PVC's are stuck to the deck units in a single skin and the joints taped with pressure-sensitive adhesive tape or welded on site. They are available in pale colours which reflect solar heat away more efficiently than felts and asphalt.

To reduce solar gain by dark finishes white stone chippings are applied. At least 20 mm thickness of white spar (from Derbyshire) is necessary for any real effect to be obtained. To maintain the effect it is necessary to wash the chippings by hosing down every year in urban atmospheres. High winds can cause chippings to blow off the roof edge and drains and roof outlets may become blocked.

FLAT ROOFS.—The first layer of felt is normally perforated and fully bonded to the decking. The two succeeding layers are fully bonded. Tongued and grooved boarding, while forming a suitable surface for felting when first laid, later tends to cup forming ridges over which the felt cracks. Plywoods, blockboards or chipboard are better substrates for felting while a screeded wood-wool roof gives a stable base allied with good thermal insulation. Several types of preformed expanded polystyrene screed blocks are available for creating falls on boarded flat roofs and these, in conjunction with a hardboard protective surface can provide adequate falls with dimensional stability and a good surface for hot applications of asphalt or felt.

TABLE 7.—WEIGHTS OF VARIOUS ROOF COMPONENTS

Materials		kg/m^2
Lead roll-cap roofing (excluding boarding and rolls)		27 to 42
Zinc and copper roofing (excl. boarding and rolls)		7·3 to 9·7
Aluminium (super purity) roofing (excl. boarding and rolls)		2·5 to 3·7
Timber boarding (incl. plywood, chipboard and blockboard)		
20 mm thick		12·2 to 14·6
15 mm thick		17·1 to 19·6
Slating with 76 mm lap (excluding battens)		
	Large Ladies	40
	Countesses	39
	Duchesses	42
Slating battens	average	7·3
Plain tiling 95 mm gauge		64 to 88
Plain tiling 102 mm gauge		58 to 83
Single lap tiling		24 to 32
Bituminous felt built-up roofing		19·6
Asphalt		39

CARPENTRY AND JOINERY

GRADING OF TIMBERS.—Timbers may be graded as to their capability to carry loads by inspection of the texture of the grain and its slope in relation to the principal axis of the member, the number of knots and the type of knots. Timbers have varying intrinsic qualities of strength and may be grouped in broad headings, but grading relates the capacity of one piece of a specific timber to that of another. For structural purposes the general run of softwoods (ie timbers deriving from coniferous trees) are classified as $5{\cdot}5\ N/mm^2$ timbers but Douglas Fir and Western Red Cedar are given a higher rating because of their consistency and few knots, as well as, in the case of cedar, the durability arising from the resinous nature of the wood. Hardwoods, on the other hand, range widely in their characteristics. For details of timbers see chapter C1.

JOINERY.—Joinery is the trade of working in wood with framed and glued joints for the making of finished timber fittings and fixtures. Joinery can be in softwood or hardwood, but all wood is wrot. Synthetic finishes are now used which are more durable and stable than traditional varnishes and polishes. Various plastics materials, particularly melamine boards have transformed working surfaces.

CARPENTRY.—Carpentry is the trade of working in wood for the making of structural frameworks, floors and roofs. The timbers used can be either softwood or hardwood but the former is the more common, and unwrot timber is widely used. The older skills of making structural joints in building frameworks still persist but are being supplanted by the use of specially designed metal fasteners, plates and connectors. These modern fastenings have resulted in substantial reductions in the sizes of members used and have permitted the design of timber trusses and girders to reach a high level of efficiency.

SIZES OF TIMBER MEMBERS.—The minimum sizes of timber members can be calculated in accordance with CP 112 'The Structural Use of Timber in Buildings', Part 2 : 1971 'Metric Units' but the Building Regulations 1985 : A1/2 Tables B1–28, include details for most of the common timber members.

CONNECTORS FOR TIMBER.—In BS 1579 1960 thirteen types of connectors for timber are described which increase the efficiency of joints.

STAIRS.—Stairs, ramps or stepped ramps are the cause of a large proportion of accidents. They are therefore more heavily controlled in their precise detailing than most other elements of building. BS 5395 'Stairs, Ladders and Walkways' in two parts, Part 1 : 1977 (1984) 'Code of Practice for the Design of Straight Stairs' and Part 2 : 1984, 'Code of Practice for the Design of Helical and Spiral Stairs' gives both general and specific advice about design. In England and Wales the requirements of Part K of the Building Regulations controls dimensions and design of stairs and ramps, while in Scotland Part S of the Building Standards (Scotland) Regulations performs a similar function. The two sets of regulations are not identical and reference must be made to the appropriate document according to the location of the site. Note that the Regulations require access to be provided for the disabled. Schedule 2 says where and how they must be given access.

Most access stairs are pitched at around 40° and have risers of around 180 mm with a going of about 225 mm. Similarly, balustrades are all about 850 to 900 mm above the pitch line of the stair unless a wide well exists in which case they have to be higher. The balustrade design is also controlled. The Approved Documents give details of handrails, guards and pedestrian and vehicle barriers. BS 6180 : 1982 Code of Practice for Protective Barriers In and About Buildings'. A 'Guide to Safety at Sports Grounds' is available from HMSO.

STUD PARTITIONS.—The studs are usually of 75 × 50 mm or 100 × 50 mm deal and are fixed to head and sole plates of similar scantlings at 400 mm centres to receive plasterboard finish. To stabilise the studs, some horizontal members are fixed between them at roughly 900 mm vertical centres. These are known as noggins.

Single stud partitions are only moderate in sound resistance. They can be filled with dry sand or rockwool or plugged with breeze blocks to improve performance but they are then not competitive with ordinary block partitions. Where sound insulation is important it is better to form a double staggered-stud partition, but it is only economic when the weight of a half-brick partition cannot be supported by the floor.

PATENT PARTITIONS.—Numerous patent forms of partitioning exist. They range from cardboard/plasterboard units with timber framings to highly complicated aluminium extrusions with expanded plastic/hardboard sandwich infill. Many claim special acoustic performance but they do not, as a rule, compare with block or brick partitions.

TIMBER ROOFS.—Many of the traditional roof forms have been superseded by standard connectored softwood trusses. They are made from small section impregnated softwood timbers, single members where in tension, double members where in compression. Spans range from 5·0 m to 12·2 m at standard pitches of 30° and 22½°, superimposed loading being adequate for normal industrial roofings and snow load. Domestic roof trusses follow similar patterns and are designed to take domestic roofings, such as interlocking tiles and concrete slates. Requirements, design and erection of Fink and Fan type trussed rafters are dealt with in CP 112 : Part 3 : 1973 'Trussed Rafters for Roofs of Dwellings'.

PATENT BEAMS.—Patent timber beams have no counterpart in traditional work. Many forms of 'warren' girder and 'N' truss fabricated in timber are available, as are I section and box beams built up from plywood and solid timber. Spans can be as great as 12·2 m when strawboard or wood wool roofing slabs are used with bituminous felt roofing.

DECKS.—Some fabricated decks of timber for roofing and flooring are designed on the stressed skin principle with the plywood upper and lower planes bonded to the framing timbers and acting as part of the structure.

STANDARD DOORS.—CP 151 : Part 1 : 1957 'Wooden Doors' deals with wooden doors of all types and BS 459 : Part 4 : 1965 with 'Matchboarded Doors'. The main type of door in use is the flush ply-faced door. Numerous others include cellular cores of coiled wood shavings, compressed fibre boards and expanded plastics as well as solid wood cores. Some cheap doors are faced with hardboard but unless the core is very good they tend to ripple. The usual run of door is hardwood lipped only on its long edges to permit planing to size of opening. Wood door frames and linings are covered by BS 1567 1953 (1960). Doors are also supplied pre-hung in their frames. Internal doors are supplied in 100 mm increments of width from 600 to 900 mm and external doors at 900, 1000, 1500 and 1800 mm, each being the dimensions of the space filled by the door and frame together.

WINDOWS.—BS 644 'Wood windows' gives sizes for double hung sash windows.

Pivot windows use sections similar to the BS 644 members but are made in large panes with horizontal pivot or hinge systems which give greater opening areas than casements. Pivot windows can be fully reversed for the cleaning of the outside surface and for painting, and when fitted with suitable stays and friction pivots are fairly stable in high wind conditions.

The maintenance of wood windows is imperative. Impregnated timbers should be used. All wood windows should be fitted with clearance gaps of at least 3 mm all round the opening portions, the rebates of the frames being quite capable of tolerating such a clearance.

Moisture Content of Timber.—The moisture content at which the timber will have to operate should be achieved in the timber before fabrication and should be between the following limits:—Internal joinery of central heated buildings, 10–12%. Internal doors, 12–15%. Other internal joinery, 14–17%. External doors, 15–18%. External joinery, 11–12%. Plywood when manufactured into joinery, 10–15%. All plywood for external use should be resin bonded.

TIMBER SHORING.—Raking Shores.—A plank Fig. 5 (C), 225 mm × 75 mm, the length varying with the height of building, is placed against the upper part of the wall to be supported. In this plank rectangular holes are cut out to admit timber 'needles', (D), from 100 mm to 150 mm × 150 mm. and about 300 mm long. These are let into the wall about 112 mm and project beyond the plank about 112 mm to receive the ends of the 'shores' (A). A cleat, (E), is usually nailed to the plank on the upper side of each needle.

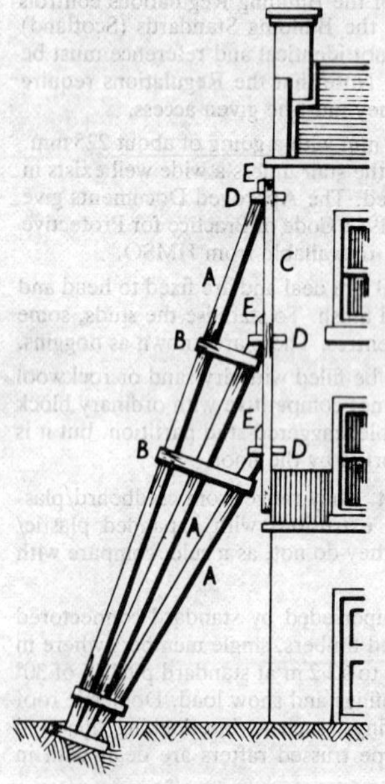

FIG. 5.—Shoring.

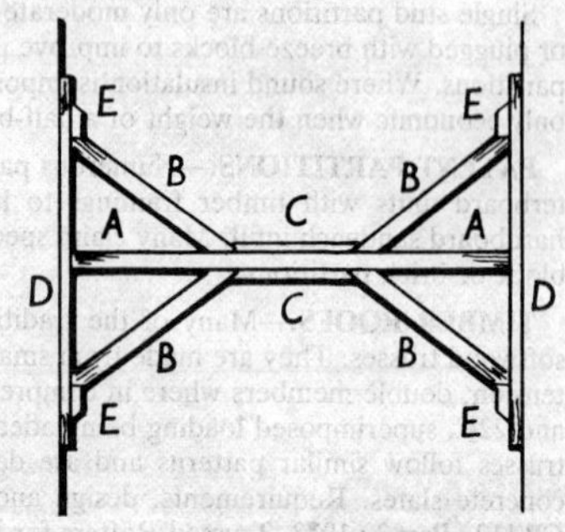

FIG. 6.—Strutting.

The shores, (A), are from 150 mm × 100 mm in very small buildings, to 300 × 225 or 300 in very large buildings. These last are usually built up from 300 × 150 half-timbers. The shores are fixed to a footing block of similar scantlings and set in the ground on a firm base at right angles to the uppermost shore. Short pieces, (B), about 25 mm thick and from 150 to 225 mm wide, are nailed on each side of the shores.

Flying Shores.—The details of assembly of struts between houses are lettered in Fig 6. Planks, (D), 225 mm × 75 mm, are fixed against each wall and the horizontal strut, (A), 150 mm × 100 mm to 225 mm × 100 mm, is lightly wedged between them. Straining pieces, (C), 150 mm × 75 mm, are bolted to the strut, and the rakers, (B), 150 mm × 100 mm are compressed by cleats, (E), spiked to and usually partly housed into the planks. The strut is usually placed at a height above ground equal to two-thirds of the height from ground to eaves level.

METALWORK

MATERIALS.—Bronze metal employed in modern commercial buildings is an alloy of copper and spelter. 9–1. For shop fronts, doors, etc., and in decorative metal interiors, sheets of 20–16 gauge are used. Drawn through dies over a core of straight grained hardwood, moulded sections of considerable length are available. Extruded bronze, 3 mm thick or more, has no core and is available in moulded sections with sharp arrises and up to 4.3 m in length.

Cast iron is used for drilled treads for fire escapes, rainwater goods, iron drains and fittings, window spandrills, balusters and newels for stairs. Cast iron vent gratings made to brickwork dimensions, are obtainable plain or galvanised, and brackets in all kinds are available.

Smith's work in timber roof trusses, in saddles, fish plates, ties and bolted connections is preferably in wrought iron. Hand rails, ornamental gates and the like are generally mild steel.

PATENT GLAZING.—Patent glazing is widely used to large factory areas. Several types of bar are used: lead coated steel, plastic-coated steel, and aluminium extrusions. Double glazing bars are available and can assist in maintaining high thermal insulation of a roof. Various methods are adopted to obtain a draught and weather seal where the bottom of the glass sheet overlaps the roofing.

METAL WINDOWS.—BS 6510 1984 'Specifications for steel windows, sills, window boards and doors' gives materials, finishes and size limits for two ranges of windows. Wood surrounds are manufactured to BS 1285 1980 'Specification for wood surrounds for steel windows and doors'.

Aluminium windows, pivot, casement and double-hung sashes are made in sizes standard only to the company producing them, but using BS alloys. Bronze windows are only used for monumental work. They are robust and durable, but very expensive. Stainless steel windows are rigid, durable and need no real maintenance.

Metal Sundries.—BS 1245 1975 'Metal door frames (steel)' gives a range of frames suitable for British Standard doors.

Staircases.—Apart from the cast-iron escape stairs which are obtainable in helical and dog-leg form, there are a number of standard metal staircases, mainly in steel which are suitable for commercial and industrial uses. Most balustrades are made in welded mild steel for painting and are fitted with extruded PVC handrails. Stainless steel and bronze handrails are also produced as standard sections.

STORAGE EQUIPMENT.—Industrial storage racks for shelved items and systematic bin storage are made in stove-enamelled steel and are available as open framework or closed pigeonhole units. Cross bracing in both elevational directions is vital where heavy parts are to be stored. Some systems of industrial storage mount the racks on tramway tracks to enable front storage racks to be slid aside to expose rear racks. Special provision must be made in the structural design of the floor for such dense storage.

Storied storage for use in lofty buildings is made in slotted angle steelwork. In certain circumstances a fire resistance may be required, particularly where the upper level of such storage is arranged with cul-de-sac gangways and where the goods stored are flammable. Stillages are useful where fork-lift trucks can operate. Clothes storage in the form of lockers for changing rooms etc is normally in standard stove-enamelled steel compartments.

Benching.—Industrial benching is usually made in steel, though for special purposes timber or lead tops can be applied. Suppliers of benching are usually also fabricators of production trackways such as roller tracks and chutes.

Rolling and Sliding Shutters.—Large industrial openings are rarely sealed by hinged doors which are vulnerable to wind and reduce vision angles for vehicles. Rolling shutters, made of hinged wood slats or S-section steel or aluminium are used. A hand hauling chain may be used for lowering and raising the curtain, or bevel gears and a winding handle/power-operated by electric motor. In either case rolling shutters are relatively slow moving.

Sliding shutters and doors are made of steel or aluminium and may run on either an overhead track or a floor track. Floor tracks are subject to fouling by rubbish and dust. Overhead tracks put the loads on to the lintel but are often easier to slide and are retained by a stud sliding in a floor groove. Sliding doors, when floor mounted, should not be tall and narrow in proportion as this can lead to 'chattering' during operation. Sliding shutters are made of a number of leaves of metal with vertical hinged joints.

DRAINAGE

For materials see chapter C8.

DRAINAGE FOR HOUSES.—Soil Drains.—The volume of sewage is based on the consumption of water, on average, 130 litres per head per day. It is generally assumed that half the daily consumption occurs within 6 hours, thus giving an average peak consumption of 11.5 litres per head per hour.

Rate of Flow.—(*a*) The maximum rate of flow should be based upon twice the average peak consumption. ie 23 litres per head per hour. Reducing this to litre per minute, gives 0.33 litre per head per min.

(*b*) In some circumstances the above peak rate of flow may be inadequate due to simultaneous use of fittings or other exceptional conditions, and due allowance should be made in such cases.

SURFACE WATER DRAINS.—Volume of Rainwater.—The usual minimum allowance is a rainfall intensity of 40 mm per hour. This is equivalent to 64 litre m^2 per min.

Rate of Flow.—This is obtained by multiplying the plan area of the surfaces to be drained by the volume per unit area per minute. If necessary, calculate separately the areas drained by each gully or other collecting point. The cumulative totals will give the information required to decide changes in fall or diameter of the drain.

GRADIENTS AND PIPE SIZES.—Normal gradients where flow is irregular (eg branch drains) are: 100 mm pipes, 1 in 40: 150 mm pipes, 1 in 60: and 225 mm pipes, 1 in 90.

The minimum self-clearing velocity for drains with a steady flow is 750 mm/sec when flowing at one quarter depth. While it is most important that the velocity should not fall below the minimum, a velocity exceeding 3 m/s should also be avoided. The latter velocity in pipes flowing full or half-full is given by the following gradients: 150 mm pipes, 1 in 9; and for 225 mm pipes, 1 in 16.

Large diameter pipes should not be used purely to justify laying at a flatter gradient; this does not increase the velocity but reduces the depth of flow and the drain may be no longer self-cleansing.

Most drainage around buildings is now carried out in fired clay or plastic. Both are readily and quickly flexibly jointed with plastic couplings. Clay pipes may be socket and spigot with plastic fairings and a rubber 'O' ring joint or plain ended jointed with polypropylene couplings. Drains under buildings must be of the flexibly jointed type laid in proper bedding materials with liberal separation where the drain passes through foundation walls ie there must be rigid arches over the pipes.

Other materials used for underground drainage include heavy duty asbestos-cement pipes, and pitch fibre pipes and certain plastics extrusions. Asbestos-cement pipes require great care in laying and backfilling to prevent damage but can, when encased in concrete give satisfactory service. Pitch-fibre pipes, though sometimes not popular with local authorities, may be useful where ground movements, such as mining settlement are expected. Perforated land drain pipes in pitch-fibre are available. Plastic land drain pipes are used in drum-supplied mole plough laying machines to lay small bore drains in a continuous operation without significant disturbance to the soil. Polyvinyl chloride pipes are suitable in suspended runs in service ducts where their flexibility, though demanding frequent or continuous support, permits tortuous routes to be followed. They are jointed either by screwed unions (for small bores) or hot-air welded joints. Clay or plastic pipes must be used for corrosive effluents although most laboratory effluents are treated by dilution pots and can then safely be run in ordinary drains.

Where drains run under buildings they should either be of cast iron or clayware fully encased in concrete. Though only soil drain manholes within a building must have double-seal covers, it is good practice to provide them for surface water manholes also, to ensure that unpleasant odours do not escape.

The Public Health Acts lay down requirements for connections to sewers and the responsibility of Local Authorities and building owners in respect of drainage. In isolated sites it can be permissible for soil drains to run to cesspools or septic tanks and for surface water to discharge to soakaways. Cesspools and septic tanks must conform with certain requirements as to overflows and vents as well as distances from buildings or watercourses.

PLUMBING & ENGINEERING INSTALLATIONS

PLUMBING GENERALLY.—Lead and iron used to dominate the trade but now the great majority of the work is carried out in copper, with inroads being made by plated steels and various plastics. For building purposes two principal types of tube are used; the normal plumbing tube and the underground quality BS 2871 : Part 1 : 1971 'Copper Tubes for Water, Gas, and Sanitation' (= ISO/R 195). The fittings used are of two main types, both in brass ware. Compression fittings rely upon the ramp compression action of a double tapered ring which is slipped over the pipe, the fitting and the union nut having female tapers which compress the ring firmly on to the pipe. Capillary fittings rely upon the fusing of a pre-inserted solder ring in the fitting. No nuts are used, the fitting being slipped over the tube up to a limiting collar and then heated by blow lamp until the solder begins to show at the point of entry of the pipe into the fitting. A wide range of fittings is available in both types, the compression fittings have the advantage of being capable of dismantling and re-use, but the capillary fittings being less obtrusive and neater. In both cases the pipe should be cut clean and square and the raw edges filed off, and for capillary fittings the surface of the pipe should be cleaned to ensure solder bond. Bending of copper tube is normally carried out by simple bending machines but tube less than 22 mm diameter can be hand-bent by the use of a long coil spring which is inserted in the tube to prevent kinking. Copper tube should never be in direct contact with galvanised products as electrolytic action is set up which causes rapid corrosion.

Plated light steel tube for domestic piped services is claimed to be lighter to handle and cheaper than copper. Plastic tubes are manufactured from polyethylene, PVC, polypropylene and nylon. The first two have achieved acceptance, the second two are rather more expensive. Nylon tube is used in mini-bore heating but its uses in plumbing are restricted to seals, glands and clips. Polypropylene is commonly used for moulded fittings (including WC pan seats) but not in pipe form. Neither polyethylene ('polythene') nor PVC are capable of withstanding temperatures above 60°C for long periods without softening and sagging, thus their use has largely been for cold or blended water supplies and for wastes. Even so they should be supported at about 600 mm intervals.

SANITARY FITTINGS.—Water closets are of three basic types, high level wash-down, low level washdown, and low level syphonic. High level WCs can be quite cheap and are commonly used in unimportant locations while the low level types are neater in appearance and more suitable for domestic purposes. The syphonic type has two traps in the soil pipe and is designed to evacuate waste by a process of emptying followed by flushing and finally refilling of the traps. This system is quiet in operation and effective. It also has the virtue of a high water level. Some continental types of closet use a dry pan and rely entirely on flushing action, but these are not favoured by sanitary authorities.

Lavatory basins are of various types including special shapes for corner mounting. Mounting can be by wall brackets or concealed clips, by pedestals, or by suspension in a flat counter. The development of thermostatically controlled water supplies has resulted in the single tap basin, the tap being a spray nozzle which can be controlled by foot pedal, while the basin has no waste plug. The use of this system can give substantial water economies. Trough basins for factory use are common but can be expensive. Circular or regular polygonal washing fountains of metal or terrazzo with a number of temperature controlled water outlets operated by pedals are better. Large numbers can be served by fountains and it is important to ensure that drying facilities are adequate to handle the flow of persons. Paper towels are hygienic but can be unsightly, endless roller towels have largely been superseded by the continuous long roll machine and these, if properly served, can be highly efficient. Blown warm air hand dryers are less efficient in terms of time taken but are hygienic and not vulnerable to vandalism. Soap in tablet form is only suitable in domestic or low usage lavatories; for continuous high-density use, soap dispensers are invaluable. In factories and workshops it is also desirable to have dispensers for grease absorbing detergents, and for certain barrier creams.

Showers are useful for rapid body cleansing in certain industrial processes. Baths are available in various sizes and some special types are made for disabled persons. Traps for baths are often difficult of access and shallow in the water seal. Durabilities of sinks vary but stainless steel is generally regarded as the best material being free from the risk of chipping and able to withstand great heat.
British Standard specifications for sanitary ware are given in chapter C8.

Wastes and soil drains must always be trapped to prevent odours rising from the foul drains. The flow of material down the soil pipe from a large fitting can cause low pressures in traps of other fittings and so anti-syphonage pipes are connected to relieve pressure drops through a second stack. Investigation has shown however, that with correct falls and lengths of runs a single stack pipe can cope with domestic drainage even on multistorey work. Special fittings are available for this system which requires swept entries and precise relationships of various connections. Laboratory wastes are now usually run in plastic pipe which must be supported at frequent intervals. Other wastes are usually run in copper.

EXTERNAL PLUMBING.—Surface water plumbing is usually carried externally and wastes and soil pipes may be. Often the materials used must be considered in the light of the roof covering, where this is metallic. Incompatible roof sheeting and gutters can lead to electrolytic corrosion.

GUTTERS.—Available in cast iron, pressed steel, asbestos cement, aluminium, fibreglass-reinforced polyesters, pvc and vitreous enamelled cast iron, and in a wide range of sections for various purposes. Gutters fall into three types, eaves, boundary wall (or parapet) and valley. Eaves gutters should be so designed that the inner edge is never lower than the outer, and preferably higher. This forms a weir over which collected water may spill if the rainwater pipes become choked. Spillage over the inner edge is liable to cause damage to wood fascias and damp penetration of walls. Boundary wall gutters are akin to valley gutters and being within the building, should always be provided with at least two outlets to rainwater pipes as a protection against overflowing and consequent damage to goods below. If the gutter length extends to the end of a building it is good practice to cut down the top edge of the end stop to form a deliberate weir overflow. For both types of gutter a large section is desirable, especially in atmospheres subject to fly ash or dust pollution or where there are tall trees. The Building Research Station has shown that even small gradients in gutters can have marked effects on water carrying capacity and recommend a fall of 1:50 as giving about double the flow as compared with a flat gutter. Gutters with swept outlet nozzles also improve flow, and straight runs of downpipe without sharp bends ensure rapid clearance of storm water.

Traps are not necessary at the foot of rainwater pipes unless the surface water drains are connected to the foul without a reverse action interceptor, and plain easy bends with some provision for rodding are the most satisfactory termination of the downpipe, but plain shoes with rodding eye are satisfactory in most circumstances. Heavy storms can, if the drains are tortuous or obstructed, cause such back pressures in manholes as to lift the covers, and even gully plates can be forced off so adequate provision in size of drains and care in laying may repay the cost in safety. Gutters, particularly valley gutters, are often suspended from the light flexible purlins and have been known to cause sagging of the members to the extent that water is puddled in subsided sections, reducing the freeboard for storms as well as affecting the self-cleansing qualities of the waterway. Erosion of fibreglass reinforced polyester gutters has been experienced and selection should be made with care.

Rainwater Pipes.—Available in the same range of materials as gutters. They are fixed to walls or stanchions by clips or, in the case of cast iron, occasionally by ears cast on to the sockets. Ferrous metal goods should be so fixed that the pipe is clear of the walls by at least 38 mm to facilitate painting of the whole surface.

BUILDING SERVICES

SERVICES.—Some standardisation of hot and cold water services is apparent in 'heat units' and harness 'plumbing units' which comprise the cold water storage tank, cylinder and all interconnections and valves. They can also include a feed and expansion tank for central heating systems. In some areas all cold fittings are connected direct to the main supply, but it is regarded as good practice, particularly in educational, catering and some industrial buildings, to provide a reserve storage tank in case of mains failure, which could cause serious difficulties. In other areas, the water authority will permit only two connections direct off the main, tank connections and a kitchen sink tap.

For domestic purposes it may be sufficient to use an instantaneous gas water heater with an appropriate rate of flow, or a storage type electrical water heater of adequate capacity, but water heating is often a by-product of the central heating system in winter while an immersion heater in the cylinder takes over the summer load providing a set amount of hot water to be available at all times. The quantity can, by using double-element heaters, be either small (for washing-up, etc.) or large (for bathing). Water heating for open discharge through taps should always be indirect, particularly in hard water areas, as continuous changing of central heating water greatly accelerates furring of the pipes and heating elements.

HEATING, VENTILATING AND AIR CONDITIONING.—Calculation of thermal and ventilation loads for any complex building requires care. Design information and details of systems are given in chapter K1. However, for quick computation on a very approximate basis for industrial building, a load of 40–55 W/m^3 will give a guide. Domestic hot water loads vary widely according to the building function but a dwelling requires, for constant hot water, about 1.2 kW. This loading is not the requirement for an immersion heater whose output may be double in order to provide a suitable recovery period in a storage cylinder. Hospital hot water demands can rise to three times the domestic load per patient.

ELECTRICAL SERVICES.—These include lighting, heating and power supplies and ancilliaries such as telephone and call systems, fire alarms and lightning conductors. Ancilliary services will be installed by specialist contractors.

ENERGY EFFICIENCY.—BS 8207 : 1985 'Code of Practice for Energy Efficiency in Buildings' recommends procedures to ensure the efficient use of energy in design and management of all types of buildings including housing. It applies to new buildings and to rehabilitation of old and includes both operation and maintenance.

PLASTERWORK, RENDERING, WALL AND FLOOR FINISHINGS

FINISHING.—The trade of plasterer includes plastering and the rendering of walls and ceilings, externally and internally as well as the laying of screeds and the making good of concrete fair-faced surfaces. Tiling on walls and floors is normally carried out by specialised tradesmen. Terrazzo is again a specialised trade but often draws its labour from the plastering trade for training in the special techniques of the material.

INTERNAL PLASTERING.—Very few plasterers now mix their own plasters. Pre-mixed bagged plaster is almost universally used. A number of combinations of undercoats and finishing coats for plaster-work using traditional methods and associated defects and remedies were given in earlier editions of 'Kempe' but now almost all work is in lightweight vermiculite plasters or dry-lining using gypsum plasterboard.

Part 1 of BS 1191 : 1973 (≠ISO 3048-9, ISO 3051) covers gypsum building plasters, excluding the premixed lightweight plasters. Gypsum plasters may vary widely in their properties, partly because methods of manufacture differ, and partly because adjustments are made to suit users' requirements. The properties required for undercoat work differ from those required for finishing, whilst in some cases a hard surface is required and in others not.

Gypsum plasters tend to expand slightly on setting and, unlike Portland cement, do not shrink appreciably thereafter. They are, therefore, less likely to break bond, or crack. Gypsum is, however, slightly soluble and in damp conditions liable to continue slow hydration, with resulting excessive expansion and failure. They should, therefore, never be used when exposed to moisture. Gypsum should never be mixed with Portland cement, or even used in contact with it in damp conditions, for it reacts with the latter to form calcium sulpho-aluminate, which expands and causes disruption. It may, however, normally be blended with lime.

Gypsum itself is the dihydrate of calcium sulphate, $CaSO_4.2H_2O$, the raw material from which the plasters are made, and the final stage when they have set. Part 1 of BS 1191 deals with four grades of plasters, giving chemical and physical properties, with methods for the determination of these properties.

(*A*) Plaster of Paris made by calcining gypsum and grinding the product. The resulting powder when mixed with water forms a smooth white paste which sets to a solid mass. No retarder or other additive is included.

(*B*) Retarded hemi-hydrate gypsum plaster is partly dehydrated gypsum, $2CaSO_4.H_2O$, to which a retarder has been added to delay the setting time for 30 to 60 minutes.

(*C*) Anhydrous gypsum plaster consists essentially of fully dehydrated gypsum with additives to control the setting time as required.

(*D*) Keene's plaster is anhydrous plaster specially prepared to produce a smooth finish with a slow set. Lime should not be added to this type.

Part 2 of BS 1191 deals with premixed lightweight plasters which are divided into two types: (*a*) *Undercoat plasters*, comprising (1) Browning plaster; (2) Metal lathing plaster; (3) Bonding plaster. (*b*) *Final coat plaster* as finishing plaster.

Internal plastering differs from rendering in that normally it does not have to withstand moisture and extreme climatic conditions. In addition to the mixes used in rendering (*qv*) which may be used where conditions warrant, lime–sand plasters may be used with or without the addition of hair. These, however, are weak and soft and take a long time to harden and so are seldom used today. Gypsum (*qv*) in any of its forms, Class B, C and D, may also be used by itself or with sand and Class B with lime and sand. Class A, plaster of Paris, is quick setting and only used for small repair work. Both cement and lime shrink on drying out, so that strong mixes tend to crack at regular intervals. The addition of sand reduces the shrinkage and also, by weakening the plaster, enables it to yield all over without visible cracking. Gypsum tends to expand on setting and a lime admixture reduces this tendency.

Plaster mixes divide themselves into 'coarse stuff' used for backing courses and 'fine stuff' for the finishing coat. Wood and steel laths and rough surfaces require two backing coats, smoother surfaces only one, whilst some sheet and slab materials in general use are specially designed to take a finished coat without a backing.

Mixes for the backing coats vary from 1:1:6 to 1:2:9 cement:lime:sand: or gypsum plaster:lime:sand, according to strength required, sometimes a 1:3 Class B gypsum and sand, or cement and sand, or hydraulic lime and sand mix is used.

The finishing coat may be any of the gypsum plasters used neat or with lime and sand as required. Class C gypsum plasters are harder than Class B and Class D are hardest of all.

Gypsum plasterboard drylining is now the usual finish in new construction. It is less labour intensive than wet plastering and less water needs to be dried out before decorating can begin. BS 1230: Part 1: 1985 'Plasterboard excluding materials submitted to secondary operations' (≠ISO 6308) gives requirements and methods of test for lining materials for various applications. BS 6214: 1982 'Jointing materials for plasterboard' specifies requirements for jointing compounds and tapes for use with tapered edge gypsum plasterboard.

EXTERNAL RENDERING.—Gypsum plaster is never used externally. An external rendering must be durable, resist moisture penetration, weather uniformly and have a good appearance. BS 5262: 1976 'Code of Practice for external rendered finishes' gives guidance on rendering old and new substrates and the maintenance and repair of existing work. If the mortar used is too strong it will crack on drying out and shrinking if the key with the backing is strong or, otherwise, it will break bond with the backing. For this reason lime-cement mortars similar to those used for laying bricks but with rather finer sand (BS 1199 1976) are commonly used, though a 1:3 by volume mix of Portland cement and sand may be used for specially watertight work where the backing is strong and also provides a good mechanical key. Where the backing is strong and dense as in structural concrete and some brickwork, a key may be provided by means of a spatter dash coat. This consists of a mixture of one part cement to two or three parts of fairly coarse sand mixed to the consistency of a thick slurry and thrown against the surface of the backing so as to adhere thereto in a thin rough coating. After this has set it should be wetted down at intervals until the normal rendering is applied. A key may also be provided by means of a bonding agent as supplied under various proprietary names. This is generally a synthetic resin such as polyvinyl acetate emulsion, which is mixed with water, cement and sand and applied by dabbing with a brush so as to produce an irregular multi-pointed surface. This is best left for four to five days before the next coat is applied.

Two coats of rendering are normally sufficient, a first or straightening coat 10 to 15 mm thick and a final coat at between 3 and 10 mm in thickness depending on the texture. In exposed conditions, however, three coats may be necessary. For the first coat, a 1:½:4½ cement:sand or, 1:1:6, cement:lime:sand mix may be used. It should be smoothed with a floating rule. When the coat has begun to dry and harden, it should be combed with a wire comb to provide a key for the next coat. It should be left for as long as possible before applying this. The final coat for normal smooth surfaced rendering may be 1:1:6 or in less exposed positions 1:2:9 cement:lime:sand by volume. Types of special finishing coat include:—

Roughcast.—First coat 1:½:4½ as above, final coat, 1 part cement, ½ lime, 1½ shingle (5 to 15 mm), 3 sand, thrown onto the wall with a trowel.

Spatterdash.—Coarse and fine grit mixed with cement and thrown onto the wall. Mixing must be continuous to maintain a consistent texture.

Pebble Dash.—First coat, 1:4½ water-repellent cement, and sand; and final coat, 1 cement, 1 lime, 5 sand, applied approximately 10 mm thick; pebbles etc. (5 to 15 mm), are dashed on to the surface while it is still soft.

Scraped.—Surface scraped some hours after application with an old saw blade or similar tool.

Ornamental Textures.—A variety of these can be applied using sash tools, wide-toothed comb, corrugated rubber and other means.

Machine Applied.—These are finishes applied by hand-operated 'flick-on' machines, cement guns and sprays. They produce a rendering of even texture, highly resistant to weathering. They include Tyrolean finish which is available as a bagged material in off-white and a number of pastel shades. It produces a knobly texture which can be left rough or rubbed down and has the advantage that paint treatment is not necessary at least for some time. It is useful for renovating old rendered walls which would not retain harder denser renderings.

WALL TILING.—Glazed earthenware tiles should comply with the standards described in chapter C8.

Ceramic tile adhesives have been developed which avoid the necessity to render and apply soaked tiles to the wet surface. The adhesives are gap-filling mastic compounds, cream or white in colour and applied either in dabs to a rough surface or combed on a smooth surface, the dry tiles being pressed back and spaced in the usual manner before pointing with conventional cements.

Cement-glazes are applied surface coatings of a synthetic resin on smooth hard renderings. They are usually finished with a coarse spray or 'splatter' of contrasting colours and form a useful continuous durable finish, particularly suitable to industrial and educational work where their low-cost and good performance are necessary.

Terrazo Wall Finish.—Marble chippings are used as aggregate, ground smooth after 3 days hardening. It may be plastered to a wall, or formed in slabs and set like marble. Coloured marble chips 12 mm down, and/or coloured cements, as well as various gradings, provide a wide variety. The mix should not be richer than 1:2½.

FLOORING.—Floor finishes have to perform various functions ranging from impression of soft luxury given by carpets, to hard durability of a factory floor. All floor finishes however must possess some durability and the finish itself is selected according to the type of duty it will have to withstand.

Ground Floor Finishes.—For domestic use the finishes to a concrete floor may be diverse but in almost all cases a levelling screed is applied to the base concrete to provide a suitable surface. The screed is usually composed of cement and sand in proportions 1:4. It should be thoroughly mixed, preferably by machine, and the sand should be tested for moisture 'bulking' so as to obtain correct mix proportions and water-cement ratio. This ratio should be as low as possible to reduce shrinkage, but inadequate water can result in unslaked cement and badly mixed screed with as bad results as excessive water which results in a weak surface and high shrinkage.

Ideally, the screed should be laid while the base concrete is still 'green' (ie within a day), but the difficulties of this operation and the damage which occurs due to working over the finished screed by following trades usually preclude it. For later application the surface of the slab must be thoroughly cleaned to remove all oils, dust, rubbish or other matter and the surface wetted by spray before application.

FLOOR SCREEDS AND TOPPINGS.—Where the screed is to have a thin or flexible covering such as thermoplastic, rubber, linoleum or carpet, the mix should be 1:3 cement and sand. Under strong rigid coverings such as terrazzo or ceramic tiles, a 1:4 cement and sand mix may be used. If exposed, however, such mixes would not withstand wear and would cause dusting. Mixes too strong to yield on drying out and shrinking will tend to crack at intervals. Since the surface dries first they also tend to curl and break bond with the sub-floor. Screed and toppings, therefore, should be avoided wherever it is possible to use the structural floor as the wear surface. If a special surface is required, it should be laid monolithically before the concrete of the sub-floor has set, so as to ensure bond with it. Where this cannot be done the problem should be approached from the point of view of the engineer rather than that of the plasterer, and every precaution should be taken to prevent failure by providing adequate key, minimising shrinkage, curing thoroughly, and limiting the size of the bays, so that too much stress cannot build up in any given area.

To provide key, it is recommended that the surface of the sub-floor should be hacked over, that it should be soaked 24 hours beforehand but not be wet, and that neat creamy grout should be brushed in just before the topping is applied. Better results may, however, be achieved if the surface of the aggregate in the sub-floor is fully exposed. The surest method of all is to provide a positive mechanical key, such as steel studs or wire loops, let into the sub-floor concrete when it is laid and left protruding to bond with the topping. They should be placed round the edges of the proposed bays.

In order to resist wear a granolithic topping is commonly used. A 1:1:2 mix of cement:sand:10 mm aggregate is suitable. If granite is used, it is better to use natural sand than granite dust as the fine aggregate because less water is necessary for a given workability. In order to reduce shrinkage the minimum of water should be used in the mix compatible with full compaction, which should be achieved by heavy tamping or vibrating before finishing with a float. The topping should be thoroughly cured for at least 7 days. This delays the shrinkage until the concrete has gained strength in bond and also prevents dusting.

Joints should be provided over all joints in the sub-base. Bonded toppings should also be divided into bays 3 to 4 m wide and not exceeding 25 m^2 for 20 to 30 mm thick toppings, or 15 mm^2 for 30 to 40 mm thick toppings. The maximum length/width ratio of bays should be 1·5:1. Where thin flexible floor coverings are to be used, the area and length of bay is unimportant as transverse cracks generally show less through these coverings than joints.

FACTORY FLOORS.—Cement-sand screeds are not in themselves suitable for use as a wearing surface. Industrial floors are therefore usually surfaced with 'granolithic' screeds which provide a durable, though dusty, surface capable of taking heavy impact loads and wheeled traffic. The application of these to the green base concrete is the best way of achieving a crack-free surface which will not lift or curl.

In lighter factory-work these may be 1–2–4 mix, 100 mm thick, finished with granolithic or other specified surface. Where heavy loading is expected the thickness should be 150 mm and reinforcement in mesh form placed 40 mm from the bottom of the concrete. The floor should be laid in 9 m^2 rectangles, alternately, with dry joints to minimise shrinkage cracks, and expansion joints, using 12 mm thickness of a resilient jointing, should be employed to divide the floor into areas not exceeding 100 m^2.

Where the floor is to be subjected to continual trucking by industrial trucks it is desirable to arrange that floor panels are laid diagonally to reduce wheel shock against the panel edges. Where steel wheel trucks are to be used the expansion joints should be more numerous but only 3 mm thick.

When the granolithic topping is incorporated in the floor as the work proceeds this can be reduced to 12 mm thickness but should be 60 mm thick if laid after. A suitable mix would be 5 parts of clean washed whin or granite chips, graded 6 mm down, containing not more than 10% of fine grit passing a 76 by 76 sieve: 2 parts of Portland cement; clean, pure water to a consistency as dry as practicable. Surface steel trowelled when initial set begins.

Floors used in some industrial buildings are particularly liable to corrosion in addition to ordinary wear and tear. Such floors should not undergo changes in volume or form shrinkage-cracks (produced in drying); for the sake of comfort, the floor should not be too hard, or too cold, slippery or noisy and should also look well and be easy to clean. To resist very severe abrasion, steel plates, clay tiles, paving brick, dense concrete, or heavy asphalt, reinforced with steel or iron grids are often used. Dust is highly objectionable in certain trades, for example, in painting shops and in food manufacture. Concrete floors are liable to be dusty unless suitably treated. Wear is greatly reduced if factory trucks are fitted with rubber tyres with ball bearings and some means of steering; they also economise human effort and are quieter in service.

Where the destructive agents are mainly organic acids and fats, the best construction appears to be a hard, acid-resistant granite asphalt-mastic, quarry tiles with a thin, neat Portland cement joint, or blue bricks set in and jointed with aluminous cement mortar. Timber is not likely to be attacked chemically but will absorb fats etc and be liable to become very slippery and unhygienic. The presence of salt makes it necessary to protect a reinforced concrete sub-floor by an impermeable surface, such as asphalt. Sheet rubber, blocked up and rubber on hard backing have been used for floor surfacing.

JOINTLESS FLOORS.—For concrete floors and granolithic topping, see section 'Concrete Work' of this chapter, see also section 'Asphalt Work'. Concrete floors may be covered with linoleum; rubber; bitumen sheet (which resembles linoleum) or with plastic rubber latex flooring consisting of a rubber latex with cement, aggregates and pigments, which are mixed on site and floated on concrete. The proprietary brands of this type of flooring have to be laid by specialist workmen.

SYNTHETIC FLOORS are made from various resins, the more common being polyesters and epoxy. The two-pack mix is brought together on site and when laid, hardens rapidly to give a floor surface with considerable elasticity and durability. Similar types of material are also used for jointing of clay floor tiles in particularly onerous conditions.

SHEET FLOORS.—Linoleum can refer to a wide range of products varying from painted bituminised papers to thick cork lino on heavy fabric bases. The former are not durable but with the extensive range of linoleums in a number of thicknesses and grades, all normal flooring requirements can be met. Linoleum is laid on a previously applied adhesive and rolled flat.

Plastic roll flooring, usually of PVC, can be obtained in varying widths and laid as linoleum. Joints can be welded together with hot air welding to give a jointless floor covering.

Rubber sheet flooring can be obtained in several textured surface finishes. Ribbing of various grades is used for entrance matting while a type composed of raised circular studs is widely used for passages particularly where ramped. Black is the usual colour because of better ultra violet light resistance but grey is also available.

TILE FLOORS.—Terrazzo tiles can be made in various shapes and sizes to order and a wide range of mixes is available. They are laid on a wet screed base, allowed to become firm and are then ground down to a smooth almost glassy polish. They suffer less from cracking than jointless terrazzo but should be laid with metallic or ebonite dividers in bays of about 1·8 m square if movement is to be concealed.

Clay tiles include quarry tiles and others such as encaustic and acid resisting tiles. They are all laid in wet or semi-dry screeds and are usually pointed up in neat cement though synthetic resins are sometimes used. Clay tiles can be very durable and when properly maintained are an attractive finish, especially when decorative patterns of tesselated tiles are used. Textured surfaces are sometimes formed on clay tiles to improve slip resistance and to permit water to flow along channels in the surface in such locations as shower rooms and kitchens. Many special shapes are available to form coves and skirtings.

Concrete tiles are more commonly used for areas and external pavings. They can be hydraulically-pressed heavy-duty pavings or thinner, coloured light-duty slabs.

Plastic tiles include 'thermoplastic' (basically bituminous material with fillers and pigment) pvc-asbestos compounds and pvc. Thermoplastic tiles are widely used for commercial and domestic flooring as they are cheap, reasonably durable and easy to keep clean. Their colours, however, tend to be dull owing to the nature of the base material and for light colours the pvc-asbestos or the pvc tiles are more suitable. The durability of these last is also greater and they tend to be less brittle, but owing to the superior formulation they are more costly. Rubber tiles and linoleum tiles are basically the same as the sheet material described above but supplied in tiles 228 or 306 mm square for patterned or chequerboard laying.

Cork tiles provide a fairly durable resilient floor surface of warm brown colour, eminently suitable for domestic and most commercial uses but not durable enough for industrial floors. Tiles are made in square or rectangular shapes rarely exceeding 228 × 228 mm, and are laid on adhesive to a smooth substrate and sanded by machine. Polishing brings up varied tones and shades in the material to form a mellow brown finish akin to wood.

Wood tiles take several forms, some being complex shapes designed to interlock to form a herringbone pattern, others (more common) being square and formed of small billets of hardwood 12 mm thick and 100 mm by 25 mm in area, laid in a basket-weave pattern on a paper facing. The tile is laid on bituminous emulsion adhesive with the paper side uppermost, the paper (glued with water soluble glue) stripped off, and the resultant floor is sanded and polished.

Asbestos tiles are rarely used for flooring but form a good surfacing for asphalt roof decks. They are dense asbestos-cement tiles which are laid on a bituminous emulsion and stand up to external conditions very well, while preventing damage to the asphalt from foot traffic and reducing the ageing and embrittling of the asphalt due to exposure to solar radiation.

Chemical resistant tiles are usually clay specially formulated to give high resistance to acid or alkaline attack. Used for floorings and tank linings the important factor is the prevention of movement of the structure as the tiles and jointings are hard and inelastic and the formation of cracks in the linings presents great problems in making good.

PAVINGS.—External pavings are also used internally particularly in vestibules and patios. Used externally, pavings must be laid to falls to prevent puddling and should be adequately drained. Footways should have a cross fall of 10 mm per metre width for asphalt, 20 mm per metre for flags and 30 mm per metre for bricks and similar small-unit pavings.

Standard hydraulically-pressed concrete flags are made in sizes 50 mm by 610 by 457; 610; 762; and 915 mm long. Coloured flags are available in a range of about a dozen colours and in various shapes and sizes designed to permit complicated patterns to be built up without cutting. Hexagonal flags can be obtained from some sources.

Granite setts are often used decoratively in conjunction with other pavings, as are cobbles. Granite setts are usually 228 × 76 × 152 mm deep; but cobbled flints are irregular in size.

Clay and calcium silicate pavers are being more widely used for their attractive appearance. BS 6677: 1986 'Clay and calcium silicate pavers for flexible pavements' gives details of pavers and the design and construction of pavements.

GLAZING

BRITISH STANDARDS.—

BS 952	'Glass for Glazing' Part 1 1978 'Classification'; Part 2 1980 'Terminology for work on glass'.
BS 5051	'Security Glazing' Part 1 1973; 'bullet-resistant glazing for interior use'; Part 2 1979 'Specification for bullet-resistant glazing for external use'.
BS 5357 1976 (1985)	'Code of Practice for the installation of security glazing'.
BS 5516 1977	'Code of Practice for patent glazing'.
BS 5544 1978 (1985)	'Specification for anti-bandit glazing (glazing resistant to manual attack)'.
BS 5713 1979	'Specification for hermetically sealed flat double-glazing units'.
BS 6206 1981	'Specification for impact performance requirements for flat safety glass and safety plastics for use in buildings'.
BS 6262 1982	'Code of Practice for glazing for buildings'.
BS 8200 1985	'Code of Practice for the design of non-load bearing external vertical enclosures of buildings.'

GLAZING.—Glass has high resistance to abrasion allied with good light transmission. Plastics may possess higher rates of light transmission but they scratch easily and some tend to discolour under the action of ultra-violet light. Nevertheless plastics are preferable to glass in buildings where vandalism is rife and toughened glass may be too expensive. The Code of Practice BS 6262 1982 gives recommendations for the design, installation and maintenance of vertically glazed glass and plastic sheet materials for glazing. The other British Standards listed above cover specialised uses.

GLAZING PUTTIES.—In Wood.—Putty made from raw linseed oil and powdered whiting. Red lead or litharge may be added for hardening and powdered pigment for colouring. Plastic or non-hardening putty is made by adding tallow, fish oil and salt to ordinary putty.

In Metal.—Metal putty as above with white lead or manganese dioxide added for rapid hardening.

In Stone.—Sand, litharge, gypsum and boiled linseed oil freshly mixed. Portland cement, sand and oil may also be used.

In Lead.—Pure pig lead, cast and hand drawn to cores of H section with heart 2·5 to 12 mm, and leaf 3·0 to 38 mm. Steel cores obviate use of iron saddle bars. Solder of 50 per cent tin is used to 'weld' joints.

In Copper.—Copper electrically deposited on a framework of copper strips soldered with glass in place, forms bead-like flanges which hold the panes and fill the interstices.

In Glass.—Canada Balsam dissolved in pure spirit to consistency of treacle used to 'weld' glass butted together, dries in 3 days.

ROOF GLAZING.—Glazing Bars.—These are designed to deflect under working load no more than one-ninetieth of the span. (*a*) Lead-clothed steel bar with wing extruded integrally with the covering 1 mm thick. The steel core may be coated with bitumen or galvanised. (*b*) Galvanised steel bar (zinc coating not less than 0·6 kg/m^2 with a non-ferrous capping. (*c*) Aluminum alloy bar with capping and weathering integral of lead. (*d*) Timber bar with non-ferrous capping section. (*e*) Reinforced concrete with suitable capping. (*f*) Bronze bar for special conditions.

Glass to BS 952, 6 mm thick, preferably wired 610 mm wide, preferably 2·03 m long, but not exceeding 3·04 m. Pitch not less than 20°.

OPAQUE GLASS SHEATHING.—In interiors, rough back permits putty adhesion to walls. On exteriors, copper clips are used at the joints. The size of pane is governed by the relative thermal movements of sheathing and backing, but projecting copper clips across an air space provide useful flexibility.

REFLECTIVE AND OTHER GLASS CLADDINGS.—Various forms of special glasses are available for external sheathing and glazing. The reflective glasses are usually used in sealed double glazing where the inner (cavity) surface of the outer sheet is coated with a thin deposit of noble metal to provide a calculated proportion of reflectance of high-frequency radiant heat energy. Different grades are available—the higher the reflectance of heat energy the lower the transmission of light through the glazing. Colours range from deep bronze to very pale yellow and silver. Heat-absorbing glasses are also combined in double glazing but depend upon a reasonable flow of air to conduct away absorbed heat from the tinted outer glass. Usually these glasses are grey in colour. Non-actinic glasses are green in colour and are designed to prevent entry of ultraviolet energy by absorption. This energy heats the glass as in other heat-absorbing types and therefore is better used in double glazing.

All these solar control glasses reduce the transmission of light energy to a greater or lesser degree, in inverse ratio to their energy rejection characteristics. Thus fully glazed walls in such materials tend to produce a 'dull-day' condition internally, and the overall drabness should be foreseen and combatted either by the introduction of clear glass panes in calculated proportion or by creation of brighter surfaces internally by colour selection with high intensity illumination.

REFLECTIVE FILMS.—Clear glass can be modified to produce reduced solar gain by the application of special films to the interior surface. The films are of plastic coated with metallic deposits similar to those used in the reflective glasses. Similarly they reduce light transmission, but are more vulnerable to physical damage from cleaning or abrasion than the glasses. Where it is intended to apply internal double glazing to existing single glazing the film can be applied to the cavity face of the outer pane.

PHOTO-SENSITIVE GLASSES.—Glasses are available which are responsive to intensity of incident light. Usually the colour is grey and the depth of tint increases with the increase of external light. The major use is in illumination control but the thermal absorption also varies as the depth of tint.

NOTES ON REFLECTIVE GLASSES.—Three aspects of the use of reflective glasses should be borne in mind:

(1) The 'mirror' effect of the use of these glasses aggravates the problem of accuracy of alignment of the glass when other objects are reflected to the observer. Flaws in the glass or its fixing are amplified and intensive supervision is necessary.

(2) The 'mirror' effect has been accepted by some planning authorities as providing a solution to the siting of buildings in historic areas and even in rural areas, on the basis that the image of the immediate environment provides a harmonious repetition of the existing ambience.

(3) The 'mirror' effect can, in traffic areas, cause dangerous confusion for drivers, by day or night, if the glass is used at low level.

PAINTING AND DECORATING

PAINTING.—The properties of paint and method of application are detailed in Chapter C7. BS 6150 1982 'Code of Practice for painting of buildings' gives recommendations for initial and maintenance painting.

Covering Capacity of Paints and Enamels.

READY-MIXED PAINT IN OIL.

First coat on wood or plaster. 9–10 m^2 per litre.
Second coat on wood or plaster. 11–12 m^2 per litre.
Finishing coat on wood or plaster. 13–15 m^2 per litre.

READY-MIXED PAINT IN TURPS.

When used on an oil undercoating, 15–16 m^2 per litre.

UNDERCOATING.
Ordinary Flatting type, 15–16 m^2 per litre.

VARNISH.
Easy-bodied, 16–18 m^2 per litre.
Full-bodied, 15–16 m^2 per litre.

ENAMEL.
Easy-bodied, 13–14 m^2 per litre.
Full-bodied, 13 m^2 per litre.

WATER PAINTS.
3·2 kg (reduced on bare plaster) covers 6 m^2 per litre.

Paperhanging.—Paste can be made from rye flour sometimes with glue size added for heavy papers, but it is common to use synthetic pastes, factory-made and packed as a granular material for cold-water mixing. The paper is pasted thoroughly and folded, paste-to-paste, to stretch before hanging. The heavier the paper the stronger the paste mix should be and the more thorough the stretching allowed.

Wallpapers.—British papers are 11½ yd × 21 in. (10·5 × 0·53 m), covering 60·4 ft^2 (5·6 m^2).
French papers are approx. 9 yd. × 18 in. (8·5 × 0·45 m), covering 40·5 ft^2 (3·75 m^2).
American papers are 8 yd. × 18 in. (7·3 × 0·45 m) covering 36 ft^2 (3·35 m^2).
Japanese papers are 12 yd × 12 in. (11·0 × 0·3 m) covering 36 ft^2 (3·35 m^2).

Papers are made in various forms, from light printed patterns to heavily embossed or flock finished damasks and include plastic faced materials, usually of PVC on a paper backing, though some are on fabric. Such 'papers' are durable, washable and suitable for hard wear and long life.

FABRICS.—A number of fabrics, particularly hessians and sackings, are hung on walls as decoration, a wide range of colours being available. Woven grasses are also made for wall applications and must be hung with care using only synthetic pastes.

Hanging Generally.—10 percent extra should be allowed for cutting and waste if the pattern repeat is small, but where the pattern repeat is large a more precise calculation should be made, particularly in expensive papers. Butt jointing is superior to lap jointing. Lap-joint edges should face the windows on side walls.

CEILING PAPERS.—Various textures are made in papers and plastic faced papers for use on ceilings. Ceiling strips should run away from windows rather than parallel with them.

FENCING

Fencing.—Fencing performs two functions, privacy and security. These objectives often militate against amenity and thus most domestic fences strike a compromise by being not so tall, nor yet so solid, as to give a prison-like appearance. Common law allows a property owner to enclose his property by fences or walls 7 ft high, but this is sometimes overriden by covenants in the deeds, or by conditions of a planning permission.

Factory fences have a clear security function but are not always full security fences, whereas many government establishments use steel angle fencing with outcurved spiked ends. No fence is completely secure, and if necessary must be backed up by patrols, dogs, etc. BS 1722 'Specification for fences' is in 13 parts.

Stock fences provide a different kind of security; that of control of animals to ensure their pasturing where desired. Cattle are weighty animals with tough hides and stock fences have therefore to be robust, with frequent posts and a reasonable weight of wire. Electrified stock fences are designed to give a small corrective shock to the animals. It is not legal to install fences with lethal currents for any purpose without other protective fences and notices.

GATES.—Gates are as various as the fences they serve. The normal sidehung gate serves most purposes, but where a very wide opening must be dealt with gates may either have long tension rods or be supported by a wheel at the outer edge running on a quadrant track. Dropping arms or gates are frequently used, not so much for security as for traffic control, at factory entrances. These are long arms, pivoted and counterweighted. They often seat in a crutch at the free end. Power-operated versions are available.

Materials.—Domestic fences are normally of timber or chain link wire with timber or concrete posts. Traditional forms include the close-boarded feather-edge boards, fixed to arris rails tenoned into the posts, in softwood or oak; and the split-chestnut paling fence on whole chestnut posts. These have been overtaken by interwoven panels in softwood or cedar which can be bought in standard units for quick erection. Hollow section plastic fenceposts and rails are increasingly used in domestic situations. The initial cost is high but they need no maintenance.

Domestic gates are obtainable in softwoods and hardwoods, mainly oak, as well as in 'wrought iron'. Most wrought iron is now, in fact, welded mild steel. Standard patterns of gates of various types of design are available from numerous suppliers, together with matching fencing panels. They are normally supplied primed with red lead, and should be painted carefully as soon as possible after erection to avoid rusting. BS 4092 1966 'Domestic front entrance gates' is in 2 parts for metal and wooden gates.

Industrial fences are commonly of chain link wire mesh on concrete or steel angle posts. Plastic-coated chain-link fencing in a strong green colour is available and is more reliable than the usual run of galvanised fencing. Posts are made with a turned out section at the top and strands of barbed wire are strained on these to discourage entry. Gates can be standard steel angle frames with chain link mesh.

BIBLIOGRAPHY

HAMILTON, R. N. D. *A Guide to Development and Planning*. 7th Edition. Oyez. London. 1981.

CULLINGWORTH, J. B. *Town and Country Planning in Britain*. 9th Edition. Allen & Unwin. London. 1985.

BARRICK, J. *Town and Country Planning*. Library Services Information Series No. 6. DoE. London. 1979.

CLARKE, H. W., NELSON, J. L'A. and THOMPSON, E., *Knights Building Regulations with Approved Documents*. Charles Knight & Co. Ltd. Croydon. 1985.

Fire Protection Design Guide Sheets for Architects. Nos. 1–16. Fire Protection Association. London.

MALHOTRA, H. L. *Design of Fire Resisting Structures*. Surrey University Press. Glasgow. 1982.

Brick Development Association, *Low Rise Domestic Construction in Brick*. Part 1 Structural Design. Feb. 1979. *Part 3 Thermal and Sound Insulation*. April 1979. Prepared for BDA by Jenkins & Potter and the National Building Agency.

REYNOLDS, C. E. and STEEDMAN, J. C. *Reinforced Concrete Designers Handbook*. Eyre & Spottiswoode Viewpoint Publications. Leatherhead. 1981.

ROBERTS, J. J., TOVEY, A. K., CRANSTON, W. B. and BEEBY, A. W. *The Concrete Masonry Designer's Handbook*, Viewpoint Publications, London, 1983.

HANDISYDE, C. C. *Everyday Details*. Architectural Press. London. 1979.

MARTIN, D. (ED), *Specification* (in Five Volumes). Published annually by Architectural Press. London.

NEVILLE, A. *Properties of Concrete*. (3rd Ed.) Pitman. London. 1981.

Steel Designers Manual. 4th Edition, Collins, London. 1985.

ROBERTS, J. J., EDGELL, G. J. and RATHBONE, A. J., *Handbook to BS 5628 Part 2*. Viewpoint Publications, London, 1986.

National Water Council Standing Technical Committee on Sewers and Water Mains. *Materials and Standards Information Guidance sheets*.

The Hepworth Handbook. Hepworth Iron Co. Ltd. Hazlehead. Stocksbridge. Sheffield. S30 5HG.

'Mitchells' Building Series. Batsford, London.

Various Titles *eg:*

BURBERRY, P. *Environment and Services*. New Edition 1984.

EVERETT, A. *Materials*. Revised Edition, 1986.

STROUD-FOSTER, J. and HARRINGTON, P. *Structure and Fabric, Parts 1 & 2*. 2nd Edition (revised), 1984.

MOXLEY, R. *Mitchells Elementary Building Construction*, Batsford, London.

BRITISH CERAMIC RESEARCH ASSOCIATION, *Model Specification for Clay and Calcium Silicate Brickwork*, Spec. Publ. 56. B. Ceram. R.A., Stoke on Trent, 1980.

WEST, H. W. H., HODGKINSON, H. R., and HASELTINE, B. A., *The Resistance of Brickwork to Lateral Loading*., Parts 1 & 2 The Structural Engineer, 55, No. 10, Oct. 1977.

WEST, H. W. H., et al., *The Resistance of Masonry to Lateral Loading—Research since 1977*. The Structural Engineer, 64, No. 11, 1986.

WATER ENGINEERING

Water Supply—Consumption—Pipes and Valves—Measurement of Flow—River Schemes—Underground Schemes—Rainfall—Run-off—Percolation—Storage and Yield—Treatment and Quality—Filtration—Dams—Embankments—Impounding Schemes—Spillways and Weirs—Water Power—Aqueducts—Penstocks—Control Gates—Wind and Tidal Power—Land Drainage—Outfalls and Sluices—Irrigation—Bibliography

By B. H. Rofe, MA (Cantab), FICE, FIWEM

WATER SUPPLY

The organisation of public water supplies in Great Britain has evolved in a framework created by successive Acts of Parliament beginning in 1874 with the Waterworks Clauses Act and continuing up to the Water Act of 1973 (England and Wales) and the Local Government (Scotland) Act 1973. In England and Wales, ten regional Water Authorities are now responsible for the entire water cycle, including conservation, resource development, water supply, sewerage and sewage treatment. In Scotland, water supply and sewerage are the responsibility of the twelve regional and islands councils, together with the Central Scotland Water Development Board (a bulk supply authority). River purification is also a responsibility of the three islands councils, but on the mainland this duty is exercised by River Purification Boards. The Reservoirs (Safety Provisions) Act 1930 and the Reservoirs Act 1975, apply to the whole of Great Britain.

Metrication.—SI units (as set out in the chapter 'Units of measurement') are used in British water engineering practice generally, except that the litre (l) and megalitre (Ml) are frequently used as units of volume, as well as the cubic metre.

Planning and Environmental Aspects.—These aspects of schemes have become increasingly important in the promotion of major projects. Normally a planning application has to be submitted at the same time as the application for power to carry out the proposed works, and, in cases where a public inquiry is held by a government inspector, the applications are often considered together.

Environmental considerations may be wide-ranging, covering such subjects as ecological disturbance, interference with public access to recreational areas, and encroachment on National Parks and areas of outstanding natural beauty. The fact that such areas, and especially the National Parks, are located in areas of high rainfall has led to conflicts of interest in a number of major proposals in recent years.

CONSUMPTION.—Consumption of water varies in different ways according to the area under consideration. In all cases there are hourly variations during each day, daily variations during each week and seasonal variations during the year. The seasonal variations are the least predictable in Great Britain due to the unreliable weather conditions and the pattern of consumption during the year is also dependent on the type of area; seaside resorts tend to have a high summer peak whilst industrial towns often show lower consumption in summer than in winter, especially where annual works holidays result in an exodus of population. A peak hourly rate of the order of three times average may be anticipated.

Daily Consumption per Head.—Consumption of water in Great Britain is usually divided into three categories: domestic, industrial and agricultural. (a) Domestic consumption in England and Wales varies between 140 and 330 litres per head per day (l/pd) with a mean of about 200 l/pd. In Scotland the range is from 240 to 350 l/pd. with a mean of 275 l/pd. Due to re-organisation into larger groupings, comparison of urban and rural areas is difficult in most cases, but for the Thames Water Authority area, London domestic consumption is 260 l/pd., the figure for the remaining predominantly rural areas being 210 l/pd. (All figures are approximate and relate to the period 1976–78.) (b) Industrial: the expressing of industrial consumption on a per-capita basis is unrealistic as it varies with the degree of industrialisation and the extent to which industry depends on public water supplies; the range in the case of Statutory Companies is between 30 and 330 l/pd. (c) Agricultural: here, again, consumption is affected by seasonal variations in rainfall, the availability of surface water, and the type of agriculture to such an extent that it cannot readily be related to the human population alone.

In arid or developing countries the consumption per head will be largely a function of availability or cost. Where water is supplied only to standpipes it is generally considered that consumption will not exceed 50 l/pd provided adequate precautions are taken to avoid waste (e.g. self-closing taps, regular maintenance and control). If however house connections are made these are usually metered with consequent costs leading often to exploitation and the temptation to make illegal connections. Under these conditions consumption can increase above the rates noted for developed countries as described above.

APPROXIMATE REQUIREMENTS OF INDUSTRY.—Industrial use of water may be divided broadly into consumptive and non-consumptive uses of which cooling water forms a major part, amounting to about 70% of the total amount used. In England and Wales electricity generation uses about twice as much water as all other industry. Approximate consumptions for a number of industries are set out below:

TABLE. 1.—INDUSTRIAL WATER CONSUMPTION.

Product	Unit	Water consumed m^3	Water recycled m^3
Oil refining	tonne of oil	0·3	2
Thermal power generation	MWh	5–10	0–200
Steel	tonne	1–50	1–15
Brickmaking	1,000	1·5	—
Paper (newsprint)			
Pulp	tonne	350	700
Paper (from pulp)	tonne	80	110
Nylon fibre	tonne	500	5,000
Wool washing	tonne	45	—
Bakeries	tonne	2–5	—
Cheese	tonne	6	3
Breweries	100 l	2	1
Soft drinks	100 l	1	0·5

AGRICULTURAL REQUIREMENTS.—(*a*) Ordinary dairy farming areas may require 55 litres per day per hectare; intensive farming may require up to 110 litres per day per hectare. A cow in milk has been found to take 130 litres per day. *Horned Cattle*: 45 litre/day. *Bottling*: 2 litres per litre of milk bottled. *Dried Milk*: 1 litre per kg dried. *Cheese*: 2 litres per kg of cheese. (*b*) *Glass Houses*, eg tomatoes, require up to 2×10^5 litres per day per hectare of glass during the growing season, the annual average may be 20,000–30,000 litres per hectare. (*c*) For irrigation of crops per hectare about 4×10^6 litres per day is suggested for about three months in the year. 100,000 litres could irrigate one hectare to a depth of 10 mm. (*d*) Watercress 3·5–5·5 $\times 10^6$ litres per day per hectare (more may be required in winter to keep it from freezing than in summer to keep it from scorching).

Agricultural requirements, like those of industry, cannot be readily related to human population. Domestic requirements in Rural Districts may be 150–300 l/pd, while agricultural and horticultural purposes may account for 50–100 l/pd.

WASTE AND WASTE CONTROL.—Waste is an important factor for which allowance must be made in all estimates as it may amount to 50% of total supply (25% is common, 10% is rare). From consideration of resource conservation, it is possible to argue that waste should be avoided at all costs; however, this may result in expenditure outweighing any financial savings and it is important that waste control work should be as cost-effective as possible and the work should be so organised that sources of leakage are located in order of size (to ensure the maximum savings) and quickly (to minimise the water loss).

Factors which can affect waste in a distribution system and which should be considered at the design stage include: pressure, corrosion, poor materials and workmanship, subsidence and traffic loads. The age of an existing system has a bearing on the amount of any corrosion and the condition of fittings. Outside the actual distribution system, excessive water consumption may occur in the operation of filters and sludge disposal; reservoirs may also leak through structural settlement or lack of waterproofing. When considering a waste control programme it is advisable to attempt to estimate the costs and the resultant benefits. Savings from waste control include not only running costs, but also deferment of future capital expenditure by reducing the rate of increase in consumption. The evaluation of costs and benefits will also assist to show when the cost of reducing waste below a certain level becomes uneconomic.

NETWORK ANALYSIS AND LEAKAGE CONTROL.—Apart from major leakages such as a burst main, revealed by surface flooding and possibly reduction of supplies over a considerable area, waste control involves systematic monitoring of the system to detect abnormal flow conditions.

As a first step a detailed plan of the water distribution pipe network should be drawn up, based on existing records, site surveys and checks on significant valves and connections. If not already installed it is nearly always worth while installing meters in each district, so that the flows into and out of a particular part of the system can be monitored. By measuring night flows these can be compared with normally accepted standards, and if over (say) 5 litres/head in a domestic area or an assessed industrial metered demand it is worth controlling leaks. The next stage in the procedure could involve a detailed analysis of the network on a computer network program such as 'WATNET' or 'GENYS' which requires calibration by simultaneous measurement of flows and pressures throughout the system. This will generally reveal the presence of bad leaks, closed valves or redundant mains.

Consideration can then be given to installation of local waste control meters in suspect areas, and the possibility of pressure reduction in a zone (often a practical and economical step). Some techniques for locating individual points of leakage are outlined below and can be brought into play if justified in economic terms, or if there is a shortage of water resources necessitating tighter control of wastage at higher cost.

Tracing Leakages.—To identify and trace the source of underground water, such as leakages from canals, reservoirs, pipes, etc: *Fluorescin*—Add fluorescin near the supposed source of leakage. One gramme is sufficient to colour 1,500 m^3 of water. *Indigo*—One gramme of indigo dissolved in sulphuric acid will colour 15 m^3 of water. The colouration is more easily detected by placing the water in a very long test-tube and looking through the latter endways. Halogen gas and nitrous oxide are being used to detect leakage. Sulphur hexafluoride has been used in place of nitrous oxide and has the advantage that the mains do not have to be taken out of service. For testing mains, see p. **I7**/7.

Stethoscope.—Proceeding along the line of the main in the hours of least consumption at night, the patrol nearly closes the valves at principal branches, each in turn, and listens with an instrument which is essentially a stethoscope. Portable amplifiers are available which make it possible to detect leakage without direct contact with the mains, but these are susceptible to interference and wind noise.

Leak Noise Correlation.—A method originally developed at Water Research Centre which is now in common use. The correlator is connected to two transducers which may be inserted at convenient available fittings such as valves, hydrants or stop taps. The distance to each transducer from a point of leakage can be established by correlating the noise level to within 1 metre. It is most effective on metal or AC pipes and is used to pinpoint leaks already established by the methods described above.

FIRE PROTECTION.—Hydrants, usually sited by the Fire Authority, are fixed either directly over the mains where these are laid up in highways or on branches where the mains are laid in easement off the highways. In built-up areas the discharge required is of the order of 4,000–7,000 l/min, and hydrants are normally provided at intervals of 150 m or thereabouts. The diameters of the branch pipes should be at least 80 mm, increased to 100 mm for branches over 100 m long. BS 750 covers fire hydrants and surface box openings; hydrants of two types are available, screwdown type, for fixing directly over the main, and sluice valve type. See also chapter 'Fire Protection'.

HOUSE SERVICES.—The approximate sizes of the bore diameters of the pipes for a 6-bedroom house are as follows. The service pipe should be 15–25 mm, with a rising pipe of 32 mm to the storage cistern in the roof. From the cistern a 25–32 mm pipe goes to the ground floor, with 20 mm branches to bath, boiler and hot water system; also 15 mm branches to lavatory basins and wc cisterns. The carrying capacities of pipes for house services are approximately as follows (the flow in l/min is given in parentheses after the relative sizes in mm):—15 mm (9); 20 mm (18); 25 mm (27); 40 mm (67); 50 mm (112).

Hot water pipes from boiler to hot water tank are usually 25–40 mm; outlet pipes from the tank are 32 mm, with branches of 20 mm to baths and 15 mm to basins. For central heating, see chapter 'Heating, Ventilation etc'.

SERVICE PIPES, ETC.—Current British Standards for tubes used in service connections, embrace both imperial and metric sizes and the relevant standard should be consulted.

Mixing Valves.—These valves provide a water supply at a controlled temperature by mixing the hot and cold supply. This supply is often necessary for industrial processes, and also for washing facilities, showers, etc. Thermostatic control of mixing valves protects personnel and apparatus, and also saves fuel by limiting water temperature.

Ferrules.—The right-angled, screw-down 'Talbot' type in non-ferrous metal, is in general use, nominal sizes range between 15 mm and 50 mm. The ferrule size is limited to 15 mm for 80 mm mains; 20 mm for 100 mm mains; and 30 mm for 150 mm mains. Cast iron saddles are used on asbestos cement and PVC mains. Ferrules can be inserted under pressure using a suitable drilling and tapping machine. As the maximum stress occurs at the top and bottom of a pipe, the tapping may be made at 45° to the vertical.

Types of Service Pipes.—Galvanised iron or steel tubes, although initially cheaper, have a shorter life than lead or copper pipes, due to corrosion and internal incrustation. As a substitute for galvanising, pipes with bitumen linings and coatings are available. Underground copper pipes employ type 'B' compression joints (BS 864). Polythene tubing is being used increasingly, both under and above ground. It is resistant to freezing, light in weight and easily bent to shape, does not corrode, but is liable to damage because of its softness. BS 1972 specifies polythene tubing for cold water service; the normal gauge employs type 'A' compression fittings (BS 864), with internal sleeve to take the coupling pressure. The heavy gauge may have screwed taper for normal pipe fittings or used with type 'A' compression fittings. Sizes vary from one material to another as shown below.

Lead Piping (BS 602 and 1085).—This standard for lead and lead alloy pipes for other than chemical purposes covers service and distributing pipes laid underground; and also service pipes laid above ground. For sizes and working pressures the standard should be consulted. See also BSCP 310. The use of lead pipes should be avoided where water is acid (pH value less than 7·0) and/or low in bicarbonates of calcium or magnesium.

Copper Piping (BS 2871: Part 1).—Copper tubes for water etc, specifies in metric terms tubes of nominal bore of 6–108 mm, for working pressures between 188 bar for 6 mm and 29 bar for 108 mm.

Polythene Piping (BS 1972, 3284 and 6572).—Covering polythene pipe for cold water services. Sizes 10–150 mm and for working pressures up to 12 bar.

Stop Taps (BS 1010).—Part 1 (Imperial) and Part 2 (Metric) both cover 0·25–2 in nominal sizes (6–50 mm). Part 2 specifies metric dimensions and test data. The sizes are usually ½ in; ¾ in; or 1 in; screw-down type; made of non-ferrous metal, matched with guard pipe (BS 1185) and surface box.

Meters.—These are usually fitted at consumer's boundary between two stop taps and housed in a suitable chamber with surface box.

Pressure Reducing Valves.—These are fixed where the static pressure exceeds about 120 m or 12 bar. Talbot-Young service pressure reducing valves (3:1 or 2:1 pressure reduction) may be used for individual properties. Larger types of valve are available for groups of consumers.

WATER MAINS

PIPES AND FITTINGS.—These (including 'specials') in general use for water distribution, comprise grey iron; ductile iron; steel; asbestos cement; concrete (plain, reinforced or prestressed); and unplasticised polyvinyl chloride (uPVC). Some standards are in inches with metric equivalents. BS CP 2010 should be referred to when designing pipelines in land. It defines '*in land*' as including above ground, below ground and overhead locations; estuary and water-course crossings; but excluding the bed of the sea below low-water mark.

BRITISH STANDARD PIPE SIZES.—The standards should be referred to for Test Pressures, etc. Some BS sizes may not be readily available, and some sizes may be available, outside the BS range. The entries under BS 534 and BS 3505 (which are in inch sizes), indicate the nearest metric equivalent size, the other standards are:

Pipe Materials Selection.—This depends on a number of criteria including working pressure, water quality and relative costs. Iron or steel pipes are suitable for the higher pressures but may need special provision to prevent corrosion; asbestos cement pipes are less liable to corrosion but more prone to breakage; uPVC pipes are easily handled but more easily distorted if not properly stacked, and their strength decreases with temperature. GRP pipes can be manufactured to particular conditions.

Grey Iron Pipes and Fittings (BS 4622).—This metric standard gives extracts from BS 10 (flanges) and interconnection details for metric to imperial spigots and sockets. Spigot and socket pipes in Grey Iron, Classes 1, 2 and 3, are suitable for maximum working pressures of 10, 12·5 and 16 bar respectively.

Ductile Iron Pipes and Fittings (BS 4772).—This standard, and BS 4622, each cover pipes and fittings with both spigot and socket, and flanged joints. Spigot and socket joints are predominantly of the mechanical type, in which a joint ring of rubber or other material is compressed either by means of an iron gland tightened by bolts, or as, in the Tyton joint, merely by the insertion of the spigot of the next pipe. Standard pipe lengths range up to 5·5 m; normally bitumen coated internally and externally, but may be supplied concrete lined. The working pressures for Ductile Iron pipes (Class K9), and fittings (Class K12), are 40 bar, up to 300 mm; 25 bar, for 350–600 mm; and 16 bar, for 700–1,200 mm sizes. BS CP 2010 Part 3, should be referred to when designing iron pipelines in land.

Steel Pipes and Fittings (BS 534 and BS 3600).—The standards covers seamless and welded pipes and fittings suitable for several types of joint including welded, flanged and screwed, or for jointing with slip on couplings, of which the Viking Johnson is the most widely used. Pipes are usually supplied in random lengths up to about 7·5 m. Linings may be bitumen, asphalt or concrete, and external sheathings include bitumen impregnated hessian and bitumen with asbestos or glass-fibre filler. Due to their liability to corrosion steel pipelines are usually protected by impressed current or sacrificial anodes, but the quality and continuity of the lining and sheathing are of primary importance. Test pressures vary with size and method of manufacture, from approximately 70 bar in a 90 mm outside diameter pipe, to 20 bar in the case of a 184 mm od pipe. BS CP 2010 Part 2, should be referred to when designing steel pipelines in land. CIRIA Report 78 covers the design and construction of buried thin-wall pipes and is generally used in the design of steel pipelines.

Asbestos-Cement Pipes (BS 486).—Pipes of nominal bore range 50 mm–900 mm are supplied with plain turned ends for jointing with detachable joints. Between these turned ends the outside diameter is variable and cut pipes may require to be turned on site before joints can be fixed. The joints available include slip-on couplings either in asbestos-cement or cast iron. Pipes may be supplied bitumen coated internally and externally. The Works test pressures for Classes 15, 20 and 25 are respectively, 15, 20 and 25 bar; sustained operating pressures should be half these figures. Most fittings for asbestos-cement pipes are made of cast iron, BS CP 2010 Part 4, should be referred to when designing asbestos-cement pipelines in land.

Concrete Pipes: Plain and Reinforced (BS 5911) and Prestressed (BS 4625).—Plain and reinforced concrete pipes are used in certain cases where the water is not under pressure. Joints are generally of the spigot and socket flexible type, incorporating a rubber gasket.

BS 4625 covers prestressed concrete pipes from 400 mm–1,800 mm nominal bore, and are generally available in U.K. between 600 mm and 400 mm. Joints are of the spigot and socket type with rubber sealing ring. Works test pressures range between 6–18 bar; under normal conditions, working pressure should not exceed two-thirds of works test pressure. BS CP2010 Part 5, should be referred to when designing prestressed concrete pipelines in land. They are heavy to handle, but useful in high stress situations.

Unplasticized PVC Pipes (BS 3505).—BS 3505 covers nominal sizes from 75 mm–610 mm in five pressure ratings, not all of which apply to the larger sizes. However, Class D pipes (working pressure 12·0 bar), of 487–610 mm nominal size, are available outside the BS 3505 range. Lengths of 6 m and 9 m are supplied; specials of the same material, or in some cases of cast iron, are available. Joints are either solvent-welded, or mechanical type, incorporating a rubber sealing ring.

GRP (Glass Reinforced Plastic).—BS 5480 is available in sizes between 300 mm and 2,500 mm dia, generally in 6 m lengths, and is corrosion resistant and light in weight. It requires careful handling and adequate support in the trench as a flexible pipe. Collar joints with rubber rings and fins are generally used.

MDPE (Medium Density Polyethylene).—BS 1972 applies—recently introduced following earlier Low and High Density versions. Rated for pressures of 6 or 10 bar for all nominal sizes from 355 mm dia to 500 mm dia—some available up to 1,000 mm dia by butt-fusion welding which is a skilled task under controlled conditions. Corrosion resistant but subject to attack by organic compounds and ultra-violet light. Currently limited to low pressure use, but scope for other applications provided care is taken in handling and ground support.

PIPELAYING.—See BS Code of Practice 2010 Pipelines (Four Parts). To avoid high friction losses and risk of air-lock it is important that pipes are laid to even gradients; they are normally laid to a minimum grade of 1 in 500, properly boned-in to the correct gradient and are covered with about 1 m of earth. Before excavation of the trench, strong painted sight rails should be fixed at each change of inclination and direction (also along the route, where necessary), with clear markings of the centre line and level to which the pipe is to be laid. If special surface materials are encountered (roads, etc) they should be kept separate for replacement. The size of the trench must allow ample room to work on the pipe, and efficient ramming round the pipe when back-filling. The bed of the trench should allow the pipe to rest its full length on undisturbed ground, and if socket joints have to be made, with adequate holes for jointing. Where necessary, the trench must be timbered and protected against slips. Where the bed of the trench is in rock, the excavation is made 80 mm deeper and well consolidated soft material placed under the pipe. In bad ground, lean concrete can be laid to provide an even bed.

When pipes have been cleaned and metal pipes sounded with a hammer, they are lowered into position with hemp-rope slings, carefully set in line, firmly bedded so that each length rests on the solid ground or on piers, and then driven home. All pipes should be laid in straight lines between the several angles and changes of inclination along the route. Changes in direction of a few degrees can be accommodated in most pipelines at the joints, the permissible angle varying with the material and size. Standard bends are available for angles of 11¼° and upwards. Where possible the pipes should be laid with the sockets uphill, commencing from washouts. The bore of the pipe should be kept free from dirt, stones, etc, and each length cleaned out immediately before laying. Pipe cutting is carried out by special pipe cutting machine, and flanges have a rubber joint ring between faces. At all times when work is not in progress, every part of the main should be effectively closed with temporary caps to prevent ingress of material.

Vertical bends should be supported by concrete from the bottom of the trench (for the full width of the trench and the full length of the bend) to the middle of the horizontal pipe. Horizontal bends are similarly supported but are also tightly packed with concrete between the outside of the bend and trench wall, to the top of the bend and for its full width. (See 'Unbalanced Pressure on Bends'.) Where pipes are laid at a steeper slope than 1 in 12, concrete stop walls are built across the trench and keyed into the sides to prevent the pipes from sliding. For slopes greater than 1 in 6, the trench bottom is stepped and filled with concrete.

In refilling trenches, selected fine material is firmly punned in joint holes and round the barrel, and 150 mm layers, each well consolidated by hand punners, follow until the fine material is 300 mm above the pipe. Thereafter, 200 mm layers of material are rammed by power or hand, and the surface materials replaced. Frozen material should not be used. Where hand ramming is used, best results are obtained from two men ramming to one filling. In public roads the trench should be filled to within 50 mm of the surface and then temporarily sealed with bituminous macadam until the permanent reinstatement is done by the highway authority.

FLOW IN PIPES: FRICTION LOSSES.—Basic principles are dealt with in the chapter 'Hydraulics (Mechanics of Fluids)'. The universal pipe friction diagram, based on the Hazen-Williams formula, with V in ft/sec;

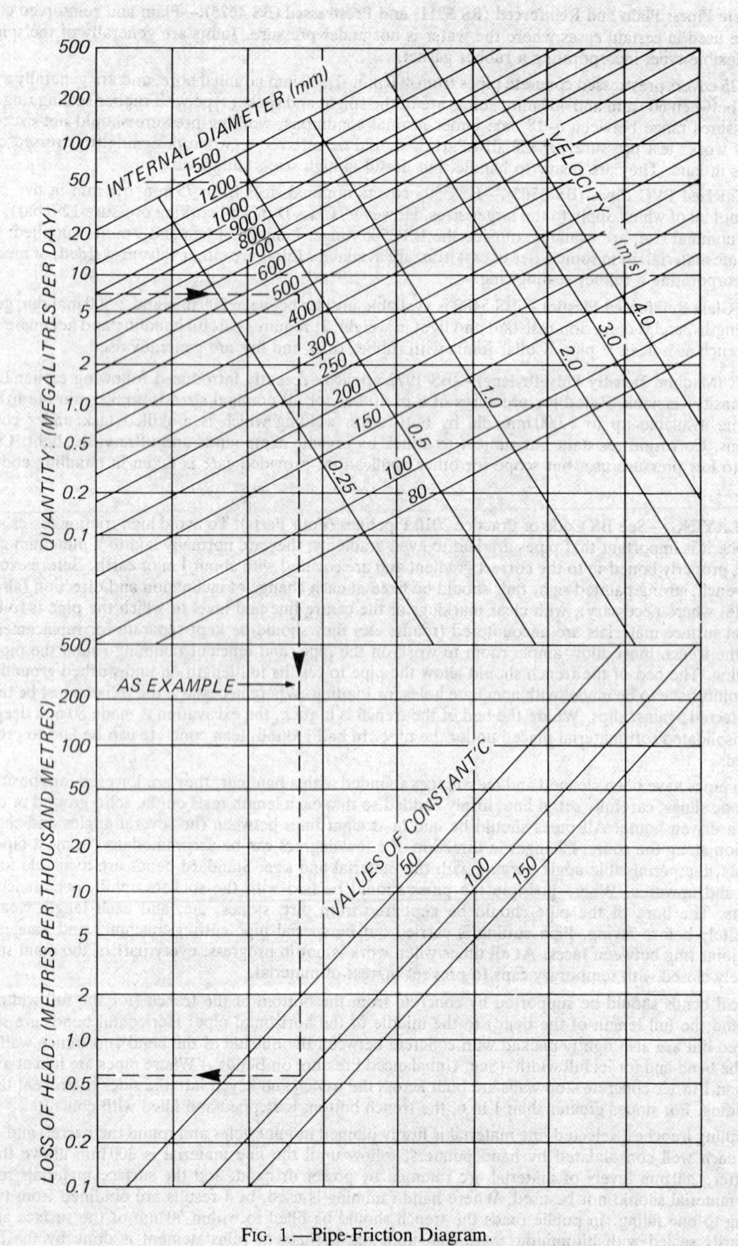

Fig. 1.—Pipe-Friction Diagram.

(*Example of Use.*—A 500 mm pipe is required to carry 7 megalitre/day; what would be the velocity and head loss? On top half of diagram, read across from rate of flow to size, and velocity reads off at 0·4 m/s approx. Then read downwards to selected value of constant *C* (in this case 100) and back to loss of head scale which reads 0·6 m per 1,000 m (see broken line).

and other dimensions in feet,

$$V = 1{\cdot}318C(D/4)^{0{\cdot}63}(H/L)^{0{\cdot}54}$$

is included in the 'Manual of British Water Engineering Practice' as Chart D. A simplified reproduction, in metric units, is given in Fig. 1. The values of C in the formula are:—150 for new mains; 100 for average mains; and 50 for old mains. This is sufficient for general design purposes but it is now generally considered that the charts prepared by the Hydraulics Research Station, based on the Colebrook-White Formula, are more accurate over the full range of flows.

Application to Compound Mains and Networks.—The lengthy calculations, sometimes involving successive approximations needed to estimate flows and pressures in compound mains of differing sizes (in series or in parallel), and in distribution networks, are nowadays performed by computer or one of the programmable desk-top calculators.

TESTING AND DISINFECTION OF MAINS.—After the completion of laying each section of main (between sluice valves or otherwise as convenient), pipe lines should be tested, for a period of not less than 6 hours, with clean chlorinated water at a pressure of 1–3 bar above the working head of the main. The length of main should be completely filled with water, and allowed to stand as long as possible to allow for liberation of air. A test pump with stop cock, tank and pressure gauge, is connected and operated until the gauge shows the required test pressure, the time and amount of water in the tank is noted. An hour later, test pressure on the gauge is restored by means of the pump, and this is repeated at hourly intervals during the test period. The total quantity of water pumped to maintain the pressure during the test is noted; this is the 'apparent leakage'.

When testing, a check should be made on all valves and washouts for leakage. The apparent leakage should not normally exceed 1 litre per centimetre of diameter per kilometre of length per 24 hours, although larger losses (of the order of 3–6 litres) are sometimes allowed where such factors as time, unskilled labour and climatic conditions apply, and leakage is not of paramount importance. With large steel mains, the effect of dilation can be avoided by allowing the main to stand at test pressure for some time, before the test commences. After each section of pipe has passed the test it should be emptied and washed clear of sediment by repeated refilling until the water is clear. The main should then be refilled and flushed with heavily chlorinated water (at least 10 ppm), and when completely filled and chlorine appears at remote branches, the section is closed for a contact time of at least two hours. The main is then flushed out and refilled with the normal chlorinated water supply (with a chlorine residual of 0·2 ppm).

CATHODIC PROTECTION OF MAINS.—An underground steel or cast iron main, however well protected, cannot be completely insulated from the moist corrosive ground. Corrosion can occur at the points where the base metal is in contact with the chemical salts in the soil; this is due to an electrolytic action set up, in which the pipe metal is normally the anode. The product of electrolysis is the corrosion of the anode. Cathodic protection of mains transfers the electrolytic action (the corrosive activity at the anode), to magnesium anodes which are sunk in the earth, and connected to the main with insulated wire. The resulting electric currents through the soil give protection to the main, and the magnesium anodes are corroded. The rate of destruction (corrosion) of the anodes, is reduced by polarisation of the main. The anodes are sited in permanently moist ground, at the same depth and about 3 m from the main. For new small diameter pipes, the average spacing is 250 m, and the average life of an anode is ten years; the latter can be closely estimated after measuring the flow of electric current. Where cathodic protection is employed, certain mechanical pipe joints (eg Viking-Johnson couplings), have to be bridged to ensure electrical continuity along the main.

The above remarks refer to the magnesium or zinc anode method of protection. A more economic method is 'power impressed', in which a current is passed through the main by means of a graphite anode. The supply of current can be provided from a transformer/rectifier. Cathodic protection may adversely affect adjacent buried structures, unless it is properly applied.

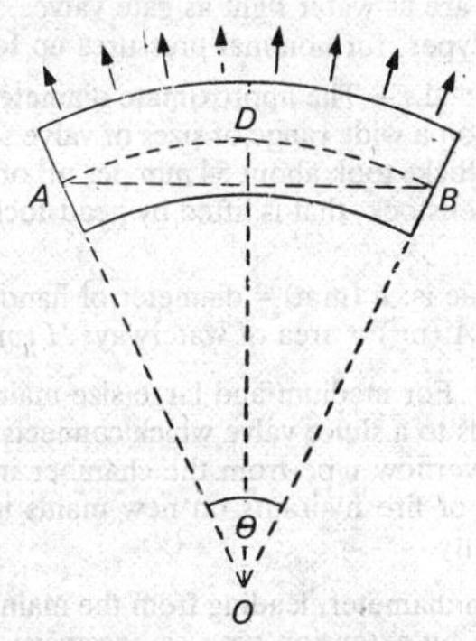

FIG. 2.—Unbalanced Pressure on Circular Bends.

Corrosional Surveys.—The resistivity of the soil is a measure of its corrosive effect and the following is an approximate guide. Four typical conditions are given together with the corresponding soil resistivity (ohm cm):—Not usually corrosive (greater than 10,000 ohm cm); Mildly corrosive (4,000–10,000 ohm cm); Corrosive (2,000–4,000 ohm cm); Very corrosive (0–2,000 ohm cm).

UNBALANCED PRESSURE ON BENDS.—For circular bends (see Fig. 2), the displacing force in the direction OD, or the resultant of the unbalanced pressures on the internal surfaces of the bend AB is given by the formula: $T = 2P \sin \theta/2$.

T = unbalanced thrust (tonnes); θ = angle subtended by bend; P = total pressure (tonnes) in pipe = $pd^2\pi/4$, where p = water pressure (tonne/mm²), and d = pipe bore (mm). If the water pressure is taken as 100 m head, p becomes 10^{-4} tonne/mm². Then $T = 2 \times 10^{-4}\pi/4d^2 \sin \theta/2$, or, $= 10^{-4}\pi d^2/2 \sin \theta/2$. Table 2 gives the unbalanced thrust on bends from 100 mm to 1,000 mm bore, for angles of 11·25 to 90 degrees, using standard bends. For example:—The thrust from a 500 mm, 45 degree bend at 60 m head is $15{\cdot}02 \times 0{\cdot}6 = 9{\cdot}01$ tonne. To convert this to kilonewtons, multiply by 9·81. Thus 1t = 9·81 kN.

TABLE 2.—UNBALANCED THRUST ON BENDS.

Nominal bore mm	Unbalanced thrust (tonnes) at 100 m head of water (10 bar). Degrees of angle bend				
	11·25	22·5	45·0	67·5	90·0
100	0·15	0·30	0·60	0·87	1·11
150	0·34	0·68	1·35	1·96	2·50
200	0·61	1·22	2·40	3·49	4·44
250	0·96	1·91	3·75	5·45	6·94
300	1·38	2·75	5·40	7·85	9·99
350	1·88	3·74	7·36	10·69	13·61
400	2·46	4·89	9·61	13·96	17·77
450	3·11	6·19	12·17	17·67	22·49
500	3·84	7·65	15·02	21·82	27·77
600	5·54	11·01	21·63	31·42	39·99
700	7·54	14·99	29·44	42·77	54·43
800	9·85	19·58	38·46	55·87	71·10
900	12·46	24·78	48·68	70·71	89·99
1,000	15·39	30·60	60·10	87·30	111·10

VALVES

Sluice Valves.—See Fig. 3. Usual water works patterns are: (1) provided with flanges (to facilitate removal from pipe-line); (2) of the non-rising spindle type; (3) operated by a key, by turning clockwise to close; (4) made in various strengths for use with pipes of different pressure ratings. Other types of ordinary valves procurable have spigots and sockets, double spigots for Victaulic joints, clockwise opening, indicators to indicate the amount of opening, rising spindles, hand wheels, locking devices. Larger sizes may be geared to assist operation and/or have by-pass valves, the size of by-pass varying between 25 mm bore for a 200 mm valve, to 100–150 mm for a 1,200 mm valve. BS 5163 covers the range 50–600 mm in pressure ratings of 10–16 bar. Sluice valves are also known as gate valves.

Butterfly valves are now often used as an alternative to sluice valves. They are compact, easily operated and, if suitably resilient seatings are used, are as water tight as gate valves. BS 5155 covers a range from 40 mm to 2,000 mm double-flanged and wafer types, for nominal pressures up to 25 bar and 16 bar, respectively.

POWER REQUIRED: VALVE HANDWHEELS.—The approximate diameter of a handwheel can be determined by the formula: $d = 30\sqrt{D}$. Tests made on a wide range of sizes of valve showed that the hand opening or closing of geared or ungeared valves or penstocks took about 54 min per m² of waterway, or $t = D^2/23{,}600$. The direct pull on a spindle to open a valve or penstock, that is lifted by headstock set at a higher level, is given (approx) by the formula: $P = 350A(H + 1)$.

The notation for the above formulae is: d (mm) = diameter of handwheel; D (mm) = internal diameter of valve; t (min) = time; P (kg) = pull; A (m²) = area of waterway; H (m) = unbalanced head.

Hydrants.—See Fig. 4 and BS 750. For medium and large size mains, a branch 80–150 mm diameter from a flanged tee on the main usually leads to a sluice valve which connects to a duck foot on which rests the screw down hydrant and stand pipe. An overflow pipe from the chamber in which the hydrant is placed acts as a washout for the main. The location of fire hydrants on new mains is carried out by the Fire Authority in collaboration with the Water Authority.

Washouts.—Usually are 80–150 mm diameter, leading from the main from a flanged tee branch with a sluice valve control and thence discharging by extension pipe as necessary to the ditch. Washout branch specials

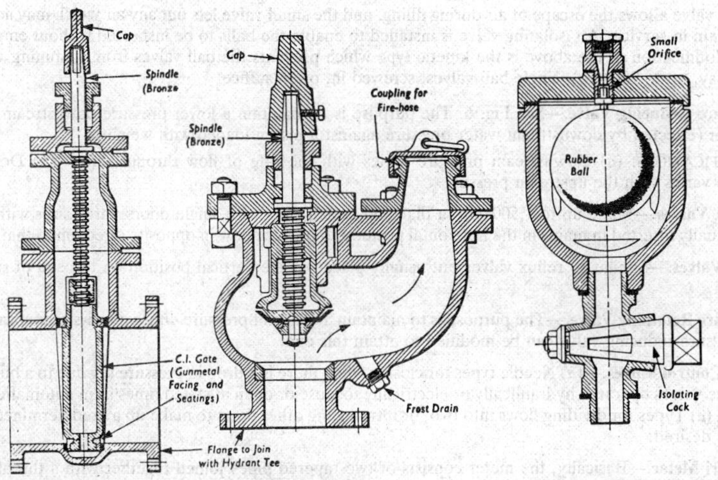

FIG. 3.—Standard Double Flanged Sluice Valve with inside screw and cap. Sizes over 200 mm dia.

FIG. 4.—Hydrant.

FIG. 5.—Single Air Valve for Small Mains.

should have the invert of the branch at the same level as that of the main to enable all sediment to be washed out.

Air Valves.—For single air valve see Fig. 5. For large mains (above 450 mm) and medium size mains (300–450 mm), these are usually the double air valve type, and installed at the high points of the main. The

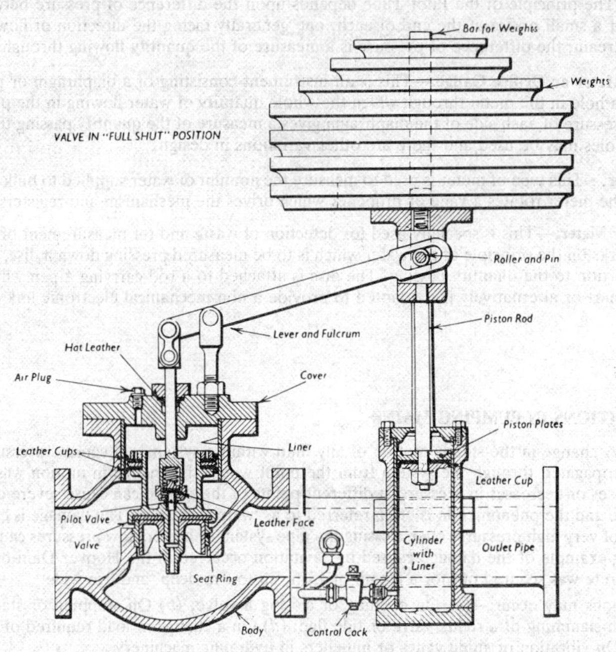

FIG. 6.—Pressure Reducing Valve suitable for cases where flow in the main may be reduced to zero. This valve is drop tight when closed.

large air valve allows the escape of air during filling, and the small valve lets out any air which may accumulate in the main in service. An isolating valve is installed to enable the balls to be inspected without emptying the main. Modification of the above is the kinetic type which prevents the ball valves from slamming. For small mains (say, up to 200 mm), single ball valves, screwed in, often suffice.

Pressure Reducing Valve.—See Fig. 6. The purpose is to maintain a lower pressure downstream than that upstream (effected by downstream water pressure against a piston loaded with weights).

MODIFICATIONS: (*a*) Downstream pressure varies with the rate of flow through valve. (*b*) Downstream pressure varies with the upstream pressure.

Reflux Valves.—Made up to 1,500 mm in diameter, small sizes with single doors, large sizes with multiple doors usually inserted in mains in the horizontal position to prevent flow in opposite direction to that required.

Foot Valves.—Similar to reflux valves but usually placed in the vertical position on the end of suctions of pumps.

Pressure Retaining Valve.—The purpose is to maintain a constant pressure either down-stream or upstream. The pressure reducing valve can be modified to attain this end.

Flow Control Valves.—(*a*) Needle types for closing when there is a drop in pressure (eg due to a burst main). (*b*) Sluice valves operated hydraulically or electrically to close or open at stated times as in automatic pumping stations. (*c*) Types for dividing flows into two, or introducing other flows to make up a predetermined quantity of water desired.

Venturi Meter.—Basically, the meter consists of two tapered pipes joined together with a throat, and the difference of head between the two ends of the taper gives a measure of the quantity of water through the pipes. This difference of pressure can be transferred, conveniently by small copper pipes a distance of 5–10 m, to a direct-reading manometer, or pen and paper chart, to give a record of the flow. The flow can be integrated, instrumentally, to record the total quantity, usually per day, passing through the pipe.

It is important to have 10 or 12 diameters of *straight* pipe upstream of the meter (eg 3–4 m for a 300 mm pipe before the water enters the meter) to ensure accurate readings; after the water has passed through the meter there are no particular practical conditions to be taken care of, but most meters require to work under approximately 5 m water pressure.

Pitot Tube.—The principle of the Pitot Tube depends upon the difference of pressure between two small pointed tubes or a small orifice at the end of each, one generally facing the direction of flow and the other pointing downstream; the difference of pressure is a measure of the quantity flowing through the pipe.

Diaphragm Meter or Orifice Gauge.—This is an instrument consisting of a diaphragm or plate inserted in the pipe, with a hole in the metal through which the whole quantity of water flowing in the pipe, passes. The difference of pressure of each side of the diaphragm gives a measure of the quantity passing through the hole. One or more holes may be used and there are other variations in design.

Rotary Meter.—This type of meter is used to measure the amount of water supplied to bulk consumers. The flow through the meter rotates a vane or propeller which drives the mechanism and registers on a dial.

Waste Water Meter.—This is specially used for detection of waste and for measurement of small quantities of water. It works on the principle of the water which is to be measured pressing down a disc, which is pressed down in proportion to the quantity passing. The disc is attached to a rod carrying a pen which records on a moving time chart or alternatively it is adapted to provide a non-mechanical electronic link direct to a data-logger.

SURGE CONDITIONS IN PUMPING MAINS

Definition.—A change in the steady motion of any fluid within a system will cause a pressure transient or 'surge' to be propagated through the system from the point where the change in motion was initiated. The resultant increases or decreases in pressure at different points of the system can cause severe damage or even complete failure and the phenomenon is often referred to as 'water hammer'. The damage is caused by either the generation of very high pressures overstressing the pipe system or by very low pressures causing cavitation. An outstanding example of the damage caused by cavitation occurred in the Hoover Dam overflow tunnel, where the concrete was scoured out for a length of 45 m, up to 8 m deep, and 9 m wide.

Surge conditions may occur:—(*a*) On opening or closing a valve; (*b*) On stopping or starting pumps or turbines; (*c*) On slamming of a reflux valve or tide flap; (*d*) On a change in load required of a hydroelectric generator; (*e*) On vibration of guide vanes or impellers in hydraulic machinery.

The velocity of propagation of the transients is affected by the density and bulk modulus of the fluid, the ratio of pipe diameter to wall thickness, and the elastic modulus of the pipe wall material. Once a pressure transient has been generated in a particular system, pressure variations occur at every point and are governed by the distance from the point of origin, the time from origin and any effects that the system may have had on the transient while travelling to the point in question. These may include the effects due to reflections at bends, junctions, changes in cross-section of the pipe, etc. In whatever curcumstances they are encountered, pressure transients can be defined by two equations: the equation of motion and the equation of continuity. The behaviour is controlled by the boundary conditions of the particular system.

SURGE CONTROL.—Where the rise or drop in pressure is found to be excessive, some method of surge control must be provided. The device should effectively reduce the rate of change of flow, the following are the most common methods:—

(1) Slower valve closure. Time should not be shorter than the reflection period of the pipe line (reference, *Paper* by Livingstone and Wilson).

(2) Increased pump inertia. By fitting a large flywheel—not generally possible for borehole pumps or large installations.

(3) Surge Shafts. Often used in hydro-electric schemes, seldom in water supply due to risk of contamination.

(4) Air Vessel. This damps the surge effect by the elasticity of the air in the vessel. Size required increases with the initial velocity, and water content of the pipe line must also be sufficient to prevent air being drawn into the pipe when the minimum pressure is experienced.

(5) Air Admission Valves. If the pressure in the pipe line is liable to drop below the vapour pressure of the liquid, thus causing cavitation, valves may be fitted that will open and admit air to the system under these circumstances.

(6) Release Valves. Open at a set maximum pressure to allow liquid to escape from the system.

(7) By-passes. Fitted around the pump to permit water to flow from the sump into the delivery pipe when the discharge pressure drops below sump pressure.

(8) Surge Suppressors. Complex valves with weights or spring devices, commonly used in USA but not often in Britain.

Evaluation of Surge Pressures.—The velocity (a) of a pressure wave within a system may be calculated from the formula:

$$a = 1\bigg/\left[\frac{\rho}{g}\left\{\frac{1}{K}+\frac{d(1-\sigma^2)}{tE}\right\}\right]^{0\cdot5}$$

where ρ = density of water; g = acceleration due to gravity; K = bulk modulus of water; d = internal diameter of pipe; t = thickness of pipe; E = Young's modulus for the material of pipe; σ = Poisson's ratio for the material of pipe.

Typical values of a, resulting from the use of this formula, would be as follows: Small cast iron pipe, 1,250 m/s; large thin-walled steel pipe, 900 m/s; small PVC pipe, 300–400 m/s.

The time taken by the pressure wave to travel to the end of the pipe and back again, $2L/a$ is known as the reflection time; L being the length of pipe involved. If a valve is closed within the reflection time, pressure on the upstream side of the valve will rise above the static pressure by a head, H_{max}, equal to aV_0/g, where V_0 is the steady velocity before closure. After the end of the reflection period, the pressure of the valve will drop by aV_0/g below the static pressure for an equal period.

For a simple system comprising a pump raising water from a stream through a direct pumping main to a service reservoir, assume the initial static head is 80 m, the velocity of the pressure wave a is 1,250 m/s, the initial velocity in the pumping main is 0·3 m/s, and g is 9·8 m/s. Then the surge pressure rise or fall on instantaneous shut-off, $(H_{max}) = aV_0/g = 38{\cdot}4$ m. The minimum pressure = 41.6 m. The maximum pressure = 118·4 m. To avoid the cost of increasing the working pressure of the pipe line, it would probably be more economic to instal an air vessel in this instance.

The principles of this calculation can be applied to more complex systems and can be evaluated by the graphical method developed by Bergeron. Alternatively, the mathematical 'Method of Characteristics', which utilises the same equations, but is more appropriate if it is necessary to evaluate the pressures at a number of points on the pipe line, can easily be calculated on a computer programme and at the same time the effect of various surge control devices analysed. Detailed descriptions of these methods are available in the references and a range of computer programs enable an analysis to be made of a number of different solutions to control surge and the most economical method selected even in complex systems.

SERVICE RESERVOIRS

The function of a service reservoir is to store potable water at the head of a distribution system, in order to meet fluctuations in daily demand and provide a reserve to meet sudden additional demands arising from a burst main, breakdown of pumps, fire, etc. It should hold from one to three days of average daily demand, and should be roofed to avoid pollution by birds, vermin, access by people, or by a polluted atmosphere.

The reservoir is usually sited on the highest ground available to meet all requirements by gravity, unless it is found to be uneconomical to pump the total demand to so high an elevation which may justify the cost of two smaller reservoirs instead of the single large one. Alternatively, the higher area may be served by booster pumping and/or a water tower. The design of the structure should generally be in accordance with BS 5337 'Code of Practice for the Structural Use of Concrete for Retaining Liquids'; and BS 8110 'Structural Use of Concrete'. The economic depth varies with the capacity, approximately as follows (Table 3).

TABLE 3.—RESERVOIR CAPACITY V. ECONOMIC DEPTH.

Capacity, megalitres	2	5	10	20	50	100
Economic Depth, metres	4	4	5.5	6	7	8

WALLS.—In recent years these have generally been formed in reinforced concrete designed as cantilevers off reinforced footings, but may also be constructed in mass concrete designed as a 'gravity dam' section. Prestressed concrete has been adopted for circular tanks, the walls being precompressed by wrapping a tensioned steel cable around the outside; the cable then being protected by a coating of pneumatically applied mortar ('Gunite'). See chapter 'Concrete: Reinforced and Prestressed'. The walls are generally covered externally by an earthen embankment which also gives some external support, the extent of which is not precise or determinate. In cases where only a light roof structure is required, it may be possible to form the walls as earthen embankments with an impermeable core, if materials are economically available. The reservoir is frequently divided into two or more compartments, by part, or full height dividing walls, to facilitate cleaning and maintenance whilst still maintaining operation. This can be achieved on small reservoirs by installing a by-pass pipe to maintain supply whilst the whole reservoir drains down.

FLOORS.—On firm ground the floor is usually formed by two layers of concrete each 100–150 mm thick, with an impermeable membrane laid between; the bottom layer is generally mass concrete but the top layer is reinforced with one or two layers of mesh fabric. Each layer is laid in squares or rectangles, equivalent in size to the column spacings, but not exceeding 7 m in width to allow for tamping, or 10 m in length. The bays are cast alternately and the joints between the top layer bays, which should be displaced from those in the bottom layer, are sealed with a non-toxic or plastic sealing compound.

COLUMNS.—Are usually formed in reinforced concrete, square or circular in cross section, and may be either cast *in situ* or precast, according to the roof structure. Steel joists coated with protective bitumen may be considered in areas subject to ground subsidence. The spacing of columns should be as wide as possible to give an economical roof design.

ROOF.—Where access is required over the roof, or a covering of earth is required for aesthetic reasons, it is formed in reinforced concrete either as a flat slab or beam-and-slab structure, generally cast *in situ*, unless speed of construction justifies the extra cost of precast units. The roof can then be covered with a layer of 300 mm of topsoil, laid over 75 mm of free draining gravel; this covering helps to maintain the roof at an even temperature. Where no covering or heavy access is required, a light barrel vault roofing may be used in corrugated aluminium sheeting; this is also advantageous where it is necessary to keep the loading on the columns to a minimum. Ventilators with gauze covers, to exclude birds and vermin, should be installed to ensure a flow of air across the surface of the water.

PIPEWORK AND INSTRUMENTATION.—The draw-off pipe should be sited as low as possible to avoid wasting any storage and the inlet should be sited as far as possible from it to avoid short-circuit flow within the reservoir. A washout sump and pipe should be provided connected to an overflow discharge pipe leading to a free discharge point—the overflow pipe itself being connected below the wash-out control valve. An overflow, normally consisting of a bellmouth or concrete weir, should be capable of discharging the maximum rate of inflow into the reservoir without the water overtopping the walls of the reservoir. A water level recorder should be provided to record the depth of water. The inlet and outlet pipes to each compartment should each have a guard valve and control valve. These are preferably sited within one valve chamber attached to the walls with easy access—however, sometimes it is necessary for site reasons to have separate inlet and outlet chambers. Self-closing valves are generally provided in the outlet pipe to close in the event of a burst main below the site to prevent the whole reservoir discharging.

WATER TOWERS.—There are several types of water towers (see also chapter 'Concrete: Reinforced and Prestressed'); typical examples are: (*a*) elevated steel tanks built up in modular sections bolted together, usually rectangular. (*b*) Reinforced concrete structures lined with asphalt, usually cylindrical but sometimes spherical or hyperbolic in outline. (*c*) Glass coated steel or fibre-glass, sectional or cylindrical tanks.

Towers range from 0·1 to 4·5 Ml in capacity, and from 12 to 40 m height. Their function is to provide limited storage at an adequate elevation to meet the needs of the area; with sufficient storage to meet the fluctuation in demand between peak and average rates, whilst maintaining a steady inflow, thus avoiding oversizing of trunk transmission mains.

STORAGE SCHEMES

The term storage scheme implies storing a large quantity of water in a reservoir for use when needed. The reservoir may be filled by: (*a*) impounding a stream by an earthen embankment or concrete dam across the valley; (*b*) pumping water from another river valley into the reservoir which is enclosed either by an earthen embankment or a concrete wall; (*c*) a mixture of (*a*) and (*b*) whereby the reservoir is filled by water flowing into it naturally from its own gathering ground as well as by pumping from an external source; (*d*) regulating the flow of water in a river by a reservoir of any of the above types (*a*), (*b*) or (*c*).

COSTS OF STORAGE AND IMPOUNDING RESERVOIRS.—The costs of a number of typical dams are given below. The types of dams are as follows: DS, direct supply; R, regulating; PS, pumped storage.

TABLE 4.—COSTS OF TYPICAL DAMS.

Name	Type	Date	Capacity (Ml)	Gross yield (Ml/d)	Approx equivalent cost 1987 £ million
Concrete gravity dams					
Clatworthy (Taunton)	DS	1960	5,000	25·0	6·1
Stithians (Cornwall)	DS	1965	5,410	15·9	2·7
Siblyback (Cornwall)	R	1970	3,180	—	3·1
Meldon (Devon)	DS	1972	3,090	29·1	6·3
Llysyfran (Pembroke)	R	1972	9,100	—	12·2
Concrete buttress dams					
Haweswater (Cumbria)	DS	1941	84,830	162·3	12·4
Lamaload (Cheshire)	DS	1963	1,980	6·8	3·5
Clywedog (Powys)	R	1968	50,000	—	16·3
Wimbleball (Somerset)	R/DS	1980	19,300	86·8	18·5
Earth and rockfill dams					
Selset (Tees Valley)	DS	1962	10,150	90·9	24·3
Llandegfedd (Cardiff)	PS	1963	24,500	115·9	6·6
Balderhead (Tees Valley)	R	1965	18,180	—	16·3
Grafham Water (Great Ouse)	PS	1966	57,730	184·1	12·4
Bough Beech (East Surrey)	PS	1967	9,100	22·7	11·9
Draycote Water (Rugby)	PS	1969	22,730	45·5	8·9
Scammonden (Huddersfield)*	DS	1970	8,180	37·3	20·4
Brianne (West Glamorgan)	R	1972	60,920	—	24·5

* Crest carries a six lane motorway about 14 m above top water level.

IMPOUNDING RESERVOIR.—Where the reservoir is to be filled from its own gathering ground the initial problems for finding the cost of a scheme are concerned with the records of run-off for several years (ideally 30); many river gaugings are recorded in the Surface Water Year Books. If the run-off is not known, then it must be deduced from records of average annual rainfall (from Air Ministry Meteorological Office) and an estimate of loss according to the locality (eg by Penman formula).

From these data the characteristics of any site may be represented by four curves showing the relationship between:

(1) Height of dam and storage (this may be obtained from ground or aerial surveys).
(2) Storage and yield (details given later at Figs. 7, 8 and 9). See pp I7/21, I7/22 and I7/25.
(3) Height of dam and relative cost, may be obtained from formulae. See pp I7/38 and I7/43.
(4) Cost and yield is easily obtained from (1), (2) and (3) and from this the cost of development for any gross yield can be found. The cost per unit yield can be calculated for various yields and plotted in the form of a graph, which will clearly show the most economical size of reservoir; in many cases the cost per unit yield falls as the size of reservoir is increased, reaches a minimum, and then increases again.

These methods may be used to compare a number of alternative sites, to enable the most economical site to be chosen. However, they give the comparative costs of raw water at the reservoir site only, the actual cost to the consumer is dependent on many other factors, such as the elevation of the site, distance to the point of supply, quality of the water, and type of treatment.

For impounding schemes it is generally necessary to build the dam having the full ultimate storage capacity, although only a fraction of the water would be required for the first few years. It is difficult to enlarge earthen embankments, although concrete dams can be enlarged fairly easily. The site conditions will determine whether the dam will be of earth or concrete, and straight or curved.

PUMPED STORAGE RESERVOIR.—Where the reservoir is to be filled from an external source, the initial problem for ascertaining the size and cost of a reservoir is to determine the conditions imposed on abstraction, ie: (*a*) the months in which abstraction is permitted; (*b*) the flow to be left in the river; (*c*) the maximum flow which may be taken.

The difficulty is to ascertain the run-off at the intake selected; generally it is determined with known data elsewhere on the river or by collation with rainfall, so that the generally more reliable and extensive rainfall records may be used. The site for the intake should be as near the reservoir as possible, whilst also taking advantage of the largest catchment available—this requirement often being met by abstracting from the nearest conjunction of a large tributary with the main river. The optimum capacity of the pumps, pipelines and reservoir can then be determined by assessing alternative schemes and plotting the cost against yield for a determined drought severity.

COMBINED IMPOUNDING AND PUMPED STORAGE SCHEME.—The cost of a partially pumped storage reservoir has some advantages over the wholly pumped storage of equivalent yield inasmuch as the reservoir is being replenished during the summer months, when pumping may be prohibited; also, on occasions, it may be able to collect more storm water from the gathering ground than would be possible from a natural gathering ground which results in a substantial saving in pumping cost. The technical data are determined by both methods outlined above.

REGULATING RESERVOIR.—This may be constructed on the lines of the Impounding, Pumped or Combined Supply schemes given above, but it performs a different function, inasmuch as its purpose is merely to 'top up' the flow of the river during periods of low flow. Its purpose is to supply a variable demand flow in the river. To estimate the required volume for the reservoir storage, it is necessary to assess the minimum and maintained flows in the river and the total volume of releases to meet these criteria over a draught period. A further normal criterion is a requirement that the reservoir should be full again within 2 or 3 years of average rainfall following the drought sequence.

CATCHWATERS.—In order to augment the yield from an impounding reservoir, water may be led into it from another gathering ground by means of catchwaters or open channels with impervious bottoms, constructed round the contours of hillsides bringing water from other gathering grounds. Catchwaters, including tunnels and pipes, may be designed in accordance with the Chezy formula $V = C\sqrt{(RS)}$. It is not economical to design a catchwater to carry more than 80–90% of the total annual flow.

In practice, in the absence of flow data, economic catchwaters should carry at the rate of some 5 times the average flow; thus if the average annual flow is 1 Ml/d the catchwater might be designed to take a flow at the rate of 5 Ml/d or 60 l/sec. Knowledge of the flow-variation for a potential catchwater area for several years is essential to be considered in relation to the available storage in the reservoir (or the cost of its enlargement).

As topography, distance, silting, ownership, maintenance, also affect the cost of the catchwater, it is best to design several capacities of catchwater (within any known data of flow), from which to select the one giving a reasonable cost.

DRAW OFF TOWERS.—For taking the water into supply where dams are at a greater height than say 15 m it is desirable to provide draw-offs at different levels, as generally water near the surface is of better quality than that at greater depths. Hence, for high dams with four draw-offs the top draw-off may be 3 m below top water level; intermediate draw-offs spaced at 8 m vertical intervals and two draw-offs at the bottom, one purely for purposes of scour and the other for supply. There are two control valves at each level, one operated by a wheel from a platform at that level, and the other by a spindle brought up to top bank level Alternatively, the latter can be hydraulically, electrically or pneumatically operated. In the case of an earthen embankment it is generally necessary to have a valve tower in the reservoir itself because it is impracticable to lay the draw-off pipes in the embankment: access being obtained by a bridge from the top of the embankment or side of the valley. In the case of a concrete dam the valve tower can be conveniently incorporated in the dam and contain siphons of different levels to act as draw-offs. For depths of over 20 m of water impounded for water supply, pumps may be installed in the base of valve towers to circulate and aerate bottom stagnant water.

Overflows consist either of a weir of the right capacity, or a bellmouth and tunnel designed to take the maximum floods (see 'Maximum Flow').

Treatment.—The treatment of surface water is of special importance owing to the corrosive nature of many upland waters. For purely gravity installations the rate of flow through the treatment plant is usually constant throughout the 24 hours and hence the pipeline is designed to carry this uniform rate to the covered service reservoirs near the town, which will balance the fluctuating daily demands. (See 'Treatment and Quality of Water', p. I7/26.)

GEOLOGY OF DAM SITES.—('C', denotes generally suitable for concrete dams and 'E', generally suitable for earth dams.) The siting of dams and reservoirs is dependent for stability and water tightness on the geological formations which, in Britain, include The Cambrian and pre-Cambrian of Leicestershire (C and E); The grits and shales of the Ordovician are Silurian of Wales, Lake District and Scotland (C and E); Granites of Scotland, Cornwall and Devonshire (C); The Old Red Sandstone in Wales; the Carboniferous Series, the Yoredales, and grits and shales of the Lower Coal Measures (giving rise to some 200 dams) in Yorkshire and Lancashire (E); The Keuper Marl and Forest Marble of Somerset and the Midlands (E); The Lias Clay of the Midlands (E); The Ashdown Beds of Sussex (E).

TYPICAL IMPOUNDING SCHEMES

South West Water Authority (River Exe Scheme).—Based on a reservoir, Wimbleball Lake, formed by the buttress dam of that name across the River Haddeo tributary. The reservoir has a capacity of 19,300 Ml and provides supplies totalling 86·8 Ml/d comprising a direct abstraction by Wessex Water Authority for the Taunton area (31·8 Ml/d) and abstraction from the Exe by the SW Authority of 8·2 Ml/d for Tiverton, 24·1 Ml/d for Exeter and 22·7 Ml/d for Torbay. When the natural flow at Thorverton Gauge on the main river is 273 Ml/d (60 mgd) or less, water must be released from the reservoir to augment the flow by an appropriate amount to permit abstraction for the areas mentioned. Minimum flow downstream of the dam is 9 Ml/d with provision for freshets of 45 Ml/d; the maximum release is 900 Ml/d to draw off bottom water and prevent accumulations of detrimental elements such as manganese.

Cardiff and South Wales.—Supply is from impounding reservoirs, Beacons (1,569 Ml), Cantref (1,464 Ml) and Llwyn On (5,505 Ml) on the River Taff Fawr. The yield is 82 Ml/d and the compensation varies between 35 and 27 Ml/d. The water is filtered near the reservoirs and is led to Cardiff in two mains 600–760 mm in diameter, distance 56 km. Other similar schemes in South Wales are based on the Taf Fechan reservoirs (17,338 Ml) for the Merthyr district; on the Talybont reservoir (11,365 Ml) for Newport and the Cray reservoir (4,546 Ml) for Swansea. The reservoir on the Usk for Swansea was completed in 1955.

A (1965) scheme for Cardiff, Newport, Abertillery and Pontypool (whose requirements are 91 Ml/d) is based on a reservoir at Llandegfedd, 3 km east of Pontypool. The reservoir (24,500 Ml) is used as a pumped storage reservoir into which the water is pumped from the River Usk (5 km north of Usk) through 3·6 km of 1,060 mm diameter, prestressed concrete pipe; the permissible pumping rate depends on the river flow. The dam has a height of 37 m and is composed entirely of rolled clay with horizontal sand blankets 600 mm thick every 6 m.

Southern Water Authority (Ardingly).—This scheme is based on the storage of 4,800 Ml provided by Ardingly Reservoir which is formed by an earth dam constructed across the Shell Brook, a tributary of the River Ouse in Sussex. The gross yield of the reservoir is 53·6 Ml/d and it permits abstraction by the Mid-Sussex Water Company of 4·5 Ml/d at their Shell Brook works and 49·1 Ml/d at Barcombe. The catchment runoff provides 90% of the reservoir yield, the remainder being obtained by pumping from the Ouse at rates up to 45 Ml/d.

SURFACE WATER SCHEMES

Rivers.—The chief factors affecting the design of river schemes are: (1) the minimum flow in the river in times of drought; (2) the quantity of water to be abstracted; (3) whether storage is possible or not; and (4) the quality of the water. (These are dealt with later in this chapter.)

Lakes.—The necessity for storage will depend on individual circumstances but if the dry weather flow of the river is not sufficient to maintain the water supply plus acceptable river flows, storage must be provided. This may be available in an existing lake but in other cases a reservoir is necessary.

INTAKES.—These usually consist of a simple masonry or concrete chamber built on the bank of the river (sufficiently large for the requisite quantity of water to flow by gravity through gratings and screens to the pump suction well). The purpose of the bars, which may be 25 mm diameter and spaced 150 mm apart, is to prevent floating debris entering the suction well. The straining arrangements may consist of rectangular, manually operated wire mesh screens in duplicate, which are usually satisfactory. Whether grids are placed parallel to the flow of the stream or at 45° facing upstream or downstream is a matter of model experiments to prevent accumulation of debris at the intake. Power driven band screens or drums with 5 mm holes, cleaned with jets of water, are also used.

PUMPING AND FILTRATION.—The pumping machinery, for transporting the crude water from the river, generally at a low elevation, through treatment works and filters to service reservoirs at the necessary high elevation is generally electrically driven, the pumps being vertical or the horizontal type (see chapter 'Liquid Pumps'). It may be necessary to have several pumping sets to synchronise with the variable flow of the stream. The filtration works either consist of slow sand filters or rapid gravity sand filters of the open type. The treatment follows the general lines described later in this Chapter, having particular regard for plumbo-solvency and sterilisation. In addition, however, some lowland river waters may be so hard that it is desirable to soften them and this is sometimes convenient because it can be linked up with the filtration process. (See 'Water Treatment', p. I7/26.)

TYPICAL SURFACE WATER SCHEMES

River Ancholme (Humberside).—(1975) The intake is sited on the Ancholme which also receives water transferred from the Rivers Trent and Witham. Initial rating is 72·7 Ml/d with ultimate rating 145·5 Ml/d. After passing through bar and drum screens the raw water is chlorinated to prevent mussel growth and flows through an 1,800 mm concrete pipeline, 2 km long to a storage reservoir of 910 Ml capacity from which it is pumped to the treatment works, a distance of 10 km, through a 1,220 mm steel pipeline. Treatment comprises partial softening by lime dosage, coagulation using chlorinated copperas, sedimentation and rapid gravity filtration. For the initial plant rating, there are 4–18 m diameter 'Accentrifloc' clarifiers and 8–6·9 × 7·0 m filters. Pre-chlorination is provided at the plant inlet and final chlorination at the filter outlet sump. The scheme affords industrial supplies but provides for modifications to secure a potable water output after the Trent water quality has been improved.

Restormel.—(1975) Present rating is 30 Ml/d. The intake is on the River Fowey in Cornwall, 1 km above the tidal limit. Twin concrete channels convey the water through a bar screen (which also acts as an electronic fish screen), and a bandscreen to the raw water pumping station whence it is pumped into a mixing chamber, where it is dosed with alum and sodium carbonate. Settlement takes place in 20 hopper-bottomed tanks 6.1 m square and 6·5 m deep, and the settled water then flows on to 9 rapid gravity filters each 5·3 × 5·6 × 4·3 m deep. The filtrate passes on to a storage tank of 6·8 Ml capacity. Sterilisation is by gaseous chlorine, with de-chlorination by sulphur dioxide. The fluoride is adjusted to 1 mg/l by injecting fluorosilicic acid, and lime is added as required for final pH correction.

Ullswater and Windermere Scheme.—(1968–72) Promoted by Manchester Corporation (now part of North West Water Authority), this major scheme includes pumping stations to draw water from both lakes, and on amenity grounds these stations have been constructed underground. From Ullswater, up to 363 Ml/d is pumped to Haweswater (another reservoir of the Manchester Water Supply System). Water is drawn from the lake by means of an intake on the lake bed and passes through a 2 m diameter conduit to the pumping station situated about 400 m from the lake. The pumping mains (twin 1,320 mm outside diameter steel pipes) are 1,030 m long and discharge into the Tarn Moor Tunnel (2,680 m) from which the water passes into the Heltondale catchwater aqueduct constructed at an earlier stage. From Windermere, up to 204 Ml/d is pumped to Watchgate Treatment Works via a balancing reservoir at Banner Rigg. The Windermere intake is 230 m from the shore, at a depth of 20 m to minimise pollution, the intake mains being twin 1,220 mm high density polyethylene. The delivery main is a 1,400 mm outside diameter steel pipeline 3,080 m long to the balancing reservoir from which a 1,400 mm gravity main 8,930 m long leads to Watchgate.

UNDERGROUND WATER SCHEMES

The chief problem in developing an underground source is to determine the quantity of water available at any one spot; the problem is one of inference often based on complex geological conditions. Although the total amount of rainfall (and when it falls) is important, it is of lesser significance in Britain than in some places abroad from the standpoint of underground water. The percentage of rainfall which percolates and the percentage of rainfall that may be retrieved theoretically should be the same, but are usually not so in practice. The geological conditions are of basic importance not only on account of the difference and extent of permeable and impermeable strata, their arrangement, and the presence or absence of faults, but also the extent and thickness of the permeable rocks underground which store the rainfall throughout drought periods.

GEOLOGY.—In Britain, particularly, where the position and extent of the geological formations, permeable and impermeable strata, are very well known, the conditions are ideal for prophesying where water may be found and in what quantity. This may also be the case in the United States, France and Europe generally, but it is by no means so in Africa or Asia where the geological conditions are not so well known. In Britain, however, the geological arrangement of the strata is complex for it is often broken by faults and unconformities underground, and, north of a line between London and Cardiff, may be seriously interfered with by the carving of glaciers when they travelled over the country or from deposits which they left when melting. Recent evidence from a reservoir works indicates that glaciation effects extended to the south coast of Britain, between Kent and Dorset. The main water-bearing formations in England in order of importance are:

THE CHALK (including all three divisions, Upper, Middle and Lower), with overlying and shelly Crags, in Yorkshire, Lincolnshire, East Anglia (Norfolk and Suffolk). Also with overlying porous gravels, Thanet Sand (and other Lower London Tertiaries) in the Home Counties (Buckinghamshire, Berkshire, Surrey, Middlesex, Hertfordshire and Essex), London, Kent, Sussex, Hampshire, and with underlying Upper Greensand in Wiltshire and Dorset.

THE BUNTER AND KEUPER SANDSTONES, of South Lancashire, Cheshire, Yorkshire, Nottinghamshire, Staffordshire, Warwickshire and certain areas of Somerset and Dorset.

THE OOLITES—Lower Oolites in East Yorkshire and Lincolnshire, Northamptonshire, Oxfordshire, the

Cotswold Hills of Gloucestershire and Worcestershire, and the somewhat arenaceous limestones of Somerset and Dorset.

THE LOWER GREENSAND beneath the Gault of the North and South Downs, and in Bedfordshire and Hertfordshire, and parts of Surrey and Hampshire.

THE CARBONIFEROUS.—This is a general term under which may be included the Carboniferous Limestone which collects water in large fissures, as in the Mendips of Somerset, and in Derbyshire and Yorkshire; the Millstone Grit and other grits with small outcrops of the Yoredales and Coal Measures in Lancashire, Yorkshire and Wales; grits in the Upper Coal Measures near Coventry, and small supplies in the Culm Measures of Devonshire.

THE PERMIAN AND MAGNESIAN LIMESTONE of the north-eastern counties.

THE ASHDOWN SAND AND TUNBRIDGE WELLS SAND of the Kent and Sussex Weald.

THE OLD RED SANDSTONE of South Wales, Forest of Dean, Herefordshire and Devon.

Quantity Pumped.—Approximate quantities (in megalitre/day) pumped from chief British formations for domestic and industrial use are: Chalk 2,000; Bunter and Keuper Sandstones (Triassic) 1,000; Oolites (Jurassic) 200; Lower Greensand 300.

Underground Water Contours.—The direction of flow of underground water has been indicated broadly by contours, showing water levels, from records of water levels referred to Ordnance datum in existing wells. These contours can be plotted on geological maps and an estimate made of the likelihood of success by reading these maps, bearing in mind known faults, rolls, anticlines and synclines and thinning out of the water-bearing strata.

PERCOLATION.—With an average rainfall of 600–900 mm per annum it is often possible to obtain 200–300 mm of useful water, but where conditions are not well known, a figure of 250 mm is often assumed; this is equivalent to 7,000 litre/day/hectare, or 700 m^3/day/km^2 of gathering ground; the area being determined from the underground contours flowing to the site of the well in permeable strata. For the basis of calculation of the annual rechange to ground water see Rainfall Section.

Springs.—Springs are often unreliable during or after dry periods. There are not many large springs in Britain, but there is a group of unique springs at Bedhampton, developed by the Portsmouth Water Company, which yield a minimum of 64 Ml/d. Other large springs from the Chalk occur under the bed of the Humber; the Hessle Whelps; in St. Margaret's Bay, Kent, and there are many in Hampshire developed for the watercress industry.

Wells.—These are usually sunk to about 60 m deep and from 2 to 4 m diameter, unlined in the hard (water-bearing) part of the strata, but lined with pre-cast concrete segments, cast iron or brickwork, for 12–30 m below the surface, to prevent surface water entering the well and where there are clay seams or unstable patches of material. The advantage of the well is that more than one pump may be inserted within it and adits may be driven in hard strata such as the Chalk or Bunter Sandstone to increase the yield, but in most common cases boreholes are preferable due to the high cost of well construction.

Boreholes.—Preliminary holes, to ascertain geological conditions, are often 100–300 mm diameter; production boreholes are 300–1,200 mm diameter BS 879 'Steel Tubes for Water Well Casing' covers three types of butting joints: screwed and socketed with V-thread, 4–24 in nominal bore; screwed flush, with square thread, 4–48 in; and butt-welded, 4–48 in nominal bore. An appendix gives metric values corresponding to the original inch units, retaining the nominal bores in inches.

Except for some cases in Chalk strata, it is desirable that boreholes be lined throughout, plain lining where in clay or other non water-bearing material or material likely to collapse such as running sand; the top 10–30 m should be similarly lined to prevent surface contamination. In water-bearing strata the lining may be perforated, with 10–25 mm diameter holes at 50–100 mm spacing, or slots 3–12 mm wide and 150 mm long, at 100–150 mm centres. Boreholes over 300 mm nominal bore may be inspected by means of a TV camera.

Specific Yield.—For comparing the yields of different boreholes it is convenient to compare their specific yields, ie pumping rate divided by the difference between rest level and stabilised pumping level. Typical specific yields are: under 20 m^3/day per metre of difference, poor; 40–100, fair; 100–200, good; over 200, very good. In homogeneous strata the yield of a well or borehole varies as the logarithm of the diameter, but the lack of such conditions precludes the use of this theory in Britain.

Tests on the new sources should be carried out for at least 14 days, of 24 hours each, non-stop. Where pumping levels are stabilised often an hour or two from the commencement of the test site is probably a good one; where, however, the pumping level does not appear to stabilise until after a few days and even then seems to be lowering as far as the measuring devices appear to show, then the site may not be very reliable and the test should be extended, or repeated for a less quantity of water. If it is not possible to conduct a full length test, information on the aquifer characteristics can be obtained by two-hour step-drawdown tests; the rate of pumping being increased after each 2-hour period.

Acidisation.—In Chalk or other limestone strata, where the borehole is sited in considerable depth and area of limestone, acid treatment may increase the yield substantially. For boreholes over 635 mm diameter, 30–50 tonnes of hydrochloric acid are injected at those parts of the borehole which appear most promising.

(These are detected at the time of drilling, or by a resistivity test on the borehole.) If the water is sufficiently clear, the strata can be inspected by the borehole camera. The acid is injected in a sealed tube under pressure for 2 or 3 hours, and after use must be disposed of under control, to avoid toxic effluents affecting vegetation, fish, water supply, etc. The process is not expensive, but due to hazards it must be handled by experts (see Bibliography).

Quality.—At least two analyses, both chemical and bacteriological, should be taken during a 14-day test and the analyst's attention should be called especially to the fact that it is a new source of supply he is investigating, and that the samples should be examined especially for plumbo-solvency, excess iron, CO_2, pH, alkalinity, and in some cases fluorine, as well as the routine examination (see 'Treatment').

Economic Diameter of Pumping Main for 16–24 Hours Pumping Daily.—The nominal bore (mm) is shown in brackets, following various rates of flow in litre/hour. The approximate flow velocity is one metre/sec: 30,000 (150); 50,000 (200); 100,000 (250); 170,000 (300); 220,000 (350); 300,000 (400); 480,000 (500); 680,000 (600); 900,000 (700). These relationships take into account the estimated annual costs of the pumping main, electrically-driven plant and building, including loan repayment and operating costs. However if a source is only used intermittently (eg in conjunction with a river source), a higher flow velocity of 1·5 m/s may be accepted with consequent reduction in pipe size for a given flow.

RAINFALL

1 mm of rain on 1 hectare = 10,000 litres, or 10 cubic metres.

The first known rainfall record in the British Isles was made at Townley near Burnley from 1677 to 1703 and, by the year 1788, simultaneous records were only ten in number. In 1854 the Meteorological Department of the Board of Trade was established. In 1861 G. J. Symons obtained about 500 records and did much to encourage the taking of observations to be made under standard conditions. The British Association furthered the work by making grants and encouraged the use of standard instruments. In 1900 Dr Mill became Director of the British Rainfall Organisation which included 3,500 observers, with observations being coordinated by Carl Salter, Dr J. Glasspoole, and E. G. Bilham. Since 1919 the Organisation has been part of the Meteorological Office.

***'British Rainfall'* was published annually from 1861 until 1970 and gave the monthly rainfall, maximum day's** rainfall and average annual rainfalls of about 5,000 listed stations. Additional informaition and maps were provided but this information can now be obtained directly from the Meteorological Office at Bracknell, which provides a full hydrometeorological advisory service. For a stated area in the British Isles, records of average monthly, annual and seasonal rainfalls can be supplied, together with estimates of evaporation, percolation and potential evapotranspiration for most areas. Typical overall figures for rainfall are given in Table 5.

TABLE 5.—AVERAGE ANNUAL RAINFALL 1916–1950 (MILLIMETRES).

	England	Wales	England & Wales	Scotland	Great Britain
January	83	149	92	154	112
February	60	105	66	106	80
March	52	85	57	89	68
April	57	82	60	88	70
May	59	86	64	87	72
June	52	79	55	87	66
July	75	106	79	114	92
August	75	116	81	122	95
September	69	114	76	128	93
October	83	148	92	158	114
November	88	145	95	143	113
December	79	142	88	143	106
Year	832	1,357	904	1,419	1,081
Winter (Oct./Mar.)	444	774	490	793	592
Summer (Apr./Sept.)	388	583	414	626	489

AVERAGE ANNUAL RAINFALL.—The average annual rainfall of the British Isles ranges from about 5,000 mm (Snowdon) to about 500 mm (Essex). For all practical purposes it has been found that the long average annual rainfall can be taken as the average rainfall over a period of 35 years, although the standard period at present used (1916–1950) showed a slight increase over the earlier 1881–1915 period. Percentage deviations for shorter periods vary from 50% for 1 year to 16% for 5 years, 8% for 10 years and 5% for 15 years, the deviation at 35 years being 1·5%.

Average annual rainfall for Great Britain during the period 1916–1950 was 1,081 mm; for England it was 832 mm, for Wales 1,357 mm, and for Scotland 1,419 mm. About 55% of the total rainfall occurred during the winter half-years (October–March).

AVERAGE NUMBER OF WET AND DRY SPELLS.—The periods for the rainfall, as defined by the British Rainfall Organisation, are of 24 hours which usually begin at 9 am, viz: *Rain day* = Over 0·2 mm per 24 hours. *Wet day* = Over 1·0 mm per 24 hours. *Absolute drought* = Under 0·2 mm on every day of 24 hours for periods longer than 29 consecutive days. *Partial drought* = Under 0·2 mm average per 24 hours for periods longer than 15 consecutive days. *Dry spell* = Under 1·0 mm on every day of 24 hours for longer than 15 days. *Rain spell* = Over 0·2 mm on every day of 24 hours for periods longer than 15 consecutive days. *Wet spell* = Over 1·0 mm on every day of 24 hours for periods londer than 15 days.

MINIMUM RAINFALL.—The incidence of the rainfall varies from place to place, thus in 1887 East Kent had a rainfall of 90% of the average for the district, whereas in 1921, it was only 50% of the average. In 1887 the rainfall in North Wales was 70% of the average for the district, whereas in 1921 it was 90% of the average. Droughts which covered a large part of the British Isles took place in the years 1887, 1921, 1932, 1933, 1934, 1943, 1944, 1949, 1959 and 1976. The minimum rainfall which occurred was under 50% of the average in East Kent. Rainfall under 50% of the average was recorded in East Kent during the year 1921, and in parts of the Midlands and south west England during the 16 month period May 1975–August 1976. In most of the south-eastern counties some 50% of the average annual rainfall has been recorded as a minimum. In the Midlands, south west England, south and eastern Ireland, and east Scotland, is recorded 60–70% of the average. Elsewhere the minimum rainfall is about 70–80% of the average, ie in Wales, northern England, and the greater part of Scotland and Northern Ireland.

Minimum Rainfall of Consecutive Months.—Anxiety may be caused by prolonged droughts, and many records are available of the amount of rainfall to be expected in periods of maximum drought. For example, from 40 stations in the British Isles, (England 15; Wales 5; Scotland 11; Ireland 9); some 62% of the average annual rainfall occurred during a drought of 12 months. This percentage is higher than that to be expected at many *individual* stations, for example, in 1921, East Kent had only 47% of its average annual rainfall, while the driest year in the British Isles, generally, had 62% of the average annual rainfall. The driest consecutive two years had 75·5% of the average and the three driest consecutive years had 81·5% of the average.

For minimum annual rainfall estimates; therefore, although 62% may suffice in many places in Britain, it may be prudent to adopt 50% of the average annual rainfall for some localities. For the driest two consecutive years 75% of the average annual rainfall for each of the two years, and for the driest three consecutive years 80% of the average annual rainfall for each of the three years may be taken.

MAXIMUM RAINFALL.—The wettest individual year recorded to date was that of 1872 when the rainfall over England and Wales as a whole was 1,295 mm, nearly twice the very dry year of 1887. For some individual localities the wettest year may be much more than 154% of the average (the average of 40 stations), for at some stations more than 3 times (300%) of the average has been recorded.

It is, however, the maximum rainfall of a few *hours* duration which determines the magnitude of floods, and the following data have been recorded: 239 mm in 24 hours; 89 mm in 1 hour; 75 mm in 45 min; 74 mm in 30 min; and 38 mm in 15 mins. Dr Glasspoole gives the following for catastrophic storms: 102 mm in 1 hour; 132 mm in 2 hours; and 178 mm in 7 hours.

Localities of Intense Daily Rainfall.—Actual records show many local areas of intense rainfall including figures of 150–230 mm per day, but readings of individual rain gauges, however interesting, do not indicate the area of land upon which such maximum intensities of rainfall may fall. Hence some estimate has been made of some heavy single falls over large areas, viz: London, whole area, 64 mm in 24 hours; Lake District (1,850 km^2) 143 mm; Eastern Ireland (3,000 km^2) 121 mm (single fall in less than 3 days).

In the south of England storm of June, 1917, the falls and areas covered were: more than 230 mm on 5 km^2; 203 mm on 34 km^2; 178 mm on 75 km^2; 152 mm on 220 km^2; 127 mm on 745 km^2; and 102 mm on 2,095 km^2. The storm lasted from 2¼–20 hours, and is classed as a 16-hour storm. For average conditions (Glasspoole) the amount of the maximum rainfall is reduced to 90% for an area of 3,000 hectares (ha); 80% for about 6,000 ha, and 70% for about 12,000 ha.

RAIN GAUGES.—The standard rain gauge for measuring daily flows consists of a 130 mm collecting tank 115 mm deep, with a brass bevelled rim. This tank has a funnel or hopper bottom with a small pipe leading into a copper receiver 300 mm deep, half buried in the ground within an outer casing which mitigates freezing. The lip of the gauge is 300 mm above the ground. A glass bottle may be inserted in the copper receiver to facilitate pouring into the graduated glass measuring gauges. There are several different types which are chiefly concerned with the capacities of the containers suitable for wet localities. In addition, there are self-recording gauges such as the Dines tilting siphon and other refinements connected therewith such as an electrical heater for melting snow and ice. An electrical translever with data logger can be added to provide a continuous recording on tape or chart so that the movement of storms can be assessed.

DISTRIBUTION OF RAIN GAUGES.—It has been shown, in the USA, that 1 rain gauge per 250 km^2 on a gathering ground of 1,250 km^2 (ie 5 gauges) would give an error of ± 15% on the average rainfall; whereas if there were only 1 gauge the error would be 33%.

EVAPORATION occurs from both water and land surfaces. Measurements have been made from evaporation tanks but these are usually regarded as only a check on theoretical work. Evapotranspiration takes place through vegetation and can be divided into 'potential' and 'actual'. The 'potential' would occur when the soil is saturated and the air temperature, sunshine and wind are contributory. 'Actual' is the 'potential' adjusted by the occasions when the above factors do not lead to full potential evaporation or evapotranspiration.

The first full evaluation of evaporation was carried out by Penman and others, who set out the factors in an equation taking into account incoming shortwave solar radiation, outgoing longwave radiation and the drying power of the air, including the factors of wind speed, saturation vapour pressure and vapour pressure. Other equations have included air temperature including the simplified formula by Thornthwaite which is useful when mean temperatures have been recorded.

Applications of the Penman equation have been programmed using different 'root' constants for different types of land use and can now be applied relatively easily by using a small computer. The concept of 'soil moisture deficit' is used which is defined as the equivalent depth of applied water (ie rainfall or irrigation water) which is needed to restore the soil to field capacity (ie full potential evapotranspiration).

Calculations of soil moisture deficit, with actual land use data and current rainfall data, can be obtained from the Meteorological Office. Root constants used vary from woodlands (200 mm) to grassland (75–25 mm).

INFILTRATION AND PERCOLATION.—Infiltration is the process by which rain enters the soil, and percolation is generally taken as the movement of water downwards through the unsaturated zone of soil into the lower saturated zone. Infiltration rates can be grouped in the following ranges:

TABLE 6.—INFILTRATION RATES FOR ENGLAND AND WALES.

Soil type/classification		Infiltration rate (mm/h)
Sands and gravels	A	8 to 12
Sandy loams	B	4 to 8
Clay loams and silty clays	C	1·5 to 4
Clays	D	<1·5

For percolation in chalk soils, Lapworth derived from empirical data the formula

$$I = 0{\cdot}9\ R - 343\ \text{mm}$$

where I = average annual percolation, R = average annual rainfall. This formula gives realistic results on areas covered by short grass (eg down land) but must not be used where there is clay cover, when alternative formulae approximate to

$$I = 0{\cdot}2\ R - 75\ \text{mm}$$

By calculation of the actual evaporation using the Penman formula it is possible to assess the amount of water percolating to ground water and thus providing recharge. This must be done in the context of an overall water balance taking into account surface water run-off.

RUN-OFF

The intensity and quantity of rainfall are much greater than the resulting flow or run-off in a river. The rain from the hills may take a long time to reach the river, especially if the gathering ground is flat or has much vegetation, or many hedges or walls; some of the rain soaks into the soil and penetrates the underlying rocks and may never enter the river at all. The loss is due to many causes, the chief of which are the geology of the gathering ground, evaporation from the surface of the ground, temperature, size and shape of the gathering ground, elevation of the gathering ground, the valley slope or the thalweg of the stream, formation of ice and artificial drainage and transpiration of plants.

In some cases streams may disappear underground and reappear, wholly or in part, in other surface gathering grounds. In all matters of water supply thorough acquaintance with geological, geographical and meteorological conditions are of paramount importance for the design of any successful scheme. The study of run-off, therefore, is directed specially in three directions:

Average Flow: Storage and Yield of a Reservoir.—The assessment of the average flow of a river is made in order that the necessary capacity of a storage reservoir can be calculated to guarantee a minimum yield for supply and compensation, throughout the driest periods without damaging the ecology of the stream.

Dry Weather Flow: Permissible 'Take' from a River.—The assessment of the minimum flow of a river from which it is proposed to extract water without building storage reservoirs, and hence the assessment of the amount of water which may be safely abstracted without damaging the ecology of the stream.

Flood Flow: Reservoir Overflow Weir Design.—The assessment of the natural maximum flood of a river, which may be expected ever to occur, in order that the overflow works may be designed large enough, but not extravagantly large, to carry such a flood without damaging the embankment or dam. In reservoir construction the study of floods is directed especially to determining the length of overflow weirs. With land drainage and irrigation the study is directed towards the capacities of culverts, channels, and pumping plant to cope with maximum floods.

Storage and Yield from Flow Records.—The quantity of water which has flowed in a stream for the driest period in question (say 1–5 years) must be known. If the daily, weekly or monthly quantities (as the case may be) of water in megalitres or mm of gathering ground are added up and plotted cumulatively as ordinate (vertical) and time (days, weeks, months) as abscissa (horizontal), the slope of the straight line tangential to the humps of the cumulative flow curve will give the *average* yield obtainable, and the longest vertical line between the straight line and flow curve will give the storage necessary to guarantee the average yield.

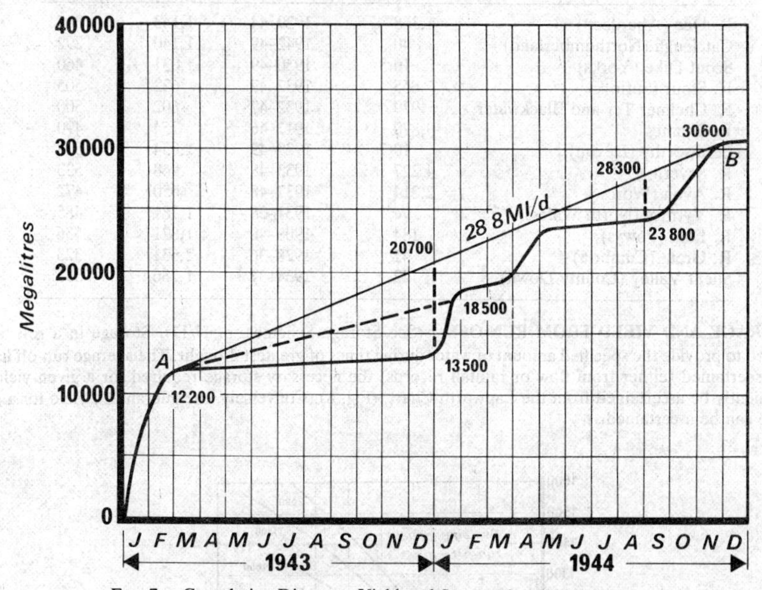

FIG. 7.—Cumulative Diagram: Yield and Storage from Flow Records.

Example.—In the mass diagram (Fig. 7):—(*a*) The wavy line *AB* represents the cumulative runoff during a 24-month dry period. The straight line *AB* represents the average yield which could be obtained during this period, namely 3,0600 − 1,2200 = 1,8400 megalitres (Ml) in 21 months or 639 days (28·8 Ml/d). The storage necessary to maintain this yield is given by the vertical line, 20,700 − 13,500 = 7,200 Ml. (*b*) If, for example, the storage given by the vertical line 28,300 − 23,800 had been taken (4,500 Ml), then the 28·8 Ml/d yield could not have been maintained. (*c*) If only the 4,500 Ml storage were available; to determine the yield for the period 1943–44, set up the 4,500 Ml at points 13,500–18,000 (near end of 1943) and draw the sloping line 1,9000 − 12,200, giving the yield of 6,800 Ml for 335 days, viz 20·3 Ml/d.

Surface Water Year Book of Great Britain.—First published for the water year (October–September) 1935–36, the series up to 1966 gave monthly mean flows and rainfall, together with mean rainfall for the 'standard' period (1881–1915 and later 1916–50), for each station, of which there were initially 28, increasing to 435 by 1965–66. Due to the progress made in computer-archiving of records by the Water Resources Board, the format of the Year Book was changed in the 1966–70 edition, and this was continued by Water Data Unit until 1982, when it was taken over by the Institute of Hydrology and published as 'Hydrological Data; United Kingdom', with a more comprehensive collation of data.

Storage and Yield from Rainfall Records.—The average annual rainfall (R) on a gathering ground can be estimated from data supplied by the Meteorological Office. The average annual evaporation, loss (L), is determined by experience. The average annual 'available rain', or average 'flow', or average 'run-off', is therefore $R - L$. The average run-off in litres per day (l/d) = area in hectares × $(R - L) \times 27{\cdot}4$, where R and L are in millimetres.

Estimation of Catchment Losses.—Penman obtained estimates of losses by deducting long-term averages of run-off from rainfall, for about 40 catchment areas. The two kinds of estimate agree and were plotted on a map to show geographical variation of evaporation. Along the South coast of England, Essex, the lower Thames and Severn valleys, and South-west Ireland, the annual average evaporation loss is about 500 mm. In South-east and South-west England and Wales the loss is about 480 mm; in the Midlands, East Anglia and

West Ireland, about 430 mm; in Northern England, Scotland and Eastern Ireland, about 370 mm. For particular catchment areas, Penman gives the following figures for average rainfall and losses.

TABLE 7.—AVERAGE RAINFALL AND LOSSES.

Locality	Area km²	Period	Rainfall mm	Loss mm
R. Dee (Aberdeen)	1,368	1929–44	1,143	305
Catcleugh (Northumberland)	40	1942–49	1,140	292
Scout Dike (Yorks)	10·5	1930–49	1,031	460
R. Stour (Suffolk)	855	1932–47	622	505
R. Chelmer Ter and Blackwater	979	1932–47	602	500
R. Thames	9,870	1917–46	754	490
Fernworthy (Devon)	10·7	1929–49	1,854	528
R. Severn	4,227	1933–48	968	533
R. Avon (Worcs.)	2,214	1937–48	650	472
R. Vyrnwy (North Wales)	94	1931–38	1,781	485
R. Elan (Powys)	184	1908–48	1,821	536
R. Greta (Cumbria)	41	1928–36	2,631	323
Silent Valley (County Down)	22	1934–37	1,786	351

STORAGE AND YIELD FROM RUN-OFF.—(See Storage Schemes, p. I7/13). Storage in a reservoir is designed to provide the specified amount of water during times of greatest drought. The average run-off having been ascertained (either from flow or rainfall records) the necessary storage required for a given yield can conveniently be ascertained from the Lapworth Chart, (Fig. 8). Conversely, the guaranteed yield for a given storage can be ascertained.

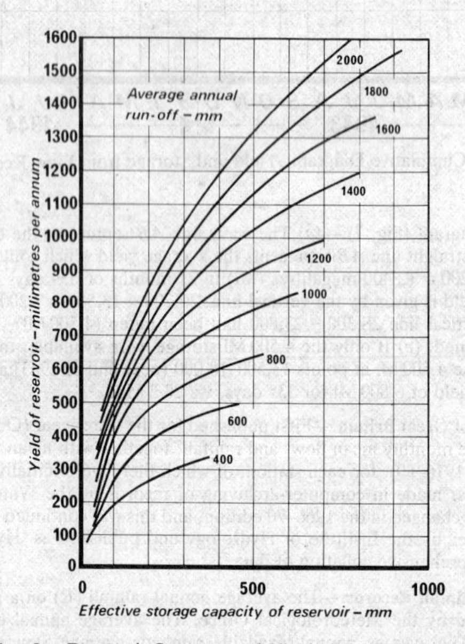

FIG. 8.—Reservoir Storages and Yields for different Run-offs.

LAPWORTH CHART.—Figure 8 shows a series of curved lines representing various average annual run-offs from various gathering grounds, expressed in millimeters. (See 'Manual of British Water Engineering Practice'. Chart A. Institute of Water Engineers.) From the curved lines on the Chart of run-off, the storage or capacities of reservoirs are given in millimeters at the base of the Chart and the reliable yields in mm per annum as ordinates.

To convert millimetres of storage, from the chart into litres and millimetres per annum of yield, into litres per day, proceed as follows:—

FOR STORAGE.—Litres—Storage in mm × catchment area in hectares × 10,000.

FOR YIELD.—Litres per day—Yield in mm × catchment area in hectares × 27·40.

Example of Use of Chart.—For four alternative schemes with a run-off of 762 mm (30 in) per annum, from a gathering ground of 2,000 hectares (5,000 acres).

Consider, *storages* of 500, 375, 250, and 125 mm, and *annual yields* of 600, 560, 500 and 375 mm. Tables 8A and 8B refer. The *constants* are headed *K* in the two tables and are defined as follows:

10,000 = Litres per hectare per annum with one millimetre depth of water.

27·4 = Litres per hectare per day with 1 mm depth of water per annum.

Table 8C shows the storage and yield for the run-offs shown in Fig. 8, and also some values in addition to those on Fig. 8. The latter may be useful for unusual or uneconomic schemes.

TABLE 8A.—FOR STORAGE.

mm	Area ha	*K* (constant)	Litres × 10^6
500	2,000	10,000	10,000
375	2,000	10,000	7,500
250	2,000	10,000	5,000
125	2,000	10,000	2,500

TABLE 8B.—FOR YIELD.

mm	Area ha	*K* (constant)	Litres/day × 10^6
600	2,000	27·4	32·9
560	2,000	27·4	30·1
500	2,000	27·4	27·4
375	2,000	27·4	20·6

TABLE 8C.—YIELD OF RESERVOIR (mm).

Run off	Storage—mm					
mm	125	250	375	500	625	750
250	125	185	225	250	—	—
500	260	350	400	450	500	—
750	375	490	560	610	660	700
1,000	460	610	710	775	825	885
1,250	525	725	845	925	1,000	1,060
1,500	575	805	965	1,085	1,175	1,250
1,750	625	875	1,070	1,210	1,325	1,425
2,000	675	955	1,150	1,325	1,450	1,575

Typical Storage and Yield for varying Run-offs during the Three Driest Consecutive Years.—For economy, it is possible to provide storage to utilise only a proportion of the run-off, usually between 60 and 80%, because otherwise the reservoir would have to be large enough to equalise the run-off of several consecutive years. For many years therefore it has been the practice to design reservoirs to 'balance' the rain for the three driest consecutive years, and even when considering a river regulation scheme, it is useful to know the potential storage and yield that may be possible, if the available run-off from a catchment is known.

MINIMUM FLOW.—The dry weather flow is particularly important for river schemes when the water is to be abstracted without storage. Dry weather flows vary from 0·3 litre/s km^2 for large catchments (with small catchments, of course, dry weather flow may be nil). In certain Sussex rivers the dry weather flow may be

0·3–0·7 litre/s km^2; in Hampshire rivers on Chalk supplied from springs, 7 litre/s km^2; in Cumbria rivers, up to 3·5 litre/s km^2; in Cornish rivers, up to 3 litre/s km^2; Thames, 1·5 litre/s km^2. The period of dry weather flow may be over a short period such as an hour or a day, but the average flow during the driest week is often taken as a reasonable period in waterworks practice.

Water Available from River.—There is no recognised proportion of the lowest flow of a river which may be taken for water supply; every case being treated on its own merits. The above examples (approximate) show wide variation of the proportion of dry weather flow abstracted where little or no storage (ie under a weeks supply) is available.

Many places take or are empowered to take practically the whole of the dry weather flow; eg Shrewsbury (Severn 490 Ml/d); Reading (Kennet 40 Ml/d); Irvine WB (Garnoch 18 Ml/d); Southend (Blackwater 20 Ml/d); Chelmer 9 Ml/d; Ter, 1·8 Ml/d.

COMPENSATION WATER.—Before the 1963 Water Resources Act, this was generally a matter of negotiation between interested persons, ie between the water works promoters and the river boards and riparian and industrial users of the water in the stream for a distance of 30 km below the point of abstraction. Very commonly the maximum allowance is one-third of the run-off of the three driest consecutive years, irrespective of whether the reservoir is designed to yield more or less than the yield of the three driest consecutive years. The amount of compensation water is also often fixed at 1/4, 1/5 or 1/6 of the designed yield of the reservoir in question. In later years the concept of 'compensation water' was supplemented as a criterion, by that of minimum acceptable flow in a river, and releases from storage were not necessarily at a fixed rate, as previously.

TABLE 9.—PERCENTAGE TAKEN FROM RIVERS FOR SUPPLY

Locality		Dry weather approx flow Ml/d	Authorised amount taken Ml/d	Dry weather flow % taken	Remarks
River	Place				
Severn	Upton-on-Severn	730	45	6·2	
Severn	Tewkesbury	730	55	7·5	
Thames	Eynsham (Oxon)	320	32	10	
Dee	Aberdeen	564	68	12	
Itchen	Otterbourne (Hants)	273	45	16·5	
Exe	Exeter	84	25	29	
Duddon	For Barrow	33	14	42	
Tees	For Tees Valley	86	39	45	
Stour	For Bournemouth	64	32	50	
Newlyn	Near Penzance	3	1·5	50	
Thames	For London	1,580	809	51	Storage
Avon	Coventry	13	7	54	
Stour	For South Essex	45	27	60	Storage
Lea	For London	124	101	82	Storage

PEAK DESIGN FLOWS.—The 1975 Flood Studies Report contains the result of over 10 years study of floods, and is now used as the basis for considering most flooding problems. It introduced the concepts of PMP (Probable Maximum Precipitation) and PMF (Probable Maximum Flood). PMP is the theoretical greatest depth of precipitation (ie rain, sleet, snow and hail) for a given duration meteorologically possible for a given basin at a particular time. The flood hydrograph resulting from PMP is called the PMF.

In the ICE Guide to Floods and Reservoir Safety (1978) it is recommended that the PMF should only be used in considering flood inflows to reservoirs where a failure would endanger lives in a community. This situation would be combined with a full reservoir and a maximum hourly wind speed of once in ten years. This and other categories are defined in Table 10.

It should be noted that the decision on Dam Category can only be taken by an Engineer appointed as a member of Panels of Engineers under the Reservoirs (Safety Provisions) Act, 1930 or Reservoirs Act 1975. The Reservoir Panel Engineer will also assess the effect of flood routing through the reservoir, the capacity of the spillway and the amount of freeboard available to prevent a dam over topping.

Typical curves have been prepared to assist in obtaining an approximate estimate of the PMF for an undulating impermeable reservoired catchment. For other types of terrain: add 15% for mountainous areas: add 5% for hilly areas: deduct 5% for flat areas. Some figures derived from these curves are shown in Table 11 below to indicate the range of requirements. The catchment area is the area which drains to the reservoir or point on the river. RSMD is an index defined as the one day rainfall of 5 year return period less effective mean soil moisture deficit. Tables of this are available in the Flood Studies Report indicating a variation from 25 to 35 in the Midlands and South East, up to 70 in the Lake District, Wales, the South West and West Ireland; and up to 90 in the Scottish Highlands. Some reduction on the flood peak figures will be obtained by reservoir routing.

TABLE 10.—DAM CATEGORIES OF FLOOD INFLOWS

Category	Initial Reservoir Condition	Dam Flood Inflow General Standard	Wind Speed	Minimum Wave Surcharge
A. Lives in a community endanged	Spilling	PMF	1-in-10 yr max: hour	0.6m
B. Extensive damages or lives not in a community	Just Full	0·5 PMF or 10,000 yr flood	1-in-10 yr max: hour	0·6m
C. Negligible risk and little damage	Just Full	0·3 PMF or 1,000 yr flood	Average annual max: hour	0·4m
D. Special case. No loss of life foreseen. Limited damage	Spilling	0·2 PMF or 150 yr flood	Average annual max: hour	0·3m

TABLE 11.—APPROXIMATE PMF SETTING

Catchment Area (km^2)	RSMD (mm)	PMF Peak Flow cumecs per sq km
1	25	9·2
	40	14·5
	70	26·0
5	25	6·5
	50	13·5
	75	20·5
	100	27·5
10	25	5·7
	50	11·5
	75	17·7
	100	23·6
50	25	4·1
	50	8·4
	75	12·9
	100	17·2

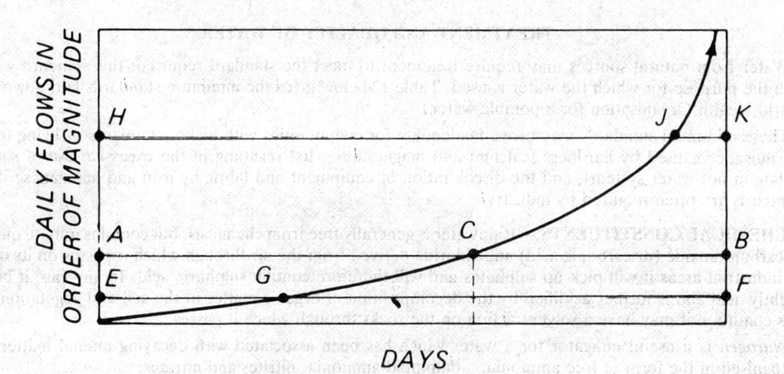

FIG. 9.—Duration Hydrograph.

HYDROGRAPHS OF STREAMS.—A natural hydrograph is defined as a graph showing the direct relationship between flow and time.

Duration Hydrograph.—If, for example, the daily flows of a river are plotted in *order of magnitude*, a duration curve is obtained:—Fig. 9. From such a curve the following data are at once apparent. The average daily flow of the stream, being the sum of all the flows ÷ 365 can be drawn by the horizontal line *ACB*.

(1) Hence *AC* is the number of days in the year when the flow is below the average.

(2) Where compensation water of a known value is given the line *EGF* can be drawn, *EG* being the number of days when the stream flow is less.

(3) When flood damage occurs at the value *H*, the horizontal line *HJK* can be drawn and *JK* will give the number of days on which flooding occurs.

(4) As the average flow is represented by the line *AB*, the area under the straight line AB represents the total annual flow of the stream and the stream has flowed for *AC* days at less than the average. The ratio of the total flow of the stream to the average flow of the stream for the period (*AC*) has been defined as the *characteristic* of the stream.

Summation Hydrograph.—If the daily flows of a river are placed in order and added, cumulatively, a summation curve is obtained. See Fig. 10. This curve readily gives:—(1) Total annual flow (ordinate at *F*). (2) Total annual compensation (ordinate *C*). (3) Total flow *y* for *x* days. (4) Total compensation *y* for *x* days. (5) Number of days (300) to supply compensation water. (6) Number of days flow less than compensation water (from *L*). (7) If *PT* is parallel to *OF*, *PN* is the sum of all flows below average daily flow. (8) Ratio *MN*/*MP* is a measure of how far river departs from the ideal. Hydrographs are particularly useful in the estimate of quantities which may be taken from a river for storage reservoirs in pumped storage schemes for water supply and hydro-electric work.

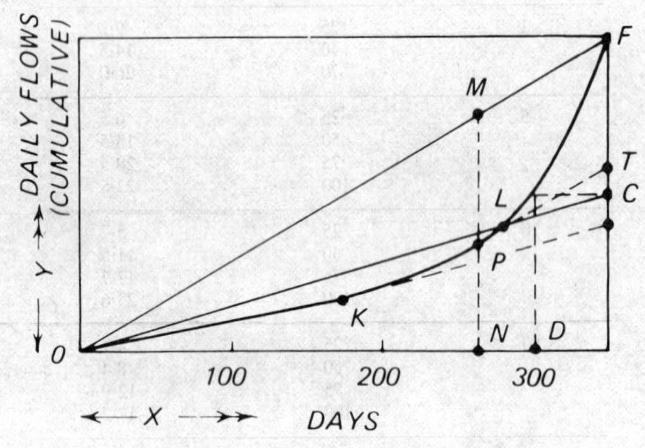

FIG. 10.—Summation Hydrograph.

TREATMENT AND QUALITY OF WATER

Water from natural sources may require treatment to meet the standard required; this standard will vary with the purpose for which the water is used. Table 12 below gives the minimum standards laid down by the World Health Organisation for a potable water.

These minimum standards may prove inadequate for communities with higher standards of living to avoid the nuisance caused by hardness (calcium and magnesium salts) resulting in the excessive use of soap and scaling in hot water systems, and the discoloration of equipment and fabric by iron and manganese. Special standards are often required by industry.

CHEMICAL CONSTITUENTS.—Rainwater is generally free from chemicals, but contains minute quantities of carbon dioxide (or carbonic acid) and chloride derived from the air through which it passes on its descent. In industrial areas it will pick up sulphates and will therefore contain sulphuric acid. In any case it becomes slightly acid and is further acidified by the decomposition of organic matter in the soil and vegetation and in this condition it may have a solvent action on the rocks through which it passes.

Nitrogen is a useful indicator for a water which has been associated with decaying animal matter and is recognised in the form of free ammonia, albuminoid ammonia, nitrites and nitrates.

Free Ammonia (ie freed when the water is distilled) should not exceed 0·03 mg/l from springs or shallow

TABLE 12.—INTERNATIONAL STANDARDS FOR DRINKING WATER

	Permissible mg/l	Excessive mg/l		Permissible mg/l	Excessive mg/l
Total solids	500	1,500	Chloride (Cl)	200	600
Colour (Hazen)	4	50	pH Range	7·0/8·5	6·5/9·2
Turbidity (SiO_2 Scale)	5	25	$MgSO_4 + Na_2SO_4$	500	1,000
Iron (Fe)	0·3	1·0	Phenols (as C_6H_3CH)	0·001	0·002
Manganese (Mn)	0·1	0·5	Lead (Pb)	0·1 max	max allowable
Copper (Cu)	1·0	1·5	Selenium (Se)	0·05 max	max allowable
Zinc (Zn)	5·0	15·0	Arsenic (As)	0·2 max	max allowable
Calcium (as $CaCO_3$)	187·5	500·0	Chromium (Cr)	0·05 max	max allowable
Magnesium (as $MgCO_3$)	208·3	625·0	Cyanide (CN)	0·01 max	max allowable
Sulphate (SO_4)	200	400	Fluoride	0·5/1·0	1·5

wells, or sewage contamination is indicated. *Albuminoid ammonia* (result of distilling water with potassium permanganate). Not more than 0·05 mg/l is very pure, but exceeding 0·15 mg/l is probably unfit. *Nitrites* indicate recent sewage contamination if they exceed 3·0 mg/l. *Nitrates*.—Water is considered pure with 5·0 mg/l, but impure with 20 mg/l.

Oxygen Deficiency.—Ground water drawn directly from boreholes often contains no oxygen. This does not indicate pollution, but aeration will be necessary to precipitate iron and manganese if these are present in solution. *Biochemical oxygen demand* (BOD) is used to classify rivers. Very clean, being 1 mg/l of oxygen absorbed, and bad, over 5 mg/l absorbed.

Chlorine.—About 20 mg/l is usual in Chalk water supplies on the outcrop. Sodium chloride is common but other chlorides are rare. *Fluorine*.—Natural waters contain 0–10 mg/l and it is desirable to have a fluorine content of 0·5–1·0 mg/l. *Iodine*.—Natural waters contain 0–5 mg/l, it is desirable that all waters should have over 3·0 mg/l. *Sodium* is rare by comparison with Calcium, but is found in some Chalk waters combined with chlorine. The chloride, carbonate, sulphate and nitrate occur in water; the nitrate in small quantities. *Magnesium* is rare in Chalk waters, but common in Coal and Limestone districts. It has marked corrosive properties. *Potassium* is rare in water supplies, the effect of its salts are similar to Sodium. *Calcium*.—A very common substance and the main source of hardness of water.

Silicon natural waters may contain 10–30 mg/l of silica (SiO_2). Excess may cause deposits of metals in steam installations. *Phosphorus* and phosphates are found in some natural waters, but are of little significance. *Iron* is common in underground waters; if over 0·3 mg/l it has to be removed or it is liable to mould linen, produce an inky taste and discolour tea. *Manganese* is often associated with iron, and may have to be removed if over 0·1 mg/l. Together they should not exceed 0·3 mg/l for similar reasons.

Aluminium occurs only in small quantities as a sulphate. It does not appear to be objectionable in hot water systems. An excessive amount would be over 30 mg/l. *Zinc*.—Remarks are as for Aluminium, innocuous up to 15 mg/l. *Lead* rarely occurs in natural waters, but if over 0·1 mg/l it should be removed. Soft and acid water, or water with a deficiency of silica can absorb lead at 30 mg/l per min (a lethal dose). *Arsenic* appears in some places in nature; below 0·1 mg/l appears to be innocuous. *Mineralised waters* are generally unsuitable for public supply.

HARDNESS.—Hardness is due to the presence of salts of Magnesium and Calcium, which react with soap and inhibit the formation of a lather. It is expressed as the equivalent of Calcium Carbonate.

The Total Hardness is the sum of the amounts of Calcium and Magnesium present in solution. This is divided into Carbonate Hardness and Non-carbonate Hardness, depending on whether or not the Calcium or the Magnesium is combined with one of the stronger acids to form a sulphate or chloride.

The Carbonate Hardness can be largely deposited by boiling the water and so driving off the loosely combined CO_2. For this reason the Carbonate Hardness is sometimes referred to as Temporary Hardness.

Carbonate Hardness is the main cause of deposits in hot water systems. Non-carbonate Hardness, precipitated by concentration, can be a major source of trouble in steam-raising installations.

ACIDITY.—The acidity of water is often expressed as the equivalent alkalinity necessary to raise the pH to 8·3 At this pH all but a trace of CO_2 is eliminated. If the pH is less than 4·2 free mineral acid is present. Between these two limits 8·3 and 4·2 the pH is largely determined by the ratio of the alkalinity, ie combined CO_2 and the acidity, ie the free CO_2 present.

While a pure distilled water with no free CO_2 present has a pH of 7, the pH of a natural water which is neither corrosive nor scale forming when in contact with a metal surface, is referred to as the 'pHs' of that water. The pHs is a function of the alkalinity and the calcium present in solution in the water. If the actual pH differs from the pHs, the difference is referred to as the saturation index. A negative index indicates a corrosive water and a positive index indicates a water which will deposit calcium carbonate. The pH value is a measure of the hydrogen in concentration (H^+) and is measured approximately by the colour developed by suitable indicating solutions or, more accurately, by potentiometric means using suitable electrodes. Electrical conductivity is used as an approximate measure of the total dissolved salts.

$$pH = \log (1/(H^+))$$

PHYSICAL IMPURITIES.—*Turbidity*, which indicates the presence of suspended matter in the water, is measured by visual or photometric comparison of a sample with a suspension of colloidal silica. It is expressed as ppm of silica. *Suspended Matter* is measured directly by a gravimetric technique. It does not correspond with turbidity measurement which is affected by the particle size of the matter present.

Colour in natural water is caused by a colloidal suspension of humic or fluvic acid and is measured by visual or photometric comparison of a sample with a solution of platinic chloride. It is expressed as ppm of platinum and is often known as the 'Hazen' Scale. *Taste and Odour* are observed directly. The degree is sometimes expressed as the *Threshold* value, ie the number of dilutions with taste and odour free water, which makes the taste or odour only just detectable. Salt can be detected by most people at 800 ppm. See also 'Acidity'.

BIOLOGICAL IMPURITIES.—These are defined as organisms which grow in water and whose presence is objectionable. Pathogenic bacteria are dealt with separately. For biological growth to occur the water must contain the food to support the growth and the environment must be suitable for the organism to flourish. The elements essential for plant growth are carbon, nitrogen, oxygen, calcium, silica and phosphorous, which must be present in a suitable form. In general therefore the more dissolved salts present in the water the more readily will growths occur. The conditions necessary for growth are warmth, generally the higher the temperature the more vigorous the growth, and, in the majority of cases, light.

The larger plants, *water weeds*, attach themselves to the bottom and sides of reservoirs and obtain part of their food through roots embedded in the silt. Smaller organisms which are freely suspended in the water are referred to as *plankton*. If the organism tends to form slimy layers on surfaces, they are referred to as *sessile*. These in turn can form part of one of the following groups:—*Algae* which are basically plants and occur as '*green*', '*yellow-green*' or '*blue-green*' *algae* or as *diatoms* which feed mainly on inorganic matter in solution. *Protozoa* which can be classed as animals, and include *Amoeba*, feed on organic matter including bacteria. *Rotifera* which are classed as animals. *Crustacea* which include the water fleas (Daphnia) and the *Cyclops*. *Polyzoa* which grow on underwater surfaces including pipes.

The troubles caused by micro-organisms in water are numerous. Their presence in numbers can impart colour and turbidity, they can produce objectionable tastes and odours, they can block filters. On the other hand they can have a good effect and contribute considerably to the natural purification of contaminated water. Extensive growths of algae, by removing carbon dioxide can soften a water and, by consuming nitrates improve the quality. Protozoa can materially reduce the bacterial population.

Drastic growths of algae and other micro-organisms are generally seasonal and often associated with the spring and autumn 'turnover' of reservoirs when nutrients, normally confined to the bottom, are brought to the top where light and oxygen are present. The increasing use of fertilizers on the fields, which can be washed out into the streams and rivers, contributes to the more abundant growths.

The growth of algae can be partially controlled in raw water reservoirs by the use of *copper sulphate* in doses varying from 0·5 to 1·0 mg/l but trout can be killed by doses of 0·2 mg/l. *Chlorine* can be used to inhibit growths in treatment plants and clear water reservoirs, but it should be used with caution where they occur upstream of the plant as dead growths may be even more of a nuisance. Raw water reservoirs are often stocked with *fish*, usually trout, as they will control the growth of the micro-organism while not being themselves objectionable.

BACTERIAL IMPURITIES.—Bacteria are small, of the order of 1 μm (1/1,000 mm). They may be classed as *Bacilli* (rod shaped), *cocci* (spherical), or *spirillum* (spiral).

The bacteria which are of concern are the pathogenic (harmful) bacteria which are not native to water and are introduced by animal or human contamination. It is assumed therefore that if a group of bacteria known to be present in all human and animal excreta is found in the water then the water must be regarded as suspect, even though that bacteria is itself relatively harmless. Such a group is the *Coli-aerogenes* group, and a standard routine method has been developed to enable the presence of these bacteria to be detected. The normal requirement for a potable water supply is the absence of *E. Coli* in 100 ml.

WATER-BORNE DISEASES.—In certain areas of the tropics, outbreaks of typhoid, cholera, dysentery, paratyphoid, etc are liable to occur due to contamination and pollution of water supplies, or to flies, contaminated food and lack of sanitation. In Britain these diseases are either unknown or of rare occurrence, and are seldom waterborne. Inadequately purified swimming pool water can carry infections of ears, eyes and nose. *E. Coli*.—Water containing this hardy germ does not seem to produce death, but it may aggravate the condition patients who are suffering from colon infections, for whom even tap water is forbidden. This is an 'Indicate organism' for testing the quality of water because it is hardier than most germs. Paradoxically the pathogenic germ cannot live long in polluted water and this is why swimming in rivers, etc, is generally safe. The term *E. Coli* stands for *Escherichia Coli* which is the main bacterium in the excreta of animals. For the general protective treatment by the addition of Chlorine or Ozone, see 'Disinfection', page I7/31.

Lead Poisoning.—Certain soft and acid water passing through lead pipes can dissolve 30 mg/l of lead in

30 seconds. Lead poisoning can be brought about by consuming between 0·75–1·5 mg/l regularly. Under 0·1 mg/l is considered safe. For the inhibition of lead see Acidity, p. I7/27, and precipitation and kindred processes, p. I7/29.

Iron.—Certain natural waters (but not from public supplies, from which the iron is eliminated or reduced) may be detrimental to those with excessive blood pressure. A usual way for eliminating iron is by cascading or by Zeolite under pressure in containers.

Calcium deficiency.—Most upland waters are soft because most British gathering grounds are in 'Upland' areas composed of geological formations which do not give up lime readily. Moreover, such areas are often covered very largely with peat and other vegetation which acidify the water. On the other hand, many surface waters, particularly in 'Lowland' areas, contain high percentages of calcium because the gathering grounds are composed of chalky boulder clay.

Dental Caries.—Where the fluorine in water is less than 0·5–1·0 mg/l dental decay may occur; where the water contains more than 1·5 and up to 5·5 mg/l, mottling of teeth is caused. Doses in excess of 6 mg/l may cause decay and other problems but the connections are not well established. Many waters are slightly deficient in fluorine and a few plants have been installed in the UK. The cheapest chemical for fluoridating water is solid crystalline sodium silico-fluoride (Na_2SiF_6). Where water contains an excess of fluoride (over 1.5 mg/l) it is possible to reduce the fluoride by passing the water through activated alumina. The process is expensive and the most practical method is to add water from another source containing a lower percentage of fluoride.

Frequency of Bacteriological Analysis.—No rules can be laid down as each case must be treated on its own merits. For waterworks purposes river water analyses may be taken once a day (or more frequently in flood time). For impounding sources, analyses may be taken once a week (or daily if circumstances warrant).

For underground waters, a bacteriological examination once a month to once a quarter for deep-seated sources, but from shallower sources, where *E. Coli* has often proved to be present, once a week. The standard of purity of water (Ministry of Health Report No 71), gives the presumptive *Coli-aerogenes* count per 100 ml as follows: Less than 1, highly satisfactory; from 1 to 2, satisfactory; from 3 to 10, suspicious; and greater than 10, unsatisfactory.

WATER TREATMENT PROCESSES

The processes necessary to treat a particular water will be determined by the quality of the raw water and the required standard of the treated water. A variety of combinations of the processes available are therefore used, and there follows a brief description of the most often used processes and their main purpose.

Screening (Coarse).—This can consist of a bar screen to retain large debris at a river intake, followed by a power driven band or rotary screen with water jets for continuously flushing the debris removed into a conduit discharging to waste.

Microstraining.—This is a development from the rotary screen having a finely woven mesh which retains all but the finest plankton in the raw water. Microstrainers are used where micro-organisms are expected to be a particular problem.

PRECIPITATION.—This is the process of converting impurities which are in solution or colloidal suspension into insoluble particles, which can be subsequently removed. The commonest form of precipitation used is coagulation with *aluminium sulphate* or *chlorinated ferrous sulphate*. These coagulants are acid salts which react with alkalinity in the water to precipitate iron or aluminium hydroxide as a gelatinous particle, referred to as floc, which in turn absorbs the colour or finely divided turbidity present. Coagulant aids such as *activated silica*, or one of the *polyelectrolytes*, are sometimes used to produce larger and tougher floc particles which settle quickly.

Another example of precipitation is the lime-soda softening reaction. Lime is added to precipitate the carbonate hardness, ie bicarbonates of calcium and magnesium. The calcium is precipitated as calcium carbonate while the magnesium is precipitated as the hydroxide.

$$Ca(OH)_2 + Ca(HCO_3)_2 \rightarrow 2CaCO_3 + H_2O$$

$$2Ca(OH)_2 + Mg(HCO_3)_2 \rightarrow 2CaCO_3 + Mg(OH)_2 + 2H_2O$$

Mixing.—This is the process of rapid dispersion of the added chemicals in the water preferably in the presence of performed precipitate. Power driven impellers or jets are normally used although mixing downstream of a weir may give adequate turbulence if the variation in flow rate is small.

Flocculation.—This process is a continuation of the mixing process but at much slower speeds, the object being to produce relative movement of the floc particles and so increase the occurrence of collisions which cause the particles to unite to form larger and faster settling floc. Flocculation is only used with a settling tank and is often integral with the tank, eg in a vertical flow tank, where eddy currents in the base produce the flocculating effect. Flocculating times vary from 10 to 30 minutes. A new method incorporating magnetite as a flocculent, which is then attracted to the base by magnetic attraction shows considerable promise in certain applications with colour problems. The magnetite is then recovered from the sludge by a complicated process and recycled into treatment.

SEDIMENTATION.—This process involves solid/liquid separation using gravity as the separating force. It is necessary as a pretreatment before filtration, where the amount of suspended matter to be removed exceeds 25–50 mg/l. The rating of a particular tank is based on the rate of flow of the water per unit area at the separation zone, and this applies whether the flow is horizontal or vertical. This may be expressed as m^3/hour m^2, or merely as a linear velocity, eg mm/sec. In a well designed tank the flow is evenly divided over the area provided, and is preferably *laminar* (not turbulent).

Rates of flow can vary between 1·2 and 5 m^3/hour m^2 (0·3–1·3 mm/sec) depending on the water to be treated, and the efficiency of the tank.

The method of removal of the separated impurities (sludge) from the tank is important. Many tanks have a concentrating vessel within the tank from which the sludge is withdrawn as a fluid. Others allow the sludge to concentrate on a substantially flat floor and are equipped with power driven scrapers to move the sludge to a point of withdrawal.

Sludge Disposal.—The sludge from the settling tanks is often run direct to lagoons where it is dewatered by drainage and evaporation. If the area required is not available within a distance which would allow the liquid sludge to be piped to the lagoons, then it may be concentrated still further by settlement, with or without the use of a conditioning chemical such as one of the polyelectrolytes, and then dewatered in filter presses.

Lagoons.—The amount of sludge to be disposed of from the sedimentation and filter treatment works varies considerably not only between one river and another but also for seasonal variation in the river itself. Hence it is necessary to make some estimate of the amount of sludge in each individual case, not only to budget for the amount of land required for the lagoons but also to provide for the disposal of the sludge from the lagoons. The quality of all liquid, wash water discharged, from the lagoons is generally subject to the approval of the water authority, although the quantity may be much reduced if the wash water is pumped back to the sedimentation tank. As a rough guide a yield of one Ml/d might need an area of 50 m^2, with another 50 m^2 to allow for emptying and cleaning. Sometimes it is possible to find vacant land, such as a large disused quarry, within a reasonable distance of the works, into which the sludge can be pumped.

FLOTATION/UPWARD FLOW.—Where there are problems related to floating contaminants or algae in the raw water, systems using upward flow skimming and flotation by dissolved air (DAF) are now frequently incorporated as a first stage of treatment. Their particular advantage is the ability to switch the units on or off over a short period, and they also utilise the natural propensity of certain materials to float.

FILTRATION.—The process used in almost all water treatment plants involves granular filters, ie *sand or anthracite* media or a combination of the two. *Slow sand filters* were the original type used in water treatment. Rates of flow were low, of the order of 0·1 $m^3/h/m^2$. After pretreatment rates of up to 0·2 $m^3/h/m^2$ or higher have been used. Apart from the large areas required the major disadvantage of slow sand filters is the cost of labour involved in cleaning the beds but this is offset by negligible material costs in chemicals and fail-safe operation. Small units have been developed for use in rural areas and in undeveloped countries where they can be operated with local unskilled labour without import costs. New developments incorporating filter fabrics should enable *ssf* to be a serious proposition when land is available.

The introduction of *rapid sand filters* became possible because means were provided for cleaning the sand *in situ*. Rates of 5 m^3/h m^2 were normal a few years ago, and with improved methods of pre-treatment now available, rates of up to 10 m^3/h. m^2 are currently used. With these higher rates it is important to control the flow carefully, so as to avoid sudden increases which can cause floc to penetrate through the bed. In general, a filter is as good as the system provided for cleaning it. The major operation in the cleaning process is the *backwash* using clean water to flush the impurities to the surface and away to waste. Before the backwash is applied it is necessary to loosen the bed by some form of agitation, and except in the smallest filters, this is effected by blowing *air* into the bottom of the bed.

The *sand* media often used is graded between 1·2–0·6 mm (BS 14–25 mesh). The depth varies from 60–75 cm. Coarser media can be used effectively in many cases and results in longer filter runs, but the penetration is greater and the safety factor is reduced. This is overcome by using a light coarse media, anthracite, on top of the normal sand which gives the advantage of the coarse media, while the sand provides the safety factor. The lighter *anthracite*, graded between 2·4–1·2 mm (BS 7–14 mesh) remains on top of the bed when backwashed. Dirty washwater from the filter is often discharged to a holding tank and then pumped to the intake if settling tanks are used. Otherwise the washwater is discharged either to a settling tank and thence to lagoons, or direct to lagoons. Where there are taste or odour problems, Granulated Activated Carbon (GAC) can be used as a filter media or added in powered form. This involves higher maintenance and running costs and is seldom justified unless there is a specific problem of taste or removal of toxic trace elements.

The water delivered from a rapid gravity filter can usually be guaranteed to have a turbidity of less than 1 mg/l, and with adequate chemical treatment a colour of less than 5 mg/l. Instruments provided in a rapid filter normally include a rate of flow indicator, and a loss of head indicator, to show when the sand in the filter requires cleaning.

Where the filter bed is contained in an open tank and the flow caused by the difference in level between the tank and the outlet sump, the filter is referred to as a *Gravity Filter*. Where the bed is contained in a pressure vessel, and the flow caused by a difference in pressure between the inlet and outlet connections, the filter is called a *Pressure Filter*. The basic function is the same and the type used generally depends on the location of the plant relative to the hydraulic level in the system.

Figure 11 shows a typical section of a treatment works dealing with water drawn from a lowland impounding

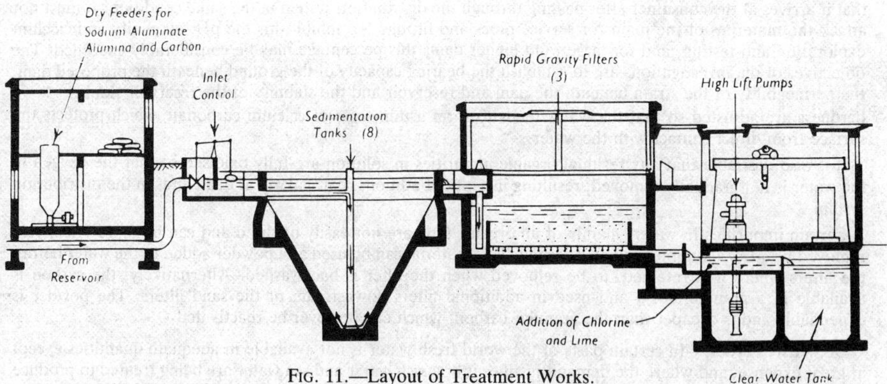

FIG. 11.—Layout of Treatment Works.

reservoir. The raw water is coagulated with Alumina and Sodium Aluminate and powdered carbon is added to absorb taste and odour. The water is then flocculated and settled in vertical flow tanks. It is then filtered through rapid sand filters. Chlorine is then added for final sterilisation and lime added to correct the pH for corrosion control. Finally the treated water is pumped from the clear water tank into the supply.

DISINFECTION.—It is generally assumed that however pure a water is, as a rule, contamination may occur. Some means of disinfection should always be provided for a potable water. *Chlorine* in some form is used for this purpose almost universally, although, *ozone* and *ultra-violet radiation* are sometimes employed. Chlorine is a powerful oxidising agent and reacts with inorganic and organic substances sometimes present in water. Since disinfection takes a finite time to complete, its effectiveness depends on maintaining an adequate *residual*, usually 0·2 mg/l over a period of not less than 30 minutes. This may require a considerably higher initial dose of chlorine.

Apparatus is available for automatically recording residual chlorine. Where a water of variable quality is being treated the dose necessary to maintain an adequate residual will vary, and in such cases it is usual to add a high enough dose to cover the worst conditions, and then to remove the excess chlorine with a reducing agent, usually *sulphur dioxide*. The SO_2 dose is often under automatic control from a *chlorine residual* detecting device.

Chlorine added to water containing ammonia will form *chloramines*, a loose combination of the two chemicals. chemicals. The disinfecting and oxidising effect of chloramines is weaker than chlorine itself, and takes longer to be effective. If however, the quantity of chlorine is some 7–8 times that of the ammonia present, the reaction is irreversible and any further chlorine is uninhibited. This is referred to as '*Break-point' chlorination*.

Chlorine can be reacted with sodium chlorite solution to form *chlorine dioxide*. This is an even more powerful oxidising agent, and is often used to remove taste and odour in water particularly where these are due to *Phenolic* compounds. As chlorine gas can be a potential health hazard if not properly handled, there is a suitable alternative using hypochlorite prepared from brine by electrodialysis at high pressures. The process gives off hydrogen which has to be vented to atmosphere.

Degassing.—Some waters, particularly ground waters, contain an excessive quantity of *carbon dioxide* which makes them corrosive. In many cases corrosion can be inhibited by removing some of the CO_2. This can be effected by *spraying* into the atmosphere or by passing through a *packed tower* with a forced draught of air blown in a counter-current direction. The same process can be used partially to remove objectionable gases such as H_2S or any others which cause taste and odour.

Aeration.—Oxygenation of water is employed in the removal of *iron and manganese*. Water drawn from large impounding reservoirs, particularly where the water is over 15 m deep so that an anaerobic zone forms at the bottom in the summer months, may also require some aeration. The same processes as used for degassing can be employed and in addition, because the efficiency does not normally have to be as great, a *cascade* aerator may be employed, or the water from the bottom of the reservoir may be maintained in an aerobic condition by circulation pumping or transfer from the bottom to the top; surprisingly little energy being required to effect this.

Ion Exchange.—Dissolved salts can be modified by bringing the water into contact with ion exchange *resin beads*. A common example of this is in the softening of water where the calcium and magnesium salts give up their calcium and magnesium in exchange for sodium associated with the beads. When exhausted the beads are regenerated with a strong solution of common salt. A wide variety of resins are now available and processes available which enable the dissolved salts to be completely eliminated, producing the equivalent of distilled water.

STABILISATION.—The final water leaving a treatment plant is of the quality required, and it is desirable

that it arrives at the consumer after passing through the distribution system in the same condition. It must not attack the materials of the mains or service pipes and fittings. To inhibit this the pH, alkalinity and calcium exploration and testing, and for larger and higher dams this percentage may be considerably exceeded. The objectives of the investigations are to establish the bearing capacity of the ground beneath the proposed dam, the permeability of the strata beneath the dam and reservoir and the stability of the reservoir slopes.
hardness are adjusted so that the water tends to form a thin scale of calcium carbonate which protects the surface from direct contact with the water.

It is also desirable that any residual organic impurities in solution are fully oxidised so that the oxygen in the water is not gradually removed, resulting in septic conditions, particularly at dead ends in the distribution system.

Certain impurities in water, mainly of an organic type are not easily oxidised and can be more effectively removed by *adsorption* into *activated carbon*. This material can be used as a powder added to the water before the filters where it is retained, to be removed when the filter is backwashed. Alternatively, the carbon is available in a granular form and used in additional filters downstream of the sand filters. The powder is expendable and is cheaper than the granular carbon, which can however be reactivated.

DESALINATION.—In certain parts of the world fresh water is not available in adequate quantities except at great expense, and where the demand justifies it brackish water and sea water are being treated to produce fresh water. The most highly developed process to date is *distillation* using a *multi-stage flash-evaporation* technique. Other processes which show promise in this field are, *electrodialysis* where electric potentials are used to cause the ions to pass through a perm-selective membrane, *reverse osmosis* where high pressure across a semi-permeable membrane causes the water to pass through, leaving the salts behind and *freezing* where ice granules are formed, separated from the brine and then thawed. The cost of fresh water (1977) from distillation plants in Great Britain has been estimated at between 40p and 60p/m^3, depending on whether the supply of energy can be used to produce electricity at the same time. Plants for the purification of sea-water exist in the Channel Islands, Gibraltar, Bermuda, and elsewhere.

OPERATIONAL TESTS.—A water that is treated so that it is clear, and contains an adequate chlorine residual and a pH within close limits, can in general be regarded as satisfactory. For routine control of a treatment works, it is essential that these three qualities are checked frequently.

In most modern works the clarity is measured continuously by a photometric technique, the residual chlorine by an ampereometric technique and pH using a calomel electrode. The results are recorded on a chart and so provide continuously evidence that the water delivered is satisfactory. Other qualities have to be tested at longer intervals and these determinations are usually carried out in a laboratory.

Radiation.—The tolerable limits are:—*Alpha emitters*, 10^{-12} curie/litre (ie one picocurie per litre). *Beta emitters*, 10^{-11} curie/litre (ie ten picocurie per litre). In particular cases reference should be made to the International Commission on Radiological Protection.

DAMS

Although the siting and use for which impounding reservoirs are established may differ between water supply and hydro-electric power respectively, the principles of construction of a dam are the same. The fundamental object of impounding water in a valley for *water supply* is that of economy, ie to make use of the valley itself for giving the highest possible *capacity* without constructing long artificial embankments, and to site such a dam on high ground to save pumping. In *hydro-electric* work the dam is sited in a valley to give economical capacity, but, particularly *head*. Hence wide flat sites giving large capacities are favoured for water supply; such sites are usually of clay material and suited for the construction of earthen dams and embankments.

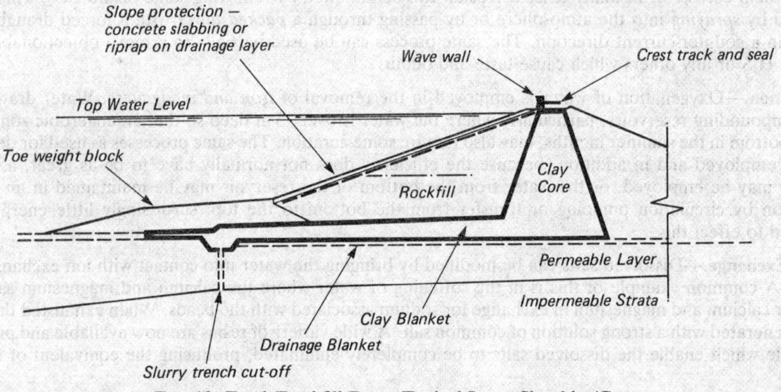

FIG. 12. Earth/Rockfill Dam. Typical Inner Shoulder/Core.

Rocky narrow gorges and steep gradients ('thalwegs') of streams are preferred for hydro-electric schemes; such sites are often best suited for high dams of concrete or masonry capable of utilising the high heads.

SITE INVESTIGATIONS.—It is essential to carry out extensive investigations at an early stage in the design of a dam. It is considered justifiable to spend up to 7% of the total cost of permanent works on preliminary

Initially the main features can be established by a geological appreciation from maps and surface features. This would be followed by:—

(*a*) Trial Pits—to check the surface strata by visual inspection, obtain samples in borrow areas and check for excavation parameters.

(*b*) Boreholes—drilled to total depth considered possible for grouting or cut-off works, and to obtain cores and samples at depth. Also to carry out *in situ* permeability and water tests.

(*c*) Geophysical—both resistivity and seismic surveys are useful for obtaining information correlated between boreholes, but should not be used without confirmatory drilling. Seismic rates can be used as a guide to permeability.

(*d*) Laboratory testing and analysis of cores and samples.

Foundation Treatment.—The foundation of the dam must be strong enough to withstand the pressure of the structure and sufficiently impermeable to prevent excessive leakage around or under the structure. In earlier dams it was customary to try and prevent leakage by constructing a cut-off trench to considerable depths up to 50 m below the dam. If the trench was in soft clay it would be refilled with consolidated clay; but if in shale, mudstone or rock, with 5:2½:1 concrete including movement joints. Due to excessive cost of such work it is now seldom done except for small shallow embankments and the cut-off is achieved either by constructing a bentonite–cement wall in a slurry trench (as at Bewl Bridge Dam in Kent), by grouting, or by construction of a rolled clay fill cut-off trench down to a low permeability layer.

The ground beneath the dam may be strengthened by providing adequate vertical or horizontal drainage. Vertical drainage can be achieved by constructing relief wells, sand drains or various proprietary methods involving the insertion of a porous membrane through a split auger tube. Horizontal drainage is achieved by laying a drainage layer protected with filter layers above and below to enable excess pore pressures to be released from the surface clays and silts while the foundation layers are consolidating during construction. If this is not possible, weak material must be removed and replaced by suitable fill.

EMBANKMENT DAMS—CONSTITUENT PARTS

GROUTING.—(*a*) It is often necessary to grout under the trench and/or core, particularly where rock seams occur (revealed below the trench bottom by deep boreholes) that may have outcrops in the reservoir floor under the submerged area, particularly in cases where the dip of the rocks is downstream. Boreholes are usually about 50 mm in diameter; grout (consisting of liquid cement, with varying quantities of water or of one part cement and one part sand) is applied under a pressure which is specified according to the nature of the strata. In rock, pressure may vary with the depth, but in alternating gritstones and shales pressures should be moderate in order to prevent uplift. A minimum pressure P, given by the formula $P = 0{\cdot}45D$ (where D is the Depth in metres over that part) is used as a guide, and can be increased in the light of experience on site. Care should be taken not to increase pressures merely to achieve greater inputs of grout, which can split the strata and cause surface heave and break out. The geological conditions may also greatly affect the watertightness of the reservoir as well as the trench; pervious formations may appear in the valley bottom under the submerged area. Thus, seams in the Ashdown Beds proved below the bottom of the trench at the Powdermill reservoir

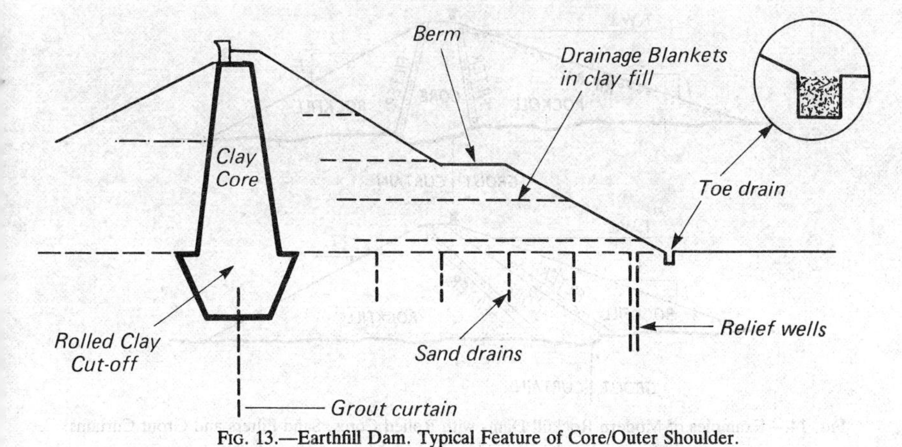

FIG. 13.—Earthfill Dam. Typical Feature of Core/Outer Shoulder.

(Hastings) came to the surface in the reservoir area and additional grouting was done there. See Fig. 14 for typical positions of grout curtains.

If grouting is considered necessary 50 mm tubes would be cast into a concrete cut-off about 2 m apart, or 50 mm dia holes drilled through a clay-filled cut-off trench when it has reached a level about 1 m above ground level. Grouting is then carried out through these holes to the base of the cut-off trench. When no more grout can be taken the hole is drilled another 3 m, ie to a depth of 6 m below the bottom of the trench. Grouting is again repeated. A third and fourth 3 m is drilled and the operation is repeated. As the efficiency of the whole process is a matter of inference, especial experience is required to avoid—(*a*) ineffectual grouting and hence subsequent leakage; (*b*) waste of cement; (*c*) damage to puddle in trench. The quantity of cement used for grouting depends on the nature of the strata and on recent dams has varied from 5 to 1,100 kg/m of borehole.

The foregoing refers to ordinary fissured rock and for economising in cement, fly ash up to 50% in volume of the cement may be used. Where fussures are large, sand may be added and what is virtually a mortar may be injected. Where fissures are fine, various clay substitutes such as bentonite may be used; the general principle is to insert grout of a finer mechanical analysis than the strata to be injected. The efficacy of the operation is determined by inference based on experience.

GROUTING.—(*b*) For grouting in alluvial soils, the tube-a-manchette method may be used as an alternative to the descending stage method described in the preceding paragraphs. In this system a borehole, cased if necessary, and of approximately 115 mm diameter is put down for the full depth to be treated. The hole is then filled with a sleeve grout consisting of bentonite, cement and water, and the manchette tube is installed to the full depth. The tube consists of a 38 mm diameter uPVC pipe having sets of holes at 300 mm intervals of depth, each set of holes being covered by a rubber sleeve. After the sleeve grout has set, a double packer grout tube is inserted down the manchette tube to any chosen level. Water for water testing, or grout is then pumped through the perforations between the packers and under the sleeves into the ground. Water or grout cannot return into the tube since the rubber sleeves act as one-way valves. Injections may be carried out at any level, and injection at any particular level can be repeated as often as desired. Provided the tubes are left undisturbed, re-injection can be carried out at a later date after the performance of the original grouting operation has been assessed.

BROAD FOUNDATION.—This foundation, that is, the whole area on which the embankment is to rest, is usually stripped of top soil, often stock-piled for covering the downstream slope; the depth of stripping is usually about 250 mm, but a greater depth may be necessary to eliminate tree roots, much weathered material and particularly boggy ground. If the latter is deep, a greater depth may have to be removed or special treatment such as the insertion of vertical drains may be necessary.

PUGGED CLAY CORE.—Most old British earth dams have a thin core (1–2 m in thickness) of clay, prepared in a pug-mill where all extraneous matter such as stones would be eliminated, and for some clays, 20% of sand might be added to reduce shrinkage. Such a clay was then 'heeled' (tramped) in along the axis of the dam and well compacted by large gangs of men. This thin puddled clay would be supported by soil known as 'selected clay material' which would act as a filter to prevent it penetrating into the stony clay. Outside the 'selected clay material' might be stony material, which according to its nature and from experience would determine the slope of the embankment between 2 and 6 horizontal to 1 vertical.

Numerous dams of this type are to be seen on the Carboniferous shales and grits of the Pennines, the Lias and Trias clays of the Midlands and the soft sandy formations in the south of England.

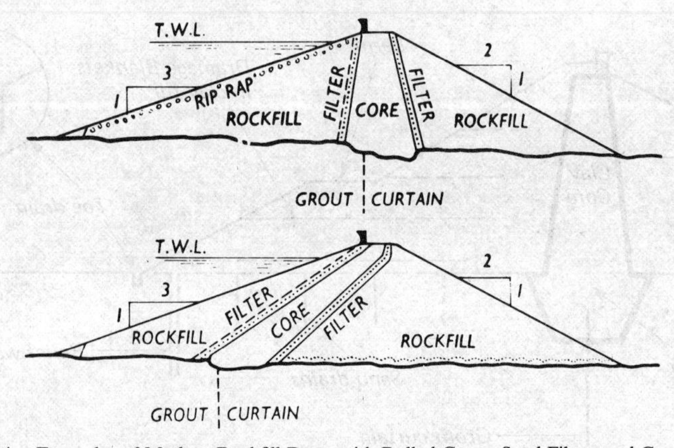

FIG. 14.—Examples of Modern Rockfill Dams with Rolled Cores, Sand Filters and Grout Curtains.

COMPACTED CLAY CORE.—The design and construction of embankment dams has changed owing to:—(*a*) the development in earth moving machinery, such as large excavators, large motorised tip wagons and dumpers, tracked and wheeled scrapers, rooters and bulldozers, smooth and rubber tyred rollers, 5–15 tonne vibrating rollers, 50–100 tonne sheepsfoot rollers; (*b*) better knowledge of the properties of clay (soil mechanics); (*c*) better knowledge of the properties of rock (soil and rock mechanics); (*d*) better appreciation of the implications of geology and conditions of the dam site. In addition, dam sites are becoming scarcer and sites formerly considered unsuitable cannot now be ruled out and reservoirs are tending to become larger and dams higher. Such rolled vibrated cores may be 10 m or more in width, varying with the height of the embankment. An empirical width at the base is half the depth of water impounded; the minimum top width would be about 4 m.

It seems, therefore, that the thin central 'pugged' core has fallen into disuse in Britain and elsewhere where labour is expensive and that the rolled fill dam, under strict soil control has taken its place. Thus, such types which are now sharply differentiated as earth fill embankments (with thin central pugged clay cores) on the one hand, and rockfill dams with thick sloping cores on the other, are becoming merely 'species' of embankment dams.

WATERTIGHT CORE OR MEMBRANE.—(For dams of granular fill.) The practice of a central core 'heeled' in clay has been referred to; this is being superseded by the desirability of using the materials at the dam site with the minimum of labour. It has been found that most materials can be utilised by the help of modern moving and compacting plant, and the basic design of the dam may be entirely a matter of utilising the materials on site. Thus, if there are clay, sandstone and rock at the site the conditions are probably ideal.

The basic types of core now being adopted are shown on Fig. 14, either a rolled central core or a rolled sloping core. The width in metres of such cores varies from one-tenth to three-tenths of the depth of water, plus 8 m. The core may safely contain small 'plums' of material other than clay. The core and filter in Fig. 14 are supported by compacted rockfill.

Asphaltic concrete is also used in cores or it may be laid as a membrane on the upstream face of a dam using pavers hauled by winches at the crest. The impermeable layer so formed is continued below the heel of the dam by a cut-off wall and grout curtain.

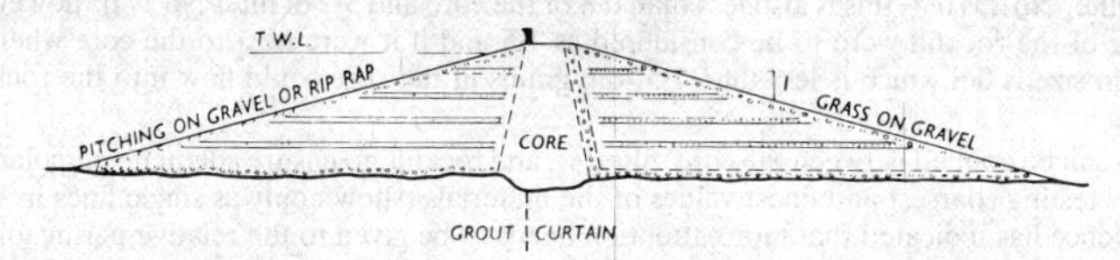

FIG. 15.—Clay Dam with Granular Blankets to Release Pore Pressure.

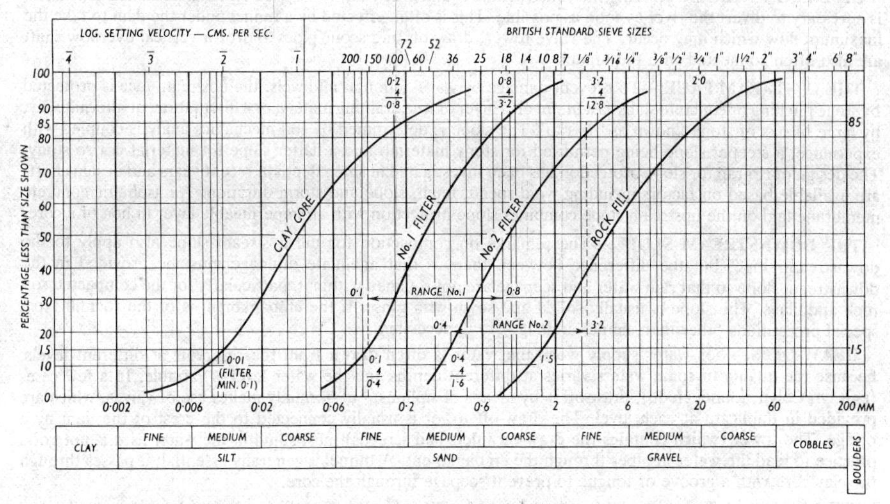

FIG. 16. Rockfill Dam. Example of Grading Curves for Core, Filter, and Rockfill. (For clarity, the lines do not give the range of particles in core, filters and rockfill; see text.)

EMBANKMENT FILL.—Where the fill available on site is hard rock, the type of dam which might be adopted is as shown in Fig. 14. If the rock is soft and could be compacted to a clay, then the type of dam shown in Fig. 15 might be considered. In these cases it is necessary to control pore pressures by incorporating a free draining layer or 'drainage blanket' (a sandwich of stone between filter layers). With all rockfill it is essential to saturate the fill during placement, and water up to 20% by volume of the fill is often added before compaction by vibrating roller. If the site is on clay and the embankment is of clay, drainage blankets should be laid to falls to toe drains to assist in relieving pore pressures in the foundation materials and fill during compaction and consolidation from the embankment. The supporting rock also affects the design of the filters for if the rock consists of large blocks of over 250 mm in width, more than one grade of filter may be required between it and the core. A filter may consist of more than one material of different grades, as shown in Fig. 16.

FILTER.—The core must be protected on both upstream and downstream sides with a layer of sand or other suitable material, to prevent the clay or other core material from entering the main embankment material. The filter must be suitably graded, as described below. See Figs. 14 and 16.

Terzaghi found, from experiment, that the main object of properly grading embanking material between filter and core, is to ensure: (*a*) adequate drainage between the clay-core and sand-filter or filters (if more than one) and rockfill, and (*b*) to prevent finer material flowing into coarser material. This principle still applies, although more complex rules have been developed for different combinations of materials, which can sometimes be replaced by synthetic filter fabrics.

(*a*) *Therefore, to ensure adequate drainage, the filter at its* 15% *range,* FINEST *size, should be* 4 *or* 5 *times more than the* COARSEST *size of core on the* 15% *range*. Thus, from Fig. 16, if 0·1 is assumed to be the FINEST size in the 15% range of No 1 filter, this value should be at least 4 or 5 times more than the COARSEST size of the clay core, which is 0·01 × 4, if assumed to be the COARSEST value on the diagram. The drainage would, therefore, be satisfactory. Similarly, if FINEST size in filter No 2 is 0·4 this is 4 times *coarser* than No 1 filter, but the *finest* rockfill of 1·5 is not quite satisfactory as it is less than 4 times coarser than that in No 2.

(*b*) *To prevent finer material flowing into coarser material*, the filter at the 15% COARSEST size should be less than 4 times the 85% grain size of the FINEST layer of the core. Thus, on Fig. 16 if 0·1 is assumed to be the COARSEST size in the 15% range of No 1 filter, this value should be less than 4 times the FINEST layer in the 85% range of the core, namely 4 × 0·2 = 0·8 which would be a very efficient filter. Similarly, if the COARSEST size in the 15% range of filter No 2 is 0·4, this is also less than 0·8 of the core and 3·2 of filter No 1. If, however, the 15% COARSEST value of the rockfill were to be considered as 1·5 and if it were next to the core where 4 times the finest 85% grain size is 0·8 which is less than 1·5, the grains in the core could flow into the rockfill if the filter were omitted.

These two main criteria can be applied between the core, filter(s), and rockfill, to ensure adequate percolation and retention of grains by testing coarsest and finest values of the materials (shown only as single lines in Fig. 16). However recent evidence has indicated that more attention needs to be given to the relative permeability of the clay and fine filter material, and the reservoir water chemistry should be taken into account.

DIVERSION WORKS.—During the construction of an earth dam, to be used on an impounding scheme, it is necessary to divert the river as soon as possible. This is often effected by a tunnel under the dam to take the maximum flow which may occur. The valve tower, draw-off and scour pipes and/or a vertical overflow shaft are also often connected with the tunnel.

THE UPSTREAM FACE.—To prevent damage by wave-action at all levels, the upstream face is protected by stone pitching or concrete slabs cast *in situ* on a layer of free draining mateial or a filter fabric, or alternatively, by large blocks of stone known as 'rip rap'. The slope is determined by soil mechanics analysis coupled with experience; a steeper slope being permitted for stony material, and a flatter slope for material not so stony. The design of rip-rap for slope protection has been investigated at some depth in recent years and design charts are available based on factors including wind speed, fetch, slope and storm duration. An asphaltic concrete membrane laid on the upstream slope combines slope protection with an impermeable layer in lieu of a core.

THE DOWNSTREAM SLOPE.—The remarks on compaction for the upstream slope also apply to the downstream slope, but the difference between them is that adequate drainage must be provided in the downstream slope so that rain water and seepage are not retained within it, particularly for the compacted soft rock and clays. The slope is usually soiled and sown with grass. If the embankment is of the rockfill type, special precautions other than simple drainage are unnecessary.

DRAW-OFFS.—For water supply work the water is often drawn from the reservoir at different levels, because the quality of some waters varies at different depths and the water level is variable. In a few cases (eg Llyn Celyn, Llandegfedd), draw-off is by means of siphons, but normally makes use of valves, which are provided in duplicate at each level. The draw-off tower is usually connected to the crest of the dam by a bridge. The tower (which contains the draw-off inlets and screens) must stand in the water as it is not good practice to lead the water in pipes through the embankment. A tunnel is generally essential; it passes through the clay core with a groove or tongue to prevent seepage through the core.

SPILLWAYS.—Where a tunnel has been made for diverting the river water during the construction of a dam, savings in cost can result from using this tunnel to carry away flood water after the dam is constructed. A vertical shaft takes the overflow into the tunnel which also does duty by taking the draw-off pipes.

A metre head over the weir may be allowed for a catastrophic storm, but it is important (*a*) to prevent whirlpool action (which reduces the discharge, say by 50%), and (*b*) to prevent the tunnel from being 'gorged', model experiments are desirable. (See chapter 'Hydraulics, Mechanics of Fluids'.) Two examples of Bellmouth weirs are as follows:

Ladybower Reservoir (Severn-Trent Water Authority). There are two identical weirs. The rim is 25 m in diameter, and the shaft curves to a horizontal tunnel 4·5 m in diameter. To prevent whirlpool formation, 12 cutwaters are disposed radially in the lip and guide walls beyond them. These have recently (1985) been model tested and proved to be satisfactory with an increased surcharge arising from the containment of a probable maximum flood within raised wavewalls under construction in 1987.

Burnhope Reservoir (Northumbrian Water Authority). A weir about 60 m long with its crest 2 m below the top of the embankment, and a cell-mouth, 15 m in diameter at the top, reducing in a depth of 7·5 m to a vertical shaft 3·5 m in diameter, which connects, by a bend constructed of cast-iron segments, to a horizontal tunnel.

CREST.—The crest is usually 1·5–2 m above the top water level, this distance is often called the 'Freeboard'. Where there is no road over the dam, the crest is often designed wide enough, say 6 m, to take a vehicle. There is generally a wave wall, particularly where the distance from the dam to the end of the water surface of the reservoir is considerable. This distance is termed the 'fetch'. The height of a potential wave in metres is sometimes taken as $0{\cdot}36F^{0{\cdot}5} + 0{\cdot}68F^{0{\cdot}25}$, where F, is the fetch, in km. Thus, if $F = 1$ km, the wave height is 1·04 m. Where for environmental or economic reasons show that a wave wall is unacceptable, the required freeboard can be incorporated into the crest of the dam in the form of a raised earth or stone wall section.

The unique crest of the Scammonden Dam, which takes the M62 motorway, is 55 m in width and comes 13·7 m above top water level.

STABILITY.—Developments in soil mechanics enable earth dams to be designed on a more scientific basis. An embankment may fail either by slip or settlement, and it is necessary to investigate the soil properties of the ground on which an embankment is to be built as well as the soil to be used in its construction. The settlement of an embankment, apart from the compaction of the bank itself, may be due to the consolidation of the underlying material due to the weight of the bank. Laboratory tests may be carried out to determine soil parameters such as shear strength, cohesion, moisture content, liquid limit, compaction and permeability. (See BS1377:1975 'Methods of Testing Soils for Civil Engineering Purposes'.)

Having tentatively fixed the height and slopes of the dam and estimated the weight and shear strength of the material of the bank, and the bearing and shear strength of the ground upon which the bank is to be placed, a typical analysis of the stability of the section of an embankment can be made as follows:

Example.—Figure 17 shows a typical cross section of the downstream slope of an embankment dam (there would also be a similar analysis for the upstream slope). There is a layer of soft material about 5 m deep under the dam, having a shear strength of 1,050 kg/m². Calculations are made assuming a slip-plane through the dam and bad ground. This plane is found by trial and for most practical purposes may be part of a circle embracing (1) the highest part of the dam; (2) the junction of the good and bad material; (3) the bad ground beyond the downstream toe, and making L, the length of the slip-plane (1-2-3), as short as possible. The process of determining the worst case (that with the lowest factor of safety) is made easier by the use of a computer program which will enable the designer to assess a complete spectrum of possible slipcircles, or alternative shapes. In this example, let us assume:

The radius of the slip-plane $R = 35{\cdot}4$ m.

Length of slip-plane $= L = R \times \theta$ radians $= 35{\cdot}4 \times \pi/2 = 55{\cdot}5$ m.

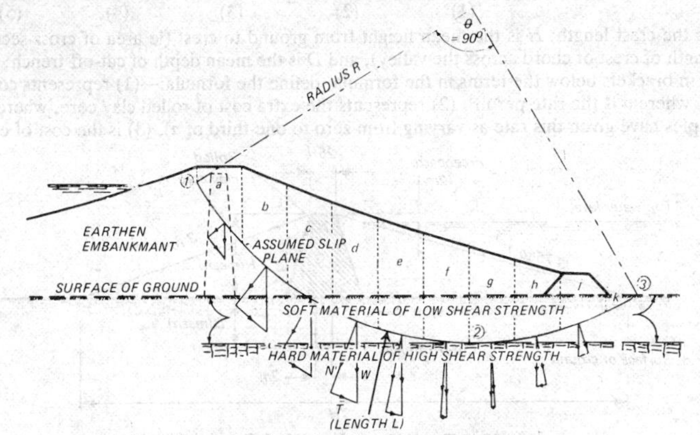

FIG. 17.—Analysis of the Stability of an Embankment Dam.

Assumed density of embanking material = 1,920 kg/m^3.

Consider a slice of the embankment 1 m thick and divide the section into strips (*a*, *b*, *c*, etc). The mass (*W*) of each strip = area × density, and the mass of each strip (*W*) is resolved by the vector method into its normal component (*N*) and tangential component (*T*), with + or − signs.

ΣT = 155,000 kg. For stability (ignoring friction),

$$\text{Cohesion, } (C)\text{, required} = \frac{\Sigma T}{L} = \frac{155{,}000}{55{\cdot}5} = 2{,}790 \text{ kg/m}^2$$

As the shear strength is only 1,050 kg/m^2 under the embankment, the bad material must be excavated and replaced with that having a higher shear strength. To provide a factor of safety of 1·5 which is usual, the material to be used for the embankment should have a shear strength of 1·5 × 2,790 = 4,200 kg/m^2.

In the case of the upstream embankment, the stability is calculated for the reservoir empty, this being the critical condition of stability. This method gives a higher value for the shear strength of the material required, and therefore provides an additional factor of safety. If the friction of the material is taken into account, say clay having an angle of friction, ϕ, of 5°, then the cohesion or shear strength required is

$$\frac{\Sigma T - (\Sigma N \times \text{tan angle of friction})}{\text{Length of slip-plane}}$$

In this example ΣN = 591,500 kg and $\Sigma N \times \tan 5°$ = 51,800 kg

Hence shear strength required is (155,000 − 51,800)/55·5 = 1,860 kg/m^2

CONTROL TESTS.—To avoid failures during construction it is necessary to maintain a constant programme of measurement and testing. Foundation pore pressures can be monitored by piezometers or standpipes, movements checked by constant checking of toe movements, and the soil parameters checked by continuous representative sampling of material combined with *in situ* and laboratory testing. The shear strength of cohesive materials can be checked by carrying out quick undrained compressive tests on 40 mm dia samples, *in situ* vane testing, and triaxial tests on 100 mm dia samples to obtain the effective stress parameters. The density should be checked by the Proctor test with a value of 95% of optimum normally being accepted as adequate. A check on air voids in the compacted fill is easy to assess, with a maximum of 10% being acceptable.

COMPACTION OF ROCKFILL DAMS.—Gravels, sands and shales when conveyed in heavy end-tip wagons and spread by heavy scrapers and/or bulldozers in layers of up to 0·5 m are generally found to be very well compacted in a preliminary sense of the order of 95% of the proctor optimum.

Sluicing with water may have to be used to ensure maximum density during dry weather. After the material has been spread and partly compacted, with sands, gravels and granular material generally, rubber tyred rollers to give pressure of 70 t/m^2 with 3–4 passes have proved satisfactory, and 5–8 tonne (t) vibrating rollers with 2 or 3 passes give good compaction for sands and gravels such as those suitable for clay core filters. Sheepsfoot rollers, 50 and 100 t in weight with projecting feet giving pressures of 700 t/m^2 with 3 or 8 passes are generally considered best for compacting clay for cores, compaction however is largely a matter of experiment to get the greatest density and stability (weight and shear strength) with the material and plant available.

COST OF EMBANKMENT DAMS.—The following formula, applicable to embankment dams of section similar to Fig. 18, is particularly useful when comparing alternative sites in preliminary investigations. Some inflationary adjustment would be necessary to the absolute values.

$$\text{Cost (£)} \quad + \underset{(1)}{3.6\,aLH^2} + \underset{(2)}{0.6\,bLH^2} + \underset{(3)}{2{\cdot}0\,cLD} + \underset{(4)}{66{,}000H} + \underset{(5)}{202{,}000}$$

Where *L* is the crest length; *H* is the mean height from ground to crest (ie area of cross-section of valley divided by length of crest of chord across the valley); and *D* is the mean depth of cut-off trench; all in metres. The numbers in brackets below the terms in the formula, define the formula:—(1) represents cost of forming embankment, where *a* is the rate per m^3. (2) represents the extra cost of rolled clay core, where *b* is the rate per m^3 (examples have given this rate as varying from zero to one-third of *a*). (3) is the cost of concrete-filled

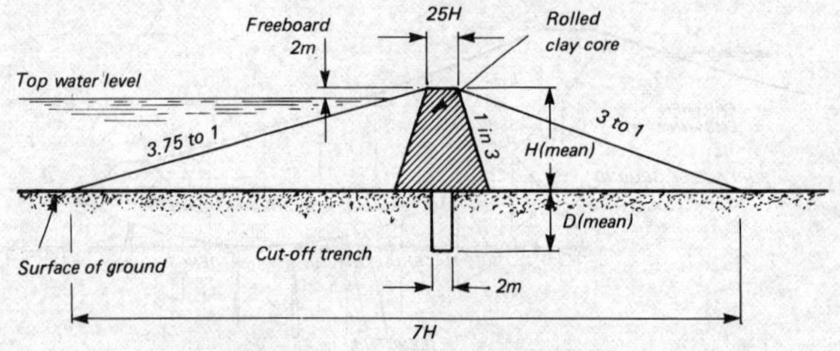

FIG. 18.—Earth Dam: Simplified Cross-section.

cut-off trench, 2 m wide, where c, is the rate per m^3. (*Note.* In many cases this would not be necessary, and shallow rolled clay cut-off substituted). (4) is the cost of stream diversions, overflow and valve shaft. (5) is the cost of miscellaneous items such as pipework and valves, footbridge to valve shaft, reinforcement and steelwork, recording instruments for water level, overflow and discharge below dam. Items (4) and (5) are based on 1985 prices, and typical 1985 values of a, b and c would be: a, £16·50; b, zero to £5·50; and c, £124·00.

This formula for cost of embankment dams, (as for concrete gravity dams) does not include for: (1) Contingencies. (2) Engineer's fees, resident engineer, and staff. (3) Land and easements, legal and loan charges. (4) Diversion of railways, roads, and other public utilities. (5) Acquisition and demolition of buildings and the provision of alternative housing accommodation. (6) Clearing the reservoir site (including felling timber), spreading lime and fencing. (7) Access roads and bridges. (8) Excavation of soft material unsuitable as a foundation for the dam (in the case of earthen dams only) and replacement with selected materials. (9) Grout curtain below the cut-off trench. (10) Camp accommodation and, or alternatively, transport of men to the site daily, if the site is isolated.

It is suggested that items (1), (2) and (3) are covered by the addition of 25% to the cost as given by the formulae (10% for contingencies, 10% for engineering and 5% for land and easements, etc); but for the other items, each site must be considered separately, and suitable additions made to the cost as given by the formula. These formulae enable a curve to be plotted quickly for any site showing the relationship between the height of the dam and its cost.

PORE WATER PRESSURE.—For banks of dams constructed with clay, over 12 m high, it is now standard practice to record the pore pressures. The conditions of placing and compaction during construction of high dams with clay materials, can therefore be controlled by testing pore pressures during construction, which vary with the weight of material above the registering apparatus. The latter consists of specially made piezometers placed in the clay fill at strategic points and connected to the downstream toe of the embankment. The piezometers may operate by hydraulic, pneumatic or electrical transfer systems, but the most common are hydraulic ones connected by flexible tubing to vacuum gauges or monometers. De-airing equipment is provided to remove air drawn in through the piezometer tips.

Regular readings are taken during the placing of material. At the time of recording pore pressures, the relative thickness of the overburden over each point is also recorded. The permissible maximum pore pressures depend on the shear strength of the material, and on the calculated factor of safety. It can be calculated, therefore, after taking a reading, whether or not this maximum has been exceeded. If so, the rate of placing may have to be slowed down to allow pore pressures to dissipate.

At the Usk reservoir for Swansea, completed 1955, the bank was constructed with a rather impervious boulder clay. Due to climatic conditions, it was placed at a moisture content slightly wetter than the optimum, and pore water pressure recorders indicated that the pressure was unusually high. Tubes were then driven vertically into the bank, and were found to have water standing in them 2–3 m above the top of the uncompleted bank, thus confirming the readings. To obtain more rapid dissipation of the pressures, and enable the rate of building to be maintained, two horizontal drainage blankets were put in at levels of one-third and two-thirds of the total height of the bank. These consisted of a drainage layer of broken stone 150–225 mm thick, blinded above and below by about 300 mm of river gravel, to prevent clay squeezing in and clogging the drainage layer. Such provisions are now standard procedure in clay embankments.

An extensive investigation into the pore-water pressure was made for the foundations of the Selset reservoir. The embankment 39 m high, had to be placed on Boulder Clay, over 30 m in thickness; the resultant seepage, due to the pressure of the dam wall, was relieved by constructing 4,000 vertical drains in the clay, and constructing horizontal drainage blankets at various levels in the embankment.

DETAILS OF EMBANKMENT DAMS IN BRITAIN (from published data)

LADYBOWER DAM.—Severn-Trent Water Authority: completed September, 1945. Length, 381 m; maximum height, above river bed, 43 m; volume about 700,000 m^3. Upstream slope about 1 in 3, the lower part protected by a stone 'beaching' and the upper part by stone pitching. Downstream slopes (beached), upper part 2 in 3; lower part 2 in 5. The greatest width at base is 203 m, crest width 5·2 m. The capacity of the reservoir is 28,600 Ml. The dam is founded on alternating Grits and Shales of Lower Carboniferous formation in which some 1,625 t of cement were pumped in 13 km of boreholes.

CHEW VALLEY DAM.—Water supply for Bristol, West Gloucestershire, Bath and North Somerset, 1955. Catchment 5,800 ha; average rainfall 1,030 mm; capacity 20,500 Ml; yield 45 Ml/d. Embankment height 13 m, 11 m wide at top; base width 95 m, inner slope 3 to 1 with berm 15 m wide; outer slope 2·5 to 1. Cut-off brench 478 m long, 1·5 m wide, maximum depth 15 m. Cementation was applied below the cut-off trench to seal small fissures in the marl; 50 mm boreholes were drilled at 4·5 m intervals and grouting was carried out to a depth of 12 m; cement injected 228 tonnes. The spill weir is semicircular and leads to a channel 16 m wide.

WINSCAR DAM.—1975. Constructed for water supply in West Yorkshire, this dam impounds 8,200 Ml. It was built immediately downstream of an existing dam and provides an increase in yield of 21 Ml/d. The dam has a crest length of 520 m, maximum height of 53 m and contains 900,000 m^3 of rockfill. This is the first dam in Great Britain to have an asphaltic concrete membrane laid on the upstream face, the membrane being 120 mm thick, placed in two layers, and having an area of 25,000 m^2. The membrane replaces the more usual clay core.

LLANDEGFEDD DAM.—Cardiff water supply, 1963 (pumped storage); capacity 24,500 Ml; yield (direct supply) 115 Ml/d. Embankment: length 350 m, maximum height 39 m, top width 8·5 m; base width 253 m; inner slopes 3 to 1, outer slopes 1·5 to 1, 2·5 to 1, 3 to 1 and 4 to 1. Concrete cut-off trench 1·8 m wide, maximum depth 13 m with grout curtain below to 24 m depth. Diversion tunnel 2·3 m wide; overflow by bellmouth. Draw off tower with air siphons instead of valves. Rolled clay core, shale in shoulders with drainage blankets.

SELSET DAM.—Built 1961, this is an earth embankment with a core of puddle clay, crest 928 m, maximum height 40 m. It is built on Boulder Clay and other drift deposits in which over 4,000 vertical drains. 450 mm diameter and 6 m deep on an average, sunk by pile driving methods and filled with Whinstone rock. These drains dried out the clay from pore pressure water and thus increased the bearing and shear pressure.

BALDERHEAD DAM.—Built 1965, is an earth dam, with a core of rolled boulder clay, the shoulders being of shale; crest length 925 m, height 48 m. It is built on a foundation of carboniferous shale with thin beds of limestone and sandstone.

SCAMMONDEN DAM.—Huddersfield water supply 1970. This was the first dam in Britain designed to carry a motorway on its crest, forming part of the M62 route. The direct catchment area is 502 ha with indirect catchment areas of 1,520 ha feeding the reservoir through catchwaters. Average annual rainfall is 1,320 mm and the gross yield 37·3 Ml/d. The capacity of the reservoir is 8,200 Ml. The dam is of rockfill construction with a three-zone clay core below which is a grout curtain. Dimensions are: crest length 625 m, maximum height above valley bottom 66 m, crest width 55 m. Downstream slope 1·8 to 1, upstream slopes 1·8 to 1 above top water level, 2·7 to 1 below. Due to motorway requirements the height and width of the dam were considerably increased and the freeboard is no less than 13·7 m. The dam is founded on alternating shales and gritstones in the Millstone Grit Series of the Upper Carboniferous System. The curtain grouting involved drilling three lines of holes totalling 57 km, and the injection of 5,450 tonnes of cement and sand.

LOCH QUOICH DAM.—This is a rockfill dam, the rockfill consisting of mica schists placed in layers 600 mm in thickness and rolled with 20 passes of a 10 ton roller and sluiced with twice the volume of the layer with water and rolled with 10 passes of a vibrating roller. The upstream slope is protected by vacuum concrete process. The clay core is protected by a layer of sand, as a filter, to prevent the clay seeping into the rockfill. This dam is 37 m high and 300 m long. Another rockfill dam in Scotland is that of Breachlaich, near Loch Tay, 24 m in height and 400 m crest length.

EARTH AND ROCKFILL DAMS ABROAD.—Between 1945 and 1957 over 600 earth and 24 rockfill dams were constructed in the United States, as well as 114 composite dams. The chief criteria were that all these dams were constructed on soft strata and of such materials were available near the sites. In Europe, noteworthy earth rockfill dams have been constructed at Serre Ponçon in France and Sylvenstein in Germany. These dams were built on over 90 m of soft moraine with embankments containing clay cores some 40 m in height, with grouted cut off curtains through the moraines. Such clay cores are protected by sand 'filters' supported by selected fill and, in turn, rockfill externally.

Two recent dams, completed in 1985 at Dhypotamosand Kalauasos in Cyprus, are good examples of modern practice in the efficient use of available materials. They are 53 m and 58 m in height respectively and the core consists of clay.

Hydraulic-Fill Dams.—This type of dam is essentially an earth dam in the construction of which the materials are transported on to the site by water and distributed to their final position in the dam by water; a pond of mud and water being maintained on the top of the dam during construction. Difficulties have been experienced in segregation and the formation of permeable layers.

CONCRETE DAMS

The use of concrete in dams is a natural development from the construction of dams in masonry which is now seldom, if ever, carried out. Concrete (or masonry) dams are suitable where there is a rock foundation within, say, 10 metres of the surface. The cement content is kept as low as possible, with consequent reduction in the strength of the concrete, to avoid excessive heat being generated within the mass by the hydration of cement during construction. It is common practice to face the concrete with a layer of rich concrete, masonry, brickwork or an applied coat of epoxy resin or bitumen if the impounded water is of such a quality that it is likely to attack concrete.

There are three main types of dam:—(1) Gravity: (2) Arch: (3) Buttress. In Britain they are usually of the gravity type by reason of the foundation conditions.

GRAVITY DAMS.—The name implies that any section of the dam will stand by reason of its own weight. It may be sited on plan straight across a valley, but is frequently curved to improve the appearance or make better use of the topography—however no reduction in section can be achieved by this means. The following factors are significant in the design of a gravity dam:

(*a*) The foundation rock must be capable of withstanding a bearing pressure of about 100 t/m^3, or alternatively must be strengthened to achieve this resistance by concreting and grouting and/or excavation of bad material and replacement by concrete.

(*b*) The resultant pressure of all factors (weight of dam, water pressure, uplift water pressure, ice, shape of dam), must pass within the 'middle third' of any horizontal section of the dam and its foundation. This condition, which must be fulfilled whether the reservoir is full or empty, ensures that no tensile stress shall occur and provides a factor of safety against overturning. (If for example, a section of the dam is 15 m wide, the line of pressure must pass at least 5 m away from the upstream face (heel) and 5 m away from the downstream face (toe)).

(*c*) Provision must be made for uplift pressures both within the dam structure and underneath the foundations. The uplift pore pressure should be taken as 100% upstream head at the upstream or reservoir face at any section, decreasing linearly to the maximum tailwater level or zero at the downstream or outer face. If an easily maintained drainage system (with pipes of 200 mm diameter or larger at centres not exceeding 3 m) is installed then the uplift pressure could be taken as being graded to 25% of the maximum at this point. For smaller drains this should be increased to 40% but where the drainage cannot be maintained then no relief should be allowed for in the design. A check on stability for the 'no drainage' condition should always be carried out.

(*d*) The dam must not slide on its foundation and the friction between the dam and the rock must be sufficient to prevent sliding. The width of the dam itself and the strength of the concrete must also be sufficient to resist shear at all horizontal sections.

The following calculations and checks should be carried out:—(1) Take an initial estimate of the base width, (W), where the overall height = h; the density of water = D_W; and the density of concrete = D_c, from the formula:

$$W = hD_W/\sqrt{(D_c - 0{\cdot}67D_W)}$$

This assumes a simple triangular profile with approx two-thirds average uplift and is generally sufficient to give a good starting point subject to later checks. Typical values of the densities of water, and concrete, would be 1,000 and 2,400 kg/m^3 respectively.

(2) To allow for a roadway on top, increase the width at the crest by steepening the downstream batter (often to vertical) from a point 10–15 m down. This will affect the line of resultant pressure but offers a considerable saving in concrete over the alternative of increasing the width of the whole structure. The batter of the downstream face depends on the weight of the concrete but normally varies between 0·7 and 0·8

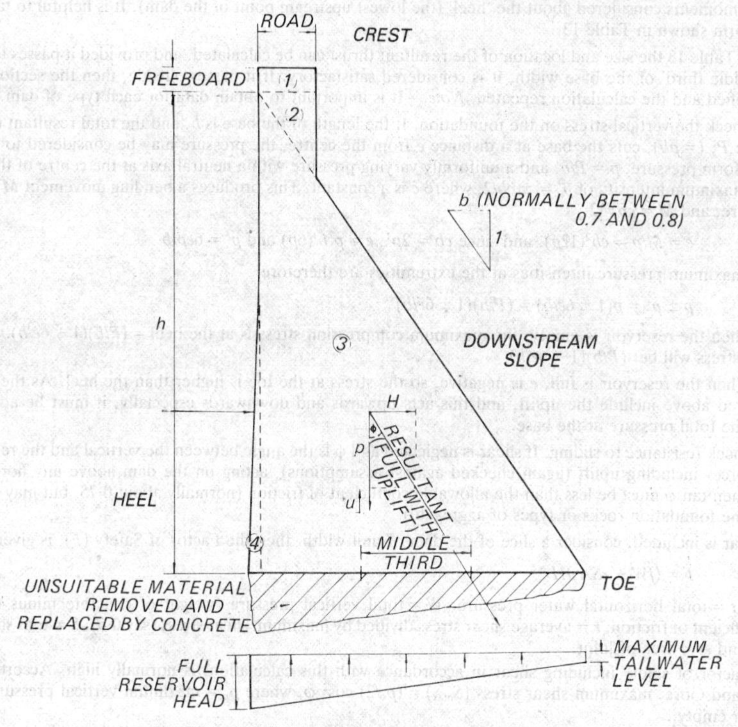

FIG. 19.—Stability Analysis of Concrete Gravity Dam.

TABLE 13.

Descriptions and dimensions	Force (t)		Lever arms about heel (m)	Moment (t − m)
	Horizontal H	Vertical P		
Concrete sections:				
(1) See Fig. 19				
(2)				
(3)				
(4)				
Total forces (reservoir empty)				
Horizontal water force				
Uplift (a) As design detail.				
(b) 100%.				
(c) Nil.				
TOTALS. Reservoir full (a)				
(b)				
(c)				

horizontal to 1 vertical. The upstream face can be vertical but a slight batter of (say) 1 horizontal to 25 vertical may be necessary to satisfy the 'middle third' rule.

(3) For Overturning—Analyse a slice of the dam of unit width by considering each of the forces producing an overturning movement. The calculation should be checked for different assumptions in regard to the uplift, and the moments considered about the 'heel' (the lowest upstream point of the dam). It is helpful to tabulate in the form shown in Table 13.

From Table 13 the size and location of the resultant thrust can be calculated, and provided it passes through the 'middle third' of the base width, it is considered satisfactory. If it passes outside, then the section must be modified and the calculation repeated. *Note.*—It is important to obtain data for each type of dam.

(4) Check the vertical stress on the foundation. If the length of the base is b, and the total resultant normal pressure P, $(= pb)$, cuts the base at a distance e from the centre, the pressure may be considered to consist of a uniform pressure, $p = P/b$, and a uniformly varying pressure with a neutral axis at the centre of the base with a maximum intensity of $p' = \pm cb/2$, where c is a constant. This produces a bending movement M, about the centre, and $M = cb^3/12$.

$$e = M/p = cb^2(12p), \text{ and since } cb = 2p', \; e = p'b/(6p) \text{ and } p' = 6ep/b$$

The maximum pressure intensities at the extremities are therefore:

$$p \pm p' = p(1 \pm 6e/b) = (P/b)(1 \pm 6e/b)$$

(i) When the reservoir is empty, the maximum compression stress is at the heel $= (P/b)(1 + 6e/b)$. At the toe the stress will be: $(P/b)(1 - 6e/b)$.

(ii) When the reservoir is full, e is negative, so the stress at the toe is higher than the heel. As the forces considered above include the uplift, and this acts upwards and downwards especially, it must be added to obtain the total pressure at the base.

(5) Check resistance to sliding. If shear is neglected and ϕ is the angle between the vertical and the resultant of all forces including uplift (again checked against assumptions), acting on the dam above any horizontal plane, then $\tan \phi$ must be less than the allowable coefficient of friction (normally about 0·75, but may be less with some foundation rocks or types of aggregate).

If shear is included, consider a slice of the dam of unit width, then the Factor of Safety (F), is given by:

$$F = (fW + rSA)/H$$

where H = total horizontal water pressure; W = total vertical pressure (weight of concrete minus uplift); f = coefficient of friction; r = average shear stress divided by maximum shear stress (say 0·5); S = unit shearing stress; and A = area of joint.

The factor of safety including shear in accordance with this calculation, is normally high. According to Wilson and Gore, maximum shear stress $(S_{max}) = (p_v/2)\cos^2\phi$, where p_v = maximum vertical pressure with reservoir empty.

(6) The maximum inclined vertical stress p_i, at the downstream toe, may be checked by Unwin's formula,

where p_v = maximum vertical pressure; and θ = angle between the downstream face and the vertical.

$$p_i = p_v \sec^2 \theta = p_v(1 + \tan^2 \theta)$$

The stress should of course be within the allowable bearing pressure calculated from the initial site investigation.

Gravity Dams Slightly Curved in Plan.—These have the following advantages: (i) Increased stability due to slight arching effect (not taken into account in the calculations). (ii) Reduced stresses due to changes in temperature. (iii) Tendency to greater watertightness. Curved dams are, of course, only practicable if a suitable rock foundation extends some distance upstream and downstream of the centre line across the site.

Low Gravity Dams.—For low concrete walls to retain water. Rankine states that the thickness at the base should be about 0·6 of the height, either for a rectangular section, or a trapezoidal section where the thickness at the top is 0·25 that of the base. Another rule is: Thickness at the top, 0·3 × height; Thickness at the middle, 0·5 × height; Thickness at the bottom, 0·7 × height.

ANCHORING OF GRAVITY DAMS.—The Cheurfas dam, in Algeria, was anchored, in order to add to the downward pressure, by vertical cables carried through sandstone, limestone and, again, sandstone, to argillaceous marl, at a depth about 30 m below the river bed and some 20 m below the bottom of a concrete base on which the dam, which is 22 m high, stands. The cables have caps bearing on the crest of the dam and were sealed at and near their lower ends. Each is composed of 630 galvanised steel wires, laid parallel and sheathed with a 'sandwich' of grease and bitumen between wrappings of sail-cloth. In Cornwall, the Argal dam (see below), was anchored by a similar method to permit raising.

STEENBRAS DAM.—Capetown, S. Africa. This dam was strengthened and raised 2 m by the Coyne process of anchoring the dam by post-tensioned cables. Holes of 60 mm diameter (minimum) were drilled through the 30 m high concrete gravity dam into the rock foundation, the anchorage being percussion drilled. Cables 35 mm in diameter were used (each of 37 wires of 5 mm diameter); the calculated prestress required was 70 t (initial tension to allow for creep was 77 t). The cables were grouted by special methods (1954).

ALLT-NA-LAIRIGE DAM.—Scotland. Height 25 m. This dam is anchored by steel rods in tension, embedded in the concrete near the up-stream face, and taken down to the rock below; this reduces the amount of concrete required by 40%, compared with a normal gravity dam.

COST OF CONCRETE GRAVITY DAMS.—For comparing alternative sites during preliminary investigations, the following formula may be used to obtain the approximate cost of concrete gravity dams of section similar to Fig. 20. Some adjustment of absolute cost values need to be made to compensate for inflation.

$$\text{Cost (£)} \quad \underset{(1)}{0{\cdot}375pLH^2} + \underset{(2)}{0{\cdot}675pLW^2} + \underset{(3)}{0{\cdot}75qLD_1H} + \underset{(4)}{2rLD_2} + \underset{(5)}{152{,}000}$$

where, L = crest length; H = mean height from broad foundation to crest (ie area of cross-section of valley divided by length of crest or chord across valley); W = width at crest of dam; D_1 = mean depth of broad foundation; and D_2 = mean depth of cut-off trench below broad foundation; all in metres.

The numbers under the formula, in brackets, refer to the terms above them. (1) = Cost of concrete dam, at rate of £p per m³. (2) = Cost of concrete, or equivalent, in crest road or footpath, at £p per m³. (3) = Cost of excavating broad foundation, at £q per m³. (4) = Cost of concrete-filled cut-off trench, 2 m wide, at £r

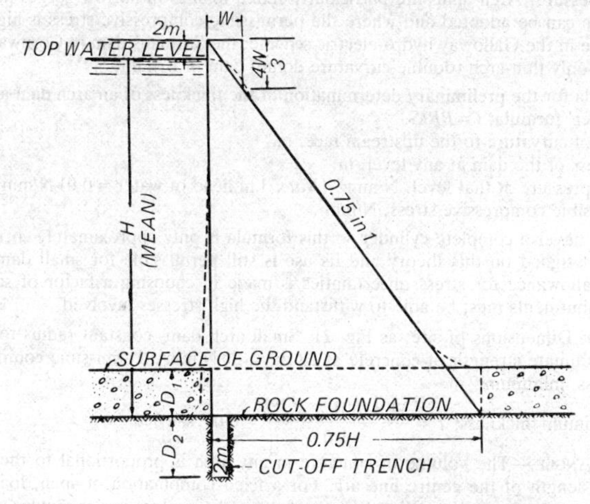

FIG. 20.—Cross-section (simplified) of Concrete Gravity Dam.

per m^3. (5) = Cost of ancillary works such as pipework and valves; reinforcement and steelwork; recording instruments for water level, overflow and discharge below dam. Item (5) is based on 1985 prices, and typical 1985 values of p, q and r would be: p, £82·50, q, £8·00; and r, £99·00

The values of p, q and r may be based on experience and the lump-sum allowance in term (5) may be varied as necessary. In addition to the above, there will be further items to allow for engineering, land acquisition, etc.

DETAILS OF CONCRETE GRAVITY DAMS IN BRITAIN (from published data)

ARGAL DAM.—Completed in 1942, Falmouth water supply. Impounds 640 Ml; catchment area, 510 ha; average annual rainfall, 1,120 mm; estimated yield, 3·6 Ml/d. Maximum height of dam (broad foundation to footpath level), 14 m; maximum depth of water to top water level, 8·5 m. Gravity section, curved in plan, having a radius of 150 m to the upstream face, with a concrete cut-off trench in the granite foundation. Grouting was used to obtain water tightness below the cut-off trench, an average of only 55 kg cement per metre of 50 mm borehole being taken. The upstream and downstream faces were faced with pre-cast concrete blocks 915 × 455 × 305 mm, thereby saving shuttering. Weight of mass concrete (vibrated), 2,400 kg/m^3. The Argal dam was raised 3 m in 1961 by prestressing, a total of 47 cables being inserted in the dam; the Les Cheurfas dam in Algeria was strengthened in 1935 by a similar method.

DRIFT DAM (1961).—Water supply of West Cornwall. This dam, near Penzance, is a curved mass concrete gravity dam on granite and a stratum of China Clay. It commands a gathering ground of 1,927 ha on which the average annual rainfall is 1,180 mm. The capacity of the reservoir is 1,300 Ml and the gross yield is 12 Ml/d. The lowest dry weather flow is 2·3 Ml/d or 1·38 l/s km^2. The maximum height of the dam is 22 m and it impounds a depth of 16 m of water. Over the China Clay part of the valley the footing of the dam was widened to reduce the pressure from 400 to 250 kN/m^2. The overflow is designed to take 113 m^3/s with a depth of water 1,220 mm over the overflow weir 41 m in length. The grout curtain of 4,750 m^2 was covered by 5,500 m of borehole into which 340 tonnes of cement was injected, equivalent to 62 kg per metre of borehole or 72 kg per square metre of grout curtain.

MELDON DAM.—1972. Constructed for water supply in North Devon, this dam impounds 3,090 Ml. Average annual rainfall on the 1,680 ha catchment area is 1,850 mm and the estimated gross yield is 30·5 Ml/d. The dam, 202 m long, and 44 m high above river level, contains 100,000 m^3 of concrete. A grout curtain was formed below the dam to a maximum depth of 20 m below the heel. Total length of grout holes was 1,900 m and 74 tonnes of cement were injected. Blanket grouting under the broad foundation required the further injection of 19 tonnes of cement. All water for supply has to be pumped to the treatment plant and the pumping station was incorporated in the dam for aesthetic reasons, avoiding an additional structure and access road.

LLYSYFRAN DAM.—1972. This dam was built for river regulation and water supply in Pembrokeshire (now Dyfed). Catchment area is 2,800 ha with an average rainfall of 1,550 mm. The storage of 9,110 Ml provides a yield of 61 Ml/d. The dam is 335 km long at the crest, 32 m high above river bed level and 52 m high above base of foundation; the volume of concrete is 245,000 m^3. A grout curtain below the dam was taken to a depth of 30 m. The original structure was designed for an ultimate raising of 12 m increasing the yield to 107 Ml/d.

ARCH DAMS (DESIGN).—In arch dams the water pressure on the face of the dam is transmitted to the abutments and the cross-section can be reduced very considerably; any cracks which may occur will tend to close under the pressure. Arch dams are particularly suited to sites in narrow gorges in rock, where a small radius of curvature can be adopted and where the permissible compressive stress is high. Examples of arch dams in Britain are in the Galloway hydro-electric scheme; the Stithians dam in Cornwall; and the Chliostair dam, which is the only thin-arch (double-curvature dome) dam in Britain.

The basic formula for the preliminary determination of the thickness of an arch dam at various levels is the simple 'thin cylinder' formula: $t = PR/S$

where R = radius of curvature to the upstream face, m.
t = thickness of the dam at any level, m.
P = water pressure at that level, N/mm^2. (*Note:* 1 m head of water = 0·01 N/mm^2 (approx).)
S = permissible compressive stress, N/mm^2.

An arch dam is never a complete cylinder so this formula is only approximately correct. However, many dams have been designed on this theory and its use is still permissible for small dams in simple settings, provided a large allowance for stress uncertainties is made in choosing a factor of safety. The geological formation of the abutments must be able to withstand the high stresses involved.

Example.—Data: Dimensions of site, as Fig. 21. Small arch dam, constant radius to upstream face, thin cylinder theory. Ultimate strength of concrete at 28 days, 20 N/mm^2. Permissible compressive stress, 1·0 N/mm^2. Top thickness, minimum 2 m.

$$\text{Maximum thickness, } T = \frac{30 \times 0{\cdot}01 \times 20{\cdot}12}{1{\cdot}0} = 6{\cdot}04, \text{ say 6 m.}$$

BEST CENTRAL ANGLE.—The volume of concrete in any arch is proportional to the product of the arch thickness and the length of the centre line arc. For a fixed combination of span, loading and permissible cylinder-theory stress it can be shown that the arc of the arch, in plan, is a minimum when $2\alpha = 133° 34'$ or

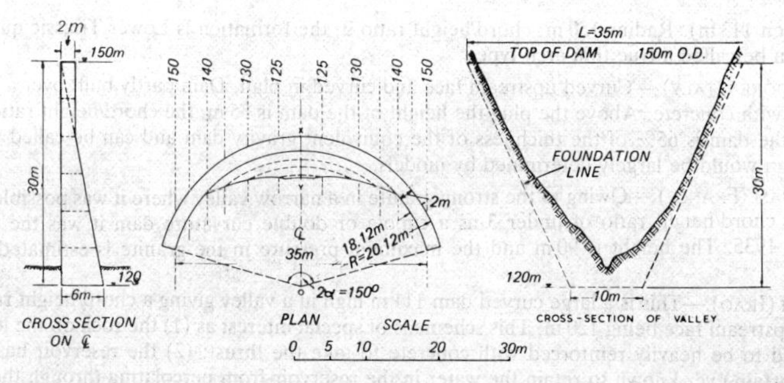

FIG. 21.—Simple Arch Dam.

when $r = 0{\cdot}544l$, where 2α = the total angle subtended by the arc of the arch, r = radius (upstream, downstream, or central), and l = arch span corresponding to the radius.

In a site with a variable span length a constant-radius dam can have the correct central angle only at one elevation. However, an appreciable variation from the best angle makes only a small change in the volume of concrete. Assume 2α has a maximum value of 150° at the top. The downstream radius corresponding to the clear top width of 35 m (Fig. 21), is 18·12 m. The minimum top thickness being fixed at 2 m, the upstream radius $R = 18{\cdot}12 + 2{\cdot}00 = 20{\cdot}12$ m. The theoretical thickness below the top is $t = PR/S$, where $P = 0{\cdot}01h$ h = height of dam in metres; $R = 20{\cdot}12$ and $S = 1{\cdot}0$. Therefore $t = 0{\cdot}01h \times 20{\cdot}12 = 0{\cdot}2h$ which varies as a straight line from zero at the top to 6 m at the bottom.

To set out the plan of the dam: (1) Draw the excavated rock contours as shown in Fig. 21. (2) Draw the centre line and locate the centre O. (3) Draw the extrados and intrados curves for the top of the dam. (4) From point X set off the arch thickness at successive contour intervals towards point Y. (5) With centre at O draw arcs through these points to the respective contours and join up the points of intersection.

For larger dams, the final design should be carried out by making detailed analyses, having regard not only to the horizontal arch elements but also the vertical cantilever elements of the dam, ie by assuming that the dam is sliced horizontally for the former and vertically for the latter analysis. When R exceeds 250 m, the section approaches that of a gravity dam and for larger radii, the advantages of the arch effect in the saving of materials largely disappear.

VARIATIONS OF GRAVITY AND ARCH DAMS.—There is a good deal of variation in the design of gravity and arch dams and the foregoing calculations give a broad indication of the pure gravity on the one hand and pure arch types on the other. It will be appreciated that the gravity type of dam whether built straight across a valley or curved (on plan), is suitable for any valley, however wide it may be, whereas the thin arch is suitable only for valleys where the chord/height ratio is under 3 approximately. (The chord is the distance between the two abutments at the crest; and the height, the maximum height of the dam from crest to footings).

Between the extremes of gravity and thin arch types of dams, there are thick arch dams, which are thinner than gravity dams and thicker than true arch dams, and the design of these are the subject of extremely complicated mathematical analysis. Model tests are being increasingly employed.

In most concrete dams reduction in thickness of concrete is the most important economy and such reduction in concrete on the gravity dam, providing good foundations are available where the chord/height ratio is under 5 or 6, can be effected. In recent years in narrow valleys and gorges (where the chord/height ratios of under 3 are possible, and the foundation rock is abundantly sound and able to withstand high thrust pressures on the abutment), the thickness of the thin arch dam can be further reduced by curving it in a vertical direction. These dams are generally known as cupola, dome or double curvature dams as they are curved both in the horizontal and vertical planes. These dams can be compared to an egg shell which is extremely strong for its thickness. In practice, however, the irregular shapes of valleys have to be shaped by mass concrete, either to plug an unsymmetrical gorge in the bottom of the valley, or else to make the abutments on each side of the valley more or less similar, on which to place a symmetrical cupola.

An alternative approach has been the use of rolled dry lean concrete, utilising a placing technique with travelling shutters used in road base construction. Trial embankments have proved the viability of the method which has been used for at least two dams in America.

EXAMPLES OF CURVED DAMS.—There are a few curved gravity dams in Britain but arch dams are rare. Stithians dam, Cornwall (1967), has a thick arch section between two gravity sections of the dam. If the gravity section had been continued across the valley where solid rock was deeper, extra cost would have been incurred owing to the extra thickness of concrete in the gravity section, as compared with the arch section. Model tests were carried out to determine the probable stresses in the arch section and its effect on the adjacent gravity sections. Noteworthy dams abroad are:

TIGNES (FRANCE).—Vertical upstream face. Height 168 m. Width of base 43 m (the equivalent gravity section would have been 113 m). Radius 150 m, chord/height ratio 2; the formation is Lower Triassic quartzite. The Tignes dam can be called a true thin arch type.

PIAVE-DI-CADORE (ITALY).—Curved upstream face and curved in plan. Dam partly built over a gorge (57 m deep) plugged with concrete. Above the plug the height of the dam is 55 m, the chord/height ratio being 5·5. Nevertheless, the dam is 65% of the thichness of the equivalent gravity dam and can be called a thick arch dam. The design would be largely determined by models.

MARÈGES DAM (FRANCE).—Owing to the strong granite in a narrow valley where it was possible to construct a dam with a chord/height ratio of under 3 as a cupola or double curvature dam it was the first example to be built in 1935. The height is 90 m and the maximum pressure in the granite is estimated to be about 650 t/m^2.

DOKAN DAM (IRAQ).—This is a large curved dam 111 m high in a valley giving a chord/height ratio of 3, the radius of the upstream face being 120 m. This scheme is of special interest as (1) the rock on the left abutment of the dam had to be heavily reinforced with concrete to take the thrust; (2) the reservoir has the longest (2 km) wing curtain ever known to retain the water in the reservoir from percolating through the Dolomite.

KARIBA DAM (ZIMBABWE).—This is a double curvature dam in a valley having a crest/height ratio of about 3½ and is founded on quartzite and gneiss. The height is 128 m, radius at crest level 245 m, and the thickness of the base is only 25 m. These dimensions were arrived at from 16 models and tested theoretically by 'trial load' analysis.

VAIONT DAM (ITALY).—This is a unique dam on the Jurassic Dolomite limestone in the Italian Alps. It is situated in a gorge giving a chord/height ratio of 0·7, the dam being 265·5 m high and the chord only 168·6 m in length. The pressure of the abutments when impounding 260 m of water, is 650 t/m^2. The thickness of the dam where it rests on the plug, at 170 m below the crest, is only 16·5 m. The dam was little damaged by the great rock-fall and overflow in October, 1963.

BUTTRESS AND MULTIPLE-ARCH DAMS.—These usually consist of a relatively thin facing supported by a series of buttresses, and are therefore a form of gravity dam, made hollow to permit the more efficient development of the latent strength of the concrete or masonry. The upstream face is inclined, in contrast to the almost vertical upstream face of the normal gravity dam. In overflow dams a downstream deck is also provided in the spillway section.

ADVANTAGES.—(1) Economy of materials, particularly advantageous where materials have to be transported long distances. It has been estimated that, for a dam 35 to 40 m high, the quantity of concrete required for a buttress dam is only about two-thirds of that required for the normal gravity type. This saving in cost is

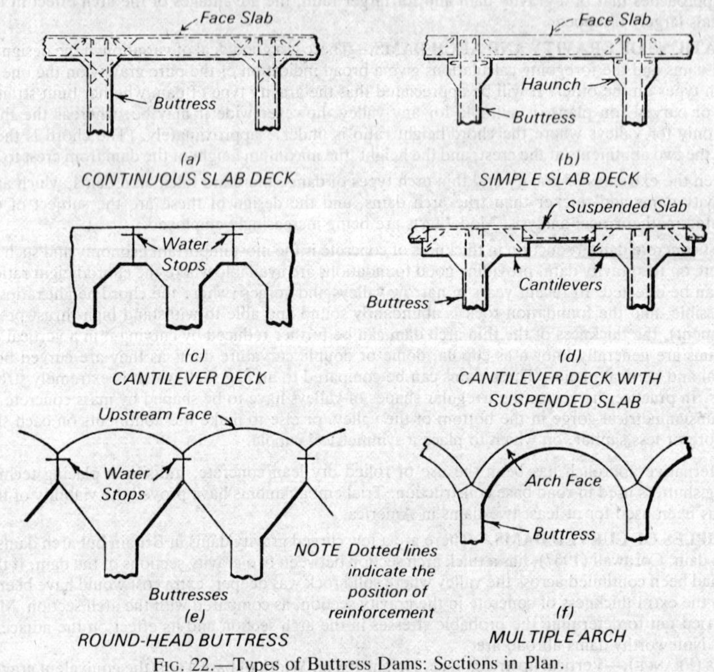

FIG. 22.—Types of Buttress Dams: Sections in Plan.

partially offset by the need for additional formwork reinforcing steel, and the higher class concrete required in thin and reinforced members. (2) Speed of construction, owing to the smaller quantity of concrete to be placed and the improved heat dissipation from the many exposed surfaces. (3) Reduced uplift pressure on the base, the pressure being relieved between the buttresses. (4) Improved access for inspection of the upstream face and foundations. (5) The utilisation of the vertical component of the water pressure on the sloping upstream face to obtain a suitable factor of safety against sliding. The inclination of the upstream face to the horizontal is usually between 45° and 55°, but slopes up to 77° have been used. (6) Lower intensity of loading on foundations. (7) Greater flexibility allowing for slight settlement under full load.

DISADVANTAGES.—(1) The thin sections, often with reinforcement, are more liable to damage by frost or prolonged weathering, causing seepage, and greater care is required in their construction. The present tendency is towards the use of thicker sections requiring no reinforcement or in which the reinforcement is deeply embedded. (2) This type of dam is more subject to destruction by sabotage or military attack. (3) The multiple arch type must have particularly unyielding foundations for the buttresses, otherwise the arches will be unduly stressed.

SUITABILITY.—This type of construction is suitable for dams of medium height, in wide valleys and particularly where the foundations may be pervious. Buttress dams have been built having heights ranging from 30 to 90 m, and lengths from 100 to 2,550 m.

TYPES OF BUTTRESS DAMS.—Figure 22 shows the main types.

CONTINUOUS SLAB DECK.—Figure 22 (*a*). The flat decking slab is built into the buttresses. This type is not used extensively. Joints are required to minimise shrinkage and temperature effects, and it is more expedient to use a design which takes full advantage of the necessary inclusion of these joints. It is also necessary to provide reinforcement at the upstream face. Another disadvantage is that the action of the deck is uncertain if there is any unequal settlement of foundations.

SIMPLE SLAB DECK.—Figure 22(*b*). The most common type of flat decking slab. The decking rests on haunches at the upstream end of the buttresses. Reinforcement near the upstream face is not required since the behaviour of the decking approximates to that of a simply supported beam. The effects of temperature differences between the slab and buttress, of deck shrinkage during construction, and of unequal settlement of foundations are largely eliminated.

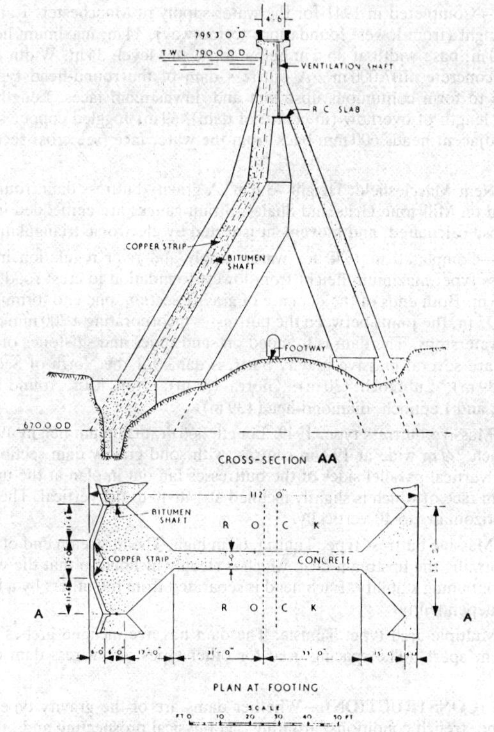

FIG. 23.—Haweswater Dam. (Dimensions in imperial units, as published.)

CANTILEVER DECK.—Figure 22(*c*) and (*d*). This type requires reinforcement at the upstream face and the monolithic construction tends to cause temperature, shrinkage and settlement strains. No actual use of this type is known.

ROUND-HEAD BUTTRESS.—Figure 22(*e*). This is a development proposed by F. A. Noetzli about 1925. The buttress heads are enlarged to full span width and the faces are curved or otherwise shaped in such a manner that the water pressure is transmitted to the buttress in compression. The buttress heads are not reinforced. Noetzli recommends the following buttress spacings: (1) 11 m for dams 25–50 m high. (2) 15 m for dams 50–80 m high. (3) 18 m for dams over 80 m in height. The Haweswater Dam is of this type. See Fig. 23.

MULTIPLE ARCH.—Figure 22(*f*). The multiple arch is a well-known type of buttress dam, in which the upstream face consists of a series of inclined barrel arches spanning the buttresses. The economic spacing of the buttresses is usually greater than that for other types of buttress dam, and a more advantageous type of buttress construction is possible. Ordinarily, the buttresses are relatively slender and they are often braced by horizontal struts spanning between them. In multiple arch dams, however, with larger spans, the need for struts may be eliminated by using double-wall or hollow buttresses, each stable within itself. A system of tie walls and struts between the webs assures unity of action. Double-walled buttresses also have a distinct advantage in appearance, particularly in high dams.

The arches are usually relatively slender and of regularly varying form top to bottom. A closer fit between the centre line of the arch and the line of pressure may be effected by means of a non-circular or multi-centred arch. Also the moment at the springing is usually greater than at the crown, for which reason a thickening towards the haunches is desirable. This may be obtained by using a single-centred extrados and a three-centred intrados. Central angles as small as 100° have been used but the recent tendency is towards central angles approaching 180°, thereby reducing the lateral pressure on the buttresses.

BUTTRESS SPACING.—It is usually cheaper to construct one large buttress than two thin ones half the thickness. For long spans, the cost of falsework for the facing may be high and secondary stresses in the haunches may give trouble. Buttress spacings vary from 5–8 m for the thin type and up to 15–20 m for the thicker or double-wall type.

DETAILS OF BUTTRESS AND MULTIPLE-ARCH DAMS (as published)

HAWESWATER DAM.—Completed in 1941 for the water supply of Manchester. Raised the level of the lake by 29 m. Maximum height (from lowest foundations to footway), 44 m; maximum height (from ground level to top water level), 30 m; base width at 36·5 m below top water level, 34 m. Width at top water level, 2·5 m estimated volume of concrete, 107,000 m^3. A buttress dam of the round-head type, having 44 buttresses widened at their ends to form continuous upstream and downstream faces. Length of each block, 10·7 m; overall length, 469 m; length of overflow (in centre of dam), 69 m; Joggled copper stops 250 × 2·5 mm thick were concreted into adjacent heads 600 mm back from the water face (see cross-section and plan at footing; Fig. 23).

LAMALOAD DAM.—Near Macclesfield. Height 43·6 m. A gravity buttress dam, round-head type. Storage is 1,977 Ml. It is founded on Millstone Grits and Shales. Strain gauges are embedded in some of the buttresses to test strains with those calculated, and movement is tested by electronic triangulation methods.

WIMBLEBALL DAM.—Completed in 1978 for water supply and river regulation in Devon and Somerset. Diamond-head buttress type: maximum height from lowest foundation to crest road, 59 m; maximum width, 55 m; crest length, 296 m. Both ends of the dam are of gravity section, one end forming the overflow spillway. Buttress spacing is 13·75 m, the joints between the buttresses incorporating a 200 mm diameter 'Paracore' plug between two rubber waterstops. The dam is founded on sandstones and siltstones of varying quality.

SCOTLAND.—There are several massive gravity buttress dams for the North of Scotland Hydro-Electricity Board, eg Lawers (39 m); Lubreoch (30 m); Giorra (30 m); Sron Mor, round-head (45 m); Errochty, diamond-head (39 m); and Lednoch, diamond-head (39 m).

LOCH SLOY DAM.—Massive buttress type, 1949. Length 366 m; maximum height 49 m. The dam consists of 13 solid buttresses, each 7·9 m wide at 19·8 m centres, with solid gravity dam sections at each end, running into the hillsides. The vertical parallel sides of the buttresses fan out in plan at the upstream end to form the dam wall, the upstream face of which is slightly inclined at 1 in 40 to the vertical. The downstream face of the buttresses slopes 8 horizontally to 10 vertically.

BEN-METIR DAM.—Massive buttress type. Tunisia, 60 m high. The upstream end of each pier is in the shape of a diamond head, forming the upstream face, which is steeply inclined so that the water pressure assists the weight of concrete in obtaining stability. Each head is separated from the others by a bituminous joint, so that the piers can settle independently.

MELLEGUE DAM.—Multiple-arch type. Tunisia. The dam has five inclined arches supported by triangular buttresses, approx 50 m apart. (The spacing used for other types of buttress dam does not usually exceed 20 m.)

CONCRETE DAMS (CONSTRUCTION).—Whether dams are of the gravity type (straight or curved) or the arch or buttress type, trench conditions, grouting, geophysical prospecting and other exploratory work as well as the river diversion, valve tower, etc, may be similar to those described in the foregoing paragraphs.

Concrete is now almost universally used as a basic material, either with ordinary aggregate, or with 150 mm aggregate and is generally vibrated.

The upstream face of a dam may be of plain concrete placed *in situ* with shuttering, or faced with pre-cast concrete blocks, or, where acid waters are a special consideration, with blue brindled bricks. As in the case of earth embankments it is desirable to bring up the main thickness of the dam fairly slowly or else consider the use of low heat cement to avoid the high temperatures of setting. Further useful data is given below.

TABLE 14.—QUANTITIES OF GROUT.

The numbered columns refer to data as follows: (1) Total lengths of borehole in metres: (2) Cement and chemical products used, in tonnes; (3) Amount of cement, etc, in kilos, per lineal metre; (4) estimated area of cut-off curtain or screen under dam in m²; (5) Amount of cement etc, in kilos per m² of grout curtain or screen.

	(1)	(2)	(3)	(4)	(5)
Piave de Cadore	73,392	6,264	85.5	37,000	170
Gallina	30,000	28,647	950	20,000	1,432
Pontesei (Mae)	18,000	700	39	16,500	42·5
Barcis	14,413	982	68·2	22,692	43·3
St. Pierre Cognet	2,117	300	137	10,000	30
Castillon	10,225	5,195	520	46,450	112
Ghrib	25,500	2,930	115	32,000	90
Sarno (Earth)	30,000	2,900	320	34,600	85

The geological formation at the first four sites are Trias Dolomite; No 5 is Upper Lias limestone; No 6 is Upper Jurassic limestone; No 7 Miocene grits and marls; and No 8 Pliocene conglomerate.

CONTRACTION JOINTS.—Rubber or plastic rubber insertion is generally used; it can be welded on site.

GROUTING.—The use of grout of cement clay, bentonite, silica gels, sodium silicate, or other materials has been perfected for: (*a*) Securing impermeability under a dam at depths up to 100 m; (*b*) Strengthening weak strata at depths up to 10 m to increase the bearing strength under the dam and its abutments; (*c*) Securing homogeneity at construction joints in arch or cupola dams. Table 14 gives examples of quantities of grout used. The first four are in Italy, and the others in France and Algeria:

INSTRUMENTS.—It is common practice to install thermometers (electrical resistance type), and strain gauges to measure strains in concrete of dams, and electronic survey methods and pendulums for measuring deformation in dams. These are valuable aids for testing the performance of dams in comparison with the forecasts made from models. In addition, instruments may be installed for long term records of behaviour of high dams. Measurements are made to check the amount of *pore-pressure*, ascertain if water pressure under the dam

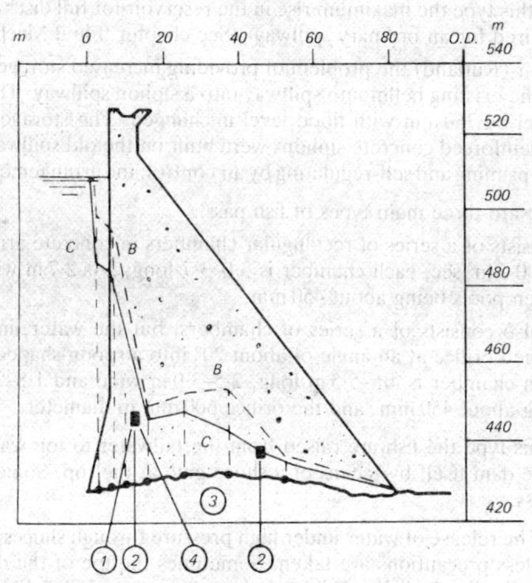

FIG. 24.—Fontana Dam. (*Notes*: *B*, denotes pressure uplift from cells before drilling slanting holes, in 1956. *C*, denotes uplift pressure after drilling holes, 1956. (1) = Grout curtain. (2) = Drain reliefs, 1944. (3) = Uplift cells, 1944. (4) = new slanting drains, 1956.)

increases, threatening dangerous uplift and to record any variation of leakage, which varies inversely as the pore pressure. Measurements are also made of the *deformation*, to ascertain any variation in settlement or tilting of a high dam due to weakness of strata, structure, or extraneous cause such as earthquakes.

Pore Pressure.—Typical records are available of excessive uplift pressure under several dams in the Tennessee Valley, one of which, Fontana, 147 m in height, constructed in 1944, was found to have excessive pore-pressure in 1952, for the pressure had doubled in some parts under the dam and the drains under the dam were choked by nearly 50% of mud. By 1955, additional drains had been dug and the pore-pressure was reduced to normal. See Fig. 24.

Deviation.—Pendulums installed inside the Spitallamm Dam (Switzerland), 114 m in height, had shown that the deviation or tilt downstream, for 18 years up to 1950, was 5 mm when the reservoir was full. In 1950, another large dam and reservoir was built, 92 m in height, distant 1,000–1,900 m from the Spitallamm, when its deviation was increased to 7 mm. Both dams are on hard granite. See Fig. 25.

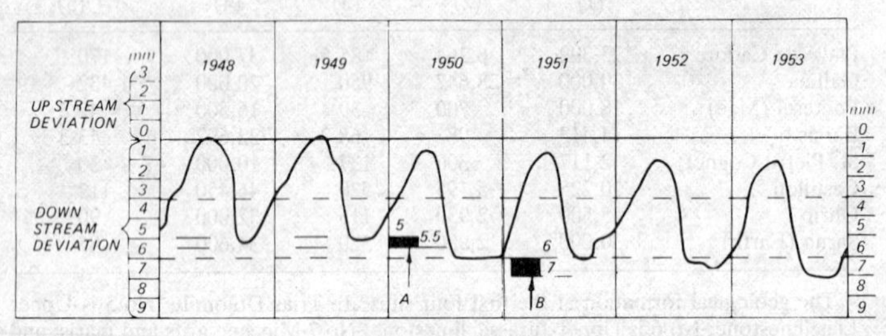

FIG. 25.—Spitallamm Dam. (*A* = Range of Maximum Deviation, 1932 to 1950. *B* = Range of Maximum Deviation, 1950 to 1966†.)

SIPHON SPILLWAYS.—These may be used (*a*) to reduce the height to which the water in a reservoir rises above normal top water level during floods, or (*b*) to increase the effective storage without reducing the flood discharge capacity.

They operate as follows: when the water rises to the level of the siphon crest, it flows over it. Air is prevented from entering the downstream leg either by a water seal or by the falling water striking the opposite side of the tube and forming a curtain across it. The current of air caused by the flow of water over the crest exhausts some of the air in the siphon barrel, producing a rise in the level of the water in the siphon, which in turn increases the flow and intensifies the priming action. More air is drawn out until it is all exhausted and the siphon runs at full capacity. When the water level in the reservoir falls sufficiently to allow air to enter the siphon the action is broken and the flow ceases.

In a siphon spillway of this type the maximum rise in the reservoir for full discharge is usually about 300 mm, as against 1·2–1·5 m required for an ordinary spillway. (See chapter 'Fluid Mechanics'.)

At Eye Brook Reservoir (Rutland) the problem of providing increased storage without raising the dam was overcome by converting the existing bellmouth spillway into a siphon spillway. This alteration made it possible to raise the overflow level by 760 mm with flood level unchanged. The storage was thereby increased from 6,900–8,100 Ml. Sixteen reinforced concrete siphons were built on the old spillway, the design being based on model tests. They are self-priming and self-regulating by air control: the arrangement is known as 'partialisation'.

FISH PASSES.—There are three main types of fish pass.

OVERFALL TYPE.—Consists of a series of rectangular chambers in concrete arranged one above another up an incline. For a flow of 0·5 m³/sec, each chamber is 3·0–3·7 long, 2·0–2·7 m wide, and 1·8–2·1 m deep, the difference in level between pools being about 450 mm.

ORIFICE TYPE.—This also consists of a series of chambers, but the water, instead of falling over a weir, passes through a submerged orifice at an angle of about 20° into a spoon-shaped depression in the floor. For a flow of 0·8 m³/sec, each chamber is 4·5–5·5 m long, 2·5–3·0 m wide and 1·8–2·0 m deep, the difference in level between pools being about 450 mm, and the orifice 600 mm in diameter.

BORLAND TYPE.—In this type the fish are raised from the tailwater to top water level in one operation by flooding a chamber in the dam itself by means of a sluice gate at the top. Sometimes compensation water is used to operate a fish pass.

JET DISPERSERS.—The release of water under high pressure through sluices or valves at the foot of a high dam may cause scour unless precautions are taken. Sometimes the toe of the dam is curved upwards to act as a deflector and a cushioning pool may be provided. A jet disperser, containing internal radial vanes, is often fixed to the end of the outlet pipe, which breaks up the jet into a conical shower of small drops, so that their energy is absorbed by the air.

SCREENS OR RACKS.—These are used for the removal of the debris carried by water flow to intakes and scour pipes. The small installations are usually manually operated, and the attendant inserts a duplicate screen before lifting a foul screen for cleaning. Larger installations employ power operated band screens, which slowly rotate and the screens are continually cleaned by water jets.

WATER POWER

GENERAL CONSIDERATIONS.—The water wheel has been used for centuries for driving millstones and its modern equivalent, the water turbine, is still sometimes used direct-coupled to industrial machinery. However, water power is now mainly used for the generation of electricity. The introduciton of high-voltage transmission over long distances has made many sites economically attractive for water-power development, which previously were considered unsuitable owing to their remoteness from the consumer. See chapter 'Water Turbines'.

ADVANTAGES OF HYDRO-ELECTRIC POWER SCHEMES.—They possess the following advantages over 'thermal' stations using steam or diesel-driven generators:-

(1) No Fuel Costs.—This is particularly important at the present time, with rising costs of coal and oil, and shortages in the supply of coal. Apart from the actual cost of the fuel saved, the use of water often reduces costs of transport, handling and storage.

(2) Longer Life.—The amortisation period for the civil engineering works is usually about 80 years and the *effective life* is probably much longer. The usual period for the mechanical plant is about 35 years, but after this time it can often continue in service for the cost of maintenance only; efficiency in larger plant has reached nearly 100% and it is therefore unlikely to become obsolete.

(3) Low Cost of Maintenance.—Water-power machinery is simple, robust and reliable. The speed is relatively low and high temperatures are not encountered. There is little auxiliary equipment to maintain.

(4) Small Labour Costs.—A hydro-electric station requires only a small operating staff, three or four men being sufficient for quite a large installation. Automatic control is often used.

(5) Quick Starting.—Hydro-electric plant can be run up and synchronised in a few minutes. The load on the station can be increased or decreased rapidly and when the plant is shut down there are no standby losses.

MULTI-PURPOSE SCHEMES.—Schemes based on storage reservoirs are often designed to fulfil other purposes besides power production, such as flood control, irrigation, water supply and navigational improvements. Much hydro-electric development is likely to take place in the near future, particularly in Africa and Asia. The hydro-electric scheme can supply a regulated flow of water to be used for irrigation, which in turn leads to a thriving community which provides the market for the power.

TYPES OF DEVELOPMENT

In order to develop hydro-electric power a fall is essential. This may be provided naturally by a river flowing over a cliff, a series of rapids in a stream, or by the difference in level between a lake situated at a high altitude and the bottom of a valley. Alternatively, an artificial fall may be created by the construction of a dam; the fall may be at the dam itself or the water may be led by a tunnel, pipe or canal to a point where there is a steep natural fall.

CLASSIFICATION.—Hydro-electric schemes are usually classified according to the height of the fall, ie the 'head', as follows: (1) *Low head*—below 30 m; (2) *Medium head*—between 30–150 m; (3) *High head*—over 150 m. These figures are quite arbitrary as there are of course no rigid boundaries.

There are two main types of schemes: (1) *Run-of-river schemes*, where no storage is provided and the reliable power is limited to the minimum or 'dry weather flow' of the river. (2) *Storage schemes*, where storage is provided by building a dam, to balance the seasonal and annual variations of flow.

High head schemes are feasible only in very mountainous countries such as Norway and Switzerland, but river flows are usually very variable and storage is usually required. This is often possible since comparatively small quantities of water are needed and the steep-sided valleys provide suitable sites for relatively inexpensive dams.

Low head schemes with large barrages and head race canals are usually found in the lower reaches of a river, particularly a large continental river, where it is difficult to find suitable sites for a high dam. Usually little storage is provided other than pondage to provide daily regulation of the flow. The reliable daily output is therefore limited to that which can be obtained from the minimum flow. However a substantial minimum flow can usually be relied upon as such rivers do not have the wide fluctuations of a mountain river. The St. Lawrence river from Lake Ontario to the sea, has a gathering ground of approximately 750 Mm^2, with an average rainfall of 840 mm per annum. The average flow is 6,825 m^3/sec, with maximum and minimum of 9,150 and 4,360 m^3/sec.

Multiple Development.—Frequently a river may be developed at a number of places along its course and any particular scheme should be considered as part of a scheme for development of the river as a whole. A storage scheme near the head of a catchment area can often provide a run-of-river station further downstream with a reliable minimum supply of water. It way be advantageous to restrict the operation of the upper station to periods of heavy flow and to replenish its reservoir whilst the lower station is operated to its full extent by the unregulated flow from the lower part of the catchment area. Sometimes a river provides good sites for storage but has no suitable fall. In such cases it may be possible to take the water into an adjacent catchment area where a greater head is available.

WATER POWER SCHEMES: COMPONENT PARTS.—A scheme is made up of some or all of the following component parts, depending on the lay-out.

HEADWORKS.—These may consist of a dam forming a reservoir (in a storage scheme) or a low weir or 'barrage' across a river or stream (in a run-of-river scheme) with the necessary intakes and control gear to divert the water into an aqueduct.

AQUEDUCT OR CONDUIT.—Required when the headworks are some distance away from the power station, to convey the water (usually under little or no pressure) from the headworks to the forebay. May be an open channel, flume, pipeline or tunnel, or a combination of these. In low head schemes this conduit may lead directly to the power house, when it is known as the 'head race'.

FOREBAY.—A reservoir at the head of the penstock providing adequate storage to meet hour-to-hour load fluctuations on the station.

INTAKE.—The entrance to the penstock from the forebay. Contains screens to prevent debris from entering the penstock, and a sluice gate to enable the penstock to be emptied for maintenance work or to stop the flow of water in case of an emergency.

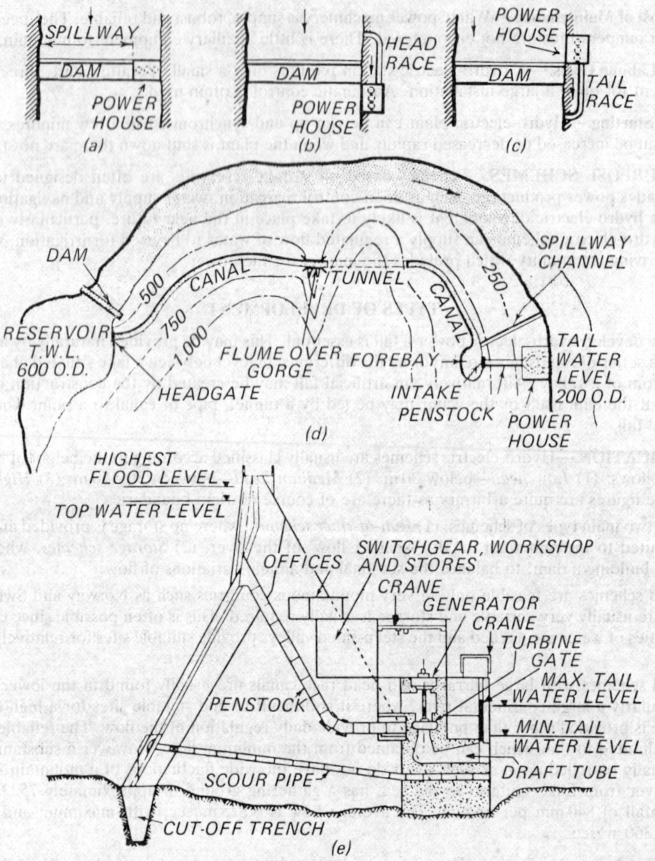

FIG. 26.—Types of Layout for Hydro-electric Power Schemes (with definitions of integral parts).

PENSTOCK.—A pipeline or tunnel which conveys the water under pressure from the forebay to the power station.

POWER HOUSE.—Contains the turbines, generators, switchgear and transformers, etc.

TAIL RACE.—A channel below the power station into which the turbines discharge, leading back into the river. If the power station is underground, the tail race may be in a tunnel.

TYPES OF LAY-OUT.—The type of layout depends mainly on the topography of the district and the head available. Usually the maximum possible head is aimed at, consistent with economy and provision against floods and droughts. Usually several alternative layouts have to be worked out in detail to determine which is the most economical. Fig. 26 shows the various alternative layouts in common use; (*a*), (*b*) and (*c*) show layouts suitable for low-head schemes. In all three cases the dam creates a head by raising the water level in the river.

(*a*) This is the simplest form of all, the power house being built at one end of the dam which forms a spillway for excess water. Water is delivered direct to the turbines and is discharged back into the river directly through the draft tubes. Sometimes when a particularly long spillway is required a hollow dam is built and the power plant placed inside it.

(*b*) The power house is constructed on the bank downstream of the dam and water is conveyed to the turbines by a head race. This provides a longer spillway, the whole of the crest of the dam being utilised.

(*c*) An alternative to (*b*), the power house being on the bank upstream of the dam, with a tail race discharging water back into the river below the dam.

(*d*) This layout is applicable to low, medium or high-head schemes. Water from a river or reservoir flows through a gradually sloping open channel, a flume over a narrow gorge, and a non-pressure tunnel through a mountain spur to a forebay at a point where there is a steep fall. From here the water flows through the penstock to the power house situated at the foot of the hill on the river bank.

(*e*) This shows a typical round-headed buttress dam with generating station immediately below it.

Sometimes a scheme contains a network of collecting aqueducts intercepting several streams in neighbouring catchments, the flows of which are added to that of the main river or to the yield of a reservoir. (Many of the schemes in Scotland include such networks.)

PUMPED-STORAGE SCHEME.—The term 'pumped-storage' describes an installation where surplus, off-peak electrical energy is used to pump water back into a reservoir to increase the output at times of peak load. The water pumped may be supplemented by natural run-off but a pure pumped storage scheme is unique in requiring only sufficient run-off to make good evaporation and seepage losses. The essential components of a pumped-storage scheme are upper and lower storage basins with a pressure conduit between them, generating plant and pumping plant. The upper storage basin should hold sufficient water for full capacity operation of the generating plant during the peak load period plus a reserve. The lower storage basin or tail pond must provide sufficient water to enable the upper reservoir to be replenished during off-peak hours.

The pumping plant may be quite independent of the generating plant or pumps may be direct-coupled to the alternators which run as motors when pumping. Turbines have been developed which also run as pumps. These require electrical units in which the number of stator poles in the circuit can be varied to obtain a higher speed of rotation when pumping. Examples are found in the Glen Shira project in Scotland, the Ffestiniog Scheme in Wales and the Hiwassee Scheme (TVA) in the USA. See chapter 'Water Turbines'.

A very large pumped storage scheme utilises the night flow over Niagara Falls; water is diverted from the Falls and stored in reservoirs of 6×10^9 gallons (US) capacity (22,700 ML). This water generates electric power through a fall of approximately 45 m.

HYDRAULIC DESIGN.—ESTIMATION OF THE AVAILABLE POWER.—The theoretical power of 1 l/sec falling 1 m is 9·81 Nm/sec, ie 9·81 watts. Hence, for 1 m^3/sec falling 1 m, the theoretical power is 9·81 kW or 13·1 hp.

If Q = flow in m^3/sec; h = head of water in m; and e = overall efficiency of the turbine and generator; the power output will be 9·81 Qhe kW. The overall efficiency, e, varies from about 70–95%, being higher for larger plant; 85% is quite usual.

For calculating the power output of a hydro-electric scheme the following two formulae are convenient: (1) Theoretical kW available = Flow in m^3/sec × head in m × 9·81. (2) Assuming 80% efficiency for the turbine, and 95% efficiency for the generator (an overall efficiency of 76%), the power output in kW = flow in m^3/sec × head in m × 7·46.

Rainfall and Run-off.—The design of a scheme should, ideally, be based on at least 30 years of run-off records, but unfortunately river flow records are rarely available. Gaugings should, however, be commenced as soon as possible. Sometimes the behaviour of a river may be assessed from records of flow in an adjacent river or one having a similar catchment area and slopes. In the absence of river gaugings river flows have to be determined from a study of rainfall records of the catchment area, which are usually available. (See paragraphs Rainfall and Run-off, p. **I7**/63.)

In the design of hydro-electric schemes it is customary to state the run-off as a percentage of the rainfall. In temperate climates the losses due to evaporation and absorption by vegetation may be 300–450 mm per annum—less than 30% of the total rainfall. In tropical climates, however, losses are much greater and evaporation as high as 92% of the total rainfall has been known. When gaugings are available they are usually re-arranged in order of magnitude and plotted as a 'duration hydrograph' (see Fig. 9), from which the average flow can be obtained. Catchments having similar topography and climate have very similar duration hydrographs if these are plotted from records covering a fairly long period, say, 10 years. Thus, in the absence of gaugings, the flow of a river can often be predicted with reasonable accuracy from the duration hydrograph of another but similar catchment.

If the cumulative discharge is plotted against time, the 'mass diagram' or 'summation hydrograph' is obtained (see Figs. 9 and 10) from which can be found the storage necessary to provide for various constant rates of draw-off. (See paragraph 'Storage and Yield', p. **I7**/21.)

Catchment Areas and Storage Capacity of Reservoirs.—For large schemes in difficult country, where contoured maps are not available, an aerial survey is much more rapid than a ground survey and is usually sufficiently accurate. The true catchment area may be larger than the apparent one in certain geological formations, such as limestone, due to the existence of underground channels. Such channels provide storage which damps out the effects of fluctuating rainfall and provides favourable conditions for small run-of-river schemes. Under these conditions correlation between rainfall and run-off is almost impossible, as there may be a time lag of several months between the rain falling and its appearance at a spring.

In calculation for large hydro-electric schemes, the catchment area is usually given in square kilometres rather than hectares. The following constant is useful: 1,000 mm (ie 1 m) of annual runoff from an area of 1 km^2, is equivalent to a flow of 31·5 l/sec.

'RUN-OF-RIVER' SCHEMES.—The most economical development of a catchment by a 'run-of-river' scheme without storage may be determined from the duration hydrograph. It is not unusual for such curves to show a flood flow rising to 30 or 40 times the average and a dry weather flow as low as 1 l/s km^2.

It is usual to install a conduit with a carrying capacity several times greater than the average flow. In the typical duration hydrograph in Fig. 27, the area under the curve gives the total run-off. If a conduit is installed with a carrying capacity of twice the average flow, all the water represented by the shaded area can be utilised (in this case 80% of the total run-off). Similarly, conduits of larger capacity would enable the following proportions of the run-off to be utilised: Three times average flow—89%; four times average flow—94%; and five times average flow—96%. (*Note.*—These figures are higher than would be obtained for a 'flashy' stream.)

In this way, a 'utilisation curve' can be obtained from the duration hydrograph showing the relationship between conduit capacity (in terms of average flow) and the percentage of water which can be utilised. Generally it is uneconomical to construct a conduit with a capacity more than 4½ times the average flow (to use between 80 and 90% of the total run-off), unless it is a very short one. The same principle applies to the diversion of water by a conduit from one catchment to another. This is most frequently resorted to in areas with a heavy rainfall where high heads are available but there are few sites available for storage, as in Scotland. This is worthwhile only if the extra revenue produced by the diverted water covers the annual charges on the extra cost of the conduit.

STORAGE SCHEMES.—If practicable these are usually more economical than 'run-of-river' schemes. In water-supply schemes where the maximum reliable yield is required, the corresponding storage consistent with economy is found. For many valleys this storage often corresponds to the flow of the three driest consecutive years, or about 70–80% of the average annual run-off. In hydro-electric schemes, however, it is usual to provide storage to utilise the flow of the driest year, or less.

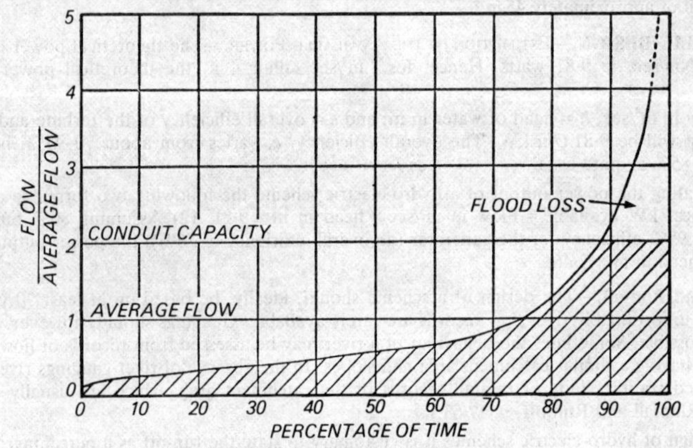

FIG. 27.—Duration Hydrograph showing Utilisation.

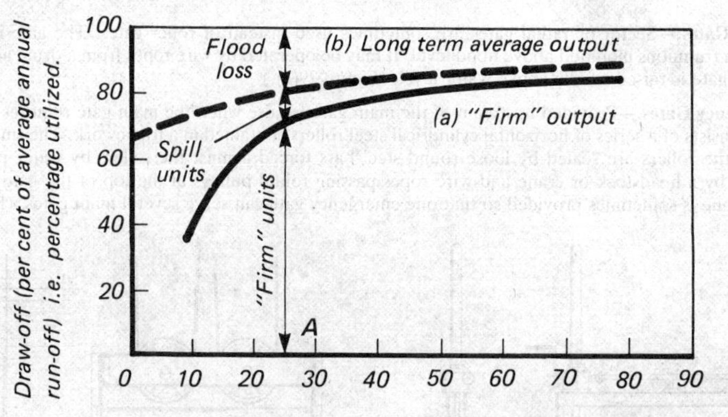

FIG. 28.—Utilisation Curve for Storage Scheme.

From the mass-diagram, by plotting the values of storage required against several corresponding rates of draw-off expressed as a percentage of the average run-off, ie against the percentage of the run-off which is utilised, a utilisation curve is obtained similar to Fig. 28 (curve (*a*)). This curve if plotted from a mass-curve covering a long period, will show the quantity of water which can be guaranteed every year for a given storage, and hence the 'firm' output of the scheme. See also p. **I7**/24.

The value of even a small amount of storage is indicated by the steep lower part of the curve, where a small increase in storage gives a considerable increase in the guaranteed minimum utilisation of water. A point is reached, however, at the beginning of the flat upper part of the curve, when the provision of large extra storage, probably at great expense, has little value in improving the 'firm' output. For example, in Fig. 28, if the storage is increased from 50–75% or $1\frac{1}{2}$ times, 'firm' output is increased only by 3%.

The following figures show the relation between storage and yield (or guaranteed draw-off) as given by W. J. E. Binnie (which may be used in the absence of a mass diagram from which a utilisation curve could be obtained): The storage (% of annual average run-off), for 15, 20, 25, 30 and 35% are related to a yield or guaranteed draw-off (% of average annual run-off) of 57, 66, 71, 75 and 77% respectively. These figures are normally used for water supply, but for water power the yield may be taken as slightly higher because the demand usually eases off when the natural run-off is at its lowest. For storages of 20–30% the yields (or guaranteed draw-offs) may be about 5% higher and the available flow in an average year may be 15% higher than the figures given.

By installing additional generating plant, the output may therefore often be increased above the firm output during the average or wet years, but this is practicable only if the grid system can absorb the extra output, eg by shutting down thermal stations. Curve (*b*) in Fig. 28 is a typical utilisation curve for a scheme of this kind, giving the 'long-term average output' for a given storage. In any ordinate such as AD, AB represents the percentage available for producing 'firm' units, BC that for producing 'spill' units and CD the percentage lost in floods.

The yearly electrical output of a hydro-electric scheme can therefore be defined as X firm units, plus Y spill units. The extra plant may often be required in any case, to provide for daily peak output in periods of normal or low run-off, and the arrangement may therefore be quite economical.

CONTROL GATES.—Various types of control gates are used for regulating the flow at intakes, in aqueducts and penstocks and for flood control. (See Fig. 29.)

Sliding Sluice Gates.—Used for small work. Consists of an iron or steel gate sliding in guides on a framework, operated by a handwheel, sometimes with bevel reduction gear. The working faces are often made of gun-metal to prevent rusting. (Figure 29(*a*).)

Fixed Roller Sluice Gates.—Used for larger work. Rollers rotate on axles fixed to the gate and travel over paths on the frame; this reduces the frictional resistance. The gate is counterbalanced by weights hung by pulleys from chains which pass over sprocket wheels on a horizontal shaft. Operated by a handle or motor geared to the sprocket wheel shaft. (Figure 29(*b*).)

Free Roller Sluice Gates.—Suitable for large work, eg gates 7·5 m square for flood control in dams. Rollers are freely suspended in protected grooves between the end posts of the gate and the piers. Usually operated electrically with automatic control by the flood water level. The power for closing, if not provided by the motor, is obtained by the out-of-balance between the gate and its counterweight. When closed by gravity suitable braking is provided by oil-pump retarders or solenoid brakes.

Sector Gates.—Sector or radial gates are sometimes used instead of roller gates. The gate is curved and rotates on trunnions mounted above flood level. It may be operated by wire ropes from a drum and when fully open the gate is raised wholly above water level. (Figure 29(*c*).)

Emergency Gates.—Provided upstream of the main gate for use when the main gate requires maintenance work. Consists of a series of horizontal cylindrical steel rollers contained in a framework. The small clearances between the rollers are sealed by loose round steel bars forced against the rollers by water pressure. It is operated by a headstock or crane and wire ropes passing round pulleys at the top of the gate. A travelling gantry crane is sometimes provided so that one emergency gate can serve several main gates. (Figure 29(*d*).)

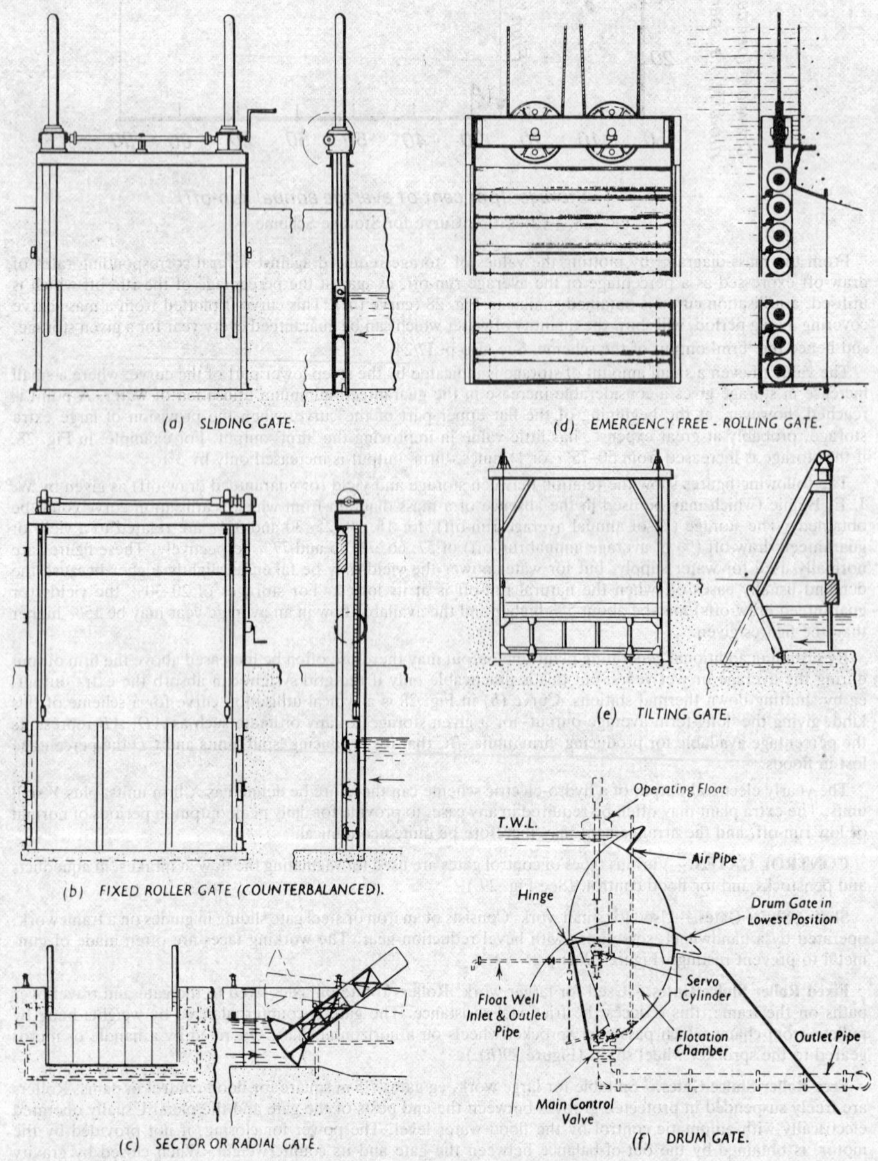

FIG. 29.—Types of Control Gates.

Tilting Sluice Gates.—Sometimes used for flood control on a dam where a permanent spillway of sufficient area is impracticable. The foot of the gate is hinged and, when fully lowered, the gate lies flush with the cill. When fully raised it makes an angle of about 70° with the horizontal. Normally the gate is kept raised by a counterweight, but if the water level increases the extra load depresses the gate, creating a spillway area proportional to the flood. The gate gradually rises again as the water level drops. (Figure 29(*e*).)

Drum Gates.—Used for flood control on dams, having a neater appearance than roller or tilting types, there being no unsightly gearing or gantries. The gate is triangular, hinged at the upstream end, and kept in equilibrium by a flotation chamber in the crest of the dam. The water pressure on the upstream side of the gate is balanced by the slightly greater water pressure in the flotation chamber. The chamber is connected with the reservoir by an opening which can be adjusted to control the quantity of water entering; it also has a pipe which discharges downstream. When the water level in the reservoir rises a few inches during floods, a float controlled valve opens and water from the flotation chamber is discharged and the gate is lowered. When fully opened the gate forms an arc of a circle in continuation of the crest of the dam, thus giving a high discharge coefficient (Figure 29(*f*).)

Two gates of this type, each 27·4 m long, by 4·9 m deep, were used at the Pitlochry dam to discharge automatically up to 1,130 m^3/sec, with a rise in reservoir level of only 300 mm. An ordinary spillway would have had to be 457 m long, even allowing a 1·2 m rise in the reservoir.

AQUEDUCTS, FOREBAY, PENSTOCKS, TAIL RACE, ETC.

AQUEDUCTS.—Aqueducts or conduits are used when the headworks are some distance away from the power station, to convey water from the headworks to the forebay. The type depends on local conditions and may be an open channel or flume, a pipeline or occasionally a tunnel. A long aqueduct may consist of a combination of some or all of these different types. Collecting aqueducts require spill points if the intakes at the streams they intercept do not provide for the release of flows in excess of the aqueduct's capacity. Open channels are nearly always provided with spillways as they collect drainage from the country through which they pass.

CHANNELS.—Channels are used mostly for low-level surface aqueducts to carry large quantities of water. They are usually of open trapezoidal form, lined with concrete to prevent erosion, reduce leakage and improve the discharge coefficient, and having a gradual slope so that the loss of head is small. Open jointed drains should be provided to prevent water pressure being set up behind the lining when the channel is emptied for maintenance work. (See chapter 'Fluid Mechanics'.)

FLUMES.—A flume is a trough of concrete, steel or wood, used instead of a channel under certain conditions, eg to cross a gorge or over ground where excavation of a channel would be difficult.

PIPELINES.—Reinforced concrete pipes are often used as aqueducts particularly at high elevations, where in winter snow and ice are liable to choke open channels. They are suitable for pressures up to about 25 m of water, and therefore loss of head can be minimised; maintenance costs are low and entry of leaves and debris is prevented. Precast spun pipes up to 1·5–1·8 m diameter are obtainable but transport of the larger pipes may be difficult to high and remote sites. Larger pipelines up to about 5 m diameter are constructed *in situ* using travelling shutters. Sometimes these are covered with an earth bank; this minimises expansion and contraction due to temperature changes and gives a good appearance.

TUNNELS.—A tunnel through a mountain or spur of land may save a long channel or pipeline. A non-pressure tunnel acts merely as a channel but a pressure tunnel may be used as a penstock enabling the fall to be utilised for power production. (See p. **I7**/59.)

FOREBAY.—The forebay consists of a reservoir at the end of the aqueduct and at the head of the penstock. Its capacity should be sufficient to take the incoming flow without spilling immediately if the load is suddenly reduced; and at the same time there should be sufficient water to cope with a sudden increase in load. It is provided with a spillway to allow excess water to escape.

If the aqueduct is long, any adjustment of the sluices at the headworks may not affect the inflow into the forebay until several hours afterwards. In a high-head scheme the water consumption per unit generated is relatively small and in times of heavy rain a long open aqueduct may collect sufficient water *en route* to operate the plant with the sluice at the headworks completely closed.

INTAKE.—The intake to the penstock from the forebay contains screens to prevent debris from entering the penstock, and a sluice gate. The screens usually slide into double vertical grooves, so that they can be lifted by a crane for cleaning. If the screens have only to exclude the size of trash which cannot pass through the turbine runner, the spacing is usually wide (especially with Kaplan turbines), and the intake dimensions are scarcely affected. If, however, descending fish have to be excluded, the spacing between bars must be not greater than 40 mm for salmon, and 25 mm horizontally by 12 mm vertically for smolts (young salmon about 15 cm long.) Also the velocity through the screen should not exceed 150–300 mm/sec, or fish may be pinned against the screen and killed. This often means very large screens and a correspondingly large intake structure.

The sluice gate is usually of the fixed or free-roller type, operated by a motor; closing is sometimes effected by counter weights or by gravity with suitable braking either by oil-pump retarder or solenoid brakes. Leakage is prevented by rubber-covered bars bearing against machined faces. Usually an automatic trip is provided to close the gate if the velocity in the penstock exceeds the normal maximum by about 30%, eg in the event of a burst. An opening is provided downstream of the gate to allow access of air when filling and emptying the penstock.

Where the penstock runs direct from a reservoir to the power house (without an aqueduct) a small forebay is usually formed in the reservoir in front of the intake by building concrete walls with gaps which can be closed by the insertion of temporary wooden gates. This enables the forebay to be emptied for maintenance work on the intake without having to empty the whole reservoir. An intake in a river is usually placed above a low dam at an angle of about 90° to the direction of flow, to prevent entry of debris; a boom of logs may also be provided.

PENSTOCKS.—The penstock which conveys the water under pressure from the forebay to the turbines may be a pressure tunnel, or a pipeline of reinforced or pre-stressed concrete, steel, or wood staves, depending on minimum thickness required.

Economic Diameter.—This depends on the velocity; a high velocity requires a small penstock with low capital charges, but on the other hand friction losses are higher; which increases running costs. A penstock may contain several diameters of pipe, often being larger at the upstream end than at the downstream end. This reduces the thickness and weight of pipes to be handled at the lower end.

In low-head schemes a low velocity up to about 1·5 m/s is preferable, because the friction loss represents a high proportion of the total head. In medium-head schemes maximum velocities vary from about 1·5 to 4·5 m/s. In high-head schemes higher velocities are not uncommon (although high velocities make governing more difficult). High velocities are permissible in short penstocks.

If the annual cost (based on capital charges and running cost, taking into account the units lost by friction) is calculated for several diameters, and plotted against diameter as a graph, a minimum point is obtained showing the most economical size. As an example, in the case of a lined steel penstock 125 m long to carry 5 m^3/s under a gross head of 120 m, such an investigation gave an economic diameter of 1·5 m. Sometimes it may be found more economical to use several smaller pipes instead of one larger one. This also provides for flexibility of operation if there are several turbines.

LOSS OF HEAD DUE TO FRICTION.—The loss of head in a penstock may be calculated from the formula

$$h = 4flv^2/(2gd)$$

where, h = loss of head (m); l = length of panstock (m); d = internal diameter of penstock (m); v = velocity in penstock (m/sec); g = 9·81 m/sec^2; and f = coefficient of friction, depending on the roughness of the pipe (0·012, for welded steel or wood stave pipes, and 0·024, for riveted steel plate pipes.)

The formula applies only to straight pipes and allowance must be made in addition for losses in bends, branches, inlet and exit, etc. Sharp bends and sudden changes in diameter should be avoided and a bellmouth inlet should be provided.

Reinforced Concrete Pipes are suitable for the penstock provided the head does not exceed about 25 m. They are designed under the assumption that the steel takes care of all longitudinal or transverse stresses in the pipe whilst the concrete acts as a waterproof shell. It is evident that, in this case, the steel thickness can be reduced in respect to the head and lay-out.

The permissible tensile stress in the steel can be taken as 110 N/mm^2. The area of steel required for the circumferential reinforcement is determined as follows: Let p be the total internal pressure in N/mm^2 (1 m head of water = 0·01 N/mm^2 approx), d = pipe bore in mm, A_s = area (mm^2) of steel per metre run of pipe, and f_T = allowable tensile stress (N/mm^2) in steel above, then:

$$A_s = 1{,}000\ pd/(2f_T)$$

The area of the longitudinal steel, per metre of circumference, is taken as half the area per metre run of pipe, as given by the formula.

Steel Pipes.—These are usually of mild steel, seamless or welded up to about 400 mm diameter, and welded for larger sizes. For low-head penstocks, riveted pipes may be used. The thickness of the pipes is usually graded from the top to the bottom of the penstock according to the head. The thickness of steel pipe required may be calculated from the formula:

$$t = K + PDF/2Se$$

where, t = nominal thickness (mm); D = external diameter of pipe (mm); P = pressure (static pressure plus surge pressure) (N/mm^2) (*Note*: 1 m head = 0·01 N/mm^2 approx); F = factor of safety (minimum 4); and S = ultimate tensile strength of steel (usually 370–400 N/mm^2).

e = efficiency of joint. The constants for this are as follows: 1·0 for weldless pipes; 0·9 for welded pipes of nominal thickness up to and including 22 mm; 0·85 for welded pipes of nominal thickness over 22 mm, up to and including 28 mm; 0·80 for welded pipes of nominal thickness over 28 mm; 0·70 for double riveted pipe; and 0·55 for single riveted pipe.

K = maximum minus tolerance required by manufacturers, and is as follows: 10–15% on roll-welded and weldless pipe; 1·2 mm for hydraulic welded pipes under 9 mm thick; 1·6 mm for hydraulic welded pipes 9 mm up to and including 22 mm thick and 2·4 mm for hydraulic welded pipes over 22 mm thick.

The nominal thickness obtained as above is generally increased by about 1·5 mm to allow for corrosion, and rounded up to the next standard thickness. In large pipes under low pressure, the thickness has to be increased still further to give the pipe the necessary stiffness (unless it is surrounded by reinforcing bands or concrete). In Britain welded steel pipes are manufactured in diameters up to 2 m (or larger), and in thickness up to about 40 mm; in lengths up to about 10 m. Riveted pipes have a higher frictional loss and require more maintenance due to 'weeping' rivets and seams. They can, however, be transported easily in the form of plates and riveted up on site.

PENSTOCK ACCESSORIES

Pipe Supports.—Penstocks are usually laid just above ground level because excavation and laying underground is expensive. They are often supported on concrete or masonry piers which must rest on a firm foundation. The spacing of the piers is determined by considering the pipe as a circular beam resting freely on supports and carrying a uniformly distributed load consisting of the weight of the pipe plus the weight of the water. This load determines a longitudinal tension in the lower side of the pipe, and this stress added to the longitudinal tension of the pressure of water caused by the static head, plus the extra head due to surge, should not be allowed to exceed f, the safe tensile strength of the material.

The stress, f_b, in N/mm^2, due to the bending $= 9{\cdot}81 \times 10^3 \times WL^2/Z$.

The longitudinal fibre stress f_t due to water pressure is, $f_t = pd/4t$ N/mm^2, where, L = distance between supports (m); W = total load (kg per m); Z = section modulus of pipe (mm^3); p = water pressure (N/mm^2); d = inside diameter of pipe (mm); and t = thickness of pipe (mm).

ANCHORAGE AT BENDS.—Tie rods or concrete anchor blocks must be provided to take the unbalanced pressure (see para 'Unbalanced Pressure on Bends' p. I7/7).

PROTECTIVE COATING.—Steel pipes are usually coated internally and externally with bitumen.

JOINTS.—Steel pipes are usually connected by flanged, welded or riveted joints or by mechanical joints such as Viking–Johnson Couplings. The most suitable type depends on site conditions and the type of labour available for making the joints.

EXPANSION JOINTS.—Special joints to allow for expansion and contraction of steel pipes are provided at suitable intervals, generally on the downstream side of each anchor block. In the type most frequently used a special socket on one pipe allows freedom of movement of the spigot end of the next pipe; leakage is prevented by rubber rings held in place by clamps.

ANTI-VACUUM VALVES.—To prevent the formation of a vacuum in the penstock (due to a burst pipe, sudden change of load in the turbines or shutting of a valve) automatic anti-vacuum valves are provided at all changes of gradient and on the downstream side of shut-down valves.

CYLINDRICAL BALANCED VALVES, or needle valves, consisting of a streamlined sliding piston, are sometimes used instead of disc valves. They do not require a by-pass and occupy less space.

AIR VALVES, SCOUR VALVES AND MANHOLES, must also be provided as in pipelines used for water supply purposes (see 'Valves' p. I7/2).

BALANCED DISC OR BUTTERFLY VALVES are much used in penstocks, both at the top end and just above the turbines. The valve consists of a streamlined disc pivoted either vertically or horizontally so that it can be moved into a position parallel to the flow (fully open) or at right angles to the flow (closed). The valve may be operated manually or by hydraulic rams using water or sometimes oil. It may be fitted with over-velocity and/or remote trip controls. A by-pass is provided so that the pressure on either side can be equalised before opening. These valves are suitable for high or low heads and can be built in large sizes. The loss of head is almost negligible.

SURGE SHAFTS.—A surge shaft or tank often has to be provided in the penstock to prevent excessive pressure changes when load changes take place. It may consist of a vertical concrete-lined shaft (with a pressure-tunnel) or a steel tank (with a pipeline). The top end must be open and above the flood water level at the headworks; it is generally sited as near to the power station as practicable. An overflow pipe is usually provided. When the load on the turbine drops and the governors close the gates, the water level in the shaft rises and excessive pressures are thus prevented. When the load increases, the sudden demand for water while the water in the penstock is accelerating is met by the shaft and pressure drops are therefore reduced.

Surge shafts are usually large and costly structures. For example, the Clunie tunnel (equivalent diameter 7 m) has a surge shaft 33·5 m diameter. Their size may sometimes be reduced if stations are interlinked in such a way that any particular station cannot get a sudden substantial addition to the load it is already carrying.

TUNNELS.—By driving a tunnel through high ground a long open aqueduct or pipeline can often be avoided. Tunnels are of two types; the non-pressure type used as an aqueduct or tail race, and the pressure type, used as a penstock. Pressure tunnels are usually lined with concrete or steel to prevent leakage and reduce friction losses. The thickness of concrete lining is usually between 200 and 300 mm.

Diameters smaller than 2·5 m are not usually economic owing to the restricted working space for either hand or mechanical loading, although smaller tunnels have been driven. The concrete lining is now often placed by pump or by pneumatic placers. Its cost per cubic metre is high (particularly for larger diameters) but the quantity of concrete lining increases only with the diameter whereas the quantity of excavation increases with the square of the diameter.

TAIL RACE.—The tail race (if any) below the turbines is usually an open channel but may occasionally be a tunnel. Screens are required at the outlet of the tail race to keep ascending fish out of the station; the spacing between bars being generally 40 mm. (Where there is no tail race and the draft tubes discharge direct into the river, the turbulence of the water may deter fish, without screens.)

DETAILS OF HYDRO-ELECTRIC SCHEMES.—THE LOCHABER PLANT.—In the second stage, for the utilisation of waters brought into the system from Loch Laggan and the upper Spey, a three-pipe line was constructed. The fall is about 245 m. The pipes are 884 m long, and make three changes of inclination, requiring, at the change points, massive concrete thrust blocks. The internal diameter of 2 m, in the upper sections, is reduced toward the bottom end to allow for the increased wall thickness, to a maximum of 30 mm. The pipes, of the spigot and socket type, were shop-fabricated in lengths of about 9 m, formed of a single plate with the longitudinal seam forge lap welded. They were joined by electric fillet welding of the inner and outer joints.

RIVER RHÔNE, FRANCE.—The Compagnie Nationale du Rhône has control over the river from the Swiss border to the Mediterranean Sea, for the threefold purpose of power development, navigation and irrigation. The Rhône has the largest volume of any of the rivers in France and has a steep slope. The general project includes 20 power stations as well as making the river navigable above Lyon as far as the Lake of Geneva; the power generated will reach about 14,000 million kWh per year. Details of the two plants are as follows:

GÉNISSIAT.—Average flow of river 370 m^3/sec; gradient about 1 in 330; head 70 m. There are six vertical shaft Francis turbines; maximum power 75 MW each; weight of runner 40 tonnes; normal speed 150 rpm. The intake is through towers attached to the upstream face of the dam, there being one tower for each machine, with a steel pressure pipe passing through the body of the dam to the turbine; the flow is controlled by a vertical sluice gate 7 × 5·5 m on the upstream face of the dam. Each turbo-alternator unit has a capacity of 65,000 kW, giving a total ultimate capacity of 390,000 kW or about 1,800 million kWh per year. A stop butterfly valve, diameter 5·2 m is provided between each turbine and the penstock, operated by three oil operated servomotors. Ventilation of the three-phase alternators is through a closed circuit with two ventilators and eight refrigerators, the cooling water being supplied from any one of the turbine penstocks.

The alternators are supported by two lines of massive concrete arches, between which the turbine room is situated. The alternators are some 10 m above the turbines; this arrangement makes it possible to erect and dismantle the turbines, using special cranes installed in the turbine room, without disturbing the alternators. Control is semi-automatic; the generators produce at 15,000 volts, which is immediately stepped up to 220,000 volts by three-phase transformers. Total volume of concrete 7 × 10^5 m^3. A navigation canal has been excavated through the plateau on the right bank.

DONZÈRE-MONDRAGON.—The diversion canal begins at the end of the Donzère gorge; about 1 km below the canal entrance, a dam equipped with six movable gates maintains the water level at about 5 m above normal. The canal runs practically level for 18 km to the power station, spillway and lock group, where there is a drop of 27 m; the tail race canal rejoins the river 11 km futher downstream, near Mondragon. Maximum flow in canal 1,500 m^3/sec, at a mean velocity of 1·5 m/sec. The dimensions of the canal in cross-section are almost equal to those of the Suez Canal, being 10 × 160 m for the head race canal and 16 × 140 m for the tail race canal. The power station is equipped with six Kaplan turbines of 50 MW. Total excavation on the scheme was 50 Mm^3.

Large locks operated at high speed are provided for navigation. The dimensions are 210 × 13 m with a drop of 28 m. During filling and emptying, when the maximum rise or fall is 2·5 m/min, the maximum flow is 100 m^3/sec. Extensive model tests were carried out to ensure that turbulence would not endanger craft.

WIND POWER

WINDMILLS.—Windmills are sometimes used for driving small pumps or generators. The power of a windmill varies approximately as the square of the diameter of the wheel and as the cube of wind velocity, but other factors must also be considered. The power P, may be calculated from the following formula: $P = AV^3/3{,}800$ kW; where, A = total area of sails (m^2), and V = velocity of wind (m/sec).

Inland the UK mean wind velocity is usually 1·5–3 m/s but may be more in exposed positions or on the coast. Windmills are usually designed to run with a wind velocity of from 2 to 10 m/s, with their highest efficiency when driven by a wind of, say 7–10 m/s. Typical outputs of windmills based on a wind velocity of 7 m/s (a pleasant breeze), blowing with a force of about 50 N/m^2, are given in Table 15.

Ample storage (either a reservoir if used for pumping, or batteries if used for generating electricity) must be provided to tide over those periods when the windmill may be out of action either due to lack of wind (say

TABLE 15.—TYPICAL OUTPUT OF WINDMILLS (7 m/s WIND)

Diameter of Wheel (m)	1·2	1·8	2·4	2·7	3·0	3·7	4·3	4·9
Power of Wheel (kW)	0·06	0·15	0·22	0·3	0·4	0·7	1·2	1·7

for 2 or 3 weeks) or excessively high winds. When used for pumping the need for water is often greatest during dry periods of the year when light winds are prevalent and windmills required for this purpose should therefore be specially designed to run in light winds. Sizes of windmills for various quantities and heads, are given in Table 16, which gives wheel diameters (m), quantity of water (l/h), and height of lift (m).

TABLE 16.—WINDMILLS: SIZES/OUTPUTS

Wheel Diameter m	Quantity (litres/hour)			
	Lift.	7·5 m	15 m	30 m
1·6		2,400	1,400	600
2·4		2,600	2,200	1,000
3·0		4,000	2,900	1,700
3·7		11,000	6,000	3,000

Windmills are fitted with a vane to keep the sails facing the wind, and with an automatic governor which regulates the angle of the wheel to the direction of the wind according to the wind velocity and also applies a brake to stop the wheel and keep it at rest when turned out of the wind (this prevents damage by high winds). The height of the tower depends on the altitude of the site and the position of surrounding buildings, trees, etc; it should be high enough to keep the lower part of the wheel at least 5 m above all surrounding obstructions within a distance of, say, 200 m. In open country a 10 or 15 m tower may be used.

Wind Turbines.—The latest developments in wind turbines show promise in producing light compliant structures instead of the heavy standard windmill designs. Using these light structures the wind turbines may be economic with much lower average annual wind speeds of 5–6 m/s, instead of the previous higher rates up to 10 m/s. Costs (at 1980 prices) could be 5 to 6p/kWh including much lower capital costs. These developments indicate that wind turbines should be seriously considered for small power supplies in remote areas with the consequent savings in the use of fossil fuels.

TIDAL POWER

TIDES.—The tide rises and falls twice in 24 hours 50 min and the power available depends on the range of the tide, which varies considerably from time to time and from place to place. Details of tidal ranges and the variations which occur, are dealt with in chapter 'Harbours and Ports', p **M3**/1.

Round the coast of Britain the average range is 5 m at spring tides and 2·6 m at neap tides. The approximate range in metres at various places are as follows (the figures are for spring tides with the neap tide in parentheses): Portishead, River Severn, 13 (6·5); River Dee, 8·0 (3·7); St. Malo, France, 13 (5·5); Bay of Fundy, Nova Scotia, 15; Deseado River, Argentine, 8·2; Adriatic Sea, 0·15.

Methods of Development.—(1) The simplest method is to build a dam across a tidal creek or estuary, so that water can be impounded and used to drive turbines installed in the dam. The incoming tide is allowed to pass through sluice gates installed in the dam, which are closed at high water. When the tide has fallen sufficiently to create a difference in level between the water above and below the dam, the water in the basin is discharged through the turbines into the sea. Finally the sluices are re-opened so that the incoming tide can refill the basin, and the cycle is repeated. This system is used for several small tide mills which are still in operation; sometimes the dam is built across a stream where it enters an estuary so that the mill works partly on tidal and partly on fresh water. This system is simple but the operating time is short. (2) The installation may be designed to work on the incoming tide as well as the outgoing tide, the tide being prevented from entering the basin until the head is sufficient to work the turbines. This system increases the number of hours the turbines can run and therefore gives a greater output, but operation is more complicated. Neither of these two methods will give continuous power. (3) To provide continuous power, eg for the generation of electricity, a proportion of the energy produced during periods of maximum output is used to pump water into a supplementary high level reservoir. This water is used to drive secondary turbines to produce power at times when the main plant is not in operation. (4) Another method for continuous power is to use two or more tidal basins in conjunction with a single power station.

Available Power.—Unless specially developed by methods (3) or (4) above, the power that can be produced directly from the tide is inevitably variable and intermittent, but this may not matter for certain industrial loads. Apart from variations in range there are periods at high and low water when the water is practically still. Also the operating periods of a tidal plant change daily with the time of high water. If turbines are installed with sufficient capacity to utilise the energy of a spring tide, they will be only partly loaded on neap tides; the load factor with therefore be low and the costs high. If smaller turbines are used, some energy will be wasted at spring tides.

Assuming a mean tidal range of only 6 m at spring tides and 3 m at neap tides, and adopting the single-basin method of development with operation on both rising and falling tides, each square metre of basin area would be capable, without storage, of giving an average daily output of approximately 80 MWh. The potential value of tidal power schemes is considerable if they can be developed economically. Proposals have been made for tidal power in Britain, using the Severn estuary, Morecambe Bay, the Humber, the Wash and Solway Firth.

Tidal Power.—RANCE ESTUARY, BRITTANY.—See Fig. 30(*a*). This scheme, completed 1968 is situated on the estuary of the River Rance. The barrage, 750 m in length, carries a two lane carriageway (each of 7 m) with a central reservation of 2·6 m. The barrage also includes, the power station (24 units of 10 MW); a lock for navigation between sea and river; the spillway for disposal of natural floods of the river; and the system of sluices which are operated to let water into the reservoir, and to provide for the reversed flow operation of the turbines, and to be closed during the time of their normal operation.

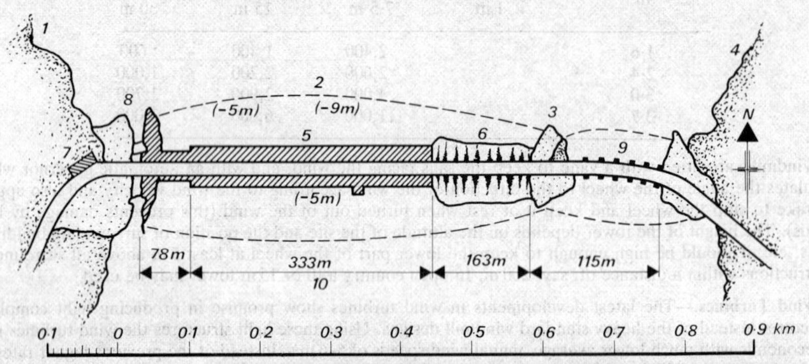

FIG. 30(*a*).—Tidal Power Scheme. Layout Plan. Rance River, Brittany. *Legend:*—(1) Pointe de la Brébis. (2) Sea—St. Malo Bay (Typical Sea Bottom Levels). (3) Chalibert rock. (4) Pointe de la Briantais. (5) Power House with road above. (6) Embankment (Dike). (7) Access shaft to power house. (8) Lock. (9) Spillway and sluice gates. (10) Rance River estuary.

The site, between St. Malo and Dinard, has an exceptional high range of tide; the highest (at equinox), 13·5 m; average full tide, 10·9 m; average normal tide, 8·5 m: average neap tide 5·0 m. The bed of the river is 13 m below mean sea level datum and the top water level in the reservoir is 13·5 m above datum, giving a total depth of water of 26·5 m. The area of the water surface of the reservoir is 2,200 hectares, and the water volume between highest and lowest tides is 18 million m^3.

The continual variation in the times of high tide causes difficulties with the regular disposal of the power output, and peak load periods of the electricity system often coincide with the dormant periods of the generating plant. However, the whole plant is designed for a net output of approx 540 GWh per year (Reservoir to Sea, 537 GWh; Sea to Reservoir (reversed turbines), 71·5 GWh; less power for pumping periods to Reservoir, 64·5 GWh).

When the turbines operate solely on the flow from the reservoir to the sea, the period of operation is approx 4·5 hours per tide. When the turbines operate due to both the discharge and also the inflow to the reservoir, the period of useful operation per tide is approx 5·75 hours. Figure 30(*b*) is an operating cycle diagram: A = period of turbines lowering water in reservoir. B = continued emptying. Sluices opened to lower the head for in-coming sea water to utilise the reverse flow turbine. C = Sea-water entering reservoir, and waiting period until there is an adequate difference of head to enable starting reverse flow turbines. D = Reverse flow turbines working under a reasonable head. E = Filling period to obtain a high head for next lowering of reservoir.

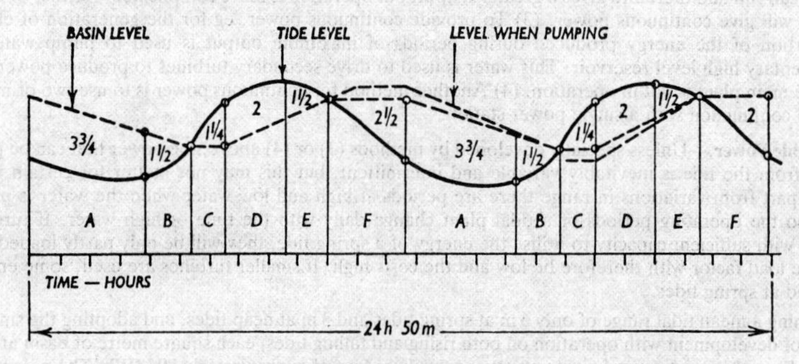

FIG. 30(*b*).—Tidal Power Operating Cycle, Rance River, Brittany.

F = Waiting period for fall of sea-level to increase head for emptying reservoir. In addition, during system off-peak hours, sea-water can be pumped to reservoir, thus providing additional power at discharge period.

LAND DRAINAGE

A distinction is made between *Land Drainage* and *Field Drainage*. The former term covers all aspects including hydrological studies, flood relief and river improvement schemes, and stormwater disposal, while the latter term is confined to measures for removing subsoil water from waterlogged land.

RAINFALL AND RUN-OFF (see section 'Rainfall', p **17**/18).—In land drainage extremes of rainfall are important, ie long periods of drought or continuous rain. 'Long periods' vary with the catchment area and may be three days for small areas, up to three weeks or more in larger areas. Snow is also of special interest. Run-off is of primary importance in the design of drainage schemes, and depends on the following factors: (i) Size, shape, topography and geology of the catchment area; (ii) Length of the river; (iii) Season of year; (iv) Weather; (v) Duration, intensity and direction of the particular rainstorm.

The run-off resulting from any period of rain in the six summer months April–Sept (the growing season), is only about two thirds that in the winter months. The difference is due not to evaporation (which is comparatively small even on hot days), but to absorption by growing vegetation, eg a hectare of corn absorbs about 2·5 Ml in a season and a single tree may absorb up to 360 l/day. The effect of a particular rainstorm depends on the weather conditions and rainfall preceding it particularly if there was a drought or snow. The discharge from snow depends on the rate of thaw (which is independent of rainfall) rather than on the amount of snow.

The peak discharge in the main river is determined by the relative times of peak discharge in the tributaries feeding it, and these depend on the direction of the rainstorm and its distribution over the whole catchment area. For short storms (up to, say, 4 hrs duration) the run-off may be calculated from: $-Q = 0{\cdot}276CAI/(T+2)$, where, Q is the run-off, (m^3/sec); C = run-off factor (often assumed to be 0·5 in England); A = area of catchment, (km^2); I = intensity of rainfall (mm/hour); and T = duration of storm (hours).

For longer periods of rain, conditions change; the run-off increases slightly for periods of rain exceeding 4 hrs and remains almost constant for rain lasting 24 hrs or more. Foi the design of internal land drainage schemes in England Table 17 may be used:

TABLE 17.—RAIN DURATION—RUN-OFF TABLE.

	Once a year			Once in 10 years			Once in 50 years		
Rainfall duration hours	Total rainfall mm	Intensity mm/hr	Run-off per km^2 m^3/sec	Total rainfall mm	Intensity mm/hr	Run-off per km^2 m^3/sec	Total Rainfa-ll mm	Intensity mm/hr	Run-off per km^2 m^3/sec
1	12·5	12·5	0·58	25	25	1·15	38	38	1·75
2	15	7·5	0·26	30	15	0·52	46	23	0·80
3	18	6·0	0·17	33	11	0·30	52	17·5	0·48
4	18·5	4·5	0·11	35	9	0·20	55	13·5	0·32
12	23	1·9	0·13	42·5	3·5	0·21	65	5·5	0·35
24	25	1·0	0·14	50	2·0	0·28	75	3·1	0·42

The main drain and outfall are usually designed to carry the maximum flow given by a storm of one hour's duration, but adjustments may be made for storms of longer duration. Other methods of calculating peak run-off are described in Road Note 35 (published by HMSO 1976). These comprise the TRRL Hydrograph Method, which is widely used, and the 'Rational' or Lloyd-Davies formula, which is considered satisfactory for small areas, where sewer sizes are unlikely to exceed 600 mm.

MEASUREMENTS OF RIVER DISCHARGE AND LEVELS.—The object of flood relief works is to control river levels. To enable the maximum height of the river after completion of the works to be calculated, the probable maximum discharge and hydraulic conditions of the river at this discharge must be obtained. The only satisfactory method of estimating the maximum discharge is, by actual measurements, to obtain a 'stage-discharge' curve showing the relation between the discharge and the level of the river at the point of measurement. River discharges are usually measured by making a survey of the cross section of the river at some convenient point, eg a single span bridge, and using a current meter to measure the velocity. Alternative methods, eg dilution and ultrasonic gauging are described under 'Flow Measurement' (p **17**/68).

Water levels are best taken continuously by an automatic float or pressure operated recorder, checked by a gauge board. Each measured discharge is plotted against its corresponding level to obtain the 'stage-discharge' curve, which for any level gives the corresponding discharge. The curve may then be extended to allow estimation of the discharge at levels higher than those so far recorded. In a large catchment area several gauging stations will be required, both on the main river and on its tributaries.

The 'stage-discharge' curve will allow previously known flood levels to be interpreted as discharges, which can be compared with the corresponding rainfall. From rainfall records the worst possible rainfall conditions can be estimated, and the maximum discharge estimated at various points in the river. From the 'stage-discharge' curve the level reached by the maximum discharge can be estimated. Also the value of C in Chezy's formula $V = C\sqrt{(RS)}$ can be calculated. The effect of the proposed works on the levels can then be estimated.

CATCHMENT AREAS AND SURVEYS.—Catchment area boundaries can be obtained from contoured Ordnance Survey maps (1:10,000; 1:25,000; 1:50,000; and also the earlier 6-inch and 1-inch to a mile), by following the ridge contours between the highest points of adjacent hills. Areas can be found by using a planimeter. Rivers are usually 'mileposted' along their centre line, starting at some arbitrary point at the mouth or confluence with another river. For convenience of reference the 'right' and 'left' banks of a river are designated looking downstream.

For river improvement or flood relief schemes, surveys should include: (1) Cross sections of the river itself at suitable equal intervals. These can be plotted looking upstream, one above another, the downstream section at the bottom of the paper, so as to give a visual picture of the river. Sections should be plotted to the same scale horizontally and vertically so that the wetted perimeter can be determined. (2) Cross sections of the land adjoining the river up to about 10 ft above flood level. (3) Details of the size and levels of bridges and culverts, weirs and other obstructions.

For internal land drainage schemes a detailed contour survey of the area should be made, with 0·5 m intervals in flat low-lying places and 2 m intervals on higher and steeper ground. Invert and soffit levels should be taken at bridges and culverts, with spot levels along roads, existing main drains, etc.

FLOOD RELIEF WORKS.—These may consist of one or more of the following:

(1) Enlargement of the existing channel. (2) Construction of a by-pass channel, to divert part of the flow above the area subject to flooding, to rejoin the river lower downstream. (3) Construction of flood banks. These should be set well back from the river so that erosion of the river bank will not weaken the flood banks.

(4) Removal of the cause of flooding. Local flooding may be caused by obstructions such as weirs or narrow bridges or culverts which may be removed or widened. (The effect of narrow bridges or culverts is generally not important unless they have an area less than 50% of the free flow area.)

Retention basins or balancing lakes perform a vital function in many drainage schemes in urban areas by storing floodwater resulting from storms, the water being released subsequently at a rate of flow within the capacity of the drainage system.

In order to evaluate the relative benefits of different flood relief works it is often useful to simulate the reaction of the stream by a mathematical model. The physical parameters are put in mathematical form incorporating flood plains, storage areas and existing channels and then a known hydrograph is run through and checked against a recorded situation to calibrate the model. The hydrograph or channel can then be varied mathematically and the effect on flooding calculated for a number of combinations in a short time.

The total capacity of the channel between the flood banks may be estimated with sufficient accuracy by considering it as made up of two channels, eg in Fig. 31 a channel of area $ABCDEF$ (wetted perimeter $BC + CD + DE$), and a channel of area $ABGH + EFJK$ (wetted perimeter $GH + GB + EK + KJ$); the Chezy formula can be applied to each separately. All dimensions are minimum. See Fig. 31 and text.

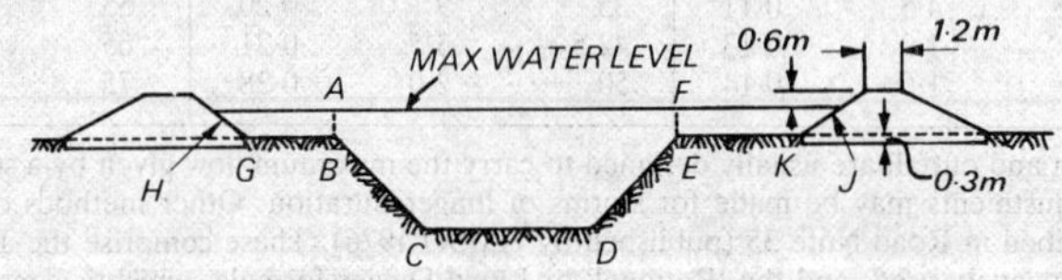

FIG. 31.—Section of Channel with Flood Banks.

Flood banks are constructed of the most suitable material available locally. Suitable batters for the river face and the land face for various materials are given in Table 18:

TABLE 18.—BATTERS FOR FLOOD BANKS.

Material	Batter	
	River Face	Land Face
Clay	1½:1	2:1
Loam	2:1	2½:1 to 3:1
Sandy clay and loam	2:1	3:1 to 4:1

The top should be 600 mm above the maximum water level, with a width of at least 1·2 m. The site of the bank should first be stripped of topsoil, etc, to a depth of at least 300 mm (see Fig. 31). The banks should be covered with topsoil and the river face should be turfed. If sand or ballast is used for the banks a clay core should be provided.

DRAINS

Field Drains.—Waterlogged land can be drained by using field drains to carry subsoil water to the field ditches. The type of field drain most commonly used is the 'tile drain'. This consists of open jointed porous stoneware pipes, 75 or 100 mm diameter, laid in the bottom of a trench about 0·3 m wide and surrounded by graded stones. The open joints should be covered with hessian to prevent soil from entering the pipes (porous concrete or perforated plastic pipes are also used). In clay or heavy soils 'mole drains' may be formed by pulling a torpedo-shaped tool through the ground by means of a plough, displacing the earth and leaving a hole, but these have only a limited life. Table 19 may be used as a general guide to the depths and spacing of field drains for various types of subsoil.

TABLE 19.—DEPTH AND SPACING OF FIELD DRAINS.

Subsoil	Depth to Invert m	Distance apart m
Clay	0·8	7–10
Sandy clay	0·9	10–12
Clay loam	0·9	12–15
Loam	0·9	20–25
Sandy loam	1·0	25–35
Sand	1·1	35–45
Coarse gravelly sand	1·2	45–75

Field drains may be laid—(*a*) Parallel; (*b*) Following the contours of the field; (*c*) In a herring-bone pattern; or (*d*) In a grid of squares. In clay soils (*c*) or (*d*) are preferable.

Field Ditches.—Field ditches collect surface water and percolation water from the field drains. The maximum surface run-off may be calculated from the formula: $Q = 17{\cdot}5\,CA$, where Q = run-off (l/s); A = area (hectare); and C = the run-off factor (for clay soils, 0·5–0·8 tilled, and 0·4–0·7 pasture; for loam soils, 0·1–0·3 tilled, and 0·2–0·5 pasture).

The maximum percolation water from the field drains will not be discharged until 5 or 6 hours after a storm so the ditches do not have to carry both surface water and percolation water at the same time. The bottom of the ditch must be below the field drains, ie about 1–1·5 m deep, and its size is determined by this, rather than by its discharge capacity. For example, if the bottom is 0·5 m wide, the cross-sectional area will be approximately 1 m^2, so that when running full, the average velocity of discharge from a 5 ha field will not exceed 30 mm/s.

Subsidiary or Feeder Drains.—These are channels collecting the water from the field ditches and conveying it to the main drains. The flows in field ditches and feeder drains are comparatively small and their gradients are very flat.

Main Drains.—These convey water from the subsidiary drains to the outfall and thence into the river. They are usually channels of trapezoidal section, and the gradient is fixed by the levels of the outfall and the feeder most remote from the outfall. They are usually designed to keep the water level for maximum flow at least 0·45 m below ground level at all points, by the Chezy formula (*qv*). Values of Kutter's N frequently used are 0·0225 for large earthen channels maintained with care, and 0·025 for smaller channels. These values are also frequently used for irrigation canals.

Surface Water Drains.—To be self-cleansing the minimum gradients of surface water drains should be such as will give a velocity of flow of not less than 0·75 m/s when running quarter full. The maximum velocity should not exceed 3 m/s. Surface water drains should not be less than 100 mm in diameter.

PUMPING SCHEMES.—Pumping may be necessary if it is not possible for the water to flow by gravity. Where either a gravity or a pumping scheme is practicable the most economical scheme may be chosen by comparing estimated capital and running costs.

Pumps for land drainage have to pump large quantities at low heads (usually less than 6 m).

The screw pump, a modified axial-flow type, has now mainly superseded the centrifugal type for land drainage work, being more economical. Its 'end-on' drive also takes up less space, thereby saving building costs. It is an economy to select a pump with a flat efficiency curve, ie a high efficiency over a wide range of head, even if the maximum efficiency is less. The pumps are usually electrically driven.

OUTFALLS AND SLUICE GATES.—Figure 32 shows a typical outfall where a drain discharges into a river provided with flood banks. It should be as high above the bed of the river as possible. The flap valve only allows flow from the drain to the river and therefore prevents the river when high from flowing up the drain. The vertical lifting sluice gate at the inlet to the outfall controls the water level in the drain, and enables water to be retained in the drain in dry periods. If control of river levels cannot be obtained by a weir, sluice gates are used. An area may at times suffer from severe flooding and yet at other times be short of water. Thus, while at one time it is necessary to allow the maximum possible discharge, at other times the maximum possible storage must be provided, but a weir providing adequate storage might be too high to pass the maximum discharge with safety.

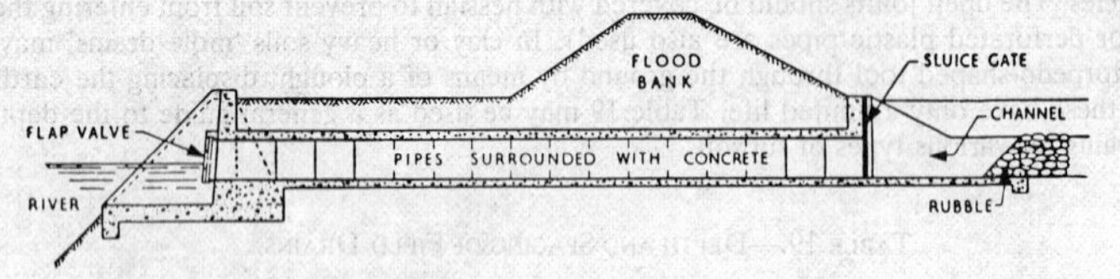

FIG. 32.—Drain Outfall.

The size of an outfall or sluice opening should be not less than 50% of the free flow area of the drain at maximum discharge for velocities up to 1·2 m/s, and not less than 75% for velocities of 1·8 m/s; for velocities over 1·8 m/s, the restriction should be as small as possible. Vertical lifting gates can be obtained in almost any size and to withstand a head in one or both directions. Larger gates are usually fitted with rollers and counter-weights and are power operated. The loss of head is small. Radial gates may be used on the top of weirs.

Flap valves and gates slope a few degrees to the vertical, and are loose hinged or double hinged to allow easy seating on closure. They are self-acting, and if the level behind exceeds that outside, water passes out; if the level outside exceeds that inside the valve is held down on its seating and water cannot pass in or out. They can be obtained in any size from the smallest diameter drain up to about 4×2 m, or more. They are suitable for tidal outfalls, and if counterbalanced the loss of head is small; usually about 25–75 mm (see Fig. 33).

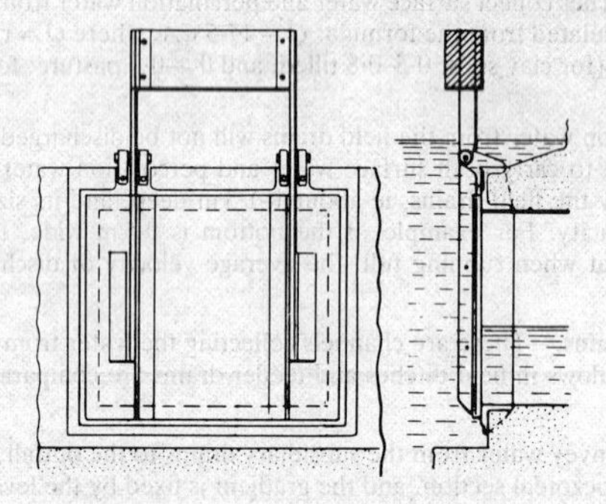

FIG. 33.—Flap Gate (Counter-balanced).

BANK REINSTATEMENT.

FAGGOTING.—Brushwood, in bundles, is placed end on to the river, along the line reinstatement. Each layer is set back and the area behind backfilled. This method is quick and cheap, but the brushwood eventually rots away. It is mainly used for the emergency protection of flood banks.

WITHY PILING.—This is suitable in slower flowing streams in areas where withies (3 year old rooted willows) are available. Stakes 100–150 mm diameter, are driven into the river bed at an angle of 20–30° to the vertical about 0·5 m apart and reaching to the top of the bank. The withies are woven in and out of the stakes, the roots being left at the back, and are pressed down the stakes to the river bed by means of a wooden fork. The area behind is backfilled, and the roots are well embedded. In time the withies root and sprout and bind the bank together; they should, however, be trimmed back each autumn.

CONCRETE BAGGING.—This is suitable for any river, however fast the current, particularly if ballast is available locally. Dry concrete in bags is lowered into the water along the line required to form a footing at least three bags wide. Further bags are then laid in courses, with broken bonds, to the surface. Above the surface each course should be set back 150–200 mm, and the backfilling brought up course by course. Eventually the bags rot away and leave the rough concrete surface exposed. This method will withstand very severe erosive conditions.

GABIONS AND MATTRESSES.—Stone filled wire crates (called gabions) laid in stepped courses, and wire mattresses, laid on the bank slopes are frequently used in bank protection. Fabric mattresses, laid on the slope and grouted with mortar have been developed in recent years.

SLABBING.—Interlocking concrete slabs form another type of revetment. The subgrade material varies with the conditions, a filter layer being incorporated where flash floods or tides occur.

EXCAVATION.—For land drainage work the dragline excavator is mostly used. In river improvement work, maximum outputs are rarely attained as the quantity of excavation is often small (sometimes less than 4 m^3 per metre length of channel), and much of the working time is taken up in moving the machine; also the ground may be soft and the machine may have to work on mats. For excavation under water the excavator bucket may have holes drilled in it to release the water. For smaller quantities hand excavation may be cheaper owing to the high cost of transporting a machine to and from the site.

PILING.—Structures in land drainage works often have to be built on poor bearing soils, and bearing piles may be required. Pumping stations and sluices may be situated between two widely differing water levels and sheet piling may be required to prevent percolation and undermining of the foundations by scour.

The length of the piles should be such that the shortest path to be taken by the percolation water is at least 10 times the maximum difference in level of the water on each side of the structure. Heavy steel sheet piling may have a useful life of up to 100 years. When driving steel sheet piling in running water the driver should commence at the upstream end. (See chapter 'Foundations and Earthwork'—Piling.)

CONCRETE IN WATER.—Concrete can only be successfully placed in still water. The use of rapid hardening cement is preferable but not essential. The mix should be dry with a high cement content and should be lowered carefully below the water surface and placed with as little disturbance as possible—it should not be dropped.

IRRIGATION

NEED FOR IRRIGATION.—Irrigation is needed for several purposes including; supplying water to replace or supplement rainfall, improving soil conditions before sowing and when harvesting, preventing frost damage and distributing solutions of fertiliser or pesticide. The patterm of irrigation need varies with climate between countries such as Iraq where the summer rainfall is nil and the winter rainfall small and unreliable, and eastern England where many crops can be grown without irrigation but where yields can be increased in some years by irrigation—the criteria in this case being financial rather than political or social.

Water Required by Crops.—The quantities of water (mm/day), required by various crops are: Wheat, 2·7; Oats, 3·5–5·0; Rye, 2·3; Maize, 2·7–4·0; Clover, 3·5; Meadow grass, 3·2–6·5; Potatoes, 1·0–1·4; Oak trees, 1·0; Fir trees, 0·5–1·0; Vineyard, 1·0. If this water is not supplied in the growing season by the natural rainfall, irrigation water is required.

DUTY OF IRRIGATION WATER.—The 'duty' of irrigation water is the relation between a volume of water and the area of crop matured by it. The 'base' of a duty is the time of continuous flow of water required to mature the crop. The volume of water required is given by $V = 86{,}400B/D$; where, V = volume of water in litres; D = duty of water, ie number of hectares of crop matured by 1 l/s flowing continuously for a specified time; and B = base of duty, ie number of days during which 1 l/s flows in order to mature the crop.

The duty depends on nature of crop, initial soil moisture content, rate of evaporation, and rainfall in the irrigation season. Typical duties for various crops in India (expressed as depths in mm) are: Wheat 225–375; Barley 225–275; Cotton 275–500; Great Millet 150–225; Poppy 275; Kharif 750–1,140; Rabi 225–500; Charki 180; Senji 275–500; Toria 150–250; Maize 275–450; Rice 900–1,015; Sugar Cane 635–1,140.

Typical duties for crops in India, expressed in ha m^3/sec, are: Rice, 650–950; Cotton, 1,200; Kharif 1,280–1,570; Rabi 2,800–4,000.

Typical duties of existing irrigation schemes, (in ha m^3/sec), in various countries, are: India 900–2,500; Transvaal 2,000; California 2,150–4,300; Southern Arizona 1,420–2,150; New Mexico 850–1,150; Utah 850–1,750; Colorado 1,150–1,700; Northern Italy 850–2,150.

Owing to losses from canals due to evaporation, etc, more water leaves the headworks than arrives at the area of crop irrigated, ie the duty in ha m^3/sec is lower when measured at the headworks than at the area irrigated. The 'duties' are best used as a guide for *relative* conditions in different places, rather than as a precise guide to quantities.

WATER QUALITY CRITERIA.—Important parameters include soluble salts, sodium, boron and bicarbonate; high salinities can be tolerated by certain crops, but only on well drained permeable soils. Unless adequate drainage is provided, salts may build up in the soil until crop yield is reduced.

WATER QUALITY TESTS.—Exploratory tests to ascertain the approximate quality of water in springs, streams and rivers, in places where laboratory tests are not readily available, may be made by the methods described below.

pH.—This measures the acidity/alkalinity, recorded by the numbers 0–14 with 7 showing neutral solutions, and the lower numbers indicate the acid properties. The pH value is measured by various instruments employing such indicators as Methyl red (4·64–6), Phenol red (6·6–8·4), Bromothymol blue (6·0–7·6). These indicators change in colour with acid and alkaline waters and are matched with standard coloured glasses.

Colour.—Colour is matched either with coloured glasses, yellow, blue, and red (Lovibond method) or with the Hazen or Burgess solutions. One degree on the Hazen scale being equal to 2·4° on the Burgess scale. One hundred and fifty to 200 on the Hazen scale represents a highly stained peaty water.

Turbidity.—Relative values of very turbid waters can easily be measured by the depth (30–80 cm) at which a 1 mm platinum wire becomes invisible in the shade in the open. Photoelectric instruments are made for less turbid waters. A neat little instrument is made having a standard electric torch bulb and battery, and a comparator on the silica scale.

Alkalinity.—This may be determined by the number of drops of decinormal nitric acid required to change the colour of a methyl orange indicator from yellow to pink.

Hardness.—For approximate values, the lather or Wanklyn test is still used, whereby the number of cc's of standard soap solution indicates the degree of total hardness. Otherwise the palmitate test is in general use.

Chlorides.—Combined chlorine is determined by the amount of silver nitrate required, using potassium chromate as an indicator.

Free or Residual Chlorine.—The standard test in the UK is the DPD test. This chemical is added to the sample and if free available chlorine is present produces a red colour the intensity of which is compared with standard discs to give measure of the amount of chlorine present. The further addition of potassium iodide will indicate the total available chlorine present.

Sewage and Organic Matter.—Four drops of a solution of permanganate of potash (Condy's Fluid), to a small glass of water. The colour turns pale or yellow if decomposed organic matter is present.

Minerals.—*Lead.*—Six drops of sulphuric acid in a small glass of water. White precipitate will be formed if lead is present. *Zinc.*—Six drops of potassium ferrocyanide to a small glass of water gives a green colour if zinc is present. *Copper.*—Eight drops of ammonia in a small glass of water will turn it blue if copper is present.

FLOW MEASUREMENT—Current Meter.—The quantity of water flowing in a river (in the absence of any weir) can be obtained by (*a*) measuring the cross sectional area; (*b*) measuring the velocity at many points in the cross section by current meter. The current meter has a propeller-screw on ball bearings which is turned at a variable rate by the varying velocity of the water; the number of turns in a unit time being proportional to that velocity. It is conveniently clamped to gas pipe tubing where cross sections up to 5 or 6 m deep, in normal flowing rivers, can generally be measured satisfactorily. The mean of the velocities multiplied by the cross-sectional area of the water is a measure of the quantity.

Although the principle of measurement is simple, many physical difficulties often arise. Thus for obtaining a cross section, if the river cannot be waded, or the current is too fast for a boat to be kept in line, sighting the meter in line from the bank may be necessary or a guiding line stretched across the river, or for wide rivers a theodolite may be used. For the points of measurement, these are best judged from the variation of velocity between one point and another, not only between different depths, but between different places across the width of the river. It may be necessary to space the velocity measurements somewhat closely where a stream develops a reverse current near the bank, or where a well defined main current flows through relatively slow moving water. The mean velocity of the cross section is at 0·6–0·7 of the depth, that is, at a third of the depth from the surface, hence for approximate estimates, where saving of time is important, the average velocity of a cross section would be the mean of all the velocities taken across the section at one-third of the depth from the surface.

Approximate Measurement By Floats.—Rough values of the flow in streams and rivers are given by timing the speed of travel of a single float in the centre of a stream and multiplying by the cross section of the stream, assuming that the mean velocity is half that of the central float. The value of half is, at least, safe. More exact approximation, for various hydraulic mean depths is given in Chapter 'Fluid Mechanics'.

Flumes.—For permanently recording flows, eg compensation water from reservoirs, a flume is often constructed. It is based on the principle of a venturi meter, but is in the form of a taper in an open channel, which increases the velocity, resulting in a difference in head, between the upstream side and throat of the flume, and thus measures the quantity flowing. These differences of head can be transmitted to an automatic recorder chart to measure quantity.

Dilution Gauging.—The dilution method consists of adding a concentrated salt solution at a constant known rate to the stream and measuring the dilution at a distance downstream sufficient to produce a uniform concentration. The natural salt content (if any) of the stream must be taken into account in the calculation. No measurements of area or velocity are required.

Ultrasonic Gauging.—In this method, two transducers are located on opposite sides of a stream but staggered so that the pulse path is inclined to the stream flow at an angle of 30–60°. The difference between times of travel of pulses in the upstream and downstream directions is directly related to the average flow velocity at the depth of the transducers.

Measuring Cylinders.—For the approximate gauging of small quantities of water (eg springs, flow from taps), various apparatus are procurable, among them a cylinder with a hole or holes in the bottom; the height of the water in the cylinder is a measure of the quantity flowing. In testing pumps at manufacturers works this method is sometimes used on a large scale.

FLOW IN STREAMS—90° V NOTCH.—Especially useful in the field for quantities up to 10^5 l/hr is the formula for sharp-edged notches: $Q = 0{\cdot}1573 \tan(\theta/2)H^{2{\cdot}5}$, where Q = flow in l/hr, with coefficient of discharge, 0·585; and H = head of water (mm), measured 1 m upstream of notch. See also, chapter 'Hydraulic Engineering' (**B1**).

RECTANGULAR NOTCH.—Applicable for large quantities, and for weirs measureable in terms of metres in length. Calculation is based on the formula for sharp-edged weirs, ignoring end contractions: $Q = 0{\cdot}2084LH^{1{\cdot}5}$, where, H = head of water (mm), measured 1 m upstream of the notch; Q = flow in l/hr, with coefficient of discharge, 0·62; and L = length of weir (mm), in the above formula, the length L, is taken as 1,000 mm, to give discharges per metre length of weir. For approximate estimates, if the depth of water is measured at the notch instead of 1 m upstream, add 10 mm to the depth if the velocity is 0·5 m/s; or, 20 mm if the velocity is 1 m/s.

For overflows of impounding reservoirs special calibration with models is desirable, but using the formula $Q = 0{\cdot}0579H^{1{\cdot}5}$, the approximate discharges per metre of length are obtained. A higher coefficient, of the order of 0·07, is possible with a well-designed crest. The head, H, is in mm (see Table 20 below).

TABLE 20.—APPROXIMATE RESERVOIR OVERFLOWS.

Head mm	Flow (Q) m³/sec	Head mm	Flow (Q) m³/sec
200	0·16	1,000	1·83
400	0·46	1,200	2·41
600	0·85	1,500	3·36
800	1·31	—	—

DESIGN OF CHANNELS

Channels are usually designed by the Chezy formula $V = C\sqrt{(RS)}$, the value of C being obtained from Kutter's formula chapter 'Hydraulic Engineering'. For irrigation canals, under favourable conditions N in Kutter's formula is frequently taken as 0·0225, and this value has been adopted in the design of very important works. For less favourable conditions the value of 0·0250 is often used. These two values are of most importance in irrigation engineering.

For the same *actual R* (such as 3·28 ft or 1 m), coefficient C for metric units is the coefficient for British units multiplied by $1/\sqrt{(3{\cdot}28)}$, or 0·552, V being expressed in m/s. Other values of N sometimes used are; Canals in conditions below average 0·0275; Canals in 'defective condition' and some rivers 0·030; Canals much obstructed 0·035; Canals in rubble masonry 0·017–0·020; Canals in ashlar and brickwork 0·013.

VELOCITY IN CHANNELS.—It is important, particularly in irrigation, that a sufficiently high velocity is maintained to prevent silting and to carry the fertilising silt to the irrigated fields. It is however, equally important that there should be no scouring of the bed. The 'critical velocity' is that *mean* velocity at which, for a channel of given depth, the current will neither deposit much silt nor unduly erode the bed. Parker gives the following mean velocities allowable in channels with various hydraulic mean depths (HMD) to prevent scour in beds of various materials (see Table 21).

Generally, a mean velocity of 1 m/s is the minimum allowable to prevent the deposition of silt or the growth of aquatic weeds and velocities up to about 2 m/s are quite frequent.

WATER LOSSES FROM IRRIGATION CANALS.—No general rule can be given for estimating the rate at which water is lost from irrigation canals. Some are practically watertight, and lose water only by evaporation, while others lose a large proportion by leakage. In India, on the Ganges Canal, at one period the water sent

TABLE 21.—CRITICAL VELOCITIES IN CHANNELS.

For:	Fine Silt			Heavy Silt and Fine Sand			Coarse sand			Small Pebbles (Peas) and Gravel			Large Pebbles (50 mm) and Coarse Gravel				Large Stones	
No scour in channel of HMD (metres)	0·3	0·8	1·5	0·3	0·8	1·5	0·3	0·8	1·5	0·3	0·8	1·5	0·3	0·8	1·5	3·0	0·3	3·0
Until a mean velocity of (m/sec)	0·1	0·2	0·3	0·3	0·5	0·5	0·5	0·7	1·0	0·7	1·0	1·0	1·5	1·8	2·1	2·8	4·5	7·0

down was accounted for as follows: irrigation 56%; loss in canal 15%; in distributaries, 7%; in village watercourses 22%. In the Punjab, a loss as high as 8 cusecs per million ft^2, (2·4 m^3/sec per km^2), of water surface has been allowed. Certain canals with discharges from 10 to 12 m^3/sec were found to lose about 20 l/s per km.

The leakage from the Donzère Mondragon canal on the River Rhône (17 km) was 1 m^3/s per km, or, 3% of the dry weather flow. This loss was reduced after 3 years through warping.

Many canals lose a great deal of water for some time after their construction, and afterwards become reasonably watertight. The deposit of silt at a reasonable rate for some time after the canal is in service may be facilitated by suitable design of the cross-sections and temporary adjustments of levels at the falls. When L is the loss from a canal, measured in the first km, the loss up to a further distance of D km is LDx, where x varies from 5/6 to 6/7. For losses due to evaporation only (excluding leakage etc) the following rule has been suggested: Mean daily loss (England) = 2 mm = 2 litre/m^2 of surface water. Mean daily loss (India) = 5 mm = 5 l/m^2 of water surface. The loss in the upper Donzère canal, in Rhone alluvium, was 1 m^3/s per km of canal.

BIBLIOGRAPHY

Water Supply

The Transactions and Journals of the Institution of Water Engineers and Scientists (IWES), formerly The Institution of Water Engineers (IWE).

The Proceedings and Journals of the Institution of Civil Engineers give accounts of Water Works.

Manual of British Water Engineering Practice. I.W.E. Volumes I, II and III 1969.

IWES Water Practice Manuals.—

Book 1. *The Structure and Practice of the British Water Industry.*

Book 2. *Recreation, Water and Land.*

Book 3. *Water Supply and Sanitation in Developing Countries.*

ACTS OF PARLIAMENT. Water Acts, 1945 and 1973. Water Resources Act, 1963. (Other Acts referring to water, 1847, 1863, 1875, 1944, 1947, and 1948). H.M.S.O.

NATIONAL WATER COUNCIL. *Water Supply Hygiene; Safeguards to be adopted in the Operation and Management of Waterworks* 1979.

Surface Water Year Books of Great Britain (from 1935). H.M.S.O.

Ground Water Year Books of England and Wales (from 1964). H.M.S.O.

Water Services Yearbook. Fuel and Metallurgical Journals.

Water Resources in England and Wales. Water Resources Board 1973.

'A Measure of Plenty'—Water Resources in Scotland. Scottish Development Department 1973.

TWORT, A.C., HOATHER, R. C. and LAW, F. M. *Water Supply.* Arnold 1974.

WALTERS, R. C. S. *The Nation's Water Supply.* Nicholson and Watson 1936.

UNITED NATIONS DEPT. OF SOCIAL AND ECONOMIC AFFAIRS (1958). *Water for Industrial Use.*

BS CODE OF PRACTICE, CP 310; 1965. *Water Supply.*

Hydraulics.—Flow in Pipes, Channels

CHOW, V. T. *Open Channel Hydraulics.* McGraw-Hill 1959.

IRELAND, J. W. *Mechanics of Fluids:* SI Units. Butterworth 1971.

LAW, F. *Alignment Charts for the Design of Sewers and other Open Channels.* I.C.E. 1942.

LEWITT, E. H. *Hydraulics.* Pitman 1962.

ADDISON, H. A. *Text Book of Applied Hydraulics.* Chapman and Hall 1964.

THOMSON, D, HALTON. *The Alignment Diagram Applied to the Flow of Water in Uniform and Compound Mains.* I.W.E. 1916.

HYDRAULICS RESEARCH STATION. Hydraulics Research Papers Nos. 1, 2 and 4.

Mains and Aqueducts

IWES Water Practice Manual Book 4. *Water Distribution Systems* 1985.
BURGESS, D. E. *Design Planning and Construction of a 45 inch Main.* I.W.E. 1973.
DUNSTAN, M. R. H. and LAWSON, W. R. *Analysing and Planning a Water Distribution Network in a Developing Country*. I.W.E. 1972.
ROBERTS, K. F. & THOMAS, E. H. *Laying and Maintaining Prestressed Concrete Pipelines*. I.W.E. 1967.
CUTHBERT, E. W. and WOOD, F. *The Thames–Lee Tunnel Water Main.* I.C.E. 1961.
BATCHELOR, T. G. *Polythene Water Pipes*. I.W.E. 1960.
WAA/WRC—*Water Mains Rehabilitation Manual* 1986.
DOE/NWC.—STC Report No. 26. *Leakage Control Policy & Practice* 1980.

Pumps and Pumping

LAPWORTH, C. F. *Surge Control in Pipe Lines*. I.W.E. 1944.
LUPTON, H. R. *Automatic Operation of Waterworks Plant.* I.W.E. 1956.
Symposium on Surges in Pipe Lines. I Mech E Proceedings 1965.
Water Hammer in Hydraulics and Wave Surges in Electricity. Louis Bergeron. John Wiley & Sons 1961.
Pressure Transients. Course, by Dept. of Mech. Eng'g. City University—A. R. D. Thorley, K. J. Enever 1973.
Note on Pressure Surge Calculations by the Graphical Method. TN.447.—P. Linton—B.H.R.A. Fluid Engineering.
Estimation of the Size of Air Vessels. 7th Conference on Hydromechanics. B.H.R.A. 1960, Paper SP670.

Rainfall, Hydrology

BILHAM, E. G. *The Climate of the British Isles*. Macmillan 1938.
GLASSPOOLE, J. *Reliability of Rainfall over the British Isles*. I.W.E. 1930 and 1947.
GLASSPOOLE, J. *Drought over England and Wales 1932–35 and Symposium*. I.W.E. 1935.
GLASSPOOLE, J. *The Realiability of Rainfall over the British Isles* (*Frequency Distribution*). I.W.E. 1951.
TODD, T. K. *Ground Water Hydrology*. Wiley 1959.
ROWNTREE, N. A. F. *Rainfall and Run-off of Reservoired Catchments in 1959*. I.W.E. 1961.
Conservation of Water Resources. I.C.E. 1962.
Symposium of Papers on Water Resources. I.W.E. 1964.
Hydrological Surveys of Various Rivers (1960–67). H.M.S.O.
Proceedings of Seminar on Operational Aspects of Drought 1975–76 I.W.E.S. and I.C.E. 1977.
IWES Water Practice Manual Book 5, *Groundwater* 1986.

Floods

BINNIE, W. J. E. *Interim Report on Floods in Relation to Reservoir Practice*. I.C.E. 1933.
ALLARD, W., GLASSPOOLE, J. and WOLFE, P. O. *Floods in the British Isles*. I.C.E. 1960.
RICHARDS, B. D. *Flood Estimation and Control.* Chapman and Hall 1950.
Flood Studies Report. Natural Environment Research Council 1975.
Floods and Reservoir Safety—An Engineering Guide. I.C.E. 1978.

River Flow, Land Drainage, Irrigation

IWES Water Practice Manuals Books 7 and 8, *River Engineering* 1986/87.
STEPHEN, G. D. *Hydraulic Calculations for Channel Improvement Schemes*. I.W.E. 1952.
MCLEOD, G. *Recent Land Drainage Pumping Stations*. Journal Inst. W.E. 1950.
AYRES, Q. C. and SCOATES, D. *Land Drainage and Reclamation*.
Ministry of Agriculture and Fisheries: Bulletins No. 138. *Irrigation* and No. 202. *Water for Irrigation: Supply and storage*. H.M.S.O.
MORGAN, W. H. *Augment of Supply by Sea-Water Distillation*. I.W.E. 1961.
MANSELL-MOULIN, M. *Flow Frequency Curves for Design of Catchwater*. I.W.E. 1966.
THORN, R. B. (Ed.) *River Engineering and Water Conservation Works*. Butterworth 1966.
PARKER, P. A. M. *The Control of Water*. Routledge & Kegan Paul 1949.
BS CODE OF PRACTICE CP 2005 1968. *Sewerage*.
Transport & Road Research Laboratory. Road Note 35. *Guide for Engineers to the Design of Storm Sewer Systems*. 1976.
WITHERS, B. AND VIPOND, S. *Irrigation: Design and Practice*. Batsford 1974.
STERN, P. H. *Small Scale Irrigation*. Intermediate Technology Publications. 1979.

Dams—Design and Geology

LAPWORTH, H. *The Geology of Dam Trenches*. I.W.E. 1911.
MORTON, E. *Influence of Geology on Dams*. I.W.E. 1973.
LANE, R. G. T. *Seismic Activity at Man-made Reservoirs*. I.C.E. 1971.
SMETHURST, G. *A Valveless Draw-off Tower*. I.W.E. 1960.
CREAGER, W. P., HINDS, J. and JUSTIN, J. D. *Engineering for Dams*. (3 Vols.) Wiley 1945.
BEDSON, P. G. *The Design of Buttress Dams*. I.C.E. 1948.

COYNE, A. *New Dam Techniques*. I.C.E. 1959.
JAEGER C. *Pumped-Storage Capacity, A Simplified Mathematical Approach*. I.C.E. 1959.
WALTERS, R. C. S. *Dam Geology*. Butterworth. 1971.
Design of Small Dams. U.S. Dept. of Interior: Bureau of Reclamation. 1974.
KENNARD, M. F. & KNILL, J. L. *Reservoirs on Limestone: The Cow Green Scheme* (*Tees Valley & Cleveland WB*). I.W.E. 1969.
ISCHY, E. and GLOSSOP R. *An Introduction to Alluvial Grouting*. I.C.E. Vol. 21. 1962.
SCRIMGEOUR, J. and ROCKE, G. *Tubes´a Manchettes* (*valve grouting pipes*), *at Backwater Reservoir, Dundee*. I.W.E. 1966.
GRUNER, E. *Dam Disasters*. I.C.E. Vol. 24. 1963.
Transactions of International Congress on Large Dams (3-yearly form 1955); and *British Section* ('BNCOLD') I.C.E. 1967 *et seq.*
BNCOLD/University of Newcastle-upon-Tyne. *Proceedings of Symposium on inspection, operation and improvement of existing dams*. 1975.
Publications by Austrian, Swiss and Turkish Committees on Large Dams.
ICOLD Meetings and Proceedings. 1976/80/84.

Dams—(Earth and Rockfill)

RUFFLE, N. J., BUCHANAN, N. and ROWE, P. W. *Derwent Dam.—Design, Construction and Embankment Stability* I.C.E. 1970.
WALTERS, R. C. S. and WALTON, R. J. C. *Yeovil Water Supply* (*Sutton Bingham*). I.C.E. 1957.
GEDDES, W. G. N., ROCKE, G. and SCRIMGEOUR, J. *Blackwater Dam*. I.C.E. 1972.
KENNARD, J. and M. F. *Selset Reservoir* (*Construction*). I.C.E. Vol. 21, 1962.
BISHOP, A. W. and VAUGHAN, P. R. *Selset Reservoir Embankment*. I.C.E. Vol. 21, 1962.
Grouts and Drilling Muds in Engineering Practice. ICE (*Symposium*) Butterworth. 1963.
LOVELL, S. MAYNARD, *Report on Rock Excavation and Specification Trials*. W.R.C.C. 1965.
HAMMOND, T. G. and WINDER, A. J. H. *Problems of Design and Construction of Great Ouse Water Scheme* (Grafham Water) I.W.E. 1967.
COLLINS, P. G. M. and HUMPHREYS, J. D. *Winscar Reservoir*. I.W.E. 1974.
WILLIAMS, H. and STOTHARD, J. H. *Rock Excavation and Trials for Scammonden Dam*. I.C.E. 1967.

Dams—(Concrete)

TAYLOR, G. E. *The Haweswater Reservoir*. I.W.E. 1951. (Buttress type).
BANKS, J. A. *Allt-na-Lairige prestressed Concrete Dams*. I.C.E. 1957.
BODDINGTON, T. J. and FARRAR, R. E. S. *Promotion of Meldon Dam*. I.W.E.S. (1975).
FORDHAM, A. E., *et al. The Clywedog Reservoir Project*. I.W.E. 1970. (Buttress type).
LACY, F. P. and VAN SCHOICK, G. L. *Concrete Gravity Dams: Uplift Observations and Remedial Measures*. ICOLD 1967.
Arch Dams. Proceedings of Symposium: Inst. C.E. 1968.
PATON, G. *The Glen Shira Hydro-Electric Project*. I.C.E. 1956.
ALLEN, A. C. *Features of the Lednoch Dam, including the Use of Fly Ash*. I.C.E. 1958.
ROBERTS, C. M. (and others). *The Garry and Moriston Hydro-Electric Schemes*. I.C.E. 1958.
BINNIE, G. M. (and others). *The Dokan Dam Project*. I.C.E. 1959.
BOGLE, J. M. (and others). *The Avon Dam*. I.C.E. 1959.
ANDERSON, PATON and BLACKBURN. *Zambesi Hydro-electric at Kariba*. I.C.E. 1960.
BASS, K. T., BATTERSBY, D., READER, R. A., EVANS, K. W., *Promotion, Design and Construction of Wimbleball* I.W.E.S. 1979 (Buttress type).
MOFFAT, A. I. B. *Review of Pore Pressure and Internal Uplift in Massive Concrete Dams*. CIRIA Technical Note No. 63. 1975.

Percolation and Evaporation

BOSWELL, P. G. H. *The Assessment of Percolation*. I.W.E. 1943.
LAPWORTH, C. F. *Percolation in the Chalk*. I.W.E. 1948.
LLOYD, D. *Evaporation Loss from Land Areas*. I.W.E. 1942.
Report on Standard Methods of Measurement of Evaporation. I.W.E. 1948.
PENMAN, H. L. *Evaporation over the British Isles*. I.W.E. 1954.

Storage and Yield

LAPWORTH, C. F. *Reservoir Storage and Yield*. I.W.E. 1949.
MITCHELL, P. B. *Reservoir Site Investigations and Economics*. I.W.E. 1951.
Deacon Diagram. See Encyclopaedia Brit. 13th Ed. Article *Water Supply*. 1926.

Groundwater

The Maps and Memoirs and Publications of the British Geological Survey (formerly the Geological Survey) and the Institute of Geological Sciences give details of local geology and hydrogeology.

Walters, R. C. S. *The Hydro-Geology of the Chalk of England*. I.W.E. 1929.
Walters, R. C. S. *The Hydro-Geology of the Lower Oolites*. I.W.E. 1936.
Edmunds, F. H. *Outlines of Underground Water Supply in England and Wales*. I.W.E. 1941.
Ineson, J. *Development of Ground Water Resources in England and Wales*. I.W.E. 1970.
Kean, O. *The Development of Pangbourne Pumping Station*. I.W.E. 1949.
Wilson, H. B. *Construction and Operation of Gravel Well Sources*. I.W.E.S. 1975.
Rofe, B. H., Durrant, P. S. & Egerton, R. H. L. *Some Aspects of the Use and Management of Ground Water Resources*. I.W.E.S. 1977.
Hetherington, H. A. P. *The Sinking of Borings*. I.W.E. 1951.
Stow, G. R. S. *Modern Water Well Drilling techniques in the U.K.* I.C.E. Vol. 23 1962.
Stow, A. H. and Renner, L. *Acidizing Boreholes*. I.W.E. Vol. 19 1965.
Slater, R. J. *Use of Television Camera for Inspection of Wells and Boreholes*. I.W.E. 1966.

River and Pumping Schemes

Mercer, C. H. H. *The Abstraction of Water Supplies from Rivers*. I.W.E. 1949.
Hetherington, R. le G., and Roseveare, J. C. A. *The River Severn Scheme for the Water Supply of Coventry*. I.C.E. 1954.
Stuckey, P. J. *The River Tavy Scheme for Plymouth*. I.W.E. 1954.
Adams, R. W. *et al. The River Derwent Scheme of Nottingham Corpn*. I.W.E. 1973.

Water Power

Gerrard, G. *Hydro-Electric Engineering*. Pitman 1949.
Roberts, C. M. *Fundamental Economics in Hydro-Electric Design*. I.C.E. 1951.
Richards, B. D. *Economic Development and Utilisation of Water Power*. I.C.E. 1946.
Roberts, C. M. *Special Features of the Affric Hydro-Electro Scheme (Scotland)*. I.C.E. 1953.
Creager, W. P. and Justin, J. D. *Hydroelectric Handbook*. Wiley 1954.
Fulton, A. A. *Civil Engineering Hydro-Electric Development in Scotland*. I.C.E. 1952.
Haldane, T. G. N. and Blackstone, P. L. *Problems of Hydro-Electric Design in Mixed Thermal Hydro-Electric Systems*. I.C.E. 1955.
Addison. *Pumping Problems—Present and Future*. I.C.E. 1956.
Brown, J. Guthrie, (Ed). *Hydro-Electric Engineering Practice*. (3 Vols). Blackie.
Roberts, C. M. *et al. Design Aspects of the Strathfarrar and Kilmorack Hydro-Electric Scheme*. I.C.E. 1965.
Allary, R. '*The Tidal Power Station in the Rance Estuary*'. La Technique des Travaux. Vol. 42, Translated by M. K. Perl; Cement & Concrete Assn., 1968.

Water Quality and Treatment

Fuller, J. R. (Ed.) *Water Pollution Manual*. Thunderbird Enterprises 1972.
Holden, W. S. (Ed.) *Water Treatment and Examination*. J. & A. Churchill 1970.
Silver, R. S. *Desalination*. H.M.S.O.
Fluoridation Studies in the UK and Results Achieved after Eleven Years. Min. of H, & L.G. 1969.
Desalination. 1977. National Water Council.
Morgan, W. H. *Augmentation of Supply by Sea-Water Distillation*. I.W.E. 1961.
Analysis of Raw, Potable and Waste Waters. H.M.S.O. 1972.
Shinner, J. S. & Davison, A. S. *Development of Bough Beech as Source of Supply (E. Surrey Water Co.)* I.W.E. 1971.
Titford, A. R. and Reader, R. A. *Design and Construction of the R. Ancholme Scheme for N. Lindsey W. Bd*. I.W.E. 1974.
White, G. C., *Handbook of Chlorination*. Van Nostrand Reinhold. 1972.
Clough, J. *Water Treatment Operation, Maintenance and Costs*. I.W.E. 1949.
The Physical and Chemical Examination of Water. I.W.E. 1949.
Oliver, G. C. S. *Biology of Eye Brook Reservoir*. I.W.E. 1948.
Gardiner, A. C., Greenshields, F. and Pearsall, W. H. *Freshwater Biology and Water Supply in Britain. Freshwater Biological Association* 1946.
Huisman, L. and Wood, W. E. *Slow Sand Filtration*. WHO. 1974.
Waterton, T. and Wood, J. Noel. *Pressure Filtration Practice*. I.W.E. 1942.
Pugh, N. J. *Treatment of Doubtful Waters for Public Supplies*. I.W.E. 1947–1949 and 1957.
Annual Reports of the Freshwater Biological Association. Windermere.
The Bacteriological Examination of Water Supplies. Ministry of Health, Report No. 71, 1969.
Maier, F. J. *Manual of Water Fluoridation Practice (USA)* McGraw-Hill, 1963.
Robinson, M. *Technical Aspects of Water Fluoridation*. Water Research Centre, 1964.
Technical Papers and Technical Reports Series. Water Research Centre (Medmenham Laboratory).

HEATING, VENTILATION AND AIR CONDITIONING

Design Temperatures—Heat Loss Calculations—Heating Systems—Boilers—Heat Distribution Systems—Pipe Sizing—Radiators—Panels—Convectors—Electric Heating—Hot Water Supply—Ventilation Systems—Rate of Air Change—Filters—Fans Air Conditioning—Heat Gains—Air Flow Calculations—Ducts—Bibliography

By D. L. Cobb, MSc, MCSI, Assoc IPHE

HEATING

The principal objective of heating a space is to provide a suitable environment for the occupants of that space to efficiently undertake their activities. This efficiency will not be forthcoming unless due regard is paid to 'comfort' and associated physiological conditions. In practice, it will be necessary to assess the whole working environment of thermal, acoustic and visual conditions in order to form a full concept of comfort. Only occasionally will there be more specialised circumstances, under which human occupation is secondary to other requirements, eg a plant or process.

HUMAN COMFORT.—Human comfort will only be attained when a person's rate of natural heat loss equals the heat required to be dissipated. Further, this bodily heat is liberated in approximate proportions of 30% convection, 25% evaporation and 45% radiation, and thus a proper balance must be maintained between these modes of heat loss. The precise situation is governed by several inter-dependent environmental factors, the principal being: (*a*) The effective Air Temperature. (*b*) The Radiant Temperature. (*c*) The Air Movement. (*d*) The Relative Humidity.

This means that a change in activity, producing more or less heat will require the above conditions to respond appropriately and so strike a satisfactory 'comfort' balance. Recent research coupled with the widespread use of convective type heating systems, has tended to cast doubt on the validity of fixed air temperatures as being an indication of thermal comfort. The result is an '*Environmental Temperature*' concept, which forms the keystone, together with Freshness, Air Velocities, Temperature Gradients, Humidity, etc, of total comfort. Initially, it is usual to approach the problem of maintaining human thermal comfort by raising the temperature of a building space to a higher temperature than the outside. Table 1 shows currently acceptable environmental temperatures for various classes of activity. It should be remembered that, ultimately, the heating scheme adopted may call for some adjustments to air temperatures, as shown later.

TABLE 1.—ACCEPTABLE TEMPERATURES FOR VARIOUS CLASSES OF ACTIVITY

Activity	Temperature °C
Seated at Rest	20
Sedentary Work	19
Light Work	16
Heavy Work	13

For maximum comfort it is always worth considering the advantages which can be offered by a well designed air conditioning installation. An exception is where space to be heated is large, relative to occupancy, such as in a store or warehouse. In this instance, subject to certain height-power limitations, localised heat, beamed directly on the occupants from radiant panels, can be most effective.

HEAT LOSS FROM BUILDINGS.—When a building is at a higher temperature than its surroundings, heat is lost by: (1) Through the building fabric, by conduction and subsequently being dissipated by radiation and convection on the outside. This is referred to as '*Fabric Loss*',—(Qf.); heat is also lost by (2): through cold air infiltrating into a building for ventilation purposes, with resulting expelled air at the building temperature. This loss is referred to as '*Ventilation Loss*',—(Qv.). Table 2 gives design values of environmental temperatures, infiltration and ventilation allowances for various buildings in the United Kingdom, as recommended by the CIBS.

OUTSIDE TEMPERATURE.—The outside temperature is taken as the lowest expected temperature which may be obtained for a definite period. The fixing of this temperature (defined as the '*design outside temperature*')

TABLE 2.—ENVIRONMENTAL TEMPERATURES, AIR CHANGE RATES, AND VENTILATION ALLOWANCES

Type of Building	Temp °C	Air Change Infiltration rates per hour	Ventilation allowance (W/m³ °C)
Flats, residences:			
Living rooms	21	1	0·33
Bedrooms	18	½	0·17
Bed-sitting rooms	21	1	0·33
Bathrooms	22	2	0·67
Lavatories and cloakrooms	18	1½	0·50
Service rooms	16	½	0·17
Staircase and corridors	16	1½	0·50
Entrance halls and foyers	16	1½	0·50
Hospitals:			
Corridors	16	1	0·33
Offices	20	1	0·33
Operating theatre suite	18–21	½	0·17
Stores	15	½	0.17
Wards and patient areas	18	2	0·67
Waiting rooms	18	1	0·33
Hotels:			
Bedrooms (standard)	22	1	0·33
Bedrooms (luxury)	24	1	0·33
Public rooms	21	1	0·33
Corridors	18	1½	0·50
Foyers	18	1½	0·50
Offices:			
General	20	1	0·33
Private	20	1	0·33
Stores	15	½	0·17
Schools and colleges:			
Classrooms	18	2	0·67
Lecture rooms	18	1	0·33
Studios	18	1	0·33
Shops and showrooms:			
Small	18	1	0·33
Large	18	½	0·17
Department store	18	¼	0·08
Store rooms	15	½	0·17
Sports pavilions:			
Dressing rooms	21	1	0·33
Warehouses:			
Working and packing spaces	16	½	0·17
Storage space	13	¼	0·08

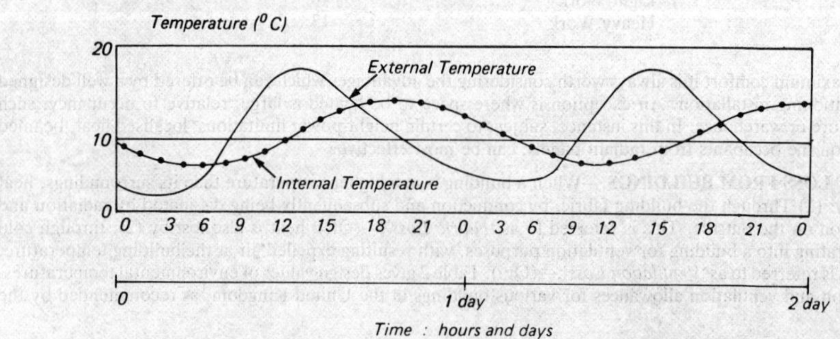

FIG. 1.—Diurnal Temperature Cycle.

is mainly a matter of economics and it is usual to ignore abnormally low temperatures which occur only rarely for short periods. It follows therefore that when the actual outside temperature is below the design outside temperature, the internal temperature will be below the nominated figure. However, the building shell will tend to modify the external environmental conditions as shown in Fig. 1.

This diurnal cycle effect, shown in Fig. 1, will ultimately depend on the building construction. Massive, well insulated buildings have the most marked effect, whereas more lightweight constructions show amplitude and time of internal temperature cycles, closely approaching the external conditions. A further factor is the inherent overload margin of the heating system which can meet exceptional outside temperatures for limited periods. It is, however, an undesirable practice to allow these margins to be too excessive and they in turn, are influenced by the method of operating the heating plant (extremes being highly intermittent, or continuous in operation).

Table 3 lists the CIBS recommendations for winter external design temperatures for the United Kingdom, against appropriate overload margins.

TABLE 3.—DESIGN TEMPERATURES AND MARGINS

Type of Building	System overload (%) capacity	Design temperature (°C) external
Multi-storey buildings with solid intermediate floors and partitions	20 0	−1 −4
Single-storey buildings	20 0	−3 −5

FABRIC LOSSES.—The fabric loss, Q_f, of a building or room space, is calculated by estimating the heat loss for each surface enclosing the space, and summating (Σ) the total.

$$Q_f = UA(T_1 - T_2)$$

where, Q_f = Rate of heat transfer to fabric in Watts.
A = Area of element losing heat in m^2.
T_1 = Internal environmental temperature in °C (from Table 2).
T_2 = Design outside temperature in °C (from Table 3).
U = Overall thermal transmittance co-efficient in W/m^2 °C.
Typical values for standard constructions are given in Table 4.

Total $\Sigma\ Q_f = Qa + Qb + \ldots + Qn$.

Where $Qa + Qb$, etc. = Loss from individual elements, using formula above.

TABLE 4.—'U' VALUES OF VARIOUS CONSTRUCTIONS. For details of exposure and other constructions, reference should be made to the CIBS Guide A.

Construction		'U' (W/m² °C)
Walls: Brickwork solid unplastered	105 mm	3·3
solid unplastered	220 mm	2·3
solid with 16 mm plaster on inside face	105 mm	3·0
solid with 16 mm plaster on inside face	220 mm	2·1
unventilated cavity, 105 mm inner and outer leaves and 16 mm internal plaster	260 mm	1·5
as above, foam-filled cavity of 50 mm (approx.)		0·6
Lightweight concrete block, solid 150 mm aerated concrete block and 16 mm internal plaster		0·97
concrete Cast	150 mm	3·5
concrete Cast	200 mm	3·1
Pre-cast panels	75 mm	4·3
Windows: Single glazed		5·6
Double glazed with air space	6 mm	3·4
Double glazed with air space	12 mm	3·0
Floors: Wood: 20 mm wood floor on joists, ventilated one side, solid concrete on ground, or		1·7
hardcore fill, and 50 mm screed		1·13
Intermediate floor 20 mm wood on joists and 10 mm plasterboard ceiling		1·6

(*continued*)

'U' Values Construction—*contd*	'U' (W/m² °C)
Ceilings and roofs: flat: 19 mm asphalt or felt/bitumen on 150 mm solid concrete	3·4
As above but 16 mm plaster ceiling and 50 mm lightweight screed	2·2
35° pitched: tiles on battens, felt and rafters with aluminium backed 10 mm plaster board ceiling on joists	1·5
As above with 50 mm glass fibre insulation between joists and boards	0·5

Conventional calculation of U values may be made from appropriate conductivities (k) and resistances (R) of materials where

$$U = \frac{1}{\Sigma R} \text{ and } \Sigma R = \frac{L_1}{k_1} + \frac{L_2}{k_2} + Ra + \ldots \frac{Ln}{kn} + Rn$$

Where L = Thickness of individual component in m.
K = Respective thermal conductivity in W/m°C (see Table 5).
Ra = Resistance of surface of component, cavity etc, in m² °C/W. This takes into account the retarding effect of surfaces and adjacent static gas films, etc. (see Table 6).

AIR INFILTRATION LOSSES.—Heat losses to ventilating air infiltrating into a building can be calculated from the general formula:

$$Qv = 0{\cdot}33\, NV(T_1 - T_2)$$

where: Qv = Rate of heat transfer to ventilating air in Watts.
$0{\cdot}33N$ = Ventilation allowance, from Table 2.
V = Volume of room or space in m³.
T_1 = Internal *AIR* temperature in °C, but *note*, this may be substantially different to the *Environmental Temperature*, as below.
T_2 = Design outside temperature in °C, from Table 3.

MEAN RADIANT TEMPERATURES.— In practice the surface areas of the enclosure acts as both reflector and emitter, by re-radiating some of the heat absorbed.

The mean inside surface temperature of a structure radiating or absorbing heat may differ considerably to the internal air temperature, depending on the proportion of radiant heat emitted from the heating apparatus. Thus for a given environmental temperature the effective air and mean radiant temperatures depend on a correct balance being maintained:

(*a*) *For convective heating*, on the insulation of the structure; and
(*b*) *For radiant heating*, on the ventilation loss alone.

The heating system and building environment both contribute to this balance.

ENVIRONMENTAL TEMPERATURE.—Although not a parameter of comfort, this is a better measure of the surrounding thermal environment than the internal air temperature alone. At the design stage, it may be necessary to adjust the heat loss equations, in particular where buildings are fairly well exposed and the standard of insulation is poor.

Space does not permit the complete derivation of adjustments necessary, but the following summarises the calculation procedure adopted by the CIBS based on a broad classification of heating schemes.

CONVECTIVE HEATING.—Using forced or natural convection air heaters, hot water radiators, etc. With this type of installation the difference between air and mean radiant temperature is likely to be significant, and calculations are as follows:

(*a*) From fabric loss formula $Q_f = UA(T_1 - T_2)$; Tables of '*U*' values (see Table 4); environmental temperatures, (Table 2); and external design temperatures, (Table 3); calculate fabric heat losses for element and summate to give total fabric losses: ΣQ_f.

(*b*) Determine the total surface area of the entire enclosure, irrespective of whether losing or gaining heat to give ΣA.

(*c*) From the Nomogram, Fig. 2, determine the value of $\Sigma Q_f/\Sigma A$; this is the excess value of air temperature over environmental temperature; this excess is *added* to the environmental temperature for the infiltration stage of the calculation.

(*d*) From air infiltration loss formula, $Qv = 0{\cdot}33\, NV\ (T_1 - T_2)$, tables of ventilation allowance (Table 2), the corrected internal air temperature from (*c*) previously, and external design temperatures (Table 3), calculate air infiltration.

(*e*) Add results of (*a*), (ΣQ_f); and (*d*), (Qv); to give total rate of heat loss and hence power required to maintain the loss against the temperatures specified.

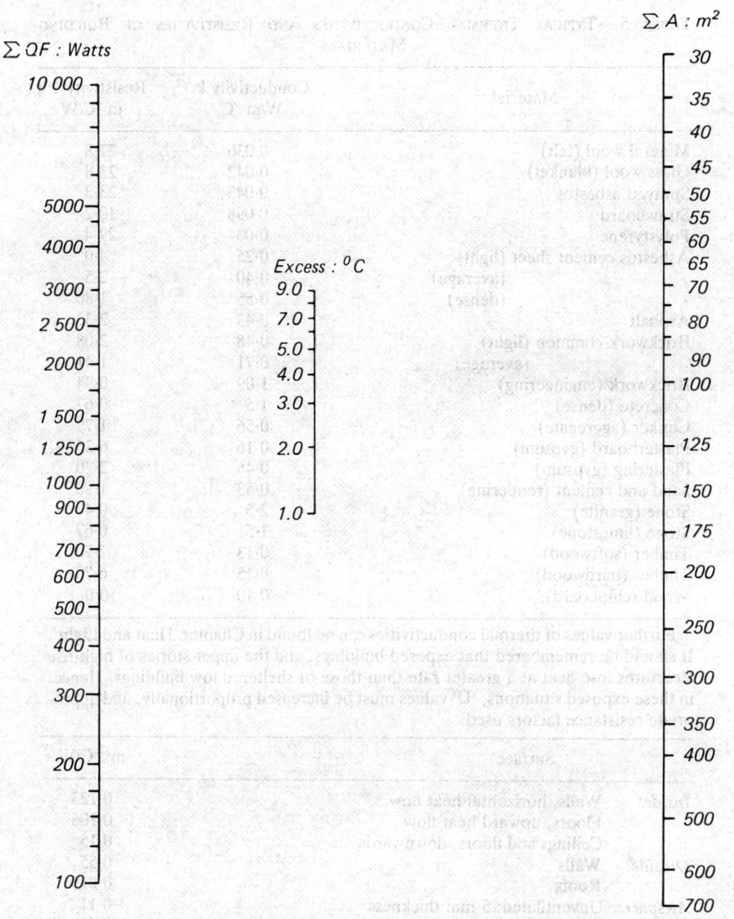

FIG. 2.—Nomogram of Air–Environmental Excess of Temperature.

RADIANT HEATING.—The inclusion of warmed surfaces in a room adjusts the design mean radiant temperature from that determined for convective heating. Radiant systems are usually those associated with commercial and industrial heating where overhead wall radiant panels or tubes are used. Heat loss calculation procedure is similar to that for convective systems:

(*a*) Calculate fabric losses as before: and total ΣQ_f.

(*b*) Total surface areas = ΣA.

(*c*) Infiltration loss may be calculated using a modified equation taking environental temperature direct:

$$Qv = Cv(T_1 - T_2)$$

where T_1 = Environmental temperature, °C from Table 2, and
T_2 = Outside design temperature, °C from Table 3.

$$\frac{1}{Cv} = \frac{1}{0.33NV} + \frac{1}{4{\cdot}8\,\Sigma A}$$

$0{\cdot}33N$ = Ventilation allowance from Table 2.
V = Volume of room or space in m³.

(*d*) Add results of (*a*), (ΣQ_f) to (Qv), to give total rate of loss, and hence, the power requirements.

TABLE 5.—TYPICAL THERMAL CONDUCTIVITIES AND RESISTIVITIES OF BUILDING MATERIALS

Material	Conductivity k W/m °C	Resistivity 1/k m °C/W
Mineral wool (felt)	0·036	27·8
Glass wool (blanket)	0·042	23·8
Sprayed asbestos	0·043	23·3
Strawboard	0·098	10·2
Polystyrene	0·034	29·4
Asbestos cement sheet (light)	0·25	4·0
(average)	0·40	2·5
(dense)	0·55	1·80
Asphalt	0·43	2·33
Brickwork-common (light)	0·48	2·08
(average)	0·71	1·41
Brickwork (engineering)	1·09	0·94
Concrete (dense)	1·5	0·67
Clinker (aggregate)	0·56	1·79
Plasterboard (gypsum)	0·16	6·25
Plastering (gypsum)	0·46	2·20
Sand and cement (rendering)	0·53	1·90
Stone (granite)	2·5	0·40
Stone (limestone)	1·5	0·67
Timber (softwood)	0·13	7·70
Timber (hardwood)	0·15	6·70
Wood (chipboard)	0·10	10·0

Further values of thermal conductivities can be found in Chapter 'Heat and Light'. It should be remembered that exposed buildings, and the upper stories of high rise structures lose heat at a greater rate than those of sheltered low buildings. Hence, in these exposed situations, 'U' values must be increased proportionally, and appropriate resistance factors used.

Surface		m^2 °C/W
Inside:	Walls, horizontal heat flow	0·123
	Floors, upward heat flow	0·106
	Ceilings and floors, downwards	0·15
Outside:	Walls	0·55
	Roofs	0·045
Airspaces:	Unventilated: 5 mm thickness	0·11
	Cavity: 20 mm or more	0·18
	Ventilated loft space between flat ceilings and pitched roofs	0·11

ALLOWANCE FOR HEIGHT.—A further necessary addition to the calculated heat loss is an allowance for height, as upper surfaces create a 'stack' effect and lose heat more rapidly. (Table 7 summarises appropriate allowances.)

INSULATION.—The adequate insulation of any building will reduce 'U' values and heat losses, thereby leading to considerable economics in running costs and fuel consumption.

The current edition of the Building Regulations specifies maximum 'U' values permitted, together with 'Deemed to Satisfy' provisions.

In general for domestic buildings, fabric 'U' values must not exceed W/m^2 °C within the context of an average perimeter 'U' value not exceeding 1·8 W/m^2 °C.

In commercial and industrial buildings the requirements are more stringent. The maximum permissible fabric 'U' value being 0·6 W/m^2 °C. Vulnerable areas of the building structure which are particularly influenced by insulation, include:

(*a*) **Walls.**—Plastic filled cavities provide approximately 50 mm of insulation (by one of the patent processes available). For solid walls, 12 mm internal insulating boards on battens with polystyrene infill is quite effective.

(*b*) **Ceilings and Roofs.**—Up to 100 mm backing of quilted glass fibre, or aluminium foil and suitable infill.

(*c*) **Windows.**—Provision of double glazing; 20 mm wide gaps are most effective.

(*d*) **Miscellaneous.**—General weather stripping to control air change; floor edge insulation in new buildings, etc.

All the above, taken either collectively, or individually, increase the internal surface temperatures and thus contribute to the overall comfort of the environment. Due care, however, must be taken to prevent condensation occurring, as a consequence of reducing the fabric temperature gradients; if this risk is likely, a vapour barrier, correctly positioned, is the effective answer.

TABLE 7.—ALLOWANCES FOR HEIGHT OF HEATED SPACE

Method of Heating and Type or Disposition of Heaters	Addition % for Height of Heated Space		
	Up to 5 m	5 to 10 m	Above 10 m
Mainly Radiant			
Warm floor	Nil	Nil	Nil
Warm ceiling	Nil	0 to 5	*
Medium and high temperature downward radiation from high level	Nil	Nil	0 to 5
Mainly Convective			
Natural warm air convection	Nil	0 to 5	*
Forced warm air			
Cross flow at low level	0 to 5	5 to 15	15 to 30
Downward from high level	0 to 5	5 to 15	15 to 30
Medium and high temperature cross radiation from intermediate level	Nil	0 to 5	5 to 10

* Not appropriate to this application.

SYSTEMS CAPACITY.—Once the heat requirement of a building or room is known, and suitable contingency margins (*M*) added, the output power (*H*) of the heating unit is known, ie $H = \Sigma Q_t + Qv + M$ (note that hot water demands for other than heating purposes are additional to *H*).

HEATING SYSTEMS.—The methods of heat release may be by: (*a*) '*Local Emitter*', where fuel is burned (or energy is used), within the space being heated. (*b*) '*Central Heating Unit*', where fuel is burned at a central location, and heat distributed by steam, water, or air, to the various spaces. (*c*) '*Thermal Storage System*', where the heat distribution medium has reserve capacity, and also where part of the building fabric acts as a heat store.

LOCAL EMITTERS.—These range from simple stoves to forced draught, thermostatically controlled heaters. Generally, local units are used where a simple, and not too large a space, requires heating. Forced draught units have efficiencies in the 70% range and consist essentially of a fuel burner and heat exchanger. Cold air is blown over this by means of a fan and thus heated air is discharged directly into the space. They are a useful form of heating for industrial premises and other specialist applications, such as providing an air curtain across a door opening. High temperature gas radiant panels are an effective form of local heating and particularly suited to industrial space heating. The units are suspended from the roof or walls and radiant heat is beamed directly on the occupants. Ratings vary across the range, 5–15 kW, whilst at floor level maximum radiant intensity of 80 W/m^2 is used for design purposes.

CENTRAL HEATING SYSTEMS.—Correctly defined, the term 'central heating' implies both a centralised heat source and a suitable distributing system, coupled with local heat emitting units. By convention, the *type* of heating system is designated by the distributing medium and the main types are:

Low Pressure Hot Water.—The most common form of central heating, due to its ease of adaption to existing buildings. Heat distribution is effected, at atmospheric pressure, by water flow through steel or copper pipework. The system usually operates at a maximum flow temperature of 80°C with return temperatures of 60–70°C. Normally, water flow is pumped, although thermo-syphonic action may provide the small circulatory effect for the ancillary hot water side.

High Pressure Hot Water.—With this system a pressure is imposed on the water so that it can operate at higher than atmospheric boiling point. This can be done by using steam boilers, the required pressure being maintained 10–16° below boiling point by mixing some of the colder return water with water from the boiler before circulating it to the heating unit.

Alternatively, the pressure can be imposed by an inert gas contained in an expansion cylinder, when the pressure is kept equivalent to about 16°C above the actual required flow temperature so that mixing of the return water is not necessary. Water at flow temperatures up to 180°C can be used with temperature drops between flow and return of up to 80°C, resulting in smaller heating units and smaller pipework. The capital cost of the boiler plant and attendant equipment, for feedwater treatment, etc, is high, and such systems are only economical for the larger industrial heating systems.

Steam Heating Systems.—These are particularly attractive if steam is already available from other process work. The steam is distributed at low pressure and the heating units are usually low temperature radiant panels or unit air heaters which extract the latent heat of steam. Secondary heating systems for associated offices, etc, are usually low pressure hot water, using steam-to-water calorifiers as the heat source.

Warm Air Heating Systems.—The use of heated air as a distributing medium can have considerable advantages over the hydraulic types of system, previously, and a well designed system is very flexible in its response to temperature changes. Basically the system is a re-circulated and filtered air ventilation system with supply air sufficiently warmed (at about 40–60°C) to make good structure heat losses and prevent uncomfortable air circulating currents. The design is essentially that of a ventilation system, covered later.

Centralised Heat Sources.—The primary heat source for a central heating system should be capable of supplying the basic heat loss of the buildings served, *plus* the heat loss from pipework outside the heated spaces *plus* a margin of the order of 20–30% to allow for quick heating-up from cold. This margin is necessary if a heating system is to operate intermittently, ie shut-down at night and over the weekend, when the building is unoccupied. It is necssary to replace the heat lost from the structure during the period of no heat input, and at the same time pre-heat the spaces to a comfortable temperature before occupation.

With the margins given, and at the design outside conditions, a pre-heat period of 3 hours on normal weekdays and 5 hours on Monday would be adequate, although some variation may occur from building to building, depending on the thermal capacity of the structure. If the heating plant is equipped with inside/outside thermostats and is linked to time-control, the system pre-heat period can be varied according to prevailing conditions. This type of sequenced, or 'optimum' starting of plant can achieve savings in running costs. Where a building structure does not lend itself to intermittent plant operation, then the fabric may be used for thermal storage. This may be useful in cases where the fuel for the heating medium is offered on an attractive 'out of hours' tariff.

CENTRAL HEATING BOILERS

LOW-PRESSURE HOT WATER BOILERS.—Boilers for central heating purposes may be of cast iron or mild steel. Cast iron sectional boilers consist of standard sections in a range of sizes, and may be fitted with automatic stoker and controls, and may burn solid fuel, oil, or gas. Mild steel sectional boilers are similar to cast iron types and are capable of withstanding higher water pressures such as may occur in multi-storey buildings. Steel rectangular boilers comprise an external water-filled shell with one or two passes of internal convection tubes; fired with one of the fuels as above; with ratings up to 3 MW and working pressures of 10 bar. Special boiler fronts and furnaces are designed for use with the types of fuel-burners employed.

The operating efficiency of boilers is directly related to the type of firing, ie hand-firing 50–60%; automatic stokers 70%; and oil or gas 75%. These efficiencies are under test conditions, and with actual working conditions they may be 10% to 20% lower, depending on the cleanliness of the boiler and the degree of automatic control. Solid fuel automatic stokers used with cast iron sectional boilers are usually of the forced draught underfeed type, with a worm feed from a hopper, or direct from a fuel bunker or magazine. The latter type is more convenient, as once the fuel is delivered to the bunker or magazine, handling is reduced to a minimum. The use of pulverised fuel brings the control and efficiency of solid fuel equipment near to that for gas and oil.

Oil burners for central heating boilers are of the pressure jet automatic type, the control being on/off, or of the modulating atomising type. The grade of oil used for heating boilers varies with the size of plant. Generally, Class 'D' oil is used for boilers up to 100 kW; Class 'E' oil for boilers between 100–200 kW; and Class 'F' oil for boilers over 200 kW. Heavier oils are used for larger plants. Oil-fired packaged boilers are integral units comprising boiler, oil burner and controls, usually contained with an insulated enclosing jacket. The units are available in a range of sizes, 15 kW to 1·5 MW, with efficiencies around 75%.

Gas-fired boilers are usually fired with natural gas and are available over the above ranges. The packaged system of burners and controls lends to close control and corresponding high efficiencies in operation. Where several small units are banked together in modular fashion, and operated in a sequential manner, it is possible to effect high firing. Dual-fuel gas/oil burning boilers are available and their use may attract tariff concessions.

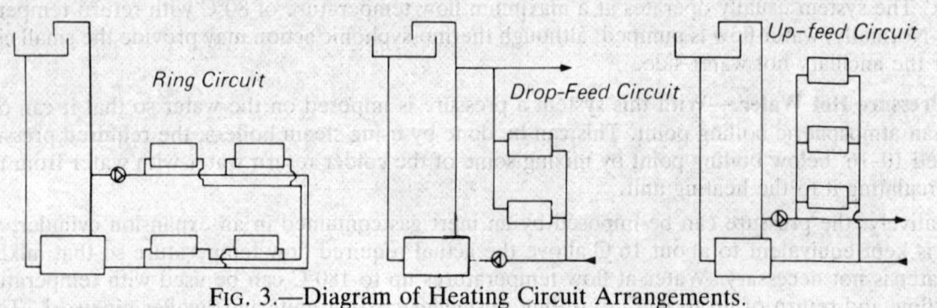

FIG. 3.—Diagram of Heating Circuit Arrangements.

Low Pressure Hot Water.—Steel or copper pipework may be used to distribute heated water from boiler or calorifier to emitting units in the various rooms or spaces. Steel pipework should comply with BS 1387, medium or heavyweight grade, with joints and fittings, either welded or screwed. Standard fittings are available and cover most requirements.

Copper pipework should comply with BS 2871, with capillary or compression fittings. This is particularly appropriate for smaller installations with pipe sizes below 28 mm. In all cases fittings should be of the 'sweep' type and square type bends should be avoided.

LPHW installations are of the 2-pipe system, where the water, after passing through a radiator or other emitting unit, is returned to the boiler without serving any other heating appliances. The size of the pipework is related to the quantity of water being circulated which itself is related to the emission of the individual heating units and the temperature drop of the water. Accelerated systems operate at a temperature differential of 11°C and gravity systems at 22°C.

Accelerated Systems.—An accelerated system uses a pump to provide the differential pressure necessary to circulate the water around the system against the resistance head of the pipework, etc. Electric motors driving centrifugal pumps are usually installed in the flow pipe from the boiler; this ensures satisfactory air-venting of radiators, heating circuits, etc.

The quantity of water to be circulated is found by dividing the total emission of the system including losses from pipes, by the temperature drop, eg 11°C, and it is good practice to allow a margin of 25% to cover water bypassing through the nearest circuits.

The pump head is either determined by sizing the pipework and calculating the resistance head or, alternatively, deciding a suitable head, when the pipework must then be sized to absorb this head. In either case it is advisable to keep the pump head between 1·8 m for small systems, and not greater than 15 m for large, widely dispersed systems. The basic calculation for the pump is based on the *index circuit* which is the longest circuit, in terms of frictional resistance. Other circuits are then sized to absorb the same head, or regulating valves installed to dissipate the surplus head.

PIPE SIZING.—It is usual to size the pipework for accelerated heating systems at a resistance of 150–200 N/m^2 per metre of pipe run. Higher or lower resistance can, however, be used, the top limit being a velocity head of 1·5 m/s above which water is noticeable. An important exception to this is the domestic microbore systems where velocities up to 4·5 m/s are acceptable, mainly due to the use of thick-walled copper pipe and its small water content.

Where the pump head is already determined, the average resistance can be obtained from the index circuit length, which should include an allowance for fittings ('the equivalent length'). Preliminary calculations necessary are:

(*a*) *Determination of water flow rates* in kg/s. This is the unit power (H) plus pipe emission power divided by systems temperature drop and heat capacity of water (4·194 kJ/kg°C).

(*b*) *Determination of pressure drop.* Adopting a pressure drop of, say 150 N/m^2 per m (or equivalent water velocity), determine the total pressure drop by dividing by the total equivalent length of index circuit.

(*c*) *Select pipe diameters from pipe sizing charts.* See Table 9. The CIBS Guide provides comprehensive tables for copper and steel piping to current SI standards, of which Table 9 is an extract. With this method of sizing the frictional allowance for fittings is usually taken into account by adding one third of the actual measured pipe length to obtain the 'equivalent length'. Any out of balance of the circuit branches are then taken up by site adjustment of lockshield valves.

For accurate pipe-sizing precise heat loads are estimated for every section of circuit taking into account pipework emission, and pressure drops per unit length of pipe obtained for selected diameters. Local resistances of fittings, etc, are extracted from Table 8 and, with EL, see Table 9, the total equivalent length per section established. The total pipe length for the index circuit is thus estimated and corresponding pressure differentials established.

By interpolation with pipe sizing tables, branch pressure drops and pipe diameters are checked and adjusted. The limited range of pipe sizes available would normally mean that the system in its final form is oversized, and excess pressure may be 'valve' absorbed as before.

TABLE 8.—'K' FACTORS OF FITTINGS

Fitting	K	Fitting	K
Elbow (average)	0·7	Radiator	5·0
Bend (average)	0·5	Entry loss	1·0
Gate valve	0·2	Exit loss	0·4
Angle valve	5·0		

When the pump head is not chosen beforehand the pipework is sized on the basis of a pre-determined resistance per metre and the pump head is then the summation of the pipework and fittings resistances.

TABLE 9.—FLOW OF WATER AT 75°C IN STEEL PIPES (Medium Grade to BS 1387) (Notation: M = Mass flow rate (kg/s); EL = Equivalent length of pipe in metres for $k = 1$; Δp = pressure loss per metre run of pipe (N/m²); and v = velocity (m/s)). (*Data from IHVE Guide.*)

Δp	v	10 mm		15 mm		20 mm		25 mm		32 mm		40 mm		50 mm		v	Δp
		⅜ in		½ in		¾ in		1 in		1¼ in		1½ in		2 in			
		M	EL	M	M	M	EL	M	EL	M	EL	M	EL	M	EL		
0·1								0·005	*0·4*	0·011	*0·6*	0·016	*0·7*	0·032	*1·0*		0·1
0·2						0·004	*0·3*	0·007	*0·4*	0·16	*0·6*	0·025	*0·8*	0·048	*1·2*		0·2
0·3						0·005	*0·3*	0·009	*0·4*	0·021	*0·7*	0·031	*0·9*	0·060	*1·3*		0·3
0·4						0·006	*0·3*	0·011	*0·5*	0·024	*0·7*	0·037	*0·9*	0·071	*1·3*		0·4
0·5						0·007	*0·3*	0·013	*0·5*	0·028	*0·8*	0·042	*1·0*	0·081	*1·4*		0·5
0·6						0·007	*0·4*	0·014	*0·5*	0·031	*0·8*	0·047	*1·0*	0·090	*1·4*		0·6
0·7				0·004	*0·2*	0·008	*0·4*	0·016	*0·5*	0·034	*0·8*	0·052	*1·0*	0·098	*1·5*		0·7
0·8				0·004	*0·2*	0·009	*0·4*	0·017	*0·5*	0·037	*0·8*	0·056	*1·1*	0·106	*1·5*	0·05	0·8
0·9				0·004	*0·2*	0·010	*0·4*	0·018	*0·6*	0·039	*0·9*	0·060	*1·1*	0·114	*1·5*		0·9
1·0				0·004	*0·2*	0·010	*0·4*	0·019	*0·6*	0·042	*0·9*	0·063	*1·1*	0·121	*1·5*		1·0
1·5				0·006	*0·3*	0·013	*0·4*	0·025	*0·6*	0·053	*0·9*	0·080	*1·1*	0·152	*1·6*		1·5
2·0				0·007	*0·3*	0·015	*0·5*	0·029	*0·6*	0·062	*1·0*	0·094	*1·2*	0·179	*1·7*		2·0
2·5		0·004	*0·2*	0·008	*0·3*	0·017	*0·5*	0·033	*0·7*	0·071	*1·0*	0·107	*1·2*	0·203	*1·7*		2·5
3·0		0·004	*0·2*	0·009	*0·3*	0·019	*0·5*	0·037	*0·7*	0·078	*1·0*	0·119	*1·3*	0·225	*1·8*		3·0
3·5		0·005	*0·2*	0·009	*0·3*	0·021	*0·5*	0·040	*0·7*	0·086	*1·0*	0·130	*1·3*	0·245	*1·8*		3·5
4·0		0·005	*0·2*	0·010	*0·3*	0·023	*0·5*	0·043	*0·7*	0·092	*1·1*	0·140	*1·3*	0·264	*1·8*		4·0
4·5		0·005	*0·2*	0·011	*0·3*	0·024	*0·5*	0·046	*0·7*	0·099	*1·1*	0·149	*1·3*	0·282	*1·9*		4·5
5·0		0·006	*0·2*	0·012	*0·3*	0·026	*0·5*	0·049	*0·7*	0·105	*1·1*	0·158	*1·4*	0·299	*1·9*		5·0
5·5	0·05	0·006	*0·2*	0·012	*0·3*	0·027	*0·5*	0·052	*0·7*	0·110	*1·1*	0·167	*1·4*	0·315	*1·9*	0·15	5·5
6·0		0·006	*0·2*	0·013	*0·3*	0·029	*0·5*	0·055	*0·8*	0·116	*1·1*	0·175	*1·4*	0·331	*1·9*		6·0
6·5		0·007	*0·2*	0·013	*0·3*	0·030	*0·5*	0·057	*0·8*	0·121	*1·1*	0·183	*1·4*	0·346	*2·0*		6·5
7·0		0·007	*0·2*	0·014	*0·4*	0·032	*0·5*	0·060	*0·8*	0·127	*1·1*	0·191	*1·4*	0·361	*2·0*		7·0
7·5		0·007	*0·2*	0·015	*0·4*	0·033	*0·6*	0·062	*0·8*	0·131	*1·2*	0·198	*1·4*	0·375	*2·0*		7·5
8·0		0·007	*0·2*	0·015	*0·4*	0·034	*0·6*	0·064	*0·8*	0·136	*1·2*	0·206	*1·4*	0·388	*2·0*		8·0
8·5		0·008	*0·2*	0·016	*0·4*	0·035	*0·6*	0·066	*0·8*	0·141	*1·2*	0·213	*1·4*	0·401	*2·0*		8·5

9·0		0·008	0·2	0·016	0·4	0·036	0·6	0·069	0·8	0·146	1·2	0·220	1·5	0·414	2·0		9·0
9·5		0·008	0·2	0·017	0·4	0·037	0·6	0·071	0·8	0·150	1·2	0·226	1·5	0·427	2·0		9·5
10·0		0·008	0·3	0·017	0·4	0·039	0·6	0·073	0·8	0·154	1·2	0·233	1·5	0·439	2·0		10·0
12·5		0·010	0·3	0·020	0·4	0·044	0·6	0·082	0·8	0·175	1·2	0·263	1·5	0·496	2·1		12·5
15·0		0·011	0·3	0·022	0·4	0·049	0·6	0·091	0·8	0·193	1·2	0·291	1·5	0·548	2·1		15·0
17·5		0·012	0·3	0·024	0·4	0·053	0·6	0·099	0·9	0·210	1·3	0·317	1·6	0·596	2·2		17·5
20·0		0·012	0·3	0·026	0·4	0·057	0·6	0·107	0·9	0·226	1·3	0·341	1·6	0·641	2·2	0·30	20·0
22·5		0·013	0·3	0·027	0·4	0·061	0·6	0·114	0·9	0·242	1·3	0·363	1·6	0·683	2·2		22·5
25·0		0·014	0·3	0·029	0·4	0·065	0·6	0·121	0·9	0·256	1·3	0·385	1·6	0·723	2·2		25·0
27·5		0·015	0·3	0·031	0·4	0·068	0·6	0·128	0·9	0·270	1·3	0·405	1·6	0·761	2·2		27·5
30·0		0·016	0·3	0·032	0·4	0·071	0·7	0·134	0·9	0·283	1·3	0·425	1·6	0·798	2·2		30·0
32·5		0·016	0·3	0·034	0·4	0·075	0·7	0·140	0·9	0·295	1·3	0·444	1·6	0·833	2·3		32·5
35·0		0·017	0·3	0·035	0·4	0·078	0·7	0·146	0·9	0·307	1·3	0·462	1·7	0·867	2·3		35·0
37·5	0·15	0·018	0·3	0·036	0·4	0·081	0·7	0·151	0·9	0·319	1·4	0·479	1·7	0·899	2·3		37·5
40·0		0·018	0·3	0·038	0·4	0·084	0·7	0·157	0·9	0·330	1·4	0·496	1·7	0·931	2·3		40·0
42·5		0·019	0·3	0·039	0·4	0·087	0·7	0·162	0·9	0·341	1·4	0·513	1·7	0·962	2·3		42·5
45·0		0·020	0·3	0·040	0·5	0·089	0·7	0·167	0·9	0·352	1·4	0·529	1·7	0·992	2·3		45·0
47·5		0·020	0·3	0·041	0·5	0·092	0·7	0·172	0·9	0·363	1·4	0·545	1·7	1·02	2·3		47·5
50·0		0·021	0·3	0·043	0·5	0·095	0·7	0·177	1·0	0·373	1·4	0·560	1·7	1·05	2·3	0·50	50·0
52·5		0·022	0·3	0·044	0·5	0·097	0·7	0·182	1·0	0·383	1·4	0·575	1·7	1·08	2·3		52·5
55·0		0·022	0·3	0·045	0·5	0·100	0·7	0·187	1·0	0·392	1·4	0·589	1·7	1·10	2·3		55·0
57·5		0·023	0·3	0·046	0·5	0·102	0·7	0·191	1·0	0·402	1·4	0·603	1·7	1·13	2·4		57·5
60·0		0·023	0·3	0·047	0·5	0·105	0·7	0·196	1·0	0·411	1·4	0·617	1·7	1·16	2·4		60·0
62·5		0·024	0·3	0·048	0·5	0·107	0·7	0·200	1·0	0·420	1·4	0·631	1·7	1·18	2·4		62·5
65·0		0·024	0·3	0·049	0·5	0·109	0·7	0·204	1·0	0·429	1·4	0·644	1·7	1·21	2·4		65·0
67·5		0·025	0·3	0·050	0·5	0·112	0·7	0·208	1·0	0·438	1·4	0·657	1·7	1·23	2·4		67·5
70·0		0·025	0·3	0·051	0·5	0·114	0·7	0·213	1·0	0·447	1·4	0·670	1·7	1·26	2·4		70·0
72·5		0·026	0·3	0·052	0·5	0·116	0·7	0·217	1·0	0·455	1·4	0·683	1·7	1·28	2·4		72·5
75·0		0·026	0·3	0·053	0·5	0·118	0·7	0·221	1·0	0·464	1·4	0·696	1·8	1·30	2·4		75·0
77·5		0·027	0·3	0·054	0·5	0·120	0·7	0·225	1·0	0·472	1·4	0·708	1·8	1·32	2·4		77·5

TABLE 9 (continued).—FLOW OF WATER AT 75°C IN STEEL PIPES (Medium Grade to BS 1387) (Notation: M = Mass flow rate (kg/s); EL = Equivalent length of pipe in metres for $k = 1$; Δp = pressure loss per metre run of pipe (N/m^2); and v = velocity (m/s)). (*Data from IHVE Guide.*)

Δp	v	10 mm		15 mm		20 mm		25 mm		32 mm		40 mm		50 mm		v	Δp
		⅜ in		½ in		¾ in		1 in		1¼ in		1½ in		2 in			
		M	EL	M	M	M	EL	M	EL	M	EL	M	EL	M	EL		
80·0		0·027	0·3	0·055	0·5	0·122	0·7	0·228	1·0	0·480	1·4	0·720	1·8	1·35	2·4		80·0
82·5		0·028	0·3	0·056	0·5	0·124	0·7	0·232	1·0	0·488	1·4	0·732	1·8	1·37	2·4		82·5
85·0		0·028	0·3	0·057	0·5	0·126	0·7	0·236	1·0	0·496	1·4	0·743	1·8	1·39	2·4		85·0
87·5		0·029	0·3	0·058	0·5	0·128	0·7	0·240	1·0	0·503	1·4	0·755	1·8	1·41	2·4		87·5
90·0		0·029	0·3	0·059	0·5	0·130	0·7	0·243	1·0	0·511	1·4	0·766	1·8	1·43	2·4		90·0
92·5		0·029	0·3	0·060	0·5	0·132	0·7	0·247	1·0	0·518	1·5	0·778	1·8	1·45	2·4		92·5
95·0		0·030	0·3	0·061	0·5	0·134	0·7	0·251	1·0	0·526	1·5	0·789	1·8	1·48	2·4		95·0
97·5		0·030	0·3	0·062	0·5	0·136	0·7	0·254	1·0	0·533	1·5	0·800	1·8	1·50	2·4		97·5
100·0		0·031	0·3	0·062	0·5	0·138	0·7	0·258	1·0	0·540	1·5	0·810	1·8	1·52	2·4		100·0
120·0	0·30	0·034	0·3	0·069	0·5	0·152	0·7	0·284	1·0	0·595	1·5	0·893	1·8	1·67	2·4		120·0
140·0		0·037	0·3	0·075	0·5	0·165	0·8	0·308	1·0	0·646	1·5	0·968	1·8	1·81	2·5		140·0
160·0		0·040	0·4	0·081	0·5	0·178	0·8	0·331	1·0	0·693	1·5	1·04	1·8	1·94	2·5		160·0
180·0		0·042	0·4	0·086	0·5	0·189	0·8	0·353	1·0	0·738	1·5	1·11	1·8	2·06	2·5	1·0	180·0
200·0		0·045	0·4	0·091	0·5	0·200	0·8	0·373	1·1	0·780	1·5	1·17	1·9	2·18	2·5		200·0
220·0		0·047	0·4	0·096	0·5	0·211	0·8	0·392	1·1	0·820	1·5	1·28	1·9	2·29	2·5		220·0
240·0		0·050	0·4	0·100	0·5	0·221	0·8	0·411	1·1	0·858	1·5	1·29	1·9	2·40	2·5		240·0
260·0		0·052	0·4	0·105	0·5	0·230	0·8	0·428	1·1	0·895	1·5	1·34	1·9	2·50	2·5		260·0
280·0		0·054	0·4	0·109	0·5	0·239	0·8	0·445	1·1	0·931	1·5	1·39	1·9	2·60	2·6		280·0
300·0		0·056	0·4	0·113	0·5	0·248	0·8	0·462	1·1	0·965	1·5	1·44	1·9	2·69	2·6		300·0
320·0	0·50	0·058	0·4	0·117	0·5	0·257	0·8	0·478	1·1	0·998	1·6	1·49	1·9	2·78	2·6		320·0
340·0		0·060	0·4	0·121	0·5	0·265	0·8	0·493	1·1	1·03	1·6	1·54	1·9	2·87	2·6		340·0
360·0		0·062	0·4	0·125	0·5	0·273	0·8	0·508	1·1	1·06	1·6	1·59	1·9	2·96	2·6		360·0
380·0		0·064	0·4	0·128	0·5	0·281	0·8	0·523	1·1	1·09	1·6	1·63	1·9	3·04	2·6		380·0
400·0		0·065	0·4	0·132	0·5	0·289	0·8	0·537	1·1	1·12	1·6	1·68	1·9	3·12	2·6		400·0
420·0		0·067	0·4	0·135	0·5	0·297	0·8	0·551	1·1	1·15	1·6	1·72	1·9	3·20	2·6	1·5	420·0
440·0		0·069	0·4	0·139	0·5	0·304	0·8	0·564	1·1	1·18	1·6	1·76	1·9	3·28	2·6		440·0
460·0		0·070	0·4	0·142	0·5	0·311	0·8	0·578	1·1	1·21	1·6	1·80	1·9	3·36	2·6		460·0
480·0		0·072	0·4	0·145	0·5	0·318	0·8	0·591	1·1	1·23	1·6	1·84	1·9	3·43	2·6		480·0
500·0		0·074	0·4	0·138	0·5	0·325	0·8	0·603	1·1	1·25	1·6	1·88	1·9	3·51	2·6		500·0
520·0		0·075	0·4	0·151	0·5	0·332	0·8	0·616	1·1	1·29	1·6	1·92	1·9	3·58	2·6	2.6	520·0

540·0		0·077	0·4	0·154	0·6	0·338	0·8	0·628	1·1	1·31	1·6	1·96	1·9	3·65	2·6		540·0
560·0		0·078	0·4	0·157	0·6	0·345	0·8	0·640	1·1	1·34	1·6	2·00	1·9	3·72	2·6		560·0
580·0		0·080	0·4	0·160	0·6	0·351	0·8	0·652	1·1	1·36	1·6	2·03	1·9	3·78	2·6		580·0
600·0		0·081	0·4	0·163	0·6	0·355	0·8	0·664	1·1	1·38	1·6	2·07	1·9	3·85	2·6		600·0
620·0		0·082	0·4	0·166	0·6	0·364	0·8	0·675	1·1	1·41	1·6	2·10	1·9	3·92	2·6		620·0
640·0		0·084	0·4	0·169	0·6	0·370	0·8	0·686	1·1	1·43	1·6	2·14	1·9	3·98	2·6		640·0
660·0		0·085	0·4	0·172	0·6	0·376	0·8	0·697	1·1	1·45	1·6	2·17	1·9	4·04	2·6		660·0
680·0		0·087	0·4	0·174	0·6	0·382	0·8	0·708	1·1	1·48	1·6	2·21	1·9	4·11	2·6		680·0
700·0		0·088	0·4	0·177	0·6	0·388	0·8	0·719	1·1	1·50	1·6	2·24	1·9	4·17	2·6		700·0
720·0		0·089	0·4	0·180	0·6	0·393	0·8	0·730	1·1	1·52	1·6	2·27	1·9	4·23	2·6		720·0
740·0		0·091	0·4	0·182	0·6	0·399	0·8	0·740	1·1	1·54	1·6	2·31	2·0	4·29	2·6	2·0	740·0
760·0		0·092	0·4	0·185	0·6	0·405	0·8	0·750	1·1	1·56	1·6	2·34	2·0	4·35	2·6		760·0
780·0		0·093	0·4	0·187	0·6	0·410	0·8	0·761	1·1	1·59	1·6	2·37	2·0	4·41	2·6		780·0
800·0		0·094	0·4	0·190	0·6	0·416	0·8	0·771	1·1	1·61	1·6	2·40	2·0	4·46	2·6		800·0
820·0		0·096	0·4	0·192	0·6	0·421	0·8	0·780	1·1	1·63	1·6	2·43	2·0	4·52	2·6		820·0
840·0		0·097	0·4	0·195	0·6	0·426	0·8	0·790	1·1	1·65	1·6	2·46	2·0	4·58	2·6		840·0
860·0		0·098	0·4	0·197	0·6	0·431	0·8	0·800	1·1	1·67	1·6	2·49	2·0	4·63	2·6		860·0
880·0		0·099	0·4	0·200	0·6	0·437	0·8	0·810	1·1	1·69	1·6	2·52	2·0	4·69	2·6		880·0
900·0		0·100	0·4	0·202	0·6	0·442	0·8	0·819	1·1	1·71	1·6	2·55	2·0	4·74	2·6		900·0
920·0		0·102	0·4	0·204	0·6	0·447	0·8	0·828	1·1	1·73	1·6	2·58	2·0	4·80	2·6		920·0
940·0		0·103	0·4	0·207	0·6	0·452	0·8	0·838	1·1	1·75	1·6	2·61	2·0	4·85	2·6		940·0
960·0		0·104	0·4	0·209	0·6	0·457	0·8	0·847	1·1	1·76	1·6	2·64	2·0	4·90	2·6		960·0
980·0		0·105	0·4	0·211	0·6	0·462	0·8	0·856	1·1	1·78	1·6	2·66	2·0	4·95	2·6		980·0
1,000·0		0·106	0·4	0·213	0·6	0·467	0·8	0·865	1·1	1·80	1·6	2·69	2·0	5·00	2·6		1,000·0
1,100·0		0·112	0·4	0·224	0·6	0·490	0·8	0·909	1·1	1·89	1·6	2·83	2·0	5·26	2·7		1,100·0
1,200·0	1·0	0·117	0·4	0·235	0·6	0·513	0·8	0·950	1·1	1·98	1·6	2·96	2·0	5·49	2·7		1,200·0
1,300·0		0·122	0·4	0·245	0·6	0·535	0·8	0·990	1·1	2·06	1·6	3·08	2·0	5·72	2·7		1,300·0
1,400·0		0·127	0·4	0·254	0·6	0·555	0·8	1·03	1·1	2·14	1·6	3·20	2·0	5·94	2·7		1,400·0
1,500·0		0·131	0·4	0·263	0·6	0·576	0·8	1·07	1·1	2·22	1·6	3·31	2·0	6·16	2·7		1,500·0
1,600·0		0·136	0·4	0·272	0·6	0·595	0·9	1·10	1·1	2·29	1·6	3·42	2·0	6·36	2·7	3·0	1,600·0
1,700·0		0·140	0·4	0·281	0·6	0·614	0·9	1·14	1·2	2·37	1·6	3·53	2·0	6·56	2·7		1,700·0
1,800·0		0·144	0·4	0·290	0·6	0·632	0·9	1·17	1·2	2·44	1·6	3·64	2·0	6·76	2·7		1,800·0
1,900·0		0·148	0·4	0·298	0·6	0·650	0·9	1·20	1·2	2·50	1·6	3·75	2·0	6·94	2·7		1,900·0

TABLE 10.—CIRCULATING PRESSURES FOR GRAVITY HOT-WATER SYSTEMS. (N/m^2 per metre height)

*°C	Temperature Differences between Flow and Return °C							
	8	10	12	14	16	18	20	22
40	27·63	33·73	35·90	44·90	49·94	54·59	58·83	62·66
45	30·60	37·51	44·11	50·39	56·32	61·91	67·13	71·97
50	33·35	41·01	48·37	55·44	62·20	68·64	74·74	80·51
55	35·93	44·28	52·35	60·15	67·66	74·88	81·79	88·39
60	38·38	47·36	56·10	64·57	72·78	80·72	88·37	95·74
65	40·71	50·31	59·66	68·78	77·64	86·24	94·58	102·66
70	42·96	53·14	63·09	72·80	82·28	91·52	100·50	109·24
75	45·14	55·88	66·40	76·69	86·76	96·59	106·19	115·54
80	47·25	58·54	69·61	80·46	91·09	101·50	111·68	121·62
85	49·29	61·10	72·71	84·10	95·28	106·24	116·98	127·50
90	51·25	63·57	75·69	87·61	99·32	110·82	122·11	133·18

* Flow Temperature.

Gravity Systems.—Gravity circulation systems can only operate when the boiler can be placed below the heat emitting units, and hence are only suitable for buildings with a large ratio of height to floor area, even so, the circulating pressure is comparatively low, and the pipe sizes must be correspondingly large. This inflexibility is not suited to modern building construction and thus pumped systems are used. The circulating pressure available from a gravity system is: $P = 9{\cdot}806(p_1 - p_2)$

where, P = circulating pressure per metre of system height (N/m^3); p_1 = density of water at flow temperature (kg/m^3); and p_2 = density of water at return temperature (kg/m^3).

Feed and Expansion.—All low-pressure hot water systems must be provided with an open tank above the highest circuit to absorb the expansion of water on heating. Water expands by $\frac{1}{23}$ in volume when heated from cold to operating temperature and the tank should be capable of taking this amount of water without overflowing. For example, an average system, 70 kW requires a tank of 90 litres capacity and a system of 600 kW a tank of 440 litres capacity.

Replacement water to balance that lost through glands, etc, is provided to the system through a ball valve in the tank, so arranged with an arm allowing the valve ball to be approximately 100 mm above the bottom of the tank, while the valve itself is above the top water level.

Air Venting.—Pipework must be arranged to ensure that entrained and dissolved air in the raw water does not accumulate and cause an air-lock. All pipework should be graded to suitable high points from which it can be vented either through an open vent, or if this is impossible, an automatic air vent or air bottle. In the latter case the air bottle must be regularly checked and air removed. These vents, etc, are additional to the permanent open vent which must be carried to above the feed tank. There must be no valves fixed on this open vent pipe, which could isolate the boiler.

High-pressure Hot Water Systems.—All HPHW installations must be 2-pipe forced systems. The procedure for pipe sizing is the same as that for LPHW systems except that the temperature drop is greater and the pipe sizing resistances must allow for the higher temperature of the water. The CIBS Tables give correction factors for flow of water at 150°C in steel pipes.

STEAM HEATING SYSTEMS.—The motive force necessary for steam distribution is derived from the reduction in steam volume from condensation; hence no pressure head is required to maintain flow as with hot water systems. Steam heating systems may be sub-divided into the major groupings as follows:

Vacuum Steam Systems.—Using steam at less than atmospheric pressure. A special vacuum pump unit is necessary to enable the system to operate satisfactorily.

Low-pressure Steam Systems.—Using steam pressures between 0·4 and 1·0 bar. Small installations may operate on a closed gravity return without the use of traps, but the general practice is to provide steam traps and an open hot-well with mechanically pumped feed to the boiler. Pipe sizing depends upon the length of main, initial pressure and maximum pressure drop which can be allowed, which in the case of gravity return systems should not exceed 17 mbar. Steam trap systems may lose up to one-third of the initial pressure in pipe resistance. Figure 4 indicates the size of pipes necessary for average sized systems together with condensate return sizes.

High-pressure Systems.—The steam is at a pressure of over 2 bar. The use of steam at high pressure usually pre-supposes that steam is being distributed for other purposes and the arrangement and sizing of pipework is as normal for steam distribution systems.

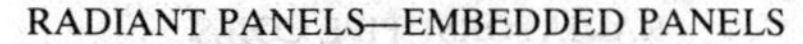

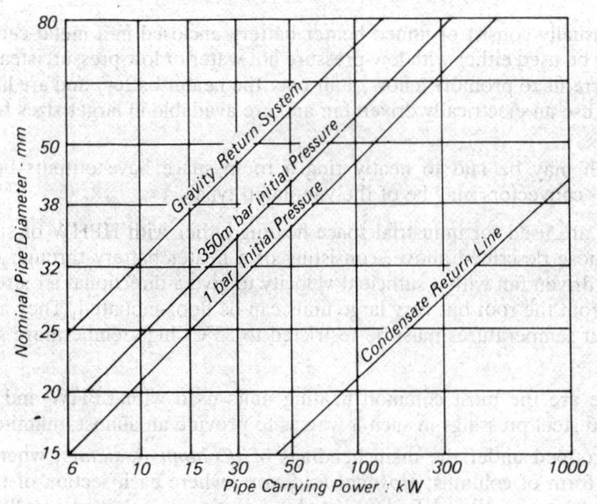

FIG. 4.—Low Pressure Steam Pipe Sizes.

LOCAL HEAT EMITTING UNITS.—These release the heat from the distribution medium at the correct rate, into individual spaces, in accordance with the calculated heat loss ($Q_f + Qv$) for that space.

In the case of water systems, the heat release is accompanied by a temperature drop in the water, whilst steam systems utilize the latent heat of condensing steam in the emitting unit. Heat is then transmitted to the space either by radiation or convection or a combination of the two. All systems can be reasonably grouped into either 'mainly radiant' comprising metal radiant panels, embedded floors or ceiling panels, etc, or 'mainly convective' units, comprising natural and forced draught convectors, unit heaters, hot water radiators and pipe coils, etc.

METAL RADIANT PANELS.—These consist of a flat metal plate to the back of which is attached a matrix of cast-iron waterways or a pipe coil. They are manufactured to be used either with low-pressure hot water, high-pressure hot water or steam. The former units are generally used for domestic work and the latter for industrial space-heating. The emission from the units is related to the surface temperature and should be obtained from the manufacturers' catalogues. As a guide, Table 11 gives the emission from heated plane surfaces in W/m^2.

TABLE 11.—EMISSION FROM PLANE SURFACES: W/m^2

Surface Temperature °C	Radiation MRT of Enclosure For E = 0·9			Convection Horizontal—Down Air Temp °C			Convection Vertical Air Temp °C			Convection Horizontal—Up Air Temp °C		
	10	15	20	10	15	20	10	15	20	10	15	20
20	48	24	0	23	10	0	34	14	0	45	20	0
40	160	140	120	91	73	55	130	110	80	180	140	110
60	300	280	250	170	150	130	250	220	190	330	300	250
80	470	440	420	260	240	220	390	350	320	500	460	420
100	660	640	620	360	340	310	530	490	460	700	650	600

EMBEDDED PANELS.—These can only be used with very low-temperature hot water and consist of steel or copper pipes embedded in the structure of the building, usually the floor or ceiling, and using the actual floor or ceiling as the emitting surface. Panels consist of a continuous length of pipe formed into a coil with the pipes at 150–200 mm centres, and for floors, the pipe panel is usually laid on a structural slab and covered with a screed at least 75 mm thick.

Ceiling panels are cast in the soffit of the slab or embedded in the plaster of a suspended ceiling. Various proprietary suspended heated ceilings exist which utilise preformed ceiling panels. The emission from embedded panels varies with the pipe diameter, pipe spacing, thickness of cover, type of surface finish and temperature of the water. As an indication, however, 12 mm pipe coils at 150 mm centres embedded in a concrete ceiling with 12 mm plaster cover, emit 190 W/m^2 to a room at 18°C when provided with water at 50°C mean temperature.

Similar panels, but at 230 mm centres, embedded in a 75 mm floor screed would emit 75 W/m^2 with water at 40°C mean temperature. In all embedded panel installations care must be taken to avoid discomfort to occupants and the surface temperature of floors must not be above 25°C or embedded ceiling panels installed in rooms less than approximately 3 m high.

Convectors.—These usually consist of finned heater battery enclosed in a metal cabine with grilles at the top and bottom and may be used either with low-pressure hot water or low-pressure steam. Natural convectors rely upon convection currents to promote a flow of air over the heater battery and are limited to about 20 kW, while forced convectors use an electrically driven fan and are available in larger sizes from about 1·5 kW and upwards.

Skirting heaters which may be laid to neatly ring a room space have outputs between 300 W/m^2 and 1300 W/m^2. Some forced convectors may be of the ventilated type.

Unit Heaters.—These are used for industrial space-heating either with HPHW or steam. They are forced convectors, similar to those described above, consisting of a heater battery through which air is forced by means of an electrically driven fan with a sufficient velocity to give a directional air stream. Units are usually made to be suspended from the roof but very large units can be floor-mounted. They are made in sizes up to 300 kW, although exit air temperatures must be restricted to 55°C; high temperature gradients must also be avoided.

RADIATORS.—These are the most common heating units used with LPHW and are constructed from cast-iron sections or mild steel pressings in such a way as to provide an almost unlimited range of sizes.

Radiator types are grouped under the main headings of: *Column Radiators*, where each section of the radiator is made in the form of columns; *Hospital Radiators*, where each section of the radiator is a single smooth unit to facilitate cleaning; *Panel Radiators*, where sections are joined parallel to the length of the radiator, and banked in single, double or triple configurations. Because of different heat release rates, it is good practice to keep heating circuits of radiators from those of convectors.

Emission from radiators is based on the manufacturers stated heating surface, as determined in BS 3528. The actual emission is not necessarily exactly equal to surface area, particularly in double and triple panel configurations, due to cross-radiation losses. Table 12 gives typical radiator emissions for 60°C between air and mean water temperatures, although manufacturers' specific figures vary.

TABLE 12.—TYPICAL HEAT EMISSION FROM RADIATORS

Type of Radiator	Width: mm	Emission: W/m^2
Column	90	643
	140	592
	190	558
Hospital	90	643
	140	552
	190	527
Single panel (cast)	—	596
(steel)	—	668
Double panel (steel)	—	622

Pipe Coils.—Heat is emitted from pipes whether specially formed as a heating coil or as pipework serving other heating appliances. Figure 5, is a graph of typical emissions from exposed horizontal steel pipes, fixed adjacent to a wall, with room air temperature between 10–20°C. In the case of horizontal pipes fixed one above the other, the percentage total emission is reduced as follows: two pipes, 95% of two single pipes; three pipes, 90% of three single pipes; four pipes, 85% of four single pipes. The emission from vertical should be reduced to 98% of the figure for equivalent horizontal pipes. Grilled or finned pipes are sometimes used to increase the heat output per linear metre, as in skirting heaters.

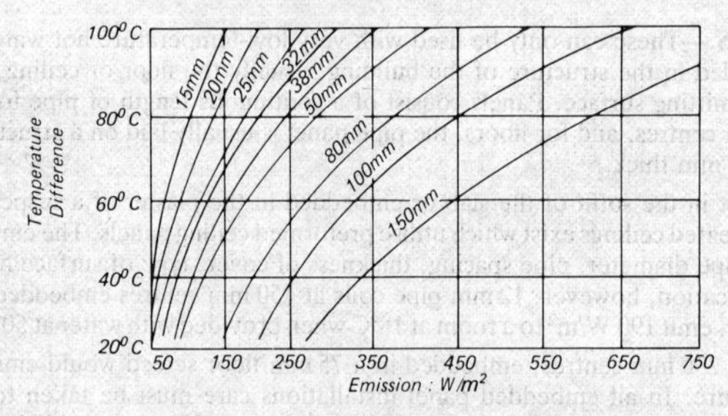

FIG. 5.—Heat Emission from Surface of Pipe (W/m^2). The graph shows curves of nominal bore: 15 mm to 150 mm.

ELECTRICAL HEATING.—The electrical heating of buildings has many attractions, requiring no labour to run, easily thermostatically and time controlled, requiring the minimum of space for its installation and in general, is of low capital cost. The actual cost of electricity, however, is high relative to other fuels, and even when off-peak tariffs can be obtained for the storage type of heater, the running costs are usually greater than other installations. Electricity can be used for heating either directly, with convectors or radiant panels, or indirectly, in storage-type heaters. Here the electricity is taken during an off-peak period at a preferential tariff, and heat released at an almost constant rate through the day. Heat losses for the space to be heated should be taken as those given previously and the rating of the unit based on these heat losses. Storage block heaters consist of a heating element embedded in refractory blocks and mounted in a metal cabinet.

Electric storage heating should be sized on the basis of heat being released for a longer period than the heating element is operative and should be over rated accordingly. A considerable refinement on the basic system above is the fan operated type. The forced warm air produces a more comfortable environment and flexible heating medium but the system is correspondingly more bulky than other types. An alternative form of storage heating is to embed the heating element in the floor screed. It is usually impossible to store sufficient heat by this method to cover the whole of the daytime period without an unduly high floor temperature, and boosting is necessary at midday. (A floor temperature of 27°C should not be exceeded at any time).

The principal disadvantage of electrical storage systems is their inflexibility in response to external environmental changes. This may be relatively simply overcome by an external anticipatory control, such as the 'Satchwell Ratiomatic' which loads the units in advance of changes pending. In addition, the high cost of electricity makes it economic to insulate the structure to the highest degree possible.

HOT WATER SUPPLY.—The quantity of hot water required for domestic use varies between 70 and 90 litres per person, per day for residential type buildings, houses, hospitals, hotels, etc, and around 24 litres per day per person, for non-residential buildings. For small domestic installations solid fuel independent boilers, gas-fired circulators or electrical immersion heaters are all suitable, one system often being used to supplement another. Gas-fired 'instantaneous'-type water heaters also offer an economic alternative to the storage-system principle.

In hard water districts, arrangements should be made for periodic inspection and removal of scale deposits which occur. It is particularly advantageous in these areas to employ an indirect method of heating the water. Here the hot water supply, ie the water actually drawn off from the taps, is heated in an *indirect cylinder* or *calorifer*, the primary of which, is in turn, heated by an ordinary heating boiler.

Thus the primary water, ie the water actually in contact with the hot surface of the boiler, is not changed, and the amount of deposit is limited. In addition, the heating surface in the indirect cylinder or calorifier is at a much lower temperature that that of the boiler plates with which the water is in contact when heated directly, and there is much less tendency for scale to form on the surfaces.

Where steam, either live or exhaust, is available, steam calorifiers are the most common means of providing the hot water supply, and lend themselves to simple thermostatic control. In small or medium-sized installations, the water may be heated by gas or electricity, the system being entirely automatic. These two methods are generally found to be too expensive for large installations, but they do, however, provide an easy and convenient means of obtaining small quantities of hot water at irregular intervals.

BOILERS AND BOILER POWER REQUIRED.—Boilers for direct heating of the water should be as simple as possible and designed so that all parts are easily accessible for cleaning, especially in hard water districts. In soft water districts special attention should be paid to the material of which the boiler is constructed. In some places the only material suitable for the boiler, and the whole system, is copper. In determining the size of boiler required it may be assumed in all cases that the water will need to be raised from 10–60°C, or through a 50°C temperature rise. Thus, if the quantity of water required is n litres, the heat loading Q, in kW, will be approximately $0{\cdot}06\,n/t$, where t, is the time in hours, allowed for obtaining the required 50°C temperature rise.

The boiler power should be related to the storage capacity and the demand on the system. As a guide on domestic installations, recovery capable of providing equivalent of two baths in $\frac{1}{2}$ hour is ideal. On other installations, if the demand is steady, the boiler power should be able to reheat the store in one hour; while a system with irregular draw-off periods of low demand and then peak demand for a short time, can have a recovery time of 2–3 hours.

STORAGE AND DISTRIBUTION SYSTEMS.—It cannot be too well stressed that whatever system is employed for heating the water, ample storage should be allowed. This provides a good reserve in case of heavy demands on the system, and has the advantage that the load on the boilers is levelled out, tending towards higher efficiency.

Storage cylinder size should be based on $\frac{1}{3}$–$\frac{1}{6}$ of the daily demand, the higher figure being used when the demand has regular peaks of draw-off with long periods of low draw-off, eg hotels, and the lower figure for systems of steady demand.

All storage vessels and circulations should be adequately lagged to prevent heat losses. The temperature of water circulated should not exceed 60°C to reduce scale formation, although this should be ample for all normal purposes. In large systems where really hot water may be required at certain points, eg kitchen, sterilizing sink, it is often advantageous to boost up at these points with gas, electricity or steam, maintaining the general supply at the lower temperature.

To guard against undue wastage of water the circulations should be run as near the actual taps as practicable, thus avoiding long draw-off pipes with 'dead' water which must be run to waste before hot water is obtained. The Water Supply Regulations give guidance on this, based on pipe diameter. The following draw-off rates may be taken as average figures in determining pipe sizes: Bath (private), 0·3 litres/s; Bath (public), 0·6 litres/s; Sink, 0·2–0·3 litres/s; Basin, 0·15 litres/s; and Shower nozzle (spray type), 0·12 litres/s.

In designing the circulation for hot water supply, it should be remembered that the pipes must be sized to supply the quantity of water necessary to meet the *maximum demand* at the taps. This maximum demand in the case of a small installation, will be when all taps are open together, but in larger installations when diversity of supply may be assumed, the *simultaneous demand* at any one time is likely to be less than the maximum possible.

Demand Units.—It is possible to assess the probable demand of various appliances by the use of Tables of grouping and usage. Conversion graphs are available for the extraction of design flow rates.

TABLE 13.—DEMAND UNITS

Fitting	Application		
	Congested	Public	Private
Basin	10	5	3
Bath	47	25	12
Sink	43	22	11
WC	35	10	5

VENTILATION AND AIR CONDITIONING

TYPES OF SYSTEM.—'*Air Conditioning*' is the supplying and maintaining of a desirable internal atmospheric condition irrespective of external conditions.

'*Ventilation*' involves delivery of air, which may be filtered, and warmed, whilst 'Air Conditioning' involves delivery of air which can be warmed or cooled and have its humidity raised or lowered. The rise in the standard of living and the design of buildings with large areas of glass, has led to the necessity of providing equipment capable of removing heat gains. Apart from the comfort of persons, the increasing complexity of many modern processes renders the necessity of accurate control of temperature and humidity in the working space and air conditioning has become increasingly important for this application.

Warm air 'Plenum' heating consists of blowing air into the occupied space at a higher temperature than 35°C, to offset the fabric losses, etc, and is used extensively in both domestic and commerical applications.

TABLE 14.—MECHANICAL VENTILATION RATES FOR TYPES OF BUILDINGS

Type of Building	Air Changes/Hour
Boiler house/engine room	15–30
Canteens	8–12
Hospitals—general rooms and wards	6
Hospitals—operating theatres	15–17
Lavatories and toilets (internal)	6–8
Offices	4–6
*Factories, Laundries, etc	over 4

* Subject to Regulations, depending on use.

AMOUNT OF AIR NECESSARY.—Ventilation provides for three main functions: (*a*) Provision for a continuous supply of oxygen for breathing. (*b*) Removal of products of respiration and occupation. (*c*) Removal of artificial contaminants produced within the ventilated space by process work, cooking, etc.

The simplest method of providing this ventilation is by natural measures, by opening of windows, but this is haphazard, and the air introduced is not properly warmed and is consequently liable to cause complaints of draught at the points of inlet. The air is also unfiltered and introduces dust and dirt into the space. With mechanical ventilation the necessary outdoor air supply per person need only be 1·0 litre/s to prevent the CO_2 produced by respiration from increasing the CO_2 concentration in the space beyond the threshold limit value.

However, the minimum outdoor air supply required to dilute the odours created by occupation to an acceptable level is a more significant factor as shown on Table 15.

TABLE 15.—MINIMUM VENTILATION RATES FOR KNOWN DENSITY OF OCCUPATION

Air space per person m^3	Outdoor air supply per person (litre/s)		
	Minimum	Recommended minimum	
		Smoking not permitted	Smoking permitted
3	11·3	17·0	22·6
6	7·1	10·7	14·2
9	5·2	7·8	10·4
12	4·0	6·0	8·0

For air conditioning, the problem is somewhat different. The total amount of air introduced is calculated from the sensible heat gains so that the temperature difference between inlet and outlet is not excessive (maximum 11°C), and this consideration generally calls for a great deal more air than the minimum ventilation rates quoted. Nevertheless, it is permissible to restrict the 'fresh air' to the minimum ventilation rates per person, and to recirculate a certain part of the used air to make up the total quantity of circulated air required. With air conditioning the used air recirculated from the space is generally at a temperature lower than the external air temperature. The higher the proportion of recirculated air the lower the amount of work done by the air conditioning equipment.

There may be cases where the number of occupants is unknown at the time of design, and in such cases it is usual to work on a basis of the number of air changes per hour. Tables 14 and 15 give typical air changes, found satisfactory for various classes of buildings with mechanical ventilation, as recommended by the CIBS.

AIR DISTRIBUTION.—The admission of fresh air to a room should be such that:

(*a*) it is evenly distributed over the whole area at a breathing level.
(*b*) it should not strike directly on the occupants.
(*c*) it should give a feeling of air movement and prevent stagnant pockets.

This calls for skill in the layout of the equipment and in the selection of air inlet grills or diffusers. Undue low velocities should be avoided, just as much as excessively high ones, and distribution above head level, not directly discharging towards the occupants, will give draught-free air movement to ensure proper distribution over the whole area.

With a mechanical supply air system, the air may be extracted by mechanical means through grills or diffusers, which may be either at high or low level, provided there is no tendency for air to short circuit from the inlet to the extract grille. Alternatively, the air may be allowed to find its own way out under the pressure of the supply fan; this is the principle adopted in domestic plenum heating systems. In the case of mechanical extract systems, it is usual to design for extracting 75–80% of the quantity of air introduced, so that any air leaks through doors, windows, etc, tend to be outwards rather than inwards. It is very unusual to find a room or space of any size whose construction is so air-tight as to preclude this leakage taking place.

Mechanical extract is sometimes used without a mechanical inlet system. This method is satisfactory for relieving conditions in such spaces as foundries, where large amounts of fumes or steam are liberated, and where a certain amount of draught is not objectionable. It must be remembered that all the air extracted must come into the building by one means or another, and in default of proper inlet system, the air will enter unheated.

AIR FILTRATION.—What is generally referred to as atmospheric dust, is a mixture of smokes and fumes which are solid particulate matter, and vapours and gases which are non-particulate. Particles are not generally called dust unless they are smaller than 80 μm. 'Smokes' are suspensions of fine particles produced by incomplete combustion or by release of chemical compounds in a finely divided state. They vary considerably in size from 0·3 μm downwards. Fumes are solid particles, predominantly smaller than 1·0 μm, formed by the condensation of vapours. It will be clear that it is important to have as high a filtering efficiency as possible, since if the air change to a building is six per hour instead of about two (as by natural means), then even if the filter removes two-thirds of the amount of dirt in the incoming air, there will still be as much dirt introduced into the building as there would be by natural ventilation. Thus, air filters may be divided into groups according to their filtering efficiency, although the type of filter to be used for a given installation depends on the characteristics of the dirt and fine dust to be removed. Almost any filter will be efficient with large particles, but filtration efficiency decreases rapidly with smaller particles. The electrostatic type is particularly efficient in this respect, removing particles as small as 0·01 μm, which includes tobacco smoke.

Dry Filters.—Consist essentially of a pad of matted material such as glass wool; the pad is contained between sheets of perforated or expanded metal. There are various refinements on this type, such as grading the material from inlet to outlet, providing it in two separate pads, etc. Some filters of this type are cleaned by shaking, or replacing the pad; pressure or time advanced automatic types of filter are available.

Viscous Filters.—These are of a similar type to the above, but the filtering material is coated with mineral oil or other viscous substance so that the dust sticks to it. The filters are cleaned by washing the oil off with a solvent, and re-oiling. A further type consists of a series of oil-coated plates or baffles so that the direction of the air is continually changed as it passes through the filter, and the dust is left sticking to the surface. The filter unit may be washed and re-coated with oil; in some types arrangements are made to flood the unit with clean oil, thus washing down the dirt, after which the plates are left to drain before re-use. As before, automatic cleaning filters are available in a wide range of sizes.

Fabric Filters.—The air passes through muslin, canvas or cotton wool stretched over frames or spacers. The velocity of the air through the fabric must be low, involving a large superficial area of fabric, but the filter units can be reduced to a relatively small size by arranging the fabric in concertina fashion. A variant on this method is to have the filtering material in long cylindrical bags, closed at one end, and with the air entering at the other. The bags are thus blown up by the air passing through them. This form of filter is efficient but bulky.

Adsorption Filters.—These consist of activated charcoal elements and are effective in the removal of odours. After use the elements can be re-activated by the manufacturer.

Electrostatic Precipitator.—The precipitator type of filter is an entirely different principle to all others. There is practically no resistance to air flow when clean, nor does the resistance of the filter increase progressively as it becomes dirty. The filter consists of series of ionising wires kept at a high potential so that the dirt particles become positively charged and are then attracted to earthed plates, down-stream from the wires. The filter needs an electrical supply which is obtained from an air-cooled power-pack with an output at about 12 kV, dc. Appropriate safety precautions must be taken to prevent access to the high-tension parts of the power-pack, or to the interior of the filter chamber while the filter is in use. It is also necessary to arrange that the fan cannot run without the filter being in use, otherwise the collected dirt tends to be blown off the collector plates. To overcome this, some simple type of viscous filter is sometimes provided down-stream of the main filter, and it may also be the practice to have the collector plates coated with oil to the same end. Electrostatic filters are cleaned by washing the dirt off the plates with hot water. Such filters are relatively expensive compared with other types, but are much more efficient.

It is often considered that an air washer constitutes a suitable filter. The air washer consists of a chamber filled with a fine water spray from a series of jets. It may well be relatively efficient as a filter to remove sand and similar materials, but it is not efficient in industrial atmospheres containing a large proportion of soot and other greasy material, which is not wetted by the water spray. The real use of an air washer is for humidifying, or dehumidifying as in an air conditioning process. If used with warm water in winter, it will act as a humidifier for an ordinary ventilating system, and will incidentally do a certain amount of air cleaning, but this is not its prime function.

AIR HEATERS.—Heating of the air may be carried out through the medium of steam, water, electricity or gas. The steam or water heaters consist of a bank of tubes containing the heating medium and round which the air passes. For ease of cleaning and maintenance, the best type of heaters are those formed of plain tube, but these are necessarily bulky. For a given length of tube more compact heaters are made possible by the use of finned tube, the emission of which may be from 3 to 5 times that of the same length of plain tube. The air heater must be designed for transferring a specified quantity of heat to a stated temperature and leaving the heater at some higher temperature.

The specified temperature rise governs the depth of the heater and the disposition of the tubes. An air heater for a small temperature rise may consist of only one bank of widely spaced tubes, whereas one for large temperature rise will have closely spaced tubes, in two or three banks. If steam is used for air heaters, it should be at a relatively low pressure, eg 350–700 mbar, and be provided with thermostatic control.

High-pressure hot water is also used for air heating, but is difficult to control to close limits, resulting in consequential 'hunting' of temperature values. Probably the most satisfactory medium is low-pressure hot water at a design temperature of 80°C or even lower. In practice, water at 50°C may give the simplest and most satisfactory operation, even though the system has been designed for a higher water temperature.

Electric air heaters are a convenient source of heat for small systems, and thermostatic control can easily be applied by means of a proportioning or modulating-type thermostat, acting upon a motorised sequence switch bringing off sections of the heater, generally through contractors.

For very small heaters on a limited temperature rise, a variant of this is to have three separate thermostats, each switching on one phase, or one section of the heater, in sequence. If a heater designed, for example, for 9° rise is switched on in three sections, then each section will be equivalent to a 3° rise, and such jumps as this in the control point are not generally permissible. It is, therefore, necessary to subdivide the heater further, with consequent complication of wiring and control equipment. When electric air heaters are used it is necessary to arrange by means of electrical interlocks, that the heater cannot be energised unless the fan is running, otherwise the heater, being rated for moving air, will be overheated and suffer damage.

A further point to bear in mind is that despite the air movement there is considerable radiation from electric heaters and cases have arisen where this has adversely affected the insulation of the plant casing and the accuracy of thermostats and thermometers placed within the plant near the heater.

Gas air heaters are usually only used in industrial applications, and may be obtained in large sizes. They consist of a series of vertical tubes placed across the air stream, each tube having its own gas burner at the base, and the top of the tubes connecting to a fume box, which requires a flue and down draught diverter to conduct the fumes out of the building.

Heat Recovery.—An increasingly popular method of reheating air in an air-conditioning system, is to use the condenser cooling water, thus recovering heat which is otherwise wasted. Where the compressors are always running and can therefore be relied upon as a source of heat, this method has advantages even though the water is generally at a relatively low temperature, and the heater must be correspondingly large. The waste heat from other sources can similarly be used, provided it is in a controllable form, eg heat from the lighting installation.

AIR COOLERS.—These are generally in a form of a battery of finned tubes, the material of which they are made depending upon the cooling medium. This is usually chilled water, but where brine is used and it is desired to have the tubes of the heater of steel, the tubular elements are built up by an inner steel tube with an outer one of copper shrunk onto it, and with copper fins attached to the outer tube. Where direct expansion cooling is used, eg a refrigeration unit evaporator, the tubes are of copper, sometimes tinned.

The considerations regarding the proportioning of cooler batteries are similar to those already referred to in regard to air heaters, with the additional complication that one cooler battery is generally called upon to fulfil two functions, ie sensible cooling and/or dehumidification.

When warm humid air is exposed to the chilled surfaces of the cooler, part of the air comes into contact with the surface either of the tubes or the fins, and may be assumed to be cooled to the mean surface temperature. If this is below its dew point, then moisture is deposited. The rest of the air, however, may be considered to pass unaltered through the spaces between the surfaces. If such spaces are relatively large in proportion to the total face of the cooler, a considerable part of the air will pass through unchanged. Down-stream from the cooler, the two proportions of air may be assumed to mix again, giving an air supply both cooler and dryer than it was originally, but not necessarily 100% saturated. Generally, air leaves the cooler battery at about 90% saturated. The 'performance' of a cooler may be assessed as the ratio of the total amount of heat (sensible and latent), extracted from the air, to the amount of heat which would have to be extracted if all that air were reduced to the mean surface temperature of the cooler and at 100% relative humidity.

It is imperative that coolers should be under thermostatic control, which in the simplest case, is achieved by starting and stopping or partially unloading the compressor, in accordance with the dictates of a thermostat in the space. It will be seen that if any dehumidifying is required, then there must be some part of the cooler surface below the dew point, and that it is not satisfactory to work the cooler at light load merely by raising its surface temperature. On the contrary, it is necessary to cut out part of the cooler completely, operating the rest at full duty (or low surface temperature). Coolers are, therefore, generally sectionalised, and in the case of water coolers, control takes the form of a step controller switching the sections on and off, in sequence. By making the sections of the cooler of unequal size, fineness of control is improved at the expense of certain complications in the wiring of the control circuits.

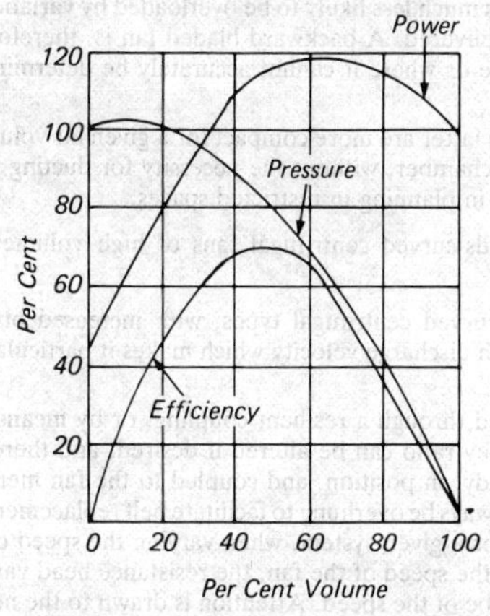

FIG. 6.—Characteristic Curves for Backward-bladed Centrifugal Fan.

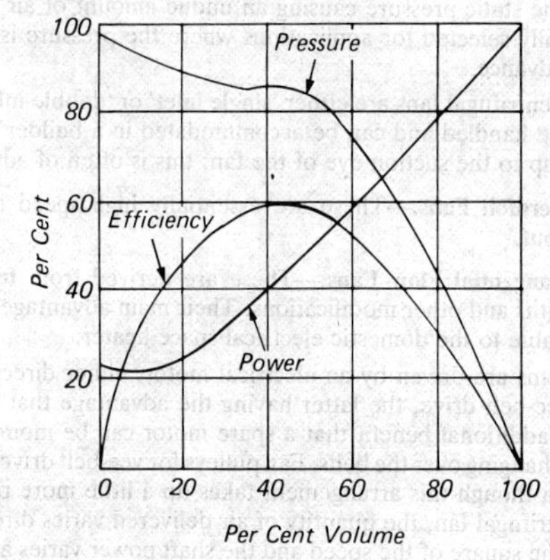

FIG. 7.—Characteristic Curves for Forward-bladed Centrifugal Fan.

Under certain conditions, when the dehumidifying load is high, the temperature of the air leaving the latent cooler can be less than is required, and a certain amount of reheat will be necessary. The temperature control in such cases, therefore, consists of a two-way thermostat, one end of which controls the sensible cooler and the other the reheater. There are certain applications, where very fine control of humidity is desired, where it may be justifiable to provide separate sensible and latent coolers, the former being placed after the latter to do such additional sensible cooling as has not been achieved inherently in dehumidifying process. The sensible cooler may then be controlled by varying the temperature of the coolant supply to it.

Air coolers must be provided with adequate means of draining away the moisture condensing upon them, otherwise this moisture may be re-entrained in the air stream. It is often considered necessary to provide eliminator plates to catch and remove from the airstream any drops of water carried over off the cooler, although the tendency is to proportion the face area of the coolers generously, and so minimise the danger of carry-over and dispensing with the need for eliminator plates.

FANS.—Essential in any system of mechanical ventilation, there are three main types of fans:

Propeller Fans.—Essentially for non-ducted applications. These fans can be obtained from the smallest units, suitable for removing vitiated air from private offices, to very large sizes. A characteristic of propeller fans is that they are not suitable for working against any appreciable pressure head.

Axial Flow Fans.—These are the modern developments of propeller fans and consist of a rotor in the air stream, having blades of efficient aerofoil section. Fans of this type are very compact and capable of working against much higher pressure heads than ordinary propeller fans.

There exist various refinements in design, such as two-stage fans and double contra-rotating units, which lead to high volume-pressure applications. The higher pressure fans of the above types tend to be noisy; the criterion being mainly one of tip-speed and even then, depending on application, some duct attenuation will probably be necessary.

TABLE 16.—SELECTION OF AXIAL FLOW FANS

Performance	Application	Max tip speed m/s
Quiet	Drawing-offices and similar rooms	900
Fairly quiet	Entrances. Vestibules and spaces away from continuous occupation	1,200
Fairly noisy	Workshops, etc	1,500

Centrifugal Fans.—These fans consist of metal casing in which revolves a multi-bladed impeller. The blading may be either forward, radial or backward, in relation to the direction of rotation, and the choice of blading has an important effect on the fan performance. Figures 6 and 7 show typical characteristic curves for a forward and for a backward bladed fan; the forward-bladed fan has a maximum efficiency of approximately 50% of its full opening volume, and at this point the static pressure also reaches the maximum.

This is the operating point usually selected for such a fan. If, however, the fan is opened up too much then the efficiency drops off quickly and power increases continuously. In the case of the backward bladed fan, however, the power characteristic is self-limiting: that is to say that at maximum efficiency power consumed is about the same as at full opening, and, therefore, the motor is much less likely to be overloaded by variations in the static pressure causing an undue amount of air to be delivered. A backward-bladed fan is, therefore, usually selected for applications where the pressure is variable or where it cannot accurately be determined in advance.

Centrifugal fans are either 'single inlet' or 'double inlet'. The latter are more compact for a given air volume to be handled and can be accommodated in a builder's work chamber, without the necessity for ducting the air up to the suction eye of the fan; this is often of advantage in planning in restricted spaces.

Aerofoil Fans.—These are essentially high speed backwards-curved centrifugal fans of high volumetric output.

Tangential Flow Fans.—These are derived from forward-curved centrifugal types, with increased blade lengths and other modifications. Their main advantage is a high discharge velocity which makes it particularly suitable to the domestic electrical space heater.

Fans are driven by an electrical motor, either direct coupled through a resilient coupling, or by means of a vee-belt drive, the latter having the advantage that the pulley ratio can be altered if desired, and there is the additional benefit that a spare motor can be mounted ready, in position, and coupled to the fan merely by changing over the belts. Fan pulleys for vee-belt drive must always be overhung to facilitate belt replacements, even though this arrangement takes up a little more room. For a given system, when varying the speed of a centrifugal fan, the quantity of air delivered varies directly as the speed of the fan, the resistance head varies as the square of the speed and the shaft power varies as the cube of the speed. Attention is drawn to the need or special calculations for the performance of the fan when working at high altitudes or in other locations where the atmospheric pressure is not standard.

Air Terminal Units.—In areas of differing heat gain patterns, air conditioning may still be supplied from a central plant, and the variations in temperature for volume may be achieved in the ductwork or at the terminal units feeding the room. Volume control may be achieved by a simple damper unit or pressure regulating valve, etc. Temperature control may be achieved: (1) By blending two airstreams in a terminal unit, with supply air temperature trimmed to offset desired cooling or heating loads. (2) By controlled reheat of pre-conditioned low temperature air supply, by hot water, steam or electricity, to design requirements.

Outlets.—These vary depending on application, etc, from simple grilles and adjustable aerofoil louvres to diffuser types.

Where simplification of ductwork is required, combined supply and extract diffusing fittings may be employed. Integrated ceiling units embodying the luminaire, also provide for simplified and uniform air-supply extraction, as well as air temperature control over the lighting fitting.

AIR CONDITIONING CALCULATIONS.—The hygrometric state of air is defined by any two of the following: (1) Dry bulb temperature (db). (2) Wet bulb temperature (wb). (3) Absolute humidity (or dew point). (4) Relative humidity.

The db temperature is the ordinary reading of a thermometer exposed to air. The wb temperature is generally determined from a sling hygrometer—the instrument comprises a thermometer bulb permanently wetted, as well as a normal thermometer (which reads db temperature).

Hygrometric tables of the CIBS are based on actual wet bulb readings, taken for certain specified conditions and therefore determined by experiment. These temperatures are not a true criteria of total heat, and the absolute humidity is expressed in the mass of water per unit mass of dry air and the dew point of this air is another way of stating the same quantity.

Relative humidity of air at a given temperature is properly defined under conditions of vapour pressure. This is very nearly the same thing as the 'percentage saturation' in which the ratio of grams of moisture per kilogram of air at the given condition is compared to the saturated condition for the same temperature.

Figure 8 shows a simplified psychrometric chart on which the various quantities referred to, above, are set out diagrammatically.

Two co-ordinates of moisture content (or mass) and enthalpy (energy) are used, with db and wb lines superimposed. This chart is based on the CIBS data referred to above.

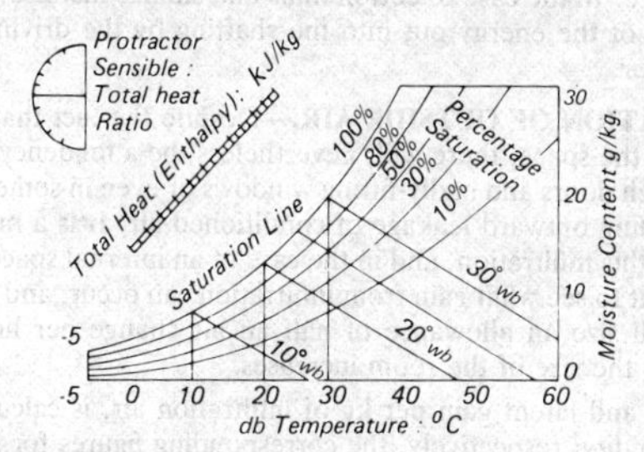

FIG. 8.—Psychrometric Chart. (The moisture content is in grams of water per kilogram of dry air.)

HEAT GAINS.—In designing an air conditioning system, the first step after determining the inside conditions required and the outside conditions relevant to the locality, is to ascertain the total heat and moisture gain to the building, with a view to providing equipment adequate for the removal of these gains. Taking first the '*Sensible Gains*', these can be sub-divided as follows: (*a*) Direct and transmitted heat gains through the building structure (walls; glazing; etc). (*b*) Gain due to fresh ventilating air at plant, and any other infiltrating air. (*c*) Gains from occupants. (*d*) Gains from process equipment; lighting and other electrical plant and equipment. The '*Latent Gains*' are those contributing water vapour to the space, ie ventilating and infiltrating air; occupants; and certain process equipment, cookers, etc.

The object of the calculation is to arrive at the simultaneous maximum heat gain, and judgment is necessary as to the relative time of incidence of the various portions of the load. For instance, when the sun is highest, over the building the gain through a flat roof or horizontal skylight is at a maximum, and direct solar radiation on to windows at a minimum. The Building Research Stations' overlays of sunpath diagrams are a valuable aid to computation of solar gain for all building orientations at various latitudes.

In addition, to this solar heat absorption, the time when the radiation falls upon a surface is not the same, in all cases, as the time of the effect being felt within the space. For a massive construction, of, eg concrete, there will be a time lag of several hours (a diurnal temperature cycle similar to Fig. 1), and this must be allowed for. In contrast, modern lightweight constructions, dominated by glass, are highly susceptible to a rapid rise in temperature.

GAINS FROM OCCUPANTS.—The human body, even when at rest, emits a certain quantity of heat and moisture, and these quantities increase rapidly soon as the person becomes active. The relative proportion of sensible to latent heat varies according to the temperature of the environment; the higher the temperature, the greater the proportion of heat that will be emitted as latent heat. Table 17 gives approximate values of the sensible and latent heat emission for various states of activity. The density of occupation should also be considered. The average density of office type area is about 8–10 m^2 per person over the whole of the conditioned floor area.

TABLE 17.—SENSIBLE AND LATENT HEAT EMISSION FROM OCCUPANTS

Occupation	Average Metabolic Rate W	% Emission at 21°C–Watts	
		Sensible	Latent
Seated at rest	115	70	30
Light work (office)	140	62	38
Light work (bench)	235	50	50
Medium work	265	47	53
Heavy work	440	—	—

GAINS FROM LIGHTING AND EQUIPMENT.—The functioning of the electrical installation (lighting, switchgear, motors), will add to the internal heat gains. Generally, in the absence of other data this can be 25–35 W per m^2 of floor area; the heating effect of the lighting being switched on is not felt immediately by the air conditioning system. In some instances a reduction may be made in the case of lighting systems above lay-lights where part of the heat is removed directly by the extract system and does not affect the conditioned space.

Gas-fired apparatus sometimes represents a serious load because it not only emits heat, but there is a considerable quantity of moisture formed by the combustion of the gas. In the case of restaurants, an allowance should be made for the gain due to the hot food brought in. A figure of 10 W and 12 grams per meal served being an approximate allowance. In the case of cotton mills and similar factories, it should not be overlooked that ultimately the larger part of the energy put into the shafting by the driving engine is transformed into heat, which must be allowed for.

GAINS DUE TO INFILTRATION OF OUTSIDE AIR.—Despite the fact that the system will be designed for a small net pressure inside the space, there will, nevertheless, be a tendency for warm untreated air from outside to find its way in through doors and badly-fitting windows or even in some cases, through the structure, and there will be a corresponding outward leakage of conditioned air. It is a matter of judgment as to what allowance should be made for this infiltration, and in the case of an internal space wholly surrounded by other conditioned spaces, it is difficult to see what gain from infiltration can occur, and in fact it is generally ignored. For an external room of small size an allowance of half an air change per hour would cover most cases, reduced to a quarter or less as the size of the room increases.

The amount of the sensible and latent gain per kg of infiltration air, is calculated by subtracting from its temperature and absolute humidity, respectively, the corresponding figures for the room condition.

TOTAL GAINS.—The amount of the sensible and latent gains are totalled separately, and probably the most convenient way of relating them to the conditioning load is by means of a ratio chart of sensible heat: total heat. The ratio is calculated and plotted from the protractor on the psychrometric chart. The slope of this protractor gives the *Room Ratio Line* which is an indication of the ratio of latent and sensible heat exchanges taking place within the space. This sloping line is plotted through the state point of the room and normally sloping downwards.

Figure 9 shows a skeleton chart with a typical calculation drawn upon it, point A–B being the ratio line. Air introduced into the space at any point on this ratio line will gain heat and moisture at the proper rate to

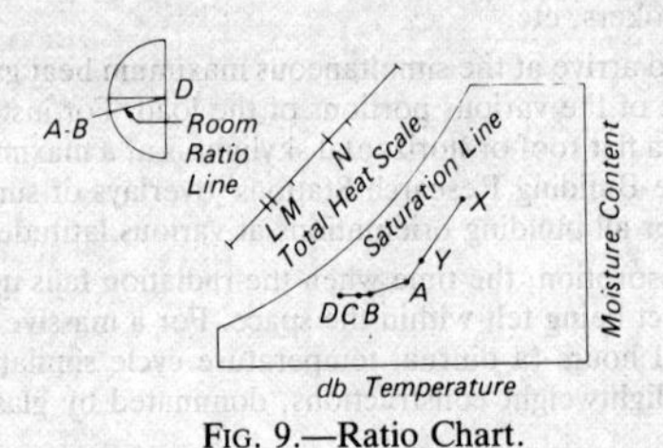

FIG. 9.—Ratio Chart.

satisfy the required room condition and it is thus a question of selecting the correct point on A–B, depending upon the temperature differential permissible in the space.

This temperature differential must be decided upon by the designer. A figure of between 8–11°C will minimise the risk of draughts and the quantity of air required is calculated by dividing the sensible heat gain by the product of the permissible differential and the specific heat of air. The quantity thus arrived at, will be in kg of air per second.

The 11° or other figure selected is plotted on the chart horizontally and determines the point B on the ratio line, this point being the room inlet condition. From point B a line B–C is drawn to the left horizontally representing duct and/or fan motor gains (these gains are wholly sensible so that the line B–C is horizontal) and the point C then represents the plant outlet condition.

Another convenience of graphical methods of calculation is in the determination of the condition of the mixture of fresh and recirculated air passing to the plant for conditioning. If the point *X* on the chart represents the outside condition, then it can be shown that if point *X* is joined to point *A* (the room condition and therefore, the recirculation air condition also), and the line *X–A* be divided at *Y* inversely in proportion to the quantities of fresh and recirculated air, then point *Y* represents the state point of the mixture. In the particular case drawn, $XY = 2YA$, which is typical for recirculation, although other economic criteria may govern this.

By projecting points *Y* and *C* on to the total heat scale, the total heat extracted from the space is determined by the length *MN* to scale. This is not, however, the cooling load required of the compressor, since the plant may not be physically capable of producing air precisely at the point *C*. In many cases, particularly in temperate zones, it will be found that in order to get the air dry enough, it must be cooled to a temperature lower than that required, and subsequently reheated. It is assumed for the purpose of the diagram that for the particular cooler selected the outlet, or off-coil condition at the required dew point is represented by the point *D* at 92% saturation. The difference in total heat between the points *D* and *C* then represents the amount of reheating per kg of air.

The total output required of the refrigeration plant is then the net cooling load *M–N* plus the reheat load *L–M*. This is the *net* compressor load. The duty of the compressor plant when calculated is thus in kg per kW of refrigeration. *Note*—1 ton refrigeration = 3·517 kW.

In designing the reheater battery an examination should be made of conditions in the space when the heat gains are not at their maximum and sometimes it is necessary to carry out a complete heat and moisture gain calculation for the partial load condition. Where the heat gain in the space is due entirely to occupants, the ratio will be constant and the state point of the inlet air will move up the line *B–A* towards *A* as the occupancy decreases. This condition is applicable to large public halls substantially surrounded by other conditioned spaces, so that the gains are almost independent of outside temperature and vary solely with the occupancy. It will sometimes be found that a bigger reheat battery is required for partial load conditions that for the design condition. In addition, the surrounding spaces may be designed to act as 'transition zones' to reduce the 'thermal shock' effect on persons entering the cool building interior, from outside.

VELOCITIES OF AIR FLOW AND DUCT SIZES

LOW VELOCITY SYSTEMS.—Where mechanical ventilation only is required and where quietness in operation is important, low velocities varying from 4 to 5 m/s are suitable. For main ducts this figure may be increased to 5 to 6 m/s according to the size of the duct, and for factories, speeds up to 9 m/s may be permissible. Where the air is used for the conveyance of dust, wood chips and similar materials, very much higher velocities are necessary to keep the material entrained in the air stream.

In order to obtain an even distribution of air throughout the system, the design of the ductwork is important. Changes in direction and section should be as gradual as possible, particular care being taken to avoid sudden changes. The finish of the ducts should always be of the best, as roughness and irregularities immensely increase the resistance to the flow of air. The ducts may be constructed of sheet metal or in builders' work. When made by the builders the ducts should be lined with glazed bricks, or, if this is too expensive, finished with Keene's cement or some similar hard smooth finish. The importance of the foregoing will be appreciated when it is realised that in mechanical ventilation where silence is essential the fan should not work against a resistance exceeding 250 N/m^2 and in other general work is advisable not to exceed 500 N/m^2 except for dust extraction and other similar industrial processes.

The IHVE charts for fluid flow are derived from the Colebrook-White equation; an approximate formula by Fritzsche (where $\Delta p/L$ = pressure drop in N/m^2 per metre; v = air velocity in m/s; and d = diameter of duct in mm) is:

$$\Delta p/L = \frac{91{\cdot}16 v^{1{\cdot}852}}{d^{1{\cdot}269}}$$

For resistance in ducts of other materials than sheet metal, multiply the result obtained from the diagram or by the above formula by the following factors:

Smooth concrete	1·5	Brickwork	2·0

When arriving at the total resistance in a duct, allowance must be made for bends and loss due to entry and egress at registers. These losses are often assessed by multiplying the velocity head through the duct fitting by a factor 'k'. Values of the velocity head factor for the more common duct fittings are as follows:

Sharp elbow (90°)	$k = 1{\cdot}25$	Expander 10° slope	$k = 0{\cdot}2$
Easy bend (90°)	$k = 0{\cdot}25$	Grille 50% free area	$k = 0{\cdot}5$
Reducer, splayed	$k = 0{\cdot}2$	Branch piece (radiused into main)	$k = 0{\cdot}32$

To obtain the total head against which the fan has to work, the velocity head at the outlet must be added to the resistance in the duct; this is obtained from the formula: $h = 0{\cdot}5\,pv^2$, where p = density of air ($1{\cdot}2\ \mathrm{kg/m^3}$); v = velocity of the air (m/s); and h = the air pressure ($\mathrm{N/m^2}$). As with pipe sizing, it is usual to employ a 'duct pressure drop' per metre run; a typical figure is $1\ \mathrm{N/m^2/m}$, and from Tables (Fig. 10) extract appropriate duct diameters. Other sizing methods are available (such as 'static region'), and may be used where appropriate.

All the above is based on circular ducts. In the case of rectangular ducts, find the equivalent circular duct to give equal discharge for equal resistance, from the following formula, and then using Fig. 10, to find the resistance to flow:

$$D = 1{\cdot}265\sqrt[5]{\left[\frac{(AB)^3}{(A+B)}\right]}$$

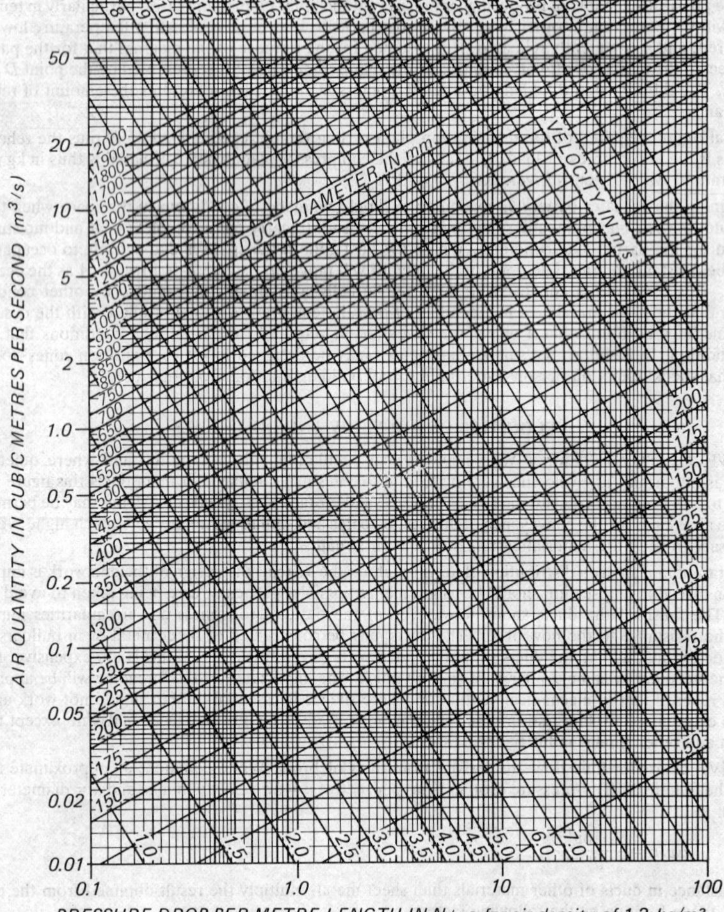

FIG. 10.—Air Flow in Round Ducts.

where A = long side of rectangular duct; B = short side of rectangular duct; and D = diameter of equivalent round duct, which can be found by means of Fig. 11.

Early consideration should be given to the position and size of ducts when mechanical ventilation is to be employed in a building. Assuming a building in which there are, say, 3,000 people, and taking 28 m^3/h, this means about 1,400 m^3/min. The velocity permissible in the ducts will depend to some extent on their length but 4·5 m/s may be taken as a good maximum average. This means that the inlet and the distributing duct should have an area of not less than 5 m^2.

As a streamline section must be maintained, it follows that where a change of direction in a duct of this size takes place considerable space is taken up, and unless provision has been made for same, difficulties may be encountered. Steel work is often a very important factor, especially in connection with the vertical subsidiary ducts, and is very difficult to modify. This trouble can only be avoided by close collaboration between the various parties concerned in the early stages of the building. It must be remembered that high air velocities and high speed fans are a potential source of trouble and expense, however attractive it may be at the the time to install small ducts that are easily adapted to the building.

HIGH VELOCITY SYSTEMS.—These are used in multi-storey buildings where space is at a premium and utilising small ducts and high air velocities. This system is of particular value where air conditioning is employed since, in order to keep the temperature differential within reasonable limits a considerable quantity of air is re-circulated from the building and mixed with the required fresh air, resulting in much larger volumes of air to be handled, and therefore larger ducts, if low velocities are used. Maximum air velocities about 20 m/s can be employed with fan resistances varying from 1,000 to 1,400 N/m^2. This requires several times the fan power which is necessary in an orthodox ventilating system where air velocities vary from 4–5 m/s.

Because of the higher pressure in the ducts, particular care must be taken to ensure air-tightness which necessitates special fabrication techniques. For the same reason, ducts of circular section are usually employed. Air at these velocities produces noise, so sound attenuators are an essential part of the system. They consist of specially constructed boxes lined with acoustic material placed on the fan outlet, and also before the terminals through which the air enters the room. These terminals also serve to reduce the entry air velocity.

The capital cost of high velocity systems is greater than orthodox systems, due to the larger motors required to drive the fans, the heavier gauge material required for constructing fans and ducts and the provision of sound absorbers. This cost must be set against the reduction in building costs when comparing the relative merits of alternative systems. Developments of high velocity systems include Single duct, Double duct, Induction, and Variable air volume, etc.

Single Duct System.—Here, only the fresh air necessary to meet the requirements of the occupants is delivered through the duct. This air is conditioned for both temperature and humidity at central plant and then enters the room through specially designed units, usually placed on the perimeter of the building, under the windows. The units are so designed that the velocity of the fresh air entering through the unit, entrains two to three times its volume of room air and the two mix together before being again discharged into the room.

Double Duct System.—In this, warm and cool air are both ducted to the units through which the air is delivered to the room, the temperature being controlled by proportioning warm and cool air automatically

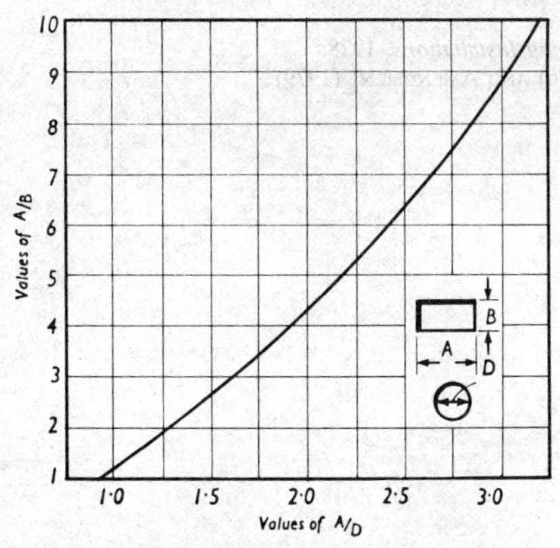

FIG. 11.—Diagram of Equivalent Round Duct Diameter (carrying the same quantity of air for the same loss as a rectangular duct).

by suitable thermostatic controls. Main advantages are that there are no pipes for conveying warm or chilled water, or for removing condensation. In both cases, mechanical extract is provided to remove the air which will be replaced by fresh air, and in case of the double duct system, also to convey the air required for recirculation to the main plant.

Induction System.—A central air plant supplies conditioned air to induction units in the rooms and water from a separate plant. This conditioned air induces air through induction units where it is heated (or cooled). The system is particularly suitable for modular building layouts; the central plant only handles part of the air treated.

Fan Coil Systems.—These are a variation of an induction system, whereby recirculation ducting from primary plant is dispensed with. Various arrangements are possible for the introduction of fresh air into room units, which also house supply fans, and the elimination of certain sections of ducting offers an element of flexibility in installation. Hence this system has advantages where air conditioning is required in an existing building with the minimum of structural alterations.

Variable Air-Volume System.—A relatively new method of air conditioning where less air is supplied at the original supply temperature to the conditioned space. This dispenses with central plant re-heat and takes minimum fan-supply power. The system is limited in terms of turn down and cannot deal with heat loss without either a perimeter system of compensating LPHW heating, or terminal re-heaters, eg the permanent lighting of an 'open plan' office layout.

Ceiling Systems.—The ceiling void above a suspended ceiling can be used as a plenum chamber to supply air conditioning. The air supply may be through ceiling or linear diffusers, and the ceiling may be cooled or heated. Alternatively, air may be extracted through special luminaires (lighting fittings), thus removing unwanted heat at source.

BS CODES OF PRACTICE

CP 3 'Basic data for design of buildings'.
CP 341 'Central heating by low pressure hot water'.
CP 352 'Mechanical ventilation and air conditioning in buildings'.
CP 413 'Ducts for building services'.

BIBLIOGRAPHY

BURBERRY. *Environment and Services*. 1977.
CHALKLEY AND CARTER. *Thermal Environment*. 1968.
FABER AND KELL. *Heating and Air Conditioning of Buildings*. 1978.
FRANCIS. *Fuels and Fuel Technology*. 1965.
JONES. *Air Conditioning Engineering*. 1976.
LOMAX. *Insulation Handbook* (1974).
PORGES. *Handbook of Heating, Ventilating and Air Conditioning*. 1976.
PETHERBRIDGE. *Sunpath Diagrams and Overlays*. 1969.
PRITCHARD. *Environmental Physics.—Heating*. 1975.
SHAW. *Heating and Hot Water Services*. 1970.
CIBS. *Guides (A, B and C)*
IOP. *Design Data for Plumbing Installations*. 1978.
BUILDING REGULATIONS (1976) AND AMENDMENT (1979).

LIGHT AND LIGHTING

Basic Principles—Definition of Lighting Terms—Design Considerations—Electric Lamps—Circuit Data—Fluorescent Tubes and Circuits—Luminaires (Lighting Fittings)—Lumen Method of Design—Illumination—Integrated Lighting, Heating and Ventilation

By R. L. C. Tate, FCIBSE

NATURE OF LIGHT.—Light is generally considered as a form of electro-magnetic radiation covering a wave-band between 380 to 760 nanometres, to which the eye is sensitive. These wavelengths are usually expressed in one of the following units:—

1 micron (μm) $= 10^{-6}$ m or 10^{-4} cm

1 nanometre (nm) = 1 millimicron $= 10^{-9}$ m or 10^{-7} cm

1 ångstrom (Å) $= 10^{-10}$ m or 10^{-8} cm

Light of different wavelengths differs in colour, as shown in Fig 1. This affects the luminous efficiency of light sources.

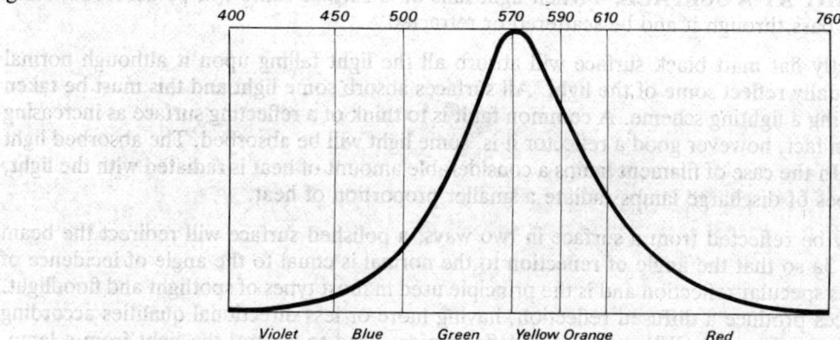

FIG. 1.—The visible spectrum and eye sensitivity curve; wavelengths are shown in nanometres.

Units of light measurement.—The basic SI units of light measurement are as follows:—

LUMINOUS INTENSITY; *The candela*; defined as the luminous intensity, in a perpendicular direction, of a surface of $1/600{,}000\,m^2$ of a black body at the temperature of freezing platinum under a pressure of 101,325 newtons per m^2.

LUMINOUS FLUX; *The Lumen*; defined as the flux emitted within unit solid angle of one steradian by a point source having a uniform intensity of one candela (Fig. 2).

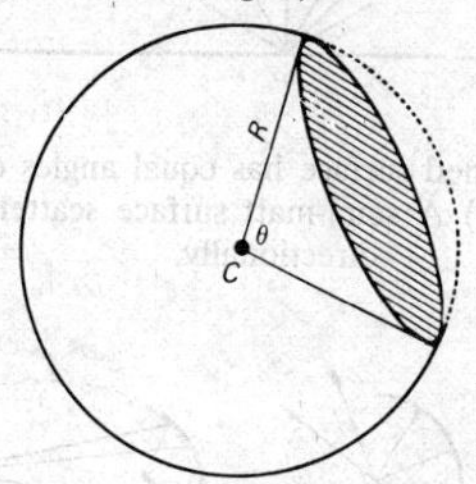

FIG. 2.—The derivation of a lumen. A source of one candela at the centre of the sphere of unit radius gives light in the solid angle 0; the shaded area being also of unit radius.

ILLUMINATION; *The Lux*; defined as one lumen per square metre (the Footcandle, or lumen per square foot is an obsolete term).

N.B—Measured illumination is referred to as *Illuminance.*

LUMINANCE (measured brightness); one candela per square metre, sometimes termed the *nit*.

It is important to distinguish between 'luminance' and 'luminosity' or apparent brightness, that is, the relative appearance of two surfaces seen together. The luminance of a motor car headlamp is the same by day or night, but at night its luminosity, compared to its surroundings, is far higher than by day.

Other, less commonly used units are the 'footcandle' or lumen per square foot, referred to above, which is equivalent to 10.7639 lux, the stilb, a unit of luminence which is 1 cd/cm², the lambert, 1/π cd/cm² and the foot-lambert, 1/π cd/ft².

Mechanical equivalent of light.—The energy in one lumen has been calculated as 0.00147 watts, but this is purely of academic interest. For practical purposes the luminous efficiency of lamps is expressed in lumens per watt, and this is known as the *efficacy* of the lamp.

Eye response curve.—To produce white light approximately equal amounts of energy must be dissipated in each of the seven colour-bands which can be distinguished in the visible spectrum, that is to say, the top horizontal line in Fig. 1 can be taken as an approximation of the energy available in light from a north sky. The eye is most sensitive to frequencies in the middle of the visible spectrum, and this is represented by the curve on the diagram. From this it will be seen that more energy must be exerted to produce the same effect on the eye in the red and blue, than in the yellow and green parts of the spectrum. The practical result of this is that the lamps which produce the maximum effect on the eye for a given power consumption are those which give predominantly green or yellow light, but are deficient in blue and red. From this it will be seen that to describe a lamp's efficiency in terms of the proportion of energy emitted as visible light to the total energy consumed is misleading unless the reaction of the eye is taken into account. This is why the 'efficacy' of lamps is expressed in lumens per watt, and why lamps of good colour-rendering properties, such as the 'Northlight' or 'colour-matching' fluorescent tubes have a lower efficacy than 'white', 'coolwhite' or 'warm-white' tubes.

BEHAVIOUR OF LIGHT AT A SURFACE.—When light falls on a surface some will be absorbed, some reflected, and some may pass through it and be scattered or refracted.

Absorbtion.—A perfectly flat matt black surface will absorb all the light falling upon it although normal black painted surfaces usually reflect some of the light. All surfaces absorb some light and this must be taken into account when designing a lighting scheme. A common fault is to think of a reflecting surface as increasing the light falling upon it, in fact, however good a reflector it is, some light will be absorbed. The absorbed light is transformed into heat. In the case of filament lamps a considerable amount of heat is radiated with the light, fluorescent and other types of discharge lamps radiate a smaller proportion of heat.

Reflection.—Light may be reflected from a surface in two ways: a polished surface will redirect the beam of light as shown in Fig. 3a so that the angle of reflection to the normal is equal to the angle of incidence of the light. This is known as specular reflection and is the principle used in most types of spotlight and floodlight. Matt or semi-matt surfaces produce a diffused reflection, having more or less directional qualities according to the nature of the surfaces (Fig. 3b). Where specular reflectors are used to control the light from a lamp, they are usually parabolic in cross-section, the light-source, which must be as compact as possible being placed at the focal point of the parabola (Fig 4a); a reflector of elliptical cross section will focus the light from a source placed at one focus of the ellipse through the second focus (Fig. 4c); this principle is much used in cinema and slide projectors. Reflectors of spherical cross section reflect light back through the focal position; they are used to avoid 'spill light' in floodlights and spotlights (Fig. 4b).

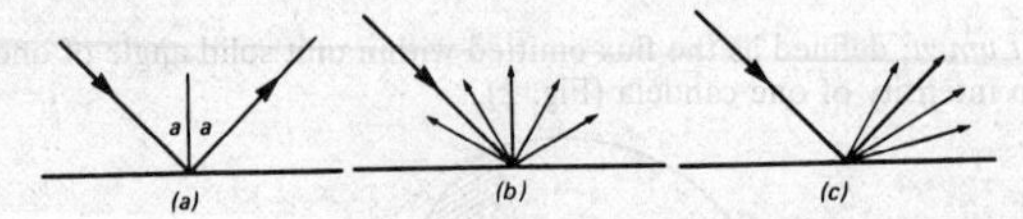

FIG. 3.—(*a*) Light reflected from a polished surface has equal angles of incidence and escape. (*b*) A matt surface reflects light in all directions. (*c*) A semi-matt surface scatters some light and also reflects some directionally.

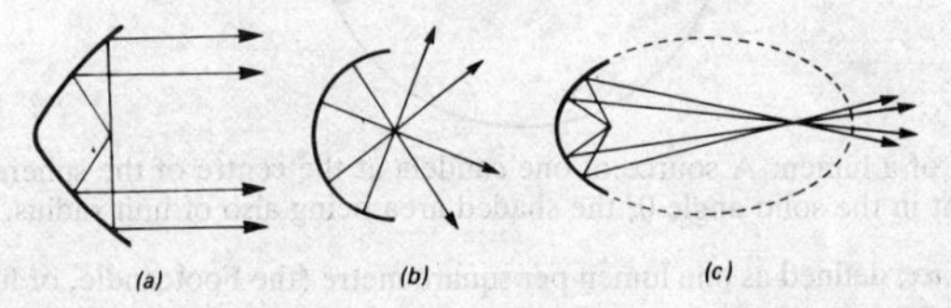

FIG. 4.—(*a*) Parabolic reflector; light from focal point reflected in a parallel beam. (*b*) Hemispherical reflector; light reflected back through focal point. (*c*) Elliptical reflector; light reflected to cross at second focus of ellipse.

Refraction.—When a beam of light passes through the junction between two dissimilar transparent surfaces, eg air and glass, it is 'bent' or refracted (Fig. 5). The angle of refraction varies with the material and the

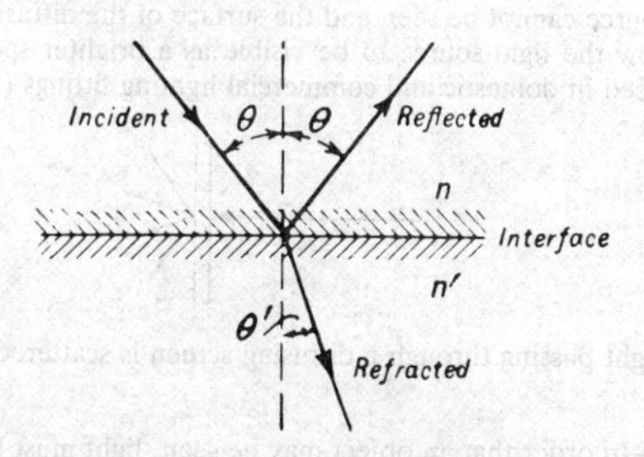

FIG. 5.—Refraction of light.

wavelength of the light, violet and blue light being deflected more than red or orange. Thus white light when passed through a prism is split up into all the spectral colours when it emerges from it. The amount of deflection is called the refractive index of the material and is measured against that of air, which is considered as unity. Table 1 shows the refractive indices of various materials for monochromatic yellow light from a low-pressure sodium source. The extent of variation is called 'dispersion' and is of importance in the design of optical instruments. An example of the use of refraction in lenses is shown in Fig. 6, a diagrammatic representation of a microscope.

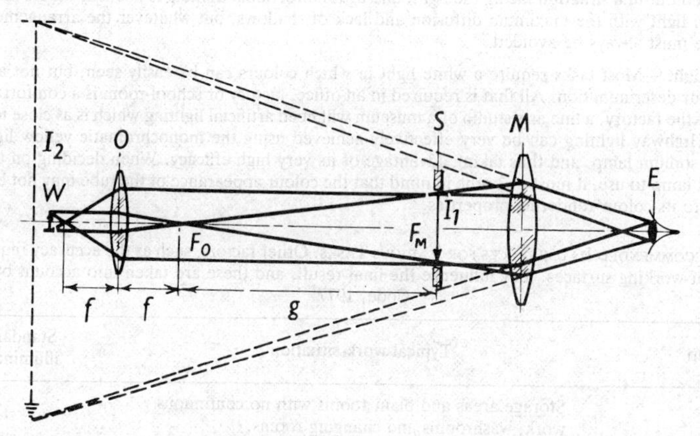

FIG. 6.—The principle of the microscope; lenses refract the light to produce magnification. Note that some light is absorbed by the lenses.

TABLE 1.—REFRACTIVE INDICES (AGAINST AIR)

Substance	Refractive Index	Substance	Refractive Index	Substance	Refractive Index
Alum	1·46	Ruby	1·76	Carbon tetrachloride	1·46
Diamond	2·42	Silica, fused	1·46	Glycerine	1·47
Glass, crown	1·52	Sugar	1·56	Nitrobenzene	1·55
Glass, flint	1·65	Topaz	1·63	Oil, cedar	1·52
Ice	1·31	Alcohol, amyl	1·41	Oil, cinnamon	1·60
Mica	1·58	Alcohol, ethyl	1·36	Oil, olive	1·46
Perspex	1·49	Alcohol, methyl	1·33	Oil, paraffin	1·44
Polystyrene	1·59	Aniline	1·59	Sulphuric acid	1·43
Quartz	1·55	Benzene	1·50	Turpentine	1·47
Rock salt	1·54	Carbon bisulphide	1·63	Water	1·33

The refractive index of air against a vacuum is 1.00029. The refractive indices of all gases are equal to unity within a fraction of one per cent.

Diffusion.—This term is used to describe the scattering of light passing through a translucent but not transparent surface such as opal acrylic or glass. The light is scattered in all directions in the case of a 'perfect' diffuser so that the light source cannot be seen and the surface of the diffusing material appears to be evenly lighted. Semi-diffusers allow the light-source to be visible as a brighter spot in the middle of the diffusing surface. This principle is used in domestic and commercial lighting fittings (Fig. 7).

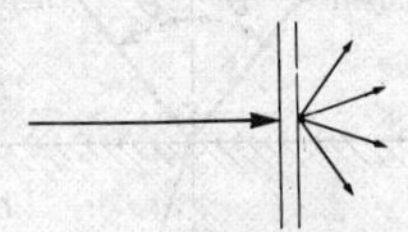

FIG. 7.—Light passing through a diffusing screen is scattered in all directions.

LIGHT AND SEEING.—In order that an object may be seen, light must be reflected from it or emitted by it and enter the eye. The pattern of light, shade and colour appearing on the retina is interpreted by the brain so that we recognise what we see. One of the principal functions of lighting is to produce a brightness and colour pattern that immediately identifies the object of regard. The colour, intensity and direction of the light all play their part in this and a 'good' lighting scheme is one that takes all the possibilities of colour, texture and modelling into account as well as avoiding direct and indirect glare.

The degree of modelling required varies considerably with the visual task; natural daylight at temperate latitudes comes predominantly from one side and where lighting is designed to provide a flattering effect or to emphasise architectural features in a building this must be taken into account. Some manufacturing processes are best carried out in a situation facing the light, and again directional lighting is needed; others may require a flat uniform light with the maximum diffusion and lack of shadows, but whatever the arrangement of the lighting, glare must always be avoided.

Colour of light.—Most tasks require a white light in which colours can be easily seen, but not all require accurate colour descrimination. All that is required in an office, factory or school-room is a comfortable light, although a textile factory, a fine arts studio or a museum will need artificial lighting which is as close to daylight as possible. Highway lighting can be very effectively achieved using the monochromatic yellow light of the low-pressure sodium lamp, and thus taking advantage of its very high efficacy. When deciding on the colour of fluorescent lamp to use, it must be borne in mind that the colour appearance of the tube may not bear much resemblance to its colour-rendering properties.

TABLE 2.—RECOMMENDED ILLUMINANCES FOR VARIOUS TASKS. Other factors, such as the accuracy required and reflectances of working surfaces, may influence the final result, and these are taken into account by the IES Code, 1977

Task group	Typical work situation	Standard service illuminance (lux)
0	Storage areas and plant rooms with no continuous work, washrooms and changing rooms.	150
1 Rough work	Rough machining and assembly.	300
2 Routine work	Offices and teaching spaces. Control rooms. Medium machining and assembly (engines). Showrooms. Inspection of rough machining.	500
3 Demanding work	Open plan, drawing and business machine offices. Inspection of medium machining.	750
4 Fine work	Colour discrimination work. Textile processing. Fine machining and assembly (electronics).	1,000
5 Very fine work	Hand engraving. Inspection of fine machinery and assembly. Very fine machining and assembly (instruments).	1,500
6 Minute work	Inspection of very fine assembly.	3,000 localised

Recommended intensities of light.—The optimum value of illumination for a given task varies with the size of the components, the length of time available to complete the task, the contrast between the work and its background and the age of the operatives. It is not always realised that speed of vision increases with illumination, as well as the ability to perceive fine detail, and that as people age, their eyesight becomes less acute, and they need more light for such tasks as reading and sewing. Table 2 shows the recommended illuminance for a variety of tasks; it is taken from the IES Code, which should be consulted for more detailed recommendations.

Glare.—Glare is caused by too high a brightness contrast between adjacent objects. In its extreme form, it makes seeing impossible, as in the case of looking directly at the sun or being caught in the full beam of a motor car headlight. Even when it is not blinding, it can much reduce the ability to see clearly. This is partly because the excess light causes the pupil of the eye to contract, reducing the amount of light on the retina and partly because the perception of lower brightness contrasts become less easy in the presence of high ones. Direct glare from bright light-sources is, of course, the commonest form, but reflected glare from light-coloured or specular surfaces must also be avoided. Glare may be experienced not only from a small source of high brightness, but from a large diffuse source of comparatively low luminance, as for example a bright sky near the horizon in winter, even when the sun is obscured by cloud.

LIGHTING DESIGN CONSIDERATIONS.

The Inverse Square Law and the Cosine Law: The average illuminance of a surface lit by a point source of light will diminish as the square of the distance from it. If light strikes a surface at an angle the illuminance is proportional to the cosine of the angle of incidence.

The inverse square law can also be used to estimate the illumination from a single lighting fitting of which the polar distribution curve is known, if reflections from walls and ceiling are ignored, and is used extensively in designing floodlighting installations.

POLAR CURVES.—A polar curve shows how the distribution of light varies with angle in a single plane. A single diagram is all that is necessary for symmetrical luminaries housing incandescent or discharge lamps, but more than one is needed for a linear lamp or luminaire.

It is important to realise that the area enclosed by the polar curve is no indication of the total light output of the lamp or luminaire. To obtain this, the intensities (in candelas) at the Russell Angles shown in Table 3 below are taken, the mean of the results found, and multiplied by 12·57. This will give the light-output of the lamp or luminaire in lumens.

TABLE 3.—RUSSELL ANGLES

10 Angles (degrees)			6 Angles (degrees)	
25·8	84·3	120·0	33·6	99·6
45·6	95·7	134·4	60·0	120·0
60·0	107·5	154·2	80·4	146·4
72·5	—	—	—	—

Light Output Ratios and Light Distribution of Fittings (Luminaires).—The ratio between the lumens emitted by the lamp and those from the luminaire is called the Light Output Ratio, (LOR). As the LOR is virtually useless unless considered with the solar distribution of the fitting, it is divided into two parts, the upward and downward LOR. For this reason it should not be used as a figure of merit when comparing luminaires. Luminaires with a high upward component are suitable for use as pendants in rooms with light-coloured ceilings but if they are used in industrial situations where the ceilings may be dirty or where there are skylights a great deal of their light will be wasted. The sideways distribution of the light must also be taken into account, and this is related to the proportions of the room they are lighting.

Utilance: Effect of Room Proportions.—A tall, narrow room more light will be required from the luminaires to provide a given illuminance than will be needed in a wider one with a lower ceiling. This is because the proportion of light falling upon the walls to that on the floor is higher in the former, and consequently more light is absorbed. If the walls are dark, or contain large areas of uncurtained windows, they may be regarded as non-reflecting surfaces. Painting the walls white, or providing light-coloured blinds over the windows, will improve the utilance of the room.

ELECTRIC LAMPS

FILAMENT LAMPS.—The basic components of any incandescent lamp are a metal filament enclosed in a glass bulb. In a few very low powered lamps the filament operates in vacuo, but for the most part the bulb contains an inert gas, the function of which is to retard the rate of evaporation of the filament by applying pressure to it. Standard lamps, with filaments operating at about 2,700°K have a rated 'life' of 1,000 hours, laid down by BS 161, which is arrived at by balancing the cost of current throughout the lamp life against the cost of lamp replacements. A 'double life' lamp with a life of 2,000 hours has been introduced, and the coiled coil version compares well with the single-coil GLS lamps. (Table 4.)

Coiling the filament reduces heat losses due to convection currents in the gas filling: double coiling can result in a larger surface area, and consequently more light than would be produced by a single coil filament. Improvements in capping cements have resulted in smaller bulbs, and this may lead to overheating where lamps are used in situations where the original size of bulb was used for a filament of lower power than it houses today.

TABLE 4.—STANDARD TUNGSTEN FILAMENT LAMPS

Watts	Average Design Lumens					Cap
	Coiled coil lamp 240 V	(Thorn) double life* 240 V	Mushroom type lamp 240 V	GLS lamps 240 V	GLS lamps 110 V	
25	—	—	—	200	205	BC (B22)
40	400	355	365	325	410	BC (B22)
60	665	595	630	575	710	BC (B22)
75	890	—	—	780	—	BC (B22)
100	1,260	1,140	1,160	1,160	1,300	BC (B22)
150	2,075	1,840	1,800	1,960	2,100	BC (B22)
200	—	—	—	2,720	2,980	ES/BC (E27 B22)
300	4,500	—	—	4,300	4,710	ES/GES (E27 E40)
500	—	—	—	7,700	8,270	GES (E40)
750	—	—	—	12,400	13,800	GES (E40)
1,000	—	—	—	17,300	19,000	GES (E40)
1,500	—	—	—	27,500	—	GES (E40)

* With coiled-coil filaments.

FACTORS AFFECTING LAMP LIFE.—Lamp life is almost always a function of filament temperature and is thus closely related to voltage. As can be seen from Fig. 8, 5% increase in the lamp voltage will result in about 20% increase in lumen output, but will approximately halve the 'life' of the lamp. Conversely, a 5% decrease will almost double the 'life' but reduce the light output by about 20%. It is important therefore to check the supply voltage in cases where lamps appear to be failing prematurely.

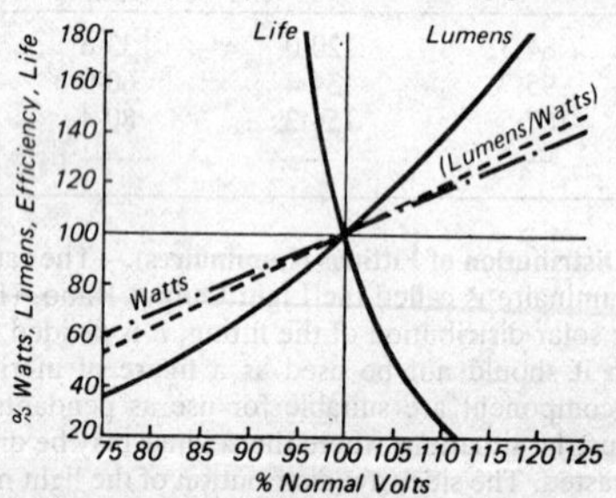

FIG. 8.—Effect of Voltage Variation on the Performance Characteristics of the Incandescent Lamp.

Thermal or mechanical shock are other likely causes of failure. Bare lamps above 60 W should not be used outdoors, or where they can be exposed to dripping water; excessive vibration from machinery or traffic should also be avoided as far as possible. Lamps are designed to be operated in the cap-up position. Any deviation will result in some loss of life depending upon lamp wattage, type of filament construction, etc. Rough service lamps, specially designed for use where there is heavy vibration, are available, they have longer filaments with more support wires than standard general service types.

REFLECTOR LAMPS.—Lamps in which the reflecting surface is laid on the inside of the bulb are available in pressed and blown-glass types. Rather more expensive than the blown glass lamps the pressed glass type (PAR38), has considerable advantages over it. Since the reflector is more accurately formed and the filament can be located more closely at the focal point, the latter can be run at a slightly lower temperature without loss of light in the beam, giving a life of 2,000 hours. In addition, the borosilicate glass of which the bulb is made is resistant to thermal shock and these lamps may be used in open housings out of doors even under really adverse weather conditions. 200 W (PAR46) and 300 W (PAR56) lamps are now available in both wide-beam and narrow-beam types.

Coloured PAR Lamps.—Special multilayer reflector coatings are now available and are used on PAR38 lamps. By varying the thickness of the layers of the material a 'dichroic' filter can be produced, which will reflect selected colours and transmit their complementaries. Four coloured 'dichroic' lamps rated at 150 W, and four ordinary lamps with coloured lacquered front glasses at 100 W, are available.

Dichroic Reflector.—Another use of dichroic filters is seen in the 150 W PAR38 in which the reflector is treated so as to reflect light but allow heat from the filament to pass through it. By this means about 80% of the heat normally reflected in the beam of light is eliminated.

Decor Lamps.—A very large number of special purpose and decorative filament lamps are available. Many of these are vacuum lamps and they are of tubular and other shapes, or have large spherical coloured glass bulbs.

TABLE 5.—LINEAR TUNGSTEN HALOGEN LAMPS

Lamp Type	K9	K1	K3	K4	K5	K8	K6
Watts	300	500	750	1,000	1,500	2,000	2,000
Caps	R7s	R7s	R7s	R7s	R7s	R7s	Fa4
Dimensions:							
Diam (max)	9·0	11·0	11·0	11·0	11·0	11·0	12·0
o/a length							
(max)	115·8	115·8	187·3	187·3	252·3	329·0	334·2
(min)	117·6	117·6	189·1	189·1	254·1	331·0	324·4
Filament							
HV	66·0	66·0	117·0	112·0	175·0	249·0	225·0
LV	62·0	57·0	—	107·0	—	—	—
Life (hrs)	2,000	2,000	2,000	2,000	2,000	2,000	2,000
Lumens:							
110 V	—	10,500	—	20,000	—	—	—
110/115 V	5,250	—	—	—	—	—	—
120/125 V	—	10,500	—	—	—	—	—
130 V	—	—	—	22,000	—	—	—
200/230 V	5,000	9,500	15,000	21,000	33,000	44,000	44,000
240/250 V	5,000	9,500	15,000	21,000	33,000	44,000	44,000
Colour Temp. °K	2,900	3,000	3,000	3,000	3,000	3,000	3,000
Filament							
HV	sc	sc	sc	sc	sc	sc	sc
LV	cc	cc	—	—	—	—	—

TUNGSTEN HALOGEN LAMPS.—These lamps use a very much smaller bulb of heat resisting glass and consequently the gas pressure can be raised very considerably without heavy blackening of the bulb. This has been done by adding a trace of a halogen, usually iodine or bromine, to the argon filling. The halogen vaporises and combines with tungsten atoms from the filament to form an unstable gaseous compound, tungsten halide, thus preventing the deposit of tungsten on the glass. The halide is carried back to the filament where it separates into its original parts to repeat the cycle. The increased gas pressure allows the filament to be run at a higher temperature without increasing the rate of evaporation, and in consequence tungsten halogen lamps give more and whiter light and can still have twice the life of most conventional lamps.

The main advantages of tungsten halogen lamps are their long life, improved light output, very compact dimensions and colour and light output maintenance throughout life. The reduction in size of the lamps has led to their use in a number of special applications such as slide and film projectors and narrow beam display lighting equipment. Their colour-rendering and maintenance qualities are especially valuable in film and TV studios. The range of lamps is very extensive: mains voltage types are shown in Table 6 and there are dozens of types of projector and studio lamps. New types are constantly being added among which is an important range of miniature display lamps in which the tungsten halogen element is mounted at the focal point of a dichroic glass parabolic reflector. These lamps give a powerful controlled beam of light with very little radiant heat, and, mounted in appropriate housings, are increasingly used for display and shop lighting. They are especially useful for lighting heat-sensitive goods, such as chocolates (Table 7). It seems likely that tungsten halogen lamps will supersede most conventional types of filament lamps in all but the domestic field in the foreseeable future.

TABLE 6.—SINGLE ENDED TUNGSTEN HALOGEN LAMPS. All types can be operated in any position, except M28 and M36 which must be Vertical, Base Down, within ±90°. Type M28 can be operated in any position if heat sinks are used! Type M35 can be operated at 13·2V (characteristics are given in Table). Types M39 and M37 have ellipsoidal mirror. Type M41 (Table 7) has a parabolic mirror. Dimensions in mm (max) for Tables 6 and 7.

Lamp Type	Voltage	Watts	Base	Maximum Overall Length	Maximum Bulb Diameter	Nominal Lumens	Rated Average Life (hrs)
M29	6	10	G4	30·0	8·5	210	100
M30	6	20	G4	30·0	8·5	420	100
M35*	12	20	G4	30·0	8·5	400	250
	(13·2)	(23)				(500)	(100)
M39	6	20	2 Tab	39·0	50·0	—	—
M32	12	50	GY6·35	44·0	12·0	850	3,000
M37	12	55	GY6·35	42·0	50·0	—	
M28	12	100	GY6·35	44·0	11·0	2,400	2,000
M67	24	100	GY6·35	44·0	11·0	1,800	2,000
M33	24	250	GY6·35	55·0	13·5	8,400	300
M36	24	250	GY6·35	58·0	15·0	5,750	2,000
M38	240/250	300	GY9·5	80·0	30·0	5,000	2,000
M40	240/250	500	GY9·5	85·0	30·0	8,500	2,000

* M35 lamp can be operated at 13·2V.

TABLE 7.—SINGLE ENDED HALOGEN DISPLAY LAMPS.

Lamp Ref	Voltage	Watts	Cap	Maximum Overall Length	Maximum Flange Diameter	Nominal Lumens or Peak Intensity (cds)
M64	12	12	GZ4	35·0	35·3	9,000
M34	6	20	G4	30·0	8·5	350
M41	6	20	2 Tab	40·0	56·0	12,500
M47	12	20	G4	30·0	8·5	350
M48	12	20	G4	36·0	48·0	7,500
M51	12	20	GZ4	35·0	35·3	1,760
M52	12	20	GZ4	35·0	35·3	5,500
M53	12	12	SBC	40·0	48·0	3,870
M54	12	12	SBC	42·0	35·3	1,760
M55	12	12	SBC	42·0	35·3	5,500
M62	12	20	GZ4	35·0	35·3	600
M63	12	20	SBC	42·0	35·3	600
M65	12	35	GZ4	35·0	35·3	9,000
M66	12	35	GZ4	35·0	35·3	3,000
M49	12	50	GX5·3	44·5	50·7	10,000
M50	12	50	GX5·3	44·5	50·7	3,700
M56	12	50	SBC	50·0	50·7	3,700
M57	12	50	SBC	50·0	50·7	10,000
M58	12	50	GX5·3	44·5	50·7	1,550
M60	12	70	GX5·3	44·5	50·7	16,000
M61	12	70	GX5·3	44·5	50·7	2,250

Rated average life 12–35W 2,000 hours
50–70W 3,000 hours

Dichroic coated mirrors reduce by 60% the heat forward. Consequently higher temperatures can be generated behind the lamp than for comparable aluminised reflectors.

All dimensions in mm.

DISCHARGE LAMPS.—Discharge lamps produce light by excitation of gas contained in a sealed arc tube. The gases commonly used are sodium vapour, mercury vapour and a combination of mercury vapour with the halides of certain rare metals.

LOW PRESSURE SODIUM LAMPS.—A sodium lamp operating at low pressure emits monochromatic light at about 580 nanometres in the characteristic sodium 'doublet'. The discharge tube is made of glass with a high resistance to the attack of sodium vapour and is enclosed in a vacuum flask. Neon is used to initiate the discharge until the sodium has vaporised completely. During the run-up period the light changes colour and increases in intensity. Each lamp must be connected to the ac mains via a leakage transformer which provides the high starting voltage necessary and thereafter acts as a choke. A power-factor capacitor is also needed.

HIGH PRESSURE SODIUM (SON).—The very high efficacy of low pressure sodium lamps loses some of its value because the monochromatic yellow light makes them unsuitable for some situations. In the SON lamp, the sodium vapour is enclosed in a smaller arc tube in which the pressure builds up to about half an atmosphere. The typical 'doublet' is broadened and flattened to include colour on either side of it. The result is a warm golden light in which colours can easily be distinguished although anything approaching colour matching is impossible. The lamps have an efficacy of over 100 lumen/watt, and are finding a great many applications, in street and industrial lighting, swimming baths, offices, shops, gymnasia and even churches. The cooling off and restriking delay in a high pressure sodium (SON) lamp is much shorter than that of the other two. The spectra of these three lamps are shown in Fig. 9, and their electrical and physical characteristics are given in Table 7.

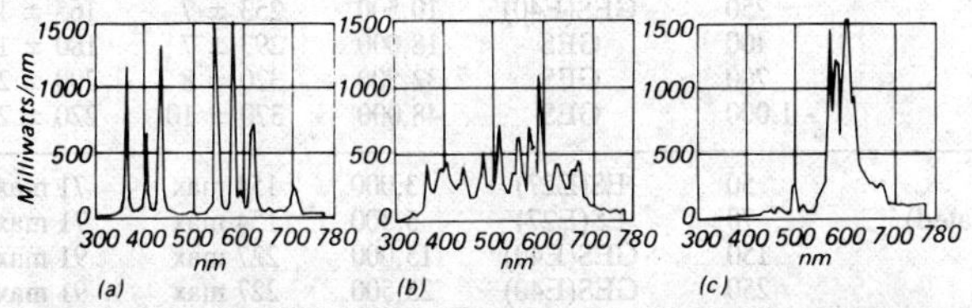

FIG. 9.—Spectra of Discharge lamps. (*a*) MBF, (*b*) MBIF, (*c*) SON. *Note.*—The vertical component refers to emitted power per unit wavelength interval. The horizontal component is the wavelength in nanometers.

A horizontal burning SON lamp in a small diameter outer tube is now available in 400 W and 250 W sizes. Designed especially for floodlighting it has the same overall length and similar caps to the standard tungsten halogen lamp and can be accommodated in floodlighting projectors designed for them. Its main application is in floodlighting but it has been used for high-bay lighting in a steel mill.

De Luxe High-pressure Sodium.—The 'De-luxe High Pressure Sodium' lamp or SONDL lamp operates at a higher arc-tube pressure than the standard lamp. Consequently it emits a whiter light (colour temperature 2300 K instead of 2100 K) with considerably better colour-rendering properties (better, in fact than those of standard 'white' fluorescent tubes). The penalty that must be paid for this is shorter life and lower efficacy than those of the standard lamps, but since the latter have the longest life and highest efficacies of any 'white' source, it is still good where the new lamps are concerned.

SONDL lamps are well suited to both industrial and commercial lighting. They are being widely used in areas where colour is important, such as sales areas and some art galleries. Most manufacturers' SONDL lamps are interchangeable with standard SON lamps.

Outer Bulb Shape.—High-pressure sodium lamps are available in two common bulb shapes; clear tubular and coated (diffuse) elliptical. The latter can be used in optical systems originally designed for MBF lamps. In the tubular type the clear outer bulb results in the arc tube becoming the light centre, permitting the design of small, highly efficient reflector systems. The correct lamp must always be used in either case to allow efficient light distribution without glare.

SON lamps with internal snap starters.—Some high-pressure sodium lamps contain a 'snap starter' similar in principle to the starter used for fluorescent tubes, but this method of starting is not recommended by all manufacturers. Three lamps of this type are marketted as direct replacements for existing MBF lamps. They may be operated from the same choke, and consume rather less power than the MBF lamps they replace.

Plug-in SON Lamps.—Philips & GEC market plug-in SON lamps which are operated on existing 250W and 400W mercury lamp circuits. The GEC also markets a range of SON reflector lamps (see Table 8).

Mercury discharge lamps need no external starting device but they must, of course, be wired in series with a choke and a power factor correcting capacitor must be included in the circuit. Like all high-pressure discharge lamps they take a little time to 'run-up' to full brightness and if switched off will not restrike immediately. The time taken to recover full brightness after restriking is considerably less than that of the initial run-up. Their sizes range from 50 to 1,000 W, the smaller lamps are especially useful in commercial installations and bulkhead fittings.

TABLE 8.—DISCHARGE LAMPS

Lamp type	Watts	Cap	Design lumens	Dimensions (mm) Length	Dimensions (mm) Diameter	Burning position
MBF	50	ES(E27)	1,800	129 ± 4	56 ± 1	U
	80	ES(E27)*	3,350	154 ± 4	71 ± 1	U
	125	ES(E27)*	5,550	175 ± 5	76 ± 1	U
	250	GES(E40)	12,000	227 ± 7	91 ± 1	U
	400	GES(E40)	21,500	286 ± 6	122 ± 2	U
	700	GES(E40)	38,000	328 ± 8	143 ± 2	U
	1,000	GES(E40)	54,000	410 ± 10	167 ± 2	U
MBIF	250	GES(E40)	16,000	227 max	91 max	BU
MBIF	400	GES(E40)	24,000	286 max	122 max	BU
MBI	400	GES(E40)	215,000	286 max	122 max	BU †
MBIF	1,000	GES(E40)	85,000	410 max	167 max	BU
MBI	1,000	GES(E40)	85,000	410 max	167 max	BU
Reflector Type MBFR	250	GES(E40)	10,500	253 ± 7	165 ± 1	BU
	400	GES	18,000	293 ± 7	180 ± 1	BU
	700	GES	32,500	320 ± 8	200 ± 2	BU
	1,000	GES	48,000	370 ± 10	220 ± 2	BU
	50	ES(E27)	3,000	154 max	71 max	U
SON (Eliptical, coated)	70	ES(E27)	5,300	154 max	71 max	U
	150	GES(E40)	15,000	227 max	91 max	U
	250	GES(E40)	25,500	227 max	91 max	U
	400	GES(E40)	45,000	286 max	122 max	U
	1,000	GES(E40)	110,000	410 max	167 max	U †
SONDL-E	150	GES	1,150	227 max	91 max	U
	250	GES	20,000	227 max	91 max	U
	400	GES	34,000	286 max	122 max	U
SON T (Tubular, clear)	250	GES(E40)	27,000	256 max	53 max	U
	400	GES(E40)	47,000	286 max	53 max	U
	1,000	GES(E40)	123,000	390 max	67 max	U
SON TD (Linear)	250	2 × RX7s	25,000	186 max	24 max	H
	400	2 × RX7s	46,000	254 max	24 max	H
SON H 'plug-in' Type	210	GES(E40)	17,250	227 max	91 max	U
	350	GES(E40)	32,600	290 max	122 max	U
SON R (Reflector lamp)	70	ES	4,000	138 max	96 max	U
SON R Reflector lamp	250	GES(E40)	18,900	260 max	167 max	U
	400	GES(E40)	33,000	260 max	167 max	U
	†310/360 at 310	GES(E40)	24,000	260 max	167 max	U
	†310/360 at 360	GES(E40)	27,000	260 max	167 max	U
Linear-Sodium SLI/H	140	Bi-pin	20,000	908·8	39·5	H
	200	Bi-pin	25,000	908·8	39·5	H
	200 (HO)	Bi-pin	27,500		39·5	
Sodium SOX	35	BC(B22)	4,350	311	53	U
	55	BC(B22)	7,500	425	53	U
	90	BC(B22)	12,500	528	67	H ± 20°
	135	BC(B22)	21,500	775	67	H ± 20°

* Also available with BC. † Ignitor required. ‡ No control gear.
† Plug in to tapped 400W mercury choke.

MBF reflector lamps are available in the higher wattages and are designed for use in unusually dirty situations, such as foundries. The full range of lamps is shown in Table 7. In column 'Burning position'. U = Universal burning, ie the lamp will burn in any position: H = Horizontal; and BU = Base upward.

MERCURY TUNGSTEN LAMPS.—Mercury lamps containing a tungsten filament wired in series with the arc tube have long been available.

METAL HALIDE—(MBI; MBI/F).—A more fundamental method of improving the colour rendering of a mercury discharge lamp is to add the halides of certain rare elements to the mercury arc. By this means a large number of spectral lines are added to those of the mercury arc so that a virtually continuous spectrum is produced. The addition of fluorescent powders on the inside of the outer glass jacket still further improves the colour of the light (Table 9).

MBIF lamps are only available in the higher wattage ratings, but their long life, excellent colour-rendering and high efficacy (in the order of 80 lm/watt), make them a likely choice in situations where there is a reasonable mounting-height. A 250 W lamp is available. They are not made in the reflector lamp shape.

TABLE 9.—CIRCUIT DATA FOR MB; MBF; MBI; AND MBI/L LAMPS ON PRECISION-WOUND BALLASTS, 240 V, 50 Hz. (Starting current for low-pressure sodium lamps is less than running current and is omitted from Table)

Lamp	Ballast G	Capacitor GC	μF	Amps (start)	Amps (run)	VA	PF	Lamp volts	Amps	% Third harmonic
MERCURY AND METAL HALIDE LAMPS										
MB, MB/F										
250 W	53193·4*	2214	13	2·5	1·41	338	0·85	130	2·13	11
400 W	53193·4*	2218	20	3.25	2·2	523	0·86	135	3·25	12
700 W	53193·4*	2235	30	6·0	3·5	840	0·87	140	5·10	11
1,000 W	2 × 53243·4*	2 × 2218	40	9·5	5·45	1,310	0·85	145	7·5	11
MBI, MBI/F										
250 W	53251T**	2386	30	1·4	1·34	291	0·90	135	0·94	1·2
400 W	53195·T**	2 × 2278	30	4·7	2·13	510	0·90†	135	3·28	1·2
400 W	53193·T**	2218	20	3·6	2·2	530	0·84	135	3·25	13
1,000 W	53247·4	4 × 2236	100	7·2	5·2	1,250	0·90	250	4·2	15
MBI/L										
750 W	53231·4	3 × 2236	75	7·0	4·9	1,180	0·83	500	1·85	14
1,200 W	2 × 53254	8 × 2236	200	9·0	7·8	1,870	0·84	350	4·0	17
1,600 W	2 × 53254	7 × 2236	175	9·5	8·7	2,080	0·87	450	3·7	14
1,800 W	2 × 53254	8 × 2236	200	9·0	8·1	1,950	0·93	450	3·7	15
SODIUM LAMPS										
SL1										
140 W	53232·4*	2218	20	—	0·8	192	0·9	175	0·93	18
200 W	53261·T*	2 × 2232	36	—	1·2	288	0·87	145	1·54	27
SOX										
90 W	53232·4*	2236	25	—	0·59	138	0·92	108	0·96	21
135 W	53260·T*	2281	13	—	0·85	204	0·94	161	0·95	17
180 W	53250·T*	2281	13	—	1·02	245	0·97	240	0·91	17
SON										
70 W	53320·T††	2383	8	0·65	0·45	107	0·81	95	0·93	—
250 W	53251·T††	2235	30	1·5	1·39	334	0·90	100	3·0	6
400 W	53239·T††	2 × 2218	40	2·8	2·2	528	0·86	105	4·4	15
SON TD										
250 W	G53251·T*	2386	30	1·8	1·44	—	0·9	100	1·44	—
400 W	G53230·T*	2 × 2331	40	3·0	2·4	—	0·85	105	2·4	—

* Control gear bears BSI Kite Mark. † Leading power factor. ** Ignitor 53283. †† Ignitor 53282.

N.B. The Ballast and Capacitor data are for Thorn Lighting Ltd products. Other manufacturers of lighting equipment use different catalogue codes.

LINEAR METAL HALIDE LAMPS.—Linear metal halide lamps are made in the UK in 750, 1,200, 1,500 and 1,600 W sizes. The first and last two types are used for floodlighting, the 1,200 W size, which has a slightly different gas filling, gives maximum radiation in the 360–450 nanometre region and is used in photo-printing. A 400 W photo-printing lamp, the MBI PAR 64, in which the arc tube is encapsulated in a pressed glass reflector, has recently been introduced.

COMPACT-SOURCE METAL HALIDE (CSI) LAMPS.—An important development is in the compact discharge lamps used for projection purposes in film and television studios and for high tower floodlighting of stadia. They are made in 400 W and 1,000 W sizes and the latter type can be encapsulated in a 205 mm dia pressed-glass reflector, giving a very powerful and concentrated beam and extending the rated life to 1,000 hours. Both sizes require an external pulse starter. A new type, the CID lamp, with similar electrical and physical characteristics to the CSI, but improved colour rendering has recently been introduced for use in colour TV studios.

CHARACTERISTICS OF DISCHARGE LAMPS

Supply Voltage Variations.—A reduction of voltage can cause instability and reduced light-output in mercury and metal halide lamps but does not much affect their life. The life of low pressure sodium lamps, however, may be shortened by a consistently low supply voltage. See Fig. 10.

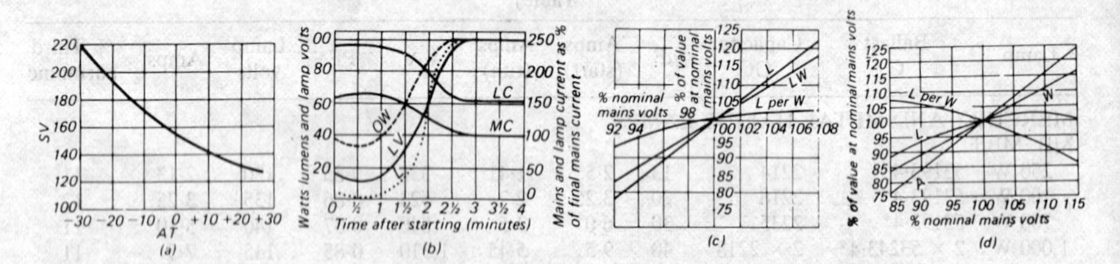

FIG. 10.—Effect of Supply Voltage Variations on Lamp Life; Current; and Light Output. Graph (*a*)—Variation of Striking Voltage (SV) and Ambient Temperature, °C (AT). Graph (*b*) Run-up Characteristics. Right-hand vertical values = % values of overall watts (OW); lamp volts (LV); lumens (L). Right-hand vertical values = mains current, with capacitor (MC); and lamp current (LC); as % of final mains current (A). Horizontal values in graph (*b*) = time after starting (minutes) (T). Graph (*c*). Effect of Variation of Mains Voltage on the Lamp. Vertical values = % of value at nominal mains volts. Horizontal values = % nominal Mains volts. As against lumens per watt (L per W); lumens (L); and lamp watts (LW). Graph (*d*). Effect of Variation of Mains Voltage on Sodium Lamp Chracteristics. Vertical values = % of value at nominal Mains volts. Horizontal values = % nominal mains volts. As against total watts (W); lumens (L); lumens per watt (L per W); and mains current (A).

Operating Position.—Mercury, or metal halide, and high pressure sodium lamps can normally be operated in any position, but most low pressure sodium lamps must be run horizontally. The 35 and 50 W ratings may be operated cap-up.

CONTROL GEAR.—Lamps which will start at mains voltage are usually operated in series with simple choke ballasts; each lamp must have its own ballast. Lamps requiring a higher starting voltage may use ignitors or step-up transformers. Because of the high frequency of the high-voltage pulses of the former, the length of cable between lamp and ignitor may be limited, and cables must be suitably insulated. A high starting voltage may be provided by the ballast itself in the form of a high-reactance step-up auto-transformer. Power-factor correcting capacitors are used in circuits incorporating chokes or leakage reactance transformers. In some of the latter types the capacitor is connected to a tapping on the ballast and serves to increase the starting voltage in which case higher voltage, close tolerance, capacitors are used. Except in such cases, bulk power-factor correction may usually be effected at the supply point.

It is important to note that if power-factor correction capacitors are wired incorrectly in series with the lamp, semi-resonant conditions may result with very heavy currents shortening the life of the lamp.

Temperature of Control Gear.—Ballast case temperatures should not exceed 15°C below their 'tw' marking. The 'tw' marking shows the maximum temperature of the winding at which the ballast will have an average life of 10 years' continuous use. The other marking Δt, is the permitted temperature-rise of the windings due to self-heating of the ballast, when it is operated under the test conditions specified in BS 4782.

The average life of control-gear, based on the endurance test specified in the relevant BS, is ten years. If gear has been in use longer than this, replacement is recommended to avoid risk of ultimate overheating. BS

4782 covers HPMV and low-pressure sodium ballasts previously covered by separate specifications. SON, and MBI(F), and MBIL discharge lamps, are not covered by BS 4782.

FLUORESCENT TUBES.—A fluorescent tube is a low-pressure mercury discharge lamp in which the inside or the arc-tube itself is coated with fluorescent powders. The reduction of vapour pressure increases the percentage emission of ultra-violet to visible radiation, so that almost all of the light comes from the fluorescent powders, giving virtually complete control of the colour of the light emitted. Different phosphors emit light of almost any desired colour, some having their maximum light output in the green-yellow region of the spectrum giving high efficacy but poor colour-rendering, others giving good colour rendering at the expense of reduced lumen output.

The standard fluorescent lamp is a 'hot cathode' discharge lamp. A cathode consisting of a hollow cylinder of tungsten wire containing electron emitting metal oxides is placed at each end of the tube and heated by passing a current through it. The heated cathodes ionise the argon in their immediate vicinity and the ionisation is then extended to the whole length of the tube, so that an arc strikes between the cathodes. The mercury then vaporises and takes over the discharge, which provides the UV radiation to energise the phosphors. The slow loss of the metal oxides from the cathodes due to electrical bombardment causes eventual failure of the lamp, but after about 6,000 hours 'life', light-output will usually have depreciated to the point where it is more economic to change the tubes than leave them in use. When the stripping of the electrodes is complete, the ends of the lamp will glow yellow, and there is likely to be considerable difficulty in starting. The damage to the electrodes occurs when the lamp is switched on, so that an increase in life can result from reducing the frequency of switching. Light output is directly related to the diameter, length and watts loading of the tube.

Voltage Variations.—Although voltage variations have little effect on tube life, they can affect light-output, tube and circuit watts. Over-voltage causes a sharp rise in tube current, leading to overheating and probable damage to control gear. Some energy management systems, (so called) apply full mains potential for starting the lamps and then underrun them. Reliable operation cannot be guaranteed in such a case and the lamp manufacturers' warranties are invalidated. Efficacy is far less, so that there is no gain, and the use of fewer fittings would be preferable. The excuse that over lighting is necessary to allow for the loss of light due to accumulation of dirt is a poor one. Cleaning the fittings regularly is cheaper.

Effect of Operating Temperature.—All discharges in mercury vapour emit the same range of wavelengths, but an increase in gas pressure results in the partial suppression of the UV content and augmentation of the visible radiation bands. Raising the ambient temperature around a fluorescent tube thus affects its light output. The consequent increase in vapour pressure reduces the UV so it will also reduce the light contributed by the fluorescent powders, and at the same time the visible mercury line-spectrum will become more powerful. The result will be a lamp of lower efficacy, giving light with ill balanced colour-rendering properties.

Standard fluorescent tubes are designed to operate at ambient temperatures of 25°C, with a lamp-wall temperature of about 40°C. This is based on their use in open industrial fittings, but today at least half the tubes are used in enclosed plastic or recessed lighting fittings in which ambient temperatures of up to 70°C are not uncommon. In such cases a bulb-wall temperature may be as high as 65°C reducing the light output by 25%. Ventilating the lighting fitting will bring the temperature down to a more acceptable level, but unless it forms part of the extract system of an air conditioned room, it is seldom practicable. The only viable solution is the use of 'Amalgam' tubes.

T8 Multi-phosphor Tubes.—A range of 26 mm diameter tubes using three or more rare earth phosphors and with Krypton filling has recently been introduced by the principal manufacturers. These lamps are made in four colours, corresponding approximately in colour appearance to Warm White, White, Cool White and Tropical daylight tubes but with rather better colour rendering properties. Thorn lighting designates these tubes 'Pluslux' and 'Polylux' according to their colour-rendering properties; Phillips name is 'Powerslimmer' TLD 84 and TLD 83. Table 10 compares the light-output of standard 'Natural and Polylux 4,000' (Powerslimmer 83).

OTHER TYPES OF TUBE.

(1) *Krypton Filled Lamps.*—If a lamp uses krypton instead of the usual argon filling it will operate at a lower wattage on a conventional circuit, eg, the 1,250 mm krypton filled white tube operates at 100 W on a conventional 125 W circuit.

(2) *The '12 M', 40 W, 1,050 mm Tube.*—A 25 mm diameter tube designed to fit within a 1,200 mm modular luminaire, operates on the same control gear as a standard 1,200 mm 40 K tube and has the same light output as that tube.

(3) *The 40 W U-Tube.*—A 25 mm diameter tube bent into a U shape. Its overall length of 532 mm allows it to fit easily into a 600 mm square modular luminaire, from which the ends of a conventional 38 mm U-tube or two 20 W straight lamps would project.

Compact Fluorescent Lamps.—Two important lighting companies have introduced specially designed fluorescent lamps intended eventually to replace the familiar tungsten filament lamp. Philips Electrical has worked on the assumption that a lamp approximately the same size and shape as the lamp it is to replace, which can be inserted in an existing BC or ES lampholder is required. Consequently their range of 'SL' lamps contain

TABLE 10.—COMPARISON OF SLIM AND STANDARD TUBES

	1,500 mm 65 W natural	1,500 mm 58 W Polylux 4,000 (Powerslimmer 83)	Advantage of slim tube
Tube diameter	38 mm	25 mm	—
Correlated colour temperature	K4,000	K4,000	Cool appearance
Ra Index	85	85	—
Initial lumens at 100 Hrs	3,700	5,400	+46%
Circuit watts at 240 V	78	72	−9%
Initial lumens/circuit watts	47	75	+60%

Note that these tubes can only be operated on switch-start on the latest electronic circuits.

the choke, as well as the starter. They allow direct replacement of the equivalent filament lamp but result in a rather heavy and clumsy design, with the added disadvantage that at the end of the lamp's life, the whole assembly must be scrapped, adding to the cost of lamp replacement.

The Thorn approach has been to design the 2D lamp which is quite different in appearance from its tungsten-filament equivalent. It is a flat lamp, made in two sizes, and is deliberately designed to meet the requirements of contemporary fittings designers who have long found the conventional filament lamp too bulky and too hot.

The choke is separate from the lamp. It is, however, very compact and can be mounted in a ceiling rose, the base of a table lamp or in a special adaptor to fit an existing socket. Once installed the choke does not have to be replaced with the lamp.

Thorn has recently introduced a single-ended 40 W fluorescent tube, especially suitable for use in 2,400 mm square modular fittings. It has a life of 10,000 hours and can only be operated on an electronic ballast.

Philips lamps come in four sizes, with approximately equivalent lumen output to standard 40 W, 60 W, 75 W and 100 W GLS lamp. The Thorn lamp is made in two sizes, with total circuit loadings of 21 W and 42 W.

Technical details are shown in Table 11. Both the Philips SL and the Thorn 2D lamps employ the new phosphors developed for the slim ranges of fluorescent tubes and have a warm colour-appearance and colour rendering. The life of both types is given as 5,000 hours.

Low-Temperature Operation.—Two major difficulties emerge when using fluorescent lamps at temperatures below 0°C. Starting becomes more difficult and light output falls very rapidly, so that at −40°C, the advantage of using a fluorescent tube is lost. The normal solution to this difficulty is to enclose the tube in a plastic sleeve which allows its ambient temperature to rise to a value in which the lamp will give full light-output and the correct colour. In very severe conditions a double plastic sleeve may be needed.

FLUORESCENT TUBE CIRCUITS.—Three basic starting circuits are commonly used; switch-start, quick-start, and semi-resonant start, but a new type of electronic starter is now available. The operation of the switch-type starter is shown in Fig. 11.

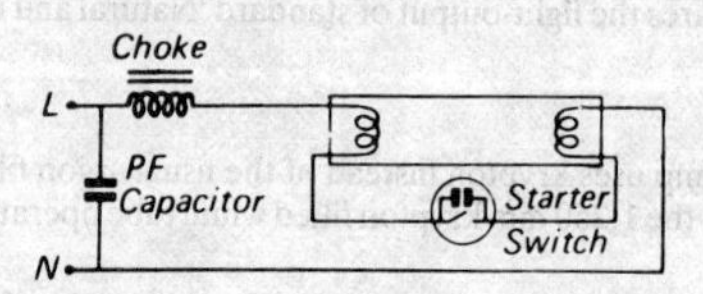

FIG. 11.—Starting Circuits for Tubular Fluorescent Lamps on a Glow-Starter switch circuit.

SWITCHED CIRCUITS: Glow Starter.—Two bimetallic electrodes are enclosed in a glass bulb containing an inert gas. When the master switch is closed full voltage is developed across them and because they are close together a glow discharge takes place between them. This warms them up and they bend towards each other until they touch, allowing current to flow through and warm the main electrodes of the lamp, so that the argon around them is ionised. The starter-switch contacts start to cool and after a few seconds spring apart. Since there is a choke in series with the lamp, the breaking of the inductive circuit causes a voltage surge across the tube, and the main arc strikes, or the process is repeated until it does so.

TABLE 11.—COMPACT FLUORESCENT LAMPS

	THORN				PHILIPS			
	2L		2D		SL9	SL13	SL18	SL25
Total circuit watts	39	21	36	38	11	13	18	25
GLS Equivalent	200 W	100 W	150 W	200 W	40 W	60 W	75 W	100 W
Lumens	3,300	1,050	1,200	3,050	450	600	900	1,200
GLS Lumens at 2,000 hours	2,900	1,260	1,960	2,270	420	710	940	1,260
Horizontal measurements	500 mm	134 mm × 134 mm	205 mm × 205 mm	205 mm × 205 mm	73 mm Dia	73 mm Dia	73 mm Dia	73 mm Dia
Vertical measurements	40 mm	27 mm	35 mm	35 mm	141 mm	161 mm	171 mm	181 mm
Weight	200 g	25 g*	130 g*	130 g	430 g	460 g	560 g	710 g
Colour-rendering index	Ra 28	Ra 82	Ra 82	Ra 82	Ra 80	Ra 80	Ra 80	Ra 80
Colour temperature	2,700 K–3,500 K and 4,100 K	2,700 K	2,700 K	2,700 K	2,900 K	2,900 K	2,900 K	2,900 K
Life (hours)	10,000	5,000	5,000	5,000	5,000	5,000	5,000	5,000
Operating position	Cap down/ Horizontal	Any	Any	Any		Any, suitably supported		

* The weight of the choke with its attachments is approximately 450g.

TABLE 12.—STANDARD FLUORESCENT TUBES, LIGHT OUTPUT DATA AND COLOURS FOR GENERALUSE

Length (mm)	2,400	2,400	2,400 Super 8	1,800 Super 6	1,800 Super 6	1,500 Super 5	1,500 Super 5	1,500†	1,200	1,050	900	900†	600	600	450	450†
Watts	125	100	85	85	75*	80*	65*	50	40	40	30	30	40	20	15	15
LIGHTING DESIGN LUMENS (2,000 hours) (THORN)																
White	8,800	8,000	6,850	6,300	5,750	5,200	4,750	3,600	2,800	2,800	1,850	2,150	1,700	1,100	750	800
Plus White	8,350	—	6,500	5,850	5,450	4,950	4,500	—	2,700	2,700	—	—	—	1,050	—	—
Warm White	8,700	—	6,750	6,100	5,650	5,100	4,600	3,550	2,700	2,700	1,850	2,150	1,700	1,100	750	800
Daylight	8,400	—	6,500	5,750	5,450	4,950	4,450	—	2,650	—	1,750	2,050	1,600	1,050	700	750
Home-lite	—	—	—	—	—	3,900	3,600	—	2,200	—	—	—	—	—	—	—
Natural	6,500	—	5,000	4,350	4,000	3,900	3,400	2,400	2,100	—	1,400	1,600	1,300	800	—	500
DL Warm White	6,200	—	4,700	—	—	—	—	—	—	—	1,250	1,450	1,200	750	500	—
'Kolor-rite'	5,700	—	4,400	3,850	3,500	—	3,000	—	1,800	—	—	1,300	1,100	750	—	—
Northlite/Colour Matching	5,300	—	4,100	3,600	3,200	3,100	2,700	—	1,700	—	—	1,250	1,050	700	450	500
De Luxe Natural	4,800	—	3,800	3,200	2,900	2,700	2,500	1,900	1,500	—	—	1,100	900	600	400	450
Artificial Daylight	3,800	—	—	2,600	2,400	2,300	2,100	—	1,200	—	—	—	—	500	—	—
LIGHTING DESIGN LUMENS (PHILIPS)																
Colour 84	9,400	—	7,200	6,300	—	4,900	—	—	3,000	—	—	2,350	—	1,200	—	—
White 35	8,000	—	6,800	6,100	—	4,700	—	—	2,800	—	—	2,200	—	1,106	—	800
Natural 25	7,000	—	5,300	4,700	—	3,600	—	—	2,300	—	—	1,700	—	850	—	700
Softone 32	5,000	—	4,000	3,400	—	2,800	—	—	1,800	—	—	1,200	—	700	—	500
Warm White 29	8,800	—	6,700	6,100	—	4,800	—	—	2,800	—	—	2,150	—	1,100	—	800
Daylight 33	8,800	—	6,500	5,800	—	4,700	—	—	2,200	—	—	2,150	—	1,100	—	800
Trucolor 37	—	—	—	—	—	2,500	—	—	1,500	—	—	—	—	600	—	—
Northlight	5,600	—	—	3,800	—	3,000	—	—	1,900	—	—	2,300	1,200	—	—	—
LIGHTING DESIGN LUMENS (GEC)																
White	8,900	8,000	6,800	6,000	5,400	5,100	4,550	—	2,800	—	—	—	1,850	1,090	—	700
Warm-white 35	9,000	—	6,750	6,050	5,400	5,100	4,600	—	2,850	—	—	—	1,800	1,120	—	700
Daylight	8,600	—	6,500	5,800	5,200	5,000	4,400	—	2,700	—	—	—	1,750	1,100	—	700
Natural	6,250	—	4,800	4,100	3,700	3,800	3,400	—	1,900	—	—	—	—	770	—	500
Colour-matching	5,800	—	—	3,900	3,500	3,400	3,000	—	1,800	—	—	—	—	—	—	—
Deluxe Natural	8,000	—	3,600	3,200	2,875	2,600	2,400	—	1,500	—	—	—	—	—	—	—
Deluxe Warm-white	—	—	—	—	—	3,730	3,500	—	2,250	—	—	—	—	890	—	—

† These tubes are 26 mm (1 in) diameter. All others are 38 mm (1·5 in) diameter. * The Super 5 tube is a dual purpose 65/80 W tube suitable for use in all 65 W or 80 W bi-pin fittings and the Super 6 tube is dual 75 W and 85 W rated. 1,500 mm (5 ft) 80 W tubes BC are still available in a limited range of standard colours. *U-Tube-(40 W)*—White, (*a*) 2,825; (*b*) 2,575. Plus White, (*a*) 2,725; (*b*) 2,500. ** This appears to be an average for the two wattage ratings.

If the starter-switch opens too soon, the lamp may start 'cold', damaging the electrodes by tearing material from them. This will seriously shorten the 'life' of the lamp. Occasionally the electrodes stick together and will not open. This can easily be diagnosed as both ends of the fluorescent tube will glow white. Note that it is important to use the correct starter. The use of one designed for a different lamp can result in false starts and consequent damage to the cathodes.

SWITCHLESS CIRCUITS

Quickstart and Semi-resonant start.—Both these circuits employ a cathode-heating transformer wired in series with the choke, and necessitate earthing of metalwork in close proximity to the tube. This provides a capacitive effect that assists in the striking of the arc. If it is not present, the ends of the lamp will glow, but the arc will not strike. Touching the tube will often make it strike and at the same time indicate that the reason for its failure to do so is a bad earth.

Semi-resonant starting circuits have a leading power-factor and are used mainly in situations such as cold stores where the low temperature makes conventional starting difficult.

Electronic starters.—This type of starter uses semi-conductors. They are principally intended for use on the slim T8 tubes, and are in effect starter switches in which the moving parts that may cause failure have been eliminated. They are of small cross-section to accord with the chokes for this type of lamp.

High-frequency Electronic Control Systems.—The efficacy of fluorescent tubes increases with the frequency of the supply, the maximum gain being at frequencies in the region of 30 kHz. This is due to reduction in electrode loss voltage and of current and consequently power for a given power rating. In addition the stroboscopic flicker associated with discharge lamps operating at mains frequency is eliminated. Since the lamp starts immediately it is switched on, life, too, is prolonged.

This can be achieved by the use of electronic control gear which, in addition to being lighter in weight than conventional gear using a wire wound choke, runs a great deal cooler, because no power is dissipated in the choke, a considerable advantage in unventilated fittings where over-heating can much reduce the light output of the tubes.

FAULT FINDING: Switch-Start Lamps.—Either the lamp or the starter are the likely cause of the fault. No attempt to start may indicate a faulty choke, but if the ends of the tube glow but the lamp does not strike, it is probably a faulty starter switch. Flashing on and off, especially if accompanied by 'shimmering' usually indicates the end of lamp life, but may be caused by a faulty starter switch or one that is loose in its holder. An infallible indication of the end of lamp life is when one cathode glows yellow instead of white.

Noise from Fluorescent Gear.—In most standard chokes the noise level is extremely low, but in some of these of smaller cross-section it can be a nuisance. Where silence is important fittings using the larger type of choke should be used. Chokes made in accordance with BS 2818:1932 have a permitted noise level of 30 dB.

RADIO INTERFERENCE.—This usually occurs towards the end of lamp life. If it happens in a new lamp it may be cured by reversing the lamp in the lamp-holder. Poor electrical contact between lamp pins and lampholders may cause interference. If it is serious a smoothing circuit may have to be used.

TABLE 13.—ELECTRICAL DATA FOR STANDARD 240V. 50 Hz FLUORESCENT TUBE CIRCUITS. Average performance tested at 25°C to BS 2818 specification. *Code for Column* 2.—Nom W = Nominal tube watts. Actual W = Actual lamp watts. Average V = Average tube volts. Average A = Average tube amps. Total W = Total circuit watts. Lag PF = Lagging power factor. Total VA = Total volt amps. Mains A = Mains current at 240 V. Start temp = Min starting temperature. %H = Third harmonics per phase.

TUBE RATING	Tube Size	8 ft	8 ft	6 ft	5 ft	5 ft	4 ft
	Diameter	1½ in	1½ in	1½ in	1½ in	1½ in	1½ in
	Nom W	125	85	85	80	65	40
	Lamp Cap	Bi-pin	BP	BP	BC or BP	BP	BP
	Actual W	123	85	84	76	64	39½
	Average V	150	184	120	100	110	102
	Average A	0·91	0·55	0·80	0·87	0·67	0·44
SINGLE TUBE SWITCH START	Total W	144*	—	95*	94*†	80*	50*
	Lag PF	0·64‡	—	0·87	0·85	0·85	0·85
	Total VA	226	—	108	110	91	60
	Mains A	0·94	—	0·45	0·46	0·38	0·25
	Start Temp	0°C	—	+5°C	0°C	0°C	0°C
	%H	15%	—	17%	17%	17%	17%

TABLE 13—(*Continued*)

SINGLE TUBE SWITCHLESS START	Total W	154*	100*	98*	99*	79*	53*
	Lag PF	0·98	0·99	0·86	0·85	0·91	0·85
	Total VA	158	100	110	116	87	62
	Mains A	0·66	0·42	0·48	0·48	0·36	0·26
	Start Temp	+6°C	+5°C	−5°C	+5°C	−5°C	+5°C
	%H	8%	7%	25%	17%	25%	17%
TUBE RATING	Tube Size	3 ft	3 ft	2 ft	2 ft	18 in	18 in
	Diameter	1½ in	1 in	1½ in	1½ in	1½ in	1 in
	Nom W	30	30	40	20	15	15
	Lamp Cap	BP	BP	BP	BP	BP	BP
	Actual W	29½	30	37	19½	15	15
	Average V	85	93	47	58	48	57
	Average A	0·39	0·36	0·88	0·37	0·36	0·24
SINGLE TUBE SWITCH START	Total W	39	39	58*	30*	25*	25*
	Lag PF	0·85	0·85	0·85	0·34**	0·30**	0·31**
	Total VA	46	46	69	90	85	81
	Mains A	0·19	0·19	0·29	0·37	0·36	0·34
	Start Temp	0°C	0°C	0°C	0°C	0°C	0°C
	%H	17%	17%	17%	17%	17%	17%
SINGLE TUBE SWITCHLESS START	Total W	42*	42*	—	—	—	—
	Lag PF	0·85	0·85	—	—	—	—
	Total VA	50	50	—	—	—	—
	Mains A	0·21	0·21	—	—	—	—
	Start Temp	+5°C	+5°C	—	—	—	—
	%H	17%	17%	—	—	—	—
SERIES PAIR SWITCH START	Total W	—	—	91*	50*	40*	40*
	Lag PF	—	—	0·85	0·85	0·85	0·85
	Total VA	—	—	110	59	47	47
	Mains A	—	—	0·40	0·25	0·20	0·20
	Start Temp	—	—	0°C	0°C	0°C	0°C
	%H	—	—	17%	17%	17%	17%
SERIES PAIR SWITCHLESS START	Total W	—	—	100*	54*	44*	44*
	Lag PF	—	—	0·85	0·85	0·85	0·85
	Total VA	—	—	118	63	52	52
	Mains A	—	—	0·49	0·26	0·22	0·22
	Start Temp	—	—	+5°C	+5°C	+5°C	+5°C
	%H	—	—	17%	17%	17%	17%

* The above circuit watts for control gear tested in accordance with BS 2818 may be reduced by up to 5% when operating in some fittings, ie the circuit watts reduce as the lamp operating temperature increases.

† Special 80 W cold store circuit operates at 0·91 amps with 0·49 leading power factor.

‡ 8 ft 125 W and 5 ft 50 W start switch circuits operate with a series type capacitor at a lagging power factor.

** Uncorrected value. Allow 0·85 if power factor capacitor is fitted.

DIMMING SYSTEMS AND EQUIPMENT.—Until recently almost all dimming systems were effected by means of variable resistors wired in series with the lighting load. This method was clumsy and awkward to control and posed a serious heat problem. The alternatives of variable transformers, saturable reactors, magnetic amplifiers, etc while allowing remote electrical control were costly and bulky. Thyratron dimmers were introduced before the war, but considerations of cost and bulk confined their use to large theatre and similar installations.

The development of solid state devices has made it possible to design very compact dimming equipment which has the added advantage of negligible power loss, and can be controlled from very small units. Power losses are very small so that efficiencies as high as 98% can be achieved, but an appropriate filter network must be incorporated to minimise radio and audio frequency interference caused by the distorted wave-form producing mains harmonics. The electronic control circuit is controlled by a low voltage signal from a variable potentiometer which can be placed in any convenient position.

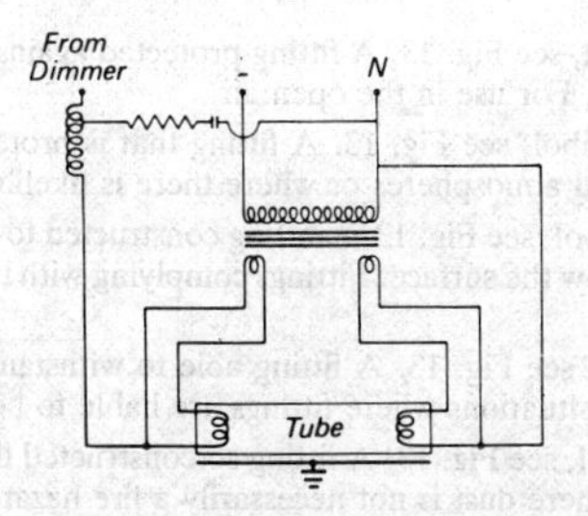

FIG. 12.—Dimmer Circuit for Fluorescent Lamp.

Dimming Fluorescent Lamps.—If a dimmer is put in series with a fluorescent lamp it must be arranged to control only the current in the main arc, the cathodes being kept hot in order to facilitate restriking at low operating voltages. This is done by means of a cathode-heating transformer with separately wound secondaries to supply the heating current to the cathodes and its primary winding connected across the mains. A tapped choke is used and a small capacitor and resistor connected between a tap on the choke winding and neutral. This circuit, which is called a 'tickler', produces a high-voltage starting pulse using the rest of the choke coil as the secondary of a step-up auto transformer (see Fig. 12).

LUMINAIRES (LIGHTING FITTINGS).—Luminaires are required to fulfil the following basic requirements:—(1) Provide support, mechanical protection and electrical connection to the lamps. (2) Control the light from lamps or tubes. (3) Maintain lamps and associated equipment at the correct temperature. (4) Be easily installed and maintained. (5) Stand up to normal atmospheric conditions, or in special cases to corrosive atmospheres or to be waterproof or proof against heavy vibrations or attack by vandals. (6) Have a pleasing appearance. (7) Have an economic selling price. (8) Be good value for money.

The electrical and mechanical characteristics of well-made lighting fittings as well as the limiting temperatures for lamps, luminaires and control-gear are laid down in BS 4533 which replaces the earlier BS 3820. This specification covers all the points listed under 1, 3, and 5 above, and lays down specific limits. Luminaires confirming to its requirements and those designed to withstand special types of atmosphere will be marked according to the code shown below.

Luminaires (Lighting Fittings) are divided, in BS 4533, into five classes according to the type of protection they afford against electric shock. (Classes 0, and 01 are not permitted by IEE Regulations).

Class 0.—Functional insulation throughout. No earthing terminal.

Class 01.—Functional insulation with earthing terminal and unearthed flexible cable and plug.

Class 1.—Functional insulation throughout with earthing terminal or earthed cable and plug.

Class 2.—Double and/or reinforced insulation throughout and no provision for earthing. This class may be of these types: (*a*) Insulation encased with reinforced insulation to protect live parts. (*b*) Metal encased with double insulation to protect live parts. (*c*) A combination of (*a*) and (*b*).

Class 3.—Extra-low-voltage Luminaires. Maximum voltage to earth: ac phase to earth, 30V. For dc, 50V.

These five classes are further divided into eight categories (classified in accordance with the 'IP' number system as in Appendix 'B' of BS 775. The relative international symbols for each number are shown in Fig. 13. The eight categories are as follows:

(1) ORDINARY IP 20.—No symbol. A fitting which complies with the general electrical and mechanical requirements of the specification but has no special provision against moisture, dust or corrosion. For use in clean indoor, normal atmospheres.

(2) DRIP PROOF IP 22.—Symbol, see Fig. 13. A fitting so constructed that when mounted in its designed position it will withstand drops of water falling in a substantially vertical direction. For use in damp rooms or under cover in the open air.

FIG. 13.—Luminaires (Lighting Fittings); 'IP' Numbers and Symbols.

(3) RAINPROOF IP 23.—Symbol, see Fig. 13. A fitting protected against drops of water falling on it from above up to 30° from the horizontal. For use in the open air.

(4) SPLASHPROOF IP 34.—Symbol, see Fig. 13. A fitting that is protected from drops of water coming from any direction. For use in humid atmospheres or where there is likelihood of water spray.

(5) WATERTIGHT IP 57.—Symbol, see Fig. 13. A fitting constructed to withstand submersion in water for 30 minutes to a depth of 150 mm below the surface. Fittings complying with this test are not necessarily suitable for continuous use under water.

(6) JET-PROOF IP 55.—Symbol, see Fig. 13. A fitting able to withstand a jet of water coming from any direction. For use in wet rooms, or situations where fittings are liable to be hosed down.

(7) DUSTPROOF IP 54.—Symbol, see Fig. 13. A fitting so constructed that dust will not penetrate it if not under pressure. For use in rooms where dust is not necessarily a fire hazard.

(8) DUST-TIGHT IP 67.—Symbol, see Fig. 13. A fitting constructed to withstand dust under pressure. For use in rooms where dust constitutes a hazard.

PROOF FITTINGS and HAZARDOUS ATMOSPHERES.—Lighting fittings made to conform to the relevant BSS are available for use in hazardous atmospheres. These atmospheres are classified as follows: (BS 4533, Part 2.1, abridged).

Zone 0.—An area in which an explosive/flammable atmosphere is *always* present. In such an area the use of any sort of electrical apparatus should be avoided. The area may be lit from outside through suitable sealed windows or pressurised lighting fittings may be used.

Zone 1.—An area where an explosive/flammable atmosphere may occur under normal working conditions. Only fittings certified by the British Approval Service for Electrical Equipment in Flammable Atmospheres, (BASEEFA), for use in Groups 1 to 3 (see BS 889), or, Groups 1 to 2c (see BS 4683) may be used.

Zone 2.—An area within which any flammable or explosive substance is so well under control that its production or release in sufficient quantity to constitute a hazard is only likely under abnormal conditions.

MATERIALS USED FOR LIGHT CONTROL IN LUMINAIRES.—The basic principles of light control and photometry have been explained above (pp. **J2**/3–5). The majority of fluorescent luminaires are provided with painted (stoved-enamel) reflectors and/or plastic diffusers, prismatic controllers or polarising plastic panels. Some designed to have low surface brightness with the maximum downward light flux, have louvered anodised aluminium reflectors of parabolic cross section.

Luminaires designed for filament lamps may be intended primarily for decoration, in which case they may be of glass or plastic or polished metal; if they are used for display lighting they usually take the form of spun or cast aluminium housings carrying polished anodised aluminium reflectors; in such cases some photometric data are usually provided.

THE LUMEN METHOD OF DESIGN.—Planning a lighting scheme consisting of a regular array of luminaires producing an average illumination at the working plane is much simplified by the use of Utilisation Tables. These are calculated from the photometric data of the lighting fitting and take into account such factors as room proportions and reflectances of walls, ceiling and floor as well as the light output ratio of the fittings. From the tables a utilisation factor (or co-efficient of utilisation) can easily be selected and this allows the total lamp lumens required to provide a given illumination to be calculated. The formula also takes into account depreciation due to the deposit of dust on lamps, fittings and reflecting surfaces:

$$F = \text{Total lamp Lumens required} = \frac{E_{av} \times A}{C \times M}$$

where, E_{av} = average illumination in lux; A = area to be lighted, in square metres; C = utilance factor (or coefficient of utilisation); M = maintenance factor (this is usually taken as 0·8, except in very dirty situations, where it may be 0·6).

The steps in the calculation are first to select the correct illuminance for the task. See Table 2. Then to select a suitable lamp and lighting fitting. The choice of lamp apart from aesthetics will be based on lamp efficacy and the light distribution wanted, the colour of light and considerations of maintenance. One would not specify filament lamps in a situation where it was difficult to reach the fittings, or where very long periods of use were involved, such as in a hospital corridor. On the other hand, fluorescent lamps cannot be used where a high concentration of light is needed over a small area, but other discharge lamps, although they give a 'livelier' light than fluorescent, cannot be dimmed.

The selection of a suitable fitting will be governed by the following considerations: (*a*) What light distribution is required. (*b*) How much direct glare is tolerable. (*c*) The lighted effect required. (*d*) The light output ratio of the fitting. (*e*) The ease of cleaning and re-lamping. (*f*) Appearance. (*g*) Suitability for the location (rain-proof or anticorrosive fittings may be required).

The mounting-height of the fittings should next be decided. This is defined as their height above the working plane. (0·85 m above floor level). Normally they are mounted as close to the ceiling as possible, but in a high narrow room they may be suspended to reduced light losses on walls. The 'Room Index' can now be calculated from the formula $(L \times W)/[\mathrm{Hm}(L + W)]$, where, L = length of room. W = width of room. H_m = mounting height of fittings above working plane.

The utilance factor will be taken from a Table provided by the manufacturer. This will take into account the reflectance of ceilings, walls and floor together with the Room Index. The total lamp lumens, F, can now be calculated from the formula.

SPACING: MOUNTING HEIGHT RATIO.—To calculate the lamps and fittings required to obtain reasonably uniform illuminance, a ratio of 1½–1 above the working plane is usually acceptable, but this may have to be reduced to 1:1 in the case of low-brightness, concentrating, recessed luminaires. From this the maximum distance of the fittings from one another can be decided, and a provisional arrangement plotted on the plan of the room. The theoretical minimum number of fittings can be found by applying the formula $(L \times W)/(\mathrm{MS}^2)$, and the number of fittings shown on the plan should not fall below this figure.

The theoretical lamp lumens required per fitting can then be found and the size and number of lamps determined from the designs lumens in Tables 5, 6, 7, 10 and 11. This will seldom work out exactly, and it is better either to choose the next size up, or, if the gap is too great, to increase the number of fittings. On no account should the number of fittings be reduced below the theoretical minimum, or an uneven light distribution will result.

LOCAL OR LOCALISED LIGHTING.—Local lighting involves raising the brightness of a small area above the surrounding level. It is used in display lighting to obtain dramatic effects, If used to light areas where severe visual tasks are carried out, such as reading or fine assembly, general lighting must also be provided to avoid eye-strain and should have an illuminance of at least as high as the square root of that of the local lighting.

Local lighting values can be calculated from the polar curves of a spotlight or reflector lamp, using the inverse square law and cosine law. In some cases manufacturers publish simplified diagrams showing the beam spread of spotlights and illuminances at stated distances from them.

Localised lighting is used in some industrial processes to raise the illuminance in a bench or special working area. Table 14 gives bench illumination from a single row of 1,500mm 65W white lamps in industrial reflectors mounted lengthways centrally over the bench. It will be appreciated that where the height above the working plane exceeds 1·5m, a general lighting scheme is preferable.

TABLE 14.—BENCH ILLUMINATION. Approximate illuminances on a bench 1,200 mm wide from a single row of 1,500 mm 65 W white fluorescent lamps in trough reflectors mounted lengthways centrally over the bench

Height above working plane mm	Spacing centres m	Illumination (lux)			Maximum distance between rows (m)
		max	min	mean	
900	1·8	819	364	606	3·5
1,200	1·8	543	364	455	4·2
1,200	2·4	485	276	378	3·9
1,500	1·8	394	333	364	4·5
1,500	2·4	333	243	303	4·2
1,500	3·0	303	184	243	3·9

An important consideration where fluorescent lighting is used in this way, is that heavy shadows may be cast by long narrow objects oriented in line with the lamps. A typical obstruction of this type might be the frame of a sewing machine. Careful placing of lamps over the bench, or arranging them diagonally over it, will overcome this.

INTEGRATED LIGHTING, HEATING and VENTILATION.—Where lighting is in use for long hours, especially in rooms of considerable size, it is common practice to install air-handling luminaires recessed in a false ceiling. These are used in conjunction with air ducts and usually form part of the air extraction system, thus serving the dual purpose of avoiding ceiling clutter and keeping the fluorescent tubes at their correct operating temperature and thus obtaining maximum light output and correct colour rendering from them.

A number of propriatory systems incorporating such fittings with standard suspended ceiling systems are available. Either square, circular or linear air diffusers may be used; in some cases they form part of the design of the lighting–air-handling system.

Indirect lighting systems.—Until comparatively recently, indirect lighting systems were confined to cornice lighting using fluorecent tubes, usually in buildings of classical design where their light was supplemented by that from decorative pendants. The introduction of high-pressure (SON) Lamps has led to a renewed interest in indirect lighting from large reflectors, usually mounted as floor standards to provide localised lighting in offices and shops, as well as in their use in standard floodlighting projectors to light the high vaults of large churches and cathedrals.

Panel lighting and luminous ceilings.—The use of overall luminous ceilings is rare today, but occasionally areas of wall and ceiling luminous panels are seen. It is important in such cases to keep the cavities as shallow as possible and to maintain them white inside. Where tubes are mounted under a skylight admitting natural daylight, the glass above them must be considered as a black area at night, so that their positions will be visible from below. The provision of a white blind below the glass can reduce this effect.

ACKNOWLEDGEMENT.—We thank Thorn Lighting Ltd for their kind assistance with the preparation of the above text.

BIBLIOGRAPHY

HENDERSON & MARSDEN. *Lamps and Lighting.* (Second edition). Edward Arnold, London.
Interior Design Handbook. (Electrical Development Council).
Technical Pocket Book. (Thorn Lighting Ltd).
Photometric Data. Vols. 1, 2 and 3 (Thorn Lighting Ltd).

CIBS Lighting Division (formerly IES) Publications
The IES Code.
The Calculation of Coefficients of Utilisation.
The British Zonal Method.
CIBS Lighting Division Technical Reports.

HMSO Publications.
The Factories Act, 1961. Sections 5, 69, 121, 128.
The Offices, Shops and Railway Premises Act, 1963. (Chap 41, Section 8).

Lighting Industry Federation
Lamp Guide LIF 3 Factfinder.

URBAN DRAINAGE

Urban Stormwater Modelling—Pollutants in Stormwater—Lloyd Davies Storm Sewer Design Method—TRRL Method—Foul Sewer Design—Sewer Materials—Structural Design of Buried Pipelines—Flow Over Side Weirs—Bibliography and References.

by R. E. Featherstone.

INTRODUCTION.—The term 'sewer' defines a pipe or conduit conveying wastewater and/or stormwater; the necessity for such artificial drainage conduits arises directly from the development of concentrated populations requiring the disposal of waterbone wastes and runoff of stormwater from the impervious surfaces.

While the earliest sewers conveyed both wastewater and stormwater, and hence are termed 'combined sewers', the need for separate storm and wastewater sewers arose initially with the development of fairly universal wastewater treatment and the present trend in the U.K. in areas of new development is towards a totally separate system. It may be argued that the combined system has some advantages in that (a), it is less expensive than the separate systems and (b), at least some of the stormwater is treated. On the other hand, the mixed stormwater and wastewater diverted past treatment works under storm conditions will be of poorer quality than that of the stormwater alone.

The philosophy of the design of stormwater sewerage systems has traditionally been to make the pipes sufficiently large that, under storm conditions of a specified frequency of occurrence, they will convey the resulting flow under open channel hydraulic conditions, to minimise the risk of surface flooding. The stormwater is thus passed directly downstream and may overload existing sewers which have to receive it or augment natural flood flows in the receiving stream. In the latter cases the downstream impact can be reduced by providing some form of temporary storage either by making the pipes larger than hydraulically necessary, or by constructing on-line, or off-line storage tanks or lakes. CIRIA[1] carried out a survey of storage ponds on urban stormwater systems in the U.K. and reported on the size and type of 235 such ponds. In the case of off-line tanks the water can be directed to treatment works before eventual disposal in a watercourse. Permanent lakes with spillway crests set at appropriate levels can be formed from the flood storage ponds; in several cases these are used for aquatic recreation, e.g. sailing, fishing, canoeing, etc., as well as forming a habitat for wildfowl.

STORMWATER MANAGEMENT MODELS.—The most dramatic hydrological effect of urbanisation caused by the replacement of natural soil cover by essentially impermeable surfaces such as roofs, roads, parking areas etc., and the improved hydraulic flow characteristics of these surfaces and the artificial drainage network, is the change in the process of the conversion of rainfall to runoff. The result is an increase in the peak rate of runoff and a decrease in the time to peak compared with the rural state.

Urban runoff models can fall into three objective categories: planning, analysis/design and operation.

Planning Models.—These give an overall assessment of the hydrological effect of a proposed urbanisation scheme, or extension thereof, without the necessity for detailed design of the stormwater drainage network. An approximation of the Rational Method may be used to estimate the peak runoff from the urban area itself from the T-year storm.

Other models, called 'prediction models' based on a statistical analysis of long-term streamflow records in partly urbanised catchments and incorporating catchment characteristics can be used to assess the effect of increased urbanisation on the T-year flood of the receiving streams.

NERC (1979)[5] presented a method for adjusting the rural mean annual flood, calculated from a regression equation expressed in terms of catchment characteristics:[3]

$$\bar{Q}_r = F \times AREA^{0{\cdot}94}\ STMFRQ^{0{\cdot}27}\ SOIL^{1{\cdot}23}\ RSMD^{1{\cdot}03}\ (1 + LAKE)^{-0{\cdot}85}\ S1085^{0{\cdot}16}$$

where F = regional multiplier
A = catchment area (km^2)
STMFRQ = stream frequency, the number of stream junctions divided by area
SOIL = soil index (0·15 for chalk, 0·5 for clay)
RSMD = one day effective rainfall of 5-year return period
LAKE = proportion of catchment draining through a lake
S1085 = main channel slope between points 0·1 and 0·85 of main channel length upstream of the design point.

TABLE 1.

Urban	Return Period, T					
	2	5	10	20	25	50
0·00	0·37	1·50	2·25	2·97	3·20	3·90
0·25	0·52	1·55	2·20	2·76	2·93	3·35
0·50	0·65	1·60	2·12	2·55	2·67	3·00
0·75	0·78	1·65	2·04	2·35	2·43	2·67

TABLE 2. REGIONAL GROWTH FACTORS $Q/\bar{Q}$ AT INTERVALS OF y

Region	y								
	0	0·5	1·0	1·5	2·0	2·5	3·0	3·5	4·0
1	0·82	0·94	1·06	1·20	1·36	1·53	1·72	1·94	2·17
2	0·84	0·94	1·05	1·18	1·33	1·51	1·72	1·95	2·23
3	0·84	0·98	1·11	1·25	1·38	1·52	1·65	1·79	1·92
4	0·80	0·93	1·07	1·23	1·40	1·58	1·79	2·01	2·25
5	0·79	0·93	1·10	1·29	1·52	1·79	2·11	2·49	2·93
6/7	0·77	0·92	1·09	1·28	1·50	1·74	2·02	2·34	2·69
8	0·78	0·92	1·07	1·23	1·40	1·58	1·76	1·95	2·16
9	0·84	0·96	1·08	1·21	1·35	1·49	1·64	1·80	1·97
10	0·85	0·96	1·07	1·19	1·31	1·45	1·58	1·73	1·88

$\bar{Q}_r$ is adjusted for the effects of urbanisation using Fig. 1. PR_r is the typical percentage rural runoff from storm rainfall and URBAN is the proportion of urbanisation in the catchment (in general URBAN = 1 is equivalent to 30% imperviousness) PR_r is estimated by:

$$PR_r = 102{\cdot}4\ \text{SOIL} + 0{\cdot}28\ (\text{CWI} - 125),$$

where CWI is the median catchment antecedent wetness index.

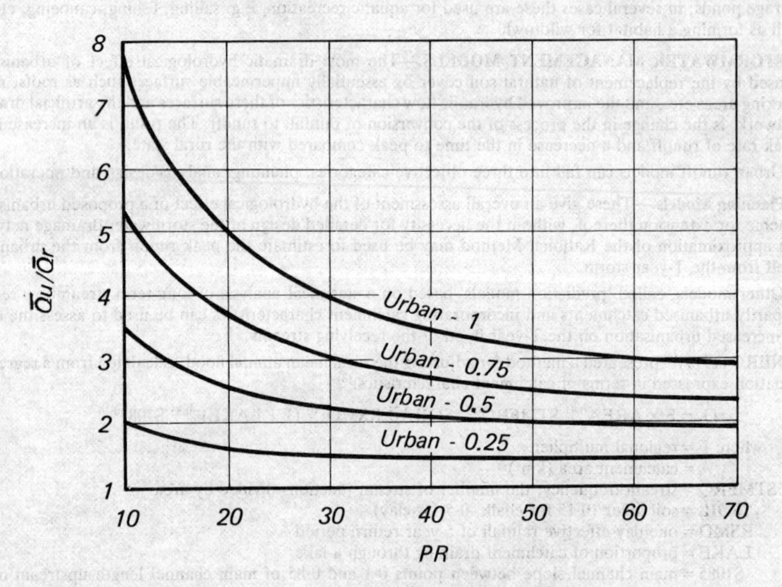

FIG. 1.—The Effect of URBAN on Growth Curve.

The T-year flood on an urban catchment is obtained from the Flood Studies Report (FSR) region rural growth curves which relate $Q/\bar{Q}$ to return periods and Gumbel y values. However the effect of urbanisation is to alter the slope of the growth curves and the approach adopted was to consider an equivalent return period so that the growth factor for the T-year flood on the urban catchment was found at an equivalent return period on the rural growth curve. The associated equivalent y value is obtained from Table 1 and used with the FSR region curves (FSR Vol 1, Fig. 2.14, p 174) or by interpolation in Table 2 to obtain $Q_T/\bar{Q}$.

Analysis/Design Models.—These models are used to simulate the outflow hydrograph resulting from a specified storm profile of an urban catchment, the details of the drainage network of which are known. Since the hydrograph of flow in each pipe in turn is generated the same models can also be used to select appropriate pipe diameters.

The urban runoff process involves several phases: depression storage, infiltration, overland flow, gutter flow and subsurface flow. Recent design and analysis models treat the surface and subsurface flow phases separately, the surface, or overland flow component, converting the rainfall profile into an inlet hydrograph to the sewer system. The overland flow models are commonly based on the continuity equation: $I - Q = dS/dt$ and a storage function of the type: $S = KQ^n$ where,

S = volume of surface storage
I = inflow rate (from nett rain)
Q = simultaneous outflow rate
K is based on slope and area while n is obtained from a typical uniform open channel flow equation. (See Ref. 6).

The solution of the equations necessitates a numerical procedure using a digital computer.

The underground flow phase involves routing the inlet hydrographs through the pipe network. Non-linear reservoir models ($S = KQ^n$), or the Muskingum-Cunge routing method have been used for this phase.[7,8]

Since this type of model simulates the hydrograph of flow along each pipe in turn, proceeding downstream along the network, they can be used both for the analysis of an existing system and design of the pipes.

Further details of the computational techniques involved will not be given in this text.

The Hydraulics Research Station in collaboration with the Institute of Hydrology have developed a computer based sewer network design package which incorporates the above principles, as well as a modified Rational procedure. Further details of the package, known as the 'Wallingford Procedure' are given on page **K4**/21.

Operational Models.—These are used for assisting control decisions during a storm event. They are basically simulation models with telemetered rain and gauged flows, as inputs, future system responses being projected; diversions into storage, etc., represent typical control options.

POLLUTANTS IN STORMWATER.—Urban stormwater discharges can have a deleterious effect on the receiving waters due to the pollutants present in the water. The pollutants originate both in atmospheric washout and from within the urban area itself, e.g. solids from building activities, wearing of road surfaces, rubber and oil deposits or roads and surface organic matter and litter. Suspended solids loads can be quite high and to avoid reduction in carrying capacity by deposition and resulting secondary biochemical problems the sewers should be self-cleansing.

Since the levels of atmospheric pollution and generation of pollutants within the area vary considerably from one area to another, it is not possible to develop a generalised water quality model to be incorporated within a hydraulic model. Observation of the relevant quality parameters, together with the associated meteorological and hydraulic parameters are needed in a particular locality in order to derive a regression type relationship. However, some idea of the range of concentrations of various pollutants is given in Table 3.

TABLE 3.—POLLUTANTS IN STORMWATER

Pollutant	Concentration Range (mg/1)
BOD	30 – 300
COD	50 –1,200
Suspended solids	20 –7,000
Total nitrogen	6 – 70
Lead	0·08– 1·9
Oils	0 – 110

See also Refs. (9), (10), (11).

HYDRAULICS OF SEWER FLOW.—Sewers are generally designed to convey the stormwater and/or wastewater under open channel flow conditions, i.e. with the pipes not running full under pressure.

TABLE 4.—VELOCITIES AND DISCHARGE RATES FOR WATER (OR SEWAGE) AT 15°C (k_s = 0·15 mm)

i. Gradient	Full-bore conditions	Pipe diameters (mm)											
		50	75	80	100	125	150	175	200	225	250	275	300
0·00400 1/ 250	Velocity m/s Discharge l/s	0·346 0·680	0·458 2.023	0·478 2.404	0·556 4.366	0·645 7.914	0·727 12.848	0·804 19.339	0·877 27·544	0·946 37·611	1.012 49·682	1.076 63.891	1·137 80·367
0·00420 1/ 238	m/s l/s	0·355 0·698	0·470 2·076	0·491 2·468	0·570 4·481	0·662 8·120	0·746 13·182	0·825 19·840	0·899 28·255	0·970 38·579	1·038 50·958	1·103 65·529	1·166 82·425
0·00440 1/ 227	m/s l/s	0·365 0·716	0·482 2·128	0·503 2·530	0·585 4·592	0·678 8·321	0·764 13·508	0·845 20·329	0·921 28·949	0·994 39·525	1·064 52·205	1·130 67·130	1·195 84·435
0·00460 1/ 217	m/s l/s	0·373 0·733	0·493 2·179	0·515 2·591	0·599 4·702	0·694 8·519	0·782 13·826	0·865 20·807	0·943 29·628	1·017 40·450	1·088 53·424	1·157 68·695	1·222 86·401
0·00480 1/ 208	m/s l/s	0·382 0·750	0·505 2·230	0·527 2·650	0·612 4·809	0·710 8·712	0·800 14·138	0·884 21·274	0·964 30·292	1·040 41·355	1·113 54·618	1·182 70·227	1·250 88·325
0·00500 1/ 200	m/s l/s	0·391 0·767	0·516 2·279	0·539 2·708	0·626 4·914	0·725 8·901	0·817 14·444	0·904 21·733	0·985 30·943	1·062 42·242	1·136 55·786	1·208 71·727	1·276 90·209
0·00550 1/ 182	m/s l/s	0·411 0·807	0·543 2·397	0·567 2·849	0·658 5·168	0·763 9·358	0·859 15·183	0·950 22·841	1·035 32·517	1·116 44·385	1·194 58·611	1·269 75·353	1·341 94·763
0·00600 1/ 167	m/s l/s	0·431 0·846	0·568 2·510	0·593 2·983	0·689 5·410	0·798 9·795	0·899 15·889	0·994 23·900	1·083 34·021	1·168 46·434	1·249 61·312	1·327 78·820	1·402 99·116
0·00650 1/ 154	m/s l/s	0·450 0·833	0·593 2·619	0·619 3·112	0·719 5·643	0·832 10·214	0·937 16·567	1·036 24·917	1·129 35·464	1·217 48·400	1·302 63·903	1·383 82·145	1·461 103·293
0·00700 1/ 143	m/s l/s	0·468 0·919	0·617 2·724	0·644 3·237	0·747 5·867	0·865 10·618	0·974 17·220	1·077 25·895	1·173 36·854	1·265 50·292	1·353 66·397	1·437 85·347	1·518 107·313
0·00750 1/ 133	m/s l/s	0·486 0·953	0·640 2·825	0·668 3·357	0·775 6·084	0·897 11·008	1·010 17·850	1·116 26·840	1·216 38·195	1·311 52·119	1·402 68·804	1·489 88·436	1·573 111·192
0·00800 1/ 125	m/s l/s	0·503 0·987	0·662 2·924	0·691 3·473	0·801 6·294	0·928 11·386	1·045 18·459	1·154 27·754	1·257 39·492	1·355 53·886	1·449 71·133	1·539 91·425	1·626 114·946

Gradient													
0·00850 1/ 118	m/s l/s	0·519 1·019	0·683 3·019	0·713 3·586	0·827 6·497	0·958 11·751	1·078 19·050	1·191 28·640	1·297 40·750	1·398 55·599	1·495 73·391	1·588 94·323	1·678 118·584
0·00900 1/ 111	m/s l/s	0·535 1·051	0·704 3·111	0·735 3·695	0·852 6·694	0·987 12·107	1·111 19·624	1·226 29·501	1·336 41·972	1·440 57·263	1·540 75·584	1·635 97·137	1·728 122·118
0·00950 1/ 105	m/s l/s	0·551 1·081	0·725 3·201	0·756 3·802	0·877 6·886	1·015 12·453	1·142 20·183	1·261 30·338	1·374 43·161	1·481 58·881	1·583 77·717	1·682 99·875	1·776 125·556
0·01000 1/ 100	m/s l/s	0·566 1·111	0·744 3·288	0·777 3·906	0·901 7·074	1·042 12·790	1·173 20·727	1·295 31·154	1·411 44·319	1·521 60·458	1·626 79·795	1·726 102·542	1·824 128·904
0·01100 1/ 91	m/s l/s	0·595 1·169	0·783 3·457	0·817 4·106	0·947 7·435	1·095 13·439	1·232 21·776	1·361 32·727	1·482 46·552	1·597 63·499	1·707 83·801	1·813 107·684	1·915 135·361
0·01200 1/ 83	m/s l/s	0·624 1·224	0·819 3·619	0·855 4·298	0·991 7·780	1·146 14·060	1·289 22·780	1·423 34·230	1·550 48·686	1·670 66·405	1·785 87·631	1·896 112·598	2·002 141·531
0·01300 1/ 77	m/s l/s	0·651 1·277	0·854 3·774	0·892 4·482	1·033 8·111	1·194 14·656	1·344 23·742	1·483 35·673	1·615 50·734	1·740 69·193	1·860 91·305	1·975 117·313	2·086 147·451
0·01400 1/ 71	m/s l/s	0·677 1·328	0·888 3·923	0·927 4·659	1·073 8·430	1·241 15·230	1·396 24·669	1·541 37·062	1·678 52·705	1·808 71·876	1·932 94·841	2·052 121·850	2·167 153·148
0·01500 1/ 67	m/s l/s	0·702 1·378	0·921 4·067	0·961 4·830	1·112 8·738	1·286 15·784	1·447 25·563	1·597 38·402	1·738 54·607	1·873 74·466	2·002 98·253	2·125 126·229	2·244 158·645
0·01600 1/ 62	m/s l/s	0·726 1·425	0·952 4·207	0·994 4·995	1·150 9·035	1·330 16·320	1·496 26·428	1·650 39·698	1·797 56·447	1·936 76·971	2·069 101·554	2·197 130·465	2·320 163·963
0·01700 1/ 59	m/s l/s	0·749 1·472	0·983 4·342	1·026 5·155	1·187 9·324	1·372 16·839	1·543 27·266	1·703 40·955	1·854 58·230	1·997 79·399	2·134 104·753	2·266 134·571	2·393 169·118
0·01800 1/ 56	m/s l/s	0·772 1·516	1·013 4·473	1·057 5·311	1·223 9·604	1·413 17·344	1·589 28·081	1·753 42·175	1·909 59·962	2·056 81·757	2·197 107·861	2·333 138·558	2·463 174·124
0·01900 1/ 53	m/s l/s	0·795 1·560	1·041 4·601	1·087 5·462	1·258 9·877	1·453 17·834	1·634 28·873	1·803 43·363	1·962 61·647	2·114 84·051	2·259 110·383	2·398 142·436	2·532 178·994
Coefficient for part full pipes		35	50	50	70	80	100	120	130	150	150	200	200

Extracted from 'Tables for the Hydraulic Design of Pipes'. Reproduced by permission Controller HMSO, courtesy Hydraulics Research Station, Wallingford, England. Crown Copyright.

TABLE 5.—RECOMMENDED ROUGHNESS VALUES k_s (mm).

Classification (assumed clean and new unless otherwise stated)	Suitable values of k_s (mm)		
	Good	Normal	Poor
Smooth materials			
Drawn non-ferrous pipes of aluminium, brass, copper, lead etc., and non metallic pipes of Alkathene, glass, perspex, etc.	—	0·003	—
Asbestos cement	0·015	0·03	—
Metal			
Spun bitumen lined	—	0·03	—
Spun concrete lined	—	0·03	—
Wrought iron	0·03	0·06	0·15
Rusty wrought iron	0·15	0·6	3·0
Uncoated steel	0·015	0·03	0·06
Coated steel	0·03	0·06	0·15
Galvanised iron, coated cast iron	0·06	0·15	0·3
Uncoated cast iron	0·15	0·3	0·6
Tate relined pipes	0·15	0·3	0·6
Old tuberculated water mains with the following degrees of attack:			
Slight	0·6	1·5	3·0
Moderate	1·5	3·0	6·0
Appreciable	6·0	15	30
Severe	15	30	60
(Good: Up to 20 years' use; Normal: 40 to 50 years' use; Poor: 80 to 100 years' use.)			
Wood			
Wood stave pipes, planed plank flumes	0·3	0·6	1.5
Concrete			
Precast concrete pipes with 'O' ring joints	0·06	0·15	0·6
Spun precast concrete pipes with 'O' ring joints	0·06	0·15	0·3
Clayware			
Glazed or unglazed pipes:			
With sleeve joints and 'O' ring seals	0·03	0·06	0·15
With spigot and socket joints and 'O' ring seals—dia. <150 mm	—	0·03	—
With spigot and socket joints and 'O' ring seals—dia. >150 mm	—	0·06	—
Pitch fibre (lower values refer to full bore flow)	0·003	0·03	—
Glass fibre	—	0·06	—
U.P.V.C.			
With chemically cemented joints	—	0·03	—
With spigot and socket joints 'O' ring seals at 6 to 9 m intervals	—	0·06	—
Slimed sewers (Pipe full roughness on sewers slimed to about half depth and running at velocities around 0·75m/s):			
Concrete	—	6·0	—
Asbestos cement	—	3·0	—
Clayware	—	3·0	—
U.P.V.C.	—	1.5	—
Sewer rising mains All materials, operating as follows:			
Normal operating velocity 1·1 m/s	—	—	3·0
Normal operating velocity 1·3 m/s	—	—	1·5
Normal operating velocity 1.5 m/s	—	—	0·6

Extracted from 'Tables for the Hydraulic Design of Pipes'. Reproduced by permission Controller HMSO, courtesy Hydraulics Research Station, Wallingford, England. Crown Copyright.

Although the flows in the sewers is generally unsteady and hence non-uniform, many analysis/design models incorporate elements of steady uniform flow either in determining times of concentration or in the storage/discharge functions. The steady uniform flow discharge in an open channel is given by:—

$$Q = A\sqrt{\frac{8g}{\lambda} . RS_0} \quad (m^3/s) \text{ (Darcy-Weisbach equation)}$$

where A = area of flow (m^2)

R = hydraulic radius (=A/p) (m)

P = wetted perimeter (m)
S_0 = slope of bed
λ is the friction factor expressed by the Colebrook-White equation:

$$\frac{1}{\sqrt{\lambda}} = -2\log\left(\frac{k}{14{\cdot}8R} + \frac{2.51\nu}{4VR\sqrt{\lambda}}\right)$$

in which K = effective roughness size (m)
ν = kinematic viscosity of water (m^2/s) ($1{\cdot}13 \times 10^{-6}$ at 15 °C)
V = mean velocity of flow.

The above equations can be combined to give:

$$Q = -A\sqrt{32gRS_0}\log\left[\frac{k}{14{\cdot}8R} + \frac{1{\cdot}255\nu}{R\sqrt{32gRS_0}}\right]$$

This is the basis of the tables and charts for the hydraulic design of pipes devised at the Hydraulics Research Station and published by HMSO.[12,13] The reproduced table (Table 4) gives full bore pipe discharges and velocities at the listed slopes for a roughness size, k_s = 0·15 mm. Table 5 shows recommended roughness sizes (k_s) for different materials of construction.

The Rational and Lloyd Davies Sewerage Design Methods.—These methods have been widely used since 1890 for the design of urban drainage systems, the Lloyd Davies method being a version of the Rational method adopted extensively in the U.K. They are not mathematical models of the urban rainfall runoff process but taking a 'time of entry' as a simplified overland flow model give the peak rate of runoff from a sewered catchment receiving rainfall at a constant intensity for a minimum duration, which depends upon the time of flow along the sewer system.

Road Note 35 recommends that the use of the rational formula be confined to the design of small areas, such as housing estates and villages, where the diameter of the largest sewer is unlikely to exceed 600 mm.[14]

The Standing Technical Committee on Sewers and Water Mains in the 1977 report[15] summarised the results of a survey on existing sewers in England and Wales and water mains from data provided by the Regional Water Authorities. 25 per cent of the length of existing sewers were between 300 mm and 1,000 mm inclusive while 70 per cent were less than 300 mm.

The Working Party on Hydraulic Design of Storm Sewers (established 1974; DOE) reported on a survey carried out during 1974 on current design practice, used by local authorities, water authorities, etc: 90 per cent used the Rational (Lloyd Davies) method and 62 per cent the TRRL method (in some cases both methods were used; hence total > 100 per cent. Most frequently used rainfall return periods were 1 year (65%), 5 year (20%) and 2 year (17%).

The concept of the Rational Method of determining surface runoff from a steady rainfall intensity is expressed by:

$$Q = KCAi \qquad (m^3/s)$$

where A = area of catchment (ha)
i = rainfall intensity (mm/hr)
C = runoff coefficient (impermeability coefficient)
$K = \frac{1}{360} = (0{\cdot}002778)$, a factor to convert the units of the product of A and i to m^3/s.

Table 4 lists values of impermeability coefficient derived from American practice.

The Lloyd Davies version of the rational method for the design of storm sewers uses the actual impermeable area (A_p) with the coefficient C = 1·0, i.e. $Q = KA_pi$. The peak rate of runoff from a catchment receiving a steady rainfall occurs when flow from all parts of the catchment appears at the outfall. Since it is known that the average rainfall intensity during a storm of specified average return period declines with storm duration, the critical storm is therefore that which has a duration equal to the time of concentration (T_c), i.e. the maximum time of overland and pipe flow along the various pipe routes to the outfall.

The intensity, duration frequency relationship was expressed by Bilham; this has been modified by later data obtained by the Meteorological Office and published in tabular form in Road Note 35 (Table 7). This shows that, for example, the average intensity of the 12 minute duration, 1 year return period storm is 35 mm/hr. The peak runoff from a sewerage network having a T_c of 12 minutes and receiving surface runoff from an impermeable area of 4·5 ha is

$$Q = \frac{1}{360}4{\cdot}5 \times 35 = 0{\cdot}437\ m^3/s.$$

The following example shows the Lloyd Davies method used in the design mode. Each pipe is treated in turn in a particular order working downstream along the system. The lengths, slopes and pipe material have been prescribed; the objective is to determine the pipe diameters for no surcharging under the 2-year storm. Although the method is applied easily using desk calculation with the aid of the hydraulic flow tables[12] and tabulated rainfall intensities[14] it is capable of being programmed on a small machine; the example shown was executed by computer.

Pipe numbering is according to the system recommended in Road Note 35, i.e. the trunk sewer pipes being numbered 1·0, 1·1, 1·2, etc., and the branch pipes 2·0, 2·1, 3·0, etc. (Fig. 2). Table 8 gives the final

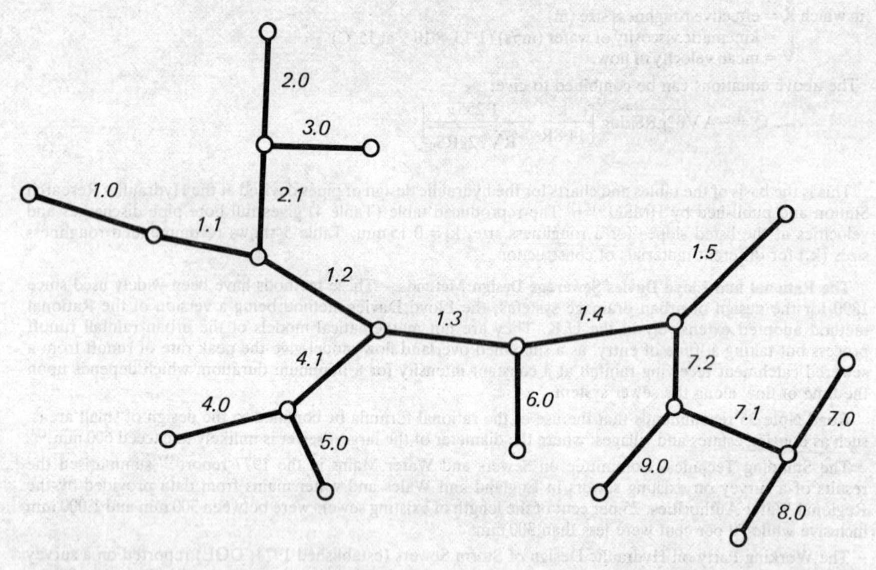

FIG. 2.—Storm Sewer Network for Rational (Lloyd Davies) Design Example (see Table 6).

design together with the times of concentration, rainfall intensities and sewer velocities at peak flow. Note that although each pipe is designed to convey the 2-year storm the duration of the storm is generally different for each pipe due to the different times of concentration.

Unproductive lengths: the effect of unproductive lengths, or carrier sewers, is to increase the time of concentration while leaving the cumulative contributing area unaltered, resulting in a reduction in rate of flow (Road Note 35). To compensate for this the time of concentration should be that which includes times of flow only for those lengths which have impermeable areas directly connected to them.

TABLE 6.—IMPERMEABILITY COEFFICIENTS

Description of Area	Impermeability Coefficient	Surface Type	Run off Coefficient
Business—Downtown	0.7 –0.95	Pavement—asphaltic and concrete	0.7 –0.95
—Neighbourhood	0.5 –0.7	—brick	0.7 –0.85
Residential—single family	0.3 –0.5	Roofs	0.75–0.95
—Multi-units detached	0.4 –0.6	Lawns—sandy soil—flat 2% or less	0.05–0.10
—Multi-units attached	0.6 –0.75	—average 2–7%	0.10–0.15
Residential (suburban)	0.25–0.4	—steep 7% or more	0.15–0.20
Apartment	0.5 –0.7	Fields—heavy soil—flat 2% or less	0.13–0.17
Industrial—Light	0.5 –0.8	—average 2–7%	0.18–0.23
—Heavy	0.6 –0.9	—steep 7% or more	0.25–0.35
Parks, cemeteries	0.1 –0.25		
Playgrounds	0.2 –0.35		

TABLE 7.—RATES OF RAINFALL IN mm/h FOR A RANGE OF DURATION AND RETURN PERIOD FOR A SPECIFIED LOCATION IN THE UNITED KINGDOM. NATIONAL GRID REFERENCE 4833E 1633N

Duration	Return Period (Years)						
	1	2	5	10	20	50	100
2·0 mins	75·6	93·4	120·5	138·3	158	187	213
2·5 mins	76·5	87·5	113·4	130·4	149	177	202
3·0 mins	66·3	82·3	107·2	123·4	141	168	192
3·5 mins	62·8	77·8	101·7	117·3	135	161	184
4·0 mins	59·6	73·8	96·8	111·8	128	154	176
4·1 mins	59·1	73·1	95·9	110·8	127	152	174
4·2 mins	58·5	72·3	95·0	109·8	126	151	173
4·3 mins	57·9	71·6	94·1	108·8	125	150	172
4·4 mins	57·4	71·0	93·2	107·9	124	149	170
4·5 mins	56·9	70·3	92·4	106·9	123	148	169
4·6 mins	56·3	69·6	91·6	106·0	122	146	168
4·7 mins	55·8	69·0	90·8	105·1	121	145	166
4·8 mins	55·3	68·3	90·0	104·2	120	144	165
4·9 mins	54·8	67·7	89·2	103·4	119	143	164
5·0 mins	54·3	67·1	88·5	102·5	118	142	163
5·1 mins	53·9	66·5	87·7	101·7	117	141	162
5·2 mins	53·4	65·9	87·0	100·9	116	140	160
5·3 mins	53·0	65·4	86·3	100·1	115	139	159
5·4 mins	52·5	64·8	85·6	99·3	115	138	158
5·5 mins	52·1	64·3	84·9	98·5	114	137	157
5·6 mins	51·7	63·7	84·2	97·8	113	136	156
5·7 mins	51·2	63·2	83·5	97·0	112	135	155
5·8 mins	50·8	62·7	82·9	96·3	111	134	154
5·9 mins	50·4	62·2	82·3	95·6	110	133	153
6·0 mins	50·0	61·7	81·6	94·9	110	132	152
6·2 mins	49·3	60·7	80·4	93·5	108	130	150
6·4 mins	48·5	59·8	79·2	92·2	107	129	148
6·6 mins	47·8	58·9	78·1	90·9	105	127	146
6·8 mins	47·1	58·0	77·0	89·6	104	125	144
7·0 mins	46·4	57·2	75·9	88·4	102	124	143
7·2 mins	45·8	56·4	74·9	87·3	101	122	141
7·4 mins	45·2	55·6	73·9	86·1	100	121	139
7·6 mins	44·5	54·8	72·9	85·0	99	119	138
7·8 mins	44·0	54·1	71·9	84·0	97	118	136
8·0 mins	43·4	53·4	71·0	82·9	96	117	135
8·2 mins	42·8	52·7	70·1	81·9	95	115	133
8·4 mins	42·3	52·0	69·3	81·0	94	114	132
8·6 mins	41·8	51·4	68·4	80·0	93	113	131
8·8 mins	41·2	50·7	67·6	79·1	92	112	129
9·0 mins	40·8	50·1	66·8	78·2	91	110	128
9·2 mins	40·3	49·5	66·0	77·3	90	109	127
9·4 mins	39·9	49·0	65·3	76·4	89	108	125
9·6 mins	39·4	48·4	64·6	75·6	88	107	124
9·8 mins	39·0	47·9	63·8	74·8	87	106	123
10·0 mins	38·6	47·4	63·1	74·0	86	105	121

Abbreviated extract from Road Note 35 'A guide for engineers to the design of storm sewer systems'. Reproduced by permission Controller HMSO, courtesy Transport and Road Research Laboratory.

Remarks on design procedure:
Pipe Number 1·0, Length: 75 m, Slope 0·0133 Impermeable area = 0·3 ha
Try diameter of 150 mm:

Full bore discharge (Q_F) = 24 l/s Full bore velocity (V_F) = 1·36 m/s
Time of flow = 0·917 min Time of concentration (T_c) = 2·917 min
Rainfall intensity for storm duration = T_c = 83·32 mm/hr
Rate of flow = 0·3 × 83·32/360 = 69·34 l/s ($> Q_F$)
Increment diameter until rate of flow $< Q_F$ Required diameter = 300mm (see table 8)

TABLE 8.—STORM DRAINAGE NETWORK DESIGN. Lloyd Davies Method. Time of entry −2·0 min. Storm Frequency 1 in 2 years. Pipe roughness size = 0·15 mm

Pipe Number	Length (m)	Gradient (1 in)	Diameter (mm)	Capacity (l/s)	Velocity (m/s)	Time Of Flow (min)	Time Of Concentration (min)	Rate of Rainfall (mm/hr)	Impermeable Area (ha)	Cumulative Impermeable Area (ha)	Rate of Flow (l/s)
1·0	75	75	300	149	2·11	0·59	2·59	86·84	0·30	0·30	72·4
1·1	50	100	300	129	1·82	0·54	3·05	81·89	0·15	0·45	102·4
2·0	100	80	225	67·9	1·71	0·98	2·98	82·56	0·20	0·20	45·9
3·0	75	120	225	55·1	1·39	0·90	2·90	83·39	0·14	0·14	32·4
2·1	75	80	300	144·6	2·04	0·61	3·59	77·31	0·15	0·49	105·2
1·2	90	120	450	340·6	2·14	0·70	4·29	71·87	0·18	1·12	223·6
4·0	100	90	225	63·8	1·60	1·04	3·04	81·98	0·25	0·25	56·9
5·0	80	100	225	60·5	1·52	0·87	2·87	83·67	0·20	0·20	46·5
4·1	75	90	375	244·0	2·21	0·56	3·60	77·18	0·25	0·70	150·0
1·3	100	120	525	510·0	2·36	0·70	4·99	67·13	0·15	1·97	367·0
6·0	75	100	225	60·5	0·52	0·82	2·82	84·28	0·20	0·20	46·8
1·4	120	150	525	455·1	2·10	0·93	5·92	61·99	0·16	2·33	401·2
7·0	60	100	225	60·5	1·52	0·66	2·66	86·11	0·25	0·25	59·8
8·0	75	100	225	60·5	1·52	0·82	2·82	84·28	0·20	0·20	46·8
7·1	100	120	375	211·0	1·91	0·87	3·69	76·41	0·15	0·60	127·1
9·0	75	90	225	63·9	1·61	0·78	2·78	84·76	0·20	0·20	47·1
7·2	60	100	375	231·8	2·10	0·48	4·17	72·66	0·13	0·93	87·7
1·5	120	150	600	645·5	2·28	0·90	6·82	58·00	0·15	3·41	549·4

Further down the system, e.g. pipe 1·2, the area contributing = total upstream area + local area connected to 1·2 = A(1·1)+A(2·1)+A(1·2) = 1·2 ha.

Time of concentration (450 mm pipe) = time of flow (1·2) + maximum time of concentration of upstream branches = 0·70 + 3·59 = 4·29 min.

The TRRL Hydrograph Method.—The Transport and Road Research Laboratory Hydrograph method was developed in the 1960's for simulation and design. It is an approximation to a simulation model: For each pipe an outflow hydrograph is generated by application of a time variant rainfall profile to the impermeable area directly connected to the pipeline by the use of a time-area diagram.

Any upstream hydrographs are displaced in time by the time of full-bore travel along the pipe and added to the locally generated hydrograph. The resulting hydrograph is routed through the pipe to allow for storage effects using a non-linear storage model. Because of the large number of calculations involved in the hydrograph generation and routing procedures a digital computer is necessary; however the programming

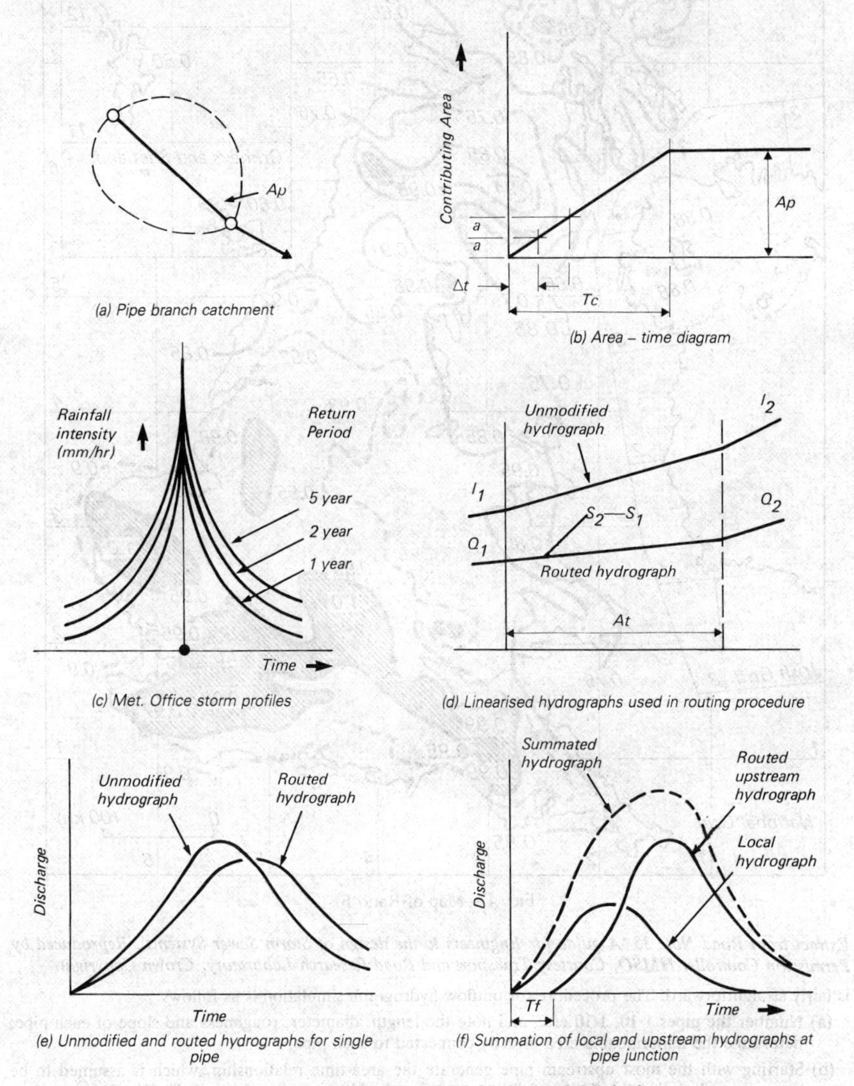

FIG. 3.—Elements of the TRRL Hydrograph Method.

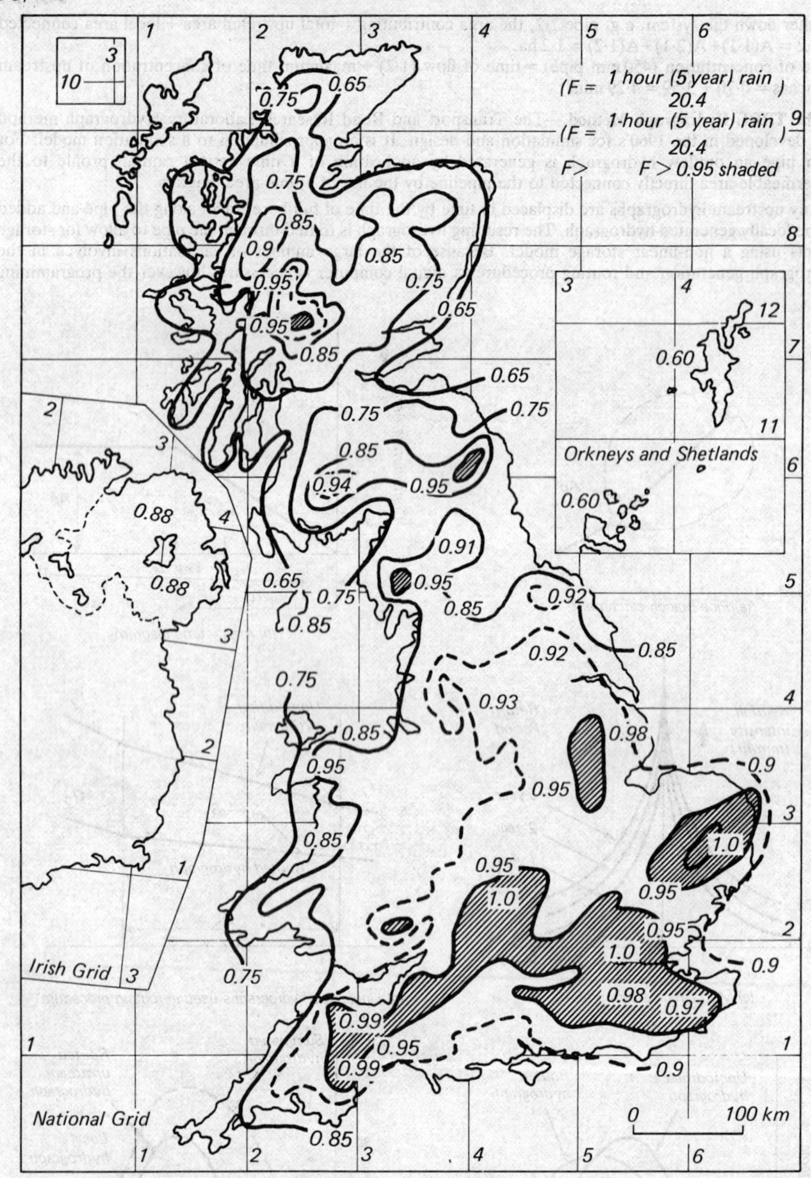

FIG. 4.—Map of Ratio F.

Extract from Road Note 35 'A guide for Engineers to the design of Storm Sewer Systems'. Reproduced by Permission Controller HMSO, Courtesy Transport and Road Research Laboratory, Crown Copyright.

is fairly straightforward. The procedure for outflow hydrograph simulation is as follows:

(a) Number the pipes 1·10, 1·10 etc., and note the length, diameter, roughness and slope of each pipe; determine the impermeable area directly connected to each pipe.

(b) Starting with the most upstream pipe generate the area-time relationship, which is assumed to be linear, by calculating the time of full-bore travel and adding a 'time of entry', Fig 3b. The area-time diagram shows the total impermeable area contributing flow at the downstream end of the pipe at any time.

Generate the unmodified hydrograph by superimposing the storm profile on the impermeable area using the rational concept. The rainfall input can be a measured hyetograph or a synthetic profile such as one of the return-period related profiles developed by the Meteorological Office, reproduced in table and shown conceptually in Fig 3c. These profiles are not suitable for the determination of flow volumes, as opposed to peak flows, nor for areas having long times of concentration, for example in excess of 1 hour. The ordinates of published profiles are multiplied by a reduction factor F depending on location; Fig. 4 shows a map giving the values of F.

Since the increments in contributing impermeable area, a, in each time interval, of say 1 minute, are equal to the ordinates of the hydrograph are:

$$I_1 = \frac{ai_1}{360}; \; I_2 = \frac{a}{360}(i_1 + i_2) \text{ and so on (Fig. 3d)}$$

(c) Route the hydrograph using the continuity relationship $I - Q = dS/dt$ where Q is the routed outflow and I the unmodified flow rate. S is the volume in storage.

The above equation is solved by assuming that the discharge rate Q is related to the storage S as though the flow in the pipe were uniform.

$$\text{Thus } S = AL \qquad \text{(i)}$$

$$\text{and } Q = -A\sqrt{32gRS_0}\log\left[\frac{k}{14{\cdot}8R} + \frac{1{\cdot}255\nu}{R\sqrt{32gRS_0}}\right] \qquad \text{(ii)}$$

Assuming a linear variation of I and Q in the 1-minute time interval, Δt, the continuity equation can be expressed as:

$$(I_2 + I_1)\frac{\Delta t}{2} - (Q_2 + Q_1)\frac{\Delta t}{2} = S_2 - S_1$$

where S_1 and S_2 are the values in storage at the beginning and end of the time interval (Fig. 3d).

$$\text{i.e. } (I_1 + I_2 - Q_1)\frac{\Delta t}{2} + S_1 = \frac{Q_2\Delta t}{2} + S_2$$

The value of the left-hand side is known (=Z) and Q_2 and S_2 can be found by generating a function $(Q\Delta t/2) + S$ vs depth over a range of depths of flow using equations (i) and (ii) and interrogating it to find the depth at which the function is equal to Z. This procedure is repeated for all time steps.

(d) In the cases of pipes with upstream pipes, e.g. 1·10 generate the unmodified local hydrograph as above. Shift the ordinates of the upstream routed hydrograph/s back in time by the time of full-bore travel along the pipe, add the local hydrograph and route the summated hydrograph as in (b). (Fig 3f).

In the design mode the procedure is identical with that described above except that the pipe diameter for each of the branches is allocated and incremented as necessary until the full-bore pipe capacity exceeds the peak of the routed hydrograph in that pipe.

THE WALLINGFORD PROCEDURE.—In 1974 the UK Department of the Environment established a Working Party on the Hydraulic Design of Storm Sewers. Its terms of reference were 'to examine all aspects of the hydraulic design of systems for the conveyance of storm water from developed areas; to assess and coordinate research projects in progress; to promote any necessary new research both in the laboratory and in the field; and to publish guidance and produce a manual of good practice for the design of such systems'. The end result of research at the Hydraulics Research Station, the Institute of Hydrology and the Meteorological Office has been the production of a manual describing a new approach to storm drainage design and associated design and analysis methods and an accompanying package of computer programs for user application (Ref. 29).

In previous design procedures, as earlier described, the smallest commercially available sewer size is selected which will convey the design discharge without surcharging. Higher discharges resulting from more intense, and less frequent, storms may cause parts of the sewerage system to surcharge but without causing surface flooding. Such design practice therefore inherently includes an unknown factor of safety against surface flooding. The new design philosophy is based on an assessment of the performance of a system designed on traditional procedure and where possible a minimisation of the construction, maintenance and flood damage costs. These methods were made possible by extensive analysis of UK storm drainage data and new computing techniques. The options available within the computer packages, which are available to designers, are—

(i) Wallingford Modified Rational method (WASSP–RAT) — to size pipes and/or calculate discharges using the Rational (Lloyd Davies) method modified by the percentage runoff from the contributing area and by a routing coefficient. The system may include storm overflow and bifurcations.

(ii) Wallingford Hydrograph method (WASSP–HYD)—to size pipes and/or simulate discharge hydrographs for observed or design rainfall events in a prescribed network layout which may include storm overflows, bifurcations, on- or off-line tanks and pumping stations.

(iii) Wallingford Optimising method (WASSP–OPT) — to design pipe diameters, depths and gradients for a minimum construction cost using the Modified Rational formula in a prescribed sewerage network layout not including overflows, bifurcations, storage tanks or pumping stations.

(iv) Wallingford Simulation method (WASSP–SIM) — to simulate time dependent flow with or without surface flooding and/or surcharging for observed or design rainfall events in an existing or designed sewer network which may include storm overflows, bifurcations, inverted siphons, on- or off-line tanks, pumping stations and outfall flaps.

Design rainfall intensity–duration curves relating to the catchment location and storm return period and duration are obtained from formulae developed by the Meteorological Office. A rainfall hyetograph is generated using the 50 per cent summer profile (Ref. 3).

The overland flow component providing the surface hydrograph as input to the sewer system is calculated using the non-linear reservoir model as developed by the Institute of Hydrology. For free sewer flow routing the fixed parameter Muskingum–Cunge model is used. Where surcharging in a group of sewers is identified a set of implicit finite difference equations is solved.

SOIL SEWERAGE.—Separate sanitary (or soil) sewers are provided primarily to convey the wastewater of a community to a point of treatment or ultimate disposal. It is essential that the sewer has adequate capacity for the peak flow and that it should be capable of transporting solids so that there is no accumulation of deposited sediment, in other words the sewer should be 'self-cleansing'. Due to variations in flowrate during the day the depth and velocity will also vary. Since the peak flow of sewage may be at least twice the average (or 2 d.w.f.) this discharge can be used as the criterion for the self-cleansing velocity; a value of 2·0 ft/s (0·61 m/s) is commonly adopted. According to Escritt[16] the practice of present day engineers is to lay sewers to gradients sufficient to ensure velocities of 0·7 m/s when they are flowing full or half-full so that when the sewer is flowing between one quarter and one fifth of its total capacity the velocity is =0·61 m/s. However, the flow in soil sewers supplied by a small number of houses may be less that this ratio and the design for self-cleansing should be based on the actual 2 d.w.f.

The quantity of sewage discharged from a built up area is approximately the water supply to the area together with an infiltration into the sewer from the surrounding ground. From investigations of infiltration by the Water Research Centre[18] it was suggested that most sewer systems have as much as 30% of the flow composed of infiltration and some as much as 50%. The infiltration flow is at present not accurately predictable since it depends on the ground conditions, the standard of construction and will vary with the age of the system. For the design of new soil sewerage systems it is sufficient to design for the water demand and make the sewers sufficiently large to convey four or six times the d.w.f.

Design Procedure.—Uniform flow is assumed at the design flows; the hydraulic flow tables[12] can be used to determine the full-bore discharges and velocities. For computer aided design the Darcy-Colebrook-White equation:

$$Q = -A\sqrt{32gRS_0}\log\left[\frac{k}{14 \cdot 8R} + \frac{1 \cdot 255\nu}{R\sqrt{32gRS_0}}\right]$$

where R = hydraulic radius (A/P)
A = area of flow
P = wetted perimeter
V = Q/A (mean velocity)
S_0 = pipe gradient.

may be incorporated. Fig. 5 shows the variation in proportional discharge and velocity with proportional flow depth in circular sewers. Note that it is not possible to generate a single curve of y/D v V/V_F and Q/Q_T for all pipe sizes, roughness sizes and slopes due to the component,

$$\log\left[\frac{k}{14 \cdot 8R} + \frac{1.255\nu}{R\sqrt{32gRS_0}}\right]$$

Each curve is identified therefore by the parameter

$$\theta = \left[\frac{k}{D} + \frac{1}{3600DS^{1/3}}\right]^{-1}$$

(S.I. units) for water at 15°C.

The tables (Table 4) give relevant values of θ for the pipe, roughness, slope and diameter in question.

The slope has the greatest influence on velocity at any proportional depth; if the combination of pipe slope and diameter is insufficient to give the 'self-cleansing' velocity the slope should be increased, not the diameter.

Effective Roughness Size of Slimed Sewers.—Although the Working Party on Sewers and Water Mains in their first report (1975) recommended a roughness size of 0·6 mm for slimed sewers with good joint alignment, the latest edition of 'tables for the hydraulic design of pipes and channels' recommend a figure of 6·0 mm for concrete pipes and 3·0 mm for clay pipes.

Flow Rates.—The flow of wastewater into the sewerage system is calculated from the product of the number of houses, the number of persons per house and the per capita dry weather flow. The per capita flows and the number of persons per house will vary with the area but typical figures are 3·5 persons/house and 200 litres (45 gall/head/day).

The discharge in sewers receiving wastewater from a small number of houses is very low and unless the pipe is very steep it is difficult to achieve self-cleansing velocities. In such cases periodic flushing from siphonic tanks receiving mains water or the connection of a proportion of surface water, e.g. from house roofs only (partially separate system) may be adopted. Some Water Authorities accept that the discharge of individual appliances can give a flushing discharge of about 3ft^3/s (1·4 l/s); such flowrates have been verified by tests by the Building Research Establishment[19].

Example: Design a sewer length receiving wastewater from 180 houses with an average of 3·5 persons per house. 1 d.w.f. = 200 l/h/day.

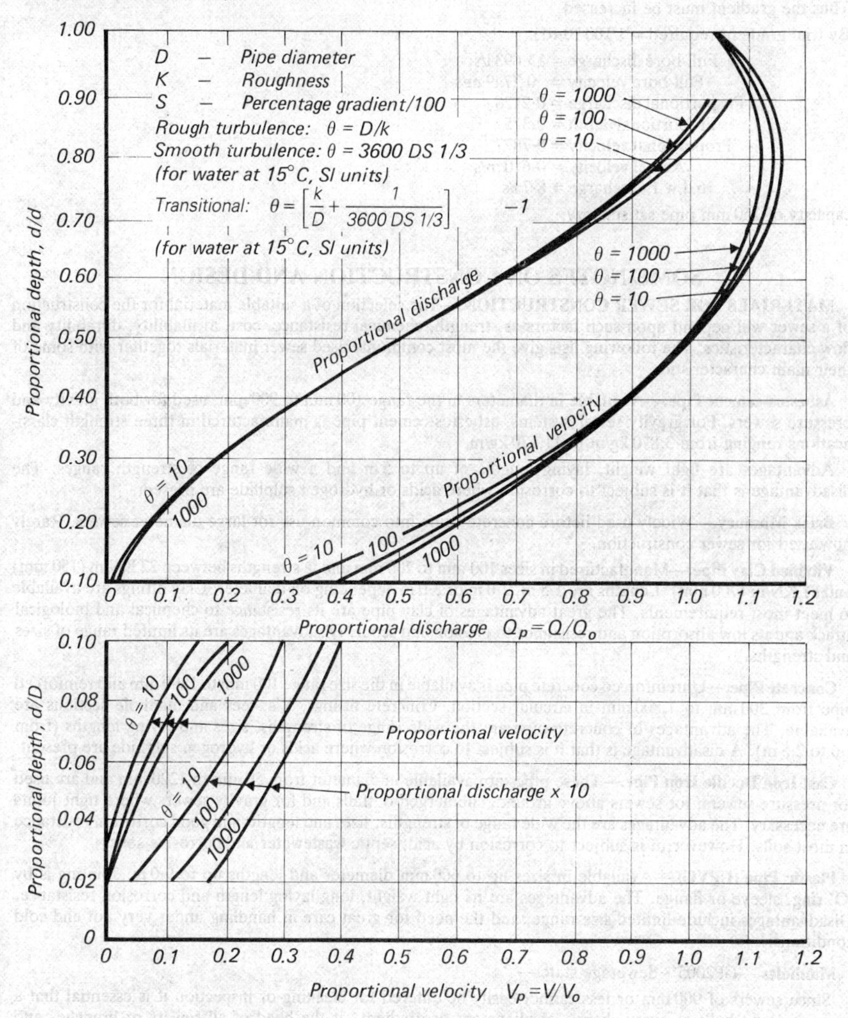

FIG. 5.—Proportional Velocity and Discharge in Part-full Circular Sections.

Extract from Road Note 35 'A Guide for Engineers to the Design of Storm Sewer Systems.' Reproduced by Permission Controller HMSO, Courtesy Transport and Road Research Laboratory, Crown Copyright.

Try pipe diameter 150 mm, k = 3·0 mm, Slope = 1/120

$$(2\text{ d.w.f.})\text{ discharge} = \frac{180 \times 3{\cdot}5 \times 200 \times 2}{24 \times 3600} = 2{\cdot}90\text{ l/s}$$

$$S_0 = \frac{1}{120} = 0{\cdot}00833$$

Full-bore discharge = 12·49 l/s
Full-bore velocity = 0·7071 m/s
Proportional discharge = 0·2327
Proportional depth = 0·33
Proportional velocity = 0·8088
Actual velocity = 0·572 m/s

Thus the gradient must be increased.

By trial gradient required = 1/100 (0·01)

Full-bore discharge = 13·693 l/s
Full-bore velocity = 0·7749 m/s
Proportional discharge = 0·2126
Proportional depth = 0·315
Proportional velocity = 0·7877
Actual velocity = 0·610 m/s
6 d.w.f. discharge = 8·7 l/s

capacity of 150 mm pipe satisfactory.

SOME NOTES ON CONSTRUCTION AND DESIGN

MATERIALS FOR SEWER CONSTRUCTION.—The selection of a suitable material for the construction of a sewer will depend upon such factors as strength, chemical resistance, cost, availability, durability and flow characteristics. The following lists give the most commonly used sewer materials together with some of their main characteristics.

Asbestos-cement Pipe.—Available in diameters in the range 100 mm to 900 mm, used for both gravity and pressure sewers. For gravity sewer systems, asbestos-cement pipe is manufactured in three strength classifications ranging from 3,870 kg/m to 11,170 kg/m.

Advantages are light weight, laying lengths of up to 5 m and a wide range of strength ranges. The disadvantage is that it is subject to corrosion where acids or hydrogen sulphide are present.

Brick Masonry.—Widely used before concrete came into common use for large diameter sewers. Rarely now used for sewer construction.

Vitrified Clay Pipe.—Manufactured in sizes 100 mm to 700 mm and in strengths between 22 KN/m (150 mm) and 81 KN/m (700 mm). Lengths are 1·5 m, 2·0 m or 3·0 m depending on diameter. Clay fittings are available to meet most requirements. The great advantages of clay pipe are its resistance to chemical and biological attack and its low absorption and resistance to erosion and scour. Disadvantages are its limited range of sizes and strengths.

Concrete Pipe.—Unreinforced concrete pipe is available in the size range 100 mm to 1800 mm and reinforced pipe from 300 mm to 1,800 mm in circular section. Concrete fittings, Y's, tees and manhole sections are available. The advantages of concrete pipe are the wide range of strengths, sizes and laying lengths (from 1·0 to 2·5 m). A disadvantage is that it is subject to corrosion where acids or hydrogen sulphide are present.

Cast Iron/Ductile Iron Pipe.—These pipes are available in diameter from 50 mm to 1220 mm and are used for pressure sewers, for sewers above ground, submerged outfalls and for gravity sewers where tight joints are necessary. The advantages are the wide range of strengths, sizes and lengths and good corrosion resistance in most soils. However, it is subject to corrosion by acid, septic wastewater and corrosive soils.

Plastic Pipe (UPVC).—Available in sizes up to 600 mm diameter and lengths up to 9·0 m. Jointing is by 'O' ring, sleeve or flange. The advantages are its light weight, long laying length and corrosion resistance. Disadvantages include limited size range, and the need for great care in handling under very hot and cold conditions.

Manholes.—CP2005 – Sewerage states—

'Since sewers of 900 mm or less cannot easily be entered for cleaning or inspection it is essential that a manhole be built at every change of alignment or gradient, at the head of all sewers or branches and wherever there is a change in size of sewer. Manholes should not be further apart than it is practicable to operate drain rods or some form of pipe scraper, i.e. about 90 to 100 m.'

On sewers which a man can enter for inspection it is not essential to have a manhole at every change of alignment. A spacing of 180 m to 240 m on straight runs is suitable.

To avoid the backwater from downstream pipes causing surcharging upstream the crowns of pipes at intersections or changes of diameter are kept level with one another rather than the inverts; the change of diameter causes a step or slope-down in the invert at the point of connection.

Maximum Permitted Velocity.—Research sponsored by CIRIA and carried out at Imperial College[21] showed that up to 7·6 m/s in straight pipelines the amount of erosion was related to the total amount of abrasive material transported rather than the velocity of flow. At bends and other changes of direction the erosion was markedly affected by velocity. (See CP2005)

BRITISH STANDARDS ON PIPELINES

Product	**Standards and Codes**
Asbestos-Cement pressure pipes	BS 486, 3656
Pitch fibre drain pipes	BS 2760
Concrete pipes	BS 556, 1194, 4101, 4625, 5178
Clay pipes	BS 65, 540, 539, 1143
C.I. pipes	BS 78, 1211, 4622, 2035, 4772
Steel pipes and iron pipes	BS 1965
Plastics pipes	CP 312
Pipelines	CP 2010
Sewerage	CP 2005

STRUCTURAL DESIGN OF PIPELINES.—Loads on buried pipelines result from the weight of earth in the trench backfill (or fill for embankment conditions) and any superimposed loads. The structural design of a sewer requires that the strength of the pipe must withstand these loads with an appropriate safety factor: the supporting capacity of a buried pipeline is a function of both the strength of the pipe itself and the type of pipe bedding.

The classical theory of gravity earth loads on pipes was developed by Marston (see reference No. 22) and this theory has achieved acceptance in the U.S.A. and the U.K. Marston's formula for the earth load on a rigid pipeline is:

$$W_f = C\rho B^2 \quad (\text{kg/m})$$

$$\text{or } W_f = C\rho g B^2 \quad (\text{N/m})$$

where W_f is load/unit length, ρ is the density of the fill (kg/m^3), g is the gravitational acceleration, C is a dimensionless load coefficient which is a function of the ratio of height of fill to width of trench and the friction coefficient between the backfill and the sides of the trench. B_d is the width between the friction planes.

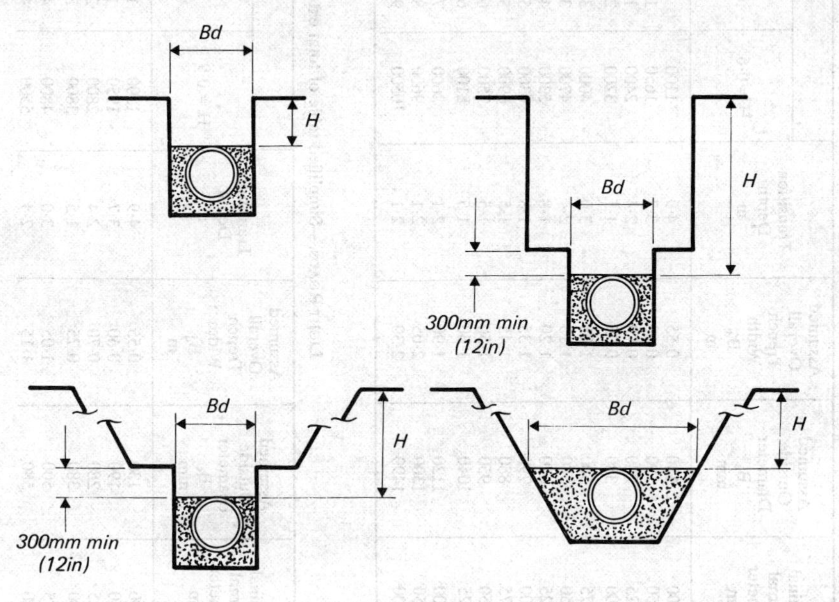

FIG. 6.—Trench Widths.

FIELDS ETC.—Simplified table of total external design loads on pipes under fields, gardens and access tracks

Nominal Internal Diameter mm	Assumed Outside Diameter B_c mm	Assumed Overall Trench Width B_d m	Transition Depth m	Total design load W_e in kg/m of pipe length for cover depth H m									
				H = 0·6	0·9	1·2	1·5	1·8	2·4	3·0	4·6	6·1	7·6
100	130	0·55	4·9	1100	910	850	850	940	1100	1300	1850	2100	2100
150	190	0·60	3·7	1650	1350	1300	1300	1400	1650	1950	2500	2600	2700
225	280	0·70	2·4	2400	1950	1850	1900	2000	2400	2600	3000	3300	3400
300	380	0·75	1·5	3200	2700	2500	2600	2600	2900	3100	3600	4000	4100
375	500	1·05	3·0	4000	3300	3200	3200	3400	4000	4800	6000	6800	7400
450	580	1·15	2·4	4700	3800	3800	3800	4000	4700	5400	6600	7600	8300
525	670	1·20	1·8	5300	4300	4200	4300	4600	5200	5900	7300	8400	9200
600	790	1·35	1·8	6300	5200	5000	5300	5600	6300	7000	8800	10500	11500
675	880	1·45	1·5	6900	5700	5500	5800	6100	6800	7600	9500	11000	12500
750	950	1·50	1·5	7500	6200	5900	6200	6500	7300	8100	10500	12000	13500
825	1040	1·60	1·5	8100	6800	6400	6700	7000	7800	8700	11000	13000	14500
900	1120	1·90	2·1	8600	7200	6900	7100	7800	9400	10500	13500	16500	18500
1050	1300	2·05	2·1	9600	8300	7900	8100	8800	10500	12000	15500	18000	21000
1200	1490	2·30	2·1	10500	9400	9000	9200	9900	12000	13500	17500	21000	24000

LIGHT ROADS.—Simplified table of total external design loads under roads carrying light traffic only

Nominal Internal Diameter mm	Assumed Outside Diameter B_c mm	Assumed Overall Trench Width B_d m	Transition Depth m	Total design load W_e in kg/m of pipe length for cover depth H m								
				H = 0·9	1·2	1·5	1·8	2·4	3·0	4·6	6·2	7·6
100	130	0·55	4·9	1300	1100	1050	1050	1150	1350	1900	2100	2100
150	190	0·60	3·7	1950	1650	1550	1600	1750	2100	2600	2700	2700
225	280	0·70	2·4	2800	2400	2300	2300	2600	2800	3100	3300	3400
300	380	0·75	1·5	3800	3300	3100	3000	3100	3300	3700	4000	4200
375	500	1·05	3·0	4800	4100	3900	3900	4400	5000	6100	6900	7500
450	580	1·15	2·4	5500	4800	4600	4600	5100	5600	6800	7700	8400

525	670	1·20	1·8	6300	5600	5300	5300	5700	6100	7400	8500	9300
600	790	1·35	1·8	7400	6500	6400	6400	6800	7400	9000	10500	11500
675	880	1·45	1·5	8200	7200	7000	7000	7300	8000	9700	11000	12500
750	950	1·50	1·5	8900	7700	7500	7500	7800	8500	10500	12000	13500
825	1040	1·60	1·5	9700	8400	8100	8100	8400	9200	11000	13000	14500
900	1120	1·90	2·1	10500	9000	8600	8900	10000	11000	14000	16500	18500
1050	1300	2·05	2·1	12000	10500	9900	10000	11000	12500	15500	18500	21000
1200	1490	2·30	2·1	13500	11500	11000	11500	13000	14000	18000	21000	24000

MAIN ROADS.—Simplified table of total external design loads on pipes under main traffic routes and under roads that are liable to be used for temporary diversion of heavy traffic

Nominal Internal Diameter mm	Assumed Outside Diameter B_c mm	Assumed Overall Trench Width B_d m	Transition Depth m	Total design load W_e in kg/m of pipe length for cover depth H m								
				H = 0·9	1·2	1·5	1·8	2·4	3·0	4·6	6·1	7·6
100	130	0·55	4·9	1500	1350	1300	1350	1450	1600	2100	2200	2200
150	190	0·60	3·7	2300	2000	2000	2000	2200	2400	2800	2900	2900
225	280	0·70	2·4	3300	3000	2900	2900	3200	3300	3400	3500	3600
300	380	0·75	1·5	4500	4100	4000	3900	3900	4000	4200	4300	4400
375	500	1·05	3·0	5700	5100	5000	5000	5400	5900	6700	7300	7700
450	580	1·15	2·4	6600	6000	5800	5900	6300	6700	7400	8100	8700
525	670	1·20	1·8	7500	6900	6700	6800	7000	7300	8200	9000	9600
600	790	1·35	1·8	8800	8100	8000	8200	8400	8800	9900	11000	12000
675	880	1·45	1·5	9800	8900	8900	8900	9100	9500	10500	12000	13000
750	950	1·50	1·5	10500	9600	9500	9600	9800	10000	11500	13000	14000
825	1040	1·60	1·5	11500	10500	10500	10500	10500	11000	12500	14000	15000
900	1120	1·90	2·1	12500	11500	11000	11500	12500	13000	15000	17500	19000
1050	1300	2·05	2·1	14000	13000	13000	13000	14000	14500	17000	19500	22000
1220	1490	2·30	2·1	16000	15000	14500	15000	16000	17000	19500	22000	25000

TABLE 9.—LOADS ON BURIED PIPELINES DUE TO BACKFILL AND SURFACE LOADS.

Extracted from 'Simplified Tables of External Loads on Buried Pipelines'. Reproduced by Permission Controller HMSO, courtesy Building Research Establishment, Watford.

Two basic trench conditions, the narrow trench case and the wide trench case, are identified. As the trench width for a pipe of given outside diameter B_c with a given cover depth increases, the backfill load also increased but only up to a certain trench width called the 'transition width'.

At a depth less that the 'transition depth' the pipe is in the 'wide trench' condition and for greater depths the pipe is in the 'narrow trench' condition. The transition depth is dependent upon the ratio of B_d to B_c. For given values of diameter and depth loads are always higher in the wide trench case. An arbitary method for deciding whether the wide or narrow trench case is relevant is to calculate W_f for both cases and to use the lower value in design.

The equations giving C for the narrow and wide trench cases are given in Ref. (25), and these may be incorporated in computer programs, basically intended for hydraulic design, to enable pipe loadings to be calculated automatically.

In addition to fill loads, surcharge loads resulting from traffic and buildings may occur. For example pipelines under main roads are assumed to be subjected to loads resulting from a group of eight wheels arranged as in BS 153, Type HB loading. The equations of Boussinesq are used to determine the effective load on the pipeline at the appropriate cover depth.

The Building Research Establishment have produced two booklets published by HMSO: Special Report 37 'Loading charts for the design of buried rigid pipes', and 'Simplified tables of external loads on buried pipelines'[23, 24] which faciliate easy determination of the external loads.

A copy of a typical table from 'Simplified tables of external loads on buried pipelines' reproduced by permission of the Controller, HMSO, shows combined backfill and surcharge loads due to light, heavy traffic and in fields. The tables also show the transition depths for the various trench widths (Table 9).

PIPE STRENGTH AND BEDDING FACTORS.—The pipe strength required to sustain the external load W_f is obtained from:

$$W_T > \frac{W_f \times F_s}{F_m}$$

Where W_T = test strength of pipe; F_s = safety factor (1·25); F_m = bedding factor.

Bedding Class	Type	F_m	
Class A (R.C.)	120° reinforced concrete cradle	3·4	
Class A (plain)	120° plain concrete cradle	2·6	
Class B	Granular bed	1·5, 1·9, 2·5	See Ref. 24.
Class C	Hand-shaped trench bottom	1·5	
Class D	Hand-trimmed flat-bottomed trench	1·1	

Example: A 300 mm concrete pipe is laid in a trench of minimum width in Class B bedding (F_m = 1·9) with a cover of 3·0 m under a main road. From the table[24] the total external design load is 4000 kg/m.

$$\text{Required pipe strength } W_T > \frac{4000 \times 1{\cdot}25}{1{\cdot}9} > 2632 \text{ kg/m (ult).}$$

A reinforced concrete pipe Class H is required. (BS 556)

FLOW OVER SIDE WEIRS.—Side weirs are most commonly used as stormwater overflows in sewerage networks. The variety of types of flow which can occur along the crest and the different methods available

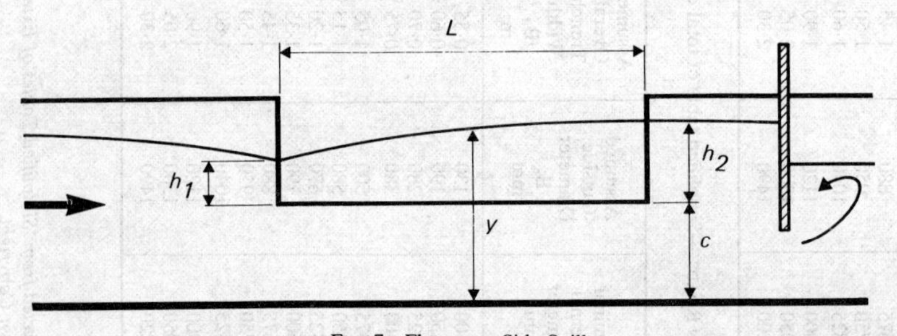

FIG. 7—Flow over Side Spillway.

for computing discharges can lead to errors in design. Five possible flow profiles which depend upon the channel slope and the existence of downstream control, have been identified (Ref. 26). A commonly occuring profile with gate control is shown in Figure 7.

Discharge per unit crest length: $q = 2/3\, C_d \sqrt{2g}\,(y - c)^{3/2}$ (iii)

The existing analytical/design methods are summarised:

(a) The Coleman-Smith empirical formula

$$L = 0{\cdot}1074\, B\, V\, h_1^{\,0{\cdot}13}\left(\frac{1}{\sqrt{h_2}} - \frac{1}{\sqrt{h_1}}\right) \text{(S.I. units)}$$

where L is the crest length, B the channel width, V the average velocity along the channel, h_1 and h_2 the incoming and outgoing heads over the crest respectively. It was usual in design to assume $h_2 = 0{\cdot}019$ m. The formula suffers from several drawbacks due to the inherent assumptions.

(b) The 'constant head method' assumes that the head over the crest is constant along the length. This requires a channel with a linear taper given by,

$$\frac{db}{dx} = \frac{2\, C_d \sqrt{2g}\,(y - c)^{3/2}}{3\, V_y}$$

(c) De Marchi's method—assuming a horizontal rectangular channel and that specific energy remains constant along the side weir the following equation for the length of the weir is obtained:

$$L = \frac{b}{2/3 C_d}\left[\phi\left[\frac{y_2}{E}\right] - \phi\left[\frac{y_1}{E}\right]\right] \quad \text{(iv)}$$

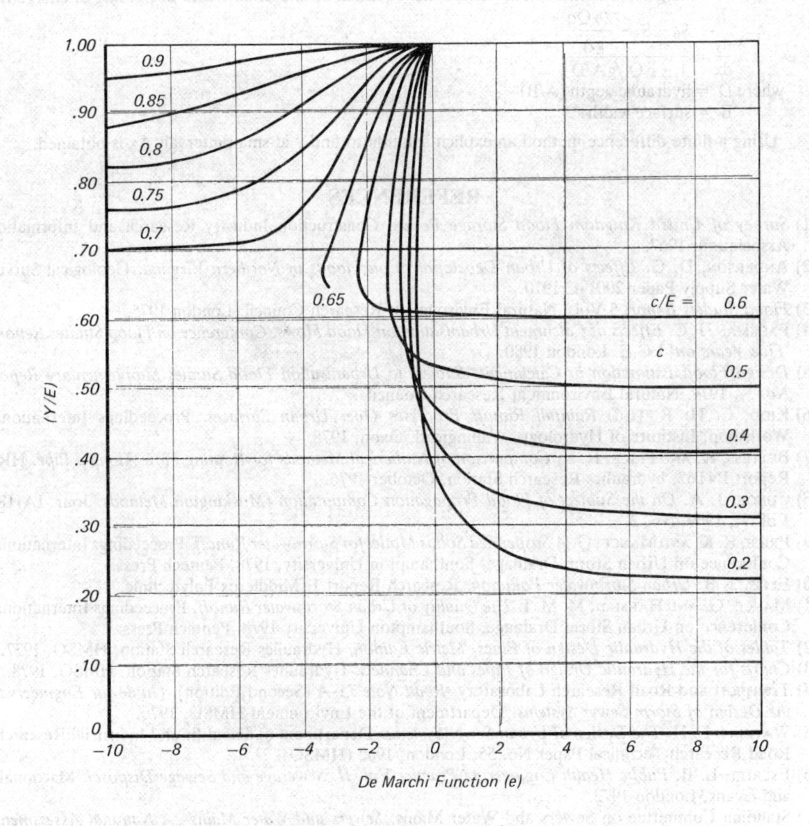

FIG. 8—The De Marchi Function ϕ(y/E).

where E = specific energy $(y + (dV^2/2g))$; b = channel width; y_2 and y_1 = depth at downstream and upstream ends of weir respectively; ϕ (y/E) is the varied flow function evaluated by De Marchi:

$$\phi\left(\frac{y}{E}\right) = \frac{2E - 3c}{E - c}\sqrt{\frac{E - y}{y - c}} - 3\sin^{-1}\sqrt{\frac{E - y}{E - c}}$$

Starting at the end of the weir at which the depth is known calculate $E = y + (\alpha V^2/2g)$: From Fig. 8 obtain $\phi(y/E)$; calculate $\phi(y/E)$ at the other end of L from equation (iv). Hence obtain the depth at this end. The velocities at each end are obtained from $V = \sqrt{2g(E - y)/\alpha}$ and Q = by V. Hence the discharges at each end are determined; the difference is the side spillage.

(d) A finite difference solution of the governing differential equation can be expressed in the form:

$$\Delta y = \frac{\alpha Q_1 (V_1 + V_2)}{g(Q_1 + Q_2)} \Delta V \left(1 - \frac{\Delta Q}{2Q_1}\right) - S_f \Delta x \qquad \text{(v)}$$

giving the rise in water surface in the downstream direction over the small distance Δx. Subscripts 1 and 2 relate to quantities at the upstream and downstream ends of Δx at each step. S_f is the friction slope given by $S_f = n^2 V^2/R^{4/3}$; α = velocity energy coefficient $(1{\cdot}0 < \alpha < 1{\cdot}3)$.

Computational procedure: Divide the distance over the weir crest into equal intervals Δx. Starting from the end of the weir where the depth is known, calculate V and Q. Estimate the first increment Δy, hence calculate y_1 and A at the end of Δx. Using an average depth calculate $\Delta Q = q\Delta x$ (lateral discharge over Δx) from equation (iii). Hence calculate Q and V at the other end of Δx. Substitute into equation (v) and calculate Δy. Compare the estimated and calculated values of Δy and re-estimate and re-compute until reasonable equality is obtained. Proceed to end of the weir in similar manner. The total lateral discharge is obtained by summing the ΔQ values.

(e) Numerical integration method: The differential equation of lateral flow with decreasing discharge is:

$$\frac{dy}{dx} = \frac{S_0 - S_f - \dfrac{2\alpha Qq}{gA^2}}{1 - \alpha Q^2/gA^2D}$$

where D = hydraulic depth (A/B)
B = surface width

Using a finite difference method an explicit solution to find y at small intervals Δx is obtained.

REFERENCES

(1) *Survey of United Kingdom Flood Storage Ponds.* Construction Industry Research and Information Association, 1967.

(2) Anderson, D. G. *Effects of Urban Development on Floods in Northern Virginia.* Geological Survey Water Supply Paper 2001–C 1970.

(3) *Flood Studies Report* 5 Vols. Natural Environment Research Council. London 1975.

(4) Packman, J. C. *Effects of Catchment Urbanisation on Flood Flows. Conference on Flood Studies Report. 'Five Years on'* I.C.E. London 1980.

(5) *Design Flood Estimation in Catchments Subject to Urbanisation Flood Studies Supplementary Report No. 5.*, 1979. Natural Environment Research Council.

(6) Kidd, C. H. R. (Ed) *Rainfall Runoff Processes Over Urban Surfaces.* Proceedings International Workshop, Institute of Hydrology, Wallingford, Oxon, 1978.

(7) Bettess, R. and Price, R. K. *Comparison of Numerical Methods for Routing Flow Along a Pipe.* HRS Report INT62. hydraulics Research Station. October 1976.

(8) Cunge, J. A. *On the Subject of Flood Propagation Computation (Muskingum Method).* Jour. IAHR, Vol. 7., 1969, No. 2.

(9) Price, R. K. and Mance, G. *A Suspended Solids Model for Stormwater Runoff.* Proceedings International Conference on Urban Storm Drainage. Southampton University, 1978, Pentech Press.

(10) Ellis, J. B. *Urban Stormwater Pollution.* Research Report 1. Middlesex Polytechnic.

(11) Mance, G. and Harman, M. M. I. *The Quality of Urban Stormwater Runoff.* Proceedings International Conference on Urban Storm Drainage, Southampton University 1978, Pentech Press.

(12) *Tables of the Hydraulic Design of Pipes, Metric Edition,* Hydraulics Research Station, HMSO, 1977.

(13) *Charts for the Hydraulic Design of Pipes and Channels.* Hydraulics Research Station, HMSO, 1978.

(14) Transport and Road Research Laboratory. *Road Note 35–A* (Second Edition). *Guide for Engineers to the Design of Storm Sewer Systems.* Department of the Environment HMSO, 1976.

(15) Watkins, L. H. *The Design of Urban Sewer Systems.* Department of Scientific and Industrial Research, Road Research Technical Paper No. 55, London, 1962 (HMSO).

(16) Escritt, L. B. *Public Health Engineering Practice Vol. II. Sewerage and Sewage Disposal.* Macdonald and Evans, London 1972.

(17) Standing Committee on Sewers and Water Mains. *Sewers and Water Mains—A National Assessment.* Department of the Environment/National Water Council. 1977.

(18) Newport, R. *A Strategy for Investigating Infiltration into Sewers.* Conference on Opportunities for Innovation in Sewerage. University of Reading. Water Research Council, 1977.
(19) Pink, B. J. *Laboratory Investigation of the Discharge Characteristics of Sanitary Appliances.* Building Research Establishment. 1973.
(20) *Sewage.* British Standard Code of Practice. CP 2005.
(21) *Erosion of Sewers and Drains.* Construction Industry Research and Information Association. Report No. 24, 1968.
(22) Marston, A. *The Theory of External Loads on Closed Conduits in the Light of the Latest Experiments.* Iowa Engineering Experimental Station, Bull. No. 96, 1930.
(23) Clarke, N. W. B. *Loading Charts for the Design of Buried Pipes. National Building Studies. Special Report 37.* HMSO, 1966.
(24) *Simplified Tables of External Loads on Buried Pipelines.* Building Research Station. HMSO, 1970.
(25) Walton, J. H. *The Structural Design of the Cros Section of Buried Vitrified Clay Pipelines.* Clay Pipe Development Association, 1970.
(26) Frazer, W. *The Behaviour of Side Weirs in Rectangular Channels.* I.C.E., Hydraulics Engineering Division Meeting—Symposium of Four Papers on Side Spillways. Oct. 1956.
(27) Collinge, V. K. *The Discharge Capacity of Side Weirs.* I.C.E. Symposium. Ibid.
(28) Chow, Ven Te. *Open Channel Hydraulics.* McGraw Hill Book Co. Inc., New York.
(29) *The Wallingford Procedure.* National Water Council/Department of the Environment, 1981.

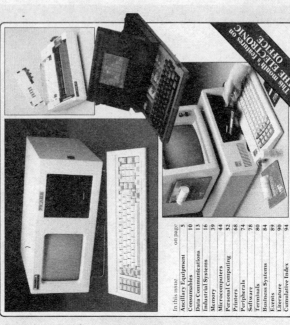

WASTEWATER TREATMENT

Legislation—Wastewater Characteristics—Surveys—Primary Treatment—Biological Treatment—Tertiary Treatment—Sludge Disposal—Bibliography.

by G. K. Anderson

LEGISLATION.—The discharge of wastewaters has been subject to increasingly effective control since the Rivers Pollution Prevention Act, 1876. It is an offence to discharge any matter which is poisonous, noxious or polluting to a non-tidal surface water although the definition of what is poisonous, noxious or polluting is left to the Courts. The Rivers (Prevention of Pollution) Acts of 1951 and 1961 require dischargers to apply to the regulatory agency (the Regional Water Authorities in England & Wales) before making new or altered discharges to non-tidal surface waters. This requirement continues under section 32 and 34 of the Control of Pollution Act 1974. Section 34 lays down that a consent may not be unreasonably withheld and that it may include the following conditions:—

(i) location of discharge and design of outfall
(ii) nature, composition, temperature, volume and rate of discharge
(iii) facilities for sampling
(iv) provision and maintenance of meters
(v) records of nature, composition, temperature, volume and rate of discharge
(vi) making of returns about the discharge; and
(vii) (new) steps to be taken to prevent the discharge coming into contact with specified groundwater

The consent may be varied at not less than two-yearly intervals.

Generally, water authorities apply the so-called 'Royal Commission Standard' requiring the BOD not to exceed 20 mg/l and suspended solids not to exceed 30 mg/l but where dilution is low it is not uncommon to have substantially more stringent standards. Typical consent conditions for discharge to a fishing stream (dilution at least 8:1) are:—

BOD (5 days at 20°C)	max. 20 mg/l
Suspended Solids	max. 30 mg/l
pH	5–9
Sulphide (as S)	max. 1 mg/l
Cyanide (as CN)	max. 0.1 mg/l
Arsenic, cadmium, chromium, copper lead, nickel, zinc	max. 1 mg/l (total)
Free chlorine	max. 1 mg/l
Oil and Grease	max. 10 mg/l
Temperature	max. 25–30°C
Insecticides or radioactive matter	none.

Under the Clean Rivers (Estuaries and Tidal Waters) Act, 1960 all new or altered discharges to estuaries and other specified tidal waters became subject to the consent procedure of the 1951 and 1961 Acts. Under the 1974 Act the water authorities will be provided with an effective means of control of the discharge of all effluents to estuaries within a three-mile limit.

The discharge of effluents to groundwater first came under formal control following the Water Resources Act, 1963, which dealt only with discharges by means of well, borehole or pipe but the 1974 Act applies to all discharges to specified groundwaters.

All discharges to sewers were effectively brought under the control of the water authorities by the 1974 Act, with a deemed consent applying to discharges carried by the Public Health (Drainage of Trade Premises) Act, 1937.

Reasonable conditions of consent to a sewer discharge may, under the Public Health Act, 1961 include:—

(i) period of day when discharge may be made
(ii) exclusion of condensate,
(iii) pretreatment required
(iv) temperature

(v) acidity or alkalinity
(vi) charges for reception and treatment;
(vii) provision and maintenance of inspection chamber and meter;
(viii) analytical monitoring of effluent;
(ix) keeping of records of volume, rate and nature of discharge; and
(x) making of returns on above matters.

A water authority is entitled to charge for the cost of receiving, carrying, treating and disposing of the effluent and the cost governed by volume and strength.

A typical formula used is:

$$C = R + V + \left[\frac{O_t}{O_s}\right] B + \left[\frac{S_t}{S_s}\right] S$$

C is charge in pence per m^3 for an effluent,
R is the reception charge, V is volume charge,
B is cost of biological treatment $+\frac{1}{3}$ cost of sludge treatment,
S is $\frac{2}{3}$ cost of sludge treatment
O_t and O_s are oxygen demands of waste and combined sewage,
S_t and S_s are *settleable* solids of effluent and combined sewage.

WASTEWATER TREATMENT AND DISPOSAL

WASTEWATER CHARACTERICS.—Almost any substance can get into a wastewater and therefore the effects on receiving waters are varied and occasionally disastrous. It is convenient to consider the effects of polluting substances in three groups:—

(i) TOXIC WASTES.—Typical examples include chromium from plating, pesticides from agriculture and radioactive materials. Measureable quantities of such pollutants can make the receiving water unfit for use as a water supply as well as destroying the plant and animal life of the stream.

(ii) OXYGEN DEMANDING WASTES.—These wastes may be conveniently sub-divided into chemical reducing agents such as sulphides, biologically degradable wastes for whose biochemical stabilization oxygen is essential and surface-active agents which interfere with oxygen transfer at the air-water interface.

(iii) NON-TOXIC WASTES.—Inert suspended solids and dissolved salts may destroy plant and animal life or make waters unsuitable for some purposes.

The increased emphasis on water quality for multipurpose use had defined a number of parameters of special significance which are used as a means of characterizing a wastewater. These are:

(i) The Biochemical Oxygen Demand (BOD), which defines the biodegradable organic content of a waste,
(ii) The Chemical Oxygen Demand (COD) which gives a measure of the total organic content, both degradable and refractory.
(iii) Suspended, Settleable and Volatile Solids
(iv) Total solids
(v) pH alkalinity and acidity
(vi) Nitrogen and Phosphorous
(vii) Heavy metals and inorganic salts.

The polluting strength of an effluent is best defined simply in terms of those organic substances which will affect the dissolved oxygen, (DO) of the receiving water which is best estimated by the five day BOD and by the concentration of suspended solids.

BODs may be used not only to indicate the strength of a wastewater but also of a treated effluent and the efficiency of the various stages during a treatment plant. The BOD_5 of domestic sewage may be expected to lie in the range of 150 to 600 mg/l whereas for industrial wastes from 0 to 100,000 mg/l may be found depending on the nature of the industry. In the absence of sewage and wastewater analyses the following may be of use:—

WASTEWATER	BOD RANGE	BOD LOAD
Domestic waste	150–600	0.045–0.06 kg/person/day
Meat Packing	200–3,000	1.4–1.8/hog
Sugar Refining	210–1,700	9–18 /tonne beet
Dairy (Milk)	1,000–2,000	0.07–0.12 /m³ milk
Distillery (Whisky)	7,500	0.08–0.93 /bushel grain
Brewery	500–1,300	0.9–3.2 /barrel;
Canning Fruit/Peas	700–2,150	9–21 /tonne
Chips	480–4,000	10–18 /tonne
Green Beans	520–3,030	4.5–10 /tonne

Dairy Cow	–	0.88 kg/cow/day
Pig	–	0.14 kg/pig/day
Poultry	–	0.15 kg/100/day

The suspended solids content of a wastewater is an indication of the amount of sludge which may be expected and is used in the design of those parts of a treatment plant dealing with the separation, treatment and disposal of sludge.

Surveys.—Surveys of wastewater discharges are required for a variety of reasons. Where the waste is being discharged into a sewer a survey is required for the calculation of charges and to test acceptibility; thereafter, periodic monitoring is needed to check on any changes in volume or nature.

In cases where pre-treatment or complete treatment of a wastewater is being undertaken at the factory, a survey is required for the design of treatment plant and afterwards monitoring is needed of both influent and effluent. Where industrial wastes are being discharged to natural waters without prior treatment, regular surveys are required to see that consent conditions are not being exceeded.

In planning and designing surveys it is therefore important to have a clear aim. The main types of surveys may be classified as follows:—

(a) Design Surveys—intensive, short-term surveys which aim to provide the basic data on volume, strength, settleability, oxidizability etc. needed to design the treatment plant.
(b) Effluent Charge Surveys—a medium-term survey aimed at characterizing the additional treatment facilities required at the local treatment plant for the treatment and disposal of that waste.
(c) Operational Monitoring—a long-term survey aimed at optimizing the efficiency of the treatment process.
(d) Routine Monitoring—a long-term survey aimed at recording variations in influent and effluent quality.

The number of samples required to establish some statistic (such as the mean) for a chemical parameter (BOD for example) depends upon the variability of the parameter and the level of precision required. The variability depends upon any number of factors and is not usually predictable, therefore a small number of short pilot surveys may be required to calculate this variability. The result of these can then be used to determine the category of variability, i.e. the type of frequency distribution. The types most commonly occurring are normal and log-normal although occasionally 3- or 4-parameter distributions occur when there is an upper limit or lower limit or both.

GENERAL OUTLINE OF WASTEWATER TREATMENT

The general purpose of a wastewater treatment plant is to efficiently and economically remove those constituents which either prevent a wastewater from achieving those standards laid down for it or cause an unacceptable amount of damage to the aquatic environment. As a rule, in the United Kingdom, this consists of the physical, chemical and biological removal of organic and inorganic solids and soluble and colloidal organic matter. In addition it may be necessary to control the discharge of the various forms of nitrogen and phosphorous and also to reduce the levels of toxic and harmful matter. Furthermore, if circumstances warrant it, the following may also be considered;

disinfection
taste and odour causing compounds
pH control
and temperature control

PRELIMINARY TREATMENT.—The aim of preliminary treatment is to protect the principal treatment processes which follow and consequently should be considered as a protective stage where no more material than necessary is removed at this stage. There is a diversity of practice as to the sequence of the preliminary unit processes, e.g. should grit removal precede or follow comminutors or macerators? Provision should also be made for measuring and recording the rate of flow arriving at the sewage works and it should be considered that storm water overflow and storm settlement tanks be part of preliminary processes.

A sewage treatment plant is not normally designed to provide full treatment for all the storm sewage delivered to it in wet weather. Provision is generally made for storing, or partially treating, that portion which cannot be given biological treatment at the time. It is therefore necessary to proportion the storm sewage between that receiving biological treatment and that being stored for treatment later, or receiving partial treatment before discharge to a water course.

At a treatment works site, the usual point of diversion is downstream of the preliminary treatment plant so that some solids are removed or disintegrated and grit is removed from the total flow.

In dry weather the flow arriving at a treatment plant is composed of domestic sewage, industrial wastes and infiltration water. During wet weather, the maximum rate of flow to the biological treatment plant is expressed in terms of the Dry Weather Flow (DWF). Where the sewage is mainly domestic, the overflow is usually set at 3 × DWF.

Since industrial wastes are often discharged to the sewers over a limited period each day it is recommended that a factor of 4 should be used when calculating the maximum rate of flow to receive full biological treatment.

The suggested maximum rate of flow to receive complete treatment is:—

$$0{\cdot}003PG + I + 3E$$

where P = Population served by sewerage system
G = Average domestic water consumption l/hd/d
I = Infiltration (m^3/d)
E = Volume of industrial waste discharged in 24 hours (m^3/d)

With small treatment plants it may be better for the total plow to receive biological treatment.

The method of storm water separation for storage or partial treatment should not operate until the full design flow is reaching the biological unit and be so designed that the flow to the biological unit does not increase as the by-passed flow increases, and it must also be self cleansing. The most usual method for achieving this is by means of a weir on one or both sides of the sewage channel with the rate of flow receiving full treatment being controlled by an electrically operated downstream penstock. Other devices include a multiple trough overflow, a float operated regulating valve and siphons. Separation may also take place at the pumping station.

In general it is not necessary to fully treat storm sewage other than by removal of suspended solids. A storm tank capacity of 6 hours DWF is considered to be the best design criterion, with rectangular, horizontal flow tanks being the most popular method of design.

Screening and Disintegration.—Crude wastewaters contain gross solids which are either organic or inorganic in nature and which could create difficulties in the pipes and mechanical parts of subsequent treatment units. These problems may be overcome by:—

(a) direct removal
(b) removal followed by disintegration and return to the flow
or (c) size reduction without removal from the flow,

(a) and (b) may be achieved by screening. This may be at the pumping station with 75 mm to 150 mm aperture screens or with screens as small as 15 mm at the treatment plant. It may often be desirable to use two screens in series the first of large aperture, followed by small aperture screens.

If the flow is less than 1,000 m^3/day manually raked bar screens at 60° to the flow should suffice and mechanically raked curved or inclined are recommended for flows in excess of this. The velocity of flow through the screens should preferably not be less than 0·3 m/sec nor greater than 0·9 m/sec. The difference in upstream and downstream levels caused by the accumulation of screenings may be used as a means of activating the automatic cleaning system.

About 0·01 to 0·03 m^3/d/1,000 population screenings will normally be produced with a weight to 600–1,000 kg/m^3 and a moisture content of 75–90%. The volatile content of dry matter is usually between 80 and 90%. They are objectionable in both appearance and odour, consequently should be either disintegrated and returned to the flow or disposed of, on or off-site, as soon as possible.

Various methods of disintegration of screenings may be used with the most common being a macerating pump. Barminuters and Comminutors both intercept large particles and macerate them without removal from the flow line. Comminutors are widely used but have many inherent problems such as the need for periodic cleaning, especially of floating cork and plastics and their abrasion by inorganic materials. Shredded rags often tend to reform into strings or 'ball-up' causing choking in pipes and pumps downstream. In common with most mechanical systems some standby and by-pass facility should be provided.

Grit Removal.—Grit is generally defined as heavy mineral matter which may cause wear of pumps and other equipment if not removed, with reported volumes of 0·005 to 0·095 m^3/1,000 m^3 and 40 to 80% moisture content.

It is theoretically possible to remove grit from the wastewater flow and yet at the same time retain the organic matter for subsequent removal. The solution is one of flow control. The optimum velocity for sewage for settlement is 0·3 m/sec which may be achieved in theoretically parabolic cross-section channels maintaining a constant velocity at all rates of flow. This method was in favour for many years but more recently mechanical devices have been preferred.

Aerated grit channels use compressed air to keep the organics in suspension while allowing grit to settle and subsequently be removed by air-lift or other pumps. Also common are detritors which consist of a square tank of shallow depth which allows all grit plus some organics to settle into a hopper from where it passes to a counter-current cleansing channel thus returning the organics to the flow with a resultant clean grit. Other methods include a vortex separator and Pista grit trap for removing grit from sewage and a cyclone separator which separates grit from primary sludge if grit is allowed to pass directly to the primary sedimentation tank.

The organic content of grit varies widely according to the provision (or not) of washing facilities. It is generally used for land-fill or disposed of by burial.

Flow Measurement.—Flow measurement should be considered as an essential part of a wastewater treatment plant and is generally a feature of the preliminary works. For most situations a Venturi flume is the most practical means of providing a single depth measurement upstream of the throat. The depth measurement is made either by means of a side float chamber, a dip tube or an ultrasonic system. Occasionally a V-notch weir may be used to measure flow at small works but this would be better after secondary treatment and just prior to discharge in order to prevent accumulation of solids upstream of the restriction.

SEDIMENTATION.—Sedimentation is widely employed in wastewater treatment either as a primary stage to remove settleable solids in the wastewater or as a secondary stage to remove biological solids following biological oxidation.

The basic design criteria for sedimentation tank design are the surface loading rate expressed in terms of the maximum flow rate per day per unit area of tank surface, the hydraulic retention period in hours, the weir loading rate expressed in volumetric loading per day per unit length of overflow weir and the settling velocity of the solid particles.

Horizontal Flow Tanks.—Horizontal flow tanks are rectangular in shape, generally with a scraper and scum blade, economical in the use of land with little or no dead space between tanks. The surface loading for primary sedimentation tanks is usually about 30 m^3/m^2d at maximum flow rate although values of up to 45 may be used if the design flow exceeds 3 DWF. At peak flow rates a hydraulic retention of 2 hours should be used with provision being made for storing sludge and account being taken of withdrawal of one tank at a time for maintenance or manual desludging. The tanks are normally between 1·5 and 3·0 m deep with a width : length ratio of about 1 : 4. The preferred weir loading is about 300 $m^3/m.d$ although up to 400 may be acceptable. In order to achieve this, double sides or even H-weirs may be necessary.

Radial Flow Tanks.—The surface loading of a radial flow tank should not exceed 45 m^3/m^2d at maximum flow with a hydraulic retention time of 2 hours at maximum flow. The minimum depth of the vertical wall should be 1·5 m and the diameter varies from 5 m to 50 m depending upon the type of scraper used. The slope of the tank floor will again depend upon the type of sludge removal mechanism and can vary from 3° to 15°.

Sludge collection is of considerable importance, being normally affected by sludge scrapers which force the sludge into a hopper, beneath the inlet in horizontal flow tanks and centrally located in radial flow tanks.

In terms of overall efficiency, it should be possible, under most circumstances and within accepted design criteria, to achieve 65 to 70% reduction in suspended solids while at the same time, reducing the BOD by 30 to 40%. This latter reason considerably reduces the load on the biological treatment unit, producing a lower moisture content sludge and generally being an economic, efficient process.

Additional care should be taken with the design of inlet and outlet systems to achieve adequate distribution of flow without short-circuiting. The selection of the type of primary tank depends on the available space, the desired efficiency and a cost analysis of all viable alternatives.

The use of chemicals to enhance settling has long been suggested and may also be used for the precipitation of soluble phosphates and other soluble inorganic chemicals from industrial wastewaters. Conversion of these by chemical reaction may be a useful treatment process and in some cases no viable alternative is available. Chemicals used include lime, alum, ferrous sulphate, ferric chloride, aluminium chlor-hydrate and a range of organic polyelectrolytes. High BOD and suspended solids reduction may be achieved but further treatment is generally necessary on order to produce an effluent satisfactory for discharge into a high quality receiving water.

BIOLOGICAL TREATMENT.—Biological oxidation techniques have found wide application in the purification of domestic and industrial wastewaters. All biological processes depend upon the growth of micro-organisms contained either in a suspended biomass or in a fixed biological slime which utilize the organic material for growth and thus have the ability to remove dissolved or suspended and collodial organics from the liquid wastewater.

The basic method of assessment of the strength of a waste and its biological treatability is the biochemical oxygen demand BOD_5 but it may also be of value to measure the chemical oxygen demand (COD) and the concentration of essential nutrients such as nitrogen and phosphorus. These latter two should always be present and in an available form so that the BOD : N : P ratio is not more that 100 : 5 : 1. If the wastewater is deficient then the possibility of adding them artificially must be considered, for example as liquid ammonia and phosphoric acid or as ammonium phosphate.

Other pre-requisites for biological treatment include the adjustment of pH to between 6.0 and 8.0 using sulphuric acid or sodium hydroxide or lime. Flow balancing (or even load balancing) of industrial wastes may be necessary, especially if the industry concerned operates on an intermittent basis such as 8 hours work per day, 5 days per week. Flow balancing will reduce the size of subsequent settling tanks, pumps and other equipment and may simplify plant operation. It is normally achieved by containing the effluent flow in a variable level tank with constant discharge and mixing is recommended by aeration which has the added benefit of increasing the dissolved oxygen. Consideration should also be given to the segregation of very strong or potentially toxic waste streams as this may affect the biological process, as will excessive settleable solids and mineral oils.

Biological Filters.—The biological or percolating filter consists essentially of a bed packed with stone or plastic media over which the wastewater is irrigated. In order to achieve a 30:20 (SS:BOD) effluent using stone medium the following guidelines may be used:—

(i) BOD 50–150 mg/l loading rate of 0·08 to 0·15 kg BOD_5 per m^3d with 25–50 mm medium at 2 m depth.

(ii) BOD 150–250 mg/l loading rate of 0·15 to 0·2 kg BOD_5 per m^3d with 1:1 recirculation using 35–65 mm medium at 2 m depth.

(iii) BOD 250–1000 mg/l two stage or alternate double filtration using 60–150 mm and 25–50 mm medium for 2 stage and 37–60 mm for ADF systems, alternating at 3–7 day frequencies.

Plastic media may often be used as a partial treatment (roughing filter) to achieve 50–70% reduction i.e. 50% removal may be achieved at 5·0 kg BOD/m^3d increasing to 85% removal at 1·0 kg BOD/m^3d. The plastic may be packed to a greater depth but must be loaded at a minimum irrigation rate of 36 m^3/m^2d and may require recirculation to achieve this. Recently systems using pre-biological filtration in combination with the activated sludge process have proved successful.

A further modification of fixed film reactor systems is in the use of rotating biological contactors (RBCs) using either plastic or polystyrene discs or plastic packed drums which rotate through a tank containing the wastewater. RBCs have a lower power demand than comparable high rate plastic medium systems but appear to be restricted so far to relatively small applications in the U.K.

Activated Sludge Systems.—In the activated sludge process the wastewater is aerated in the presence of an 'activated sludge' which consists of flocs of bacteria, protozoa etc. The oxygen required by the process is introduced into the unit by either surface or diffused air aeration devices. Table 1 provides an indication of the design parameter to be used for various modifications.

TABLE 1.—ACTIVATED SLUDGE DESIGN PARAMETERS.

System	Organic Loading (kg BOD/kg MLSS d)	MLSS (mg/l)	HRT (hr)	Sludge Return %
High rate	1 –2	2,500	1– 2	33
Conventional	0·4 –0·5	2,000	6– 8	33
Conventional/Nitrification	0·15–0.2	3,000–4,000	8–10	50
Extended Aeration	0·05–0·15	3,000–6,000	18–24	100

The process organic loading is related to the biodegradability of the wastewater and is the food micro-organism ratio expressed as kg BOD_5 applied per kg Mixed Liquor Suspended Solids per day (kg BOD/kg MLSS d).

Aeration Capacity.—For most wastewaters with a high proportion of biodegradable matter (i.e. COD:BOD_5 greater than 2:1) and loaded at 0·2 to 0·5 kg BOD_5/kg MLSS d every kg BOD_5 removal requires about 1 kg dissolved oxygen. Most aeration systems can transfer about 1–4 kg oxygen per kwh (air to water) at 10–20°C. In practise a transfer efficiency of 1·5 O_2/kwh is necessary since a DO concentration of 1 mg/l in the reactor is sufficient to maintain aerobic conditions.

Mixed Liquor Solids Concentration.—The maximum MLSS that can be maintained is a function of the settling qualities of the sludge and relates to the size of the clarifiers and rate of return sludge. It is essential to optimize on MLSS to minimize the aeration tank capacity whilst maintaining an effective sludge settling rate. Hence for conventional operation 1,500 to 2,500 mg/l is used whereas for extended aeration 3,000–6,000 mg/l is used.

Process Modifications.—Modifications to the conventional process include *extended aeration* which is characterized by a long retention time, a high MLSS and very low excess sludge production; *contact stabilization* which consists of a short aeration period for adsorption of BOD, settlement of the sludge and sludge reaeration to oxidize the BOD; and a number of variations of operation including *tapered aeration* and *step aeration* and *Pasveer Oxidation Ditch* systems. More fundamental changes in process concept include the recent development of high intensity aeration capacity systems such as the Deep Shaft process which introduces air under pressure at depths of up to 100 m and pure oxygen systems, both of which allow operation at much higher tank loadings than was possible before. It is, however, felt that the high rate nature of both processes could tend to limit their applications to the full treatment of readily biodegradable wastes or as a partial pretreatment system.

Stabilization Pond Systems.—If adequate land area is available, it is possible to effect treatment in specially designed pond systems. In warm climates, the high temperature and light intensities result in relatively high organic load removal rates and algal oxygen generation capacity. Loading rates of 50–100 kg/ha/day are frequently applied for aerobic systems. However, in the U.K. pond treatment will most likely be limited to mechanically aerated lagoons or for 'polishing' treated effluent in maturation lagoons.

Anaerobic Processes.—Almost all naturally occurring organic matter and many synthetic organic compounds can be fermented anaerobically and if the process is carried to completion, the end products are usually CH_4 and CO_2 from carbonaceous matter and NH_3 from organically combined nitrogen. The process is, in many ways, ideal for industrial wastewater treatment, having several significant advantages over the available methods. The energy yield for cell synthesis is lower than in aerobic systems thereby resulting in much lower sludge yields and the energy intensive aeration process is absent, consequently operating costs are reduced. In fact excess energy, in the form of methane is produced which in turn may be used for either heating the reactor to its optimum temperature of about 35°C or used as process heat in the industry producing the original wastewater. The solids produced in the anaerobic activated sludge process do not settle readily but a number of patented systems have recently been introduced including that of the Bioenergy Process which have enabled high strength soluble industrial wastes to be treated efficiently with a BOD_5 of as high as 10,000 mg/l. Alternatively such wastes may also be treated by the anaerobic filter. Wastes successfully treated by anaerobic processes include starch-gluten, creameries, slaughterhouses, distilleries, wine production, cider and pectin and many others.

Tertiary Treatment.—It is now becoming necessary in many parts of the U.K. for effluents discharging into non-tidal waters to be of a quality higher than the usual 30:20, SS:BOD. This is largely due to the increasing use and indirect reuse of greater volumes of water. The additional processes required to reach such standards are termed tertiary treatment and are often similar to those used in raw water treatment. Much of the BOD in an effluent from secondary treatment is due to the residual suspended solids, its removal therefore will reduce both the BOD and suspended solids. Microstraining is one such process, retaining solids of diameter greater than about 0·045 mm although this system has reduced in popularity to the advantage of rapid gravity sand filters with the upward flow type appearing to be the most efficient and economical. Lagooning may also be used but the larger land requirements often make this system unacceptable as does the use of grass plots.

A summary of design data for tertiary treatment processes is as follows:—

Lagoons
3,500 to 5,000 m³/ha day
0·8 to 2·6 m deep
50 to 150 hours hydraulic retention

Grass Plots (normally for small works only)
2,000 to 5,000 m³/ha day
1:60 to 1:100 land slope
0·1 to 3·0 ha plots of land

Microstainers
300 to 700 m³/m² fabric/day
1 to 3 m diameter drums
15 to 65 microm mesh

Rapid Gravity Sand Filters (downward)
3 to 4 m head
up to 250 m³/m² d
0·8 to 1·7 mm nominal diameter, Leighton Buzzard sand
1·5 m depth

Rapid Gravity Sand Filters (upward)
up to 400 m³/m² d
0.15 m depth of 40–50 mm gravel
0·25 m depth of 8–12 mm gravel
0·25 m depth of 2–3 mm sand
1·5 m depth of 1–2 mm sand

Advanced Wastewater Treatment.—It is highly likely that in the future, effluents of even better quality than those from tertiary treatment will be demanded. For example both ammonia and nitrate-nitrogen may have to be removed. This may be achieved by ammonia stripping in an air tower at high pH or by biological nitrification with biological denitrification being used to reduce the nitrate to nitrogen gas. The objectionable orthophosphate may be reduced to less than 1 mg/l (as P) by chemical precipitation using lime, alum or ferric salts. Residual organic carbon in solution is efficiently, if not at low cost, removed by the use of activated carbon in either the granular or powdered form.

Sludge Treatment and Disposal.—Sludge is removed from both primary and secondary sedimentation tanks at sewage treatment works and as yet, remains the greatest problem to both designer and plant operator. It is estimated that up to 50% of the total capital and operating costs result from the collection, treatment and disposal of sludges. The quantity and nature of sludge is a function of the quantity of wastewater treated and the type of wastewater treatment plant used. Table 2 indicates typical values in the U.K.

TABLE 2.—VOLUME, SOLIDS AND MOISTURE CONTENT OF SLUDGES FROM DOMESTIC WASTEWATER.

Type of Sludge	Quantity (l/h/d)	Dry Solids (kg/h/d)	Moisture Content %
Primary	1·1	0·05	94–96
Low Rate Percolating Filter	0·23	0·14	89–98
High Rate Percolating Filter	0·30	0·18	98
Surplus Activated Sludge	2·40	0·36	99

Sludge, especially that from domestic waste treatment plants is a foul smelling, high organic and high moisture content material while sludges from industrial wastes may vary from inorganic, such as those from metal and mineral based industrial wastes to organic such as those from food and drink industries. In particular, industrial waste sludges may contain toxic materials which should then reflect in the type of treatment afforded and the ultimate disposal method selected.

Sludge may be spread on land, dumped at sea or burnt in incinerators. It has been estimated that approximately 20% of the sludge in the United Kingdom is dumped at sea, 40% applied to agricultural land and 20% disposed of elsewhere. However, before ultimate disposal is considered it is often necessary to first dewater and then dry the sludge to an acceptable moisture content.

Pretreatment.—Some form of pretreatment is generally necessary and in the United Kingdom this is most commonly by anaerobic digestion which (i) reduces the quantity of sludge, (ii) renders the sludge inoffensive with regards odour, (iii) may improve its dewatering characteristics, (iv) decreases the number of pathogenic organisms and (v) makes the sludge more acceptable onto agricultural land.

At an operating temperature of 35°C and a loading of about 2 kg volatile matter per m^3 per day a 50% reduction in volatile matter can be achieved. About 15 days minimum hydraulic retention time is required and the digester will produce about 1 m^3 gas per kg solids destroyed (this is equivalent to about 0·02 m^3 gas per capita per day at 70% methane and a calorific value of 33,000 kilojoules per m^3). At very large works sufficient energy is produced for all the works requirements and at smaller works sufficient heat should be produced for heating both the digester and the plant buildings.

The presence of synthetic detergents and toxic matter such as heavy metals may inhibit the digestion process while an overload of organic matter may result in the production of excess volatile acids. These problems have, in the past, resulted in the belief that the process should be replaced by some or other form of pretreatment, however, careful control and good operating procedures should make digestion the ideal system.

Dewatering.—If possible, sludge should be dewatered before ultimate disposal in order to make its transport and handling more economic. The traditional method is by air drying in open *drying beds*, which consist of large areas of low walled tanks containing sand, gravel and an underdrain system. About 0·5 m^2 surface area per person is required and after two weeks to three months depending upon the season and climate the sludge may be lifted manually or mechanically. The large area and labour intensity operation has recently seen a reduction in their use.

Many mechanical processes are available for dewatering sludge, all of which require the use of either chemical conditioners or a heat treatment process in order to readily release the bound and free water. Chemical conditioning is generally carried out using lime with iron salts, or aluminium salts, although recently a large number of organic polyelectrolytes have also been introduced for this purpose. 'Heat Treatment' consists of heating the wet sludge under pressure to about 200°C. About 35 such plants have been constructed in the United Kingdom but many operating problems and the total cost will probably see a decreased application in the future.

The major dewatering system in use, and much favoured by operators is that of pressure filtration in which moisture is removed by the application of high pressures to filter cloths containing the wet sludge. Most such filters are batch systems although a number of continuously operated systems have been introduced. Solid-bowl centrifuges and vacuum filters, common in the United States, have found little application in the United Kingdom, especially at municipal wastewater treatment plants. One problem common to all dewatering systems is the very high BOD of the resultant liquors which, when returned to the treatment plant may cause a shock organic load on the process.

Ultimate Disposal of Sludge.—The traditional, and possibly ideal method of disposal is that of land spreading. The sludge contains organic matter, useful as a soil conditioner, plus some nitrogen (2–3%) phosphate (1–2%) and potash (0·3–0·5%). Up to 120 m^3 wet sludge per hectare may be applied but this figure is affected by soil type, sludge type and agricultural use of the land. Dumping of wet sludge at sea is favoured by many large authorities since it is final and independent of climatic conditions. However, stricter controls are being applied by EEC and MAFF and alternative methods may have to be found in the future. Finally incineration may be used but high costs and the resultant pollution problems frequently limit its use unless specific reasons can be found.

BIBLIOGRAPHY

Technical Committee on Storm Overflows and the Disposal of Storm Sewage: Final Report. Ministry of Housing and Local Government HMSO London, 1970.
Some Short Investigations by the Water Pollution Research Laboratory. Notes on Water Pollution No. 20 Water Pollution Research Laboratory, Stevenage, 1963. Department of Scienfific and Industrial Research.
HAZEN, A. *On Sedimentation.* Trans. A.S.C.E., **53**, 1904.
TEBBUTT, T. H. Y. *The Performance of Circular Sedimentation Tanks.* Water Pollution Control, **68**, 1969, (4) 467.
BRADLEY, R. M. and ISAAC, P. C. G. *The Cost of Sewage Treatment.* Water Pollution Control, **68**, 1969 (4) 368.
HAMLIN, M. J. and MARCH, R. P. *Rectangular Settling Tanks for Sewage.* CIRIA, Report 11, 1968.
CLEMENTS, M. S. *Design of Radial-Flow Sedimentation Tanks on Velocity Principles.* Survey; Local government Technology, **134** No. 4041, Nov. 1969 28–31.
Domestic Sewage: Load per Person per Day. Water Pollution Control, 66. 1967, (2) 193. Institute of Water Pollution Control and Water Pollution Research Laboratory.
Small Sewage Treatment Works: BS Code of Practice CP 302, 1972. British Standards Institution.
Treatment of Secondary Effluents in Lagoons. Notes on Water Pollution No. 63 Water Pollution Research Laboratory, Stevenage 1973. Department of the Environment.
TRUESDALE, G. A., BIRKBECK, A. E., SHAW, D. *A Critical Examination of Some Methods of Further Treatment of Effluents from Percolating Filters.* J. Proc. Institute of Sewage Purification, 1964, (1) 81–101
FISH, H. *Some Investigations of Tertiary Methods of Treatment* I.P.H.E.J. **65**, 1966, (1) 33.
BANKS, D. H. *Upward-Flow Clarifier for use in Treating Sewage Effluents.* Survey Local Government Technology, **123**, 1964, No. 3745, 21–23.
BAYLEY, R. W. *Nutrient Removal from Wastewaters.* I.P.H.E.J. **70**, 1971, 150.
MCCARTY, P. L., BECK, L. & ST. AMENT, P. *Biological Denitrification of Wastewaters by Addition of Organic Materials.* Proc. 24th Industrial Waste Conference, Purdue University, 1969, 1271.
BAILEY, D. A., BAYLEY, R. W. & WAGGOTT, A. *Treatment of Wastewaters with the Aid of Activated Carbon.* Conference on Activated Carbon in Water Treatment, Water Research Association, University of Reading, 1972.
CLAYTON, M. B., WOOD, A. A. and ROSS, A. H. *Disposal of Municipal Sludges to Agriculture.* Disposal of Municipal and industrial Sludges and Solid Toxic Wastes. Institute of Water Pollution Control, London 26–27 Nov. 1973. 74–102.
Report of Working Party to Standing Committee on the Disposal of Sewage Sludge. Department of the Environment, London, 1977.
Manual of British Practice in Water Pollution Control. Institute of Water Pollution Control.
Unit Processes. Sewage Sludge III Utilization and Disposal.
Tertiary Treatment and Advanced Wastewater Treatment.
Primary Sedimentation.
Preliminary Processes.
BARTLETT, R. E. *Public Health Engineering Design in Sewage.* Applied Science, 1970.
KLEIN, L. *River Pollution Control, Vol. 3,* Butterworth (1966).
ESCRITT, L. B. *Public Health Engineering Practice: Water Supply and Building Sanitation, Vol. I.* Macdonald and Evans, London, 1972.

WASTES MANAGEMENT

Analysis—Storage—Bins and Containers—Collection Organisation—Disposal Plant—Incineration—Controlled Tipping—Composting—Street Cleansing.

By E. A. Mossey, CEng, MIMechE, FInstWM, MBIM, MCIT

REFUSE COLLECTION

ANALYSIS OF REFUSE.—When assessing wastes management services and organisation from economic, environmental and technological aspects it is of paramount importance that a detailed and reliable knowledge of the quantities and composition of the wastes is obtained. The storage, collection and subsequent disposal are all equally affected, but when consideration is being given to such matters as waste derived fuel, materials recovery and waste generated methane it is essential to know both the chemical and physical characteristics of the wastes concerned. It is possible that in the future wastes may be used to supplement the present fuels used and it will be essential to know of potential environmental and health risks in addition to corrosive and other effects on plant and buildings.

If wastes arising from domestic premises were constant in quantity and analysis, wastes disposal methods and their comparison with other areas and methods would be relatively straightforward. Unfortunately this is not so and until a uniform method of quantifying and classifying the various components of wastes is carried out under a standard procedure, design criteria for collection methods and final disposal methods must remain comparatively inefficient.

The financial burden on public funds required for wastes management services requires that the fullest consideration be given to a detailed analysis of the wastes involved. Due to the regular analyses of wastes being carried out less frequently a serious gap in the data on changes in density, trends and calorific values could have an adverse effect on future methods of both collection and disposal of all wastes.

Legislation now defines controlled waste as household, industrial and commercial wastes and further detailed definitions may be obtained from The Control of Pollution Act 1974.

At present the only reliable sources of national information are from C.I.P.F.A. and The Society of County Treasurers and The Surveyors Society.

ANALYSIS OF HOUSE REFUSE.—Analysis is undertaken to obtain data relating to yield, composition, seasonal variation, salvage potential and calorific value. Due to season variations tests must extend over a full year.

The procedure for making analysis of refuse is detailed in a Monograph published by the Institute of Wastes Management. Any analysis should be made annually during the third week in October, and every four years approximately the third week in January, April, July and October.

All premises from which domestic refuse is collected should be classified as follows:

1. Multi-storey flats or block consisting of 4 or more floors.
2. Houses, chalets and bungalows.
3. Tenement and other type property.

It may be appropriate to vary the above classifications to take account of any local conditions providing the classifications represent any factors which may affect refuse composition.

A separate classification would only be justified if the premises concerned formed a significant proportion of the whole e.g. premises used seasonally for holiday purposes.

Density.—This is ascertained by measuring volume against known weight prior to screening.

Analysis.—It is recommended that the minimum number of premises per sample is 100. Samples should be taken from the same premises each collection occasion and should be representative of the refuse normally collected each week.

Each sample should be weighed and its volume measured in a cubic metre box. Notes should be made of each weight and its volume and collated on an appropriate form.

The first stage is to screen the refuse using a 2 cm mesh, the second stage requires the manual extraction of the following:

putrescible and vegetable matter, paper, ferrous and non-ferrous metals, textiles, glass and plastic, and a note made of the remaining items if any.

Each of the above groups are then weighed, and each individual weight divided by the number of dwellings and the results noted.

The weight of each constituent group per dwelling is multiplied by the number of premises in the group of premises and the results summarised. This procedure is repeated for the sample of refuse collected from each group of premises.

The following table gives a sample of refuse data for one year.

Constituent		Percentage by weight
2 cm Screenings		10·3 – 7·1
Putrescible		25·3 –23·4
Paper		29·9 –33·9
Metals		8·1 – 7·1
Textiles		2·7 – 4·1
Glass		11·3 –14·4
Plastic		4·5 – 4·2
Other		7·9 – 5·8
Density	kg/cubic metre	14·9 14·4
	Cwts/cubic yard	2·25 2·17

The Department of the Environment has carried out analyses of domestic refuse with the co-operation of County and District Councils since 1974 and the Institute of Wastes Management has published a 38 page booklet entitled "The Analysis of Domestic Waste".

Reference.—Proc. I.W.M. Oct 1987 – The effects of the introduction of large wheeled bins on the composition of domestic waste.

STORAGE OF HOUSE REFUSE.—Householders normally store refuse in the kitchen for a short time prior to depositing it in a receptacle from which it will be collected by the local authority. BS 1577 1949, 'Mild Steel Refuse or Food Waste Containers' gives details for a galvanised binette having 0·5 ft^3 capacity; this container is intended for immediate storage purposes, or in instances where the output of refuse is low and when collections are frequent.

Although a variety of receptacles is available, the galvanised and other loose-lidded bins are likely to continue to be produced for the immediate future. BS 792 1947, 'Mild Steel Dustbins', gives specifications for a variety of sizes of galvanised steel tapered bins with plain sides, domed and seamless removable lids and dished bottoms. Rubber rings may be fitted to the base and rubber lids may be used with these bins to minimise noise. Paper or plastic sacks are now being used by an increasing number of local authorities, and the British Standards Institution have under consideration the preparation of a standard for plastic sacks for refuse storage. A number of collection authorities are using a continental style of plastic bin which has two wheels fitted to the base, this will assist householders to site the bin at a collection point where a 'kerb side' collection is given.

Reference.—Proc. I.W.M. Oct 1987 – Research into the effects of the introduction of continental style wheeled containers on the generation and collection of household waste.

REFUSE STORAGE AT FLATS.—For blocks of flats of no more than a few storeys high the use of dustbins, paper or plastic sacks normally suffices. When the quantity of refuse produced warrants the use of larger storage receptacles, then 1·25 yd^3 containers may be used. Larger skip type containers of up to 15 yd^3 may also be used.

In taller blocks of flats vertical chutes discharging into containers offer an economical method of refuse transfer. In office buildings, goods lifts and hoists are often used to move refuse. Guidance on storage and collection methods for flats and design criteria for chutes is contained in BS 1703 'Refuse Chutes', and also in Code of Practice BS CP 306, 'The Storage and On-Site Treatment of Refuse from Buildings'. Other systems which dispose on site of as much refuse as possible include the following.

(*a*) **Garchey System.**—This is essentially a water borne system which enables refuse to be transferred from the flats to a central collection point or points. Refuse is placed in a cylindrical container and when released the waste water stored in a special container under the sink conveys the refuse to a storage chamber normally below ground level. From this chamber refuse is either transferred to an incinerator after treatment in an hydro extractor or, as in later installations, is collected by a specialist tanker. ***NOTE***—Building Research Station, Building Digest (2nd series), No 40, summarises a study of experiences by flat dwellers on the use of dustbins, containers, with and without chutes and the Garchey System. There is unlikely to be any extensive use of this system due to high maintenance costs.

(*b*) **Refuse Compression Systems.**—A variety of these devices are now available and may be used in blocks of flats or in any other building in which a high output of refuse is created. These devices reduce the volume of storage space required to store refuse between collections—there may also be less fire risk.

(*c*) **On-site Incineration.**—These small incinerators which may be assisted by gas are usually fed by chutes. They may be automatically or manually controlled. An essential feature is for the flue to be separate from the chute and to include an after burner and a grit collection chamber. Care must be exercised by the users when aerosol and other similar containers are disposed of; articles which are too big to be conveyed by the chute may be collected manually and later loaded into the rear of the incinerator.

(*d*) **Pneumatic Suction.**—This method has been developed in Sweden and one London local authority has installed such a system in a large housing project. The system comprises a number of vertical chutes in which refuse is deposited and rests on a valve which is opened at predetermined times and allows the refuse to travel through a horizontal transporter tube to a storage silo from where it may be either fed into an incinerator or compression device before final removal.

REFUSE COLLECTION ORGANISATION.—First it is necessary to determine the frequency of refuse collection in order to establish collection costs and service criteria. Household refuse from average residential districts is normally collected once per week: in areas of high output and where storage space is restricted, daily or twice weekly collections may be required. Consideration must be given to collections from hotels, canteens and restaurants and sources of large quantities of putrescible wastes. Special collections of bulky household and trade refuse on a rechargeable basis must be taken into account.

The collection area is normally divided into rounds the size of which is determined by the output and frequency of collection. The system for collection will be either (*a*) continuous or (*b*) task.

(*a*) *Continuous*.—Refuse is collected from premises in strict rotation, work ends irrespective of last collection point daily, and restarts on next collection day at this same point.

(*b*) *Task*.—Work load is pre-set either by agreement or by work study; employees cease work as each daily termination point is reached; this system has the advantage of a known area of collection and is favoured by householders who have responsibility for providing any access to the bin or where there is a need to place the bin out for collection.

Costs.—There are two main elements, labour and transport, and it is essential to establish the correct ratio. Transport costs per bin are lowest with large collection crews, while labour costs are lowest with small crews. Team or crew size should be established after tests controlled by work study methods. The number of loaders required varies with bin site, collection system, low density, vehicle organisation and type—length of haul (ie to disposal point) and all unproductive mileage. Output of bin collection may vary widely over seasons from approximately 50 to 25 bins per man/day. Overall labour costs may be reduced by the use of incentive bonus schemes, but considerable care should be taken in preparing a scheme before its introduction, as other problems may arise which could adversely affect costs.

TRANSPORT ORGANISATION.—The choice lies between the single vehicle system (ie one vehicle per team) and a relay service. The adoption of either method depends on the following factors determined by method study: (*a*) vehicle capacity; (*b*) team loading rate; (*c*) length of haul (travelling time). The correct relay for any given set of conditions is indicated in the following Table:

Type of relay	Required when
2 vehicles: 1 team	travelling time equals loading time
3 vehicles: 2 teams	travelling time equals one-half of loading time
4 vehicles: 3 teams	travelling time equals one-third of loading time

The single vehicle system is not normally used when haul to disposal point is uneconomic. Relay systems provide a consistent feed to disposal point and reduce lost time due to vehicle unavailability (breakdown and other delays). Vehicles may be of compression or non-compression type. Compression vehicles may be continuous or manually operated.

VEHICLE CAPACITIES RELATED TO NORMAL BS BINS

Vehicle capacity		Number of BS Bins		
yd³	m³	Non-compression	Gravity compression	Continuous compression
10	7·5	100	130	200–250
16	12		210	275–410
30	15		270	400–600

REFUSAL DISPOSAL.—The following are the main methods in use at the present time:

(1) Controlled Tipping/Land Reclamation.
(2) Pulverisation.
(3) Direct Incineration.
(4) Separation/Incineration (ie the extraction of dust, cinders and uncombustible items followed by the incineration of the remainder.)

(5) Composting.
(6) High Density Baling.

Landfill.—If sufficient reclaimable land is available within economic range, the cheapest method is controlled tipping, this system being employed by the majority of local authorities. The term 'controlled tipping' is gradually giving way to the more accurate and constructive term 'land reclamation'.

Landfill should be carried out in accordance with the Department of the Environment recommendations. Refuse is deposited in layers approximately 2 m deep and consolidated by earth moving equipment. Approximately 23 cm of primary cover should be applied to the surface and sloping sides to avoid odour and wind disturbances; screens should also be provided in areas of high wind. Final cover and treatment should be in accordance with plans for the ultimate use of the completed site. After removal of hardcore access, scarify area with deep tines for drainage, apply minimum 7 cm top soil for grass cultivation or minimum 30 cm together with 30 cm subsoil or substrata for agricultural use. Settlement takes place at approximately 7½–22½% over five years, the majority taking place during the first two years.

The use of suitably designed Transfer Stations whereby refuse may be transferred from collection vehicles to large capacity vehicles or river barges will reduce transport costs where long distances to the final deposit site are involved.

Rodent Control.—Surface to tip should be inspected daily and treatment applied where necessary. Good covering applied quickly reduces need for insecticides.

TIP CAPACITY PER ACRE (4,047 m²) (approx)

Depth	feet	6	12	30	50
	metres	1·83	3·67	9·16	15·2
Capacity	tons	3,000	6,000	16,000	27,000
	tonnes	3,050	6,110	16,290	27,500

PULVERISATION.—Since pulverised refuse is approximately twice the density of crude refuse there are economic advantages so far as transport is concerned, the need for compaction is reduced and pay loads are higher in relation to vehicle unladen weight.

The homogeneous nature of refuse prevents voids when tipping and assists in even consolidation; the tip life is extended and the amounts of cover required are reduced. There are further advantages in respect of rodent and insect nuisances and the fire hazard is virtually non-existent. Refuse may be pulverised by (*a*) drums or (*b*) hammer mills.

Drums Method.—Refuse with addition of water is fed to a slowly rotating drum; the fibrous strength of materials is reduced; refuse is later screened to separate pulverised matter from rejects. Covering material is not required for appearance providing rejects are deposited first and covered by pulverised matter; cover is necessary to prevent odour in hot weather. Wheeled vehicles cannot travel over surface as easily as on a controlled tipping site.

Hammer-mills Method.—Refuse with a small addition of water is fed into a very strong chamber through which is mounted a shaft to which the hammers are fitted. These rotate at high speed (500–3,000+ rev/min) reducing the refuse passing through a combined process of impaction and shredding. Hammer mills require a continuous flow and may be fed by vibrating feeder, plate conveyor or elevating belt. At transfer stations the use of articulated trailers dispenses with the use of final storage hoppers.

DIRECT INCINERATION.—All modern direct incineration plants are fitted with mechanical grates and normally no full separation is carried out. Storage is usually in a concrete bunker and approximately 25× the grate capacity (tonne/h) minimum for a five day week. Charging is carried out by overhead grab crane and discharges to an almost vertical feed chute. A number of gates have the grate area divided into a large number of small segments between which dust falls and air is forced through the feed bed. Flow of refuse through the gate is effected by the slope and the amount of agitation caused by the movement of grate segments or, in the case of chain grates, by movement of the whole grate. Clinker residue can be delivered from quench pits by drag bar or conveyor direct to a disposal container. Magnetic extraction of ferrous metals from the clinker may be profitable. Flue gas cooling may be carried out by fine water sprays, the addition of cold air in a mixing chamber or by use of steam. Flue gas cleaning may be effected by multi-cyclones, gas scrubber or electrostatic precipitation, the last being the most efficient.

Separation and Incineration.—Refuse is deposited in a storage hopper and elevated to a sufficient height for gravity feed to a screen where dust is removed; refuse is conveyed from the screen to a picking belt and finally to grates. Horizontal rotary screens fitted with internal helix are preferred. Picking belts from which salvageable materials are extracted have a maximum speed of 25 cm/sec. Magnetic extraction of ferrous metals is normally carried out by overhead type magnet. Furnaces of top feed type range from two to eight cells with a common combustion chamber into which large items are hand fed. Grates are sometimes troughed to assist in the mechanical clinker extraction; modern refuse seldom results in hard one piece clinker and therefore flat grates are more common in which clinker may be extracted into skips or adjacent quench pits.

Combustion.—The design of the plant depends on the calorific value of the refuse which must be ascertained by refuse analysis and allowances made for estimated future changes. Chimneys may be constructed in mild steel, engineering brick or reinforced concrete and must be of sufficient height to avoid nuisance.

COMPOSTING.—The composting of refuse has not met with the success that was originally anticipated due probably to the changes which have taken place in refuse. Refuse may be pulverised by drum or hammer mill or rasp in order to: (1) Reduce the particle size and thus expose a larger area to bio-chemical treatment. (2) Assist by mixing organisms and food sources. (3) Add water for fermentation. The pulverised refuse can then be composted by the following methods.

(*a*) **Drum.**—A combination of pulverisation and fermentation by retention in a rotating drum for 5/6 days during which moisture and air are provided.

(*b*) **Tower (Gravity Chamber).**—Fermentation takes place in a closed tower with a number of floors; refuse which is delivered to the top floor is tumbled from floor to floor by gravity over several days, during which moisture and air are provided. Capacity of cells is dependent on input of refuse and can be up to 475 tons.

(*c*) **Windrows.**—Refuse is stacked in continuous heaps not more than 6 ft (2 m) high. Aeration is provided by turning over at intervals with temperature normal. The process can take several months.

(*d*) **Aerated Windrows.**— Refuse is stacked in a building and aerated by air passing through floor orifices—the maturing time is reduced to approximately four weeks.

(*e*) **Cell.**—Material is stored in cells with purpose built aeration inlets.

HIGH DENSITY BALING.—High Density Baling is a comparatively recent concept in European Solid Wastes processing. Refuse is collected in the normal manner and may be partially compressed in the collection vehicle. On discharge at the primary disposal point the refuse is fed by a conveyor, or other mechanical means, to a press of such construction that it reduces the refuse to between a fifth and an eighth of its original volume. This produces an almost solid block of refuse which will be bound with wire prior to the final transportation to the landfill site. Among the advantages claimed for this method are:

(i) a reduction in the number of vehicles required for transport to final disposal point
(ii) a simpler type of vehicle may be used for a given weight
(iii) a better use of landfill sites with higher consolidation rates, less absorbance and a significant reduction in wind blown, bird and rodent nuisances.

KITCHEN WASTE DISPOSAL UNITS.—These units consist of an electrically driven compact grinder which is fitted to a kitchen sink designed with a suitable outlet to waste. A special waste pipe is required and is flushed in the normal way. The units will disintegrate most kitchen waste and are designed to avoid damage by accidental inclusion of cutlery. It is some decades since these units were first used in Britain and they are now well established especially in snack bars and restaurants. It is possible that if sales increase the amount of refuse removed by cleansing departments will be reduced, but the amount of suspended objects in domestic sewage will increase pro rata.

NEW METHODS.—Although the traditional methods of solid waste disposal (incineration, composting, landfill etc) have been practiced for many years, they are not without operational problems, consequently a need exists for either upgrading the above disposal methods, or developing innovations, or disposal techniques.

Three recently developed innovations in solid waste disposal, which appear to hold some promise, are the medium temperature and high temperature incineration process and landfill with leachate recirculation process. The third method is by compressing solid wastes before final disposal and is normally termed high density baling. Two plants are in operation in Britain.

Although landfill is still regarded as the most viable method of refuse disposal, in areas where there are problems involving a shortage of disposal sites and where transport to the final disposal site is uneconomic, consideration has been given to alternative methods whereby the volume may be reduced. Such methods include the production of fuel pellets or RDF (refuse derived fuel) as in Eastbourne; the incineration of refuse with heat recovery as in the GLC plant at Edmonton, and also in Coventry. Other attempts to reduce the volume of refuse to be disposed of at source include the provision of bottle banks, whilst the use of specially designated sites (Civic Amenity Sites) where domestic refuse of a bulky nature, and refuse not normally collected by the collection authority may be disposed, will reduce collection costs and reduce the amount of wilfully dumped refuse.

LANDFILL GAS RECOVERY.—The production of landfill gas, approximately 1:1 mixture of methane and carbon dioxide, is an inevitable by-product of the anaerobic decomposition of refuse in the natural 'bioreactor' provided by a landfill site. First reported abroad in the 1960's, landfill gas only became an issue in the U.K. in 1970's with the move towards larger landfill sites, tighter control of landfill practices and the increase in the value of energy. The first two points resulted in higher gas production rates at larger sites, with the consequently increased problems of odour, vegetation dieback and fire risk. The idea of recovering the energy for profit was immediately attractive, transforming, as it did, a liability into an asset. Development of this resource is a good example of environmental credits resulting from the exploitation of a source of energy.

A recent survey of U.K. sites identified some 650 sites able to receive wastes likely to generate gas, of which about 50% may be capable of producing gas in significant quantities. A study is underway to establish the range of gas production rates at different sites, but these are currently known to vary by up to a factor of 10 according to such variables as:—site hydrogeology, refuse packing density, refuse composition and age, climate, type of covering material, and site geometry.

Until this study has been reported, a typical gas yield can be taken as two therms per tonne of refuse per annum over a period of about thirteen years. Applying this figure to the larger sites i.e. over 200,000 tonnes gives a national technical potential of around 1·3 mtcepa using present day landfilling practices.

At present our knowledge of the biochemical processes at work in a landfill site is fairly rudimentary, but the scope for enhancing gas production is felt to be considerable. The Department of Energy is supporting research and development on landfill gas production and utilization under its Biofuels Programme and providing funds for demonstration projects under its Energy Efficiency Demonstration Scheme. These programmes are formulated and managed for the Department by the Energy Technology Support Unit at Harwell. Close liaison is maintained with the relevant waste management programmes of the Department of the Environment. A U.S./U.K. collaborative agreement on energy research and development was signed in 1984. Subsequent bilateral discussions on landfill gas technologies have identified specific topics suitable for collaborative effort. These fall under two headings (a) Generic studies to improve understanding of the microbiological and chemical processes occurring in landfill and (b) improvements in technology to increase gas yields and improve overall economics.

A successful outcome to these research and development projects may double or possibly treble the gas yields presently obtained, thus increasing the national technical potential to over 3 mtcepa.

The 11th Report by the Royal Commission on Environmental Pollution—Managing Waste, The Duty and Care is now published Cmnd 9675.

STREET CLEANSING

The regulations concerning Street Cleansing are contained in The Public Health Act, 1936, Sec 77, 78, 81 and 82; and The Highways Act, 1959, Sec 106, 127, 128, 129, 130.

STREET SWEEPING.—Street sweeping may be carried out by manual and/or mechanical methods.

Manual.—Individual beats, the output per man/day ranges from 185 m to 5 km and should be established by method study and allow for frequency of sweep, weed control, channel cleaning, emptying of litter bins, traffic both pedestrian and vehicular. Frequency depends on local conditions and may vary from more than once per day in high pedestrian density areas to once per week in open residential developments. Street sweepers are normally equipped with a metal framed truck which can carry one or two bins which may take plastic bin liners. Brooms for sweeping channel and footpath surfaces are adapted to suit local conditions. Stocks are usually of beech which can be re-bristled. Shafts, 150 to 170 cm long, are of ash and may be fitted with a light alloy shaft socket. The filling material may be of bahia, the various types of bass, polypropylene, gumati or mixtures of these materials. The life depends on use and varies from 12 to about 65 days.

Mechanical.—Approximately 50% of street sweeping operations are mechanical and basically three types of mechanical sweepers are used: viz: heavy road, light road and footpath and footpath/precinct; vacuum assisted sweeping machines are available with driver control mechanism and dual sweep facilities for use on dual carriageways and one-way street systems. The effective channel mileage covered depends on the type of road surface, geographical details of district, traffic density and movement conditions and the amount of street parking and ranges from 96 km to 240 km per week. The machines are normally equipped with a water tank for dust arrestation and brushes which may be of either natural or synthetic fibre will provide approximately 160 km to 1,600 km, while high tensile steel fillings will give approximately 2,000 km to 2,400 km.

GULLY CLEANSING.—Normally carried out by diesel engined vehicles of 3·5 m^3 to 5·5 m^3 capacity. The detritus is lifted from the gully pot by suction and the contents of the tank are discharged by a hydraulic tipping device, plate compression or by use of the pump as an exhauster. The output per machine varies considerably and depends on gully type and size, travelling time and other unproductive mileage, access to gully (car parking and other carriageway obstructions) and frequency. Frequency varies from once per week in wholesale market areas to three to six times per annum. Work study results show that the number of gullies cleaned varies from 70 to over 200 gullies per working day. Gully machines may be adapted for cleansing of cesspools, collection of night soil and sewer and street washing. Where gully machines cannot obtain access to gully pots then manual methods are used; a scoop is employed to extract the maximum of solids which must be conveyed to a disposal point and the gully sealed from a water supply.

GRITTING AND SALTING.—Due to the high cost of the removal of snow by manual labour the maximum use of crystal or rock salt is used. The salt should be free-flowing, not be too coarse and able to be stored for long periods. (See BS 3247 and Road Research Laboratory Note No 18). The salt should be applied as soon as possible to avoid compaction. The amount of salt applied must depend on local conditions, the rate of application may vary from 2·5 cwt/mile (80 kg/km) to 1 ton/mile (640 kg/km) depending on the severity of the snowfall. Gritting machines may be used to treat compacted snow or ice or in frosty conditions. Grit used should range from 6 mm to less than 10 mm. See BS 1622. A wide variety of mechanical equipment is available and includes spreading machines for salt and/or grit for footpaths, pedestrian precincts, etc (Refer to Vehicles Regulations S 12126/163 and S 1864/1966); ploughs—either 'Vee', or rotary type—may be used where snow is of sufficient depth to warrant their use. (See MOT Memorandum H4/69). Thermal snow melting machines can be used to disperse snow at the rate of 25 to 73 tonne/hour. In areas of high road traffic density with particular hazards recourse may be had to under-surface road heating.

TOXIC AND HAZARDOUS WASTES

In the event of any type of nuclear waste requiring disposal contact must in the first instance be made by the producer, user or carrier to the Department of the Environment when direction will be given.

The temporary storage, collection and final disposal of both toxic and hazardous wastes is a very complex and wide ranging subject involving the scientific knowledge required to deal with each type of waste. Due regard must be paid to the effect a particular type of waste may have on another and to the economics of disposal. Unlike general non-toxic wastes there is unfortunately no one method which can deal with this type of waste and the subject cannot be dealt with adequately in one chapter of one book.

Sites which have been used for the disposal of toxic and, or, hazardous wastes and have not been properly managed in the past may now give rise to serious threats to human life and the environment; and those persons who are charged with the responsibility of managing both new and old sites must pay attention to this aspect of wastes disposal.

An idea of the complexity of the subject may be obtained from publications listed under references, which also will be of assistance to site managers.

REFERENCES FOR WASTE MANAGEMENT

1. *Reclamation, Treatment and Disposal of Wastes—An Evaluation of Options*, HMSO 1976.
6. *Polychlorinated Biphenyl (PCB) Wastes*, HMSO 1976.
7. *Mineral Oil Wastes*, HMSO 1976.
8. *Heat Treatment Cyanide Wastes*, HMSO 1976.
9. *Halogenated Hydrocarbon Solvent Wastes from Cleaning Processes*, HMSO 1976.
11. *Metal Finishing Wastes*, HMSO 1976.
12. *Mercury Bearing Wastes*, HMSO 1977.
13. *Tarry and Distillation Wastes and Other Chemical Based Residue*, HMSO 1977.
14. *Solvent Wastes (excluding Halogenated Hydrocarbons)*, HMSO 1977.
15. *Halogenated Organic Wastes*, HMSO 1978.
16. *Wood Preserving Wastes*, HMSO 1980.
17. *Wastes from Tanning Leather Dressing and Fellmongering*, HMSO 1978.
18. *Asbestos Wastes*, HMSO 1979.
19. *Wastes from the Manufacture of Pharmaceuticals, Toiletries and Cosmetics*, HMSO 1978.
20. *Arsenic Bearing Wastes*, HMSO 1980.
21. *Pesticide Wastes*, HMSO 1980.
23. *Special Wastes: A technical memorandum providing guidance on their definition*, HMSO 1981.
24. *Cadmium-Bearing Wastes*, HMSO 1984.
25. *Clinical Wastes*, HMSO 1983.

In addition to the above papers the following HMSO publications may be of interest.

Hazardous Waste Problem Sites (OECD).
Hazardous Wastes in Landfill Sites.
Laboratory Decontamination and Destruction of Aflatoxins B_1, B_2, G_1, G_2, in Laboratory Wastes, WHO.
Laboratory Decontamination and Destruction of Carcinogens in Laboratory Wastes: Some N-Nitrosamines, WHO.

(Note these two last publications are the first arising from a special programme to develop, validate and publish methods for the destruction and disposal of laboratory waste containing carcinogens).

Control of Pollution (Special Wastes) Regulations 1980 Part 1, Shedule 1.

WASTE MANAGEMENT BULLETINS published at 4 monthly intervals (these Bulletins cover not only toxic and hazardous wastes but waste management generally).

FIRE PROTECTION

Brigade Organisation—Appliances—Fire Prevention—Legislation—Building Regulations—Structural Fire Protection—Fire Prevention on Ships—Protection of Buildings—Portable Fire Extinguishers—Fire Hose—Industrial Hazards.

By E. H. Whitaker, QFSM, FIFireE.

FIRE BRIGADE ORGANISATION

The Fire Services Act 1947 places on Fire Authorities which are County and Fire and Civil Defence Authorities (as prescribed by the Local Government Act 1985) in England and Wales and Regional Councils in Scotland a statutory responsibility for the maintenance of an efficient Fire Brigade in their area. Guidance as to the standards of the Fire Brigade and its size is given through the Home Office Fire Service Department, at Queen Anne's Gate, London. Standards of Fire Cover have been laid down by the Secretary of State on the basis of graded Fire Risk Categories within areas and the numbers of pumping appliances that should attend initial calls to incidents in those areas. Following the publication of the Report of the Joint Committee on Standards of Fire Cover, of the Central Fire Brigades Advisory Council, a survey is taking place to ensure uniformity, nationally, regarding risk categorisation.

Risk Category	No of Pumps to attend the initial call to an incident.	Time limits for attendance of pumps at the scene of the incident (minutes)		
		1st	2nd	3rd
A	3	5	5	8
B	2	5	8	–
C	1	8–10		
D	1	20	–	–

The fire risk categories range from areas of buildings of extra high risk through categories A, B, C and D in descending order of risk. Category D including for instance, remote rural areas and A the dock side areas of large ports. The number of appliances and the time limits for these attendances is shown in the table above. Areas defined as extra high risks have special attendances over and above those for risk category A. The types of appliances used by the Local Authority Fire Brigades fall into the following categories:

PUMPING APPLIANCES.—Self propelled pumps are powered by petrol or diesel engines and range in pumping capacity from 1,575/2,250 to 2,150/4,050 litres/min. The pumps are either single or multi-stage centrifugal being provided with a priming device to lift the water to the pump inlet when it is not connected to a pressure main. Many pumping appliances are designed to serve a dual purpose and are named according to their dual function, eg Pump/Ladder (carrying a 13·5 m extension ladder). Pumps may also carry a tank of water containing 1,800/2,250 litres. Such pumps then bear the designation 'Water Tender'. These appliances may in addition also carry out the dual function as above and be then designated Water Tender/Escape or Water Tender/Ladder.

SPECIAL APPLIANCES.—Fire Brigades have available to meet abnormal risks in their areas appliances designed to fulfil functions other than those of pumping appliances. These special appliances include:

(a) Turntable Ladders.—These comprise a heavy duty petrol or diesel powered vehicle on which is mounted a four or five section power operated ladder of extending range of up to 30 m. The ladders are of metal construction and can be rotated through 360°.

(b) Hydraulic Platform.—These appliances have a double or triple jointed power operated boom with a cage or platform at the upper end. Elevation of the boom is by built-in hydraulic rams and the lifting cage or platform can reach up to a vertical height of 19·5–25·5m.

(c) Emergency Tenders.—These appliances carry a range of power operated tools, lifting equipment and breathing apparatus. They are intended to supplement the limited equipment of the standard pumping appliances.

(d) Foam Tenders.—The large quantity of foam making compound and the mixing equipment carried makes these appliances capable of dealing with major fires in oil risks.

(e) Salvage Tenders/Damage Prevention Units.—The vehicle carries such items as waterproof sheets, smoke odour removers and roofing materials. Its purpose is to minimise the effects of fire and damage by water from fire fighting operations to a building and/or contents thus reducing financial loss.

(f) Decontamination/Chemical Incident Units.—Units designed for dealing with the increasing occurrence of chemical incidents in industrial premises and on roads and motorways.

(g) Specification Standard of Appliances and Equipment.—The Central Fire Brigades Advisory Councils Committee on Design and Development have issued detailed specifications covering all aspects of the above appliances and most other Fire Brigade equipment. As a result, national standards are achieved in all major items of Fire Brigade equipment. National Coal Board fire and rescue stations throughout Great Britain and many engineering, chemical and other industrial works use the same sort of modern equipment as the public authority fire brigades and manufactured to meet the same specifications. Thus interchangeability can take place at an incident.

(h) Portable Pumping Appliances.—Portable and Trailer pumps are extensively used in industrial Brigades. An enormous range of such appliances exist but basically, portable pumps are either mounted on skids or in a tubular carrying frame, sometimes with removable wheels, and range through the Ultra Light 110/270 litres/min type to a 1,575 litres/min Medium Pump. Trailer pump sizes also vary the more common size being the Light 450/675 litres/min and Large 1,575/2,250 litres/min types. The light trailer pump is usually designed to allow for the removal of the pump from the chassis, to allow man-handling over obstacles.

FIRE PREVENTION

Section 1(i)f of the Fire Services Act 1947 requires Fire Authorities to give advice when requested on matters relating to fire prevention. All authorities have established Fire Prevention departments, whose officers carry out inspections, enforce the legislative responsibilities of the Authority and are available to advise architects and engineers on Fire Precaution matters on request. No charge is made.

FIRE PREVENTION LEGISLATION.—Legislation is primarily concerned with ensuring adequate means of escape and giving an alarm in case of fire, in places of work and in buildings in use by the general public. Factories, offices, shops and hotels used by the public over a specified occupancy figure are required to have a certificate from the fire authority, certifying that the means of escape and other fire precautions are satisfactory. Generally speaking the requirement to hold a fire certificate is governed by the number of persons employed or the number of persons using the building.

The primary fire prevention legislation in the United Kingdom dealing with general fire precautions is contained in the Fire Precautions Act 1971. Other legislation having a bearing on fire safety is listed below. These Acts of Parliament contain a fire safety requirement. Local County Council Acts of Parliament also contain some fire safety provisions. Check with the appropriate County or Metropolitan County Council.

Licensing Act 1964—All premises selling intoxicating liquor.
Gaming Act 1968—All gaming and bingo premises.
Betting, Gaming and Lotteries Act 1963—Betting shops.
Caravan Sites and Control of Development Act 1960—All caravan sites.
Children and Young Persons Acts—Homes where they are in care.
Cinematograph Acts 1909 and 1962—All cinemas (not clubs).
Consumer Protection Act 1961 and Consumer Safety Act 1978—General public.
Education Act 1944—Local authority and private schools.
Explosives Act 1875—Regulating and Licensing of Stores.
Housing Acts 1961, 1969 and 1980—Houses in multiple occupancies.
Mental Health Act 1959—Mental hospitals and homes.
National Assistance Act 1948—Old Person's Homes.
Nurseries and Childminders Act 1948—Nurseries and Homes.
Nursing Homes Acts 1963 and 1975—Private and Public Nursing Homes.
Petroleum Consolidation Acts 1928 and 1936—Storage and transport of petrol.
Private Places of Entertainment Act 1967—Private Clubs, etc.
Public Health Act 1936—High buildings and buildings used by the public.
Animal Boarding Establishments Act 1963—Safety of animals boarded out.
Pet Animals Act 1951—Safety of animals for sale or on display.
Riding Establishments Act 1964 (and Amendment 1970)—Horse riding establishments.
Child Care Act 1980 and Children's Homes Act 1982—Regulations of children's homes.
Residential Homes Act 1980—Registration of homes for the disabled, the elderly and the mentally disordered.

BUILDING REGULATIONS

Building regulations apply to new or altered buildings and where there is a 'change of use' in an existing building.

STRUCTURAL FIRE PRECAUTIONS.—The Building Act 1984 came into operation on 11 November 1985. It consists of the Manual to the Building Regulations 1985, Mandatory rules for means of escape in case of fire and 12 approved documents. The most important, as far as the Fire Service is concerned, is approved document B Fire Spread.

BASIC PRINCIPLES.—The regulations are made to safeguard public health and safety including the risk from fire and are aimed at limiting the spread of fire either within a building or from one building to another. The risk of spread depends on:

(*a*) The use of the building;
(*b*) The fire resistance of elements of structure and the resistance of surface finishes to the spread of flame;
(*c*) The size of the building or compartments;
(*d*) The degree of space or structural separation between buildings or parts of buildings.

These four risks are recognised as follows.

(a) Use of Building.—All building or compartments are classified in purpose groups according to the use to which they are put. The operation of the regulations may be more or less stringent according to the classification, eg Group II includes buildings such as hospitals, old persons and young childrens homes, where, due to the occupancy characteristics, life risk is high, although fire loading can usually be expected to be low. In this grouping therefore, the regulations strictly control fire spread within the building and require only a moderate fire resistance in elements of structure, eg one hour fire resistance in the majority of cases.

(b) Fire Resistance and Surface Spread of Flame.—Requirements as to the periods of fire resistance are given in the Building Regulations. BS 476 Part 8 gives the method of test by which the fire resistance is measured and vary according to the 'purpose group', size and height of the building. Surface Spread of Flame requirements are also in the Regulations and BS 476 Part 7 gives the method of surface spread of flame tests for materials.

(c) Size of Building.—The maximum size of buildings or compartment of a building is controlled according to its 'purpose group' and is limited by imposing maximum compartment sizes. Vertical and horizontal shafts or openings between or passing through compartments must be fire protected or fire separated according to the type, size of buildings, fire resistance and other factors in the regulations which are all inter-related.

(d) Degree of Separation.—The degree of space or structual separation between buildings or compartments is imposed in relation to the fire resistance of external walls, separating walls, compartment walls and floors and roof classifications.

(e) Precautions against fire in high buildings.—BS Code of Practice CP3: Chapter (IV) (1948) has been replaced by the following.—

Dwelling Houses.—British Standard 5588 Fire Precautions in the design and construction of buildings section 1.1:1984 code of practice for single family dwellings.

Flats.—British Standard code of practice CP 3 code of basic data for the design of buildings, Chapter IV. Precautions against fire Part I: 1971 Flats and maisonettes (in blocks over two storeys).

Shops.—British Standard 5588 Fire Precautions in the design and construction of buildings, Part 2: 1985 code of practice for shops.

Offices.—British Standard 5588 Fire Precautions in the design and construction of buildings, Part 3: 1983 code of practice for office buildings.

References include the recent Home Office Circular. 'New arrangements for Building Control' and 'New British Standards', also the D of E Circular (DOE 22/85: WO 53/85) which includes reference to the (Approved Inspectors etc) Regulations 1985.

STRUCTURAL FIRE PROTECTION

Modern buildings are subjected to controls which are designed to retard the spread of fire both within them and between them.

British Standard 476 Part 3 is applicable to materials and structures used in buildings and tests are carried out by the Fire Insurers Research and Testing Organization. The full title is "Fire Tests on Building Materials and Structures" and is in 6 parts: Part 3 'External fire exposure roof tests', Part 4 'Non-combustibility test for materials', Part 5 'Ignitability', Part 6 'Fire propagation test for materials', Part 7 'Surface spread of flame tests for materials', Part 8 'Test materials and criteria for the fire resistance of elements of building construction'.

Elements of Structure.—Each element of structure (ie building frame, floor, wall, shaft or stairway enclosure) has an inherent degree of fire resistance, the grading of which depends upon, amongst other things, its constituent parts, its thickness and its construction. Grades of fire resistance for elements are contained in BS 476 Part 8 'Fire Resistance of Elements of Building Construction'. An element of structure may consist of one or more building components. National periods of fire resistance for elements of structure is given in the Building Regulations when tested in accordance with BS 476 Part 8.

Shafts.—Details of fire resisting construction for enclosing shaft walls of stairways, goods and passenger lifts and hoists are set out in the Building Regulations but in general, stairways shafts and access shafts for fire fighting should have a fire resistance not less than that of the building in which they are contained.

Doors.—There are many types of construction for fire resisting doors, eg (1) Metal cored, ie core of flanged steel strips interlocked and sheathed with 3 mm asbestos millboard, then covered overall with thin steel plate, giving 4 hours' fire resistance. (2) Core of teak or yellow pine boards creosoted and sheathed with sheet steel or iron sheets lock jointed giving 2 hours' fire resistance. Many are now 'custom made'.

It is essential that the frames are of a material having at least the same fire resistance as the doors.

Special attention should be given to the fitting of the doors to prevent the passage of flame and smoke around the edges. Poor workmanship seriously affects fire resistance.

The maximum opening which can be effectively protected by a fire resisting door is considered to be 5·2 m^2 provided that the specifications of the door(s) and frame(s) conform to the Rules of the Fire Offices Committee.

All fire resisting doors which cannot be kept locked shut should be rendered self closing.

BS 459 1951 Part 3 specifies the construction of ½ hour and 1 hour fire check doors and frames.

The Building Regulations specify fire resistance of doors and their positioning.

Glazing.—The British Standard Code of Practice CP 153 Part 4 recommends the following types and areas of glazing and associated frames and for the positioning of glazing in internal and external walls for fire resistance purposes:

(1) Wire in glass in panes, 6 mm thick and not exceeding 1·2 m^2 in area.
(2) Copper light glazing with unwired glass 6 mm thick with the individual panes not exceeding 0·015 m^2 in area. Panels of copper lights should not exceed 0·4 m^2 in area but composite panels may be assembled by the use of metal dividing bars.
(3) Single vision panels in fire resisting doors of unwired glass at least 6 mm thick and not exceeding 0·065 m^2 in area.
(4) Special glazing passing British Standard Tests 476 part 8 for stability, integrity and insulation for up to 60 minutes with glass panel sizes up to 1,983 mm by 800 mm.

The determination of the melting and ignition temperatures of plastics used as roof lights, wall and ceiling linings is referred to in BS 2782.

Fire Retardant Paints and Solutions.—Modern fire retardants for use on timber etc are of two main groups, those applied during production and those for surface applications of elements *in situ*. Impregnation is carried out with water soluble salts such as ammonium phosphate, monoammonium phosphate, ammonium sulphate, ammonium or zinc chloride or phosphoric acid which give an improved surface spread of flame rating. Surface coatings are usually flat paints and can provide coatings which intumesce on exposure to flame while others contain soluble silicate which improve the surface spread of flame rating. The intumescent type of coating also improves the fire resistance of the timber so treated.

FIRE PREVENTION ON SHIPS

Fire Prevention at Sea.—Uniform measures established by international agreement for prevention, detection and extinction of fires in cargo and passenger ships are contained in a Convention.

The 1960 International Convention for the Safety of Life at Sea, is now obsolete and has been replaced by the 1974 International Convention for the Safety of Life at Sea. The regulations annexed to the Convention have been amended in 1978, 1981 and 1983. Copies of these publications are available from HMSO or the International Maritime Organisation.

M Notices are now available from the Department of Transport or HMSO. M Notices 268, 516 and 527 are obsolete and no longer available. Fire Prevention M Notices current on 30 April 1985 are 852; 765; 694; 528; 1075; 393; 709; 1090; 764; 1117; 681; 825; 1118; 946; 1136; 443; 651; 750; 1022; 707; 984; 986; 750; 782; 957.

The Statutory Instrument 1965 No 1106, has been replaced by Statutory Instrument 1980 No 544, Statutory Instrument 1981 No 574 and Statutory Instrument 1985 No 1194.

FIRE PROTECTION OF BUILDINGS

(a) Fixed Fire Fighting Installations.—This heading refers to the wide variety of equipment fitted in buildings which, on the outbreak of a fire, automatically detects the fire and allows an appropriate extinguishing medium to be applied. At the same time, through an electronic relay a warning system may be sounded indicating that an automatic fire extinguishing system is operating. Arrangements can be made for the audible warning associated with this system to operate external to the protected machine or building, in a place where it can be continually monitored, such as a works gate-house, a control room, an alarm signalling centre or the Control Room of the works or the local authority fire brigade.

The more common types of automatic systems are:

(i) Sprinkler and drencher systems, designed to discharge water in the form of a dense spray over the protected area. Water drenchers can also be fitted external to buildings to protect the premises from adjacent fire risks. Systems can be maintained as 'wet' or 'dry' systems, depending on climatic conditions, eg a 'dry' system would be situated in premises prone to frost. All the systems usually have a dual water supply, such as town mains plus a pressure tank. FOC rules and BS 5306 lay down strict standards of installation and water supplies.

(ii) Foam generating systems. These can use either a liquid foam solution or a two-powder solution, the powders being brought together at the point of mixing with water and being aerated. These installations are found on chemical plants, highly flammable liquid tanks and certain processing plants where there is a major flammable liquid risk.

(iii) Dry or wet risers. These are vertical pipes up the face or stair-well of a building with valved fire brigade outlets at each upper floor level and, in the case of a wet riser, fitted to a pressure water supply and, in the case of a dry riser, having a fire brigade inlet at ground level to which hoses can be connected.

(iv) Dry powder or inert gas flooding systems. These will be found protecting spraying booths, gantries and loading bays of flammable liquids, some storage areas, basements, in fact any installation where sudden outbreak requires an equally swift response in extinguishment. The gases usually used are Halon 1211, Halon 1301, CO_2, CB or BCF. The choice of system would depend on the risk. These systems must conform to BS 5306 and in the case of sprinkler installations, with the very comprehensive rules of the Fire Offices Committee for Automatic Sprinkler Installations, available from the Fire Offices Committee, Aldermary House, Queen Street, London EC4P 4JD.

(b) Automatic Fire Detection/Alarm Systems.—There has over the last few years been a major growth in the range of types and method of operation of automatic fire alarm systems. As with intruder alarm systems, microchip technology and microcomputer technology has made a tremendous impact.

There are five main functions of any AFA system:

(i) To detect the outbreak of fire or the condition leading to a likely outbreak. Detector types include smoke detection by obscuration or ionisation, heat detection by preset heat operated switches using bimetallic strips, vacuum chambers, heat sensitive resistors. Light sensitive systems such as photo telemetry and low temperature fuses. Many detectors combine a number of different principles of operation.

(ii) To give a warning of the outbreak of fire to people resorting in the building. By the provision of relays which, depending on the requirement would simply indicate a visual warning or an audible warning either at the monitoring station or throughout a building as the case may be.

(iii) To bring into operation an extinguishing system if so provided under certain conditions (ie not allowed in places of public resort or in certain places of work).

(iv) To give an alarm to a point from which outside support may be forthcoming, ie the county Fire Control of the local authority fire brigade, a works fire brigade Control Room, a building services Control Room or a commercial alarm switching centre.

(v) To indicate to an appropriate centre that the system has a defect. Some systems are now sufficiently sophisticated to indicate the type and location of the defect.

A new and interesting development is the continuous monitoring of electrical circuits of a system by a computer to continually read out conditions prevailing and report any changes in those conditions as they occur. This new development will considerably reduce the incidence of false calls compared to those of genuine calls, currently the ratio of 40 to 1.

(c) Portable Firefighting Equipment.—First aid firefighting precautions include the provision of firefighting equipment designed to be used by people resorting to or working in a building in the initial stages of a fire. Equipment includes portable fire extinguishers, water or sand in buckets or special containers, glass fibre or woollen fire blankets in suitable containers, hose reels, and exceptionally in larger buildings flaked lengths of hose in cradles connected direct to valved water supplies.

(d) Manual Alarm Systems.—Current fire safety standards require many places of work or of public resort to have installed facilities whereby in the event of the outbreak of fire an alarm can be sounded simultaneously throughout the building. These manual systems must have a power supply independent of the normal supply to the building (ie batteries). These systems usually consist of 'break glass' alarms located on exit routes from buildings. The actual alarm itself can be bells, siren, hooters etc. BS 5839 Part 1 1980 gives acceptable standards for the design of fire detection and alarm systems in buildings.

PORTABLE FIRE EXTINGUISHERS

A great number of portable extinguishers of various types and designs are in use today, but in general they are covered by the following four categories:

(1) Those expelling water or dilute chemical solutions.
(2) Those expelling foam.

(3) Those expelling gas or vapour forming liquid.
(4) Those expelling dry powder.

These extinguishers have been developed to combat specific types of fires and when providing extinguishers it is essential that the correct type of appliance to deal with the risk should be obtained. Some of the dry powders used in extinguishers are claimed to be all purpose extinguishers, negating the need for different types in different locations.

The BSI has defined a portable fire extinguisher as a first aid fire fighting appliance which can be carried by hand. BS 5423 has been issued for portable extinguishers in 5 parts, namely.—

(1) For water type (soda acid); for water type (gas pressure) and for water type (stored pressure).
(2) Chemical foam extinguishers; gas expelled foam extinguisher.
(3) Halogenated hydrocarbon extinguishers.
(4) Carbon dioxide (CO_2) extinguishers.
(5) Dry powder type extinguishers.

BS 5306 Part 3 1980 deals with the general considerations, siting, suitability, distribution, inspection and maintenance, periodical testing by discharge and recharging as applicable to portable extinguishers for building and plant. More detailed advice on the matter is given in BS 5306 and the guides to the Fire Precautions Act and Portable Fire Extinguishing Appliances Booklet No 6 published by the Fire Protection Association.

The Fire Officers Committee (FOC) has adopted these standards and strict compliance with FOC Rules and Regulations is essential in the equipment installed in industrial and commercial premises in order to qualify them for rebates on premiums or (Tariff) Fire Insurance Policies.

The provisions of fire extinguishers for installation on marine passenger carrying vessels is governed by the Merchant Shipping (Fire Appliances) Rules, Statutory Instrument 1980 No 544, Statutory Instrument 1981 No 574 and Statutory Instrument 1985 No 1194.

The essential requirements to be noted in the BS specifications are:

(*a*) Regulation markings.
(*b*) Standard tests.
(*c*) Capacity and expansion space.
(*d*) Nature of dynamic or chemical charge.
(*e*) Method of actuation.
(*f*) Velocity and throw of jet.
(*g*) Materials, dimensions and construction.

The regulation markings to be indelibly printed or etched on the exterior of a liquid type extinguisher operated by gas or air pressure are as follows:

(*a*) A declaration that it has been tested by internal hydraulic pressure to 24 bar for a continuous period of 2½ min without leakage or visible distortion.
(*b*) Its liquid charge capacity.
(*c*) The name and address of the manufacturer or responsible vendor.
(*d*) The year of manufacture.
(*e*) The type of extinguisher.
(*f*) The liquid level to which the extinguisher should be charged.
(*g*) The number of the British Standard with which it conforms.
(*h*) Any relevant instructions regarding actuation or recharging.

The capacity of types (1) and (2) shall not be less than 4·5 and not more than 9 litres and type (4) shall be manufactured in 5 standard sizes holding 0·5 litres, 1 litre, 2·5 litres, 4·5 litres or 9 litres respectively. The expansion space in a gas pressure type liquid extinguisher shall be of sufficient volume to ensure that when the discharge nozzle is temporarily closed and the extinguisher is put into operation at a temperature of 21°C the pressure exerted shall not exceed 17 bar.

There are fundamental differences in the effect of the types of extinguishers named on different classes of fires, resulting from differences in the extinguishing media and differences in the dynamic or chemical charges, but different methods adopted for actuating a given type of extinguisher do not affect in any way the working efficiency of that type but only the manner of operating it. Chemical hand extinguisher bodies are now being manufactured with a plastic lining and discharge tube: this considerably reduced internal corrosion.

Soda Acid Extinguishers (Type 1).—Soda acid extinguishers discharge a dilute alkaline solution resulting from the chemical action of an acid in conjunction with a carbonate and/or bicarbonate solution. The proportion of acid to alkali in the chemical charge varies to some extent for different makes of extinguisher but a standard commonly recognised for an extinguisher of 9 litres capacity is 70 ml sulphuric acid (H_2SO_4) strength 78% to 0·5 kg bicarbonate of soda.

The soda acid type of extinguisher may be operated by breaking a hermetically sealed bottle containing an acid and thereby permitting the acid to come in contact with the carbonate or bicarbonate solution, or, by turning over the extinguisher, the acid bottle being tipped thereby spilling the acid into the carbonate or bicarbonate solution. Operation may alternatively be performed by striking a knob on the extinguisher or by a blow on its side. This type whilst generally known as a chemical extinguisher is so only in the sense of producing by chemical reaction the pressure required to expel the liquid contents. Chemicals employed for this purpose have no value as fire extinguishing media, for in properly proportioned charges the acid/alkali reaction produces a neutral weak dilute solution. These extinguishers have, in the main, been replaced by water (gas pressure) type.

Water (Gas Pressure) Extinguishers (Type 1).—Water type (gas pressure) extinguishers discharge water at high pressure exerted by the expellation of a compressed gas, usually CO_2 from liquified formation to atmospheric formation upon release from a small disc sealed cylinder (alternatively cartridge or capsule). In a typical extinguisher of this type of 9 litre capacity, the liquified CO_2 has been compressed to 60 bar in a cartridge 230 × 25 mm in diameter and will on release expand to 330 mm at atmospheric pressure and temperature. This is 450 times its original volume when liquified and equal to 2¼ times the capacity of the water container in which the expansion occurs, hence the high velocity of water upon discharge. This type of extinguisher is usually operated by striking a knob on the head cap, the knob being connected to a piercing pin which pierces the sealing disc of the gas cartridge. In a more recent type of water extinguisher known as the 'stored pressure' type, air is compressed into the water container by hand or foot pump or mechanical compressor.

Foam Extinguishers (Type 2).—Foam extinguishers discharge a closely knit stream of cohesive bubbles of gas formed by chemical action of an acid which is stored in an inner receptacle in conjunction with an alkaline carbonate or bicarbonate solution, in combination with a stabiliser, stored in the outer container of the extinguisher. The function of the stabiliser is to affect the surface tension of bubbles resulting from the conjunction of the two solutions so as to provide a cohesive wall structure for each bubble, thereby permitting expansion of the gas therein to its normal capacity at any temperature without causing the bubbles to burst, as they otherwise would. The expansion of these bubbles creates a pressure within the extinguisher whereby a stream is propelled a distance of upwards of 6 m in a specified period of time. In the case of a 9 litre extinguisher this is from 30 to 90 seconds according to the prevailing temperature conditions. The lower the temperature, the slower the reaction, which becomes nil at temperatures close to freezing point.

In an alternative method of expelling foam liquid the container is filled to the correct level with a solution which is expelled by carbon dioxide gas from a cartridge or cylinder which is placed inside the body in a similar way to that used in water gas pressure extinguishers. The solution is aerated at the discharge nozzle. The average rate of expansion of the solution to produce the foam is 8 to 1 at a temperature of 10°C extinguishers should not be exposed to frost and preferably placed where the temperature does not fall below 10°C.

The foam (chemical mixtures) type extinguisher may be actuated by conjoining the inner and outer solution in one of the following ways:

(*a*) by turning over the extinguisher;
(*b*) by unlocking or piercing a sealing device and turning over the extinguisher, or turning over the extinguisher otherwise, causing a hermetically sealed bottle containing the inner solution to be broken.
The gas pressure type of foam extinguisher may be actuated by:
(*i*) turning the extinguisher over.
(*ii*) releasing or piercing the sealing device.
(*iii*) by releasing or piercing the sealing device and maintaining the extinguisher upright.

Chlorobromomethane Extinguishers (CH_2ClBr).—These extinguishers, commonly referred to as CB or CBM are now banned and any still found in use should be replaced and returned to the manufacture.

Bromochlorodifluoromethane Extinguishers (CF_2BrCl) (Type 3).—(commonly referred to as BCF or halon 1211) is a heavy colourless non flammable gas at normal temperatures. The gas is about 5·3 times as heavy as air and when cool condenses to a liquid with a boiling point of −4°C. It is also liquified by pressure and it is as a liquid under pressure used as a fire extinguishing medium. The liquid has a specific gravity of 1·83 at 20°C. Because of its toxic properties it should not be used where there is any risk of its vapours or those of the decomposition products being inhaled. Extinguishers containing BCF are available in 350 gm, 3 kg, 5 kg and 11·5 kg sizes.

Carbon Dioxide Extinguishers (Type 4).—Carbon dioxide extinguishers consist of a standard CO_2 cylinder (BS 401 or BS 1288) with CO_2 capacity of 2½ (1·1 kg), 5 (2·2 kg), 7 (3·1 kg), 10 (4·5 kg) and 15 lb (7 kg) fitted with a syphon tube large valve opening, quick opening valve, nonfreezing nozzle and conical entrainment shield to limit the amount of air entrained by the CO_2 at the point of discharge. These are charged with liquified CO_2 which on rapid release is particularly effective in dealing with electrical hazards and flammable liquids. The method of operation of CO_2 extinguishers is by releasing or piercing a sealing device and keeping the extinguisher reasonably upright.

Dry Powder Extinguishers (Type 5).—The extinguishing medium of these appliances consists of a finely divided powder usually sodium of potassium bicarbonate with agents designed to ensure free flowing non-caking and non-moisture absorbing properties.

The powder is contained within the extinguisher body constructed of either metal or plastic and expelled by the release of CO_2 from a small pressure vessel into the extinguisher. The powder can be discharged through a discharge hose and a hand controlled nozzle or in the case of the smaller extinguishers, directly from a discharge orifice set into the extinguisher body. Dry powder extinguishers have gained in popularity in recent years. They are 'all purpose' in that they are effective in all classes of fire. Special powders are also available for use in combating fires involving the hazardous metals—magnesium, sodium, potassium, etc.

The effects of water type 1 when discharged upon materials in combustion are:

(*a*) to cool them so that flammable gases are no longer given off;
(*b*) to damp them so that the vapour (steam) may arise to assist in their extinction by smothering; and,
(*c*) by a forcible jet of water to reach the seat of the fire.

Type 2 when used on fires involving flammable liquids blankets the surface of the liquid, creating a barrier:

(*a*) between the oxygen in the atmosphere; and,
(*b*) between the heat of the burning gaseous vapour and the liquid fuel from which the vapour is produced.

Types 3 and 4 act on a different principle. They have no appreciable cooling or damping effect nor do they rely on a forcible jet, but smother combustion by the exclusion of oxygen and in the case of type 3 by an inhibiting action on the fire reaction taking place. Type 5 has a smothering effect and with certain powders, a solid is formed, securely enclosing the burning material.

FIRE HOSE

The hose used by fire brigades is of 45, 70 or 90 mm internal diameter and is suitable for use at working pressures of up to 10 bar. Mixtures of cotton or flax and synthetic fibres or synthetic fibres alone are now in general use for the jackets of fire hose onto which it is now usual to fit an internal impervious lining. Plastic impregnated extruded hoses are also now available and are being increasingly used.

Hose is generally lined to provide a smooth internal surface, so reducing friction to the water passing through and to prevent water seepage inside a building. The loss of pressure due to friction in delivering 450 litres/min through a 25 m length of 65 mm rubber hose is approximately 0·2 bar. Through 300 m of hose the friction loss is therefore approximately 2–3 bars. Assuming the pressure available at the pump to be 8–10 bar there would be around 7 bar available at the jet.

In order to reduce friction loss where large quantities of water must be pumped through hose over considerable distances, twin lines of hose need to be laid out and several pumps arranged along the line in relay to maintain adequate working pressure.

National standards are laid down covering the general characteristics of good hose in the Specification issued by the Joint Committee on Design and Development of Appliances and Equipment of the Central Fire Brigades Advisory Council.

Fire Hose Couplings—BS 336 1980 gives full details of the dimensions of instantaneous Fire Hose Couplings as used by all the Fire Authorities in the UK. These couplings are manufactured in light alloy and also in gunmetal.

INDUSTRIAL HAZARDS

NITRATE BATHS.—These present a serious risk of explosion and fire. The baths should be constructed of steel of low carbon content and be placed on a non-combustible base, in a well ventilated and fire resisting building. A catch pit should be provided of sufficient capacity to contain the whole of the contents should a fracture of the bath occur. The interior of the pit should be kept clean and dry and the bath provided with a steel lid capable of being quickly closed down. Normal operating temperature for nitrate baths is 500–600°C.

The bath should be cleaned every 7–14 days and daily whenever metal with magnesium content is being treated, and foreign matters should be removed. The bath should be emptied every six months and examined for pitting and corrosion. Electric heating is preferable but where heating is by flame, the flame must not come into contact with the contents, heating must be carefully controlled as nitrates begin to decompose at about 600°C and above this temperature the reaction can be violently explosive. Articles to be treated must be dry and free from grease. As water boils at 100°C and expands 1,700 times its volume when turning to steam, no water must be near the baths. In workshops where nitrate baths are situated, the installation of any type of water extinguisher should be prohibited. Dry powder is the only satisfactory extinguisher agent for nitrate fires. Dry sand may be used to dam the flow of the escaping molten nitrate. Further information is given in a memorandum issued by the Health and Safety Executive, Safety Health and Welfare Booklet No 27 entitled Precautions in the Use of Nitrate Salt Baths (HMSO).

CYANIDE CASE HARDENING.—Hot molten cyanides used for case hardening processes present serious risks. Fire and explosion may be brought about by the following conditions:

(1) Immersing damp components in the molten liquid.
(2) Failure of the bath allowing molten liquid to leak onto other materials.
(3) Accidental mixing of molten cyanide and nitrate salts.

At fires involving cyanide, prussic acid fumes may be evolved and breathing apparatus must be worn by firemen. Cyanide solutions are harmful to the skin by absorbtion and rubber boots and gloves should be worn. The most suitable extinguishing and damming agent is dry sand.

All such baths should be provided with a steel cover capable of being quickly closed down. Further information on the precautions necessary in connection with cyanide baths is given in the Health and Safety Executive Form 850 Memorandum on the Use of Cyanide Compounds for the Treatment of Steel and Form 385 Precautions in the Use of Cyanide Poisons (HMSO). Normal temperature for cyanide baths is 800–900°C.

DISSOLVED ACETYLENE CYLINDERS.—These become dangerous when heated as the result of being involved in a fire, as the result of a backfire, careless handling or the decomposition of acetylene and acetylene solvent contained in the cylinder. Once decomposition within the cylinder has begun the most effective action is to turn off the cylinder valve whenever possible and cool the cylinder with copious supplies of water in the form of a spray, leaving the cylinder in position until it is cooled sufficiently when it should be immersed in water for at least 12 hours. Treat the cylinder as an explosive missile and keep people as far away as possible. Notify the Police and Fire Brigade immediately.

FLAMMABLE and DANGEROUS METALS.—The machining of light alloys especially those containing magnesium presents fire risks because of the flammability of the resultant swarf and dust. The main precautions to be observed are as follows:

(*a*) the machines and surrounding to be kept dry;
(*b*) strict cleanliness around machines. Dust and swarf should be removed frequently and kept in safe receptacles away from the production materials and not allowed to accumulate;
(*c*) tools should be kept sharp, as blunt tools are frequently a cause of friction and sparks;
(*d*) water must not be used for extinguishing purposes.
(*e*) powdered talc, rock dust and dry sand in plentiful quantities are the only safe extinguishing agents for metal swarf and powders. Further information on the hazards and precautions necessary in connection with light alloy dust is given by the Department of Energy (Research Report No 3) and Department of Employment (Forms 830 and 896).

Metal Fires.—Metals normally accepted as non-combustible and associated with everyday life are frequently readily combustible at high temperatures or in finely divided form. Causes of fire include:

(*a*) Metallic spark from ferrous metals.
(*b*) 'Pyrophoric' or self-heating properties of certain metals where in given temperature and humidity conditions, experience a rise in temperature by rapid oxidation.
(*c*) The ability of 'alkali metals' to chemically react in contact with water, or in some cases, with air.

Aluminium.—Gives off hydrogen when in contact with solutions of potassium hydroxide or sodium hydroxide. Can ignite spontaneously in contact with sodium peroxide.

Beryllium.—Gives off hydrogen in contact with water. Is highly toxic.

Brass.—Reacts with oxidising agents.

Cadmium.—Reacts vigorously with oxidising agents. Emits poisonous fumes when heated.

Caesium.—Reacts with oxidising agents. Can ignite spontaneously in moist air.

Cobalt.—Can be ignited by heat or flame. In finely divided form will heat and ignite by chemical reaction.

Iron.—Iron pyrites present a spontaneous heating risk.

Lead.—Reacts violently with oxidising agents.

Lithium.—Fire hazard if exposed to heat or flame. Reacts violently with water, acids or oxidising agents. Will explode by chemical reaction.

Magnesium.—Readily ignitable in fine form. Reacts with water when heated.

Manganese.—Decomposes water. Dissolves in dilute acids. Reacts with oxidising agent.

Potassium.—Very dangerous fire hazard. Reacts violently with all moisture, producing heat. Also with oxidising agents. Forms explosive compound with carbon dioxide.

Sodium.—Very reactive. Ignites in air if heated. Will decompose violently with oxidising agents. Reacts with halogens, acids and hydrocarbons. Has violent reaction with carbon dioxide and water.

Titanium.—Easily ignited in chips or dust form. Has been known to ignite spontaneously with oil.

Zirconium.—Similar to titanium, but fire and explosion hazard more severe.

Metal fires are difficult to extinguish. They should be allowed to burn out if possible. In the great majority of industrial fires it will be necessary to apply the correct extinguishing technique to the burning metal. Suitable agents include powdered graphite, talc, soda ash, limestone and dry sand. All work by smothering.

ANIMAL AND VEGETABLE OILS.—These oils are those classed as fatty oils of animal or vegetable origin. Animal fatty oils include cod liver oil, lard oil, menhaden (fish) oil and whale oil. Vegetable fatty oils include castor oil, ground nut oil, olive oil, palm oil and rapeseed oil (all non-drying oils), cottonseed oil and maize oil (semi-drying) and linseed oil, soya bean oil and tung oil (drying oils).

Drying oils have a strong tendency to absorb oxygen and therefore a tendency to self-heat. In many industrial processes in which fatty oils are employed they are mixed with solvents which, unlike the addition of mineral oils, effect a sharp reduction in the flash point of the mixture and thus increase considerably its fire hazard.

There is a severe spontaneous ignition hazard attached to fatty oils, particularly those referred to as 'drying oils'.

The correct fire fighting medium for use on all oils is foam. The application of water is liable to produce reactions of explosive violence, the instant evaporation of the water into steam with the consequence of rapid expansion being liable to throw quantities of burning oil in all directions.

FIRE INVOLVING PLASTICS.—The growth in the use of plastics over the last 20 years has been phenomenal and with that growth the introduction of a new kind of fire hazard. Whilst many plastics are, to all intents and purposes, non-combustible or have slow burning rates, the materials used are in many cases of higher fire and explosion hazard than the end product and give off extremely dangerous fumes (the products of decomposition) when involved in fire.

Plastics comprise organic materials, chiefly carbon in combination with other chemicals such as hydrogen, oxygen and nitrogen. They are either semi-synthetic in origin, these mainly being from the cellulose derivatives or synthetic in origin, these mostly being the polyester, polystyrene or polyvinyl derivatives. Plastics are either thermosetting (those which are plastic during the process of manufacture and on being heated become permanently set on reaching quite moderate temperatures) or thermoplastic (being of such a composition that they may be softened on heating and hardened on cooling as often as may be desired).

When dealing with fires involving plastics the toxic hazards of the process of combustion should be noted. In general, fires involving plastics can be adequately dealt with by water. In the plastics manufacturing industries, substantial quantities of flammable liquids are likely to be involved, such as analine, styrene or ethylene. Invariably foam will be required on such fires, however small fires will usually respond to the use of water in a form of spray or the use of carbon dioxide or dry powder.

FIRES INVOLVING FUELS.—This brief chapter does not attempt to cover all the known fire risks of fuels. Some are so well known they do not require specific mention. Fuels treated in this section are solid fuels such as coal, coke and wood, heavy oils, vehicle fuels and liquified petroleum gases.

(*a*) **Coal, Coke and Wood Fuels.**—Stored coal, whether in a small layer or a large stack will oxidise and self-heat. To prevent ignition coal stacks should be kept under water or some other way designed to keep out air. Alternatively sufficient ventilation should be provided to carry off heat as fast as it is generated. Stacks should be checked regularly for temperature rise. Coke is normally unlikely to fire by spontaneous combustion. Timber is not subject to oxidisation but will readily ignite, particularly if in finely divided form. Hard woods are more difficult to ignite than soft woods.

(*b*) **Petrol and Fuel Oils.**—The main types of fuel referred to under this heading are paraffin hydrocarbons (petroleum derivatives) and aromatic hydrocarbons (coal tar derivatives). Petroleum products as a whole are classified according to flash point. Class A have a flash point below 23°C, Class B between 23°C and 66°C and Class C above 66°C. All those in Class A are defined as petroleum mixtures and are subjected to conditions of licence.

(*c*) **Liquified Petroleum Gases.**—This term refers to varieties of hydrocarbons derived from crude petroleum processes or from natural gas. LPG is a gas at normal temperature and pressure but becomes liquid with either a moderate increase in pressure or a moderate drop in temperature or both. Included in this list are propane, propylene, butane and iso-butane butylene. The more readily liquifiable gases of this group are commercial propane and commercial butane. However each may contain, in various amounts, several of the other hydrocarbons mentioned.

LPG's are odourless. A stenching agent is added to detect its presence, except where the intended use requires a gas free from odour, for example in the manufacture of aerosols. Butane is the LPG commonly used for domestic use in both lighting and heating. It is usually stored in light gauge steel bottles, the commonest type holding 14·52 kg. British Standard Code of Practice BC9 gives details on storage. Guidance on cylinder storage is given in Guidance Notes CS4 and CS8 published by the HSE and in Code of Practice No 7 published by the Liquefied Petroleum Gas Industries Technical Association (LPGITA).

LPG is also stored in large quantities at refineries and other major installations and distributing depots of the oil industry. Also at producer and holder stations of the Gas Board and premises of large industrial users. Containers are usually cylindrical (both vertical and horizontal) or spheres. Quantities in excess of three million litres in one container is not unusual. Catchment areas are provided to contain spillage and direct it away from the containers. Large tanks are protected by various types of automatic water spray installations. In the event of fire, every endeavour should be made to extinguish small leaks and turn off the source of supply. Large leaks should be allowed to burn until the source of supply has been turned off. Every endeavour should be made to ensure storage cylinders are not heated by any heat source. If there is a serious leak without ignition it should not be ignited but all possible steps taken to prevent ignition and disperse the gas safely. All vehicles and other engines should be stopped, electrical equipment should be switched off, fires extinguished and the use of other kinds of heating appliances should cease. Telephone or radio equipment should not be used unless flameproof. The leaking gas is heavier than air and so a careful check should be made at low level, including basements, water ditches and similar channels.

RADIOACTIVE MATERIALS.—The fact that a material is radioactive does not in itself increase the fire hazard of the material. The increased risk from dealing with fires involving radioactive materials emanates from the radioactivity given off which would consist of either alpha particles, beta particles or gamma rays. It is essential fire fighting is carried out within the limits of safety imposed by the degree of radiation. (For Radiation Hazards, see Health Physics p. F1/22.)

DUST EXPLOSIONS.—Term used to denote the very rapid propagation of flame which can occur when finely divided particles of a combustible solid are suspended in air or in a gas. It resembles an explosion, and is sufficient in power to raze a building to the ground. Dust explosions are common in grinding and pulverising mills—especially in dust extraction plants.

Usual causes are outside heat source, foreign body causing spark, heat from friction or overheated motor or static electricity.

Dusts are divided into three classes.

Class I.—Dusts which ignite and propagate flame readily, the source of heat required for ignition being small.

Aluminium	Cotton	Magnesium	Shellac
Bronze	Dextrene	Malt	Starch
Cellulose acetate	Ebonite	Paper	Sugar
Chicory	Ferromanganese	Phenolformaldehyde	Sulphur
Coal	Flax	Polythene	Tea
Cocoa	Flour	Potato	Titanium
Cork	Grass (dried)	Rice bran	Tobacco
Cornflour	Grains	Rubber	Wood dust

Class II.—Dusts which ignite readily but require a large source of ignition.

Barley	Herring meal	Prussian blue	Shoddy
Castor oil meal	Yellow meal	Seaweed	Steel grindings

Class III.—Dusts which do not ignite in the tests applied.

Bonemeal	Graphite	Mineral black	
Charcoal	Insect powder (pyrethrum)	Kelp	
Detergent powders	Ivory	Lamp black	Plumbago

EXPLOSIVES.—Every factory in which explosives are manufactured must be licensed by the Health and Safety Executive.

STORAGE OF EXPLOSIVES

Explosives may be stored in five different ways under existing legislation and the methods of storage are generally based on the quantity of explosives to be stored. The five methods of storage are as follows:—

(1) In a factory licensed by the Health and Safety Executive.

(2) In magazines licensed by the Health and Safety Executive. A magazine licence indicates the types and quantities of explosives which may be kept and lays down the distances which may be maintained by the magazine from certain buildings, roads, works etc.

(3) In stores licensed by the Local Authority under the Explosives Act 1875.

For quantities more than 30 kg but not exceeding 2000 kg of "blasting" explosives, application must be made to the County Council for a Store Licence for mixed explosives. Licensed stores are divided into five divisions, (A, B, C, D and E) depending upon the amount to be stored and the available distance from any "protected work".

The minimum distance from any store to a "protected work" must not be less than 23 m and in certain cases can be as far as 215 m.

(4) In premises registered with the Local Authority under the Explosives Act 1875 for quantites above 5 kg but not exceeding 30 kg, premises must be registered with the County Council. There are two modes of keeping "blasting" explosives in "registered" premises, depending upon the circumstances under which the storage is proposed.

MODE A up to 30 kg of "blasting" explosives.
MODE B up to 7 kg of "blasting" explosives.

(5) Explosives for private use and not for sale, explosives and detonators in quantities not more than those stated in the Police certificate and/or Police licence, but in no case may they exceed:—

a) For "blasting" explosives generally, 5 kg together with 100 detonators, or
b) for gunpowder 15 kg together with 100 detonators; or
c) for gunpowder and "blasting" explosive 15 kg gunpowder, but every 3 kg of gunpoweder not so kept, 1 kg of "blasting" explosive; together with 100 detonators.

Storgage under this heading requires the acquisition of a Police Licence or Certificate but does not require the premises to be licensed or registered.

For the purposes of the Explosives Act 1875 Order in Council divide explosives into seven classes.

Class 1	Gunpowder	(black powder, black blasting powder)
Class 2	Nitrate mixtures	(amatol, TNT – trinitrotoluene)
Class 3	Nitrate compounds	(dynamite, gelatines)
Class 4	Chlorate mixtures	(usually the salts of sodium or potassium)
Class 5	Fulminates	(Azides, styphnates, not explosive alone)
Class 6	Ammunition	
Class 7	Fireworks	

For fire fighting purposes on Ministry of Defence Establishments or property, explosives are divided into fire fighting divisions.

Division 1.1	Will explode en masse as soon as fire reaches them.
Division 2.2	Readily ignited. Burn with great violence without exploding.
Division 3.3	Do not explode en masse, even after exposure to fire for a considerable period of time.
Division 4.4	Explosives which present no significant hazard.

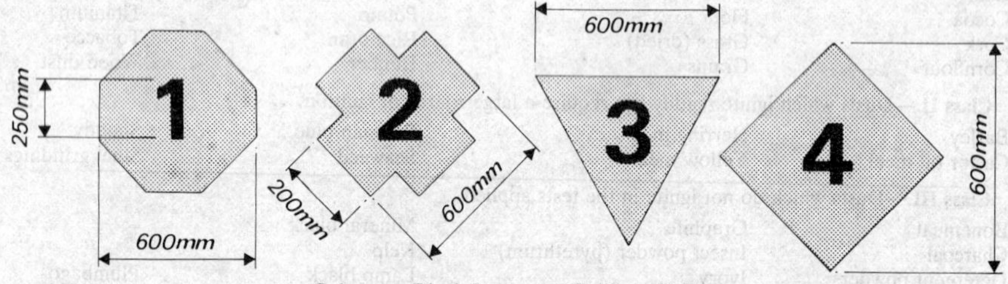

Colours.—Black Letters on Brilliant Yellow.
FIG. 1.—Fire Division Symbols (for use on Buildings or Stacks).

Symbols.—Stores may display a symbol to warn of hazardous contents (see Fig. 1). Symbols for road transport are shown in Fig. 2. Supplementary symbols advising the type of hazard are given in Fig. 3. They are printed in bright eye striking colours.

Colours.—Black Letters on Brilliant Yellow.
FIG. 2.—Fire Division Symbols (Road and Rail Transport).

CONVEYANCE OF DANGEROUS SUBSTANCES BY ROAD.—The Dangerous Substance (Conveyance by Road in Road Tankers and Tank Containers) Regulations 1981 came into operation on 1st January 1982. These replace the Hazardous Substances Regulations 1978.

The new regulations cover the movement of dangerous substances and require the vehicle carrying to display in the form of a hazardous warning sign, a U.N. identification number of the material, the emergency action to be taken in the event of a leak, fire or explosion (Hazechem), the name of the substance being carried and an emergency contact telephone number. The regulations also impose certain duties on operators and drivers. In the case of a multi-load, a hazard warning sign will only be permitted to be displayed if all the substances being carried are in the approved list.

The regulations impose a duty on the operators of the vehicle to obtain from the consignor of the substance information about the risks created by the load. The driver must have with him details of the product, its risks and the action he should take in an emergency.

FIG. 3.—Supplementary Fire Symbols.

Further regulations in respect of driver training and information came into operation on 1st January 1983. As from 1st January 1984 further regulations dealing with examination and testing of tanks will be introduced.

The Health & Safety Commission has issued a booklet entitled 'Approved Substance Identification Numbers, Emergency Action Codes and Classifications for Dangerous Substances conveyed in Road Tankers and Tank Containers as Amended from Time to Time'. The Chemical Industries Association Ltd., Alembic House, 93 Albert Embankment, London SE1 7TU will provide details about a voluntary scheme for the marking of vehicles conveying substances of low hazard. This is known as the "Black and White Marking Scheme".

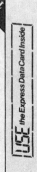

OCCUPATIONAL SAFETY AND PROTECTION

Safety Organisation—Accidents—Manual and Power Handling—Tools—Traffic—Machinery Guarding—Ladders—Lifts and Lifting Tackle—Stacking and Lifting—Electricity—Personal Safety and Equipment—Clothing—Dermatitis—Reading List

By RoSPA (The Royal Society for the Prevention of Accidents)
(Occupational Safety Division)

Early attempts to reduce the toll of industrial accidents originated from motives which were almost without exception humanitarian. The growth of the social problems engendered by industry led to a series of legal instruments empowering factory inspectors to enforce minimum standards of safety, as well as other measures affecting the well-being of factory workers. In the present century the culmination of these early statutes has been reached in The Health and Safety at Work Etc Act, 1974. Nowadays, too, the desire to reduce the numbers and lessen the effects of accidents at the work place is backed by a realisation that accidents cause needless waste of men, materials and time.

SAFETY ORGANISATION.—A sound safety organisation is necessary before work to reduce accidents can begin. The size of the department responsible for safety depends on the size of the plant and the nature of the process. No hard and fast rule can be laid down; the exigencies of the individual situation are the ruling factors in the number to be employed in the safety department.

The Safety Officer.—It is desirable that the safety officer should be responsible to the works manager and should not be concerned, primarily, with production. His status should be such that he may work on a similar plane to his administrative and executive colleagues. The safety officer's duties are most effectively performed if he functions in an advisory capacity. Safety on the shop floor rests with those who supervise the work in hand. A safety officer's responsibility, and that of his department, is to encourage designers, engineers, chemists, technicians and supervisors of all grades, to accept safe working as an essential principle affecting their respective jobs, besides influencing their approach to each safety problem.

Safety Representative.—Regulations which came into force on 1st October 1978, prescribe the cases in which recognised trade unions may appoint safety representatives and in which the employer shall establish a safety committee. The main theme of the regulations is consultation and communication right through the workplace. The principal duties of representatives are accident investigation, safety inspections, and safety complaints from their workgroup. Detailed explanation of the Safety Representatives and Safety Committees Regulations may be seen in RoSPA's publication 'Safety Reps'.

Safety Committees.—The Safety Committee composed of representatives of management, foremen and workers, has been found to be a useful adjunct to the implementation of a safety programme. The safety committee also serves to acquaint management with matters of safety from the shop floor. In the composition of a committee it is inadvisable to give workers less than equal representation with the management. In the majority of successful committees the workers predominate. Total membership is best limited to a maximum of 15. Three members is the smallest number for practical purposes. In large works the committee may prove more valuable if sectionalised by departments. Where Joint Consultation or other Works Committees exist they may usefully act as Safety Committees, so long as proper time for consideration of safety problems is allocated.

The works safety committee is not an alternative to a trained safety officer. A good safety committee can be of enormous help to the safety officer—especially in small works where the safety officer has to combine accident prevention with other duties—but it does not remove the need for the co-ordination of the safety effort by one person. Like the safety officer, the safety committee must act as an advisory body without executive powers.

Within the context of the Safety Representatives and Safety Committees Regulations, 'safety committee' has a legal connotation; a statutory safety committee is one set up in response to a written request from two or more union-appointed safety representatives and in consultation with the unions and with the safety representatives who asked for it. But the employer is then accorded the right to set up the committee as he thinks fit, and to appoint whatever people he considers suitable—there is no obligation to include safety representatives.

In establishments which have a mixed union/non-union workforce, the safety committee can provide the means for giving protection to groups of employees who are not entitled to statutory safety representation.

Management may decide that in the interests of good industrial relations it is worth consulting the recognised trade unions about the proposed measures to protect those groups.

Management Support.—The effort of the safety officer, the safety committee, and all those who implement their policies will be stultified if unqualified support for the principles of accident prevention is not provided by management. Management must always be ready to consider the suggestions of the safety officer or the safety committee and whenever necessary, allocate technical staff for the further study of safety problems in order to exercise the same control over accident producing conditions as is exercised over straightforward production methods. A fundamental task of the Safety Officer is to create the conviction amongst operatives that all management grades consider the production of safe working conditions and methods as vital to their work.

Implementing a Safety Programme.—The implementation of a safety programme where hitherto there has been none of the essential components mentioned above might well begin with a survey of the existing problems by specialist bodies competent to give advice and make recommendations on the subject. A good deal of published material on this subject is already available. The survey can be followed up by an intensive programme of publicity and safety education. This, coupled with a fundamental improvement in the general standard of works tidiness—usually termed 'industrial housekeeping'—would establish the conditions upon which a more developed safety programme can be maintained.

These are first steps, the logical development of which is a planned course of action which takes account of the special technical needs of the industry and makes thorough investigation of the causes of accidents followed by recommendations for remedial measures. Essential to the pursuit of this course of action are, 'frank studies and reports on the real basic causes of injuries; the support of the management and technical staff in reducing the technical causes of accidents to a minimum; proper safety training as part of the training for the job (not in most cases, special safety training); increased influence of joint safety committees; and a specialised service, particularly in larger industries, of propaganda, publicity or safety education designed specifically for the needs of the individual units.' (H. R. Payne: *Journal of the Royal Society of Arts*, 19th Sept. 1952, pp. 740–52).

Ideally, the safe operation of plant and machinery begins at the design stage of each item, whether a building, part of a building—such as a floor or staircase—a machine, or a complete process. Much of this work is capable of codification and there are in existence numerous examples of professional and trade organisations' work in this respect. These codes are to the advantage of designers, engineers, industrial chemists and operators alike.

ACCIDENTS.—On a percentage basis the causes of accidents follow a similar pattern year by year, as reference to the figures published annually by H.M. Chief Inspector of Factories shows. Approximate percentages are as follows: Handling goods 25%; Falls of persons 17%; Falls of objects 9%; Hand tools 7%; Transport 7%; Machinery 18%; Stepping on and striking against objects 8%; Others 9%. The causes of various accidents are briefly recorded below, together with some guidance on accident prevention.

ACCIDENT STATISTICS.—In Britain many firms measure their accident prevention performance by the frequency rate calculated from a formula originally used by the Royal Society for the Prevention of Accidents. The factors used are the number of man-hours worked and the number of lost-time accidents. The number of man hours means time worked, including overtime, by all employees except office staff and foremen. Lost time accidents are all accidental injuries involving absence from normal work beyond the day or shift on which they occur.

$$\text{Frequency Rate} = \frac{\text{Lost-time accidents} \times 100{,}000}{\text{man-hours worked}}$$

H.M. Chief Inspector of Factories in his Annual Report utilises the Incidence Rate in order to give a series of figures by which industries can compare their accident rate against the 'national average'. The factors used are the number of reported accidents per 100,000 employees.

$$\text{Incidence Rate} = \frac{\text{Number of reported accidents} \times 100{,}000}{\text{Number of employees}}$$

HANDLING GOODS.—(Man Handling)

Hands and arms.—Mainly due to splinters, punctures by sharp materials and nails; traps between goods or between goods and doorways or projections; cuts by sharp-edged goods, iron bands on bales or boxes, wires on packages. Prevention is mainly a matter of teaching the correct manner of grasping, carrying and placing, though many types of goods can be handled more safely if gloves or special holders are supplied, and in some cases alteration to packages is the proper solution, alertness of the worker is at all times a factor.

Back injuries and hernia.—Most back accidents are due to incorrect lifting, ie failure to take up such a position and use such a method that the weight of the object lifted moves smoothly over the muscles best fitted to support the strain without imposing a sudden load or jerk on any of them. Feet should be placed approximately 12 inches apart. The chin should be tucked in and the back kept straight. Hernia is only likely to be caused if a natural weakness exists and undue strain is put on the part.

FIG. 1.—Foot-operated Press Guard.

FIG. 2.—Electrically interlocked Milling Machine Guard.

A correct method of lifting is far more important in industry than great muscular strength. Mere weight is not always the determining factor. Bulk or awkward shape may make a comparatively light article dangerous to lift.

Feet.—Accidents are mostly due to dropping goods on feet. Also encountered in team lifting owing to a misunderstanding (see 'Team Lifting' below). Intelligent choice of method of holding awkward, slippery and ill-balanced objects is important; also in choosing a suitable place for putting down goods. Battens to raise objects above the floor are often useful and in many occupations safety footwear is invaluable.

Body and head.—Typical accidents are due to tools and materials falling from above, leaking acid or caustic overhead lines and valves, the carrying of containers without proper regard for their type or contents, and walking into projections.

Team lifting.—Awkward shaped or heavy objects can only be safely handled by a gang when one person in a position to see every movement gives orders, which are promptly and properly obeyed.

Hand trucks, sack barrows, etc.—Proper piling of the load, being able to see ahead, watching for finger traps in doorways, taking corners wide are all important.

Collisions.—Usually due to lack of vision. Either because of unsuitable pathways, or too high a load, or pushing instead of pulling.

HANDLING GOODS.—(Power Handling)

Fingers and hands may be trapped when inserting the sling in the hook, lifting the safety catch on the hook, attaching or detaching the sling dogs or case hooks, hardening down the bight, or steadying the sling, whilst taking the weight. The use of a wrong method of slinging may result in disaster, eg if case hooks are put on a case with heavy contents the bottom of the case may fall out, or failure to knock down the bight may result in goods falling out of the sling. Knocking down the bight with a crow-bar instead of a piece of wood is a serious offence against good practice, as it may easily damage a sling. The bight can be knocked down too far and strain the sling; this is not as generally known as it should be. The weight of every load should be known and should be within the safe load of the lifting gear.

Goods should be lifted a few inches at first and the security of the load tested before the full lift is taken. Other hazards are due to lifting goods off or on to insecure foundations or leaving them in an unstable condition. Packing should be used to protect slings from sharp-edged loads. This applies to chains as well as to ropes. A bent chain link or a kinked wire rope is seriously weakened. Planed hardwood is sharp enough to cut a fibre rope sling.

Visible or audible signals should be standardised and clearly given. Goods are often lowered on to the feet or hands when attention is concentrated on placing them exactly in a certain position. Loads pulled up on the slew not only strain the crane and tackle but introduce the danger of swinging. High winds can also make loads difficult to manage. Loads which must travel over or close to workers should be directed by a slinger or chargehand who can see the whole route.

The introduction of conveyors of all kinds constantly introduces new hazards into works; their mechanism should be guarded completely, and special attention be given to the design of attachments for suspended loads.

FALLS OF PERSONS.—About half of these accidents happen, surprisingly enough, when people are walking on the level. Common causes are uneven floors; presence of water or oil on floor, projections of stacked material into walkways, nails, tools, bits of wood, etc, left lying about; bad or unsuitable footwear, defective eyesight uncorrected by glasses; sudden clouds of steam, smoke or dust; bad lighting, especially glare and shadows; failure to adapt pace and method of walking to floor surface. Falls near machinery involve an additional hazard as they may result in contact with moving parts or in the inadvertent starting of machines.

Falls from heights are due to similar fundamental causes with the addition of insecure or incomplete scaffolds, planks, ladders, ramps and handrails; to standing on unstable foundations such as piles of boxes and drums, to climbing when a ladder should be used, to curved surfaces like tank wagons and boilers. Many falls are from ladders and through glass or asbestos sheet roofs or corroded metal sheeting; sometimes also stepping on glass which has become so dirty that it doesn't look like glass any longer.

At heights and in hoppers and chutes, safety belts save many accidents. Handrails should always be fixed where possible even on jobs of short duration. Mid-rails, as well as top-rails are desirable. Holes and excavations should be fenced.

FALLS OF OBJECTS.—There are roughly three main sources of these falling dangers. There are things being handled, such as tools, which slip out of the hands; there are tools or parts left about which are kicked or fall by vibration or wind pressure; there are ill-fixed or worn-out parts of structures, such as bolts, which fall because they have not been inspected or renewed. Elevated gangways and walkways should have toe-boards. They will often prevent objects from falling.

Other causes of falls of tools or materials from work-benches; falls of objects on to the feet when being carried; collapse of trench sides; materials improperly stacked or supported; objects not secured against the effects of wind; greasy objects or greasy hands; badly loaded trucks; throwing tools from one man to another instead of passing (or hauling up on a line if one man is aloft); trying to carry something too heavy or too awkward for one man, or trying to carry too many things at once.

HAND TOOLS.—(Defective Tools)

Hammers, hatchets, axes, adzes, picks, sledges.—Loose heads, split or chipped handles involve a double risk; the head flying off and a mis-hit. A split handle may lacerate the hand. Rounded faces on hammers and blunt edges on cutting tools also cause mis-hits. There are many methods of securing heads on tools. Accurate fit of the handle is fundamental—whatever method is adopted for actual fixing. A loose head is best dealt with by fitting a new handle.

Cold chisels.—Cold chisels; wedges; caulking tools; punches; drifts, etc, all become work-hardened when in use, and cracks develop and pieces are liable to fly off with great force when they are struck. It is desirable to 'safeend' these tools by depositing one-eighth inch of bronze on the top 1 in of the tool, after suitably reducing the diameter. Such tools outlast normal tools by about three times.

Files, carpenters' chisels, screwdrivers.—Files should be fitted with sound handles as many permanently disabling hand and foot injuries have been caused by the tang of a bare file which has ripped through the palm of a hand when the file has encountered an obstruction on the workpiece, or has fallen from a bench or lathe. Even greater danger to the chest and stomach exists when a bare file is used in conjunction with a lathe. Loose or broken handles on screwdrivers and chisels should be replaced; avoid makeshift repairs.

Spanners.—Splayed out and cracked jaws often result from misuse. The use of a spanner in bad condition damages the nut (bad craftsmanship) and may slip off causing the user to bark his knuckles, or lose his balance and fall off a ladder.

General Notes on the Use of Tools.—Accidents are often the result of misuse of a tool or selection of the wrong kind of tool. Examples are: the use of a file as a lever or its tang as a reamer, a spanner or wrench which does not fit the nut, cutting towards the hand or body with a knife or chisel. As a rule such practices tend to damage the work also and cannot, therefore, be regarded as good craftsmanship. Tools should be properly stored when not in use. Sharp-edged tools such as axes should have the edges buried or encased in wood. Hand tools should be put away in drawers or boxes.

TRANSPORT.—In factories, main hazards are due to ordinary road vehicles moving about the works, to small hand and power trucks, to railway locos and trucks, to locomotive cranes and even to goods being carried by hand, eg ladders. Keeping a good look-out, especially when coming into or out of doorways, round corners and crossing roads, tracks and alleys is the method of avoiding injury from traffic. Good design of route in the first place and constant alertness is needed because traffic moves comparatively fast.

When being overtaken it is necessary to watch that one is not trapped between vehicle and wall. This applies specially to trailers. Trailers should also be watched for when crossing behind vehicles especially in the dark. Many people have been badly hurt by walking into the side of a trailer. Avoid passing behind a vehicle that is being backed. Loads may project beyond the width of a vehicle. Improperly loaded goods may fall, especially on bumps or at corners.

Railways are a special hazard. Step over lines, not on them, especially at points, which may trap feet. Always go round a train of trucks, never duck under. This applies even if no loco is about because something else, such as gravity or wind, may cause a truck to move.

All the ordinary rules of safe driving apply with redoubled force in a works. There are not usually any pavements; doorways open directly on to roads; there are unfenced level crossings; there are hundreds of regular activities not encountered in the ordinary roads; there may be overhead obstructions such as low pipe bridges. The various kinds of fork-lift trucks have introduced a new hazard into works not designed for their use and special attention should be paid to them because of their comparatively bad visibility.

Shunting.—A shunting pole should not be used for any purpose other than coupling trucks. Riding on a shunting pole is illegal. When coupling, the pole should be rested on the buffer housing, not on the spindle where it may be pinched and cause severe injury to the shunter. Hands and feet should be kept clear of buffers, and buffers should not be ridden on. Proper scotches and sprags should be used to keep trucks stationary. Small trucks and narrow gauge tubs should be coupled from below.

Leading wagons should be accompanied or led except where this is absolutely impossible. Shunters riding on wagons being pushed should ride in sight of the driver. Vehicles should be left clear of points, tracks, paths and crossings and secured with sprags or brakes and by both when on inclines. Leading wagons should be braked before going down an incline.

MACHINERY

Machinery, eg engines, motors, machine tools, woodworking machinery and transmission machinery, accounts for about 19% of all industrial accidents. Machinery deserves the utmost respect as a hazard because of the relative severity of the injuries caused by it. The permanent disability rate must be very high indeed.

FIG. 3.—Lathe with Guard and Screen.

The intrinsically dangerous parts of machinery have been classified into 17 groups based on records and experience of the Factory Inspectorate of the Health and Safety Executive. The following parts or combination of parts are, therefore, regarded as being intrinsically dangerous. The examples given are not necessarily comprehensive.

(1) Revolving Shafts, Couplings, Spindles, Mandrels and Bars.—eg line and counter shafts; machine shafts; drill spindles; chucks and drills etc; boring bars; stock bars; traverse shafts.

(2) In-running Nips Between Pairs or Rotating Parts.—eg gear wheels: friction wheels: calender bowls: mangle rolls: metal manufacturing rolls: rubber washing, breaking and mixing rolls: dough brakes: printing machines: paper-making machines.

(3) In-running Nips of the Belt and Pulley Type.—eg belts and pulleys, plain, flanged or grooved; chain and sprocket gears; conveyor belts and pulleys; metal coiling and the like.

(4) Projections on Revolving Parts.—eg key-heads; set screws; cotter pins; coupling bolts.

(5) Discontinuous Rotating Parts.—eg open arm pulleys; fan blades; spoked gear wheels, and spoked flywheels.

(6) Revolving Beaters, Spiked Cylinders, and Revolving Drums.—eg scutchers; rag-flock teasers; cotton openers; carding engines; laundry washing machines.

(7) Revolving Mixer Arms in Casings.—eg dough mixers; rubber solution mixers.

(8) Revolving Worms and Spirals in Casings.—eg meat mincers; rubber extruders; spiral conveyors.

(9) Revolving High-Speed Cages in Casings.—eg hydro-extractors; centrifuges.

(10) Abrasive Wheels.—eg manufactured wheels, natural sand stones.

(11) Revolving Cutting Tools.—eg circular saws; milling cutters; circular shears; wood slicers; routers; chaff cutters; woodworking machines, eg spindle moulders, planing machines and tenoning machines.

(12) Reciprocating Tools and Dies.—eg power presses; drop stamps; relief stamps; hydraulic and pneumatic presses; bending presses; hand presses; revolution presses.

(13) Reciprocating Knives and Saws.—eg guillotines for metal, rubber and paper; trimmers; corner cutters; perforators.

(14) Closing Nips Between Platen Motions.—eg letterpress platen printing machines; paper and cardboard platen machine cutters; some power presses; foundry moulding machines.

(15) Projecting Belt Fasteners and Fast Running Belts.—eg bolt and nut fasteners; wire pin fasteners and the like; woodworking machinery belts; centrifuge belts; textile machinery side belting.

(16) Nips Between Connecting Rods or Links, and Rotating Wheels, Cranks or Discs.—eg side motions of certain flat-bed printing machines; jacquard motions on looms.

(17) Traps Arising From the Traversing Carriages of Self-Acting Machines.—eg metal planing machines.

Further information on this subject is given in BS 5304. 'Safeguarding of machinery.

Fig. 4.—Protective Guards, Screens and Goggles.

MAIN CAUSES OF MACHINERY ACCIDENTS.—Machinery accidents can be divided roughly into six classes. First, those due to machinery that is completely, and deliberately, unfenced such as high shafting. The presumption is that it is 'safe by position' . . . until someone approaches it owing to inexperience, over-enthusiasm, disobedience, lack of supervision, lack of plain orders or something similar. Secondly, there is machinery that is partly unfenced. Its condition may be due to a presumption that the unfenced side will not be approached, or a genuine but unjustified, idea that the unfenced side is unapproachable. Thirdly, there is the removal of the fencing. This removal may be unauthorised. Sometimes, however, it is justified by work that has to be done, such as examination, lubrication and adjustment, and the accident is due to lack of the other precautions that become necessary in such circumstances. Guards which have been damaged in use or have not been repaired are sometimes removed. Fourthly, there are automatic and interlocking guards. Many accidents result from inadequate guards, improper setting, failure to test regularly during use, deliberate interference, insufficient maintenance, and, occasionally, mechanical failure. Fifthly, it must be admitted that there are a few machines for which no guards can yet be universally applied that conform to the ideal of 'complete enclosure'. Examples are certain power presses, milling machines, and machines used in trades such as textiles, rubber manufacture, papermaking and woodworking. There is also the difficulty of contact with work being turned by a machine, eg in a lathe. Sixthly, there is inadvertent starting, often by a person other than the injured, or by belt creep from the loose to the driving pulley. The provision of one of the simple mechanisms which exist to prevent this, is obligatory.

General Precautions.—The prevention of machinery accidents is still very much a technical and managerial matter. The first and most important precaution is therefore a better appreciation, particularly in smaller works, of the fact that a guard must be a 'complete enclosure' preventing the access of even fingers to dangerous parts and must be robust. The second is to set up a system of testing and maintenance to prevent deterioration of the guards and their mechanisms. The third is to ensure that the guards provided are always in use. The fourth is to provide a substitute by training in those few cases when guards are literally impossible. Even so, operatives who work with or near machinery will always have to respect it. The general lines of defence are neat and tidy clothing without loose ends; sleeves buttoned up at the cuffs or, better still, cut off above the elbow; hair—all of it—under caps; no finger rings; respect for works rules about mounting belts and approaching machinery supposed to be 'safe by position'. (Actually no machinery is safe by position. It is the person near it who is, or is not, safe by position. When he gets too near he becomes 'unsafe by position'.) There are incidental hazards which lead to machinery accidents such as untidiness, slippery floors, attempts to clean or oil while in motion and inadequate light or glare.

MACHINE GUARDING

Standards of machine guarding will tend to be influenced by legal requirements and it is reasonable to state that in factories where there is no marked inclination towards the adoption of positive safety measures, the standard of guarding, if any guarding exists at all, will be about the minimum required by the law. Very often the deficiencies of a guard will remain undetected until the occurrence of an accident. It is for this reason that the employment of a safety organisation to advise and make recommendations on such subjects is increasing in industry. In broad terms the requirements of any type of guard are that it should afford maximum protection to the machine operator with the minimum interference with his work. In practice these desiderata may be difficult to fulfil, but the knowledge of those firms with the most experience of the difficulties likely to be encountered, indicates that a combination of determination and sound engineering principles can overcome many of the problems, in much the same way as more commonplace difficulties are overcome.

The guarding of a machine is influenced considerably by its design and age. Designers of modern machinery are paying increasing attention to the desirability of incorporating safeguards into the general layout of their machines. This tendency is partly due to a certain legal obligation under the Factories Act and partly due to demands of machinery buyers. Safety in design is not confined to guards alone. Machines can be so designed that the physical barrier between the operator and the hazard is necessarily imposed to enable power to be hooked up, examples of this type of machinery are found in modern laundries. Hydro-extractors are a case in point. The machinery cannot be set in motion until the operator's hands are clear of working parts and the top cover of the machine has been put in position.

In his report for 1959, H.M. Chief Inspector of Factories drew the attention of machine manufacturers and designers to the most important safety principles which should be borne in mind if machines were to be efficient both from the point of view of safety and of function, for no machine should rightly be called efficient if it is capable of endangering the life or limb of the person who has to operate it or work near it. These safety principles are:

1. *To be safe during maintenance and cleaning*, eg, methods of lubrication designed so as to eliminate the need for operators to approach dangerous parts.

2. *The elimination of dangerous parts*, eg, the use of a totally enclosed electric motor and vee belt and pulley drive, obviating overhead revolving shafting and long belt drives.

3. *Failure to safety*, eg, if a workpiece is held in position on, say, a revolving table by an electric clamping arrangement, care should be taken that the object cannot fly off the table and injure the operator should there be a failure in the electric supply.

4. *Correct placing of control devices*. These should be so placed that they cannot be accidentally operated, and so that the different kinds of controls are easily distinguishable from each other, even—if necessary—in the darkness. There should be uniformity in the design of such controls. Stop buttons should stand well above the surrounding surface, have a mushroom head and be coloured red. Other buttons should be sunk or shrouded to prevent accidental contact.

5. *The danger of fatigue*. The designer should remember that fatigue is often a contributory cause of accidents. Close observation and study of the operation is necessary if the machine design is to permit ease of operation, thereby increasing efficiency and contributing to safety.

In contrast there is the more common type of machine such as the drill, grinding wheel, power press on which a guard is superimposed. In some cases the guard may be of fixed design; in others it will be necessary for it to be provided with a range of adjustment.

Where repetitive work is passing through a machine to any degree, the design and setting of a guard to meet safety requirements presents less of a problem than in those situations where a small run of a particular component is passed through a machine to be quickly followed by one of perhaps an entirely different size or shape, for which the existing guard may be unsuitable. In some cases guards equally suitable to all jobs can be designed but in most cases difficulties such as these should be largely overcome by production staff. The design of the necessary guard should be included in the production instructions. In any event it will be seen that matters affecting safety in works are bound up inevitably with the production staff. The need for the closest attention to safeguards by supervisory staff at a time when a machine is being set-up or reset to undertake fresh work must be emphasised.

The safe operation of some particular types of machinery has been the subject of special study by committees of experts set up to examine the special problems involved. The principles laid down in their recommendations deserve consideration. The most detailed work has been with regard to power presses, although milling machines have also been the subject of a report.

POWER PRESSES.—A comprehensive study of the guarding of power presses has been made by an official Committee; their findings have been published in the following reports:

FIG. 5.—Radiovisor Electric Press Brake Guard.

Report of the Joint Standing Committee on Safety in the Use of Power Presses. Fencing of Hydraulic Presses. (HMSO, 1952).

Fourth Report of Proceedings of the Joint Standing Committee on Safety in the Use of Power Presses. (HMSO, 1959.)

Power Press Safety Code. (Fifth Report of Proceedings of the Joint Standing Committee on Safety in the Use of Power Presses.) (HMSO, 1965.)

Power Press Toolsetting and Tool Design. (Sixth Report of the Joint Standing Committee on Safety in the Use of Power Presses. (HMSO, 1968.)

Safety in the Use of Press Brakes. (Seventh Report of the Joint Standing Committee on Safety in the Use of Power Presses. (HMSO, 1969.)

Electro-Sensitive Safety Devices for Friction-Clutch Press Brakes. (Eighth Report of the Joint Standing Committee on Safety in the Use of Power Presses.) (HMSO, 1970.)

Power Press Safety. (Standards prepared by the Joint Standing Committee on Safety in the Use of Power Presses.) (HMSO, 1979).

These reports summarise all the desirable features of press and press guard design, and it is noteworthy that, in the first of the reports listed, the Committee refers to three appropriate classes of guards for power presses, viz: Static fixed guards, interlocked fixed guards, and automatic or mechanical guards.

Whenever the nature of the operation permits, a static fixed guard should be employed. It should prevent access of the fingers to any trapping point and must be in effective position at all times when the ram is liable to descend either through the normal operation of the clutch or equivalent mechanism, or through any other cause whatever.

An interlocked fixed guard is a guard intended to ensure that: (*a*) when there is access to the parts where trapping can occur, the press clutch is prevented from making an engagement; and (*b*) when the press ram is in motion no access of the fingers to the parts where trapping can occur is possible.

An automatic guard operates on the principle of mechanical removal of the hand from danger and generally speaking its use should be limited. It should not be used on:

(1) Variable stroke presses.

(2) Presses with less than 5 in stroke. In the case of drawing and multiple acting presses the expression means the stroke of that member which has the least movement.

(3) Presses in which the crankshaft speed is greater than the equivalent of 50 rev/min in the case of multiple acting presses.

(4) Presses on which the conditions are such that the distance between any parts where trapping can occur is less than one-half of the stroke. Account shall be taken in the determination of this distance, of the minimum distance between trapping parts when inserting or removing the component.

A most useful publication for users of these machines is *Safety in the Use of Mechanical Power Presses*. Department of Employment, Health and Safety at Work Booklet No. 14.

As from July 1966, power presses became subject to The Power Presses Regulations 1965 (SI 1965 No 1441), which provide for the regular and systematic thorough examination, inspection and testing of these machines and their attached safety devices, so that any defects which render a press unsafe to operate may be promptly recognised and remedied. A Department of Employment booklet 'Power Presses Regulations 1965 and 1972—a general guide' is supplied by HMSO.

PRIME MOVERS.—Accidents on engines (steam and gas), motors of all kinds and water wheels usually occur to people who are oiling or feeling bearings. A regulation makes this illegal except when carried out under certain special conditions by specially authorised persons wearing approved clothing. Remote oiling devices are also a safeguard, and these are therefore being used more and more to replace manual oiling. Attendants should be reminded of dangers by suitable notices, and pay particular attention to their clothing and to their foot-holds and hand-holds.

SHAFTING.—Whatever its size, whatever its speed, however smooth is its surface, shafting must be regarded as dangerous. It causes some of the most appalling injuries. People are swept up by a tie, a trouser leg, a bit of waste sticking out of a pocket, even the slack at the back of an overall. They are whirled round with horrible results. Hair is torn out by the roots. All this is rather gruesome but has to be said because so many transmission machinery accidents seem to be due to ignorance of the danger that lies in an innocent-looking smooth shaft. Unless shafts are guarded they should be stopped when painting, window cleaning, electrical work, etc, is to be carried out in their immediate vicinity. Many scalping accidents, incidentally, are due to inadequately fenced shafts running under benches or forming parts of machines such as drills.

DRIVING BELTS, ROPES, CHAINS AND PULLEYS.—Apart from lack of adequate fencing the principal cause with drives is attempting to mount belts. This may be done without proper knowledge, contrary to orders, or without a proper belt pole or other appliance. Contact may be made with sharp fasteners, or when putting on belt dressing. Belts on revolving shafts cause accidents because they have a trick of suddenly lapping round the shaft. This often happens when they are touched. Great damage may occur in these cases by a belt tending to hoist, or pull over, a machine. Belt mounting gear operating from outside belt guards and belt perches should be fitted.

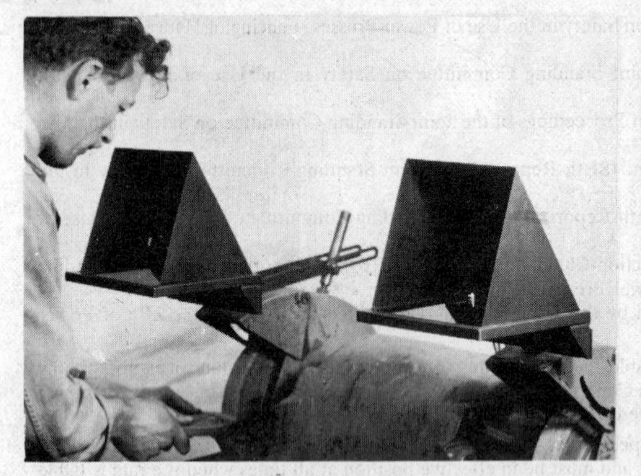

FIG. 6.—Grinder Guard complete with Visor.

FIG. 7.—Non-slip Mat for Machinists.

Gearing.—The general machinery causes apply, ie, inadequate guards and approach to gears presumed 'safe by position'.

MACHINE TOOLS

Woodworking Machinery.—Every machinist knows these can maim in a fraction of a second, but he often prefers to rely on his own undoubted skill rather than on guards, which may need frequent adjustment, and on push-sticks and jigs. Although these technical measures do not always give protection equivalent to a fixed and complete enclosure, they will generally minimise the seriousness of injuries if skill momentarily fails, if attention relaxes or if some untoward event occurs. Wood is a variable material and the most skilled man cannot always predict its behaviour. Hence the need for a better understanding that woodworking machinery guards are not a slight on skill, but a means of lessening the probability and seriousness of injury if something unexpected happens.

Drills.—The clamping down of work is essential. Otherwise, if the drill hangs up, the work will swing round and cause an injury. Thin sheet is especially dangerous because it becomes a sort of horizontal saw. The whole of the moving parts of a drill, including the tool, should be fenced.

ABRASIVE WHEELS.—There are many technical causes of abrasive wheel accidents, including improper mounting, running at wrong speed, inadequate guards or guards not strong enough to retain broken pieces of burst wheels.

In operating, many injuries (in addition to injuries due to not using goggles or the screen) are due to improper adjustment of the rest. If a tool that is being ground slips between the rest and the wheel there will be a jam. The tool may fly out violently, the wheel may burst, or both. There are also dangers in grinding on the side of a wheel not meant for side grinding, and in pressing too hard on the wheel, especially when cold. The mounting of abrasive wheels and speed of operations are governed by The Abrasive Wheels Regulations, 1970.

On dry work, efficient exhaust ventilation is necessary to prevent damage by dust to operator's lungs, and recent work has shown this to be possible. (See also Vol I, p 466B.)

LADDERS

Defects.—Ladders are given much hard use and wood is a variable material. Ladders are therefore liable to many defects such as worn or split rungs, missing rungs, missing tie-bars, split rails and warped rails. Most of these defects make the ladder liable to break in use. Missing rungs, however, cause falls because their absence is forgotten, especially when descending. Warped rails make the ladder insecure besides placing extra strain on one side or the other. A good ladder requires regular inspection, every time before it is used. A bad ladder should not be used. Ladders made of battens nailed to deals are never very reliable. Rungs may come off or the whole ladder may collapse sideways after some use.

On step ladders the cords may be too short or too long or entirely absent, and hinges may be loose. Cords of unequal length are also dangerous because they strain the ladder. A step ladder may collapse if not opened to the full extent.

Defective ladders should be clearly marked and removed as soon as possible. At the earliest possible moment they should be sawn up to make further use impossible. The fact than an obviously defective ladder has been nearer at hand than a sound one has led to many accidents. Defects may go undetected because the ladder has been painted. Paint should never be used. Ladders should be protected by one or more coats of clear varnish.

IMPROPER PLACING.—Ladders may be set at the wrong angle. If too straight up and down they are liable to fall over backwards. If too sloping they may break because of the extra strain. In any case the feet will have a greater tendency to slip. Placing at the wrong angle is sometimes due to choosing a ladder too long or too short for the job. A guide to the safe erection of a ladder is found in the ratio of 4:1. That is, the feet of the ladder should be placed away from the vertical structure against which the ladder rests by a quarter of the distance existing between the feet and the upper resting point of the ladder. If the ladder is much too short, it may not have enough purchase at the top if leant on a beam or sill. When it slips off it may not move far but the jar may throw the user to the ground. Theoretical considerations governing the stability of ladders have been discussed by H. A. Hepburn, in *The British Journal of Industrial Safety*, 1958, Vol 4, No 46, pp 155–58.

Ladders placed on uneven ground may slip unless suitable precautions are taken. Soft ground can usually be dug out to provide a level base, but when this is not possible, a partially-filled sandbag placed under both stiles will very often provide a satisfactory alternative. In either event, the ladder should be lashed or a man detailed to steady it. Ladders placed in gangways may be hit by trucks or passers-by, and a man should be stationed at the base to prevent this. Ladders placed near doorways, whether inside or outside, are much safer if the door is locked. When a ladder is used as access to a landing or working platform, too short a projection at the top may cause a slip or fall; a minimum projection of 3 ft 6 in above the landing is desirable and is, in fact, a legal requirement in the construction industry.

IMPROPER USE.—The use of a step ladder where a longer straight one would be better, the use of an extension ladder where a single long ladder is required, lashing ladders together where a longer ladder is to be had, and incorrect lashings are all improper uses. So are leaning over too far to one side, especially when pulling on a spanner or pipe grip, carrying heavy or bulky goods up or down instead of using a line (especially on vertical fixed ladders), attaching blocks or tackle to ladder rungs, using rungs as supports for planks or bracket scaffolds. Acrobatic attempts like sliding down or facing outwards lead to falls. Sliding also involves the danger of splinters.

Generally, a ladder should have a man at the foot. Even if non-slip feet of the correct type for the floor are used, it is desirable to have a man at the foot of an unlashed ladder. Ladders should be lashed at the top, after which, the man at the foot is free to act as a lookout if there is traffic. Defective footwear has caused many a fall owing to catching in the rungs. Ladders may be broken by overloading. Only one man should be on a ladder at a time.

Ladders may also be damaged in storage, eg, by exposure to weather, by extreme heat and by insufficient supports when hung horizontally.

HANDLING LADDERS.—When one man carries a ladder he has two ends to think of. The front end may hit someone coming round a corner unless kept well up in the air. The back end can swing round and knock someone's feet from under him. The back cannot be watched, but the person carrying the ladder can judge where it is, and he will remember about it when swinging round.

When erecting or lowering a long ladder attempts to do so with insufficient man-power may cause a bad crash; so may failure to use a steadying rope from the top when the ladder is long enough to need one. Ladders on trucks should be 'flagged' fore and aft and the swing on corners must be allowed for.

LIFTS AND LIFTING TACKLE

LIFTS AND HOISTS.—There are very many technical measures that can make lifts safer. Technical accident causes cover an enormous number of mechanical and structural defects, including inadequate interlocks, interlocks too easily accessible to interference, failure to inspect interlocks regularly and to keep them in good repair, inadequate fencing of well or of counterweight, limit stops improperly set or maintained, worn ropes and guide shoes, defective switchgear. The best of equipment may be abused through carelessness, ignorance or deliberate misuse, eg, using limit stops to stop at top and bottom, controlling stopping by cage gate, overloading, using goods lifts for passengers, bending gates by running trucks into them, allowing trucks to shift when inside hoist cage, allowing goods to project through gates. The unauthorised operation of lifts has frequently caused accidents, particularly to juveniles. Before the Factories Act came into force there were also many fatal accidents due to hands or feet projecting between widely spaced bars of collapsible gates.

Accidents happen also during repair and overhaul; persons may be trapped between counterweight and cage or between counterweight and bottom of well; or between cage and top or bottom of well. Inadvertent or incorrect operation when a man is on the cage or in the well may cause accidents. Trapping has also happened during attempts to climb out of the cage when it has stuck.

CRANES AND RUNWAYS.—These include jib cranes, loco cranes, guy and Scotch derricks, gantry cranes, telphers and teagles. All types may be subject to mechanical defects of various kinds. Apart from occasional defects in design, mechanical defects can nearly all be prevented by regular inspection by a competent person and by proper maintenance. Inspection and maintenance has to cover not only the lifting gear but structural members, anchorages, supports, tracks, power units and control gear, all of which can lead to accidents. Faults in operation are a common cause of crane accidents. Sometimes they are due to operation of a crane by an unauthorised person or to an authorised person being unfamiliar with the controls of the crane he is working, but mistakes sometimes occur even when a man is on his own crane.

There are many ways in which a load may be made to fall, or a crane collapse or fall over, apart from abuse of the actual lifting tackle (see below). Loads may be pulled up on the skew and put an unforeseen strain on the crane; loads so pulled up may swing and then hit persons or property; loads may hit or catch in structures on being hoisted or lowered; rail tracks may not be level causing loco cranes to tip over; loads may be snatched instead of being started or stopped gradually; a load pulled from under a pile of material may impose ten, twenty or a hundred times the expected strain on the crane; towing with a loco crane is liable to do the same; a jib may be set at the wrong radius for the load to be lifted; a crane may not be anchored to the track when it should be; mobile (road wheel) cranes are particularly liable to be taken to places where the ground does not give them a stable foundation; an attempt may be made to lift a greater load than the crane should carry; people working near runway cranes are far too frequently crushed between the crane and fixed structures either owing to the driver not knowing of or forgetting their presence; crushing accidents also happen with loco cranes owing to the overhang of the cab. Other operational causes include the abuse of limit stops and either mistakes in, or misunderstandings about signals.

Jib cranes on construction sites are frequently involved in fatal accidents through being driven too close to overhead power lines. This hazard has become so serious that the Chief Inspector of Factories found it necessary in 1965 to send a special appeal to managing directors of all construction companies, together with an explanatory leaflet showing the steps which should be taken to prevent such incidents. See BS Code of Practice CP 3010 1972 Safe Use of Cranes.

LIFTING TACKLE.—Despite the long list of operational causes of crane accidents, it is probable that the misuse of lifting tackle (eg, chains, slings, rope slings, hooks, shackles, eye-bolts) causes even more lifting machinery accidents. The usual result of such misuse is fall of the load. Hence the reason why foot passengers should always avoid walking under suspended loads and why crane drivers, especially in shops, should avoid taking loads over people's heads as far as is humanly possible. There is an additional hazard when loads are carried in grabs, buckets, nets, etc.

Rope slings may have defects caused by exposure to weather, improper storage, contact with chemicals or heat. Rope slings are particularly sensitive and defects may not always be apparent to the eye. Misuse may kink wire rope slings, thus weakening them, and chain slings may be defective owing to overloading, knotting or bending round the sharp edges of loads. Chain slings become brittle with use or frost and require periodical heat-treatment. If not regularly treated, or if not really thoroughly examined and repaired after treatment, they may break. Slings and heavy tackle may be incorrectly marked or the markings may be misunderstood. It becomes necessary to reduce the safe working load of ropes, slings and chains after wear, and regular examination and testing together with the maintenance of markings, is essential. Tables of safe working loads for slings at various angles should be provided for slingers.

Misuse is an even commoner cause of fall of load. The choice of the wrong sling may produce a fracture though it is hardly fair to blame the sling if the weight of an unknown load has been wrongly estimated. The angle of the sling legs may be miscalculated and too light a sling used in consequence especially with three- or four-legged slings. Knotting slings and knocking down the bight too hard or with a wrong implement may damage the sling or its parts. One the other hand, if the bight is not knocked down far enough, the load may be so loosely held as to fall out. There are correct methods of slinging various types of loads and the use of the wrong type of sling, or wrong methods of applying the right one, may lead to trouble. Sharp cornered loads will cut or damage slings unless properly packed (even wood can cut a rope sling). A load should not rest on a sling as the strands may be crushed and the sling rendered unsafe for further use. The use of packing will prevent this and will also enable the slings to be withdrawn from beneath the load. Hooks may not be properly secured in slings or loads may slip out. A hook with only its point in an eyebolt or hole in a load like a bedplate is sure to get strained even if the load does not actually fall. There are always extra slipping hazards with special appliances such as case and can hooks, plate clamps and dogs. The use of dogs on heavy cases introduces the further danger of the bottom of the case falling out owing to lack of support. Shackle pins may not be properly secured. When two cranes are lifting an extra heavy load the balance may not be properly kept.

Eyebolts have some special hazards of their own as they are particularly liable to damage, especially if left in place when not actually in use for lifting. They are also, for some reason, far too often of poor design or wrongly placed in the load. Even if sound and of good design, the load may be applied to them in the wrong plane or they may not be properly screwed down. Use of hooks through them instead of shackles may strain them and so may the use of a continuous sling instead of one with separate legs.

In another class are accidents in which fingers are pinched between sling and load, sling and hook or in the bight. Loads may also be lowered on to fingers or toes, or fingers may be crushed between load and structure or stacked material. In high winds loads may get out of control, and swing round. This is a particularly serious hazard in erection work.

All slings, ropes, chains, and other lifting tackle should be properly stored when not in use. This will prevent damage to the tackle and contribute to improved housekeeping.

STACKING

Goods may fall when being lifted on to the stack. This may be due to lack of a good grip, to trying to lift too heavy a load singlehanded, to bad teamwork in team lifting, to breakage of cases and containers, to tearing of bags, to slipperiness or to a sudden wound from a sharp point causing the load to be dropped. Some kinds of load, eg bales of fibrous material, are naturally awkward to handle owing to a large bulk, to their shape, or to lack of compactness. Pallets may be unsuitable or defective and fork-lift trucks may be mishandled.

Unless stacks are properly built, they may collapse or at least goods may fall from them. There is a safe method of stacking for each type of goods or materials. Bags, for instance, are laid flat, the rows or tiers are tied or bonded, and tall stacks are stepped back every so many tiers. Drums and barrels are laid on their sides with the bottom row or tier well chocked. Each successive tier is stepped back so that the stack is shaped like a pyramid. When the drums have reinforcing or rolling bands, battens should be placed between each tier to act as bearers and ensure stability. An alternative method of stacking drums is end on. Wooden battens are placed between tiers and the stack kept low and straight-sided. Modern mechanical handling methods enable the drums to be placed on end on pallets and stacked by fork-lift truck. There are special methods of stacking timber, and unevenly-shaped objects such as castings also require special treatment. All goods and materials likely to roll, such as drums and rolls of paper, need proper chocks, not just any makeshift.

Neglect of any of the principles of safe stacking (which are a firm foundation, the use of chocks and dunnage if necessary, building according to accepted safe practice for the article in question) will lead to collapse of a stack and perhaps of a building. Heavy stacks are sometimes made to lean against structural walls that have only been built to take a vertical load, not a sideways thrust. When stacking on a floor sufficient consideration is not always given to the weight of the stack in relation to the maximum safe loading of the floor. Stability, the fundamental in safe stacking, becomes even more important when the stack is on a trolley or wagon and is going to be shaken about. Stacks may also be shaken when in buildings where there is heavy machinery.

Climbing on to stacks, instead of using a ladder, leads to accidents. So does falling into gaps in the stack when it has been badly made. This is specially liable to happen when the stack is built of irregularly-shaped objects such as oak logs or boxes of unequal size. When lowering a wood stack, a neighbouring stack may fall on to men at the one being cleared. This may be due to an attempt to strut the neighbouring stack instead of lowering it.

Men on the top of stacks may also find themselves in close and dangerous proximity to unfenced machinery, to the power wires of cranes, and to the rail tracks of gantry cranes. Either the stacks should not have been built so high or the danger points should have been fenced.

Attempts to make the work of unstacking quicker by throwing down from the top or pulling out from the bottom may lead to accidents. Pulling out from below is specially dangerous. At any time, of course, something may be inadvertently knocked off the top of the stack on to men below and a badly built stack may shed some of its higher parts in quite a moderate wind.

Also related to incorrect stacking are certain of the types of spontaneous combustion.

ELECTRICITY

Many factors enter into determining whether a shock will be fatal or not, eg, extent and closeness of contact, resistance of earth or return circuit, voltage and whether ac or dc, path of current through body and moistness of skin. The main technical causes are defective equipment (eg poor insulation), incorrect installation (eg, a switch in the neutral instead of the live wire), lack of efficient earth, poor maintenance and overloading.

Trained electricians run greater risks than ordinary employees because they often have to work on live apparatus. At the same time, they do not always switch off when they can. They may even become confused about which part of the apparatus on which they are working is dead and which alive. Sometimes they fail to use the proper gloves, tools and shields for working on live apparatus.

Electricity also causes accidents to unauthorised persons who try to renew fuses or connect up tools and appliances. Perhaps the commonest electrical hazard to those who are not electricians is the portable electric tool. These accidents are almost invariably traced to a failure in maintenance at some stage. Sometimes the earth wire is missing, sometimes it is broken or giving poor continuity, sometimes it is deliberately disconnected, as when a three-way cable is connected to a two-way outlet. Electrical apparatus may become live because of an internal defect, but quite often the trouble is due to faulty connections at the terminals. Only a few wisps from the live wire have to touch the metal casing to make the whole tool live if the earth is defective. Hence the danger when unauthorised people make apparently simple looking connections instead of getting an electrician. Another danger in the unauthorised connection is the overloading of the circuit.

Some tools are intended to be completely insulated and need no earth, eg the Home Office type handlamp. Removal of a part, such as the cage from a handlamp, may make it unsafe. The use of an ordinary lamp holder on a length of flex is always hazardous, but specially so in damp situations or in metal vessels, such as boilers.

Other electrical hazards include defective switches which may finally fail at an important moment; failure to mark a switch clearly when it is off and a man is working on the equipment; failure to realise that even quite low ac voltages have caused death when the conditions were right; failure to use goggles when a blow-out is thought to be a possibility; failure to find the fault before renewing a blown fuse; failure to switch off or to insulate oneself before attempting to remove a shocked person from contact with a conductor; failure to switch

Fig. 8.—Example of well-guarded driving belts.

off before performing even simple operations like changing a lamp. Earth protection devices can guard against many of these dangers. Modern practice is to employ low-voltage equipment; or double insulated, or all insulated to BS 2754 1976 for inspection lamps and portable tools.

RADIATION.—The increasing use of X-ray apparatus, radio-active isotopes and luminous paint in industry introduces new hazards which are specially dangerous because they are unseen. Also, the pathological effects are often not apparent for a long time after exposure. If such equipment is installed, or its use is contemplated, contact should be established with the National Radiological Protection Board, Harwell, Didcot, Berkshire.

PERSONAL SAFETY EQUIPMENT AND CLOTHING

SAFETY EQUIPMENT.—This covers such equipment as safety belts, goggles, fixed and portable screens, protective devices such as masks, hats, helmets, eye veils, breathing apparatus, suits, spats, aprons, leggings, boots, gloves and palms. These are generally provided to protect against flying particles; heat and cold; hot, corrosive, poisonous and otherwise harmful substances; dusts, fumes, gases and smokes; pastes and powders; sparks and excessive light and heat rays; sharp edges and abrasives; electric shock; water and liquids not intrinsically harmful but liable to lead to discomfort; falls from heights (safety belts); falling objects (safety boots and hard hats).

Personal protective equipment is only the second line of defence: the first is to eliminate the hazard at its source if possible. Finally reference may be made to the occasions on which the use of protective appliance is actually dangerous, eg, a glove when working on a machine that can wind the glove up in it. In such cases some type of loose palm can generally be used. If it catches, it pulls off easily and does not take the hand in with it.

Accidents under this heading are mainly due to failure to wear or use safety equipment when provided. For the majority of them, however, there is little excuse. On occasions, however, there may be excusable ignorance that the equipment ought to be used, or what is provided may be unsuitable. In extreme cases the necessary provision may not have been made.

The prime remedy for accidents due to failure to use protection is in the hands of the employees. Many of the codes of Regulations for Dangerous Trades and the Welfare Orders not only require employers to provide specified equipment but place the onus for its use on employees. There is also a general provision in 'The Health and Safety at Work Etc Act', 1974, which says that employees shall use safety appliances provided under the Act. Workers should be trained to regard protective equipment as essential and it should be carefully selected and popularised.

This, however, only affects some appliances; by no means all are covered. Many excuses are given for the non-use of appliances. The fundamental cause is probably not laziness or bravado, as is sometimes said, so much as a refusal by the individual to recognise that he is as likely to be injured as anyone else. It is often said that appliances are uncomfortable. Very often the discomfort will disappear if an honest attempt at regular use is made, but even if it does not, the discomfort is better than the eventual loss of an eye or some other permanent disability.

Disregard for the safety of others leads to the non-use of certain types of appliances, eg, a screen used to protect passers-by from flying chips. Passers-by sometimes insist on looking at a welder despite the presence of a screen. See 'The Protection of Eyes Regulations', 1974. (HMSO).

Safety belts should be firmly attached to a suitable anchorage point, the anchorage rope being kept as short as possible to prevent a dangerous fall. Eye protection in the form of goggles, spectacles or face shields should be selected with care so that they will not be cast aside on the pretext of discomfort or other shortcoming.

An exhausted or wrong type of canister on a respirator and the use of a canister type when a fresh-air or self-contained apparatus is required; gloves which give a poor grip on whatever is being handled; plain goggles when a toughened or laminated glass is needed, are all examples of equipment applied incorrectly. Canister respirators should be used only for the gas they give protection against, and never in any atmosphere which might become deficient in oxygen.

Included in this class are the too frequent occasions when a safety appliance is given to a worker instead of protection against the danger being provided at its source. Examples are the provision of a respirator instead of an efficient exhaust to prevent dust or fumes coming out into the workroom and provision of protective clothing against liquids when splashes could be stopped at source.

CLOTHING.—Defective footwear leads to many accidents. Worn soles may permit penetration by sharp objects or may catch and trip the wearers. They are specially dangerous on all ladders and scaffolds. Worn heels lead to stumbling, fatigue and general unsteadiness. Fatigue caused by standing long hours in defective and ill-fitting footwear may in turn lead to accidents. It is a common mistake to try to wear out at work shoes that were never intended for rough use. (Both men and women may be seen in factories in old dance shoes.) Women's heels are dangerous if excessively high, if worn down, or if the shoes are ill-fitting so that they are liable to turn over. Sandals and 'gym' shoes are generally unsuitable for factory use.

Those who handle heavy objects should always wear safety boots.

Wherever machinery is, special care should be taken with clothing. Loose ties, open coats, scarves, long hair are all very dangerous near machinery, but hundreds of people are caught even without having taken chances such as that. The slack in the back of a one-piece overall is sufficient to wind up on an innocent looking smooth shaft.

Clothes should be close fitting, with no loose ends. Buttons should be kept fastened. Overall trousers should be properly hemmed up. Many a man has tripped himself up because he has just turned up the bottoms of a pair of new overalls instead of having them sewn. Rolled up sleeves are better than long sleeves, when working on machines, provided that they are tightly and tidily rolled. Even better are short sleeves, cut off above the elbow.

Certified machinery attendants, who may have to approach unfenced machinery in motion, have to wear special clothing as laid down in the Operations at Unfenced Machinery Regulations, 1938 and 1946. Among other things they are only allowed a hip-pocket because of the danger from cotton waste projecting and being caught by machinery. This danger may be encountered by other machine workers. Factory clothing often gets dirty quite unavoidably, but failure to keep it reasonably clean may lead to trouble. For instance, oil-soaked clothing continually rubbing on the skin is a typical cause of dermatitis.

INDUSTRIAL DERMATITIS

Industrial dermatitis is an inflammatory reaction of the skin caused by a wide variety of irritants. In industry it is one of the principal causes of disablement from industrial diseases. The condition affects workers in many trades; it can take many forms and vary in degrees of seriousness. Some people are more sensitive to skin irritants than others. Any part of the body which comes into contact with a skin irritant may be affected, but the hands and arms are the most likely areas to be attacked. If dermatitis is neglected it may spread to other parts of the body.

Almost anything can cause dermatitis and, among the well-known causes of the condition are mineral oil; chemicals; solvents and degreasers; tar, pitch and other products of coal tar; radiations; sugar; dough; cement; certain hard woods; some vegetables, fruit and flowers; and certain antibiotics. It is possible in some instances to remove or reduce the risk of dermatitis by replacing a hazardous material with a safe one, and this is obviously the best course to take. If, however, it is not possible to dispense with a hazardous material, then other means of preventing contact must be used.

The best method of protection is, of course, total enclosure or complete mechanisation of the process. Failing that, mechanical aids should be used as widely as possible. These may include tongs, scrapers, dipping trays, splash and scrap guards, chip screens, and control of oil flow. Local exhaust ventilation is important when dust, fume or oil spray are produced in a process. Good general environmental conditions, including the maintenance of reasonable standards of ventilation and temperature, are also important.

Personal Protection.—Personal protective clothing plays an important part in the prevention of dermatitis and such clothing is a specific statutory requirement in a number of industries. It is important that all protective clothing be maintained in a sound condition, cleaned or washed regularly, stored apart from other clothing when not in use, and renewed as required.

Finally, when all other possibilities have been exhausted, it may be necessary to resort to the use of a barrier cream which is rubbed into the skin before work. A wide range of such creams is available to provide protection against many substances, and the right choice of cream is most important.

After work, thorough cleansing with soap and water is essential and adequate washing facilities will be required. Soap should be chosen with care. Soaps are detergents and some are harsh on the skin. 'Soft soap' is soft in consistency but is normally too strong for use on the skin. What is generally desirable is a super-fatted soap suited for use with a particular water supply to ensure a quick and free lather. Where cleansing agents other than soap are found to be necessary, the cleanser should always be used in as weak a solution as possible, and the cleanser should be thoroughly removed with soap and water and finally rinsed from the skin with clean water.

SELECTION AND INSPECTION OF WORKERS.—Wherever possible, medical advice should be sought in the selection of workers for employment on processes known to have a dermatitis risk, and the physician concerned should be well aware of the particular hazards. The control of dermatitis requires a well-thought-out and well-executed plan to include systematic and frequent inspection of methods of work and precautionary measures, and of the skin condition of those at risk. In the absence of a works medical officer or nurse, a responsible person, preferably trained in first-aid, should be appointed to carry out these duties.

READING LIST

HAMILTON, MARGARET, *Safety Committees.* RoSPA.
Factory Accidents: Their Causes and Prevention. RoSPA.
Occupational Safety and Health. (Monthly.) RoSPA.
The Health and Safety at Work Etc Act, 1974. HMSO.
Redgrave's Health and Safety in Factories. Butterworth.
Tolley's Health and Safety at Work Handbook, RoSPA
MUNKMAN, J. H. *Employers' Liability at Common Law.* Butterworth.
SAX, N. IRVING. *Dangerous Properties of Industrial Materials.* Van Nostrand Reinhold Company.
HEINRICH, H. W. *Industrial Accident Prevention.* McGraw Hill.
Accident Prevention—A Workers' Education Manual. International Labour Office.
Annual Reports of H.M. Chief Inspector of Factories, HMSO.
Annual Reports of H.M. Chief Inspector of Mines & Quarries, HMSO.
STEEMSON, JACKY, Labourer's Law, RoSPA.
HOOPER, E., *Beckingsale's, The Safe Use of Electricity*, RoSPA.
Safety in the Stacking of Materials. (Dept of Employment, Health and Safety at Work, Booklet No 47). HMSO.
GILL, FRANK S. and ASHTON, INDIRA, *Monitoring for Health Hazards at Work*, RoSPA.
BIRD, FRANK E. JNR., and GERMAIN, GEORGE L., *Damage Control*, RoSPA.
BIRD, FRANK E. JNR., and LOFTUS, ROBERT G. *Loss Control Management*, RoSPA.
BIRD, FRANK E. JNR., *Management Guide to Loss Control*, RoSPA.
CROWE, M. JOAN and DOUGLAS, HUGH M. *Effective Loss Prevention*, RoSPA.
KUHLMAN, RAYMOND L., *Professional Accident Investigation—Investigative Methods and Techniques*, RoSPA.
FINDLAY, JAMES V., *Safety and the Executive*, RoSPA.
FINDLAY, JAMES V. and KUHLMAN, RAYMOND L., *Leadership in Safety*, RoSPA.
MACKIE, J. B. and KUHLMAN, R. L., *Safety and Health in Purchasing.* RoSPA.
RING, LEONARD, *Facts on Backs.* RoSPA.
Health and Safety in Welding and Allied Processes. The Welding Institute.

ENGINEERING MANAGEMENT; THE LAW RELATING TO EMPLOYMENT

Sources of Law—Pre-employment—Employment Contracts—Discrimination—Disciplinary Hearings—Closed Shop—Payment—Deductions—Recovery of Shortages—Time Off—Maternity—Business Transfers—Levies—Trade Union Recognition—Health and Safety at Work—Concepts of Law—Official Bodies—ACAS—Termination of Employment—Redundancy—Unfair Dismissal—Industrial Tribunals—Courts of Appeal—Trade Unions in Law—Bibliography

By Christopher Waud

SOURCE OF THE LAW

HISTORICAL.—Prior to 1963, the law covering the relationship between an employer and an employee was almost exclusively derived from the common law and in some respects was very archaic. It had been evolved over the centuries by the judges, who have declared what rights and obligations existed and enforced them.

Provided an employer complied with his strict contractual obligations, he could generally behave according to his whims. If he exceeded his powers and proceedings were brought for breach of contract in an ordinary case, the remedies available to an employee were very limited and the costs of obtaining them high; so usually the matter went by default.

It was only where the contract of employment had terms imposed on the parties by statute, as occurs for instance with some school teachers, that the common law could be invoked and used very effectively.

The Contracts of Employment Act, 1963 was the start of a long line and increasing number of statutes which regulate the rights and duties of employers and employees, and which now cover every aspect of their relationship.

An employer's rights to take legal action against a union has been limited by statutes going back to 1906. The considerable immunities have been slowly eroded in recent years and an employer is now able to obtain redress against them; again the common law remedies have been found to be very effective.

EUROPEAN LAW.—The law has been complicated by two external factors. Firstly, our membership of the European Economic Community obliges us to comply with community law as laid down in the Treaty of Rome, and with 'Directives' issued by the Commission for the European Community.

A considerable number of directives have emanated from the Commission because it is charged with the duty of promoting co-operation between Member States in regard to labour law, working conditions, employment, the right of association, and collective bargaining.

As the European law tends to be phrased in very general terms, there has been uncertainty as to what is covered. The European Court of Justice gives a ruling on each case referred to it and by this means a sort of European common law is being built through interpretation. The decisions of the European Court of Justice have to be applied in our own courts and tribunals.

Secondly, the United Kingdom is a signatory to the European Convention on Human Rights and Fundamental Freedoms. The European Court of Human Rights adjudicates on whether there has been a breach of the Convention. Although the decision of that court is not directly enforceable in this country, nevertheless our own legislation has to be interpreted, where possible, to conform with any ruling. If that is not possible then our own Acts of Parliament have to be amended to accord with it.

PRESENT POSITION.—In consequence of the development of the law from four different sources there has been a great deal of overlap, complication, and uncertainty. Further, one set of laws are administered in the ordinary courts and another in the tribunals, and there are different remedies in each.

The range of the legislation is also liable to vacillate according to the political party in power, but it is however subject to some control under our various Treaty obligations. There is a hard core that is unlikely to change.

A great deal of the legislation is so complex that its precise meaning is often difficult to ascertain. This has led to many appeals, some of them going up to the House of Lords; but there has been a lack of unanimity at every tier of the judicial process on the correct interpretation of various provisions.

Because European Community law takes precedence over our own, it is always necessary to keep a wary eye on what is coming in from across the water, and in particular on decisions given by the European Court of Justice.

Cost of Failure to Comply.—There is a great temptation to hope that an employment problem will not arise and take no action. Such a course can be catastrophic on occasions. A claim under the Equal Pay Act, where large numbers of employees are involved, may have far-reaching consequences.

Even claims by a few employees which fall foul of the closed-shop provisions can turn out to be expensive. In *Artisan Press v. Srawley and Parker [1986] IRLR 126*, the Employment Appeal Tribunal ordered employers to pay two sacked employees a total of £38,147, where they had failed to comply fully with an order to re-instate them.

Very often a little care and perhaps negotiation can avoid big claims, but some underlying knowledge of the law is essential. Consult a detailed up-to-date text book or a legal encyclopaedia if there is a serious problem (See Bibliography).

JURISDICTION OF CIVIL COURTS AND TRIBUNALS.—The High Court (and, for smaller claims, the County Court) continue to adjudicate upon the old common law rights and duties which arise out of contracts of employment and also on those relating to trade unions.

The common law claims mainly consist of actions for wrongful dismissal, for tortious acts, for declarations as to rights, and for various orders like an order of prohibition to prevent a person from following some declared course, eg, to hold a disciplinary enquiry or to dismiss an employee.

Appeals from their decisions are heard by the Court of Appeal and then by the House of Lords, with a right of reference to the European Court of Justice at any stage.

The Industrial Tribunals, which previously had existed for a number of years for certain limited purposes, have been given the task since 1963 of enforcing the statutory law in most instances. They have jurisdiction over actions for unfair dismissal, redundancy, sex and racial discrimination, equal pay, maternity rights, unlawful deduction of wages, appeals both in respect of levies, health and safety at work orders, together with a host of others.

Appeals from their decisions are heard by the Employment Appeal Tribunal, and further appeals go to the Court of Appeal and then finally to the House of Lords. Cases can be referred to the European Court of Justice at any stage where guidance is necessary on the applicability of the European law to any particular case.

PRE-EMPLOYMENT

ADVERTISEMENTS.—The employment legislation bites even before a person is taken into employment. The Sex Discrimination Act, 1975 and the Race Relations Act, 1976 prohibit discriminatory advertisements except in certain instances. An advertisement for a 'white storeman' is likely to fall foul of both statutes.

Under the Sex Discrimination Act, it is permissible to use a descriptive term like 'waiter' provided it is made clear that the job is open to both sexes. Under both Acts, discriminatory advertisements are not unlawful provided they relate to a 'genuine occupational qualification' (eg, 'a male person with negroid features is required for acting part' or 'female nurse required at girls school').

Breaches of the law are dealt with in several ways. The Equal Opportunities Commission or the Commission for Racial Equality have various powers, including the right to serve 'Non-Discrimination Notices' and/or they may bring proceedings in either the tribunals or the county court.

SIFTING OUT CANDIDATES FOR INTERVIEWS.—The two Discrimination Acts should be borne in mind when deciding which candidates should, or should not, go forward for interview. The Acts prohibit discrimination in regard to recruitment for jobs.

Although both Acts are not identically worded, they are sufficiently similar to be considered together. There is a complicated formula for ascertaining whether there has been discrimination and the circumstances are set out in which it is unlawful. Basically discrimination can occur in two ways: direct and indirect.

Direct discrimination will occur when a person says, 'I will employ no blacks or women', or where he filters out women or persons with foreign sounding names from applications forms. It also may occur if new employees are recruited by word of mouth where this is likely to have a deleterious effect upon women or ethnic minorities.

Indirect discrimination occurs where terms or conditions for employment are imposed which cannot be justified and a substantial proportion of one sex or racial group are unable to comply with it, but only a person who cannot reasonably comply with it can bring proceedings in her/his own name, although the Equal Opportunities Commission or the Commission of Racial Equality can seek a declaration that the term or condition is unlawful.

A requirement that 'all candidates must be over 6' tall, be clean shaven and wear a company hat', will be likely to affect women, and Sikhs more adversely than the rest of the population. In the absence of special circumstances it is doubtful that it could be justified.

If a number of candidates are likely to be ruled out because they do not have some qualifications, care should be taken to ensure that those qualifications are necessary for the job. A requirement that all clerks should have at least 3 'A' and 6 'O' levels would be likely to affect some ethnic minorities more severely than the indigenous white population. If it was not necessary, it would be likely to be in breach of the Acts.

Even where a person is acting under the best of motives, eg, he is seeking to protect women from jobs where violence might be anticipated or a coloured person from a position where he might be subject to racial abuse, he will fall foul of the Acts. So too even if there is no intention to discriminate, but that is the effect of any action taken. Equality of opportunity is the over-riding principle.

THE INTERVIEW.—This can be a very sensitive area; and it gives rise to many disputes. Some people 'feel' that interviewers are hostile or that questions are loaded, and that the reason must be because of their sex or colour. These 'feelings' often turn into certainty when they are rejected for employment time after time, and consequently any casual observation which is capable of various interpretations may be seized upon as proof of discrimination.

The cardinal rule is that no person must be put at a disadvantage by reason of sex or race. The same sort of questions should be put to all candidates and preferably a note taken of them and the gist of the answers. This will provide evidence to negate allegations of discrimination, should they be made at a later date.

ORAL TERMS OF EMPLOYMENT.—Memories of people are notoriously fickle even when honestly trying to recollect what had been agreed at a time when the terms of a contract were being worked out. 'You undertook to pay me commission when sales exceeded £100,000 pa.' 'Yes I did, but I added, "only if they were from new customers"'. The arguments are often incapable of being resolved and frequently end up in discord at best and in litigation at worst.

Every important part in a contract should be confirmed in writing so that each side knows the true position. Once an employee commences working, he will be deemed to have accepted the terms. If he disputes any, then he must do so immediately otherwise he will lose his right to have them altered.

If he (or even the employer) wishes to, he can apply to the tribunal for a declaration as to what terms, which by statute have to be in writing (see below), have been agreed; but in most cases the employee may find it imprudent to do so, if he wants to retain his employment.

RESTRICTIVE COVENANTS.—Sometimes the success of an employer's business depends upon secret processes or formulas which inevitably some of his staff will have to know about. If any of those staff were to leave and join a competitor or set up in business himself, then the employer's own business might be imperilled.

One way to reduce the risk of harm is to require the employee, at the commencement of the employment, to enter into a restrictive covenant precluding him from going into competition after the termination of his employment. Later on, the employee may not agree to the alteration of his contract to include such a term, and there may be difficulties in trying to force it on him.

Prima facie, every restrictive covenant is against the public interest and unenforceable, but where it can be shown that it is necessary to protect a business and is no wider than is reasonable in the circumstances, then it will be upheld by the courts.

The covenant usually relates to an undertaking not to work for a competitor, or to set up a similar business, within a certain distance of the employers' premises and for a limited length of time.

So where an interior designer, who was employed in a furniture business, covenanted not to work in a similar job in the U.K. for 12 months after leaving the company, the restraint was held to be jusified in time and area because of the untold damage she could do; and she was prevented from joining a competitor (*A & D Bedrooms Ltd. v. Michael & Hyphen Fitted Furniture Ltd., March 8, 1983, Ct. Sess.*).

THE EMPLOYMENT

THE CONTRACT OF EMPLOYMENT.—The legal relationship between an employer and his employee depends upon the 'contract of employment', part of which will (or should) be in writing; the rest will be oral or implied. It sets out the rights and obligations of each party.

It is not expected that a contract of employment would be drafted with the same sort of precision as a lease or a will, or be interpreted so strictly; the courts and tribunals apply a great deal of common sense in order to make the contract work.

However some care ought to be taken to think out important terms because a great deal may depend on them. Generally speaking the employer makes the offer of employment by setting out the particulars, and if the employee accepts, whether expressly or by implication, then there is a binding contract of employment.

Many terms are implied either by reason of sort of relationship that exists, eg, a long distance lorry driver would be expected to travel throughout the country which would necessitate him spending nights away from home, or they are imposed by the general law, eg, that an employee must faithfully work for his employer and not surreptitiously work at the same time for a rival business.

Terms that have to be in writing.—S.1 of the Employment Protection (Consolidation) Act, 1978 (as amended) requires an employer to serve on an employee within 13 weeks from the commencement of employment the following *written* statement.

(a) THE NAME OF THE EMPLOYER AND THE EMPLOYEE.—This has to be inserted in order to identify the parties. The employer is liable under many different Acts of Parliament for a number of duties, and if he defaults, then the employee knows the true identity of the company or person whom he can sue.

The identity may be important when trying to ascertain whether there are any 'associated employers' (see page 19) because certain rights will depend on it.

(b) DATE OF COMMENCEMENT OF EMPLOYMENT.—The contract must state when the contract begins, and this may vary from the date when the employee actually commences work. If the employer bought a firm which formerly employed the worker, and there was no break in the employment, then the date of commencement will relate back to the commencement of employment with the previous firm.

There is a duty on the employer to record whether any employment with a previous employer counts towards the total period of employment. Failure to do so will not necessarily prejudice the employee's rights. A tribunal will decide which date is correct in the event of the question having to be decided.

This is a most important provision, as a great deal may depend on it. Firstly, an employee may be debarred from bringing a number of claims, because he does not have the necessary qualifying period of continuous employment. Secondly, if an employee is dismissed, then the amount of his redundancy pay or the 'basic award' in an unfair dismissal claim will depend on the length of service.

Thirdly, there may be an agreement or arrangement, in a redundancy situation that selection for dismissal of employees whose circumstances are the same, will on the basis of 'last in, first out' or on some other special terms. A breach of it, in the absence of special reasons, will make the dismissal automatically unfair.

(c) JOB TITLE.—This is not the same as job description or specification, but it is important in a number of respects.

Firstly, if no further details are given other than a person is employed for instance as a 'lorry driver', then an employer might be circumscribed in the duties that he can call upon an employee to do. The employee might object to driving a van, or performing tasks other than those normally done by a lorry driver.

Secondly, a claim might be made under the Equal Pay Act, 1970 (as amended), that a woman is performing the same job as a man, but is only receiving three-quarters of his pay. If the job titles were the same in both cases, eg, 'messengers', then this would raise a *prima facie* case of discrimination; but the problem could be cured by qualifying the job title with a grade and applying a job description to each grade. This might show that the man's job was more onerous than the woman's, warranting the higher pay.

Thirdly, if a man was required to carry out work that he was not contractually required to do and the breach goes to the root of the contract, he can leave and claim that he was 'constructively dismissed' and the employer may become liable to pay him damages or compensation.

(d) SCALE OF REMUNERATION.—The contract should clearly spell out everything of importance. If an employee leaves because he claims that he is not being paid the correct amount, then the written terms will, or should establish who is right. If the employer is in default then he will be liable to pay damages or compensation.

In the event of a dismissal and in certain other cases certain calculations have to be made to establish the normal 'week's pay' of an employee. It will consist of the basic pay, any compulsory overtime, cost of living allowance, bonuses, commission and so forth but not travel allowances and matters of that kind. This is applicable in redundancy and unfair dismissal and certain other claims.

(e) NORMAL HOURS OF WORK.—There is an obligation to set out the normal hours of work, or, if flexi hours apply, the rules applicable to it. This is important because if an employee is dismissed for being habitually late and a dispute arises over what are his correct hours then the written terms will (or should) resolve the question.

It may be necessary to have compulsory overtime, in which case the contract should say so. In some industries, an overtime requirement may be implied, but it is better to state the position in black and white.

(f) INCAPACITY DUE TO SICKNESS OR INJURY.—If there are no terms or conditions in relation to pay or other benefits during absences due to sickness or injury, then the contract *must* say so.

There is nothing to prevent an employer from stipulating that any payment will be left to his discretion and however it is exercised the decisions cannot generally be impugned. The only exceptions that could arise might occur under the discrimination Acts. If an employer, for instance, in exercising his discretion always makes up the difference between sickness benefit and pay with white male employees, and not with coloured or female staff, then although he may be within his contractual rights, nevertheless, he will fall foul of the Race Relations Act, 1976 and the Sex Discrimination Act, 1975.

(g) HOLIDAYS.—Holiday entitlements must be specified. If holidays have to be taken at certain times, eg, when a factory closes down, then the contract should say so.

If holidays have to be staggered, or if a certain period of notice of the proposed dates has to be given, or holidays fitted in with other employees, then the contract should state the position.

It should be borne in mind that there is no statutory minimum for holidays, but Directive 457/1975, from the European Community has specified that 4 weeks' paid holiday should be the norm. It is likely that courts and tribunals will pay increasing attention to this provision, as our law becomes more integrated with that in Europe.

(h) PERIOD OF NOTICE.—The 1978 Act requires a minimum period of notice be given to employees who have worked for a month or more, as set out hereunder, but not to those guilty of serious misconduct who may be summarily dismissed.

(i) At least *one week's notice*, if the employee has been employed for one month or more;
(ii) at least *two weeks' notice*, if employed for two years;
(iii) one *additional weeks' notice* for each further year of service up to a maximum of 12 weeks' notice.

For certain statutory purposes, if no notice or inadequate notice is given, then the employment is 'deemed' to carry on until the end of the statutory period. This is known as the 'effective date of dismissal'. The result may be to give an employee the necessary qualifying period in order to bring a claim, or increase the amount of redundancy pay or the 'basic award' in an unfair dismissal claim.

Very frequently, employers give a longer period of notice than is required by statute, particularly to senior staff. If the employee is dismissed without being given the agreed period of notice, then under the statutory law, the contract will *only* be 'deemed' to carry on until the end of the statutory period for the purpose of ascertaining certain statutory rights. Thereafter the employment ceases.

At common law, the contract can remain in existence because such a notice will be in breach of contract and so null and void. But the employee may be prevented from working, and as he has a duty to mitigate any loss sustained by him, by, for instance, seeking other employment, he may find it better to accept the invalid notice and leave. An employer can always give a fresh notice of dismissal complying with the contractual requirements. Furthermore, damages, if recoverable, may turn out to be relatively small.

(i) PENSIONS.—If there are no pension rights, then the contract *must* say so.

(j) DISCIPLINARY RULES AND PROCEDURE.—There is sometimes a tendency for these to be elevated to the status of Queen's Regulations and Admiralty Instructions, and to be almost as compendious. This often provides a field day to barrack-room lawyers.

There is no right answer as to how detailed the procedure should be, but it is probably advisable to have a basic structure, and let common sense and practice fill in the gaps.

The importance of a breach of procedure lies in the different approach to it by the common law and the statutory law. A breach at common law may enable the aggrieved person to apply to the High Court for a declaration that a purported action by the employer is unlawful, or for an order prohibiting an employer from taking a particular course, eg, to hold a disciplinary enquiry or to dismiss. The employer will then have to start again, following the correct procedures.

Under statutory law, an employee, when he brings proceedings in the tribunal, will impliedly acknowledge that he has been dismissed. A procedural default in the dismissal process by a failure, for instance, to hold a disciplinary hearing, will normally result in a finding of unfair dismissal.

But if on the information known to the employer at the time it was patently fair and equitable to dismiss, then a procedural failing will not be fatal. Thus if an employee deliberately burnt down his employers' factory, then a hearing would generally be fruitless.

Even if there is a finding of unfair dismissal, the employee may receive little or no compensation if it is found that there was conduct which was unknown to the employer at the time he took the decision to dismiss, eg, a dismissal on the grounds of punctuality, which is found to be unfair, but a subsequent investigation showed that the employee had been embezzling considerable sums of money over a number of years.

(k) GRIEVANCE PROCEDURES.—Employers are required to give details of their grievance procedures. This is a useful requirement because it provides means whereby a person who feels strongly about something to get the matter off his chest. It may not resolve a dispute but it does provide a safety valve. How much better it is for an employer to be aware of a problem and perhaps take some action rather than carry on with the risk of an incident occurring which might ultimately lead to litigation.

The lines of complaint at every stage should be clearly set out. The probability is that they will rarely be fully used.

Terms in Several Documents.—In many instances, agreements have been made with unions, either by the employer himself or by the employer's trade association and which include some of the matters which are required by statute to be in writing. It is sufficient for the employer, when serving the written terms, to identify the document only and inform the employee where it may be seen. It must be reasonably accessible.

Similarly, there may be an entitlement to a pension, details of which are voluminous, and it is sufficient that copies are available for inspection at a reasonably convenient position. Disciplinary and grievance procedures may be displayed on a notice-board in a canteen or other suitable place, and as long as there is adequate reference to them in the written terms, then that will suffice.

Notification of Amendments.—An employer will change the terms of contract from time to time. He is required to give the employee written notice of the change within 1 month of the alteration. If a wage rise has been negotiated with the employee's union, it will generally be sufficient to post the details of the new terms on a notice-board provided that this is the agreed way (as set out in writing in the contract of employment) of notifying staff of any changes. The employer may not rely on the union to convey the information to its members.

FAILURE TO PROVIDE WRITTEN TERMS.—If the employer fails to provide the information required to be in writing, then he can apply to the tribunal to determine the terms. Usually they can be inferred from all the circumstances and this may involve seeing how the parties have subsequently behaved. Where it is impossible to arrive at a decision, then the tribunal will have to

> 'invent them for the purpose of literally writing them into the contract' (per Stephenson L J in *Mears v. Safecar Security Ltd. [1982] ICR 626, CA*)

As the terms which have to be made up are likely to be those most favourable to the employee, the failure may turn out to be expensive.

There are many terms that are not required to be in writing: but many of them are nevertheless reduced to writing, some are given orally and the rest are inferred from all the circumstances. The written terms are not necessarily the binding ones. An employer may have made a mistake or there may have been a clerical error.

If there is a dispute over what the agreed terms were and which should have been written, then either side may apply to the tribunal to declare what those terms were, and they will then become incorporated in the contract.

ALTERATIONS IN THE TERMS OF EMPLOYMENT.—It is generally permissible within limits for an employer to alter the terms of a contract, and in the course of a worker's employment, this is done on many occasions. Generally they are concerned with matters favourable to the employee, like pay rises, promotion and so forth, and so there is no opposition.

Where an employer wishes, for instance, to automate part of his business which will necessitate some of his staff learning new skills, can he force the changes? The answer has to be looked at from the common law and from the statutory law.

At common law, an employer can generally act as he pleases provided that he complies with his contractual obligations. If his employee refuses to undertake various duties, he can be dismissed with impunity providing that the requisite notice is given. He can then offer the employee the new terms to take effect at the expiration of the existing contract, and if they are refused, the employee will be out of a job. There will be strong pressure on him to accept, provided the altered terms are not too onerous.

The test applied under the statutory law, where an employee has had to be sacked because he has refused to accept the changes, is whether the dismissal was fair in all the circumstances having regard to equity and the substantial merits of the case and to the size and administrative resources of the employer. In practice this means that if the decision is taken for sound business reasons, then the dismissal is likely to be found to be fair.

Where Changes are Permissible within the Contract.—In many instances, the changes can be made within the confines of the contract itself. So where taxmen refused to use computers for the purpose of collecting PAYE because new skills to operate the machines were necessary, it was held that the requirement to use them was permissible within their existing contracts and so could be imposed without their consent. Those who refused to work and were suspended without pay had no cause for complaint because the legal principle of 'no work, no pay' applied (*Cresswell v. Board of Inland Revenue [1984] ICR 508, Ch D*).

On the other hand, where a Local Authority tried to substitute allowances, which they gave to staff for using their own cars while on official business, by providing them with transport from a pool instead, it was held to be unlawful, and of no effect (*Reg. v. Birmingham C C, ex p. NUPE & Ors. The Times, April 24, 1984, DC*).

ITEMISED PAY STATEMENT.—S.8 of the Employment Protection (Consolidation) Act, 1978 (as amended) requires every employer to provide his worker with a pay statement, *with or before* each payment, setting out:

(i) the gross pay;
(ii) the fixed deductions like tax, national insurance, pension contributions;
(iii) any variable deductions, identifying what they are; and
(iv) the net amount, and how it is paid, eg, cash or into a bank account.

Breach of this duty can result in an employer being ordered by a tribunal to pay a sum not exceeding any unnotified deductions for a period not exceeding 13 weeks before the proceedings are commenced. Proceedings must be commenced within 3 months of the last breach. There is no power to extend time.

EQUAL PAY/EQUAL VALUE OF WORK.—The Equal Pay Act, 1970 did not come into effect until 1975 (by which time it was amended by the Sex Discrimination Act, 1975), the long lapse being designed to give employers the opportunity to eradicate any discrimination in pay and conditions on the ground of sex.

The Treaty of Rome, which we joined on 1 January, 1973, provides 'men and women should receive equal pay for equal work', and since that time, a number of 'Directives' have emanated from the Commission for the European Community, amplifying how the principle should be interpreted.

Our own legislation has been subject to the scrutiny of the European Court of Justice and in some cases, found to be wanting. As the Treaty of Rome and Directives passed under it lie behind our own Acts, a litigant who feels he or she has not received redress for genuine grievances in our own Courts can apply to have his or her case referred to the European Court of Justice; and in a number of leading cases litigants have been successful.

For instance, our Equal Pay Act (as amended by the Sex Discrimination Act, 1975) precluded the operation of the Act in respect of provisions for retirement, so that discrimination in respect of pensions was outside the scope for consideration. In *Worringham & anr. v. Lloyds Bank plc [1981] ICR 558* the European Court of Justice ruled that pensions were part of the 'pay' of an employee and there had been discrimination against the female complainant who was not eligible to join a pension scheme until a later age than her male colleagues. The provision in the Equal Pay Act has had to be disregarded: subsequently it was revoked by the Sex Discrimination Act, 1986.

The same Act was found wanting in a number of other respects and as a result the Equal Pay (Amendment) Regulation, 1983 has had to be passed. It is likely to have very far reaching effects. The Sex Discrimination Act, 1986 has made further amendments in respect of matters where we had failed to fulfill our commitment to the Treaty.

The Equal Pay Act (as amended by the 1975 and 1986 Acts and the Regulations), provides that every term in a woman's (or a man's) contract of employment must not be less favourable than a man's (or a woman's) contract, and any term which offends against that requirement or is omitted is deemed, respectively, to have no effect, or to be included where the man and the woman are:

(i) doing the same work, or
(ii) work which is of a broadly similar nature and the difference is not of practical importance, or
(iii) it is rated as equivalent under a job evaluation study or scheme, or
(iv) if *none* of the above apply, then where the work is rated as of equal value.

In respect of (i)–(iii) above, it is a defence to prove that a variation between a man's contract and a woman's contract was genuinely due to a material factor which is not a difference of sex and that factor *must* be a material difference between the woman's case and the man's. In respect of (iv) above, the factor *may* be a material differences. Thus, if there are different rates of pay for men and women doing the same job, and this is due to length of service (which applies equally to both sexes) then there will be no breach of the Act.

Where a Job Evaluation Study has been carried out and accepted by the employer, it is binding on him even though it has not been implemented because of opposition from some of his staff.

A comparison must be made with a person of the opposite sex who works for the same employer, or an associated employer, at the same establishment, or, if he or she works at a different establishment there must be common terms and conditions either generally or for employees of the class being considered, eg, electricians at two sites in different parts of the country.

So where a qualified nursery minder claimed that her work was of equal value with 11 males, who were employed in a variety of jobs ranging from caretakers to clerks and administrators but at different establishments, she failed in her action because there were substantial differences in their terms in respect of hours and holiday entitlements and they were not in the same class of employment (*Leverton v. Clwyd County Council, The Times, March 29, 1988, CA*).

But the fact that a person of the opposite sex is employed in the same capacity and remuneration as the complainant does not preclude a complaint being made that another person of the opposite sex is employed in another area of operations in the same undertaking but is being paid more for work of equal value. That would constitute a breach of Article 119 of the Treaty of Rome.

Discrimination occurs if a member of one sex does not receive the same basic pay as a person of the opposite sex where the work is of equal value; and this applies depsite the fact that the other additional benefits balance up the shortfall. If there is any variation in terms, then under the Equal Pay Act, they must be independently justified (*Hayward v. Cammell Laird Shipbuilders Ltd., The Times, April 6, 1988, HL*).

Where a person of one sex does work of **greater** value than a person of the opposite sex at the same establishment or service whether public or private, but is paid **less**, then prima facie that would breach the no discrimination requirement contained in Article 119 of the Treaty and our tribunals and courts would have to provide a remedy within the context of our indigenous legislation (*Murphy & Ors. v. Bord Telecom Eirann, The Times, Feb. 6, 1988, ECJ*).

It would follow that if they were paid *the same* it would still amount to actionable discrimination, but our adjudicating bodies are not empowered to determine what the differential should be (or the rate for the job), although a nominal difference would probably fall foul of the Article.

To whom the Act applies.—The Act applies to any person, irrespective of length of service, whether working full or part time, or whether an employee or one who works under a contract personally to execute any service or labour (e.g., an independent accountant) but not to those who work wholly or mainly outside Great Britain.

DISCRIMINATION ON GROUNDS OF SEX OR RACE.—There always has been discrimination in the employment field, and there probably always will be. What the Acts try to do is to contain it within acceptable limits.

It is a highly sensitive area with a strong emotive content. An employer may dislike a person (purely as an individual) and genuinely feel that he is not up to the standard required for promotion, and if that person is from an ethnic minority, he may also genuinely think that the reason for not being promoted is racial. Few people are able to see their own short-comings.

The definition of 'discrimination' is set out at page 2. Not all discrimination offends against the law. In broad terms, what is prohibited is to deny a person, on the grounds of her/his sex or race, promotion, training, benefits or facilities, or dismiss or subject him/her to any other detriment.

There can also be discrimination by way of victimisation, that is to say, by an employer treating a person less favourably than in the circumstances he would treat someone else, because that person had brought proceedings or given evidence or information in any proceedings connected with sex or racial discrimination, or made allegations in respect of it, *provided* it was made in good faith.

In order to prove that there has been discrimination, a comparison must be made with a person of the opposite sex whose relevant circumstances are the same or not materially different. Thus, it may be necessary to compare a married woman with a married man or a middle aged coloured man with a middle aged white man, where the question would be relevant.

There are a number of exceptions to the operation of the Act. It does not apply where a question of decency or privacy arises, e.g., where there is only one dormitory reasonably available to sleep in, so that only one sex can be sent on a course or be promoted; or where there is a genuine occupational qualification, which could arise where a coloured actor is not transferred to another and better paid part in a play because a white person is necessary to provide authenticity for it.

The Sex Discrimination Act 1975 exempts from its provisions discrimination which relates to pregnancy and childbirth. Both under this Act and the Race Relations Act, positive discrimination is permissible by certain training bodies with a veiw to redressing any imbalance that has existed in a particular area during the previous 12 months.

Questionnaire.—In order to assist employees in ascertaining whether there has been discrimination, the Secretary of State for Employment has prepared a questionnaire (available at any Job Centre, or from the Equal Opportunities Commission or the Commission for Racial Equality) which may be served on an employer requiring him to provide various particulars and to explain the circumstances in which, for instance, a particular employee has not been promoted.

If an employer has never promoted a woman or a coloured employee, although there have been a number of suitable candidates, then that would tend to raise a *prima facie* case of discrimination; but it could be rebutted by showing that there were other non-sexual or non-racist reasons why this was so.

The employer is not obliged to complete and return the form, but if he fails to do so, then a tribunal or court considering a case is likely to take an adverse view unless there is a credible explanation. Similarly, an uninformative, evasive or untruthful answer is likely to have the same consequence.

Other who are caught.—An aider and abettor of another to breach the Acts is liable provided it is done knowingly, but it is a defence to show that the person acted on a statement from that other that the action was lawful and it was reasonable to rely on that assertion.

Those who give instructions to discriminate or pressurise others to do so are also caught, and an employer is vicariously liable for the acts of his employees unless he can prove that he has taken such steps as were reasonably practical to avoid the discrimination.

Those who are Protected.—The same persons who can bring an equal pay claim (see page 7) may apply under these Acts; the same exceptions also apply.

The penalty for a breach is an award not exceeding that which may be given in an unfair dismissal claim (see page 27). The figure is generally raised annually and the maximum amount from 1 April, 1987 is £8,500*. In practice, the award is likely to be under £3,000 but a tribunal may impose other conditions on the employer as well, eg, that the employee should be sent on a training course or be promoted to the post he had applied for within 3 months.

Time Limits.—Due to a lacuna in the Equal Pay Act (as amended) it would seem that there is no time limit for claims brought for equal pay although the compensation is limited to losses incurred during the two years prior to the commencement of proceedings.

DISCIPLINARY HEARINGS.—Practically every company has to hold disciplinary proceedings from time to time. Some are very formal, almost following the procedures of a court; others, usually conducted by small employers, are very casual and rudimentary.

It should be borne in mind that these proceedings may come under the scrutiny of the tribunals or courts on occasions, and it is as well to keep an eye on some aspects of them. What is essential is that those who

* The amount is generally increased on 1st February or 1st April.

adjudicate must act fairly and justly; but there are a number of circumstances in which an employer can still come to grief.

A hearing may be attacked on the basis that the holding of one at all constitutes a breach of an agreement, or it may be affected by extraneous events; or there may be some breach of a procedural requirement, or a breach of natural justice.

The difficulty facing an employer is that there are a number of ways that an employee can challenge his decisions. The employee may rely on remedies in the civil courts, by seeking declarations or orders by means of an ordinary writ or by special procedures known as 'judicial review'; or he may invoke the statutory law, by taking proceedings in the tribunals. Different principles apply in each. To add to the complications, the remedies vary according to where the case is heard. It is necessary to look at the law generally, so as to identify the main pitfalls.

The Hearing.—The written statement setting out the terms of contract (see pages 3 to 6) will (or should) have contained particulars of the disciplinary procedure. It does not have to be in any particular form, but it must provide a fair forum in which the facts can be established and for there to be an impartial adjudication.

It is important that an employee should know what is alleged against him in sufficient detail so as to be able to answer the charge. This may involve giving him particulars of the allegations together with copies of witnesses' statements and any relevant documents in sufficient time before the hearing to enable him to study them and prepare his case.

So if a cashier is alleged to have unlawfully taken money from the tills on four occasions, then she should be given the dates and times, and, if it is known, the amount. She cannot be expected to answer the charges, other than to deny she had committed them, unless she knows the precise allegations. She might be able to prove that she was not on duty on one of the occasions.

Those employers who do not have a proper disciplinary procedure may adopt the one produced by ACAS. It may be incorporated into the contract of employment having been suitably adapted where necessary.

Employer's Default.—If the employer has defaulted in the proceedings by for instance allowing the employee to be dismissed by someone who was not authorised to take that action, he can be attacked from two directions, and with different consequences. Firstly, an action can be started in the High Court for a declaration that the employers are in breach of their contractual duty, and seek an order for the notice of dismissal to be set aside or for some other remedy which may have the effect of causing the employment to continue (for some purposes), or on the other hand to accept the dismissal and claim damages instead.

Secondly, an employee may accept that he has been dismissed and bring a claim in the Industrial Tribunal, alleging that the dismissal was unfair (see pages 24 to 26). If proved the tribunal can order re-instatement or alternatively award compensation (see pages 26 to 28).

Period of Notice.—Another way an employer can become unstuck relates to a failure to comply with the terms of the contract. If an employee is entitled to 6 months notice (except where guilty of gross misconduct warranting summary dismissal), then if the employer, whether through error or intentionally, only gives him a lesser period of notice, then the employee can apply to the High Court for the notice to be set aside on the grounds that it is a nullity. If an order is made then the employer will have to give a fresh notice of dismissal of the correct length.

The fact that inadequate notice has been given is irrelevant in the tribunals, because by bringing proceedings the employee is impliedly acknowledging that he has been effectively dismissed. The only issue will be whether the dismissal was fair and if it was not, whether he is entitled to an order of re-instatement or to an award of compensation.

Judge in own Cause.—It is important to bear in mind that generally no man should be a judge in his own cause. This was how it was put in a leading case:

> 'Even if he was impartial as could be, nevertheless if right minded persons would think that, in the circumstances, there was a real likelihood of bias on his part then he should not sit. And if he does sit, his decision cannot stand . . . The court will not enquire whether he did, in fact, favour one side unfairly . . . Suffice it that reasonable people might think he did' (*Metropolitan Properties Ltd. v. Lannon [1968] 3 AER 304*).

So where a school-master was dismissed by the governors of a voluntary aided school maintained by the council, and that council, pursuant to its powers, held an enquiry into his conduct and agreed that he should be sacked, that decision was overturned on the grounds that three members who adjudicated at that enquiry were governors of the school, even though they had not taken part in the original decision to dismiss (*Hannam v. Bradford City Council [1970] 2 AER 690*).

A disciplinary body is required to exercise its discretion reasonably as to how a hearing is conducted, what evidence is taken into account, and what is the appropriate penalty. It has been put this way in another leading case:

> '. . . a person entrusted with a discretion must, so to speak, direct himself properly in law. He must call his own attention to matters which he is bound to consider. He must exclude from consideration

matters which are irrelevant to what he has to consider. If he does not obey these rules, he may truly be said . . . to be acting 'unreasonably'. Similarly, there may be something so absurd that no sensible person could ever dream that it lay within the powers of the authority. . . . [For] example . . . the red-haired teacher, dismissed because she had red hair. . . . It is so unreasonable that it might almost be described as being done in bad faith' (*Associated Provincial Picture Houses Ltd. v. Wednesbury Corporation [1948] 1 KB 223*).

Right to Cross-Examine.—There is no absolute necessity to give an employee an opportunity to cross-examine witnesses who have made allegations against him, but where this is possible without great inconvenience and expense and will assist in arriving at the truth, then it should be allowed.

Where patients at a hospital made written complaints against a sister, and were not present at a discplinary enquiry, there was no breach of natural justice because there was no procedure by which the employers could have forced them to attend, and in any event there was no application for them to be called at the hearing (*Khanum v. Mid-Glamoran H. A. [1979] ICR 40, EAT*).

Opportunity to be Heard.—Under the common law, where there is a contractual duty to hold a disciplinary enquiry before dismissing, and this may be inferred in certain instances, then a failure to afford the employee an opportunity to state his case, will generally be a breach of natural justice.

There will be cases where this is not only impractical but unnecessary. If an employee deliberately sets his employer's premises on fire and is sent to prison for 3 years, it would be absurd to suggest that he should be invited to give his reasons before being dismissed. In any event, he would be precluded from attending any disciplinary hearing. It would be likely that the contract would be frustrated, eg, it would come to an end automatically without any action being taken by either party (see page 18).

Under the statutory law, a failure to allow an employee to give his side of the story is likely to make a dismissal unfair. But if on the information available to the employer, it is obvious that nothing that the employee could say would make any difference then the dismissal may be adjudged to be fair.

Internal Appeals.—It is one of the cardinal principles of our law that not only must justice be done but that it must be seen to be done. This can give rise to difficulty when conducting an internal appeal against a decision to dismiss.

Generally speaking, a person who has taken the decision to dismiss should not participate in the appeal; but this may not be possible in a small company, where the boss takes all the decisions. The principle to be applied on internal appeals was set out in *Rowe v. Radio Rentals Ltd. [1982] IRLR 177, EAT*

'It is very important that internal appeals procedure run by commercial companies (which usually involve consideration of the decision to dismiss by one person in line management by his superior) should not be cramped by legal requirements imposing impossible burdens on companies in the conduct of their personnel affairs. There may be some exceptional case in which the rule that justice must appear to be done might apply to the full extent that it applies to a judicial hearing. But in general, it is inevitable that those involved in the original dismissal must be in daily contact with their superiors who will be responsible for deciding the appeal: therefore the appearance of total disconnection between the two cannot be achieved. Moreover, at the so-called appeal hearing (which in this and many other cases is of a very informal nature) the initial dismisser is very often required to give information as to the facts to the person hearing the appeal. It is therefore obvious that rules about total separation of functions and lack of contact between the appellate court and those involved in the original decision cannot be applied in the majority of cases'.

Defects in Disciplinary Process.—Sometimes there is a defect at an earlier disciplinary hearing. Under the common law, it may be possible to put right that error or defect on an appeal; but this cannot be done where the contract is underpinned by statutory obligations, eg, where some of the terms and conditions of employment are imposed by statute as occurs for instance to people holding public offices.

If the initial hearing was acting in excess of its jurisdiction, or those adjudicating were blatantly biassed, then providing that the body hearing the appeal was not similarly tainted and had power to deal with the person in the manner in which it did, *and*, at the end of those proceedings a fair result was reached by fair methods, then the decision will stand.

Under the statutory law, the tribunals are not so much concerned with the contractual position than with whether the decision was fair and equitable in all the circumstances, having regard to the size and administrative resources of the employer. Accordingly, if there was a defect at an earlier stage, then that matter would be weighed up as well as the rest of the evidence.

CLOSED SHOP.—A closed-shop agreement, sometimes referred to as a union membership agreement, may be expressly agreed or arise as a result of custom or practice. To come within the statutory definition there must be an agreement or arrangement between an *independent* union, or a number of them, and an employer, or his association, whereby the employer agrees to employ only staff who are members of a union or of a particular one. It must relate to an identifiable class of employees, eg, all the manual workers, the drivers, or the electricians, etc.

In order to have an *approved* closed shop agreement, which will provide immunity to employers and unions in respect of claims made by employees, the following must have been observed:

(i) where the original closed shop agreement came into effect prior to 15 August, 1980, a review ballot has been held, and not less than 80% of those entitled to vote *or* 85% of those who voted, were in favour of it, or

(ii) where the first ballot to have a closed shop took place after 14 August, 1980, it has been approved by not less than 80% of those entitled to vote

(iii) there has been *no* subsequent ballot in which the result is less than 80% of those entitled to vote *and* 85% of those who voted, and

(iv) all those entitled to vote must have been given the opportunity to do so in secret, and if it was done over a period of days, then a qualifying date must have been specified being a date not later than the last day for voting and only the votes of those who were employed on the specified date were counted, *and*

(v) the last ballot approved the closed shop was carried out within 5 years of any claim.

ACTION SHORT OF DISMISSAL.—This provision was originally enacted to protect an employee from a vindictive employer, but it has now been extended to enable him to obtain redress against a union or a person(s) (eg, a shop steward) where they (or he) are bringing pressure on an employer to take action against him short of dismissal. He is also able to take action directly against the union (or the person(s) bringing pressure) in conjunction with proceedings against the employer.

'Action short of dismissal' means any penalty imposed by an employer on an employee such as laying him off from work, demotion, refusing to put him on overtime, giving him the worst jobs and so forth.

Employers may normally take any action of this kind against an employee, but it becomes unlawful when the *reason* is that he is seeking to prevent or deter an employee, as an individual, from becoming a member of an independent trade union or taking part in its activities at the appropriate time, or, for the purpose of compelling him to become a member of a trade union or of a particular trade union. It is in respect of this last matter that the provisions now have a far-reaching effect.

Liability can be avoided if it can be shown that there was an *approved* closed shop union agreement, that is to say, there has been full compliance with all the requirements in regard to ballotting, *and* the statutory exemptions do not apply.*

The main exemptions relate to an objection to joining a union on the grounds of conscience or other deeply held personal conviction, or where a person has never been a member of the union since the closed shop agreement came into force, or where there is in existence a Declaration from a tribunal that the employee has been unreasonably excluded from the union or proceedings are pending before the tribunal for one, or where the employee holds qualifications necessary for his job which preclude him from striking or taking industrial action and he is expelled from his union because of his refusal to do so.

Compensation.—An employee against whom the action has been taken is entitlted to an award consisting not only compensation for any losses sustained by him, but also for damages for frustration and stress.

Proceedings are taken in the tribunals, by claiming against the employer in the first instance, and if that employer so wishes, he may 'join' in the same action the union or person(s) bringing the pressure on him. If the tribunal found that the fault lay entirely with the union or the person(s) bringing the pressure, then they (or he) would have to pay the compensation and any costs, if ordered.

Previously many employers hesitated in 'joining' a union, and would often pay up where they were innocent parties; and the employee would not be able to obtain redress from the party who had caused him the loss. The Employment Act, 1982 amended the law by enabling the employee to join the union and/or person(s) causing the loss in the same action. He could then ask the tribunal to order the true culprit to pay the compensation.

Formerly, provisions were sometimes written into contracts under which contractors undertook to use union-only staff on various work sites, but such provisions are deemed null and void under the 1982 Act. If adverse action is taken against an employee because he is not a member of a union (other than where there is a valid closed shop agreement, *and*, he does not come within the exemptions*) then he can obtain redress against his employer.

Time Limits.—A claim must be presented to the tribunal within 3 months of the incident about which complaint is made; there is power vested in the tribunal to extend the time when it was not reasonably practically to have brought the proceedings in time (see page 20).

PAYMENT BY CHEQUE/CREDIT TRANSFER.—The Wages Act, 1986 allows an employer to pay his existing staff by means other than cash, eg, by cheque or credit transfer, but the actual method will be a matter for negotiation.

---

* There are proposals currently before Parliament to revoke this limitation of liability. If passed they will have the effect of making any action short of dismissal relating to the closed shop automatically unlawful.

If the employer is insistent on paying his existing staff by cheque then it may be difficult for an employee to refuse to accept it provided there are means by which he can cash it, eg, by taking it to a bank which is reasonably accessible.

An employer could make it a term of the contract with all new employees that wages would be made by credit transfer, and perhaps offer existing employees a once-and-for-all payment to accept their wages in future by such means.

DEDUCTION FROM WAGES.—An employer is entitled to make a deduction from the wages of his employee where:

(i) it is authorised by statute (eg, tax, national insurance contributions, an attachment of earnings order);
(ii) it is deducted pursuant to a contract made in writing by the employer with the employee in advance of any deduction;
(iii) it is a sum which the employee has agreed in writing to repay (eg, a loan from the employer);
(iv) an over-payment of wages or expenses is being recovered;
(v) payment is made to a third party pursuant to written instructions given by the employee (to his union, for instance);
(vi) deductions are made because the employee has taken part in a strike or other industrial action.

Wages cover all emoluments whether stated to be pay, fees, bonuses, holiday pay, commissions; but it does not include advances, loans, expenses, pensions or redundancy payments or any payments made to an employee other than in his capacity as a worker.

The right to make deductions extends to an independent contractor who is performing acts of personal service. They may be made from his gross pay but he must have agreed in advance to this in writing.

Time Limits.—Complaints that an employer has unlawfully made deductions must be made to the tribunal within 3 months of the matter about which complaint is made (or if a series, then the last of the matters) or if that is not reasonably practical, then as soon as reasonably practical thereafter (see page 20).

CASH SHORTAGES AND STOCK DEFICIENCIES.—The right of an employer to recover cash shortages and stock deficiencies is restricted to workers in retail employment. This is defined as those employed in the sale and supply of goods or services. It need not be the employee's regular or main employment, eg, it may be a garage mechanic who is temporarily serving petrol.

There is no statutory limitation on making deductions from a worker's pay packet where he has agreed to it in writing in advance provided that:

(i) the demand for the payment of a sum due has been made in writing and served on the employee personally or sent to his last known address, and
(ii) it is made within 12 months of the detection of the shortage or deficiency, and
(iii) any deduction is *not* more than 10% of the amount of his salary or wages made on any one pay-day, except the last one before he leaves the employment.

Where the total amount is in excess of the 10% ceiling, then the deductions may be spread over subsequent pay days until fully recovered. If there is still a sum outstanding after the termination of the employment, then the employer can recover the balance in the county court.

Time Limits.—Complaints that an employer has unlawfully made deductions must be made to the tribunal within 3 months of the matter about which complaint is made (or if a series, then the last of the matters) or if that is not reasonably practical, then as soon as reasonably practical thereafter (see page 20).

TIME OFF WORK.—Some employees undertake certain official duties like sitting as magistrates or as members of a tribunal, or they perform functions on behalf of their unions. In order not to penalise them, the law permits them to have reasonable time off to carry out such functions.

What is 'reasonable' has to be decided in the light of the facts of each case, which will include what time is required for the duty, how much other time the employee is allowed off for his other duties, and the circumstances of the employer's business and the effect that the absence is having on running it. Inevitably there can be a big divergence of views on what is reasonable in a particular case.

ACAS Code of Practice provides guidelines on what should be allowed, but at the end of the day, there has to be a balancing act. The time off for union business must be for *bona fide* purposes and which are concerned with enhancing industrial relations. Planning a strike or seeking to foment unrest does not qualify.

Where the time off relates to union work, a distinction is drawn between whether the employee is acting as an official of an *independent* trade union, which is recognised by the employer for bargaining purposes, where he is permitted by the employer to take time off to carry out union activities under the statute and not under some private arrangement, *and*, when he is an ordinary union member participating in union activities, eg, attending a meeting to discuss acceptance of a pay offer. For the former, he is entitled to be paid during his absence; for the latter he is not.

MATERNITY.—The provisions relating to maternity have long been a headache to all who have to understand them, be they employer, or employees or even the judiciary. They have been criticised for

'being of inordinate complexity exceeding the worst excesses of a taxing statute'

It has long been recognised that pregnancy puts women at a disadvantage in the employment field. They have to leave their jobs for many months and not many employers will normally keep their posts open, even if a woman is very good. She might not come back, and further someone would have to do her job in her absence.

The conflicting interests have been resolved in favour of women who are now given a statutory right to return to work following the birth of their child, and so employers have to use their ingenuity to overcome any difficulties.

A woman who has been continuously employed for 2 years prior to the beginning of the 11th week before the expected week of confinement is entitled to have her job back after the birth of her child provided she complies with the undermentioned formalities:

(i) she gives notice (in writing, if required by her employer) that she will be absent on account of pregnancy or confinement but intends to return to work after the birth of her child. It must be given at least 21 days before she leaves, or if that is not reasonably practical, then as soon as practical thereafter;

(ii) she produces for inspection, if required to do so by her employer, a certificate from her doctor or midwife stating the expected date of birth;

(iii) if her employer, not earlier than 7 weeks after the expected date of confinement, seeks written confirmation that she does intend to return to work, then she confirms in writing that she does within 14 days, or if that is not reasonably practical, then as soon as is reasonably practical thereafter;

(iv) she gives written notice that she intends to resume working *at least* 21 days beforehand, the date for return to work being not later than 29 weeks after the beginning of the week when the birth occurred.

The requirement to give the *written* notice prior to return to work is mandatory, and failure to comply, for whatever reason, removes her statutory right to return. But the date of return can be delayed by up to 4 weeks, by the employer, for any reason provided he specifies it, and by the mother, if she is incapable of work and produces a medical certificate to confirm it.

Where the law allows an extension of time on the grounds that it was 'not reasonably practical' to comply with the time requirements, then provided she acted reasonably promptly when she was in a position to make a decision, she would retain her statutory rights. This could arise, for instance, where she was waiting for the results of medical tests, but not where the delay was caused by her not being able to make up her mind.

If the employee has common law terms under her contract of employment which are more favourable to her, then she can rely on those terms to extend her rights. So if there is an agreement that she need not return to work for 40 weeks following the birth (as opposed to the statutory 29 weeks) then she can be absent for the 40 weeks. She will retain her *statutory* right to return to work provided she has complied with the statutory formalities such as the giving of notice etc.

The special statutory rights entitle her to return to work on the same terms and conditions as she would have been on had she not been absent through pregnancy. The job need not be precisely the same but the

> 'nature of work . . . and the capacity and the place in which [s]he is so employed'

must be not less favourable.

If her job has ceased to exist either on account of redundancy or re-organisation then she must be offered suitable and appropriate alternative employment on terms and conditions no less favourable, if this is available, either with the employer or with his successor, or with any associated employer.

Small Employers.—Those employers with not more than 5 staff including any with an associated employer at the time the women left, will be immune from any liability where it is not reasonably practical to permit her to return to her old job or to offer her other work. For instance, if a woman is employed in a shop where the owner and 3 other persons work, and it is essential to have a full quota of staff, there is no requirement that the job must be kept open for her; but if there is a vacancy at the time the woman is able to return, it must be offered to her.

MISCELLANEOUS MATTERS

BUSINESS TRANSFERS.—The law relating to the sale of businesses is complicated by the fact that part of it is derived from our indigenous legislation, (the Employment Protection (Consolidation) Act, 1978 (as amended)), and part has been imposed as a result of an EEC Directive which led to the passing of the Transfer of Undertakings (Protection of Employment) Regulations, 1981.

The Act and the Regulations are not mutually exclusive, and the interpretation of a European type of legislation, using our own common law canons of construction, has led to some unanticipated results. The Regulations have been irreverently dubbed 'the Pandora's box of ambiguities'.

Further, the European Court of Justice is itself building up its own 'common law' by a series of rulings on the meaning of this Directive. Hence it is necessary to keep a weather eye on that quarter.

Our own Legislation.—The 1978 Act provides that where a change occurs in the ownership of a business which includes a trade or profession or any activity carried on by a body of persons the new owner takes over the liabilities of the staff who are in the business at the time of transfer, or in any identifiable part of it which is transferred. Employees then continue on as though they were still employed by the same person or firm, and their rights and duties will remain unaffected.

There has to be a transfer of a going concern, which will usually include the good-will, know-how, the benefit of existing contracts, copyrights and so forth. The test that is usually applied is to ascertain whether the business remains essentially the same, but in different hands, and it matters not how the parties see it, or even how they have described it.

A purchaser is at liberty to decide which employees he takes over from the previous firm. By ensuring that there was a clear break of a day between their dismissal and the transfer of the business to him, he will avoid any liability to claims from those dismissed employees.

There are still unresolved judicial views as to when a 'transfer', for these purposes, takes place. When negotiations are complete? When there is a binding agreement to buy the business but before completion? When the new employer is let into possession of the business to run it, but before there has been an assignment of the lease of the property to him, so that he can withdraw from the sale if that assignment is blocked? The permutations are endless but it would seem that the law will finally came down in favour of the transfer occurring when completion takes place.

Position of Vendor.—A vendor who wishes to protect the position of his staff may not be in a position to do so if he is selling an ailing business. The sale may be the only way to remain solvent, or the business may be in the hands of a receiver.

If he complies with a requirement to dismiss all the staff prior to the sale of the business, he will be exposed to a claim by his own staff. But he is entitled to rely on the defences which are available to him under the 1978 Consolidation Act: eg, redundancy or some other substantial reason, which will generally restrict his liability to making a redundancy payment.

Liability under Transfer Regulations.—The Regulations apply to the transfer of 'any trade of business', or part of one, except where it 'is not in the nature of a commercial venture'. The transfer may be effected by sale or other disposition, or operation of law. This is a narrower definition than under the 1978 Act.

On such a transfer, the purchaser takes over all the vendor's rights, powers, duties and liabilities in respect of the staff provided that the employee is still employed *at the moment* of transfer.

If an employee decides to leave the job at the time of the transfer, then the purchaster will be liable for any rights the employee may have in relation to the employment, eg, unfair dismissal, redundancy pay, holiday pay, severance pay and so forth. The employment will automatically pass to him, whatever the wishes of the parties, provided that the employee is still in employment at the moment of transfer.

Practical Effect of Difference between Act & Regulations.—There are some aspects where the differences will have a practical effect. The Regulations do not apply to certain activities like employment in Local Authorities, in charities or in some types of clubs (except in the bar, which may be a severable commercial activity) and so on. In such a case the employee would still have his rights under the 1978 Act, but if the (vendor) employer was in liquidation, then the chance of him recovering his full loss will be limited. The Secretary of State underwrites certain obligations, eg, redundancy pay, money in lieu of notice, outstanding holiday pay, and a few other matters up to certain limits.

Where the Regulations apply, the employee has the additional protection in that a dismissal, if for any reason connected with the transfer, is automatically unfair, whether carried out by the vendor or the purchaser, unless it is shown that it was for:

(i) 'an economic, technical or organisational reason entailing changes in the workforce . . .', and
(ii) it was fair and equitable in all the circumstances.

This means that it is difficult for the purchaser of a business to alter the terms of an existing contract of employment of a worker in a business that he has purchased, eg, reduce his pay, remove his right to commission and so on. If he does so to any substantial extent, he takes the risk that the employee may leave, and claim that he has been constructively dismissed (see pages 21 and 22). If that is proved, then the dismissal will be automatically unfair because the employer would not be able to show that the alterations would 'entail changes in the workforce'; it would only be in the contract with the employee. Furthermore it may be difficult to prove that it was fair and equitable in the circumstances.

LEVIES.—The Secretary of State for Employment is empowered under the Industrial Training Act, 1982 (which replaced the 1964 Act) to make provision for the training of persons for employment in any activities of industry or commerce, by establishing Boards to carry out that function.

The Manpower Services Commission, having complied with various statutory requirements to consult interested parties, puts forward proposals for making an Industrial Training Order, and if accepted, the Secretary of State will make an order, by statutory instrument, setting up the Training Board. The Board submits levy proposals to the Manpower Services Commission for the raising of funds, and if approved, the matter is put to the Secretary of State. If he is satisfied that the proposals are necessary to encourage adequate training, he may impose a 'levy' on employers in the industry.

The Levy Order is made by statutory instrument and all those who come within the provisions are liable to pay. The amount is based on a figure for each grade of employee, subject to various limitations. The Board is responsible for ascertaining which employers are liable and to assess them. For these purposes the Board is empowered to require employers to provide details of their business and, in particular, information about their employees.

If there is a refusal or failure to supply the necessary information, then the Board estimates the liability and makes a demand for payment, which has to be remitted within a specified time. The assessment is likely to be on the high side, and the only way that the amount, or even liability to pay any amount, can be challenged is to appeal to the Industrial Tribunal.

A tribunal will hear the evidence of each side. This may be done by the calling of witnesses, or by the production of documents, or by making representations in writing. Normally the Board will not attend the hearing but submit its case in writing and leave it to the firm or person appealing (on whom the onus of proving the case lies) to satisfy a tribunal that there is no liability or the amount was wrong. It can be an expensive and time consuming exercise which could have been avoided by completing the questionnaire accurately and in time. A tribunal may rescind the assessment, or reduce the amount, or confirm it, or even increase it.

The tribunal will generally have to consider two key areas on an appeal. Firstly, does the employer come within the definition of a relevant employer as set out in the Levy Order? Secondly, if he does, has the assessment been made on the correct basis? In order to be liable to pay anything it will generally have to be shown that either more of the manpower deployed or the turnover is concerned with the industry to which the Order relates, and this was the position between the stipulated levy dates.

For the purposes of an appeal, it is important to present as much evidence as possible by way of documentation because a tribunal will have to determine the number of employees, what they did and what part of the turnover of the company related to the industry concerned. Accounts, contracts of employment, and so forth carry far more weight than oral evidence.

TRADE UNION RECOGNITION.—An employer may recognise an independent trade union for the purposes of collective bargaining, that is, in respect of negotiations relating to terms and conditions of employment, engagement or termination or suspension from work, allocation of work, discipline, membership of a union, facilities for union officials and machinery for negotiation or consultations. If it does so, then the union automatically acquires certain other rights, like the right for its members to have time off from work to carry out official union duties.

Whether there is 'recognition' depends on whether there is mutuality, that is to say, when the employer acknowledges the role of the union to negotiate. Mere reliance on an agreement, which had been affected by a trade association, to which the employer belongs, with a union, will not be sufficient. There must be direct negotiation between the employer and the union.

An agreement to recognise a union need not be formal, or in writing. It may have come about imperceptibly and unintentionally, and even against the avowed intention of the employer. But it cannot be imposed by a third party or by an extraneous event. So where the Secretary of State for Education granted a union the right to sit on the Burnham Committee, which fixed teachers' salaries, it did then give them the right to recognition because some of their teaching members were employed by a Local Authority. Only the actions of the employers are relevant in deciding whether there has been recognition of a union.

Inevitably, in the absence of express agreement, there is a wide grey area. There may be recognition for some purposes but not for others. The conduct of an employer may be equivocal. In order for a union to qualify, it must show that it has been clearly recognised for collective bargaining purposes over a period of time. Even if it does, the employer may withdraw that right at any time and there is no procedure by which the union can force an employer to recognise them again other than by using their industrial muscle.

SUSPENSION ON MEDICAL GROUNDS.—In some industries employees are liable to come into contact with injurious substances such as radioactive articles, lead or dangerous chemicals. Provisions have been made whereby, if an employee's health is endangered, then he must be suspended from work.

This will arise where the monitored radiation dose limit has been exceeded or if a specially appointed doctor certifies that the employee's health is endangered by, for instance, excessive contact with lead.

Any employee with more than 1 month's service, who is suspended from work must be given his normal week's pay until such time as he is certified fit to return, up to a maximum period of 26 weeks. This right is limited to instances where he is suspended as a result of the *risk* of bodily or mental disablement and *not* where he is sent home as a result of it. In the latter instance the employee may still be entitled to be paid, but not under this provision.

Complaints of a failure by the employer to make this payment, or where there is a dispute over the amount, are made to the Industrial Tribunal, but they must be lodged within 3 months of the alleged breach or if that is not reasonably practical, then as soon as reasonably practical thereafter (see page 20).

CODES OF PRACTICE.—A number of different bodies issue Codes of Practice on a variety of subjects. Even when they are produced with the authority of Parliament they do not have the force of law but they may be taken into account by a court or a tribunal when adjudicating on any case. They are rather like the Highway

Code: the intention is that they should give practical guidance on how a person or party should conduct or organise themselves in the employment field.

The conciliation service, ACAS, issue a number of codes dealing with industrial relations. They provide a procedure for settling disputes, and for conducting disciplinary hearings; they advise on what disclosures of information ought to be given to a union for the purpose of collective bargaining, what time off ought to be allowed to employees to attend to union business or carry out public duties and so forth.

The Commission for Racial Equality has produced a Code dealing with the problems of racial discrimination in the employment field and what positive acts ought to be taken to counter this problem. Similarly, the Equal Opportunities Commission has published its own Code dealing with sexual equality.

The Health and Safety Executive has issued a Code of Practice which sets out what information should be disclosed by employers to their staff or their representatives. They relate to changes which might effect the health and safety of employees, to providing technical information about any hazards, or to reports from consultants, to instructions from manufacturers, to records of accidents, to notification of any dangerous occurrences or of industrial diseases, and to the results of any routine tests.

The Secretary of State for Employment has brought out a Code on picketing. He recommends that the number of pickets at each entrance to a works should be limited to 6 and there should be consultation with the police at the time. There should be no interference with essential services and disciplinary action should not be taken against a union member for crossing an unauthorised picket line or one manned by members not at their place of work.

Another Code of Practice produced by the Secretary of State gives help on the creation and operation of closed shop agreements. It suggests that before one is brought about there should be overwhelming support for it, that basic individual rights should be respected and that it should be flexibly and tolerantly applied.

The Manpower Services Commission has produced a code covering the employment of disabled persons, in which it sets out the difficulties encountered by disabled people and how employers can help. Those with handicaps should receive fair treatment and be considered solely on their ability to do the job. They should be integrated into any job and if they have special needs then these should be carefully considered. Their ability and potential should be fully developed and every opportunity given to them to train and obtain promotion. The Code is purely for use on a voluntary basis.

HEALTH AND SAFETY AT WORK.—The Health and Safety at Work etc., Act, 1974 was passed with a view to codifying the numerous statutes and statutory instruments which regulate the obligations of employers, and to provide for a unified inspectorate service; but little progress has been made in either direction yet. The Acts and statutory instruments made under them remain and are either enforced by the Local Authority or by the Health & Safety inspectorate, depending on which Act is alleged to have been breached.

There is a general duty on employers under the Health and Safety at Work etc., Act to ensure, so far as is reasonably practical, the health and safety at work of not only all their employees, but also of others who are on their premises and who may be affected by their operations. Thus commercial travellers are usually protected.

The phrase 'reasonably practical' means that the degree of risk involved has to be weighed against the onerousness of the measures necessary to abate the danger and the frequency with which it is likely to arise. If the cost of remedial work is disproportionately high to the risk then the employer can rely on the phrase.

For instance, if the floor of a cellar beneath a warehouse is very rough but employees only visit it extremely rarely, and there is little likelihood of them doing so more frequently in the future, a requirement that it should be re-surfaced would obviously be absurd. The employer could claim that it was not 'reasonably practical'.

Notices.—Inspectors will pay routine visits to premises to ensure that the employer complies with his statutory duties. If there is an accident, then they will usually attend to establish the cause and see whether there has been a breach of the Act. If one is found, then the inspector can either orally tell the employer to put the matter right and later check that this has been done, or he can serve an 'Improvement Notice' or a 'Prohibition Notice'.

If the matter alleged is very serious, eg, guards have been removed from a circular saw which is in constant use, or the employer has been flouting the law despite frequent warnings of the consequences, then the inspector may prosecute the offender in the Magistrates' Court.

If an Improvement Notice is served, it must specify the section of the Act alleged to have been breached, give reasons for the allegation, and require the matter to be remedied within a period of not less than 21 days. That period may be extended, more than once if necessary, provided that no appeal has been lodged. It may also be withdrawn before the end of the specified period.

An appeal against a Notice must be lodged at a tribunal not later than 21 days after it has been served on the employer, or within such further period as is reasonably thereafter. In the case of an Improvement Notice, the effect of appealing is to freeze the requirements until the hearing. If the appeal is abandoned then they are automatically re-imposed. The tribunal has power to confirm, cancel or modify the notice, as it thinks fit.

Unless the employer disputes the Notice, then he must comply with the requirements within the specified time limit, or the agreed extended time limit. If he fails to comply he can be prosecuted in the Magistrates' Court, and it is no defence to prove there that it was not reasonably practical to comply with the Notice, which he could have raised in proceedings before the tribunal. The offence is failing to comply.

A Prohibition Notice is more serious. If an inspector is of the opinion that any activity which is carried on by the employer or an occupier contravenes an Act and involves a risk of serious personal injury, then he will serve a Prohibition Notice, and specify the matters which allegedly give or will give rise to the risk. He will direct that those activities shall not be carried on unless the matters specified have been remedied. If there is a time limit specified for remedying the defects, then the inspector may withdraw the Notice at any time before its expiry, or he may extend the period provided that no appeal has been lodged.

The lodging of an appeal does not have the effect of automatically suspending it. An application has to be made to the tribunal for this to be done; and this will be the subject of separate proceedings ahead of the main hearing.

SOME CONCEPTS OF LAW

WHO IS AN EMPLOYEE?.—A great many rights and duties depend on whether a person is an employee or is self-employed. Some of the Acts and statutory instruments give differing definitions on who is an 'employee', but the same common law tests are applied except in those cases where the definition is widened to include a someone who would otherwise be excluded. For instance, in the discrimination Acts it covers those who are self employed but who perform works of personal service.

At common law no one test is decisive but the question of direction and control is very important. The whole picture has to be considered. Is the person able to accept or refuse work, is he subject to disciplinary proceedings, is he paid gross or less tax, is he purporting to work on his own account or for and on behalf of the employer, must he take holidays as directed?

What a party cannot do is to put the wrong label on the relationship, whether for a genuine or for an illegal reason. But there is a wide grey area where a person could quite legitimately come under one heading or the other, and in those circumstances it is open to both sides to elect to treat the person under either. Where they do so, they will be bound by that agreement.

But where it is found that the wrong description has been attached to the relationship, eg, he is really an employee although described as self-employed, then the courts or tribunals will make a declaration to that effect. It is possible though that for some other purposes, e.g. for tax, or National Insurance, he could still be held to be the opposite.

ILLEGAL CONTRACTS.—The courts and tribunals take a tough stand on contracts which are tainted by illegality, irrespective of the hardship caused to one side or of the undeserved gain to the other. An employee may throw away considerable employment rights as a result of greed for a relatively small sum of money. The usual way this occurs is that part of his pay does not go through the books, and hence is not subject to tax. When this occurs there is a break in the continuity of employment (see pages 19 and 20) and in many cases this will deprive him of the necessary qualifying period of employment in order to bring a claim.

Although the employer benefits in a number of ways, he will be at risk under some of the penal provisions in the tax legislation.

The harshness of the rule is mitigated in some instances. An employee will not be deprived of his rights where he can show that there was no illegality on the facts as he knew them. For instance, if less than the proper amount of tax was being deducted, and this was due to the incompetence of his employer, and which was unknown to him, then he will not be debarred from bringing a claim.

Where the contract is against the public interest, the employee will also lose his employment rights. For instance, a contract to secure clients for a brothel would be illegal and any wages or commission owing would be irrecoverable.

On the other hand, where the contract is *prima facie* lawful, but is carried out in an unlawful way, the employee would not be debarred. So if a lorry driver was required to drive his vehicle in an unroadworthy condition, or where he would have to exceed the speed limit in order to reach his destination within time limits specified by the employers, then he could still bring proceedings against the employer.

FRUSTRATION OF CONTRACT.—From time to time an event occurs which makes it virtually impossible to carry out a contract because of some extraneous event. If there is an agreement to let a house but it is burnt down in the meanwhile, there would be frustration and the contract would come to an end automatically without the need for anyone to take any action. In the absence of special provisions, the rights and liabilities of each party would lapse.

The same principle applies to employment contracts. The significance is that there would be no 'dismissal' by an employer and which is generally necessary in order to found certain claims.

Frustration generally arises in imprisonment and sickness cases. If an employee is sent to prison for 5 years, then he would be unable to carry out his job for a substantial time; it would be frustrated. Similarly, if an employee has a heart attack and is unlikely to be able to return to work, then there would be frustration. A sentence of 3 weeks imprisonment for refusing to pay a fine, or absence for 3 weeks through illness would not bring the contract to an end. In between, there is inevitably a large grey area.

Where a person deliberately does an act which prevents him from carrying out his side of the bargain, then he cannot rely on the doctrine as a defence to a claim against him. He will be liable for the full consequences of the breach.

FUNDAMENTAL BREACH OF CONTRACT.—Every contract of employment has a number of different terms: the pay, the number of weeks' holiday, the job content, the normal hours of work and so forth. Some of the provisions are important and others are peripheral. If there is a breach of an important element, which goes to the root of the contract, then there would be a fundamental breach of contract, and the aggrieved party can treat the contract as being at an end and claim damages or compensation.

If the breach is not serious then the contract cannot be abrogated; and the only remediy lies in a claim for damages—a course which is rarely followed by an employee, who wishes to remain in the employment.

The borderline between the two is often hard to determine. For instance, if the right to some allowances is removed from an employee which will only have a small effect on his net income then there would probably be no fundamental breach, but if his salary is reduced by a quarter then it would obviously be serious. If the reduction is 5% it could go either way.

Thus where the contract required the employee to act as a buyer for a firm, but all the interesting parts of his job were subsequently removed leaving him with only humdrum duties, it was held that that amounted to a fundamental breach (*Coleman v Baldwin [1977] IRLR 342, EAT*).

'WITHOUT PREJUDICE'.—The law encourages parties to try and resolve their differences without having recourse to litigation, but not everyone is reasonable and consequently a large number of cases find their way into the courts and tribunals.

In order to be able to compromise an action, a party must be allowed to speak openly and freely without the risk of what he proposes being revealed to those to adjudicate in his case. An offer to settle a claim for £2,000 might be taken to be an acknowledgement of liability whereas all that is being done is to try and buy off an action in order to save further expense.

A party can ensure that any proposals to settle an action is kept confidential by marking any correspondence 'without prejudice'. The letter cannot be produced at a hearing unless he waives his 'privilege'. But it is necessary for there to be a dispute or for some negotiations to be taking place at this time; otherwise there will be no 'privilege' attached to it.

Sometimes negotiations take place through ACAS to settle a claim. All statements made to, or any advice given by, ACAS are privileged and cannot be disclosed in court or in the tribunal unless both sides agree. But where it is alleged that has been a concluded agreement, which is disputed by one side, then an ACAS official can be called to give evidence to prove the agreement.

***EX-GRATIA* PAYMENTS.**—When an employment comes to an end, there are usually some payments due to an employee: money in lieu of notice, holiday money, redundancy pay and so on. Sometimes an employer makes an '*ex-gratia*' payment as well (a sum which he is not obliged to pay under any legal requirement) for a variety of reasons. He may do so as an act of generosity, or because he anticipates trouble and he wishes to buy off any prospective claim.

If he makes an *ex-gratia* payment, which is by implication in settlement of any claim that an ex-employee may have against him, then that sum may be set-off against any liability he may have in respect of the employee. This is because any claim by the employee will arise from the cessation of the employment and will be limited to the loss he has sustained. The *ex-gratia* payment would not have been paid to him, but for his leaving the employment.

In the tribunals there is generally a limit on the amount the employee can recover, and consequently his loss may be much greater than the maximum compensation that the tribunal can award in a particular case. If that is so, then the *ex-gratia* payment will be taken off his actual loss, and he will recover the balance, up to the maximum that the tribunal can award.

MITIGATION OF DAMAGES.—There is a duty on everyone to mitigate so far as is reasonable any damage he has sustained. So if a man is sacked, he must seek suitable alternative employment as soon as possible. If he merely sits around building up his loss, then he will be unable to recover the amount attributable to his idleness.

A difference between the common and statutory law arises on a dismissal. At common law, in order to dismiss there must be compliance with the contractual obligations, eg, a requirement to give a notice of a fixed length, or follow certain formalities for disciplinary hearings before dismissing. An employee may expressly or by implication waive his rights and elect to treat the dismissal as effective.

A failure to follow the requirements may result in the contract not being lawfully terminated, and the employment carries on until as there has been full compliance provided that the employee is able to continue working.

Under the statutory employment law, the contract ceases when one employer dismisses, or, if he gave notice then when the notice expires, and it matters not whether the employee consents or not.

ORDINARILY WORKS IN GREAT BRITAIN.—The rights and duties arising out of the employment legislation are intended to apply, in the main, to those staff whose contracts of employment provide that they work in Great Britain.

In practice it is often difficult to determine in borderline cases where a person ordinarily works. For instance, a long distance lorry driver may spend most of his working life on the roads on the continent of Europe. Or a girl may be employed by an English company to run some chalets in Switzerland for a year. Are they protected under the Acts?

In deciding where a person ordinarily works a court or tribunal has to consider what was originally agreed between the parties, or the effect of any subsequent variation, and what has happened to the employee in practice. In most contracts, the employer retains a degree of discretion as to where an employee should work, and so the overall position has to be evaluated.

In marginal cases the test that is usually applied is to see where the employee's base is, and if he spends a lot of time travelling, then where it begins and ends, where his home is, in what currency he is paid, whether he pays national insurance, and the like.

There are special provisions which give protection to those who work on oil-rigs, and on U.K.-registered ships.

'ASSOCIATED EMPLOYERS'.—The phrase 'associated employers' is frequently found in the employment legislation and various rights and duties arise from it. The statutory definition is as under;

> Any two employers are to be treated as 'associated' if one is a company of which the other (directly or indirectly) has control, or if both are companies of which a third person (directly or indirectly) has control.

A 'company' must be a limited company and 'control' is limited to cases where a person is a major shareholder with voting rights so that he can impose his will in the case of a dispute.

Sometimes husbands and wives together, but not individually, are the major shareholders in two companies, but because the wife does not participate actively in their affairs, the husband in practice exercises control. It is doubtful whether in this instance the two companies would be associated in law.

CONTINUOUS EMPLOYMENT.—Under the statutory law, most rights are only acquired by employees who have the necessary 'continuous employment' with an employer. For instance, every employee, with two years continuous employment, who is dismissed because of a fall off of work, is entitled to redundancy pay, the amount of which increases with age and the length of service. If there is a break of a week or more, then that period is broken, and an employee will have to start building up the period of continuous employment again.

In order to preserve the employee's rights in a number of different situations, where the period of continuous employment would otherwise be broken, elaborate statutory provisions have to be applied. They are of such complexity that there have been a large number of appeals on the meaning of various phrases and words in different circumstances.

For the purposes of counting the period of continuous employment, the time starts when the employee commences under his contract, and not when he takes up his duties, and ceases on the date when he stops working or ceases to be paid, if later. Further, part time work is excluded unless the employee is contractually bound to work 16 hours per week or more, or does in fact work at least 16 hours per week; but where he has been employed for five years or more, then the figure is reduced to 8 hours per week.

A break of a week or more in the employment does not affect the continuity in the circumstances set out below. The more common ones are where the employee is absent:

(i) through sickness or injury, up to a maximum of 26 weeks unless there is an agreement for it to continue longer;
(ii) on account of temporary cessation of work, which must be of a transient nature;
(iii) in circumstances in which, by arrangement or custom, he is regarded in a business or trade as being continuously employed;
(iv) as a result of a lockout by the employer, or a strike by the employee, although in the latter case, the time out on strike does not count for computation purposes;
(v) through working temporarily abroad, but not for more than 26 weeks, and time spent abroad does not count for computation purposes;
(vi) there is re-instatement or re-engagement with the employer or with an associated employer in consequence of a complaint of unfair dismissal;
(vii) for employees with *less* than 5 years service, the contract is temporarily varied so as to provide for between 8 and 16 hours of work each week, up to a maximum of 26 weeks;
(viii) for a women where (a) she is absent wholly or partly because of pregnancy or confinement for a period of up to 26 weeks, or (b) where she exercises her statutory right to return to work following the birth

of her child, from up to 11 weeks before the expected week of confinement until the 29th week from the beginning of the week when the birth occurred, but this can be extended to 33 weeks in certain circumstances; or by a (common law) agreement, for a longer period;

(ix) the business in which the employee works is transferred to a new employer and the employee is employed at the time of transfer.

The parties cannot by agreement change the effect of the law relating to the status or rights of an employee which arises under the statutes. But they can privately agree on different rights and liabilities which will be enforceable under the common law in the ordinary civil courts.

For instance, an employee may have six years of service with a firm of auctioneers owned by one brother, and then transfer to another similar firm owned by a second brother. If the second brother agreed that the transfer would not break the employee's period of continuous employment and he works for a further four years before being made redundant, then because the second brother does not come within the statutory definition of an 'associated employer' (see page 19), there is only a *statutory* entitlement to redundancy pay based on 4 years of continuous employment. The second brother would have a *contractual* liability to pay it on the basis of 10 years of continuous employment.

TIME LIMITS.—The law requires various acts to be done within specified times, otherwise rights will be lost. This is strictly enforced in respect of statutory remedies, which are tried in the Industrial Tribunals.

Each Act specifies the time limits, and states whether a tribunal may extend the time, and if so what test has to be applied. It has to be proved either:

(i) that it was not reasonably practical to have presented the claim in time, and it was lodged as soon as reasonably practical thereafter, or

(ii) that it is 'just and equitable' to extend time having regard to the reason shown by the employee and to all the other relevant circumstances.

In order to prove that it was not 'reasonably practical' to have presented his claim in time, the employee must show that there was some physical or cogent reason that prevented him from doing so, ie, he was ill or abroad at the critical time, or that he had posted his 'Originating Application' (see page 29) in time to arrive within the period specified, but that for an unknown reason it was delayed in the post. Ignorance of the law is generally not good enough, as there is wide publicity given to the necessity to act within the time limits.

Further, if solicitors or other skilled advisers like the Citizens' Advice Bureau or a union are acting on behalf of a person, and they fail to take action in time, then their negligence will not save the employee from the consequences.

The 'just and equitable' test is far less stringent, and a tribunal can look into all the circumstances which they think are relevant. This would include considering the apparent strength or weakness of a case.

Claims for breach of contract of employment brought in the ordinary civil courts must be commenced within six years when they then become statute-barred. By that time the matter will generally have been settled or lapsed, and so the time factor does not usually pose a problem.

The time limits and test for extension of time for the more frequent claims are as under:

Claim	Time limit	Test
Unfair dismissal	3 months	reasonably practical
Redundancy (unless written notice to an employer has been given)	6 months	fair and equitable up to a maximum of 12 months
Discrimination	3 months	fair and equitable
Equal Pay	3 months	fair and equitable
Failure to give Written Reasons	3 months	reasonably practical
Action Short of Dismissal	3 months	reasonably practical

BURDEN OF PROOF.—Where a party makes an allegation, eg, that he was discriminated against on the grounds of race, the onus of proving it generally lies on him. Sometimes a statute switches the burden to the other side, or does not put the burden on either party to prove some element.

Where the onus does lie on a party, all that is necessary is for him to prove that on a balance of probabilities his allegation is more likely than not to be true.

OFFICIAL BODIES

ACAS.—The Advisory, Conciliation and Arbitration Service, ['ACAS'], is well known now although it was only established by statute in 1975. It is required to promote improvement in collective bargaining and the reform of collective bargaining machinery, to try and settle disputes, or to refer disputes to the Central Arbitration Committee, and to issue Codes of Practice where it thinks it appropriate.

It has acquired considerable expertise in settling employment disputes, especially those concerned with the dismissal of individual employees, and it brings about a settlement in about two-thirds of all claims commenced in the tribunals. They do not necessarily result in a cash payment. The Service is able to independently advise an employee or an employer as to whether any claim has any chance of success and whether it should be abandoned although it is no part of their duty to advise as such but merely to try and effect a settlement.

Any advice that the Service gives is confidential and cannot be divulged in any proceedings.

CENTRAL ARBITRATION COMMITTEE.—This body, which also came into existence in 1975 from the same statute, inherited the duties that were formerly carried out by other arbitration boards and bodies.

It arbitrates on disputes referred to it by ACAS.

It also deals with complaints that an employer has failed to make disclosure to recognised unions of certain information which is required for collective bargaining purposes. But an employer cannot be forced to give information about groups of employees or issues in areas where the union is not recognised nor where it relates to individuals who have not given their consent to disclosure.

CERTIFICATION OFFICER.—The Certification Officer, who is appointed by the Secretary of State, is responsible for:

(i) ensuring observance of statutory procedures governing the setting up and operation of political funds and dealing with member's complaints in respect of breaches of fund rules;

(ii) ensuring compliance with statutory procedures for mergers and transfers of engagements, and complaints about the conduct of merger ballots;

(iii) maintaining a list of unions and employer's bodies, ensuring that they keep proper accounts and that superannuation schemes conform to requirements for actuarial examination;

(iv) reimbursing unions for certain expenditures incurred in conducting secret postal ballots.

(v) approving the ballot rules of any union wishing to continue spending money on political objects, and dealing with complaints that unions have not held secret ballots for elections to certain offices.

A union whose name is on the list maintained by the Certification Officer, may apply to him for a certificate that it is independent. If, having made such inquiries as he thinks fit and taking into account relevant information, he finds that

(i) the union is not under the domination or control of the employer, and

(ii) it is not liable to interference by the employer,

then he will issue a certificate.

If he refuses to issue one, then a union may appeal to the Employment Appeal Tribunal (see page 33). If, on appeal, the Appeal Tribunal is satisfied that a certificate should have been issued, it will make a declaration to that effect and give the appropriate directions.

THE TERMINATION OF EMPLOYMENT

GENERALLY.—A great many rights depend on an employee being 'dismissed', eg, in order to be eligible to claim redundancy, to bring an action for unfair dismissal, and for certain other remedies there must have been a 'dismissal'.

How a Dismissal Occurs.—The contract of employment can come to an end in many different ways; some of them will be classified as an employer's 'dismissal', others not. The contract may be expressly terminated or the effect of action taken by an employer may amount to a 'dismissal' both under the common law as well as under the statutes.

If the contract is for a fixed term and comes to an end without being renewed, then by statute it is deemed to be a 'dismissal'; but where the employee is taken on to do a particular job of indeterminate length, and the contract comes to an end on completion of the work, there is no 'dismissal'.

If the employee resigns, there is generally no 'dismissal', because that is the employee's own decision. But sometimes a person 'resigns' in a moment of anger and not intending to, and the employer realises that it is not a genuine resignation. In such circumstances, the employment does not come to an end. On the other hand, where there is a clear and unequivocal resignation, this is binding and may not be withdrawn without the consent of the employer.

But if the employee resigns because of the conduct of the employer, it may become a 'constructive dismissal' and the employee retains his full rights. To entitle him to leave, there must have been a fundamental breach of contract by the employer, either of an express or an implied term. It is not sufficient that the employer has acted *unreasonably*.

So if an employer unilaterally decides to halve the salary of the employee that would be a breach going to the root of a contract entitling the employee to leave and claim that he has been constructively dismissed.

In every contract of employment there is an implied term that there must be mutual trust and confidence. If this is broken, it would be likely, in many instances, to amount to a fundamental breach.

Thus if an employer told the subordinates of a manager that the manager had been guilty of dishonesty, which was untrue, it would undermine his authority and destroy respect for him. The manager could leave as the employer would have behaved in a way which was inconsistent with the proper relationship between an employer and employee.

If an employer calls for volunteers for redundancy, and an employee puts his name forward, this is not a resignation, even though the employee is applying to leave, because the decision on whether he goes or not rests with the employer.

On the other hand, where an employer, in order to reduce numbers, puts forward a scheme for early retirement, leaving it up to employees to decide whether to apply or not, then those who leave under it are not 'dismissed', even though the employer has the final say on whether a person should be released, because when the circumstances are looked at overall it was not the employer who *really* brought the contract to an end.

A situation can arise where both an employee is desirous of leaving, and an employer is anxious to see the back of him; and the employer commits some act which entitles the employee to leave. The employee threatens to do so, but the employer offers him favourable terms of settlement. If *as a result of the terms* the employee leaves, there is no 'dismissal'. If he wishes to rely on the conduct, he must leave immediately, otherwise he will lose his rights.

There can be a 'dismissal' following repudiatory conduct by the employee. For instance, if an employee is refused permission to take extended leave abroad, but he nevertheless does so, then his conduct would amount to repudiatory conduct. When the employer 'accepts' this repudiatory conduct, by for instance taking his name off his books, there will then be a 'dismissal' in law by the employer.

Contracts can also terminate upon frustration, without either side taking any action at all (see page 17). They can also cease by express mutual consent or 'be to be inferred all the circumstances', eg, an employee telling his employer that he is fed up with working for him, and then going off to get another job, The employer may be glad to see him go, and send him his P.45 but there would be no dismissal.

A compulsory winding up order on a company automatically terminates the contracts of employment of all those who work for a company, except for staff kept on by the liquidator.

Notice Periods.—The statutory law requires that an employee should be given the under-mentioned periods of notice of dismissal:

(i) at least *one week's notice*, if the employee has been employed for one month or more;
(ii) at least *two weeks' notice*, if employed for two years', and
(iii) one *additional weeks' notice* for each further year of service up to a maximum of 12 weeks' notice;

but an employee is only required to give *one weeks' notice* that he is leaving.

No notice is required where an employee's conduct warrants summarily dismissal; similarly an employee may leave without giving any notice where the employer's conduct is such that he can leave immediately.

Under the common law, the notice period is that which is specified in the contract of employment. Where nothing is said, then the length has to be implied, and the test applied is that which is reasonable in the circumstances. It will not be less than the statutory periods (see page 5) and in the case of senior staff can be up to a year or more.

Qualifying Periods of Employment.—Most rights contained in the employment legislation require an employee to have been employed for a minimum length of time before he can bring a claim. That employment must be continuous, although it may not necessarily be with the same employer (see pages 19 and 20). There is a presumption that the employment, where it is with the same employer, is continuous from the moment it commences until it ends.

The following are the periods of time necessary in order to be able to bring proceedings in the more frequent cases:

Unfair dismissal	2 years (generally)
Redundancy	2 years
Discrimination	none
Equal Pay	none
Action Short of Dismissal	none
Failure to provide Written Reasons for Dismissal	6 months
Written Particulars of Employment or an Itemised Pay Statement	3 months

Date of Dismissal.—The date of dismissal is important under the statutory law in three respects. Firstly, an employee may not have the necessary length of service in order to bring his claim. Secondly the amount of compensation is dependent upon the length of his employment, and thirdly, he must bring his proceedings within the specified time after his dismissal.

An employee cannot be deprived of his rights through a failure by an employer to give him the requisite notice (except where his conduct warrants summary dismissal).

So an employee who has been employed for three weeks short of five years must be given four weeks' notice of dismissal. This would mean that he would have been deemed to have been employed for five years in all, and entitled to redundancy pay (and other rights) based on five years' service. Similarly, a worker employed for one week short of two years must be given one week's notice which would mean that he would have the necessary qualifying period to bring a claim for redundancy pay or unfair dismissal. This is known as the 'effective date of dismissal'.

But if proceedings are brought in the tribunal he must take the necessary action within the period specified in the Act. Times starts to run from the date when the employment terminated, but not when it should have ceased if notice had been given or where money in lieu of notice was given.

If he fails to do so, then his action will be lost unless the tribunal has power to extend time and the employee is able to prove that it was not reasonably practical to present his claim within the period, or that it is fair and equitable in all the circumstances that the claim should be allowed to continue.

At common law, proceedings must be issue with 6 years of a breach, but usually by that time any claim will have lapsed or settled.

REDUNDANCIES.—In 1965, Parliament introduced the concept that an employee who is dismissed as a result of redundancy should receive compensation, the amount being based on his age and length of service. The idea was not to punish the employer, although it did make him more careful in organising his business, but to compensate the employee for the loss of his job generally caused by no fault of his own.

To be entitled to redundancy pay, an employee must have at least 2 years of continuous service (see pages 19 and 20) on the effective date of dismissal, and the dismissal must be wholly or mainly due to the fact that:

(i) the employer has ceased, or intends to cease to carry on the business in which the worker was employed *or* at the place where the worker was employed, or

(ii) the requirements of the business for the employee to carry out work of a particular kind at his work-place, or elsewhere, have ceased or diminished, or it is expected that they will do so.

There is a presumption, unless the contrary be proved, that every dismissal is on account of redundancy, and this even applies where the employee starts off in one company but ends up in another, following a series of take-overs

Who is Specifically Excluded.—Generally speaking, every employee is entitled to a redundancy payment but the following are either ineligible or are excluded:

(i) dock workers, share fishermen, certain merchant seamen, Crown servants, employees in public office or in the National Health Service, and certain others where there is a private scheme of redundancy available for them;

(ii) a domestic servant who is a close relative, but not a spouse;

(iii) where a man is over 65 years of age or a woman 60;

(iv) part time workers, who normally work less than 16 hours of work each week, except those with 5 years of service or more where the figure is reduced to 8 hours;

(v) in certain cases where there is a contract to do a particular task, and there is no dismissal at the end of it;

(vi) those who normally work outside Great Britain in accordance with their contracts of employment (see page 19) unless they are in Great Britain at the time of dismissal in accordance with their employers' instructions;

(vii) where the employee is offered suitable alternative employment on the same terms by the same employer or an associated employer (see page 19) and he unreasonably refuses the offer; or on different terms or in a different place, and after a reasonable trial period of not less than 4 weeks he unreasonably refuses to continue that employment.

(viii) where the contract is for a fixed term of 2 years or more and the employee has agreed in writing to forego his right to claim redundancy.

How the Amount is Computed.—For each year of continuous service (see pages 19 and 20) the following scale is applied up to a maximum of 20 years;

(i) 18 to under 22 years	1/2 weeks' pay
(ii) 22 but under 41 years	1 weeks' pay
(iii) 41 to 65 years**	1.1/2 weeks' pay.

The payment is calculated by ascertaining the age of the employee at the effective date of dismissal (see page 22), then working out the number of week's applicable to him and multiplying that number by the week's pay (see page 24). The latter figure is subject to a maximum of £164* per week, in respect of dismissals after April 1, 1988.

Where the employee is approaching his/her 65th year** then the amount is reduced by 1/12th for each complete month, eg, a person aged 64 years and 5 months would have 5/12th of the amount deducted.

---

* The amount is generally increased on 1st February or 1st April.

** Legislation is currently being introduced to amend the provisions which previously applied the figure of 60 years for women.

Interpretation of the Law.—Originally employers sought to avoid liability under the Act by proving that the case did not come within the definition because their total liability could be quite substantial on occasions despite being entitled to a rebate of nearly a half. If was often at a time when they could least afford to pay it.

Later when the unfair dismissal provisions were enacted the argument swung the other way, namely, the dismissal was for redundancy. This could provide an answer to a claim that a dismissal was unfair, which exposed them to claims for very much larger amounts.

Each phrase or word in the Act has to be considered to see whether they affect the facts in a particular case. For instance, where an employee is engaged to do night work, he cannot normally be moved to day work without his consent. If his employer, because of shortage of work, closes down his night shift and offers the worker day work instead, which he declines and he decides to leave, then the employee will be debarred from obtaining redundancy pay *unless* he proves that he has not unreasonably refused the offer to change his shifts. The phrase 'work of a particular kind' in the Act covers this sort of situation.

If, when an employee is taken on, it is anticipated that the work will fall away, he will still be entitled to a redundancy payment when dismissed for shortage of work. But where he is recruited in anticipation that work will increase, but it fails to materialise, and this results in his being dismissed, then he will not come within the statutory definition.

Time Limits.—A claim must be brought in the tribunal within 6 months of the dismissal, but a tribunal has power to extend the time for a further 6 months only (eg, 12 months in all) where it is just and equitable (see page 20). The employee's rights are preserved in either period if he has notified the employers in writing of his claim for redundancy or if he has brought proceedings for unfair dismissal.

Rebates for Small Employers.—Only those employers with less than 10 employees, which includes any employed by an associated employer (see page 19), can recover the 35% rebate from the government in respect of a redundancy payment. In computing the numbers, up to a maximum of two domestic staff may be disregarded, provided they are employed for less than 8 hours per week.

Duty to Consult over proposed Redundancies.—An employer is obliged to consult, at the earliest opportunity, an independent union which he recognises for collective bargaining purposes when contemplating dismissing one or more employees of any description for redundancy.

Where 10 or more employees are to be dismissed, then 30 days' notice must be given, and for 100 employees or more, 90 days. If there are 'special circumstances' which render it not reasonably practical to comply, the employer must take such steps thereafter to do so as soon as it is reasonably practical in the circumstances. He must also notify the Secretary of State as well, and this applies even though there is no relevant union to consult.

'Special circumstances' is restricted to instances where there is a sudden disaster, or unforeseen event; a mere slow decline leading to insolvency will not suffice.

When giving notice to the union, an employer must disclose in writing the following:

(i) the reasons for the dismissals;
(ii) the number and description of those involved;
(iii) how the selection will be carried out;
(iv) the method by which it would be carried out;
(v) the total work-force at the establishment;

and he *must* consider any representations made to him by the union and reply in writing with his reasons if he rejects any or all of the union's contentions.

Protective Award upon Failure to Consult.—A breach of these requirements entitles a union to make a complaint to a tribunal. If the allegation is found proved, the tribunal will make a declaration to this effect. It may also grant a 'protective award' which will cover all employees of the description specified, even though some of them may not be members of the union concerned.

The effect of an award is to preserve the employment for such period as is stipulated by the tribunal, commencing with the proposed date of the first dismissals, if they have been specified (and not when they first took effect), or with the date of the award, whichever is earlier, for a maximum of:

(i) 28 days for up to 10 employees;
(ii) 30 days for up to 99 employees;
(iii) 90 days for 100 employees or more.

A complaint should be made to the tribunal before the proposed dismissals take effect; but they must be made within 3 months beginning with the date on which the dismissals take effect or within such further period as is reasonable when it was not reasonably practical to have presented the complaint in time. A late application is unlikely to be of much benefit.

UNFAIR DISMISSAL.—The provisions relating to *unfair* dismissal—not to be confused with *wrongful* dismissal (see pages 28 and 29)—were first enacted in 1971. Although there have been a number of amendments made since then, the basic structure remains much the same. Only the Industrial Tribunal has jurisdiction to adjudicate on this right and it forms the vast bulk of the work before it.

It is essential that the person responsible for dealing with staff problems should be reasonably familiar with the basic principles that govern this subject. Common sense and a feeling for natural justice are important qualities, but they must be applied within the framework of the law.

Who is Protected?.—In order to be able to bring a complaint, a person must have been an *employee* (see page 17), but certain employees are expressly excluded, eg, registered dock workers, share fishermen, servicemen, those exempted by order of Secretary of State where there are private schemes, and certain specific others.

Except where the dismissal is deemed to be *automatically unfair* (see below) the following are ineligible from bringing a claim:

(i) those with less than 2 years of continuous service;
(ii) where the employee has reached 65 years, unless there is a normal retiring age for persons in the position held by the employee, in which case that other age will apply;
(iii) where the employee is on a fixed contract of two years and has agreed in writing during that period to abandon his rights to bring a claim at the expiry of the term;
(iv) where the employee works part time with normal hours of work of less than 16 hours per week, unless he has been employed for 5 years or more, when the figure is reduced to 8 hours.

In addition, the following are excluded, namely:

(i) where the employee is ordinarily required to work outside Great Britain under the terms of his contract (see page 19);
(ii) where the employee was taking part in a strike or other industrial action, or the employer was conducting a lock-out arising out of a dispute with his work-force at the date of dismissal, then provided all those involved were also dismissed *and* were not offered re-employment within 3 months of the dismissal of the employee complaining of being unfairly dismissed. The normal time limit of 3 months for presenting a claim (see page 20) is increased to 6 months.

Automatically Unfair Dismissals.—The dismissal of an employee for the under-mentioned reasons is deemed to be automatically unfair, entitling him to a higher Basic Award and a Special Award (see page 20).

(i) because the employee is, or proposes to become a member of an independent trade union; or
(ii) because he had taken part or proposed to do so, in the activities of an independent trade union, within working hours, where this had been agreed by the employer, or outside them; or
(iii) because he was not a member of a trade union, or of a particular one; or he had refused, or proposed to refuse, to join or remain a member;

*unless** in respect of (iii) above,

(a) it was the practice in accordance with a valid union membership agreement (see pages 10 and 11), and which is *binding* between the employer and the union for employees of the same class to belong to an independent union; and
(b) the main reason for the dismissal was that he had ceased to be a member of, or refused to join a union in accordance with the union-membership agreement; and
(c) the union-membership agreement had been approved by a ballot held within 5 years of the notice of dismissal.

*and**

(iv) the employee does not object to being a member of the union on the grounds of conscience or other deeply held personal conviction; or
(v) he has not been a member of the union, where the agreement came into effect prior to August 15, 1980, or, if it took effect on or after that date and he was entitled to vote in the ballot, he has not been a member of the union since that ballot; or
(vi) there is in existence a Declaration from the tribunal that he has been unreasonably excluded or expelled from the union; or proceedings for one are pending; unless the non-membership was caused by his fault;
(vii) he holds qualifications for his job which preclude him from striking or taking other industrial action and he was expelled from his union for that reason, or he refused to comply with a requirement to make a payment to charity or to another person(s) in lieu of joining the union.

Other Automatically Unfair Dismissals.—There are two other circumstances in which a dismissal will become automatically unfair, (but it is not a 'deemed' automatically unfair dismissal and does *not* entitle the employee to a higher Basic Award and a Special Award):

(i) where an employee is dismissed for redundancy and the same circumstances apply to another employee

---

* There are proposals currently before Parliament to revoke these limitations of liability. If passed they will have the effect of making all dismissals relating to the non-membership of a union or a particular union automatically unfair.

doing similar work for the same employer and he was selected in contravention of a customary arrangement or an agreed procedure,

and

there were no special reaons to justify it;

(ii) where an undertaking (or a part of it) which is of a commercial nature is transferred from one person to another and an employee is dismissed in consequence of it, whether by the transferor or by the transferee.

But it is a defence for the employer to prove:

(a) that the dismissal was for 'an economic, technical or organisational reason which entailed changes in the workforce. . .',

and

(b) it was fair and equitable in the circumstances.

When is a Dismissal Unfair?—An employee may be lawfully dismissed on any of the following grounds:

(i) conduct;
(ii) capability;
(iii) redundancy;
(iv) some statutory restriction;
(v) 'some other substantial reason';

provided it is just and equitable having regard to all the circumstances and to the size and resources of the employer.

So if an employee is dismissed for setting fire to his employer's premises, which caused considerable damage, then a dismissal on the grounds of conduct would be patently fair. Similarly, if a person is employed as an electrician to carry out work in private homes, and he keeps on leaving a number of installations in a dangerous state despite training and warnings, a dismissal on the grounds of capability is likely to result in a finding that it was fair.

Before a person is dismissed for redundancy (see pages 23 and 24) care should be taken to see if there is an alternative post available within his job description. Failure to offer him one which is available is likely to result in a finding that the dismissal was unfair.

A statutory restriction could arise where for instance a foreigner has a work permit for employment as a maid in a hotel for a year, but it is not renewed. A dismissal on this ground would be fair, because it would be illegal to employ her without a permit.

The term 'some other substantial reason' covers a wide number of circumstances. It includes dismissals arising out of re-organisations, or where an employee, with a personality difficulty, cannot work with other staff, with whom he has to co-operate. But a dismissal as a result of a threat of a strike or other industrial action would not provide the employer with a defence because pressure on an employer for this reason cannot be taken into consideration.

There is a great mountain of case law on whether it is 'just and equitable' to dismiss, and which covers both the substantive reason for dismissing, as well as any procedural defects. The underlying principle to be applied in each case is whether the dismissal offends against a sense of fairness.

Before dismissing any employee, there should be a full investigation of all the circumstances, and the employee should normally be given the opportunity of making any representations. There should be a careful and objective evaluation of the facts and then a decision made which is reasonable in all the circumstances.

Each Side partly to Blame.—On occasions where there has been a dismissal each side may be partly at fault at different stages. If an employee was dismissed for fighting, but it was not very serious and there was considerable provocation, he may succeed on his allegation of unfair dismissal, but find his compensation being reduced on account of 'contributory fault'.

But where the dismissal is as a result of *redundancy*, then although the employee may have been responsible for bringing about a redundancy situation through striking or go-slows, no reduction is permitted for contributory fault.

Remedies for Unfair Dismissal.—There are two courses open to an employee who is found to have been unfairly dismissed. He can seek an order for re-instatement or re-engagement, or he can apply for compensation.

An order for re-instatement or re-engagement is rarely made because in most cases each side does not want it. Furthermore, the post must generally still be vacant and an order will usually only be made where there has been no or only a little contributory fault.

In practice it is only in large organisations that this sort of relief is likely to be granted, because the employee can be moved to another branch or area where he is away from the original source of conflict.

Where an order for re-instatement is made, the employee returns to his old position with the same rights that he had or would have had, but for the dismissal, including all arrears of pay. An order of re-engagement is usually made where the employee has been guilty of small percentage of contributary fault. The tribunal will decide on all the terms, including arrears of pay, if it thinks it right to grant any.

An order for *compensation* is made in all other cases on the following basis. There will be a basic award, a compensatory award, an additional award and a special award.

(a) THE BASIC AWARD.—

(i) This is computed in the same way as the redundancy payment (see page 23) except that the years below 18 may be included. It is subject to the same *pro-rata* reduction where an employee is approaching his or her 65th year. Contributory fault is taken into account except in redundancy cases (subject to the exception in (ii) below). The maximum in respect of dismissals from 1 April, 1988 is £4,920.*

(ii) For the deemed automatically unfair dismissals, the minimum award is £2,400* for dismissals from 1 April, 1988 but this may be reduced for contributory fault, and this also applies in redundancy cases, although the proportional reduction in these cases can only be applied to the difference between the normal basic award (calculated as in (i) above) and the £2,400*, if any.

(b) The COMPENSATORY AWARD, consisting of an amount which is 'just and equitable' up to a maximum of £8,500 from April 1, 1987 consisting of:

(i) the loss of wages, net of all deductions, up to the date of the hearing, less any earnings between the date of dismissal and the hearing. No credit need be given for any payment of salary received in lieu of notice, or if none has been paid, for any earnings during the notice period; and

(ii) the estimated future loss from the date of hearing; but the length of the period cannot be extended by the degree of 'unfairness' or the mental distress caused to the employee, or the manner of dismissal; and

(iii) the loss of any benefits, including pension rights, and expenses; and

(iv) the loss of industrial statutory rights, which is a nominal amount of about £100;

but

all are subject to a *pro-rata* reduction for:

(a) contributory fault, and

(b) any failure to mitigate the loss.

The final amount may be reduced by any *ex-gratia* payments given as a result of the dismissal or earnings after the expiry of the notice period (if no money in lieu of notice was given).

If an employee is dismissed for the wrong reason, but the employer subsequently discovers grounds on which he could have validly dismissed, then although a dismissal may be technically unfair, the compensation can be reduced to nil on the basis that it would be 'just and equitable' to do so;

(c) There can also be an ADDITIONAL AWARD, where the employer fails to comply with an Order for re-instatement or re-engagement, unless he proves that it was not practical for him to do so. The Award is calculated as follows.

(i) When the dismissal is unlawful under the discrimination Acts then it is not less than 26 weeks' pay nor more than 52 with a maximum of £164* for each week's pay for dismissals after 1 April, 1988 with an overall maximum of £8,500*;

(ii) in any other case *except* those where it is deemed to be automatically unfair, not less than 13 weeks' pay nor more than 26 weeks' pay, calculated as in (i) above.

(d) A SPECIAL AWARD will be made where:

(i) the dismissal is deemed to be automatically unfair,

and

(ii) where the dismissal is for *redundancy*, the employee has not unreasonably refused an offer of suitable alternative employment or unreasonably terminated a trial period for a new job, or started work under a renewed or different contract in consequence of an offer made prior to the dismissal and the new contract starts within 4 weeks of the old one ceasing,

and

(iii) the employee has sought an order for re-instatement or re-engagement and the tribunal, in its discretion, refused to make such an order.

The compensation is calculated as follows:

(i) a week's pay (but *without* an upper limit) is multiplied by 104, with a minimum of £11,950* and a maximum of £23,850* for dismissals after 1 April, 1988,

BUT where an order for re-instatement or re-engagement has been made, but not complied with, and the employer cannot prove that it was not reasonably practical to comply with it, then the compensation is increased to:

(ii) a week's pay (as in (i) above) multiplied by 156 with a minimum of £17,900* from 1 April, 1988 and *no* maximum,

but in arriving at the amount under (i) and (ii) above the tribunal will:

(iii) make a reduction for contributory fault where appropriate.

An order for re-enstatement must be complied with strictly. Where an employer, who purported to do so,

---

* The amount is generally increased each year either on 1 February or 1 April.

but in fact gave his two employees less favourable terms, it was held that that constituted a failure to reinstate in accordance with the law. He had to pay compensation of £38,147 to the two employees.

Who pays the Compensation.—Normally the employer will be responsible for paying any compensation, but where he or the employee has 'joined' a union or a person(s) bringing pressure (see page 11) in respect of claims arising from automatically unfair dismissals (see pages 24 and 25), then a tribunal has power to order the party in default to pay the award on the basis of what is 'just and equitable'.

Time Limits.—Proceedings in the tribunal must commence within 3 months (except in special circumstances) of the date on which the employment ceased (see pages 22 and 23).

A Discriminatory Dismissal.—A dismissal of an employee on the grounds of sex or race breaches the Sex Discrimination Act, 1975 or the Race Relations Act, 1976. The victim is entitled to the same sort of compensation as for unfair dismissal, but in addition he or she will receive damages for hurt feelings which usually is an amount not in excess of £3,000.

The benefit to an employee of being able to bring proceedings under either of these two Acts is that no qualifying period of service is required.

It is no defence to show that there was no *intention* to directly discriminate; and where the effect of a condition or requirement results in indirect discrimination against women or ethnic minorities (see page 3), whether it is intended or not, an employer is still liable.

Dismissal arising from Pregnancy.—Pregnant women are given special protection. If an employer dismisses an employee with more than 2 year's continuous service at the effective date of dismissal because, or mainly because, she is pregnant or for any other reason connected with her pregnancy, that would be automatically unfair (but entitling her to ordinary compensation only). Her employer can avoid liability if he proves that:—

(i) at the material time
  (a) that she was incapable of doing the work she was employed to do, or
  (b) there was some statutory prohibition against her continuing to do it,
  and
(ii) he failed to offer her a new job, if one was available, and it was suitable and appropriate to her in all the circumstances, and
(iii) it was on no less favourable terms.

Even if there had to be a dismissal because there was *no* suitable alternative employment, the tribunal would still have to consider whether the dismissal was fair and equitable in all the circumstances.

So a dismissal for events linked to hypertension which has been brought on by pregnancy, or to post-natal depression or to a miscarriage would be a reason connected with pregnancy so as to provide a woman with protection. But absenteeism made worse by pregnancy, which was unknown to the employer, would not qualify.

A woman who wishes to return to work following the birth of her child must comply with all the statutory requirements in the giving of notices. If having done so the employer fails to take her back, that will be deemed to be a dismissal in law by him.

If her job has become redundant, then she must be offered suitable alternative employment, if this is available, either with the employer, or with any successor of the employer, or with any associated employer (see page 19), and the job must be suitable and appropriate to her and the terms and conditions no less favourable, otherwise the dismissal will be unfair.

A DISMISSAL FOR BREACH OF CONTRACT

Generally.—Litigation over common law rights and duties, in the main, relates to such matters as *wrongful* dismissals, procedural breaches, and declarations as to various rights. Although the tribunals do not have jurisdiction in exactly the same spheres, a litigant can generally get adequate and quicker relief before them, and hence most actions are disposed of there.

At common law, everything depends on the ordinary law of contract, e.g. has there been a breach of the terms and conditions of employment? The law requires some of them to be in writing (see pages 4 and 5), but a great many will be orally agreed or inferred in all the circumstances, and some are imposed by the general law.

Extent of the Breach.—The remedies open to parties depend on the seriousness of any breach. If it is of importance and goes to the root of the contract, or put another way, there is a fundamental breach, then the aggrieved party may accept the breach as a repudiation of the contract by the other side, and treat the contract at an end (see page 5). Any loss sustained by him can be recovered from the other side.

If, on the other hand, it is only of marginal importance, then the contract continues and the only remedy lies in the recovery of damages for any loss. In the employment field, this is unlikely to have any significant impact, as few employers consider it worthwhile suing their staff and if an employee were to bring proceedings against his boss, then he would be unlikely to retain his employment for long, let alone get promotion.

Wrongful Dismissal.—Wrongful dismissal generally occurs in two ways. Either an employee has been given insufficient notice for the termination of his employment or there has been a defect in the procedural process leading to the dismissal. If an employee is entitled to 3 months notice and is only given 2 weeks, then that notice is a nullity. The employee may carry on working as though nothing has happened, or he may seek a declaration from the courts that it is of no effect. Or he may accept the notice, leave and sue for any loss he has sustained which is generally limited to the period of full notice, and subject to his duty to mitigate damage.

If the employer prevents the employee from working beyond the 2 weeks, then he will be in breach of contract and liable in damages for any loss sustained by the employee during the remainder of the notice period. But the employee will be under a duty to mitigate his damage by seeking other employment. Failure to do so will result in any damages being reduced to the extent to which he is in default.

The notice periods are very important. In the event of a breach by the employer of his duty to give his employee the written details of the periods, the law will imply what is a reasonable notice in a particular case. This will be not less than the minimum period of notice laid down by statute. If a person holds a very senior position, a period of up to a year might be implied.

If an employee can only be dismissed in a particular way, eg, by the Board of Directors following a disciplinary hearing, but the employer follows another course and dismisses the employee, then a declaration can be obtained in the High Court that there has been no valid dismissal. But generally speaking an employer cannot be ordered to take a sacked employee back into service (eg, the remedy of specific performance) and so if the employer ceases to provide work or pay the employee, then that person must seek employment elsewhere to mitigate his loss.

FAILURE TO PROVIDE WRITTEN REASONS FOR DISMISSAL.—An employee with 6 months service or more who is dismissed is entitled to know the reason for it. An employer, if asked for those reasons, whether orally or in writing, must provide them in writing within 14 days of the request. He need only state in broad terms what the *true* reasons are, and if he has already set them out in a letter or a note, he can enclose a copy of it.

If the employer unreasonably refuses to provide a written statement, the employee can apply to the tribunal for an award which will consist of a penal payment of two weeks gross pay without limit to the amount.

Time Limits.—The claim must be made within 3 months of the failure or if this is not reasonably practical, within such further time as is reasonable (see page 20).

PROCEEDINGS

IN THE INDUSTRIAL TRIBUNALS.—Most litigation in respect of employment is now fought out in the Industrial Tribunals. Tribunals, which are presided over by a legally qualified Chairman with one lay member drawn from the CBI and the other from the TUC, were designed to provide a quick and cheap remedy for injustices in the employment field.

They deal with an enormous volume of work, most of which arises from dismissals. An increasing amount is now concerned with equal pay and value claims and with discrimination cases. They have no jurisdiction in employer/union disputes, eg, for actions requiring a union to have a ballot before a strike, or where a party is seeking to enforce their common law rights. These can only be dealt with in the ordinary civil courts.

Although they are much more informal than the ordinary civil courts, and are not bound by same strict rules of evidence, they follow ordinary court procedures. If their decision is not unanimous then the majority view will prevail, and this applies even if it is the two lay members who are against the chairman on a point of law.

If there is only the chairman and a member sitting (which is permitted with the consent of both parties) and there is a split decision, then the chairman's decision is final. Perhaps surprisingly majority decisions are a comparative rarity.

Procedures.—In the tribunals the parties may represent themselves or be represented by anyone they wish, and the procedure is designed to enable a lay-person to put their case without being penalised through lack of knowledge. But the law has become extremely complicated and technical and consequently a person should have some knowledge not only of the law but also of the procedures.

Legal aid is not available at present but free representation may be provided by the Citizens' Advice Centre, or a Legal Advice Centre or a few other bodies. Employers are frequently represented by their Personnel Officers or their trade associations.

When there is a dispute over a dismissal the parties may invite ACAS to resolve it. In every case ACAS is sent copies of the proceedings and it will intervene of its own motion if it thinks that it will be helpful. The Service will use its considerable experience and knowledge to try and settle it. The mere fact that it is intervening does not prevent time limits from running and so proceedings may have to be started in order to preserve the position (see page 20).

The Originating Application.—Proceedings are commenced by lodging an 'Originating Application' at an office of the Industrial Tribunals. This document is obtanable from any job centre or unemployment office, from the Citizens' Advice Centre, or direct from any Industrial Tribunal Office. It has to be filled in with various formal details, and must give an outline of the nature of the complaint. If time is running short, a letter to the tribunal will usually be treated as an Originating Application and preserve a person's rights, provided it names the 'respondent', eg, the body against whom some relief is sought, and states what the claim is about.

When the Originating Application (or letter) is received at the tribunal it is said to be 'presented' and time no longer runs. The person making the application becomes the 'applicant'. A copy of it together with a blank Notice of Appearance is sent to the employer (or other body) who now becomes the 'respondent' and he must fill in the formal parts of it, and state his grounds of opposition to the allegations. This must be returned within 14 days.

A respondent cannot participate in the proceedings until he has lodged his Notice of Appearance. An action could go to a hearing with a decision being made against him, were he to delay too long.

These pleadings are not intended to be as precise as those in the ordinary civil courts; and they are not interpreted in the same strict way as a lease or a will. But they should identify what the real nature of the complaint is or the reply to it.

For instance, if a person complains that he has been unfairly selected for redundancy because someone more junior to him was not dismissed, then he would probably be debarred from alleging at the hearing that the true reason was that he was a shop steward and the respondents were dismissing him for engaging in trade union activities.

The Stopping of a Case.—Sometimes the Originating Application shows that the respondent does not have a case to meet. For instance, the applicant may not have the necessary qualifying period of service to bring the claim, or he may be seeking damages which the tribunal has no power to award. The respondent should complete the formal parts of the Notice of Appearance and merely dispute the jurisdiction.

In all probability the matter will have been spotted and the tribunal will have written to the applicant and notified him that the tribunal does not have jurisdiction. He will be invited to withdraw his application, but an applicant can insist on continuing. A respondent, who has lodged his Notice of Appearance, can apply to the tribunal for the Originating Application to be dismissed on the grounds that it is frivolous or vexatious.

The papers will be referred to a Chairman, who has power to strike out such an application. Before making an order the applicant is given an opportunity of stating why the claim should not be struck out.

Pre-Hearing Assessments.—No person can be debarred from bringing a claim unless there has been a settlement under the auspices of ACAS. In consequence, provided that there is jurisdiction, the tribunal must hear the case, however unmeritorious it may appear to be. The same applies to a hopeless defence as well. In such instances the abused party can apply to the tribunal at any stage for an order for a 'Pre-Hearing Assessment'. A chairman has discretion on whether to order one.

A Pre-Hearing Assessment is a special hearing before the full tribunal at which no evidence is given, but the tribunal will come to a decision on the basis of agreed facts as set out in all the documents and having heard oral argument from both sides. Where the circumstances warrant it, the tribunal will warn a party that if he continues with his case or with his defence then he will be at risk of having an order for costs made against him at the final hearing.

For instance, if an employee agrees that he was sent to prison for 6 months for breaking into his employer's premises and stealing a considerable amount of cash, then any claim that he was unfairly dismissed for that burglary would inevitably fail. Or if an employer sacks a man because of alleged dishonesty without any disciplinary hearing but later admits that he made a mistake over identity, this will almost certainly lead to a finding of unfair dismissal.

The second tribunal, which finally adjudicates, has to be constituted with a different chairman and members, and they are not allowed to know the outcome of the earlier proceedings until they have heard all the evidence and made a finding on liability. They can then decide whether to make the defaulting party pay costs and, if so, how much (see page 32) in the light of whether a warning had been given and on the facts elicited before them.

Further Particulars.—Sometimes it is not clear as to what precisely is the issue in a case or it may be necessary to pin a person down as to what exactly he is alleging. A person can seek to clarify the position by asking for 'Further Particulars' of the claim. The other side should be asked to supply the Particulars voluntarily first of all, and if they are not provided then an order can be sought (by letter) from the tribunal that they be given. The tribunal will make an order where they are relevant and will help to narrow the matters to be decided.

For instance, if an employer alleges that he sacked an employee because of frequent complaints about the standard of his work from the employer's clients, the employee is entitled to know the identity of those clients, the dates on which they complained, and details of their complaints. The real issue can then be ascertained. It may turn out that the complaints came from two clients, who always complained about every member of staff or that the employee did not produce the goods that were supplied to the clients.

Failure to Provide Particulars.—If either party fails or refuses to comply with an order, then the other side can apply to the tribunal (in writing) for the whole or part of an Originating Application or of a Notice of Appearance be struck out and, where appropriate, for the respondent to be debarred from defending.

The tribunal will give the erring party an opportunity to say why an order should not be made. If there is no reply or the reason given is not acceptable, then the claim will be struck out or he will be debarred from defending.

Witnesses.—Sometimes a witness can give crucial evidence but for various reasons is reluctant to appear. Perhaps he fears that his own employment may be at risk, or there may be a prohibition against a person attending without a witness order, as occurs with police officers in most forces.

A party can apply to the tribunal for a witness order, stating what the witness can say, how it will help his case, and that the witness will not attend voluntarily. The tribunal, if satisfied on these matters, will then make an order.

Preliminary Hearing.—The documents may show that there is a dispute as to whether the tribunal has jurisdiction. For instance, has the Originating Application been lodged in time, or did the employee ordinarily work outside the U.K.? Is he over-age or otherwise ineligible to bring a claim?

In order to avoid the expense and trouble of bringing all the witnesses along to fight the case on its merits, it is usual for the tribunal to direct that there be a preliminary hearing to determine the point. If it is found that there is no jurisdiction, then the case will be dismissed.

Discovery or Inspection of Documents.—Documentation is the *lynch-pin* of every good case, because, by and large, exhibits speak for themselves. An employer might allege that an employee was "always late", but this may mean many things. It may count for little if the tribunal finds that a witness who makes such a statement is unreliable. A contemporaneous record, showing his actual times of arrival, will provide the critical information and is likely to be conclusive.

A record should be made at the time of every important aspect of a person's employment, and so be available for scrutiny by the tribunal. The record will paint its own picture, especially if there is a thread going through them, eg, the employee was frequently warned about his time keeping.

Although it is not obligatory for those documents to be produced to the other side prior to the day of the hearing, it is wise to do so. If they are voluminous, there might be an application for an adjournment in order to study them. Someone may have to pay for the costs thrown away.

In order to know what papers the other side have up their sleeve, a party is entitled to seek voluntary disclosure of all relevant documents. If they are not supplied, then an application (in writing) can be made to the tribunal for an order for disclosure, and facilities granted to take copies of them. The tribunal will make an order limited to those documents that appear to be relevant for the disposal of the issues raised. The other side cannot be forced to provide copies, although in practice they usually do.

Interlocutory Hearing.—Some cases get bogged down in the paper-work with allegations and counter-allegations, and it becomes increasingly difficult to establish the real issues. A Chairman will frequently order an Interlocutory Hearing which will take place before a Chairman sitting alone, to decide all outstanding matters and give any directions necessary to bring the case to a speedy trial.

Fixing Date of main Hearing.—Normally speaking the tribunal will try and fix a hearing on a date suitable to both sides by sending out a pre-listing letter. Apart from seeking mutually convenient dates, they ask for information on how many witnesses are likely to be called and for their estimate of the length of the hearing. Tribunals are pretty shrewd at guessing the length themselves. Sometimes the information is sought and dates agreed on the telephone.

If a pre-listing letter is sent out, it is important to respond with all the information sought. If a case is not finished on the day or days specified, then it will be put off to a further date which is not only convenient to the parties, but also to the members of the tribunal, and this can often entail a delay of up to 3 months.

Some cases where the parties are not represented and which appear straightforward will be fixed without reference to either side. If the date is inconvenient they should object to it immediately.

Adjournments.—Once the case is set down after consultation with the parties, or where the parties have been given a date and they have not objected to it for a period of time, it will not be adjourned except with the consent of *both* sides.

If a party has strong grounds, eg, an important witness is ill, then the tribunal will generally grant an adjournment, but not where a witness will be away on holiday, or because witnesses have not been interviewed. A party must get his case ready well in advance, otherwise he will have to pay the penalty.

If an adjournment is necessary in the course of a case because, for instance, a party has failed to warn a witness to attend, and it is necessary in the interests of justice for that person to testify, then it is likely that the defaulting party will be ordered to pay the costs occasioned by that adjournment.

Procedure at Hearing.—The party on whom the burden of proof lies has the right to open and close his case. The opening should be kept short and confined to giving a summary of the allegations, and identifying any important documents. For instance, if the employer's case is that an employee was always late in arriving for work and he had been warned on a number of occasions, then photostats of the attendance book and copies of the letters written to him or of attendance notes relating to oral warnings should be produced and read, or better still summarised.

Witnesses will then be called to prove the matters alleged. Perhaps the manager will be able to explain how impunctuality was causing problems on the production line, and the employee had been warned but his usual excuse was that he could not get up early enough in the mornings to get to work on time, or that the traffic was bad.

Each witness may be cross-examined by the other side. The purpose is not necessarily to try and show the person up as a liar, but to identify the areas of dispute, so that the tribunal can concentrate on all the relevant evidence to help them decide whose story they prefer.

Witnesses are generally not allowed to read from written statements, unless there are special reasons and the other side does not object. They should be 'led', that is to say, they should be asked what happened at various stages, so that the whole picture of an employee's or an employer's case emerges. A representative may not put 'leading questions' to his own witness, ie, one which suggests the answer, or to cross-examine him. Where there is no dispute over some evidence, then the rule does not apply, eg, 'I think that you agree that you told Mr Smith that he was never going to make the grade and you were dismissing him?'.

Rules of Evidence.—The tribunals are not debarred from listening to 'hearsay evidence', but the weight to be attached to it will depend on all the circumstances. If first-hand evidence is available, then it should be called, because there is less chance of error. Where a decision is taken on statements made by customers, or external bodies to the employer, eg. a customer complains that a representative of a firm has misbehaved himself on their premises, it is not generally necessary to call witnesses from outside parties.

Points of Law.—The statutory law is riddled with obscure words, phrases and technicalities. There are numerous judicial pronouncements to be found in other cases on what is meant by them or what should be done in certain situations.

It is to the wording of Acts of Parliament that tribunals have to turn. Authorities can be helpful on the approach to be adopted, or the test to be applied in a particular situation, but most cases will turn on their own facts. For instance, was the applicant warned that if he was late again he would be likely to lose his job? Was it fair and equitable to dismiss for being late again, when his train was delayed? Three warnings in one case might be adequate, but not in another.

The Decision.—At the conclusion of all the evidence, each side sums up their case. It is desirable to be concise and to the point because a tribunal will have formed a view on the credibility of witnesses, and a great deal will depend on which side they believe.

The tribunal will generally retire for a period of time and then reconvene and either give their Decision in full or summary form. They will either provide full written reasons later, or in some cases an abbreviated one, depending on what is required.

A party can require the full reasons to be given, provided it is applied for within 21 days of the Decision being promulgated. In some cases, the tribunal will reserve the Decision in order to consider the case for longer. The full Decision will then generally be sent to the parties, although the rules allow a summary Decision to be given.

At the hearing, the tribunal will usually make a decision on liability first; and if in favour of the employee, it will often leave it to the parties to try and resolve the question of compensation. This is especially helpful to the employee because if the figure is agreed, he will avoid losing part of an award under the Recoupment Regulations.

If the tribunal has to access compensation, the award will be reduced by the amount received by the employee in the interim by way of unemployment pay or social security, etc. The employer will be responsible for paying this latter amount direct to the Government.

If there is insufficient time to complete the case that day, then an agreement on the amount of compensation will save the costs of a further hearing; but if there is adequate time and it appears that the parties are unlikely to agree terms then the tribunal will proceed to deal with it.

Expenses & Costs.—Litigants and their witnesses, but not a professional representative or a union official, attending a tribunal are entitled to be paid for their loss of earnings (up to certain limits), their travelling expenses and a subsistence allowance. The tribunal staff will arrange for payment of the amounts out of public funds.

Either side in the proceedings can ask for an order from the tribunal that the other side should pay their costs. Normally no order is made unless the tribunal is satisfied that the action has been brought or conducted vexatiously, frivolously or unreasonably, or where a party has caused an adjournment through their own fault. If an order is made, the amount will have to be tailored to the ability of a party to pay it.

Review.—There is a procedure whereby either side can apply to the tribunal, within 14 days of the promulgation of the Decision, for a 'Review', on the grounds that:

(i) there was an error in the Decision as a result of a mistake made by the tribunal staff;
(ii) no notice of the hearing date was received;

(iii) the Decision was made in the absence of a party who was entitled to be heard;
(iv) there is new evidence available which was not known about or could not have been reasonably foreseen at the time of the hearing and which would have effected the result;
(v) the interests of justice require a review.

The procedure cannot be used to try and re-litigate a lost case by seeking to present a better one. Tribunals are chary of granting reviews unless there are strong *prima facie* grounds: there has to be an end to litigation. Where the Chairman of the tribunal that adjudicated is of the opinion that it has no reasonable chance of success, he is empowered to refuse leave to allow the case to go forward for consideration by the full tribunal. The latter alone has the power to allow a review and then to consider it.

Appeals.—Appeals are heard by the Employment Appeal Tribunal. They have to be lodged at the Appeal Tribunal within 42 days of the promulgation of the Decision. The Appeal Tribunal only has jurisdiction on appeals over *matters of law*, and so if a tribunal has found as *a fact* that it prefers the evidence given by one witness rather than another there can be no appeal unless the decision is perverse. The test of perversity is high; it must be such as to cause the objective bystander to say "My goodness, that is wrong".

There can be further appeals by leave from the Employment Appeal Tribunal to the Court of Appeal by leave of either the Appeal Tribunal or of the Court of Appeal, but again only on a *point of law*; and similarly from the Court of Appeal finally to the House of Lords with leave from either.

THE HIGH COURT AND COUNTY COURT.—The High Court and County Court deal with all the common law actions relating to employment law, although the latter Court is restricted to claims up to £5,000 and is subject to certain other limitations.

A litigant in person may appear in either court, but a firm must be represented by solicitors and counsel in the High Court, or by a solicitor (and counsel, if they wish it) in the County Court (but with some exceptions).

The procedure is very much more formal and the rules more strictly applied than in the tribunals, but legal aid is availabe for those with limited means. A person or firm should seek advice from their solicitor if they become embroiled in litigation in these two courts, because the loser in an action generally has to pay the costs, and these can be very high.

THE EUROPEAN COURT OF JUSTICE.—This court, which was set up by the European Economic Community, is assuming increasing importance because its rulings are binding on us. They may conflict with the previous decisions of our courts or with an express provision in one of our own Acts.

If the European Court of Justice finds that a decision given by our own courts or any provision made in an Act of Parliament is in conflict with the European Law, then it will make a declaration to that effect and leave it to our own courts to enforce its rulings and to provide an appropriate remedy.

Our own courts must refer a claim to it where there is no further right of appeal available to a litigant, and where the effect of Community Law is in issue, although a Court at any stage, of its own motion, can make a reference. Parties do not have direct access to the European Court. The Commission, at the behest of an individual, is empowered to seek a ruling from the Court that a State is in breach of the European law. A Member State may take proceedings against another.

EUROPEAN COURT OF HUMAN RIGHTS.—In 1953, the United Kingdom ratified the European Convention for the Protection of Human Rights and Fundamental Freedoms. The Convention lays down the minimum rights that a person is entitled to in various spheres of activity, including those relating to employment. In 1959, the European Court of Human Rights was established and from 1966 the U.K. has recognised the rights of individuals to petition the court direct.

Unliked some E.E.C. law, the Convention is not directly enforceable in our Courts or Tribunals, but our own legislation has to be construed, if at all possible, so as not to conflict with it.

If there is an irreconcilable difference between the two laws, then it is up to the Government to pass legislation so as to accord with the Convention. The law relating to the closed shop (see page 10) came about as a result of a ruling from this court that three railwaymen, who had lost their jobs because they had ceased to be members of a union, had a valid claim for breach of the Convention because our own laws provided no remedy.

POSITION IN LAW OF UNIONS AND THEIR OFFICERS

GENERALLY.—The extent of the immunity which was initially granted to unions, their officials and members since the Trade Union Act, 1906 has been greatly reduced in recent years. It is a sensitive subject where feelings can run high and the law is unlikely to remain static for long.

There has been difficulty in understanding some of the legislation because new Acts have been superimposed on existing ones. In consequence it is generally necessary to proceed stage by stage from the initial legislation and work out the effect of various amendments. The late Lord Diplock described the process as being a 'legislative maze'.

The meaning and effect of various enactments have been the subject of much judicial scrutiny and there have been considerable differences of views on the meaning of various sections, phrases and words. This has led to uncertainty and much litigation, some of which has resulted in unforeseen consequences.

If a union, at any stage, fails to comply with any of the technical requirements of the Acts, then they may find themselves liable, even if they were unaware of an important fact which has brought about their liability and they had no intention of being in breach of the law.

No longer immune are political and sympathy strikes; nor are strikes arising out of demarcation disputes because they are not between an employee and his employer. But motive, eg, hatred of an employer, does not remove the immunity, *provided* the purpose comes with the provisions, eg, improvement of wages, *and* the person taking the action honestly and genuinely believes that his objective is likely to be achieved by the action.

Any grievance must be communicated to the employer first before any action may be taken, otherwise immunity will be lost.

Liability at Common Law.—The common law rules governing the liability of unions for the acts of its officials and members depend on the law of agency. This generally requires consideration of the 'rule book' to ascertain whether a person is acting within the authority of his union. The book itself may lack clarity, especially if there have been many amendments, not all of which have been properly recorded. In consequence the position is usually lacking in certainty, which has resulted in employers being disinclined to embark on expensive litigation under the common law.

Liability under Statute.—Under the Act, it is provided that all:

'acts shall be taken to have been done by the union if it was authorised or endorsed by a responsible person';

such acts being treated as so authorised or endorsed, if it comes from:

(i) the principle executive committee;
(ii) a person with power to authorise or endorse the acts complained of;
(iii) the president or general secretary, or equivalent;
(iv) a full time official of the union or a committee to whom he regularly reports
unless
(v) the official or committee was prevented by union rules from so acting, and the action is repudiated by the principle executive committee, president or general secretary as soon as reasonably practical, and
(vi) the official or committee are notified in writing immediately of the repudiation, and
(vii) no act inconsistent with the repudiation occurs.

A union which fails to take the appropriate action, or even if it gives clandestine approval, will be liable for the acts of a 'person', or two or more persons acting in combination (eg, a union official(s), and/or member(s)) and consequently for damages flowing from a 'tort' committed by him or them.

Immunity is preserved in the following circumstances, namely, where:

(i) the action relates to *interferences with contracts of employment*; and
(ii) it is done '*in contemplation or furtherance of a trade dispute*'; and
(iii) it does not involve certain types of '*primary*' or '*secondary action*'; and
(iv) the action taken has the '*support of members under a secret ballot*', and
(v) where there is *picketing*, it is not carried out in an unlawful manner.
(vi) where the action taken does not induce a *breach of statutory duty*.
(vii) see below*.

The usual means by which a union can attack an employer is by calling strikes, go-slows, work-to-rules, or blacking of goods, thereby preventing an employer from fulfilling his commercial contracts. Before a union takes action there must be a trade dispute between the worker and *his* employer relating wholly or mainly to the terms and conditions of employment, or to dismissals or suspensions, or to work or discipline, to membership of a union or facilities for officials of the union, or negotiations by them. The protection given extends to disputes occurring outside the United Kingdom provided that it will effect employees in one of these matters.

Fear of job losses can come within the section because it relates to the termination of employment, but it must be genuinely based on 'something definite and of real substance'. Where there is interference with a contract by unlawful means, eg, by nuisance or violence or even intimidation of employees, then the immunity is lost.

'Primary action' occurs where some action is taken by an employee directly against his employer, which is at the core of the dispute. This would happen if employees acted on union instructions to 'go-slow' in support of a wage claim. 'Secondary action' arises where a person induces another to interfere with a contract of employment when that other is not involved in the dispute.

---

* Proposals are currently before Parliament to make any industrial action taken to press for the operation of the closed shop unlawful, and remove the immunity granted to unions. This will cover situations where the action taken is because the employer employs or intends to employ non union labour or persons not of a particular union, or where the union pressurises the employer to treat employees less favourably because they are not members of a union or of a particular union.

Immunity for 'secondary action' is preserved where:

(i) the contract which will be interfered with is a contract of employment which has the effect of damaging a business or commercial contract; and

(ii) the main purpose is to directly prevent or disrupt the supply of goods or services during the dispute, between the two employers, and, the action is likely to achieve that end, or

(iii) the main purpose is to do the same as in (ii) above but with any 'associated employer' (see page 19) to the one in dispute, who was supplying or receiving the goods or services during the dispute in substitution of the employer, and, it must be likely to achieve that end,

but *not* where a trade union or individual organises, or threatens, industrial action in firm 'A', which would result in breaches of contracts of employment by employees in that firm, *and* it will have the effect of interfering with the supply of goods and services to or from firm 'B'; *and* the reason is;

(i) because firm 'B' employs non-union labour in connection with the work done relating to the supply of those goods or services, *or*

(ii) because firm 'B' does not recognise, negotiate or consult with trade unions or its officials.

Immunity from actions for tort will also be lost where a union has failed to hold a secret ballot, conducted in the specified manner, of all those entitled to vote. A majority of those voting must have voted in favour of action. This applies to industrial action as well as to strikes, and there must be a specific unequivocal question relating to each and a delay of not more than 4 weeks after the ballot before any action is taken. A fresh ballot would have to be held if the dispute was settled and another one relating to some *other* unrelated matter occurred within the 4 weeks.

Only those members whom it is reasonable for the union to believe will be called upon to strike or take other industrial action may be allowed to vote, and this will include members who may be indirectly interested in the outcome. A voting paper must be supplied to each member who must be allowed to vote in secret and without cost to himself.

A person may only picket at or near his place of work and for the purposes of peacefully persuading others to abstain from work. A union official may picket at the same premises providing some of his members work there and he is representing them. There must be no unreasonable harassment either by intimidation or even weight of numbers and this extends even to employees wishing to go to work who are accosted on the public highway.

Where there is a requirement for an employer to carry out certain statutory duties then it would be unlawful for a union or its officers to attempt to persuade employees to desist from carrying out those tasks. Such action, provided it had the effect of preventing compliance with the statutory requirements and not merely making it more difficult, would result in immunity being lost.

REMEDIES FOR UNLAWFUL ACTION.—There are two main courses open to an employer where unlawful action is taken against him. He can apply to the High Court for an injunction to order a union to desist from its action, or he can sue them for damages; or he can do both.

An injunction is generally more effective because it removes the immediate cause of conflict and may cause the trouble to go away; it also gives each side more time for reflection. Sometimes a union, in order to continue industrial action, is required first of all to carry out a ballot of its members and it finds that they are against the action recommended.

Proceedings usually commence with an application for an 'interlocutory injunction', that is a temporary one pending the hearing of the full action. The plaintiff (usually the employer) will have to show that it is a genuine case with a serious issue to be tried and which, on the balance of convenience, lies in his favour; that is to say, that if one is refused, then it would be unlikely that compensation in damages would be adequate remedy at the trial.

If the statutory defence of 'trade dispute' will probably arise and is more likely than not to succeed then an injunction is unlikely to be granted. Where the consequences to an employer will be very serious should an order not be made, the test applied is that there should be a high degree of probability that the defence will succeed.

The granting of an injunction is subject to the Judge's over-riding discretion. Even if on the facts a plaintiff is entitled to one, nevertheless it may be refused if the Judge thinks that no useful purpose will be served by granting one. He has to apply the maxim 'Equity does nothing in vain'.

If a union refuses to comply with an injunction, then it will be exposed to unlimited fines for contempt of court, and if these are not paid, then all their assets can be sequestrated in order to pay them.

A union can be made to pay damages, like any other individual, to any person or body harmed by any unlawful industrial action taken by them, subject to the limits set out in Table 1.

A party is entitled to recover the losses which were reasonably foreseeable from the unlawful action. A liberal approach is taken by the courts as to what can be ordinarily anticipated. Whether a union appreciates the fact or not, they will be deemed to realise the sort of consequences that would ordinarily follow from interference with commercial transactions.

TABLE 1.—MAXIMUM DAMAGES PAYABLE BY UNION FOR UNLAWFUL INDUSTRIAL ACTION.

Total Membership	Maximum Damages
less than 5,000	£10,000
5,000–24,999	£50,000
25,000–99,999	£125,000
100,000 or more	£250,000

Additional aggravated damages may be recovered where a person's dignity and pride are injured, but only to the extent necessary to compensate for it. Exemplary damages may be awarded in order to show a tort-feasor that blazen unlawful industrial action in breach of the law does not pay.

Time Limits.—Proceedings have to be brought within 6 years of the breach about which complaint is made.

BIBLIOGRAPHY

HARVEY, *Industrial Relations and Employment Law.* Butterworth & Co (Publishers) Ltd
HEPPLE and O'HIGGINS, *Encyclopaedia of Labour Relations Law.* Sweet & Maxwell, and W. Green & Son
KIDNER, RICHARD, *Trade Union Law.* Sweet & Maxwell
PERRINS, B., *Trade Union Law.* Butterworth & Co (Publishers) Ltd
WAUD, CHRISTOPHER, *Guide to Employment Law 1988.* Associated Magazines Ltd.

AGRICULTURAL ENGINEERING

Agricultural Prime Movers—Traction and Power Take-off Drives—Implements and Equipment—Machinery and Harvesting—Transport and Handling—Safety Regulations—Crop Drying and Storage—Animal Feeding—Manure Disposal—Environmental Control—Field Drainage—Irrigation—Bibliography.

By J. A. C. Gibb, OBE, MA, MSc, CEng, HonFIAgrE, Fellow ASAE, FRAgS; and N. W. Hudson, PhD, MSc(Eng), BSc, CEng, FICE, FIAgrE, MemASAE

INTRODUCTION.—Agricultural engineering is concerned with any application of engineering to the production of food, fibre and other crops on agricultural, horticultural and other holdings. As such, its scope includes field machinery and the related motive power, crop harvesting, drying, storage and processing, the control of environment for livestock, for crop production in enclosed environments, and in storage buildings, control of soil and water conditions, techniques of handling materials in agricultural conditions, and the disposal or re-use of waste materials without causing environmental pollution.

In many of these applications the precise character of engineering processes based on physical science has to be related to agricultural practices which are variable because of their essentially biological nature. An engineer working on agricultural applications must, therefore, be able to understand that the successful employment of engineering techniques is dependent on design which takes account of the variation in conditions likely to be encountered in practice and which also provides protection for mechanical, electrical or other systems which are to be exposed to attack from inorganic or organic chemicals, physical damage by livestock, vibration and possibly neglect and abuse by unskilled operators in at least some parts of the world.

The chapter that follows is intended to provide a guide to current data on agricultural engineering techniques and requirements under the headings listed above, which are necessarily selective. A bibliography on p. K1/29 suggests further reading.

AGRICULTURAL PRIME MOVERS.—The development of agricultural prime movers over almost a century has been marked by a gradual shift of emphasis on their function. Initially the tractor was simply a machine to pull implements as a substitute for animal power, and to drive stationary equipment for crop processing. The advent of hydraulic systems then allowed implements to be mounted on the tractor so that it could be used as a mobile machine-tool, providing control of the position of the working tools of agricultural production and power to drive them. The importance of the transport and handling activities in agriculture was then appreciated and design to facilitate these functions resulted in the manufacture of mechanical handling attachments for use with conventional tractors. Specialised prime movers for transport purposes were also introduced, fitted with wheel equipment giving full mobility on agricultural surfaces as well as permitting relatively high speeds on the public roads. Further development of hydraulic equipment for materials handling purposes, fitted to chassis based on agricultural tractors, led to the production of rough-terrain fork lift vehicles and their widespread adoption by farmers during the late 1970's.

The current position is that the prime mover requirement of agricultural production is predominantly satisfied by 4-wheel tractors powered by Diesel engines within the power range 30–300kW. Machines in the power range 30–70kW are used for general purposes, including light cultivation and harvesting work and non-specialised transport with single-axle or double-axle trailers. Larger tractors are associated with wide cultivation implements and because of their weight and size are often of limited use for other purposes. There is an increasing demand for low ground-pressure vehicles for the application of herbicides or other chemicals in the winter on land when it is in a readily-compactible state. Such vehicles have up to 8 wheels with low pressure tyres exerting a ground pressure of as little as 2.5kPa, and provide for mobility in conditions in which larger and heavier tractors would seriously damage the soil structure, to the detriment of crop yields and field drainage.

The introduction of self-propelled machines for specific functions has been confined almost entirely to harvesting operations and for the applications of spray chemicals and other materials to growing crops. The concept of a multi-purpose chassis designed to operate a range of single-purpose harvesting units has never gained acceptance to any significant extent, in spite of the obvious logic of utilising one expensive prime mover for a succession of harvesting tasks, rather than providing each harvesting machine with its own power unit, transmission and chassis.

The present-day agricultural producer has thus, after a very long period of development, the choice of a range of general-purpose prime-movers based on the mobile machine-tool concept, supplemented by specialist machines each designed to emphasise the tractive, or transport or materials handling functions of the tractor.

Some of these technical features are discussed in the following sections. Designers must bear in mind the comparatively limited size of the agricultural market and the fact that most farm tractors and machines are used un-intensively, by industrial standards, because of seasonal and climatic constraints. Rugged construction is desirable to cope with severe working conditions and, although rock-bottom price is no longer a prime requirement and the price levels of agricultural equipment in recent years have increased ahead of inflation, a realistic pricing policy is essential for commercial viability.

TRACTION.—The power available at the rear axle of an agricultural tractor cannot be transferred to the drawbar without losses, which include the rolling resistance of wheels in contact with the soil, gradient resistance, wheel slip and work done in cutting, churning and displacing the soil. According to Senkowski (*Journ I Agr E*, Vol 19, No 3) tractive efficiencies in actual work which exceed 40% can be regarded as reasonably satisfactory. Up to 15% of the loss may be due to wheel slip.

Traction can be augmented by increasing the weight of the tractor. This can be done by fixing weights to the wheel discs or by using the large, low-pressure tyres as water containers. Water ballasting of the tyres entails filling them as nearly as possible to 100% with water (which should include 25 kg of calcium chloride plus 0·5 kg of slaked lime per 50 litre of water to prevent freezing). Filling 100% also reduces the likelihood of sidewall wrinkling. The effect of adding weight W is to add approximately $\frac{1}{2}$ W to the tractive effort available at the drawbar. Other devices to increase traction include the substitution of cleated steel wheels (for use on clay soils only), the use of *tyre girdles*, retractable or non-retractable *strakes* and *cage wheels*. The latter also minimise sinkage.

A *differential lock* in a wheeled tractor transmission can reduce wheel slip appreciably in straight-line operation. Hydraulic or mechanical locking systems are used, but a means of rapid disengagement is of vital importance. *Four-wheel drive* allows more total power to be used while reducing the amount of traction at each wheel, and is of particular application to tractors of over 80kW. Double or triple wheels are virtually essential for adequate traction with engine outputs of over 150 kW.

Tyre tracks, *half tracks* and *full tracks* offer three further stages of increased tractive capacity, in proportions directly related to their additional cost compared with the standard tractor. However, all of these devices, except retractable wheel strakes, restrict the tractor to operation on agricultural surfaces only, limiting its use for transport purposes on hard roads and thus reducing its versatility. The effect of traction aids, compared with standard pneumatic tyres, depends on interacting factors such as soil type and moisture content. In light, sandy soils there is little advantage, while maximum benefit is gained in heavy clay soils at high moisture contents. The advantage offered by traction aids is further diminished by the trend towards increased speed of operation.

The tractive performance of individual tractor models is ascertained in test procedures based on BS 1744 1960 and Test Code Document 97 of the Organisation for Economic Co-operation and Development (OECD).

IMPLEMENT MOUNTING.—Large cultivation implements and harvesting machines are too heavy, with their centres of gravity too far back from the point of attachment to allow convenient mounting at the rear of the tractor. Such equipment is, therefore, towed by the tractor, although it may be powered hydraulically, or via the power take-off (pto) shaft, and its depth or height of working may be determined by controls on the tractor.

Most other farm equipment can be tractor-mounted with considerable advantage. Mounting can be at the front or rear of the tractor, or underneath the engine and transmission assemblies. No standards for front- or mid-mounting have been adopted; BS 1841 1968 and 1973 refer to rear mounting. The great majority of tractor-mounted implements now in use conform to this standard, which specifies attachment by means of an upper hitch pin and two lower hitch studs, secured at each point by a linchpin. More rapid systems of implement mounting are provided by quick coupling systems of attachment which have been developed separately in Britain, the USA and some continental countries (BS 4621 1970).

Heavy rear-mounted implements such as large multi-furrow ploughs, or load-carrying devices such as fork-lift attachments, may alter the weight distribution of the tractor to the extent that front-end instability is experienced. Methods of overcoming this difficulty include the attachment of up to about 400 kg in cast-iron weights carried on a suitable frame forward of the radiator grille, or the use of weights bolted to the front wheels. With front-mounted implements such as fore-end loaders, weighting of the rear wheels or the use of a concrete ballast block carried on the rear linkage may be necessary to maintain rear wheel adhesion.

WEIGHT TRANSFER FROM IMPLEMENTS.—Increased weight on the tractor's rear wheels can result either from the change of position of the static centre of gravity due to the mounting of an implement and/or by the transference of forces from either a mounted or a trailed implement, through its connection to the tractor. The 3-point linkage was first designed to enable a relatively light tractor, by utilising this dynamic transference of weight, to employ a larger amount of power than would otherwise have been possible. The effect of mounted implements on the tractor is discussed by P. A. Cowell (*Farm Machine Design Engg*, Vol 1, June 1967).

With trailed implements, improper hitching so that the point of attachment is above the rear axle must be avoided in the interests of safe operation, even though a measure of weight transference from front to rear

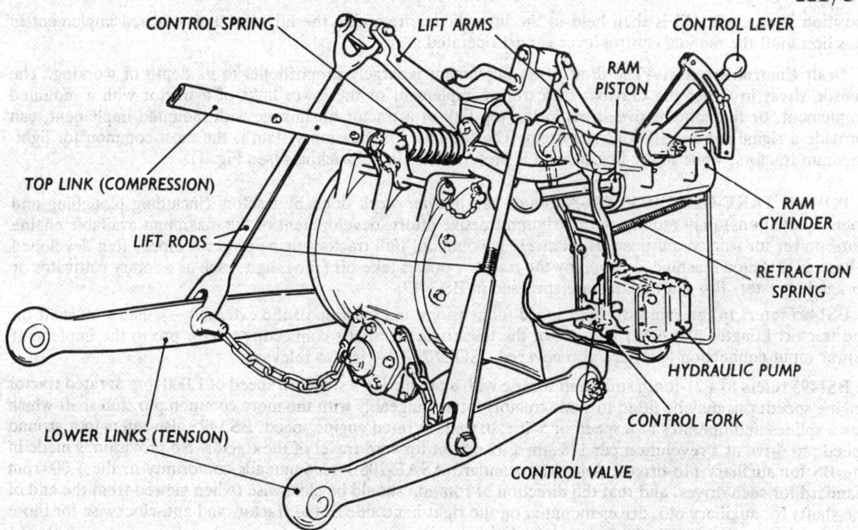

FIG. 1.—Hydraulic Draft Control of Mounted Implement (*Shell*).

wheels is obtained. Effective and safe systems of weight transference from a trailed implement are available, which depend on utilising the tractor lift system to exert an upward stress on a suitably strengthened implement towbar and tractor drawbar. In extreme conditions of wet and soft soil such devices are likely to increase the risk of bogging down the tractor rear wheels, but in all other conditions they can be of considerable value.

Position and Draft Control of Mounted Implements.—In addition to providing a means of raising and lowering mounted implements, hydraulically-actuated systems of implement mounting also allow the tractor operator to select systems of either position- or draft control. Position control enables the position of the implement in a vertical plane to be set relative to the tractor transmission housing and is normally employed for implements not in deep contact with the soil. Draft control systems embody a means of feedback to enable the depth of working of soil-engaging implements to be varied automatically, to maintain a constant draft. Electronic control systems have supplanted mechanical or hydraulic sensing systems in some designs.

A general arrangement is shown in Fig. 1. The implement is mounted at the rear ends of the lower links, with the rear end of the top link connected to the mast fitting on the implement. The angle of attack of the implement (pitch) can be altered by telescoping the top link. Its level in relation to the tractor rear axle is adjusted by means of a threaded lift rod, normally on the right-hand side. The lateral swing of the implement is restricted by check chains.

Position Control Systems (See Fig. 2).—The oil pressure control valve can be operated either by a manually-set lever or by movement of the lift arms. In practice, the hand lever is used to preset the system to a required position and downward movement of the lift arms then moves the spool valve until a neutral

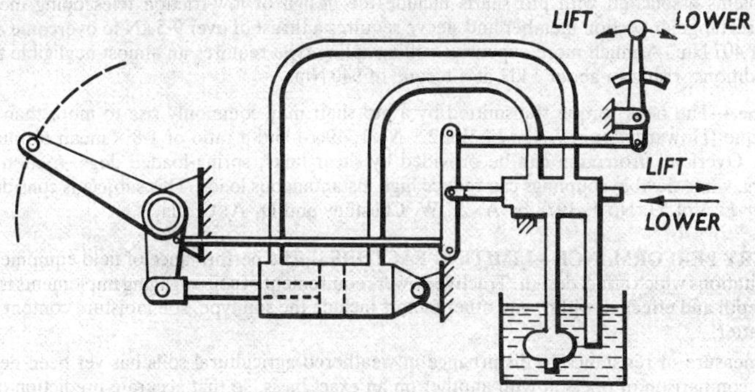

FIG. 2.—Position-Responsive Hydraulic Control System.

position is reached. Oil is then held in the lift cylinder, retaining the lift arms and attached implement in position until the manual control lever is next operated.

Draft Control Systems.—The draft of an implement is largely proportional to its depth of working. The tensile stress in either the drawbar of a trailed implement or the lower links of a tractor with a mounted implement, or the compressive stress in the top link of a tractor lift linkage with mounted implement, can provide a signal for a draft control system. The top-link compression system is the most common for light-medium tractors, while lower-link tension is preferred for large machines (see Fig. 1).

POWER TAKE-OFF DRIVES.—Although the heavier work done by tractors (including ploughing and some cultivations) may require the maximum tractive effort, development of the maximum available engine horsepower for tractive purposes is relatively uncommon. Full tractor engine power is more often developed where an attached machine is driven by the tractor's power take-off (pto) shaft, such as a rotary cultivator or forage harvester. Pto shaft guards are specified in BS 3417.

BS1495 refers to the rated working speed, dimensions and location of the externally-splined stub shaft on the tractor. Lengths and other features of the telescopic pto shafts connecting tractor pto to the implement power input connection (pic) are also covered. ISO 5673-1980 is also relevant.

BS1495 refers to a 21-tooth stub shaft for use with a pto having a standard speed of 1,000 rpm at rated tractor engine speed; this may be fitted to some tractors interchangeably with the more common pto stub shaft which has 6 splines and operates at a speed of 540 ± 10 rpm, at rated engine speed. BS 1495 also refers to a ground speed pto drive at 1 revolution per 178 mm ± 12 mm of forward travel of the tractor. No provision is made in the BS for auxiliary pto drives; American standard ASAE-206.1 recommends conformity to the 1,000 rpm standard for such drives, and that the direction of rotation should be clockwise (when viewed from the end of the shaft) for auxiliary pto drives mounted on the right-hand side of the tractor, and anti-clockwise for those mounted on the left-hand side.

Control of pto Drives.—The simplest form of control is provided by a dog clutch which engages or disengages the power train from the transmission to the pto stub shaft. If the main transmission clutch is disengaged, the pto and transmission cease to be driven simultaneously. A dual drive arrangement, whereby two clutches are provided, allows successive disengagement of the drives to the transmission and pto as the clutch pedal is depressed through two stages; a system that is provided on most modern tractors.

The extra degree of control offered by the dual clutch is of considerable value in operations where a constant pto speed but a varying ground speed is desirable. An independent pto drive, in which the power train to the pto shaft does not include the main transmission clutch, offers a further stage of control, but involves greater complexity in the pto shaft drive arrangements.

Belt Drives.—BS 1495 refers to tractor belt pulleys, which should give a belt speed of 15·75 ± 0·5 m/s, at rated engine speed. Belt drives of this type are now used only rarely.

Out-of-balance Forces in Operation.—A paper by L. H. Freeman (*Journ I Agr E*, Vol 22, No 1, 1966) presents a comprehensive review of problems associated with pto shafts. The location of the pto and pic shafts on the tractor and implement respectively and the position of the implement hitch point (in the case of a trailed implement) or the geometry of the implement mounting (in the case of an implement mounted on the 3-point linkage of the tractor), exercise a considerable effect on the velocity variations between the front and rear universal joints of the pto shaft. The design of pto-driven implements should always aim at keeping the angles of deflection of the front and rear universal joints as nearly similar as possible, not only under conditions of normal work, but also when a trailed implement negotiates corners and when a mounted implement is raised. Constant velocity joints which reduce these problems are under development.

Other problems associated with pto shafts include the design of low-friction telescoping members. The conventional rectangular-section member and sleeve requires a thrust of over 9·5 kN to overcome axial friction at a torque of 407 Nm. A much more expensive rolling-spline type requires an almost negligible thrust under the same conditions, rising to about 1 kN at a torque of 940 Nm.

Peak Torque.—The peak torque transmitted by a pto shaft may commonly rise to more than three times the mean torque (Howard, *Journ I Agr E,* Vol 22, No 1, 1966) and a ratio of 1·8 × mean torque is a useful design figure. Overload protection can be provided by shear links, spring-loaded dogs, friction clutches or torque limiters, while flexible couplings can reduce high instantaneous loads. This subject is considered further in *Journ I Agr E*, Vol 53, No 1, 1978 by A. A. W. Chestney and D. A. Crolla.

MACHINERY PERFORMANCE—LIMITING FACTORS.—The performance of field equipment is subject to various limitations which affect design. Tractive power requirement of soil-engaging implements is determined by working depth and effective width, and other factors include the soil type, soil moisture content and content of organic matter.

No single measure of resistance to disturbance in weathered agricultural soils has yet been devised which would permit comparison of one soil with another on an exact basis, so that accurate prediction of the power requirement of soil-engaging implements in the conditions in which plant growth takes place is almost impossible. The actual drawbar pull of a trailed implement in given conditions can be measured by a drawbar dynamometer or in the case of mounted implements by strain-gauge techniques.

Permissible Implement Weight.—This is limited by considerations of tractor weight distribution or balance, or by the load-bearing capacity of the soil. Scientific evidence on the effect of compaction on agricultural soils is inconclusive, but excessive pressure—particularly if allied to the smearing effect of wheel slip under traction—is thought to be deleterious to soil structure. Compaction effects can be minimised by the use of wide-section tyres or tracks, but practical considerations of furrow or inter-row width, or wheel dimensions, limit this possibility.

Implement Directional Characteristics.—These may be restrictive. A plough body turns the furrow either to the right or to the left, depending on its design. With a right-handed plough, the implement must always operate to the left of its previous work, so that in fields of finite size a complex pattern of working is necessary if a level result is to be achieved. Companion sets of left-handed and right-handed bodies can be used alternately, as in the case of reversible ploughs. Harvesting machines usually have a directional characteristic also, if only in discharging the harvested crop into transport vehicles on one particular side. Careful choice of working pattern is necessary if idle running is to be minimised.

The need to avoid overlap exists in many cases irrespective of implement type. In spraying or fertiliser spreading operations overlap gives rise to over-application, which can affect crop yield adversely as well as being intrinsically wasteful, while in harvesting work overlap implies reduction of machine capacity. Systems of markers, utilising tines suspended from an implement, or sighting poles, or foam generators to lay marks, can assist in achieving accurate operation.

TABLE 1.—WORKING CAPACITY OF SOME FARM MACHINES (Adapted from *Profitable Farm Mechanization*, by C. Culpin)

	Approx working data			Normal speed km/h	Draft kg	Field efficiency %
	Width m	Depth mm	Rate ha/day			
Plough (2-furrow)	0·6	150	1·6	5·6	500	80
Plough (6-furrow)	1·8	150	6·0	5·6	1,500	80
Rotary cultivator	1·5	150	3·0	3·2	—	85
Spring-tine harrow	4·0	75	20·0	8·0	600	85
Disc harrow	2·5	100	8·0	5·6	500	85
Grain drill	4·0	—	16·0	8·0	—	70
Fertiliser distributor	6·0	—	17·0	8·0	—	50
Crop sprayer	4·5	—	10·0	6·4	—	50
Combine harvester	3·6	—	8·0	3–7	—	75
Pick-up baler (hay)	3·0	—	6·0	6·4	—	50
Mower (finger-bar)	1·5	—	4·0	5·6	—	75
Forage harvester (flail)	1·25	—	2·5	4·8	—	65
Potato harvester	0·75	—	0·8	2·0	—	70
Sugar-beet harvester	0·5	—	0·8	4·0	—	50

Size of Implements.—Overall size may be restricted by considerations of manoeuvrability, even where weight or power requirements are not limiting. Light cultivation implements, sprayers and seed broadcasters could all be made very wide indeed if it were not for the difficulties presented by ground contours, the high peripheral speeds of wide implements when turning on a short radius and the difficulty of judging accurately the clearance between the outer end and obstructions such as hedges or trees. Also, on most farms relatively narrow gates, roadways or culverts have to be negotiated. Implements more than 3 m wide may have to be made to fold or dismantle to allow for these conditions. In some overseas territories, machines up to 30 m wide are in use.

Field Efficiency.—The theoretical rate of working of a machine, where S = speed of operation (m/s) and W = effective width of machine (m), is equal to $SW/2{\cdot}78$ ha/h. This rate is reduced in practice by factors including: pattern of field operation, size and shape of field, sub-optimal soil and crop conditions, level of crop yield, operators' rest time, machine maintenance or adjustment time and incomplete integration of interdependent operations in a multi-machine system. The *field efficiency* factor is based on such reductions.

Forward speed determines the machine working rate in conditions in which the available power is not limiting. The interaction of factors such as the poor ability of human operators to withstand the low-frequency resonance characteristics of low-pressure pneumatic tyres, ability to retain control of the vehicle, and the need for a high degree of steering accuracy in many operations, places a normal limit of approx 8 km/h on forward speed during operation with implements and machines.

Seasonal Capacity of Equipment.—This depends on theoretical working rate × field efficiency × the number of days, or hours, per season or per year, during which it can be operated. The effective operating period is determined by climatic and cropping factors and by the availability of labour on the farm. Some machines and equipment are in fact used for a very small number of hours or days during the whole year. Table 1 gives information on the performance of field equipment under 'average' conditions on British farms.

SOIL-WORKING EQUIPMENT.—Farm crops are grown only in the uppermost part of the soil, and the majority of cultivation implements operate to a depth within 150–300 mm. The design of implements has evolved on an empirical basis over a long period of time, although work in the last 30 years by P. C. J. Payne and others has thrown some light on design principles. Most non-driven implements shear the soil by a wedge action. In *ploughing*, a wedge with an upper surface lying at about 20° to the horizontal is forced through the soil so as to sever a furrow slice from the unploughed ground, turning it about a fulcrum provided by an unsevered strip, and inverting it more or less completely. In doing this, a layer of the soil is effectively made available to be worked subsequently into a seedbed, and surface weeds or extraneous matter are buried. (P. C. J. Payne, *Journ Ag Engg Res*, 1956, **1**, 1. R. J. Godwin and G. Spoor, *Journ Ag Engg Res*, 1977, **22**, 3.)

Mouldboard Ploughs.—These utilise a share to make the horizontal cut at furrow-bottom level, to make the lower part of the vertical cut at the land-side of the plough body, and to initiate the action of rotating the furrow slice. Inversion of the furrow slice is completed by the action of the mouldboard. A disc (or knife) coulter completes the vertical cut (see Fig. 3).

Disc Ploughs.—These employ dished concave discs to combine the functions of share, coulter and mouldboard. The design of a disc plough has to provide adequate bearing surfaces to accommodate the horizontal thrust against the soil resulting from inversion of the furrow slice. Disc ploughs are less effective than mouldboard ploughs in achieving complete burial of surface material and growing weeds.

Tined Implements.—These also shear the soil by a wedge action, regardless of the shape actually presented to the soil. If a flat tine passes through the soil, a wedge of soil forms in front of it, causing the soil to fail along a succession of slip planes. The soil is also disturbed along lines of weakness roughly at right-angles to the passage of the tine. By decreasing the rake angle of the tine, ie by mounting it with the base further forward than the top, the pull required for the tine to pass through the soil can be reduced. The effectiveness of soil shattering is also reduced, so that a designer has to consider whether his main object is to obtain maximum soil disturbance, or minimum draft. Horizontal 'wings' may increase the shattering efficiency of tines.

Tined implements of various sizes and weights perform a range of operations. *Chisel ploughs* and *heavy cultivators* can work to 300 mm or greater depths, shattering the soil either in the initial stages of seedbed preparation, or following ploughing. Chemical weed control methods may subsequently be necessary, since there is no weed-killing effect comparable with that of ploughing. *Spring-tine cultivators* and *harrows* may be used in subsequent operations to produce the finer aggregates and crumbs conducive to satisfactory plant growth and to restore a measure of consolidation, necessary to give plant roots adequate anchorage in the soil.

Curved tines may be used to raise clods or vegetable matter to the surface. Rotating soil-working implements may be driven only by contact with the soil, as in the case of *disc harrows* which break down clods and

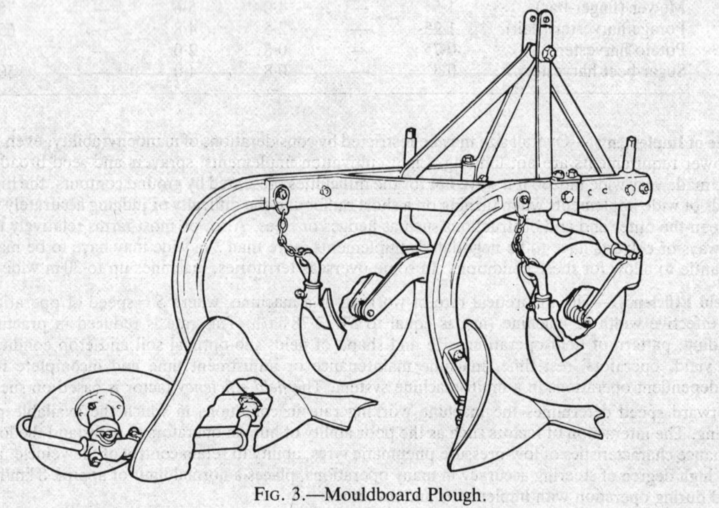

FIG. 3.—Mouldboard Plough.

consolidate the soil as well as cutting up growing weeds or crop residues. *Rotating harrows* similar in general construction to disc harrows, but with radially-mounted tines instead of dished discs, are also used.

Power-driven Implements.—These utilise an increased impact speed to enable soil aggregates to be disintegrated more effectively. These include *reciprocating harrows* and *rotary cultivators* with vertical or horizontal rotors. A power-driven digging machine employing rows of spade-shaped blades is also available. A levelling machine or grader can be used in the final stages of seedbed preparation. Precision seeding equipment and weed control operations in rowcrops demand an even and level surface, which also facilitates all subsequent machine and transport operations on the land.

MACHINES FOR CROP ESTABLISHMENT.—Sowing and planting equipment has to achieve an appropriate level of accuracy in distribution and placement of the seed. *Broadcasters* are used to distribute seed at random on to the surface of the soil, employing simple brush mechanisms to deliver seed through variable apertures in the rear wall of the seed hopper.

Seed Drills.—These utilise various kinds of feed mechanism to deliver seed, via coulter tubes, to tined or rotating coulters, which open shallow furrows. The seed is randomly distributed in the direction of forward travel and soil tends to fall inwards to cover the seed after the coulter has passed. The application rate can be altered by changing ratios in the drive train to the feed mechanism.

The seed requirement per ha varies between crops, and may also vary for a given crop, depending on time of year, variety, soil and climatic conditions, altitude and the condition of the seedbed. For many crops exact seed spacing is not required. A particular feature of cereals and most other crops is compensatory growth—ie a plant which is not competing with other plants close at hand will grow larger than it would otherwise—so that, up to a point, the crop growth tends to be self-stabilising.

For row-crops, in particular, precision sowing may well be necessary and requires a fine, level seedbed. This involves controlled seed production to obtain genetic uniformity and accurate size grading, both falling within the province of the seed supplier. For mechanical precision in sowing, necessary features include accurate seed pick-up and feed mechanisms, minimum drop height, lateral rigidity of the seed placement unit, the ability to float on the surface of the soil to cope with the minor surface unevenness and freedom from slip in the driving mechanism. Rearward acceleration of the seed can be arranged to counter the forward velocity of the seeder unit and minimise spacing errors in the direction of travel.

Many types of seeds are now available embedded in uniform spherical pellets formed from mixtures of fertilising and disease-inhibiting chemicals in an inert base.

Crop	Seed rate kg/ha	Sowing depth mm	Seed details		Approx row width mm
			Shape	Size (max) mm	
Cereals	110–220				
Grass seeds	22–23	0–13	Various		—
Sugar beet (natural)	9–11	20–40	Cluster	9·5	540
Sugar beet (rubbed)	4–7	20–25	Spherical	4·4	540
Turnips	0·6–5	13–25	Spherical	1·6	550
Carrots (normal)	3–5*	13	Flat-ovate	2·4	460–690
Carrots (in beds)	5–7	13	Flat-ovate	2·4	100 (in groups of 12 rows)
Potatoes (earlies)	2,400–3,700	50	Oval-spherical	50	710
Potatoes (main crop)	1,900–2,600	100			

* Low rates are used with spacing drills and wide rows when grown on the ridge.

Precision seeders which incorporate most, or all of the above features, are designed to deliver single seeds at a constant spacing—perhaps every 12 or 25 mm. *Spacing drills* are similar machines in which single seeds or groups of two or more seeds spaced close together, are separated by gaps of several cm along the direction of travel. The row width in which crops are sown depends on plant growth considerations and on the minimum practicable width of the sowing mechanisms. Examples of typical row widths and seed parameters are tabulated above.

In determining practical row widths the range of adjustment of tractor wheel track has to be considered, while, on a given farm, it is desirable to standardise on a single row width for the normal range of root crops. After-cultivations, characteristics of harvesting machines—including the track width of transport equipment—and the width of tractor rear wheels may also affect the decision. Narrow rear wheels, either pneumatic-tyred or steel, may be used where the size of the task warrants the cost of them and the labour of fitting and removal.

Transplanting Machines.—These are used for a number of mainly horticultural crops. All current types are hand-fed with seedlings of 200–300 mm overall length, which are placed in a shallow furrow and held either manually or mechanically until a layer of soil has been compacted over the roots by press wheels. Flexible rubber discs or cam-operated pairs of fingers may be used to receive the seedlings from the operators and carry them to the planting position. Machines for transplanting seedlings in paper pots automatically are under development.

Potato Planters.—These are designed to plant potatoes graded between screens of 50 × 32 mm mesh, as specified by the Potato Marketing Board. Potatoes may be exposed to artificial light to encourage the formation of sprouts or 'chits' up to 12 mm long at various points on the surface of the tubers. The feed mechanism must be designed to treat the tubers gently and preserve the chits intact. Potatoes are planted in a shallow furrow and normally covered immediately by dished discs or mouldboards carried on the planting machine, which form ridges 100–150 mm high above the tubers.

Most sowing and planting machines are used on flat seedbeds. In wet areas and for some overseas crops they may be modified to work on previously ridged land, usually by providing conical guide rollers to hold the coulters in place on top of the ridges. For work on flat land markers are usually essential to maintain the correct spacing of adjoining runs. With many seeders and drills it is desirable to include a monitoring system of some kind to give warning when any part of the sowing mechanism ceases to function, or the hopper needs replenishing.

FERTILISER AND MANURE APPLICATION.—Inorganic fertilisers may be applied at the time of sowing or planting. In general it is more economical to place fertiliser just below or to the side of the seed, but not in contact with it, in that a smaller quantity will be required than would be needed to cover the whole field evenly in a separate operation.

Disadvantages of simultaneous seed and fertiliser distribution include the added complication and weight of the combined machine, slower working rate because of stops to refill both fertiliser and seed hoppers, and the possibility of corrosion of the whole machine through exposure to fertiliser. The use of suitable plastics offers advantages in this latter respect.

Fertiliser Distributors.—For broadcast distribution of powdered or granular fertiliser, these machines may give a fixed width of spread approximating to the width of the fertiliser hopper, or may obtain a wider spread by feeding the material on to a spinning disc or similar mechanism. Rates of application may be from 100–1,100 kg/ha or more, while lime is spread—usually by contractors' machines—at up to 10 tonne/ha, or more.

The mechanisms commonly used include plate-and-flicker (Fig. 4(*a*)) or roller feed (Fig. 4(*b*)) mechanisms. The distribution rate is determined by the rotational speed of the mechanism in relation to a gate setting. Agitation in the hopper may be necessary to prevent bridging of the material. In the disc type (Fig. 4(*c*)) the fertiliser falls from the hopper onto the spinning disc and is thrown out in an arc by a series of vanes.

Fertiliser mechanisms combined with seed sowing mechanisms may employ a star-wheel system (Fig. 4(*d*)) or a fluted roller which feeds the material under an adjustable gate, the application rate being determined by the star-wheel tooth size and its speed of rotation. A coulter tube discharges the fertiliser adjacent to the seed coulter or into a separate coulter. Contact with the seed is normally avoided, as in dry soil conditions the fertiliser may damage the seed and inhibit germination.

Liquid and gaseous fertilisers are used in Britain only to a limited extent. Ammonia is drilled into the soil to a depth of 150–250 mm by means of knife-edged coulters and an appropriate manifold and tubing system. Other fertilisers in solution may be applied in a similar way, or merely broadcast. Injection of anhydrous ammonia at high pressures is also practised to some extent.

The handling of animal wastes, as solids or semi-solids, involves a range of *manure-spreaders*. One distribution principle for *farmyard manure*, which consists of a mixture of bedding straw and excreta, utilises two or more shredders and a spreader, rotating on horizontal axes and fed with the material by a moving belt or by a chain and slat conveyor. Land-wheel or pto drive may be employed. Another mechanism, suitable for either farmyard manure or slurry, consists of a horizontal rotor carrying a series of flail chains, situated in a long tank with the upper part of one side open. The manure is thrown out to the side by the pto-driven rotor. Application rates may vary from 25–50 tonne/ha. In areas where air or water pollution might otherwise occur, injection of macerated animal waste slurries into the soil may be practicable, using equipment based on similar principles to that for anhydrous ammonia.

Pest and Weed Control Equipment.—This includes sprayers, aerosol generators and dusting machines. Spray materials include soluble powders, wettable powders which form suspensions in water and fluids which form an emulsion which may be stable or unstable. Agitation is essential for suspensions and wettable powders.

Sprays are used for selective weed-killing or destruction of all growing material as well as for pest control. A high level of uniformity of distribution is required with fungicides, contact herbicides or insecticides, but effective results with growth regulator herbicides or stomach insecticides can be obtained with less even coverage. Application rates, in litres per hectare, are described as low (55–220), medium (220–660), and high volume (over 660). The rate of application is controlled by nozzle size, operating pressure (usually in the range 250–700 kPa) and the forward speed. Gear, roller vane, centrifugal, diaphragm or piston pumps may be used. Agitation may be hydraulic or mechanical, and a device to prevent drip from the nozzles when not spraying—usually a control valve arrangement reversing the flow through the nozzles and thus sucking in

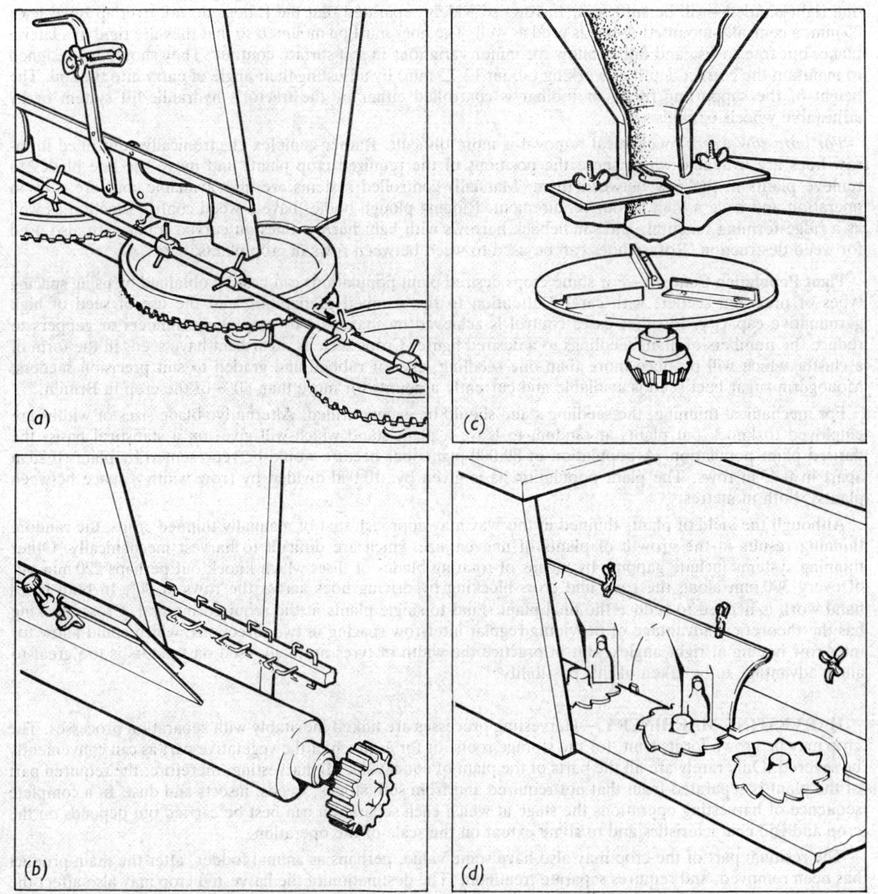

FIG. 4.—Fertiliser Distributor Mechanisms. (*a*) Plate-and-Flicker. (*b*) Roller Feed. (*c*) Disc Type. (*d*) Star-wheel or Fluted Roller Type.

air—is desirable in view of the toxic effect of even small quantities of many spray chemicals. Adequate provision must be made for filtration at the tank entry, before the pump and in the nozzles.

Sprayers may be fully-mounted, semi-mounted or trailed, depending mainly on tank size, which in turn depends on the intended application rate. Low-volume sprayers are usually mounted, with the pump driven directly by the pto stub shaft. Sprayers for use in orchards are much more complex, often using air as the vehicle for delivering small volumes of chemical, or applying volumes of over 1,100 litre/ha at pressures of up to 4 M Pa. Further information can be obtained from Bulletin No 5 of the Ministry of Agriculture.

Pre-emergence spraying may be carried out at the time of sowing to control weeds developing in the rows where the plants will come through.

Mechanical Methods of Weed Control.—Hoeing between the rows of crop plants to uproot or destroy weed seedlings is done by hoe blades carried on toolbar frames mounted at the front or rear of a tractor, or mid-mounted between front and rear axles. The rear-mounted position is most convenient in that it allows easy attachment to the tractor's hydraulic lift linkage and eliminates wheel marks and soil compaction caused by the tractor. Its steering characteristics are the reverse of what is required, however, since the toolbar moves further into the crop when a steering correction is made, and the tractor operator has to look behind him; a second operator may, therefore, be required to steer the hoe toolbar. For these reasons rear-mounted hoes cannot be set to work as closely as front- or mid-mounted implements, and a gap of 75 mm is about the minimum that is practicable.

L-shaped and A-shaped hoes are used. For narrow inter-row spaces a pair of L-hoes—one left-handed and one right-handed—will be sufficient. In rows so widely separated that the L-hoes do not overlap by at least 25 mm, a centrally-mounted A-hoe is used as well. The hoes must be mounted so that they are rigid in a lateral plane, but free to rise and fall to allow for minor variations in soil surface contour. They should be designed to maintain the correct depth of working (about 12–25 mm) by adjusting their angle of entry into the soil. The height of the supporting frame or toolbar is controlled either by the tractor's hydraulic lift system or by adjustable wheels or skids.

For intra-row weeds mechanical removal is more difficult. Rather complex electronically controlled intra-row hoes are available which sense the positions of the required crop plants and move the hoe blades to remove plants in the row between them. Manually-controlled systems are also available, but are slow in operation and have a high labour requirement. Ridging plough bodies have a weed control function as well as a ridge-forming function, and saddleback harrows with light harrow tines on curved frames are also used for weed destruction. Rotary hoes can be used to weed between rows of crop plants.

Plant Population Control.—For some crops desired plant populations can best be obtained by using spacing types of precision seeder, with careful attention to the seedbed preparation and the use of seed of high germinative capacity. In other cases control is achieved mechanically by employing thinners or gappers to reduce the numbers of plant seedlings to a desired figure. Crops such as sugar beet have seeds in the form of a cluster which will produce more than one seedling, even if rubbed and graded to suit precision seeders. Monogerm sugar beet seed is available and currently accounts for more than 80% of the crop in Britain.

For mechanical thinning, the seedling stand should be evenly drilled. Alternative blade sizes or widths are employed to knock out plants at random to leave a plant stand which will give, on a statistical basis, the desired plant population. A population of 89,000 plants per hectare would be represented by plants 0·25 m apart in 0·45 m rows. The plant population/ha is given by: 10,000 divided by (row width × space between plants), both in metres.

Although the yield of plants thinned in this way may approach that of manually thinned crops, the random thinning results in the growth of plants of uneven size which are difficult to harvest mechanically. Other thinning systems include gapping by means of rotating blades or discs which knock out perhaps 220 mm out of every 300 mm along the row, and cross-blocking by driving hoes across the rows at 90°. In both cases hand work is needed to reduce the final plant stand to single plants at the required interval. Cross-blocking has the theoretical advantage of providing regular inter-row spacing in two directions, which could allow for inter-row hoeing at right angles. But in practice the width of tyres normally used on tractors is too great to allow advantage to be taken of this possibility.

HARVESTING MACHINERY.—Harvesting processes are linked inevitably with separation processes. The crop may be grown for its fruit, for the storage roots, or for as much of the vegetative part as can conveniently be severed. Only rarely are all the parts of the plant of equal value. In harvesting, therefore, the required part of the plant is separated from that not required and from soil, stones, weeds, insects and dust. In a complete sequence of harvesting operations the stage at which each separation can best be carried out depends on the crop and soil characteristics and to some extent on the scale of the operation.

The residual part of the crop may also have some value, perhaps as animal fodder, after the main product has been removed, and requires separate treatment. The destination of the harvested crop may also affect the harvesting process, perhaps complicating it by requiring that a chopping stage be introduced, or limiting it to a certain period of time each day when the atmospheric relative humidity is below some specific level. For these reasons, harvesting operations may be quite complex, consisting of an integrated sequence of operations spaced out over time, combined in one single machine where possible, and subject to considerable variation for seasonal or climatic reasons. The provision of transport adds to the complexity of the system.

Cutting Machines for Standing Crops.—Grass crops, cereals and some fodder crops are harvested by cutting the aerial part 25 mm or more above ground level. For grass in particular, cutting may be followed by a period of moisture loss (wilting) in the field before it is collected and stored as hay or silage. The crop distribution characteristics of cutting machines are important, either in returning the crop to the ground in an organised fashion or in delivering to the next harvesting mechanism.

Shearing types of cutter include the *reciprocating mower* in which triangular knife sections (BS 1592 1965) 76 mm wide move with a horizontal stroke of 76 mm shearing the vegetation between the sharpened knife edges and ledger plates which form part of the mower knife fingers. The knife sections should register centrally with the fingers at the end of each stroke. The drive may be taken from an eccentric through a connecting rod or pitman or may be arranged hydraulically. The speed is variable, and for cutting grass ranges from 10 to 25 Hz.

The reciprocating mower will cut crops of any length, and leaves them in a swath with the butt end forwards and underneath subsequently cut heads. Inner and/or outer swath boards move the crop laterally so that it occupies a narrower swath than the width of cut, to allow tractors working subsequently to straddle the swath rather than crushing it into the stubble. Mowers are usually fully-mounted on the tractor, either at the rear or between the front and rear axles.

The *cylinder* type of mower, familiar as the domestic lawn mower, can be used for cutting grass crops not exceeding 200–300 mm in length. It may cut each blade of grass more than once. By fitting a deflector, the cut crop can be directed backwards on to a conveyor, if required.

Inertia types of cutter employ rotors revolving about either vertical or horizontal axes. The cutting surfaces strike the crop at up to 100 m/s peripheral speed, shearing the upper part of the stem against the inertia of the lower part. The vertical-rotor machines may be driven from above or below the rotors, which carry 2, 3 or 4 replaceable blades each or may be toothed like a circular saw. By arranging for pairs of rotors to contra-rotate a directional delivery pattern is established.

Horizontal-rotor machines, with the rotor axis at right-angles to the direction of travel, may be used at relatively low peripheral speeds of about 25 m/s to avoid excessive crop shattering and subsequent loss, for cutting grass intended to be returned immediately to the stubble for wilting and subsequently to be made into hay or high dry-matter silage. At about 40–50 m/s a considerable amount of laceration takes place and a substantial air current is set up which, with the energy imparted to the cut material, can be used to deliver it through ducting into a trailer drawn behind or alongside the cutting machine. The lacerating effect can be increased by bolting one or more anvils or ledger plates to the inside of the rotor housing.

With horizontal-rotor designs, the location of the main supporting wheels has to be considered. If the rotor is placed in line with wheel centres in a vertical plane, the most accurate control of stubble height will be obtained. If the wheels are behind the rotor the overall width of the machine is reduced and the wheels do not run over any uncut crop, but surface irregularities result in uneven stubble height and possibly in 'scalping' raised parts of the ground surface, introducing some soil into the crop. In addition to crop harvesting purposes, rotary cutting mechanisms are used for topping grazing pastures (cutting grass which is growing more quickly than it can be used) and for light-duty reclamation work.

Machines for Crop Movement in the Field.—To enable cut crops to dry out from their initial moisture content of up to 80% or more as quickly as possible, a wide range of equipment is used. The cut swath is rearranged into a windrow to allow more effective exposure to the wind, also reducing the area of contact with the damp soil and stubble.

Crushers and *crimpers* consist of a pair of plain or fluted rollers mounted one above the other across the direction of travel, and spring-loaded together. A feed roller to pick up the swath may be provided. The crop passes between the crushing rollers, flattening the stems and rupturing the cell structure, in part at least, to assist in the release of moisture and to increase the surface area/unit mass of the grass stems.

Crops treated in this way lose moisture very quickly in suitable weather conditions, so that reduction from 80% to under 30% moisture content may take place in little over 24 hours. Combined cutting and conditioning machines employ rotary cutting mechanisms to deliver the crop to secondary mechanisms which assist moisture loss by abrading the waxy cuticle of the crop stems. Such mechanisms consist of rotating brushes or tined drums, frequently utilising nylon, polypropylene or other plastics for the crop-impacting elements.

Aerators and *tedders* are used to pick up a swath or compacted windrow by passing it over or under a tined rotor, returning it to the ground to form a new windrow in the case of an aerator, or broadcasting it in the case of a tedder. At moisture contents above 40% the loss of leaf from grass or legume crops is small.

Swath turners are often combined with *side delivery rakes* in a single machine, which can sometimes also be used as a tedder. The mechanisms include finger-wheels of approx 1m diameter fitted with radial spring tines, or rake bars forming a cylinder mounted horizontally but at an angle of about 40° to the direction of travel, or in some cases pairs of horizontal rotors. Whatever the mechanism, the operation is intended either to invert and loosen a swath or windrow while moving it sideways on to a drier part of the crop stubble, or to assemble two or more swaths or windrows together to facilitate picking up by a baler or other machine.

Balers are used to pick up and bale hay or straw crops, to produce a package which is relatively stable, provides a measure of quantity for rationing or littering livestock, and economises in storage space. Conventional balers have a reciprocating plunger mechanism operating at up to 1·5 Hz. The crop is fed into the bale chamber by packer arms and each successive charge is severed from the remaining material by a knife on the leading edge of the ram, in conjunction with a stationary shear plate.

The length of the bales is determined by an adjustable trip mechanism driven by a toothed wheel which protrudes through the side of the bale chamber and engages with the bales as they are formed. An average length in practice is 0·9 m. The density of the bales is controlled by tension screws which pull the sides of the bale chamber closer together. Density, in kg/m^3, is defined as: low, 130; medium, 130–225; and high, over 225. Low-density and medium-density bales are normally tied with two bands of sisal twine (BS 3543 1962), although polypropylene twines are now used to some extent. Wire-tying balers, using wire to BS 3335 1961, are used for high-density baling.

Pick-up balers are normally pto-driven by the tractor pulling them, and work at rates of up to 8–10 tonne/h in hay and 4–6 tonne/h in straw. Self-propelled machines are also available. While conventional balers are efficient as machines for packaging hay and straw into bales, the labour requirement for handling these packages subsequently has prompted the development of alternative forms of package. These include large bales of 320–720 kg weight, which can be moved by tractors and other mechanical-handling machines, and cubes of about 50 mm side, which can be handled in bulk. Further development is required before cubing machines become commercially acceptable, but substantial numbers of large bale machines are now in use.

Silage Harvesting Equipment.—This often deals with wet grass, ie grass which has not had the opportunity to lose moisture by wilting in the field after being cut. The grass is cut, lacerated to some extent and delivered by the forage harvester into an accompanying trailer. The type of machine required depends on the intended storage method. If the grass is to be stored in a horizontal silo, short chopping is not as essential as if it is to be put into a tower silo from which it will be mechanically unloaded at a later stage, although even in a horizontal silo mechanical removal is facilitated by chopping.

A chop length of 50–100 mm can be obtained with machines which incorporate a flywheel-type chopper as well as primary cutting flails. This not only gives the degree of short chopping required for storage in horizontal silos, but also gives the machine a two-stage capability. It can be used to cut the grass initially and to return it to the ground for wilting, returning later to pick it up, chop and deliver into a trailer. For storage in tower silos, much shorter chopping is required, and full-chop machines with cylinder choppers having up to 10 blades and driven at 16 Hz, or other suitable mechanisms, may be used to give a chop length of 6–10 mm. The material is conveyed into tower silos by blowers with paddle-blade fans requiring up to 40 kW to drive them.

A problem likely to be met with wilted green material in the 45–55% moisture content range is gum build-up. The gum emanates from the forage and forms a coating on everything it touches. While it is quite easily removed with water, or prevented from forming by adding water to the crop, no more sophisticated remedy has been devised as yet.

Grain-harvesting Equipment.—This has to cut the standing crop, thresh out the seed from the heads and separate the grain, the yield of which ranges from 2 to 10 tonne/ha, from straw, chaff, weed-seeds and other extraneous material. Ministry of Agriculture statistics show that a limited number of *binders* are still to be found on farms in Britain, but by far the greatest acreage is harvested by *combine-harvesters*. Both types of machine use reciprocating cutter bars, although the knife speed at 6–9 Hz is lower than for cutting grass and the knife usually has a 150 mm stroke. The knife sections are normally serrated and have a self-sharpening characteristic when cutting cereal straw.

The *binder* has a reel to deliver the cut crop on to a platform, from which a conveyor carries the material to the binder deck. Here it is bunched into sheaves, each tied individually by a single band of sisal twine when it reaches a pre-set size and density. The shape of the base of each sheaf can be adjusted to allow for stable stacking of groups of six sheaves into a stook, and the position of the band can also be adjusted. After maturing in the field the sheaves are carried away into storage for subsequent threshing.

For cutting with a *combine-harvester* (or 'combine') the crop must be as nearly and evenly ripe as possible. The cut crop is passed by a feed roller into the threshing cylinder, or drum. The drum consists of a cylinder carrying a number of beater bars which rub the grain from the ears against stationary bars forming part of an arc-shaped concave. The loose grain may pass through the bars of the concave onto a reciprocating grain pan, which conveys the grain to a series of sieves. The threshed straw is assisted from the drum by a stripper roller and passes on to reciprocating straw shakers, which allow loose grain to fall through as the straw passes rearwards to a discharge point.

The sieves, in conjunction with an air blast, separate the chaff and tailings (pieces of unthreshed head) from the grain. The tailings are returned to the drum for re-threshing. The grain is delivered to a temporary storage tank, from which it is discharged by an auger into a bulk trailer drawn alongside. Alternatively, a bagging attachment may be used, with a second operator to attend to it. It is unusual to grade the grain sample on the combine, although some machines arranged for bagging have size graders fitted.

A *stationary threshing machine* has a series of mechanisms broadly similar to those of a combine, but also has a second cleaning stage and provides for de-awning barley, polishing the grain and grading it into first quality, seconds and small grains.

Important developments in combine-harvester design during the late 1970s included the introduction of a number of axial-flow threshing mechanisms, in which the crop is delivered endways to either one or a pair of threshing and separating rotors. The crop is impelled towards the rear in a spiral pattern, giving a number of opportunities for each grain to be separated from the ear as it is rubbed between the threshing section of the rotor and the stationary concave. The advantages claimed for these mechanisms include simplification of the design because no straw shakers are required, and increased efficiency of threshing. The grain is cleaned by a fan and sieves in the conventional manner.

A significant further advance in the mid-1980s was the development of a header mechanism for separating the grain from standing crops, offering the possibility of simplification and radical redesign of the harvester.

Other developments, which have resulted in the combine-harvester becoming the most complex and expensive agricultural field machine in widespread use, include the availability in some models of automatic controls for cutting height and of steering guidance while cutting. Comprehensive instrumentation of, and power-operated systems for setting, the various operating functions are provided, and ergonomic improvements include the provision of a sound-insulated and air-conditioned operator's work station.

Straw Disposal.—After grain harvesting this consists of burning it in the field, or baling it for use as bedding and litter for livestock. Other possibilities include ploughing it into the soil after spreading it and chopping it with disc harrows, or collecting and stacking it. A small amount goes for manufacture into strawboard.

Burning as a means of disposal, though popular with cereal farmers for its low cost and husbandry benefits, may give rise to environmentally unacceptable levels of smoke, smuts and smells, and practicable alternatives continue to be sought.

ROOT CROP HARVESTING.—This equipment has to contend with the removal of soil from the crop as well as other unwanted material. Root crops such as turnips are lifted out of the ground by their foliage, but for most crops the soil around the roots must be loosened by means of one or more shares, which may also lift the roots up to a conveyor of some kind. Harvesting normally proceeds one row at a time. One or more cleaning stages are provided, consisting of vibrating conveyors or tumbling drums to remove superfluous soil, while an inspection section may enable operators to remove either the crop from the remaining rubbish, or rubbish from the crop.

Potato harvesting systems, in enterprises of sufficient size, may justify the capital expense of complex machines, which remove the desiccated remains of foliage which has been chemically treated, or has died back naturally, lift the whole ridge with the potatoes, and progressively separate out the loose soil and all other unwanted material before delivering the crop into sacks, containers or an accompanying trailer.

Mobile equipment accompanying the harvester in the field is used by some farmers to clean, weigh and package potatoes for direct dispatch to wholesalers or supermarkets.

Special problems in potato harvesting include: (*a*) *Minimising damage incidence:* by design which avoids dropping potatoes more than 230 mm, by providing adjustment of agitator sections to suit prevailing conditions and by covering all components liable to bruise the tubers with a resilient material such as rubber. (*b*) *Separating stones from potatoes:* by using inclined studded rubber conveyors, adjusted so that the relatively non-spherical stones are carried upwards while the potatoes roll down. (*c*) *Separating clods from potatoes:* many different methods have been tried, including X-ray and gamma-ray discriminators to control a bank of deflector fingers, which is expensive and complex but seems to have no other disadvantage; and a flotation method in which the bulk and weight of a water tank are most undesirable and immersion adversely affects the keeping quality of the potatoes when stored subsequently.

Adverse ground conditions are often encountered, and place a limit on the permissible size and weight of potato harvesters. So does the fact that the crop is grown in rows, normally on the ridge, which means that very large machines involve either complex field layouts in which the first section of the crop must be harvested by some other, smaller equipment, or large headlands must be left unplanted, reducing the crop yield/ha of land.

For smaller acreages of potatoes, systems of lifting with ploughs, spinners or elevator diggers may be used, all of which return the tubers to the ground, on top of the loosened soil, to be picked up by hand. Yields of potatoes range from 15 to 50 tonne/ha, according to the type, variety and date of harvesting.

The *sugar beet crop*, yielding 30–40 tonne/ha, is also grown in rows. but provides scope for almost complete mechanisation. The roots are separated from the tops with a fair degree of precision. The maximum weight of sugar-bearing root is required, but the point at which the top is severed must not be so high as to include stem material, which will attract a penalty from the sugar factory.

The roots are not very susceptible to mechanical damage or frost. After lifting they are usually transported to temporary storage heaps from which they are loaded into road or rail transport to be taken to the factory. The tops have some value for cattle food, after a period of wilting during which certain undesirable chemical properties are modified to a safe form. The tops may then be fed direct or may be made into silage. Alternatively, they may be ploughed into the soil both as a means of disposal and to enrich the organic matter content of the soil.

Harvesting machines usually employ a feeler wheel or track to determine the operating level of a topping unit consisting of one or more fixed knives, or driven or undriven discs. Lifting shares loosen the roots and raise them out of the ground to a cleaning drum or conveyor and the roots are then conveyed either direct into an accompanying trailer, or into a temporary storage container. The latter may be located on the harvesting machine or—in one design—on the tractor, on a frame above the tractor driver and engine. An alternative beet harvesting system lifts the loosened beet out of the soil by means of a pair of inclined belts, which grasp the beet foliage and carry the whole plants up to a disc topping unit. Tractor-mounted versions of this machine are available, but most other types are trailed.

Carrots may be harvested by machines adapted from suitable types of potato or sugar-beet harvester. While most carrot crops are grown in rows up to 0·5 m apart, which are harvested one or two rows at a time, some machines have been designed for carrots grown in beds in rows only 100–180 mm apart, harvesting the whole width of the bed at once. Topping the carrots is a problem which has been solved most satisfactorily by a rotor with rubber flails which can remove the whole top from the root in one blow, working on one row at a time and situated on the harvester immediately before the lifting shares. Other possibilities include rotary knives or flail forage harvesters, which offer almost the only feasible method for carrots grown in beds.

Vegetable and Fruit Crops.—These have such varied characteristics that only a very few notes can be given here. A *universal vegetable* harvester has been developed by the National Institute of Agricultural Engineering, based on the twin inclined-belt referred to above. *Onion* and *bulb* harvesters are in small-scale production in Britain, working on the same basic principles as some types of potato lifting machines. Specialist machines are available for harvesting *hops*, stripping the cones from the unwanted bine either in the hop garden or at a central point to which the cut bine is transported.

In the United States, and especially in California, many different types of fruit and vegetable harvesting equipment have been developed. Tractor-mounted shakers for *apples* and other tree fruit are associated with mobile catching frames, and, for *prunes*, with collecting machines to pick up fruit from the ground. For *celery* harvesting, complete mobile plants for harvesting, washing and packaging are in use. Other machines have been produced for harvesting cherries, tomatoes, grapes, strawberries, blackcurrants, lettuce, cucumbers and many other crops. Design to minimise the incidence of damage is of prime importance.

In most cases in which these machines have been utilised successfully, their acceptability usually depends on factors such as plant breeding to produce varieties which ripen uniformly, or give a single harvest instead of a harvest continuing over a period of several successive pickings, the availability of varieties which have a high resistance to damage by impact or abrasion, or a manufacturing rather than than a fresh-crop market. Since these machines are often very complex and expensive, it is only on a large scale that they can be justified economically.

For the *frozen vegetable market*, mobile and stationary pea and bean harvesters are available on both sides of the Atlantic. A minimal delay between the field harvesting and factory freezing operations is essential in the maintenance of high quality. The harvesting machines are highly specialised and perform a difficult job of separating the peas and beans from the unwanted parts of the crop with the minimum of damage, and they have to be serviced by a rapid and efficient transport system from field to factory. Because of its high cost and complexity this equipment is usually operated by the frozen food companies, for whom farmers grow the crops under contract, or by cooperating groups of farmers.

Other crops include grass and herbage seeds, and peas and beans for drying rather than fresh consumption. Generally such crops require a two-stage harvesting process, in which the crop is first cut by a mower or a specialised cutting machine and then left lying in a windrow for a few days to reach a state of even ripeness and maturity. In the second stage a combine-harvester fitted with a pick-up attachment will thresh out the crop from the unwanted material. For some herbage seed crops a second threshing drum is fitted to the combine, so that the seed heads are removed from the straw in the main drum and the seed from the seed heads in the second drum or huller. Oil-seed rape is harvested in the same way as grain.

TRANSPORT AND HANDLING.—In agriculture as in manufacturing industry, handling enters into every facet of productive work. Handling conditions on the farm are more difficult than in a factory in that distances between field and farmstead may be relatively great, the ground conditions may be rough, muddy or on an appreciable gradient, the value of the materials is often relatively low in relation to their volume and the physical plant—in terms of production areas such as orchards or processing areas in old buildings—may offer severe limitations of layout and headroom.

Transport by means of tractors and trailers utilises relatively cheap and versatile equipment which is well adapted to the normal ground conditions, but the maximum size of load is often 3 tonne or less, and rarely exceeds 10 tonne, while methods of loading and unloading often run counter to established principles of materials handling.

Trailers, when employed in harvesting operations, are loaded in many cases directly by crop harvesting machines. But for other tasks manual loading may well be employed—as in handling seed or fertiliser in sacks or bags. Tractors equipped with front loaders may load manure and silage, while various forms of grab can be used with front loaders for bale handling. Trailers are often unloaded directly on to the ground by hydraulic tipping mechanisms operated by the tractor's hydraulic system. Two-stage high-lift trailers are available, giving a tipping height which can enable the material to be discharged into conveyors or distributors rather than on to the ground, or to place bulk materials into storage buildings.

Self-unloading trailers can deal with chopped material such as grass for silage, or silage after it has been removed from the silo, or grain, or manure. The main advantage is their ability to discharge the material under control into a limited area—such as the hopper of a conveying fan, or a cattle feed trough—rather than tipping out a large and unmanageable heap.

Self-loading trailers are available for chopped grass or for bales, while self-loading vehicles have been under development for some years at the National Institute of Agriculture Engineering, intended to load wooden containers—for grain, apples, potatoes, etc—of approx ½ tonne capacity each, to form a total load of 3 tonne.

While *bulk handling* is the most suitable method of dealing with materials which flow relatively easily, such as dry grain, liquid fertiliser and—to a lesser extent—potatoes and sugar beet, most agricultural materials do not flow easily. Fertiliser tends to cake if it becomes at all damp; grass, hay and silage are fibrous and inherently non-free flowing, as also are ground materials such as feeding-stuffs. Potatoes and fruit crops are subject to damage by impact, vibration and compression.

Most of the above materials can be made to move in bulk so long as they are kept in motion, and a great variety of elevators and conveyors is available, working on auger, oscillation, flat-belt, en-masse, vibration, bucket and pneumatic principles. The problems arise when the materials have been deposited in store. For extraction from storage of materials such as wet grain, silage and meal, augers, unloaders with rotating toothed cutting conveyors or vibrators may be used.

A problem associated with bulk handling is that of measurement, both of gross quantities harvested or stored and of smaller quantities drawn from storage for rations for livestock. The variation between varieties, and in given varieties between seasons, renders volumetric methods liable to appreciable inaccuracy, so that for large quantities integrating batch weighers are best. For the relatively small quantities measured out in compounding rations, volumetric meters or vibrator meters may be used.

Handling in *semi-bulk*, using pallets or containers ranging in capacity from 250 kg to 1 tonne, can provide a means of sub-dividing large bulks into more convenient units which may be handled mechanically. Semi-bulk loads of this kind offer a means of storage as well for potatoes and concentrate foods for livestock.

For smaller enterprises, fork-lift attachments can be mounted at the rear of farm tractors, lifting loads of up to 1·25 tonne to a height of 3·5 m. Such equipment is hydraulically operated, through appropriate spool valves connected to the tractor's external hydraulic service tapping point. It is less efficient than comparable industrial equipment, since the operator is seated facing in the wrong direction. It is possible to reverse the driving controls to correct this, but only at the expense of committing that particular tractor to single-purpose use as a handling machine. Adapted tractor-front-loaders can be fitted with handling forks for containers lifted either from the bottom or by means of shoulders formed in the sides of the containers. Their effective capacity does not normally exceed 500 kg, but systems tailored to this size of handling unit can, nevertheless, be effective for handling potatoes, orchard fruit and other commodities. A tractor equipped with such a fore-end loader can also carry two containers on a lifting frame mounted on the rear hydraulic lift linkage.

Tractors can also be used as transport vehicles when fitted with *transport boxes* mounted at the front or rear. The permitted dimensions of such attachments are limited to floor areas of 0·836 m^2 at the front and 1·4 m^2 at the rear.

Rough-terrain fork-lift trucks based on reversed tractor chassis are becoming popular on large farms and holdings where there is sufficient work in field conditions to justify their high cost. These offer lifting capacities up to 5 tonne with maximum lift heights to 7 m.

SAFETY REGULATIONS.—Some farm machines are inherently dangerous, so that safe operation depends both on providing guards for mechanisms which could otherwise present a hazard to men working near them, and on the development of a code of practice aimed at eliminating risk. Up to 100 fatal accidents and many thousand non-fatal accidents occur each year in the course of agricultural work. Tractors overturning account for one-third of the fatal accidents.

Health and Safety at Work Act 1974.—As in other industries legislation is based on this Act of Parliament. Other measures include.—

The Agriculture (Safety, Health and Welfare Provisions) Act 1956.—This introduced Regulations covering First Aid, Ladders, Power Take-off, Avoidance of Accidents to Children, Circular Saws, Safeguarding of Workplaces, Stationary Machinery, Lifting of Heavy Weights, Threshers and Balers and Field Machinery. The latest date for the fitting of guards to machines, new or already in use, was January 1st 1968.

The Agriculture (Tractor Cabs) Regulations 1974.—This requires that safety cabs or safety frames which will prevent overturning tractors from continuing to roll must be fitted to wheeled tractors weighing 560 kg or more. It is noteworthy that in Sweden only one fatal tractor overturning accident has been recorded since 1959, when similar legislation was introduced—and this was in a case in which the driver tried to jump out before the tractor came to rest. Weather cabs which pre-date the Regulation have no structural strength and may increase the danger to a tractor driver when a tractor overturns. Fully enclosed, sound-insulated cabs are normally fitted to tractors used in the UK.

The causes of tractor overturning accidents include operation on steep slopes, unbalanced rear-wheel braking systems and improper hitching of trailed implements. Attachment of implements above the proper drawbar level can exert an overturning moment about the rear axle, which, in conjunction with the rear axle torque reaction, can very quickly result in the tractor rearing and overturning backwards. Further information can be obtained from the Health and Safety Information Centre, NAC, Stoneleigh, Kenilworth, Warwicks, CV8 2LZ.

CROP DRYING.—Agricultural drying processes almost invariably depend on the use of large volumes of air passing through the crop to be dried, with a relatively small air temperature rise. Over-heating destroys the germinative capacity of seeds and spoils cereal grains for malting and bread-making. Practical heat sources include oil fuels, liquid petroleum gases, solid fuel, electricity and the waste heat from internal combustion engines. It is possible that interest in heat-pumps may develop, following the introduction of refrigeration plant for certain systems of low-temperature crop storage, and in the context of high energy costs.

Grain Drying.—For safe storage under atmospheric conditions grains must not exceed the moisture contents shown in Table 2. In a normal year, in most parts of Great Britain, the moisture content as harvested will be likely to exceed these figures. Drying (or, where applicable, chilling—see text at Fig. 10) is therefore essential if the grain is to be stored for more than very few days, and must be done immediately because damp grain in bulk rapidly heats and spoils, while moulds and insects also proliferate.

Drying processes may be continuous, using air temperature increases of 35–65°C above ambient, according to the type of grain and its intended use. Maximum permissible air temperatures, for avoidance of damage to various types of grain, are as follows: Stock feed grains, 80–105°C (*Note:* cooling difficulties may be experienced with feed grains dried at over 93°C); Milling wheat, 65°C; Seed or malting grains (<24% mc), 49°C; Oily seeds, 46°C.

Where maximum retention of germinative capacity is essential, the initial moisture content of the grain must also be taken into account, and the maximum air temperature limited. The safe air temperature, to avoid damage to germination, is given in parentheses after the following examples of moisture content %: 18 (66·7°C); 20 (61·6°C); 22 (56·7°C), 24 (52·8°C); 26 (48·9°C); 28 (45·5°C); 30 (43·3°C).

TABLE 2.—MOISTURE CONTENT (%) AND GRAIN STORAGE PERIODS. (For clean, undamaged grain stored (*a*) In bulk or closely stacked sacks, or (*b*) In bulk with aeration or turning, or in open-sack storage. Temperature <18°C. Storage period in months from harvest)

Storage Period		Months (*a*)				Months (*b*)			
		1	6	8	>8	1	6	8	>8
Moisture Content %	Feed Grains	17	15	15	14	18	17	16	15
	Seed or Malting	16	14	14	13	17	16	15	14

Automatic process control systems are based on frequent determinations of grain moisture content, using capacitance or resistance measuring techniques.

In continuous grain driers the air is passed through beds of grain 100–150 mm thick which may move in relation to the air stream vertically, horizontally or in a series of sloping cascades. It is essential to cool the grain to near ambient temperature after drying to avoid subsequent moisture uptake, which would encourage mould growth in storage. A cooling stage is, therefore, an essential part of a continuous drier; in practice two-thirds of the grain at any one time is in the drying section and about one-third in the cooling section.

The *rate of output of dried grain* will be dependent on the system characteristics, including rates of pre-cleaning and handling and capacity to move into storage. Designed outputs range from 1 to 20 tonne/h based on removal of 6% of water at a hot air inlet temperature of 65°C. *Batch drying processes* also employ air temperature values broadly similar to those quoted above. The grain layer may be up to 300 mm thick, but the arrangements for drying and cooling are the same in general. Fully-automatic control of the operation can be provided, based on comparison of ingoing and exit air temperatures rather than on direct determination of grain moisture content. After drying, grain is moved into storage containers by means of flat belt, auger or chain-and-flight conveyors, or occasionally by pneumatic conveyors.

Low-temperature drying is often associated with grain storage processes. Large volumes of air are passed slowly through large bulks of grain, the depth of which during drying will not exceed 2–3 m. The relative humidity of the air is adjusted to the required value by raising it a few degrees above the ambient temperature. On reaching an equilibrium value with the drying air no further drying of the grain takes place (see Fig. 5).

The *rate of drying in low-temperature processes* is relatively unimportant, since normally the grain will remain in storage for an appreciable period. Drying results in a moisture gradient in the whole bulk of grain, with a dry front at the equilibrium moisture content moving slowly in the direction of the airstream. Drying must, therefore, take place quickly enough to reach the outer layers of grain, whose moisture content may actually have increased as the moisture removed from lower layers reaches them, before they have begun to mould or spoil. This is the reason for the maximum depths specified for drying in bulk. In a bottom-ventilated silo the grain depth during drying must be limited to 1·5 m if the grain moisture content exceeds 20%; when this layer is dry, a further 1·5 m may be placed on top.

Under these conditions of operation a bottom-ventilated silo, given a minimum airflow rate, evenly distributed, of 4·5 m/min, warmed sufficiently (not usually exceeding 5·5°C above ambient) to reduce its RH to the required equilibrium value, can be expected to dry the whole bulk by the equivalent of 0·5% moisture reduction/24 hours. In a radial-ventilated bin, 1% daily moisture reduction can be expected with similar conditions of air humidity and a minimum airflow of 6·35 m^3/min per tonne being dried. Intermediate results are obtained from on-floor drying processes.

Driers operating on this principle include drying bins ventilated vertically from a false bottom (Fig. 7); radial ventilation bins (Fig. 8) in which air passes from a central tube of expanded steel mesh horizontally through a grain thickness of 1–1·5 m and then out through the bin walling, of expanded metal or other construction; and on-floor drying, in which a system of main and lateral ducts on or let into the floor passes the air upwards through a grain layer up to 2·4 m in depth. The ducting must be designed so that the rate of air flow does not exceed 10 m/s. Cooling after drying is not required in these cases. Automatic control of the air heating may be based on humidistat assessment of ambient air humidity.

Hay Drying.—Hay can be made in the field in the more favourable areas of Great Britain, but artificial drying provides an insurance against bad weather conditions, and is likely to involve a smaller loss of feeding value. Hay can be dried in bales, as long material dried loose and as chopped grass, dried loose.

As a natural material, grass has a very high moisture content. Most drying processes therefore economise

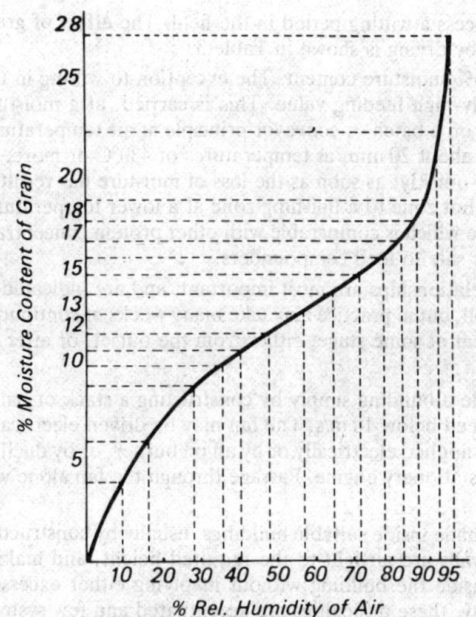

FIG 5.—Equilibrium Values for Grain and Air.

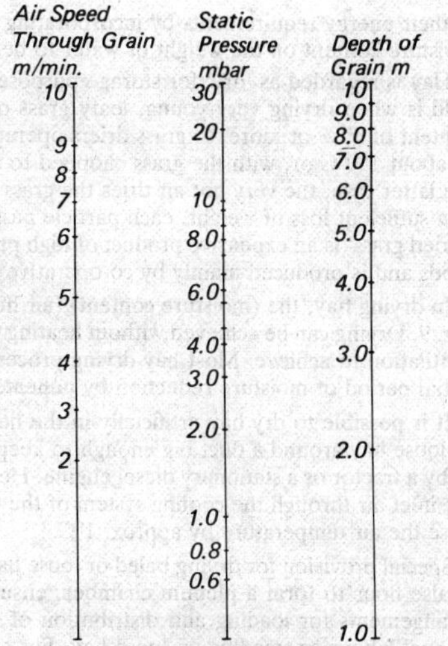

FIG. 6.—Nomogram for Relationship between Static Pressure; Depth and Air Flow through Grain (*A. S. Cromarty*).

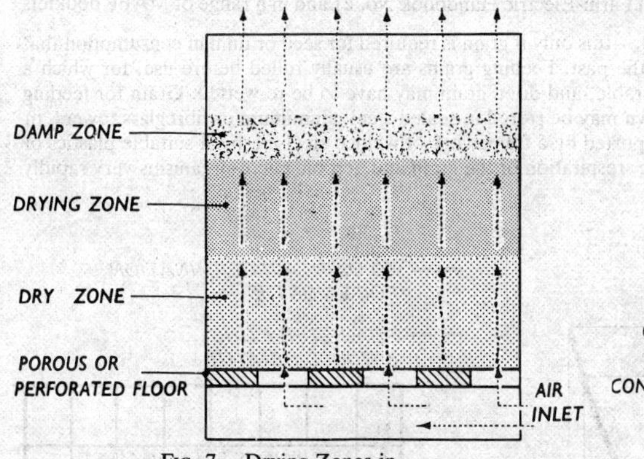

FIG. 7.—Drying Zones in Silo Ventilated from Floor.

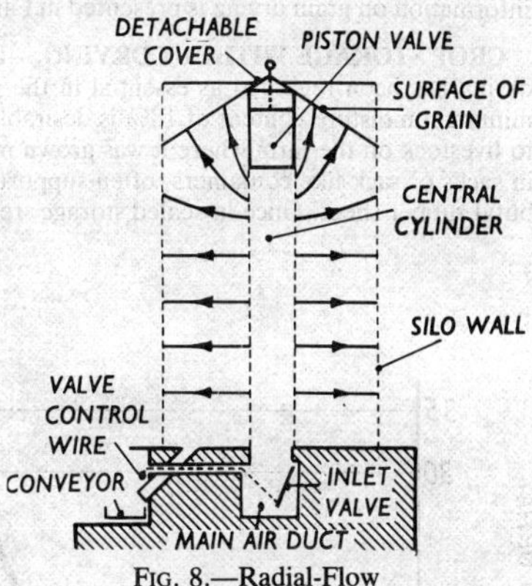

FIG. 8.—Radial-Flow Ventilated Silo.

TABLE 3.—WEIGHT OF WATER REMOVED TO PRODUCE 1 TONNE OF DRY HAY†

% Moisture content of hay*	Weight (kg) of water to be removed	% Moisture content of hay*	Weight (kg) of water to be removed
80	3,000	45	450
75	2,200	40	350
70	1,650	35	250
60	1,000	30	150
55	800	25	50
50	600	20	—

* (Wet Basis). † (At 20% Final Moisture Content).

in their energy requirements by incorporating in the process a wilting period in the field. The effect of grass moisture content on the weight of water to be removed by drying is shown in Table 3.

Hay is regarded as 'dry' for storage purposes at 20–25% moisture content. The exception to wilting in the field is when drying very young, leafy grass of especially high feeding value. This is carried, at a moisture content of 80% or more, to grass driers operating either on a batch or conveyor principle at air temperatures of about 150°C or, with the grass chopped to lengths of about 20 mm, at temperatures of 430°C or more. In the latter case, the very hot air dries the grass extremely quickly; as soon as the loss of moisture has resulted in a sufficient loss of weight, each particle passes out of hot zone to a finishing zone at a lower temperature. 'Dried grass' is an expensive product of high protein value which is comparable with other protein concentrate foods and is produced mainly by co-operative groups for sale to feed compounders.

In drying hay, the (moisture content)/(air humidity) relationships are most important, and are indicated in Fig. 9. Drying can be achieved without heating the air at all, but in practice may take many weeks of continuous ventilation to achieve. Most hay drying processes use heat at some stage, either from the outset, or after an initial period of moisture reduction by unheated air.

It is possible to dry hay artificially in the field or inside a building simply by constructing a stack of baled or loose hay around a duct big enough to keep the airspeed below 10 m/s. The fan may be driven electrically or by a tractor or a stationary diesel engine. Heat can be supplied electrically or by an oil burner, or by ducting the inlet air through the cooling system of the tractor or stationary engine. Passage through the fan alone will raise the air temperature by approx. 1°C.

Special provision for drying baled or loose hay can be made inside suitable buildings, usually by constructing a false floor to form a plenum chamber, ensuring the walls are airtight to the required height, and making arrangements for loading and distribution of the hay inside the building without involving either excessive manual labour or treading on loose hay. For chopped hay, these difficulties are accentuated and few systems of this type are now in use.

Technical information on hay drying is given in the Electricity Council's Farm-Electric Handbook No. 22, and in Mechansation Booklet 23 from the Ministry of Agriculture, Fisheries and Food (MAFF). Similar information on grain drying is presented in Farm-Electric Handbook No. 21 and in a range of MAFF booklets.

CROP STORAGE WITHOUT DRYING.—It is only if grain is required for seed or human consumption that drying has been regarded as essential in the past. Feeding grains are usually rolled before use, for which a minimum moisture content of 18% is desirable, and dried grain may have to be re-wetted. Grain for feeding to livestock on the farm where it was grown may be stored in sealed steel, aluminium or fibreglass towers, or in sacks or sack-like containers, often supported by a framework of welded steel mesh, of suitable plastics or butyl rubber sheet. Once in sealed storage, respiration of the grain and aerobic micro-organisms very rapidly

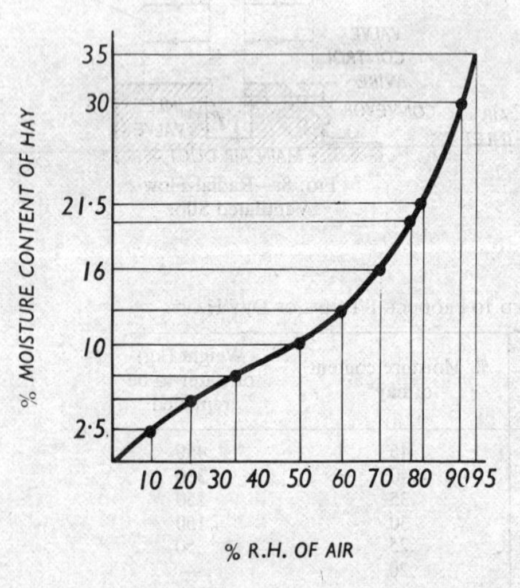

FIG. 9.—Air Humidity and Hay Moisture Content Equilibrium Values.

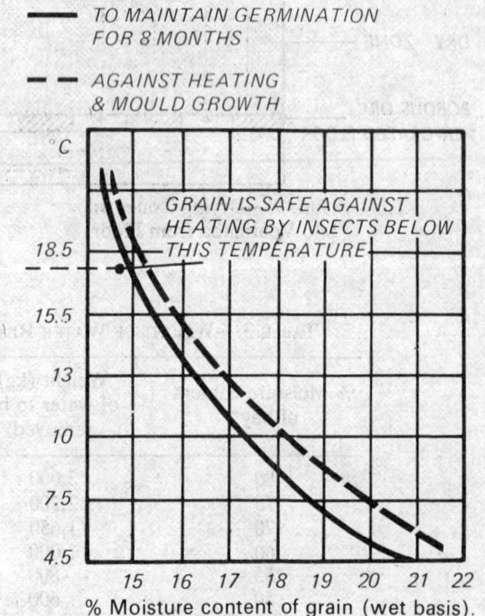

FIG. 10.—Cold Storage of Grain; Safe Temperatures.

uses up the available oxygen and raises the CO_2 level so that all such activity ceases; anaerobic organisms continue to function, but merely introduce a slight beer-like taint which is not unpalatable to livestock. Pressure-equalisation arrangements may be required, to cater for diurnal temperature variation.

The preferred moisture content for sealed storage is 18–20% although grain of 18–25% moisture content can be stored satisfactorily. In fact, grain with more than 25% water content is difficult to thresh with a combine-harvester, thus limiting the maximum value in any case. Particular attention must be given to safety regulations where men are likely to enter containers used for sealed storage to ensure adequate ventilation before and during entry. Dust in grain stores and processing buildings can also be a serious health hazard.

The main problem in *emptying a sealed silo*, apart from minimising the ingress of oxygen, is in overcoming bridging. The most effective system is undoubtedly to have a sweep-arm auger delivering to a fixed auger conveyor, both situated at the base of the silo and suitably sealed. A single rigid auger placed in one of three alternative positions, all sealed, is also used, and a flexible auger may also be successful, although effective sealing during use is sometimes difficult.

Chilling of Grain.—This is an alternative to drying for grain subsequently to be used for human consumption, seed, malting or milling. It involves chilling rapidly to a temperature of 5–10°C, depending on the incoming grain moisture content, as shown in Fig. 10. Cold storage of grain of more than 22% moisture content may not be practicable, and the preferred moisture content range is 18–20%. On-floor storage installations, similar to those for drying except that a wider spacing between lateral ducts may be used, provide a suitable means of utilising chilled air.

In calculating the required specification for a refrigeration plant for grain chilling, the following data are suggested by E. D. Munday (*Journal Inst Agr Engrs*, Vol 21, 1965): (*a*) Air temperature to be 4·5°C less than required grain temperature, allowing a temperature difference of 3°C after providing for up to 1·5°C air temperature rise due to fan and motor heating. (*b*) Air flow rate to be 1·2 m/min evenly distributed. (*c*) Specific heat capacity of grain: 1·88 kJ/kg °C. (*d*) Pressure drop through cooling coil and ducting: 3·75 mb. Other assumptions have to be made as to incoming grain temperature, atmospheric air humidity, and maximum allowable cooling time. (For the latter, a period of 24 hours would be reasonable.)

Cooling grain in store without refrigeration, by blowing in cool ambient air, eg at night, can also be valuable, not only for undried grain but also, as can be seen from Fig. 10, for dried grain stored in high ambient daytime temperatures.

Grain Storage.—Dry grain may be stored in bins of steel, aluminium, timber, glass-fibre, concrete, brick, etc, or in frameworks lined with fabric or paper, or in sacks. The following are average figures in m³/tonne, for various types of dry grain: Wheat (1·32); Barley (1·46); Oats (2·01); Rye (1·46); Peas (1·32); Beans (1·24); Linseed (1·55). Since a designer cannot predict the type of grains to be stored throughout the life of a grain store, it is usual for capacities to be calculated on an average basis of 1·45 m³/tonne.

Measurement of Grain Moisture Content.—This may be of grain in bulk or sampled and, in the latter case, either ground or dealt with as whole grains. Rapid methods make use of the electrical resistance or capacitance of the grain bulk or sample, while others include measurement of the gas pressure developed in a closed container when the moisture in a weighed sample of milled grain is mixed with calcium carbide, or the loss in weight of a standard sample when heated for a given time.

Grain Cleaning and Grading Equipment.—This includes *pre-cleaners* which are used to remove dust, particles of straw and green material and other extraneous matter from grain before it is dried or stored. Such contaminants waste drying or storage capacity, are likely to be of higher moisture content than the grain and will encourage respiration, heating and mould formation in their vicinity.

Cleaning mechanisms consist of sieves, and horizontal or vertical airstreams. The grain is fed from a supply hopper by a feed roller in order to give an even delivery of material to the separating mechanism. By suitable arrangement of the airflow pattern and choice of sieves the required grain fraction is separated from heavier, lighter, larger and smaller contaminants, for which disposal must be arranged. Throughputs of grain range from 3 to 15 tonne/h or more.

Graders are used before grain is sold off the farm for milling, malting or seed. The grain is given a second cleaning and is graded for size by means of a series of sieves, assisted by airblasts or aspirating blasts. An alternative system utilises indented cylinders to pick out the required sizes of grains. Throughputs of 2–5 tonne/h are normally obtained. Separation by specific gravity is also used for some purposes.

FOOD PREPARATION FOR LIVESTOCK.—Preparation of concentrate foods consists of grinding or crushing the grain constituents, mixing them with relatively small quantities of other materials such as high-protein foods and vitamin or mineral supplements and, possibly, compressing the mixed materials into pellets. These operations may be carried out by an agricultural milling business, or the farmer may buy in those materials he does not produce himself, and prepare rations on the farm. If the farm feed requirement is over 2 tonne/week, home food preparation is usually economically sound. Mobile contract services are also available.

Grinding.—This is invariable done with small electrically-driven hammermills (Fig. 11), in which hammers travelling at a peripheral speed of about 100 m/s break the grain into particles small enough to pass through

FIG. 11.—Interior of Small Hammermill.

holes in a circular screen. Output depends on screen size, cereal variety and horsepower applied. Moisture content also affects the output; grain wetter than 18% should not be ground with a hammermill. The approximate output from hammermills for pig/poultry meals is 50 kg/kWh with a similar power requirement for pelleting.

Small mills can be run without attention under automatic control and are especially suited to overnight operation on off-peak electricity tariffs. They also incorporate provision for pneumatic delivery of the milled material to a storage bin or mixer.

Crushing.—Grain, especially barley, may be fed in large quantities to cattle as the main part of their diet. It is crushed to improve its digestibility; grinding is neither necessary nor desirable. Crushing is carried out by mills with either plain rollers (for grain of up to 18% moisture) or corrugated rollers (for grain of 20–25% moisture content, as from a sealed store). The amount of added moisture per tonne of dried grain to raise its moisture content to 18% is given by $W = (222{\cdot}5 - 12{\cdot}36m)$, where W is litres of water and m is the initial grain moisture content. The water should be added to the grain 24–36 hours before it is to be crushed. The output of plain-roller crushing mills is 130–340 kg/kWh, and of corrugated-roller mills is 1,300–2,800 kg/kWh. Steaming machines can be used to moisten grain to about 25% moisture content to take advantage of the high throughputs of the corrugated-roller machines, which were designed primarily for use with moist grain.

Pneumatic or mechanical crushed-grain removal systems are employed. The smaller types of plain-roller machine are sometimes found in combination with small hammermills and share the same conveying system.

The storage period ('shelf life') of prepared feeding stuffs in relation to freshness is as follows: Milled and pelleted dry grain, 3–4 weeks; Milled dry grain, 1–2 weeks; Rolled grain below 18% mc, 1–2 weeks; Ditto, over 21% mc, 2–3 days; Wet-stored grain after removal from silo, 1 week in cold weather, 2–3 days in hot weather. The approximate number of m^3/tonne of ground cereals, etc are: Wheat 2·2; Barley 2·0; Oats 2·5; Beans 1·9.

Mixing.—It is accepted that a certain standard of efficiency in mixing is required, but no really scientific technique for assessment of mixing efficiency has yet been formulated. In practice, thorough mixing by hand, carried out twice, gives a mixing standard acceptable for all classes of livestock. This is obtainable by mixing in a vertical mixer for 5–10 minutes, or in a horizontal mixer for 3 minutes.

Vertical mixers consist of a vertical auger rotating inside a cylindrical hopper with a conical base mounted on a tubular leg of an internal diameter appropriate to the auger. The mixer may be filled from above or from a hopper at the lower end of the auger, which may be placed below floor level for ease of filling from sacks or bins. Discharge is normally at the base of the conical part of the mixer body, at a height of about 1 m.

Horizontal mixers have a large-diameter horizontal rotor fitted with counter-formed flights to move the material to the centre where the discharge point is situated. They must be filled from the top. Apart from more rapid mixing, the only advantage over the vertical type is their ability to mix wet materials. The disadvantages are higher power requirements, greater floor-space requirement and the need for filling and emptying at different levels.

Conveyor mixers utilise an endless chain conveyor carrying cross-slats to mix the materials. Filling and delivery are carried out on the same floor.

Combined milling and mixing.—Food preparation on the farm can easily be automated, and several types of fully-automatic plant can be obtained. Even without full automation, the process must be considered as a whole with mill, mixer and conveying arrangements matched to each other and to the farm requirements.

Conveying arrangements.—Pneumatic conveying of the freshly-ground meal from the hammermill is usually arranged, and this is particularly convenient with vertical mixers. Tangential entry of the conveying pipe into the mixer body allows the latter to act as a cyclone to separate out the meal from the airstream. Separate cyclones are required for other types of mixer, or filters of fine-weave calico may suffice, as in the case of a conveyor mixer. Particular attention should be given to dust control in all food preparation processes, and more specialised dust filters may be required in some cases. Meal does not flow freely from bins or hoppers once it has settled and vibrators or some manual work may be necessary at the removal stage, unless the hoppers are constructed with conical bases sloping at a very steep angle to the horizontal. Such hoppers are inevitably very tall in relation to their volume and may need to be situated outside the buildings they serve.

Cubing and Pelleting.—Compressing the mixed meal into 'cubes' (large pellets, of about 13 mm diameter and length) or small pellets of about 3–6 mm diameter and length, may be done in order to make the material easier to handle or to minimise wastage by the livestock. Cubers are available with either a roller and ring-die mechanism or a piston and die mechanism. Either cubes or pellets may be produced, by changing the dies. Binding additives are not normally required, unless it is intended to store the cubes for a lengthy period.

Animal Feeding.—Livestock are well equipped to feed themselves by grazing or self-feeding from a silage clamp and, where practicable, it usually pays to let the animal search out its own food. But the increased concentration of livestock which is becoming essential to economic production requires increasingly that food has to be conveyed to intensively-housed animals, often throughout the year.

Hay is still more often to be found in the baled form than loose. In either case, manual work is required to remove it from store and distribute it to the livestock. 'Easy-feeding' systems of manual distribution, using gravity to the maximum extent, enable 1 man to feed hay to 100 cattle in 12 minutes, or self-feeding systems with barriers to control the cattle may be employed.

Silage feeding can be completely mechanised if the feed is stored in towers equipped with top or bottom-unloaders. These consist of one or more cutter-conveyors or sweep augers delivering to fixed conveyors, augers or blowers which discharge the silage at the base of the silo. In the case of a top unloader, delivery may be via the external access chute. From the silo, further conveyors—either augers or belts—may deliver to extended feed-troughs or mangers, in which the silage is distributed by open augers, shrouded augers, travelling belt conveyors or reciprocating conveyors. An alternative is a circular trough round the base of the silo, either rotating or fixed and equipped with a suitable conveyor.

Mechanical unloaders mounted on tractors may be used for silage stored in clamp (horizontal) silos. With material of a suitably short chop-length, manure forks on tractor front-loaders may be used to dig out silage. Otherwise, self-feeding by the cattle is the best answer. For this reason, many horizontal silos are now built under cover in a building complex which forms a coherent system for cattle housing and self-feeding.

Supplementary foods may be added to the main bulk of silage at an appropriate point before it reaches the livestock. Where cattle are housed in yards at some distance from the silo, a self-unloading trailer with a cross-conveyor can be used to deliver the silage into a continuous feed-trough adjacent to one of the yard fences.

Complete diet feed wagons are self-unloading trailers fitted with hopper bodies mounted on sensitive weighing equipment, used to batch, mix, transport and distribute feed materials, combining silage with concentrate feeds to form balanced diets.

Dry Concentrate Food.—For poultry in a broiler house or deep litter house, a continuous chain and flight conveyor running slowly in a shallow trough at feeding height may be used. It is supplied from a hopper, through which it passes, returning uneaten food for recirculation. Other conveyor systems are used to replenish tube feeders or hoppers from which food is released in measured volumes on to the floor, either manually or automatically.

In battery systems, feed hoppers on overhead rails circulate slowly in front of the cages. Water is sometimes supplied in a similar way. Similar systems, on a larger scale, are used for pigs in yards or fattening houses. An automatic system of food dispensing to pens of pigs is also available, in which a hopper moves along an overhead conveyor in front of the pens, discharging a ration on a pen basis according to the number of pegs inserted in a rack to operate a volumetric dispenser. The feeding of *wet meal* as mash or slurry, and *water*, can also be automated.

Manure Disposal.—The removal of animal wastes is a necessary concomitant of animal feeding. Concurrently with the development of ever more intensive housed-livestock enterprises on farms, legislation (in particular the Rivers (Prevention of Pollution) Acts. 1951 and 1961, and the Water Resources Act, 1963) has required stricter control of the disposal of farm effluents. Livestock farmers thus have greater quantities of effluent than before, and have to be very careful as to how it is discharged. The methods of former days, such as soaking up the liquids and holding the solids with straw to make farmyard manure, resulting in a valuable organic fertiliser which was handled as a solid material, are often ruled out on a cost basis even if there is sufficient straw available to provide the animal bedding required. New restrictions are imposed by the Control of Pollution Act, 1974.

Effluent from livestock housing can be discharged (under the Public Health Act, 1961) into local authority sewers, provided the authority agrees and at whatever charge may be imposed. Even for the minority of farms within reach of public sewerage systems this possibility is likely to be eliminated on grounds of cost.

For enterprises of modest size (50–70 dairy cows, or 400–500 pigs), the effluent may be collected in holding tanks, diluted by 100% or more with rain or washing-water. Straw and other solids should be excluded. Tank trailers of 1,100–3,400 litre capacity are filled by auger conveyors or vacuum pumps and are used to transport the effluent to suitable fields on the farm. The tanks are discharged by flails, by gravity or air pressure to distribute the effluent on the land. Recent Ministry of Agriculture recommendations specify maximum applications of 50 m^3/ha, at intervals of not less than three weeks.

A problem with trailer spreaders occurs in some winter periods when the land may be so wet as to make the passage of vehicles over it undesirable. The maximum number of livestock are likely to be housed during this period, so that the need to dispose of effluent is also at a maximum. Holding tanks of sufficient capacity to carry over such a wet period offer almost the only simple solution. The production of various types of farm effluent is shown in Table 4.

TABLE 4.—FARM EFFLUENTS (1 m^3 = 1,000 litre)

Source			Approx. BOD (mg/l)
Arable silage	made in wet weather	270 litre/tonne	
Arable silage	10–17% dry matter content	190 litre/tonne	60,000
Arable silage	26–35% dry matter content	10 litre/tonne	
Dairy cattle	per head	14 litre of liquid/day	
Dairy cattle		51 litre of solids/day (incl. straw)	16,000
Dairy cattle (on slats)		28 litre of slurry/day	
Beef cattle		7 litre of liquid/day	
Beef cattle		35 litre solids/day (incl. straw)	16,000
Beef cattle (on slats)		23 litre of slurry/day	
Adult pigs		2·5 litre liquid/day	
Adult pigs		15 litre of solids/day (incl. straw)	8,000–40,000
Adult pigs (on slats)		7 litre of slurry/day	
Laying poultry (per 100 birds)		0·028 m^3 of solids/day	50,000

For larger enterprises, a system of pumping out the effluent through portable or semi-permanent pipelines and sprayguns can be used. Pumps are usually fitted with chopping mechanisms to deal with straw or other solids, and the sprayguns may have rubber orifices to allow any remaining large particles to pass through. Water should be added to the raw effluent to give at least 1:1 dilution, and arrangements for agitation of the effluent in the holding tank must be provided. Single-stage open-vane impeller pumps giving delivery pressures up to 830 kN/m^2 are commonly used.

Although many farmers have developed reasonably satisfactory systems for meeting their immediate manure disposal problems on the lines just described, severe difficulties still remain. In populated areas the smell which results from anaerobic storage of liquid wastes, or from spraygun distribution of effluent, can be very objectionable. Aerobic or anaerobic treatment systems may be employed to control smell and to reduce the polluting qualities of the wastes, while retaining their fertilising properties for crop growth.

Handling and Treatment of Farm Wastes.—Quite different criteria from those for town sewage apply to farm wastes. Handling and treatment methods for livestock wastes must recognise that these materials have very much higher solids contents (from 7 to 25%) than town sewage, and that it is not economically feasible to modify the Biochemical Oxygen Demand (BOD) or the mineral content sufficiently to permit discharge into watercourses. Application to the land will be inevitable in almost all cases, with the land itself acting as the main treatment medium.

While town sewage treatment technology is based on filtering out a minute proportion of solids from a very large volume of water, and then purifying the water, livestock wastes to be handled as a solid should have all unnecessary water (rainfall, yard washing water) excluded from them. Some of the water already mixed with the solids may be removed by roller presses or other mechanical means. The solids may then be composted before application to the land by conventional means, and the liquids treated separately to control smell and perhaps reduce their BOD and nitrate contents before they also are applied to the land.

Techniques associated with aerobic storage and treatment of wastes include the use of fixed or floating surface aerators. Anaerobic techniques include the possibilities of methane production in vessels kept at a temperature of about 35°C. At the time of writing neither the technical nor the economic aspects of these methods have yet become standardised.

ENVIRONMENT CONTROL.—Control of the production or storage environmental conditions is now a commercial necessity in many cases.

In *potato stores* heat is produced at up to 75 W/tonne/h after harvest, dropping to 9–12 W/tonne/h in mid-winter. Natural ventilation can disperse this heat in potatoes stored up to 3 m high, and with forced ventilation potatoes may be stored up to 4–5 m high. A fan capacity of up to 67 m^3/h per tonne, against pressures from 500–800 N/m^2 is required. Forced ventilation is also required if chemical sprout suppressants are used.

Generally, ware potatoes must be kept at temperatures of 4–5°C, after curing at 10°C, although the storage temperature depends on storage life required and the final use of the potatoes. To ensure that frost damage does not occur, walls and roofs should have 'U' values not exceeding 0·6 W/m^2 deg C.

Livestock can cope with a range of environmental conditions, largely because of their inherent adaptability. However, because of the increasing intensity of production greater attention must now be paid to ventilation and temperature control in animal houses by using suitable methods of insulation and ventilation; the main requirements are to avoid draughts and sudden changes of conditions. Supplementary space heating and controlled ventilation are necessary for some classes of stock.

For *pigs*, a general temperature of 18°C and a creep temperature of about 28°C for the young piglets is normally suitable. These can be maintained in well-insulated buildings by the heat given off by the sows and by supplementary creep heaters. Air-change rates of 10–20 m^3/h per sow in winter and up to 130 m^3/h per sow in summer are required. Heating and ventilation control systems should be designed particularly to measure temperatures at the points which affect the livestock concerned. Avoidance of draughts is of first importance. Weaners require temperatures gradually decreasing from 27°C at about 3 weeks of age to 18°C by 8 weeks of age, which is then maintained throughout the fattening stage. Fattening pigs are not very sensitive to high humidities but for the sake of the stockman it is best to prevent the humidity rising to a level of human discomfort.

Poultry also require controlled temperature and air-change conditions. 'U' values of 0·6 W/m^2 deg C should be employed for the walls and roof of poultry laying houses. The general air temperature should be in the range of 20–23°C, with air-change rates of 0·36 m^3/h per kg of live weight in winter and 4·0 m^3/h per kg of live weight in summer. The design of air inlets and outlets should provide for even air distribution throughout the poultry house at minimum practicable rates of air movement.

Cattle are less affected by environmental conditions than pigs or poultry, except that young calves may be susceptible to low temperatures, particularly if humid conditions are experienced. Temperatures of about 10°C and plenty of ventilation are required at the early stages of rearing and the avoidance of draughts and wet conditions is of paramount importance. Uneven ventilation is often experienced in wide span buildings (18 m span and over).

MICROELECTRONICS APPLICATIONS IN AGRICULTURAL ENGINEERING.—As in other technical fields, in recent years microelectronics technology has been applied in almost every kind of mechanism and control system. For detailed information the reader is referred to the book *Farm Electronics* by S. W. R. Cox (see Bibliography). The following notes indicate a range of current applications.

Tractors.—Guidance systems, monitoring of work rate, control of engine performance and economy of operation, control of implement position and function.

Drainage Equipment.—Laser control of level and microprocessor control of trenching and drain-laying machines.

Crop Production.— Control of seed distribution mechanisms to avoid gaps and obtain desired plant populations; control of spray chemical application rate by monitoring flow rate and ground speed; crop yield measurement and recording.

Crop Harvesting.—Control of header position, monitoring of grain loss and control of forward speed and threshing performance in combine-harvesters; discrimination between potatoes and extraneous material on potato harvesters and on static equipment; potential for selective harvesting of vegetable crops by size or colour discrimination techniques.

Crop Processing.—Crop moisture content measurement and drier process control; separation of ripe/unripe or healthy/diseased produce by colour discrimination.

Crop Storage and Protected Cropping.—Monitoring and control of temperature, humidity and gaseous environment.

Animal Production.—Identification of individual animals by means of transponders or signal transmitters and control of feed dispensing to individuals or groups of livestock; weighing and weight recording, associated with colour marking and batching into desired sub-groups; for poultry, control of hatching and brooding environment, weight recording, egg recording; for dairy cattle, control of milking machine vacuum level and pulsation, milk yield recording and linked feed dispensing; control of cluster removal on completion of milking (and possibly cluster attachment, now at development stage); health monitoring and oestrous detection, mastitis detection; on-line recording of production and management data; for meat animals, measurement of backfat thickness, weight-gain/feed consumption monitoring and recording.

Management.—Records and analysis of: livestock performance, insemination and parturition dates; crop varieties, seed rates, fertiliser applications, pesticide treatments, yields; financial data, profitability, depreciation, accounting and taxation returns, PAYE, staff data, selection of equipment and operating strategies.

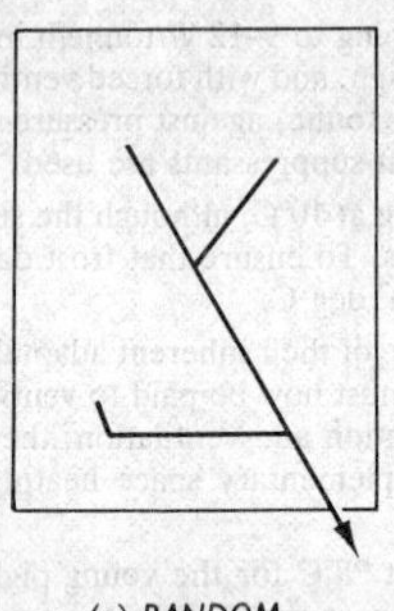

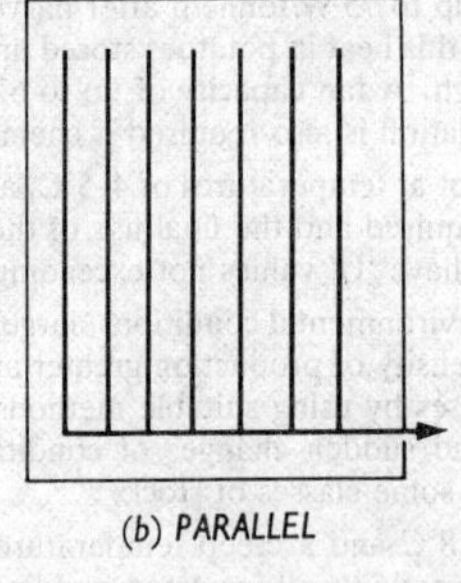

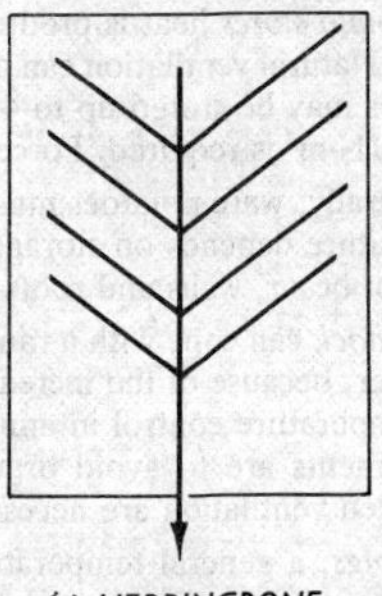

FIG. 12.—Patterns of Tile Underdrainage.

FIELD DRAINAGE.—This is the removal from agricultural land of surplus water which might otherwise restrict crop growth. The effects of excess water may be to reduce the aeration of the soil, to reduce soil temperature, to inhibit root growth, and to reduce the volume of soil suitable for root growth. The problem may be localised, for example wet patches in a field, or may be general over a large region. It may occur temporarily for a period of days or weeks, or may be a permanent condition. Crops vary greatly in their tolerance of wet conditions, both as to the amount of excess water they can stand and the duration of the flooding, but almost all commercially grown crops are adversely affected to some extent by inadequate drainage.

The surplus accumulates because incoming water, as rain or surface flow, does not drain away fast enough, and the practice of field drainage is directed towards accelerating or increasing the natural outflow, either at the surface by means of open drains or ditches, or below the ground by a system of closed underdrains. If the primary object is to avoid surface waterlogging then surface drainage is indicated, but the permanent lowering of a water table is usually attempted through a system of underdrains. The relatively low permeability of most soils in England has led to a widespread use of underdrains. (*See also* chapter 'Water Engineering', section '*Land Drainage*'.)

Surface Drains.—Surface drainage alone may be adequate if the problem is simply to remove excess surface water, or if the soil is freely permeable so that water will move laterally to the drains. One method is to excavate open ditches on a gentle gradient to carry off surface water, or the whole land surface may be shaped by ploughing into a series of corrugations so that the raised parts are drier and the depressions act as open drains. This method, known as ridge and furrow, was widely used in England for centuries before the use of clay tile drains, and can still be seen in permanent pastures where there has been no cultivation to level the ridges. The system is extensively used in Africa today as an inexpensive and simple method of draining land which either does not warrant or does not need the more thorough and more expensive permanent underdrains. The furrows usually run straight down the slope, and discharge into a collecting drain at the lower edge of the field.

Even when the field is drained by a system of sub-surface drains it is common practice for these to discharge into an open ditch. The disadvantages of open ditches are that they require regular maintenance, clearing out silt and removing vegetation, but their advantages are that they are unlikely to be blocked by roots of the trees and hedges which so frequently surround fields, and also that it is possible to see the outflow from each line of tile drains and so detect blockages. Because of these advantages many open ditches are still retained even now that the cost of laying a 150 mm tile drain is little more than the cost of cleaning out an open ditch.

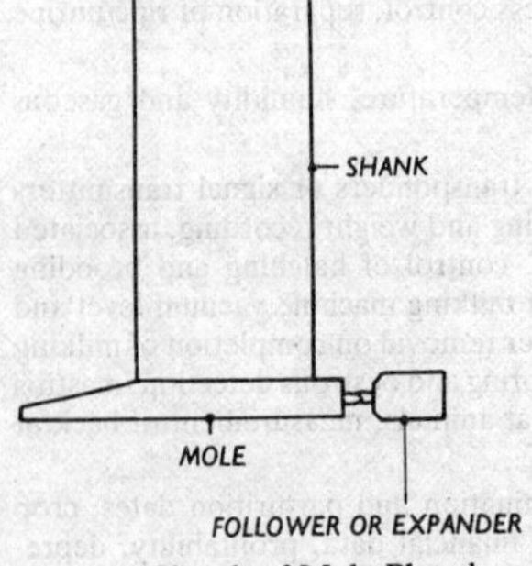

FIG. 13.—Sketch of Mole Plough.

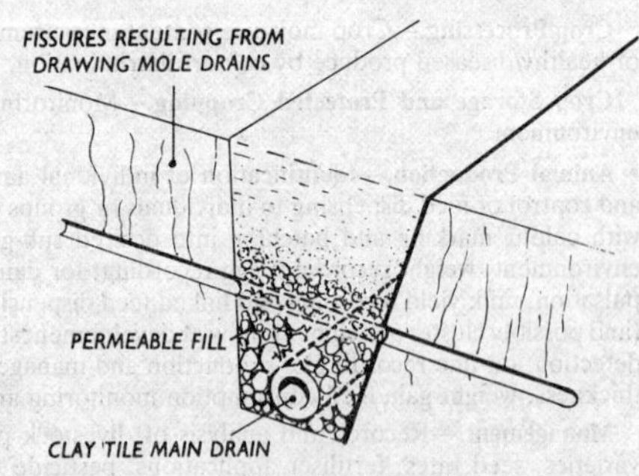

FIG. 14.—Junction of Mole Drain and Tile Main Drain.

Sub-Surface Drains.—Sub-surface drains may be lined or unlined. Lined drains are expensive and long lasting, and employ materials such as clay tiles and their modern counterparts, while unlined drains are cheaper but have a shorter life. Some common patterns of tile drains are shown in Fig. 12. Random drainage, Fig. 12(*a*), is the hit and miss approach of laying a line of tile drains from an outlet at the lowest point of the field to any noticeably wet parts. Additional lines can be added until the system eliminates all wet areas. 'Regular' or parallel drainage, Fig. 12(*b*), has closely spaced lines running down the steepest slope to a main drain or ditch along the lower edge of the field. Herringbone pattern, Fig. 12(*c*), relies on each line of tile intercepting some of the water seeping downhill below the ground surface.

Since the object of sub-surface drainage is to remove surplus water which might inhibit crop growth, an ideal design will do just this and no more. The amount to be removed is defined as the 'drainage coefficient' or the depth of water in mm which the system is expected to drain in 24 hours. This amount will vary according to the soil type and the cropping pattern. Typical values might be from 12 to 50 mm. The main variables in the design of a drainage scheme are the size of tiles and their depth and spacing. Usual sizes for pipes are 100 mm and 150 mm dia. Spacing in clay soils is 6–9 m; in sandy soils spacing is up to 60 m. Depth of drains are from 0·4 to 1·2 m. Gradient 1:300 to 1:1000.

When tiles are laid by hand the practice is to dig an open ditch to the approximate depth required, then finish off to the exact grade using sight rails and boning rods (see Chapter on Surveying). If the tiles are laid in a flat-bottomed trench they are wedged in place with soil or stones to prevent lateral displacement during backfilling, or a shallow semi-circular furrow may be scooped out of the bed of the trench for the pipe to rest in. The tiles are butted tightly together, but the unevenness in the cut ends ensures that there are small gaps through which the water can enter. Too wide a gap may allow soil to enter and silt up the pipe. To minimise the entry of soil and ensure easy entry by water the tiles are covered before the soil is replaced. A wide variety of materials are used for this including turf sods, straw, ash, gravel, tarred paper and plastic film. Where rapid movement is required, as at the junction with mole drains, a 'permeable fill' of washed and graded gravel is used.

In Britain today most tiles are laid by machines which excavate the trench by endless belt or wheel buckets and feed the tiles down a chute. In a second operation the tiles are covered and the trench refilled. On smooth ground laying by machine is straightforward and a satisfactory grade can be achieved by laying the drain at constant depth below the soil surface, but on undulating ground grade control is difficult. Recent machines employ systems of remote control guidance following a beam of light to ensure that the tiles are laid on a constant uniform grade irrespective of the ground surface level.

Mole Drains.—Cheap unlined underdrains, called mole drains, are effective in clay soils which will retain a moulded shape after a mole plough is drawn through the soil. See Fig. 13. The vertical shank and the mole shatter and and crack the soil to increase the downward movement of water, and the expander or follower shapes a circular smooth-walled tunnel which carries the water. By mounting the plough at the end of a long beam the depth becomes self-adjusting and evens out some of the surface irregularities. Crawler tractors are used to draw the drains initially, while subsequent reconditioning can be done with wheeled tractors.

For efficient operation the soil must be suitable, and the drains drawn when the soil is at the right moisture content. Mole drains are shallower and closer than tile drains—usually from 0·3 to 0·75 m deep and from 1·5 to 9·0 m apart. Gradients may be between 1 in 50 and 1 in 500. Diameters up to 200 mm have been used, but 60–90 mm are most common. A working life of 10–15 years is normal in good conditions, but this can be extended by redrawing the same drains.

Combined Systems.—The weakness of mole drains is in their outlets which are subject to collapse and vulnerable to interference. By allowing a network of mole drains to discharge into tiled main drains the advantages of both can be obtained. The tiled drains are installed first at greater depth, then shallower mole drains drawn at an angle to the tile drains. At intersections the trench carrying the tile drains is filled with gravel. See Fig. 14.

New Materials and Methods.—Much attention is being given to the use of plastic pipes as alternatives to clay tiles, and several methods are in use. An early method was to join together 6 m lengths of pipe before laying them in a trench, but this has been largely replaced by machines capable of laying a continuous pipe from a large coil carried on the machine. Another approach is to form a tube underground from a flat plastic strip with a kind of zip-fastener. This allows the strip to be fed down through a narrower slit than would be required for the pipe. The technique of drawing telephone cables after a mole plough has been successfully modified to draw drainage and water supply pipes. When continuous plastic pipe is used for drainage, some perforations in the pipe are necessary to allow entry of water. Bituminous-fibre pipes offer another effective substitute for clay tiles where weight and transport are important cost factors. Mole drains could be made more efficient if the moulded channel could be stabilised; this has been attempted using concrete mixes and various chemical stabilisers.

IRRIGATION.—Irrigation is the practice of applying water artificially to soil in order to stimulate crop growth. The usual reason is to enable crops to be grown in areas which are arid or subject to periodic drought, but today there is an ever-increasing interest in 'supplementary irrigation', applying small quantities of water to make up deficiencies in natural rainfall. In the struggle to provide the food supplies required for the increasing world population, one of the important factors is the scope for more efficient use of water resources by irrigation. Most of the land area of the world suited to rain-grown cropping has been developed, but with irrigation a vast area of land in the temperate middle latitudes could multiply its food production many times over. It is debatable whether the greater potential increases lie with the increased yields from supplementary irrigation on existing lands, or the opening up of large irrigation schemes which will bring thousands of acres of land into production. In 1975, it was estimated that 52,500 ha were under supplementary irrigation in Britain.

Estimating Water Requirement.—The object of irrigation is to supply enough water to meet the requirement of the crop; any more would be wasteful and could lead to problems of soil erosion or excessive salinity.

Water is taken up through the plant roots and some is used to build the plant tissue but most is evaporated or transpired by the leaves of the plant. The soil surface also loses water by evaporation. The total of these demands is known as the consumptive use or the *evapotranspiration* and much research has been directed towards methods for its estimation or prediction. Since the amount of water evaporated by the soil and the plant will depend upon atmospheric factors, many research workers have offered empirical formulae which enable the water requirement to be predicted from meteorological observations.

METHODS OF APPLICATION.—Irrigation water may be applied either by surface methods, ie by releasing it as a flood on to the soil surface, or by the sprinkler method, ie distributing it under pressure through nozzles so that it falls to the surface like rain. Both methods have advantages and the choice will depend on many factors. In general, surface methods require less capital expenditure on equipment, but need uniform gentle slopes and suitable soil textures. On the whole, most irrigation in arid conditions is by surface methods except on highly capitalised schemes. Sprinkler systems are usually favoured for supplementary irrigation because they are portable and do not require major land preparation or permanent works. The factors to be considered in the choice of system may be grouped under several headings; those relating to the soil, ie soil texture, depth, infiltration rate, slope and topography of the field; those relating to the crop, ie whether row-crop or broadcast, method of sowing, cultivating, fertilising and harvesting, and rooting depth; those related to climate and water supplied, ie cost of available water, wind and air temperature; and also costs relating to capital, maintenance, power, labour, etc.

Flood Irrigation.—This is the application of water so that it floods over the surface of the soil, and this may be carried out with varying degrees of control. At one end of the scale is wild flooding, the almost uncontrolled release of water over unprepared land. The water will be applied very unevenly. The opposite extreme is 'Border Strip' irrigation which is accomplished by advancing a sheet of water down a long narrow strip between low ridges or borders. The strip between borders must be carefully levelled and on a uniform grade, and the method is mainly used for forage crops. To facilitate mechanisation, the strips can be very long if portable laterals are used to apply water at more than one point down the run. The width of strip is usually 6–18 m and gradient about 1½%. When built with precision and operated with accuracy this is a very efficient method, economical in both labour and water.

Furrow Irrigation.—For any crop grown in rows it is more efficient to apply the water down furrows between the rows. An equal amount of water is released down each furrow by a syphon drawing water from a slightly elevated canal at the head of the field. A recent development is the use of gated pipes, ie pipes with small controllable outlets at spacings corresponding with the distance between furrows. Lightweight aluminium pipes started this trend, but are being replaced by collapsible thin-walled plastic pipes which roll up when not in use. Gated pipes allow the long runs essential to efficient mechanical crop handling. Variations on the basic principle are 'corrugations' or small furrows used for close-growing grain crops on steeper slopes, and broad-based furrows, which may be up to 3 m wide and are used in orchards.

IRRIGATION AND MECHANISATION.—To be efficient and economic, irrigation farming must, in most countries, be linked with mechanisation. The potential advantages of high yield and reliability can only be fully exploited when accompanied by reliable and efficient handling of the crop at all stages. Surface irrigation need not be an obstacle to mechanisation if the layout is designed with this in mind. The canal and road networks have much in common and should be planned together. There will be main supply canals bringing water into the scheme and main roads bringing supplies in and taking produce out. There will also be the branch or distribution canals taking the water into the fields, and the field roads for harvesting or reaping. Crossings must be minimised, and where unavoidable, either the canals must be bridged or sections of the canal must be piped.

For many crops, the necessity for cheap efficient mechanical handling of the product is so important that the irrigation layout is planned to suit the road network rather than the other way round. Examples are sugar cane and citrus. In cereal crops or forage crops, the main requirement is long straight runs for seeding, cultivating or harvesting equipment, and this is achieved either by sub-surface distribution pipes, or, increasingly, by lightweight portable pipes laid temporarily and removed before the next mechanical operation.

In all surface methods where the land is divided into long strips, the width of the strips must be related to the width of the machinery which will be used.

Sprinkler Irrigation.—It is obviously desirable to apply water over rectangular areas and this is achieved with several sprinkler systems. Lines of pipe with many small perforations or small nozzles will water an even strip on either side of the pipe, and in some systems a larger area is covered and uniformity of application improved by oscillating the pipe.

Rotary sprinklers are most popular in spite of the fact that some overlap of the watered area is unavoidable. Whirling sprays driven by jet reaction from the nozzles are popular in gardens, but the oscillating rotary sprinkler which revolves in a series of small jerks is used for commercial irrigation. Sprinklers of this type are available for operation at pressures from 20 to 700 kPa.

The high labour requirement for moving sprinkler lines from one position to the next is leading to increasing interest in systems which are easy to move, or move automatically. Several systems allow a complete spray line to be towed on wheels either in the direction of the pipe or at right angles. Completely automatic movement of the line can be achieved by using small hydraulic motors operated by the water which is being applied. An increasingly popular application of automatic movement is the *centre-pivot* system, in which a long pipe carrying many sprinklers slowly rotates about the central point.

Sprinkler irrigation is not suitable when the wind is very dry and likely to cause excessive evaporation losses, or strong enough to cause uneven distribution. Surface methods are also preferable where the appearance of fruit or vegetables would be spoiled by splashes of soil, or for crops particularly vulnerable to diseases which spread under humid conditions, or are spread by splashing water. Sprinkler irrigation is also finding increasing application for frost protection in orchards.

Water Supply.—Open canals supplying or distributing water may be left unlined if seepage losses are small because of the soil type, or will not have undesirable effects such as wasting expensive water or causing waterlogging. Large supply canals are usually of trapezoidal section, and lined with concrete placed *in situ* by machines with travelling slip forms. Smaller distribution canals are usually semi-circular in section and may also be lined with concrete placed and shaped by hand. Pre-cast linings of concrete or asbestos-cement are economic for sizes up to about 600 mm diameter, but casting *in situ* is cheaper for larger sizes.

Many semi-permanent linings or surface stabilising techniques have been tried. Cement-stabilised soil offers a cheap and effective alternative to concrete linings if the soil conditions are suitable. Asphaltic or bituminous membranes require a protective covering layer of soil and so are more suitable for storage reservoirs than canals. Various flexible sheet linings of plastic or rubber show promise but have not yet offered the desirable combination of low cost and long life.

Since open channels interfere with vehicle movement and require maintenance, supply by pipes has many advantages. High-pressure pipes are usually welded steel when above ground, and steel, plastic, or asbestos-cement when below ground. Pipes used for distribution within the irrigated field may be operated with only sufficient pressure to bring the water to the surface, or with additional pressure for sprinklers. Precast concrete pipes are useful for pressures up to 70 kPa and in sizes up to 600 mm diameter. For low-pressure concrete pipes of sizes larger than this a novel technique for continuous *in situ* casting has been developed in Israel. With trained and organised operators this is cheap and efficient. Asbestos-cement pipes are used from 100 to 450 mm diameter, and suitable for pressures up to 200 kPa. The joints are sealed either by hot asphalt or by the compression of rubber rings. Rigid plastic is available up to 600 mm diameter and has the advantage of extreme lightness; the joints may be simply welded on site.

SOIL CONSERVATION.—Erosion always has taken place and always will. The surface of the earth is constantly changing with mountains rising, valleys being cut deeper and wider, the coast line advancing here, receding there. The physical pattern which we see today is not the result of a single cataclysmic sculpturing but the result of changes so infinitely slow that only after centuries or millennia is the effect noticeable. Erosion is simply one of the aspects of this constant process of change. Man's activities seldom slow down the process, but it can be greatly accelerated by unwise exploitation of natural resources, and particularly by unsuitable methods of agriculture.

The two active agents causing erosion are wind and water, and of the two water erosion is the more serious problem when considered on a world scale. Wind erosion is worst in low rainfall areas, because dry soil is more prone to blowing, and where large land masses lead to sustained prevailing winds. Water erosion caused by the scouring action of surface run-off can occur anywhere, but this is of little importance compared with the damage resulting from the impact of falling rain. The severity of the rainfall greatly affects this splash erosion and so it is much more serious under the high intensity rainfall of tropical and sub-tropical climates than in temperate regions. As a first approximation the areas subject to severe rainfall erosion lie between the latitudes 45° North and 45° South.

Wind Erosion and Control.—The movement of soil particles by wind takes place in three ways. *Creep* is the movement of the large grains, of diameter greater than 0·5 mm, which are rolled along the surface of the ground by the force of the wind and other moving particles. This is the way sand dunes roll forward. *Suspension* is the movement of fine particles, less than 0·1 mm diameter, which are carried aloft and remain suspended by eddy currents so that they are carried for great distances. Dust storms and dust clouds contain particles in suspension.

But the most important movement is that of the medium-sized particles, from 0·1 mm to 0·5 mm diameter,

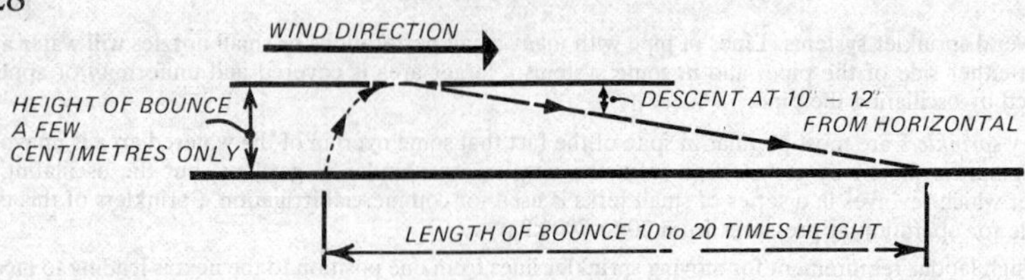

FIG. 15.—Path of a Soil Particle Moving in Saltation.

which proceed in a series of bounces known as *saltation.* Neither suspension nor creep will result in serious erosion unless saltation also occurs. Initially a particle is bounced into the air by the collision of large rolling grains. It is then swept downwind so that it descends at a flat angle and strikes the ground with considerable force, throwing up other particles. Each bounce is to a height of a few centimetres only, and the length is from 10 to 20 times the height (Fig. 15), but very large quantities of soil are moved in this way.

The first principle of wind erosion control is correct land use, and remedial measures will be of no avail if the basic problem is that an unsuitable form of cropping is being attempted. This was demonstrated in the Dust Bowl in the USA, where the wind erosion resulted from overcropping of cereals, drying out soils which had previously been stable under their natural vegetation of permanent prairie grassland. The problem has been corrected by a return to grassland farming. Given suitable land use, the most effective control is achieved by crop management which conserves moisture, for moist soil does not blow. Surface mulches of crop residues, and harvesting only grain heads, leaving the standing stalks, are also useful techniques. The wind at ground surface is also slowed down if the surface soil is composed of large clods or cultivated into ridges. Windbreaks or shelter belts are effective for small fields, but not for open prairies or where the rainfall is too low for good tree growth.

Rainfall and Erosion.—The action of raindrops striking the soil surface is to disintegrate the soil aggregates into fine particles easily splashed or washed away. This is a work process, eg involving the expenditure of energy, and strong links have been established between the kinetic energy of falling rain and its power to cause erosion. This power is directly related to the intensity or rate of rainfall, because high intensity rainfall is composed of larger drops which fall faster and thus have greater kinetic energy compared with gentler rain. The rain in tropical countries has a capacity to cause erosion of the order of twenty times that of temperate rainfall; for this reason rainfall erosion is a serious menace in the tropics.

Erosion Control.—The control of water erosion falls in two categories. Methods which directly control the surface run-off by earth-moving structures so that it is led safely off the land without causing damage are *mechanical protection* and correspond to the first line of defence. These must be reinforced by correct land management and crop management aimed primarily at ensuring that an adequate vegetative cover is maintained on the soil surface to protect it from raindrop splash. The two types of control are complementary, and neither is likely to be successful alone.

Where only a small part of the land is cultivated, as is frequently the case in less developed countries, a primary problem is to divert from the arable land the surface run-off coming from higher ground. This is done by *diversion ditches* or stormwater drains excavated on the upper side of the arable land and which lead the run-off away on a safe non-scouring grade. The surface run-off resulting from the rain which falls on the arable land is led away in similar banked ditches called *graded channel terraces* or *contour ridges* or *contour bunds.*

Contour Bands.—These can be built by hand in undeveloped countries where there is a surplus of labour. A more efficient way is to use conventional farm implements such as ploughs or disc tillers which, working along the length of the terrace, move soil from the channel or ditch and pile it up to form the bank on the downstream side. When large areas are to be terraced, it becomes economic to use heavy earthmoving equipment such as powered road graders or angle dozers. Whatever the method used for the original construction, it is important that the banks should be regularly maintained, since they tend to be worn by man, nature and animals. This maintenance can be mostly efficiently achieved when it is part of the regular tillage pattern.

Mechanical protection methods should always be supported by contour cultivation, ie carrying out all cultivation operations along a level contour instead of up and down the side of the hill. On gentle slopes, this alone may be sufficient to control erosion, or the field may be 'strip cropped', that is divided into parallel bands of different crops so that those more resistant to erosion shield those more vulnerable.

A difficulty arises if unevenness of the land causes the contour strips or the channel terraces to converge or diverge. If the width of the cultivated strip is not constant, mechanical cultivation is made more difficult. One solution is to make the banks and ditches low with gentle slopes so that tractors and implements can work over them; another is to shape the land by cutting and filling so that parallel channel terraces can be built.

The United States Soil Conservation Service pioneered a system of land classification which suggests for any particular piece of land the most appropriate agricultural use and the degree of erosion control which will be required to prevent erosion. The method is known as *Land Capability Classification* and the recommendations are arrived at after measurement of many factors which will influence the hazard of erosion, such as the slope of the land, the soil texture depth and permeability. With minor variations to suit local conditions the method is proving a valuable aid to conservation planning in many countries.

BIBLIOGRAPHY

ALCOCK, R., *Tractor-implement Systems*, AVI Pub. Co., 1986.

BISHOP, C. F. H. AND MAUNDER, W. F., *Potato Mechanisation and Storage*, Farming Press, Ipswich, 1980.

BUTTERWORTH, B., *Materials Handling in Farm Production.* Crosby-Lockwood Staples, 1979.

BUTTERWORTH, B. AND NIX, J., *Farm Mechanisation for Profit*, Granada, 1983.

COX, S. W. R., *Farm Electronics,* Collins, 1987.

CULPIN, C., *Farm Machinery*, Collins, 11th Edition, 1986.

ELECTRICITY COUNCIL: *Farm Electric Handbooks* (various dates).

HUDSON, N. W., Soil Conservation, Batsford, 2nd Edition, 1982.

McCLEAN, K. A. *Drying and Storing Combinable Crops*, Farming Press, Ipswich, 1980.

N.I.A.E., *Handbook of Agricultural Tyre Performance*, Report No. 18, 2nd Edition, 1976, National Institute of Agricultural Engineering, Silsoe, Bedford.

SCHWAB, FREVERT, EDMINSTER AND BARNES, *Soil and Water Conservation Engineering*, John Wiley (New York), 1966.

STONE, A. A., *Machines for Power Farming*, 3rd Edition, Wiley, 1977.

WELLER, J. B., *Farm Buildings*. Vol. 1. Estates Gazette, 1970.

WELLER, J. B., *Farm Buildings*. Vol. 2. Estates Gazette, 1972.

WITHERS, W. B. J. AND VIPOND, S., *Irrigation: Design and Practice*, Batsford, 1973.

WATERHOUSE, JAMES, *Water Engineering for Agriculture,* Batsford, 1982.

JOURNALS

The Agricultural Engineer, Journal and Proceedings of the Institution of Agricultural Engineers, West End Road, Silsoe, Bedford, England.

Journal of Agricultural Engineering Research, published for the British Society for Research in Agricultural Engineering by Academic Press Ltd., London.

Agricultural Engineering, Journal of the American Society of Agricultural Engineers, 2950 Niles Road, St. Joseph, Michigan, U.S.A.

Transactions of the A.S.A.E., published bi-monthly by the American Society of Agricultural Engineers, as above.

FURTHER READING

The Agricultural Engineer (Journal and Proceedings of the Institution of Agricultural Engineers):

POTTER, M. J., *Electronics on Farm Machinery*, Vol. 41, No. 2 (Summer 1986), pp. 58–61.

MATHEWS, J., *The Introduction of New Technologies*, Vol. 41, No. 3 (Autumn 1986), pp. 70–76.

ACKNOWLEDGEMENT.—Particular thanks for their kind assistance are due to the Directors and members of the AFRC Institute of Engineering (formerly the National Institute of Agricultural Engineering); the Electricity Council; the British Standards Institution; the Institution of Agricultural Engineers; and the staff of Silsoe College (formerly the National College of Agricultural Engineering).

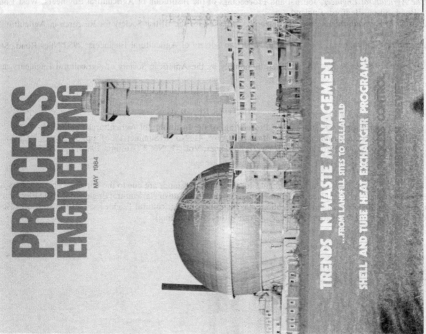

OFFSHORE ENGINEERING

Development of natural offshore resources.—Environment—Exploration—Reservoir Rocks—Geology—Seismology—Drilling—Production Development—Offshore Platforms—Fixed—Floating—Tethered Buoyant—Production Facilities—Oil and Gas Processes—Water Treatment—Power Generation—Electrical Installation—Heating and Ventilation—Fire-fighting and Safety—Accommodation—Instrumentation and Controls—Telecommunication—Supplies Handling Systems—Corrosion—Fatigue—Fire and Explosion—Acoustics—Vibration—Transport and Storage—Offshore Storage—Oil Transport—Single Point Mooring Buoys—Pipelines—Trenching—Underwater Development—Offshore Services—Derrick Ships—Submersibles—Diving—Dynamic Positioning—Inspection and Maintenance—Legislation—Codes of Practice—Economics—Abandonment—Conclusion.

By L. C. Allcock

Offshore engineering is concerned with the development of natural resources from the offshore environment. The oceans have traditionally been a source of food but in recent years, there has been a major endeavour to extract energy and minerals from the ocean itself, the seabed and the rocks below the seabed. The principal interest has been from the crude oil and natural gas industry, with the objective of extracting these mineral resources from reservoir rocks deep below the bed of the ocean.

Offshore engineering, for the oil and gas production industry, is concerned with providing installations in the sea to support drilling and production activities which are similar in many respects to the facilities used traditionally on land to achieve the same objectives. The move offshore has required the application of a very wide range of engineering disciplines in an oceanic environment, by adaptation of known technologies to take advantage of or where necessary, combat offshore environmental conditions.

ENVIRONMENT.—The offshore environment is quite different from the familiar onshore conditions in many ways. The principal difference is clearly the deep, salt water which is in constant, dynamic movement, responding as it does to wide variations in climate and providing an increasing challenge of depth, generally related to the distance offshore. Installations in this environment must be designed to resist the forces of winds, waves and currents at increasing distances offshore, with corresponding lessening of protection from nearby land masses. Great depths of water impose high ambient pressures at the seabed, which in turn affect sub sea installations and have effect on the seabed foundation conditions. The need to construct working decks far above the sea bed, on structures which must resist the broad spectrum of dynamic loading from the environment, including all possible combinations of severity and direction, is possibly the primary challenge. The maximum loading imposed by the one hundred year or fifty year statistically most severe storm condition presents the obvious design problem but the structure must also resist the cyclic forces imposed by average sea conditions, which involves the additional hazard of materials fatigue. Other important environmental considerations are the heavily salt laden atmosphere, exacerbated by the tidal range, with its continually changing wet and dry conditions and by the height to which salt spray is thrown in storm conditions. The severely corrosive conditions thereby created have a significant effect on the selection and operation of mechanical, electrical and electronic equipment. Structures offshore are also as exposed to earthquake attack. In this respect they do not differ from onshore structures, but the space geometry of the offshore structure, with its unusual slenderness, makes it peculiarly vulnerable to earthquake effects.

EXPLORATION.—An accumulation of oil and gas may have formed if reservoir rocks are present deep below the surface. These are formations containing interconnected pores or cracks and voids. The subsurface reservoir must be capped at its upper boundary by a rock formation impervious to the passage of fluids and there must also be closure of the reservoir by an impervious formation which prevents the lateral migration of fluids. This may be effected by upward convexity in the cap rock or by faulting. Typical reservoir rocks are sandstones (porous and permeable) and limestones (cracks and voids) and typical cap rocks are shales and clays. Dependent on reservoir conditions of temperature and pressure it is usual to find fluids in them in density related layers and if hydrocarbons are present it is usual to find natural gas overlying oil which in turn overlies salt water.

The origin of crude oil and natural gas is generally thought to be dependent on the earlier (in geological terms) existence of a shallow sea, rich in animal and vegetable life. The organisms, on dying, sank to the seabed and were buried by mud and sediment from rivers. Thick accumulations of mud would produce conditions of raised pressure and temperature under which, with possibly bacterial assistance, the organisms were transformed into hydrocarbon fluids. These source beds were in the course of time subjected to increasing pressure and geological movements allowing the fluids to migrate upwards and laterally. The fluid could either escape through the surface or be trapped in reservoir rocks given the conditions described above. Natural gas may be generated in a somewhat similar manner, during the formation of coal.

Hydrocarbon fluids can be generated in sedimentary rocks of almost any age but reservoirs have generally been found in sediments younger than the carboniferous epoch. The search for hydrocarbons consists primarily of endeavouring to locate the type of reservoirs in which they may be trapped. A variety of techniques is used. Exploration of a new area for prospective geological structures which might contain hydrocarbons was traditionally initiated by aerial survey using wide angle lenses and stereoscopic review. This gave opportunity for study of the main geological features. The method is only of minimal interest in the search for offshore prospects except in their relationship to adjacent onshore geological features.

The principal tool used in the search for conditions that might favour the generation and accumulation of fluid hydrocarbons, is geological study. This will extend over the whole area of the sedimentary basin, accepting or rejecting it on the understanding that drilling into the basin on the best available evidence will be the final determining factor. The exploration geological investigation is fundamentally to map the area as accurately as possible in order to determine the age and distribution of the rock formations with particular emphasis on angles of dip and strike and identification of major faulting and unconformities. Evidence of oil seepages in the form of asphalt or tars is also of value.

Geological mapping is normally followed by employment of two geophysical tools. The first of these is measurement and mapping of the gravimetric force over the area of the sedimentary basin. Sedimentary irregularities can be mapped with sensitive gravity instruments and this enables modifications to be made to the basic geological picture. It is also known that shock waves travel at slightly differing speeds through contrasting rock formations. By use of explosions or even sharp detonations at the surface and electronic measurements of the reflected shock waves at instruments set at defined distances from the explosion focal point, it is possible to map the underlying rock configurations. Prognosis of the types of rock can also be made by combining these seismic surveys with the geological mapping. Modern improvements in the science of accurate time measurement and the use of computer techniques to digest very large volumes of information, has improved greatly the value of geoseismic methods.

Other scientific tools are used in exploration investigations to corrobrate the main evidence. These include magnetic surveys to detect minor variations in the geomagnetic field, examination of fossils and microfossils (palacontology) and seeds and pollens (palynology) to determine the ages of rock formations and geochemical exploration where rocks are checked for presence of natural gas seepages in even minute amounts. Micro-seepage of hydrocarbons may also cause local increases in certain bacteria populations which are detectable.

In the offshore search, geoseismic methods of exploration have been the most successful. They are more easily applied from survey ships than the onshore equivalents and the development of more refined techniques, particularly in computer aided mapping, which has been developed to the point of producing three-dimensional portrayals of sub surface rock configurations, has significantly improved the level and quality of information available to the exploration geologist. By use of these many aids the geologist can, however, only improve the chances of the oil and gas industry making a successful hydrocarbon discovery. The final proof that a capped reservoir exists and contains producible hydrocarbons can only be obtained by drilling boreholes into the prospective rocks.

The drilling of a deep exploration well is a high cost exploration tool, and exploration drilling offshore is many times more expensive than onshore.

EXPLORATION DRILLING.—Early in the twentieth century, the rotary system of drilling was first used by the oil industry to replace the cable tool percussion system of boring wells. The modern drilling rig has been developed on the principle of rotary drilling with the application of modern engineering understanding. A modern drilling rig consists of the following major components.

A drill bit is rotated by a column of pipe called the drill string. As progress is made, the drill string is extended by adding joints of drill pipe at the top, whilst the string is held suspended in the hole. The column of pipe is suspended from a derrick by wire line. The hoisting and lowering system is based on a high speed, high power winch transmitting force by wire line strung through a fixed sheave assembly at the top of the derrick (crown block) and a large tackle sheave assembly (travelling block). The tension in the wire line is measured continuously and the weight of pipe applied to the drill bit can be adjusted by a hydraulic clutch system. The rotation of the drill pipe is achieved by using a square profile length of pipe at the top of the string which engages in a square hole in a rotary table. The square profile pipe is called the Kelly. The table applies torque to the Kelly and an arrangement of bushings in the table permits the Kelly to be moved vertically whilst torque is applied. The drill string is hollow and the drill bit bores a hole which has a larger diameter than the drill pipe. A high volume, high pressure pumping assembly forces fluid down the centre of the string through apertures in the drill bit usually equipped with jet style nozzles. This drilling fluid (mud) serves three main purposes: (a) the bit is cooled and lubricated by it, (b) it has properties of density and viscosity which can be adjusted by use of chemicals which lifts the drill cuttings up the annulus between the wall of the borehole and the drill pipe and (c) the hydrostatic pressure exerted on the borehole by the column of mud maintains control of fluid pressures in the rock formations of the borehole.

The bit may penetrate a rock formation which contains gas or oil with a higher natural *in situ* pressure than the containing pressure exerted by the drilling mud. Conversely the bit may enter a porous or fissured rock which has a lower *in situ* pressure than the pressure at the bottom of the mud column. In this latter case, the mud will flow away into the rock. This will cause a loss of control pressure and rock pressures previously controlled may become uncontrolled. In the former case of excessive pressure and in this last case of loss of mud, the well will have a tendency to blow out and tremendous forces can be unleashed in this way. To counteract this danger an assembly of specially designed, large bore valves is installed at the top of the borehole, the blowout preventer (B.O.P.). As the hole is drilled, the length of open, unprotected bore becomes excessive and it is therefore stabilised by placement of casing pipes which are cemented to the hole. The blow out preventer stack is bolted to the top of the casing pipe. As more hole is drilled, smaller diameter casing pipes are successively cemented into place and the B.O.P. stack replaced by a smaller diameter, higher pressure equivalent. The valves of the B.O.P. stack are controlled both from the driller's position on the derrick floor, and also remotely. They can be closed either around the drill pipe when it is in the borehole or across the open hole if the pipe has been withdrawn.

The mechanical engineering aspects of the drilling rig have changed radically over the past few years. Originally steam was the predominant prime source of power and continued to be used widely into the recent past. Concurrently a great deal of development work was done to produce diesel powered mobile units to drill shallow wells. Both the drilling winch, including the rotary table, and the mud pump assembly were driven independently by large diesel or gas fuelled engines. With the movement offshore, steam became unsuitable as a power medium for reasons of weight and lack of compactness. Offshore rigs are therefore principally diesel engine powered. In some cases the engines are used to generate electricity and instead of direct drive winches and pumps the diesel engines have been replaced within the rig area by electric motors. Electrically powered rigs have become widely used but are by no means universal.

The offshore drilling rig as originally used was mounted on a small platform supported on a piled foundation. These early platforms were designed to carry the derrick only. The rest of the rig was carried on a tender barge. Further developments produced the barge mounted drilling rig, with a barge which could be ballasted down to sit on the sea bottom, or more usually, a river bottom or dredged swamp location. This was soon followed by introduction of drilling from a floating rig. A variation on the fixed platform and 'sit-on-bottom' drilling rig has been the jack-up platform. This is essentially a barge mounted drilling rig complete with derrick. To the outside of the barge are mounted three, four or more tubular frame legs. These legs are up to one hundred metres or more in length. On arrival at a location, the legs are lowered to the sea bed and firmly pushed in. The barge itself is then lifted up the columns by use of large capacity jacks until the barge is clear of the highest possible wave effects. Drilling from a jack-up rig is equivalent to platform drilling and is unlike floating drilling.

The first floating drilling successes were from conventionally anchored ships and this was followed by use of larger ships with the rig mounted over the bow or the stern or in some cases through a hole in the centre of the ship called a 'moon pool'. Some drill ships had rigs mounted on turntables. This permitted the operator to rotate the ship around the drilling rig by adjustment of the anchor cables thereby heading the vessel into the seaway. This system came some way to reducing the pitch, roll and heave of the ship shaped vessel but in hostile environments downtime continued to be excessive.

A major change occurred with the introduction of the new geometry of the semi-submersible vessel. (Fig. 1). These uniquely shaped vessels consist of submerged hulls in the form of 'torpedoes' which can be ballasted or deballasted at will. The submerged hulls are connected to the work deck by vertical tubular columns which pass through the sea surface. The vessel can be deballasted and float with the hulls at the surface in which case they behave similarly to ships. With the hulls ballasted down, the vessel, having a very small water plane area, becomes transparent to wave. This small water plane area reduces heave of the vessel to as little as twenty per cent of a normal ship response, and pitch and roll are reduced to being almost unnoticeable. Under these conditions, it is possible for a drilling rig to continue drilling for a much greater proportion of the time than had ever been possible. In severe environments such as the North Sea, drilling can now be undertaken throughout the winter, whereas before the advent of the semi-submersible this would not have been possible. Clearly a good deal of other special equipment has been designed to allow drilling to be carried out from a working platform subject to marine motion, with the drill pipe rotating in contact with the bottom of the borehole and the vessel heaving and pitching around it.

For reasons of safety and blow out control, it is usual to set the blow out preventer assembly at the sea bed. The drill pipe between the rotary table at the derrick floor, and the sea bed B.O.P. stack is rotated within a marine conductor pipe. This simultaneously provides an annulus through which drilling mud is returned to the drilling rig. These marine conductors usually incorporate external small diameter piping through which hydraulic or electro-hydraulic control systems can be operated to control the valves of the B.O.P. assembly. Maintenance and repair of these control systems and the B.O.P. stack itself can be carried out by divers or remotely controlled mechanisms monitored by television cameras mounted on guide wires or themselves, free swimming, and controlled from the derrick floor.

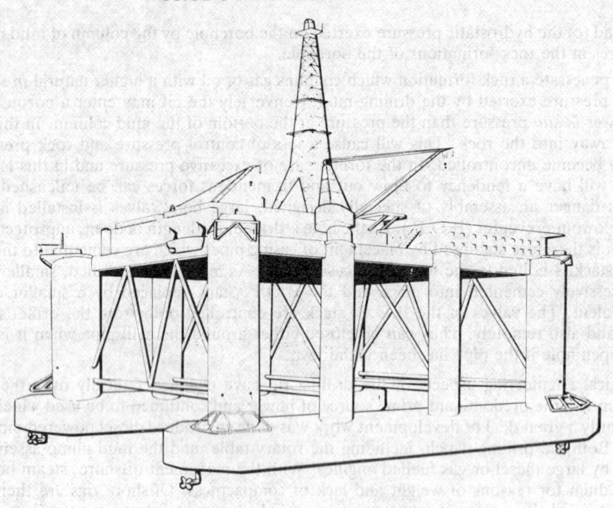

FIG. 1.—Semi-submersible Floating Drilling Rig.

The marine conductor is subjected to continuous wave and ocean current action. The pipe is latched to a flexible coupling at the top of the blow out preventer stack at its lower end and held laterally at the drilling floor level, the vessel being free to move within the scope of its anchorage. The conductor would collapse under its own weight if it was not suspended and held in tension. This is done by use of special heave compensated tensioning devices which maintain a constant tension in the conductor pipe throughout the whole scope of heave motion displayed by the drilling vessel. The marine conductor is a severely stressed element of the equipment and problems of fatigue particulary at the joints are proving difficult to overcome. Conductors have been used in water depths in excess of 700 m and designs for much greater depths are available.

One of the problems of the semi-submersible vessel is its load carrying capability which is relatively small by comparison with conventional shipshaped vessels. There is therefore the need for semi-submersible drilling rigs to be continuously supplied with material and equipment. They are therefore fitted out with special cranes and materials handling systems which can handle supplies, (principally drill pipe, casing, chemicals and cement) in rough sea conditions.

The semi-submersible has not completely displaced shipshaped and jack-up drilling rigs for exploration drilling. One of the advantages of the ship is that it has an acceptable drilling performance in the more benign sea areas and being self-propelled, is able to move rapidly between locations.

The semi-submersible usually has to be towed at relatively slow speed although some units are now equipped for self propulsion. For wide ranging exploration drilling campaigns the ship shaped rig frequently performs more economically.

A recent development in exploration drilling practice is the introduction of dynamic positioning. By this means a ship or semi-submersible vessel is able to maintain its position over a fixed point on the seabed by use of computer controlled thrusters. This facility removes the need for conventional anchorages with the economic advantage of significant time saving. This advantage increases considerably when drilling is undertaken in deeper water. Normally a semi submersible is anchored with eight or ten anchors each with a mooring wire or chain cable some two to three times the water depth in length. There is also a noticeable saving in weight which is of particular advantage to the load limited semi-submersible vessel.

PRODUCTION DEVELOPMENT DRILLING.—Should an exploration well determine the existence of a hydrocarbon reservoir, it is usually necessary to pursue the clarification of the size and geological complexity of the reservoir by drilling additional boreholes known as appraisal wells. These are drilled normally by the same floating drilling rig as was used to drill the exploration well. If these wells show that oil or gas are present in commercially exploitable quantities, an offshore platform would probably be constructed above the reservoir. These platforms vary greatly in size, but one of their primary requirements is to provide space for the installation and operation of a development drilling rig. Platform mounted rigs are similar in most respects to onshore drilling rigs. It is usual for fixed platforms to incorporate conductor tubes within the structure of the platform, to allow for the drilling of a large number of wells from a single platform. The B.O.P. assembly is therefore installed at platform deck level, as the conductor pipes are not subject to marine motion, and the B.O.P. stack can control well pressure safely from the level of the deck.

The commerciality of offshore development of hydrocarbon resources has been made possible by the introduction of techniques to drill slanted boreholes to predetermined drainage points in the reservoir. By use of wedges placed and set in the borehole, the direction followed by the drill bit can be controlled accurately in deviation from the vertical and azimuth. The weight on the drill bit also effects the deviation and must be carefully supervised. The use of these techniques enables the operator to achieve very great accuracy. The borehole is checked frequently during the drilling operation by use of electronic instruments and progress can be plotted continuously. With careful planning it is possible to drill one hundred or more wells from a single platform. Deviations up to 65° have been achieved and by use of slanted conductor tubes and specially modified drilling techniques even greater deviations are possible.

Very great accuracy is essential to the drilling of deviated boreholes (1) to preclude the possibility of drilling into an adjacent completed well and (2) to permit the drilling of a replacement well to the same drainage point, should the first hole be damaged and abandoned. There is also the risk of a drilling well getting out of control and blowing out. It is not always possible to bring a wild well under control by access at the top of the well because of incurred damage or fire, although expertise to attempt this has been highly developed. It may prove necessary to drill a relief well from a remotely anchored floating drilling vessel. Such a relief well must penetrate the same drainage point in the reservoir rock as the wild well, to permit the operator to kill the pressure source by placing a mud plug or cement. Drilling technology has been developed to an accuracy that permits successful use of this method.

PRODUCTION DEVELOPMENT.—When positive proof has been obtained that commercially exploitable quantities of oil or gas are present in a reservoir the task of the engineer can be defined in relatively simple terms. It is to provide the installations and equipment whereby production wells can be drilled and completed and the hydrocarbons safely transported from the reservoir, processed and delivered to a point where they can be sold.

Hydrocarbon reservoirs may exist at almost any depth, and can be considered accessible to the drill down to depths between 8,000 and 10,000 m. Reservoir thickness may vary from a few metres to several hundred metres and they may occur as coherent reef type rock formations or as thin layers of sand separated by strata of clays and shales. The rocks may be faulted, with layers containing hydrocarbons being present at different levels in the same basic reservoir.

TABLE 1.—COMPARISON OF PHYSICAL CHARACTERISTICS OF TYPICAL CRUDE OILS

Properties	Crude Oil A	Crude Oil B
Specific gravity	0·81	0·87
American Pet. Institute gravity	43	18
Kinematic viscosity at 100°F, cSt	1·9	107
Pourpoint °F	+15	+60
Paraffin wax, per cent	2·33	9
Sulphur	0·15	5·5
Asphaltenes	0·01	8
Hydrogen sulphide, p.p.m.	Nil	Nil
Aromatic hydrocarbons, per cent	14.4	—
Gas/Oil ratio, ft^3/barrel	1700	300

At these depths pressures in excess of 600 bar and temperatures of 150°C may be encountered. Crude oil and natural gas occur as a wide variety of physical—chemical mixtures of hydrocarbons ranging from methane (CH_4) with its single carbon atom down through the gaseous hydrocarbons into the liquid spectrum of molecules with compounds in the C20 to C30 range. It is rare to find crude oil with identical properties in more than one reservoir and crude oils with differing properties may occur at different levels in the same reservoir. One reservoir may contain methane with only minute traces of liquid (condensate) hydrocarbons entrained in it; another may contain crude oil with several hundred cubic metres of gas dissolved in each cubic metre of oil and a third may contain heavy oils with negligible quantities of gas in solution. As the fluid is produced up the borehole, pressures and temperatures are reduced, the fluid expands and at a specific pressure and temperature, which may differ from one well to another, gas will begin to bubble out of solution and separate from the liquids.

The physical properties of this fluid, which the engineer needs to know, include the specific gravity, the viscosity, the pour point, (the temperature at which the liquid begins to solidify) the relative volumes of oil and gas present throughout the range of pressures from the reservoir down to one atmosphere and the range of temperatures down to well below zero centrigrade. This last parameter applies particularly to the gas. The engineer will probably also need to know the relative volumes of the different gaseous hydrocarbons present in the associated gas.

At the wellhead process facilities must be provided by which the engineer can arrange for the separation and segregation of the oil, gas an contaminents contained in the well fluid. The contaminents may include in the gaseous phase; carbon dioxide, hydrogen sulphide and occasionally inert gases; in the liquid phase; water of high salinity, and in the solid phase; sand and silt. The oil may also contain sulphur in solution and traces of other elements. The method of segregation will vary but the general first principle is to strip the solution gas from the crude oil as near the wellhead as possible. This usually means in the case of crude oil that the process operating pressure is reduced in stages to approximately one atmosphere or slightly lower so that the residual liquid hydrocarbons can be pumped and transported by pipeline or tanker with a minimal danger of gas emerging from solution, and creating an environmental hazard, or damaging the handling equipment, particularly the pumps.

During the production process large quantities of fluid are withdrawn from the reservoir bringing about rapid changes in the physical conditions in the reservoir itself. At the high ambient pressures in these deep geological formations a great quantity of gas is usually dissolved in the oil, and as the formation pressure is progressively reduced the residual fluid expands to replace the fluid volumes that have been withdrawn. Sometimes reservoir pressures fall only slowly because of the presence of vast volumes of salt water below the layers of hydrocarbons. These volumes may be so huge that several years of hydrocarbon production may only represent a small percentage of the total fluid volume which is in communication with the drainage points created by the boreholes. These fluid volumes are so large that the very small compressibility of water becomes an important factor and the slight pressure reductions in the reservoir cause an expansion of the aquifer which fills the rock volumes after the oil has been withdrawn.

With such a natural drive the pressure in the reservoir can continue to be sustained without assistance but should this natural maintenance of pressure not occur the pressure will reduce to a point where gas emerges from solution in the reservoir itself. Production will then be disrupted by gas bubbles preventing flow through the rock pores. The engineer may be called upon to provide for the maintenance of pressure above the bubble point by artificial means either by injection of gas into the upper part of the 'oil column' or by injection of water below the hydrocarbons or around the periphery of the oil body. The pressure maintenance fluids are introduced by pumping down special boreholes strategically located within the reservoir and in an optimum position relative to the producing wells. Water and gas have much lower viscosities than oil and will migrate through the rock pores more rapidly than the oil. This may result in preferential production of injected gas or water at the expense of oil. These tendencies may be controlled and checked by reducing the flowrate and as mentioned above by careful selective placement of the perforations in the borehole casings of each well as may be required.

The efficient drainage of the reservoirs and a recognition of the explosive natural energy present at the source of the oil and gas combined with the realisation that these fluids are highly inflammable and hazardous, will continue to pose major engineering problems. The demand to provide facilities and engineering understanding of the associated problems is difficult in onshore development and the difficulties are increased by the movement to the offshore environment.

The technology of offshore development of oil and gas production has a history of rapid continual change in response to the challenges of greater water depths and more severe oceanic environments. The primary requirement has been the provision of a working deck mounted on a structure from which production wells could be drilled and on which sufficient area could be provided for the installation of production equipment, such as the oil and gas process facilities to separated oil, gas water and contaminents, oil storage, gas disposal systems, pumps, compressors, utilities, living accommodation, and connections to the seabed pipelines for transhipment of oil and gas.

In the early days of platform development it was normal for reasons of safety to complete the well drilling before production was initiated and production process equipment, utilities and living accommodation were frequently mounted on separate adjacent structures. As water depths increased different types of platform were designed and gradually the practice of concurrent drilling and production, with the operatives accommodated on the same platform, emerged as an economic requirement, dictated by the very high cost of a deep water structure. The necessary improvement of safe practice and fire prevention were effected and it is now usual to find a total offshore development taking place within the confines of a single structure.

OFFSHORE PLATFORMS—FIXED AND FLOATING.—The first essential for offshore activity has been provision of a platform on which a successful drilling and production programme can be carried out. An extensive research and development programme has been and continues to be addressed to the use of floating platforms and a few successful applications of the method have been made and are in operation: Conventionally, production has been developed offshore from fixed platforms.

Two basic types of platform are in general use, both of which have subsidiary variations in design. These are firstly piled structures and secondly gravity structures. A preference for one type of structure over another has not clearly emerged due in part to the continual change in the cost of materials, specialised labour and equipment available for the total construction; in part to the changing demands of the offshore industry with respect to total size of platform; in part due to the lack of history of the different types of structure in greater water depths and more severe environments.

Piled structures suffer from the disadvantages of uncertain and costly installation times offshore, their vulnerability to damage by adverse weather during the early period of their installation, their lack of oil storage capacity and the need to install the oil and gas drilling and process facilities and living accommodation offshore after completion at site of the base structure. Gravity structures on the other hand are more expensive to fabricate, are relatively inflexible to design modification should the foundation soil conditions vary even slightly from the foreseen, criteria, and pose soil mechanics problems which cannot be answered with absolute confidence in relation to optimum economic design objectives.

The history of offshore platforms is complex and shows the fluid response given by the engineer to the demands of offshore industry. Platforms are now being designed and installed in offshore areas which were thought, only a few years ago, to pose insurmountable problems. This rapid evolution of new technologies will no doubt continue.

PILED STRUCTURES.—The early offshore structures were designed on the basis of a small number of relatively large (24 in and 30 in) diameter tubular steel piles driven by steam hammers. The areas where platforms of this type were used were predominantly seabeds with thick deposits of soft, sedimentary silts and muds; for example the Gulf of Mexico, Lake Maracaibo, the Gulf of Paria between Trinidad and Venezuela, and the South China sea offshore Brunei and Sarawak. The platforms required four, six or eight piles and on completion of piledriving operations the platform decks were welded to the tops of the piles. It was essential that the very long piles required to penetrate the thick layers of soft mud should be driven accurately and straight. This led to the use of a pile driving template known as the jacket. A space frame structure would be prefabricated onshore which had sufficient height to provide continuous conductor pipes through which piles could be driven from above the surface of the sea whilst the jacket rested on the seabed with sufficiently small bearing pressures to ensure the jacket remained stable and vertical, at least until pile driving was completed. These jackets were carried to the offshore site mounted horizontally on a barge and launched into the sea (Fig. 2). From an initial position of horizontal floating, gradual ballasting of selective leg members would bring about upending to a vertical floating position and seabed placement would be effected by further ballasting after final positioning. These early structures did not use the jacket as an integral part of the structure but solely as a pile driving construction tool.

FIG. 2.—The 'Jacket' (pile-driving template).

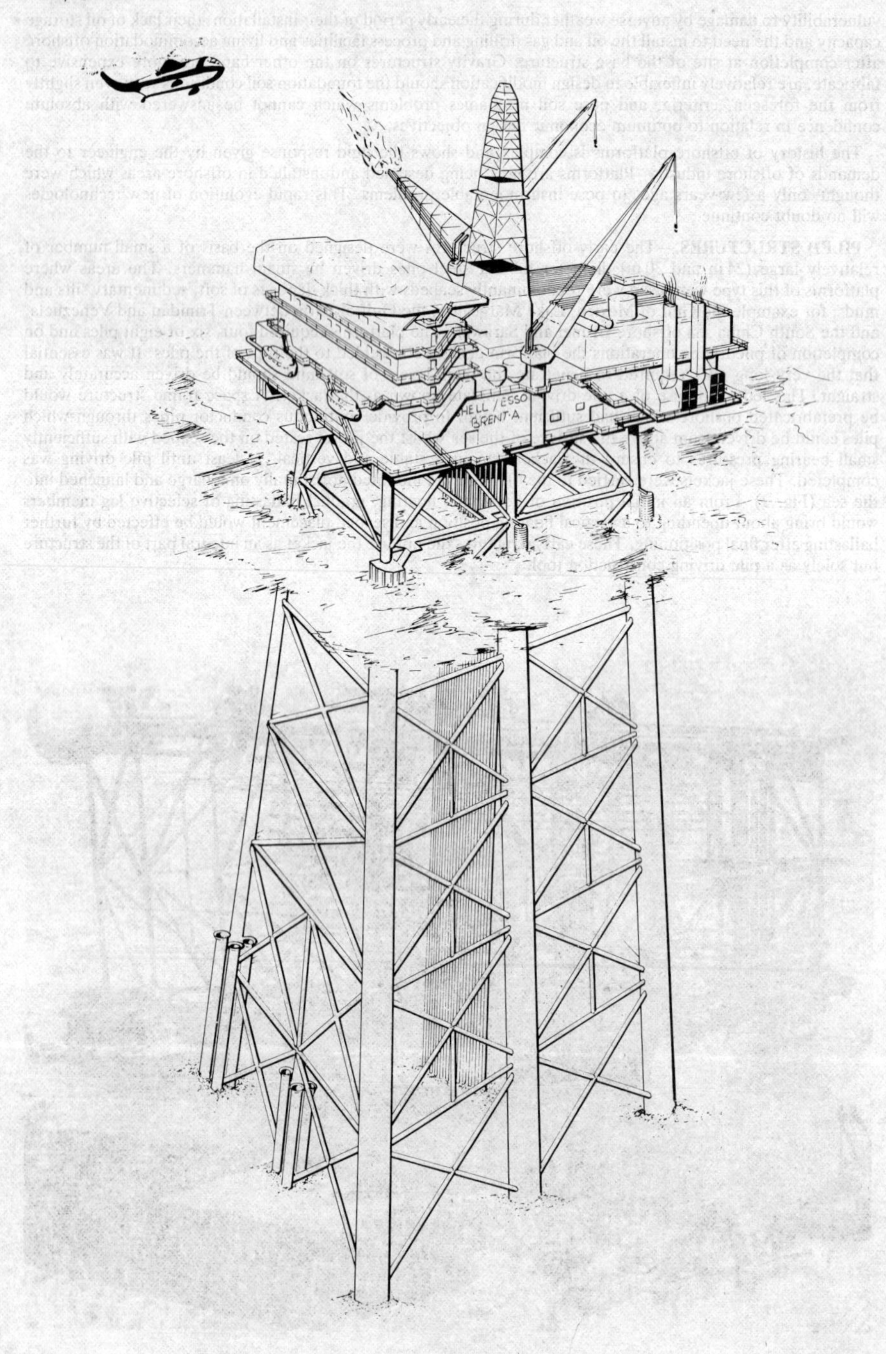

FIG. 3.—Self Floating Steel Structure.

With increasing depths of water and increasing top load carrying requirements the jacket became an essential component not only of the construction programme but also of the final structure and means were found to drive more than one pile in cluster form around the base of each jacket leg. Up to eight piles have been driven in a cluster surrounding a single jacket leg, with due attention to maintaining adequate clearance between piles. Clusters of piles act as groups not as a sum effect of single piles. Platforms using up to fifty or more piles have been constructed and piles up to 72 inches in diameter have been driven.

Many variations on the early structures have been introduced. Even in the very early days, concrete piles were substituted for the steel tubulars but did not prove fully successful due to their inflexibility in length, when an unexpected variation in the depth of an adequate foundation bearing layer occurred. The use of higher tensile strength steels for both piles and jackets was introduced with consequent savings in steel weight. With greater severity of service requirements, the problems of fatigue and stress intensification at joints in the jacket frames became more complex, and have been the subject of continuous research. More interestingly, the jackets became so large that launch barges became significant cost items in the construction budget, and the idea of self floating jackets was introduced. (Fig. 3). This made the launch barge unnecessary. Several structures of this type were constructed. In the Gulf of Alaska, (Cooke Inlet), where a major design criterion was an ability to resist impact forces imposed by masses of drifting ice, a tower type structure was developed which used a single central leg of large diameter. The complete structure takes the form of a mushroom, with the stalk rising through the water surface and spreading out into a fully cantilevered working deck above the water and into a spread footing with a large number of piles driven through the base.

The launch type structure (Fig. 4) has however retained its general popularity and jackets in excess of 20,000 tonnes have been prefabricated and successfully launched and placed. Dead loads on these structures of as much as 20,000 tonnes have been installed, equivalent to a live load imposition approaching double that amount. Water depths exceeding 125 metres have been conquered with these huge installations, and steel platforms pinned to the seabed with piling have been constructed in water depths of 250 metres.

Concurrent with the advances in designs of piled platforms there has been a comparable advance in the technology of pile driving equipment. (Fig. 5). The steam hammers which weighed possibly five tonnes and required extensive back up of steam raising plant, have been superseded by a range of diesel hammers which may weigh three hundred tonnes or more. The comparative energy per blow delivered to the pile has increased in a similar manner and there is now a much clearer insight into the optimal blow rate and the behaviour of a pile during the driving operations. A recent development is the use of hammers which perform under water.

GRAVITY STRUCTURES.—The gravity structure relies entirely on its own weight, and the ability of the seabed to carry that weight for structural stability during the design storm condition. There are a number of variations in design of gravity structures and they may be made in either concrete or steel or in a combination of both materials. The first application of the gravity structure principle in the offshore oil industry was in the Ekofisk Field, offshore Norway. Previously the theory had been applied in lighthouse construction. The Ekofisk structure, which was originally designed for use as an oil storage structure but was later modified for use as a platform for a very large gas handling and compression plant, was followed in rapid succession by the construction of several drilling and production gravity structures of basically reinforced concrete construction. It is of interest that the great demands on the onshore prefabrication sites, together with the significance of the water depths available to the constructor for the fabrication and towing of these structures near to shore, resulted in designs which showed quite wide variations, constrained as they were by the conditions of the construction site. It proved virtually impossible to make an optimised design which could be built at all the available sites.

TABLE 2.—COMPARISON OF OVERTURNING MOMENTS: GRAVITY STRUCTURES
(Similar Water Depths—c. 160 m; Wave Height—over 30 m)

Plan Dimensions of Caisson metres	Height of Caisson metres	Overturning Moment tonne metres
diameter 90	55	338·500
square 120 × 120	40	388·100
square 92 × 92	40	68·600

The gravity structure is built to a shape which tries to concentrate as much of its mass and bulk as close to the seabed as possible (Fig. 6). The objectives are to construct the platform as near to shore as possible, place the topside facilities in position at a sheltered site prior to the offshore tow, and then move the whole to its offshore location using ocean going tugs. These objectives are met as far as possible by construction of a multi celled caisson raft which may be up to 100 metres in diameter and 60 metres high. From this raft base a number of columns are carried up to the full height of the structure. After arrival at the offshore location the

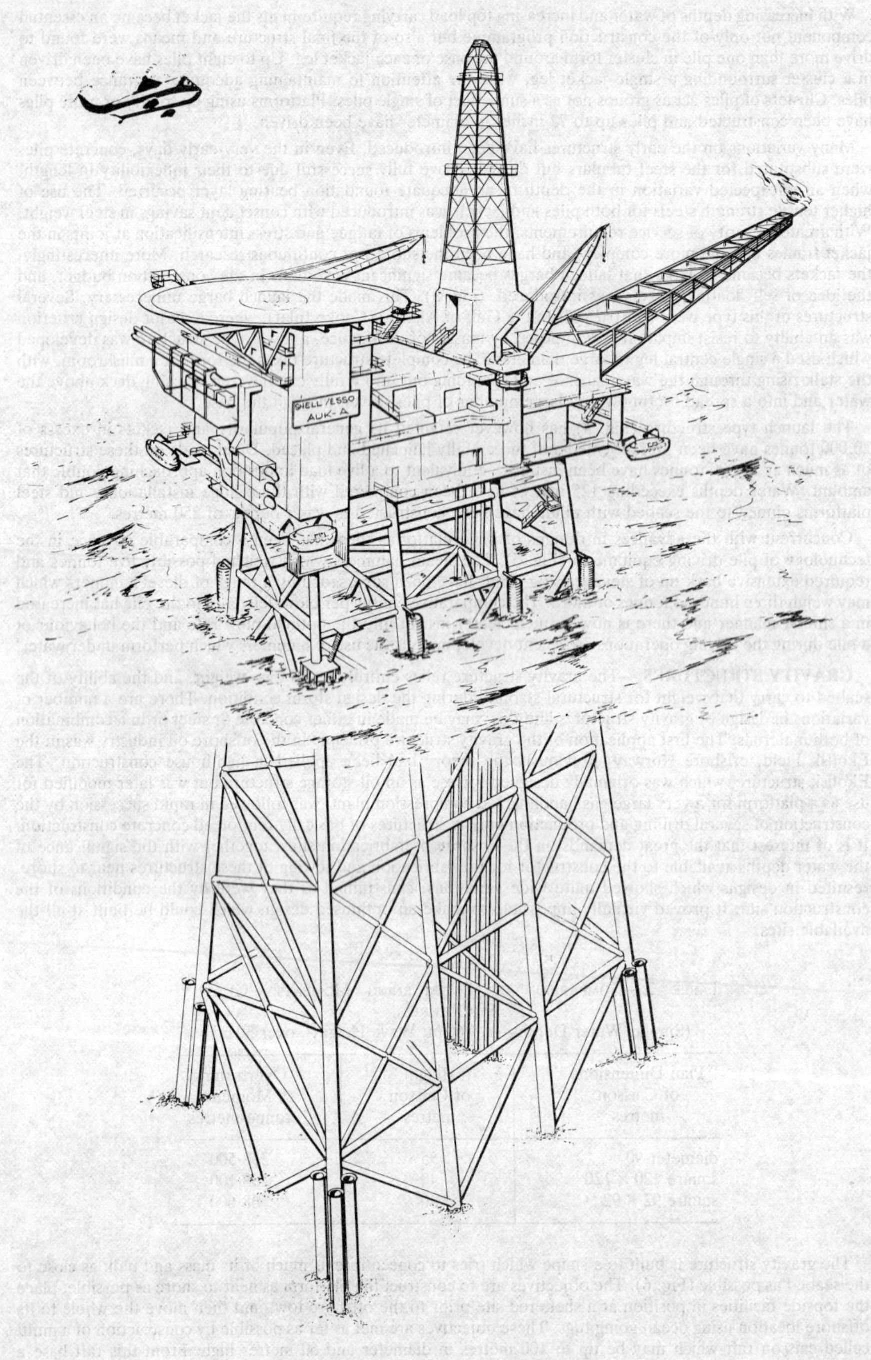

FIG. 4.—Steel Launch Type Structure.

FIG. 5.—Pile Driving Hammer.

caisson base is water ballasted and landed on the seabed. Offshore installation time can therefore be reduced to a few days which in hostile environments, with relatively short fair weather periods, gives the gravity structure a marked advantage over the piled structure. Gravity structures have been designed for 160 m water depth with weights in excess of 300,000 tonnes.

COMPARISON OF PILED AND GRAVITY STRUCTURES

WIND WAVE AND CURRENT FORCES.—An offshore environment creates dynamic, lateral loading conditions on offshore installations which are very specific to the particular location. The study of these several environmental conditions and their effects and their transference to an offshore structure has been and continues to be a major preoccupation of engineering research laboratories. A volume of data has been published on the behaviour of installations under these widely varying forces but much remains for further investigation. The random nature of wave generation and the total combined effect of waves, ocean swell, current and wind forces pose problems which are extremely difficult to quantify, analyse and determine but sufficient is known and has been translated into design codes of practice which history has tended to prove, err on the side of safety. The piled structure is comparatively transparent to waves and currents and the total combined lateral loading experienced by a piled structure is correspondingly much smaller than the environment imposed lateral forces on a gravity structure. Even within the range of piled structure designs there are wide variations. The launch type jacket platform offers the lowest obstruction to wave passage, the self floating structure which requires larger diameter legs to provide inbuilt buoyancy during the ocean tow offers a higher obstruction and the monoleg tower type being of larger diameter offers a single large obstruction whilst not presenting a profile which will retain drifting ice jammed within it. The jacket type structure however often suffers from an underestimation of lateral loading, because its final transparency after subsequent additions of pipeline and well conductor riser pipes, suffers a more significant proportional decrease than is the case with structures with less transparency from the outset.

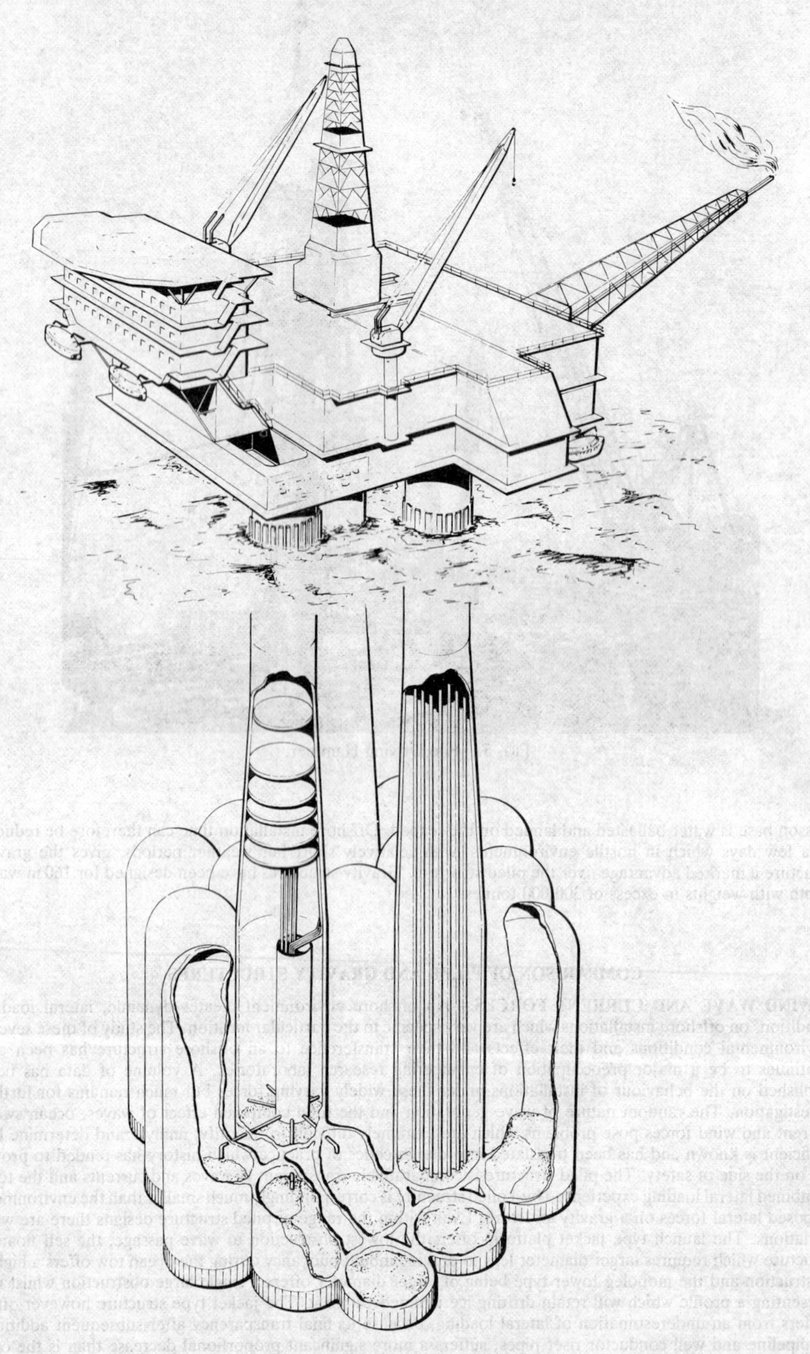

FIG. 6.—Concrete Gravity Structure.

The gravity structure presents a much greater barrier to lateral environmental force attack. A structure standing in 140 m of water may be required to resist a lateral wave load of the order of 50,000 t, and 2,000,000 tm overturning moment. The design will aim to reduce these loads as much as possible with commensurate improvement in structural stability. Wave forces on gravity structures are essentially different in nature from those on piled structures. Because of the great bulk of the caisson raft foundations which may reach up through half the water depth, it is necessary to resort to potential theory for the analysis of the loads. Analytical tools are available and comparison with model tests shows that these tools can be used with confidence. It is also noteworthy that the caisson, protruding into the wave affected surface zone of the water raises the surface elevation of the wave because of the very local bottom effect on a large wave. This effect must be investigated when establishing deck elevation above the still water sea level. A further design constraint is that although one of the advantages of the gravity structure is its ability to carry with it from inshore to location the completed deck and all facilities already in place, and although the structure has a small water plane area and responds only slightly to marine conditions, there will inevitably be some marine motion during the ocean tow. The slow harmonic sway of the great loads of the deck and facilities set high above the water impose significant dynamic bending stresses on the relatively slender but very long columns.

FOUNDATIONS.—Seabed soil properties can vary widely over short distances both horizontally and vertically. The detailed investigation of the seabed soils at the precise location of a future platform is an essential precursor of the platform design. Because economic constraints impose a need for a minimum lead time on the overall development plan, it is often necessary to conduct extensive soil investigations at several possible locations during the course of an appraisal drilling programme. The final siting of the platform is dependent on the results of the reservoir appraisal.

The seabed area of a platform will normally lie within a circle of 200 m diameter. The first difficulty is to ensure that the positioning of the soil investigations will be repeatable within allowable tolerance on all future returns to the location. During the recent past major improvements in offshore survey systems have been implemented and in areas such as the North Sea, repeatability within one or two metres can be achieved. In more remote areas such repeatability may be impossible and when determining the various factors of soils consistency, platform stability and scope of the investigation the range of surveying inaccuracy must be taken into account. There is also the need to ensure that satisfactory soil samples and measurements of acceptable accuracy are obtained. This can be most difficult in deep water and poor sea conditions. It is usual to make a geophysical survey using shallow seismic techniques to define reflection horizons down to the full depth and beyond the predicted penetration of the designed piles into the seabed. This will probably be followed by a pattern of five soil borings to a similar depth. At the same time cone penetration tests will be made. If it is not known whether the future structure is to be a piled or a gravity structure as many as fifteen cone penetration tests may be carried out. If a pile structure has already been selected then this number of C.P.T's will be much reduced. These tests usually penetrate up to 25 m into the seabed and as many samples as possible are recovered and carefully analysed at a soils laboratory. The borings and the C.P.T's are made from a specially equipped ship, although recently, small semi submersible work vessels have been introduced and are gaining acceptance because of their greater stability with the consequent advantages of lower weather down time, a lesser chance of equipment loss and the possibility of completing soil investigations even in winter.

In the case of piled structures the functions of the piles are to provide (1) lateral restraint against the horizontal loads imposed by wind, wave and current, (2) vertical support for the loads imposed by the platform itself and its facilities and (3) resistance to the overturning movements created by the horizontal forces and the dynamic response of the structure. The properties of the deep soils, evaluated from the shallow seismic surveys and the borings will provide the resistance to the vertical loads (compressive and tensile) and determine the depth to which piles must be driven. The soils properties of the seabed near the mudline will define the lateral loading resistance. The design of the jacket is relatively insensitive to the properties of the foundation soils. One of the major advantages of the piled structure is that it will permit relocation of the structure within quite wide limits right up to the time of placement, should this prove desirable for reasons of new reservoir evaluation. Unpredicted unconformity in the foundation soils can also be countered by adjustment in the pile design penetration or by modification of the pile section.

In the case of gravity structures the properties of the deeper soils will determine the long term settlement of the structure and the safety factors for vertical stability and overturning, while the properties of the shallower soils will permit the calculation of skirt penetration and factors of safety for horizontal stability. Soils profiles often show weak shallow layers overlying and mingling with stronger layers of soil. It is most important to the safety of the platform to have foundation skirts below the structure of sufficient depth to mobilise the strength of the deeper layers when the surface layers are weak. Any failure of the surface soils in shear will allow lateral movement of the structure under severe storm loading. It is therefore important that the pore water content of the soils immediately under the structure within the skirt perimeter should be maintained stable to preclude any loss of shear resistance throughout the life of the structure. The weakening of clays under cyclic loading and the liquefaction of sand with increasing water content are phenomena which are not fully understood. Foundation design for pile structures and more particularly gravity structures is essentially conservative and high factors of safety are used in practice. Until better soil testing equipment and greater knowledge of soils properties are available, this conservative approach will continue to be adopted.

It is also important in the case of piled structures to ensure the jacket will remain stable on the seabed before the piling is installed. At that stage there will be no deck and topside loads and the piling will normally be undertaken in the fair weather period. The calculated overturning moment of the jacket will be checked against the maximum expected wave height during the installation period. Ballasting of the jacket will improve its stability against lateral forces but if the seabed is soft this may cause unacceptable settlement of the legs. This possibility can be countered by the use of mud mats to spread the loads which bear on the seabed.

TRANSPORTATION AND INSTALLATION.—There are several distinct phases in the period between a structure leaving its fabrication site and its offshore completion.

(a) removal from the fabrication yard;
(b) transportation to the selected offshore location;
(c) placement on the seabed;
(d) securing to the seabed;
(e) installation of deck and modules;
(f) hook-up and commissioning of facilities and utilities.

In the case of piled structures it is important that all but the last phase should take place during the better weather season.

For gravity structures it is important to take as much advantage as possible of the inherent buoyancy of the structure and place the deck and facilities on the structure before transportation to the offshore location. If there are draught limitations over the route of the ocean tow then the first stages of the tow, until deep water is reached, may have to be completed at a lesser draught than the caisson height; the superstructure loading may have to be reduced to improve stability during the shallow submergence stage. If, on the other hand, the structure can be towed with the caisson fully submerged, the stability under tow will impose the only limit on the superstructure loads. The load that can be carried is then a function of the draught limitations and the geometry of the structure. A gravity structure usually consists of a caisson raft with a number of columns rising between the caisson and the deck. The floating stability is most critical during submergence of the caisson. The metacentric height suddenly decreases as the caisson roof submerges and the water plane area decreases. As the structure is further lowered by adding more ballast water into the caisson the metacentric height slowly increases again and more weight can then be added at the top of the columns.

OTHER CONSIDERATIONS.—When a jacket structure has been successfully piled and pinned to the seabed, the deck and the facilities and utilities can be placed on it. The deck may be a relatively simple beam assembly which is merely a support frame for the modules containing all the necessary plant and equipment. All the facilities required are prefabricated in these modules which are transported on barges and lifted into place by ship mounted cranes. Individual weights of more than 2,000 tonnes have been placed in this way. The deck contains no built-in facilities.

In gravity structures there are two types of deck. The first is essentially a bare deck which is placed on the structure before float out, and all the equipment is then placed on the deck packaged in a similar manner to the facilities on a jacket structure. The second type is called the integrated deck. This is a large, multifloored structure which is prefabricated with all the process plant and equipment installed. Integrated decks may weigh 20,000 tonnes before placement on the top of the columns of the structure. Gravity structures decks are placed by floating them in on barges over the structure while it is submerged at its deepest possible floating draught. After connection the assembly is deballasted for towing. In many cases a compromise type of deck has been used. A large deck is prefabricated, complete with some of the necessary plant equipment and set in place on the structure. The balance of the facilities are prefabricated separately in module form and are lifted into place on top of the deck by floating crane. After all the plant and equipment has been placed, the pipework, electric cabling and instrumentation must be hooked up. When modules are used this phase of the construction can be very time consuming.

SUMMARY OF COMPARISON—PILED versus GRAVITY STRUCTURES

(a) **Piled Platform**

(i) the horizontal stability is more fully understood and this allows more economy in the design.
(ii) the final selection of the platform location is less critical because pile design need not be oversensitive to changes in soil conditions and because pile make-up may be modified at a very late stage.
(iii) the combined costs of materials and fabrication are in general lower.
(iv) the site soil investigations can be less extensive and the costs lower, provided a decision to select a piled structure can be made sufficiently early and before much information about the reservoir is available.
(v) a deep water construction site is not required.
(vi) fabrication skills are principally associated with steel working and assembly experience and these are usually available in the main industrial centres associated with ship construction.
(vii) the attachment of pipeline risers to a steel jacket is relatively simple and additional risers can be installed after placement of the structure offshore.

(b) **Gravity Platform**

(i) the installation time for the platform is short, thereby reducing costly offshore operations and their exposure to weather risks.

(ii) the potential exists, although historically it has not been used very successfully, for transport of all the deck and facilities to the offshore location after installation inshore, thus avoiding costly offshore placement.

(iii) the platform has the capability for oil storage.

(iv) a larger deck area can be provided.

(v) construction relies on labour with a higher unskilled component. Work forces of this type are more readily available. On the other hand, the construction sites for gravity structures require deep water close inshore and it can be expected that the selected site may be remote from traditional construction and industrial areas.

FLOATING STRUCTURES.—Many discoveries of oil and gas cannot be exploited commercially by use of fixed structures. The water depth may be so great that a fixed structure is uneconomic and in water depths where fixed structures could be employed the oil or gas deposit may be too small or spread too thinly and widely to justify the cost of a fixed platform. These cases can be developed by using seabed completed wells connected via a production marine riser to a floating platform moored above the oil or gas field. The limiting conditions for fixed installations have not been defined and they have been used in water depths exceeding 250 m albeit in benign environments. It has also been shown however that it can be attractive to use a floating platform as the basis for an EARLY PRODUCTION SYSTEM. This is a system whereby the appraisal wells drilled from a floating drilling vessel are completed at the seabed and produced to a floating platform carrying the required process plant and other facilities. This permits production to be initiated and create income whilst a fixed platform is being designed and installed for full field development.

The first of these early production systems was developed for use in the EKOFISK field, offshore Norway. It was developed around a jack-up platform not a floating structure but the principle was identical. The jack-up platform was described in the drilling section above. Following the use of the early production scheme at Ekofisk, the ARGYLL field, offshore UK was developed in 75 m of water depth using a semi-submersible vessel as the base for the process plant.

The Argyll field development plan called for the drilling of four vertical, seabed completed oil wells. These were connected by seabed pipelines to a riser base set on the seabed. The well fluids were flowed to the deck of the semi-submersible through a marine conductor riser assembly, made up of a number of small diameter pipelines held together by horizontal spider frames. The centre pipeline of the assembly was of larger diameter and the processed crude oil was pumped down this pipe from the floating platform and through a further low pressure seabed pipeline to an oil loading buoy, to which a tanker was moored, and connected by a floating hose string. The marine conductor was fixed to the seabed riser base with a universal coupling. On the semi-submersible floating vessel the individual pipelines are all secured by heave compensated tensioning devices, which permit the vessel to heave, roll and pitch whilst keeping the vertical pipelines under constant upward tension. These devices prevent the collapse of the pipelines under their own weight. The riser assembly is designed to flex and resist the wave forces imposed upon it. The well fluids are piped from the top of the marine riser through flexible hoses to the oil processing equipment and the entrained gas, after separation, is flared off.

The Argyll development showed the commercial possibilities of this form of oil field development in 75 m water depth but in a relatively severe environment.

Similar systems are being applied elsewhere in the world and in due course it can be expected that marine risers for use in much greater depths of water will be designed and used. There are however economic barriers to the widespread application of the semi-submersible floating platform as a basis for oilfield development. One of the major drawbacks is that because of the relatively small water plane area of the semi-submersible vessel it will carry proportionately lower top loads and the construction of larger vessels to carry greater loads becomes expensive and generally less cost effective. As a result careful studies have been made of the use of conventional ship-shaped platforms. One development has been the use of a marine riser supported by a buoy at the sea surface. The well fluids are produced up the riser and through the buoy which is built in a SINGLE POINT MOORING configuration (see section on tanker loading systems). The oil is piped to process facilities mounted on the deck of a tanker, which is moored to the buoy. The gas is flared and the oil stored in the tanker itself. Smaller shuttle tankers then come alongside this field storage vessel and the cargo is transferred for onward shipment.

The future of offshore development in deeper waters, which present even more severe environmental problems, will depend largely on the successsful application of floating platforms.

TETHERED BUOYANT STRUCTURES.—Another form of offshore platform which is under active development is becoming known as the TENSION LEG PLATFORM OR TETHERED BUOYANT STRUCTURE. The proposal is aimed at development of oil and gas production from water depths greater than 400 or 500 m. This type of platform works on the same principle as a taut moored buoy, that is a buoy moored to a heavy anchor at the seabed by means of a vertical wire. The Tethered Buoyant Structure is essentially a large semi-submersible form of floating vessel moored by vertical cables to a very heavy gravity anchor at the seabed instead of using a conventional mooring and anchorage assembly. A tension force is maintained in the vertical cables by adjustment of the buoyancy in the floating platform to ensure positive tension in the mooring in all states of the sea. This combination of forces reduces marine response in the platform to a negligible movement in the vertical plane and a very minor horizontal movement. The horizontal drift excursion can also be made very small. The use of controlled buoyancy acting against a tensioned mooring system permits the use of a semi-submersible form of floating platform, but with the important advantage that the additional load can be carried on the structure and balanced by increasing the buoyancy.

There are many unanswered problems with regard to the Tethered Buoyant Structure (Fig. 7). Its future development and application will depend on the solution of these complex engineering unknowns and the economic evaluation in comparison with other systems.

OTHER VARIANT STRUCTURES.—In addition to piled and gravity fixed structures, the floating platform with conventional moorings and the tethered buoyant structure there are other variants. Among these are included the use of ship-shaped platforms with alternative types of mooring including the single point mooring buoy, the possible addition of dynamic assistance to the vessel positioning/mooring system, the use of partially tensioned mooring cables in combination with floating structures and the use of tensioned guy wire systems applied to a light weight fixed piled structure to improve its resistance to lateral wave forces in deeper waters.

FACILITIES ON THE OFFSHORE PLATFORM.—Offshore oil and gas production facilities are complex and extensive with the primary objective of converting the produced well fluids into a form and condition which will permit safe and economic handling and onward shipment to a point of sale. The principal functions of process equipment include (1) separation of the oil from gas, water and sediment; (2) separation of residual liquids from the gas stream; (3) treatment of water to remove traces of free oil and emulsified oil in water.

The secondary functions of the process plant and equipment may include (1) oil treatment to counteract hydrogen sulphide problems; (2) oil storage and pumping; (3) gas treatment for dewpoint control and special dehydration to prevent formation of loose chain mixtures known as hydrates; (4) special anticorrosion treatment particularly with regard to carbon dioxide corrosion; (5) gas compression either for onshipment by pipeline or for reinjection.

Additionally there may be water treatment and pumping plant for a water injection system, living accommodation for 150 to 250 personnel, utilities to sustain the power, water, heating and ventilation requirements for plant and personnel and a wide range of safety, fire-fighting, instrumentation, control communications systems, craneage and supplies handling systems (Fig. 8). Although each of these elements of the offshore installation is treated separately in the following discussion it will be clear that there is a considerable interaction and interrelationship between these ancillaries.

THE OIL PROCESS STREAM.—At each wellhead an assembly of high pressure valves is installed which provides control, shut down capability and access to the well. This assembly is called the Christmas Tree. From the Christmas Tree the well fluid is carried in a Flowline to a manifold which receives crude from a number of wells. The commingled stream is then piped to a train of separator vessels which usually consist of several stages. A separator is essentially a large drum vessel with a defined operating pressure. The first stage pressure will be somewhat lower than the flowing wellhead pressure, and each succeeding separator is set to operate at progressively lower pressures with the final stage, set possibly at one atmosphere, or slightly above or below, depending on the gassiness of the fluid. At each working pressure, the velocity of flow of the fluid is reduced in the wider diameter of the drum. Gas emerges upwards from the fluid stream and water gravitates to the bottom of the fluid buffer lying in the lower half of the separator. A stable fluid level is maintained in each separator by a level control device. The rate of flow is of paramount importance, in that retention time in the vessel is directly related to the flowrate and the quantity of gas emerging from solution in the oil, and the successful gravity separation of the water content is time dependant. A series of baffles are used to direct the oil and induce streamline rather than turbulent flow, and a series of screens are usually placed in the gas offtake to trap any liquids entrained in the gas stream and encourage droplet formation. The droplets will coalesce and fall back into the liquid stream. It can readily be seen that too high a fluid flowrate will not allow adequate time for gas to emerge (*Critical Liquid Throughput*) or in the case of crudes with a high gas to oil ratio, too high a gas flowrate will result in liquid droplets being carried over with the gas stream (*Critical Gas Throughput*). The sizing of the separator is therefore an important aspect of the design.

As the fluid passes through the several stages of separation there will be a progressive change in the vapour pressure of the liquid stream and several gas offtake streams will be created, all at different pressures. Produced water will be continuously withdrawn from the separators and after treatment to remove residual oil (down to below 50 to 25 parts per million oil in water) the water will be pumped to the sea or used for reinjection in the reservoir. Thus by straightforward separation the oil stream is made suitable for pumping to storage within the offshore platform, for transfer via an offshore single point loading buoy to a tanker, or for direct shipment by seabed pipeline to an onshore entrepot terminal or refinery plant.

The physical condition of the oil must be carefully controlled to ensure that its vapour pressure is not too high for safe storage or shipment, or alternatively that the oil pour-point is not so high that the viscosity increases until it is impossible to pump the oil. To overcome these problems it is not unusual to introduce oil heaters or coolers into the process to modify the crude temperature so that the final product is conditioned to meet shipment or storage requirements.

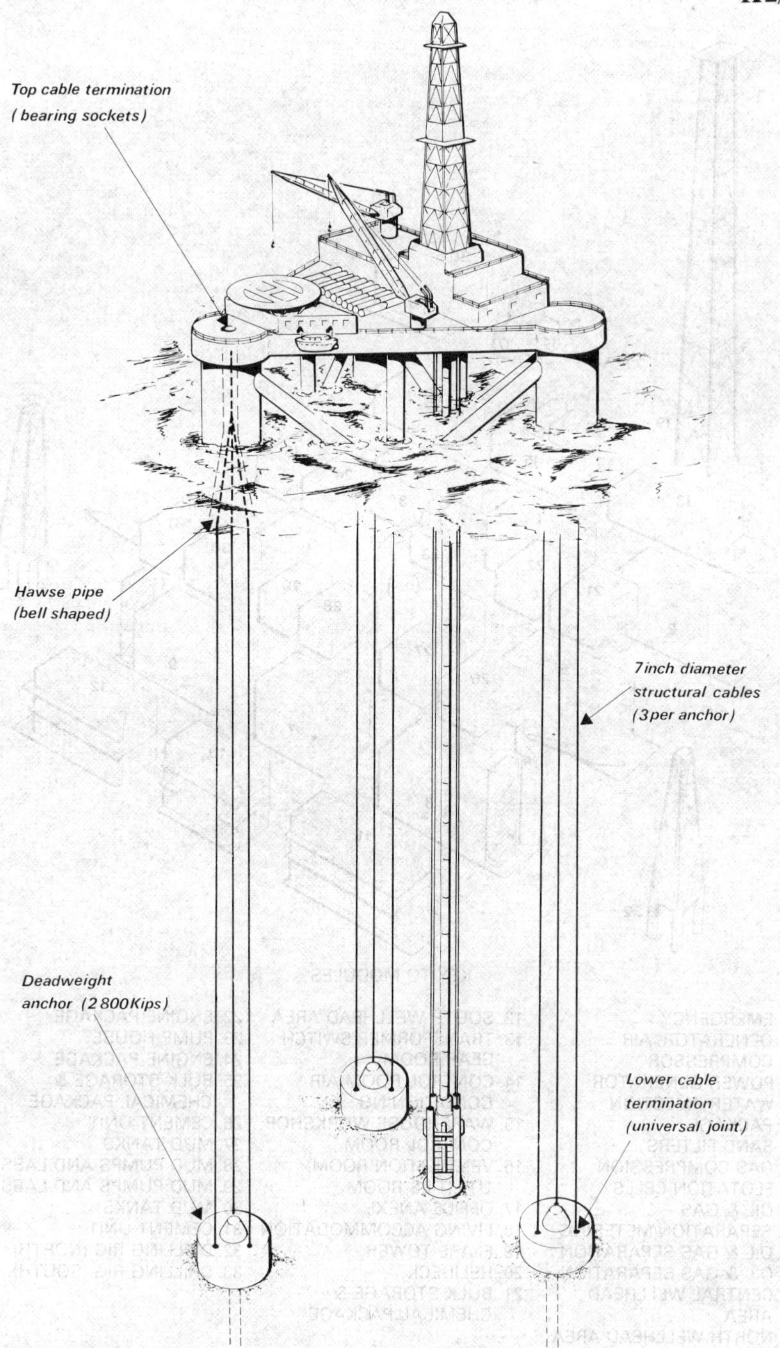

FIG. 7.—Tethered Buoyant Structure.

KEY TO MODULES

1. EMERGENCY GENERATOR, AIR COMPRESSOR
2. POWER GENERATOR
3. WATER INJECTION PACKAGE
4. SAND FILTERS
5. GAS COMPRESSION
6. FLOTATION CELLS
7. OIL & GAS SEPARATION/METERING
8. OIL & GAS SEPARATION
9. OIL & GAS SEPARATION
10. CENTRAL WELLHEAD AREA
11. NORTH WELLHEAD AREA
12. SOUTH WELLHEAD AREA
13. TRANSFORMER/SWITCH GEAR ROOM
14. CONTROL ROOM AIR CONDITIONING
15. WAREHOUSE WORKSHOP CONTROL ROOM
16. VENTILATION ROOM, UTILITIES ROOM
17. OFFICE ANEXE
18. LIVING ACCOMMODATION
19. FLARE TOWER
20. HELIDECK
21. BULK STORAGE & CHEMICAL PACKAGE
22. ENGINE PACKAGE
23. PUMP HOUSE
24. ENGINE PACKAGE
25. BULK STORAGE & CHEMICAL PACKAGE
26. CEMENT UNIT
27. MUD TANKS
28. MUD PUMPS AND LABS.
29. MUD PUMPS AND LABS.
30. MUD TANKS
31. CEMENT UNIT
32. DRILLING RIG (NORTH)
33. DRILLING RIG (SOUTH)

FIG. 8.—Topside Facilities Breakdown Showing Components.

In cases where sulphur or hydrogen sulphide is a contaminent, special precautions must be taken to preclude the possibility of steel embrittlement not only in the well casing and tubing but also throughout the process equipment. Special steels are used to combat embrittlement which can occur with only slight traces of these contaminents. Where higher percentages are present it becomes necessary to install desulphurisation plant which may make the entire process too expensive to consider. The poisonous nature of hydrogen sulphide is invariably a major hazard when this gas is present and at an offshore platform the hazard is significantly more serious.

TABLE 3.—COMPARISON OF PHYSICAL COMPOSITIONS;—CRUDE OILS AND NATURAL GASES

Composition mol per cent	Crude Oil		Natural Gas	
	Oil A	Oil B	Gas C	Gas D
Methane	0·56	1·75	95·05	88·93
Ethane	0·38	1·44	2·86	5·99
Propane	0·47	3·07	0·49	2·00
Iso butane	0·18	0·80	0·08	0·19
butane	0·64	3·21	0·09	0·35
Iso pentane	0·64	1·55	0·03	0·05
pentane	1·23	2·63	0·02	0·06
Hexane	2·95	2·50	0·00	0·02
Heptane plus	88·01	82·98	0·04	—
Nitrogen	—	—	1·26	0·75
Carbon dioxide	4·94	0·07	0·04	1·65
Sulphur	—	—	—	0·20
Helium	—	—	0·02	—

THE GAS PROCESS STREAM.—During normal operations there are two basic gas streams. (1) the stream which is to be utilised or sold and (2) the stream which is to be wasted.

Possible uses for the gas may include:

Power Generation.—Fuel either for direct drive engines or in gas turbine driven electrical generator units. This gas will require treatment to remove all liquids, some compression and possibly heating. The required pressure for turbine use is normally in the range of ten to fifteen atmospheres.

Reservoir Pressure Maintenance.—For injection into the reservoir for pressure maintenance or retention for future production to sales, it is also important that free liquid should be removed from the gas and it is usual to drop the pressure and temperature (usually as a benefit gained from the expansion process of pressure reduction) and then recompress. To minimise the compression horse power requirement the pressure reductions through the separator stages will also be tuned to generate the maximum gas at the highest possible pressure compatible with the other service requirements of the process. Typical injection pressures will be slightly higher than the subsurface reservoir pressure. Pressures in excess of 500 atmospheres may be necessary.

Pipeline Transportation to Shore.—Operating pressures for sales pipeline transmission will usually range from 70 atmospheres upwards to 150 or even 200 atmospheres.

Even more stringent specifications may be applied for gas quality than are applied for fuel or injection gas. Liquid dropout in the pipeline must be prevented and any contaminent in the form of carbon dioxide, hydrogen sulphide and water vapour must be controlled down to a minimum.

It is frequently necessary to inject dew point depressants into a sales gas pipeline such as methanol or to remove water vapour by glycol contacting plant. The combination of water vapour and carbon dioxide or hydrogen sulphide will cause rapid and dangerous corrosion.

Feedstock for a Process Plant.—Natural gas can be converted into liquefied natural gas, ammonia or methanol. It could also be used to make electrical power offshore for transmission to onshore. In general it is more economic to transport gas to shore by seabed pipeline before conversion by one or other of these processes.

Gas Lift of Production.—If reservoir pressures decline such that there is inadequate residual pressure to lift the well fluid to the surface wellhead, it is possible, by injection of measured quantities of gas at the bottom of the producing well, to lighten the gravity of the produced fluid flowing up the well tubing. When this system is in use the gas is clearly recycled, this is therefore not strictly a method of using up quantities of gas.

The second gas stream is vented or flared. From all the processes, particularly from the final stage of separation, there will be residual gas, probably at low pressure, which must be safely vented away from the platform. It is also essential to provide an emergency blowdown venting system to a remote flare in order to dispose rapidly of all process gas in the case of shut down, fire or explosion. At an offshore platform it is difficult to provide process and emergency flare systems in a safe manner. The platform and the personnel must not be exposed to excessive radiation and this means that either the flare/vent tower must be very high or the flare stack must be placed a safe distance away from the platform and the gas transported to it by seabed pipeline. A high flare stack on the platform may prove a difficulty with helicopter traffic.

WATER TREATMENT PROCESS PLANT.—There may be various requirements for water treatment systems to make raw seawater suitable for the several demands.

Potable Water for Life Support.—To provide water for drinking, laundry and sanitation it is usual to provide a desalinisation plant as an alternative to shipping fresh water from shore.

Water Injection.—Sea water is frequently used for injection into the reservoir for artificial pressure maintenance purposes. An alternative is to use water produced from the reservoir with the oil. This latter system is a method of disposing of water which would otherwise have to be de-oiled prior to disposal to the sea. In all cases the water will require treatment.

As a preliminary it is essential to ensure that the water used for injection is compatible with the water in the reservoir. It is not unusual for a chemical reaction to occur resulting in plugging of the reservoir pores and consequent failure of the injection system. In general the required water treatment includes de-oxygenisation (to minimise corrosion in the injection piping) and addition of bacteriocide to prevent the injection of anaerobic sulphate reducing bacteria which may proliferate in the reservoir and produce hydrogen sulphide from the sulphates in the reservoir water.

Disposal of Water.—All waste water at an offshore platform must be de-oiled and rendered harmless to the environment before it can be disposed to the ocean. There are various proprietary plants manufactured for these purposes based in general on the lighter gravity and coalescent properties of oil relative to water. By reduction of flow velocity and passing the water stream over and under a pack of parallel plates the oil is left floating above the water body which is drained off from below. The final oil content of the water may be further reduced by addition of chemicals.

Fire Fighting.—A highly reliable, high volume, high pressure fire fighting water system will be a necessity at every offshore platform. The water is obtained from the sea and requires little treatment apart from the addition of inhibitors to minimise corrosion in the fire fighting system pumps and piping.

POWER GENERATION.—A major offshore oil production platform may have a total power demand in excess of sixty megawatts. There are several options open to the designer in selecting the ways in which this demand can be met. For economic reasons natural gas taken from the produced well fluid will normally be the selected primary fuel although the platform will still require power when production is shut in and no gas is available. The aviation type gas turbine has also established a pre-eminent position as a first selection as a power source because of its high power-weight ratio. For major power consumer points the option remains between individual turbine drivers for pumps and compressors in the range of two megawatts of demand, or the generation of electric power and distribution to individual motor drivers at each offtake. Various permutations of the balance between direct drive and electric motor drive can be the optimum in different applications. For individual offtakes of less than two megawatts it is more usual to use electric motor drives powered from a central plant.

The primary power system will not be adequate for emergency situations and a standby power system must be provided for life support and essential platform safety systems fuelled by other than gas produced at the platform. Power generated from a secondary source is also needed for start up of the primary power generators.

Power generation systems will be decided by a number of factors:

(a) space and overall weight limitations—it is clear that the structural designers will prefer the lowest weight and space demand.
(b) the positioning and layout of fuel supply piping and exhaust ducting compared with the electric power cable distribution systems.
(c) the comparative thermal efficiency of the competing alternative systems.
(d) overall comparative cost.
(e) operational reliability and ease of maintenance and repair.

In general terms it has been found that central power generation becomes more attractive with increasing total demand for power. It has also been shown that for flexibility of use, particularly when matching high speed gas turbines to slower speed compressor offtakes, then individual drivers become clumsy to apply and central power generation is preferred. Provision of standby power for scheduled overhaul periods and breakdown is also more readily catered for in a flexible manner by the central power source alternative. An operating philosophy may be established whereby production of oil and gas can be given priority over subsidiary offtakes such as water injection, and in the event of failure of one central power source turbine, the other gas turbines can be operated in the peak mode. Certain types of aero derivative gas turbine can be operated in so called base load and peak load modes. The areas derivative turbine has proved very suitable for offshore application for several reasons. It has a very high power/weight ratio, the time between overhauls has been improved to in excess of 25,000 operation hours and it is relatively easy to remove the turbine from the platform and return it to shore for overhaul. The standard industrial gas turbine is normally over large for offshore use, and can provide major problems of maintenance and overhaul in cramped offshore platform conditions. An advantage of gas turbines is that these machines can be used on a dual fuel, gas or diesel oil, basis and the switch from one fuel to another can be accomplished quickly. One of the problems of the central power generation system is the starting of the very large individual electric motors. These can be overcome by use of special starters. The secondary power system for emergency and for start up of the main generators is normally diesel powered.

An interesting related problem is the degree of integration of the power requirements of the drilling activity with the power requirements of the production system. In the case of a platform with an oil storage and oil pumping installation it must also be considered whether this can better be powered independently or integrated with the main power system. In each case local criteria will influence the final selection.

Other matters which must be reviewed include start-up arrangements, system frequency, turbine generator control, load shedding arrangements, the distribution system, voltage levels and regulation, containment of faults within switch board capacity, switchgear selection, earthing systems for the power and also for lightning currents.

In gas turbine installations there are a number of design features which are worthy of mention. In the very rigorous saliferous conditions offshore, special attention must be given to the air intakes to reduce the salt content of the indrawn air and a system must be devised to minimise corrosion when an individual machine is idle. Recycling of exhaust gases must also be precluded. Engine cleaning, waste heat recovery, reduction of noise, access for assembly and overhaul and the minimising of air turbulence relative to helicopter operation are all points requiring attention at the design stage.

HEATING AND VENTILATION.—An offshore platform is a complex and highly compact industrial plant which is divided into individual modules separated by steel walls, roofs and floors. These different compartments must be air conditioned. They are classified into hazardous and non-hazardous areas by definitions included in various codes of practice related to the presence or absence of hydrocarbons in the particular module. The need for stringent design practice is evident and it is vital that air circulating in hazardous areas is not allowed to be drawn into non-hazardous areas. This is done by establishing a ventilation system with a slight underpressure in hazardous zones and an equivalent over pressure in non-hazardous compartments. At the same time there must be rigorous control of temperature and humidity levels.

FIRE FIGHTING AND SAFETY.—Oil and gas are hazardous substances and in combination with the high pressures associated with drilling activity and high pressure production processes, predicate a vital need for the highest quality and reliable hazard detection and warning systems backed up by complex fire-fighting installations. From the viewpoint of fire hazard, an offshore production platform can be divided into five general areas: (1) process, (2) drilling, (3) electrical, (4) utilities and (5) accommodation and control areas.

In each of the areas there is a different fire hazard. The dangers have been recognised and codes of practice and government regulations have been introduced and stringently applied. In general terms, automatic fire detection systems are deemed essential where there is no protection from an automatic sprinkler system. A flammable gas detection system is required wherever such gas may accumulate. Manually operated fire alarm systems are required; a fire main is required with pumps that operate automatically and without the main power system, and many other features.

Additionally there has been significant attention to the problem of fire weakening of stressed structural steel, particularly main deck beams, and to the segregation of fires by the use of fire resistant walls. This is given specific importance in the segregation of living accommodation from the balance of the platform. In summary the fire protection system is made up as follows:

(i) if gas can accumulate—gas detection is required;
(ii) if a fire can occur—fire detection is required;
(iii) for process and drilling areas—deluge protection;
(iv) for normal areas—sprinkler protection;
(v) for electrical and electronic areas—a halogen protection system.

There is also the danger of explosion. Wherever this possibility exists endeavours are made to limit damage by the introduction of blow off panels in outside walls, floors or roof areas. Venting of the hazard conditions is the best solution, but where this is not possible, explosion suppression must be considered. The science of explosion suppression at offshore platforms and hydrocarbon process plants is in its infancy although promising results have been obtained by use of HALON compounds in combination with ultra violet flame detectors. This is a subject of wide research.

Other safety requirements at offshore platforms include provision of lifeboats, of fire resistant quality and launching capability from very high elevation above the water (up to 40 m).

In support of these safety measures there is also the need for first level medical services and continuous training involving all personnel. Legislation in many countries also deems essential the continuous presence of a stand-by vessel near each offshore platform with capacity to rescue men from lifeboats or from the sea itself.

ACCOMMODATION.—The number of personnel must be accommodated at an offshore platform may vary between the requirements at small, unmanned platforms at minor gas fields close inshore, where the need is only for maintenance visits, and the very extensive demands of a large oil production and drilling platform located remote from shore. Accommodation may be needed for as many as 300 persons and must include for possibly one or two per cabin, catering, (restaurant, kitchen and cleaning services) sanitation and hygiene, recreation areas and probably medical services, office space and telecommunications and control centres.

INSTRUMENTATION AND CONTROLS.—A carefully integrated instrumentation and control system is required. In many instances these systems are linked via telecommunications networks to onshore display and control centres. There are several basic requirements for these installations:

(a) the process must be designed to 'fail safe'
(b) the requirements of the process operator must be met with respect to the need for knowledge of pressures, temperatures, flow rates and other basic data;
(c) the updated condition of the electrical, gas detection, fire protection and telecommunications networks must be known.

The system must operate reliably in a difficult environment with high salinity, high humidity and vibration. The final provision will probably comprise pneumatic, hydraulic and electronic instruments although full account must be paid to the hazardous and non-hazardous areas of the platform.

The major difficulty is reliability in severly corrosive conditions, combined with the sheer complexity of the systems. This can be the cause of excessive shutdown of production due to the 'fail safe' basis of design and

FIG. 9.—Offshore Platform Showing Helicopter Facilities.

the time expended in sequenced start-up procedures. These complexities are forcing the expanding use of computer assisted production in both the control and data collection aspects of the offshore operations.

TELECOMMUNICATIONS.—The offshore production industry presents two main problems to the communications engineer; (1) internal communication for operational instructions transmission, for public address and safety warnings; (2) external communications to other platforms, ships, helicopters and an onshore base.

The range of demands calls for a wide range of systems including tropospheric scatter, UHF networks, telephones, HF radio, VHF radio, homing beacons, radar to detect ships and planes, public address, closed circuit television, walkie-talkie for crane and supply boat operation, hifi (recreation area) systems and special individual demands.

Reliability under onerous environmental conditions is the most difficult aspect of these demands on the telecommunications engineer.

SUPPLIES HANDLING SYSTEMS.—Offshore platforms must be continuously supplied over periods of several years with material to support operations. The demands of the drilling activity include supplies of well casing tubulars, drill pipe and drilling tools, chemicals for drilling muds, cement for cementation of tubulars in the boreholes, diesel fuel for rig operation and sundry small supplies. The production operation and the offshore personnel create a demand for food, spare parts, tools and a wide variety of minor needs.

These are handled by use of specially designed supply ships of 2,000 to 3,000 tons capacity, having some dynamic position equipment such as bow thrusters to supplement the main propulsion system and with very high sea-keeping qualities. The vessels are frequently fitted out for special duties, such as pipe handling, bulk cement and chemicals handling employing silos and pneumatic transfer, oil transfer systems and anchor recovery and placement winches.

At the platforms much of the cargo is handled in containers hoisted by platform mounted pedestal cranes. These cranes must operate in very severe service conditions. The most hazardous service is at the moment when a supply ship in a rough sea falls from under the load at the point of lifting. The sudden impact or snatch load may be a combination of the mass of the load in a free fall condition and the strength of the connection between the load and the ship. This latter should of course be zero but the ship's cargo must be restrained from marine induced movement and snagging of loads is not uncommon.

Personnel movement between onshore base and platform is normally by helicopter (Fig. 9). The platform must therefore be fitted with navigational aids for both ship and helicopter operation which must frequently be carried out in marginal weather conditions. In the design stage platforms are frequently subjected to model scale wind tunnel investigation with a particular objective of studying the micro climate in and around the platform and its effects on helicopter operations.

GENERAL OFFSHORE INSTALLATION ASPECTS.—Development of offshore oil and gas production has challanged known technology to an unprecedented degree in many specialised disciplines. Among these can be mentioned structural engineering in general, fatigue of material under cyclic variable loading, corrosion, acoustics, noise and vibration, fire and explosion detection and suppression, soil mechanics to name but a few.

The fundamental causes for the demand to advance specialist understanding have been touched on, but it is of particular interest to review the combination of factors originating in the special offshore environment which affect the offshore structure and the installed facilities. These are as follows:

(a) the dynamic attack by wind, wave and current on the structure itself which by virtue of its non-rigid design transmits these dynamic effects to the whole of the installation.
(b) the saliferous nature of the atmosphere which may be abnormal up to heights of several hundred metres in severe weather.
(c) the high oxygen content of sea water down to significant depth in rough weather areas subject to current, and up to significant heights above the sea in the spray thrown over the offshore structure.
(d) the fire and explosion hazard associated with hydrocarbons and highly electrified installations.
(e) the build up of marine growth, both vegetable and animal which the structure will attract, thereby increasing the dynamic stressing inflicted by the environment.
(f) the noise and vibration transmitted through a coherent structure from the initial effects of the environment and added to by the installed machinery and plant, the drilling activity, and not excluding possible impact by supply ships.
(g) the complexity of the total installation and its relationship to human ability to withstand the conditions, and at the same time, understand the operations and perform safely.

HYDROCARBON TRANSPORT AND STORAGE

An oil and gas field must produce high volumes of oil or gas to ensure its commercial success. As already mentioned the raw well fluid will contain various proportions of crude oil, natural gas, condensates (natural gasolene), salt water, water vapour and various gaseous, liquid or solid contaminents.

There is a variety of solutions available for storing and transporting the commercially valuable portion of the well fluid to a point of sale and for taking care at the same time to dispose of the valueless components safely during the processing and transportation sequence.

STORAGE OF OIL.—The storage of liquid oil onshore can be accomplished by use of surface tankage, made of steel or occasionally concrete, or of underground caverns. Offshore the alternatives include:

(i) within the structure of the platform—to date, the steel piled platform has not been used to provide other than minor storage capacity whereas many of the concrete gravity structures have been constructed to store up to 50,000 m^3 of oil within the caisson foundation raft. For reasons of structural integrity this normally has to be done by maintaining the caissons full of liquid, either sea water or oil, at all times. This is to obviate the very high cost that would have to be paid to provide structural strength to counter the risk of implosion by external sea water pressure.
(ii) by use of tankers moored to special buoys adjacent to offshore platform and interconnected by seabed pipeline.
(iii) by use of purpose designed floating storage vessels which may incorporate systems for loading tankers directly.

(iv) by use of purpose designed seabed storage tankage. There have been many proposals for such systems but few applications, principally for reasons of cost effectiveness.

The general design criterion for oil storage is one of safety and explosion/fire prevention. This relies on careful control of the vapour pressure. It is also essential that the stored oil should not cool to the extent of losing its 'pumpability'.

STORAGE OF GAS.—It is virtually impossible to devise means of storing gas other than by compression and injection into reservoir rocks or by liquefaction. Offshore liquefaction systems have not as yet been developed and applied. Offshore gas for commercial application is normally transported to shore by seabed pipeline for direct onshore utilisation in industry or as feed stock for a liquefaction or a fertiliser plant.

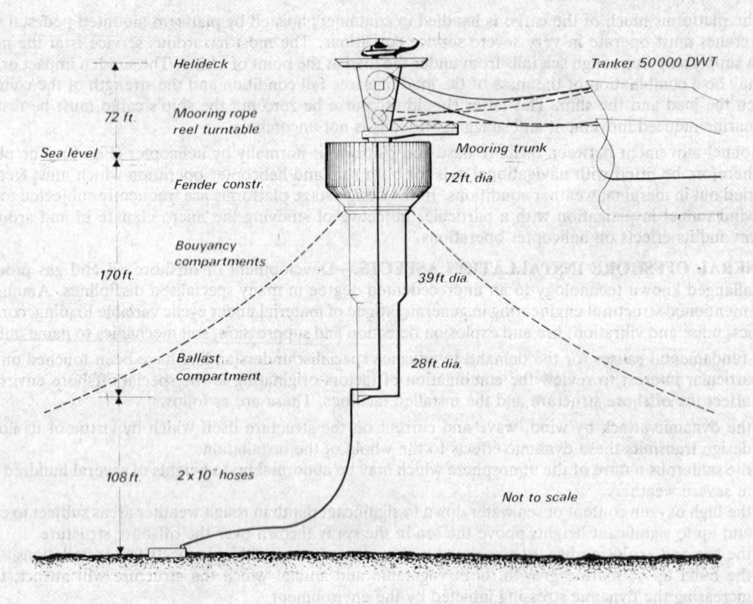

FIG. 10.—Single Point Tanker Loading Buoy.

TRANSPORT OF OIL.—There are two basic transport systems:

(i) by direct shipment by oiltanker from offshore to onshore terminal.

(ii) by seabed pipeline to an onshore terminal where oil can be loaded into tankers, or near which there is a refinery.

Both systems require that a pumping plant is available at the offshore platform and a pipeline connection to the seabed down the columns of the structures. The seabed pipeline is then constructed away from the base of the platform to a tanker loading buoy or to a landfall onshore.

SINGLE POINT MOORING BUOYS.—In the postwar period tanker sizes increased from the 12,000 and 18,000 dwt tons ships which were in general service at that time. It therefore became increasingly difficult to provide sheltered moorings with alongside berths for the loading and discharge of oil from the larger new ships. A new type of cargo handling system was therefore developed. The basis was a large buoy anchored conventionally with an eight point mooring pattern (Fig. 10). This buoy had a flexible vertical hose connection to the end of a seabed pipeline and to a central vertical pipe in the body of the buoy. The buoy was built to rotate freely around this central pipe like a turntable. Oil could pass from the centre tube through a carefully machined gland system to a delivery flange on the periphery of the turntable. From this flange a floating flexible hose carried oil along the surface of the sea to a receiving manifold on board the tanker. The tanker was moored by a single cable to the turntable adjacent to the floating hose flange connection. The environmental forces of wind, wave and current would act on the tanker and make it weathervane around the buoy so that the ship would head up into the waves, the position in which the effects of the environment cause the least response of the vessel. This **SINGLE POINT MOORING BUOY SYSTEM** was developed to the point where very large crude oil tankers could load and discharge up to 15,000 tonnes of crude oil per hour in sea states with two to three metre waves (Fig. 11). The same principle has been used to develop buoys with special configurations which permit oil loading into tankers to continue in much rougher seastates and in much greater

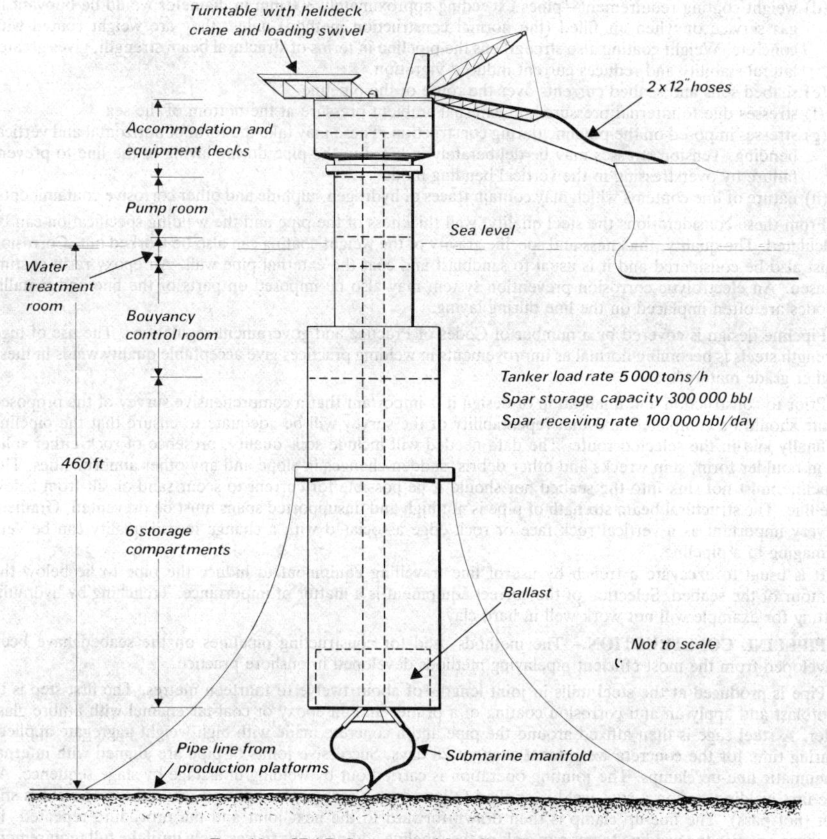

FIG. 11.—SPAR Storage and Loading Buoy Mooring.

depths of water. This is done by using a buoy body with a much greater draught and a low water plane area. One such buoy loads ships through a hose connection suspended from a crane high above the tanker bow. The crane deck rotates similarly to the earlier buoys. The rough water buoy mentioned contains oil storage capacity in a compartmented cylinder below the water (40,000 m^3) and can continue loading tankers in wave heights up to approximately six metres.

Alternative devices have also been developed which depend on a single gravity anchor with a rigid leg articulated to it with a universal coupling at the seabed. Oil flows through the anchor, up the fixed leg, which is kept vertical by buoyancy attached near the top, and thereafter to the tanker which is moored to a swivel at the top of the vertical leg. The rotating principle is retained.

Use of any of these loading devices in deeper, more severe environments near offshore platforms will predicate the use of tankers with modified oil receiving manifolds. It is also important that only low vapour pressure crudes are handled in this way; there are many unsolved problems regarding the transfer of high vapour pressure cargoes offshore. Purpose built tankers are necessary to handle this type of fluid, flexible pipe technology is scarcely adequate to this service and the hazardous nature of the fluids with their associated low flash points make a fundamentally safe operation, difficult. The transfer of gas is not considered economically or technologically viable at the present time.

PIPELINES.—The seabed pipeline is the simplest and most cost-effective method of transporting large volumes of oil and gas from an offshore field provided the volumes exceed certain levels dependent on the distance offshore. Factors which must be considered in the design of a pipeline are as follows:

(a) pressure rating—this will normally be higher for gas than for oil pipelines for commercial reasons.
(b) flow rate requirement.
(c) water depth.

(d) weight coating requirement—pipes exceeding approximately 300 mm in diameter would be buoyant in gas service or when air filled (the normal construction method) unless they are weight coated with concrete. Weight coating also strengthens the pipeline in terms of structural beam strength, gives greater lateral stability and reduces current induced vibration.
(e) seabed soils and seabed currents over the route of the pipeline.
(f) stresses due to internal pressure and external ambient pressure at the bottom of the sea.
(g) stresses imposed on the pipeline during construction. These may take the form of horizontal and vertical bending. Tension stresses may be deliberately induced in the pipe during laying of the line to prevent failure by overstressing in the vertical bending mode.
(h) nature of line contents which may contain traces of hydrogen sulphide and other corrosive contaminents.

From these considerations the steel quality, wall thickness of the pipe and the welding specification can be calculated. The quality, thickness and specific gravity of the weight coating can also be worked out. Corrosion must also be considered and it is usual to sandblast and coat the external pipe wall. An epoxy resin coating is used. An electrolytic corrosion prevention system may also be imposed on parts of the line and metallic anodes are often implaced on the line during laying.

Pipeline design is covered by a number of Codes of Practice and government regulations. The use of high strength steels is becoming normal as improvements in welding practices give acceptable quality welds in these higher grade materials.

Prior to construction and finalisation of design it is important that a comprehensive survey of the proposed route should be completed and that repeatability of the survey will be adequate to ensure that the pipeline is finally laid in the selected route. The data needed will include soils quality, presence of rock either solid or in boulder form, ship wrecks and other debris, sudden changes in slope and any other abnormalities. The pipeline must not sink into the seabed nor should it be possible for current to scour sand or silt from below the line. The structural beam strength of pipe is not high and unsupported spans must be prevented. Gradient is very important as a vertical rock face or rock edge associated with a change in soil quality can be very damaging to a pipeline.

It is usual to excavate a trench by use of line travelling equipment to induce the pipe to lie below the contour of the seabed. Selection of the correct equipment is a matter of importance. Trenching by hydraulic jetting for example will not work well in hard clay.

PIPELINE CONSTRUCTION.—The methods used for constructing pipelines on the seabed have been developed from the most efficient pipelaying methods developed in onshore practice.

Pipe is produced at the steel mills in joint lengths of about twelve to fourteen metres. The first step is to shotblast and apply an anti-corrosion coating of a primer and an epoxy or coal-tar enamel with a fibre glass filler. A steel cage is then affixed around the pipe and a concrete made with high weight aggregate applied. Curing time for the concrete weightcoat is about 28 days. Successive joints of pipe are aligned with internal pneumatic line-up clamps. The jointing operation is carried out by welding in a stage by stage sequence. At the first welding station a root weld is applied followed by a second bead put on while the root weld is still hot (hot pass). The line-up clamp is then drawn forward to the next joint and the procedure repeated. In onshore practice the welding teams move along the pipeline adding welds successively until the full requirement has been completed. Offshore the several welding stations are set up on a large barge and the barge is moved forward by winching against prelaid anchors. The barge carries the pipe on rollers to permit this forward movement. There may be five or six welding stations in use as the pipelaying barge is winched along one pipe joint (twelve metres) at a time. The jointing operation is completed with a radiograph and final inspection of each weld and a manually applied primer and epoxy coating. As can be seen the welding, radiography and field joint coating take place simultaneously.

Various systems of automatic welding are being introduced and in one or two instances double jointing of pipe is also being carried out before the pipe is transported to the laybarge. This allows the use of pipelengths of about twenty-five metres thereby speeding up the construction progress.

Central to this whole operation is the construction vessel known as the laybarge. The first of these vessels were flat bottomed barges. Joints of pipe were stacked at the bow of the vessel, the pipe ends were bevelled and then using a system of rollers, pipe would be loaded, joint by joint, to a pipe roller track mounted in many cases on outriggers over the starboard side of the craft. As the vessel moved forward the pipe followed guides over the stern down a space frame ramp equipped also with rollers in a Vee format. This frame became known as the 'stinger'. The operation was controlled from a control tower from which the eight or ten anchor winches were started and stopped. Anchor handling tugs were continuously in use moving anchors particularly forward and aft of the vessel so that the barge was always anchored and had sufficient winch cable on the drums to permit regular movement and continuous operation.

As water depths and the severity of the average seastate increased with advance offshore, new generations of pipelay vessels were designed and brought into service. Ship shaped vessels with some self propulsion were introduced but these were still responsive to wave conditions and the semi-submersible configuration soon followed. These vessels were very stable work platforms and pipelaying became possible in wave heights of five metres or more. A disadvantage of these larger craft and particularly the semi-submersibles is the height of the deck pipetrack above the water surface.

As water depths further increased and the demand for larger pipe diameters became more insistent, the length of pipe and more importantly the weight of pipe, hanging between the end of the laybarge and the seabed increased disproportionately. The length of pipeline on the stinger and the unsupported length between the toe of the stinger and the seabed (the S-bend section) became so long that self-weight of the pipe caused it to buckle and fail. This problem was overcome by introduction of tensioning devices which clutched the pipe and induced a longitudinal tension in the S-bend. The length of the stingers was also modified to improve the situation and one important improvement was the invention of a multi unit articulated stinger with adjustable buoyancy along its length. This permitted the constructor to adjust the curvature of the stinger and optimise the S-bend form relative to water depth.

As distances offshore increased pipe handling from onshore base to offshore vessel became more taxing, and in the rougher offshore conditions, pipe transfer from supply boat to laybarge became very difficult. Larger pipehaul ships were introduced, larger cranes were installed on the laybarges and some use was made of containers with ten or more joints of pipe packaged into single lifts.

Other variations of the main pipelay methods have been introduced. It was found that smaller diameter pipe could be deformed beyond the steel yield point and reformed into straight pipe. This developed into a method of pipelaying whereby pipe is constructed in long straight lengths onshore. It is then reeled up on a large diameter spool. This is mounted on a barge or ship. At the offshore location (the foot of a platform for example), the end of the reeled pipe is attached by wire cable to a seabed fixed point and the ship towed forwards. The linepipe is unreeled through a hydraulic pipe straightening assembly and delivered over a stinger to the bottom of the sea. Offshore welding is virtually reduced to joining successive reel lengths and great lengths of pipe can be laid rapidly. Reel barge systems are not suitable for concrete coated pipe although bend resistant anti corrosion coatings have been proven. The reel barge has been used to lay pipe up to 300 mm diameter and within limits it is possible to adjust the weight of the pipe by increasing the wall thickness.

PIPELINE TRENCHING.—Pipelines on the bed of the sea are subject to damage from ocean currents (vortex induced vibration and scouring), from trawling activity and from anchor dropping from passing ships. This latter problem is more serious adjacent to offshore platforms and recovery of anchors can be more damaging than the original placement. For these reasons anchor dropping near to platforms is very closely monitored. To reduce to some extent the damaging of seabed pipelines, particularly close to shore in shallower water, it is common practice to dig a trench into which the pipeline is lowered. These trenches are excavated by use of 'bury barges'. A hydraulic jetting assembly is equipped to travel along the pipeline using the line as a track. Heavy duty pumps are mounted on the ship and the jets blast a Vee shaped trench under the pipe. This system is not universally successful and other forms of equipment are used for different soil conditions. Fluidisation of seabed sands can be accomplished by pumping water into sand, causing a 'quicksand' condition into which the pipe will sink under its own weight. Near to shore ploughing of a trench is frequently used and the pipe laid in the trench afterwards. Rock blasting is also used when hard rock is encountered and cannot be avoided. A line travelling machine has also been developed with rotating cutter heads which can cut into the harder clays.

Overall the jetting system is the most commonly used. Frequent inspection of the work and measurement of the trench is necessary. This is accomplished by divers and mobile underwater television monitors.

UNDERWATER DEVELOPMENT.—The progress of the offshore search for hydrocarbons into deeper waters has been accompanied by massive increases in the cost of fixed platforms and a great interest has developed in the possibility of oilfield development using seabed installations. As mentioned previously the practice of completing wells at the bottom of the sea has already been proven.

Before discussing the progress made in this specialised technology a review of the drilling production process will be of assistance. The oil and gas flows up from the reservoir through the tubing in the bore hole. After passing the well-head christmas tree it is piped to an oil/gas separator. Thereafter the oil and gas are handled separately. As the well fluid pressure decreases through a critical level gas emerges from the liquid and the bulk of fluid in flow increases rapidly. This in turn increases the friction losses in the flow system and assuming constant pipeline diameter, reduces flowrate significantly. It is also usually essential (except in the case of dry natural gas) to reduce fluid pressure to near atmospheric to ensure full separation. Eventually, the valuable hydrocarbons must be transported to a point of sale and the valueless components wasted. Subsea installation will be required to fulfil these same process functions recognising that at some stage in the process the hydrocarbons will have to be brought through the water surface. The selection of this point in the process is a question of economics, but it does seem that a platform of some type will always be an essential feature of any field development plan.

Power requirements are a further factor, and it has been shown that to generate power on a floating platform and transmit it to the seabed by power cable is more economic than to install and operate a power generator at the seabed for other than minor power demands.

There are many different approaches to subsea development but they can be divided into three general classifications: (1) diver dependent wet systems; (ii) one atmosphere enclosed dry systems; (iii) diverless wet systems using remote operated manipulator intervention methods with, possibly, diver back up.

A further system is under evaluation which seeks to utilise a water-filled enclosed system at the seabed. This system is based on the incompressibility of water to obviate some of the clumsiness of pressuring and depressuring air or gas filled enclosed systems.

Much of the philosophy of underwater engineering is dependent on the ability of divers to approach and execute work in specific water depths. Diving technology is discussed elsewhere in this chapter. To date little progress has been made in the technology of separation underwater although one or two trials have been made.

One feature of oil production is the need to measure reservoir conditions and the need to repair wells during their service life. The operator requires to ensure vertical access to each borehole so that re-entry can be achieved at possibly frequent intervals (once or twice per year). Io recent years there has been much concern at the cost of re-entering a subsea well, merely to take simple pressure and temperature measurements, with an expensive semi-submersible drilling vessel. Systems have therefore been developed which allow the operator

FIG. 12.—Derrick Ship Lifting 1800 tons load.

to pump tools through the flow line and down the tubing in the borehole. Tools have been manufactured which measure and record pressure, temperature and flowrates and even to carry out minor repair work such as replacement of downhole safety control valves. After completion of the job, flow is reversed and the tool recovered back to the tool launching manifold. These 'through the flowline' techniques may prove invaluable to successful subsea oilfield development.

Underwater technology is in its infancy and can be compared to space technology in that man is endeavouring to operate processes and mechanical equipment and to work himself in an environment where he is unable to breathe, and in which the ambient pressure would cause death, without adequate complex measures being taken to make living and working viable in so hostile an environment.

GENERAL OFFSHORE SERVICES.—There are a number of services which must be provided in offshore development which have made remarkable technological advance in the recent past. These include offshore derrick ships (crane barges), diving, submersibles and submarines (manned and unmanned), underwater television and dynamic positioning of vessels.

DERRICK SHIPS.—From the early use of barge mounted cranes it became apparent that the offshore industry would need larger cranes which could lift heavier loads to greater heights above the water (Fig. 12). From flat bottomed vessels which could lift possibly 50 tons to heights of 15 to 20 m, the industry has progressed through ship-shaped, non-propelled derrick ships to cranes mounted on semi-submersible work ships. Vessels with dynamic assisted positioning are already in use. The cranes mounted on these vessels have rated capacities of as much as 3,000 tonnes and can lift packages to heights of 50 m or more above the sea (Fig. 13).

FIG. 13.—Semi-submersible Derrick Ship Baldur.

These semi-submersible mounted cranes can perform in sea-states far exceeding anything previously considered feasible and the real possibility is emerging of offshore construction work continuing through the North Sea winter.

SUBMERSIBLES AND SUBMARINES.—The increasing demand for engineering work at the seabed such as inspection of structures, pipelines and other installations, surveys of sites, repair of pipelines, making of pipeline connections and recovery of dropped objects, has brought about remarkable advances in the technology of manned and unmanned submersible craft, coupled with improvements in video technology, cameras, manipulators and sundry other subsea aids. Improvements are being made continually to these crafts in terms of endurance, reliability and in the launch and recovery systems used by the service mother ships handling the submersibles. Some of the most recent vessels also include for diver lockout and recovery. Not least among the achievements has been the introduction of the free swimming television camera which can be 'flown' from a surface service vessel and produce video tape records at the control room for later evaluation.

Subsea colour photography has also shown significant improvements and more use is being made of stereoscopic photography.

DIVING TECHNOLOGY.—The ability to work under water has been an ongoing challenge and objective to man down centuries of history. The advances made in diving technology over the recent past have been unprecedented. Intensive research by governments and private industry have gradually lowered the water depths in which man can overcome the physiological hazards of living and breathing in great ambient pressures. Cost effective tasks have been completed in 300 m or more of waterdepth and diving inspections have been carried out in double that depth.

At the same time tools have been developed for use by divers in these great depths, although most of the divers' work has been associated with inspection and recovery of objects from the seabed. The technology of living and working in high pressure environments has, however, also been successfully applied to work in dry chamber habitats, principally in connection with pipeline repair. A purpose constructed chamber is clamped around the damaged line, probably with the assistance of divers working in the water, and the chamber is then filled with an inert gas. Welding personnel are then lowered and locked out into the chamber from a diving bell and the repair accomplished by welding in the dry, but nevertheless in the ambient pressure. Welding in water is not a developed technology.

A further development has been the introduction of pressure resistant suits which are flexible and articulated in such a way that a man can dive and move freely in the suit whilst enjoying a one atmosphere environment inside the suit. The unit is self contained with respect to life support and the suits have a rating to carry out work in 500 m or more of water depth.

DYNAMIC POSITIONING.—The offshore industry will continue to advance its operations into deeper and rougher waters. As a result, the use of conventional ships' anchoring systems, with heavy anchors and very long and cumbersome moorings made of chain or wire cables, are becoming too expensive and time consuming to handle for a number of operations. The use of propellors, additional to the main propulsion system, distributed around the ship's hull to provide thrust in any direction is becoming a widespread practice with two general objectives.

(1) to provide added and improved manoevreability and control in the operation of vessels, principally smaller vessels, when alongside platforms or larger ships or in congested port situations.
(2) to keep a large vessel steady in a defined position above a selected seabed location.

In the first application this added control may be achieved solely by use of thruster propellors in the bow of the vessel which provide lateral force to keep the ship headed into the sea when it has negligible seaway, or when the vessle is moored, and it is desirable to reduce drift which can be achieved by keeping the mooring in tension by exerting force in a contrary direction.

In the second application eight or more thrusters may be mounted all round a ship or semi-submersible drilling vessel to enable it to remain in position whilst drilling a seabed borehole. Dynamically positioned vessels are coming into increased use in offshore floating drilling, lifting, pipelining and diving support operations. The basis of the system is to provide a method of informing the propulsion system of its position relative to the required position and using a fast response control assembly to direct and regulate the thrusters so that the ship is continually returned to the desired location.

Location definition is usually obtained by means of acoustic pingers or reflectors set on the seabed from which the ship obtains responses, and which can then be translated into exact distances by computer, or by means of a taut wire which is required to remain vertical at all times. Deviation from the vertical is measured and computed into a direct measurement of drift. Fed with this information offset from the desired location, the ships computer can determine the instructions which must be give to each propeller thruster in terms of revs/minute and direction of thrust.

INSPECTION AND MAINTENANCE.—When viewed as a highly compact, complex process plant the above water facilities installed on an offshore platform are similar to an onshore chemical plant. The need for continuous monitoring and inspection is evident and although the severe environment can provide conditions of rapid deterioration of plant and equipment, the major demands are for careful planning and scheduling of inspection and maintenance to reduce downtime to a minimum, in order to optimise returns on the very high capital investment.

Underwater inspection and repair pose a totally different problem and an area of technology with novel demands on human skills, and for tools to accomplish the tasks efficiently. The greater proportion of an offshore structure lies below the surface of the sea and seabed pipelines and underwater production installations create their own demands on mans ability to inspect and maintain them in working condition.

Underwater structures accumulate great quantities of marine growth, which must be cleaned off before inspection can proceed, and steel structures must be checked for corrosion, fatigue cracking and damage inflicted by falling objects. Each joint must be examined on a regular basis and if possible records kept of its condition, so that deterioration can be recognised.

The development of underwater TV cameras which can be remotely operated and the collateral ability to record by video tape has been a major forward step in this work, but there is still a pressing need to improve the quality and speed of underwater inspection and this is the subject of a wide ranging research effort.

Underwater repair is an area with even less background of meaningful experience. Methods of welding in dry, pressurised chambers have been introduced but the great cost of mounting a repair activity underwater, creates its own demands for improvements in the skills and equipment available for this category of work.

LEGISLATION AND CODES OF PRACTICE.—The emergence of a major industry offshore has created a number of important legal problems of interest both nationally and internationally. Industry has moved out from land far beyond the traditional and well established confines of territorial waters and into areas where the nations of the world recognised the freedom of the seas. The prior rights of international shipping and fishing industries were in general supported worldwide. The new offshore activity could not proceed and could not be allowed to proceed without regulation and as a result there are now international agreements with respect to sovereignty over the continental shelf. This is in general terms the area of the sea with water depths less than 200 m adjacent to a land mass. Complex rules exist for defining median lines between neighbouring countries. In the wake of these international agreements and conventions, the respective individual governments have introduced legislation to control offshore activity within the continental shelf areas under their jurisdiction. These regulations in principle express government concern for the health and welfare of personnel working offshore, safety of the installations and their operations with respect to preservation of life and conservation of national resources, national interest in taxation and protection of the environment from pollution and misuse.

Each country has taken its individual stance on the questions raised and many have progressed their interest into promotion and protection of home industry and into matters of direct concern to the engineer, such as scrutiny and certification by objective third party review of designs of structures and installations, inspection and operating practices and maintenance/repair activities.

In these latter areas of concern a great deal of reliance has been placed on a wide range of industry Codes of Practice and national Standards and Specifications principally the work of recognised professional institutions and controlling bodies. All offshore designers and operators must acquire familiarity with the governing legislation, codes of practice and standards specifications applicable to the discipline in which they are active.

ECONOMICS.—The costs of an offshore development programme are extremely high and, as the bulk of the investment must be completed before any oil or gas is produced, it is of paramount importance that construction times and costs incurred before income is generated must be minimised. Of equal importance is the need to plan the investment and maintain progress on time. The role of the engineer in the fields of estimating, planning and scheduling has developed a new importance to the success of offshore ventures and an understanding of economics in commercial industry is becoming essential.

The operating costs of offshore activity is also very high and an understanding of economics is again of great importance to ensure that operations are not continued beyond the point of commercial viability which must include consideration of the costs of abandonment of an offshore developed installation.

Most governments devote some part of their legislation to an insistence on removal of all offshore installations and leaving the seabed in its original condition after finalisation of commercial operations. The technology of well abandonment is well known but the removal and scrapping of major offshore constructions will be a costly project in its own right and will require significant engineering consideration when the time comes.

CONCLUSION.—It will be seen from this review of offshore engineering that the technology is in fact the application of known engineering disciplines in an unusual environment. Offshore conditions can be divided into two contrasting divisions. Above the sea surface presents a very different challenge from that which pertains below the surface and the troubled interface called traditionally 'between wind and water' is a further sub division with its own special engineering problems.

The specialist engineer from almost every engineering discipline is required to apply his intelligence, expertise and skills to the challenges presented by offshore development, and improvement and refinement of those skills will be of continuing and increasing importance.

MINING ENGINEERING

Minerals—The Metallic Minerals—The National Coal Board—Systems of Mining—Systems of Coal Mining—Mechanisation of Coal Getting—Ground Movement and Support—Shafts—Principles of Mining Subsidence—Winding—Ventilation—and Firedamp Drainage—Dust Hazards—Electrical Signalling—Underground Radio Communication—Coal Preparation—Preparation of Mineral Ores.

Mining engineering concerns the extraction of minerals from the earth's crust, and their initial treatment at the site of mining to a form suitable for further processing. This Section deals with the occurrence of minerals, and with the methods, machines and other equipment used in extracting the minerals. That includes the location and evaluation of a mineral deposit, gaining access to it, the extraction of the mineral, and its subsequent preparation. In its modern sense, mining engineering draws on many other branches of engineering and applied sciences. The professional mining engineer is required to have an understanding of geology, surveying, mineral processing, mine economics, management techniques and mining law, in addition to the planning and control of the actual mining operation. Many aspects of the day to day running of a mine, for example, ore grade control, production scheduling etc, now require a knowledge of computer techniques.

MINERALS

A mineral is defined geologically as a naturally formed substance which possesses a definite chemical composition and a definite atomic structure. But although a mineral is a definite chemical compound or element, the term is often used in a more extended sense. Many of the most commonly mined products—coal, oil, phosphates and building materials—are mixtures of several compounds and are not strictly defined as minerals. However, for practical purposes, minerals may be considered as any materials of economic value that can be extracted from the earth. The extraction of minerals can be grouped into three broad categories of activity:—(1) The mining of metals. (2) The extraction of non-metals (such as salt, sulphur, sand and gravel). (3) The mining of (or drilling for) energy materials (coal, oil, uranium ores, oil shales, tar sands, geothermal energy and gas).

The deepest mines approach depths of 3·8 km beneath the earth's surface. Oil and gas exploration wells have been drilled as deep as 6 km, but these operations are still limited to the outermost layer of the earth. From studies of earthquake phenomena, it is possible to determine the physical properties of the different layers of the earth. The thickness of the outermost *crust*, made up of the rock types apparent at the earth's surface, averages some 32 km, barely half of 1% of the radius of the earth. Extending beneath the crust is a 3,000 km thick layer of denser material termed the *mantle*. Finally, at the centre of the earth is the *core*, some 3,500 km in radius, which is thought to consist of nickel-iron at such high temperature and pressure that it behaves like a fluid.

Nearly 99% by weight of the earth's crust is made up of only eight of the 92 naturally-occurring elements. These are, in decreasing order of abundance:—oxygen (50%); silicon (26%); aluminium (7·54%); iron (4·2%); calcium (3·3%); sodium (2·5%); potassium (2·25%); and magnesium (2·25%). Hydrogen, titanium, chlorine, carbon, phosphorus and sulphur are present in quantities from 1·0% to 0·1%, in the order given. All of the remaining elements together constitute less than 1% of the earth's crust.

ROCK-FORMING MINERALS.—The majority of the rocks forming the accessible portions of the globe consist of the minerals listed below, associated in variable proportions. Some rocks are homogeneous, consisting of one mineral species only, but most are heterogeneous, containing two or more.

The common rock-forming minerals are:—quartz; feldspar group; mica group; amphibole group; pyroxene group; olivine; garnet; calcite; dolomite; rock salt; gypsum; apatite; magnetite; and pyrite. Rocks are classified according to their mode of formation into three major groups:—

IGNEOUS ROCKS.—These are formed from solidified magmas, which are molten mixtures of minerals (often rich in gases) injected into the upper layers of the crust. Igneous rocks are sub-divided according to their mineral content, origin and texture. If magmas consolidate beneath the surface they form *intrusive* rocks with typical structures that may be exposed later by erosion. Magmas reaching the surface form *extrusive* rocks, such as volcanic lavas. Igneous rocks usually contain ferromagnesian minerals (those rich in iron and magnesium, such as the amphiboles) and feldspars (or feldspar-like minerals). Many contain quartz. Igneous rocks rich in light minerals (in terms of both colour and specific gravity) such as quartz and potash feldspar, are termed acidic. Those richer in ferromagnesian minerals are called basic rocks. The texture of igneous rocks varies from coarsely crystalline to glassy rocks with no visible crystalline structure at all.

Intrusive rocks are formed as magma cools, a gradual process in which the more volatile constituents remain as fluids longer. Those that cool at depth are more coarsely crystalline than near-surface intrusions. The best known of the deeper (plutonic) intrusive rocks is *granite*, formed mainly of potash feldspar (approx. 60%), quartz (30%), together with mica or the amphibole hornblende.

A large number of rocks are extrusive, the most common being *lava*. This molten material pours out through fissures and volcanoes, to spread as lava flow or build up cones. Like intrusive rocks, they grade in colour from light (acidic) to dark (basic), and in composition from those rich in quartz to those with none. Because of rapid cooling, the textures are generally fine-grained.

SEDIMENTARY ROCKS.—Sedimentary rocks are built up of the remains of pre-existing rocks, or are deposited from solution by chemical or organic agencies. Nearly all are composed of minerals transported from their place of origin to a new place of deposition by the action of weathering—by running water, wind, waves, currents, ice or gravity. Once deposited, sediments are consolidated into layers termed beds or strata. The most common sedimentary rocks are *sandstone* (quartz grains cemented by silica, calcite or iron oxide), *shale* or *mudstone* (clays consolidated into rock), *limestone* (mostly calcite of marine origin), and *conglomerate* (rounded pebbles, usually of quartz, cemented in a matrix of finer material).

The structure of rocks is not uniform, but is commonly apparent as banding, a feature known as stratification. This layering is due to variations in the physical character of the sediments; on a smaller scale, the property of sedimentary rocks to split into layers parallel to the original bedding is termed lamination.

METAMORPHIC ROCKS.—These are those which have been modified under the influence of heat, pressure and chemical change. These changes usually bring about a new crystalline structure, the formation of new minerals and sometimes a coarsening of the texture. The main agents of metamorphism are pressure and temperature (both of which increase with depth in the earth's crust), crustal movements, igneous activity or permeation by gases and fluids from igneous material, and the percolation of mineral-bearing ground water.

Simple metamorphic rocks are those formed by the direct alteration of sedimentary rocks, where the changes are mainly recrystallisation. *Marbles* are recrystallised limestones, often tinted by iron oxides, carbon or serpentine. *Quartzites* are metamorphosed sandstones which have recrystallised, usually obliterating their original grain structure. *Slate* results from the metamorphism of shale. *Schists* are examples of more highly metamorphosed rocks. They frequently contain a considerable amount of mica, which imparts a distinct planar structure (schistosity). Schists are named after their most characteristic mineral.

CLASSIFICATION OF MINERAL DEPOSITS.—Many systems have been devised in the past to classify mineral deposits. One of the more practical mineral classification systems is that based on the economic use to which the minerals are put by man. Using these criteria, *ores* are defined strictly as metals or metal-bearing minerals that can be recovered at a profit. In common usage, however, the term includes some of the non-metallic minerals such as sulphur and fluorspar. *Ore minerals* are compounds valued for their economic content of metals. Economic minerals may be divided into the following groups:—

(*a*) Ore minerals: those valued for their economic content of metals, occurring either as compounds or in the native state.

(*b*) Energy minerals: those used as fuels. They include the different varieties of coal, asphalts, bitumen and other solid hydrocarbons, mineral oils, natural gas, oil shales and tar sands.

(*c*) Salts: the halides, sulphates, carbonates, silicates, phosphates, etc. of the alkaline and alkaline-earth metals.

(*d*) Industrial materials and building stone: members of this group should more properly be considered as rocks rather than minerals. Examples include granite, slate and limestone.

With regard to their mode of occurrence, many systems of classification of mineral deposits have been devised. Systems used in the past have emphasised form, texture and the mineral content of ore deposits, whereas modern classifications have developed around the theories of ore genesis or environments of deposition. The system that is most widely used by economic geologists is that due to Lindgren, originally propounded in 1913, and subsequently modified and extensively revised by others. The system is based on the assumption that the composition of a particular mineral association may be defined by the environmental conditions (depth and temperature) under which the minerals were deposited. Table 1 gives a revised version of the Lindgren classification.

STRATIGRAPHIC COLUMN.—Although the deposition of sedimentary rocks has been a continuous process, it is convenient to divide geological history into periods marked by the formation of distinctive groups of rock types and by the nature of the fossils they contain. From a knowledge of the sequence in which sedimentary rocks have been deposited, a *stratigraphic column* (a table of the main periods of geological history) has been compiled. The most important divisions are marked by breaks or interruptions (unconformities) in the continuity of deposition.

TABLE 1.—LINDGREN CLASSIFICATION OF MINERAL DEPOSITS

Depositional Conditions	*Temperature*	*Pressure*	*Examples*
(1) Deposits produced by chemical processes of concentration			
(A) In magmas by processes of differentiation			
1. Magmatic segregation deposits	700–1500°C	Very high	Chromite deposits of the Bushveld complex S. Africa
2. Pegmatites	Moderate to very high	Very high	Important source of some of the rarer metals
(B) In bodies of rocks			
1. Epigenetic deposits (concentration by introduction of foreign substances)			
(A) Origin dependent on igneous activity			
(i) By direct igneous emanations			
(*a*) From effusive bodies (sublimates, fumaroles)	100–600°C	Atmospheric to moderate	Stibnite (Sb_2S_3) deposits at Solfatara, Italy
(*b*) From intrusive bodies (igneous metamorphic) deposits)	500–800°C	Very high	Magnetite deposits of the Iron Springs district, Utah
(ii) By hot ascending waters			
(*a*) Hypothermal deposits (deposition and concentration at great depth)	300–500°C	Very high	Kolar gold field, India
(*b*) Mesothermal deposits (deposition and concentration at intermediate depths)	200–300°C	High	Copper deposits at Butte, Montana
(*c*) Epithermal deposits (deposition and concentration at slight depth)	50–200°C	Moderate	Almaden mercury mines, Spain
(*d*) Telethermal deposits (deposition and concentration from nearly spent solutions)	Low	Low	Zinc-lead deposits of Upper Silesia, Poland
(*e*) Xenothermal deposits (deposition and concentration at shallow depths but high temperatures)	Low to high	Atmospheric to moderate	Tin-silver deposits of Potosi, Bolivia
(B) Origin independent of igneous activity (deposited by circulating ground waters at moderate or slight depth)	Up to 100°C	Moderate	Horn silver mine, Utah
2. By concentration of substances contained in the rocks themselves			
(*a*) Concentration by dynamic and regional metamorphism	Up to 400°C	High	Marmeton iron deposit. Marmora, Ontario
(*b*) Concentration by ground water of deeper circulation	0–100°C	Moderate	Copper deposits at Miami, Arizona
(*c*) Concentration by rock decay and residual weathering near surface	0–100°C	Atmospheric to moderate	Nickel laterite deposits, New Caledonia
(C) In bodies of surface waters			
(1) By interaction of solutions	0–70°C	Moderate	
(*a*) Inorganic reactions			Phosphate beds, Black Sea, USSR
(*b*) Organic reactions			Ironstones of the East Midlands, UK
(2) Evaporite deposits (by evaporation of solvents)			Potash deposits. Boulby, Yorkshire, UK
(2) Deposits produced by mechanical processes of concentration	Moderate	Moderate	Witwatersrand gold-uranium reefs, S Africa

In this way, rocks have been divided into six main divisions, known as eras. These are successively divided into periods, series and stages. According to the scheme most commonly adopted, the principal eras and periods of the stratigraphic column are as follows:

Eras	*Periods*	Equivalent alternative systems	Age (years × 10^6)	
Quaternary	Pleistocene		1	Era of human development
Tertiary	Pliocene	Neogene	25	Development of mammals
	Miocene		60	
	Oligocene	Palaeogene	135	
	Eocene			
Mesozoic	Cretaceous			
	Jurassic		180	
	Triassic		225	
Upper Palaeozoic	Permian		270	
	Carboniferous	Pennsylvanian Mississippian	350	Development of coal measures
	Devonian		400	
Lower Palaeozoic	Silurian		440	
	Ordovician		500	
	Cambrian		600	
Proterozoic & Archaeozoic	Precambrian		3,000+	

The minerals which are extracted in mining operations may be formed by any of the geological processes which make up rocks themselves. Thus mineral deposits may be igneous, sedimentary or metamorphic in origin, and may be found in rocks of all types and ages.

THE METALLIC MINERALS

Of the many naturally-occurring minerals, only about one hundred are of economic importance. However, every mineral has its own special characteristics which determine not only the use to which its constituents are put, but also its mode of occurrence and the methods by which it is mined and processed. Some of the most important metallic minerals, (those extracted principally for their metal content), are considered below.

IRON ORES.—Iron is the fourth most plentiful element in the earth's crust. The world currently produces around 900 million metric tonnes of iron ore annually which is used in the manufacture of steel and other iron alloys. There are four principal forms of iron ore: *magnetite*—Fe_3O_4, 72·4% iron content; *hematite*—Fe_2O_3, 70·0% iron; *limonite*—$2Fe_2O_3 3H_2O$, 60 to 70% iron content according to the degree of hydration; and *siderite*—$FeCO_3$, 50% iron content.

In practice, most of these ores are adulterated by waste material (gangue) which may reduce the iron content. Depending on the location, the difficulties of mining and their proximity to shipping facilities, the economic iron content of ores may vary greatly. In the case of magnetite, which may be more easily concentrated than hematite, it may be as low as 25–35%. The typical range of iron contents in the world's major iron ore deposits is 40–50%.

The chief sources of iron ore concentrates are as follows:—USSR, 28% of world iron ore production; China, 14·5%; Brazil, 13%; Australia, 11%; USA, 5·5%; China, 14%; USA, 6·5%; India, 5%; Canada, 4·4%; and South Africa, 3%.

A number of the world's largest iron ore mining operations have been developed only in recent years. These include the deposits in the Hamersley, Pilbara and Mt Goldsworthy regions of Western Australia; the Aguas Claras deposits in Brazil; and the Knob Lake and Carol Lake operations in north-eastern Canada, all of which have been brought into production since 1945. Deposits which have been in production longer include the Mesabi Range deposits of the Lake Superior region of the USA; the limonitic Jurassic iron ores of France, Luxemburg and the UK; and the magnetite deposits of Kiruna in Sweden.

Changing economics of iron ore mining have, however, rendered several of the traditionally important iron districts of less significance. Post-war exploration for new deposits has been so successful that iron ore surpluses now exist in many countries. All of the iron ore mines now coming into production are open-cast and operate on a huge scale of production. A declining proportion of mined output is transported as *direct shipping* ore. After mining the ore, crushing and preliminary concentration, it is most frequently converted into *pellets*, whose use has revolutionised the iron and steel industry. Pellets are semi-refined iron ore, prepared by compacting with a cementing material and then baking. Being of uniform size and composition, pellets are the most convenient and economical form of iron ore used in blast furnaces. Another modern alternative to pellets as a charge for blast furnaces is *sinter*, prepared from direct shipping ore by screening a fine fraction of ore and then agglomerating it by a heating process. Well over three-quarters of the total amount of iron ore consumed in the world is agglomerated, sintered or pelletised.

COPPER ORES.—The most familiar of the *base metals* (a group of non-ferrous metals contrasted with the precious metals—gold, silver and platinum) is copper. Beacuse of its excellent thermal and electrical conducting properties, its durability and the ease with which it may be worked, copper has found applications in many industries. Some 60% of all copper is consumed in the electrical industry, and it is also widely used in alloys.

Total Western World mine production of copper (excluding the considerable tonnages of recycled secondary material) amounts to some 6·5 million metric tonnes per year. The major producers of the Western World are Chile (21% of the total), USA (17%), Canada (12%), Zambia (7·5%), Zaire (8%), Peru 6% and Australia 4%.

Some of the more important copper ore minerals are: cuprite—Cu_2O, 80% copper content; chalcopyrite (copper pyrites)—$CuFeS_2$, 34·5% copper; chalcocite (copper glance)—Cu_2S, 80% copper; covellite—CuS, 66·5% copper; bornite—Cu_5FeS_4, 63% copper; tetrahedrite—$(Cu, Fe)_{12}Sb_4S_{13}$, 35·5% copper; tennantite—$(Cu, Fe)_{12}As_4S_{13}$, 35·5% copper; enargite—Cu_3AsS_4, 48·5% copper; malachite—$CuCO_3$, $Cu(OH)_2$ 57·5% copper; azurite—$2Cu_3(CO_3)_2(OH)_2$, 35·5% copper; chrysocolla—$CuSiO_3$, $2H_2O$, 36% copper.

Of all the ore metals, copper occurs in the widest range of geological environments. Copper can occur in primary magmatic deposits (associated with both basic and acidic intrusions) or in sedimentary rocks. In the primary deposits at Sdbury, Ontario, magmatic segregation deposits of copper occur in association with nickel and platinum. In terms of economic importance, the association with acidic rocks is the most important. This association includes the vein type copper deposits (such as those at Butte, Montana), disseminations (as in the 'porphyry' copper deposits of the southern and western USA) and complex ores, frequently in association with pyrite deposits (as typified by the Cerro de Pasco deposits in Peru). In the sedimentary environment, copper deposits may show an apparent relationship with the presence of volcanic rocks (as at White Pine, Michigan) or may be wholly sedimentary in association with no igneous rocks as the source (as for example the deposits of the Copperbelt in Zambia).

LEAD AND ZINC ORES.—Lead and zinc frequently occur in intimate association. The principal ores are the sulphides, galena (PbS) and sphalerite (ZnS), although both metals also occur widely as the oxide and carbonate. Galena has a maximum lead content of 87% when pure, but the mineral frequently contains subordinate amounts of silver in extractable amounts. Production of lead is widely distributed. The major producers are the USSR, Australia, USA, Canada, Mexico and Peru. Many European countries such as Yugoslavia, Spain, Sweden and Ireland produce sizeable amounts. The total Western World mine production of lead is around 2·5 million metric tonnes per year.

Sphalerite (also known as zinc blende) contains 67% zinc when pure, but part of the zinc is usually replaced by iron and a little (up to 5%) cadmium is also present.

The largest proportion of lead production is from marine sedimentary formations ranging in age from 550 to 330 My. The lead is commonly accompanied by zinc and often carries economically significant silver. Most of the USA production is in this class. Broken Hill, Australia, the world's largest individual concentration of lead (with zinc and silver) is in much folded and altered Precambrian sediments. The largest Canadian producer, the Sullivan mine in British Columbia, is also of Precambrian age.

SILVER AND GOLD ORES.—Gold generally occurs as the native metal, often alloyed with silver and other precious metals. Although gold is a rare metal, it has been produced in many parts of the world. By far the largest producer is South Africa, whose enormous Witwatersrand and Orange Free State gold deposits produce two thirds of the world's supply. Next in importance are the USSR, Canada, USA, Brazil, the Philippines, Australia, Chile, Colombia and Papua New Guinea. China is also a significant gold producer with an output thought to be on par with the USA; it is forecast that the PRC could be producing 100 tonnes per year by the end of this decade. The South African deposits consist of gold-bearing conglomerates in which the gold occurs in the metamorphosed sandy matrix cementing the small quartz pebbles. The conglomerate bands (known as 'reefs') occur at several horizons in the Witwatersrand system. The deposits are widely held to be of placer (alluvial) origin, but the mode of emplacement of the gold remains in dispute. Gold also occurs in quartz veins and in alluvial placer deposits, as rounded masses (nuggets), flakes or grains.

Gold production (excluding Communist countries) in 1985 was 1,212·8 metric tonnes. Sizeable amounts of gold are also produced as a by-product of mining other metals such as copper. Because of the high price of gold, mining operations can be carried out economically with exceptionally low grades of ore, containing as little as 0.0001% gold, and at great mining depths. The bulk of the world's gold is now produced from deep underground mines although many new open pit gold mining operations have started up in Australia in recent years (see for example *Mining Magazine* Jan. 1986 pp 16–21, Kidston Gold Mine). In Canada three new underground gold mines have opened up in the Hemlo area of Ontario. (*Mining Magazine* July 1985, pp 20–31). This area is expected to become of increasing importance as a gold producer in future.

For further information on new gold mining projects in the Western world, see 'World Gold Projects' *Mining Magazine*, Sept. 1986, pp 184–205. A description of a gold mine in the USSR was given in this same publication, 'The Muruntau Gold Complex', pp 207–209.

Silver is now obtained largely as a by-product from the mining of copper, lead and zinc, although a few districts such as the Coeur d'Alene area in Idaho and some mining centres in Mexico and Peru are primarily silver ore mining operations. The latter two countries are the world's leading producers of silver, followed by the USSR, Canada, and the USA. Smaller quantities are produced by Australia, Bolivia, Burma, Zaire, Argentina and West Germany. Total new mine production of silver in the Western World in 1985 was 9·950 million kilograms. Silver ores can occur as veins, replacement deposits, contact metamorphic deposits or alluvial deposits. The most important primary ore is the sulphide, argentite (Ag_2S).

ALUMINIUM ORES.—Aluminium is one of the most abundant elements in the earth's crust, and concentrations of its ores are widely distributed. The most important ores are laterites, the products of weathering of tropical soils which contain aluminium in the form of the hydrated oxide, bauxite. The best known economic deposits are in Australia, Jamaica, Guinea, Surinam, Guyana, France (and French Guiana), Greece and Yugoslavia. Total world production of bauxite (excluding the Soviet bloc and China) during 1985 was 77·6 million metric tonnes. The manufacture of aluminium from its ores requires enormous amounts of electrical energy, so that smelters producing aluminium by electrolysis are usually constructed in areas with abundant supplies of cheap electricity.

TIN ORES.—Tin occurs chiefly as the oxide, cassiterite (SnO_2), which is obtained commercially from both vein deposits and alluvial placers. In veins it may be associated with arsenic, silver, copper and iron minerals while, in placers, common associates include ilmenite, monazite, tantalite and columbite. A relatively small number of countries produce the bulk of the world's tin ore. The chief producers are Malaysia,

Metal	*Ores*	*Sources*
Antimony	(Chiefly obtained as a by-product) Stibnite, Sb_2S_3	Veins in quartz
	Tetrahedrite, $(CuFe)_{12}Sb_4S_{13}$	Occurs with other copper ores
Arsenic	Arsenopyrite, FeAsS	Veins, often associated with igneous intrusions
Bismuth	Bismuthinite, Bi_2S_3	Veins, associated with copper, lead, tin and other ores
Chromium	Chromite, Cr_2O_3	Primary mineral in ultrabasic igneous rocks, as in Zimbabwe and New Caledonia. Some 80% of the worlds chromite reserves occur in South Africa's Bushveld complex.
Magnesium	Magnesium chloride, $MgCl_2$, (recovered from ocean brines) Magnesite, $MgCO_3$	Irregular veins in serpentine masses, (as in Greece), and as replacement deposits in dolomites and limestones (as in Austria)
Manganese	Pyrolusite, MnO_2 Psilomelane, $(Ba_3,H_2O)_4Mn_{10}O_{20}$	Sedimentary deposits precipitated by organic processes; also occurs in deep ocean metallic nodules
Mercury	Cinnabar, HgS	Veins or disseminations, associated with volcanic activity, as at Almaden, Spain
Molybdenum	Molybdenite, MoS_2	In granites and pegmatites, as at Climax, Colorado
Nickel	Pentlandite, (Fe,Ni)S	In primary magmatic deposits often associated with other sulphides as at Sudbury, Ontario
	Garnierite, a hydrated nickel magnesium silicate	Formed by the lateritic decay of nickeliferous serpentine, as in New Caledonia and Cuba
Tungsten	Scheelite, $CaWO_4$ Wolframite, $(Fe,Mn)WO_4$	Veins surrounding granite masses, as at King Island, Tasmania
Uranium	Uraninite, UO_2 Carnotite, $K_2O.2U_2O.V_2O_5.H_2O$	Widely distributed. Occurs in veins, disseminations or impregnations
Vanadium		Chiefly a smelter by-product

A compact summary of world geology and distribution of mineral deposits is Duncan R Derry's *'A Concise World Atlas of Geology and Mineral Deposits'* Mining Journal Books, London, 1980. See also EDWARDS, R. AND ATKINSON, K. *Ore Deposit Geology* Chapman & Hall, London, 1986.

Indonesia, Bolivia, Thailand, Brazil and Australia. Total western world production in 1984 was 174,275 tonnes of tin-in-concentrates. The main uses of tin are in the manufacture of tin-plate, and in a number of important alloys.

Many of the numerous other metals and metallic compounds of use to man are obtained as by-products in the extraction of the major metals listed above. Others are extracted separately from their ores in a wide variety of different types of mining. In some cases, certain compounds of a metal are of greater economic value than the metal itself. A list of the principal ores and sources of some of the other metallic minerals of economic importance is given below.

BRITISH COAL.—The National Coal Board (renamed British Coal 1986) was constituted in 1946 and took over the running of the collieries on 1st January, 1947. Its duties are:—(*a*) To work and get coal in Great Britain. (*b*) To secure the efficient development of the coal mining industry: (*c*) To make supplies of coal available without showing 'undue preference' to anyone, and to regulate qualities and sizes, quantities and prices so as best to further the public interest, in all respects. Its duty is also to promote the health, safety and welfare of all employees, and to utilise their practical knowledge. The British Coal board is solely responsible for managing the industry and running it on sound business lines.

For deep mining there are three levels of management, the Board, the Areas and collieries. The collieries, of which there are about 136, are managed by Colliery General Managers, Agent Managers or Colliery Managers (depending on their size and complexity), who are accountable to the Area Director for the safe and efficient management of their collieries. There are 10 Areas, each (except Kent) headed by an Area Director who is directly accountable to the Board. He is assisted by a Deputy Director (Mining) and a Deputy Director (Administration). The Deputy Director (Mining) and Production Managers assist the Area Director in holding Colliery Managers to account. Kent has a General Manager.

At Area Headquarters the main Headquarters departments are represented. The Heads of Area departments are directly responsible to the Area Director and functionally responsible to the Director General or Head of the corresponding department at Headquarters. British Coal has a chairman and from eight to fourteen members, not more than eight being full time. British Coal Headquarter's main duties are to decide on and set objectives for the industry; to lay down the general policy directives and the limitations within which management must work: to hold management to account; and to provide for the future by means of research and development, and the recruitment, training and development of staff.

The main work of Headquarters Departments is to advise British Coal board on general policy and objectives for the industry; to provide information to the Board so that they can hold Areas to account; and to set in motion the execution of policies in their respective fields.

Area	*Area Office*
Scottish	Green Park, Greenend, Edinburgh, EH17 7PZ
North East	Coal House, Team Valley, Gateshead, Tyne and Wear, NE11 0JD
North Yorkshire	PO Box 13, Allerton Bywater, Castleford, West Yorks, WF10 2AL
South Yorkshire	St George's, 46 Thorne Road, Doncaster, DN1 2JS
North Derbyshire	Bolsover, Chesterfield, Derbys, S44 6AA
Nottinghamshire	Edwinstowe, Mansfield, Notts, NG21 9PR
South Midlands	Coleorton Hall, Coleorton, Leicester, LE6 4FA
Western	Staffordshire House, Berry Hill Road, Stoke-on-Trent, ST4 2NH
South Wales	Coal House, Ty-Glas Avenue, Llanishen, Cardiff, CF4 5YS
Kent	1–3 Waterloo Crescent, Dover, Kent, CT16 1LA

HEALTH AND SAFETY LEGISLATION IN MINING.—Health and safety in mines and quarries of all kinds are governed primarily by the Health and Safety at Work etc. Act 1974, the Mines and Quarries Acts 1954 to 1971, and the regulations made under them. Of the Mines and Quarries Acts, the principal is that of 1954. Part I of the Mines and Quarries (Tips) Act 1969, governs tips that are deposits of mining or quarrying waste associated with mines or quarries that have not been abandoned. Part II of the 1969 Act applies to tips associated with abandoned mines and quarries.

For the purposes of these Acts, mines and quarries are defined by the Mines and Quarries Act 1954. This Act defines mines and quarries as excavations or systems of excavations made for the purpose of, or in connection with, the getting of minerals (whether in their natural state or in solution or suspension) or products of minerals. It is a mine where the minerals are got wholly or substantially by means involving the employment of persons below ground; otherwise it is a quarry, but a mere well or bore-hole is neither, even if it is made for getting minerals eg by brine pumping. Surface land and buildings surrounding or adjacent to a mine's shafts or outlets or to a quarry and occupied together with the mine or quarry for its purposes are generally regarded as part of the mine or quarry.

The 'Health and Safety at Work etc Act 1974' was passed to provide for the health and safety of employees at places of work of all kinds and of other persons who might be affected by the carrying on of any undertaking, whether of an employer or of a self-employed person. This Act superimposed more general requirements on the provisions of the Mines and Quarries Act 1954 and of other Acts governing health and safety at places of work of particular classes. Eventually it is envisaged that all these Acts will be replaced by regulations made under the 1974 Act. Some such regulations have been made already repealing parts of the Mines and Quarries Act 1954.

SYSTEMS OF MINING

Synopsis.—Most minerals are won from the earth by one of the following methods.—

(1) UNDERGROUND MINING, in which men work underground to extract and haul the minerals out of the mine through a shaft, drift or adit to the surface.

(2) OPENCAST MINING, also called opencut (Australia), open-pit (USA), or strip mining, in which overburden is removed to expose the seam or orebody before extraction.

(3) QUARRYING, in which an open pit, mine or excavation is used for the extraction of stone, sand, gravel or industrial minerals from open faces with or without removal of overburden.

(4) ALLUVIAL MINING, which is the exploitation of alluvial deposits by dredging, or hydraulicking—ie using high-pressure water jets. Dredging is used on near-surface deposits which lie under or close to water.

(5) OTHER METHODS—In addition to these methods of mining, within which there are numerous variations in the equipment and techniques used, there are a number of mining methods which are currently used only in a few instances, and some which will undoubtedly be used to an increasing extent in the years ahead. Such methods include the pumping of hot water or steam underground for the extraction of sulphur (Frasch process); solar evaporation, used in hot countries for recovery of salts (eg Great Salt Lake project, USA and Dead Sea potash, Israel); *in situ* leaching (this process is sometimes accompanied by a major underground explosion to fragment the orebody and in some cases this explosion may be a nuclear one); underground and surface hydraulic mining, in which high pressure water jets are used to extract soft minerals (eg coal) with transport of mineral to surface by hydraulic pipeline; heap leaching of surface deposits; and the large-scale recovery of minerals (manganese nodules) from the deep sea bed, which seems unlikely to be achieved before 1990.

Once an orebody has been located, probably by a combination of aerial and ground geophysical techniques, its detailed exploration is usually undertaken by means of an extensive drilling programme (diamond drilling, in which cores are recovered and assayed). By drilling to a particular grid pattern, a picture of the orebody with metal content is built up and the method of exploitation (opencast or underground) is decided upon with regard to such factors as depth of orebody, thickness of overburden, shape, volume, etc.

After the extent, geometry and attitude of an orebody have been determined, the selection of mining method and design of development and extraction workings require skilled engineering and planning services. S.P.

TABLE 2.—MINING DESIGN PARAMETERS. (1 = most important; 4 = least important)

Consideration Factors	Basic Design Parameters				
	Size	Config-uration	Ground Support	Arrange-ment	Inclin-ation
Depth of orebody	4	4	4	4	1
Geological characteristics of orebody	4	4	4	4	1
Proposed mining method	4	4	4	4	2
Physical characteristics of broken ore	4	4	4	2	2
Relationship of opening with orebody	4	3	3	4	1
Geology, depth, hydrology of capping	2	1	1	4	1
Rock conditions around opening	1	1	1	4	1
Ground water around opening	1	1	1	4	1
Ore and waste tonnage required	1	2	4	3	2
Surface topography	4	4	4	4	2
Flexibility for expansion or change	1	2	4	1	1
Ventilation requirements	1	2	2	3	2
Ore reserves and life of mine	1	2	2	2	1
Quantities of men & mat'ls to be handled	1	2	4	1	2
Multilevel or single-level loading	4	2	4	2	1
Weight and size of equipment to be handled	1	2	4	1	2
New opening, or deepen existing opening	1	1	1	1	1
Location, surface or underground	4	4	4	4	1
Capital cost	1	2	2	2	1
Operating cost	3	3	2	2	1
Underground ore transportation method	4	3	4	2	1
Safety requirements	4	4	4	1	1
Scheduled completion time	2	2	2	3	1
Purpose	2	2	2	2	1

Wimpfen (Chief Mining Engineer, US Bureau of Mines, 'Evolving Improvements in Underground Mining', 1976) lists 24 criteria that have to be considered and their relative importance. These are given in Table 2.

However, in the final analysis, whether an orebody will be mined by surface or underground methods will depend on the relative mining costs. In every case, total capital and operating costs must be considered. A correct decision is extremely important inasmuch as contract commitments are made for product deliveries long before the mine is placed in production. Equipment for surface and underground mining is not interchangeable. Further, investment in equipment for any mining method and pre-production stripping expense for surface mining must be made long before any returns are received and before the method has been proven successful. Thorough engineering studies are therefore essential to help establish the most favourable mining method. In general, surface mining is found to be more economical when the orebody is large and the depth of overburden is not excessive.

UNDERGROUND MINING.—In exploiting an orebody by underground mining techniques, there are two basic processes involved—development, a term used to cover all work carried out to gain access to the orebody and mine it; and stoping—a term used to describe the actual extraction technique adopted. Over the past few years, certain trends have become evident in both development and stoping practice—a much higher degree of mechanisation, such as the use of full face borers, raise borers and mechanised drill jumbos for development work; and an increasing usage of trackless equipment (highly mobile diesel powered load-haul-dump units, with rubber tyres) and mechanised stope drilling rigs.

Mechanisation of underground stoping and development operations is now at a stage where a substantial proportion of underground mine production is achieved by the use of trackless mining equipment in the form of load-haul-dump vehicles, mobile haulage units and ancillary support vehicles. The use of such trackless equipment has increased tremendously since the early 1960's and underground mines in Africa, Australia, Canada, Europe, the Middle and Far East, South America and the USA use such equipment in stoping and development. A good summary of currently available trackless mining equipment and trends is provided by an article entitled 'Mobile mining equipment—an underground mines survey' (*Mining Magazine*, September 1981, pp 187–201).

In many trackless mines, a spiral ramp or incline may extend from surface down to the orebody; this ramp may be used for transporting men and materials into the mine and ore out of it. In other mines using trackless equipment, the ramp may be combined with a shaft system which is used for transport of ore out of the mine. Examples of the latter are the Udden mine in Sweden and the Baluba mine in Zambia. (*Mining Magazine,* Nov. 1976, p 412). A detailed description of a trackless mine utilising load-haul-dump vehicles and a conveyor belt incline for transporting ore out of the mines is given in *Mining Magazine*, Dec. 1976, pp 504–519 (Rapid development of the Fukasawa mine by a trackless haulage system).

In underground mines using vertical or inclined circular shafts, sinking of such shafts by well established methods continues, but an increasing number are being constructed by mechanical boring machines. These machines have mounted cutters that break the rock by either an abrasive or a shearing action. Thrust to the head on which the cutters are mounted comes from thrust jacks, or is applied through the drill string, or by its weight.

A comprehensive review of methods of sinking and raising of shafts in underground mines by methods other than drill and blast was given in *Mining Magazine,* April 1983. This review included all highly mechanised methods such as raise borers, reaming heads, shaft drilling machines, boring without drill pipe and blind shaft boring.

The principal trends in underground mine development are summarised as follows by Wimpfen (ibid): (1)—Conventional circular concrete-lined shafts will be constructed for most new mines. (2)—Rectangular shafts with timber sets will continue to be sunk for (*a*) exploration, (*b*) deepening of existing shafts, and (*c*) internal underground shafts. (3)—The construction of bored shafts for ventilation will increase. However, their inability to handle large volumes of air, because of their small cross-sectional area, will limit their use. The present state of the art limits their diameter and depth. (4)—The spiral ramp system of development as a supplement to shaft mining is being adopted increasingly. First employed on a large scale at Kiruna, Sweden, this system is now used at International Nickel Co. operations in Canada, at the Pilot Knob iron mine in Missouri, and at the Texasgulf Kidd Creek mine in Ontario, Canada.

Some important methods of underground ore extraction are considered below:

Room and Pillar Mining.—In which ore is extracted from working places (rooms), pillars of rock being left behind for support purposes. Room and pillar is the most common underground mining method in the USA and non-coal room and pillar accounts for over 75% of all US mines that produce over 1,200 metric tonnes per day. Orebodies best suited to this extraction technique are regular stratiform types not greatly folded or deformed, which are strong or moderately strong; have moderate to strong backs and floors; are relatively flat-lying; contain ore that is relatively uniform in thickness and grade; and are of considerable extent in area.

Massive or dome type deposits (eg salt) are commonly mined by this method. Maximum practical depth for room and pillar mining depends on the strength of the pillars. The deepest such mines in the USA are about 1000 m below surface. Extraction rates range from 35% at depths below 900 m to over 90% at shallow depths where pillars can be recovered.

Sub-level Caving.—Caving systems utilise the weakness inherent in the rock mass and the force of gravity to break the ore as it moves to transportation loading points. Drilling in sub-level caving has progressed from small drifts and short drill holes to relatively large drifts that make it possible to use large machines for both long-hole drilling and loading. Mechanisation of drilling, loading and transport in sub-level caving has proved relatively easy; these methods have shown more rapid development in Sweden than elsewhere. It is applicable in large, low grade deposits of moderate strength with weak, readily caveable walls that dip in the range of 60° to 90°. Surface subsidence is inevitable with caving methods.

Sub-level Open Stoping is a technique applicable to strong orebodies that require minimal support and are surrounded by competent country rock.

Cut-and-Fill Mining.—In such methods the principal feature is that the worked out stope is back-filled; in the past, fragmented waste rock was frequently used, but now hydraulic filling with tailings from ore processing, or sand, are customary. Fill is transported to the stope by pipeline, sometimes from surface. The role of fill in mining has been described completely in 'Fill Technology in Underground Metalliferous Mines' by E. G. Thomas, 1979.

Longwall Mining.—This method of stoping is used in some South African gold mines, particularly at great depths, and is applied successfully where gold ore occurs in zones of consistent payability.

Vein Mining.—Vein deposits present problems in extraction because they are frequently irregular, steeply inclined and sinuous along both strike and dip. Mineralisation is seldom uniform, and barren or below grade zones are common. In addition, the vein structure may be displaced by faults. Vein mineralisation width may range from a few centimetres to 30 m; the mining width is usually from 1·5 m to 9 m. Most vein deposits have in the past been mined by variations of three basic methods:—shrinkage stoping, square set stoping, and cut-and-fill stoping.

The rubber-tyred, load–haul–dump (LHD) units used in underground trackless mining were originally self-contained diesel powered units, but a number of mines are now opting for electrically-powered load–haul–dump units. These have more restricted mobility and they are connected to the electrical power source by means of a cable, usually wound on a reel mounted on the vehicle. They have the advantages of lower operating costs and are environmentally much more acceptable as there are no exhaust fumes to cope with (an important consideration in restricted underground workings). Electrically powered load–haul–dump machines are made by manufacturers in the German Federal Republic and Finland. (See 'Design of electrically driven LHDs', *Mining Magazine*, October 1982, pp. 282–289).

A very comprehensive and up-to-date reference on all metalliferous mining methods is the 'Underground Mining Methods Handbook' produced by the American Institute of Mining Engineers (1982, edited by W. A. Hustrulid).

OPENCAST MINING.—This method is applicable to minerals lying in seams relatively near the surface. The soil and overburden are removed in a series of generally parallel cuts, which are progressively backfilled with overburden from subsequent cuts. The method has long been used in USA, where it now produces more than 400 million tonnes of coal a year, nearly two thirds of that country's total output. In the UK Opencast Mining Operations have been used for many years in the working of stratified ironstone and was introduced for the mining of coal in 1942. Since then the method has produced more than 450 M tonne of coal, and the British Coal Corporation has increased its output by opencast mining in recent years to 15 M tonne/year.

Before opencast working starts, accurate prospecting is essential to evaluate the extent of workable reserves and the profitability of the project. Any change necessary in the method of working, caused by unexpected changes in geological structure and extent of previous underground workings, are likely to be expensive. Prospecting is carried out by drilling, both open-hole and cored, the latter giving samples of both the overburden and mineral to be worked. Overburden cores should be examined for any weak layers such as strata discontinuities, jointing and bedding, that could affect stability. In addtion, geophysical methods of exploration are now extensively in use. With coal it is important to determine at least the calorific value and the ash, moisture, volatile matter, sulphur and chlorine percentages.

The excavation face of each cut, towards the next cut, is called the 'high wall'. Its slope depends on depth, material and strata dip but will often be about 65° to the horizontal though the slope overall in a deep pit will not exceed 45°. 'Low walls', on the spoil side of each cut, will be formed at the natural angle of the cast or tipped waste, usually 27° to 38° but is dependent upon the dip of pavement of basal seam and the nature of the material being tipped. For mixed shale and rock the immediate temporary bulking of overburden in the spoil heaps is from 25 to 35%.

Where the seams dip at no more than 1 in 7 the first cut is often made along the outcrop or basset edge and subsequent cuts parallel with this, advancing towards the deepest part of the deposit to be worked. This plan has the advantage that it will be possible to work to the deep if this becomes economic. With steeper dips the spoil (low wall) side would not be stable and cuts must be made from shallow to deep or diagonally, the latter allowing an easier gradient for haulage out of the cut. The first of these would be a 'box' cut with a deep face on both sides, the excavated material from it would have to be transported to dump rather than cast on the surface.

In most operations, the cheapest method of excavation is by dragline, which operates from the top of the bench that it is digging, and casts the material directly into the previous void. Draglines are available up to 170 m^3 capacity with booms to 100 m length, able to dig to a depth of 56 m.

When the depth is too great for a dragline alone, and particularly in multi-seam working, the upper layers of overburden are removed by face shovel and dump truck combination. Such shovels range from 5 to 46 m^3 capacity, usually either diesel or electrically driven and mounted on crawlers. Diesel powered hydraulic shovels are now being more extensively employed because of their high output and greater mobility. Dump trucks are from 50 to over 200 tonnes capacity, diesel driven with engines of about 10 to 16 horsepower per tonne of capacity. Haul roads for dump trucks should not be steeper than 1 in 12 though short ramps at 1 in 10 or steeper may have to be accepted. The large stripping shovels, once popular in the USA are being replaced by the more versatile dragline. Bucket wheel excavators, either with integral stacker or feeding a belt conveyor system, are available but suitable only in soft overburden such as Loess. In the brown-coal areas in West Germany, East Germany, South Australia and the USSR bucket wheeler excavators and very large ladder type excavators, similar to dredgers, are used.

In the UK opencast coal sites vary widely in size and depth and the machinery used varies accordingly to suit particular site conditions. A commonly used prime mover is a diesel crawler excavator that can be rigged as either a dragline to carry a $4\frac{1}{2}$ m^3 to 6 m^3 bucket on a 37 m boom or a 5 m^3 shovel. It weighs some 200 tons and is driven by an engine of 535 hp. Under favourable conditions output of this size of dragline can be up to 200 m^3 per hour. Larger, crawler mounted, draglines are now being developed so that the rate of output from each is much greater.

The largest excavator in use at present in the UK is a walking dragline with a 50 m^3 bucket on an 81 m boom. The total weight of 2,903 tonnes is carred on a 17 m dia welded steel 'tub', each of the two walking shoes is 17 m × 3 m. The triangular boom is formed of high-tensile steel tubes welded *in-situ*. Electric drives are Ward-Leonard controlled and total 6,250 hp, power being supplied by trailing cable at 11 kV, 50 Hz. The machine is controlled by one man from one of the two cabs which project forward each side at the front of the main revolving frame. The full crew is three men, driver, banksman and maintenance engineer. This dragline is moving overburden on an opencast coal site in Northumberland and its output can be up to 200,000 m^3 per week.

Hard rock must be fragmented by blasting before it is excavated by either shovel or dragline. The most commonly used explosive is ammonium nitrate–fuel oil mixture (AN–FO), but slurry or gelignite are used where wet holes or harder rock justify the extra cost. To avoid delay and to achieve good fragmentation it is necessary to fire a number of holes in each blast. The separate charges are linked by detonating fuse, or electrically. Milli-second delays, or delay detonators, are used to reduce vibration. It is generally accepted that the peak particle velocity of any vibrations reaching buildings outside the opencast site should not exceed 12 mm/sec.

For blasting, vertical holes, 120 to 300 mm dia are commonly made with rotary air-blast drills using tri-cone or tungsten carbide tipped bits. The tendency is towards larger machines with masts up to 20 m allowing single-pass drilling. Under suitable conditions larger holes at wider centres will give cheaper blasting. The burden and spacing must be sufficient enough to avoid sympathetic detonation between adjacent holes (generally not less than 3 m) but not so great as to leave unbroken rock between. From 4 m^3 of hard rock to 12 m^3 of shale will be broken for each kg of explosive used.

Once the overburden has been removed in each cut the mineral is dug and loaded. For coal, crowd-shovels, either rope or hydraulic are used in sizes from $\frac{1}{2}$ m^3 to 10 m^3. In early days, particularly in ironstone mines, transport from the cuts was by rail but the cost of moving track has prohibited its use and, except in brown-coal mines where conveyors are used, transport now is always by rubber-tyred dump trucks. In the USA, these are often articulated with bottom-dump bodies carrying 100 tonnes or more. Articulated trucks are not suitable for steep gradients and in the UK either two-axle dump trucks or normal highway vehicles are used. Where the size and location of the production sites allow, it is preferable to provide a private road from site to coal preparation plant, from which the products will usually be despatched by main-line railway.

Mineral will normally be loaded from opencast workings more cleanly than is possible underground. Rock partings in coal seams can usually be separated and discarded at the face and washing may not be needed. Recovery varies according to roof, seam and floor conditions. With careful loading, recovery should be around 85% and the ash content of coal as delivered should not be more than 2% above that inherent in the seam.

Economic ratios of overburden to mineral vary widely according to relative costs and values. In USA, and UK, coal is being worked at ratios by volume of 30 to 1 and higher, particularly for special qualities such as coking coal and anthracite. Particularly in West Virginia, USA, augers are used to win additional coal beyond the final high-wall. Holes are up to 1 m dia, and up to 50 m horizontal length.

Maximum depth, like ratio, varies with the circumstances. Extra depth, particularly beyond the reach of a dragline, is expensive. Many coal sites in USA and UK are worked to 60 m and some to more than 75 m. One coal site in Northumberland UK, is curently operating to win 12 million tonnes from more than a dozen overlapping seams to a maximum depth of 140 m. Another in Fife, Scotland has been worked to 210 m depth to win coal from a thick seam in a steep syncline.

Most countries of the world now require some restoration of worked-out opencast sites. It may be acceptable to form a lake so as to avoid having to refill the final cut but most sites are restored to some form of agriculture or forestry. In UK this is done to a very high standard. Restoration must be planned from the start so as to avoid unnecessary movement of material. The operation is to strip separately and set aside top soil and subsoil (0·6 to 1·0 m) thickness which are finally respread over the re-graded overburden by motor-scrapers. Adequate drainage must be arranged as the run-off from newly restored land is greater than normal. With overburden to mineral ratios greater than about 8 to 1 the land finishes higher than before working due to permanent bulking of the overburden which more than makes up for the volumes of mineral removed. Sand and clay do not bulk appreciably but shale and rock bulk by 8% to 17%. Settlement, about 1% of depth, is usually complete within 5 years of restoration. New settlement may occur if the surface is loaded, eg by heavy buildings, or if the ground-water conditions are changed. Where buildings or structures are proposed for a restored opencast site, it is now common practice to compact the backfill in layers during placement to minimise the effects of settlement.

In inhabited country, operators have to avoid conflict with the neighbours. During working, care must be taken to avoid nuisance; blasting, noise and dust are the main causes of complaint. Not only should restored sites be designed to be agriculturally productive, but careful thought should be given to landscaping the restored area.

In general, opencast mining operations are a low-cost method of winning minerals from the ground and they also provide an opportunity, during the restoration phase, to improve the landscape particularly in areas of dereliction.

There are several good examples of this type of land rehabilitation in the UK and these take the form of Country Parks, Golf Courses, Watersport areas and recreational facilities.

ALLUVIAL MINING (DREDGING).—This method of alluvial mining has reached a high degree of development in Malaysia, where at the beginning of 1982 there were a total of 55 alluvial tin dredges operating. Dredging is also applied to placer gold deposits. The dredge is mechanically driven and works on an artifical pond made by itself. It uses mechanical buckets to dig into tin-containing ground. It screens and washes this material on board the dredge to retain the tin (cassiterite) content; and rejects the waste material from the rear as it moves. The dredge may be sea-going (as in Thailand and Indonesia). In alluvial mines the tin-bearing quality of the ground prospected or mined may be measured in terms of the weight of the tin concentrates or the calculated weight of tin content in each cubic metre of ground.

One of the largest alluvial tin mines in Malaysia is Berjuntai Tin Dredging Berhad and the dredging methods used at this mine are fairly typical of large-scale tin dredging operations (see *Mining Magazine*, March 1982, pp 200–209). The use of underwater bucket wheel dredges rather than the bucket ladder type widely used in Malaysia is now being investigated and an experimental unit of this type is being tested at Berjuntai.

A further use of dredging is in recovery of heavy titanium and iron-bearing minerals from Australian beach sands in Queensland (for a detailed description of mining and processing heavy mineral sands off the Queensland coast, see 'Consolidated Rutile' *Mining Magazine*, August 1986 pp 82–89). This method is also used outside Australia, for example in recovery of beach sand minerals on the Natal coast (Richards Bay beach sand project in South Africa; *Mining Magazine*, Nov., 1976, pp. 425–433). The sands are mined using floating dredges which feed a floating concentrator. Initially, a dredge pond is excavated and filled with water. Usually two dredging units are emplaced and the concentrator constructed on floating pontoons. Mining proceeds by the continuous dredging away of the sand at the front of the pond and the stacking of the same sand, but after removal of the heavy minerals at the back of the pond. In this manner the pond moves forward at a rate of between one and three metres per day.

The vegetation ahead of the pond is first cleared and the thin layer of topsoil is removed for later use in restoration. The dredges undercut the banks and extract the material through a suction duct. The 'mined' slurry is then pumped directly to a trommel screen above a floating surge bin along a 500 mm diameter flexible pipe and then fed to the floating gravity concentrator. The trommel screen discards the +76 mm fraction into the pond. From such operations the heavy minerals ilmenite, rutile and zircon ('black sands') are recovered. A typical beach sand dredging rate might be 1,100tonne/h by a single dredge.

A comprehensive survey of the various types of dredges currently being used for recovery of alluvial minerals was given in *Mining Magazine* July 1985 pp 36–45. Further reading is 'Evaluation/Decision Process for Small Scale Placer Gold Mining' *Mining Magazine* April 1986, pp 312–321 and Mining Techniques for Alluvial Tin Deposits, published in 1985 by the Seatrad Centre, Ipoh, Malaysia. Another definitive work is Alluvial Mining by E H Macdonald, Chapman & Hall 1983.

OTHER MINING METHODS.—Methods of mining not currently used to any great extent but likely to attract more interest in the future are considered below.

Offshore (Deep-Sea) Mining.—The great technical challenge of marine mining, as far as exploitation of mineral resources on the continental shelves and deep ocean floor is concerned, is in the collection of ores and their transport to the surface of the sea. Most international effort has been devoted to finding a suitable high-capacity mining method for recovering manganese nodules, which contain many metal values of economic interest (notably copper, nickel and cobalt, with manganese itself, although present in concentrations of the order of 30%, being of least economic value). The current picture regarding exploitation of undersea ore deposits of all types is given in 'Offshore Mineral Resources' published by GERMINAL (Groupe d'Etude et de la Recherche de Mineralisation au Large, P.O. Box 6009, 45060 Orleans Cedex, France) in 1984.

Systems proposed for deep-sea nodule mining are the hydraulic system in which a length of pipe is suspended from a surface float or vessel; a gathering head collects and winnows the nodules from the undersea sediments and feeds them to the bottom of the pipeline while rejecting oversize material. Some means must be incorporated of causing the water inside the pipeline to flow upwards with sufficient velocity to suck the nodules into the system and transport them to surface. Power means being considered for hydraulic dredges are centrifugal dredge pumps and air lift pumps. One company has successfully tested an air-lift dredge in the Blake Plateau nodule deposit in about 760 m of water.

Systems are being planned for recovering about 1million metric tonnes of nodules per year from depths as great as 5,490 m of water. Another method devised for full-scale production of nodules is the mechanical continuous line bucket (CLB) system. This consists essentially of a loop of cable to which are attached dredge buckets at 25 to 50 m intervals and a traction machine on the surface vessel capable of moving the cable such that the buckets descend to the ocean floor along one side of the loop, skim over the bottom filling with nodules along the bottom side of the loop and return to the surface on the third side of the loop. ('Ocean Floor Mining', by J. S. Pearson, Noyes Data Corp, Park Ridge, NJ, USA, 1975). Recent opinion suggests that the problems of a large-scale, deep-sea nodule mining operation of a size comparable with land-based mines have been gravely underestimated, making such an operation unlikely before 1990 at the earliest. ('Limits and possibilities of deep-sea mining for the extraction of mineral raw material—the case of manganese nodules'. Udo Boin, *Mining Magazine*, Jan. 1980, pp 43–47).

Hydraulic Mining.—In West Germany, a mine which utilised high pressure water in the production, conveying and hoisting of coal, the Hansa mine, was producing coal by mid-1977 but this ambitious programme has now been closed down and in some respects has not been a success. A similar project is underway at the Robinson Run mine in the USA. This type of underground hydraulic mining might be increasingly applied to coal in the future, as among other advantages, fewer men are required to work underground. Hydraulic pipelines are used for transportation of many minerals, but winning by hydraulic means (water jets), is likely to be applied only to softer minerals.

With regard to coal the state-of-the-art is covered in two recent publications, 'Equipment for Hydraulic Handling of Coal' and 'Applications for Hydraulic Handling of Coal' from IEA Coal Research, 14/15 Lower Grosvenor Place, London SW1 0EX.

In-Situ Extraction and Leaching.—In situ chemical or solution mining is the in-place extraction of metals from ores located within the confines of a mine (unfractured or fractured ore, stope fill, caved material and ores in permeable zones), or in dumps and ore heaps. This type of mining covers preparation of ore for subsequent inplace leaching, flow of solution through rock masses, leaching of minerals with inexpensive, regenerable reagents and metal recovery from the solutions. The technique has been applied mainly to low-grade copper ores but it is expected to be applied in future to recovery of lead, zinc, nickel, manganese, uranium, silver, gold, molybdenum and mercury. (R. B. Bhappu in 'Economics of Minerals Engineering', Mining Journal Books Ltd, London, 1976).

Some advantages of this method are: (1)—It is environmentally attractive, as it creates less surface disturbance and results in less water and air pollution than conventional mining. (2)—Capital and operating costs are lower than a conventional mine-milling operation. (3)—It can often be used to recover metals economically from low grade ore that could not be recovered by conventional mining, milling and smelting. Disadvantages are the difficulties in effectively contacting the ore with leach solutions; recovery of the solutions without appreciable loss; testing the process short of a field operation is difficult; ground water contamination may result; and much of the data on physical, chemical and bacteriological factors involved in *in-situ* extraction have not been commercially evaluated.

The use of the method for the recovery of gold at a number of mines is described in *Mining Magazine*, May 1986, pp 405–411.

QUARRYING.—The quarrying industry in the UK mainly produces concreting aggregate and roadstone. Sand gravel, limestone and igneous rocks represent the bulk of the materials quarried for these purposes, and together account for an annual output of over 200 million tonnes.

Other quarried products include limestone, chalk and clay for the manufacture of cement, various forms of lime for industrial and agricultural applications, sands for the glass and foundry industries, clays and shales for brick making, and ball and china clay for use in pottery and paper manufacture. The traditional branch of the quarrying industry related to the production of building stone and roofing slates now represents a very small proportion of the industry's output and investment, as a result of technological and architectural changes in the building and construction industries. The total output of all quarried minerals reached a peak of 335 million tonnes in 1974. Since that time some sectors experienced a sharp downturn in demand but, by 1985, it had again reached 290 million tonnes.

Quarrying, or mineral winning, and related processing activities are normally associated with a rock 'quarry', or a sand and gravel (or clay) 'pit', although in recent years an increasing quantity of sand and gravel has been obtained by marine dredging operations in areas off the major river estuaries around the coast (16 million tonnes in 1985).

The precise form of the rock quarry is determined by the topography, the geology of the deposit, and the quantity of overburden involved. The conventional limestone or igneous rock quarry, is one in which overburden is minimal and the stone is obtained from a single face or from a series of benches. Single-lift faces of 60 metres have been developed in the past, but the trend is towards face heights of 20metres which offers safer working conditions on each bench.

When the overburden has been removed, usually by scraper, blast holes are drilled to a pre-determined pattern usually by track-mounted, hydraulic or compressed-air operated rigs which produce a rotary action at the bit, or alternatively, a mainly percussive action, as in the down-the-hole hammer drill. Drill holes, commonly 80 to 200 mm diameter may be arranged in a single row, with a spacing of 3–5 metres and a similar burden (distance from hole to free face), depending upon the characteristics of the rock and the strength of the explosive used. Benefits, particularly in terms of explosive efficiency and safety, may be gained if angled drilling is employed and many faces are inclined between 5° and 25° from the vertical.

The explosives charge may take the form of conventional nitro-glycerin based explosives or blasting agents such as free flowing ammonium nitrate/fuel oil mixtures (ANFO) or plastic sheathed slurry compounds. Rock strengths, jointing, the presence of water, and costs, are all factors affecting the choice of explosive, but ANFO mixtures have become widely used since the early 1960's and slurry explosives found increasing popularity during the 1970's. The upper section of each hole is usually stemmed with rock fines to reduce air blast and fly rock. The explosive charge may be initiated by means of an all-electrical system, or a non-electrical system but possibly having the widest application is a combination of the two in which continuous high velocity detonating fuse in each hole is initiated by electric detonator.

In place of the instantaneous initiation of all holes, special detonators can be used at each hole or delay devices can be connected into the detonating fuse line to improve efficiency and to reduce vibration levels. These devices are also used in multi-row blasting patterns which are increasingly favoured in applications which call for high volumes of fragmented rock from low faces.

With a blasting ratio of between 5 and 10 tonnes of rock/kg explosive, a quarry blast can yield many thousand tonnes of rock. Whilst yield plays a major part in blast design calculations, other considerations are the degree of fragmentation required and the shape of the rock pile. Adequate fragmentation may eliminate the need for hydraulic breaking or drop balling, while the shape of the rock pile should suit the type of loading equipment which is in use; usually a face shovel, wheeled loading shovel or hydraulic excavator.

Unconsolidated sand and gravel quarrying operations may involve working a deposit which is below the water table. This situation may call for the use of a pontoon mounted gravel pump, grab or dredge, or alternatively a dragline excavator which stands on the overburden surface, and can locally strip back this material before loading the deposit from below water. In some situations sections of the working can be dewatered by continuous pumping, to enable the deposit to be loaded visibly, and hence more efficiently, by dragline. Dry pits and clay workings may be worked by face shovel, or wheeled loading shovel digging directly from the face which should have a height to match the size and digging of the machine. China clay operations present a special case in which the clay and associated minerals are flushed from the face by high pressure hydraulic monitors.

The haulage of blasted or excavated materials from the quarry face to the processing plant is commonly effected by purpose-built dump-trucks of up to 50 tonnes capacity, although field conveyors and rail systems occur in some operations, particularly in sand and gravel workings and barge transport may be favoured in wet pits. Processing for aggregate production revolves around the crushing and screening plant with associated feeding, conveying and blending equipment. The number of crushers varies principally according to the output required, and hardness of the rock, but primary, secondary and tertiary reduction stages are common, employing compression or impact crushers.

In gravel and sand operations and in some rock production plants a washing operation is introduced to remove clay and silt and to separate the sand from the gravel. In sand production, classifiers may be used to produce several sizes of sand and dewatering of the product is commonly carried out with aid of cyclones. In the production of specialist sands for glass making and for the foundry industry this stage of production is very important and may be supplemented by drying and mineral dressing processes designed to rid the sand of deleterious material. The washing process introduces the problem of the disposal of unwanted fines smaller than 75 μm and the recirculation of wash water. This may be achieved by the use of a concentrating process involving a thickener, or the use of flocculating agents, but more commonly in the case of sand and gravel working is associated with lagoon settlement systems confined within worked out sections of the pit.

Processed materials are generally called upon to meet the requirements of a BS Specification, and quality control systems are used to check that the product meets with customers' requirements with regard to grading, flakiness, moisture content and cleanliness. BS 812 covers a variety of tests to establish aggregate properties which may be listed in specifications, and these include aggregate crushing value, 'flakiness index' and polished stone value, for aggregate used in road surfacing applications.

The market area of a quarry usually exists within a 20 mile radius because of the widespread availability of materials for aggregates and because transporting costs are high in relation to the ex-works selling price. There are exceptions to this situation where specialised products are produced such as low impurity sands for glass and foundry applications, and china clay for paper. In these instances the raw material is less widely available, processing costs are higher and therefore the haulage costs represent a smaller percentage of the selling price. In some instances the hardness or skid resistance of a road-stone may be such that it can claim a wider market. The considerable market for aggregates in the south-east of England, an area lacking suitable rock deposits, has given rise to the establishment of a number of distribution terminals which receive railborne stone, principally from quarries in the West Country and in the Midlands.

The minimisation of environmental nuisance from dust, noise and blast vibrations is an important consideration in all branches of the quarrying industry. In addition visual impact is reduced by careful screening and phased restoration. Many examples of restored sand and gravel workings exist as a result of practices such as those outlined in Opencast Mining. In some cases workings are re-filled with industrial and domestic waste, a process which calls for measures to prevent ground water pollution and to control methane discharge.

Quarrying is a potentially hazardous occupation, but the accident record steadily improves through improved plant design, training and the guidance of the Mines and Quarries Inspectorate, exercised within the statutory framework of the Mines and Quarries Act. The education and training of personnel at all levels in the industry is co-ordinated by the trade associations, and by the Institute of Quarrying, who have jointly promoted the development of the Doncaster Metropolitan Institute of Higher Education as a national and international centre for education in minerals surveying, extraction, processing and reclamation.

SURVEYING OF BOREHOLES.—A good overview of the current state-of-the-art in borehole surveying was given in *World Mining*, February 1982, pp 42–44. Borehole survey instruments vary in accuracy, complexity and application and so it is essential to have a clear idea of the requirements of the particular job in hand. The standard survey instruments available (made by various manufacturers) are the Drift Indicator, the Magnetic Single Shot, the Magnetic Multiple Shot, and the Gyroscopic Multiple Shot.

The Drift Indicator.—This is considered to be the most basic survey instrument and the most economical, providing a fast and reliable means of monitoring borehole inclination. As it is simple to operate and provides quick results, it is the most efficient tool for maintaining a straight vertical course when drilling holes in such mining applications as degassing holes, dewatering holes, blastholes, and pilot holes for ventilation shafts and raises.

The drift indicator does not however provide directional information. When strict verticality is essential the drift indicator is normally used at short regular intervals to check that the borehole remains within acceptable tolerances of drift from the vertical. When the indicator shows that the hole is deviating beyond the acceptable tolerances, an instrument which can indicate borehole direction as well as inclination is run down the hole so that the necessary hole adjustment can be made.

As regards accuracy, the drift indicator can measure a hole's inclination from vertical to within one quarter of a degree. It records each inclination survey on a calibrated paper disc, providing a permanent record. The tool consists of a timer, angle unit and running gear. As it is the tool run most often, it must be of rugged construction, simple to operate and have the ability to rapidly, reliably and accurately take numerous surveys.

For this instrument, an all-mechanical timer is generally felt to be the most durable. In situations where noise may prevent the operator from hearing the timer running, a small observation port to allow a visual check of watch operation is valuable.

To ensure reliable surveys the timer should incorporate a means of verifying survey accuracy. As an example, the timer made by the Eastman Whipstock company punches a calibrated paper disc against a plumb bob, and then rotates the disc 180° and makes a second punch. This procedure, in effect, records two inclination readings at the same depth. When the two punch marks are 180° apart and at equal distances from the centre dot, the operator knows the survey is accurate.

A variety of interchangeable angle units is necessary for straight hole drilling needs. A 0–1–½ degree unit, with a survey disc calibrated to one-quarter degree increments is best for holes that must be kept vertical. Angle units of 0–3°, 0–6°, 0–12° and 0–30° are the other most widely used as they allow a range of surveys from holes that must be vertical to holes whose change of inclination needs to be monitored.

As drift indicator surveys are usually taken at short intervals, it is imperative that each run is done as quickly as possible. The drift indicator's running gear should incorporate features which reduce survey time and make operation easier. The wireline head on the drift indicator should be designed to prevent the line from twisting. This facilitates operation of the tool safety of the drill site.

A surface watch that can be synchronised with the instrument's time should also be employed. This helps to ensure an accurate survey and also saves time. The operator will know exactly when the survey has been completed and will thus be able to retrieve the instrument from the hole without delay.

The Magnetic Single Shot.—This instrument records on a film disc the inclination and magnetic direction of the hole at a single measured depth. Armed with this information, the operator can calculate the borehole trajectory and the location of the bottom of the hole. The magnetic single shot survey instrument is fairly simple to operate and the film disc gives a permanent record of the survey.

Magnetic single shots have been used to survey deep, straight holes and holes off the vertical in such mining applications as leaching, degassing, dewatering, grouting, in-situ gasification of coal deposits and mineral exploration. With special angle units this tool can provide accurate survey data on horizontal holes drilled for degasifying coal seams and for assessing the size and extent of coal and ore deposits.

The magnetic single shot tool includes a timer, battery pack, camera, compass–angle unit and running gear. For the single shot instrument, a solid-state electronic timer is the most reliable. The camera has an optical system and a set of lights which are switched on by the instrument timer to photograph the compass–angle unit on a film disc. The film-disc loader and developing equipment should permit daylight loading, unloading and developing without the requirement of a darkroom or camera bag.

The compass–angle unit measures the direction and inclination of the borehole at a given point. A magnetic compass determines hole direction, and a plumb bob or a drift arc measures the hole's angle from the vertical. Angle units should be interchangeable and available in a variety of ranges to accommodate virtually any borehole.

The magnetic single shot can be run on a wireline, dropped down the drill string, pumped through a horizontal borehole or run through a horizontal hole on drill rod. When run in the drilling assembly the single shot instrument must be isolated from drill pipe magnetism by non-magnetic drill rod or non-magnetic collars. Otherwise the instrument must be operated in open hole.

The Magnetic Multiple Shot.—This survey instrument measures borehole inclination and magnetic direction in the same way as the magnetic single shot. However, the multi-shot instrument can take hundreds of survey pictures on one run. It is used to survey long sections of a borehole, or an entire hole, taking survey measurements at regular intervals. The survey information helps to build up complete data on the contours of subsurface geological structures, the thickness of formations, the depth and location of faults, and any other geological features.

In order to get accurate geological information, essential for effective and economic mining, precise knowledge of the course of boreholes is imperative. Exact hole paths must also be known when boreholes are drilled in mines from one underground level to another, or several other levels, so that they can be located and intersected directly without requiring time-consuming and costly search operations.

Although the magnetic, multiple shot tool uses the basic idea of the single shot instrument, the two tools vary significantly. For the multiple shot instrument a programmable electronic timer is best. This offers reliability and the greatest flexibility for survey starting delays and variable picture intervals. The heart of the multiple shot instrument is a miniature camera that uses 10mm film. The compass–angle units are virtually the same as the single shot units. The camera's lens, surrounded by three bulbs, reduces and projects the image of the angle unit on to the film. The motor-driven camera automatically advances the film and regulates the lighting of the bulbs.

Except for the protective barrel, the running gear depends on the method used to run the survey. The tool can be dropped downhole and the survey taken as the drill string is pulled, or it can be run on a wireline. It can also be placed in the drill string above the bit and the survey taken as the pipe is run in the hole. In horizontal or ascending boreholes it is usually pushed ahead by the drill rods.

Because the directional information is derived from a magnetic compass, the tool must be isolated by non-magnetic drill rods or non-magnetic collars, or run in an open hole.

Gyroscopic Multiple Shot.—In cased holes, tubing or certain ore deposits—in fact any situation where there is magnetic interference—gyroscopic surveying instruments must be used. The gyroscopic multiple shot survey instrument is much the same as the magnetic multi-shot. The difference is that the gyro instrument replaces the conventional magnetic compass with a gyroscopic compass. The reference for the survey directional data is set by orienting the gyroscope to a known direction.

Gyroscopic instruments reliably provide accurate survey data in conditions where magnetic tools cannot. However, as a result of the increased complexity of the tool, two basic requirements must be met to maximise survey accuracy and minimise the possibility of a misrun. First, the gyroscope itself must be carefully manufactured to extremely fine tolerances to ensure accuracy and reliability. Depending on the size of the gyro, constant spin rates between 18,000 and 42,000 rev/min must be maintained. The gyroscope must also be rugged to withstand the conditions down the hole.

The surveyor who uses this type of instrument must be well-trained in using the gyro and interpreting the results. Prior to the survey being run he must carefully and accurately orientate the gyro to a known direction. The operator must also monitor for drift—that is, the tendency of the gyro to move from its primary orientation. Drift can be caused by many factors including friction, gyro imbalance, and motor speed instability, or outside forces such as the impact of hitting an obstruction in the hole or rough treatment while running the survey. In addition, the gyro does not move with the earth's rotation and this will cause apparent drift. Drift must also be correctly included in the survey calculation. As gyroscopes are adversely affected by vibrations and jolts, they are normally run down the hole by wireline.

Computers.—Survey calculations are nowadays much facilitated by the use of computer programs. A computer can significantly reduce the time needed to produce a final survey report and minimise human errors.

Computer plots, in both horizontal and vertical planes, give a clear view of a borehole for analysis. Multi-hole plots, presenting the relative position of holes one to another are particularly valuable when for example freeze holes are used in a shaft sinking operation.

A recent article gives useful information on how to obtain additional valuable data from borehole surveys. See *Mining Magazine*, Sept. 1985 (pp 232–6) 'The calculation and use of two drill factors from borehole survey data', by Dr. J. R. Tweedie.

SYSTEMS OF COAL MINING

Two distinct systems of obtaining coal from underground workings are in use today. They are known in the United Kingdom as the bord and pillar and the longwall systems. The former is the older system and has largely been superseded in Britain today, although it is still widely used in France, Australia and the United States of America.

BORD AND PILLAR SYSTEM.—This mining system is variously described as 'bord and pillar', 'pillar and stall' or 'stop and room' according to the nomenclature of the particular coalfield where it is or has been practised. The system involves the drivage of pattern of intersecting roads to cut the seam into a series of pillars. The pillars support the roadways and are then extracted at a later stage when their support function is no longer necessary. In seams 1·2 to 3 m thick the whole seam thickness is usually extracted leaving the roof and floor intact. Generally the first or 'whole' working is completed in the area for extraction and the 'broken' working or pillar extraction follows later. The size of the pillars is determined by the seam depth and thickness and should always be adequate to protect the roadways for their required life. In modern practice the system has many modifications and is generally confined to the 'first' working only, in the majority of cases. With modern knowledge of pillar strengths, a symmetrical system of pillars is not essential. The pillars, or strips of coal left for support, can be planned with knowledge of the strata conditions.

The system is now used in modified form to suit mechanised extraction methods in those cases where only a limited extraction of mineral is possible eg under built-up areas, under estuaries and sea beds where subsidence of the surface must be minimised. Whilst the bord and pillar system was adopted fairly extensively in this country at the beginning of the century this was associated with hand methods of mining. Pillars were extracted by a variety of methods dependent on local conditions. This generally took the form of stripping the sides and ends of the pillars until the extraction was complete. As the thicker and shallower seams became exhausted it was necessary to work the thinner and deeper seams and the longwall system became more and more popular.

During the war period, as an emergency measure to obtain more output quickly, a renewed effort was made to adopt bord and pillar systems utilising the American heading and loading machinery which was available in the early 1940's. However this burst of activity made little impact on any attempts to revive this system of working. In suitable conditions, using modern machinery, the system of working is highly efficient. It has the advantages, over the longwall system, that the roadways are supported by the coal pillars, all packing and ripping are eliminated and the amount of unproductive face labour is reduced. To counteract these advantages the amount of plant movement is greater as is the expenditure in capital per ton of output and the total percentage extraction is smaller, even where the pillars are eventually removed, than with a longwall system. Additionally the control of the surface subsidence is more difficult and less predictable.

The system is not used in Britain except for those special cases already mentioned: it represents only about 2% of the total annual output, against 97% of the output in USA. This clearly indicates the different emphasis placed on the system of mining in these two coal producing countries. In the United States there is a preponderance of thick, unfaulted and level seams lying at relatively shallow depth and these circumstances make the use of bord and pillar system profitable.

LONGWALL SYSTEM (ADVANCING).—As the name implies this system is distinguished from the 'bord and pillar' system by the length of 'wall' from which the coal is won. Although used in certain coalfields from the beginning of the century it is now the universal system in this country. Early systems worked with long continuous faces, advancing very slowly outwards from the shaft the coal being mined by hand; transport of the mineral in tubs from the face in small roadways at 15 m to 30 m centres was universally used.

Coalcutting was initially applied to longwall faces of this type with the stall-gate transport system. With the advent of face conveyors, the longwall faces become shorter and straight, and were either of the single or double unit type. The introduction of power loading and the armoured flexible conveyor has enabled outputs to be concentrated on fewer faces and in small areas. The current tendency is therefore for faces to become shorter with faster advance per day, and generally of the single unit type where the complications of machine movement and support at a central loading gate are eliminated. Currently face lengths vary from 45 m to 230 m with an average of approximately 130 m. On the single unit faces the roadways are carried at the end of the face with two packs as roadside supports or one pack plus a solid side. Packing material is normally obtained *in situ* in average seams from roof or floor of the seam but in the case of thick seams has, exceptionally, to be imported from elsewhere. The mined area behind the face was formerly supported by a series of 'strip' packs built with fallen material from the wastes, but this area, with modern hydraulic supports on the face is now almost universally caved.

The question of control of the strata behind a longwall face is a complex subject and involves consideration of the strength of roof and floor beds, the type of face support and the extent and nature of the permanent pack or pillar support. Great progress has been made in the last 20 years or so and a great number of different techniques and practices have been tested—and are still being developed—to ensure the best possible conditions at the faces and the greatest stability and life for the roadways.

Cycle of Operations.—The introduction of coalcutters to longwall faces, together with the later adoption of conveyors, influenced the various face operations and made each dependent on the other. After the coal was cut and filled on to the conveyor the next operation was the dismantling, advancing and re-erection of the face conveyor in its new track. To complete the cycle the roadway rippings and roadside packs were extended. This so called 'cyclic system' persisted until the mid-1950s when some 80% of the output in Great Britain was produced in this way. The system had problems, essentially due to the interdependence of each operation in the cycle, and this tended to produce delays and dislocation of work which was a frequent and costly occurrence. The search for methods of reducing the unproductive and exhausting operations such as packing, conveyor moving and handfilling eventually produced the loading machine and power loader. These developments are dealt with at a later stage.

Although not the ideal mining system in many ways, advancing longwall faces account for almost 90% of all longwall faces now operating. A typical modern advancing longwall face with the equipment which could be used is shown in Fig. 1. In this illustration the roadside packing and ripping are shown as hand worked with props and bars as face supports. More advanced systems may incorporate mechanisation to undertake these tasks with the complete face supported by power operated 'chock' type supports.

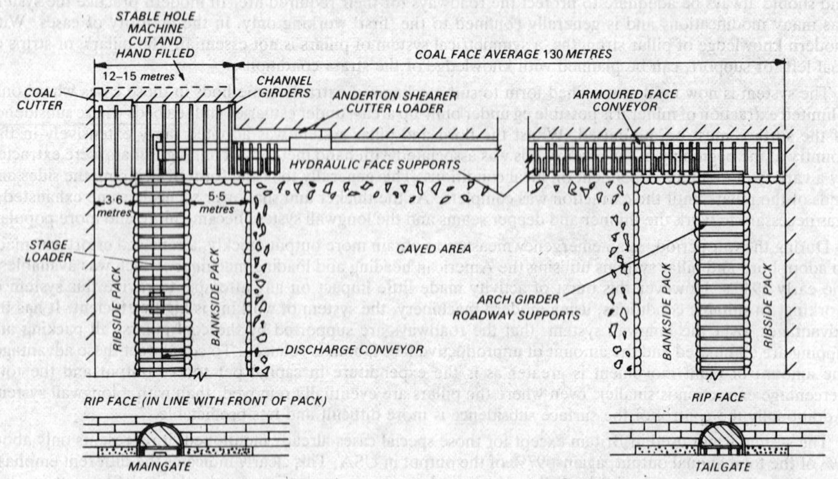

FIG. 1.—Typical Layout of an Advancing Coal Face.

LONGWALL SYSTEM (RETREATING).—For many years the practice of retreating longwall faces from the colliery boundaries after driving the initial roadways was unpopular in Britain. In a review of the British coal industry by a technical advisory committee undertaken in 1945 the report 'Coal Mining' recommended that the retreating system of mining should be the second choice after the intensive bord and pillar system. This was recommended to achieve high productivity and efficiency, but in spite of these advantages it was very little used as a mining system. Many reasons were put forward for this reluctance, including the lack of the necessary development drivage equipment, the problems of maintaining the roadways driven in solid coal and finally impatience in waiting for the completion of the required development in times of coal shortage. No doubt a combination of all these factors was responsible for the slow progress of this system of mining.

The development of power loading machines and experience of their use has clearly exposed the bottleneck of gate-end ripping and packing in the advancing system, and redirected attention to the advantages of mining on the retreat. Retreat mining is now increasingly aided by power heading machines capable of dealing with both coal and stone. Some 16% of the longwall faces operating during 1982 were retreating, and higher percentages are projected for the years ahead. Retreating eliminates the problems of gate-end support, advance stable holes or headings, ripping and packing. It also greatly increases the potential for truly continuous mining. Several 'partial' retreat systems are now in operation. Here several panels advanced to the colliery boundary and then some panels retreat using the existing roadways.

The longwall retreating system has the following definite advantages: (1) Roadways are supported by solid coal or partly by coal pillar in those cases where very wide packed headings are used. (2) The seam to be worked is proved by the development headings in advance thus locating geological problems such as faults, washouts etc at an early stage enabling plans to be modified if necessary. (3) The elimination of the 'cyclic' operations of ripping and packing enables work at the face to progress in a continuous manner.

Where properly planned and worked the system gives very high outputs and efficiences—much higher than a comparable advancing face. Fig 2 shows a modern colliery layout with retreating faces.

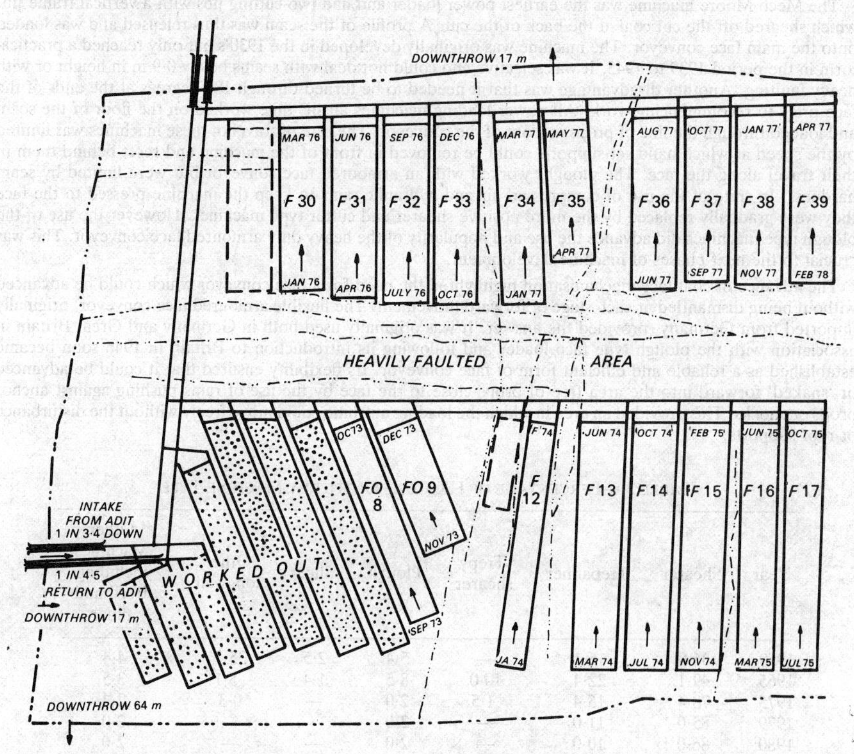

FIG.2.—Typical Layout Retreating Coal Faces. (Arrows in faces indicate direction of working. Faults are shown by dotted lines. Extraction height 0·7–1·07 m. Face length 100 m. Coal pillars 18 to 27 m)

MECHANISATION OF COAL GETTING

Historical.—The development of coal face mechanisation techniques has been a long and interesting process and is worthy of a brief description. Speed of change has been most rapid in the last 20 years or so and as a result it is now acknowledged that the face techniques in Britain are the most highly developed in the world.

The first step in the mechanisation of coal getting was the replacement of the hand pick by the coalcutter. The coal was then hand filled into tubs directly at the face. The introduction of face conveyors established the cycle of cutting, filling, packing and conveyor moving. This method of mining persisted into the 1950's. It was then that loading machines reached a sufficient state of reliability to replace the hand filling of coal onto face conveyors. The first group of machines were capable of loading cut and blasted coal on to the face conveyor. These machines were based on the standard coalcutter with the conventional picks being replaced by loading 'flights'. The Huwood loader was a slightly different type and worked on the buttock of the prepared coal. The coal was loaded onto a bottom belt type conveyor by a series of oscillating flights working on a base plate. The cycle of operations established by the face conveyor continued, the coal was cut and loaded and the packing and conveyor moving followed. The timbering or face support had to follow the passage of the loading machines as they travelled the face.

The next stage in the development was the introduction of machines which could both cut and load the coal in one operation onto the face conveyor. These power loaders can be classified according to the depth of web removed: (1) 50 mm to 250 mm web. This group comprises the plough, scraper box and slicer type of machines where the coal is wedged or scraped off the face. (2) 600 mm web. This group contains a variety of multi-jib cutters, the rotating drum shearer, the trepanner and the trepan-shearer machines. (3) 1·2 to 1·8 m web. This group of the largest web machines includes the Meco Moore cutter loader and a few developments of multi-jib cutters supplemented by chains of loading flights. During the period 1950 to 1960 only the Meco Moore and trepanner established any form of regular application throughout the country.

The Meco Moore machine was the earliest power loader and had two cutting jibs with a vertical frame jib, which sheared off the cut coal at the back of the cut. A profile of the seam was thus released and was loaded onto the main face conveyor. The machine was originally developed in the 1930's but only reached a practical form in the period 1939 to 1945. It was selective and could not deal with seams below 0·9 m in height or with heavy faulting. Another disadvantage was that it needed to be turned through 180 degrees at the ends of the face prior to recommencing work. All power loading machines at this time worked on the floor of the seam and loaded through the line of props in front of the conveyor. The rate of travel of these machines was limited by the speed at which hand set supports could be removed in front of the machine and reset behind them in their travel along the face. The ploughs worked with an armoured face conveyor but were limited by seam hardness. In spite of the use of compressed air and hydraulic rams to keep the machine pressed to the face they were gradually replaced by the more positive shearer and cutter type machines. However the use of the plough type machines did advance the use and popularity of the heavy duty armoured face conveyor. This was crucial to the next phases of machine development.

The advance of coal face mechanisation highlighted the need for a face conveyor which could be advanced without being dismantled at each stage of forward movement. The flexible armoured face conveyor, originally imported from Germany, provided the answer. It was originally used both in Germany and Great Britain in association with the plough type face loader and following its introduction to Britain in 1946 soon became established as a reliable and efficient form of face conveyor. Its flexibility ensured that it could be advanced or 'snaked' forward into the area free of props close to the face by the use of rams pushing against anchor props or chocks. This provided an area in which the loading machine could move freely without the disturbance of roof supports.

TABLE 3.—PERCENTAGE OF UK COAL OUTPUT BY MACHINE TYPE

Year	Shearer	Trepanner	Trep-shearer	Plough	Slicer	Other longwall	Other Machines including Bord and pillar
1959	36·9	15·1	—	5·4	2·5	35·7	4·4
1965	49·1	22·4	10·0	8·5	1·4	5·1	3·5
1975	78·4	15·4	1·5	2·0	—	0·3	2·4
1979	85·0	11·0	—	2·0	—	—	2·0
1980	86·0	10·0	—	2·0	—	—	2·0
1981	87·0	10·0	—	1·0	—	—	1·0
1982	88·0	10·0	—	1·0	—	—	1·0

This type of face conveyor was strong enough to carry loading machines on its structure and still be advanced by power. Coalcutters were initially used to prepare hard coal for subsequent ploughing. This was followed by mounting machines of the disc shearer type on the armoured flexible conveyor. Early machines were developed from existing coalcutters with extended transverse shafts to carry the pick drums. However developments were very rapid and hydraulic haulage was introduced with stronger chains replacing the rope haulage arrangements and machines were generally increased in strength, power and efficiency. The other machines of the medium web type, including the trepanner and trepan-shearer, also developed quickly and each new improvement in design and performance brought its wave of popularity. However the ascendency of the versatile and powerful shearer type machine was assured. The use of power loading machines in the last 20 years is illustrated by Table 3.

The extended use of power loading machines and the armoured face conveyor stimulated the use of hydraulic face props. In the early 1950's the single hydraulic prop became established and provided the answer to the need for an easily and withdrawn, strong, reliable support. Even more important was the further stimulus given to the subsequent development of frame supports, chock type supports and eventually the selfadvancing support which was a chock which could set, withdraw and move on the face by power. These later developments have revolutionised roof support at the face and allowed the elimination of packing and introduced the almost universal practice of caving the wastes behind longwall faces.

MODERN POWER LOADERS.—The rate of machine development in the last 15 to 20 years has been such that machines once considered very effective, such as the Meco Moore, have gone out of use and those machines still in operation have been improved almost beyond recognition. It is therefore only necessary to describe those power loaders which are currently producing the bulk of the annual output.

Shearer Loader.—This is undoubtedly the most popular and versatile machine in modern use and is responsible for nearly 85% of the present (Table 3). The latest machine consists of the following units:

(1) An electric drive with power up to 600 kW, from two 300 kW, water cooled motors, driving through gearboxes to the haulage and cutting units. (2) A hydraulically powered unit driving the haulage sprocket. This engages on the fixed pre-tensioned chain anchored to the face conveyor and allows the machine to haul itself along the face. Alternatively the haulage may be effected by the latest track-reactive haulage in which the sprocket of the machine is replaced by a toothed chain engaged in a fixed rack attached to the conveyor structure. Another alternative is ram propulsion. These modern developments eliminate the tensioned haulage chain on the face and its associated breakage and handling. (3) A cutting unit consisting of a drum or drums onto which the cutting picks are fixed. Machines may have either fixed or 'ranging' drums at one or both ends. The ranging drums are fixed on arms pivoting and driving from the machine through trains of gears in the ranging arms. The ranging drums are used in the thick seams where drum diameters are used in the thick seams drum diameters are approximately 2/3rds of the seam thickness. See Fig. 3. All the machines have suitably designed ploughs or cowls for diverting the cut coal onto the conveyor and cleaning up the coal left by the previous run.

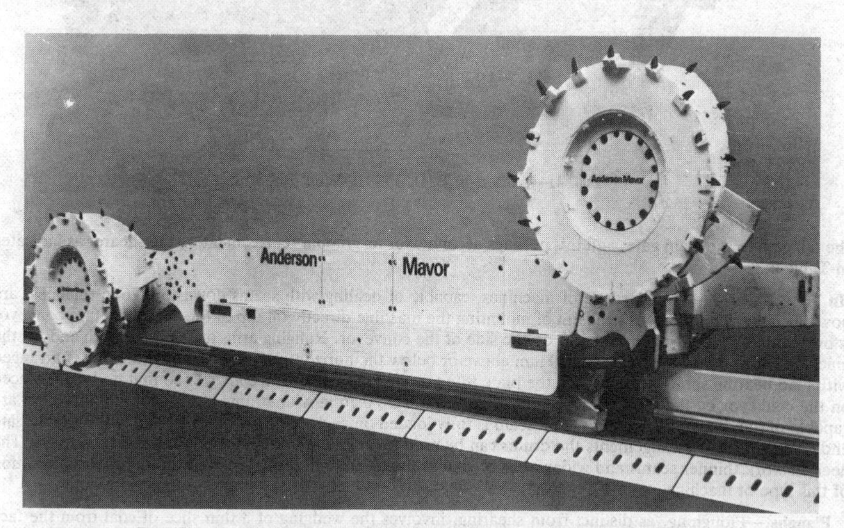

FIG. 3.—Typical Modern Cutter-Loader; the Anderson-Mavor Shearer.

The modern version of the shearer loader has many additional refinements in the drum design, variation in speed, dust suppression arrangements, 'sensing' devices for horizon control and steering arrangements. Machine control may be arranged directly from the machine or remotely by the use of either push buttons or radio signal. Most machines are now fitted with a variety of safeguards including pre-start warning devices.

Trepanner.—As indicated in Table 3 this type of machine now produces some 11% of the present output and is on the decline. The trepanner is mainly confined to the thinner, softer and cleaner seams, in the thickness ranges between 0·9 and 1·2 m. It is an auger type of machine and has the virtue of producing more large coal than the shearer. The Trepanner operates on the floor of the seam with steering and control arrangements mounted on the conveyor structure. It can be either single ended or double ended for working in both directions. The auger take the main core of coal which is broken off at the base of the auger and fed through slots in the auger drum onto the face conveyor. Additional horizontal and vertical chains and top discs trim the face section of the remaining coal. The haulage arrangements are similar to the shearer, often the fixed chain sprocket type, or the more recent track reactive system.

Trepan-shearer.—This machine comprises an auger head as with the trepanner plus the addition of a fixed drum to undertake the trimming. It combines the large coal production features of the trepanner with some of the flexibility and simplicity of the shearer. The machine is only capable of working in one direction, from

FIG. 4.—Anderton BJD-B57 'In-Web' Shearer.

the tail gate to the main gate, and this perhaps accounts for its gradual replacement by the shearer as indicated in Table 3.

'In Web' Shearer.—A new range of machines, capable of dealing with seams down to 0.76 m thickness are now available. The previous problem of mounting the machine directly on top of the armoured face conveyor is overcome by mounting the shearer on the side of the conveyor. Ranging arms are fitted at both ends of the machine which enables it to range 300 mm above or below the horizontal. The machine mounting is arranged with load bearing shoes working on a toe plate fitted to the face side of the conveyor so that no load is placed on the conveyor by the shearer. Machines of this type have 0.76 m wide drums as a standard feature but are capable of handling 0·91 m drums. The seam is fully loaded on each direction of travel and with suitable gate end conveyor drive arrangements the drums can be used to assist in the ripping and dinting of roadways. The need to work thinner seams and wider webs of coal in the future will probably result in the wider application of this type of machine.

Ploughs.—Ploughing, as distinct from shearing, involves the wedging of a thin slice of coal from the face by a series of wedge shaped picks mounted in the plough head. The depth of slice is dependant upon the coal hardness and the power available. The plough unit comprises: (1) The plough head which is a heavy casting, attached to the endless haulage chain, onto which the picks are set. (2) The drive unit fixed to the drive head of the conveyor.

TABLE 4.—ARMOURED FLEXIBLE CONVEYOR OUTPUT

Conveyor Width metres	Chain Loading Kg/metre	Conveyor speed, metres/min				
		36·6	51·5	57·0	64·6	77·4
		Conveyor output, tonnes/hour				
0·61	99	216	305	339	381	457
0·76	149	326	457	508	579	686

Ploughing is effected by pulling the head along the face with guides and chain tubes on the face side of the armoured conveyor controlling and guiding the plough.

The plough is an attractively simple device and whilst it is widely used in the softer coal seams on the Continent, and in spite of much research and modification, it has never made a major breakthrough in the UK. It is expected to evenutally disappear in favour of the more positive machines now available for working thin seams.

ARMOURED FLEXIBLE CONVEYOR.—It will have already become apparent that the armoured flexible face conveyor has played a crucial role in the development of power loading machines. It has been progressively improved and strengthened since its introduction over 20 years ago. This has been a necessary development as the machines mounted upon it have grown in size and weight.

The size and construction of the pans, connectors, chains etc are controlled by NCB Standards. The depths have tended to become standardised at either 128 or 222 mm, with variable chain speeds and widths of 0·61, 0·76 and 0·91 m. The chain size used is either 18, 19, 22 or 26 mm, dependent upon the size and power of the conveyor. The use of twin outboard chains with connecting flights is almost universal with only a few centre strand (single or double chain) applications. The manufacture of the line pans is also controlled as to the type of steel used, the rolling, welding and tolerances. The pans consist of a horizontal deck plate welded between side rollings with joints to allow the conveyor to 'snake' whilst being advanced. To increase the conveyor capacity, and prevent spillage, goaf side plates can be bolted to the pans. The channels and brackets need to carry electric cable, water hoses etc are also attached to the goafside of the pans. Ramp or toe plates can also be attached to the face side of the pans to assist in the loading of spillage as the conveyor is pushed forward. The conveyors are moved over mechanically by the hydraulic rams attached to the self advancing supports or, where these are not used, from other anchor props.

Driving arrangements for AFCs are also standardised in Great Britain. Motors can drive at right angle to, or parallel to, the line of pans on each side of the gearhead and tail end and can be interchangeable. For 18 mm chains, drive motors of 65, 150 and 300 hp are available, transmitting their power through traction type fluid couplings and gearboxes. The various combinations of width and speed available produce a wide range of carrying capacity to suit a wide range of powerleading capacities. Table 4 illustrates the range of conveyor capacities using outboard chains. This type of conveyor has also a fairly wide application in other areas apart from the coal face. It is used as a stage loader and in steep drifts where it can operate on gradients of 1 in 1 in either direction.

BORD AND PILLAR AND HEADING MACHINERY.—Although the tonnage obtained by bord and pillar mechanised methods is small in UK, this mining technique produces the bulk of the output in both the USA and Australia. This involves either a separate cutting machine followed by loaders or a combined cutting-loading machine. A similar range of equipment is used in heading work for longwall developments and retreat mining. The heading size influences the choice of machine rather than the system of mining.

LOADING MACHINES.—Machines for loading broken minerals, coal, ore etc. have been used in headings and tunnels of all kinds for a long time. They can be broadly classified into two groups: (1) Bucket or Shovel Loaders: (2) Gathering Arm Loaders.

Bucket or Shovel Loaders.—This type of loader is not necessarily confined to mining work and is widely used on the surface. The surface machines tend to be less compact in design since there are no roadway size limitations involved. For mining applications the machine is commonly rail or tyre mounted and the bucket

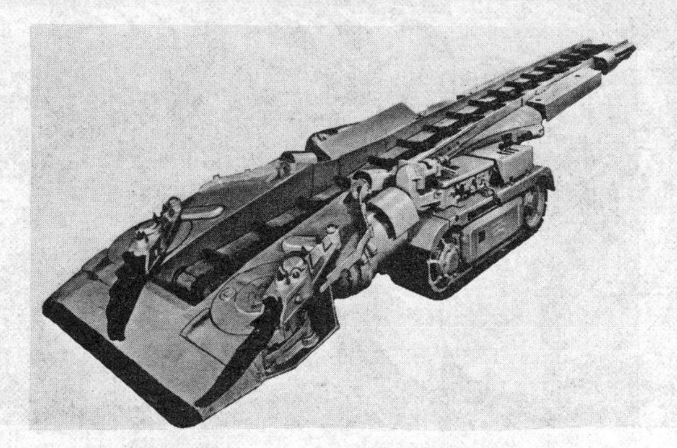

FIG. 5.—Caterpillar-mounted Gathering-arm Loader (*Joy Manufacturing Co*).

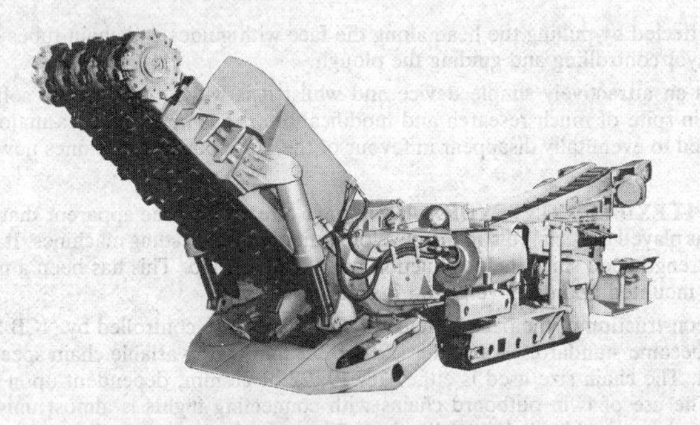

FIG. 6.—Caterpillar-mounted Continuous Miner. (*Joy Manufacturing Co*).

FIG. 7.—Dosco-NCB Dint Header.

FIG. 8.—NCB/Dosco In-Seam Miner.

is loaded by crowding forward into the material to be moved. The bucket is then raised by a form of 'link and chain' mechanism to tip over the top of the machine into a car or conveyor. Side discharge models are also available where height is limited or where other physical considerations make the normal machine unsuitable. Loading capacity is dependent upon both the bucket size and the skill of the operator. However, it is possible to load at the rate of up to 1 tonne per minute based on three lifts per minute. This type of machine is not widely used in coal mining but has a role to play in stone tunnels and in wet conditions where other machines would not be suitable.

Gathering Arm Loaders.—This type of loader is generally caterpillar mounted with a gathering head projecting forward to an apron plate several metres wide. The mineral is loaded by oscillating arms, working on either side of the apron plate, which sweep the material onto a flexible chain conveyor which runs from the apron plate, up and over the machine and onto a boom. This boom can be swivelled in a horizontal plane which gives flexibility in the final discharge arrangements. Hydraulic controls operate the movement of the caterpillars, the apron plate and the boom. The drive power is either by individual electric motors or by hydraulics via a large central drive. Figure 5 shows a typical machine which can have a loading capacity between 1 and 4 tonne/min dependent upon the material and site conditions. This type of loader is very suitable where the material is loose and well prepared. However, its use is declining in the UK due to the increased application of machines which both cut and load the mineral.

CONTINUOUS MINERS.—As in longwall mining the advantages of having one machine to 'get' and load the coal is enormous. A great deal of manoeuvring of the coalcutter and loading machine is avoided and the combined cutting-loading machine can stay in the heading at all times and becomes a continuous miner. Machines of this type are made by several manufacturers and they vary in size, design and method of movement to suit a range of seam heights and conditions. They basically comprise a pick type cutting apparatus with the coal loaded either through or around the machine by an inbuilt conveyor. A typical 'continuous miner' is shown in Fig. 6. The model illustrated is mounted on caterpillar tracks and is capable of driving roadways 3·6 to 6·7 m wide in seam heights which can vary between 1·5 and 3 m.

The chain ripper bar tears the coal from the face on the upward motion and discharges it onto the intermediate conveyor which feeds the centrally located hopper. The coal is then carried by a rear conveyor to the main transportation system. The ripper head and rear conveyor are capable of swinging through an arc of 45 degrees on each side of the centre line of the machine and the gathering arm deals with material which is spilled below the ripper bars. The advance of 0·46 m is made by a series of 'sumps' and upward cuts whilst the machine is traversed across the width of the heading.

DINT HEADERS.—During the extraction of coal a situation eventually arises where stone or dirt partially or completely replaces the coal due to a fault, washout or similar geological discontinuity. If the machine, in use at that time, cannot cut the new material then it has to be removed and replaced by a new machine. This causes delays and additional expense. The 'dint header' was designed to overcome this problem and is capable of extracting stone with a compressive strength of up to 844 kg/cm^2 as well as coal. It also has sufficient power and strength to cut below the floor and tackle floor repair problems. Figure 7 illustrates the machine, which

FIG. 9.—Dosco-MK2A Road-header Tunnelling Machine.

also has caterpillar tracks, ripping chains, a central conveyor and hydraulic jacks to raise and lower its height. It is designed to operate in rectangular roadways which can vary in height between 1·5 and 2·1 m.

IN-SEAM MINER (British Coal/Dosco).—Whilst this machine was originally designed for working in headings in seams from 1·07 m at 50 mm increments up to 1·4 m, it is also capable of dealing with dirt and soft stone. The machine is based on the endless chain system with picks spaced at 0·2 m centres, with scoops to collect and deliver the mined material onto a central conveyor. The machine is illustrated in Fig. 8 and the positive steering arrangements make it ideal for drivages within the seam including headings and stable hole elimination on Longwall faces.

RIPPING AND TUNNELLING MACHINES.—Although 80% of rippings are still broken down by the use of explosives there has been considerable progress in the mechanisation of this mining operation. Unfortunately the wider applications of mechanical aids to ripping lips is dependent upon a corresponding mechanisation of the disposal of the ripping debris into the pack area. In certain circumstances the two operations are very closely linked. Figure 9 illustrates the boom type roadheader which has become widely used. The boom is adjustable for cutting profiled roadways and capable of dealing with strata with compressive strengths up to 1,054 kg/cm^2. Machines of this type, with the disposal conveyor removed and platforms or scaffolding added, can be used in mechanical packing systems. Such an application is shown, schematically, in Figure 10 where a slusher is used for the packing.

The technical progress in the fields of mechanisation of coal getting and heading drivage has resulted in the development of a range of machines for use around the coal face, heading or tunnel. This is a field where further progress is still required. Work is currently being undertaken in such areas as cable handling, ripping scaffolds, packing arrangements, power packs, yielding supports and the removal of small coal ahead of the face conveyor. The reader is referred to the reports and publications of British Coal's Mining Research and Development Establishment for full descriptions of these and other developments.

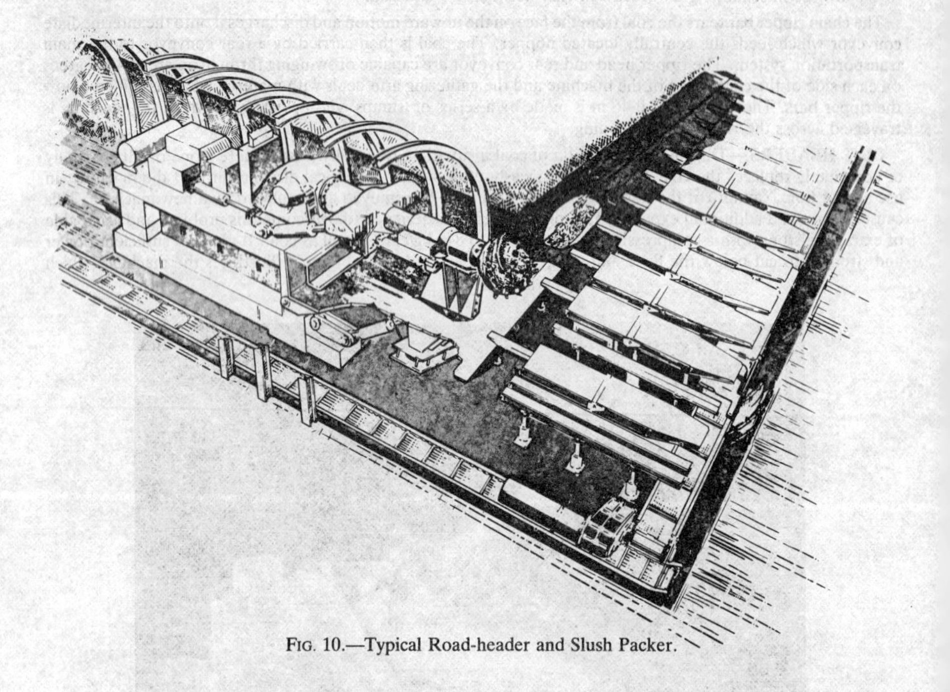

Fig. 10.—Typical Road-header and Slush Packer.

GROUND MOVEMENT AND SUPPORT

The extraction of coal from underground workings causes a stress redistribution in the strata, from the original virgin conditions, and an associated amount of movement. The term 'strata control' covers the study of the stress in the strata, rock movement and the means of supporting the undermined mineral. No subject has received more attention and investigation in the last 30 years. This is understandable considering how

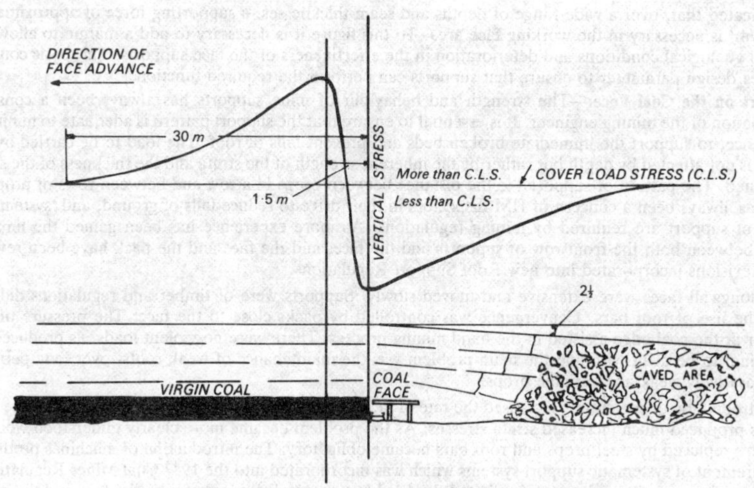

FIG. 11.—Typical Stress Distribution at Coal Face.

important it is to the mining process. The success of any mining operation depends on the effectiveness of the methods adopted to control and support the undermined strata. Strata control can be subdivided into two main sections: (1) The study of the strata characteristics *per se*, their strengths and behaviour under stress; (2) the support of the strata by artificial methods, their strength characteristics and reactions to the forces induced by mining.

STRATA BEHAVIOUR.—As a result of long investigations and much practical research and experience the principles of strata movement are now fairly well understood. The stresses and movements underground can be measured with modern instruments and the eventual surface subsidence can be fairly accurately predicted.

It is generally accepted that when coal support is withdrawn at a longwall face, the overlying strata forms a cantilever over the face and waste. This cantilever gradually hinges down from a fulcrum near the face edge to a point some 30 to 45 m back in the waste, the actual distance beingd ependent upon the strength of the strata, its geological condition and the type of packing or caving adopted. The beds immediately overlying the seam break up as the coal face supports are withdrawn, then bulk up after breaking and so eventually provide support for the upper layers of the cantilever. Movement of the cantilever is inevitable but total collapse is prevented by the contact of the upper beds with the consolidated packs or waste material. The immediate beds above the seam, to the point where breakage ceases, are carried on the artificial supports at the face. It is their function to maintain the lower beds, against the upper beds, and so prevent bed separation and also yield with the subsiding cantilever. This theory has been widely investigated and confirmed by research workers of different countries over a long period. The results are generally as shown in Fig. 11.

The coal extraction causes a concentration of stress just ahead of the face and at the solid sides and corner of the panel being extracted. Normal stress is taken as that appropriate to the depth of the seam. From the face the beds converge as shown and the lower beds collapse in the area behind the face. The lower beds in breaking bulk up and the extent or height of caving is determined by the manner of this break up or bulking. For normal coal measure shales the ratio of the density of solid to broken material averages about 1·5. Tests have shown that the height of caving can be determined from the following formula: $C = h(K - 1)$, where c = Height in metres of caving above roof level; h = Seam height in metres; and K = 1·5 average.

CONVERGENCE.—It is not possible to influence the slope of the upper beds of the cantilever of strata owing to the weight of rock involved. Therefore the slope of these upper beds governs the minimum rate of convergence, ie the angle of inclination of the roof relative to the floor. Tests and experience have shown that the convergence can be calculated using the formula: $C = 11{\cdot}83H + 28{\cdot}7$, where C = convergence in mm per metre of face advance; and H = height in metres of the seam extracted. This is, of course, only applicable in normal mining conditions. In practical terms it is about 40 mm per metre of face advance for the medium face thicknesses. At a distance of 2 m from the face the convergence would therefore be about 80 mm minimum for a medium thickness seam.

As already mentioned, the function of the face supports is to hold the lower beds of the cantilever over the working area up against the upper beds and so prevent bed separation and increased convergence. Many tests have indicated that, over a wide range of depths and seam thicknesses, a supporting force of approximately 11 tonne/m^2 is necessary in the working face area. To this figure it is necessary to add a margin to allow for abnormal geological conditions and deterioration in the effectiveness of the face supports. This basic concept provides a design parameter to ensure that supports can perform the required function.

Support on the Coal Face.—The strength and behaviour of mine supports has always been a constant preoccupation of the mining engineer. It is essential to ensure that the support pattern is adequate to minimise convergence, to support the immediate broken beds and prevent falls of roof. The load to be carried by ths supports is not affected by depth but rather by the inherent strength of the strata and the thickness of the seam being mined. The pattern of supports, ie the distance between props in a row and between rows of props in a face, has always been a concern of HM Inspectors in their drive to reduce falls of ground, and 'systematic' patterns of support are required by mining regulations. As more experience has been gained the limiting distance between both the front row of supports and the face, and the face and the pack have been revised and the revisions incorporated into new Roof Support Regulations.

Early longwall faces were extensive and moved slowly. Supports were of timber and regulations did not require the use of roof bars. Convergence was controlled by packs close to the face. The pressure of the cantilever at the coal edge assisted in the hand mining process. There were no violent loads, as produced by coal cutting, to be dealt with and the main problem was the maintenance of weak roofs, over long periods, on comparatively weak and variable props.

The introduction of coalcutters increased the rate of face advance and it soon became apparent that the new machines produced much increased strata stresses. As the problem became more clearly understood wooden props were replaced by steel props and roof bars became obligatory. The introduction of machines produced the requirement of systematic support systems which was incorporated into the 1947 Coal Mines Regulations. The introduction of face conveyors necessitated the need for greater distances between the face and the packs and a maximum limit of 2 m was stipulated. Following a great deal of investigation at this time into packing, caving and various support patterns the distances between props, rows of props and the face to packs were extended and revised. These new dimensions together with the requirement that any support system had to be 'approved' by HM Inspectorate was incorporated into the 1956 Mines Support Regulations. Similarly and for the first time the actual supports to be used needed the approval of the Mines Department as it was then called. A testing facility was set up in order that new supports could be submitted for test and approval.

The widespread introduction of the armoured flexible conveyor and the increased use of power loaders resulted in the development of the 'prop free front face'. This involved long spans of roof being temporarily left exposed and the frequent removal and resetting of supports to allow the free passage of machines along the coal face. Hydraulic supports became popular as they were more easily removed and reset and were capable of developing an initial setting load. The 'frame' and 'chock' type of supports were a logical development. These latter units are heavy and cumbersome and clearly would need to be moved by power. This led to the 'Self Advancing Power Operated Support' where the setting, withdrawal and movement of the support system is integrated into the movement of the conveyor and functions from a power source.

The complete concept of roof support at the longwall face has thus changed in the period under consideration. This is clearly shown by the following details of the growth of 'powered' supports on British longwall faces at five yearly intervals: The number of installations in 1958 was 26; there were 176 in 1963; 700 in 1968; and 695 in 1973. The latest figures show that the trend has continued and today only minor faces, such as those used for training, are supported by props and bars.

FACE SUPPORTS

Timber Props.—Timber props are rarely used today in large-scale mining operations except for temporary and emergency situations. However, they are very useful and versatile with application in the support and strutting of many types of excavation and cavities. The strength of an individual prop depends upon the relationship of its diameter to its length, the type of timber, its condition and length of seasoning, moisture content and freedom from flaws. As an approximate rule of thumb soft wood props have a bearing strength of 157 kg/cm^2 of the area of the narrow end and hardwood props have a bearing strength of 196 kg/cm^2. These bearings strengths are greatly increased if the props have been seasoned and air dried.

The 1966 Coal and Other Mines (Support) Regulations recognise timber props as a temporary support and requires that they be replaced when broken or unstable. It also specifies the dimension of the 'lids' to be used with the timber supports and since they are not 'approved supports' it stipulates that their use is limited to 7 days.

Chocks.—Chocks are used as temporary support in those situations where stability is very important. They tend to replace several props for reasons of either strength or the need to have a greater area of surface contact with the roof and floor. Their chief field of use is at the waste edge of longwall faces. The use of chocks, to support the waste edge and control its collapse, was considered indispensable in caving situations prior to the introduction of the power-operated chock type of face supports.

Chocks built of prepared softwood timber, 100 to 150 mm square, will carry loads of 21 to 31 kg/cm^2 of contact area when compressed by about 3%. This loading will increase to a maximum of 42 to 56 kg/cm^2 at 20% compression. If the chocks are built of hardwood the loads increase to some 56 to 70 kg/cm^2 at 3% and

105 kg/cm^2 at 20% compression. At a loading of 70 kg/cm^2 the actual loads carried by a chock built with wood of 10, 12·5, and 15 cm sections, using two pieces per layer, are 29, 46 and 65 tonne respectively.

Chocks have to be made to fit tightly to the roof when they are set. They are then released, withdrawn and eventually reset. This cycle can produce a compression of 5, 10 or even 15% dependent upon the initial height of the chock. In order to facilitate the resetting, timber wedges are used to bring the chock tight to the roof. The chock is dismantled using a form of chock 'release', the most simple of which consists of four pairs of cast steel wedges. Each pair of wedges has a simple trip device incorporated which, when struck with a long-handled hammer, allows the upper wedge to slide off the lower wedge. They are placed over each corner of the chock and so arranged that two pairs can be tripped and freed on one side of the chock and the other two on the opposite side. This causes the collapse of the chock above the release devices.

Chocks are also made with steel frames and integral release devices. A typical chock of this type has four 'H' sections forming columns standing at the corners of a flat base plate. Each of the four releases has a transverse wedge to enable it to be set tightly. The release mechanism is similar to that described earlier with the exception that the trip device is operated by a cam which is turned by a remotely operated pulling device. The chock can be advanced by merely continuing to pull the chain of the release device which is a further safety factor.

Steel Props.—The rigid steel prop provides a stronger and more uniform support than the timber prop. It also has the advantage of a longer effective life which reduces the transport costs, and the ability to be repaired and rehabilitated after damage. However, they have the disadvantage of being of a fixed length without any yielding properties, except when driven into the floor by excessive pressure.

Steel props are normally of 'H' section rolled steel with a tensile strength of 30 to 40 tons per sq in. Carbon and manganese are added to ensure deformation without sudden fracture. Table 5 shows the strength properties and data for the various sections normally used for face supports.

The floor end of a rigid steel prop may be open or closed depending on the strength of the floor on which it is to stand and the bearing area required to induce a satisfactory resistance. To a large extent, penetration of the floor is necessary to give the load-yield characteristics to support the roof and yet allow for its inevitable subsidence. If penetration is too easy the support may offer less than its effective strength, causing roof troubles which can only be corrected by increasing the floor bearing area. Lack of height adjustment is a great disadvantage in the rigid prop and to overcome this problem, some props have been fitted with special heads incorporating a large wedge device. The use of the wedge ensures that there is an initial setting load, it also provides a small height adjustment and makes for an easier release under load.

TABLE 5.—STRENGTH CHARACTERISTICS FOR STEEL PROPS AND ARCHES. (Sections *b, d, f,* and *h* are of mild steel; sections *a, c, e* and *i* are of medium carbon steel; section *g* is of 1·7% manganese1steel.)

Reference	Section Data			Strength Properties		
	Dimensions mm	Area mm^2	Mass kg/m	Max Loading kg/mm^2	Max Strength tonnes	Av Strength tonnes
a	127 × 127	3980	31·3	55·6	117	61
b	127 × 114	3412	27·0	45·2	91	51
c	108 × 89	2703	21·2	60·8	81	41
d	127 × 76	2696	21·1	49·0	66	30
e	89 × 89	2522	19·8	66·3	83	41
f	102 × 102	2387	18·8	45·7	64	30
g	102 × 64	2277	17·9	67·6	75	36
h	102 × 64	2277	17·9	45·8	61	25
i	83 × 76	1896	14·9	59·7	57	25

Many attempts were made to produce a satisfactory yielding prop which would incorporate the important features required by a coal face support. These can be summarised as: (1) Adjustability in length to cope with seam height variations and allow for yield. (2) Provision for setting tightly with an initial load of at least 3 tonnes. (3) Capacity to yield or shorten while maintaining adequate resistance of 20, 30 or 40 tonnes according to the local conditions, the full resistance being offered with a yield of up to 25 mm.

The most successful props of this type were developed on the Continent and were dependent upon the friction between the prop members which were held together by a wedge and clamp arrangement. These type of props were both heavy and cumbersome and experience showed that their performance was erratic. The critical friction coefficient was affected by both dust and water and often by combinations of each. In addition, their success was too dependent upon the human factor. The initial tightness was determined by the operator and in practice it was found that often only some 75% of the initial setting resistance was achieved. This provided too great a local variability and the friction prop was eventually replaced by the hydraulic prop.

Hydraulic Props.—The first attempts at hydraulic prop design were undertaken around 1924 in Germany. The first full face installation was undertaken in Great Britain during 1947 and this led to a period of rapid development. The hydraulic prop has all the advantages required from a yielding support. A typical prop comprises two steel tubes, of about 89 and 100 mm diameter, the lower one forming a pressure cylinder and the upper one a ram. Both tubes contain oil and the prop is extented by pumping the oil from the ram tube into the cylinder tube by means of a pump built into the ram. This pump is operated manually by a detachable handle engaging a transverse crankshaft near the top of the ram. In this way the prop is extended and set tight to the roof, with an initial setting load of 5 tonnes, all in one operation. At a predetermined loading of about 20 tonnes the prop yields by passing oil from the cylinder into the ram. This is achieved by a pipe, inside the ram, which connects the piston head to a spring-loaded control valve mounted in a housing above the pump shaft. This valve can also be pulled off its seat by hand either by the use of a chain hooked to a shackle in the valve housing or by means of the pump handle being used as a lever to release the load on the pump prior to the withdrawal of the prop.

A guard tube, of the same diameter as the end cap of the prop, is fitted around the cylinder to protect it from damage. Prop heads vary in design depending upon the type of roof bars in use at the particular face. Mineral oil was initially used in the props, but this has now been replaced by hydraulic fluid, a 5% soluble oil and water solution, to reduce the fire risk. Modern props usually have setting loads of 5 to 10 tonnes with release at 25 to 30 tonnes. Fig 12 shows the various components.

Roof Bars.—As in the case of props, steel eventually replaced wood as the material used in roof bars. Typical steel bars are corrugated or 'W' section approximately 127 mm wide, 10 to 13 mm thick, and with a length varied to suit the particular support system. In mining systems which involve the movement of supports

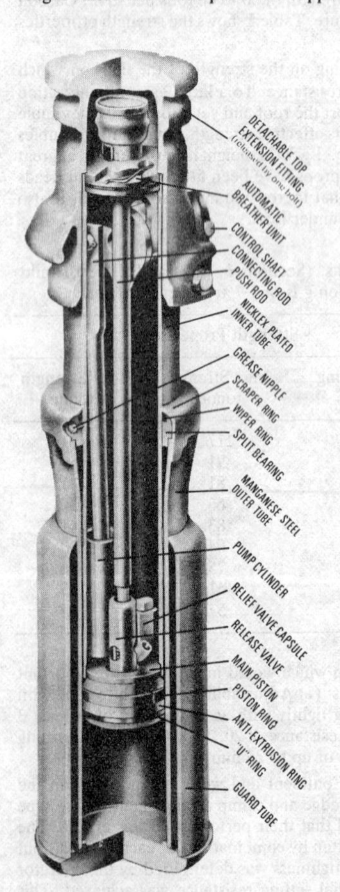

FIG. 12.—Hand-set Hydraulic Prop (*Dowty*).

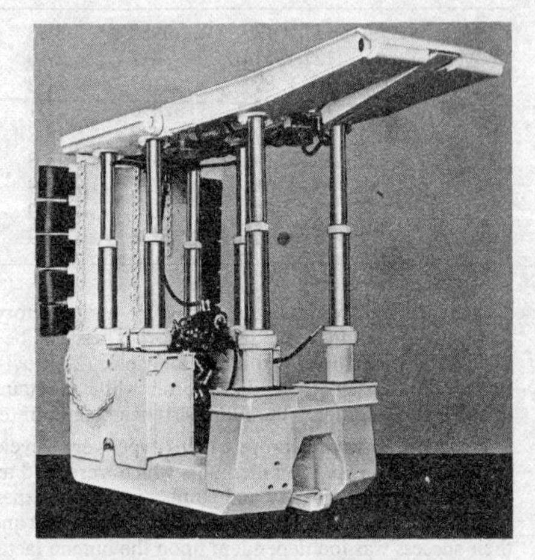

FIG. 13.—Self-Advancing, 240 tonne, 6-Leg Hydraulic Roof Support (*Gullick*).

or a prop-free front area, a hinged bar is used. These bars vary from 0·9 to 1·2 m long, with a width of 102 to 127 mm, and a section depth of 76 to 102 mm. The ends are adapted to form a hinge having one forked and the other reduced, so that the bars can couple end to end. The connecting joint is completed with a steel pin about 38 mm diameter. The joint can be locked so that one bar is held in cantilever. To lock the joint a wedge is inserted near the hinge pin and this then allows a degree of adjustment of the cantilever bare to meet the slope of the roof.

At junctions, such as roadheads and stable holes, where longer roof spans have to be supported over machinery, heavier roof bars are needed; channel sections or special 'H' sections are used, following the approval of the design and steel quality.

Hydraulic Chocks.—These were the natural development from the hydraulic prop and by 1955 several types were undergoing field trials. Initially the development tended either towards a grouping of props on a steel base with a roof canopy, or the enlargement of a single prop fitted with a suitable base and roof plate. This latter type was widely used as a waste edge support and where coupled to the conveyor, by a hydraulic ram, could be moved forward and then used as an anchor during the moving of the conveyor.

The most popular type of hydraulic chock was that designed by Desford, which operated on a hydraulic closed circuit from a power pack in the gate. Models ranged in various sizes and loads form 30 to 102 tonnes. Modern chocks, involving a variety of ram arrangements and design modifications, are widely used underground at ripping lips, for machinery anchors and pack hole supports, as well as on the coal face.

Power Operated Self-Advancing Supports.—The increased application of power loading in the UK revealed the need to have a much faster method of operating face supports. This led to the development of power setting as well as power movement of supports. In Britain, two manufacturers, following different lines of research, led the development of these supports. The Dowty Company evolved the 'frame' type of support which consisted of pairs of their 'Roofmaster' units, with either 2 or 3 legs, set at 0·76 m centres. The units were moved alternately by power, one frame holding the roof whilst the other advanced. A 'chock' type unit comprising 4 props set on a baseplate, with box section roof bars as a canopy, was developed by Gullick.

Experience proved that the chock type unit was more popular and eventually replaced the frame type unit. Over the past 15 years substantial changes in design have taken place. Higher fluid pressures were used, and improved canopies, bases and control gear were developed. A wide range of 4, 5 and 6 leg units are now available from both British and Continental equipment manufacturers, with specification ranges of from 0·76 to 3·66 m in height and loadings of up to 325 tonnes per unit. Special 4-leg units capable of loadings up to 711 tonnes are being prepared for use in Australian mines. These will be the strongest yet manufactured. A typical modern 240-tonne roof support of this type is shown in Fig 13. This is a standard 6-leg support with an articulated roof canopy and extensible slide bars as well as a telescopic flushing shield; it is self-advancing and each leg carries 40 tonnes.

SPECIAL APPLICATIONS OF POWERED SUPPORTS.—Whilst a wide range of powered supports are available to suit most mining conditions, a range of additional features are required for special conditions.

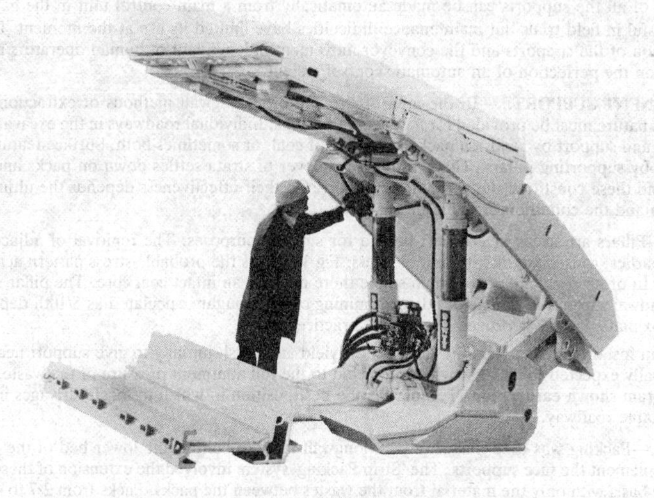

FIG. 14.—Caliper Canopy Shield Support, 2-Leg (*Dowty*).

Steep Seam Supports.—Supports used in very steep seams require some form of anchoring or stabilisation to prevent them slipping downhill when they are moved forward. This is achieved by providing a self-steering master chock at intervals down the face. This enables the other chocks to be accurately positioned either by rubbing on the adjacent lower chock or by a limited length of chain acting as a link from the adjacent higher chock. Alternatively steering rams can be attached to each support. Double acting legs are normally incorporated to give positive lowering from the roof which is necessary in steep gradients where the lowering of props tends to be sluggish. Supports of this type can be used successfully in gradients up to 1 in 1.

Thin Seam Supports.—Units for thin seams require special design considerations to provide adequate travelling clearances on the face. The required travel in the telescopic legs is achieved by the use of double telescopic legs. Clearances are improved by the use of plate type canopies or by spring steel floor and roof members.

Thick Seam Supports.—Special heavy duty units are required for seams with a thickness of 2·1 m and over. These incorporate 4, 5 or 6 legs and have been successfully used in seams up to 3·66 m height.

Shield Supports.—In thick seams with friable roofs the intrusion of broken waste material into the chock track can impede movement and access for maintenance purposes. This is generally overcome by the use of flushing shields behind and at the sides of the chocks. This problem can also be solved by the use of 'shield' type supports which is a relatively new development. Here the flushing guard is incorporated in the canopy. The support embodies an articulated caliper type canopy covering the top and rear between which the prop legs operate. This type of support is illustrated in Fig 14 and the use of fewer legs reduces obstructions as well as maintenance. It is now in use on a trial basis in Britain.

Operation of Powered Supports.—The spacing of the powered supports on a coal face is determined by their size and load-bearing capacity together with the type of roof which can be left exposed. Distances vary between 0·76 and 1·22 m centres. Fluid pressures range from 70 to 140 kg/cm^2 and the supply is by 'power packs' in one or both gates through flexible hoses to each unit. The setting loads are a function of the prop diameter and applied pressure. Yield loads are determined by valve settings within the chock.

The sequence of operational movements is generally controlled by the position of the operating valve rather than by the use of a series of valves. The use of valve gears ensures that the correct sequence of operations is followed and that no mistakes are made. The power packs which supply the hydraulic fluid under pressure are now highly efficient and incorporate pumps, sealed tanks and a series of devices for ensuring the correct proportioning of oil and water at the right level, filtration equipment and a sludge removal device.

Control Systems.—Various arrangements are currently in use for controlling the movements of chocks to ensure both greater speed and safety. This can be achieved by a simple manual system involving the movement of the chock by its own controls. In the 'adjacent chock' system the control of the moving chock is made from the adjacent unit. This gives a certain degree of operator protection. The 'batch or bank' method is effected by initiating a sequence from a master unit in each batch or bank of chocks.

A further sophistication of these control systems is the sequential arrangement which provides a degree of automation. An example of this is the 'Remotely Operated Longwall Face' (ROLF) system, where the movement of all the supports can be made automatically from a main control unit in the gate. This system was successful in field trials but maintenance difficulties have limited its use at the moment. Efforts to make the operation of the supports and the conveyor movement independent of human operators must, in future, depend upon the perfection of an automatic control system.

PERMANENT SUPPORTS.—In the area of excavation in longwall methods of extraction, supports of a permanent nature must be provided for a variety of reasons. Individual roadways in the excavated area require protection and support by roadside packs, or pillars of coal, or sometimes both. Surface features may require protection by supporting pillars. The subsiding cantilever of strata settles down on packs and broken caved material and these constitute the permanent support. On their effectiveness depends the ultimate subsidence of the area and the condition of the mine roadways.

Pillars.—Pillars are areas of coal left behind for support purposes. The removal of adjacent support, as indicated earlier, causes a redistribution of stress. Fig 15 shows the probable stress pattern across a pillar and pack area. In order for a pillar to remain stable there must be an intact coal core. The pillar size required to protect roadways from the effects of adjacent mining can be roughly calculated as 1/10th depth +14 metres. This approximate guide has proved effective in practice.

In certain instances, the pillars are designed to yield and crush initially to give support near a ribside, but are evenutally expected to collapse when subjected to the full abutment pressure of the waste. A study of the stress diagram shown earlier, Fig 11, indicates the best position in which to locate drivages in such pillars to obtain a stable roadway.

Packing.—Packing was used universally on longwall faces to control the lower bed of the subsiding strata and to supplement the face supports. The 'Strip Packing' system involved the extension of these packs by hand on a cyclic basis with only the material from the wastes between the packs. Packs from 2·7 to 4·6 m long were built over 30 to 80% of the face length with the individual wastes between the packs being encouraged to cave.

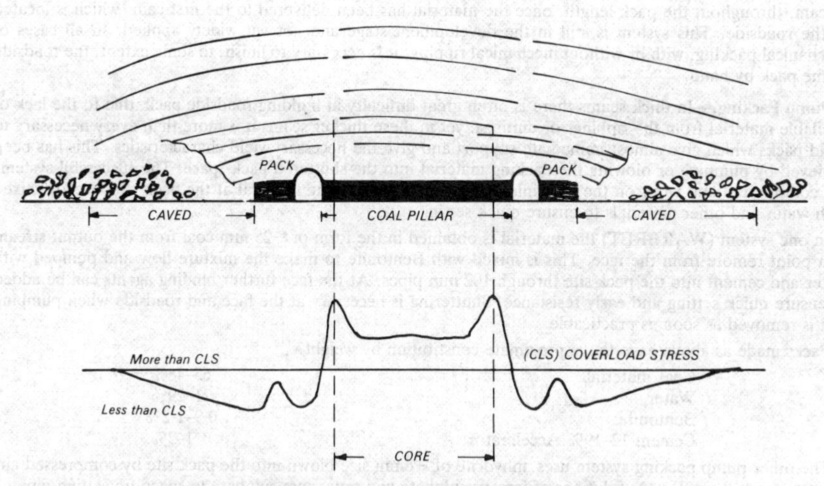

FIG. 15.—Probable Stress Distribution across Coal Pillar.

The use of more powerful supports to carry the nether roof beds and allow them to cave and break up behind the conveyor, has made it possible to practice caving throughout the complete face length. Packing is now confined to the areas adjacent to the roadways which are required to be maintained in the advancing system.

Solid Packing.—In order to either limit surface subsidence, or because of gas emission or spontaneous combustion problems, it was the practice at some collieries to completely stow the waste by pneumatic methods. This has few applications now and other methods are employed to solve these mining problems. In pneumatic stowing the general practice is to provide material crushed to less than 50 mm in size to a general collection station, located either on the surface or underground, and then transport it to the stowing machine which is usually situated in the tail gate. The material is then blown by compressed air onto the face. A solid web of packing is thus added from one end of the face to the other following the extraction of a similar web of coal from the face. The system is slow and costly in both air and transportation and limits the extraction rate from the face. The use of caving has overtaken this cumbersome packing practice.

Caving.—Full face caving is now standard practice on longwall faces. It is now accepted that the broken material, behind the face supports, bulks up to about $1\frac{1}{2}$ times its volume. Therefore, with a 1·5 m seam extraction, applying the formula detailed earlier, the caving height will be approximately 4·6 m above the floor, and here the broken material would contact the subsiding upper beds. Whilst strata above this level will still fracture, it will remain largely in place, supported by the caved material below. The most difficult mining condition in which to adopt this practice is where the lower beds are very strong and do not fragment easily, or alternatively, break off erratically.

ROADSIDE PACKING.—Advancing longwall roadways require side support packings; these transmit the upper forces, caused by movement, through to the floor beds and in so doing protect the roadway from major loads. As well as providing support, the roadside packs absorb the debris produced in ripping the roadway to it necessary height and profile. Hand-packing is a laborious and time-consuming operation and limits the rate of face advance, since this operation must be completed at the same speed as the rate of coal removal. Whilst many attempts at mechanisation have been made during the past, the only really successful device has been the mechanised ripping development. Here the material is excavated at a constant rate and can be fed to a separate packing appliance.

Slusher Packing.—In suitable cases, slusher packing can be very successful, even with hand ripping. Here the ripped material is transported by a slusher bucket and compacted into the pack. The drive is by a rope haulage system situated in the gate. The quality of the pack produced has been found to be acceptable in the thinner seams, but tends to deteriorate with increase in seam height.

Plough Packing.—Several types of plough arrangements, working with a small belt or chain, have had some success. In these systems the material is ploughed off the conveyor into the pack and the plough is removed when the packing is completed.

Cam Packing.—A recent mechanical system using large cams, anchored to the powered supports and operated by the power pack, has been developed. A series of these cams transport the material, from cam to cam, throughout the pack length, once the material has been delivered to the first cam, which is located at the roadside. This system is still in the development stage and not yet widely applied. In all cases of mechanical packing, with or without mechanical ripping, it is necessary to finish, to some extent, the roadside of the pack by hand.

Pump Packing.—In thick seams there is often great difficulty in building roadside pack, due to the lack of available material from the rippings or dintings, yet in these thicker seams it is more than every necessary to build packs which give almost immediate support and give the necessary yield characteristics. This has been achieved by pumping or blowing the packing material into the shuttered pack space. The successful systems are complicated and work on the principle of providing the packing material at the pack site already mixed with water and other materials to ensure quick setting.

In one system (WARBRET) the material is obtained in the form of −25 mm coal from the output stream at a point remote from the face. This is mixed with Bentonite to make the mixture flow and pumped with water and cement into the pack site through 102 mm pipes. At the face further binding agents can be added to ensure quick setting and early resistance. Shuttering is necessary at the face and roadside when pumping and is removed as soon as practicable.

Packs made as above have the approximate constitution by weight

Coal material	65–48%
Water	21–29%
Bentonite	0·9–1·2%
Cement 12–19% Accelerator	1–2%

The other pump packing system uses anhydrite of −6mm size blown into the pack site by compressed air, using water and accelerator solutions of ferrous sulphate and potassium sulphate to speed up setting time.

Both systems are used in the thicker seams in Great Britain, but only to the extent of 3·3% of all roadside packing sites.

ROADWAY SUPPORTS.—Coal Mining Regulations require some form of systematic roadway support.

Whilst many systems can be used to support the roof and sides of a roadway, the most popular and practical support for roadways is the steel arch. In retreat mining, where rectangular roadways are preferred, straight H-section girders and props are used.

Arches.—BS 227 1970, 'H-Section Steel Arches for Use in Mines', specifies the material and physical properties of the arch section, fish plates, size, splay, weight and preferred size. The strength of an arch varies with the section, quality of steel, and size of the arch. The supporting value depends on not only the foregoing features, but also on the method of strutting and how well the arch fits naturally, or following *in-situ* local packing, to the profile of the roadway. In short the supporting strength must take account of the arch form as a whole and the load application.

Tests have indicated that supporting values can be increased up to 2½ times by continuous strutting, such as a 76 mm brick lining. For normal conditions, straight legged arches set at 0.9 m centres, when subjected to loads evenly distributed over the crown, with the sides firmly supported, can carry average loads of 11 tonne/m^2 of supported area. This is the figure already quoted for the supporting value required on a coal face.

Roof Bolts.—These have made little progress as a recognized form of roadway support except as additional or supplementary to existing support systems. This was not the case in USA, where 48 km of roadway were supported on bolts in 1949, and this had increased to about 1435 km by 1951, and the progress is still continuing. Roof bolts are used not only in roadways, but also in the rooms of their room and pillar system of extraction. Rooms up to 27·4 m in width are supported entirely by roof bolts, and these give the additional advantage of increasing the clearance height, and providing greater freedom for movement and transportation.

The current theory is that a roof requires reinforcement rather than support to prevent its collapse. This distinction is very important and fundamental. When weakness occurs, chiefly from poor bonding along the bedding planes, ie from pronounced lamination, it is stated that the roof bolts bind the laminations together to form them into one homogeneous beam. This provides strength and stability, since the capacity of a beam to sustain its own weight varies in proportion to the square of its thickness. In addition disintegration of the lower and exposed surface is inhibited.

The roof bolts commonly in use, vary from 19 to 32 mm in diameter, and in length from 0·9 to about 2·4 m. They are set in holes drilled to the required length but of a slightly larger diameter than the anchor device at the end of the bolt. Several types of anchor are in use, the most popular being a split at the end of the bolt of about 120 to 150 mm in length, which is flared enough to allow a steel wedge to be introduced. To set the bolt, it is merely pushed up the hole until the wedge touches the end and the bolt is then hammered into place. This causes the wedge to enter the slot, the bolt end to expand, and thus become securely anchored in the hole. A roof plate is then fitted over several bolts, or a steel bar, and the nuts tightened at the exposed end of the bolt. In another type the wedge is drawn forward in the bolt by a mechanical wrench, which has the advantage of regulating the load applied to each bolt.

In spite of the fact that roof bolting has not been widely used in this country for roadway support, its use has been extended in other locations such as faulty ground, or on coal faces as a form or reinforcement. Further developments include the application of epoxy resins to the field of roof bolting and the use of wooden dowels which are set in drilled holes using either resin or cement. The use of dowels and bolts, their length and support pattern are still a matter of experience and field trials. During 1975, approximately 500,000 bolts, or dowels, were used in Britain for strengthening strata at the coal face, supporting fall areas, and minimising floor lift.

SHAFTS

Shafts are necessary to reach mineral deposits and the modern tendency is for them to become deeper and deeper. Deep shafts take some time to sink and occupy a considerable amount of the development period of a new mine. In view of the long time that is involved in a deep sinking, it is important to choose a fast and efficient method of not only sinking, but also lining of the completed shaft.

SHAPE AND SIZE.—The shaft section can vary between rectangular and circular. Whilst the former shape is easily divided into compartments, by frame supports, the shape is not suitable in either weak ground, or where special sinking precautions are necessary. Circular sections are most popular since this involves the minimum excavation for a given cross section, and the maximum strength to resist lateral pressure. They are also more suitable for a simultaneous sinking and lining process.

Very large rectangular shafts of 15·9 × 3·7 m and 14 × 4·3 m have been sunk in the USA, in order to accommodate cage and skip winders in each shaft. In some cases rectangular sections have been used with the addition of rounded ends which will allow compartments in the rectangular sections and services at the ends. The complications of framing, supporting and lining such a shape are obvious. Except for the case of particularly strong strata it is doubtful whether a large rectangular shaft would be sunk today in preference to a circular one. Small shafts in metal mines still tend to be rectangular for this reason. Recent shafts sunk by the National Coal Board have been circular in shape and 7·3 m internal finished diameter, requiring and excavated diameter from 8·2 to 9·1 m to allow for the lining.

LINING.—The type of lining used in a shaft is determined by the nature of the strata, whether it is wet or dry, the depth of the shaft and whether or not water or strata pressure has to be resisted. The function of a lining is to provide a smooth surface, prevent rock disintegration and at the same time, resist lateral pressure which may be created when beds of different strengths and geological conditions are penetrated. Water under pressure may need to be held back to reduce heavy inflow into the excavation and reduce the cost of pumping.

These functions can best be performed by a monolithic concrete or brick lining. Concrete is generally preferred on the grounds of strength, ease of installation and the fact that it can be supplemented by inner and outer cylinders of steel to provide additional strength. In order to avoid excessively thick concrete walls, in conditions where extremely high water pressures exist, cast iron 'tubbing' is used. This comprises heavily ribbed segments which are bolted together with water tight joints and then injected with cement to fill the voids which may exist behind the segments to ensure water-tightness. In order to shorten the sinking time, which forms a large part of the initial development programme, it is now normal practice to sink and line the shaft simultaneously. The lining is installed from a multi-deck scaffold suspended some 24 to 30 m above the shaft bottom.

SINKING.—The initial surface excavation is normally carried out to some distance below the rock head using a form of temporary crane and headgear. At this stage the sinking winder, sinking headframe and scaffold winch are installed. A double-drum, or Koepe, winders is used during the sinking, and the 'hoppits' are then drawn to the surface where suitable arrangements are made for the disposal of the debris. The strata conditions determine the type and extent of temporary lining required to support loose material. Also whether or not skeleton rings, boards, sheets or bolts are needed and if so, at what particular spacings.

As the sinking deepens the scaffold is erected in the shaft and onto this a 'mucking' machine is installed to load out the debris. This usually incorporates a clam shell, or similar, type of grab. The buckets are guided through the aperture in the scaffold decks and from this scaffold the lining can be extended upwards whilst sinking continues downwards with all the personnel in the shaft having full protection. Generally, the strata at the bottom of the shaft are broken by simultaneous rounds of shots once the complete drilling pattern is finished. Where it is necessary to pump water, a sump is created below the shaft bottom. This also provides a relief face for the blasting round.

Lining is started from a selected strong bed where a 'crib' is excavated and the foundations laid, once the correct level and alignment with the shaft centre is established. Shuttering is erected, and the concrete lining then poured. All erections and removals are undertaken from the scaffold which is raised and lowered by the winch. In good average ground shaft sinking is a straight forward process. The necessary pumping and ventilation are carried out in much the same way as with a horizontal drivage. It is only when the water flow is excessive, and beyond the normal pumping capacities, that special sinking methods have to be employed. These are necessary in order to reduce or if possible stop the influx of water so that sinking and lining can proceed normally.

SPECIAL SINKING PROCESSES

CEMENTATION PROCESS.—This process was first used in Britain at Hatfield Main Colliery, Yorkshire, and has been successfully used in many sinkings throughout the world since then. It is used in wet strata where injection of cement can close the pores and fissures to stop the inflow of water. In this process it is necessary to make the cementation preparations prior to reaching the water bearing strats. It is usual to drill, from the shaft bottom, a series of 38 to 51 mm diameter holes to lengths up to 61 m below the shaft bottom. The holes are then fitted with glands through which the rods work and which can be closed when they are withdrawn. These injection holes are then filled with cement grout under pressure until tests show that the sealing of the pores and fissures has been effective.

The holes are first injected with solutions of sulphate of soda and silicate of alumina which react to form a colloidal solution which blocks the very fine rock pores and lubricates the larger ones for the subsequent cement injection. When the section of strata has been successfully treated and the water inflow reduced the normal sinking process is continued. The amount of cement grout, length of pumping, grouting pressures etc. are all functions of the particular fissure size and frequency. The cementation process is normally undertaken by specialists experienced in this type of work.

FREEZING PROCESS.—This process has been used, during many sinkings in both Britain and the Continent, where water bearing strata had been encountered, and where the success of the injection process did not seem assured, due to the size of the pores and fissures. The system is basically the creation of an ice wall around the area in which the shaft is to be sunk. Sections of wet strata have been successfully treated by this process in recent years, including the shafts in Britain at Lea Hall, Bevercotes, Kellingley and Cotgrave collieries.

To form the ice wall, a series of holes, at about 1·2 m centres, are drilled in a circle around the shaft, to create the ice wall through which the sinking excavation can proceed. The diameter of the freezing hole circle is dependent upon not only the shaft size, but also the depth of strata to be frozen, since the deeper the length to be treated the thicker the ice wall. It is important to have sufficient margin of error, to ensure that the blasting does not fracture either the ice wall or the freezing tubes. The water bearing strata are frozen by circulating cold calcium chloride brine in concentric freezing tubes. The water returning brine solution is then recooled and recycled. The absorption of heat from the strata produces small cylinders of cold frozen ground, which grow from each freezing tube and eventually meet to form a continuous ice wall. Once this is completed sinking can proceed in the normal way.

Normal freezing plant is used except that a number of small units are preferred to a large central plant, in order to reduce the risk of breakdown once the freezing process has started. This also gives additional capacity should it be required. The coolant normally used is ammonia or Freon 12. The time required to drill the holes and complete the freezing process will essentially depend on the depth of strata to be frozen, but usually it takes 6–12 months. After the sinking and lining are complete, the frozen ground is allowed to thaw out, and any water leaks sealed by injections behind the lining.

HONIGMANN PROCESS.—This is essentially a drilling process where the shaft if drilled in one section as a large hole. It is best suited to soft ground and wet conditions, where it is less expensive than the freezing method. Cast iron tubbing lining is used, built up on the surface, and allowed to sink or is forced down into the shaft as more lengths are added at the surface. The leading ring has a cutting edge to facilitate penetration. Ready access is gained on the surface and operations such as caulking on the outside of the lining can be undertaken at the surface.

The shaft is not excavated to its full diameter in one operation. A pilot hole 1·8 to 2·44 m in diameter is first drilled to the complete depth. This is subsequently enlarged by one or more cuts using larger tools with steel cutters which are rotated from the surface by means of a tubular stem which is extended as drilling proceeds. The shaft is filled with emulsion of clay or bentonite to a level above that of the ground water in order to support the walls of the excavation. Compressed air is passed down a pipe in the stem, into which it is released above the bottom of the excavation. The stem thus becomes a pump up which the drilled material is carried in a mud suspension prior to being discharged at the surface. The mud is then treated, clarified and recirculated. The process has been used during the shaft sinking at Emma and Beatrix Collieries in Holland where suitable conditions were found. It is safer than other sinking methods, due to the fact that most of the work is undertaken on the surface. It is also relatively cheap. The method has not been applied to shaft sinking in Great Britain.

Rates of Sinking.—Using mechanical methods of debris disposal at the shaft bottom, sinking rates of 50–60 m per monthe are not uncommon. In one recent sinking of a 7·3 m shaft a monthly progress of 154 m was recorded, and in another case 122 m of progress was made in a 6 m shaft in 30 days. It must be noted when considering these figures, that no depths are quoted, and this factor is very important when considering the rates of sinking. Obviously, the sinking of a length of shaft at 150 m depth is much easier than achieving a similar rate at a depth of 600 m.

The rates of sinking achieved must take into account all the factors involved. It is important to stipulate whether or not weekends were worked, lining was undertaken simultaneously, and how much mechanisation was employed.

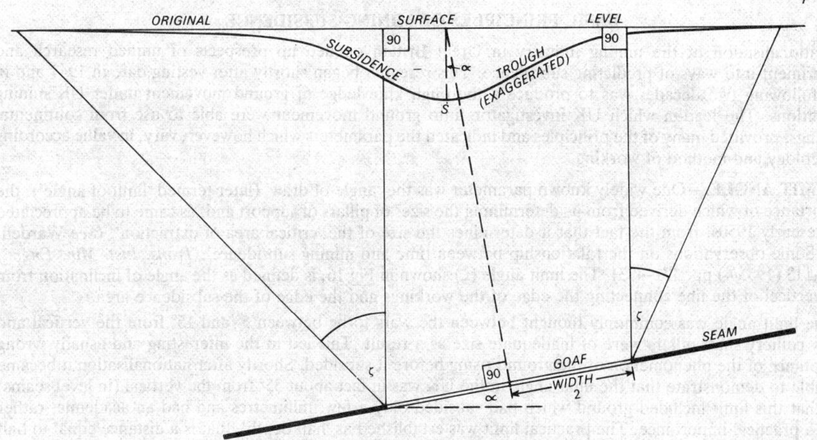

FIG. 16.—Effect of Inclination on Subsidence Profile (Seam Inclinations up to 18°).

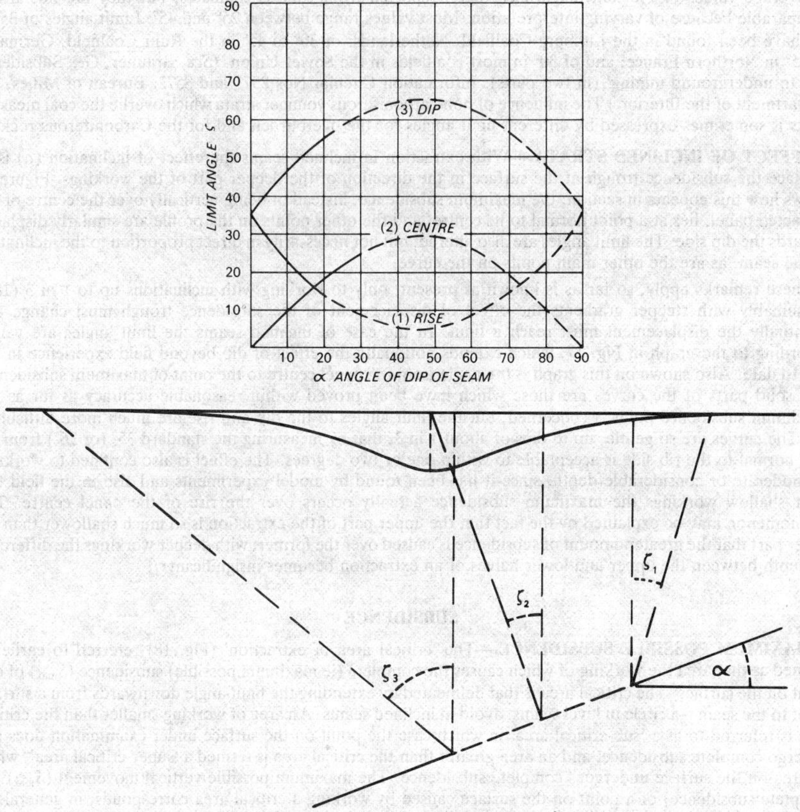

FIG. 17.—Effect of Seam Inclination on Limit Angles. (*See*, Rom, H., 'A limit angle system', Mitteilungen aus dem Markscheidewesen 71, 4, 1964 pp. 197–199.)

BASIC PRINCIPLES OF MINING SUBSIDENCE

Nationalisation of the mining industry in Great Britain openeu up prospects of unified research and experiment into ways of predicting subsidence. This research began shortly after vesting date in 1947 and in the following two decades was to produce a thorough knowledge of ground movement under UK mining conditions. The lead-in which UK investigators into ground movement were able to use from continental findings, provided many of the principles and indicated the parameters which however, vary, in value according to geology and method of working.

LIMIT ANGLE.—One widely known parameter was the 'angle of draw' (later termed 'limit of angle'), the importance of which derived from its determining the sizes of pillars of support and, as came to be appreciated in the early 1950s, from the fact that it determines the size of the 'critical area of extraction'. (*See* Wardell, K., 'Some observations on the ralationship between time and mining subsidence'. *Trans. Inst. Min. Engrs.*, Vol. 113 (1953/4) pp. 471–483). The limit angle (ζ) shown in Fig 16, is defined as the angle of inclination from the vertical of the line connecting the edge of the workings and the edge of the subsidence area.

The limit angle was commonly thought between the wars to be between 5° and 15° from the vertical and many colliery shaft pillars were of inadequate size as a result. This led to the interesting and usually wrong acceptance of the phenomenon of the ground rising before it subsided. Shortly after nationalisation it became possible to demonstrate that the limit angle in the UK was in fact about 35° from the vertical (in level seams) but that this limit included ground which had subsided only a few millimetres and had an academic, rather than a practical importance. The practical limit was established as 'half depth', that is a distance equal to half the seam depth. This distance subtends an angle of 26½° and the 'half depth' support area was already enshrined in the Mine (Working Facilities and Support) Act 1923, and is the area considered sufficiently wide for the purpose of protecting railway viaducts, tunnels or other works.

Average values of the limit angle have been reported from various coalfields, but they are not always comparable because of varying interpretation. Most values range between 25° and 45°. Limit angles of 35° to 45° have been found in the Limburg Coalfield, Netherlands: of 30° to 45° in the Ruhr Coalfield, Germany; of 35° in Northern France; and of 30° in most coalfields in the Soviet Union. (*See*, Brauner, G., 'Subsidence due to underground mining' (in two parts), Information Circular Nos 8571 and 8572, Bureau of Mines, US Department of the Interior.) The influence of non-carboniferous younger strata which overlie the coal measure rocks is sometimes expressed by different limit angles for the overburden and for the Carboniferous rocks.

EFFECT OF INCLINED STRATA.—With extraction in inclined seams the effect of inclination (α) is to displace the subsidence trough at the surface in the direction of the deeper part of the workings. Figure 16 shows how this appears in section; the maximum subsidence, instead of being vertically over the centre of the extracted panel, lies at a point normal to its centre, and the other points on the profile are similarly displaced towards the dip side. The limit angles are also altered, but not necessarily in direct proportion to the inclination of the seam, as are the other main points on the curve.

These remarks apply, so far as is known at present, only to working with inclinations up to 1 in 3 (18°). Presumably with steeper gradients the effect of displacement of the subsidence trough must change and eventually the displacement must reach a limit. In the case of inclined seams the limit angles are varied according to the graph in Fig. 17, which extends notionally the effect of dip beyond field experience in the UK to date. Also shown on this graph is the angle from the panel centre to the point of maximum subsidence. The solid parts of the curves are those which have been proved within reasonable accuracy as far as the maximum subsidence point is concerned, but the limit angles to the dip and rise are much more difficult to fix. The curves are so gentle, up to dips of about 1 in 3, that by measuring the standard 35° (or 26°) from the line normal to the rib side is acceptable to within one or two degrees. The effect is also confined to workings at moderate or considerable depth, since it has been found by model experiments and also in the field that over shallow workings the maximum subsidence actually occurs over the rise of the panel centre. This phenomenon may be explained by the fact that the upper part of the extraction is so much shallower than the other part that the greater amount of subsidence is caused over the former; with deeper workings the difference in depth between the upper and lower halves of an extraction becomes insignificant.

SUBSIDENCE

MAXIMUM POSSIBLE SUBSIDENCE.—The 'critical area of extraction' (Fig. 18) referred to earlier is defined as that area the working of which causes the complete (ie maximum possible) subsidence (S_{max}) of one point on the surface. The critical area is that delineated by extending the limit angle downwards from a surface point to the seam—a circle in level seams, avoid in inclined seams. An area of working smaller than the critical area is referred to as a 'sub-critical area' in which case the point on the surface under examination does not undergo complete subsidence, and an area greater than the critical area is termed a 'super-critical area', when an area on the surface undergoes complete subsidence. The maximum possible vertical movement (S_{max}) (or complete subsidence) of a point on the surface caused by working a critical area corresponds, in general, to the thickness of seam extracted (m) multiplied by the subsidence factor (a), ie $S_{max} = m \times a$. The subsidence factor in Great Britain is found to be normally between 80 and 90% of the extracted thickness in cases where longwall workings are caved or strip packed and when the working panels have no centre gates or other zones of special packing apart from those at the main and tail gates. Strip packing (except in very shallow seams)

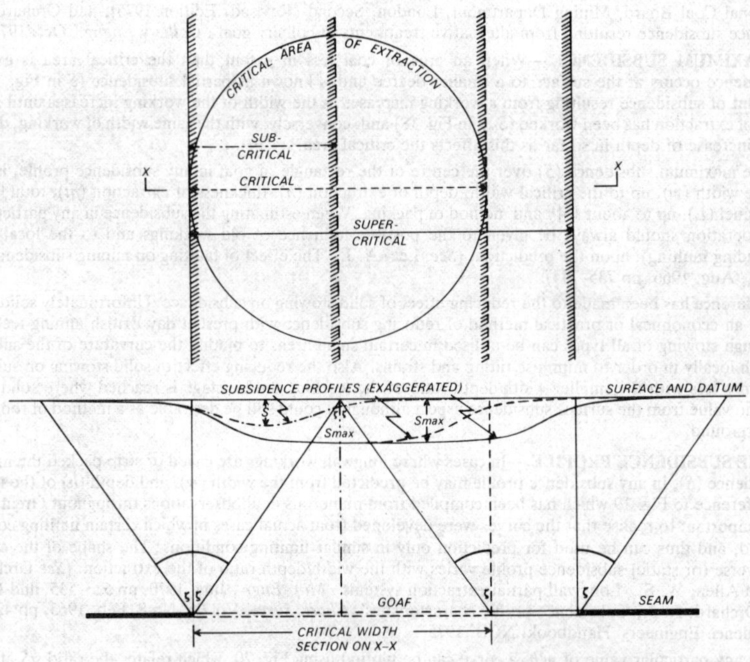

FIG. 18.—Critical Width of Extraction to produce Maximum Subsidence.

has no practical value in minimising subsidence. When considering the subsidence factor in a virgin area the smaller subsidence factor is generally used (ie approximately 80%). Solid stowing has a moderating effect on the amount of subsidence in proportion to its efficiency; the most efficient solid stowing in Great Britain has been pneumatic stowing which can reduce the subsidence by 50%. (*See*, 'Subsidence Engineers' Handbook',

Subsidence factors reported from different mining districts vary considerably, and some values of the subsidence factor (a) are as follows:

COALFIELD AND METHOD OF PACKING	SUBSIDENCE FACTOR (a)	REFERENCES
Ruhr Coalfield, Germany		Brauner, G., *Bulletins* 8571 and 8572, US Bureau of Mines.
Pneumatic stowing	0·45	
Other solid stowing	0·50	
Caving	0·90	
Pas de Calais Coalfield, France		
Hydraulic stowing	0·25–0·35	
Pneumatic stowing	0·45–0·55	
Caving	0·85–0·90	
Upper Silesia, Poland		
Hydraulic stowing	0·12	
Caving	0·70	
USSR		Muller, Jushin, & Karavaev, Leningrad, 1968.*
Lizelow District	0·4–0·8	
Other districts	0·65–0·9	
USA Pennsylvania		
Caving	0·5—0·6	Brauner, G.

* Muller, R. A., Jushin, A. I., and Karavaev, J. I. (editors) 'Manual for calculation of buildings and construction in mining areas'. p 278 (in Russian). Publishers of Construction Literature, Leningrad, 1968.

National Coal Board, Mining Department, London, Second (Revised) Edition 1975); and Orchard, R. J., 'Surface subsidence resulting from alternative treatments of colliery goaf'. *Colliery Engng.*, Oct. 1974.)

MAXIMUM SUBSIDENCE.—When an area of coal less in extent than the critical area is extracted, subsidence occurs at the surface to a smaller degree and is known as partial subsidence (S in Fig. 18). The amount of subsidence resulting from a working increases as the width of the working increases until a critical area of extraction has been worked (S_{max} in Fig. 18) and, conversely, with the same width of working, decreases with increase of depth in so far as this affects the critical area.

The maximum subsidence (S) over the centre of the rectangle of goaf in any subsidence profile, is related to the width (w), up to the critical width, depth of extraction (h), thickness of extraction (m), total length of the panel (L), up to about $1{\cdot}4h$ and method of packing. When estimating the subsidence in any particular case consideration should always be given to the possible influence of old workings and to the local geology (including faulting), upon the prediction. (*See*, Lee, A. J., 'The effect of faulting on mining subsidence'. *Min. Engr.*, Aug. 1966, pp 735–744).

Reference has been made to the reducing effect of solid stowing on subsidence. Unfortunately solid stowing is not an economical or practical method of reducing subsidence with present day British mining techniques, although stowing of all types can be utilised in certain small areas to modify the curvature of the subsidence trough locally in order to minimise tilting and strains. Also the reducing effect of solid stowing on subsidence becomes less with the smaller width/depth ratio of the working until a stage is reached where solid stowing is of no value from the surface subsidence aspect although it could still be desirable as a method of roof control underground.

THE SUBSIDENCE PROFILE.—In cases where longwall workings are caved or strip packed the maximum subsidence (S), in any subsidence profile may be predicted from the width (w), and depth (h) of the workings by reference to Fig. 19 which has been compiled from numerous field observations throughout Great Britain. It is important to realise that the curves were developed from actual cases in which certain limiting conditions existed, and thus can be used for prediction only in similar limiting conditions. The shape of the complete transverse (or static) subsidence profile varies with the width/depth ratio of the extraction. (*See* Orchard, R. J. and Allen, W. S., 'Longwall partial extraction systems'. *Min. Engr.*, June 1970, pp 523–535; and Hall, M. and Orchard, R. J., 'Subsidence profile characteristics'. *Chart. Surv.*, Vol 95, No 8, Feb. 1963, pp 422–428). Subsidence Engineers' Handbook, NCB, 1975.

For any particular value of w/h, a curve can be plotted using Fig. 20, which relates the ratio s/S at various points, with d/h the distance of those points from the centre of the panel in terms of depth. Where deep seams are concerned, critical areas are large and two or three panels may be needed to cover the critical area; in these conditions several gateroads and packs occur close together within the area. Over each of these support zones a hump—or at least a flattening—occurs in the subsidence profile. (As regards centre gates even in sub-critical widths of panel, these are often encountered because in deeper seams even a wide panel can still be sub-critical). The maximum subsidence is often reduced as a result of the centre gate packs. As often happens between consecutive panels a pillar of solid coal is left, which will reduce S to zero when of critical

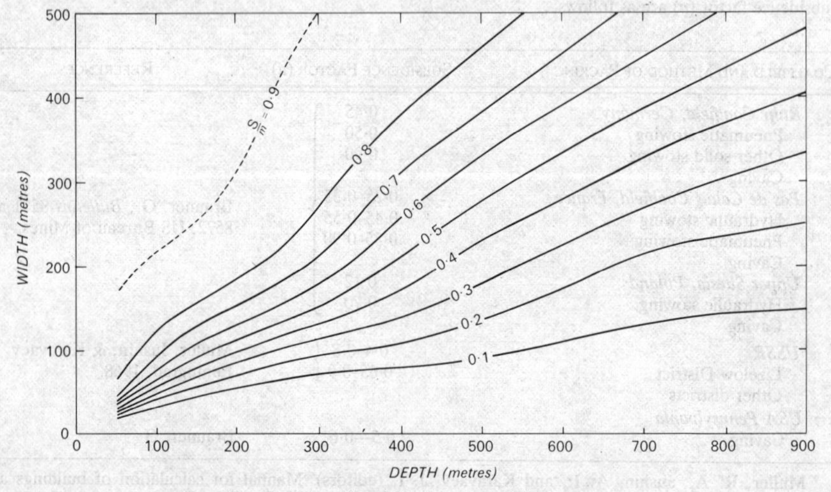

FIG. 19.—Relationship of Subsidence to Width and Depth.

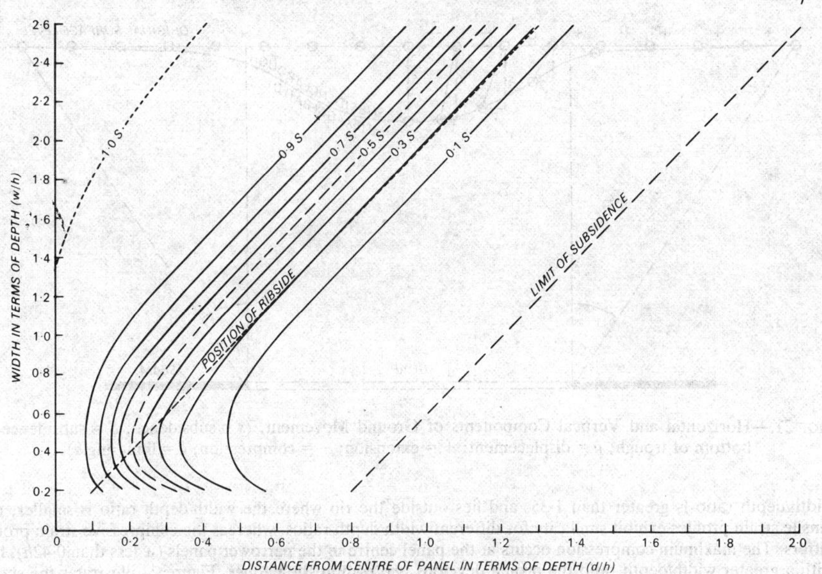

FIG. 20.—Graph for Predicting Subsidence Profiles.

width, but have no effect where it is too narrow. (*See* Orchard, R. J. and Allen, W. S., 'Ground curvature due to coal mining'. *Chart. Surv.*, May 1965, pp 622–621). Subsidence Engineers' Handbook, NCB, 1975.

HORIZONTAL MOVEMENT.—When a subsidence trough is formed at the surface the central part subsides vertically and the remainder moves inwards as well as downwards. The vertical component of the resultant movement is called subsidence, and the horizontal component is called displacement. When adjacent points on the earth's surface are displaced horizontally at different rates the ground must be either extended or compressed horizontally, according to whether the inner or the outer point is moving more rapidly. It follows that since the centre point is not moving horizontally, the points on either side of it, having moved inwards, cause the ground over the centre of the extracted area to be compressed. Similarly, since the limit points on the subsidence trough are not moving horizontally, there must be a zone between the limit points and the zone of compression which is extended horizontally.

In subsidence engineering terminology, 'strain' (e), is the change in length over a piece of ground or structure expressed either as a dimension over the length or as a fraction of the unit length. Thus we may express a strain of 0·01 m in 10 m, as one part per thousand, or 1 mm per m, or simply as 0·001. The sense of the strain is always specified, extensions and compressions being indicated by a + and − sign respectively.

Figure 21 illustrates the incidence of the zones of horizontal strain occurring along the subsidence profile. In the example the components of vertical displacement (S), and horizontal displacement (V), are shown, together with the resultant movements downwards and inwards of each point except the limit points and the centre point.

The amount of strain occurring in the subsidence profile is indicated by the curvature of the profile, which, in turn, depends upon the amount of subsidence occurring and the distance over which the basin or trough of subsidence is spread. Generally, the thicker the seam the greater the subsidence; the shallower the seam the shorter the distance over which subsidence is spread, both factors tending to produce greater curvature in the subsidence profile. From this it can be seen that strain is proportional to subsidence and inversely proportional to depth. Thus as seen earlier, it is customary to refer to subsidence in terms of seam thickness, so it is customary to refer to strain in terms of subsidence/depth. The relationship between strain in terms of subsidence/depth and the width/depth ratio is illustrated on Fig. 22.

THE STRAIN PROFILE.—In the same way, that 'contours' joining the points of equal subsidence can be drawn on a graph (see Fig. 20), a graph can be made showing lines joining the points where the horizontal strains are similar at various width/depth ratios (Fig. 23). Using Fig. 22 and 23, the strain profile for any width/depth ratio can be calculated and plotted together with the subsidence profile obtained from Figs. 19 and 20. The distances in Fig. 23 which shows only half a profile are again measured from the panel centre. Although the position of the maximum extension (+E) coincides with the position of the rib side where the

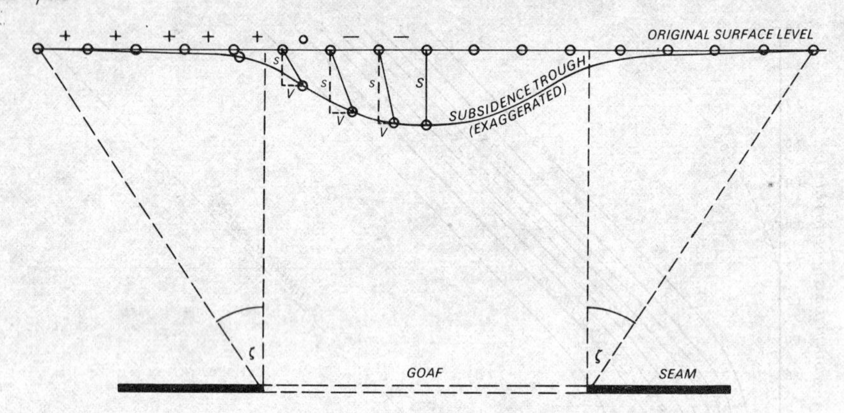

FIG. 21.—Horizontal and Vertical Components of Ground Movement. (s = subsidence; S = subsidence at bottom of trough; v = displacement; + = extension; − = compression; ζ = limit angle).

width/depth ratio is greater than 1·35, and lies outside the rib where the width/depth ratio is smaller, the tensile strain profiles exhibit similarity for different width/depth ratios, whereas the compressive strain profile differs. The maximum compression occurs at the panel centre in the narrower panels (w less than $0{\cdot}42h$), but with a greater width/depth ratio the profile develops two compression zones. Figure 24 illustrates the shape of the strain profile at the different states: when $w = 0{\cdot}42h$, when the single compression zone has a greater intensity than the extension; when $w = 0{\cdot}9h$, when a hump occurs in the compression curve; and when $w = 1{\cdot}5h$, when two separate compression zones occur. The middle diagram encompasses a range of width/depth ratios from about $w = 0{\cdot}5h$, to about $w = 1{\cdot}4h$. Where the surface is level but the seam is dipping the tensile strain on the dip side of the panel is increased and on the rise side decreased.

SURFACE SLOPE DUE TO SUBSIDENCE.—Ground slope due to mining subsidence is related to the strain profile. The maximum slope occurs at the transition point which is the position where the strain profile passes from tensile to compressive, the position of maximum horizontal displacement and where half the maximum subsidence occurs. The value of maximum slope (G_{max}) for a critical width of extraction, is $G_{max} = 2{\cdot}75S_{max}/h$; the value of the constant is dependent upon the width/depth ratio (see Fig. 22).

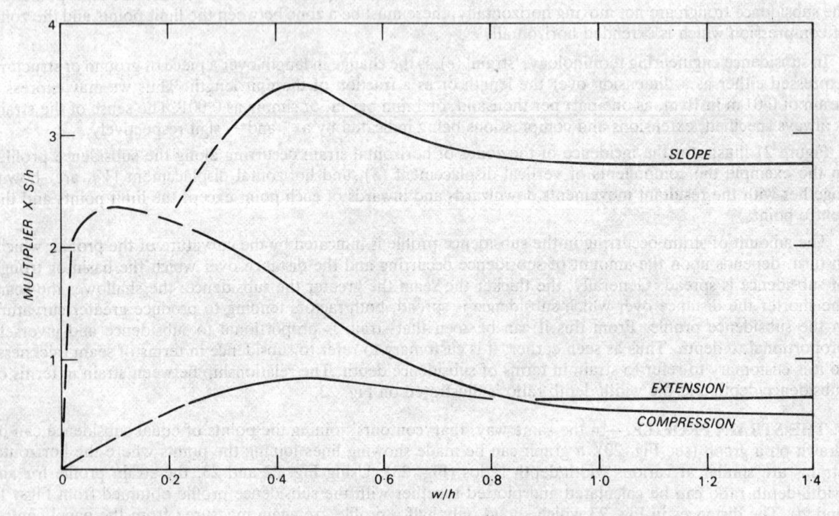

FIG. 22.—Relationship of Slope and Strain at various Width/Depth Ratios to Maximum Subsidence and Depth.

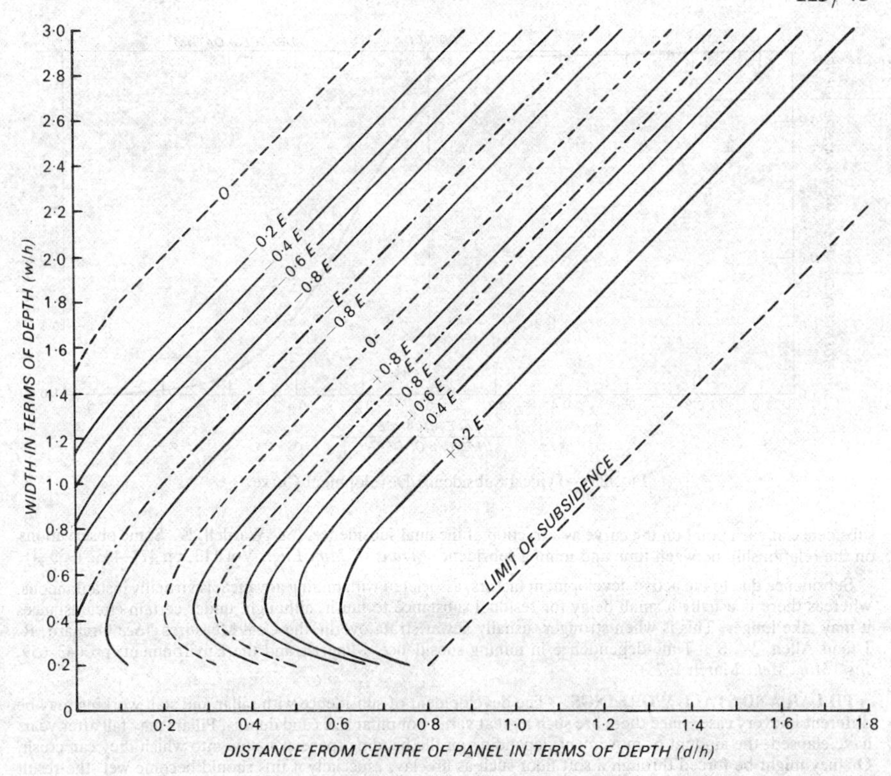

FIG. 23.—Graph for Predicting Strain Profiles.

SUBSIDENCE DEVELOPMENT.—The subsidence of a point at the surface begins when a face enters the critical area and on average 95% of the total subsidence occurs while the face is within the critical area, the average 5% residual subsidence is a time-dependent part of the whole, although it can be demonstrated that some time-dependent subsidence is taking place continually and is embraced by the development curve. The subsidence development curve (dynamic subsidence curve), is a line on a graph depicting the changing subsidence of a surface point in relation to the position of the face of an extraction passing through the critical area of that point. Figure 25 shows the typical subsidence development of a point in dimensionless terms—the

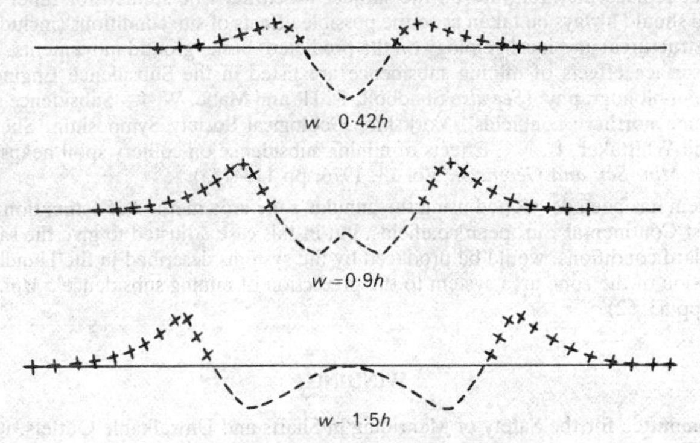

FIG. 24.—Three Principal Types of Strain Profiles.

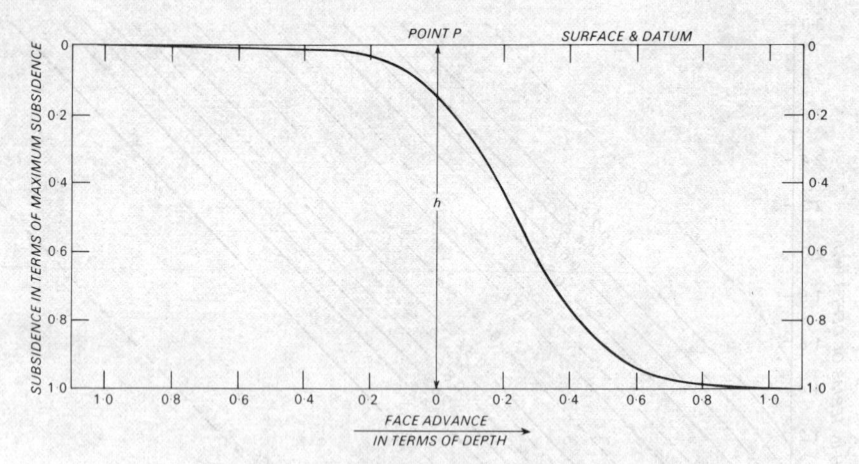

FIG. 25.—Typical Subsidence Development Curve.

subsidence at each point on the curve as a fraction of the final subsidence. (*See* Wardell, K., Some observations on the relationship between time and mining subsidence. *Trans. I. Min. Eng.*, Vol 113, pp 471–483, 1953–4).

Subsidence due to the active development factors, associated with mining advance, is virtually instantaneous, whereas there is usually a small delay for residual substance to finish, although, under certain circumstances it may take longer. This is when stronger, usually newer strata overlie the Coal Measures. (*See* Orchard, R. J. and Allen, W. S., 'Time-dependence in mining subsidence' Minerals and the Environment, pp 643–659, *Inst. Min. Met.*, March 1975).

PILLAR AND STALL WORKINGS.—The development of subsidence with pillar and stall working may be different in every case, since there are such a great variety of pillar sizes and depths. Pillars may fail after years have elapsed, the amount of movement depending on the heading space available into which they can crush. Or they might be forced through a soft floor such as fireclay, especially if this should become wet, the result being to lower the surface just as effectively as though the pillars had crushed and spread. Where the floor is soft the limiting factors are the thickness of the soft floor stratum and the space available in the headings into which the floor can be forced. With properly designed pillars the roof subsidence may not reach the surface in measurable amounts. (Subsidence Engineers' Handbook, NCB, 1975.)

The graphical method for predicting the basic ground movements associated with mining trough subsidence outlined above is commonly referred to as the National Coal Board method, and has been practised for many years. Consequently, substantial confidence can now be placed in this method of prediction. A complete treatise of this method is set out in a publication by the National Coal Board, entitled 'Subsidence Engineers' Handbook', although this publication is intended as a reference for those engineers and surveyors who are concerned with subsidence engineering and who are acquiring a specialist knowledge in the subject. The Handbook does not replace the literature on the subject which must be studied for fuller knowledge to be gained. Due regard should always be taken as to the possible effects of site conditions (including the condition and design of any structures) and local gelology on the predicted, basic, ground movements. Various methods of mitigating the surface effects of mining subsidence are listed in the Subsidence Engineers' Handbook, together with a useful bibliography. (*See also* Shadbolt, C. H. and Mabe, W. J., 'Subsidence aspects of mining development in some northern coalfields'. Yorkshire Geological Society Symposium, Sheffield, 1970; and Forrester, D. J. and Whittaker, B. N., 'Effects of mining subsidence on colliery spoil heaps'. (In two parts). *Int. J. Rock. Mech. Min. Sci. and Geomech.* Vol 13, 1976, pp 113–133).

A computer system has been developed using the annular zone area method of estimation which is used on a wide scale in most Continental European coalfields, but in this case adjusted to give the same result as that which, under standard conditions, would be produced by the systems described in the Handbook. (*See* Marr, J. E., 'The application of the zone area system to the prediction of mining subsidence'. *Min. Engr.*, Vol 135, No 176 Oct 1975, pp 53–62).

WINDING

The National Committee for the Safety of Manriding in Shafts and Unwalkable Outlets, was set up by the Health and Safety Executive, as a result of the Markham Colliery winding accident in July 1973. The final report of this Committee is expected by the end of 1979, and may be a major review of winding practice. The revision of this text under title 'Winding' has been deferred therefore and will be published in the 1985 edition of the Year Book.

Standard British practice for winding in main shafts is always on a balanced system, the shaft has two divisions in which one cage ascends while another descends, and their deadweights therefore balance each other. Each cage is suspended on a separate rope. The two ropes pass over head-pulleys, mounted in a head frame vertically over the shaft, to the winding engine house. A single drum-winder is usual, the ends of the two ropes being made fast to a common drum and sychronous movements of the cages thus assured.

WINDING ENGINES.—The development of winding engines has proceeded in step with improvements in the design and manufacture of winding ropes, and with the increased depth and better construction of shafts. Between 1850 and 1900, sizes and speeds of engines increased rapidly, when rope speeds of 90 ft per sec were permitted to be used in conjunction with over-wind prevention gear.

Winding engines in the UK are mostly between 3,000 and 7,000 hp, and the maximum speed during a wind is about 5,000 ft per min, or 57 mph. For example, the time is 52 sec for a wind 2,200 ft deep, an average of 2,562 ft per min; and a speed of 5,100 ft per min is on record. In a Kimberley SA, diamond mine, for a shaft 1,560 ft deep, the average speed of wind is 2,230 ft and maximum 3,770 ft per min, the acceleration period is 16 sec, retardation 13 sec, total 42 sec.

Electric winders did not compete with steam until 1906. Both ac motors with rheostatic control, and Ward-Leonard controlled dc motors were used at first. The Ward-Leonard-Ilgner system was introduced to equalise the energy fluctuations in the winding cycle, by means of a fly-wheel. Improvements in geared drives about 1920 enabled high-speed motors driving through Wellman-Bibby couplings to be used. Electric winders are being increasingly used at collieries and metalliferous mines.

The considerations governing the type and power of engine or motor required to equip a given shaft are as follows. First, the daily output required; it is determined by the useful load per wind times the number of winds per shift. The latter depends on the depth of the shaft, the type of winding plant to be installed, and the allowances for delays at each end, and for winding men and stores of all kinds. The nett winding time for mineral may be found by deducting 20–40% for man-winding. The gross load is the sum of the useful load, the weight of tubs and cage, and the weight of rope, and guide friction and windage (which are taken at about 10% of above).

With cage winding of tubs and cars as commonly practised in this country and elsewhere, the time taken in decking, ie, at the surface, discharging full tubs from the cage and replacing them with empties, and the reverse operations at the pit bottom, is between 5 and 10 sec when track and decking arrangements are in fair average condition and manually operated. To an increasing extent these operations are being controlled by pneumatic or hydraulic power, with consequent reduction of time and men engaged.

For example of pneumatic control, at Bold Colliery the lower deck is cleared first, and the cage is then dropped into position on a lower set of keps so that the tubs on the second deck can be cleared. The shaft is 900 yd deep, and although each cage has to be decked twice, 50 winds per hr are made. This is done with two men only on the bank. Decking time is further reduced when multi-deck cages are discharged simultaneously. At Brookhouse Colliery the cage is stopped at the bank for 7 secs with this system in use, and 73 winds are made per hour. The type of pneumatic ram for tub loading consists of a heavy steel cylinder of 5 in diameter with heads of ample size and without projections on which tub chains may catch. Inside the cylinder moves the piston tube, which is of smaller diameter but strong enough to withstand the hard use it will have. A combined crosshead and pusher is bolted to the piston tube.

DRUM WINDERS.—Three main types of drums are used; namely, cylindrical, conical, and cylindro-conical. Reel type winders are now obsolte. The object of this type, as of the conical type, was to equalise the driving torque by using a smaller diameter of drum when exerting maximum rope pull to lift and accelerate the loaded cage. In practice the cylindro-conical type, or a variation, the bi-cylindro-conical type, are most widely used in deep mining. In the latter design each half of the drum comprises two cylindrical portions of about 1:2 ratio of diameters linked by a conical portion. The smaller cylinders are at the ends, and the portions of larger diameter lie together in the middle of the drum. This type has the advantage that both ropes can use the central parallel portion of the drum surface, and the whole drum is simpler, more compact and cheaper than the purely conical type. But it has the serious disadvantage that with multi-deck cages simultaneous decking is necessary. The cylindrical drum type (or the Koepe wheel) will be more widely used with electric-driven winders, in conjunction with a tail or balance rope under the cages.

Drums are made of cast steel entirely or fabricated from steel castings, forgings, and rolled sections. The winding surface of the cylindrical portion may be grooved or smooth, or lagged with wood in which the rope makes its own grove. The diameter of drum or sheave should not be less than 100 times the diameter of the winding rope, in order to avoid excessive flexion and consequent wear of the rope. For similar reasons the angle of fleet of the rope should be less than 2°. This angle is derived from the travel of the rope across the drum relative to its position at the crown of the head pulley. It is measured, on a plane containing the axles of both, by the projected angle the rope makes between its position on the centre-line of the pulley and its extreme travel on the drum.

KOEPE WINDERS.—Drum winders are in world wide use; the Koepe system is also accepted as an economical, safe, simple and flexible method of winding. For mining conditions in Germany, it has the advantage over drum winders in the ease with which it can be adapted to wind from various depths. Because the coal seams in Germany are seldom flat and often steeply inclined (up to 90°), horizon mining is almost universal. In this system a main shaft is sunk to full depth at the outset and horizontal roads or levels are driven across the tilted strata to intersect the inclined seams. Staple shafts are sunk within the mining zone to connect higher roads with a lower one, which is the main haulage road. These staple shafts are equipped with rope hoists or spiral chutes to lower coal from the overlying levels, and all the coal is wound up the shaft from one level. Hence the winding equipment installed at the outset has to be capable of raising a large output from one level, and must also be readily adaptable for raising coal from a greater depth when seams are worked from deeper levels at later data.

A drum winder to meet these requirements and accommodate the final length of rope would be relatively large and heavy for immediate purposes and the Koepe system is a cheap and simple alternative. At first the massive drum was replaced by a wheel with one groove in its periphery. A single winding rope lay in this groove. But at many mines in Britain and elsewhere, it has been shown that multi-rope friction winders are as efficient and safe, and more conomical than single-rope systems. In both systems the friction wheel has to be lagged to provide adequate friction for the ropes. Multi-ropes are naturally of much smaller diameter than a single rope to carry the same total load, so the friction wheel also can be of smaller diameter.

The Koepe wheel may be mounted in an engine house at ground level, or in a tower built over the shaft, in which case it replaces the usual pithead pulleys. If it is in an engine house, two pithead pulleys are needed, and care must be taken to ensure that the fleet angle of the rope on the Koepe wheel is not more than 1·5°. The wheel itself is built like a narrow drum; in Germany fabricated construction is used. The usual single-rope wheel is from 5 to 8 m diameter; it is at least 100 times the diameter of the largest rope to be used, and the pressure in the tread must not exceed 18 kg/cm^2. Wooden blocks are fastened in a recess in the rim of the wheel. In Germany, inserts of leather, rubber, or bonded fibre, are set in the wooden blocks.

The cages or skips are suspended one on each end of the ropes which pass over the Koepe wheel; the arc of contact of the rope around the wheel is always less than 360°, and usually between 180° and 230°. To effect complete balance of the system, a tail rope is used, joining the bottoms of the cages. This rope, which is usually heavier than the winding rope and may be flat or round, hangs freely in the shaft and passes round a guide pulley (of a mere timber baulk) set at a position below the lowest winding position of the cages. The ratio of total suspended load to the useful or out-of balance load is 3·2 to 1 minimum. Hence all weights other than the useful load are balanced, and the power required is that to raise the load, overcome friction and accelerate the moving and revolving masses; the latter are, of course, much less than with drum winders. (See also chapter 'Wire Ropes'.)

The Koepe system is best suited for winding heavy nett loads from deep levels (not less than 1,000 ft) and is not suitable for multi-level winding. It is, however, more readily adaptable to winding from deeper levels in the same shaft than is drum winding. Multi-rope suspension has to be considered when the loads and depths create forces beyond the capacity of a single rope of the maximum size used, which is 77 mm/diameter. One Koepe winder using four ropes each of 47 mm/diameter has been made to wind useful loads of 12,000 kg from a depth of 1,350 m. To ensure equal distribution of load to the four ropes special means of attachment to the cage are used.

The risk of slip or creep between the Koepe wheel and the winding rope can be effectively guarded against; first, by using suitable material in the rope groove (eg, wood and leather, rubber, bonded fibre or special aluminium alloy inserts); secondly, by limiting the rates of acceleration and retardation to induce frictional forces not exceeding 0·2 compared with 0·3–0·8 coefficients of friction given by the linings named above; and thirdly, by the right choice of rope and proper attention to its treatment and cleaning. Langs lay ropes are nearly always used, ie ropes in which the wires in the individual strands are twisted in the same direction as the strands in the rope. This construction gives bigger contact area and better adhesion between rope and tread than ordinary lay or locked coil.

Regulations in Germany allow a statutory life of 2 years for a rope on a Koepe winder, as compared with 3 years and 6 months under British regulations for a rope on a drum winder, but the latter uses two ropes and the former only one normally. See 'Modern Trends in Winding Technique', by A. W. Kidd and H. M. Hughes, *Trans. I. Min. E.*, Vol 114, 1955.

WINDING ROPES.—(See also chapter 'Wire Ropes'.) For winding ropes, the ratio of the full strength of the new rope to the 'dead load' it has to carry is called the Factor of Safety. The 'dead load' is the sum of the weights of the cage (and all its attachments) when fully loaded, and the weight of the rope itself applicable. The 'live load' induced by upward acceleration may be over three times the 'dead load', but between 1·3 and 1·7 is the usual range. The smaller figure is for deep winds, because a long rope acts as an elastic cord to reduce the forces. This action alleviates the effect of the weight of the rope mentioned above. In practice the Factor of Safety as defined is between 7 and 10; the smaller figure is for deep winds.

But the real factor of safety is much less; partly because of accelerating forces but chiefly because the fatigue limit of the wires comprising the rope is about 25% of their ultimate tensile strength when new. Under corrosive conditions the fatigue limit is reduced indefinitely: galvanising is the best means of protecting a wire rope from corrosion.

The effect of fatigue is shown as transverse cracks in their wires after a few years' service. Hence three-and-a-half years is the maximum length of life permitted for a winding rope for use in mines in Britain. Ropes which have been on light duty only may be granted extensions of service at six-monthly intervals on application through the Inspectorate. A daily and monthly examination by an experienced ropeman of every winding rope is compulsory. Haulage ropes are not subject to regulations as to length of service.

The standards of practice are now such that travel in mine shafts is one of the safest forms of transport. Some 100 years ago, when winding ropes were made of fibre or of iron, about 20% of such ropes broke in service. Fifty years later the number had fallen to 1%, steel than being in general use for rope making.

All winding rope breakages in Great Britain are investigated by the Safety in Mines Research Establishment, and the responsible officer has given the following analysis of 32 failures he has investigated, between 1938 and 1950. (*See* 'Winding Ropes—Safety and Control', by A. E. McClelland, MSc MIMinE, *Colliery Guardian*, Overseas Supplement, 1951). The following list gives the predominant causes of the breakages of the winding ropes, with the number of cases of each cause: corrosion—fatigue (11); corrosion (9); faulty capping, including seven bent-back-wire cappels (9); fatigue (1); kink, resulting in fatigue (1); damage as a result of fouling and obstruction (1). Total 32. Mr McClelland gives the following summary for the proper selection, inspection and maintenance of ropes to secure safety in winding.

(1) The first essential for safety in winding rope practice is careful and enlightened visual examination. Non-destructive testing devices cannot, at present, replace such examination. Mechanical tests form a very useful method of aiding visual examination, but, again, in no way replace it.

(2) The condition of a drum rope can, nearly always, be determined by careful and intelligent examination of the rope exterior together with examination of the interiors of all recapping samples, the latter supplying information as to the type of deterioration at work and the former giving information as to the degree. Internal examination of previously discarded ropes is also extremely useful, particularly in the case of Koepe ropes which do not yield regular recapping samples.

(3) Since the ropeman has a most responsible job, more attention should be given to his selection and training. He should be kept up to date by means of information bulletins, etc.

(4) A valuable second line of defence against serious accidents is provided by the practice of employing the same rope for winding men and mineral, the load and speed with men being kept below those employed for mineral. This amounts to regular proof testing of the rope with regard to its capacity to carry men in safety.

(5) Consideration should be given to making the drawn-galvanised rope the standard article in countries such as the UK, where corrosion is the most widespread form of deterioration, ungalvanised ropes being used only when the conditions are known to be suitable.

(6) Both ungalvanised and galvanised ropes should be kept well lubricated at all times.

(7) The bent-back-wire type of capping is prone to incorrect fabrication and consequent failure. Its discontinuance should therefore be considered.

(8) Copper coatings on wires, as sometimes used in the drawing process, can greatly accentuate corrosion. Thus all manufacturers should debar such 'copperised' wire.

(9) The need for the use of very large ropes and the use of steels above 130 tons/in^2 tensile strength should be avoided by the employment of light alloy conveyance, skip winding, and eventually, multi-rope winding.

Some 500,000 persons are lowered and raised daily, in this country alone, and there may be 100 men in a shaft at one time. Hence the risk of accident by overwinding or other cause is one of the greatest potential sources of disaster in mining. Such accidents are rare because of the excellent design and construction of all components and precautionary devices, and the stringent recent amendments in The Coal Mines General Regulations (Winding and Haulage) 1937, 1948.

As a precaution against overwinds it is compulsory to fit a detaching hook between the cap of a winding rope and the cage chains. The device operates when the detaching hook reaches a cone-shaped 'bell' which surrounds the rope and is mounted at a suitable height in the head-frame. Impact with the bell causes the detaching hook to open by shearing a safety rivet whereupon the cage is left suspended in the head-frame.

When winding persons another automatic control device (a slower banker) has to be engaged, which will prevent the descending cage from being landed at pit bottom at a speed exceeding 5 ft per sec. This device has to be rested at weekly and three-monthly intervals. A centrifugal governor is ued to control the maximum speed during a wind. The same governor may serve for slow banking by an arrangement which integrates the speed of the drum with its angular position during the last few revolutions: eg, a nut travelling on a screwed shaft geared to the drum shaft. The automatic control may work continuously or at the end of the wind only; most of them cut off power and apply the brakes in the event of overtravel or excess speed.

BRAKES.—Brakes operate by friction on plain cylindrical surfaces usually made integral with the rope drum or wheel. The post-brake, which is preferred on large winders, has two shoes mounted one on each side of the brake surface; each embraces an angle of about 90° and is suitably lined. The shoes are pivoted at their centres on posts which transmit all the friction forces direct to the foundations. They are operated by a link mechanism attached to their ends, which is designed to endure parallel motion and uniform pressure from both shoes. The brake mechanism is designed so that the brake is automatically applied on the event of failure of power or other cause. Normally it is worked by a weighted level under manual control by means of steam or air or oil operated pistons.

CAGE AND SKIP WINDING.—A major part of the output of coal in Great Britain is still cage wound, the tubs ascending with their loads of coal. The policy of British Coal is to apply skip winding where practicable in new sinkings and conversions. This system is already used on a small scale in this country, and on a large scale in the Ruhr, Poland, and in USA where skips of up to 12 tons capacity are used, as compared with 10 tons in this country. For a description of one of the first plants in this country, see 'Skip Winding at Barnborough Main Colliery.' G. C. Payne, BSc, MIMinE, *NACM*, 1944; also, 'Seven Years' Experience of Skip Winding,' Col E. Hart, MC, *Trans. I. Min. E.*, Vol 105, pt 6, 1946.

Where cage winding is giving satisfactory service there is little to be gained in applying skip winding. But in cases where an increase in output is not possible with cage winding, then skip winding shows the following advantages.

In Britain the weight of coal relative to total weight of coal and cage etc, is 34% for cage winding, and 48% for skip winding. On the Continent lighter equipment using light alloys enables these figures to be increased to about 40% and 55%. Thus the proportion of pay load to total load is raised by nearly 40% by substituting skip for cage winding, and loading and unloading are faster, thus increasing the capacity of the shaft; less labour is required at decking levels; simpler lay-out of pit at top and bottom result; fewer tubs or cars are needed, and the size of car used underground is not restricted by the size of cage; also, the rope is in tension always and not subject to snatch. The chief disadvantages are the difficulty of keeping separate, different qualities of coals and that of winding men and supplies with a skip; the latter may often require one shaft to be equipped with cages, or a cage is substituted for one skip after a winding shift. Anti-breakage devices appear competent to prevent excessive breakage of coal with skip winding. Plants with capacities for winding up to 3,000 tons in a 7 hour shift from depths exceeding 2,000 ft are at work in this country, and much higher capacities, up to 1,000 tons per hour from a depth of 600 ft are used in USA.

Many skips used in collieries in the UK are adapted to shafts designed for cage winding with the object of increasing the shaft capacity, and their design has been influenced thereby. The plan dimensions are similar to those of an equivalent cage, but the length may be greater. The length has to accommodate the side discharge chute and its control doors, as well as the side loading aperture. Ordinary structural steel sections and plates ¼ in–⅜ in are used for the body, with welded or riveted construction. On the Continent, skips made almost entirely of light alloys are in use, and one is also working at Gresford Colliery.

Anti-breakage devices are usually in the form of hinged flaps operated by spring and dashpot gear, or the latter combined with counterpoises. These devices also reduce the shock on the rope when the skip is loaded. The bottom doors of the skip are operated and locked by levers with spring catches; and in the Ruhr an improperly closed door trips a catch in the shaft which stops the wind.

When a rope haulage system is retained, with tubs holding 10 cwt to 20 cwt, tipplers are used to load the skip. The tubs are picked up by a creeper elevator and passed on at a regular rate into the tippler, two tubs at a time. The coal enters a pair of hoppers or measuring pockets, of which one feeds each of the skips. One onsetter attends to all these operations at pit bottom. The empty tubs pass from the tippler back to a standing line for redistribution to the districts. At the bank, the coal is discharged automatically into a bunker, from which it is fed on to a belt conveyor and passed to the screens.

When feasible, a haulage system using large drop-bottom cars holding 3 to 6 tons is preferred. Loading arrangements comprise a dumping hopper of rather greater capacity than the skip at each loading level. The cars are moved over the hopper by a creeper or a retarder, or by air or oil operated piston pushers. The operation of these devices is interlinked with that of the auxiliary equipment, such as door trips and anti-spillage plates, and is placed under the control of one man.

Locomotives for haulage have come into more general use in recent years. The total number was 383 in 1950, 520 in 1953, 900 in 1956 and at June 1969, there were 1,071 in use underground. Of these, 691 were diesel, 286 were electric battery and, 12 were electric trolley; the first electric trolley haulage was installed in 1953. This comprised four locomotives each of 8 tons weight, and 62 hp with axle-hung motors driving the two axles by single-reduction gears; a mercury-arc rectifier supplied current at 250 volts.

VENTILATION AND FIREDAMP DRAINAGE

The broad objectives in ventilating a coal mine can be stated as being to provide constantly, in all travelling and working parts below ground, air flow rates and facilities to: (1) Give an adequate oxygen supply. (2) Dilute and render harmless noxious and inflammable gases. (3) Achieve and maintain conditions of temperature and humidity which are not prejudicial to health, safety, and the winning of coal. (4) Assist in diluting and controlling airborne dust concentrations to acceptable levels.

QUANTITIES OF AIR PROVIDED.—Air supply rates need to satisfy the requirements of men at work and the safety and security of the mine itself and operating electrical machinery. The levels of air supply depend also on; the volume rates of emission of gases evolved from the worked seam, in workings, from the adjacent strata and sometimes from old workings, and the effectiveness of firedamp drainage systems (where applicable); the extent, depth and inclination of workings; coal production levels; methods of working (advancing or retreating longwall, pillar and stall, narrow drivages); the amount and intensity of development work; the amount and nature of dust made; sometimes on certain methods of transport (eg free steered vehicles in drivages and certain airways); the liability, if any, to spontaneous combustion; the requirements of old districts; and other local and special environmental needs and considerations. In specific parts of mines, the quantity of air provided depends on: whether longwall workings or narrow drivages are being considered; the number of such workings; the method of working them and level of production; whether or not electricity is used; whether diesel or battery locomotives are employed and whether, and at what rate, particular noxious or inflammable gases may be produced. In workings liable to abnormal situations associated with spontaneous gas emissions or spontaneous outbursts of coal and gas, additional emergency air supply systems may be provided. (See I. H. Morris, 'Substantial Spontaneous Firedamp Emissions' Mining Engineer, June 1974).

Physiologists commonly quote the basic air requirements of a man at work as about 1·2 l/s. The total quantities of air supplied in modern coal mines, however, significantly exceed those required by the relevant number of men and are usually governed by methane emission levels or levels of other gases produced in mine workings, the extent of workings, operational requirements (such as in headings), good ventilation practice, mine climate and other environmental needs, and statutory requirements. Air supply rates for many longwall faces may exceed 35m^3/s or about 13m^3/s per meter of working thickness. In British mines some of the basic statutory needs for the general body of air are:— the oxygen content must not fall below 19%; the carbon dioxide concentrations must not exceed 1¼%; and carbon monoxide concentrations in locomotive roadways must not exceed 100ppm. Numerous statutory levels of firedamp are specified according to general and particular situations involving the working district, the particular working area, the use of electricity, explosives, diesel and other locomotives, firedamp drainage and other considerations. The Coal Mines (Respirable Dust) Regulations 1975 identify the airborne dust requirements. (See also Mines and Quarries Act 1954–1971; Health and Safety at Work 1974 and the Law relating to Health and Safety in Mines and Quarries Part 2 1970 and amendments.)

Fresh air is a mixture of gases containing by volume 20·93% oxygen, 78·10% nitrogen, 0·94% argon and 0.03% carbon dioxide, with some small proportions of the rare gases such as helium, krypton and neon. The common concentration given for nitrogen (79·04%) includes the argon figure. The atmosphere also contains physical matter such as water vapour, dust, products of combustion, as well as heat. Mine air is also a mixture of dry air and water vapour, the latter exerting a pressure which is independent of the pressures of the other gases. Water vapour normally accounts for only 1 or 2% of the total pressure of the atmosphere. The relative humidity of the air is usually in the range 35–95% and has a direct effect on the density of air. The density of dry air is of the order of 1·2 kg/m^3 at 101·3 kPa and 288 K (15°C).

The composition of mine air can vary significantly in passing through a mine. The oxygen content is reduced (for example, by breathing and oxidation of coal and other materials), and noxious and inflammable gases, dust and some other products of combustion may be added. Significant quantities of heat may flow into the air stream from strata and machinery, particularly at moderately deep and deep mines. The principal mine gases and some of their properties are given in Table 6.

Firedamp (mainly methane with some ethane, propane, butane and small volumes of, helium), held, mostly by adsorption, in the worked and adjacent coal seams and strata, is released when coal is won and strata adjacent to the worked seam is fractured and microfractured by mining. Sometimes it is released suddenly as in spontaneous gas emissions or spontaneous outbursts of coal and gas (See R. Williams and I. H. Morris: 'Emissions and Outbursts in Coal Mining': Symposium in Environmental Engineering in Coal Mining IME 1972).

Firedamp is lighter than air. At atmospheric pressure, methane has an explosive range of approximately 5 to 14% with air, and can be ignited by frictional heat or sparks, explosives, electricity and other causes. Ignition temperatures of methane range from 650 to 750°C and the most easily ignitable mixture occurs at 650°C. The most easily ignited methane concentration in air is 6·6% and the most violent 9·5%. The flammability range of methane decreases with reduction in oxygen content in air and increases with elevated pressures.

Firedamp is emitted continuously in coal mines, and, in general, firedamp emission rates increase as coal production is raised. Many practical factors govern the operational level of firedamp emission in longwall workings and headings (see I. H. Morris 'Firedamp: from Coal Face to Energy', Access, Cardiff, 1980), and these include worked seam thickness and rank; seam gas contents (m^3/t); coal density in adjacent strata (ie cms of coal per metre of strata in the roof and floor, say within 60/100 m in the roof and 30/50 m in the floor of the worked seam); moisture content of coal; depth of working; whether a virgin or previously worked area is under consideration; method, level and rate of coal production; width of excavation; and whether certain geological factors (such as faults, folds, whins, splitting or converging of seams, cap rocks, abnormal coals) are involved. Firedamp emission rates may be of the order of 2 to 250 l/s in coal headings and from about 10 to 250 l/s from coal fronts of longwall faces. In longwall districts, firedamp emission rates may range from approximately 10 to 1,500 l/s. Rates may exceed 4,500 l/s, however, when sudden abnormal firedamp emissions occur from the floor or roof, or from roof and floor of the worked seam.

The other principal inflammable gases in mines are carbon monoxide (from oxidation, spontaneous combustion, fires, explosive and exhaust gases from diesel engines) and hydrogen as a product of spontaneous combustion, heatings, battery charging, action of water on a red hot fire and as a constituent of firedamp in some cases.

TABLE 6.—PRINCIPAL GASES FOUND IN COAL MINES

Gas	Symbol	Relative Density	Flammability* Limits at Atmospheric Pressure: %	Gross Calorific Value kJ/m^3	Long Term Exposure† Limit Values ppm
Air	—	1	—	—	—
Oxygen	O_2	1·11	—	—	—
Nitrogen	N_2	0·97	—	—	—
Carbon Dioxide	CO_2	1·53	—	—	5,000
Methane	CH_4	0·55	5–14	37,110	—
Ethane	C_2H_6	1·05	3–12·5	64,530	—
Propane	C_3H_8	1·56	2–9·5	96,600	—
Butane	C_4H_{10}	2·09	1·8–8·5	125,700	—
Iso Butane	C_4H_{10}	2·07	1·8–8·5	125,700	—
Carbon Monoxide	CO	0·97	12·5–72	11,860	50
Hydrogen	H_2	0·07	4–75	11,940	—
Hydrogen Sulphide	H_2S	1·18	4–45	23,500	10
Nitric Oxide	NO	1·04	—	—	25
Nitrogen Dioxide	NO_2	1·5	—	—	5

* Depends on direction of propagation and other factors.

† *See* Occupational Exposure Limits 1984, Guidance Note EH 10, Health and Safety Executive April 1984.

The long term exposure limit is concerned with total intake of airborne substances hazardous to health over a period of eight hours.

The toxic gases include carbon monoxide, oxides of nitrogen and hydrogen sulphide. Very small concentrations (a few parts per million-ppm) of carbon monoxide are commonly found in mine air. Higher general body carbon monoxide concentrations are experienced during spontaneous heatings of coal, mine fires, and also after explosions of firedamp and/or coal dust when it may be present in concentrations which are very poisonous. Sixty minute self rescuers are issued to every person going underground in British mines as a protection against carbon monoxide and these convert the carbon monoxide to carbon dioxide. Higher carbon monoxide concentrations are found also in firedamp drainage boreholes and systems, diesel engine exhausts and in stopped off districts.

Oxides of nitrogen (NO_x) comprising nitric oxide, nitrogen dioxide and its dimer nitrogen tetroxide (N_2O_4) occur in shotfiring fumes and the exhaust of diesel engines and is a term used to describe the sum of those two toxic nitrogen oxides. Nitric oxide (NO) is a colourless, odourless gas, slightly heavier than air which reacts with atmospheric oxygen to produce nitrogen dioxide (NO_2). The latter is a reddish brown pungent gas which dissolves in water to form nitrous and nitric acids. Nitrogen dioxide is much more toxic than nitric oxide, and has a long term exposure limit of 5 ppm compared with 25 ppm for nitric oxide. Low concentrations of nitrogen dioxide may cause irritation but serious illness (lung oedema, bronchitis) can develop at higher concentrations. Concentrations above about 30 ppm nitrogen dioxide are generally considered highly significant.

Hydrogen sulphide is encountered on occasions in certain geological formations above the carboniferous coal measures and may therefore be encountered in some shafts or drifts passing through such measures. It is also found occasionally in floor measures below a worked seam. The gas is toxic, has a long term exposure limit of 10 ppm, a distinguishing smell of rotten eggs, may result from the action of acidic mine waters on naturally occurring pyrites, and may be found during spontaneous combustion.

Methane, carbon dioxide and nitrogen may become suffocating gases, with a deficiency of oxygen in a mine environment in which those gases are present in abnormal concentrations. Carbon dioxide and nitrogen are the main (inert) constituents of blackdamp, which may be present in or emanate from old workings.

DETECTION OF MINE GASES BY HAND METHODS.—The flame safety lamp has been used for the detection of firedamp and oxygen deficiency in coal mines for about 160 years, and provides a visual guide as to the methane concentrations present and the presence of oxygen. Firedamp is detected using the lowered (testing) flame and observing the height of a blue cap above the yellow fuel cap. The height of the blue cap increases with rise in methane concentration until the flame spires. At about 1½% a pale blue cap is just visible above the fuel cap, at above 2% a gas cap of some two-thirds of a complete triangle is visible, compared with a larger height at 3%. The flame smokes or flickers in methane concentrations of about 5% when the flame is extinguished. The flame is also extinguished in oxygen deficient situations. Modifications of the basic flame safety lamp have been evolved to enable probes and other devices to be applied to test for methane at roof level and other places. The Garforth lamp, which provides facilities for gas to be supplied from the bottom of the lamp from a small aspirator bulb, can be used to test samples from roof level or from places which are difficult of access. Standard gas caps in the range nil to 20% firedamp can be obtained. (*See* 'Mine Gases', Booklet, Industrial Training Branch of the National Coal Board, 1974 and 'Beware Firedamp' NCB 1977).

A large number of approved, portable electric hand methanometers are used in British mines, which are calibrated and tested regularly in laboratories for accuracy, repeatability, and operational suitability. Some 9,000 portable low concentration methanometers are employed by colliery and other officials to detect and/or measure methane concentrations. These instruments are specially approved for underground use and contain a heated pellistor filament coated with a catalyst on which methane is caused to burn. As a result, the heated filament increases in temperature, causes a change in the electrical resistance of the filament, and produces an out-of-balance voltage in a Wheatstone bridge network of which it forms a part. The out-of-balance voltage is proportional to the percentage methane present. These instruments have a range of 0 to 5% methane by volume, an analogue meter or digital display and are required to be in error by not more than ±0·1% methane or 8% of the true methane concentration whichever is the greater. Remote sampling may be carried out by means of a probe which is attached to the methanometer or by mounting a digital methanometer on the end of a support rod. The D6 Methanometer is small, compact, weighs 472 gms, of the diffusion type, hand operated, and can be provided with an aspirator bulb/probe attachment. The D6D, three digit, methanometer is a digital version of the D6 which can be employed for remote sampling using a probe or by supporting the D6D methanometer in a cradle at the end of a rod. The SM1, three digit, methanometer has; a range of 0 to 5 per cent; a rechargeable battery and externally accessible recharging socket; and calibration setting potentiometers under a tamper proof sliding cover.

In addition to the above, over 4,500 diffusion type, automatic, firedamp detectors (AFD's) are used in British mines which indicate continuously by meter or digital readout the concentration of methane in mine air. Modern automatic firedamp detectors are small, robust and employ the pellistor detector/Wheatstone bridge principle. They are powered by rechargeable batteries which enable the AFD to be used continuously for about 8 to 10 hours. They are fully approved for underground use, have a range of 0 to 3 or 0 to 5% methane, and are provided with a red visual alarm which flashes regularly at the rate of once per 15 seconds if firedamp concentrations are below a pre-set value, and once every second if concentrations are above the pre-set value. The latter can be arranged to give a warning within the range 0·2 to 3% firedamp. Automatic firedamp detectors are used by workmen and certain officials particularly in headings and at longwall faces.

High concentrations of methane are measured by an approved hand held, HC111 methane tester, of which there are about 1,000 in use in British mines. This tester also consists essentially of a Wheatstone bridge and meter calibrated 0 to 100% methane. In this monitor, methane cools the working filament due to greater thermal conductivity of methane compared with air. The presence of methane causes a change in filament resistance and creates an out-of-balance of the bridge containing the 0 to 100% meter. This methane tester weighs 980 gms and is widely used for firedamp drainage work and for the measurement of high concentrations in boreholes. They are also used in degassing operations, assessing concentrations in methane layers and in special situations (e.g. abnormal firedamp emissions) where higher methane concentrations are encountered.

A number of approved hand held monitors is available for coal mines. These monitors are based on the electrochemical cell, and indicate oxygen present in partial pressure (kPa) or percentage oxygen. The OX1 consists of a temperature compensated galvanic cell, an electronic amplification and alarm circuit, a meter and a rechargeable battery housed in a black, anti static, plastic case. It weighs about 470 gms. Oxygen in the atmosphere diffuses to the working electrode of the galvanic oxygen cell, and is reduced causing an electric current to flow in the cell. The amount of current flowing is proportional to the number of molecules of oxygen in the atmosphere ie to the partial pressure of oxygen, is amplified, to allow an analogue meter display with a range of 14 to 24 kPa (red band 14–15·5 kPa, yellow 15·5–17 kPa, and green 17–24 kPa). An audible alarm circuit is triggered by the signal level and can be set to operate in the range 15–19 kPa. The maximum error is of the order of ±1·5 kPa. The OXD1, weighs 660 gms, has a LCD digital display (0–25% by volume O_2 equivalent), audible alarm for oxygen deficiency, rechargeable batteries, uses an electrochemical cell, has an alarm range of 14–23% oxygen equivalent, a stainless steel case, fault and low battery indicators, relevant electronics, and is unaffected by pressure fluctuations. The E14 oxygen monitor employs electrochemical cells of the cassette design, weighs 450 gms, measures oxygen partial pressure, has an analogue meter display with a range 14 to 24 kPa oxygen partial pressure, audible alarm range within the operating range, is powered by two Mallory batteries, has a metal case, will fail safe in event of battery failure, cause the alarm to sound in the event of cell failure and a tagged plastic pin which selects the low and normal polarising voltage and acts as an on/off switch for the alarm.

The estimation of carbon monoxide concentrations at site is commonly carried out using glass stain tubes. For measurement, both ends of the tube are broken, the tube is inserted in a hand gas sampling pump, and a prescribed number of strokes made. This action produces a length of coloured stain proportional to the carbon monoxide present. The reading is obtained by comparing the stain edge with a scale provided on the glass tube which commonly have ranges of 5 to 150, 100 to 700, 10 to 300, or 100 to 3,000 ppm carbon monoxide. Considerable use is made of hand held CO monitors based on two or three electrode electrochemical cells.

The SCO1 is an approved, diffusion type, hand monitor with a range of 0–200 ppm carbon monoxide, and is based on the use of a three electrode electrochemical cell, from the working electrode of which a current is generated on exposure to carbon monoxide. This current is amplified, and used to drive a liquid crystal digital display. The monitor is powered by nickel-cadmium cells or dry battery and used for general body work.

The CO Tracer is a hand (or portable) monitor which determines carbon monoxide within the range 0–2000 ppm and which uses a three electrode electrochemical cell. It is provided with a 3 digit display, an electric sampling pump, a rechargeable battery for 120 hours continuous use, weighs about 1·5kg, and is employed for spontaneous combustion work. Other hand monitors are also used for spontaneous combustion work, such as thermal imagers (for example, Probeye) to locate hot spots (for instance at road sides) and non contact infra red thermometers.

Stain tubes are usually employed for direct determinations of nitric oxide (NO) and/or nitrogen dioxide (NO_2) underground. A manual bellows type, gas sampling pump is used to which is attached a stain tube selected to cover the rangs 0·5 to 5000 ppm NO_X (2 tubes) or 0·5 to 5000 ppm NO_X (5 tubes). Electrochemical cells or organic semiconductors may be used in the future. Gas detection tubes are used also for on site determinations of hydrogen sulphide (0·5 to 77 ppm) and carbon dioxide (0·5 to 10 per cent). In rare situations, gas detection tubes have been used below ground to determine concentrations of formaldehyde, hydrocyanic acid and oxygn also. Smoke tubes are used to indicate flow directions and give coarse values of air velocity, leak detection and sometimes movement of gas streams and layers.

MINE VENTILATION SYSTEMS.—Conventional mine ventilation systems usually involve exhaust ventilation by main, booster and auxiliary fans, singly operating in series and/or parallel; parallel airways extensive main airways systems, probably firedamp drainage and possibly some local air conditioning. Large airflow rates may be involved. Some evidence exists to indicate that conventional ventilation systems may have a number of limitations in relation to the size of the royalty, for example, undersea workings and relative remoteness of workings, say over 15 km from the shafts. Such limitations may include limiting pressure tolerance per fan installation (about 7 kPa for human beings), excess energy losses and air speeds, inability to provide required coal face and development air flow rates and environmental conditions, and very high costs. For these and other reasons, consideration is being given to booster fan controlled recirculation systems in which a pre-arranged, continuously monitored, proportion of the total air quantity handled by an inbye booster fan installation would be recirculated, and used again in inbye workings with 'fresh' air. (See I. H. Morris and G. Walker 'Changes in the Approach to Ventilation in Recent Years'. *Mining Engineer*, January, 1982, pp 401–417, and R. Robinson, 'Trials with a Controlled Recirculation System in an Advance Heading' *Mining Engineer* 1972 also, I. H. Morris, 'Ventilation Systems and Spontaneous Emissions and Outbursts' pp 51–1 to 15–19. Symposium; Ventilation of Coal Mines. Australian Institute of Mining and Metallurgy, Illawara Branch, May 1983.)

AIR FLOW FORMULAE—VENTILATION.—Mine roadways offer resistance to air flow due mainly to surface drag between air and roadway sides which depends mainly on length of airways, their free cross sectional area, type of lining, shape and direction. Nearly all the applied ventilation pressure is used to overcome airway resistance. Effective cross sectional area, length of airways and air quantities flowing are predominant factors in mine roadway pressure losses. Atkinson's equation for these losses is:

$$P = \frac{ksV^2}{A} = \frac{ksQ^2}{A^3} = \frac{lkOQ^2}{A^3}\ \mathrm{N/m^2} \qquad (1)$$

in which it is shown that the ventilating pressure difference P across a length of airway depends directly on the 'friction factor' k, the rubbing surface s in square meters (equal to the product of the length of airway l and its periphery O), the square of the mean air velocity V in m/s, and inversely on the cube of the airway cross sectional area, A, in square metres. Significantly, the pressure difference is shown to be proportional to the square of the air quantity flowing, Q, in m^3/s, and inversely proportional to the cube of the airway cross sectional area, A. For typical straight underground airways, the values of k, the 'friction factor', may range from 0·007 Ns^2m^4 for a smooth concrete lined roadway to about 0·016 Ns^2m^4 for rough airway conditions. Energy losses are directly proportional to the cube of the air quantity flowing.

A simpler pressure difference relationship is used which is derived from basic fluid flow principles and which can be related to Atkinson's equation. In this case,

$$P = RQ^2 \qquad (2)$$

where P is the friction pressure difference across a length of airway in Pascals (N/m^2), R is the roadway resistance in Gauls (Ns^2m^{-8}) and Q the air flow rate in m^3/s. Roadway resistances are expressed in Gauls per 100 m of airway (relative to a standard density of 1·2 kg/m^3) and can be of the order of 0·009 Gauls per 100 m for a slabbed roadway with a cross sectional area of 10 m^2 to about 0·020 Gauls per 100m for a rough airway of the same cross sectional area.

The above considerations relate to straight airways. Additional pressure and energy losses occur if: bends are present; obstructions lie in roadways; rapid changes in cross sectional area, gradients, or alignment take place; and sudden reductions in size of roadway arise. Such losses are usually expressed as $P = CV^2/(2g)$ or as: $P = C_1V_1^2 - C_2V_2^2/2g$ where C_1 and C_2 are friction factors (for example, for bends of various angles); V is the mean air velocity in m/s; and V_1 and V_2 are mean air speeds (m/s) at two reference stations.

Mine workings form simple and complex combinations of individual airways in series, parallel, series/parallel and various mesh arrangements. The air flows in such circuits are interdependent in that changes in one mesh or part may lead to significant changes in others. Calculation of fan duties by hand calculator, desk calculator or computer is undertaken in the simplest cases by direct application of simple pro forma based on the modified $P = RQ^2$ Atkinson formula. Common ventilation problems, however call for the forecasting of requirements and the effects of undertaking circuit changes; introduction of additional roadways and/or booster fans and/or new main fans; extending underground workings; introducing new seams; interconnecting and enlarging mines or complexes; changing coal production levels and centres of production; changes in method of working; and identification of the most effective and most economical methods and arrangements of satisfying certain requirements, and the limiting conditions associated with existing systems. For these and other reasons, networks of airways are constructed for analysis, limbs of which are given appropriate values of airway resistance and air quantity flowing. Each loop is subsequently balanced (using the modified Atkinson equation) to satisfy Kirchoff's Laws: the entire network system is also required to satisfy the same conditions. Successive approximation (iterative) methods are used in which meshes of airways are considered in turn so that each mesh and the entire network is in balance. Manual methods of successive approximations can be laborious and time consuming for fairly extensive problems or large mines or mine complexes, and as such can be inhibitive especially where various combinations or arrangements need to be expeditiously assessed in relation to alternative demands or solutions, fan duties, layouts emergencies and other matters. Analogue (electrical and water) methods were formerly applied but common digital computer programs have been employed for about twenty years as a routine to solve all network problems using standard pro forma input forms. Main frame computers are generally used

Originally the batch process, involving prior completion of proforma covering basic network data for a main frame computer, was widely employed. The advent of relatively cheap, high capacity, high speed personal computers, considerable experience of practising ventilation engineers with personal computers, and relatively large choice of full and simplified software programs have led to the use of desk top personal computers with floppy or Winchester discs. Upward capacity expansion and compatibility with a main frame computer are desirable or required depending on the type, size and frequency, and number of collieries involved.

Assessment of energy losses are of prime importance in analyses of mine ventilation systems. Roadway air power loss (RAPL) is given by $RAPL = PQ = RQ^3 Nms^{-1}$ or watts where the symbols have the usual meanings. Roadway air power losses are directly proportional to air density and, significantly, to airway resistance and the cube of the air quantities flowing. Expression of roadway air power loss in watts per standard length of 100 metres provides a simple, quick, effective and easy practical method of assessing comparative airway loads and energy deployment in mine ventilation circuits. Recurring increases in unit energy prices indicate that energy expenditure will remain of predominating importance and lead in appropriate cases to the evolution of alternative lower energy expenditure methods, such as booster fan controlled recirculation systems mentioned above. Total fan ventilation costs can vary from about 30 to 60% of the individual colliery total power costs.

SURFACE AND UNDERGROUND BOOSTER FANS.—Over the last thirty years or so, the modern centrifugal (radial) fan has superseded the conventional variable pitch, multi stage, axial machine as the main ventilator at most collieries because, in addition to its high efficiency, it provides stable operation, relatively low noise levels, is simple, robust and has relatively minor or indiscernable stall effects and non-overloading power characteristic. Single or double inlet, backward, aerofoil bladed radial fans are commonly employed mainly with vee belt, gear box, or direct drive. The maximum static efficiencies of such fans are of the order of 86/88%. (See I. H. Morris and F. B. Hinsley: 'Some Factors Affecting the Choice of Fans for Mine Ventilation' Transactions of the Institution of Mining Engineers, London, Vol III, 1952). The flexibility of radial fans has been increased by partial blading, using extensible tips aerofoil vanes or adding tips to existing aerofoil vanes, and by the use of inlet guide vanes which, however, reduce efficiencies. Such fans vary from about 1 to 10 metres in diameter and operate at fan shaft speeds from about 61 to 30 rad/s. Surface fan duties up to 7 kPa at 500 m^3/s have been installed with powers of about 3000 kW.

Numerous developments have taken place with axial main fans. Advances in the design of blade profiles and local or remote auto electro hydraulic adjustment of pitch (AVP) of fan blades during operation provide advantages of: improved operating efficiencies by matching current mine requirements and mine resistance to blade position; reduced running costs; direct drive and wide relatively high efficiency operating range. These fans have higher pressure production capabilities and higher tip speeds than conventional axial machines, are driven directly at ac speeds (for example 103 rad/s), give a non overloading power characteristic, and high static efficiencies of 86% over a comparatively wide range of mine resistance. Silencers are usually required with AVP fans. Where appropriate, additional advantages of small nominal size, reduced weight, lower rotor inertia, smaller foundations and civil works and reduced capital outlay can be attained with such axial machines. The relative importance of possible stall conditions, mine planning uncertainties, local noise levels and increased silencing costs always need to be assessed for each application. Another development involves the use of mixed flow fans. In these machines, air is accelerated substantially whilst passing through the fan rotor, after which a high degree of pressure recovery is achieved in a downstream diffuser. One of the principal advantages of such fans is higher pressure production per stage. Vertical and horizontal axial fan installations have been employed. Main fans may be directly coupled to single, two speed or four speed electric motors. Direct drives have the benefits of minimum drive losses compared with gearbox and vee belt drive. Variable speed motors, however, are relatively expensive and not always economically justifiable.

Booster fans are generally of the axial type though 'tailor made' backward bladed radial fan installations, which may require larger underground excavations, are employed also. Large, single high efficiency axial flow booster fans or clusters of in line axial fans in a series/parallel arrangement are used in the United Kingdom. Typical booster fan installations are often based on 1·22m diameter axial machines running at 154 rad/s, each taking about 55 kW with fan maximum efficiencies of 60/65%. Typical installations may comprise two or three such fans in series connected to a single tube or up to four tubes making series/parallel combinations of up to nine fans. A typical duty for a single tube fan installation is 1·5 kPa for 21 m^3/s with a peak load of 51 kW, compared with 2·8 kPa for 23 m^3/s and 98 kW power demand for a two stage, single tube arrangement. At larger installations outputs may rise to over 5 kPa at 100 m^3/s and booster fans with total installed power of up to 1,000 kW have been employed. One two or three installations may be applied in large modern mines. Mixed flow booster fans have been used also, as typified by a 1·2 m 154 rad/s machine provided with the rotor direct mounted on a 112 kW motor shaft giving an output of 25 m^3/s at a pressure of 2·5 kPa. In recent years, substantial advances have been made in the installation of booster fans within treated roadways, with local and remote continuous monitoring of the local environment for methane and smoke; fans for pressure temperature and vibration; and operation by air reversal doors position, electrical load and sometimes by TV monitoring: (See E. R. Wastell and S. J. Robson: 'Remote Monitoring of Underground Fans'. Mining Engineer, London, Vol 138, 1976). Investigations have shown that rotor out of balance can be covered by vibration monitoring in the frequency range of 15 to 60 Hz whereas vibration within the higher frequency range of 250 Hz to 10 kHz is indicative of bearing deterioration. Extended periods (8 to 48 hours) between examinations of some 100 booster fans have been obtained in UK mines, when comprehensive local and remote monitoring of the environment, booster fan, and site are undertaken. Such installations are provided with remote (surface) fan stop and restart facilities. Remote restart of underground booster fans is permitted in certain circumstances, for example, within a prescribed time interval (such as 30 minutes) of booster fan stoppage.

AUXILIARY VENTILATION SYSTEMS AND FANS.—Events over the last thirty years or so have demonstrated a predominant role for auxiliary ventilation systems from the stand points of modern mining demands, continuity of ventilation and accident rates and trends. Auxiliary fans are generally employed to ventilate headings or blind ends in forcing, exhausting, or overlap systems, generally through flexible wire, reinforced flexible, glass reinforced plastic (GRP) or rigid steel tubing.

Traditionally, common auxiliary fan systems have employed 510, 610 or 760 mm diameter fans rated at 7·5, 25 and 27·5 kW. They are of the in line axial type, bifurcated axial, or the in line radial type. The in-line axial fan has been used for decades, and has an impeller directly located on the shaft of a motor in the air stream. In the bifurcated axial machine, the electric motor is enclosed in a 'pod'. A typical 760 mm diameter in-line axial fan operating at 307 rad/s provides an output of 1·75 kPa at 7 m^3/s at a peak efficiency of about 53%. A typical 760 mm diameter bifurcated axial fan operating at 307 rad/s provides an output of 2 kPa at 7 m^3/s at a peak efficiency of about 52%. The in line radial auxiliary fan is made in diameters of 610 mm and 760 mm with powers of 18·5 kW and 37 kW respectively. This fan has the advantages of larger pressure development, quieter operation and power economy arising from higher efficiency. The motor is installed within a pod to give the bifurcated design. A 760 mm diameter in line radial fan, for example, gives an output of about 6 m^3/s at 3·3 kPa at a fan shaft speed of 307 rad/s with a peak efficiency of about 63%. A 610 mm in line radial fan, running at a speed of 307 rad/s handles 3·2 m/s at 3·3 kPa at its peak efficiency of 59%. Many auxiliary fan installations are provided with silencers upstream and downstream the fan itself and, depending on the installation, may be associated with static extractors or overlap systems for dust control. Larger axial and radial fans (over 120 kW rating) have been applied to ducting up to 400 mm diameter. Single or dual duct systems may be employed.

Some recent incidents have re-emphasised the importance of continuous ventilation and auxiliary ventilation systems (see 'Report on Explosion at Houghton Main Colliery, Yorkshire, June 1975' HMSO, 1978. 'The Explosion at Golborne Colliery, Greater Manchester County, 18th March 1979', HMSO 1979, and 'The Explosion at Cardowan Colliery, Stepps, Strathclyde Region 27 January 1982' HMSO, 1982; 'The Outbreak of Fire and Explosion at Coventry Mine, Kersley, Warwickshire, 10 December 1982, HSE 1983'). Design modifications to auxiliary fans have included the use of flange mounted motors, solid blades, bifurcated fan bodies, thicker fan casings, and means of reducing the risk of incendive sparking from rotating fan blades and the acceptance of designs to prescribed standards.

Manager's rules for auxiliary ventilation systems cover normal operation and other situations, such as planned stoppages, (e.g. for maintenance) and degassing operations. The monitoring of auxiliary ventilation systems is being done on an increasing scale, and may include one or more of the following parameters: firedamp; airflow; smoke; fan ventilation; fan pressure; and fan motor carcase temperature.

Controlled and monitored air recirculation systems are adopted at many mines to reduce airborne advance drivages whilst maintaining the required ventilation standards. (See A. J. Pickering and R. Aldred, Controlled Recirculation of Ventilation; A Means of Dust Control in some Drivages, *Mining Engineer*, March 1977).

FIREDAMP EMISSION AND FORECASTING.—The basic gas (firedamp and higher hydrocarbons) content of coal seams is related to coal composition and rank (per cent carbon and volatile matter), moisture and ash content, depth of working and other factors. Thus, for British coals, typical gas contents are about 1 m^3/t for high volatile coals, 2 to 8m^3/t for medium volatile coals, and 17 to 22m^3/t for anthracites. Elsewhere, the gas content of high ranking anthracites exceeds 35m^3/t.

Blackshales and dark inert formations may have gas contents of about 0·1m^3/t. The practical forecasting of mean firedamp emission levels in longwall workings and drivages is carried out regularly to ascertain firedamp emission levels (l/s) when certain production levels and advance rates are anticipated. These assessments take into account desorption rates from coals up to 100m above and down to 50m below the worked seam using the available geological data. Use is also made of the gas content, thickness, and the position of each seam relative to the worked seam, face length, nature and disposition of adjacent strata, depth of working, geological discontinuities, level of production and certain local factors (for example, whether a virgin or previously worked area is being considered). Using these basic facts, the principles of relaxed cores in roof and floor strata around the worked excavation are applied recognising the facts that strata movement, fracturing and micro-fracturing and degassing of adjacent strata occurs slightly ahead of an over the face area, and decreases beyond certain times and distances behind faces and with incrasing height above and depth below the worked seam. Experience shows that in British mines, most activity and emission (depending on the seam content of the sequence) often occurs within about 60m in the roof above and approximately 30m in the floor below the worked seam in established districts. Many practical methods of forecasting can be used and experience shows that a unique relationship has not been identified between percentage degassing (the percentage of the total gas content desorbed) and vertical distance above and below the worked seam. A number of basic curves and relationships are employed depending mainly on the seam densities, predominance of hard and/or soft formation inthe affected area above and below the worked seam, and practical experience. (See I. H. Morris: 'Some Factors Affecting Rates of Methane Emission' *Mining Engineer* 1965/66; I. H. Morris loc. cit. Access 1980; I. H. Morris and G. Walker loc. cit. *Mining Engineer* 1981). It needs to be recognised, however, that these methods provide mean estimates, are commonly within 10 per cent of mean emission rates but may be less accurate in situations, for example where insufficient is known about the local geology and physical characteristics of the adjacent strata, where geological changes are taking place or geological discontinuities are present, and where significant variations occur in face advance rates. The forecasts, however, are invaluable in ventilation planning, in the design of ventilation, firedamp extraction and utilisation systems, and the solution of practical problems.

FIREDAMP DRAINAGE AND UTILISATION.—The drainage of firedamp from strata associated with current and old mine workings is practised throughout the world, particularly in Europe, and is extending as an essential part of coal mining. About 500 million m^3 of pure methane are drained annually in the United Kingdom where gas is extracted from about 350 productive districts and some headings, and 3,000 boreholes.

Firedamp drainage is employed for one or more reasons in: longwall advancing or retreating districts; old districts; coal headings; or cross measure drivages. It is used to reduce firedamp concentrations in return gates, at the coal face, and in intake gates of longwall productive districts. It may be employed to deal with local firedamp problems, such as those which might be present near return gateside packs; ripping lips; roadway sides and other places; and may be adopted to remove and/or prevent the layering of gas. It is applied to control and reduce the amount of firedamp released into the air stream from faults; feeders or blowers; firedamp reservoirs; and old districts. It is also used successfully to prevent, limit, and deal with firedamp associated with gas outbursts from roof and/or floor strata. It can be employed to improve environmental conditions, particularly at the coal face, by enabling firedamp in coal producing districts to be controlled without having to resort to exceptionally large or prohibitive air quantities at the working face which would otherwise be necessary if dilution only was practised. In some cases, it can limit running costs of machinery, such as fans, used for the environment by applying a direct and effective method of dealing with firedamp. It can make high gas emission or high gas risk areas, which would otherwise be sterilised, available for exploitation. Firedamp drainage has the advantage that, in satisfying underground environmental requirements it also can provide a lucrative source of gaseous fuel.

Firedamp is drained at some 90 collieries, or about 70% of the total of British mines, at which it forms an essential part of the environment control system. The method is simple, direct and one of the most effective means of controlling and limiting the amount of firedamp which enters the underground ventilating stream from adjacent strata and sometimes from the worked seam also (See I. H. Morris 'Firedamp Drainage in Mines' Iron and Coal Trades Review, December 1961).

Firedamp drainage is commonly based on the cross measure method in which boreholes of 35 to 70 mm diameter are drilled above and/or below the worked seam usually just behind advancing or retreating longwall faces. New boreholes are drilled continually near the working face, the nearest borehole being kept within 10 to 40 m from the face. Boreholes are drilled at intervals of 5 to 25 m and at angles of 40 to 60 degrees to the horizontal. Each borehole is provided with a standpipe, which is usually 3 to 10 m long, to reduce air inleakage and provide support for borehole fittings. The standpipe is sealed using Denso tape and drill cuttings, or by resin, or bentonite, or high alumina cement in certain floorholes. The length of individual boreholes ranges from about 15 to 100 m depending on local circumstances and conditions, strata sections and the type of problem encountered. Firedamp is drained either in return gates or in intake and return gates of longwall districts. Individual boreholes yield from 2 to 250 l/s and extraction rates from individual productive districts are usually in the range of 10 to 1,500 l/s. Most colliery firedamp extraction rates range from about 50 to 2,000 l/s (See I. H. Morris 'Substantial Spontaneous Firedamp Emissions' *The Mining Engineer*, 1974 and E. Bumstead and W. Greenwell 'Firedamp Emission at Yorkshire Main Colliery'. *The Mining Engineer*, 1979 also Firedamp Drainage; Handbook for the Coalmining Industry in the European Community, *Verlag Gluckauf*, 1980).

From 30 to 95% of the total firedamp emission in a longwall district may be captured by a firedamp drainage system. Sometimes firedamp is drained from the worked seam at the ends of longwall faces, or in coal headings. In the latter, 50 mm diameter holes are drilled in the worked seam and/or adjacent strata from manholes on each side of the heading for a length of about 30/40 m in advance of the heading. Large quantities of firedamp may be drained from old districts also, sometimes to reduce or eliminate intake and/or return airway contamination. Substantial quantities of firedamp are drained from old shafts (See B. G. Morgan 'Developments in Methane Drainage Techniques in South Wales Area'. Mining Engineer, 1974).

Where conditions are suitable (for example more permeable, well cleated, or disturbed coal seams, with moderate to high gas contents), firedamp drainage from the worked seam itself prior to working has been very successful and effective in reducing the gas content of the seam to be worked and decreasing the number of outbursts. Long boreholes (average length about 100 m), 50 mm diameter, are drilled in the worked seam using resin sealed standpipes to drain firedamp for some four months prior to working, say a block of coal by retreat mining (See P. Marshall, R. Lama and E. Tomlinson 'Experiences on Pre Drainage of Gas at West Cliff Colliery' Proceedings of the Symposium 'Seam Gas Drainage with particular reference to the Working Seam'. May 1982 *The Australian Institute of Mining and Metallurgy*—Illawara Branch).

In the United Kingdom, the largest quantity of firedamp drained from one colliery is about 40 million m^3 per annum. About thirty collieries drain more than 4 million m^3 firedamp annually. Gas is extracted from the workings through steel pipes, to which boreholes are connected, using either underground water seal extractors, or water seal extractors located and connected up in parallel at the surface of the mine. Such approved extractors may be of a design in which the rotor is mounted centrally within an elliptical casing, or of the current type in which the rotor is mounted eccentrically within a circular casing. The latter are more efficient (maximum about 50%), quieter, have a non overloading power characteristic, are suitable for direct ac motor drive, cheaper per litre/second of mixture handled, and more stable in operation. Typical extractor performances are: 300 l/s at 65 kPa suction and 50 kPa delivery pressure with a power demand of 32 kW at a speed of 103 rad/s; and 480 l/s at a suction of 65 kPa and a delivery pressure of 50 kPa for a power of 45 kW at a speed of 77 rad/s. The largest water seal extractor used for firedamp drainage work handles 820 l/s at a suction of 50 kPa and a delivery pressure of 50 kPa for a power of 173 kW at a speed of 52 rad/s.

About 240 million m^3 of drained firedamp are utilised annually in the United Kingdom. Of this, approximately 110 million m^3 are utilised at collieries compared with about 130 million m^3 sold to external customers. Most of the internal utilisation takes place in colliery boilers for the production of hot water or steam, mainly for space heating, by burning drained firedamp down to a purity of 30%. Drained gas is employed also in 0·5, 0·7 and 1·25 MW dual fuel reciprocating engine sets for power generation and steam production, and in a 1·3 MW gas turbine set for power generation and hot water for space heating. Drained gas is used to heat downcast air at collieries. External customers are supplied with drained firedamp through gas grids and long pipe lines. The 130 million m^3 of drained firedamp is utilised externally in brickworks, clay industries, a tilery, glass works, tyre factory, chemical works, small plastics factory, small coal drying plant, distillery and at a trading estate (See I. H. Morris loc. cit Access 1980; S. F. Smith 'The Parkside Colliery Methane Gas Disposal Project' *Mining Engineer* 1982).

ENVIRONMENTAL MONITORING.—Pitwide systematic and continuous monitoring forms part of routine managerial systems in British coal mines. Traditionally, methods of monitoring the mine environment have been based on periodic, spot observations using hand monitors. Such methods contribute greatly to the monitoring of the mine environment, but provide a limited amount of information. Sometimes they suffer from the disadvantage that a comparatively long time may elapse between taking samples and measurements and the availability of results, and can be labour intensive and costly. Successful developments of suitable transducers and monitors, integrated circuits, approved and certified, intrinsically safe, digital time division multiplexing data transmission systems, and the application of small, on line micro computers and data handling equipment have enabled remote monitoring of the mine environment to be achieved to give continuous indication of state, early warning of abnormal and adverse environmental trends and automatic power isolation in prescribed conditions. Such systems can be applied to monitor necessary elements of the environment over distances in excess of 15km and any machinery (main, booster and auxiliary fans, firedamp extractors and utilisation plants and air conditioning units) that forms an essential part of the mine environmental system. (See: R. B. Dunn 'Mining Systems and the Development', Mining Technology, 1974, and I. H. Morris and G. W. Gray 'Environmental Monitoring and Control in the United Kingdom', International Conference on Remote Control and Monitoring in Mining, Birmingham, 1977 and 'Changes in the Approach to Ventilation in Recent Years' by I. H. Morris and G. Walker, *Mining Engineer*, January 1982).

The principle of management by exception is employed in routine real time, mine environmental monitoring schemes in which a continuous stream of data is fed to a surface central station for assessment of current

Parameter	Monitor	Range(s)	Number of Channels/ Detectors	Application	Location	Typical Use
Methane	BMI	0–3% v/v	1	General Body	S + U	Airways and Ducts
	MM1	0–50% v/v	1	General Body	S + U	Airways and Headings
		or 0–100% v/v	1		S + U	
	1350	0–5% v/v	Up to 8	General Body	S	Firedamp Extraction Plant
	BM2H	0–100% v/v	1	Pipe Systems	S + U	Firedamp drainage
	Infra Red	0–3%, 0–10% v/v	1	General Body	S + U	Airways, Tube Bundles
		0–75% v/v	Multi	Pipe Systems	S	Firedamp Extraction/Utilisation Plant
Air Velocity	BA2	0–2, 0–5, 0–10 m/s	1	General Body	S + U	Airways and Ducts
	BA4	0–2, 0–5, 0–10 m/s	2	General Body	S + U	Airways and Ducts
Suction/ Pressure/ Differential Pressure	BP1	Typical suction { 0–5 kPa, 0–100 kPa	2	Pipes duct systems and General Body	S + U	Airways, Pipes and Ducts
	BP2	0–1000 Pa Differential	1			
	BP3	0–100 kPa (absolute)	1	General		Airways
Carbon Monoxide	Emcor III	0–50 ppm 0–500 ppm	1	General Body	S & U	Airways, Stoppings and Pipes
	BCO 1	0–200 ppm	1	General Body	S & U	Airways, Stoppings and Pipes
	COSEC	0–200 ppm	1	General Body	S & U	Airways and Stoppings
Products of Combustion	P3270	On/Off	1	General Body	S & U	Airways and Headings
	Fides	On/Off	1	General Body	S & U	Airways and Headings
		(CO:0–200 ppm	1			
	Fidesco	(POC: On/Off	1	General Body	S & U	Airways and Headings
	Firant	On/Off Analogue	1 or 2	Local General Body	S & U	Airways and Headings
Oxygen	BO1	0–30% V/V	1	General Body	S & U	Airways, Headings and Stoppings
Methane, Oxygen, Carbon monoxide	Multi Gas	Methane: 0–3% V/V Oxygen: 0–25% V/V Carbon monoxide: 0–1000 ppm	3	General Body	S & U	Airways, Stoppings and Drivages
Fan Vibration	MAVIS	On/Off	up to 12	Booster Fans	S & U	Airways
	FIFFI	On/Off		Auxiliary Fans	S & U	Airways and Drivages

'S' denotes Surface 'U' denotes Underground

positions, verification of early warning and alarm states, identification of adverse trends and for logging, treatment and presentation of data including that on abnormal states (date, times, location, type etc), faults and duration of abnormalities. Such continuous monitoring is seen as a prerequisite to the use of certain other transducers, transmission facilities and selected machine operation during working and supervisory (week end, holidays etc) periods. Thus, the condition of an environment containing machinery, such as water pumps, can be continuously monitored for suitability, prior to, and during, remote starting, running and stopping. Significant security benefits and savings on manshifts and power demands can be realised.

Continuous interrogation of selected environmental parameters by fixed monitors at a large number of strategic positions (over 100 in a large environmental monitoring system) can be achieved by regular and rapid scanning of such positions, so that current values can be determined, variations detected and evaluated, abnormal values and adverse trends identified and discretionary early warnings given and electric power automatically isolated according to prescribed micro computer configurable programs. Action can then be considered by management and, if necessary, steps taken, sooner than previously praticable, to correct or ameliorate the effects of abnormal conditions. However, remote environmental monitoring is not intended to replace systematic local searches being conducted by experienced underground mining personnel, but is seen as a means of initiating limited remedial action. Increasing use is being made of control units and control equipment, such as approved actuator valves, initially in an incident preventive role (such as isolation of electric power, when one or more prescribed levels, such as firedamp are exceeded or other levels, such as airflow, are not attained). Concurrently, automatic corrective systems are employed to counter or compensate for natural changes (such as falling atmospheric pressure), as in the control of stopped off areas and certain parts of firedamp extraction plants and systems.

Continuous monitoring of the mine environment would include general body and drained firedamp concentrations, air, drained gas and methane flow rates, pressures, carbon monoxide, smoke and products of combustion. Details of some fixed monitors are given in Table 7. Developments are continuing for wet and dry bulb temperatures, or relative humidity and dry bulb temperature, and airborne dust monitors. Most fixed monitors serve a single function (for example methane) but developments are continuing for multi purpose monitors, such as multi gas (methane, oxygen and carbon monoxide) or multi purpose (for example, methane, airflow, carbon monoxide, pressure).

Recent developments include environmental transducer centres in which a number (up to four initially) of different sensors with their dedicated power supplies, control units and liquid crystal displays, battery etc are operated from a single module, central control unit. Alarm and electric power trip facilities are provided for each channel also. Thus, in a mine airway, a single module with sensors for general body methane, carbon monoxide, oxygen and air flow might be chosen whereas, at a firedamp drainage monitoring station, drained firedamp purity, pipe suction, flow differential pressure, and general body methane may be selected. Such environmental transducer centres have many other applications including: drivages; auxiliary ventilation systems; booster fan and underground firedamp extractor installations; and air conditioning monitoring and control.

Pitwide environmental monitoring systems are designed around underground and surface monitoring and control centres, at which one or more outstations may be located. These outstations are usually connected in parallel to a two or four wire dedicated data transmission cable which relays digital information to a surface data information, control and communications centre. Real time microcomputers with 256 k or more memory capacity are employed in that centre to collect, organise and present data and information (programmed to meet specific needs of colliery management) on local and remote visual display units and line printers. Additional off-line storage and data recall and presentation facilities are often provided by secondary computers. Advances continue to be made in environmental monitoring systems and in the design and specification of data transmission systems such as low speed digital signals and high speed data highways to cater for large volume data transfer (See K. Jones 'The Environmental Monitoring and Remote Control Scheme for Manton Colliery'. The Mining Engineer, 1976. A. W. Corbett: 'The Use of Computers for the Continuous Monitoring of the Environment at Brodsworth Colliery', *Mining Engineer*, 1979 and I. H. Morris and G. Walker 'Changes in the Approach to Ventilation in Recent Years' Mining Engineer 1982 also 'An Advanced Environmental Monitoring System' by R. J. Waddle, *The Mining Engineer*, June 1985 pp 703–705 and 'A Review of Industry; Problems and Current Developments' by G. Cooper *Mining Technology*, Jan 1986).

Typical local monitoring and control centres are sited at or for: main fans; booster fans; auxiliary fans and systems; surface and underground firedamp extraction plants; surface and underground air conditioning plants; inbye (and outbye) ends of drivages; inbye end of intake gates and inbye and outbye end of return gates; at stopping sites; water pumping sites; measuring stations along gate and main airways for ventilation, firedamp extraction, air conditioning, and at surface firedamp utilisation plants. On/off or analogue data is relayed from fixed monitors at such centres to a local outstation where analogue inputs are digitised and all data transmitted to the surface on demand using a time division multiplexing data transmission system. Each monitoring and control centre is equipped with one, two or three outstations, though at larger centres (such as surface firedamp extraction plants) over ten outstations may be applied.

Requirements at individual monitoring and control centres vary widely. At booster fan sites, for example, pressures, firedamp, smoke, airflow, vibration and/or equipment temperatures, and many on/off states are monitored, manual facilities provided for remote stop and start, with automatic power isolation facilities for some abnormal states such as excess vibration and high methane. Auxiliary ventilation systems may be monitored (with alarms) at the inbye end of a drivage for one or more of the following parameters (methane, air flow, carbon monoxide, products of combustion, oxygen) and at the outbye end for one or more of methane, airflow, fan pressure, vibration, smoke, machinery temperature, electrical load depending on the system and local requirements. Main ventilation systems are monitored along trunk airways and in gate roadways where monitoring of airflow and general body methane and carbon monoxide is undertaken. Conveyor roadways and systems may be monitored (with alarms) for smoke, products of combustion, carbon monoxide, abnormal heat at fixed machinery sites and sometimes methane depending on the layout. Continuous scrutiny of firedamp drainage systems is achieved either by analogue or on/off devices monitoring vacuum, pressure, differential pressure across orifice plates or venturi devices, purities of drained gas, seal water temperature and flow, operating states and other parameters. Automatic trip facilities provided for certain eventualities, (such as low purities of drained gas) and remote stop and start facilities incorporating actuator valve and other controls are employed. Stopping sites are monitored for methane, flow rates, suction and smoke, and automatic control facilities are used when firedamp extraction and/or pressure balancing is needed. Absolute pressure monitors are available for this purpose and for ventilation pressure surveying of large or combined mines. The total number of outstations in typical environmental monitoring and control schemes ranges from about four to thirty.

An essential part of numerous environmental monitoring schemes is the tube bundle system, now employed for whole mine monitoring or shaft monitoring at about 90 British coal and at many overseas mines. In this system, mine air is drawn continuously through 4·3, 6·3, 8·6, or 11·8 mm bore polythene tubers installed throughout (or part of) a mine by small scavenger and sampling vacuum pumps situated at the surface. A number of tubes (up to 19 in one bundle) is assembled within one overall PVC cover, which may also be armoured. Samples are extracted from the various sampling points (up to 65 at some collieries and complexes) according to a prescribed sequence. Continuous gas analysis is then carried out by colliery infra red analysers and other sensors (electrochemical cells, semi conductors etc), and associated equipment provides data on concentrations and records of carbon monoxide, methane (high and low concentrations), carbon dioxide, oxygen, and other mine gases. Micro computer driven, two (or more) analyser stream, tube bundle systems with V.D.U. display and line printers are being widely applied. These systems give continuous routine mine air sample results to laboratory standards; automatic warning of changing situations; presentation of all data (including early warnings and alarm) on a visual display unit and line printer; and direct management information, including trends and CO/O_2 deficiency ratios for districts liable to spontaneous combustion. Automatic transfer of micro computer data to a colliery environmental mini computer system is readily achieved. (See I. H. Morris and G. W. Gray 'Environmental Monitoring and Control in the United Kingdom': International Conference, Birmingham, UK, 1977 and A. C. Hurworth: 'The Application of a Microcomputer to Mine Gas Analysis'. Symposium on Dedicated Digital Control. Institute of Measurement and Control, Aston, Birmingham, 1977).

MINE CLIMATE.—In moderately deep and deep mines, one of the principal functions of ventilation is providing acceptable environmental conditions using many methods, including significant local air speeds. Normal mouth temperature is about 310 K but body temperatures vary, among other factors, with rate of work and the temperature of the working environment. Higher body temperatures may lead to additional heat stress and possibly to heat stroke. Heat may be acquired by the human body from strata, by radiation from machinery and by convection from air at temperatures higher than the skin. It is essential, if near normal body temperatures are to be maintained, that adequate heat losses occur from the body, particularly by increased evaporation of sweat. Some evidence indicates in general that human performance decreases at American Effective Temperatures of about 301 K (See below). Some countries have prescribed limiting environment (comfort) values related to effective temperatures of about 301 K, with cessation of work at effective temperatues of 305 K. Other countries give dry bulb temperature limitations of 299, 301 and 310 K respectively or temperature limitations of 309 K (dry bulb) and 303 K (wet bulb).

The principal sources of moisture and water are: the strata itself; natural water 'make'; and water used for cooling machines and dust control. Some of the water is evaporated causing an increase in enthalpy (heat content per unit mass flow) of mine air, manifested as a rise in wet bulb temperature of the environment. Geothermic gradients vary significantly in different parts of the world, being relatively small in South African mines (about 1°C per 100 m) compared with 1°C per 35 m below a depth of 15 m in the United Kingdom and other European coalfields. In the United Kingdom, virgin rock temperatures (VRT) at the same depth vary significantly between coalfields and sometimes within relatively small distances in the same coalfield. For example, at a depth of 1000 m, VRT readings of approximately 308 K (35°C) and 311 K (38°C) have been obtained in the North Staffordshire coalfield whereas temperatures of about 306 K (33°C) have been obtained at a depth of 700 m in Derbyshire. Virgin rock temperatures over 331 K (58°C) have been measured in European coal mines. V.R.T.'s in excess of 337 K (64°C) are anticipated in West German Coal Mines at depths of about 1300 m, compared with 343 K (70°C) in South African gold mines at depths of about 5000 m. In modern mechanised mines, machines can make significant and important contributions to the heat in the working environment especially in moderately deep and deep mines. Apart from work done against gravity, power consumed by machinery manifests itself as heat in the environment causing evaporation of local moisture and rise in wet bulb temperature. Long distances also may contribute to significant increases in dry and wet bulb temperatures at working places.

A comfort index widely used in coal mines to describe the environment is the American (basic) Effective Temperature (ETA) obtained from a nomogram or sets of tables. This index relates the three predominant variables of an environment in a single figure. Thus, a dry bulb temperature of 301 K, a wet bulb temperature of 297 K, and an air velocity of 2 m/s would give the environment an ETA of 294 K, compared with an ETA of 299 K for an environment with a dry temperature of 303 K, a wet bulb temperature of 300 K and an air speed of 0·75 m/s. The conditions of a given underground environment, and hence its ETA often are improved locally by increasing air speeds and improving the control of moisture sources and enthalpy.

The comfort of an underground environment may be enhanced in a number of ways. Basic practical measures include: the application of unit ventilation; provision of higher air quantities (and therefore higher air velocities) at working places consistent with acceptable practical limits; the application of ascensional or decensinal homotropal ventilation (ie air flowing in the same direction as the coal) where practicable; local air recirculation; restricting the number, dimensions, and form of blind ends and provision of positive ventilation in them; minimising the size of (return) ripping lips where practicable; giving special consideration to the maximum length of return gate roadways and air velocities in them; separation of parallel intake roadways; adoption of latest dust control measures and advances to reduce, where practicable, both amounts of airborne dust and the amount of water used; increasing adoption of retreat mining; careful siting of electrical equipment especially in intake airways; early stopping off of old districts; and regular monitoring of variables (wet bulb and dry bulb temperatures, air velocities, energy and water consumption etc) directly related to the comfort of the working environment.

Surface and underground (including local) air conditioning plants have been used in coal mines for many years and large plants have been used in metal mines for over seventy years. The estimated total cooling capacities in West European Coal Mines are of the order of 200 MW, including about 170 MW in West Germany and 15 MW in the United Kingdom. The maximum cooling capacity of such plants is about 10 MW. Local air conditioning plants are of the direct or chilled water type involving; an evaporator (in which the air is cooled and the heat acquired by a refrigerant); a compressor for the refrigerant; a condenser (where heat from the refrigerant is transferred to cooling water); and an after cooler in which heat is exchanged from water to the return ventilating stream. Small 50 kW local direct air conditioning units rated at 135,000 k cal/h are employed in inbye drivages and near return ripping lips and 750 kW chilled water units, rated up to 650,000 k cal/hr in districts for improved environmental conditions at the face, return ends, and in return gates, and for cooling water for dust control and machine motors. Increasing use is being made of systems in which chilled water is distributed throughout a mine through insulated pipes of steel or other materials. Continuous monitoring and automatic control of chilled water systems will enable coolth to be distributed and redistributed according to the temporal and prevailing demands at working places.

Centralised air conditioning plants are employed both underground and at the surface of British and West German mines with cooling capacities up to 6 and 10 MW respectively. (See 'Mine Climate in the Coal Mining Industry'. *Gluckauf Essen*. Vol. 118 (1982) No. 19 also J. M. Anderson and I. Longson 'The Optimisation of Ventilation and Refrigeration in British Coal Mines, *The Mining Engineer* Aug. 1986 pp 115–120). The application of such plants is expected to increase significantly in West European (German and British) coal mines as they become deeper and the need to maintain or improve production levels continues.

COMPUTERS IN THE MINING ENVIRONMENT.—Computers are widely applied in three principal areas for routine; computation, collation and recall of data; monitors; and operation, discrimination, alarm and routine monitoring and control. In the office, terminals provide direct access to remote main frame computers which are employed for routine solutions of ventilation networks (analysis of existing, future, proposed, partly hypothetical networks, colliery mergers, demergers, main and booster fan duties etc) and forecasting of underground climatic conditions for a mine or part of a mine. Each of these applications may involve large numbers of separate computations and, in the climate program, large numbers of relatively short lengths of roadways, numerous variables with many alternative choice of constants for each, variable heat sources and sinks, heat storage and other factors for which a main frame computer is necessary. There are, however, some limitations in main frame computer work—for example, sometimes in delay to available solutions because of time sharing or other higher priority work, and the lack of immediate availability of computer facilities to deal with incident, urgent, or transient problems, or to test various potential transient solutions, ideas, and hypotheses; main frame computer capacity is not needed for a high proportion of mundane tasks. In many office applications for example, on the spot limited computer power is needed to: collate, organise and reorganise routine data; input, store, and recall local technical data and information; undertaking costs and budget analyses; and various other routine and repetitive applications. Graphics, programmable and interactive features are considered essential for routine analytical and other work. Environmental engineers and others are exploiting so called 'Expert' systems in which experienced practising engineers are applying fundamental knowledge, expertise, intuition, inference and above all, judgement to provide solutions to day to day problems.

Modern desk top, relatively cheap, personal computers have ample capacity to meet the demands of most applications particularly when the facility of ready access to a compatible mainframe computer is available. A typical personal computer for most of the above applications, therefore, would comprise an 8 or 16 bit microcomputer with 40k bytes ROM, 64/640k bytes RAM, 160k bytes per surface floppy disc capacity or 10,404k bytes per fixed (Winchester) disc, visual display unit, line printer and link to a mainframe computer. Such personal computers are easily operated, user friendly, cope easily with networks consisting of over 500 roadways of various types, and satisfy the aforementioned and other requirements, such as assessments, solutions and forecasting of auxiliary ventilation, firedamp emission and drainage, and air conditioning problems, forecasting (real time and off line) trends in incidents (of excess firedamp emissions, spontaneous heatings, mine fires at one or more locations, or locations involving interconnected collieries); forecasting changes in the local (and/or pitwide) environment which would accompany system reorganisations, plant stoppages (for example, main, booster, or auxiliary fans or methane extractor plants) and other situations and circumstances. Further practical simplification of certain software programs (for example mine climate and ventilation network) would increase the application of personal computers.

The second area in which microcomputers and microprocessors are used on an increasing scale is within environmental monitors themselves. In these applications for example, they are used to: present data and alarm, scan multi function monitors (e.g. multi gas monitors); discriminate and organise data prior to presentation; compute certain bench mark values and current values of indices (for example, ratios); initiate preventive or protective action (e.g. isolation of power supplies), particularly when one or more multiple inputs (for example, methane, airflow carbon monoxide) can reach significant or unacceptable levels individually or collectively.

Microcomputers are also widely used in dedicated (for example carbon monoxide and fire) or pit wide environmental monitoring systems. Microcomputers can be installed in underground and surface outstations to discriminate the mass of data being inputted from various fixed monitors and relay selected data (and alarms) to the surface according to the software program. Real time microcomputers can be used at the surface to scan the outstations of existing time division multiplexing systems (capacity 500bits/sec) or of systems designed to the BS56556 low speed digital standard, and collect, process and present data and information from a continuous stream of data obtained from fixed monitors. Downstream (secondary) off line computers also enable data and information from the real time system to be treated, stored, recalled and presented according to prescribed software management programs.

Increasingly microcomputers are being applied in automatic control of simple and complex equipment and plants, such as fans (main and booster) and underground and surface firedamp extraction plants. In such applications, increased amount of continuous monitoring, control equipment (approved and certified where necessary), and software is adopted for overall control including early (programmed) identification of system needs, pending or actual faults and changing trends, controlled adjustment, compensation or rectification, and programmed response to continuously changing situations.

MINING DUST HAZARDS.—The dust hazards in mining are of two sorts; dusts which cause respiratory diseases (respirable dust) and those which form explosive or combustible mixtures with air (inflammable dust). In both cases the very fine particles are the most dangerous. Their suppression at source is the best remedy if their generation cannot be prevented.

The Coal Mines (Respirable Dust) Regulations, 1975, impose requirements with respect to respirable dust in all British coal mines at which more than 30 persons are employed underground. The requirements include the obtaining and evaluating of airborne dust samples; the prevention and suppression of dust; the maximum permitted concentrations of respirable dust at working places underground; and medical supervision of men who have been, are, or may be, exposed to dust while at work. Also, dust respirators need to be made available. In this respect, the dust helmet originally developed by the SMRE is now being used with success in some mines. It gives protection to the head, eyes and lungs. Disposable dust respirators have undergone successful trials and are being widely used. The maximum permitted respirable dust index (average respirable dust content from a series of samples) varies according to the working place as follows: (1) Operations on a longwall face, 7·0mg/m^3. (2) Operations in a drivage where the average quartz content exceeds 0·45mg/m^3, 3·0mg/m^3. (3) Any other operations, 5·0mg/m^3.

Considerable work has been done by the Safety in Mines Research Establishment in conjunction with British Coal in connection with dust sampling and measuring instruments. In particular, OSIRIS (Optical Scattering Instantaneous Respirable dust Indication System) has been developed to provide a direct reading respirable dust measuring system for coal mining and other industries. Underground trials are continuing.

British Coal has also produced an instrument which gives on-site read-outs of gravimetric dust concentrations on a shift basis. The instrument known as a Gravimetric Dust Monitor uses beta-ray absorption techniques. These apparatus are becoming more useful and they give readings with a high degree of accuracy.

The long term research work carried out to combat mine dusts and the implementation of new and improved methods over a period of 30 years has resulted in a very considerable reduction in the numbers of men contracting dust disease.

Dust prevention measures include the use of sharp cutting tools, efficient loading out arrangements, and the avoidance, as far as practicable, of cutting roof or floor rock. It is a fact that cutting in roof or floor stone, can produce up to 20 times more dust than cutting in coal. Even so, dust is formed during every operation of cutting, blasting, breaking or loading of coal and its transport out of the mine. Consequently, wetting the coal and dirt, before, during and after each of these operations is good practice. Wet cutting and drilling are universal. The most common method in British Coal mines is the internal feed system with the water released close to the cutting tool. This system makes efficient use of water and gives up to about 30% improvement in dust conditions compared with external sprays. Water powered venturi extractors are now being used on coal cutting machines. They are attached to cowls or dozer doors and act in reverse of hollow shaft ventilation in that the air–dust mixture is drawn from the cutting zone, whilst with hollow shaft ventilation air is directed into the cutting zone. These machine mounted scrubbers on shearers or trepanners can give an additional 20% reduction in dust in the air. Manufacturers now design the most sophisticated methods of dust suppression into their machines and equipment.

Dust which is not suppressed at source and becomes airborne is dealt with in two ways: (*a*) Dilution by the ventilation. (*b*) Extraction from the ventilation. Dilution by the ventilation of a dust concentration takes place on almost a *pro rata* basis, but only so long as the air velocity in itself is not high enough to raise appreciable amounts of dust. This 'threshold' velocity at which there is a significant pick up of dust varies considerably from about 180 m/min to above 240 m/min according to the conditions, such as type of dust, fineness and moisture content. Dust is extracted in a variety of ways. In mechanised headings or drivages the dust is normally extracted by an exhausting type of auxiliary ventilation system incorporating a dust filter, and this method is extensively practised in British Coal mines. Other methods of extraction include the use of free standing filters, and water-powered venturi type dust scrubbers. Improved methods are constantly being developed.

British Coal has recently developed a dust extractor drum for use on shearer loaders. The drum incorporates mine water powered venturi dust scrubber tubes. Early tests are encouraging.

COAL DUST.—Most coal dust explosions have originated at or near the coal face after initiation by a firedamp explosion, however, there have been exceptions. One example is the explosion at Markham colliery in 1938 where the source of ignition was attributed to an electric arc. Also, in other countries, coal dust explosions have occurred due to diverse causes. In France at Courrières (1948) and Béthune (1949) explosions in the compressed air line ignited coal dust in and near the downcast shaft and these two incidents serve as a reminder that the coal dust explosion hazard is not confined to the vicinity of the coal face.

The minimum amount of coal dust which is capable of propagating an explosion is very small, of the order of 35g/m^3. This represents no more than a very thin layer over the periphery of a roadway and, in fact, in certain circumstances a layer as thin as 0·1mm may be enough to propagate an explosion. The explosibility of coal dust depends on a number of factors, principally its volatile matter content, fineness, disposition and dispersibility, and the strength of the initiating explosion. Coals with a volatile content of not more than 10% (anthracites), are generally considered to be non-explosive, whereas the explosibility of bituminous coals increases linearly with volatile content, up to a point where any increase in volatiles ceases to have a significant effect on the explosibility of the dust. In the UK, this point is taken as 35% volatiles. With regard to dust size, it is generally assumed, for practical purposes, that explosive coal dust is finer than 250 micrometre (0·25mm). Also, the presence of firedamp increases the explosibility of a coal dust mixture. For example, with 1% firedamp, the combustible content of the dust needs to be reduced by about one fifth to give the same explosibility factor for the hybrid firedamp mixture, ie the inert content of the dust needs to be raised.

The basic requirements to effectively combat coal dust explosions are: (1) To prevent an ignition of firedamp which may lead to an explosion. (2) To neutralise coal dust so that it cannot explode. (3) In the ultimate, suppress an explosion should one occur.

In British mines, general stone dusting is the method universally adopted for the neutralisation of coal dust. It involves spreading sufficient inert dust to mix thoroughly with the coal dust, so that the mixture is non-flammable, and the amount required depends primarily on the volatile content of the coal. For example, for a coal dust having a volatile content in excess of 35% it is a statutory requirement, in British mines, for the dust mixture to contain not less than 75% incombustible matter. The type of dust used is limestone and this must comply with specified requirements with respect to composition (not more than 3% free silica), fineness and dispersibility. The total amount of limestone dust currently used in British Coal mines is equivalent to about 1¼kg of dust per tonne of coal mined.

Dust binding by means of highly hygroscopic salts, is an alternative way of neutralising coal dust and this method is now widely practised in West German coal mines. The principle of dust binding is for the dust which settles on the roof, floor and sides of a roadway, to be moistened by hygroscopic salts so that it is retained and rendered indispersible. This action is continuous so long as sufficient hygroscopic salt solution remains on the surface to moisten the dust, and when this is not so, then retreatment is necessary. The hygroscopic salts used are either calcium or magnesium chloride, together with a wetting agent, and they are applied to the whole periphery of the roadway in the form of either powder, paste or flakes; powder or paste are normally used on the roof and sides whereas flakes are invariably used on the floor. In addition to powder or flake calcium chloride a solution of calcium chloride is now available which avoids degradation storage of flakes. One of the main disadvantages of hygroscopic salts is corrosion, and this applies particularly to electrical equipment.

It has to be recognised however, that there is no one method of neutralisation which will give complete protection against the risk of a coal dust explosion. As an example, sufficient coal dust to propagate an explosion could be present on a conveyor belt and structure even if the remaining parts of the roadway were properly treated. Also, in the case of general stone dusting, there is the chance, in extreme circumstances, of a thin layer of coal dust forming on the surface, sufficient in itself to propagate an explosion. As extra protection in such circumstances, it is now a statutory requirement, in most coal mining countries, to install explosion barriers at specified places. These barriers comprise a series of shelves, installed near to the roof of the roadway, loaded with either limestone dust or water in containers and designed to collapse and thereby be operated by the blast of an explosion. In British Coal mines, the stone dust barrier is, at present, the type generally in use, whereas in other West European countries, the water barrier is more popular.

MINING FIRE HAZARDS.—Fires are amongst the greatest potential hazards in mining, particularly underground where most of them occur and where special features make it more difficult to deal with them. The means of dealing with underground fires are very similar to those used for surface fires. The features include:—

(1) The roadways act as airways and act as flues which increase the intensity of any outbreak, particularly where the ventilation quantities are high.

(2) The resulting fumes may move through the workings downwind of the fire and endanger men remote from the outbreak.

(3) Gas and coal dust are usually present and may result in explosions causing loss of life and serious damage.

(4) In some mines, there is a risk of spontaneous combustion which can be followed by open fires.

(5) Access to underground fires can be very difficult and dangerous and may involve long distances from the shafts to the seat of the fire.

If fires are not discovered and dealt with quickly they may get out of hand with danger to workmen, loss of equipment and even the loss of part of a mine by having to seal it off or flood it with water.

Fires underground may broadly be classified into (1) open fires and (2) spontaneous combustion fires.

An open type of fire can vary from one which is small and localised, to a severe fire in which the main combustion zone can, according to the circumstances, either spread along an underground road, or alternatively remain localised in one place. With spontaneous combustion the fire zone (ie heating) normally moves back towards its intake supply, whereas the fumes travel in the opposite direction towards the return. A very important point is that spontaneous combustion, if not controlled, can ultimately break out into an open fire and this represents a serious situation. A severe underground fire can present a complex and hazardous condition and, in such circumstances, it is essential to be able to assess the overall position quickly and decide on appropriate action. The factors to be considered are the location, type and intensity of the fire; the materials involved or likely to become involved; and the distribution and particularly the stability of the ventilation.

The statutory requirements for British Coal mines are laid down in the Coal and Other Mines (Fire and Rescue) Order, 1956.

Effects of Underground Fires.—Smoke, toxic gases, damage and ventilation disruption may result. The smoke produced may vary in density and amount according to the type of materials burning and is only dissipated by travelling along the airways and eventually to the surface of the mine. Toxic gases produced depend on the intensity of the fire and the materials involved, the principal gas being the deadly carbon-monoxide. All men underground carry self-rescuers which will protect them against carbon-monoxide but not against shortage of oxygen. A large open fire may have a profound effect on the ventilation. Excessive damage, such as roof falls which may be extensive, can seriously impair fire-fighting and even prevent it altogether. The constriction effect may reduce the flow of ventilation whilst the buoyancy effect in an inclined roadway caused by the heat from the fire raising the temperature and lowering the density of the atmosphere on the downwind side may further destabilize the ventilation.

PRECAUTIONS AGAINST FIRE.—*Prevention* must be the first objective, but it has to be recognised that it will never be possible to eliminate completely the risk of underground fire, and the requirements therefore, are twofold: (1) To reduce to an absolute minimum the risk of initiation of fire. (2) To *prevent* a small fire from developing into a severe one.

Mechanical and electrical equipment for use in mining should be so designed, built and installed to reduce the risk of fire and, after installation, it cannot be over-emphasised that it is essential for the equipment to be regularly inspected and properly maintained. This applies particularly to such equipment as belt conveyor systems, hydraulic circuits, compressors, and diesels all of which have an above-average fire risk. Also, protective devices should be used wherever possible; for example, sensitive earth leakage and overload protection for electrical equipment and temperature protection (eg fusible plugs, links and thermostatic switches) for such equipment as fluid couplings, air compressors and electric motors used in coal mining machines.

The use of combustible materials underground should be minimised but where they are used they should, wherever practicable, be fire resistant (ie self extinguishing) and if not fire resistant should be very strictly controlled. Fire resistant materials available include conveyor belt, flexible ventilation ducting, brattice cloth, electric cable covering, timber, hoses, and vee belts. In British Coal mines, the policy regarding hydraulic fluids has been to replace mineral oil with fire resistant fluid in hydrostatic and hydrodynamic applications.

Mechanical friction on belt-conveyor systems is one of the main causes of fire in coal mines. Fires initiated by conveyor rollers have generally been caused by bearing failure giving rise to frictional heat, which eventually ignites coal dust in close proximity. A very fine, volatile coal dust can ignite at a temperature as low as 150°C, the risk being inversely proportional to the size of the dust. In the UK, considerable progress has been made towards reducing the fire risk associated with conveyor systems.

With regard to spontaneous combustion, the mining layout should be designed to minimise risk. Simple layouts, capable of being quickly isolated and stopped off, should be used and, in this connection, it is prudent to prepare sites beforehand, for stopping off a district. The key to the solution of the problem of spontaneous combustion lies in the control of air leakage and this requires attention to be given to the distribution of the ventilation pressures and the sealing of potential leakage paths.

FIRE FIGHTING.—Fires invariably start from small beginnings and if fought promptly and efficiently can often be extinguished with little damage or danger. It is therefore, important that suitable equipment is provided, and properly sited and maintained, with trained men available to use it.

Every mine has its own specific fire-fighting arrangements made in accordance with current regulations and instructions and under the "Coal and Other Mines (Fire & Rescue Regulations, 1956)", it is the duty of every Mine Manager to secure the provision of suitable and sufficient means of extinguishing fire.

Water must be provided underground at sufficient pressure and in adequate quantities to all places where men work (with very few exceptions). In addition, where machinery for cutting or getting mineral is in use effective means of preventing ignitions must be provided or suitable extinguishing facilities carried on the machine or at suitable intervals in proximity to the machines.

Properly constructed fire stations are provided near to the downcast shafts or outlets. These are equipped with fire hoses, couplings, branch pipes, nozzles, dividing & collecting trenchings, portable fire extinguishers and supplies of sand and stonedust.

Fire ranges with water under pressure are installed throughout the mines with fire points and hydrants at vulnerable places, such as conveyor loading and transfer points. Suitable portable extinguishers are kept at all places where electric motors, transformers and switchgear are in use. Certain tests are carried out at intervals of not more than 30 days following examination of all equipment.

Automatic water spray systems (water curtains) are now extensively used in British Coal mines, as also is protein foam equipment. The main application for protein foam is for fighting fires involving flammable fluids, and it is therefore the practice for it to be kept on the intake side of places where there is a risk of an oil type fire, eg air-compressor stations.

The use of inert gas (nitrogen) for combating underground fires can be very effective in certain types of underground fire situation, and when used, the nitrogen is supplied to the mine as a liquid and then converted into gas by an evaporator. This method has been successful in several instances.

MINING RESCUE AND EQUIPMENT.—Rescue depends chiefly on discipline and strict adherence to a prearranged method of evacuation. The first requirement is to evacuate any affected district without risk to personnel. In the event of fire and as a last resort there should be a way of isolating the ventilation from the fire. If men are cut off, then rescue apparatus and methods must be used.

When a mining accident is caused by explosion or fire, or inrush of gas or water, rescue work has often to be done in a poisonous atmosphere or one deficient in oxygen. Regulations require that suitable rescue equipment be maintained at every mine producing coal and employing more than 100 men below ground. These regulations are contained in the Coal and Other Mines (Fire and Rescue) Order, 1956. To comply with the regulations 15 Central Rescue Stations are maintained by British Coal, where breathing apparatus and additional rescue equipment are serviced and maintained. The rescue stations are of two types: (1) With a permanent brigade, usually with a resident rescue corps of from 14 to 16 men, to provide teams that co-operate with the men from the mine. (2) With rescue officers and instructors only, who co-operate with the teams from the mine.

A rescue team has at least 5 men. Each station is equipped with breathing apparatus of an officially approved type which enables rescue workers to remain for up to two hours in an irrespirable atmosphere. Such apparatus may be worn only by trained, qualified rescue workers who have had instruction and exercise in its use—a qualified rescue worker being one who has been medically examined, passed fit to a high standard, completed a lengthy training course and had at least 6 practices in the previous 12 months.

Central Rescue Stations are geographically situated so as to be up to 32 km of the mines which they serve and under the control of qualified superintendents and officers.

The minimum amount of apparatus and equipment to be kept at each Central Rescue Station includes the following: (*a*) Twenty complete suits of breathing apparatus with means of supply to enable them to be used for at least 48h. (*b*) Four smoke helmets, or other apparatus serving the same purpose, with not less than 37m of tubing for each. (*c*) Four reviving apparatuses not of a forced breathing type. (*d*) Two portable signalling devices. Among other items to be kept are: electric and flame safety lamps; a motor vehicle; means for training persons to test for flammable gas with a flame safety lamp; cages of small birds; and first aid boxes.

At coal mines, rescue rooms are provided containing tube breathing apparatus and reviving apparatus to enable emergency work to commence pending the arrival of resources from a Central Rescue Station. Plans of the workings (Rescue Plans) have to be kept and up-dated at three-monthly intervals so that rescue teams can find their way underground to the site of an emergency. Trained teams of rescue workers attached to the mine and teams from other mines operate from these rooms in an emergency.

The regulations also lay down in detail certain conditions relative to the conduct of rescue work underground.

BREATHING APPARATUS.—Breathing apparatus and respirators for rescue work into three main classes:

(1) Self-contained.—The wearer is made independent of the surrounding atmosphere and of any other persons for air supply. He carries with him a supply of oxygen in the form of compressed oxygen, compressed air, liquid oxygen, liquid air or a chemical that yields oxygen.

(2) Smoke Helmets and Masks.—Air is supplied to the wearer through a tube with the inlet end in fresh air. Air is drawn through the tube of one type by the effort of the wearer's own lungs. In other types the air is forced through the tube by a pump, fan, bellows etc. Compressed air line equipment is also used.

(3) Filter Type Respirators or Gas Masks.—As in military gas masks, air is inhaled from the surrounding atmosphere through canisters of chemical absorbents which remove or neutralise certain specific gases. They are of no avail if the oxygen content of the atmosphere is too low.

Filter type respirators of Class (3), ie self-rescuers, are carried by all men in mines. One such appliance of Class (2) must be kept at each mine where more than 100 men work underground. Self-contained breathing apparatus of Class (1) uses one of two systems, ie closed, or open circuit. In the closed or regenerative system, the breath exhaled is purified and recirculated. The CO_2 is absorbed by specially prepared soda lime, and its oxygen content is replenished fit for inhaling. The oxygen supply may be carried in steel cylinders at high pressure or in the form of liquid; the liquid occupies one eight-hundreth part of its gaseous equivalent at normal temperature and pressure. In the open-circuit system, the air supplied from a cylinder is exhaled by the wearer to the atmosphere.

The weight of an apparatus of Class (1) ranges from about 2 to 37 kg. Of the several types of apparatus officially approved for use in mines, either the 'Proto Mk IV', compressed oxygen, or the 'Aerorlox' liquid oxygen, are used at all rescue stations in the UK. One of the most important developments for many years is a new self-contained compressed oxygen breathing apparatus. This has been designed and developed by the manufacturers in conjunction with British Coal. The main objective was to design a two-hours duration positive pressure breathing apparatus suitable for use in a wide variety of conditions which may be encountered in mines rescue and thereby capable of replacing both the 'Proto' and 'Aerorlox' apparatus. Development has been over a number of years and the apparatus has been thoroughly tested for compliance with British and Euro-standards. It is relatively simple in design and easy to maintain and test and is suitable for immediate use. It has the further advantages of being self-purging, suitable for intermittent use and for use under water.

The apparatus is normally for two-hours duration, but will also be available as a one hour apparatus for special purposes. Initially, it will be fitted with a mouthpiece, but the development of a face mask with speech facility is proceeding, British Coal has ordered 50 apparatus for extended tests at two rescue stations and the intention eventually is to replace all existing apparatus over a period of some years. The apparatus is code named 'SEFA' (selected elevated flow apparatus). Results have exceeded expectations and the apparatus is very popular with users.

Self Rescue Apparatus.—This can be divided into two types: (*a*) Self-contained type, ie Class (1), and (*b*) Filter type respirators, ie Class (3). Self-contained escape apparatus has been developed and is now used in this and other countries. Such an apparatus can enable a trapped man to effect his own escape, or to be carried through unbreathable air.

By comparison, the filter type respirator, (ie self-rescuer), has been developed to afford protection against carbon monoxide (CO), and can only be used safely in atmospheres where there is sufficient oxygen. With this apparatus the air breathed passes through a filter containing the chemical 'Hopcalite', which converts CO to CO_2. This type of self-rescuer is now used in most mining countries and, in Britain, it is mandatory that every man going underground should carry one with him at all times. A new type 275 has an increased life of up to 1½ hours.

FIRE DETECTION.—Detection of underground fires is concerned with two types of incident (1) slowly developing heatings resulting from spontaneous combustion and (2) fires developing more quickly very often caused by machinery. Much work has been carried out in respect of methods of detection and considerable success has resulted. In British Coal mines, and particularly those liable to spontaneous combustion, the most widely used portable CO detector has been the stain tube type, in which a fixed volume of air sample is drawn through a glass tube containing chemicals. The CO in the air reacts with the chemicals to form a coloured stain, the length of which indicates the concentration of CO. Other types of portable instrument include the ecolyser which is based on an electro-chemical cell with the CO concentration indicated on a meter. In fact, smaller instruments of this type for the detection of both carbon monoxide and oxygen have been developed and are now being used underground.

Hand held carbon monoxide meters have been developed (EMCOR and SCOI) and are being used instead of stain tubes in some cases. Another development (FIDES) is being tested for locating incipient fires. This is a total products of combustion detector. A thermal noise monitor (FIRANT) is also used as a general fire detector but it needs to be sited close to the source.

A fixed point, mains-powered instrument for measuring the CO reading is the Unor. It works on the infra-red radiation principle and can give a continuous recording of the concentration. There are at present many of these instruments in use in British Coal mines. The other type of CO monitoring equipment, widely used in British Coal mines, is the tube bundle system; with this system tubes extend from the sampling points underground and/or in the upcast shaft to an infra-red analyser located on the surface. Samples are analysed and recorded from each measuring point in accordance with a predetermined sequence and currently most British Coal mines are equipped with this type of installation.

Development work to improve existing methods of detection is constantly being carried out covering a wide variety of methods. These include heat detectors, ionisation smoke detectors, electro-mechanical cells for carbon monoxide and semi-conductor sensors for the detection of products of combustion.

In the past, small birds (canaries) were used for detecting the CO concentration due to the fact that such birds are usually affected by the gas much quicker than man. However, this does not apply in all types of underground environmental circumstances, and although canaries are still kept at rescue stations and at mines in the UK, they are not now considered to be sufficiently reliable, and therefore rarely used although they still have to be provided by law.

ELECTRICAL SIGNALLING IN COAL MINES.—UK legislation requires all electrical apparatus which is to be connected, in a coal mine, into any circuit used for signalling, whether by telephone or otherwise, to be of a type approved by the Health and Safety Executive (HSE). Approval is granted normally only to signalling apparatus which has been certified, following testing by the Mining Certification Service, H.S.E.(M) at their Explosion and Flame Laboratories, Buxton, as being intrinsically safe for use in mines. Additionally, apparatus which has been certified intrinsically safe to harmonised European Standards by other European test houses nominated in accordance with article 14 of the Mining Directive 82/130/EEC may also receive approval.

The latest standards relating to intrinsically safe apparatus are harmonised European Standards: BS5501Pt 1 (General Requirements) and Pt 7 (Standard of Protection '1'). Whilst electrical signalling apparatus for use in coal mines is still certified intrinsically safe in accordance with the earlier standard BS1259, it is designed generally to BS5501.

FIG. 26.—Leaky Feeder Installed in Mine Roadway. An in-line repeater is shown at the top right.

Over the last two decades there has been a radical change in the design of signalling equipment used in coal mines. Signalling systems almost invariably form part of a combined signalling and lockout circuit, the latter providing a means of automatically stopping a haulage or conveyor motor from any point along the roadway in which the equipment is installed. Lockout circuits are generally loop circuits with a current flowing in series through all lock-out stop contacts, and are designed to fail safe against a short circuit of the loop. On alternating current systems this is achieved by the use of a diode at the end of the loop circuit and a DC sensitive relay at the control point. On direct current systems, it is common practice to use a transistor oscillator as a termination unit, and at the control point an alternating current detector incorporating a transistor amplifier driving a diode pump. On coal-face signalling systems, an additional feature is generally incorporated to provide a number indication at the control point of the particular lockout stop button which has been operated and an indication of the lockout circuit, whether 'healthy', or 'lockout', or 'fault'.

The majority of signalling systems provide a means of speech communication. On the simplest systems, a pair of conductors is provided and each lockout station or signalling key incorporates a jack socket to allow a portable sound-powered hand set to be plugged in. Such systems generally have an amplifier and loudspeaker at the control point. The vast majority of signalling systems, however, provide complete loudspeaker communications over the full length of the system. Due to the very limited current available in an intrinsically safe circuit, it is standard practice for each loudspeaker amplifier to contain its own rechargeable battery, which is trickle-charged from a common current supply. The total power output of the loudspeaker system can be several times greater than the maximum power available from the intrinsically safe supply. This is possible because the batteries are recharged over a full 24h period, whilst the speech system is seldom used for more than 4h during the 24h day.

The fact that most signalling systems incorporate loudspeaker amplifiers has led to the use of transistor oscillators which produce tones on the loudspeakers instead of the bells used earlier. Further use is made of the loudspeaking system to broadcast a prestart warning automatically before machinery is started. It is fairly standard practice to generate two tones of different frequency, broadcast alternately at a repetition rate of one to five times per second. Operational safety of this system is obtained by siting the prestart warning at the remote end of the signalling system and incorporating a monitoring circuit at the control unit to detect the essential characteristics of the prestart warning for a period of about 5s before allowing a start sequence to continue.

The coal mining industry is now using more fast rope hauled manriding trains, and this has led to the development of very-high-frequency radio signalling from the manriding car to the haulage house. Current design of equipment provides for a continuous signal to be transmitted from the moving car, which must be received at the haulage to permit the haulage to continue to run. This allows a manriding train to have an emergency stop facility on every car in the train. Coded signals for stopping and starting the haulage can be transmitted over the same radio link, and a second radio link provides speech between the haulage driver and the train guard.

Modern systems of signalling in vertical shafts now employ data transmission techniques. The enhanced signalling and interlock features required for winding men through unwalkable mine outlets together with the need for high reliability and the requirement for intrinsic safety are difficult to meet with conventional circuits.

RADIO COMMUNICATION IN MINES.—Radio waves at practical mobile communication frequencies will not propagate naturally in mines or tunnels to any generally useful extent. Over the years a variety of techniques have been proposed to overcome the problem, but the present-day universal solution is to use what has come to be known as the 'leaky feeder' technique or one of its variants in order to propagate very-high-frequency (VHF) signals artificially wherever they are required. The techniques involve installing throughout the mine or tunnel a special cable—the 'leaky feeder'—which in its simplest form is a coaxial radio-frequency cable that has been deliberately provided with a controlled degree of leakage as a distributor of signal energy. In its usual and most generally useful form, this comprises a coaxial cable in which the normal wire-braided outer conductor or screen has been opened out in a loose weave to give a cover of only 67% or so instead of the 93–95% that is usual for normal use. While not impairing significantly the still-important capability of the feeder to transmit signals internally over long distances, it does introduce a carefully determined amount of 'leakage' to provide coupling to and from any mobile radio sets in the vicinity.

Such a line may be used in a purely passive mode to assist direct communication between two or more personal radio sets: the mere presence of the line in the tunnel or mine roadway, completely unconnected, can typically extend an unassisted natural range of 200 metres to 500 metres or more. Generally, however, the line is connected electrically to a conventional radio base station (in lieu of a normal aerial), and reliable ranges of up to 2 km are then typical. Conversation between mobile sets is then provided by 'talk-through' operation, in which the base station automatically re-transmits all signals it receives but on its own transmission frequency.

To extend the range further, early leaky-feeder systems simply deployed additional base stations, under a common control with the first and linked by telephone lines. Nowadays, this practice is considered obsolete: a more consistent and reliable performance is obtained, and more economically, by the inclusion of small amplifiers or 'repeaters' in the line to compensate for the losses as they arise. Such repeaters are spaced typically at intervals of 300–500 metres, and are powered over the line itself.

Several available techniques allow such repeaters to be simple one-way devices, even though communication must usually be two-way and often simultaneously so (as, for example, in talk-through operation). An early NCB system, as installed in many UK coal mines, used a 'split' base station with the separated transmitter and receiver linked by a parallel telephone line to complete the path for audio-frequency and dc-control signals. Later developments avoid the separate telephone line by using the feeder itself to double as the link, normally at a lower radio frequency where the line losses are low with little or no need for intermediate in-line amplification in this direction; in such systems every remote extremity is simply terminated in a small line-powered frequency converter.

There have also been developments following the more straightforward approach of a true two-way repeater. However, such devices are inevitably complex and comparatively expensive and are best avoided. The simpler one-way devices now recommended are usually specially designed and manufactured for the purpose and even the largest systems can be made intrinsically safe if necessary; but if intrinsic safety is not a requirement it can be a useful expedient to employ amplifiers designed originally for community television distribution systems.

Leaky-feeder systems are best suited to the VHF waveband, say between 30 and 200 MHz. Standard types of personal or mobile radio set are suitable, subject to their meeting any requirement there may be for intrinsic safety.

Radio communication may be extended on to the working faces of a mine by the same principles. In these situations, however, it is sometimes preferable to use a different type of feeder, and a very cheap and expendable 'ribbon feeder' is particularly useful and effective provided conditions are dry. Short-distance radio control of cutting machinery is possible without recourse to leaky feeders, and frequencies in the region of 150 MHz have been used successively for this purpose in Europe. Another area where leaky-feeder assistance is not required is in vertical shafts, where standard UK practice now is to use frequencies in the region of 170 MHz for direct set-to-set communication over depths of 1000 m; in such situations any necessary guidance is provided by winding and balance ropes, and by metal cage guides.

Development of radio communication in overseas mining has followed diverse approaches to suit differing conditions and mining methods. In Belgium, a preferred alternative to continuous leaky-feeder assistance is the 'INIEX-Delogne' principle, in which a standard non-leaky coaxial cable is interrupted at intervals with a simple radiating device; the claimed advantage is a lower optimum frequency (between 1 and 10 MHz), giving an improved range without use of repeaters; a technique using alternate leaky and non-leaky sections in a cable is also advocated and gives similar performance with greater practical convenience. In France, the same objective is achieved by use of extremely leaky cables having a braid cover as low as 30%; personal radio equipment has been specially designed for coalmining use, working on frequencies near 7 MHz, and ranges up to 5 km are claimed without recourse to repeaters. German preference has largely remained with the older inductive-loop principle using low frequencies, but an easing of radio regulations has prompted an interest in leaky feeders.

In the United States, the leaky feeder technique is being applied, but at UHF (ultra-high frequencies) rather than VHF, with consequent reduced range capability and higher feeder costs. The reason for this choice is the predominance of room-and-pillar mining, where the use of UHF may be expected to provide more effective lateral penetration from the leaky feeder into workings not themselves directly equipped with feeder; in practice, this advantage rarely compensates for the severe penalties incurred. Apart from this application and a continuing use of low-frequency inductive systems, the main interest in radio has been for possible communication with trapped miners, through the overburden from the surface. It has been shown that low frequencies are the most promising for this purpose—even below 10 kHz, where speech modulation becomes impossible—and suitable equipment has been developed. Similar work has been carried out in South Africa.

In many countries the use of radio even wholly underground is subject to licensing considerations. In the UK, the licensing and regulatory body is the Radio Regulatory Department, Waterloo Bridge House, London SE1. For NCB mines, any necessary clearances should be obtained through the Board's Chief Electrical Engineer.

For all types of underground radio communication a specialist consultancy service is available from Martin, Davis and Partners, 21 Gilmais, Great Bookham, Surrey KT23 4RP; a similar service is available in the USA from R. A. Isberg, Inc., 1215 Henry Street, Berkeley, CA 94709. Complete systems are available from Mine Radio Systems, Sunderland, Ontario L0C 1H0, Canada; from Illawarra Communications, PO Box 1181, Wollongong 2500, NSW, Australia; and from Emcom Communications, PO Box 3985, Durban 4000, South Africa.

Further information can be obtained from the following.—

(1) Delogne, P., *Leaky Feeders and Sub-Surface Radio Communication*, Peter Peregrinus (for IEE). 1982.

(2) Martin, D. J. R., *Leaky Feeder Communication in Tunnels*, Wireless World, Vol. 88, No. 1557, pp 70–75 and No. 1558, pp 33–37, June and July, 1982.

CONSPECTUS OF UK COAL PREPARATION

MINING INFLUENCES.—In the UK there is general support for a policy of maximising the use of indigenous coal resources. However, in setting down a future plan for coal, British Coal realised that, while new good reserves were being found for exploitation, nevertheless in the near/middle term future there would be a large dependence on increased capacity at existing mines. The result will be that many seams will be developed which are not first choices either for mineability or quality, and the difficulties of preparing coal satisfactorily for markets will be increased. More important, the raw feed will become fine. It will also become wetter as a result of the application of water sprays underground to reduce dust concentration levels to less than 6mg/m^3. While developments are in hand to offset some of the problems, it is unlikely that there will be any significant improvement in the quality of deep mined run-of-mine coal within the forseeable future.

Associated with the development of new capacity at existing mines has been a policy of rationalisation, which has resulted in the joining of some neighbouring collieries underground with common delivery of raw coal to the surface via a new drift conveyor. Quite obviously the seams mined at adjacent collieries are generally the same, but for the coal preparation engineer these changes do mean that the input feed rate to the preparation plant is often considerably higher than when the mineral was lifted via the shaft in skips or mine cars. If geological and economic conditions are unfavourable for joining neighbouring collieries underground, raw coal is sometimes transported overland from one pit to another, which again increases the need for preparation plant facilities to be of higher capacity than hitherto for deep mined coal in the UK. In a programme of construction of new plants therefore, some plants will be designed to handle input feed capacities of 1,200–1,500 t/h or even 2000 t/h.

Between 1977 and 1981 seventeen new plants were commissioned and six more between 1981 and 1984. The result is that almost 25% of British Coal's cleaning plant with a total throughput capacity of approximately 12,000–14,000t/h, will have been newly constructed within a 7–8 year period. The construction of completely new plants is expected to continue at the rate of about two per year at least into the late 1980s, but beyond that the situation is uncertain.

PREPARATION PHILOSOPHY.—Apart from ensuring that the quality and consistency of products meet customers' needs, while at the same time achieving maximum proceeds for British Coal, the programme for construction of new plants contains five main aims. These are.

(*a*) Correct choice of plant for raw coal treatment,
(*b*) Maximum utilisation of high cost capital equipment,
(*c*) Simplification of plant,
(*d*) Where possible a reduction in manpower, with control of plants being maintained automatically by computer systems, and
(*e*) Concern for the environment, particularly in respect of the disposal of tailings and effluents.

In general, and particularly for the next ten years or so, no major changes are envisaged in the main processing units to separate run-of-mine coal into clean coal, middlings and reject. Dense medium processors and Baum jigs, and froth flotation for the fines will still be used. Recent plant performance tests, such as are

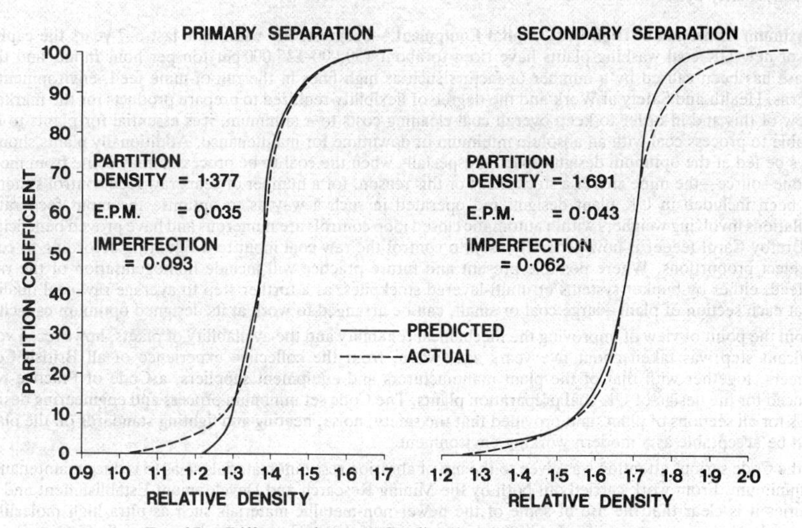

FIG. 27.—Difference between Predicted and Actual Performance.

always carried out to prove operational performance, have indicated a high degree of efficiency of separation for these processors when they are correctly applied within their feed capacity limits. That is not meant to imply that the performance in these main processors is considered totally acceptable, and indeed it is a main objective of British Coal's research and development in coal preparation to improve operations and thereby to improve product consistency. For example, for the dense medium process, and especially for small coal, effort is devoted to the control of the magnetite medium circuit, and to the correct specification of the medium solids, including non-magnetic contaminants, particularly for separations at very low and very high relative densities. Similarly, a microcomputer-based control system has been applied to speed the interrogation and integration of an electronic pressure transducer signal of bed conditions in a Baum jig to control the evacuation of reject. It would appear that this technique has allowed a far quicker anticipation of change of jig bed conditions, and performance results available to date indicate that at least a 1% reduction in the coal misplaced to the reject product has been achieved.

How therefore have the five main aims of the philosophy for coal preparation in the UK been implemented?

Correct Choice of Plant.—It is hoped and expected that the market trend for coal will be towards expansion in the industrial market for graded larger coals, and for more select products of smaller size for customers who have possibly converted from other forms of energy and who require lesser tonnages but of more regular supply. For these purposes it is possible that a far tighter specification for products will be required, with smaller standard deviations in ash and other quality criteria, than for coal used in larger quantities for power generation. It is therefore imperative that the best system or combination of systems is selected for the treatment of the raw coal to produce the necessary quality of products. In order to assist the selection of plant, therefore, and to allow 'searches' to be made of the raw coal washability data, British Coal has developed computer programs to enable predictions to be made quickly and reliably of the practical performance in all the major cleaning processors.

These programs have been prepared from the wealth of data available within British Coal of actual plant performance tests, and it has been proved that the information obtained is truly factual, inclusive of the actual errors of separation on the plant. For example Fig. 27 shows the difference between the predicted and actual performance for a prime coking coal sized 12 mm–0·5 mm treated in British Coal Vorsyl separators in the South Yorkshire Area; and in another example where a special test wash of a South American coal was carried out in a Baum jig plant in the North East of England, the difference between the predicted and actual yield and sulphur content of a clean coal product of predetermined ash, was 0·6% and 0·05% respectively. The computer prediction is not therefore purely an academic exercise.

Naturally, from the results of computer analysis of the raw coal data and information on the operating costs per ton incurred by the various processors, taking into account interest and depreciation charges, comparative assessments can be made of the annual profits from each system or combination of systems. The latter technique is comparatively new, but is beginning to be applied and with significant benefits at an early stage in the design of all the new preparation plants for British Coal. The uniqueness of these overall facilities have been recognised worldwide and quite a number of contracts for coal cleaning performance predictions have been undertaken on a consultancy basis.

Maximum Utilisation of High Cost Capital Equipment.—Progressively within the last 6–7 years the capital costs of new UK coal washing plants have risen to about £30,000–£35,000 per ton per hour input, and this increase has been caused by a number of factors such as high fines in the run-of-mine feed, environmental concerns, Health and Safety at Work and the degree of flexibility required to prepare products for the market. In view of this and in order to keep overall coal cleaning costs to a minimum, it is essential for plants to be available to process coal with an absolute minimum of downtime for maintenance. Additionally plants should always be fed at the optimum design capacity, especially when the coal to be processed may come from more than one source—the mine and/or a stockpile. For this reason, for a number of years raw feed control systems have been included in UK plant designs and operated in such a way as to optimise the input feed rate. Installations involving weighers within automatic closed loop controls are numerous and have proved beneficial. The Bretby Carol feeder is now generally used to control the raw coal input to a Baum jig according to coal and reject proportions. Where possible present and future practice will include homogenisation of the raw coal feed, either by bunker systems or multi-layered stockpiles, as a further step to average raw coal quality so that each section of plant—large coal or small, can be arranged to work at its designed optimum capacity.

From the point of view of improving the mechanical reliability and the availability of plants, however, a very significant step was taken about five years ago, when, from the collective experience of all British Coal engineers, together with that of the plant manufacturers and equipment suppliers, a Code of Practice was produced for the design of UK coal preparation plants. The Code set minimum process and engineering design details for all sections of plant, and provided that the safety, noise, heating and lighting standards on the plant would be acceptable as a modern working environment.

In the Code serious attention was given to the use of abrasion resistant materials so as to reduce maintenance to a minimum. From work carried out both by the Mining Research and Development Establishment and at Collieries it is clear that the use of some of the newer non-metallic materials such as ultra high molecular weight polyethylene can give extended life and can be cost effective. Cast basalt tiles, especially for pipe lining and bunkers, have also proved attractive, for while the initial capital cost may be approximately 3 times that for basic cast iron, if the wear life can be up to 20 years, as has been predicted for certain installations, the extra initial costs can be more than justified. The evaluation of new materials continues, but it is considered that major steps have already been taken to improve the availability of the plant and therefore maximise utilisation.

As another example, the Code has set down parameters for bunker design in order to avoid hang up or 'ratholing', and so that material will discharge under control at the required rate. It is most probable that with the deterioration in raw feed quality, especially increased fine clay content and higher moistures, control of flow from bunkers has in the past perhaps been one of the major causes of unavailability of plant. However,

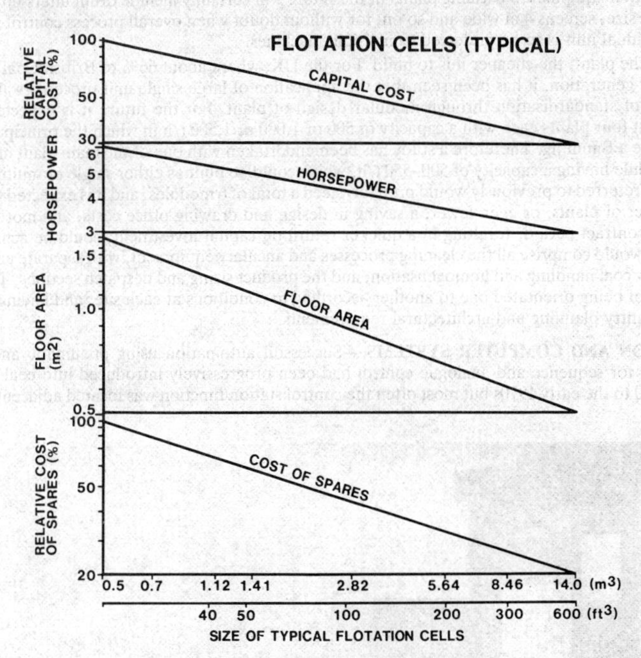

FIG. 28.—Typical Benefits of Larger Unit Processes

from basic analyses of the handlability characteristics of coal types, designs for bunkers can now be produced which will ensure mass flow even for the worst conditions. There have been beneficial repercussive effects from this development. For example, difficulties experienced in the past with the reliable operation of bunker level indicators, have now been overcome with bunkers of mass flow design. Many commercially available bunker level transducers are now perfectly satisfactory for continuous plant operation.

In addition to the Code of Practice, a list of acceptable coal preparation equipment has been produced, which, from exhaustive trials at collieries, identifies those items which have proved to match British Coal standards both in process performance and mechanical and electrical reliability. The list includes all equipment used, process machines, transducers, and ancillary plant, and it constitutes British Coal's 'shopping guide', since only proven proprietary items from that list may be installed on UK plants. The list is regularly reviewed and new equipment is added after a full assessment of a one-off installation over a 6–12 month trial period. Similarly, any item of plant that may subsequently be found unsatisfactory in continuous commercial operation is removed from the list.

Simplification of Plant.—Although in the past views have differed as to whether it is better to use one large-capacity or two or more smaller-capacity units, it is gradually being accepted that process performance efficiency and engineering standards can be maintained with larger machines. In the UK, therefore, while at one time it was thought for example that the maximum washing width for a conventional Baum jig for 125 mm–0 raw coal was 2·6–2·7 m, a number of machines 3·66 m wide have now been installed as at Cwm, Frickley and Oakdale Collieries. Plant tests have proved that performance is completely satisfactory, and typically values of Imperfection for 25–12·5; 12·5–4; 4–2; 2–0·5 mm sizes are 0·117, 0·137, 0·163, and 0·193, respectively, which are equal to those obtained in machines of smaller size. It is expected that quite soon a 5m wide conventional Baum jig will be installed for commercial operation.

Similarly, froth flotation cells three to four times the capacity of earlier units and up to 14–15 m^3 in size have been installed in the UK and operate continuously and entirely satisfactory on an hour by hour, day by day basis. It will be appreciated that not only can plants be simplified by the use of larger, higher-capacity machines, and problems avoided in the division of both solids and liquid flows to multiple streams, but many other advantages can accrue. While the graphs in Fig. 28 relate to typical benefits from the use of larger froth flotation cells they are indicative equally of the kind of savings which can be made in terms of reduction in floor space, capital costs of plant, lower power consumption, and reduced costs of spares for any other item of coal preparation equipment. Washing plants of the future will certainly include drum filters up to 74 m^2 and possibly 110 m^2 size, screens 4 m wide and so on, for without doubt when overall process control is considered one large individual unit is to be preferred to multiple machines.

The simpler the plant, the cheaper it is to build. For the UK, where about 66% of British Coal's production is for electricity generation, it has been seen that the application of large single unit processors also leads to a further degree of standardisation through modular design of plant. For the future it is expected that there might be at least four plants each with a capacity of 500 or 1,000 or 1,500 t/h in which the principal coal/reject separator will be a Baum jig. Therefore a study has been undertaken with one of the main plant manufacturers to design a module having a capacity of 500–550 t/h, which could be built as either single or multiple modules. The four plants referred to previously would probably need a total of 6 modules, and it is expected that certainly over this number of plants, or even fewer, a saving in design and drawing office costs, and more particularly a reduction of contract period, resulting in a quicker return on capital investment, could be achieved.

The modules would comprise all the cleaning processes and ancillary equipment, with separate arrangements provided for raw coal handling and homogensation, and the product sizing and despatch sections. The modules will be capable of being orientated one to another according to conditions at each site, and having due regard to town and country planning and architectural requirements.

AUTOMATION AND COMPUTER SYSTEMS.—Successful automation using pneumatic and electronic instrumentation for sequence and analogue control had been progressively introduced into coal preparation plants from 1960 to the early 1970s but most often the control station/function was located adjacent to the item

FIG. 29.—Microprocessor Centralised Control.

of plant being controlled. However, for some time computer-based systems had been installed in a variety of process industries, including the chemical and oil industries, and it was natural that investigations of the possibilities of similarly controlling all operations in the preparation plant by microprocessor or minicomputer should follow. Based on evidence from the other industries, a number of advantages could be expected such as:

(*a*) More efficient utilisation of manpower
(*b*) Better utilisation of plant
(*c*) Improved performance and quality control
(*d*) Improved information availability
(*e*) System flexibility

but it was decided that whether or not these could be realised in practice for coal preparation could only be confirmed through experience of installation and evaluation of systems at colliery sites.

During the late 1970's, therefore, a number of existing and new coal preparation plants were equipped with process computers to provide the experience of several different approaches. The installations ranged from powerful minicomputer-based systems covering all aspects of monitoring, display control, logging and reporting for a large plant by a single processor, to programmable logic or microprocessor control systems of smaller capacity but equally capable of sequence and analogue control and event logging for management information. The exploitation and application of this technology in coal preparation has proceeded quickly to the point where at the present a total of 19 plants are controlled by computers in some form.

Of particular interest has been the retrofitting of microprocessor systems to older existing plants such as those at Rawdon and Bold Collieries. Equally important is the manner in which the systems have been completely accepted by plant personnel. Application of this technology to coal preparation is not difficult and it is clear that, with a small amount of training, operators conditioned to old hardwired systems can quickly adapt. For example, the easily understood programming facilities at both plants have been used by colliery staff without assistance to modify and improve the systems. Undoubtedly the installations at Rawdon and Bold have been particularly successful, providing new centralised control facilities (Fig. 29) and all the associated transducers within about 14 months from conception to completion of the installation and commissioning.

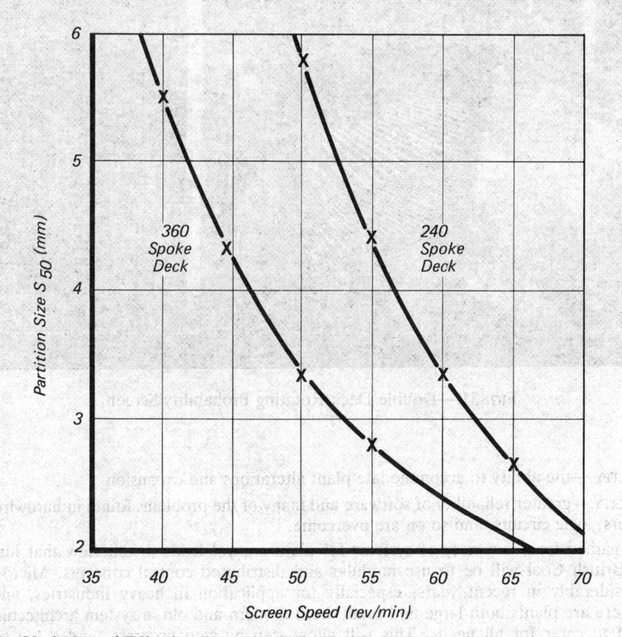

FIG. 30.—Variation of Effective Screening Size with Deck Speed—240 and 360 Spoke Decks.

The application of minicomputers to coal preparation control in the UK is intended to be from firm evidence of the benefits to be obtained and not just as a result of fashion or trend. While assessments of the advantages continue, it is nevertheless true that all systems installed so far, whether of the larger minicomputer for central control of all the operations on a complex plant as at Lea Hall, South Kirkby, Askern and others, or microprocessor or PLC systems as at Rawdon, Bold, Thurcroft, Dinnington and so on, have been accepted as real improvements on previous systems. Immediate advantages are derived through the installation of transducers, which obviously would have been equally effective with either a computer based or conventional control system. There are benefits, however, which can already be directly attributed to the computer systems, and these results from the advantages of the power and flexibility of software for handling logic and process control, and the presentation of information. These benefits are briefly as follows:

(*a*) Simplification of Control.—operation of plants is now less complex with much of the thinking carried out by the computer system. Protection of both equipment and manpower is safer.

(*b*) Improved Displays.—information presented by visual display units (VDUs) is clear and concise. An item failed in alarm is quickly brought to the attention of the operator by message and display with simultaneous action to prevent spillage or damage.

(*c*) Logging.—simple event logs and records of failures have assisted in highlighting priority work to improve general plant availability.

Fig. 31.—Double Deck Rotating Probability Screen.

(*d*) Flexibility.—the ability to accommodate plant alterations and expansion.

(*e*) Reliability.—greater reliability of software and many of the problems found in hardwired systems such as relays, timers, logic circuits, and so on are overcome.

Experience gained from a variety of systems for plant control leads to the view that for the future the approach by British Coal will be to use modular and distributed control concepts. Micro-technology has improved considerably in recent years, especially for application in heavy industries, and since in coal preparation there are plants both large and small, both modern and old, a system architecture for control is to be adopted to cater for all needs. This will allow step by step progress, and a big reduction in the commissioning difficulties which occur with fully integrated systems and which can take a very long time to locate even by specialist computer system and software engineers.

NEW DEVELOPMENTS.—To a large extent current development work in coal preparation is associated with measuring or control devices which will then ultimately be used via a microcomputer in the overall monitoring and control of plants.

Rotating Probability Screen.—The Rotating Probability Screen is now becoming internationally recognised as the only effective means of extracting dry fines at about 6 mm size and below from raw feeds containing sometimes in excess of 8–10% free moisture. The principle of design with a horizontal circular screen deck comprising individual stainless steel rods radiating from a central vertical rotating shaft is unique. Fine particles can be removed continuously from damp feeds without blinding of the deck and change in sizing point can readily be made merely by changing the speed of rotation. Evidence of this is given in Fig. 30 which shows typical performance curves for a production installation of a 2·4 m diameter machine capable of accepting feed rates up to 150 t/h. Such a facility readily lends itself to the full automatic control of the process.

Over the last 3–4 years a total of 19 machines have been installed by British Coal, and with the successful development and testing of a double-deck machine to accept 100 mm–0 raw coal (Fig. 31) it is expected that the exploitation rate will increase. Other countries and industries have already appreciated the commercial value of the Rotating Probability Screen, and units are in operation or have been ordered for the USA, China, Australia, Ireland, South Africa and The British Steel Corporation.

Coal Quality Monitoring.—Fundamental to all coal preparation operations is the requirement to know coal quality, and the development of ash, moisture and sulphur monitors has been a priority in the UK just as in other countries. At the present there are 31 radiometric ash monitors installed particularly to monitor blends or blend proportions, and on some of these installations as in Scotland, microwave moisture measurement has also been added to the same presentation unit. The Phase 3A Monitor is not strictly an on-line transducer, but even though an associated sampling system is necessary, the material size for presentation is 5 mm at the rate of 20 kg per minute. By correct design of the ash monitor circuit a continuous signal can be provided only 3–4 minutes delayed from the time of sampling. Integration of the signal will provide a value of trend in ash content which can then be used effectively in process control. Where coal feeds contain less than 6–8% free moisture, significant commercial advantages have been obtained from ash monitor installations. However, because of difficulties with wet coal, development work is now proceeding to measure ash content of coal up to 50 mm size directly on line.

Trials are being made also with a Phase 3A Ash Monitor presentation unit to measure the pyritic sulphur in coal via iron fluorescence. The effective accuracy of the measurement of total sulphur content is better than ±0·01%, and facilities are available therefore to measure ash, moisture and sulphur with the one machine. From the ash and moisture signals calorific value has been computed as a further stage of development, and at the Longannet and Monktonhall sites in Scottish Region the accuracy has been ±800 kJ/kg on a shift bais.

Flocculant Mixing and Addition.—For more efficient mixing and automatic control of the addition of flocculant to the feed to thickeners in order to obtain maximum use from high cost reagents, two other developments, the Bretby Autex and 'Clarometer' have been introduced in recent years. The Bretby Autex flocculant mixer rapidly 'wets' and disperses individual particles of the reagent before hydration causes balling. The 'Clarometer' automatically controls the rate of addition of this correctly mixed flocculant solution according to a relationship between the actual settling rate of the suspended solids and a predetermined optimum rate. Experiences from a large number of automatic flocculant mixing systems operating throughout the Industry show that there can be a reduction of about one-third in the amount of flocculant used in addition to manpower savings.

Other new developments currently being pursued include a monitor to measure the ash content of flotation tailings on line, and a machine for the intimate mixing of components of coal blends, particularly to disperse higher proportions of filter cake.

FINES CLEANING AND DEWATERING.—Currently run-of-mine coal in the UK contains up to 20% minus 500 μm size, but, more important, one-third of this is minus 10 μm size and has a relatively high ash content of 40–45%. The accurate specification of equipment for fines treatment, whether for flotation, filtration or flocculation is essential, for on the one hand more equipment than necessary must be avoided in view of high capital costs, and on the other if too little is provided the problems and costs of retrofitting are disastrous. In order to gather necessary basic data a pilot rig has been built at MRDE to allow complete and continuous processing of minus 500 μm fines at a rate of 0·5 t/h. The rig enables investigations into how the capacity for unit machine size can be increased while maintaining standards of performance, identification of particular features of any special coal flotation or filtration, and examination of how one of the main fines treatment process may interact with another. Examinations of bench, pilot and commercial installations have identified that results from the pilot plant can be scaled directly to full size commercial machines. Results from the use of this facility can be used for the correct selection and sizing of equipment for new plants, and to identify how optimum use can be made of machines in existing washeries. For most new fines treatment plants built by British Coal, preliminary trials are carried out on the pilot plant, preferably with actual coal samples. If such samples are not available other coal is used of a raw quality as near as possible to that expected.

Obviously the pilot rig offers opportunities for basic research also, and if for example the new conversion processes should require coal with a preponderance of a certain maceral type—such as vitrinite or exinite to improve process reactivity, this too can be studied, including choice of reagent for optimum selectivity.

A main area of concern however is the dewatering of flotation concentrates without thermal drying to give a product of acceptable handlability. Although from a size distribution of the clean coal froth and its solids concentration, accurate specification can be made of the filtration area required for a particular coal treatment duty, nevertheless for bituminous coal the moisture content in the cake so produced often is typically 30%. All new preparation plants include continuous vacuum filter belt drums whereby after cake discharge the cloth is thoroughly washed to provide a clean filtering medium each revolution. This has resulted in a reduction in filter cake moisture content by about 2% to 28%. The application of screenbowl centrifuges operating in the region of 700–800 g may achieve a further reduction of possibly 3–4%, although investigations continue into establishing whether these machines alone can satisfactorily close a wash water circuit without the back up of vacuum filter machines.

NEEDS FOR PELLETISATION.—In the preparation of fines a major concern has always been the improvement of calorific value, but it now seems that quite a different characteristic, that is handlability, has to be considered if complete inmixing of fines produced by mining operations is to be allowed. The reconstitution of fines minus 500 µm into granules of coarser size capable of withstanding shear in storage and handling, possibly flame contact on entering a combustion chanber, and without complete breakdown to dust is essential. Preliminary investigations of extrusion techniques using limited binder addition have shown it to be possible to pelletise jigged slurries and filter cake, and information is being obtained of the limiting parameters for all the different ranks of coal mined in the UK, together with estimates of likely total costs. It is certain now that a technical solution is possible, but because of possible low machine throughput rates and high associated operating charges the pelletisation of coal will be costly. There may not be an alternative, however, if the newer smaller industrial customers who are expected to return to coal from other forms of energy are to be completely satisfied. In the past these customers have controlled energy at the turn of a switch, and it is envisaged that within limits this is how coal will similarly have to be supplied. Rapid loading either of complete train loads or of individual wagons for these customers will become standard practice, just as it has for the electricity supply industry with its far bigger requirements. Investigations are also being made into the containerisation of coal and the provision of a service for the supply and removal of containers from customers on a regular basis, especially in town and city sites where storage facilities for coal are seriously limited. Good handlability and the facility for controlling coal flow from either a large storage bunker or a small service hopper are therefore very important.

DISPOSAL OF TAILINGS AND EFFLUENT.—A trend is developing in the UK, particularly in the large coal producing regions of the Midlands and Yorkshire, for combining coal preparation facilities for a number

FIG. 32.—A Filter-press Tailings Treatment Plant.

of mines in one large central plant capable of treating up to 1,500–2,000 t/h. It is also the policy of British Coal to design fines treatment plants for 20% of the run-of-mine input, and the problems of tailings disposal are therefore quite severe. For large discard greater than ½ mm size, secondary screening to remove as much water as possible is always carried out and typically the free moisture content in the material discharged to the tip is about 2%. Civil Engineers have agreed however that it is preferable in many cases for large discard and tailings to be delivered separately to the tip where better control of layering and/or mixing can be carried out.

Various techniques for tailings treatment have been applied with varying degrees of success. For example, deep cone thickeners using high molecular weight polyelectrolyte reagents at the rate of about 0·5 kg/ton can effectively produce a thickened discharge of about 60% solids wt/wt such that no more treatment is necessary. There are plants operating where 12 cones have been installed to process about 35–40 t/h of dry solids. In South Wales, where topographical difficulties prevent disposal of such a thickened product, further stabilisation is achieved by the addition of about 2% cement. Trials with solid bowl decanter type centrifuges have shown that with the correct choice of flocculant these machines can also produce a dewatered product of about 60% solids wt/wt and a clear effluent. Cement can be used effectively to stabilise this material further and in a particular feasibility study the combined process of thickening and solid bowl centrifuges with cement appears to be a cost effective alternative to pressure filters. The total cost per ton of dry solids using the centrifuges has been estimated to be below the £7·50 for pressure filters and therefore an installation has been completed to confirm costs and consistency of operating performance. Without doubt, however, the pressure plate filter is recognised as the most effective means of disposing of tailings, although costs per ton of dry solids can be between £3 and £6·50 depending on the length of cycle time. The large central washeries have upwards of 100 t/h of tailings to be treated and the pressure filter sections can in themselves be significantly sized plants (Fig. 32). For example at a new plant recently commissioned there are 24–150 chamber 2 m×1·5 m machines. As a new development of pressure filters, however, membrane plates have recently been used. Membrane plates allow pressure to be applied directly to each cake in a press via a rubber diaphragm or membrane and it is unnecessary to fill the whole of the recess with cake as in normal pressure filter operation. The result has been to improve output in some cases by a factor of 25%, and also to reduce moisture by 2–3% from that obtained by conventional pressure filters operating at the same pressure (10 bar). All presses used by British Coal are as near automatic as can be possible, and the introduction of membranes and automatic cloth washing equipment has certainly been of assistance towards the automatic release of cakes. Nevertheless research and development work continues on this particular feature which will have to be resolved completely before pressure filter operations can be fully automatic.

Land available at colliery sites for the tipping of discard and tailings is becoming scarce and examinations are being made of how in future the total plant reject can be disposed of remotely from the mine, and in districts where environmental considerations are less severe.

CONCLUSION.—It is important to ensure that, in whatever form coal is produced from the mine, consistent products can be prepared for power generation, for the smaller industrial users, or for the new conversion processes of the future. It is to be hoped, therefore, that this review of coal preparation has highlighted the current philosophy of plant design and construction, also the issues of major concern where research, development and investigational work is being undertaken in order to achieve this objective.

A sudden change at all coal preparation plants to complete control by a mini-computer, or micro-processor, is unlikely to occur, but the pattern of change in coal preparation projects is in this direction. With raw coal stockpiling and homogenisation, rapid single track loading of one product from each plant, the use of television cameras and other aids, it is perhaps not unrealistic to visualise that the plants of future will be managed by one attendant printing his instructions to the plant, in a central processing control room, with 2 or 3 other staff periodically on patrol. Such developments will make it easier to comply with the legislation that is imminent both in this country and abroad, to control environmental pollution, such as noise at places of work.

THE PREPARATION OF MINERAL ORES

The preparation of ores, also known as mineral dressing or beneficiation, is the series of processes by which they are rendered suitable for the extractive metallurgist to obtain the valuable metals therefrom. According to present thinking the domain of the ore dresser, mineral engineer or mineral technologist, extends from comminution (a general term for size reduction embracing breaking, crushing, and grinding) through screening and classification; gravity concentration methods; to magnetic and electrical separation methods, flotation and liquid/solid separation.

Certain processes which in the past were relatively important—for example hand picking or sorting are now used to a much lesser extent due to higher labour costs and the fact that many modern ore dressing mills have very high throughputs, particularly as lower grade ores are now being processed. Hand picking was used for selecting valuable lumps of ore, obvious by their appearance, from conveyor belts; sometimes for discarding lumps of waste, also obvious by appearance; or for removal of tramp metal which could damage crushing installations. Hand picking, although one of the most ancient mineral processing techniques, has still its place in ore beneficiation particularly in the less developed countries. (See Hand Sorting and Modern Milling Practice, *Mining Magazine*, Dec. 1984, p 602.) Today, the removal of tramp metal is usually done by a powerful electro-magnet suspended above the ore-carrying conveyor belt. Mechanical ore-sorters, based on detecting differences in optical or other characteristics of ore and waste, now exist. A new type of ore sorting system which makes use of a remote form of detector to measure variations in electrical conductivity and/or magnetic characteristics as individual rocks pass through the sorter was described in *Mining Journal*, Dec. 11, 1981, p 446.

A further advance is a microprocessor-based optical ore sorting system made by RTZ Ore Sorters of South Africa. One of these units has been installed underground at a limestone mine in Finland. The feed, consisting of mixed run-of-mine material passes through the sorter; each piece of ore or waste is separately evaluated using a special optical scanning system and compared with a reference standard. High speed air valves route the rock to the correct destination. Another innovation in the sorting field is the 'Precon' from Outokumpu Oy of Finland which separates waste rock from the ore before it is fed to the concentrator. This device works on the principle of irradiating the feed material and measuring the scattered gamma radiation; this is calculated by microprocessor and sends the mineral to the correct destination by air blast. See 'Mineral processing developments at Hammaslahti, Finland, *Mining Magazine*, February 1985, pp 122–129.

The entire process from feeding in of raw ore at one end to production of concentrates at the other is usually considered in terms of a flowsheet. Selection of crushing and grinding equipment (the first stage of the flowsheet) will depend on such factors as hardness, degree of wetness and grain size at which the valuable mineral is liberated; also the ore throughput rates required. Further planning of the flowsheet depends on how many valuable metals are to be recovered from the ore, and the physical and chemical characteristics of the ore. E. J. Pryor in 'Mineral Processing' (Elsevier Publishing Co. 1965), lists the principal exploitable characteristics of minerals which can be utilised in devising a flowsheet. See Table 8.

COMMINUTION.—The size reduction of the ore in modern mill flowsheets usually incorporates two crushing stages (primary and secondary—in some cases a tertiary crushing stage is used) followed by grinding of the ore. A preliminary size reduction process sometimes occurs when large lumps of ore result from the mining process—for this purpose hydraulic breakers are usual (see 'Impact hammers' *Mining Magazine*,

TABLE 8.—PRINCIPLE EXPLOITABLE CHARACTERISTICS OF MINERAL ORES

Selective Mineral Characteristic	Type of Separating Force	Operation
Colour, lustre	Visual, manual, automated	Hand sorting of graded ore, to remove detritus, waste rock, special constituents. May use fluorescent lighting, or impulses triggered by reflected light
Specific gravity	Differential movement due to mass effects, usually in hydraulic currents	'Gravity' separation of sands and gravels by dense media separation, jig, sluice, shaking table, spiral
Surface reactivity	Differential surface tension in water	Removal of relatively aerophilic minerals as froth from aerated pulp by froth-flotation. Widely used process.
Chemical reactivity	Solvation by appropriate chemicals	Hydrometallurgy. Ore exposed to solvating chemicals with heat and pressure, then filtered. Dissolved element/s recovered from filtrate, chemically, electrolytically or by ion exchange
Ferro-magnetism	Magnetic	Magnetic devices remove the preferred mineral. Also used to remove "tramp" iron
Conductivity	Electrostatic charge	Particles pass through high-voltage zone. Rate of dissipation of induced charge influences subsequent deflection. Differential conductivity
Radio-activity	Alpha or beta rays	Signalled by Geiger-Muller valve which also activates a separating or 'picking' device
Shape	Frictional	Sliding force is opposed by 'cling' of particle, resultant movement depending on cross-section and area, hence on shape
Texture	Crushing Screening Classifying	Characteristic shapes and surfaces are developed during comminution

Dec. 1985, pp 499–509 for a comprehensive review of this equipment and its applications). The main type of primary crusher is the jaw crusher, which consists essentially of one fixed and one moving jaw. In modern underground mines it is becoming increasingly common to have a primary crusher underground, as this offers a number of advantages in transporting the ore out of the mine. At the Baluba copper mine in Zambia, a German-made Wedag 1,500 mm×1,200 mm jaw crusher is installed on the 255 m level of the mine.

In open pit mines also there is a trend towards use of a primary crushing unit actually within the pit—usually a mobile crusher which can be shifted about as work proceeds. The in-pit crusher is usually related to the means of transporting the ore out of the pit—by conveyor, rather than truck haulage. See 'Giant mobile crusher', *Mining Magazine*, July 1985, pp 8–9, and 'Portable Crusher at Sierrita, Arizona shows substantial cost savings in first year', *Mining Magazine*, January 1985, pp 95–96.

TABLE 9.—DETAILS OF A-1 JAW CRUSHERS. (*Allis-Chalmers*)

Approx Feed Size (metres)	Capacity Range metric tonne/h	Product Size Range (mm)	Makers Number	Maximum hp
1.12	450–660	140–250	4,860	250
0.92	380–580	125–250	4,248	150
0.66	250-400	100–200	3,242	100

Gyratory crushers also are used as primary crushers. The gyratory crusher consists of a hollow, cone-shaped fixed surface or anvil, containing a cone-shaped spindle or hammer which gyrates around the vertical axis of the fixed surface. Thus the annular space between the hammer and anvil changes in width as the spindle revolves. Material feeds in as the gap opens, is crushed as it closes and falls through as it opens again. Table 10 gives details of a range of gyratory crushers.

Cone crushers are similar in principle to gyratory crushers. The crushing head may be a short frustrum and gyrates eccentrically. Cone crushers are designed to deal with feed material up to about 38cm, reducing this to 3.75–6.25cm, at a rate of 950–1,300tonne/h. Models at the lower end of the cone crushing range take a feed size of about 2.5cm and reduce it to 3mm to 6mm; throughput rate is about 10–13metric tonne/h for this size of crusher. Other types of crusher used in ore processing include impact crushers. A recent increasing trend is the choice of a gyratory crusher for primary crushing at many mines.

TABLE 10.—DETAILS OF PRIMARY GYRATORY CRUSHERS. (*Allis-Chalmers*)

Approx Feed Size (metres)	Capacity Range (metric tonne/h)	Product Size Range (mm)	Makers Number	Maximum hp
1.37	4,300–6,600	216–304	60–109	1,000
1.37	2,500–3,600	152–228	60–89	600
1.12	1,800–2,550	140–200	54–74	500
1.02	1,700–2,700	127–200	48–74	500
0.92	880–1,650	114–178	42–65	400
0.76	600–850	102–140	36–55	300
0.64	420–900	64–140	30–55	300

GRINDING.—In most modern mills this is carried out using ball, rod or autogenous mills, or combinations of these. In most concentration plants requiring fine grinding of the ore, the largest power consumption invariably occurs in the grinding section. Much attention has therefore been paid to developing different milling methods and machinery to reduce power, capital and associated running costs.

In the past the problem of dealing with large tonnages of ore was dealt with by the installation of a large number of moderately-sized mills. An example of this is the Nchanga copper concentrator, in Zambia, in which grinding was accomplished in eleven 2·75×2·45m ball mills each handling 48metric tonne/h of feed. Now, several approaches are possible; the use of very much larger ball mills, on their own or in combination with rod mills; the use of autogenous and semi-autogenous milling techniques; the use of multi-stage and combination grinding circuits; and the use of specialised milling techniques. (*See* 'Economics of Mineral Engineering', Mining Journal Books, London. 1976).

At the Panguna concentrator of the Bougainville copper mine in Papua New Guinea, 78,000metric tonne/

day of ore can be dealt with in eight primary ball mills of 5·5m diameter ×6·4m long. Each mill is fed with 406metric tonne/h, grinding to 45% minus 200 mesh.

Autogenous grinding is accomplished in large diameter, short length mills fed with run-of-mine ore (ie no preliminary crushing stage). The diameter: length ratio of the mill is between 2 and 3 to 1, recent practice favouring the 2:1 ratio. In pure autogenous milling the ore acts as its own grinding medium; in semi-autogenous milling, a small proportion of steel balls is added. Achieving true autogenous milling is not easy, as several important requirements have to be met; the mill must be large enough to lift the ore to a suitable height so that sufficient energy is developed for crushing; the ore fragments entering the mill must be of sufficient size to accomplish crushing; and most importantly, the ore must be hard enough so that there is always an adequate supply of correctly sized particles in the mill to achieve the correct grind.

Rod and ball mills are essentially a cylindrical drum charged with the crushing medium, either steel balls or rods, the cylinder revolving about its horizontal axis; they are usually run wet in view of the dust problems resulting from dry grinding. Many mills of this type now have wear-resistant rubber linings, which have been shown to give better service than metallic ones. The trend today is towards larger crushing and grinding equipment and towards the most simple and economical single-stage grinding. An example of current practice is a new taconite plant in Minnesota, which uses six 11 m diameter by 4.6 m long autogenous mills, driven by two 6,000hp motors. Current practice in grinding and equipment currently available is given in the survey 'Grinding mills.—Rod, Ball and Autogenous', *Mining Magazine*, Sept. 1982, pp 197–225. A more recent article in *Mining Magazine*, April 1986 covers the complete range of crushing and grinding equipment currently available worldwide and includes roll and hammer mills which are used in some special mineral processing applications.

For a clear overview of the fundamental principles of comminution, the most recent research advances and modern methods involved in the process the reader is referred to a comprehensive new text Crushing and Grinding Process Handbook by C. L. Prasher published by John Wiley & Sons, Chichester, England 1987.

SCREENING AND CLASSIFICATION.—Sizing of the crushed ore as it progresses through the flowsheet is an essential part of the ore preparation process, and this is usually done on wire mesh screens; for very large sizes of ore, 'grizzlies' (a series of steel bars forming a grid) are used; it is also becoming increasingly common for screens to be made of such materials as reinforced rubber or polyurethane, these materials giving considerably longer life with abrasive ores. The Trelleborg Company of Sweden manufactures a very wide range of rubber screen cloths. Shaking or vibrating screens are usual and sometimes revolving screens or trommels.

The Mogensen Sizer.—A multideck inclined screening device being used increasingly exploits the basic engineering concept that the effective aperture of an inclined mesh as far as vertically falling materials is concerned, is the horizontal projection of the actual aperture.

The Rotating Probability Screen.—Developed in Britain by the Mining Research & Development Establishment of the National Coal Board, is described on p K3/75. When used for mineral processing, the raw mineral falls onto the rotating rods, the fines passing through and the coarser particles being thrown off. The sizing point is determined by the speed of rotation. Since there are no supporting members, there is nowhere for fines to build up on the screening surface—a problem with conventional screens leading to 'blinding' ie, blockage of the screen holes.

In sizing on screens, the mineral particles are presented to a rigid system of gauging meshes which cause separation in terms of one or two dimensions of their cross-section. However, in the process of classification, no such physical restraint is at work; instead, the rate of fall of each particle through a fluid medium is exploited under controllable conditions, so as to direct it into either the 'oversize' or 'undersize' class. The factors influencing movement of particles relative to a surrounding fluid are summarised by Pryor (*ibid*).

In modern mill flowsheets, cyclones are used as classifiers, frequently in closed circuit with ball mills in the grinding circuit. The growth in the use of cyclones as classifiers in grinding circuits is due to several facts. First, by its use of centrifugal force, the cyclone can speed up settlement rate and therefore either handle larger tonnages with light equipment in a smaller space, or make a separation at finer meshes than is possible for a mechanical classifier. Capital cost and installation are cheaper. A point of importance where flotation is subsequently used, is that it keeps only a small tonnage in circulation and thus reduces oxidation effects in the grinding circuit.

The liquid-solid hydrocyclone (usually referred to as the cyclone), when used as a classifying device in ore dressing circuits, consists of a cone with a cylinder at the top; when mineral pulp is fed tangentially into the cyclone at the top, a vortex is generated about the longitudinal axis. The accompanying centrifugal acceleration increases the settling rates of the particles, the coarser of which reach the wall of the cone. Here they enter a zone of reduced pressure and flow downward to the apex, through which they are discharged. The percentage of feed leaving as coarse product depends on the apertures of the inlet and vortex finder, provided the underflow does not exceed some 30% of the feed. At the centre of the cyclone is a zone of low pressure and low centrifugal force which surrounds an air-filled vortex. Part of the pulp, carrying the finer particles, moves inward toward this vortex and reaches the gathering zone surrounding the air pocket. Here it is picked up by the tube called the vortex finder and removed through a central overflow orifice. The vortex finder is adjusted so as to project into the cylindrical section of the cyclone, and short-circuiting of newly-arrived pulp is thus minimised. The main factors controlling cyclone operation are feed inlet diameter; feed pressure; feed rate; solid/liquid ratio; position and diameter of vortex finder; diameter of apex; specific gravity of solids in feed. A recent account of factors affecting hydrocyclone performance in mineral processing was given by B. A. Wills in *Mining Magazine*, Feb. 1980, pp 142–146.

FROTH FLOTATION.—If a particle is to be held in a mineralised froth, it must be ground to a fineness at which the downward pull of gravity is insufficient to overcome its adhesion to an air-interface. The usual commercial separation entails the lifting of a heavy metal sulphide away from a relatively light gangue by the agency of air bubbles rising through a pulp. This buoyancy results from the adhesion of the particle to a comparatively large bubble. The adhesive force with which a particle clings to the air-water interface is opposed by the gravitational drag due to its mass. For successful exploitation of differences in surface properties most ore minerals must be ground finer than 48–65 mesh.

The process of flotation is carried out in a cell which is basically a tank containing a pulp consisting of the finely ground mineral slurry to which various reagents have been added to produce the froth and promote particle-bubble attachment. The importance of flotation in the ore dressing process can be gauged from the fact that in the United States alone, some 500 million metric tonnes of ore are concentrated by this means each year. The largest concentrators are designed to process up to 100,000 metric tonnes per day of ore and some mills contain over 1,000 flotation cells.

A complete survey of modern flotation machines appeared in *Mining Magazine* January 1982 pp 35–59, ('Flotation Machines') by Peter Young. Young notes that flotation machines now in use can be divided into four classes:

(1) *Mechanical:* The most common type characterised by a mechanically driven impeller which agitates the pulp and disperses air into it. Each impeller produces nearly ideal mixing in its vessel. It is normal to have a number of impellers in series. Within this class there are two sub divisions:

(*a*) *Pulp flow:* 'Cell-to cell' machines have weirs between each impeller, 'open flow' machines do not.

(*b*) *Aeration:* 'Supercharged' machines receive air from a blower, 'self aerating' machines use the depression created by the impeller to induce air.

(2) *Pneumatic:* Machines in this class have no impeller and rely upon compressed air to agitate and/or aerate the pulp.

(3) *Froth separators:* In these, the incoming feed is introduced from above, onto the froth bed, and not into the pulp zone.

(4) *Column:* The essential feature of column machines is a countercurrent flow of air bubbles and slurry, or of pulp and wash water.

A few machines do not fall neatly into any of these classes.

Design, manufacturers, specifications and operating characteristics of all these types of machine are given in Young's article.

As with most mineral processing and mining equipment the trend in flotation in towards larger and larger sizes: about ten years ago flotation cells were limited to volumes of 2·8m^3, but are now being designed in much larger volumes. In 1987, the Copperton concentrator near Salt Lake City in the USA, which processes copper ore from the famous Bingham Canyon open pit mine, was supplied with flotation cells having a capacity (one single cell) of 85 m^3 (3000 ft^3); the largest yet built in the World. (*Mining Journal*, Feb. 13, 1987 p. 109).

A comprehensive review of chemical reagents used in flotation for the recovery of various minerals is given in *Mining Magazine*, Sept. 1984, pp 202–219.

GRAVITY CONCENTRATION PROCESSES.—These are a wide range of processes whose effectiveness depends on the difference in specific gravity between the valuable mineral and the gangue or waste. They cannot be considered in detail but include jigs, in which a pulsating current of water is utilised; shaking tables; spitzkasten; spirals etc.

Gravity concentration methods are capable of treating minerals in a very wide size range, but a recent trend has been to look at gravity concentration processes which can treat fine material. As an example, the tin-bearing mineral cassiterite is not easily concentrated by flotation, hence some 85% of the world's tin is produced by gravity concentration.

Gravity separation processes are not restricted to the use of water as a separating medium. A series of processes are available utilising various forms of dense media separation. In the laboratory, organic heavy liquids have been used for many years to achieve very precise separation of minerals, but there are a number of drawbacks to the use of many of these liquids on a large scale. At plant level, commonly used heavy media include suspensions of ferrosilicon or finely divided magnetite in water.

Complete information on gravity concentration processes including theoretical aspects and plant practice is given in 'Gravity Concentration Technology' by R. O. Burt and C. Mills, *Elsevier* 1984.

MAGNETIC, ELECTROSTATIC AND ASSOCIATED METHODS.—Magnetic separation is applicable to minerals in which a natural or induced degree of polarity can be sustained during passage through a magnetic field. High intensity or electrostatic separation is applicable where one particle species is relatively non-conducting and the feed to the system is sufficiently mobile and close-sized to allow the delicate electrical forces of repulsion and attraction to act on particles gathering charge as they move through a field of high electrical intensity, and on into one where insulation is suitably controlled and charge dissipation becomes a discriminating force.

THICKENERS.—In a conventional thickener—usually a large, shallow cylindrical tank into which mill pulp carrying finely ground solids in suspension is fed centrally, the entering pulp displaces part of its volume as a peripheral overflow of moderately clean water. During gentle radial drift of this overflowing water from centre to sides, the solids fall slowly, either individually, or as aggregates. Coarse material reaches a zone where a rake, revolving very slowly at the tank bottom, sweeps slurry to a discharge well. Typical uses of thickeners in mineral processing are to reclaim water from a muddy effluent by allowing silt to settle; to remove a suspended mineral product from a pulp; to thicken (ie increase the solid/liquid ratio of) a pulp; and to reclaim some mill water before discarding the solids from a tailings pulp.

The use of the world's largest thickeners in a counter-current decantation system at the Twin Buttes copper mine in Arizona was described in *Mining Magazine,* Jan. 1977, pp 38–43. These giant thickeners, of which there are four, are each 122 m in diameter.

A new approach to thickening is the lamella thickener. The principle of thickening by installing inclined plates in tanks has been in use for some time and the lamella thickener has been developed on this principle, mainly for applications in the mineral industry. Principles underlying these thickeners and their application are given in *Mining Magazine*, April 1976, pp 291–7. A new development in the thickening field is the Magnetic Hydrocyclone Thickener. This device consists basically of a magnetic field surrounding a cyclone. It is considered to have wide application in the minerals processing industry and was described in *Mining Journal*, January 7, 1983, p. 6.

The principles underlying some mineral processing operations are described in considerable detail in *Mineral Processing, Volume 1.—Fundamentals, Comminution, Sizing and Classification* by Gusztav Tarjan, published by Akademiai Kiado, Budapest, 1981. (English text)

The subject of ore preparation is now such a complex science that only an outline of the many processes has been given here. Suggested further reading is: E. J. Pryor, *Mineral Processing*, 3rd edition 1965, Elsevier Publishing Co.; *Mineral Processing Technology* by B. A. Wills, Pergamon Press, 2nd Edition 1981; *Mineral Processing Plant Design*, American Institute of Mining Engineers, 1978; and Mining Annual Review 1986 'Mineral Processing'. (*Mining Journal Ltd*).

AIRCRAFT PROPULSION

Definitions—Engine Performance—Human Limits of Flight—Climb and Range—Jet and Propeller Propulsion—Reheat—Fuel Consumption—High-velocity Combustion—Ramjets—Pulsejets—Gas Dynamics—Compressors and Burners—Propellers—Supersonic Aircraft—Rocket Engines and Fuels—Rockets Theory

By J. L. Nayler, M.A., C.Eng., F.R.Ae.S., F.A.I.A.A., F.B.I.S.

DEFINITIONS

Turbojet Engine.—An air-swallowing engine, composed of a compressor, combustion chambers and a gas turbine, which generates thrust by a jet of hot gases from a nozzle.

Turbofan Engine.—A turbojet engine in which air passing over the engine is accelerated by a fan, resulting in increased mass flow and propulsion efficiency.

Bypass Engine.—A turbojet engine in which excess air from the L.P. compressor is by-passed into the propelling nozzle.

Turboprop Engine. —An air-swallowing turbojet engine coupled to a propeller, and providing thrust mainly by a propeller and partly by a jet.

Ramjet Engine.—An air-swallowing engine, composed of a diffuser, a combustion chamber and a nozzle, which generates thrust by its jet of hot gases.

Pulsejet Engine.—An air-swallowing engine, composed of a combustion chamber to which air is admitted through valves that are opened or shut by the pressure in the chamber, and of a nozzle which generates thrust by its jet of hot gases.

Rocket Engine.—A liquid-propellant engine carrying its own oxidant.

Rocket Motor.—A solid-propellant engine carrying its own oxidant.

Turborocket Engine.—An engine combining the properties of turbojet and a rocket engine.

Pressure-jet Engine.—A flame tube, to which compressed air and fuel are supplied, together with a propelling nozzle.

Auxiliary Power Plant.—An independent engine and ancillary equipment to provide power for auxiliary services.

Specific Consumption.—The quantity of fuel or oil consumed per horse-power per hour, or per lb. of thrust per hour.

Centrifugal Compressor.—A compressor in which the pressure rise is caused by centrifugal forces set up by a rotating impeller.

Axial-flow Compressor.—A compressor with alternate rows of fixed and rotating blades, radially mounted, with the flow through the compressor in the direction of the axis.

Radial-flow Compressor.—A compressor with alternate rows of fixed and rotating blades, axially mounted, the general direction of flow being radial.

Impeller.—The rotating member of a centrifugal compressor.

Compressor Casing.—A casing enclosing the impeller or rotating member.

Compressor Drum.—A cylinder or series of discs upon which the rotating blades of an axial-flow compressor are mounted.

Diffuser.—A passage or passages for converting the velocity of the air into pressure; for example, the compressor delivery to the combustion system.

Flame Tube.—A tube within a combustion chamber in which combustion occurs.

Primary Holes.—Holes through which air flow is passed into a flame tube for the early stage of combustion.

Secondary Holes.—Holes, downstream of the primary holes, to pass extra air into a flame tube to stabilise the flame, and to complete combustion.

Tertiary Holes.—Holes, downstream of the secondary holes, to pass air into a flame tube to dilute the hot gas, and so reduce its temperature.

Swirl Vane.—A vane for imparting a swirling motion to the air passing into a flame tube or combustion chamber.

Interconnector.—A pipe connecting adjacent flame tubes or combustion chambers.

Nozzle Guide Vanes.—A ring of stationary vanes for accelerating the combustion gases and directing them on to the first row of rotating turbine blades.

Burner.—A device, with a fixed or variable orifice, for injecting a spray of fuel into the combustion chamber.

Spill Burner.—A burner in which some of the entering fuel is recirculated instead of passing direct into the combustion chamber.

Radial-flow Turbine.—A turbine in which the general direction of flow is radial.

Inward-flow Turbine.—A turbine in which the general flow is radially inwards with axial outlet.

Turbine Shroud Ring.—The ring which prevents the escape of gas past the tips of the blades of an axial-flow turbine.

Nozzle or Propelling Nozzle.—The nozzle attached to the rear end of a jet pipe, or rocket, or exhaust cone.

Thrust Spoiler.—A controllable device connected with the propelling nozzle, to reduce or to reverse the jet thrust.

Reheat.—The combustion of extra fuel introduced between the gas turbine and the exit nozzle of a jet engine, in a part of the engine termed the afterburner.

Specific Impulse.—The thrust of a rocket engine per unit rate of propellant consumption, usually stated in lb. per lb. per sec.

Stalling.—When the relative angle between the flow direction and the compressor blades becomes excessive, the blades lose lift, as in the case of an isolated aerofoil.

Surging.—A sudden drop in delivery pressure accompanied by excessive aerodynamic pulsing throughout the engine.

HUMAN LIMITS OF FLIGHT.—In some ways it is misleading to measure height arithmetically, since the density and pressure of the air decrease in geometrical progression. A better physical aspect is obtained by defining height in terms of the percentage mass of the atmosphere left above the ceiling. Experimental research aircraft have flown to a height of 120,000 ft, where there is more than 99% of the mass of the atmosphere below them, and less than 1% above. This means that flight has begun between the atmosphere and outer space, and any higher flights are gradually blending into space flight where there is no atmosphere. Such flights mean drastic changes in the environment of man and his aircraft. In this region various functions for both begin to cease and what is called the 'Aeropause' signifies the region between the 10 mile and 120 mile levels, that is, above 52,800 ft, a region equivalent to the last 12% of the atmospheric mass. In this region explosive decompression (the result of sudden exposure to low pressure at these heights) is extremely critical, and pressure suits are worn by pilots. At these heights the aircraft must be driven by a rocket engine owing to the absence of sufficient atmospheric oxygen for combustion.

The following table defining the functional borders of space, due to *Haber*, gives the limits of flight from the above aspect:

Function	Altitude Miles	% Atmospheric Mass above Ceiling
Contributing to respiration	10	13
Preventing boiling of body fluids	12	8
Sustaining combustion of fuels	13–15	5·5–3·5
Absorbing cosmic ray particles	13–23	5·5–0·5
Absorbing solar ultra-violet (210–300 mμ)	22–28	0·6–0·15
Supplying aerodynamic lift	50–60	0·0045 –0·00045
Supplying diffuse daylight	60–90	0·00045–0·000017
Absorbing meteors	65–95	0·00020–0·000010

It is hard to realise that aerodynamic lift and drag vanish at heights of about 50–60 miles based on a speed of 5 miles per sec., and are equally negligible at much lower heights at lower speeds. The speed of 5 miles per sec. is quoted because, for various reasons, this is when aviation will develop rapidly into space flight. The actual escape velocity from the earth's gravity is 6·96 miles per sec.

It seems likely that for a long time to come manned flight will be restricted to the aeropause and will last a few minutes only. At lower heights, say, 200,000 ft, the maximum sustained speed is about Mach 5·0. Flying faster will produce too much aerodynamic heat. An aircraft can operate in sustained flight at a maximum altitude of 100,000 ft. In the above table, this is a height of about 20 miles. Rocket propelled aircraft, of course, have reached higher altitudes in coasting flight.

NOISE AND VIBRATION.—In 1958 British European Airways defined an acceptable noise level as one which varied from 90 decibels at 75 vibrations per sec. to 60 decibels at the high frequency of 7,200 c.p.s. The vibration limits decrease from an amplitude of 0·005 in. at 10 c.p.s. to 0·0015 in. at higher frequencies. For V.T.O.L. aircraft the limitation on noise level for taking off and landing was not to exceed 90 decibels at a distance of 200 ft. Noise is essentially a question concerning aircraft propulsion, since any reduction must affect the power unit which is the prime source of the noise. Noise attenuation is related to the rate at which the hot gases mix with the surrounding air. Many aircraft manufacturers are working on the problem of noise reduction. This is becoming increasingly important as the thrust of engines, and speed of aircraft, get steadily higher. Among the important developments have been multiple jet nozzles, teeth on the exit circumference of the jet nozzle, and corrugations in the nozzle. A reduction of 5 to 10 decibels was obtained with several existing engines; the small corrugated nozzle adopted by Rolls-Royce has met with some success, and loss in thrust is approximately 1%. Noise rating has been reduced by designing for a lower jet velocity, and the bypass and turbofan engines have been the most successful. These engines give a lower specific fuel consumption than small ratio bypass engines, and still lower than the normal turbojet engine, but bypassing increases engine weight.

ENGINE PERFORMANCE

The power plant in an aircraft is needed to propel the aircraft through the air. In the case of piston engines, the power plant (rated in horse-power) drives a propeller and the propeller gives a thrust. In the case of a jet engine, the jet of hot gases delivers a thrust which is usually measured in pounds. When the aircraft is in steady horizontal flight the thrust balances the drag.

The speed of an aircraft in steady flight can be varied over wide limits by changing the angle of incidence of the wings, which alters the total drag of the aircraft. The thrust of the engine has to be adjustable so that it balances the drag of the aircraft over this speed range. The thrust and the drag both vary in different ways with the altitude of the aircraft since the air density and the temperature decrease with height. All these changes affect the problem of aircraft propulsion.

The most important conditions of flight are those of top speed; cruising speed; stalling speed; and to a much less extent, the approach speed. The first is very important for racing and military aircraft, the second for determining the range of the aircraft, and the third as a measure of the slowest speed at which the aircraft can fly and also as that at which it touches down to land. The remaining case has no great bearing on the propulsion problem, being usually 10 to 15% greater than the stalling speed so that the pilot has a little reserve of speed in hand for emergencies.

The specification for taking off an aircraft is that it shall, after starting from rest on a runway in no wind, clear a 35 foot screen in a given measured distance. In the case of multi-engined civil aircraft a successful take-off with one engine cut must be possible. Plenty of engine power meets the requirement to take off quickly, but with the incentive of competition there is always an aim to carry larger loads for longer distances at faster speeds with the consequence that runways are being extended at most airports. The runway distance depends on a number of characteristics of the aircraft and its engine; such as power loading (which is the all-up-weight of the aircraft divided by the engine power); the wing loading(which is the total weight divided by the wing area); the drag; and the cruising speed. The length of runway for take-off decreases rapidly with more powerful engines and increases when heavier loads are carried by the same aircraft. An aircraft designed to cruise at greater height needs a shorter runway to take-off. The length of the landing run is specified after clearing a 50 ft screen at a measured distance, and is longer for aeroplanes with higher wing loading.

The above is true for all kinds of aircraft and engines. Jet engines differ from piston engines in that the thrust is nearly independent of the speed, whereas the thrust of a propeller during take-off is much greater than its cruising thrust. Jet aircraft need, therefore, a longer take off; on the other hand, most jet aircraft are so much faster, having much more powerful engines, that the take-off is not usually a serious limitation. Piston-engined aircraft can have reversible pitch propellers, decreasing the landing run. The landing run of jet aircraft is reduced by using parachutes and also reversed thrust. To help the aircraft designer to meet the varying conditions of flight the engine constructor provides data for the power or thrust developed under a variety of conditions. It is specified for different altitudes defined by the 'International Standard Atmosphere' by means of a table defining the density, pressure and temperature for all heights based on the average atmospheric conditions; for example, for a temperate or a tropical climate. (See Altitude Table, p. L1/32).

The rate of climb of an aeroplane depends on the excess thrust. This usually decreases with height, except when power plants are designed to give a greater power at some altitude above sea level. The rate of climb decreases as altitude increases until it is zero, which defines a height that is called the absolute ceiling of the aircraft. At this height the thrust balances the drag and there is no reserve power. The maximum rate of steady climb occurs at that forward speed when there is the greatest excess power and that speed is called the speed for best climb. The actual least time to a given height is not always obtained by flying at the maximum rate of climb, because modern jet aircraft have engines with such a powerful thrust that the kinetic energy from speed can be turned very quickly into height by zooming. The climb rate of any particular aircraft depends on its drag.

CLIMB OF JET AIRCRAFT.—The longitudinal or forward motion of an aircraft in flight in still air is given by the equation:

$$T - D - W \sin \delta = \frac{W}{g} \cdot \frac{dV}{dt}$$

where T = thrust, V = air speed, D = total drag of aircraft, W = its weight, δ is the angle of the flight path to the horizontal and t is time.

To allow for the effect of the induced drag due to the lift, let the drag in straight level flight be D_h and the induced drag in this condition KD_h. The total drag along the inclined path will then be:

$$(1 - K)D_h + KD_h \cos^2 \delta = D_h - KD_h \sin^2 \delta.$$

If H is the altitude of the aircraft, $\sin \delta = \frac{1}{V} \cdot \frac{dH}{dT}$.

From these three equations we find the climb $\frac{dH}{dT}$ is given by:

$$\frac{dH}{dt} = \frac{V}{W}(T - D_h) + K\frac{V}{W}\sin^2 \delta;$$

and the second term on the right hand side is small except perhaps in steep dives or zooms, so that

$$\frac{dH}{dt} = \frac{V}{W}(T - D_h).$$

A symbol H_e, called the energy height, is the height at which the potential energy of the aircraft is equal to the sum of its potential and kinetic energies at height H and speed V. At high speeds such as those of jet aircraft the difference $\frac{1}{2}V^2/g$ between H_e and H will amount to several thousand feet. For a speed of 600 ft per sec. it will be 5,500 ft. In practice this means that aircraft with top speeds that are very high can turn their speed into height and the opposite. As these aircraft can accelerate very fast, the time to a given height is appreciably reduced by spending a greater time at low altitudes to gain speed and then using a zoom. The saving in time, say, to reach 45,000 ft is of the order of 10% compared with the steady climb given by the last equation.

RANGE OF AIRCRAFT.—The power plant and its characteristics affect the range of an aircraft. Some engines have a greater weight per horse-power or per pound of thrust than others, but the heavier engines often have a lower fuel consumption. Range is the distance flown when all the fuel has been burnt, and it is estimated for the case of no wind and called the Still Air Range. In practice, an aircraft carries a large reserve of fuel at the commencement of its flight in case it meets headwinds, to allow for delays after reaching the vicinity of an airport and for other contingencies.

Rate of fuel consumption of the power plant in the air is checked by flights of each new aircraft type under a variety of conditions, since it cannot be expected to be the same as under bench tests in the laboratory. Other measurements and estimates are made of the engine performance in the aircraft during the same series of flights and frequently the thrust is measured direct by a pitot comb located in the jet stream behind the aircraft. A good estimate of the thrust is obtainable from a single pitot reading when the general characteristics of the particular engine are known.

JET ENGINE DESIGN.—There are three main objects in the design of gas turbines for aircraft: (1) low fuel consumption; (2) low weight; and (3) small frontal area. The specific fuel consumption is expressed as pounds of fuel consumed per hour per pound of thrust given by the engine, the specific weight is defined as pounds weight per pound of thrust, and the frontal area is specified as the maximum frontal area presented by the engine per pound of thrust. Weight is a primary consideration in aircraft so that it is important both to keep down the weight of the engine and the fuel that is needed. The most important as regards the latter is to have a low specific consumption under cruising conditions. The total weight of engine plus fuel for a given duty should be as low as possible. The third consideration, that of low frontal area, is a feature which helps in the reduction of drag of the aircraft, which is also a primary consideration and is important in determining the maximum speed with maximum power. The question of the drag of the aircraft is dealt with in the chapter, 'Aerodynamics'.

A jet engine can be improved by increasing the efficiency of its component parts. The stage has now been reached where only small improvements in the aerodynamic efficiencies of compressors and turbines can be expected, the practical limit being of the order of 90% for both these components. Greater accuracy in the engineering details with less sensitivity to damage will give some further improvement of the power plant as a whole, but a greater improvement has come by increasing the pressure ratio of the compressor as this is an effective way of reducing both consumption and frontal area. An increase of pressure means a larger number of stages in the compressor and this increases the difficulty of matching the components over a wide range of operating conditions, because it is essential to ensure that none of the compressor blades is either stalled or choked. When the blades stall in a manner similar to the stalling of an aeroplane wing, the flow becomes unstable and breaks down to give rise to surging. Choking means that the speed of sound is reached in some part of the compressor, which fact limits the total flow through it with a consequent drop in its efficiency.

Many compressors are split into L.P. and H.P. sections which are mechanically independent in order to increase the pressure ratio. The ratio of the speeds of rotation of the two sections can be varied and this helps to extend the range of the engine, since this ratio is independent of other factors in the engine. The low pressure section can be used to pass air direct to the exhaust nozzle, as in the bypass engine.

The power of a jet engine is the kinetic energy of the exhaust gases, but the thrust given to an aircraft is due to the momentum of the gases issuing in the jet. Thus if the kinetic energy is doubled the momentum is only increased by the factor—$\sqrt{2}$, that is by about 40%. An increase of the maximum temperature of the engine increases its efficiency; it also increases the specific consumption calculated on the thrust produced for propulsion.

TURBOPROPS.—For moderate speeds of operation of civil aircraft and likewise for some military transport, a combination of turbine and propeller is more efficient than using the turbojet only, but at the highest speeds the jet alone is the best because it is impossible to design a propeller of sufficiently high efficiency when its blade tips are moving through the air at supersonic speeds. Some improvement is possible in what is known as the supersonic propeller; that is, a propeller in which all the working portion of its blades meets the air at speeds above that of sound; but there are other difficulties such as noise and blade strength, apart from a lower efficiency.

Some idea of the relative efficiency of the two methods of propulsion can be got from the diagram, which shows curves for jet, fixed pitch and constant pitch propellers on a basis of thrust plotted against speed. At speeds above about 550 miles per hour the jet is the most efficient. The constant speed propeller used with the turboprop combination comes in at lower speeds and the fixed pitch propeller is the least efficient. With a free turbine type of engine there can be a larger variation in speed without much loss in power and this variation can be matched by some complications in the control of the constant speed propeller.

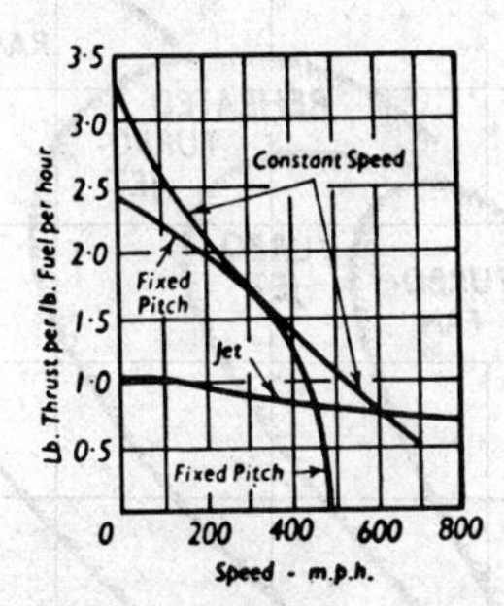

Relative Efficiencies of jet and propeller propulsion.

TURBOFAN ENGINE.—In the turbofan (or ducted fan) engine the fan, which is smaller in diameter than a normal propeller, is located in a duct. The smaller diameter produces a resulting propulsive efficiency that will be lower than for propellers used for aircraft of medium speeds. At higher speeds turbofan engines will be theoretically more efficient than propellers because the speed of the blade tips will be less. A typical arrangement is shown in Fig. 1; the fan is sometimes forward of the compressor.

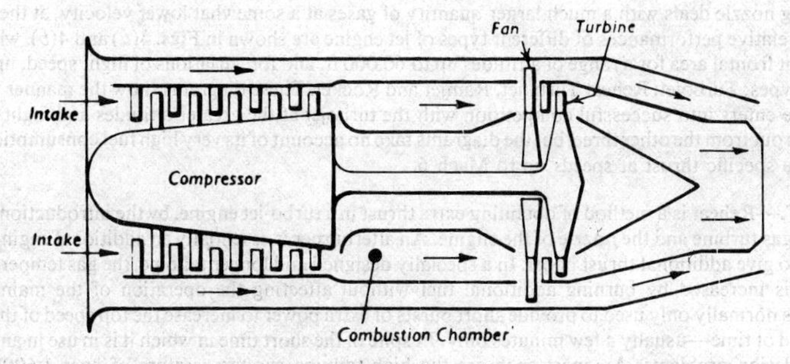

FIG. 1.—Turbofan engine.

EFFICIENCY OF AIRCRAFT GAS TURBINES.—Although the efficiency of gas turbines continues to improve, the types of engine which prove most efficient must depend upon the duty for which they are required. Fig 3 gives the appropriate zones of operation of different types of jet engine, as follows:—(1) Turbines of light weight and low cost for low speeds: (2) Turboprop and turbofan engines for freighter aircraft; (3) Turbofan engines in the transonic speed range, for better take-off, reduced fuel consumption, and less noise; (4) Turbofan engines for V.T.O.L. supersonic aircraft; (5) Ramjets above Mach 2 with special intake design and high-temperature operation; (6) Ramjets and turbojets with reheat after Mach 2·5 with a variable geometry for propelling nozzle; Ramjets or turbo-rocket engines after Mach 3, with assistance for take-off and acceleration.

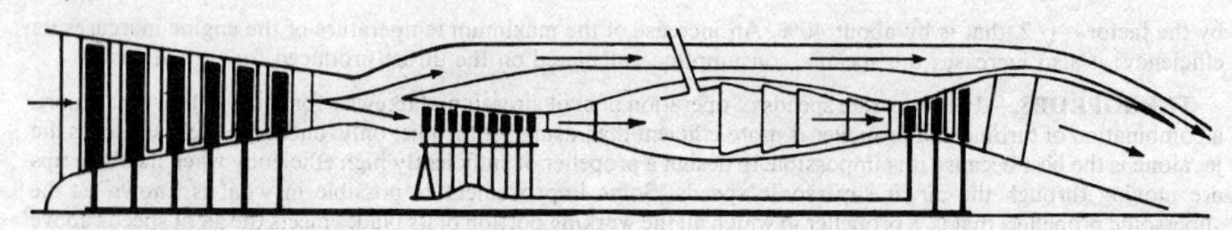

FIG. 2.—Typical bypass engine.

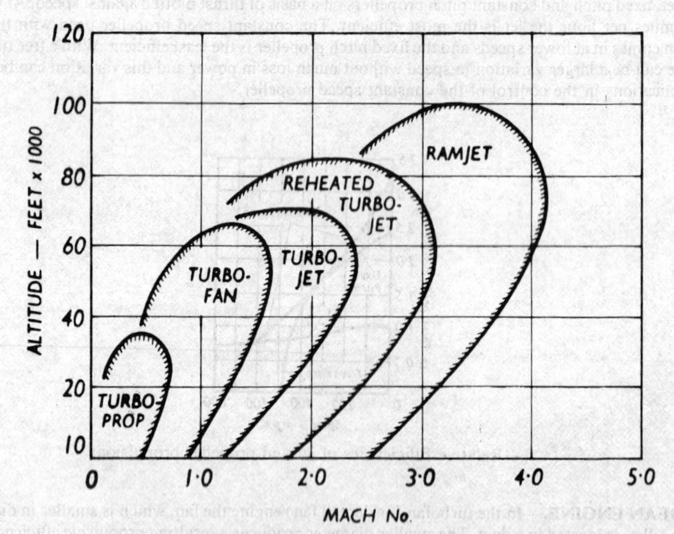

FIG. 3.—Turbojet Performance.

In the above selection it should be noted that bypassing air (Figs. 1 and 2) gives efficient performance because the propelling nozzle deals with a much larger quantity of gases at a somewhat lower velocity, at the lower flight speeds. The relative performances of different types of jet engine are shown in Figs. 4(*a*) and 4(*b*), which give the thrust per unit frontal area for a range of altitudes up to 60,000 ft, and for variations of flight speed, up to Mach 4, for the four types: Turbojet, Reheat Turbojet, Ramjet and Rocket. These diagrams show the manner in which the ramjet engine enters into successful competition with the turbojet at the greater altitudes and flight speeds. The rocket stands out from the other three, but the diagrams take no account of its very high fuel consumption. Fig. 4 (*c*) compares the specific thrust at speeds up to Mach 6.

REHEAT.—Reheat is a method of obtaining extra thrust in a turbo-jet engine, by the introduction of extra fuel between the gas turbine and the nozzle of the engine. An afterburner is essentially an additional engine attached to the exhaust to give additional thrust boost. In a specially designed and longer tailpipe, the gas temperature behind the turbine is increased by burning additional fuel without affecting the operation of the main engine. An afterburner is normally only used to provide short bursts of extra power to increase the top speed of the aircraft for a short period of time—usually a few minutes only. In spite of the short time in which it is in use in any flight there are special design problems. Amongst such are the high tailpipe gas temperature of over 1,600°C which is considerably hotter than the melting point of most alloys. This leads to severe problems of reliability and serviceability. Efficient combustion is required and at the same time the hottest areas must be cooled. For good aerodynamic efficiency the nozzle has to be variable. to adjust the jet area for the two conditions of with and without reheat.

The nozzle converts the available pressure energy in the tailpipe into useful momentum in the jet and has to give good efficiency for the wide range of flight conditions. Early afterburner nozzles were of a two-position type, but these have developed into nozzles whose diameter can be varied by flaps. The actuators to vary these flaps are moved by power, which may be in a form that uses an electrical, hydraulic or pneumatic source. The last can come from a tapping on the compressor. The problem is not simple, because the actuating rods may need a cooling shroud and all parts, especially the flaps, have to withstand high temperatures.

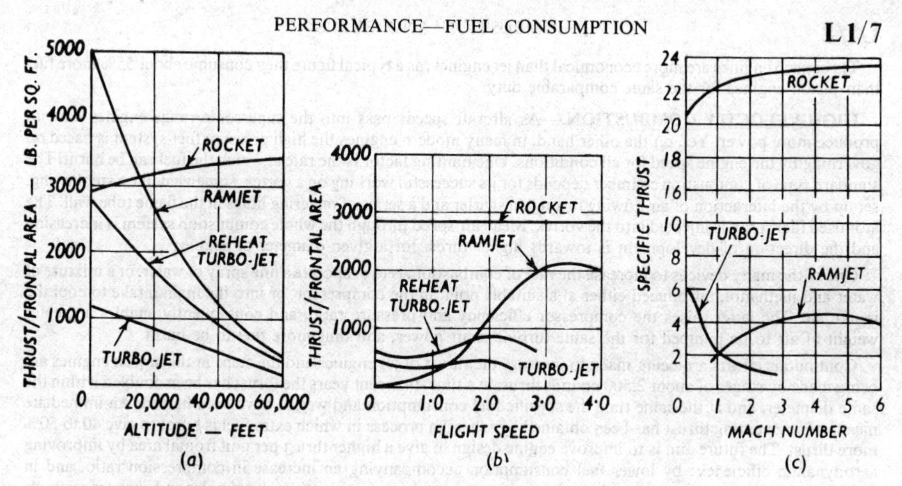

FIG. 4.—Thrust Variation of different types of jet Engine. (*a*) At Various Altitudes. (*b*) Thrust per Unit Frontal Area. (*c*) Thrust for a range of Mach Numbers.

The importance of reheat for boosting aircraft performance increases with the speed of flight, especially when the speed has become supersonic. A subsonic afterburner often gives an increase of thrust of 40%; at Mach 3, 75% of the propulsive thrust can be provided by the afterburner. With the trend for higher exhaust temperatures from the jet portion of the engine, and the demand for increased temperatures of reheat, there is need for materials having greater strength at high temperatures. Nimonic alloys are used extensively in the flame tubes and afterburners of British aircraft.

FUEL CONSUMPTION.—A main difference between jet and piston engines for aircraft operation is in their fuel consumption. Propulsion by jet engines is more expensive in this respect. A comparison between two airliners of about 100,000 lb weight, the one fitted with jet and the other with piston engines shows that the former consumes twice as much fuel per hour as the latter in cruising flight. The narrow relationship between thrust and r.p.m. for the gas turbine is well illustrated by the fuel wasted in a stack while an aircraft is waiting to land at an airport. The figure is relatively worse under these conditions because a piston engine can run at low engine speeds with consequent low fuel consumption.

Air temperature is a primary factor for jet engines and a 10°C rise in temperature can reduce the cruising height by 2,000 ft, the air speed by 13 knots, and the range by 2%.

The maximum fuel economy is at a speed about 15% greater than the minimum drag speed. The turbojet airliner is flown by cruising at a constant engine speed and at indicated airspeeds which are reduced every half hour as the aircraft weight decreases with the steady consumption of its fuel. This latter means that the aircraft climbs slowly during the whole of its cruise and finishes at about 40,000 ft, which is 8,000 to 10,000 ft higher than at its commencement. The procedure differs from the piston-engined aircraft which flies at a given altitude during its cruise. The lower air temperature and density at the greater altitudes means that the airspeed indicator reads a low figure compared with its true airspeed: for example, 200 knots at 40,000 ft means 370 knots true air speed.

AIRCRAFT GAS TURBINE FUELS

Specification No.	S.G. at 15·5° C min.	S.G. at 15·5° C max.	Flash Point °C	Freeze Point −°C	B.Th.U.
R.D. 2482	—	—	38·8	40	18,300
R.D. 2486	·751	·802	—	60	18,400
F/KER/210	·739	·825	—	60	18,400
R.D. 2488	·78	·85	60	40	18,300
J.P.1.*	—	·85	43·3	60	—
J.P.4.*	45	57	—	60	18,400
J.P.5.*	36	48	60	40	18,300

* American Specification (A.P.I.)

Turboprop engines are more economical than jet engines; as a typical figure they consume about 55% more fuel than piston engines for the same comparable duty.

HIGH-VELOCITY COMBUSTION.—As aircraft speeds pass into the supersonic range engines have to produce more power. Yet, on the other hand, in many modern engines the high pressure fuel-system is based on governing by the engine speed for all conditions. One limiting factor is the rate at which the fuel can be burnt. The standard type of combustion chamber depends for its successful working on a vortex, somewhat like a smoke ring, set up by the interaction of air flowing through a swirler and a series of metering holes in the flame tube wall. The atomised fuel spray is injected into the vortex. Mean air speed through the whole combustion system is increasing and the direction of development is towards higher thrust for a given diameter of engine.

One of the many devices to increase the rate of combustion, is to evaporate a fine spray of water, or a mixture of water and methanol, introduced either at a suitable point in the compressor, or into the main intake to cool the intake air. The latter raises the compressor efficiency and pressure ratio, and consequently enables a greater weight of air to be pumped for the same turbine shaft power, and thus more fuel to be burnt.

Continuous efforts are being made to increase the thrust of jet engines and the steps in the largest engines are being made by stages of about 2,500 pounds thrust at a time. In recent years the thrust has been doubled within the same diameter, and at the same time the specific fuel consumption and weight have been halved. An immediate means of augmenting thrust has been obtained by reheat; a process in which extra fuel is burnt to give 40 to 50% more thrust. The future aim is to improve engine design to give a higher thrust per unit frontal area by improving aerodynamic efficiency; by lower fuel consumption accompanying an increase in compression ratio, and in turbine temperatures; by reducing the weight with new metals such as titanium; by simpler and cheaper methods of construction; and to decrease noise.

HIGH ENERGY FUELS.—The fuels used by aircraft should possess high energy content per unit of weight or per unit of volume, and much research has been directed towards new types of fuels. Experiments have been made with rocket fuels in short range aircraft, and although the performance was satisfactory, the rate of fuel consumption was very high. The principal fuel requirement is a better fuel for an air-breathing engine.

The specific energies of possible chemical fuels is known. Hydrogen is supreme in terms of heat release per unit weight, but even when liquefied its density is very low. Its heat per unit weight is 2·8 times that of kerosine and 1·8 times that of pentaborane.

Boron and beryllium are substances which are theoretically very suitable for the production of fuels. Boron gives the greater heat per unit weight, but has a slightly greater volume. Beryllium has been discarded as a fuel because of the malignant toxicity of many of its compounds, and the corrosive action of its combustion products. Much work has been done in America on investigation of boron and the borates, including plans for large scale production. If a performance index is calculated on the product of the heat per given weight, and the heat per given volume, the following boron fuels are promising:

Fuel	Perf. Index	Heat/Weight*	Heat/Volume*
Boron	5·17	1·26	3·80
Boron-Pentaborane	3·50	1·36	2·50
Boron-Kerosine	3·10	1·40	2·40
Pentaborane.	1·85	1·60	1·1

* Kerosine as unity.

Boron is a stable substance which does not burn below 700°C, is second only to the diamond in hardness and exceedingly abrasive. If used it would be as a slurry with kerosine, or possibly in the form of pentaborane, which is a mobile liquid freezing at −47°C and boiling at 65°C. It is not spontaneously inflammable in cold air, but may explode in hot air. It is toxic and burns almost completely to boric oxide which would erode turbine blades, so that it appears to be more suitable for ramjets, or as an afterburner fuel for turbojet engines. In America ramjet engines have been extensively tested on high energy fuels which include pentaborane. The SW-110A specification calls for a supersonic aircraft with a dash performance of Mach 2, the intention being to use a fuel, such as pentaborane, in the afterburner at full thrust. The U.S. Air Force figure for the heat release of pentaborane is 29,127 B.Th.U per lb., compared with kerosine at 18,000. This fuel weighs 38 lb per cu ft compared with 42 for aviation petrol and 51·2 for kerosine; it melts at −46·7°C and boils at +60°C.

MATERIALS FOR AIRCRAFT GAS TURBINES

The development of the gas turbine depends upon the available materials which have to withstand the conditions of temperature, stress and corrosion. Vacuum induction melting and consumable electrode vacuum arc melting are having a marked effect on the production and properties of turbine blade and disc materials; the refractory material silicon nitride has also improved future prospects.

Taking first the axial-flow compressor, aluminium alloys were at first widely and successfully used for the blades while the temperature was in the neighbourhood of 200°C but they have become unsuitable now that the temperature exceeds 300°C with the increase of compression ratio. The choice of material is 12% chromium steels or 18–2% chromium-nickel steels, which have a higher proof stress than the austenitic stainless steels, do not rust like the low alloy steels and are not pitted and eroded by the dust particles carried in the air stream. These two classes of materials cannot be used in the unmachined forged state, as is possible in the alternative of the aluminium bronzes. The low density and corrosion resistance of titanium have shown an improvement on steel alloys. In all cases the ultimate choice of material will depend not only on its specific strength (strength for a given weight) but also on its capacity for economical large-scale production.

Combustion chambers are made primarily of formed sheet metal parts welded together. The flame tube is subjected to the biggest stress due to radiation from the flame, and needs adequate strength at a temperature of 900°C as well as adequate resistance to thermal shock. The earlier austenitic steels have been superseded by steels containing a high percentage of chromium (up to 25%), or of nickel (up to 30%), and steels with up to 1% titanium. A great number of flame tubes are made of either Nimonic 75 (chromium 20, titanium 0·3, carbon 0·1%, balance nickel); or Inconel (chromium 15, iron 8% and balance nickel). Alloys with a higher strength at the working temperatures, such as Nimonic 80 (Nimonic 75 with $2\frac{1}{2}$% titanium and 1% aluminium); and Inconel X (Inconel with these same additions), give a further improvement on the earlier materials. The two former materials as coatings on both sides of an inner layer of copper give an improved material for resistance to thermal shock.

Turbine discs, which carry the rows of turbine blades, vary in temperature from about 150°C. at the centre to 600°C at the rim which induces stresses additional to those due to centrifugal forces. A steel commonly used in the United Kingdom for discs is G18B, 13% chromium, 13% nickel and 10% cobalt matrix, with additions of carbide-forming elements for hardening such as molybdenum, tungsten and niobium. These steels are treated by 'warm working' at a temperature below the normal forging temperature to increase their proof stress and creep properties. U.S.A. engine manufacturers use a steel 16% chromium, 25% nickel and 6% molybdenum. Ferritic steels which are inferior regarding creep properties but have a higher proof stress are also used, their composition being similar to the 12% chromium steels with additions of the same three hardening elements. The ferritic steels are only satisfactory if the discs have adequate air cooling, so that when rim temperatures rise above 600°C austenitic steels will be required. They are being replaced by 12% chromium martensitic steels.

The materials for nozzle guide vanes and stator blades must be resistant to oxidation and thermal shock and have satisfactory creep properties at high temperatures, but relatively low stresses. Most stator blades are precision-cast and made either of cobalt base alloys containing 28% chromium and 5% molybdenum, or austenitic steels with chromium 23%, nickel 12% and tungsten 3%. Nimonic alloys have also been used. These components in service distort or crack at the trailing edges due to thermal shock. Hollow blades are stated to be an improvement and may be air-cooled or internally cooled.

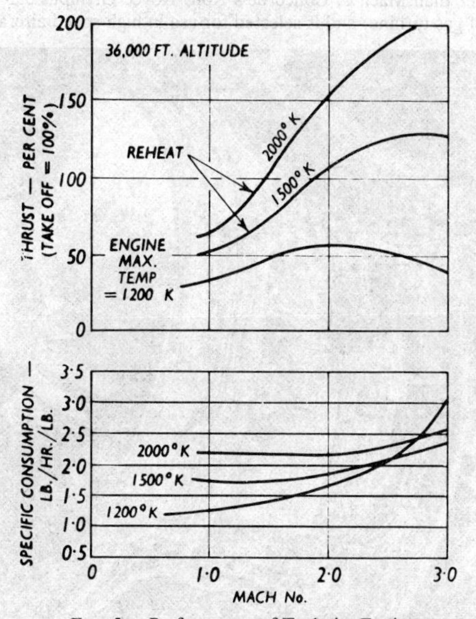

FIG. 5.—Performance of Turbojet Engines.

Turbine rotor blades have to be resistant to creep and rupture and with a high fatigue strength. Future development will be in materials with resistance to corrosion and oxidation than those now experienced, and they must have adequate resistance to corrosion and oxidation. The use of wrought blades is common, the materials being one of the Nimonic alloys or similar to S816 which is a cobalt base alloy containing chromium and nickel and hardened by carbides. The forgings are machined to size, thus removing the layer of oxidised material formed during forging. S816 and Vitallium, which are cobalt base alloys, have flatter curves of creep resistance plotted against temperature, and on this account are preferable for use at the highest temperatures. There are alloys which have a better creep resistance at very high temperatures, but they are difficult to forge satisfactorily and are almost invariably brittle and have a low ductility.

Outer casings are normally made of aluminium or magnesium alloy castings as the temperatures to which they are subjected are relatively low. The centre casing inside the ring of combustion chambers reaches much higher temperatures and is usually made of 18–8 chromium-nickel steel. The cast flanges to which the steel metal parts are welded are often made of austenitic steel such as H.R. Crown Max. Hotter turbine castings are of the 25–20 chromium-nickel type of steel. The general aim in materials is to meet the coming requirements of still higher temperatures of operation and the need for economical methods of production.

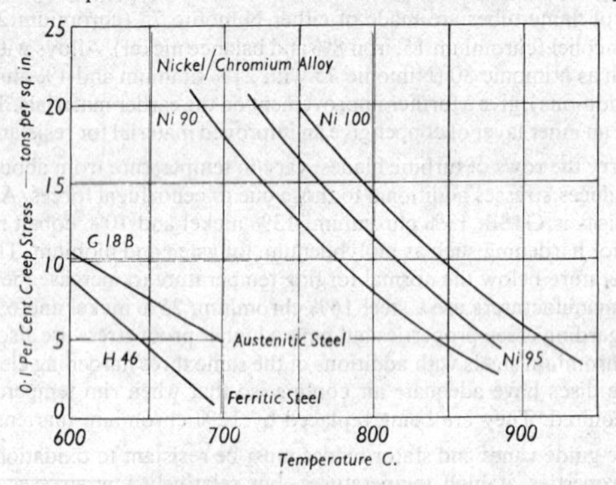

FIG. 6.—High temperature Materials for Turbojet Engines.

ENGINES FOR SUPERSONIC FLIGHT.—Whilst military aircraft in the eighties have veen flying at speeds in excess of Mach 3, passenger carrying aircraft, in the shape of the British Aerospace/Aerospatiale Concorde supersonic airliner, flys faster than Mach 2. Concorde's Rolls Royce Olympus 593 engine is a turbojet, the simplest and earliest form of gas turbine, and is selected for use in high-speed aircraft because its low frontal

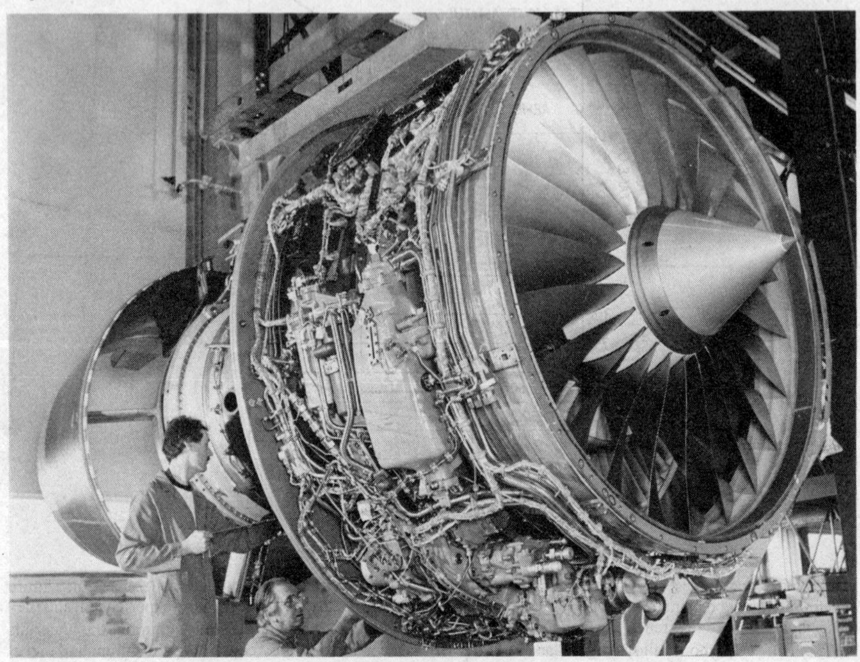

FIG. 7.—The turbofan 535E4 which is used on the Boeing 757.

area and high jet velocity offer advantages. The turbojet is referred to as a 'reaction' engine due to the fact that it derives its power from the reaction to the jet. Basic features of the design include a two-spool compressor driven by high and low pressure turbines which have a cannular type combustion chamber with ten flame tubes.

The faster an aircraft flies the more an air-breathing engine takes on the characteristics of a ramjet engine, and a centre-body intake becomes essential. The propelling nozzle must be of the convergent–divergent type fitted to the afterburner of the engine and the throat is in many engines automatically adjusted to maintain a constant turbine temperature over a range of jet temperatures between 1,000°K and over 2,000°K. A sufficient margin of jet velocity is maintained at flight speeds of Mach 2·5 and over by using reheat without going to prohibitive temperatures in the turbine. The performance of a turbojet engine increases with different amounts of reheat over a range of speeds up to Mach 3. A reheated turbojet can show an overall efficiency at this speed (measured as work done against drag divided by the calories in the fuel burnt) as high as 40%. Also, at this speed, the air inlet temperature is 300°C, so that the compressor and turbine are little needed, in fact 75% of the propulsive thrust is provided by the afterburner acting like a ramjet. At the time of the introduction of the Olympus 593, the General Electric Co. has the GE4/J5, a single shaft turbojet, which was larger and more powerful than the Olympus with a rating of 63,200 lb; and there was also the Pratt and Whitney and Kuznetsov large turbofan engines, the former's JTF17A–21 having a thrust of 61,000 lb.

ROLLS ROYCE ENGINES FOR AIRCRAFT.—Many of the engines produced by Rolls Royce for aircraft flying in the mid-eighties are of the turbofan variety. The turbofan is probably the most common derivative of the gas turbine for aircraft propulsion. It is a 'bypass' engine, where part of the air is compressed fully and passes into the combustion chamber, while the remainder is compressed to a lesser extent and ducted around

FIG. 8.—Assembling a RB211, 524D4 version: engine powers TriStars and Boeing 747s.

the hot section. The bypass either rejoins the hot flow downstream of the turbine, or is exhausted to atmosphere through an anulus surrounding the hot exhaust. In both cases the result is reduced overall jet velocity, giving better propulsive efficiency at lower aircraft speeds, lower noise levels and improved specific fuel consumption.

The 535 turbofan, Fig. 7, has a thrust range of 37,400 lb (166·4 kN) to 42,000 lb (186·8 kN), and is said to have further growth potential. It entered service as the 535C on the Boeing 757 in January 1983. An improved version, the 535E4, was brought out in October 1984 and embodies additional advanced technology which includes a hollow wide-chord fan, improved '3D' aerodynamics, and integrated final nozzle to provide even lower cost running.

However, for greater thrust it is necessary to turn towards the RB211, a turbofan producing up to 56,000 lb (249 kN), Fig. 8. It is in service with the Lockheed TriStar and Boeing 747. Well established, having first flown commercially in 1972, the engine with its three-shaft, high bypass ratio set new standards of efficiency and quietness. The latest version, the RB211-524D, is currently the most fuel efficient engine in service on the Boeing 747.

The turbofan, Fig. 9, has military aircraft applications. Known as the Ardour, the Rolls Royce engine has a thrust range of 5,200 lb (23·1 kN) to 8,400 lb (37·4 kN) with afterburning. It is used to power the SEPCAT Jaguar, British Aerospace Hawk, and the Japan T-2 and F-1 aircraft. A non-afterburning Ardour powers a version of the Hawk selected by the US Navy to form the basis of their undergraduate pilot training programme from 1990 onwards.

Amongst the latest R-R turbofan projects is the V2500, a medium-thrust high bypass ratio (5·5:1) under development for the new generation of 150-seat airliners. This engine is the product of the combined skills of British, European, American and Japanese aero-engine manufacturers. It is scheduled to enter service in 1989 on the Airbus Industrie A320. Another advanced project, and just gone into service, is the Tay, Fig. 10. This also is a turbofan which has a two-spool fan and combines advanced technology with the best features of the well-proven Spey. The engine produces 13,500 lb (60 kN) of thrust and was chosen for the Gulfstream IV executive transport and the Fokker 100 short/medium-haul airliner. It is also under consideration by other manufacturers of new aircraft and re-engined versions of current products.

All gas turbine engines have their special arrangements for lubrication, fuel supply, etc., to give satisfactory working. The systems for the 'Spey' have been chosen for illustration, and Fig. 12 shows the ramifications of

FIG. 9.—A military aircraft turbofan, the Ardour, which powers the Hawk and Jaguar.

the lubrication system, indicated by arrows. The fuel supply and its control are complex, but some idea can be obtained from the diagram Fig. 14. All this is necessary to the satisfactory working of the engine. Fig. 13 is a diagram of the flow of air and of the products of combustion.

AUXILIARY POWER SYSTEMS.—The main aircraft engine has, in the past, been the basic source of motive power for driving alternators, generators, hydraulic pumps and air compressors, thus providing the power requirements for retraction of undercarriage, for movement of control surfaces and flaps, and for operation of air brakes and tail parachutes. In certain types of aircraft, the auxiliary power is being supplied by a separate gas turbine, which can supply either shaft torque, or compressed air, or a combination of both in one unit. In large aircraft the auxiliary engine is a separate installation, either operating continuously or when desired. The auxiliary engine may lead to an all-pneumatic auxiliary powered aircraft, compressed air being used to start the main engines, and to drive constant speed air turbines; the latter will drive the electrical and hydraulic accessories.

The facilities for bleeding air from the compressor of the main engine, or from the auxiliary gas turbine, has led to a 'bleed air' turbine accessory drive unit of constant speed, sutiable for a constant frequency a.c. electrical system. The constant speed is achieved by governor control of the turbine inlet nozzles, or through a butterfly valve in the turbine inlet.

An air turbine accessory unit is also used as an emergency source of power, being driven by ram air after being automatically lowered into the airstream when the main aircraft accessory power system fails. It is installed close to the outer skin of the aircraft for ease of lowering when required.

RAMJET.—The ramjet engine has no compressor or turbine as in the case of the turbojet engine. The air is led to the fuel injectors where the fuel is burnt in the combustion chamber (see Fig. 15). There is no convergent–divergent nozzle for the jet, the exit of which is nearly equal to the maximum diameter of the engine and is cooled by air holes just before the exit. An adequate speed through the air is necessary to ram the air into the entry and the pointed pressure head, and this provides air pressure for control of the air-fuel ratio. The propulsive jet is discharged at a greater speed than the forward speed of the engine and thus provides thrust. The propulsive force is equal to the change in momentum of the gases flowing through the engine. The ramjet is more efficient than a turbojet engine at speeds above Mach 2. The overall propulsion efficiency is often expressed as the ratio of speed.

FIG. 10.—One of R-R's latest turbofans, the Tay, for the Gulfstream and Fokker 100.

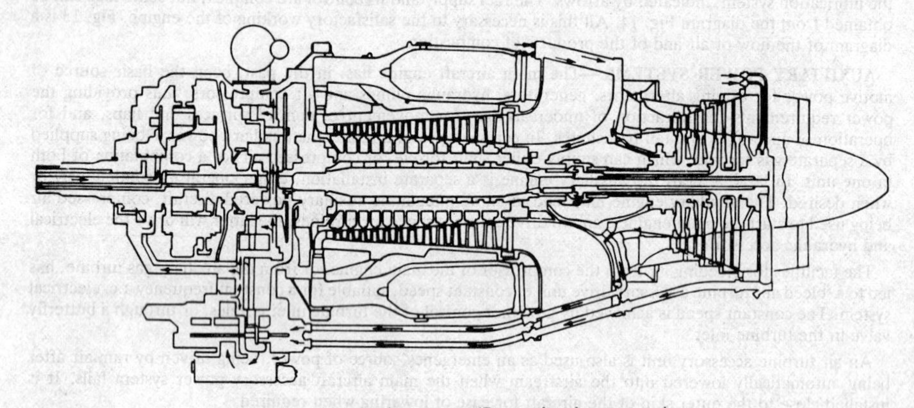

FIG. 12.—Lubrication system 'Proteus' turboprop engine.

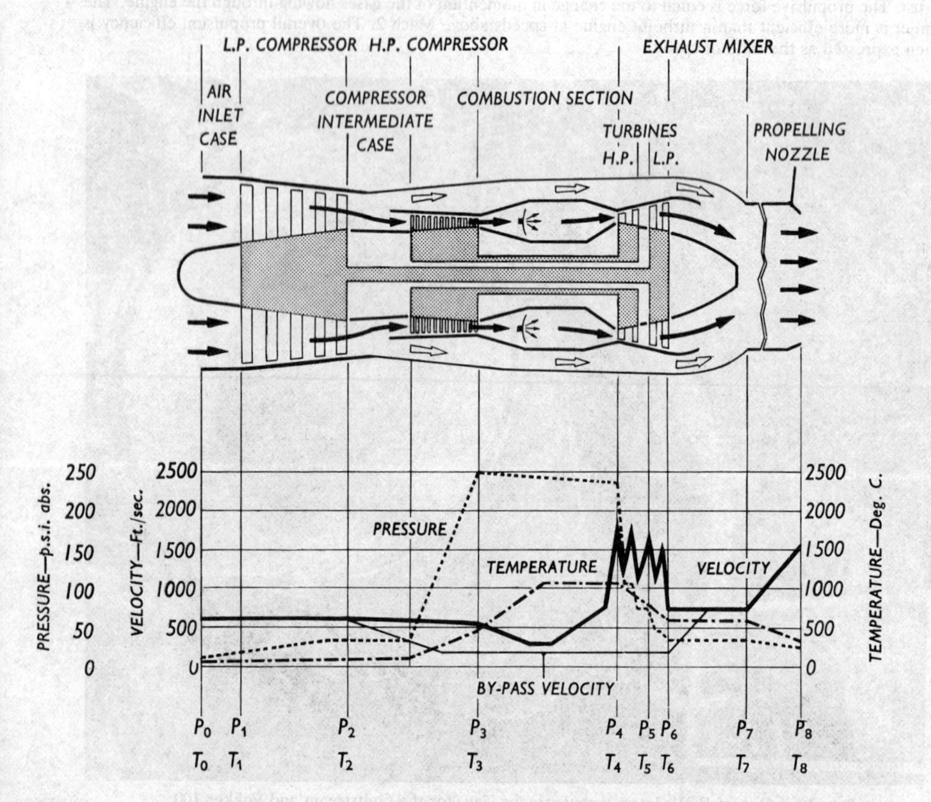

FIG. 13.—Rolls-Royce 'Spey' Turbofan Gas Flow Diagram.

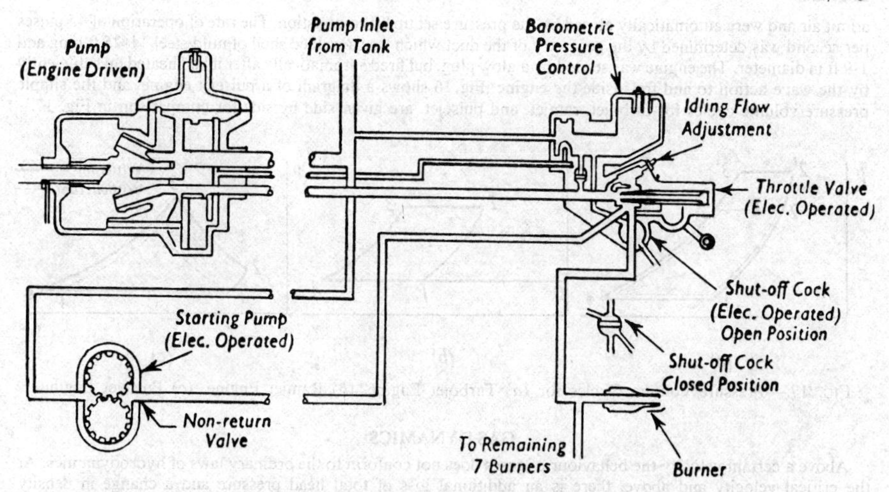

FIG. 14.—Fuel System Diagram—Turboprop Engine.

to specific fuel consumption. At the same tail-pipe temperature the efficiency curve for the ramjet crosses that for the turbojet with reheat after Mach 2·5 and is much greater, exceeding 50% overall efficiency, at Mach 5. One factor is the high compression ratio obtainable at the intake of the ramjet, viz:—6 at M = 2; 27 at M = 3; 65 at M = 4; and 100 at M = 5.

The design of the ramjet intake will vary with the design speed. Above Mach 3 the nose of the body becomes a closely fitting double cone with a small annular gap that is narrowed at still higher speeds.

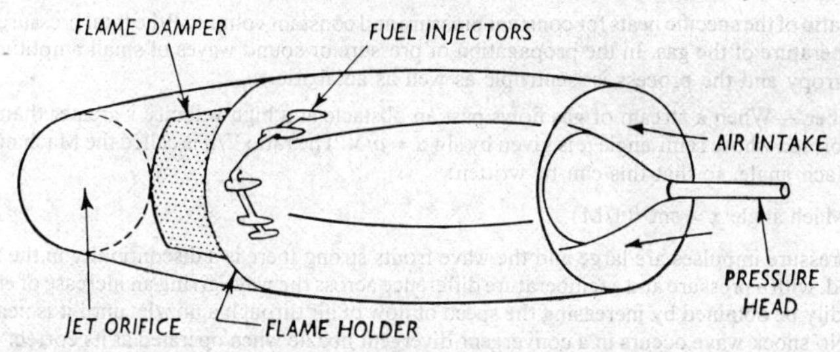

FIG. 15.—Diagram of Ramjet engine.

PULSEJET.—This is similar to a ramjet but the thrust is given by intermittent pulses instead of continuously. The best known pulsejet was that used by the Germans to power the V–1 flying bomb. The front of the engine unit consisted of a grid which controlled the admission of air to the combustion chamber. There were sixty-three valves composed of pairs of rectangular flap plates, each operated by two steel springs. The valves opened to

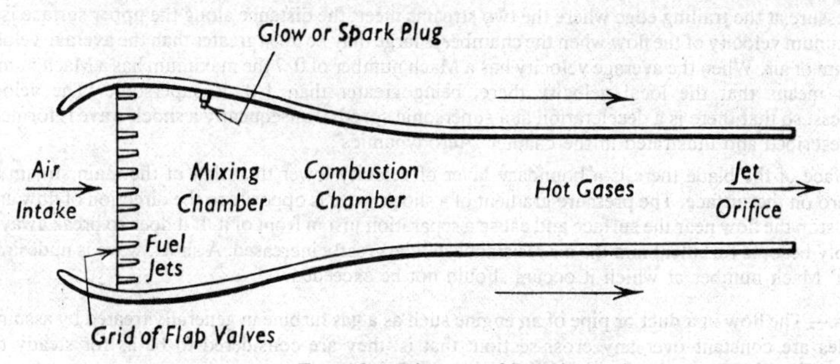

FIG. 16.—Diagram of Pulsejet engine.

admit air and were automatically closed by the pressure set up by combustion. The rate of operation of 45 pulses per second was determined by the geometry of the duct which was a welded shell of mild steel 11·25 ft long and 1·9 ft in diameter. The engine was started by a glow plug, but fired automatically after it had heated up sufficiently by the wave action to and fro inside the engine. Fig. 16 shows a diagram of a pulsejet engine, and the simple pressure/volume cycles for turbojet, ramjet, and pulsejet, are given side by side for comparison in Fig. 17.

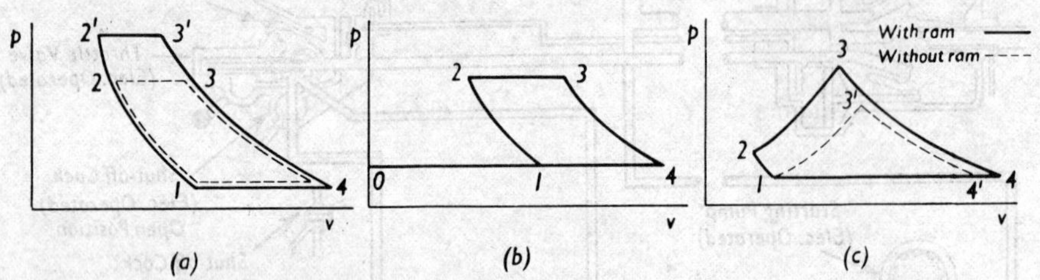

FIG. 17.—Pressure/Volume Cycles for (*a*) Turbojet Engine. (*b*) Ramjet Engine. (*c*) Pulsejet Engine.

GAS DYNAMICS

Above a certain velocity the behaviour of gases does not conform to the ordinary laws of hydrodynamics. At the critical velocity and above, there is an additional loss of total head pressure and a change in density accompanying a change in pressure of the gas. The effect is known as a compressibility phenomenon. It starts at a certain velocity when small shock waves begin to appear, and can be made visible by passing a strong light through a gas and observing the shadow on a screen. These phenomena occur long before the velocity of the gas reaches the speed at which sound is transmitted through it, and become more prominent as that speed is reached and exceeded. A pressure wave is propagated through the gas at a velocity which depends on both the pressure and density of the gas and its value, usually signified by the symbol 'a', is given by the formula

$$a = \sqrt{(\gamma P/\rho)} = \sqrt{(\gamma . R . T.)};$$

where γ is the ratio of the specific heats for constant pressure and constant volume, P the total pressure, ρ the density and T the temperature of the gas. In the propagation of pressure or sound waves of small amplitude, there is no increase of entropy and the process is isentropic as well as adiabatic.

Mach Number.—When a stream of gas flows past an obstacle at a high velocity v greater than 'a', a conical wave front is formed whose semi-angle α is given by $\sin \alpha = a/V$. The ratio V/a is called the Mach number and the angle α the Mach angle, so that this can be written:

$$\text{Mach angle } \alpha = \sin^{-1}(1/M)$$

When the pressure impulses are large and the wave fronts strong there is a discontinuity in the flow; a 'shock wave' is formed, with a pressure and a temperature difference across the wave giving an increase of entropy. Shock waves can readily be obtained by increasing the speed of flow of air through a nozzle, until it is near the speed of sound in air. No shock wave occurs in a convergent-divergent nozzle when operated at its correct pressure ratio because the flow accelerates under the influence of the pressure drop, but if the output pressure is increased beyond its design figure a shock wave is formed in the nozzle. The total-head pressure is less on the down-stream side of the pressure wave; the static pressure and temperature are higher on the same side because the shock wave is a compression wave. Part of the lost kinetic energy is converted into thermal energy with a consequent increase of entropy.

The flow over a compressor or turbine blade shows a region of high velocity and low pressure over the front highly cambered part of the top surface because after the air has flowed over both surfaces it must have the same velocity and pressure at the trailing edge where the two streams meet; the distance along the upper surface is the longer. The maximum velocity of the flow when the chamber is large may be 50% greater than the average velocity in the main stream of air. When the average velocity has a Mach number of 0·7 the maximum has a Mach number of 1·05, which means that the local velocity there, being greater than 1·0, is supersonic. The velocity further back is less, so that there is a deceleration at a supersonic speed. Consequently a shock wave is formed at that point, as described and illustrated in the chapter 'Aerodynamics'.

Near the surface of the blade there is a boundary layer of velocity lower than that of the main stream and decreasing to zero on the surface. The pressure gradient of a shock wave is opposite to the direction of flow and a shock wave will stop the flow near the surface and cause a separation just in front of it. If it does so break away the flow will probably become turbulent and the air resistance will be greatly increased. A shock wave is undesirable and the 'critical' Mach number at which it occurs should not be exceeded.

Gas Turbines.—The flow in a duct or pipe of an engine such as a gas turbine in generally treated by assuming that the variables are constant over any cross-section, that is, they are considered to be as for steady one-dimensional flow. The three equations which have to be satisfied are:

(1) CONSERVATION OF MASS; $\rho A V =$ constant; or $d\rho/\rho + dA/A + dV/V = 0$
where σ, A and V are respectively the density, cross-sectional area and velocity:

(2) CONSERVATION OF MOMENTUM:

$$dP/\rho + VdV/g + dZ + dF = 0$$

where P, Z, F, represent pressure, height from datum and frictional force.

(3) CONSERVATION OF ENERGY (for a gas):

$$C_p\,dT + VdV/(g\,J) + dZ/J + dH + dW/J = 0$$

where T is temperature, H is heat, W is work done and J is the mechanical equivalent of heat. For air, $C_p = 0{\cdot}240$ and $\gamma = 1{\cdot}40$, during compression; and $C_p = 0{\cdot}276$ and $\gamma = 1{\cdot}33$, during heating and expansion.

THEORY OF THE GAS TURBINE.—The gas turbine or jet engine is a heat engine in which compression and expansion are effected by rotary machinery by contrast with the piston engine where the machinery is reciprocating. Modern aircraft gas turbines are consequently of greater simplicity and lighter construction. There are three stages in the ordinary jet engine. Air is compressed in a compressor, the air is burnt with fuel and the products of combustion drive a turbine. The air is cool when drawn in through the intake, it is heated by compression, it is still further heated and the total volume of gases increased greatly in the combustion chamber. The gases expand in passing through the blades of the turbine and finally pass out through the jet pipe as a stream of very fast moving hot gas. In many jet engines a proportion of the hot gases bypass the turbine and enter straight into the jet pipe.

The volume of the working fluid and its temperature determine the amount of work that can be got out of an engine. In the gas turbine we increase the volume and temperature of the gases, which are the working fluid, and more work is got out of the air during expansion than has been put in during compression, so that there is a surplus to do useful work.

In the cylinder of a piston engine the fuel-air mixture is compressed, burnt and expanded, all in one part of the engine. In the gas turbine there is a much greater flexibility because these three processes of compression, combustion and expansion occur in three separate component parts of the engine. Each component has been developed and improved and the overall performance of the complete engine made up of these three essential parts can be predicted when the performance of each separate part is known. The component parts must, however, be matched for a given engine although an engine can, on account of this flexibility, be designed for a wide range of duties. The great need in the aircraft gas turbine is for compactness and so the components are put together in a single unit which is relatively simple. Complications are being added with further development of the aircraft jet engine, of which the most important is reheat. The large excess of air which is not burnt with fuel in the combustion chamber, mixes and combines with extra fuel injected after the turbine. This increases still further the volume of hot gases in the jet pipe and thus increases the thrust from the jet engine. The excess air that has passed through the engine has helped to keep it cool and there is usually on this account no necessity for special cooling as is arranged in the liquid-cooled piston engine. Improved design and new materials have enabled gas turbines to run at higher temperatures, and necessitated special arrangements for air cooling the turbine blades.

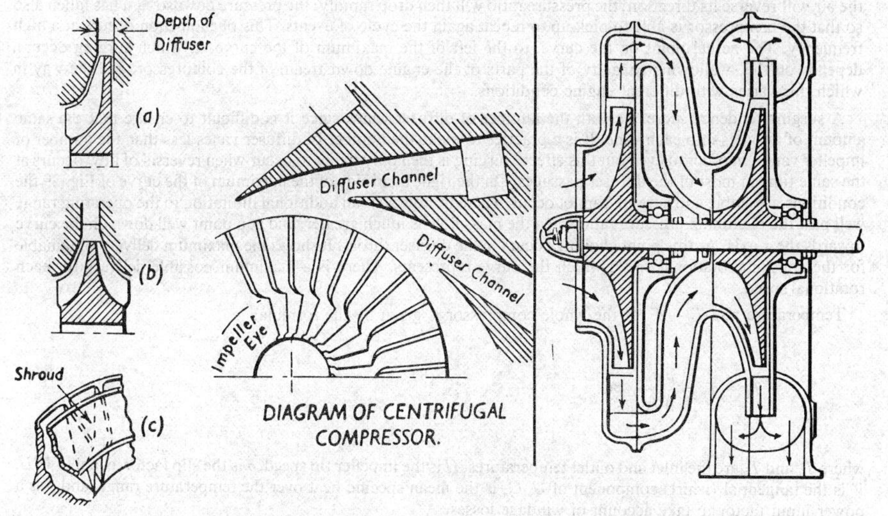

FIG. 18.

FIG. 19.—Two-stage Compressor (section).

CENTRIFUGAL COMPRESSORS.—The function of a compressor is to supply compressed air to the combustion chamber. This can be done by two completely different types of compressor, respectively centrifugal and axial (Figs. 18 and 20). Very rapid progress in early development of the jet engine was made with the centrifugal type, but later developments are all tending to the use of the axial compressor because it has a smaller overall diameter and can be made, aerodynamically, more efficient.

The centrifugal compressor consists essentially of a rotating impeller and a number of fixed diverging passages, called the 'diffuser', in which the air is decelerated. Some of the kinetic energy given to the air by the impeller is converted into pressure energy in the divergent passages by what is called 'diffusion'. The impeller may be single- or double-sided, the air being admitted to one or both sides respectively (Figs. 18(*a*) and (*b*)). Air is sucked into the impeller eye, whirled round at high speed by the vanes on the impeller disc and flung out into the diffuser channels by centrifugal force. The air tends to flow round the edges of the vanes in the space between the impeller and the outside of the casing so that a shroud, as shown in Fig. 18(*c*) is sometimes attached to the vanes. The shroud increases the manufacturing difficulties and has not come into general use on impellers for aircraft gas turbines. Straight radial vanes are normally used because the impellers are highly stressed.

Centrifugal compressors in aircraft engines have usually only one stage of compression. The Rolls-Royce 'Dart' has a two-stage compressor. Fig. 19 shows a two-stage compressor with two single-sided impellers.

A pressure ratio of 4 to 1 can be obtained with a single-stage centrifugal compressor and, with some lowering of efficiency, a higher pressure can be achieved. It is preferable to keep the stage ratio reasonably low and to obtain higher pressures by increasing the number of stages. This increases the axial length of the unit because it necessitates interstage passages to transfer the air from the diffuser of one stage to the intake eye of the next stage, as shown in Fig. 19. There will be interstage losses that will reduce the overall efficiency. The pressure ratio per stage increases as the square of the peripheral velocity, but this velocity must be kept below that of the speed of sound because of the loss of aerodynamic efficiency and the very high mechanical stressing of the impeller.

It is important to avoid a breakdown of flow which will occur if the speed of sound in the fluid is approached, and it has to be remembered that the speed of sound increases with temperature so that higher actual speeds are possible in the hot gases after combustion. What matters is the *Mach* number, or the ratio of actual speed to the speed of sound. In the diffusing channels there is always a tendency for the flow to break away from the boundary even at low speeds, and to get the maximum possible flow in the smallest possible compressor as in the design of aircraft gas turbines, the air speeds are high. The actual Mach numbers for the flow must not exceed that value at which the losses increase rapidly due to the formation of shock waves, especially at the entry of the diffuser and at the points of maximum velocity in the impeller passages. A maximum efficiency of about 80% may fall by 3 or 4% at the highest running speeds of a typical compressor for a turbo-jet engine.

The characteristics of a compressor are shown diagrammatically in Fig. 29 for a constant speed of operation. With no flow the pressure ratio is given by the cutting of the curve with the *y* axis. As the mass flow increases the pressure rises gradually to a maximum and then decreases. What is known as the phenomenon of 'surging' can occur on the first part of the curve before this maximum, when the flow conditions are not stable. Surging occurs with a sudden drop in pressure and an excessive pulsation throughout the compressor. With a decrease in mass flow the delivery pressure falls; if the pressure of the air downstream from the compressor does not fall fast enough the air will reverse its direction; the pressure ratio will then drop rapidly; the pressure downstream has fallen also so that the compressor is able to pick up to repeat again the cycle of events. This phenomenon occurs at a high frequency. The actual point on the curve, to the left of the maximum of the curve, at which surging occurs, depends on the swallowing capacity of the parts of the engine downstream of the compressor, and the way in which this varies with different engine conditions.

A surging tendency increases with the number of diffuser vanes since it is difficult to ensure that the same amount of air goes into each vane. It is a practice to make the number of diffuser vanes less than the number of impeller vanes, in order to even out this effect. Surging is then only likely to occur when reversal of flow occurs at the same time in most of the diffuser passages. On the right-hand side of the maximum of the curve of Fig. 29 the conditions are stable and surging cannot occur. There is, however, an additional limitation to the operating range well past the maximum pressure ratio when the mass flow is much greater, and at a point well down on the curve towards the *x* axis. At this point choking occurs in the diffuser throat. It shows the maximum delivery obtainable for the constant rotational speed which the curve represents. There is a maximum possible delivery for each rotational speed.

Temperature rise $T_2 - T_2$ of the whole compressor is given by the formula:

$$T_2 - T_1 = \frac{\rho.\sigma.U^2}{g.J.Cp}\ °\mathrm{C}.$$

where T_1 and T_2 are the inlet and outlet temperatures, U is the impeller tip speed, σ is the slip factor, equal to V/U, V is the tangential (whirl) component of U, C_p is the mean specific heat over the temperature range, and ρ is a power input factor to take account of windage losses.

The total-head pressure ratio is given by:

$$\frac{P_2}{P_1} = 1 + \eta\left(\frac{(T_2 - T_1)}{T_1}\right)^{\gamma/(\gamma-1)}$$

where P_1 and P_2 are the intake and delivery pressures, and η is the total-head isentropic efficiency.

Total-head isentropic efficiency is given by:

$$\eta = \frac{[(P_2/P_1) - 1]^{(\gamma-1)/\gamma}}{(T_2/T_1) - 1}$$

AXIAL COMPRESSOR.—The principal advantage of an axial compressor is that it can be designed to have a higher efficiency than any other type. It has a smaller cross sectional area than a centrifugal type, which is an advantage in an aircraft where frontal area is of great importance. The axial type is expensive to make because of the very large number of blades used in its construction. The highest pressure ratio which gives in practice a flexible aircraft engine is about 6 to 1 and in the large engines a low and a high pressure compressor are installed.

In essentials the axial compressor consists of alternate rows of moving and fixed blades attached to a rotor and its casing respectively. The two forms of rotor in general use are the drum and disc types illustrated in Fig. 20. There is usually a set of fixed blades before the first and there may be one after the last row of rotating blades. The first set of fixed blades are called inlet guide vanes. One set of rotor and stator blades together comprise a stage; different engines have various numbers of stages in their axial compressors. It is not practical to obtain the same pressure ratio for every stage and 1·25 to 1 can be obtained in a single stage. It is this small ratio which is responsible for the large number of stages in an axial compressor.

The air flows in through the inlet guide vanes along the annulus between the rotor and the casing. The size of the annulus decreases from the low- (inlet) to the high-pressure (outlet) end of the compressor in order to keep the axial velocity constant throughout the length of the compressor. If this were not done the increasing density along the compressor would result in a steadily decreasing velocity. The constant axial velocity throughout the axial compressor simplifies the design since one stage may be repeated for the others.

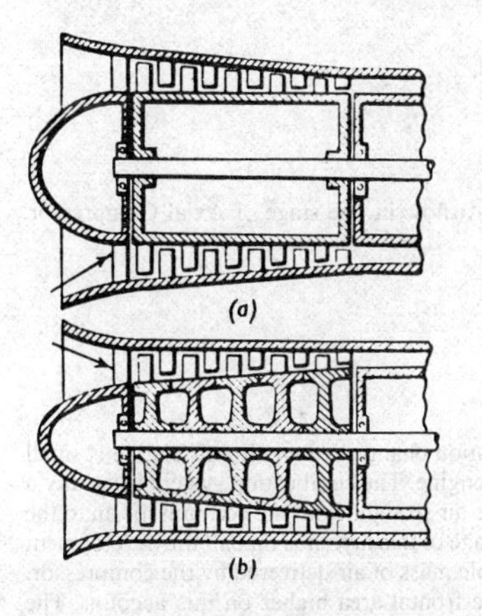

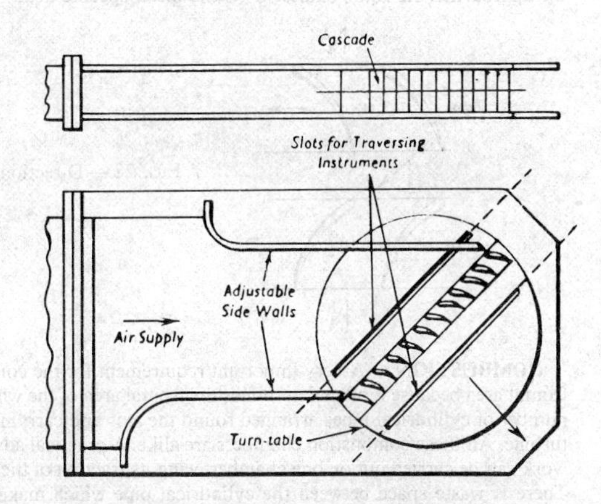

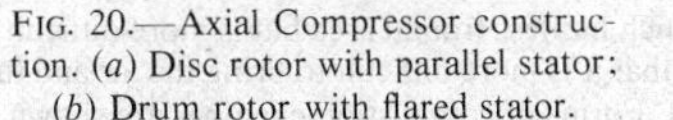

FIG. 20.—Axial Compressor construction. (*a*) Disc rotor with parallel stator: (*b*) Drum rotor with flared stator.

FIG. 21.—Elevation and Plan of simple Cascade Tunnel. (Traversing paths indicated by dotted lines).

As in the centrifugal compressor the kinetic energy of the air is converted by diffusion into pressure energy. The air is acted on by the individual blades which are aerofoils in section; that is, the general characteristics are similar to those of an aeroplane's wing. The performance of a single blade can be either calculated or measured in a cascade wind tunnel. This tunnel is an arrangement for testing a number of blades set out in the form of a straight cascade in a stream of air, the speed of which can be varied. Special instruments measure the direction of flow of the air stream and its pressure. A blade is tested as one of a number of aerofoils placed in a cascade and the forces on it are measured. Cascade tests give the angle, called the deflection, through which the air is turned for a minimum loss, and the drag coefficient of the profile or section from which the efficiency of the cascade can be calculated. The cascade is mounted on a turn-table as shown in Fig. 21. Tests on variations in the shape, spacing and angles of the blades give a mass of data from which the choice of design of the blades and their position on the rotor can be made. Each rotor blade does work on the air and increases its absolute velocity and also, because the passages between consecutive rotor blades are divergent, there is some diffusion and a rise of pressure. The air next goes through the passages between the stator blades, where it is further diffused and turned through an angle to give it the correct entry for the next stage, and also the correct velocity. In addition to the constant axial velocity, there is a constant work input per pound at all radii.

The axial compressor must not be run at too high an axial speed because compressibility effects will reduce its efficiency. The Mach number of the flow at the entry to a blade row must not be much greater than a certain critical value for the flow over the individual blade or else the compressibility losses will cancel the pressure rise and the blade row will cease to be any use as a diffuser.

The limits of operation of an axial compressor to avoid surging and choking are relatively smaller than for a centrifugal compressor. The range of stable operation is narrow and calls for greater care in matching the individual components of the jet engine.

If the same blade form is used throughout a compressor the overall pressure ratio is approximately given by the equation: $R = (R_s)^n$; where R_s is pressure ratio for one stage and n the number of stages and

$$R_s = \left(1 + \frac{\eta_s T_s}{T}\right)^{\gamma/(\gamma-1)}$$

where T is the inlet temperature, T_s the temperature rise per stage, and η_s the isentropic efficiency at each stage.

The overall static pressure ratio can be calculated from the formula:

$$R = \frac{P_2}{P_1} = \left(\frac{T_2}{T_1}\right)^{\eta_s\gamma/(\gamma-1)}$$

where P_1 and P_2 are the intake and delivery pressures, and T_1 and T_2 are the inlet and final temperatures.

$$\text{Also, } T_2 - T_1 = n\,T_s\text{; and, } T_1 = T_a - \frac{(V_a \sec \alpha_0)^2}{2gJCp}$$

where T_a is the ambient temperature, V_a is the axial component of the air velocity and α_0 is the angle at which the air approaches the rotor blades. C_p is the mean specific heat.

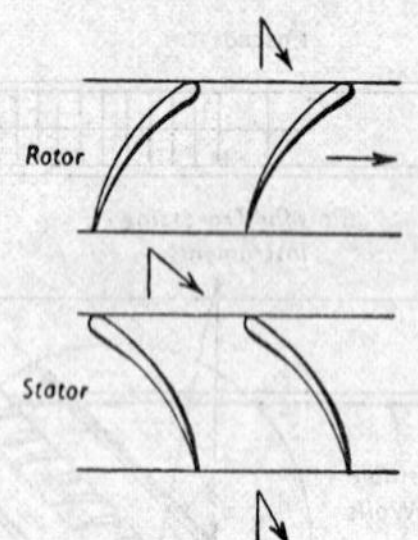

FIG. 22.—Direction of Airflow in one stage of Axial Compressor.

COMBUSTION.—A very important requirement for the combustion chamber of an aircraft engine is small frontal area because it often determines the frontal area of the whole engine. The combustion system is usually a number of cylindrical pipes arranged round the axis and carrying the air straight from the compressor on to the turbine. All these combustion chambers are alike. A practical advantage of this layout is that all the development work can be carried out on one chamber using its fraction of the whole mass of air delivered by the compressor. There is waste space between the cylindrical pipe which makes the frontal area higher on this account. The modern alternative is an annular form of combustion chamber which has less frontal area but is more difficult to make and develop. The natural form of a jet of fuel is circular so that it is more difficult to bring the air and fuel together in an annular casing to give an even fuel-air distribution. Forms of combustion chamber are shown in Fig. 23.

Aircraft gas turbines must have a low weight as well as occupy a small space, but their endurance requirements are much less than for other types of gas turbines. The temperature level of the gases after combustion must be low to suit the highly stressed materials in the turbine and the temperature distribution must be as uniform as possible to avoid local overheating and to get high turbine performance. The combustion has to be maintained in a stream of air with a velocity of about 200 ft/sec. and operation must be stable over a wide range of air/fuel ratios from full load to idling conditions from about 60 to 1 up to 120 to 1, the high dilution helping to keep down the temperature level. The need for operation in aircraft at high altitudes requires flexibility over a wide range of working conditions. Combustion takes place at a much richer mixture strength than that quoted and the hot gases are diluted with secondary air to give the lower temperature necessary before entry into the turbine. The region in which combustion takes place is called the primary zone into which the fuel is injected by a burner directed either up or down stream. The diluent air is added in the secondary or mixing zone. About 15 to 20% of the air is introduced in the primary zone where the fuel burns almost completely in a very short time. Another 30% of the air is added in the secondary zone to complete the combustion. Finally, in the tertiary zone the remaining air is mixed with the hot gases to cool them to the correct temperature. (See Fig. 23).

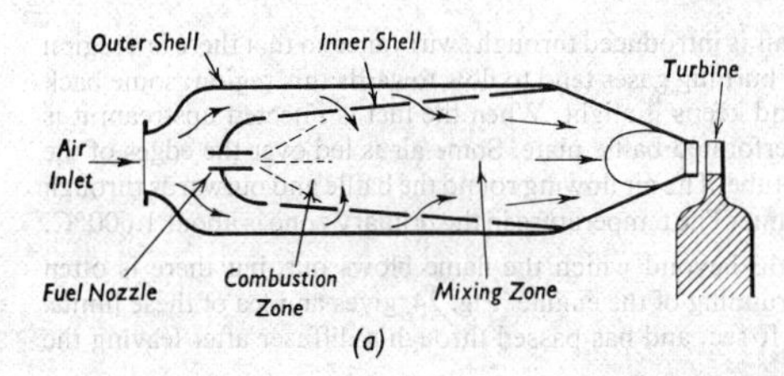

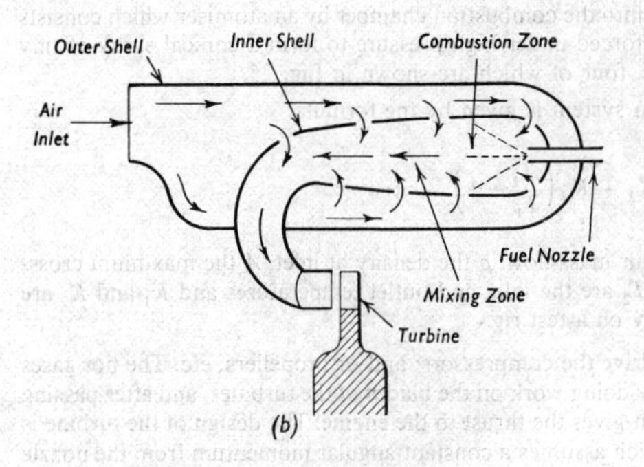

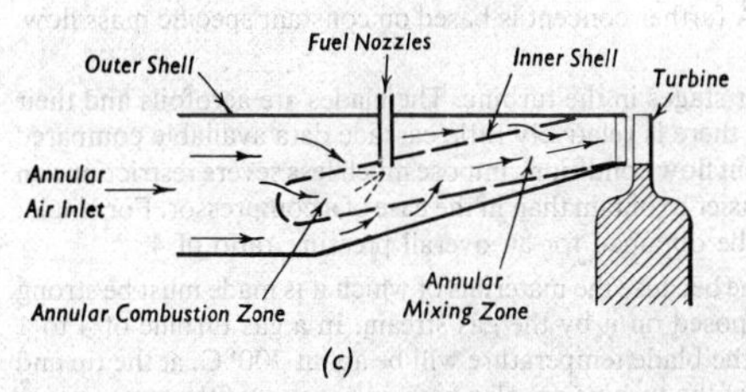

FIG. 23.—Combustion Chambers. (*a*) Cannular. (*b*) Reverse-Flow. (*c*) Annular.

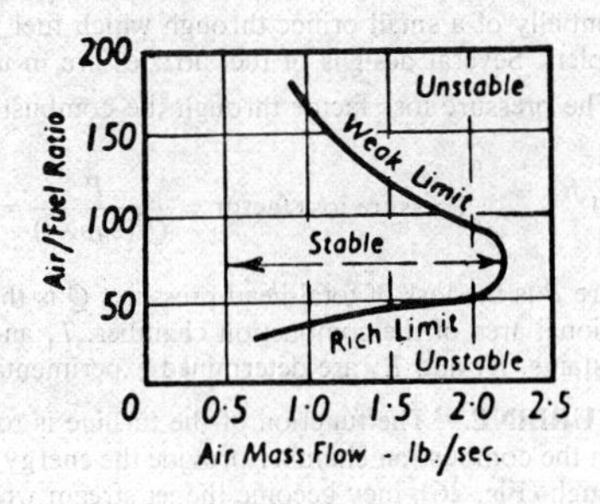

FIG. 24.—Stability loop. Air/Fuel Mixtures.

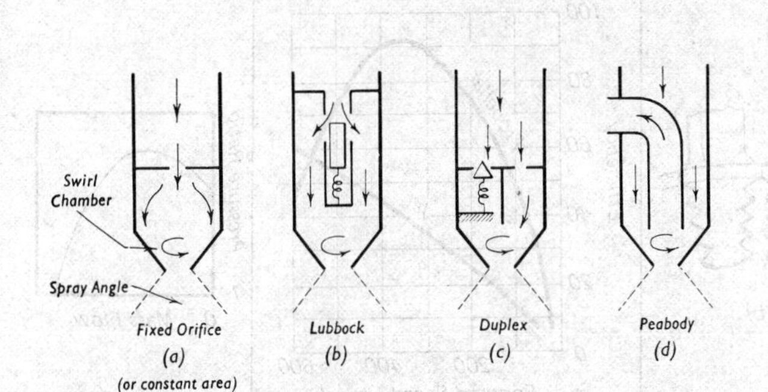

FIG. 25.—Types of Fuel Nozzles.

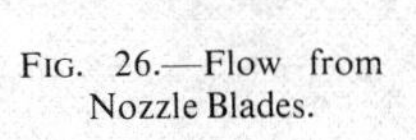

FIG. 26.—Flow from Nozzle Blades.

When the fuel is injected downstream, the primary air is introduced through swirl vanes so that there is a region of low pressure along the axis of the chamber and the burning gases tend to flow towards this region; some back flow of the hot gases feeds back into the jet of fuel and keeps it alight. When the fuel is injected upstream it is sprayed around a sheet metal cone supported by a perforated baffle plate. Some air is led over the edges of the baffle plate to flow along the inner surface of the flame tube. The air flowing round the baffle and outwards through the cone combine to produce the recirculation of the flame. The temperature in the primary zone is about 1,600°C.

There are rich and weak limits to the air/fuel ratio beyond which the flame blows out, but there is often instability within narrower limits as shown by rough running of the engine. Fig. 24 gives an idea of these limits. The inlet air velocity is usually not greater than 250 ft/sec. and has passed through a diffuser after leaving the compressor to reduce its value to about half.

British jet engines burn kerosine. This is injected into the combustion chamber by an atomiser which consists essentially of a small orifice through which fuel is forced under high pressure to form a conical spray of tiny droplets. Several designs of fuel nozzles are in use, four of which are shown in Fig. 25.

The pressure loss factor through the combustion system is given by the formula:

$$\text{Pressure loss factor} = \frac{P}{Q^2(2g\rho A^2)} = K_1 + K_2\left(\frac{T_2}{T_1} - 1\right)$$

where P is the loss of total-head pressure, Q is the air mass flow, ρ the density at inlet, A the maximum cross-sectional area of the combustion chamber, T_1 and T_2 are the inlet and outlet temperatures and K_1 and K_2 are constants. K_1 and K_2 are determined experimentally on a test rig.

TURBINE.—The function of the turbine is to drive the compressors, and/or propellers, etc. The hot gases from the combustion chamber provide the energy by doing work on the blades of the turbines, and after passing through (Fig. 26), they become the jet stream which gives the thrust to the engine. The design of the turbine is based on a concept of so-called free vortex flow, which assumes a constant angular momentum from the nozzle and a constant axial velocity at all radii of the blades. A further concept is based on constant specific mass flow, that is, the mass flow per unit area is constant.

In aircraft engines there are usually only two to four stages in the turbine. The blades are aerofoils and their performance is calculated from aerodynamic data, but there is relatively little cascade data available compared with that for compressor cascades. The largely convergent flow conditions impose much less severe restrictions on the design and the high efficiency of a turbine is much easier to obtain than in the case of a compressor. For single-stage turbines a static efficiency of 87% to 90% can be obtained for an overall pressure ratio of 4.

Blade temperature is a limiting condition in the turbine because the materials of which it is made must be strong enough at that temperature to withstand the forces imposed on it by the gas stream. In a gas turbine of 4 to 1 pressure ratio and a maximum temperature of 800°C. the blade temperature will be about 700°C. at the tip and 20° to 30°C. lower at the root. The stresses in the disc of the turbine are also high on account of the temperature and the requirement of a high power/weight ratio to give the maximum work output at high speed and high temperature. Single-stage turbine discs for aircraft engines are stressed as high as 15 tons/in with a rim temperature of 500°C. and over.

Blade vibration is also a factor limiting the life of the turbine and there are many modes of vibration which are not accurately calculable. Experience has so far been more fruitful than theory in solving the vibration problems of gas turbines. The attachment of the blade to the disc is of importance and two methods are shown in Fig. 27; alternatively the blades have fixed fins.

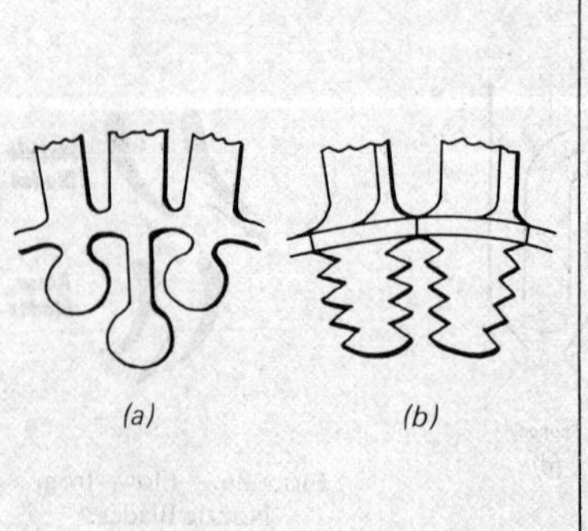

FIG. 27.—Turbine blade Root Fittings. (*a*) Modified De Laval type; (*b*) Fir-tree type.

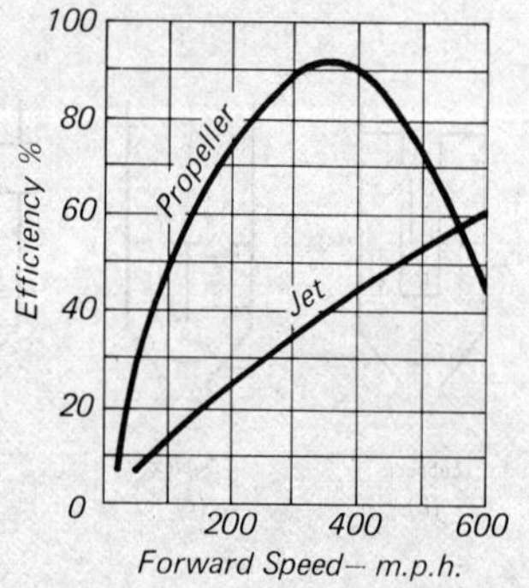

FIG. 28.—Propulsion efficiency.

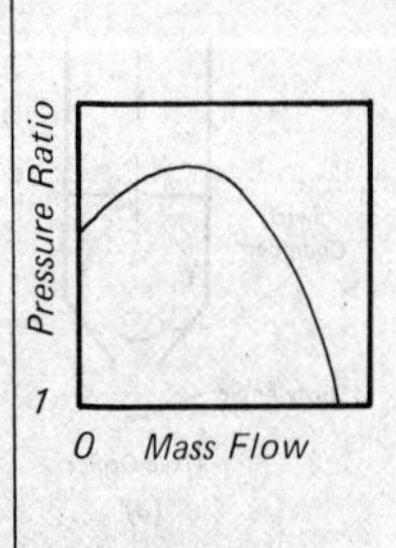

FIG. 29.—Theoretical characteristic.

SUPERSONIC FLIGHT.—A jet engine for subsonic flight differs from that for supersonic flight. The modifications include a supersonic diffuser to precede the subsonic diffuser in front of the axial flow compressor, the inlet area of the engine is variable to cover the much wider range of inflow conditions, the tail pipe is generally equipped with an afterburner for reheat, and the exhaust nozzle area must be variable. The compressor has to operate over a much wider range of conditions and have a much larger air capacity, while still maintaining a small frontal area. It is of the two-spool axial type. The turbine must operate with the highest possible inlet temperature. As the supersonic flight speeds increase, the stagnation temperature of the air increases rapidly, which affects the temperature in the compressor. At Mach 3, at an altitude of 35,000 ft, the outlet temperature of the compressor will reach about 500°C for a pressure ratio of 6, and 600°C, for a pressure ratio of 12, so that the blades of the compressor will be subjected to increasingly higher temperatures. Ignition of the combustible mixture becomes more critical when the static pressure of the combustion air is reduced; the range of ignitable mixtures decreases and the rich and lean inflammability limits approach each other. This problem during flight at the highest altitudes is corrected by the increase in the Mach number, which tends to raise the inlet static pressure to satisfactory values. Also, increasing the temperature of the air entering the combustion chamber, helps to vaporise the fuel, with the result that the combustion efficiency is increased. There will be a wide range of air-inlet velocities to the combustion chambers, ranging from 120 to 250 ft per sec, and lower inlet air pressures; the higher speed makes the achievement of good combustion efficiency difficult at the higher supersonic flight speeds. A converging-diverging type of exhaust nozzle is essential, and with reheat it must be possible to vary the throat and exhaust areas independently.

PROPULSIVE EFFICIENCY.—Both jet propulsion and propeller drive are fundamentally the same. The former uses a very high-speed jet of small diameter and the latter a lower speed jet of air of much larger diameter. A mass of air is expelled rearwards and there is a change of momentum. The power supplied in the two cases may be the same, but the energy—$\frac{1}{2}mv^2$—is utilised to produce different amounts of momentum, mv, depending on the relative proportions of m and v. The efficiency of propulsion is dependent on the ratio of the velocity, v, of the fluid expelled to the velocity, u, of the aircraft. The Froude efficiency is

$$\eta_f = 2u/(u + v)$$

The jet velocity is at least 1,700–1,800 ft per sec. so that its efficiency is small at low speeds and rapidly increases at high speeds as shown in Fig. 28. The propeller efficiency becomes low at speeds of the order of 550 m.p.h., but a gas turbine increases in efficiency due to the ram effect of high forward speed so that the intake air provides an appreciable supercharging effect.

The biggest factor in the use of the gas turbine is the possibility of very large powers. An increase of power is obtained by an increase of general dimensions and a large gas turbine involves no more complication than a small one. The rapid development in size and power has been great; for example, the early 'Welland' with a thrust of 1,600 lb has successors with over 50,000 lb thrust.

The equation governing the mass flow through the turbine is of the form:

$$\frac{Q\sqrt{(T_3)}}{P_3} = A\sqrt{\left\{\frac{\gamma g}{R}\left(\frac{2}{(\gamma + 1)}\right)^{(\gamma+1)/(\gamma-1)}\right\}}$$

where A is the total area of the nozzle throats and R is the gas constant.

NON-DIMENSIONAL PARAMETERS.—The non-dimensional parameters normally used for plotting compressor characteristics are P_2/P_1, T_2/T_1, $Q\sqrt{T_1}/P_1$ and $N/\sqrt{T_1}$ and for turbine characteristics are P_3/P_4, T_3/T_4, $Q\sqrt{T_3}/P_3$ and $N/\sqrt{T_2}$ where P is pressure and T is temperature and the suffixes 1, 2 refer to the inlet and outlet of the compressor and 3 and 4 to the inlet and outlet of the turbine; Q is the mass flow and N the rotational speed. A linear dimension should be included in the last two parameters to make them truly non-dimensional. Typical curves for the pressure ratios of an axial compressor and a turbine are given in Figs. 30 and 31 for different values of $N/\sqrt{T}$, the limitation in the former case being the surge line as shown and in the other the ordinate 1·0 corresponding with choking. The total-head efficiency curves for different values of $N/\sqrt{T}$ are shown in Figs. 31 and 33.

JET ENGINE TECHNOLOGY.—The trend in jet engine technology has always been towards higher turbine engine temperatures (T.E.T.'s), higher reheat temperatures, and higher overall pressure ratios; there has also been a trend to use high bypass ratios. The chosen configuration will often be a three-shaft engine in preference to a plain fan two-shaft engine or a coupled fan intermediate compressor two-shaft engine, depending on a particular company's experience.The three-shaft engine will have three spools, the intermediate compressor and H.P. compressor being driven by the corresponding turbine units and the fan by the L.P. turbine. The common bypass ratio in 1976 was 5·0, the overall pressure ratio 20:1, and the design T.E.T. about 1,600 K. Since then, the overall pressure ratio has been raised to 25, the T.E.T. to 1,800 K, and the reheat temperature from about 1,850 K, to 2,100 K.

A smaller engine will result from the advanced technology with the fan diameter being reduced from 33·0 in. to 27·5 in.; the tail-pipe diameter from 38·5 in. to 28 in.; the nozzle diameter maximum from 32 in. to 24 in.; the basic engine length from 95 in. to 60 in.; the tail-pipe length from 85 in. to 40 in.; giving overall lengths of 180 in.

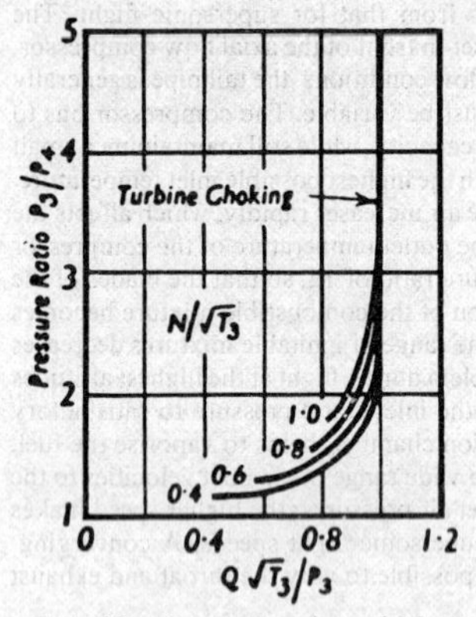

FIG. 30.—Pressure ratio and Mass Flow Characteristics. Axial Compressor.

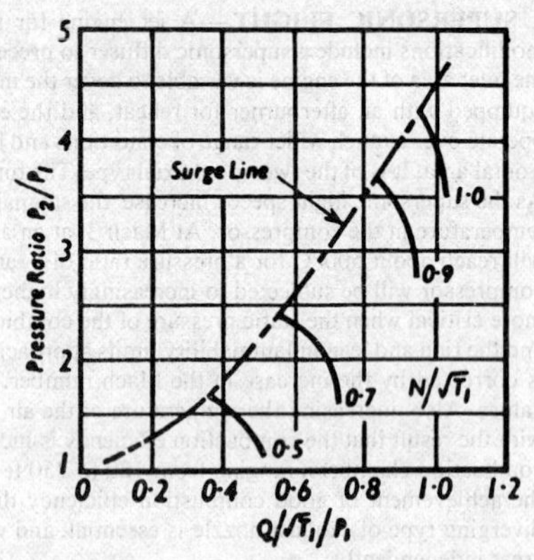

FIG. 31.—Pressure ratio/Mass Flow Characteristics. Turbine.

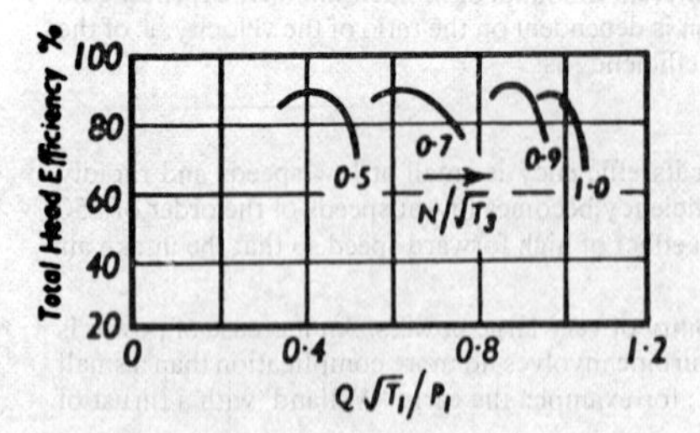

FIG. 32.—Axial Compressor Characteristics.

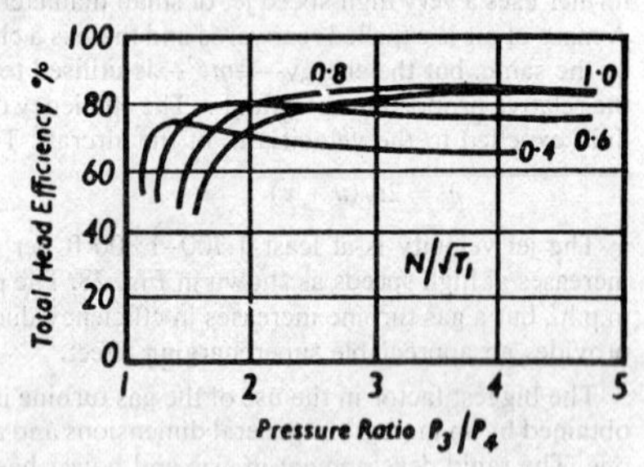

FIG. 33.—Turbine characteristics. Total-head efficiency/pressure ratio.

and 100 in. respectively. The thrust/weight ratio will increase from 6 to 10 lb/lb. and the thrust/frontal area ratio from 14·3 to 27·2 lb/in².

The T.E.T. increase has been obtained by the use of better materials; increased cooling air, quantity and quality, perhaps with a heat exchanger; and improved blade cooling techniques leading up to transpiration cooling. The achievement of higher reheat temperatures may be unstable at altitude if 'reheat buzz' is present; the high performance must be obtained within a minimum volume reheat chamber, the burning length must be small, and to keep the frontal area small, the combustion must accept high entry flow Mach numbers. The overall pressure ratio for the advanced engine of 25:1 will have the fan compressor as the key component; for a given bypass ratio, the design fan pressure ratio will increase to over 3:1 with an increase in T.E.T.; the aerodynamic design of the higher pressure spools provides for minimum weight while matching turbine requirements, which means a minimum number of stages and a good surge margin; the ultimate objective is to get the maximum aerodynamic work out of slower running units in order to gain lighter and more reliable high temperature engines.

In conclusion the high overall pressure engine, and the high T.E.T., lead to small combustion chambers which are easier to cool and result in a shorter engine length; the size of the chamber being dictated by its ability to generate sufficient heat energy to accelerate the engine from a windmilling condition at high altitude.

BYPASS ENGINES.—Turbo-fan engines are capable of giving high efficiencies since a large amount of air can be taken through the outer part of the engine and then mixed with the hot gases from the turbine, after the turbine. This gives a greater mass flow through the engine at a lower speed and a lower temperature to provide a more powerful and a quieter propulsive jet. The bypass air can be several times the volume of the hot gases and designers have considered ratios up to 15 to 1. The General Electric TF-39 has a bypass ratio of 8 : 1; the highest bypass ratio current in 1969 of any high efficiency subsonic engine. It is described in some detail to show the recent trend of design.

The stimulus for the development of this engine came from the need to provide the world's largest transport, C-5, with a demonstrable long life engine, plus reliability for 30,000 hours, for the cold parts including all structural frames, and half that life for the hot section parts when flown in typical 4·5 hour missions. In view of the length of the mission it was necessary to have superior fuel economy. In parallel with this military engine, a commercial CF-6 engine was derived, utilising the same core engine with a modified low pressure turbine and a new smaller diameter, high pressure ratio, quieter fan. For both a low smoke combustor was developed. Fig. 34. is a diagram of a typical high bypass ratio turbofan, such as TF-39, in which the fan thrust generates about 85% of the total jet thrust.

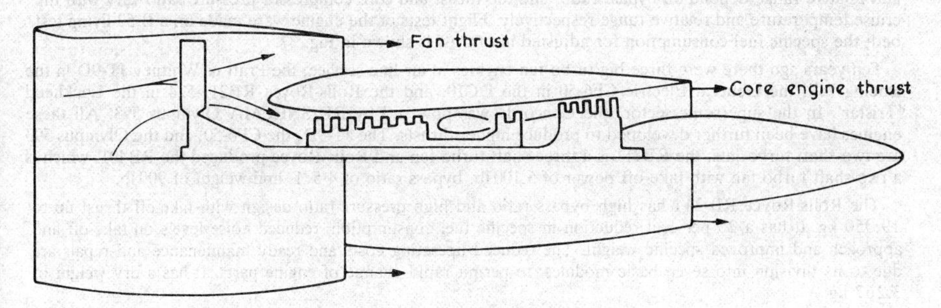

FIG. 34.—Typical High-Bypass Ratio Turbofan.

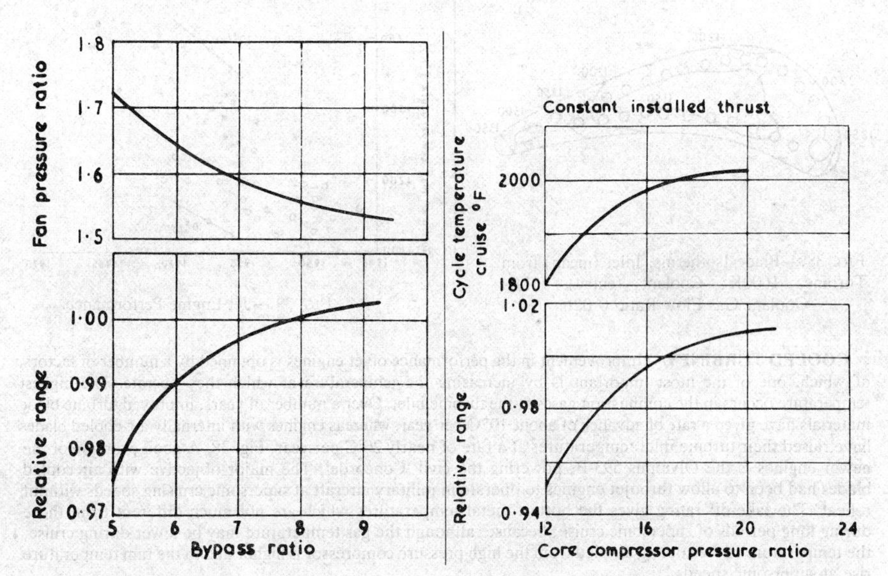

FIG. 35.—Fan Pressure Ratio and Relative Range vs Bypass Ratio.

FIG. 36.—Effect of Core Compressor-Pressure Ratio on Relative Range.

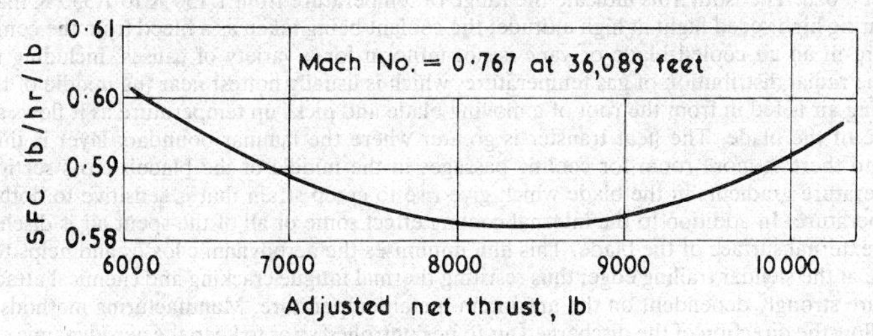

FIG. 37.—Altitude Performance.

Modern gas producers are very efficient so that the majority of the total propulsive thrust can come from the fan which is driven from the low pressure turbine spool, as shown. The fan pressure ratio is established on propulsive efficiency considerations for the aircraft mission and for speed requirements, and then the total fan flow is established to meet the required thrust levels. The bypass ratio of 8 : 1, and fan pressure of 1·55, was selected as a near optimum combination based on Fig. 35, and Fig. 36. These figures indicate how the fan pressure ratio and relative range depend on bypass ratio, and the thrust and core compressor pressure ratio vary with the cruise temperature and relative range respectively. Flight tests of the engine were made on a B-52 flying test bed; the specific fuel consumption for adjusted net thrust is shown in Fig. 37.

Ten years ago there were three big turbo-fan engines in air-line service; the Pratt & Whitney JT-9D in the Boeing 747; the General Electric CF6-50 in the DC10; and the Rolls-Royce RB211-524 in the Lockheed 'Tristar'. In the supersonic sector, the Concorde was powered by RR/SNECMA Olympus 593. All these engines have been further developed to produce higher thrusts. The JT-9D, the CF6-50, and the Olympus 593 are two-shaft turbo-jets; the RB211 is a three-shaft turbo-fan and Rolls-Royce produced the RB401, which is a two-shaft turbo-fan with take-off power of 5,100 lb. bypass ratio of 4·5 : 1, and weight of 900 lb.

The Rolls-Royce RB-211 has high bypass ratio and high pressure-ratio design with take-off thrust up to 19,050 kg. It has a 25 per cent reduction in specific fuel consumption, reduced noise levels on take-off and approach and improved specific weight. The reduced operating costs and ready maintenance and repair are due to its division into seven basic modules, to permit rapid change of engine parts. It has a dry weight of 3,267 kg.

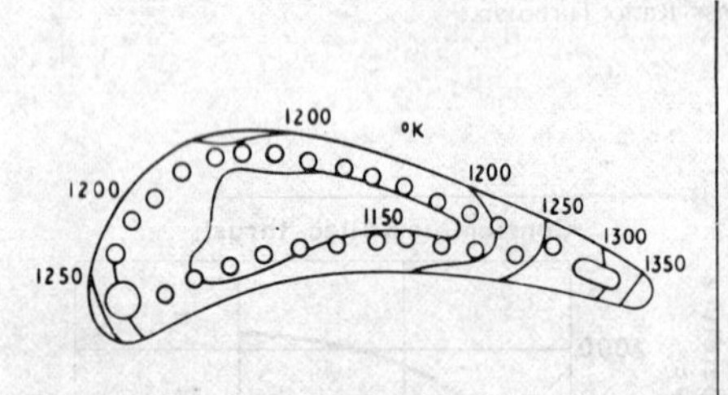

FIG. 38.—Blade Isotherms. Inlet (mean) from Turbine. 1600K; Coolant (entry) 773K: Coolant/Gas Flow Ratio 0·026.

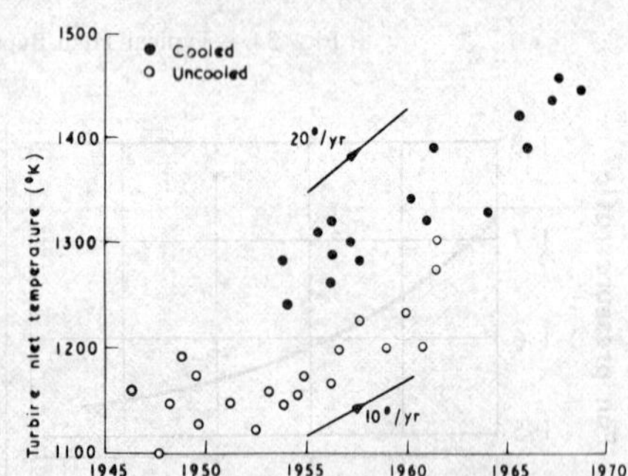

FIG. 39.—Jet Engine Performance.

COOLED TURBINES.—Improvement in the performance of jet engines is obtained by a number of factors, of which, one of the most important is by increasing the temperature at which they operate. The highest temperature occurs in the combustion gases at the turbine inlet. Over a number of years, improved turbine blade materials have given a rate of advance of about 10°C per year, whereas engines with internally air-cooled blades have raised their turbine inlet temperatures at a rate of nearly 20°C per year, Fig. 38. A good example of the newer engines is the Olympus 593-B, powering the civil 'Concorde'. The major objective with air cooled blades had been to allow turbojet engines to operate in military aircraft at supersonic cruising speeds without reheat. The take-off rating gives the hottest metal temperatures which are not much different from those during long periods of supersonic cruise, because, although the gas temperature may be lower during cruise, the temperature of the cooling air bled from the high pressure compressor is higher due to the ram temperature rise at supersonic speeds.

It can be observed in Fig. 39 the results of a computation of the heat flow in a typical turbine blade for a mean inlet temperature of 1,600°K, a coolant supply temperature of 773°K in the blade root, and a coolant gas flow ratio of 0·026. The isotherms indicate the range of temperature from 1,150°K to 1,350°K that can be encountered during high speed flight at high altitude; the coolant being taken as a bleed from the compressor. The temperature in an air-cooled blade or vane is not uniform for a variety of causes, including the non-uniformity in the radial distribution of gas temperature, which is usually hottest near the middle of the blade span. The cooling air is fed in from the root of a moving blade and picks up temperature as it flows spanwise along the inside of the blade. The heat transfer is greater where the laminar boundary layer is thin at the leading edge and there is more room for cooling passages in the middle of the blade's cross section. Thus there are temperature gradients in the blade which give rise to creep strain that is sensitive to both applied stress and temperature. In addition to the internal cooling effect some or all of the spent air is discharged as a film over the external surface of the blade. This film minimises the aerodynamic losses and helps to reduce the temperature at the slender trailing edge; thus resisting thermal fatigue cracking and chemical attack there, both of which are strongly dependent on the maximum metal temperature. Manufacturing methods need to be evolved to allow the direction of the discharged air to be controlled so as to keep the aerodynamic efficiency penalty to a minimum. Fig. 40 indicates what can be achieved with a transpiration cooled turbine in a bypass engine intended for supersonic flight.

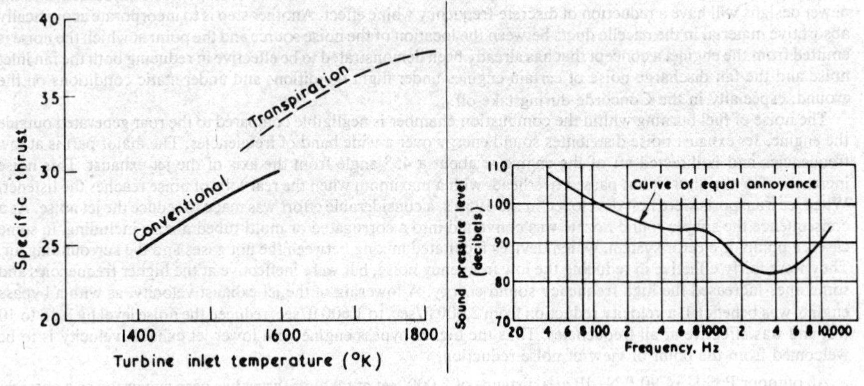

FIG. 40.—Specific Thrust at Mach 2·2 (Engine Bypass Ratio = 1).

FIG. 41.—Equal Noisiness Curve.

The upward trend of the graph in Fig. 40 indicates what could be obtained with higher turbine inlet gas pressures by using transpiration cooling techniques that will need adequate cooling air supply pressure to drive the coolant through the very fine passages forming a porous surface. At present it is only the turbine blades in the first stages that need cooling, but, as temperatures increase, more and more rows of vanes and blades will need to have cooling air passed through them. It is also probable that further advances will come with nickel-base alloys that have better creep strength accompanied by more resistance to corrosion, impact damage and fatigue.

ENGINE NOISE.—With the steadily increasing power of airliners the problem of noise in the neighbourhood of airports has assumed increasing importance. Moreover, as the power of an aircraft's engine increases, so will the noise, unless something is done to ameliorate it. The ear is most sensitive to noise in the 3,000 to 4,000 Hz region; for example, the human ear finds a noise of 100 decibels (dB) at 100 vibrations a second (Hz) to be as noisy as one of only 90 dB at 1,000 Hz, or one of 80 dB at 4,000 Hz. The relative loudness of noise at different frequencies has been based on listener's response tests. It is measured in what is known as the P.N.L. unit, of the International Standards Organisation, as a basic unit of annoyance for aircraft flyover noise, rated at different distances from, and heights above, the observer. Fig. 41 shows a curve of equal annoyance for a range of frequencies.

The question of noise has influenced considerably the design of the aircraft engine, and for this and other reasons, engines of higher bypass ratios are being designed for civil aircraft. The next generation of engines will have a low tip speed for the fan, no fan-inlet guide vanes, large axial spacing between the fan blades and the outlet guide vanes, and a high ratio of outlet guide vanes to fan blades. However, much has already been done with the present generation of engines to reduce noise. The sources of noise are several (see Fig. 42). They include fan noise directed forward of the engine; fan noise from the fan exhaust directed backwards; compressor noise projected forwards; combustion noise; turbine noise directed backwards; and jet exhaust noise from the mixing of the hot gases and the ambient air directed backwards and sideways. An indication has been given above of what can be done concerning fan noise, but other factors contribute to the total engine noise, as described below.

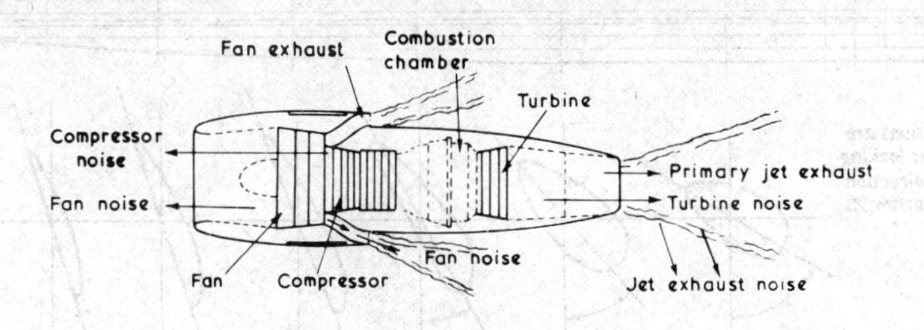

FIG. 42.—Turbofan Engine Noise Sources.

In some of the low bypass ratio turbofans, the fan whine or screech generated by the fan stages, was higher in noise level than either the compressor or turbine noises, and the P.N.L. value rated the fan noise to be more annoying than the jet exhaust noise even at take-off thrust. The blade/fan relationships will be modified, and the newer designs will have a reduction of discrete-frequency whine effect. Another step is to incorporate acoustically absorptive material in the nacelle ducts between the location of the noise source and the point at which the noise is emitted from the engine, a concept that has already been demonstrated to be effective in reducing both the fan inlet noise and the fan discharge noise of certain engines under flight conditions and under static conditions on the ground, especially in the Concorde during take-off.

The noise of fuel burning within the combustion chamber is negligible compared to the roar generated outside the engine. Jet exhaust noise distributes sound energy over a wide band of frequencies. The major part is at low frequencies and is directed aft of the engine at about a 45° angle from the axis of the jet exhaust. This noise increases after the aircraft has passed overhead, with a maximum when the rear lobe of noise reaches the listener. When jet transports were first developed in the 1950's, a considerable effort was made to reduce the jet noise. As a consequence the simple round nozzle was converted into a corrugated or multi-tubed nozzle including, in some cases, a pump or ejector system, which devices facilitated mixing between the hot gases and the surrounding air. They were fairly effective in reducing the low frequency noise, but were ineffective at the higher frequencies and sometimes increased the high frequency sound energy. A lowering of the jet-exhaust velocity, as with a bypass engine, was beneficial: a velocity reduction from 2,000 ft/sec. to 1,600 ft/sec. reduced the noise level by 8 dB to 10 dB, and was effective at all frequencies. Thus the higher bypass engine with lower jet exhaust velocity is to be welcomed from the point of view of noise reduction.

An outdoor P.N.L. of 90 P.N. dB at a distance of 8,000 feet at take-off thrust has been suggested as a possible threshold of serious annoyance in airport neighbourhoods, and the same value at approach thrust at 3,400 feet, but this may be difficult to realise so that aircraft, especially supersonic airliners, will have to fly at much less than full power rating near airports and surrounding country, to reach anything approaching this low level of noise.

The problem of fuel for the aircraft of the future, and the depletion of the world's hydrocarbon fuel reserves, has led to the search for alternatives. Manned space projects have demonstrated that liquid hydrogen can be manufactured, handled and used safely in large quantities. Leading manufacturers of air-liners have worked out the basic configurations and designs for aircraft run on liquid hydrogen. McDonnell Douglas have made models for wind tunnel tests, to demonstrate that passengers can be carried in air-liners with this fuel, within the next decade. Moreover, liquid hydrogen is the cleanest burning of all fuels.

PROPULSION BY PROPELLER

This is still the most common form of aircraft propulsion. The jet is gradually replacing it in the faster aircraft types, but there will always be a field of usefulness for the propeller in the slower machines. Descriptions have been given of turboprop propulsion, the combination of the jet engine with the propeller, which has ousted the piston-propeller combination for aircraft of the intermediate speeds used for transport purposes. There will, however, always remain aircraft which will retain piston engines. The small personal plane will mostly be designed to fly at low speeds and land in small areas, for which the jet-propelled plane is not suitable.

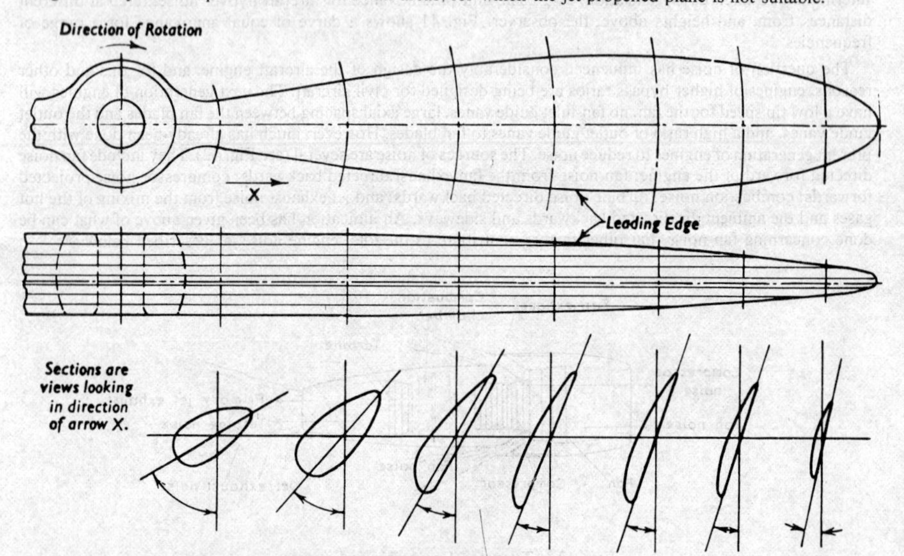

FIG. 43.—Typical Wooden Propeller showing Laminations.

The propeller is the means whereby the torque of the engine is converted into thrust, the propeller giving a large slipstream of air at low velocity compared with the much smaller jet of air of very greatly increased speed from the gas turbine.

THE PROPELLER.—See Fig. 43. The shape of the blade changes continually along its length as shown for a wooden propeller. The sections for a metal propeller are much thinner. The performance of the propeller can be calculated from each cross section bearing in mind the angle at which each aerofoil meets the relative wind as indicated in Fig. 44. A typical set of characteristic curves is shown in Fig. 45.

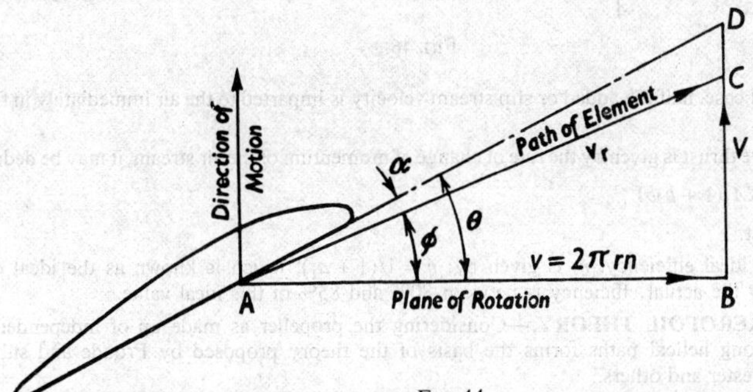

FIG. 44.

PROPELLER THEORIES.—A number of theories have been put forward by means of which expressions for thrust, torque and efficiency may be obtained. Among the most important are: (*a*) the Froude momentum theory; (*b*) the simple aerofoil theory; (*c*) the inflow theory.

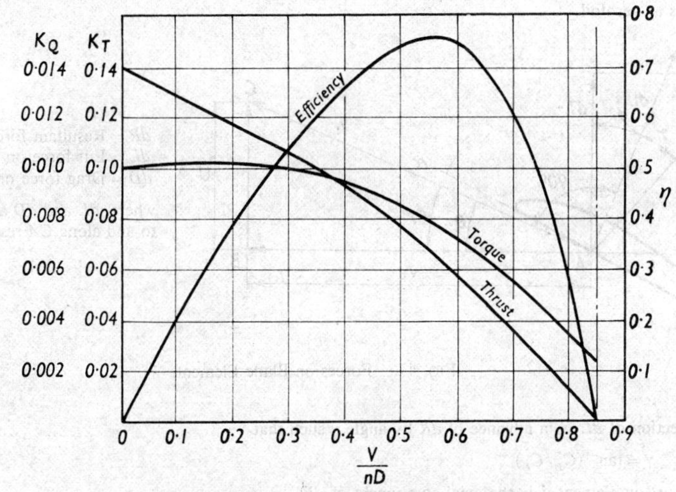

FIG. 45.—Characteristic Curves for a Propeller.

THE FROUDE MOMENTUM THEORY.—In propounding this theory Froude supposed the actual propeller replaced by an ideal one consisting of an imaginary disc in whose plane an instantaneous change of pressure occurred under working conditions.

Regarding the propeller as stationary, the ingoing and outgoing streams are indicated in Fig. 46. On the upstream face of the disc there is a region of negative pressure which causes acceleration, and on the downstream face the pressure changes to a positive value which increases the velocity of air in the outgoing slip-stream of smaller diameter.

The outgoing stream contracts, making the slipstream velocity V_2 greater than V_1.

Thus $V_2 = V_1(1 + b)$, where b is the outflow factor.

Neglecting losses, it may be shown that.

$$V_0 = V_1(1 + b/2) = V_1(1 + a_1)$$

where a_1 is the inflow factor.

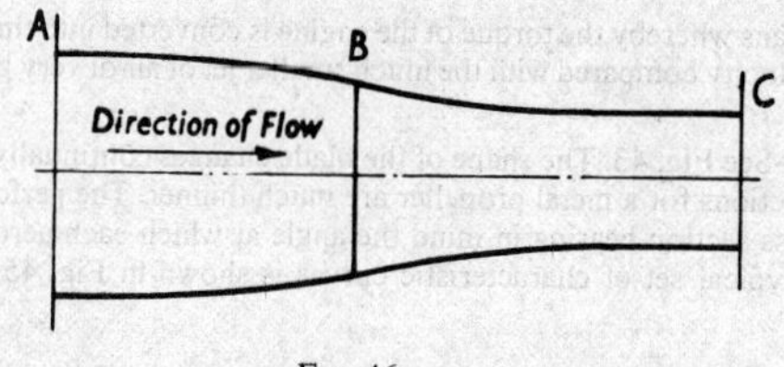

FIG. 46.

Hence in the ideal case, half the added or slip stream velocity is imparted to the air immediately in front of the propeller.

Thrust.—Since the thrust is given by the rate of change of momentum of the air stream, it may be deduced that,

$$T = \rho K A_0(1 + b)bV_1^2$$

where T is the thrust.

Efficiency.—The ideal efficiency, η, is given by: $\eta = 1/(1 + a_1)$, which is known as the ideal or Froude efficiency. Generally the actual efficiency is between 80% and 85% of this ideal value.

THE SIMPLE AEROFOIL THEORY.—Considering the propeller as made up of independent aerofoil elements moving along helical paths forms the basis of the theory proposed by Froude and subsequently developed by Lanchester and others.

Axial inflow as indicated in the momentum theory is neglected, the velocity of air relative to the propeller and immediately in front of its plane being taken as V, the translational speed of the aircraft.

Forces Acting on Blade Element.—Fig. 47 shows the forces acting on an element of blade at radius r from the axis and substituting V for U and ϕ for ϕ_1, the diagram is applicable to the present case. We have, treating the element as an aerofoil,

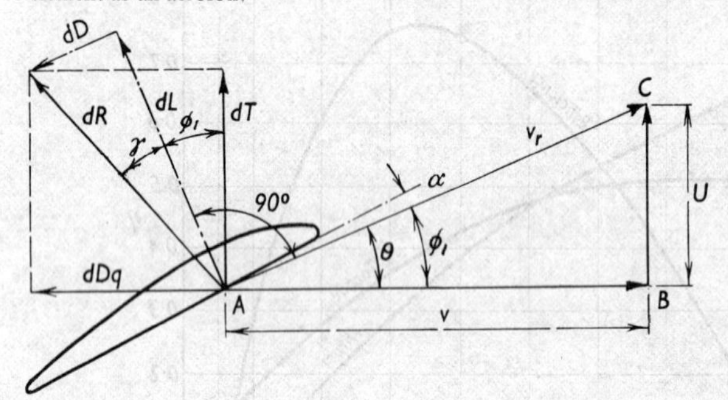

dR = Resultant force on element
dL = Lift force on element
dD = Drag force on element

where, dL and dD act normal to and along CA respectively.

FIG. 47.—Forces on Blade Element.

The direction of dL is in advance of dR by angle γ such that

$$\gamma = \tan^{-1}(C_D/C_L)$$

dT = thrust on element, i.e., the axial component of dR,
dD_q = transverse component acting at radius r from axis of rotation,
dQ = torque reaction on element,

then

$$dT = dR \cos(\phi + \gamma)$$
$$dD_q = dR \sin(\phi + \gamma)$$
$$dQ = rdR \sin(\phi + \gamma)$$

Efficiency of Whole Propeller.—The efficiency of the whole propeller is given by:

$$\eta = \text{work done by propeller/work done by engine}$$

which reduces to

$$\eta = \frac{\tan\phi}{\tan(\phi + \gamma)}$$

On this basis, the efficiency of the element is maximum when $\phi = 45° - \gamma/2$.

Since $\gamma/2$ is small, this means that the maximum efficiency occurs when the rotational and translational speeds of the element are approximately equal.

The efficiency may be taken to be that of an element situated at a distance from the axis of about two-thirds tip radius. Thus, if an element so situated is working under the above condition, the propeller would be working approximately at its maximum efficiency.

THE INFLOW THEORY.—The simple theory, which was the first to be applied to design, generally gave efficiencies which were in excess of those obtained in practice. This led to the adoption of the inflow theory which allowed for the fact that the air immediately in front of the propeller has a velocity greater than that of its translation.

The axial inflow factor a_1 may be obtained experimentally for any given model or it may be calculated.

There is experimental evidence that in addition to axial flow, a rotational inflow also exists, acting towards the boss. This is, however, small and is generally neglected.

Helix Angle of Blade Element.—Fig. 47 shows the forces acting on an element of blade, as already described, but in arriving at the helix angle ϕ_1, the velocity of the air passing the propeller disc is now given by

$$U = V(1 + a_1)$$

and

$$\tan\phi_1 = \frac{U}{\omega r} = \frac{V(1 + a_1)}{2\pi rn}.$$

Efficiency of Blade Element.—The efficiency of the element now becomes

$$\eta_a = \frac{1}{1 + a_1} \cdot \frac{\tan\phi_1}{\tan(\phi_1 + \gamma)}$$

The Total Thrust and Torque per Blade.—For any element of blade having chord c, treating the element as an aerofoil the resultant force dR on it is $dR = c_l \rho\, c\, dr\, v_r^2 \sec\gamma$

$$\text{Total thrust/blade } T_b = \int_0^R pc \sec\gamma \cos(\phi_1 + \gamma)\, dr$$

$$\text{Total torque/blade } Q_b = \int_0^R pcr \sec\gamma \sin(\phi_1 + \gamma)\, dr$$

where pressure/ft^2 or air loading of blade $= C_L - \rho vr$

The efficiency of the whole blade is,

$$\eta_b = \frac{V}{\omega} \cdot \frac{T_b}{Q_b}.$$

The efficiency of the best propellers is in the region of 93%.

VARIABLE PITCH PROPELLERS.—The variable pitch, constant speed propeller is an essential feature of aircraft using either piston or gas turbine engines. The pitch or inclination of the blades is adjusted in flight, whilst maintaining a constant speed, to absorb the power generated by the engine. The constant speed propeller may be controlled manually or by automatic feathering and reversing, but there is a safety lock to guard against the inadvertent operation of the latter. Propellers on turbo-propeller aircraft usually have hydraulic operation for the pitch control, although electrical forms have been used, and there are additional automatic safety lock features to avoid dangerous overspeeding in the event of control system failure. The engine and propeller r.p.m. are automatically synchronised to eliminate 'beats' in modern multi-engined aircraft. Electric de-icing of the propeller and spinner is common practice.

Three and four-bladed propellers are in general use, and propellers with a great number of blades have been manufactured for special aircraft. The tendency is to develop the four-bladed propeller. Contra-rotating propellers are paired on a common axis and were introduced to absorb greater horse-power with the same overall diameter. Two three-bladed contra-rotating propellers are more efficient than a six bladed for the reason that the rear propeller rotates in the opposite direction, and reduces rotational losses. Special engine reduction gear for the contra-rotating pair of propellers adds considerably to weight, complication and cost, but they are fitted to some aircraft.

The power that has to be absorbed by a propeller continues to increase. The piston engine has reached a maximum of 4,000 b.h.p., but the limit for turbo-propeller power unit is much higher and, in America, units have been designed with outputs up to 15,000 b.h.p. The turboprop is replacing the piston engine except for

horse-powers below about 1,000. In general, for aircraft speeds of up to 500 m.p.h., a propeller combination is more efficient than a jet engine; but turbofans with high by-pass ratio are becoming predominant.

BLADE MATERIALS.—Solid duralumin and hollow steel blades are the main materials used for sections of the N.A.C.A. 16 and 65 Aerofoil Series. The blades have a thickness/chord of 4% at the tip and of 6% at the 0·7 radius, which give a cruising efficiency of 85% at 450 m.p.h., and a little less at 500 m.p.h. The strength of these materials tends to limit a further reduction in the thickness/chord ratio to obtain higher efficiencies as the cruising speeds of aircraft increase.

Hollow steel blades are used where high engine powers and high cruising speeds demand a wide chord for the blade. The hollow construction decreases the blade weight and consequent centrifugal loads on the hub compared to solid duralumin blades, but is expensive in development and manufacture. Hollow duralumin blades are now being used with the wide blade chords. For other purposes the solid duralumin blade is predominant in propeller manufacture and is fitted to a large number of civil and military types of aircraft.

The propeller has to be strong to withstand not only the normal steady stress arising from power absorption and from the centrifugal loads, but also the alternating stresses arising from the aerodynamic excitations in torsion and in flexure. Cases have been known of propellers working satisfactorily at a stress of 27,500 lb/in^2 corresponding with a factor of safety of 2. The design has also to avoid serious resonances at the operational speed of the engine, and be strong enough for the vibration stresses due to asymmetric airflow into the propeller disc, due to proximity of the nacelle and the wing. Many tests are made on prototypes of a new propeller 55design, including spinning on a special spinning tower at the R.A.E.; strain gauge tests in an engine hangar; and in flight and engine hangar development tests. Functional and performance tests in an aircraft follow.

ALTITUDE TABLE—I.C.A.O. STANDARD ATMOSPHERE

Calculated from tables for every 100 ft. given in N.A.C.A. Report No. 1235: 1955.

Height ft. × 10^3	Pressure mb.	Pressure lb./ft.^{2}	Density lb. (mass/ft.^{3} × 10^4)	Relative Pressure × 10^3	Relative Density × 10^3	√(Relative Density) × 10^2	Temperature °C.
0	1,013	2,116	765	1,000	1,000	100	15·0
1	977	2,040	743	964	971	98·5	12·5
2	942	1,967	721	930	943	97·1	11·0
3	908	1,897	700	896	915	95·6	8·5
4	875	1,828	679	864	888	94·1	7·0
5	843	1,760	659	832	862	92·7	5·1
6	812	1,696	639	801	836	91·3	3·1
7	781	1,632	620	772	811	89·9	1·1
8	752	1,572	601	743	786	88·5	− 0·9
9	724	1,513	583	715	762	87·1	− 2·8
10	697	1,455	565	688	736	85·7	− 4·8
12	644	1,346	530	636	693	83·1	− 8·8
14	595	1,243	497	587	650	80·6	− 12·7
16	549	1,147	466	542	609	78·0	− 16·7
18	506	1,057	436	499	570	75·4	− 20·6
20	466	972	407	460	533	72·8	− 22·4
25	376	785	343	371	448	66·9	− 34·5
30	301	628	286	297	374	61·1	− 44·4
35	238	498	237	235	310	55·3	− 54·3
40	188	392	188	185	246	49·6	− 56·5
45	147	308	148	146	194	44·0	− 56·5
50	116	242	116	114	152	39·0	− 56·5
55	91	196	92	90	119	34·5	− 56·5
60	72	150	72	71	94	30·6	− 56·5
65	57	118	57	56	74	27·2	− 56·5
80	27·5	57	27·6	27	36	18·9	− 46·3
100	10·8	22·6	10·1	11	13·2	11·5	− 40·0
120	4·6	9·6	3·96	4·5	5·18	7·19	− 21·6
140	2·06	4·3	1·66	2·03	2·17	4·66	− 3·3
160	0·97	2·0	0·75	0·96	0·98	3·13	+ 9·7
180	0·46	0·97	0·364	0·46	0·48	2·19	+ 3·1
200	0·212	0·44	0·181	0·21	0·24	1·54	− 18·2
250	0·0218	0·045	·23(10^{-1})	0·021	·30(10^{-1})	0·55	− 71·5
300	1·68(10^{-3})	3·5(10^{-3})	·47(10^{-2})	1·7(10^{-3})	·62(10^{-2})	0·25	(− 70)
400	3·4(10^{-5})	7·0(10^{-5})	·21(10^{-4})	3·3(10^{-5})	·28(10^{-4})	0·02	(+ 68)

SUPERSONIC PROPELLERS.—In quite a number of cases propellers have been successfully flown, whose tip speed has exceeded the speed of sound. At such high tip speeds, the propeller becomes appreciably noisier. There are no operational aircraft in which the propeller is wholly supersonic, and unless some solution is found to reduce the prohibitive noise level, supersonic propellers are very unlikely to be fitted to civil aircraft. By 'wholly supersonic' is meant that the whole of the blade, from the spinner to the tip, is operating under supersonic conditions. Nevertheless, work has been done in more than one country on the development of a supersonic propeller made of solid steel, to give adequate strength for the thin blade (2%) that will be necessary at the propeller tip. Efficiencies of 79% are attainable for a supersonic propeller at, say, 600 m.p.h., but for operational propellers in aircraft of lower speeds, efficiencies have risen above 90%.

THE STANDARD ATMOSPHERE.—In order to afford a basis of comparison of full scale tests, an International Standard Atmosphere has been defined which corresponds with the average conditions in Western Europe. It is assumed that:

(i) The air is dry and its chemical composition the same at all altitudes, by volume being 78·03% nitrogen, 20·99% oxygen, 0·94% argon, and 0·04% carbon dioxide.

(ii) The temperature at mean sea-level is 15°C, and the barometric height reduced to 0°C. is 760 mm.

(iii) The weight of air under these conditions is 1·2257 kg/m³ (0·07656 lb/ft³). The value of 'g' is taken to be uniform at 980·62 cm/sec.² (32·17 ft/sec.²). The mass density ρ_0 of air at mean sea-level is therefore 0·00238 slug/ft³.

(iv) For any altitude Z metres above mean sea-level up to a limit of 11,000 metres, i.e. to the bottom of the stratosphere, the temperature (°C) varies thus:

$$\theta_Z = 15 - 0{\cdot}0065Z$$

(v) Above 11,000 metres θ is constant and equals to $-56{\cdot}5°C$.

(vi) It follows that for any altitude Z is less than 11,000 metres, where the barometric pressure is p_z and specific weight a_z and specific mass ρ_z, these quantities are connected by the equations:

$$\frac{p_z}{p_0} = \left(\frac{T_z}{T_0}\right)^{5\cdot256} = \left(\frac{288 - 0{\cdot}0065Z}{288}\right)^{5\cdot256}$$

and

$$\frac{\rho}{\rho_0} = \frac{a_z}{a_0} = \left(\frac{T_z}{T_0}\right)^{4\cdot256} = \left(\frac{288 - 0{\cdot}0065Z}{288}\right)^{5\cdot256}$$

(vii) For altitudes above 11,000 metres the relations are:

$$\log_{10}\frac{p_1}{p_z} = \log_{10}\frac{\rho_1}{\rho_z} = \log_{10}\frac{a_1}{a_z} = \frac{Z - 11{,}000}{14{,}600}$$

where suffix 1 refers to conditions at Z = 11,000 metres.

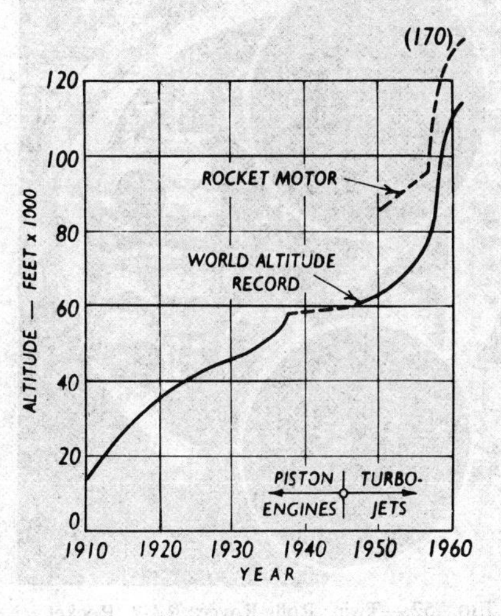

FIG. 48.

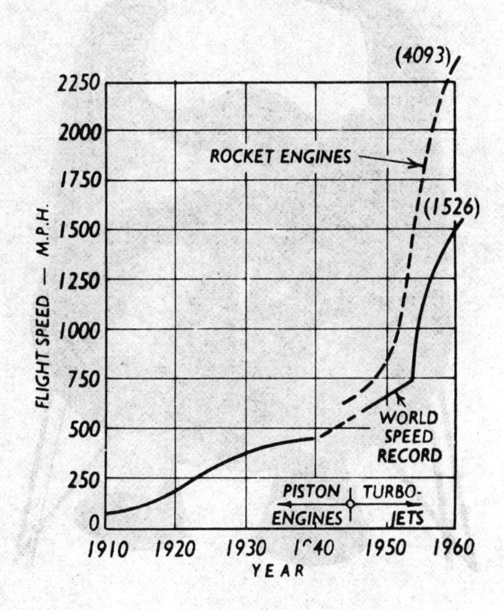

FIG. 49.

ROCKET ENGINES

Basically, a rocket consists of a cylindrical chamber, closed at one end and open at the other, which is maintained at a higher temperature than the surrounding atmosphere. This pressure acts on the closed end to provide a propulsive thrust which drives the cylinder forward. At the same time the pressure in the chamber forces the substance inside, usually a gas, out of the open end and a continuous supply of new material must be provided to maintain the thrust. A rocket carries with it a complete supply of chemicals for combustion which, when burnt, provide the gases for propulsion. The chemicals are either carried in separate tanks to save space as in the liquid-propellant rocket engines, or in a solid-propellant rocket motor in the cylindrical combustion chamber.

A rocket is inherently simple and consequently weighs very little in comparison with the thrust it produces. Unlike other forms of power units, it tends to consume its supply of propellants exceedingly quickly and provides a very high thrust for a relatively short time. Where a very high thrust is needed, a rocket has no competitor amongst other forms of motive power. Its adoption for special purposes has increased greatly in recent years, first in increasing the take-off power of aeroplanes and for powering fighter aircraft, more recently for military missiles and for astronautical purposes. Rocket propulsion has also been used experimentally for the propulsion of special sleds to investigate the effects of accelerations on human beings and on instruments as well as to propel motor vehicles, this last with little success because of the high power and short duration of the propulsive jet.

LIQUID PROPELLANT ROCKETS.—The first large rocket was the German V-2 rocket of 1939–45 war, which produced a thrust of 56,000 lbf when fed with liquid oxygen and a mixture of ethyl alcohol and water at the

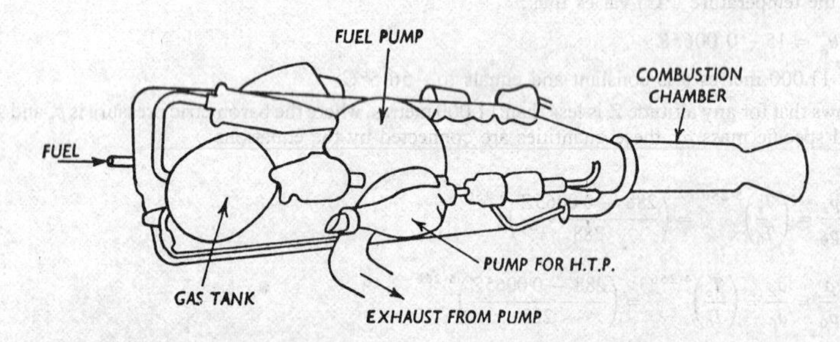

FIG. 50.—Rocket Engine.

FIG. 51.—Bristol Siddeley 'Gamma' Mk. 304.

FIG. 52.—Twin Rolls-Royce RZ-2 Rocket Engines.

rate of nearly 280 lb per second. Smaller rocket engines powered the short range German fighter aeroplane Me-163. The V-2 rocket engine was taken as a prototype after the war and one firm, the Rocketdyne Division of North American Aviation Inc., had developed, by 1961, kerosine burning units to thrusts exceeding one million pounds. A Reactions Motors Inc. rocket unit powered the first truly supersonic aeroplane, the XS-1, and rockets have been used in all the American research aircraft which have flown up to speeds with a Mach number greater than 6, and reached a height of 67 miles above the earth's surface. These performances, and even more the flights of space vehicles, are not possible except with rocket power. In addition, research rockets, using one or more stages and fired vertically from the ground, have reached speeds of over Mach 7 within two seconds of firing. The importance of rocket engines in enabling aircraft to improve performances can be seen from Figs. 48 and 49.

Fig. 50 shows a typical rocket engine for a fuel such as kerosine with the oxidant highly-concentrated peroxide (H.T.P.) as used in the Bristol Siddeley, Mk. 304, 'Gamma'. It has an oxidant to fuel ratio of 8·2 : 1, and S.I. of 250·5 *in vacuo* (see Fig. 51). Fig. 53 shows in diagrammatic form the working of this and other rocket engines. Turbines driven by high pressure gas or by gases from the main propellants at very high speeds drive centrifugal pumps to supply the oxidant and the fuel separately from their supply tanks to the combustion chamber. In order to cool the walls of the combustion chamber some, or all, of the fuel passes en route through a cooling jacket (Fig. 54) before entering the combustion chamber from the ejector. The fuel and oxidant mix in this chamber, sometimes igniting spontaneously on mixing and in other cases using a hyperbolic substance or other means to initiate ignition. The hot gases then pass through a convergent-divergent nozzle to form the exhaust jet of the rocket.

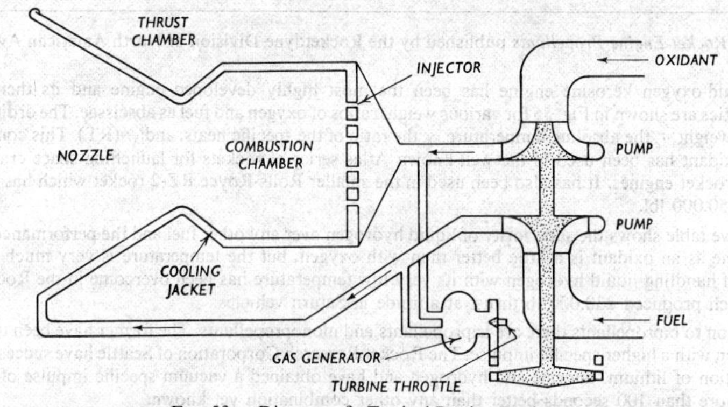

FIG. 53.—Diagram of a Typical Rocket Engine

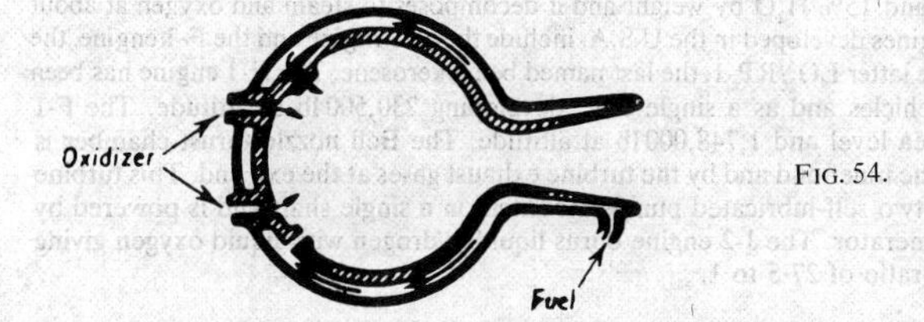

FIG. 54.

A variety of fuels and oxidants have been used in rockets. The fuels have included the hydrocarbons:—methane, propane and kerosine; compounds containing hydrogen and nitrogen; ammonia, hydrazine, unsymmetrical dimethyl hydrazine (U.D.M.H.), diethylenetriamine; the alcohols: methyl, ethyl and furfuryl alcohol; the boranes: diborane and pentaborane; and aluminium borohydride. The oxidising compounds have included oxygen, hydrogen peroxide, nitrogen tetroxide, nitric acid and fluorine with some of its compounds. The relatively low temperature obtained with alcohol fuels was an advantage in the early days of rocket development but their inferior performance led to their disuse. The amine compounds (those containing NH_2 groups) were cheap but their performance was not much better. This left aviation kerosine as an important and cheap liquid fuel and since methods of dealing with liquid hydrogen have been learnt this last fuel has been preferred to kerosine, hydrazine and liquid methane. The thrust of a rocket using any fuel is rated by its specific impulse (S.I.), which is the thrust per unit of propellant and can be thought of as the impulse (thrust multiplied by time) produced per unti mass of propellant. The S.I. is measured in pounds force seconds per pound mass (lbf s/lbm) and is often quoted as so many seconds. In the following table*, the S.I. is given for the four more important fuels and oxidants with the chamber temperatures in degrees Kelvin (°K), calculated on the bases of expansions at equilibrium (*e*) and frozen (*f*) compositions from a chamber pressure of 1,000 psia to atmospheric pressure at outlet.

Fuel/Oxidant	95% H_2O_2 +5% H_2O	Nitrogen tetroxide	Oxygen	Fluorine
Kerosine	266 (*f*) 273 (*e*) 2900°K	263 (*f*) 276 (*e*) 3250°K	286 (*f*) 300 (*e*) 3500°K	317 (*f*) for 79% F_2 + 21% O_2
Hydrazine	277 (*f*) 282(*e*) 3400°K	283 (*f*) 292(*e*) 3500°K	301 (*f*) 313(*e*) 3350°K	334 (*f*) 363(*e*) 4600°K
Liquid Methane			298 (*f*) 3300°K	332 (*f*) for 79% F_2 + 21% O_2 4400°K
Liquid Hydrogen			388 (*f*) 2700°*K* 391 (*e*) 3000°*K*	398 (*f*) 3100°*K* 410 (*e*) 3900°*K*

* From *Rocket Engine Propellants* published by the Rocketdyne Division of North American Aviation.

The liquid-oxygen kerosine engine has been the most highly developed engine and its thermodynamic characteristics are shown in Fig. 55 for various weight ratios of oxygen and fuel as abscissae. The ordinates are the molecular weight, t_c the absolute temperature, γ, the ratio of the specific heats, and $\sqrt{(RT)}$. This combination of fuel and oxidant has been used in the well-known Atlas series of rockets for launching space craft and other American rocket engines. It has also been used in the smaller Rolls-Royce RZ-2 rocket which has a maximum thrust of 150,000 lbf.

The above table shows the superiority of liquid hydrogen over any other fuel and the performance of any fuel with fluorine as an oxidant is a little better than with oxygen, but the temperature is very much higher. The difficulty of handling liquid hydrogen with its very low temperature has been overcome in the Rocketdyne J-2 engine which produced 230,000 lb thrust at altitude in Saturn vehicles.

In addition to bipropellants there are tripropellants and monopropellants. The former have been tried to find a combination with a higher specific impulse. The Rocket Research Corporation of Seattle have successfully tested a combination of lithium, fluorine and hydrogen and have obtained a vacuum specific impulse of almost 600 seconds, more than 100 seconds better than any other combination yet known.

The best known monopropellant is hydrogen peroxide (H.T.P.), already mentioned as an oxidant. Commercially supplied H.T.P. is 85% H_2O_2 and 15% H_2O by weight and it decomposes to steam and oxygen at about 900°K. The most powerful rocket engines developed in the U.S.A. include the H-1 engine and the F-1 engine, the former using oxygen/kerosine and the latter LO_2/RP-1, the last named being kerosene. The H-1 engine has been used in clusters on larger launch vehicles and as a single unit, developing 230,500 lb at altitude. The F-1 provides thrusts of 1,552,000 lb at sea level and 1,748,000 lb at altitude. The Bell nozzle thrust chamber is regeneratively cooled by the fuel at the inner end and by the turbine exhaust gases at the exit end. This turbine of approximately 60,000 h.p. drives two self-lubricated pumps mounted on a single shaft and is powered by hot gases from a bipropellant gas generator. The J-2 engine burns liquid hydrogen with liquid oxygen giving 230,000 lb thrust with an expansion ratio of 27·5 to 1.

ROCKET THEORY.—The theory of rocket propulsion is based on the combustion of the propellant which generates gas at high pressure, density and temperature; the gas then expands through the nozzle to emerge at high speed but at lower pressure, density and temperature. It is the rearward momentum which provides the thrust, the magnitude of which is largely determined by the pressure of the gas in the chamber and by the geometry of the nozzle.

The Equation of State must hold, namely

$$P/\rho = R\theta/m$$

where P is the pressure, ρ the density, θ the absolute temperature, m the mean molecular weight of the gas and R the Universal Gas constant equal to 2777 ft lbf/lb deg. C. Let C=constant, be the energy obtained from the combustion of unit mass of propellant, V the gas velocity, γ the ratio of the specific heats and g the gravity constant, then this constant can be written in the following form

$$C = (\gamma/\gamma - 1)(p/\rho) + V^2/2g$$

If p_0, ρ_0 and θ_0 are the stagnation pressures, density and temperature, that is, the values of these quantities when the gas velocity is zero, then for isentropic flow the pressure is given by

$$\frac{p}{p_0} = \left[1 - \frac{V^2}{2Cg}\right]^{\gamma/(\gamma-1)} = \left[1 + \frac{\gamma - 1}{2} M^2\right]^{\gamma/(\gamma-1)}$$

where M is the Mach number of the flow.

Similarly

$$\frac{\rho_0}{\rho} = \left[1 + \frac{\gamma - 1}{2} M^2\right]^{1/(\gamma-1)}$$

and

$$\frac{\theta_0}{\theta} = 1 + \frac{\gamma - 1}{2} M^2$$

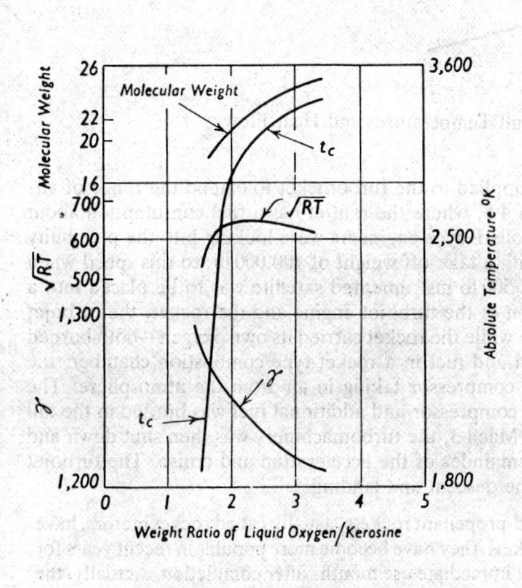

FIG. 55.—Thermodynamic Characteristics of a Liquid Oxygen Kerosine Rocket Engine.

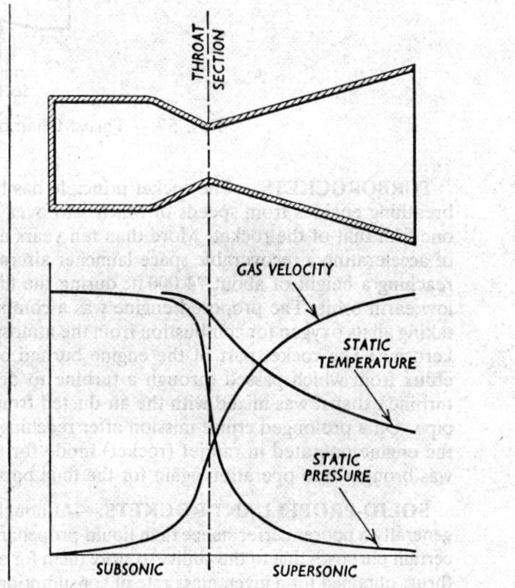

THROAT SECTION

GAS VELOCITY

STATIC TEMPERATURE

STATIC PRESSURE

SUBSONIC

SUPERSONIC

FIG. 56.—Expansion in a Supersonic Nozzle.

Considering the flow through the nozzle, the mass flow rate must be the same at all positions along the nozzle. At the throat the Mach number must be unity and the values of pressure, density and temperatures at the throat are given by putting $M = 1$ in the three preceding equations. In addition, it can be shown that the velocity at any position along the nozzle, V, to that at the throat V_T can be obtained from

$$V/V_T = M \sqrt{\left\{(\gamma + 1)/2 \left(1 + \frac{\gamma - 1}{2} M^2\right)\right\}}$$

The flow through a typical nozzle can thus be calculated and the typical values of the ratios of gas velocity, V/V_T of static temperature, θ/θ_0, and of static pressure, p/p_0, are shown in Fig. 56. The temperature through the nozzle decreases steadily, the pressure decreases rapidly just before and less rapidly after the throat is passed, and the gas velocity increases rapidly up to Mach 1 at the throat and continues to increase further, though at a decreasing rate right up to the nozzle exit.

Fig. 57 shows the heat flow and the calculated change of wall temperature down a typical chamber. The peak values at the throat section should be noted. The rates of heat transfer are of the order of 200 calories per square centimetre per second, much higher than in the operation of gas turbines and very much higher than in other types of engine. This is in spite of the cooling of the chamber profile by a coolant flowing through tubes inside the surface. The following simple formula has been put forward for the maximum possible heat transfer rate at the throat; namely, $0{\cdot}0034\ p_c C^x$, where p_c is the chamber pressure, in atmospheres and C^x is the characteristic velocity of the gases in feet per second based on the cross sectional area of the throat, the pressure under stagnation conditions and the mass flow rate. This theoretical formula is based on various approximations and overestimates the heat transfer rate in the practical case by a factor of about three.

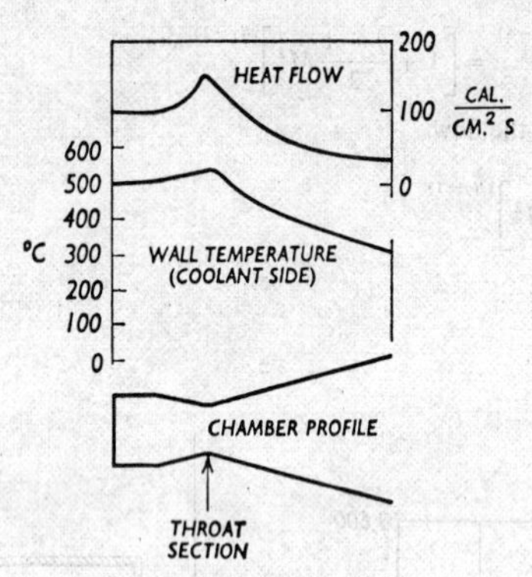

FIG. 57.—Thrust Chamber Wall Temperatures and Heat Flow.

TURBOROCKETS.—The rocket principle has been applied to the turborocket to extend the range of air-breathing engines from speeds of Mach 3 to over Mach 4·5, where the ramjet has a fuel consumption about one fifth that of the rocket. More than ten years ago Rolls-Royce engineers were looking into the possibility of accelerating a recoverable space launcher aircraft, with a take-off weight of 100,000 lb, to this speed when reaching a height of about 74,000 ft; during the flight a 500 lb instrumented satellite was to be placed into a low earth orbit. The proposed engine was a combination of the turbojet engine and the rocket, the turbojet taking all its oxygen for combustion from the atmosphere while the rocket carried its own oxygen—both burned kerosine. The rocket part of the engine burned oxygen and fuel in a rocket-type combustion chamber, the efflux from which passed through a turbine to drive a compressor taking in air from the atmosphere. The turbine exhaust was mixed with the air ducted from the compressor and additional fuel was burned in the tail pipe. On a prolonged cruise mission after reaching, say Mach 3, the turbomachinery was then shut down and the engine operated in ramjet (rocket) mode for the remainder of the acceleration and cruise. The turbojet was brought into operation again for the final part of the descent and landing.

SOLID-PROPELLANT ROCKETS.—Although solid-propellant rockets, usually called rocket motors, have generally a poorer performance than liquid-propellant rockets, they have become more popular in recent years for certain purposes due to the ability to store them for almost immediate use months after completion. Actually, the thrust obtained for a given mass rate of consumption of propellant (i.e. the specific impulse) may be 10 to 20 per cent lower than for a rocket engine. Long storage, ease of handling and readiness are, however, important operational factors. Successful solid motors measure up to 260 in. dia.

The principle of the rocket motor is shown in Fig. 58. It consists basically of a propellant charge and a motor body, the latter comprising the case containing the propellant charge, the nozzle and various other components. The case has to be strong enough to stand the pressure which builds up while the propellant is burning in the combustion chamber. There is often a plate at the one end to hold the charge in place. An igniter lights the charge and the direction of burning is indicated by the arrows. A nozzle closure plug ruptures when the pressure reaches some preset pre-determined value and if the pressure becomes excessive it is released by the safety cap. The nozzle is held firmly in place by a retaining ring. In one common type the nozzle is secured to the combustion chamber by an end-closure in the form of a truncated cylinder that fits over the end. On to this end-closure is fixed a blast tube through which the burnt gases pass to the expansion core at the end as in Fig. 58. In this more advanced type of rocket, the igniter is entirely enclosed in the combustion chamber and not far from the face of the propellant charge. An obturator, or seal, to prevent the flow of gas backwards is found encircling the end of the unburnt charge. To prevent the overheating of the convergent part of the nozzle or of the end-enclosure a lining of thermal insulation is essential. After the convergent part the nozzle is a cone of rapidly expanding diameter and the general description is that of a convergent-divergent nozzle in accordance with the best practice for supersonic flow.

The propellant charge almost fills the combustion chamber and it is required to burn in a particular manner since the magnitude of the rocket's thrust depends on the area of the surfaces where burning is taking place. The thrust duration will continue until the propellant is all burnt, a duration dependent on the depth of the propellant in the direction normal to the burning surface. Once the charge is ignited it will burn on all its exposed surfaces and consequently the cross section of the charge is given various shapes and burning is inhibited on certain surfaces usually including the outer cylindrical surface. As indicated in Fig. 58 a solid charge will burn only on the end face and the burning surface will recede in a longitudinal direction. This type of burning is called "cigar-burning". More commonly there is a perforation through the charge along the longitudinal axis, and the perforation will maintain the same cross section throughout, such as a cross or a many-pointed star. The charge is, in this case, inhibited at the end so that burning takes place radially outwards on the surface of the perforation or conduit throughout the length of the charge.

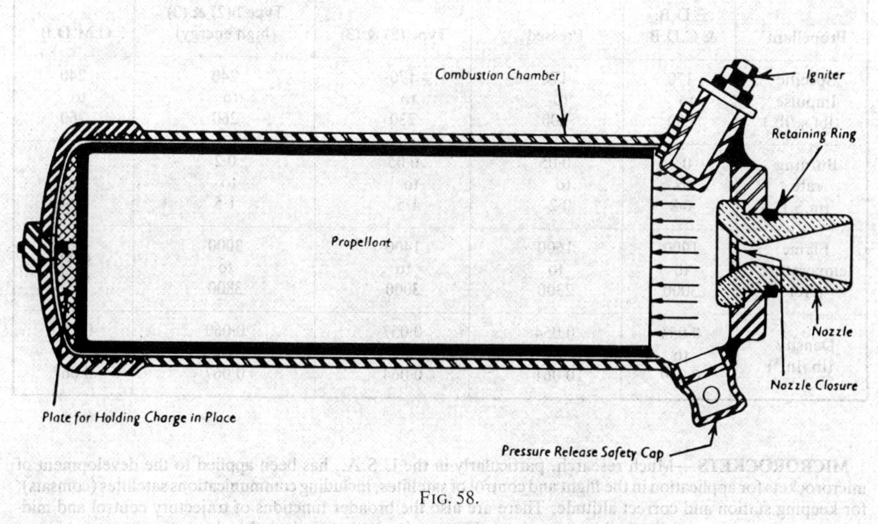

FIG. 58.

Some charges are manufactured separately and placed in the combustion chamber through the open end of the case, a process termed "cartridge insertion". Other types of solid propellant are cast or moulded direct into the chamber when they become bonded to the case and accordingly do not require an inhibitor on the outer surface: they are called "case-bonded".

The combustion of the charge is initiated by the igniter, which contains a small amount of pyrotechnic composition and is fired electrically. The burning of the propellant generates gas at high pressure and high temperature so that the case is usually made of steel, although sometimes of a high tensile aluminium alloy. The whole of the casing may be lined with thermal insulating material. Gas seals prevent leakage of gas through joints between components.

The burnt gases exhaust through the nozzle and the narrowest part of its profile is called the throat. Erosion by the hot high-velocity gas occurs and is particularly severe at the throat. On this account special throat inserts of hard refractory material are a normal practice in rocket motors, where the problem of erosion is more acute than in rocket engines.

Solid propellants are classified as follows:

(*a*) Colloidal or double base: (1) cordite or extruded double base (E.D.B.); (2) cast double base (C.D.B.)

(*b*) Composite: (1) pressed; (2) plastic; (3) propellants with polymerizable binders.

(*c*) Composite modified double base (C.M.D.B.).

Double base propellants are a colloidal gel of the two nitric esters, nitrocellulose and nitro glycerine. The composition of cordite and case double base propellants are similar, but the manufacture is different and the former has been largely supplanted by the latter, in which the charge is manufactured by casting into a tube of inhibiting material since they are not very suitable for case-bonding. Colloidal propellants have nitrocellulose 50–60%, nitroglycerine 25–45% and 5–15% other ingredients.

Composite propellants are a mixture of ingredients, some of which function as oxidants and others serve as fuels. Dry ingredients are consolidated under high pressure to form pressed charges which are unsuitable for case-bonding and therefore of limited use. Other charges are manufactured by moulding or casting direct into the case and consist of a high proportion of crystalline salts containing oxygen with a small amount of liquid binder as the fuel. The oxidant is commonly ammonium perchlorate and the binder-fuels are either rubbery or resinous polymers or nitropolymers. Plastic propellants have a viscous liquid binder. The third type (c) refers to a cross between (a) and (b) such as when nitropolymers are used in composite propellants.

In addition to the above types, aluminium powder has been used up to 15% as an additional fuel in high energy types, and beryllium or lithium are possible future ingredients. A good modern solid propellant contains ammonium perchlorate, aluminium, and viscous or polymerizable binders. The general characteristics of the propellants are given on the next page:

SOLID PROPELLANTS: PERFORMANCE CHARACTERISTICS

Propellant	E.D.B. & C.D.B.	Pressed	Type (2) & (3)	Type b(2) & (3) (high energy)	C.M.D.B.
Specific Impulse (lbf.s./lb.)	170 to 200	170 to 200	170 to 230	240 to 260	240 to 260
Burning rate (in.S.)	0·2 to 0·8	0·05 to 0·2	0·05 to 1·5	0·2 to 1·5	0·3 to 1·0
Flame temperature (°K)	1900 to 3000	1600 to 2300	1400 to 3000	3000 to 3800	over 4000
Density (lb./in.^{3})	0·054 to 0·059	0·054 to 0·061	0·057 to 0·064	0·060 to 0·067	0·060 to 0·067

MICROROCKETS.—Much research, particularly in the U.S.A., has been applied to the development of microrockets for application in the flight and control of satellites, including communications satellites (comsats), for keeping station and correct altitude. There are also the broader functions of trajectory control and mid-course manoeuvres as well as orbit corrections. The requirements may include a large thrust required once or only for a few times or a very low thrust for a very large number of times.

The very low-level thrust required may be as small as 10^{-4} lbf and here the requirement can be met by a subliming solid microrocket; a type of rocket used on the OV2-1 satellite for spin control. This rocket has a solid crystalline mass in a tank and the solid-vapour equilibrium maintains the vapour pressure in the tank. When a propellant valve is opened, the vapour escapes through a nozzle to provide thrust and the solid sublimes rapidly to replace the vapour that has been released. Other methods are likewise used to obtain sublimation of mono-propellant and bipropellant solids.

Vaporizing liquids, such as ammonia, hydrazine and certain liquid bipropellants are also used in microrockets and their type of performance does not differ much in principle from the large rockets described earlier in this chapter with limitations imposed by the small Reynolds and Knudsen numbers of the exhaust flow into the very low pressure and temperature of space by small nozzles. Cold-gas systems from gas stored at high pressure and various gaseous bipropellant systems are also used for certain microrocket applications but do not replace the subliming solid rocket for the latter's special applications; nor do electrochemical systems some of which rely on nuclear isotopes. These references to different methods indicate what a wide field has opened up in microrocketry.

BIBLIOGRAPHY

BRAGG. *Rocket Engineers.* Newnes.
COHEN AND ROGERS. *Gas Turbine Theory.* Longmans.
CONSTANT. *Gas Turbines and their Problems.* Todd.
DABOO. *Solid Fuel Rocket Propulsion.* Temple Press.
GLAUERT. *Elements of Aerofoils and Airscrew Theory.* Cambridge University Press.
GODSEY AND YOUNG. *Gas Turbines for Aircraft,* McGraw-Hill.
HARDY AND LAIDLAW. *Aeronautical Science.* Oxford University Press.
HODGE. *Gas Turbine Cycle and Performance Estimation.* Butterworths.
JUDGE. *Modern Gas Turbines.* Chapman Hall.
KEENAN. *Gas Turbines and Jet Propulsion.* Oxford University Press.
KUCHEMANN AND WEBER. *Aerodynamics of Propulsion.* McGraw-Hill.
KYD. *Variable-pitch Propellers.* Pitman.
NAYLER. *Dictionary of Astronautics.* Newnes.
OWER AND NAYLER. *High Speed Flight.* Hutchinson.
SHEPHERD. *Introduction to Gas Turbines.* Constable.
SMITH. *Gas Turbines and Jet Propulsion.* Iliffe.

AIRPORTS AND AIR TRANSPORT

Airports in the total transportation system—Glossary—Forecasting Air Transport Demands—Site Selection—Airport Geometry and Concept—International Standards and Recommended Practices—Pavement Design—Aeronautical Ground Lighting and Visual Aids—Telecommunications—Navigational and Landing Aids—Electronic Services—Air Traffic Control—Airport Ground Operations and Equipment—Commercial Facilities—Trends in Aircraft Design—V/STOL Operations—Bibliography.

By A. D. Townend, BSc(Eng), ACGI, DIC, CEng, FICE, MConsE *et al* of Sir Frederick Snow and Partners

INTRODUCTION

An airport is a very complex undertaking which comprises many disciplines. The great majority of these are of an engineering character but substantial contributions are made by economists, architects and others.

In general, the engineering problems and solutions are not unique to airports. For instance, drainage, structural design, building services etc within an airport are no different, in essence, from other projects. There are, however, some engineering aspects which are found only on airports and these include aircraft pavement design (and some features of construction), aeronautical ground lighting, landing aids etc.

The three dimensional nature of flying requires particular attention in regard to aircraft safety for a considerable distance round an airport and within the operational areas of the airport. There are international standards and recommended practices for these aspects at airports handling international services and many countries have adopted similar standards and practices for domestic airports.

Other parts of the airport associated with passenger handling, the air traffic control building, airport management etc are not subject to the same sort of regulation and the airport planner and designer has scope for individual skill.

This chapter sets out information on the major factors in airport planning, design and operations together with those parts of airline and aircraft operations which are closely related. The chapter has been divided into discrete sections, each dealing with a particular aspect of the overall subject, in order to assist reference, but the divisions are, in a sense, artificial since there is considerable interrelation between the parts. Airport planning, in particular, is an iterative process.

THE AIRPORT AS A PART OF THE TOTAL TRANSPORTATION SYSTEM

In the 1950's and 1960's an airport was considered as a unit, which was relatively self contained, and whose basic function began and ended at the boundary. It is now recognised that an airport is one part of the overall transportation system which should be integrated into that system. This ideal cannot always be met since there are always some constraints, even at the most suitable of new sites, and compromise is necessary.

TABLE 1.—INTERNATIONAL AND DOMESTIC SCHEDULED TRAFFIC FOR ICAO STATES (*Source*: ICAO)

Year	Passengers Carried (Thousands)	Passenger Kilometres (Millions)
1950	31,000	28,000
1960	105,562	108,814
1970	382,954	460,481
1980	643,659	927,728
1985	778,611	1,173,771
1986	838,103	1,255,844

Note: Figures exclude USSR except for 1970. This was the first year they reported but the figures for that year cannot be isolated.

The airport is an interchange point, albeit large and complex in the case of a major international airport, from one mode of transport to another. The transfer is from surface to air or air to surface and the surface mode of transport is predominantly road although there are a few airports with direct rail (including underground) links, eg Heathrow, Gatwick. The economics of a rail link will rarely be favourable enough to justify construction since it can serve only a limited number of population centres whereas the road system will be able to provide access from many more points.

The scale of the operations is enormous. The International Civil Aviation Organisation (ICAO) collects world wide statistics from the 150 reporting states. Table 1 summarises the growth from 1950 to 1983.

Each passenger (see Table 1) with the exception of transfer passengers, has had to be transported to and from an airport, no matter what size it is. The impact of each airport on the transportation system of the surrounding area or region varies with the size of airport and some idea of the problem at the top of the scale can be gained from the annual passenger totals at the twenty-five busiest airports in the world which handled more than 14 million terminal passengers each in 1985. These are given in Table 2.

TABLE 2.—TRAFFIC AT WORLD AIRPORTS IN 1986 (*Source*: ICAO and BAA statistics)

Location	Airport	ATM's (000)	Terminal Pax (000)	International Terminal Pax (000)	Cargo Tonnes (000)
Chicago	O'Hare	706·3	53,338	3,369	589·9
Atlanta	Hartsfield	569·6	45,192	1,416	279·5
Los Angeles	Los Angeles Intl	507·5	41,418	6,450	785·3
Dallas	Dallas/Ft Worth	552·0	39,945	500	359·2
Denver	Stapleton	373·6	34,686	200	149·6
London	Heathrow	293·9	31,310	25,734	537·1
New York	Newark	369·9	29,433	1,307	271·2
San Francisco	San Francisco Intl	385·7	27,814	2,814	388·7
New York	Kennedy	267·1	27,224	15,395	992·5
Tokyo	Tokyo Intl (Haneda)	262·3	27,245	500	352·2
New York	La Guardia	323·2	22,189	136	45·8
Miami	Miami Intl	243·1	21,948	7,668	520·3
Boston	Logan	361·8	21,792	2,450	239·7
St Louis	Lambert	398·9	20,352	93	64·7
Frankfurt	Frankfurt Main	231·9	19,753	14,544	784·3
Paris	Orly	164·1	18,544	7,206	202·2
Honolulu	Honolulu Intl	261·8	18,235	2,775	218·3
Osaka	Osaka Intl	121·9	17,695	3,523	319·1
Detroit	Metropolitan	350·7	17,605	800	92·2
Toronto	Pearson	220·4	17,360	7,986	245·3
Minneapolis/St Paul	Intl	250·0	17,073	265	N/A
London	Gatwick	157·7	16,309	15,195	163·8
Pittsburgh	Pittsburgh Intl	357·5	15,990	N/A	41·3
Paris	Charles de Gaulle	144·9	14,427	12,899	510·6
Washington	National	246·5	14,308	N/A	57·8

The effect on the surface transport system is clearly significant whether the airport site has been specifically selected and integrated into the overall system or whether it is, so to speak, an 'historical' site which has evolved (of which there are many, particularly in the developed countries). The surface system has to cater for passengers travelling to and from the catchment area for the particular airport and direct city centre links are not generally effective since the expansion of motor car ownership has given freedom to travel from any point within the area.

Air transport on the short haul routes is subject to competition from surface modes of transport both road and rail and the scene is never static. An improvement in the surface system is met by shorter flight times due to faster aircraft, by special passenger facilities to reduce time at the airport or, in a few instances on high density routes by a shuttle service. Air transport on the medium and long haul routes, by contrast, competes only within itself as airlines strive to win passengers from their competitors by in flight standards and service, types of aircraft etc. Competition by frequency is less likely since international routes are controlled. International agreement covers the 'Freedoms of the Air' which are defined as:

For the aircraft of State A, the freedoms are:

First Freedom.—The privilege of flying over the territory of State B without landing.

Second Freedom.—The privilege of landing in State B for technical reasons only, i.e. for such purposes as refuelling but not to pick up or set down any passengers, cargo or mail.

Third Freedom.—The privilege to set down in State B traffic (*i.e.* passengers, cargo or mail) picked up in State A.

Fourth Freedom.—The privilege of picking up in State B traffic destined for State A. This is closely linked with the third freedom.

Fifth Freedom.—The privilege of picking up or setting down in State B traffic which is destined for or has come from State C. As an example, if British Airways operates on route London–Athens–Beirut with full traffic rights; it is entitled to carry third and fourth freedom traffic between Athens and Beirut.

For descriptive purposes the first and second freedoms are known as 'technical rights', as distinct from the third, fourth and fifth freedoms, which are known as 'traffic rights'.

Sixth Freedom.—Sometimes used to describe the combination of third and fourth freedom services on either side of State A so as to provide a service between States B and C via State A. For example, a West German airline is able to carry traffic between London and Athens by operating a service from London to Frankfurt and thence from Frankfurt to Athens. This may be done by the connection of two separate services or by the creation of a through service. Although at first glance the sixth freedom appears to be little different from the fifth freedom, most countries (the United States is one of the exceptions) make a distinction between the two, and the opportunities for sixth freedom may be an important consideration in assessing the balance of opportunity in the exchange of traffic rights.

In addition, the operation of scheduled air services between UK and US territory and of non-scheduled services on the North Atlantic is covered by the Bermuda 2 Agreement of 1977 (amended in 1980).

Internal routes may also be the subject of competition between airlines particularly in developed countries on the same basis as the international, ie in flight standards and service, types of aircraft etc, but they may also be the subject of a licencing system administered by a Civil Aviation Authority or Government Department. The USA has led the way in de-regulation.

Within the airport boundary, there has to be provision of extensive car parks, both short and long term, which sterilise large areas but which generate significant income for the airport authority.

It should not be thought that an airport can be planned and designed to a fixed set of principles or round a particular type of user since there are many different interests involved. In the terminal building, for instance, there are at least five 'populations' involved:

(*a*) passengers
(*b*) airline staff
(*c*) airport management staff
(*d*) concessionaires providing services, eg duty free, catering, newsagency/magazines etc.
(*e*) statutory bodies, eg customs and excise, immigration

There will be conflicting requirements and interests between these 'populations', eg greater capital expenditure by the airport management may result in lower operational costs for airlines or provision by airport management of more concessions to generate income may impede passenger flows.

The solution adopted in airport terms to the problems posed will inevitably be a compromise and the skill and expertise of the airport planner and designer lie in establishing the compromise which best meets the varying needs.

GLOSSARY

This glossary is intended to provide a quick reference for the more commonly used terms, including abbreviations. Reference is made to other sections of the chapter if the subject is dealt with in greater detail.

AFTN (Aeronautical Fixed Telecommunications Network)—A world wide system of radio and cable links for transmitting and recording messages (TELECOMMUNICATIONS, NAVIGATIONAL AND LANDING AIDS).

AGL (Aeronautical Ground Lighting)—The operational lighting system for an airport (AERONAUTICAL GROUND LIGHTING AND VISUAL AIDS).

AGNIS (Aircraft Guidance Nose-in System)—A pilot aid for parking aircraft on stands equipped with air bridges (or jetties) or nose loaders giving exact guidance for alignment and stopping.

ASDE (Airport Surface Detection Equipment)—A radar system for use at busy airports to assist air traffic controllers in the safe manoeuvring of aircraft and vehicles on the ground.

ATC (Air Traffic Control)—A general description covering the services provided to ensure the safe, orderly and expeditious flow of air traffic movements.

AOCI (Airport Operators Council International)—An American organisation serving the interests of airport operators.

Aerodrome elevation—The elevation of the highest point of landing area.

Aerodrome reference point—The designated geographical location of an aerodrome.

Airspace—A defined volume of space above the earth's surface under the jurisdiction of an aviation authority.

Airway—Controlled airspace (*qv*) in the form of a corridor equipped with radio navigational aids.

Apron—A defined area on a land aerodrome, intended to accommodate aircraft for the purpose of loading or unloading passengers or cargo, refuelling, parking or maintenance.

BAA (British Airport Authority)—The Authority set up by statute to manage and develop certain specified airports in UK. These are Heathrow, Gatwick, Stansted, Prestwick, Glasgow, Edinburgh, and Aberdeen.

BALPA (British Airlines Pilot Association)—The professional organisation for commercial pilots in the UK.

CAA (Civil Aviation Authority)—The statutory body in UK for the controlling, regulating and licensing of aircraft, (and airship), airline and airport operations.

CNR (Composite noise rating)—An American method of assessing the impact of aircraft noise which includes aircraft noise levels, numbers of landings, take offs and engine runups, time of day and runway utilisation.

CTR (Control zone)—A zone established about an individual aerodrome to afford protection to aircraft arriving from or entering the terminal area (TMA) (*qv*) (AIR TRAFFIC CONTROL).

Clearway—A rectangular area at the end of the take-off run available and under the control of the aerodrome licensee, selected or prepared as a suitable area over which an aircraft may make a portion of its initial climb to a specified height.

Controlled Airspace—An airspace of defined dimensions within which air traffic control services are provided to controlled flights.

Crosswind component—The velocity component of the wind measured at, or corrected to a height of, 10 m above ground level at right angles to the direction of take-off or landing.

DME (Distance measuring equipment)—A radio aid which gives the pilot continuous information on his distance from the equipment (TELECOMMUNICATIONS, NAVIGATIONAL AND LANDING AIDS)

DOC (Direct operating costs)—The operating costs of an aircraft which are related directly to flying.

DVOR (Doppler very high frequency omni-directional radio beacon)—A radio aid which gives the pilot guidance in azimuth (TELECOMMUNICATIONS, NAVIGATIONAL AND LANDING AIDS).

EPNdB (Effective perceived noise decibel)—The unit of measurement of effective perceived noise level (EPNL) (*qv*).

EPNL (Effective perceived noise level)—A modification of perceived noise level (PNL) (*qv*) involving a discrete frequency correction factor and a duration correction factor. EPNL has been adopted by the International Civil Aviation Organisation as the standard measurement for aircraft noise.

Environmental impact statement—A requirement of the US Department of Transportation by which applicants for federal aid for an airport development must submit a statement describing the effect of the development on the quality of the environment.

FAA (Federal Aviation Administration)—The US Government Agency for controlling, regulating, and licensing of aircraft, airlines and airport operations.

FAR (Federal Aviation Regulation)—A regulation issued by the FAA in relation to a specific requirement, eg Part 36—Aircraft noise.

Gate—An aircraft parking space adjacent to a terminal building for the loading and unloading of passengers, baggage, mail and hold cargo. It also describes the point in a terminal building where airport coaches serving remote aircraft stands (*qv*) embark and disembark passengers.

GA (General aviation)—All civil aviation operations other than scheduled air services and non-scheduled air transport operations for remuneration or hire.

IATA (International Air Transport Association)—An association of scheduled international airlines whose role is to foster the interests of civil aviation, to provide a forum for industry views and to establish industry practices.

ICAA (International Civil Airports Association)—An association of civil airport authorities.

ICAO (International Civil Aviation Organisation)—An international body with member states whose main objects are to establish standards and recommended practices and to facilitate air transport by the reduction of formalities.

IFR (Instrument flight rules)—A set of rules governing the conduct of flight under instrument meteorological conditions (IMC) (*qv*).

ILS (Instrument landing system)—A radio approach and landing aid which identifies an approach path in azimuth and descent angle together with information on distance from the runway (TELECOMMUNICATIONS, NAVIGATIONAL AND LANDING AIDS).

IMC (Instrument meteorological conditions)—Meteorological conditions expressed in terms of visibility, distance from cloud, and ceiling, less than the minimum specified for visual meteorological conditions (VMC) (*qv*) IMC prevail if any one of the following criteria are not met: 5 n.m visibility, cloud clearance horizontally of 1 n.m and vertically of 1,000 ft.

ITA (Institute of Air Transport)—An association of individuals and organisations with interests in civil aviation.

Instrument runway—A runway intended for the operation of aircraft using instrument approach procedures. There are two main types: a nonprecision approach runway which is served by visual aids and a non-visual (ie radio) aid providing at least directional guidance adequate for a straight-in approach and secondly a precision approach runway which is served by an instrument landing system (ILS) (*qv*) and visual aids intended for operations down to specified decision heights and runway visibility range depending on the category of ILS (TELECOMMUNICATIONS, NAVIGATIONAL AND LANDING AIDS).

LCG (Load classification group)—A grouping of aircraft and pavement load classification numbers (LCN) (*qv*) into broad bands to group together aircraft imposing similar stress levels on pavements in reasonable and regular increments of pavement thickness.

LCN (Load classification number)—In the UK aircraft are classified in a numerical scale representing the severity of load and there is a similar related scale to represent the strength of the pavement. This method of classification is known as the load classification number (LCN) system.

MLS (Microwave Landing System)—A recent development of ILS (*qv*) which permits a curved approach and gives continuous distance information. The system adopted by ICAO for use after 1985 works on a time reference scanning beam principle but some existing systems use the Doppler principle.

NEF (Noise Exposure Forecast)—A refinement of the composite noise rating (CNR) (*qv*).

NNI (Noise and Number Index)—A measure of the noise effect of aircraft which takes account of the average peak noise level received at the point from a group of aircraft of similar noise generating level and the number of aircraft. The annoyance caused by the noise effect was measured in a social survey round Heathrow Airport, London.

Noise contour—A line joining points of equal noise level. The noise level can be measured in various ways, eg CNR, NEF or NNI (*qv*).

Non-Instrument runway—A runway intended for the operation of aircraft using visual approach procedures.

Obstacle—All fixed (whether temporary or permanent) and mobile objects, or parts thereof, that are located on an area intended for the surface movement of aircraft or that extend above a defined surface intended to protect aircraft in flight.

PANCAP (Practical annual capacity)—A measure of practical annual capacity for runways for long range planning purposes published by FAA. Factors influencing PANCAP include runway configuration, weather and aircraft mix.

PHOCAP (Practical hourly capacity)—The hourly capacity of a runway on similar lines to the annual capacity (PANCAP) (*qv*). It should be noted that PANCAP is not PHOCAP × 24 × 365.

PNL (perceived noise level)—A method of measuring the noise level of jet aircraft based on the instantaneous measurement of sound pressure levels in the various octave bands for each half second increment of time during the period of the noise. The calculations weight the octave band levels of the noise according to the degree of annoyance caused.

PNdB (Perceived noise decibels)—The unit of measurement of perceived noise level (PNL) (*qv*).

Precision approach runway—A particular type of instrument runway (*qv*).

SBH (Standard busy hour)—The hour in which the standard busy rate (SBR) (*qv*) occurs.

SBR (Standard busy rate)—The hourly flow rate (of passengers or aircraft) which is used for design purposes. It is an empirical factor and is defined as that rate which is exceeded 29 times in the year. It has been found to give a reasonable basis for design (FORECASTING AIR TRANSPORT DEMANDS).

SSR (Secondary surveillance radar)—A system of secondary radar using ground transmitters/receivers (interrogators) and airborne transponders conforming to specifications developed by ICAO. The air traffic controllers' display shows the flight number, altitude and bearing.

STOL (Short take off and landing)—A term applied to aircraft which are designed to operate from short runways. All the present examples are turboprop and they are characterised by low wing loadings and special flaps.

Shoulder—An area adjacent to the edge of a pavement so prepared as to provide a transition between the pavement and the adjacent surface.

Stand—An aircraft parking space adjacent to or remote from, a terminal building for the loading and unloading of passengers, baggage, mail and cargo. Similar to, but not synonymous with, gate (*qv*).

Stopway—A defined rectangular area on the ground at the end of the take off run available prepared as a suitable area in which an aircraft can be stopped in the event of an abandoned take off.

TMA (Terminal control area)—An area established about one or more busy aerodromes to afford protection to aircraft entering and departing from the airways (*qv*) system (AIR TRAFFIC CONTROL).

TPHP (Typical peak hour passenger)—A method developed in America from data at US airports relating annual passenger throughput to typical peak hours, ie not the absolute peak (FORECASTING AIR TRANSPORT DEMAND). It is analogous to the standard busy hour (SBR) (*qv*).

Taxiway—A defined path on a land aerodrome established for the taxiing of aircraft and intended to provide a link between one part of the aerodrome and another.

Threshold—The beginning of that portion of runway usable for landing.

Touchdown zone—The position of a runway, beyond the threshold, where it is intended landing aeroplanes first contact the runway.

VASIS (Visual approach slope indicator system)—The standard approach system consisting of light units positioned up wind of the runway threshold and close to the runway edge which give slope guidance during the approach by means of colour coding; there are many variations of the basic system (AERONAUTICAL GROUND LIGHTING AND VISUAL AIDS).

VCR (Visual control room)—The room at the top of a control tower where the air traffic controllers are positioned (AIR TRAFFIC CONTROL).

VFR (Visual flight rules)—A set of rules governing the conduct of flight under visual meteorological conditions (VMC) (*qv*).

VMC (Visual meteorological conditions)—Meteorological conditions expressed in terms of visibility, distance from cloud, and ceiling, equal to or better than the following criteria:— 5n.m visibility, cloud clearance horizontally of 1n.m and vertically of 1,000 ft.

VOR (Very high frequency omnidirectional radio beacon)—A radio aid which gives the pilot guidance in azimuth (TELECOMMUNICATIONS, NAVIGATIONAL AND LANDING AIDS).

V/STOL (Vertical and short take off and landing)—A term used to embrace helicopters and short take off and landing aircraft (STOL) (*qv*) (V/STOL OPERATIONS).

VTOL (Vertical take off and landing)—A term used to describe all aircraft that have the capability of landing and taking off vertically. They are all helicopters in the civil field but the Harrier is a military example with tilting jets (V/STOL OPERATIONS).

FORECASTING AIR TRANSPORT DEMANDS

DEMAND ANALYSIS.—Projections of air travel demand for passengers, cargo, airline routes, load factors and aircraft sizes are essential for the process of airport planning and form an important input to decision making and policy information by governments and aviation authorities. This activity requires a large number of forecasts, such as passenger by type and route, freight, aircraft technology, aircraft load factors, choice of access modes, number of 'meeters and greeters' per passenger, airport visitors, etc.

There is a widely held belief that 'forecasts are always wrong' and 'the accuracy does not really matter, it only shifts the time scale to plus or minus a few years' but forecasts are essential because they provide a firm basis on which decisions about airport development can be made at defined times. The type and accuracy of forecasts depend greatly on the purpose to which they will be put. The feasibility of a project can often be examined adequately in the light of relatively crude maximum forecasts, or range of forecast such as were adopted by the UK Civil Aviation Authority in the study for the National Airports Plan and such forecasts are often quite appropriate to systems planning.

However, detailed master planning tasks such as site selection, land use planning, terminal area layout and access planning, together with environmental impact and financial planning to assess the economic feasibility, require a set of demand forecasts to acceptable levels of accuracy at defined times. The accuracy inevitably deteriorates with time, but this is consistent with the needs of short term detailed facilities planning within the long term requirements including the safeguard of long term options. There are three broad time bands: short term up to 5 years, medium term up to 10 years and long term up to 20 years. It is not realistic to look beyond that period.

A serious problem associated especially with the short and medium term time scales is the lead time, that is the time between the initial planning and the commissioning of the project, so that a 20 year plan may not even cover the expected medium term of the project if the planning process due to public inquiries, acquisitions and other legal procedures require 5 to 10 years as in the cases of the new Munich II airport, the second runway at Frankfurt and the third London airport. London's need of a third airport was first recognised as far back as 1957.

All forecasts should be kept under review over the period to which they relate to ensure that there has been no fundamental change in any of the factors affecting them.

TYPES OF FORECASTS.—Forecasts for annual passenger throughput, annual freight and mail, transport movements and aircraft types form the basis on which the scale of the system is estimated, the impact on the environment (or other system) is assessed and the financial viability is verified.

The most important parameters for detailed planning however are the number of passengers and aircraft and volume of cargo during the busy periods. Hence, two types of forecasts are required:

Annual figures—to assess the scale of operation and the financial considerations.

Hourly flows—for facility design.

METHOD OF ANALYSIS.—The choice of method of analysis will depend largely on the time scale of the forecast, the purpose of the forecast and the availability of suitable data. Experience has shown that in most cases available data (especially in developing countries) is not in a form suitable for forecasting.

The complexity of the method is a function of historic stability of the situation to be analysed, the availability of a data base and the budget cost for the study. The shorter term forecasts even in less stable environments can usually be met adequately with simple trend methods which may not need to be unduly concerned with causality and uncertainty. The choice of method will be influenced by:

(i) Purpose and use of the forcasts.—Lead time, ie the period before forecasts come to fruition—range and sensitivity analysis are not necessarily helpful to the decision maker, hence the penalty for being wrong, ie investing too soon or too late, must be examined.

(ii) Reliability and Credibility.—Mathematical techniques may appear to be non-biassed but they are not necessarily more accurate.

(iii) Mathematical ease.

(iv) Availability of data.

Time Series and Trend Extrapolation.—These are the simplest techniques requiring no broad data base nor consideration of causality, but they may be modified to take into consideration expected variations from the base case. They assume basically that air travel demand will follow its established pattern of growth and that future demand is a time function of the past experience.

Time series analysis differs from extrapolation of historical trends by the use of mathematical curves, such as the Logistic and Gompertz curves (sometimes known as intrinsic models), in which time is taken to be the only variable on which prediction is based and a mathematical growth curve is selected to fit the actual historical data. Although such methods will suffice for certain applications such as annual budget forecasts and short term development, these methods are not considered satisfactory for any other forecasts, especially cases involving turning points and long term planning.

Judgemental Methods.—The judgemental or subjective method requires an educated guess of the travel demand to be made based on past experience of traffic volume and intuition of the future. Although no demand models are used, factors that may influence demand are taken into account.

Judgemental forecasts can be produced by a single analyst or a panel of experts. The latter is known as the Delphi technique, the aim of which is to narrow the wide band of the individual forecasts by a carefully designed programme of questionnaires and feedback following which the participants either re-affirm their original opinions or revise them. Although this method has the advantage of low cost and ease of production, it is limited to short term forecasting only or where limited data exists, such as in the case of new airline routes.

Market Research Method.—This is sometimes known as Category Analysis or Cross Classification method and relates the travel patterns of a given segment of the population to its demographic and economic characteristics. The production of trips is primarily attributed to households and their trip behaviour is dependent on the location and the characteristics of the household such as occupation and income, family size and structure, car ownership, number of workers, population, etc.

There are three critical assumptions bearing on the validity of this method:

The behaviour of homogeneous categories in the population is different between the categories and constant within them.

A realistic assumption is needed on the projected growth of the traffic group within an individual cell.

The model should take into account expected changes in the socio-economic structure of the population.

The advantages of this method are that it is not mechanistic like trend curves and it is not an averaging process, providing the categories used are well defined.

The disadvantages are the large input of data required (indeed category analysis in practice is mainly concerned with forecasting a number of variables in each of the above mentioned categories) and the relatively short validity of the intermediate forecasts.

Econometric Methods.—The econometric method relates the traffic to underlying economic parameters such as GDP, income per capita and service variables such as fare levels and trip time, and it shows an economic relationship through one or more equations between demand (dependent variable) and a number of predictor or independent variables.

The initial step which is also common in producing any forecast of air passenger traffic is the review of past trends. This will provide a reasonable indication of the general characteristics for a forecasting model. The next step is to identify factors such as population, income and income distribution, fare levels and how they may have influenced demand in the past. In general, the selection of variables will be determined by the availability of data, consistency, reliability, the size of the base and perhaps most important, the availability of projected growth values of the independent variables selected. It is worth noting that forecasting the GNP or other indices may not be easier than forecasting traffic growth itself.

Factors affecting air traffic demand can be grouped in two broad categories, socio-economic and transport related. The first group includes general economic activities, geographic and political environment and demography; transport related variables are cost of travel time, comfort, safety, accessibility and reliability. Demand may be influenced by a complex interaction of one or more of these variables.

The choice of the general form of the demand equation will depend on historical traffic trends, data, period of forecast, price elasticity etc, and it could be a linear form, log-linear, exponential or semi-logarithmic, or some combination of these forms. A functional relationship between the dependent and independent variables can be derived from the data collected and this relationship is then calibrated by testing the equation over the base period. The object of the calibration test is to find the relationship that gives the least discrepancy between the computed demand and actual observed demand using multiple regression analysis.

The final step in model development is evaluation in terms of its effectiveness to explain and forecast travel demand. This step may lead to reformulation of the model and hence repetition of previous steps.

The use of this technique tends to be limited to established mature markets where data, indices and growth rates are readily available.

HOURLY FLOW DESIGN.—The hourly flows for passengers, aircraft movements and cargo are determined from the corresponding annual forecasts. Hourly passenger throughput determines the size of terminal buildings, car parks and the requirements for airport access. Aircraft movements during busy periods determine the number of runways required, taxiways and apron gates together with the level of sophistication of the landing aids.

Hourly flows can be derived from annual volumes by applying calibrated factors or ratios. However, wide variations can be expected between airports because passenger flows depend on the type of traffic, ie short, medium, long haul, domestic or international and the nature of the traffic, business or leisure. Other practical influences are the size of the facility and particular ways that airlines may operate from an airport.

The measure of hourly flow has to be defined since it would be uneconomical to design a terminal building to the absolute peak hour flow as it would then be fully utilized only during one hour in a given year. Hence, in common with the design of other transport facilities, airports are designed to handle, in comfort, traffic which occurs during the defined busy periods, but congestion or overcrowding is accepted for only short periods at the busier times. In this way, an acceptable balance between comfort and cost can be made. This is shown diagrammatically in Figure 1.

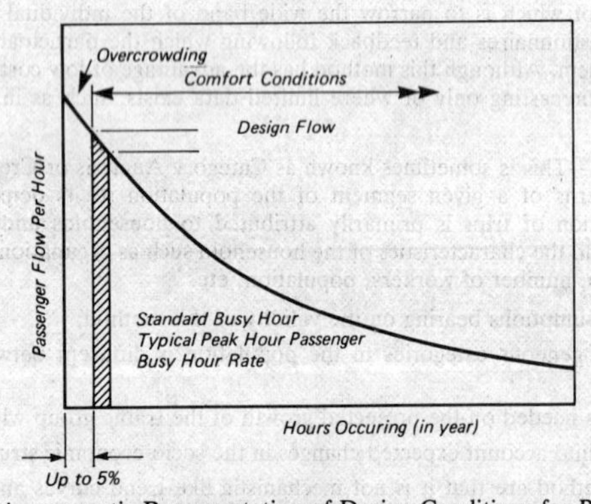

FIG. 1.—Diagrammatic Representation of Design Conditions for Passenger Flows.

Some busy hour measures which have been developed by various authorities are (i) Standard Busy Rate, (ii) 5% Busy Hour, and (iii) Typical Peak Hour Passenger.

Standard Busy Rate (SBR).—SBR is defined as the thirtieth busiest hour in the year and it is mainly used in the UK. Figure 2 shows the empirical relationship between SBR and annual passenger throughput based on selected UK Airports. The relationship is less reliable below 0·4 m to 0·5 m passengers per annum as particular factors begin to predominate. The critical design parameter for the terminal building at these levels would be its ability to process the full load of passengers of the largest aircraft, over a reasonable time period: this is particularly important in relation to arrivals, as disembarkation occurs over a relatively short period

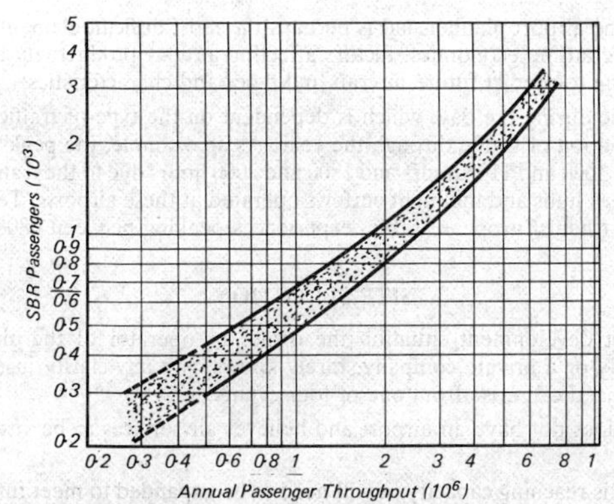

FIG. 2.—Relationship between Annual Passenger throughput and SBR. (*CAA and Sir Frederick Snow & Partners*).

compared to departing passengers whose arrival at the airport can be spread up to 2 hours before the scheduled time of departure.

Busy Hour Rate (BHR).—This standard measures the percentage of passengers that experience conditions worse than the comfort conditions during a given year. This level is set by the airport authority concerned, as for example, in the UK, BAA has adopted 5% and in France, Aeroport de Paris Autorité uses 3%.

Typical Peak Hour Passenger (TPHP).—This method has been developed by the U.S. Federal Aviation Administration (FAA) using data from US airports, and the relationship between annual passengers and TPHP is given in Table 3.

TABLE 3.—RELATIONSHIP BETWEEN ANNUAL PASSENGER THROUGHPUT AND TPHP (*Source*: FAA—Facility Requirement Forecasts for Medium Air Transport Hubs through 1980 dated January 1964)

Annual Passengers (millions)	TPHP percentage of annual flows
over 20	0·030
10 to 19·9	0·035
1 to 9·9	0·040
0·5 to 0·9	0·050
0·1 to 0·49	0·065
under 0·1	0·120

Other methods of defining hourly flows include Busiest Hour, Average Daily Peak Hour/Peak Profile Hour etc. There is no universal measure that can be used in establishing passenger flows during busy periods, and no matter what method is used it has to be recognised that establishing hourly flows is relatively imprecise.

Aircraft Movements.—The relationship between passenger movements and aircraft movements in the busy hour is determined by two factors; the aircraft fleet mix and the load factor.

The load factor is the ratio of passengers carried to seats available. High average load factors make operations of aircraft more profitable but they imply that during peak periods passengers would be turned away. Experience has shown that scheduled services cannot operate satisfactorily with average load factors greater than 0·75 but inclusive tour services could be as high as 0·95 and 1·0 in the busy season.

Aircraft fleet mix is more difficult to forecast because it depends on the type of operation, sectors operated and aircraft technology. Airlines are very reluctant to forecast aircraft fleets mainly because of the changing technology of aircraft and a general unwillingness to reveal their fleet plans to possible competitors. The planner has to rely almost exclusively on his experience and knowledge of the aviation scene to determine 'average' plane sizes and seating configurations.

Present trends indicate that the number of propeller and turboprop aircraft will be reduced considerably (except in the special cases of very short field lengths) and the number of the more productive wide body and large jets will be increased. Judging what aircraft will be available and timing their introduction is one of the most important tasks of the airport planner and is perhaps the most difficult element of demand forecasting. An understanding of basic airline economics, factors affecting aircraft productivity and future technology is therefore essential in trying to predict future aircraft and types and characteristics.

The fluctuation of traffic during the day, which is dependent on the type of traffic handled at the airport, is as important as the variation of traffic through the year. As an example, the peak hour at Heathrow's No. 3 terminal occurs between 1000 and 1100 hours and 1800 and 2000 hours due to the transatlantic routes between London and the US Eastern hubs and the night curfews operated at these airports. Terminal 1, which handles mainly domestic and short haul European traffic, experiences peaking between 0800 and 0930 and between 1600 to 1800 hours.

SITE SELECTION

In almost every airport development situation the owner or operator of the airport, whether it is the Government, an Authority or a private company, rarely knows with any clarity just what is required in the particular situation. The need can arise from one of four events:

(i) the city or region does not have an airport and believes air services to be vital to its future economic development.

(ii) the existing airport is reaching capacity, it will need to be expanded to meet future demand, and it may be more advantageous to find an entirely new site.

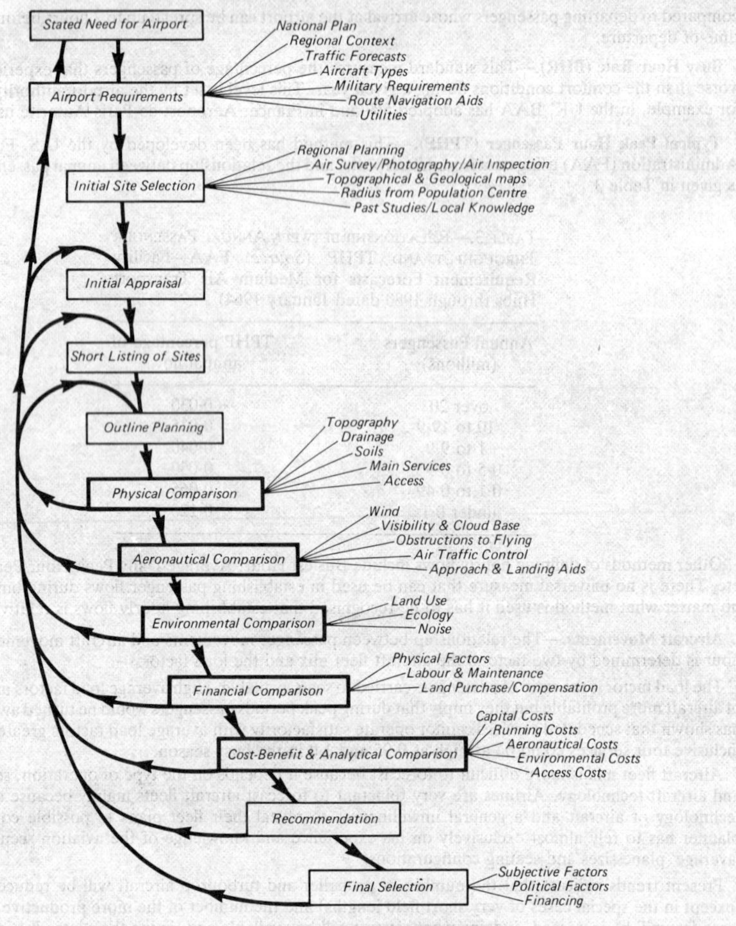

FIG. 3.—Site Selection Cascade.

(iii) the existing airport is reaching capacity, it cannot be expanded and a second airport is needed.

(iv) the existing airport creates so many noise and other disturbance problems that an alternative is wanted.

The problem can be as true for the developing countries where the improvement of air communications is a vital key in the countries' advance, as for the highly developed countries where the airports are frequently competing with urban growth in terms of land space and infrastructure demands and are also a nuisance to the peace of the community.

The owner will seek advice either from within his own airport authority and technical services or from international, public and private consulting organisations. Whoever it is has to consider the alternatives in a logical manner and study the factors to be taken into account in the process of evaluating future developments of an airport and selecting appropriate sites. The US FAA sets out master planning procedures and lists the following nine factors which should be included in a minimum site selection analysis, but the method of analysis has not been identified.

- Airspace Analysis
- Obstructions
- Environmental impact and nature of surrounding development
- Proximity to areas of aviation trip generation
- Ground access
- Physical site characteristics, including atmospheric conditions
- Utilities
- Land cost and availability
- Comparative analysis of alternative sites.

The process can be seen as a series of descending steps where, at each one, the studies that are made and the conclusions reached not only affect the subsequent step but may also modify the previous ones. The whole process is iterative and it can be so several times over. The analyst has to conceive, in successively more precise steps, what is required of the airport. Then he has to find a number of sites which can accept his concept, judging each site and comparing one another in physical, aeronautical, environmental, financial and economic terms to reduce the list initially to a few and finally to one.

The whole process is shown in diagrammatic form in Figure 3 and can be called the Site Selection Cascade. The main flow of the cascade starts from the owner's or operator's stated need for the airport. The analyst has to take this need, find out all possible factors that can contribute to the airport's future and develop a clear understanding of the basic requirements of the airport in the short, medium and long term.

Having determined the airport requirements mainly in terms of the length and number of runways, the overall size of the terminal area and other major facilities and the category of instrumentation of the airport, the analyst has to find the initial set of alternative sites of which the existing airport, if there is such, has to be one. Even if event (iii) or (iv) referred to in the first paragraph above is applicable, the existing airport should still be analysed for comparative purposes.

The list of sites has to be reduced to a short list by producing airport layout plans, firstly in broad terms, for all sites which then have to be compared to reduce the number. The method has then to be repeated in more detail for the smaller number of sites.

The cascade shows five steps of comparison but it is emphasised it is not necessary that all the steps will have to be considered every time. It is quite likely that a physical comparison would remove some of the sites as being worse than others, but it may be that aeronautical and environmental situations have to be applied before such a reduction is possible. No two studies will be alike and each airport site within a study will have to be considered individually. As the diagram indicates, every comparative step can make one reconsider the initial planning for that airport site and the process has to be repeated. It may, in certain exteme circumstances even affect the initial airport requirements and the process would have to be repeated again.

Finally, a short list of sites will have been achieved, perhaps 3 or 4. In the light of the previous work a more detailed scheme for the development of each of the short listed sites has to be drawn up so that the whole process of comparison in each of the necessary steps can be repeated.

To the right of the main cascade are given the many factors that have to be considered at each step in the process. These pointers are not necessarily comprehensive nor in every case is each item relevant. In some situations some of the items mentioned in one step have to be used; in others, for example, noise (usually included in the environmental comparison) might have to be considered in the physical comparison if it affects runway alignment, but the items indicated are intended to give the broad pattern of approach.

The airport owner or operator has to make a final selection once a recommendation has been made. It has to take into account the recommendation and all the investigations that have led to that, and it also has to take into account political factors, subjective factors and the potential financing problems.

Some particular points are:

Airport Requirements.—Essentially, the most important requirements are the length and direction of the runway or runways, the overall area for all the terminal facilities and the overall area for land needed for the whole airport. National or regional planning can help to define the scale of the airport but the traffic forecasts, involving an assessment of the aircraft types and taking into account any military requirement, will lead to the assessment of these fundamental needs.

For subsequent involvement after shortlisting sites, it may be necessary to assess the electrical power demand or other energy needs and utility service requirements, such as sewerage demand, as the availability for dealing with, or providing these services may be significant in the site comparison.

A knowledge of the air routes and associated aids for operating the airport will be needed for the more detailed comparison considerations.

Initial Site Selection.—In seeking a site for a new airport, the process of finding the sites to consider may either be the easiest or the hardest step of all in the site selection process. In urban environments in highly developed countries, which lack space, it may be that there is no such thing as an entirely new site and the planner has no choice but to compare existing airfields or disused military airfields. This has certainly been the situation in the United Kingdom for more than 30 years where all airport development has been on pre-war or old wartime airfields, but in the developing countries, the problem can be entirely different since potential new sites will exist. The airport planner might have immense difficulty in picking one particular location from another and he could, for example, face a variety of desert areas or, at the other extreme, mountainous, jungle areas.

The best way to begin is to seek the views of the local population and aviation interests, who will also have views on where the airport should be sited. Some may, to the planner, appear unacceptable, but it is essential not to discard any at this stage. The next step is to study all available mapping which can be supplemented by any available aerial photography and past studies or reports. Only when an initial set of sites has been selected, should an inspection by air or on the ground be considered and the choice of either or both will depend very much on the ease of access.

Population Centre.—It is essential to preset a journey time limit from the source or destination of most of the passenger traffic in making an initial selection. If the source is a single centre, such as a city, then it is relatively easy to draw a 'contour' from the city centre which should be in terms of ground travel time, say 45 minutes, rather than in measured distance. This 'contour' must have regard to road improvements or new access systems. The same principle should apply if there is more than one population centre. It will serve to eliminate any sites suggested which are too far away from the source of the traffic.

Physical Comparison.—The purpose in a physical comparison of several sites is not, initially, to quantify the total amount of work necessary to construct the airport on that site, but to compare the difficulties of construction on the one site with the others. Therefore, the first consideration in physical comparison is to determine what aspects of the construction will be similar on all sites for these can then be discarded from the preliminary reckoning. For example, if several sites are in similar desert country, there is no need to consider the topography, whereas if the sites are in thick, hilly country, the topography will probably be the most significant item. Complete assessment of work will be needed for the shortlisted sites for the financial comparison.

Some outline planning will have to be carried out for each site, in order to compare the volume of earthwork, drainage work, the provision of main services, the extent of the access systems and the soils and geology of the site on which the airport is to be constructed.

The comparison will generally be in qualitative terms, that is, one site in one particular aspect will be easier and cost less than the other, but it may be necessary to quantify some aspects in financial terms and this will link the physical comparison to the financial comparison.

Aeronautical Comparison.—While site A, for example, might be simpler to construct than site B, the ease with which aircraft operations might be handled on one site rather than the other may be quite the reverse. A comparison of the factors affecting aircraft operations may then be necessary.

In terms of meteorology, two factors must be studied, wind (direction, strengths and frequency) and visibility (visual range and cloudbase). Analyses will have to be based on recorded meteorological data whenever it is available. Frequently it has to be assessed from nearby meteorological stations; the data should be long-term, 10 years or more if possible. Wind analyses will indicate the value to aircraft operations of the runway bearing appropriate to the site under study by determining the crosswind usability and preferential direction of operation. Visibility analyses, combined with an obstacle survey, will determine the appropriate standard of navigation and approach aids.

Frequently the most important aspect to consider is the potential interference to safe flying by obstructions of high ground, buildings, overhead lines, pylons and radio masts. Guidance for obstacle assessment is given in the ICAO Annexe 14 and this should be sufficient for an aeronautical comparison. (See INTERNATIONAL STANDARDS AND PRACTICES).

Air traffic control services can usually be developed and adapted to meet the differing requirements for airports constructed on different sites and, generally, will not need to be studied in an aeronautical comparison. The exception is when aircraft operations from the particular site will conflict with other operations from an adjacent airport.

Environmental Comparison.—There are three factors on the cascade—land use, ecology and noise and of these the most important in almost all circumstances is land use; not only an assessment of the use to which the land is currently being put, but also an assessment of the potential use of the land, if it were not taken for the airport site. Thus the land use comparison might be in two parts and it may be necessary to quantify it in financial terms. If, for example, the land on one site was valuable to the economy in food production, the fact may be so very significant as to outweigh almost all other comparisons.

In certain other situations, the natural balance of ecology can be seen as an extremely important factor, for example, the ecology of the site of the proposed third London Airport of Maplin was one of the leading considerations that finally overturned the Commission's report on that study.

In the developed world in the 1960's and early 1970's, the consideration of environmental nuisance from aircraft noise became one of the most important aspects of airport planning, and engendered the subsequent introduction of quieter jet aircraft, noise abatement procedures and night curfews at major airports in the industrialised countries which has substantially reduced the noise nuisance. The social concern with aircraft noise has reduced in importance. Nevertheless, in a site comparison for airports in an urban environment, a simple comparison of whether one airport would cause more noise nuisance than another is valuable. In the USA, it would be essential as part of an environmental impact statement required by the FAA.

A number of methods of measuring noise nuisance have been developed in many countries for validity in their relevant social environment; these include the Noise Exposure Forecast (NEF) and the Composite Noise Rating (CNR) used in the USA, the Weighted Equivalent Continuous Perceived Noise Level (WECPNL) of the ICAO, the Noise and Number Index (NNI) used in the UK, and similar scales used in France, Germany and Canada; they can all be used comparatively and environmental considerations may dictate the use of one of them, but in practical terms, it will probably be sufficient to compare the EPNdB contour plan associated with one of the noisier, and more frequent, aircraft.

Financial Comparison.—The financial comparison of one site against another is a measurement of the differential cost of constructing an airport on the sites. It may be necessary to determine the total capital cost of physically constructing on each site, adding to this the cost to the Airport Authority of maintaining the construction over a period of say twenty years, and the cost of purchasing the land and any compensation involved. The financial comparison is thus a direct comparison between the costs of establishing the airport on different sites.

Cost Benefit and Analytical Comparison.—The results of the four methods of comparison have to be considered together since it is more than likely that different sites will emerge as the prior selection in each comparison above. Some items may carry greater weight than others and it is practical to use a scoring method with each comparison. It is not possible to evaluate in numerical or mathematical terms one comparison with another. For example, it is not possible to directly balance an environmental comparison against the physical comparison.

Attempts have been made to carry out such assessments by means of cost benefit analysis, where every item has been given a cost value. This has been compared to the benefits arising from development, and the benefits have also been priced in the same cost values. In a cost benefit comparison, the capital costs of providing the airport, the total running costs, including those by the Airport Authority, the airlines, concessionaires, etc, the aeronautical costs of flying into and out of the airport, the environmental costs and the notional costs of access time to and from the airport, have all to be taken into account.

The Roskill Commission in carrying out the Third London Airport Study attempted to do this in the extreme, but it did not ultimately succeed, for the simple reason that these costs and benefits cannot all be quantified sensibly in equivalent money terms. How can one compare, for example, the loss of a 400 year old church with the benefit gained by saving 5 minutes off the journey time of a million passengers?

Cost-benefit or any type of analytical comparison is valuable if it is considered as one other form of comparison alongside the less precise methods and all have to be judged together.

Recommendation and Final Selection.—The penultimate step in the cascade is labelled 'recommendation' which is the amalgam and conclusion of those who have carried out the previous comparisons and all the steps in the cascade. Since the consideration of four or five methods of comparison, not directly interquantifiable, must almost certainly be a matter of judgement, the weighting of priorities is best carried out at first individually, and then by the group of experts to reach a combined conclusion and recommendation for the preferential order of alternative sites.

The analyst's recommendation must then be presented to the person or organisation who commissioned the study and who has to make the final decision or selection. Obviously, he can accept the recommendation given to him, but he may weigh the comparisons differently, even subjectively. It may only be possible to consider finance at this step; for example, he may conclude that the difficulty of finding the capital for development would predominate. Political factors are frequently most important of all, but cannot be judged until this final step in the cascade.

So the process of site selection can have a scientific or logical basis to the method, but the final choice is usually dictated by other typical, but rarely scientific, considerations.

AIRPORT GEOMETRY AND CONCEPT

PLANNING SYSTEMS.—The airport is an interchange area, the means whereby people and goods can change from one mode of travel on the ground to another mode of travel in the air (and vice-versa) and where all the services to effect this change are provided. All airports have common factors, yet all are different. The differences are in the layout or geometry of one part of the airport in relation to another; in the geometry or arrangement of its individual parts; in scale or in concept.

Every airport, however small or large, has people and goods arriving by road, being managed by other people and services and leaving by aircraft. This, of course, also happens in the reverse direction and there are many variations to this basic flow system.

This simple idea can be expanded, as a whole range of factors, influences, conditions, resources and methods affect it and cause the endless variety in airports. It is easiest to consider the airport as four planning systems surrounding a core, as shown in Figure 4.

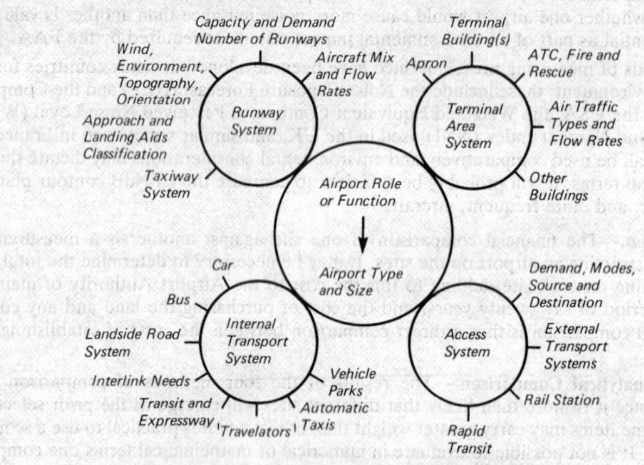

FIG. 4.—The Planning Systems.

The core is the concept of the role or function of the airport and all the planning has to keep this constantly in view. Surrounding the core are the four planning systems, namely, the runway system, the terminal area system, the access system and the internal transport system. The four are interdependent and are related to the core role; in small airports the runway system is the most important of the four and in large airports the fourth system, that of internal transport becomes much more significant in the planning. The physical relationship of these parts of the airport are determined, not only by the needs of the airport itself, but by outside constraints, such as topography, the location or direction of the access system, etc. It has been stressed that every airport is a compromise of many factors.

THE ROLE OF THE AIRPORT.—The core concept requires the planner to understand the function of the airport, its relationship with the types of aircraft that are using the airport and the resulting type of airport. It introduces the concept of size or degree of magnitude of the airport.

At the smallest or first degree, the airport is an airfield with a role in general aviation, flying training, agricultural aviation, small scale air taxi operations and business flying.

The second degree handles commercial air transport from local, feeder and commuter air services. Substantial air taxi and business operations increase demands of this level of airport and a military airfield can also be thought of as being at this level.

The third degree of airport serves a major city or a region with mainly domestic airline operations and probably with a few international operations. Major military bases, many joint user with civil operations, come into this level.

Finally, the fourth degree of magnitude handles international operations on a major scale and this level can be thought of in terms of single and multiterminal airports, or in another way, as hub, interchange and termination or base airports.

These conceptual roles of the airport must not be confused with any other form of classification, coding and categorisation. For example, for the purposes of applying its recommendations and standards, the International Civil Aviation Organisation (ICAO) codes airports by the length of its main runway, together with the wing span and wheel base of the aircraft capable of using the airport. The FAA categorises airports into general aviation airports, hub airports and transport airports mainly for the purpose of its own financing programme and it is quite possible for a large US general aviation airport to be larger than a hub airport in another country.

THE RUNWAY SYSTEM.—The runway system comprises the runway or runways, the taxiways linking the parking aprons to the runways, the underrun and overshoot areas, the strips of unobstructed ground surrounding the runway, in fact, the whole of the paved and protected areas provided to allow the aircraft to move under their own power when on the ground.

The major items which have to be determined are (i) runway length, (ii) runway direction or orientation, (iii) number of runways, (iv) operational category of the runways, and (v) capacity of the system.

Decisions on these lead on to the width of the runways, the size and nature of the strip and other associated areas, the size and location of taxiways and the provision of safety areas. Standards and practices are given in ICAO Annex 14, in the UK CAP 168, in the USA FAA Advisory Circular Subject No. 150 and in similar documents of other countries. The major requirements are summarised in INTERNATIONAL STANDARDS AND PRACTICES.

Runway Length.—The runway length is normally based on the critical aircraft either for maximum take-off weight or the take-off weight for a defined stage sector and it is calculated using either the manufacturers aircraft performance charts or the US FAA publication 'Runway Length Requirements for Airport Design' AC 150/5325-4.

Factors that influence the runway length of the aircraft performance characteristics are (1) elevation of the airport, (2) temperature, (3) runway gradient, and (4) wind strength and direction.

An example of an aircraft performance chart is given in Figure 5 and relates the runway length requirement basically to take-off gross weight, but it also brings in other parameters, ie the aircraft flap setting, the airport reference temperature (or temperature of operating) and the pressure altitude which can approximate to the elevation of the airport. The chart demonstrates that at higher temperatures the runway length requirement is substantially greater than at the standard day temperature. Generally, but not always, the take-off distance requirement for the critical aircraft will be greater than the landing distance but both have to be determined in a similar manner.

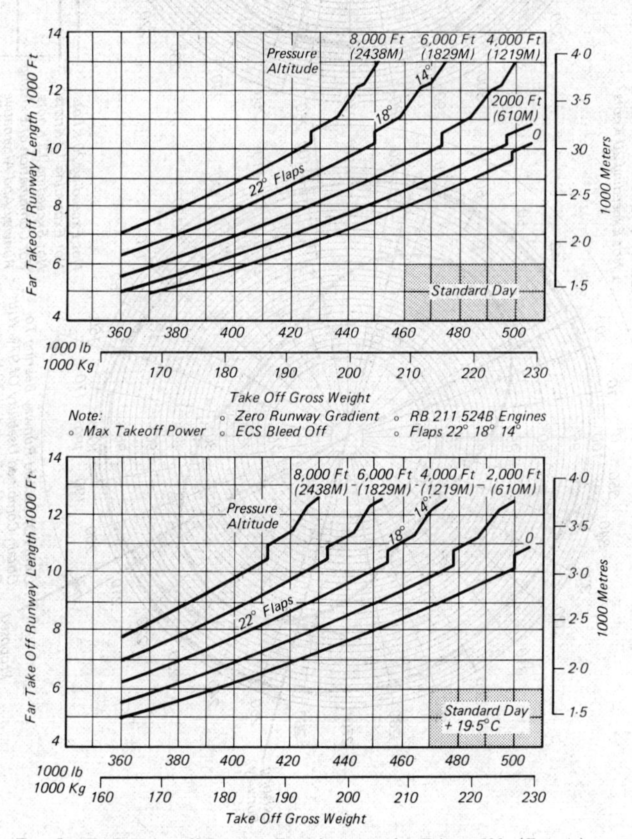

FIG. 5.—FAR Take-off Runway Requirements for Tristar 500. (*F.A.A.*)

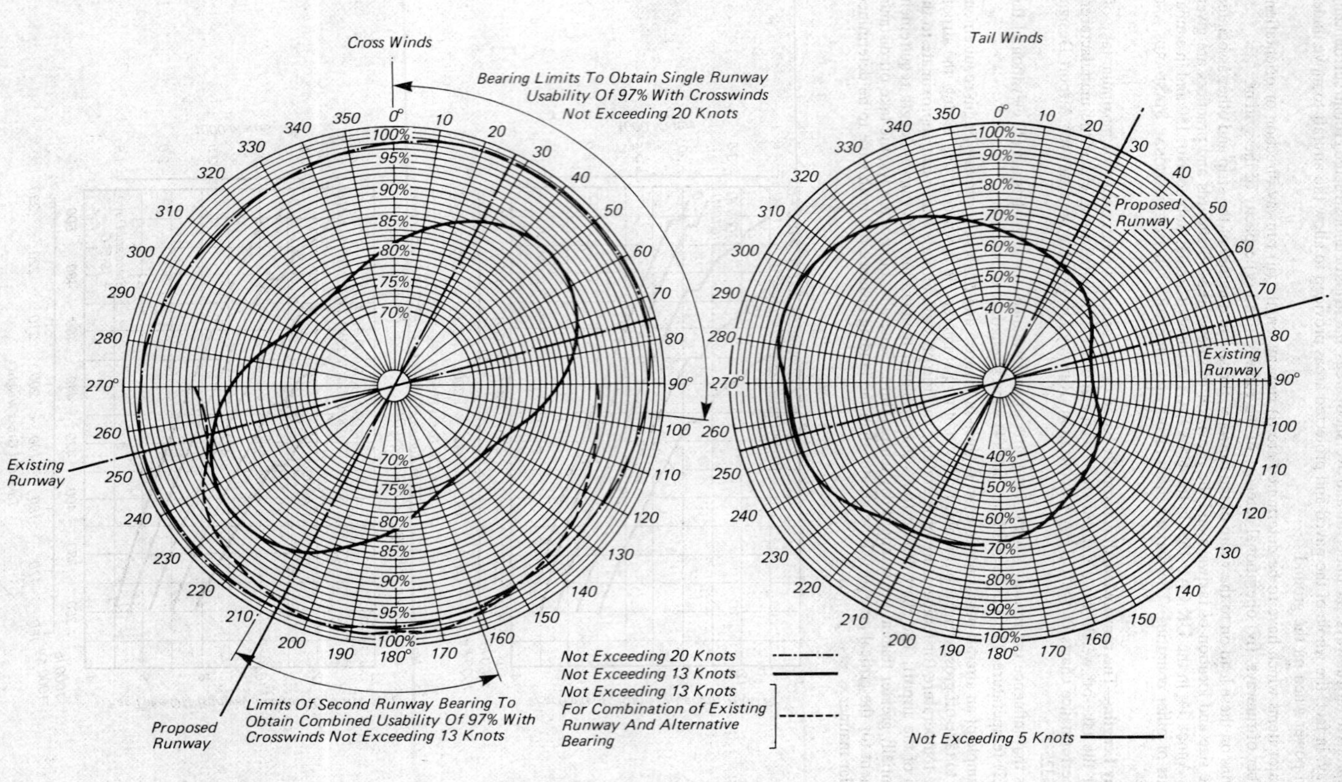

FIG. 6.—Polar Diagrams of Runway Usability.

The requirement must then be met by the runway and its associated areas but it does not have to be provided totally in paved runway. In certain circumstances, stopway at both ends of the runway and, or, clearway, which is clear flying space, can meet part of the aircraft runway length need. In all cases, the minimum length of emergency distance available has to be calculated and the limiting take-off run of the aircraft requirement has to be provided in paved runway. A general understanding of the take-off path of the aircraft's flight in its various segments is a basic essential to the planning and determination of the runway length.

Runway Orientation.—It used to be most important to direct the runway in line with the prevailing wind, but today's jet aircraft are stable even in fairly severe cross winds and can land and take off with tail winds up to about 5 knots, with the result that the topography and environment frequently becomes of much greater importance than the wind strengths and directions. Nevertheless, it is essential to plot a wind rose of the wind frequency and direction that have been analysed for a period of at least five years. The geometrical method of plotting a wind rose can now be replaced by computer analysis for the whole 360° and plotted, if necessary, as a polar diagram as shown in Figure 6. The optimum direction from the point of view of the wind is that which suffers the least effect of cross wind components. The limiting cross wind component strengths normally taken are 10 knots for very light aircraft, 13 knots for small propeller driven transport aircraft and 20 knots for jet commercial aircraft but in certain situations, it may be better to consider an individual critical aircraft.

The head and tail wind components can also be calculated in a similar way enabling the preferred direction of operation on the runway to be determined.

Number of Runways.—There are two conditions, capacity and crosswind, necessitating the provision of more than one runway. At large airports it is the frequency and total number of operations that cause a single runway to be insufficient and for that situation some capacity calculations are necessary in relation to an estimate of the future demand in terms of aircraft movements. At smaller airfields or major airports where smaller aircraft are likely to operate, the meteorological conditions become more significant and an analysis of the component of cross winds is essential in order to determine whether the smaller aircraft, which are more susceptible to cross winds, will require one or more subsidiary runways. Various forms of runway systems are shown in Figure 7.

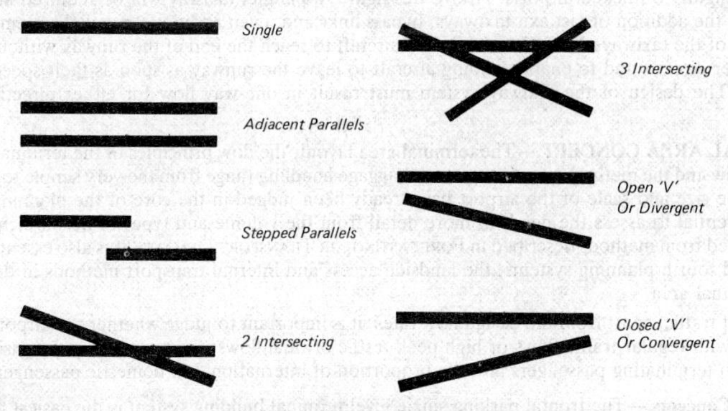

FIG. 7.—Runway Systems.

The capacity of a runway is determined by the maximum sustained rate at which it can be used by aircraft without significant delay to aircraft movements. Airport runways handling transport aircraft operations are generally considered to have reached capacity when delays to departures average 4 minutes during the two adjacent normal peak hours of the week. For general aviation operations the average delay level is two minutes in the peak hour of the week.

Capacity is dependent upon weather, ATC procedures, experience of controllers, visual aids, navaids, aircraft mix, surface condition, adequacy of taxiways and aprons, and arrival/departure mix.

The capacity depends to a large degree on the ability of the taxiway system to facilitate the movement of aircraft traffic to and from the runway. Minimising occupancy times by aircraft through the provision of a parallel taxiway and the location of exit taxiways will increase the capacity of the runway. The exit taxiways should be located to provide easy and rapid flow to a point where the aircraft is considered clear of the runways. Holding bays where aircraft taking off can wait near the runway will also enhance airport capacity. Each part of the runway system has to be balanced with the others.

The annual capacity of a single runway will exceed 150,000 transport operations providing the taxiway facilities are appropriate.

Runway Classification.—The standards associated with the runway which determine strip width, clearances (both on the ground and in the air), gradients and so on are affected by the sophistication of the equipment to be installed to assist the aircraft to approach to land.

There are three basic classifications.—The first is where simple visual aids, often but not necessarily including aeronautical ground lighting, are provided to aid the pilot; the aircraft operate under Visual Flight Rules (VFR), the runway is classified as a 'visual runway' and the appropriate standards are set out in the various documents.

The second is where simple radio aids, such as a non-directional beacon (NDB) or a VHF omni-directional radio range aid (VOR), are installed; the aircraft may operate under Instrument Flight Rules (IFR), the airport may be used in slightly less clear weather conditions 'lower minima', and the runway is classified as an 'Instrument approach runway' with its appropriate standards.

The third classification is that of a 'precision instrument approach runway' where more sophisticated aids, including an instrument landing system (ILS), are installed enabling the aircraft to approach and land in poor or even bad weather. Due to the high cost of such installations, including appropriate ground levelling, lighting, electrical supplies and so on, it is only worth providing precision instrument runways at major airports, where all aircraft are almost certain to be operated under IFR. There are five categories of aircraft operation to such runways, depending on the degree of accuracy, reliability, duplication etc both of the equipment on the ground and in the aircraft. The categories are expressed in the following five values of weather minima below which the pilot has to be able to see the runway, and complete the landing and taxiing operations.

Category 1: 60 m decision height and about 800 m runway visual range (RVR). Visual landing and taxiing.
Category 2: 30 m decision height and about 400 m RVR. Visual landing and taxiing.
Category 3A: Zero height and about 200 m RVR. Visual final phase landing and taxiing.
Category 3B: Zero height and about 50 m RVR. Visual taxiing.
Category 3C: Zero visual reference.

Taxiways.—The taxiways enabling the aircraft to manoeuvre between the parking aprons and the runway are a key part of the runway system. Single entry taxiways, which necessitate aircraft to backtrack along the runway before and after landing, will allow up to 10 operations per hour (depending on the type of aircraft) at relatively lightly trafficked airports. Above this figure, a parallel taxiway will be required and this can be improved by the addition of fast exit taxiways, bypass links and, even additional parallel systems. Essentially, the function of the taxiways is to allow taking-off aircraft to reach the end of the runway without interference to or by other aircraft and to enable landing aircraft to leave the runway as soon as their speed has reduced sufficiently. The design of the taxiway system must result in one-way flow for either direction of runway operation.

TERMINAL AREA CONCEPT.—The terminal area layout, the flow principles of the terminal building, the passenger flow and the methods of passenger and baggage handling range from the very simple to the extremely complex. The size and scale of the airport has already been judged in the core of the planning systems and it is then essential to assess the needs in more detail from the volume and types of flow which have already been estimated from methods described in FORECASTING AIR TRANSPORT DEMAND. It is also essential to consider the third and fourth planning systems, the landside access and internal transport methods in deciding on the type of terminal area.

In terms of traffic, apart from the design flow rates, it is important to judge whether the airport is one which has to cope with regular traffic flows or high peak traffic or tidal flows; the proportion of transit and transfer passengers to terminating passengers and the proportion of international to domestic passengers.

Terminal Concepts.—The frontal parking single level terminal building system is the easiest to understand. It is shown diagrammatically in Figure 8 and is satisfactory for small flows and few aircraft. Passenger movements are carried out by walking and baggage handling either by hand or by simple trolley. Probably, more than 90% of the world's airports have simple terminal systems like this, but these airports will handle much less than 90% of the total passengers worldwide.

A slight upgrading of this simple system introduces 1½ or 2 level operation (Figures 9 and 10). Newcastle Airport in the UK is a good example of the 1½ level system.

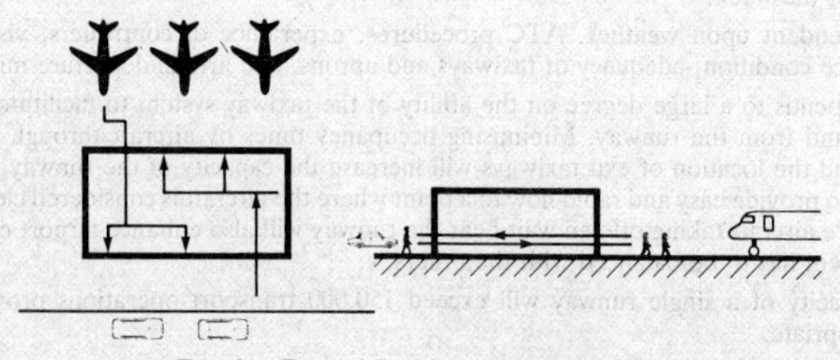

FIG. 8.—Frontal Parking—Single Level.

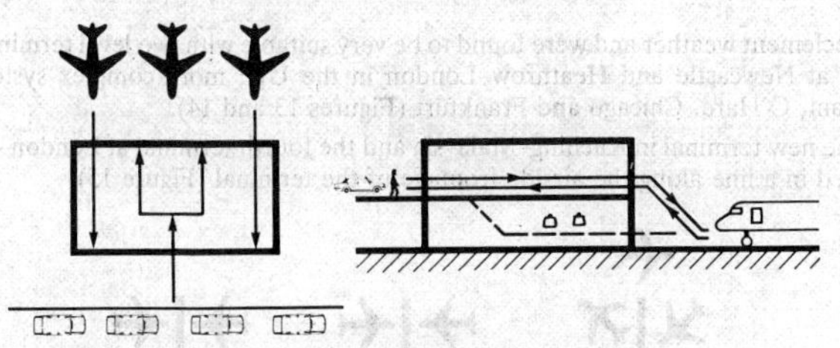

FIG. 9.—Frontal Parking—1½ Level.

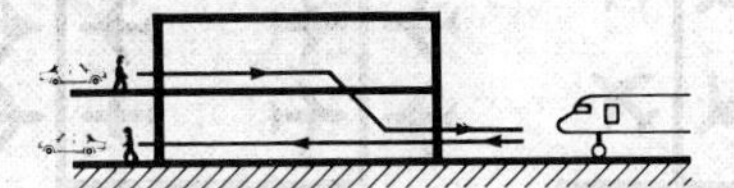

FIG. 10.—Frontal Parking—2 Level.

A very efficient variation of frontal parking is the terminal system at Hanover, Germany which has shaped the terminal in the form of a triangle (Figure 11). The aircraft are parked frontally on two sides with vehicular and passenger access on the third side.

Simple frontal parking terminal systems handle up to a million passenger movements a year in a fairly straightforward manner. Two level buildings, larger aircraft, apron congestion and the need for protection from weather has led to the use of passenger loading devices, such as noseloaders and airbridges and these are in use in all terminal concepts (Figure 12).

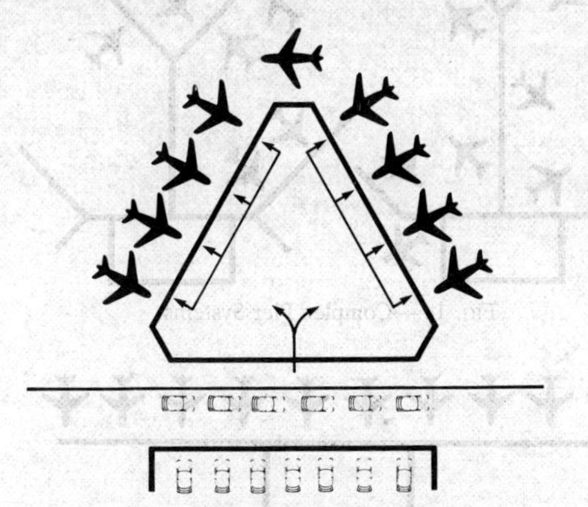

FIG. 11.—Frontal Parking—2 Level Triangular.

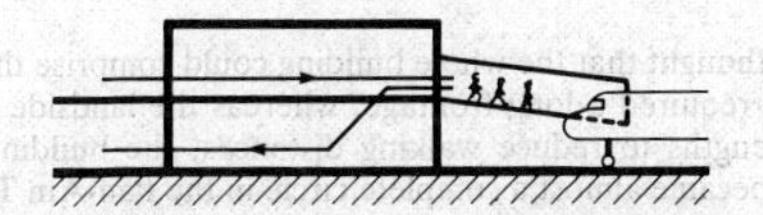

FIG. 12.—Frontal Parking—2 Level with Air Bridge.

The next step from walking between terminal and aircraft was the use of buses and the method is still by far the most common of all concepts. It has, in parallel with others, been developed with improved bus type vehicles, scissor lift vehicles, airport lounges and various hybrids; examples of this are Dulles–Washington, Mirabel–Montreal and Jeddah. Another use for buses and vehicles of this type for all terminal area concepts is to cater for excessive peaks and overflows.

Larger aircraft and more aircraft led to longer walking distances and apron congestion by buses, other vehicles and equipment. Piers or terminal fingers were introduced to avoid these problems and to protect passengers from inclement weather and were found to be very suitable with two level terminal building systems. Simple forms are at Newcastle and Heathrow–London in the UK; more complex systems of piers are at Schipol, Amsterdam, O'Hare, Chicago and Frankfurt (Figures 13 and 14).

At Orly–Sud, the new terminal in Kuching–Malaysia and the fourth terminal at London–Heathrow the piers have been extended in a line along the airside frontage of the terminal (Figure 15).

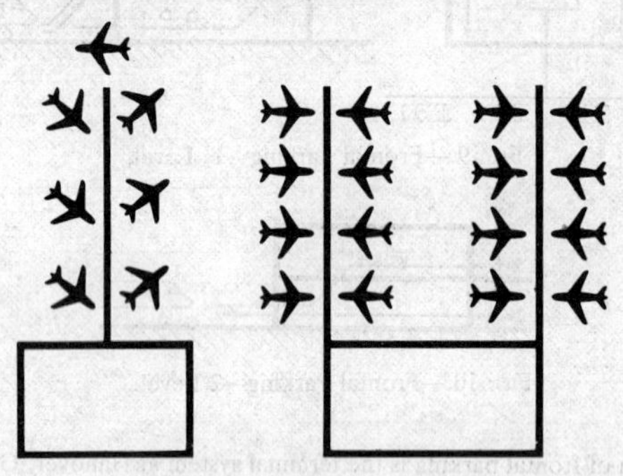

FIG. 13.—Simple Pier Systems.

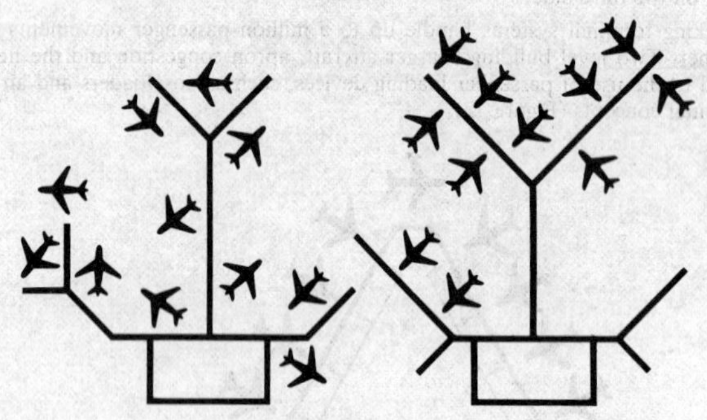

FIG. 14.—Complex Pier Systems.

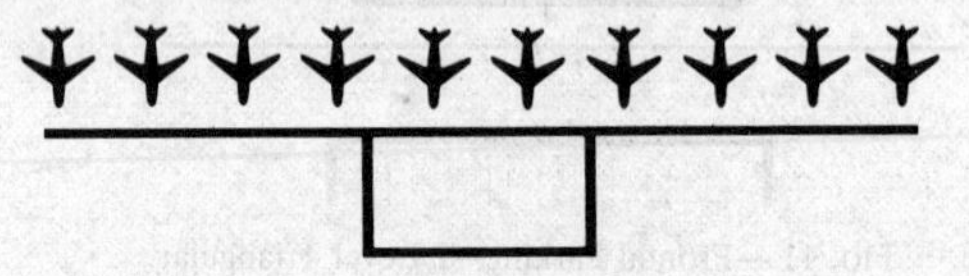

FIG. 15.—Linear Parking.

This last arrangement led to the thought that the whole building could comprise the airside pier (Figure 15), but, as the aircraft and the airside required a long frontage, whereas the landside vehicle picking up/setting down area needed shorter kerb lengths to reduce walking distances, the building became curved and an example of this is Berlin–Tegel. It became almost a complete circle in the Pan-Am Terminal in Kennedy–New York, and more recently at Kansas City, and completely in Toronto where the airside pier became an annular ring. The common services, facilities and car parks had then to change from horizontal distribution to vertical distribution in a multi-storey central block (Figure 16.)

In parallel with the pier to arc to ring development, the airside facilities were separated from the landside and passenger handling facilities became a satellite to the main central terminal building. One of the earliest of these was at Geneva and a similar example is at Los Angeles: each satellite is linked underground at these airports by a subway, but with a little loss of flexibility in aircraft operation. The satellite can be linked above ground as at Koln–Bonn, Abu Dhabi and San Francisco (Fig. 17).

The central aim (but not always the achievement) in all systems has been to facilitate passenger, baggage and cargo flow but it has often been at the expense of restraining similar freedom of movement by the aircraft.

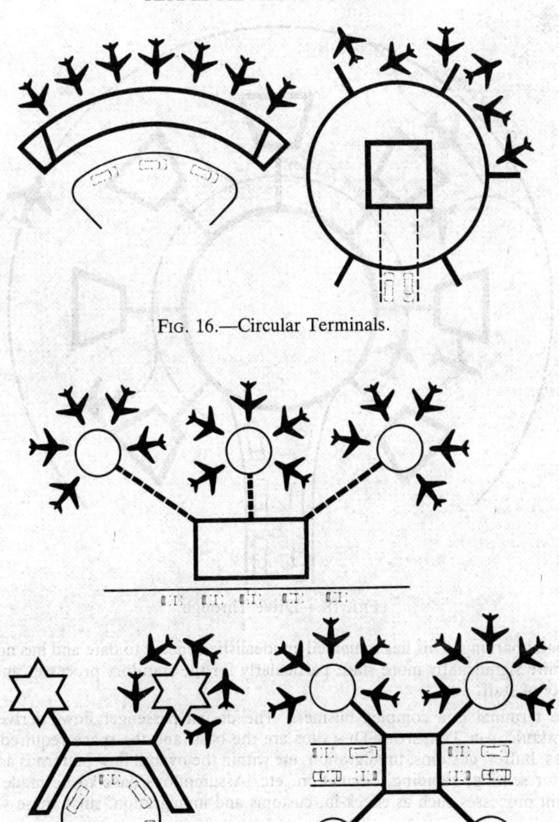

FIG. 16.—Circular Terminals.

FIG. 17.—Satellite Systems.

A determined and innovative attempt to redress the balance was taken in the design of the first terminal at Paris–Charles de Gaulle, providing the drivethrough concept (Fig. 18).

All terminal systems then are of the frontal parking, pier access parking, linear parking, satellite parking or remote parking principles, or they are combinations or variants of two, three or four of these fundamental concepts.

Transit between terminal and aircraft in the simple systems of all the four concepts has been and will continue to be by walking. As walking lengths have increased, travelators have been put into pier systems, as at Frankfurt, Heathrow–London and many others. Automatic trains have been put into satellite systems, as in Miami, Tampa and Tacoma–Seattle and Dallas–Fort Worth.

Centralisation and Decentralisation.—With any variation of the five concepts outlined above, the necessary airline and governmental passenger handling control operations within the terminals can be grouped in one or more central areas or they can be dispersed, or decentralised, to points close to each aircraft gate. The vast majority of airport terminals have centralised passenger handling, eg Heathrow Terminal 3–London, all small airports, e.g. Newcastle Airport, but the airline procedures can be carried out at the aircraft gates giving partial decentralisation as at Heathrow Terminal 1–London on domestic flights, where a heavy baggage drop facility retains the centralised part of the operation.

Immigration and hand baggage customs checks can be carried out at the gate, leaving only heavy baggage collection and customs inspection centralised. The West German Airports, eg Koln–Bonn and Hanover are clear examples of this form. Decentralisation allows for later checking in and greater reassurance to the passenger regarding the destination of his baggage but it does require more staff to operate. The principle has led to the unit terminal concept where all the operations are related to individual aircraft gates and of necessity

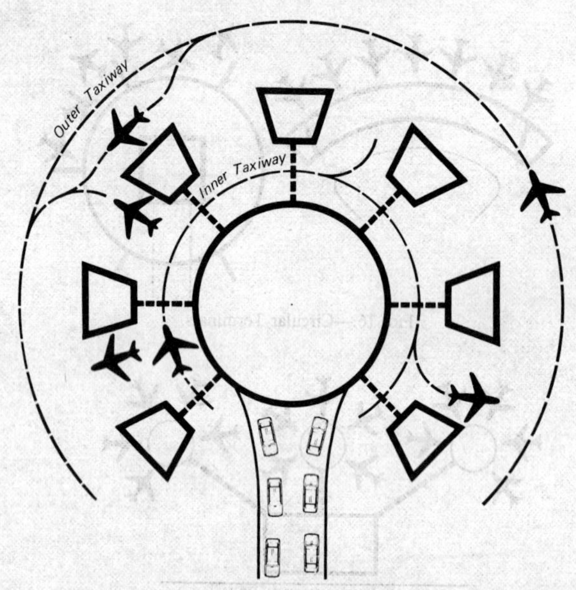

FIG. 18.—Drive Through.

involves aircraft frontal parking. This has remained an idealistic concept to date and has not yet been put into practice. It will require significantly more staff, particularly for the statutory processes and airlines, together with greater mobility of staff.

The sizing of the terminal is a complex business. The design passenger flows derived by the methods described in FORECASTING AIR TRANSPORT DEMANDS are the basis and the space required for each function, eg departure lounges, buffet, customs, immigration, etc within the overall flow pattern is assessed on a normal architectural basis for seating, standing, circulation, etc. Assumptions have to be made also for the times required for different processes such as check-in, customs and immigration, since these will affect the space needed.

There is no general planning figure to relate terminal area to the passengers handled due to the many variables, eg centralised or decentralised concept, rates of domestic to international passengers, etc, but it is likely that the area needed will be in the range of 10 m^2 to 25 m^2 of building per passenger movement in the standard busy hour but these figures exclude airline offices.

Apron Layout.—The layout of the apron is directly tied to the terminal building principle which, itself, is linked intrinsically to the aircraft handling method, of which there are basically two: the aircraft can either manoeuvre under its own power or it can park under power and be pushed out backwards by aircraft tractor. The use of tractors or tugs has increased for two reasons; the first is that increased numbers of aircraft can be handled on less apron by being pushed out, since a self-manoeuvring aircraft requires very much greater space in which to turn on entry and on exit. The second reason is that jet aircraft are able to idle their engines

TABLE 4.—CLEARANCES AT AIRCRAFT STANDS

Aerodrome Code Letter*	Clearance in metres
A	3
B	3
C	4·5
D	7·5
E	7·5

* See INTERNATIONAL STANDARDS AND RECOMMENDED PRACTICES for explanation.

without giving any forward thrust to the aircraft and so the aircraft tug is able to move a 'freewheeling' aircraft. The disadvantages of using aircraft tugs is that the pilot has to rely on yet another service rather than being in direct control of the parking operation and the airline costs increase.

The area of apron required will depend upon the terminal concept method of handling aircraft, etc. The aircraft stand clearances given in ICAO Annex 14 and reproduced in Table 4 are used as the basis for planning and taxiway clearances are given in INTERNATIONAL STANDARDS AND RECOMMENDED PRACTICES.

Other Buildings.—Other buildings and facilities have to be included with the terminal and the terminal apron in order to complete the terminal area. Air traffic control, fire and rescue and cargo buildings are usually associated with the terminal by function and, therefore, location in the general terminal area, but there are examples where some or all of these facilities have been located remotely.

Buildings indirectly associated with the terminal area, include aircraft maintenance hangars, aircraft catering, hotels, airport maintenance, fuel installations, aircraft sanitation, electrical sub-stations, communication buildings, security services and administration buildings. These are normally separated from the terminal area.

ACCESS SYSTEM.—Road access will be the main method and, as with normal road planning, it will be necessary to assess the traffic demand: for this, road traffic source and destination surveys may be needed, together with an analysis from the air traffic forecasts. The designer must not forget that it may be necessary to provide special facilities for buses or coaches, taxis and airport service vehicles. Road access for small airports will obviously be simple, but for larger airports, it may terminate in a single or multi level system. In planning the access to the airport, one principle to bear in mind is to aim to guide the driver to his desired destination within the airport by giving him easy directions allowing him to make one decision in terms of route at one time. The type of road access will to some extent depend on the nearby external road systems which may be of local roads or of motorway type. Rail systems can be very useful at large airports as an addition to access to the airport by road, but they probably need to serve at least two million passenger movements a year before a rail access system should be considered.

Examples where rail access has been extensively used are Gatwick–London, Frankfurt and Brussels, whereas the system into Charles de Gaulle–Paris, while it provides a valuable service, has not yet made a major contribution to travel to the airport. It may well be that the major single users of rail access between the airport and the local city are the airport staff.

Rapid transit or forms of subway systems, such as the London Underground have also been installed to serve airports, but as with rail systems, their capacity is so large and the service has limited destinations, that very careful study of its potential viability is essential.

INTERNAL TRANSPORT SYSTEMS

Landside Road System.—The landside road system extends from the road access to provide links between all the buildings and functions of the airport in all but the very large airports. It is again important to provide simple routing allowing route decisions to be made one at a time; for example, the car driver taking friends to the airport only wishes to know where to set down his passengers. Once he has done so, he may then wish to park his car and he should be able to see directions at that point: he should not be confused with the choice of car parking or setting down at the same time as he approaches the terminal. Segregation of vehicles for arriving and departing passengers is important and both should be segregated from cargo and all other airport service vehicles. The system should also allow vehicles leaving from vehicle parks, either to leave the airport or to drive to the picking up and setting down areas for arriving and departing passengers.

Though the demand for public car parking spaces can be related directly to the annual passenger throughput of the airport, this parameter varies considerably as indicated in Table 5.

TABLE 5.—PARKING SPACES PER MILLION ANNUAL PASSENGERS

Heathrow	550
Paris	735
Frankfurt	415
J. F. Kennedy	696
Orlando	200
Los Angeles	490
Tampa	550
Kansas City	770

Interlinks.—The terminal facilities at very large airports are separated by large distances or into several terminal buildings and interlinking between these buildings for passengers, staff and goods is essential. The variety of desired links between terminals, vehicle parks, rail stations, bus stations and so on can become very great and the internal transport system designed to provide such a multi-link system is critical to the basic terminal concept.

For example, if a road system is to provide the internal links, that road system may have to serve a complex bus system as well as use by private vehicles. In a multi-terminal airport, a passenger may leave his car in a car park adjacent to one terminal and arrive back a few days later at another terminal, whence he has to get back to the original car park.

The most common system of interlinking is that of internal buses, but there have been other systems installed at major airports and this may become more common as airports get larger in the future.

Travelators.—The use of travelators to transport people along lengthy corridors, such as in the piers at London–Heathrow and Amsterdam, has gained popularity in the last decade, but they have also been installed to transfer people from one terminal to another as at Frankfurt and Heathrow and they could be provided to link terminals to vehicle parks and other airport facilities. The concept of high speed travelators may one day be seen at a future airport.

Automatic Trains.—The concept of an automatic carriage or lift moving horizontally has been developed and installed to provide a rapid link between main terminal and satellite terminals. The system developed by Westinghouse has been installed at several airports in the USA and is currently being installed at Gatwick–London. Its limitation is inflexibility in that it can only run between a few points and, as mentioned earlier, the movement demand at airports leads to a need for multi-routing.

Automatic Taxis.—One possible solution to this problem is the introduction of small computer controlled vehicles moving on concrete multi tracks. The system has been under study for many years and is known as the automatic taxi system and it will be interesting to see if it is eventually developed for practical installation. If it is, it should meet airports' need more than all the other systems which have been installed to date.

INTERNATIONAL STANDARDS AND RECOMMENDED PRACTICES

The International Civil Aviation Organisation (ICAO) was established in 1947 following the Chicago Convention on International Civil Aviation held in 1944.

The Organisation is responsible for the establishment of international recommended practices and the facilitation of air transport by the reduction of formalities for customs and immigration. The work covers technical, economic, statistical, legal and technical assistance fields which are recorded in the ICAO publications.

The technical publications which relate particularly to airport design and planning are contained in a series of Annexes to the Convention on International Civil Aviation, and a series of manuals. The most important of these are:

ANNEXES TO THE CONVENTION ON INTERNATIONAL CIVIL AVIATION

Annex 10	Aeronautical Telecommunications	Vol. 1 Part 1: Equipment and Systems
Annex 14	Aerodromes	
Annex 16	Environmental Protection	Vol. 1, Aircraft Noise

MANUALS

Aerodrome Design Manual; Part 1; Runways, Part 2; Taxiways, Aprons & Holding Bays, Part 3; Pavements, Part 4; Visual Aids.

Airport Planning Manual; Part 1; Master Planning.

Airport Services Manual; Part 1, Rescue and Fire Fighting; Part 2, Pavement Surface Conditions.

Heliport Manual

Stolport Manual

The requirements for the operational areas of airports are covered by Annex 14 to the Convention on International Civil Aviation and reference should be made to this for the detailed standards and recommended practices. Excerpts in relation to obstacle limitation surfaces, are given in Figure 19 and Tables 6 and 7. Excerpts in relation to widths, clearances, vertical alignment of runways and taxiways are given in Tables 9 to 14. These excerpts are for guidance only and reference should be made to Annex 14 for full details.

Obstacle Limitation Surfaces.—Imaginary surfaces which extend over the area occupied by the airport and beyond its limits are defined. It is necessary to restrict the creation of new objects and to remove or mark existing objects (whether man made or naturally occurring) which project above these imaginary surfaces. A plan view of them is shown in Figure 19 and dimensions are given in Tables 6 and 7. The main components are:

(1) An inner horizontal surface located 45 m above the airport elevation extending to a horizontal distance *a* measured from the aerodrome reference point.
(2) A conical surface with a slope of 5% above the horizontal, a lower edge coincident with the periphery of the inner horizontal surface and an upper edge located at a height *b* above the inner horizontal surface.
(3) Transitional surfaces along the side of the strip and part of the side of the approach surface (*qv*) that slopes upward and outwards at *c*% to the inner horizontal surface.

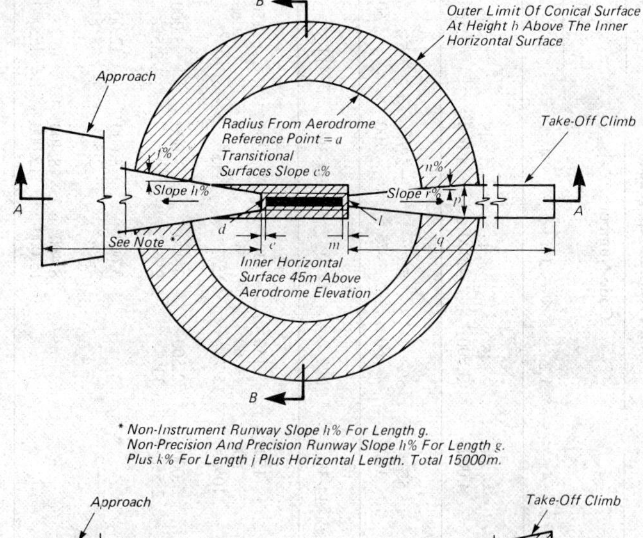

* Non-Instrument Runway Slope h% For Length g.
Non-Precision And Precision Runway Slope h% For Length g.
Plus k% For Length j Plus Horizontal Length. Total 15000m.

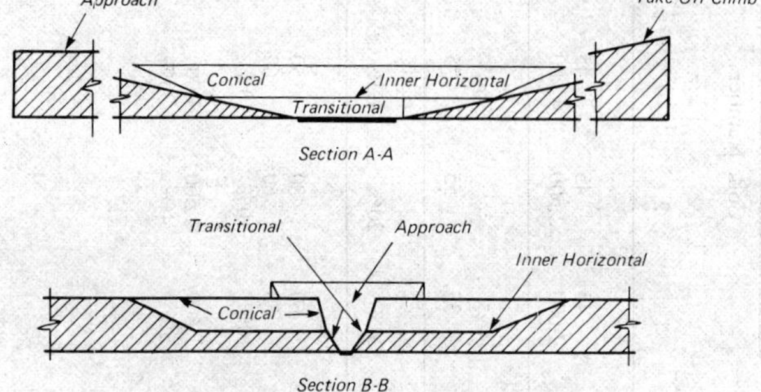

FIG. 19.—Obstacle Limitation Surfaces. (*ICAO*).

(4) Approach surfaces established for each runway direction used for the landing of aeroplanes. The limits of the approach surfaces are determined by an inner edge, two diverging sides (when viewed from the runway end) and an outer edge, the inner and outer edges being perpendicular to the flight path. The inner edge of length *d* is located at a distance *e* from the runway threshold. Each side diverges at a rate *f*% from the extended centreline of the runway to the outer edge and the length to the outer edge is *g*. The slope of the surface above the horizontal is *h*%. Non-precision approach and precision approach runways have an approach surface in which the outer section of length *j* is at a flatter slope *k*% and with a horizontal section beyond.
(5) Take-off surfaces established for each runway direction used for the take off of aeroplanes. The limits of the take-off surfaces are determined by an inner edge, two sides which initially are diverging and then parallel and an outer edge, the inner and outer edges being perpendicular to the flight path. The inner edge has a length *l* and is at the end of the clearway if provided (and if it exceeds the specified distance)

TABLE 6.—APPROACH RUNWAYS: DIMENSIONS FOR OBSTACLE LIMITATION SURFACES

		Runway Classification									
		Non-Instrument				Non-Precision Approach			Precision Approach		
		Code Number				Code Number			Category I		Category II or III
Surface and Dimensions[a]		1	2	3	4	1,2	3	4	1,2	3,4	3,4
INNER HORIZONTAL											
Height		45	45	45	45	45	45	45	45	45	45
Radius	*a*	2,000	2,500	4,000	4,000	3,500	4,000	4,000	3,500	4,000	4,000
CONICAL											
Slope		5%	5%	5%	5%	5%	5%	5%	5%	5%	5%
Height	*b*	35	55	75	100	60	75	100	60	100	100
TRANSITIONAL											
Slope	*c*	20%	20%	14·3%	14·3%	20%	14·3%	14·3%	14·3%	14·3%	14·3%
APPROACH											
Length of inner edge	*d*	60	80	150	150	150	300	300	150	300	300
Distance from threshold	*e*	30	60	60	60	60	60	60	60	60	60
Divergence (each side)	*f*	10%	10%	10%	10%	15%	15%	15%	15%	15%	15%
First section											
Length	*g*	1,600	2,500	3,000	3,000	2,500	3,000	3,000	3,000	3,000	3,000
Slope	*h*	5%	4%	3·33%	2·5%	3·33%	2%	2%	2·5%	2%	2%
Second section											
Length	*i*						3,600[b]	3,600[b]	12,000	3,600[b]	3,000[b]
Slope	*j*						2·5%	2·5%	3%	2·5%	2·5%
Horizontal section											
Length							8,400[b]	8,400[b]		8,400[b]	8,400[b]
Total Length							15,000	15,000	15,000	15,000	15,000

[a] All dimensions are measured horizontally.

[b] Variable length. Under certain circumstances the length of the second section may be increased but the length of the horizontal section will be reduced by the same amount.

NOTE.—Inner horizontal, inner transitional and balked landing surface omitted.

TABLE 7.—DIMENSIONS AND SLOPES OF OBSTACLE LIMITATION SURFACES

Surface and Dimensions[a]	Take-Off Runways Code Number 1	 2	 3 or 4
TAKE-OFF CLIMB			
Length of inner edge	60 m	80 m	180 m
Distance from runway end[b]	30 m	60 m	60 m
Divergence (each side)	10%	10%	12·5%
Final width	380 m	580 m	1,200 m 1,800 m[c]
Length	1,600 m	2,500 m	15,000 m
Slope	5%	4%	2%

[a] All dimensions are measured horizontally unless specified otherwise.
[b] The take-off climb surface starts at the end of the clearway if the clearway length exceeds the specified distance.
[c] 1,800 m when the intended track changes of heading greater than 15° for operations conducted in IMC, VMC by night.

or at a distance m from the end of the runway. Each side diverges at a rate of $n\%$ relative to the extended centre line of the runway until a specified maximum width p is reached, continuing thereafter at that width to the outer edge. The distance between the inner and outer edges, or length of take off surface, is q and the surface slopes up at $r\%$ to the horizontal.

Aerodrome reference codes.—These are assigned to airports depending on the main runway length, aircraft wing span and outer main gear wheel span in accordance with Table 8.

Runway Lengths.—The actual runway length to be provided for a primary runway should be adequate to meet the operational requirements of the aeroplanes for which the runway is intended and should be not less than the longest length determined by applying the corrections for local conditions to the operations and

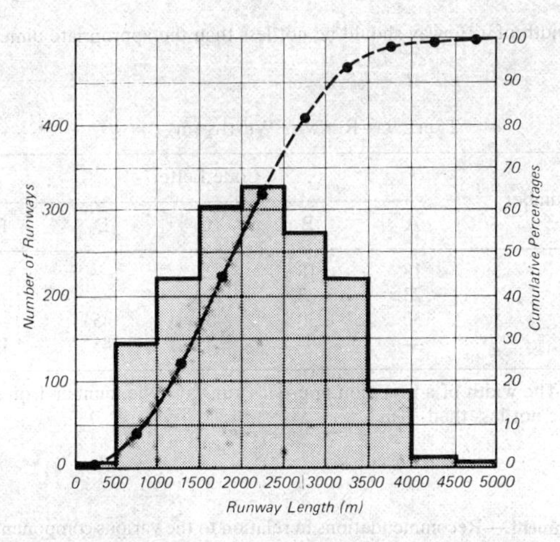

FIG. 20.—Runway Lengths at Aerodromes used for International Civil Aviation. (*ICAO*).

performance characteristics of the relevant aeroplanes. Runway lengths at aerodromes used for international civil aviation are shown in Figure 20. A typical graph for aircraft take off runway length requirements is shown in AIRPORT GEOMETRY AND CONCEPT. The actual runway length can be reduced within certain limits if a stopway or clearway is provided.

TABLE 8.—AERODROME REFERENCE CODE

Code Element 1		Code Element 2		
Code No.	Aeroplane Reference Field length	Code letter	Wing Span	Outer Main Gear Wheel Span
1	Less than 800 m	A	Up to but not including 15 m	Up to but not including 4·5 m
2	800 m up to but not including 1200 m	B	15 m up to but not including 24 m	4·5 m up to but not including 6 m
3	1200 m up to but not including 1800 m	C	24 m up to but not including 36 m	6 m up to but not including 9 m
4	1800 m and over	D	36 m up to but not including 52 m	9 m up to but not including 14 m
		E	52 m up to but not including 60 m	9 m up to but not including 14 m

Notes

(a) The aeroplane reference field length is the minimum field length required for take-off at maximum certificated take off weight, sea level, standard atmospheric conditions, still air and zero runway slope, as shown in the appropriate aeroplane flight manual prescribed by the certificating authority or equivalent data from the aeroplane manufacturer.

(b) The outer main gear wheel span is measured between the outside edges of the main gear wheels.

Runway widths.—The width of a runway should be not less than the appropriate dimension in Table 9.

TABLE 9.—RUNWAY WIDTHS (m)

Code Number	Code Letter				
	A	B	C	D	E
1	18	18	23	—	—
2	23	23	30	—	—
3	30	30	30	45	—
4	—	—	45	45	45

Note: The width of a precision approach runway code number 1 or 2 should be not less than 30 m.

Runway Vertical Alignment.—Recommendations in relation to the various components of vertical alignment are given in Table 10.

TABLE 10.—RUNWAY VERTICAL ALIGNMENT

	Code Number			
	4	3	2	1
Maximum effective slope	1%	1%	2%	2%
Maximum slope	1·25%	1·5%	2%	2%
Maximum change between consecutive slopes	1·5%	1·5%	2%	2%
Maximum rate of change of slope per 30 m	0·1%	0·2%	0·4%	0·4%
Minimum radius of curvature in metres	30,000	15,000	7,500	7,500
Minimum distance betweeen successive points of intersection of vertical curves is the sum of the absolute numerical values of the corresponding slope changes multiplied by the factor given in metres	30,000	15,000	5,000	5,000

Notes: (1) The effective slope is obtained by dividing the difference between the maximum and minimum elevation by the runway length.

(2) The maximum slope for a runway code number 4 should not exceed 0·8% for the first and last quarters.

(3) The maximum slope for a runway code number 3, precision approach Category 2 or 3 should not exceed 0·8% for the first and last quarters.

Runway Transverse Slopes.—Recommendations for the transverse slopes are given in Table 11.

TABLE 11.—RUNWAY TRANSVERSE SLOPES

Code Letter				
E	D	C	B	A
1·5%	1·5%	1·5%	2%	2%

Note: The transverse slopes should not exceed 1·5% or 2% as applicable nor be less than 1% except at runway or taxiway intersections where flatter slopes may be necessary.

Taxiway widths.—The width of a straight portion of a taxiway should be not less than that given in Table 12.

TABLE 12.—TAXIWAY WIDTHS

Code Letter	Taxiway Width
A	7.5 m.
B	10.5 m.
C	15 m if the taxiway is intended to be used by aeroplanes with a wheel base less than 18 m;
	18 m if the taxiway is intended to be used by aeroplanes with a wheel base equal to or greater than 18 m.
D	18 m if the taxiway is intended to be used by aeroplanes with an outer main gear wheel span of less than 9 m;
	23 m if the taxiway is intended to be used by aeroplanes with an outer main gear wheel span equal to or greater than 9 m.
E	23 m.

Taxiway Vertical Alignment.—Recommendations in relation to the various components are given in Table 13.

TABLE 13.—TAXIWAY VERTICAL ALIGNMENT

	Code Letter				
	A	B	C	D	E
Maximum slope	3%	3%	1·5%	1·5%	1·5%
Maximum change of slope per 30 m	—	—	1%	1%	1%
Minimum radius of curvature in metres	—	—	3,000	3,000	3,000
Maximum change of slope per 25 m	1%	1%	—	—	—
Minimum radius of curvature in metres	2,500	2,500	—	—	—
Maximum transverse slope	2%	2%	1·5%	1·5%	1·5%

Taxiway Minimum Separation Distances.—These are given in Table 14.

PAVEMENT DESIGN

GENERAL CONSIDERATIONS.—The concept of pavement design is generally restricted to that of the pavement structure but the study of local conditions, the availability of construction materials and the facilities for construction and maintenance are of equal importance.

Pavement design is not an exact science due to the many variables and imprecise factors that need to be taken into account in various degrees during the process of design. This process can be summarised as the logical assembly and consideration of the relevant ground and weather conditions, the material resources, the construction and maintenance equipment, and the labour resources, in the determination of the type, quantity and configuration of the materials to be used to satisfy the requirements, *i.e.*:

(*a*) Providing sufficient strength for all the aircraft likely to use the airport over the design life of the pavement.
(*b*) Protecting against surface, base or foundation damage through the action of traffic and weather.
(*c*) Ensuring against the absence of loose particles and damage to aircraft.
(*d*) Providing resistance to jet blast, hot air from jet efflux and fuel spillage (especially on aprons and the ends of runways).
(*e*) Protecting against damage arising from temperature movements.
(*f*) Providing high friction characteristics and a good riding surface in wet and dry conditions.
(*g*) Providing ease and economy in construction and maintenance.

Although some of the problems which occur on aircraft pavements arise from some of the other factors, the subject of this section is the design of the various structural layers that make up the pavement to ensure that the pavement is capable of withstanding the moving and static loads applied by the aircraft main wheels without failure.

It is important to realise what is meant, in this context, by failure. In respect of the concrete or 'rigid' pavement, it means the breaking up of the surface, the cracking of the concrete layer or excessive deformation of the concrete slabs providing an irregular running surface. In the case of a bituminous or 'flexible' pavement, it means excessive cracking and deformation with ingress of water exacerbating those effects.

PAVEMENT TYPES.—The basic design methods recognise two types of pavement:

(i) Rigid—of concrete material in which the aircraft load is spread from the wheels through a fairly thin layer of uniform, relatively non-elastic material, so that the soil or layer below the construction can accept the resulting stress without permanent deformation.

TABLE 14.—TAXIWAY MINIMUM SEPARATION DISTANCES

Code Letter \ Code Number	Distance between Taxiway Centre line and Runway Centre Line								Taxiway Centre Line to Taxiway Centre Line	Taxiway, other than Aircraft Stand, Taxilane Centre Line to Object	Aircraft Stand Taxilane Centre Line to Object
	Instrument Runways [a]				Non-instrument Runways [a]						
	1	2	3	4	1	2	3	4			
A	82·5	82·5			37·5	47·5			21	13·5	12
B	87	87			42	52			31·5	19·5	16·5
C			168				93		46·5	28·5	24·5
D			176	176			101	101	68·5	42·5	36
E				180				105	76·5	46·5	40

a. The separation distances shown in columns 2 and 3 represent ordinary combinations of runways and taxiways. The basis for development of these distances is given in the Aerodrome Design Manual, Part 2.

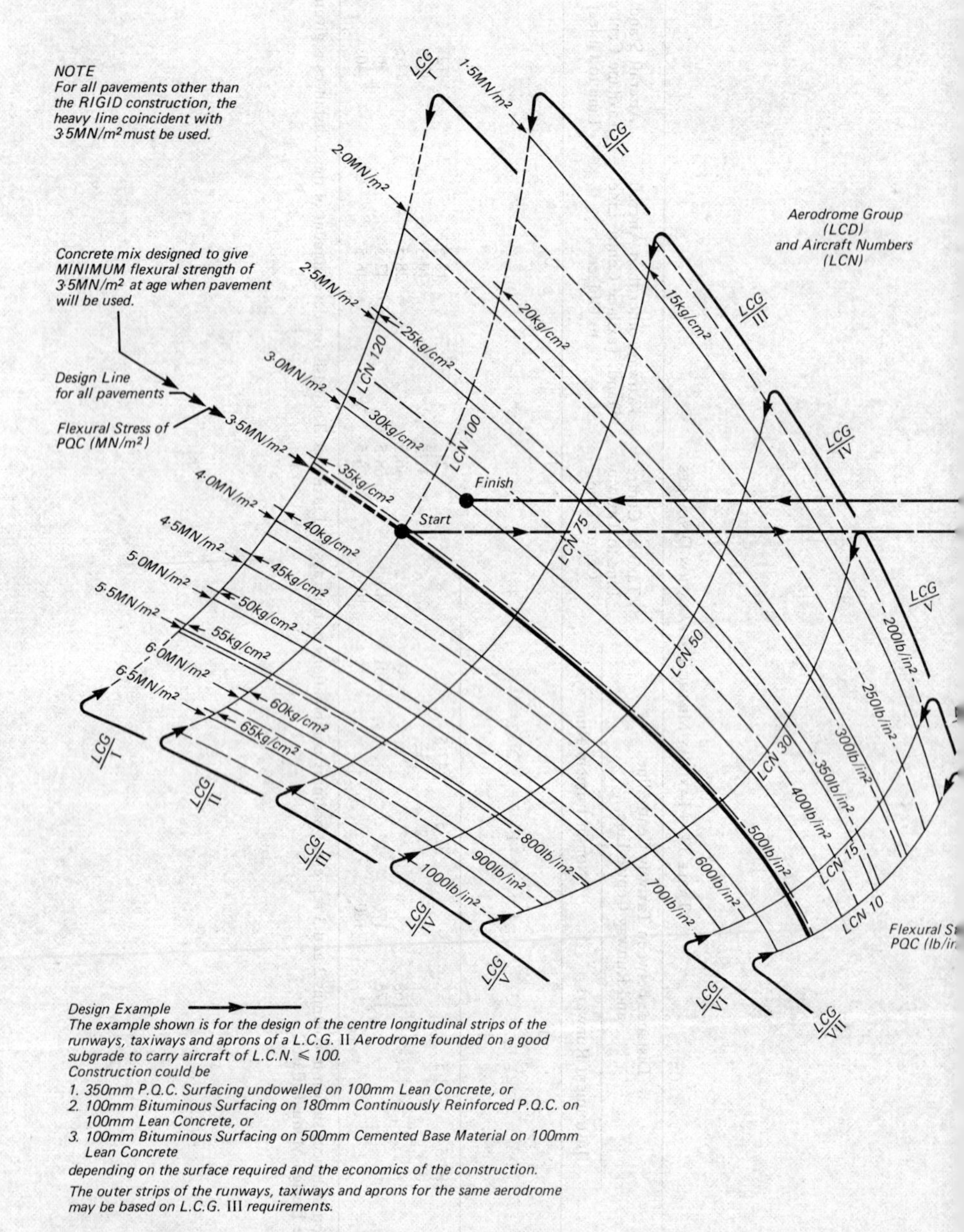
NOTE
For all pavements other than the RIGID construction, the heavy line coincident with 3·5MN/m² must be used.
Concrete mix designed to give MINIMUM flexural strength of 3·5MN/m² at age when pavement will be used.
Design Line for all pavements
Flexural Stress of PQC (MN/m²)
Aerodrome Group (LCD) and Aircraft Numbers (LCN)
Finish
Start
LCN 120
LCN 100
LCN 75
LCN 50
LCN 30
LCN 15
LCN 10
1·5MN/m²
2·0MN/m²
2·5MN/m²
3·0MN/m²
3·5MN/m²
4·0MN/m²
4·5MN/m²
5·0MN/m²
5·5MN/m²
6·0MN/m²
6·5MN/m²
15kg/cm²
20kg/cm²
25kg/cm²
30kg/cm²
35kg/cm²
40kg/cm²
45kg/cm²
50kg/cm²
55kg/cm²
60kg/cm²
65kg/cm²
200lb/in²
250lb/in²
300lb/in²
350lb/in²
400lb/in²
500lb/in²
600lb/in²
700lb/in²
800lb/in²
900lb/in²
1000lb/in²
LCG I
LCG II
LCG III
LCG IV
LCG V
LCG VI
LCG VII
Design Example
The example shown is for the design of the centre longitudinal strips of the runways, taxiways and aprons of a L.C.G. II Aerodrome founded on a good subgrade to carry aircraft of L.C.N. ≤ 100.
Construction could be
1. 350mm P.Q.C. Surfacing undowelled on 100mm Lean Concrete, or
2. 100mm Bituminous Surfacing on 180mm Continuously Reinforced P.Q.C. on 100mm Lean Concrete, or
3. 100mm Bituminous Surfacing on 500mm Cemented Base Material on 100mm Lean Concrete
depending on the surface required and the economics of the construction.
The outer strips of the runways, taxiways and aprons for the same aerodrome may be based on L.C.G. III requirements.

FIG. 21.—Design and Evaluation of Rigid Composite and Flexible Aircraft Pavements. (*Department of the Environment, UK*).

NOTE
The recommended equivalent construction in Chart 1 is related to D O E Standard Specification.

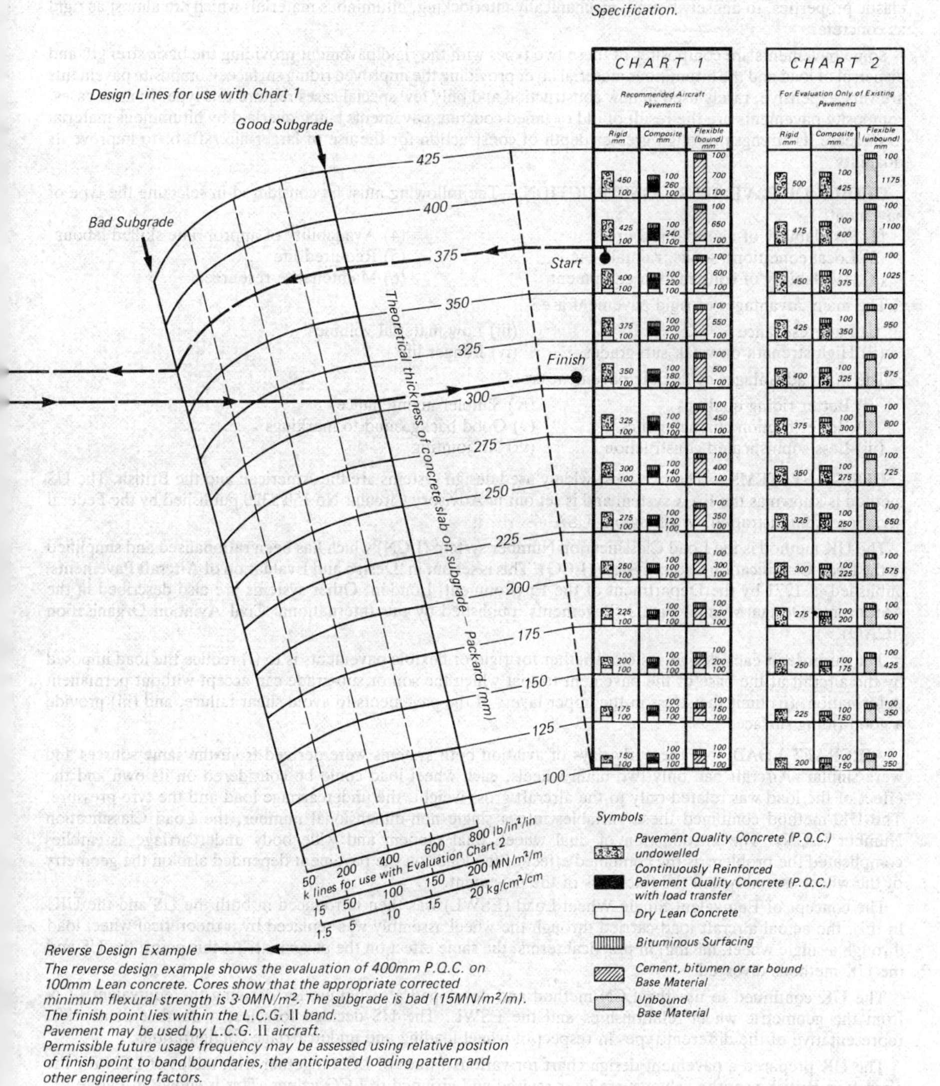

Reverse Design Example
The reverse design example shows the evaluation of 400mm P.Q.C. on 100mm Lean concrete. Cores show that the appropriate corrected minimum flexural strength is 3·0MN/m². The subgrade is bad (15MN/m²/m). The finish point lies within the L.C.G. II band. Pavement may be used by L.C.G. II aircraft. Permissible future usage frequency may be assessed using relative position of finish point to band boundaries, the anticipated loading pattern and other engineering factors.

(ii) Flexible—of relatively elastic material in which the elastic deformation of the material under load is successsively transferred to lower layers of decreasing strength so that the soil or layer below can accept the resulting stress without permanent deformation.

It must be recognised that neither material is ideal in these respects. Concrete layers have a certain elasticity and, indeed, many of the problems associated with this type of pavement result from its deflection. Flexible pavements range from soils and unbound stone material, highly susceptible to deflection with little or no elastic properties, to densely bound, mechanically interlocking, bituminous materials which are almost as rigid as concrete.

Some pavements are composites of these two types with the rigid pavement providing the basic strength and dispersal of load and the bituminous material layer providing the improved riding surface. Composite pavements are very expensive, rarely used in new construction and only few special cases require this type. In most cases, composite pavements are the result of old or failed concrete pavements being overlaid by bituminous material to increase its strength through greater depth of construction for the use of larger aircraft, or to improve its ridability.

CHOICE OF PAVEMENT CONSTRUCTION.—The following must be considered in selecting the type of pavement:

(1) Availability of material resources
(2) Local conditions—soils, rainfall, etc.
(3) Availability of construction equipment
(4) Availability of appropriate skilled labour
(5) Required life
(6) Maintenance resources

The main advantages of rigid pavement are:

(i) Fuel resistance
(ii) High strength on weak sub-grades
(iii) Low material volumes
(iv) Longer life

The main advantages of flexible pavement are:

(i) Better riding qualities
(ii) Better friction characteristics
(iii) Less sophisticated construction
(iv) Simpler maintenance
(v) Good background to markings
(vi) No jointing

DESIGN SYSTEMS.—The two most widely used design systems are the American and the British. The US method is known as the FAA system and is set out in Advisory Circular No 150/5320 published by the Federal Aviation Administration, Washington, USA.

The UK method is the Load Classification Number system (LCN) which has been rationalised and simplified to the Load Classification Group system (LCG). This is set out in 'Design and Evaluation of Aircraft Pavements' published in 1971 by the Department of the Environment, London. Other systems are also described in the Aerodrome Design Manual Part 3 'Pavements' published by the International Civil Aviation Organisation (ICAO).

The purpose of each design system whether for rigid or flexible pavements is to (i) reduce the load imposed by the aircraft at the base of the pavement to that which the soil or sub-grade can accept without permanent deformation, (ii) limit the stress in the upper layers of the pavements to avoid shear failure, and (iii) provide a good riding surface.

AIRCRAFT LOAD.—In the early days of aviation both systems were derived from the same sources and were similar. Aircraft had only two main wheels, each wheel load could be considered on its own and the effect of the load was related only to the aircraft gross weight, the undercarriage load and the tyre pressure. The UK method combined these variables into a single non-dimensional number, the Load Classification Number (LCN). The introduction of dual wheel, dual tandem and wide body undercarriage assemblies complicated the problem as the combined effect of the loads on the pavement depended also on the geometry of the wheel assembly and the thickness of the pavement.

The concept of Equivalent Single Wheel Load (ESWL) was then introduced in both the US and the UK. In this, the actual aircraft load carried through the wheel assembly was replaced by a theoretical wheel load through a single wheel, having, in practical terms, the same effect on the pavement. At this point, the US and the UK methods diverged.

The UK continued to use the LCN method and developed a technique for deriving the equivalent LCN from the geometric wheel relationships and the ESWL. The US decided to select a number of aircraft, representative of the different types in respect of wheel loading and undercarriage configurations.

The UK prepared a pavement design chart for various values of LCN together with tables of LCN for the aircraft in British use: the values were later revised and grouped to LCG values. This is shown in Figure 21.

The FAA prepared pavement design charts for several typical aircraft. These were refined to design charts for three types of wheel assembly single, dual and dual tandem. Further charts were introduced with the advent of wide body aircraft to include the B747, DC10 and L-1011 Tristar. Typical FAA charts are shown in Figures 22 and 23.

SUB-GRADE STRENGTH.—It is essential to determine the strength characteristics and behaviour under varying moisture content of the soil or sub-grade on which the pavement is to be placed. For the design of

Table 15 tabulates soils by the Unified Soil Classification System with appropriate ranges of CBR and *k* values.

TABLE 15.—UNIFIED SOIL CLASSIFICATION SYSTEM: CBR AND SUBGRADE MODULUS RELATIONSHIPS (*Source*: FAA)

USC Divisions		USC Reference Letter	Soil Description	Field CBR	Subgrade Modulus *k* (pci)
	Gravel & gravelly soils	GW	Gravel or sandy gravel well graded	60–80	300 or more
		GP	Gravel or sandy gravel poorly graded	35–60	300 or more
		GU	Gravel or sandy gravel uniformly graded	25–60	300 or more
		GM	Silty gravel or silty sandy gravel	40–80	300 or more
Coarse-grained soils		GC	Clayey gravel or clayey sandy gravel	20–40	200–300
		SW	Sand or gravelly sand well graded	20–40	200–300
		SP	Sand or gravelly sand poorly graded	15–25	200–300
	Sand & sandy soils	SU	Sand or gravelly sand uniformly graded	10–20	200–300
		SM	Silty sand or silty gravelly sand	20–40	200–300
		SC	Clayey sand or clayey gravelly sand	10–20	200–300
		ML	Silts, sandy silts, gravelly silts or dintomaceous soils	5–15	100–200
	Low compressibility	CL	Lean clays, sand clays or gravelly clays	5–15	100–200
Fine-grained soils		OL	Organic silts or lean organic clays	4–8	100–200
		MH	Micaceous clays or diatomaceous soils	4–8	100–200
	High compressibility LL 50	CH	Fat clays	3–5	50–100
		OH	Fat organic clays	3–5	50–100
Peat and other fibrous organic soils		PL	Peat, humus and other		

rigid pavements, both systems require the soil strength in terms of the modulus of sub-grade reaction (*k*). The units are lbs/in^2/in in imperial units: kg/cm^2/cm in metric units and MN/m.^{2}/m in SI Units.

For the design of flexible pavements, the FAA system and the original LCN system both require the soil strength to be assessed or measured in non-dimensional values of CBR (California Bearing Ratio). The LCG method designs fully bound 'flexible' pavements only by an empirical comparison with rigid pavements.

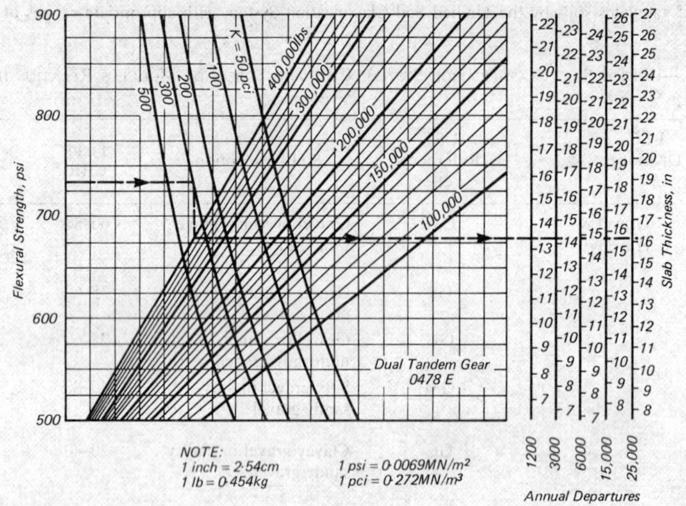

FIG. 22.—Rigid Pavement Design. Curves—Dual Tandem. (*FAA*).

Soil Classification.—The adoption of the ASTM-D-2487 method of soil classification in 1978 (Unified Soil Classification System) represented a radical change in FAA standards. This change was based on research studies which concluded that this unified system is superior in detecting properties of soils which affect airport pavement performance.

The primary purpose in determining the soil classification is to enable the engineer to predict the probable field behaviour of the soil that supports the pavement, eg volume/moisture variation in clay soils. This indicator of behaviour is, however, approximate due to a variety of reasons such as degree of compaction, saturation, overburden etc. Soil strength should be measured using CBR tests for flexible pavements and plate bearing tests for rigid pavements as early as possible in the design/construction process.

PAVEMENT STRENGTH REPORTING—THE ACN/PCN SYSTEM.—The ICAO recommends that aircraft authorities declare pavement strengths in terms of pavement classification numbers (PCN) whatever the design method or strength assessment method is used. Aircraft are evaluated in corresponding classification numbers (ACN). The ACN/PCN system and ACN values are given in the Aerodrome Design Manual part 3.

THE AMERICAN SYSTEM OF PAVEMENT DESIGN

Criticial and Non-critical areas.—The FAA design method is based on the gross weight of the critical aircraft which is assumed to be operating at the maximum take-off weight. The design recognises the concept of 'concentration of traffic'. The areas of traffic concentration are considered as 'critical areas', which comprises the central portion of the runway, aprons, taxiways and runway ends, where departing traffic will load the pavement.

The design charts produce a pavement thickness T which is appropriate to critical areas. Non-critical areas needing $0{\cdot}9T$ include the runway adjacent to the central strip and taxiways used only by landing aircraft: a further reduction of pavement thickness to $0{\cdot}7T$ can be provided where pavement is required but traffic is unlikely, such as along the extreme edges of the runway.

A few representatives of the large number of design charts are given (Figures 22 and 23).

Equivalent Design Aircraft Departures.—The design method requires the following initial steps:

(1) an estimate of the annual departures (half the total movements) of all aircraft forecast to use the pavement.
(2) determination of the design aircraft.
(3) calculation of the equivalent number of departures of the design aircraft.

It should be noted that arrivals are neglected since the landing weight of an aircraft is less than the take-off weight. The design method provides a pavement life of 20 years with the forecast annual departures.

The aircraft mix and numbers of annual departures will have been forecast by methods described in FORECASTING AIR TRANSPORT DEMAND. The various types of aircraft together with the relevant number of departures, maximum take-off weights and types of undercarriage gear have to be listed. The pavement thickness for each aircraft type is then determined from the appropriate design chart described in the next two paragraphs (see Figures 22 and 23 for examples) and the aircraft requiring the thickest pavement is the design aircraft.

The departures of all the aircraft are then converted to equivalent departures of the design aircraft by use of the following relationship based on the undercarriage configuration:

$$\log R_1 = \log R_2 \times \left(\frac{W_2}{W_1}\right)^{\frac{1}{2}}$$

where R_1 is the equivalent design aircraft departures; R_2 is the departures after conversion for gear type for each aircraft in turn; W_1 and W_2 are loads per wheel for the respective aircraft. It is assumed that the nose wheel takes 5% of the total load.

R_2 is obtained by multiplying the departures of each aircraft by the factors; 0·80 for converting single to dual wheel; 0·60 for converting dual wheel to dual tandem or double dual tandem; 0·50 for converting single to dual tandem.

The factors given are those more commonly required, but it is possible that conversions have to be made in the opposite sense, eg dual tandem to dual wheel and the reciprocal values will be used.

The values of the calculated R_1 can then be totalled to determine the equivalent departures of the design aircraft.

Rigid Pavement Thickness Design.—The FAA Advisory Circular gives design charts for the following groups and individual aircraft:

Single Wheel Gear	Douglas DC10-10
Dual Wheel Gear	Douglas DC10-30 and 40
Dual Tandem Gear (Figure 22)	Lockheed Tristar—L-1011 Series 100 & 200
Boeing 747-100 and 200	
Boeing 747-SP	

Use of the charts requires the following data:

Concrete flexural strength.	Gross weight.
Sub-grade modulus.	Number of the equivalent annual departures of the design aircraft.

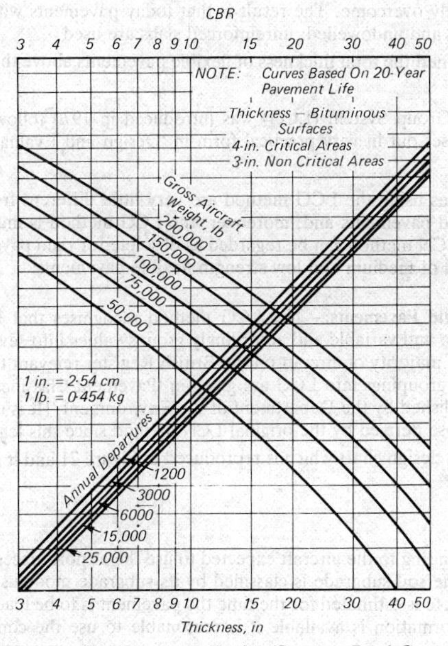

FIG. 23.—Flexible Pavement Design Curves—Dual Gear. (*FAA*).

Concrete flexural strength is taken as the value which can be readily produced with the available concrete materials at 90 days.

The sub-grade modulus should be determined by plate testing sample areas of sub-grade, but frequently at the time of design this is not practical and so it is assessed from the soil classifications. The *k* value is required on the sub-base and the FAA have produced a chart to indicate increases in this value for different thickness of stabilized sub-base.

The charts give the total concrete slab thickness for critical areas, which can then be reduced by the appropriate factors for non-critical areas.

Flexible Pavement Thickness Design.—The FAA Advisory Circular gives flexible pavement design charts for the same aircraft groups and aircraft as listed above, for the rigid pavements. Figure 23 shows the chart for dual wheel gear. Use of the figures requires the following data:

The CBR value of the sub-grade
The gross weight
The annual departures of the design aircraft.

The figures give the total pavement thickness of a three-layer construction. They also give the thickness for the critical and non-critical areas of the bituminous surface or wearing course, the thickness of the granular base course and, by deduction, the thickness of the granular sub-base. It is the FAA policy to require stabilised sub-base and base courses for new pavements which are to accommodate aircraft weights of 100,000 lbs or more. The thickness of the stabilised layer is equivalent to a granular layer at a ratio of up to 1 to 1½.

In addition to the design charts the FAA present a further chart which shows the minimum base course thickness and this has to be calculated as a check against the thickness determined from the main charts.

Pavement Evaluation.—The advisory circular contains separate charts for evaluating the strength of an existing pavement.

THE BRITISH SYSTEM OF PAVEMENT DESIGN

Historical.—The Load Classification Number (LCN) system of design determined the thickness of 'rigid' or concrete pavement, where the concrete slabs are.—

a) undowelled, that is without any method of transferring load from one to the other, or
b) dowelled, that is having devices to transfer loads across the slab joints.

For many years it was thought that the second method was going to be the most reliable and used less concrete but the resulting problems, despite the most sophisticated machines and devices for laying the concrete, were never properly overcome. The result is that today pavements with load transfer devices are generally avoided in the UK and undowelled, unreinforced slabs are used.

The LCN method determined the total thickness of flexible pavements above the subgrade of given strength in CBR values.

The Load Classification Group System (LCG) was introduced in 1970 following many years of testing, analysis and research. It is set out in very practical form in 'Design and Evaluation of Aircraft Pavements' published in 1971.

Rigid pavement thicknesses using the LCG method are very little different from those using the original LCN method for undowelled pavements and, moreover, the LCG method is much more straightforward to use; for these reasons, the LCN method can be regarded as obsolete for rigid pavement design. It is still used in many countries for design of medium and low strength flexible pavements.

The LCG Method for Rigid Pavements.—The LCG method recognises that LCN values and the other relevant factors are imprecise and variable and accordingly groups values into seven bands from Groups I to VII. The LCN values for the majority of aircraft on the British Register relevant to the particular parameters used in the design and their groupings into LCG are given in 'Pavement Classification for Civil and Military Aircraft Volume I 1971' published by the Department of the Environment. (It is unfortunate that these LCN values are different from those derived by the original LCN method since this leads to confusion.)

This publication contains a design chart which is reproduced in Figure 21 and it requires the following data:

Aircraft LCG
Sub-grade modulus
concrete flexural strength

The highest LCG corresponding to the aircraft expected to use the airport, excepting the occasional visitor, is selected for the design. The soil subgrade is classified by its subgrade modulus or *k* value. The minimum flexural strength of the concrete is estimated for the time the pavement is to be loaded; this may be six months after construction. If no information is available it is reasonable to use the common value of 3·5 MN/m^2 (500 lbs/in^2).

The design chart is entered at the upper value of the LCG band and the pavement quality concrete thickness is then read off the corresponding band of the 'Rigid' column. An example is given on the published chart.

Some points should be noted:

(i) The LCG grouping for the aircraft or the LCN value must be taken from the corresponding volume as the LCN values differ from that calculated by the original LCN method or which are given in the ICAO Aerodrome Design Manual Part 3.

(ii) The LCG system and design method is more generalised than that of the FAA. It is basically related to UK practice and to the soils commonly found in the UK. Not only are these often clay soils with low strength, but with all the year round rainfall it is normally advantageous to prepare a working surface on which to lay the pavement quality concrete. For these reasons the LCG method always incorporates a 100 mm (4 in) layer of dry lean concrete but it is not taken into account in the design calculations.

The LCG system recognises the concept of 'channelisation'. Studies on airports have indicated that over 95% of aircraft operate on the central 30 m of runway and almost all taxi along the centreline of taxiways. Thus the central strips of runways and taxiways, to which must be added all the aprons or holding areas, can be considered as channelised areas.

For 'non-channelised areas' one group lower can be selected to reduce the required design thickness. The designer should recognise that the construction processes may cancel the economies resulting from this refinement of design.

The strength of an existing pavement can be determined from the same chart using a reverse process to design. An example is given on the chart.

Composite Pavements.—The LCG method is also appropriate to design a pavement which is a composite of a reinforced concrete slab to spread the aircraft load with a bituminous surface to provide the good riding qualities and water shedding. The design process is exactly similar to that of unreinforced rigid pavements except that the composite column of Chart 1 is used.

The LCG Method of Flexible Pavements.—The simplest way of designing a flexible pavement is to use a similar process as for unreinforced rigid pavements except that the flexible column of Figure 21 is used.

A flexible pavement constructed to such a design would be satisfactory, for the whole construction is in bound material. There is only one system of construction accepted which comprises a 100 mm layer of bitumen bound surfacing, a thick layer of cement, bitumen or tar bound base material on the standard 100 mm of dry lean concrete.

The completely bound construction is based on the concept, arising from past experience, of its being equivalent to the rigid pavement design on which the LCG system is based. With the possible exception of

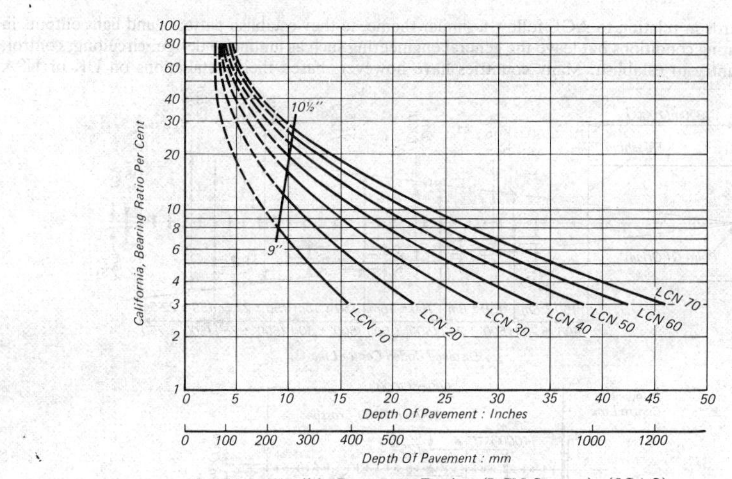

FIG. 24.—Flexible Pavement Design (LCN System). (*ICAO*).

construction on very poor sub-grade soils this type of pavement will be entirely satisfactory but it will also be expensive and, in some circumstances, may be considered even as extravagant.

The LCN Method for Flexible Pavements.—In many countries the availability of bitumen or other binder material is limited and the production capacity of satisfactory mixing plant for bound materials may also be very low. Consequently, there has to be restraint in the use of bound materials to obtain the most economic design in the circumstances.

For this purpose, the original Load Classification Number (LCN) system (where the base can be constructed in several layers of increasing strength and the lower layers can be of unbound material) can be used.

The process involves the selection of the LCN of the critical aircraft, for the total thickness of pavement. This is matched against the LCN of the pavement which is obtained by relating the thickness of the pavement to the strength of the soil sub-grade measured in terms of the California Bearing Ratio (CBR).

The design method is given in the ICAO Manual Part 3 (1st Edition 1977 only) and the design chart is given in Figure 24.

AERONAUTICAL GROUND LIGHTING AND VISUAL AIDS

A pilot making a visual landing depends on visual markings on the runway and surrounding area. Natural landmarks are normally very limited and therefore positive identification in the most effective positions must be provided by day and by night. This is achieved by lighting and painted markings. Aeronautical ground lighting (AGL) is provided for the pilot in the form of visual signals which are quickly and easily understood. This section deals first with AGL, and concludes with painted markings.

STANDARDS.—When a pilot approaches any aerodrome it is essential that he recognises immediately what he sees and standardisation is of paramount importance. A large measure of standardisation has been achieved internationally: for civil aerodromes this has been done through the International Civil Aviation Organisation (ICAO) and for military aerodromes through NATO and the Aviation Standardisation Coordinating Committee (ASCC). Standards are contained in the following documents.—

Annex 14		— Aerodromes (ICAO)
Part 4		— Aerodrome Manual Doc 9157-AN/901 (ICAO)
CAP 168		— Licensing of Aerodromes (CAA UK only)
Advisory Circular	150/5340-4C	— Installation Details for Runway Centreline and Touchdown Zone Lighting
	150/5340-19	— Taxiway Centreline Lighting System
	150/5340-24	— Runway & Taxiway Edge Lighting System (FAA US only)
STANAGS		— Airfield Marking and Lighting (NATO)*
Standards		— Airfield Lighting and Marking (ASCC)*

* These are not classified but copies are extremely difficult to obtain.

All the standards in relation to AGL follow a similar theme, ie they establish patterns and light outputs in relation to operating conditions but leave the general engineering such as luminaire design, circuiting, control, etc, to each country to establish. Many countries have however, based their installations on UK or USA

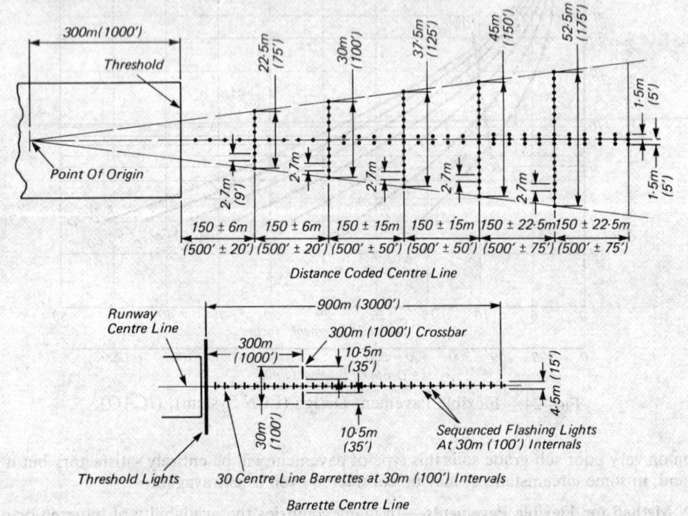

FIG. 25.—Precision Approach Category I Lighting Systems. (*ICAO*).

practice so there is a large measure of standardisation of equipment and installations throughout the world. Visual aids for aerodromes is however, a living subject so all the Standards are reviewed and updated regularly.

APPROACH LIGHTING.—As the pilot approaches the runway the first lighting pattern visible to him will be the approach lighting system which is installed before the runway threshold. ICAO recognise two systems, the first is the British Calvert system and the second is the American Federal Aviation Agency (FAA) system.

Both systems use a line of lights placed at equal intervals on the line of the extended runway centre line with one or more light 'bars' at right angles to the centre line at specified, equal intervals.

The Calvert system (or distance coded centre line) for a precision approach Category 1 runway shown in Figure 25 employs a geometric pattern of lighting leading towards an origin—the touchdown point—on the runway centre line and 300 m in from the threshold. The lights are arranged so that, when a pilot approaches in a straight line towards the runway touchdown point, they appear to move radially away from it due to the relative motion of the pilot and the lights. A symmetrical pattern indicates to the pilot that he is on the correct approach, ie on the extended centre line of the runway. The pattern seen by the pilot also gives guidance in

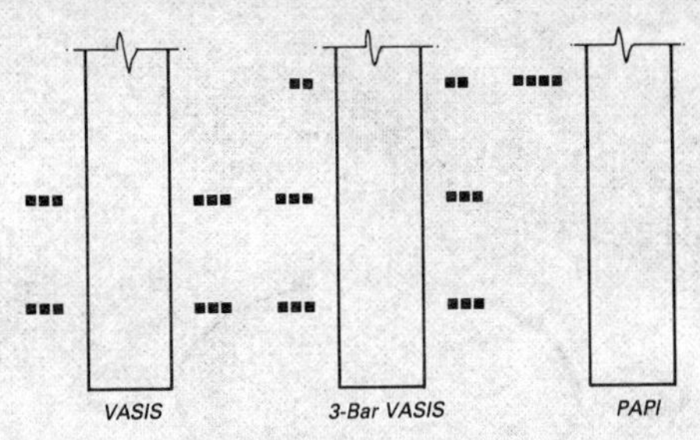

FIG. 26.—Typical Visual Approach Slope Indicator Systems & Precision Approach Path Indicators. (*ICAO*).

level and in angle of descent. The cross bars appear horizontal across the windscreen when the aircraft is level; if the cross bars move slowly down the windscreen the angle of descent is right and approach is correct, but if the approach is too steep the cross bars will move up the windscreen.

The FAA system (or barrette centre line) for a precision approach Category 1 runway also shown in Figure 25 employs short cross bars of lights (barrettes) arranged across the extended runway centre line at specified equal intervals together with one longer cross bar close to the runway threshold and additional sequenced strobe lights on the extended centre line. There is no radial effect with this system but the strobe lights appear to give a moving line of light towards the runway.

Variations on both the full, basic systems are employed depending upon the runway classification of the aerodrome. Full details are given in ICAO Annex 14 and CAP 168.

VISUAL APPROACH SLOPE INDICATORS.—The angle of descent indication provided by the approach lighting is not accurate and visual approach slope indicators (VASIS) are provided to give more precise guidance to the pilot. The locations of the lights in typical installations are shown diagrammatically in Figure 26. The basic system comprises four units each of three lights set as wing bars—two on each side of the runway—which indicate combinations of red and white lights to the pilot depending on his position relative to the correct—normally 3°—angle of descent. The correct angle is indicated by a red/white combination; all red indicates 'fly up' as the pilot is below the correct angle and all white indicates 'fly down' as he is above the correct approach.

It is anticipated that VASIS will be replaced by precision approach path indicators (PAPI) shown in Figure 26 as the official ICAO guidance system and the changeover will be effected by 1995. PAPI consists of a single wing bar of 4 number sharp transition multi-lamp paired units located on the left side of the runway (unless it is physically impracticable). PAPI also gives colour coded information in red and white. Full details of VASI and PAPI installations are given in ICAO Annex 14.

RUNWAY, TAXIWAY AND APRON EDGE LIGHTING.—Threshold (start of runway), runway end, runway edge, taxiway centre line and/or edge lighting and apron edge lighting are normally employed where an aeronautical ground lighting system is provided.

Runway centre line and/or touchdown zone (TDZ) lighting may be provided on the runway depending upon the classification of runway and lead-in lighting may be employed on the apron for aircraft guidance to the stands.

ICAO publication Annex 14 together with ICAO Aerodrome Manual Part 4 define the requirements for all types of aerodromes. In the United Kingdom, reference must also be made to the Civil Aviation Authority Publication CAP 168.

TYPE OF LUMINAIRES.—Two basic types of luminaires, namely 'elevated' and 'semi flush', have been developed for the AGL services mentioned above.

Elevated lights are normally used for approach lights and taxiway edge services although any or all can be of the semi flush type dependent on the aerodrome. Approach lights may be mounted on masts, the heights of which are determined by the ground configuration. The runway threshold touchdown zone, runway centre line, runway end, taxiway centre line, and stop bars are usually of the semi flush type fittings. The location colour and optical criteria of all AGL fittings is laid down in ICAO Annex 14/CAP 168 together with ICAO Aerodrome Manual Part 4.

DESIGN OF LUMINAIRES.—Most aerodromes today utilise a mixture of elevated and semi flush luminaires in the aircraft pavements/shoulders. Elevated lights must be capable of withstanding jet efflux but if struck by an aircraft they must cause minimum damage. All elevated fittings must have frangible mountings, which break readily if struck by an aircraft.

FIG. 27.—Typical Semi-Flush Lighting Fitting. (*Thorn EMI Lighting*).

The required lighting levels are normally produced by incandescent or tungsten halogen lamps with prismatic glass diffusers and/or parabolic reflectors.

Over the years it has been far more difficult to develop the semi flush type luminaires, since the diameter and projection above aircraft pavement level must be as small as possible to minimise obstruction to aircraft wheels and snow ploughs, and to withstand crushing and vibration forces set up by aircraft landing and taking off. Since the introduction of the tungsten halogen lamp with its higher luminous efficiency it has been possible to reduce drastically the size of these fittings and to increase the required light outputs to meet the ever higher standards imposed by ICAO to meet objectives such as blind landing.

Most semi flush fittings comprise a cast metal base with an easily removable light unit housing the lamp, reflectors and lense, and an overlapping cast metal cover. An example of a typical fitting is shown in Figure 27.

ELECTRICITY SUPPLIES.—ICAO Annex 14 and CAP 168 necessitate the availability of two independent electricity supplies, and the permissible time to change over from one to the other in the event of a supply failure varies from 1 second upwards depending upon the runway classification and the particular section of the installation. For example, Precision Approach Category II or III runways require a maximum break of 1 second for approach, threshold, runway end, runway centre line and runway touchdown zone lights and 15 seconds for runway edge, essential taxiway and obstacle lights.

The source of electricity supply and its distribution throughout the aerodrome is of such importance that it is normal to provide standby generating plant regardless of how many incoming supplies are available.

For major aerodromes operating in runway categories I, II and III visibility conditions, two independent incoming electricity supplies taken from widely separated sections of the supply authority network are desirable. For maximum security a high voltage, closed ring system is recommended with balanced feeder protection to isolate immediately any faults which may occur together with local low voltage standby facilities. The following methods of restoration of supply are recommended to protect against failure of the normal electricity supply each relating to the acceptable non-operational time limit:

(a) Where a break of 1 second is allowed, automatic changeover between two independent supplies, for example, two normal incoming supplies feeding a closed ring would be satisfactory. Alternatively, a standby diesel generating set can supply the load under Category II or III conditions with automatic changeover to the normal incoming supply in the event of failure of the generating set. This method may not be acceptable, however, where Category II or III conditions exceed 500 hours per annum since this will hasten the standby plant towards a major overhaul with all its attendant difficulties.

(b) For a break time of between 10 and 90 seconds an automatic start standby diesel generating set is sufficient.

The maximum switchover times for the AGL services are as follows:

Runway Classification	Switchover Times
Non instrument	Generally 2 minutes except where the operation is essential for safety of flight operations.
Instrument approach	Generally 15 seconds.
Precision approach category I	Generally 15 seconds.
Precision approach category II	Generally 1 second except for runway edge, essential taxiway, stop bars other than those at holding positions, and obstacle lights which may be 15 seconds.
Precision approach category III	As category II except that all stop-bars must be 1 second.

THE LIGHTING CIRCUITS.—The design of the luminaire demands a low voltage lamp whereas the length of cable feeding them, which is often over several kilometres, necessitates high voltage distribution. It is important that the intensity of all lights are the same and remain unaffected by the failure or burning out of one or more lamps usually up to a limit of 10% of the circuit. It follows, therefore, that on the grounds of monitoring uniform light intensity, control, economy and reliability, all AGL circuits should be designed as high voltage series circuit loops with a series isolating transformer feeding each luminaire, from a sub-station preferably adjacent to each end of the runway. Lighting circuits such as runway edge lighting should be fed by two or more interleaved circuits. When two circuits are used to feed the same service, alternate luminaires should be connected to the same circuit.

Services requiring separate interleaved circuits—

(*a*) approach lighting
(*b*) supplementary approach lighting
(*c*) runway edge lighting
(*d*) runway centre line lighting
(*e*) touchdown zone lighting
(*f*) high intensity taxiway centreline lighting

Services requiring separate circuits—

(*a*) low intensity taxiway centreline lighting
(*b*) low intensity taxiway edge lighting
(*c*) threshold bars and runway end lights
(*d*) edge lighting of paved areas

Other services required are:

(*a*) taxiway stop bars—depending upon traffic operation, on separate circuits or in groups or with taxiway lighting.

(*b*) VASI (or equivalent)—two circuits per runway end and all luminaires on the same side of the runway should be connected to the same circuit. This arrangement ensures that even when a circuit is lost, a complete VASI pattern at one side of the runway will continue to operate.

(*c*) runway visual range lights (RVR)—circuited with runway edge or centre line lights.

All the equipment in the control/distribution centre should be bonded to earth. An earth wire should also be run from the distribution centre with the HV series circuit cables and bonded to the secondary side of all isolating transformers.

CONSTANT CURRENT REGULATORS.—Aeronautical ground lighting is used over a wide range of visibility conditions from bright sunlight to dark clear nights and it is necessary to be able to control the intensity from 100% to less than 1% of maximum light intensity. Changes in steps are required, rather than infinite control, because the air traffic controller needs to be able to choose specific settings and the eye only notices changes in brightness of the order of 3 times. High intensity lights therefore require at least 6 stages of intensity control whereas low intensity require only maximum and one stage of dimming. Lighting circuits requiring three or more stages of luminance control should be supplied through constant current series circuit regulators which accurately control the output current within plus or minus 2% of any setting regardless of load changes or supply voltage fluctuations, indicate an earth fault whilst permitting the system to continue to operate, respond to circuit changes within 15 cycles, provide back indication and have a high degree of reliability. The CCR operates on the principle of the Boucherot bridge circuit where, in an ideal case, the output current does not depend upon the size or the nature of the load impedance. The latest types of thyristor control regulators are now coming into use progressively. Lighting circuits which require two or less stages of luminance control may be supplied through tapped mains transformers saving the cost of constant current regulators.

ISOLATING TRANSFORMERS.—Isolating transformers should have a double winding and be encapsulated or enclosed in a cast iron compound filled box. One end of the secondary winding should be bonded internally to the transformer core and brought out to an external earthing terminal. These transformers should be solidly connected in the HV series loop circuit.

CABLES.—Single core primary cables should be used to feed the isolating transformers in an airfield ground lighting circuit with 2 core secondary leads from each isolating transformer to the luminaire terminating in a watertight socket. The luminaire electrical circuit terminates in a matching watertight plug. Any circuit loop current can be chosen provided that the current ratio of the isolating transformers is chosen to match the loop current and the lamp current. The most common loop currents used throughout the world at the moment are 6, 6·6, 8·3, 12 and 20 amperes. When calculating the loop current the following should be considered: the lower the loop current for a given number of luminaires in the circuit, the higher is the loop voltage; for loop voltages up to 2 kV, single core plastic insulated and plastic sheathed cables can be used without suffering damage; above 2 kV, the electrical stresses set up in the cable sheath may cause breakdown dependent upon the load in each circuit and a metal screen may be required in the cable between the insulation and the sheath to prevent electrical stress in the sheath, further, the cables may require to be upgraded in voltage rating.

REMOTE CONTROL.—The remote control system provides the air traffic controller with a ready means of switching on or off and of changing the levels of illumination of the various lighting services. The two main principles used are either 'direct wire' or 'multiplex'. Systems using direct wire principles are usually restricted to aerodromes with only a few lighting services to control and which are unlikely to be subject to extensive developments. Multiplex type systems are used for major aerodromes so as to provide greater flexibility for extensions and variations to lighting patterns and any new control requirements which may arise. Furthermore, locational geographical changes to sub-stations, control centres, etc, often become necessary on major aerodromes and need to be taken into account in basic design philosophies of the control system.

CONTROL DESK.—This should be designed to provide the operator with on/off and intensity controls and their associated positive back and fault indicating features which are easily identifiable under all conditions of illumination in the control room for AGL services. For this purpose it is necessary to provide a self illuminated mimic diagram, control equipment and brilliancy selection switches for the AGL services. The recent use of fibre optics has greatly helped in the manufacture of the mimic diagram. The layout of the mimic and the colour of the lights should be designed to give the controller precise information of the AGL services selected.

CONTROL APPARATUS.—All equipment should be designed to give a high degree of operational reliability, to provide as far as possible any lighting pattern selected regardless of control cable faults or equipment failures. Solid state equipment should be used where practicable although relays may be more desirable at the interface between the apparatus and external cables. Modular construction to facilitate maintenance work and rack mounted apparatus is recommended. Provision should be made for the manual control of airfield ground lighting circuits locally in the control centres to enable lighting patterns to be established at times when the control system is out of commission.

RUNWAY, TAXIWAY AND APRON MARKINGS.—White painted markings are used to assist the pilot and full details are given in Annex 14, CAP 168 and 150 Series. Typical runway markings are shown in Figure 28.

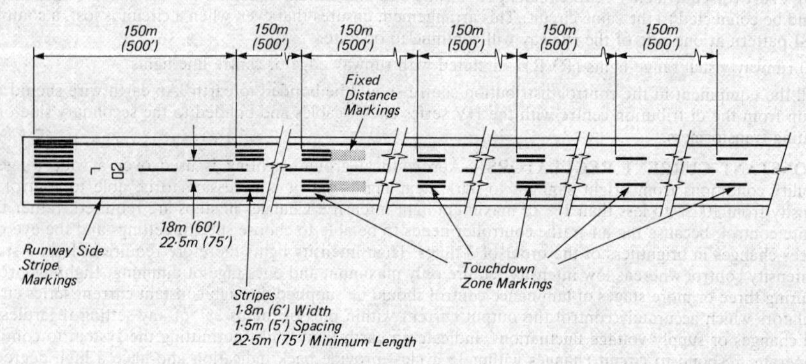

FIG. 28.—Typical Runway Markings. (*ICAO*).

APRON SERVICES.—Two items of importance are the apron floodlights for night working and pilot guidance systems for parking aircraft.

Floodlights should give an adquate level of illumination for safe operations at ground level to the Standards required in Aerodrome Manual, Part 4, and the cut off must be such as not to cause interference to pilots in aircraft which are approaching and taking off.

There are several systems for assisting pilots in parking aircraft in relation to airbridges and jetties but all give guidance in the line of approach and the position to stop so that the aircraft doors are in the correct position. Nearly all employ optical means but at least one uses a pressure pad in the pavement for the stop indication and induction systems are available.

TELECOMMUNICATIONS

Telecommunications is a generic term covering radio navigational aids and radar as well as voice and data communications by both landline and radio. The complementary equipment carried in aircraft generally comes under the term 'Avionics'.

The telecommunication requirements of a modern airport can be quite extensive and consist of some or all of the following:

Air Ground Radio Communication	Public Communication Services
Direct Speech Communication	Navigational Aids
Direct Data Communication	Final Approach & Landing Aids
Land Mobile Radio	Radar

The needs, which the telecommunication system has to meet, are established from the Operational Requirement of the airport. This document sets out how the airport will be operated, based on the individual criteria involved. These include, not necessarily in order of importance, the position of the airport with respect to other air traffic patterns, the surrounding terrain, availability of outside services, estimated traffic density, weather minima to be applied, together with the capital costs and running costs of the telecommunications installation.

Once the telecommunication requirements are determined, specifications for equipment and guidance on the siting of various navigational and landing aids, can be found in the International Civil Aviation Organisation (ICAO) publication 'International Standards and Recommended Practices Aeronautical Telecommunications, Annex 10, Volumes 1 & 2', more commonly known as 'ICAO Annex 10'.

The following paragraphs give further information on the items listed at the beginning of this section.

AIR GROUND RADIO.—The first essential for efficient control of air traffic is a communication link between the pilots and the air traffic controllers. This is provided by Very High Frequency (VHF) radio telephony (R/T) equipment installed in the aircraft and on the ground, utilising a special frequency band (117·975 MHz to 136 MHz). Tho ground equipment, depending upon the amount and type of traffic involved, can vary from a single transceiver (combined transmitter and receiver) installed in the control room to a large multi-channel installation using remote transmitter and receiver sites and employing sophisticated micro-processor controlled operating equipment in the tower.

There is a mandatory requirement to keep a log of communication between aircraft and controllers in order that reference can be made to it in the event of an aircraft accident or incident; each entry must be maintained for at least thirty days. The most efficient method of maintaining such a log is to record the conversations on magnetic tape and store the individual reels for at least thirty days before wiping them clean ready for use again.

DIRECT SPEECH COMMUNICATION.—Rapid and reliable speech communication is required between air traffic control officers both within an airport and between airports and the appropriate air traffic control centre (ATCC). In addition the same type of circuit is required between air traffic control on an airport and other interested airport organisations including the fire & crash station, apron control and the meteorological office. These speech circuits are normally provided by direct landline links but where this is either not possible or is uneconomical, any other medium, capable of providing direct speech access, can be used.

The termination of these direct circuits can vary from a simple telephone to sophisticated keyboard equipment sharing a common operating instrument with the air ground radio and associated with the same microprocessor controlled equipment.

DIRECT DATA COMMUNICATION.—In civil aviation operational data communication is handled by the aeronautical fixed telecommunication network (AFTN). This is a worldwide communication system utilising cable, radio or satellite links for the exchange of messages between fixed aeronautical stations such as airports and air traffic control centres.

The common method of sending and receiving messages on the network is by means of teletypewriter equipment. Usually, each country operates its own AFTN with a main or national switching centre communicating with the national switching centres of adjoining countries to form the worldwide system.

Depending upon the amount of communication traffic handled, switching centre techniques can vary from manual re-transmission of messages by keyboard, to re-transmission via perforated tape, to manual switching of stored messages and, finally, to fully automatic processor controlled switching by means of the message address heading. An international standard message format is used which enables messages to be accepted by all recognised forms of switching centre throughout the world. Only those messages concerned with the safety of air navigation and for the regular and economical operation of air services are accepted on the AFTN system; this includes appropriate meteorological information.

Studies are now taking place within ICAO concerning the introduction of a high speed data network called common ICAO data interchange network (CIDIN). It is proposed that this type of network will eventually replace the AFTN in heavy traffic areas but still make it possible to interface with those sections of the AFTN remaining in the lighter traffic areas. Some AFTN electronic switching centres now in use, and certainly those installed in the future, will permit the transmission of high speed data as envisaged for CIDIN.

A similar worldwide network known as the Societe de Internationale Telecommunications Aeronautiques (SITA) is operated on behalf of the world air lines for commercial and administrative messages.

LAND MOBILE RADIO.—Control of both aircraft and vehicles within the aircraft manoeuvring areas on an airport is exercised by ATC ground movement control (GMC) from the tower visual control room (VCR). An appropriate VHF radio channel in the aeronautical band, between 121·60 MHz and 121·975 MHz inclusive, is used for this purpose.

The control of vehicles outside aircraft manoeuvring areas, for example, those concerned with maintenance and with the servicing of aircraft on the apron, is usually carried out by the various agencies concerned over a UHF frequency in the business band, eg 450 MHz to 470 MHz. It is usual for both GMC and management apron control to also have access to these radio channels (but not to monitor them), in order to maintain vehicle movement discipline over the areas under their respective control.

PUBLIC COMMUNICATION SERVICES.—An aerodrome like any other organisation has to be administered and kept in touch with the outside world. An essential to this end is connection to the national telephone system via the local public exchange. This connection can vary from a single telephone terminated exchange line to a large private electronic exchange (EPABX) with many lines to the public exchange depending upon the size of the aerodrome.

The aerodrome PABX also provides interconnection within the aerodrome and frequently has direct tie lines to airline PABX's, area control centres, hospitals and local fire brigades.

A public telex service is usually installed at an aerodrome for general purpose use and also, at the smaller aerodromes, to handle messages which would normally be carried on the AFTN.

NAVIGATIONAL AIDS.—The main civil aviation navigational aids are the very high frequency omnidirectional range (VOR), with its variant the Doppler VOR (DVOR) and the non-directional beacon (NDB).

The VOR normally operates within the VHF radio band, 111·975 MHz to 117·975 MHz and provides the pilot with a 'line of sight' compass bearing from the site to the aircraft. VOR's are generally used as en-route aids to give track guidance down an approved route or airway. In conditions where site difficulties could cause multi-path propagation problems, a DVOR can be used as the Doppler system tends to minimise such effects as well as improving accuracy and stability.

In addition to providing bearing information, VOR's usually have distance measuring equipment (DME) co-located on the site. As the name implies, this provides the pilot with continuous information of the distance between his aircraft and the VOR/DME site. The DME operates within the UHF band 960 MHz to 1215 MHz.

The NDB radiates an omni-directional signal, within the frequency band 200 kHz to 1750 kHz, which does not, in itself, provide bearing information. Complementary direction finding equipment is fitted in the aircraft to give a pilot the compass bearing to the NDB site: NDB's are used as en-route navigational aids where the provision of the more costly VOR could not be justified.

Where a track or airways system is in operation, reporting points along the route can be identified by the use of en-route VHF marker beacons which operate at 75 MHz and radiate a narrow, vertical beam.

The radio carriers of VOR's, NDB's and Marker Beacons are normally modulated with two or three letter morse code identification signals. In certain circumstances, the VOR transmission may also be modulated by speech to provide flight information.

FINAL APPROACH AND LANDING AIDS.—Lower power versions of the VOR and the NDB are frequently used as final approach aids where they provide an instrument approach service giving guidance in azimuth only. Used in this context they are usually referred to as terminal VOR (TVOR) and locator respectively.

The most widely used precision approach and landing aid is the Instrument Landing System (ILS). This is shown diagrammatically in Figure 29. The ILS ground equipment consists of:

(a) A localiser transmitter (LOC), operating in the VHF frequency band 108 MHz to 111·975 MHz, situated at the far end of the runway in use, to give accurate guidance in azimuth to the pilot.

(b) A glide path transmitter (GP), operating in the UHF frequency band 328·6 MHz to 335·4 MHz, situated at the side of the runway towards the threshold, to give accurate guidance in angle of descent to the pilot.

(c) A middle marker transmitter (MM), situated on the runway centre line at approximately 1050 m from threshold.

(d) An outer marker transmitter (OM), again situated on the centre line but at a distance between 3·5 and

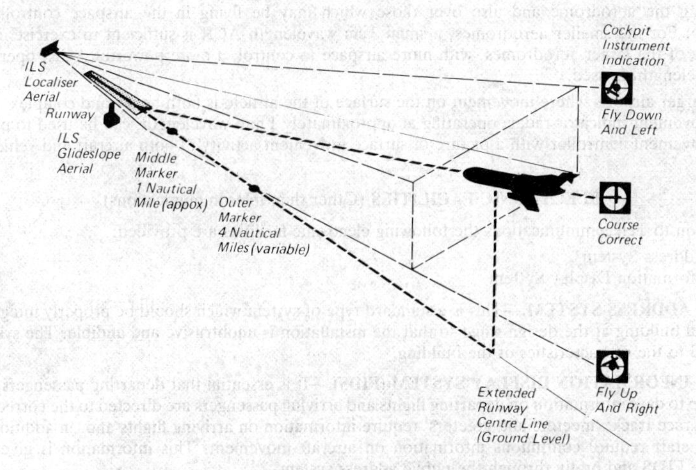

FIG. 29.—Simplified Diagram of the Instrument Landing System. (*ICAO*).

6 nautical miles from threshold. Both the MM and the OM operate at 75 MHz, but with different modulation signals, and radiate a narrow vertical beam to mark the progress of the aircraft towards the runway.

A DME can be co-located with the GP where there is difficulty in siting ILS markers to give the pilot continuous information on 'distance to go' to runway threshold.

The LOC and GP transmissions are converted by the aircraft equipment into instrument needle readings which show 'fly left/fly right' and 'fly up/fly down' indications respectively. When the aircraft passes through the transmissions of either the OM or the MM, an appropriate light is activated on the ILS needle instrument.

ILS will, as planned, eventually be replaced by the microwave landing system (MLS) which enables multi approach paths to be flown and which can also operate in difficult sites where ILS would not. Separate equipment is required in the aircraft from that provided for ILS approaches.

A few MLS installations are already in service in North America and more are being ordered. The UK Civil Aviation Authority has an experimental system in operation for evaluation and flight testing purposes and two systems are proposed for the London Dockland Stolport.

However, it is anticipated that ILS wil be 'protected' until 1995 after which signatories to ICAO will be free to replace it by MLS. There will probably have to be an overlap period of some ten years when both systems will operate alongside each other. In the meantime a new generation of digitally controlled ILS is appearing that could be usefully employed until the end of that period.

More information on MLS installations is being incorporated in ICAO Annex 10, Attachment C to Part 1 of that publication. Final details concerning the ideal siting of antennae have yet to be determined.

In certain circumstances where it is not possible to provide an ILS installation, a 3 cm wavelength precision approach radar (PAR), sometimes known as a talk-down radar, can be provided as an alternative precision approach aid. However, the cost of such an installation is high and a team of specially trained and licensed air traffic control staff is required whenever it is in use.

RADAR.—Apart from the precision approach radar mentioned earlier as a landing aid, the radar systems used in civil aviation can be divided into three categories:

(*a*) Long range radar system (LRRS)
(*b*) Airfield control radar (ACR)
(*c*) Airfield surface movement indicator (ASMI)

Long range radar systems are normally used to provide radar cover over airway sectors, particularly along busy routes, to enable positive control to be exercised over aircraft flying along those routes. They are also used to enable control to be maintained in the upper air space, above airways sectors, normally used by overflying aircraft. In addition LRRSs are frequently employed to provide radar cover over whole areas of a country where a flight information service (FIS) is operating. This service, along with general flight information, provides a pilot with information on his position and the position of other aircraft in the vicinity without exercising positive control of aircraft. A wavelength of 23 cm is in common usage for this type of equipment.

Airfield control radar is used, as the name implies, to enable positive control to be exercised over aircraft approaching the aerodrome and also over those which may be flying in the airspace controlled by the aerodrome. For the smaller aerodromes, a small 3 cm wavelength ACR is sufficient to exercise control but in the case of the larger aerodromes, with more airspace to control, a more powerful ACR, operating on a 10 cm wavelength, is used.

In the larger airports where movement on the surface of the airfield is both heavy and complex, an airfield surface movement indicator radar, operating at approximately 1 mm wavelength, can be used to provide the ground movement controller with a picture of surface movement activity of both aircraft and vehicles.

ELECTRONIC FACILITIES (Other than telecommunications)

In addition to Telecommunications the following electronic facilities are provided:

Public Address System
Flight Information Display System

PUBLIC ADDRESS SYSTEM.—This is a standard type of system which should be properly integrated into the terminal building at the design stage so that the installation is unobtrusive and audible. The system must be matched to the characteristics of the building.

FLIGHT INFORMATION DISPLAY SYSTEM (FIDS).—It is essential that departing passengers are given clear and up to date information on departing flights and arriving passengers are directed to the correct baggage carousel or race track; 'meeters and greeters' require information on arriving flights and, in addition, airport and airline staff require continuous information on aircraft movement. This information is given visually through the FIDS and orally through the public address system.

The FIDS usually consists of two elements—large display boards and TV screens—linked to a central data unit which will be microprocessor controlled at all but the smallest airports.

The display boards vary in the principle of operation and include mechanical split flapboards, rotating disc dot matrix, fibreoptic and light emitting diode systems.

The positioning of the boards and screens needs careful planning having regard to the areas where they are required, sight lines and ceiling heights.

METEOROLOGICAL SYSTEMS.—The meteorological systems are responsible for providing meteorological services at designated airports. The types of service provided include periodic weather forecasts for departure, destination and alternate airports including en route segments. Actual periodic weather information is reported by observations at the designated airports.

The extent of the provision of these services depends upon the size of the airport and the scale and type of air transport services provided.

The type of essential meteorological information provided to pilots, for flight planning purposes can be split under two headings, namely for airports and en route use.

The major items of airport information will include:—

(a) Surface wind speed, direction and peak gusts.
(*b*) Visibility.
(*c*) Barometric pressure.
(*d*) Air temperature.
(*e*) Dew point.
(*f*) Cloud types, base, tops and amount of cloud covering the sky for each type.
(*g*) Precipitation, i.e. rain, snow, sleet and hail.
(*h*) Runway surface condition, i.e. dry, wet, snow deposits/ice and braking action.

The major items of en route information for varying attitudes will include:—

(*i*) Wind speed and direction.
(*j*) Visibility.
(*k*) Air temperature, including icing levels.
(*l*) Cloud types, base, tops and amount of cloud cover.
(*m*) Position of jet stream, electrical storms and turbulence.

The meteorological offices, by use of satellites technology, are now able to provide very accurate weather forecasts and advanced automated weather observations are provided at major airports, the information being disseminated to the various operational locations. Additionally, these observations are recorded.

SECURITY SYSTEMS.—Some thirty years ago airport security was much less onerous than today as the scope was restricted to protecting persons and property and preventing unauthorised entry to operationally sensitive areas. Security was provided by static or mobile uniformed staff, with manual search of selected passengers' hand baggage and closed circuit television to monitor remote areas.

It became necessary to provide more sophisticated systems as time progressed to combat the new risks. The smuggling of arms, explosives, drugs and major theft are a source of prime concern to security experts. Hijacking, and more recently, extreme acts of terrorism by various terrorist organisations, have infiltrated many airport security nets causing numerous deaths and substantial damage to aircraft and airport terminals.

The cost of installing and running modern security systems has become a major element of airport finance. The prime objective of airport security is access control and the various methods used are listed below:—

(a) Airport perimeter fencing.
(*b*) Fencing of other airport areas, such as power stations and operational areas.
(*c*) Closed circuit television, including night vision cameras.
(*d*) X ray equipment.
(*e*) Metal detectors, static and hand held.
(*f*) Drug sniffing equipment; specially trained dogs are frequently used.
(*g*) Electronic fences and detectors.
(*h*) Intruder alarms.
(*i*) Personnel and vehicle entry/exit card control.
(*j*) Fire detection, other than aircraft fire/crash services.
(*k*) Vehicular and foot patrols.
(*l*) Centralised monitoring and control of all security services.

Apart from various forms of security services provided at the majority of airports, at international airports, Customs are responsible for the control of the entry/exit of hold baggage and freight. Immigration services are responsible for the control of persons departing/arriving.

AIR TRAFFIC CONTROL

In the early days of commercial aviation, some sixty years ago, aircraft movements were such that very little control was necessary and aircraft flew more or less at random, in the knowledge that there was little likelihood of conflict with other aircraft. However, at areas where aviation was more concentrated, between London and Paris for example, measures had to be adopted to ensure that aircraft flight paths were safe and not in conflict. The measures in terms of todays technology, were very crude, but were necessary to afford safe operations within defined areas about the early aerodromes.

Aircraft in those early days flew in straight lines between airports whenever possible since this was the most cost effective route structure. This route structure, however, had to be adapted to avoid mountain ranges; in addition, long tracks over the sea were not possible due to the lack of aircraft range and the inability to fix position by reference to the ground. It was also necessary on occasions to deviate from the straight line track to take on fuel at centralised refuelling points. As aircraft movements increased, they tended to follow the same tracks and authorities realised that some separation and control was required. Air Traffic Control (ATC) became a necessity.

ELEMENTS OF AIR TRAFFIC CONTROL.—The aim of ATC is to provide a safe, orderly and expeditious flow of traffic, both in the air and on the ground. Various methods have been developed to achieve this aim and these have had to keep pace with technological and aircraft development to provide a unified Air Traffic Service (ATS). The three main methods are the application of separation standards, provision of controlled airspace and telecommunications. Units responsible for the provision of ATS are aerodrome control, approach control and area control.

Separation Standards.—The provision of separation standards involves a three dimensional problem, namely geographical location of the aircraft, both in the air and on the ground, time and height. The problem is an international one and most contracting States of the International Civil Aviation Organisation (ICAO) have agreed to unified separation standards. Most countries of the world are members of ICAO and those that are not tend to follow ICAO standards. Within ICAO, States can and do use differing standards, however they are obliged to notify these differences to other members, for obvious flight safety reasons. It is ATC that applies the separation standards which are designed to keep aircraft separate from one another by applying vertical and horizontal separation techniques.

Separation distances vary but, for example, an aircraft flying along an airway (*qv*) under radar surveillance may not pass within 5 nautical miles of another at the same height; alternatively, if two aircraft are less than 5 nautical miles apart horizontally, they must be at least 1,000 feet apart vertically. This separation is increased to 2,000 feet at heights above 29,000 feet.

Controlled Airspace.—In addition to providing acceptable separation methods for aircraft flying along busy air lanes and landing and taking-off at busy airports, it became necessary to protect these operations from other aircraft not so engaged and so airspace of specific dimensions was developed about these various flight operations to provide the necessary degree of protection and all flights within these areas are controlled.

Rules of the air were introduced, applicable to both pilots and controllers, regarding the use of controlled airspace. One fundamental rule is that no aircraft may enter controlled airspace, without having first filed a flight plan of intention and, secondly, having received an ATC clearance from the specific ATS unit responsible. Thousands of ATC clearances are issued every day, and as a specific flight proceeds these clearances are often amended in the interest of flight safety as instructions are issued to conform with the separation standards already discussed.

Aircraft on each individual flight are protected by the various means discussed above, from the departure aerodrome to the destination aerodrome and on the route between them, although many of the flight paths cross international borders.

The world's airspace is divided into areas of national responsibility by international agreement. The UK's airspace, for example, extends over the land and surrounding seas where it meets the airspace of adjacent countries. These areas of responsibility are known as Flight Information Regions (FIRs), within which controlled airspace has been established. The UK has two FIRs, namely the Scottish FIR and London FIR and air traffic services are provided to aircraft within their boundaries (Figure 30).

The airspace within an FIR is separated vertically into lower, middle and upper airspace and Figure 31 illustrates the vertical division of UK airspace.

The types of controlled airspace are Control zones, Terminal control areas, and Airways.

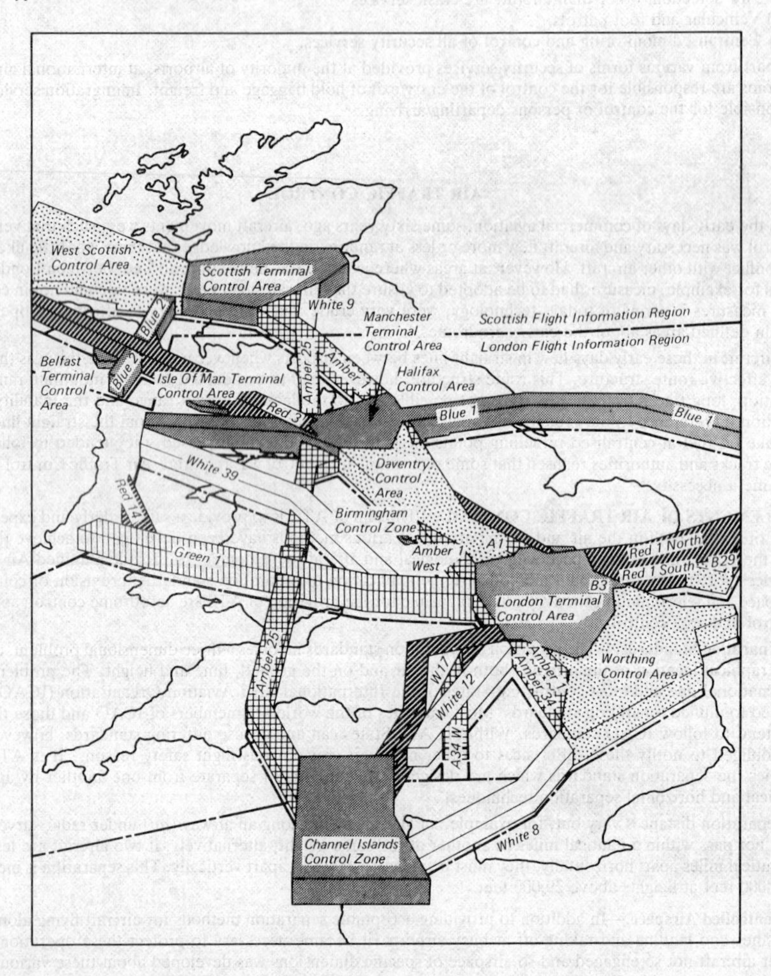

FIG. 30.—Airways in UK Airspace. (*CAA*).

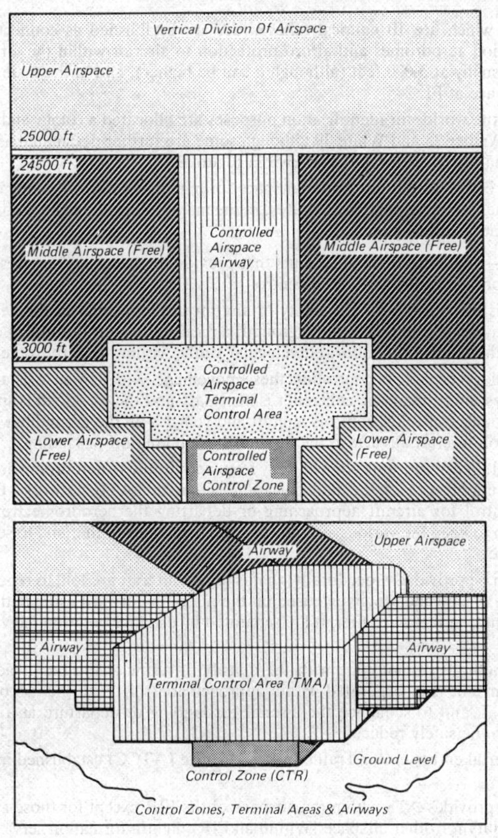

FIG. 31.—Vertical Division of Airspace. Control Zones, Terminal Areas and Airways. (*CAA*).

The airspace outside controlled airspace, in the lower and middle airspaces, is an area where aircraft are free to fly without any control. They must comply, however, with basic separation rules and avoid the traffic zones of aerodromes that are not protected by controlled airspace.

All flights above an agreed datum, which is usually 3,000 feet (although it can be higher), are conducted on a fixed altimeter pressure setting and pressure changes en-route can be ignored. This ensures that all aircraft are flying at their designated heights by reference to one datum and this designated height under these operational conditions is referred to as a flight level (FL).

Control Zones.—A control zone is established about an individual aerodrome where the traffic density warrants it, and it is usually situated within a terminal control area where there are one or more active aerodromes. The control zone dimensions are usually from ground level to 2,500 feet above the aerodrome and it affords protection to aircraft arriving from, or entering, the terminal control area as shown in Figure 31.

Terminal Control Area.—Terminal control areas are designed to protect one or more busy aerodromes and when there are two or more aerodromes, one of the aerodromes will be designated as responsible for the overall co-ordination of traffic movements between the two aerodromes. Alternatively, an area control unit, which is not necessarily situated at either of the aerodromes, may control the area. The terminal control area base is usually at 2,500 feet, the tope of the control zone, and extends upwards to the base of the upper airspace, FL 245 as shown in Figure 31.

A terminal control area is connected to the various airways which cross it and affords protection to aircraft entering and departing the airways system for the aerodromes within the terminal area, or bound for en-route destinations as shown in Figure 31.

Airways.—Airways, which are 10 nautical miles wide, are established as connecting corridors between departure and destination aerodromes and afford protection to aircraft within the airspace. Airways extend upwards from a base usually at 3,000 feet (although it can be higher), and in the main extend upwards to the base of the upper airspace at FL 245.

Airways throughout the world, for identification purposes are allocated a colour and a number designation. Examples are Blue 1, Amber 25 and White 39 although some are further designated as Red 1 North and Red 1 South. The airways pattern over the UK is shown in Figure 30.

Upper air routes are established in the upper airspace for high flying aircraft, many of which are transitting national airspace to other countries and these routes, in the main, follow the delineation of the airways system within the lower and middle air spaces.

Air Traffic Services.—There are three ATS units that provide the necessary services for ATC and they are aerodrome control, approach control and area control.

Aerodrome control is responsible for the safety of aircraft in the vicinity of the aerodrome, that is those aircraft that are flying by visual reference to the ground, aircraft taking-off or landing or manoeuvring on the ground, together with the control of authorised vehicular traffic within the aerodrome boundary.

Normally one controller is capable of controlling these movements, aided by an assistant controller; however, at very busy aerodromes, more than one controller is necessary and the workload is split into ground control and air control. The ground controller controls aircraft and vehicles on the ground but not on the runway and the air controller controls aircraft already in the air and those taking-off or landing.

Approach control will, like aerodrome control, vary from aerodrome to aerodrome depending on the density of the traffic and the importance of the units location within the ATC network. Basically, an approach controller provides control for aircraft approaching or departing the aerodrome from adjacent controlled airspace and it is his job to keep the various aircraft separate from one another and to sequence them correctly for landing or departure.

Approach control can be provided procedurally; that is to say, aircraft are told to report at various positions, and clearances to climb or descend are given based on the aircrafts' forward estimated time of arrival (ETA) at the next reporting point; in this way, aircraft are separated by distance between the various reporting points and by height.

Procedural control methods cannot cope with the density of traffic at the busier aerodromes and, in this case, an approach radar unit is incorporated within approach control. With the use of radar, the controller is able to identify aircraft and to sequence the aircraft for landing or departure at a much quicker rate, as separation standards can be safely reduced.

Area Control is undertaken by an Air Traffic Control Centre (ATCC) established in each FIR throughout the world.

Basically, the ATCC provides ATS within the airspace of the FIR except for those aerodromes which have an additional responsibility for other airspace. Within an FIR, flight information services are provided by the ATCC together with an alerting service which provides for co-ordination of facilities in the event of an aircraft being in distress or any other emergency, eg need for medical facilities on landing.

Telecommunications.—Telecommunications is a generic term, which includes amongst others all the necessary operational facilities specifically needed at each airport, or ATS unit, to enable the pilot and controller to carry out their various activities in an efficient manner. A separate section deals in greater detail with the full range of telecommunications services but those services required essentially for ATC purposes are:

(i) Radio telephony—Air/ground. This provides circuits between the pilot and controller, for the passing of instructions and reporting by aircraft.

(ii) Line Communications—Ground/ground. This provides speech and telegraphic circuits between ATS units, for the passing of ATC messages and data.

(iii) Navigational Aids. Navigational aids (Navaids) provide guidance information to pilots enabling them to navigate their aircraft accurately and to carry out let down procedures to make visual contact with a runway.

AIRPORT GROUND OPERATIONS AND EQUIPMENT

This section is concerned only with airside operations and outlines the ground support facilities necessary to support aircraft ground operations. The amount and degree of sophistication of ground support necessary will differ between airports and will depend upon the role of the airport and the type and number of aircraft operating at peak hours.

AIRCRAFT GROUND SUPPORT REQUIREMENTS.—Aircraft ground support requirements will include: Hangarage/parking/turn round facilities; Engineering maintenance; Freight handling; Emergency services; Other ground support services.

Hangarage/parking/turn round facilities.—Facilities for the hangarage and parking of aircraft is made available at airports, the size of hangars and number of aircraft parking stands will vary between airports and will depend upon the number of resident airlines operating and the type and number of aeroplanes used and whether aerodromes provide domestic services or a mix of international/domestic services (see TRAFFIC FORECASTING)

Hangars are necessary to provide under cover facilities either for the garaging of aircraft, a mixture of garaging and engineering, or solely for engineering maintenance purposes.

Airlines providing passenger and freight services to and from airports will require parking facilities for their passenger aircraft as close as possible to the terminal building. Freight aircraft should be adjacent to the freight building or handling facilities.

The parking facilities, including parking guidance systems and tow and push requirements, will vary with the intensity of traffic; busy international airports will require sophisticated methods to achieve fast aircraft turn round times, nose in guidance systems for docking, passenger air bridges connecting aircraft directly with the terminal and fixed hydrant re-fuelling systems. At smaller airports aircraft would self manoeuvre to and from the terminal building and passengers would either walk or be transported to and from the terminal.

The term 'turn round' in respect of aircraft concerns the disembarkation of the arriving passengers and their baggage, servicing and replenishment of the aircraft systems and the embarkation of the departing passengers and loading of their baggage. Freight will also be loaded and unloaded and it should be noted that a significant volume of freight is carried in the holds of passenger aircraft.

It is in the interest of both the airlines and the airport authority to achieve fast turn round times so ensuring minimum down time for the aircraft and the release of the parking space for other aircraft. Turn round times of less than an hour can be achieved with large aircraft, although the norm is 60 to 75 minutes. Activities during turn round, in addition to passenger, freight and baggage handling, will include replenishment of the aircraft's systems, eg re-fuelling by fuel tanker or underground hydrant system, topping up of oxygen, potable water and oils, servicing of toilets, re-provisioning of in flight meals and aircraft cleaning. Figure 32 shows a typical aircraft under turn round conditions.

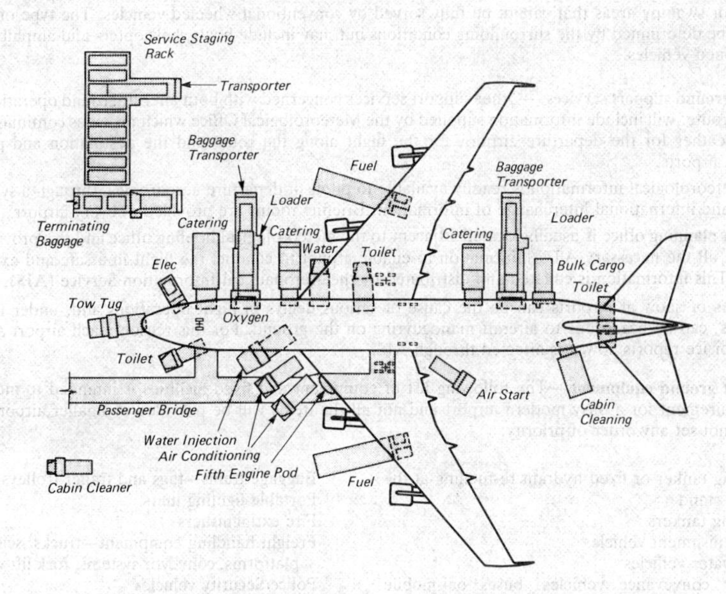

FIG. 32.—Boeing 747 Servicing Arrangement. Typical Turn Round. (*Boeing*).

Systems of baggage retrieval by arriving passengers and baggage check for departing passengers will vary in terms of sophistication between airports and are important factors in achieving quick turn round times discussed above. Systems will vary from the movement of every individual piece of luggage by hand to and from the aircraft by single truck, to containerised baggage conveyed by baggage trains to automated baggage conveyor and terminal systems.

Engineering maintenance.—Where airlines are 'in residence' at airports, it is usual practice for the airline to establish an engineering maintenance base for the phased servicing of their aircraft. Examples of this are British Caledonian's maintenance base at Gatwick Airport, London and British Airway's at Heathrow Airport, London. The larger airlines have also established maintenance bases throughout the world, within their route structure, to ensure minimum aircraft down time, by recovering aircraft for maintenance locally.

Freight Handling.—Air freight aircraft have been developed to the extent that they are capable of carrying 250,000 lb which can be loaded or unloaded by two men in 30 minutes. Other aircraft have been developed to carry a mix of passenger/freight on the main deck and other freight in the hold, whilst other solely passenger aircraft carry freight in the hold, together with passenger baggage. Most freight is either containerised to custom fit modern wide bodied aircraft, or at least palletised to facilitate handling of bulk loads.

Separate parking facilities are usually provided for all freight aircraft associated with a freight terminal complex, where containers and pallets are broken down or made up as applicable. Customs bonded facilities for storage and processing of freight is provided at international airports.

Emergency services.—Emergency fire/crash/rescue services are provided at all airports, these services are categorised according to the number of aircraft movements and the size of the critical aircraft.

The number of fire engines, and the output of their extinguishing agents, provided at an airport is detemined by the category nominated by the competent authority. The main aim of these emergency services is to save lives and it is therefore necessary to achieve rapid response and control times. This is achieved by a high degree of vehicle serviceability and practice drills to ensure high efficiency of the fire crews.

Response time is the time between receipt of the alarm call to the emergency services first effective intervention at the aircraft incident. Control time is the time required from the arrival of the first fire tender to reduce the initial intensity of the fire by 90%. It should be the operational objective of the emergency services to achieve response times not exceeding two minutes, to any part of the aircraft movement area and a control time of one minute.

Usually included with the emergency services is one or more ambulances to provide a nucleus of medical aid, together with a first aid room and resident nursing attendant usually located in the terminal building. Back up facilities for both medical and fire services are provided by the local authorities and the overall facilities are co-ordinated to provide emergency services both on and off the airport.

In addition to the above, suitable rescue equipment and services should be available at airports adjacent to water or swampy areas that cannot be fully served by conventional wheeled vehicles. The type of rescue craft will be determined by the surrounding conditions but may include boats, helicopters and amphibious or air-cushioned vehicles.

Other ground support services.—Other support services concerned with both aircraft ground operations and those en-route, will include information supplied by the Meteorological Office which provides continuous data on the weather for the departure airport, for the flight along the route and the destination and possible diversion airports.

The meteorological information is readily available to pilots at departure aerodromes, through a system of national and international interchange of information. Briefing rooms are provided at every airport.

A flight planning office is usually located adjacent to the meteorological briefing office and this provides the pilot with all the necessary ATC information to enable a pilot to conduct the flight in a safe and expedient manner. This information is collated and distributed by the Aeronautical Information Service (AIS).

Deposits of snow at airports can be the cause of serious delays in flight operations and, under freezing conditions, can be hazardous to aircraft manoeuvring on the ground. For this reason, each airport affected by snow or ice reports how it is affected through AIS.

Airport ground equipment.—The following list of equipment and fixed facilities is intended to indicate a total requirement for a busy modern airport and not all the items will be provided at smaller airports. The list does not set any order of priority:

Re-fuelling tanker or fixed hydrant re-fuelling at the aircraft stand
De-fuelling tankers
Oils replenishment vehicles
Potable water vehicles
Passenger conveyance vehicles, buses or mobile lounges (people movers)
Passenger air bridges
Ground electrical power units (mobile or fixed installations)
Conveyor belt units
Air starter units
Oxygen replenishment units
Airport and airline personnel carrying vehicles
Toilet servicing vehicles
Refuse collection vehicles
Cabin servicing vehicles—catering and cleansing
Baggage trains—tugs and trailer trolleys
Portable lighting units
Fire extinguishers
Freight handling equipment—trucks, scissor lift platforms, conveyor systems, fork lift vehicles
Police/Security vehicles
Mobile cranes
Runway sweepers
Passenger and crew aircraft steps
Aircraft tugs and tractors
Avionics servicing vehicle
Airport maintenance vehicles
Wheel chocks
Jet blast fences
'Follow me' vehicle
Line maintenance vehicles and servicing stands or platforms

The following equipment may have to be provided and this will depend on the circumstances and climatic conditions:

Water methanol replenishment unit	Aircraft de-icing equipment
Ground air conditioning units for aircraft cabins	Snow clearance vehicles and equipment
Ground heating units for aircraft cabins	Bird scaring equipment

COMMERCIAL FACILITIES

There are a large number of ancillary activities at an airport which are essential for the operational or commercial viability. Airports gain a significant proportion of their total income from commercial activities on the airport, and these fall into several categories:

(*a*) those activities where the airport benefits from the turnover, usually referred to as concessions, which might include within the terminal building.

Cafeteria	Ice cream kiosk
Cocktail Lounge	Newstand
Coffee and Snack Shop	Pharmacy
Duty Free Shop	Restaurant
Gift Shop	Vending Machines

and on the airport itself—Aircraft refuelling; Car parks.

(*b*) rented accommodation or space, for example, within the terminal buildings:

Advertising	Games
Airline administration offices	Hotel information & reservation
Airline ticket sales	Insurance sales
Airline check-in desks	Post office
Baggage handling service	Public lockers
Bank	Shoeshine
Barber shop	Taxi stand
Car hire	Ticket sale for rail, bus & coach
Currency exchange	Tourist information

or on the airport—Cargo handling; Maintenance hangars:

(*c*) accommodation for essential services by Government departments, such as Customs & Excise; Immigration

In addition, the airport has to provide and pay for essential services for which there is no return, such as:

(*d*) for the operation of the airport:

Air traffic control	Police
Fire brigade	Security
Meteorological	

(*e*) for the convenience of the passengers and visitors:

First aid	Nursing mothers room
Information service	Public telephones

The importance of the income from concessions and rents is shown in Table 16.

The income from a duty free shop is of particular value to the airport operator and forms a significant proportion of the commercial income on airports where one is provided.

TABLE 16.—INCOME FROM CONCESSIONS: (*Source*: BAA—1981/82)

Airport	Total Income £ million	Commercial Income	
		£ million	%
BAA overall	277·49	117·06	42·19
Heathrow	186·76	79·13	42·37
Gatwick	52·33	25·33	48·40
Stansted	2·36	1·60	67·80
Glasgow	13·70	4·21	30·73
Edinburgh	6·13	1·67	27·24
Prestwick	7·91	2·24	28·32
Aberdeen	8·29	2·35	28·35

Whilst the income from non-aeronautical facilities are of great benefit for the operator, these facilities derive from services which are essential for the passengers, such as car parking, or from amenities which the passenger expects, such as a gift shop, or for international flights, a duty free shop. They are planned upon marketing analysis, or preferences indicated by past experience or judgement. The accessibility and accommodation for them must be arranged so that maximum exposure to the passenger and visitor can be accomplished without interfering with the airports main function, which is to provide facilities. It is also clearly important that the airport operator has the means of regulating the commercial activities.

TRENDS IN AIRCRAFT DESIGN

Aircraft design has been in a state of continuous evolution since the first powered flight by the Wright brothers in 1903 and the two world wars were powerful stimuli. The following identifies those aspects of airport planning and design that are affected by changes in the physical characteristics of aircraft. There have been two major aircraft developments in the last twenty-five years which have had far reaching effects on airport planning and design. These were the introduction of the Boeing 707 in 1958, which required runways in excess of 3,000 m and the introduction of the wide bodied Boeing 747 in 1970, which required more space on the aircraft stand and terminal buildings capable of handling 500 passengers in short periods of time.

The development of the aircraft industry was directed entirely towards the needs of the airlines, that is reduction of the direct operating costs, and no consideration was given to the increasing airport and ATC costs which constitute part of the total air transport system costs. However, although this trend for larger and more productive aircraft will continue, the present attitudes in the industry point towards designs that compromise between aerodynamic efficiency and existing ground facilities.

Aircraft design will continue to develop and affect airport planning and design and the following aircraft characteristics should be considered for the future.

(i) Increased wing span, less sweep and winglets
(ii) Landing gear dimensions, brakes and tyres
(iii) Increased fuselage length
(iv) Increased all up weight
(v) Engine efficiency and noise.

The International Civil Aviation Organisation has put forward possible dimensions for the largest air transport aircraft in 1995 and these are shown in Table 17 together with the corresponding figures for the Boeing 747, which is the largest existing air transport aircraft.

TABLE 17.—FORECAST DIMENSIONS OF AIR TRANSPORT AIRCRAFT
(*Source*: ICAO)

	Forecast for 1995	Boeing 747
Wing span	84 m	60 m
Main gear span	20 m	14 m
Length	84 m	70 m
Tail height	23 m	20 m
All up weight	1,250,000 lb	750,000 lb

The effects of these larger characteristics together with passenger numbers and engine noise, are outlined in this section.

WING SPAN.—Wing span has a major effect on runway and taxiway clearance requirements and aircraft stand widths with a consequent effect on fixed installations such as aprons (particularly cul de sacs), nose loaders and air bridges. ICAO Annex 14 recommends a taxiway separation for Code E aerodromes of 76·5 m (see Table 14 in INTERNATIONAL STANDARDS AND RECOMMENDED PRACTICES) and this would be inadequate for the 1995 aircraft with a wing span of 84 m. It is likely that the separation would be of the order of 100 m—a significant increase. There would have to be reconstruction of existing terminal buildings, piers and satellite terminals together with wider spacing of aircraft stands remote from these facilities. Maintenance hangars will also need to be larger. The growth of wing spans is shown in Figure 33.

MAIN GEAR SPAN.—The recommended maximum width of taxiway for Code E aerodromes is 23 m and it is unlikely that this will be adequate for a main gear span of 20 m. There would be a need for taxiways of approx. 29 m width on the straight portions and a greater widening on curves to accommodate the tracking effect, which will be increased both by the wider main gear and the larger wheel base (which will be inevitable).

LENGTH.—The length of fuselage will mean an increase in aircraft stand length and this, in turn, will require a re-alignment of taxiways in order to maintain clearances. This will be difficult on existing airports

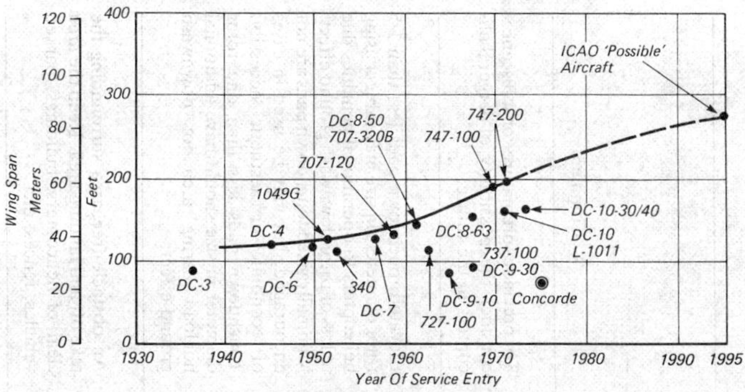

FIG. 33.—Growth in Aircraft Wing Span. (*Based on Commission for the Third London Airport*).

and particularly where there are constraints due to existing buildings etc. The increased length will also affect maintenance facilities such as hangars.

ALL UP WEIGHT.—The effect of all up weight is, perhaps, less easy to forecast. The Boeing 747 caused relatively few problems in regard to pavement strength since it has sixteen main gear wheels and the imposed loading on the pavement is not significantly greater than that for the previous generation which were the Boeing 707 and Douglas DC8. The growth of all up weight is shown in Figure 34. There is a greater awareness now by aircraft designers of the interrelation between aircraft weight and pavement strength and it may be that careful design of the undercarriage involving numbers of wheels, wheel size, wheel spacing and tyre pressure could result in only relatively small increases in the pavement loading.

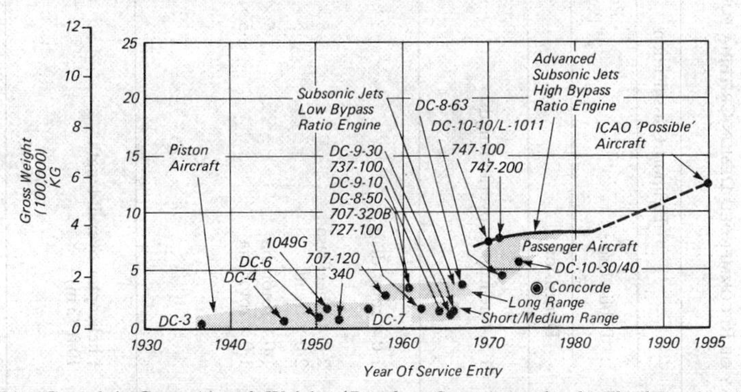

FIG. 34.—Growth in Gross Aircraft Weight. (*Based on Commission for the Third London Airport*).

NUMBERS OF PASSENGERS.—ICAO did not forecast the number of passengers in the 1995 aircraft but it is possible that there could be 900 to 1,000. This will result in major increases in the areas for passenger handling including check-in, immigration, customs, lounges and baggage handling.

AIRCRAFT NOISE.—New noise certification limits came into effect in January 1986 for UK registered aircraft and 1987 for foreign registered aircraft. The regulations effectively take older, noisy aircraft out of operation unless engines are replaced or modified to reduce noise. Advances in engine technology have also resulted in a significant reduction in aircraft noise in the last twenty years but this will not continue at the same rate and, indeed, is probably reaching the limit. Moreover, as engine noise diminishes other factors such as airframe noise become relatively more significant. The main improvement in aircraft noise will result from the phasing out of the older noisier aircraft and the predominance of modern, quieter aircraft.

V/STOL OPERATIONS

Definition.—V/STOL is a term used to describe aircraft which are capable of 'vertical/short take off and landing'. The description covers VTOL, STOL and V/STOL aircraft characteristics. The VTOL classification includes aircraft capable of vertical take off and landing; helicopters and the military Harrier come into this classification.

TABLE 18.—SUMMARY OF RECOMMENDED DESIGN CRITERIA FOR HELICOPTER FACILITIES (*Source*: FAA)

Design Feature	Heliport Classification: Public Use	Heliport Classification: Private Use, Personal Use	Comment
	Dimension		
Take off and landing area			
Length, width, diameter	1·5 × helicopter overall length		To preclude premature obsolescence, consider the possibility of larger helicopters in the future.
Touchdown pad			Elevated touchdown pads less than 1·5 rotor diameters in size may subject using helicopters to operational penalties due to loss of rotor downwash ground effect. Minimally sized touchdown pads are not encouraged, but may be used in cases of economic or aesthetic necessity. Touchdown pads less than one rotor diameter in size should have additional nonload-bearing area for downwash ground effect.
Length, width, diameter	1·0 × rotor dia		
Minimum ground-level			
Length, diameter	2·0 × wheelbase	1·5 × wheelbase	
Width	2·0 × tread	1·5 × tread	
Minimum elevated			
Length, diameter	1·0 × rotor dia	1·5 × wheelbase	
Width	1·0 × rotor dia	1·5 × tread	
Peripheral area			An obstacle-free area surrounding the take off and landing area. Keep the area clear of helicopters, buildings, parked vehicles, fences, etc.
Recommended width	¼ helicopter overall length		
Minimum width	10 ft (3 m)		
Taxiway			
Paved width	Variable, 20 ft (6 m) minimum		Paved taxiways are not required if helicopters hover taxi.

Parking position Length, width, diameter	1·0 × helicopter overall length	Parking position should be beyond the edge of the peripheral area. Parked helicopters should not violate the 2:1 transitional surface.
Pavement grades Touchdown pad, taxiways, parking positions	2·0% maximum	
Other grades Turf shoulders, infield area, etc.	Variable, 1½ to 3%	A 10 ft (3 m) wide rapid runoff shoulder of 5% slope is permitted adjacent to all paved surfaces.
Clearances, rotor tip to object Taxiways, parking positions	10 ft (3 m) minimum	Consider possibility of larger helicopters in the future.
Helicopter primary surface Length, width, diameter Elevation	1·5 × helicopter overall length Elevation highest point take off & landing area.	Imaginary plane overlying the takeoff and landing area. Area to be free of all obstacles.
Helicopter approach surface Number of surfaces Angular separation Length Inner width Outer width Slope	Two 90° min, 180° preferred 4,000 ft (1,220 m) 1·5 × helicopter overall length 500 ft (152 m) 8:1	Protection for helicopter approaches and departures. The surface should not be penetrated by any objects that are determined to be hazards to air navigation.
Helicopter transitional surface Length Width Slope	Full length of approaches and primary surface. 250 ft (76 m) measured from approach & primary surface centerline. 2:1	Surface should not be penetrated by objects.

Note: Above criteria do not apply to offshore helicopter facilities.

The STOL classification includes fixed wing conventional aircraft specifically designed for short take off and landing at congested and inaccessible areas, where larger aircraft are incapable of operating and also provides a feeder service to the larger airports. Typical examples are the Pilatus Britten-Norman BN-2B Islander and the de Havilland DHC-7 Dash 7.

The V/STOL classification includes aircraft which are capable of being operated in the vertical mode, but which can also operate in certain circumstances using an ultra short take-off and landing run. Helicopters can achieve a lower fuel consumption at lift off and a higher pay load, by adopting forward flight early during take off. In the same way the military Harrier can achieve the transition from vertical flight to conventional flight by using an ultra short take off run.

These descriptions are used in comparison with CTOL (conventional take-off and landing) and RTOL (reduced take-off and landing).

Aircraft in these various categories have differing demands for runway length, which are illustrated broadly in Table 19.

TABLE 19.—TYPICAL RUNWAY LENGTHS

Aircraft Definition	Runway Length (m)
VTOL	0–
V/STOL	0–500
STOL	500–800
RTOL	800–1,400
CTOL	1,400–

Whilst the characteristics of aircraft are being constantly improved in terms of increased power, reduced noise levels, increases in payload and fuel economy, CTOL aircraft are still designed to descend on a 3° glide path, in the final approach to the runway section. STOL aircraft, on the other hand, are capable of steep approach glide path angles in the order of 6° to 7½°.

Airports worldwide have been designed to accommodate CTOL aircraft types, for both short haul and long haul flights. V/STOL aircraft characteristics have for some time been confined to aircraft with 12–25 passenger seats and with a range of say 500 nautical miles, although recent developments include the Boeing Chinook-243 helicopter with a 44 seat capacity with a range of 545 nautical miles and the de Havilland DHC-7 Dash 7 with 50 seats and a range of 1,160 nautical miles.

In the past, V/STOL aircraft operations were tolerated at the larger international airports as a welcome passenger feeder service from the smaller aerodromes, but currently most of the larger airports are actively discouraging V/STOL operations where airports are operating close to maximum capacity. This is mainly due to the nuisance value of the smaller aircraft which are difficult to integrate into the air traffic patterns where faster jet aircraft are operating and the fact that they are taking up space on the ground at the airport, where considerably larger aircraft and passenger revenues could be expected.

TABLE 20.—PRINCIPAL AIRCRAFT WITH V/STOL CHARACTERISTICS

Characteristics	Aircraft Type	*Take Off Length (metres)	No. of Passengers
VTOL	All helicopters (too numerous to list)	—	2–44
	largest Boeing Chinook-234		
	Military Harrier	—	crew only
V/STOL	Military Harrier	200	crew only
	All Helicopters	200	2–44
STOL	Pilatus Britten-Norman		
	BN-2B Islander	335	9
	BN-2A MK III Trilander	595	17
	Shorts SC-7 Skyvan	485	19
	De Havilland Canada DHC-6 Twin Otter	365	20
	DHC-7 Dash 7	690	50

TABLE 21.—PRINCIPAL AIRCRAFT WITH RTOL CHARACTERISTICS

RTOL	British Aerospace		
	BAe 146 Series 100	1,085	93
	BAe HS 748 Series 2B	927	58
	Fokker F27-200 Friendship	988	48

* Take off and climb to 35 feet

There is therefore a move to segregate V/STOL and CTOL operations, by providing V/STOL airports throughout the world, particularly this applies in the USA, although there is a need within Europe and some have already been provided.

Advantages of STOL operation.—The advantages of STOL operation are directly related to airport requirements. STOL aircraft operate on take off and landing with steep gradient flight, and require considerably shorter field lengths than conventional aircraft. An airport suitable for V/STOL aircraft requires a smaller area of land than an airport handling conventional aircraft, and the noise 'footpoint' is very much less than a conventional aircraft of similar size. It is, therefore, possible to build a new STOL airport closer to existing conurbations and also in geographically more difficult terrain.

For shorthaul journeys there can be an improvement in the access to the airport, and the costs to the passenger can be shown to be advantageous over other modes of transport.

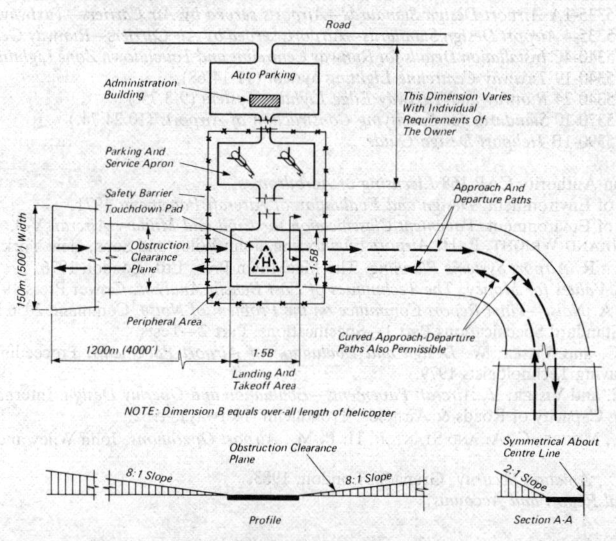

FIG. 35.—Typical Heliport Layout. (*FAA*).

Characteristics of VTOL Airport.—A VTOL airport serves the needs of helicopters. It should be recognised that although a helicopter will land on a pad, the normal approach and take off runs are conventionally to STOL characteristics.

The dimensional requirement of pads are such that they can be provided on roof tops, as is common in cities in the USA, or on barges, or platforms moored in rivers, as can be seen on the River Thames in London. Perhaps the most significant provision of helicopter landing pads is on the North Sea oil rigs.

A typical heliport installation, with landing pad and associated hoverway and apron is shown in Figure 35.

BIBLIOGRAPHY

International Civil Aviation Organisation (ICAO)

(a) *International Standards and Recommended Practices—Aerodromes* Annex 14 7th edition.

(b) *International Standards and Recommended Practices—Aeronautical Telecommunications* Annex 10 Vol. 1 Part 1 3rd edition.
(c) *International Standards and Recommended Practices—Environmental Protection* Annex 16 Vol. 1 1st edition.
(d) *Aerodrome Design Manual* (Doc. 9157) Part 1—*Runways* 1st edition.
(e) *Aerodrome Design Manual* (Doc. 9157) Part 2—*Taxiways Aprons and Holding Bays* 1st edition.
(f) *Aerodrome Design Manual* (Doc. 9157) Part 3—*Pavements* 1st edition.
(g) *Aerodrome Design Manual* (Doc. 9157) Part 4—*Visual Aids* 1st edition.
(h) *Airport Planning Manual* (Doc. 9184) Part 1—*Master Planning* 1st edition.
(j) *Airport Services Manual* (Doc. 9137) Part 1—*Rescue and Fire Fighting* 1st edition.
(k) *Airport Services Manual* (Doc. 9137) Part 2—*Pavement Surface Conditions* 1st edition.
(l) *Manual on Air Traffic Forecasting* (Doc. 8991) 1st edition.
(m) *Heliport Manual*(Doc. 9261) 1st edition.
(n) *Stolport Manual* (Doc 9150) 1st edition.

US Federal Aviation Administration. *Advisory Circulars.*
(a) 150/5300-6A *Airport Design Standards, General Aviation Airports, Basic and General Transport* (2.24.81).
(b) 150/5200-8 *Planning and Design Criteria for Metropolitan STOL Ports* (11.5.70).
(c) 150/5320-6c *Airport Pavement Design and Evaluation* (12.7.78).
(d) 150/5325-2c *Airport Design Standards—Airport served by Air Carriers—Surface Gradient and Line of Sight* (2.6.75).
(e) 150/5325-4 *Runway Length Requirements for Airport Design* (4.5.65).
(f) 150/5325-5B *Aircraft Data* (7.30.75).
(g) 150/5335-1A *Airport Design Standards—Airports served by Air Carriers—Taxiways* (5.15.70).
(h) 150/5335-4 *Airport Design Standards—Airports served by Air Carriers—Runway Geometrics* (7.21.75).
(j) 150/5340-4C *Installation Details for Runway Centreline and Touchdown Zone Lighting Systems* (5.6.75).
(k) 150/5340-19 *Taxiway Centreline Lighting System* (11.14.68).
(l) 150/5340-24 *Runway and Taxiway Edge Lighting System* (9.3.75.)
(m) 150/5370-10 *Standards for Specifying Construction of Airports* (10.24.74.)
(n) 150/5390-1B *Heliport Design Guide.*

Civil Aviation Authority CAP 168 *Licensing of Aerodromes.*
Department of Environment. *Design and Evaluation of Aircraft Pavements* 1971.
Department of Environment. *Pavement Classification for Civil and Military Aircraft* Vol. 1 1971.
ASHFORD, N. AND WRIGHT, P. H. *Airport Engineering.* John Wiley and Sons, New York, 2nd edition 1984.
DE NEUFVILLE R. *Airport Systems Planning.* The MacMillan Press Ltd. London 1976.
FROST, M. J. *Values for Money. The Techniques of Cost Benefit Analysis.* Gower Press 1971.
WILSON, SIR A. *Noise—Final Report Committee on the Problem of Noise.* Command 2056 HMSO July, 1963.
AASHTO. Standard Specifications Part 1—Specifications; Part 2—Tests.
KOOLE, R. C. and VISSER, W. *Design and Evaluation of Airport Pavements.* Proceedings, Association of Asphalt Paving Technologists 1979.
KOOLE, R. C. and VISSER, V. *Aircraft Pavements—Evaluation and Overlay Design.* International Symposium on Bearing Capacity of Roads & Airfields, Trondheim (Norway), 1982.
ASHFORD, N., MOORE, C. A. AND STANTON, H. P. M., *Airport Operations*, John Wiley and Sons, New York, 1984.
DOREY, F. C., *Aviation Security*, Granada, London, 1983.
BAA, *Annual Report and Accounts.*

MECHANISED HANDLING OF MATERIALS

Belt Conveyors—Elevators—Scraper Chain Conveyors—Roller Conveyors—Overhead Conveyors—Skip Hoists—Screw Conveyors—Other Load Handling Equipment—Ship Loaders/Unloaders—Airport Luggage Handling—Mail Handling—Hydraulic & Pneumatic Applications—Industrial Trucks—Mechanised Warehousing—British Standards—Bibliography.

By John W. Kyle, CEng, MIMechE

It has been estimated that two thirds of the cost of manufactured goods arises from movement, handling and storage. Storage philosophy is now therefore closely associated with materials handling and a mechanical handling system may be used to provide temporary storage between stages of production. The subject can only be outlined in this chapter. The bibliography should provide further reading.

GENERAL CLASSIFICATION

Conveyors and elevators may be broadly classified into two main groups: for the handling of either bulk materials, or unit loads. BS 3810 'Glossary of Terms used in Materials Handling' Part 2 covers conveyors and elevators (excluding pneumatic and hydraulic handling).

CONVEYORS AND ELEVATORS FOR BULK MATERIALS.—These may be grouped as follows:

(*a*) **Belt Conveyors** (including fixed, portable and mobile).—Troughed; walled; chain or wire rope/belt; closed; blanket; steel band; and wire mesh.

(*b*) **Chain Conveyors.**—Apron and slat; apron with pans; scraper; drag-bar, or drag-link; en-masse conveyors/elevators; disc or button conveyors; gravity bucket conveyors/elevators.

(*c*) **Screw Conveyors.**—Full-bladed; ribbon; paddle types; tube conveyors; vertical; auger.

(*d*) **Vibratory Conveyors.**—Vibratory; vibrating; oscillating (grasshopper).

(*e*) **Elevators.**—Vertical belt and bucket; centrifugal discharge type; inclined belt and bucket type; chain and bucket type, positive discharge type chain and bucket elevators; continuous bucket elevators; vertical internal discharge chain and bucket elevators.

(*f*) **Skip Hoists.**—Inclined; vertical; stockpiling.

(*g*) **Feeders.**—Belt; apron; drag-bar (scraper); chain-curtain; horizontal paddle-wheel; screw; vibrating; shaking or reciprocating; rotary drum; rotary vane; rotary table feeders.

UNIT LOAD CONVEYORS AND ELEVATORS.—These may be grouped as follows:

(*a*) **Belt Conveyors.**—Flat.

(*b*) **Chain Conveyors.**—Raised link, or offset roller chain type; chain conveyors with driving dogs; slat elevators/conveyors; push-bar conveyors; horizontal circulating plate/tray conveyors (carousel); sling or pocket elevators/conveyors; fixed tray (corner hung) elevators/conveyors; crossbar elevators/conveyors; accumulating conveyors.

(*c*) **Overhead Conveyors.**—Chain or rope haulage conveyors; fixed suspension type; chain or rope haulage conveyors; suspension pushing type; enclosed track type; overhead towing conveyors.

(*d*) **Underfloor.**—Towing chain conveyors.

(*e*) **Elevators.**—Swing tray; barrel or drum type; sack elevators; magnetic elevators/conveyors.

(*f*) **Roller Conveyors and Chutes.**—Gravity roller type, roller conveyors—transfer (right angle) or turntable type, two-way (Y junction), ball transfer tables, spiral roller conveyors, wheel conveyors, powered or live roller conveyors; gravity chutes.

BELT CONVEYORS

These are used for a wide range of applications in commerce and industry, from the light, flat belts used in offices and small assembly plants for unit loads, to heavy troughed conveyors used in docks, quarries, mines and heavy industry for bulk materials. The latter are in most cases troughed on the carrying side by suitably designed idlers which support the belt and the load (Fig. 1). The troughing increases the capacity of the conveyor

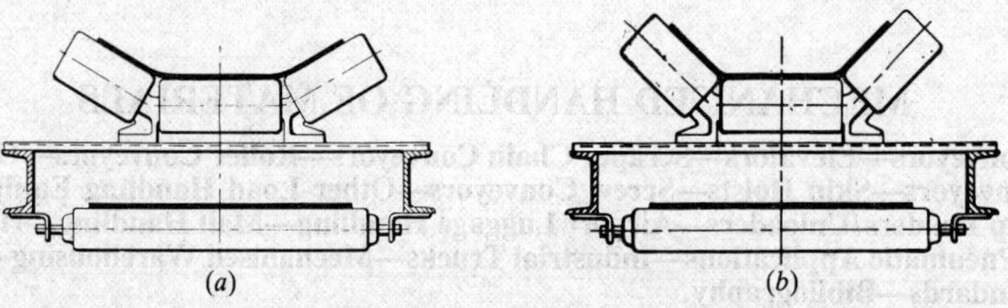

FIG. 1.—Cross-sections of Troughed Idlers. (*a*) 25° Trough. (*b*) 45° Trough.

and obviates spillage. The conveyor is driven through a pulley or pulleys and the driving gear or gears. For some particular applications belt conveyors driven at both ends are available. Another variant is provided with a supporting driving belt. BS 2890 gives basic information on troughed belt conveyors incorporating rubber and fabric belting manufactured in accordance with BS 490 Part 1 for handling materials in bulk within the range of belt widths from 400 to 2,000 mm. BS 2890 does not apply to underground mining conveyors and to conveyors for materials which do not behave as solids. BS 3289 covers belting for mines. Portable and mobile conveyors are covered by BS 4531.

The material may be loaded on the belt by hand, shovel, chute, mechanical feeder or other means; it is removed by discharging over the end pulley or by deflecting it at some intermediate point in the length of the conveyor.

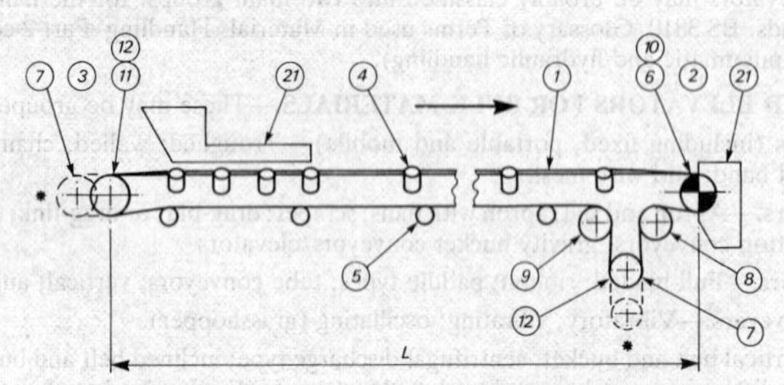

FIG. 2.—Typical Troughed Belt Conveyor and Components. Numbers correspond to the text.
* = alternative tensioning device. L = conveyor length.

The following definitions generally conform to BS 2890 (see Fig. 2).

1. *The Belt.* Carries the material and transmits the power.
2. *Head of Conveyor.* The discharge end of the conveyor.
3. *Tail of Conveyor.* The loading end of the conveyor.
4. *Carrying Idlers.* Idlers which support the loaded belt.
   An assembly of one or more carrying idlers, suitably mounted, comprises a carrying idler set.
5. *Return Idlers.* Idlers which support the empty side of the belt.
   An assembly of one or more return idlers, suitably mounted, comprises a return idler set.
6. *Drive.* The equipment which drives the belt, comprising power unit, transmission and driving pulley or pulleys.
   Power Unit. Motor or engine.
   Transmission. An assembly of devices coupling the power unit to the drive pulley/pulleys to drive the belt at the desired speed.
   Driving Pulley. A pulley which drives the belt.
7. *Take-up Device.* A device for taking up slack and applying tension to the belt. Also for storing excess belt, ie storage loop.
8. *Snub Pulley.* A pulley used to increase the arc of contact of the belt on the drive pulley.
9. *Bend Pulley.* A pulley used to change the direction of the belt.
10. *Head Pulley.* The terminal pulley at the head end of a conveyor. This may be a drive pulley.
11. *Tail Pulley.* The terminal pulley at the tail end of a conveyor. This may be a take-up pulley.
12. *Take-up Pulley.* The travelling pulley used in the take-up device.
13. *Anti Run Back.* An automatic device for preventing a loaded elevating conveyor running backwards when the power source is removed.
14. *Retarder.* A device for preventing the over-speeding of a regenerative conveyor.
15. *Brake.* A device for bringing conveyor to rest and maintaining it at rest.
16. *Cleaner.* A device for removing material which may adhere to the belt or pulley.

17. *Handing of Conveyor.* The sides of a unidirectional belt conveyor are left-hand or right-hand when looking from the tail towards the head of the conveyor.
18. *Tripper.* A device usually comprising two or more pulleys, mounted either in a fixed position or on a travelling carriage, for discharging material from a belt conveyor continuously or at selected points or at any point along the length.
19. *Shuttle Conveyor.* A unidirectional or reversible belt conveyor having over-end discharge, the whole being mounted on a travelling carriage capable of being shuttled backwards and forwards along a track, discharging continuously or at selected points.
20. *Plough.* A blade or blades mounted obliquely across the belt to discharge the material by deflecting it from the belt.
    Note: Can be useful where headroom and space is limited, but is not recommended for any duty other than slow speed conveyors handling non-abrasive free flowing materials.
21. *Chute.* A straight, curved or spiral, open topped or enclosed smooth trough, by which materials are directed and lowered by gravity.
22. *Safeguard.* A guard or device designed to protect persons from danger.

CONVEYOR BELTING

The principal components are (a) the carcass, or re-inforcement, to transmit the power and support the material load, and (b) the cover to protect the carcass and transmit the drive by friction.

The Carcass may be of woven fabric in the form of multiple layers (plies) or an integral mat (solid woven) or a single layer (cords). Objectives of the design are to provide longitudinal strength, transverse load support, troughability, controlled elasticity, and resistance to damage by impact, ripping or tearing. It must also offer the facility to make joints on site.

Cotton duck was the original textile fabric, but the subsequent use of synthetic fibres has greatly improved strength and flexibility.

Steel cord is now well established for high tensile strength, where a single flight, long centre, high lift, conveyor can replace two or more units and transfer points. Obviously, the widely differing physical properties of steel compared to textile necessitate specific conveyor design practice (BTR, Clouth).

The Cover may be of natural or synthetic rubber (BS 490 Part 1) depending on the degree of abrasion, cutting, gouging, heat, etc anticipated with the material being carried. PVC (Dunlop 'Vinyplast', Fenner 'Fenaplast') can be made fire resistant to British Coal specification for underground mines. Other polymers are available at extra cost for special conditions, eg hot materials (BTR 'Pyrotex', Dunlop 'Betahete').

Deep Troughing as shown in Fig. 1 can achieve additional carrying capacity and/or less spillage. The belt itself must be capable of conforming to the trough section, and care taken to avoid creasing along the line of the idler junction; synthetic fibres and steel cord are ideal for the purpose. Over-stressing or buckling at the transition from troughed to flat at terminal pulleys and the design of vertical curves become more critical.

Selection of Belt BS 490 Part 1 deals with rubber and plastic conveyor belting of textile construction for general use and specifies construction, dimensions, properties of cover, carcass and complete belt. It includes tensile strength, adhesion, and troughability; making of samples and methods of test. BS 2890 deals with troughed belt conveyors incorporating belting to BS 490 Part 1, covering belt widths 400 to 2000 mm.

The belt is a high cost item and it is therefore important that the most efficient and cost effective one is selected. For this reason, questionnaires issued by the belt manufacturers should be submitted and their recommendations sought. Influencing factors are: width, thickness, weight, carcass and cover to suit the material being conveyed, tensile strength and factor of safety related to service conditions, troughability, load support, elongation under working loads, method of jointing.

Belt Rating and Designation can be selected from the standard ranges, see Table 1. From this, the belt type is designated—eg 'Type 600/3' carcass strength 600 kN/m width of three ply construction. 'Type ST 2000' steel cord strength 2000 kN/m width. Further designation gives cover thicknesses and quality, see Table 2—eg '5 × 1.5 Grade M'.

TABLE 1.—WHOLE BELT TENSILE STRENGTH IN kN/METRE WIDTH

For textile carcass:

160, 180, 200, 224, 250, 280, 315, 355, 400, 450, 500, 560, 630, 710, 800, 900, 1000, 1120, 1250, 1400, 1600, 1800, 2000, 2240, 2500

Underlined are preferred values, and should be specified wherever possible. (BS 490 Part 1)

For steel cord:

ST 500, 630, 800, 900, 1000, 1150, 1250, 1400, 1600, 1800, 2000, 2250, 2500, 2750, 3150, 3500, 3750, 4000, 4250, 4500, 4750, 5000, 6000, 7000

(DIN 22131)

BELT COVER MATERIAL PROPERTIES

TABLE 2.—BELT COVER QUALITY AND THICKNESS

For textile carcass:

Conveyed Materials		Covers		
			Thickness (mm)	
Category	Examples	Quality	Top	Bottom
Non-abrasive	wood chips, pulp, flue dust, ground cement, very fine coal	N 17	1·0/1·5	1·0
Slightly abrasive	sand, earth, gravel, bituminous coal (up to 75 mm lump size)	N 17	1·5/3·0	1·5
Abrasive	anthracite coal, coke, sinter, overburden (up to 250 mm lump size)	N 17S	3·0/5·0	1·5
	ores (up to 150 mm lump size)			
Heavy and abrasive	limestone, slag, ores (up to 250 mm lump size)	M 24	5·0/6·0	1·5
Heavy, sharp and abrasive	ores (over 250 mm lump size)	M 24	6·0/9·0	2·0/3·0
	trap rock, quartz, glass cullet			
Moderate hot (up to 120°C)	coke, cement, foundry sand	N 17S	3·0/5·0	1·5
Hot (120–150°C)	coke wharf, sinter, slag	BUTYL	5·0/6·0	1·5
Very hot (over 150°C)	ditto, red hot lumps	BUTYL	6·0/10·0	2·0/3·0
Oily	oiled coal, artificial fertilisers	NITRILE	3·0	1·5
		PVC	1·5	1·5
Sticky	wet clay	PVC	1·5	1·5
Run-of-Mine (underground)	coal, gypsum rock	*NEOPRENE	3·0	1·5
		*PVC	1·5	1·5

* = fire resistant quality (MHEA)

For steel cord:

Type	Recommended top cover thickness			Minimum bottom cover thickness
	Non-abrasive materials	Heavy abrasive materials	Sharp, heavy abrasive materials	
	mm	mm	mm	mm
ST 500	5	8	9–12	5
ST 630	5	8	9–12	5
ST 800	5	8	9–12	5
ST 900	5	8	9–12	5
ST 1000	5	8	9–12	5

ST 1150	5	8	9–12	5
ST 1250	5	8	9–12	5
ST 1400	5	8	9–12	5
ST 1600	5	8	9–12	5
ST 1800	5	8	9–12	5
ST 2000	5	8	9–12	5
ST 2250	5	8	9–12	5
ST 2500	5	8	9–12	5
ST 2750	6	9	10–13	6
ST 3150	6	9	10–13	6
ST 3500	7	10	11–14	7
ST 3750	7	10	11–14	7
ST 4000	7	10	11–14	7
ST 4250	8	11	12–15	8
ST 4500	8	11	12–15	8
ST 4750	8	11	12–15	8
ST 5000	9	12	13–16	9
ST 6000	9	12	13–16	9
ST 7000	10	13	14–16	10

(BTR)

Belt Widths are standardised in a range of metric sizes as follows: 400, 500, 600, 650, 750, 800, 900, 1000, 1050, 1200, 1350, 1400, 1600, 1800, 2000 mm. The underlined are preferred sizes, and should be specified wherever possible (BS 490 Part 1).

Belt Joints made in situ can be either mechanical fastener or vulcanised splice. In each case, the resultant joint stregth is less than the whole belt, and although an appropriate factor of safety is applied, failures often occur due to poor workmanship or abuse in service. Therefore, inspect and maintain joints regularly.

Mechanical Fasteners are easily made and replaced. Their strength is less than a vulcanised splice and fine materials can spill through. Used on smaller and temporary installations.

Vulcanised splicing is a specialist service provided by belt manufacturers and contractors, using expensive, purpose-made equipment. When correctly done, the joint has a long life, good flexibility, and presents a smooth belt surface. Always specified for steel cord belting. See BS 6593 'Code of Practice for On-Site Splicing'.

SELECTING A TROUGHED BELT CONVEYOR.—This problem may be approached in two ways: (1) Basic characteristics which the proposed conveyor must satisfy, will be known. These include: *C*, the maximum capacity (or output) or peak load anticipated/required (tonne/hour); *w*, the density of material carried (tonne/m^3); the character of the material (sticky, powdery, hot, acid or oil-contaminated, etc); the maximum size of lumps (mm); *L*, the horizontal length measured between centres of terminal pulleys (m); and *H*, the vertical difference in level (m), ie the lift or fall (according to the direction of travel with load). Knowing *C* and *w*, and the size of lumps, a suitable belt width can be found from Table 3 (see Example below), keeping in mind that Table 3 is based on a load surcharge angle of 20°, and a speed of 1 m/s. Table 4 indicates the recommended

TABLE 4.—RECOMMENDED MAXIMUM BELT SPEEDS FOR NORMAL USE

Material to be conveyed	Belt width (mm)				
	Up to 500	600 to 650	750 to 800	900 to 1,050	1,200 to 2,000
	Belt speed (m/s)				
Grain and other liquid flowing and non-abrasive materials	2·5	3·0	3·5	4·0	4·5
Coal, crushed stone and similar lump materials	2·0	2·5	3·0	3·5	4·0
Heavy abrasive ore, coarse, sharp stone etc	1·75	2·0	2·25	2·75	3·0
Prepared damp foundry sand without ploughs	1·5 (for all belt widths)				
Prepared foundry sand and similar abrasive materials with ploughs	0·75 (for all belt widths)				
Non-abrasive materials with ploughs	1·0 (for all belt widths)				
Shake-out foundry sand with small cores and castings	1·0 (for all belt widths)				

(Dunlop)

TABLE 3.—CAPACITIES OF TROUGHED BELT CONVEYORS
(Expressed in tonnes/hour based on speed of 1 m/s and and load surcharge angle of 20°)

Belt width (mm)	Rec max lump (mm)		Troughing angle (degrees)	Area of load (sq m)	Average density of material carried (tonnes/m²)							
	Sized	Unsized			0·5	0·75	1·0	1·25	1·5	2·0	2·5	3·0
500	100	160	20	0·0191	34	51	69	86	103	138	172	207
			27½	0·0220	39	59	79	99	119	158	198	238
			30	0·0228	41	61	82	102	123	164	205	246
			35	0·0243	43	65	87	109	131	175	218	262
			45	0·0263	47	71	94	118	142	189	237	284
600	125	200	20	0·0291	52	78	104	131	157	209	262	314
			27½	0·0334	60	90	120	150	180	241	301	361
			30	0·0347	62	93	125	156	187	250	312	375
			35	0·0369	66	99	132	166	199	265	332	389
			45	0·0399	71	107	143	179	215	287	359	431
650	125	200	20	0·0348	62	94	125	156	188	251	313	376
			27½	0·0400	72	108	144	180	216	288	360	432
			30	0·0415	74	112	149	187	224	299	374	448
			35	0·0441	79	119	159	198	238	318	397	477
			45	0·0477	85	128	171	214	257	343	429	515
750	150	250	20	0·0486	87	131	175	219	262	350	437	525
			27½	0·0555	100	150	200	250	300	400	500	599
			30	0·0581	105	157	209	261	314	418	523	627
			35	0·0620	112	167	223	279	335	446	558	670
			45	0·0665	120	180	239	299	359	479	599	718
800	160	250	20	0·0551	99	148	198	248	297	397	496	595
			27½	0·0634	114	171	228	285	342	456	570	684
			30	0·0657	118	177	236	295	355	473	591	710
			35	0·0698	125	188	251	314	377	503	628	754
			45	0·0753	135	203	271	339	407	542	678	814

900	175	300	20	0·0719	129	194	259	324	388	518	647	777
			27½	0·0820	148	221	295	369	443	590	738	886
			30	0·0859	155	232	309	387	464	618	773	928
			35	0·0917	165	248	330	413	495	660	825	990
			45	0·0984	177	266	354	443	531	708	886	1,063
1,000	200	300	20	0·0893	160	241	321	402	482	643	804	964
			27½	0·1027	184	277	369	462	554	739	924	1,109
			30	0·1065	191	287	383	479	575	676	959	1,151
			35	0·1131	203	305	407	509	611	814	1,018	1,222
			45	0·1219	219	329	439	548	658	878	1,097	1,317
1,050	225	350	20	0·0997	179	269	359	449	538	718	897	1,077
			27½	0·1138	205	307	410	512	615	819	1,024	1,229
			30	0·1192	215	322	429	536	644	858	1,073	1,287
			35	0·1272	229	343	458	572	687	916	1,145	1,374
			45	0·1365	246	369	491	614	737	983	1,229	1,474
1,200	250	400	20	0·1317	237	355	474	592	711	948	1,185	1,422
			27½	0·1515	272	409	545	681	818	1,091	1,363	1,636
			30	0·1571	282	424	565	707	848	1,131	1,414	1,697
			35	0·1668	300	450	600	750	901	1,201	1,501	1,802
			45	0·1796	323	485	646	808	970	1,293	1,617	1,940
1,350	275	450	20	0·1690	304	456	608	761	913	1,217	1,521	1,825
			27½	0·1928	347	521	694	868	1,041	1,388	1,735	2,082
			30	0·2019	363	545	727	909	1,090	1,454	1,817	2,181
			35	0·2155	388	582	776	970	1,164	1,552	1,940	2,327
			45	0·2313	416	625	833	1,041	1,249	1,665	2,082	2,498
1,400	275	450	20	0·1823	328	492	656	820	984	1,312	1,641	1,969
			27½	0·2097	377	566	755	943	1,132	1,510	1,887	2,265
			30	0·2175	391	587	873	978	1,174	1,566	1,957	2,349
			35	0·2308	415	623	831	1,039	1,246	1,662	2,078	2,493
			45	0·2484	447	670	894	1,118	1,341	1,788	2,236	2,683

Cont. on L3/8

TABLE 3.—*continued*

Belt width (mm)	Rec max lump (mm)		Troughing angle (degrees)	Area of load (sq m)	Average density of material carried (tonnes/m^2)							
	Sized	Unsized			0·5	0·75	1·0	1·25	1·5	2·0	2·5	3·0
1,500	300	500	20	0·2104	379	568	757	947	1,136	1,515	1,894	2,272
			27½	0·2401	432	648	864	1,080	1,297	1,729	2,161	2,593
			30	0·2514	453	679	905	1,131	1,358	1,810	2,263	2,715
			35	0·2684	483	725	966	1,208	1,449	1,932	2,416	2,899
			45	0·2880	518	778	1,037	1,296	1,555	2,074	2,592	3,110
1,600	325	500	20	0·2404	432	649	865	1,082	1,298	1,731	2,164	2,597
			27½	0·2766	497	746	995	1,244	1,493	1,991	2,489	2,987
			30	0·2868	516	774	1,032	1,290	1,549	2,065	2,581	3,098
			35	0·3045	548	822	1,096	1,370	1,644	2,192	2,740	3,288
			45	0·3277	589	884	1,179	1,474	1,769	2,359	2,949	3,539
1,800	350	600	20	0·3074	553	830	1,106	1,383	1,660	2,213	2,766	3,320
			27½	0·3535	636	954	1,272	1,591	1,909	2,545	3,182	3,818
			30	0·3666	660	990	1,320	1,650	1,980	2,640	3,300	3,960
			35	0·3891	700	1,050	1,401	1,751	2,101	2,802	3,502	4,203
			45	0·4186	753	1,130	1,507	1,884	2,260	3,014	3,768	4,521
2,000	400	700	20	0·3825	688	1,032	1,377	1,721	2,065	2,754	3,442	4,131
			27½	0·4399	791	1,187	1,583	1,979	2,375	3,167	3,959	4,751
			30	0·4562	821	1,231	1,642	2,053	2,463	3,285	4,106	4,927
			35	0·4842	871	1,307	1,743	2,179	2,614	3,486	4,358	5,229
			45	0·5207	937	1,405	1,874	2,343	2,811	3,749	4,686	5,623

(Dunlop)

Notes

(1) The capacities given in the table are based on 3 equal length roll idlers. For long centre idlers the capacity is approximately 80% of that shown.
(2) For free flowing material such as grain, dry cement etc, the maximum surcharge angle will be of the order of 5° and the capacity can be estimated as 60% of the values shown if 20° troughing is used and 80% of the values shown if 45° troughing is used.
(3) For belts operating at angles of inclination in excess of 15°, the capacities obtained from the above table should be reduced by 10%.

maximum belt speeds, v (m/s) for typical selected material for normal use. (2) Alternatively, if the width of the belt is known the maximum expected capacity could be found.

Notes

(1) In the case of belts loaded on inclines of 10° for more it may be necessary to reduce the above speeds to achieve maximum capacity.

(2) High belt speeds should be treated with caution; they can create turbulence at loading points, accelerate cover wear, encourage low density materials to become airborne, increase the risk of product size degradation, and reduce the life of chutes, etc.

Example.—(1) Required, a belt conveyor to be used for handling 500 t/h of coal, unsized, having density of 1·0 t/m^3. Assume belt speed of 2 m/s. Table 4 indicates that 3·0 m/s would be the recommended maximum speed for a belt 800 mm wide. Table 3 shows that for a belt 800 mm wide, and for 'average density of material' of 1·0 t/m^3, the required capacity (251 t/h at 1 m/s) is reached; for a belt speed of 2 m/s, 251 × 2 = 502; then follow the same line to the left, the maximum unsized lump size allowed (250 mm), and troughing angle recommended (35°) are given; area of load stream, S, will then be 0·0698 m^2 for the width of 800 mm.

(2) Alternatively, if the width of belt is known, Table 3 will indicate the maximum capacity expected for the given material at a certain speed. The example given above could be used for checking: find 800 in the column 'Belt width', follow this line towards the right and the column 'Average density of material' (1·0 in our example), running down the 800 mm (width), the capacity of 251 t/h will be found for a conveyor running at 1 m/s. See also BS 2890.

CAPACITY.—This can be calculated from the formula:

$$C = 3{,}600Swv$$

where C = capacity (t/h); S = area of load stream (m^2); v = belt speed (m/s); and w = density of material carried (t/m^3). The formula will give the speed or the area of load stream if the other three items in the formula are known.

CALCULATION OF BELT TENSION.—Knowledge of the pull at the driving pulley or the effective tension (T_E), developed at the driving pulley during normal working conditions, is necessary in order to calculate the maximum belt tension (T_M), then to select the best belt construction, and, also, power required:

$$T_E = A + B + D$$

where T_E = effective tension; A = tension (or force) necessary to move the empty belt along the conveyor; B = force to move the load along the conveyor; and D = force required to raise (or to lower) the load, if the conveyor is not horizontal. All in newtons; the values of these three components are as follows:

$$A = F_B \times L_1 \times W_1 \times 9{\cdot}81 \qquad B = F_L \times L_1 \times W_2 \times 9{\cdot}81 \qquad D = \pm W_2 \times H \times 9{\cdot}81$$

Where, F_B = factor of friction for empty belt; F_L = factor of friction for load on level (values for F_B and F_L are: average, 0·03; exceptionally good, 0·022).

Assuming $F_B = F_L = F$: $T_E = A + B + D$ (see above)

$$T_E = 9{\cdot}81L_1 \times F \times (W_1 + W_2) \pm (9{\cdot}81 \times W_2 \times H.)$$

L_1 = adjusted length, ie conveyor length L(m), plus 45 m for normal driving conditions, or 150 m for regenerative conditions; W_1 = weight of moving parts (kg/m), see Table 5; W_2 = weight of load = $0{\cdot}278C/v$ (kg/m), where C is capacity or peak load t/h, and v is belt speed (m/s); H = vertical lift or fall (m).

TABLE 5.—WEIGHT OF MOVING PARTS (W_1)

Belt width (mm)	Light duty idlers 102 mm	Medium duty idlers 127 mm	Medium duty idlers 152 mm	Heavy duty idlers 152 mm	Heavy duty idlers and belt
	(kg/m)	(kg/m)	(kg/m)	(kg/m)	(kg/m)
500	24	28	36		
600	28	36	45	49	58
650	30	38	47	52	62
750	37	46	56	62	73
800	39	48	60	65	77
900	45	55	70	79	91
1,000	49	60	77	88	102
1,050	52	64	82	94	109
1,200	63	71	95	110	128
1,350	70	82	107	126	144
1,400	71	84	110	129	148
1,500		91	120	143	164

1,600	96	127	151	173
1,800		142	170	198
2,000		155	190	220

(Dunlop)

Notes
(1) The above values are derived from the sum of twice the belt weight plus idler weights per unit length, and are sufficiently accurate for most calculations of effective tension/power requirements.
(2) In some instances, eg a long, horizontal conveyor, the effective tension/power attributable to the moving parts may be a significant proportion of the total. In such cases, the actual mass of components should be used in the final calculations.

TABLE 6.—DRIVE FACTOR (K)

Angle of wrap (degrees)	Drive factor (K): Gravity take-up, Bare drum	Gravity take-up, Lagged drum	Screw take-up, Bare drum	Screw take-up, Lagged drum
160	2·00	1·60	2·45	2·05
170	1·92	1·55	2·32	1·97
180	1·85	1·50	2·20	1·90
190	1·78	1·46	2·08	1·85
200	1·72	1·42	2·00	1·78
210	1·67	1·38	1·94	1·73
220	1·62	1·35	1·90	1·68
230	1·58	1·32	1·85	1·65
240	1·54	1·30	1·80	1·60
250	1·50	1·28	1·77	1·57
360	1·26	1·13	1·52	1·32
380	1·23	1·11	1·50	1·30
400	1·21	1·09	1·48	1·28
420	1·19	1·08	1·45	1·26
440	1·17	1·07	1·43	1·24
460	1·15	1·06	1·41	1·21

(Dunlop)

Power Required for Conveyor Drive $P = \dfrac{T_E \cdot v}{1000}$

Where: P is in kW; T_E is in newtons; and v in m/s. Conversely, if the output of the installed motor drive is known, then T_E may be obtained from the above formula.

If the conveyor is equipped with a tripper, additional power will be required.

Induced, or Slack-side, tension is the minimum tension induced into the belt as it leaves the driving pulley: $T_2 = T_E(K - 1)$, where T_2 is in newtons; K is the drive factor (See Table 6).

Tight-side tension is in the belt as it enters the driving pulley: $T_1 = T_E + T_2$ newtons.

Usually, T_1 calculated as above is satisfactory to ensure that sufficient tension exists at all points along the conveyor belt. However, conditions can arise where it is insufficient to support the load, often at the tail end of the conveyor, and excessive belt sag may occur. In such cases, additional tension has to be added (see MHEA 'Recommended Practice' or manufacturers' catalogues).

The ratio T_1 to T_2 is independent of the diameter of the pulley. The co-efficient of friction can be increased by lagging the driving pulley; the angle of wrap can be increased either by the use of a snub pulley, or by adopting tandem driving pulleys, thereby increasing the capacity of the drive without increasing the maximum belt tension (see Fig. 3).

There are alternative methods of belt tension calculation (eg Dunlop, BTR, MHEA), and for proper results the various factors and values should always be taken from one source.

TYPES OF BELTING FOR PARTICULAR APPLICATIONS.—They are too numerous to be treated here at length. Only examples are given below, but the list is not exhaustive; neither all manufacturers nor all belt types listed.

(*a*) *Steep-angle* conveyor belting for handling loose materials (sand, cement, earth, coal), sacks, and lumps.

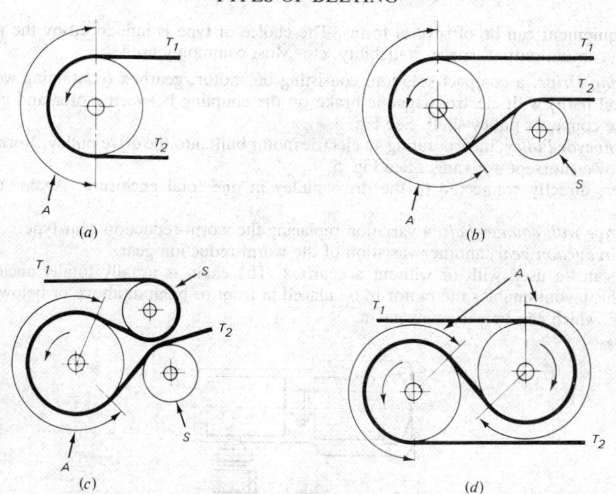

FIG. 3.—Pulley Drive Arrangements. (*a*) Plain single drive pulley. (*b*) Single drive pulley with a snub sheave. (*c*) Single drive pulley with double snub. (*d*) Tandem drive.
A = arc of contact. S = Snub pulley. T_1 = Tight side tension. T_2 = Slack side tension.

Achieved by 25 mm high bars in chevron formation integrally moulded with the face cover. (*Dunlop 'Chevron'; Uniroyal 'Steepgrade'* and others). (*b*) *Cleated belting* is also produced by *Dawson*. (*c*) *Woven-glass coated belt* with a special non-sticking substance (*Tygaflor*) recommended for handling certain chemicals and in cases where dialectric properties are useful (eg, for drying, cooking, processing, etc). (*d*) *Grid-shaped belting* made of glass-filled polyamide has a low noise level and is resistant to micro-organisms, to humidity and heat (*Bayer*). (*e*) Another *grid-shaped belting* is recommended for wet and dry materials in cooling plants (eg, in the rubber industry); for drying tunnels and for moving materials through water baths, spray tunnels, washing plants, etc; suitable for temperatures from −20°C to +140°C (*McInnes, Wiese*). (*f*) *Wire belting*, particularly suitable for handling materials in low temperatures, down to −40°C, also recommended for draining and spraying operations, drying, sterilising, washing, heating, cooling, etc, while in transit; one manufacturer (*Metal Belts Ltd*) offers a selection of about 50 designs of wire conveyor belting; they are calculated in the same way as other beltings, but wire belting is, of course, much heavier. (*g*) *Steel cord belting* is typically composed of high-strength steel wire and neoprene; eg, a 915 mm wide belt composed of 97 steel cords, 4 mm in diameter with 9 mm spacing (*BTR 'Silvercord'*). (*h*) *Silicon rubber belts* employed for handling hot sticky substance, such as dough, chocolate, toffees, etc. (*Dawson*). (*i*) *Belting reinforced with nylon and terylene* (*ICI*) permits it to be used for deep troughing and longer hauls. (*j*) *Rubberised polystyrene belting* is characterised by silent conveying and is used for cereals and other granulated materials (*Law Denis*) (*k*) For oily and greasy materials or waste, etc, Semperit 'G' belting is recommended; it is rot-resistant, constructed uo to 1,200 mm wide *synthetic duck piles*. (*l*) Troughed belts provided *with skirt boards* allow the prevention of spillage and waste of the material carried, some constructors (eg, *Semperit*, or *SIG/Flexbord*) offer belts provided with elevated flexible sides, fulfilling the same role; it is claimed that a 1,200 mm wide belt would allow the capacity to be doubled at least. (*m*) Rubber chain conveying and driving medium (*McInnes, Wiese*, and others) is recommended for silent running; it does not need any greasing, and is not subject to corrosion.

CONVEYOR DRIVING GEAR

Electricity is the usual power supply. Electric motors for driving conveyors are mostly of the squirrel cage induction type, totally enclosed, with direct-on-line starting. If a fluid coupling is not fitted between the motor and the gearbox (as recommended for large conveyors), then a slip-ring induction motor is preferred. BS 3979 gives details of output (kW) and metric dimensions of electric motors.

The drive is usually located near the head (ie discharge) end of the conveyor, but in some cases it can be located underneath the conveyor working on the return belt. The latter arrangment is particularly convenient if material is transferred from one conveyor to another at the head-end of the first. On long, high horsepower conveyors it is usual to provide more than one drive to assist in reducing the maximum belt tension.

Drive pulleys are single or tandem (see Fig. 3). Single drives may be up to 800 mm diameter and transmit up to 100 kW at belt speeds up to 3 m/s. A more powerful and efficient tandem drive has pulleys 1,370 mm diameter with 480° arc of contact with the belt (the most that can be achieved on the two drums), supplied for belt widths from 900 to 1,500 mm, the drive is rated up to 317 kW at a belt speed of 2·3 m/s, but other models in the range cater for ratings up to 720 kW at a belt speed of 5·08 m/s (Anderson).

CONVEYOR DRIVING GEAR

The driving equipment can be of several forms. The choice of type is influenced by the power required, conveyor size, maximum output, space availability, etc. Most commonly used are:

1. *Worm Reducing Drive*, a compact solution, consisting of: motor, gearbox (containing worm and geared wheel in an oil bath) with electro-magnetic brake on the coupling between motor and gearbox, directly coupled to the conveyor pulley shaft. See Fig. 4.
2. *Motorised Conveyor Pulley*, incorporating an electric motor built into the drive pulley. Normally considered only for the lower horsepower range. See Fig. 5.
3. *Geared Motor*, directly connected to the drive pulley in one total enclosure. Again, used on smaller conveyors.
4. *Spur-wheel drive with countershaft*, a variation replacing the worm-reduction gear type.
5. *Parallel-shaft reduction gear*, another variation of the worm-reduction gear.
6. *Chain Drive* can be used with or without a gearbox. The chain is usually totally enclosed and splash lubricated. This layout enables the motor to be placed in front or behind, above or below, the axis of the driving pulley, which can be very convenient.

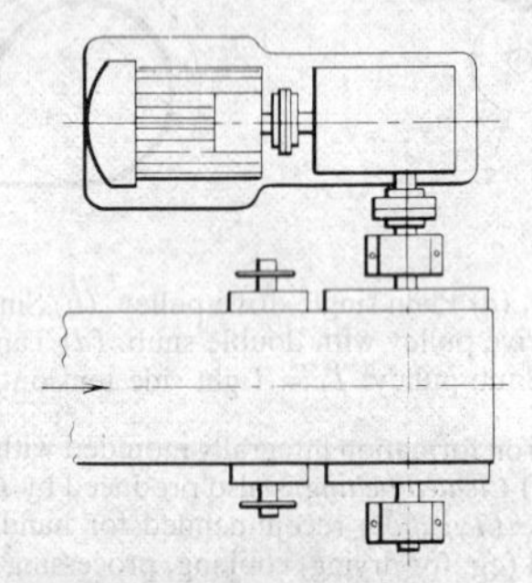

FIG. 4.—Plan of Typical Single Pulley 'open' type Driving Gear using Worm or Helical Gearbox.

FIG. 5.—Motorised Conveyor Drum (*Jokimotor*).

PULLEYS

It is important that pulley diameters should not be too small for the belt selected and flexing stresses in the belt must be held to safe values. The current use of synthetic fibres has brought about a significant reduction in required pulley diameters. Keep in mind that larger diameters are beneficial and therefore preferable to the minimum listed. See Table 7.

IDLERS

It is recommended (BS 2890) that tube material for idler construction should be electric resistance welded (ERW) or seamless, or cast iron is sometimes used. Based on available tube sizes, the following nominal diameters are stated 101.6, 108, 127, 133, 152.4, 159, 168.3 mm. Other standardised information laid down in BS 2890 includes length of idler face, its relation to belt width, configuration of centre and wing idlers, frame mounting dimensions, etc.

There are many factors affecting the life of idlers, but in many applications idler life is governed by the ingress of water and/or solid contaminants causing premature failure of the bearings. The type of bearing seal must be consistent for the duty—eg dusty conditions, a wet atmosphere (CMC sealed cartridge end caps, SKF seize-resistant). Considering the large quantity of idler sets on a conveyor installation and their effect on cost and efficiency, care in the specification and maintenance of this component will by amply repaid.

The spacing of troughing and return idler sets along the length of a conveyor depends on the tension in the belt and the weight of material on it. Too great a pitch can result in excessive belt sag and disturbance of the load. A guide to current practice is given in Table 8.

TABLE 7.—RECOMMENDED MINIMUM PULLEY DIAMETERS FOR TEXTILE BELTS (PULLEY DIAMETERS EXPRESSED IN MM)

Anticipated maximum belt tension (kN/m belt width)	Nominal belt carcass thickness (mm)																							
	Up to 3			Above 3 and up to 4			Above 4 and up to 5			Above 5 and up to 6·5			Above 6·5 and up to 8			Above 8 and up to 10			Above 10 and up to 12·5			Above 12·5 and up to 16		
	A	B	C	A	B	C	A	B	C	A	B	C	A	B	C	A	B	C	A	B	C	A	B	C
10	200	200	200	250	200	200	250	200	200															
12·5	200	200	200	250	200	200	250	250	200															
16	200	200	200	250	250	200	315	250	200	315	250	250												
20	250	200	200	315	250	200	315	250	250	315	315	250	400	315	315									
25	250	250	200	315	250	250	315	315	250	400	315	250	400	400	315	500	400	400						
32	315	250	200	315	315	250	400	315	250	400	315	315				500	400	315	500	500	400	630	500	500
40	315	315	250	400	315	250	400	315	315	400	400	315	500	400	400	630	500	400	630	630	500	800	630	630
50	400	315	250	400	315	315	400	400	315	500	400	315	500	500	400	630	500	500	800	630	500	800	800	630
63				400	400	315	500	400	315	500	400	400	630	500	400	630	630	500	800	630	630	1,000	800	630
80							500	400	400	500	500	400	630	500	500	800	630	500	800	800	630	1,000	800	800
100										630	500	400	630	630	500	800	630	630	1,000	800	630	1,000	1,000	800
125										630	630	500	800	630	500	800	800	630	1,000	800	800	1,250	1,000	800
160													800	630	630	1,000	800	800	1,000	1,000	800	1,250	1,000	1,000
200																1,000	1,000	800	1,250	1,000	1,000	1,250	1,250	1,000

A = Driving pulleys

B = Non-driving pulleys (terminal, tripper, take-up, snub and bend pulleys) located where the belt tension may exceed 60% of the anticipated belt tension

C = Non-driving pulleys (terminal, take-up, snub and bend pulleys) located where the belt tension will not exceed 60% of the anticipated belt tension

(MHEA)

RECOMMENDED MINIMUM PULLEY DIAMETERS FOR STEEL CORD BELTS
(PULLEY DIAMETERS EXPRESSED IN MM)

Belt type	Drive pulley	Tail and high tension snub	Low tension snub
ST 500	630	500	400
ST 630	630	500	400
ST 800	630	500	400
ST 900	630	500	400
ST 1000	630	500	400
ST 1150	630	500	400
ST 1250	630	500	400
ST 1400	800	630	400
ST 1600	800	630	500
ST 1800	800	630	500
ST 2000	800	630	500
ST 2250	1,000	800	630
ST 2500	1,000	800	630
ST 2750	1,250	800	630
ST 3150	1,250	1,000	630
ST 3500	1,400	1,000	630
ST 3750	1,400	1,000	630
ST 4000	1,400	1,000	630
ST 4250	1,400	1,250	800
ST 4750	1,600	1,400	800
ST 5000	1,800	1,600	1,000
ST 6000	2,000	1,800	1,250
ST 7000	2,250	2,000	1,600

(BTR)

For purposes of standardisation, pulleys should be selected from the following nominal diameters (BS 2890): 200, 250, 315, 355, 400, 455, 500, 610, 630, 760, 800, 915, 1,000, 1,060, 1,220, 1,250, 1,400, 1,600 mm.

ANGLE OF INCLINATION

The maximum gradient, in favour or against, on which material can be conveyed on a belt without rolling or slipping is governed by the shape, size, assortment and condition of the material; belt speed; loading arrangements; and whether the feed is continuous or intermittent. Definite figures meeting all conditions cannot be given, but see Table 9 for a guide. The figures are for a smooth surface rubber belt, with a continuous feed and well-filled capacity.

A raised pattern, cleats or bars moulded on to the carrying surface of the belt permits a significant increase

TABLE 8.—TYPICAL PITCH OF IDLER SETS FOR TROUGHING ANGLES UP TO 35°
(BS 2890)

	Carrying idler sets			Return idler sets
	Density of material t/m³			
	0·5 to 1·2	1·3 to 1·9	2·0 to 3·0	
Belt width (mm)	Pitch (mm)			
400, 500, 600, 650	1,600	1,500	1,400	3,000
750, 800, 900	1,500	1,400	1,300	3,000

1,000 1,050 1,200 1,350	1,400	1,300	1,200	3,000
1,400 1,600 1,800 2,000	1,200	1,000	800	3,000

Note: For wing idler inclinations greater than 35° it may be necessary to decrease the pitch in order to maintain the troughed shape of the belt.

in the angle of inclination, although the capacity may be reduced. Useful where ground space is restricted (*Dunlop 'Chevron'*).

VERTICAL CURVES occur in belt conveyors to connect tangentially two straight sections, which may be partially inclined and horizontal, or at two differing angles of inclination. Two basic curves can occur (see Fig. 6). Radius R must be large enough to prevent the belt buckling or being over-stressed under any working condition of start-up or loading. Analysis of the problem and methods of calculating the minimum radius are given in MHEA 'Recommended Practice' and abridged versions appear in manufacturers' catalogues.

CURVED CONVEYORS having major curves in the horizontal plane are advantageous in cases where a straight line would otherwise require intermediate transfer stations. However, such installations require great expertise in their design, installation and operation to maintain stability, and projects of this nature should always be considered in collaboration with an experienced manufacturer (Dowty Meco).

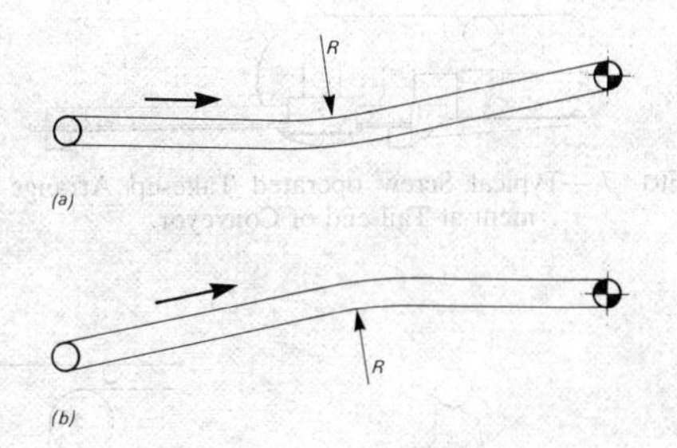

FIG. 6.—Vertical Curves
(*a*) Concave. (*b*) Convex. R = Minimum Radius

TABLE 9.—MAX ANGLE OF INCLINE FOR BELT CONVEYORS WITH VARIOUS MATERIALS

Material	Max angle of incline (degrees)	Average weight (t/m³)	Material	Max angle of incline (degrees)	Average weight (t/m³)
Alumina	12	0·9	Iron ore	18	1·6
Asbestos ore or rock	18	1·3	Lead ore	15	3·8
Ashes, coal, dry	23	0·6	Limestone, crushed	18	1·4
Asphalt	30	1·3	Manganese ore	20	2·15
Barley	12	0·6	Mortar, wet	20	2·4
Bauxite, crushed	20	1·3	Oats	10	0·42
Brewers grain, dry/wet	27	0·45/0·9	Phosphate rock, broken, dry	14	1·3
Brick	27	1·76	Phosphate rock, pulverised	25	0·96
Cement, Portland	20	1·5	Quartz	15	1·36
Chalk, lumpy	15	1·3	Rice	8	0·65
Charcoal	22	0·35	Rye	8	0·7
Clay, dry, lump	20	1·1	Salt, dry fine	11	1·2
Coal, anthracite (under 3 mm)	18	0·96	Salt, dry, coarse	20	0·75
Coal, anthracite sized	16	0·9	Sand, bank, damp	22	1·9
Coal, bituminous, run of mine	18	0·8	Sand, bank, dry	18	1·6
			Sand, foundry	24	1·56

Material			Material		
Coal, lignite	22	0·75	Sand, silica, dry	12	1·5
Coke, loose	18	0·48	Sawdust	22	0·2
Copper ore	20	2·17	Slate	18	1·36
Earth dug, dry	20	1·2	Sugar, granulated	15	0·83
Earth wet, with clay	23	1·7	Sugar, raw, cane	22	0·96
Granite, broken	18	1·44	Talc, powdered	12	0·9
Gravel, bank run	20	1·52	Wheat	12	0·77
Gravel, dry, sharp	16	1·52	Woodchips	27	0·32
Gravel, pebbles	12	1·52	Zinc ore, crushed	22	2·6
Gypsum, 12 mm screened	21	1·2			

TENSIONING OR TAKE-UP DEVICES.—A take-up device performs three functions: (1) Enables the belt to be initially stressed to that tension at which the pulley will drive; (2) Enables excessive sag and any unwanted accumulation of slack to be removed; and (3) allows for belt stretch and shrinkage. Such a device should be incorporated into every belt conveyor. The main types in use are (*a*) screw operated (see Fig. 7); (*b*) weight or gravity-operated (see Fig. 8) which may be placed anywhere along the line, and is preferred for long conveyors; (*c*) electrically-loaded winch-type; and (*d*) hydraulically-loaded winch-type.

Special care must be taken analysing the take-up design on downhill and reversible conveyors, or conveyors of irregular contour. The recommended allowances for belt stretch, ie pulley movement based on the centre-to-centre length of the conveyor, are given in BS 2890. Table 10 gives the recommended minimum amount of take-up for belt tensioning, suitable for conveyors up to 300 m centres; take-up for longer conveyors should be discussed with the manufacturer.

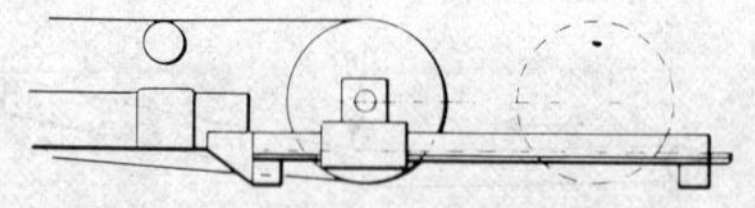

FIG. 7.—Typical Screw operated Take-up Arrangement at Tail-end of Conveyor.

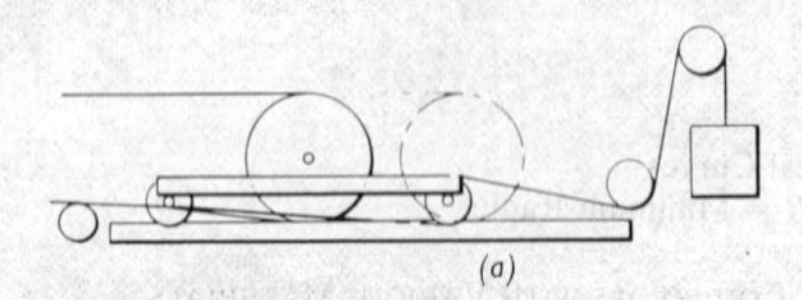

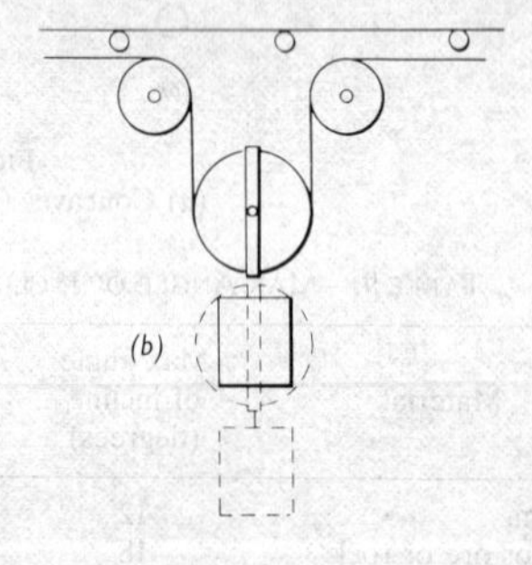

FIG. 8.—Diagrammatic Lay-out of Gravity Weight operated Take up.
(*a*) Horizontal type. (*b*) Vertical type.

CHUTES AND HOPPERS.—There are many methods by which the material can be fed onto the belt. Ideally, the chute, or transfer hopper (etc) should ensure that the material is transferred onto the belt at the same speed and in the same direction. This free flow being achieved without material breakage, without spill or overloading the belt; the material being positioned on the receiving belt correctly. Dust should be suppressed by suitable protection; and it is advisable to have the chute corners sufficiently steep to ensure self-cleaning.

The idlers on the receiving belt, adjacent to the chute or tansfer hopper, should be more closely spaced, with the first idler 150 to 225 mm behind the loading point, but never directly under the point where the material first touches the belt.

FEEDERS.—This is a system of feeding the material onto the belt, giving a regular flow of material, so that a full and uniform load cross-section is obtained along the whole length of the conveyor. A feeder serves to eliminate surges; to obviate spillage; to prevent overloading; and to maintain full capacity.

Feeder Types.—There is no all-purpose feeder, but several types are available to suit the given application, ie the required capacity; the type and condition of the material to be handled; and the site layout. In cases of fine, or free flowing material a simple plate-type gate, or rack-and-pinion door, can often be used to control the feed from a hopper to the belt. Where the material is lumpy, or sluggish, then some system of regulating the feed is a necessity. Figure 9 illustrates four types of feeders for conveyors in common use:

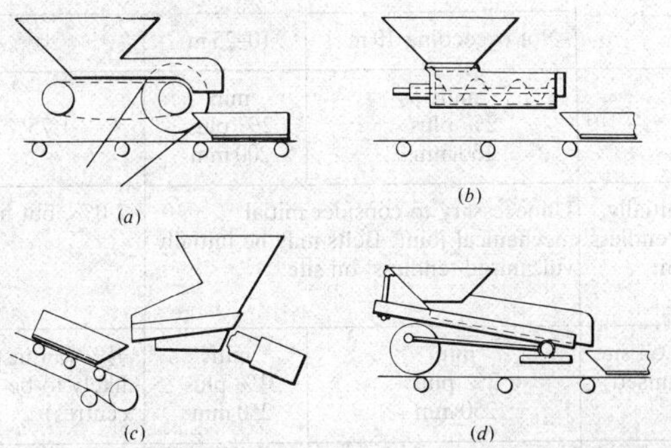

FIG. 9.—Conveyor Feeders. (*a*) Belt or Apron. (*b*) Screw. (*c*) Shaker. (*d*) Electro-magnetic Vibrating.

(*a*) belt- or apron-feeder; both may be horizontal or inclined. Belt-feeders are used for granular and small-lump materials, and apron-feeders for heavy and larger-lump materials; (*b*) screw feeders are used for bulk materials such as powdered, small-lump and granular materials (the latter should not be friable); (*c*) a shaking or oscillating feeder is usually provided with a table set in reciprocating motion, so that when the table moves forward, the material from the hopper fills the free space formed below the outlet; when the table moves back, the material spills over the front edge of the table, onto the conveyor; (*d*) electromagnetic vibrating feeder is suitable for capacities up to 1,200 t/hr; it is also preferred for handling small lumps. Other types are disc feeders and chain feeders.

There are several types of vibratory bowl feeders 150–900 mm diameter used for heavy components or food and pharmaceutical products. An electronic control system maintains and regulates the flow rates (PSM Automated Systems).

Skirt Plates.—Are fitted to feed chutes to guide the material into the centre of the belt and avoid spillage. Except on feeder conveyors, the average width between them should not be more than two-thirds of the belt width. See BS 2890. Their purpose is to guide the material along the receiving belt. Two plates are mounted symmetrically about the centre of the conveyor. Skirt boards should be vertical wherever possible. In cramped positions they can be sloped but the angle of slope should not exceed 60°.

DISCHARGING AND UNLOADING.—The simplest method of discharging material from a belt conveyor is to allow the load to flow over the head pulley. The position of the chute bottom should be such that, theoretically, the upper lip of the chute reaches a position higher than the horizontal centre line. The following solution is used to find for each material the trajectory or discharge curve, which would reduce degradation of material and impact upon the chute bottom, due to a local change in slope at the point of impact.

This method is shown in Fig. 10. The centre of gravity of the load lies approximately at radius R from the

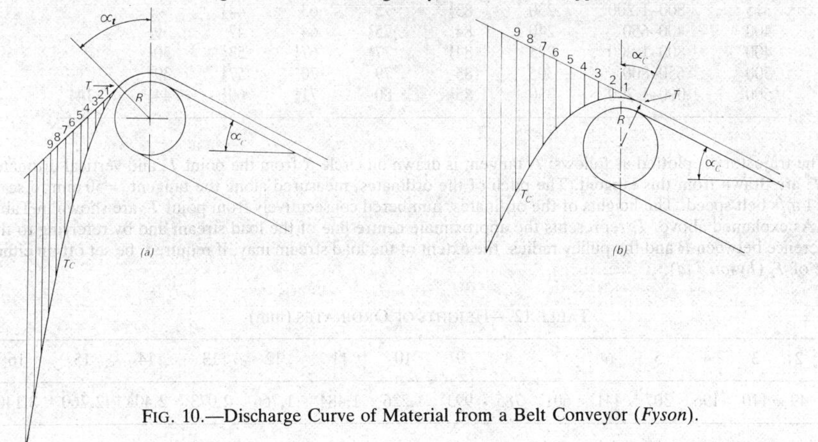

FIG. 10.—Discharge Curve of Material from a Belt Conveyor (*Fyson*).

TABLE 10.—CONVEYOR RECOMMENDED TAKE-UP FOR BELT TENSIONING (BS 2890)

Type of belt joining (for belts with . . .)	Centre to centre—Length of conveyor (no allowance included for the take-up)		
	Not exceeding 10 m	10–25 m	25–300 m
Permanent mechanical fasteners	min 2% plus 150 mm	min 2% plus 200 mm	min 1.75%, but not less than 700 mm
Mechanical fasteners initially, but finally to be made 'endless' on site with a permanent vulcanised spliced joint	Unnecessary to consider initial mechanical joint. Belts may be initially vulcanised 'endless' on site		2·0%, but not less than 1 m
Initially made 'endless' on site with a permanent vulcanised spliced joint	min 2% plus 250 mm	min 3½% plus 250 mm	4½% (an installation condition not likely to be required above 200 m centres)
Ordered and fitted endless at the minimum length of the conveyor circuit plus 0·5%	min 4½% plus 150 mm	min 5% plus 250 mm	6%, but such an installation condition is not likely to be required

centre of the head pulley. The centre line of the discharged load follows a trajectory (T_c), from the point T, where the load leaves the conveyor. In the case of a low speed conveyor, point T lies at an angle α_t beyond the vertical centre line of the head pulley, Fig. 10(a). In the case of a high speed conveyor, point T lies at an angle α_c, behind the vertical centre line of the head pulley, Fig. 10(b), where α_c is the angle of elevation of the conveyor. In the case, therefore, where $\alpha_c = 0$, point T lies on the centre line of the pulley. Table 11 shows values of R for various typical pulley diameters, and the angle α_t, for selected belt speeds. For higher belt speeds, α_c applies as above. When angle α_t is larger than α_c, then point T is indicated by α_t, as shown in Fig. 10(a). When angle α_t is smaller than α_c, then point T is indicated in Fig. 10(b).

TABLE 11.—RELATIONSHIPS: CENTRE OF GRAVITY RADIUS AND PULLEY DIAMETER; TRAJECTORY ANGLE AND BELT SPEED

Pulley dia (mm)	Belt width (mm)	Radius R (mm)	Angle α_t (in degrees) at belt-speed m/s 0·51	0·76	1·02	1·27	1·52	1·78
200	400 and 500	130	78½	63	36			
250	400–650	165	81	69	50	30		
315	400–650	195	82	72½	57½	32½		
315	800–1,200	230	83½	75	63	44½		
400	400–650	240	84	75½	64	47	9½	
400	800–1,200	275	84½	77½	67½	53½	30½	
500	650–800	305	85	79	70	57½	39	
500	1,000–1,200	330	85½	80	71½	60½	44½	14½

The trajectory is plotted as follows: A tangent is drawn on circle R from the point T, and vertical ordinates to T_c are drawn from this tangent. The pitch of the ordinates, measured along the tangent, =50 mm to scale per 1 m/s belt speed. The heights of the ordinates, numbered consecutively from point T, are shown in Table 12. As explained above, T_c represents the approximate centre line of the load stream and by referring to the difference between R and the pulley radius, the extent of the load stream may, if required, be set off on either side of T_c (*Fyson Ltd*).

TABLE 12.—HEIGHTS OF ORDINATES (mm)

1	2	3	4	5	6	7	8	9	10	11	12	13	14	15	16
12	49	110	196	307	441	601	785	993	1,226	1,484	1,766	2,073	2,404	2,760	3,140

TRIPPERS.—This is a device used when discharge is required at a point or points along a conveyor. A tripper comprises two bend pulleys; these may be fixed, or travelling. The latter is positioned on a carriage over which the material is unloaded. A fixed tripper delivers the material to a two-way chute equipped with a flap valve, so that when the desired volume of material has been discharged at a given point, the gate is thrown over (Fig. 11). This permits the material to return to the conveyor belt and to be carried forward to a following tripper, or to the end of conveyor. A travelling (or movable) tripper can be moved to any position along the conveyor. Travelling trippers may be: (1) hand-driven through gearing; (2) hand-operated by a friction drive from belt (Fig. 12); (3) operated by automatic reversing friction drive from belt; or (4) operated by independent motor; chutes so arranged that material is delivered to one or both sides of the belt, or back to the belt again. Discharge chutes can be arranged on the tripper to provide discharge to one or both sides of a belt. Additional power is required if the conveyor is equipped with one or more trippers. The amount of this addition is influenced by the belt width and length, as well as conveyor inclination. The manufacturer will provide details of the type of equipment selected.

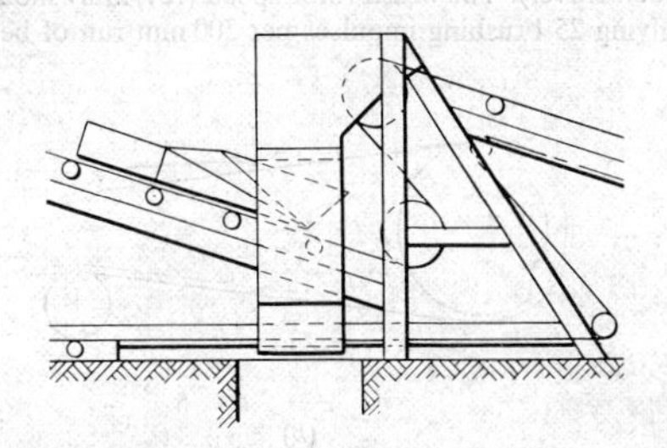

FIG. 11.—Typical Arrangement of Fixed Tripper.

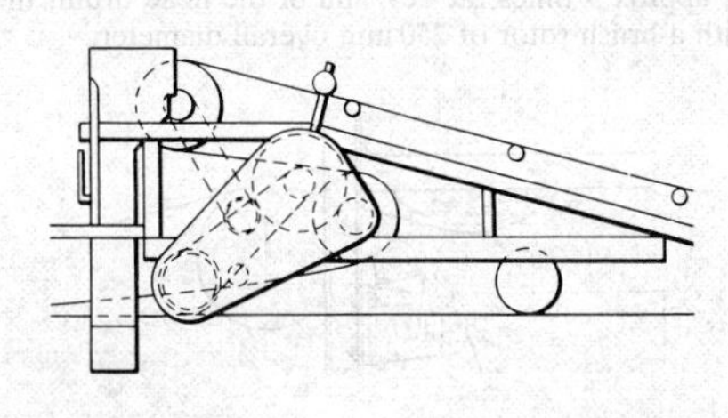

FIG. 12.—Typical Travelling Tripper moved by Power supplied by the Conveyor Belt.

ANCILLARY EQUIPMENT

AUTOMATIC BRAKES.—When a belt conveyor lifts or lowers material and the power required for the operation exceeds the power to drive the empty belt plus that to convey the material horizontally, a suitable mechanical holdback or power-operated brake should be fitted. Otherwise once the power is cut-off, the weight of material will cause the belt to move due to gravitational forces and the gradient.

SAFETY-TRIP SYSTEM.—This consists of a cable running parallel with the belt for the whole length of the conveyor. This cable, when pulled, automatically trips out the drive, and stops the conveyor. It is essential that trip systems be fitted on all conveyors in tunnels, gantries, and enclosed spaces.

GUARDING.—The Health and Safety at Work Act 1974 (Section 6) creates legal responsibilities regarding the safe working of machines (conveyors). The protection of hazard points by guards, handrails, etc is described in MHEA 'Code of Practice on Safeguarding of Hazard Points on Troughed Belt Conveyors'.

BELT WEIGHERS.—The material carried on conveyors and elevators can be weighed and recorded automatically. There are various weighing systems indicating the weight of individual loads and/or cumulative totals. On belt conveyors, the weighers should preferably be positioned where the belt tension is lowest, but not too close to the loading points (See *MHEA 'Recommended Practice'*).

Many applications are possible. For instance, in some installations the weigher, in addition to providing weight information, can also initiate closed-loop control of a process-flow rate by signalling the amount to be supplied by each of several belts, and adjusting their rate of feed. Weighers are used in automatic checking systems, etc.

Continuous weighers can weigh, blend and proportion accurately flows from 10 to 10,000 t/h. (eg, *Mitchen Process Engineering Ltd*); load-cells are used for hopper weighing and batching systems, belt weighers and feeders, etc. (*Hymatic Control and others*) from 30 to 2,500 kg.

BELT CLEANERS.—It depends entirely on the type of material being carried and particularly on its moisture content as to whether the problem of cleaning the belt is easy or difficult. Materials which are dry, or comparatively so, do not adhere to a belt to any degree and can be easily removed. On the other hand, wet fines tend to adhere firmly to the belt and can be difficult to clean off. Unless the fines are removed, they tend to build up on return pulleys and idlers and ultimately cause belt mis-alignment and damage. Also they may create a nuisance by dropping beneath the conveyor run. Many aspects of this important accessory are covered in MHEA 'Conveyor Belt Cleaning Devices'.

Two main types of cleaning device are (a) Static, comprising scraper blades of polyurethane or rubber, with pressure applied against the belt surface by means of counterweights, springs or torsion units (care should be taken not to overdo the pressure); and (b) Dynamic, comprising a rotating brush or blades, either independently driven or belt driven, running in the opposite direction to the belt surface.

The open brush type is best for most purposes and conditions at little extra cost for mechanisation where facilities are not available for direct motivation. The open brush core cannot clog and requires tip pressure only. Figure 13(*b*) indicates the ideal position for all cleaner units in relation to the head drum; the brush rotation being the same as the head drum (ie contrary to belt travel). The brush rotor speed (rev/min) should be approx 9 times the rev/min of the head drum, thus giving 25 brushing impulses per 300 mm run of belt, with a brush rotor of 250 mm overall diameter.

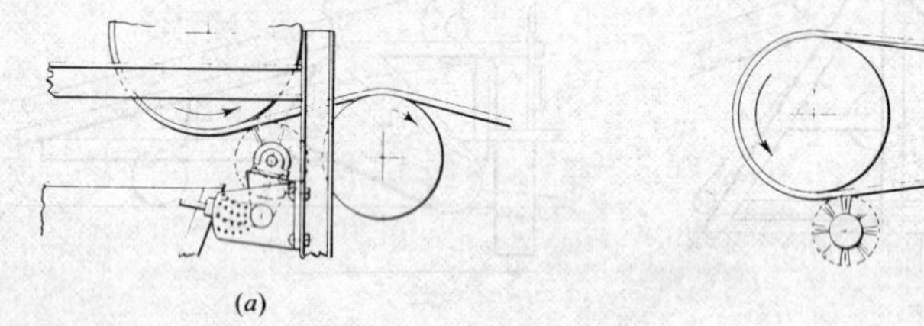

FIG. 13.—Conveyor Belt Cleaners. (*a*) Rotor with Geared Motor and Micro-adjustment. (*b*) Open brush type.

MAGNETIC SEPARATORS.—There are various systems of removing metal particles from the conveyed material; these particles may be ferrous or non-ferrous. For ferrous particles, electro-magnets may be positioned above the conveyor belt, or set at an angle above the head pulley, or be mounted inside the head pulley. For non-ferrous particles, electronic devices of various types can be employed (see Fig. 14).

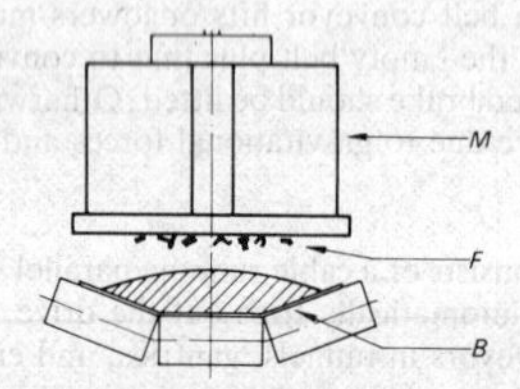

FIG. 14.—Electro-magnet over Belt Conveyor; M = Electro-magnet. B = Belt conveyor. F = Tramp iron.

OTHER TYPES OF CONVEYOR

MOBILE AND PORTABLE CONVEYORS.—The term 'portable' usually implies a conveyor designed to be lifted, and moved manually as a unit, from one position to another. A conveyor is 'mobile' if it is on wheels, crawlers or pontoons, ie towed, or pulled mechanically. Both types are versatile and can be constructed for transport of materials in bulk or unit loads; can be self-driven; and can be adjusted by means of hydraulic power. BS 4351 'Portable and Mobile Troughed Belt Conveyors', specified belt widths as follows: 300, 400, 500, 600, 650, 800, 1,000 and 1,200 mm; and idler roller diameters: 25, 51, 57, 76, 89, 102, 108 and 127 mm.

APRON CONVEYORS.—These are mainly used for handling heavy abrasive materials, eg ores, stone, etc. They consist of one or more endless chains, attached to interlocking or overlapping plates which form a continuous moving belt or apron which operates overhead and foot terminals with the necessary intermediate structure to support the load, etc (*Ewart*). To select an apron conveyor suitable for the material to be carried and the capacity required; guide-lines will be found in manufacturers' catalogues.

SLAT CONVEYORS.—These are primarily used for unit load handling, such as boxes, crates, castings, etc.

These conveyors are similar in construction to apron conveyors, but in this case slabs are non-overlapping and non-interlocking, they are made of hardwood, steel or plastics—according to material to be carried. It is recommended that the slats should be at least 100 mm wider than the largest unit carried, allowing for it being out of square, should there be a possibility for it to occur.

'EN MASSE' CONVEYORS/ELEVATORS.—These are used for handling grain or any other similar bulk materials (particulary such which should be kept clean) and characterised by an endless chain composed of shaped flights moving material inside an enclosed duct. Mixing and blending operations are easily carried out in this type of conveyor.

DISC or BUTTON CONVEYORS.—These are used for moving bulk materials along a V-shaped trough. In this type the chain (as above) may be replaced by a rope with discs or 'buttons' attached to this main hauling component.

WIRE CONVEYORS.—These are mentioned under 'Types of Belting'.

CHAIN CONVEYORS.—A few variants of the types described above. (*a*) Designed for handling grain, etc, this type is provided with cleaning flights (consisting of rubberised polystyrene pads) (*Law Denis*). (*b*) Designed for handling hot ashes (etc) this installation allows them to cool during transit; it is provided with distribution to several outlets, selection of the latter being controlled fully by remote instruction; there are also self-cleaning arrangements, as above (eg, *Louis GmbH*).

BELT-ON-ROLLER CONVEYORS.—As the name implies, these conveyors are characterised by a friction-back rubber belt (or similar) placed over mild-steel tubular rollers, 50 mm in diameter. Drives for one or two way operation are available giving a standard speed of 20 m/min. This conveyor can be used for horizontal or inclined handling of boxes, crates, etc. (*Fenamec*).

SLIDER-BED CONVEYORS.—The basic unit of this type consists of a friction-back rubber belt supported on a flat surface forming part of a box section with steel sides. Geared motors are used to give a speed of 20 m/min. This conveyor can also be used for horizontal or inclined transport even of fragile packages, eg when it is used as an assembly table for continuous manufacture. (*Fenamec*).

AIR-SUPPORTED BELT CONVEYORS.—The hovercraft principle has been applied for handling containers and packages. It is possible to support loads on a conveyor which is itself resting on an air table with low friction (*UKAEA Laboratories* at Springfields). Air valves of simple design release air only when the loaded belt presses on the valve ball (*Transferro*). This system may be applied with advantage to loading and unloading railway cargo/containers.

AIR-CUSHION CONVEYOR.—Another method of using air pressure for conveying, suitable for all forms of scrap (swarf, paper, cardboard, wood, plastic shavings, etc), cartons, tubes, tiles, etc, is based on low-pressure air issuing from a series of louvres punched in the conveying surface plates, which lifts and propels the materials. Air pressure generated by centrifugal fans ducted to the louvred plates. Air pressure from below varies according to the type of material being handled from 80 mm water gauge for paper and cardboard to 200 mm for swarf. Air flow rates vary from 1,200 to 2,000 $m^3/hour/m^2$. ('Jet Stream', *Ling Systems*).

Aerobelt.—In this system the belt is supported on a film of air which is blown into the tubular trough sections by a small fan; one such fan is adequate for several hundred metres of conveyor. Carrying idler rollers are not required (there are only guide rollers at the transition points at the head and tail). Few moving parts mean less wear and tear, and, therefore, less maintenance is needed. The belt is noiseless in operation. It is claimed that to transport (for instance) 75 t/h of corn over a distance of 100 m Aerobelt requires 4·5 kW while a chain conveyor requires 13 kW (*Numec Ltd*) (Fig. 15).

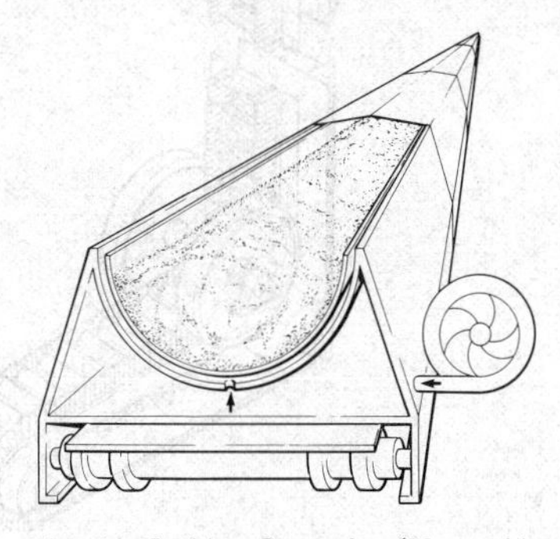

FIG. 15.—Air Cushion Conveying (*Numec 'Aerobelt'*).

VIBRATING CONVEYORS.—Also referred to as oscillating or shaking conveyors or feeders, used to handle bulk materials in form of powder, granules or lump. They are usually powered by electric motor vibrators.

CABLE BELT (registered trademark) is a conveyor design whereby the carrying and driving functions are separated. Driving tension is transmitted by two endless drive cables, one at each side of the belt. The belt then becomes a carrying platform, suitably stiffened laterally to develop an in-built troughing effect when loaded, and positively located on the drive cables by moulded V section shoe forms. The drive cables run on regularly spaced pulleys. The ability to take very high driving tensions through the cables to a drive unit located anywhere adjacent to the system and the inherent low frictional losses, enables very long centre installations to be achieved, incorporating horizontal and vertical curves if necessary. Belt width from 600 to 1,600 mm. See Fig. 16. (*Cable Belt Ltd*). Example: *Aluminium Partners*, Jamaica: 14·5 km long, descending 580 m at 18°, conveying 1,425 t/h bauxite at 4 m/s.

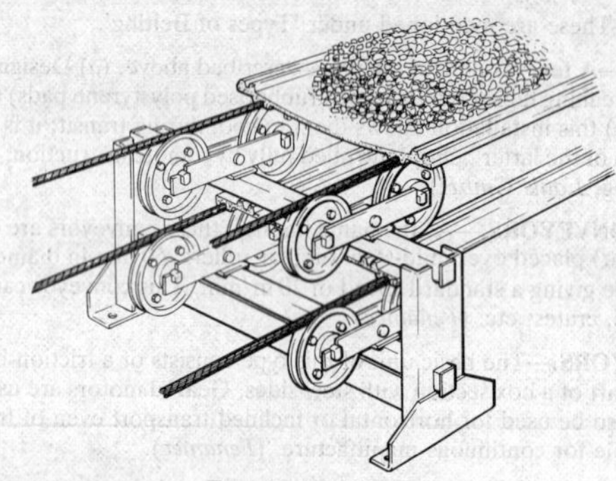

FIG. 16.—Cable Belt.

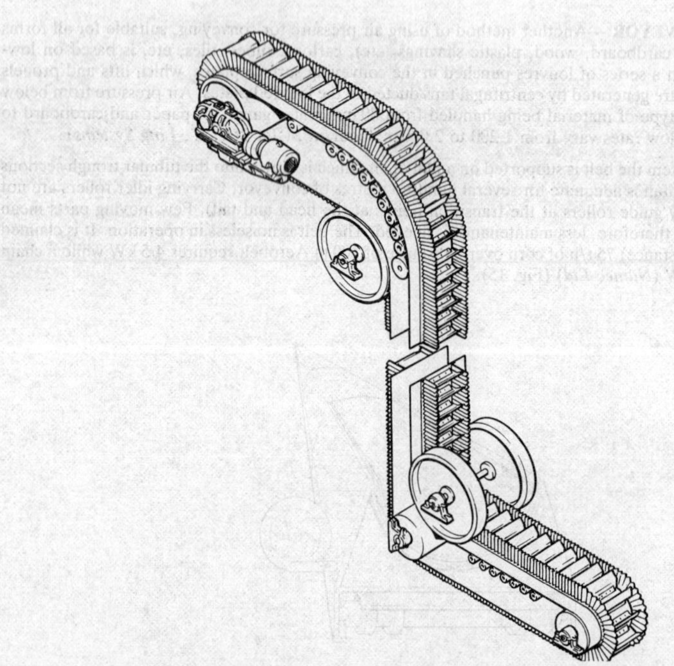

FIG. 17.—Sidewall Belt. Vertical and Horizontal Conveying (*Scholtz 'Flexowell'*).

SIDEWALL BELTING consists of a rigidly designed base belt with flexible corrugated sidewalls fitted to each side. Special cross-cleats spaced at regular intervals fit between these sidewalls. The resultant closed pockets lift the conveyed material at angles up to 90° at full capacity, without spillage or degradation, and with an efficient head pulley discharge. The design permits a wide choice of conveyor route configurations. Belt width up to 3,200 mm. See Fig. 17. (*Conrad Scholtz GB Ltd 'Flexowell'*). Example: *Turris Coal Co*, Elkhart Mine, Springfield, Illinois, USA: 1,600 mm wide steel cord reinforced base belt, 100 m vertical lift, 650 t/h of coal at 2·3 m/s.

TYPICAL LARGE INSTALLATIONS.—(1) A conveyor 14·9 km long in single flight (at British Coal, Selby Mine, UK), 980 m lift, capacity 3,200 t/h (10,000,000 t/year), 9,000 kW (*BTR/Anderson*). (2) A 17 km long conveyor to transport up to 8,000,000 t/year from 2 underground mines in Mexico. (*Kaiser Engrg*, a subsidiary of *Raymond International*). (3) A 19 km steel-cord conveyor, 900 mm wide, to transport up to 2,000 t/h in Peru, (constructed by *Yokohama*, belt replaced in 1980 by *Dunlop, Australia*). (4) A 3,000 mm wide conveyor, constructed in West Germany, carries 40,000 t/h (*PHB/RWB*).

ELEVATORS

An elevator is a mechanical means of raising or lowering bulk materials or unit loads (eg packages) along a vertical or steeply inclined path. It consists generally of an endless belt or one or two strands of chain to which are fixed buckets, arms, swing trays, or some other form of attachments, depending upon the type of materials to be elevated. Elevators follow a simple line of continuous motion—up one side, round a pulley or sprocket at the head and down the other side to the tail, or vice-versa.

Bucket elevators will handle practically all loose materials provided the lumps are not too large for the buckets. As a general guide, the size of the largest lump should not exceed two-thirds of the projection of the bucket. Special care must be taken in the selection of the type used if the material is of a sticky nature or will not flow readily.

The essentials of an elevator are (see Fig. 18):

(1) The buckets or some other form of attachment to carry the material or cargo.
(2) The belt or chain to which the buckets or attachments are fixed and which also transmits the drive.
(3) The drive (for typical driving arrangements see Fig. 27).
(4) Accessories for loading the elevator or picking up the material, for receiving the discharged material, for maintaining adequate tension, and for enclosing and protecting the elevator.

CENTRIFUGAL DISCHARGE ELEVATOR (Fig. 19).—The material is discharged by centrifugal action as the buckets pass over the head pulley and therefore this type of elevator is a high-speed unit. The buckets are bolted at intervals to the chain or belt. The material is delivered to the elevator either by flowing into the boot from where it is dredged by the digging action of the buckets as they round the tail pulley or sprocket, or by some form of feeder unit such as Rotary Feeder (Fig. 26(*a*)), or a Shaking Chute (Fig. 26(*b*)).

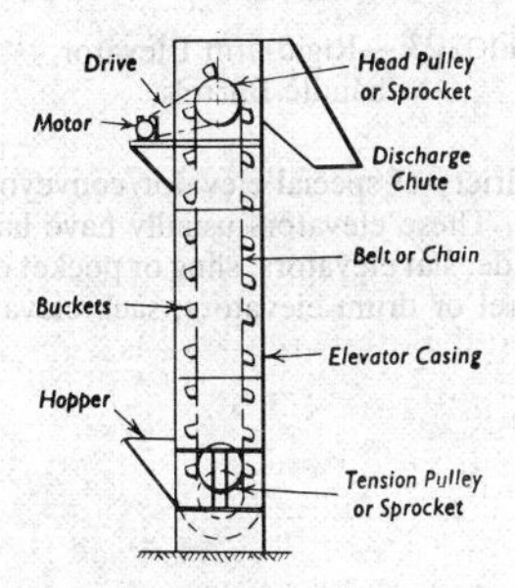

FIG. 18.—Diagram of Essential Arrangement of typical Elevator.

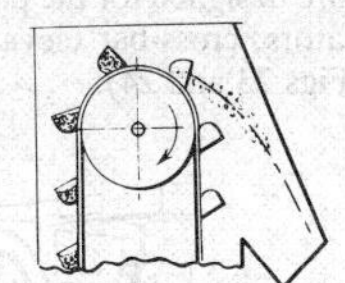

FIG. 19.—Centrifugal Discharge Belt or Chain and Bucket Elevator.

CONTINUOUS BUCKET ELEVATOR (Fig. 20).—This is a slow-speed unit. The buckets are bolted adjacent to one another along the single strand of chain or belt and each bucket discharges over the front of the preceding bucket which forms a chute or guide for the material to the main discharge chute. The material is fed to the buckets after they have come round the tail pulley or sprocket and have started to ascend. The chain speeds normally range from 25 to 40 m/min, while belt speeds from 30 to 80 m/min will cover the usual range.

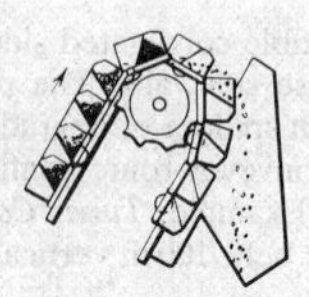

FIG. 20.—Continuous Belt or Chain and Bucket Elevator.

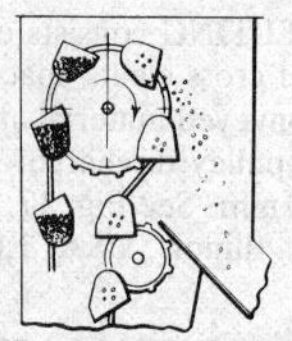

FIG. 21.—Positive Discharge type Chain and Bucket Elevator.

POSITIVE DISCHARGE ELEVATOR (Fig. 21).—This is a slow-speed unit for friable, sticky or slow-flowing materials. The buckets are bolted between two strands of chain which are snubbed after passing over the head sprockets to bring the buckets into an inverted position above the discharge chute. The feeding arrangement is similar to that used with a centrifugal discharge elevator. Normally the chain speeds range from 40 to 50 m/min.

HEAVY-DUTY ELEVATOR (Fig. 22).—This type of elevator in respect to feed and discharge resembles the continuous bucket. However, the employment of two strands of chain enables the use of larger buckets which may extend outwards on both sides of the chain and it is from this increased handling ability that the name is derived. The normal range of chain speed is from 10 to 30 m/min.

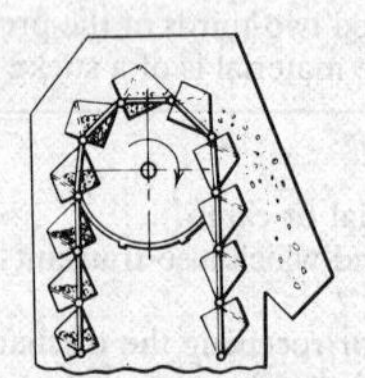

FIG. 22.—Heavy-duty Chain and Bucket Elevator.

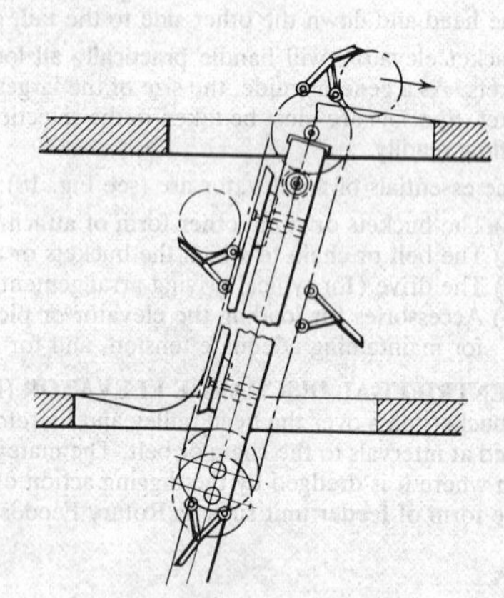

FIG. 23.—Rigid-arm Elevator to handle Barrels.

UNIT LOAD ELEVATORS.—This group comprises the wide variety of special elevator/conveyor devices for handling specific units, containers, components, materials, etc. These elevators usually have hangers on carriers which are designed for the particular application. They include: slat elevators, sling or pocket elevators; fixed-tray elevators; cross-bar elevators; swing-tray elevators; barrel or drum elevators; sack elevators, and many others (Figs 23 and 24).

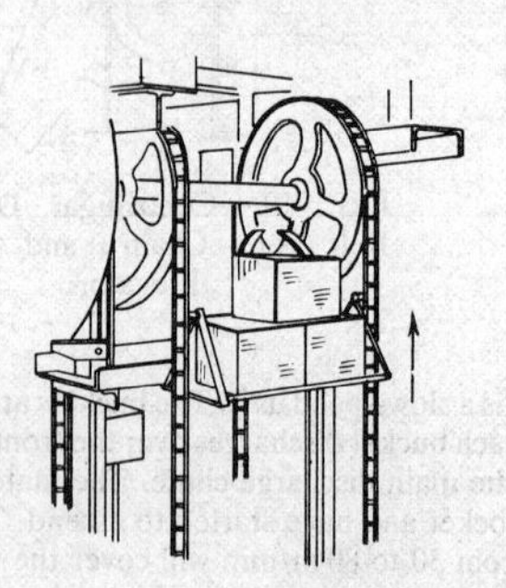

FIG. 24.—Top of a Swing-tray Elevator.

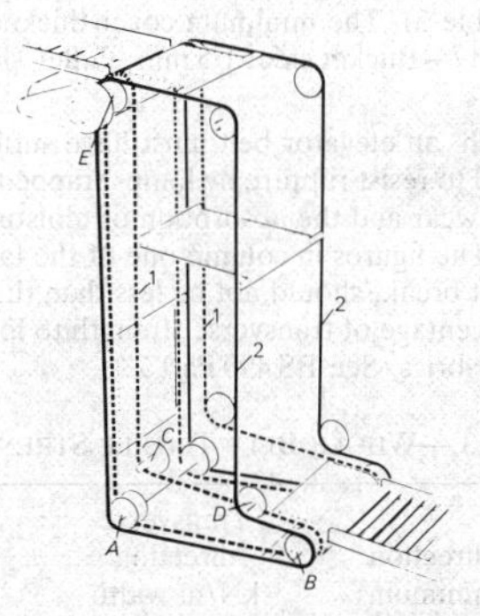

FIG. 25.—'Escaveyor' conveyor/elevator. 1 and 2 = Paths of two chains; *A* and *B* = Through shafts; *C* and *D* = Stub shafts; *E* = Drive shaft (*Paterson Hughes*).

ELEVATOR BELTING.—BS 490 Part 2 specifies elevator belting, which consists of a carcass with or without covers. The carcass is composed of either one or more plies or woven fabric, or is of solid woven fabric, impregnated with rubber or a plastics mix. As for conveyor belts (*qv*), the whole is either fused or vulcanised together. The carcass may be protected by a breaker ply.

As with conveyor belts, elevator belting is designated according to the grade of the cover (if present), and the type of belting, defined by the full thickness tensile strength. The grades of rubber cover are similar to

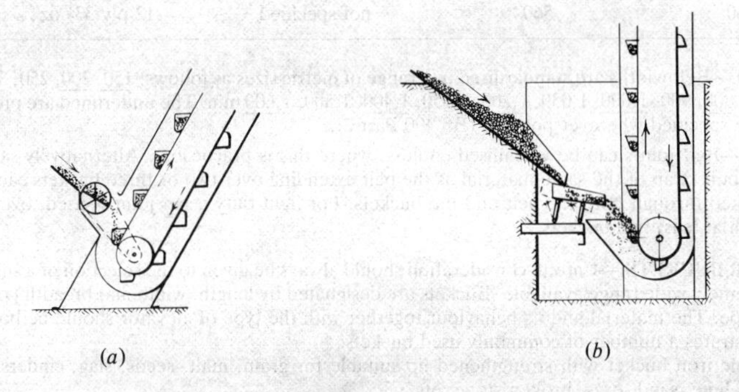

FIG. 26.—Diagrams of Feeder Arrangements for Bucket Elevators. (*a*) Rotary type. (*b*) Shaking Chute.

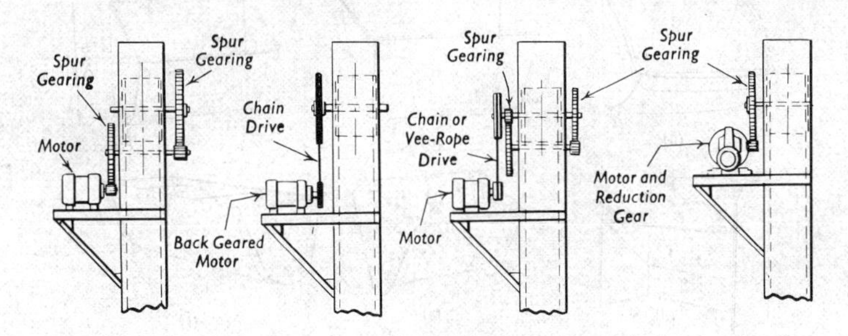

FIG. 27.—Typical Driving Gears for Elevators.

those described for conveyors (see Table 2). The minimum cover thicknesses are: Grade M24—Bucket side, 1·5 mm; Pulley side, 3·0 mm. Grade N17—Bucket side, 1·5 mm; Pulley side, 2·5 mm. Grade N17—both sides, 0·8 mm.

In addition to having tensile strength, an elevator belt must have sufficient body to prevent the bucket or fastener bolts from pulling through and to resist rupture by lumps trapped between the tail pulley and the belt. It should also have good resistance to wear and the absorption of moisture. Table 13 gives the maximum full thickness designated tensile strength. The figures in column one of the table mean that for each metre of belt width, at its full thickness, the force, at break, should not be less than that stated, eg 190 kN. The figure after the solidus (40 or 60) indicates the percentage of transverse strength to longitudinal strength. Table 13 applies to man-made fibres as well as cotton fabrics. See BS 490 Part 2.

TABLE 13.—WHOLE BELT TENSILE STRENGTH.

Type	Longitudinal direction kN/m width (minimum)	Transverse direction kN/m width (minimum)	For cotton fabrics the data below is a guide to strength requirements
190/40	190	75	3 ply 32 oz
190/60	190	110	3 ply 33½ oz
240/40	240	95	4 ply 32 oz
240/60	240	140	4 ply 33½ oz
290/40	290	115	5 ply 32 oz
290/60	290	175	5 ply 33½ oz
340/40	340	130	6 ply 32 oz
340/60	340	200	6 ply 33½ oz
385/60	385	225	7 ply 33½ oz
425/60	425	250	8 ply 33½ oz
450	450	not specified	9 ply 33½ oz
500	500	not specified	10 ply 33½ oz
560	560	not specified	12 ply 33½ oz

Belt Widths.—Belt widths are standardised in a range of metric sizes as follows: 150, 200, 250, 300, 400, 500, 600, 650, 750, 800, 900, 1,000, 1,050, 1,200, 1,350, 1,400, 1,500, 1,600 mm. The underlined are preferred sizes, and should be specified wherever possible (BS 490 Part 2).

Belt Joints.—Belt joints can be vulcanised endless, where this is practicable. Alternatively, a butt joint is made, with a butt strap of the same material as the belt extending over two or three buckets each side of the joint, and bolted through both the belt and the buckets. For light duty a lap joint is used, overlapping and bolted through at least two buckets.

ELEVATOR BUCKETS.—Careful consideration should always be given to the selection of a suitable bucket from the extremely wide range available. Buckets are designated by length, width and breadth (projection) in addition to type. The material and its behaviour together with the type of elevator should be borne in mind. Figure 28 illustrates a number of commonly used buckets:

(*a*) Malleable iron bucket with strengthened lip suitable for grain, malt, seeds, slag, cinders, coal, coke, cement, lime, sand, ores, broken stone, etc.

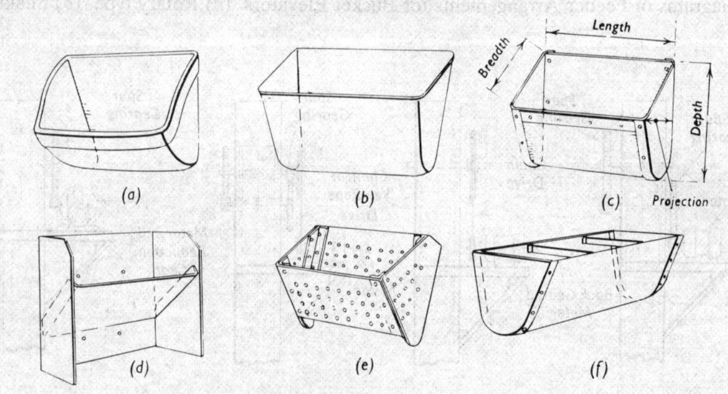

FIG. 28.—Selection of typical Elevator Buckets.

(*b*) Deep seamless steel bucket suitable for grain, malt, cinders, coke, coal, slag, cement, ground lime, ores, sand, broken stone, etc.
(*c*) Riveted steel bucket.
(*d*) Riveted or welded bucket for continuous bucket elevator.
(*e*) Perforated riveted steel bucket for water-laden gravel or coal.
(*f*) Long steel bucket with stay pieces and seamless flanged ends for flour mills.

In addition there are buckets made of rubber and plastic materials, as well as those made in all the familiar ferrous and non-ferrous alloys, and lined with rubber or plastics.

ELEVATOR CHAIN.—Buckets up to 50 cm wide are commonly bolted to a single strand of chain. With wider buckets two strands of chain are normally used. A wide range of chain is available. The chain divides into two groups: (*a*) cast chain (normally used at slow and medium speeds); (*b*) Precision chain (normally used at medium and high speeds).

In selecting the chain a number of points must be established: (1) pitch of chain; (2) size of sprocket; (3) load to be carried; (4) nature of material; (5) operating conditions.

The selection of chain pitch is related to the size of buckets, roller loading, etc. It is advantageous to aim at a reduced number of chain components per unit of length.

Figure 29 illustrates examples of some of the many types of standard chain available.

(*a*) Steel elevator (roller) chain with attachments suitable for a centrifugal discharge elevator.
(*b*) Steel roller chain with attachments suitable for a dump type (positive discharge) elevator.
(*c*) Steel bushed, chain.
(*d*) Combination chain.
(*e*) and (*f*) Lay bushed chain.

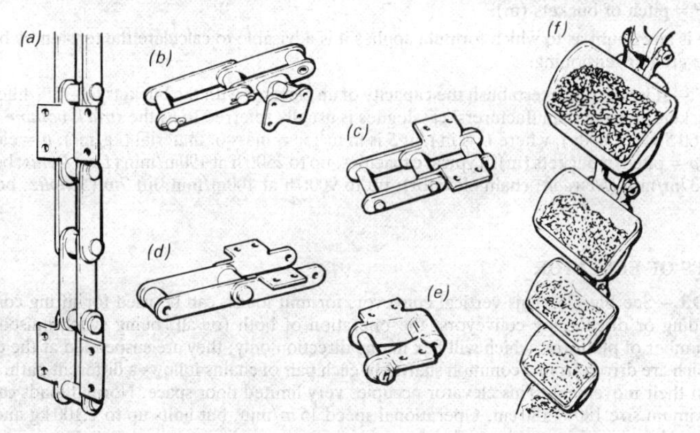

FIG. 29.—Selection of typical Elevator Chains (*Ewart*).

It is customary to run chain elevators at much lower speeds than belt elevators; the normal range of chain speed being from 60 to 100 m/min for a vertical elevator with one or two chains. Medium chain speeds can be employed on inclined spaced bucket elevators where the incline allows discharge by gravity—such medium speeds range from 34 to 55 m/min with one or two chains.

POWER REQUIRED TO DRIVE AN ELEVATOR

Chain and Bucket.—

Vertical elevators: $P = v[W_2 + K(W_1 + W_2)]/100$

Inclined elevators: $P = v[W_2 \sin\theta + K(W_1 + W_2)\cos\theta]/100$

where, P = power (kW); v = elevator speed (m/s); W_1 = mass of one side of chain and buckets (kg); W_2 = mass of material in buckets (kg); K = constant (0·2 for skidder bars, and 0·1 for rollers); and θ = angle of elevator gradient with the horizontal.

Belt and Bucket.—

Spaced bucket: $P = w[v(H + 9{\cdot}144)]/100p$

Continuous bucket: $P = w[v(H + 3{\cdot}04)]/100p$

where, P = power (kW); H = vertical height of elevator (m); w = mass of material in each bucket (kg); v = belt speed (m/s); and p = pitch of buckets (m).

Centrifugal Discharge Elevator.—The power requirements of this type are generally similar to the above types with the additional considerations of speed. The actual force acting on the material carried in the bucket as it moves round the head pulley of the elevator is the resultant of the constant vertical force due to gravity and of the radial force due to centrifugal action. The centrifugal force, due to the bucket load, is equal to W_2v^2/rg, where, W_2 = mass of material in bucket (kg); v = speed of load in bucket (at centre of gravity of load) (m/s); r = radius from centre of head pulley to centre of gravity of load (m); and g = acceleration due to gravity (9·81 m/s²).

At a speed governed by the diameter of the head pulley the centrifugal force is equal to the weight of the bucket load so that $W_2v^2/rg = W_2$, or $v^2 = rg$.

TENSION IN BELT.—In some instances the weight of the belt and the empty buckets on the down side provides sufficient slack side tension without adding tension at the tail shaft. In such cases the total tension is:

(*a*) On a spaced bucket elevator $T = BH + [bH + w(H + 9{\cdot}144)] \div P$

(*b*) On a continuous bucket elevator $T = BH + [bH + w(H + 3{\cdot}04)] \div P$

In other cases where added tension is necessary to make up the required slack side tension the total tension is:

(*a*) On a spaced bucket elevator $T = (1 + K)\left[BH + \dfrac{bH + w(H + 9{\cdot}144)}{P}\right]$

(*b*) On a continuous bucket elevator $T = (1 + K)\left[BH + \dfrac{bH + w(H + 3{\cdot}04)}{P}\right]$

where, T = total tension (kgf); B = mass of belt (kg/m); H = vertical height of elevator (m); b = mass of each bucket (kg); w = mass of material in each bucket (kg); K = coefficient (1·0 for bare pulley, 0·84 for lagged pulley); and P = pitch of buckets (m).

When there is any doubt as to which formula applies it is advisable to calculate the tension by both methods and to use the greater tensioning.

CAPACITY.—It is practice to establish the capacity of an elevator with the buckets 60–75% filled. The rated capacity of buckets given in manufacturers' catalogues is usually referred to as the *struck volume*, *S*. The *peak capacity*, $C = 60\,Swv/(1{,}000p)$, where C is in t/h; S is in m³; w = mass of material (kg/m³); v = elevator speed (m/min); and p = pitch of buckets (m). Typical capacities: up to 250t/h at 190m/min (*Law Denis*; belt elevator); say 80t/h at 137m/min (*Newcon*; chain elevator); up to 900t/h at 100m/min, lift 7m (*Scholtz*; belt elevator).

OTHER TYPES OF ELEVATOR

ESCAVEYOR.—See Fig. 25. This vertical conveyor, for unit loads, can be used for lifting combined with horizontal feeding or discharging conveyors, the operation of both (or all) being synchronised. Escaveyor consists of a number of platforms which will flex in one direction only; they are suspended at the corners from four chains which are driven from a common shaft; but each pair of chains follows a different path, thus guiding the platform in their movement. This elevator occupies very limited floor space. Normal loads carried are up to 270 kg, maximum size 180 × 180 cm. Operational speed 15 m/min, but units up to 1,100 kg and sizes up to 106 × 122 cm can be carried at a reduced height.

ELEVATOR/LOWERATOR.—'Speedlift' (*Fenamec*), another type of continuous vertical handling comprises two pairs of endless chains. Two basic models are available: (1) for boxes or cases and (2) for pallets. Throughput (T) depends on maximum height and length of loads handled, as the carrier pitch = load length + height + 380mm = P (m).

'BOTTOMLESS BUCKET' ELEVATOR.—The principle of 'bottomless bucket' consists in having a series of 10 such buckets fastened to a continuously elevating belt; the last in each series is a complete bucket with a bottom. In this way each series of 'bottomless buckets' forms a vertical column of material (grain, sand, sugar, salt, various chemicals) elevated without spillage. It is claimed that this method allows up to double the output (as stated by *Law Denis/Gautier*; or *Kamas*). Output of up to 250t/h at a speed of 150m/min is possible.

VERTICON.—This vertical elevator system comprises a series of folding slats (fixed in one direction and bending in the other) which lock together to form a solid platform when operating on horizontal plane. Supported by linked chains, the unit is enclosed within a light, steel, self-contained tower. In operation the Verticon can be incorporated with a feeder or accumulator-conveyor. (*Gough & Co.*)

WIESE BUCKET ELEVATOR.—This type consists of plastic buckets fitted one behind the other and fixed between two parallel rubber conveying chains. Each rubber chain/belt is provided with drive teeth incorporating high-tensile steel wires which are the load carrying members. The buckets are connected closely to each other by flexible joining strips. By virtue of this design it is possible to use this conveying equipment in dusty or wet enclosing trunking or in open iron structure; it is corrosion free, non-toxic and chemically inert (*McInnes Wiese*).

THRUST-MOTION RIGID CHAIN.—This system is useful when precise positioning of loads and their non-shifting is required, and when floor space is limited. The principle consists in using a specially-designed chain which can transmit thrust motion as well as tractive force; in a way the chain acts like a knee-joint which can bend in one direction only. This thrust-motion rigid chain therefore acts as a jack, the rod of which can be coiled. The chain itself has links with shoulders which rest against each other as they appear from the driving gear; the chain is then made rigid when thrusting as well as when pulling. (Serapid chain originating from France, marketed by *Oldham & Newton*).

VACUUM BELT CONVEYOR/ELEVATOR.—This type is used for lifting and transporting various products have reasonably flat surface, eg up to 150 sheets/min, up to 500 × 500mm in size. The vacuum belt is a modification of the conventional belt conveyor.

It consists of two layers. The inner layer is a conventional conveyor belt perforated to allow air to be drawn through it. The outer layer, which adheres to the inner layer, is an open-cell type elastomeric foam belt. The principle applied is a low-pressure differential across the porous belt surface. A series of conveyor rollers span the open side and act as a support for the vacuum belt. A centrifugal blower is used to create a vacuum. In practice the lifting force is exerted on practically the whole surface area. The maximum lifting capacity of this conveyor is determined not by the weight of the material carried, but by the weight per unit of area contacting the belt surface. (*Salem*).

SCRAPER CHAIN CONVEYORS

The scraper chain conveyor is a fairly loose fitting name for a unit in which non- or semi-abrasive materials in bulk are pushed, pulled or dragged along a trough. It may be divided into two main types: (*a*) the push-plate; (*b*) the drag-link.

Push-plate Conveyor.—This is also called push-bar, suspended flight or roller-flight; the conveyor comprises a series of metal or wooden flights or scrapers attached at a pre-selected pitch to one or two chains passing round sprockets at each end of the run. The flights push the material before them along a trough. The conveyor may be loaded at any point along its run and the discharge may be through controlled openings in the bottom of the trough or over the end of the run (Fig. 30).

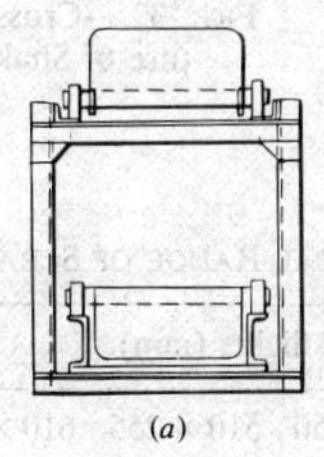
(*a*)

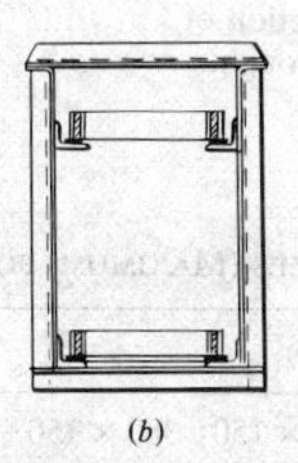
(*b*)

FIG. 30.—Cross-sections of typical Single-chain Scraper Conveyors. (*a*) Scraper Flight Conveyor. (*b*) Suspended Flight Conveyor with conveying element supported by Skidder Bars. (*c*) Suspended Flight Conveyor with conveying element supported by Rollers.

Drag-link Conveyor.—This is also called the drag-chain, drag-flight or 'U' link conveyor, and comprises one or two strands of chain, with or without flights, sliding along in the trough and dragging the material along either by the links themselves or aided by the flights. This conveyor may be loaded and discharged in the same manner as the push-plate type. Fig. 31(*b*).

When used on surface or industrial type applications it is common for the return chain to be elevated above the material, ample clearance being provided. Suspended flight conveyors always convey on the lower run while centrally hung or double flights can convey on either run or both runs simultaneously if required. If the upper run is not used for conveying, guides, tracks or spaced idler rollers (or sprockets) are provided to support the chain. Fig. 31(*a*).

Scraper chain conveyors will operate on gradients up to 40–45° but at greatly reduced capacity. If the slope is greater than 20–25° the flight depth may have to be increased to prevent the material flowing back. Conversely this conveyor may be used to retard or control the flow of material down gradients too steep or long for a chute. Here again, deeper flights may be necessary.

The troughs may be made of metal, wood or some other material suitable to special circumstances. It is common to fit renewable liners to the troughs if the material is at all abrasive. The pitch of the flights is usually from 380 to 610 mm, with single-strand chain, and from 255 mm to 1 m, with double-strand chain.

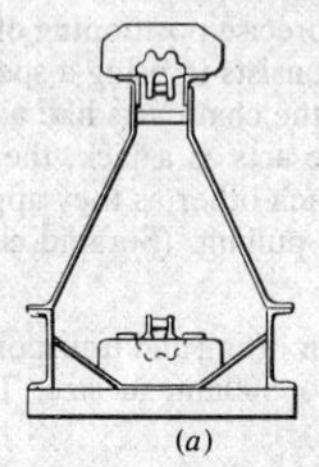
(a)

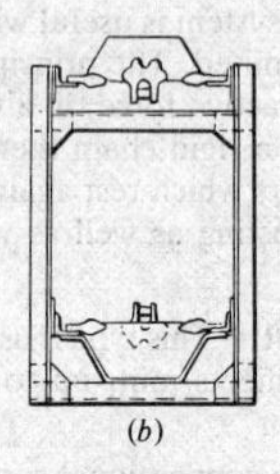
(b)

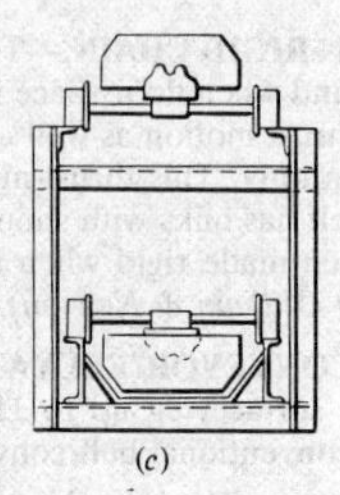
(c)

FIG. 31.—Cross-sections of Typical Double-chain Scraper Conveyors. (*a*) Suspended Flight Conveyor using rollers. (*b*) Drag-link Conveyor.

Chains speeds range up to 45 m/min. The drive is usually applied at the delivery end, generally through the medium of spur gearing, or transmission chains, or a standard reduction gearbox, or a combination of such units. A simple take-up device is usually fitted at the tail end.

Table 14 gives a guide to the maximum lump sizes handled by a typical range of conveyors of the type illustrated by Figs. 32 and 33.

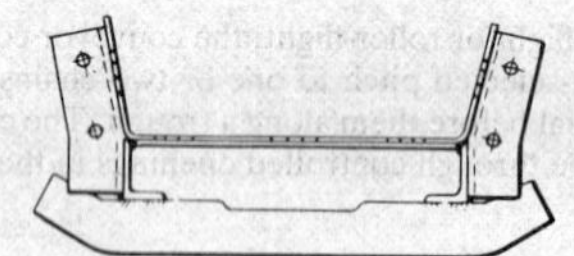

FIG. 32.—Cross-section of Scraper Chain Trough.

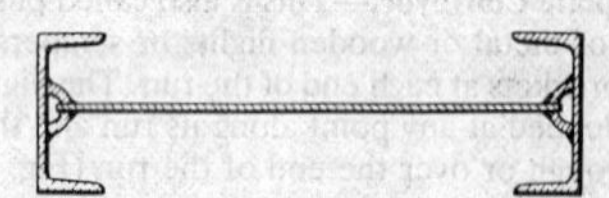

FIG. 33.—Cross-section of Structure of Shaking Conveyor.

TABLE 14.—LUMP SIZES (MAXIMUM) FOR TYPICAL RANGE OF SCRAPER CONVEYORS.

Type	Size of flights (mm)							
	254 × 100	305 × 150	380 × 150	450 × 150	510 × 255	610 × 255	760 × 305	915 × 255
Single-strand chain	76	90	115	127				
Double-strand chain			127	200	254	305	355	400

POWER REQUIREMENTS.—The pull on the chain or resistance to turning (kg) at the pitch radius of the head sprocket may be determined from the following formulae:

LEVEL CONVEYOR WITH CHAIN AND MATERIAL SLIDING:

Chain pull = $(2 \times C \times L \times F_c) + (M \times L \times F_m)$.

LEVEL CONVEYOR WITH ROLLERS SUPPORTING CHAIN OR FLIGHTS AND MATERIAL SLIDING:

Chain pull = $(2 \times C \times L \times F_r) + (M \times L \times F_m)$.

INCLINED CONVEYOR WITH CHAIN AND MATERIAL SLIDING:

Chain pull = $(C \times L)[(\cos\theta \times F_c) + \sin\theta] + (M \times L)[(\cos\theta \times F_m) + \sin\theta] + (C \times L)[(\cos\theta \times F_c) - \sin\theta]$.

INCLINED CONVEYOR WITH ROLLERS SUPPORTING CHAIN OR FLIGHTS AND MATERIAL SLIDING:

Chain pull = $(C \times L)[(\cos\theta \times F_r) + \sin\theta] + (M \times L)[(\cos\theta \times F_m) + \sin\theta] + (C \times L)[(\cos\theta \times F_r) - \sin\theta]$.

where, C = mass of chain and flights (kg/m); M = mass of material load on conveyor (kg/m); L = conveyor length (m); F_c = friction coefficient between chain and slides, and trough (0·33 for metal on metal); F_m = friction coefficient between material and trough (eg 0·35 for coal); F_r = coefficient of rolling friction (average value 0·05). The sliding friction of material on metal varies considerably with the material and its conditions, and manufacturers' advice should be sought.

To determine the motor power, allowance should be made for transmission losses, starting loads, and surges, depending upon conditions. Thus 10% for losses at the head and tail ends, 10% for losses in the drive plus 10–20% for starting, etc, should be added to the chain pull to establish what may be called the 'gross turning effort'.

Then: Motor Power (kW) = Gross turning effort (kg) × Chain speed (m/sec) ÷ 100.

CAPACITY.—The following formula will enable the capacity for a level conveyor to be approximated:

$$\text{Capacity } (C) = BDwv/16{\cdot}6$$

where, C is in t/h; B = breadth of trough (m); D = depth of trough (m); w = mass of material (kg/m^3); and v = chain speed (m/min).

When operating on an incline of 20° and steeper, the capacity given by the above formula should be multiplied by the factors given in Table 15.

TABLE 15.—FACTORS FOR INCLINE IN EXCESS OF 20°

Gradient	Pitch of flight mm	
	380–610	611–1000
20–25°	0·98	0·90
26–30°	0·91	0·81
31–35°	0·84	0·70
36–40°	0·70	0·65
40–45°	0·60	0·55

SCRAPER CONVEYORS FOR COAL MINING.—Underground coal mining is probably the greatest application of scraper conveyors. Several forms of the conveyor are to be found, each developed to perform a particular duty or range of duties, but all conveying on the top run with the return strand of chain travelling back under the material carrying trough.

For either the 'Room and Pillar' or 'Longwall System' of mining, there is a range of scraper conveyors of approximately 300, 380 and 500 mm widths which are easily and speedily built up from sectionalised unit lengths; usually approximately 2 m long; of intermediate, single or double piece structure and employing single or double strand chain of the types illustrated in Fig. 34—*g*, *h*, and *i*. Figure 32 shows a typical cross-section of a one-piece scraper chain trough. See chapter O1, 'Mining Engineering'.

CHAIN FOR SCRAPER CONVEYORS.—A wide range of chain is available and may be divided into three groups: (*a*) cast chain; (*b*) precision chain; (*c*) forged chain. When selecting a chain for a particular application a number of points must be established: (1) pitch of chain; (2) size of sprocket; (3) load to be carried; (4) nature of material; (5) operating conditions.

Figure 34 illustrates examples of some of the many types of standard chain available:

(*a*) Ewart type detachable chain.
(*b*) Steel bushed chain with renewable pins and bushes of either carbon or manganese steel. The illustration shows a 'C' type attachment link.
(*c*) Renold heavy-duty precision chain with steel rollers. The rollers are available with or without flanges.
(*d*) Steel roller and malleable link chain.
(*e*) Climax improved drag link chain.
(*f*) Fabricated steel drag or 'U' link chain.
(*g*) Combination steel pin and flight and malleable iron link chain. (This type is also used with drop forged steel links.)
(*h*) Riveted pintle chain with malleable iron and steel flights and pins. The illustration shows the flight bolted or riveted to an attachment link.
(*i*) Double strand steel flat link riveted or bolted chain with pitched scraper bars.
(*j*) Double strand short link chain made of carbon steel, electrically welded, heat treated, tempered and calibrated for length. The illustration shows a 15 link unit length complete with alloy steel connecting link and rolled steel scraper bar.

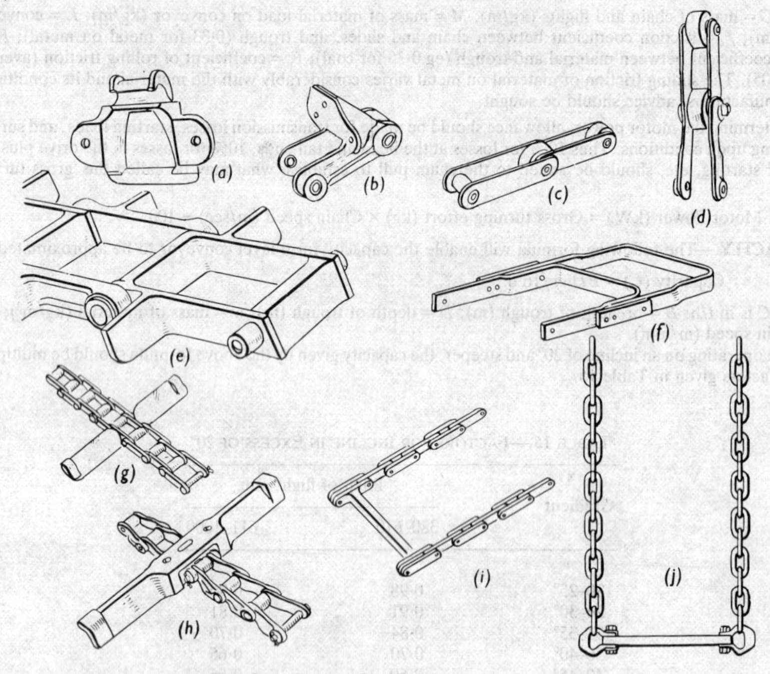

FIG. 34.—Typical Chains for Scraper Conveyors.

ROLLER CONVEYORS

Roller conveyors, of one type or another, may solve the problem of moving unit loads having a flat base of regular shape (but it does not prevent handling of sacks, wire baskets or containers with rims but care should be taken when choosing roller diameter pitch, width; guide rails may be required); roller conveyors are also useful when an accumulation of products is required on a horizontal conveyor with a controlled line pressure and product release rate (eg System 2000 *Fenamec*), capable of handling loads up to 2000 kg; a positive accumulation system, incorporating sprockets allowing conveyed loads to accelerate and decelerate as well as accumulate. Another system (Q50; produced by *CMC*) achieves accumulation by the 25 mm diameter line shaft being completely shrouded by a series of 32 mm diameter tubes; when a carton is stopped on the conveyor, the rollers beneath it will be prevented from rotating, and, therefore, the belts will act as a brake on the friction-driven tube; the rollers behind will also be braked, thereby forming a short section of dead track; each grooved roller is independently driven from the common line shaft by a polyurethane belt. Bends and curves are possible in the design of these conveyors. Three main types of roller conveyors are available:

Gravity.—This type comprises a series of freely rotating tubular rollers mounted at a preselected pitch in a fabricated frame usually of sectionalised unit length and slightly inclined along which the load is moved by the force of gravity acting upon it.

Powered or Live.—This type comprises a series of tubular rollers mounted at a preselected pitch in a fabricated frame in which each of a selected number of the rollers is driven by a chain or belt. Powered roller conveyors are usually employed where the fall required by the gravity roller type is unattainable or where level or slightly rising sections have to be accommodated. They are commonly used in conjunction with gravity roller conveyors. Another type of roller conveyor can negotiate bends and curves, and return underneath to form a complete loop. This eliminates separately driven sections at corners and bends. Steel rollers are driven by a special braided rope carried on pulleys (*Alvey Conveyor* (*UK*) *Ltd*). It is advisable to consult the manufacturer when such conveyors are required (Fig. 35).

Wheel-roller.—This type comprises wheels and a driving belt. (Fig. 36).

FIG. 35.—Wheel Conveyor (*Fenamec*).

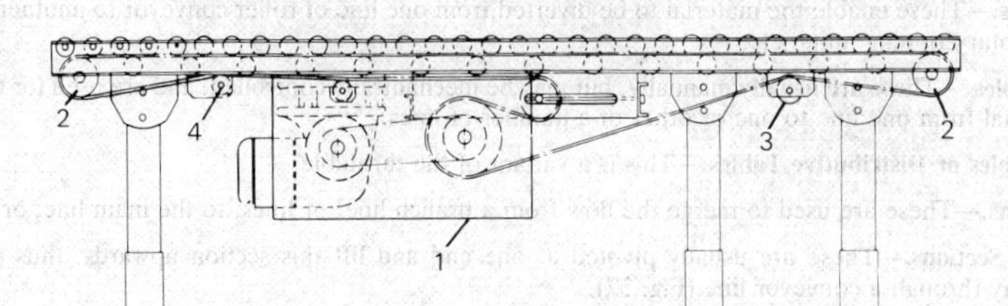

FIG. 36.—Typical Live Roller Conveyor with Belt Drive. 1 = Drive unit. 2 = End roller. 3 = Snub roller. 4 = Belt return idlers. (*Matthews/Rexnord*).

ESSENTIAL PARTS OF A GRAVITY CONVEYOR

Rollers.—The diameter of the rollers used for a specific duty depends upon the manufacturer's design and load rating. Rollers are usually made from ERW (electric resistance welded) steel tubes (to BS 6328).

Roller Pitch.—The standard pitch is the distance between centres of consecutive rollers. It should be approximately one-third of the length of the cargo, so that it is supported by at least three rollers. Usually the width of the roller should be 50–75 mm longer than the width of the widest unit load. In cases of very wide loads it is usual to employ either two parallel conveyors of narrow width or a special multiple unit with two or more rollers transversely placed to make up the required overall width.

Standard pitch values are: 37·5, 50, 75, 100, and 200 mm. Typical standard length of rollers are: 300, 350, 400, 450, 600, 750, and 900 mm. Standardised dimensions are given in BS 2567.

Frame.—The frames in which the rollers are mounted are fabricated from suitable rolled steel angle or channel section rigidly braced. The section used is related to the duty and span. Simple interlocking devices are fitted at the frame ends. Guide rails are on occasion fitted to the frames—commonly on curved sections or highly elevated runs.

TABLE 16.—THICKNESS OF ROLLER TUBING AND MINIMUM CURVE RADIUS (BS 2567).

Roller diameter (mm)	Roller tubing thickness (mm)	Min radius of curve, *R*, of roller track (mm)	Spindle diameter (mm)
25·4	1·2	630, 800	6·5
38·0	1·2	630, 800	10·0
51·0	1·6	800, 1,000	10·0
57·0	1·6	800, 1,000	10·0
63·5	3·2	800, 1,000	16·0–20·0
76·1	3·2	800, 1,000	22·0
88·9	5·4	1,250	25·0

Note.—R is measured to the inside face of the inner frame rail. Manufacturers should be consulted concerning loads, radii, etc.

Stands or Trestles.—A range of fixed or adjustable height stationary or travelling stands is available, to enable the required degree of slope to be achieved. Fixed stationary stands are usually employed when neither the load nor the route varies. Adjustable stands are usually employed when a wide variety of weight or size of loads is being handled. Travelling stands are useful when the route of the material is changed frequently. Stands should be positioned as close to the conveyor unit joint as possible to give stability. The stands may be made of wood or metal.

In addition to the straight sections of a roller conveyor, other component units are available. Typical of these are:

Curved Sections.—These are commonly available in 45° bends and 90° bends with taper or parallel rollers. Table 16 lists minimum radii.

Switches.—These enable the material to be diverted from one line of roller conveyor to another line; there are also rotary tipping units, etc.

Turntables.—These are usually manually, but may be mechanically controlled, and are used for transferring the material from one line to one or other of a number of lines.

Ball Tables or Distributive Tables.—This is a variant of the turntable.

Junctions.—These are used to merge the flow from a branch line, or lines, to the main line, or vice versa.

Hinged Sections.—These are usually pivoted at one end and lift this section upwards, thus providing a passageway through a conveyor line (Fig. 37).

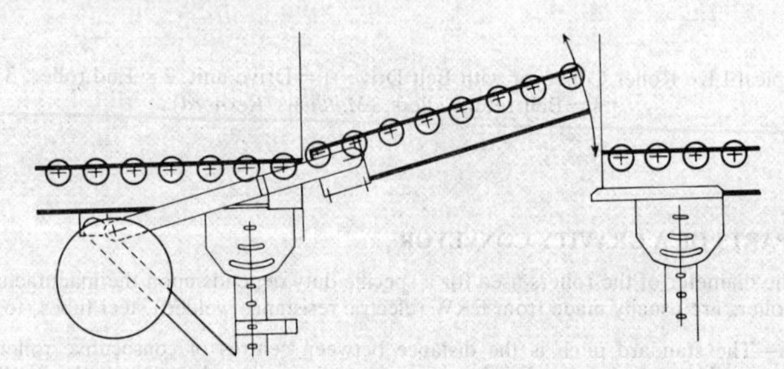

FIG. 37.—Roller Conveyor Counterweight Hinge (*Matthews/Rexnord*)

Gate Section.—This is an alternative method of providing a passageway through a conveyor line; the section swings open sideways, like a gate.

Weighers.—These units permit visual, or recorded, details of the material in transit.

Chutes.—It may be that the drop available between start and finish is so great that the resultant average conveyor gradient would be too steep. In such circumstances chutes are employed. Three types of chutes are: (1) plain straight chute; (2) plain spiral chute; (3) roller spiral chute.

ANGLE OF INCLINATION.—The slope safely allowed on a gravity roller conveyor depends upon the nature, and weight, of the items to be conveyed; it is therefore advisable to consult the manufacturer when considering a specific application. As a guide, the following are examples of commonly employed gradients for a number of typical weights with a hard flat riding surface: For a weight of 2–9 kg, the gradient is 7–4%; for 9–22 kg, it is 4%; for 22–70 kg, it is 4–3%; and from 70–110 kg, it is 3–2·5%.

At curves, or when using plain-bushed rollers, it is usual to double the gradient. Soft loads may need a gradient of 10% or more. In some cases these loads are first placed on pallets to enable the normal grades to be employed. Where there is a considerable length of run, it is sometimes necessary to provide extra elevation either at the start or at some intermediate point. For this purpose power operated elevators, lifters or humpers are employed; usually they take the form of flat belt, slat or push-bar conveyor; they may be fixed, or portable.

Capacity.—This depends on roller pitch, roller width, etc.

OVERHEAD CONVEYORS

By reason of its almost infinite possibilities in length, flexibility and capacity, the power-driven overhead conveyor is capable of wide application in numerous industries. Space that would otherwise be wasted can be used by the conveyor because of its flexible nature. High runs leave the floor space below free and can be used to provide mobile storage for work in transit. The clear space on the floors made available by the overhead suspension of loads can be used as a work area or for storage. The cross section of the conveyor is relatively small, and in most cases, with the attachments and carriers, does not take up much more space than the loads themselves. See BS 2853 'Design and Testing of Steel Overhead Runway Beams'.

TYPICAL APPLICATIONS.—Work can be done on the material whilst it is in transit. Trolley conveyors are used to:

(*a*) Move incoming parts and raw materials from receiving points to storage and outgoing parts to despatching bays.
(*b*) Handle commodities in the food industry and stores.
(*c*) Carry loads between storage and manufacturing and from one department to another.
(*d*) Carry work in process from one operation to another, possible through assembly and inspection to packing.
(*e*) Provide mobile storage in warehouses, also between operations.
(*f*) Effect transport between buildings over short or long distances.
(*g*) Handle parts through processing, such as spray or dip painting, rust-proofing, sanding, washing, degreasing, drying, baking, cooling, sand blasting, and through enamelling, annealing, heat treatment ovens, etc.
(*h*) Facilitate foundry work such as assembly of moulds, casting operations, cooling castings, baking cores and drying moulds.
(*i*) Tow trucks in warehouses, etc.
(*j*) Push carriers running on adjacent non-powered monorail tracks, with optional automatic or manual engagement and release devices.
(*k*) Accommodate a weighing machine for materials in transit.
(*l*) Transport personnel in underground mines.

CONSTRUCTIONAL DETAILS.—Figure 38 shows a typical arrangement. The essential parts of an overhead installation are:

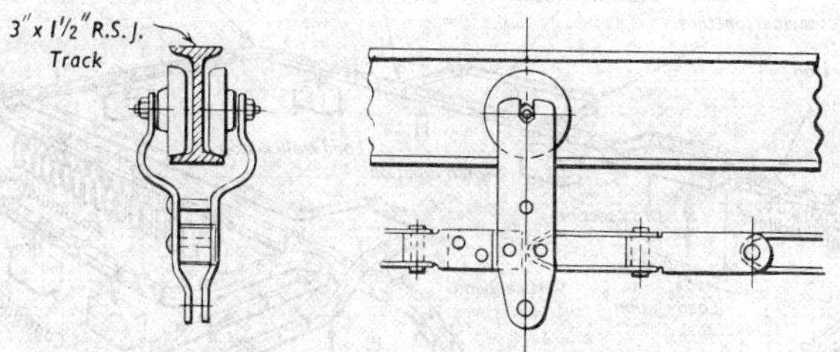

FIG. 38.—Constructional Details of Overhead Installation.

Suspended Track, usually a rolled steel joist, double angles, a tee, or a beam having a suitably designed cross-section. A dual track is used for heavy duty transport and storage (up to 1000 kg load is usual). The track may be enclosed in box-type or tubular enclosure (see Fig. 39). The path of motion can be almost any irregular combination of horizontal runs, ups and down, inclines, bends and curves, to meet requirements over any distance. Being commonly suspended from existing roof members, conveyors can be laid out to clear existing equipment, to rise over passageways and to come down to loading and unloading stations. Switches, turntables and crosstracks allow for variations in constructional arrangements.

The use of square-box construction track as shown in Fig. 39, obviates the necessity for wheel corners for bends of 60 cm radius and upwards. It is common practice to weld track-joints *in situ*. Normally the maximum angle of slope at vertical curves is 45°, but on units of the types shown in Figs. 38 and 39, the use of a double point suspension load-bar may be conveyed vertically (Fig. 43).

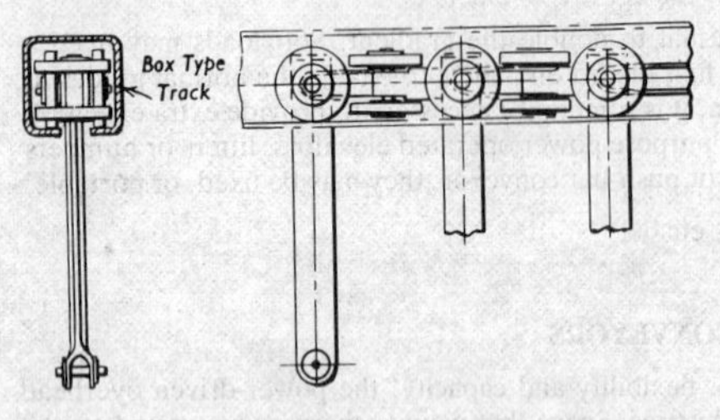

FIG. 39.—Typical Arrangement of Box-Type Track.

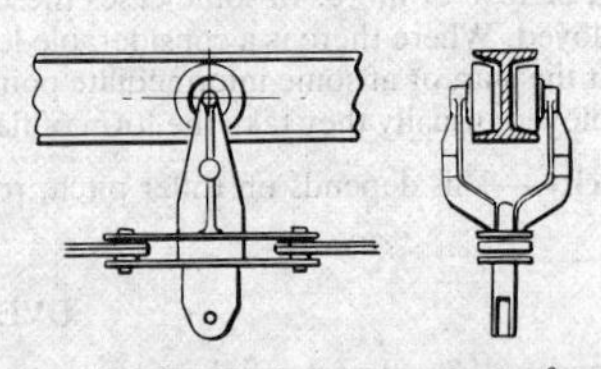

FIG. 40.—Typical Arrangement of Medium-duty Trolley Conveyor.

The clearance between two carriers is reduced when they travel on an inclined track. To plan the installation, the actual carrier spacing, L is given by the formula: $L = (l + c)/\cos \alpha$, where L is in cm; l (cm) = overall length of carrier (or load, if it is longer than the carrier); c (cm) = clearance required; and α (degrees) = angle of the slope.

Trolleys, also called carriages, single-, or multi-wheeled, rolling along the track. Trolleys are normally of fabricated, drop forged, pressed, or cast construction. Figures 38–47 show a number of typical arrangements.

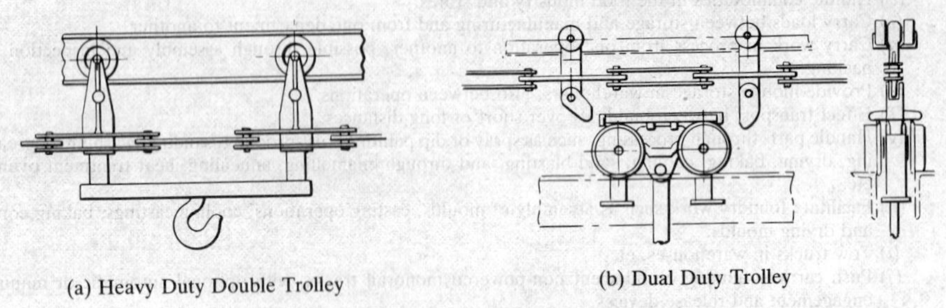

(a) Heavy Duty Double Trolley (b) Dual Duty Trolley

FIG. 41.—Other types of Trolley Conveyor.

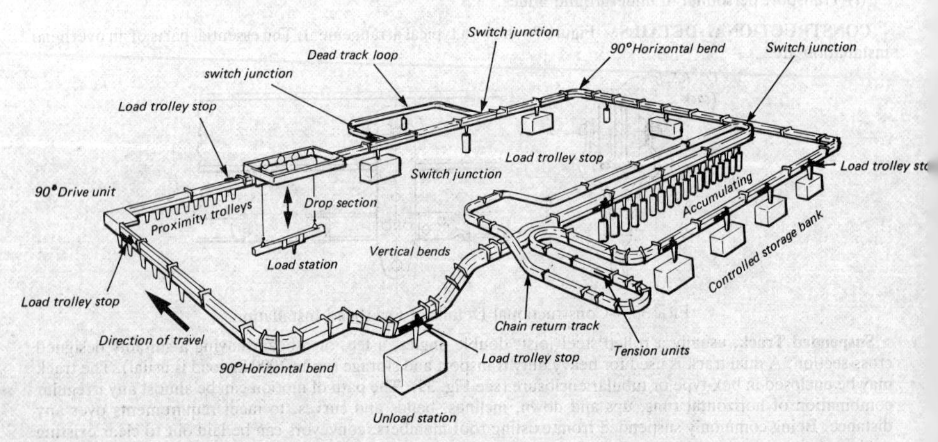

FIG. 42.—Typical Overhead Conveyor Layout (standard units make up a conveyor system assembled together to form a complete circuit). *'Flowmaster'-Torvale Fisher.*

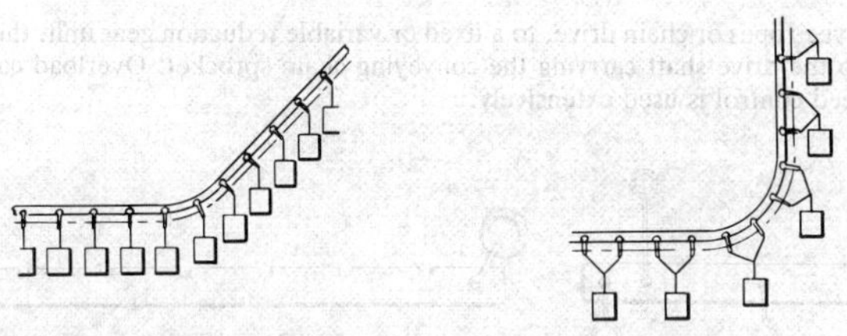

FIG. 43.—Arrangements of 45° and Vertical Installations.

Load Carriers are of various types to suit specific requirements, depending upon type and size of load and the proposed capacity. Figure 48 shows a selection of typical carriers: baskets, hooks, pans, trays, racks, slings, or load-bars coupling two trolleys for heavy-duty installations, say handling 5000 kg loads. Figure 47 shows load-bars hung from clevis attachments by using pins or links to carry certain types of loads.

Hangers or Attachments from which are hung the loads to be transported. According to the purpose of the installation attachments are combined with load carriers (eg hooks). *Clevis Attachment.*—Figures 38, 39, and 45 show a simple method of suspending the load which hangs in a vertical position at all times. The connection between the tongue of the carrier in the clevis and the clevis bolts should be a loose fit.

Figure 46 shows such a typical and commonly used attachment when removable hooks carry the loads. The hole in this attachment is made large enough to allow the carrier to be easily connected or removed. Pendant-type attachments are sometimes used when carriers must be rigidly connected to trolleys. In such cases each attachment has two bolt holes for this connection. Double suspension is used for heavier loads. Hangers are attached at each carriage or selected carriages. Idler or dummy attachments are intermediate chain (or rope) supports positioned between load-carrying attachments.

Haulage is provided by a continuous chain (or rope) which connects the trolleys (carriages). Fig. 44 shows examples of the many types of chain used on overhead chain conveyors in addition to those already shown on Figs. 38–41, which incorporate King's 'Pluplanar' and 'Flat-Flex' chains. Figure 45 shows a malleable iron 'Ewart' detachable chain. Figure 41 shows a Renold chain of the bushed-roller type, with either solid or hollow bearing pins.

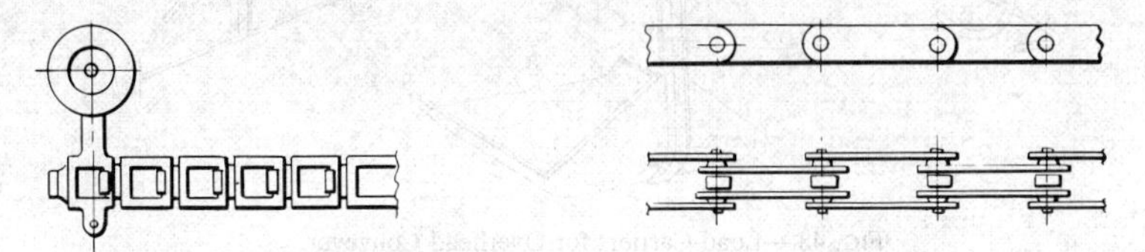

FIG. 44.—Typical Chain Designs for Overhead Conveyor.

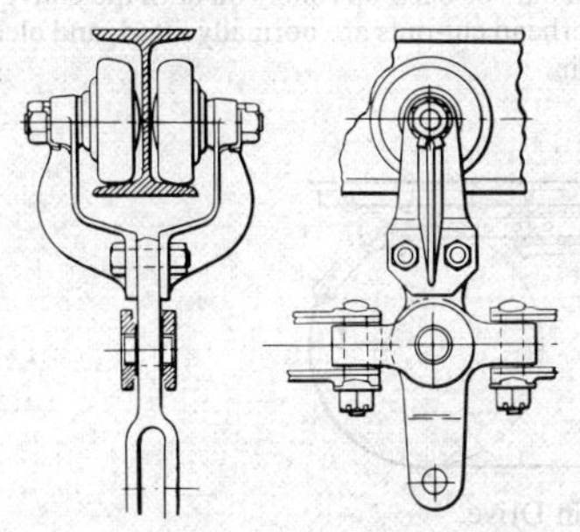

FIG. 45.—Clevis Attachment.

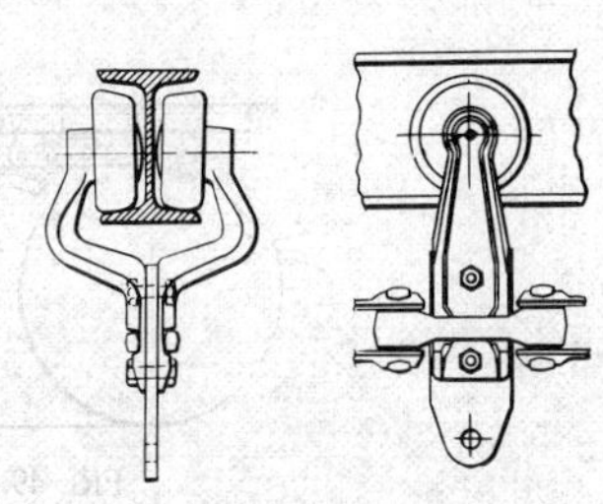

FIG. 46.—Pendant Attachment.

Drives.—Three general types of drives are employed:

Sprocket Drive.—This conforms to the conventional type of chain conveyor, where the conveying chain is wrapped round and driven by a sprocket on the drive shaft. It is located invariably at a 90°, or 180°, horizontal bend corner. The drive is usually from a motor, sometimes through an electro-magnetic, hydraulic or eddy current coupling, by vee ropes or chain drive, to a fixed or variable reduction gear unit, then by a final straight cut spur reduction to the drive shaft carrying the conveying chain sprocket. Overload cut-outs are normally fitted. Electronic speed control is used extensively.

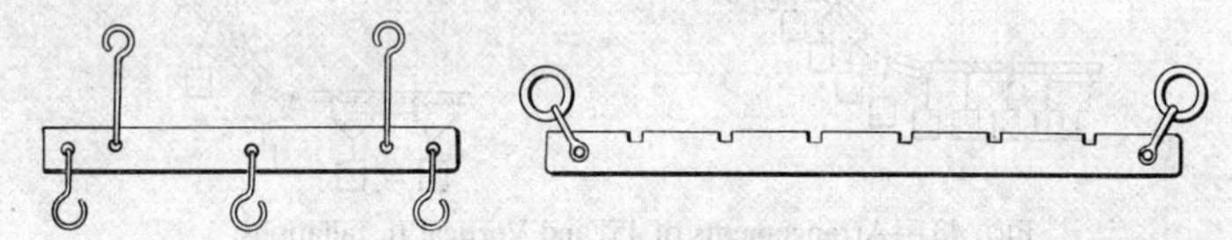

FIG. 47.—Load-Bars.

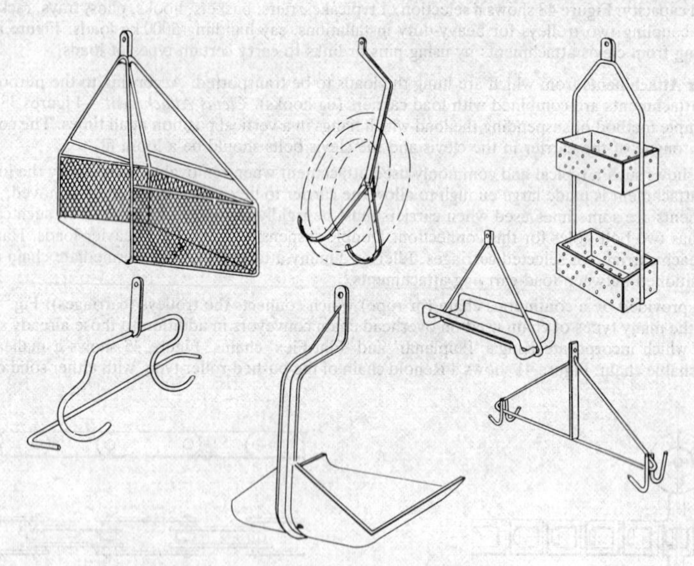

FIG. 48.—Load Carriers for Overhead Conveyor.

Caterpillar Chain Drive.—Figure 49 shows a drive of this type consisting of a short loop of auxiliary driving chain running alongside and parallel to the conveying chain. Skid bars or back-up rollers on both the conveying chain and the caterpillar track maintain the drive in contact. Overhead cut-outs are normally fitted, and electric limit switches ensure correct engagement of the caterpillar chain.

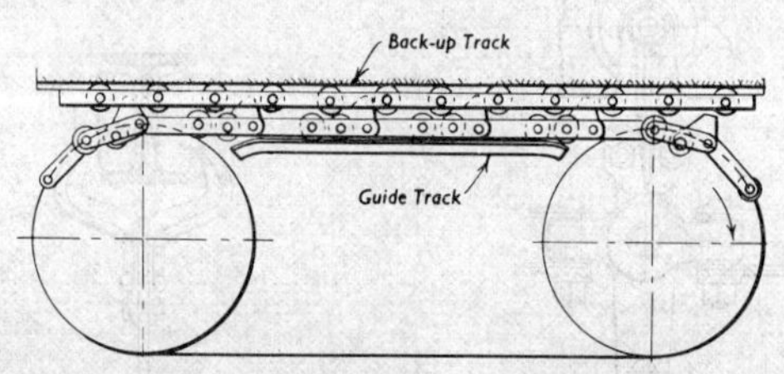

FIG. 49.—Caterpillar Chain Drive.

Chain Pull and Power.—The chain size is determined by multiplying the sum of the total weight of chain, trolleys, carriers and load, by a friction coefficient which varies according to the type of chain or trolley used. Allowances must also be made for lifts, and for losses at vertical and horizontal curves; these losses vary depending on the chain pull, spacing of trolleys, and radius of the curve. With trolley conveyors of the type shown on Figs. 38 and 39, the following constants may be used to approximate the chain pull (but it is advisable to consult manufacturers' catalogues and tables, as these factors vary and affect the final results).

Tractive effort to move load = static load × 0·05.

Added load due to frictional loss at 90° horizontal bend = loading at bend × 0·05.

Added load due to frictional loss at 180° horizontal bend = loading at bend × 0·10.

Added load due to frictional loss at vertical bend = loading at bend × 0·10.

Theoretical power, P (kW) = $FS \div 6000$, where F is the chain pull (kgf); and S is conveyor speed (m/min).

'Monotractor' (*British Monorail*) allows a speed of up to 108 m/min moving loads up to 3 t, but 5 t loads would be moved at a speed of 85 m/min max.

Take-ups.—Chain Tension Control.—Automatic tensioning devices for conveying chains are incorporated in some sprocket-type drives. On other arrangements of sprocket-type drives, and when using a chain-type drive or when the track conditions warrant it, separate automatic tension units are provided.

Safety Devices.—These ensure safety of operation and also reduce maintenance costs by ensuring correct spacing between the loads. In case of overload a shear-pin device is used; it cuts out the drive and operation cannot be restarted until the accumulation is attended to and a new pin fixed in place.

SKIP HOISTS

The skip hoist is a mechanical means of raising bulk materials along a vertical or normally steeply inclined path. In its simplest form it comprises a guided bucket or skip, usually of rectangular section, which is raised and lowered by a wire rope and operated through appropriate controls by a powered winch.

The skip is filled in a loading pit at the bottom of the track, and then elevated. At the discharge point the track usually curves into a horizontal position so that the top of the bucket travels over dumping area. The bottom of the skip is pivotable in the hoisting frame; it continues to travel upwards causing the cargo to be emptied from the inverted skip. The various operations may be either manually controlled, partly automatic, or fully automatic. Guides or tracks determine the path of travel which must be arranged to suit site conditions and the duties to be performed. Typical paths for skip hoists are shown on Fig. 50.

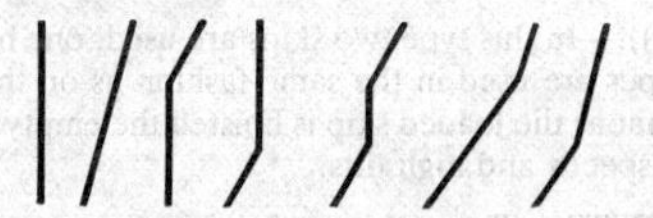

FIG. 50.—Typical Paths for Skip Hoists.

Usually the skip is a simple rectangular box, open at the top, fabricated from steel plates and sometimes fitted with renewable liners. It is mounted on four flanged wheels which guide it along the track. In addition, it commonly has a hoisting frame pivotally fixed to the bottom, but extending slightly above the top of the skip where connection is made to the wire rope (see Fig. 51). If the loading is automatic, then control arms to engage the feeder may also be provided. The skip does not 'bottom' when loading, but is always suspended on the rope.

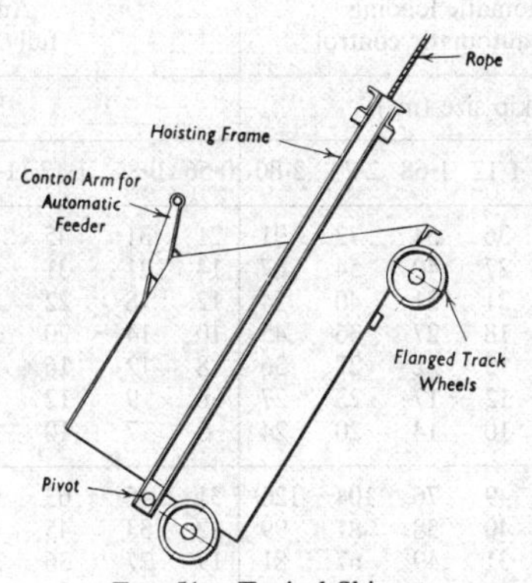

FIG. 51.—Typical Skip.

The skip hoist is especially suitable where it is required to raise, sometimes to quite considerable heights of up to say 70 m, and even more, bulk materials which contain large lumps, or which are abrasive or corrosive or at high temperature. It may also be used on occasion to raise sticky materials which might clog elevator buckets and adhere to conveyor belts, or to raise friable materials which might otherwise suffer excessive degradation if handled by a bucket elevator. In short, the skip hoist may be, under such circumstances, better suited to a specific application than a bucket elevator or an inclined belt conveyor. There are three types of skip hoists: (*a*) Single unbalanced skip; (*b*) Single balanced skip; (*c*) Double balanced skip.

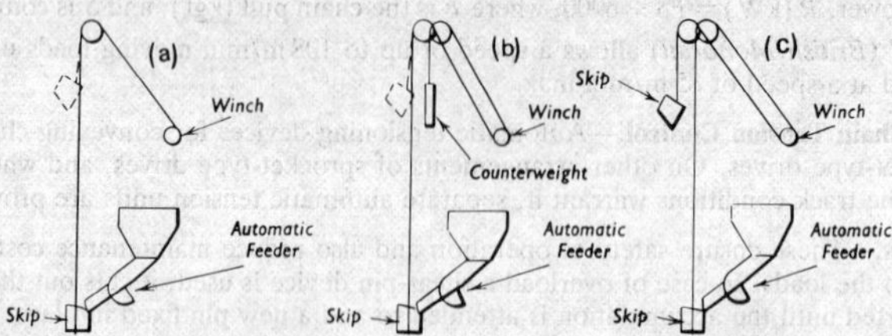

FIG. 52.—Types of Skip Hoist. (*a*) Single Unbalanced Skip. (*b*) Single Balanced Skip. (*c*) Double Balanced Skip.

Single Unbalanced Skip (Fig. 52(*a*)).—The winch has sufficient power to elevate the total weight of the skip and its cargo. The empty skip descends by gravity, overhauling the gearing, and the speed is controlled either electrically or mechanically, depending upon considerations of the electric supply, etc. This arrangement is usually restricted to small capacities at slow speeds and moderate lifts.

Single Balanced Skip (Fig. 52(*b*)).—In this type the single skip is counterweighted. Two wire ropes are used, one being attached to the skip and the other to the counterweight. The ropes are wound on to the winch drum in opposite directions so that as one is taken in the other is let out. The weight of the counterweight is usually equal to the dead weight of the skip plus half of the weight of the cargo so that a positive load is imposed on the motor at all times. This arrangement is usually applied to medium to high capacities at medium to high speeds and fairly high lifts.

Double Balanced Skip (Fig. 52(*c*)).—In this type two skips are used, one balancing the other and ascending, while the other descends. Two ropes are used in the same fashion as on the single balanced skip but in this case each is fastened to a skip so that as the loaded skip is hoisted the empty one is lowered. This arrangement is used for high capacities at high speeds and high lifts.

PERFORMANCE OF SKIP HOISTS.—The capacity of a skip hoist is dependent upon the following: (1) speed of travel of skip; (2) distance of travel of skip; (3) method of loading (manual or automatic); (4) capacity of skip; (5) loading and discharging time of skip; (6) the use of single or double skips.

As a guide Table 17 gives capacities in tons per hour for a range of typical vertical skip hoists when handling automatically loaded material weighing 800 kg/m^3 and operating at commonly selected speeds. The capacities are proportionate when handling materials of different mass per cubic metre.

TABLE 17.—CAPACITIES OF SKIP HOISTS (t/h) WHEN HANDLING MATERIALS OF DENSITY 800 kg/m^3

Type of skip hoist		Automatic loading partly automatic control						Automatic loading fully automatic control								
		Skip size (m^3)						Skip size (m^3)								
		0·56	0·84	1·12	1·68	2·24	2·80	0·56	0·84	1·12	1·68	2·24	2·80	3·36	4·20	5·60
	12	18	27	36	54	72	91	21	31	45	67	85	108	131	166	222
Single un-	18	13	20	27	40	54	67	14	21	31	45	58	73	91	113	149
balanced or	24	10	16	21	31	40	54	12	18	22	36	49	58	72	91	121
single balanced	30	9	13	18	27	36	45	10	14	20	27	40	49	58	77	100
slow speed	36	7	10	15	22	27	36	8	12	16	22	31	40	49	62	86
(24 m/min)	48	5	8	12	17	23	27	6	9	12	19	27	31	40	49	62
	60	4	7	10	14	20	24	5	7	10	15	20	26	31	40	49
	12	25	36	49	76	104	126	31	45	63	95	126	156	190	239	316
Single un-	18	20	31	40	58	81	99	22	33	45	67	91	113	136	167	225
balanced or	24	16	24	31	49	67	81	19	27	36	58	77	95	113	140	190
single balanced	30	14	20	27	40	54	67	15	23	31	45	63	77	95	118	154
medium speed	36	12	18	24	36	49	58	14	20	27	40	54	67	81	99	136
(43 m/min)	48	9	14	19	27	36	45	10	14	20	31	40	49	58	77	99
	60	8	12	16	24	31	40	8	12	16	24	31	40	49	58	81

Single un-balanced or single balanced (two-speed) high speed (80 m/min)	24		54	86	108	136	163	202	271
	30		45	67	91	113	140	172	231
	36		40	58	81	99	121	149	202
	48		31	49	67	77	99	122	167
	60		27	40	54	67	86	104	140
Double bal-anced (two speed) high speed (80 m/min)	24		104	158	213	267	321	400	530
	30		91	140	185	231	275	344	459
	36		81	122	163	202	243	304	404
	48		67	99	132	152	199	248	334
	60		54	81	113	140	167	212	279

SKIP SPEEDS.—Depending upon the capacity required and the length of travel and, to a certain extent, the type of skip hoist, the speed of the skip may range from 15 to 150 m/min. When operating at the higher speeds it is necessary to arrange for slowing down the speed of the skip as it approaches its loading and discharging positions in order to relieve the brake of excessive duty, to lessen shock loads and to facilitate accurate positioning of the skip. Where a change in direction of the track occurs either adjacent to the loading or the discharge positions the reduction in the hoisting or lowering speed should take place before that point is reached by the skip.

LOADING SKIP HOISTS.—The skip may be loaded manually or automatically. With manual feeding this may be direct or indirect. When the capacity is small the material may be brought to the loading pit in small hand-pushed carts or barrows and dumped or shovelled direct or down a chute into the skip—this is known as direct manual feeding. With indirect manual feeding, the material is first dumped into a receiving hopper, and the feed controlled by a hand-operated gate to the skip.

AUTOMATIC FEEDING.—This is always indirect and can be applied to all types of skip hoists. There are three main types of automatic feeders or loaders: (*a*) Damming type; (*b*) Full bucket control type; (*c*) Weight of load in bucket type.

Damming Type.—In this type of automatic feeder the skip engages and opens a gate and chute as it moves into the loading position, thus allowing the material to flow into the skip. The material continues to flow until the skip is full and then it backs into the chute, thereby damming the flow. As the skip leaves the loading position it closes the gate and chute again. If, however, the control of the travel of the skip is automatic, the skip may hoist away after a predetermined time lag, whether the bucket is full or not.

Full Bucket Control Type.—This type is similar in automatic loading action to the damming type, but the skip will only start upwards when full. It remains inoperative when empty or only partially filled. This type therefore obviates unnecessary trips by the skip.

Weight of Load in Bucket Type.—This type of automatic feeder is used if materials differing widely in weight are handled successively. The skip starts its upwards travel, cutting off the feed, as soon as it is loaded with a predetermined weight of material. The load on the winch remains the same regardless of the weight per cubic foot of the cargo. The size of the bucket should be such as will accommodate in volume the required amount in weight per trip of the lightest of the various materials to be handled.

CONTROL.—There are two control methods: *partly automatic*, in which the skip makes one round trip and stops, or, *fully automatic*, in which the skip continues to repeat the cycle until stopped. The method of control is linked with the method of feeding; thus with manual feeding, full automatic control is never used.

In addition, a number of appliances and features are available to ensure continuous safe working of skip hoists. Typical of these features are:

(1) BRAKE (commonly solenoid operated), incorporated in the winch, usually between the motor and the reduction gear, and capable of sustaining the skip at any point in the run in the event of a power failure.
(2) SLACK ROPE SWITCH, which will stop the skip should the rope for any reason become slack.
(3) TRACK LIMIT SWITCHES, which will stop down the skip hoist should either the skip or the counterweight travel beyond their selected stops.
(4) OVER-RUN TRACK LIMIT SWITCHES, which operate if either the upper or lower track limit switch fails.
(5) ADJUSTABLE ROPE TAKE-UP, on single and double balanced skips.
(6) AUTOMATIC ROPE TAKE-UP, on automatically loaded skip hoists.
(7) OVERLOAD TRIPS, on the electric motor controls.
(8) OVERFLOW SWITCHES, stopping the skip hoist when the upper receiving bunker is full.

POWER REQUIREMENTS.—As there as so many varying factors to be taken into consideration in designing a skip hoist, such as path of travel, rope layout, material handling, two-speed operation, etc, it is advisable to consult the manufacturer concerning the power of the motor, its rating, etc.

SCREW CONVEYORS

These are also called 'Helicoidal' or 'Helix' Conveyors.

BS 4409 Screw Conveyors Part 1, deals with 'Trough-Type for Industrial Use'. Part 2, deals with 'Portable and Mobile Tubular Type (Augers) for Agricultural and Light Industrial Use'.

Nominal diameter of a trough-type is the outside diameter of the helical screw; *nominal diameter* of a tubular is the external diameter of the tube. The normal *pitch* (or *flight*), of the helical screw for both types is usually equal to the nominal diameter, so that, for example, in one revolution of a 30 cm normal pitch screw conveyor, the cargo travels forward approximately 30 cm. *Shaft height* is the vertical distance between the shaft centre-line above the foot of the trough support, and the *height* above shaft is the distance from the centre-line of the shaft to the top of the trough; these two definitions apply to the trough type. *Radial clearance* is the distance between the helical screw and the interior of the cylindrical part of the trough or the interior of the tube.

Figure 53 shows the essential parts of a screw conveyor; these are: the screw and shaft; the trough and hanger; the feed and discharge chute; and the drive. The usual length of the screw and shaft is in standard unit lengths of 2–3 m; special lengths are available, but the length is related to the torque which can be transmitted safely by the screw shaft and couplings. The manufacturers will be able to assist in each particular case. Standard diameters are: 100, 125, 160, 200, 250, 315, 400, 500, 630, 800, 1,000, and 1,250 mm. Typical flights are (Fig. 55):

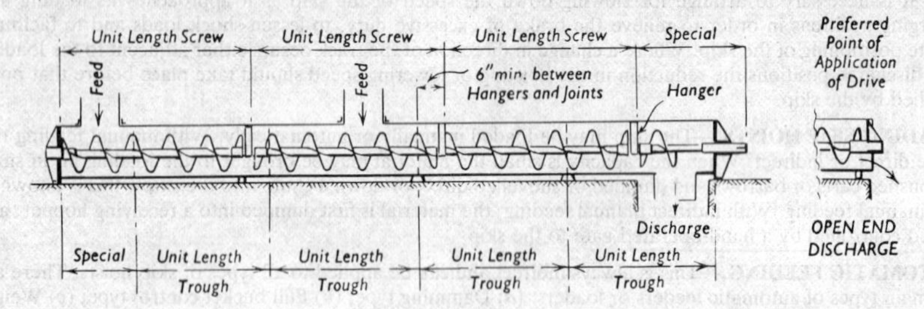

FIG. 53.—Essentials of a Screw Conveyor.

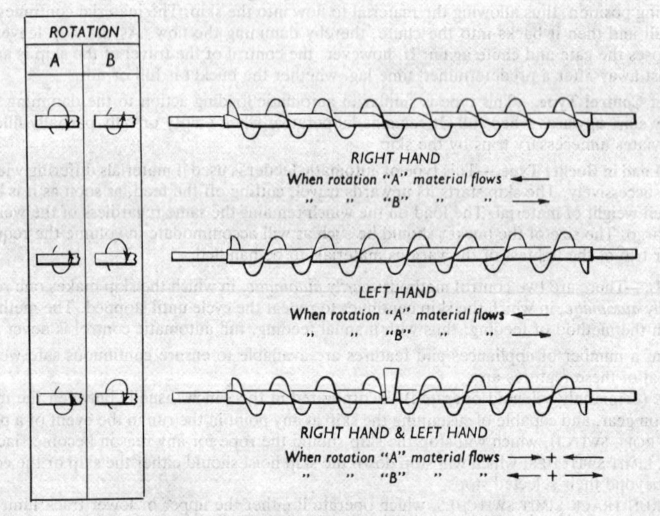

FIG. 54.—Rotation and Travel of Material.

(1) **Full-Bladed Type** (or normal single pitch flight, or Archimedean spiral) for general purpose, usually for powdery and/or abrasive materials. It consists of either a continuous spiral of individual flights, bolted or riveted together and secured to the shaft or a number of cast or forged flights mounted on and keyed or welded in sections to a solid shaft. The pitch is equal in this type to the outside diameter of the flights.

(2) **Double Flight** is used where very smooth conveying action and discharge are required, but maximum recommended lump size is less than for the equivalent diameter of single pitch flight. This flight consists of two sets of normal pitch flights mounted on the shaft to form a double screw.

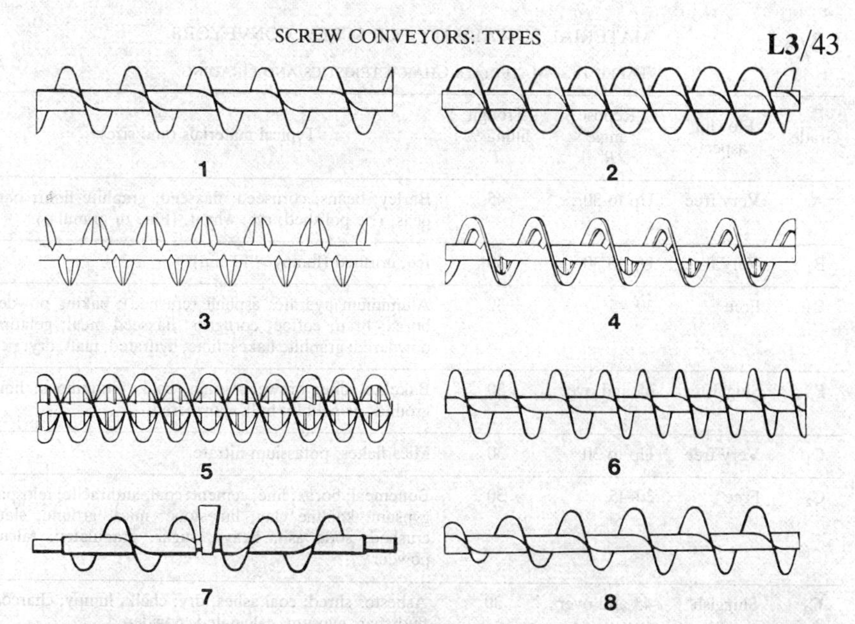

FIG. 55.—Screw Conveyor Flights. (1) Full-bladed, single pitch. (2) Full-bladed, double pitch. (3) Paddle. (4) Ribbon. (5) Double ribbon. (6) Variable pitch. (7) Double-handed. (8) Taper screw (*Ajax Fairway Engineering*).

(3) **Paddle Type** (or cut flight) recommended for conveying and mixing light, free-flowing materials. It is similar in construction to the normal single pitch flight, but with paddles or notches cut in the edges of the flight.

(4) **Cut and Folded Flight** resembles the cut flight with the exception that the material is not completely removed from the notch, but folded back to form an agitator which lifts or stirs the material to achieve a more thorough mixing action.

(5) **Ribbon Flight** is used when the material is wet or sticky, and for granular, powdery or fine material when some mixing is required. This type consists of a flat bar formed into a spiral and rigidly fixed by usually forged spokes to the shaft.

(6) **Double-Handed Screws** are right- and left-hand screws, or spirals, mounted on a common shaft, thus allowing materials to be conveyed in opposite directions simultaneously.

(7) **Variable-Pitch Screw** is used where the feed from a hopper has to be regulated, or to use a portion of the conveyor capacity for filling up from another inlet, provided further on. This type consists of screws of different pitches mounted on a common shaft.

(8) **Taper Screw** is mainly used in feeder and hopper dischargers. The progressive increase in conveying capacity avoids dead pockets in a storage bin by agitating material, usually vertically.

(9) **Mixing Paddle Types,** these are of full-bladed type or paddle type, based on the types described above in (1) and (3).

(10) **Screw Tube Conveyor,** in this type the conveying element is in the form of a ribbon helix attached to the inside of a revolving tube.

The screw units can be obtained not only in the commonly employed materials, steel and iron, but in aluminium, brass, bronze, copper, galvanised steel, monel metal, stainless steel and tinned steel for special, purpose applications.

The direction of travel of the material depends upon the hand of the flight and the direction of rotation (Fig. 54).

GRADE OF MATERIAL.—The nature of the material being handled determines the operating speed and the depth to which a screw conveyor may be loaded. Generally, free flowing materials may be loaded to greater depths and conveyed at higher speeds than abrasive materials, but in addition some materials are deliberately kept low in the troughs and away from the hangers to reduce breakage and possible discoloration. To this end materials are divided into nine grades—A to D, and care should be taken to ensure that the corresponding load rating and the maximum speed of the screw conveyor is not greater than the recommendation for the grade of the particular material being handled (see Table 18 and Fig. 56).

TABLE 18.—MATERIALS CHARACTERISTICS AND GRADING.

Grade	Flowing aspect	Repose angle $R°$	Trough filling % T	Typical materials (and size)
A	Very free	Up to 30	45	Barley; beans; cornseed; flaxseed; graphite flour; oats; peas; rice polished; rye; wheat. (Fine or granular).
B_1	Very free	Up to 30	30	Ice, crushed (lumpy > 12 mm).
B_2	Free	30–45	30	Aluminium hydrate; asphalt (crushed); baking powder; borax; bran; coffee; corngrits; flaxseed meal; gelatine, powdered; graphite flakes; lime, hydrated; malt, dry; rice.
B_3	Sluggish	45 and over	30	Bakelite, fine; brewer's grain; coal, bituminous; lime, ground, or pebble; milk, powdered.
C_1	Very free	Up to 30	30	Mica flakes; potassium nitrate.
C_2	Free	30–45	30	Bonemeal; borax, fine; cement; coal, anthracite; feldspar; gypsum; kaoline clay; limestone; mica, ground; slate, crushed; soda ash, heavy; sugar, granulated; talcum powder.
C_3	Sluggish	45 and over	30	Asbestos shred; coal ashes, dry; chalk, lumpy; charcoal; fluorspar; gypsum, calcinated, powdered.
D_2	Free	30–45	15	Alumina; bauxite, crushed; manganese sulphate; slag; granule.
D_3	Sluggish	Over 45	15	Coke breeze; steel chips, crushed.

Notes: 1) (The textures of Grades A and B are non-abrasive; of Grades C, mildly abrasive; and Grades D, are very abrasive. 2) The recommended angle of repose (R) is in degrees, 3) recommended trough filling (T)%).

TROUGHS AND HANGERS.—The troughs are normally 'U'-shaped, made of metal or wood (or a combination of both materials) in unit or special lengths. The materials commonly used are steel or cast iron, but others may be employed for special-purpose applications. The troughs are easy to enclose and make dust tight by the use of removable covers. They may be jacketed for the purpose of heating or cooling the cargo.

The hanger frame which carries the bearings in which the screw units are mounted should offer the minimum amount of obstruction to the material moving along the trough, it should be strong enough to support the weight of the screw unit, etc, and sufficiently rigid to resist both the side thrust caused by the rotation of the screw in the material and vibration. The type of material used in the bearings themselves depends upon the character of the cargo.

LUMP SIZE.—Care should be taken to ensure that the maximum size of lumps to be handled do not exceed the manufacturers' recommended limits (see Table 19).

FEED AND DISCHARGE CHUTES.—When the feed to the conveyor is comparatively uniform and free of pressure an ordinary chute may be used but care should be taken not to position the feed point above or within several feet in front of a hanger. The conveyor should have ample capacity to take the peak feed whether one or more permanent feed points are located along its length. Hand slides or rack and pinion gates are sometimes provided to enable the feed chutes to be opened or closed individually.

The discharge may be arranged at one or more points along the line of the conveyor by the use of curved or flat hand slides or rack and pinion doors, or it may be adjacent to the head end or through an open ended trough at the head end. When discharging to a hopper a section of the bottom of the trough may be omitted so that as the discharged material builds up, it forms its own trough along which the material is conveyed for a gradually increasing distance until the bunker is filled.

SCREW CONVEYOR DRIVE.—A thrust bearing should be used, particularly when the material is heavy or sticky and also when the conveyor is long. Whenever possible the thrust bearing and the conveyor drive should be located at the discharge end so that the screw shaft is in tension. Such an arrangement prevents undesirable end-play at the drive and ensures that the conveyor runs itself empty notwithstanding any coupling that may fail. If the drive is located at the feed end, the failure of an intermediate coupling may result in packing of the conveyor. Typical of the drives available are:

(1) Back geared motor flexibly coupled direct to screw shaft extension.

(2) Motor flexibly coupled to worm reduction gear which is in turn flexibly coupled to screw shaft extension.

(3) Chain drive from back geared motor to screw shaft extension.
(4) Chain or vee belt drive from motor to bevel gear unit mounted on discharge end of conveyor.

TABLE 19.—MATERIALS COMMONLY HANDLED BY SCREW CONVEYORS (W = approx density (kg/m^3); G = grade of material; K_2 = constant) (*Ewart*).

Material	W	G	K_2
Alumina	960	D_2	1·19
Aluminium hydrate	290	B_2	0·33
Asbestos shred	320–400	C_3	1·46
Ashes, coal, dry	560–640	C_3	1·46
Asphalt, crushed, <12 mm	720	B_2	0·33
Bakelite, fine	480–640	B_3	0·54
Baking powder	660	B_2	0·33
Barley	610	A	0·22
Bauxite, crushed, <75 mm	1,200–1,360	D_2	1·62
Beans, whole	580	A	0·22
Bonemeal	880–960	C_2	0·81
Borax, fine	850	B_2	0·33
Bran	255–320	B_2	0·33
Brewer's grain, spent, dry	400–480	B_3	0·54
Brewer's grain, spent, wet	880–960	B_3	0·54
Cement, Portland	1,040–1,360	C_2	0·87
Chalk, lumpy	1,360–1,440	C_3	1·46
Charcoal	290–400	C_3	1·46
Coal, anthracite	960	C_2	0·87
Coal, bituminous, mined	800	B_3	0·54
Coffee, green beans	510	B_2	0·33
Coffee, ground	400	B_2	0·33
Coke, breeze, <6 mm	400–560	D_3	1·62
Cork, fine ground	192–240	B_3	0·54
Corn, seed	720	A	0·22
Corn, grits	720	B_2	0·33
Feldspar, ground, <3 mm	1,030–1,120	C_2	0·87
Flax, seed	720	A	0·22
Flaxseed meal	400	B_2	0·33
Fluorspar	1,310	C_3	1·14
Gelatine, granulated	510	B_2	0·33
Graphite, flake	640	B_2	0·33
Graphite flour	450	A	0·22
Gypsum, calcinated <12 mm	850–960	C_2	0·87
Gypsum raw, <25 mm	1,460–1,600	C_2	1·14
Gypsum, calcinated, powder	960–1,280	C_3	1·14
Ice, crushed	560–720	B_1	0·33
Kaolin clay, <75 mm	2,610	C_2	1·14
Lime, ground, <3mm	960	B_3	0·54
Lime, hydrated, <3 mm	560–640	B_2	0·33
Lime pebble	850–900	B_3	0·81
Limestone, <3 mm	1,090	C_2	0·87
Malt, dry, ground, <3 mm	350	B_2	0·33
Malt, dry, whole	430–480	B_2	0·33
Malt, meal	580–640	B_2	0·33
Mica, ground	210–240	C_2	0·87
Mica, flakes	270–350	C_1	0·54
Milk, powdered	320	B_3	0·54
Oats	415	A	0·22
Pea, dried	720–800	A	0·22
Potassium nitrate	1,220	C_1	0·54
Rice, polished	720–770	A	0·22
Rice, rough	580	B_2	0·33
Rice grits	670–720	B_2	0·33
Rye	710	A	0·22
Sand, dry	1,440–1,760	D_2	1·19
Slag, furnace, granulated	960–1,040	D_2	1·19
Slate, crushed, <12 mm	1,280–1,440	C_2	0·87
Soda ash, heavy	880–1,040	C_2	0·87
Soda, ash, dry	320–560	C_2	0·87
Steel, chips, crushed	1,600–2,400	D_3	2·16
Sugar, granulated	800–880	C_2	0·87
Talcum powder	640–960	C_2	0·87
Wheat	720–770	A	0·33

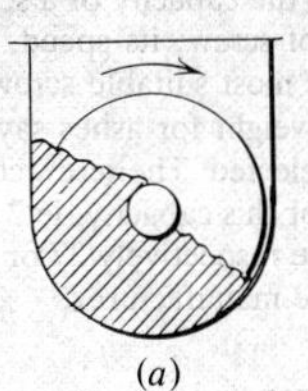

(*a*)

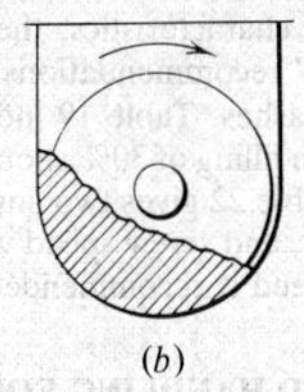

(*b*)

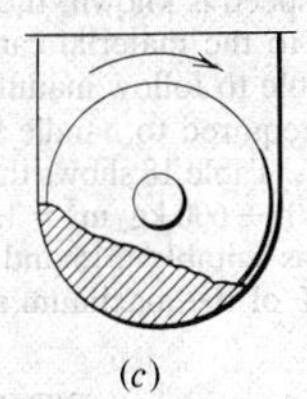

(*c*)

FIG. 56.—Loading of Screw Conveyors. (*a*) 45° Loading Grade 'A' Materials. (*b*) 30° Loading Grades 'B' and 'C' Materials. (*c*) Loading Grade 'D' Materials.

SCREW SPEEDS AND MATERIALS CHARACTERISTICS.—Table 22 gives the percentage of the maximum recommended screw speed for selected typical capacities and belt widths for the four grades of materials. Table 18 contains ranges of materials classified in grades A to D (with sub-divisions), and gives: coarseness (abrasiveness); flowing aspect; type (size); and recommended angle of repose. Table 19 lists typical materials, together with their density (kg/m^3); grade; and a constant which is a factor applying to a particular type of material when calculating the power required.

POWER CALCULATION FOR SCREW CONVEYORS.—For a standard conveyor, working on the level, under normal conditions, the power required at the drive is obtained from the formula (based on *Ewart* data):

$$P = CL(K_1 + WK_2)/10^5$$

where P is in kW; C = capacity required (m^3/h); L = length of conveyor (m); W = density of material (kg/m^3); K_1 = constant (see Table 20); and K_2 = constant (see Table 19).

TABLE 20.—VALUES OF CONSTANT K_1: FOR POWER CALCULATION FORMULA (*Ewart*).

Grade of material	Diameter of screw (mm)				
	160	200	250	315	400
A	121	78	52	44	35
B	190	113	78	60	52
C	450	277	190	155	130
D	900	560	390	310	260

When selecting the motor, allowance should be made for losses in the driving unit and momentary overloads; this is of particular importance in the small power range. The manufacturer should be consulted when a worm reduction gear is used.

TABLE 21.—CAPACITIES OF SCREW CONVEYORS. (At a maximum recommended speed, with normal pitch screws) (*Ewart*).

Dia of screw (mm)	Maximum lump size (mm)	Capacities (m^3/h) at 1 rev/min		
		Material Group 'A'	Material Groups 'B' and 'C'	Material Group 'D'
160	20	0·074	0·049	0·025
200	25	0·154	0·103	0·051
250	45	0·300	0·200	0·100
315	50	0·624	0·416	0·208
400	75	1·270	0·846	0·423

CAPACITY OF SCREW CONVEYORS.—Table 21 gives approximate capacities (in m^3/h), for a range of conveyor sizes and groups of materials listed in Table 18 at a unit speed of 1 rev/min. Thus, the approximate capacity for any given speed may be found by multiplying the unit capacity indicated in the Table by the value of the relevant speed. For example, to handle 9 m^3/h or Bran (which is grade B_2, and free flowing), a 160 mm diameter screw would require a speed of 183 rev/min (9 m^3/h ÷ 0·049 = 183·67); this speed is too high. A 200 mm diameter screw would give the required capacity with a speed of 90 rev/min (9 ÷ 0·103 = 87·38). Conversely, if the speed is known, the capacity can be found. *Note.*—As the capacity of a screw conveyor or elevator is related to the material carried, its characteristics, the type of screw, its speed, and the feeding system, it is advisable to follow manufacturers' recommendations for the most suitable screw conveyor.

Example.—It is required to handle 9 t/h of ashes. Table 19 indicates weight for ashes say 600 kg/m^3 and grade of material C_3. Table 18 shows that trough filling of 30% should be selected. The screw conveyor capacity should be 9,000 kg/h ÷ 600 kg/m^3 = 15 m^3. Table 22 gives two answers for this capacity, ie 2 screw diameters are recommended as suitable: 315 and 400 mm, and screw speed would be respectively 37 or 17 rev/min, and resp. 80% and 40% of the maximum screw speed is recommended by the manufacturer.

OTHER LOAD HANDLING EQUIPMENT

LIFTING TABLES.—These are useful when regular lifting or lowering is required of unit loads such as boxes, trays, heavy tools, etc. Standard lifting tables are usually of the scissor type, and lever operated, using

TABLE 22.—PERCENTAGE OF MAXIMUM RECOMMENDED SCREW SPEED. (*Ewart*).

Grade	Capacity m³/h	For which are suitable: Screw dia (mm)	At screw speed rev/min	% of max recom screw speed	Grade	Capacity m³/h	For which are suitable: Screw dia (mm)	At screw speed rev/min	% of max recom screw speed
A	20	250	65	50	C	5	200	48	90
	30	250	100	77		.5	250	25	50
	40	250	130	96		10	315	24	55
	40	315	64	55		15	315	37	80
	50	315	80	70		15	400	17	40
	60	315	95	82		20	400	23	60
	80	400	62	62		30	400	36	85
	100	400	80	80					
B	10	200	90	90	D	2½	200	48	80
	10	250	48	50		2½	315	12	25
	20	315	48	60		5	250	50	98
	30	315	74	85		5	315	24	50
	30	400	38	50		10	400	27	57
	40	400	48	60		15	400	38	88
	50	400	60	80					
	60	400	70	93					

hand- or foot-operated hydraulic or electro-hydraulic jacks often with roller or ball conveyor tops. Hydraulic scissor lifts are useful for cargo lifting or as dock levellers at wagon loading bays, also at airports, warehouses, etc to transfer loads between split work levels. Lifting height may reach 3 m; platform sizes up to 2·5 × 4·3 m; and loads of 30 t can be accommodated (Fig. 57). Another type can lift 50 t to a height of 6 m at a speed of 5 m/min. Safety devices such as 'dead man's' hand operated button etc. are available.

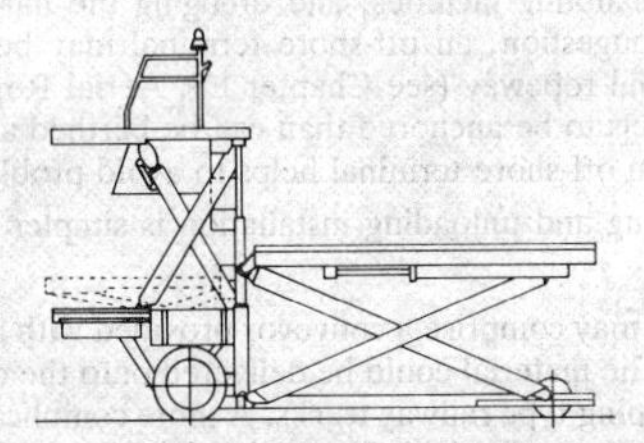

FIG. 57.—Combined Lifting Table, Travelling type (*APL-Atel Products*).

STAIR-CLIMBERS.—There are several models of these mechanised devices designed to moving packages (weighing up to 1,500 kg) and persons along stairs at a speed of 1·3 m/min, but up to 8 m/min for smaller loads. Such an installation is particularly valuable for disabled persons where no vertical lifts are available. A typical device consists of an electro-hydraulic self-levelling platform, provided with stabilizers and safety equipment (*Stair-Robots/Handling Equipment*, and others).

BUCKET-WHEEL RECLAIMERS.—Also called bucket-wheel excavator or rotary excavator, is another combined mechanical handling machine used not only for excavation in open-pit mining and highway construction, but also for stacking out and reclaiming of bulk materials in ship-loading and unloading, etc. Such installations usually comprise conveyors, hoppers, trippers in addition to wheel-reclaimers, stackers, etc. A bucket-wheel reclaimer may be mounted on a walking device or crawlers, or move on rails. The reclaiming operation is generally achieved by buckets spaced equally on the rim of a rotating wheel. Buckets are provided with steel teeth or lips. For certain materials the bucket back is formed by chains, some designs include shaking devices or means to prevent clogging or sticky materials. The number of buckets ranges from 6 to 18, the cutting speed at the lip may be from 60 to 240 m/min, and even more.

A few examples of typical installations: (1) Bucket-wheel excavator designed to excavate up to 240,000 m³/day of material; wheel diameter is 21·6 m, the conveyor belt is 3200 mm wide (*Krupp/Orenstein & Koppel*). (2) Machine equipped with a 500 mm wide conveyor belt working at a speed of 1 m/s. (*Voest Alpine, Austria*). (3) Reclaimer having a capacity of 3,000 t/h, maximum rate up to 2,000 m³/h, equipped with up to 8 buckets, belt speed is 4 m/s, belt width 1,200 mm (*REI*). (4) Excavator designed for a capacity of 16,000 m^3/h, wheel diameter 21·6 m, up to 18 buckets, each having a volume of 6·32 m^3. (*Krupp Industrietechnik*, Fig. 58). (5) Rail-mounted bucket-wheel with a stacking capacity of 3,000 t/h and reclaiming 1,500 t/h, having a 35 m long boom (*Fives-Cail Babcock*). (6) Bucket-wheel removing 6 m cuts of clay overburden and transferring to a conveyor, each section of the conveyor being directed to the new position by automatic sensors without further command. (*Rahco*). (7) Machine having a capacity of 9,000–12,000 t/h, wheel diameter up to 8 m; 10 buckets, belt speed 3·3 m/s, boom length 50 m. (*PHB, West Germany*.).

FIG. 58.—Bucket Wheel Excavator in Open Cast Mine (*Krupp-Industrietechnik*).

SHIP-LOADERS AND UNLOADERS

These installations are mostly custom built to satisfy local requirements and consist of conveyors of various types and other classic components. The development of mechanised ship-loaders and unloaders is due to the advantages of saving the operating time, reducing labour and the often recurring delays involving penalties. To these economic reasons should be added: scarcity of space at the dockside of existing ports, the cost of extending them, improving their handling facilities, and dredging the harbours. To solve the problems of shortage of space and dockside congestion, an off-shore terminal may be constructed connected with the mainland by a conveyor or an aerial ropeway (see Chapter L5; Aerial Ropeways and Cableways). Such an arrangement allows for larger vessels to be anchored than can be berthed at the dockside where the water is often too shallow. In some cases an off-shore terminal helps to avoid problems caused by tidal conditions.

The construction of a ship-loading and unloading installation is simpler if the duty is limited to one-way handling only.

SHIP-LOADERS.—A small unit may comprise a conveyor provided with a cantilever boom which loads the material direct into a ship's hold. The material could be delivered onto the conveyor from a hopper which, in turn, could be filled by lorries or tipping-type railway trucks. A more complicated plant may include a travelling loader running on rails along the jetty or the dockside; such a loader could be fed by a conveyor into which the material is loaded by a drag-scraper (eg, the installation at Takoradi, Ghana, *BRECO*). Other examples: a conveyor combined with a ship-loader, having a capacity 2,500 t/h (Fig. 59) constructed by *BRECO* at Sierra Menera, Spain; a plant capacity 2,200 t/h loading manganese ore at Pointe-Noire, Congo (*REI/COMILOG*); a 153 m long ship-loader having a capacity 11,000 t/h (*Fives-Cail Babcock & ASEA*); *ASEA* apply their *SINDAC* computer-based system for monitoring and controlling ship-loading operations and material handling.

The ship-loaders at Tees Dock (*BRECO*), loading 1,000 t/h of potash, is another good example of these installations. It includes a conveyor with a working speed of 140 m/min, equipped with belts 1,200 mm wide; the return idlers are of the rubber disc type; a portal-type ship-loader transfers potash from the travelling tripper to the ship's hold by a shuttle boom-conveyor which runs through a fixed boom gantry; at the seaward end of the shuttle conveyor a chute transfers the material from the boom to a circular telescopic chute. This loader is capable of working in winds of up to 50 km/h. The machine is mounted on a set of 4 bogies, each comprising a 4-wheeled articulated unit, two of which are driving units. A set of scissor-type rail clamps, mounted on the underside of each bogie, embrace the head of the track rails; they are operated by a toggle mechanism, this allows the ship-loader to travel along the rails as required.

Among other projects are (1) The coal export terminal at Jarrow Slake (Port of Tyne, UK) including an installation composed of rail-unloader, conveyors, stackers, reclaimers and a ship-loader handling up to 2,800 t/h. It is controlled and monitored automatically by Brown-Boveri equipment. The plant has transducers to monitor operation and fault conditions of the drives and conveyors, a central programmable logic controller for automatic and sequence control of the plant, with visual display screen and printer, and a closed circuit television system to monitor critical plant areas. (2) Ships of up to 15,000 dwt could be loaded more rapidly at

FIG. 59.—Conveyor and Ship-loading Plant at Sierra Menerva, Spain; (*BRECO*).

the Forth Ports Authority's installation (*Fyson*) using two mobile ship-loaders with 30 m long conveyors each of which can deliver 600 t/h of materials into ships. Each ship loader is provided with two integral feeder conveyors with low back hoppers, enabling two lorries to discharge into each conveyor simultaneously at road level, without the need for ramps or pits thus sharply reducing lorry turn-round time and increasing loading speed. Telescopic chutes at the head of the conveyors are fitted with rotary thrower heads with variable speeds for controlling material trajectory.

SHIP UNLOADERS.—A few typical examples. (1) A slewing-grab type portal machine with a span of 28 m and a grab lifting up to 16 t weight single items, was constructed by *PHB*. (2) A conveyor (*'Cewell'*, *Scholtz*) equipped with one single endless belt (*'Flexowell'*) installed amidship, is fed by 3 longitudinal troughed conveyors installed transversely; the material is then discharged into a hopper for transferring from the ship on a boom conveyor. This plant is able to elevate 10,000 m^3/h up a 30 m lift (Fig. 61). (3) A ship self-unloading

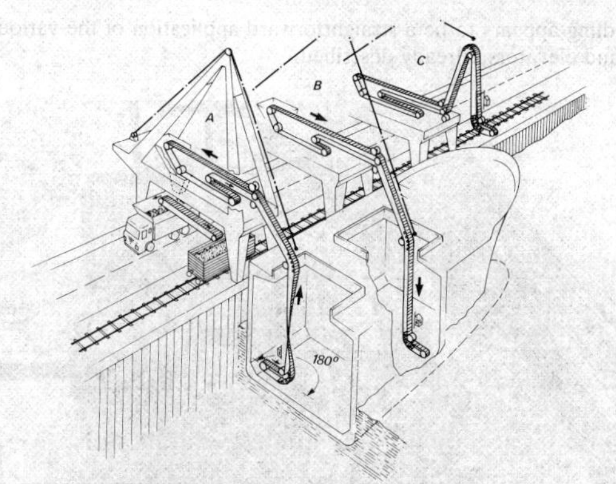

FIG. 60.—Ship-loading and unloading 'Flexoturn' System. Single 'Flexowell' belt in 3 positions; (A) Unloading operation; (B) Loading operation; (C) Stowed position (*Scholtz*).

installation (*Scholtz*) consists of 2 reclaiming tunnels, each provided with one belt conveyor and a plough, arranged in the ship's hold. The bulk material is reclaimed by wide-span ploughs which, between them, cover the entire area of the hold; the material is delivered to the conveyor belts (*Flexowell*) which run in the double bottom of the hold the full length of the ship. The material is delivered by these conveyors to the elevators, via lifting wheels to the transverse feeder-conveyor belts. It then is transferred to the vertical conveyor, and removed from the ship into a hopper and a boom conveyor.

PNEUMATIC SHIP-UNLOADERS.—The application of pneumatic machines for unloading granular materials from ships has advantages of speed of operation, avoidance of dust and loss of material by spreading,

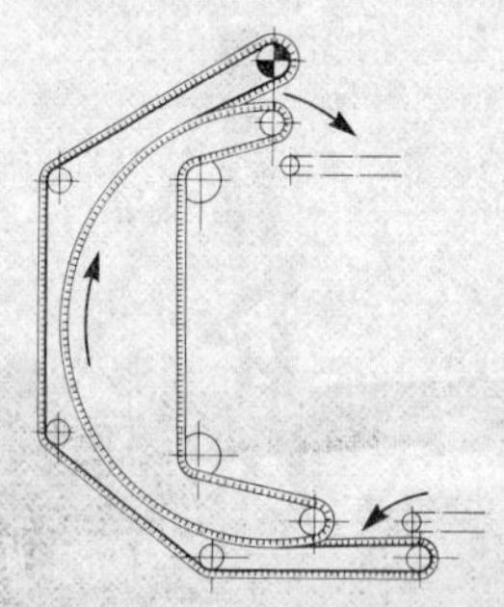

FIG. 61.—Ship-loading and Unloading 'Cewell' Conveyor based on Flexowell principle (*Scholtz*).

etc. One or more machines can be used, each fitted with a multiple suction leg. Capacities exceeding 600 t/h are possible.

SHIP-LOADERS/UNLOADERS.—Systems designed for both loading and unloading materials are also available. One such installation, developed by *Scholtz*, using their *Flexowell* belt, is shown in three positions (Fig. 60), (A) unloading operation, (B) loading operation, and (C) stowed position. In the stowed position the ship can dock or depart from the quay without difficulty. During unloading the bulk material is scooped up by the collecting device (bucket wheel or scooping rollers), the belt is then loaded at the transverse frame and the material arrives at the pulley on the gantry, and is discharged into a hopper. Capacities of up to 5,000 t/h are possible.

BARGE-LOADERS/UNLOADERS.—This is another method of coal unloading from a barge using a bucket-wheel unloader with a capacity which may exceed 1,000 t/h, rotary stacker units, bucket-wheel reclaimers, and a system of conveyors and chutes (eg, the installation supplied by *Koch* to Vitry power station Paris). Another installation was constructed for the Porcheville power plant. Higher capacities are possible, eg, at Dunkerque harbour, which consists of a feeding installation handling 6,600 t/h of iron ore, reclaiming, and loading 2,200 t/h of iron ore or 1,700 t/h of coal into railway trucks (*Koch*).

AIRPORT LUGGAGE HANDLING

Airport luggage handling appears to be a straightforward application of the various types of standard belt and roller conveyors, and elevators, already described.

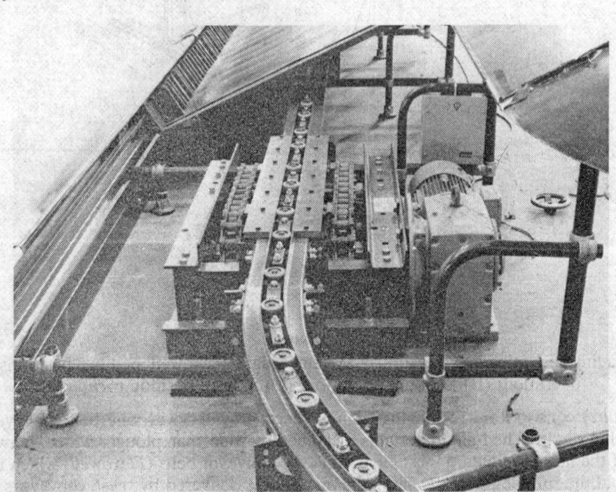

FIG. 62.—Airport Luggage Conveyor showing Mechanism Under Conveyor (*Fenamec*).

A well designed comprehensive installation of luggage handling systems is, however, a major factor in ensuring safe, efficient, reliable and prompt operation of the service (Fig. 62). Since uninterrupted (as far as possible) continuity of operation, is of paramount importance all conveyors should be designed so that they can be stopped and started when fully loaded. As the stoppage of an airport handling system due to component breakdown may have far-reaching consequences, suitable preventive measures should be taken at the design stage. The noise level must be considered at the design stage also; it is important to ensure that noise is kept to an absolute minimum. The noise level target in *Fenamec* designed installations is 65 dB.

The development and expansion of existing airports underlines the value of a modular construction of various components, as far as possible.

Designers should also keep in mind (1) great variety of sizes and shapes of various pieces handled as luggage, (2) materials these items are made of, and (3) all types of handles, straps and labels attached, which risk being trapped or torn from the luggage during its travel along conveying systems.

The handling operation is obviously different (A) at the luggage departure input end, and (B) at the luggage arrivals/reclaiming end. There is also (C) gate-room checking system.

(A) At the check-in desk the luggage is placed on a short weighing conveyor (often equipped with a load-cell); the luggage is moved backwards by means of a take-away conveyor, ie, a transverse, low-level belt conveyor and then transferred over a plate-type junction onto a longitudinal sorting conveyor. The sorting is not easy, because the bags from all the above-mentioned transverse conveyors are moved onto one common longitudinal conveyor, on which all the bags are mixed up regardless of destination. There is usually more than one check-in desk each with its own transverse conveyor (eg, 92 check-in desks at London Heathrow Terminal 3). Sorting is carried out by hand: reading the destination label on each item, although mechanical methods may help in this operation. The luggage is then directed to the 'air-side' conveyor.

One method introduced to speed up package sorting is the voice-operated conveyor control (*EMI Threshold*; *Westinghouse*). A mini-computer terminal, able to interpret spoken orders, is linked to a carousel tilt tray sorting conveyor. As packages pass the sorting position, their destination code is spoken into a microphone which activates the tilt tray at the required destination spur.

(B) At the reclaiming end, the incoming luggage is transferred from the aircraft onto conveyors bringing it to inclined reclaim conveyors in the passenger arrival hall. There are several types of reclaim conveyors. A tilted conveyor (forming a part of the *Fenamec* installation at Heathrow airport) is loaded automatically with baggage by the air-side conveyors arranged outside the hall which form a continuous circuit, this tilted conveyor transports the baggage on moving overlapped flexible slats and presents it to the passengers for reclaim. An electrically controlled system incorporates a merge control to avoid baggage colliding at the air-side in-feed, and to prevent baggage jamming in wall openings.

To enhance the operational performance and increase the efficiency of any conveyor installation, *Fenamec* and others have designed and constructed a wide range of system controls, including electromagnetic devices, solid-state logic, and fully programmable systems.

(C) The gate-room checking system is characterised by baggage spiral chutes, allowing for speedy last minute luggage dispatch.

Airport handling installations are more expensive than industrial conveying systems, as prominence is given to aesthetics, speed of maintenance, etc.

AUTOMATIC MAIL HANDLING

The Post Office handling of mail (letters, packets and bags) is an example of computerised mechanised handling of materials. It is a specialised application and two examples are given below.

The South West District Post Office at Nine Elms, inaugurated in December 1983, is the first example. The installation fulfils four functions: (1) through mails systems, conveying bags of mail; (2) packets system, conveying loose packets; (3) empty bag system and (4) despatch system, carrying bags of sorted mail. In five peak hours each evening 45,000 items are sorted for overnight despatch and delivery throughout the country early next morning. Operation is as follows.

Full bags of 'through mail' are unloaded from Post Office vans at the arrivals platform and loaded onto a belt-on-roller elevating conveyor (fitted with a 5 mm thick solid woven cotton belt). This feeds a right-angled bend and shute, delivering bags to a high level horizontal conveyor which may be run in the 'transfer' or 'store' mode. The 'transfer' mode is fitted with a delay stop facility which allows the transfer of mail from the in-feed point to the discharge shute before the system is stopped. In the 'store' mode mail is accumulated on the high level horizontal conveyor. Blockage detectors are in operation on shutes on the mail bag system and mail level detection is indicated through illuminated or flashing beacons. At the end of the high level conveyor mail bags are discharged down a shute to floor level where they are opened, loaded into skips and taken to sorters. Sorted mail in bags is then placed onto floor level belt conveyors and transported to the despatch platform for loading into vans.

This system handles up to 500 mail bags per hour, weighing between 2 and 20 kilogrammes each. The packet system is separate and can handle up to 12,000 loose packets per hour. This Post Office has an average traffic of 1,700,000 stamped letters, about 1,800,000 metered letters and about 642,000 packets (Fenamec).

The Stockholm Post Office, which handles up to two million letters and 90,000 packets per day, employs sorting operations on three levels, involving the use of highly sophisticated systems (AGV/Tellus, Digitron/ Schindler).

AUTOMATIC-SORTING.—One typical installation sorts parcels weighing up to 50 kg or bulk materials (1) direct into bags or containers and/or (2) into stepped chute, and/or (3) via a brake-hand to an accumulator roller conveyor, and/or (4) direct to a belt conveyor with or without chutes, and/or (5) to an accumulation roller conveyor with rollers mounted in herringbone pattern, and/or (6) sorting to the last destination where all slats are tilted. Five thousand parcels per hour can be sorted at a slat conveyor speed of 1.1 m/s. Encoding may be by voice, keyboard terminal, optical recognition (of codes or typewriter characters) or a micro-computer data terminal (Kosan Crisplant/American Chain and Cable Co.).

HYDRAULICS IN MATERIALS HANDLING

Hydraulics contributes to materials handling in 3 ways: Conveyance through pipes; Driving power for various types of equipment used in Direct, or Indirect applications; and Loadcells.

PIPELINE CONVEYANCE.—This method of materials conveying employs a liquid carrying medium, (eg, water). The systems available differ in details, but are based on the same principle. All of them provide a continuous, or almost so, flow of materials suitable for such transport. It is claimed, that a 20 cm diameter pipeline has a greater capacity than a twin-track railway with 20 trains a day. (Paper presented to CME by M. L. Barker). Pipelines laid underground save ground-level space; capsule-carriers may be supported on wheels to reduce friction losses of sliding contact inside a pipe. The slurry pipeline is another example of hydraulic conveyance. The solids to be handled must be of suitable type to be processed, ie by grinding, then made into slurry, pumped through the pipe itself, and, at the end of the journey, recovered. The problems involved are, of course, quite different from those met in conveyor belt transport: pipe diameter, flow velocity, particle size and distribution, solids concentration, the relation between the material carried and the fluid carrier, etc must be considered and investigated. The cost of a length of pipe is proportional to its diameter (D), whereas its carrying capacity is proportional to $D^{2\cdot5}$; doubling the diameter, therefore, reduces the handling cost to 0·35 times its former cost per unit of carrying capacity.

The formulae needed for the calculations will be found in textbooks and manufacturers' literature.

A typical example: The Black Mesa pipeline connecting a Peabody coal mine in Arizona, USA, and the Mohave generating station in Nevada, 439 km away. The line has a capacity of 4·5 million t/year of coal slurry. The pipeline is divided into 4 sections: 132, 68, 85 and 154 km long. Flow speed is 1·7 m/s (See paper by M. Swiss published in the CME February, 1981.)

HYDRAULIC POWER.—Hydraulic power is used in materials handling equipment usually for lifting but also for gripping, rotating and in situations where large forces have to be exerted with precision of positioning. (See description of conveyors, lift trucks elevators, etc.)

LOADCELLS

(*a*) **Floatpads.**—These are used for moving heavy loads over short distances by means of placing the loads on the floatpad, which has a pressurised grease bearing system to reduce the friction on its under-side. For example, two loads of 5,000 t were moved 35 m at a dockyard. Floatpads offer the advantage of being easily movable from one operation to another. Frictional resistance is minimal; when the pad is operated on a suitable steel surface, the coefficient of friction can be as low as 0·0005; other types of surface can result in coefficients of friction up to 0·01.

The floatpad consists of a steel housing faced with a layer of elastomer on the underside. This elastomer, say 6 mm thick neoprene, is vulcanised to the steel housing. Grease under high pressure is pumped through internal galleries in the housing and flows out through a pattern of feed orifices set in the elastomer face. A load-bearing grease film is formed between the elastomer and the rigid bearing surface. The elastomer dishes slightly under the pressure of the grease and a partial seal is formed around the bearing periphery, thus restricting the outflow of grease. The load capacity of a floatpad depends on: (1) the pad area; (2) the fluid supply pressure; and (3) the characteristics of the elastomer layer (*Standale Engineering*).

(*b*) **Water Skate.**—This presents the water cushion concept in load movement. The skate works on the principle of a semi-trapped volume of water under pressure contained by a compliant seal (skirt) which, due to the depth of skirt enables the 'work piece' to be jacked free of the ground and then be towed or winched by conventional means. The residual friction coefficient in the system at this stage is approximately 3% of the all-up weight on a flat and level surface, a pump being required to supply water at the equivalent of the leak of water from between the skirt and the ground surface. Changes from these basic data take place, however, and depend on the exact type of terrain and surface irregularities or slopes. The skate modules are designed to be either incorporated in, or placed beneath, structures at the build stage or shortly prior to movement. The correct number of skates should be used to suit the loading and operational conditions. Pressure can be varied from module to module, thus giving the user the ability to suit his loading conditions. Existing units allow lift up to 100 t, but a multi-modular system to suit individual requirements is possible.

PNEUMATICS IN MATERIALS HANDLING

PIPELINE CONVEYANCE.—This method is gaining popularity for its ease of handling free-running materials from bulk solids (eg, coal) to powdery materials (eg, flour). Installations fall into 2 groups: pneumatic conveyors, and pneumatic capsules. Pneumatic conveyors may have capacities of up to 500 t/h, or even more, and lengths up to 3 km, according to conditions and types. Pneumatic capsule pipelines have capacities of up to 200 t/h, but higher are possible; some are designed for handling wheeled capsules.

Generally speaking, pneumatic conveyors are of 4 systems: (1) Negative pressure vacuum system in which materials may be drawn into the pipe at several points (eg, solid wastes); (2) Positive pressure system (drawing from one point), (*a*) Dense phase (eg, sand), and (*b*) Dilute or Lean phase (eg, beans, seeds, cement, gravel); (3) Combined pressure push–pull system (ie, combination of the two previously mentioned), and (4) Closed circuit (eg, for explosives). According to type, the pipeline diameter may reach 2,000 mm (for systems with wheeled capsules), but no more than 900 mm or so for other systems.

Air-lift is a type of pneumatic conveyor having a smaller capacity (up to 200 t/h). Air-activated gravity conveyors (AAGC) have capacities of up to 2,500 t/h and are used for shorter distances (up to 0·5 km); material is transported in them either by gravity force, or using fluidisation, thus decreasing friction between the material carried and pipe walls.

Formulae giving the speed of the conveying air stream, air consumption, etc, may be found in manufacturers' literature or texts.

There are particular systems of pneumatic conveyance, using screw-feeders, bucket elevators, vibratory and/or 'en masse conveyors', with accessories as required: blowers, feeders–precipitators, etc.

Typical systems.—Denseveyor (developed by *Macawber Engineering*) is characterised by (1) dome valves (used to seal off controlled amount of incoming material from the hopper) and (2) a series of control valves and pressure monitoring devices for precise measuring and control of material levels and air flow. This installation consists basically of a pressure vessel, mild-steel pipework and a receiving hopper controlled by level switches. (See paper by B. Snowdon, CME July, 1980.) Examples of Denseveyor installations include (*i*) Iron oxide (used by foundries) conveyed at 10 t/h across 38 m from three 20 t feed hoppers to reception hopper 9·1 m above ground level, enabling it to be gravity-fed into tankers for transfer to customers. (*ii*) Activated carbon (a fine dense material, produced from peat) carried from a 700 kg surge hopper via a 100 mm inside-diameter pipeline, to a reception hopper.

Pneumatic installations, using capsules, are not new. One was built in Hamburg in 1967. It uses capsules 1·6 m long and having a 460 mm diameter, has an operating speed of 10 m/sec and carries up to one million letters per day.

PNEUMATIC MATERIALS HANDLING.—Pneumatics is used extensively in materials handling installations, in a variety of ways. There are (*a*) direct applications (conveyors, overhead chain conveyors, air-supported belt conveyors', 'Aerobelts', etc) using compressed air and (*b*) indirect applications (air-cylinders for push–pull motions and for linear motors, lifting beams, etc).

VACUUM HANDLING SYSTEMS.—One of these devices, based on the Bertin air cushion, consists of upper and lower air chambers; the upper chamber acts as a pneumatic suspension unit; the lower 'bell-shaped' chamber inflates to form the 'air cushion' itself, thus giving the ability to 'hover'. Capacity of these Air Skates is from 0·3 to 60 t. Suction pads, designed to equip handling mechanisms, have lifting power from 0·1 to 500 kg (*Condor*).

INDUSTRIAL TRUCKS

The equipment described in this section covers a wide field. Each type of truck is designed for a specific duty, eg for lifting; short distance transporting; stacking unit loads, etc. It is obviously advisable to study manufacturers' catalogues and machine characteristics.

Comparison of similar models should be made on a similar basis; for example, the capacity of a counter-balanced truck is usually established on the basis of an arbitrarily fixed load centre at a specific distance from the face of the forks; thus a truck with a 2,000 kg capacity at a 500 mm load centre is designed to carry a 2 t load so long as the centre of gravity of the load is no further than 500 mm away from the back of the forks (*Hyster*). Once the truck capacity is established on a basis equal to others being analysed, other specifications can be compared, taking then into account truck length, turning radius, speed, lifting/lowering, loaded/empty, on level/on gradient, and other factors, such as the power source to be adopted. While electric batteries do not emit smoke, an advantage in food plants or in confined, poorly ventilated areas, they require a costly battery charger and their weight has to be considered. Trucks powered by internal combustion engines are usually preferred when large trucks (say, about 5 t capacity) are required. Tyres must be considered. Pneumatic tyres are usually recommended for large trucks (say, about 7 t capacity) and for rough surface. Solid cushion tyres are used mostly for indoors working. Overall extended height, maximum fork height (so called 'top of fork'), overall lowering height, etc, are other factors to be taken into account. While the above considerations are meant for lift trucks, a similar line of approach should be used for other types of trucks.

Other aspects to be kept in mind are: weight of the whole machine, tilt range (where applicable), braking system, safety devices (eg, safe load indicator), hydraulic/pneumatic equipment (eg, hydrostatic steering), remote control, automation/programming/computer, solid-state systems, machine dimensions (track and overall width, height of mast in fully-lowered and fully-raised positions, minimum aisle width, wheel base, fork spacing maximum/minimum, etc), safety guards (eg, ensuring that, according to case, a 2 t load dropped from a height of 1·5 m would not harm anybody), reduction of noise. If a truck is driver-operated then his comfort, seat type and position, safety, visibility, etc, should be considered together with general safety. Unitary (modular) construction is often useful when bigger units of certain machines are considered, so that major components can be individually mounted, removed and replaced.

It should be noted that some manufacturers use their own terminology.

Classification.—'Truck Terminology' published by F.E.M. (Federation Europeenne de Manutention) classifies industrial trucks as follows: (1) Fork-lift trucks, (2) Pallet trucks, (3) Power trucks, (4) Elevating platform trucks, (5) Tractors and special trucks, (6) Straddle carriers, (7) Platform stackers, (8) Pallet stackers, (9) Miscellaneous power units, and (10) Hand trucks.—See also BS 3810 'Glossary of Terms Used in Materials Handling', Part 1.

The trucks described below are divided into three groups: (*a*) trucks for horizontal handling. (*b*) trucks for horizontal and vertical handling, and (*c*) trucks for vertical handling. Most of them are powered, hand operation limiting the value and range of functions; some trucks may be rider and/or pedestrian operated.

TRUCKS FOR HORIZONTAL HANDLING

FIXED-PLATFORM TRUCK.—This is usually a mechanical vehicle with a load-carrying platform permanently fixed to the front or rear. They can be 3- or 4-wheeled; powered by petrol, diesel, or electric battery; have front or rear drive or be pedestrian controlled; and have solid or pneumatic tyres. Some platform trucks are used for towing; many special attachments are available.

Figure 63 shows examples of fixed platform trucks: (*a*) Typical of the up to 4 t capacity general use range of fixed-platform trucks in which the low body facilitates loading. (*b*) Typical of general-purpose fixed-platform trucks with load capacities up to 5 t. According to design the driver sits or stands. (*c*) Having a high degree of manoeuvrability and capable of handling loads up to 3 t this typical pedestrian controlled fixed-platform truck is most useful in confined places. Available also with elevating platforms. (*d*) Powered dumper/tipping truck. (*e*) Crane truck.

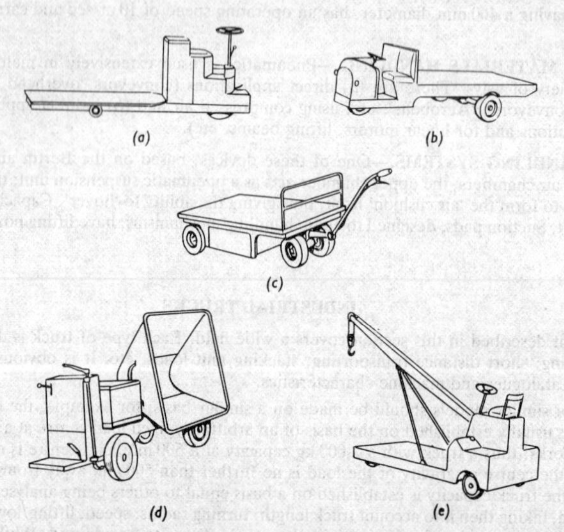

FIG. 63.—Typical Fixed Platform Trucks.

ELEVATING PLATFORM TRUCK.—This is a development of the fixed platform unit. It enables stillages to be handled and, where capable of high lifts, is useful when commodities require to be loaded or off-loading at different levels. They may be power-driven or manually pulled. When handling stillages the elevating truck is driven or pushed below the stillage, the platform is then raised mechanically or automatically (by hydraulic or electric power) until the stillage legs are a few inches clear of the floor. The truck may then be driven or pulled away complete with stillage. The range of power-driven trucks is similar in respect to availability or power units, drives, tyres, etc, as fixed platform trucks.

There are two types of these trucks: (1) low-lift (or stillage) platform trucks (not suitable for pallets), raising the load just clear of the ground, and (2) high-lift platform trucks.

Fig. 64 shows examples of elevating trucks:

(*a*) For capacity up to 5 t and lifts up to 10 cm, this elevating truck is typical of the wide variety of mechanical single- or multi-stroke hand lift units for handling stillages.

(*b*) A typical hydraulically operated hand-lift platform truck for operation with or without stillage up to 2 t capacity. There are also platformless designs with foot pedal jacking capable of capacities up to 5 t.

(*c*) Typical of petrol or electric elevating platform trucks suitable for operation with low clearance stillages. Load capacities up to 4 t.

(*d*) Typical of the range of petrol or electric elevating platform trucks built with the loading deck up to 50 cm from the ground when in the lowered position and lifting 10 cm. Load capacities up to 4 t.

(*e*) In situations where the commodities must be loaded or off-loaded at different levels the high-lift elevating platform truck is useful. Petrol or electric trucks are available capable of lifting 5 t up to 2 m. Lifting operation may be performed mechanically or hydraulically.

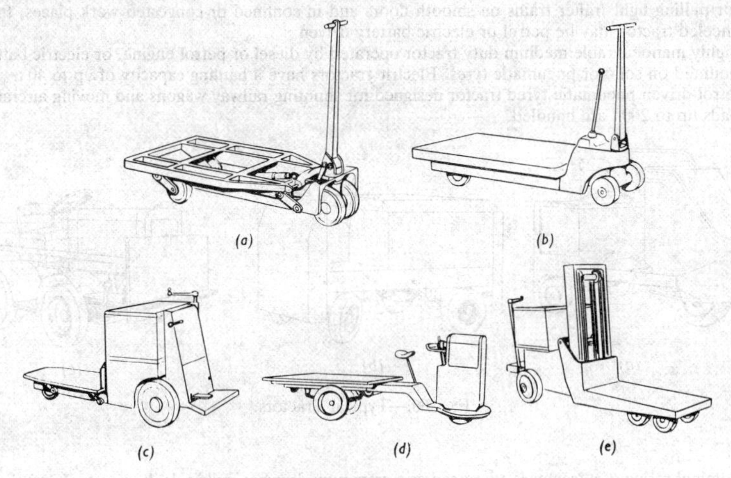

FIG. 64.—Typical Elevating Platform Trucks.

DRIVERLESS TRUCK.—Automatically controlled should be mentioned here. It is capable of carrying loads or towing trailers. Sensing elements fitted to the vehicle detect signals from control wire embedded in, or deflecting tapes or painted lines on the floor or road surface over which it operates. Routes and destinations may be preselected. These trucks may be remote controlled by radio.

PALLET TRUCK.—The forks may have extension sleeves which are inserted below the pallet. Pallet trucks of straddle design also called transporter trucks; have several uses in connection with the handling of palletised unit loads, possibly in conjunction with fork-lift trucks. For instance, pallet trucks may be employed to advantage in a level-floor works, where due to restricted floor loading space and the dimensions of the lift, it is only possible to employ a fork truck on the ground floor. Also, in cases where it would be uneconomical to hold a fork truck in readiness to move a single load unit a short distance, then a pallet truck can be used. Finger extensions may be fitted to handle palletless loads. Figure 65(*a*) shows a typical hand-manoeuvred hydraulic or mechanical pallet truck. Figure 65(*b*) shows a pedestrian-controlled pallet truck, electric-battery or internal-combustion engine driven.

TRACTORS.—(Other than crawler mounted and agricultural tractors.) Depending upon the tonnage to be handled it is not generally economical to employ fork-lift or platform trucks to transport loads for distances over 100 m. The tractor with trailers is ideal for these longer hauls and this system is frequently employed at railway stations, docks, airfields, etc, where large quantities of widely varying goods are transported relatively long distances. Under average conditions one tractor can work three trains of trailers, ie one train loading, one in transit, and one unloading. The trailers may be loaded and unloaded manually, by crane, or by fork-lift truck.

Industrial tractors of three- or four-wheel construction are available with varying draw-bar pulls, depending

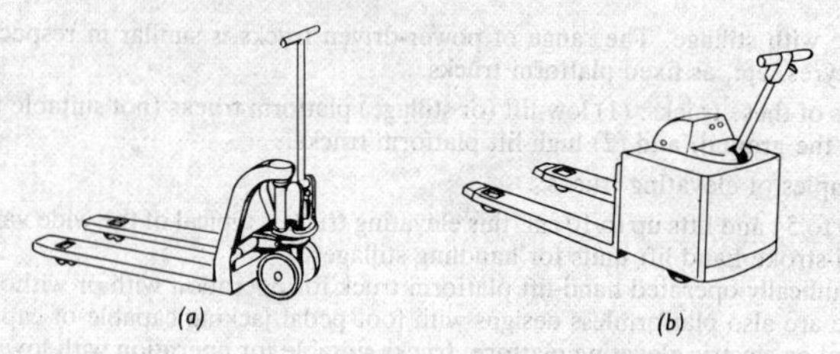

FIG. 65.—Typical Pallet Trucks.

upon the design and power unit, which may be petrol, diesel or electric battery. They may be mounted on solid or pneumatic tyres. In addition to hauling loads of materials, tractors are employed for such duties as pushing and pulling railway wagons in goods yards and for the movement of aircraft on runways. Figure 66 shows various types of tractors:

(*a*) For pulling light trailer trains on smooth floors and in confined or congested work places, this three-wheeled tractor may be petrol or electric battery driven.
(*b*) Highly manoeuvrable medium duty tractor operated by diesel or petrol engine, or electric battery, and mounted on solid or pneumatic tyres. Electric tractors have a hauling capacity of up to 40 t.
(*c*) Petrol-driven pneumatic-tyred tractor designed for shunting railway wagons and moving aircraft, where loads up to 200 t are handled.

FIG. 66.—Typical Tractors.

The nominal rating of a tractor is expressed as a maximum drawbar pull in decanewtons (ION) that can be developed at a specific coupling height while a load is moving at a uniform speed (BS 4339 Rating of Industrial Tractors).

DRIVERLESS TRACTORS.—This type of tractor may be guided by magnetic field or optically sensor-operated, and is equipped with ultrasonic detector able to feel the obstacles and stop the truck without touching them (eg, *Fenwick*). Computerisation also plays an important role in this field.

TRUCKS FOR BOTH HORIZONTAL AND VERTICAL HANDLING

FORK-LIFT TRUCK.—This is a mechanical vehicle with a high degree of manoeuvrability, which can raise, carry and lower a unit or palletised load, by means of two steel forks or other attachments, mounted on the front or side of the vehicle. The trucks are powered by battery-driven electric motors or by an internal combustion engine; the largest trucks may handle loads of up to and over 10 t and lift them at speeds up to 30 m/min, according to the maximum load capacity of the truck. Fork-lift trucks have a range of 'free lift' which enables the load to be elevated without raising the mast; this feature is of advantage where stacking is carried out under low ceilings, as well as helping the stability of the truck. They may be micro-processor controlled having all hydraulic functions controlled by buttons/switches from the driver's panel, the height selected being shown on a digital display, together with the indication of the moving load position. The control may be automatic or manual There are four basic types of fork-lift truck in use: (*a*) the counterbalanced type; (*b*) the straddle or out-rigger type; (*c*) the reach type; (*d*) the side-loading type (Figs 67, 68).

Counterbalanced Fork Truck.—This truck was first designed as a stacking unit; it carries the load ahead of the front wheel; available for lifts up to 15 m above floor level.

Straddle or Out-rigger Truck.—This is also called a 'narrow-aisle' or 'narrow-gangway' type, and has special applications in confined spaces as well as ability to handle slung loads.

FIG. 67.—Container Lift-truck handling items 12 m long (*Lancer Boss*).

Reach-type Fork Truck.—This truck combines the characteristics of the other two types and the load can be retracted to within the vehicle wheelbase, thus reducing counterbalance weight and allowing for narrow aisle stacking. There are three designs of the reach-type trucks: (1) *Moving-mast*, in which the whole mast assembly moves out towards the load and is usually carried on wheels and runners formed in the out-rigger legs. This type is preferred for long-reach travels. (2) *Pantograph system*, in which the mast remains fixed to the body of the truck, but the forks are extended outwards to the load on a scissor-type mechanism; this method offers great stability at high lifts, although its reach distance is restricted. (3) *Rotating swivel action*, this permits operation in an aisle which is only marginally wider than the load carried.

Side-loading Fork Truck.—This truck has advantages in manipulation and stability. Models are available with tilting capacity up to 25 t, and up to 50 t if jacks are used, with 1 m/min lifting speed.

Figure 68 shows a selection of typical fork-lift trucks: (*a*) A pedestrian-controlled electric counterbalanced truck. (*b*) A standard rider-controlled, electric or internal combustion engined truck. (*c*) A petrol or diesel powered truck for heavy work, including grades of 1 in 7 fully loaded; load capacity 3 t (max) with a 4 m lift. (*d*) Heavy type, solid tyred, electric truck with telescopic or non-telescopic lifting equipment. They can be fitted with forks, ram or platform; load capacity, over 3 t. (*e*) Similar type to (*d*) but pedestrian controlled.

STABILITY OF FORK-LIFT TRUCKS.—This is of prime importance and operators should guard against overloading. Where testing is necessary the procedure consists of 4 basic tests: (1) longitudinal stability; (2) stacking and travelling; (3) lateral stability; (4) limits of manoeuvrability. The operational space requirements will be specified by the manufacturer.

TRUCK CAPACITY.—This is the maximum load at a specified distance from the 'heel' (the back of the fork), say, 60 cm. But a truck having a capacity of, say, 2,000 kg at 0.6 m could safely take a concentrated load of 2,400 kg at 0.5 m, but only 1,600 kg at 0.75 m; in this example the moment $M = 2{,}000 \times 60 = 2{,}400 \times 50 = 1{,}600 \times 75 = 120$ t-m. (See BS 4338 'Rated Capacity of Fork-Lift Trucks). Some models (eg Caterpillar) have a capacity of 42 tonnes with a load centre of 900 mm or 36 tonnes with a load centre of 1500 mm.

TRUCKS FOR VERTICAL HANDLING

To meet the requirements of vertical stacking, these trucks must have stability; reach the required height for storing purposes; take as little floor space as possible, and be able to move and manoeuvre in narrow aisles; they may be rider controlled or pedestrian operated.

STACKING TRUCK.—This is also called a 'stacker' or 'pallet truck', usually powered, and is characterised by extended legs, and forks for insertion under loads. The truck is fitted with a mast, which may be telescopic; forks of various lengths are attached to a sliding carriage on the mast which can be raised or lowered within the limits of the mast design.

TURRET TRUCK.—This is used for vertical storage and distribution of goods, and has particular application in warehouses where space is limited and high lifts are required; they may be designed for lifts up to 13 m.

Other types of truck employed for high stacking include:

Straddle Stacker.—This is similar to the turret truck, but characterised by having legs wide apart to clear the base of the load or pallet, which obviously must not be wider than the space between straddle legs; space must be allowed on each side of the load for the legs.

Reach Truck.—This is used for heavy loads which have to be stacked up high. Alternative motions allow movement of the whole mast, or the pantograph mechanism extends the fork only.

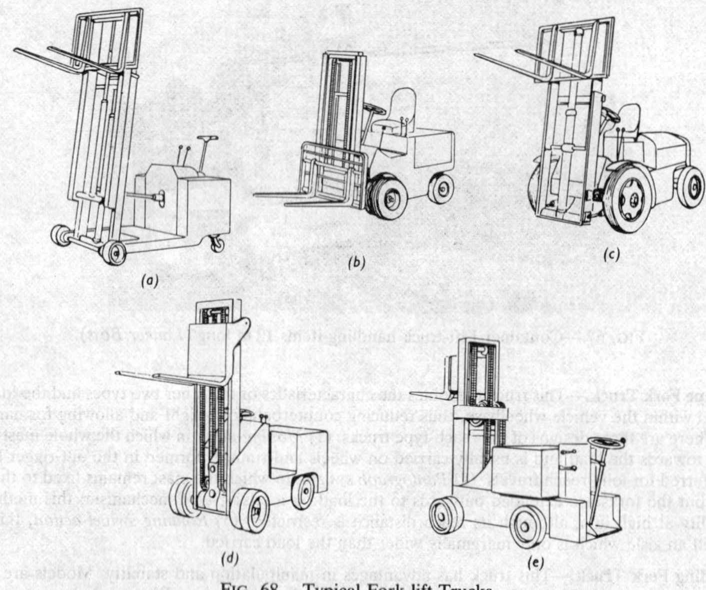

FIG. 68.—Typical Fork-lift Trucks.

Narrow-aisle Stacker.—This is a development of the reach-truck, imposed by the need to operate the machine in a narrow passage between two rows of shelving. As the saving of floor space is the primary economic requirement, the tendency to employ high-bay racking is the second condition which must be satisfied, in addition to the aisle width reduction.

High Rack Stacker.—This type travels on rails positioned on the side of each aisle. Typical capacity is 2 t, with a lift height of 10 m. Higher capacities, are available, suitable for a minimum aisle width of 110 cm.

FIG. 71.—Automatic Mini-stacker. (*Fenamec*)

SOLID STATE TECHNOLOGY.—Applied nowadays to lift trucks (and other materials handling equipment) is claimed to ensure optimum performance, long life, high reliability plus reduced maintenance requirements. For instance Hyster trucks are provided with controllers (*General Electric SCR*) which have the facility of independent adjustment of the rate of acceleration, creep speed and intensity of electrical braking (plugging) to suit the needs of the driver, in addition to other advantages: helping him during ramp start, protecting the motor, etc.

FORK-LIFT ATTACHMENTS.—In addition to the standard forks, many types of different attachments are now available while new attachments are constantly being devised which allow the fork-lift truck to be used for special applications. These attachments are quickly interchangeable. The basic design of the fork-lift truck is such that the weight of the truck itself counterbalances the load about the front axle as fulcrum point. This must be considered when attachments are added to a fork-lift truck as the load carrying capacity may be affected. It is recommended that reference should be made to the manufacturers for detailed information about any particular application. Figure 69 shows a selection of typical attachments. See also BS 3810 Part 1.

(*a*) Extension sleeves for forks which can be quickly attached to standard trucks when handling light bulky loads.
(*b*) Barrel forks comprising three small arms in place of the standard forks for handling barrels or drums horizontally.
(*c*) Drum carrier—an alternative to (*b*) comprising a four-section hood which fits over four drums and embodies hydraulic clamps.
(*d*) Ram or boom to simplify the handling of coils of wire, tyres, rolls of paper, etc.
(*e*) Jib which together with hook and slings is of use in handling awkward loads unsuitable for palletisation.

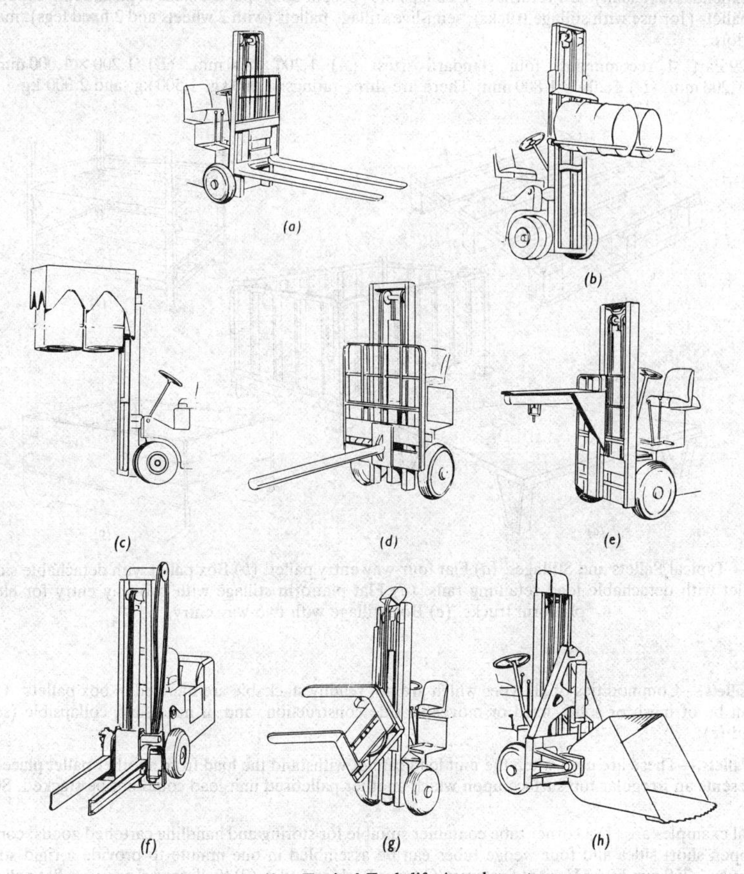

FIG. 69.—Typical Fork-lift Attachments.

(*f*) Squeeze clamp—hydraulically operated, clamping a unit load of bales, sacks, etc, for easy lifting and transporting and stacking.
(*g*) Rotating head—fully revolving this attachment enables the operator to lift, carry and elevate a suitably designed container and to discharge its contents into a hopper, lorry, railway wagon, etc.
(*h*) Shovel—with capacities up to 1 m^3 and capable of discharging at heights up to 4 m, hydraulically operated, can be used for lifting and transporting a wide range of loose materials.

There are many other special attachments designed to meet the requirements of particular industries; these include push-pull devices, vacuum pads, magnets, dumping forks, crane, jib or boom attachments, drum grips, timber claws, side shifts (for load positioning), load stabilisers, load guards, clamps, etc.

PALLETS AND STILLAGES.—Pallets and stillages (skids) are used for the handling and storage of unit loads. Generally constructed of wood or metal (or a combination of both materials), pallets are designed for stacking and with a ground clearance of 150 mm (max) under the deck which enables them to be handled by fork or pallet truck. Three main types of pallets are in general use: flat pallets, box pallets and post pallets. BS 2629 Part 1 specifies sizes, materials and marking for types of pallets. BS 2629 Part 2 refers to pallets for use in freight containers. BS 3810 Part 1 lists terms related to pallets and their components (Fig. 70). Each pallet should have the makers' identity mark; the BS number (if applicable); and the load-carrying capacity (kg).

Flat Pallets.—These are used to take unit loads which are rigid when stacked and capable of sustaining the load of other units placed on top of them. Pallets are of various types, namely: single-deck, double-deck, two-way entry pallets, four-way entry pallets (Fig. 70(*a*)), eight-way entry pallets (i.e., which permits the entry of forks from all 4 sides and diagonally), reversible (not suitable for use with pallet trucks); wing pallets (having a deck or decks projecting beyond the outer bearers to facilitate the use of lifting slings), box pallets, post pallets, expendable (usually non-returnable), collapsible (post or box type, the sides of posts being collapsible), stillage pallets (for use with stillage trucks), semi-live stillage pallets (with 2 wheels and 2 fixed legs), maritime or stevedore.

BS 2629 Part 1 recommends four standard sizes: (*A*) 1,200 × 800 mm. (*B*) 1,200 × 1,000 mm. (*C*) 1,200 × 1,200 mm. (*D*) 1,200 × 1,800 mm. There are three ratings: 1,000 kg, 1,500 kg, and 2,000 kg.

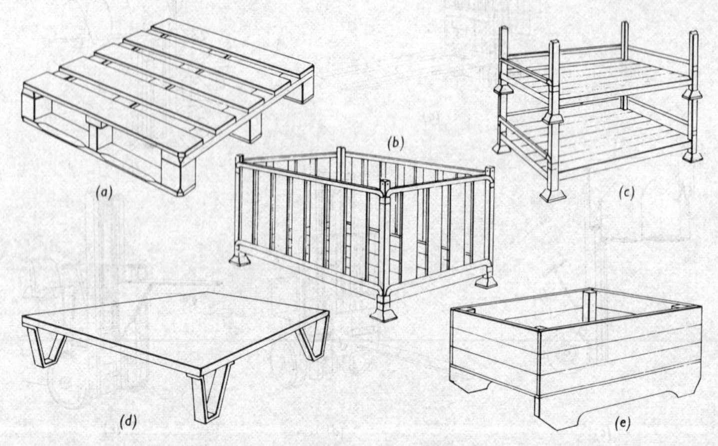

FIG. 70.—Typical Pallets and Stillages. (*a*) Flat four-way entry pallet. (*b*) Box pallet with detachable sides. (*c*) Post pallet with detachable load retaining rails. (*d*) Flat platform stillage with two-way entry for elevating platform trucks. (*e*) Box stillage with two-way entry.

Box Pallets.—Commodities of all types which are not readily stackable are handled in box pallets. The box pallet can be of mesh or solid, fixed or moveable-side construction, and, if necessary, collapsible (see Fig. 70(*b*) and (*e*)).

Post Pallets.—These are used when the unit load cannot withstand the load from another pallet placed upon it, or presents an irregular top surface upon which another palletised unit load could not be stacked. See Fig. 70(*c*)).

Typical examples are (1) a corner tube container suitable for storing and handling cartoned goods, consisting of two open short sides and four wedge tubes can be assembled in one minute to provide a rigid structure 1,250 mm or 1,750 mm high (Variant Systemet/Gilspur Packing Ltd.). (2) 'Palletower' converts flat pallets into stackable containers. These models can be of mesh, rods, solid, braced or open panels with hinged gates. They can be nested sixty to one when not in use. 'Tower racks' is characterised by tubular post pallets with removable posts. It is able to take fully laden flat pallets stacked up to four high with one tonne on each. (3) Various models of robot palletisers and automatic pallet handling systems are available. 'Robopal' (Inpac Automation Ltd.—Vickers) will carry out 360 operations per hour, depending on pack size, weight and orientation on the final stack. The lifting heads, normally suction vacuum type (alternative gripper fork and magnetic type heads are available) have a range of movement which allows operation to a pre-programmed palletisation pattern.

Stillages.—Stillages are not generally designed for stacking. They are usually of flat or box construction and handled by elevating platform trucks. They can, however, be handled by fork trucks and specially adapted pallet trucks (see Fig. 70(*d*)). See BS 4337.

SILOS AND BUNKERS.—The discharge of materials from silos and bunkers is given insufficient design attention, particularly where sticky, powdery or compacting materials are involved. Gravity flow is not always satisfactory. The problem may be solved by installing mechanical devices, eg rotating arm moving against the conical slope of the silo, mixing blades, screw devices, vibratory devices includng bin bottom shaking or air pads to aerate granular or powdered materials, etc. Typical silos are approximately 2–6·5m diameter, 2·5–12·5m high, with a capacity of 440 cubic metres (All Flow/Carter-Day). Wear resistant liners are sometimes recommended.

MISCELLANEOUS UNITS.—Under this heading can be classified other units of equipment as:

(*a*) Power barrows and their attachments such as tipping skips for bulk materials and interchangeable wood or metal platforms for sacks, cases, warehouse and works sundries, etc.
(*b*) Power shovels and their attachments such as diggers, angle and bulldozer blades, etc.
(*c*) Order pickers to assist with automatic operation of trucks and machines, leading to computerised handling of stores, etc.

HAND TRUCKS AND EQUIPMENT.—Of extremely wide variety and most useful for small intermittent light loads over short distances. The main classes are:

(*a*) One- and two-wheeled barrows, trucks and trolleys for bulk materials, cases, sacks, barrels, carboys, etc.
(*b*) Three- and four-wheeled box trucks, dollies, platform and tipping trucks, etc.
(*c*) Two-wheel tug-lift jack attachments for moving two-wheeled stillages and containers.

FREIGHT CONTAINERS FOR TRANSPORT.—The advent of the freight container for movement of cargo and merchandise has revolutionised installations at ports and the loading/unloading equipment at railway and road vehicle terminals. Travelling gantry cranes quickly handle the containers, and the 'turn round time' for ships and lorries is reduced to a minimum. The ISO recommended sizes for containers are: 2·5 m high × 2·5 m wide, and 3, 6, 9 or 12 m long.

CONTAINER HANDLING.—The large size of the containers which have to be suitable for fragile materials calls for a special approach. Ship to shore cranes (Morris) have container capacity 35 tonnes and hook beam capacity 40·6 tonnes, outreach from water side rail 39 metres, back reach 15 metres and height of lift above quay 27 metres. They have hoisting speed loaded of 30·5 metres/minute, trolley travel speed 122 metres/minute, gantry speed 46 metres/minute. Stacking gantries (rubber tyred) have a similar capacity. Bulk liquid containers have a nominal capacity up to 1,000 litres. The tanks are provided with polyethylene inner containers and welded galvanised steel plate outer containers. They may be stacked three high, (*Schütz*).

AUTOMATIC GUIDED VEHICLES (AGV).—These computerised machines can collect a load from the floor (like a forklift) and place it on a roller conveyor, rack, etc. Several models are available of which the AGV (Tellus Engineering) is a good example.

DOLLY TRUCKS.—Where heavy items have to be moved by hand (eg cases, crates, furniture, machinery, etc), these load carriers are quick and efficient, avoiding the liability to accident and damage due to rollers being placed under a load. The dolly truck usually has six wheels to a bogey, the central pair of wheels being of larger diameter to permit the truck to pivot and turn. The trucks can be adapted to suit special duties and are available with high or low wheels of large or small diameters.

MACHINE SKATES.—These are small robust load carriers, placed in suitable positions under heavy objects to enable them to be safely moved in any direction while ensuring that the load is supported without fear of jarring or damage. The types of machine skates can be briefly divided as follows: *Solid Box*, in which a number of wheels are assembled in tandem formation and covered over for protection. *Solid Plate*, in which a number of rollers are assembled, in line, and covered by a rigid plate. *Endless Track*, which consists of an assembly of rollers between two rigid side plates, the rollers being connected to each other by means of an endless roller track with side frame clearance. Each type of skate conveyor is available in a range of sizes.

WEIGHERS FOR INDUSTRIAL TRUCKS.—Some models of platform scales for industrial trucks are suitable for payloads up to 9 tonnes. With electronic weighing and digital weight indicators they assure automatic, prompt and safe operation.

MECHANISED WAREHOUSING

BASIC PLANNING.—(1) Delivery of goods from outside (by rail, lorries, conveyors, ropeways, etc) (2) Transfer to the input positions which may be on the delivery-from-outside level, or on another level. (3) Horizontal distribution (by conveyors, monorails, trucks, etc). (4) Vertical distribution (according to the size of the store: lifts, reach trucks, turret-reach- narrow aisle- or stacking-trucks, with suitable attachments, etc). (5) Despatch of goods, ie the above four groups of operations in reverse order.

COMPUTERISATION.—All the operations described are now more frequently carried out automatically and/or by automated robots directed by computer. In general procedure is as follows. The incoming items are placed on a conveyor (say, using a fork-lift truck) which takes them to a position where identification (weighing, counting, and sizing) of all items can be carried out. This function is controlled manually or by computer. This is done by a man operating, say, a reach truck, or automatically, by a driverless reach truck, as directed by a computer. The computer may also confirm the purchase order, repacking for storage, sampling, etc. Retrieval operations are carried out in the same manner. In this way a central computer is able not only to direct all handling manipulations automatically, but also to offer instantaneous information about the number of each item in stock, ie to keep an up-to-date inventory, the position of each item in the store, and in addition, the computer may be instructed to ensure that there is a sufficent number of each item in stock, as programmed in advance, and to decide the priority of operations, planning truck work, etc.

INSTALLATIONS.—Almost all the types of materials handling equipment described above, more or less automated and computerised according to requirements, find application in mechanised warehousing. In particular roller conveyors have many applications, in co-ordination with reach-trucks and narrow-aisle stackers, computer-operated, both for low storing and high warehousing. Certain types of roller conveyors may also be useful where it is desirable to accumulate goods being conveyed to relieve a build-up of line pressure, or for the removal of single items, their marking or counting. (eg, *Fenamec*, with standard bed length of up to 3 m, width up to 900 mm, typical speed 20 m/min, package weight up to 70 kg).

As each installation has its own individuality it is difficult to describe general designs, but it is useful to give typical solutions. One automated store is served by a stacker able to handle two-tonne loads on pallets, raising them to 34 m (*FATA*). A warehouse constructed for the Cambridge University Press stores 15 million books (5,000 titles) in addition to 500 different bibles and about 60 journals. This store is served by counter-balanced trucks (*Crown Lifttruck*), and Hi-Racker trucks (*Barlow*), lifting loads up to 1,700 kg, which are able to work in aisles as narrow as 1.5 m. An operator, in an elevating cab, can work at eye level, and the fork, rotating through an angle of 180°, allows him to stack complete pallet loads, each weighing 1,400 kg, in a 12 m high warehouse and/or to pick single items either side of the racking.

If space allows horizontal spreading warehouses may be less costly, and still be computerised. For instance, a cold store, its total volume exceeding 20,000 m^3, storing over 4,000 pallets, is equipped with several reach trucks having an 8 m lift (*Lansing Bagnall*) and powered pallet trucks (*Rolatruc*). Another installation is equipped by radio-controlled robot pallet trucks (*FATA* and others); the position and progress data of the trucks being recorded by a central traffic computer which allocates priorities for the trucks and plans their routes.

Stackers-load-pickers produced by several manufacturers can operate in similar conditions, eg Pacemaker with lift up to 13 m, also with an elevating cabin, and Rotareach (both *Narrow Aisle*, UK), with lift up to 8 m, load up to 1·5 t, and aisle width 1,370 mm (ie only 440 mm wider than the load it carries); travel speed 140 m/min, lift speed 20 m/min. Ministacker (*Fenamec* AMS200) is a fully automatic, computer-controlled unit of modular design, engineered to meet individual requirements. This unit is characterised by one lower and one upper carriage, which (provided with 4 guide wheels) runs along a horizontal rail bus-bar through which power is fed. A lifting unit slides along the vertical mast. This lifting unit is designed to take various attachments. Drives, with thyristor controls for travelling and lifting, are provided at the bottom of the mast near the lower carriage. It has a travelling speed of 120 m/min in normal operational conditions (160 m/min max) and a lifting travel speed of 40 m/min. Typical AMS 200 installations in operation in Scandinavia, provide automatic intermediate storage between manufacturing machines; the average weight of a load fixture is 300 kg, and 645 positions are available for storage. A computer terminal orders empty fixtures out and directs filled fixtures into specific positions in the racking, and records location, type of component/product and quantity.

One narrow-aisle truck (*URF Atlet*) is equipped with a fork turning through an angle of 180°. It has a lift capacity of up to 1,500 kg. This machine is roller guided. UHS stackers (*Nordic Cranes, Belfast/Litton*) can operate 2 pallets simultaneously to heights of up to 28 m in temperatures as low as −35°C. These units are also top-guided, running on a single-flow rail at speeds of 50 m/min horizontally and 18·5 m/min vertically. Another trailer-loader operates in conjunction with high-rise storage and handling equipment; this installation handles 5,000 pallets loaded with wine (etc)/day; the operator programmes the information required sending pallets off to any of 22,000 bins in 9 bays 20 m high storage area; a computer also plans the operation for the next day. (Tellus Maskin AS, Sweden).—Even a larger number of different items—400,000 of them in 73,000 pallet locations is dealt with by an installation supplied by Link 51.

Systems of computerised installations for automatic truck guiding, including electric battery, diesel drives etc, tailored to customers' requirements, are available. There is constant progress; new systems and machines being

introduced all the time, eg a combined pallet placer and order picker with a 180° lateral stacking turret fork designed to accommodate high rise warehouse applications up to 12 m (Combi/Narrow Aisle UK Ltd). The systems mentioned above are typical, picked at random, from: Barlow Handling/Hyster/Saxby, Lansing Bagnall, Crown, Condor, Oehler-Wyhler Lagertechnik, Atlet, Link 51, Southern Storage Group, FATA, Fenamec, PHB, Koch, Buckau-Wolf, Lancer Boss, Caterpillar and others (Figs. 71, 72 and 73).

FIG. 72.—Reach truck with Tilting Carriage equipped with 'Autosense' protecting system; Stacking height 8·6 m; Capacity 2,500 kg. (*Saxby*)

FIG. 73.—Automatic Parcel Sorter. (*Dictron-Schindler*)

TRUCK GUIDING SYSTEMS.—Truck guiding was originally achieved by rollers fixed on the trucks themselves which could engage rails fitted either to racking or to the floor. Latest designs involve wire guidance leaving the floor clear, or optical sensors situated on each side of the trucks (*Narrow Aisle Co*).

Pathfinder wire-guidance system helps the truck driver in narrow aisles to manoeuvre along the sides of aisles and between the storage racks, but it is equally useful with automated trucks. A guide wire, sending out an electronic signal, is installed 10 mm below floor level; the signal is picked up by sensors mounted on the lift-truck. The truck driver is in control, but the Pathfinder allows him to use automatically full speed forward and reverse drives with only 10 cm side clearance. (*Loghisticon*, USA)

BRITISH STANDARDS

Belt Conveyors and Elevators

BS 490 Part 1 1985 'Rubber and Plastics Conveyor Belting of Textile Construction for General Use (Multiply, Single-ply or Solid Woven Construction).
BS 490 Part 2 1975. 'Rubber and Plastics Belting of Textile Construction for Use on Bucket Elevators'.
BS 2890 1973 'Troughed Belt Conveyors' (Revision pending).
BS 3289 1982 'Conveyor Belt for Underground Use.
BS 3810 'Glossary of Terms Used in Materials Handling'. Part 2 1965 'Conveyors and Elevators'. Amend: 1967.
BS 4531 1986 'Portable and Mobile Troughed Belt Conveyors'.
BS 4890 1973 'Test Methods for Mechanical Joints in Conveyor Belting'.
BS 5667 1980 'Safety Requirements—Belt Conveyors'.
BS 5767 1979 'Guide for Storage and Handling of Conveyor Belts'.
BS 5934 1980 'Calculation of Operating Power and Tensile Forces in Belt Conveyors'.
BS 6318 Part 1 1982 'Classification of Elevating Buckets'.
BS 6318 Part 2 1982 'Dimensions of Vertical Bucket Elevators with Round Steel Links'.
BS 6318 Part 3 1982 'Dimensions of Deep Elevator Buckets'.
BS 6593 1985 'Code of Practice for On-Site Non-Mechanical Joining of Conveyor Belts.

Chain and Slat Conveyors

BS 2075 1971 'Chain and Chainwheels for Slat Conveyors'. Amend: 1979.
BS 2853 1957 'Design and Testing Overhead Runway Beams'. Amend: 1959, 1961, 1967, 1969, 1970.
BS 2969 1987 'High Tensile Steel Chains for Chain Conveyors'.
BS 4116 1971 'Steel Roller Chains, Chainwheels and Attachments for Conveyors'.
BS 5667 Parts 11, 12, 16, 17, 18 1979 'Safety Requirements—Slat and Chain Conveyors'.
BS 5801 1979 'Flat-top Chains and Chain wheels for Conveyors'.

Roller Conveyors

BS 2567 1972 'Steel Non-powered Roller Conveyors'.
BS 5667 Part 14 1979 'Safety Requirements—Live Roller Conveyors'.

Screw Conveyors

BS 4409 Part 1 1969 'Trough-type Screw Conveyors for Industrial uses'.
BS 4409 Part 2 1970 'Portable and Mobile Screw Conveyors. Tubular Type (Augers) for Agricultural and Light Industrial Use'.
BS 4409 Part 3 1982 'Calculating drive power for screw conveyors'.
BS 5667 Part 10 1979 'Safety Requirements—Vertical Screw Conveyors'.

Hydraulic and Pneumatic Conveyance

BS 3810 Part 3 1967 'Glossary of Terms—Pneumatic and Hydraulic Handling'.
BS 5667 Parts 2–7 'Safety Requirements'.

Industrial Tractors, Trucks: Pallets, etc

BS 2629 Part 1 1967 'Pallets for Materials Handling—Dimensions, Materials and Marking'. Amend: 1978.
BS 2629 Part 2 1970 'Pallets for Materials Handling for Use in Freight Containers'.
BS 2629 Part 3 1978 'Pallets, performance requirements and tests'.
BS 2800 1957 'Tests of Wheeled and Crawler Industrial Tractors'. Amend: 1960, 1962.
BS 3318 1978 'Centre of Gravity Location of Tractors'.
BS 3726 1978 'Stability Testing of Counter-balanced Lift Trucks'.
BS 3810 Part 1 1964 'Glossary of Terms—Pallets, Stillages and Powered Trucks'.
BS 4155 1986 'Dimensions of Pallet Trucks'.
BS 4337 1986 'Principal Dimensions of Hand-operated Stillage Trucks'.
BS 4430 Part 2 1986 'Safety of powered industrial trucks—Operation and maintenance'.
BS 4436 1978 'Stability of Reach and Straddle Fork-lift Trucks'.
BS 5639 Parts 1–5, 'Fork arms for Fork-lift Trucks'.
BS 5777 1979 'Verification of Stability Testing of Pallet Stackers and High Platform Lift Trucks'.

BS 5778 1979 'Verification of Stability Testing of Industrial Trucks Operating with Special Conditions of Stacking with Mast Tilted Forward'.
BS 5802 1979 'Maximum Actuating Forces for Tractor Controls'.
BS 5829 1979 'Control Symbols for Powered Industrial Trucks'.
BS 5933 1980 'High-Lift Rider Overhead Guards For Trucks'.
BS 6074 1981 'Volumetric Rating of Tractor-Scraper for Earth-Moving Machinery'.
BS 3810 Part 5:1971 'Glossary of Terms—Lifting Tackle'.
BS 5323:1980 'Scissor Lifts'.
BS 6347 Part 2 1983 'Power determination of agricultural tractors'.
BS 6347 Part 3 1983 'Turning and clearance diameter for agricultural tractors'.
BS 6347 Part 6 1983 'Centre of gravity of agricultural tractors'.
BS 6389 1983 'Determination of operator's field of vision for agricultural tractors'

BIBLIOGRAPHY

General
KOSKIN. *Modern Material Handling.* Chapman & Hall.
WOODLEY, D. R. (Editor). *Encyclopaedia of Material Handling* (2 vols). Pergamon Press, 1964.
Material Handling in Industry (3rd edition). Electrical Development Association.
Materials Handling; Selecting the Equipment. Committee for Materials Handling. Department of Industry, 1977.
Simons, M. (Ed). *Materials Handling.* Institute of Directors in collaboration with Department of Industry, 1977.

Conveyors and Elevators
Design of Belt Conveyors. Mavor & Coulson, Glasgow.
Conveyor Belt Selector Book. BTR Belting.
Recommended Practice for Troughed Belt Conveyors. M.H. Eng'rs. Association, 1986.
Starflex Conveyor Belting. Dunlop Belting Services.
Screw Conveyors. Ewart Chainbelt Co.
Vertical Bucket Elevators. Ewart Chainbelt.
Slat and Apron Conveyors. Ewart Chainbelt.
Handbook on Belt Design. Material Handling Dept. of GEC/Fraser Chalmers Engineering Works in association with Hewitt-Robins Inc, New York, 1956.
Conveyor Belting Reinforced with Nylon and Terylene. ICI Fibres, Industrial Uses Dept.
Conveyor Belt Cleaning Devices: MHEA, 1982.

Industrial Trucks, Tractors etc
ASTLEY, R. W. & LAWTON, R. H. *The Ergonomic Aspects of Fork-Lift Truck Design.* Cranfield Institute of Technology, 1971.
F.E.M. Safety Code for Powered Industrial Trucks. British Ind. Truck Assn.
F.E.M. Truck Terminology.
Materials Handling with Industrial Trucks. British Ind. Truck Assn.
Selection and Training of Fork Truck Drivers. British Ind. Truck Assn.
WILLIAMS, I. *Using Industrial Trucks for Materials Handling.* Hutchinson, 1973.

Hydraulic and Pneumatic Conveyance
Solid-Liquid Flow of Materials. BHRA Abstracts Journal, Vol 13, 1982, Cranfield.
Hydraulic Transport of Solids in Pipes. 6th International Conference 1979.
Powder Handling and Storage. Papers presented at the 1969 Symposium. Institute of Materials Handling & Liverpool Regional College of Technology (Ed A. S. Goldberg).
Hydraulic Transport of Solids. Institution of Mechanical Engineers (Sponsored by Institution of Materials Handling 1980.
Pipeline Transport of Slurries. Trans Tech Publications 1979.
Pneumotransport. Proceedings, International Conference on the Pneumatic Transport of Solids in Pipes. BHRA Fluid Engineering, 1972–78.
JAMES, J. G., *Pipelines considered as Mode of Freight Transport.* 'Minerals & the Environment', Vol 2, No 1, 1980.
KARASIK, V. M. (USSR), *Slurry Hydrotransport of Minerals and Tailings*, Translation edited by Cooley, W. C. (USA). Trans Tech Publications, 1979.
MONTFORD, J. G., *Operating Experience of the Black Mesa Pipeline.* (Ref CME, Febr 1981).
POKROVSKAYA, V. N. (USSR), *Increasing the Effectiveness of Hydrotransport.* Trans edited by Cooley, W. C. and Faddick, R. R. Trans Tech Publications.
NOLTE, C. B., *Optimum Pipe Size Selection.* Trans Tech Publ 1978.
SMOLDYREV, A. Y., & SAFONOV, Y. K., *Pipeline Transport of Slurries.* Translation edited by Cooley, W. C. Trans Tech Publications.
SNOWDON, B., *Pneumatic Conveying-Scope for Exploitation.* CME Journal, July, 1980.

SWISS, M., *Transporting Slurry in Pipelines and Ships*. CME Journal, Feb. 1981.

TRAYNIS, V. V. (USSR), *Parameters and Flow Regimes for Hydraulic Transport of Coal by Pipelines*. Translation edited by Faddick, R. R. Trans Tech Publications.

TURCHANINOV, S. P. (USSR), *The Life of Hydrotransport Pipelines*. Translation edited Cooley, W. C. Trans Tech Publications.

WASP, E. J., KENNY, J. P., & GANDHI, R. L. *Solid-Liquid Flow; Slurry Pipeline Transportation* Trans Tech Publications.

Mechanised Warehousing

BURTON, J. A. *Effective Warehousing*. Macdonald & Evans, 1973.

CHORAFAS, D. N. *Warehousing*. Macmillan Press, 3rd edition 1981.

HOEFKENS, L. F. *Material Handling in Works Stores*. Ilife, 1954.

KAY, E. *A Mathematical Model for Handling in a Warehouse*. Pergamon Press, 1968.

ZIMMER, G. F. *Mechanical Handling and Storing of Materials*. Technical Press. *The Loading Bay Handbook*. R. S. Stokvis & Sons 1981.

Miscellaneous

DALLY, H. E. (ED) *Container Handling and Transport*. C.S. Publications, 1983.

REISNER, W. ET AL *Bins and Bunkers for Handling Bulk Materials*. Trans Tech Publications, 1978.

RASPER, L. *Bucket Wheel Excavator*. Trans Tech Publications, 1975.

RUSHTON, A. & WILLIAMS, J. *The Cost of Materials Handling*. National Materials Handling Centre, 1982.

Code of Practice for the Construction and Survey of Ships' Cargo Handling Gear. Lloyd's Register of Shipping, 1967.

CASTELLANO, E. J., EMSLEY, R. M., & ADIE, J. F. *Design of a Parcel Handling Machine by Computer Simulation*. Proceedings, Institution of Mech. Engineers, 1980. Vol. 194, No. 11.

JONES, L. (Ed). *Mechanical Handling with Precision Conveyor Chains*. Hutchinson, 1971.

LIFTS, ESCALATORS AND PASSENGER CONVEYORS

Types of Lifts—Principal Lift Drives—Lift Control Systems—Recommended Lift Dimensions—Traffic Studies—Builders Work—Well Construction and Tolerances—Installation and Servicing — Escalators—Capacity—Driving Machinery—Passenger Conveyors—Surrounding and Safety—Bibliography.

By M. J. Savage, CEng, MIMechE, FBIM, FCIBSE and D. H. Weston, CEng, FIMechE, MBIM

Lifts are used for the vertical transportation of goods and people whereas escalators and passenger conveyors are used for the inclined or virtual horizontal movement of passengers in buildings. The lift industry covers the design, installation and servicing of all these products.

Great importance is attached to the planning of lifts against the requirements of the building at the earliest stage since once installed, lift configurations are permanent and extremely difficult to change, therefore, particular reference should be paid to the chapters on dimensional standards, traffic study and lift well tolerances.

The basic reference documents which greatly affect design and safety parameters of lift equipment within the UK are the British Standards, Codes of Practice and IEE regulations. See Bibliography p. L4/15.

It is most important that the recommended dimensions for loads and speeds of lifts are used for new lifts since it greatly simplifies the planning of buildings and the selection of the type of lift as well as allowing the supplier to offer rationalised products at economic prices. The lift industry however is always willing to accommodate special tailor-made installations, but these are more expensive than standard products. There are more than 100,000 lifts in service with many of these being over 20 years old. There, therefore, exists a large scope for up-grading and modernisation of such lifts to present day technology and architectural standards.

The industry is highly specialised and requires engineers with knowledge of the construction industry and the decoration and finishing of building interiors. However, it above all requires competent mechanical and electrical engineers with very specialised experience, to design, install and maintain lift equipment to conform to the necessary high standard of safety, quality and good performance.

Electronic analogue and digital systems are almost universally used today for control systems and for some drives within the industry. Due to the vast scope of engineering specialities required in the lift industry it is virtually impossible for an engineer, irrespective of his qualifications, competently to specify in detail the design and operation of lifts, until he has had considerable training and experience within the industry itself.

To be competitive in world markets, without sacrificing safety and performance, standardisation must be adopted to the maximum extent. The present policy of some consultants writing their own detailed specifications without co-ordination makes it difficult for the lift industry to achieve the necessary degree of standardisation. Nevertheless, the lift industry via the National Association of Lift Makers, supports the British Standards Institution in its efforts to provide standard specifications and a code of practice to cover the design and installation of all lifts and allied products within the UK and Europe. The universal use and the correct application of these BSI publications should go far to accommodate the purchasers' requirements.

A purchaser conforming to the appropriate British Standards specification and accepting the advice of the relevant Code of Practice is accepting the recommendation of a competent panel of experts drawn from user interests as well as manufacturers. The appropriate BSI publications are given (see Bibliography p. L4/15).

In an attempt to come to a common safety code throughout Europe many years of research and discussions have taken place with the result that a European Standard has been agreed upon for electric lifts known as EN81/1. A European standard for hydraulic lifts, EN81/2 has just been approved.

BS 5655 Part 1 1979 conforms in large to this Standard, the only exceptions being certain clauses which are subject to the Factories Act or building regulations which were already in force and which are law. It should be stressed, however, that there are very few exceptions to EN81/1 and they are all listed in Appendix V of BS 5655 Part 1. The EEC have signed a Directive in September 1984 for implementation by all member countries by September 1986. This Directive is an "optional" one which means that a country's own particular Standard can still be used in parallel to the EEC Directive but that a member state cannot refuse to accept an electric lift supplied from another member country which conforms to the EEC Directive. One of the essential features of the EEC Directive is that certain lift components need to be type tested and these are again fully listed in BS 5655/1. The EN 81/2 for hydraulic lifts has at present no Directive.

The situation of an optional Dirtective will be reviewed after 5 years to see whether it should be made a "total" Directive which means that the member states would have to make their own standard comply with the Directive and also make it law.

Since the British Standard BS 5655 complies almost totally with the EN81/1 Standard most British manufacturers have already altered their equipment in recent years to conform with its requirements apart from having the particular components officially type tested which are being undertaken at the present time. There is an officially approved BSI test authority and UK test tower.

TYPES OF LIFTS.—The type of lift required is determined by the purpose for which it is to be used and the nature of the building into which it is to be installed. The more general classifications for these lifts are as follows:

Passenger Lifts.—These are lifts for the carrying of people and are usually installed in such buildings as office blocks, apartment houses and public buildings. The passenger carrying capacity of such lifts is determined by BS 5655 Parts 1, 2 and 5. These Standards determine the recommended sizes of lift cars, door openings and shaft sizes. The relevant speed of the lift is again recommended and is usually the function of travel, number of floors height and population of the building.

The quantity, capacity and speed of lifts to suit a building is usually determined by traffic study calculations (see p. L4/5).

Goods Lifts.—These lifts are used primarily for the transportation of goods although they can be designed to accommodate passengers as well. The size of cars and shaft are a function of the load to be carried and set down in BS 5655 Parts 1, 2 and 5. The types of doors are generally manual although power operation can also be supplied. The range of loads offered for such lifts varies considerably.

Service Lifts.—These lifts may be electrically or hand-power driven and are usually applied to small loads, their major application being food carrying restaurant lifts. These lifts are not passenger carrying and their definition will be found in BS 5655 Part 1.

The present British Standard applying to these lifts is BS 2655/1. A new standard BS 5655/3 is being prepared.

Fire Fighting Lifts.—BS 5588/5 has been issued during 1986 and changes the previous concept of a firemans lift to a fire fighting lift. This means that a fire fighting lift is designated to have additional protection with controls that enable it to be used under the direct control of the Fire Brigade. The lift should be built within a fire fighting lift shaft and well, which essentially requires a fire fighting lobby in front of the lift, a separate stair-well, all enclosed in its own fire resistant enclosure. It is therefore vital, at the planning stage, that BS 5588/5 is consulted to determine the number of fire fighting lifts, together with their location and shaft construction.

Lifts for residential and personal use.—In recent years considerable attention has been given to the needs of the elderly or disabled, to enable them to continue to live independently and maintain mobility within the home. The major handicap frequently is the staircase, and if this problem can be overcome by means of a simple and economical lift, then the need for continual home help attention, or alternatively removal to hospital, is eliminated or at least postponed. Recent British Standards BS 5776 1979, BS 5900 1980 and BS 5965 1980 lay down safety guidelines for the construction of simple lifts of this type and are being adopted quite widely by individual companies and by Local Authorities as a basis for a small but important section of the market. The range covered is quite wide, extending from a simple hand-operated installation to one which has many of the features of a standard general purpose passenger lift. BS 5900 will shortly be revised. Note BS 5900 applies to single family dwellings and not nursing homes.

Lifts for the handicapped.—There is increasing legislative requirement for physically handicapped people to travel freely within multi-storey buildings. So far as lifts are concerned, it has been established that the minimum convenient size of passenger lifts in the UK is the standard 8 person lift to BS 5655, 1100 mm × 1400 mm inside car with 800 mm clear entrance width, for those in self-propelled wheelchairs, with the car and landing push-buttons in positions and heights suitable for the wheelchair occupants. Where there are special needs for the blind, then Braille symbols can be provided on push box face-plates, and for severely handicapped special low-level push boxes. In residential homes for old people, attention is necessary to the operating speed and sequence timing of the automatic doors, and special audible signals may be necessary.

PRINCIPLE LIFT DRIVES.—The type of lift drive which is necessary for particular installations is usually dependent upon the classification of the lift chosen. The customer is generally interested in the classification and the drive is of secondary importance to him. However, at the initial planning stage, the selection of the drive can be very important since it can greatly effect the structural features of the building in the vicinity of the lift shaft. The various principles of the various types of drives are therefore listed below. Namely,

Electric Traction Drive.—This is the most common type of lift drive. The lift car is suspended from a set of steel wire ropes in friction contact via V or U shaped grooves with a traction sheave connected to the lift machine which is usually mounted above the lift shaft. The other end of the rope is connected to a counterweight which travels in the lift well in the opposite direction to the car. The movement of the car is effected by the lift machine rotating the traction sheave. Drive to the traction sheave is normally from a high-speed electric motor through a worm-reduction gear box, though in high speed 'gearless' lifts a slow speed motor is used, coupled directly to the traction sheave.

To reduce power requirement, the counterweight is made equivalent to the weight of the lift car plus approximately half the rated load carried in the car.

Depending on technical circumstances, 2:1 roping is sometimes used instead of 1:1 roping, and sometimes the lift machines may require to be mounted at the side or the bottom of the lift well. In these cases the suspension ropes have to be diverted by appropriate additional pulleys and/or on the car and counterweight.

As the drive in all these cases depends completely on friction between ropes and sheave, there are strict limits on the relationship between dimensions of the ropes, sheaves, sheave grooves and the relative weight of car and counterweight so that there is no risk of uncontrolled slippage of ropes in sheave grooves.

The method of driving the traction sheave with this type of drive is usually via the use of an electric motor. The control of such motors can vary widely and is normally dependent upon the maximum nominal contract speed of the lift itself. Typical methods are:

SINGLE SPEED AC DRIVE.—In general, a single speed lift machine powered by a single speed AC motor can provide stopping within 35 mm of floor level from a running speed of about 0·5 m/s, and this is probably the maximum acceptable limits in UK for such a lift used for light passenger duty.

Stopping distance and levelling accuracy for a lift depends normally on the mechanical brake for stopping, and is related to the square of the speed at which the brake is applied. For more accurate stopping therefore, and greater comfort, it is necessary to reduce the speed of the lift electrically before applying the mechanical brake, and generally a levelling speed not exceeding 0·3 m/s is sought.

2-SPEED POLE CHANGE AC DRIVE.—The next stage of drive sophistication is the use of 2-speed pole change AC motors. These are double wound 3-phase motors having 2 synchronous speeds, generally in ratio 3:1 to 6:1. The higher speed is used for normal running and the lower speed is switched on electrically at a preset distance from floor level to provide a slower approach speed at which the mechanical brake is applied to stop the lift. Levelling accuracy of 10 mm is normally obtainable. The comfort of the speed transition from high to low speed can be adjusted and improved by a number of ways, both in the construction of the motor and in the electric circuitry which effects the transition. Lifts of this type are used for lift speeds up to 1·0 m/s, with carefully designed motors and control circuits. There is now a trend towards variable-speed a.c. with direct floor approach at speeds of 1·0 m/s and 1.6 m/s.

WARD–LEONARD DC DRIVE.—Beyond 1·0 m/s we come into the region of high-speed lifts for higher buildings, generally office or hotel, where comfort, accurate stopping and short floor-to-floor times are essential features, and a satisfactory overall speed pattern needs to be established and maintained if the system is to work effectively. For many years the answer to the problem in this speed range has been found in the use of a DC lift motor controlled on the Ward–Leonard Variable Voltage principle from an AC/DC motor–generator set. A DC motor is a variable speed unit in contrast to the fixed speed characteristics of the conventional single- or 2-speed AC machine. Therefore a smooth and flexible speed pattern can be established through suitable control equipment which can enable the lift to accelerate or decelerate smoothly at whatever rate is desired and to come to rest electrically, so that the mechanical brake can function merely as a holding brake. Geared lifts of this type are used up to speeds of at least 1·6 m/s. Levelling accuracy of 6 mm is obtainable. They are used also on lower speed lifts where a very smooth ride is essential, even though considerably more costly than 2-speed AC. A system now used as an alternative to MG set is a static convertor, which provides through thyristors an equivalent controllable DC power source for the lift motor. However, mains pollution and harmonics have to be carefully filtered with these drives.

VARIABLE SPEED AC.—The alternative to DC drive for the same speed range is the variable speed AC motor, and this has become a common means of drive for higher-speed geared lift machines. This may be fed from controlled solid state devices. Typically a preset speed pattern is established electronically and monitored, normally by means of a tachogenerator driven from the lift motor itself. The power fed to the motor produces the necessary value of torque to drive or brake the lift in accordance with the prescribed stepless speed pattern from start to stop. A levelling accuracy of 6 mm is obtainable.

GEARLESS.— For the drive of gearless lift machines the principle of motor drive is DC, similar to that for higher speed geared DC machines, although the control circuitry is generally more elaborate. Such lifts can operate up to and beyond 7 m/s, though in the UK few exceed 5 m/s since building heights do not justify this.

Electro-hydraulic Drive.—This is the main alternative means of drive generally suitable for short or medium rise lifts. The lift car is connected directly, or indirectly via a rope or chain suspension, to a long stroke hydraulic ram mounted below or at the side of the car in the lift well. Movement of the car is effected through flow of oil in or out of the hydraulic cylinder. The oil is provided under pressure from a power pack incorporating an oil pump driven by an electric motor, and a sophisticated control valve which effects a smooth starting and stopping of the lift in both directions of motion.

For some applications this means of drive is more suitable than traction drive on grounds of convenience, low shaft headroom or building cost. The machine room does not, as is necessary with traction drive, require to be located above or immediately adjacent to the lift well. As no significant loads are imposed on the lift well structure or upper floors of the building, lighter means of building construction may be possible. On the other hand the raised load of the lift is not counter-balanced and therefore such installations consume considerably more electricity than electric traction lifts. Therefore the electric motor is considerably larger than for the corresponding traction lift, requiring heavier electric cabling.

The speed of hydraulic lifts, depends directly on the flow rate of oil in and out of the hydraulic ram/cylinder unit and is usually limited to 1·0 m/s. A constant speed pump, usually screw-type for smooth action, is driven by a single-speed AC motor for upward travel. Speed control is therefore completely effected by a hydraulic valve system which feeds the oil flow to the ram at the required rate and by-passes the surplus back to the storage tank. In some cases this may be monitored by a speed-sensing device which enables a pre-determined speed pattern to be maintained under varying load conditions. For downward travel, the car descends under its own weight, the speed control system regulating the oil flow back to the tank. The levelling accuracy can be within the same range as for traction lifts detailed under Two-Speed Pole Change AC drive.

LIFT CONTROL SYSTEMS.—Lifts are mainly activated by signals from push-buttons mounted on the landings and in the car. Such signals are relayed to the lift controller which according to the algorithm of the system will eventually result in the call(s) being served. The way in which a group of lifts responds to the car and landing calls may vary widely in its complexity and will depend upon many factors such as the number of floors served, the configuration of the building and the type of drive.

Two widely used control systems are described below:

Automatic Push-button.—The lift is capable of receiving, storing and acting upon one instruction at a time. When the lift is standing at rest at a floor, a button pressed at a landing, or in the car, will cause the lift to travel to the required landing, stop there and await a further call. It cannot receive any other calls while it is travelling. Such a system is simple and generally adequate only for lifts where traffic is light and few landings served.

Collective.—In this system a lift is capable of receiving and storing calls while at rest or in motion. It then follows an established pattern of response. At each intermediate landing there are 'up' and 'down' pushes and at each terminal landing a single push. Registration of a call is normally indicated by illumination of the push. The car contains a full set of floor pushes. Pressure on a car push for a floor above the car, or an 'up' push on a landing, will cause the doors to close and the car to move upwards. On its way up, the car will answer all registered landing calls for an 'up' direction, and any further car calls registered for floors above the car.

While the car is travelling up, the 'down' calls will not be effective to stop the car 'till up calls ahead of the car have been answered, but they will be registered, becoming effective when the car has answered the uppermost call and reverses its direction of motion. Then a similar pattern of operation commences for dealing with 'down' calls and car calls registered for floors below the car.

A simplified form of collective control, 'down' collective is employed in buildings where the bulk of the traffic is between the ground floor and individual upper floors, as in a block of flats, and there is little interfloor traffic. The system does not register 'up' landing calls, only 'down' calls, and for this reason there is only one push-button located in each landing station.

Where the traffic requirements justify two lifts side-by-side, they are normally interconnected to form a duplex collective system. They share a common set of landing push-buttons, and the calls registered in the system are allocated to one or other of the cars in a way which takes into account most effectively the position and direction of motion of each car.

Typically one car, designated the 'parked car' will park at a specified 'home floor'. The second car will be a 'free car' and will park at the floor where it became free. Initially only the free car will respond to any landing calls registered, but if after a predetermined time any landing calls remain unanswered the 'parked car' will be released to assist in answering landing calls. If a car call is registered on the 'parked car', it will immediately be released to answer landing calls. The direction of intended movement of the car on arrival at a floor will be indicated by an illuminated sign generally mounted in the lift entrance frame. An audible signal announces the approach of a car.

The first lift to become free will return to the 'home floor' and if on arrival no outstanding landing calls are registered, it will become the 'parked car' until such time as it is released again because of outstanding landing calls. If one lift is out of service for any reason, all landing calls will be routed to the operative lift.

In normal operation both lifts will continue to respond to all landing calls, with either lift answering a landing call. Once a landing call has been answered by one lift, the call will be cancelled on both lifts.

Group Control.—Three or more lifts may be interconnected into a collective system. With an increasing number of cars and height of building, the system of landing call allocation to individual cars becomes increasingly complex. For 3 cars a relatively simple extension of the 2 car system may be adequate, but for 4 to 8 cars (the practical limit) some form of supervisory system is used, nowadays often making use of micro-chip technology which can swiftly analyse all the relevant information and make decisions on landing and car call allocation and the relative position of cars to optimise continually traffic handling. Such a system may also be capable of logging data on call response times, displaying call handling graphically on TV screens, and even detecting and logging intermittent deviations from optimum lift performance.

The design of lift control systems for heavy traffic in high buildings is a subject for the specialist, and much care is necessary in the selection of the size and number of lift cars and their speed. For preliminary guidance tables are available in for instance, the BS 5655 Part 6 but detailed design of the scheme depends on a thorough knowledge of the planned use of an individual building and the traffic handling capabilities of lift manufacturers' equipment. This needs to be studied at an early stage of the building project, as the number, shape and size of the lift wells is an important structural matter within the frame of a building. The features of traffic study are described on page L4/5.

EMERGENCY CONTROL.—Lifts form a vital part of the transport system of a building. In a non-fire emergency, for instance, failure of electric power in a building, it may be necessary to maintain vertical transportation by at least a portion of the lift installation, and therefore it is now common practice in larger buildings and hospitals for the lifts to function on an emergency power supply network, which is switched on automatically if mains power fails. A number of operating systems are used, some of which restrict the number and speed of lifts remaining in service, possibly returning all others sequentially to the main floor.

RECOMMENDED LIFT DIMENSIONS.—It is strongly recommended that the Architect or Consulting Engineer uses the recommended range of loads, speeds, car sizes and shaft sizes as laid down in BS 5655 Part 5. This standard reflects much of the technical content of the ISO 4190/1 and ISO 4190/3 standards and also specific requirements relevant to the UK practice.

Of particular importance are the recommendations for:

(1) the top headroom which is the dimension from the upper terminal floor level to the underside of the lift shaft ceiling
(2) the depth of the lift pit which is the dimension from the lower landing to the base of the lift shaft
(3) the height of the machine room.

These dimensions are based on the requirements of BS 5655 Part 1.

The selection of the recommended sizes of lifts are particularly advantageous to the client since there are many lift companies who use standardised components and therefore can offer more attractive prices for such sizes. However, it is also common practice in the lift industry for the lift maker to offer 'tailor-made' installations to suit special building configurations.

For the modernisation of the existing lifts in existing buildings, many parts of BS 2655/8 applies, although a replacement standard BS 5655/11/12 is being prepared.

Basic diagrams of lift arrangements will be found in BS 5655 Part 5 and this standard should be used for the initial planning of buildings although it must be stressed that the number of lifts is often the subject of a detailed traffic analysis as discussed below.

TRAFFIC STUDIES FOR PASSENGER LIFTS.—Traffic studies may be defined as a method of determining the number of lifts, their capacities, loads and speeds which are required to move a certain amount of traffic in the form of people within a building within a given time. Whilst it is advised that the lift manufacturers are individually consulted at the initial planning stage of a building due to the specialist nature of such an analysis, the BS 5655 Part 6 gives a very helpful general guide.

The most important factors which determine the final calculations may be listed as follows:

(1) the population of each floor which is served by the lifts
(2) the floor heights of the building
(3) the number of floors which the lifts have to serve within a building
(4) the maximum traffic demand by people which generally occurs morning, noon and evening.

These are not the only factors which affect the calculation since flexi-time, the type of use the lift is given, whether there are basement entrances for individual lifts of a group of lifts, all have important effect on the overall installation performance and analysis.

The final calculation which is designed to populate a building at a certain rate uses three main factors:

(1) the number of people who require lift service
(2) the interval which is a measure of the quantitive services required
(3) the handling capacity required.

The population of a building is dependent upon the type of use to which it is to be put or how it is to be let and is normally measured in square metres per person. It is imperative that this information is given to the lift maker for his calculation, to enable a meaningful study to be made.

The interval is the time taken for one round trip of one lift car defined by the number of cars which form the group system. This gives a measure of the quality of service and the average waiting time for passengers is theoretically 50% of the interval although in practice it is probably nearer 75% of the interval. It should be noted, however, that during peak periods such as morning, lunchtime, and evening the waiting times are generally longer and the interval can be considered irrelevant for these periods.

As a very general guide, one lift is required for approximately every (a) 3 floors for excellent quality service; (b) 4 floors for average quality service; (c) 5 floors for below average quality service. Furthermore, the carrying capacity of any groups of lifts should not be less than 630 kg per lift.

The individual calculations from each lift maker will differ for a particular building since they will be based on their own individual equipment which usually differs from company to company.

BUILDERS' WORK.—It is absolutely essential for a safe, good running lift installation that there is close mutual liaison between the building contractor, architect and lift maker at an early stage.

Shaft.—It is essential for the builder to provide a clean plumb shaft within the tolerances indicated in BS 5655 Part 6. It is the practice of lift makers always to state the minimum plumb shaft on the layout drawing with any out of plumb tolerances being as an addition to these minimum dimensions.

Lift shafts are very often constructed of concrete and it is common practice within the UK to have metal inserts imbedded into the wall during the shaft construction for the accommodation of guide brackets and lift entrances. When brick shafts are the method of construction then concrete blocks carrying the metal inserts are normally used and located within the shaft walls.

There has been a recent trend towards Fast Track building construction using a main supporting steel frame and dry wall linings. It is most important for the contractor to liaise directly with the lift contractor to discuss attachments of the lift to the building frame and the fire rating of entrances.

Machine Room.—With regard to the machine room it is essential that this is constructed to the relevant regulations regarding, dimensions, temperature and ventilation since failure to do so would contravene HSE regulations for the safe working of the maintenance and construction personnel as well as having a detrimental effect on the lift performance and operation.

It is usual practice that the lift maker does not commence work on site until shaft and motor rooms have been satisfactorily constructed often with the inclusion requirement of scaffolding having to be provided by the builder.

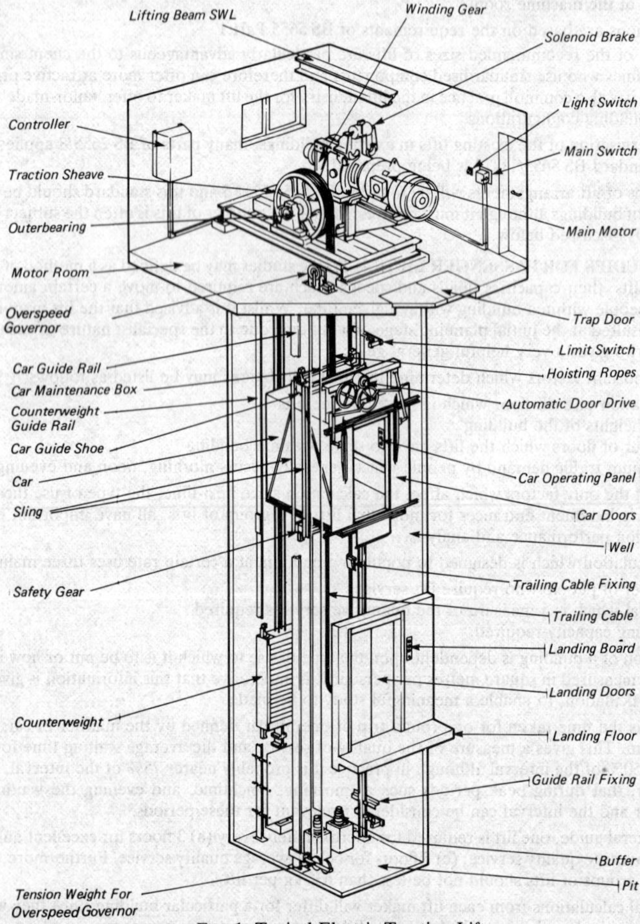

FIG. 1. Typical Electric Traction Lift.

LIFT WELL CONSTRUCTION AND TOLERANCES.—It is vital that the lift well is constructed within the tolerances laid down in BS 5655 Part 6. It is also important that the outside of the front wall is also constructed within the recommended tolerances so that architraves may be satisfactorily manufactured by the lift maker without recourse to tailor-made measurements during the construction of the lift which could cause delays and increased cost in the contract. Furthermore, when the front wall thickness is given by the architect, the thickness of the intended finish should also be detailed if architraves are to be supplied by the lift maker. If the tolerances are exceeded, it may be necessary to remanufacture all the lift brackets, lift car and architraves.

Typical electric and hydraulic lifts.—Figure 1 shows the configuration of a typical electric traction lift with machine room above. There can be many variations of where the machine room is sited. It is possible to mount it, at the bottom, adjacent to or below the shaft, or at the top at the side. This can change the arrangement of ropes quite dramatically, and in many cases, a separate overhead pulley room is required to conform with BS 5655 Part 1.

Figure 2 shows the configuration of a typical indirect acting hydraulic lift with the jack mounted in the shaft.

Figure 3 illustrates a typical direct acting hydraulic lift with machine room at the lowest level served. This lift, where the lifting jack is placed centrally under the car would normally require a well bore hole as shown. There are many other configurations and methods of lifting the car by placing the jack within the normal lift shaft depths and at the side of the car which can be discussed directly with the lift manufacturer.

INSTALLATION AND SERVICING.—A completed lift is subjected to careful check and running tests by the manufacturer before hand-over to the customer, and a detailed test certificate provided which is generally on the lines of the recommendations of BS 5655/10.

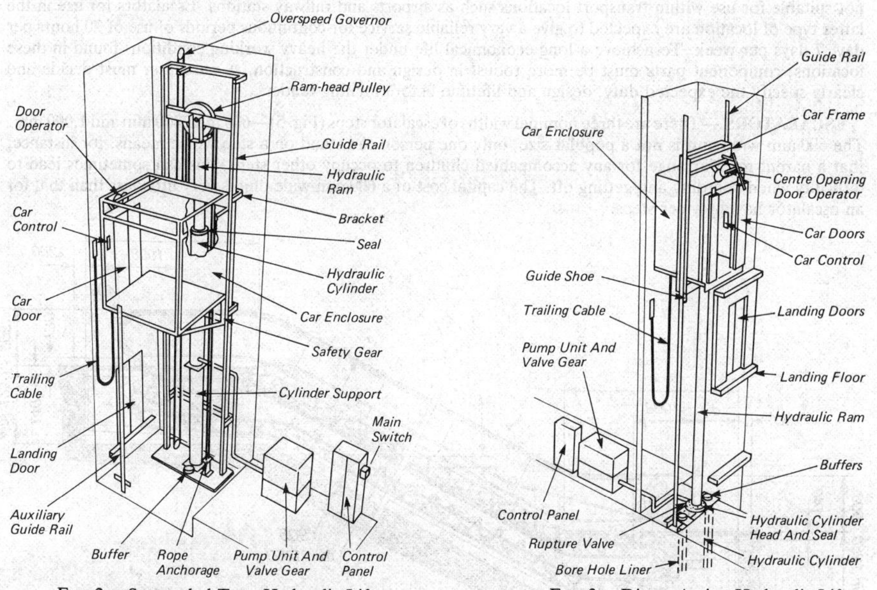

FIG. 2.—Suspended Type Hydraulic Lift.

FIG. 3.—Direct Acting Hydraulic Lift.

To satisfy legal requirements, most lifts (except mainly in private dwellings) require six-monthly checks by a competent person to confirm such items as lifting ropes and landing door locks which if defective could present hazards to the lift user. A prescribed form of report is used, which must be retained by the owner for possible Government inspection, eg in event of a dangerous incident. Apart from this legally-prescribed inspection many insurance companies require that lifts covered by their policies must be checked regularly by their own inspection engineers.

In order to keep lifts in good and safe operational order, regular servicing is necessary, and this is usually provided on a regular contractural basis, normally by the servicing organisation of the original lift installer who has specialised knowledge of the equipment. They provide as necessary, the facilities for major and minor repairs and the ability to deal promptly, frequently on a round-the-clock basis, with lift stoppages however caused. They are able to report on the condition of the lift, recommend and provide equipment for the progressive up-dating of the equipment throughout the building as the needs arise, and undertake the periodic examinations required by law.

ESCALATORS AND PASSENGER CONVEYORS.—Escalators and passenger conveyors are a form of public transport suitable for moving large numbers of people between adjacent floor levels and for relatively short horizontal distances. They find application in large department stores, shopping precincts, banks, hotels, hospitals, airports, bus stations, railway premises, exhibition halls etc.

Escalators are generally installed between all floors of Department Stores and have found uses on the lower levels of commercial buildings because of their passenger handling capabilities. When installed in offices they allow a more efficient lift service to the higher floors.

Standardisation.—British Standard No. 5656 (1983) has replaced BS 2655 Part 4. Reference should be made to the National appendix W which clearly sets out the timetable for compliance with BS 5656 and the status of BS 2655 during the interim period of 3 years from November, 1983.

It is necessary that all components (1) are properly dimensioned, of sound mechanical and electrical construction and made of material with adequate strength and of suitable quality and free from defects; (2) are kept in good repair and working order. In particular, care shall be taken that the dimensions indicated are maintained despite wear; if necessary, the worn parts shall be replaced.'

It should be realised that BS 5656 is a document which concentrates on the safety features to be incorporated in the design, construction and operation of escalators. The question of the quality of Engineering design incorporated within component parts is a separate matter. It is the responsibility of the purchaser or his engineer to specify and be satisfied that the engineering quality of component parts of a machine will be equal to the duty and life expectancy required.

A range of escalator designs from those in use in departmental stores to the very heavy duty types found in busy underground railway applications. The type of escalators used in the majority of department stores are not suitable for use within transport locations such as airports and railway stations. Escalators for use in the latter type of location are expected to give a very reliable service for continuous periods of use of 20 hours per day, 7 days per week. To achieve a long economical life under the heavy working conditions found in these locations, component parts must be more robust in design and construction. A purchaser must decide and clearly specify the expected duty, design and lifetime before inviting tenders.

ESCALATORS.—There are three nominal widths of escalator steps (Fig. 5)—600 mm, 800 mm and 1,000 mm. The 600 mm wide unit is not a popular size, only one person can stand on a step which means, for instance, that a parent must arrange for any accompanied children to occupy other steps, this can sometimes lead to difficulty when boarding and getting off. The capital cost of a 600 mm wide unit is very little less than that for an escalator having wider steps.

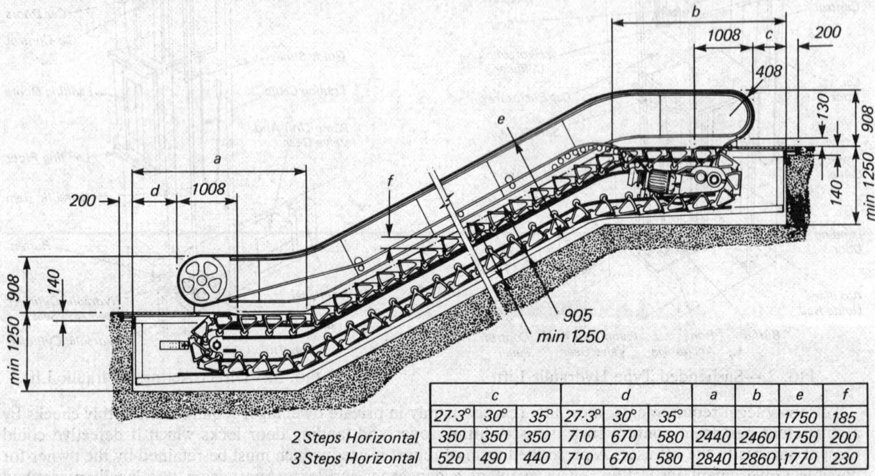

	c			d			a	b	e	f
	27·3°	30°	35°	27·3°	30°	35°			1750	185
2 Steps Horizontal	350	350	350	710	670	580	2440	2460	1750	200
3 Steps Horizontal	520	490	440	710	670	580	2840	2860	1770	230

FIG. 4.—Section Through Typical Escalator.

A popular escalator step width used in department stores is 800 mm. With this step it is possible for a parent and child to stand side by side on this size of step. However, for the lower floors of large Department Stores and other places where a heavy traffic flow is to be expected, the 1,000 mm step width is more usual. This width allows two persons with hand luggage or shopping bags to stand side by side. Also there is sufficient room for persons to walk past other passengers who are standing to one side as is usual practice in some underground railway applications.

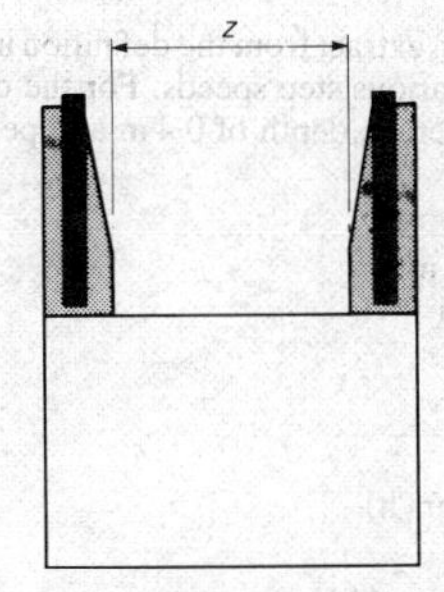

FIG. 5.—Nominal Width z of an Escalator/Passenger Conveyor.

Escalator Speed.—The maximum allowable speed of any escalator is 0·75 m/sec. provided the angle of inclination does not exceed 30°. If the angle of inclination is more than 30°, but not more than 35° then the speed must not exceed 0·50 m/sec.

Angles of Inclination.—The angle of inclination of an escalator should not exceed 30° but for rises not exceeding 6·0 m the angle of inclination is permitted to be increased to a maximum of 35° subject to the speed limitation above. Manufacturers offer standard units of 30° and 35° inclination in accordance with the above, also some manufacturers offer escalators having an angle of inclination of about 27° to match the incline of adjacent staircases, but these units are not in quantity production and are relatively expensive.

Nominal width z m	Rated speed m/s		
	0·5	0·65	0·75
0·6	4,500 pers/h	5,850 pers/h	6,750 pers/h
0·8	6,750 pers/h	8,775 pers/h	10,125 pers/h
1·0	9,000 pers/h	11,700 pers/h	13,500 pers/h

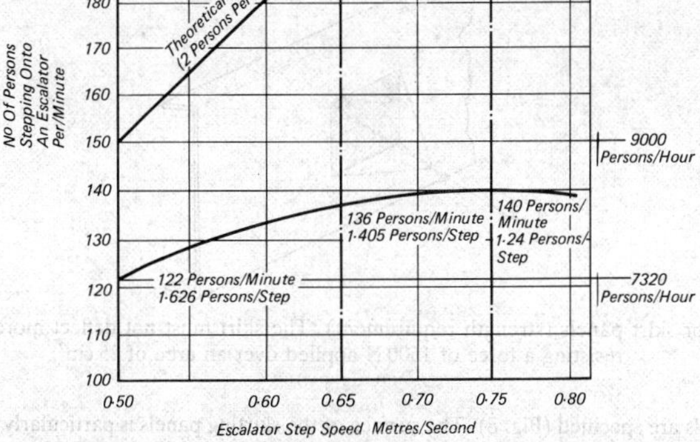

FIG. 6.—The Influence of Speed on the Carrying Capacity of Escalators. (The measured escalator capacity was achieved from a moving queue waiting to board escalators.) Ref. A. J. Mayo, Imperial College.

Escalator Capacity.—The following is an extract from the definition in BS 5656. The chart gives the theoretical capacity for each width of escalator for various step speeds. For the determination of the theoretical capacity it is assumed that on one step with an average depth of 0·4 m and per 0·4 m visible length of a pallet or belt, there are carried:

1 person at a nominal width z = 0·6 m
1·5 persons at a nominal width z = 0·8 m
2 persons at a nominal width z = 1·0 m

Theoretical capacity calculation is then:

$$c_t = \frac{v}{0{\cdot}4} \times 3600 \times k$$

c_t = theoretical capacity (pers/h)
v = Rated speed (m/s)

The K factor for the most common widths will be:

k = 1 for z = 0·6 m
k = 1·5 for z = 0·8 m
k = 2 for z = 1·0 m

With this formula the theoretical capacities will be as shown in Fig. 6 (page L4/9):

It must be noted that in practice the number of people moved on an escalator depends upon many factors not the least of which is the ability of the public at large to present themselves onto the escalator steps at the rate that steps become available. Several studies have been carried out both within the UK, Europe and the Far East and the findings are generally in agreement. The actual capacity of an escalator is less than the theoretical capacity and for step speeds higher than about 0·7 m/s, the number of passengers carried per minute decreases. Figure 6 (page L4/9) shows measured capacities against escalator speeds obtained during various studies. The usual speed for escalators in shopping malls, department stores etc is about 0·5 m/s and it has been observed that even if there is a moving queue, except in very special circumstances such as store sales, no more than 110 persons per minute board a 1·0 m wide escalator.

During normal busy periods the average number of persons boarding an escalator has been measured at 100 per minute over a 5 minute interval.

Steps.—The minimum design requirements for the strength of steps is specified in BS 5656 which document requires them to be type tested. For instance, a fatigue test has been introduced which calls for a minimum of 5 million cycles against a force fluctuating between 500 N and 3,000 N. Step and pallet designs must withstand this test together with other tests without permanent deformation and damage.

Most step designs are manufactured from aluminium alloy die castings with grooves in the step risers. These grooves overlap with extensions of the treadplate ribs so that a continuous clearance gap is not available into which some types of footwear could be drawn when a step riser moves in a vertical direction with respect to a following step, as is the case if plain risers are used. Dimensions of the tread grooves and clearances with respect to riser grooves and comb teeth are specified.

Balustrade Skirtings.—These panels are immediately adjacent to the side of the steps and the minimum strength requirement is now specified (Fig. 7). The maximum allowable running clearances between the step

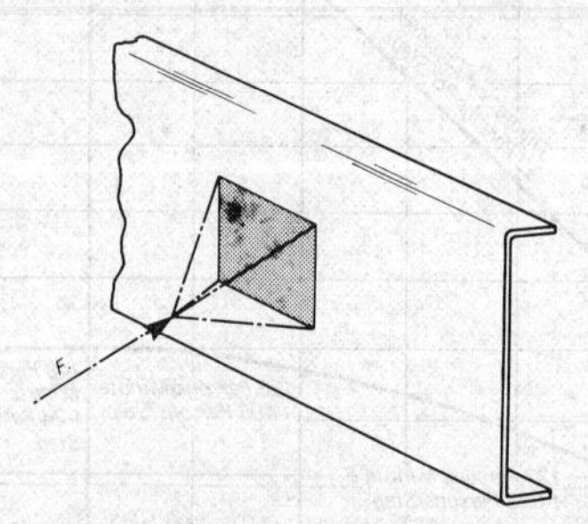

FIG. 7.— Escalator skirt panels (strength requirement). The skirt must not deflect more than 4·0 mm when resisting a force of 1500 N applied over an area of 25 cm².

and the skirt panels are specified (Fig. 8). The surface of the skirting panels is particularly important for safety reasons, it is specified that the surface should have a low coefficient of friction and this is usually achieved by coating the surface with PTFE. The low friction surface should be maintained in good condition during the life of the escalator.

Skirting Guards.—The Guidance Note PM 34 published by the Health and Safety Executive in November, 1983 requires devices to be fitted to the skirting panels to minimise the likelihood of foot-wear, particularly childrens wellington type boots coming into direct contact with the skirting panel. An extract from this Guidance Note is shown as a National Variation in appendix V of BS 5656. Suitable deflector devices should be fitted on all new escalators ordered after January 1st 1984. Retrospective fitting of deflector devices is required for all existing downward moving escalators.

Balustrading.—For indoor type locations toughened glass balustrades have become normal, for other applications such as outdoor locations, stainless steel is used. There are minimum strength and rigidity requirements to be observed by the manufacturers.

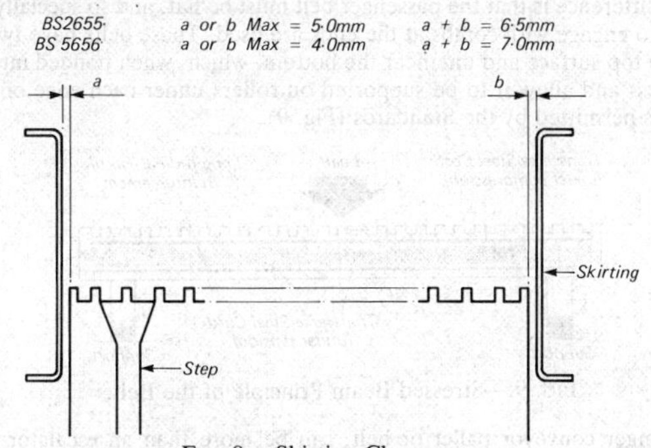

FIG. 8.—Skirting Clearances.

Driving Machinery and Brakes.—Escalators are usually driven by means of an induction type motor from an AC supply through a worm and wheel type of reduction gear and coupled either directly or through roller type duplex chains to the step chain wheel shaft.

The steps are connected together and driven by conveyor type roller chains, the minimum factor of safety of the chains according to BS 5656 is 5 based upon a theoretical passenger load of 5,000 N per m^2 of step area. This load is equivalent to 204 kg per step which is 36% more than the average weight of two people each weighing 75 kg. BS 2655 called for a factor of safety of 8/1 in relation to a smaller load and in practice approximately similar chains are required to satisfy both specifications.

The braking performance is now specified in BS 5656 and requires minimum and maximum stopping distances to be observed for unloaded and loaded downward moving escalators. For this purpose brake test loads are specified for each width of escalator and the stopping distances for different speed values are as follows:

Rated Speed	Stopping Distance Between
0·5 m/s	min 0·20 m and max 1·00 m
0·67 m/s	min 0·30 m and max 1·30 m
0·75 m/s	min 0·35 m and max 1·50 m

For intermediate speeds the stopping distances are to be interpolated. The stopping distances shall be measured from the time the electric stopping device is actuated.

Safety Requirements.—Safety requirements are comprehensively specified in BS 5656 which includes several safety features not previously covered wtihin BS 2655. There is no need for purchasers specifications to list and describe the safety devices as they are fully specified in the British Standard.

Site Installation.—Except for a few very large escalators it is now normal for an escalator to be completely manufactured and tested within the manufacturers works and despatched as a complete unit to the site by lorry. Special consideration is usually required for admitting a one piece unit into a building and early consideration must be given to the siting of escalators within buildings.

The cost of delivery and lifting them into their final positions can be very high if adequate provision has not been allowed for offloading, moving and lifting within the site, each store type unit can weigh between 8 and 9 tons. Escalators are a finished item of equipment and their delivery should be scheduled consistent with adequate time being allowed within the programme of works and a satisfactory time allowance for commissioning and completion of surrounding building finishes. The layout, planning and programme of works should be discussed with the manufacturer at an early stage.

Layout.—Decisions respecting layout arrangements are made in the initial planning stages of a project. There are several configurations of escalator layout and the arrangement is dictated by the requirements of passenger flow throughout a building.

PASSENGER CONVEYORS.—BS 5656 specifies the constructional and safety requirements of passenger conveyors and these are generally similar to escalator requirements. Passenger conveyors are used for moving people over horizontal distances, for instance in flight piers within Airports, also, many are used in supermarkets and shopping malls. If inclined, the maximum angle of inclination is restricted to 12°. two main types are manufactured:

Pallet Type.—The pallet type of treadway is similar in appearance to escalators except that steps are not formed. If the unit is designed to span different floor levels, the pallet tracks are designed with a large transition radius to facilitate the change in inclination.

Belt Type.—In passenger conveyors using belts for treadway, the belt forms a closed loop running round a drive drum at one end and a tensioning drum at the other, similar to the belt conveyors used for materials handling. The essential difference is that the passenger belt must be flat, and so specially designed belts which have a grooved surface to engage with combs at the ends are used. These belts have two layers of transverse steel cords, one near the top surface and one near the bottom, which, when bonded into the rubber, give the belt its transverse stiffness and allow it to be supported on rollers under each edge only, without exceeding the maximum deflections permitted by the Standards (Fig. 9).

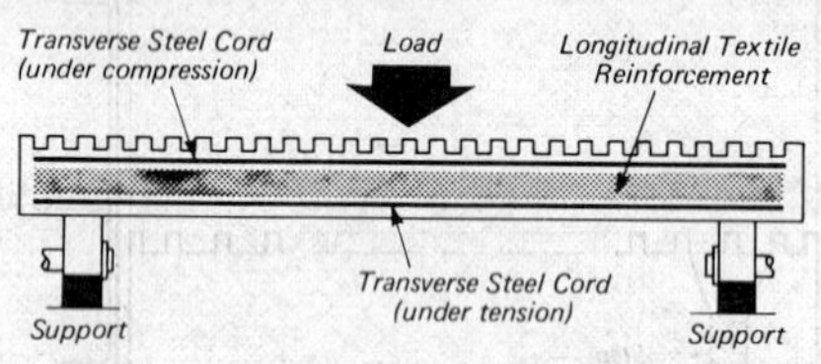

FIG. 9.—Stressed Beam Principle of the Belt.

The width of a passenger conveyor pallet or belt, can be more than an escalator step provided certain regulations are fulfilled. The maximum speed of a passenger conveyor can be increased beyond 0·75 m/s. to 0·9 m/s provided the width of the pallet is restricted to no more than 1·10 m and pallets move in a horizontal direction for at least 1·6 m before entering the combs. A newly developed type of horizontal passenger conveyor has pallets 1·4 m wide. This type is wide enough to allow passengers to pass by those in possession of heavy luggage on trolleys. They have been successfully used in airport terminal buildings and long flight piers.

Supermarket type trolleys and luggage trolleys are sometimes used in association with passenger conveyors. Some types of trolleys are not suitable for use with passenger conveyors without modification. Attention must be directed to the trolley wheels and braking system, advice should be sought to ensure compatability.

SERVICING AND PERIODIC INSPECTION.—All escalators and passenger conveyors must be serviced at regular intervals by competent persons. The service interval must be related to the intensity and duration of use of individual installations, for instance units in continuous use within Airports will require more frequent attention that units installed within Department Stores. During servicing it is important that all the clearances and features relating to the safety of users are checked and reported upon.

The Guidance Note PM45 issued by the Health and Safety Executive in June 1984 explains the position with respect to the Health and Safety at Work Act (1974) and in order to comply with this law Companies and other organisations and their service officers must ensure that escalators and passenger conveyors are safe for use at all times. The Guidance Note gives advice to legally responsible persons and to persons carrying out inspections. It specifies that in addition to the regular servicing, all installations must receive an examination at not more than six monthly intervals by a competent technician or engineer. The examination reports should be kept on the premises and be available for inspection by the inspector responsible for enforcing the Health and Safety at Work Act.

SURROUNDINGS WITHIN BUILDINGS

SAFETY REQUIREMENTS.—BS 5656 specifies the minimum clearance between Escalators and Passenger Conveyors and adjacent building obstructions, it also requires adequate circulation spaces to be provided at each end of an installation. This free area should measure at least 2·5 m from the end of the balustrade, however, if this distance is not available a minimum space 2·0 m long for a minimum width of twice the distance between the handrail centre lines should be provided (Fig. 10).

Certain circumstances demand larger circulation areas, for instance supermarkets where trolleys are in use, therefore this matter must be given adequate consideration during project planning stages. Minimum headroom clearances are required and the clear height above the steps of an escalator or of pallet and belt passenger conveyors at all points shall not be less than 2·3 m (Fig. 11).

Minimum clearances between the handrail and an obstruction such as an adjacent wall must not be less than 80 mm (Fig. 12). Headguards are required if there is an obstruction such as a vertical building column or the underside of a floor slab within 0·50 m from the centre line of a handrail (Figs. 13 and 14).

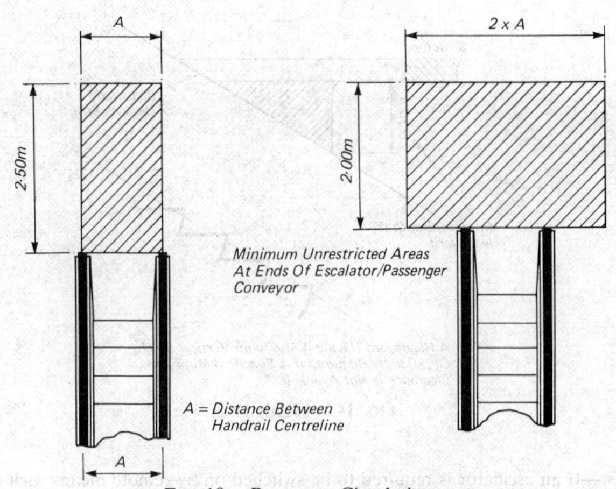

FIG. 10.—Passenger Circulation.

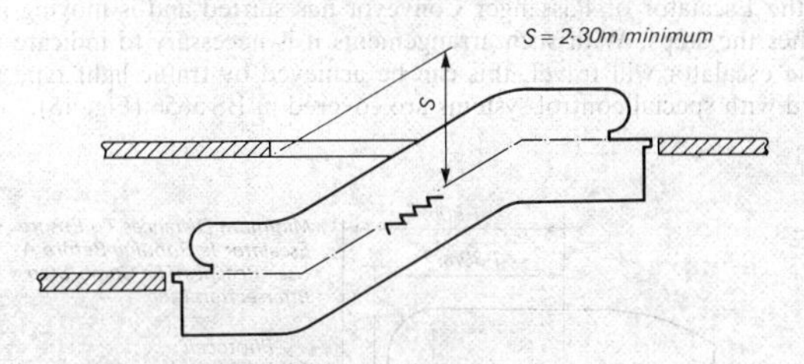

FIG. 11.—Minimum Headroom Requirement.

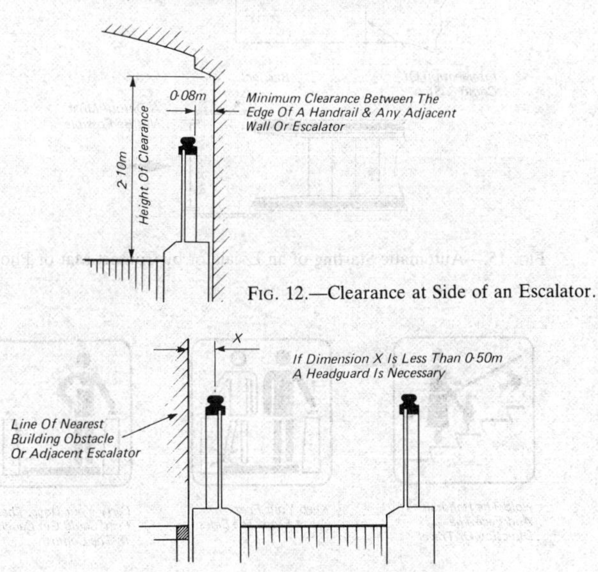

FIG. 12.—Clearance at Side of an Escalator.

FIG. 13.—Clearance at Side of an Escalator.

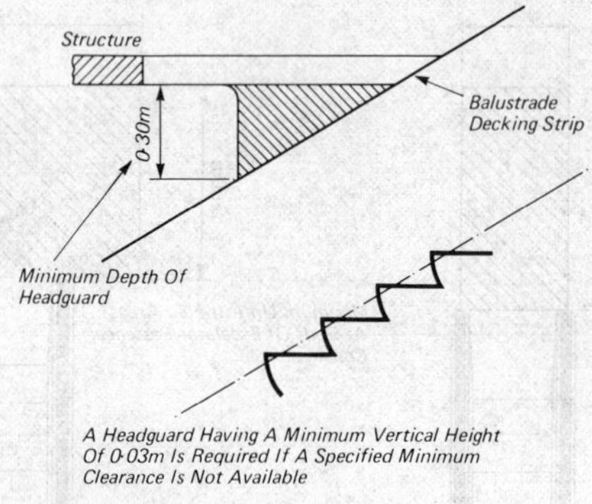

FIG. 14.—Headguard.

Special Controls.—If an escalator is required to be switched on by remote means such as a contact mat or a photo electric device, it is necessary that these devices be placed a minimum distance away from the comb lines to ensure that the Escalator or Passenger Conveyor has started and is moving in the preset direction before the user reaches the steps. With such arrangements it is necessary to indicate to intending users the direction in which the escalator will travel, this can be achieved by traffic light type indicators. The safety precautions associated with special control systems are covered in BS 5656 (Fig. 15).

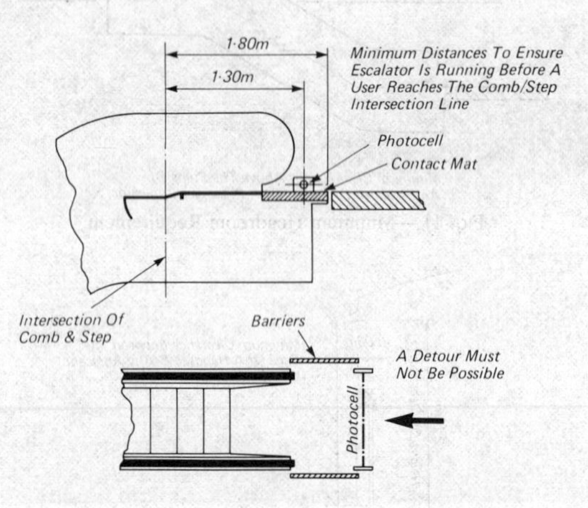

FIG. 15.—Automatic Starting of an Escalator by Contact Mat or Photocells.

FIG. 16.—Safety Notices.

Signs and Notices.—Signs or notices must be provided near to the entrances of Escalators and Passenger Conveyors. It is preferable that such signs be in the form of pictographs and should at least cover the following:

SMALL CHILDREN MUST BE HELD FIRMLY
DOGS MUST BE CARRIED
STAND FACING THE DIRECTION OF TRAVEL; KEEP FEET AWAY FROM SIDES
HOLD THE HANDRAIL

Additional notices will possibly be necessary according to local conditions. The minimum size of pictographs must be 80 mm × 80 mm and they must be manufactured of a durable material. They should be placed in positions such that they are easily seen by persons intending to use an Escalator or Passenger Conveyor (Fig. 16).

BIBLIOGRAPHY

BS 5655 Part 1 1986 Safety rules for the construction and installation of electric lifts.
BS 5655 Part 2 1983 Specification for hydraulic lifts.
*BS 5655 Part 3 Safety rules for the construction and installation of electric service lifts.
*BS 5655 Part 4 Safety rules for the construction and installation of hydraulic service lifts.
BS 5655 Part 5 1981 Specification for dimensions of standard electric lift arrangements.
BS 5655 Part 6 1985 Code of practice for selection and installation.
BS 5655 Part 7 1983 Specification for manual control devices, indicators and additional fittings.
BS 5655 Part 8 1983 Specification for eyebolts for lift suspension.
BS 5655 Part 9 1985 Specification for guide rails.
BS 5655 Part 10 Specification for testing and inspecting of electric and hydraulic lifts.
BS 5655/11 Modernisation/Construction of electric lifts.
*BS 5655/12 Modernisation/Construction of hydraulic lifts.
BS 6977 Flexible cables for lifts and other flexible connections.
*BS 5655/13 Code of Practice for safe working on lifts.
BS 2655 Part 8 1971 Modernization or reconstruction of lifts, escalators and paternosters
Note: BS 2655 is being progressively superseded by BS 5655, and BS 5656 but is still relevant for the modernisation of some existing lifts and much work in existing buildings.
BS 5656 1983 Safety rules for the construction and installation of escalators and passenger conveyors
BS 5588/5 Code of Practice for firefighting stairways and lifts.
BS 5588/8 Code of Practice for means of escape for disabled people.
BS 5965 1980 Manually driven balanced personal home lifts.
PD 6500 1986 Explanatory Supplement to BS 5655 Part 1 (latest issue 1981).
BS 5776 1979 Powered Stairlifts.
BS 5900 1980 Specification for powered home lifts.
BS 302/1/4 Stranded steel wire ropes for lifts.
BS 476/7 Method of classification of the surface flame spread of products.
BS 476 Part 8 1972: Fire Tests on Building materials and structures—fire resistance of elements.
Wiring Regulations. 15th Edition (1981) Institution of Electrical Engineers.
Health and Safety at Work etc Act 1974. HMSO.
Factories Act 1961. HMSO.
Offices, Shops & Railway Premises Act 1963. HMSO.
Building Regulations 1976. HMSO.
Construction Regulations 1961.
HSE Guidance Notes.—PM 7 (1977): Lifts, PM 8 (1977): Passenger carrying paternosters, PM 26 (1981): 'Safety at Lift Landings', PM 34. (1983) Safety in the Use of Escalators, PM 45 (1984) Escalators—Periodic Thorough Examination
Statutory Instrument.—1962: No 715 (Factories Act) Hoists Exemption Order 1962.
Statutory Instrument.—1968: No 849 (OS & RP Act) Hoists and Lifts Regulations 1968.
Statutory Instrument.—1968: No 863 (OS & RP Act) Reports Order—periodic examination form for lifts.

* Standards in the course of preparation or about to be published.

What's new in Industry
The guide to products & equipment
In this issue on page
Mechanical components and sub-assemblies 7
Factory equipment 10
Office equipment and services 18
Inspection and measurement 20
Computer systems and equipment 24
Safety, security and welfare 34
Production machines and tools 36
Environmental control 40
Process plant and control 43
Plant maintenance 48
Handling and storage 51
Finishing and materials 56
Electrical components and sub-assemblies 59
Packaging 63
Buildings and maintenance 66
Hand Tools 71
Free literature 77
Product feature: Valves & Pumps Page 26

AERIAL ROPEWAYS AND CABLEWAYS

Ropeway Types and Performance—Monocable—Bicable—Rope Sizes—Power Requirements—Loading and Labour-saving Devices—Passenger Ropeways—Cableways—Bibliography.

By Z. Frenkiel, CEng, FIMechE

AERIAL ROPEWAYS

The aerial ropeway is a form of transport in which cars of a special type, also called carriers, suspended from overhead ropes, are employed for conveying materials, goods or passengers from one station to another. The ropes are of steel wire construction and they connect the stations in a straight line, although intermediate angle stations are possible. Along the route the ropes are supported by intermediate trestles, unless the ropeway is in one span, for instance crossing a deep valley. A ropeway car consists of a carriage and a container, the latter suspended from the carriage on a pivot by means of a hanger. There are various types of carriage, their design depending on the system of the ropeway of which they form part. Generally a carriage comprises a device for gripping the hauling (or haulage) rope, and wheels to run on the carrying (or track) rope. In the monocable system, one carrying-hauling rope only is used. The hanger is swan-neck shaped; this enables the car to pass trestles and station supports. The container may be in the form of a bucket, tray, passenger cabin, etc. Buckets are usually designed for transport of materials in bulk, and may be of the tipping or bottom opening type. See Fig. 1 and Fig. 10.

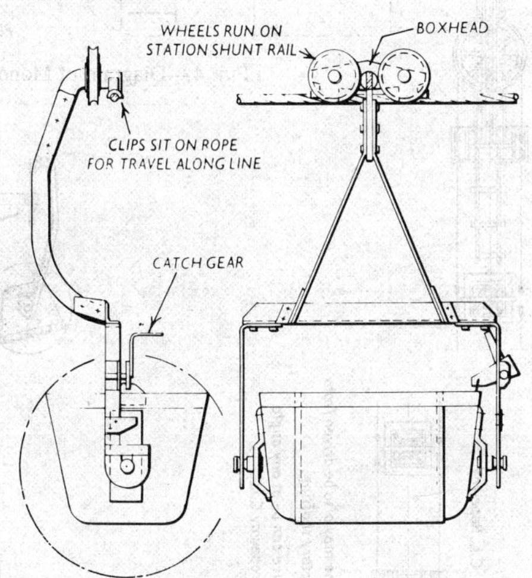

FIG. 1.—Typical Monocable Rotating Type Bucket and Hanger (*B.R.E.Co.*)

The aerial ropeway, in one form or another, can be used to transport passengers or anything that can be slung or put in a carrier or container. It has many important advantages over other means of transport, namely:—(*a*) It is not limited by adhesion between a wheel and a rail as in the case of railways, nor between rubber and road as in the case of road transport. It can therefore negotiate steeper gradients. (*b*) Being practically independent of territorial difficulties it can take the shortest route between terminals and not be concerned with those gradient problems or bridging worries which influence route selection for roads or railways. (*c*) It is not necessary to acquire the land over which a ropeway will be installed, although nominal wayleave rentals may be payable. (*d*) Visibility along the route is not a criterion for the operation of a ropeway. It can therefore operate efficiently in fog, rain or snow, or at night. (*e*) It is particularly advantageous in hilly, marshy or mountainous country since the installation cost is cheaper than for railways, road transport, or belt conveyors. (*f*) Power consumption for operating an aerial ropeway is less than for any alternative system handling the same duty over the same route.

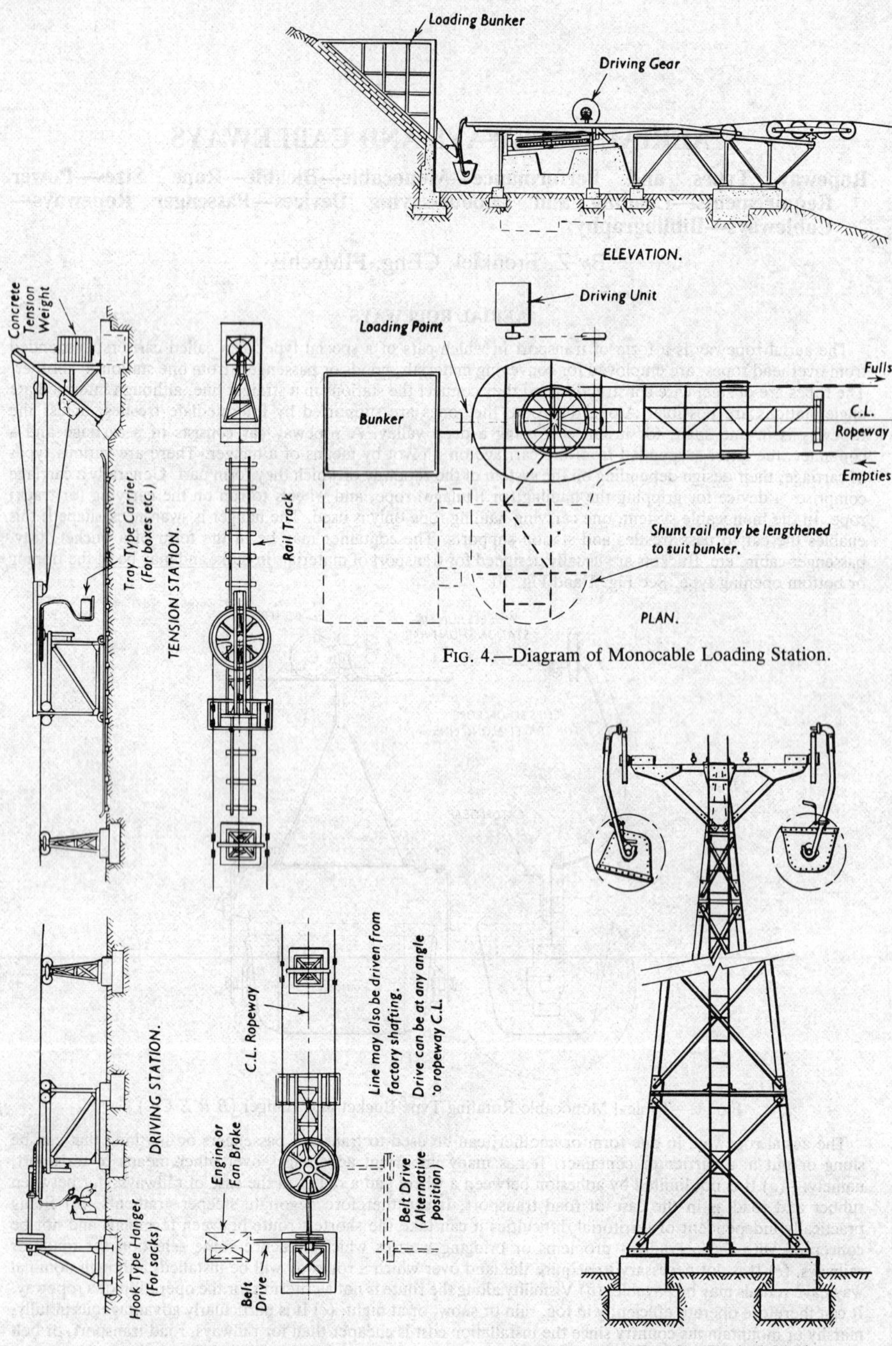

FIG. 4.—Diagram of Monocable Loading Station.

FIG. 2.—Typical Fixed-Clip Terminal Stations.

FIG. 3.—Typical Steel Monocable Trestle.

ROPEWAY LENGTH.—There is no limit to a ropeway length. This is because an aerial ropeway is composed of sections of units up to 6 miles (10 km) in length, each unit containing its own driving and tension gears. In other words, each section can be compared to an individual ropeway. These sections are connected by divide stations, where the ropeway cars are transferred automatically from one section to the next. The fact that a long ropeway is divided into sections, allows the route to be improved and difficult parts to be avoided by arranging intermediate divide stations as angle stations at no extra cost. It is also possible to provide intermediate loading and/or unloading stations for goods, and alighting or boarding stations for passengers.

In 1919 the then longest ropeway in the world was constructed by Ropeways Ltd in Dorada, Columbia. It was 73,350 m long and was split into 15 sections. It had a capacity of 20 t/h and was used for mixed cargo. A 75 km long ropeway connecting Massua and Asmara in Eritrea was built during the last war by Ceretti and Tanfani (Italy). The longest bicable ropeway is situated in Sweden and has a length of approx. 96 km with a capacity of 50 tonne/hr. The longest heavy-type monocable ropeway is in Gabon/Congo in Equatorial Africa and has a length of 77 km. Designed by BRECO (England) and constructed by an International Consortium, its speed and capacity has been increased by COMILOG engineers to 280 t/h (over 2×10^6 t/year).

ROPEWAY CLASSIFICATION.—This is generally related to the constructional systems employed, which are mainly monocable and bicable, and both can be of fixed clip and detachable grip types. Each of them can be of to-and-fro (jigback) variety, the simplest form of ropeway. These systems and types will be described in more detail and their characteristics analysed and compared.

MONOCABLE SYSTEM

The monocable system is based on the use of one single endless rope which supports and also hauls the load or loads. This rope is the 'carrying-hauling rope', or just 'the main rope'. There are two main groups of monocable ropeways:— fixed clip ropeways, and detachable grip ropeways. The endless, continuously running rope is typical for both groups. This rope passes around a large diameter sheave at each end of the line, or section of the line in case of multi-section ropeways. One of these terminal sheaves is driven by suitable gearing, while the other responds to a floating counter-weight which maintains the tension on the rope. Some installations have the driving arrangements and the tension weights at one end of the ropeway; in these cases the other terminal will be of a 'plain return' type for the rope. Along the line, the rope is supported on trestles or towers which carry pulleys on which the rope runs. The design of cars (carriers) is similar, generally, for both fixed clip and detachable grip ropeways. The individual differences and particulars of these two main groups and their variants are summarised as follows.

FIXED CLIP MONOCABLE ROPEWAYS.—The carriage of these ropeways is replaced by a clip, permanently fixing the rope to the hanger from which is suspended a carrier. There are three variations of such ropeways.

To-and-Fro ('Jigback').—This is called 'Reversible' in the USA and is one of the simplest types; a carrier travels forwards and backwards between the loading and unloading positions. Usually there are two cars, clipped to the endless rope. When one is at one terminal the other is at the opposite end terminal. The ropeway is stopped for loading and unloading. The capacity of such a plant is dependent upon the number of trips per hour that can be completed; the number of trips is in turn influenced by the distance the car has to travel. Installations of this type are normally limited to lines of a few hundred metres. Very steep gradients can be negotiated.

Continuously Running Types.—These are equipped with cars evenly spaced along the rope and permanently fixed to it. Here two alternative types are possible.—

Stop and Start System.—Here the rope is running for a few minutes, then stopped when a car arrives into the terminal station for loading and/or unloading. This system is extremely simple and cheap, but is only suitable for light units, easy to load or unload, such as sacks of tea, stems of bananas, etc. A typical example: 400 sacks per hour on a 45° slope. This system can be used for passenger transport.

Non-stop Running System.—With continuous running the ropeway must run at slow speed, say no more than 80 m/min., as passengers have to alight and board the car while the line is in motion; the same applies to loading and unloading the sacks, etc., on industrial ropeways. The length of these lines is usually limited to 3 km, and up to 40 tonne/hour.

DETACHABLE-GRIP MONOCABLE ROPEWAYS.—These are built with a continuously running endless rope to which the carriages are locked automatically when leaving a station and unlocked automatically when entering a station. The carriage enters the station on wheels, which are not used along the line, runs from the rope onto the station shunt, is unlocked from the running rope and proceeds to the loading or unloading position. The procedure is reversed on the outgoing side.

These ropeways can be divided into two groups:—(*a*) gripping type carriages of various designs, and (*b*) the English system (BRECO), characterised by an extremely simple 'carriage' called a 'boxhead'; this is provided with saddle clips, resembling an inverted 'U' which rest or 'sit' on the rope; the boxhead also incorporates wheels, as described above. The limiting factor for this type is the gradient, which must not exceed 23° on the steepest slope anywhere along the line. On a steeper line, clips must be provided with projecting 'pips' to

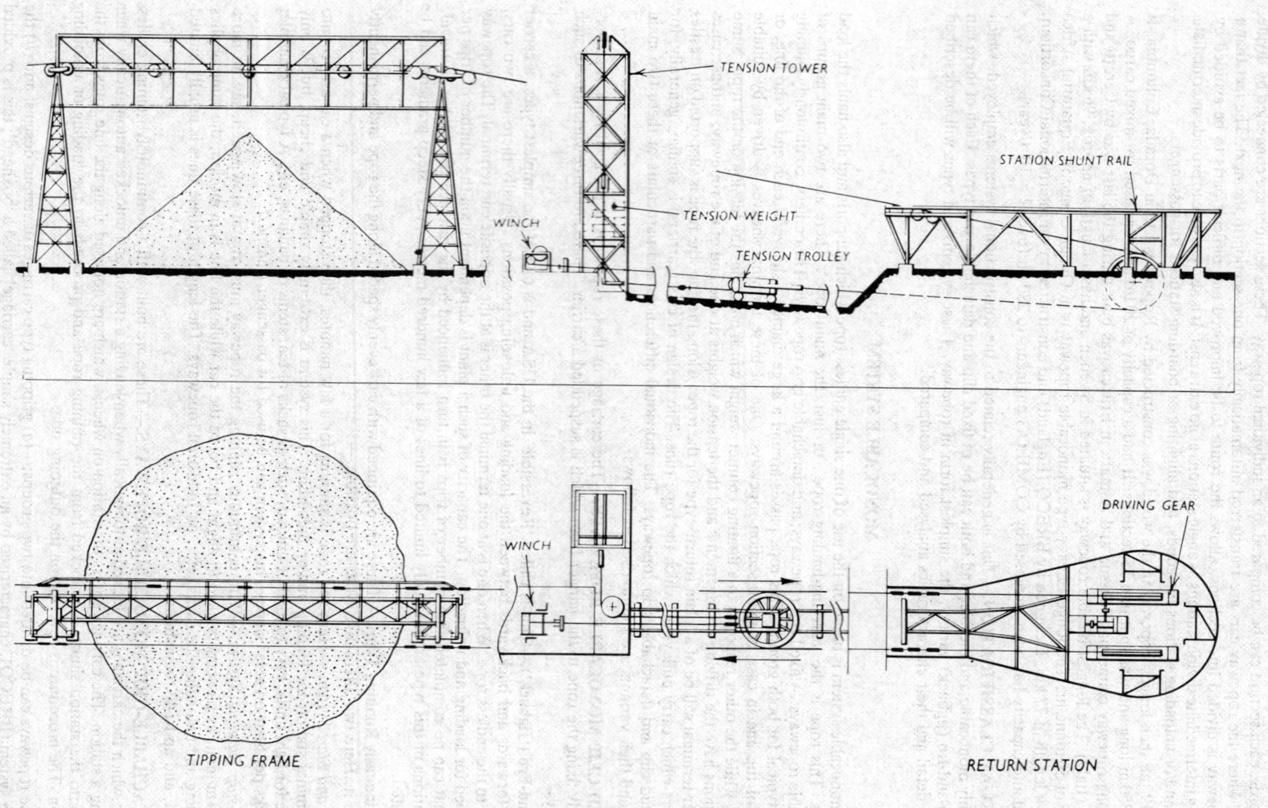

FIG. 5.—Diagram of Monocable Unloading Station, Driving Gear and Tension Tower, Steel Structure.

ensure better grip of the rope, but this may be detrimental to the rope. The capacity of both types now exceeds 200 t/h.

ROPEWAY CAPACITY AND INDIVIDUAL LOADS.—The capacity of a ropeway depends on the number of cars (carriers) sent out per hour, and the pay-load in each carrier. In other words, if a certain output per year is required, first it must be decided how many working days per year the ropeway could be in operation, and how many hours per day. It is usual to take as a base 300 days per year at 8 hours per day = 2,400 working hours per year. If, say, it is required to transport 480,000 tonne/year with the possibility that output may be doubled, then the ropeway capacity required would be 200 tonne/hour. A monocable ropeway would be recommended if the route is not too steep. The doubled output could be achieved by operating for 16 hours per day. If the line is too steep for a monocable line, or if the increase of output be expected, then a bicable ropeway would be considered; such a ropeway would be designed for 400 tonne/hour (960,000 tonne/year). At the beginning the line would be equipped with only half the carriers required to handle 400 tonne/hour and the line would give half of the above output, ie 480,000 tonne/year, as in the initial proposal.

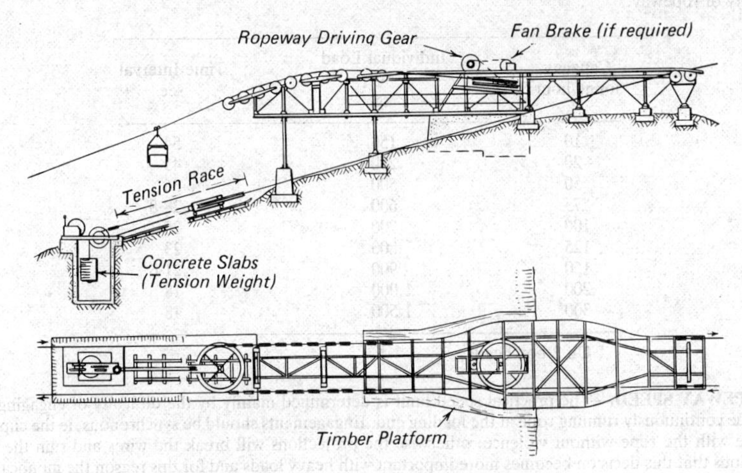

FIG. 6.—Typical Monocable Divide Station.

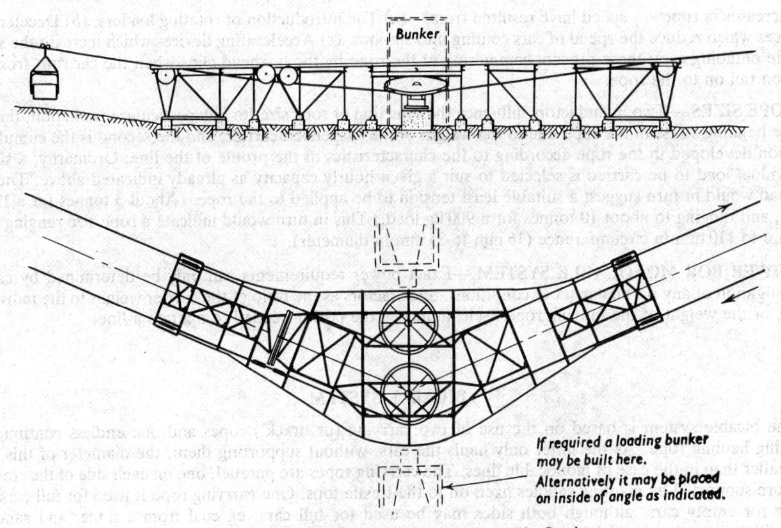

FIG. 7.—Monocable 'Through' Angle Station.

In practice the problem is more complicated as practical economic and technical aspects must be taken into consideration, keeping in mind that a monocable ropeway is approximately 40% cheaper than a bicable constructed in the same conditions for the same capacity. On the other hand, a twin monocable line with half capacity in each line may be found preferable to a single line, thus allowing for further flexibility of operation; increasing the final capacity when required; carrying various materials at the same time; shutting one line and operating on the other for economy reasons, or for maintenance. The same considerations apply to the transport of passengers.

A further factor to be taken into account is the method of loading. At 200 tons/hour for a monocable ropeway with mild steel buckets (if transport of material in bulk is considered), and 1-ton individual load per bucket as a practical limit for a certain type of ropeway, an 18-second bucket interval (3,600 seconds—200 loads) would be required. To load a bucket comfortably 20 to 30 seconds are required, but loading bunkers could be designed to fill two or three buckets at the same time, or an automatic rotating distributing hopper could be provided. See 'Methods of Loading'.

The following table gives examples of time intervals between specified individual loads for given ton/hour capacity of ropeway.

Capacity tonne/hour	Individual Load kg	Time Interval sec
10	150	54
20	250	45
50	500	36
75	600	28·8
100	700	25
125	800	23
150	900	21·6
200	1,000	18
300*	1,500	18

* On 2 box-heads.

ROPEWAY SPEED.—The practical speed limit is determined mainly by the difficulty of engaging the car with the continuously running rope at the loading end. Engagements should be synchronous, ie the clips should engage with the rope without violence, otherwise the projections will break the wires and ruin the rope. It is obvious that this decision becomes more important with heavy loads and for this reason the monocable rope gives better service on ropeways or heavy capacity but without gradients so that the clips can operate satisfactorily without the need for projections. Monocable ropeway speed has exceeded 4·0 m/sec.

Increases in ropeway speed have resulted from:—(*a*) The introduction of rotating loaders. (*b*) Decelerating devices which reduce the speed of cars coming into stations. (*c*) Accelerating devices which increase the speed of the outgoing cars; these prevent hammering of the rope by the boxhead clips when the car runs from the station rail on to the rope.

ROPE SIZES.—Two main factors influence the selection of rope size for any particular installation, the first is the bending stress in the rope due to the weight of the suspended carrier, and the second is the cumulative tension developed in the rope according to the characteristics of the profile of the line. Ordinarily, a size of individual load to be carried is selected to suit a given hourly capacity as already indicated above. The size of load would in turn suggest a suitable least tension to be applied to the rope. (About 3 tonnes for a 150 kg load, and ranging to about 10 tonnes for a 900 kg load.) This in turn would indicate a rope size ranging from 50 mm to 110 mm in circumference (16 mm to 35 mm in diameter).

POWER FOR MONOCABLE SYSTEM.—Exact power requirements can only be determined by careful investigation of any particular set of conditions. Such factors as the ratio of the carrier weight to the individual load, or the weight of the moving rope itself, influence the power needed to operate a line.

BICABLE SYSTEM

The bicable system is based on the use of two carrying (or 'track') ropes and one endless continuously running hauling rope. As the latter only hauls the cars, without supporting them, the diameter of this rope is smaller than in the case of monocable lines. The carrying ropes are parallel, one on each side of the trestles, and are supported by pivoting saddles fixed on to the trestle tops. One carrying rope is used for full cars, the other for empty cars, although both sides may be used for full cars, eg coal from a mine, and sand for back-filling, or other material in the opposite direction.

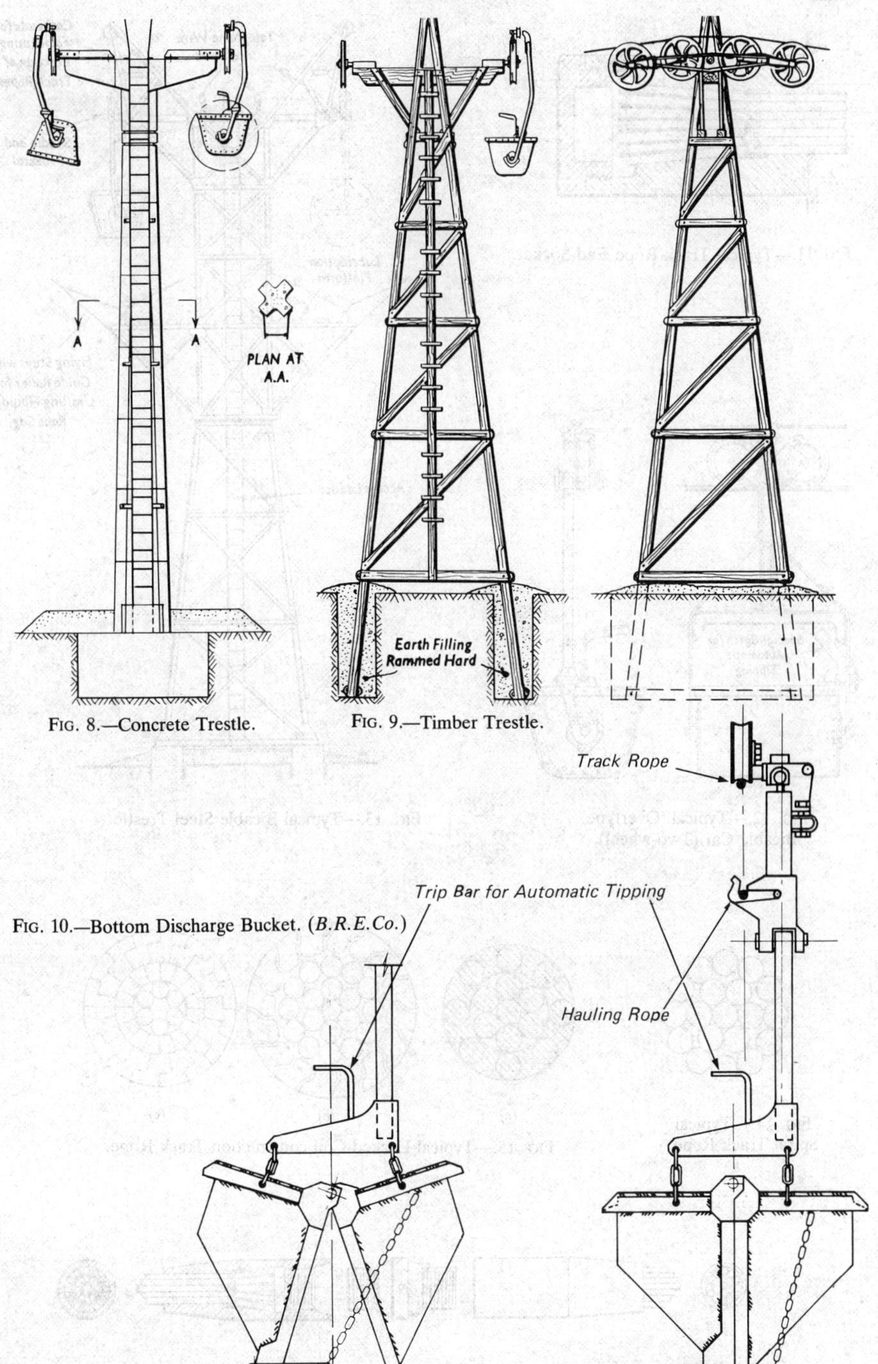

FIG. 8.—Concrete Trestle.

FIG. 9.—Timber Trestle.

FIG. 10.—Bottom Discharge Bucket. (*B.R.E.Co.*)

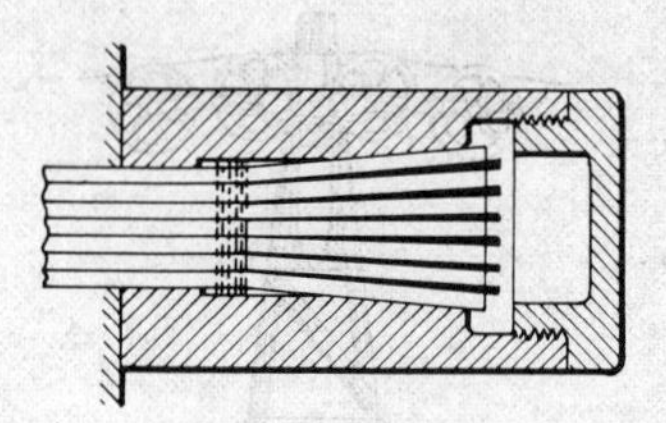

FIG. 11.—Typical Track Rope End Socket.

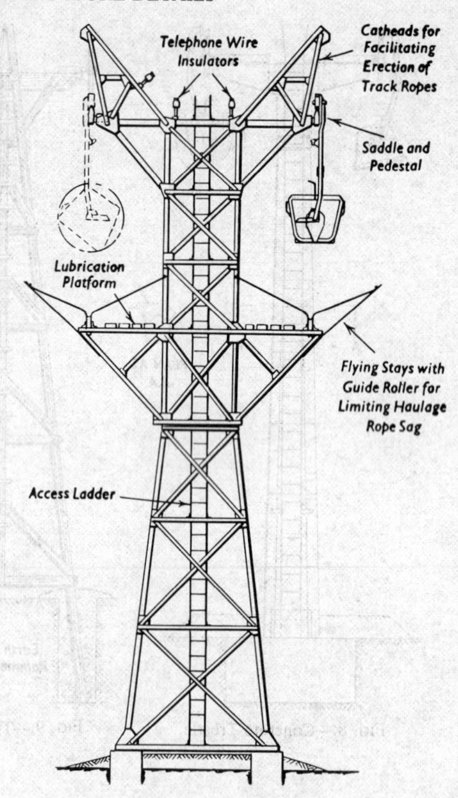

FIG. 13.—Typical Bicable Steel Trestle.

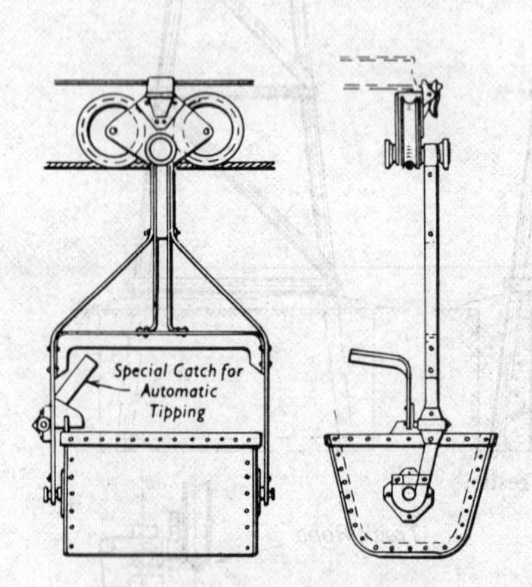

FIG. 12.—Typical 'Overtype' Bicable Car (Two-wheel).

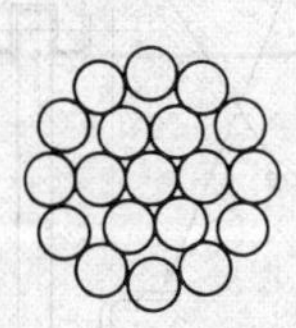

FIG. 14.—Typical Spiral Track Rope.

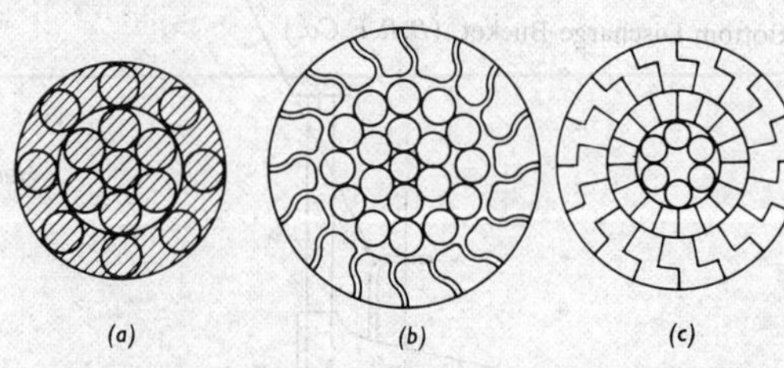

FIG. 15.—Typical Locked-Coil-construction Track Rope.

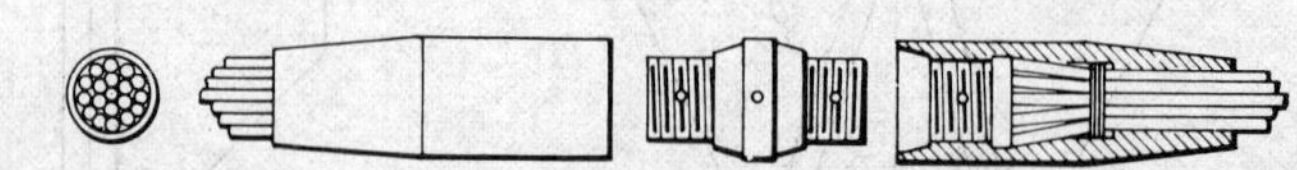

FIG. 16.—Typical Track Rope Line Coupling.

As in the case of monocable ropeways, there are two main groups of bicable ropeway:—(*a*) fixed clip ropeways, and (*b*) detachable grip ropeways. The first are very similar to those described for monocables and their capacities and applications are similarly limited, although the to-and-fro types have been developed to take cabins carrying 120 passengers. Bicable ropeways of the detachable grip type allow for heavy traffic, up to 500 tonne/hour on a single line (or double this figure on a twin line). These will be dealt with here.

The bicable car comprises the same three main components as the monocable car, but the carriage is more complicated; in particular the automatic gripping device. As a bicable line may take pay-loads reaching 5 tons, the whole carriage and its wheels must be of stronger construction. These wheels run on the rope along the line, and over pivoting steel saddles located on the trestle tops. The incoming car is automatically unlocked when entering a station, it runs on the station shunt rail, as in the case of the monocable system. Also as in the monocable system, the hauling rope passes around large diameter sheaves at each terminal station, and is driven at one end and tensioned at the opposite end.

LOAD CAPACITIES (BICABLE).—The considerations which govern the selection of loads on the monocable system apply equally to the bicable system, but greater freedom exists because the carrying rope can be varied in size to suit the load independent of the capacity. As the bicable car is much more expensive than the monocable boxhead, the loads are increased so that for the same capacity the number of cars required is fewer. A typical selection of loads and capacities would be:

Capacity tonne/hour	Individual Load kg	Time Interval sec
25	350	50·4
50	600	43·2
75	750	36·0
100	900	32·4
150	1,000	24·0
200	1,250	22·5
250	1,500	21·6
300	1,600	19·5
500	1,800	12·9
650	2,170	12·0

This table can be varied in many ways and economical selection may change according to the different costs of ropes and cars. (Depending on the commodity to be carried so the type of car may vary, also its weight and relative cost.) In certain cases the size of individual load is automatically settled by the purpose of the plant and may therefore bear no arbitrary relationship to the capacity. e.g. (1) a logging ropeway may have a capacity of only five tons per hour and have to carry logs weighing over one ton each. (2) a fully automatic bicable ropeway, 600 tonnes/h capacity, (Agudio, Brazil). Carriers (buckets) supported on 2 or 4 carrying ropes, on each side of line allow increase in capacity of ropeway to 2500 t/h.

SPEED OF LINE.—As with the monocable ropeway, the speed at which the line is to run, will considerably influence the initial cost of the plant; bicable line speed can be designed for 280 m/min or more. However, the factors to be taken into account in settling a speed are different.

TRACK ROPE.—Bicable track ropes can be of (1) spiral construction (Fig. 14) suitable for lines of moderate capacity, ie lines equipped with light loads or with loads well spaced along the line, or of (2) locked-coil construction (Fig. 15*a, b, c*), which are preferable for heavier capacities. Ropes of this latter type are much more expensive but they have the advantage of providing a better surface for wear, and if a wire should break, it cannot protrude from the texture of the rope and obstruct the passage of carriages. Long lengths of track rope are connected by taper couplings, where the ends of the rope are open out in a conical chamber and secured by wedges or by white metal (Fig. 16).

At the points where the ropes are anchored and where they are tensioned, they are socketed in a similar manner (Fig. 11). The cost of these track ropes is considerable and they should be well looked after. From the time of their delivery to the site, they should be well greased, for if surface corrosion is once allowed to set in, it will lead to cracks in the surface, which will eventually cause broken wires.

Whilst monocable track ropes can conveniently be oiled and inspected as they pass through one of the stations, it is necessary for a bicable track rope to be oiled from a special oiling car which drips the oil on to the rope and spreads it by means of a brush. For inspection of the rope a man must travel along the line in a bucket, or in a special inspection car. It is usual on long lines to be driven at a slow speed while inspection is taking place. Oiling should be done about once a month and rope inspection about once a fortnight.

The amount of tension required in track ropes is considerable and calls for a rigid and massive tension gear.

HAULING ROPE.—Selection of a haulage rope is an involved process needing investigations into cumulative tensions and horse-power. The hauling rope is normally of round strand 6/7 Langs Lay construction, with a hemp or fibre core. This construction gives sufficient flexibility for passing round the driving and tension sheaves, and the various deflection sheaves and rollers, and it also gives a good area for wear on the outer wires. When the hauling rope is gripped to the carriages at regular intervals it moves along parallel to the track rope but when there are no carriages at some sections of the line, it falls down into rollers fixed on the trestles, and is thus prevented from trailing on the ground, or on the trestle steelwork.

CARRIAGES.—The carriages used on a bicable ropeway are provided with two or more wheels according to the weight of the load.

The hauling rope is attached by a gripping mechanism which is generally applied by the weight of the load, so that the pressure on the rope is greater with a full load than with an empty bucket. Some makers, however,

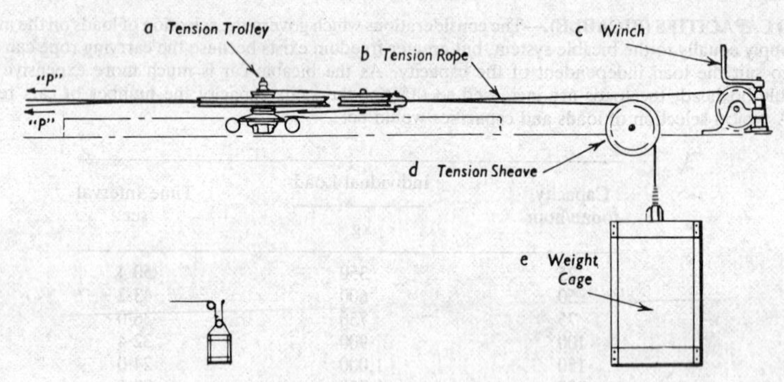

FIG. 17.—Typical Bicable Hauling Rope Tension Gear.

use a screw grip. In either case, where a bucket is moved from the line on to the station rail for loading or unloading, the rope has to be freed from the grip at the unlocking frames and re-engaged at locking frames arranged at the station.

In one form of carriage the hauling rope is situated above the track rope (Fig. 12). This type is suitable for passing round angle stations, but is best employed to fairly level lines. More often, the hauling rope is placed below the track rope (Fig. 10).

Some carriages of this type are adaptable to all conditions. They are able to pass through angle stations while gripped to the rope, they can climb steep gradients; and can pass over pressure frames or groups of trestles situated at peaks on the line. These universal carriages are somewhat expensive; and when the site conditions are not severe, simpler and cheaper types can be used.

LENGTH OF BICABLE ROPEWAY.—There is no limit to the length which can be constructed, but, as with the monocable system, it would be composed of a number of units linked together. Cars would run straight through from one unit to the next.

CAPACITY.—The greatest capacity carried on a single bicable ropeway is 500 tons per hour, but much higher capacities, even up to 1,000 tons per hour, can be transported by appropriate design.

COMPARISON OF ROPEWAY SYSTEMS.—Each ropeway is specially designed and built to provide a particular service. This means that capital charges (interest and amortisation) as well as running costs (operation and maintenance), play an important part in the choice of the more suitable systems. Capacities and loads of both monocable and bicable types have been detailed in earlier paragraphs.

In such cases, for instance, as the construction of a dam, or working a limited ore field, the first cost may be the deciding factor, as the recovery value of a ropeway in a remote region is not easy to ascertain. In deciding on the system most suited to a particular transport problem, the experienced ropeway engineer must take into consideration not only the many and often difficult technical features involved, but also the economic factors.

STRUCTURES.—Normally the structural work for the stations and trestles is fabricated from standard mild steel sections, but where timber is plentiful the structures may be economically constructed on site from that material. In some cases, mass concrete, or reinforced concrete structures are adopted. They may form part or the whole of the structural work but usually will be more expensive than the equivalent steel or timber structures. Where the ropeway is built for a cement works or a gravel pit, concrete structures will be economic as the cost of materials and transport will be reduced and local labour would be employed.

METHODS OF LOADING MONOCABLE AND BICABLE.—Incoming cars upon arrival at a loading station will run freely on a rigid rail and automatically become disengaged from the moving rope. The loading operation may therefore be carried out before the car reaches the exit side of the station and departs on its journey along the line. The method of loading will depend upon the material being conveyed.

(*a*) **Hopper and Chute Loading.**—Bulk materials, such as coal, limestone, sand, etc, which will flow freely, would be delivered to ropeway buckets through shoots attached to a storage bunker. The shoots would be fitted with hand or power-operated gates for controlling the flow of material and would be correctly related in position to the ropeway station to allow buckets to be filled while the cars are at rest momentarily on the shunt rail.

(*b*) **Unit Loading.**—Where the ropeway is carrying particular loads such as heavy tree trunks, sacks of tea, packed goods etc., special loading arrangements are employed. These may be entirely manual or may be power assisted. Long tree trunks, lengths of pipe, bundles of planks etc, are usually carried by twin carriers with slings. Chain blocks are frequently incorporated with the carriers for enabling the load to be raised clear of the ground or delivery ramp. Sacks packed goods etc, are usually carried on tray or platform carriers. They are brought to rest with the tray adjacent to and level with the edge of the loading bay floor on which the loads are waiting. The loads can then be slid on to a ropeway carrier without the effort of lifting.

(*c*) **Rotary Distributor Loading.**—The automatic loading of the buckets of an aerial ropeway can be performed by a rotary distributor. On arriving at the loading point the buckets are uncoupled from the loading rope and connected to a chain haulage, which moves the buckets along the rails to the rotary distributor. Here the buckets are filled and passed to the locking frame for connection to the hauling rope; the whole process is automatic and a bucket interval of 10 sec can be achieved without difficulty.

METHODS OF UNLOADING.—Unloading is usually automatic, by means of a trip lever placed at the required position over a bunker or pile; the trip lever acts on the bucket lever catch and causes the contents to be tipped or emptied.

Shiploading Plant.—One of the more elaborate applications is a shiploading plant. This is employed where conditions do not allow a vessel to come alongside a wharf. In such cases it is advantageous to build a sea terminal on a caisson fixed on to the sea bed at a certain distance from the shore, so that vessels may anchor for loading or unloading. An aerial ropeway connects the shore with this sea terminal; thus demurrage, harbour duties etc, are reduced. This solution is also useful in view of the overcrowding of ports.

LABOUR-SAVING DEVICES.—The demand for greater ropeway capacities and also the need for a greater degree of automatic running, has led to improvements in ropeway designs and to the introduction of auxiliary equipment for eliminating operative labour.

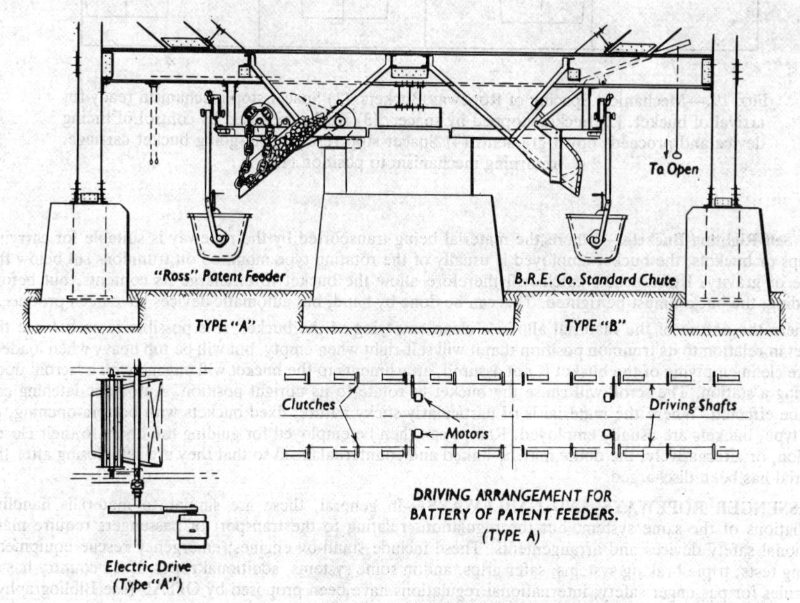

FIG. 18.—Typical Bucket Loading Station.

(*a*) **Auxiliary Haulages.**—Auxiliary haulages have been perfected for ensuring the continued movement of cars round the free shunt rail of the stations. The haulage may be by rope or chain and operates at a slow speed. At loading stations the cars will automatically disengage and come to rest at a preselected loading position. After loading, re-engagement with the auxiliary haulage will take place and the car will proceed to the exit side of the station.

(*b*) **Automatic Spacing Gear.**—To handle a given capacity a ropeway carries a certain size of load every so many seconds. This time interval should be maintained carefully for smooth running and maximum rope life. Normally, the cars are despatched by hand against a visual or audible signal. Automatic spacers have been produced to receive a car or cars and to despatch them one at a time at predetermined intervals. This ensures accuracy and eliminates labour. Figure 19 gives an outline arrangement of the operation of a bucket spacer. The device consists of a mechanism with a pawl which stops the travel of the bucket along a rail with a falling gradient. The carriage supporting the bucket is released by means of a solenoid operation of the pawl, and the mechanism resets to stop the following bucket. The timing switch can be mounted on the shunt rail or be carried by the track rope; alternatively, the timing can be operated by a gear drive from the driving sheave or other constant contact with the hauling rope.

(*c*) **Automatic Bucket Loading.**—Various manufacturers have produced their own solutions of the problem of loading buckets automatically. Some treatments are partially automatic and some completely automatic. The devices include power-operated shoot gates; balanced hoppers which pre-weigh a correct bucket load and discharge it automatically when a bucket arrives; rotary or rocking valves which measure by volume correct bucket loads and discharge them to the buckets as they arrive; a revolving hopper divided into compartments each with a shoot, and rotating at such a speed that passing buckets are in contact with a shoot long enough to receive their correct capacity; electrically interlocked feeders which are set in operation by arrival of a bucket and switched off when bucket is full as indicated either by a weigh-rail or a time switch.

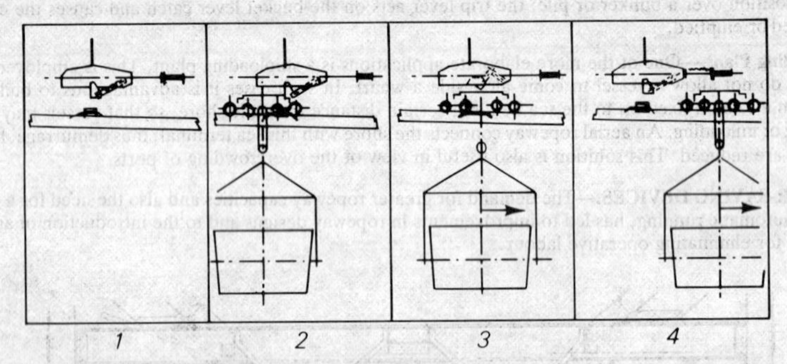

FIG. 19.—Mechanical Spacing of Ropeway Buckets. (1) Spacer stop mechanism ready for arrival of bucket. (2) bucket stopped by spacer. (3) Bucket released by control of timing device and proceeds down gradient. (4) Spacer stop reset by out-going bucket carriage, returning mechanism to position (1).

(*d*) **Self-Righting Buckets.**—Where the material being transported by the ropeway is suitable for carrying in skips or buckets, the bucket employed is usually of the rotating type mounted on trunnions set below the centre of gravity. Release of a catch will therefore allow the bucket to discharge its contents, but before reloading, the bucket must be righted. This can be done by hand, but automatic devices have been produced.

Where the nature of the material allows a clean emptying of the bucket, it is possible to so balance the bucket in relation to its trunnion position that it will self-right when empty, but will be top heavy when loaded. Where clean emptying of the bucket is not assured, attachments to the bucket will engage with a 'scroll' upon entering a station. The scroll will cause the bucket to rotate to its upright position. Automatic latching can then be effected. Where the material is of particularly sticky nature, fixed buckets with bottom-opening, or shell type, buckets are usually employed. Ramps can then be employed for guiding the doors to their closed position, or alternatively, the doors may be linked and counterbalanced so that they are self-closing after the material has been discharged.

PASSENGER ROPEWAYS AND CABLEWAYS.—In general, these are similar to materials handling installations of the same system, but the regulations relating to the transport of passengers require many additional safety devices and arrangements. These include stand-by engines; emergency rescue equipment; loading tests; triple braking systems; safer grips, and in some systems, additional ropes. Each country has its own rules for passenger safety; international regulations have been proposed by OITAF (see Bibliography). Passenger ropeways may broadly be grouped as follows.

Winter Sports Installations.—To these belong the installations in which the passenger never leaves the ground, eg *ski-tows*, enabling skiers to slide up snow slopes by means of an extending tow bar, and also *ski-lifts* provided with towing seats. These installations can be fixed-clip or detachable grip type.

Chairlifts and Cabinlifts.—These may operate both in summer and in winter. Chairlifts are equipped with one to four seats; cabins take up to six persons. Monocable chairlifts and cabinlifts can be of fixed clip or detachable grip types with one or two grips; the former operate at slower speeds, as the passengers usually board their seats or alight while the chairs or cabins are moving. Detachable-grip cabinlifts may be operated at higher speeds (300 m/minute) and they reach high capacities; the twin installation at 'Expo 67' dealt with 2,800 persons/h (BRECo). Grips of special design are available and have been used on gradients exceeding 45 degrees. The ordinary monocable grip used for industrial purposes, is limited to about 23 degrees.

A recently developed monocable cabinlift with carriers supported by 2 ropes (on each side of line) allows up to 20 passengers per cabin (*Pomagalski*).

Bicable Passenger Ropeways or Cable-Cars are also fixed-clip or detachable-grip types; the cabins can be for up to six persons, or on large installations, with cabins for up to 150 passengers. They may be two-cabin type with a cabin starting from each terminal at the same time, and crossing mid-way. Two-cabin installations can be compared with to-and-fro ropeways, but the cableway principle enables the cabin to be lowered at intermediate stations. Often 2 track ropes are used on each side of the line. Single spans have reached 3,600 m and the difference in level between terminals 1000 m (van Roll; Agudio). Aluminium has been used successfully for large cabin construction.

ROPEWAY APPLICATIONS

(*a*) **Automatic Ropeways.**—Automatic ('push button') control is applied to installations of ropeways. The advantages are the reduced labour costs for operation and the avoidance of some risk of human error. On the other hand, automatic installations are expensive to install and to maintain, particularly when a skilled engineer is required to be in attendance to deal with an emergency or break-down on passenger ropeways.

(*b*) **Cargo Handling Ropeways.**—Although a ropeway can be used to handle ship's cargo at the dockside, in some cases it is preferable to construct an offshore terminal to the ropeway. Where the materials handled and the local conditions favour this arrangement, there can be advantages from the use of bigger vessels, increased loading speed, etc.

(*c*) **Suspension Railways.**—These are a variant of a bicable ropeway in which the carrying rope is replaced by a rail, curved as required and supported from roof or wall to save ground space. Capacities, for passengers or freight, of up to 1,000 tons per hour are possible.

(*d*) **Funicular Railways.**—These are in fact ropeways with cars travelling in rail tracks, or sometimes over snow. They are usually of the to-and-fro type and can be constructed for passenger and material transport. Operating speeds on passenger funicular railways may reach speeds of over 600 m/min.

(*e*) **Self-driven Ropeway or Cableway Cars.**—This is a variant particularly useful for temporary or erection installations as well as for forest industry.

CABLEWAYS

A cableway is a machine having operating motions similar to a transporter overhead crane but with larger lengths outside the economic limits of usual crane design. The main essentials required to form a cableway comprise the following:—(1) One main track rope. (2) Means of supporting the track rope at either end at a suitable height. (3) One load carriage complete with lifting blocks. (4) One double drum winch complete with operating ropes for travelling the load carriage in either direction and hoisting and lowering the suspended load.

Figure 20 shows a typical cableway of the fixed type, and also a typical cableway of the travelling type.

CABLEWAY APPLICATIONS.—Figure 20 shows that cableways provide a means of handling loads at all points between the track cable supports. As spans up to 1,050 m have been successfully operated and loads up to 25 tons lifted on one track rope, their practical use is extensive. One of the main advantages of a cableway is its ability to operate without interfering with any other work that may be in progress inside the operating area. This feature makes a cableway the ideal means of handling materials for the construction industry. The 'aerial ferry' is an application of the cableway used for transporting vehicles across a river or other stretches of water. An installation consisting of three spans, and 1 km in length, is in service.

CLASSIFICATION AND SYSTEMS.—The three cableway systems in general use are the 'American'; the 'English'; and the 'Travelift'. They are briefly described below.

THE AMERICAN SYSTEM is that shown in Fig. 26 where the hoisting rope is reeved through the fall blocks and is anchored on the load carriage. This system operates with a single motor-driven winch and provides only a rectangular trajectory for the load across the span.

THE ENGLISH SYSTEM differs in that the hoisting rope passes through the fall blocks on the load carriage but is anchored at the end cable support remote from the operating winch. The winch is fitted with separate motors for each motion of hoisting and traversing, whereby allowing a diagonal trajectory being carried out, if required across the span.

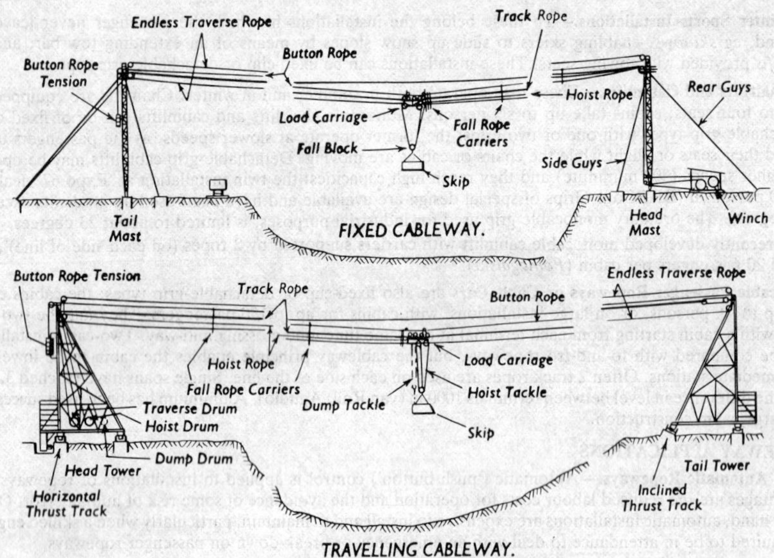

FIG. 20.—Examples of Fixed and Travelling Cableways.

NOTE.—With both the above systems a button rope operating fall-rope carriers is required on spans exceeding 150 m, to prevent tangling of the hoist and traverse ropes. In the case of the 'English' system, duplicate sets are required on each side of the load carriage.

THE 'TRAVELIFT' SYSTEM operates with a single-motor winch and enables both motions to operate simultaneously and provides a diagonal trajectory if required, but without the need of fall-rope carriers and button rope. Three operating ropes are used—the transmission, hoisting and conveying ropes. Both the transmission and the conveying ropes are endless. The transmission rope passes around three operating sheaves geared to a hoisting drum on the load carriage. A two-part fall block arrangement from the hoisting drum completes the system.

In addition to the above systems, cableways have been built having the complete winch unit mounted on the load carriage enabling grabs and similar appliances to be effectively employed.

It is of interest to mention that the cableway capacity is quoted differently in this country and in the USA. In the UK the hook-load capacity means the normal working load which the cableway carries. Under test conditions it will carry 25% in excess of this figure (possibly at reduced speed). In North America it is normal to quote the test or maximum load as the 'size' of cableway.

MAIN TRACK ROPE SUPPORTS.—These are of a general standard type or either timber or steel construction.

FIXED MASTS are of the 'needle' type requiring side supporting guy ropes in addition to the main rear anchorages, or the 'pyramid' type which require rear anchorages only.

MOVABLE MASTS OR TOWERS are of the 'pyramid' type, self-supporting by means of rear counter-ballast, all mounted complete on wheeled bogies suitable for moving on rail tracks. Power travelling can be affected by either rope haulage or by power gearing on the bogies themselves. Horizontal thrust loading applied to the towers by the main track cable etc is resisted by inclining the forward rail tracks, or alternatively by means of additional horizontally mounted bogies running on a rail at the rear of the towers. The two methods are shown in Fig. 20.

Load Carriages.—All load carriages are of the fully articulated pattern and vary from 3-wheeled units for small loading up to 12-wheeled units for suspended loads for 25 tonnes. Track wheels and rope sheaves are usually mounted on ball or roller anti-friction bearings.

Track Ropes.—Track ropes for light duties may be of flattened strand flexible construction, but for the larger loads lock coil construction is usual. On occasions means of turning the track rope are provided to evenly distribute the wear from the load carriage track wheels.

Operating Ropes.—Hoisting and travelling ropes are of flexible construction and of suitable steel, having six strands of 19 wires per strand.

Winches.—Winches may be of the single-motor or two-motor type, having a hoisting drum preferably able to coil the operating rope in a single lap without over-riding, a travelling drum of the fleeting type, or alternatively a full coiling drum similar to the hoisting motion. On installations where skip dumping is used an additional drum similar to the hoist will be required for the dumping rope.

TRACK ROPE TENSIONS.—Maximum conditions of tension occur with the concentrated load at the centre of span, and experience has proved that an allowance for sag or deflection of 4¼%–5½% of the span between rope supports is practical.

Leading Particulars of Some Typical Cableway Installations

CASTELDO DO BODE DAM, PORTUGAL.—Four radial travelling cableways (American Standard System). 10 tons load. 506 m span.

ROXBURGH DAM, NEW ZEALAND.—Two 3·3 m^3 travelling cableways (English System). 10 tons load. 490 m span.

NORRIS DAM, UNITED STATES OF AMERICA.—Two 4·5 m^3 travelling cableways (American Standard System). 15 tons load. 587 m span.

ORKNEY ISLANDS, SCOTLAND.—Five luffing type cableways (American Standard System). 10¾ tons load. 520 to 777 m spans.

DETROIT RIVER DAM, USA—Two 6·3 m^3 travelling cableways (Travelift System), 25 ton load. 603 m span.

PERIBONKA RIVER DAM, CANADA.—One 6·3 m^3 radial travelling cableway. (Travelift System.) 25 ton load. 652 m span.

SOLINA DAM, POLAND.—Two cableways, hook load 20-tons, capacity of concentrating bucket 6 cu metres, span between masts 701 m.

SEFID ROUD DAM, IRAN.—Three cableways, radial type, 11-ton hook load each, 610 m span each, two-motor design.

TIGRIS RIVER, IRAQ.—Ropeway transporter carrying vehicles, etc, up to 24 tons gross. Total length 700 m.

BRITISH STANDARDS

BS 463 Part 1: 1958, Sockets for Wire Ropes. Part 2: 1970 Sockets for Wire Ropes (Metric units).
BS 464: 1958, Thimbles for Wire Ropes.
BS 643 1970 'White-metal Ingots for Capping Steel Wire Rope'.
BS 1290: 1983, Wire Rope Slings.
BS 3810: Part 7. Glossary of Terms. Aerial Ropeways and Cableways.
BS 5281: 1975, Ferrule Secured Eye Terminations for Wire Ropes.

BIBLIOGRAPHY

SCHNEIGERT, Z. *Aerial Ropeways and Funicular Railways.* (Z. Frenkiel, Ed.) Pergamon Press (Oxford 1966).
SPAIN, R. E. *Aerial Cableways.* (London 1948).
DEAN, F. E. *Famous Cableways of the World.* Fred Muller (London 1958).
GIORDIANO, G. *Logging Cableways.* UN Food and Agriculture Organisation (1959).
PUBLICATIONS OF OITAF (*International Organisation for Ropeway Transportation, Rome).*
Technical Recommendations for Construction of Continuous Movement Monocable Passenger Ropeways of Fixed-clip and Detachable-grip Types (*Rome, 1968*).
Magnetic Inspection of Ropes (report by Prof. G. Greco, Dr. F. Winkler, and Dr. J. Wolff).
Technical Recommendations for Construction of To-and-fro Bicable Passenger Ropeways (Rome 1966).
KAWECKI, Z., and STACHURSKI, J. *Report about the State of Investigation in the Field of Steel Ropes* (1975).
International Illustrated Dictionary. Mechanical Handling Engineers Association. (In English, French, German, Italian, Russian and Spanish).
Illustrated Terminology of Ropeways, Cableways and Dragscrapers (FEM). Federation Europèene de la Manutention (In German, English, French, Italian, Spanish and Swedish).
Safety Code for Operation and Maintenance of Powered Industrial Trucks (FEM)
Logging Cableways. UN Economic Commission for Europe. Food and Agriculture Organisation of the United Nations (Geneva, 1959).
DWYER, C. F., *Aerial Tramways, Ski Lifts and Tows. Description and Terminology.* Forest Service, US. Department of Agriculture (1975).
How Safe is a Rope—OIPEEC (International Organisation for the Study of the Endurance of Wire Ropes) Conference, Cracow, 1981.

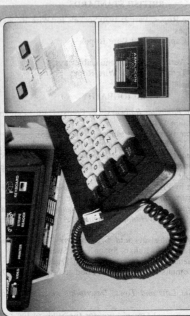

RAILWAY PERMANENT WAY*

Rails—Fishplates—Sleepers—Ballast—Rail Fastenings—Rail Lubricators—Mechanical Maintenance Appliances—Track Laying Machines—Continuous Welded Rail—Switches & Crossings—Clearances—Curves—Crossings—Track Formulae

By C. Lockwood

RAILS.—The flat-bottom design of rail is now universal for main-line tracks, although for some years it is probable that bull-head rails will still be used to some extent in Great Britain where the flat-bottom rail was adopted as standard after extensive trials.

The general increase in speeds and axle loads in the years prior to 1939 had emphasised the necessity for a very high standard of track maintenance and there was a tendency to increase the weight of new rails everywhere. In Great Britain some miles of 50 kg bull-head rail were laid. The heaviest British locomotives had maximum axle weights of about 23 tons. Other factors also need to be taken into consideration. For instance, in Great Britain track maintenance is normally possible throughout the year whereas thousands of miles of American track receive no attention for months on end due to the extremes of temperature making it unsafe or impossible to fettle the track, and the permanent way must therefore be designed to withstand this lack of attention, particularly the stresses associated with the heaving of the road bed during the winter months.

PERMANENT WAY ON BRITISH RAILWAYS.—The standard rail for main lines from 1949 until July 1960 was the 109 lb flat-bottom rail in 60-ft lengths joined by four-bolt fishplates 20 in long (Fig. 4). In July 1960, however, the British Rail (BR) 109 lb rail was replaced by the BS 110A section (Fig. 2(*a*)). For less important routes the BR 98lb rail section was also introduced in 1949 (Fig. 4). The rails were supported in double shouldered cast iron baseplates weighing 39 lb each and secured to creosoted softwood sleepers (8 ft 6 in long, 10 in wide and 5 in deep) by means of spring steel spikes. One such fastening is the Elastic Rail Spike (6 per sleeper Figs. 4 and 6) and another is the Macbeth Spring Spike (4 per sleeper). Small nibs are cast on the undersides of the baseplates to assist in preventing gauge spread on curves (Figs. 4 and 5).

Other types of fastenings designed to enable rails to be changed or turned without disturbing the fastenings between baseplate and sleeper have been introduced. Figure 7a illustrates the Mills 'C' Clip assembly, employing a cast iron baseplate and two spring steel clips which are driven into position by means of a platelayer's hammer. In the same category is the Pandrol Spring Clip which is driven into position by a special tool in a direction parallel to the rail. The Pandrol clip has become the standard BR fastening for all tracks with wood, concrete or steel sleepers and switch and crossing bearers. (Figs. 9 and 13). With both these assemblies resilient pads may be used between the rail foot and baseplate seating. Rubber-bonded cork has proved to be satisfactory for this purpose and has been used in large numbers. The two spring clip assemblies described have one very important feature in common. In each case the full load on the rail foot is immediately applied as the clip is driven into position, no other nut or bolt or other tensioning device being required.

In Great Britain the basic number of sleepers used per mile of track was 2,112, but since increased to 2,288, or 2,464 on difficult formations, or on some curves 1320, 1432 and 1540 per km.

RAILS.—The steel for flat-bottom and bull-head rail shall be of the best quality. The source of the steel and the manufacturing process employed for the production of both Bull-head and Flat-Bottom rails shall be the responsibility of the manufacturer. The purchaser may request the supply of a broad outline description of the steelmaking and casting processes and steel supplies to be provided at the time of tender. The chemical composition of the steel set out in BS 11:1985 are shown in Table 1.

TABLE 1.—COMPOSITION OF RAIL STEEL

Steel Grade	Alloying elements (% by mass)				
	C	Si	Mn	P	S
Normal	0·45–0·60	0·05–0·35	0·95–1·25	0·040 max	0·040 max
Wear Resisting	0·65–0·80	0·10–0·50	0·80–1·30	0·040 max	0·040 max
	0·55–0·75	0·10–0·50	1·30–1·70	0·040 max	0·040 max

***Note on Units etc.**—Where reference is made to former British Specifications and obsolescent track components where Imperial Units were used, it is considered inappropriate to convert to metric equivalents.*

Note.—The mechanical properties of the rails shall be: Normal grade shall have a minimum tensile strength of 710 N/mm^2 and a minimum elongation of 9%. Wear resisting grade shall have a minimum tensile strength of 880 N/mm^2 and a minimum elongation of 8%.

In this country Sequence Continuous Casting is now used for the production of all rails. A sequence of casts of the same grade of steel is poured through a continuous casting machine without interruption in flow of liquid steel into the moulds and strands. The pouring of the next cast commences before the flow of the steel from the previous cast has terminated, leading to an intermixing of some liquid steel from the two successive casts. The minimum rolling reduction of cross sectional area for rails up to 60 kg/m (120 lb/yard) rolled from continuously cast blooms of square or rectangular cross section shall be 8:1. If cast ingots are used, the cross sectional area at the larger end shall not be less than 25 times that of the rail to be produced.

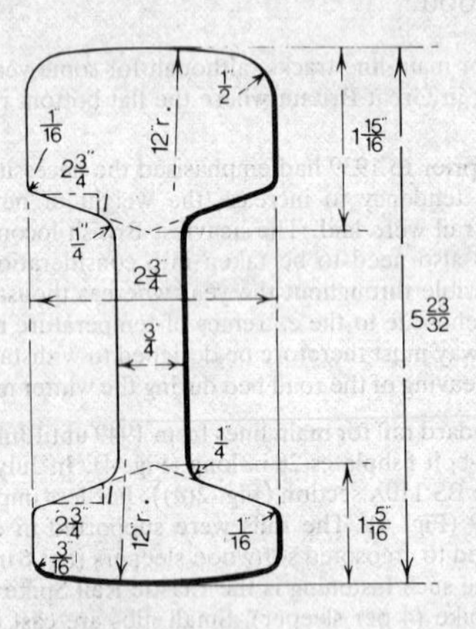

Metric Equivalents of inch dimensions

$\frac{1}{16}$in = 1·59 mm $\frac{1}{2}$in = 12·7 mm $1\frac{15}{16}$in = 49·21 mm
$\frac{3}{16}$in = 4·76 mm $\frac{3}{4}$in = 19·05 mm $2\frac{3}{4}$in = 69·85 mm
$\frac{1}{4}$in = 6·35 mm $1\frac{5}{16}$in = 33·34 mm $5\frac{23}{32}$in = 145·26 mm

FIG. 1.—95RBH Bull-head rail section weighing 95lb per yard is the only Bull-Head rail used by British Rail.

FLAT-BOTTOM RAILS.—Following earlier trials with flat-bottom rail sections of various weights, two new designs were introduced as British Rail standards in 1949. The salient features of the two sections are given in the following table.

TABLE 2. FLAT-BOTTOM RAIL DIMENSIONS (BRITISH RAIL DESIGN).

			109lb	98lb
Rail—	Overall depth	in	$6\frac{1}{4}$	$5\frac{5}{8}$
	Width of foot	in	$5\frac{1}{2}$	$5\frac{1}{2}$
	Width of head	in	$2\frac{3}{4}$	$2\frac{3}{4}$
	Depth of head	in	$1\frac{15}{16}$	$1\frac{13}{16}$
	Depth of foot	in	$1\frac{3}{16}$	$1\frac{1}{8}$
	Min web thickness	in	$\frac{5}{8}$	$\frac{9}{16}$
	Fishing Angles—*Top*	1 in	$2\frac{3}{4}$	$2\frac{3}{4}$
	Bottom	1 in	$2\frac{3}{4}$	$2\frac{3}{4}$

Area of rail in sq inches multiplied by 10·209 equals weight in lb per yard. Weight of rail per yard in lb multiplied by 11/7 equals tons per mile of single track. Weight of rail in kg per metre multiplied by 2 equals weight in lb per yard (approximately).

Apart from the two British Rail standards now obsolete there is a series of British Standard Rail Sections. A new range of flat-bottom rail sections in the sizes 60-lb to 110-lb inclusive, suffixed 'A' was introduced in the 1959 edition of BS 11. The leading dimensions for the rail sections given in the 1955, 1959, 1978 and 1985 revisions of BS 11, are contained in Table 3 (see also Figs. 1, 2 and 3). The leading dimensions for the range of FB sections currently available, given in the 1985 revision of BS 11 are detailed in Table 4. See also Figs. 2(*b*) and 2(*c*).

Variation in Dimensions.—The following tolerances shall be allowed for rails up to and including 60 kg/m (120 lb/yd) section mass with a height up to 165 mm ($6\frac{1}{2}$ in) a foot width of 140 mm ($5\frac{1}{2}$ in) and a head width of up to 70 mm ($2\frac{3}{4}$ in)

Overall Height of Rail $+\frac{1}{32}$ in $-\frac{1}{64}$ in (±0·50 mm)

Width of Head $\pm\frac{1}{64}$ in (±0·50 mm)

Width of Foot $\pm\frac{1}{32}$ in (±1·00 mm) (BH Rail $\pm\frac{1}{64}$ in)

Thickness of Web $\pm\frac{1}{64}$ in (+1·00 mm −0·50 mm)

Verticality, the deviation from verticality at the rail head shall not exceed $\frac{1}{64}$ in (0·50 mm)

The Base of all flat bottom rails shall be true and flat but a slight concavity not exceeding $\frac{1}{64}$ in (0·50 mm) shall be permissible.

Fishing surfaces; if the rail fishing template touches the web the clearance at the fishing surfaces shall not exceed 0·005 in (0·15 mm) at any one point. On the other hand the template shall not stand away from the contour of the web by more than $\frac{3}{64}$in (1·20 mm), and in doing so, the template must touch both fishing surfaces.

The Imperial dimensions given above apply to rails designed in Imperial units. The metric tolerances apply to rails designed in metric units.

TABLE 3.—PAST AND PRESENT BRITISH STANDARD RAILS—IMPERIAL UNITS.

BS Rail Section No.	A in	B in	C in	D in	E in	F in	G in	J in	K in	L in	M in	T in	V in
50'O'	$3\frac{15}{16}$	$3\frac{15}{16}$	$2\frac{1}{16}$	$\frac{13}{32}$	$1\frac{5}{16}$	$\frac{41}{64}$	—	$\frac{11}{32}$	$\frac{7}{32}$	$\frac{7}{32}$	—	—	—
60A	$4\frac{1}{2}$	$4\frac{5}{16}$	$2\frac{1}{4}$	$\frac{7}{16}$	$1\frac{13}{32}$	$\frac{7}{8}$	$2\frac{7}{32}$	$\frac{3}{8}$	—	$\frac{3}{8}$	—	$\frac{21}{32}$	$\frac{19}{64}$
60R	$4\frac{1}{2}$	$4\frac{5}{16}$	$2\frac{1}{4}$	$\frac{7}{16}$	$1\frac{13}{32}$	$\frac{21}{32}$	$1\frac{7}{8}$	$\frac{3}{8}$	$\frac{7}{32}$	$\frac{11}{32}$	9	—	—
65A	$4\frac{11}{16}$	$4\frac{5}{16}$	$2\frac{5}{16}$	$\frac{15}{32}$	$1\frac{15}{32}$	$\frac{7}{8}$	$2\frac{11}{32}$	$\frac{3}{8}$	—	$\frac{3}{8}$	—	$\frac{37}{64}$	$\frac{5}{16}$
65R	$4\frac{11}{16}$	$4\frac{7}{16}$	$2\frac{5}{16}$	$\frac{15}{32}$	$1\frac{29}{64}$	$\frac{11}{16}$	$1\frac{31}{32}$	$\frac{7}{16}$	$\frac{1}{4}$	$\frac{3}{8}$	12	—	—
70A	$4\frac{7}{8}$	$4\frac{3}{8}$	$2\frac{3}{8}$	$\frac{31}{64}$	$1\frac{9}{16}$	$\frac{29}{32}$	$2\frac{7}{16}$	$\frac{3}{8}$	—	$\frac{7}{16}$	—	$\frac{19}{32}$	$\frac{5}{16}$
70N	$4\frac{7}{8}$	$4\frac{5}{8}$	$2\frac{3}{8}$	$\frac{31}{64}$	$1\frac{1}{2}$	$\frac{29}{32}$	$2\frac{7}{16}$	$\frac{3}{8}$	—	—	—	$\frac{9}{16}$	$\frac{11}{32}$
75A	$5\frac{1}{16}$	$4\frac{1}{2}$	$2\frac{7}{16}$	$\frac{1}{2}$	$1\frac{21}{32}$	$\frac{15}{16}$	$2\frac{17}{32}$	$\frac{7}{16}$	—	$\frac{7}{16}$	—	$\frac{39}{64}$	$\frac{21}{64}$
75R	$5\frac{1}{16}$	$4\frac{13}{16}$	$2\frac{7}{16}$	$\frac{33}{64}$	$1\frac{9}{16}$	$\frac{47}{64}$	$2\frac{1}{8}$	$\frac{7}{16}$	$\frac{1}{4}$	$\frac{3}{8}$	12	—	—
80A	$5\frac{1}{4}$	$4\frac{5}{8}$	$2\frac{1}{2}$	$\frac{33}{64}$	$1\frac{43}{64}$	$\frac{53}{64}$	$2\frac{5}{8}$	$\frac{7}{16}$	—	$\frac{1}{2}$	—	$\frac{41}{64}$	$\frac{11}{32}$
80R	$5\frac{1}{4}$	5	$2\frac{1}{2}$	$\frac{17}{32}$	$1\frac{39}{64}$	$\frac{49}{64}$	$2\frac{13}{64}$	$\frac{7}{16}$	$\frac{5}{16}$	$\frac{3}{8}$	12	—	—
80'O'	5	5	$2\frac{1}{2}$	$\frac{35}{64}$	$1\frac{19}{64}$	$\frac{27}{32}$	—	$\frac{3}{8}$	$\frac{1}{4}$	$\frac{1}{4}$	—	—	—
85A	$5\frac{7}{16}$	$4\frac{3}{16}$	$2\frac{9}{16}$	$\frac{17}{32}$	$1\frac{3}{4}$	1	$2\frac{23}{32}$	$\frac{7}{16}$	—	$\frac{1}{2}$	—	$\frac{41}{64}$	$\frac{11}{32}$
85R	$5\frac{7}{16}$	$5\frac{3}{16}$	$2\frac{9}{16}$	$\frac{35}{64}$	$1\frac{43}{64}$	$\frac{25}{32}$	$2\frac{9}{32}$	$\frac{7}{16}$	$\frac{5}{16}$	$\frac{3}{8}$	12	—	—
90A	$5\frac{5}{8}$	5	$2\frac{5}{8}$	$\frac{35}{64}$	$1\frac{13}{16}$	$1\frac{1}{32}$	$2\frac{13}{16}$	$\frac{1}{2}$	—	$\frac{1}{2}$	—	$\frac{43}{64}$	$\frac{23}{64}$
90R	$5\frac{5}{8}$	$5\frac{3}{8}$	$2\frac{5}{8}$	$\frac{35}{64}$	$1\frac{23}{32}$	$\frac{13}{16}$	$2\frac{23}{64}$	$\frac{1}{2}$	$\frac{3}{8}$	$\frac{3}{8}$	15	—	—
95A	$5\frac{13}{16}$	$5\frac{1}{8}$	$2\frac{3}{4}$	$\frac{37}{64}$	$1\frac{27}{32}$	$1\frac{1}{32}$	$2\frac{29}{32}$	$\frac{1}{2}$	—	$\frac{1}{2}$	—	$\frac{5}{8}$	$\frac{23}{64}$
95R	$5\frac{13}{16}$	$5\frac{9}{16}$	$2\frac{11}{16}$	$\frac{9}{16}$	$1\frac{25}{32}$	$5\frac{3}{64}$	$2\frac{7}{16}$	$\frac{1}{2}$	$\frac{3}{8}$	$\frac{3}{8}$	15	—	—
95RBH	$5\frac{23}{32}$	$2\frac{3}{4}$	$2\frac{3}{4}$	$\frac{3}{4}$	$1\frac{15}{16}$	$1\frac{5}{16}$	—	$\frac{1}{2}$	$\frac{1}{4}$	$\frac{1}{4}$	—	—	—
95N	$5\frac{13}{16}$	$5\frac{1}{2}$	$2\frac{3}{4}$	$\frac{35}{64}$	$1\frac{25}{32}$	$1\frac{1}{32}$	3	$\frac{1}{2}$	—	—	—	$\frac{11}{16}$	$\frac{23}{64}$
100A	6	$5\frac{1}{4}$	$2\frac{3}{4}$	$\frac{19}{32}$	$1\frac{59}{64}$	$1\frac{5}{64}$	3	$\frac{1}{2}$	—	$\frac{9}{16}$	—	$\frac{41}{64}$	$\frac{3}{8}$
100R	6	$5\frac{3}{4}$	$2\frac{3}{4}$	$\frac{9}{16}$	$1\frac{27}{32}$	$\frac{27}{32}$	$2\frac{1}{2}$	$\frac{1}{2}$	$\frac{3}{8}$	$\frac{3}{8}$	15	—	—
105A	$6\frac{1}{8}$	$5\frac{3}{8}$	$2\frac{3}{4}$	$\frac{5}{8}$	$1\frac{59}{64}$	$1\frac{7}{64}$	$3\frac{1}{16}$	$\frac{1}{2}$	—	$\frac{9}{16}$	—	$\frac{11}{16}$	$\frac{13}{32}$
110	$6\frac{1}{4}$	6	$2\frac{7}{8}$	$\frac{19}{32}$	$1\frac{29}{32}$	$\frac{29}{32}$	$2\frac{5}{8}$	$\frac{9}{16}$	$\frac{3}{8}$	$\frac{3}{8}$	15	—	—
110A	$6\frac{1}{4}$	$5\frac{1}{2}$	$2\frac{3}{4}$	$\frac{5}{8}$	$1\frac{15}{16}$	$1\frac{3}{16}$	3	$\frac{1}{2}$	—	$\frac{5}{8}$	20	$\frac{23}{32}$	$\frac{7}{16}$
113A	$6\frac{1}{4}$	$5\frac{1}{2}$	$2\frac{3}{4}$	*	$1\frac{15}{16}$	$1\frac{3}{16}$	—	$\frac{1}{2}$	*	*	—	$\frac{23}{32}$	$\frac{7}{16}$

* True metric dimensions—see table 4

Falling Weight Test.—Brief details of this test for various flat bottom rail sections are as follows: A short unnotched rail of at least 1·3 m long is placed on its base on two bearers 1·0 m between centres. A single blow is applied with a guided falling weight of normally 1000 kg. The height of the fall varies in relation to the rail section and is determined by the formula $H = 150\,R \div W$ where H is the height of the fall in metres, R is the mass per unit length of rail (kg/m), and W is the mass of the falling weight (kg). For the test the test piece shall normally be at ambient temperature but if this is below 10°C the test piece temperature may be increased to between 10°C and 25°C.

Straightening.—The finished rail after cold straightening shall, when standing on its base or lying on its side, be capable of being pulled by hand into straight line and of retaining that position.

In the case of jointed track the fracture of rail ends, commencing from cracks initiated at the fishbolt holes in the rail webs, has become a major problem under modern traffic conditions. Work carried out by the Research Department indicated that stresses in rail fishbolt holes varied directly with the thickness of rail web and consequently in 1970 it was decided that considerable advantage lay in the thickening of the web of the BS 110A rail. This was achieved by changing to a parallel web 20 mm in thickness, and this resulted in the use of a new rail section BS 113A. This rail has a similar head and foot profile to the BS 110A rail (See Fig. 2(*d*)). At the same time a new heavier section fishplate was introduced having round drilled fishbolt holes in contrast to the punched pear-shaped holes previously used (Fig. 3).

SPECIAL STEELS FOR RAILWAY RAILS.—Experiments are continually being carried out in endeavours to produce rails capable of giving a longer life in the track before their removal is indicated owing to loss of weight by abrasion, corrosion, etc. Rails rolled from steel containing from 12 to 14% manganese appear to meet the requirement for a greater abrasive resistance but owing to their comparatively high initial cost are

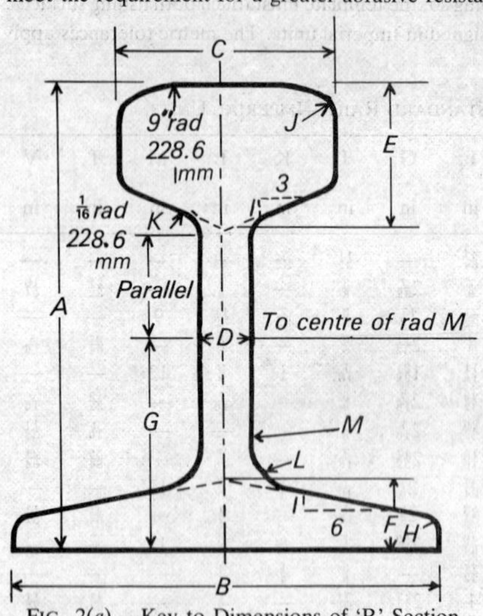

FIG. 2(*a*).—Key to Dimensions of 'R' Section Rails. Also 110 Section.

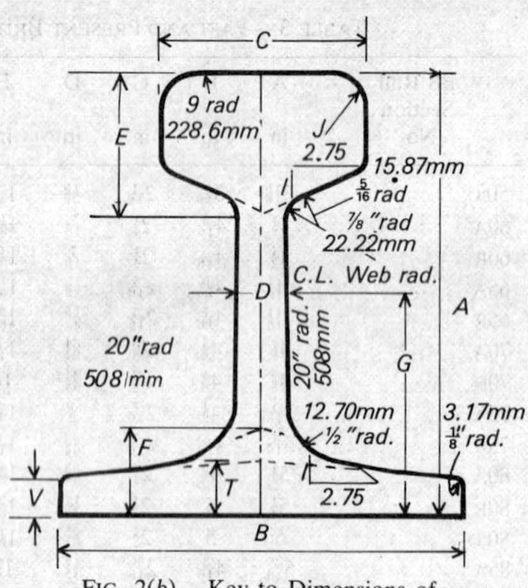

FIG. 2(*b*).—Key to Dimensions of 'N' Section Rails.

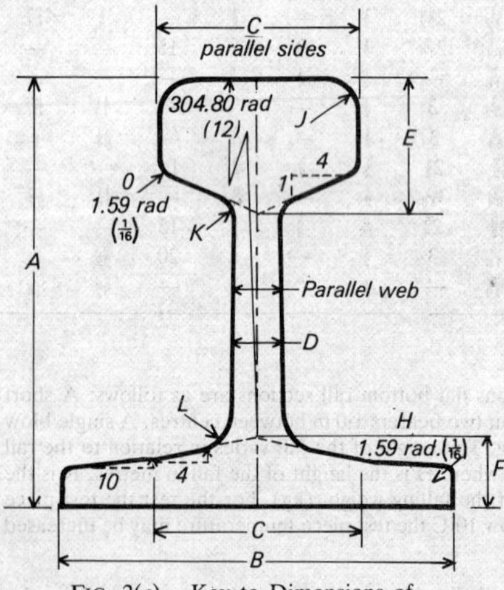

FIG. 2(*c*).—Key to Dimensions of 'O' Section Rails.

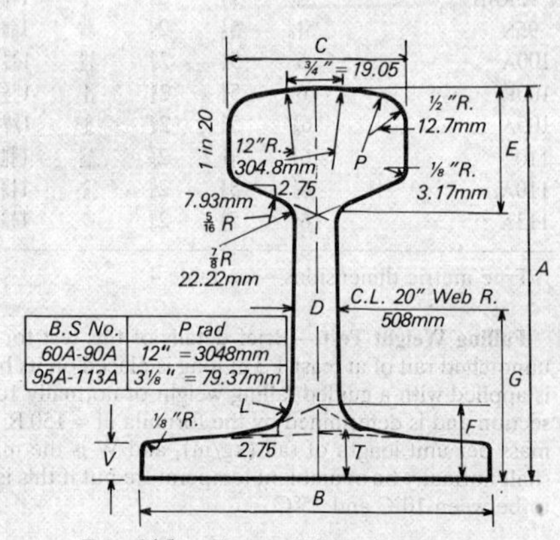

FIG. 2(*d*).—Key to Dimensions of 'A' Section Rails, except 113A.

TABLE 4.—BRITISH STANDARDS RAILWAY RAILS: TABLE OF DIMENSIONS OF SECTIONS IN METRICATED UNITS

BS rail section no.	A mm	B mm	C mm	D mm	E mm	F mm	G mm	J mm	K mm	L mm	M mm	T mm	V mm
50'O'	100·01	100·01	52·39	10·32	33·34	16·27	*	8·73	5·56	5·56	*	12·34	7·34
60A	114·30	109·54	57·15	11·11	35·72	22·22	56·36	9·53	—	9·53	508·00	16·67	7·54
60R	114·30	109·54	57·15	11·11	35·72	16·67	47·63	9·53	5·56	8·73	228·60	—	7·54
70A	123·82	111·12	60·32	12·30	39·69	23·02	61·91	9·53	—	11·11	508·00	15·08	7·94
75A	128·59	114·30	61·91	12·70	42·07	23·81	64·29	11·11	—	11·11	508·00	15·48	8·33
75R	128·59	122·24	61·91	13·10	39·69	18·65	53·98	11·11	6·35	9·53	304·80	—	8·47
80A	133·35	117·47	63·50	13·10	42·47	25·00	66·67	11·11	—	12·70	508·00	16·27	8·73
80R	133·35	127·00	63·50	13·49	40·88	19·45	55·96	11·11	7·94	9·53	304·80	—	8·86
80'O'	127·00	127·00	63·50	13·89	40·48	21·43	*	9·53	6·35	6·35	*	16·67	10·32
90A	142·88	127·00	66·67	13·89	46·04	26·19	71·44	12·70	—	12·70	508·00	17·07	9·13
90R	142·88	136·53	66·67	13·89	43·66	20·64	59·93	12·70	9·53	9·53	381·00	—	9·26
95A	147·64	130·17	69·85	14·68	46·83	26·19	73·82	12·70	—	12·70	508·00	15·87	9·13
95R	147·64	141·29	68·26	14·29	45·24	21·03	61·91	12·70	9·53	9·53	381·00	—	9·26
95RBH	145·26	69·85	69·85	19·05	49·21	33·34	*	12·70	6·35	6·35	*	—	—
95N	147·64	139·70	69·85	13·89	45·24	26·19	76·20	12·70	—	12·70	508·00	17·46	9·13
100A	152·40	133·35	69·85	15·08	48·82	27·38	76·20	12·70	—	14·29	508·00	16·27	9·53
100R	152·40	146·05	69·85	14·29	46·83	21·43	63·50	12·70	9·53	9·53	381·00	—	9·26
110A	158·75	139·70	69·85	15·87	49·21	30·16	76·20	12·70	—	15·87	508·00	18·28	11·11
113A	158·75	139·70	69·85	20·00	49·21	30·16	*	12·70	8·00	15·00	*	18·26	11·11

* Parallel web, therefore, no web radius M or dimension G

only economical when, in the ordinary course, the rails have a very short life and their frequent renewal entails heavy labour charges, such as in the case of complicated blocks of crossing work or in electrified lines.

For situations in which they are subjected to the action of chemical fumes, water, etc, rails containing from 0·25–0·30% copper have been tried, and in one instance where such rails were laid in the vicinity of water troughs, the records show that after two and one-third years' life they had lost in weight about 20% less than ordinary Bessemer Acid steel rails laid at the same time for comparison.

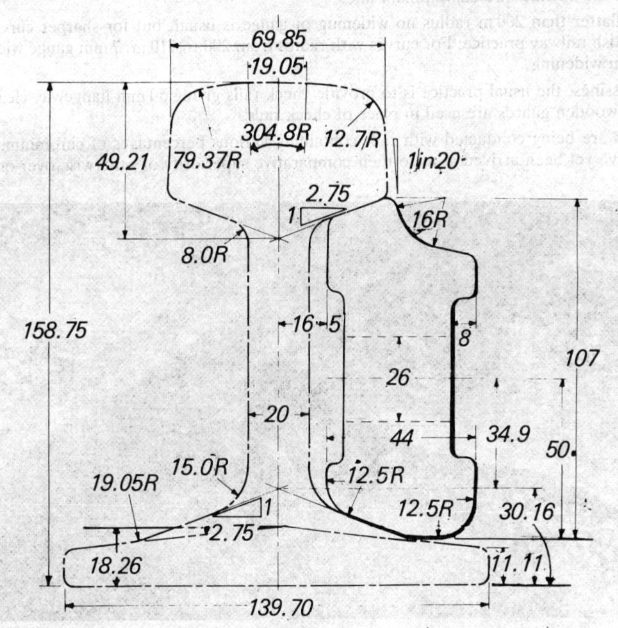

FIG. 3.—Rail Section 113A (Weight 113·69lb/yard—56·39kg/m).

TABLE 5.—CALCULATED MASSES AND PROPERTIES FOR RAILWAY RAILS IN METRICATED UNITS BS 11:1985.

BS rail section no.	Calculated mass lb/yd	Calculated mass kg/m	Moment of inertia I_{xx} cm^4	Section modulus cm^3	Distance from top of rail to neutral axis mm	Area of whole section mm^2
50'O'	50·0587	24·833	424·30	84·77	50·051	3163·47
60A	61·7189	30·618	695·85	117·31	59·320	3900·34
60R	60·1141	29·822	680·85	115·98	58·704	3798·92
70A	70·1637	34·807	910·69	145·74	62·487	4434·01
75A	75·5007	37·455	1048·8	161·82	64·812	4771·28
75R	74·6678	37·041	1061·3	159·09	66·709	4718·65
80A	80·1502	39·761	1204·7	177·46	67·887	5065·11
80R	79·9736	39·674	1224·5	175·99	69·575	5053·95
80'O'	80·0894	39·731	1100·5	166·88	65·943	5061·27
90A	90·9104	45·099	1563·8	214·83	72·794	5745·10
90R	89·7147	44·506	1584·3	211·85	74·784	5669·54
95A	95·3671	47·310	1741·8	233·32	74·655	6026·74
95R	95·0277	47·142	1791·3	232·30	77·113	6005·30
95RBH	94·8820	47·069	1458·0	188·46	67·893	5996·09
95N	94·6425	46·951	1774·8	233·20	76·105	5980·96
100A	101·1566	50·182	1961·0	252·42	77·688	6392·61
100R	99·8467	49·532	2013·1	253·73	79·342	6309·83
110A	109·9081	54·523	2323·4	277·07	83·856	6945·66
113A	113·6874	56·398	2332·4	277·95	83·914	7184·50

CHECK RAILS AND WIDENING OF GAUGE ON CURVES.—In accordance with the Ministry of Transport Requirements (1950), curves of 200 m radius or under in passenger lines are provided with continuous check rails. Flatter curves are sometimes similarly checked if the speeds over them are high and if they have superelevation adverse to the curvature which, although undesirable, is occasionally necessary in the case of turn-outs from the outside of a curved main line.

For curves flatter than 200 m radius no widening of gauge is usual, but for sharper curves the following represents British railway practice: For curves with radius from 200 to 110 m, 7 mm gauge widening, from 110 to 70 m, 19 mm widening.

At level crossings, the usual practice is to provide check rails giving 50 mm flangeway clearance, although in some cases wooden guards are used in place of check rails.

Experiments are being conducted with rails containing various percentages of chromium, but no definite conclusions have yet been arrived at as to their comparative superiority or otherwise over ordinary rails.

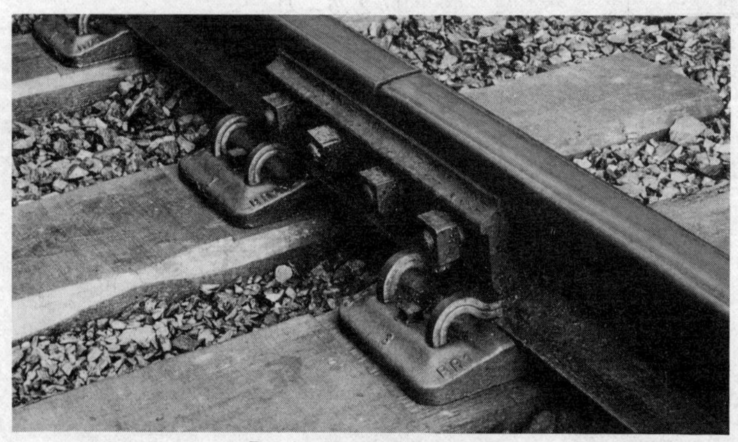

FIG. 4.—Elastic Rail Spike.

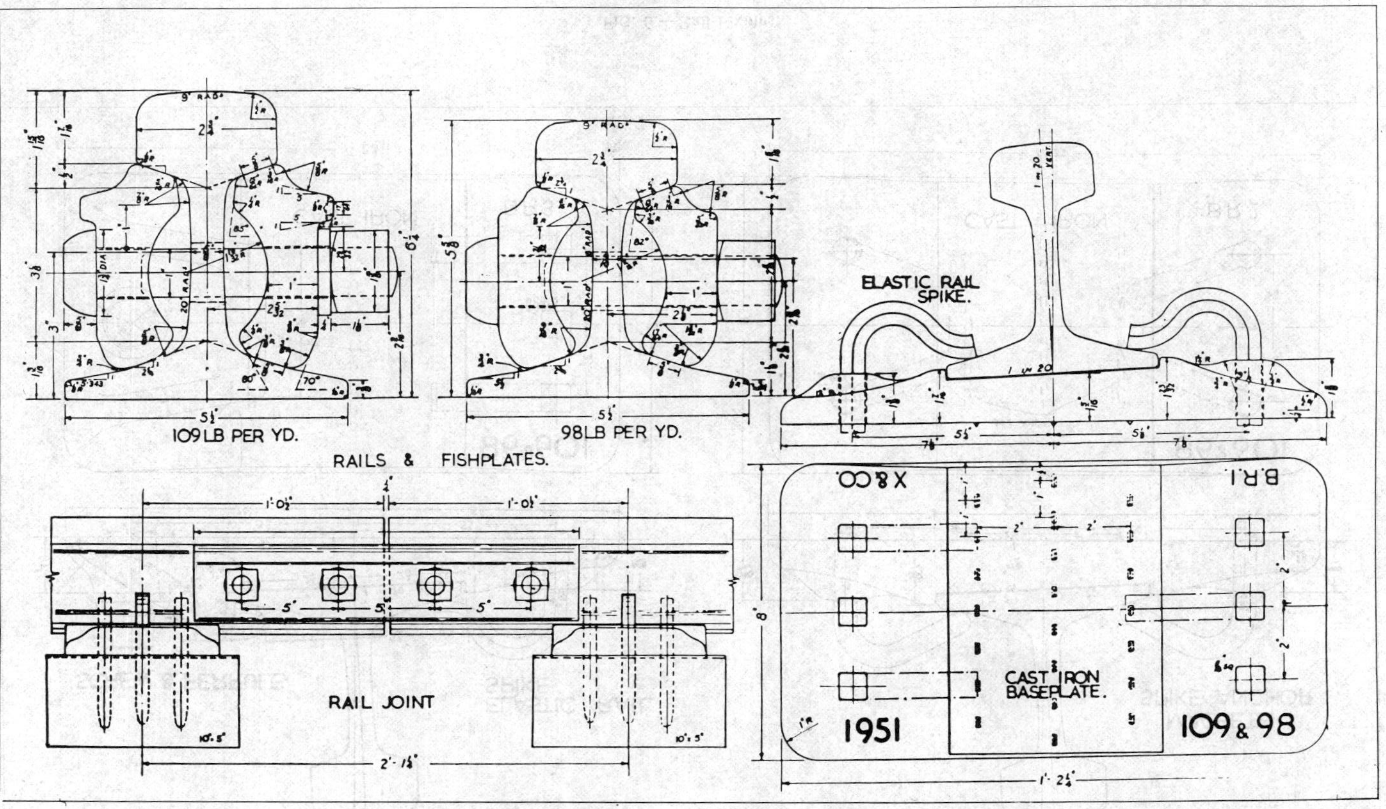

FIG. 5.—British Rail Standard Track (1949).

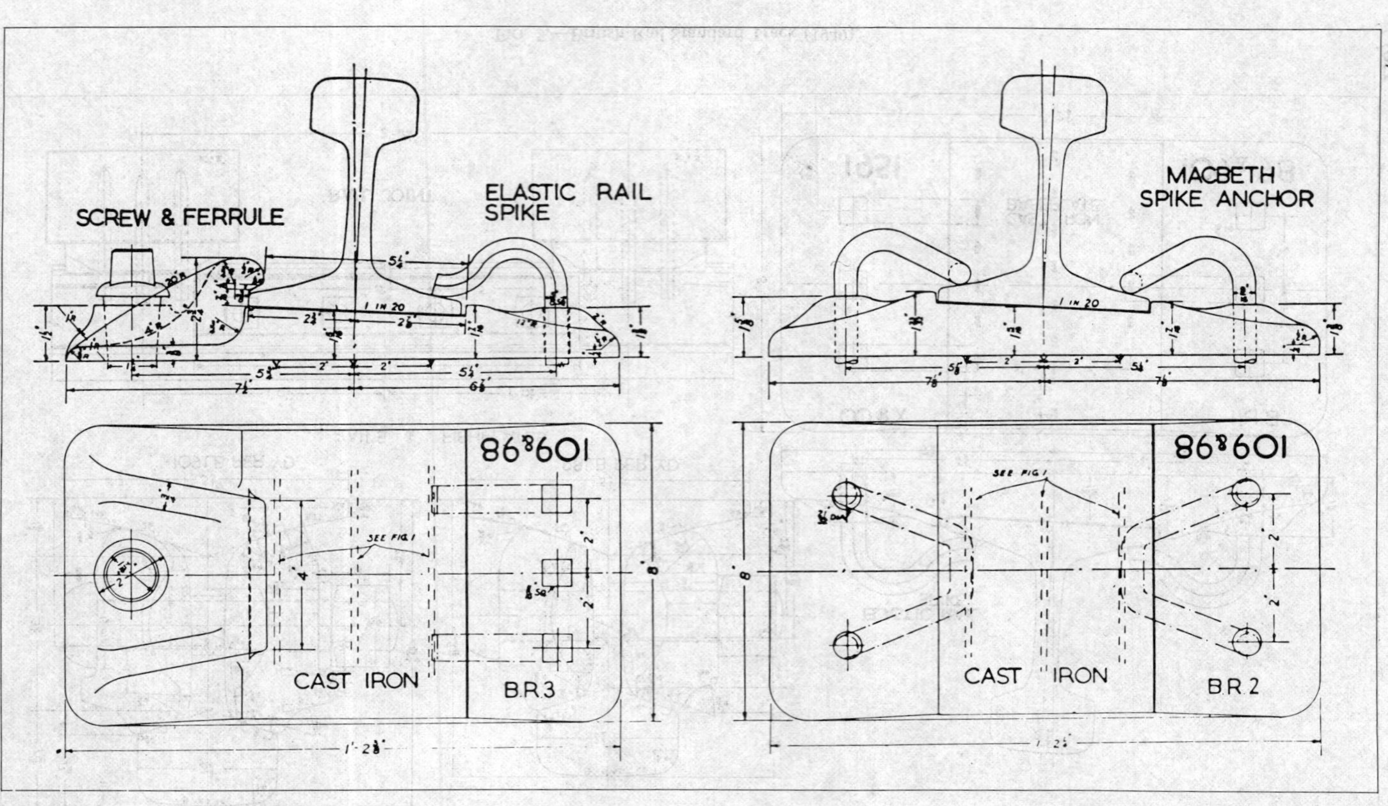

FIG. 6.—Rail Fixings.

FIG. 7.—Mills 'C' Clip.

HEAT TREATMENT.—Many railways specify the Sandberg Regulated Sorbitizing process for rails to be used in situations where rapid wear is experienced. Briefly this treatment comprises a partial quenching of the treads of the rails, after rolling, by means of an atomized water spray followed by retarded cooling from about

FIG. 8.—Pandrol Clips on Concrete Sleepers.

FIG. 9.—Pandrol Clips in Switches and Crossings on Concrete Bearers.

550 to 300°C, after which the rails are allowed to cool out in the normal manner. The Sandberg treatment has the effect of considerably hardening the treads of the rails whilst the webs and feet retain their normal structure, but experience has shown that such rails are prone to develop a corrugated surface unless laid in lines carrying intensive traffic where rate of wear by abrasion is more rapid than loss by corrosion.

It is contended that rails are particularly prone to develop incipient internal fissures whilst cooling between the above-mentioned range since the tensile strength of the metal has been shown to be at its lowest at a temperature of about 400°C. The effect of slow cooling is to even out the temperature as between the external and internal metal of the rails until they are sufficiently cool to resist this tendency. Retarded cooling is now specified by British railways for ordinary rails and undoubtedly reduces internal residual stresses in the steel.

STEEL CONDUCTOR RAILS FOR ELECTRIFIED TRACK.—Typical modern specification per cent: Carbon, 0·06 max; Silicon, 0·05 max; Manganese, 0·10–0·20; Sulphur, 0·03 max; Phosphorus, 0·04 max.

Resistance not exceeding 16 microhms per 100 lb/yd (6·5 times that of pure copper of equal length and section area) at 60°. The tensile breaking strength of such rails is approximately 20 tons per sq in.

SHORT RAILS IN CURVES.—Owing to the length of the outer rail of a curve exceeding that of the inner, it is necessary in order to keep the rail joints square to insert at intervals on the inside of the curve special rails, usually from 2 in to 5 in shorter than the standard length. Where G = gauge of track, L = length of outer rail, R = radius of outer rail (all in feet). The necessary decrease in rail length is given by: $d = GL/R$, also $R = GL/d$. For 60 ft rails and 4 ft $8\frac{1}{2}$ in gauge, d in inches = 3,390/R. In metric terms—rails 18·3 m, gauge 1·432 m (1·5 m rail centres), $d = (1{\cdot}5 \times 18{\cdot}3)/R$ m.

FISHPLATES.—BS 47:1959. The steel must show on analysis that it conforms to the following: Carbon, 0·20–0·30% for Class A Steel, and 0·30–0·42% for Class B Steel; Manganese, not to exceed 0·80%; Silicon, not to exceed 0·15%; Phosphorus, not to exceed 0·075%; Sulphur, not to exceed 0·075%.

Standard C or D tensile test pieces must give the following results: Breaking strength (kg/mm^2), 44 to 55 for Class A Steel, and 57 to 66 for Class B Steel; Minimum elongation, 22% (Class A) and 20% (Class B).

Worn and Reconditioned Fishplates.—Some use of Tapered Rail Joint Shims is made in this country and America in connection with the maintenance of worn rail ends and fishplates. To meet the various conditions of wear usually encountered these shims or packings are made in several lengths, from 9 to 16 in (229 to 306 mm), and vary in thickness at the centre from 0·03 to 0·15 in (0·76 to 3·8 mm), tapering towards two ends. A special stepped type of shim is also available for use in cases of unequal wear. (Fig. 10).

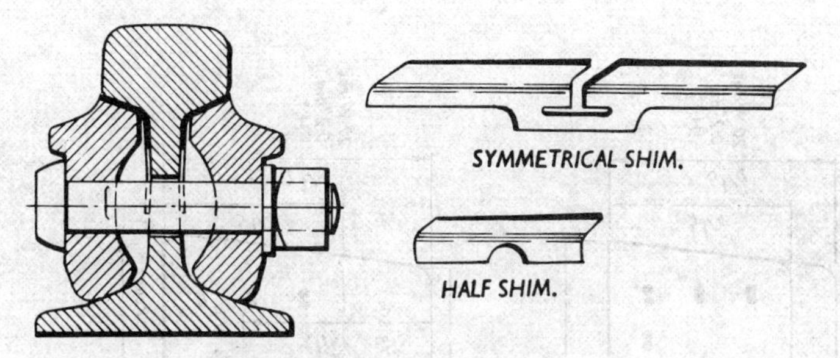

FIG. 10.—Rail Joint Shims.

FISHBOLTS AND NUTS (Abstract from BS 64 1946).—A tensile test shall be made either on a test piece taken from the bar or on a test piece turned from the finished bolts. The test shall be carried out in accordance with the provisions of BS 18 and shall comply with the requirements set out in Table 6.

TABLE 6.—TENSILE STRENGTH FOR FISHBOLTS AND NUTS.

Material	Tensile Stress Tons per sq in	Min elongation Per Cent on			
		Test Piece A	Test Piece B	Test Piece B1	Test Piece C or Subs
Material for bolts. Test piece cut from bar	35–40	—	18	22	23
Test piece from finished bolt	35–42	—	—	—	20
Material for nuts	35–40	20	—	—	25

BEND TEST.—The bend test piece shall when cold be capable of being bent, either by pressure or by blows from a hammer, round a bar equal to its diameter or thickness until its sides are parallel without showing any signs of fracture.

SCREW THREADS.—Shall be either BSW or BSF as specified by the purchaser. Threads shall be cut either to BSW or BSF form and shall conform to the 'medium fit' tolerances specified in BS 84 1940.

WOODEN SLEEPERS.—British Rail has made use of creosoted softwood sleepers, Baltic Redwood (*Pinus Sylvestris*) or Douglas Fir (*Pseudotsuga taxifolia*), and hardwoods such as Jarrah. The standard sizes are 8 ft 6 in long, 10 in wide, 5 in thick, and where special jointed sleepers are used they are 12 in wide. Metric sizes.—250 mm × 125 mm × 2,600 mm. Joint sleepers 300 mm wide

The early difficulties with the ordinary pressure creosoting process when treating Canadian Douglas Fir sleepers were overcome by incising before treatment together with a more rigid specification.

The incising operation consists in passing the sleepers through a machine provided with four rollers each equipped with removable cutters, designed to part the fibres of the wood without crushing or breaking, and if creosoting is carried out immediately, it is found that uniform penetration results with this otherwise refractory timber. Incising and creosoting are carried out in accordance with BS 913 1954 (see chapter 'Timber').

Crossing timber is usually 12 × 6 in (300 × 150 mm) and varies in length from 8 ft 6 in to 40 ft (2·6–12·4 m), whilst longitudinal bridge timbers may be 16 × 7 in (400 × 180 mm) and upwards where they are required to take chaired or base plated track.

On main lines where the standard plain track now consists of continuous welded rails on concrete sleepers, Jarrah hardwood timbers are used under the switches and crossings. The timbers are 125 mm in depth as against the 150 mm of softwood. Very few softwood sleepers are now used by British Rail.

CONCRETE SLEEPERS.—In recent years extensive use has been made in Great Britain of reinforced concrete sleepers. For sidings, goods loops and lightly operated branch lines independent block sleepers have

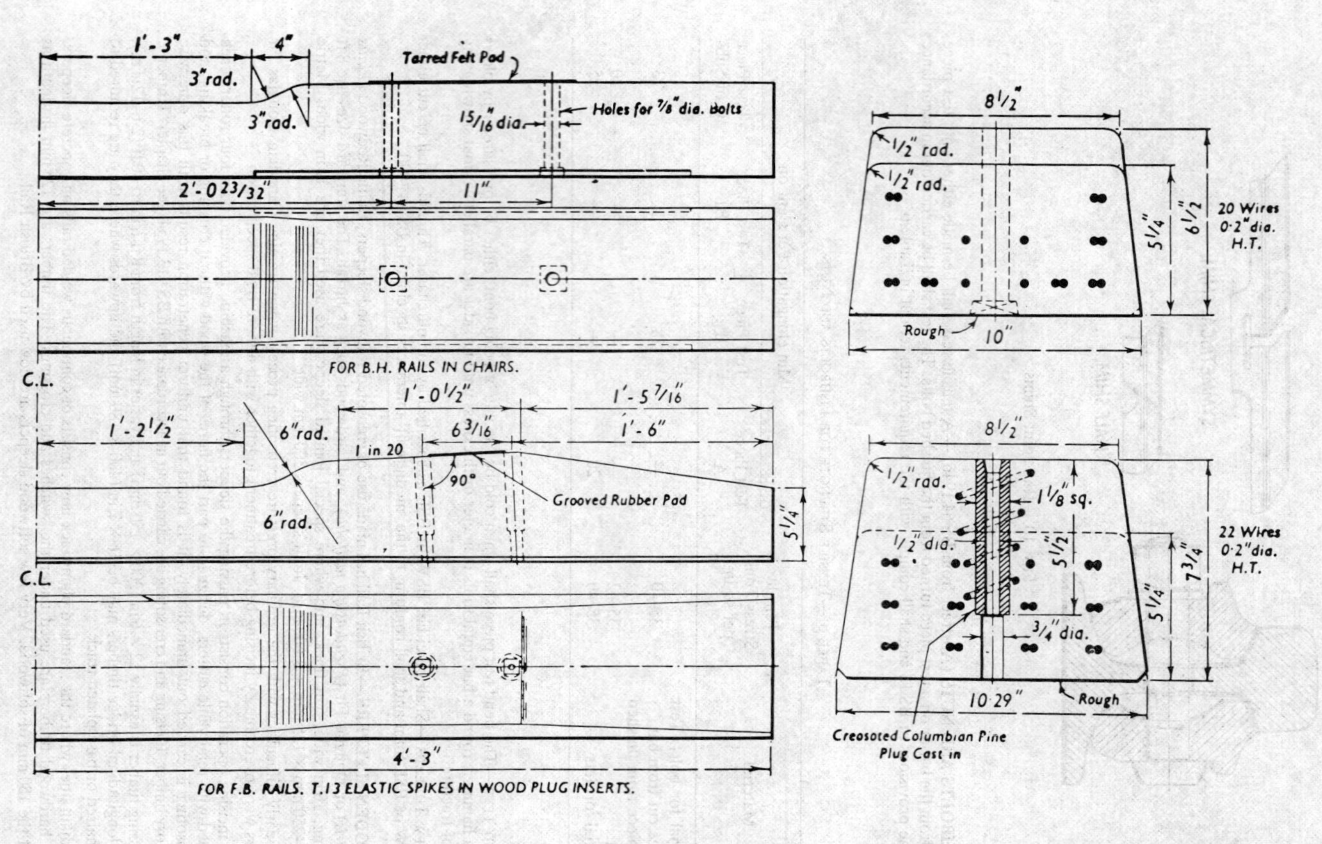

FIG. 11.—Concrete Sleepers (Early types).

been used, every third or fourth pair being connected together by steel gauge ties or replaced by transverse sleepers. The reinforcement of such blocks may consist of a single sheet of steel mesh fabric.

Numerous types of transverse concrete sleepers have been designed and track tested but for running lines where speeds are fairly high only prestressed concrete has been found to be suitable. Figure 11 shows early types of concrete sleepers for bull-head rails in chairs; the other for flat-bottom rails without baseplates but resting on resilient pads. The latter design provides for the use of type T Elastic Rail spikes as rail fastenings, driven into wood inserts cast in the sleeper. Variations of this type of sleeper provide for the use of resilient clip fastenings of several types. In general concrete sleepers are about four times as heavy as wooden sleepers but once laid in the track this additional weight is an advantage, particularly with long welded rails.

Pre-stressed concrete sleepers have now become the standard for welded-rail track in Main Lines of British railways. As from 1966, the 'Pandrol Clip' becomes the standard fastening for use with these concrete sleepers. Special malleable iron shoulders designed to take the Pandrol clips are cast-in the sleepers (Figs. 8 and 12). The rail rests on a resilient pad of rubber or rubber-bonded cork, which in turn rests directly on the concrete sleeper. For electrical insulation purposes a small nylon insulator is placed between the Pandrol clip and the rail foot.

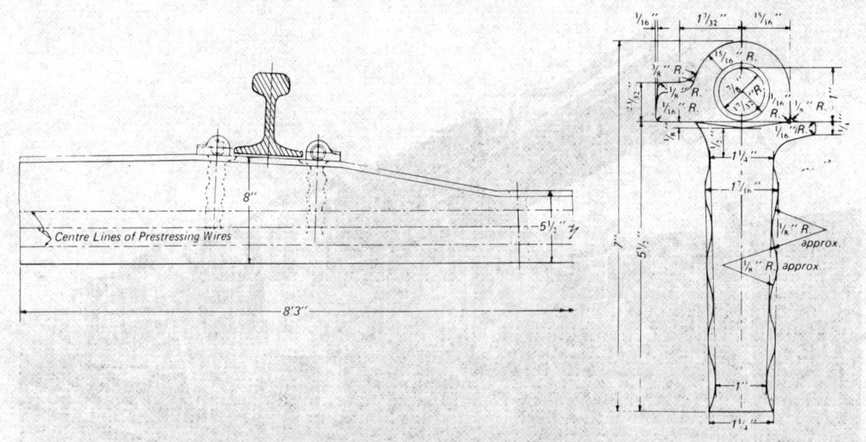

FIG. 12.—Prestressed Concrete Sleeper with 'Pandrol' Insert.

Alterations in the shape of the Pandrol Insert are currently being tested for greater stability in the concrete.

BALLAST.—The purpose of ballast is (*a*) to distribute the load over a larger area of the formation, (*b*) to provide a more or less uniform elastic medium between the track and the bed, (*c*) to provide rapid and efficient drainage of surface water, and (*d*) to hold the sleepers in position. The size of ballast, consisting of crushed stone varies from 7 to 63 mm, but the tendency is to confine it to the limits between 25 and 50 mm. For sidings, unimportant branch lines, and for clay cuttings and banks, ashes have been used for ballast; also for lines subject to mining subsidence. The ballast should extend from at least 180 mm beyond the ends of the sleepers with a slope of about 40° at the sides.

In modern railway practice, the formation is 600 mm below rail level, and is cambered 150 mm, dry stone cross-drains being formed as required into open jointed pipes of 'U' shaped drains (in the case of cuttings) laid in the cesses. In course of time ballast becomes dirty and consolidated so that it interferes with the drainage and on this account should be periodically cleaned by screening. This is usually done by the use of ballast forks or screens but in recent years increasing use is being made of self-propelled mechanical ballast cleaning machine, the Plasser (Fig. 13).

RAIL AND FLANGE LUBRICATORS.—Owing to the guiding force exerted by wheel flanges on sharp curves, both the flanges and the running face of the high rails tend to become worn more rapidly, depending upon the radius of the curve, wheelbase of vehicle, etc. Extensive use is now made of automatic rail and flange lubricators installed at suitable situations, generally at the commencement of a curve, and in many instances these appliances will be at least double the life of a rail subjected to side-wear. In the Portec type, Figure 18a, the grease is forced out by means of small plunger pumps operated by the outside of the wheel treads. Figure 18b shows another type of rail lubricator (Mills-Hurcol). This machine is operated by vertical movement of the rail under traffic. Where necessary, provisions can also be made for the lubrication of continuous check rails, to reduce noise and wear.

MECHANICAL MAINTENANCE APPLIANCES.—The ever-increasing necessity for economy in maintenance and renewal expenditure combined with labour shortages has inevitably led to a more extended use of mechanical tools, etc, for various platelaying operations and the following are some of the appliances being used on British Rail today.

Ballast Cleaning Machines.—In order to keep the track formation well drained, it is necessary periodically to clean the ballast to allow water to pass freely through it. On-track ballast cleaning machines have been developed to achieve this by removing the ballast to a depth of up to 150mm below the sleepers and returning any reusable stone after discarding dirt, stone, dust, etc.

Ballast cleaning leaves the track somewhat deficient in ballast and this is rectified with the passage of a ballast hopper train. Incorporated in this operation a Ballast Regulator Machine provides the correct spreading of the extra ballast in the "four-foot" and on the shoulders. Ballast tamping and consolidating machines provide the necessary final ballast profile.

FIG. 13.—Plasser Ballast Cleaning Machine.

Ballast Tamping Machines.—In 1960 the first automatic lifting and levelling tamping machine was introduced. The top level of the track was automatically adjusted and each sleeper individually tamped to suit this level. In the years that followed, improvements in design were achieved.

Figure 14 illustrates one of the early Plasser tamping machines fitted with four pairs of tamping tools to each rail, thus enabling two sleepers to be dealt with simultaneously. Automatic track lining machines were also being developed and brought into use in order to correct any misalignment of the track on both the straight and the curves (Fig. 21). Within a comparatively short time the lifting, tamping, levelling and lining operations were incorporated in one large machine and Fig. 15 shows one of the more modern versions now in use. Electric hand tampers, operating in groups of four, supplied with power from a 3kw portable generator are used in the vicinity of points and crossings, see Fig. 18.

RAIL RECTIFICATION MACHINES.—Rails in the running tracks can suffer periodic damage such as corrugations, wheel burns, side-cutting, lipping and crushing and in order to preserve smooth running conditions it becomes necessary to correct these faults. To obviate the necessity for the very costly replacement of the faulty rails a Plasser machine has been developed to plane the running surfaces of the rails while still in the track and to produce as far as possible the original contour of the rail head (Fig. 16). Following the Rectification

FIG. 14.—Plasser Duomatic Tamping Machine.

FIG. 15.—Tamping, Levelling and Lining Machine.

machine, and attached to it, is a Swarf Machine fitted with rotating magnetic drums which pick up the steel cuttings left by the planing process and deposit them in a storage bin.

Ballast Scarifiers.—Used for breaking up hard ballast prior to laying of new track. A tractor-hauled scarifier can deal with 2·5 km of ballast in 10 hours and releases about 8 men for other duties. Rubber-tyred or caterpillar track tractors are employed.

Track Relaying Machines.—Where practicable, track relaying is carried out in complete prefabricated 18·3m lengths. The old track is also lifted out in similar lengths. Rail mounted cranes travelling on the adjoining line are often used for this purpose. Special track laying machines have also been designed for this work and consist of large self-propelled vehicles which have sideways extending jibs from which the 18·3m lengths of track are raised or lowered (see Fig. 19). When it is not possible to obtain possession of two parallel tracks for the relaying operation, or on single track lines, these machines cannot of course be used. In these cases a single line track laying unit is required, as illustrated in Figure 20.

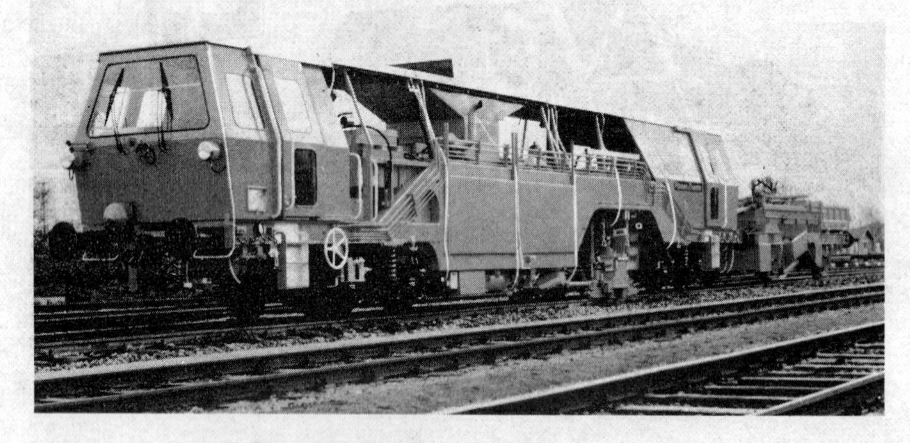

FIG 16.—Rail Rectification Machine with Swarf Collector.

FIG. 17(*a*).—'Portec' Rail and Flange Lubricator (*Portec* (*U.K.*) *Ltd*).

Rail Barrows, Track Liners, Lifting Jacks, etc.—Rail barrows mounted on a rubber-tyred wheel and with self retaining jaw to grip the rail head enable six men to lift a 18·3 m rail—saving 18 men. Two lever operated track liners enable small gangs to carry out slewing without assistance from adjoining gangs. Two men with liners can do the work previously performed by six to eight men equipped with slewing bars.

Ratchet and hydraulic lifting jacks with quick release have been specially developed for lifting heavy crossingwork, etc. Rail creep adjusters operated by means of right- and left-hand screw threads enable up to 200 m of rail to be pulled or released at a time.

Fly spanners, impact wrenches, portable rail saws and drilling machines, chain saws, motor scythes and hoes, electric hedge trimmers, trench diggers, bulldozers, and heavy frog rammers are other developments now used extensively in connection with on- and off-track maintenance.

AUTOMATIC LINING MACHINES.—Plasser automatic track lining machines are used to correct misalignment of straight track and to regularise curved track. The machines measure the amount of slue required to correct the alignment and then push the track sideways as necessary (Fig. 21).

FIG. 17(*b*).—'Mills-Hurcol' Rail and Flange Lubricator.

FIG. 18.—Electric Hand Tampers (*Kango Ltd.*)

FIG. 19.—Track Relaying Machine.

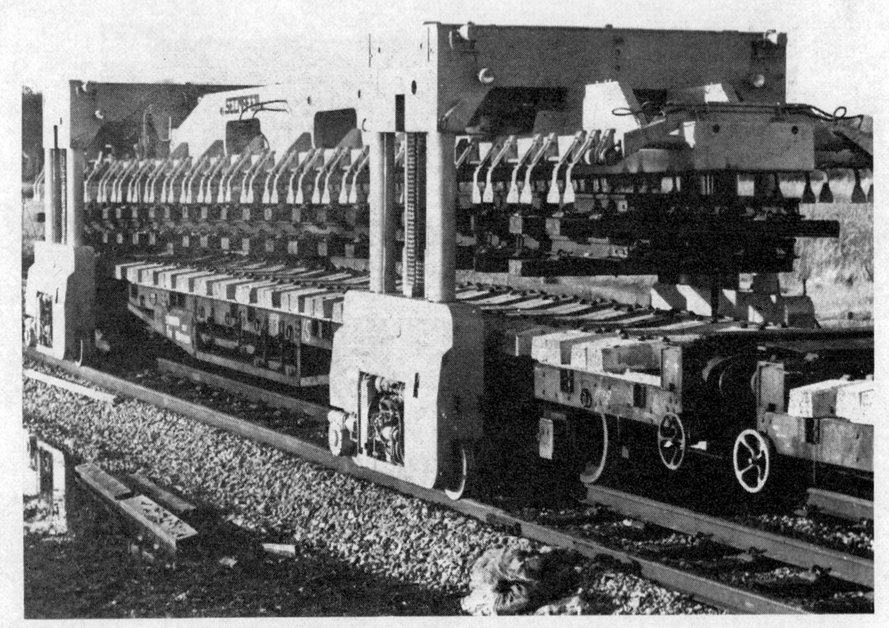

FIG. 20.—Secmafer Tracklaying Machine.

FIG. 21.—Track Lining Machine.

TRACK RECORDING VEHICLES.—For a number of years past, developments have taken place in the design of special vehicles for continuously recording the physical state of the track under load by means of various mechanisms. Three types of such vehicles are the Sperry (USA), Amsler (Switzerland) and Mauzin (France). The Matisa-Mauzin Coach records the following data on a chart 21 cm wide: Irregularities in cross level: Irregularities in level of both rails separately; Variations in cant; Versines of both rails separately; and Variation of gauge from standard. In France the information obtained from the Mauzin charts is used to formulate maintenance and renewal programmes. On British railways several Matisa Track Recording cars are now in use. These machines are smaller and simpler versions of the Mauzin coach. They are self-propelled and at 20 mph produce a reliable record of track data (Fig. 22a). A new high-speed track recording car has been designed and built by British Rail, and is now in use. It can operate at speeds up to 125 mph (200 km/h) (Fig. 22b).

CONTINUOUS WELDED RAIL.—In most countries considerable attention is now being given to the elimination of rail joints by the use of continuously welded rails. By so doing a considerable reduction in track maintenance is achieved, rail end failures reduced and smoother running obtained. The greatest problems encountered in the installation of long rails are those associated with the high internal stresses which are bound to occur when the free thermal expansion or contraction is restricted. It has been established that irrespective of the length of a continuously welded rail, movement due to rise or fall of temperature only takes

FIG. 22a.—Matisa Track Recording Trolley.

place in the 60 to 90 m at each end of the length. It therefore follows that very high tensile or compressive stresses are likely to occur in the rail between these end zones. In order to contain these stresses and to prevent buckling of the track when temperatures are high it is essential that adequate numbers of sleepers, good rail fastenings and first class ballasting conditions are provided. In this respect the heavy weight of concrete sleepers makes their use attractive in giving increased stability to the track. On British railways extensive use has also been made of Jarrah sleepers in connection with continuous-welded rails. This hardwood, grown in Western Australia, is heavy enough to give the required stability, is extremely resistant to decay and requires no treatment with creosote or other preservative solution. Longitudinal splitting of the timber is rare. Cast iron baseplates incorporating quick release fastenings such as the Mills 'C' and Pandrol clips are used with the Jarrah sleepers and the rails are supported on rubber pads resting on the baseplate seatings.

FIG. 22b.—High Speed Recording Car.

Before the installation of continuous-welded rails it is customary to renew the track in standard 18·3 m prefabricated lengths, and to provide a uniform bed of clean ballast to a depth of 220–300 mm below the sleepers. The track is brought to a high standard as regards alignment and longitudinal level and after a suitable period for consolidation, the continuous-welded rails are then installed in place of the 18·3 m lengths used in the relaying operation. Changing these rails can be carried out easily and speedily by making use of rail changing trolleys.

When the continuous-welded rails have been put in the track it is necessary to ensure that they are in a regularised stress-free condition at a suitable temperature before they are finally fastened down. To do this the rails are placed on small steel rollers which are mounted on the baseplates at 9 m intervals, and consequently they are able to freely expand or contract according to temperature variations. The required fixing down temperature is in the range 70–80°F (21–27°C) this being approximately mid-way between the highest and lowest temperatures the rails have to withstand in service. When the rail temperature at the time of installation is below the required range it is necessary to warm the rails before fastening them down. This is done by artificially expanding the rails to obtain a correct stress-free condition within the correct installation temperature range, a method which has largely replaced the gas rail warmers. This method utilises a hydraulic tensor or rail puller attached to the free end of the welded rail and also to the adjoining fixed rail or the middle of the length to be stressed (Fig. 25). The free rail is then stretched until it is the correct calculated and measured length to suit the temperature rise required. At this moment the rollers are removed and the rail clipped down to the sleepers. In order to accommodate the limited amount of movement at each end of a welded length it is customary to install a set of expansion switches or a pair of expansion joints (Fig. 23).

When it is necessary to install catchpoints in continuous welded rail track special switches have to be used to withstand the very high longitudinal stresses experienced in such track due to temperature changes (Fig. 26).

The welded joints are usually made by the electric flash-butt, thermit or electric-arc methods. It is customary to weld standard length rails into longer lengths in the depot, transport to the relaying site and then to site-weld these lengths to form the desired continuously welded section. On British railways it is usual to depot-weld by the flash-butt method into 90, 180 and 220 or 360 m lengths which can be transported to the site and subsequently welded into longer lengths either at the lineside or alternatively when laid in the track. The thermit method is used for the site welds. Extensive use is now made of welded joints in switches and crossings in main lines, motive power depots, and marshalling yards, where the elimination of standard rail joints has effected a very great reduction in maintenance costs.

RESURFACING WORN RAILS BY WELDING.—The practice of building up *in situ* worn switch and crossing rails is now universal; portable electric arc welding plant is used almost exclusively.

CLEARANCES ON CURVES.—The greatest distance by which the end of a vehicle or load overhangs the running face of the rail on the outside of a curve is termed the End Throw. If R = radius of curve; G = gauge of track; W = width of vehicle or load; L = overall length of vehicle or load; B = wheelbase or distance between bogie centres (all in metres).

$$\text{End throw} = \frac{W - G}{2} + \frac{L^2 - B^2}{8R}.$$

FIG. 23.—Expansion Joints.

FIG. 24.—Rail Heating Trolley for Continuous-Welded Rails.

The overhang of the centre of the vehicle on the inside of a curve is known as the Centre Throw, and with the same notation:

$$\text{Centre Throw} = \frac{W - G}{2} + \frac{B^2}{8R}.$$

In the case of structures adjoining the inner rail of a curve having superelevation, additional clearance should be allowed.

PERMANENT WAY—HEIGHTS AND WIDTHS.—Ministry of Transport Requirement or Recommendations are shown in Fig. 27.

FIG. 25.—Hydraulic Tensor.

FIG. 26.—Catchpoints strengthened for CWR.

FIG. 26(a).—Welded Rail Train Leaving Depot.

PLATFORMS.—The minimum clear width of any platform throughout its length is to be 2 m. At important stations the width to be not less than 3·6 m, except for short distances at either end in any case of difficulty. In the case of island platforms, the minimum width for an adequate distance on each side of the centre of its length to be 3·6 m. The descent at the ends of platforms to be by ramps and not by steps.

The edges of the platforms to overhang not less than 0·3 m, and the recess so formed to be kept clear as far as possible of permanent obstruction (Fig. 27).

GRADIENTS.—It is desirable to avoid constructing a station on, or providing a siding in connection with a line which is laid upon a gradient steeper than 1 in 260.

CHEMICAL WEED KILLING.—The control of weeds on railway tracks today is usually done by spraying with chemical solutions. In Britain, 'Atlacide' weedkillers are in general use and are obtainable as either liquid concentrates or dusting powder (the latter is used in places inaccessible by spraying, eg cable runs, etc). The liquid concentrate is diluted for use with from three to six parts of water, but the active chemical application rate (approx 200 lb dry weight per acre) is constant. The action of 'Atlacide' depends largely on the absorption of the chemical by foilage and stem, hence spraying is carried out, as far as practicable, when weeds have made sufficient growth to enable the foliage to be well covered by the fine spray. In most districts, best results are obtained by spraying in spring and early summer (in some cases, in the autumn also). Brushwood on railway banks requires special treatment and trials are being undertaken with various preparations.

INTERNATIONAL UNION OF RAILWAYS (U.I.C.).—Many years ago the Railway Administrations of all the European countries set up a joint organisation for the purpose of discussion and mutual exchange of views on all aspects of Railway development. The headquarters of the organisation is in Paris and the Members Committee have regular discussions on any particular problems raised by individual administrations and the solutions to which are of mutual benefit to all. Any particular problem is then referred to a specialist committee of representatives of those administrations particularly interested, for extended deliberations, research and experiment culminating in a final report on findings and solutions. The Office of Research and Experiment (O.R.E.) is permanently situated in Utrecht and from that Office are issued the reports of the numerous committees for submission to U.I.C.—Paris.

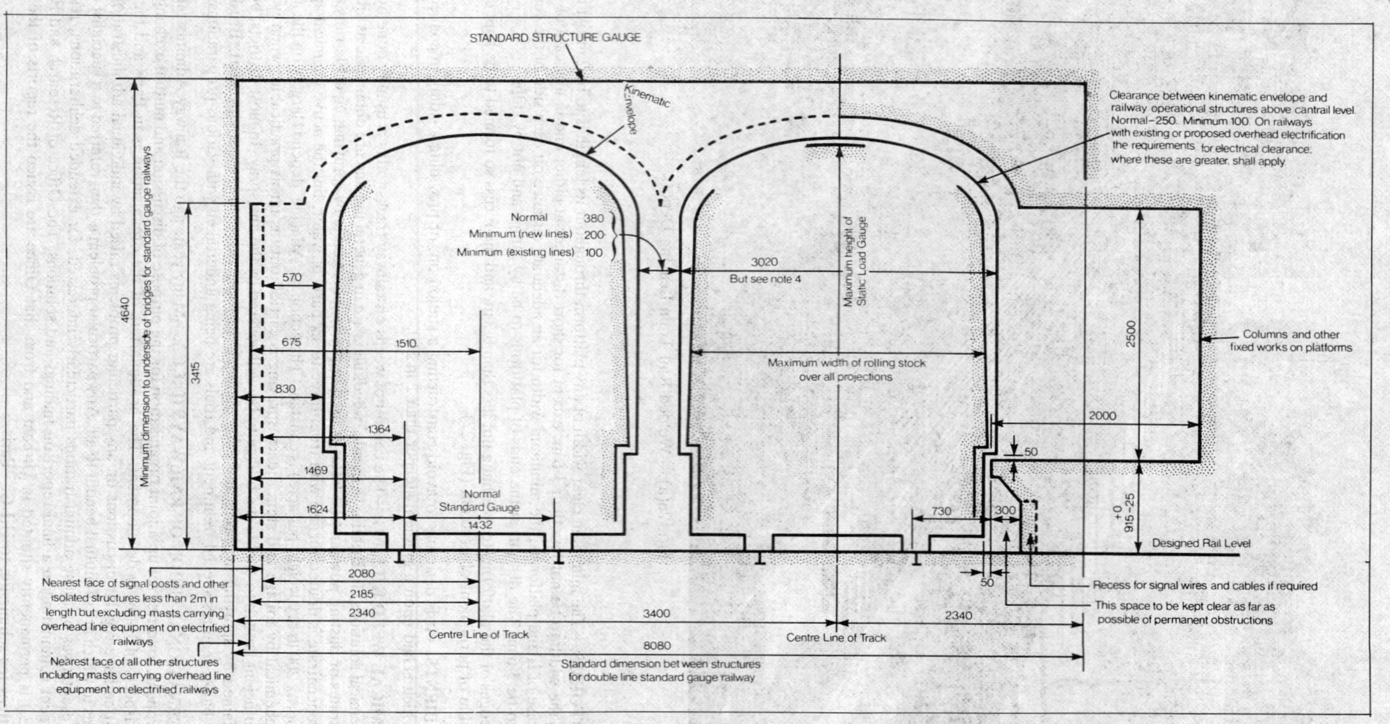

FIG. 27.—MOT Clearances.

One such problem was the design and standardisation of switches and crossings for future high speeds up to at least 300 km/hr. British Rail designs meet the standards recommended.

SWITCHES AND CROSSINGS.—British Rail designs for switches include both straight and curved planing of the switch blade. Built-up crossings are made in the range 1 in 4 to 1 in 21 (CLM) and cast high manganese crossings in the range 1 in 7 to 1 in 28. In the past, rails were mounted on baseplates with a 1 in 20 inclination. However, current designs have vertical rails, improved geometrical layout and switches having much finer entry angles (see Table 8 and Figs. 28, 29, 30). Transitional turnouts using the new designs make it possible to install crossovers and double junctions for higher speeds than were previously possible. The swing-nose common crossing has been designed for future use for main line speeds in excess of 160 km/h. It gives an uninterrupted path for the wheels over the crossing and requires no check rails (Fig. 31).

TABLE 8.—TURNOUTS.

Switch Type	Crossing Angle	Lead Length to Crossing Nose	Radius of Turnout	Max Speed
AV	1 in 7	18·6 m	141 m	30 km/h
BV	1 in 8	21·5 m	184 m	35 km/h
CV	1 in $9\frac{1}{4}$	25·0 m	246 m	45 km/h
DV	1 in $10\frac{3}{4}$	29·3 m	332 m	50 km/h
EV	1 in 15	40·7 m	645 m	70 km/h
FV	1 in $18\frac{1}{2}$	50·1 m	981 m	85 km/h
SGV	1 in 21	57·3 m	1,264 m	100 km/h
GV	1 in 24	65·5 m	1,650 m	115 km/h

FIG. 28.—Vertical Type Switches.

SUPERELEVATION OF OUTER RAIL ON CURVES.—The effect of centrifugal force on vehicles travelling round a curve is usually counteracted, at least partially, by raising the outer rail of the curve above the level of the inner rail, thus giving the track a transverse slope.

When this superelevation exactly counteracts the centrifugal force, the speed at which the vehicle is moving is the Equilibrium Speed. If the vehicle travels at a higher speed, then the amount of extra superelevation

FIG. 29.—Common Crossing.

FIG. 31.—Swing Nose Crossing Being Assembled.

FIG. 30.—Cast Manganese Crossing.

which would be required to regain equilibrium is the Cant Deficiency. The maximum speed at which a vehicle may negotiate a curve is given by:

$$V_m = 0{\cdot}29\sqrt{[R(E + D)]}$$

where V_m is in km/h; R in metres; E and D in millimetres.

Maximum value for $E = 150$ mm; maximum value for $D = 110$ mm.

Crossing Angle by CLM

$\theta = 2\cot^{-1}2N \qquad N = 0{\cdot}5\cot\theta/2$

$$\sin\theta = \frac{N}{N^2 + 1/4} \qquad \sin\frac{\theta}{2} = \frac{1}{2\sqrt{(N^2 + 1/4)}}$$

$$\cos\theta = \frac{N^2 - 1/4}{N^2 + 1/4} \qquad \cos\frac{\theta}{2} = \frac{N}{\sqrt{(N^2 + 1/4)}}$$

$$\tan\theta = \frac{N}{N^2 - 1/4} \qquad \tan\frac{\theta}{2} = \frac{1}{2N}.$$

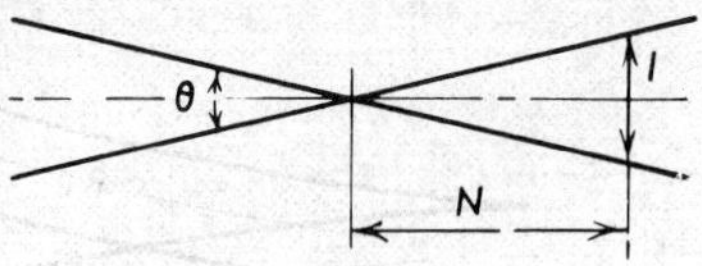

FIG. 32.

Straight Track with Straight Switch and Curved Crossing

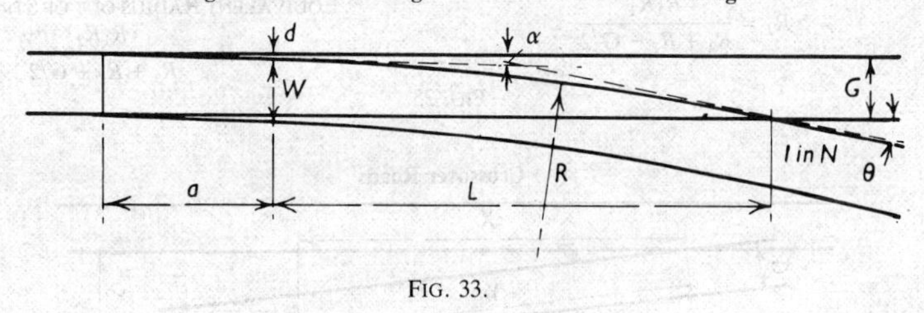

FIG. 33.

d = switch heal divergence. $\qquad M = a \div d.$

$W = G - d. \qquad a$ = switch length = Md.

$$L = W\cot\frac{\alpha + \theta}{2} = 2W\left(\frac{MN - \frac{1}{4}}{M + N}\right)$$

$$R = \frac{W}{\cos a - \cos\theta} = \frac{2WM^2N^2}{M^2 - N^2}\text{ (approximately)} \quad = \frac{LMN}{M - N}\text{ approximately}$$

$$\cos\theta = \cos\alpha - \frac{W}{R}$$

$$N = M\sqrt{\left(\frac{R - \frac{1}{4}W}{R + 2WM^2}\right)}\text{ approximately.} \qquad N = \tfrac{1}{2}\cot\tfrac{1}{2}\theta$$

$$= \frac{LM + \frac{1}{2}W}{2WM - L}\text{ (approximately).}$$

Straight Track with Straight Switch and Straight Crossing

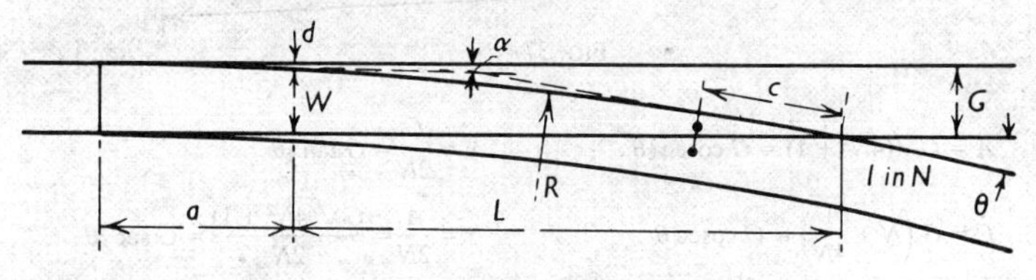

FIG. 34.

$$W_1 = W - c\sin\theta = G - \left(d + \frac{c}{N + (1/4N)}\right)$$

$$L = W_1 \cot\frac{a+\theta}{2} + c\cos\theta = 2W_1\left(\frac{MN - (1/4)}{M+N}\right) + c\left(\frac{N - (1/4N)}{N + (1/4N)}\right)$$

$$R = \frac{W_1}{\cos\alpha - \cos\theta} = \frac{2W_1 M^2 N^2}{M^2 - N^2} \text{ approximately.}$$

$$\cos\theta = \cos\alpha - \frac{W_1}{R} \qquad N = M\sqrt{\left(\frac{R - \frac{1}{2}W_1}{R + 2W_1M^2}\right)} = \tfrac{1}{2}\cot\tfrac{1}{2}\theta$$

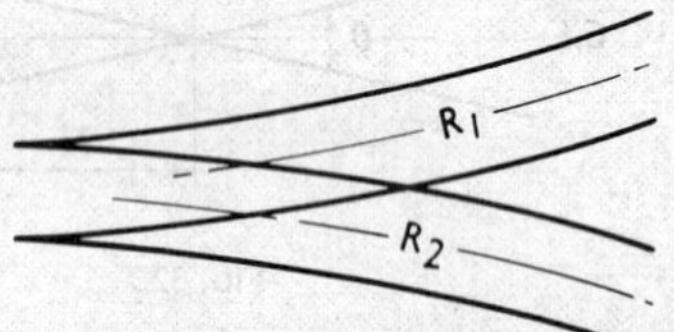

CONTRA FLEXURE

$$R_E = \frac{R_1R_2}{R_1 + R_2 - G/2}$$

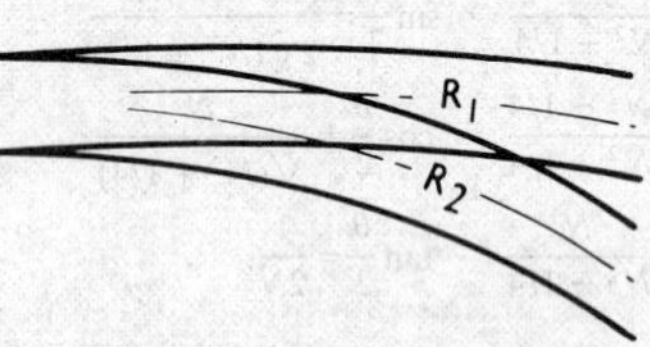

SIMILAR FLEXURE
EQUIVALENT RADIUS OUT OF STRAIGHT

$$R_E = \frac{R_1R_2}{R_1 + R_2 + G/2}$$

FIG. 35.

Crossover Roads

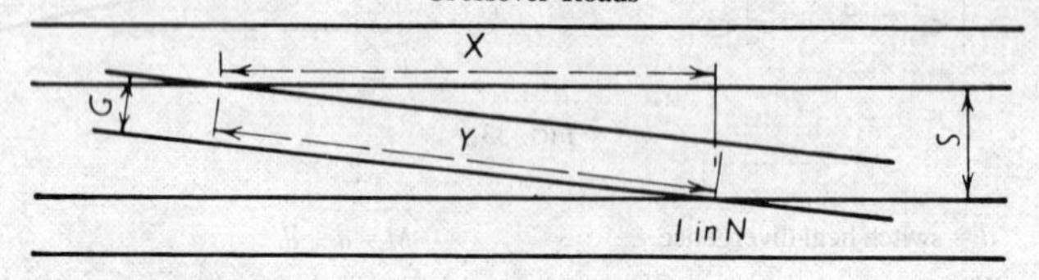

FIG. 36.

$$X = N(S - G) - \frac{S+G}{4N} \qquad Y = N(S - G) + \frac{S+G}{4N}$$

This also applies when the tracks are curved if the length Y is curved to the same radius and the same sense as the main lines.

Diamond Crossing with both Tracks Straight

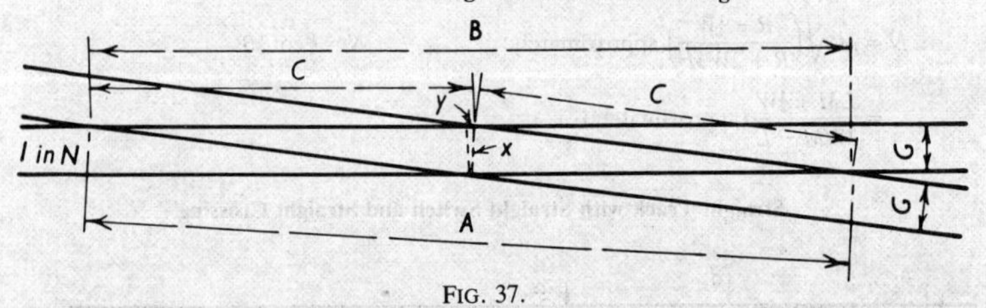

FIG. 37.

$$A = G\sqrt{(4N^2 + 1)} = G\operatorname{cosec}\tfrac{1}{2}\theta \qquad y = \frac{G}{2N} = G\tan\tfrac{1}{2}\theta$$

$$C = G\left(N + \frac{1}{4N}\right) = G\operatorname{cosec}\theta \qquad x = \frac{A}{2N} = \frac{G\sqrt{(4N^2+1)}}{2N} = G\sec\tfrac{1}{2}\theta$$

$$B = 2GN = G\cot\tfrac{1}{2}\theta$$

Scissors Crossing—Straight Tracks

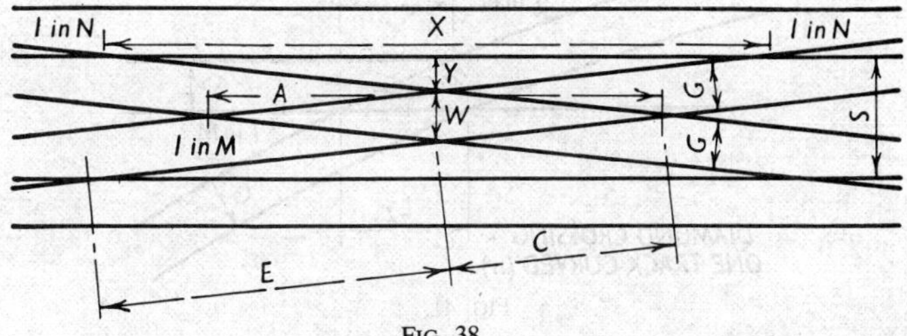

FIG. 38.

$$M = \frac{N}{2} - \frac{1}{8N} \qquad X = N(S - G) - \frac{S + G}{4N} \qquad W = \frac{A}{2M} = S - 2Y$$

$$C = G\left(M + \frac{1}{4M}\right) \qquad A = G\sqrt{(4M^2 + 1)}$$

$$E = \frac{X}{2}\left(\frac{N + (1/4N)}{N - (1/4N)}\right) \qquad Y = \frac{X}{2}\left(\frac{1}{N - (1/4N)}\right)$$

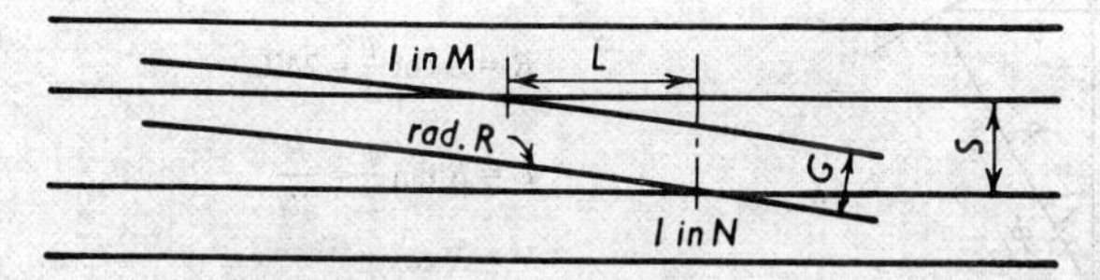

FIG. 39.

$$R = \frac{(4N^2 + 1)}{8(M^2 - N^2)}[(4M^2 + 1)(S - G) + 2G]$$

$$L = 2M(S - G) - \frac{(4M^2 + 1)(S - G) + 2G}{2(M + N)}$$

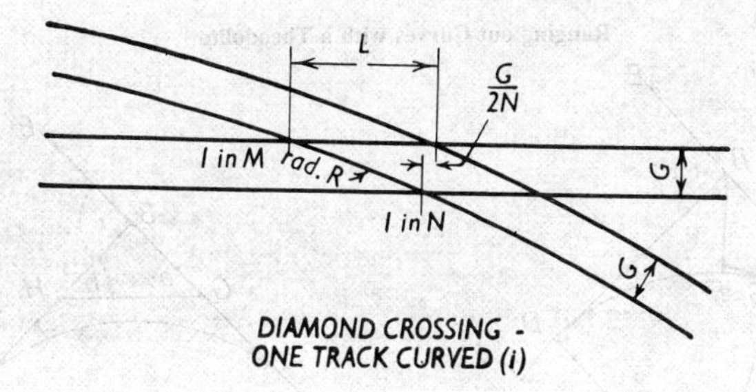

FIG. 40.

$$R = \frac{G(4M^2 + 1)(4N^2 + 1)}{8(M^2 - N^2)} \qquad L = G\left(\frac{4MN - 1}{2(M + N)} + \frac{1}{2N}\right)$$

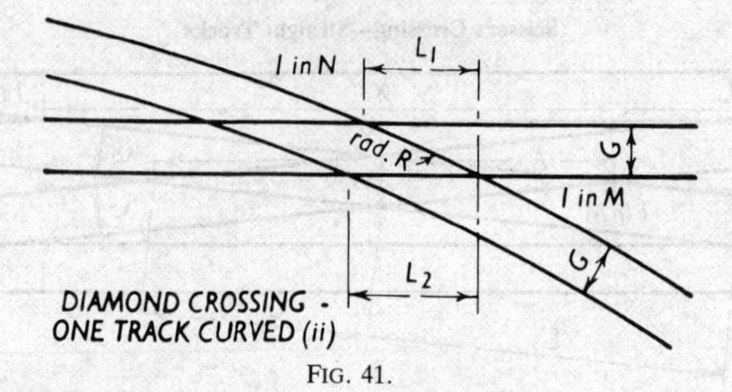

FIG. 41.

$$R = \frac{G(4M^2+1)(4N^2+1)}{8(N^2-M^2)} \qquad L_1 = G\left[2M - \frac{4M^2+1}{(2N+M)}\right] \qquad L_2 = L_1 + \frac{G}{2N}$$

USEFUL FORMULAE

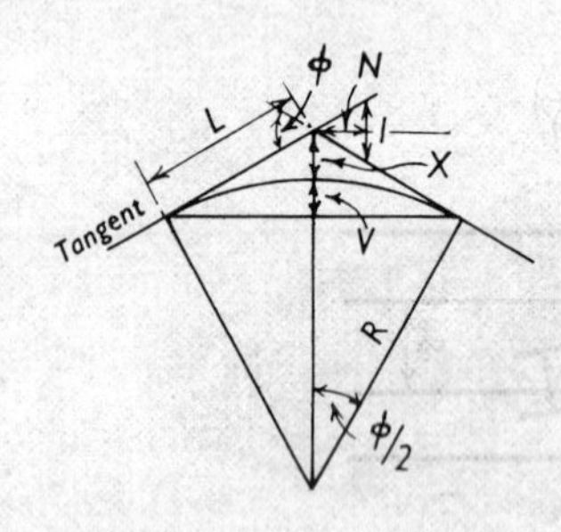

$$X = R\left(\sec\frac{\varphi}{2} - 1\right) = R\left[\frac{\sqrt{(4N^2+1)}}{2N} - 1\right]$$

$$V = R\left(1 - \cos\frac{\varphi}{2}\right) = R\left[1 - \frac{2N}{\sqrt{(4N^2+1)}}\right]$$

$$R = L\cot\frac{\varphi}{2} = 2NL$$

$$L = R\tan\frac{\varphi}{2} = \frac{R}{2N}$$

$$V = X\cos\varphi$$

(When N is >10, $V = X$ (approximately)).

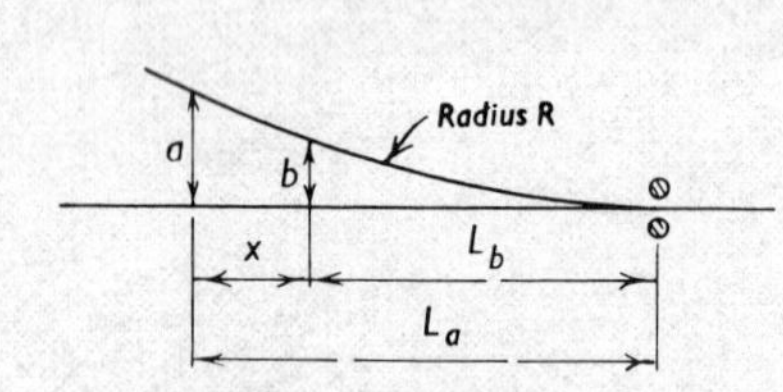

$$R = \frac{1}{2(a-b)^2}\{B(a+b) + \sqrt{B[(a+b)^2B - (a-b)^2A]}\}$$

$$A = [x^2 + (a+b)^2]$$

$$B = [x^2 + (a-b)^2]$$

Approx.

$$R = \frac{1}{2}\left[\frac{x}{\sqrt{a} - \sqrt{b}}\right]^2$$

Ranging out Curves with a Theodolite

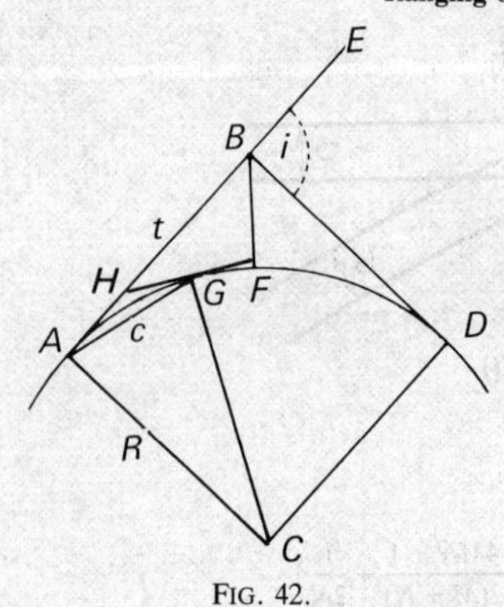

FIG. 42.

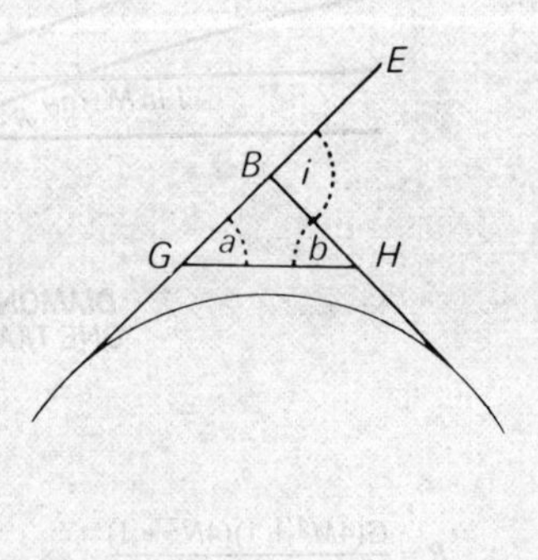

FIG. 43.

R = radius of curve = AC; i = angle of inclination of intersection = EBD; t = tangent AB or $BD = R \tan i/2$.

Length of curve = $AFD = 0{\cdot}0002909\ Ri$.

Tangential (or 'setting off') angle (angle between c and (t) in minutes for any chord c).

$= 171{\cdot}873\ c/R$.

R and c being expressed in feet or chains and i in minutes.

The angle ACG is called the 'deflection' angle, and is twice the tangential angle GHB, ie the tangential angle is one-half the deflection angle.

To find the Angle of Intersection and Point of Intersection where the latter is inaccessible (Fig. 41)

If B is the inaccessible point, then—
Range the line GH.

$$i = a + b,$$

$$GB = \frac{GH \sin b}{\sin l} \qquad HB = \frac{GH \sin a}{\sin i}$$

Setting out Curves by Offsets

First offset BD from the tangent line.

$$DB = \frac{AD^2}{2 \text{ radius}}.$$

Offset from any chord AB produced

$$\text{to } E = EC = \frac{AE \times EB}{2 \text{ radius}}$$

Or where $AB = BE$, then

$$EC = \frac{AB^2}{\text{radius}}.$$

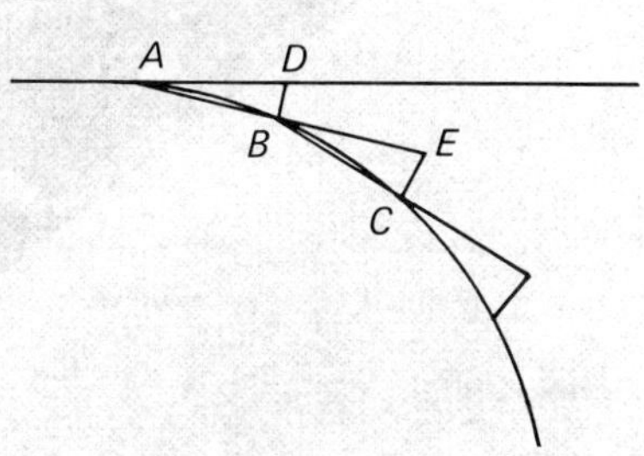

FIG. 44.

TRANSITION CURVES.—When a train travels round a circular curve radial acceleration varies directly as the square of the speed and inversely as the radius, disappearing entirely when the radius is infinite, that is, when the track is straight. A transition curve or easement spiral (Fig. 45), is, therefore, inserted between a tangent and a regular circular curve or between two curves of the same 'hand' but differing in radius in order that the radial acceleration shall be attained gradually in the length of the transition curve. The absence of suitable transition curves not only gives rise to very uncomfortable running conditions but also makes it impossible to maintain the track in its proper alignment.

Many forms of spiral have been advocated for this purpose but the curve which best fulfils all the requirements of a true transition is the spiral, the intrinsic equation of which is:

$$1 = m\sqrt{\varphi}$$

It can be shown, however, that for the majority of railway purposes the cubic parabola is a very close approximation and can be set out by means of a rectangular offset from the tangent by the formulae shown in Fig. 45.

When using the formulae of Fig. 45 it will be found that where the ratio R/L is much less than say 4, difficulties in setting out arise, especially near the junction of the transition with the circular curve. This is due to the approximations employed in the derivation of the usual formulae and in such instances more accurate formulae should be used to ensure the best results. Such formulae are not difficult to derive from the equation to the cubic parabola but are somewhat cumbersome. If, however, 'c' is substituted for the ratio R/L the following simple relations can be established.

$$p = \frac{(4c^2 - 1)^{1 \cdot 5}}{8c^2} \qquad D = \frac{c}{\sqrt{(1 - 4p^2)}} L = mL \qquad Y = \frac{1}{6p} L = qL$$

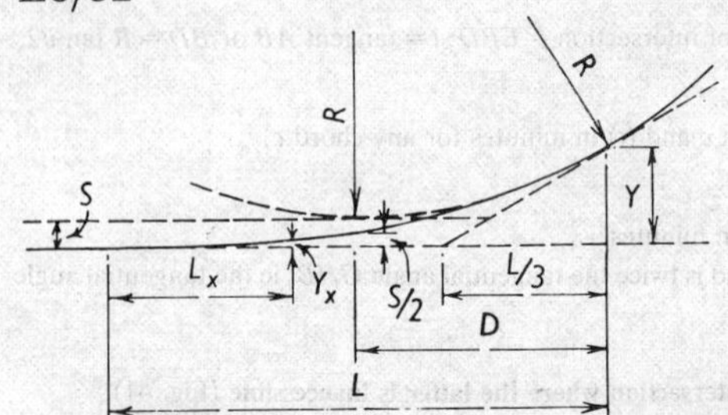

$$S = (q + 2mp - c)L = nL$$

$$S = L^2/24R \qquad Y_x = L_x^3/6LR$$

$$Y = 4S \qquad D = L/2$$

FIG. 45.—Transition Spiral.

FIG. 46.—Glued Insulated Joint.

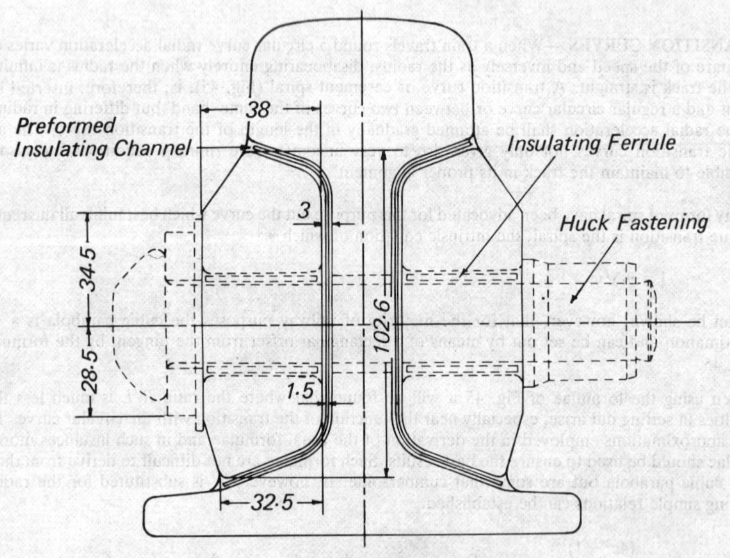

FIG. 47.—Glued Joint.

INSULATED RAIL JOINTS.—The steadily increasing mileage of track circuits installed in recent years has resulted in the necessity for providing a larger number of insulated rail joints.

Numerous arrangements have been experimented with from time to time but until a few years ago block joints on the whole consisted of ordinary steel fishplates machined on the bearing surfaces to permit the insertion of thin fibre channels between the plates and rails, the gap between adjoining rails being filled by a suitably shaped fibre end post. The fishbolt holes in the rails were enlarged to take fibre ferrules surrounding the bolts. Nylon and similar plastic insulations have now replaced the fibre, giving much increased working life (Fig. 46). Now that continuous welded rails are used for all main lines it has become necessary to design insulated joints capable of withstanding longitudinal forces of at least 100 tons without the rail joint opening. This is achieved by the glued joint (Fig. 47). The insulating channel is of glass fibre and the adhesive is epoxy resin.

BRITISH STANDARDS

BS 11	Railway Rails
BS 47	Fishplates
BS 64	Fishbolts and Nuts
BS 84	Screw Threads and Tolerances
BS 2856	Conversion of Inch and Metric Sizes

FURTHER READING

British Railway Track, Design, Construction and Maintenance; Published by the Permanent Way Institution.

RAILWAY SIGNALLING

Colour-Light Signalling—Track Circuits—Systems of Operation—The British Fail-Safe Relay—Train Description—Rapid Transit Developments—Single Line Railways—British Standards

By J. S. Hawkes, BSc(Eng), CEng, MIEE, FIRSE

From a number of points of view the science of Railway Signalling is conservative in the extreme, but developments are continually being engineered to cater for the changing requirements in other departments of the railway. In Britain the Modernisation Plan brought about considerable advancement and generally in most parts of the world, traffic growth patterns and financial considerations have necessitated new methods of control. Again, advances in techniques have wrought their own changes and the broadening field of the science has embraced technologies never associated with signalling hitherto.

Signalling in the strict and original sense of interlocking, route holding and conveyance of 'stop' command to the train continues to demand the highest standards of safety—it is a product of Safety Engineering and this is a subject which should never be treated lightly both when considering expenditure and the skill of engineers involved. In a wider sense, however, the subject is covering a field expanding into supervision of traffic movements in general and into an ever increasing range of systems and devices aimed at presenting data to the signalmen in the most easily assimilated form and assisting the Operating Department of a railway by giving them the means of having an ever widening view of the traffic position under their direction. Whilst great reliability is still a necessary requirement in this field, it is the speedy handling of data, often in considerable quantities, which is the making of these schemes so that here electronic techniques and computers are coming well to the fore, but not without the greatest care being taken in their use and application so as to achieve the reliability demanded. Some of the recent applications and techniques are described later.

FIG. 1. Typical Colour-light Signal.

In the meantime signalling in the more strict sense is considered, and it is to be noted that, second only to the essential provision of safety in traffic movements, is its capability of facilitating the maximum utilisation of the track along any route and of providing for fast high density services wherever needed. Continuous colour-light signalling is a principal means of attaining such goals and it is some of the associated electrical methods of operation and control which are described here. However, it should not be thought that this is a single complete system just recently designed, as it has of course been evolved step by step from the earliest application of electricity to signalling. Indeed, it was the application to mechanical signalling which formed the early basis in so far as establishing a form of train control, namely the block system; from that stage railways have grown so as to handle increasing traffic with greater efficiency. Some railways having a low traffic density or where the supply of electrical power is difficult over much of the long distances covered are still adequately served by mechanical signalling systems, whereas others are at an intermediate stage having, for example, a few power operated points at the far end of passing loop stations, some primary cell track circuits to protect such points or to detect trains otherwise out of view or, perhaps, colour-light signals at a station for much improved visibility but with mechanically operated points as power operation could not be justified. Such signalling schemes as these are referred to again later under 'Signalling Overseas', in which possible steps in the advancement of schemes are described. Electrical forms of single line block operation are covered here, both with and without tokens, and also steps towards greater efficiency of signalling, possibly complete with remote control and supervision.

It is not possible in an article of the present length to explain, or to offer guidance on, details of signalling circuits and equipment involved in these various schemes and techniques, but for those engineers and students who have need of further information on this topic they are strongly recommended to make a study of the series of instructional booklets published by the Institution of Railway Signal Engineers. A greatly extended version of these is also available in the form of a single book entitled 'Railway Signalling', published in 1980 by A & C Black of London, covering signalling philosophy, principles of interlocking, control systems and equipment, etc and profusely illustrated with diagrams and circuits.

COLOUR-LIGHT SIGNALLING.—In semaphore signalling practice the location of signals along the line was largely determined by the position of stations, and the frequency of traffic was therefore determined by the longest distance between two block posts. To provide for a more frequent service the signals must be more precisely located and the electrical nature of colour-light signals enables this to be done with comparative ease. Thus, three- or four-aspect signals, according to the nature of the traffic are spaced more or less uniformly along the line. Figure 2 shows the layout of signals and the sequence of aspects for two successive trains, with three- and four-aspect signals. The signals are spaced to provide for uniform time interval between trains; thus the spacing would be closer together on the slower running sections of the line, as for example where there are steep adverse gradients, and farther apart on the high speed stretches.

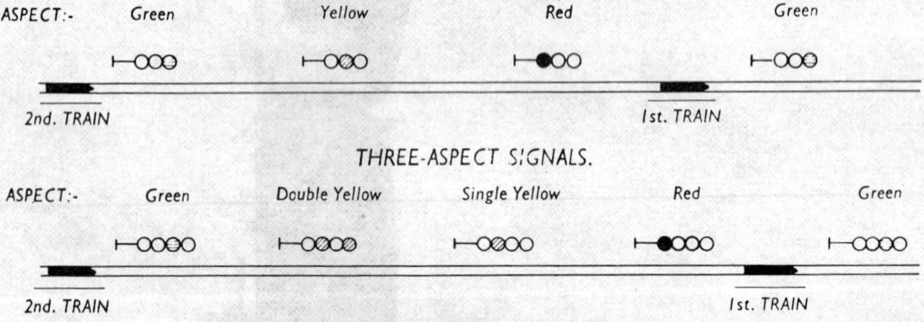

FIG. 2.—Aspect Sequences.

In this section British methods only are discussed and it should be appreciated that the code of signal aspects used in this country is much simpler than many of the systems in general use abroad. Great Britain pioneered the use of colour-light signalling in Europe, and developed a very important principle of the fourth aspect. A joint Committee was set up by the Ministry of Transport and the Institution of Railway Signal Engineers to consider three-position signalling in both semaphore and colour-light systems, and not only was the latter favoured by far the most strongly but also the fourth aspect was added in the form of the double-yellow aspect to provide a preliminary warning. This sequence of aspects was first introduced on the Southern Railway in 1925 and has become the standard for British Rail. Although it was the first system of four-aspect signalling and is still by far the simplest, it has proved extremely satisfactory in service and has been adopted for the fastest running, electrically operated main lines in this country.

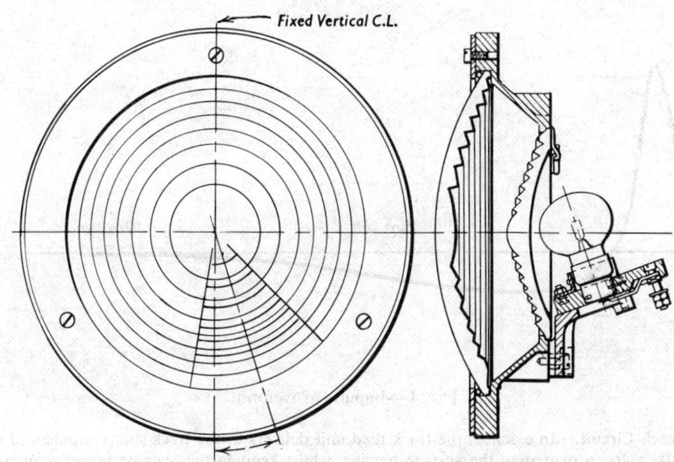

FIG. 3.—Light Unit of Multi-unit Signal.

MAIN SIGNALS.—One of the great benefits of the colour-light signal is its tremendously improved visibility as compared with the oil-lit roundels of semaphores. This is of special advantage in bad weather or fog when it is particularly appreciated by all enginemen and results in distinct improvements in running times.

The light unit of a modern multi-unit colour-light signal is shown in Fig. 3, and with a standard signalling lamp of maybe 25 watts (see BS 469), such a lens combination gives a concentrated beam of light rendering the indications clearly visible up to a mile away in bright sunshine. To achieve this range 'beam spread' has to be set to no more than 2½° and this does introduce certain problems in design and in the siting of a signal for best visibility around curved approach tracks etc. In such a situation it is possible to add a specially ribbed cover glass which does spread the beam a few degrees to the right or left only, but of course the range is reduced correspondingly. Also to provide a close-up indication for a driver stopping close to and almost underneath the signal a deflecting sector can be moulded into the front lens, as indicated; by rotation of the glass the angle to left or right can be varied. The coloured glass of the inner lens of the unit provides the required signal indication colour and units are mounted together to form the complete multi-aspect signal required, as is illustrated in Fig. 1

SUBSIDIARY SIGNALS.—To ensure that there can be no confusion, especially at night, with the main colour signals, the subsidiary and ground shunt signals operate on the 'position-light' principle. Two lights displayed horizontally (one red and one white) form the stop aspect of a shunt signal and two white lights displayed diagonally indicate 'proceed'. 'Draw-ahead' signals, mounted below a main signal as in Fig. 1, are normally extinquished; when a train is required to draw forward, two white lights are displayed diagonally with the main signal kept at 'red'.

TRACK CIRCUITS.—Positive detection of the presence of trains on the track is a very necessary feature of all but the simplest of signalling systems, and a method by which not only will a single vehicle always show its presence, but will continue to do so even when stationary, is bound to be attractive. Such a method uses the very long established simple track circuit, which in its basic form applies a low voltage across one end of a pair of rails, this voltage then energising a track relay connected across the other end of the section of rails. Of course these rails must be reasonably insulated from one another, such as by the use of wood sleepers or concrete with insulations and the section ends must be defined by insulating rail joints to confine the track circuit current to the section in question; the track relay being energised will then show that the relevant section of track is clear of vehicles since the presence of any wheel pair and axle will electrically short circuit the relay and de-energise it.

Simple systems still utilise a steady dc feed supply, often from batteries, whilst others, for numerous reasons, use coded current to pass more information, or again, ac to provide immunity to stray effects of dc electrification of the line. These basic forms of track circuit have been dealt with in previous editions of this handbook, to which reference should be made, but in recent years some other track circuit designs have been introduced to overcome problems arising from track conditions or construction, or from ac electrification. A brief mention of some of these would be of value here.

A toublesome cause of track circuit unreliability is that due to deterioration of rail contact conditions resulting from rusting of the rail surface or from deposits of sand on it. The normal low voltage of the track cicruit is often insufficient to break down this surface barrier but higher voltages would be uneconomic and possibly dangerous to personnel, so a very useful compromise has been found in the development of the:

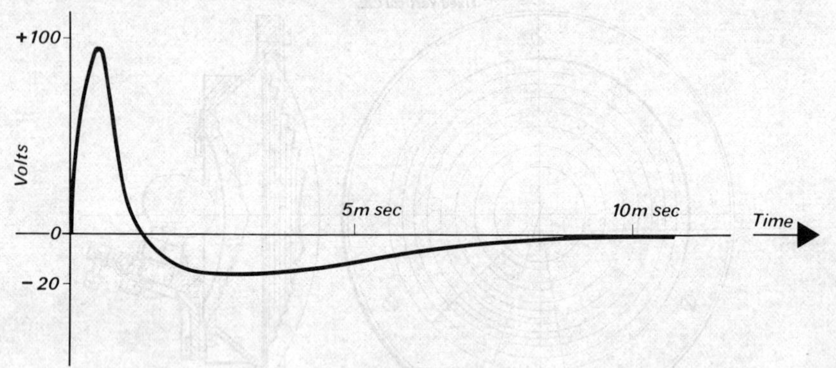

FIG. 4.—Impulse Waveform.

Impulse Track Circuit.—In essence, the track feed unit delivers to the track sharp impulses of voltage, of perhaps 80–100 volts to overcome the surface barrier, whilst keeping the average power demand down to normal levels, and the receiver integrates the pulses to energise a track relay in the normal manner.

A more sophisticated equipment generates a special impulse waveform as shown in Fig. 4 having positive and negative components, and these pulses, transmitted at about 3 per second, are checked by the receiver and its double wound relay for these component shapes and polarity. The relay does not respond to incorrect polarity nor to symmetrical waveforms so that the track circuit is thereby inherently protected from false energisation both through break-down of rail joint insulation, since contiguous track circuits are given alternate polarities, and by stray traction currents. This equipment can be used in both ac or dc electrified territory, where the track circuit length can be up to 1 km or 2 km according to application, and considerably longer in non-electrified areas.

Track construction can well affect track circuit design and in particular the fast increasing use of Continuous Welded Rail by the Permanent Way Department is in direct conflict with the Signal Engineer's requirement of insulated rail joints for track circuit operation. One patented solution to this problem is to replace the joint insulation by the creation of a short zone of 'high' impedance to track circuit current. This is achieved by using an audio frequency ac track circuit current and 'resonating' the required zones of rail to this frequency by means of capacitors. Known as a:

Jointless Type Track Circuit, it has been developed for operation over 1 km or 2 km according to circumstances and for use in both ac and dc electric traction areas in a number of countries. In this case, tuning is achieved by inductors and capacitors connected across the rails in the manner shown in Fig. 5.

Here, frequencies of 1,700 Hz and 2,300 Hz are used alternately, with two other frequencies being used for an adjacent line of track. The centre-tapped track transformers provide cross-bonding points at X and Y if required, and operate the track circuit receivers (Rx). The L/C filters are series tuned so as to pass their respective frequencies, viz 'A LIM' set at 2,300 Hz limits the extent of TC 'A', and 'B LIM' defines the extremities of TC 'B', and it is to be noted that loss of shunt at these filter locations is compensated for by an overlapping of track circuits amounting to about 1 metre. In addition, the capacitor of 'C LIM', together with the rails and transformer coil, forms a transmitting (Tx) loop resonant at 1,700 Hz for TC 'B' and similarly that of 'A LIM' a receiver loop. The trimmers E and F likewise tune relevant feed and receiver loops to 2,300 Hz. Other forms of jointless track circuit are described in a paper by B. H. Grose 'Jointless Track Circuits and Electrified Railways' *Proc Inst Railway Signal Engineers*, November, 1972.

Most railway electrification systems use the rails for traction current return and therefore the track circuits must be rendered safely immune to the effects of fundamental and harmonic frequencies present. Several of the long established track circuit designs are immune to dc traction only or to ac only, but where both forms of traction occur in the same locality the choice of track circuit is limited. The Impulse track circuit already mentioned is one, and the:

Reed Track Circuit is another. Here the required immunity is achieved by using a track circuit operating at an audio frequency so chosen as to avoid the fundamental and harmonics of the traction supply. The essential feature however, is the use of a special filter which not only ensures response solely to the chosen frequency but which is so highly selective, in this function, that six fully distinguishable frequencies are available in the range of 363–378 Hz.

It is the double reed filter which gives the track circuit its name, and the diagrammatic view in Fig. 6 shows the two tuned metallic reeds connected by a coupling plate. Reed 1 is vibrated at its natural frequency by oscillations in coil 1, and through the coupling plate the identically tuned second reed vibrates in resonant

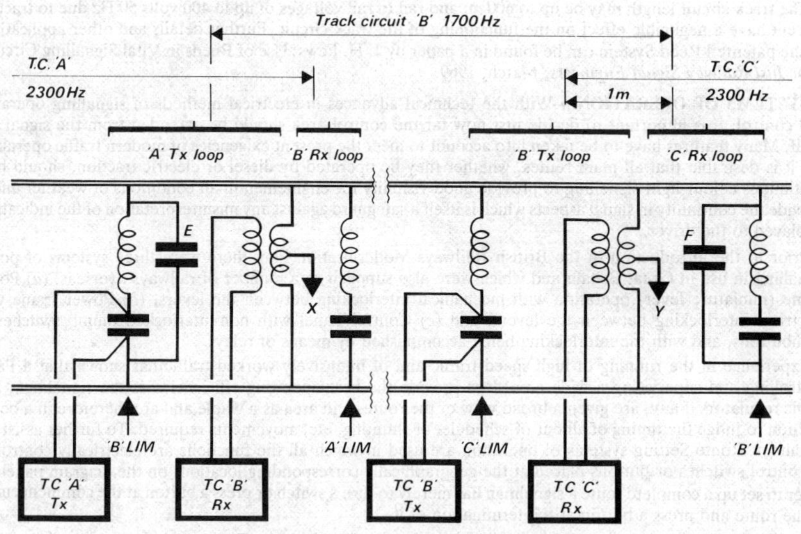

FIG. 5.—The Patented Aster Track Circuit.

response. This is picked up by coil 2 and is passed on via an amplifier. It can be seen that no dc effects can be conveyed through such a filter, and track connections to the receiver would be destroyed long before traction currents or harmonics could force sufficient energy through both out-of-tune reeds to falsely energise the track relay. Futhermore the filter construction renders it fail-safe, as any damage resulting in alteration of the tuning of a reed would not cause the same change in the other reed and consequently, no frequency would pass through.

The track circuit itself is generally conventional with an oscillator, reed filter and feed resistor at the feed end, and with a similar reed filter, amplifier and track relay at the other end. As before, the presence of a vehicle shunts the power away from the relay end to give detection, but here adjacent track circuits and those on a parallel track use the six different reed frequencies in rotation so that there will be no possibility of falsely energising a receiver from an incorrect feed set through a broken-down rail joint insulation.

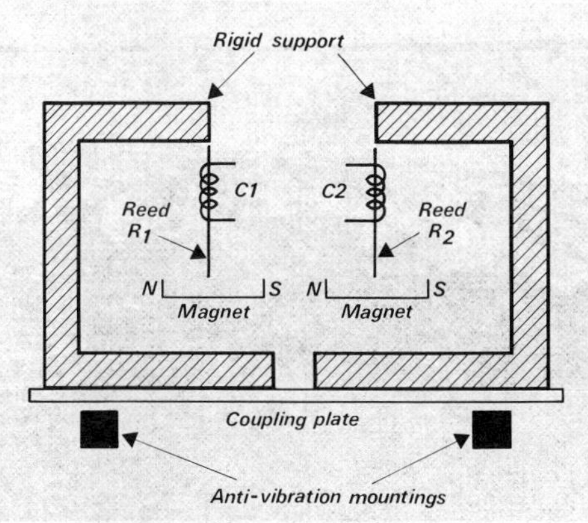

FIG. 6.—The Double Reed Filter.

The track circuit length may be up to 600 m, and rail to rail voltages of up to 400 volts 50 Hz due to traction current have a negligible effect on the functioning of the track circuit. Further details and other applications of the patented Reed System can be found in a paper by J. H. Fews 'Use of Reeds in Vital Signalling Circuits' *Proc Inst Railway Signal Engineers*, March, 1969.

SYSTEMS OF OPERATION.—With the technical advances in electrical methods of signalling operation and control, it is important to decide just how far the control area should be extended from the signal box itself. Many features have to be taken into account to meet the present exigencies of modern traffic operation, but it is desirable that all main routes, whether they be operated by diesel or electric traction, should have continuous colour-light signalling to provide good visibility for enginemen in all conditions of weather and to provide the continuity in signal aspects which is itself a safeguard against any misinterpretation of the indications displayed to the driver.

Prior to the introduction of the British Railways Modernisation Plan there were three systems of power signalling in use in Great Britain and which were also supplied to a number of railways overseas: (*a*) Power frame (miniature lever) operation with mechanical interlocking between the levers, (*b*) Power frame with electrical interlocking between the levers, and (*c*) Control Panel with non-interlocked thumb switches or pushbuttons, and with the interlocking being accomplished by means of relays.

Experience in the running of high speed traffic and of intensively worked traffic has shown that a Panel controlling and supervising a wide area does provide the best operating efficiencies as the signalmen, and traffic regulators if any, are given a broad view of the routes and area as a whole and are therefore in a better position to judge the timing of all out-of-schedule, or shunting, etc, movements required. To further assist the signalmen Route-Setting systems of operation are used in which all the functions are electrically controlled by control switches or buttons placed at the geographically corresponding locations on the diagram panel. In order to set up a complete route a signalman has merely to turn a switch or press a button at the commencement of the route and press a button at the termination of it.

The larger the area of control the more advantageous it is to include traffic regulating staff in the control room so as to facilitate the co-ordination of functions and traffic movements. In turn this leads to having the illuminated track diagram in a curved form to ensure clarity of view for the increased number of personnel, which often goes further to include an operator of the public address system for the station platform announcements. One recent example of the panel control of a large area is that of London Bridge, commissioned in 1976, and a view of part of the control room is shown in Fig. 7. The very dense traffic of 2,000 trains per day is controlled through the route-setting pushbuttons on the miniature panel which is positioned in front of the 18 m (60 ft.) long main illuminated track diagram so as to allow the signalmen a clear view of the 240 track-kms.

THE BRITISH FAIL-SAFE RELAY.—It is the fail-safe principle of railway signal engineering that any failure, however diverse, of the constituent vital elements on which safety of trains and life depend shall result in a warning or danger indication being displayed to the driver of a train. Just as semaphore arms are designed

FIG. 7.—Part of the Control Centre at London Bridge.

so that they return to the danger position in the event of a breakage of wire or other connection, so the electric relays used for track circuits and other safety purposes in an electric interlocking are designed so that any interruption of the operating current will result in the armature returning with certainty to the normal de-energised position. Much detailed research and development work on the part of both British Rail and the manufacturers, working in close collaboration, was needed to produce the specifications on which British Rail has standardised for its safety signalling relay requirements. Figure 8 shows an example of a safety-type line relay complying with the British Rail Specification, in this case one especially immunised against false operation due to induction or leakage effects from alternating current sources such as traction catenaries, etc.

FIG. 8.—The British Signalling Safety Line Relay.

The circuits in which these relays are used are concerned with the interlocking of signals and points and with the display of aspects in the colour-light-signals—these are the safety circuits in which the use of safety relays and components is essential. In the non-safety circuits, such as perhaps route set-up button circuits and panel indications generally, and also remote control and indication whether by electronic means or direct wire, other forms of relays and switching devices can be used, often of very small dimensions, providing of course that they do meet the requirements of reliability and long-life.

TRAIN DESCRIPTION.—The illuminated track diagram in the control room of a power signalling scheme shows the movement of the traffic by the changing red track occupancy lamps as a train proceeds and areas of traffic congestion are easily picked out. However, the Regulator needs one further piece of information and that is the identity of the train represented by each group of red lights. The train's timetable head-code is therefore also displayed on the diagram, with these numbers being advanced from signal to signal in step with the movements of the track indications. The amount of information to be handled for such an area as that above is large, so that a separate train describer system has been designed to deal with this independently from the signalling but receiving all the necessary data from it. The system at West Hamstead is electronic for speed and reliability, and is operated entirely by computers.

The system is divided into four main parts whose functions are as follows: Data collection; Data processing; Information display; and Communication with fringe signal boxes. Block diagrams, Figs. 9, 11 and 13, outline the arrangement of the hardware for these functions.

Data Collection.—Data is collected from the signalling system and from control units (Fig. 12) at both the main signal box and the fringe boxes associated with the adjacent control areas whether large or small. The data is made available to the computers through two identical systems of input cards, one for each computer. The input systems receive the same input data but are independently connected to their associated computer

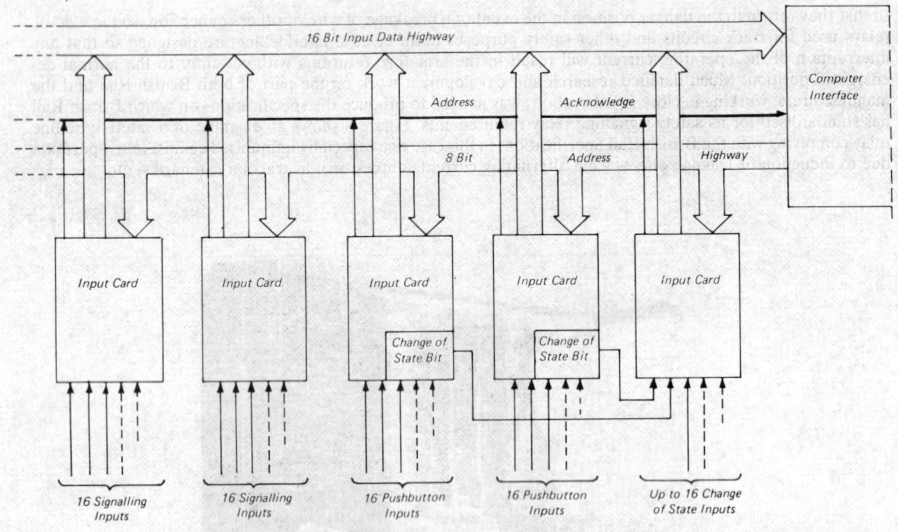

FIG. 9.—Block Diagram of Input to Computer.

via address and data highways, as indicated in Fig. 9. A reed relay interface transfers the state of signalling relays and operator's push-buttons to Data Input printed-circuit cards and data received from fringe boxes is stored by Data Set Receiver cards. When each of these cards is addressed, its input information is transferred to the computer via the input data highway.

The computers perform all system functions regularly and at frequent intervals. During each of these major scans the states of all signalling inputs are read, updating the computers with the states of track sections, points and signals within the control area. The interval between successive scans is short enough to be sure of seeing all train movements. Many minor scans of certain input cards take place during each major scan. When they occur a check is made for changes of state of the inputs from signalman's set-up pushbuttons and from fringe boxes and if these are present the data is transferred to the computers. Because of the small interval between minor scans, these inputs are accepted by the computers almost as soon as they arrive, providing a seemingly instantaneous response to the signalman's pushbuttons at both main and fringe boxes.

Data Processing.—The West Hampstead installation uses duplicate processing computers, though this need not always be so, and Fig. 10 shows the suite of cubicles concerned. The manner in which the computer outputs are interleaved so as to have both computers normally on line and yet have either as standby for the other is indicated in Fig. 11.

Compact computers of the programmable general purpose type are used for the processing function. The various software tasks are carried out by a modular software system assembled from proven modules which are common to all installations having the same operating facilities. To enable the system to operate in a particular installation, additional information dependent on the geography of the area, steps required and other fixed parameters, is introduced into the system in the form of data tables and stored by the computer memory.

This approach to the processing function allows: (*a*) Modification or expansion of the area, or the train movements required therein, to be achieved by the relatively straightforward process of modification of the data tables only. (*b*) Modification of a single operating facility to be made by modifying the relevant programme module only, without affecting the operation of other modules. (*c*) The introduction of further software tasks, such as the control of platform indicators or communication with a supervisory system, by the addition of further programme modules capable of operating with the data used by existing modules.

Each programme module, performing a particular task, is allocated a priority depending on the response time required, the length of the task and its relation to other tasks it may generate. The lowest programme module in order of priority is the background checking module which runs continuously when no other tasks are outstanding. Only one programme module can run at any one time. The Real Time Executive schedules the programme modules according to the requests outstanding for each module and their relative priorities.

FIG. 10.—Computer-based Train-Describer at West Hampstead, London.

Further control is provided by a Clock Routine module which runs as a result of the real time clock interrupt and performs two basic tasks. It keeps account of time and thus requests all programme modules which run at regular intervals, the request interval for a programme being determined by the nature of the task performed. It also carries out primary scanning of some inputs to determine whether processing is required, generating the requests for programme modules accordingly. Thus, some modules run at regular intervals (eg scan signalling inputs) and some only when their particular tasks are required (eg service an operator's set-up keyboard when a change of state of the input is detected).

During each major scan the signalling inputs are scanned. When a change of state is detected and this is attempting to trigger a step, the state of the inputs acting as conditions to that step are checked. These being correct, the information is passed to the step processing routine. Thus the signalling inputs are processed before being used to initiate the stepping of train descriptions. In this processing, 'software noise filtering' is introduced to give the following benefits: (1) Immunity from the effects of closing relay bounce of up to 0·5 sec duration. (2) Immunity from the effect of false indication of track occupancy, provided that this indication has a duration of less than 0·5 sec. (3) Immunity from the effects of discontinuities of up to 2·5 sec in an indication of track occupancy. When a step does take place, then the binary coded train description is moved from the 'from' berth storage cell to the 'to' berth storage cell associated with the particular step.

In addition to initiating the up-dating of displays at main and fringe boxes, the step processing routine

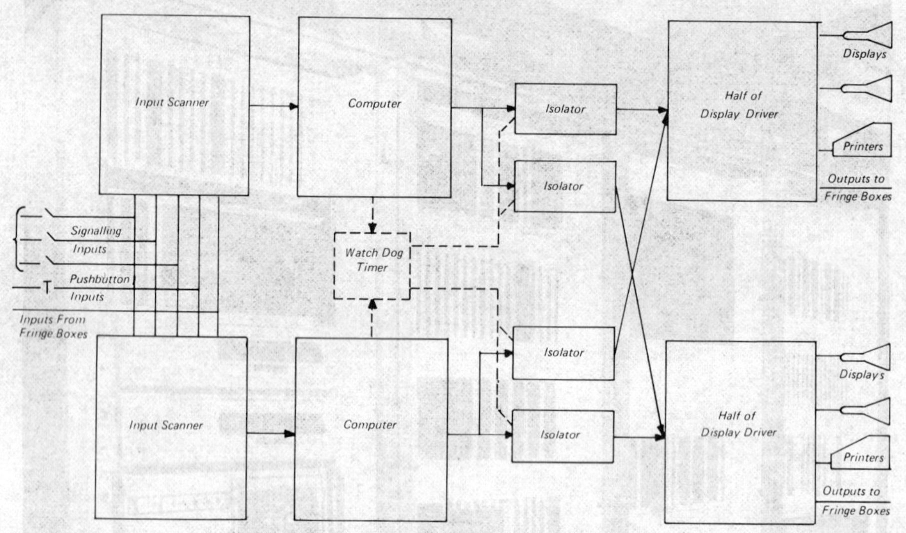

FIG. 11.—Duplicated Computer-based Train-describer.

generates information for other facilities as required and may include, for example, train reporting and speed reporting.

Information Display.—Train descriptions are displayed on the main box illuminated diagram by miniature cathode ray tubes or, more recently, by means of Light Emitting Diode (LED) display modules. Each module contains, typically, four 5 × 7 LED matrices for the four characters which appear as illustrated in Fig. 12, and which can be read clearly and without strain from a distance of over 6 metres. Mounted behind the diagram are distribution units, each feeding 32 of the display modules with the required low voltage supplies and with a screened control line pair deriving from the computer equipment.

The display modules are divided into groups (maximum of 64 per group), each group being controlled through separate Display Processing Cards (DPC) as illustrated in Fig. 13, to reduce the possibility of a single fault leading to the loss of all displays. The effect of the loss of one group is further alleviated by ensuring wherever possible that adjacent displays are not of the same group.

The DPC and two Display Routing Cards are housed in the describer equipment cubicles and perform the functions of highway interfacing, data storage, decoding and line driving. Train descriptions are stored in the processor in ASCII coded form and whenever the displayed information is to be modified or refreshed the processor presents to the DPC the characters of the description in ASCII code and the address of the required display module. This is accomplished by successive transfers of parallel data via the output highway.

The data is decoded from ASCII to dot pattern data and a clock signal impressed upon it. The composite message is then transmitted to the appropriate display module (determined by the address) by the associated Display Routing Card via the Distribution Unit and over a screened twisted pair cable to ensure a high degree of noise immunity. The display module receives the serial composite signal, separates the clock and data components and clocks the data into an internal shift register store to display the new description. The changing of a train description in this way takes place in a fraction of a second so that the change appears instantaneous. Since the processor regenerates the display data whenever a step takes place and also each time it refreshes a display, which it does at regular and frequent intervals, mutilated descriptions cannot be carried forward from berth to berth or displayed for prolonged periods.

As a possible back-up to the main display system, Video Display Units consisting of large screen CRT Monitors and electronic control modules can be incorporated. These can also display other information relevant to possible extensions to the system facilities. For example, displays in connection with Platform Indicator Control, Platform Allocation and Supervisory Systems can be readily provided in this manner.

Each signalman has a pushbutton control unit as in Fig. 12 with which a new description can be interposed into any display (eg a Bay Platform for commencement of a journey). Alternatively, it can be used for interrogation purposes should doubts arise as to any indication; by setting up a signal number the computer responds by displaying the description of a train approaching that signal or conversely by setting up a description the response is the number of the signal which the train is currently approaching. The Regulators also have similar pushbutton units to enable them likewise to interrogate the computer, but they also have the Automatic

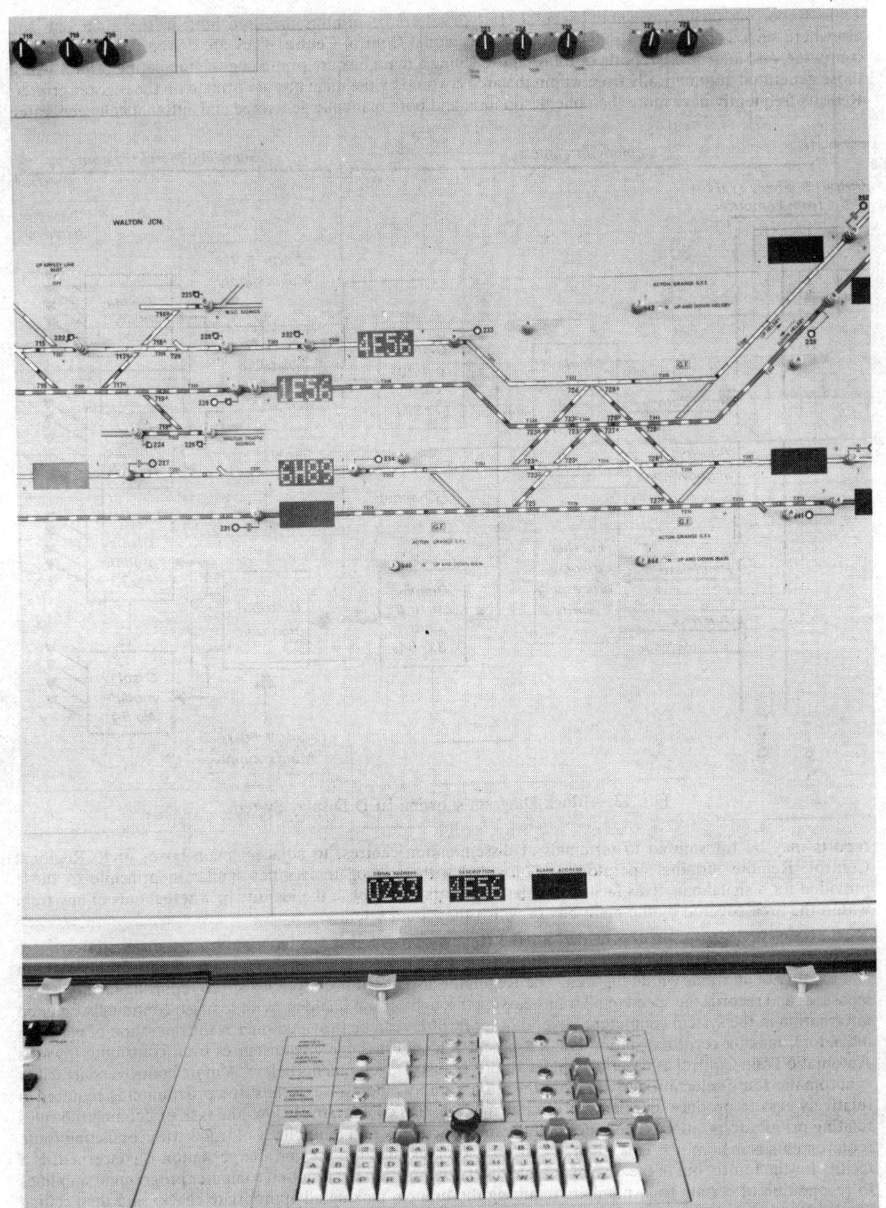

FIG. 12.—Part of Signalling Control Desk showing Signalman's Push-button Control Unit and a Section of the Illuminated Diagram.

Train Reporting facility available. Several teletypewriters or printers are used both in the main box and elsewhere such as at adjacent signal boxes or a Regional Control Centre. They are driven directly from the computer, and in general, reports of trains approaching a main box are printed on the regulating printer whilst those generated automatically from within the area covered by the main box are printed on the register printer. Reports frequently have more than one destination and both manually generated and automatically generated

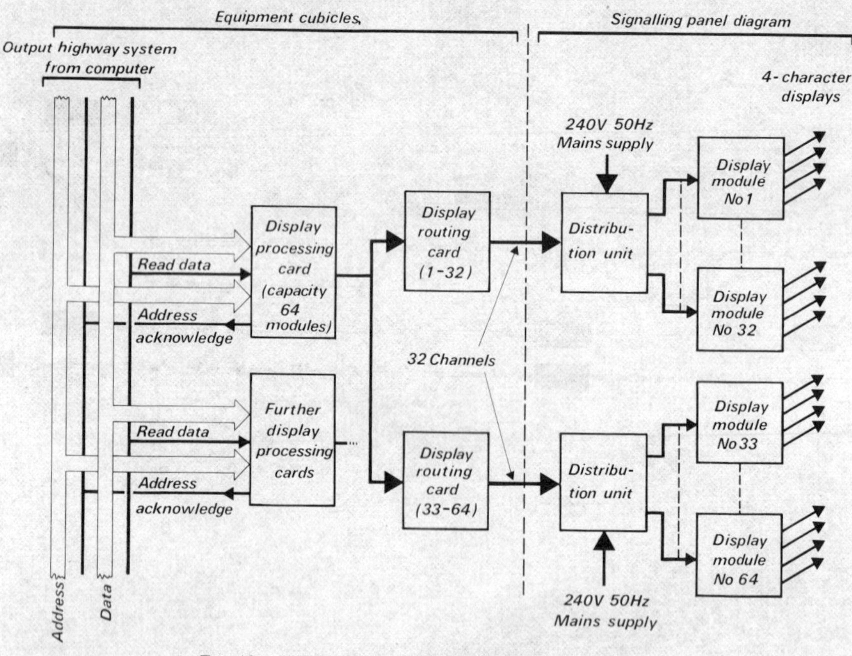

FIG. 13.—Block Diagram showing LED Display System.

reports may be transmitted to terminals at dissemination centres, to adjacent main boxes or to Regional Control. Remote terminal operators are provided with interrogate facilities similar in principle to those provided for a signalman. This facility enables operators to establish the identity or whereabouts of any train within the area covered by the main box of which they are a satellite.

The train reporting printers provided for the Regulator's use at the main boxes have the same interrogate facilities and in addition the Regulator may, with a single command, generate a complete list of the position and identity of all trains within his area. The Regulator also has at his disposal a speed reporting facility which measures and records the speed of all trains passing through certain sections. With so much continually updated information in the system computers, several other facilities can be provided such as the operation of platform indicators, making recorded station announcements etc and in some circumstances even contribute towards Automatic Train Control as described under Rapid Transit Developments below. A more controversial facility is automatic route selection derived from the train numbers themselves; whilst the programming required is relatively easy to produce and the cost of implementing it is comparatively low, the task of defining the rules relating priority to position, speed, destination and punctuality of a multiplicity of trains with conflicting route requirements is mammoth. This, then, as far as a complex junction area or a large station is concerned, is a facility for the future, but in the case of a single diverging junction the required computer programme simplifies to recognition of certain train numbers requiring the branch, making all appropriate checks and then calling for the junction to be set accordingly. The reader is referred to R. C. Jones's paper, *Inst Rly Signal Eng'rs*, Feb 1974, for futher details of the diverging and converging junction operation at Pirbright on the Southern Region of British Rail.

Fringe Boxes.—The Fringe Box equipment includes projection indicator displays, lamp indications, alarm acknowledgement pushbuttons and a signalman's set-up keyboard. The set-up pushbuttons enable the signalman to send information to the main box computer via a high-speed time division multiplex (TDM) data transmission link and as each character of a train description is set-up by the fringe box signalman it is sent to the computer and returned for display at the fringe box. Operation of the 'transmit' button confirms that the description displayed in the set-up berth has been visually checked and is satisfactory, and the computer then steps the description into the 'last sent' display.

RAPID TRANSIT DEVELOPMENTS.—Many city transport authorities around the world are now calling for the latest techniques for their rapid transit systems. Automatic driving and automatic supervision of operations can provide the best possible service with greatest flexibility to cater for large fluctuations in passenger demands, and can maintain a best service in the face of day-to-day changes in the availability of operating personnel, rolling stock, etc. The computer of the train describer already dealt with above is well able to be expanded to deal with optimisation of the train running programmes and this, when integrated with the signalling control system, forms the major part of the modern conception of Rapid Transit operation.

The entire control system can be classed as Automatic Train Control (ATC), which, in the main, divides into the three following sub-systems:

(1) The ATS (Automatic Train Supervision) system—remote control and indication for traffic supervision with computer drive and using software programmes for traffic optimisation, time-table production etc.

(2) The ATP (Automatic Train Protection) system—The fundamental safety control of the trains—signalling in the strict sense and enforcement of train stops.

(3) The ATO (Automatic Train Operation) system—The automatic driving function, anticipating the safety commands and ensuring correct and smooth stops at station platforms and elsewhere.

Although interdependent, the three systems perform well-defined functions within the overall system, and their description below can be seen as relating to a typical installation in which manual driving as well as automatic is required under differing conditions.

Considering **ATP** first, this is the system which provides the fundamental safety control of train running. It makes use of the principles of 'coded track circuits' in which modulated carrier signals flow in the track and are transmitted inductively to ATP equipment on the train. Speed restrictions which, for reasons of safety, are imposed over a section of track according to the local track conditions and occupancy ahead, are defined by the ATP code applied to the track circuit. The system ensures that collisions do not occur by providing for absolute overlaps so that there is always sufficient unoccupied track for an emergency brake application to stop the train. Should the speed of the train exceed the maximum safe speed indicated by the ATP code on the track, application of the emergency brake takes place.

The table of typical ATP codes (Fig. 14) shows the code meaning and the response from the train ATO equipment. Figure 15 then shows a typical sequence of codes behind a train with a number of absolute overlap distances pointed out. For any position of train A, the code received by a following train, such as at B, can be determined and reference to the table will define its ATO response. Code 1 (stop) is overridden by 'station stop' so as to extend travel along the braking profile to platform end.

A target speed, for display on a speedometer in the cab, is also conveyed to the train by the ATP code, and indicates the speed to which the train is to be regulated by manual or automatic means. A manual driving mode can be selected in which the ATP equipment warns the train attendant and inhibits motoring while the train speed is above the target speed that is being demanded. Because the inherent functions of the ATP are concerned with operational safety, it uses circuits based on long established signalling principles and fail-safe equipment throughout. The train attendant will always be present in the leading driving cab of the train, and can if necessay drive the train manually, with ATP operative, but with a reduced frequency of service.

ATO is the normal mode of service operation. It accomplishes automatically the regulation of train speed between stations and accurate station stopping and enables short station running times with minimum headway to be achieved. Additionally, the ATO equipment controls auto-shunting moves at terminal stations and can indicate which doors are to be opened when the train stops at a station. When, for operational reasons, it is necessary to modify the running programme, appropriate commands from the Train Supervision System are implemented by the ATO equipment. In this way, a train can be instructed not to stop at a station or to coast for a period between stations. Headway, inter-station running times and power consumption are all affected by such strategies.

To enable it to carry out these functions, the train carried ATO control equipment receives data from three sources—ATP codes from the ATP equipment, ATO commands from loop aerials by the track and train speeds from axle driven tachogenerators. From this data motoring and braking commands and other control signals are generated by the ATO equipment. When the train is running in this mode, it always has the fail-safe back-up of the ATP system, which causes an emergency brake application if incorrect operation of the ATO equipment has caused the safe speed to be exceeded.

The **ATS** system provides a means by which train and track information is centralised and displayed on a panel and diagram in the central control room. This data, which indicates the identity and position of the train and also route, signal and point conditions, is then used to control the lines either automatically or, if required, manually. Under manual control the running of the lines is manually supervised and controlled over electronic Time Division Multiplex (TDM) communication links to the local relay rooms where the safety interlockings for particular areas of the lines are situated. The supervisor, therefore, has a comprehensive picture of the

Code No.	ATP maximum safe speed km/h	Cab indication maximum target speed km/h	ATO controller response	
			Nominal speed km/h	Action
0 Code	0	STOP	0	APPLY EMERGENCY BRAKE AND MAINTAIN ON
1	35	STOP	0	BRAKE TO ZERO (Unless station stop command received—then follow profile)
2	35	35	32	MOTOR TO 32 km/h AND MAINTAIN SPEED
3	55	35	32	BRAKE TO 32 km/h AND MAINTAIN SPEED
4	55	55	50	MOTOR TO 50 km/h AND MAINTAIN SPEED
5	70	55	50	BRAKE TO 50 km/h AND MAINTAIN SPEED
6	70	70	63	MOTOR TO 63 km/h AND MAINTAIN SPEED

FIG. 14—Table of Typical ATP Codes.

line. Local area panels similar to that at the central control room, are situated in the relay rooms to enable the local signalling to be manually controlled from there, if required.

As an aid to manual train supervision the train number display and storage equipment already described is used to display the train number, relative to occupation of selected tracks, on the control panel. The supervisor has to key-in the train identity, part of which is the train number, before the train leaves the terminal station. Thereafter, the train number steps automatically across the diagram as the train progresses along the line. Facilities are incorporated which allow the supervisor to interrogate the computer of the train describer regarding a particular train number and have the remainder of the data associated with the train displayed for reference. The train identity data within the computer is also used to provide passengers with train length, if this may vary, and destination information.

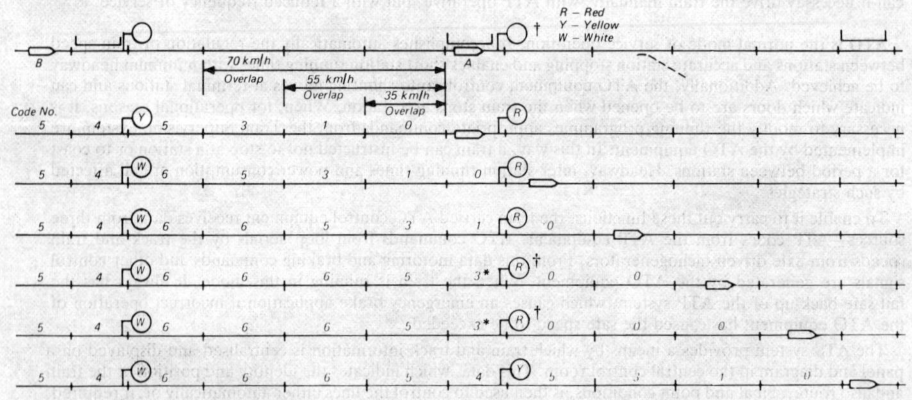

FIG. 15.—Typical Code Sequence behind a Train († Certain signals may be controlled to Red for junction or schedule reasons, then code 3* changes to 1 when platform track is occupied and preceding track clear.)

In full automatic operation the train number display equipment, with its computer, is considerably enlarged such that, acting on the information obtained, it can exercise automatic control over the running of trains. The computer is programmed to regulate the flow of traffic, maintaining the pre-selected running times and headway by adjusting coasting points and station departure times. When running times and headway cannot be maintained, the computer implements either pre-programmed or manually requested corrective procedures to modify the time accordingly. A printer is provided on which the status of the system is indicated to the supervisor. The programmes used to control the running of the trains are stored in the computer and are made up of programme modules and data tables. The data tables contain the variable parameters, depending on the geography of the area, number of signalling inputs and controls, etc. This modular arrangement of programmes and data simplifies the building up of the train supervision system stage by stage and allows for straightforward expansion of the area supervised by additions to the data tables only. Particular attention has to be given to the design of the programmes to achieve high resistance to failures due to errors in, or faulty manipulation of, the input data. The four programmes used for traffic control are described below:

Monitor Programme.—The monitor programme determines the train running intervals by noting track circuit occupancy. Where these times differ from the selected times by more than a predetermined tolerance the monitor programme calls in the traffic organisation programme. The monitor programme also alerts the supervisor if the system malfunctions and if a block shows random occupancy or does not clear after a train has passed. Faults on the train or in trackside equipment will be evident if the signalling is restrictive and a train does not maintain the correct running time between stations.

Traffic Organisation Programme.—The traffic organisation programme performs the headway control, and attempts to maintain the headways selected by the supervisor. A number of running conditions which vary train coasting points and departure intervals from stations can be selected, thus enabling the train to arrive at a station at the correct moment, and in this way the optimum conditions can be chosen in the interests of power economy. The supervisor can select manually the running conditions between any pair of stations and this gives him the means to control the running of a single train.

Strategy Selection and Re-timing Programmes.—When a serious delay or hold-up occurs the monitor programme calls in the strategy selection and re-timing programmes. The strategy selection programme considers the type, location and time of failure and evaluates a train running routine which can best minimise the delays. The new routine can include such measures as station skipping, taking trains out of or bringing trains into service, reversing trains and altering station to station intervals. The re-timing programme examines these routines and selects the optimum taking into account passenger delays, train utilisation etc. This optimum routine is used to replace the running conditions which are in operation at the time.

The strategy selection and re-timing programmes can be used off-line to simulate alternative strategies and routines. However, the extra programming and storage costs involved in increasing the complexity of these programmes may outweigh the benefits associated with this facility. Since the programme tapes will be available, a more economical method may be to load the programmes into another suitable computer and use this for simulation purposes.

SINGLE LINE RAILWAYS.—In the majority of cases a railway is built as a single line so as to keep construction costs down to be in keeping with the expected returns from what is initially a low traffic density. However, it so often happens that after a decade of operation the traffic demand has built up to such an extent that the facilities for progressing the trains through the system become saturated. The result then is that the railway becomes a bottleneck to the flow of trade and in consequence any opening of alternative means of transport to overcome this may well lead to the decline of the railway and a waste of its assets.

Fortunately there are a variety of ways of increasing the traffic carrying capacity of a single line railway which are considerably less expensive than doubling of the track, for instance, and two such methods are Tokenless Block Working and Centralised Traffic Control (CTC).

Tokenless Block Working.—An all-electric system of block control can be used to safeguard the movement of trains through the single line sections. The starting signals reading into a block section are electrically controlled by the system which also automatically detects the entry of trains into the section and their departure from it. It is therefore in a position to control access to the section from either direction.

A recent Tokenless block system uses the floor-standing unit illustrated in Fig. 16, and is known as the Tokenless Relay Block system in view of the use of signalling-type Safety, or Vital, relays to provide the essential interlocking function. The system uses a dc line circuit and, after an exchange of bell code signals, operation of the 'train coming' button or key-switch at the receiving station releases the circuits in the despatching station to permit the 'train going' button to give clearance to its associated starter signal. This 'out of phase' condition is positively retained by the use of latched relays, which lock the circuits at both ends of the block section and thereby provide the safety interlocking between the opposing starter signals at each end.

An immediate benefit in time saving accrues from tokenless operation since not only can the block and signals be cleared prior to the arrival of the train but there is also no need for the train to stop to be handed a proceed order or a physical token. The trains enter the block section on the authority of the starter signal alone and it is arranged that the starter is replaced to normal automatically as the train enters the section. This is usually achieved by installing a short track circuit in advance of the signal and occupation of this track circuit de-energises the signal relay (or the signal replacer) by breaking a stick circuit which cannot be made up again until the system has been restored to normal and a further release obtained.

At the receiving station a short rail circuit and contiguous track circuit are installed at the station entrance and as the train arrives and passes over them, the sequential occupation and clearance of this pair of circuits is registered by an 'arrival' relay. The operators are thus enabled to normalise the block which can then be

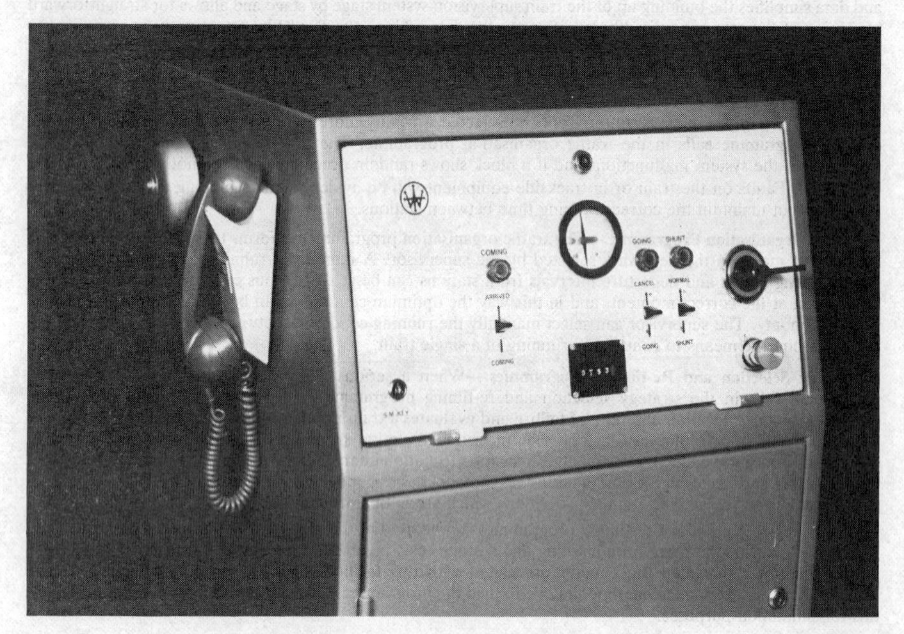

FIG. 16.—Tokenless Relay Block.

set again in either direction. Before completing this normalisation however, it is the duty of the operator at the receiving station to satisfy himself that the train has arrived complete, and he can be assisted in this by such devices as 'tail of train' detectors, etc.

In the event of a train being unable to accept a block section which had been set up for it, a cancellation feature is provided. This is the equivalent of restoring a token to the sending instrument, and is effected by operation of the cancel switch. Provided that the starter signal is normal and that its replacing track circuit has not been occupied, a time delay cycle of 60 seconds is initiated, at the end of which the cancellation counter advances by one, for security check purposes, and the equipment is freed for co-operative normalisation by the operators.

Should a train which has moved into the block section be required to return to the despatching station, operation of the 'arrival' switch brings the rail and track circuit into use to register the train's return. Thereafter the block is again normalised, providing the operator has observed the train to be complete. Railways running through isolated tracts of country frequently have no access to power supplies and the relay block is specially designed for such conditions, taking only 0·5AH for handling 30 trains, which clearly suits primary cell operation.

If relay type signalling with a control panel has been installed at a station then the relay block panel can be built into that for the signalling, as illustrated in Fig. 17, its relays being rack mounted with the others. The relay block can easily be extended to double track situations, still using only a single pair of line wires, and if electrical interference is anticipated from power lines or traction then a frequency modulated carrier system can be used. Other extensions include 'shunt permission' facilities, and also intermediate siding control with a 'shut-in' feature.

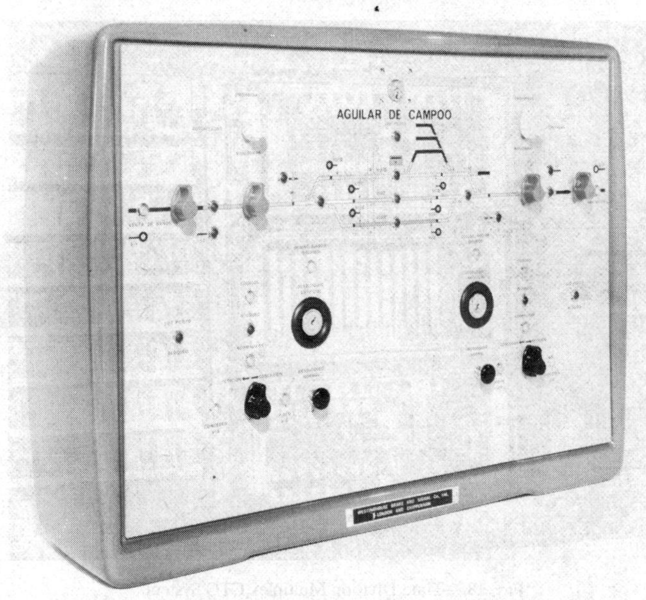

FIG. 17.—Station Control Panel with Relay Block Operation.

It is to be noted that with these systems of tokenless block operation, a train registers its presence at the ends of the block section only. The occupation of the block occurs as the train is detected passing the starter and the block is taken to be clear again when an exit is registered; the system relies on the receiving operator observing that the train is complete. The only foolproof way of proving the section to be clear is by track circuiting it throughout, and if this is done then a fairly simple block system can be provided, since it will not involve a sequence of 'one shot' operations as do the tokenless block systems.

Track Circuit Block Systems.—The track circuit through the block would be of the directional type, that is, it has feed and relay equipment at each end and also at each end a directional control relay, which, energised or de-energised, will determine whether the track feed or the track relay respectively, is connected to the rails. A simple line circuit is required between stations so that the operators may exchange bell signals, and an operator accepting a train would operate a thumb-switch or push button to energise his directional relay, which would pick up provided his starter signal was normal. The block track relay at the despatching end would thus be energised, this then constituting proof that the section is clear and that there is no train signalled in the opposing direction. The block track relay energised would permit the despatching operator to clear his starter signal.

The block track circuit would be sub-divided into lengths depending upon ballast resistance, and feed and relay equipment would be required at each cut section location. The block track circuits would be de-energised in the 'line closed' condition, and primary cells would therefore be used to feed them without requiring frequent replacement. Coded track circuits have also been used for this type of block working. These enable longer track circuits to be used, and also can convey additional information between the operators whereby 'ask', 'accept' and 'train on line' indications can be provided. A mains power supply is essential for such track circuits however.

Centralised Traffic Control (CTC).—The overall management of traffic movements along a single line railway is best conducted by one person having a direct and continuous view of the position and progress of the various trains in the area. From this he is able to vary the time-table crossings and by-pass movements to best overall advantage in the light of current performance, day-to-day delays, etc. Once all the passing-loop stations have been equipped with electric signals and points and a relay-type interlocking then a CTC system can rapidly and continuously collect all the data on train movements etc. from the stations and display it to the CTC operator on a track diagram representing the whole line. Equally important, however, is the fact that the same system can then transmit directly to the stations each of the oeprators' commands to control the signalling and hence the traffic movements, without any intermediary stages or personnel.

For speed of transmission and reliability the CTC systems are electronic and of the time division multiplex

FIG. 18.—Time Division Multiplex CTC System.

type. Each signalling function in turn has sole use of the line circuit for a very short period during which control and indication information for that function is passed between CTC office and the station. The data transmission link is usually just one pair of line wires along the whole route but may be a quad arrangement with line amplifiers should the section be a long one. A radio transmission link could equally well be used and may be appropriate in particular cases but the physical line circuit is more often preferred in view of its simplicity of construction, low power requirements and freedom from electrical interference.

A typical wayside station CTC equipment is illustrated in Fig. 18 and this operates the local relay interlocking

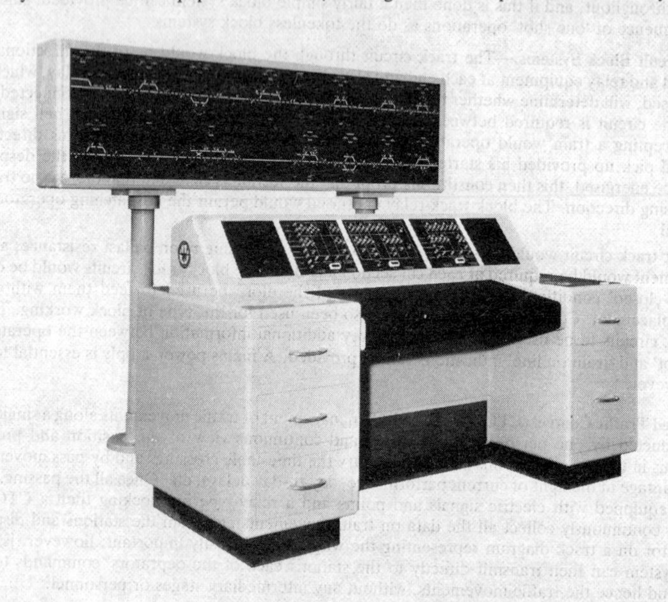

FIG. 19.—CTC Desk, Master Panel Type.

which provides the guard against any conflicting movements being set up if called in error. This equipment also detects the state of the signals, the position of the points, occupancy of the track circuits, etc for transmission back to the CTC office. The CTC operator sets the points and signals by means of thumb-switches or pushbuttons. He also sets up the block between the stations, but since he is in control of both ends of the block there is obviously no need for an exchange of bell signals and an 'ask' and 'acceptance' procedure. The block section is track circuited, and steady energy or coded track circuits may be used. In some cases one or more intermediate automatic signals are provided so that a closer headway can be achieved with following trains.

Instead of each function having its own switch or button, which on a large scheme may put some out of easy reach, the control pushbuttons may be grouped together on a master panel where there are enough pushbuttons to operate the largest station, as shown in Fig. 19. When the controller wishes to operate a signalling function at a particular station, he first operates a station selection button on the master panel followed by the function button with the appropriate identification number.

A useful adjunct to the CTC system is an automatic traingraph recorder which registers on a moving chart the occupation and clearance of selected track circuits to enable a graph of the day's movement to be built up. The size and complexity of some recent CTC schemes has, however, led to the use of computer-aided control combined with Train Description as in Figs. 10 and 12. In these cases the recorder is a teleprinter which is driven by the computer to print out the train number, time and place as each station in the route is passed, thus listing all train movements in detail for future reference without needing any specific operator participation.

Another feature frequently met in CTC schemes is the provision of local control panels. The controller can hand over the operation of a station to local staff when required, especially for shunting movements.

STANDARDS

A Selection of Standards applicable to Railway Signalling

BRITISH STANDARD SPECIFICATIONS

BS 376 'Railway Signalling Symbols' Part 1 'Schematic' Part 2 'Wiring & Circuits'.
BS 456 'Dimensions of Track Circuit Insulation'.
BS 469 'Electric Lamps for Railway Signalling'.
BS 561 'AC Line Relays, 2-Element (3 position)'.
BS 581 'Electric Point Operating Mechanism'.
BS 714 'Cartridge Fuse Links'.
BS 1745 'AC Track and Line Relays, 2-Element (2 position)'.
BS 3347 'Capacitors for Track Circuits'.

BRITISH RAIL SPECIFICATIONS

BR 820 'Colours of Light Signals, Filters and Lenses'.
BR 865 'Transformer-Rectifier Units'.
BR 895 'Screening for Cables subject to high Electro-magnetic Induction'.
BR 902 'Electrical Requirements for HV Point Machines'.
BR 904 'Feed Set for AC immune DC Track Circuit having a BR 939A Track Relay'.
BR 930A 'DC Neutral Relay, Plug-In Type'.
BR 932A 'DC Biased Relay, AC immune, Plug-In Type'.
BR 933A 'DC Slow Pick-up Neutral Relay, AC immune, Plug-In Type'.
BR 935A 'DC Magnetically Latched Relay, Plug-In Type'.
BR 939A 'DC Neutral Track Relay, AC immune, Plug-In Type'.
BR 943 'DC Biased Contactor Relay, AC immune, Plug-In Type'.
BR 949 'DC Time Relay Unit, Plug-In Type, for Point Control Circuit'.
BR 963 'Twin DC Slow-acting Neutral Relay Unit, Plug-In Type'.

PASSENGER CARRYING RAIL VEHICLES

Definitions—Rail Transit Systems—System Requirements—Design Criteria—Train Performance—Reliability—Design Proving—Vehicle Body Design—Materials—Structural Design—Structural Materials—Weight Reduction—Bogie Design—Suspension—Springs and Dampers—Interior Design—Traction Equipment—Diesel Traction—Electric Traction—Brake Systems and Performance—Brake Equipment—Magnetic Track Brakes—Heating and Ventilating—Manufacture and Production—Bibliography.

By P. J. Allender

INTRODUCTION

In this revision of the Railway Rolling Stock chapter (Chapter L8, 1987 edition; J L Koffman) the opportunity has been taken to revise the format, incorporate a substantial part of the diesel railcar chapter, eliminate inessential mathematical content by quoting sources, and to build a bibliography into the chapter. Much of the content of previous rolling stock chapters was strongly biassed toward British Rail technology. Reference will also be made to vehicles using lift systems without wheel and rail contact.

DEFINITIONS

To clarify international terminology a few special terms will be defined, mostly taken from US vehicle technology.

Adhesion, Coefficient of.—The coefficient of rolling friction in wheel to rail rolling contact.

It is the ratio between the longitudinal force, acting tangentially to the wheel, at the wheel-rail interface and the component of vehicle weight acting perpendicularly, through the wheel radius, to the rail.

Blending.—Where motion resisting forces due to current reversal on electrical traction equipment are simultaneously combined with mechanical braking to produce a required braking force.

Coasting.—Where accelerating forces are no longer operating and only minimal braking forces are in use to control speed reduction to required levels.

Drive.—A complete traction system containing one or more motors or engines, their controlling equipment, and the associated devices required to transmit motor or engine power to driving wheels or other motion-producing equipment.

Failsafe.—Design of the traction, control, signalling, or other components of vehicle operational systems so that the occurrence of one or more failures can not result in an operational condition which puts passengers or crew at risk of harm.

Fixed Guideway.—A description which includes rail and wheel systems, but also covers other guided systems where a fixed route is used. Thus, monorail, cable, maglev, and other systems are included. High technology systems may also be known as AGT (Advanced Ground Transport) systems if AGT uses guideways.

Interface.—A point or points where two or more separate systems meet for transferring energy or information.

Jerk.—The rate of change with respect to time of acceleration or deceleration, produced, for instance, by a vehicle entering a curve, change in track level, control unit steps, etc.

Load Weighing.—A means of achieving a relatively constant ratio of tractive force (or effort) to vehicle gross weight by measuring axle loads and using the result to control traction energy.

Maglev.—Vehicles in which magnetic forces acting vertically are used to lift the loaded vehicle a small distance sufficient to permit movement along a fixed guideway without friction. Traction is normally achieved by linear motors.

Quality Assurance.—In the context of this chapter, quality assurance implies the steps taken, and proof of compliance, to ensure that a vehicle supplied and commissioned ready for operational use is fit for the user purpose, taking into account all environmental, human and engineering adverse influences outside the direct control of the vehicle supplier.

Reliability.—The probability that a vehicle, functional system or component will continue to operate within its designed parameters without failure for an estimated minimum period of time. In practice, the probability is determined by studying the reported number of failures actually occurring and using statistical methods to derive mean times before failure values.

Slide, Wheel.—Also linked to wheel slip. A condition occurring during vehicle braking when the vehicle is moving at a speed greater than that indicated by the rotational speed of the wheels. Devices to increase friction or adjust wheel speeds may be used to control slip/slide effects.

Speed, Balancing.—A relatively constant speed at which a vehicle or train will run when the traction energy input is equal to the forces resisting motion on straight level track.

Speed, Scheduled.—The effective average speed of a vehicle or train between commencing motion at one station or terminal to recommencing motion at some subsequent station or terminal. In practice this is determined by measuring the time for a specified journey, including all scheduled stops within the journey, and dividing by the distance between starting and finishing stations.

Spin, Wheel.—Also related to wheel slide or slip. Wheel spin occurs when, due to a lack of wheel to rail adhesion, driving wheels are unable to induce the acceleration indicated by their rotational speed. Here also, devices which increase friction or adjust wheel speeds until traction occurs may be used.

Stop, Emergency.—Also called Emergency Braking. Deceleration of a vehicle or train as rapidly as is safely possible by applying a specified or controlled maximum braking effort. Normally an emergency stop procedure will continue until the vehicle or train is halted, but in some circumstances a manual over-ride at a very low speed may be possible.

Stop, Service.—Also known as Full Service Braking. Deceleration of a vehicle or train at a predetermined rate designed to bring a vehicle or train to a halt in accordance with the journey requirements. This can also be used to reduce vehicle speeds in accordance with variable service conditions by limited application dictated by safety requirements.

Traction System.—The whole system of wheels, motors or engines, drive transmissions, brakes, control devices, and other elements which propel or retard a vehicle in response to input command actions. In automatic systems track to vehicle interfaces are provided for vehicle control from stationary control centres.

Truck.—US term for bogie.

Weight.—In vehicle designs four weight categories are assigned both for vehicle weight limitation in build and for the height response of suspension systems to ensure coupling, structure clearance and platform alignment. These are conventionally designated:

AWO Vehicle empty of passengers and crew but ready to run, including any fuel for engines, water for toilets, etc.

AW1 Vehicle with crew and all passenger seats full, ready to run.

AW2 Vehicle with crew, all seats filled, and an estimated operational load of standing passengers, ready to run.

AW3 Vehicle with crew, all seats filled, and all possible standing areas filled in a maximum calculated standing density, ready to run. This is crush load condition. Sometimes the weights above tare are designated M1 to M3.

RAIL TRANSIT SYSTEMS.—It is not possible here to describe transit systems in any detail. There are two basic groups, inter-city and urban. Inter-city systems are designed for trains capable of travelling at a relatively high schedule speed between urban centres, and their journey may include intermediate stops. Passenger facilities will vary according to the distances and time involved, including at least toilet facilities rising to buffet, restaurant and sleeping capacities. Communications and signalling will vary with the rail sytem and its location. In developed countries complex signalling and communications systems capable of partial automatic train control may be found, the complexity depending to a large extent on local and environmental conditions. Less developed regions, including well separated urban centres, may use single-track working and only fuel or food stops on very long journeys. Urban, including suburban, systems operate within the bounds of a town, city or conurbation. Urban systems are variously described as mass transit or rapid transit, as light, heavy or intermediate, and as trams and trains. The most important factor is the capacity of the system to move a specified number of passengers per hour in any single direction. Vehicle and train design will be based on the most cost-effective way of providing this capacity and dealing with daily peaks and valleys of demand. Light, heavy and intermediate refer mainly to passenger flow capacities and not to the vehicle weight, other factors include that (1) light rail may be segregated from road traffic, but operate frequently on suitable roads. Driving is commonly visual, so that signalling is not necessarily sophisticated. (2) heavy rail is always segregated and has full signalling and communications.

SYSTEM REQUIREMENTS

GENERAL DESIGN CRITERIA.—It will be obvious that rail vehicles will be designed to be suitable for all aspects of their operational environment. This may include coupling with existing vehicles, and compatability with existing track, stations, signalling, tunnels, curves and other constraints.

An important factor will be Fail Safe Design where either no failure within a safety critical system can lead to harm to pasengers, or self-correcting systems using redundant elements are used to by-pass faults. Fail safe means that in safety critical areas all foreseeable failures result in isolation of a potential hazard. At one time passenger emergency alarms were designed to operate train brakes to bring a train to a halt. In heavily used systems this is no longer regarded as safe, so that a stop command must be confirmed by a crew action. Brake systems will, therefore, have two independent circuits so that failure of one still permits a train to be brought to a halt. One vitally important consideration will be harm to, or death of, the train driver; careful provision is essential to avoid a dangerous accident.

Design life of a normal passenger rail vehicle will be 30 years, representing around two million kilometres of travel. Most vehicles last well beyond 30 years, a classic case being the Glasgow underground cars built in 1896 and still in service in 1976.

Operational environments are of crucial importance in designing vehicle structures, and traction systems. Train performance is normally specified for standard temperature and pressure conditions in dry air. One example might be 30°C and 1 bar pressure. Then loss of performance might be expected not to exceed 0·5% per degree change in temperature, or 1·3% for every 100 metre rise in altitude above the height at which the specified standard conditions apply. Climatic conditions, mainly daily ranges and annual ranges of temperature and humidity, will be needed to decide on heating and ventilation as well as corrosion preventive measures. The latter need particular attention if temperatures can fall below the condensation or dew point. Condensation is an important factor needing consideration during export transportation. A design brief should also include rainfall and snow data, wind and dust data, possible flood conditions, track and air contamination, and any local electromagnetic interference.

Vehicle designers will need to be aware of minimum curve radii measured at the centre line of the track, maximum superelevation or cant, track gauge, vertical curves, gradients and their length, track condition and permitted rail wear, types and positions of rail switches, and platform heights. Clearance requirements will dictate many vehicle dimension tolerances. Main features will be vehicle lengths, widths, and heights; the latter will vary with passenger loading and wheel wear. Positions of station platform edges and canopies, tunnels and tunnel roofs, power and signal gantry and equipment must be specified relative to track centre line and rail level. If this information is not available it must be measured on site. Old data should be checked so that earth movement effects are dealt with.

The four categories of vehicle weight are given in the Definitions. Opinions vary, but for many purposes passenger weight is assessed at 80 kgs per person. Low standing densities usually assume four standing passengers per square metre of free floor area, and high densities assume eight per square metre. For example, if the vehicle tare weight is 30 tonnes, that is the AWO condition, seating for 100 passengers adds 8,000 kgs, i.e. 8 tonnes giving AW1 = 38 tonnes. If the free floor area is 30 square metres, then

$$AW2 = 38 + (4 \times 30 \times 80)/1{,}000 = 47{\cdot}6 \text{ tonnes and}$$
$$AW3 = 38 + (8 \times 30 \times 80)/1{,}000 = 57{\cdot}2 \text{ tonnes.}$$

During the operation of passenger rail vehicles vibration will be inevitable. The important considerations include restricting ranges of vibration frequency amplitude and acceleration to ensure acceptable passenger comfort, and to protect axle bogie and body mounted equipment from damage. A rail vehicle is free to vibrate about and along each of the three principal axes which pass through the vehicle centre of gravity. The nature of these movements can be extremely complex to analyse. Vertical vibration impulses originate in variations in rail height, such as at rail joints and track irregularities. Most of the lateral vibration is associated with wheel conicity, variations in track gauge, flange clearances and rail straightness variables. Vehicle mass and the elastic characteristics of suspension related components introduce their own effects. Design criteria will depend on the anticipated period of exposure to train motion. Typical vibration exposure criteria are given in Fig. 1, but for full details ISO 2631 should be referred to. British Rail prefer a Ride Index obtained from accelerometer measurements of amplitude and duration during tests on dry track with straight, left and right curves of specified minimum lengths. Curves defining Ride Index Values are illustrated in Fig. 2 and Table 1 describes the acceptability ascribed to a range of indices. For full details refer to Koffman (See Bibliography).

TABLE 1.—RIDE INDEX VALUES

Index Number	Operational Description	Human Tolerance Period in Hours
1	Excellent	More than 24
1·5	Very good	More than 24
2	Good	More than 24
2·5	Fairly good	About 13
3	Satisfactory	About 5·6

TABLE 1.—*continued*

Index Number	Operational Description	Human Tolerance Period in Hours
3·5	Fairly Satisfactory	About 2·8
4	Acceptable	About 1·5
4·5	Unacceptable	About 1·1
5	Harmful	About 0.6

As far as equipment is concerned, some typical design criteria are given in Table 2. These will depend on track conditions and both wheelset and suspension design. Actual conditions should be checked by instrumental measurement, preferably using continuous recording.

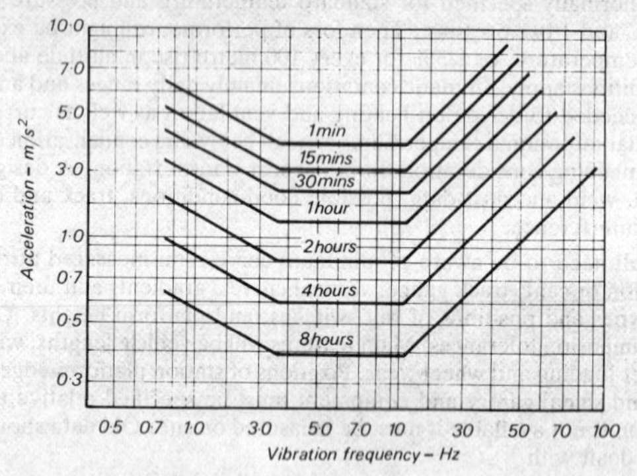

FIG. 1.—Vibration Exposure Criteria; each curve denotes the maximum tolerable exposure for various combinations of frequency and vertical or horizontal acceleration.

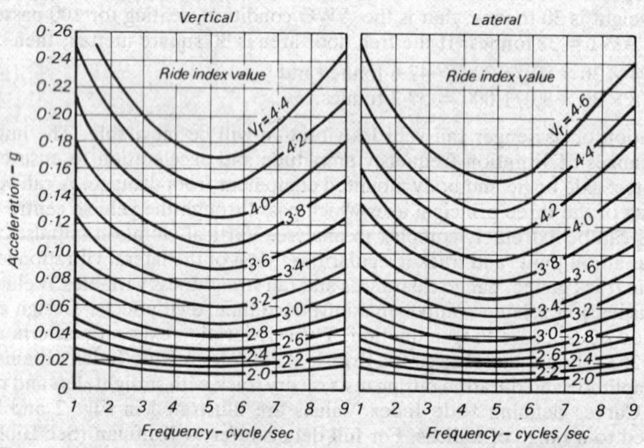

FIG. 2.—Ride Index Values for Vertical and Lateral Oscillations.

TABLE 2.—SHOCK CRITERIA FOR EQUIPMENT

	Max. Acceleration m/s²	Max. Frequency H2	Random Shock Load m/s²
Axle Mounted	200	100	300
Bogie Mounted	40	100	80
Body Mounted	2	100	20

Train Performance.—It is not feasible to provide operational performance criteria for single powered vehicles unless these are intended to function individually. Normally, complete trains of specified vehicle combinations are given criteria capable of monitoring potential speeds, acceleration and braking, body vibration and noise, and in recent times maintainability and reliability. A set of vehicles making up a train may be referred to as a 'rake'.

Acceleration and braking will normally be specified for dry, level straight (also called 'tangent') track. In addition, both acceleration and braking criteria will be expressed in terms of the weight condition (assuming all vehicles in the train are at the same weight condition within the range AW0 to AW3, see Definitions). Usually, criteria are not given for acceleration in the crush load (AW3) condition. Typical values for a light rail vehicle are:

Maximum acceleration at AW2 weight 1·52 m/s²

Time to reach 80 km/h from rest not more than 60 seconds at AW2 weight.

Speeds will vary slightly as wheel wear occurs, but are usually a design maximum assuming AW2 weight, a mean speed between specified stops, and a minimum speed for train marshalling. In general, urban mass transit aims at high accelerations and decelerations with a maximum speed around 100 km/h, intercity services may accelerate and decelerate more slowly but have high maximum speeds. Much depends on the services operation requirements.

Wheelslip and wheelslide depend on the condition of the wheel-rail interface. Wet conditions reduce adhesion, the dynamic characteristics of the vehicle alter wheel loadings, axle driving mechanisms and running gear have significant effects, and the geometry of the wheel to rail contact is critical.

The coefficient of adhesion reduces with vehicle speed, being about 10–15 per cent lower for every 100 km/h increase in speed. Wheel wear above 4 mm reduces adhesion by about 5 per cent per millimetre of additional wear of the tread. Brake calculations should assume a coefficient of adhesion of 0·15. Electronic slip-slide sensors are currently available to control wheel speeds automatically.

Tractive resistance formulas follow the general pattern:

$$R = K + LV + MV^2$$

where R is total tractive resistance in Newtons and K, L and M are constants which depend on the exterior surface parameters of the train.

A typical formula for diesel railcars is:

$$R(N) = 1000 + 5{\cdot}7V + 0{\cdot}27V^2 \text{ (}V\text{ in km/h).}$$

Tractive resistance increases during coasting by about 30 per cent. Specific values for K, L and M should be discussed with traction equipment suppliers. Some formulas calculate tractive resistance in Newtons per vehicle tonne.

The original Davis formula is:

$$R = WN(A + B/W + uV + CSV^2/WN)$$

where R is tractive resistance
W is axle load.
N is number of axles
A and B are constants
U is wheel to rail adhesion (or friction) coefficient
V is vehicle speed
C is drag coefficient
S is front end cross-sectional area

For further details refer to standard texts.

Impulse or Jerk is controlled by specifying that rates of change of acceleration, including constant acceleration round curves, should fall within the limits 1·1 to 1·4 m/s² at AW2 and normal operational conditions. Jerk limitation may be electronically controlled, and can be operated in conjunction with slip-slide controls. Normal brake operation is jerk controlled.

To adjust braking effort for varying passenger loads it is common for suspension systems to be fitted with load sensors. Where load weighing is required the system produces signals which adjust propulsion and braking forces. A fail-safe mode ensures that the control signal cannot fall below that appropriate to the AO weight.

Noise.—Essentially, there are three aspects to noise control:

(a) vehicle interior limitation of train induced noise
(b) limitation of train noise to the exterior environment
(c) control of exterior noise entering vehicles.

Noise is dealt with in chapter B4. It is intended, therefore, to discuss ony those aspects relevant to railway vehicles. Audible effects of noise vary with frequency so that at very low frequencies around 30 Hz the tolerable sound pressure level is much higher than that at high frequencies around 8,000 Hz. Sound level meters are usually designed to compensate for this frequency effect, and for most purposes a weighting scale A is used. A change of 3 decibels corresponds to a doubling (or halving) of the sound pressure level. In practice the sound pressure level is:

$$L(dB(A)) = 10\log(p/p_0)$$

p_0 is a reference pressure of 20 micropascals. Recommended values are given in Table 3.

A particular problem with metal bodied rail vehicles is drumming of exterior panels. air pressure variations due to holes, inadequate bedding of panels on frames, loose doors and improperly fitted frames can be considerable. Two common means of reducing panel drumming are to apply an anti-drumming coating consisting of a heavily filled elastic membrane capable of being sprayed and to sandwich an elastic membrane between an internal and external panel. Glass or mineral wool compressed about 25 per cent is quite effective in the second method, but more efficient proprietary products are available. Noise transmission varies inversely with panel mass so that increased thickness or denser materials will transmit less noise. Expert guidance should be sought in dealing with noise insulation problems.

TABLE 3.—RECOMMENDED NOISE LEVEL MAXIMA.

Application	Max. dB(A)
Sleeping Cars	60
Dining Cars	65
Intercity Compartment	65
Urban/Suburban Cars	70
Driving Cabs	75
External Train Induced Noise at 7·5 m	90
Stationary Motored Vehicle	65
Train at 65 km/h	75
Traction System Noise	85

Reliability.—Maintainability and reliability are two closely related topics of increasing concern. Reliability implies that the whole vehicle, as well as its components, will operate satisfactorily for not less than a specified minimum period or mileage. A 'mean time between failures' (MTBF) is usually specified. Full details are given in BS 5760 (Reliability of Systems, Equipments and Components). In very simple terms reliability theory is based on recognising three normal failure zones:

(1) Initially high, but decreasing prototype, test and commissioning failure rate.
(2) Relatively level useful life interval with a stable mean time between failures.
(3) A final increasing failure rate due to wearing out.

Consider a simple example, an urban mass transit train accelerates then brakes to a halt ten times an hour over a 20 hour day for 300 days each year over a 30 year life. A brake lever will, therefore, be subject to just under two million fatigue cycles. Assuming a factor of safety of ten, the lever material must have an endurance life at its maximum working stress of not less than 20 million cycles.

A considerable body of information is available about electronic components, but relatively little published data on rail vehicle mechanical parts. There has been reluctance on the part of vehicle operators to provide failure feedback to vehicle builders unless very significant early failures occur. It will be evident that reliability estimates depend on:

(1) Availability of both major and minor failure feedback.
(2) Estimates of intrinsic reliability from studies of all possible failure modes.
(3) Careful and cautious estimation of combined systems or assembly failure modes.
(4) Satisfactory quality assurance requirements realistically based on achievable standards from routine production.

Maintainability has been described after reliability because the shorter the interval mean time between failures the more important it will be to ensure that failed items are quickly replaced to avoid loss of service revenue.

There are six vital principles to be considered:

(1) System, assembly and component choices should minimise failures as far as possible.
(2) The cost of maintenance and adjustments should be minimised in terms of manpower, replacement items and maintenance equipment.
(3) Loss of revenue due to vehicle breakdown should be minimised.
(4) Available manpower skills should be investigated and taken into consideration in devising repair and maintenance schedules and instructions.

(5) All components requiring regular servicing and maintenance should be readily accessible, and access for workshop tools should be considered in realistic operations.
(6) Fitting requirements should take account both of the interchangeability of original equipment as well as the possible need for alternative replacement over long periods if original items cease to be available.

Ongoing quality assurance programmes should, of course, be designed so that developing faults can be easily diagnosed. In safety critical electronic circuits and systems where electronic fault detection is possible it may be desirable to include a fault indication board in a convenient place.

Design Proving.—Strictly, design proving falls into the province of quality assurance which is covered more fully in Chapter D10 and in BS 5750: Quality Systems.

Three aspects will be outlined here, components and systems initial proving, pre-delivery examintion of vehicles and trains, post-delivery commissioning.

With very large numbers of individual items entering into the construction of a rail vehicle it is impossible to examine each in detail. Many items, in particular structural and decorative products will be inspected on the basis of:

(1) Supplier competence and the presence of acceptable quality systems.
(2) Statistically based sampling and examination of delivered products.
(3) Comparison of submitted design information with the best available records of performance of comparable products or applications.

Safety critical items, such as brake equipment, should be studied in great detail. In many cases corrosion prevention has been found to be lacking and can lead to early failure. New designs should be fitted into operational mock-ups capable of simulating operational conditions at extreme design parameters. Care does need to be applied in using high rates of test to simulate lifetime operational cycles. In addition, realistic environmental conditions need to be considered, including any export transit conditions.

Completed vehicles are usually required to be submitted to static end load crushing tests simulating the maximum anticipated load in the event of a crash. Some specifications do, in fact, require a simulated full speed crash into solid buffers. Passenger overloads should be tested with uniformly distributed weights, underframe deflections being measured, usually with strain gauges in appropriate positions. Vehicle systems are normally bench tested as well as being examined after fitting. Thus, traction equipment may be operated on roller test beds or on track. Both individual vehicles and coupled vehicles will be checked both to ensure that drawings showing anticipated fixed obstacle positions are confirmed by the railway civil engineers. Several cases of unexpected tunnel subsidence not recorded on drawings leading to vehicle fouling of fixed structures have been reported.

On-site commissioning of trains involves trial running for representative periods long enough to detect early faults. Automatic couplers will be repeatedly coupled and uncoupled. Service drivers will be trained and used in running trials. Real passengers may be invited to test the new vehicles and comment. Continuous and fast feedback of faults between commissioning engineers and vehicle builders will occur to permit rectification during build. As an example, freak weather conditions on site revealed a minor, but unsightly adhesive failure on a decorative panel. Two vehicles per week, were being delivered, taking five weeks for delivery. A further three weeks elapsed before the cause of the fault was identified and rectified. Another five weeks elapsed for the delivery of replacements for 26 vehicles. In contracts where continual delivery is imperative even minor problems can lead to very considerable logistics problems. Usually, commissioning will continue on a goodwill basis over the whole period from initial delivery until the last vehicle has been commissioned. Contractural liability for rectification will, however, be on an agreed basis. Legal product liability to the travelling public tends to last the lifetime of the vehicle and is a very difficult problem.

VEHICLE BODY DESIGN

GENERAL FACTORS.—Passenger rail vehicle bodies vary considerably in dimensions and construction, but for most practical purposes consist of a cladding mounted on a strong framework. The interior is suitably insulated and lined to meet passenger comfort requirements. Figure 3 illustrates the general nature of the body frame. Body, length, width, overall height and floor height above rail are dictated by fixed structure limitations. summarised as a loading gauge. A fairly simple example of a loading gauge is given in Fig. 4, and designers normally check that this includes compensation for vehicle lengths when transverse body centre shifts transversely when negotiating curves. Figure 5 illustrates a typical body size related to its loading gauge, and Table 4 covers a number of body parameters. Articulated bodies use a leading and trailing bogie and a central pivot bogie with a wide flexible gangway between each body. Bodies of this kind are common on light rapid transit vehicles where smaller rail curves may occur.

Choice of Materials.—Modern passenger rail vehicles are most commonly built as substantially steel or substantially aluminium alloy, with a vast range of combinations. Body end claddings may be metal or reinforced plastics. Steel bodies generally fall into three categories:

(1) primarily structural grade mild steel framing clad with mild steel sheet
(2) higher strength structural grade steel framing clad with mild steel or a low alloy steel sheet, frequently frames are specified in low alloy high tensile slow rusting steels.

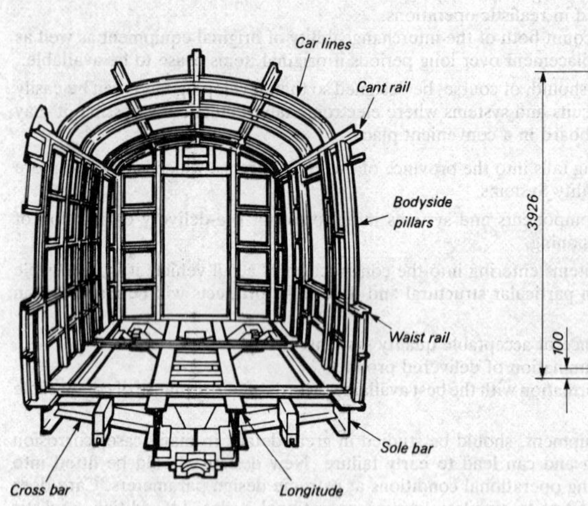

FIG. 3.—General Nature of Body Frame.

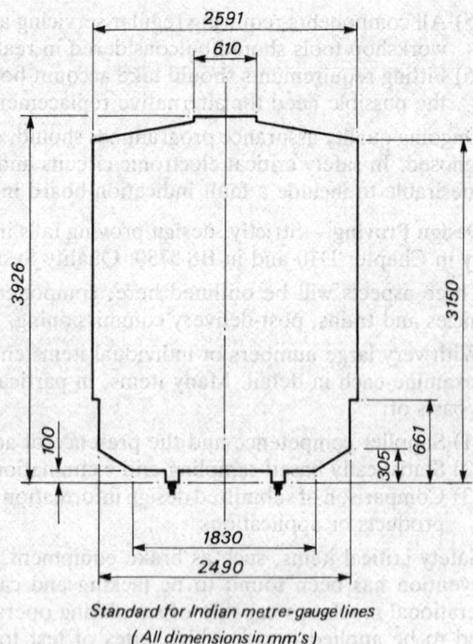

FIG. 4.—Typical Simple Loading Gauge.

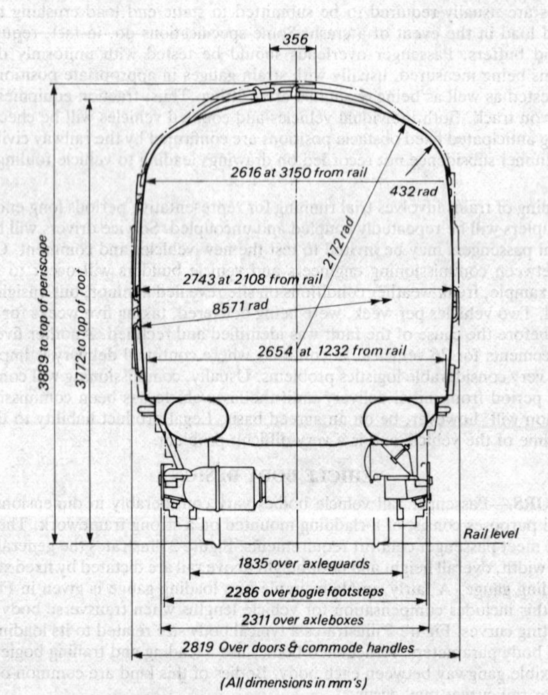

FIG. 5.—Typical British Rail Car in Loading Gauge.

(3) stainless or low alloy high tensile steel framing with relatively thin stiffened stainless steel sheet cladding.

Non-stainless steels need careful attention to painting and protective coating. A vital factor to minimising maintenance painting is to ensure first that the coating is applied to a properly prepared surface, and second that coatings are chosen to meet the worst anticipated operating and transport environments. Paints and other protective coatings are dealt with elsewhere in the Yearbook, and a systematic approach is recommended.

Aluminium alloy bodies may be built on an aluminium underframe or, if flexing must be reduced, on a steel underframe. Structural grade alloys are used for body framing, depending on whether cold forming operations are needed. Cladding is usually in a simple alloy chosen to be compatible with fixing processes. A relatively modern concept is to use wide extruded aluminium alloy planks designed to be joined by welding. This concept largely eliminates the need for a separate body frame but needs great care in design and production.

The most popular reinforced plastics are polyester resins using chopped strand glass fibre mat reinforcement. These may be hand laid or vacuum impregnation formed to give products of excellent surface finish and in a vast range of colours. Fire safety requirements need to be considered carefully, in particular an increasing demand for reduction in output of smoke and harmful combustion products. Current guidelines will be available in BS 6853 briefly outlined in a recent article.

Structural Design.—Body shells are designed to be capable of supporting a uniformly distributed minimum vertical load:

$$L\ (\text{tonnes}) = 1{\cdot}3\,(B + 0{\cdot}16P)$$

where B is the weight of the body in tonnes in a ready to run condition, and $0{\cdot}16P$ represents twice the number of passengers (P) at maximum load AW3 assuming each passenger to weigh 80 kg (0·08 tonnes).

Calculated or experimentally determined stresses in structural members and cladding panels should not be allowed to exceed 80 per cent of the elastic limit or proof stress of the materials involved.

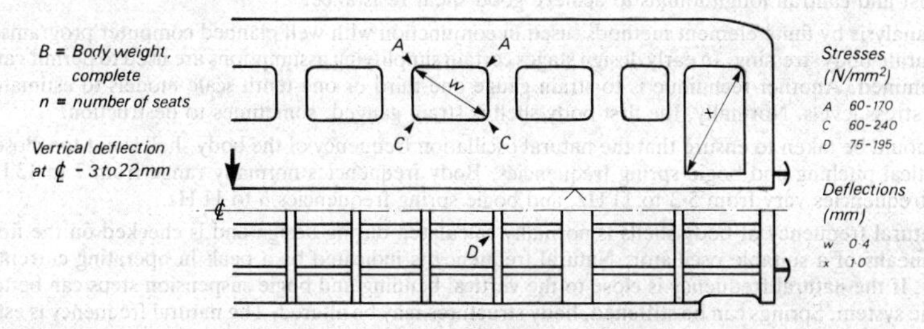

FIG. 6.—Stresses of a Body Shell under a Uniformly Distributed Vertical Load $L = 1{\cdot}3\,(B + 0{\cdot}16P)$.

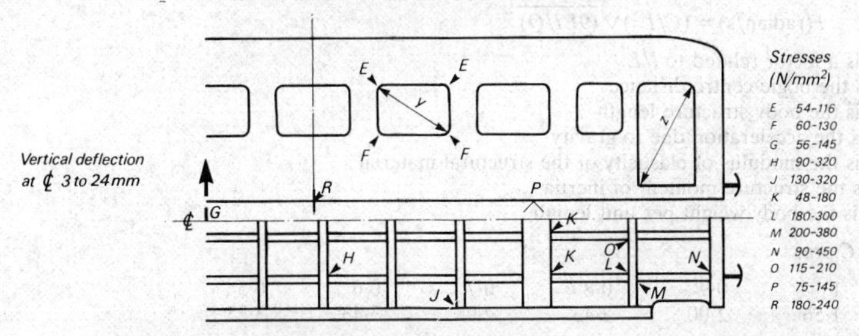

FIG. 7.—Stresses of a Body Shell Subjected to a 2 MN End Load at Buffer Level.

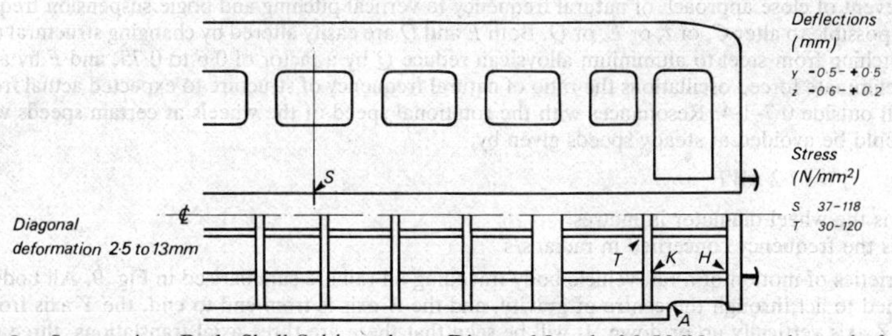

FIG. 8.—Stresses in a Body Shell Subjected to a Diagonal Load of 0·5 MN across the underframe.

Tests on modern coach body shells subjected to vertical load L are summarised in Fig. 6. This shows the highest stresses at places of stress concentration, the range of deflections at the body centre and the diagonal distortions at doors and windows. Stresses are stated in MN/m² and deflections in mm. Ranges are the result of differences in design.

A conventional rule is that at maximum load with an allowance for dynamic effects the elastic deflection between bogie centres should nowhere exceed 0·1% of the bogie centre distance. Other effects are that, under vertical load, the body width at waist level will reduce by up to 1.6 mm, and the height from floor to roof will increase by 0·4–0·8 mm. The body shell of vehicles used on inter-city routes in Britain is required to withstand an end buffing load of 200 tonnes without permanent deflection. In addition, in separate tests, the body must withstand a diagonal compressive load of 50 tonnes at buffer level, 40 tonnes at 350 mm above buffer centre-line level, 30 tonnes at waist and cantrail level. The results of the 200 tonne end buffing load is summarised in Fig. 7, and those of the 50 tonne diagonal load in Fig. 8.

Railcars and railbuses are usually subjected to 120 tonnes end load test. Buffing loads depend on the energy available in collisions. Since collision energy is in proportion to MV^2, the buffing load should be related to the speed V and the mass in motion M. Elastic reduction in body length will usually be due to impact decelerations of 4g for steel underframes and 2g for aluminium alloys. Steel vehicles will probably reduce in length by 1·7%, aluminium ones by 2·1%.

Underframes and body superstructures are designed to ensure as uniform a transmission of stress as possible without introducing stress concentration as far as possible. Sudden changes of cross-sectional area, section shape and directions of load path are avoided at all costs. Doors are preferable at ends only, any used between bogie centres need stiffening to avoid excessive loss of vertical load strength. Smooth connections need to be designed to fix longitudinal and cross members of the body frame to verticals. Side pillars should be fixed to floor, waist and cantrail longitudinals to achieve good shear resistance.

Stress analysis by finite element methods, used in conjunction with well planned computer programs permit quite accurate body stressing. In early design stages certain simplifying assumptions are used to permit variations to be examined. Another technique is to strain gauge one-third or one-tenth scale models to estimate stress flow and stress levels. Normally, the first body shell is strain gauged, sometimes to destruction.

Care should be taken to ensure that the natural oscillation frequency of the body shell is not too close to the body vertical pitching and bogie spring frequencies. Body frequencies normally range from 7 to 13 Hz, and pitching frequencies vary from 5·3 to 11 Hz, and bogie spring frequencies 6 to 11 Hz.

The natural frequency of body shells is normally calculated during design and is checked on the first body shell by means of a suitable oscillator. Natural frequency is indicated by a peak in operating current of the oscillator. If the natural frequency is close to the vertical bending and bogie suspension steps can be taken to detune the system. Springs can be stiffened, body structures may be altered. The natural frequency is estimated by:

$$F(\text{radian/s}) = (C/L^2)\sqrt{(9EI/Q)}$$

where, C is a factor related to l/L.
l is the bogie centre distance
L is the body structure length
g is the acceleration due to gravity
E is the modulus of elasticity of the structural material
I is the structure moment of inertia
Q is the body weight per unit length

Values of C are:

l/L	1	0·9	0·8	0·7	0·6	0·5
C	1·56	2·00	2·43	2·95	3·43	3·25

In the event of close approach of natural frequency to vertical pitching and bogie suspension frequencies it is usually possible to alter C, or I, or E, or Q. Both E and Q are easily altered by changing structural materials. Thus, switching from steel to aluminium alloys can reduce Q by a factor of 0·6 to 0·75, and F by a factor of 0·75. To eliminate forced oscillations the ratio of natural frequency of structure to expected actual frequencies should fall outside 0·7–1·4. Resonances with the rotational speed of the wheels at certain speeds will occur. These should be avoided at steady speeds given by:

$$V = 7{\cdot}2\,\pi WF$$

where W is the wheel diameter in metres
F is the frequency concerned in radians/s

The varieties of motion of a rail vehicle body travelling on rail are summarised in Fig. 9. All body motions are assumed to act through the centre of gravity, and the X axis is from end to end, the Y axis from side to side, the Z axis vertically up or down. It will be seen that there are three axial translations, three rotational translations and six combined axial-rotational motions. Data for typical European vehicles is summarised in Table 4.

Constructional Materials.—Vehicle underframes are invariably constructed of metal sections using various combinations of welding, rivetting and bolting to transmit stresses between members. Many underframes are

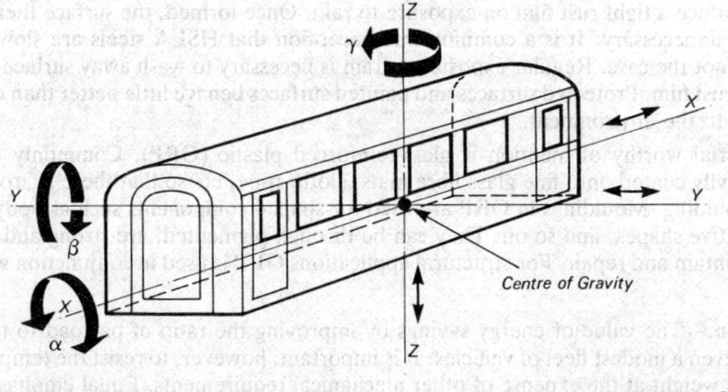

FIG. 9.—Fundamental Modes of Vehicle Oscillations and Coupled Modes.

TABLE 4.—TYPICAL EUROPEAN INTERCITY ROLLING STOCK.

Railway	Body Length	Tare Weight	Body Shell	Bogie Centres	Bogie Weight	Wheel Base	Wheel Diam.	No. of Seats	Wt. Seat	Wt. per Metre
	m	t	t	m	t	m	m	—	t	t
British	19·67	42·0	7·3	14·18	10·1	2·59	0·92	64	0·66	2·14
French	22·88	40·5	11·2	15·56	11·0	2·30	0·93	80	0·51	1·77
German	25·09	37·0	9·8	18·99	10·0	2·53	0·95	66	0·56	1·47
Italian	23·20	38·3	9·9	16·60	10·4	2·70	0·92	54	0·71	1·65
Netherlands	21·35	47·0	11·0	15·66	17·2	3·00	1·00	72	0·65	2·20
Switzerland	23·36	32·5	10·0	16·32	8·6	2·70	0·91	72	0·45	1·39
Denmark	20·74	34·5	—	14·44	11·8	3·00	0·97		—	1·66
Austria	24·98	37·8	9·5	18·99	10·1	2·53	0·95	60	0·63	1·51
Belgium	22·01	35·7	12·5	15·45	10·0	2·71	1·00	108	0·33	1·62
Sweden	23·64	45·2	10·7	16·62	13·0	2·57	1·00	48	0·94	1·91

made of lower carbon structural steels, primarily to BS 4360 Grade 43A a weldable 430 MN/m^2 mild steel. This always needs painting for corrosion protection, and the key to durability is the best possible surface preparation followed as quickly as possible by a good primer. Primers containing zinc chromate were formerly very popular, but many rail vehicles builders prefer the less toxic zinc phosphate. For areas difficult to clean fully because of limited access there are now ranges of softer coatings based on hardened oxidized petrolatum which are tolerant of surface condition. The primer will permit some delay before overcoating with undercoats to build film thickness and a finish which is normally a gloss paint to minize dirt pick-up. Using commercial alkyd paints, such a system should require maintenance every five years, with damage repair as soon as possible after accidents.

To reduce weight it is now common to find higher strength structural steels being used such as BS 4360 Grade 50B (even 55B), a weldable 500 MN/m^2 steel. End units carrying the first impact of buffing and drawgear loads are quite often made in this type of steel and inserted into underframes of other materials. Painting is normal, but flame-sprayed aluminium has been used with considerable success for long-term durability.

In the USA and Japan various stainless steels have been used. These are the stronger austenite and ferritic grades, usually of weldable composition. To avoid weld decay problems, rivetting is often used for joints. Stainless steel is accepted as non-corroding, but in underframes where regular cleaning is not possible a coating is necessary to avoid localised and crevice corrosion.

Aluminium alloys are used extensively for rapid transit urban vehicles. The strong alloys, 6083 in particular, are available in shaped extrusions capable of meeting almost any design structural purpose. Although it is true that aluminium has a much lower melting point than steel it can withstand fire very well because of the high thermal conductivity. Almost the only problem with aluminium is its relatively high deflection under load. Design to minimise deflection removes a substantial part of any weight savings. (For properties of aluminium alloys, see Chapter C6).

High Strength Low Alloy (HSLA) steels, such as the Corten range of British Steel, are higher strength structural steels classified in BS 4360 as 'Weather Resistant'. These contain small amounts of copper and chromium which induce a tight rust film on exposure to rain. Once formed, the surface then rusts very slowly so that painting is unnecessary. It is a common misconception that HSLA steels are slow rusting under all conditions. This is not the case. Regular exposure to rain is necessary to wash away surface contaminants and maintain an intact rust film. Protected surfaces and painted surfaces behave little better than ordinary structural steels on exposure to the environment.

One other material worthy of mention is glass-reinforced plastic (GRP). Commonly these consist of a polyester resin heavily coated onto fine glass fibre mats, cloth, rope, etc so that there is around 25–30% glass in the resultant moulding. Mouldings in GRP are used for shaped components such as body ends, equipment box covers, decorative shapes, and so on. They can be through-pigmented, are strong and damage-resistant, and are easy to maintain and repair. For structural applications GRP is used in conjunction with a load bearing metal framework.

Weight Reduction.—The value of energy savings by improving the ratio of payload to tare weight can be considerable over even a modest fleet of vehicles. It is important, however, to resist the temptation to minimise only the body shell weight at the expense of other mechanical requirements. Equal emphasis shuld be placed on reducing the weight of running gear, equipment, furnishing and traction equipment. Some typical weight proportions are summarised in Table 5.

TABLE 5.—WEIGHT OF COMPONENTS IN TERMS OF TARE WEIGHT.

Vehicle	Body Shell %	Running Gear %	Equipt. %	Furnishing %	Traction %
British Rail Coach	23·0	32·0	17·5	12·5	0
London Underground	19·0	33·0	16·0	13·0	19·0
German Rheingold	27·2	21·9	21·1	29·8	0
German Coach	32·8	24·6	16·9	25·7	0
3-car Diesel Train	27.0	20·9	9·4	27·3	15·4
3-car Electric Train	22·8	26·2	8·0	18·8	24·2

Ideally, comparable reductions should be made in the weight of each main area of weight. Furnishings dictate the *comfort ratio*, that is the proportion of seats in the maximum passenger capacity. This is likely to be around 30% for urban and suburban vehicles, exceptionally low proportions around 15% have been found. Higher proportions are normal for intercity vehicles averaging 50% or more. Care must be taken in minimising seat cushion weights that the risk of rapid fire spread is not increased.

One area of weight reduction has been the use of aluminium alloys for body shell construction. In addition to reducing energy demand for traction there were also significant reductions in wheel and brake wear. Although there is some annual cleaning cost, the need to paint is no longer essential. On average about 1·2% of the tare weight of a steel vehicle is paint. Every five years the normal rail vehicle paint needs cutting back thoroughly, refinishing and varnishing.

Strong heat treated aluminium alloys such as 6061, 6063, 6082 have been in common use. A serious problem is that to reach maximum design strength the best condition is solution heat treated to dissolve randomly dispersed precipitates, followed by controlled low temperature precipitation to produce a well-ordered dispersion. Unfortunately, this full thermal treatment cycle leaves the metal inadequate in ductility to withstand cold forming. Warm forming is possible, but needs great care to avoid loss of strength. The best condition for forming is solution treated, but this remains stable for only 24–36 hours without refrigeration. In the absence of refrigeration, precipitation will occur naturally but resulting in a lower strength than that from thermal precipitation. For this reason some designers prefer slightly lower strength alloys which are normally naturally aged (precipitated).

Aluminium alloys corrode at a rate which depends on their purity and on the nature of their alloying elements. Copper has a great influence on the rate at which aluminium corrodes, magnesium the least effect. Generally, the closer to commercially pure aluminium the better is the resistance to corrosion. In practice, weaknesses in the natural aluminium oxide film near inclusions and imperfections lead to cracks in the oxide film. The film is normally micro-cracked due to thermal shrinkage, but larger, mechanical cracks attract moisture which forms aluminium hydroxide which fills the cracks. Aluminium hydroxide is soft and takes up dirt readily. For this reason aluminium presents a grey appearance after exposure, with clumps of hydroxide forming *white rust*. Periodical weak acid or alkaline cleaning is required to eliminate the aluminium oxide and hydroxide, carrying soiling with it.

Although the density of aluminium is one-third that of steel, the saving is less owing to the lower elastic modulus and fatigue strength. Against this, the energy absorbing characteristic of aluminium is better than that of steel. Aluminium alloys are tolerant of indifferent workshop practices, and with modern equipment sound welds are easily achieved.

Much competition against aluminium alloys for rail vehicle bodies has come from the use of stainless steel.

Sections are normally cold formed, and exterior body panels are thin—they are normally corrugated for stiffness. The Budd Company in the USA has specialised in stainless steel rail vehicles for many years. Painting is not necessary to prevent corrosion, and water-detergent cleaning is adequate. Production is less simple than carbon steel, HSLA or aluminium alloy.

BOGIE DESIGN.—The essential objective of a bogie is to transmit a variable total body weight to rails without exceeding permissible axle loads, and to minimise track and other deviations from a smooth, comfortable ride. Bogie frames usually consist of a framework at each side supported vertically upon axleboxes, and a horizontal frame attached by a suspension system to the vertical frame and having means whereby the vehicle body can pivot around a point on the longitudinal centre-line of the bogie.

Bogie weight is normally kept as low as possible. It consists of two elements: Unsprung weight—carrying forces directly to or from rails, and sprung weight which is all other bogie items supported by metal, plastic, rubber or air springs. Low unsprung weight improves riding by minimizing vertical oscillation. Wheels are usually as small in diameter as possible, consistent with wear—usually 800–900 mm. Lightweight wheel centres have been used, but opinion on their performance varies widely. Bogie weight is normally not more than 30% of the total weight.

Earlier bogies had axleboxes sliding freely up and down within a wear-resistant lined slot in the bogie sideframes. Bearing life is improved and torsional stresses are reduced by having a positive connection between axlebox and sideframe in line with the sideframe. Spring and damper systems need space outside or inside the sideframes. The in-line philosophy is now achieved by using primary rubber-steel laminate springs. Bogie moments of inertia about vertical and lateral axes through the centre of gravity should be minimised to reduce inertial forces and improve riding behaviour. Riding is improved by minimum bogie wheelbase, minimum total weight and elimination of headstocks of substantial weight. To avoid excessive lateral acceleration on tangent track, and poor angle of attack between wheel flange and rail on curves wheelbases usually fall within the range 2,300–2,600 mm.

Heavy rail vehicles commonly use helical coil spring primary suspensions with suitable oscillation damping devices. Primary suspension between unspring and sprung parts of a bogie require a damping factor of 0·4–0·5 to deal with oscillations over switches, crossings and rail joints. Coil springs require hydraulic damping systems matched to the spring characteristics. Secondary suspension supports the bogie bolster, and requires a damping factor of 0·2–0·25. Particulars of some passenger vehicle bogies are given in Table 6.

TABLE 6.—PASSENGER COACH BOGIES.

Railway	Wheel-base mm	Sprung Weight t	Unspring Weight t	Tare Load Deflection		Distance between suspension elements across bogie		Link	
				Primary Suspension mm	Secondary Suspension mm	Primary mm	Secondary mm	Length mm	Angle
British Rail Mk 1	2591	3·5	2·7	81	71	1970	1500	452	2°25′
British Rail B4	2591	2·95	2·1	40	90	1980	1980	—	—
French Railways	2300	2·3	3·2	65	122	1970	1970	—	—
Belgian Railways	2700	2·34	2·53	71	110	1956	2021	275	6°40′
German Railways	2500	3	2·5	62	116	2000	1970	610	0
Italian Railways	2400	3	2·7	92·5	89	2000	1590	435	0
Swiss Railways	2500	1·95	1·95	95	76	1956	1840	380	7°
Danish Railways	2500	3	2·7	64	113	2000	1950	600	8°30′
Dutch Railways	2750	3	2·7	86	70	1956	1700	500	11°20′

Total deflection at tare when static should range between 150–180 mm. The distribution of deflection between primary and secondary suspension elements is chosen to suit the bogie and body weights and the lateral spacings of primary (l_1) and secondary (l_2) suspension elements. Usually between 100–125 mm (around 60%) of the total deflection is allocated to the secondary suspension. When maximum body loads are high it is essential to ensure that bogie or body components do not foul loading gauge or platform limits. This may entail non-linear suspension characteristics.

For passenger comfort the natural frequency of the secondary suspension is best at one Hertz. It is now common to achieve this by using air-bag springs. These are particularly effective with the high payload to tare ratios such as are found on urban and suburban vehicles. Swing links are not laterally restrained at their points of support, hence knife-edge supports are used. Free lateral and fore-and-aft motion permits meeting bolster to check plate clearances. Links at each side should be as close as feasible, possibly replaced by a single link at each side to minimize fore-and-aft body shuttle oscillation due to bogie pitching. A swing link length l of about 500 mm has ben found best. An inevitable difference between the knife-edge radius r_k and the supporting bearing surface R_b produces a significant effect on the *effective* link length l_e.

$$l_e = \frac{(l + R_b - r_k)^2}{[l + (R_b^2/e) + (r_k^2/e)]}$$

where $e = R_b - r_k$.

If $l = 500$ mm, $r_k = 5$ mm and $R_b = 6$ mm, then:

$$l_e = (500 + 6 - 5)^2/(500 + 6^2/l + 5^2/l) = 447 \text{ mm}.$$

Provided stressing permits, the lateral elasticity of the secondary suspension may increase the effective length of swing links by up to 120 mm. As shown in Fig. 10, if a king pin is fitted in a suitable position in the bogie

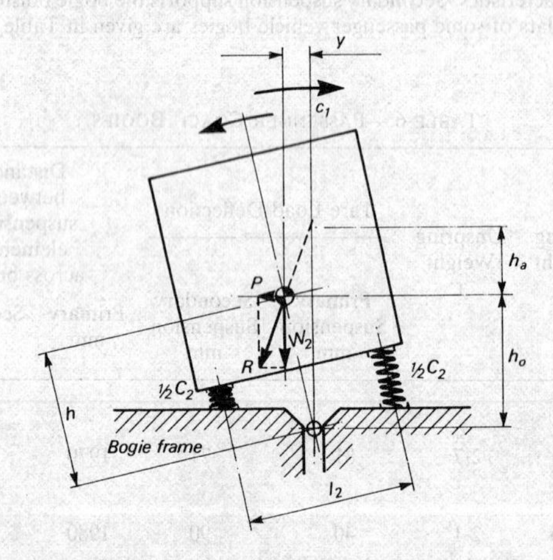

FIG. 10.—Simple Secondary Suspension Design Relying on Body Roll to Deal with Lateral Forces.

frame then the lateral suspension elasticity can replace swing links due to the effect of the distance from the king pin to the body centre of gravity. Here, helical springs can deal with vertical, lateral and rotational motions caused both by bogie nosing and running through curves. This is simple, reduces weight and minimises maintenance. Some effects on excitation of tuning suspension systems are shown in Fig. 11.

The fore-and-aft motion of bolsters is normally restrained by check plates. Loading on the swing links holds the bolster in an equilibrium position when the vehicle is stationary. If the check plates are properly located, contact with the bolster does not occur often. Improperly located check plates lead to frequent contact and body judder. Lateral excitation can usually be minimised by maintaining leading and trailing axles parallel as far as possible.

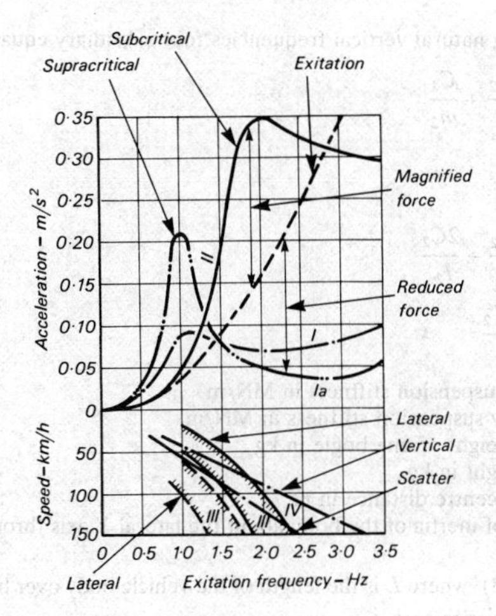

FIG. 11.—Action of Sub-critical and Supra-critical Suspension Design. (I.—Acceleration of Sprung Mass with Normal Frequency of 1 Hz. Ia. Unduly low damping. II.—Acceleration of sprung mass with natural frequency of 2 Hz. III.—Wheelset frequencies. IV.—Vertical excitation frequency.)

Bogie to body rotational torque is determined by:

$$\text{Torque} = [(0{\cdot}03 \text{ to } 0{\cdot}04) \text{ Axle load}(KN) \times \text{Wheelbase}(m)] \text{ in kNm.}$$

This has been found to give adequate rotational damping with minimal wheel flange wear and no significant risks of derailment on curve or on twisted track at low payloads.

Suspension Design.—Good suspension design aims for comfortable riding, no perceptible resonances at operational speeds and smooth damping of transient accelerations. Vertical excitation occurs at rail joints and at welds and at mid-length of rail lengths. If the track is made of 12·5 m lengths of rail about 40% of the vertical excitation is due to joints. Rail lengths 25 m have about 30% mid-length excitation, with 17% rail joint excitation and 10% excitation at one-third and two-thirds along the rail between joints. Maximum vertical excitation amplitude is about 6 mm on good track and 15 mm on poor track. The nature of vertical excitations is illustrated in Fig. 12, and is complicated by changes in tyre conicity with wheel wear.

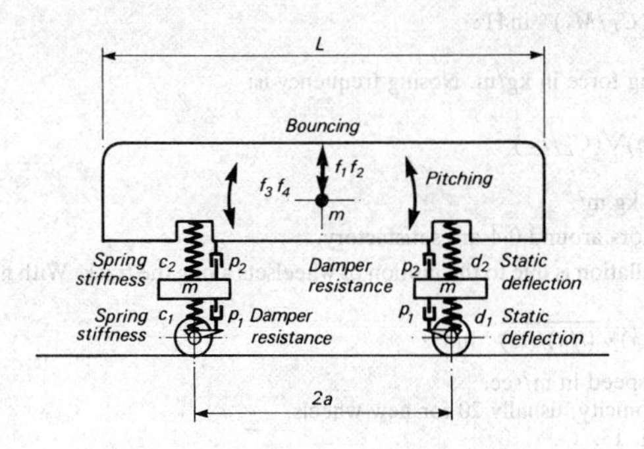

FIG. 12.—Bouncing and Pitching of Vehicle Body.

As an aid to calculating natural vertical frequencies four subsidiary equations are used.

$$A = \frac{C_1 + C_2}{2m_1} + \frac{C_2}{m_2}$$

$$B = \frac{2C_1C_2}{m_1m_2}$$

$$C = \frac{C_1 + C_2}{2m_1} + \frac{2C_2}{I_{2y}}$$

$$D = \frac{2a^2C_1C_2}{m_1I_{2y}}$$

where C_1 is the primary suspension stiffness in MN/m
C_2 is the secondary suspension stiffness in MN/m
m_1 is the sprung weight of one bogie in kg
m_2 is the body weight in kg
a is half the bogie centre distance in m
I_{2y} is the moment of inertia of the body about the lateral Y axis through the centre of gravity in kg m^2. Its value is

$I_{2y} = m_2(L/3)^2$ where L is the length of the vehicle body over headstocks in metres.

Then the bouncing frequencies are:

$$f_1 = \frac{1}{2\pi}\sqrt{A + (A - B)^{1/2}} \quad \text{in Hz}$$

$$f_2 = \frac{1}{2\pi}\sqrt{A - (A - B)^{1/2}} \quad \text{in Hz}$$

and the pitching frequencies are:

$$f_3 = \frac{1}{2\pi}\sqrt{C + (C - D)^{1/2}} \quad \text{in Hz}$$

$$f_4 = \frac{1}{2\pi}\sqrt{C - (C - D)^{1/2}} \quad \text{in Hz}$$

Best performance will be achieved when a primary damping factor of 0·4–0·5 is used with a secondary damping factor of 0·2–0·25. These give a total sprung damping factor of 0·15–0·25 for the whole vehicle.

It has been observed by test running that the side-to-side wavelength of the wheel and bogie path varies between 15 and 25 metres. In addition, if the bogie centre distance is around 18 metres the body oscillates laterally, but when the bogie centre distance reaches 20 metres nosing begins.

Coach bodies oscillate on the swing links about radius r in Fig. 13. Using the lengths shown in Fig. 13 this radius is:

$$r = a(al - 2bh)^2/(l^2f^2 - b^3l - 4ab^2h)$$

The natural frequency of lateral body oscillation is

$$f = \frac{1}{2\pi}\sqrt{(C_L/M_1)} \quad \text{in Hz}$$

and C_L is total centering force in kg/m. Nosing frequency is:

$$\frac{F}{N} = (a/2\pi)\sqrt{(C_L/I_{22})}$$

where $I_{22} = m_2(l/3)^2$ in kg m^2.

Lateral damping factors around 0·4 are satisfactory.

Horizontal plane oscillation is due to the motion of wheelsets along the track. With new wheels the frequency is:

$$f_w = (v/2\pi)\sqrt{(l/n)/(rs)} \quad \text{in Hz}$$

where v is the vehicle speed in m/sec.
n is the wheel conicity, usually 20 for new wheels.
l is shown in Fig. 13.
r is also shown in Fig. 13.
s is half the distance between the rolling circles of the wheels in m.

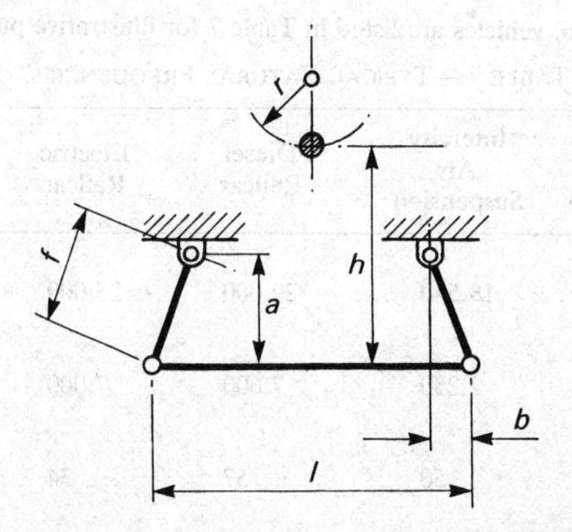

FIG. 13.—Effective Swing Link Length of Inclined Links.

After 30,000–50,000 km wear on the tyre treads varies the conicity. Lateral and vertical displacements must be considered in relation to the railway loading gauge. Wheel and bogie component wear may influence vehicle clearances in operation. Maximum body roll displacement, illustrated in Fig. 14, is normally 125 mm on each

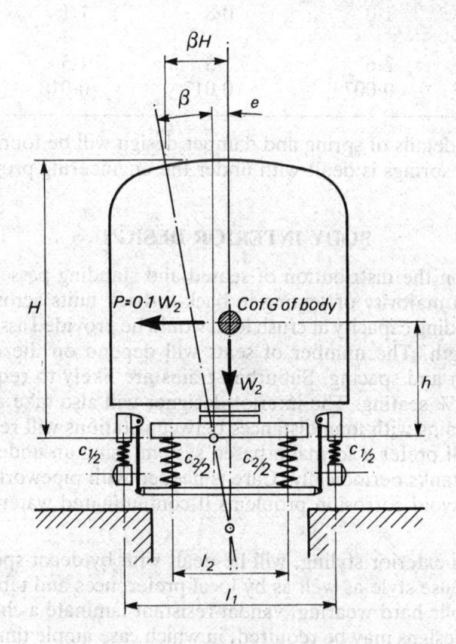

FIG. 14.—Body Roll Displacement.

side of the vertical centre-line. Wear of about 20 mm will reduce this tolerance to 105 mm. Body roll displacement implies an unbalanced lateral load equivalent to one-tenth of the body weight. This acts through the body centre of gravity.

Body roll is resisted by both primary and secondary suspension elastic elements. Primary suspension roll resistance component is:

$$C_a = C_2 l_1/2 \text{ in kg } m/\text{rad.}$$

Similarly, secondary suspension roll resistance component is:

$$C_b = C_2 l_2/2 \text{ also in kg } m/\text{rad.}$$

Here, C_1 is the vertical stiffness of the primary suspension, C_2 that of the secondary suspension, Lengths l_1 and l_2 are shown in Fig. 14. Combined stiffness, including both bogies is:

$$C_t = (\tfrac{1}{2})(C_1 l_1^2)^2/(C_1 l_1^2 + C2 l_1^2) \text{ in kg } m/\text{rad.}$$

Natural frequencies of typical vehicles are listed in Table 7 for illustrative purposes.

TABLE 7.—TYPICAL NATURAL FREQUENCIES.

	Intercity Air Suspension	Diesel Railcar	Electric Railcar	Unmotored Trailer
Body Weight (kg)	18,540	29,000	25,000	18,300
Bogie Sprung Weight (kg)	2,250	7,600	7,000	3,100
Primary Deflection (mm)	50	57	34	51
Secondary Deflection (mm)	125	93	100	77
Maximum Bouncing (H2)	5·6	4·5	5·0	5·5
Maximum Pitching (H2)	5·8	4·5	5·1	5·6
Nosing (H2)	1·0	0·8	1·1	1·0
Maximum Sway (H2)	2·6	1·5	1·5	1·6
Roll (radian)	0·007	0·017	0·018	0·016

Springs and Dampers.—Full details of spring and damper design will be found elsewhere in this Yearbook. Rubber used in springs and air springs is dealt with under the engineering properties of rubber.

BODY INTERIOR DESIGN

Initially, a decision is made on the distribution of seated and standing passengers. Trains carrying people for long distances will require a majority of seating in back-to-back units across the vehicle with a gangway space for access. Additional standing capacity at crush load would be provided assuming, probably, 2 passengers per metre of compartment length. The number of seats will depend on the compartment dimensions and railway standards for seat width and spacing. Suburban trains are likely to require about 50% seating area. Mass transit trains may have 25% seating. The interior designer will also take account of any requirement to carry wheelchair passengers. Trains with long distances between stations will require vehicle fitted lavatories. Modern sanitary regulations will prefer a formalin based system using an underframe mounted settling tank fitted with means for emptying tanks periodically. Care is needed with pipework, pumps, fittings and tanks to minimise leakage risks and to avoid corrosion problems if contaminated water (such as seawater) is used to refill flush tanks.

Interior design, together with exterior styling, will be dealt with by decor specialists. Colour combinations may be dictated by a railway house style as well as by local preferences and taboos. Where large surfaces are covered with a melamine-phenolic hard-wearing, vandal-resistant laminate a choice may be made of standard designs. Alternatively, special designs may be required, in which case ample time must be allowed for printing the coloured paper laminated immediately below the clear melamine layer. In view of long term maintenance over about 30 years it is wise to consider simple standard colours and designs to assist maintenance colour matching. Similar considerations will apply to painted and self-coloured surfaces. Painted surfaces should use materials resistant to damage and cleaning. Self-colour plastics should be chosen so that methods of repair are simple and damage-resistant. The edge of a coin firmly scraped along a surface is a common means of selection.

Floor coverings must be extremely hard-wearing. Carpet is popular in some countries and railways, usually wool or a wool-composite. Flame-retardant rubbers are used in many railways. Polyvinylchloride (PVC) is a very practical type of floor covering, but its use is being challenged in view of both the release of hydrogen chloride by fire or modest heat and the migration of pigments in certain environmental conditions. Where fire was rigidly controlled a floor covering consisting of heavily sand filled rubber proved acceptable.

Seating used on trains implies consideration of the contribution of seat elasticity and comfort to passenger satisfaction. An un-upholstered stainless steel bench type seat used longitudinally on a mass transit train was surprisingly comfortable. Metal or reinforced plastic seat frames are now common. From then, a choice tends to be one of springs with padding, similar with an upper foam layer, block foam (possibly with a flame-retardant interlayer around), relatively thin strong foam, etc. With foams two factors are important, maximum fatigue behaviour to BS 3157, and an acceptable fire behaviour to BS 5852 using large wood crib fire sources. Seat coverings vary considerably, wool moquettes being popular, although more easily cleaned versions are also used. Leather is still in use, and simulated leather-cloths are also used. The natural frequency of seated passengers is normally restricted to 3Hz, with a damping factor of 0·25.

Vehicle lighting is a specialist subject. (See chapter J2).

TRACTION EQUIPMENT

Passenger vehicle mounted traction equipment is either underfloor mounted diesel engines or wholly electric motor traction. The choice of traction system, that is, motive power, control and transmission elements must depend on the local conditions and resources of the railway. Conventionally, a consultant specializing in railway engineering makes a systems study of the economics of operating the rail system and recommends a traction system.

Electric traction has many economic advantages, but necessitates a high capital investment in fixed electrical equipment. Fixed installations need to be amortized over an operational lifetime of 20–30 years. Another factor is that the high investment in track equipment implies that electric traction has less route versatility than diesel. A common economic measure of operating efficiency is:

Train Productivity (passenger annual kilometres)
= Average Passengers per Train
× Average Train Speed (km/hr) × Percent Availability
× Annual Working Days.

Most of these factors will be the same for both electric and for diesel traction. The availability of electric traction, however, is about 90%, compared to diesel of 80%. Some studies suggested that operationally 25 electric trains are equivalent to 40 diesel trains of the same passenger capacity.

Diesel Traction.—The rugged simplicity of diesel-engined trains and their initial capital outlay economy are attractive to new railways and where limited resources must be spent wisely. Traction diesel engines are usually defined by reference to BS 2953 and UIC 623-OR. There is a tendency to emphasise long operational life and high reliability at the expense of low running costs and easy maintainability.

On diesel multiple units the engines are controlled to achieve an optimum combination of driving power and de-clutched idling to take advantage of fuel economy by coasting.

Diesel traction is commonly by horizontal 6-cylinder engines of 375 kW output. Power is normally taken directly from the crankshaft through a fluid connection and reduction gearbox. A cardan shaft is usually interposed to compensate for relative suspension motion between engine and bogie frame mounted gearbox. Another cardan shaft connects to the axle-mounted final drive. Drive for auxiliary equipment may be taken from a suitable point by belt, shaft or electrical systems.

Intake air speed needs to be controlled not to exceed 60 m/s to avoid significant loss of output power. Cylinder compressions of 10 MPa have been found best. This is taken into account in engine design since there is also a high thermal load to be dissipated by cooling. Efficient cooling is essential to remove some 60% of the cylinder energy lost as waste heat. Restrictions on size and weight dictate a compact cooling system. Pressurisation to 0·3–0·7 bar increases heat capacity and permits substantial space savings. To avoid erosion the cooling water flow is limited to one litre per minute, and water temperatures are aimed at 80°C. Corrosion inhibitors are added to the cooling water. To increase cooling efficiency fans fitted downstream of the cooler/radiator save 40% fan power while giving 50% more cooling capacity.

Main engine lubricant oil is usually pumped at 200–400 kPa. Valve gear is lubricated at 30–70 kPa. Oil and air are filtered to reduce wear, in the case of oil particles greater than 10–15 microns are filtered out. Water entry into the engine is minimised by siting engine air intake as high as feasible above rail level.

Electric Traction.—The main feature of motors for electric multiple-unit trains is a relatively small size for the power output and low weight. Motors must operate in very arduous environments with high reliability. It is usual to use the highest input voltage consistent with power supply limitations.

Power supply choices depend on system requirements. Alternating current is superior for high energy and long transmission distances, and voltages are quite easy to change. Direct current requires generating capacity, but has superior power development. Voltages are limited, but where start and stop occurs frequently DC gives excellent traction quickly.

Voltage choices vary, but 600 volts DC is often found. 1500 volts AC is also common. There is, of course, more readily available AC than DC. DC motors are limited to 2,500 kW; above this AC must be used.

Power to the train is collected by pantograph from overhead catenary wires on AC systems. Some AC and all DC power is collected by sliding collector shoes at, or near rail level. Linear motors carry the traction power items on a linear track, and lower energy demand magnets in the motor and lift magnets on the vehicle. Linear motors are considerably less efficient than conventional motors. Their use is now mainly confined to magnetically levitated vehicles, although during winter linear motor traction is more certain than wheel on rail.

A common configuration is for one side of traction motors to be flexibly mounted on the bogie frame. To maintain gearbox contact the other side of the motor is pivoted on the axle, or mounted on an axle-tube (quill) around the axle between the wheels.

Class H electrical insultion is used in traction motors. Armature design is, of course, dictated by the rail gauge. Traction performance is defined in IEC 165.

BRAKE SYSTEMS

A well designed brake system is essential to the safe operation of a train and to its overall performance. Excessive acceleration or deceleration forces, often in combination with gravity, can take control of a train with disastrous effects on stability. Passenger trains were legally required to have automatic brake systems since a non-automatic brake failure at Armagh in 1889 caused part of a train to separate and run away on a slope, finally colliding with the remainder of the train.

Steel wheels on steel track depend upon the adhesion between wheels and track surfaces. This is equivalent to the coefficient of friction and varies slightly, but is normally taken to be 0·15. An implication of this is that any force opposing wheel rotation must not cause decelerations which lead to wheel to rail longitudinal forces which exceed the downward force of friction. Excessive horizontal force in the running direction leads to wheel *slide*. The converse is where rotational forces exceed frictional forces and result in wheel *slip*. Braking forces need to be controlled so that neither wheel slip nor slide occurs.

Brake system designers have two primary considerations in mind:

(1) to provide automatic brake operation in the event of a sytem failure or accidental damage.
(2) to provide means for controlling brake application forces capable of controlling wheel rotational forces or deceleration forces.

A generalised stopping distance graph is shown in Fig. 15. The maximum retardation achievable from a given brake power at full operational pressure will be subject to limitation by the available adhesion. To ensure acceptably smooth braking and also to minimise stresses, due to braking differences between vehicles in a train, brake application and release timings must be carefully phased. On a short close-coupled train the time to maximum brake pressure may be 5 seconds, while on a longer train elastically coupled pressure build may take up to 30 seconds for even retardation.

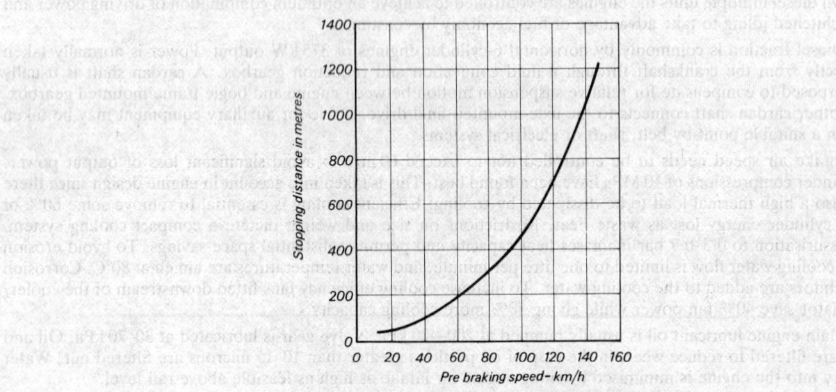

FIG. 15.—Typical Electro-pneumatic Braking Curve.

Rates of application and release of brakes influence passenger comfort. Even standing passengers can adapt to high uniform retardation rates. Sudden changes of deceleration rate cause considerable discomfort, particularly to standing or moving passengers. Changes in rates of acceleration or deceleration are called '*jerk*'. Maximum jerk is usually accepted to be 0·45 m/s^3, although much lower values are common in design practice. Electronic systems can be programmed to control both retardation and changes in acceleration/deceleration within required acceptance limits. Modern electronic control systems permit simultaneous operation of brakes throughout a train. On mass transit systems brake operation tends to be electro-pneumatic, where trains run at short headways.

Vacuum braking made use of the natural vacuum used in steam locomotives. It is gradually disappearing, but is still in use in some countries and on private steam hauled railways. Modern passenger trains are compressed air braked. It is not intended to discuss vacuum brakes here.

In both vacuum and air brakes kinetic energy is converted into heat energy by friction of brake shoes or pads. Earlier cast iron brake shoes have now been replaced by proprietary friction compounds. Separate axle-mounted discs are being discontinued in favour of pads acting on the wheel rim.

Brake Forces and Performance.—The brake operating pressure must be matched to the retardation rate required, or to the specified stopping distance. Drivers can regulate the maximum level of braking power of the train. Distribution of the brake power along the train is automatically controlled in accordance with the load condition of each vehicle, and in accordance with the speed of the train. Precautions are taken during brake system design so that at no time can the wheels be locked by applying too much brake power.

Low power braking is called *single stage* braking, and is driver operated for low rate braking or minor speed adjustments. The brake power is such that the wheels will not lock when the vehicle is empty. As the loading of the vehicle increases the ratio of brake force to total vehicle weight reduces, and this increases stopping distances. Increase of vehicle weight raises the adhesion and hence reduces risk of wheel slide.

When the brake power falls below 35% of the total weight of the vehicle provision is usually made for increasing the braking force in accordance with the weight to be stopped. Figure 16 indicates how an automatic load-weighing device increase the brake force back to its original value above 80% of the vehicle weight. This is of particular importance when designing brake systems for mass transit trains.

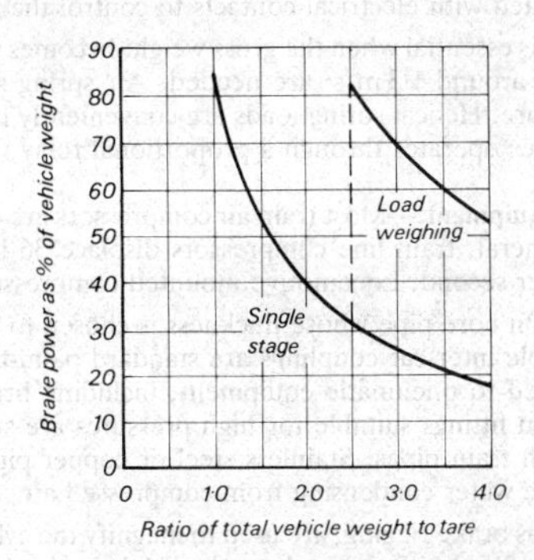

FIG. 16.—Effect of Vehicle Weight on Brake Power to Weight Proportion.

Speed control of brake power was inconsistent with cast iron brake blocks whose coefficient of friction on steel wheels varied between 0·3 and 0·06, depending on vehicle speed. Frictional composites based on synthetic resins with fibre filling having much more uniform friction coefficients have now superseded cast iron on passenger rolling stock. Another feature of speed controlled braking is that loss of adhesion is eliminated during high speed braking so that damage to wheels and rails is minimised. By absorbing energy in electric traction equipment operated in reverse (dynamic braking) it is possible to brake very fast trains.

Air Brake Systems.—In the simplest air brake system, originally invented by George Westinghouse in 1872 compressed air was fed into a reservoir, and from there into a train pipe which operated the brake cylinders under manual control. The response time was slow and further equipment was needed to improve braking performance.

Passenger trains used on main lines use a graduated release automatic brake capable of allowing small adjustments in brake cylinder pressure (brake power or force). Auxiliary reservoirs are used so that main brake pipe pressure is maintained. To overcome slightly slow response a second air pipe is added so that better control of brake function can be achieved. Through pipe systems, whether one-pipe or two-pipe, do result in some loss of brake power along the train.

With multiple-unit trains which are firmly coupled precise control of braking is essential to avoid overstressing underframe components. Fortunately it is easy to provide interconnections for electrical control of the pneumatic systems. Simultaneous operation of brakes is carried out by one of two systems of EP (electro-pneumatic) braking. The indirect system uses the main through train pipe air pressure to open individual vehicle brakes. Instead of opening the train pipe to atmosphere to apply brakes, each vehicle has an electrically operated valve which isolates the train pipe and opens the individual vehicle brake pipes to air. In the other, direct system each vehicle carries an air reservoir charged from the main train pipe. Electrical controls are used to admit air for vehicle reservoirs and to isolate reservoirs while opening the brake cylinder piping to air.

Controls on direct systems can be very sophisticated, using electronic systems to provide accurate control of brake pressures. This permits vehicle load weighing to be used in conjunction with train speed sensors to provide coded signals to the brake controller.

Dynamic Braking.—In dynamic braking electric traction motors are electrically organised so that they become, in effect, generators feeding current back into the traction power system. This absorbs energy and slows a train, but friction brakes are still needed to halt a train. Dynamic braking is normal on multiple-unit rolling stock to provide control during coasting. To bring a train to a controlled halt at a station the brake pressure on friction brakes must be reduced to avoid wheel locking. For safe operation the current generated by the dynamic braking is measured and its retardation effect used to control the pneumatic pressure necessary for a specified rate of deceleration. Blending of dynamic and friction brake effects is carried out by either detecting the presence of a rheostatic brake capable of considerable retardation and then applying just sufficient air pressure for the brake shoes to contact wheel or disc surfaces; or if the dynamic retardation is limited then it is monitored so that supplementary air pressure can be controlled. Blending is then carried out by electronically converting regenerated current levels into equivalent friction brake pressures and controlling air pressure to give the remaining brake force needed.

Load Composition.—Mass transit trains operate on short headways (time between trains) so changes in gross to tare weight ratio are important. One technique is to monitor the retardation on the basis that high brake forces equate to high retardations.

Then by setting maximum limit on retardation it is possible to prevent wheel slide. Retardation is measured by mercury in a toroidal tube fitted with electrical contacts to control the air pressure.

Separate weighing of each car is essential when the gross weight becomes more than 1·5 times the tare weight of the vehicle, and retardations around 1·3 m/s^2 are needed. Air spring secondary suspensions permit load weighing by measuring air pressure. Helical spring loads are conveniently monitored by measuring deflection. Stepwise control of braking forces operates through a proportional relay valve or code system.

Air Compressors and Brake Equipment.—Most train air compressors are either driven from the diesel engine or from electrical power. In general, train line compressors displace 36 litres per second and multiple unit compressors displace 12 litres per second. Locomotive mounted compressors are much larger.

Air brake piping is often 25 mm bore pipe whose thickness is chosen to give about 2·5 times the maximum brake operating pressure. Flexible inter-car couplings are standard palm-type fittings. Smaller pipes, usually 12 mm bore are used for air feed to pneumatic equipment, including brake cylinders where vehicle brake reservoirs are used. Compression fittings suitable for high pressures are suitable for small pipes, but brazed fittings are preferred for through train pipes. Stainless steel or copper pipes are common. Pipe systems are fitted with water traps to remove water condensing from compressed air.

Lever mechanisms, described as brake rigging, are used to magnify the cylinder pressure. These are normally heavy steel components, probably fitted with sintered metal self-lubricating bearings. Brake shoes were formerly white cast iron, but are now almost exclusively filled resin compositions to reduce noise and iron-dust pollution. Separate brake discs are usually parallel cast iron rings mounted on an axle-mounted steel hub.

Magnetic Track Brakes.—On high speed trains where there could be difficulty in decelerating without wheel slide it is becoming common to use magnetic track brakes. A battery of electromagnets is mounted on each side of the bogies on a bar immediately above the track running surfaces. In operation the magnets are energised and pneumatically lowered on to the track. Power consumption for a 24 V magnet system is between 1·0 and 1·2 kW/m length of linked magnets. At train speeds above 100 kilometres per hour the braking force is a fairly constant 5 kN.

HEATING AND VENTILATION

The internal environment within a rail vehicle will depend on the requirements of a railway and the ability of heating and ventilation equipment to deal with extremes of external environment. For illustrative purposes a passenger coach 20 m long, 2·5 m body width and 2 m internal body height will be used. This has an interior volume of 100 cubic metres. It is proposed to use an internal temperature of 16°C and a minimum exterior temperature of −4°C. The temperature difference is, therefore, 20°C.

Heat losses occur by thermal energy interactive transfer in which heat reaches surfaces predominantly by convection and radiation and is then conducted to a cooler region by conduction through bounding surfaces. At normal ambient temperature the thermal properties of constructional materials are sufficiently constant for design calculation. When radiated energy is low compared to convection and conduction it is possible to use heat flow rate $\dot{Q}$ in proportional to the temperature difference across a bounding surface ΔT and to the thermally exposed area A. The proportionally constant, or heat transfer coefficient, is now described as a U value. Then:

$$\dot{Q} = U \, . \, A \, . \, \Delta T$$

where U is in W/m^{2}C.

In the absence of accurately calculated U-values, (See Chapter J1), approximations are permissible for early design estimates. It is taken that for the vehicle roof U = 0·35 W/m^2 °C. About 15% of wall surface area may be assumed to be glazed, for single thickness glazing U = 5·7 w/M^2 °C, and for double glazing U = 3·0 W/m^2 °C. Thus, an initial estimate for the illustrative example would be:

Situation	U-Value W/m^2 °C	Area m^2	ΔT °C	Heat Flow kW
Roof	0·35	50	20	0·35
Walls and Ends	0·6	90	20	1·08
Double Glazing	3·0	14	20	0·84
Floor	1·0	50	10	0·50
				2·77

In addition, heat is lost from air removed from the vehicle by ventilation. An absolute minimum for breathing is 7 cubic metres per person per hour. Higher values are actually used as will be noted later. If there are 2 persons per square metre, then the vehicle of 50 m^2 floor area will carry 100 passengers. These will need 700 cubic metres of air per hour to replace breathed air. The vehicle volume is 100 m^3, so the ventilation requirement is 7 air changes per hour (ach). Respiration contaminants such as carbon dioxide, water vapour and odorous vapours require an additional 0·00004 cubic metres per hour per passenger. Safety demands an ample clearance, particularly during hot weather:

Pollutants	Air Change/Hour
Non-smoking	10–15
Smoking	15–20
Equipment Rooms	20
Vestibules	10
Cooking	60
Restaurant	20

The normal theoretical volume of the vehicle interior needs to be multiplied by a *permeability* value, usually 0·8, to compensate for the volume of furniture and fittings. The example, with 100 m^3 volume, has an effective volume for calculating air changes of 80 m^3. Vehicles for tropical railways will require greater air change values.

Atmospheric air contains 20·35% oxygen by volume, and 0·03% carbon dioxide. Expired air contains 16·2% oxygen and 3·4% carbon dioxide. For personal comfort carbon dioxide should not exceed 0·08%.

A stationary person breathes about one cubic metre of air per hour. This air volume would imply that 0·034 m^3/hr is expired as carbon dioxide, per passenger. The tabulated recommendations include allowances for expiration.

Heat requirements for air changes must be added to the values already calculated. Assuming 10 ach in the example the volume is 100 m^3, so the air moved amounts to 100 m^3/hr (About 1·2 tonnes per hour). The specific heat capacity of air is 1·26 kJ/m^3, from this it can be calculated that the heating requirement is 2 kW per air change per hour. For non-smoking, cool, occupancy the recommendation is 10 ach that is 20 kW. It is normally assumed that space heating is 25% efficient, so installed heating would be 80 kW.

People evolve body heat at 0·1 kW/hr, so 100 passengers give out 10 kW. To heat one air change per hour requires 2 kW, hence, conversely to remove 2 kW requires one air change per hour. Removal of 10 kW will need 5 air changes per hour during summer months.

Air conditioning controls humidity also, and guidance should be sought from the chapter on heating and ventilation in this Yearbook. Generally, a minimum humidity of 35% and maximum 60% is comfortable, although a slightly lower minimum may be acceptable in winter. Seated passengers on long journeys will find temperatures in the range 21 to 26°C acceptable.

The effect of vehicle speed is to increase heat transfer from the vehicle by a factor

$$F = 0{\cdot}6\ V^{0{\cdot}25}$$

Where V is in km/hr. For 120 km/hr $F = 1{\cdot}98$, that is, heat transfer is doubled and hence the power to compensate for heat loss is also doubled. The illustrative example gave power to allow for heat transfer when stationary as 2·77 kW, at 120 km per hour this is doubled to 5·54 kW, say 6 kW. Then the value of 80 kW for air changes rises to 86 kW at peak demand.

Heating is controlled by either room or duct thermostats. Room thermostats operate through thermally sensitive elements to reduce or increase heater ouput. Some are feedback controlled by a small resistance heater which warms the sensor slightly to avoid excessive rise in compartment temperature before the thermostat cuts off power to heaters. Duct thermostats are either rod type sensor controlled or use a contact sensor. It is important to use accurate thermostats since one degree excess temperature increases the power demand by about 0·5 kW.

For advice on the location and size of ducts and grilles, etc, see chapter J1 on Heating and Ventilation and Air Conditioning.

REVIEW OF VEHICLE MANUFACTURE

On receipt of an enquiry for vehicles the specification is studied in detail. The feasibility of complying with the specification requirements at a competitive cost and within specified time limits is examined. When it is clear that the specification and commercial considerations can be met, further study of the manufacturing technologies is made to lay the foundations for cost estimates. At this point the objective is to prepare a formal descriptive and priced tender for the contract involved.

Based on the specification, sufficient preliminary design is carried out to determine vehicle dimensions, loading parameters, outline structural design and stress estimates, interior layout and important cross-sections. General arrangement drawings are prepared and decor schemes sketched out. Simultaneously, by interchange between departments cost estimates for materials, manpower and resources are carried on. Production route planning and method studies are organised, and preliminary project management documentation is prepared. Detailed analyses are made of resources for management, design, production and financing. Decisions are made on the use of models and mock-ups to aid aesthetic and ergonomic design and to support tendering. Outline quality plans are prepared.

After award of the contract more detailed project planning begins. More design planning is commenced.

Outline network drawing and production plans are prepared and co-ordinated, and purchase lead times are incorporated. Once a project manager or coordinator is appointed the procedures necessary to control design and production change, and for monitoring progress and quality, are established.

The project manager/coordinator keeps track continuously of all documented aspects of the contract, design, production, quality and delivery of vehicles. All letters, reports and other documents relevant to the project are noted and filed. Project review meetings are held periodically.

Drawing Office Procedure.—Before detail design drawings are commenced the drawing office planner and production controller coordinate on critical path networks so that drawings needed for production will be available on time, and to advise buyers when materials, components and assemblies should be ordered to ensure their delivery on time. Schedules of required drawings are prepared, lists of jigs, fixtures and templates are prepared.

Beginning from the planned delivery dates, production and quality control measures are planned from the last operation progressively to the first operation using the critical path network. The time from the end of one operation to its starting point is the basis for the end point of the preceding operation and so on. Account is taken of operations which can be carried out in parallel so that items to be assembled are ready together. Deliveries, with an allowance for delays, are planned so that subcontract supplies arrive in time to be fitted at appropriate stages. Allowance is made for possible quality control rejections. It should be apreciated that planning allows for batches of vehicles to be delivered at suitable intervals throughout the contract.

Plans are made for the availability of draughtsmen (including women) and seniors/supervisors required to produce the planned number of drawings and materials lists to be available at required dates. Supplementary information such as purchasing specifications, works procedures, test procedures, health and safety product data sheets, standard item schedule/specifications, and so on, is prepared continuously as required.

Production Procedure.—Sub-contract work is coordinated with in-house work so that all anticipated assembly problems are clarified. Major machined and formed items are commenced on machines proved to be capable of meeting quality control requirements. Accuracy and repeatability are ensured by templates or numerically controlled machine tools. As far as possible computer aided design and manufacture (CAD-CAM) are used.

Welded sub-assemblies are produced within geometric tolerance envelopes (BS 308 Part 3). Roll-over jigs are used to aid accuracy and accessibility for the optimum type of weld and for fitting sub-assemblies and equipment. Procedures detailing welding data, such as current, speed, wirefeed, etc are used to minimise distortion.

Production depends on a smooth flow of items to the appropriate positions in assembly, and from one assembly stage to the next. Flexible mechanical handling is essential, particularly since many sub-assemblies will weigh more than a tonne. Standardization of components used in bulk is intended to minimise costs as well as to ensure maintenance available.

The earliest stage in assembly is completion of the underframe structure. This is often carried out inverted to aid accessibility. In addition, the fitting of equipment is simplified. Turning the underframe over then permits fitting floor panels. Bodyside, body end and roof sub-assemblies are constructed meanwhile, so that all may arrive simultaneously at a suitable time to produce an assembled body shell.

Glazing, insulation, linings, floor coverings, seats and other interior fittings are added progressively. At planned times wiring and piping are fitted, usually using pre-formed items. Doors are fitted and testing of operation is carried out. Before undue costs have been incurred a high-pressure water-spray test is carried out and any leaks rectified before they become inaccessible.

Painting or other exterior finishing processes are carried out on a planned basis. Early protection of steelwork and assemblies proceeds by stages, initially to protect a carefully prepared surface from oxidation. Later coats are added both to seal joints against moisture penetration and to build film thickness. Finish coats of the correct colour, thickness, gloss, hardness and durability are added, possibly with a consumable overcoating of clear varnish or other protective coating.

Quality control procedures and criteria are imposed at planned states in production. Once final quality clearance has been given, the vehicle is thoroughly cleaned, identification lettering, labels and transfers are added. Finally, the vehicle is prepared for despatch.

Quality Assurance.—Former concepts of product inspection as a collection of imposed tolerances and tests are no longer used. Today, quality assurance in accordance with BS 5750 coupled with reliability assessment in accordance with BS 5760 is normal. (See Chapter D10, Quality Assurance). Briefly, quality assurance accepts that quality begins with the interpretation of customer requirements. All stages of design and information flow are critical to quality. The operative phrase is that quality cannot be inspected into a product after it has been made; quality is designed and controlled by observation of operational processes and personnel skills.

Ultimately, the objectives are to ensure that the vehicle can be operated within the dimensional constraints of the railway structure, and that the vehicle consistently meets operational criteria over the design life of the vehicle. The final quality control stage is commissioning the vehicle by carrying out long-term operating trials and rectifying faults observed during commissioning trials. When the customer has agreed that commissioning is satisfactory, a batch of vehicles is formally handed over for revenue operation. Such acceptance may, at agreed periods, trigger part payment of contract moneys.

CONCLUDING REMARKS.—It will be understood that the present treatment of the engineering aspects of rail vehicle construction is not intended as a comprehensive design manual. As far as has been possible, the objective has been to produce an aide-memoire using the best available background information.

Broadly, the plan adopted was to proceed by outlining the effects of rail systems on train performance for passenger service. Various aspects of design follow. Traction is dealt with briefly, mainly based on railcar methods. Locomotives are not covered here. Braking and train formation are also dealt with briefly. The interior environment is dealt with in accordance with recognised standards.

Safety and reliability are dealt with in outline form. A short description of vehicle services is included.

Finally, a review of vehicle manufacture is given. This is based on an analysis carried out for a vehicle builder. Quality assurance is briefly described since it is now accepted practice.

It has not been possible to deal with some topics in adequate detail but further information may be found in the Bibliography. The References included have been chosen primarily either for their treatment of a topic, or because of their historical interest. No claim is made that the References are by any means comprehensive. Much valuable contemporary information is usually well reported in *Railway Gazette*.

BIBLIOGRAPHY

ALBERT, H. and RAQUET, E., '*Testing Noise-damped Wheels on Hamburger Hochbahn*,' Railway Engineer International, 5 (6) 51; 1980.

ALLENDER, P. J., '*A Survey of the Development of Fire Safety Regulations for Railways*,' Fire Safety Journal, 8 (1), 15; 1984.

BAKER, R. G., '*Testing for quality and reliability*,' Metals and Materials, 2 (5), 262; 1986.

BARWELL, F. T., '*Tribology of the Action of Wheel upon Rail*,' Railway Engineer Intermnational, 8 (4), 101; 1979.

BOTHAM, G. J. M., '*The Glasgow Underground—Design, Development and Construction of the New Cars*,' Railway Engineer, 3 (3), 23; 1978.

BROCKWAY, K. P. '*Aluminium Technology and Railway Rolling Stock*,' J. I. Loco. E., 50 (272); 1960.

BROWN, J. and DAVIDSON, R., '*Effects of Track Construction on Vibration and Noise in the Glasgow Underground*,' Railway Engineer, 4 (2), 43; 1979.

CHAPRONT, P., '*Automatic Train Driving—the Jeumont-Schneider System*,' Railway Engineer, 4 (5), 55; 1979.

COLLINS, A. M., '*The Environmental Impact of Railways*,' Railway Engineer, 4 (5), 49; 1979.

COOK, B. E., WARD, R. J. and SILVERLOCK, P. P., '*The Cleaning of Railway Rolling Stock*', I. Mech. E. Railway Division Journal, 1 (1), 62; 1970.

COX, E. S., '*Some Problems in Vehicle Riding*,' J. I. Loco. E., 52 (283), 574; 1962.

DAVIS, B., '*Rubber rides on Europe's rails*,' European Rubber Journal, 168 (5) 9; 1986.

DAVIS, W. J., '*Train Resistance Formulae*,' General Electric Review, 29, 685; 1926.

FOSTER, G., '*Welding of Cast Iron and Steel Components in Locomotive Manufacture and Maintenance*,' J. I. Loco. E, 45 (2), 158; 1955.

GABB, W. C. and LEIGH, M. J., '*The Glasgow Underground—Automatic Propulsion and Braking Control System*,' Railway Engineer, 3 (6), 43; 1978.

GAWTHORPE, R. G., '*Aerodynamics of Trains in the Open Air*,' Railway Engineer, 3 (3), 7; 1978.

GAWTHORPE, R. G., '*Aerodynamic Problems with Overhead Line Equipment*,' Railway Engineer, 3 (4), 38; 1978.

GRANT, J. C., '*Rapid Transit Energy Demand*,' Railway Engineer, 1 (4), 14; 1976.

HAWTHORNE, B. J., '*Development of the Use of Plastics in Railways Rolling Stock*,' I. Mech. E. Railway Division Journal, 1 (5), 491; 1970.

HIGTON, J. A. '*Bogie Design for Rapid Transit Vehicles*,' Railway Engineer, 4 (3) 47; 1979.

HILL, R. F. and ALLENDER, P. J., '*Developments in Construction and Materials used in Passenger-Carrying Rolling Stock*,' Railway Engineer International 5 (3), 22; 1984.

HOLLINGBURY, P. L., '*Acceleration and Passenger Comfort in High-Performance Rapid Transit Vehicles*,' Railway Engineer, 4 (2), 51; 1979.

HORNE, J. R. and SHOOTER, A., '*High Speed Trains Present Maintenance and Servicing Problems*,' Railway Engineer, 3 (4), 33; 1978.

HURST, J. K., '*Control of Welding Standards: Construction of Locomotives and Rolling Stock*,' Railway Engineer, 4 (1), 52; 1979.

JARVIS, J. M., '*Fire precautions in Locomotives and Rolling Stock*,' I. Mech. E. Railway Division Journal, 2 (2), 94; 1971.

KILSHAW, N. C. and STABLES, J. R., '*Inspection and Testing for New Railway Locomotives and Rolling Stock*,' Railway Engineer, 4 (1), 49; 1979.

KOFFMAN, J. L., '*Air Springs as Applied to Heavy Suburban Multiple-Unit Vehicles*,' J. I. Loco. E. 53 (295); 1964.

KOFFMAN, J. L., '*Design for Comfort*,' J. I. Loco. E, 57 (319); 1968.

KREISSIG, E., '*The Design of Light-Weight Railway Rolling Stock*,' J. I. Loco. E., 40 (216), 4; 1950.

LEA, N. D. and ASSOCIATES INC. 'Light Rail Transit Car Specification Guide,' Report UMTA-MA-06-0025-81-4, Washington: Urban Mass Transportation Administration; 1981.

MACLEOD, W. H., '*Some Features of Rail Curving*,' J. I. Loco. E., 45 (2), 204; 1955.

MARSH, G. M. and SHARP, A. C., '*The Development of Railway Brakes*,' Railway Engineering Journal, 2 (1), 46; 1973.

Ministry of Transport, *Railway Construction and Operation Requirements for Passenger Lines and Recommendations for Goods Lines*, London: HMSO; 1950.

MURRAY, C. L., '*Wheelslip and the APT*,' Railway Engineer, 3 (2), 22; 1978.

NFPA 130, *Standard for Fixed Guideway Transit Systems*, Quincy Mass. USA National Fire Protection Association; 1982.

NOUVION, F., '*The Problems of High-Speed Transport on French Railways*,' J. Mech. E. Railway Division Journal, 1 (5), 595; 1970.

POCKINGTON, A. R. and ALLEN, R. A., '*Improved Data from Load-measuring Wheels*,' Railway Engineer, 2 (4), 37; 1977.

RAWLE, D. L., '*Recent Traction Motor Developments*,' Railway Engineer, 2 (6), 36; 1977.

ROBERTSON, A. S., '*Trends in Electric Traction*,' J. I. Loco. E., 40 (215), 304; 1950.

SERGEANT, V., '*Auxiliary Electrical Supplies for Passenger Coaches*,' Railway Engineering Journal, 2(1), 14; 1973.

SIMPSON, T. F. B., '*Diesel Locomotive Building and Maintenance*,' J. I. Loco. E., 47 (2), 131; 1957.

TAYLOR, D. R. and SCHOLES, A., '*Computer Aided Design of Railway Vehicles*,' Railway Engineering Journal, 4 (6), 63; 1975.

THOMPSON, W. T., '*Rolling Bearings—their Contribution to Modern Rolling-Stock Design*,' J. I. Loco. E., 40 (216), 343; 1950.

VAN DORP, S. D. and GRAHAM, G. W., '*Modern Methods of Train Performance Calculation*,' J. I. Loco. E., 47 (2), 195; 1957.

WEBSTER, E., '*Design Considerations for New Rolling Stock for the Victoria Line, London Transport Railways*,' J. I. Loco. E., 50 (326), 576; 1969.

WICKENS, E. G. M., '*The Appearance and Amenity Design of Rolling Stock*,' J. I. Loco. E., 55; 1965.

RAILWAY ELECTRIC TRACTION

Systems of Electrification—Project Planning & Development—Power Supplies—Power Transmission—A.C. Feeder Stations—D.C. Substations—Conductor Rails—Overhead Contact Lines—Electric Locomotives—Multiple Unit Coaches—Traction Motors—Circuits—Auxiliaries

By T. R. Hume, CEng, MIMechE, MIEE

GENERAL CONSIDERATIONS.—Before considering details, it is important to realise that within quite close limits, all the systems of electrification partake of similar characteristics, both operational and economic. The low voltage dc conductor rail system generally associated with urban and suburban railways, has been used effectively in the Southern Region of British Rail for high-speed passenger and heavy freight service. Similarly the high voltage overhead ac systems, generally held to be most suitable for less dense main line traffic, are used satisfactorily to provide dense suburban multiple unit services in Britain, France, Germany, Sweden, America and India. This fact has tended to become obscured by the great amount of argument over the years about the choice of systems.

Before the advent of practical diesel traction, electrification had to be justified in comparison with steam traction having very different operating characteristics. Diesels share many of the operating characteristics of electric vehicles, like instant readiness, reversibility, easy multiple unit working, continuous use over long period without servicing and absence of stand-by losses, so the distinctions are now rather more difficult. There are a few cases, such as underground lines, which dictate the use of electricity, but in general the case has to be made on economic grounds.

The cost of the fixed installation to convey power from the generating station to the vehicle is high, whatever system of electrification is used and the routeing is necessarily rather inflexible, since it is too expensive to contemplate electrification of every single yard of track, particularly in sidings, where it is sometimes unsafe in any case. The problem is therefore to find advantages adequate to compensate these disadvantages.

An electric locomotive or motor coach will cost less to build than its diesel equivalent (or a more powerful vehicle can be built for the same cost). It should have a longer life, cost less to maintain and have a higher availability but its fuel costs are likely to be about the same at present, unless exceptionally favourable prices for electricity can be negotiated. As oil becomes scarcer, however, its price must be expected to rise in relation to that of electricity. The price of diesel fuel varies little but the charges for electricity vary with considerations of time, peak demand, etc, which are calculated against the tariff structure. The part of the charge for the kilowatt-hours consumed will be at quite a low rate compared with diesel fuel: especially so if there is a lower rate for power taken at times when the whole load can be supplied by the most efficient base load generating stations: but the charge for the maximum kilowatt demand can represent a high proportion of the whole fuel cost, particularly in suburban operation where the heaviest traffic usually coincides with the peak loads on the electricity supply.

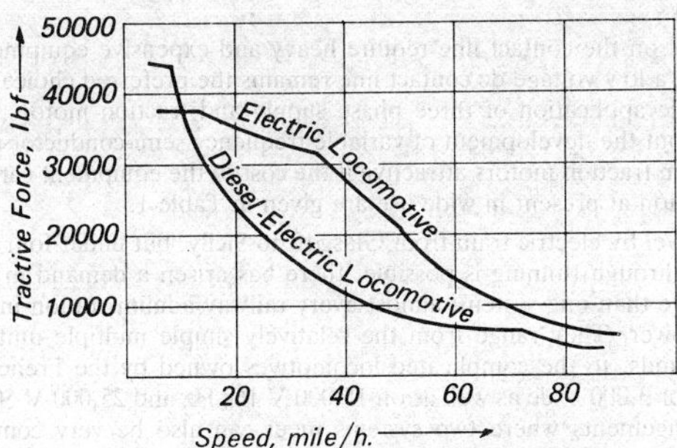

Fig. 1.—Locomotive Characteristics; Diesel and Electric.

The haulage characteristics of diesel and electric locomotives differ widely in nature as is shown by the curves in Fig. 1. These are for locomotives of similar size and weight designed for similar duties. Each will be able to start about the same load since their weights are about the same, but the electric locomotive will have the better acceleration and higher speed up gradients. It will, however, not be able to reach a significantly greater top speed. Overall performance will therefore be similar on long start to stop runs over fairly level routes. The electric locomotive has an advantage which grows with the shortening of the distance between stops or slowings. This shows up most clearly in suburban service. The characteristics are for a diesel-electric locomotive of 1,550 hp and an electric locomotive rated at 1,600 hp but these figures should not be regarded as meaning the same thing. That for the diesel is the power which the engine is capable of delivering into its generator whereas that for the electric is the one hour rating of its traction motors. There is no direct relation between the characteristic of a traction motor and its rating, so this figure gives only a rough indication of haulage capacity. As a broad practical indication, an electric locomotive is usually able to deliver at the rails between one and a half times and twice its rated power, but this may be over only a narrow band of speed. The comparison given is representative, but should not be taken as an accurate guide in every case.

Taken together, the differences between diesel and electric traction are sufficient to mean that an optimised diesel solution will differ substantially from an optimised electric solution to meet the same broad traffic requirement, and a fair comparison between the two can only be made on this basis. A crude comparison of total annual costs does not however complete the study. A great part of the electric annual costs are for servicing the investment and so are fixed for its term. A relatively much smaller part of the diesel costs are fixed in the same way so it is necessary to assess the likely trends in traffic levels and running costs over the years. An increase in traffic will obviously make an electrification more profitable, as will a rise in the general standard of living resulting in higher wages. A comparison published by BR in 1978 gives total costs per train-mile in Inter-City service of £1.82 for diesel haulage and £1.26 for electric. Maintenance costs are £0.89 for diesel and £0.21 for electric. Diesel fuel is £0.49 and electric current at the supply point is £0.40. These figures should only be regarded as typical. The actual values will vary in different cases with duty cycles, and age, condition and design of units.

SYSTEMS OF ELECTRIFICATION.—In the early developments the dc series motor, operating at approximately 500 V, was used for traction work. It was supplied with power by dc generators, and when the scope of systems grew, by ac-fed substations equipped with rotary converter or other apparatus to provide dc power. The substations were sited a few miles apart, the distance being determined by maximum load demand, conductivity in contact line and return, permissible voltage drop at the train and fault current level. Such systems require a heavy investment in lineside equipment and a good deal of manpower attending the equipment in the substations, at any rate in the early times before the development of unattended substations. There was therefore soon a move to extend the scope of electrification by reducing these costs.

This took two directions, both aimed at extending the substation spacing by increasing the voltage of the contact line. The first was a straightforward increase in the dc voltage, for safety reasons necessarily on an overhead contact line. It was found that 1,500 V was about the maximum that could be practically applied between the brush arms of a motor of the required size, but that insulation to earth for 3,000 V was practicable, permitting two motors to be permanently connected in series across a 3,000 V contact line. Both 1,500 V and 3,000 V dc overhead contact systems are in widespread use and continue to expand.

The second approach was to apply a much higher ac voltage to the contact line, stepped down by a transformer on the train before feeding to the traction equipment. Early attempts to use the 50 or 60 Hz general industrial supply were unsuccessful but prompted investigation into ac traction motor design. The problems were found to be tractable if a sub-standard frequency, 15 (later 16⅔)Hz in Europe and 25 Hz in America were used. The systems remaining in widespread use are 15 kV 16⅔ Hz and 11 kV 25 Hz. The later development of rectifiers which could be carried on trains made possible the use of dc traction motors and of 50 Hz on the contact line, which had become much more attractive with the spread of the general supply networks at this frequency.

All the systems using ac on the contact line require heavy and expensive equipment on the trains, so the original system employing a low voltage dc contact line remains the preferred choice for urban and suburban work. The only large scale application of three phase supply and traction motors, in Italy, has now been converted to 3,000 V dc, but the development of variable frequency semi-conductor inverters may eventually make three phase induction traction motors attractive if the cost of the equipment can be reduced sufficiently. The systems of electrification at present in wide use are given in Table 1.

It is now possible to travel by electric train from Glasgow to Sicily, but under four or five different systems of electrification. Where through running is possible, there has arisen a demand in recent years for motive power able to run on more than one system; almost every railway administration in Europe can boast of at least one type of such power. They range from the relatively simple multiple units sets working between Belgium and the Netherlands, to the complicated locomotives owned by the French and German railways which can work on 1,500 or 3,000 V dc as well as on 15,000 V 16⅔ Hz and 25,000 V 50 Hz. The operating and contact line feeding arrangements where two systems meet can also be very complicated. Despite these difficulties in only very few cases has it been considered justified to convert an older installation when it is extended or is joined by a different system, so small is the economic or operational advantage of one system over another. Indeed the French, who have been the most enthusiastic advocates of the 50 Hz system, are still adding to their substantial 1,500 V dc network

The systems in use in any given country are usually the result of Government decision. The standard for British Rail is the 25,000 V 50 Hz system approved by the Ministry of Transport in 1956, with dispensation

TABLE 1.—ELECTRIFICATION SYSTEMS (CR = Conductor Rail; OH = Overhead)

Contact Line			Where Principally Used
Voltage	Frequency	Type	
500–800	dc	CR	Urban and suburban, worldwide. Main lines Britain (S. Region)
1,500	dc	OH	Australia; Britain (Tyne and Wear Metro); Denmark; France; India; Japan; Netherlands; New Zealand; Spain
3,000	dc	OH	Algeria; Belgium; Brazil; Czechoslovakia; Italy; Jugoslavia; Morocco; Poland; Russia; S. Africa
15,000	16⅔	OH	Austria; Germany; Norway; Sweden; Switzerland
11,000	25	OH	America (Conrail)
25,000	50–60	OH	Britain; Zaire; France; Hungary (initially 15 kV on contact line); India; Japan (25 kV on contact line for standard gauge; 20 kV for 42 in gauge); Jugoslavia; Pakistan; Portugal; Russia; Turkey

to use 6,250 V 50 Hz, where it is difficult to provide clearance for 25,000 V and to use the 750 V dc conductor rail system for limited extensions of existing systems, principally the large Southern Region electrified area. This regulation reversed previous decisions to adopt the 1,500 V dc, system as the British standard, with a similar dispensation for the Southern Region. This change was largely the result of the progress made by the French in demonstrating the ability of the ac system to meet all requirements at attractive cost without causing difficulties to the general supply system. This development work was founded on pioneer work with locomotive borne rectifiers and 50 Hz series traction motors in the 1930's in Germany; this work was not followed up, due to the decision to retain and extend their substantial 16⅔ Hz network.

There have also been numerous experiments with battery-electric traction throughout the world. Only in the case of Germany has there been service application on a significant scale, where the secret of success seems to have been a combination of low cost energy and very careful attention to battery technology to achieve the greatest possible life. In Britain, London Transport make use of battery locomotives for works trains, and the Southern Region has ten motor luggage vans for use with Continental boat trains; these have traction batteries to enable them to work away from the conductor rail on quayside or sidings. These are, of course, cases of special operating need and economy is not the prime consideration. Virtually all examples of battery-electric traction use conventional lead acid batteries, but of special rugged construction and capable of withstanding heavy charge and discharge cycles. The rising price and impending scarcity of oil have prompted much development work throughout the world on new types of storage battery. It seems likely that this must, relatively soon, bear fruit in the form of rugged cells of high energy density and efficiency as well as long life which would revolutionise battery traction.

Although not strictly a system of electrification, diesel-electric traction deserves a mention here since the electrical manufacturers have been pioneers in its development and much of the equipment is similar to or even interchangeable with that for pure electric traction. The great majority of main line diesel locomotives in the world have electrical transmission although in the lower powered range, up to about 800 hp, and mainly for shunting or secondary duty, mechanical or hydraulic transmission is favoured. In general, electric transmission is heavier than either mechanical or hydraulic transmission and more expensive than mechanical. Its attraction lies in its controllability and ease of transfer of power between the engine and the independent driving axles, but above all to the complete independence of engine and axle speeds. This enables the engine to be run at the best combination of speed and torque to meet any given power demand regardless of the track speed, which promotes good fuel efficiency and low maintenance in the engine.

Despite the recent construction of a couple of 50 kV systems, the future is unlikely to see the wide scale application of any new system of electrification, at any rate on conventional railways. The advance of semiconductor technology may in due course make a high voltage dc system attractive, considered in isolation, because line reactance is now the limiting factor in spacing of feeding points, but the advantages are unlikely to be sufficient where through running to any existing electrification could ever arise. A non-contact system appears attractive but it does not seem possible that the line equipment for it could ever be other than relatively expensive and it remains to be seen whether speeds can usefully be pushed high enough on conventional railways to make it essential.

PROJECT PLANNING AND DEVELOPMENT.—The planning of an electrification (or comprehensive dieselisation) requires a team including commercial, operating and engineering skills. The engineer has much to contribute since he alone can be expected to understand the relation between variations in the traffic specification and costs which are vital to the success of the project. Furthermore this must be considered imaginatively in the light of probable future trends in traffic and technology since, once the investment has been made, it cannot easily or cheaply be altered.

Energy consumption and maintenance costs rise very sharply at the higher speeds, as does the maximum power demand and hence the size of the installation required to meet it. The capital cost rises much less than linearly with power capacity, so reserve against possible future increases in demand may be a worthwhile investment. Increase in maximum speed will however lead to a proportionately lesser increase in overall service speed. This will have a commercial attraction as well as making somewhat better use of operating manpower and rolling stock. The problem therefore is to evaluate incremental changes in service speed and to compare them with the value of the increment in commercial attraction. The system should then be designed around the greatest performance beyond which the prospective gains in commercial attraction produced by further increase would be outweighed by increased costs. This cannot of course be done with objective accuracy, particularly as allowance has to be made for probable future trends, but an informed act of judgement is required.

The basic tool used in this process is the speed/time/distance calculation, in which the fundamental data of traction characteristics, loads, gradients and speed restrictions are used to produce sets of timings from which a timetable can be built up. These calculations can be repeated with varying postulated data until the most satisfactory balance is reached. The calculations are usually done by a 'step-by-step' method. Each step of the calculation is taken by finding the gross tractive effort available at the speed already reached and deducting from it the resistance to motion and the gradient resistance. The resulting net tractive effort will produce an acceleration which is assumed to be reasonably linear over the next speed increment, for which the time and distance are then calculated and added to those already amassed. When done manually this is a tedious process, so digital computers are now usually employed. Special purpose analogue computers have also been built using both mechanical and electrical analogues.

Energy consumption can be calculated at the same time, but must be regarded as approximate (except when used for comparison with calculated consumptions for different conditions) since traffic delays and driving technique can cause wide variations in day to day consumption, especially when the distance between stops is short. In this lies much of the attraction of automatic driving for urban railways.

POWER SUPPLY

GENERATION.—Power is now usually purchased, even when it has to be specially generated as in the case of the low frequency systems. Generation for a purely railway load is necessarily on a relatively small scale with the prime requirements of reliability and continuity. Generating sets are therefore modest in size and the general techniques, conventional and conservative. Low frequency supplies are usually generated and transmitted as single phase to the feeding points where they are stepped down to the contact line voltage. Use is also made of the public supply in the central three-phase standard frequency to single-phase, low frequency converting stations, which again supply the feeding points over high voltage transmission lines.

TRANSMISSION.—Power is taken by the railway from the supply authorities at a number of points spread strategically over the electrified network. In the case of the dc systems, these points are generally joined together by a secondary, railway owned, distribution network which follows the route and is looped in to the substations which feed the contact line. There is thus a ring main, but, to avoid paralleling the supply authority's network, a switch is left normally open about midway between feeding points. A typical modern railway transmission network is at 33 kV, using oil filled cable laid in surface concrete troughing by the lineside. Transmission to the low frequency systems is by overhead line to and between the feeding points by the most direct routes. The pattern is decided by the need to provide a secure supply. The distribution system of the electricity supply authority eliminates the need for a railway electricity transmission network for 50 Hz systems, and in most cases it is possible to secure a supply with little need of special railway feeders.

AC FEEDER STATIONS.—These consist essentially of a transformer stepping down to the contact line voltage, with circuit breakers on the incoming feeds and between the traction busbars and the sections of the contact line. These breakers are usually remote controlled in modern installations. The industrial frequency electrifications are fed from three phase transmission systems, and in some early examples, Scott connected transformers were used with the two output phases feeding the contact line in opposite directions to minimise the unbalance. More recently, two of the three incoming phases have been used in the same way, but experience has shown these precautions to be unnecessary when the connection is made to a high capacity network. In addition the transformers themselves have proved sufficiently reliable to allow the use of a solitary single phase transformer at each feeder station.

Spacing of feeder stations is a function of loading, permissible voltage drop, short circuit protection, as well as convenience of access to the supply network for 50 Hz systems, but it is of the order of 20 miles. Such long sections require to be broken up for operational reasons, and this is done by track sectioning points with remote controlled circuit breakers etc.

DC SUBSTATIONS.—The main ac ring supply is led into and out of the substation through circuit breakers, one of which may be replaced by a powered isolator to reduce costs. The supply to the transformer is taken through a further circuit breaker. Since the general change over to mercury arc rectifiers in the 1930's no new rotary converters have been installed. The early mercury arc rectifiers were of the continuously pumped water cooled type, but in recent practice, sealed air cooled types have been used, either in steel tank or glass bulb form. These have now given way in turn to the almost universal use of silicon semiconductor rectifiers.

Six, double-six or twelve-phase connection was usual in transformers, feeding rotary converters or mercury arc rectifiers but a simple three phase connection suffices with the semiconductor rectifiers. Many of them are however being used to replace early rectifiers without replacing the original transformers, so the multi-phase arrangements continue in use with advantage to the smoothing of the dc output. Off-load tap changers are provided in the transformers to permit fine adjustments to the substation output voltage which ensures that adjacent substations share the load properly. Apart from the special windings, transformers are conventional oil immersed naturally cooled units as a rule but some authorities have special requirements. London Transport, for instance, prefers units with closed circuit air blast cooling, to minimise fire risk in the built up areas, where many of their substations are situated.

The rectifier feeds through a dc circuit-breaker to the main dc busbar, which is connected in turn to the contact line sections through similar breakers. All breakers are normally closed so that all sections of the contact line are normally paralleled. Furthermore, all substations usually feed in parallel, in distinction from ac feeder stations each of which feeds only the sections radiating from it, to avoid paralleling the main transmission system. Ac switchgear is of normal air- or oil-break type, with vacuum switches finding increasing favour, but the dc breakers are specialised. They are now usually of a high speed type mechanically or electrically latched, and with overload tripping sometimes operating on a rate of rising current or falling voltage. Usually all switchgear is remote controlled and there is some degree of telemetering. The more powerful substations often have more than one transformer and rectifier, but the principles are the same.

It is common also with dc systems to break the continuity of the contact lines between substations at a track sectioning point, connecting the ends through circuit breakers to a common busbar, but here the purpose is to improve the conductivity of the contact line by paralleling its sections on multi-track routes, more than to provide convenient operational sections. This is particularly true of the low voltage conductor rail systems, where the relatively short distance between substations is not too long for operating convenience. Substation spacing is determined by the same factors as with ac and varies from about 1½ miles with a heavily loaded 600 V system to about 20 miles with a moderately loaded 3,000 V system.

CONDUCTOR RAIL CONTACT LINES.—The train shoes may make contact with either the top, the inside or the underside of the conductor rail; top contact was adopted on all British systems but one, because it is fitted in most easily where clearances are tight. It is however, the most vulnerable to interference from snow and ice, the most hazardous to men on the track, and the most liable to short circuit from stray material. It is generally accepted that the maximum safe voltage for a conductor rail is about 900 V to earth or running rail, but there are exceptions, notably the 1,200 V side contact system between Manchester and Bury. Except for this and the small Glasgow Underground, all systems in this country have their outside conductor rails in the standard position, with the top of the conductor rail 3 in above the level of the running rails and its centre line 16 in from the inside face of the nearer running rail. Nominal voltages for the largest systems are 630 V for London Transport, and 660 to 750 V for different sections of the Southern Region.

The rails are usually 100 to 150 lb wt per yard and rolled in high conductivity steel; welded together in lengths up to about half a mile, flash butt being the preferred method. Top contact rails normally simply rest on porcelain or glass insulators carried on the ends of the sleepers about eight feet apart. Lateral movement is restrained by shoulders on the insulator cap and longitudinal movement is normally only controlled by a single anchor point in each continuous welded length. Protection varies between the continuous timber sheathing (apart from the contact surface) of the Manchester–Bury system or the continuous timber cover spaced away from the top of the top contact rail of the Stockholm Underground to the single, or double, side protection boards used where men are frequently on the track by London Transport and British Rail.

The return path is normally through the running rails which are at about earth potential but are not earthed. Because of the high currents, both rails are used as far as possible which introduces the complication of impedance bonds when track circuits are employed for signalling. These bonds permit the dc traction currents to pass through them freely, but are insulators to the ac of the signal track circuits. Where there are many short track circuits a single rail may be used for the traction return and may be reinforced with a return feeder. Heavy traction bonds are fitted across all discontinuities in the running rails such as joints, crossings and points blades and parallel tracks are bonded together at intervals, which may call for large numbers of impedance bonds. There is no bonding to structures such as bridges or signal posts.

London Transport have complex signalling and use a separate return conductor rail which is midway between the running rails, with its top surface 1½ in above running rail level. No special measures are taken to control its potential which floats at about 100 to 150 V below earth. The running rails are not connected to the traction circuit in any way, except through instrumentation. It is the general habit to connect the positive to the conductor rail and the negative to the return but some administrations claim advantage to the balance of wear by doing the reverse.

OVERHEAD CONTACT LINES.—These are generally wire systems with some degree of vertical resilience, but there have been one or two examples of overhead rails. The wire systems are used for both high voltage dc and ac systems and the principles are similar for all; each administration however has its own preferred detailed arrangements. The chief design requirement is to provide for adequate conductivity of the system and to ensure contact at all times and at all speeds. Heavy wear and/or burning will rapidly destroy the contact wires. The equivalent copper cross-sectional areas of the overhead lines vary from (approx.) 600 mm^2 for 1500 V dc. to 130 mm^2 for 15–25 kV, ac.

The simple 'tramway' overhead wires, suspended from semi-resilient supports attached to pasts, are generally considered suitable for speeds up to 40 mile/h. The limitation is due to sag problems and abrupt change of direction at suspension points which make conditions which the pantograph cannot follow. Simple catenary suspension is usual for speeds above 40 mile/h; for the highest speeds, a compound catenary or stitch wire construction are used.

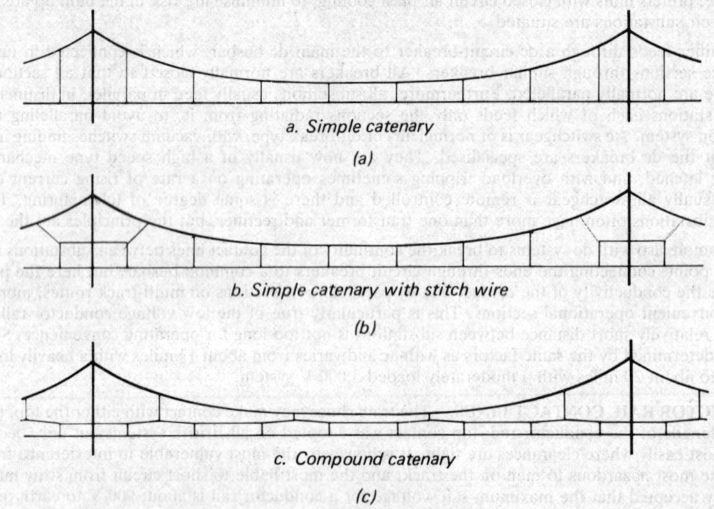

FIG. 2.—Forms of Overhead Catenary Construction. *(a)* Simple. *(b)* Simple with Stitch Wires. *(c)* Compound.

Investigations into the dynamics of overhead lines and pantograph systems have led to designs of simple catenary suspensions suitable for speeds over 100 mile/h. The simple tramway system may similarly be designed for much higher speeds. Contact wires are usually single although some systems use two wires; the wire is of hard-drawn grooved copper. Catenary wires are of stranded HD copper, aluminium steel composite, or of galvanised steel. On open line sections the overhead line is usually staggered from side to side to even the wear on pantograph contact strips. Spacing of structures is approx 75 m apart; where possible these are simple masts, but gantries or headspans may have to be used over multiple tracks.

The overhead system is usually divided into tension lengths of about 1,000 m, anchored in the middle, and tensioned to approximately 500 kg weight at each end by a pulley and weight, or recently, a hydro-pneumatic device. At the tensioning ends, the contact wire is taken up while the overlapping end of the next length is brought down so that the pantograph transfers smoothly from one to the other. The free end is then led to the side of the track where the tensioning device is attached to a stayed structure. Wires over turnouts, crossings etc, are taken in and out of running in the same way, but there, as in sidings, the tensioning device may be omitted.

At electrical sectioning points, a neutral, or normally dead, section of wire is interposed in the same way to prevent pantographs from connecting the two sections together. The complexities of this arrangement can now be avoided by the development of lightweight insulators made up of epoxy/glass rods threaded through ceramic and PTFE collars which can be spliced into the contact wire without introducing a significant discontinuity to the running. At such sectioning points it has been traditional to expect the driver to open the locomotive main circuit breaker to avoid drawing an arc from the contact wire but BR practice is to provide trackside magnets acting on receivers carried on the locomotive, for this purpose. Similar magnets initiate reclosure of the breakers after passage of the section.

A major source of cost and delay in the construction of overhead systems is the need to enlarge clearances in many bridges, tunnels etc, which may involve complete reconstruction. Present British regulations require a minimum of 270 mm static and 200 mm passing clearance for 25 kV 50 Hz, but special reduced clearances of 150 mm static and 125 mm passing now permitted in certain circumstances, have greatly reduced installation problems. Return is invariably to the running rails and similar arrangements to those for conductor rail systems are made except that the lower currents make the provision of adequate conductivity simpler. The high voltage ac systems have no need of more than signalling bonds over joints. On the other hand, the greater distance between feeding points causes a greater proportion of the current to find its way back through earth; this leaves the outward feed fields less balanced and more prone to interfere with telecommunications circuits. Interference is in any event liable to be high with high voltage ac systems, so special screening of telecommunications cables and other measures are usually necessary, extending frequently to paralleling the rails by return feeders into which the current is drained by booster transformers, located at intervals.

ROLLING STOCK

LOCOMOTIVES.—The primary requirements in a locomotive are ability to exert sufficient traction force to start the specified load and haul it up the steepest gradient, and provision of sufficiently powerful equipment to enable it to work that load at the required speeds. The first is a function of the total weight on the driven wheels and the effective coefficient of friction between them and the rails. Modern line haul locomotives are invariably mounted on bogies with all axles driven, usually by independent motors, and the designer aims to put an equal weight on each axle so that each will contribute an equal share of the tractive effort. Exertion of effort at the drawbar however, imposes a pitching moment on the whole locomotive, and similarly each bogie will tend to pitch under the traction force it passes to the body. The result is unloading of the axles towards the front of the locomotive proportional to the effort, together with unloading of the front axle(s) of each bogie, which is more serious, since the bogie has a relatively short wheelbase. This latter is counteracted by passing the tractive force from the bogie to the body at as low a level as possible, or by designing the attachment of the bogie so that it cannot tilt or, occasionally, by a special air cylinder which forces down the headstock of the bogie while the locomotive is starting. Present French practice is to drive all axles on each bogie through a gear train from a single motor, but this arrangement has found little favour elsewhere Electrically it is sometimes arranged that the fields of the motors driving the leading axles are weakened during starting so that they exert less effort than the others.

If one axle does slip momentarily, either because of unloading or because of local poor adhesion, circuit conditions in the locomotive will determine whether it runs away, continues more or less steadily or, the slip disappears. A motor characteristic falling steeply with speed will help, but in any event the motors should be connected in such a way that when one of them slips, the voltage on the others should rise as little as possible. A popular arrangement on the newest locomotives, with silicon rectifiers, is to feed each motor from its own transformer secondary winding and bridge connected rectifier. Slip is less likely to develop when the incremental power steps are small, that is, there are many notches. As economic semi-conductor technology develops, increasing use is being made of notchless control in which power increase is stepless and the best possible use of adhesion is made. This also lends itself to new forms of control by the driver, such as the setting of current limits, or speed limits, with automatic compliance by the locomotive equipment as running conditions permit.

TABLE 2.—LEADING PARTICULARS OF REPRESENTATIVE ELECTRIC LOCOMOTIVES.

	Railway Authority					
	Brit. Rail	Swiss Federal		German Federal		French
Supply Voltage	25kV	15kV	15kV	15kV	15kV	1,500 (dc)
Supply Frequency	50Hz	16⅔Hz	16⅔Hz	16⅔Hz	16⅔Hz	—
Type or Class	87	Ae 6/6	Re 4/4II	103 (E.03)	110 (E.10)*	BB8500†
Year	1972	1962	1967	1965	1957	1965
Wheel Arrangement	Bo–Bo	Co–Co	Bo–Bo	Co–Co	Bo–Bo	B–B
Traffic Duty	Mixed	Mixed/ Mountain	Mixed	High-Speed/ Passenger	Mixed	Mixed
Max Speed, km/h	160	125	140	200	150	150 & 90‡
Output hp (cont rating)	5000	5,300	6,050	8,000	5,000	3,500
Total Wt (tonnes)	81	120	80	112	85	79
Length (mm)	17,830	18,400	14,800	19,500	16,490	14,700
No of Traction Motors	4	6	4	6	4	2
Type of Control	HT Tap§ Changer; Rectifier dc Motors	HT Tap Changer; Direct ac Motors	HT Tap Changer; Direct ac Motors	HT Tap Changer; Direct ac Motors	HT Tap Changer; Direct ac Motors	Series/ Parallel & Resistance

* Primarily for passenger service. Other versions low-geared for freight, or with higher gears for high speed passenger traffic.
† There are also ac (25kV–50 Hz), and ac/dc versions, of same power.
‡ Alternative gear ratios can be selected with the loco at rest.
§ One locomotive has thyristor control.

If a slip does develop it may be arrested by sanding the rails, applying a small braking effort, or reducing the tractive effort from the slipping (or all) motor(s)—or by any combination of these measures. The crudest method of improving pulling power is simply to increase the weight of the locomotive, by providing a heavier structure, a greater number of driven axles, or even ballast. Despite its lack of sophisticated appeal, this is a valid solution so long as account is taken of the operating and economic disadvantages of using a heavier locomotive.

In earlier times the weight of equipment required to provide for high power output was great enough to make necessary carrying axles over and above the number which had to be driven to provide the required tractive effort. Nothing more than modest mixed traffic or freight duties were within the range of the total adhesion locomotive. Development led to the first high performance locomotives of this type appearing about 1940 and the position now is that it is readily possible to incorporate far greater power in a locomotive than can ever be used unless the route characteristics permit running at very high speeds. This has been brought about partly by more refined and calculated design, but perhaps mostly by modern materials, particularly for insulation. Fortunately the possibility of thus providing high power at reasonable cost has coincided with a rising demand for higher speeds both in passenger and freight service. The same trends are evident with diesel locomotives but they inevitably lag some way behind, because of the substantial weight of reliable and economic prime movers.

MULTIPLE UNIT COACHES.—Multiple unit applications divide into two fairly distinct classes, urban and suburban and, loosely, main line. These determine the nature and scope of the equipment required, although there can be much common ground between them. Urban and suburban duties are characterised by heavy loads, frequent stops, and often barely adequate stations and track facilities, particularly at terminals. To make the best use of these facilities and to provide an attractive service, high acceleration and braking rates, and a minimum of the train length devoted to non-revenue earning equipment or accommodation are required. Ready access from the platforms is also needed to keep stopping times to the minimum. There is little need for a high proportion of seating since journey times are short and seats tend to be in conflict with the needs for maximum total capacity and for ready access. Nor does the maximum speed need to be very high since it can have little influence on journey time: it can in fact be a disadvantage in that it requires high energy consumption. High acceleration requires a high proportion of motored axles although 50 per cent is adequate to produce the highest acceleration which is generally regarded as being comfortable particularly for standing passengers, that is about $0.1\,g$. This is the proportion used on London Transport's Victoria Line, although later LT (and some BR) stock has two out of three of the axles motored.

Main line multiple unit duties in general can be fulfilled just as well by locomotives and hauled coaches, working push/pull if necessary, except where special needs have to be met; as, for instance, in the Southern Region of BR, where the best possible used must be made of short platforms in the London terminals, or on the Japanese 'Shin Kansen', where the very high speeds demand a power capacity which could not be provided in a locomotive of reasonable size. Nevertheless, multiple units can still be attractive for such duties because the locomotive as a vehicle exists purely to carry its equipment. It is obviously attractive if the equipment can instead be dispersed among vehicles fulfilling some other purpose as well, and this is likely to be the cheapest arrangement unless the power is dispersed among too many individual equipments. This is unlikely to be the case with main line units except for very high speed duties. Locomotives are only really attractive when a substantial part of their time has to be spent on non-passenger duties or for very high speed trains when the power can most economically be provided in what are, in effect, light highly specialised locomotives, as in BR's. 'Advanced Passenger Train'.

The distinction between locomotive and main line multiple unit working can become very blurred. The Swiss, for instance, have replaced locomotives on some of their trains which have traditionally been worked push/pull by motor coaches of the same power. Again, the Bournemouth services on the Southern Region are worked by what appears to be a twelve car train, made up of three 4-car units of the usual kind. All the traction power is however concentrated in the two motor coaches of one of these units. At the end of the electrified route one or both of the other two, unpowered, units is worked forward to Weymouth by a diesel-electric locomotive as a push/pull train. If one of the specially equipped diesel locomotives is not available, the train can be worked as an ordinary hauled train. Similarly, either these 4-car motor units or the Swiss motor coaches, can be used as locomotives with ordinary hauled stock, even including freight vehicles, if the occasion demands. Apart from the use of the body for load carrying, the distinction between light locomotives and main line motor coaches is thus slight, and the equipment can be very similar; in the same way, the distinction between less powerful main line motor coaches and those for suburban duties can be small.

There is therefore a continuous spectrum of equipment to meet requirements from one end of the scale to the other, and it is wiser to take this flexible view than to observe rigid but artificial divisions. This extends to the principles of remote multiple unit control, by which the power units receive their commands from a position which may be on any vehicle, powered or unpowered, or even off the train altogether. There is no difficulty in devising a scheme covering the specialised needs of each class of use as well as their common needs and this can also embrace diesel power. It is accepted that it is desirable for all vehicles to have compatible couplings and power brake systems unless there are very good reasons to do otherwise. It is an extension of this principle that all motive power units should respond to common control commands.

TRACTION MOTORS.—Despite many attempts to use other characteristics, the series machine remains in virtually universal use, because it is most easily controllable, shares the load well and makes the most reasonable demands on the power supply system. Field weakening is often employed to give additional characteristics for speed flexibility. Now that electronic technology is beginning to lead to the use of separately excited and also induction motors, it is interesting that the control systems are arranged to conserve the series characteristic. Dc machines are usually saturated at the high currents but ac machines are not. Early study of the requirements for working on ac showed that a low flux per pole (and therefore a large number of poles) and full compensation were necessary and that the lower the supply frequency, the more tractable would the problems be. This is largely because of the 'transformer voltage' induced in the short-circuited armature coils undergoing commutation. Ripple in the rectified supply and surges in a dc supply can have similar, although smaller effects, in dc motors.

Field systems are fully laminated in ac and some dc motors used on 50 Hz vehicles. Laminated main and interpole pieces are usual for all duties. Motor frames are either cast or fabricated steel. Broadly, wave-wound armatures are used in dc motor coaches; lapwound armatures everywhere else, occasionally compensated in dc applications, and usually in ac Locomotive motors are usually force ventilated, and those for motor coaches self-ventilated, except at the lower end of the power scale where they may often be totally enclosed. Dust is a besetting trouble with all motors and particularly with those of motor coaches; except on a leading motor coach, there is no point on the periphery of the coach from which clean air may be drawn and filtration necessitates heavy maintenance.

The most common suspension arrangement is the nose-suspended or axle-hung, in which one side of the motor is carried through bearings on the axle and the other by a bracket, normally with some resilience, on a bogie transom. Drive is through reduction gearing. It has long been widely held that this arrangement is hard on the track, although research has failed to show that up to approx 100 mile/h, it is the unsprung rather than the total weight on the axle which damages the track. A multitude of arrangements for supporting the motor fully in the bogie frame with drives able to take up the resulting misalignment has been evolved over the years; the drive is often resilient as well and complications can result. Perhaps the simplest arrangement is that widely used by German Federal Railways. This is like the axle-hung arrangement except that instead of bearing directly on the axle, the motor and gearwheel are carried on a tube surrounding the axle, and itself carried on rubber rings attached to the roadwheels. Another common arrangement similarly uses a hollow (quill) shaft surrounding the axle to carry the gearwheel and journalled in the motor frame, but in this case with the motor fully supported by the bogie so that the hollow shaft is supported by the motor; the drive is taken to the axle through a link or spider assembly. Cardan shafts are also used, either hollow and surrounding the axle or passing through a hollow armature shaft. With very small motors there is room to fit a cardan shaft between the armature and the pinion. A whole similar family of devices has been used with the motor shaft at right angles to the axle, sometimes with the drive taken from both ends of the motor to two axles; these are generally associated with light motor coaches or tramcars.

Modern practice is to use class B, or class H, insulation with vacuum impregnation of field and armature coils. Field coils may be bonded to their pole pieces. Split or multi-part brushes have long been used in ac motors and are now spreading in dc motors. The linear motor has received a good deal of attention in recent years but so far there have been no service applications. It has the merits of mechanical simplicity and exerting its tractive effort independently of wheel to rail adhesion but this has to be set against the inflexibility which has always restricted the use of traditional induction motors in traction applications as well as low efficiency and poor power factor. The apparent mechanical simplicity may also be offset by the need to guide the motor in close relationship to its reaction rail.

POWER CIRCUITS.—Collector shoes are generally paralleled within the unit or motor vehicle, but not beyond. The same is true of pantographs with lower overhead voltages, but modern high voltage practice is to use only one pantograph per motor equipment, or even per train. United Kingdom regulations do not in any case permit power cables to be connected between vehicles whose routes include significant lengths of single line tunnels. A main circuit breaker is provided almost invariably in ac practice and sometimes in dc, particularly at the higher voltages. In their absence line switches are adapted to give protection, often two or more in series.

The usual dc practice is to group motors in series at starting with resistance in circuit. The resistances are shorted out in steps during acceleration and then the motors are regrouped in parallel with resistance re-inserted, and the process repeated; with multi-motor equipments this may be done more than once. Transition between the motor groupings may be by a bridge method which maintains tractive effort, or by a shunt method which reduces it but uses simpler equipment. The final stage in acceleration is normally by weakening the motor fields, by tapping or by shunting. Inductive shunts are often used despite their weight and cost, because they produce the most stable conditions during and after the circuit change.

Most modern resistances are made of a stainless alloy and are liberally rated; they are often force-ventilated in locomotives. Electrically interlocked contactors or unit switches are now giving way to cam-operated switches which are inherently mechanically inter-locked but can be slow in action. They are driven by electric motors or by air/hydraulic motors. In tramcars or light motor coaches the low currents permit the use of motor driven commutator devices. Some examples of motor-generator control have been built, notably in this country the 27 locomotives of the Southern Region, now all withdrawn, in which the generator is connected in series with the traction motors across the line. Its excitation is varied by the driver, to buck or boost the line voltage.

An arrangement becoming widespread in recently built stock uses thyristors to feed pulses at full line voltage to the motors at a high repetition rate. The average motor current is controlled either by varying the repetition rate of pulses of constant width or, by varying the width at constant rate. This almost eliminates starting losses but increases the small running losses. However it still requires commutator motors. The ideal, the first examples of which are beginning to enter general service, is to use a variable-frequency thyristor inverter to feed squirrel-cage induction motors.

Traditional ac control is by on-load tap-changing on the main transformer, usually with separate load breaking switches. Either the low-voltage secondary may be tapped, or a separate auto-transformer with high voltage tapping may be provided in the same tank; the latter method is preferred with high powers. To keep the number of taps down, resistance switching has been used to divide the tapping steps. It is becoming standard practice to use thyristors in the main rectifier arms with variable phase-angle delay or cycle selection for the same purpose, or even to eliminate tapping altogether. This gives stepless control over tractive effort making the best possible use of adhesion and the practice is spreading even to the low frequency ac systems. There have also been some examples of simple single-ratio transformers feeding conventional dc power circuits, mainly in equipments converted from dc service, or to permit inter-working between dc and ac sections of the route.

Dynamic braking is common where its use can be justified by the saving in brake block wear or by the avoidance of overstressing the power brakes on long descents. Saving of energy by regeneration is hardly worthwhile in view of the complications in both vehicle and track equipment and the small proportion of energy recovered, so the emphasis is on rheostatic braking in which the electrical energy is dissipated in resistances aboard the vehicle. It can often be justified on tramcars and urban multiple units making frequent stops particularly if the heat produced can be used to warm the passenger accommodation. While braking the motors are connected as separately excited generators, the excitation being provided by one of their number, by a special tapping on the transformer on ac stock, or by a separate exciter. The simplest systems are controlled in steps by varying the value of the loading resistance. The rating of the motors must be increased to cover braking duty, as must that of starting resistances where they are used for braking.

Transformers are generally oil immersed with forced circulation, conforming to standard power supply practice, apart from the need to cope with higher fault levels than normal for transformers of their size; BR's latest multiple unit stock uses natural cooling. Silicon diode and thyristor bridge-connected rectifiers are now normal practice. They may be air-cooled or share the transformer coolant circuit. Air blast main circuit breakers are used together with contactors and grouping switches.

CONTROL CIRCUITS.—Remote control is normal practice and only signal currents link the driving position with the point at which the switching is done, whether it is on the same vehicle or not. This is done by using the control circuits to apply a number of power limits, usually three or four, to which each of the power equipments conforms in its own time according to its local conditions of current loading etc. The driver's master controller is therefore only a selector switch by which he may set the power limit he wishes the train to reach. Usually he may arrest the progression at any point, which may of course mean that different equipments rest at different states, but he is not normally able to notch back from a higher to a lower preset limit; only to shut off completely. It is not however very difficult to add the ability to notch back if needed, as it might be for locomotive applications. All BR multiple unit stock, ac and dc as well as London Transport's and most of that in the rest of the world, uses this principle of control, although the detailed applications rarely permit direct coupling outside their own families. The Southern Region for instance has two blocks of incompatible stock. Apart from the latest suburban stock all stock including electric and diesel-electric locomotives can couple and run in multiple together.

Each equipment should be made self-protecting so that there is no need for indicating back; it is rarely worth the driver's while to attend to a fault while running unless it is so gross as to indicate itself by slowing the train a great deal, or even stopping it.

There is a tendency at present to replace the driver's act of selection by automatic equipment, governed for instance by the driver pre-setting the required speed or, by impulses from the track. The commands to the individual equipments are still however transmitted in the same way. Present systems require a substantial number of train line wires but electronic development is now making possible economical coded systems using radio or only a single pair of conductors along the train. An example of the latter is used on the push/pull trains worked by BR in Scotland. BR coaches have for many years been fitted with train wires for remote control of lighting and it has proved possible to superimpose the control and indication signals on them in addition to the old and the other new use for public address. These developments facilitate the extension of multiple unit or push/pull working to any kind of service, passenger or freight, wherever good use can be made of their flexibility. Radio links have been used for some years now in America to control helper locomotives in the middle of extra long freight trains.

AUXILIARIES.—Most auxiliary equipment and control systems operate at 50; 70; or 110 V. The source is a special winding on the main transformer on ac vehicles, rectified and backed up by a battery where necessary and from a motor-generator or motor-alternator with floating battery on dc vehicles. Thyristor inverters have not yet found much application except in small units to feed fluorescent lamps from a battery supply. The heavier auxiliaries on ac vehicles are sometimes driven by induction motors. All vehicles, except some tramcars and related light motor coaches, require a supply of compressed air, for braking, control and such ancillary purposes as horns, window wipers and power doors; the compressors are motor driven. Fluorescent lighting is now general in new stock. Modern phosphors and the advent of reliable high frequency inverters have improved the efficiency to the point where it is now economic.

Electric heating is the rule on electric locomotive hauled, as well as on multiple unit, trains. It is generally fed at line voltage on dc systems and at similar voltage from a special winding on the traction transformer, on ac systems. Convection or radiant heaters are usual but there is increasing use of pressure ventilation and air conditioning. Power operated doors, operated by compressed air or electric power, are widely use; they are sometimes interlocked with power circuits to prevent movement when doors are not fully closed.

Further Reading.—The records and indexes of the IEE and the IMechE contain much information on railway electric traction. There is a wide range of Standards, both British and foreign; see also the relevant sections of the technical press.

THE ENGINEER
The Weekly for Engineering Management
19 January 1984

MOTOR VEHICLE ENGINEERING

Conceiving the Whole Vehicle—Engines and Related Systems—Transmission and Drive-Line—Suspension, Steering and Running Gear—Body/Chassis Design—System Controls and Displays—References and Bibliography.

By John Fenton, MSc, CEng, MIMechE

Motor vehicle engineering affects both passenger cars produced in very high volumes and the manufacture of special-purpose vehicles in relatively small batches. The approach to the automotive engineering of these different categories could be affected for example by the relative investment made in CAE equipment by different manufacturers and/or design houses. Nearly all sectors are taking on more CAE equipment in recent times and thus the new interest in analytical techniques: they allow designs to be simulated and performance in its widest sense, to be predicted.

Vehicle engineers are required either to conceive new vehicles, which are very closely evolved from their predecessors or, conversely, provide clean-sheet designs for new markets. Even though in other instances engineers are conceiving vehicles almost entirely from brought-out assemblies, rather than being involved in engineering each and every system of the vehicle it is nevertheless more evident than ever before that there is a need to simulate vehicle and system behaviour and predict performance. The stimulus follows, of course, from increased competitiveness in the market and rising costs of development.

CONCEIVING THE WHOLE VEHICLE

Before considering the vehicle's four main constituent systems—power unit, drive-train, suspension/running-gear, body structure/equipment—it is necessary to predict performance and simulate behaviour of the vehicle as a whole.

Within large-scale production volume car, or commercial vehicle companies, Product Planning Departments engineer a broad 'specification' for a new vehicle which is a condensation of much searching and planning of market preferences; consideration of developing-product and manufacturing technologies, plant capabilities and future-projected custom tastes. The small-scale producer is likely to engineer vehicles to meet changing market preferences in a more directly-reactive way, but his scale of operation may limit his ability to make many innovative changes at low cost. Both categories of producer need to measure the performance of projected designs to gauge their effectiveness in meeting market specifications, prior to build.

VEHICLE PERFORMANCE PREDICTION

Tractive Force Distribution.—Vehicle performance is defined by the simple equation $P = W\mu$, where P = tractive force; W = load on driving axle; μ = coefficient of friction between wheel and road. The value of W for a stationary vehicle may be found by simple moment calculation once the static weight distribution has been determined but the value for a moving vehicle is more difficult. In work by Taborek (Ref. 1) the loads on moving axles are termed dynamic axle reactions, designated here by W_{df}, W_{dr} for front and rear axles, respectively. Whatever the dynamic axle reactions may be, they must sum to the total vehicle weight, W. In a two-axle vehicle any dynamic weight transfer will load one axle at the expense of the other. If dynamic weight transfer = W_d then:

$$W_{df} = W_f - \Delta W_d \text{ and vice versa.} \tag{1}$$

To determine ΔW_d in any particular case the tractive force P is required. It can be calculated from M_d, the torque at the driving axle. This is a function of engine torque M_e, total reduction ζ, transmission efficiency η and rolling radius r:

$$P = (M_e \zeta \eta)/r \quad \text{and} \quad \Delta W_d = (H/L)(M_d/r - fW). \tag{2}$$

Where H is height of centre of gravity above the ground, L the wheelbase and f is rolling resistance.

Front and Rear-Wheel Drive.—Substituting $P_{f\,max} = W_{df}\mu$ in (1) and rearranging

$$W_{df} = W(L_r + fH)/(L + \mu H) \tag{3}$$

Where L_r is the distance from the centre of gravity to the rear axle. Maximum transferable tractive force is then

$$P_{f\max} = \mu W[(L_r + fH)/(L + \mu H)] \quad (4)$$

The square bracketed term may be interpreted as the weight distribution factor W_d/W; let this = w, then eq. (3) becomes $W_{df} = W_{wf}$ and eq. (4) becomes $P_{max} = \mu W_{wf}$. In the same way, for rear wheel drive $P_{r\max} = \mu W_{dr}$.

Four-wheel Drive.—In this case $P_{4\max} = \mu W$ and the weight distribution factor, $w_4 = 1$. This means that in the four-wheel-drive configuration full vehicle weight is theoretically utilized in producing tractive forces. Such a condition is realized, however, only when tractive forces (and engine torque) are distributed to the axles in the same proportion as are the dynamic weights on the respective axles.

Tractive Force Chart.—The interrelationship of tractive force, coefficient of friction and weight distribution can be plotted in the form shown in Fig. 1(a). As the chart contains only dimensionless factors, it has a general validity for all rigid vehicles.

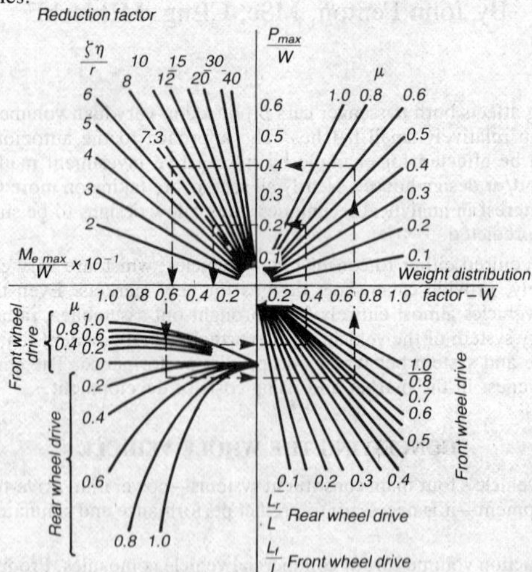

FIG. 1(*a*).—Tractive force chart: lower LH quadrant represents C-of-G height/wheelbase (h/L).

The following assumptions and simplifications have been made: Influence of rolling resistance on dynamic axle weight is neglected. Weight distribution factors are dimensionless as absolute geometrical dimensions of wheelbase and centre of gravity position are avoided by use of dimensionless ratios. Weight of the vehicle is eliminated by dividing the tractive force equation by $WP_{max}/W = w\mu$. Values of maximum engine torque per unit vehicle weight are given by:

$$M_{e\max}/W = (P_{max}/W)/(\zeta\eta/r).$$

WORKED EXAMPLE FOR USE OF CHART.—For a vehicle having centre of gravity (CG) position given by $h/L = 0.35$, $L_f/L = 0.45$, find the maximum transferable tractive effort (μ front and rear = 0.60 and the maximum engine torque for a low gear reduction factor: $\zeta\eta/r = 7{\cdot}3$.

SOLUTION. Starting at the lowest left-hand quadrant project the $\mu = 0.60$ ordinate vertically downwards to intersect the h/L curve at value of 0.35 for both front- and rear-wheel drive. From these intersection points follow the broken lines to the vertical P_{max}/W scale to get values of maximum transferable traction. $P_{f\max} = 0.21\ W$ and $P_{r\max} = 0.405\ W$. Continuing round the example lines to the left-hand abscissa gives the maximum engine torques as 0.056 W for the front-wheel drive and 0.028 W for the rear-wheel drive. Assuming a vehicle weight of 4000 kg, $P_{max} = 1620$ kg and $M_{e\max} = 224$ kNm for front-wheel drive; $P_{max} = 840$ kg and $M_{e\max} = 112$ kNm for the rear-wheel drive.

Transmission Inertia Resistance.—In determining the accelerative performance of a vehicle at the drawing-board stage, consideration of translatory mass inertia is straightforward. The estimation of rotary inertia however, is more difficult and it is necessary to sum the rotating inertia of the separate transmission components by relating respective torque to the driving axle as $M_i = \Sigma Ia\zeta$ where I = moment of inertia, a = angular acceleration and ζ = reduction ratio.

Taborek (Ref. 1) rewrites this equation as $M_i = a_d\Sigma I\zeta^2$ where d refers to the driving axle. Use is then made of the equality of the wheel circumferential speed to the vehicle translatory velocity to postulate an equivalent mass m_e hypothetically concentrated at the rolling radius r. This mass has the same effect on the inertia of translatory motion as the summation of inertia torques of individual rotary parts. Thus, $M_i = m_e r^2 a_d = {}_d\Sigma I\zeta^2$ where $m_e = (\Sigma I\zeta^2)/r^2$ the effective mass being:

$$m^1 = m + m_e = m\gamma \tag{5}$$

where γ is called the dimensionless 'rotary mass factor'. To find the value of γ the rotating parts are divided into two groups: (a) the front and rear wheels, (b) the parts rotating at engine speed. The latter gains in importance in the lower gear range• since m_e is proportional to the square of the reduction ratio. Average values of γ collected from existing literature are given for fully laden commercial vehicles as follows: fourth gear 1.09 then 1.20, 1.60 through to 2.50 in first gear. Calculation of γ is possible by rearranging eq. (5) as:

$$\gamma = 1 + m_e/m = [(\Sigma I_w/mr^2) + (\Sigma I\zeta^2/mr^2)]$$

where I_w is 'wheels' inertia and I is 'engine speed parts' inertia at speed ratio ζ with respect to driving axle. Based on a number of sample calculations:

$$\gamma = 1 + (0.04 + 0.0025\zeta^2)$$

PERFORMANCE CALCULATIONS.—Rolling resistance is primarily affected by tyre carcase construction and a dimensionless co-efficient f is used to express resistance in terms of vehicle running weight. ($f = 0.018$ for radial and 0.013 for cross-ply tyres).

Transmission resistance is obtained from a summation of the power consumed at various stages along the power train and normally expressed as an overall power-train efficiency η. This is made up typically of 0.99 for clutch, 0.98 for gearbox in direct drive and 0.95 in lower gears; differential and final drive is usually assumed as 0.95 and an allowance for joints and bearings of 0.98. Thus the product of these provides $\eta = 0.90$ in direct drive and 0.85 in lower gears.

Air resistance is determined from the equation $R_a = C_D . A\rho V^2/2g$ for vehicle speed V, projected area A and air density ρ. The drag co-efficient C_D ranges from 0.30 for a 'good' saloon body to 0.8 for a 'bluff' box van.

Gradient resistance, Rg, is the component of gravitational force parallel to vehicle attitude in $Rg = W \sin\theta$. This is of particular significance in relation to drive disposition and vehicle C of G position in establishing conditions of limiting adhesion, Fig. 1(b).

Since $Wd\mu = fW + W . \tan\theta_{max}$, maximum gradient $= w\mu - f$.

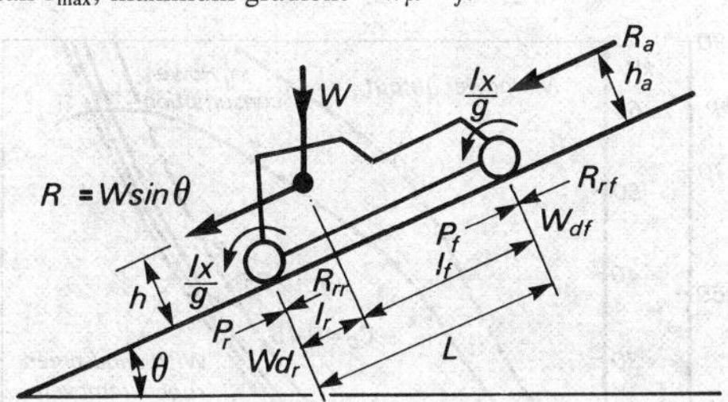

FIG. 1(*b*).—Forces applying to a vehicle accelerating uphill.

Accelerative Performance.—Selection of gear ratio may be on the basis of cruise efficiency or other criteria but a useful equation given by Barnacle (Ref. 2) shows gear ratio for maximum acceleration in:

$$G_{max} = \frac{R . r}{T_e} \pm \sqrt{\left[\frac{R . r^2}{T_e} + \left(\frac{W . r^2}{g} + \frac{I_w}{r}\right) \Big/ I_e\right]}$$

where $R = R_r + R_a$ and I_e, I_W are respectively moments of inertia of parts acting at engine speed and wheel speed. Engine speed is related to vehicle speed according to:

$$V = \frac{2\pi . Ne . r}{12 \times 60 . \eta_{sl} . G} \cdot \frac{3600}{5280} = \frac{Ne . r}{168 . G . \eta_s}$$

where η_{sl} is a tyre slip factor assumed = 0.965.

So N_e and T_e for each gear reduction may be tabulated against road speed by means of the engine torque/speed characteristic curve. Motion resistance forces are subtracted from P to give Pf the 'free tractive force', then 'transferable' tractive force based on dynamic weight transfer effects and adhesion co-efficients is found.

To calculate acceleration, the equation $a = Tf . g/\gamma W$ is used so that acceleration may be plotted against vehicle speed and by graphical integration a time/speed curve, Fig. 1(c), becomes available to obtain times for accelerating up to (and between) given speeds.

AUTOMOTIVE AERODYNAMICS.—The noted performance-car designer, Frank Costin (Ref. 3) has shown, Fig. 2, the effects of changes in drag coefficient on power requirement. The effect of tyre rolling drag is comparatively small; note also the significant change in power requirement in changing from 0.45 to 0.55 drag coefficient. Even the effect of removing a rubber windscreen surround, standing proud by 12.7 mm, and taking off two wing mirrors measuring 27 × 76 mm is quite significant.

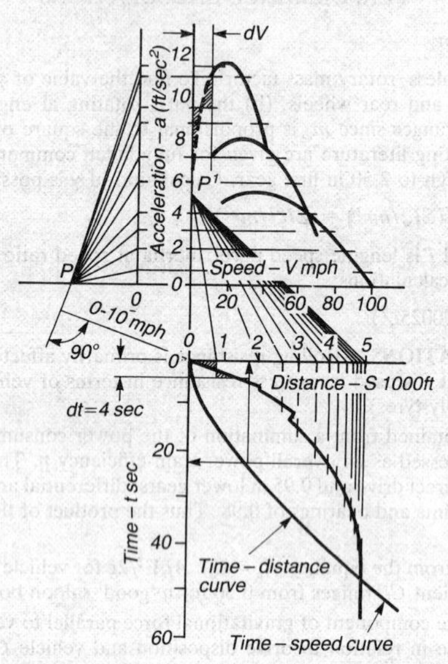

FIG. 1.(*c*)—Taborek performance graph for a particular vehicle design where accelerative performance is plotted (at given speeds).

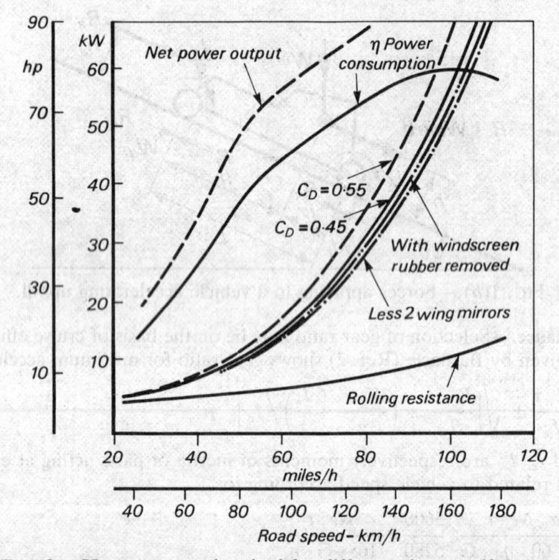

FIG. 2.—Horse-power absorbed for different drag coefficients.

Reducing Air Drag.—Areas of conventional car bodies considered to offer considerable scope for drag reduction are the 'sunken-rectangle' type radiator grille, the flight-deck type bonnet top, some designs of which actually cause reverse air flow, windscreen layout, particularly surround mouldings, rain gutters, and the rear of the 'top block', which normally is only a location for the rear window. The important area of radiator intake requires an appreciation of the air flow characteristics at the radiator. Flow through it is at relatively low speed and during the cooling process there is a change in pressure. The desired condition is high pressure and low velocity at the front face of the matrix and a low pressure at the rear face. Also the air should be speeded up from that at the intake so that it can be returned to the outside air at the same or a higher speed.

For the design of undertrays it is recommended to allow as great a distance between the undertray and the road as possible, the shortest possible transverse span of flat surface, the largest practicable side radii, and a slight nose down incidence of the entire undertray. Fig. 3 shows the profile of a car assumed to have no front air intake. As the air approaches the body it has to divide to flow around it; this point of diversion is termed

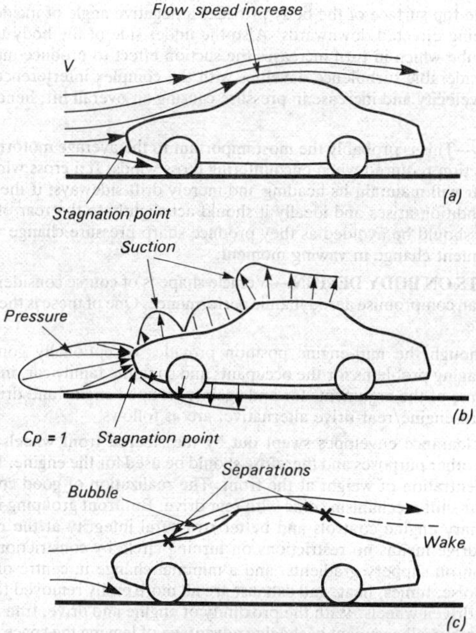

FIG. 3.—Air flow and distribution around a typical saloon car.

the stagnation point, Fig. 3(*a*), where the 'dynamic pressure head' is $\frac{1}{2}\rho V^2$ where ρ is air density and V its relative velocity with the vehicle. As the air flows around the body a pressure distribution is developed as indicated. As the air velocity is increased over the roof a pressure drop occurs to cause a suction zone. Conversely, at the base of the windscreen the streamlines separate and a pressure results from the low velocity. Starting again at the stagnation point, as the air moves around the curved nose it speeds up and the pressure falls until at Fig. 3(*b*), atmospheric pressure is reached. The drag force is of course the summation of the horizontal components of the arrows around the pressure distribution. The contribution diminishes very rapidly as the distance from the stagnation point increases and therefore the nose shape is critical to the drag; surrounding lips which trap air should especially be avoided and careful rounding of flat surfaces such as headlamp mounts should be employed.

Drag reduction can also be obtained by reducing the 'wake' size, that is, maintaining unseparated air flow much further back on the body. Whereas the flow around a smooth aerofoil section, say, is streamline from nose to tail, a bluff car body inevitably causes a break up of the flow into turbulence. While flow remains streamline, air adheres to the car over a thin boundary layer whereafter it is sheared until the air velocity builds up to that of the main stream. Tangential viscous friction forces arises which add to air resistance whenever smooth flow is distorted by surface roughness or protuberances. Severe discontinuities in the surface profile can cause a separation of flow which is the commencing point for the turbulent wake. When flow reaches the corner of a windscreen, for example, it must slow down causing the pressure to rise, thus producing a separation. In this particular case flow would probably re-attach itself further down the vehicle and a bubble would form, Fig. 3(*c*).

Means should be provided for maintaining boundary layer as far back along the body as possible. Very gentle curvature can maintain attached flow right up to the rear of the vehicle. It is important to remember that the car is a three-dimensional shape and there is a flow around the sides as well as over the top. If the side windows on a saloon car are sloped well inwards not only will the blending in of the windscreen be easier but air will make its way around the sides to sweep the separation point further towards the tail of the car.

AERODYNAMIC STABILITY.—Roll stability aspects can be achieved by ensuring that centre of pressure (point of application of wind side force) is close to the roll axis of the car. Small deviations from the ideal can be tolerated if the vehicle does not have pronounced roll-steer characteristics. Distribution of lift forces acting on a vehicle determines the magnitude of the pitching moment which tends to vary the wheel loading with speed. A tail-end spoiler used to form the top edge of a drag-reducing cut-off tail also causes negative lift on the rear wheels and can be useful in increasing lift stability. Lightweight cars with centre of gravity well aft are less easy to control and are susceptible to zero or small negative lift at the front. Techniques such as drooping the nose can be helpful, which is equivalent to reducing the angle of incidence of an aerofoil.

In wedge-shape cars the top surface of the body provides a negative angle of incidence which results in the aerodynamic lift force being directed downwards. Also the under side of the body together with the ground forms a kind of venturi tube which in turn increases the suction effect to produce more negative lift. But for a very low slung car considerable turbulence develops with the complex interference of the boundary layers with reduced mean flow velocity and increase in pressure causing an overall lift; hence the use of negative lift devices on racing cars.

Yawing Plane Stability.—This is probably the most important to the average motorist since it will govern the amount of steering correction required when encountering cross winds. If a cross wind force acts through the neutral steer point the car will maintain its heading and merely drift sideways; if the side force acts ahead of this point an unstable condition arises and ideally it should act slightly to the rear of the neutral steer point. Sharp corners on a body should be avoided as they produce sharp pressure change which can be aggravated by side gusts with consequent change in yawing moment.

OTHER CONSTRAINTS ON BODY DESIGN.—Vehicle shape is of course considerably influenced by other factors than those which can compromise aerodynamic performance. One of these is the layout of the mechanical components in the vehicle.

Engine Position.—Although the mid-engine position provides exceptionally good weight distribution it obviously can cause packaging problems for the occupants and so in the family car, in particular, front or rear-layouts are preferred. Some of the arguments for and against grouped engine and drive layouts, front or rear, and the conventional front-engine/rear-drive alternative, are as follows.

Because of the large clearance envelopes swept out by the steered front wheels, space between them is comparatively useless for other purposes and therefore should be used for the engine. Basic stability in handling too, follows from a concentration of weight at the front. The realization of good cooling and engine access, and generally a better gear shift mechanism come with rear drive. But front grouping is preferred for proximity of the driver to the primary engine controls and better structural integrity at the rear of the vehicle. Rear grouping of engine and drive means no restrictions on turning circle by constriction of steered wheel swept clearances, better traction on slippery gradients, and a minimal change in centre of gravity position for the unladen and laden car. Noise, fumes, heat, and exhaust are all more easily removed together with the problem of steering the otherwise driven wheels. With the proximity of engine and drive, transmission power losses can be reduced and there is an overall occupant packaging advantage of leaving the space between the wheels clear for passengers.

With once conventional front engine rear drive configurations there is a critical packaging problem, particularly in low height sports saloons, in the areas of the rear seat and drive axle differential unit. This problem can be overcome by the use of short rear axle radius rods which rotate the axle at full bump to ensure that the nose of the pinion clears the rear seat profile.

In an experimental Ford project, the Techna car has a different approach to drive line arrangement by utilising an offset and canted configuration, Fig. 4 showing the considerable gains in occupant space without increasing the low silhouette of the vehicle. The solution complied with the usual constraints of economical manufacture and also involved forward location of the engine-gearbox.

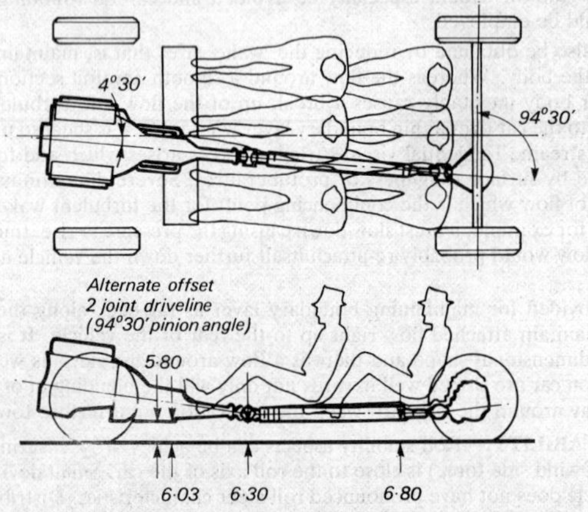

FIG. 4.—Offset drive line arrangement of Ford Techna car.

ERGONOMICS TECHNIQUES FOR OCCUPANT PACKAGING.—A common word used by ergonomists is the 'percentile' which describes the stature of a man or woman according to his or her place in the graph of percentage of population against overall stature dimensions. It is usual to design within percentile extremes on the basis that there are very few women, say, smaller than the 5th percentile and very few men larger than the 95th, these corresponding, respectively, to 58 and 72 inch statures. Hywell Murrell (Ref. 5) shows in Table 1 and Fig. 5 the factoring of data to accommodate the percentile variations. He goes on to show how the vehicle controls can be fitted to the driver. Foot controls are divided between those like brakes, needing considerable force, for which free leg movement is required, and the 'precise' control of throttle, say, where use of ankle articulation is better suited. For braking and declutching a situation of progressive force with virtually zero movement is ideal.

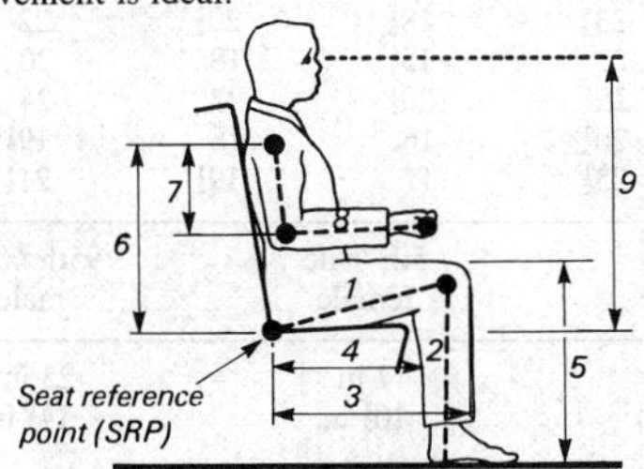

FIG. 5.—Key dimensions, seated man; see Table 1.

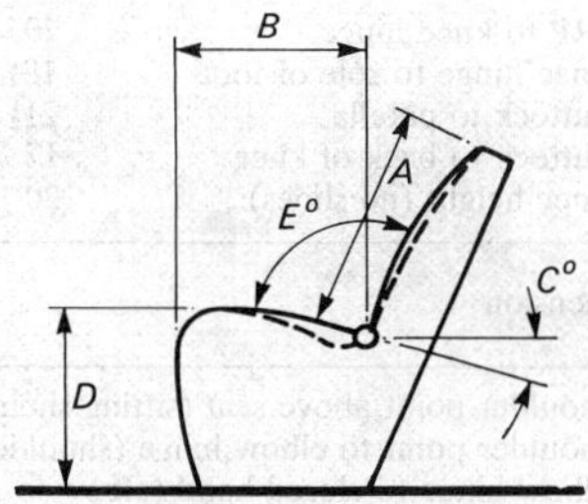

FIG. 6.—Seat control dimensions; see Table 2.

Pedal Force and Movement.—Critical factors are: knee angle in leg operation optimum 160–165 degrees, with the most comfortable relaxed range 120–130 degrees; and ankle angle, in leg and ankle operation, within 90–125 degrees and 75 degrees absolute minimum. Optimum lateral offset of pedals from body midline is 2–5 in (50–130 mm); at 6·5 in (165 mm) offset, leg force potential is reduced by 75 per cent.

Alternative approaches in calculation are either to determine seating/pedal position, given the force required hence knee angle from Fig. 5; or given seat/pedal position to determine maximum allowable force. Optimum seat parameters are shown in Fig. 6 and Table 2.

Ankle controls like throttle are best with pedals hinged at their base. Optimum and maximum angles for barefoot are given by Fig. 7 and Table 3. When pedal is hinged at heel floor contact point, angle E should be increased, to allow for heels, by 5 degrees for men and 10 degrees for women compared with 'no-shoes' condition. For example, in Fig. 7, $E = 45$ degrees (55 degrees with shoes) for women and $E = 55$ degrees (58 degrees with shoes) for men (also $E = 71$ degrees and 73 degrees for men and women with 7 in (180 mm) seat height) so an acceptable pedal can be arranged.

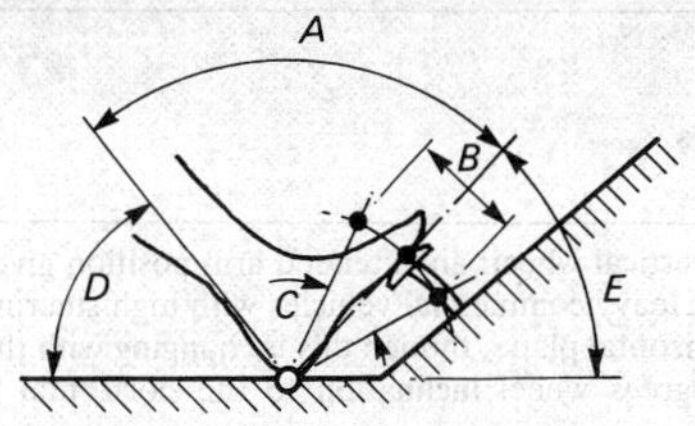

FIG. 7.—Foot control dimensions; see Table 3.

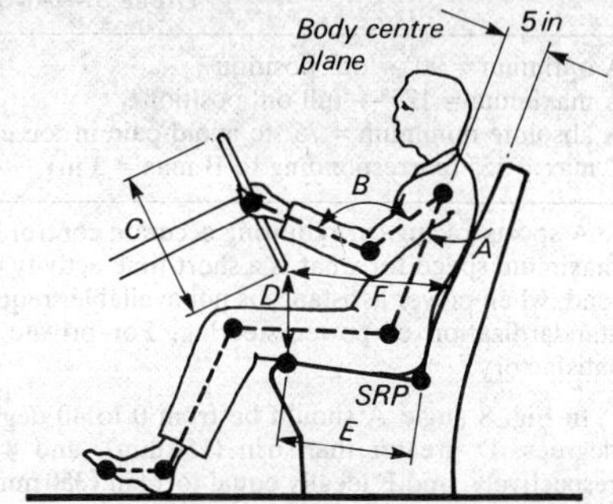

FIG. 8.—Seat and hand control parameters measured from Seat Reference Point.

Ankle Functions.—Designing controls for ankle operation starts with the determination, from Table 2, of seat heights for population extremes and finding corresponding D in Fig. 7. A pedal angle is then selected to lie within allowable range. Throttle and brake pedal surfaces are then aligned for quick foot interchange, so the throttle pedal is mounted closer to the Seat Reference Point (SRP) than the depressed brake pedal. Sufficient throttle spring loading is required to support the foot. As an example, when E = 55 degrees to suit the smallest woman on an 11 in (280 mm) seat, A is 115 degrees for the largest man on a 7 in (180 mm) seat. If depression is 15 degrees, this gives an unacceptable maximum for A of 130 degrees. Remedy is to increase E to 60 degrees and reduce the depression.

Hand Operations.—For hand controls like the steering wheel, applied hand force depends on column rake, perpendicular distance from SRP to wheel centre, and seat back inclination. Maximum force is available pulling longitudinally with forearm and shoulder acting together while faster, but lower efficiency motion is obtained with movement across the body. A wheel tilted 30 degrees to the vertical could have a rim force 1·7 times that with a vertical wheel but the rate of turning is halved and the energy expended reduced considerably.

TABLE 1.—PERCENTILE VARIATIONS

Dimension (inches)	Percentile male			Percentile female		
	5th	50th	95th	5th	50th	95th
1 SRP to knee hinge	20	22	23½	18½	20½	22½
2 Knee hinge to sole of foot	18½	20	22	15½	18	20
3 Buttock to patella	21½	23½	25	20½	22	24
4 Buttock to back of knee	17	19	20½	16	18	19½
5 Knee height (no shoes)	20	21½	23½	17	19½	21½

Dimension	5th %ile female	95th %ile male
6 Shoulder point above seat (sitting shoulder height less 2 in)	17 in	23 in
7 Shoulder point to elbow hinge (shoulder to elbow less 1½ in)	10½ in	14½ in
8 Elbow hinge to closed hand (elbow to fingertip less 1 in for hinge and 4 in for closed hand)	11 in	15 in
9 Sitting eye level above seat	25½ in	33½ in

TABLE 2.—OPTIMUM SEAT PARAMETERS (see Fig. 6)

SEAT PARAMETERS
optimum E = 105° (90% acceptable, 102°–108°)
C = 6° (90% acceptable, 5°–8°)
B ⩽ 16 in for small women
= 17 in as compromise (provided knee pivot of small woman > 2½ in above seat front edge, to allow full pedal depression)
A = 18–24 in
D < 15–16 in

TABLE 3.—ANGLES FOR FOOT CONTROLS

A optimum = 90°—'off' position
A maximum = 125°—'full on' position
A absolute minimum = 75° to avoid pain in toe extensor muscles
C max = 15° (corresponding to B max = 3 in)

A sports/racing car requiring accurate control is suited by a vertical wheel; an extended arm position gives maximum speed for what is a short time activity of high stress. Heavy commercial vehicles with high steering load, when power assistance is not available, require a more horizontal plane, though this is changing with the standardization of power steering. For private cars 40–60 degrees wheel inclination to the horizontal is satisfactory.

In Fig. 8 angle A should be from 0 to 40 degrees, B between 80 and 125 degrees, C between 14 and 19 degrees, D greater than 6 in (150 mm), and 8 in (200 mm) for E = 12 in (300 mm) and 15 in (380 mm), respectively, and F ideally equal to 14 in (350 mm). These dimensions are based on hands gripping the wheel at extreme width on a horizontal axis.

Ergonomics Techniques in Ride and Handling Evaluation.—In order to engineer satisfactory vehicle performance in terms of ride comfort and handling control it is useful to adopt an ergonomic approach in finding the design criteria which give preferred human responses. Both ride and handling are characteristics of road/vehicle/occupant combinations and this should be realised before modelling simulations. Different stimuli received by drivers on the one hand, and passengers on the other, should also be taken into account.

Human sense organs involved in ride vibration perception include the vestibular systems—those near the ear for detecting linear and angular accelerations of the head—and the proprioceptors, throughout the body, which respond to pressure changes. Hence, mechanical responses of the body to vibratory energies has to be considered (Ref. 6).

For handling control Wohl (Ref. 7) has proposed two possible transfer functions for the driver:

$$\frac{F}{\psi} = \frac{W}{TkV} \quad (1) \quad \text{and} \quad \frac{F}{x} = \frac{W}{kT^2v^2} \quad (2)$$

where F = force applied to the steering wheel, W = wheelbase, v = speed, T = driver's response time, ψ = direction of motion relative to reference line (eg the road lane), and x = distance from reference line. Whether equation (1) or (2) applies depends on whether the driver is steering mainly by ψ or by x. In each case, or even if there is some weighted combination of the two, it appears that the driver's gain must be velocity modulated; however, we know from many other studies that the human operator performs best when acting in a servo loop as a simple amplifier with a high constant gain. To create this situation for the driver, a given steering wheel torque must result in the same rate of change of vehicle direction regardless of speed. This is the case if:

$$\text{Front wheel angle } \theta = k \,.\, F \,.\, \frac{W}{V} \text{ and it then follows that } \frac{F}{\psi} = \frac{1}{Tk}$$

Such a system results in high gain at low speed, as when parking, and low gain at high speed when over-correction is more likely to result in instability. It also means that the lateral acceleration of the vehicle can be limited by the choice of k.

THE POWER UNIT

POWER TRAIN.—Basic thermodynamic theory and the piston engine are discussed in chapters A4 and F6. Here, the engine and drive-train (transmission and drive line) are considered together as the power-train, Figs. 9, 10 and 11. In the majority of cars and on some commercial vehicles the engine is grouped with the transmission and drive shafts in the increasingly popular front wheel drive layouts (on cars) and rear wheel drive layouts (on buses). Trucks still favour the traditional layout of engine, gearbox, propellor shaft and 'rigid' drive axle in-line along the chassis of the vehicle. In all categories, on-board computers are increasingly specified and control both engine and automatic transmission management as an integrated system.

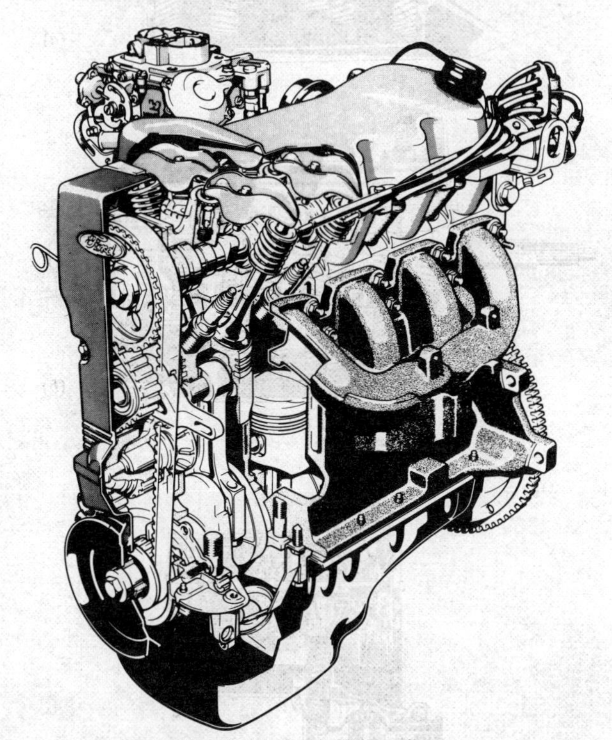

FIG. 9.—Ford 1·3 CVH engine.

Computer Modelling.—The computer has also radically altered the design of the power train and it is possible to predict engine performance using thermodynamic models, Fig. 12 (see page L10/12), and The Ford Motor Company is one of the manufacturers using this method. Revised versions of the engine can be conceived 'on paper' by feeding appropriate data to the company's central computer installation. A thermodynamic model of the engine is drawn up, and using the so-called 'filling and emptying' technique, the performance of derived versions of the engine can be computed by feeding in changes to the basic design parameters.

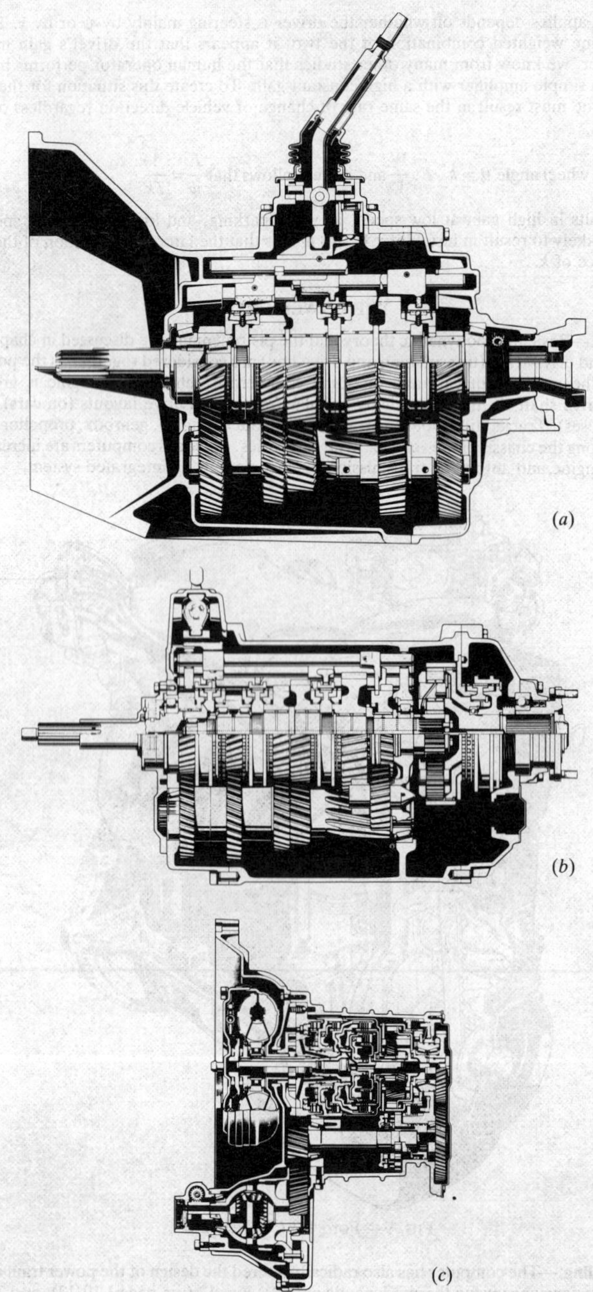

FIG. 10.—ZF gearboxes. (*a*) Ecolite for medium range commercial vehicles; max input torque 560 Nm. (*b*) Ecosplit gearbox has integrated splitter group and 16 gear ratios for heavy-duty commercial vehicles. (*c*) Automatic transmission for cars and light commercial vehicles with front-wheel drive, comprises torque converter with integral torsion damper, planetary gearbox, and hydrostatic control.

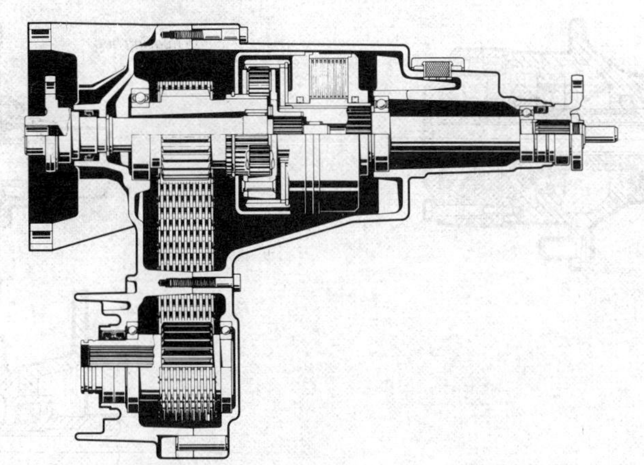

FIG. 10(d).—Transfer gearbox for passenger cars and light commercial vehicles with all-wheel drive. Consists of gear chain drive, planetary gear, and visco-drive.

Input data for the computation include engine geometry, valve effective areas, turbocharger characteristics, heat release rate, component temperature estimates, intake and exhaust conditions, speed and fuelling. The computation will then reveal indicated and brake mean-effective-pressure, power and fuel consumption, air flow, heat transfer, gas pressures and temperatures, and mass flow.

The various volumes of the engine are: compressor, charge cooler, inlet manifold, intake valve flow, gas properties, heat transfer, combustion, gas exchange, exhaust flow, exhaust manifold, turbine, and engine friction. Flow between the volumes can be calculated from the pressure temperature characteristics in each volume and a knowledge of the interconnecting effective areas between the volumes. Heat released from combustion is the basis for calculations showing how much energy is used in powering the piston and how much is released to coolant and to the exhaust. Turbocharger characteristics are supplied by the component manufacturer and exhaust systems are allowed for in the calculations.

The computation can provide performance parameters at each degree of crank rotation for a given load and speed, so a full understanding of a complete combustion cycle can be obtained. The pressure development throughout one cycle is, of course, crucial to the combustion characteristics, mechanical loads, and the noise emitted from the engine.

Effects of changes in valve timing, cam profile, and lift can be evaluated, and the prediction of the overall breathing characteristics (volumetric efficiency) of the engine saves considerable time otherwise spent with 'in the metal' development programmes. Turbocharger matching is another facility of the system that saves extensive development time and cost; even the effect of charge cooling can be predicted. Effects of changes in fuelling, injection pump cam form and inlet porting can also be studied.

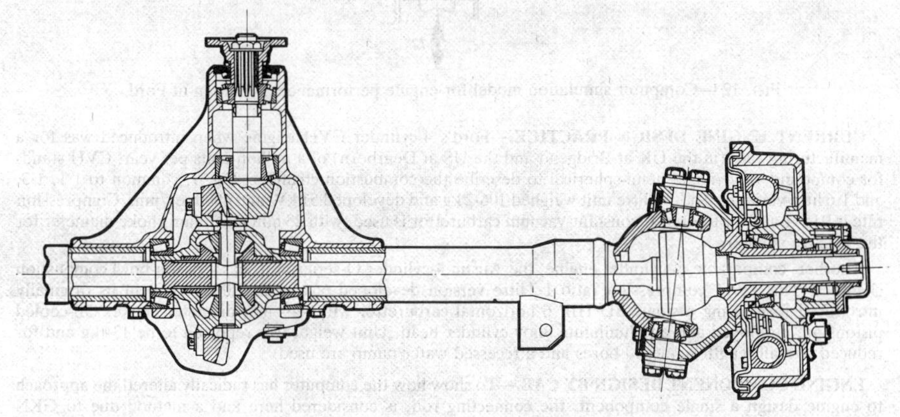

FIG. 11(a).—GKN final drive system: input reduction, steer-drive axle.

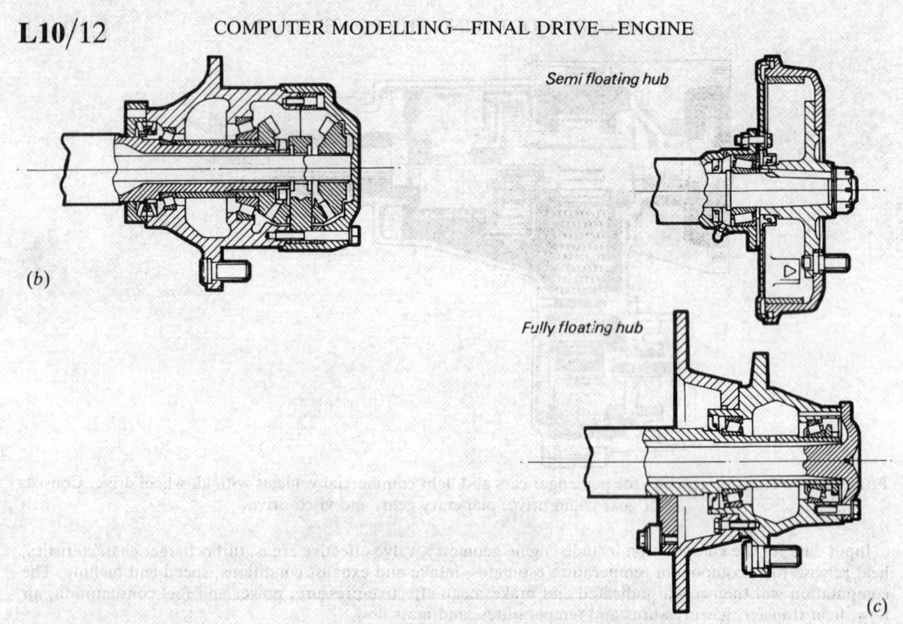

FIG. 11.—GKN final drives: (*b*) Wheel hub reduction for beam axle. (*c*) Floating hub designs for beam axle.

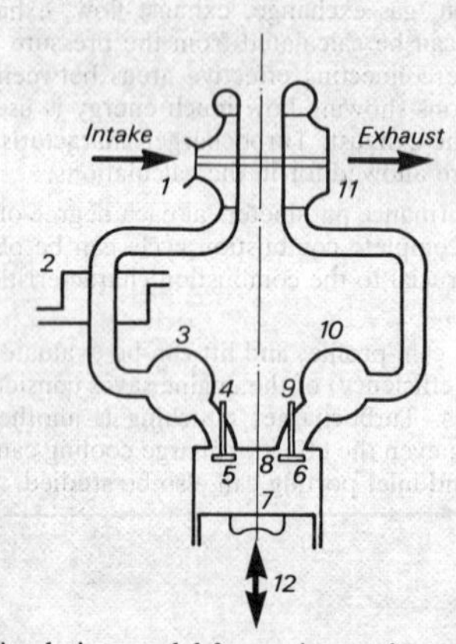

FIG. 12.—Computer simulation model for engine performance prediction at Ford.

CURRENT ENGINE DESIGN PRACTICE.—Ford's 4-cylinder CVH engine when introduced was for a manufacturing rate (in the UK at Bridgend and the US at Dearborn) of a million units per year. CVH stands for compound valve-angle hemi-spherical to describe the combustion chamber, Fig. 9, common to 1·1, 1·3, and 1·6 litre variants. The 1·3 litre unit weighed 106·2 kg and developed 51 kW and 6000 rev/min. Compression rate is 9:5:1 and a Motorcraft constant-vacuum carburettor is used, with 23 mm maximum choke diameter for the 1·3 litre version.

Another, comparable, 4-cylinder engine, the Austin 4-cylinder O-series unit, has a piston-bowl combustion chamber. The 9:0:1 compression ratio 1·7 litre version developed 65 kW at 5200 rev/min in its originally introduced form using a single SU HIF 6 horizontal carburettor with 44·4 mm diameter choke. Oil-cooled pistons are employed and an aluminium alloy cylinder head. Unit weight was reported to be 134 kg and for reduced overall length siamesed bores and a recessed water pump are used.

ENGINE COMPONENT DESIGN BY CAE.—To show how the computer has radically altered the approach to engine design a single component, the connecting rod, is considered here and a method due to GKN described for predicting the life of the part. This is also made possible by the ability to measure and statistically describe in-service loading and by the refinement of strain-life fatigue analysis techniques. Both allow a useful interpretation of design load histories for design calculation. This is backed by improved methods for cyclic measurement of material properties coupled with finite-element and related methods of studying internal stresses in components.

A continuous design and evaluation 'loop' is linked to rig testing and in-service monitoring and a system approach to the interaction of components like pistons, connecting rods and crankshafts had now been realised. Strain gauges at the critical areas provide data for building accurate Finite Element Method (FEM) models. Subsequent analysis reveals areas of redundant metal which when removed, without referring additional stress to the critical areas, can lead to equivalent strain distributions, before and after modification. A CAD system can then describe the new shape, from which NC machining of forging dies can be arranged with an associated CAM program. Service loads are held in a data bank where they are digitised in amplitude vs time form as an event corresponding to, say, an engine condition. The solid models of forgings are built up from brick-shaped elements which are analysed from a point of maximum stress in the model that will lead to a fatigue failure—while low stress areas point to opportunities for weight saving.

FEM for Optimised Con-rod.—FEM analysis can also be used to determine overall deformation, as well as stress level, and even buckling failures can be examined. With a con-rod, for example, the conventional form of column has an H-section, which is designed traditionally for buckling resistance. With the modern trend to shorter con-rods, this factor is of lesser significance and an easier-to-forge more rounded section becomes feasible, Fig. 13. In this design, material has actually been added to the big-end region, for improved bearing support. However, overall life is much a function of surface condition and, for example, suitably shaped sinter-forged rods produce a longer life. The computer reads an in-house developed contour-plotting program to generate an FEM mesh for these analyses.

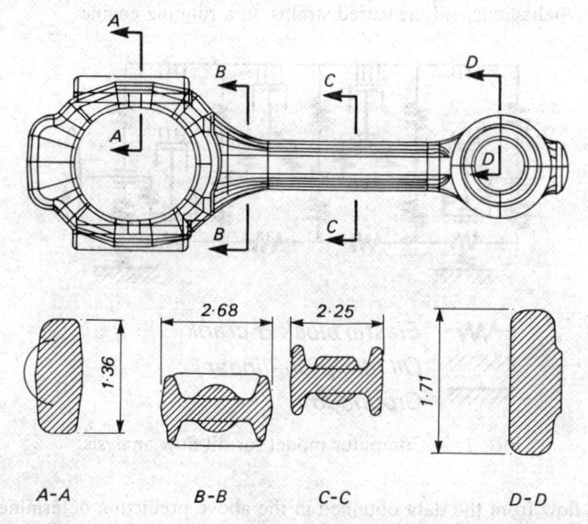

FIG. 13.—Buckling, as well as direct stress analysis can lead to refined cross sections.

Specimens are sinusoidally stroked in cyclic test machines which monitor strain and load. Both strain/life and dynamic stress/strain characteristics are obtained for different materials. Total strain is derived from a combination of plastic and elastic strains, and results taken when evaluating materials are in the form of scattered points which must lie in a strain band for acceptance. In the eventual design analysis a stress strain product rather than a modulus is used; another parameter needed is the stress concentration factor.

ENGINE SYSTEM DESIGN.—CAE techniques have also been developed to design systems such as engine-cooling and engine lubrication.

Modelling lubrication systems.—A program which has been developed by Perkins to model the entire oil circulation system of a high speed diesel engine can predict flow in both steady-rate and transient conditions. The pie-chart of steady-state oil flow in Fig. 14 is of particular significance. It shows not just that the engine oil pump has a high reserve of flow capacity, dumped (or routed to piston spray-cooling) by the relief valve above a certain speed, to cater for increased flow as clearances increase throughout engine life—but also shows the dominant effect of the crankshaft bearings. An understanding of crankshaft bearing behaviour is thus of key importance in the design of the engine lubrication system. The ability to apply computer techniques in this area shows that the textbook method for calculating oil-flow through the idealised hydrodynamically lubricated bearing are now inappropriate.

Dynamic changes in loading within a single crankshaft cycle destroy the concept of the journal rotating on a fixed wedge of oil; cyclic displacement of the journal within the bearing actually causes oil to be 'pumped'

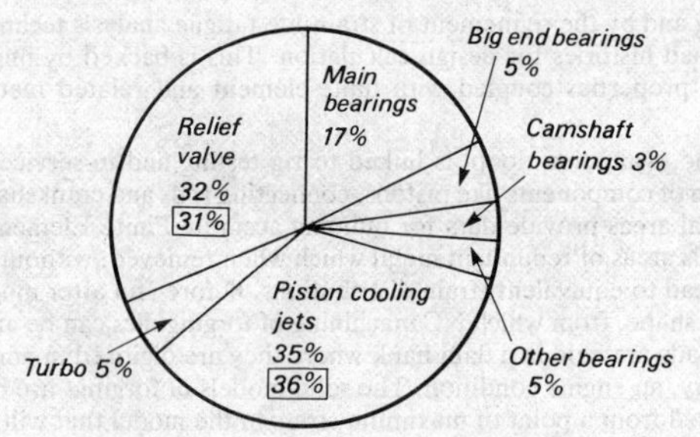

FIG. 14.—Steady-state oil flow in an engine.

in and out of the bearing at a higher rate than suggested by equating prevailing line oil-pressure with journal clearance. In fact peak oil pressure within the bearing clearance volume may be up to one thousand times the supply pressure. In the procedure for predicting crankshaft bearing loading, sequential solution of the hydrodynamic and structural equations has been found to correctly describe a real engine situation.

Sophisticated FEM techniques, for crankshaft and crankcase, are used to obtain the structural equations while the hydrodynamic operation of the main bearings is modelled by the 'mobility' method. Non-linear oil-film stiffnesses are elements of an overall crankshaft model, Fig. 15. Tests have shown that a good co-relation exists between predicted behaviour and measured strains on a running engine.

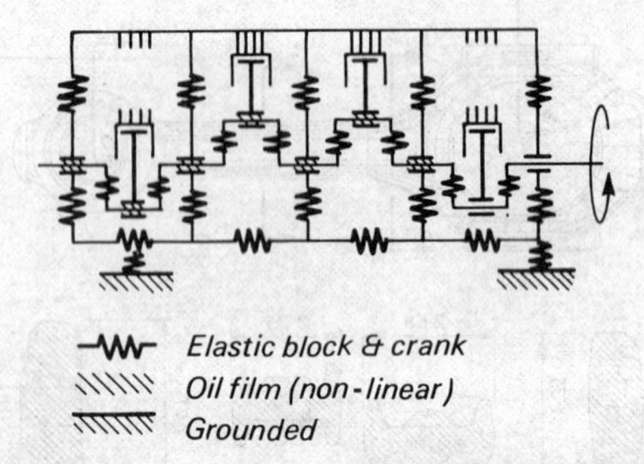

FIG. 15.—Computer model for oil-flow analysis.

The derivation of oil flow from the data obtained in the above prediction determines the size of the main gallery and feed pipes for the crankshaft bearings. The distributed oil flow prediction program can then be brought into use to determine the relative feed rates to other parts of the engine. The camshaft requirement is likely to be only 5 per cent that of the crankshaft, using hole rather than groove-fed bearings. For the valve rocker gear, non-hydrodynamic conditions apply in the bearings and much development know-how goes into designing the overall shape of the rockers in order to route oil along them for drip feeding the valve guides. Feed to the rockers is usually achieved by a flat on one of the camshaft journals, allowing an intermittent supply once every revolution.

ENGINE NOISE REDUCTION.—Other aspects of engine system design affect the whole vehicle. Engine structure design and exhaust silencer design are crucial to the reduction of noise throughout the whole vehicle.

Engine structural noise.—While engine vibration usually originates in the crankshaft assembly, noise generally comes from piston and valve gear, plus the resonance of engine panels excited by the crankshaft assembly. Besides the means to achieve best balance of the assembly, other considerations are the overhang of the torsional vibration damper (fitted to smooth out irregular gas loadings) and that of the even heavier flywheel and clutch assembly. Crankcases are usually stiff enough in the plane of the cylinders but may be five times less stiff in a perpendicular plane. Deep skirt designs and sidewall ribbing can alleviate the problem.

The main noise source of the valve gear is most probably the camshaft. It is hit a series of irregularly spaced blows on every lift and drop, yet slender camshafts are commonly provided with bearings only on each side of every two cylinders, or every four cams. Experience has shown that overhead camshafts with bearings straddling every cam, and light valve gear, do not get noisy at high speeds. In a pushrod engine having an unfavourable rocker-arm ratio, the equivalent mass at the cam is equal to the tappet and pushrod plus two valves. With pushrods, too, insufficient ramp on the closing side of the cam to allow for the collapse of the valve gear under the closing load, permits the valve to hit the seat at much more than the designed velocity.

A rocker shaft and its brackets are subject to the sum of the pushrod load and that required to accelerate the valve. For high-speed operation they should be designed on a comparative deflexion basis. As a criterion of valve-gear rigidity, the deflexions should be small compared with the ramps of quietening curves. They can be measured by applying double the maximum high-speed inertia load to the valve head, with the valve gear in compression. Valve springs with many coils and a low rate, surge and clash at high speeds, and do not remain as quiet as those with only three or four working coils. Rocker-gear covers should be attached directly to the cylinder head rather than to the valve gear or rocker-shaft brackets, to avoid noise amplification. For minimal noise these covers should be made of non-metallic and non-resonating material. Also, integral panels enclosing valve gear should be ribbed or have a compound curvature rather than flat surfaces. See case study below.

EXHAUST SYSTEM ANALYSIS

Smith (Ref. 8) has pointed out that the trend in petrol engine design is to arrange for maximum charge induction per stroke and to obtain fullest possible burning from the charge. This usually involves considerable valve overlap and, therefore, gives the engine a high sensitivity to back pressure and to the exhaust system design in general; for example, the problem of inter-cylinder interference in a short-stub manifold is an important one, Fig. 16, and Smith warns against the over-simplified approach of designing on the basis of mean back pressure.

Cyclic variations in back pressure for a variety of systems, measured on a single-cylinder research engine are shown in Fig. 17: the ideal solid curve (left) is compared to practical results, shown dotted. It should be noted that, of the two straight-through pipes compared, although the shorter (full line) had a lower mean back pressure, the particular length of the longer (dotted line) caused a negative pressure at the end of the exhaust stroke, at the engine speed concerned. An interesting point is that the depth of the velocity gradient in exhaust pipes due to wall friction is by no means insignificant and is measurable in millimetres.

Smith and others describe the basic kinetic energy theory of scavenging, before super-imposition of sonic wave effects, as a pressure 'slug' acting as shown in Fig. 18, whereby the gas column moves at an average speed of 60–90 m/s. The superimposed waves, moving at about 400–500 m/s, arise from the sudden pressure impulse brought about by the particular combination of valve opening rate and timing, in association with the cylinder pressure. There was also evidence to suggest that the high-velocity head of the gas as it enters the pipe is partially converted into a static head in order to accelerate the residual gas.

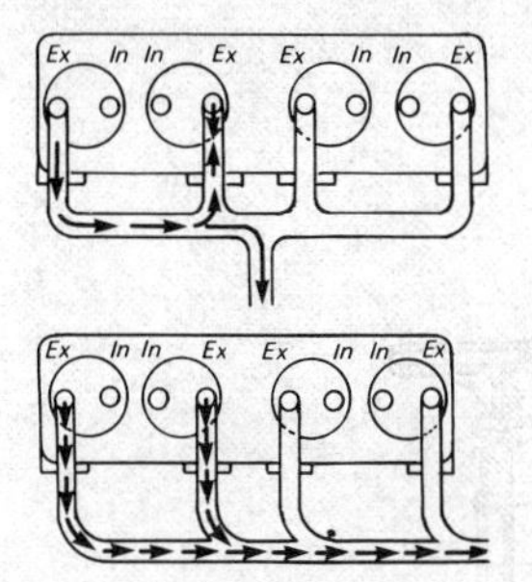

FIG. 16.—Avoiding inter-cylinder interference in an exhaust manifold.

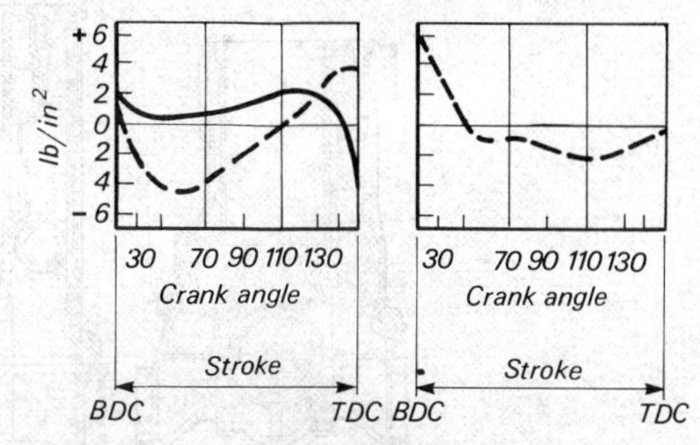

FIG. 17.—Cyclic variations in back pressure on single cylinder engine comparing short (full line) and long (dotted line) exhaust pipes (left) against ideal curve (right) for comparison.

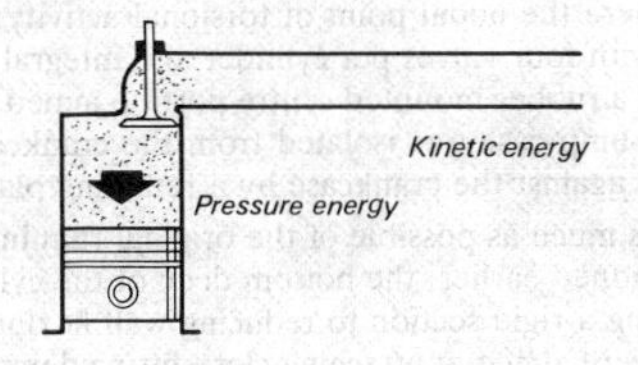

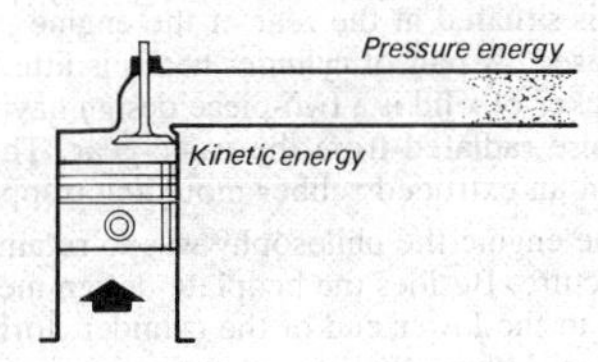

FIG. 18.—Formation of pressure slug (pulse) in exhaust.

Case Study in Noise Control.—The UK-government sponsored Quiet Heavy Goods Vehicle (QHGV) Programme, shows how a systems approach to the whole vehicle has led to an understanding of which are the best routes to noise reduction. The vehicle concerned was a 238 kW Rolls-Royce engined 38-tonne Foden S83 tractor which was demonstrated at the Transport and Road Research Laboratory to have a drive-by noise level of 81 dB(A) which is quieter than current truck designs, at the time of writing.

Tyler (Ref. 9) show the allocation of work to the contracting research organizations and the target sound pressure levels, in Table 4. The general design philosophy was to reduce sound emission from the engine by means of structural changes and to provide a structural enclosure around the engine and transmission to isolate airborne noise transmitted from the engine structure and its ancillaries. Thirdly, the cooling system is totally ducted and employs a mixed-flow fan and, finally, the exhaust system was redesigned.

TABLE 4.—SOURCE OF ENGINE NOISE

Research organisation	Source	Maximum level (dB(A) at 1 m	at 7·5 m
ISVR	Engine including gearbox	92	77
	Air intake, exhaust system (computer modelling)	84	
MIRA	Cab noise		69
	Cooling system	84	69
	Exhaust system (development of practical systems)	84	69
NEL	Final cooling fan design		(Additional target of 90 dB(C))
TRRL	Tyre road surface noise	—	75–77

ISVR Research Engine.—In the original design the engine was modified to use gear drives for all accessories and auxiliaries. Essentially the 13·05 litre unit (135 mm bore × 152 mm stroke) embodies a two-piece crankcase split on the crankshaft axis, the lower 'bed plate' structure of which imparts significant stiffness to the assembly. The upper part of the crankcase is of dry-liner design, and the whole assembly is arranged to have as many of its external surfaces as possible covered by flat sound deadening panels, Fig. 19, attached to the crankcase in regions of low vibration levels. These comprise neoprene and perforated steel sandwich panels.

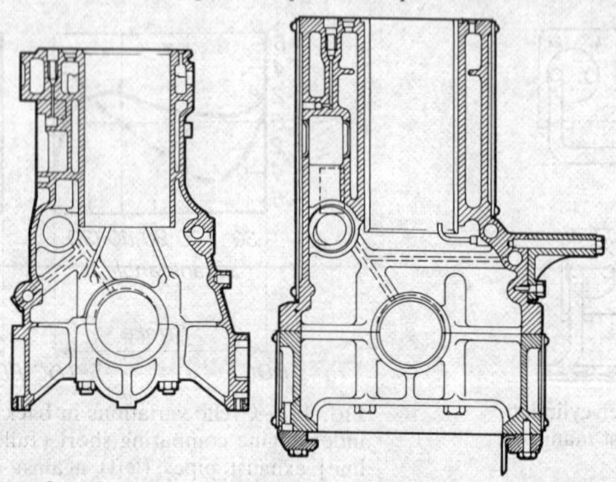

FIG. 19.—Comparison of engine structures before and after modification to improve sound insulation.

The gear train is situated at the rear of the engine, where the nodal point of torsional activity is low, and helical gears are used. A pair of cylinder heads is fitted with four valves per cylinder and integral rocker-box pedestals. The rocker-box lid is a two-piece design having a rubber mounted centre portion aimed at reducing the amount of noise radiated from the valve gear. The sump casing is isolated from the crankcase skirt by suspending it from an extruded rubber moulding trapped against the crankcase by a retaining plate.

In modifying the engine the philosophy was to retain as much as possible of the original running gear, in a strengthened structure. Besides the bedplate design mentioned earlier, the bottom deck of the cylinder block was moved down to the lower end of the cylinder, forming a rigid section to reducing wall flexing caused by crankcase distortion. Other crankcase structure changes were aimed at attaching close-fitting damping panels, including a single flat panel to cover the offside of the structure and arrangement of the ancillaries on the nearside. Panels were also fitted along the sides of the bedplate and oil galleries grouped on the nearside.

Computer predictions suggested that 2 mm offset of the gudgeon pin to the thrust side would reduce impact severity at full load and this was incorporated. Removal of the timing gear train to the rear of the engine involved the use of a compound drive. Pressure angle of the gears was reduced from 25 degrees to 20 degrees, and the teeth were also helically cut to reduce noise. Laminated, damped panels fitted to either side of the cylinder block and bedplate consisted of a central sheet of steel perforate and outer plain mild steel sheets, sandwiched together with neoprene.

Contributions to overall noise reduction from the constituent elements amounted to 2·5 dB(A) for moving timing gear from front to rear, 3 dB(A) for the damped panels, 4 dB(A) for the block structural modification, and 2 dB(A) for the isolation of the covers.

EXHAUST SILENCER CONSTRUCTION.—A MIRA designed silencer assembly, Fig. 20, built for the QHV prototype, is entirely reactive and consists of two cylindrical boxes with a total volume of 186 litres. It produces a back pressure of 39 mm of mercury and a noise level within 2 dB(A) of the target of 69 dB(A) at 7·5 m. The overall length is 4·27 m at 254 mm diameter, which compares with a standard production silencer for the equivalent vehicle of 1·08 m with a 254 × 330 mm oval section.

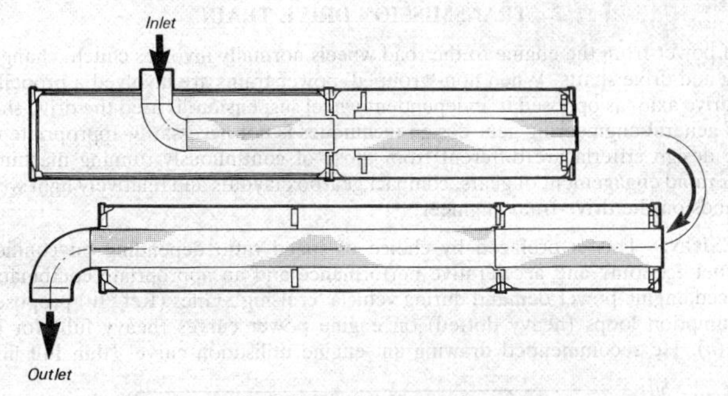

FIG. 20.—QHV silencer configuration.

Silencer Design Criteria.—The silencer maker normally receives a brief from a vehicle manufacturer governing the physical size, noise level required below the legal maximum, and back pressure limit. The last factor is also governed, in the case of trucks, by engines certified to BS Au 141a, which specifies maximum back pressure and inlet depression values beyond which unacceptable smoke emission could take place; this is at the 4·4 kW/t minimum installed power requirement for the engine in the vehicle. Principal silencer materials are mild steel, aluminised steel, and stainless steel. Aluminised steel is generally used for rear silencers on cars and for internal components; on trucks and buses both cases and end plates are produced in aluminised steel.

The general approach to design is one of allowing the exhaust gases to expand into chambers of large cross-sectional area. Recent research suggests that the energised column of gas, following an exhaust valve opening, with its noise (or shock wave) front creates the sound emitted at the tail pipe. Associated with this are 'gas noise characteristics' which need to be damped out or eliminated acoustically. Two different methods of approach are required for these different frequencies and types of noise, according to TI Chiswick Silencers.

Gases leaving the combustion chamber have a velocity of around 100 m/s generating a shock wave velocity of up to 400 m/s. At these speeds there is an appreciable distance differential between the noise created by the valve opening and the slug of gas with which it was originally associated. Expansion of the relatively low frequency wave fronts, successively, into volumes adding up to one-third engine capacity is general practice. 'Roughness' following in the wake of the wave front is reduced by the use of louvred tubes within closed portions of the silencer, acting as Helmholtz resonators to attenuate the high frequencies.

Shape of Expansion Chambers.—This is a critical area of silencer design, and a typical example for a present-day large car is a chamber having a 14·75 litre single cavity of large cross-section and overall length of 400 mm giving good low-frequency attenuation with offset pipe connections. Should the case diameter be reduced to 100 mm, the resulting 1830 mm length to achieve the same volume would result in negligible low frequency attenuation. In cars it is not usually possible to obtain all the volume in one place; hence the development of multi-box systems. The first is usually placed a quarter-wave length of the predominant frequency from the manifold. More often a large silencer, particularly for commercial vehicles, has several expansion chambers arranged so that there is a flow reversal between one and the next. The reversals cause out-of-phase pulsing at the same frequency with an accompanying attenuating effect.

One peak frequency in the combustion exhaust spectrum is loosely termed 'boom' and is often dealt with by a separate Helmholtz resonator. Here a resonating chamber with a narrow neck or tube inserted can be calibrated so that the resonating frequency is out of phase with the predominant exhaust frequency. It has been shown that the noise response before and after the insertion of a short tuning tube, 50 mm long and 40 mm in diameter is a 10·5 dB reduction in boom peak around 145 Hz, as well as a general reduction in noise level. Given adequate resonator volume, the boom frequency can be completely removed.

Over-run 'Rasp'.—The second problem of gas-induced noise is largely one exhibiting itself as 'pipe noise', case rattle, plate vibration, or 'over-run rasp'. The first three are usually overcome by such measures as laminated pipes, damped end-plates, increased number of bulkheads, and insulated case structures. The exact cause of rasp is uncertain, save that it is certainly affected by manifold design in respect of manifold outlet positioning in relation to exhaust ports. Without recourse to manifold redesign, the normal approach is to provide a resonator within 1070 mm of the exhaust ports. An alternative approach is to pass the gas through an 'absorption chamber' prior to expansion for eliminating higher frequencies.

Use of absorption materials should be treated with reserve owing to their tendency to deteriorate in service. The process of attenuation involves absorbing the sound waves in mineral wool packing and converting them into heat energy. The problem is to ensure proper packing of the material, type approval regulations requiring a durability cycle of 10,000 km. Long-strand glass silk is the most popular material, with basalt fibre as an alternative for high temperature applications.

TRANSMISSION DRIVE TRAIN

Transmission of power from the engine to the road wheels normally involves clutch, change-speed gearbox, final-drive gearing and drive shafts. When non-'grouped' power trains are involved a propellor shaft is added and when a rigid drive axle, as opposed to independent wheel suspension, is used the drive shafts become half-shafts. The use of general-engineering gear design techniques is not necessarily appropriate to an automotive drive train as the design criteria are different from those of continuously running machine gearboxes, for example. Need for rapid engagement of gears, compact gearbox layouts and relatively light weight construction puts special demands on the drive-train engineer.

GEARBOX DESIGN.—This is prefaced by choice of speed ratio depending on conflicting operational requirements of fuel economy and accelerative performance and an appropriate combination will result in substantially reduced engine power demand during vehicle 'cruising'. Giles (Ref. 10) proposed the plotting of specific fuel consumption loops (heavy dotted) on engine power curves (heavy full) for different throttle openings, Fig. 21(*a*). He recommended drawing an 'engine utilisation curve' (thin full lines), for cruising

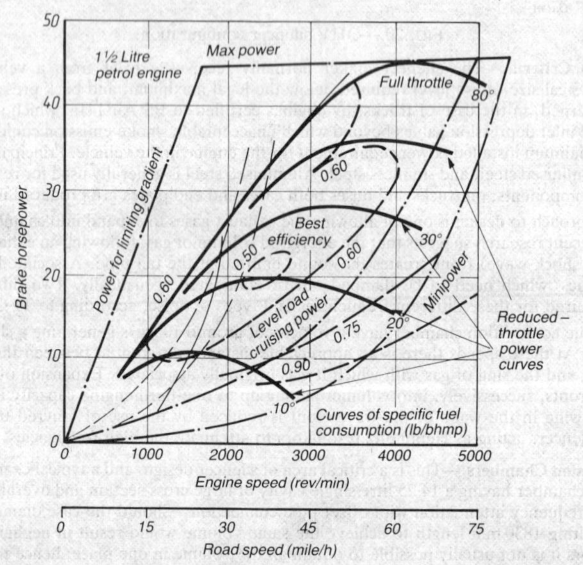

FIG. 21(*a*).—Specific fuel consumption loops plotted over engine power curves to determine zones of economical running.

economy, through the highest-lowest points of each consumption loop then, subsequently, to construct 'power requirement' lines (heavy chain-dotted) and 'ratio' envelopes. For a minimum power requirement curve, around half of the power required for level-road cruising can be used. This could be equivalent to a downhill cruise of 1:25, say, and power demands below this can be ignored. The 'requirement' envelope is then closed by the limiting gradient or road adhesion requirement, shown in Fig. 21(*b*) by a horizontal line indicating the requirement for maximum power at all road speeds so that best accelerative performance is available. Giles gives the following procedure for determining ratio envelopes:

(i) Calculate power absorbed in overcoming level-road resistances and hence find maximum level-road speed for given power.
(ii) Choose minimum power criterion and find corresponding engine-speed increments, from the curve, up to maximum speed.
(iii) Write down engine speed for distance travelled per maximum engine output, for fractions of the maximum engine speed, up to the point where power required = power available.
(iv) Similarly, write down engine speed/distance travelled relationship for minimum power requirement.
(v) Obtain the lowest gear by relating the maximum gradient or the limiting traction, to available engine torque.

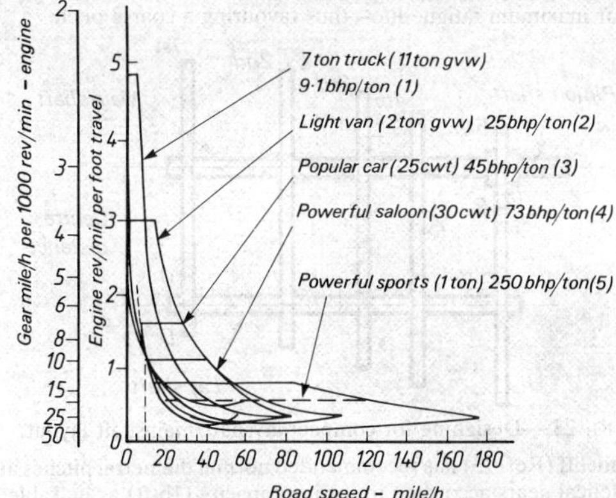

FIG. 21(*b*).—Engine utilisation curve drawn to obtain power requirement.

The envelopes shown superimposed in Fig. 21(*b*) are plotted from those calculated by Giles for theoretical vehicles in different type categories. They show at any given speed what useful ratio limits can be employed by the particular vehicles considered. He suggested that, at the time of writing, actual ratios chosen for real vehicles were generally lower than those he calculated, and that full advantage was not being gained from recently increased engine powers and reduced vehicle weights, a situation that no longer applies in the current vogue for fuel economy.

Ratio Stepping.—Abinett (Ref. 11) has pointed out that in order to obtain even down changes (and to make up changes possible at all) then torque/speed curves in each ratio must overlap the maximum torque point on adjacent curves. In general, he felt that ratio spacing should be such that undue strain is not put on the engine by either too low or too high an engine speed at the time of gear engagement. Referring to the practice of

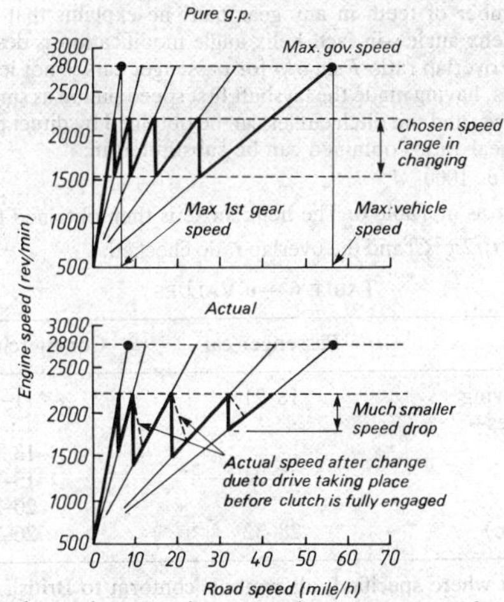

FIG. 22.—Theoretical and actual geometric progression arrangement for determining gear ratios.

arranging the ratios in geometric progression on commercial vehicles, he gave diagrams, Fig. 22, comparing theoretical and actual systems, to demonstrate that it was usual to arrange a close step between the upper two ratios for traffic conditions. This in turn adjusted the position of the lower ratios.

Lowest Gear Ratio.—Stott (Ref. 12) has referred to conflict between lowest gear ratio and shaft centre distance—a vital dimension in the overall compactness of the gearbox, Fig. 23. Since the higher intermediate gear pairs A cannot cope with a large 'step-up' speed, the first-reduction constant-mesh pair B is limited in degree of 'step-down'. In turn, this means that for first gear, the major part of the speed reduction is in the first-gear pair C, and the tooth strength of the smallest layshaft pinion D becomes the design criterion. He also pointed out that centre distance also affected choice of tooth pitch, since too fine a pitch necessitated a large centre distance for keeping tooth stresses within acceptable limits. Too coarse a pitch, on the other hand, gives rise to roughness, but Stott explained that, since case-hardened steels seldom suffered from surface failure, they could be designed for maximum fatigue life—thus favouring a coarse pitch.

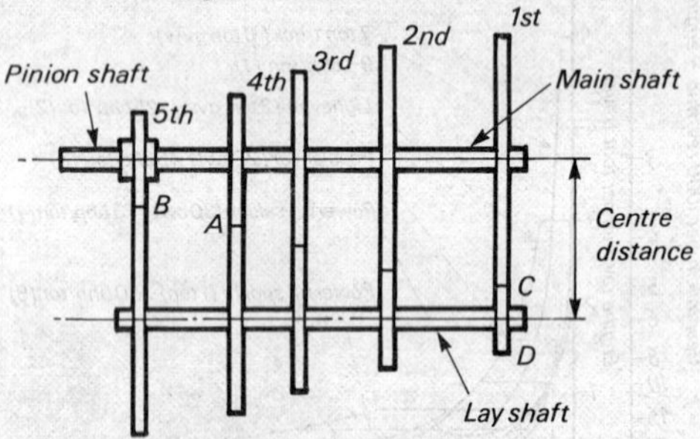

FIG. 23.—Designing for compact layshaft/mainshaft layout.

Exact speed ratios.—Radcliff (Ref. 13) has recommended normal diametral pitches and shaft centre distances (inches) for automotive helical gears according to torque capacity (1b-ft) as in Table 5.

TABLE 5.—HELICAL GEARS

	Torque range	Diametral pitch	Centre distances
Private car	<200	12DP	$0{\cdot}5 + 0{\cdot}5\sqrt[3]{T}$
	>200	10DP	
Commercial vehicle	<200	8DP	$0.8\sqrt[3]{T}$
	200–250	7DP	
	>250	6DP	

In considering the total number of teeth in any gear pair, he explains that this number can be reduced increasing circular pitch and helix angle—in fact, helix angle modification is desirable in each pair to reduce gear thrust. In this respect the overlap ratio $F \sin \sigma/p$ for passenger cars is not less than 1 and for commercial vehicles not less than 0·75. Thus, having made the layshaft first speed pinion as small as possible, the calculation of exact numbers of teeth follows, and the pitch circles can be obtained by direct proportioning. He then points out that the resulting overall gear ratios obtained can be substituted in:

$$F = 2P \,.\, m_e \,.\, R_{go}/v \,.\, 1000 \,.\, d$$

Where v is an undefined factor as in Table 6. The helix angle is then obtained from:

$\sigma = \cos^{-1}[P(T+t)/2\pi^2 C]$ and the overlap ratio checked.

TABLE 6.—v VALUES

Gear pair	Passenger car	Commercial vehicle
Layshaft driving	18–21	11–13
Intermediates—		
4th		13 15
3rd	21–24	15–17
2nd		20–22
Low (bottom)	28–32	26–30

Note: except where specified, all symbols conform to British Standard 2519: 1954.

Load Capacity of Gears.—SMMT advisers to the BSI have stated that the British Standard stressing procedures for gear teeth were not really applicable to passenger-car transmission gearboxes. In general, such procedures were too conservative in allowable load/life values and would result in excessively large teeth and gears to meet a gear operating life that is essentially only a fraction of that of the vehicle as a whole. Initial gear-teeth calculations on new car gearboxes involved service factors based on extensive study of past failure records of similar gears, together with accelerated fatigue test rig results.

Passenger-car Tooth Profiles.—Stott (Ref. 12) has stated that the British Standard involute tooth profile is more closely conformed with in heavy-duty trucks and tractors whose operation calls for frequent use of intermediate gears. For cars and light trucks, he explained that as full torque is transmitted through the gears for but a small part of total vehicle running time, required life can be comparatively short and stresses correspondingly high. On this proviso he considered bending fatigue rather than surface deterioration to be the criterion of failure.

For automobile gearboxes in general Stott argued, too, that since universal interchangeability of gears was obviously not required, standard tooth proportioning and tooth correction systems were therefore not called for. A drawing of meshing tooth profiles, which can be provided by CAD is thus used to correct the tooth forms so as to achieve simultaneous failure on both gears in a pair. Maximum tooth correction is applied particularly to the smallest layshaft pinion so as to assist the high stress tolerance on this sparsely toothed gear.

In automotive gearing, bending stresses were arranged such that relative cycles to failure are approximately in the inverse ratio to the numbers of teeth. Stott explained that, for stressing purposes, tooth spacing accuracy with modern production methods was such that the load application point on helical gears was midway along the line of contact. The life cycles of a gear can be written in terms of mainshaft cycles, the examples given in Table 7 being those which might serve as a target for initial development. Since the truck speed ratios are appreciably lower than the car ratios, corresponding input shaft cycles show a greater life between cars and trucks.

TABLE 7.—MINIMUM LIFE REQUIREMENTS AT MAXIMUM INPUT TORQUE (MAIN SHAFT CYCLES ÷ 10^6)

Gear pair	Light truck	Passenger car
1st	0·75	0·5
2nd	3·5	2·0
3rd	7·0	3·0

In general, Stott set the limit of tooth correction on a very small pinion as an increase in root width up to 0·125 in each side in excess of the face width of the mating gear. Modern techniques allow very small pinions of only 12 or 13 teeth to be made satisfactorily. Practical hints given by Stott include:

(i) The modification of helix angle to offset the detrimental effects of shaft deflexions and general gearbox compliances,

(ii) Slight lateral offset of mating helical gears to avoid corner fracture of teeth,

(iii) Limiting compliance of the gear wheel itself by using centrally located webs and approximating rim thickness to tooth depth,

(iv) Providing protective tooth-tip chamfers to avoid accidental deformations in handling gears in their unhardened state,

(v) Centre mounting of first speed gears in a three-speed box, to minimise tooth corner-loading effect arising from shaft deflexions,

(vi Helping to reduce noise by limiting: (i) helical overlap $>1·0$, (ii) pitch circle and o/dia. runout within 0·0002 in total indicator reading, (iii) 0·00025 in maximum variation from true involute, (iv) tooth spacing errors $<0·0005$ in tooth to tooth (maximum accumulated = 0·001 in), (v) 0·003 in maximum lead error.

COMMERCIAL-VEHICLE TOOTH PROFILES

Abinett (Ref. 11) summarizes the failure causes of commercial-vehicle gearbox teeth as:

(i) *Wear.* (a) Pitting—sub-surface shear stresses leading to oil ingress into resulting cracks and then hydraulical failure;
(b) Flaking (spalling) due to resonant dynamic loading during tooth insertion, or maldistribution of tooth load;
(c) Scuffing—breakdown of boundary lubrication leading to drastic failure.

(ii) *Bending.* (a) Inferior metals. (b) Bad heat treatment. (c) heavy overload. (d) High dynamic loading.

(iii) *Rim failure.* Fig. 24—stress reversals at points shown can propagate cracks. As rim thickness decreases, the two points approach one another.

He then calculates gear load capacity on the basis of BS 436 (Ref. 14).

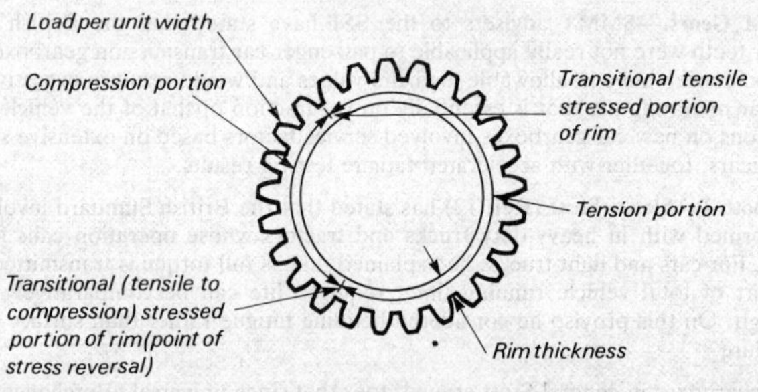

FIG. 24.—Rim failure nomenclature.

Tooth Correction.—The requirements for tooth correction of British Standards teeth has been given by Dean-Averns (Ref. 15), who describes the basic process as one of increasing addendum and decreasing dedendum in the pinion of any gear pair, and vice versa in the wheel. Fig. 25 shows uncorrected teeth for which the pinion has had to be undercut; the top portion of the wheel tooth is clearly redundant. This portion can be removed together with a corresponding reduction in pinion tooth dedendum. He emphasises though, that continuity of tooth engagement must be ensured, whereby line contact XY must be greater than the base pitch (circular pitch × cos ψ). Fig. 25 also shows the corrected profiles, for which the type of contact at various positions on the tooth flank is indicated; dark lines on the pinion represent portions of working by equi-spaced (and equi-sized) portions of the wheel. The figure shows that true rolling must take place at the pitch circle, but sliding occurs at the tips of the tooth flanks and can compromise the amount of correction desirable.

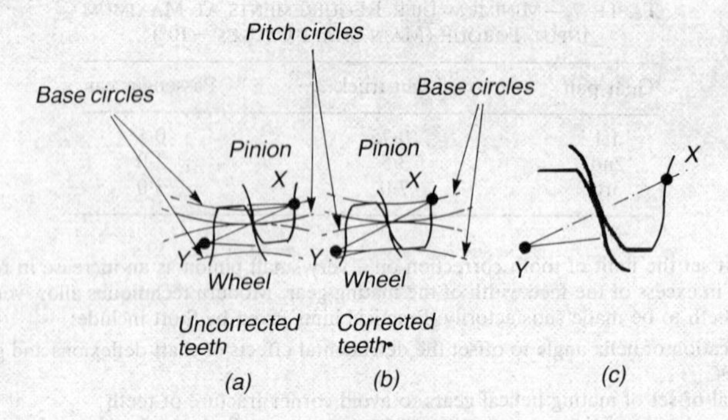

FIG. 25.—Uncorrected and corrected pinion teeth compared.

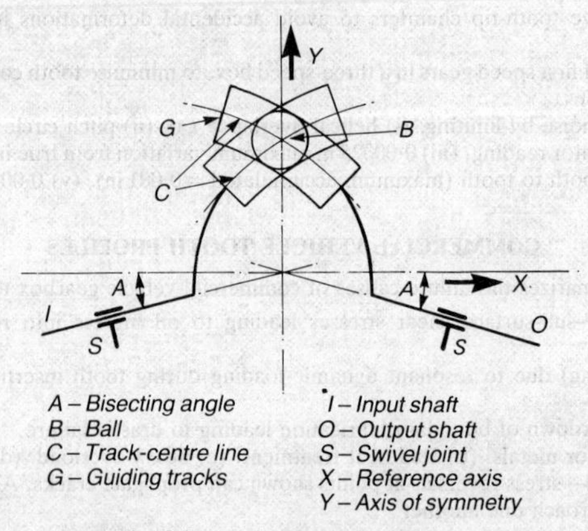

FIG. 26.—Geometry of constant-velocity joint. Balls always lie in a plane between input and output shafts.

Recommended addendum values are derived from:

$$Pn(1+k)/\pi$$

where correction coefficient

$$K_{wheel} = K_{pinion} = 0{\cdot}4(1 - t/T \quad \text{if} \quad (t+T)S^3 \not< 60;$$

but

$$K_{pinion} = 0{\cdot}02(30 - t\sec^3\sigma)$$

and $$K_{wheel} = 0{\cdot}02(30 - T\sec^3 v) \quad \text{if} \quad (t+T)\sec^3\sigma < 60.$$

DYNAMIC LOADING OF GEAR TEETH—Modern transaxle gearboxes often involve a gear pair running continuously under load in top gear. The superimposition of fluctuating input torques from the crankshaft and oscillations, reflected back from the drive-line, sometimes necessitate an analysis of gears under dynamic loading. Abinett (Ref. 11) recommended Buckingham's (Ref. 16) early approach to the study of dynamic loading, based on the analysis of results of an extensive test programme sponsored by ASME at MIT. He found that the well-known Lewis formula (Ref. 17) was inadequate to predict tooth loads even at low speeds, because, under 'dynamic' conditions, teeth were suffering from surface pitting at the pitch point, rather than failure in bending. Buckingham also concluded that, since dynamic loads were not proportional to applied loads, the use of velocity factors was incorrect and misleading. By applying elementary equations of uniform acceleration to the meshing of gears, and factoring the resulting expressions according to graphical relationships revealed in the practical tests, he derived expressions for the following: (a) Effective mass at pitch line of gears (b) Acceleration (c) Amount of tooth separation (d) Impact load.

These were combined and simplified to give a working equation of dynamic increment to be added to the tooth load W on helical teeth as

$$W_{dyn} = \frac{0{\cdot}05\,V_p\,(W + f\,.\,J\,.\cos^2\sigma)\cos\sigma}{0{\cdot}05\,V_p + \surd(W + f\,.\,J\,.\cos^2\sigma)}$$

where the factor J takes values according to tooth-to-tooth error e, as in Table 8.

TABLE 8.—'J' FACTOR FOR STEEL GEARS ($\psi = 20°$)

e (in)	0·0005	0·001	0·002	0·003
Full depth	830	1600	3320	4980
Stub	860	1720	3440	5160

In applying this formula to an actual commercial-vehicle type gearbox, Abinett (Ref. 11) selects a 'B-10' life for which the maximum number of failure is not greater than 10 per cent (average 5 per cent). He then determines maximum specific pressure intensity, S lb/in^2, induced by the calculated dynamic load, from the Hertz formula which, for steel gears, is simplified to:

$$S = 2290\surd[W_{dyn}(r_1 + r_2)/(r_1 r_2 \sin\psi)]$$

for meshing radii r_1 and r_2.

Cycles to failure are then read off a fatigue curve for 'B-10' wear life at 58 Rockwell 'C'. He then recommends minimum (cycles to failure) values for each gear pair on a typical five-speed commercial-vehicle gearbox as in Table 9.

TABLE 9.—RECOMMENDED MINIMUM CYCLES TO FAILURE ('B-10' LIFE) ÷ 10^6

Gear	1st	2nd	3rd	4th	Primaries	Reverse
Cycles	1·0	3·0	6·0	12·0	25·0	1·0

THE DRIVE-LINE

Loading Conditions.—Beyond the gearbox, the clutch and final drive gearing are amenable to analysis by fairly conventional engineering techniques. Fatigue loading must be taken into account, however; as it also should be in the design of drive shafts and associated universal joints. Macielinski (Ref. 18) has provided a design procedure for load/life calculations on both traditional Hookes type joints and constant velocity joints covered by the Rzeppa patent. The homokinetic behaviour of the latter types is shown by the author to depend on the torque-transmitting balls being guided in such a manner that they always lie in the plane bisecting the angle between driving and driven axles, Fig. 26. Two basic loading conditions are classified: momentary loading caused by sudden application of driving torque against stationary components, and fatigue loading caused by continuous variation of torque and speed when in motion. First criterion is the one normally employed in design and is arrived at by factoring a static torque capacity by 1·2 to 1·8.

Static Torque Capacity.—The Hertzian theory of contact between loaded curved surfaces can be utilised to obtain maximum contact pressure (in tonf/in²):

$$P_{max} = 1{\cdot}5\,P_{mean} = \frac{23600}{2240\,\mu v}[P_a(\Sigma p)^2]^{\frac{1}{3}}$$

(μ and v are Hertzian shape co-efficients and

$$\Sigma p = \left(\frac{1}{r_{11}} + \frac{1}{r_{12}} + \frac{1}{r_{21}} + \frac{1}{r_{22}}\right)$$

respective subscripts of r refer to radii of torque-transmitting bodies in direction of rolling and in the plane 90° to it; prefix 1 refers to the ball and 2 the track. Σp is conveniently expressed in terms of conformity ψ, depending on track type and shape. For straight track $\Sigma p = 2(2\psi - 1)/\psi d$, when d = ball diameter. Combining and rearranging these expressions:

$$P^3_{max} = \left(\frac{23600}{2240}\right)^3 \cdot \frac{1}{(\mu v)^3} \cdot \frac{4(2\psi - 1)^2}{\psi 2d2}$$

which may be written as $[1/K]P_a$.

Torque transmitted $T = P_a \,.\, n \,.\, R \,.\, \sin\Delta$ for ball number(s) and pitch circle radius R(Δ = pressure angle). Extensive testing has shown P_{max} to be 242 tonf/in² (ultimate).

Joint Life.—Values for joint life (L) have been determined using techniques developed by investigators into bearing fatigue who give $L \propto 1/T^3$; subsequent work on $C.V.$ joints gives $L \propto 1/N$ for speeds above 1000 rev/min. An angular factor has also been determined as $A = (1 - \sin\alpha)\cos^2\alpha$ and, empirically, $L \propto A^3$ so that:

$$L = \frac{396580\,T^3_{100}A^3_x}{T^3_x N_x}$$

where subscript refers to 'working values' and T_{100} is a joint 'application' torque available from the manufacturers.

From a working torque T_x, working life is obtained from:

$$\frac{L_x}{400} = \frac{T^3_{100}A^3_x}{T^3_x + 0{\cdot}094^3} \cdot \frac{1000}{N_x}$$

for steady conditions where N_x is working speed.

FATIGUE CONSIDERATIONS IN DRIVE SHAFT DESIGN.—Russell (Ref. 20) shows that, for design purposes:

Direct stress—alternating fatigue—limit = $0{\cdot}36u$ (for $u \leqslant 56$) = $0{\cdot}5u$ to 8 (for $56 < u \leqslant 96$) and =40 (for $u > 96$) where u is the ultimate tensile stress in tons/in². This postulates a maximum fatigue limit of 40 tons/in² for normal commercial steel qualities. With the absence of stress-raisers, fatigue-strength of case-hardened shafts can be factored up by $d/(d - 2c)$ for shaft diameter d and case depth c. Notch sensitivity for torsion is recommended as:

$$0{\cdot}9/\{[1 + 2{\cdot}16(175 - u)^4 \times 10^{10}]/\sqrt{r}$$

for notch radius r, in terms of torsional fatigue.

An interesting comment is made on the supposed 'strengthening effect' of splines: referring to the practice of cutting splines into a 'head' of greater diameter. The universality of this assumption is challenged (Ref. 19) by illustrating the case of a 440–450 Brinell number steel shaft with permissible stress at the mean diameter, d (approximately 45,000 lbf/in²), whereas permissible stress on the root diameter, d, without splines, would be about 90,000 lbf/in². The splined shaft could take greater torque at full load if:

$$\frac{d^3_m \times 45 \times 10^3}{5{\cdot}09} > \frac{d^3_r \times 90 \times 10^3}{5{\cdot}09}$$

that is $d_m > 1{\cdot}26\,d_r$ a condition which would fall outside the recommended BS splines.

Analysis of Sound Wave Phenomenon.—Other authorities in the area of fatigue loading suggest that gear-excited vibration of the drive train results in amplification of the pitching motion of the axle housing which when transmitted through the suspension to the body initiates a standing sound wave in the vehicle.

Computer analysis of this phenomenon involved a mathematical model developed to treat the drive-line as three independent dynamic groups, Fig. 27, in which a 'motion-generator' is used to simulate gear tooth excitation. Prominent parameters chosen to study driveline response are torsional acceleration of axle housing centre section and torsional input impedances of the pinion ring and housing groups. A computer program was used to obtain typical responses from which a velocity-ratio graph could be drawn and thereby define the

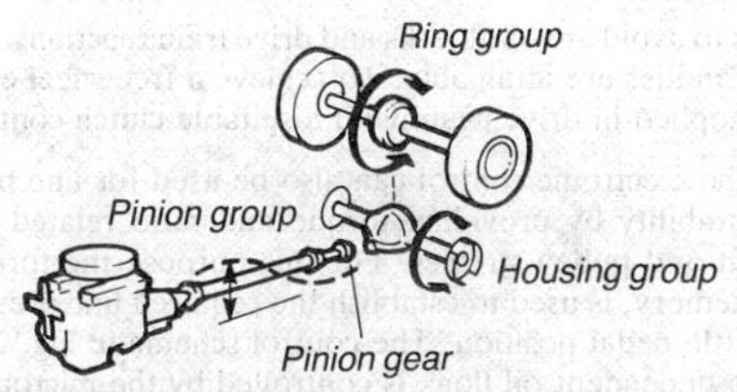

FIG. 27.—Drive line as three independent dynamic groups.

problem frequencies; other curves produced by the program served to isolate the effects of the different impedances for the pinion, ring and housing groups. A further program was used to indicate how curing devices, such as torsionally tuned dampers, can be made effective by generating torsional and bending mode shapes of the drive train at any frequency selection between 300–1200 Hz; then, by means of amplitude plots, optimum positioning of curative devices can be indicated.

AUTOMATED, AUTOMATIC AND CONSTANTLY VARIABLE TRANSMISSIONS.—In cars and buses, and increasingly on trucks, forms of non-manual gear-shifting are introduced to satisfy particular market requirements. These may be servo-shift (power assistance given to the manual lever effort), or automated 'hot' shift where the lever is actuated by 'remote' control to demands on load and speed sensors. Such systems of course involve speed ratios that apply to the gearbox and which is automated. A further refinement is an automatic transmission, in which fewer ratio steps are provided between, conventionally, epicyclic gear trains, engaged servo-hydraulically, and a torque convertor coupling replaces the clutch to provide a limited measure of continuously variable ratio changing. Much attention nowadays is focussed on transmissions which have continuously variable ratios right across the speed range. These are controlled by on-board computers and will probably become more attractive as the cost of micro-electronic systems falls and scarcer fuel supplies dictate a need to meet more economical running.

The Fiat Uno-matic CVT.—The underlying principle behind this continuously variable transmission (CVT) is the use of a trapezoidal section metallic belt and two variable diameter pulleys to transmit power. From the time the engine is switched on to the point where the desired speed is reached, pulley diameter varies in a continuous process that creates a continuously variable transmission ratio. The gear train includes two hydraulically controlled multiple disc clutches, one for forward gear, the other for reverse. Both are mounted on the main shaft and rotate the drive (or main) pulley via an epicycloid unit as soon as the engine is speeded up. This gets the car moving. Power is then transmitted by the belt to the driven (or secondary) pulley and from there to the differential via an intermediate double reduction unit consisting of two helicoidal toothed gear pairs, one on the layshaft, the other on an intermediate shaft. As the car starts, belt wind diameter on the drive pulley is at its lowest and the pulley is wide open, so that the variator works on a low ratio. Acceleration increases belt wind diameter and gradually closes the drive pulley. At the same time the driven pulley opens, thus gradually raising the transmission ratio to the corresponding high ratio value.

The two pulleys are opened and closed by a hydraulic control unit fed by a gear pump driven by the engine. The unit, affected by four different parameters (instant transmission ratio, accelerator pedal position, gear level position, engine revs), regulates and modulates the pressure on the mobile half pulleys. In particular the hydraulic valves vary belt block compression by the pulleys in response to variation in the drive torque ratio. Specifically, compression increases as the ratio drops and/or torque increases. The hydraulic control unit also governs the two clutches (one for forward take off, one for reverse), forced lubrication of the various rotary couplings, and oil delivery to the heat exchanger outside the gearbox. From one end to the other of the transmission ratio, the Uno-matic has a total spread gear ratio of 5·55 : 1. At low engine power (light throttle), the transmission quickly reaches high ratios with lower fuel consumption. Harder acceleration for higher speeds holds the transmission at low ratios with excellent acceleration and pick up. Kick-down will give maximum performance (pick up and acceleration) since the engine reaches 5000 rev/min at the lowest possible ratios required for instant speed.

Uno-matic Transmission Design Features.—This unit consists essentially of the following parts. A front unit contains an epicyclic gear train operated by a multi-disc oil-bathed clutch; this handles take-off and forward-neutral-reverse gear functions. Next is a continuous variator in which the drive and driven pulleys linked by the metallic belt are mounted on two parallel shafts. It is followed by a final drive unit incorporating a differential. Finally there is a hydraulic control unit including a gear pump supplying the pressurised oil used both to activate the pulleys and to lubricate and cool all transmission parts.

FORD CVT CONTROL SYSTEM.—Ford has shown that the power train matching capability of a CVT can be considerably enhanced by applying electronic controls to the transmission ratio control. The basic functions of the Ford CTX 811 hydraulic control system are: automatic start-up clutch control; line pressure control to provide adequate clamping forces and belt tension; and stepless ratio change control. An electronic control concept offers a variety of calibration potentials on top of the conventional hydraulic system. On the automatic start-up clutch control, the shift engagements for neutral-drive, neutral-reverse selection can be optimised for low and high idle engine speeds to avoid any shift jerks and drive train reactions. Different clutch characteristics tuned to the individual driving modes are attainable. To achieve a freewheel effect when coasting, the clutch can easily be disengaged and applied in drive again with a suitable clutch control strategy.

Microprocessor Control.—The electronic control can also be used for line pressure calibration to improve transmission efficiency and durability by providing torque and ratio related clamping forces and reducing thereby unnecessarily high belt and pulley stresses. For this purpose the torque versus speed engine map, stored in the microprocessor memory, is used to establish the required line pressure to transmit the torque for a given engine speed and throttle pedal position. The control schematic Fig. 28 shows that the ratio control valve, which provides the ratio-dependent oil flow, is controlled by the microprocessor output.

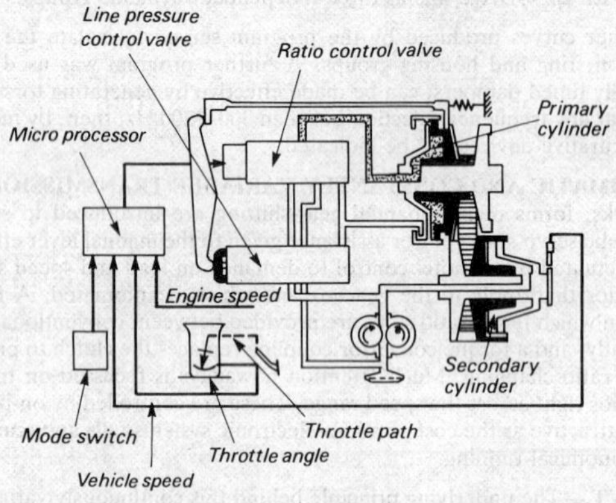

FIG. 28.—Ford continuous variable transmission (CVT) control system.

The control module functions from the following inputs: engine speed derived from the ignition coil; vehicle speed picked-up by an inductive speed sensor installed in the speedometer cable; throttle angle provided by a throttle position potentiometer and mode signal, supplied from the mode selector switch operated by the driver. The ratio control strategy is determined from mathematical algorithms and data files stored within the microprocessor. With the hydraulic control system only one control line tailored either for economy of performance can be established. The application of an electronic ratio control concept provides the flexibility of at least two different calibrations, avoiding compromise penalties of a single control strategy.

ALL WHEEL DRIVE.—Drive to more than two wheels of a four- or multi-wheel vehicle is now commonplace in both cars and commercial vehicles. The Audi Quattro permanent four-wheel drive system is well established for production cars.

Audi argue that the advantage of four-wheel drive in distributing the driving forces uniformly to all four

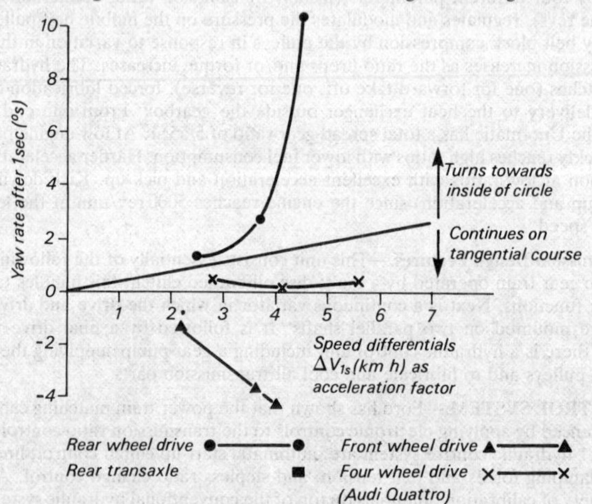

FIG. 29.—Cornering with fixed steering input at an accelerating speed.

wheels is not merely that it gives better traction. The total force that a tyre can transmit to the road surface (resulting from traction force and cornering force) is limited by the grip available. Therefore, a large amount of tractive force on one wheel necessarily means that this wheel can only develop a reduced amount of cornering force. Fig. 29 shows a comparison of front-wheel drive and four-wheel drive cars when cornering at a steady speed on a constant radius. The plot shows the amount of additional steering lock that must be applied to maintain the cornering radius at increasing speed, or lateral acceleration. The necessary steering lock application and thus the understeer tendency, is less for four-wheel drive than for front-wheel drive. In addition, the variations in steering response between driving on a wet or dry road and driving on ice are particularly small in the case of four-wheel drive.

Shared Differential.—In converting the Audi to 4WD the output shaft inside the gearbox, being the output gears, was made tubular on the Quattro, Fig. 30. The rear end of this shaft is splined, coupling it with a small

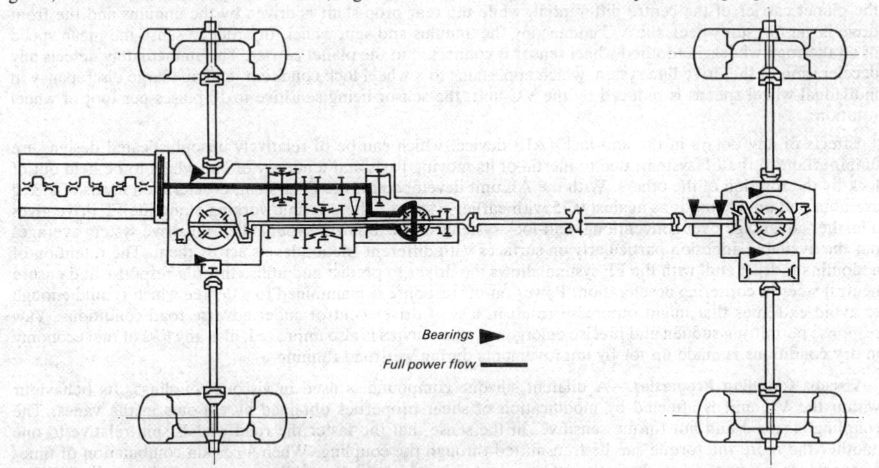

FIG. 30.—Four-wheel drive mechanical configuration used on Audi Quattro.

differential whose pinions then distribute the torque to the front and rear axles. When the car is on a straight course, the differential housing and the pinions inside it rotate together. When negotiating a corner or manoeuvring, the differential allows relative movement of the pinions, thus preventing wind-up between the axles. If this differential is not provided, the consequent tyre slip under fast cornering can reduce the possible cornering forces, and increase tyre-wear.

For these reasons a certain amount of relative motion between the front and rear final drives is desirable, but it must be possible to prevent this if necessary when the front or rear wheels are on a slippery surface, snow, ice or gravel. For this purpose the differential housing can be coupled with the rear take-off flange; in other words the differential can be locked. The differential on the rear axle can also be locked in a similar way, so progress is assured even in the worst road conditions.

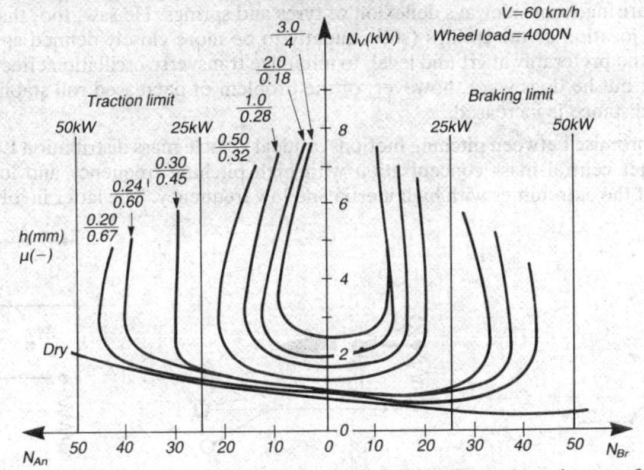

FIG. 31.—Power loss vs tractive power as a function of road water film.

Tyre Traction.—The vertical axis, Nv, in Fig. 31 shows the power loss in kW and the horizontal axis the tractive power—either propulsion, N_{An}, or retardation—at 60 km/h and as a function of the water film thickness on the road surface. The μ values given only apply accurately for the tyres used here (size 175/170HR 14) and for these test conditions. Due to the non-linear shape of the curves, it can be calculated that, when comparing for example 2 × 50 kW tractive power and 2 × 0 kW (rear wheels on over-run) with 4 × 25 kW on a dry road, the power loss is 11 per cent greater for the layout with two driven wheels. The diagram also shows, for instance, that 25 kW tractive power per wheel can just be transmitted with a water film thickness of 0·4 mm whereas with four-wheel drive the same power can be transmitted with a film thickness up to 2 mm. Taken overall, therefore, fuel consumption is not a decisive factor in opting for or against four-wheel drive.

Viscous Coupling System.—While the Audi Quattro gives even front/rear axle torque split, the Ferguson Formula system uses a viscous coupling (VC) between front and rear axles. The gearbox output shaft drives the planet carrier of the centre differential, while the rear prop-shaft is driven by the annulus and the front drive is via the sun wheel, the VC connecting the annulus and sum wheel. In order to sense the mean speed of all the road wheels, a toothed wheel sensor is connected to the planet carrier. This immediately detects any deceleration in the drive line system which appertains to a wheel lock condition, and any large discrepancy in individual wheel speeds is reduced by the VC unit, the sensor being sensitive to 10 pulses per foot of wheel rotation.

Effects of any delays in the anti-lock (AL) device, which can be of relatively unsophisticated design, are unimportant to the FF system, due to inertia of its moving parts and tendency of one wheel to be held out of lock by the rotation of the others. With the AL unit developed for the FF system, deceleration levels of 0.85 g are obtained on dry roads as against 0.75 with earlier systems. The AL unit working alongside FF drive gives a further advantage over conventional anti-lock systems of the 'bolt-on' type, in that the drive system averages out the available adhesion particularly on surfaces with different friction levels across them. The retention of a 'dominant drive end' with the FF system allows the driver to predict and utilise throttle response and ensure neutral steer in cornering acceleration. Power on-off response is maintained to a degree which is mild enough to avoid extremes that might otherwise result in loss of driver control under adverse road conditions. Yaw response permitting sudden and precise emergency manoeuvres is also improved; also any loss of fuel economy in dry conditions is made up for by improvements during wet-road running.

Viscous Coupling Properties.—A dilatent silicone compound is used in viscous couplings. Its behaviour within the VC unit is affected by modification of shear properties obtained by cut-outs in the vanes. The coupling is speed and not torque sensitive, in the sense that the faster the road wheels spin relative to one another the more the torque can be transmitted through the coupling. When a certain combination of time/temperature/pressure is reached, the VC torque capacity increases rapidly with virtual elimination of slip, almost a 'lock-up' condition, but without shock loading. This rapid torque-rise characteristic is known as the 'hump', and is plotted at a constant speed difference of 155 rev/min. As soon as the slip speed ceases, the 'hump' collapses and the VC unit reverts to its normal behaviour.

SUSPENSION AND RUNNING GEAR

SUSPENSION DESIGN FOR IMPROVED RIDE.—One of the observations of Lanchester (Ref. 19) pioneer researcher in vehicle ride, was that whereas vertical ride motions were essentially direct-related to road contour the superimposed lateral motions had an important secondary relationship with centre of gravity height, as simply expressed in Fig. 32. In this motion, resulting from negotiation of the kind of obstacles illustrated, he propounded a lateral reaction at the tyres, proportional to the centre of gravity height, causing a 'hustling' of the tyres on the road arising from sideways deflexion of tyres and springs. He saw, too, that the height, above ground, of the lateral location of the springs (subsequently to be more closely defined as roll centre) should be as low as possible, and preferably at ground level, to minimize transverse oscillation effects—with a tolerably high centre of gravity; but he does warn, however, of the problem of decreased roll stability as the centre of gravity-to-roll-centre distance is increased.

On the second compromise between pitching motions *vs* ideal vehicle mass distribution Lanchester preferred the 'extremes' of either central mass concentration with high pitching frequency and low inertia, or, concentration of masses at the extremities with high inertia and low frequency. The latter involved acquiring much

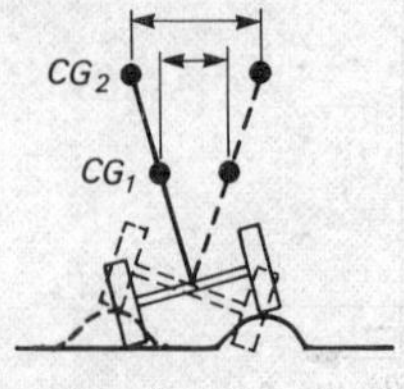

FIG. 32.—Cross-wise road motions.

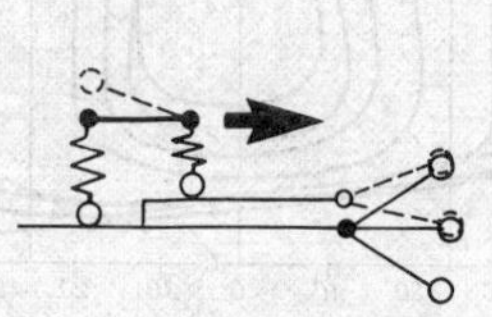
FIG. 33.—Pendulum analogy.

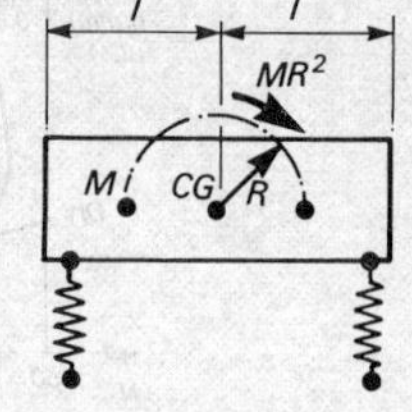

FIG. 34.—Simplified ride model.

lower pitch energy to be lost, than the former.

A simple pendulum analogy can be used to represent the sudden discontinuity in road level as horizontal displacement of the pendulum fulcrum. In the example shown in Fig. 33 of a step in road height the suspended body has no time to respond to the change, during the change. Then, as the swing begins, if, after a half-swing the original fulcrum position is restored, oscillations pile up on one another and the ride is bad. The importance of the pitching period to wheelbase relationships, for rough-road operation, is thus established.

Road wheel disturbance.—In the case of a single bump in the road, following sudden displacement of the fulcrum and its sudden return, the suspended body will be in 'midswing' and possessed of impulse velocity, with direction according to striking front or rear wheels. If the rear-wheel disturbance is a complete period later, the front-wheel disturbance is annihilated; for a half-period interval between disturbances, an amplification takes place. As the same critical velocities thus apply for both road condition, Lanchester considers the analogue justified; he pointed out, however, that magnitude of impulse (energy imparted) $\propto$ (time of application)^2, which is $1/\propto$ (velocity)^2. This showed how speed (in ironing out roughness) was to be an additional parameter, to be used as well as those describing the analogy.

He uses the simplified ride model, Fig. 34, to show equality of pitch and bounce frequencies for $l = R$. Instead of resorting to the more generalized analysis, he merely states that as the wheelbase is inevitably longer than the idealized spring base, the pitch frequency is too high on all but the most soft-spring vehicles; hence the need for coupled suspension systems. In roll, however, the opposite problem occurs and the spring base being too narrow, in respect of the transverse moment of inertia, it creates the need for an anti-roll bar; hence, the righting moment varies as (springbase)^2.

The presence of quite high levels of spring and suspension friction in commerial vehicles might justify Lanchester's consideration of vehicle suspension as two uncoupled single-degree-of-freedom systems, front and rear, justified by the opposite end suspension acting as a pivot when the one end was being worked. The normal difference in front and rear spring ratio provides two distinct oscillation periods, up to the limit of friction anchorage, and thus adds validity to the argument.

In vehicles such as highly laden commercial vehicles with high differential front/rear spring rates, when conditions are severe enough to remove vertical load on the rear springs in negotiating a road bump, an effect is caused of a falling beam hinged at one end. Since only the centre of percussion of the beam falls with g acceleration, points backward of it have greater acceleration and the supported passengers (or payload) at this point may suffer levitation! Vehicle layout involving load concentration at rear extremity (grouped rear-engine/drive units for example) favour this situation as well as providing a high pitching moment of inertia.

Ripple Effects.—Campbell's (Ref. 20) idealized vehicle model gives the equations for a ripple input, from the road to the suspension, Fig. 35. For ripple/span S, depth x (and time of $\frac{1}{2}$-oscillation induced by ripple = S/V), tyre/ground contact is maintained for the relationship shown in the following equation which gives the half suspension period under action of the unsprung mass for vehicle front end:

$$\frac{S}{V} > \frac{T_f}{2} \frac{(W_f)^2}{(W_f)^2}$$

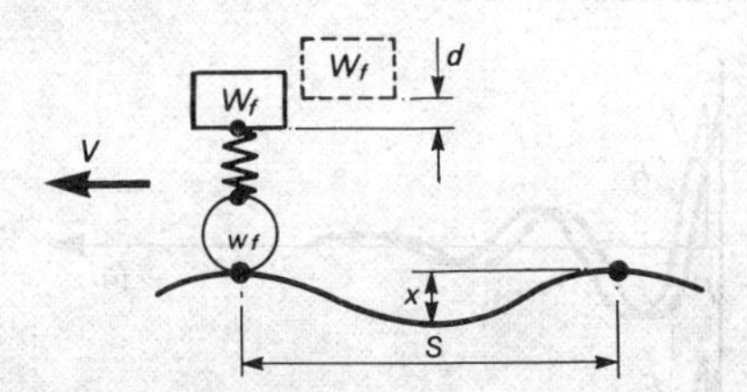

FIG. 35.—Road ripple W_f is Sprung Mass and w_f Unsprung Mass as Shown.

For initial static spring deflexion d, maximum ripple depth for maintained contact is related in:

$$x = d(1 + w_f/W_f)$$

These expressions show that, whereas sprung rate should be as low as possible, a limit is set by value of unsprung mass, which should also be as low as possible.

For a ripple frequency not coinciding with spring frequency, Campbell showed that input force to the suspended mass:

$$P = (W_f/g)a_f = (W_f/g)A_f \quad \text{so that} \quad A_f = (w_f/W_f)a_f$$

for accelerations A and a.

Hence, he suggests that for ripples corresponding to frequency of suspension excited by unsprung mass there is no body movement, yet when excited by sprung mass there is maximum body movement.

Case for Equal Pitch/Bounce Frequency.—Using only a very slightly more generalized version of the model in Fig. 34, having l expressed as l_2 and l_1 (to front and rear), Campbell states the simplified pitching equation:

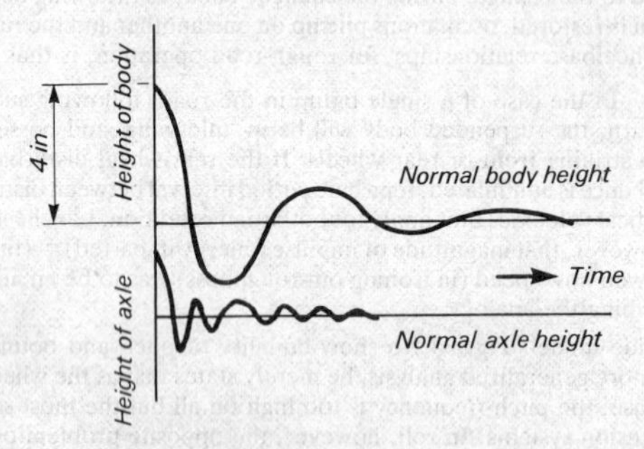

FIG. 36.—Vertical mode vibration test of sprung and unsprung masses.

$$t = 2\pi\sqrt{\left[\frac{dR^2}{al_1l_2}\right]}$$

to compare with

$$T = 2\pi\sqrt{(d/a)}$$

for bounce. Then he shows that for a certain disposition of road ripples, such that adjacent peak-to-trough equals wheelbase, resonance pitching occurs; a critical speed exists also for resonance bouncing and the interferences of frequencies l/T and l/t causes heterodyning (common on vehicles with engine amidships and low overhangs) resulting in R^2/l_1l_2 as low as 0.6.

Good Ride Characteristics.—Cain (Ref. 21) has used the results of laboratory-controlled experiments, on the free vibration of an actual vehicle wheel and suspension, to propose desirable data for good ride. Fig 36 is a plot of the corresponding motions of sprung and unsprung masses. As well as showing the need for spring/damper frequency low enough to prevent discomfort, other recommendations were:

(i) suspension rebound movement as small as possible to avoid the additive effect of successive bumps;
(ii) avoidance of sharp changes in body motion due, for example, to instantaneous accelerations at full bump;
(iii) well-damped wheel motion to present loss of adhesion of steered wheels and avoid crash-through arising from anti-phase peaks of wheel/body motions.

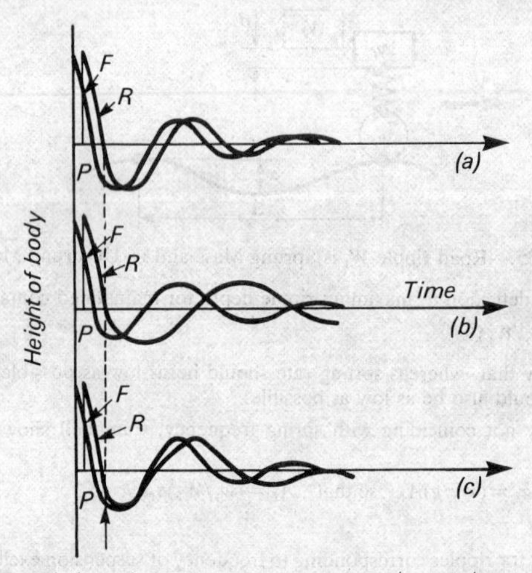

FIG. 37.—Pitch mode in vibration tests on front/rear (F/R) suspension.

Pitch Characteristics.—Fig. 37 shows the results of further plots of free-vibration tests incorporating a phasing device to simulate front/rear suspension motion relationships, as a vehicle passes over a single obstacle. (Speed is 100 km/h for a 3 m wheelbase vehicle's rear wheels hitting obstacle 1/8.8 s after fronts; a—equal spring frequencies, b—lower rear, c—lower front. Ordinates *p* describe the extent of pitching motion in the three cases with a clear preference for the latter). In order to minimise free pitching Cain recommends the use of near equal front/rear suspension frequency, with front slightly less than the rear, to compensate for phase difference in road bumps.

Damping Considerations.—Suspension analysts normally express damping force as a damping coefficient—a constant of proportionality multiplied by the vertical velocity of the vehicle sprung mass. On the other hand, the conventional performance curve given by the manufacturer is the work diagram—a plot of damping force times displacement as the damper is cycled with simple harmonic motion. From the expressions $x = X \sin \omega t$ describing simple harmonic motion and $F = cx$ describing the force characteristic, the theoretical work diagram is an ellipse having the equation $F = X\omega c/(\sin^{-1} x/X)$ where F = damping force; x = displacement (+ve bump, −ve rebound); ω = cycling frequency × $1/2\pi$; c = damping coefficient; X = stroke.

To meet the compromise between controlling body resonance on the one hand and avoiding axle excitation at the wheel hop frequency on the other, various departures from the elliptical work diagram shapes have been tried. The velocity rate is often reduced at the ends of the strokes and the rate on rebound is often quite different from the bump rate. Sideways displacement of practical work diagrams within the co-ordinate axis also occurs due to static friction.

RIDE FREQUENCY CLASSIFICATION.—Sylvester (Ref. 22) provides a valuable breakdown of the predominant ride frequencies, Table 10; they apply particularly to light vehicles but include on- and off-road types.

TABLE 10.—RIDE FREQUENCIES

Source	Range (Hz)
Main suspension:	0·5–2·5
bounce	lower range
pitch	upper range
roll	1·5–2·0
Boulevard jerk	3·0–5·0
Wheel bounce	7·0–16·0
Engine on mounts	7–18
Body structural	13–40
Engine internal	10–200
Drive line beaming	8–300
Road 'noise'	40–400

Main Suspension.—Sylvester underlines the classic view that the lower the frequency, the greater the comfort, but points out that bounce frequency had settled around 1.167 Hz for most cars—further reduction being limited, in conventional designs, by bump/rebound clearances; this was particularly the case for high laden/unladen weight ratios. In roll, particularly for light vehicles, frequencies have settled near the top end of the range in the table, due to the limits imposed on roll angles; it is also explained that anti-roll bars nowadays take the 'lion's share' of roll stiffness from the main springs. Owing to the inevitability of the radius-of-gyration-in-pitch being shorter than half wheelbase, pitch frequencies are invariably higher than bounce; exceptions are, of course, coupled front/rear suspension systems.

Tyre Springing.—Both the whole body (with friction-locked main suspension) and separate wheel assembly vibration, respectively 'boulevard jerk' and 'wheel bounce', are the two vibration modes arising from the tyre spring rate.

COMPONENT VIBRATIONS.—Some engines transmit troublesome amplitudes (around ±0·002 in) to the body structure, involving a 'booming' vibration above 100 Hz. 'Booming' vibration is also a result of drive-line beaming resonances, and, in the case of the monocoque vehicle, to the whole critical band of audible energy induced from road irregularities. This part of the spectrum involves 'rumble', 'thump' and 'harshness' below 100 Hz and, above it, 'road roar'. The vehicle parameters affecting vehicle response to these vibrations are given by Sylvester as:

(i) input impedance of suspension links, number of anchorages, their individual characteristics of the use of flexibly-mounted sub-frames;
(ii) body input impedance—as governed both by local reinforcements around the suspension anchorages and by the vibration-transmission properties of the whole body;
(iii) vibration modes of passenger compartment surface and the sound pressure pattern due to standing waves.

Structural Flexures.—In contrast to the vibrations of localized areas, the overall beaming (and torsion) of monocoque bodies—normally involving frequencies above 20 Hz—is not subject to regular excitation, that is except by wheel unbalance in high-speed cars. With commercial vehicles involving separate chassis structures, however, beaming modes are prominent. These have been examined by Smith (Ref. 23) and their effects illustrated in Fig. 38.

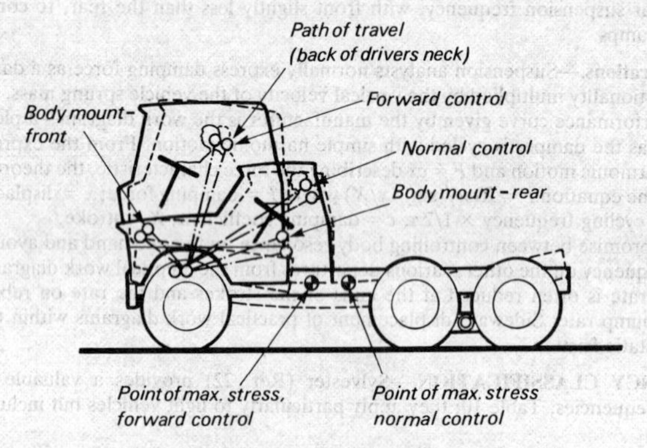

FIG. 38.—Truck ride motions.

Smith points out that, apart from the obvious solution of raising flexure resonance by deepening frame section, a more subtle approach was to increase frame-moment-of-inertia. This is arranged by sufficient and strategically located, rigid, body mounts; recommended spacing is 300–355 mm, with end-mount location not less than 127 mm in from the body ends.

Body-shake vibration is categorized in relation to 'harshness' by Boden (Ref. 24), who quotes corresponding frequency ranges as 5–25 and 25–200 Hz, respectively. To find changes in vehicle parameters which reduce shake without increasing harshness and vice-versa he proposed a hypothetical representation of the relationship between the two modes, based on subjective impressions.

Janeway (Ref. 25) concluded that 'Jerk', or rate of change or acceleration, was the critical criterion of comfort in the lower frequencies associated with vehicle ride, giving values of 700 in/s^3 and 150 in/s^3 as the discomfort threshold for vertical and fore/aft motion, respectively. Elsewhere he had provided dimensionless forms of the equations for pitch and bounce vibration which were an important milestone in the design analysis of vehicle ride. Using 'lumped-masses' at radius *i* in Fig. 39, he showed large static deflections δ (front or rear of his idealised vehicle) that:

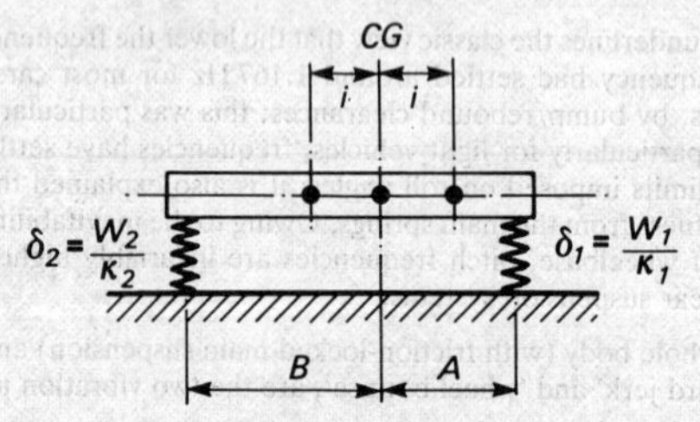

FIG. 39.—Using 'lumped masses' at radius *i* for equation of pitch and bounce.

Bounce frequency $fb = \left\{\frac{4{\cdot}9}{\delta}\left[C + \sqrt{(D^2 + E)}\right]\right\}^{\frac{1}{2}}$ and

Pitch frequency $fp = \left\{\frac{4{\cdot}9}{\delta}\left[C + \sqrt{(D^2 + E)}\right]\right\}^{\frac{1}{2}}$

for $C = a\left(\frac{1}{d} - 1\right)(\tau - 1) + \frac{1}{d} + \tau$

$$D = a\left(\frac{1}{d} + 1\right)(\tau - 1),\ E = \frac{4a}{d}(1 + a)(\tau - 1)^2$$

where $a = A/(A+B)$, d = dynamic index = i^2/AB, k = radius of gyration = $\sqrt{(I/M)}$ and $\tau = \delta_2/\delta_1$ where $\delta_2 \geqslant \delta_1$. Then a subsequent equation (see Fig. 40 for notation), derived by Janeway, gives jerk value at the driver's head:

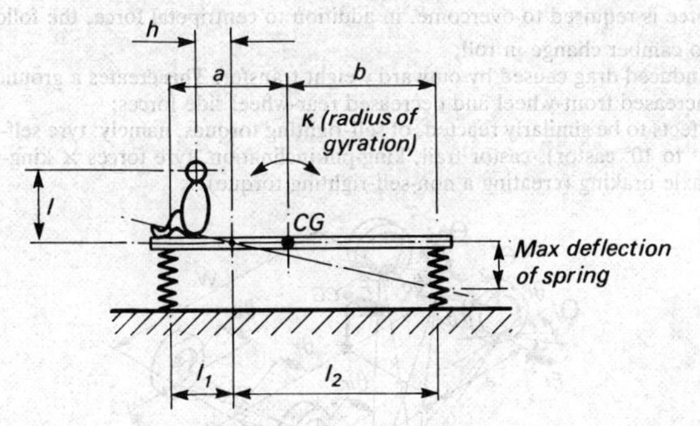

FIG. 40.—Notation for equation of jerk value at the driver's head.

$$= 8\pi^3 \cdot \delta \cdot fp^3 \cdot \frac{h}{l^2}$$

$= 8 \times 31 \times 5{\cdot}04 \times 2.19^3 \frac{h}{l^2}$; so for $l_2 = 80$ in and $h = 50$ in, horizontal jerk $= 158.50 = 7400$ in/sec^3

STEERING AND HANDLING

WHEEL GEOMETRY AND TYRE CHARACTERISTICS.—The expression 'Steer angle = heading angle + rear slip angle—front slip angle' can be used in conjunction with tyre-characteristic graphs of cornering force versus slip angle to obtain vehicle handling characteristics in steady-state turns. The slip (or drift) angle is conveniently understood by considering an analogous spring system, due to Ellis (Ref. 26), representing the cornering stiffness of a tyre, Fig. 41: a row of n (say 10) springs with fixed ends on ground and free ends attached to rigid member AB (also fixed in ground plane) subject to cornering force. If, for example, $L = 9$ in, $CF = 500$ lb and pneumatic trail = 0.152 ft and taking each spring to have stiffness $\delta S = 200$ lb/in, then, drift angle $\theta = 3{\cdot}2°$, $d = 0{\cdot}5$ in and aligning torque $AT = 76$ lb ft (this is equivalent to a castor angle of 8° with $RR = 13$ in, since $\tan 8° = 12 \times 0{\cdot}152/13$).

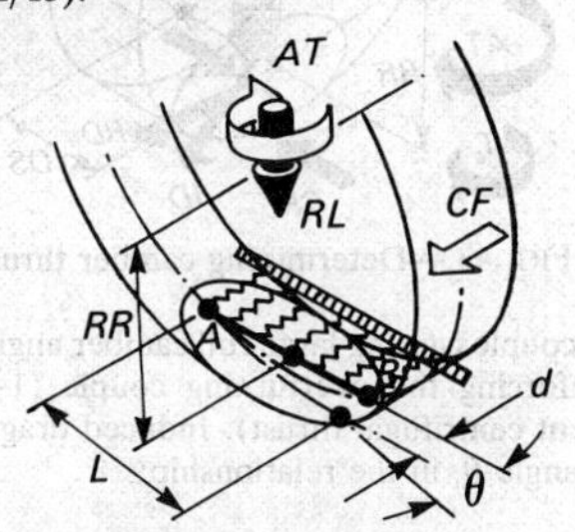

FIG. 41.—Cornering stiffness simulation.

The linear relationship holds until CF is large enough for slip to occur at B then θ increases rapidly and AT decreases. Effects of change in radial load RL, for the normal rated load of the tyre RL_0 are as follows: for $RL < RL_0$, L and n decreases and d increases, at constant CF; therefore θ also increases. For $RL > RL_0$, although L and n increase, $\Sigma\delta S$ actually decreases; d therefore again increases with θ.

Development of Cornering Force.—Fig. 42 can be used to differentiate between slip angle θ and steer angle Θ. At very low speeds the vehicle turns about a centre O on the axis of the rear contact-pitch centres; inner/outer steer angles are then related by:

$$\cot \Theta_0 - \cot \Theta_i = T/W$$

As speed is increased, there is a build-up of slip angles and drift forces which, in the case of a steady-state turn, correspond to those required to balance centripetal force, as follows:

$$F_{\mathrm{f}} = \frac{F \, . \, b}{W}, F_{\mathrm{r}} = \frac{F \, . \, a}{W}$$

Cornering (drift) force is required to overcome, in addition to centripetal force, the following effects:

(i) Thrust due to camber change in roll;
(ii) Differential induced drag caused by outward weight transfer. This creates a ground-plane couple to be reacted by increased front-wheel and decreased rear-wheel side forces;
(iii) Combined effects to be similarly reacted, of self-righting torques, namely: tyre self-aligning torque (can be equivalent to 10° castor), castor trail, king-pin inclination, tyre forces × king-pin offset moments, and steered axle braking (creating a non-self-righting torque).

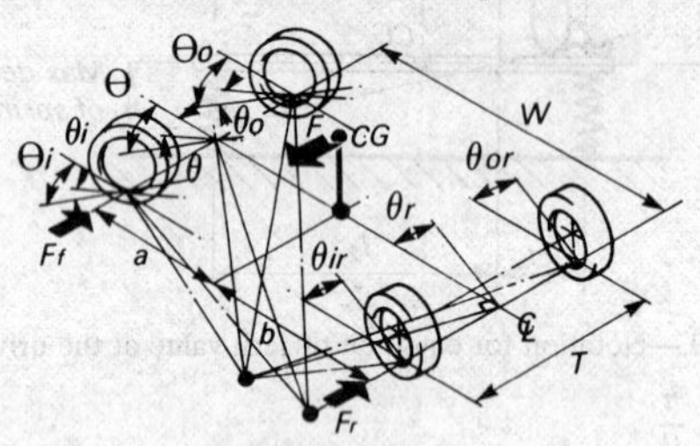

FIG. 42.—Identifying slip and steer angle.

The interrelation of these tyre and wheel parameters is illustrated in Fig. 43. Camber angle, C, causes camber thrust F_c in the ground plane, for radial load RL, up to the normal rated radial load RL_0 on the tyre. The relationship is:

$$F_c = RL \tan C$$

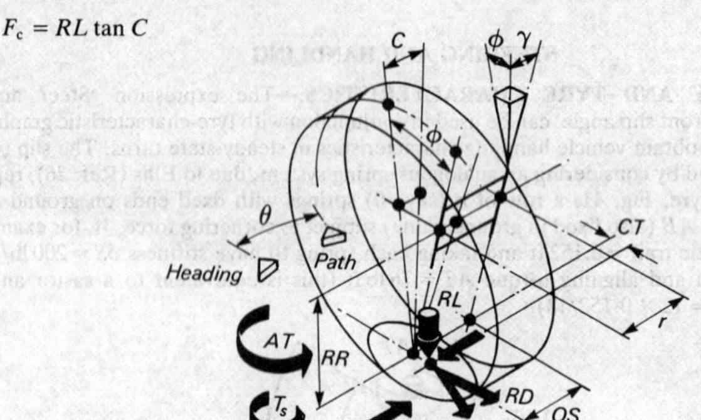

FIG. 43.—Determining camber thrust.

In the presence of an overturning couple causing large roll camber angle C_r, a powerful drift force is exerted, in the direction of the force, reinforcing the overturning couple (1–1½° camber change, at 0·5 g lateral acceleration, gives thrust = 5 per cent centrifugal thrust). Induced drag, ID, in addition to rolling drag RD, exists under a heading-to-path slip angle θ, in the relationship:

$$ID = R \tan \theta$$

Self-aligning torque, AT, due to the combination of castor trail CT and pneumatic trail—a value for the latter torque has been suggested as $\cong \frac{1}{6}$ of contact patch length (Ref. 27) is derived by:

$$CT = RR \, . \tan \theta$$
$$AT = CF[(L/6) + RR \, . \tan \theta]$$

King-pin offset, OS, causes a torque (created by tyre/ground friction coefficient, μ) in the static condition:

$$T_s = \mu \, . \, RL\sqrt{(OS^2 + k^2)}$$

k, the radius of gyration, can be approximated (if the contact patch is assumed circular):

$$k^2 = (\text{tread width})^2/8$$

King-pin inclination, γ, when neglecting the effect of vehicle rolling due to king-pin rotation, causes self-centring torque:

$$T_{KP} = RL \,.\, OS \,.\, \sin\theta \,.\, \sin\gamma.$$

Camber angle, Fig. 44, can also change with steer angle Θ, due to king-pin inclination, to value C' and also to a new value C'', due to castor trail. Thus, taking into account:

(i) King-pin inclination effect only. Because $H = r \sin C$, when angle $\Theta = 0$, then for any other value of Θ:

$$h_4 = r\cos(\gamma + C) \,.\, (1 - \cos\Theta) \,.\, \sin\gamma$$

Therefore, new camber

$$C' = \sin^{-1}(\sin C + \cos\gamma + C)(1 - \cos\Theta \sin\gamma).$$

(ii) Castor, ϕ, effect only.
Again at $\Theta = 0$, $h = r \sin C$, but for other values of Θ: $h_2 = r \sin\Theta \,.\, \sin\phi$

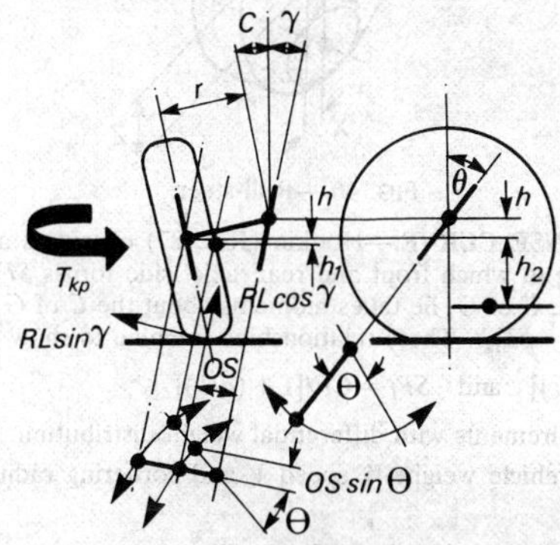

FIG. 44.—Camber change with steer.

In this case the new camber angle $C'' = \sin^{-1}(\sin C + \sin\Theta \sin\phi)$. For the combined effect C' and C'' are added algebraically.

Roll Effects.—Roll modifies inter-axle weight distribution according to roll-axis position and relative front/rear roll stiffnesses. Fig. 45 shows a vehicle with unequal-length parallel-link front suspension and trailing-spring beam-axle rear suspension. For a lateral acceleration a, the total couple about the roll axis:

$$\text{Total Couple} = a \,.\, W \,.\, H \,.\, + H \,.\, \tan\varepsilon.$$

For small angles of roll, the respective axle couples are:

$$\text{Front Couple} = \frac{S_F}{S_F + S_R}(a + \varepsilon)W \,.\, H$$

$$\text{Rear Couple} = \frac{S_R}{S_F + S_R}(a + \varepsilon)\, W \,.\, H + F_R \,.\, h,$$

(including those of the ground-plane rear tyre forces about the roll axis).

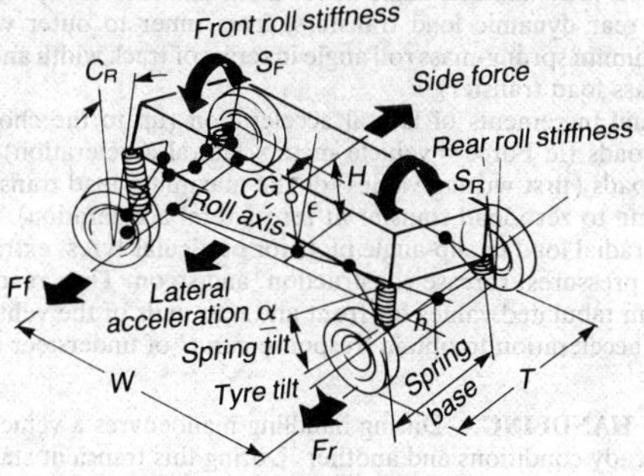

FIG. 45.—Roll motions.

Roll stiffness S relates spring and tyre tilt with spring base and track.

Rear roll-steer angles are related to roll angle and effective 'spring link' length. For a 'spring link' tilted downward at all times during suspension travel, Fig. 46, the roll steer angle:

$$\tan \delta = \frac{x}{z} = \frac{x/T/2}{z/T/2} = \frac{\psi}{\varepsilon}$$

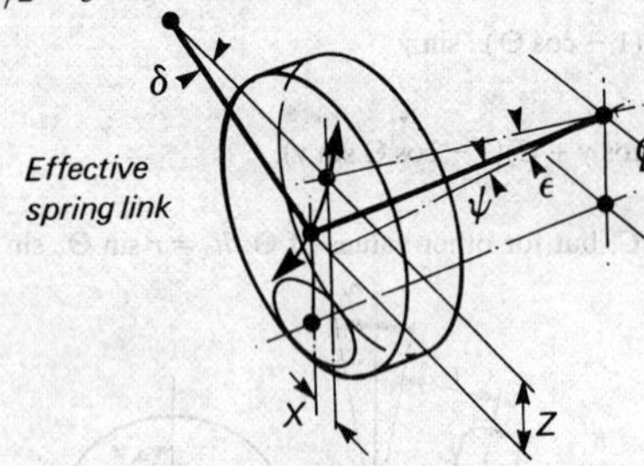

FIG. 46.—Roll-steer.

CONSTRUCTING A RESPONSE CURVE.—Hodkin (Ref. 27) considers a simplified load system for a vehicle in steady state cornering in which front and rear 'axle' side forces SF_f and SF_τ sum to the value of centrifugal force CF acting at the C of G, he takes moments about the C of G (set at distances a and b from front/rear axles) to obtain $SF_f a = SF_\tau b$. These relationships combine to show

$$SF_\tau + CF/[1 + (b/\varepsilon)] \quad \text{and} \quad SF_f = CF/[1 + (a/b)]$$

directly equating side force requirements with differential weight distribution.

$CF = (w/g) - (V^2/\tau)$ relates vehicle weight W speed V and cornering radius τ; therefore, by expressing centripetal acceleration as:

$$V^2/T \text{ as a percentage } (n) \text{ of } g, \text{ then } CF = n \,.\, W.$$

Slip angles β, being related to CF by the tyre characteristics and the degree of understeer $(\beta_f - \beta_\tau)$, can be plotted against n to obtain the steady state response characteristic of the vehicle. It is then necessary to see how tyre forces can be modified by such factors as differential tyre inflation pressures, cambering the tyres to produce extra side thrust during roll (by adjusting roll stiffness and suspension geometry), creating differential dynamic load transfer by varying roll centre height through suspension geometry manipulation and/or the use of anti-roll bars with predetermined front/rear stiffness ratio. The degree of load transfer depends on C of G height, and magnitude of sprung mass; and the extent of front/rear differential distribution depends (without anti-roll bars) on limits set by the sometimes conflicting sprung rate requirements for desired ride comfort.

The following procedure is recommended when constructing response curves to balance the effects of varying load factors acting on the vehicle:

(i) Write down from a gravitational analysis the sprung-mass weight, centre-of-gravity height, and fore/aft position, with respect to wheelbase.

(ii) Determine by geometry the heights of the front and rear suspension roll centres; obtain the position of the roll axis and find the distance x from it to the sprung mass C of G.

(iii) Express the sprung mass tilting moment in terms of $x \,.\, n \,.\, g$ (where $n \,.\, g$ is the percentage maximum lateral acceleration chosen) and equate it against the suspension restoring moments based on spring rate, spring installation ratio and roll angle θ, for front and rear ends, then solve for θ.

(iv) Calculate front and rear dynamic load transfers, from inner to outer wheels, for maximum lateral acceleration and maximum sprung-mass roll angle in terms of track width and tyre rolling radius (allowing also for unsprung mass load transfer).

(v) Tabulate against equal increments of lateral acceleration (up to the chosen maximum) a column of corresponding side loads (ie Force = vehicle mass × lateral acceleration), then columns of inner and outer wheel radius loads (first writing values for the maximum load transfer condition and decreasing linearly up the column to zero load transfer at zero lateral acceleration).

(vi) Obtain side force *vs* radial load *vs* slip-angle plots for particular tyres, extrapolating curves for different rim widths, inflation pressures, carcase construction, and so on. Then read off mean slip angles, that is $\frac{1}{2}$ (inner + outer) from tabulated values for front and rear ends of the vehicle. Then plot front-rear slip angle against lateral acceleration to obtain 'response curve' of understeer against percentage g-turn for the vehicle.

TRANSIENT STAGE IN HANDLING.—During handling manoeuvres a vehicle passes through a transient stage between one set of steady conditions and another. During this transient stage, the steering behaviour of the car is influenced by factors additional to those considered for steady-state turns.

If the moment of inertia of the car about a vertical axis through its centre of gravity is such that k^2/ab is unity (k being its radius of gyration), Fig. 47, the vehicle can be represented by masses W_f and W_r—equal to the loads carried by front and rear wheels—placed at those wheel centres. The centripetal acceleration of the front end of the car due to the drift angle produces no reaction at the rear wheels, and the sideways reaction at the rear will only build up gradually as the car goes on to a curved path. In much more common condition, where the k^2/ab ratio is less than unity, then the equivalent masses W_f and W_r will lie within the wheelbase, and the immediate effect of the angular acceleration is to induce at the rear wheels an inward force, which will then as before gradually build up to the final steady value. In both cases, the force at the rear wheels during the transient stage is in one direction only.

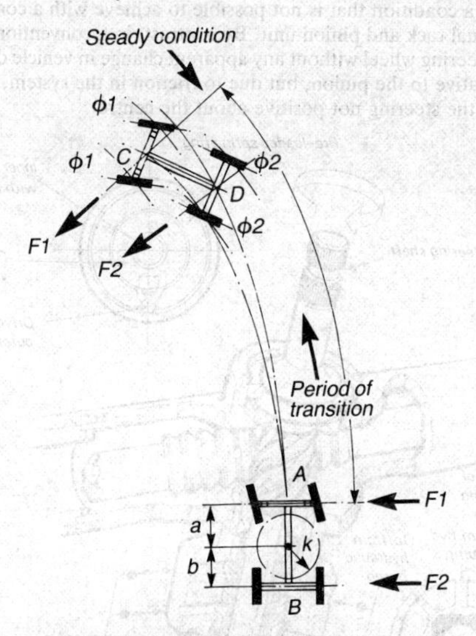

FIG. 47.—Transient handling.

Cornering Force Effects.—While a car is entering a bend, a higher load is required at the front wheels than that to produce the centripetal acceleration of the front-end mass, because rotational acceleration must also be given to the vehicle. This tends to compensate for the lagging 'tyre tread effects', and the car behaviour is roughly comparable with its normal steady-cornering behaviour. When a car is leaving a bend, a different situation exists. Front-wheel steering angle has to be let off so that centrifugal force can provide the necessary torque to destroy the rotational velocity of the vehicle round its centre of gravity. Drift angle of the front tyres is either eliminated or, in cases where steering angle is let off very rapidly, even reversed in direction. There is a corresponding increase in the inward force that must be supplied by the rear tyres, and hence in the rear drift angle.

The transient response of a vehicle can be either disturbance response or control response. Disturbance response is caused by the application of an external force to the vehicle at its centre of gravity or centre of pressure. Control response results from an input to the steering system in the form of steering-wheel displacement. These external and internal inputs excite the same dynamic system, and therefore the responses produced are closely related to each other.

During cornering both of these inputs are applied simultaneously. The application of steering input causes an external force to act on the dynamic system, namely centrifugal force. The resultant vehicle response is the combination of control and disturbance responses; it is observed by the driver, who then steers the vehicle to maintain the intended path. The corrective action of the driver clearly depends on the nature of the vehicle response. This can be understeering response, over-steering response, or neutral-steering response.

The difference between these responses is indicated by the path the vehicle pursues during or after the disturbance: whereas the path of an understeering vehicle turns in the direction of the disturbing force, an over-steering one turns in the opposite direction. A neutral-steering vehicle follows a straight path away from the disturbing force.

Under/Over-Steer Response.—During cornering, the resultant yawing moment produced about the C-of-G opposes the turn of the vehicle for an understeering condition, therefore tending to increase the path radius of curvature. A decreasing radius of curvature is produced by an over-steering vehicle, though, because the resultant yawing moment helps the vehicle to turn. The inertia forces developed by the understeering vehicle oppose the disturbance forces, so the vehicle tends to stabilize its motion. In the case of oversteering, the inertia force produced acts in the same direction as the disturbing force and therefore magnifies the disturbance. This clearly indicates an unstable condition.

STEERING AND SUSPENSION SYSTEMS

Rack-and-pinion steering, now almost universal on cars, is also making inroads into commercial vehicles. Refinements such as 'positive centre feel' have been developed for cars. The system on the Rover 800, Fig 48, includes a power valve which has been redesigned so that it does not operate for small input forces at the steering wheel. A circa-spring ring is pre-loaded into position so the valve will not operate until the input forces exceed the spring pre-load, a condition that is not possible to achieve with a conventional torsion bar. Thus, the valve operates as a manual rack and pinion unit. By contrast, in a conventional power valve, it is possible to have small inputs at the steering wheel without any apparent change in vehicle direction. This occurs because the torsion bar can twist relative to the pinion, but due to friction in the system, the rack may not necessarily move; thus the driver finds the steering not positive about the centre.

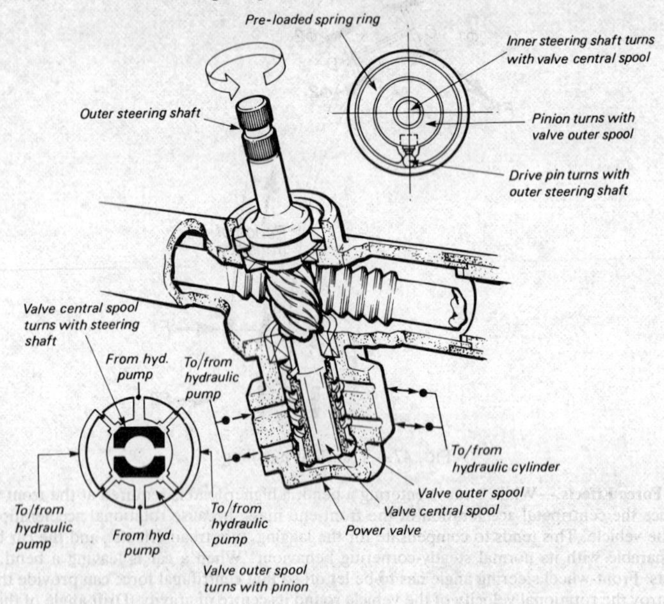

FIG. 48.—Positive centre feel (PCF) steering on Rover 800.

The circa-spring provides the torsional resistance at the steering wheel. When power assistance is required, an increase in effort at the steering wheel overcomes the pre-load of the spring. The valve begins to operate and the steering rack operates with a progressive performance. It is possible to tailor the system to a particular vehicle requirement by varying the amount of pre-load of the spring, its stiffness and rate of generation of power assistance.

SUSPENSION-DAMPER DEVELOPMENTS.—The modern telescopic shock absorber is velocity sensitive but detail design changes can affect the response and make the unit frequency and amplitude sensitive. Force at low velocity is controlled by the leak setting. In a 'twin-tube' construction this is individual to the compression and rebound stroke; a monotube, or 'gas' shock absorber normally has leak setting which is common to both compression and rebound. As the velocity rises, the increasing pressure forces the blow-off valve to progressively open. The fully open position of this valve or other orifices in the valve will restrict the oil flow at very high velocities causing the PV curve to steepen. The shape of the PV curve is used to identify the shock absorber characteristic, as previously discussed.

The Armstrong Adaptive Suspension Control System involves controlling damper and spring rate. The spring rates for a vehicle are determined taking into account the variation in wheel load between driver only and the gross vehicle weight (GVW). With conventional springs even if of variable rate, or if used with spring aids, there is a substantial amount of the suspension travel taken up by the change in vehicle mass. There is also a considerable change to the natural frequency over the range of load. Optimum ride frequency can be maintained if the spring rate is adjusted to suit the load. Also, if control is applied to the position of the suspension the full amount of travel in both compression and rebound is available for smoothing road irregularities. A further advantage of variable spring rates giving near constant ride frequency is that the relative front to rear frequencies can be matched without compromise, improving pitch control and steering characteristic.

TRENDS IN LINKAGE AND HUB LAYOUT.—On cars the MacPherson suspension strut layout is now the norm, with steering arms from the rack and pinion controlling the angular position of the hub. Typically, on buses, an independent linkage system is used; whilst on trucks, rigid beam axles and leaf springs are preferred. In multi-axle vehicles, additional axles, to that located at the front, may be steered; the IVECO 220.38 truck being an example, Fig. 49. In this design, air suspension is used for the second and third axles—a possible future pointer for other vehicles in this category.

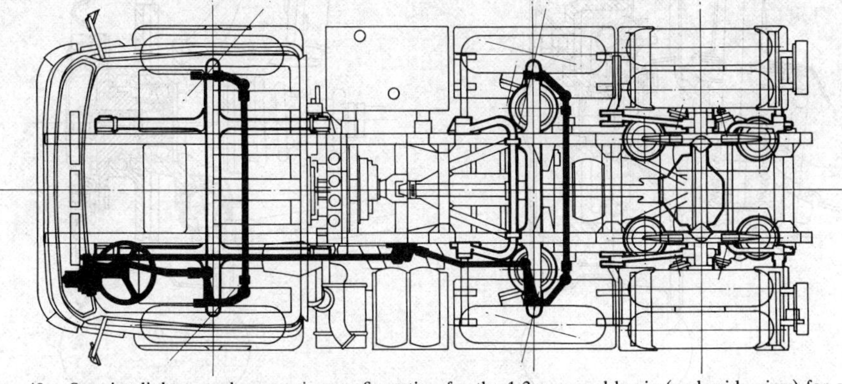

FIG. 49.—Steering linkage and suspension configuration for the 1·3 m-spread bogie (underside view) for an IVECO twin-steer tractor. Air suspension is applied to the second and third axles.

Multi-wheeled trucks also involve special linkages for wheel suspension. Three commonly used suspension linkages for tandem axles are the 'four spring' rocking beam and non-reactive types also the increasingly used 'two spring' type, Fig. 50. On articulated semi-trailers both air and rubber-spring suspension are strongly challenging steel leaf-sprung systems. There is also a challenge to steel springs from composite leaf springs, already fitted on some panel vans.

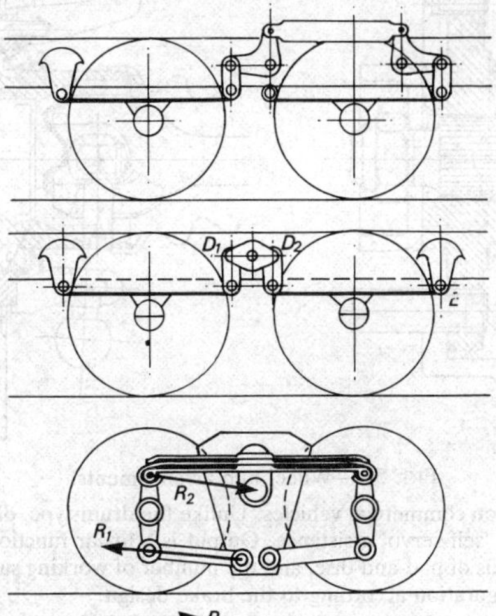

FIG. 50.—Tandem bogie suspensions.

Wheel hubs are supported by angular-contact ball bearings and taper-roller bearings, both providing reaction to thrust loads (from cornering or kerbing) as well as radial loading. There is a trend in cars towards non-separable bearings, to reduce handling damage, and even to double row integral bearings instead of a pair, Fig. 51.

BRAKES AND BRAKE OPERATING SYSTEMS.—Car brakes are now predominantly of disc-type while

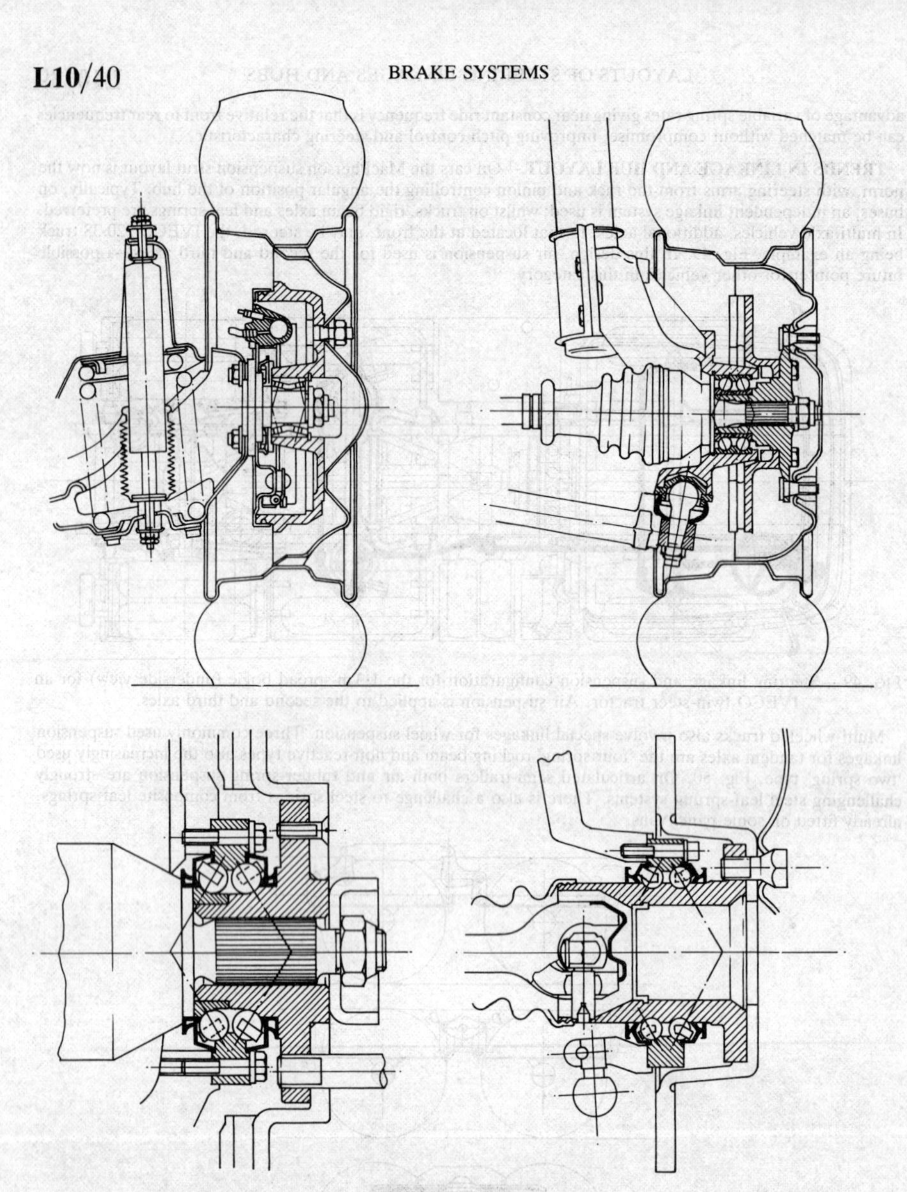

FIG. 51.—Wheel hub arrangements.

drum brakes are still the rule on commercial vehicles. Unlike the drum-type, disc brakes have little geometric effect so there is no inherent 'self-servo' assistance. Output is a linear function of clamping force, frictional coefficient, mean contact radius of pad-and-disc, and the number of working surfaces. Drum brake shoes may be of leading or trailing configuration according to the brake design.

Actuation of disc brakes is tending towards the single-sided 'first' caliper mechanism which has its piston and cylinder in a well ventilated area inboard of the disc. With high friction disc materials, a pedal load of 400 N would be required to decelerate a light vehicle at around 8·5 m/s^2 without servo assistance for the system in Fig. 52. For medium to heavy cars servo assistance is now the norm.

Commercial Vehicle Brakes.—For commercial vehicle disc brakes single sided calipers are preferred, in packaging terms, for their ability to incorporate hydraulic and mechanical operation. The reaction beam principle was first used in this type of caliper in which tie-bars extend across the edge of the disc to ensure

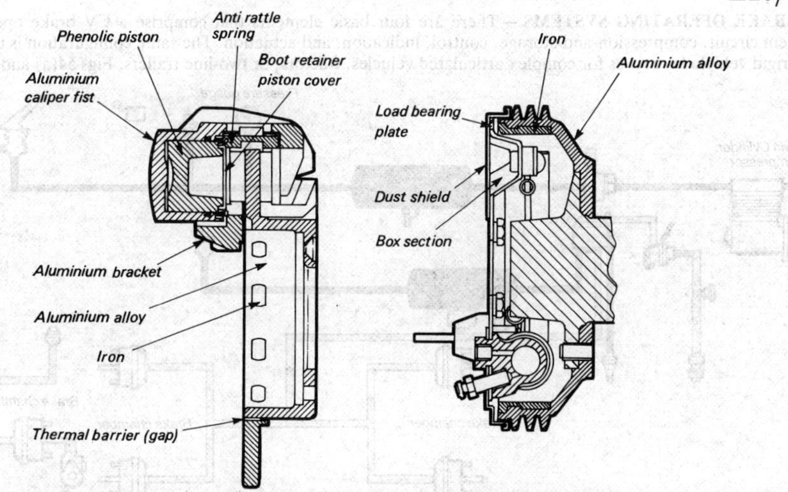

FIG. 52.—Lightweight front caliper and disc (left) and rear brake assembly and drum designs by Automotive Products.

clamp load is applied on the centreline of the outboard lining. Equal loading of the disc from inner and outer pads is achieved as drag loads of the pads are reacted against the fixed mounting bracket and not the siding clamp structure.

To incorporate a means of efficient mechanical parking within the clamping head, the parking brake must recognise state of adjustment of the service brake and so be integral with it. Minimum running clearance is necessary to overcome the inherently low factor of the disc brake and its reduced effective radius to meet high pad force × travel requirement in actuation. Auto adjustment is thus incorporated which senses clamp load as well as travel. An alternative to single disc brakes is necessary above 16 tonnes gross vehicle weight.

Air wedge actuation of the sliding caliper brake hub has proved to be an acceptable layout for heavy goods vehicle (HGV) builders. A typical Rockwell air-wedge brake with auto-adjust incorporates a 44 mm thick disc (rotor) which provides a swept area of 1250 cm^2, the ventilated design having 10 per cent greater power capacity (by giving 13 kW dissipation at 315 °C) than competitive designs, and 30 per cent more than solid discs. The use of optionally available offset rotors is a convenient way of adapting the brake to different axle layouts, but the use of extended hub members is now being considered as an alternative. A two-leading shoe configuration contributes to high efficiency and, it is said, that the integral auto-adjuster, by maintaining a constant low running clearance, provides good stability considering the high brake factor involved. For parking, a spring chamber actuates one of the air brake's two wedges, Fig. 53.

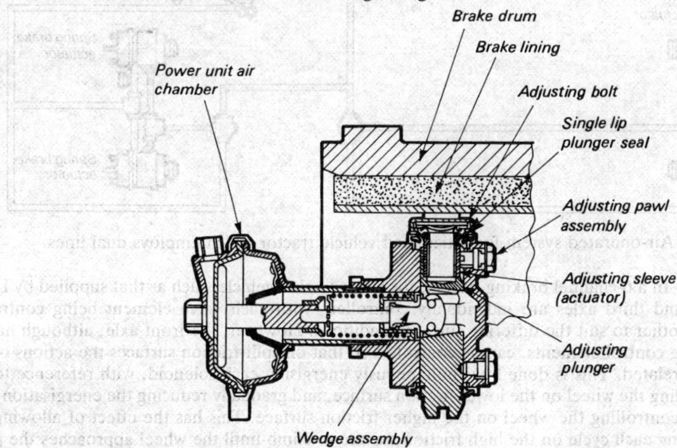

FIG. 53.—Wedge brake with integral automatic adjustment, from Rockwell International, with auto-slack adjuster.

BRAKE OPERATING SYSTEMS.—There are four basic elements that comprise a CV brake operating system circuit: compression-and-storage, control, indication, and actuation. The same configuration is utilised for rigid vehicle layouts as for complex articulated vehicles, tractors, or two-line trailers, Figs 54(a) and 54(b).

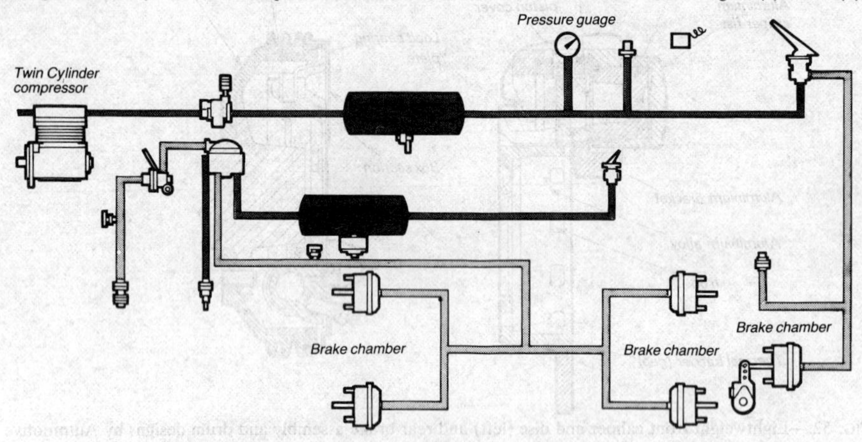

FIG. 54(*a*).—Air-operated braking system for rigid vehicle: main elements are compression-and-storage, control, indication and actuation.

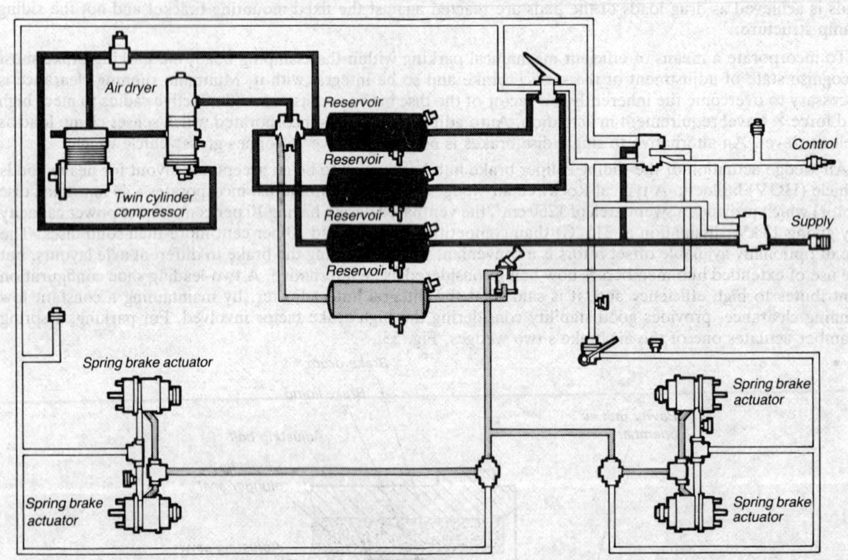

FIG. 54(*b*).—Air-operated system for articulated vehicle tractor which employs dual lines.

Anti-lock braking.—In a 6-channel braking system, for a three-axled vehicle, such as that supplied by Lucas Girling, the second and third axles are individually controlled, with each valve element being controlled independently of the other to suit the differing surface conditions. However, the front axle, although having two independent valve control elements, can be controlled so that on split-friction surfaces the actions of the control elements are related. This is done by simultaneously energising each solenoid, with reference to the valve element controlling the wheel on the lower friction surface, and gradually reducing the energisation time of the valve element controlling the wheel on the higher friction surface. This has the effect of allowing the pressure reached during each cycle on the high friction surface to climb until the wheel approaches the point of slip after which it is controlled independently. The slip pressure is retained in a pneumatic memory on each cycle and the knee point between the two rates can be a function of solenoid energisation time or provided as a percentage of the stored slip pressure. A 4-channel module variant by the same company has four sensor inputs, fed via amplifiers, to the custom interface. This interface reads all four sensor inputs every 16 ms and the information is fed to the microprocessor in serial form.

In order to prevent a vehicle from skidding in any driving condition a low drive wheel slip has to be ensured, as well as an optimum wheel slip during brake applications. This task is fulfilled by a drive slip control integrated in the WABCO auto-braking system, (ABS), Fig 55. Using the ABS wheel sensor information the electronic

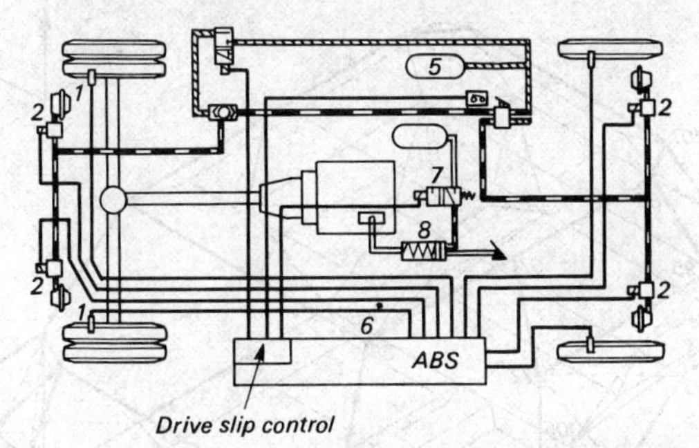

FIG. 55.—WABCO braking system with anti-spin feature.

unit controls the wheel behaviour. If during acceleration, when using a split drive arrangement, increased drive wheel slip occurs at one wheel, a controlled brake application is made automatically at that wheel. As a result, the drive wheel on the high friction coefficient can transmit the corresponding full drive force without the assistance of a differential lock. If both wheels show increased drive slip, the engine torque is automatically controlled.

BODY/CHASSIS DESIGN

While the basic structure of a car differs from that of the commercial/industrial/passenger-service vehicle, it shares the task of carrying the system controls for the whole vehicle. In all but a few specialist cars the separate ladder-chassis frame has given way to monocoque or integral construction in which the skins and/or integral space-framework take or share the main structural loads. Trucks and many buses/coaches retain the ladder frame and it, like the integral body/structure of the car, carries the increasingly complex vehicle system controls.

The shape of the car body is thus compromised, from an ideal structural shape, in its need to accommodate doors, latching and locking systems; windscreen, side and back-lights; instrument/display panel with associated harnesses and/or mechanical cable controls; engine, transmission, suspension and steering system and foot pedal controls; seat mounts and sides; engine fuel, cooling and exhaust system; and brake cooling too is beginning to make its demands on body shape. Another factor is the rapidly increasing number of servo-motors used to perform former manual functions like seat and mirror adjustment, window-opening and cover panel unlatching. The physical volume of conventional electric wiring to serve these motors, and the control systems for engine/transmission management, is also beginning to affect the size of cut-outs within the body shell.

BODY AND CHASSIS SHAPE CONSTRAINTS.—The ladder frame of the typical goods or passenger-service vehicle, while having principal longitudinal beam members to withstand the loading from a whole variety of body types, while using a common chassis-design, is also affected by supporting vehicle systems. Those which can affect the associated structure include saddle-mounted fuel-tanks; multi-axle bogies suspensions; cab tilt systems; engine and drive train mounts; air brake reservoirs; body tipping gear.

Pressure from the market to provide the numerous vehicle systems naturally compromises the structural designer who must optimise a body or chassis design around these constraints on shape. He has also to provide a minimum weight structure of adequate strength, stiffness, corrosion and fatigue resistance, within an exterior envelope increasingly influenced by stylists and aerodynamicists. The truck chassis designer has the additional constraint of building-in torsional flexibility to allow both on- and off-road operation, with a variety of body types, while using simple robust leaf spring beam axle suspensions.

Design by Finite Element Analysis.—With some special exceptions most car body designers are therefore confronted with a shape of shell which they must idealise for analysis, by the finite-element method (FEM), to determine its deflection under load, progressively modifying the member properties to increase structural efficiency. The coarseness of the mesh chosen for the FEM analysis, is still a question for debate. Against the greater accuracy (and of course computation cost) of a finer mesh is the argument that a coarser 'mesh' based on the idealisation of the shell into beam and (shear) panel elements leads to a better understanding of structural behaviour and therefore better design optimisation of future model developments.

Moore (Ref. 28) has described the latter approach in which numbered nodes are used to represent beam and panel intersections defined in spatial position by a co-ordinate axis system, Fig. 56. Six equilibrium equations are obtained at each node for the three orthogonal force and moment systems applying. Node displacements (and thus structural deflection) are obtained by solving the equations. Individual panel and beam forces and bending-moments are calculated by back-substitution of the displacements, so as to calculate resulting stresses.

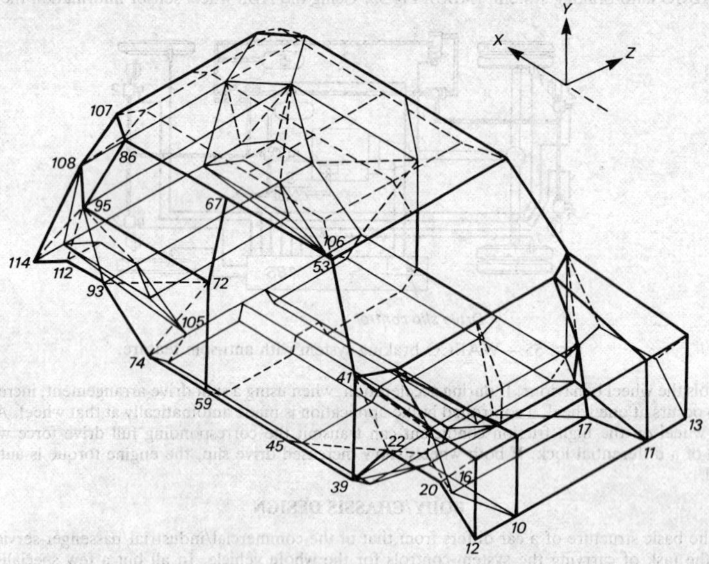

FIG. 56.—Coarse mesh analysis of beam and panel intersections defined in spatial position co-ordinates.

The car body types recognised by Moore apply to transverse-engine/front-drive and longitudinal-engine/rear-drive layouts. The first has virtually flat-floor and suspension sub-frames feeding road loads almost directly into the relatively stiff side-frame. The second has a more substantial floor structure with front-rear pairs of longitudinals for reacting axle loads, a deep propshaft tunnel and under-seat crossmembers linking them. But, like the truck chassis, the second type suffers from the limitation of low torsional rigidity due to the insignificant rotational stiffnesss of the crossmember to side-rail joint.

Design of Thin Wall Sections.—Beyond analysis of the overall shell the necessity arises to study individual sections of the body for high localised deformations or stress concentrations. Here the design rules for sheet (thin wall) structures apply. In beam calculations, for example, it is necessary to ensure that cross section shape remains constant to minimise bending deflections: hence the need for bulkhead rings and web stiffeners. A useful simplification in the analysis is to eliminate all loads on a strained element with respect to whose direction the thin-wall is flexible; this leads to complimentary shear flows in the wall being equal. A useful generalised expression for estimating twist θ per unit length l of thin-wall open section members is:

$$\theta/l = T/(G/3)\,.\,\alpha\,.\,(\Sigma hi)\,.\,ti^3$$

for torque T and shear modulus G; where t is thickness and h width of elements of the section, numbered from one to i; shape coefficient $\alpha = 0{\cdot}83$ for angles, 1·10 for C-shapes, 1·17 for Z-sections and 1·0 for T-sections.

To simplify analysis of shear panels, 'tension-field' conditions can be assumed. By assuming the elemental direct compressive stress is zero, a tensile stress (factored for safety) is taken as the criterion for failure. A 'real' body panel may be idealised as one in pure shear plus a set of bars around the edges which take all the end load. The end load carrying members comprise 20 to 60 times the thickness of adjacent sheet in the concentrated boom area.

Panel Construction.—For a stiffened panel (using vertical swages, distance d apart, for buckling resistance R under shearing force S, it can be shown that spot weld (number N at pitch p) load per unit length is $N.d.s/p$ at the top and bottom edges of the panel. In a curved panel under bending loads, Fig. 57, direct stress in the web, which again can be stiffened by swages, is M/hRt. A general guidance for swaging is that all swages should be straight and not intersect, and that they should run along the shortest distance between supported edges of panel. Stiffness of swages depends mainly on depth and axial load capacity and it can be estimated by considering the buckling resistance of an equivalent width and depth channel section.

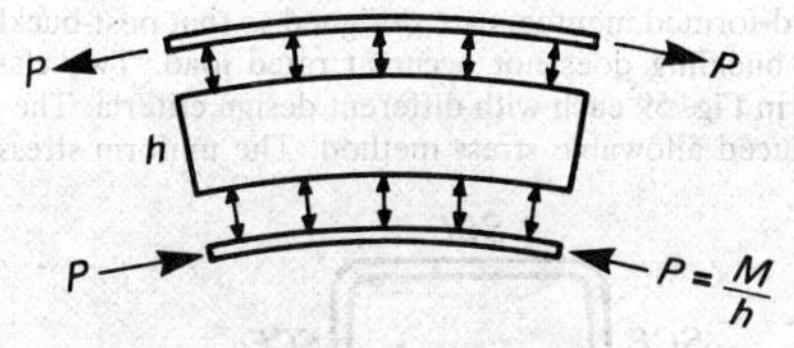

FIG. 57.—Curved beam load system.

Typical metal thicknesses used in car construction are 1·0 mm for large area panels such as roofs, quarters, doors and floors; these can reduce down to between 0·75 and 0·65 mm where curved contours add stiffness and 'tightness'. In major structural parts such as cross members, sills, rails and pillars, thicknesses of 1–1·25 mm are common with 1·625 mm used for local reinforcements.

Panels are normally spot-welded together, typical strengths for given panel thickness being shown in Table 11. Pitch for spot-welds normally varies between 25 and 65 mm according to strength and sealing requirements; minimum pitch is three times the spot-weld diameter. A spot-welded flange will normally be subject to twist because the shear load, Q, in the panel is unlikely to be applied through the centroid of the joint, Fig. 58. Each weld will be subject to load $Q \,.\, d_i^2/\Sigma d_i^2$ in the direction of loading together with a force $Q \,.\, L \,.\, r_i \,.\, d_i^2/\Sigma r_i \,.\, d_i^2$ (for spot-weld diameter d_i) perpendicular to the line between the weld centre and the centroid, due to the torque of the applied load about the centroid.

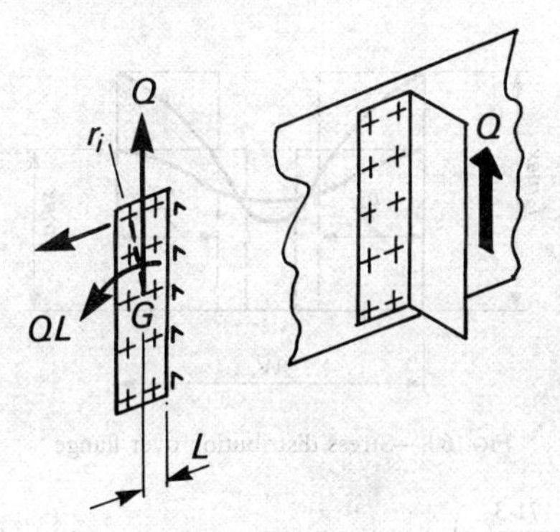

FIG. 58.—Spot-welded flange forces.

TABLE 11.—STRENGTH OF SPOT-WELDED PANELS

SWG	Thickness (in)	(mm)	Spot weld dia. (in)	(mm)	Average shear failing load (ton)	(tonne)
20	0·036	(0·915)	0·18	(4·575)	0·63	(0·64)
18	0·048	(1·22)	0·22	(5·6)	0·80	(0·813)
16	0·064	(1·62)	0·25	(6·35)	0·88	(0·895)

Car structures are usually made from extra deep drawing mild steel to EN 2A/1 with an ultimate tensile strength (UTS) of 310 MN/m^2 and 0·5 per cent proof stress between 186–263 MN/m^2. Work hardening in forming structural elements can raise UTS to 371 MN/m^2 and 0·5 per cent proof stress to 310 MN/m^2. Modulus of elasticity is 210 GN/m^2 for most steel. Minimum sheet-metal gauges are set by considerations of in-factory handling and susceptibility to damage. Above these values, gauges of loaded members will be fixed to ensure resistance to compressive buckling or shear instability.

Post Buckling Strength.—The American Iron and Steel Institute has published a guide showing techniques for exploiting post-buckling strength of compression elements in beams and struts, cold-rolled from strip. These use the concept of 'effective width' by predicting the performance of compression flanges, in design. The work is an extension of the theory of thin walled sectioned members in bending which indicates that the top flange of say, a top-hat section member, buckles in waves having a length equal to twice that of the flange width. Due to edge constraint on the flange from the side webs only the centre of the flange is free to buckle out of plane, and a non uniform stress distribution therefore exists across it. Experiments show the flange can carry increased load up until the edge stresses reach their yield point.

AISI explain that most cold-formed members are designed so that post-buckling strength is part or all of the safety factor and that local buckling does not occur at rated load. Two classes of flanges are considered, stiffened and unstiffened, as in Fig. 59 each with different design criteria. The former uses the effective-width concept and the latter a reduced allowable stress method. The uniform stress distribution across a stiffened

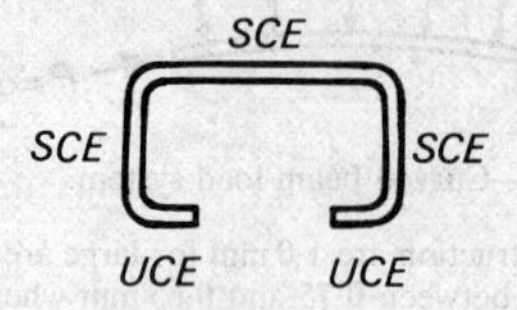

FIG. 59.—Stiffened and unstiffened flanges.

compression flange is replaced by a uniform stress distribution of the magnitude of the edge stresses acting across the edge strips width $b/2$, where b is the effective width, Fig. 60. Effective width b (in inches) is obtained from:

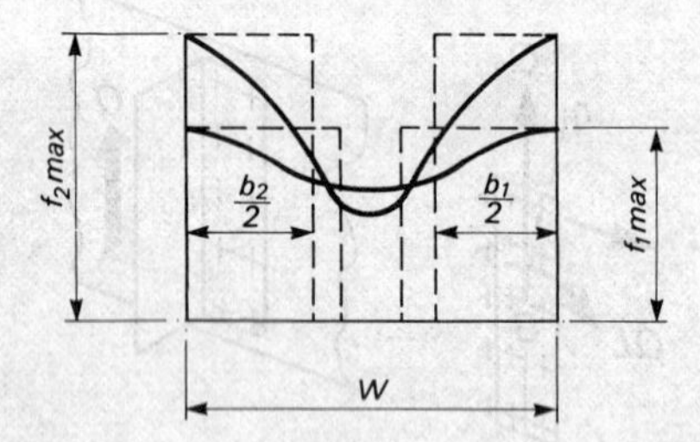

FIG. 60.—Stress distribution over flange.

$$\frac{b}{t} = \frac{326}{(f)^{1/2}} \cdot \left(1 - \frac{71 \cdot 3}{(w/t)(f)^{1/2}}\right)$$

with W = total width of flange, t = thickness of material, and stress f in units of thousands lbs/in^2. For a flat compression element to behave as a stiffened flange it must have an edge stiffener with section transverse second moment of area = $1{\cdot}83\ wt^3$.

CONCEIVING A NEW VEHICLE BODY.—The highly competitive car market has forced vehicle makers into shorter lead times for new body-style introductions. An OEM now, typically, puts out new body styles to specialist design and prototyping houses: these employ expert staff and free the OEM from programming new introductions, at irregular intervals, into his design and experimental engineering schedules. Under these conditions a total styling programme might take as little as 45 weeks—culminating in a fully finished but nonrunning styling model with opening doors and complete interior.

Specialist Design and Production Teams.—The elements of the programme overlap considerably, involving several specialist teams. The latter include styling, scale model making, production-engineering, product-engineering, digitising: then prototype-building experts in GRP, paint, drape-forming and trim. Designers are allocated for each project, supervised by the styling director and typically work on the exterior sketches (renderings) concluded by a client presentation. These are then re-drawn and represented, as necessary. At the end of the initial period, work is also likely to start on interior sketches—to complete the presentation within the time-scale indicated above. A scale exterior model will be presented to the client by the end of this programme.

From the same start-point, Product Engineering will spend time on a preliminary package and feasibility study and within that time a separate team works on exterior steel 'armature' drawings, passing to Production Engineering who then build the exterior armature within weeks. The model makers then build a full-scale exterior clay model using inputs from the digitisers' computer-study of scale-renderings. In this last period, Product Engineering carry out packaging and structural feasibility studies; the interior clay is then produced. The working to develop the final design whilst attending to seats, sidewalls, carpet and headlining. At about this time, Manufacturing will have spent overlapping periods making the wooden interior armature and a wire cage model.

Final Feasibility Stages.—Product Engineering, meanwhile, will have commenced a third packaging and feasibility study overlapping the commencement of body-engineering proper on detail body design, after final acceptance by the client. During this final feasibility-period items like instrument panels are developed, in detail, and an egg-box former will be constructed for panel making. A team from Manufacturing Engineering also inspects the design at this stage for its tooling feasibility. The former is set up on a surface table after the exterior panels are made so these can be first tacked then spot-welded together. Within this period stylists prepare 'show car' exterior and interiors in conjunction with the model-makers, manufacturing supplying a steel chassis and exterior brightware for this. A team of vacuum drape forming specialists obtains the interior surface development of screens and lights. Immediately before the commencement of body engineering, the digitisers collect the skin-lines from the approved interior/exterior models.

The procedure described for producing the full size styling model represents a major step in the process of designing a car for production. Such a styling model gives the senior management of a company an opportunity to see the proposed vehicle at an early stage and they can then suggest changes and refinements. These styling models can also be used as a marketing aid by holding a clinic to check the public's reaction to the general design and features.

Whilst the styling model is being prepared the detail design of 'body in white' (an unpainted shell) and trim will be proceeding, and the tooling to enable the first phase of prototypes to be made will be under course of manufacture. On completion of the phase-one prototypes a test programme will be undertaken and any necessary modifications will be made to the design. A second phase of prototypes will be manufactured, incorporating modifications necessary for final test and evaluation. These phase-2 prototypes will be closely resembling the car that will eventually run off the production line build.

CONTROL SYSTEMS AND DISPLAYS

The reducing cost of micro-electronics is making possible the introduction of sophisticated control systems even on moderately priced cars. It is quite possible that systems on today's luxury cars could be featured on tomorrow's popular cars. Micro-electronics are increasingly taking over control functions on cars and are likely soon to affect commercial vehicles in an increasing extent. Nevertheless, power-electrical feeds are still required for the various systems actuators. As this chapter is being written the conventional wiring harness might be giving way to multiplex wiring involving a power ring main, local actuator circuits, and multiplexing the signal wires into a data-bus ring to control them.

STATE-OF-THE-ART VEHICLE ELECTRONICS.—The Jaguar XJ6 has gone some way towards multiplexing by reducing signal wire cross section area from 1·0 to 0·5 mm^2 and using compact multi-way connectors of 1·5 mm pin diameter. The objective in creating the system was to double the complexity in response to market requirements but at the same time to improve reliability by an order of five times with a mean failure rate of 1 per cent being demonstrated to a 90 ± per cent confidence level. It was decided that a signal wire earth switching technology would be used. New multi-way connectors were devised, with between two and 36-way connections, and these are positive-mate anti-backout systems which will either latch or reject upon making.

Microprocessor Controlled Systems.—The system encompasses some seven microprocessors driving earth-line switching systems for: engine management, air conditioning and heating, driver information systems, levelling management, cruise control, ABS and the central microprocessor. The central microprocessor, in addition to providing overall control, also controls all time-based systems. It has 30 outputs, having 1 kbyte of ROM, 64 kbytes of RAM and controlling functions from 1 ms to 20 min. CMOS technology is used throughout in order to reduce quiescent drain which is down to 50 mA. Cross-polarity and voltage surge protection is provided on all microprocessors and logic units with watch-dogging on all microprocessors which reset in the unlikely event of microprocessor crash.

The system is protected through a multiple load dump system using zener ring technology. Features of the system include: hot and cold bulb failure detection; automatic air conditioner operation; automatic seat heating; automatic rear screen and mirror operation and timing; automatic sequence locking of doors, windows and sliding roof; lighting logic systems.

DIAGNOSTIC AND SYSTEM DISPLAYS.—A vacuum fluorescent dot matrix (32 × 32) display is used to present to the driver the eleven types of warning signals emanating from different control units and sensors on the car. Below the matrix are two lines of 20 characters, which may either describe an ISO warning symbol or present journey or fuel consumption information. The trip computer is operated by nine keys to give nine possible items of display information and the facility to input the intended journey length. The fuel quantity in the tank, the oil pressure, cooling temperature and battery voltage are presented as bar graphs in vacuum fluorescent technology. The odometer is in the same display technology, the information being held and updated in EPROM within the panel. The speedometer is driven by a speed signal originating from a variable reluctance sensor, excited by a toothed wheel on the rear axle assembly.

Engine Control.—The engine management systems control both fuel and ignition timing: primary sensors, air mass flow, and engine speed. A toothed wheel on the crankshaft behind the pulley excites a sensor to generate an engine speed signal and a missing tooth on that wheel indicates the crankshaft position, Fig. 61. Secondary analogue sensors detect cooling temperature and throttle position.

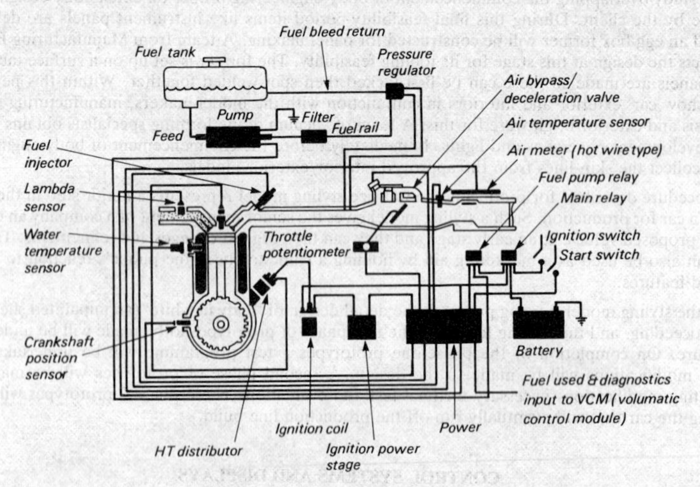

FIG. 61.—Lucas engine-management system.

Lighting System Controls.—The switches, which control the exterior lamps, are also of the low-current form, acting as signals to a circuit in the facial panel. The logic circuit prevents the selection of certain combinations of lamps, prohibited by legislation. The outputs from the lighting logic circuit energize relays located within modules at the four corners of the vehicle, the relays providing current to the adjacent lamps. The four relay modules also contain electronic circuits which can detect current flow to the bulbs and will locate a failed bulb whether it is illuminated or not, provided the ignition is turned on. Outputs from the four modules are arranged in a 'wired OR' configuration, and will activate bulb failure warning signals on the dot matrix display of the instrument panel.

The turn indicator is an electronic version, where the steering column stalk switch does not latch but is only momentarily depressed by the driver and returns to the central position. The low-current switch signal activates the central timing processor and the appropriate lamps are operated through the relay modules. The microprocessor cancels the turn indicator by sensing the position of a magnet on the steering column with three reed relays.

Comfort Control.—Air conditioning is based on a system of two rotary flaps to control the mixing of hot and cold air. The flaps are operated by servo motors and feedback potentiometers linked to a microprocessor. The driver can select the range and distribution of temperature and humidity conditions within the vehicle using the control panel on the centre console. The last conditions selected are retained while the ignition is turned off. The temperature within the car, and of the induced air, is measured by active semi-conductor sensors, which yield a voltage proportional to absolute temperature.

REFERENCES AND BIBLIOGRAPHY

(1) TABOREK J. J., *Mechanics of Vehicles*, Machine Design, May 20 to Dec 26, 1957.
(2) BARNACLE, H. F., *Mechanics of Automobiles*, Pergamon.
(3) COSTIN, Automotive Engineer, Dec 1975.
(4) WHITE, *A Rating Method for Assessing Vehicle Drag Coefficients*, MIRA Report 1967/9.
(5) MURELL, H., Automotive Design Engineering, Oct 1983.
(6) MAGID E. B. and COERMANN, R. R., (1963), *Human Response to Vibration*, Chapter 5 in Human Factors in Technology (Ed BENNETT, E. et al), McGraw-Hill.
(7) WOHL, J. G., (1961), *Man-machine Steering Dynamics—Human Factors*, Vol 3, No 4, pp 222–228.
(8) SMITH, *Scientific Design of Exhaust Intake Systems*, Foulis.
(9) TYLER, *The TRRL Quiet Heavy Vehicle Project*, Proceedings IMechE 1979.
(10) GILES, J. G., *Transmission Ratio Requirements of Road Vehicles*, MIRA Report 1957–54.
(11) ABINETT, R. E., *Important Design Criteria for a 5-speed Automotive Gearbox*, The Engineering Designer, Nov 1963.

(12) STOTT, T. C., *Problems in the Design and Development of an Economical Automotive Gearbox*, Proceedings IMechE (AD), No 1, 1953–54.
(13) RADCLIFFE, T. A., *Gearing and Gearboxes*, Automotive Engineers Reference Book, Newnes.
(14) *Machine Cut Helical Spur Gears*, BS 436: 1940.
(15) DEAN-AVERNS, *Automobile Chassis Design*, Iliffe.
(16) BUCKINGHAM, E., *Dynamic Loads on Gear Teeth*, ASME Special Research Report, 1931.
(17) ABBOTT, W., *Machine Drawing and Design*, Blackie, p 110.
(18) MACIELINSKI, J. W., Paper 29, IMechE Drive-line Engineering Conference 1970.
(19) LANCHESTER, *Motor Car Suspension and Independent Springing*, Proceedings I.A.E. 1935–36.
(20) CAMBELL, *The Sports Car, its Design and Performance*, Chapman and Hall, 1954.
(21) CAIN, *Vibration of Rail and Road Vehicles*, Pitman, 1949.
(22) SYLVESTER, *Vibration Reductions in Motor Cars*, Society of Environmental Engineers, 1966 Symposium, Vol 4.
(23) SMITH, *Frame Beaming, Fifth-wheel Location—Special Body Mounting and Loading Problems*. SAE SP-260, 1965.
(24) BODEN, *Some Aspects of Vehicle Ride*, ASAE Sympsium, Advances in Automobile Engineering—Vehicle Ride, Pergamon, 1963.
(25) JANEWAY, R. N., *Ride and Vibration*, HS—6 Data Sheets, SAE 1950.
(26) ELLIS, *Tyre Mechanics and Vehicle Handling*, Automotive Design Engineering, Sept, 1963.
(27) HODKIN, R. K., *Vehicle Handling*, Chapter 8 in Vol 1 of Automotive Technology Series, Iliffe—Butterworth.
(28) MOORE, G. G., Paper 5, IMechE/ASAE Symposium on Body Engineering, 1970.

FENTON, J., The following books, by the author of this chapter, provide further reading on aspects of vehicle engineering:
Handbook of Automotive Design Analysis, Business Books, 1973.
Vehicle Body Layout and Analysis, MEP, 1980.
Gasoline Engine Analysis for CAD, MEP, 1973.

Design Engineering
The ideas journal for Design Engineers
May 1984
Cylindrical bearings
Hydrostatic transmissions
Switched reluctance motors
SPECIAL REPORT: Transmission drive belts and pulleys

INLAND WATERWAYS

Introduction—Definitions and Classification of Waterways—Some Basic Principles of Open Channel Flow—River Engineering—Canalisation and Navigation Canals—Multipurpose Utilisation of Waterways—Transport on Inland Waterways—Locks—Thrift Locks—Lifts and Inclined Planes—Lock Approaches—Inland Ports—Notes on Some Existing UK and Major World Waterways—Scale Models of Inland Waterways—References and Bibliography.

By P. Novak, B.Sc., Ph.D., Dr.Sc., C.Eng., FICE, FIWEM
Emeritus Professor; University of Newcastle upon Tyne

INTRODUCTION

Navigation on inland waterways is the oldest mode of continental transport. Although during its long history it has passed through many stages of technological development and in some countries from prosperity through stagnation to depression and almost oblivion, there is at present a clear renaissance of inland navigation. There is no doubt that it forms nowadays an important and integral part of the transport infrastructure of many countries in the world.

Inland navigation was one of the grounds for ancient civilisations developing and flourishing in the valleys of great rivers—the Nile, Eufrates, Ganges, Jang-c-tiang etc. Even artificial waterways were known in ancient Egypt (the Ta Tenant canal connecting the Nile and the Red Sea 1900 B.C.), Mesopotamia and China (the over 1700 km long Ta–jun–cha canal from Peking started in 500 B.C.).

In Europe the emperor Charles the Great started as early as 793 the building of a canal intended to link the Rhine and the Danube (Fossa Carolina), an attempt soon to be abandoned. The first clearly documented navigation lock dates from 1439 and was constructed on the canal Naviglio Grande in Northern Italy.

Industrialisation was the prime mover of modern waterways development in the 18th and 19th century and with the network of navigable rivers and canals in England was at the forefront of this type of development; e.g. the Bridgewater canal built by James Brindley and the Ellesmere canal built by Thomas Telford.

The present great European network of inland waterways is based on modernised and expanded navigation facilities with origins in the era of industrial revolution. The same applies to the navigation facilities on the great American waterways, e.g. on the Mississippi, Ohio River etc. Although in the 20th century inland waterways often could not compete with the railway and later motorway networks they retained, and even increased their role in the provision of a highly effective means of transport, particularly of bulk material.

The role of inland waterways in water resources management, in the provision of modern recreational facilities and in the enhancement of the environment has further contributed to this new perception.

In spite of the rapid development of other modes of transport there are some universally valid advantages in transport by inland navigation (Ref. 1). These are:

(a) Low energy requirements; the specific energy consumption for navigation is about 80% of that for rail and less than 30% of the consumption for road transport,

(b) High productivity of labour per unit of transport output,

(c) Low material requirement per unit of transport volume; the corresponding values for rail and highway transport are two and four times higher respectively,

(d) Lowest interference with the environment (low noise, low exhaust fume generation),

(e) Very low land requirement (in case of navigable rivers),

(f) Low accident incidence in comparison with other transport modes,

(g) Capability of easily transporting bulk cargo and large industrial products.

DEFINITIONS AND CLASSIFICATION OF WATERWAYS

Waterways can be divided into three classes:

(1) Natural channels, i.e. rivers, or part of rivers, whose flow is not modified; the river channel may be improved by river training works.

(2) Canalised rivers, i.e. rivers whose flow is to a greater or smaller degree controlled by engineering works.

(3) Canals, i.e. entirely artificial waterways whose water is obtained by diversion from rivers, by pumping or from reservoirs.

In the endeavour to ensure gradual unification of European waterways and the standardisation of their parameters, the Economic Commission for Europe (ECE) adopted, in 1961, a uniform classification of inland waterways. This classification is based on the dimensions and the tonnage of traditional standard vessels and classifies the waterways into six classes (Refs. 1 and 2).

For every class the necessary parameters of the waterways and its structures were deduced from the parameters of standard vessels, i.e. the depth of water in the fairway of the canal or navigable river, the widths of a one-way and two-way fairway, the minimum radius of curvature of the fairway axis, the widening of the fairway in curves, minimum clearances, the clear navigation spans of bridges, useful dimensions of locks, etc. (Refs. 3 and 4).

Simultaneously with the adoption of the above classification it was agreed that the European waterways of international importance would be so built or reconstructed as to ensure that their parameters would correspond with the requirements of at least the IVth class and permit continuous passage to vessels of a tonnage between 1350 and 1500 tons. Classes I to III waterways have a regional character.

Big European rivers, such as the Rhine, the Danube and others, are being made navigable at present mostly to the parameters of the Vth class (1500–3000 tons). The VIth class (>3000 tons) includes primarily the Soviet navigable rivers and canals or the lowland stretches of the biggest European rivers. Similar or even larger dimensions are found in navigable rivers of other continents, notably in North and South America.

The above mentioned international classification of inland waterways was adopted in the period when, with the exception of motorboats, towing by tug boats was used almost exclusively. In the past two decades, however, this traditional navigation technology was almost completely replaced in Europe (in USA already much earlier) by the economically and operationally more advantageous pushing of the barges by push-boats. (see pp. L11/11 and L11/12).

The introduction of this new technology resulted in proposals for the amendment of the existing waterway classification (Ref. 1). Originally a 'Europe I' barge with maximum tonnage 1240t was considered as a basic unit for class IV waterways but eventually an economic 'Europe II' pushed barge type was introduced with the dimensions of 76·5 × 11·4 × 2·5m and a tonnage of 1660t. This standard barge is built also for Class V waterways (draft 3·5m, tonnage 2520t) and Class VI waterways (draft 4·0m and tonnage 2940t). Therefore, Seiler (Ref. 5) recommended that the type Europe II barge be used as standard barge for waterways of international importance, together with recommendation that Class IV to Class VI waterways should be designated according to the number and arrangement of these barges in pushed trains (Fig. 1). For Class IV waterways he assumes

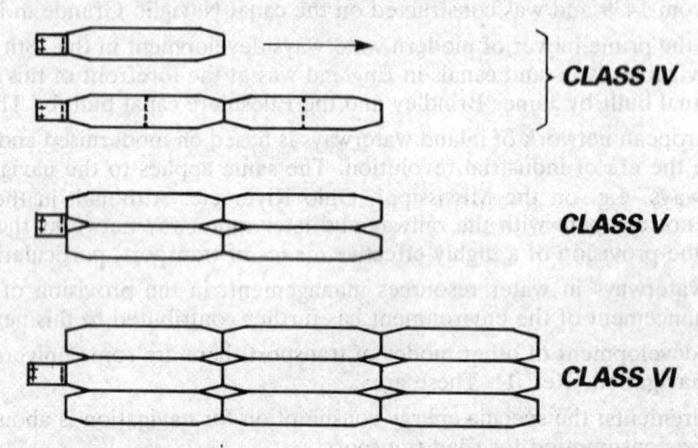

FIG. 1.—Push-trains used on European Waterways (Ref. 1).

the use of 1 + 1 pushed trains of the tonnage of 3320t and the corresponding lock dimensions of 190 × 12 × 3·5m. For Class V waterways Seiler suggests a 1 + 4 pushed train as standard which has a tonnage of 10080t for the draft of 3·5m. and the corresponding lock dimensions of 190 × 24 × 4·5m. For Class VI waterways he recommends a 1 + 9 pushed train as standard, which has a tonnage of 26460t for the draft of 4·0m and requires the construction of locks of the dimensions (260–300) × 36m in plan.

More wide ranging changes are contained in the proposal of waterway classification prepared in Czechoslovakia (Ref.6), which is based on the endeavour to homogenise maximally the European navigation network and to achieve its operational integrity.

This proposal differentiates two waterways categories:

(1) Waterways of international importance, whose fundamental parameters are determined by the type I pushed barge with the dimensions of 82·0 × 11·4 (2·2–4·0)m;

(2) Waterways of local importance, whose fundamental parameters are determined by the type L pushed barge with the dimensions of 41·0 × 5·7 × (1·8–3·0)m.

The pushed barges and their push boats can be arranged next to one another or in series, in accordance with the character of the waterway. Some of the possible compositions of pushed trains are illustrated in Fig. 1. On their dimensions all the waterway parameters and the dimensions of their locks are based.

The above-mentioned proposals for the revision of waterways classification differentiate more sharply the waterway classes, defining more accurately their fundamental parameters; however, no international agreement on this amendment of waterway classification has been concluded so far.

Before proceeding with a more detailed discussion of modes of transport on inland waterways and design and operation of associated hydraulic structures (commencing p. L10/11) it is necessary to state at least some concepts and equations for flow in open channels and discuss briefly some types of river engineering works of relevance to inland navigation.

SOME BASIC PRINCIPLES OF OPEN CHANNEL FLOW.

Definitions.—Open channel flow may be laminar or turbulent depending on the value of Reynolds number Re $= (vR/\nu)$ where v is the mean flow velocity, R the hydraulic radius A/P, A the cross-sectional area of flow, P the wetted perimeter and ν the coefficient of kinematic viscosity. In rivers and canals there is invariably turbulent flow. Further, open channel flow may be steady with the discharge Q only a function of distance (or constant) and unsteady with Q also a function of time t. Steady flow may further be uniform (with Q and depth y and hence velocity v constant or non-uniform). Non-uniform flow may be rapidly or gradually varied (Q constant, with v and y varying with position x) or spatially varied [$Q = f(X)$]. In natural rivers we normally have unsteady flow; in canalised rivers and canals predominantly steady non-uniform or uniform flow. The flow can be supercritical (Fr > 1) or subcritical (Fr < 1) where the Froude number is defined by:

$$\mathrm{Fr}^2 = \frac{\alpha Q^2 B}{gA^3} \tag{1}$$

where B is the water surface width.

In navigable rivers and navigation canals the flow is invariably subcritical.

Canals are usually prismatic open channels; rivers are generally non-prismatic. The boundaries of open channels formed by the bed and sides may be fixed, e.g. in artificial concrete lined channels, or movable as in rivers or unlined canals in alluvium.

Some basic equations.—Only a few basic concepts can be touched upon here. For further and more detailed treatment the reader is referred to books on the subject, e.g. Ref. 7.

The energy of flow between two sections distance x with hydrostatic pressure distribution is given by the Bernoulli equation:

$$z_1 + y_1 + \frac{\alpha_1 v_1^2}{2g} = z_2 + y_2 + \frac{\alpha_2 v_2^2}{2g} + h_e \tag{2}$$

where z is the height of the lowest point of the bed above datum, α the Coriolis coefficient derived from the velocity distribution in the section and h_e the energy head loss due to friction and local losses. If H is the total energy head, $(H + z + y + \alpha v^2/2g)$ S_0 the slope of the bed, and S_e the slope of the energy line then $S_0 = \frac{\Delta z}{\Delta x}$ and $S_e = -\Delta H/\Delta x$. For flow with losses due to friction only

$$h_e = h_f \quad \text{and} \quad S_e = -\frac{h_f}{\Delta x} = S_f$$

Evidently for uniform flow

$$S_0 = S_e = S_f \tag{3}$$

Denoting τ_0 the mean shear stress on the channel perimeter P and R the ratio A/P (the hydraulic radius), from the balance between gravity and frictional resistance we get:

$$\tau_0 = \rho g R S_0 = \rho v_*^2 \tag{4}$$

where v is the shear velocity, and ρ the density of the fluid.

Since in fully turbulent flow $\tau_0 \propto v_*^2$, equation 4 leads to the well-known Chezy equation for uniform flow:

$$v = C\sqrt{RS_0} \tag{5}$$

(Units of C are $L^{1/2}T^{-1}$).

The 'coefficient' C can be expressed as:

$$C = \sqrt{\frac{8g}{\lambda}} \tag{6}$$

where λ is the friction coefficient in the Darcy–Weisbach equation:

$$h_f = \frac{\lambda l v^2}{2gD} = \frac{\lambda l v^2}{8gR} \tag{7}$$

λ can be expressed from boundary layer theory as:

$$\frac{1}{\sqrt{\lambda}} = 2\log\frac{6R}{a + \delta'/7} \tag{8}$$

where a is a length characterising the roughness ($a = k/2$ where k is the roughness 'size') and $\delta' = 116\nu/v_*$ is the thickness of the laminar sublayer, (ν is the kinematic viscosity).

Another frequently used expression is the Manning equation using a constant n which is a function of roughness:

$$v = \frac{R^{2/3}}{n}\sqrt{S_0} \tag{9}$$

(i.e. $C = R^{1/6}/n$; units of n are $TL^{-1/3}$).

From equations 4, 5 and 6 it follows that

$$v_* = v\sqrt{\frac{\lambda}{8}} \tag{10}$$

From Bernoulli's equation 2 it follows that for a general *non-prismatic* channel and *non-uniform* flow:

$$-S_0 + \frac{dy}{dx} - \frac{\alpha Q^2}{gA^3}\left(B\frac{dy}{dx} + \frac{\partial A}{\partial b}\cdot\frac{db}{dx}\right) + S_f = 0$$

and thus

$$\frac{dy}{dx} = \frac{S_0 - S_f + \dfrac{\alpha Q^2}{gA^3}\cdot\dfrac{\partial A}{\partial b}\cdot\dfrac{db}{dx}}{1 - \dfrac{\alpha Q^2 B}{gA^3}} \tag{11}$$

For a *prismatic* channel $db/dx = 0$ and equation 11 reduces to:

$$\frac{dy}{dx} = \frac{S_0 - S_f}{1 - \mathrm{Fr}^2} \tag{12}$$

Introducing the *channel conveyance* $K = CA\sqrt{R}$ (i.e. the discharge for a slope 1) equation 12 becomes

$$\frac{dy}{dx} = S_0\frac{1 - \left(\dfrac{K_0}{K}\right)^2}{1 - \mathrm{Fr}^2} \tag{13}$$

Equation 13 implies that $\tau_0 = \rho gRS_f$ (see equation 4) as well as $\tau_0 = \rho gR_0S_0$.

Equation 13 can be conveniently used to analyse and compute various surface profiles in non-uniform flow as generally $K^2 \propto y^N$ where the exponent N is called the *hydraulic exponent.* Numerical methods may also be used to solve equations 2 or 13 for prismatic channels and must be used for nonprismatic channels.

For *unsteady* flow the treatment of continuity and equation 2 yields:

$$S_f = -\frac{\partial H}{\partial x} = -\frac{\partial z}{\partial x} - \frac{\partial y}{\partial x} - \frac{v}{g}\frac{\partial v}{\partial t}\frac{dt}{dx} - \frac{v}{g}\frac{\partial v}{\partial x}$$

and thus the Saint-Venant equation:

$$S_f = S_0 - \frac{\partial y}{\partial x} - \frac{v}{g}\frac{\partial v}{\partial x} - \frac{1}{g}\frac{\partial v}{\partial t} \tag{14}$$

The first term on the RHS of equation 14 signifies uniform flow and the first three terms nonuniform flow. From continuity it follows that a change of discharge in Δx must be accompanied by a change in depth in Δt:

$$\frac{\partial Q}{\partial x} + B\frac{\partial y}{\partial t} = 0 \tag{15}$$

(for no lateral discharge in Δx); thus

$$A\frac{\partial v}{\partial x} + v\frac{\partial A}{\partial x} + B\frac{\partial y}{\partial t} = 0 \tag{16}$$

The first term on LHS of equation 16 represents the prism storage and the second the wedge storage.

For $Q = Av$ and $dA = B\,dy$, equation 14 yields for a *general channel shape*

$$\frac{\partial Q}{\partial t} - \frac{2QB}{A}\frac{\partial y}{\partial t} + gA\left(1 - \frac{Q^2B}{gA^3}\right)\frac{\partial y}{\partial x} - gAS_0 + gAS_f = 0 \tag{17}$$

For a *rectangular* channel equation 16 becomes

$$y\frac{\partial v}{\partial x} + v\frac{\partial y}{\partial x} + \frac{\partial y}{\partial t} = 0 \tag{18}$$

The solution of the above equations can be achieved only by numerical techniques applied e.g. to their finite difference form (Ref. 8).

In the case of *rapidly varied unsteady* flow a *surge* is formed which has a steep front with substantial energy dissipation (analogous to a moving hydraulic jump). From the momentum and continuity equations y_1, v_1 refer to the section ahead of the surge height Δy (moving with celerity c), thus

$$c = -v_1 \pm \sqrt{g\left(\frac{A_1 + \Delta A}{\Delta A}\Delta y + \frac{A_1 + \Delta A}{A_1}y_1\right)} \tag{19}$$

For a rectangular section equation 19 converts into

$$c = -v_1 \pm \sqrt{g\left(y_1 + \frac{3}{2}\Delta y + \frac{\Delta y^2}{2y_1}\right)} \tag{20}$$

which for small surges (common in navigation canals) results in

$$c \cong -v_1 \pm \sqrt{g\left(y_1 + \frac{3}{2}\Delta y\right)} \cong -v_1 \pm \sqrt{gy_1} \tag{21}$$

For the flow velocity $v = 0$ equation 21 reduces to $c = \sqrt{gy_1}$

SEDIMENT TRANSPORT.—A fuller discussion of sediment transport in open channels is clearly outside the scope of this brief text, but a few aspects of particular relevance to inland navigation have to be included here.

From the point of view of source, sediment transported by flow can be divided into washload, comprising very fine material moving in rivers and canals in suspension, and bed material load, moving as bed load and suspended load depending on sediment size and velocity. For river engineering and navigation canals, bed load is the important element of sediment transport as it determines the morphological erosion and sedimentation aspects; suspended load may be important in river engineering; sedimentation only in reservoirs and exceptionally at canal intakes.

The important properties of sediment and sediment transport are the sediment size (d), shape, density (usually 2650kg/m^3), fall velocity (w), bulk density and porosity and sediment concentration (C) (volumetric or ppm or mg/litre). It is usual to distinguish clay ($0{\cdot}5 < d < 5\ \mu$m), silt ($5 < d < 60\ \mu$m), sand ($0{\cdot}06 < d < 2$ mm) and gravel ($2 < d < 60$mm) according to size.

The fall velocity can be approximately expressed by the equation

$$w = \left(\frac{4}{3}\frac{gd}{C_D}\Delta\right)^{1/2} \tag{22}$$

where $\Delta = (\rho_s - \rho)/\rho$ and C_D is a drag coefficient dependent on the Reynolds number $\mathrm{Re} = \dfrac{wd}{\nu}$. For values of $\mathrm{Re} < 1$ (very fine sediment) $C_D = \dfrac{24}{\mathrm{Re}}$ which leads to Stokes law; for large sizes with $\mathrm{Re} > 10^3$, C_D becomes constant and is a function of grain shape only (usually $C_D \cong 1{\cdot}3$ for sand particles). The fall velocity varies therefore, with $d^{1/2}$ to d^2. The threshold of sediment motion (incipient motion) is given by a critical value of the shear stress which for a plane sediment bed is given by the Shields criterion:

$$\tau_c = c(\rho_s - \rho)gd \tag{23}$$

where c according to various authors varies between 0·4 and 0·6. The condition of validity of equation 23 is that $\mathrm{Re} = \dfrac{v_* d}{\nu} > 10^3$. As from equation 5 $\dfrac{\tau_0}{\rho} = v_*^2$, equation 23 can also be written as

$$\mathrm{Fr}_d^2 = \frac{v_*^2}{gd\Delta} = c. \tag{23a}$$

For a sediment particle on a slope (e.g. side slope of a canal) inclined at an angle β to the horizontal the critical shear stress is reduced by a factor:

$$\cos\beta\sqrt{1 - \frac{\tan^2\beta}{\tan^2\phi}} = \sqrt{1 - \frac{\sin^2\beta}{\sin^2\phi}}$$

where ϕ is the natural angle of stability of the non-cohesive material. (For stability naturally $\beta < \phi$). The average value of ϕ is about 35°. On the other hand the maximum shear stress induced by the flow on a side slope of the canal is usually only about 0·75 ρgys (instead of ρgys—see equation 5). Thus in designing a stable canal in alluvium it is necessary to ascertain whether the bed or side slope stability is the critical one for channel stability. In a channel which is not straight the critical shear stress is further reduced by a factor between 0·6 and 0·9 (0·6 applies to very sinuous channels).

Investigations into bed load transport have been going on for decades without a really satisfactory all embracing equation connecting the fluid and sediment properties being available. This is due mainly to the complexity of the problem including the effect of different bed forms on the mode and magnitude of bedload transport, the stochastic nature of the problem and the difficulty of verifying laboratory investigation in prototype. Nevertheless substantial advances have been made. Most of the used approaches can be reduced to a correlation between the sediment transport parameter $\phi = q_s\, d^{3/2}\sqrt{g\Delta}$ where q_s is the sediment transport in $m^3/s/m$ and the flow parameter $\psi = v_*/\Delta gd$. The power of ψ in many correlations varies between 2 and 3, i.e. q_s varies as v^n with $4 < n < 6$ demonstrating the importance of a good knowledge of the velocity field in modelling and computation of bed load transport.

RIVER ENGINEERING

River morphology and regime.—River morphology is concerned with channel configuration and geometry and with longitudinal profile; it is time dependent and varies particularly with discharge, sediment input and characteristics and bank material. River morphology can be substantially influenced by engineering works, although this influence is not necessarily beneficial. Natural river channels are either straight—usually only very short reaches—meandering, i.e. consisting of a series of bends of alternative curvature connected by short, straight reaches, or braided, i.e. the river divides into several channels which continuously join and separate.

Bends can be divided into free (surface), limited (entrenched) and forced (deformed) with ratios of radius of curvature to width from about 3 (forced) to about 7·5 (limited); (5 for free bends). In free and limited bends the depth gradually increases to a maximum downstream of the apex of the bend; bends are characterised by spiral flow and triangular sections with the maximum depth and velocity at the concave bank and maximum sediment transport at the convex bank. Crossings are relatively straight reaches between alternative bends and are approximately rectangular in section.

Meandering rivers usually have a ratio of channel to valley length bigger than 1·5 (Ref. 9) with meander length (distance between vertices of alternate bends) about 10 times the stream width. The ratio of meander length to width varies between 2 and 4.

In rivers the mean cross sectional velocity varies from usually about 0·5m/s at low flows to 4·0m/s at floods—but there are exceptions to these values. The maximum, velocity in a section usually exceeds the mean by 25–30%.

River regime is concerned with the channel geometry. A river in alluvium is considered to be in regime if its channel is stable on a long-term average. Short term changes will occur with changes of discharge and sediment transport and the concept of 'stability' is here clearly different from the one defined by the critical limiting tractive force implying no motion of sediment on the bed and banks.

The cross section and longitudinal slope for a regime channel will primarily be a function of discharge with the width B depth y and slope S providing three degrees of freedom for selfadjustment of the channel. The relationship between these three parameters and discharge, proceeding in a river system in the downstream direction, has been based mainly on measurements carried out on the Indian subcontinent and is usually expressed as:

$$B \propto Q^{1/2};\ y \propto Q^{1/3};\ S \propto Q^{-1/6} \qquad (24a\text{–}c)$$

Lacey and Pemberton (Ref. 10) generalised the basic regime equation into

$$v = aR^{\frac{b+1}{2}}S^b \qquad (25)$$

where a and b vary with sediment diameter. The power b is $\frac{1}{4} < b < 1$ with the lower limit for $d > 2$ mm and the upper for $d > 0{\cdot}1$ mm. Lacey's original equation

$$v = 0{\cdot}635\sqrt{fR} \qquad (26)$$

where $f = \sqrt{2500d}$ (d in m, v in m/s) combined with equation 25 or equation 24(a–c) leads to the basic regime statement

$$R^{1/2}S \propto d \qquad (27)$$

In contrast the critical tractive force theory leads to (see equation 23)

$$B \propto Q^{0{\cdot}46}\ y \propto Q^{0{\cdot}46}\ S \propto Q^{-0{\cdot}46} \qquad (28a\text{–}c)$$

and

$$SR \propto d \qquad (29)$$

Both the regime concept and critical tractive force theory lead to a relatively weak dependence of velocity on discharge. The regime concept results in:

$$v \propto Q^{1/6} \qquad (30)$$

and the critical tractive force theory in:

$$v \propto Q^{0{\cdot}08} \qquad (31)$$

Generally the critical tractive force approach would be more associated with coarse material (gravel) and upland river reaches and the regime concept with the fine material in lowland river reaches and canals. The above relationships apply to changes in cross section in the downstream direction. At any one river section different 'at a station' relationships apply. Characteristically they are:

$$B \propto Q^{0\cdot26};\quad y \propto Q^{0\cdot4};\quad v \propto Q^{0\cdot34};\quad S \propto Q^{0\cdot14} \tag{32a–d}$$

Braided river reaches are usually steeper, wider and shallower than individual reaches with the same Q; indeed braiding may be regarded as the incipient form of meandering.

Data and their measurement.—The basic data required in river engineering are cross-section characteristics, plan form and slope of channel, bed and bank material, water discharge and quality, sediment characteristics and discharge, groundwater levels, land use, etc.

Apart from standard surveying techniques, different types of non-recording and recording (analogue, digital) water level gauges, the latter sometimes in conjunction with various telemetering systems, are being used. Depth measurement is usually carried out by rods, lines and on larger rivers by echo sounding devices. In tidal estuaries it is necessary to reduce all soundings to a standard datum (usually mean low water level).

Discharge measurement is carried out by means of velocity measurement using various types of current meters for point or depth integrated measurement or approximately by float measurements; ultrasonic velocity meters can also be used in special cases. Discharge can also be measured by means of flumes, weirs (sharp-crested, broad-crested), by using tracers (dilution techniques) or ultrasonic velocity meters. Sediment for further analysis of size, shape, etc., is collected from the bed of various types of grabs.

Suspended sediment samples can be in the simplest form collected by spring loaded flap valve traps; point integrating or depth integrating sediment samplers with nozzles oriented against and parallel to the flow and samplers shaped to achieve a true undistorted stream velocity at the intake are used for measuring suspended sediment discharge. Measurement of bed load is extremely difficult and there is probably no universally satisfactory method, although some well functioning samplers have been developed. Their efficiency has to be tested in the laboratory for the range of field conditions in which they are to be used. Continuous pumped suspended load (and in some cases bed load) samplers are also being used.

River improvement.—The objective of river improvement works is to aid navigation, to prevent flooding, to reclaim or protect land or to provide water supply for irrigation, hydropower development or domestic and industrial use.

For navigation purposes the main river improvement works are those which provide sufficient depth and/or stabilise the river channel in a suitable form. The minimum depth of the waterway is given by the maximum draft of the vessel and a clearance which should exceed 0·30m. The principal methods used to improve navigable channels are river regulation, dredging, canalisation, construction of lateral canals, and flow improvement by reservoir construction and operation. Only the first two will be briefly dealt with here.

In river regulation or training the river may be encouraged to pursue its natural course or it may be straightened. The latter requires great sensitivity and should be used only with caution and due regard to environmental constraints. In the upstream reaches the main problem is the short term and seasonal variation of flow, high velocity, channel instability and shoal formation. In the middle and lower reaches it is often necessary to raise river banks. In estuaries dredging may be necessary together with the construction of works reducing the channel width, e.g. groynes, longitudinal training walls etc.

An efficient river training system will try to maintain and improve the natural sequence of bends in a meandering river whilst preserving sufficient depth for navigation at low flows and suppressing unduly sharp bends and excessive velocities. This is mainly achieved by groynes, jetties, longitudinal dykes and embankments and ground sills. Groynes are small jetties, solid or permeable, constructed of timber, sheet piling, vegetation, stone rubble, etc. They usually project into the stream perpendicularly to the bank, but sometimes are inclined in the upstream or downstream direction. Their main purpose is to reduce channel width and remove the danger of scour from the banks; their ends in the stream are liable to scour with sediment accumulation between them. As their effect is mainly local the spacing between groynes should not exceed about five groyne lengths, but usually is appreciably smaller, a spacing of about two lengths results in a well defined channel for navigation.

Longitudinal dykes (or training walls) are usually more economical than groynes and if properly positioned equally or even more effective. The material used is again rubble, stone, fascine work (on soft river beds).

Training walls may be single, i.e. on one side of the channel; or double. In some instances a series of stream deflectors (vanes) constructed of wood panels or metal, placed at a suitable angle (often almost parallel to the bank) and depth can be used to either divert an eroding flow from the river bank (which is to be protected) or on the other hand to induce bed erosion and local deepening of the flow. Details of their location are best determined by model studies or experiments in situ.

Dredging using mechanical or hydraulic suction dredgers is the most effective means of navigation channel regulation, but its impact is often only temporary.

Bank protection is carried out by planting, faggotting (faggots or fascines are bundles of branches—usually willow), thatching, wattling, mattresses, rubble, stone pitching, gabions, bagged concrete, concrete slabs, asphalt slabs, prefabricated concrete interblocking units with or without vegetation, articulated concrete mattresses, soil-cement blocks, geotextiles, used tires, etc.

The choice of material is influenced by the extent of the area to be protected, material availability, material and labour cost, access to site, mechanisation available, soil conditions, design life, etc. Channel bed liable to extensive erosion can be stabilised by ground sills or, more extensively (and expensively), by a series of drop structures.

Ground sills usually span the whole width of the river channel with the greatest height at each bank and a gentle slope to the stream centre. Rubble mounds, cribs filled with rubble and concrete are some of the materials most frequently used for ground sills.

Some special inland navigation problems.—Two problems of importance in inland navigation have to be mentioned here:

(i) CONSTRICTED WATERWAYS. Navigation on constricted waterways whether rivers or canals, presents two problems from the river engineering point of view; increased local velocities and danger of erosion of banks.

As a vessel moves along a waterway a backflow of water occurs filling the space vacated by the submerged volume. In a restricted space the velocities of this back flow can be considerable. Furthermore the water level along the vessel is depressed with the greatest depression occurring near midship. The bank protection required on constricted waterways has to withstand these velocities as well as the effect of waves generated by the movement of the vessels. Effective bank drainage is essential (Ref. 11).

Generally it is desirable, particularly on commercially used waterways, to have a ratio of waterway cross-section to the immersed section of the barges (total immersed section of a train) bigger than 4 to 1. The limiting ratio is of course also speed dependent.

The minimum width B of a waterway in a straight section with simultaneous navigation in both directions is $B = 3b$ or $B = 2b + 3\Delta b$ where b is the width of a barge (or a group of barges) and Δb the side clearance with $\Delta b \geq 5$m. If navigation is in one direction only $B = (1{\cdot}5 \text{ to } 2)b$.

The maximum flow velocity for upstream navigation to be economically viable is about 2·5m/s.

(ii) CURVES. The design of regulated river curves has to take into account the size of the barges, method of haulage as well as the speed of navigation (see p. L11/11).

The minimum radius of a curved waterway is given by the length L of a typical barge multiplied by a constant which is about 3 for push boats and 4·5 for towed barges. The width of the waterway in a bend with two-way traffic has to be increased to $B_0 = B + \Delta B$ (Fig. 3) where

$$\Delta B = \frac{L^2}{2R + B} \cong \frac{L^2}{2R} \qquad (33)$$

Aspects of the above problems will be further dealt with in the following section.

CANALISATION AND NAVIGATION.

Canalisation.—A free flowing river can be canalised by a series of barrages with navigation locks. Canalisation becomes necessary from the navigation point of view if the free flowing river has too small a depth and too high a velocity to permit navigation.

The advantages of canalisation are:

(i) Opportunity for multi-purpose utilisation of water resources;
(ii) Sufficient depth for navigation throughout the year, even at times of low river flows;
(iii) Reduced velocities of flow;
(iv) Increased width of waterways;
(v) Safer and cheaper navigation;
(vi) Often reduced need for bank protection and its maintenance compared with regulated rivers.

The main disadvantages are:

(i) High capital cost;
(ii) Need for protection of adjacent land;
(iii) Drainage problems;
(iv) Delay of traffic passing through locks;
(v) Possible deposition of sediments at the upstream end;
(vi) Possible winter regime complications.

The upper reaches of most of the major navigable rivers are canalised or in the process of being canalised (Rhine, Danube, Dniepr, Volga, Mississippi, Ohio, etc). The height of individual steps in the cascade of barrages, i.e. the difference of water levels, varies greatly according to hydrological, morphological and geological conditions, but is usually between 5 and 15m.

Navigation Canals.—Navigation canals can be used to bypass a river section difficult to navigate and can be used in conjunction with a single barrage or several barrages spaced wider apart than in case of river canalisation. Furthermore they are an essential part of inland navigation where they connect two watersheds. They require suitably shaped intakes, often a separate flow regulation structure and navigation locks (e.g. the Rhone canal).

The position and layout of canals can, within the traffic and geological constraints, be adapted to general transport, land use and industrial demands. The canal is usually appreciably shorter than a canalised river would be which, together with low (or zero) flow velocities, aids navigation in both directions. Their main disadvantage is use of land, and disruption of communications; thus when planning a canal maximum use should be made of existing rivers as far as their canalisation is feasible.

Navigation canals can have a fall in one direction only or in both directions with a top water reservoir. They may connect two river systems or branch off a navigable waterway to give access to an industrial centre. The crossing of a canal with a navigable river, the branching of a canal from the river or branching of canals may create special traffic and construction problems, (Fig. 2.) Canals may be without flowing water or with a flow if they serve another purpose simultaneously with navigation (see also p. L11/10).

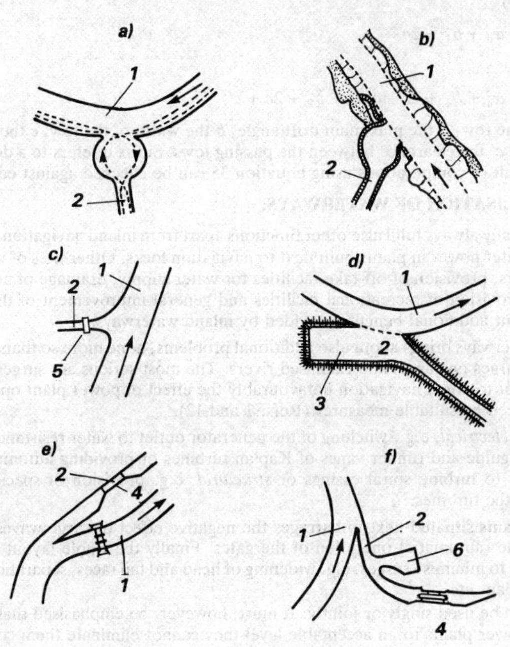

FIG. 2.—Branching of a canal from a navigable river: (Ref. 2) 1–river, 2–canal, 3–turning of barges, 4–locks, 5–flood gate, 6–basin.

Sections of canals which are either temporarily or permanently above the surrounding groundwater table need, apart from erosion protection, some means of protection against loss of water by seepage. Proper underdrainage and protection of the impermeable or seepage resistant layer against back pressure in case of an increase of the ground water level are also essential. Materials used are clay, concrete, plastics, etc. Bank protection on canalised rivers and canals is of the same type and variety as on trained rivers.

Adequate canal depth and width are required as on regulated rivers and, because of the drift of tows passing through bends, a bigger width is required there.

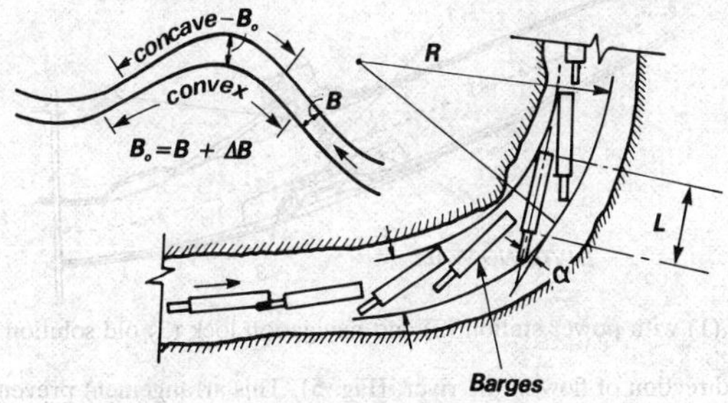

FIG. 3.—Bends and tow drift on a waterway.

The drift (deflection) angle α is the inclination of the tow to the tangent of the radius of curvature passing through the centre of the tow (Fig. 3). The drift depends on the radius of the bend, the speed, power and design of the tow (tug), loading of the tow, wind forces and the flow pattern. The drift angle is larger for tows travelling in the downstream than upstream direction.

The US Army Corps of Engineers extrapolated German drift angle data from the Rhine up to a tow length of 180 m and obtained for the downstream direction values $2° < \alpha < 15°$ for radii of curvature $400 < R < 2500$m (the larger the radius the smaller is the angle α). For the upstream direction the values of α are halved.

According to US Army Corps Engineers the following equations apply for the channel width B_0 in bends for one-way traffic (Ref. 9).

$$B_{01} = L_1 \sin \alpha_d + b_1 + 2c \tag{34}$$

and for two-way traffic:

$$B_{02} = L_1 \sin \alpha_u + b_1 + L_2 \sin \alpha_d + b_2 + 2c + c' \tag{35}$$

where L is the length of the tow, α the maximum drift angle, b the width of the tow, c the clearance between tow and channel bank and c' the clearance between the passing tows. Suffix d refers to a downbound and u to an upbound tow. The result of computations using equation 35 can be checked against equation 33.

MULTIPURPOSE UTILISATION OF WATERWAYS.

Modern waterways practically always fulfil also other functions apart from inland navigation. The most common case is the utilisation of water power in plants built next to navigation locks. Other uses of waterways are flood protection on trained rivers, provision of off-take facilities for water supply, drainage of adjacent land, waste water disposal etc. The provision of recreational facilities and general improvement of the environment are some of the most important additional benefits provided by inland waterways.

Multipurpose use of waterways brings about also additional problems, none more so than the peak operation of power plants causing surges on canals and canalised rivers. The most serious are surges caused by sudden load rejection. In order not to affect navigation unfavourably the effect of power plant operation must in the majority of cases be reduced by suitable measures (Refs. 1 and 12).

These measures may be *electrical*, e.g. switching of the generator outlet to water resistance, *mechanical*, e.g. disconnecting the linkage guide and runner vanes of Kaplan turbines or providing automatic gate controlled outlets connected directly to turbine spiral casings or *structural*, e.g. provision of special auxiliary outlets designed as by-passes for the turbines.

In the case of power plants situated next to barrages the negative effect of surge waves on navigation can also be reduced by suitable (automatic) operation of the gates. Finally the whole layout of the barrage and plant can be so designed as to minimise surges, e.g. widening of head and tail races, separation of the navigation channel from the power plant etc.

The above measures can be used singly or jointly. It must, however, be emphasised that although they can reduce the surges from power plants to an acceptable level they cannot eliminate them completely.

The optimum control of a whole cascade of plants is usually best developed by the use of mathematical modelling combined with field measurements. Winter regime has also to be taken into account in these studies.

The layout of a barrage with a power plant, navigation lock(s) and their approaches requires careful consideration of the respective functions of the individual components of a complex hydraulic structure. This may result in different layouts on small and large navigable rivers and on navigation canals, (Ref. 13).

On smaller rivers and at older works the general layout usually followed a scheme with the navigation lock and power plant having parallel axes and situated on either side of the weir or barrage. The lock was separated from the river flow by a long narrow dividing wall, (Fig. 4). A better solution adopted in newer structures is one where the lock is separated from the river by an island and the turbine axes (forebay and tail race) are

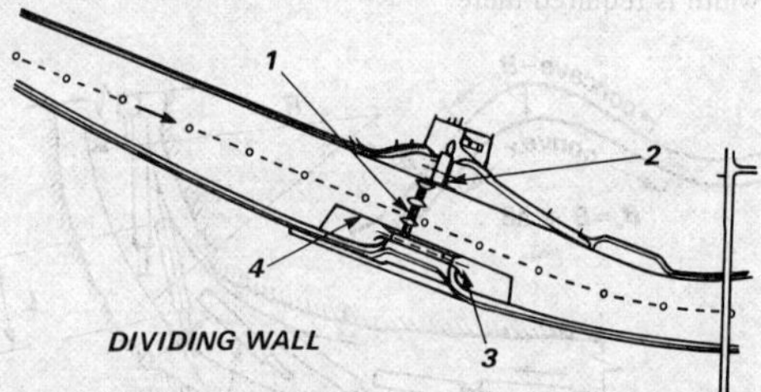

FIG. 4.—Barrage (1) with power station (2) and navigation lock (3) old solution of layout (Ref. 2).

set at an angle to the direction of flow in the river, (Fig. 5). This arrangement prevents scour at the dividing walls of the power plant and lock and results in improved efficiency both of navigation and of the power plant.

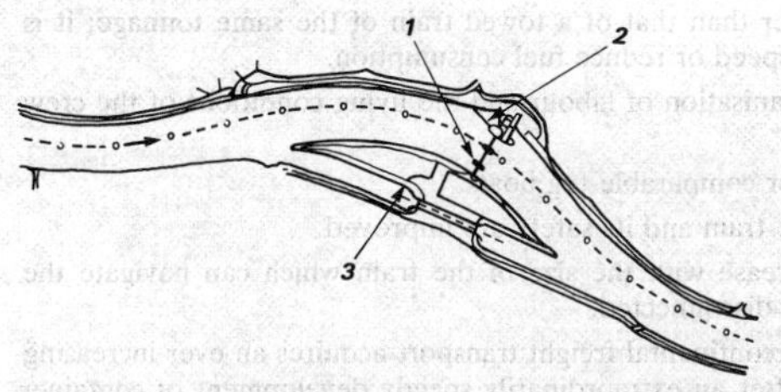

FIG. 5.—Barrage (1) with power station (2) and navigation lock (3) new solution of layout (Ref. 2).

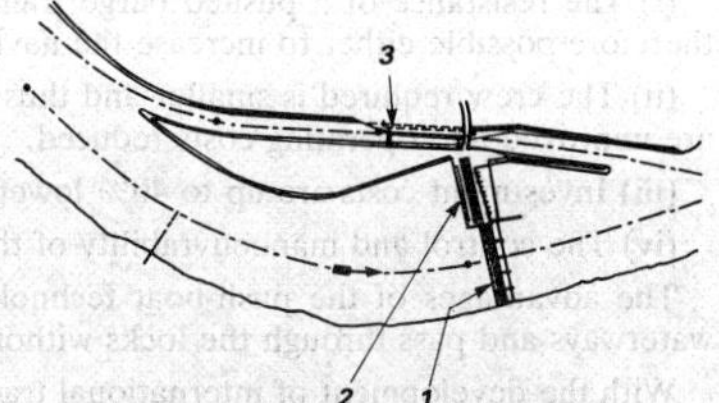

FIG. 6.—Layout of the barrage (1), power station (2) and navigation locks (3) at Birsfelden on the Rhine (Ref. 2).

On large navigable rivers the considerations governing the layout are complex and usually have to take into account also problems of sediment transport, ice, etc.

The design of a barrage with power plant(s) and lock(s) (Fig. 6) on a river forming an international boundary may even call for a symmetrical arrangement with two power plants and two sets of locks on either side of the river.

Details of a suitable layout of a complex water resources utilisation particularly one involving hydropower development and navigation are best studied on scale models.

TRANSPORT ON INLAND WATERWAYS

Utilisation of Inland Waterways.—The influence of inland navigation in various countries is very varied pending primarily on their geographical position and economic factors. Although it is difficult to get accurate data due to different methods of registering freight on inland waterways (all freight or only that transported by the respective country) and the difficulty of distinguishing between coastal and inland navigation in some countries. Table 1 gives at least a general overview (relating to 1980/83) for some countries both in absolute (length and utilisation of waterway) and relative terms when compared with rail and road transport.

TABLE 1.—FREIGHT ON INLAND WATERWAYS: ANNUAL THROUGHPUT OF SHIPPING

Country	Length of waterways	Utilisation of waterways		Fraction of total transport capacity	
	km	Volume 10^6 t/year	Output 10^9 tkm/year	Volume %	Output %
GFR	4,322	222	49	14·5	29·5
Switzerland	21	8	0·05	2·3	0·4
Netherlands	4,387	241	31	48·3	63·1
Belgium	1,961	91	5	31.3	22·3
France	8,568	76	10	10·7	8·0
GDR	2,319	17	2	2·8	3·2
Poland	3,898	17	2	3·1	1·3
Austria	358	3	2	4·1	12·9
Hungary	1,622	11	2	2·7	6·3
Jugoslavia	2,001	29	7	9·7	13·9
Roumania	1,659	19	3	2·4	3·0
Bulgaria	471	9	2	2·1	7·2
Czechoslovakia	476	12	4	1·8	4·5
Italy	596	2	0·2	1·0	0·4
UK	3,328	5	0·01	0·6	0·6
Sweden	1,165	5	0·5	1·6	1·6
Finland	15,000	8	2	2·1	5·7
USSR	150,000	605	262	5·5	6·8
USA	41,403	1,761	234		22·2
China	107,800	312	57	14·4	8·7

Traction, push tow and lighters.—Barges may be self-propelled or towed or pushed by tugs. On some continental canals diesel or electric tractors or engines on a track along the canal have replaced the original form of traction by horses. On larger canals and navigable waterways the traditional method of using tug boats pulling a number of barges was replaced almost universally by 1970 by the control of a group of barges by push boats (see p. L11/2). This development has been mainly due to the following advantages of the push tow:

(i) The resistance of a pushed barge train is lower than that of a towed train of the same tonnage; it is therefore possible either to increase the navigation speed or reduce fuel consumption.

(ii) The crew required is smaller and thus the organisation of labour and the living conditions of the crew are improved and operating costs reduced.

(iii) Investment costs are up to 40% lower than for comparable tug boats.

(iv) The control and manoeuvrability of the whole train and its safety are improved.

The advantages of the push-boat technology increase with the size of the train which can navigate the waterways and pass through the locks without being disconnected.

With the development of international trade, intercontinental freight transport acquires an ever increasing importance on the principal waterways (Ref. 6). After an extraordinarily speedy development of container transport the progressive method of international transport by means of floating containers, called lighters, has begun to assert itself (Ref. 10).

This system is intended above all for the transport of goods whose consigner and recipient are situated on navigable waterways of different continents. Lighters, grouped on inland waterways into pushed trains, are transported across the sea in special marine carriers provided with loading and unloading equipment of their own: a marine lighter carrier can handle 1500–2000 tons of freight per hour, (Refs. 14, 21). At present there are four systems of this transport; the BACAT system with lighters of 140 tons, suitable for navigation on British small waterways, the LASH system with lighters of 375 tons, the SEA BEE system with lighters of 850 tons, and the INTERLIGHTER system with lighters of up to 1100 tons used by the Danubian states.

The size of the push trains varies according to the characteristics of the waterway (see p. L11/2); on some larger ones, e.g. the lower Mississippi, 48 barge push-tows with towboats exerting a power over 5000 kW are not uncommon.

Resistance of Ships.—The interaction of a ship with the surrounding body of water is a complicated one, particularly in a constricted waterway where, furthermore, the interaction of the flow and waves generated by navigation with the banks and bed of the waterway has to be taken into account (see p. L11/8). These factors together with the power and speed requirements of the tow determine the design of the navigation fairway, which also has to take into account the various bottlenecks encountered, e.g. fixed and movable bridges, offtakes and intakes, harbour entrances and exits, navigation locks, river and canal crossings, ferries, bypasses, crossing of lakes used for recreation, etc. (see p. L11/11).

The resistance of ships on restricted waters is influenced by many factors, the most important being their speed, flow velocity, shape of bow and stern, length, squat and draught (both at bow and stern), keel clearance and distance from canal banks (Ref. 15).

A general expression for the resistance R of a towed vessel is (Ref. 16):

$$R = C_F \tfrac{1}{2}\rho(v+u)^2 A' + \rho g B T z_s + \tfrac{1}{2}\rho g B z_B^2 + C_p' \tfrac{1}{2}\rho v^2 B(T + z_B) - C_p'' \tfrac{1}{2}\rho B T(v + u_s)^2 \quad (36)$$

where

v = the ship's speed
u = the velocity of the return flow (u_s at the stern)
z = depression of the water level (equal to the squat) (at stern or bow)
C_F = frictional resistance coefficient
A' = wetted hull area
B = width of the ship
T = draught
C_p', C_p'' = coefficients depending on speed and draught.

Equation 36 can be simplified by neglecting small terms to

$$R \cong C_F \tfrac{1}{2}\rho(v+\mu)^2 A' + \rho g B T z + C_p \tfrac{1}{2}\rho v^2 B T \quad (37)$$

The return flow velocity u and squat z in equation 37 can be computed from Bernoulli's equation and continuity:

$$2gz = (v+u)^2 - v^2 \quad (38)$$

$$vA = (v+u)(A_c - A_M - \Delta A_c) \quad (39)$$

where A_c is the canal cross section and A_M the midship sectional area. A good approximation for ΔA_c is given by:

$$\Delta A_c = B_c z \quad (40)$$

where B_c is the undisturbed canal width.

The resistance augmentation for push tows over a single ship of the same dimensions and parameters is only moderate.

The resistance decreases with the ratio n of the canal cross-sectional area A_c and the immersed section of the barge(s) A_M. As an example, Fig. 7 gives the appropriate variation of the resistance R for a 1350t barge

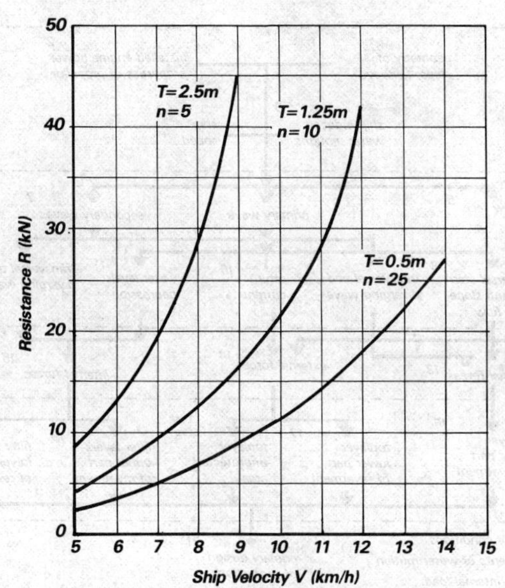

FIG. 7.—Resistance as a function of velocity.

as a function of v for three values of n and T (full draught $T = 2{\cdot}50$ m at $n = 5$). The curves have been computed from the simple equation due to Gebers:

$$R = (\lambda A' + kBT)v^{2\cdot25} \tag{41}$$

where $k = 0{\cdot}14$ for steel hulls and $0{\cdot}28$ for wooden ones; $k = 1{\cdot}7$ for small boats and empty barges and $3{\cdot}5$ for full barges. The results of equation 41 agree quite well with measurements from models. Figure 8 shows R as a function of n for 3 values of v for $T = 2{\cdot}5$ m.

A ship navigating a bend of radius r encounters an increased resistance due to the centrifugal force acting on the side of the ship passing through the bend at a drift angle α (see pp. L11/9 and L11/10).

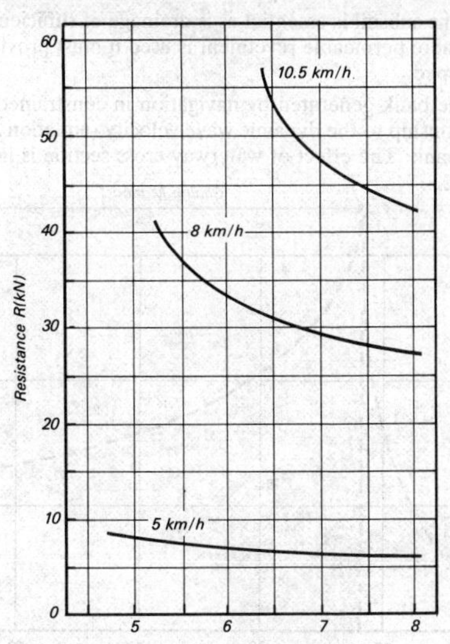

FIG. 8.—Resistance as a function of n.

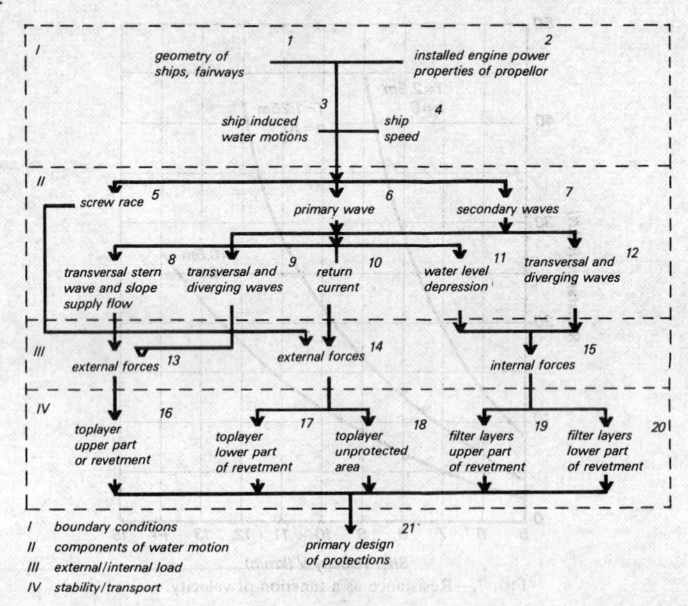

FIG. 9.—Bank protection of navigable waterways (Ref. 23) *Delft Hydraulics Laboratory.*

Wave action on banks.—The ship induced water motion causes waves attacking the banks of the waterway which requires suitable bank protection (see also p. L11/7). The whole complex interaction between boundary conditions, components of water motion, the forces acting and the bank revetment design for stability is shown schematically on Fig. 9.

It is important (Bowmeester et al 1977) to appreciate that the protective facing of banks must reach down below the water surface to a sufficiently low level and its bottom edge must be flexible enough to ensure permanent contact with the subsoil.

A good filter adapted to suit the subsoil is essential as is drainage of sufficient capacity underneath more or less impermeable revetment. Where permeable revetment is used it must provide sufficient drainage from the slope without any air being trapped.

The height of the waves at the bank generated by navigation in constrained waterways depends primarily on the ship's speed and its relationship to the dynamic wave velocity (equation 21), size and form of the vessel and its position relative to the bank. The effect of waterway cross-section is implicitly contained in the wave

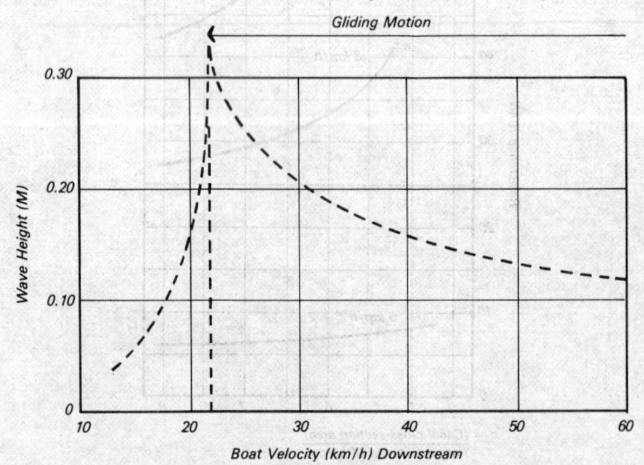

FIG. 10.—Wave height generated by fast boats (Ref. 17).

velocity. The boat speed is the most important factor and the generated wave height rises quite steeply with the speed until a maximum is reached corresponding to the speed at which the sailing motion becomes a gliding one with the bow above the water surface. This speed corresponds to the surge velocity and is rarely attained by commercial shipping or larger pleasure boats. Figure 10 is an example of the wave height generated by fast (police) boats on the upper Rhine (Ref. 17).

LOCKS

General.—Concentrated heads on canalised rivers and canals are usually overcome by navigation locks. The main components of locks are the lock gates, the lock chamber and the lock valves and filling (emptying) systems. The lock gates are of different types: mitre, hinged, sliding, vertical lift, submerged tainter (horizontal axis), sector (vertical axis), reversed tainter, etc.

The valves in the lock filling system are usually vertical lift, butterfly or cylindrical valves. Stop logs or vertical lift gates are used as emergency closure gates.

The lock chambers must be designed with sufficient stability against surface and ground water and earth pressures and have sufficient resistance against ship impact.

Clearances of up to 0/9m are usually allowed on either side of the largest vessel with the effective length of a lock usually 1 to 5m greater than the longest vessel the lock is intended to accommodate. Because of the difference in elevation of gate sills the upstream gate is nearly always smaller (lower) than the downstream one. The gate sill elevation controls the draft of tows that can use the lock; usually 1 to 2m is added to the required design depth as a provision for future development of the waterway.

The lock sizes (length L, width B and particularly their head H) together with the selected system of lock filling and emptying, determine the design of the lock as well as the type and function of its gates. In the course of the filling and emptying of the lock a complicated unsteady flow occurs not only in the lock itself but also in its approach basins. This flow exerts considerable forces on the barges. These forces must not exceed a permissible limit and their effect must be eliminated by the tying of the vessels with mooring ropes in the lock or in its approach basin. During emptying of the locks the vessels are usually affected by smaller forces than during filling because of the greater initial depth of water in the lock.

According to the size and type of filling we can divide locks into these categories:

(a) Locks with direct filling and emptying through their gates; this method is used mainly for small and medium lock sizes;

(b) Locks with indirect filling by means of long culverts situated either in the lateral lock walls or in their bottom and connected with the lock chamber by means of suitably designed outlets;

(c) Locks of large dimensions in plan and high heads with more complex filling and emptying systems, designed to ensure regular distribution of water during the filling and emptying along the whole lock area;

(d) Locks with combined direct and indirect filling.

Locks with direct filling.—In the case of low and medium head locks ($H < 12$m), of small to medium dimensions in plan ($B = 12$–24m, $L = 190$–230m) the locks have the shape of a prismatic trough with vertical walls and a solid bottom, constructed of suitable reinforced concrete precast components or as an in situ RC open frame, (Fig. 11b), or of anchored steel sheet piles, (Fig. 11a), or concrete walls braced at the lock bottom.

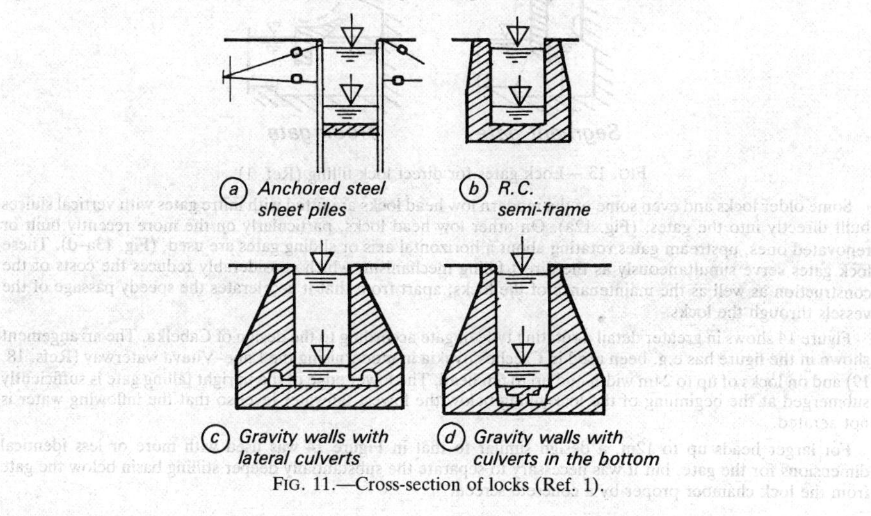

FIG. 11.—Cross-section of locks (Ref. 1).

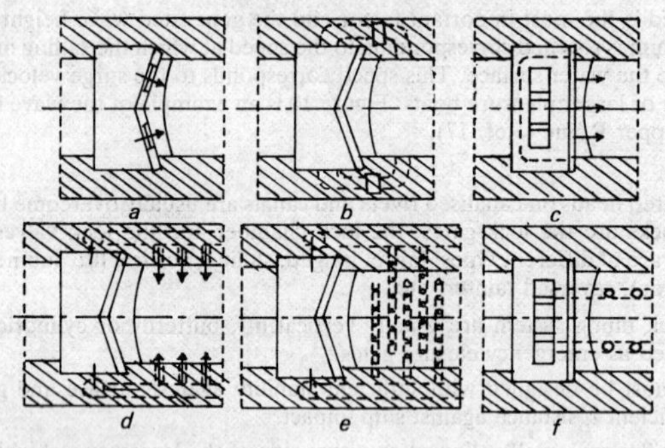

FIG. 12.—Filing systems for locks:
(a) Direct filling through sluices in gates.
(b) Indirect filling through short culverts in lateral walls.
(c) Indirect filling through culverts under the gate sill.
(d) and (e) Indirect filling through long culverts in the lateral walls.
(f) Indirect filling through long culverts in the bottom.

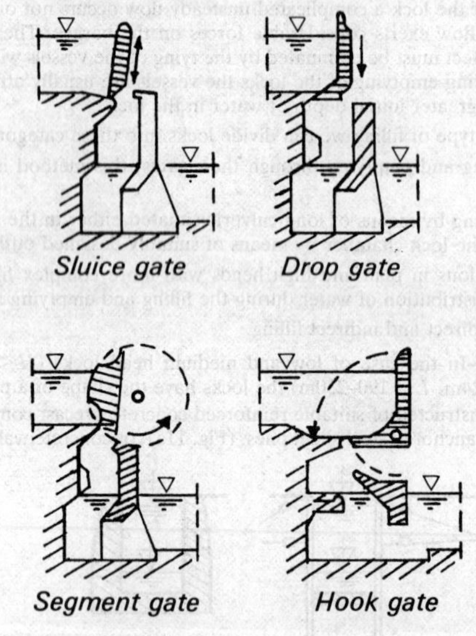

FIG. 13.—Lock gates for direct lock filling (Ref. 1).

Some older locks and even some of the modern low head locks are fitted with mitre gates with vertical sluices built directly into the gates, (Fig. 12a). On other low head locks, particularly on the more recently built or renovated ones, upstream gates rotating about a horizontal axis or sliding gates are used, (Fig. 13a–d). These lock gates serve simultaneously as the direct filling mechanism, which considerably reduces the costs of the construction as well as the maintenance of the locks; apart from that it accelerates the speedy passage of the vessels through the locks.

Figure 14 shows in greater detail a rotating type of gate according to the design of Cabelka. The arrangement shown in the figure has e.g. been used in Czechoslovakia in modernising the Labe–Vltava waterway (Refs. 18, 19) and on locks of up to 24m width and up to 6m head. The lower edge of the upright falling gate is sufficiently submerged at the beginning of the lock filling below the lowest tailwater level so that the inflowing water is not aerated.

For larger heads up to 12m, a design similar to that in Figure 14 was used with more or less identical dimensions for the gate, but it was necessary to separate the substantially deeper stilling basin below the gate from the lock chamber proper by a concrete screen.

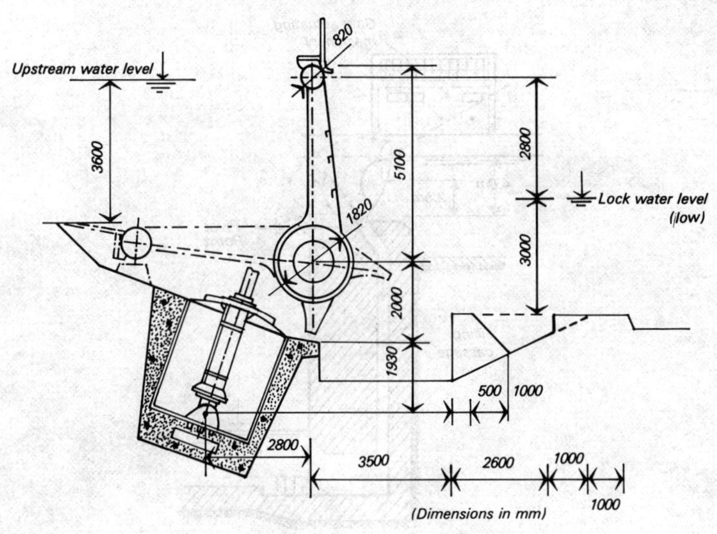

FIG. 14.—Rotating gate of Cabelka type (Ref. 1).

The installation of this type of gate is substantially eased by floating it into its position; made possible by the two horizontal tubes forming an integral part of its structure, which are hermetically sealed and act as floats. The motion of the tilting gate is ensured by a hydraulic motor, mounted at the bottom of the upper gate recess in a protective casing with sliding cover.

For direct filling of locks 12m wide, with an initial water depth of 3·5m–4·0m, an incremental inflow below the gate at the beginning of its filling $dQ/dt = 0{\cdot}2\,m^3/s^2$ is permissible without the forces in the mooring ropes of the handled ships exceeding their permissible values. The rate of rise of the water level varies within the limits of $0{\cdot}8 < v < 1{\cdot}2$m/min.

Directly filled locks may be emptied either by means of short culverts or directly below the downstream lifting gates or even through openings in the gates, closed with sluice, butterfly or flap valves.

Another type of direct filling system with sector gates turning along vertical axes is shown on Fig. 15 with

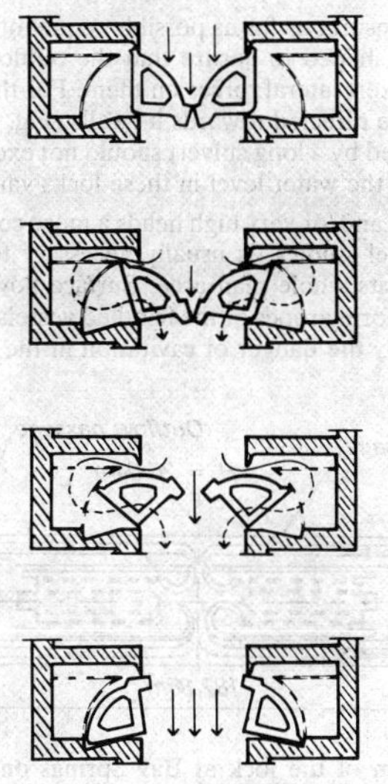

FIG. 15.—Various stages of head gates positions for direct filling of locks (Ref. 2).

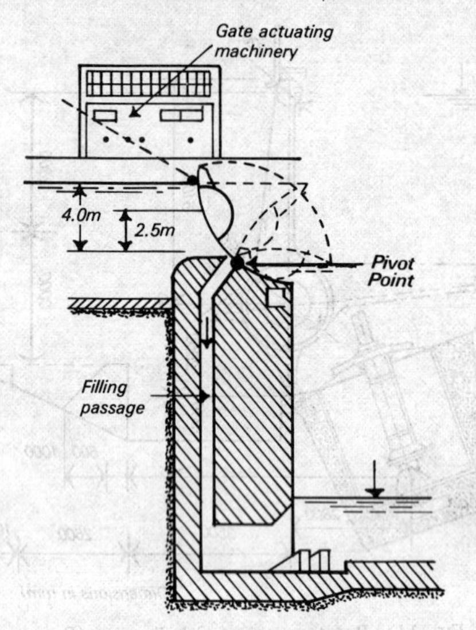

FIG. 16.—Direct filling of high head locks (Ref. 2).

the various stages of opening of the gates. The system is suitable for low heads only; the gates turn slowly through the initial stages of opening increasing their opening speed as the water level difference decreases. For larger heads the filling system using a leaf gate as shown on Fig. 16 can be used. The filling system is designed to prevent air entrainment in the filing passage below the gate contributing thus to a calmer filling.

Locks with indirect filling and emptying.—Indirect filling and emptying of high head locks ($H > 12$m) and minor dimensions in plan ($B = 12$m) is best achieved by means of long culverts, situated either in the lateral walls (Figs. 11c, 12d, e) or in the bottom (Figs. 11d, 12f). At the upstream and downstream end of the lock the culverts are provided with gates (sluice or segment), which must be situated below the lowest possible water level. To reduce outlet losses the overall cross-sectional area of all outlet ports should be 1·3–1·5 times as large as the cross-sectional area of the fully opened culvert gate.

The outlet ports are distributed to ensure, as far as possible, equal outflow along the culvert length and are usually staggered and positioned and shaped to ensure that the outflow into the lock is directed below the bottom of the vessels in order not to exert lateral forces on them. For the same reason the outlet ports of long culverts situated in the lock bottom are directed towards its walls (Fig. 11d). The permissible rate of increase of the inflow of water into the locks filled by a long culvert should not exceed $dQ/dt < 0{\cdot}6\text{m}^3/\text{s}^2$ at the beginning of the filling. The mean rate of rise of the water level in these locks varies between 1·5m/min and 2·0m/min.

For locks of large dimensions in plan and/or very high heads a more complicated filling and emptying system, usually designed on the basis of model studies, is usually necessary to ensure uniformly distributed inflow (outflow) of water into the lock over its whole plan area. Surface flow and translation waves, which would generate unacceptable forces in the mooring ropes of the handled vessels, must be eliminated as far as possible. The filling velocity is usually limited by the danger of cavitation in the filling system.

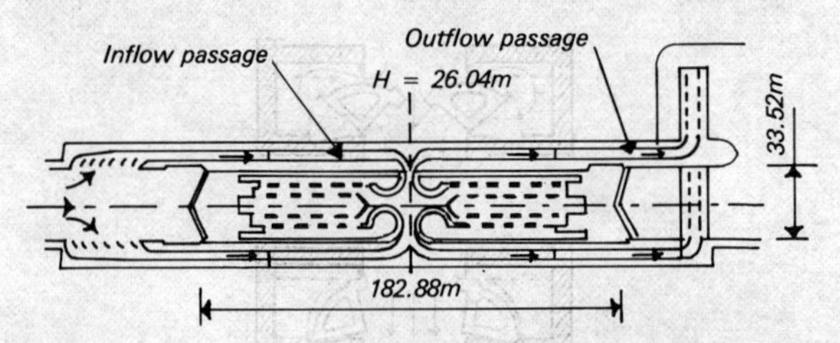

FIG. 17.—Filling and emptying system of the lock at Bay Springs on the Tennessee–Tombigbee waterway (USA) (Ref. 9).

There are many locks in existence with various designs of filling and emptying systems. Figure 17 is an example of such a system used in the lock at Bay Springs on the Tennessee–Tombigbee waterway, USA. (L = 183m, B = 33·50m and H = 26m).

The maximum head for which single stage locks can be used is determined basically by the limit for which a rational filling and emptying system—feasible technically and viable from the economic and water resources point of view—can be designed. Examples of very high heads used for a single stage lock are H = 42·5m on the Ust–Kamenogorsk scheme on the Irtysh river, USSR (lock dimensions 100 × 18m, minimum water depth 2·5m), then H = 35m at the Carrapatelo dam on the Duero river, Portugal and H = 34·5m at the John Day Dam on the Columbia River, USA.

On canalised rivers used for power generating purposes as well, where water requirements for navigation must be minimised, high heads are overcome by means of either coupled locks (e.g. on the Gabcikovo scheme on the Danube), two-stage locks (e.g. on the Djerdab scheme on the Danube), three-stage locks (e.g. in the Dnicprogress scheme on the Dniepr river, USSR), or a whole cascade of locks with intermediate reservoirs. The economy of handling water is achieved, at the cost of increased capital outlay and longer time of the passage of vessels through the given step.

Hydraulics of locks.—The design parameters of major interest are the time of filling (emptying) T, the maximum discharge Q and the maximum forces acting on a vessel during lockage. If we assume that the lock is filled from a large forebay with constant water level we can write:

$$Q\,dt = ca\sqrt{2gh}\,dt = -A\,dh \tag{42}$$

where A is the lock area in plan, h the instantaneous head (the difference between the forebay and lock water levels), c a coefficient and a the filling system area (valve area); both c and a are functions of time but c is usually taken as a constant.

For an instantaneous complete opening of the filling system equation 42 yields:

$$T = \int_0^T dt = -\frac{A}{Ca\sqrt{2g}}\int_H^0 \frac{dh}{\sqrt{h}} = \frac{2A\sqrt{H}}{Ca\sqrt{2g}} \tag{43}$$

For a linear opening of the system in time T_1 ($a = a_t T_1/t$)

$$\int_0^{T_1} dt = -\frac{A}{Ca\sqrt{2g}}\int_H^{h_{T_1}} \frac{dh}{a_t\sqrt{h}} = -\frac{AT_1}{Cat\sqrt{2g}}\int_H^{h_{T_1}} \frac{dh}{\sqrt{h}}$$

Thus

$$\int_0^{T_1} t\,dt = \frac{2AT_1}{Ca\sqrt{2g}}(\sqrt{H} - \sqrt{h_{T_1}})$$

and

$$T_1 = \frac{4A(\sqrt{H} - \sqrt{h_{T_1}})}{Ca\sqrt{2g}} \tag{44}$$

The total time of filling from equations 43 and 44 is then

$$T = T_1 + \frac{2A\sqrt{h_{T_1}}}{Ca\sqrt{2g}} = \frac{T_1}{2} + \frac{2A\sqrt{H}}{Ca\sqrt{2g}} \tag{45}$$

(Generally the opening of the filling system is non-linear). In the same way we could derive the equation for the time to equalise the water levels between two locks areas A_1 and A_2. For an instantaneous full opening of the filling system

$$T = \frac{2A_1A_2\sqrt{H}}{(A_1 + A_2)Ca\sqrt{2g}} \tag{46}$$

If $A_1 = A_2$

$$T = \frac{A\sqrt{H}}{Ca\sqrt{2g}} \tag{47}$$

and for $A_1 = \infty$ we get again equation 43.

The time of filling of a lock by an overfall height h_1 over a gate width B is given approximately by

$$T = \frac{AH}{\frac{2}{3}C_d B\sqrt{2g}h_1^{3/2}} \tag{48}$$

(equation 48 neglects the change from a modular to non-modular overflow at the end of the filling).

If the opening of the filling system is gradual but not linear we have to compute the time of filling by a step method; e.g. from equation 43 it follows:

$$\Delta t = \frac{2A}{Ca\sqrt{2g}}(\sqrt{h_{i-1}} - \sqrt{h_i}) \tag{49}$$

thus:

$$h_i = \left(\sqrt{h_{i-1}} - \frac{C\sqrt{2g}}{2A}a\Delta t\right)^2 \tag{50}$$

Equation 50 gives us the change with time of the depth $h_i^1 (h_i^1 = H - h_i)$ in the lock and it also permits us to compute the change of discharge with time from equation 42:

$$Q_i = ca_i\sqrt{2gh_i} \tag{42}$$

(In equations 49 and 50, a is a function of time).

Of particular interest is of course the maximum discharge Qmax. In the special case of a linear opening of the filling (emptying) system we can determine Qmax and the head at which it occurs analytically from the two equations

$$t^2 = \frac{4AT_1}{Ca\sqrt{2g}}(\sqrt{H} - \sqrt{h_t})$$

and

$$Q = \frac{Cat\sqrt{2gh_t}}{T_1}$$

For Qmax $d\theta/dh_t = 0$ giving

$$h_t = \frac{4}{9}H \tag{51}$$

The maximum discharge occurs at $\frac{4}{9}H$ if the filling system is not fully open yet by the time this level is reached; i.e. the criterion is the value of h_{T_1} computed from equation 44. If $h_{T_1} < \frac{4}{9}H$ the maximum discharge occurs at $\frac{4}{9}H$; if $h_{T_1} > \frac{4}{9}H$ then the maximum discharge occurs at the head of h_{T_1} corresponding to the end of opening the filling (emptying) system.

The real time of filling can be up to 12% shorter than the computed one due to inertia effects in the filling system.

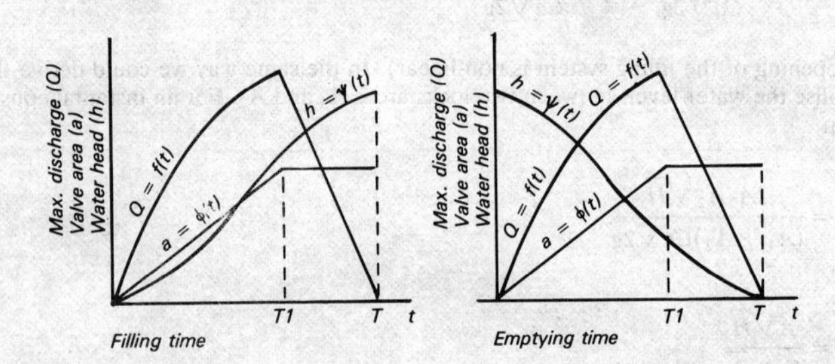

FIG. 18.—Variation of $Q.a$ and h with time (Ref. 2).

The coefficient of discharge usually varies between 0·6 and 0·9 and is a function of the geometry of the system. Although also a function of time an average value of c, best determined by field or model experiments (Ref. 35), is usually used in the computation. Figure 18 shows typical shapes of the Q, a and h values as a function of time. During lockage the vessel is tied by hawsers to bollards with the ropes at an angle between 20° and 40° to the longitudinal axis of the lock (vessel). Due to inertia during the small movements of the vessel the force in the ropes is about 35% bigger than the force P acting on the vessel. The resultant tension in the rope is then:

$$R = \frac{1{\cdot}35P}{\cos 40^\circ} = 1{\cdot}75P \tag{52}$$

For safety the permissible tension is limited by:

$$R_{\text{per}} = \frac{D}{600} \tag{53}$$

where D is the displacement of the vessel. In Eastern Europe (Ref. 2) the relationship equation 54 is used.

$$R_{\text{per}} = \frac{D^{3/5}}{20} \tag{54}$$

The force P has three main components:

P_1—resistance of the vessel,
P_2—force due to the longitudinal slope of water surface in the lock;
P_3—force due to translatory wave action caused mainly by 'sudden' changes of inflow into (outflow from) the lock.

P_1 and P_2 act against each other and to a great extent eliminate themselves.

The value of P_3 which is about 80% of P is mainly influenced by the value of dQ/dt. Thus the force acting on the vessel during lockage can be limited by imposing a permissible limit on dQ/dt during the filling (emptying) operation. This is best achieved by controlling the rate of opening of the valves on the filling system and/or by the shape of the culverts at the valves. The limiting value of the transverse component of the horizontal forces acting on the vessel should not exceed 50% of the longitudinal component P (Refs. 18 and 19).

THRIFT LOCKS.—On canals where there is water shortage high heads may be overcome by lifts (see p. L11/22) or by locks with thrift basins; the latter have the advantage that they permit simultaneous handling of large tows but require bigger land use than lifts.

In the thrift locks considerable reduction of water is achieved by conveying by gravity part of the water during lock emptying to thrift basins to be returned to the lock during its subsequent filling, (Fig. 19).

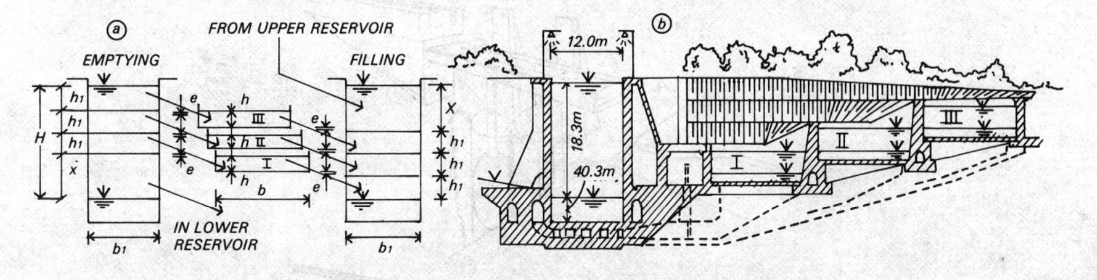

FIG. 19.—Thrift basins (Ref. 1).

Thrift basins are usually constructed next to the lateral lock wall, either as open (Fig. 19) or as superimposed closed reservoirs. Every basin is connected with the lock by its own conduit provided with two-way gates. By increasing the number of basins to more than four, only a very small additional reduction of water consumption can be achieved and the handling time increases disproportionately in comparison with simple locks. Locks with thrift basins are used for heads of up to 30m. For these heads they can still be designed so that their efficiency is comparable with standard types of boat lifts.

If b and b_1 are the thrift basin and lock widths and h and h_1 the basin and lock depth increments, n the number of thrift basins and e the excess head allowed during the operation (it would take too long to wait for complete level equalisation) and x the residual depth to be filled from (during filling) or discharged to (during emptying) the canal, then, assuming the lock and basin to have equal lengths:

$$b_1 h_1 = bh \quad \text{or } K = b_1/b = h/h_1 \ (<1)$$

$$x = (e + h) + (e + h_1) = 2e + h_1 + h = 2e + (K + 1)h_1 \tag{55}$$

For a total lift H and the lift provided by the basins nh_1:

$$H = x + nh_1$$

$$h_1 = \frac{H - x}{n} \tag{56}$$

thus from equations 55 and 56 the head loss x

$$x = \frac{2en + (K+1)H}{n+K+1} \tag{57}$$

or the relative head loss

$$\frac{x}{H} = V = \frac{K + 1 + \dfrac{2en}{H}}{n+K+1} \cong \frac{K+1}{K+n+1} \tag{58}$$

The efficiency E of the thrift lock is

$$E = 1 - V = \frac{n - \dfrac{2en}{H}}{K+n+1} \cong \frac{n}{K+n+1} \tag{59}$$

E and V are not strongly dependent on H as usually $2en \ll H$. The value of K is usually 0·5 to 0·7. Little is gained by increasing n (beyond 4 or 5) or decreasing K. A larger number of narrow basins is often cheaper than a smaller number of broader ones.

LIFTS AND INCLINED PLANES

If the provision of water for the operation of high head locks causes major problems, it is possible to use boat lifts for the operation of which the water requirements are almost zero. To overcome very great heads (as much as 100m) only boat lifts are really feasible. Boat lifts consist, as a rule, of a horizontal water-filled trough provided at both ends with gates.

The troughs of the boat lifts have a maximum length of about 100m. Therefore, they are suitable for the handling of barges and short 1 + 1 push trains; major push trains have to be disconnected. However, because of the great travelling speed of the trough, the capacity of the boat lifts is relatively high.

According to the direction of motion of the trough lifts can be either vertical or inclined.

According to the principle used for balancing and moving the boat trough filled with water vertical lifts use pistons, floats (Fig. 20a), counterweight balances (Fig. 20b) or other special mechanisms. Inclined boat lifts

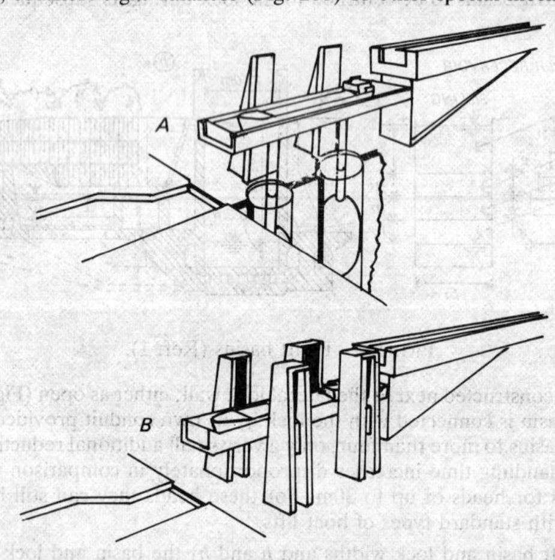

FIG. 20.—Vertical boat lifts with floats (A) or counterweights (B) (Ref. 1).

usually have the boat trough mounted on a special undercarriage travelling on a track on an inclined plane, either in the direction of the longitudinal trough axis or normal to it (Figs. 21a, b, 22). The trough is, as a rule, counterbalanced by a suspended weight travelling on an inclined track below the undercarriage of the boat trough. The acceleration of the trough during starting and the deceleration during braking must be small

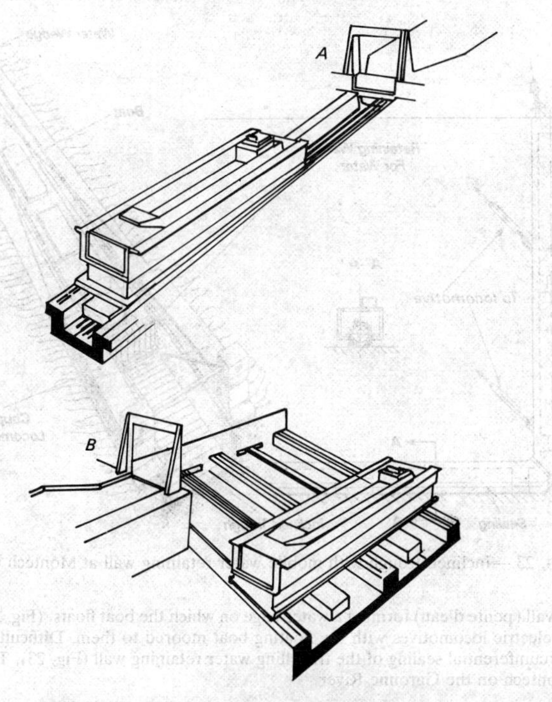

FIG. 21.—Inclined boat lifts (Ref. 1).

enough to maintain the variations of the water level in the trough within permissible limits in order to reduce the forces in the mooring ropes of the boat to acceptable magnitude. To reduce these forces, part of the water is sometimes let out of the trough before its lifting to settle the boat at the bottom of the trough and thus stabilise it. Boat lifts are more sensitive in operation than the locks and more prone to damage. A special type of inclined boat lift is a design developed by J. Aubert (Ref. 20). It consists of an inclined trough with a mobile

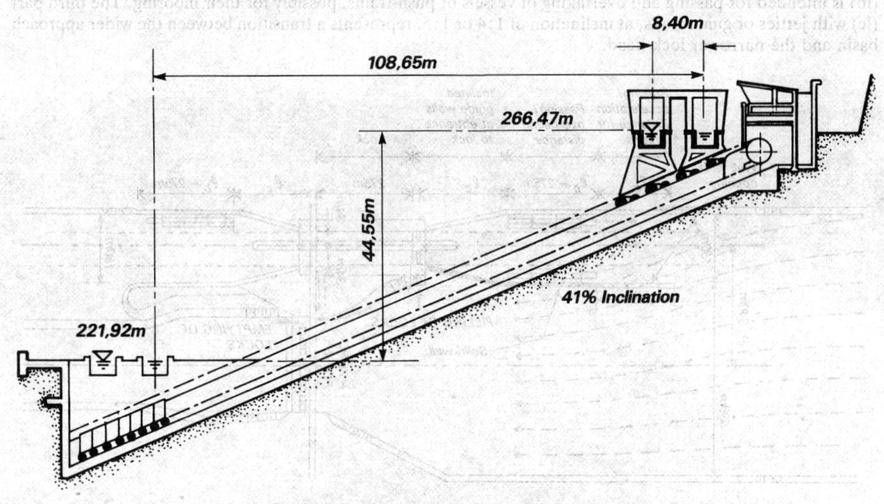

FIG. 22.—Inclined boat lift at Arzviller (Ref. 1).

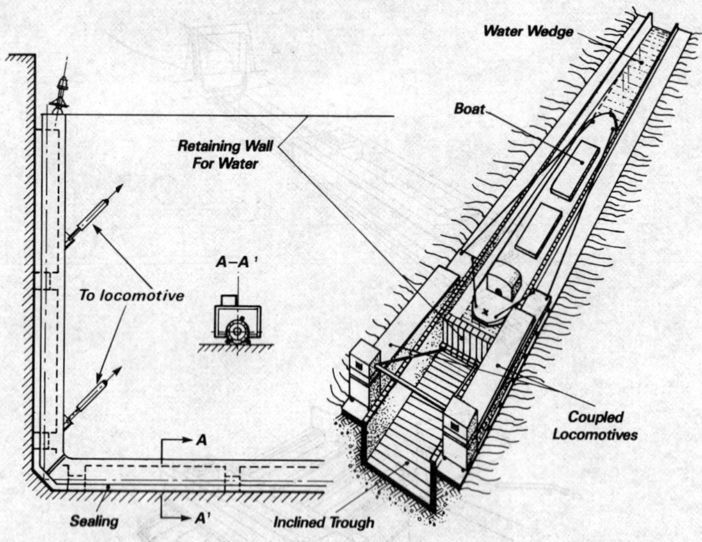

FIG. 23.—Inclined trough with mobile water retaining wall at Montech (Ref. 1).

water retaining wall (pente d'eau) forming a water edge on which the boat floats, (Fig. 23). The 'wall' is moved by two coupled electric locomotives with the floating boat moored to them. Difficulties in operation can be caused by the circumferential sealing of the travelling water retaining wall (Fig. 23). This type of boat lift has been built in Montech on the Garonne River.

LOCK APPROACHES.—Lock approaches provide the transition between the navigable river and the lock and must be designed both to ensure a safe and speedy entry into the approach basin and the lock and to permit the mooring of boats waiting to enter the lock whilst this is operating to pass other vessels down or upstream. The approach basin width will thus depend on the above factors as well as on the number of locks (single, twin, etc.,) and the likely number of push trains waiting for handling.

On a waterway with flowing water the approach basin is divided into three parts (Fig. 24). The first part (la) is intended for the braking of the vessels entering the lock or for their accelerating at departure. The next part (lb) is intended for passing and overtaking of vessels or push-trains, possibly for their mooring. The third part (lc) with jetties or guide walls, at inclination of 1:4 or 1:5, represents a transition between the wider approach basin and the narrower lock head.

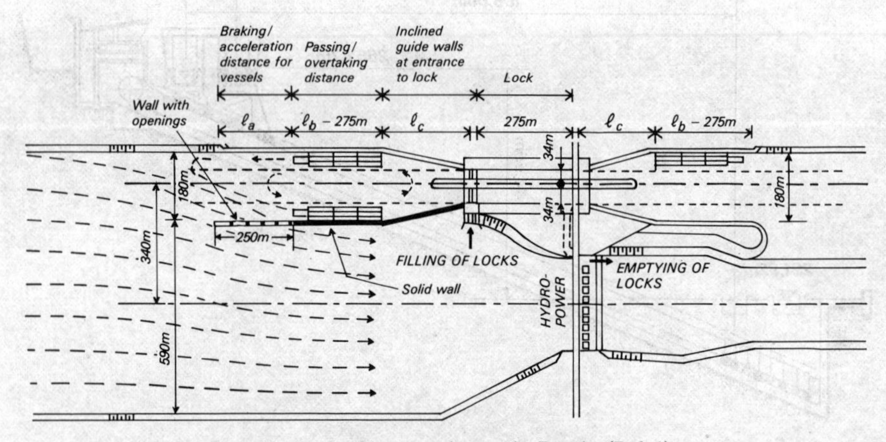

FIG. 24.—Lock with approaches on the Danube (Ref. 1).

The approach basins of locks on canalised rivers are usually separated from the power plant or weir by a long dividing wall or an island. A sudden change of the width and cross-section here results in critical flow regions with lateral contraction and transverse or even reverse flow. These conditions are very unfavourable for navigation and may cause accidents.

To reduce the transverse velocity in the critical area below the permissible value of about 0·35m/s, it is advisable to provide a water passage in the dividing wall near its head (Fig. 24).

The approach basins of navigation locks on still water canals may be symmetrical or asymmetrical in plan and are usually relatively short, since no braking length is required, because vessels can reduce their speed before entering the approach basin. The same applies to the downstream approach basins of the locks on waterways with flowing water, since the vessels enter them against the flow direction.

Downstream lock approaches have to be, however, protected against undesirable currents arising from spillway and/or power plant discharges and from the lock emptying system.

When designing fender structures, dolphins, jetties, etc., it is necessary to account for the forces and displacements which are likely to occur due to the impact of ships during mooring or collisions (Ref. 21). The resultant force will depend on the velocity of the ship and its angle with the fender structure as well as, of course, on the ship displacement. Generally, loaded push-tows have smaller velocities and angles of collision than unloaded ones. The theoretical computation is fairly complicated, but measurement in prototype indicates that the collision can be schenatized as a linear damped mass spring system. The contribution of the dolphin and ground to damping is considerable (Ref. 22).

INLAND PORTS.—Inland ports serving loading and unloading of vessels, transfer of goods and their further handling are connected with their further handling are connected with their hinterland by water, highway and/ or pipeline transport routes. The ports can have specialised zones or basins intended for the transfer of certain cargoes (ore, coal, aggregates, sand, individual shipments, containers, etc, (Ref. 23).

The extent, location and layout of an inland port are determined by its transfer capacity (Ref. 24). For a small capacity a port can be built directly on the bank of a navigable river or canal by widening it by at least two or three standard boat widths or by the width required for barge turning.

For a medium transfer capacity it is more advantageous to build one or two port basins outside the waterway, connected with the fairway by a suitable designed entry (Fig. 25).

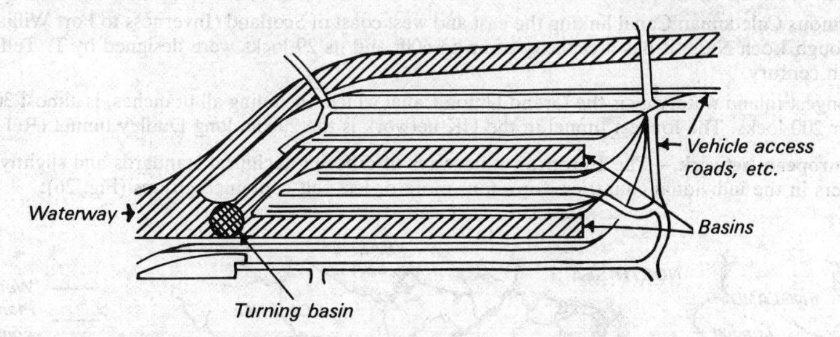

FIG. 25.—Medium capacity port (Ref. 1).

A large transfer capacity port should be as compact as possible; it has several basins connected with the waterway by means of an approach canal, extended beyond the entry into a port approach basin intended for the formation of push-trains or for vessels waiting for unloading. A turning basin is usually situated in the proximity of the port approach basin.

The port layout depends above all on local conditions and the purpose which the port should serve.

Manual or semi-mechanical transfer of freight in ports has been almost fully replaced by discontinuous or continuous mechanical handling (conveyor belts, pneumatic conveyors, pumps) particularly for the conveyance of liquid substances. Automated continuous transfer suitable for large quantities of freight, in particular for bulk and liquid cargo, is the most productive form.

Gantry cranes have their rail tracks laid along the waterfront, as close to the water as possible, to ensure that at least two barges are within reach of their jibs. In the interest of efficiency the cranes should not travel over too long distances but they must have a large action radius (Ref. 25).

Some ports have large capacity stationary gantry cranes with travelling trolleys intended for the transfer of very heavy and bulky goods. In their vicinity concrete assembly surfaces are provided, intended for the assembly of large size products which could not be transported to the port on the highway or railway owing to their large dimensions. For products of excessive weight and dimensions, which cannot be handled otherwise, the roll-on roll-off transfer system has to be used.

For goods sensitive to moisture, roofed berths are used, provided with overhead travelling cranes. Apart from that ports are provided with modern storage capacities for packaged goods, dumps for temporary storage of bulk and grain silos. Separate from the port territory are large capacity tanks for the storage of inflammable substances, situated in the proximity of tanker berths.

The ever increasing intensity of utilisation of inland waterways and the mechanisation of transfer operations necessitates automated control of ports and transfer operations. This is particularly so in the rapidly developing container transport system (Ref. 26). Automatic container terminal control systems are based on a suitable combination of computer data processing and remote control of man-operated transfer of goods (Ref. 27).

NOTES ON SOME EXISTING UK AND MAJOR WORLD WATERWAYS

UK waterways.—Although the building of inland waterways in UK was at the forefront of European development in the late 18th and during the 19th century, the English canals fell into disuse towards the close of the 19th and in the first half of the 20th century, mainly due to the rapid development of rail and road links joining inland industrial centres to the coastal ports. After all, no major English town is further than about 150km from a coastal region, an obvious reason for the importance of coastal navigation.

The last twenty years or so, however, have seen a renaissance in the use of inland waterways even in Great Britain, as their role in water resources management, provision of modern recreational facilities and enhancement of the environment, quite apart from their commercial value, has become more widely appreciated.

The total length of usable inland waterways in UK amounts to almost 4000km. The largest part is owned by the British Waterways Board, a substantial share is held by the British Transport Docks and Port Authorities, whilst the regional Water Authorities are responsible for about 15% of the total.

The most important inland waterways are those connected to the estuaries and the rivers Mersey, Severn, Thames and Humber.

The major UK canal is undoubtedly the Manchester Ship Canal constructed between 1887 and 1893 which has parameters in class VI (see section 2). It is 50km long, 36·5m wide (bottom) and 8·5m deep; its five locks can take vessels of up to 12000 tons. The Avon is navigable to Bristol for boats of a capacity up to 5000 tons (also class VI). Examples of some other major inland waterways (other than estuaries) of class III (up to 10000 tons) are the Gloucester Ship Canal, the Weaver up to Northwick, the Ouse to Selby and the Tay to Perth. The Trent up to Newark falls into class II (up to 600t).

The famous Caledonian Canal linking the east and west coast of Scotland (Inverness to Fort William) passes right through Loch Ness; it has a capacity of up to 600t and its 29 locks were designed by T. Telford in the early 19th century.

The longest inland waterway is the Grand Union Canal which, including all branches, is almost 300km long with over 200 locks. The longest tunnel in the UK network is the 2900m long Dudley tunnel (Ref. 28).

The European Network.—The European waterways of differing technical standards and slightly diverging parameters in the individual countries, form four more or less self-contained groups (Fig. 26):

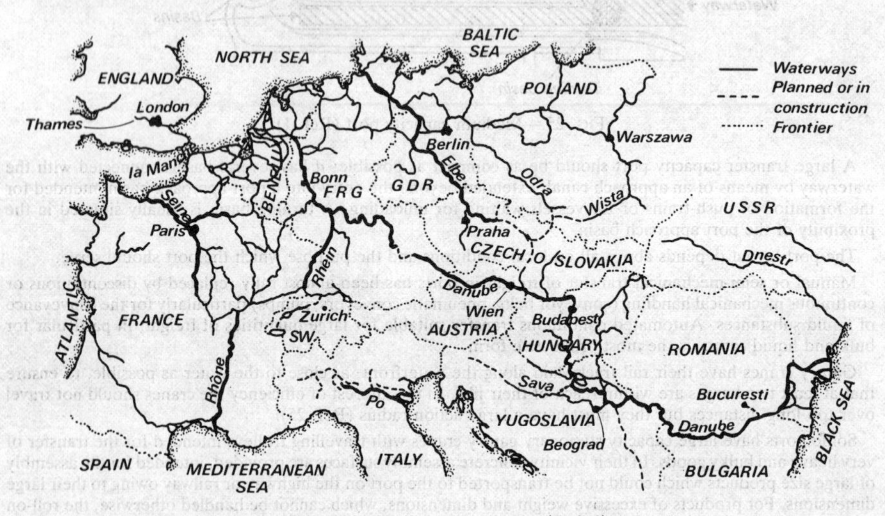

FIG. 26.—European waterways (Ref. 1).

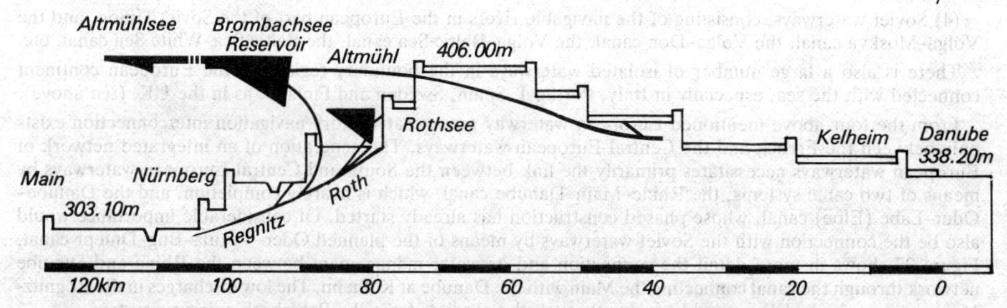

FIG. 27.—Rhine–Danube connection (showing how a system of locks links the Main to the Danube at Kelheim).

(1) French waterways;

(2) Central European waterways between the Rhine in the West and the Vistula in the East, consisting of navigable rivers flowing to the North and the canals inter-connecting them in an east-west direction;

(3) South European waterways, comprising the Danube, the navigable sections of its tributaries and accompanying canals;

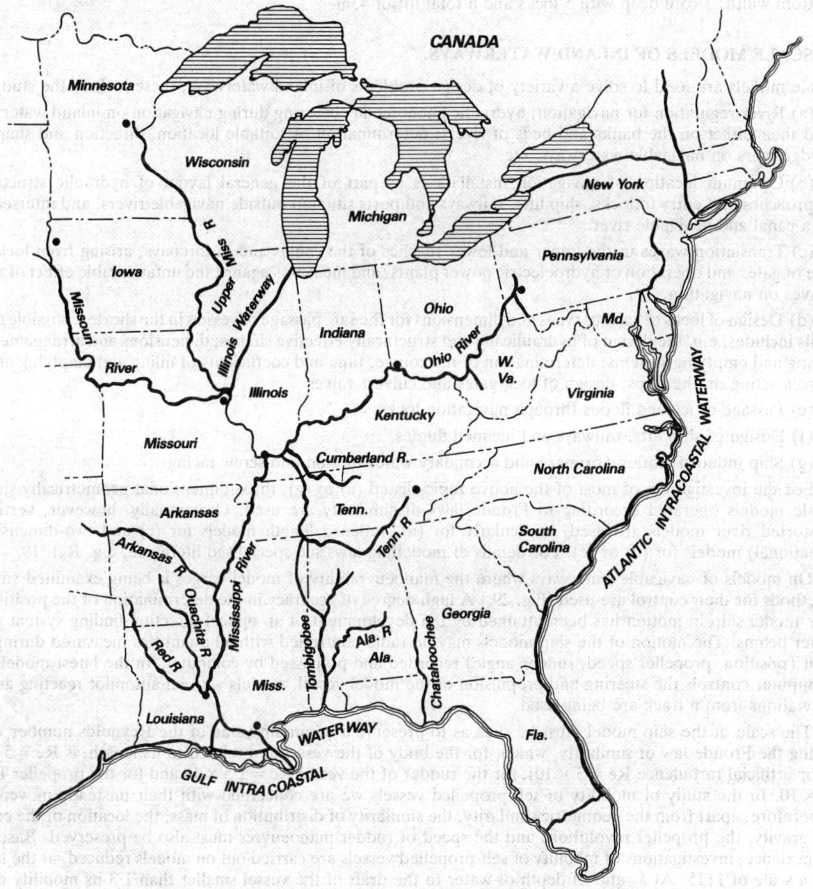

FIG. 28.—Waterways in the central and eastern USA (Ref. 9).

(4) Soviet waterways, consisting of the navigable rivers in the European part of the Soviet Union, and the Volga–Moskva canal, the Volga–Don canal, the Volga–Baltic Sea canal, the Baltic Sea–White Sea canal, etc.

There is also a large number of isolated waterways in the boundary regions of the European continent connected with the sea, especially in Italy, Portugal, Spain, Sweden and Finland, as in the UK, (see above).

From the four above mentioned European waterway groups satisfactory navigation interconnection exists only between the French and the Central European waterways. The generation of an integrated network of European waterways necessitates primarily the link between the South and Central European waterways by means of two canal systems; the Rhine–Main–Danube canal, which is nearing completion, and the Danube–Oder–Labe (Elbe) canal, whose phased construction has already started. Of considerable importance would also be the connection with the Soviet waterways by means of the planned Oder–Vistula–Bug–Dniepr canal. Figure 27 shows in more detail the connection and its water management between the Rhine and Danube network through the canal connecting the Main with the Danube at Kelheim. The low discharges in the Regnitz-Main area can be supplemented by water through the canal or from the Brombach reservoir system.

United States of America.—There is an important network of navigable rivers and canals particularly in the central and eastern United States. Figure 28 shows schematically some of the most important waterways including open river navigation on the Middle and Lower Mississippi from St. Louis to the Gulf of Mexico and on the Missouri River from Sioux City in Iowa downstream, major canalised rivers such as the Upper Mississippi, Ohio, Tennessee, Lower Columbia and Arkansas Rivers and canals, e.g. the Chain of Rocks Canal on the Mississippi, the Arkansas Post Canal and the Tennessee–Tombigbee Waterway (opened in 1985) with a watershed section 65km long (including the Bay Springs Lock, Fig. 14) and a canal section 70km long, 91m bottom width, 3·65m deep with 5 locks and a total lift of 43m.

SCALE MODELS OF INLAND WATERWAYS.

Scale models are used to solve a variety of design problems of inland waterways; these include the study of:

(a) River regulation for navigation; hydraulic phenomena occurring during navigation on inland waterways and their effect on the banks and beds of rivers; determination of suitable location, direction and shape of bridge piers on navigable waterways, etc.

(b) Optimum location of navigation installations as part of the general layout of hydraulic structures; approaches and entry to locks, ship lifts, railways and ports situated outside navigable rivers, and intersection of a canal and navigable river.

(c) Translation waves in the upper and lower reaches of the canals and in forebays, arising from lockage, use of gates and operation of hydroelectric power plants, and measures against the unfavourable effect of these waves on navigation.

(d) Design of locks of various types and dimensions for the safe passage of vessels in the shortest possible time. This includes, e.g. the design of hydraulically and structurally effective shapes; dimensions and arrangement of filling and emptying systems; determination of the course, time and coefficients of filling and emptying and of forces acting on the ships; design of lock gates and culvert valves.

(e) Passage of ice and floods through navigation locks.

(f) Design of ship lifts, railways and inclined flumes.

(g) Ship induced motion (primary and secondary water motion and screw racing).

For the investigation of most of the above topics listed (a) to (g), three dimensional geometrically similar scale models operated according to Froude laws of similarity are used. Occasionally, however, vertically distorted river models are used, particularly for (a), reduced length models for (c) and two-dimensional (sectional) models for (d) or (e). For details of modelling laws see specialised literature, e.g. Ref. 19.

On models of navigable waterways where the manoeuvrability of model barges is being examined various methods for their control are used (Fig. 29.) A high degree of accuracy in the determination of the position of the model ship in motion has been attained by the development of an optical direction-finding system using laser beams. The motion of the ship models may be radio controlled with all quantities measured during the test (position, propeller speed, rudder angle) recorded and processed by computer. In the latest models the computer controls the steering and propulsion of the model vessel, models with an autopilot reacting and to deviations from a track are being used.

The scale of the ship model must be such as to preserve a minimum value of the Reynolds number when using the Froude law of similarity, which, for the body of the vessel and related to its length, is $Re = 5 \times 10$ (for artificial turbulence $Re = 3 \times 10$); for the rudder of the vessel $Re = 1{\cdot}5 \times 10$ and for the propeller $Re = 7 \times 10$. In the study of mobility of self-propelled vessels we are concerned with their unsteady movement. Therefore, apart from the geometric similarity, the similarity of distribution of mass, the location of the centre of gravity, the propeller revolutions and the speed of rudder manoeuvres must also be preserved. Based on experience, investigations of mobility of self-propelled vessels are carried out on models reduced, at the most, to a scale of 1:15. At a ratio of depth of water to the draft of the vessel smaller than 1·3 its mobility drops sharply. Tests on ship manoeuvring models are often used to calibrate mathematical simulation models.

FIG. 29.—Investigating the manoeuvrability of model barges (scale 1:25) *Delft Hydraulics Laboratory.*

Experimental studies of locks may be divided into three groups:

(a) study of locks with unsteady flow;

(b) study of locks under steady flow conditions;

(c) study of horizontal forces acting on vessels passing through the lock.

(a) Investigation of locks with unsteady flow concentrates on the mode and time of filling (emptying) the lock, the value of the coefficient of filling (emptying) and on alternate solutions of filling (emptying) systems. It is necessary to measure continuously the change of the water level in the lock and of the position of the gates in the filling (emptying) culverts as well as the time or filling (emptying). The water level in the lock should be measured at several points placed so as to record the longitudinal slope of the water level and the amplitude of the waves moving along the lock.

(b) The study of the lock under steady flow conditions is used mainly for the determination of the discharge coefficients and the effectiveness of energy dissipation for individual phases of filling and emptying. During measurement it is necessary to maintain on the model not only a constant discharge but also the corresponding water levels in the lock (deduced from the unsteady flow experiments).

(c) The horizontal forces acting on the vessel during the filling or emptying of the lock are investigated experimentally on models of vessels both inside the lock and in its (downstream) approach by measuring the reactive effects of water on the vessel and the changes of these forces with time during filling or emptying the lock, $P = f(t)$. The magnitude and usually also the direction of the horizontal forces acting on the vessel change during the filling (emptying) of the lock and the vessel is pulled alternately to the upstream and downstream gates by the dynamic effect of waves passing from one end of the lock to the other.

The dynamometers for the measurement of horizontal forces are usually connected to recorders with a time base where the opening of the gates and the water levels in the lock and the approaches are simultaneously recorded. To eliminate forces of inertia and friction the dynamometers must prevent substantial movement of the model vessels, which must be stabilised at a chosen point. The horizontal plane in which the forces are measured lies either in the variable level of the deck of the vessel or is at a constant level above the upstream water surface. In the latter method, which has been used almost exclusively until recently, the horizontal forces acting on the vessel are transmitted by two vertical masts to two rings placed in the horizontal measuring plane. The masts, which are fixed to the bow and stern of the vessel, pass without resistance through the rings to which dynamometers of various types are fixed.

The complete exclusion of inertia is achieved by the use of strain gauges stabilizing the vessel almost at one point.

A common disadvantage of all dynamometers placed on a horizontal measuring plane above the model of the lock are the moments caused by the long arm of the masts especially at the beginning of the filling of the lock, when the water level is at its lowest and when the greatest horizontal forces usually act on the vessel. It is therefore more advantageous to place the dynamometers directly on the level of the deck of the vessel.

Finally, in another device for measuring horizontal forces consisting of a set of three dynamometers at the bow and stern of the model vessel the recording points of each set touch vertical rods which are not firmly connected to the vessel, but rest on it and follow its rise or fall. Both rods pass freely through long sockets on a fixed frame placed above the model of the lock.

REFERENCES

(1) CABELKA, J. and GABRIEL, P., *Inland Waterways.* Developments in Hydraulic Engineering—3 NOVAK, P. (Ed.), Elsevier Applied Science Publishers, London 1985.

(2) CABELKA, J., *Inland Waterways and Inland Navigation* (In Czech). SNTL Praha—Alfa Bratislava 1976.

(3) BLAAUW, H. G., KOEMAN, J. W. and STRATING, J., *Nautical Studies in Port and Channel Design.* Dock and Harbour Authority 63 May 1982 (Part I) and August 1982 (Part 2).

(4) BLAAUW, H. G. and VERHEY, H. J., *Design of Inland Navigation Fairways.* ASCE Journal of Waterway, Port, Coastal and Ocean Engineering, Vo. 109, No. 1, February 1983.

(5) SEILER E., *Die Schubschiffahrt als Integrationsfaktor zwischen Rhein und Donau.* Zeitschrift für Binnenschiffahrt und Wasserstrassen, N.8, 1972.

(6) KUBEC, J., *Improvement of the Integration of Ocean and Inland Navigation by Means of a Unified System of Dimensions of Barges and Lighters.* 25th International Navigation Congress PIANC, Edinburgh, 1981, S.I.-4.

(7) NOVAK, P., *Applied Hydraulics.* International Institute for Hydraulic and Environmental Engineering, Delft. 2nd revised edition 1986.

(8) CUNGE, J., HOLLY, F. and VERWEY, A., *Practical Aspects of Computational River Hyudraulics.* Pitman, London 1980.

(9) PETERSEN, M. S., *River Engineering.* Prentice Hall, New Jersey, 1986.

(10) ACKERS, P., *Sediment Transport Problem in Irrigation Systems Design:* Developments in Hydraulic Engineering—1 NOVAK, P. (Ed.), Applied Science Publishers, London, 1983.

(11) *Principles Governing the Design and Construction of Economic Revetments for Protecting the Banks of Rivers and Canals.* XXXIInd International Navigation Congress, Pianc, Paris, 1969, S.I.—S.6.40.

(12) GABRIEL, P., *Regelung von Frequenz und Uebergabeleistung in Kanalkraftwerken.* Oesterreichische Zeitschrift fur Elektrizitätswirtschaft, 2, 1969.

(13) CABELKA, J. ET AL., *Rational Design of Locks and Weirs on Waterways in Czechoslovakia.* 26th International Navigation Congress, Brussels, 1985, S, I-2.

(14) HILLING, D., *Barge Carrier Systems—Inventory and Prospects,* Benn Publications, London 1977.

(15) FUEHRER, M., *Wechselbeziehungen zwischen Schiff und beschränktem Fahrwasser.* Mitteilungen der Forschungsanstalt für Schiffahrt, Wasser und Grundbau, Berlin 1985.

(16) KAA VAN DE, E. J., *Power and Speed of Push-tows in Canals.* Proceedings symposium of Aspects of Navigability of Constraint Waterways including Harbour Entrances. Delft Hydraulic Laboratory 1978.

(17) HUBER, A. and WEISS, H. W., *Wellenerosion am Rhein.* Wasser, Energie, Luft, 78, Heft 9, 1986.

(18) JONG, DE R. J. and VRIJER, A., *Mathematical and Hydraulic Model Investigation of Longitudinal Forces on Ships in Locks with Door Filling Systems.* XIXth IAHR Congress, New Delhi, February 1981.

(19) NOVAK, P. and CABELKA, J., *Models in Hydraulic Engineering, Physical Principles and Design Application.* Pitman, London, 1981.

(20) AUBERT, J. ET AL, *La pente d'eau a Montech,* Navigation, ports et industries, Paris, 1973.

(21) FONTIJN, H. L., *The Berthing of a Ship to a Jetty.* Proc. ASCE J. Waterw, PortT., Coast and Ocean Div. 106, WW2, pp 239–259, 1980.

(22) VRIJER, A., *Fender Forces caused by Ship Impacts.* 8th International Harbour Congress, Antwerp, June, 1983.

(23) PORTEOUS, J. D., *Canal Ports.* Academic Press, London, 1977.

(24) BOURRIERES, P. and CHAMEROY, *Ports et Navigation Modernes,* Eyrolles, Paris 1977.

(25) CORNICK, H. J., *Dock and Harbour Engineering*. Griffen, 1968.
(26) WHITTAKER, J. R., *Containerisation*. John Wiley, New York, 1975 (2nd edition).
(27) KOUDSTAAL, R. and WEIDE VAN DER, J., *System Approach in Integrated Harbour Planning*. Seatech III Conference on Asian Ports Development and Dredging, Singapore, March 1981.
(28) EDWARDS, L. A., *Inland Waterways of Great Britain*. Imray, Laurie, Norie and Wilson, 1972.

BIBLIOGRAPHY

BOUWMEESTOR, J., KAA, E. J. VAN DE, NUHOFF, H. A. and ORDEN, R. G. J. VAN. *Recent Studies on Push Towing as a Base for Dimensioning Waterways*. 24th International Navigation Congress PIANC, Leningrad 1977.

CABELKA, J. ET AL. *Modern Equipment of Locks Raising the Traffic Capacity and Security of Navigation on Inland Waterways in CSSR*. 24th International Navigation Congress PIANC, Leningrad 1977, S.I.-1.

CABELKA, J. and KUBEC, J. *Construction et Modernisation des Ecluses sur l'Elbe en Tchecoslavaquie*. 22nd International Navigation Congress. PIANC, Paris, 1969, s.I.-1.

GABRIEL, P. ET AL. *Improvement of the Conditions of Navigation on the Canalised Rivers in Czechoslovakia*. 24th International Navigation Congress PIANC, Leningrad 1977, S.I.-4.

WHITTAKER, J. R. *Containerisation*. John Wiley, New York, 1975 (2nd edition).

KOLKMAN, P. A. *Low Head Navigation Lock Door Filling and Emptying Systems Developed by Hydraulic Investigations*. Delft Hydraulics Laboratory, Publication No. 111, Delft, 1973.

KOLKMAN, P. A. *Ships Meeting and Generating Currents*. Proceedings Symposium of Aspects of Navigability of Constraint Waterways including Harbour Entrances. Delft Hydraulic Laboratory 1978.

Hydro Delft. Delft Hydraulics Laboratory, No. 71, 1985.

GABRIEL, P. ET AL. *Technical and Economical Aspects of Upgraded Utilisation of the Labe-Vltava Waterway*. 26th International Navigation Congress PIANC, Brussels 1985, S.I.-1.

HAGER, ET AL, *Methods of Increasing the Capacity and Safety of Waterways*. 24th International Navigation Congress, PIANC, Leningrad, 1977.

KING, J. *Navigable Waterways*. Kempe's Engineer Yearbook 1983 Edn.

KOESMAN, J. W., STRATING, J. and WITT, F. G. J. *Ships in Cross-currents*. Proceedings Symposium of Aspects of Navigability of Constraint Waterways including Harbour Entrances. Delft Hydraulic Laboratory 1978.

KUHN, R. *Binnenverkehrswasserbau*. Verlag Ernst & Sohn, Berlin 1985.

MICHAJLOV, A. V. *Inland Waterways (in Russian)*. Stroizdat, Moskva, 1973.

La voie navigable—une voie d'avenir. L'Office National de la Navigation, Paris, 1980.

PARTENSCKY, H. W. *Grenzen der Leistungsfähigkeit von Binnenschiffschleusen*. Jahrbuch der Hafenbautechnischen Gesellschaft. Hamburg 39. Band, 1982.

RENNER, D. *Schiffartstechnische Modellversuche für Binnenwasserstrassen, ein neues Messsystem und neue Auswertungsmöglichkeiten*. Bericht No. 48, Versuchsanstalt für Wasserbau der Technischen Universität München, 1984.

ROEHLE, W., ADOLF, E. and FRUHWIRT, K. *Measures against Damage to Locks and Ships and Measures During Winter Operations on the Austrian Danube*. 24th International Navigation Congress PIANC. Leningrad, 1977.

US Army, Corps of Engineers, Engineer Manual 1110-2-1611. *Layout and Design of Shallow Draft Waterways*, 1980.

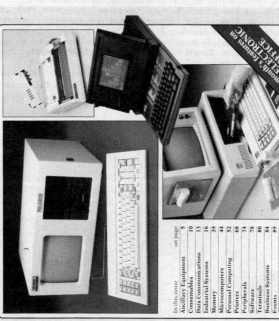

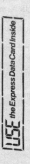

NAVAL ARCHITECTURE AND SHIP DESIGN

Definitions—Dimensions—Displacement—Coefficients—Hydrostatic Particulars—Inclining Experiment—Transverse Stability—Trim—Flooding—Weights—Resistance and Power—Trials—Costing—Contracts—Regulations—Classification Societies—References.

by P. William Penney, M.Sc., C. Eng., M.R.I.N.A., C.Dip.A.F.

DEFINITIONS AND DIMENSIONS

The forward perpendicular (F.P.) is a vertical line generally taken through the intersection of the fore edge of the stem and the summer load line.

The after perpendicular (A.P.) is taken where the aft side of the sternpost meets the summer load line, or, if there is no sternpost, at the centre of the rudder stock.

Amidships between perpendiculars, is the centre between perpendiculars and is denoted by ⏀.

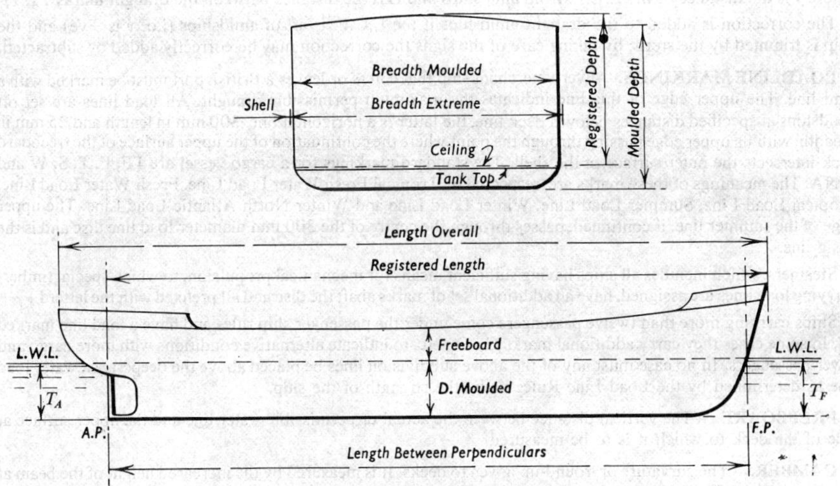

FIG. 1.—Principal Dimensions

MOULDED DIMENSIONS.—Length between perpendiculars (L.B.P.) is the length usually referred to by the Builders. See Fig. 1.

The moulded breadth (B) is measured at amidships and is the maximum breadth over the frames.

The moulded depth (D) is the depth at amidships from top of keel to the top of the deck beam at side. The name of the deck to which the depth is measured should always be stated.

OVERALL DIMENSIONS.—Length overall (L.O.A.) is the greatest length of vessel from the extreme fore end to the extreme after end.

Breadth extreme is the greatest breadth to the outside of shell plating.

Depth is measured from the underside of keel to the top of a specified deck at amidships.

REGISTER DIMENSIONS.—To enable a ship to be identified by the Authorities the length, breadth, and depth are shown on the ship's register and are referred to as the register dimensions. The register length is the length of the ship measured from the fore side of the stem at the uppermost point to the after side of the sternpost or rudder stock.

The register breadth is the extreme breadth of the ship to the outside of shell plating.

The register depth is taken at the middle of the register length and is measured from the top of the upper deck beam at the middle line to the top of the tank top or floors, or to the ceiling if fitted at the half length.

DRAUGHTS OF A SHIP.—The draught of a ship is the distance between the lowest point or keel of a ship and the waterline. Draught marks are scrieved in a vertical line up the ship close to the bow and the stern at intervals of 20 centimetres. The marks are placed on both port and starboard sides of the ship so that an average may be taken if the ship is heeled.

Mean draught is the average of the bow (T_F) and stern (T_A) readings, but allowance should be made for any hog or sag especially for long ships.

Sag occurs if the draught measured at amidships ($T_{⊠}$) is greater than the average of the draughts at the ends of the ship i.e. $T_{⊠} > \frac{1}{2}(T_A + T_F)$.

Hog occurs if the draught amidships is less than the average.

The draught at amidships ($T_{⊠}$) can be determined by measuring the distance of the Load Line above the waterline and subtracting the measurement from the quoted Summer Load Line draught (maximum permissible draught).

Corrected mean draught at amidships $= \frac{1}{6}(T_A + T_F + 4T_{⊠})$.

A further correction must be made to calculate the draught at the Centre of Flotation (L.C.F. or C.F.), the position along the length of a ship at which the draught remains constant for small changes of trim. This is known as the Layer Correction and equals

$$\frac{y \times (T_A - T_F)}{L}$$

where y is the distance of the L.C.F. from amidships and L is the distance between the draught marks T_A, T_F.

The correction is added to the draught amidships if the L.C.F. is aft of amidships (i.e. y is +ve) and the ship is trimmed by the stern; by taking care of the signs the correction may be correctly added or subtracted.

LOADLINE MARKINGS.—Every merchant ship that enters or leaves a British port must be marked with a load line. The upper edge of this line indicates the maximum permissible draught. All load lines are set off amidships at specified distances below a deck line, the latter is a horizontal line, 300 mm in length and 25 mm in breadth, with its upper edge passing through the point where the continuation of the upper surface of the freeboard deck intersects the outer surface of the shell. The standard markings for a cargo vessel are TF, F, T, S, W and WNA. The meanings of these marks are, respectively, Tropical Fresh Water Load Line, Fresh Water Load Line, Tropical Load Line, Summer Load Line, Winter Load Line and Winter North Atlantic Load Line. The upper edge of the summer line, if continued, passes through the centre of the 300 mm diameter load line disc and is the basic line.

Steamers, which includes all ships having sufficient means for mechanical propulsion, to which special timber-carrying load lines are assigned, have an additional set of marks abaft the disc and all prefixed with the letter L.

Ships carrying more than twelve passengers come under the passenger ship rules and have a load line marked C_1. In some cases they carry additional marks C_2, C_3, etc. to indicate alternative conditions with more cargo and fewer passengers. In no case must any of the above subdivision lines be placed above the deepest sea water load line as determined by the Load Line Rules or by the strength of the ship.

FREEBOARD.—The vertical distance between the actual or permissible water line and the upper surface at side of the deck to which it is to be measured.

CAMBER.—The curvature or 'round-up' given to decks. It is measured by the increased height of the beam at the centre. The difference in height at any station of the deck at centre and at side is the amount of camber at that place. The camber of the weather deck is generally one-fiftieth of the breadth of the ship. Camber is desirable for all weather decks but can be dispensed with on lower decks.

SHEER.—The longitudinal curvature given to decks. It is measured by the difference in height of side at any point above the height at side amidships, i.e. above the moulded depth. Generally the sheer at the F.P. is twice the sheer at the A.P. with a zero value at amidships. The ordinates in millimetres of the standard sheer profile of the Load Line Rules are as follows, where L is the length of the ship in metres.

Station	*Ordinate*	*Station*	*Ordinate*
A.P.	25 (0·33L + 10)	F.P.	50 (0·33L + 10)
$\frac{1}{6}$L from A.P.	11·1 (0·33L + 10)	$\frac{1}{6}$L from F.P.	22·2 (0·33L + 10)
$\frac{1}{3}$L from A.P.	2·8 (0·33L + 10)	$\frac{1}{3}$L from F.P.	5.6 (0·33L + 10)

The sheer curve is presumed to be a parabola and the mean sheer is one-sixth of the total sheer forward and sheer aft.

RISE OF FLOOR.—The run up of the bottom plating measured transversely at amidships. In a cargo vessel there is only a small rise of floor.

FLARE.—The outward curvature of the hull surface above the waterline. Flare gives increased buoyancy in pitching and rolling and promotes dryness.

LINES DRAWING.—The delineation of the ship's form in three planes or views. The longitudinal elevation is known as the profile and shows the contour of the stem and stern. The half breadth plan shows the shapes of decks and waterplanes. The transverse sections are shown in the body plan.

BOW LINES.—The trace on the moulded surface of the fore body caused by the intersection with vertical planes running parallel to the middle line plane. In the after body these traces are known as buttocks. It is now common to use the latter term throughout the ship without distinction. Bow and buttock lines appear in their true form on the profile of the lines drawing and as horizontal and vertical lines on the half-breadth and body plan respectively. They are particularly useful in fairing up the half-breadth plan.

PARALLEL BODY (P.M.B.).—That portion of the immersed body any transverse section of which has the same area and the same shape. Its length is denoted by L_p. See Fig. 2.

FORE BODY.—The immersed body forward of the midship section, the latter being placed midway between the fore and aft perpendiculars. *AFTER BODY* is the immersed body aft of the midship section.

ENTRANCE.—The immersed body forward of the parallel body, or if the latter does not exist, forward of the cross section of greatest area. Its length is denoted by L_e.

ANGLE OF ENTRANCE.—The angle between the tangent to the load waterline at the fore end and the middle line of the ship.

RUN.—The immersed body aft of the parallel body, or if the latter does not exist, aft of the cross section of greatest area. Its length is denoted by L_r.

CURVE OF AREAS.—The base of the curve is the length of the ship and the ordinates at any point along it represent the transverse area of the immersed section at that point. The area under the curve is equal to the volume of displacement.

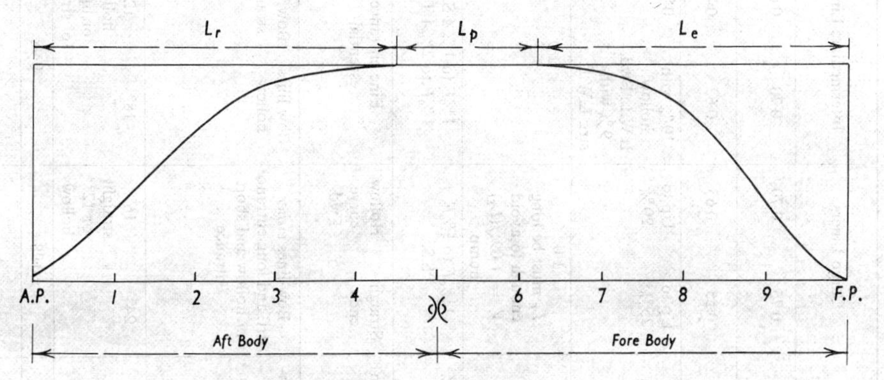

FIG. 2.—Curve of Areas of Immersed Sections.

TRIM.—The longitudinal inclination of a ship. It is measured by the difference between the forward and after draughts. A ship is said to be 'on even keel' when the draughts are the same forward and aft. It is said to be 'down by the head' when the draught forward is greater than the draught aft, and 'down by the stern' when the draught aft is greater. *CHANGE OF TRIM* is the arithmetical sum of the changes of draught forward and aft produced by shifting weights on board.

CENTRE OF FLOTATION (C.F.).—The centroid of the waterplane. When a ship changes trim without change in displacement the vessel turns about a transverse axis through the centre of flotation. Consequently the draught at C.F. will remain unchanged so long as the displacement is unchanged. If the C.F. is abaft amidships, the changes of draught will be greater forward than aft, and *vice versa*.

EXAMPLE: A ship of length 92 m floats initially on an even keel at 3·65 m draught. Due to a redistribution of loads on board, the ship trims 380 mm by the head. The C.F. is 3 m abaft amidships. What are the new draughts forward and aft?

The distance of the pivot from the fore end = 46 + 3 = 49 m.

Change of draught forward $= \frac{49}{92} \times 380 = 202$ mm Change of draught aft $= \frac{43}{92} \times 380 = 178$ mm.

thus the correct draughts are: Forward 3·85 m; Aft, 3·47 m.

DISPLACEMENT.—The displacement of a vessel is the quantity of water displaced by the ship and is usually expressed in tonnes, (1 tonne = 1000 kg) but sometimes in cubic metres. If a ship is floating freely in still water, the weight of water displaced must exactly equal the weight of the ship with everything that is on board. If the vessel is floating in sea water, the displacement in tonnes (Δ), is equal to the volume of the displacement (∇), in cubic metres multiplied by 1·025. For fresh water (F.W.) the displacement in tonnes is equal to the volume of

TABLE 1.

Type of Ship	Slow Speed Cargo Ships		Medium Speed Cargo Ships		Cargo Liners		Intermediate Liners		High Speed Liners and Fast Coastal Passenger Ships		Cross Channel Ships	
Cp	0·82	0·78	0·78	0·75	0·75	0·70	0·70	0·65	0·65 and below		0·65 and below (best results 0·57)	
$P = 0{\cdot}746 \frac{V}{\sqrt{CpL}}$	0·4	0·6	0·5	0·6	0·55	0·65	0·6	0·8	0·7	0·9	1·05	1·40
Length of parallel body	34%		Up to 25% depending on beam		Up to 25%	Up to 20%	10% with hollow L.W.L. Fwd. 9% with strt. L.W.L.	0%	None		None	
$\frac{\text{Entrance}}{\text{Run}}$	0·6	0·8	0·8 to 0·9	1·00	1·0 L_E must be long enough to avoid $V = 1{\cdot}09\sqrt{(L_E)}$ hump		1·0		1·1		1·2	
L.C.B. as $\%L$ from amidships	2% Fwd.	1% Fwd. S.S.	2% Fwd.	1·0% Fwd. S.S.	$1\frac{1}{2}\%F$ to $\frac{1}{2}\%F$ S.S.		$1\%F$ to $1\%A$ S.S. $1\%F$ to $2\%A$ T.S.		$1\frac{1}{2}\%A$ to $2\%A$ T.S.		2% to $3\%A$ T.S.	
Shape of Area Curve	Straight ends		Straight ends	Medium hollow Fwd.	Straight ends	Hollow curve Fwd.	Fine entrance essential		Fine ended curve of areas. Bulbous bow useful above P = 0·75		Fine ended	Fuller ends using bulbous form
Shape of L.W.L.	Bow: slightly convex throughout Stern: fairly strt. slope not greater than 20°		Bow convex	Bow convex to straight	Bow lines *either* strt. and long entrance *or* hollow and short entrance		Bow lines hollow	Bow lines straight	Fine L.W.L. Fwd. hollow		Fine end Fwd.	Fuller ends by making W.L. endings strt. or hollow with bulb
$\frac{1}{2}\alpha_E$ on L.W.L.	35°	32°	30°	27°	24°	16° straight or 12° hollow	18°	12° hollow or up to 16° straight	Down to 6° with hollow		6° to 7°	6° with hollow 9° with straight
Cm	0·98	0·99	0·98		0·98		0·98		0·95		0·90	0·95
Cruiser stern	Reduces resistance up to 6%										Essential to increase length	

displacement in cubic metres ($1 m^3 = 1$ tonne). The mass density for sea water (S.W.), is 1·025 tonne/m^3, or 0·975 m^3/tonne. Thus for sea water:

Displacement in tonnes = under water volume (m^3) × 1·025
or = under water volume (m^3) ÷ 0·975.

The density of sea water varies according to the locality and even according to the season of the year or the state of the tide.

TONNES PER CENTIMETRE (T.P.C.).—At any waterline, this is the number of tonnes that must be placed on board in order to sink the vessel 1 cm or the number of tonnes taken out to lighten the vessel 1 cm. If A is the area of a given waterplane in square metres then the displacement of a layer 1 cm thick at this waterplane, assuming the ship parallel-sided in its neighbourhood is $0{\cdot}01A m^3$ or, $0{\cdot}01A \times 1{\cdot}025$ tonnes in sea water; and $0{\cdot}01A$ tonnes in fresh water.

COEFFICIENTS OF FINENESS

The *BLOCK COEFFICIENT* (C_B) is the ratio of the volume of displacement to the volume of a block having the same length, breadth and mean draught as the vessel.

$$C_B = \frac{\nabla}{LBT} = \frac{0{\cdot}975\Delta}{LBT} \text{ in sea water,}$$

where
∇ = Immersed volume of displacement in cubic metres.
Δ = Displacement in tonnes
L = Length of ship in metres between perpendiculars
B = Breadth of ship in metres to outside of shell plating
T = Draught in metres

The *PRISMATIC COEFFICIENT* (C_P) is the ratio of the immersed volume of displacement to the volume of a prismatic solid the same length between perpendiculars as the ship and having a constant cross-section equal in area to the immersed midship section.

$$C_P = \frac{\nabla}{LA_M} = \frac{0{\cdot}975\Delta}{LA_M} \text{ for sea water,}$$

where A_M is the immersed area of the midship section in square metres.

The *MIDSHIP SECTION AREA COEFFICIENT* (C_M) is the ratio of the immersed area of the midship section to the area of the circumscribing rectangle.

$$C_M = A_M/BT$$

From the above it will be observed that $C_B = C_P \times C_M$.

The *WATERPLANE AREA COEFFICIENT* (C_W) is the ratio of the area of the waterplane to the area of the circumscribing rectangle.

$C_W = A_W/LB$, where A_W = area of waterplane in m^2.

Table 1 gives the salient features known to be necessary to ensure a good performance for various types of ships working over different speed ranges. This information has been developed as the result of many years of experience with models in tanks and with actual ships and was given in imperial units by F. H. Todd. (Trans. Marine Engineers, Vol. 57).

The length and fullness of a ship for economical propulsion at a given speed are closely associated and the block coefficient can be selected from the large amount of published data available. An expression originally due to F. H. Alexander relates the block coefficient, service speed and length by the expression:

$$C_B = 1{\cdot}24 - V/2\sqrt{L}, \text{ for } V/\sqrt{L} = 0{\cdot}9 \text{ to } 1{\cdot}1$$

This expression normally indicates the maximum block coefficient that should be used. Sir Amos Ayre (Trans. Inst. Marine Engineers, Vol. 57) gives values for higher values of $V/\sqrt{L}$ and they can be expressed as $C_B = 1{\cdot}00 - 0{\cdot}23\, V/\sqrt{L}$ where the block coefficient derived is the maximum that should be used for service conditions.

S. B. Ralston (Trans. Inst. of Engrs. & Shipbuilders in Scotland, Vol. 91) gives data in a diagram which relates the length and breadth to the block coefficient involving service speed. Table 2 giving block coefficients has been derived from this diagram.

It is frequently desired that the block coefficient at draughts other than the load draught be known and this can be done by the expression: Change in C_B per metre of draught = $1/(10H)$.

Thus if $C_B = 0{\cdot}72$ and $H = 7{\cdot}33$ m, then C_B at 6·1m draught $= 0{\cdot}72 - 1{\cdot}23 \times 0{\cdot}0136 = 0{\cdot}72 - 0{\cdot}017 = 0{\cdot}703$.

TABLE 2.

L/B	$V/\sqrt{L}$								
	0·905	0·996	1·087	1·177	1·268	1·358	1·449	1·539	1·630
5	0·720	0·706	0·680	0·660	0·634	0·612	0·591	0·567	0·550
6	0·740	0·728	0·711	0·688	0·665	0·640	0·616	0·592	0·572
7	0·760	0·751	0·736	0·716	0·694	0·670	0·646	0·623	0·601
8	0·780	0·774	0·761	0·744	0·725	0·703	0·680	0·657	0·636

HYDROSTATIC CURVES.—As the draught of a ship changes, the displacement, area of waterplane, coefficients, centre of buoyancy, metacentres, etc., also vary and it is customary to show these changes by means of curves on a vertical scale of draught while the horizontal ordinates represent displacement, area of waterplane etc. These items depend wholly on the shape of the underwater form of the vessel and are therefore most important basic curves. Such a displacement curve will give at any mean draught the displacement of the vessel at that draught but this will not be quite accurate if the ship is floating at a waterplane not parallel to the designed load waterplane.

In the early stages of the design of a ship, the displacement, KB, BM_T, BM_L, T.P.C. and M.C.T. 1 cm are frequently desired at intermediate draughts in addition to the load draught. The present writer, in the *Shipbuilder*, Feb. 1957, described how these values may be estimated without a body plan being available and based on the length, breadth, draught and load displacement of the design concerned.

CENTRE OF BUOYANCY.—The centre of buoyancy B is the centroid of the immersed volume. The vertical position of the centre of buoyancy can be determined and estimated in several ways. The area above the displacement curve and bounded by the vertical draught line and any required waterline represents the moment of displacement about that waterline. Consequently the distance of the centre of buoyance below the waterline can be determined by dividing the area by the displacement.

The height of the centre of buoyancy above the keel (KB) can be estimated from Morrish's Rule as follows:

$$KB = H - 1/3\left[\frac{H}{2} + \frac{V}{A}\right] = 1/3\left[\frac{5H}{2} - \frac{V}{A}\right]$$

On the substitution of displacement and waterplane area equivalents the formula becomes:

$$KB = H[(5C_W - 2C_B)/(6C_W)],$$

where H = the draught in m, V = volume of displacement in cu m, and A = area of waterplane in sq m.

The height of the centre of buoyancy above the keel may also be estimated with considerable accuracy from the expression:

$$KB = H/[1 + (C_B/C_W)]$$

The value of C_W for normal ships is very closely given by the expression $C_W = C_B + 0{\cdot}1$.

WETTED SURFACE.—The wetted surface (S) of a ship is the total area of the surface of the shell plating and appendages to the waterline at which the vessel is floating. Reliable formulae for the assessment of the wetted surface are as follows:

$S = 1{\cdot}7LH + LBC_B$ (Mumford) $\qquad S = 2{\cdot}58\sqrt{(\Delta L)}$ (Taylor)

where S = wetted surface in sq m, H = draught in m, Δ = displacement in tonnes, and C_B = block coefficient.

BONJEAN CURVES.—Bonjean curves were first proposed at the beginning of the nineteenth century by Bonjean, a French naval engineer, for the purpose of readily obtaining for any given waterline, the area of the immersed portion of each selected transverse section throughout the vessel's length. They are simply curves of transverse sectional area on a vertical scale of draught and are drawn generally for the same stations as are used for the sheer draught and displacement sheet calculation. Such curves are extremely useful in determining the displacement of a ship to a waterline having an excessive trim as during launching and to an irregular waterline such as the surface of a wave used in standard strength calculations.

CURVE OF AREAS.—This is a curve in which the horizontal base represents to scale the length of the ship and the ordinates represent the immersed area of the corresponding transverse sections of the vessel. The load waterplane curve is usually drawn in association with the curve of areas. In order to standardise such curves they are frequently drawn within a rectangle. The sectional area curve has several exceptional features and can be prepared by comparison with ships similar in form to the design under consideration. It gives the area below the load waterline of all transverse sections and thus fixes the longitudinal distribution of the ship's buoyancy. Since the ordinate at the midship section gives the area at that section and the curve is plotted on the ship's length as a base, the ratio of the area under the curve to that of the circumscribing rectangle will be the prismatic coefficient.

Thus the sectional area curve and load waterplane curve together give the prismatic coefficient, block coefficient, waterplane area coefficient and longitudinal position of the centre of buoyancy. The only element not provided by these curves directly is the position of the centre of buoyancy above the keel. This can be determined with sufficient accuracy by one of the expressions previously given. For any sectional area curve in which the midship area is taken as unity

$$\overline{X} = \frac{X_F \times C_{Pf} \times L/2 - X_A \times C_{PA} \times L/2}{L \times C_P}$$

where $\overline{X}$ is the distance of the centre of buoyancy forward of amidships and X_F and X_A are the distances of the centroids of fore and aft bodies respectively from amidships.

Also if r = length of run and C_{Pr} = prismatic coefficient of run

$$C_{Pa} = \frac{C_{Pr} \times r + L/2 - r}{L/2} = \frac{r(C_{Pr} - 1)}{L/2} + 1$$

$$C_{Pa} - 1 = \frac{r(C_{Pr} - 1)}{L/2} \text{ and } \frac{C_a - 1}{C_{Pr} - 1} = \frac{r}{L/2} \text{ or } \frac{1 - C_{Pa}}{1 - C_{Pr}} = \frac{r}{L/2}$$

If the length of entrance e is equal to length of run r and the length of parallel body is denoted by m, then the following relationship exists:—$\Delta/1{\cdot}025 = L \times A_M \times C_P$
also $\Delta/1{\cdot}025 = e \times A_M \times C_{Pe} + m \times A_M + r \times A_M \times C_{Pr}$
then $L \times C_P = (e \times C_{Pe} + m + (r \times C_{Pr})$
Since $e = r$

$$L \times C_P = e(C_{pe} + C_{Pr}) + m. \text{ But } m = L - 2e.$$

Hence $L \times C_P = L - e[2 - (C_{Pe} + C_{Pr})]$

and
$$\frac{e}{L} = \frac{1 - C_P}{2 - (C_{Pe} + C_{Pr})}$$

In using the curve of areas from a previous design it may well be that the position of the centre of buoyancy so obtained is not suitable for the new design. By altering the curve as shown below the necessary modification to the position of the longitudinal centre of buoyancy may be secured.

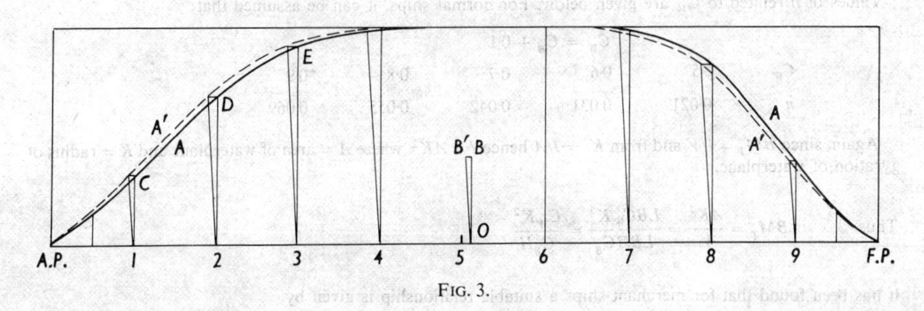

FIG. 3.

In Fig. 3 AA is the original curve of areas and B its centroid. BB' is the movement of centre of buoyancy desired. Draw the triangle $BB'O$; through C, D, E, etc., draw lines parallel to base. From 1, 2, 3, etc., draw lines parallel to OB' to meet the parallels through C, D, E, etc. The intersection of these lines give spots for new curve $A'A'$, which will be found to have the same total displacement and total prismatic coefficient and the desired position of the centre of buoyancy.

If the sectional area curve is drawn, as is usual, within a rectangle whose area is reckoned as unity, then the area under the curve is equal to the prismatic coefficient C_p and the remaining areas to $1 - C_P$. If all such distances as OY (Fig. 4) be reduced or increased to OY′ in the ratio $(- C_P')/(1 - C_P)$, where C_P' is the prismatic coefficient desired for a new design to be derived from the basis, then the spots Y′ will define a new curve of areas having the prismatic coefficient C_P'. In this way, the new curve corrected for prismatic is obtained, but not for the longitudinal positions of the centre of buoyancy. Hence, to derive a curve from a basis which will be correct both for prismatic coefficient and for all the longitudinal positions of the centre of buoyancy proceed as follows:

Apply the method given above to obtain the curve having the desired prismatic coefficient. Calculate this curve both longitudinally and vertically, and then modify this curve to give the desired longitudinal position of the centre of buoyancy as shown in Fig. 4.

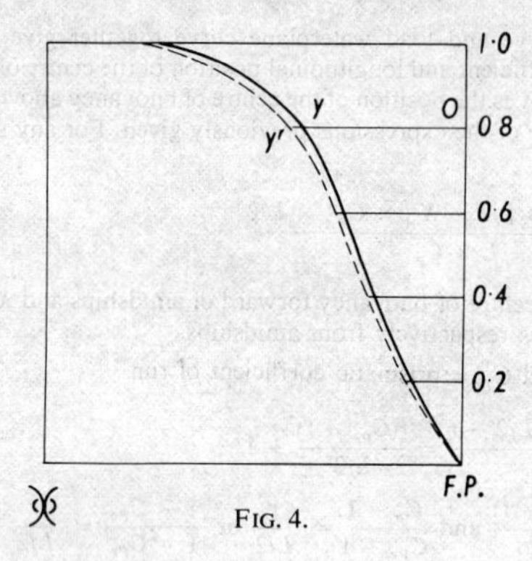

FIG. 4.

TRANSVERSE METACENTRE.—If a ship is inclined transversely through a small angle, the centre of buoyancy B will move slightly from the middle line towards that side, say to B', and the vertical through B' representing the upward thrust of the water will cut the inclined middle line at a point M called the 'Transverse Metacentre'.

$$BM_T = I/V$$

where BM_T = height of transverse metacentre above the centre of buoyancy in m, I = transverse moment of inertia of the waterplane about its middle line in $m^2 \times m^2$, and V = volume of displacement in cu m.

The height of the transverse metacentre above the centre of buoyancy may be estimated by the following expressions.

$$BM_T = \frac{I}{V} = \frac{nLB^3}{LBHC_B} = \frac{nB^3}{HC_B}$$

where n is the inertia coefficient.

Values of n related to C_W are given below. For normal ships, it can be assumed that:

$$C_W = C_B + 0{\cdot}1$$

C_W	0·5	0·6	0·7	0·8	0·9
n	0·021	0·031	0·042	0·055	0·069

Again, since $BM_T = I/V$ and from $K^2 = I/A$ hence $I = AK^2$, where A = area of waterplane and K = radius of gyration of waterplane.

Thus $$BM_T = \frac{AK^2}{V} = \frac{LBC_WK^2}{LBHC_B} = \frac{C_WK^2}{C_BH}$$

It has been found that for merchant ships a suitable relationship is given by

$$K^2 = (0{\cdot}17\, C_W + 0{\cdot}13)^2B^2$$

Consequently inserting this in above expression

$$BM_T = C_W(0{\cdot}17\, C_W + 0{\cdot}13)^2B^2/C_BH$$

METACENTRIC HEIGHT.—The metacentric height (GM) in any condition of loading of the ship is the distance between the transverse metacentre M and the centre of gravity G of the vessel in the condition under consideration. For all practical purposes in normal ships the point M does not change in position for inclinations up to as large as 10 degrees, but beyond this it takes up different positions.

As far as a ship's initial stability or stability in the upright condition is concerned, it can be stated that:—(*a*) If G is below M the ship is in stable equilibrium, (*b*) If G is above M the ship is in unstable equilibrium, (*c*) If G coincides with M the ship is in neutral equilibrium. In (*a*) the ship will return to the upright position, if slightly inclined and set free. In (*b*) the ship will not remain upright.

The value of GM can be obtained either by separate calculation of the position of G and M, or by an inclining experiment.

INCLINING EXPERIMENT.—The immediate purpose of the inclining experiment is to determine the metacentric height. The ultimate purpose is to determine the position of the centre of gravity for a definite condition of the ship—the '*Light Condition*'.

The inclining experiment is carried out as the vessel approaches completion, when weights that have yet to be put on board can be determined together with their final positions. The principle upon which the experiment is based can be indicated by a summary of the essential steps in the performance of the experiment. With the ship floating freely in still water, a known weight on the ship is shifted a measured distance in an athwartship direction. This causes the ship to list. The precise angle of list is measured by means of a pendulum or stabilograph. The *GM* in feet may then be calculated by one of the following equations:

$$GM = \frac{w \times a}{\Delta \times \tan\phi} \text{ or } GM = \frac{w \times a \times l}{\Delta \times d}$$

where w = mass moved in tonnes; a = distance mass moved athwartships in m; l = length of pendulum in m; d = deflection of pendulum in m; ϕ = inclination in degrees; Δ = displacement in tonnes.

It is important that certain precautions be taken in the inclining experiment and these are as follows: (1) A survey should be made of the weights to come off and go on, with their centroids, to bring the vessel to the required condition. (2) All tanks in the ship should be empty or full. There should be nothing which will move when the ship heels. (3) The vessel must be free to incline. Gangways should be cast off and only for and aft moorings allowed to remain. (4) If possible a fine day should be chosen, with the water calm and little wind. All personnel not employed in the experiment should be sent ashore. (5) The ship should be upright. (6) The weights employed should be so arranged that they can be shifted quickly across the deck to a predetermined position. Their weight should be such as to cause a small angle of heel. (7) The pendulum should be as long as possible, and hung so as to swing freely. (8) The density of the water should be taken by a hydrometer and the draughts measured forward and aft. From this data the displacement and position of the centre of buoyancy can be obtained from the hydrostatic curves.

The *KM* can also be obtained from the hydrostatic curves so that

Any liquid free surface present during the Experiment has the effect of lowering the value of *KG* (as inclined). The free surface correction (*FSC*) is such that

$$FSC(\text{m}) = \frac{\text{second moment of area of free surface (m}^4) \times \text{liquid density (t/m}^3)}{\text{displacement of ship in tonnes}}$$

Finally the mass of the ship and its corrected centroid *KG* must be modified by subtracting the weights to come off and adding the weights to go on. The result gives the Lightship mass of the ship and its centroid above the keel. A similar calculation is made to determine the position of the longitudinal centre of gravity of the Lightship.

STABILITY BOOKLET.—All ships are required to carry on board an approved Stability Information Booklet to comply with the Merchant Shipping (Load Line) Rules 1968. A document setting out a recommended presentation is available from the Department of Trade. The booklet should contain General Particulars of the ship, plans showing cargo spaces and tanks, hydrostatic particulars, capacities and centroids of cargo spaces and of tanks, Cross Curves of Stability (*KN*), Deadweight loading scale, a set of typical loading

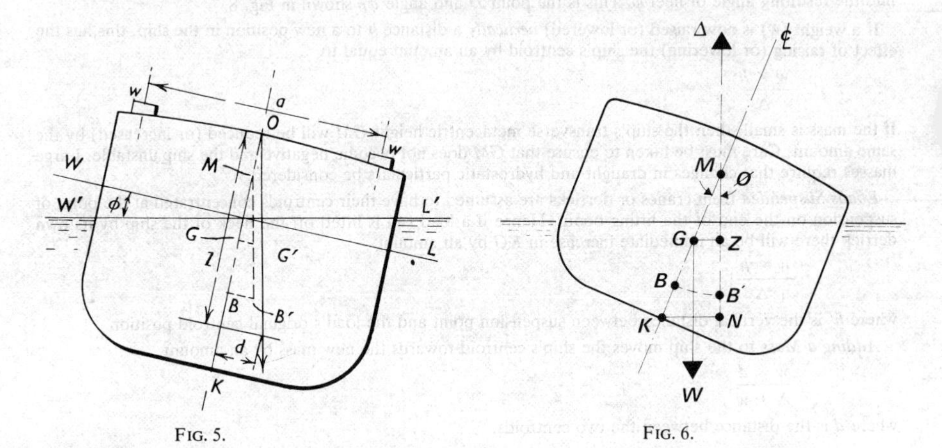

FIG. 5. FIG. 6.

conditions expected for the ship in service including the Lightship condition. One of those conditions must show the result of the ship being completely full of cargo, consumable liquids and stores as well as loaded down to its deepest permitted load waterline.

Loading Condition Statements are required in pairs for both departure and arrival states, where on arrival consumables and stores are reduced to 10% of their departure quantity. Accordingly salt water ballast may need to be shown as added during the voyage in order that the ship meets the stability criteria upon arrival. Statements must give ship's draught, displacement, loading arrangement, metacentric height corrected for any free surfaces and a Curve of Statical Stability. One pair of statements must show a satisfactory water ballast condition without any cargo on board.

STABILITY

A ship floating in still water is supported by a force equal to the weight of the ship. This supporting force is called Buoyancy. The centroid of the displaced water is called the centre of buoyancy. The buoyancy of a ship may be taken as a single force acting upwards through the centre of buoyancy. The weight of the ship may be regarded as a single force acting at the ship's centre of gravity, and directed vertically downwards. These forces are equal in amount, vertical and opposite in direction. As the vessel is at rest under the action of these forces, the resultant weight and buoyancy must act along the same vertical line. The ship is then in equilibrium.

If the ship is now inclined by an external force such as wind, the resultant forces of weight and buoyancy may no longer act along the same vertical, but will tend to rotate the ship. The turning effort is measured by the product $\Delta \times GZ$ called the righting moment. GZ is the righting lever. If the external force is removed, the righting moment returns the ship to its initial upright position. See Fig. 6.

For angles of heel up to about 10°,

$$GZ = GM \sin \phi$$

and Righting Moment $= \Delta . GZ = \Delta . GM \sin \phi$.

MOVEMENTS OF WEIGHTS ON BOARD SHIP.—Moving a weight *horizontally* across the ship is the action during the Inclining Experiment. The centroid G moves to G', and B moves to B'. See Fig. 5.

$$GG' = \frac{w \times a}{\Delta}$$

and

$$GG' = GM \tan \phi$$

so that Heeling Moment $= w \times a = \Delta \cdot GG' = \Delta . GM \tan \phi$.

If the expression for the righting moment is now introduced in the form

$$\Delta . GZ = \Delta . GM \tan \phi . \cos \phi$$

we find that:

$$\text{Heeling Moment} \times \cos \phi = \Delta . GZ$$

This expression is used when larger angles of heel occur and a Curve of Statical Stability must be drawn to find the resulting angle of heel ϕ. This is the point D and angle ϕ_D shown in Fig. 8.

If a weight (w) is now raised (or lowered) *vertically* a distance h to a new position in the ship, this has the effect of raising (or lowering) the ship's centroid by an amount equal to

$$\frac{w \times h}{\Delta}$$

If the mass is small, then the ship's transverse metacentric height GM will be reduced (or increased) by the same amount. Care must be taken to ensure that GM does not become negative and the ship unstable. Large masses require that changes in draught and hydrostatic particulars be considered.

Loads Suspended from cranes or derricks are assumed to have their centroids concentrated at the point of suspension on the end of the lifting boom. Hence if a load (w) is lifted off the deck of the ship by its own derrick there will be an immediate increase in KG by an amount

$$\frac{w \times h'}{\Delta}$$

where h' is the vertical distance between suspension point and the load's original centroid position.

Adding a Mass to the ship moves the ship's centroid towards the new mass by an amount

$$\frac{w \times d}{\Delta + w},$$

where d is the distance between the two centroids.

This shift may be horizontal, vertical or a combination of the two. Discharging a mass has the opposite effect, the shift being equal to

$$\frac{w \times d}{\Delta - w}$$

CROSS CURVES AND CURVE OF STATICAL STABILITY.—Providing the angle of heel ϕ is small, then the righting lever GZ may be taken equal to $GM \sin \phi$. (Fig. 6). At the larger angles of heel the shape of the underwater volume changes especially when the deck edge becomes submerged and the position of the metacentre M can no longer be assumed a fixed point. The changes in righting levers are obtained from *Cross Curves of Stability*, otherwise known as *KN-curves* which plot KN against displacement for particular angles of heel ϕ. Fig. 7.

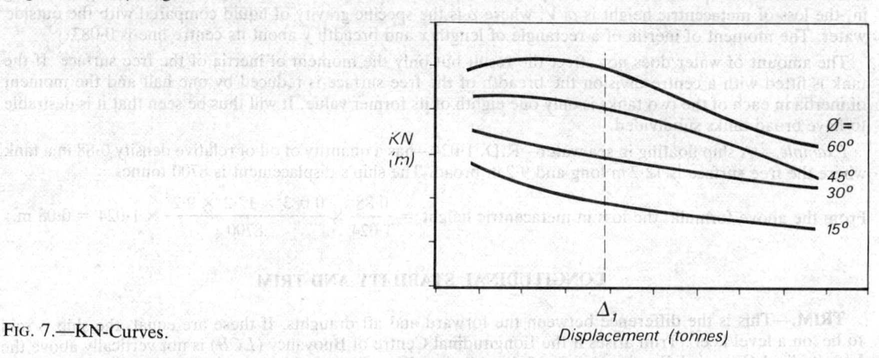

FIG. 7.—KN-Curves.

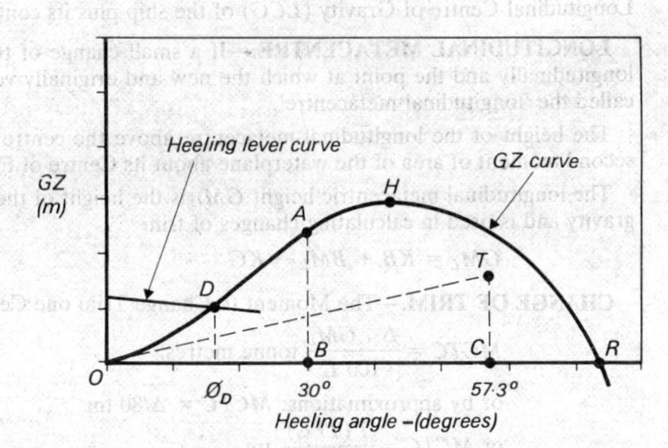

FIG. 8.—Statical Stability Curve.

To obtain the *Statical Stability Curve*, Fig. 8, which shows the change in GZ with angle of heel, draw a line at the required ship displacement Δ_1 and lift off values of KN for each ϕ.

Then from Fig. 6 it will be seen that:

$$GZ = KN - KG \sin \phi$$

where KG = Ship's centroid + Free Surface Correction.

In Fig. 8, the point T is at a height TC above the axis equal to the metacentric height (GM) corrected for any free surface. A line joining T to the origin O provides a tangent to the GZ curve. The point R is the Angle of Vanishing Stability and the length OR the Range of Stability.

Certain minimum stability criteria are required to satisfy the United Kingdom's *Load Line Rules*:—

Initial GM ($=TC$) $\geqslant$ 0.15 m
Area under GZ-curve up to 30° (Δ' OAB) $\geqslant$ 0·055 m radians
Area under GZ-curve up to 40°* $\geqslant$ 0·09 m radians
Area between 30° and 40°* $\geqslant$ 0·03 m radians
Value of the Maximum GZ (point H) $\geqslant$ 0·20 m and to occur at an angle not less than 30 degrees.

* or lesser angle at which water could enter hull.

The statical stability curve assumes that no water enters the ship and that the ship heels without changing trim. In some instances it is necessary to make allowance for the change in trim as the ship heels in which case the curve is said to have 'free trimming'.

FREE LIQUID.—In the section dealing with the inclining experiment special attention is drawn to the necessity to make certain that no free water is permitted to remain in the ship during the experiment. By free water is meant water having a free surface. If a compartment, such as a double bottom ballast tank, then the water will have precisely the same effect in the ship as if it were a solid body having the same weight and position of centre of gravity as the water. If, however, the water does not completely fill the tank, but has a free surface, then if the ship is heeled, the water in the tank must adjust itself so that its surface is parallel to the level waterline of the ship. Thus the centroid of the liquid changes its position and it can be shown that this has a detrimental effect upon the metacentric height.

The loss in metacentric height is given by the expression i/V where i is the moment of inertia of the free surface of the liquid about a fore and aft axis through the point of intersection of its two surfaces; and V is the volume of displacement of the ship. If the liquid in the tank is other than the water the ship is floating in, the loss of metacentric height is $\rho i/V$, where ρ is the specific gravity of liquid compared with the outside water. The moment of inertia of a rectangle of length x and breadth y about its centre line is $0{\cdot}083xy^3$.

The amount of water does not affect the result but only the moment of inertia of the free surface. If the tank is fitted with a centre division the breadth of the free surface is reduced by one half and the moment of inertia in each of the two tanks is only one eighth of its former value. It will thus be seen that it is desirable to have broad tanks subdivided.

Example.—A ship floating in sea water—R.D. 1·024—has a quantity of oil of relative density 0·88 in a tank where the free surface is 12·2 m long and 9·2 m broad. The ship's displacement is 8700 tonnes.

From the above formula, the loss in metacentric height $= \dfrac{0{\cdot}88}{1{\cdot}024} \times \dfrac{0{\cdot}083 \times 12{\cdot}2 \times 9{\cdot}2^3}{8700} \times 1{\cdot}024 = 0{\cdot}08$ m.

LONGITUDINAL STABILITY AND TRIM

TRIM.—This is the difference between the forward and aft draughts. If these are equal, the ship is said to be 'on a level keel'. Trim arises if the Longitudinal Centre of Buoyancy (*LCB*) is not vertically above the Longitudinal Centre of Gravity (*LCG*) of the ship plus its contents.

LONGITUDINAL METACENTRE.—If a small change of trim occurs the centre of buoyancy will move longitudinally and the point at which the new and originally vertical lines of action of buoyancy intersect is called the 'longitudinal metacentre'.

The height of the longitudinal metacentre above the centre of buoyancy $= BM_L = I_L/\nabla$ where I_L is the second moment of area of the waterplane about its Centre of Flotation and ∇ is the volume of displacement.

The longitudinal metacentric height GM_L is the height of the longitudinal metacentre above the centre of gravity and is used in calculating changes of trim

$$GM_L = KB + BM_L - KG$$

CHANGE OF TRIM.—The Moment to Change Trim one Centimetre (*MCTC*) is given by the expression:

$$MCTC = \frac{\Delta \,.\, GM_L}{100\,L} \text{ tonne metres.}$$

or by approximations: $MCTC = \Delta/80$ tm

or $MCTC = \dfrac{7\,(TPC)^2}{B}$ tm

where Δ = displacement in tonnes; B = ship's breadth in metres; TPC = tonnes per centimetre.

If a mass (w) which is already on board is moved forward (or aft) a distance χ, then the moment changing trim is $w.\chi$ and the change of trim $= \dfrac{w\chi}{MCTC}$ centimetres.

If the centre of flotation is assumed to be at amidships, then half this change is added to the draught forward (T_F) and half subtracted from the draught aft (T_A).

If a small mass w' is added to the ship at a distance d aft of the Centre of Flotation (F), the draughts will be affected by both a parallel sinkage as well as a change of trim:

$$\text{New } T_A = \text{Original } T_A + \frac{w'}{TPC} + \tfrac{1}{2}\frac{w'd}{MCTC}$$

and

$$\text{New } T_F = \text{Original } T_F + \frac{w'}{TPC} - \tfrac{1}{2}\frac{w'd}{MCTC}$$

If the mass is discharged or it is positioned forward of F, there will merely be changes in signs. Note that the accuracy of these expressions diminishes as F moves from amidships.

LOADING/DISCHARGING LARGE WEIGHTS.—The above method becomes inaccurate with large alterations in displacement. It is necessary to proceed as follows:

(*a*) Determine the draught at the Centre of Flotation (T_{LCF}) using draughts T_A, T_F.

(*b*) Use Hydrostatic Curves at T_{LCF} to obtain values for Δ, LCB, $MCTC$.

(*c*) Calculate the position of the ship's original Longitudinal Centre of Gravity from the expression:

$$\text{Trim in metres } (= T_A - T_F) = \frac{\Delta \times \text{Separation of } LCB \text{ and } LCG \text{ (m)}}{MCTC \times 100}$$

(*d*) Calculate the movement of the LCG when the weight is added (or subtracted), and so the ship's new LCG position.

(*e*) For the new displacement obtain T_{LCF}, LCB, $MCTC$ values.

(*f*) Calculate the new trim using the expression in (*c*) above and this is proportioned around the new T_{LCF} to give the final ship draughts.

FLOODING.—If a compartment in a ship becomes damaged and open to the sea, water will flood in until its level inside the compartment is the same as in the sea outside. The ship may experience merely bodily sinkage, but trim and heel can also occur to give an unsymmetrical condition. Accurate calculations are difficult and tedious and often need to be done with a computer.

If the damaged compartment is located at amidships and has a volume v. m^3 (the lost buoyancy) up to the pre-damaged waterline, then the bodily sinkage will equal v divided by the intact waterplane area, where Intact Waterplane area = pre-damaged 'complete' waterplate − waterplane area inside the compartment.

This is known as the *Lost Buoyancy* method.

Should cargo be present in the damaged compartment an allowance for permeability (μ) must be made, the multiplication factor decreasing down from 1·00 as less water is able to enter the compartment.

If the damaged compartment is not at amidships a change of trim as well as bodily sinkage must be considered. The moment (m^4) causing change of trim is approximately the lost buoyancy (m^3) times its distance to the centre of flotation (m) and the change of trim is that moment divided by the new second moment of area of the damage waterplane (m^4) and multiplied by the length of the ship.

WEIGHTS

The total weight or displacement of a merchant ship is made up as follows: (1) Displacement = Lightweight + Deadweight. (2) Lightweight = Hull + Propelling Machinery. (3) Hull = Steel + Wood and Outfit.

LIGHTWEIGHT.—Generally defined as that in which the vessel is complete and ready for sea, but no fuel, feed water, fresh water, stores, provisions, ballast—other than permanent ballast—passengers, baggage, and cargo on board. It is accepted that in the completed ship, the propelling machinery is ready for immediate operation. In a steamship, the boilers are filled to working level, the condensers, lubricating oil systems, and coolers are in working conditions. In a motorship, all cooling water and lubricating oil systems are full.

HULL.—The Weight of Steel includes steel plates and sections of all kinds. Rivets where involved. Hull castings and forgings.

The Weight of Wood and Outfit includes: Carpenter work; joiner work; plumber work; upholstery; boats and davits; smithwork; deck machinery and pipings; electric lighting installation; heating installation; ventilation; insulation; refrigerating machinery; galley outfit; paint; awnings; fire fighting apparatus; wireless and radar equipment, etc.

PROPELLING MACHINERY.—The weight includes main propelling unit, shafting and propellers; main boilers and auxiliaries, uptakes and funnels; all pumps and auxiliary plant in machinery space; piping; ladders and gratings, etc.

DEADWEIGHT.—The total deadweight of a ship is the difference between the load displacement and the lightweight. Thus the total deadweight includes cargo, fuel, feed and fresh water, stores, provisions, passengers and baggage.

The magnitude of some of these items are as follows: *Fuel in Bunkers:* This depends on the radius of action of the ship, and should include a margin for emergencies of about 15%. *Feed Water:* Allow about 15% of fuel oil. *Fresh Water:* Allow about 25 person days per tonne. *Stores:* Allow about 150 person days per tonne. *Passengers, Crew and Effects:* Allow about 115 kg per person.

The estimate of a ship's weight is an important factor in ship design. In the early stages of the design the weight can be only roughly approximated. The designer is dependent on accumulated data and initially the total weight is proportioned from similar vessels already built. The naval architect collects, classifies and preserves finished weight data.

Hull weight data may be estimated either in detail or as a whole. Detail calculation requires that plans of the vessel are available together with reference lists giving weight rates or actual weights of all varieties of fittings. For preliminary work, where a rapid estimate of weights is required, the method of coefficients is frequently used. By this method, the entire weight of the hull or of certain portions is compared with an arbitrary parameter of simple form depending upon the principal dimensions of the ship. Such a parameter, to be used only for purely preliminary investigations, is the cubic number, which is the product of the length, breadth and depth divided by 10.

$$\text{Cubic number } CN = L \times B \times D/10$$

where L = Length between perpendiculars in m, B = Breadth moulded in m, and D = Depth moulded in m to uppermost continuous deck, then

Weight of Hull = $CN \times$ Coefficient of hull weight = $CN \times CH$
Weight of Steel = $CN \times CS$
Weight of Wood and Outfit = $CN \times C_w$ & o.

The use of coefficients and other approximations must of necessity cause the values so obtained to be subject to a certain amount of error. As the design proceeds the weight estimate is revised and made increasingly more accurate. The following table gives average values of the hull, steel and wood and outfit coefficients to be used in association with the cubic number method for various types of ships.

Ship Type	C_S	C_W & 0	C
Tug	1·34	0·56	1·90
Trawler	1·70	0·88	2·58
Cross Channel Ship	0·92	0·56	1·48
Cargo Ship	1·10	0·24	1·34
Intermediate Liner	1·55	0·75	2·30
Atlantic Liner	1·23	0·75	1·98
Oil Tanker	1·06	0·28	1·34

WEIGHT OF MACHINERY.—In making preliminary estimates the weight of propelling machinery is frequently taken as proportional to the horse power, the number of horse power per ton of total machinery weight being recorded for all ships built. It must be remembered, however, that although propelling machinery weight varies with power, it is not necessarily proportional to power as large installations will be lighter per horse power than small installations. The weight also varies with the type of machinery. Reciprocating machinery is in the region of 4–6 P_I per tonne for installations from 2,000 to 5,000 P_I. Geared turbines with watertube boilers are about 7 to 13 P_S per tonne for installations ranging from 4,000 to 30,000 shaft power. For preliminary design work, data from strictly comparable actual ships are needed. Details of the propelling machinery are given in the *Trans. Inst. Marine Engrs.* (Vols. 56 and 59).

The make up of the machinery weight, in Tons, for a cross channel passenger ship of 10,740 P_S (trial); 21·64 knots (trial) with two sets geared turbines as given in imperial units by E. L. Denny, before the Inst. Mech. Engineers, in 1958, is as follows: Boilers complete, 78·1; Uptakes, casings, air heaters, 38·2; Funnel, 15·4; Turbines and manoeuvring gear, 23·8; Condensers, 21·6; Piping systems, 61·6; Lagging, 10·0; Floors, ladders, gratings, lifting gear, 37·6; Gearing, 47·3; Tunnel, 65·1; Miscellaneous, 36·3; Auxiliaries, 96·0; Generators, 90·0. Total Weight (dry), 621·0, water and oil, 40·0. Total Weight (steam up), 661·0.

RESISTANCE AND POWER.—The knowledge of ship resistance has evolved largely from the exhaustive experimental inquiry made by W. Froude into the resistance of thin planks towed through the water at varying speeds. Others who have contributed greatly in this field are R. E. Froude, Tideman, Geber, Taylor and Schoenherr. The resistance of a ship is generally considered to be the force necessary to tow the vessel through perfectly smooth water, no account being taken of any interaction between hull and propeller or of the resistance of appendages. The power necessary to overcome this resistance is called the tow-rope or effective power (P_E).

The main elements contributing to the resistance of a ship in smooth water are: (1) Skin-friction resistance due to the motion of the hull through the water. (2) Wave making resistance due to the energy continually being supplied by the ship to the wave system created by the vessel on the surface of the water. (3) Eddy resistance due to the energy carried by eddies formed around stern fittings and bossings. (4) Air resistance experienced by the structure of the vessel above water as it advances through the air. The term 'residuary resistance' is applied to the sum of the effects of items (2), (3) and (4) above. It denotes the whole of the resistance of the ship less the skin friction resistance. The wave making resistance is the largest component of the residuary resistance.

A great deal of the knowledge on ship resistance has been derived from experiments with models. Such small scale work is quicker and cheaper to carry out than experiments with full size ships. All maritime nations now possess model ship testing tanks in which such work is carried out. The models are made of paraffin wax or wood, may be 3 to 7 m in length and when ballasted to represent to scale the loaded ship, weigh from 900 to 1300 kg. They are towed by means of a travelling bridge from which they are suspended. An automatic record is taken of the total resistance and speed. The results are corrected to apply to the ship, as indicated later.

From the experiments carried out by W. Froude he concluded that frictional resistance could be expressed by a formula of the type $Rf = fSV$ where Rf = frictional resistance in N, S = wetted surface in square m. V = speed in m/s. f = a coefficient depending upon length (L) of surface and its nature. n = speed index.

The value of n is taken as equal to 1·825. The values of f in sea water are given below.

Length m	f	Length m	f	Length m	f
2·0	1·966	11	1·589	40	1·464
2·5	1·913	12	1·577	45	1·459
3·0	1·867	13	1·566	50	1·454
3·5	1·826	14	1·556	60	1·447
4·0	1·791	15	1·547	70	1·441
4·5	1·761	16	1·539	80	1·437
5·0	1·736	17	1·532	90	1·432
5·5	1·715	18	1·526	100	1·428
6·0	1·696	19	1·520	120	1·421
6·5	1·681	20	1·515	140	1·415
7·0	1·667	22	1·506	160	1·410
7·5	1·654	24	1·499	180	1·404
8·0	1·643	26	1·492	200	1·399
8·5	1·632	28	1·487	250	1·389
9·0	1·622	30	1·482	300	1·386
9·5	1·613	35	1·472	350	1·376
10·0	1·604	—	—	—	—

The Law of Comparison enables the residuary resistance of a ship to be estimated from that of the model or from that of a ship of different size but of the same form. The law is as follows. The residuary resistances of similar ships will vary as the cube of the linear dimensions provided the speeds are in the ratio of the square root of the linear dimensions. L and l being the length (m) of ship and model.

Thus $r_r/r_r = L^3/l^3$ if $V/v = \sqrt{(L/l)}$ where R_r = residuary resistance of ship, and r_r = residuary resistance of model, that is, $R_r \propto L^3$ if $V/\sqrt{L}$ is constant.

Also since for similar ships the displacement will also vary as the cube of the linear dimensions then

$$R_r/r_r = W/w \text{ if } V/\sqrt{L} \text{ is constant;}$$

where, W = displacement of ship, and w = displacement of model.

When $V/\sqrt{L}$ is constant the ships are running at their corresponding speeds.

With models the procedure is as follows:

(1) The model is run at the corresponding speed (v); $v = V\sqrt{(l/L)}$ where v and l are for the model and V and L for the ship.

(2) The total resistance for the model (r) is recorded during the experiment.

(3) The frictional resistance for the model is calculated by the expression $r_f = fsv^{1·825}$ where s = wetted surface of model.

(4) The resistance of the model is given by $r_r = r - r_f$.

(5) The residuary resistance of the ship R_r is obtained as shown above by $R_r = r_r(L/l)^3$.

(6) The frictional resistance of the ship is obtained from $R_f = fSV^{1·825}$.

(7) Total resistance of ship $= R = R_r + R_f$.

(8) The effective power $(P_E) = R \times V \times 0·5144$ = kW. where V is in knots.

(9) The ratio P_E/P_S is called the propulsive coefficient and has values from about 0·50 to 0·75.

The bare hull effective power must be increased for the added resistance of the appendages such as rudder and bilge keel in a single screw ship by about 6% and in a twin screw ship the allowance is about 10% due to the effect of bossing. The shaft power determined by the propulsive coefficient is increased by about 15% for 'sea conditions' in order to allow a margin for wind and waves.

TAYLOR METHOD.—The effective horse power may be estimated from a 'Standard Series' such as given by D. W. Taylor in his book *Speed and Power of Ships*. The results of a comprehensive series of models towed at Washington are embodied in a set of charts giving the residuary resistance in pounds per ton of displacement for a range of speed-length ratio, prismatic coefficient and displacement-length coefficient covering the practical proportions of ships. The data is given for two ratios of breadth (B) to draught (H) and it is assumed that for intermediate ratios of B/H the residual resistance will vary in a straight line between the values obtained for the given ratios of B/H. The information given in this work has been used for many years and with consistent success. A re-analysis of the original test data for the Taylor standard series has been published by M. Gertler. *T.M.B. Report* 806.

AYRE METHOD.—In a paper read to the N.E. Coast Inst. of Engineers and Shipbuilders (Vol. 64) details are given in imperial units of a method for estimating P_E.

$$P_E = \Delta^{0\cdot 64}V^3/C_2$$

where Δ = displacement in tons; V = speed in knots; C_2 = constant, at given values of $V/\sqrt{L}$.

Charts for the values of C_2 are given in the paper. Various corrections are required for block coefficients, breadth-draught ratio, longitudinal position of the centre of buoyancy and length factor, and these are detailed in the paper. A great amount of research work with models has been carried out and much of the data has been made available in the transactions of the Inst. of Naval Architects; Society of Naval Architects and Marine Engineers; Inst. of Engineers and Shipbuilders in Scotland; and N.E. Coast Inst. of Engineers and Shipbuilders.

ADMIRALTY COEFFICIENT.—A method which can give guidance values, although not precise results, for power estimations is the use of the Admiralty coefficient. This is the value

$$A_C = \Delta^{0\cdot 66}V^3/P_I \text{ or } = \Delta^{0\cdot 66}V^3/P_S$$

depending upon the type of propelling machinery installed. Δ = displacement in tonnes; V = speed in knots.

The coefficients of performance, A_C vary for different ships and vary for different speeds in the same ship and also for different displacements. In estimating preliminary power by this method great care is essemtial. Before a reliable A_C value can be assumed, data from a similar ship must be available and the operating conditions must not be greatly different from that of the known vessel.

The assumptions made in the Admiralty coefficient method are as follows:

(*a*) Resistance varies as the square of the speed or $R \propto V^2$

(*b*) Resistance varies as the wetted surface or $R \propto S$

(*c*) The P_I or P_S varies as the P_E or, $P_I \propto P_E$

Thus $\quad R \propto V^2 \times S$ or $R \times V \propto V^3 \times S$ ....(1)

But $R \times V$ is a measure of work done, hence $R \times V \propto P_E$

from (1) $V^3 \times S \propto P_E$ and from (*c*) $V^3 \times s \propto P_I$

or $\quad P_I = SV^3/C$ where C is a constant ....(2)

Again in similar ships $\Delta \propto L^3$ and $S \propto L^2$

thus $\quad L \propto \Delta^{0\cdot 33}$ and $L \propto S^{0\cdot 5}$

Consquently $\quad S^{0\cdot 5} \propto \Delta^{0\cdot 33}$ $\therefore S \propto \Delta^{0\cdot 66}$ i.e. $S = C\Delta^{0\cdot 66}$

Substituting for S in (2) and introducing a new constant $P_I = \Delta^{0\cdot 66}V^3/C$ or, $A_C = \Delta^{0\cdot 66}V^3/P_I$ where A_C is a coefficient of performance.

Admiralty Coefficient applied to Fuel Consumption.—a variation of the Admiralty coefficient frequently used by marine engineers when comparing service performances consists of substituting the daily fuel consumption in tonnes for the power in the expression $A_C = \Delta^{0\cdot 66}V^3/P_I$.

The power developed must be proportional to the fuel consumption per unit of time and thus $P_I \quad \Delta^{0\cdot 66}V^3$ so also will the fuel consumption. It is usual to write fuel consumption per 24 hours = $\Delta^{0\cdot 66}V^3/K$, or, $K = \Delta^{0\cdot 66}V^3$/(Fuel Consumption per 24 hours).

ESTIMATE SHEET.—When making tentative estimates of weights, power etc., for a design it is desirable to use a form such as is indicated by the following example: Ship to be 134 m by 18 m by 12 m to weather deck. Tween deck height 2·75 m. Draught 8·1 m, and total deadweight 9,650 tonnes. Diesel machinery. Service speed $14\frac{1}{2}$ knots.

From data of similar ships, assume that $C_S = 1\cdot 10$; C_W & O = 0·26; Machinery weight = 5 P_B tonnes; A_C = 425; C_B = 0·72. Then, Cubic Number = 134 × 18 × 12/10 = 2895.

		Tonnes
Steel = 2895 × 1·1	=	3200
Wood and Outfit = 2895 × 0·26	=	750
Machinery = 4000/5	=	800
Light Weight	=	4750
Deadweight	=	9650
Margin ($\frac{1}{2}$% Dwt.)	=	50
Displacement	=	14,450

Displacement = 134 × 18 × 8·1 × 0·72 × 1·025
= 14,450 tonnes

$$P_B = \frac{14{,}450^{0\cdot 66} \times 14\cdot 5^3}{425}$$

= 4000 kW.

ENQUIRY FOR NEW TONNAGE.—An enquiry should state

(*a*) Type of ship and service: Cargo tramp, cargo liner, intermediate, passenger ship, cross channel, tanker, fruit carrier, meat carrier, etc.

(*b*) Type of propelling machinery and fuel.

(*c*) Total deadweight.

(*d*) Radius of action—fuel one way or out and home; fuel margin desired; fuel for port use.

(*e*) Speed, trial condition; deadweight or draught on trial, duration of trial.

(*f*) Harbour or other limitations.

(*g*) If passenger ship: number of passengers and class, number of passengers per cabin, and number of public rooms.

RUDDERS.—The area of a ship's rudder is commonly determined by dividing the product of the ship's length and load draught by about 60 to 70 for moderate speed cargo vessels.

The maximum angle of helm for efficiency of turning depends upon the speed of the ship and the ship form but is about 38 degrees from the middle line plane and stops are fitted to arrest the rudder at this angle.

The force on the rudder can be estimated from the formula: $\phi = kAV^2\theta$ where ϕ is in N. A in sq m, V in m per sec and θ in degrees.

From experiments carried out by Baker and Bottomley the following formula was derived:

For middle line rudders behind single screws: $\phi = 18{\cdot}0AV^2\theta$ Newtons

R. W. L. Gawn (I.N.A. 1943) suggested the following:

For middle line rudders behind twin screws: $\phi = 15{\cdot}5AV^2\theta$ Newtons

In addition to knowing the force on the rudder it is necessary to know the position of the centre of pressure. It is generally assumed that for a rectangular rudder the centre of pressure is 0·35 the breadth of the rudder abaft the leading edge if behind deadwood and 0·31 the breadth if the rudder is in the open. For rudder shapes other than rectangular the position of the centre of pressure would require to be calculated in more detail.

The product of the maximum force (P) on the rudder and the distance of the centre of pressure abaft the axis (h) is the torque or twisting moment (T); that is, $T = P \times h$ where P is in newtons and h is in metres.

The diameter of the rudder head may be determined from the expression:

$$d = \sqrt[3]{[16T/(\pi f)]}$$

where d = dia of rudder head in m, and $f = 77{\cdot}2 \times 10^6$ N/m² for cast steel.

The classification societies have rules for the determination of the diameter of rudder stocks. In Lloyd's Register of Shipping the diameter of the rudder stock, D_S, is given by the formula:

$$d_S = 83{\cdot}3\, k \sqrt[3]{[(V+3)^2 \sqrt{(A^2S^2 + a^2)}]}\ \text{mm}$$

where, A = rudder area in m²; S = distance in metres from centre line of rudder pintles to the centre of pressure; V = maximum service speed in knots when loaded; k = 0·248 for rudders in propeller slipstream, and 0·235 for rudders on centre line of twin screw ships; a = zero when two or more pintles are fitted. Further details are given in Lloyds Rules, chapter D, section 22.

TRIALS.—Ship trials are usually carried out before the vessel is accepted by the owners and during such trials the vessel must meet the specified requirements. Trials generally consist of (a) speed trials over a measured mile course, (b) fuel consumption trials, (c) steering trials, and (d) equipment trials.

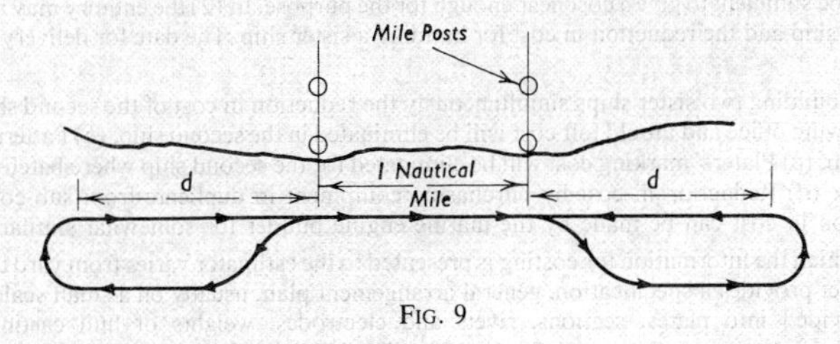

FIG. 9

Measured Mile trials.—For the accurate determination of the ship's speed through the water from the observed times of successive runs over a measured mile (1852 m.) course the following precautions should be observed. See Fig. 9. In the diagram d is a distance of about 2 miles for the acceleration of the vessel after turning so that speed on the mile is uniform.

(1) The successive runs in opposite directions should be made over the same course which must be at right angles to each of the pairs of mile posts.

(2) On completing each run the vessel should be immediately turned off the course with an angle of helm not exceeding 15 degrees. It is essential that the speed of the vessel on the mile is uniform. Whilst on the course leading to the mile as well as on the mile itself the helm should not exceed 5 degrees.

(3) The intervals of time between the runs on the mile should be uniform and as short as possible.

(4) The revolutions of the propeller should be noted.

(5) At least two observers should time the vessel independently over the course on stop watches.

(6) The mean speed and the mean values of rev/min should be determined by the mean of means method or from the following formula:

V_1, V_2, V_3, V_4 are the successive speeds with and against the tide, the mean speed (V) is given as follows:

For four runs $V = (V_1 + 3V_2 + 3V_3 + V_4)/8$

For rev/min substitute r_1, r_2, R_3, R_4 for V_1, V_2, V_3, V_4.

TONNAGE.—The measurement of tonnage is an economic problem and in the past an aspect of ship design which has exercised a controlling influence on design and has been to some extent responsible for the production of several types of ships. Tonnage measurement is required to establish the gross and net tonnages upon which port and harbour dues, etc. are levied.

The principle on which tonnage measurement should be based has been the subject of controversy for generations. Over the years Commissions were appointed and rules for tonnage formulated. To produce a unified system for tonnage measurement of ships was assigned to the Inter-Governmental Maritime Consultative Organization, or I.M.C.O. as it is more generally called. The Sub-Committee on tonnage measurement started its work in 1959 and in 1969, I.M.C.O. convened in London, an International Conference on Tonnage Measurement of Ships, 1969; this was the first international agreement ever made in this field.

The Convention provides for gross and net tonnages of ships to be computed independently. The gross tonnage is determined from a formula as a function of the total moulded volume of all enclosed spaces. The net tonnage is derived from a formula, as a function of the total moulded volume of all cargo spaces with corrections for draught and number of passengers. The net tonnage so calculated must not be less than 30% of the gross tonnage. The significance of the new convention is not only that it provides a unified system of tonnage measurement, but also that it simplifies to a great extent, the determination of gross net tonnage in comparison with the previous national tonnage measurement regulations.

COST ESTIMATING.—In the negotiations leading up to a contract for the construction of a new ship, the estimated cost to the shipbuilder of carrying out the proposed work is of primary consideration. Cost is of such importance that personnel are maintained to provide the management with the information desired. The cost to the shipbuilder must be lower than the price quoted, the difference being the profit from that particular contract. The total profit arising from the ships completely in any one year should be such that after deducting taxation, the remainder is adequate to meet the following; (*a*) Pay an appropriate dividend on the capital invested in the shipyard. (*b*) Cost of replacement of plant and machinery from year to year. (*c*) Contribution to a reserve fund for future expenditure on new plant and new buildings brought about by changes in methods of production.

For both new construction and repair work the estimating department is called upon to provide cost figures in two main categories: (1) Where either time or specification data or both are very limited and a guidance cost only is expected. (2) Where sufficient time and information are available for the preparation of a reliable quotation.

In (1) costs are submitted informally at the request of a shipowner who is interested in a ship for a particular service and desires to know the limits within which the cost may fall. This makes it possible to determine what the overall operating costs might be as related to the initial investment in the ship. A cost so proposed generally obligates neither the owner nor the builder. The application of a few rates based upon the type of ship, deadweight, power, etc., will be sufficient to give a cost near enough for the purpose. In (2) the enquiry may request a quotation for building one ship and the reduction in cost for building a sister ship. The date for delivery is also a matter of great importance.

In the case of building two sister ships simultaneously the reduction in cost of the second ship will be made as follows; (*a*) Drawing office and mould loft cost will be eliminated in the second ship. (*b*) Patterns will be available from the first ship. (*c*) Platers' marking cost will be eliminated for the second ship where batch drilling is adopted for riveted work. (*d*) Reduction in cost by purchasing equipment in duplicate from sub-contractors. Corresponding reduction in cost can be made by the marine engine builder for somewhat similar reasons.

The form in which the information for costing is presented to the estimator varies from yard to yard. In all cases the naval architect provides a specification, general arrangement plan, usually on a small scale, gross weights of hull steel subdivided into plates, sections, rivets and electrodes, weights of hull castings, deck castings and smithwork. In certain cases this is supplemented by detailed lists of carpenters' timber quantities for decks, hatch covers, sparring, ceiling, etc.; area of deck coverings other than wood; particulars of auxiliary deck machinery, derricks, lifeboats, sanitary fittings, windows, sidelights and other outfit items. In other cases the estimators have to obtain this information from the specification and plan provided.

The hull cost for estimating purposes is generally subdivided as follows: (1) Material, (2) Labour. (3) Establishment charges. To the sum of these must be added the cost of propelling machinery and the profit to arrive at the quotation cost.

The labour indicated in item (2) above is generally put into two sections: (*a*) Ironworker trades: platers, welders, riveters, drillers, caulkers, loftsmen, and shipwrights. (*b*) Fitting out trades: carpenters, joiners, polishers, blacksmiths, painters, redleaders, plumbers, mechanics, electricians, sheet-metal workers, riggers, and labourers. The total cost for (*a*) is obtained by multiplying the gross steel weight by the appropriate labour cost per tonne of steel determined by results suitably adjusted from similar ships previously built. In (*b*) the cost is determined by quantities estimated from plans and specifications multiplied by a price per m^2 or lineal metre obtained from sectional cost records of similar ships previously built.

Establishment Charges.—All charges of material and labour should be directly applied to the product with which they are concerned. There are, however, certain costs which cannot be treated in this way. Such items are included as a percentage of labour or of labour plus material. These items are grouped under the heading of 'Establishment Charges', and include plant and tool maintenance, cost of fuel—coal, coke and oil—electricity, gas, water, medical services, personnel department, apprentice training, commercial department, garden, watchmen, insurance, rates, rents, cost of storekeeping and timekeeping.

The make-up of the cost for material, labour and establishment charges of a 9,500 tonnes dead weight diesel cargo ship, on a percentage basis is approximately 62% for the hull and 38% for the propelling machinery. The total cost of the hull can be divided into: Material 64%; Labour 25%, and Establishment Charges 11%.

SHIP CONTRACTS.—The most important feature of a shipbuilding contract, like most contracts, does not appear from the wording of the specification or the contract itself; it is the mutual confidence that exists between the builder and the purchaser. It must be remembered that in spite of all that is done by the naval architects, marine engineers, and lawyers, in preparing documents, matters will arise during the construction of the ship, such as changes in design or alterations in equipment and machinery, which can only be resolved by discussion between the parties motivated by a mutual desire to produce the best ship for the intended purpose.

The contract is an agreement for a stated sum to construct a ship by a specific time in accordance with plans, specifications and contract conditions. The memorandum of agreement generally takes the following form:

(1) The builders agree to build, launch, complete and sell, and the purchasers agree to purchase a . . . vessel, with machinery and equipment, to be called, until named, the builders' No. . . . and which shall have the following leading dimensions of Hull and specified machinery. (Here follow the hull dimensions for: L.B.P.; Breadth; Depth; and Draught; also the details of the Machinery, Engines and Boilers.) All as per signed specifications.

(2) *Classification.*—The builder shall obtain a certificate of classification for . . . class, and shall build the vessel in accordance with D. of T. Regulations for the type of vessel specified. The builders pay all classification and D. of T. fees. (3) *Survey.* The purchasers have the right to send a surveyor to the premises of the builder during working hours, to inspect the vessel and machinery. Any defect found shall be made good. (4) *Delivery.*—The vessel to be completed ready for sea trial not later than . . . and if not so completed, by . . . the builders shall be liable to pay the purchasers, unless exempted by clause (5), £ . . . per working day for each day of later completion. The purchasers shall pay the builders the same amount for each day of earlier completion. (D. of T. = Department of Trade).

(5) *Strikes, Accidents, etc.*—If the delivery of the vessel is delayed by fire, storm, trade dispute, or accident, or any cause not within the absolute control of the builder, or by any additions or alterations ordered by the purchaser, or if delay takes place in paying any instalment of purchase price, prior to delivery, the builder shall be allowed one working day's extension for each day lost by these causes.

(6) *Insurance.*—The builders shall, during building, and until delivery, fully insure the vessel against all risks. If the vessel be destroyed by fire or lost otherwise before delivery, then the contract shall cease and the builders shall repay all instalments of the purchase price paid, but without interest. If the vessel be damaged by fire, collision, or otherwise before delivery, the purchasers shall not be entitled to refuse to accept delivery, but the builders shall make good such damage as speedily as possible to the satisfaction of the classification society. The time occupied shall be allowed before any claim can be made under Clause (4).

(7) *Default by Builders.*—Should the builders fail to finish the vessel in accordance with the contract, the purchasers shall have power to enter the yard, and use the builders plant and all materials provided for the vessel, in finishing her. The cost involved shall be deducted from the purchase price then unpaid, and if the balance of unpaid purchase price is insufficient, the deficiency shall be made good by the builders. The exercise of such powers shall be without prejudice to any claim for delay under Clause (4). (8) *Security.*—The vessel shall, from first instalment being paid, until final delivery, be considered the property of the purchasers subject only to the builders' rights, with respect to any unpaid balance due to them. (9) *Default by Purchasers.*—If the purchasers default for 14 days in the payment of any instalment, the whole balance of the purchase price shall immediately become due, and payable with interest at the rate of . . . per cent per annum. (10) *Payment.*—The purchasers shall pay to the builders the sum of £ . . . , as the purchase price of the vessel. One-sixth part of the purchase price shall be paid over on each of the following occasions: (*a*) On signing the memorandum of agreement. (*b*) When keel is laid. (*c*) When the vessel is framed. (*d*) When the vessel is plated. (*e*) When the vessel is launched. (*f*) When the vessel is delivered.

(11) *The Trials.*—Immediately on completion, the vessel shall make a trial at . . . For the trial the builders shall provide the crew for navigation, the engine room staff, and the fuel for the trial. Any further weights the purchaser desires on board beyond water ballast, are to be provided by the purchaser, who shall pay all expenses

for loading and insuring such cargo. If the purchasers are dissatisfied with the trial trip, they shall notify the builders in writing immediately after the trial trip, specifying the grounds for dissatisfaction. In default of such notice the trial trip shall be deemed satisfactory in all results.

(12) *Guarantee.*—The builders are to guarantee the machinery for a period of six months from the completion of the trial trip, against defective material or workmanship in the original construction. Should any such be discovered the builders shall supply and fit in a port in Gt. Britain, new materials to replace the defect. The engineers, during the period of the guarantee, shall be appointed by the Builders, but paid by the Purchasers, whose employees they shall be.

[*13*] *Right to Alter.*—The Purchaser shall be at liberty to require alterations to be made in the vessel and machinery, provided such alterations are ordered in writing, and provided an addition or abatement from the purchase price, and time if necessary, be allowed. All such alterations are to be mutually agreed.

(14) *Discrepancies.*—If any difference exists between the contract and the specifications, it is agreed that the contract shall express the intention of the parties and shall be adopted.

(15) *Arbitration.*—Any dispute arising between the parties in connection with the vessel shall be referred to a single arbitrator in . . . to be appointed by the parties. All the provisions of the Arbitration Act shall apply to this agreement.

COMPUTERS.—The routine ship calculations for the hydrostatical properties of the vessel's hull form, stability, capacity, launching etc., are lengthy and tedious. Over the years many approaches have been made and methods employed to reduce the labour involved, such as desk calculating machines, and mechanical integrators in the form of the planimeter, integrator and intergraph. Now a new tool is available in the electronic computer and most of the routine ship calculations are amenable to straightforward programmes. In the past many items in the field of naval architecture, including ship design, have been neglected because of the amount of laborious mathematical calculation required and the prohibitive cost and time involved. The computer reduces the time of measure computation to a matter of minutes, and as a result of this, repetitive solutions of a calculation can be made and an optimum solution obtained instead of, as previously, just an acceptable solution.

The British Ship Research Association (B.S.R.A.) has done a great deal to assist in the operation of programmes for Shipbuilders and in the development of new programmes that might be required. The B.S.R.A. has a computing unit in Glasgow, at Strathclyde University; this unit provides services for Scottish and Northern Ireland shipyards. Lloyd's Register of Shipping has a computer service which falls into two main sections: (*a*) Provision to clients of a comprehensive programme library relating to engineering and naval architecture computations, such programmes having been written and developed by the Society's staff. (*b*) The writing, testing, development and, if required, the running of programmes to a client's specification. The service which the Society offers both to internal departments and to the designer and builder, has a library of over 100 programmes. Foremost among these are the classification programmes for tankers and cargo ships intended to facilitate approach of these vessels in accordance with the Society's Rules.

The Danish Ship Research Institute has, since 1958, computed a wide variety of ships and new programmes have been developed in close collaboration with Regnecentralin and the Danish Towing Tank. Det Norske Veritas, the third largest classification society in the world has for a decade made regular and rapidly increasing use of the computer. The society has programmes on hydrostatic calculations, stability, flooding etc., which are available for the shipbuilding industry.

The use of computers can make revolutionary changes but it is important to bear in mind that computers cannot exercise selective judgement and no answer they give can be any better than the data with which they are fed.

AUTOMATION.–Automation in ships is a very important development. The term automation is an all-embracing one which can be misleading since it is used to cover anything from a simple instrument and control loop to a highly complex control system for a complete plant.

For many years ships have been equipped with an appreciable amount of instrumentation mounted adjacent to the point of measurement. Simple automatic control loops have also been adopted. The tendency recently has been to centralise the instruments and to provide remote control at a central point. The grouping of engine controls and instrumentation in sound-proofed glassed-in and air-conditioned control rooms located in the engine room of the ship is the main feature of centralised control. In this way watch-keeping is simplified and overall visual observation of the installation still possible. Remote control, in general terms, is a system of direct control of the propelling power from the navigating bridge. This system has been for some years, applied to ferries, tugs, trawlers, coasters etc. In broad terms the instrumentation and control schemes for ships are in three categories, Navigation; Cargo Handling; and Propelling Machinery and Auxiliaries:

NAVIGATION.—The instruments contained in an average wheelhouse and chartroom can be divided into three classes as follows:—(*a*) *Acting instruments;* Gyro and magnetic compass indicators; propeller speed and direction indicator, rudder angle indicator, radar screen, ship speed indicator. (*b*) *Preferation instruments:* Navigator; direction finder; echo sounder; course recorder. (*c*) *General equipment:* Charts; barometer.

Navigational aids are by necessity centralized on the bridge and the acting instruments should be within easy vision of watch-keeping officers. Maximum angle of visibility is an important facility and this should not be impaired by the lay-out of navigational aids.

Cargo Handling.—Some tankers are fitted with an automated cargo handling system which can be used for either remote control or programmed as a fully automated system for the control of loading and discharging operations.

Propelling Machinery and Auxiliaries.—The control of the propelling unit and its auxiliaries is more complex. Nevertheless the development work on centralised engine room instrumentation and bridge machinery control has now reached such a stage that it is now possible to move the generally accepted machinery control centre from the engine room to the bridge. The propeller speed and direction is controlled by a deck officer. All movements are indicated in the control centre on the bridge and from this centre the watch-engineer can scan the unattended engine room by means of television cameras. Conventional engine room controls are fitted, as part of the system, in case of an emergency.

STATUTORY REGULATIONS.—The two bodies concerned with maintaining standards in building British ships are the Government and the Classification Societies. The statutory regulations as laid down by the Government are dealt with by the Department of Trade and have the primary object of promoting safety of life at sea. Classification is not compulsory, but ships not built to the rules of a classification society would have to be surveyed and approved by the Department of Trade. Insurance of Ships and their cargoes is not the concern of a classification society.

The Marine Division of the Department of Trade issues rules with which ships must comply, enforced by the various Merchant Shipping Acts. Regulations are revised or amended from time to time so it is important to make enquiry through the Department of Trade's Marine Library for the latest effective regulations:

Merchant Shipping Notice No. M 943 lists the principal Statutory Instruments (SI) and their subsequent amendments at September 1980. Some of the more important 'Merchant Shipping Regulations' (or rules) which are used by naval architects include:

SI 1980 No. 686 Code of Safe Working Practices.
SI 1978 No. 795 Crew Accommodation.
SI 1978 No. 1543 Dangerous Goods Rules.
SI 1980 No. 536 Grain.
SI 1980 No. 538 Lifesaving Appliances.
SI 1980 No. 544 Fire Appliances.
SI 1968 No. 1053 Load Line Rules.
SI 1980 No. 535 Passenger Ship Construction.
SI 1980 No. 537 Cargo Ship Construction and Survey.
SI 1967 No. 172 Tonnage.

CLASSIFICATION SOCIETIES.—The purpose of classification of ships, their equipment and material and certain onshore marine installations (e.g. refrigerated plant) is to ensure that these are built to a high standard. If the ship is to remain in class regular inspection and surveys are carried out during its lifetime to ensure it will be maintained in a seaworthy condition and operate reliably. Classification is not obligatory but there is a preference and benefit when underwriters consider the ship for insurance purposes.

There are eight principal and independent classification societies supported by the larger maritime nations but generally operating completely free of government control.

Lloyd's Register of Shipping	(United Kingdom)
American Bureau of Shipping	(U.S.A.)
Bureau Veritas	(France)
Det Norske Veritas	(Norway)
Germanischer Lloyd	(Germany)
Nippon Kaiji Kyokai	(Japan)
Registro Italiano	(Italy)
Russian Register of Shipping	(Russia)

Shipowners may choose to have their ships classed by any society and indeed on occasions elect to have dual classification. Rules and regulations are similar, much depending on the reputation and services offered by each society. A forum for discussion and working parties is provided within the International Association of Classification Societies.

Lloyd's Register require that ships be examined at intervals not exceeding five years. Since this needs time out of service which increases with age, shipowners often elect for a continuous survey with some inspections being carried out annually as mutually convenient. Repairs and replacements are advised by the local surveyor whose reports to Head Office may contribute to an overall monitoring of existing rules and help in any subsequent rule development.

If a classed ship becomes damaged it must be inspected and the repairs certified by the surveyor before it is allowed to proceed in service. Class may be temporarily suspended or withdrawn.

When seeking classification certain detailed plans of the ship must be submitted for society approval. Since modifications may be demanded it is advisable that plans be submitted well in advance of any commitment to shipyard production. This applies especially to new ship types and novel concepts in structure and operation.

In new areas of technology Provisional Rules give guidance until they can be substantiated by service performance and surveyors reports. The societies have a research and development department which can examine new equipment, techniques and materials for the general improvement of ships. Consultancy services are usually available for individual enquiries.

The highest class given by Lloyd's is 100A. and this is given to all sea-going ships built in accordance with. or by standards equivalent to. the rules and regulations for the draught required. The material to be used in construction is tested at the place of manufacture before despatch to the shipyard. and if satisfying the test requirements. is marked with Lloyd's brand. Should. however. the material show defects in the process of being worked into the ship it can be rejected by the society. New ships are required to be built under the society's special survey. and are given the Mark ✠ in front of the classification numeral. During the course of construction. the surveyors examine the material and workmanship. and require the rectification of any items not in accordance with the rules or the approved plans. or of any defective material or workmanship.

The figure 1 after the character of classification of a ship indicates that the equipment of anchors. cables and hawsers is in good and efficient condition. Another notification in the Register Book is the letters L.M.C. which means Lloyd's Machinery Certificate. and indicates that the Machinery has been built in accordance with the rules and regulations prescribed.

OTHER ORGANISATIONS

The Inter-Governmental Maritime Consultative Organisation (IMCO) is a forum for the consideration of international maritime problems. It does not possess direct regulatory powers. However, agreements reached at its international conventions, when brought into effect by assent of the required number of participating national governments, do become binding upon mariners of those nations through the respective national legislative processes. IMCO also functions as a source of information and counsel to other parts of the United Nations having an interest in maritime affairs.

Significant agreements achieved recently include:

International Convention for Prevention of Pollution of the Seas by Oil 1973.
Revision of the Safety of Life at Sea Convention (SOLAS) 1974.
International Regulation for Preventing Collisions at Sea 1972.
Code for the Construction of Chemical Ships.
Code for the Construction of Gas Carriers.

The United States Coast Guard (USCG) is a near-equivalent to the British government's Department of Trade. It lays down standards and physically controls all shipping activities in American waters, with which British vessels must comply if operating there.

Other countries have their own national organisations to which ship designers would be advised to turn for information on local requirements and procedures.

REFERENCE PUBLICATIONS AND OTHER SOURCES OF INFORMATION

Embarking on a new engineering project may require collection of data from a wide range of sources. This section provides references which contain further details about individual ship types, marine operations, technical analysis and ship calculations.

TRANSACTIONS OF PROFESSIONAL INSTITUTIONS

Royal Institution of Naval Architects—bi-monthly journal 'The Naval Architect', contains review articles as well as formal technical papers which are gathered into the Annual 'Transactions'.

Institute of Marine Engineers—monthly 'Marine Engineers Review' and 'Transactions' in three series.

Society of Naval Architects and Marine Engineers (of America) (SNAME)—quarterly journal 'Marine Technology' and annual 'Transactions'.

North East Coast Institution of Engineers and Shipbuilders—annual 'Transactions' published in four (originally six) parts.

CLASSIFICATION SOCIETIES—LLOYD'S REGISTER OF SHIPPING

All societies publish their annual Register of Ships and Classification regulations as well as other intermittent reports. Those issued by the Committee of Lloyd's Register of Shipping include:

'Rules and Regulations for the Classification of Ships', printed in seven parts—Regulations; Materials; Structural Details; Ship Structures; Main and Auxiliary Machinery; Control, Electrical, Refrigeration and Fire; Special Ship Types.

'Register of Ships' in three volumes (A–G, H–O, P–Z) includes particulars of all known ocean-going merchant ships in the world of 100 tons gross and upwards. A 'Subsidiary Section' covers shipborne barges, docking installations, liquefied gas carriers, refrigerated cargo installations, refrigerated cargo containers classed with Lloyd's Register. The Register is kept up to date by means of cumulative monthly 'Supplements'.

An 'Appendix' to the Register contains lists of shipbuilders and engine builders, wet and dry docks, telegraphic addresses and telex numbers. A 'List of Shipowners' includes former names of ships. There is a 'Register of Offshore Units, Submersibles and Diving Systems' and 'Lloyd's Register of Yachts'.

Other Rules Published

Inland Waterways Vessels.
Floating Docks.
Mobile Offshore Units.
Submersibles.
Ships for Liquefied Gases.
Yachts.
Reinforced Plastic Yachts (provisional).

Other Publications

Guide to Machinery and Electrical Equipment in Yachts.
Geometric Properties of Rolled Sections and Built Girders (in 3 volumes).
Cargo Handling Gear Code.
Guidance Notes and Requirements for the Classification of Air Cushion Vehicles.
Test Requirements for Approval of Control and Electrical Equipment.

TRADE JOURNALS

'Cargo Systems International' (monthly).
'Fairplay International Shipping Weekly' (with supplements).
'Lloyds List' (daily).
'Motor Ship' (monthly, with supplements).
'Shipping World and Shipbuilder' (monthly).

TRADE ORGANISATIONS

British Ship Research Association's monthly 'Journal of Abstracts' gives brief summaries of most of the technical papers and important articles appearing in the marine press. There is an 'Annual Index' of subjects, authors and ships' names.

H. P. Drewry (Shipping Consultants) Ltd.—'Shipping Studies' and 'surveys', published intermittently and available to subscribers only.

Other consultants publish reports but at less frequent intervals.

International Cargo Handling Co-ordination Association—technical reports and surveys available to member companies and private subscribers.

GOVERNMENT PUBLICATIONS. (other than Statutory Regulations listed previously)

'Marine Activities: Guide to the Responsibilities of Government Departments and Agencies'—HMSO. 1977.
'The Carriage of Dangerous Goods in Ships' (The Blue Book)—HMSO. 1978 with later amendments.
'Instructions for the Guidance of Surveyors'—several issues relating to different ships and their equipment—HMSO.
'Merchant Shipping Notices'—(M-Notices)—Series of important advisory pamphlets published by the Department of Trade. Listed in M 914.

Inter-Governmental Maritime Consultative Organisation, publications list for 1980 issued by IMCO Publications Section.

BOOKS

COMSTOCK, J. P., (ED)., *Principles of Naval Architecture*, SNAME, 1967.
TAGGART, R. (Ed) *Ship Design and Construction*, SNAME, 1980.
RAWSON, K. J. AND TUPPER, E. C., *Basic Ship Theory*, (2nd edn) Longman, 1976.
DERRETT, D. R., *Ship Stability for Masters and Mates*, (3rd edn) Maritime Press, 1975.
MUCKLE, W., *Strength of Ships Structures*, Arnold, 1967.
TAYLOR, D. A., *Merchant Ship Construction*, Butterworths, 1979.
BHATTACHARYYA, R., *Dynamics of Marine Vehicles*, Wiley, 1978.
O'BRIEN, T. P., *The Design of Marine Screw Propellers*, Hutchinson, 1962.
TODD, F. H., *Ship Hull Vibration*, Arnold, 1961.
ROBB, A. M., *Theory of Naval Architecture*, Griffin, 1952.

CONFERENCES

International conferences and symposia are sponsored by professional bodies, universities or trade organisations. The published proceedings often include 'state-of-the-art' presentations as well as technical developments and innovations.

MARINE PROPULSION

Prime Mover—Steam Cycles—Boilers—Developments in Coal Fired Steam Plant—Marine Diesels—Types—Construction Details—Performance—Slow and Medium Speed Diesel Engines—Support Systems—Fuels—Gas Turbine Propulsion—Shock Resistance—Noise—GT Module Types—Performance—Heat Recovery—Bibliography.

By G. Armstrong, BSc, PhD, C.Eng., M.I.Mar.E., and I Thorp, BSc, M.Phil., C.Eng., F.I.Mar.E.

Fundamenally, the choice of prime mover for marine propulsion plant is governed by the following general characteristics.

Main Engine	Broad Characteristics
Steam turbine	Output up to 70 MW.
	Best attainable fuel consumption 240–250 kg/MWh (decreasing with increasing power).
	4 hours to start from cold.
	Can accept coal and the lowest quality liquid fuels.
	Reversible.
Diesel	Output up to 45 MW.
	Fuel consumption 160–200 kg/MWh.
	2–4 hours to start from cold.
	Can accept low quality fuels but not as low as steam plant and not solid fuel.
Gas turbine	Output up to 21 MW/engine.
	High fuel consumption 300 kg/MWh.
	High power/weight ratio.
	Can deliver full power 2 minutes from start-up.
	Irreversible.

The diesel category can be further subdivided into medium speed and slow speed engines:

Medium speed	RPM	:	400–600
	Bore	:	up to 620 mm
	Power	:	up to 16 MW
	4-stroke		cycle/irreversible
Slow speed	RPM	:	55–200
	Bore	:	up to 900 mm
	Power	:	up to 45 MW
	2-stroke		cycle/reversible

In general, medium speed engines have a 10–15% greater specific fuel consumption, are cheaper in terms of first cost per kilowatt output but cannot tolerate as low a quality fuel as the slow speed engine.

The above chararacteristics, broad as they are, are nonetheless sufficient to eliminate almost completely some prime mover types from certain applications and to cause major changes of emphasis within a given application in response to economic pressures.

Warship and Merchant Ship Propulsion.—The propulsion requirements for these applications are quite distinct. Warships are required to be highly manoeuvrable and capable of putting to sea at short notice, whereas engine selection for merchant ships is governed almost entirely by overall costs. For warship applications, the slow speed diesel is eliminated primarily on grounds of manoeuvrability. The engine and propeller are directly coupled and astern running is achieved by stopping the engine and restarting it in reverse. Not only can that process in itself take up to two minutes but the engine is started by admitting compressed air to the cylinders and the number of starts is, therefore, limited by the size of the compressed air reservoirs. The relatively large engine height and length required for slow speed engines is a further disadvantage.

Steam turbines are usually reversed by fitting an astern turbine on the same shaft as the low pressure ahead turbine. Astern running merely involves shutting-off steam to the ahead turbine and admitting it to the astern turbine, and the shaft can thus be turning in the opposite direction in less than 15 seconds. The disadvantage of steam plant for warships is, of course, the time taken to start from cold: although the normal period of around 4 hours can be reduced in an emergency. The low thermal inertia of the lightweight aero-derived marine gas turbine means that it is always instantly available. Gas turbines however, in common with medium speed diesels, are unidirectional and manoeuvring must be achieved either by a reversing gearbox or controllable pitch propeller. Gas turbines are also the least fuel efficient prime mover; a disadvantage which is further compounded by the specific fuel consumption increasing if the engine is operated other than at full power. This problem may be overcome by providing alternative smaller power units, either gas turbine (COCOG: Combined gas or gas) or diesel (CODOG: Combined diesel or gas) for reduced speed operation. Overall, the propulsion plant becomes complicated, but a desirable level of standby capacity is also introduced.

Discounting the very specialised option of nuclear propulsion for submarines, modern surface warships are almost exclusively propelled by combinations of medium speed diesels and/or gas turbines. The operating conditions for merchant ships however, lead to rather different conclusions and considerable changes have taken place over the past ten years.

Before 1973 fuel accounted for only about 11% of shipowners costs: both diesel and steam plant had been adapted to consume the poorer grades of residual fuel. Crew costs were a larger factor and the emphasis was on reduced manning, automation and unmanned machinery operation. This situation changed almost overnight in 1973 with the increase in crude oil price and fuel costs now account for some 55% of shipowners expenditure. The effect of this is twofold. First, fuel economy of propulsion plant assumes a far greater importance, and, secondly, it can be shown by transport economic theory that as fuel costs increase the economic ship speed decreases. To a first approximation.—

$$P \propto V^3$$

Where P is power required and V the ship speed, and hence a small reduction in ship speed greatly reduces the power required. (A 70,000 dwt bulk carrier requires about 15,000 kW for a ship speed of 17 knots. The same ship with an installed power of only 6,000 kW could achieve almost 13 knots).

Both of these effects favour the diesel engine with its lower specific fuel consumption compared to steam plant, and of course, eliminate the gas turbine. Steam plant had been the traditional high power option, and although its proponents were not slow to point out the advantages of steam plant.—

(1) Steam plant fuel consumption figures probably included the auxiliary load (about 5% of propulsive power);
(2) maintenance costs and lubricating oil consumption of steam plant were generally lower than those for diesel plant of equivalent power;
(3) steam plant has a greater tolerance of poor quality residual fuels than diesel;

The overwhelming trend over the last twelve years has been towards diesel plant even to the extent of steam to diesel conversions proving to be economic. However, studies of ship operation economics undertaken three or four years ago indicated that with the likely increasing price of oil there were trade routes where a coal fired steam plant offered economic advantages over a diesel plant. Some coal fired ships have been built, notably for the Far Eastern coal trade, but the relative stability of oil prices since that time has not encouraged widespread adoption of coal firing.

Although the ability of diesel engines to burn poorer grades of liquid fuel has improved and experiments have been undertaken by engine manufacturers to investigate the combustion of coal/oil mixtures, the problems caused by abrasive wear of cylinder liners and injection equipment by coal and ash particles mean that the direct combustion of solid fuels in diesel engines is unlikely to be offered commercially in the forseeable future. Other than for special applications the only advantage of steam plant is its ability to burn solid fuel, and this in turn depends on the future price of coal relative to that of oil.

STEAM PLANT

Ideal and Practical Cycles.—It can be shown as a consequence of the Second Law of Thermodynamics that the maximum efficiency of a heat engine working between a heat source at temperature T_B and a heat sink at temperature T_A is given by

$$\eta = 1 - \frac{T_A}{T_B}.$$

In the case of marine steam plant, where heat is rejected to the sea, T_A is, of course, fixed and it follows that in order to increase the cycle efficiency the temperature at which heat is transferred to the cycle T_B must be increased.

Figure 1(*a*) shows a simple Carnot cycle (without superheat) applied to the steam cycle in Fig 1. This cycle would have an ideal efficiency of.—

$$\eta\,\text{car} = 1 - \frac{T_A}{T_B}.$$

As all heat transfer takes place (process $1 \rightarrow 2$) at the highest temperature T_B and heat is rejected at the lowest temperature T_A. The Carnot cycle is however, not applicable to practical cycles for the following reasons.—

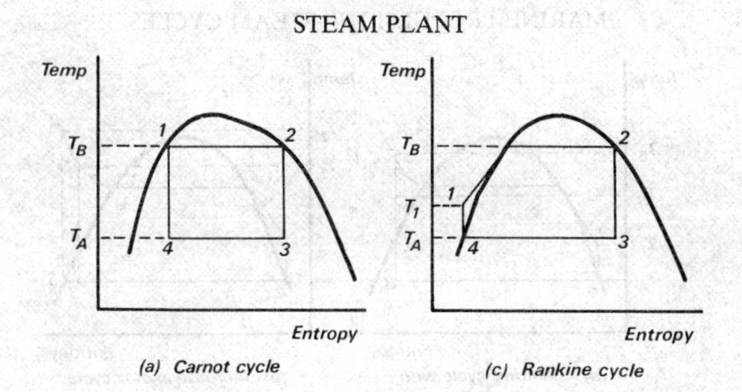

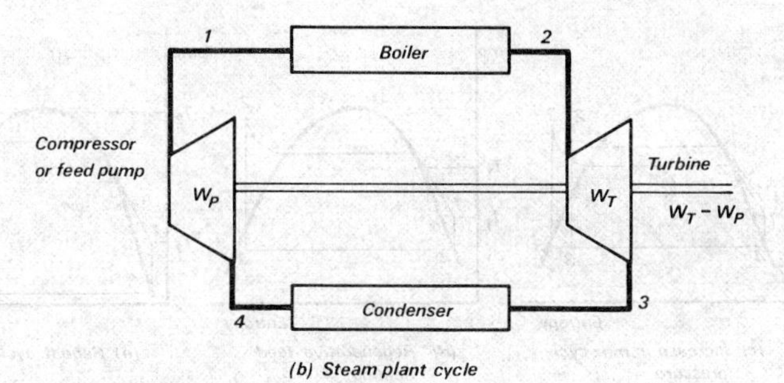

FIG. 1.—Thermodynamic Cycles.

(1) It would be very difficult to arrest the condensation process 3–4 at the point 4, which is defined merely as that point at temperature T_A which has the same entropy as point 1.

(2) The process 4-1 on the Carnot cycle indicates compression of a wet vapour (which is itself difficult in practice) with a final condition on the saturated liquid line. Compressor input power Wp is then larger than the equivalent 4-1 process in the Rankine cycle, Fig. 1(*c*) which takes place entirely in the liquid region, and hence the work ratio r_w defined as.—

$$\frac{\text{net work output}}{\text{positive work in cycle}} = \frac{W_T - Wp}{W_T}$$

is lower. The lower the work ratio of a cycle, the more sensitive the cycle efficiency becomes to irreversibilities in the expander and compressor, and it can be shown that although the ideal Carnot cycle efficiency is higher than that of the ideal Rankine cycle, the efficiency of a real Rankine cycle may exceed that of the equivalent real Carnot cycle, where process efficiencies of less than 100% are included in both cases.

These disadvantages of the Carnot cycle lead to the adoption of the Rankine cycle for practical steam plant. However, the ideal Rankine cycle efficiency will always be less than that of the ideal Carnot cycle operating between the same two temperatures as not all the heat in the Rankine cycle is transferred at T_B: part is transferred between T_1 and T_B. The efficiency of the ideal Rankine cycle is thus.—

$$\eta \,\text{Ran} = 1 - \frac{T_A}{\bar{T}_B}$$

where $\bar{T}_B$ is the mean temperature of heat transfer and is always less than T_B.

The same concept can, of course, be applied to cycles with superheat, Fig. 2(*a*) where T_B is defined as the maximum superheat temperature, and it is seen that the cycle efficiency will be.—

$$\eta \,\text{Ran} = 1 - \frac{T_A}{\bar{T}_B}$$

as heat is transferred throughout the temperature range T_1 to T_B.

Development of Steam Plant: Increase in efficiency.—There are four methods described below by which the efficiency of steam plant can be increased, and all four fundamentally are methods of raising $\bar{T}_b$.

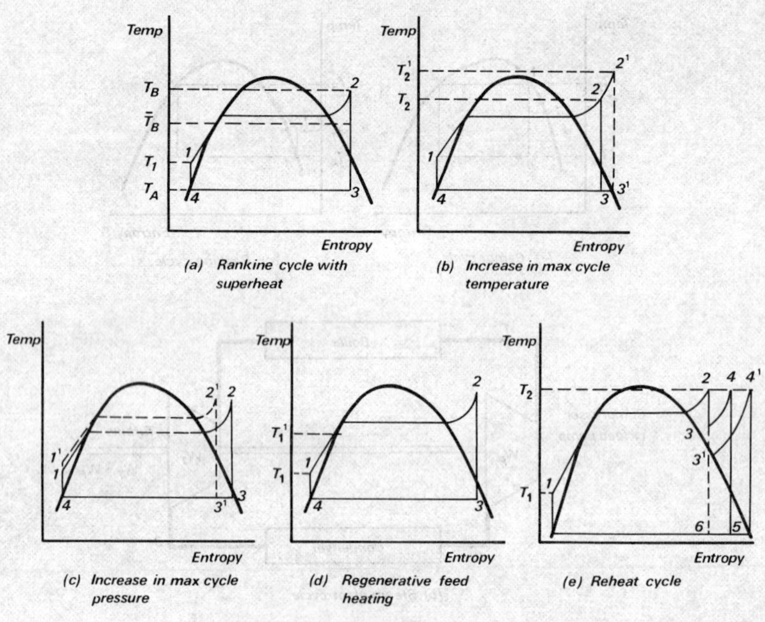

FIG. 2.—Superheat and Reheat Cycles.

(1) **Increase in maximum cycle temperature.**—Fig. 2(*b*) shows a Rankine cycle with a maximum temperature of T_2. It is seen that if the maximum temperature is raised to $T2^1$, and expansion thus takes place from 2^1 to 3^1 in place of 2 to 3 then more heat is transferred to the working fluid at the higher end of the temperature range, and hence the mean temperature of heat addition $\overline{T}_b$ is increased.

(2) **Increase in cycle pressure.**—The line 1–2 in Fig. 2(*c*) is a line of constant pressure, and represents the heat transfer process in the boiler. If the boiler pressure is raised to the line 1^1–2^1 (with the maximum cycle temperature remaining constant) then it can be seen that heat transfer takes place at a correspondingly higher temperature, thus increasing $\overline{T}_b$.

(3) **Regenerative feed heating.**—In the basic Rankine cycle, the temperature of the feed water inlet to the boiler is T_1 and heat is transferred to raise the water temperature to Tsat whereupon evaporation commences.

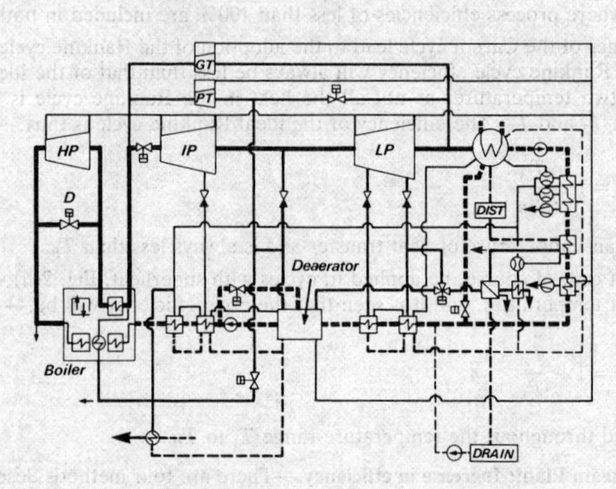

FIG. 3.—Steam Cycle 5CR *Stal-Laval*.

If means can be found from within the cycle (ie, regeneratively) to raise the feed water temperature to say $T1^1$ Fig. 2(*d*) then the mean temperature of external heat transfer to the cycle ($\overline{T}_b$) will have been increased. Up to five stages of feed water heating are common in marine steam plant, using steam bled from the main turbine at an appropriate pressure as the heat source.

(4) **Reheat cycles.**—High pressure plants commonly employ a reheat cycle (Fig. 2(*e*)) where expansion takes place in a high pressure turbine (2–3) and is then reheated either in the boiler or in a separately fired reheater to the same initial temperature (3–4) before expansion in the low pressure turbine (4–5).

There are two reasons for adopting reheat cycles. Firstly, in high pressure plants expansion without reheating (2–3–6) could result in the dryness fraction of the steam at point 6 being below the normal minimum of about 85%, which in turn increases the erosion of low pressure blading by water droplets. Secondly, providing reheating is done at a sufficiently high pressure (3–4) then reheating represents additional heat transfer to the cycle at the higher end of the temperature range T_1 to T_2 and hence $\overline{T}_b$ is increased. Clearly if reheating takes place at too low a pressure, say 3^1–4^1, the additional heat transfer place between T_3^1 and T_4^1 and $\overline{T}_b$ may not increase. It does not however, follow (for other reasons) that the reheat process should be at the highest possible pressure, and reheat pressures of about one fifth boiler pressure reflect typical practice.

MARINE STEAM PLANT EXAMPLES.—Practical marine steam cycles have developed over the last twenty years towards increasing pressure, temperature and number of feed heating stages, and the introduction of reheating cycles, although fuel economy was much less important before the 1973 fuel price increases than it is today. In 1965 Stal Laval introduced the AP (Advanced Propulsion) standard designs with superheater outlet steam conditions of 513°C and pressures of either 64.3 bar or 82.0 bar (abs). These were designated by the following code.—

2–5 : No. of feed heaters
B,C : Electric generator drive
  B : back pressure turbines
  C : condensing turbines
R : Reheat cycle

Figure 4 shows the corresponding fuel rates for the various cycles and indicates the increase in cycle efficiency with increasing sophistication in terms of temperature, pressure, feed heating and reheating.

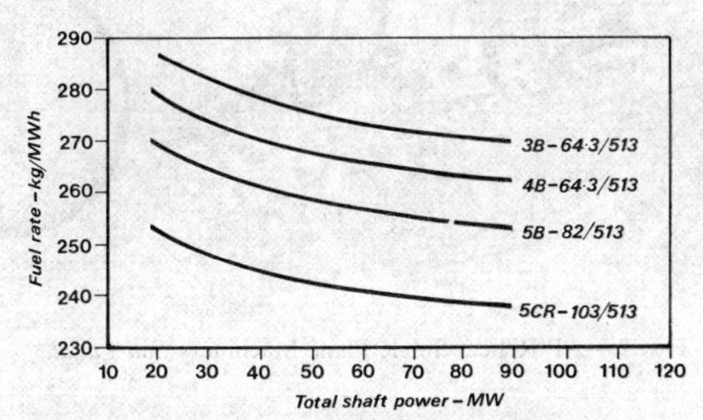

FIG. 4.—Fuel Rate of the Various Steam Cycles.

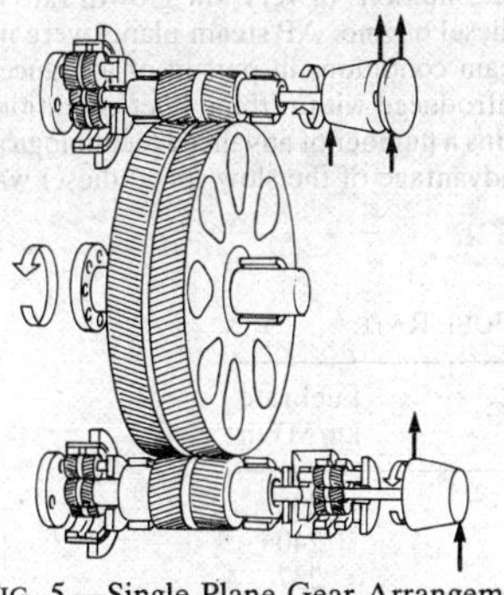

FIG. 5.—Single Plane Gear Arrangement with Triple Reduction on HP Side.

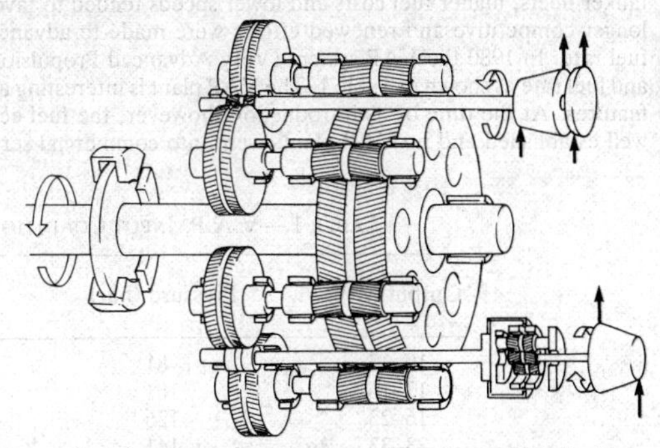

FIG. 6.—Gear Arrangement of the Locked Train Gear.

AP Turbine Machinery.—Up to a torque of 4 MNm (420 kw/rpm) a single plane cross compound arrangement is used. The primary reductions are epicyclics with a parallel final reduction. The LP side has a double reduction and the HP side can have either double or triple reduction (Fig. 5). The triple reduction is used for low propeller speeds (up to 110 rpm) at high powers and the double reduction for the higher propeller speeds common in fast container shps.

At torque above 4 MNm a locked train gear with four gear meshes in the final reduction has to be used (Fig. 6) and the condenser is positioned beneath the HP and LP turbines.

The low torque configuration (with epicyclic gears) can also be employed with an underhung condenser in designs where engine room length is more important than height. The single plane arrangement, of course, permits a lower engine room height (Fig. 7).

The HP turbines are of impulse type with a single impulse governing wheel as first stage and three nozzle groups. Depending on size either nine or ten stages are applied. Both the LP and the built-in astern turbine exhaust axially in the same direction to the condenser (single plane or underhung)—a feature which avoids heating the ahead blading when running astern. Final stage blades are protected against erosion by stellite shields.

FIG. 7.—AP Reheat Single Plane Machinery *Stal-Laval.*

VAP Turbine Cycles.—After the 1973 fuel price rise the new market conditions of very low growth rate in tanker fleets, higher fuel costs and lower speeds tended to favour the diesel engine. AP steam plants were no longer competitive and renewed efforts were made to advance the steam conditions in pursuit of a reduced fuel rate. In 1980 the VAP system (Very Advanced Propulsion) was introduced with turbine inlet conditions and fuel rate as shown in Table 1. The VAP plant is interesting and contains a number of advanced technological features. At the time of its introduction, however, the fuel economy advantage of the slow speed diesel was well established and no VAP plants went into commercial service.

TABLE 1.—V.A.P. INPUT CONDITIONS AND FUEL RATE

Output MW	Pressure (bar)	Temp °C	Fuel rate kg/MWh
10–13	81	600	245
13–16	101	600	240
16–23	126	600	237
23–33	141	600	232

The high pressures required the adoption of a reheat cycle and the temperature of 600°C required a major change in boiler technology: the adoption, as a final stage superheater and reheater, of a fluidised bed combustion unit. In conventional boiler designs, high temperature gas-side corrosion by sodium and vanadium compounds in the fuel limit the steam temperature to about 540°C. The characteristics of fluidised bed combustion however, are such that a steam temperature of 600°C can be achieved with a bed temperature of only 850°C. A conventional boiler would require a gas temperature in the region of 1500°C under similar circumstances whereupon the risk of high temperature corrosion is very much greater.

The main boiler is of conventional non-reheat marine radiant type, the technology of which is well established. Superheated steam is, therefore, produced at the relatively moderate temperature of 500°C. The steam temperature is then further increased to 600°C in the topping superheater side of the fluidised bed unit. On exit from the HP turbine, the steam is reheated (at 23% of the turbine inlet pressure) to 600°C in the reheater section of the fluidised bed unit.

Although the fluidised bed unit adds to the complexity of the cycle there is a considerable advantage in having a unit which is independent of the main boiler. Designers of integral reheat boilers have to solve the problem of reheater protection when running astern when there is no steam flow through the reheater, but superheated steam must be supplied to the astern turbine, Fig. 8. Under these circumstances it is imperative that flue gases be not admitted to the reheater side of the boiler. A separately fired reheater can simply be shut-down during manoeuvring.

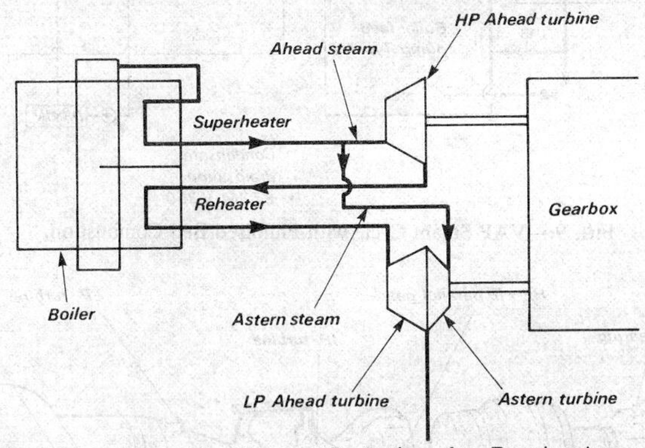

FIG. 8.—Requirement for Reheater Protection when Running Astern.

After the fluidised bed unit, the 5CR VAP cycle, with two LP heaters, one deaerator and two HP heaters as well as a rotary gas air heater, follows a similar pattern to the AP cycles, Fig. 9. From an economic point of view, six feed heaters would have been justified at the high pressures conceived but it was deemed preferable to have a fully symmetrical HP turbine entirely free of extraction points, and only one bleed point in the IP turbine. Separate turbine driven auxiliaries are used: the turbo alternator being a condensing turbine, and the feed pump turbine a back pressure type exhausting to the deaerator. Steam for both these turbines is extracted from between the main boiler and the FBC unit at a temperature of 500°C. Partial load characteristics are claimed to be superior to non-reheat plant.

VAP Machinery.—The layout of VAP machinery, Fig. 10 is fundamentally different to the previous AP series. The primary reduction gear casing supports the HP and IP turbines and the unit comprises an epicyclic gear for the LP turbine and parallel shaft gears for the HP and IP turbines. The primary reduction unit drives a double reduction planetary gear immediately forward of the thrust block. The LP and astern turbine is of conventional axial exhaust type taken from the AP series but the HP and IP turbine speeds are approximately double those of the AP series. Operating at 600°C required materials which are highly resistant to creep, and high temperature nickel based alloys are used for the casings, rotors and blades of the first stages.

MARINE BOILERS

(1) **Bi-drum Boilers.**—The Babcock M21 boiler is typical of this traditional design (Fig. 11) which offers the following range of output

Output tonnes/h	34 to 113
Superheater outlet pressure kg/cm^2	35 to 83
—outlet temperature °C	400 to 538

A wide choice of features is available to suit particular requirements and a total of eight combinations of options incorporating single or double superheater arrangements, conventional expanded tangent tubes or membrane tube panel construction and either roof or front mounted burners can be chosen.

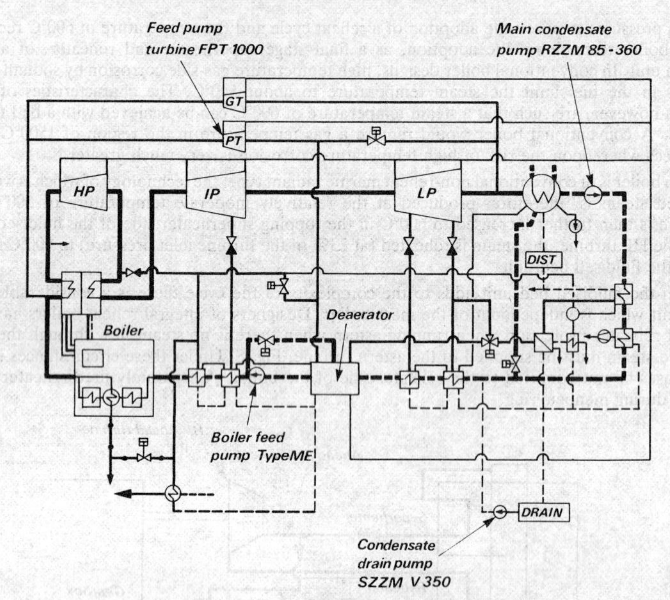

FIG. 9.—VAP Steam Cycle with Fluidised Bed Combustion.

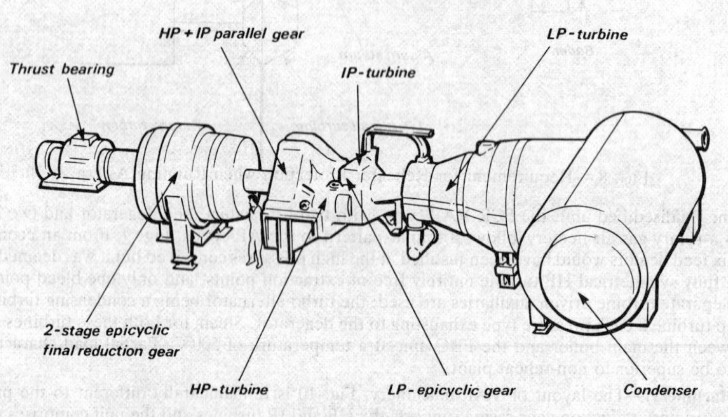

FIG. 10.—Layout of VAP Turbine Plant.

Membrane tube panel construction represents a relatively modern simplification in boiler design whereby the longitudinally finned water wall tubes are welded together to form fully water-cooled gas tight panels. These are used to form the enclosure and screen walls of the furnace and convection surface chamber and hence the use of refractory is eliminated. The furnace panels can be works prefabricated and a separate gas-tight steel casing is not required.

(2) **Marine Radiant Boilers.**—The Marine Radiant boiler, Fig. 12 is of membrane wall construction and consists of two connected parts: a fully water cooled furnace and a fully water cooled chamber containing the integral convection heating surfaces. These two parts are separated by a membrane screen wall which is gas-tight apart from an opening at its lower end through which the gases leave the furnace. The oil burners are mounted in the roof of the boiler, giving long flame travel to ensure that combustion is completed within the furnace. Combustion gases leaving the furnace pass through the open lower portion of the screen wall and turn in a cavity before flowing upwards over superheater and economiser surfaces. Superheating is done in primary and secondary stages and final steam temperature is controlled by interposing an attemperator, with

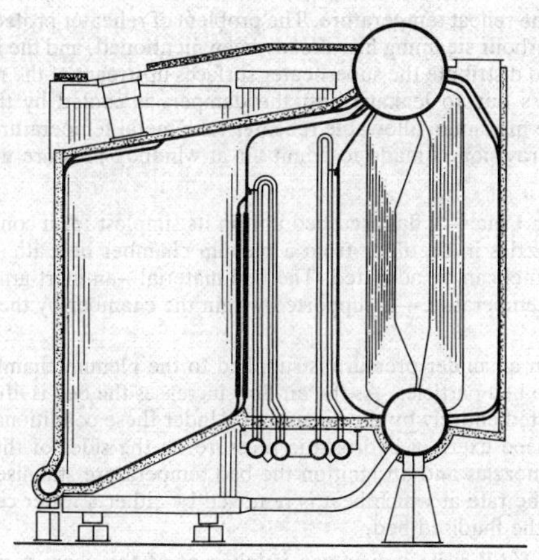

FIG. 11.—Babcock M21 Marine Type Boiler.

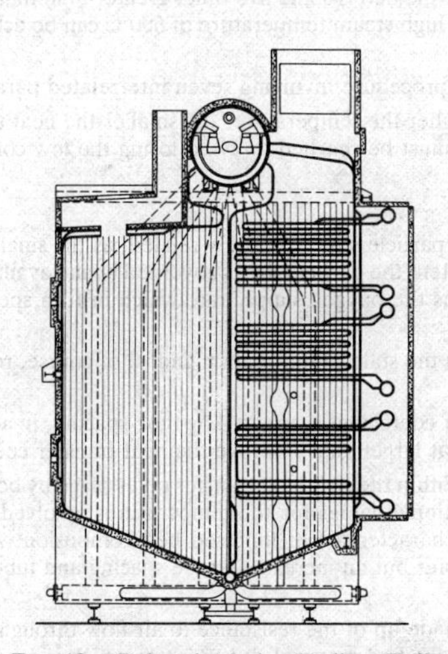

FIG. 12.—Babcock Marine Radiant Boiler.

by pass, between the first and second stages. The attemperator consists of a tubular heat exchanger located in the steam drum.

All boiler tubes are welded to drum and headers, and water cooled tubes bent round the burner openings eliminate the need for firebrick quarls.

The following range of output is available.—

Output tonnes/h	40–226
Superheater outlet pressure kg/cm^2	48–145
—outlet temperature °C	470–538

(3) **Marine Radiant Reheat Boiler.**—The marine radiant reheat boiler is a version of the radiant boiler for application to reheat cycles. In external appearance both types are very similar incorporating complete membrane wall construction and roof firing. In the reheat boiler however, the convection chamber is divided by a further membrane wall, into two parallel vertical gas paths each of which, in the direction of gas flow, contains a primary and secondary superheater followed by the reheater in one pass and the economisers in the other. The proportion of gas flowing through the two passes is regulated by dampers above the reheater and

economiser which control the reheat temperature. The problem of reheater protection in integral reheat boilers during manoeuvring and harbour steaming has already been mentioned, and the Babcock solution (in addition to the control dampers) is to distribute the superheater surfaces upstream of the reheater so that any flue gases admitted to the reheat pass due to leakage past the dampers is cooled by the superheater surfaces to a temperature well below the maximum allowable reheater tube metal temperature. As an added precaution to reduce leakage gas flow, provision is made to admit air at windbox pressure upstream of the closed reheat dampers.

Fluidised Bed Combusion Unit.—A fluidised bed unit in its simplest form consists of a chamber into which air is admitted through nozzles in the floor from a plenum chamber beneath. Amongst the air nozzles are nozzles through which oil fuel can be admitted. The bed material—an inert granular material which will not melt at the bed operating temperature—is supported within the chamber by the distribution plate containing the fuel and air nozzles.

In operation, combustion air under pressure is supplied to the plenum chamber and flows up through the air nozzles and between the bed particles. As the air flow increases the bed is lifted and alternatively becomes fully fluidised being supported entirely by the air stream. Under these conditions, the bed has the appearance of a boiling liquid and indeed exerts a hydrostatic pressure on the sides of the chamber. Fuel can now be admitted through the fuel nozzles and on ignition the bed temperature stabilises at a value dependent upon the rate of fuel input and the rate at which heat is removed by either a water cooled enclosure and/or steam cooled tubes immersed in the fluidised bed.

In its application to the VAP cycle, advantage is taken of of the characteristic that the convective heat transfer coefficient to the tubes in the bed is some five times greater than that obtained in a normal convection bank superheater, and hence the high steam temperature of 600°C can be achieved with a bed temperature of only 850°C.

Detailed design is an iterative procedure involving seven interrelated parameters

(1) Bed temperature.—The higher the temperature, the smaller the heat transfer surface area required for a given duty, but a compromise must be reached to avoid losing the low combustion temperature advantage of the unit.

(2) Bed particle size,

(3) Fluidising velocity and bed particle size are closely related, as the smaller the particle size the lower the fluidising velocity. To a certain extent the particle size is governed by the availability of a suitable inert material, and the fluidising velocity governs the oxygen supply rate which in turn specifies the fuel flow-rate and heat release per unit of bed area.

(4) Bed depth. This varies with the state of fluidisation and is, of course, related to the spacing and number of tubes in the bed.

(5) Tube spacing. Heat transfer coefficient is affected by tube spacing, in addition to the number of tubes in a given bed depth. It is found that larger gaps improve the heat transfer coefficient.

(6) Heat transfer coefficient. Within the unit heat transfer takes place by both convection and radiation. The radiative component has conventional values for the temperatures involved, but the much greater values of the convective component is a characteristic of fluidised bed combustion. An increase in particle diameter reduces the convective heat transfer but an increase in tube spacing and tube temperature both increase heat transfer.

(7) Bed draught loss. This is made up of the resistance to air flow through the distribution nozzles plus the air pressure necessary to support the bed material. It is a factor which is considered in relation to the disposal of the flue gases and the point at which these can be combined with the gas stream from the main boiler.

FUTURE DEVELOPMENTS

Coal Fired Marine Steam Plant.—In response to economic pressure a number of studies conducted in the late 70's and early 80's investigated the feasibility of returning to coal firing. On certain trade routes it was shown that coal could be advantageous, with an increasing margin in favour of the coal burner as the oil/price ratio increased.

There are three methods by which coal can be burned to provide propulsive power at sea:

(1) Spreader stoker.
(2) Pulverised fuel.
(3) Fluidised bed combustion.

(1) **Spreader Stoker.**—Fig. 13 shows the mode of operation of a spreader stoker and travelling grate in which the grate moves at between one and five metres per hour in the opposite direction to that in which the coal is being thrown from the overthrow rotor. Between 60% and 80% of the total ash is deposited in the grate dump hopper beneath the grate, with the remainder leaving the furnace with the flue gases as fly-ash. This is collected by a cyclone separator. It is likely that due to port restrictions facilities for ash storage must be provided to await disposal at sea.

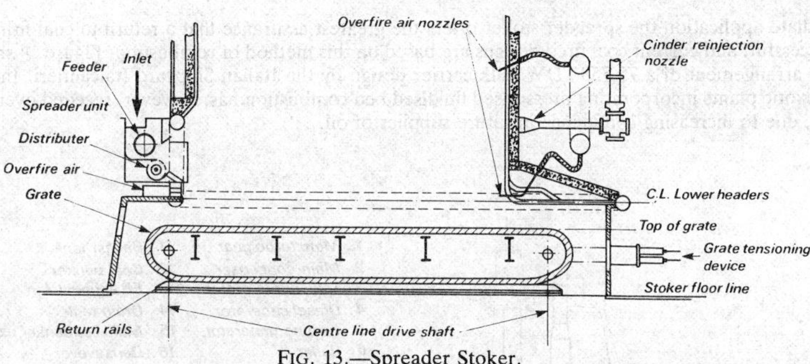

FIG. 13.—Spreader Stoker.

Combustion air, in direct proportion to the amount of coal being burned, is delivered beneath the upper portion of the grate and as overfire air above the coal bed. This latter creates turbulence to cut down unburned coal loss from the furnace. Residual carbon which does escape is collected after the superheaters and reinjected into the overfire air.

The forced draught fans are sized to overcome all the air side losses from the forced draught fan discharge through the stoker to the furnace. The furnace and flue gas side are kept at a pressure slightly below atmospheric by induced draught fans to eliminate the infiltration of soot and flyash into the engine room. This is referred to as a balanced draught system.

Boiler control is based on modulation of undergrate air which controls the heat release. Changes in coal fuel rates rapidly affect the heat release from the furnace as up to 50% of the coal burnt is injected as coal fines and burns in suspension. It is likely, however, that steam dumping would be required to accommodate very rapid load changes.

Excess air varies from about 25% at maximum output to 90% at 20% output and this, together with the requirement to limit gas side velocities to between 15 and 20 m/sec (compared to 30 m/sec in an oil fired boiler) leads to a furnace volume of about three times that of the equivalent oil fired boiler.

(2) **Pulverised Fuel.**—The general characteristics of this method of firing are similar to those of oil. The coal is crushed from 30 mm lumps to very fine particles, typically 70% through 75 micron BS sieve, and injected into the boiler where the particles burn in suspension.

Although pulverised fuel firing is the commonest means of solid fuel combusion ashore, for two reasons it is possibly the least likely method to be employed at sea. Firstly, the method is the least tolerant of variation in coal quality: a relatively unimportant point for land based plant whose fuel supply is on a long term contract from a constant source. A ship, however, must ideally be capable of accepting different qualities of fuel from several bunkering stations situated worldwide. The second reason concerns the question of safety, and the risk of spontaneous combustion of pulverised fuel. This problem can be ameliorated by pulverising the fuel immediately prior to combustion and thus eliminate the need for pulverising facilities ashore or the requirement to inert the pulverised fuel bunkers.

Pulverised fuel firing gives a similar rate of response to load changes as oil fuel, but turndown is iimited to about 5:1. Below 25% MCR, therefore, an alternative fuel such as oil would be needed.

(3) **Fluidised Bed Combustion.**—The principle of the coal fired fluidised bed unit is identical to that already described with reference to the VAP propulsion plant. Recently it has received considerable publicity by virtue of its ability to burn low quality fuels in a manner which permits economical control of nitrogen and sulphur emissions. Such emission restrictions are not yet applied to ships at sea but, more significantly, fluidised bed units can accept wide variations in fuel quality due to the lower combustion temperatures and rapid mixing of the fuel and air. In particular, in terms of total bed content, less than 1% is combustible and inert material in the fuel is no disadvantage: an 18%–20% ash content merely maintains the bed depth by offsetting losses by elutriation.

Looking further into the future, the fluidised bed unit can be applied in several forms which fall broadly into two groups:

(1) Atmospheric fluid beds, in which the pressure of 1,250 mm w.g. in the bed arises from normal system resistance over heating surfaces and through the bed and the unit merely acts as a combustor for steam generation. Prototype designs include bed containment walls of the fully water cooled membrane type with evaporative surfaces, superheater and reheater (if applicable) being immersed in the beds. Some heat exchange surfaces would be necessary in convection zones to cool the flue gases before the economiser.

(2) Pressurised fluid beds, operating at 6–8 bars, which may incorporate gas turbines or a combination of steam and gas turbines.

For immediate application the spreader stoker offers the greatest assurance that a return to coal firing at sea will be successful, and current coal fired designs are based on this method of combustion. Figure 14 shows the machinery arrangement of a 75,750 TDW bulk carrier design by the Italian Shipyard Italcantieri. Interest in the more exotic plants incorporating pressurised fluidised bed combustion has, however, receded over the last four years, due to increasing confidence in future supplies of oil.

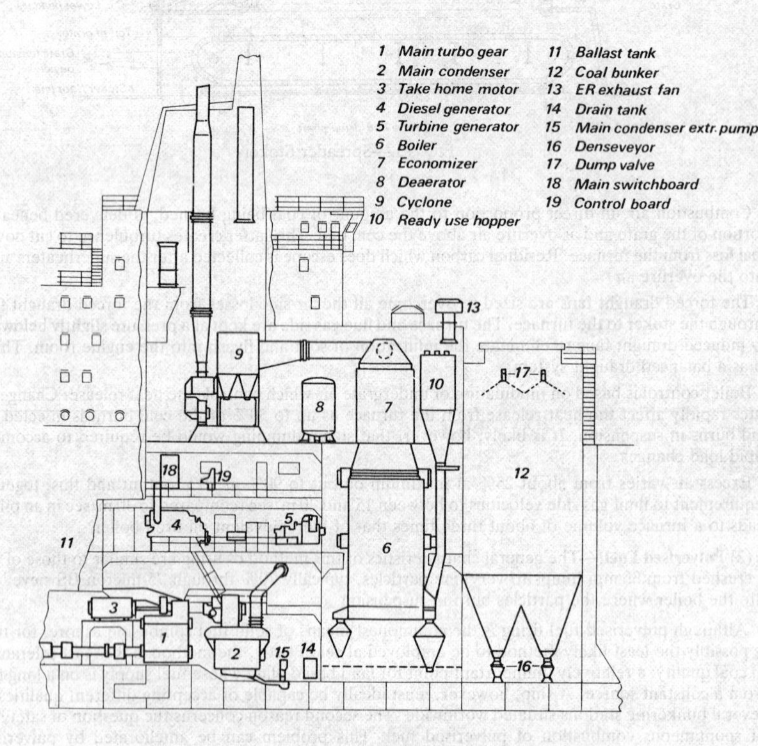

FIG. 14.—Machinery Arrangement for 75,750 TDW Bulk Carrier.

MARINE DIESEL ENGINES

Although diesel engines were installed in ships for propulsion purposes long before the Second World War, it is only in the period since that conflict that these engines have come into their own as ship's main machinery.

The major application has been in commercial ships rather than naval vessels. The diesel engine provides the efficiency in fuel consumption desirable for minimsation of operating costs with the consequent increase of competitive trading prospects. On the other hand, diesel engines have a relatively poor power to weight ratio, significant for naval vessels where reduction of weight and space requirements are important. Typical naval installations are described elsewhere in this chapter.

The main reason for the increase in the use of the diesel engine to the complete exclusion of the steam reciprocating engine and the relegation of the steam turbine to a few specialist applications is the ability of the larger engines to burn residual fuel of high viscosity and low price ie similar to that used in boiler furnaces. Since the specific fuel consumption of the diesel engine, and particularly of the slow speed directly coupled version, is superior to steam engines and gas turbines, this facility for burning heavy fuels gives the diesel a clear advantage.

Consideration of figures published in 'The Motor Ship', February 1986, entirely support this conclusion. The following tables are extracts from those figures.

TABLE 2.—MAIN PROPULSION PLANT INSTALLED IN SHIPS COMPLETED IN 1985 OF 2000 TONNES AND ABOVE.

Engine Type	No. of Ships Installed	No. of Engines	bhp	%
Diesel	878	980	8,292,736	98·38
Diesel-Electric	10	27	96,796	1·15
Steam Turbine	1	1	40,000	0·47
TOTALS	889	1,008	8,429,532	100·00

TABLE 3.—ANALYSIS OF LOW SPEED ENGINES INSTALLED IN 1985.

Engine Type	No. of Ships Installed	No. of Engines	bhp	%
MAN—B & W	342	345	3,791,440	55·42
Sulzer	194	195	2,379,129	34·78
Mitsibushi	108	108	626,380	9·17
Others	6	9	43,720	0·63
TOTALS	650	657	6,840,669	100·00

TABLE 4.—ANALYSIS OF MEDIUM AND HIGH SPEED ENGINES INSTALLED IN 1985 FOR MARINE PROPULSION PLANT.

Engine Type	No. of Ships Installed	No. of Engines	bhp	%
Pielstick	34	54	360,630	23·28
Wartsila	37	64	297,738	19·22
MaK	25	32	153,968	9·94
Sulzer	15	18	121,222	7·84
MAN—B & W	16	24	117,642	7·60
SWD	9	15	110,978	7·16
Hanshin	18	18	67,100	4·33
Deutz	27	18	65,856	4·26
Others (21)	57	97	253,729	16·37
TOTALS	238	350	1,548,863	100·00

ENGINE TYPES.—Diesel engines for marine use fall into three categories. These categories tend to be based on power and rpm considerations.

Slow speed diesel engines provide the highest power ranges available from any one engine, the largest versions being capable of over 3 MW per cylinder with up to twelve cylinders in-line giving in excess of 40 MW at Maximum Continuous Rating (MCR). At the time of writing, ship's sizes and speed, having reached a peak in the early seventies, have gradually been reduced to the point where the larger versions of this type of diesel engine are very rarely required and new ranges of very efficient engines of more moderate ratings have been designed and are being fitted. These are described in a later section. Because these engines are slow revving ie, between 60 and 200 rpm, they are used directly coupled to the propeller, with astern passage provided by reversing the direction of rotation of the engine.

Medium speed engines cover a wide range of speed and power with 400 rpm to 800 rpm depending on design and power requirements. Increasing use is being made of this type of diesel engine for main propulsion purposes. Since all engines in this category rotate at too high a speed for direct connection to the propeller and in the majority of designs are also uni-directional, rpm must be reduced by gearing and a controllable pitch propeller is used for manouevring.

Faster running engines are used for the propulsion of smaller craft and for providing electrical power generation in larger diesel engine propelled vessels. This category provides a very wide range of choice in the low to medium power ranges, a relatively large number of designs being available, both in the in-line and V form.

SLOW SPEED ENGINES.—Many different types of slow speed diesel engines have been designed and developed over the years since their first inception as a propulsive device for ships. These have ranged from four-stroke normally aspirated engines through double-acting versions and opposed piston engines to the present day very efficient single-acting, two-stroke, turbocharged multi-cylinder engines.

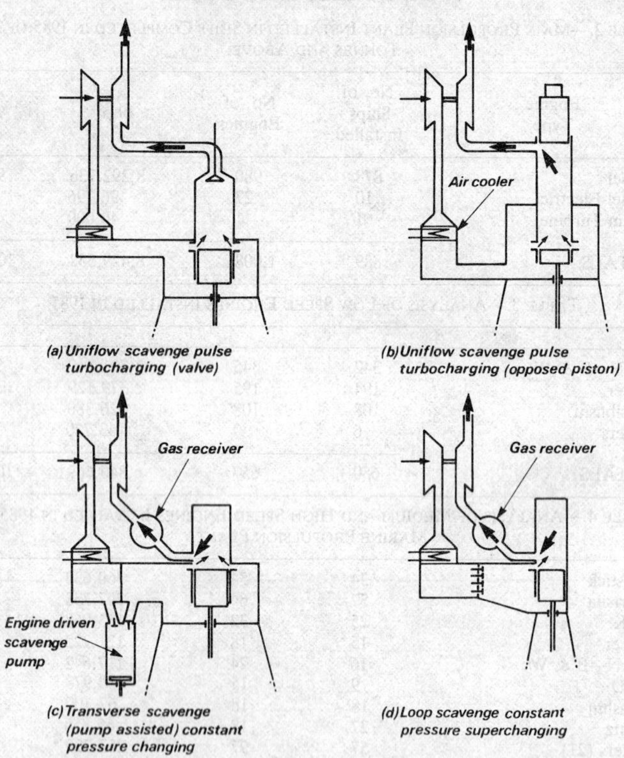

FIG. 15.—Scavenging and Supercharging of 2-Stroke Marine Diesel Engines.

The process of scavenging ie, cleansing the cylinders of the products of combustion and recharging those cylinders with a fresh charge of air, is done by either uniflow, cross or loop scavenging. This is illustrated diagrammatically in Fig. 15. Other combinations are possible.

Table 5 gives leading particulars of some of the more popular types of these high powered diesel engines. All are of the crosshead type, turbocharged and capable of burning fuel of viscosity up to 3500 secs. Redwood No. 1 at 100°F, ie 400 cSt at 50°C.

TABLE 5. DETAILS OF SOME HIGH POWERED SLOW SPEED 2-STROKE DIESEL ENGINES

Engine Make and Type	Bore mm	Stroke mm	rpm	bph/cyl (metric)	Type of scavenging
MAN-B & W					
K90MC	900	2,588	90–67	5,360–3,216	uniflow
L90MC	900	2,916	78–59	5,310–3,190	uniflow
S80MC	800	3,056	77–58	4,560–2,780	uniflow
SULZER					
RTA84M	840	2,900	78–56	4,700–2,580	uniflow
RTA84	840	2,400	90–65	4,500–2,480	uniflow
RTA76	760	2,200	98–71	3,680–2,020	uniflow

MAN-B & W Engines.—Like other leading designers, MAN-B & W have responded to the challenge of higher oil prices by progressively reducing the specific fuel consumption of their engines. A cross-sectional view of one of the latest designs, the long-stroke K-MC engines, is shown in Fig. 16.

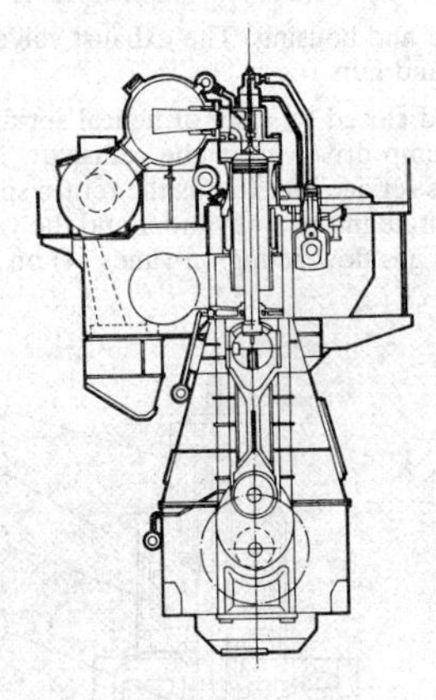

FIG. 16.—Cross Section of MAN-B & W K80 MC 2-Stroke Diesel Engine.

GENERAL CONSTRUCTION.—The bedplate is fabricated in one piece and is extremely rigid with overall dimensions being kept to a minimum. It is assembled using longitudinal side girders and welded cross girders with cast steel bearing supports.

The bedplate is designed for long, elastic holding-down bolts, arranged in a single row and tightened hydraulically. Because these bolts are placed inside the longitudinal girders the overall engine width is reduced leading to simpler installation. Epoxy chocking can be used if desired.

The frame box is a single welded fabrication leading to increased engine rigidity. It is fitted with relief valves and hinged doors in way of each cylinder. These doors give good access to crankcase components.

Braced staybolts, hydraulically tightened, connect the bedplate, frame box and cast iron cylinder frames to form a rigid unit.

The scavenge box is large enough to ensure uniform admission of air into the cylinder. All walls of the scavenge box are water cooled, including the double structure between scavenge box and crankcase top.

Crankshaft.—The crankshaft of the MC is of the welded type leading to a saving in weight. Alternatively, the more traditional semi-built type can be supplied using forged steel crank throws with cold rolled fillets.

The thrust shaft forms an integral part of the crankshaft. By fitting the sprocket rim for the camshaft chain drive onto the outer circumference of the thrust collar the thrust bearing and chain drive are combined reducing the overall engine length.

The main bearings are traditional using steel shells lined with white metal.

Running Gear.—Long stroke engines inevitably increase the overall engine height. In order to compensate for this a relatively short connecting rod with few principal parts has been adopted. The large area of the lower crosshead bearing unit allows the use of white metal in this heavily loaded area. Floating guide shoes facilitate alignment. The crankpin bearings are thin shells again lined with white metal.

Oil cooling is used for the pistons which consist of a chrome molybdenum steel crown rigidly bolted to the piston rod. Piston rods are surface treated to minimise friction at the piston rod glands and assist in providing an efficient seal at the crankcase top.

Cylinder Liners and Covers.—The liners are symmetrical and of a simple well-proven design, cooled by water. Temperature control of liner surfaces safeguards against cold corrosion and ensures stable lubrication conditions by also avoiding excessively high temperatures. The cylinder liner and piston rings are lubricated by timed cylinder lubricating oil injection.

The cylinder covers are one piece steel forgings with bored passages for cooling water. A central bore is provided for the exhaust valve with bores suitably placed to house fuel valves, cylinder relief valve, starting air valve and indicator cock. The covers are attached to the cylinder frame by hydraulically tightened studs.

Camshaft Drive.—The camshaft is driven by two single chains from the crankshaft providing engine operation even should a break in one of the chains occur. Use of chain drive allows the camshaft to be positioned high on the engine giving shorter hydraulic connections to fuel injectors and exhaust valves thus minimising timing errors.

Exhaust Valve.—An important component in any diesel engine but of central importance in a uniflow scavenged engine. The water cooled, cast iron housing contains a rotating valve spindle made of heat resistant steel with Stellite seatings to both valve and housing. The exhaust valve assembly is fastened to the cylinder cover by hydraulically tightened studs and nuts.

The valve is opened hydraulically and closed by a set of helical springs. The hydraulic system is operated via a high pressure pipe by a piston pump driven from the camshaft. Latest designs (Fig.17) incorporate a pneumatic rotating valve which prolongs service life. In this the return springs are replaced by a piston (1) and air cylinder (2). The piston can freely rotate in the air cylinder and the valve spindle (3) rotates relative to the valve seat. Rotation is produced by the gas flow acting on vanes (4) on the flame guard (5).

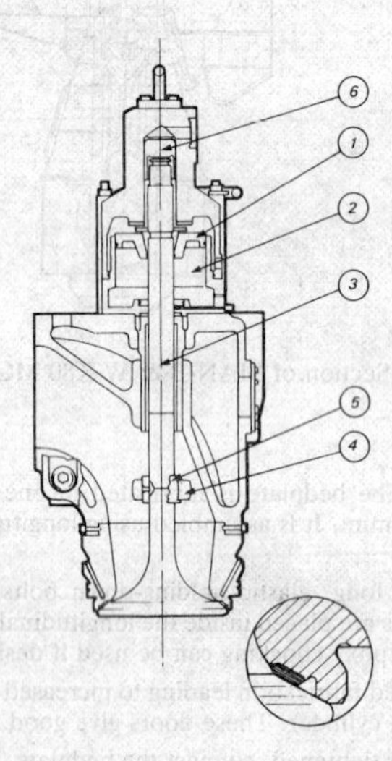

FIG. 17.—Detail of Exhaust Valve Seat for MC Engine.

Opening of the valve is by the hydraulically operated piston (6). When the valve is opened, air under the piston is compressed and this compression pressure then closes the valve at the appropriate time, as dictated by the exhaust cam. The air system is precharged to about 5 bar prior to engine start-up.

Fuel System.—The fuel system on the engine is closed and pressurised to avoid the possibilities of boil-off with open stand pipe systems and cavitation on the suction side of the supply pump.

The fuel injection valves are uncooled lightweight valves the temperature being controlled by constantly circulating fuel. The injectors are opened by fuel oil pressure and closed by a spring when the fuel pump spills. The stellite nozzles give long service life despite the low quality of present-day marine fuels.

The fuel pump has a nodular cast iron housing with a central pump cylinder of steel. The actual pump sleeve and plunger are of nitrided steel. The pumps incorporate variable injection timing for optimising fuel economy at part load.

Most engine types, other than the two smallest engines (L35MC & L42MC) use the governer output shaft position as the controlling parameter for VIT. The start of fuel injection is controlled by alteration of the pump barrel position, this being actuated by a toothed rack. Individual adjustments can be made on each cylinder. A collective adjustment of the maximum pressure level of the engine can also be carried out to correct for varying fuel quality, wear etc. Both of these types of adjustment can be carried out while the engine is running. See Fig. 18.

Reversing is achieved using a mechanism which incorporates an angularly displaceable roller in the fuel pump drive to each cylinder. The link connecting the roller guide and the roller is self-locking in the "ahead and astern" positions without the aid of external forces. The link is actuated by compressed air. Fig. 19.

Exhaust System & Turbocharger.—Air intake to the turbocharger is direct from the engine room through the intake silencer. Air delivered from the turbocharger is led via an air cooler to the scavenge ports in the lower portion of the cylinder liner. Up to three turbochargers may be fitted depending on the size of the engine and the number of cylinders.

After the turbocharger the exhaust gas may then be led to an exhaust gas economiser for low pressure steam generation used for auxiliary power generation or heating requirements. Alternatively options are available to utilise part of the exhaust gas energy in Turbo Compound. System (TCS) where a gas turbine, driven by an

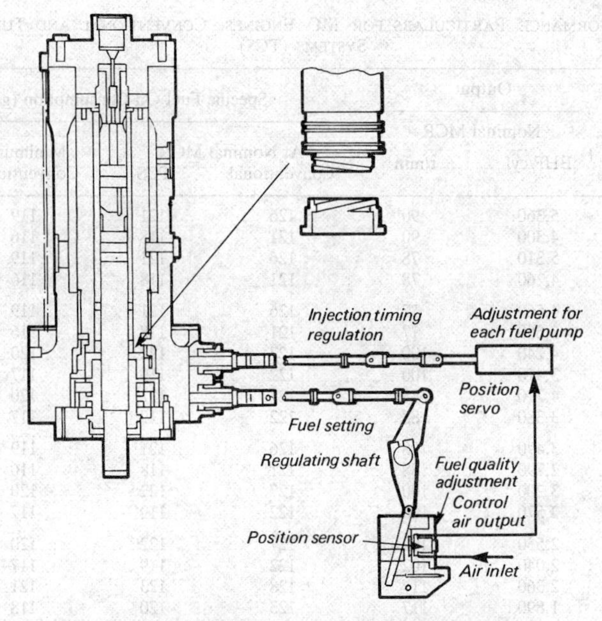

FIG. 18.—L-MC VIT System and Fuel Pump Cross Section.

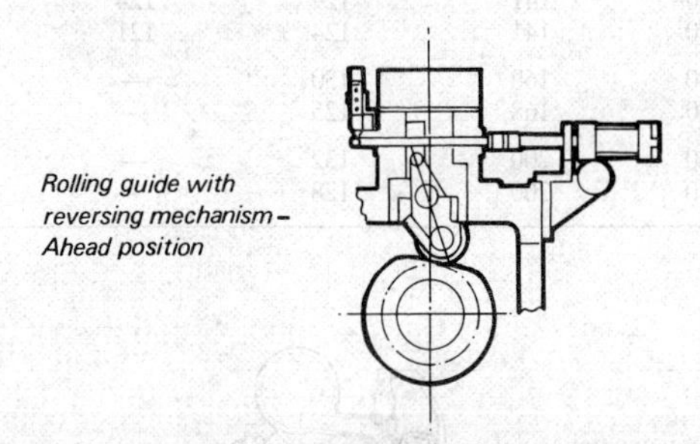

FIG. 19.—Reversing Mechanism for MC Engines Showing the Roller Guide with Reversing Mechanism in the Ahead Position.

exhaust gas by-pass can input power back to the main shaft through mechanical gearing, or be used to provide electrical auxiliary energy directly.

The full MAN—B & W engine programme is shown in Table 6. Specific fuel consumption figures are based on ISO ambient reference conditions with a fuel having a lower calorific value of 10,200 kcal/kg (42,707 kJ/kg).

SULZER Engine.—Another leading slow speed diesel engine manufacturer for the marine market, Sulzer Brothers Ltd. of Winterthur, Switzerland offer a range of this type of engine built by themselves and many licencees throughout the world. The relatively new RTA series, offering great fuel economy will be described.

RTA SERIES—GENERAL CONSTRUCTION.—The rigid box-like bedplate consists of thick single wall fabricated longitudinal girders and welded-in rigid cross-members. The thick walled centre pieces of these cross-members are of cast or forged steel and carry the main bearings as well as providing anchor points for the rods. The tie rods which effectively "clamp" the cylinder blocks, engine columns and bedplate together transmit the inertia and combustion loads thus relieving the welded columns.

TABLE 6.—PERFORMANCE PARTICULARS FOR MC ENGINES; CONVENTIONAL AND TURBO-COMPOUND SYSTEMS (TCS)

Engine Type	Output Nominal MCR BHP/cyl	r/min	Specific Fuel Oil Consumption (g/BHPh) At Nominal MCR Conventional	TCS	Minimum at Part Load Conventional	TCS
K90MC	5,360	90	126	121	119	117
K90MCE	4,300	90	121	118	116	114
L90MC	5,310	78	126	121	119	117
L90MCE	4,260	78	121	118	116	114
S80MC	4,560	77	126	121	119	117
S80MCE	3,650	77	121	118	116	114
K80MC	4,240	100	127	122	120	118
K80MCE	3,410	100	122	119	117	115
L80MC	4,210	88	127	122	120	118
L80MCE	3,380	88	122	119	117	115
S70MC	3,490	88	126	121	119	117
S70MCE	2,790	88	121	118	116	114
L70MC	3,200	100	127	122	120	118
L70MCE	2,570	100	122	119	117	115
S60MC	2,550	102	127	122	120	118
S60MCE	2,040	102	122	119	117	115
L60MC	2,360	117	128	123	121	119
L60MCE	1,890	117	123	120	118	116
S50MC	1,780	123	128	123	121	119
S50MCE	1,420	123	123	120	118	116
L50MC	1,650	141	129	124	122	120
L50MCE	1,320	141	124	121	119	117
L42MC	1,160	168	130	—	123	—
L42MCE	930	168	125	—	120	—
L35MC	760	200	132	—	127	—
L35MCE	610	200	128	—	125	—

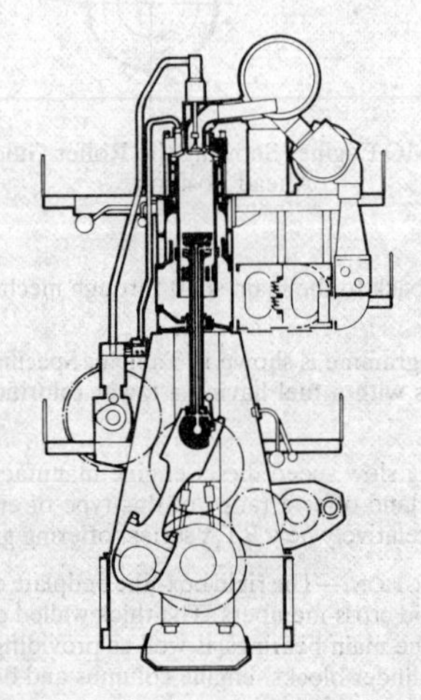

FIG. 20.—Cross Section of the RTA 84M Engine.

Figure 20 shows the general arrangement of the RTA84M engine. The main bearings, steel shells lined with white metal are held in position by two jack bolts, hydraulically tightened against the underside of the columns.

The welded engine columns are assembled with stiffening side plates for longer-bore models or as part of a fabricated monobloc frame in the smaller and medium bore engines. Access to the totally enclosed crankcase is by large doors on either side of the engine. The crankcase is provided with explosion relief valves as required by the Classification Societies.

CYLINDER.—The jackets, of fine lamellar cast iron, form either a multi-cylinder monobloc unit for smaller sizes or are bolted together individually to form a rigid cylinder block. The cylinder block is completely dry simplifying its design with cooling water restricted to the individual cylinder jackets mounted on top of the block.

The cast iron cylinder liners themselves are bore-cooled and have load dependent cylinder lubrication. The bore cooled cylinder covers are machined from solid forgings or castings and carry the exhaust valve cages, fuel injectors, starting air valves, etc.

CRANKSHAFT AND RUNNING GEAR.—The crankshaft is semi-built of normalised steel. For larger engines with more than 6 cylinders the crankshaft is made in two parts with the thrust shaft bolted on.

Gear drive for the camshaft is housed in a double column and offers an elegant connection for an optional power take off drive and for the efficiency boosting power turbine, if fitted.

The camshaft is assembled from a number of sections connected by sleeve couplings. Individual camshaft lengths serve each combined fuel pump unit. Reversing engine timing is accomplished by a rotational hydraulic servomotor for each fuel cam with positive locking in ahead and astern positions. Exhaust valve timing is symmetric and needs no special reversing arrangements.

Connecting rods and bottom end bearing bodies are of forged normalised steel with white metal lining. A short connecting rod is used to reduce overall engine height, its top end being forged integral with the crosshead bearing.

The crosshead is of forged steel directly connected to the piston rod by a flange. Cast steel, white metal lined guide slippers are fitted either side of the crosshead, these slippers running in cast iron double faced guides fitted to the engine columns. The single full width crosshead pin bearing of large surface area is supplied with high pressure lubrication through a swinging link mechanism (See Figure 22). The piston assembly consists of an oil cooled cast steel piston crown and short cast iron piston skirt attached to a forged steel piston rod. The cooling oil is supplied to the crosshead via swinging links (Fig. 22) and thence to the piston through a drilled passage in the rod. The incoming oil is directed as jets into the blind cooling bores of the crown to give positive circulation in the most heated zones. (See Fig. 21).

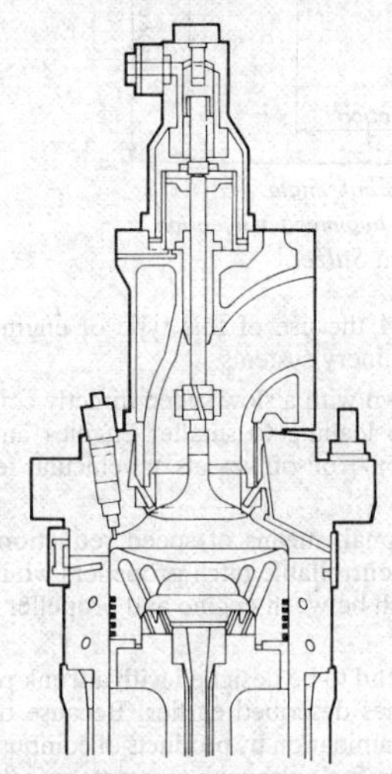

FIG. 21.—Cross Section of the RTA 62 Combustion Space Showing the Fully Bore-cooled Elements of Piston Crown, Cylinder Liner, Cylinder Cover, and Exhaust Valve Seat Ring. (The single Nimonic exhaust valve is hydraulically actuated, has an air spring and is rotated by a vane impeller.

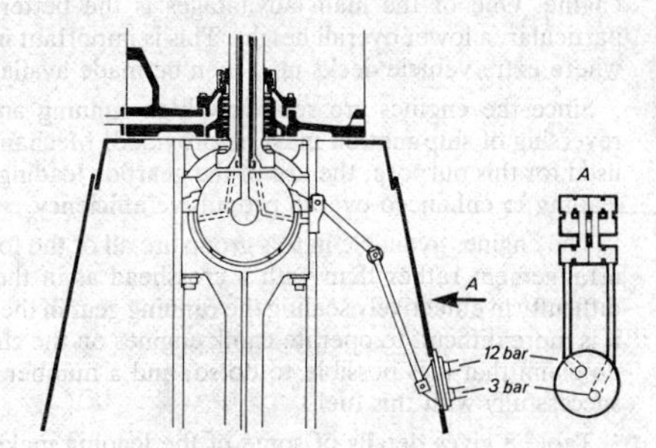

FIG. 22.—Piston Cooling Oil and Crosshead Lubricating Oil are Delivered via Swinging Links; Sulzer RTA.

EXHAUST SYSTEM AND TURBOCHARGERS. These engines use the uniflow system of scavenging and gas exchange. This is achieved by using a single Nimonic exhaust valve mounted in a separate cage with bore-cooled valve seat (See Fig. 21). Valve rotation is ensured simply by vanes on the valve stem. Valve opening is hydraulically actuated from the camshaft and it is closed by a pneumatic spring.

High efficiency uncooled turbochargers working on the constant pressure system are assisted at low-load conditions by auxiliary blowers.

FUEL INJECTION.—The RTA engine uses highly accurate double valve-controlled fuel pumps with provision for variable injection timing (VIT). This gives a high level of flexibility for load-dependent and fuel dependent injection timing. One advantage of VIT is the ability to control the permissible maximum combustion pressure. This enables fuel consumption to be lowered—particularly at part load. The combustion pressure at part load is lifted to its nominal full load value by advancing the timing of the fuel injection. Variations in fuel quality can also be allowed for. Burning heavy fuel can lead to a drop in maximum combustion pressure and hence a rise in specific fuel consumption. By adjusting the fuel quality setting, the nominal combustion pressure curve can be re-achieved. Figures 23 and 24 illustrate diagrammatically how this is achieved and the consequent savings to be made.

The RTA range of two-stroke engines for marine propulsion is given in Table 7. Performance curves for an RTA62 are given in Fig. 25.

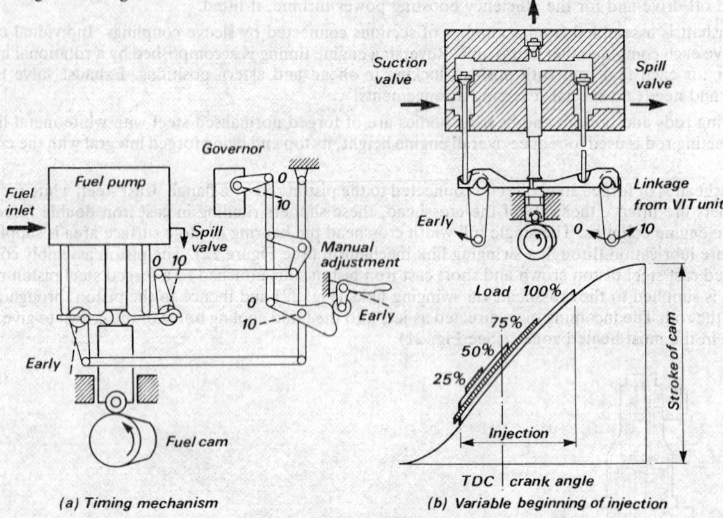

FIG. 23.—Variable Injection Timing (VIT) Mechanism *Sulzer*.

MEDIUM SPEED ENGINES.—As can be seen from Tables 2 and 4 the use of this type of engine for propulsion purposes forms a significant proportion of modern ship machinery systems.

A number of advantages can be seen when a direct comparison is drawn with a slow speed directly coupled engine. One of the main advantages is the better power/weight ratio leading to smaller engines and, in particular, a lower overall height. This is important in ships such as Roll-on/Roll-off vessels or vehicular ferries where extra vehicle decks may then be made available.

Since the engines are relatively high running and usually unidirectional, means of speed reduction and reversing of ship motion must be provided. Mechanical gearboxes and controllable pitch propellers would be used for this purpose, the use of the gearbox leading to a very good match between engine and propeller rpm, leading to enhanced overall propulsive efficiency.

The engines available in this group are all of the four-stroke type and tend to be designed with a trunk piston arrangement rather than with a crosshead as in the slower speed engines described earlier. Because of the difficulty in effiectively sealing the running gear in the crankcase from contamination by products of combustion, it is more difficult to operate trunk engines on the cheaper residual quality fuels although many manufacturers do claim that it is possible to do so, and a number of the larger versions of some designs have worked very successfully with this fuel.

Table 8 gives details of some of the leading makes of medium speed diesels for ship propulsion. Many of these engines have industrial applications and the smaller versions—bordering on the high speed range—can be found being used as generator drives, particularly on ships which require large auxiliary powers eg, refrigerated ships etc.

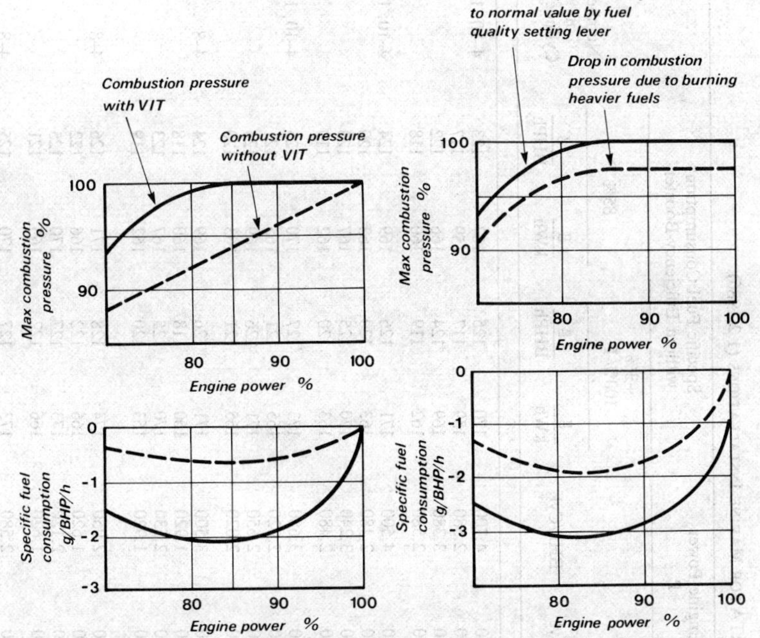

FIG. 24.—Effects of Variable Injection on Fuel Consumption and Maximum Combustion Pressure.

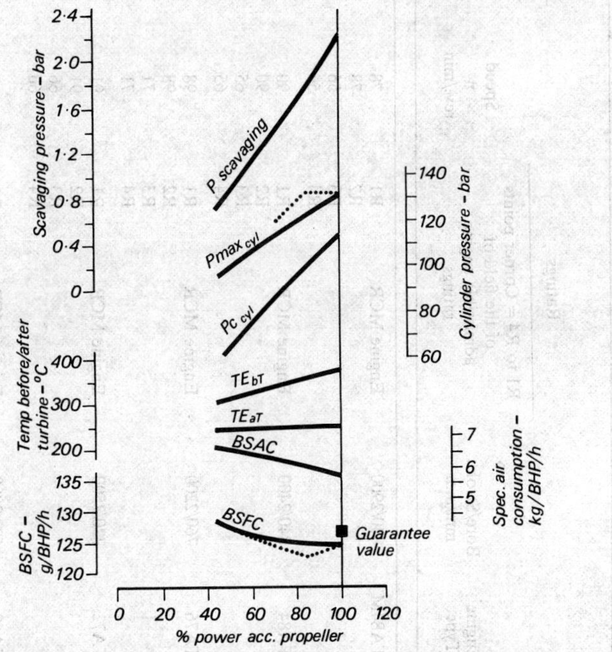

FIG. 25.—Test Results from the First SULZER RTA 62. (The effect of VIT is shown by dotted lines).

TABLE 7.—TWO STROKE DIESEL ENGINES TYPE RTA FOR MARINE INSTALLATIONS (1.2.1986)

Engine Type	Bore/Stroke mm/mm	Ratings: R1 to R4 = Corner points of the field of admissible engine ratings		Speed n rev./min	Engine Power P kW/Cyl.	Engine Power P BHP/Cyl.	Specific Fuel Consumption* without Efficiency-Booster: +3% 100% P g/kWh	+3% 100% P g/BHPh	85% P g/kWh	85% P g/BHPh	Number of Cylinders
RTA84M	840/2900	Engine MCR	R1	78	3,460	4,700	170	125	167	123	4–10, 12
			R2	78	1,900	2,580	159	117	159	117	
			R3	56	2,490	3,380	169	124	166	122	
			R4	56	1,900	2,580	162	119	160	118	
RTA84	840/2400	Engine MCR	R1	90	3,310	4,500	171	126	169	124	4–10, 12
			R2	90	1,820	2,480	163	120	163	120	
			R3	65	2,380	3,240	170	125	167	123	
			R4	65	1,820	2,480	163	120	162	119	
RTA76	760/2200	Engine MCR	R1	98	2,710	3,680	173	127	170	125	4–10, 12
			R2	98	1,490	2,020	165	121	165	121	
			R3	71	1,950	2,650	171	126	169	124	
			R4	71	1,490	2,020	165	121	163	120	
RTA72	720/2500	Engine MCR	R1	91	2,570	3,500	171	126	169	124	4–8
			R2	91	1,410	1,920	160	118	160	118	
			R3	66	1,860	2,530	170	125	167	123	
			R4	66	1,410	1,920	163	120	162	119	
RTA68	680/2000	Engine MCR	R1	108	2,170	2,950	174	128	171	126	4–8
			R2	108	1,190	1,620	166	122	166	122	
			R3	78	1,560	2,120	173	127	170	125	
			R4	78	1,190	1,620	166	122	165	121	
RTA62	620/2150	Engine MCR	R1	106	1,900	2,580	173	127	170	125	4–8
			R2	106	1,050	1,430	162	119	162	119	
			R3	76	1,360	1,850	171	126	169	124	
			R4	76	1,050	1,430	165	121	163	120	

RTA58	580/1700	Engine MCR	R1	127	1,590	2,160	175	129	173	127	4–9
			R2	127	870	1,180	167	123	167	123	
			R3	92	1,140	1,550	174	128	171	126	
			R4	92	870	1,180	167	123	166	122	
RTA52	520/1800	Engine MCR	R1	126	1,330	1,810	174	128	171	126	4–8
			R2	126	740	1,000	163	120	163	120	
			R3	91	960	1,300	173	127	170	125	
			R4	91	740	1,000	166	122	165	121	
RTA48	480/1400	Engine MCR	R1	154	1,090	1,480	178	131	175	129	4–9
			R2	154	600	810	170	125	170	125	
			R3	111	780	1,060	177	130	174	128	
			R4	111	600	810	170	125	169	124	
RTA38	380/1100	Engine MCR	R1	196	680	930	181	133	178	131	4–9
			R2	196	370	500	173	127	173	127	
			R3	141	490	660	179	132	177	130	
			R4	141	370	500	173	127	171	126	

* Specific fuel consumptions are for ISO Standard Reference Conditions and fuel with net calorific value of 10,200 kcal/kg.

TABLE 8.—TYPICAL ENGINE DETAILS OF SOME MEDIUM SPEED MARINE DIESEL ENGINES.

Engine Builder	Bore mm	Stroke mm	rpm	bhp/cyl metric
MAN-B & W	400	450	600	748
Pielstick	570	620	400	1,650
Sulzer	400	480	600	900
SWD	620	660	428	1,830
APE Allen	325	370	750	355

S.E.M.T. Pielstick.—This design is made under licence by a number of builders worldwide as well as by the parent company in France. A range of PC engines covers a wide spectrum of powers at different rpm. Table 9 illustrates this range

TABLE 9.—S.E.M.T. PIELSTICK MEDIUM SPEED ENGINE RANGE.

Engine Type	Bore mm	Stroke mm	Speed rpm	Power/cyl BHP/cyl	bmep bar	Specific fuel consump gm/BHph
PC 2–5	400	400	520	650	19·1	147
PC 2–6	400	400	520	747	22	135
PC 3	480	520	470	950	18·9	150
PC 4	570	620	400	1,500	21·3	142
PC 4–2	570	620	400	1,650	23·4	139

GENERAL ENGINE DETAILS.—As an example of the Pielstick PC range the successful PC 4 will be described. As can be seen from Table 11 above, recent developments have uprated this engine type (ie to the PC 4–2 version). Fundamental structural details remain much the same in the two types with the PC 4–2 being more compact and having higher power/weight ratio. The PC 4 is supplied in both in-line and V versions. In-line engines have 6, 7, 8 or 9 cylinders whilst the V at 45° engines have 10, 12, 14, 16 or 18 cylinders. Clearly the larger powered engines providing as they do up to 27,000 bhp overlap considerably with the slow speed versions described earlier. For example, it is possible to provide a 40 MW marine propulsion unit using two medium speed engines.

The engines are designed to burn heavy fuel with viscosities up to 420 cST at 50°C (4,000 secs Redwood No. 1 at 100°F) and with a vanadium content of up to 400 ppm.

The crankcase is of one piece welded construction with the crankshaft underslung in bearings secured by hydraulically tightened vertical and horizontal bolts. The crankshaft itself is forged in one piece from Chromium-molybdenum steel. The camshafts are driven through flexible couplings from the crankshaft.

Cast iron water jackets isolate the crankcase from the cylinder cooling water, the cylinder liners being bore cooled. The pistons are of the composite type with a light alloy skirt and a steel crown. Operating temperatures are of the order of 300°C on the piston crown and 160°C in the top ring groove.

As the engines are of the four-stroke type, both inlet and exhaust valves are contained in the cylinder head. The head itself contains one centrally mounted fuel injector, two exhaust valves, two inlet valves, a starting air valve and a cylinder relief valve. The exhaust valve seats are water-cooled.

High performance turbochargers deliver air through water cooled heat exchangers or air-to-air radiators to the inlet manifold. Figure 26 shows a cross section of the PC4-2 V engine.

APE-Allen.—A wide range of four-stroke engines are made by this organisation for industrial, marine auxiliary and marine propulsion use. The larger powers are outlined in Table 10.

TABLE 10.—SOME OF THE LARGER ENGINES FROM THE APE-ALLEN RANGE.

Engine Type	rpm	No. of cylinders	bhp	BMEP bar (full load)
S37-G	720/750	6	2,534/2,640	17·2
S37-G	720/750	8	3,379/3,520	17·2
S37-G	720/750	9	3,802/3,960	17·2
VS37-G	720/750	12	5,069/5,280	17·2
VS37-G	720/750	16	6,578/7,040	17·2

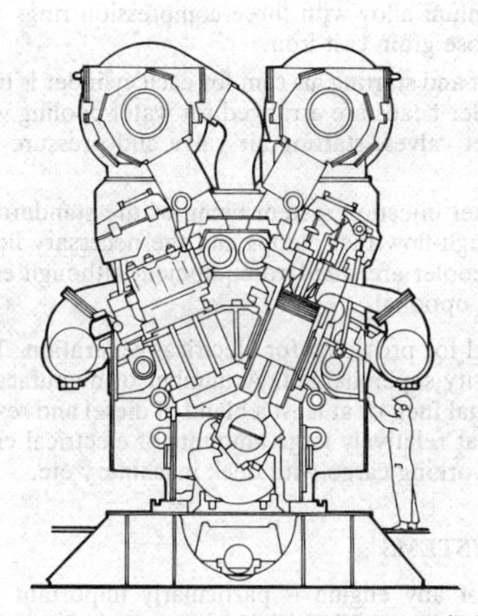

FIG. 26.—Cross Section of SEMT Pielstick (PC4-2V) Medium Speed Diesel Engine.

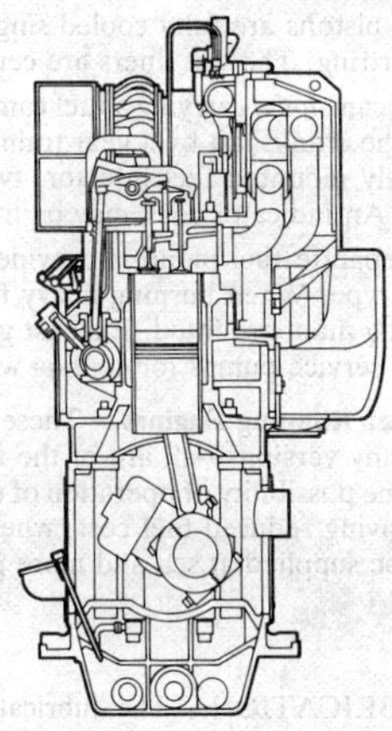

FIG. 27.—Cross Section of APE-Allen Type (S37-G) Medium Speed in-line Diesel Engine.

An in-line S37-G engine will be described. As can be seen from Table 10 these engines are available with 6, 8 or 9 cylinders in-line. It is pressure charged and intercooled with bore and stroke of 325 mm and 370 mm, respectively.

The main structure of the engine consists of a deep sided cast iron bedplate with integral sump attached to the cast iron cylinder block by long through bolts which are hydraulically tensioned. The main bearings are of the thin walled steel backed type lined with aluminium tin and overlay plated. Each main bearing cap is also secured by hydraulically tensioned bolts. See Fig. 27 and Fig. 28.

The cylinder block, camshaft housing and air manifold form an integral casting. The crankshaft is a one piece forging of medium carbon steel. Oil from each main bearing is fed through drillings to the connecting rod bearings. The connecting rods are of two piece construction in alloy steel. The big end is diagonally split to enable the rod to be withdrawn through the cylinder liner, the bearing itself being a thin wall shell lined with aluminium tin and overlay plated. The 'H' sectioned rod is drilled to provide lubrication to the renewable small end bush and case-hardened fully floating gudgeon pin.

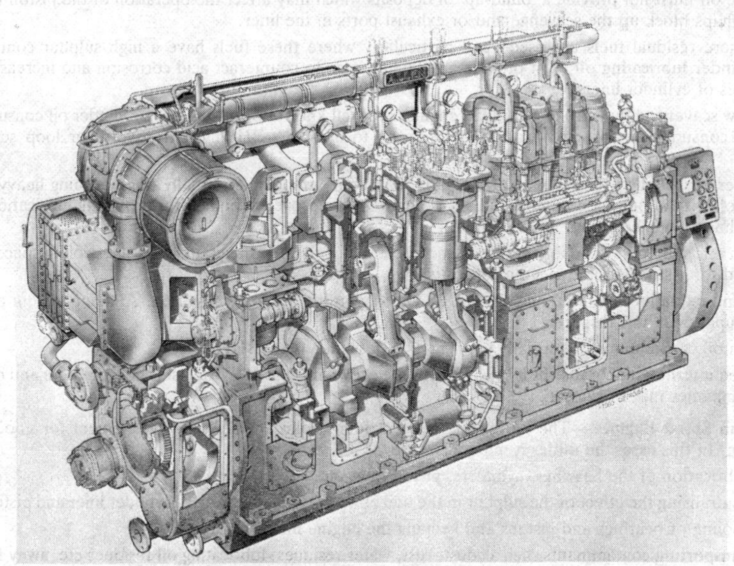

FIG. 28.—APE-Allen S37-G Medium Speed Diesel Engine.

The pistons are fully cooled single piece made from aluminium alloy with three compression rings and a scraper ring. The wet liners are centrifugally cast in special close grain cast-iron.

The camshaft, carrying a fuel cam, an inlet cam, exhaust cam and starting air cam for each cylinder is driven from the crankshaft by a gear train. Individual cast-iron cylinder heads are arranged for water cooling with a centrally mounted fuel injector, two exhaust valves, two inlet valves, starting air valve and pressure relief valve. An indicator cock may be fitted if required.

A separate fuel pump is provided for each cylinder, the fuel injection system being of the standard jerk pump type. When burning heavy fuel, cooled injectors, through-flow fuel pumps and the necessary heaters and ring main are fitted. Exhaust gas turbo-charger and intercooler are standard equipment although engine driven service pumps for cooling water and lubricating oil are optional.

Faster Running Engines.—These engines are used in general for providing for electrical generation. These are many versions—all are of the four-stroke type, the majority supercharged. A number of manufacturers offer the possibility of operation of even these engines on residual fuel, or at least a blend of diesel and residual fuel, giving reduced fuel costs where circumstances dictate that relatively large amounts of electrical energy must be supplied at sea and more particularly in port whilst working cargo with deck machinery etc.

ENGINE SUPPORT SYSTEMS

LUBRICATION.—The lubrication of the running gear of any engine is particularly important when considering mechanical efficiency. In addition, the problems associated with the lubrication of piston rings and cylinder liners must also be overcome. It is easier to deal with the slow speed two-stroke crosshead engines initially. The medium speed four-stroke engines have problems associated with the contamination of system oil by combustion products and due allowance must be given to this.

Slow Speed Engines.—Consideration of all the available types, indicates that they are all 'crosshead' engines. This means that a piston rod is used to connect the piston to the crosshead and as such provides a convenient means for an effective seal between any leakage of combustion products past the piston rings, and the crankcase itself.

At the same time, lubrication must be provided for the cylinder liner walls and piston rings. To this end a special cylinder oil is used. This oil is injected into the cylinder through a series of quills in the cylinder liner. A number of properties are required of this oil and in general various additives are used to improve the oil quality to acceptable levels.

Since the oil is being injected onto the cylinder walls and piston rings it must be able to:

(a) Provide lubrication even at the high temperatures and pressures encountered in the combustion space.

(b) In the process of burning, the lubricating oil must not leave deposits (of say unburned carbon).

(c) The oil must not provide a 'build-up' of deposits which may affect the operation of the piston rings, or perhaps block-up the scavenge and/or exhaust ports in the liner.

(d) Where residual fuels are used—and particularly where these fuels have a high sulphur content, the cylinder lubricating oil must provide an alkaline base to counteract acid corrosion and increased wear rates of cylinder liners.

Uniflow scavenged two-stroke crosshead engines are well known for having a low cylinder oil consumption. Average consumptions are some 0·5 g/BHPh rising to 0·7–0·8 g/BHPh for transverse or loop scavenged engines.

Cylinder oils should preferably be of the SAE 50 viscosity grade and normally when burning heavy fuels, a cylinder oil with a total base number (TBN) of about 70 has proved adequate for providing lubrication of the cylinder liners coupled with a low wear rate.

System oils should have adequate dispersance/detergency to keep the crankcase (and cooling spaces where oil is used for piston cooling) clean of deposits.

Rust and oxidation inhibited oils of SAE 30 viscosity grade are generally used. Alkaline system oils have proved superior in this respect.

System oil consumption is normally very small ie, less than 0·1 g/BHPh.

Selected international brands of lubricating oils are shown in Table 11. The list is not complete and oils from other companies may be chosen.

Medium Speed Engines.—The lubricating oil of a four-stroke engine is a vital element for good engine operation. In this case, the duties it must serve are

(a) Lubrication of the bearings, cylinders, piston rings etc.

(b) Neutralising the effect of the sulphur in the fuel oil to prevent corrosion of cylinder liner and piston rings.

(c) Cooling of bearings and pistons and keeping the engine interior clean.

(d) Transporting contaminants such as dust, rust, water residues, lubricating oil residues etc. away from the engine to the filters and separators.

TABLE 11.—TYPICAL LUBRICATING OILS FOR SLOW SPEED ENGINES.

Company	System Oil SAE 30/TBN 5–9	Cylinder Oil SAE 50/TBN 70
BP	Energol DL-MD 30	CLO50-M
Castrol	Marine MPX 30	S/DZ 65
Chevron	800 Marine Oil	Delo Special
Esso	Tromar AS 30	Tromar SV
Gulf	Veritas AC 30	Cyloil 700
Mobil	Mobilgard 300	Mobilgard 570
Shell	Melina 30	Alexia 50
Texaco	Doro AR 30	Taro Special

Thus the system lubricating oil must be a mixture of suitable base oil to provide lubrication and cooling, and a series of additives to perform the neutralisation, cleaning & transportation of contaminants and the stabilisation of these properties.

Because of the method of operation in all of these engines ie. using the trunk piston, gudgeon pin, connecting rod mechanism, it is not possible to provide a really effective seal once the piston rings begin to wear. Scraper rings are fitted at the bottom of cylinder liners to provide some means of draining off contaminated oil and are adjusted to provide a certain amount of cylinder wall lubrication. (Only one manufacturer—Sulzer with their ZA40 has cylinder lubrication on a four-stroke medium speed engine).

Consumptions vary but average figures are in excess of 1g/BHPh. With some of the larger medium speed engines the system oil is centrifuged continuously and the majority of these engines have their own engine-driven lubricating oil pumps.

Piston and Jacket Cooling.—All engines, two-stroke and four-stroke, crosshead and trunk, use water as the cooling medium for circulating through the cylinder jackets and cylinder covers. Requirements vary as to pressures and temperatures. The larger engine with high thermal inertias also require some method of heating the circulating water in order to warm the engine through prior to starting. This may take several hours but will prevent excessive thermal stresses being incurred. It is common practice to utilise some of the energy which the jacket water carries from the engine in a fresh water generator. This evaporates sea water at a temperature and pressure below atmospheric, and in many cases can make the ship self-sufficient in fresh water.

As has been described in the section dealing with slow speed engines, some makes use oil for piston cooling whilst some use water for this purpose. The advantage of oil is that leaks in the supply system do not contaminate the crankcase oil. On the other hand, the thermal capacity of oil is only half that of water thus requiring twice the flow for the same amount of cooling duty.

FUELS & FUEL TREATMENT

Characteristics of Diesel Engine Fuels.—Diesel engine fuels can be subdivided into two distinct groups ie, distillate fuels and residual fuels.

Distillate fuels such as gas oil and diesel oil are refined products deriving their name from the refining process ie, distillation.

Residual or heavy fuels contain a large portion of the residue of the refining process. They are basically the left-overs of the refinery and are of lower quality than diesel but also of lower price.

Clearly the main criteria to be satisfied by any marine fuel will be associated with combustion quality, the amount of impurities present and the handling of the fuel, ie, storage, pumping and treatment.

Combustion Quality.—Within the last decade increasingly sophisticated processes such as catalytic cracking and visbreaking have been adopted by refineries in order to increase the proportion of high quality distillate products extracted from a given crude source. This has inevitably reduced the quality of the residual fuel grades by reducing the content of more readily combustible components.

Research on the ignition and combustion of residual fuels has received a lot of attention during the last three or four years, particularly as the traditional indicators of ignition performance, cetane number, cetane index etc. cannot be applied to residual fuels.

There is support for the Calculated Carbon Aromaticity Index (CCAI) proposed by Shell, and the Calculated Ignition Index 1 (CII-1) proposed by BP. Both indices are calculated from the density and viscosity of the fuel.

(i) $CCAI = \rho - 140{\cdot}7 \log_{10} \log_{10} (\nu + 0{\cdot}85) - 80{\cdot}6$

where ρ = density of fuel at 15°C, kg/m^3

ν = viscosity of fuel at 50°C, cSt

CCAI ranges from about 790 to 950. A higher figure indicating a lower ignition quality.

In general terms fuels with a CCAI of less than 850 are likely to be satisfactory, whereas those having a CCAI of greater than 870 may cause ignition problems and lead to unacceptably high rates of cylinder pressure rise.

(ii) $CII\text{-}1 = 294{\cdot}26 - 277{\cdot}3D + 13{\cdot}263 \log_{10} \log_{10} (\nu + 0{\cdot}7)$

where D = density of fuel at 15°C, kg/l

ν = viscosity of fuel at 100°C, cSt

The coefficients of CII-1 are chosen so that the value relates to the cetane number range of poor ignition quality fuels. Hence, the lower the value of CII-1, the lower the ignition quality.

Impurity Content.—Clearly this should be kept as low as possible and harmful impurities should be removed if possible by pre-treatment of the oil before use. The impurities are present in the fuel as a result of natural occurrence in the crude oil from the refining process, or as a result of the storage in the ship. Some impurities are oil soluble and almost impossible to remove by standard treatment systems. These include sulphur and vanadium. Water and solids such as sand, rust, metal oxides and catalyst particles can be removed, or at least reduced, by filtration and centrifuging.

Some solid particles are produced during combustion and this ash can cause mechanical wear of engine components. The catalyst particles, formed from silicium and aluminium oxides used in the refining process can form very abrasive particles and this increases cylinder liner wear.

Vanadium and sodium help to form a high temperature corrosive ash which can attack exhaust valves and turbocharger blades whilst the sulphur content can lead to low temperature corrosion of combustion chamber components by the formation of sulphuric acid.

Handling and Storage.—Storage, pumping etc is affected by the physical properties of the oil such as viscosity, density, flash point and pour point. The viscosity dictates the temperature to which high viscous fuels must be raised to ensure the correct viscosity for pumping, settling, centrifuging and injection.

Table 14 summarises the fuel properties which affect the design of diesel engines and their fuel oil systems.

TABLE 12.—FUEL PROPERTIES WHICH EFFECT THE DESIGN OF ENGINE AND FUEL HANDLING SYSTEMS.

Quality Criteria	Fuel Oil Characteristics	Main Effects
Combustion Quality	Conradson Carbon Asphaltenes	Ignition ability Combustion conditions Fouling of gas passages
Impurity Content	Sulphur Vanadium Sodium	Corrosive wear Formation of deposits High temperature corrosion Exhaust valves and turbochargers.
	Water	Interference with the combustion process. Increased heat load of combustion chamber components. Possible mechanical wear of fuel injection system.
	Ash	Mechanical and corrosive wear Formation of deposits
	Catalyst Fines	Mechanical wear of fuel injection systems.
Handling Properties	Viscosity Density Pour Point	Temperatures, pressures and capacities of fuel oil systems for storage pumping and treatment.
	Flash Point	Safety requirements.

Fuel Oil Standards.—Whilst no detailed international standard for marine fuel exists at the time of writing, the British Standards Institution (BSI) has recently (1983) issued a set of standards which will probably form the basis for a fully international specification.

The new standard, BSMA 100: Petroleum fuels for marine oil engines and boilers, covers 12 grades of fuels. Table 13 shows the main features of the standard.

As can be seen there are two distillate grades M1 and M2 and seven grades M3 to M9 are quoted for fuels containing residual components for use where density has to be limited to suit handling and treatment requirements. Three additional grades are designated without density limitations. Three properties are not included in the table but are currently under consideration. Suitably acceptable tests have yet to be devised for ignition quality, total sediment and aluminium content although a value of 30 ppm for this latter component should be regarded as a maximum for the intermediate fuels M3 through to M9.

TABLE 13.—BRITISH STANDARD MARINE FUELS.
Properties of marine fuels in BSMA Petroleum fuels for marine oil engines and boilers

Property	Grade											
	Class M1	Class M2	Class M3	Class M4	Class M5	Class M6	Class M7	Class M8	Class M9	Class M10	Class M11	Class M12
Density at 15·C, max	—	0·9000	0·9200	0·9910	0·9910	0·9910	0·9910	0·9910	0·9910	—	—	—
Viscosity kinematic cSt*, at 40°C												
Min	1·50	—	—	—	—	—	—	—	—	—	—	—
Max	5·50	11·00	14·00	—	—	—	—	—	—	—	—	—
Viscosity kinematic cSt*, at 80°C max	—	—	—	15·00	25·00	45·00	75·00	100·00	130·00	75·00	100·00	130·00
Cetane index, min	45·00	35·00	—	—	—	—	—	—	—	—	—	—
Carbon residue, Ramsbotton, % (wt), max	—	0·25	2·50	—	—	—	—	—	—	—	—	—
Carbon residue, Ramsbottom on 10% residue, % (wt), max	0·20	—	—	—	—	—	—	—	—	—	—	—
Carbon residue, Conradson, % (wt), max	—	—	—	12·00	14·00	20·00	22·00	22·00	22·00	—	—	—
Flash point, closed, Pensky-Martens, °C, min	43·00	60·00	60·00	60·00	60·00	60·00	60·00	60·00	60·00	60·00	60·00	60·00
Water content, % (vol), max	0·05	0·25	0·30	0·50	0·80	1·00	1·00	1·00	1·00	1·00	1·00	1·00
Sediment by extraction, % (wt), max	0·01	0·02	—	—	—	—	—	—	—	—	—	—
Ash, % (wt), max	0·01	0·01	0·05	0·10	0·10	0·15	0·20	0·20	0·20	0·20	0·20	0·20
Sulphur content, % (wt), max	1·00	2·00	2·00	3·50	4·00	5·00	5·00	5·00	5·00	5·00	5·00	5·00
Cloud point, °C, max	−16	—	—	—	—	—	—	—	—	—	—	—
Pour point, upper†, °C, max												
December 1 to March 31	—	0·00	0·00	24·00	30·00	30·00	30·00	30·00	30·00	30·00	30·00	30·00
April 1 to November 30	—	6·00	6·00	24·00	30·00	30·00	30·00	30·00	30·00	30·00	30·00	30·00
Vanadium content, ppm, max	—	—	100·00	250·00	350·00	500·00	600·00	600·00	600·00	600·00	600·00	600·00

* 1 cSt = 1 mm^2/sec
† The word 'upper' does not apply to classes M2 and M3.

Further Comments on Individual Analysis Data

CARBON RESIDUE indicates the coke-forming tendencv of fuel oil. The higher the value, the higher will be the tendency to form deposits in the combustion space and gas passages. It is possible that high Conradson carbon numbers may in some cases be linked with a lowering of maximum pressures. The value is measured by standardised carbonising tests such as the Conradson and Ramsbottom tests.

SULPHUR is present in fuel oil mainly in organic compounds. The amount is measured by chemical means and is expressed as a weight percentage of the sample tested.

Sulphur burns and contributes to the calorific value of the oil although its specific energy is lower than that of carbon and hydrogen. The sulphur oxides produced by combustion may in themselves not be harmful provided they can be got rid of as a gas. Because of the combustion of hydrogen, water vapour is present and at low temperature conditions, combination of sulphur oxides and water can occur with a consequent deposition of sulphuric acid. The effect can be diminished by keeping higher temperatures in the system and by using alkaline cylinder lubricating oil to neutralise the acid.

It is not usually possible to remove or decrease the sulphur content of fuel oil by conventional treatment methods.

ASH is a measure of inorganic non-combustible material present in the fuel oil. The ash content is found from a combustion test and expressed as a weight percentage residue from complete combustion of the sample. Some ash forming materials can be reduced by centrifuging.

VANADIUM AND SODIUM are constituents of the ash content and can be found by analysing the results of the ash combustion test. Vanadium is oil soluble in the crude oil itself and cannot be removed from the fuel oil. Sodium derives from the crude oil and also from contamination by sea water during the storage and handling of the oil. It is possible to remove most of the water-soluble sodium by water-washing, if required.

During combustion, vanadium and sodium form corrosive ash which is exacerbated if the weight ratio of sodium to vanadium exceeds 1:3.

VISCOSITY is a measure of the internal friction or resistance of an oil to flow. The common unit of kinematic viscosity is the Stoke (St) or its derivative the centistoke (cSt) although other methods of assessing viscosity are widely used. These include Redwood No. 1 or No. 2, Saybolt Universal (SSU), Saybolt Furol (SSF) and Engler.

Traditionally viscosities have been expressed in seconds Redwood No. 1 at a specified temperature. In 1977 this scale was officially superseded by the metric unit of kinematic viscosity ie, the centistoke. It is probable that all three standards will continue to be used in marine parlance ie, Redwood No. 1 at 100°F, cSt at 50°C and cSt at 80°C (the standard for intermediate oils in the British Standard).

Table 14 gives the comparison necessary for any conversion.

TABLE 14. COMPARATIVE MEASURES OF VISCOSITY.

Seconds Redwood No. 1/100°F	cSt/50°C	cSt/80°C
200	IF 30	IF 12
300	IF 40	IF 15
400	IF 60	IF 20
600	IF 80	IF 25
800	IF100	IF 30
1,000	IF120	IF 35
1,200	IF150	IF 40
1,500	IF180	IF 45
2,000	IF240	IF 55
3,500	IF380	IF 75
4,500	IF460	IF 90
6,000	IF600	IF115

All grades of residual oil are now given a number corresponding to the viscosity in cSt at 50°C or 80°C preceded by the letters IF (for intermediate fuel). Marine diesel oil (MDO) is expressed in centistokes at 40°C. It remains to be seen whether this system will give way to the BSI classifications described earlier.

DENSITY is an important parameter in the centrifuging process where water and water soluble impurities must be removed. Since the efficiency of the separation process depends upon the difference between densities of the oil and the water, high density oil is more difficult to treat in this way. Usually this will require a much reduced flowrate through the centrifuges with a consequent increase in centrifuge capacity.

FLASH-POINT is defined as the temperature at which the oil gives off enough vapour to create an inflammable air fuel mixture. This effects the temperature at which the fuel can be stored, handled and transported. Classification society requirements limit the flash point of most fuels to a minimum value of 60°C.

POUR-POINT is the lowest temperature at which an oil will flow (or can be poured). Clearly fuel oils must be stored and handled at temperatures above the pour points to avoid crystallisation which may block filters etc, and inhibit pumping. Generally the temperature required to reduce the viscosity to a pumpable level is greater than the pour point.

FUEL OIL TREATMENT

Fuel Oil System.—The fuel oil installation can be subdivided into the following systems.

(i) Storage and handling system.
(ii) Cleaning system.
(iii) Service system.

(i) The storage and handling system consists of the filling pipe system, bunker tanks and transfer pump with pipe system. For residual fuels it is usually necessary to provide heating coils in the bunkers to ensure pumpability. This requires that temperatures in bunker tanks should not fall below 5°C above the pour point and that the viscosity should be below 1,000 cSt. Temperatures ranging from 15–40°C depending on the fuel are usually required.

(ii) The cleaning system consists of settling tank(s), appropriate pipe system and some form of cleaning equipment. The most popular, and generally regarded as the most efficacious, method is by centrifugal separators although homogenizers and self cleaning filters have occasionally been used.

(iii) The service system which is used for final fuel preparation and its delivery to the engine, comprises service tank(s), priming pumps, filters and heaters for adjusting the final oil viscosity prior to injection into the cylinders.

Where residual oil is used as a fuel there will usually be a separate diesel oil system and an appropriate change-over device to enable the engines to operate on diesel oil when necessary. Diesel oil is often used for manoeuvring since the relatively complex heating system need not be used in such circumstances resulting in easier shipboard operation during this busy time in the machinery space.

The settling tank, acting as a buffer store heats the oil to a temperature in the range of 50–70°C and some water and sludge which settles out due to gravity forces can be removed. From the settling tank the oil is taken to the centrifuges where it is preheated to a temperature of 80–90°C to reduce its viscosity and also its density relative to water.

A common method is to arrange for residual oil to be subjected to two centrifuges—the first arranged as a purifier to remove water and water solubles, the second, to remove any remaining solid particles. Diesel oil does not require heating and it is usual to arrange for a once through centrifuging for this distillate fuel. Figures 29(*a*) and 29(*b*) show two possible arrangements.

From the centrifuges the oil is pumped to the daily service tanks whence it is taken via booster pumps and heaters to the main engine. In order to obtain correct atomisation it is important to maintain a value at the injector of the order of 10–15 cSt. This viscosity will vary from engine design to engine design, the figure

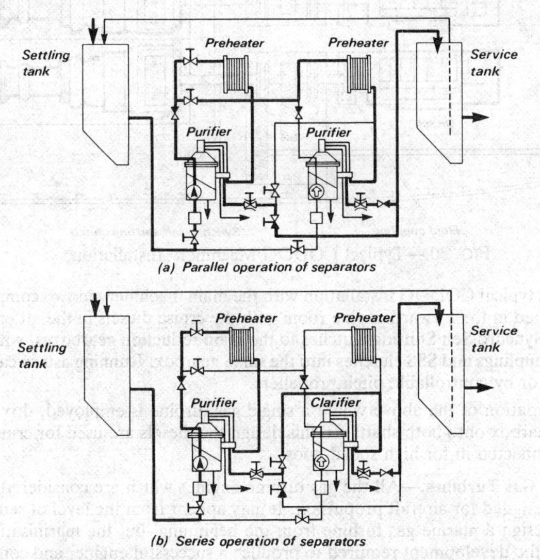

FIG. 29.—Methods of Centrifuging Fuel for Marine Use.

mentioned being a typical range. Since pressurising usually increases the viscosity slightly it is necessary to adjust the viscosity in the low pressure system to say 7–10 cSt. To this end many ships now use an automatic viscosity controller which maintains the required viscosity by adjusting energy flow to a steam or electric final heater.

To enable temperatures to be maintained and hence correct viscosities, all fuel lines carrying residual fuel are traced again with either steam pipes or electric resistance elements. With the modern trend towards higher and higher viscosity fuels, main engines, particularly of the large two-stroke types can run on IF 600 (6,000 secs Redwood No. 1 at 100°F) although more popularly at say IF 380 (about 3,500 secs Redwood No. 1 at 100°F), whilst auxiliary engines will use better quality fuel, often distillate.

There is a trend towards designing the smaller auxiliary engines to burn heavier fuels thus moving towards the concept of a 'unifuel' ship, but more likely is the possibility of running these auxiliary diesels on a blend of heavy fuel and marine diesel oil, blending being done onboard ship. This reduces the cost of providing auxiliary power considerably but will almost certainly lead to increased maintenance.

GAS TURBINE PROPULSION

Since the mid 1960's virtually all British warship designs have used gas turbines for their main propulsion machinery. The features of gas turbine plant in relation to warship and merchant ship propulsion are discussed in section 1.

The Royal Navy Type 21 frigates, and Types 42 and 22 destroyers are all COGOG, with Rolls Royce Olympus gas turbines being used for boost power, and Tyne gas turbines for cruising. The Invincible class aircraft carriers are propelled by four Olympus gas turbines in a COGAG configuration (combined gas and gas) in which the ship can operate with either one or two gas turbines connected to each of two propeller shafts.

Many warships, mainly found in foreign Navies, use a CODOG configuration. This arrangement uses a diesel as the cruise engine and takes advantage of the better fuel economy of the diesel with the higher power gas turbine available for boost.

The modern 3,000 tonne frigate would require about 40,000 kW total shaft power for a maximum speed of 30 knts, and this can be achieved by two boost gas turbines. A cruising speed of 20 knts would require about 7,000 kW, well within the capability of one or two diesel engines. Although economical, diesels produce considerable underwater noise: a disadvantage for warships engaged in anti-submarine warfare.

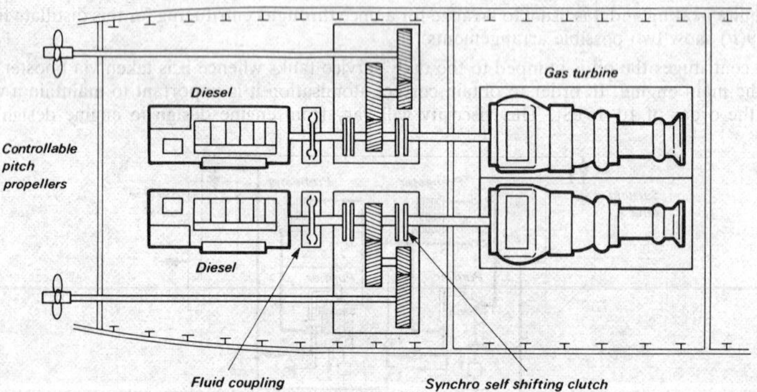

FIG. 30.—Typical CODOG Machinery Installation.

Figure 30 illustrates a typical CODOG installation with the main machinery in two compartments, the boost gas turbines being situated in the forward engine room with the cruise diesels in the aft engine room. The gas turbines drive through Synchro Self Shifting clutches to the main reduction gearboxes, with the diesels driving forward through fluid couplings and SSS clutches into the same gearbox. Running astern can be achieved either by a reversing gearbox or by controllable pitch propellers.

Figure 31 shows a variation of the above where a single gas turbine is employed, driving through a single input, double output gearbox onto both shafts. In this design the diesels are used for cruise and manoeuvring with the gas turbine connected in for high speed boost.

Marinisation of Aero Gas Turbines.—All the gas turbine engines which are considered for warship designs today were originally designed for aircraft propulsion. It may appear from the level of redesign necessary that it would be easier to design a marine gas turbine from the beginning, but the marinisation process is only a relatively small part of the development required to produce a successful engine, and considerable advantage can be taken of the extensive operational experience of the aircraft engines.

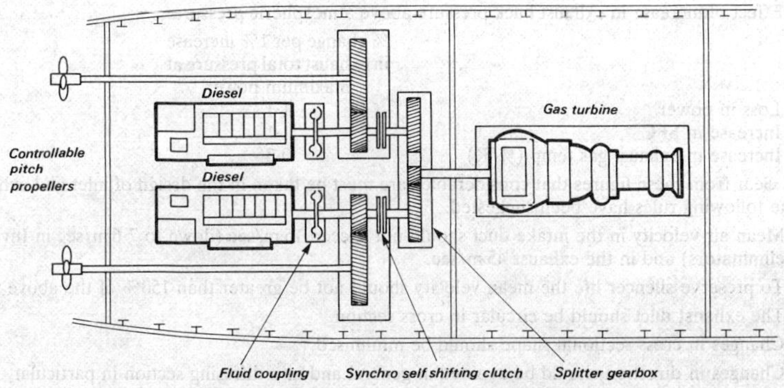

FIG. 31.—CODOG Machinery Installation (Single Gas Turbine).

Fundamentally, marinisation involves the redesign of the jet engine to provide rotational power in a corrosive environment at sea level. The engine may be required to burn fuel of a different quality, additional noise and shock requirements must be met, and air and exhaust gas has to be ducted to and from the engine over substantial distances.

Corrosion.—In the early days of gas turbine marine propulsion the problem of hot corrosion of the turbine blades was less serious as turbine entry temperatures (at 1050°K) were low by modern standards. Little attempt was made to exclude water from the engine beyond siting the air intakes facing aft and using a plenum chamber in the (vain) hope that the lower velocities would prevent the water from being entrained in the airflow.

Over the last twenty years, of course, there have been considerable advances in the development of blade materials and coatings, together with developments in air filtration systems. Blade cooling allows the use of higher turbine entry temperatures (1,300–1,350°K) but it should be noted that in aero engines the concern is with creep life limitations and therefore, mean metal temperatures, whereas in the marine engine it is corrosion, which is governed by surface temperature. It has been shown experimentally that, amongst other factors, the rate of corrosion increases with gas velocity, concentration of sea salt and thermal cycling.

Compressor corrosion and erosion can be minimised by suitable choice of materials (titanium or stainless steel) or the use of various coatings. The injection of water repellent fluids into the engine after shut-down has also been shown to reduce the rate of corrosion.

Combustion.—In warships, it is highly desirable to have low exhaust smoke levels, both for cosmetic reasons and in order to minimise the infra-red signature, which increases with smoke density. Invisible exhaust smoke (Bacharach 3 or under) is aimed for and this depends, amongst other parameters, on the quality of fuel burned. Aero engines burn kerosene, and the heavier distillates used in marine gas turbines for reasons of cost and availability produce more smoke, higher luminosity and hence more radiation.

The combustion cans and burners must, therefore, be designed to produce a high degree of fuel atomisation and fuel air mixing in order to achieve complete combustion. Higher radiation characteristics of the fuel may demand more sophisticated cooling techniques in order to keep the combustion can temperatures to an acceptable level and attention must be paid to the design of the combustion can inter-connectors to ensure good light-around. Different fuel spray patterns will also affect the positioning of the ignitors.

It is important that the temperature profile at the inlet to the HP turbine is reasonably flat for reasons of blade creep life and a maximum deviation from the mean of about 5% is acceptable with the peak temperature occurring at about mid height. This does however, involve a compromise as a flat temperature profile leads to high combustion can temperatures.

Ducting.—The specific air consumption of a gas turbine is approximately twice that of the equivalent diesel engine and the performance is very sensitive to inlet pressure loss and increase in exhaust back pressure. The following figures apply to the Olympus TM3 module:

(a) Effect of pressure loss relative to atmospheric pressure at compressor inlet:

	% change per 1% intake pressure loss at maximum power
Loss in power	2·2
Increase in SFC	1·2
Decrease in engine mass flow	1·0
Increase in exhaust gas temp (%°K)	0·3

(b) Effect of increase in exhaust back pressure above atmospheric pressure:

	% change per 1% increase in exhaust total pressure at maximum power
Loss in power	1·1
Increase in SFC	1·1
Increase in exhaust gas temp (%°K)	0·3

It is clear from these figures that considerable care must be taken in the design of inlet and exhaust ducting and the following rules have been suggested.

(1) Mean air velocity in the intake duct should not exceed 15 m/sec (down to 7·6 m/sec in Invincible's salt eliminators) and in the exhaust 45 m/sec.

(2) To preserve silencer life the mean velocity should not be greater than 150% of the above values.

(3) The exhaust duct should be circular in cross section.

(4) Changes in cross sectional shape should be minimised.

(5) Changes in direction should be avoided in general and in a diffusing section in particular.

These limitations and the overall spaces required for ducting can have far-reaching effects the total ship design. Although the power to weight ratio of gas turbine plant is low, when taking the volume of ducting into consideration, the power to volume ratio in some designs may not appear quite so attractive. Figure 32 shows the substantial internal space devoted to the ducting arrangements of the propulsion machinery in the 'Invincible' class aircraft carriers.

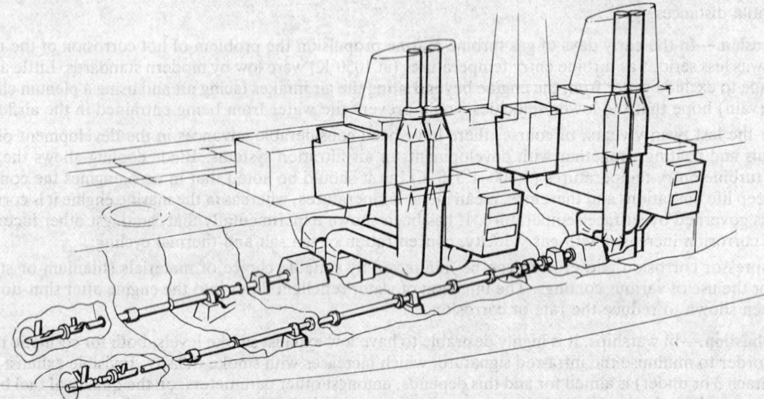

FIG. 32.—HMS Invincible Propulsion Machinery.

In addition to the pressure loss requirements the ducting must satisfy further parameters. Some of which are peculiar to warships:

(1) House three stages of air intake infiltration required to minimise salt ingestion.

(2) House the splitter silencers required to minimise airborne noise levels.

(3) Sufficiently blast resistant to withstand a pressure fluctuation of 1 bar within two seconds.

(4) Prevent ingestion of foreign objects.

(5) Prevent panel resonances and vibration.

(6) Accommodate thermal expansion.

(7) Provide satisfactory disposal of the high temperature exhaust gases in relation to upper deck fittings, helicopter operations etc.

As a way of overcoming ducting problems, consideration has been given to siting the gas turbines closer to the upper deck and employing electrical transmission. The use of superconducting electrical equipment may be applied within the foreseeable future.

Shock resistance and noise levels.—Warship propulsion machinery must, of course, be able to withstand shock caused by underwater explosion. Allied with this the engine supports must minimise, as far as possible, the contribution of the engine to underwater noise.

The normal aero engine is stressed for acceleration of no more than 10–12 g, but these figures refer to continuous acceleration and the engine will withstand considerably higher shock loads which are applied for only a few milliseconds. The weak points in the aero engine, in relation to shock, are the engine casings—

particularly in way of the bearing supports. By strengthening the casing and distributing the load through ring mounts the Rolls Royce range of marine gas turbines can withstand the following vertical shock loads for a period of 12·5 milliseconds:

Olympus	50 g
Tyne	40 g
SMIA	40 g

In addition, the engine will be flexibly mounted in order to absorb the difference between the maximum shock input from the seat and the maximum shock resistance of the engine. In practice, this is a formidable design task, and involves a compromise between satisfactory alignment and shock and noise attenuation. For good alignment and a stable mounting system the stiffness of the rubber should be high, but in that case the shock absorption and noise attenuation is low.

Airborne noise levels of less than Nr 82 (82 dB at 1 kH_z) are desirable for reasons of habitability and it is thought that airborne noise levels below Nr 100 would not contribute significantly to underwater noise. The greater contribution to underwater noise is through the engine supports and satisfactory attenuation requires mountings of low stiffness. This in turn may cause alignment problems and the possibility of large resonant movements due to external low frequency (<10 H_z) oscillations.

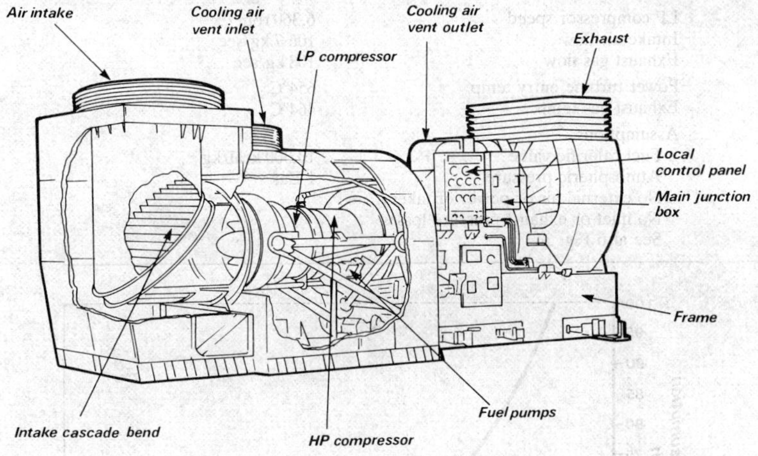

FIG. 33.—Marine Olympus Module *Rolls Royce.*

ROLLS ROYCE MARINE OLYMPUS TM 3B MODULE

The Marine Olympus module Fig. 33 consists of an Olympus 2017 gas generator, power turbine with exhaust volute, air intake enclosure and cascade bend, and gas generator accoustic enclosure. The power turbine is designed to last the life of the ship, but the gas generator is an exchange unit and can usually be replaced within 24 hours.

Olympus Gas Generator.—The type 2017 gas generator is a straight flow high pressure ratio unit, with a five stage axial LP compressor and a seven stage axial HP compressor. Each compressor is driven independently by its own single stage turbine.

The combustion system consists of eight combustion chambers formed as an annulus. Each chamber is fitted with a duplex burner located within a swirler. Igniters are fitted in two of the lower chambers and ignition is distributed by tubes connecting adjacent chambers. The gas generator is carried by stiff rings on tubular struts mounted through struts to the power turbine support frame. To avoid alignment problems and the application of shock or thermal loads, connection to the power turbine is through a bellows joint.

Mounted on the gas generator and driven through auxiliary gearboxes are the pressure and scavenge lubricating oil and fuel pumps. Starting is by a pneumatic starter motor driving the HP compressor.

Power Turbine.—The Olympus power turbine has a single stage rotor disk available with either clockwise or anticlockwise rotation. The rotor shaft is supported in two plain journal bearings and located axially by double acting thrust bearings. Lubricating oil is normally supplied from the ships main gearing.

The rotor assemply is mounted on a fabricated steel support pedestal. Sockets are mounted at the forward end for the ball ends of the struts which form the gas generator mounting frame. The pedestal also supports the stainless steel exhaust volute which is flexibly connected to the ships uptake system.

TABLE 15.—PERFORMANCE AND DIMENSIONS OF ROLLS-ROYCE OLYMPUS 3B MODULE.

Weights	
Module	28,760 kg inc gas generator
Gas generator	3,039 kg (engine change unit)
Dimensions	
Length	9,170 mm
Width	2,641 mm
Height	3,530 mm
Shock capability	
Vertical	50 g
Horizontal	25 g
Fore and Aft	7 g
Power output	21 MW at 15°C
Power turbine speed	5,660 rpm
Fuel consumption	0·214 kg/kW/h
LP compressor speed	6,360 rpm
Intake air flow	106·7 kg/sec
Exhaust gas flow	108 kg/sec
Power turbine entry temp	654°C
Exhaust gas temp.	464°C
Assumptions.—	
Fuel calorific value	10,300 kcal/kg
Atmospheric pressure	1 Bar
No external air or power offtakes	
No inlet or exhaust pressure losses	
See also Fig. 34.	

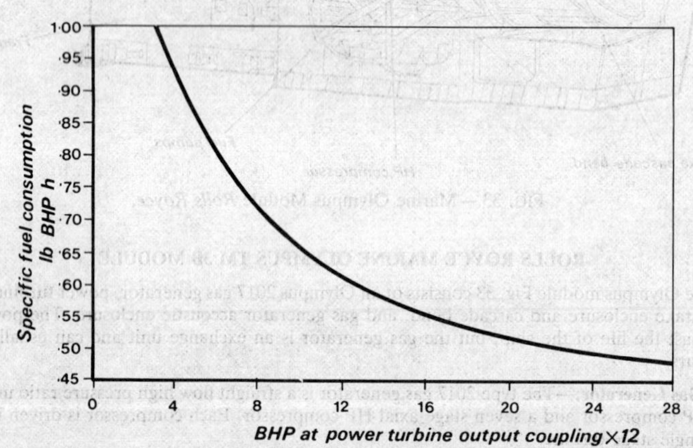

Atmospheric Pressure 14·7LBF/SqInABS (1·03KGF/SqCm)ABS. Air Inlet Temperature 15°C. No inlet or Exhaust Ducting Pressure Losses. Fuel Lower Calorific Value 10300 CHU/LB (10300KCAL/KG). Nominal Performance. Power Varies With Turbine Speed Along a Cube Law. Load Line Passing Through 28000BHP at 5660Rev/Min.

FIG. 34.—Variation of Specific Fuel Consumption with Brake Horsepower (Marine Olympus TM3B Module).

Rolls Royce SM Series Marine Propulsion Turbines.—Rolls Royce present three versions of the SM series, all of which are derived from the Spey aero gas turbine. The Spey gas generator and two stage free power turbine are mounted on a common base frame. This gives a module of 12·75 MW at continuous rating, and a sprint rating of 14 MW.

The unit is available in three configurations (Fig. 35). For frigates and destroyers requiring shock protection and designed to operate in conditions of nuclear, biological and chemical warfare a self contained enclosed module (the SM1) is available mounted on its own base frame.

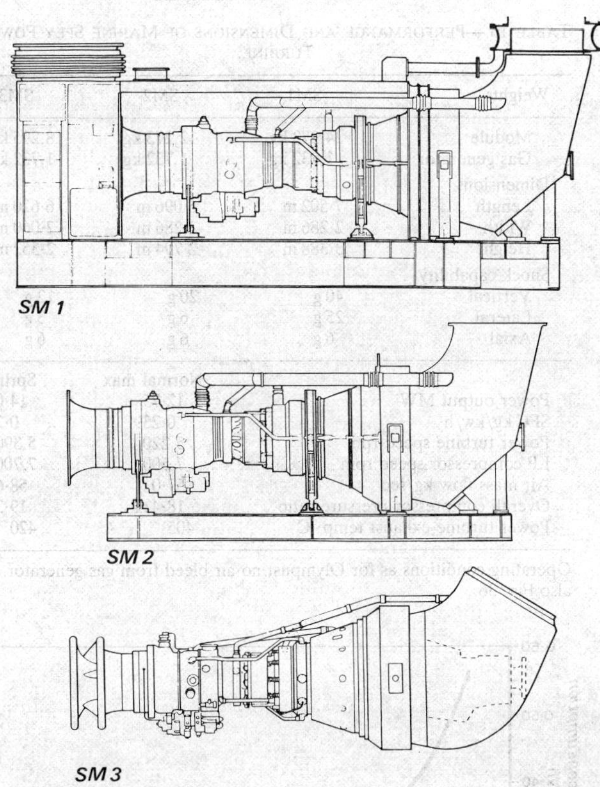

FIG. 35.—Marine Spey Propulsion Units *Rolls Royce*.

A lighter weight version, designated the SM2 is available for strike missile craft, corvettes and surface effect ships. This is similar to the SM1 but without the accoustic enclosure and cascade bend. The base frame is lighter.

A third version, suitable for small craft, SWATH (small waterplane area twin hull) vessels and hydrofoils is designated the SM3. The gas generator, power turbine and exhaust volute are retained, but there is no base frame and the gas generator is rigidly connected to the power turbine. The complete unit has three mounting points for integration into the ships structure.

Marine Spey Gas Generator.—The marine Spey gas generator is a twin spool high pressure ratio axial flow unit with a five stage LP and an eleven stage HP compressor in tandem, each driven independently by its own two stage turbine.

A gearbox on the compressor casing provides drives for oil pressure and scavenge pumps, hydraulic pump, fuel pump, speed signal generators and starter.

Marine Spey Power Turbine.—The turbine is an overhung two stage unit incorporating tilting pad thrust bearings mounted in a steel support ring and surrounded by the exhaust volute. In the SM1 and SM2 the gas generator and power turbine are secured to base frames and connected by a bellows section. In the SM3 the gas generator is rigidly connected to the power turbine and both items are intended to be supported from the ship's structure.

Rolls Royce Marine RB 211 Engines.—The RB 211 aero unit is a triple spooled turbofan engine, from which the RB 211 gas generator Fig. 37 is derived by removal of the fan, fan casing, fan turbine and shaft. The power turbine is a two stage unit, manufactured by Cooper Energy Services. The marine version is intended primarily for merchant ship applications.

RB 211 Gas Generator and Power Turbine.—In order that component designations remain common with the aero engine, the two spools are termed intermediate pressure (IP) and high pressure (HP). The IP compressor consists of seven axial stages drive by a single IP turbine and the HP compressor consists of six stages drive by

TABLE 16.—PERFORMANCE AND DIMENSIONS OF MARINE SPEY POWER TURBINE.

Weights	SM1	SM2	SM3
Module	24,373 kg	12,273 kg	8,295 kg
Gas generator	1,732 kg	1,732 kg	1,732 kg
Dimensions			
Length	7·502 m	6·096 m	6·620 m
Width	2·286 m	2·286 m	2·060 m
Height	3·388 m	2·794 m	2·352 m
Shock capability			
Vertical	40 g	20 g	12 g
Lateral	25 g	6 g	3 g
Axial	6 g	6 g	6 g

	Normal max	Sprint
Power output MW	12·75	14·0
SFC kg/kw/h	0·239	0·235
Power turbine speed rpm	5,220	5,390
LP compressor speed rpm	7,500	7,700
Air mass flow kg/sec	57·0	58·6
Overall compressor pressure ratio	18·4:1	19·3:1
Power turbine exhaust temp °C	405	420

Operating conditions as for Olympus; no air bleed from gas generator. See also Fig. 36.

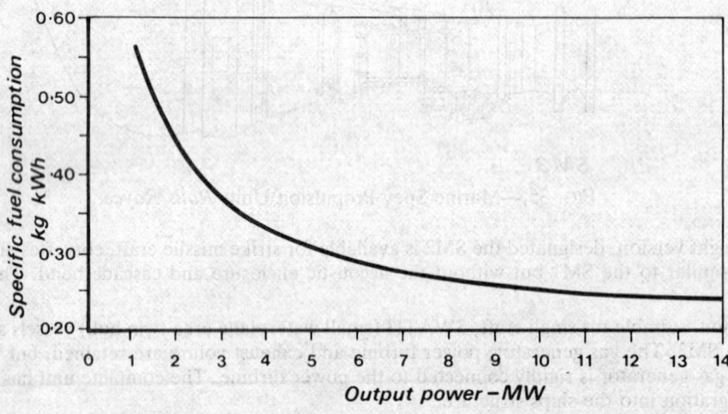

FIG. 36.—Variation of Specific Fuel Consumption with Output Power (SM1, SM2 & SM3) *Rolls Royce*.

a single stage HP turbine. Bleed valves are fitted to the IP and HP compressors to give stable engine handling and low starting power. Variable intake guide vanes are fitted forward of the first row of IP compressor blades to give optimum performance through the power range.

The gas generator is of modular construction and major maintenance is undertaken by means of module change outs. This reduces the need for holdings of spare gas generators as the five main modules are completely interchangeable with similar new or reconditioned units. Details of the complete assembly are shown in Fig. 38.

Assumptions as for Olympus; no air bleed from the engine other than that released by the compressor blow-off valves.

Rolls Royce Marine Tyne (RM Series) Engines.—In the aero version the Tyne engine was a turboprop with the propeller drive by the LP compressor. In the marine version the last two turbine stages are separated after the removal of the propeller to form the power turbine. In consequence, the power turbine forms part of the gas turbine change unit and the high output speed of up to 13,000 rpm makes a separate 4:1 reduction gearbox necessary.

COCOG machinery layouts, with separate cruise and boost engines, were developed mainly because of the

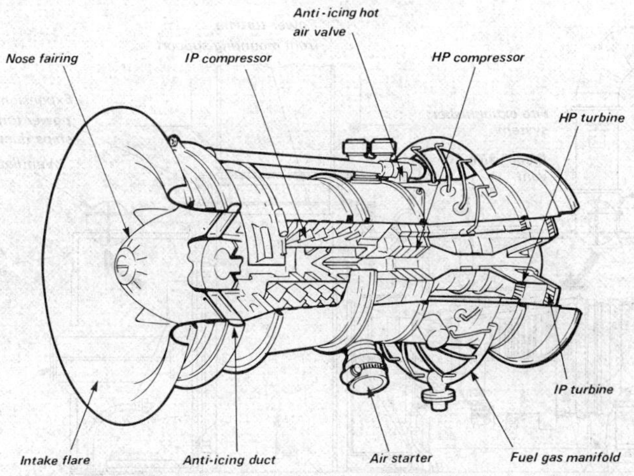

FIG. 37.—RB211 Gas Generator (Internal Construction) *Rolls Royce.*

TABLE 17.—PERFORMANCE AND DIMENSIONS OF ROLLS-ROYCE RB11 MARINE ENGINES.

Weight (excluding intake plenum chamber and silencer Fig. 37)	41,288 kg
Dimensions	
Length	7·04 m
Width	4·2 m
Height	3·9 m
Power output (15°C air temp)	21·56 MW
Power turbine speed	4,800 rpm
Fuel consumption	0·243 kg/kW/h
IP compressor speed	6,420
Air mass flow	87·5 kg/sec
Power turbine exhaust temp	454°C

absence at the time of a suitable mid range engine. With the development of the Spey SM series, Rolls Royce expect sales of the Marine Tyne for frigate applications to fall with preference being given to COGAG layouts offered by the SM.

TABLE 18.—PERFORMANCE AND DIMENSIONS OF ROLLS-ROYCE MARINE TYPE (RM SERIES) ENGINES.

Tyne RM1C	
Module Weight	14,061 kg
Dimensions	
Length	5·56 m
Width	2·12 m
Height	2·61 m
Power output	3,980 kW
Output shaft speed	3,425 rpm
Fuel consumption	0·285 kg/kW/h
Exhaust gas temp	441°C
Exhaust gas mass flowrate	21·8 kg/sec
Assumptions	
Air inlet temp	15°C
Atmospheric pressure	1 Bar
No intake or exhaust ducting pressure losses	
Fuel calorific value	43,000 kJ/kg

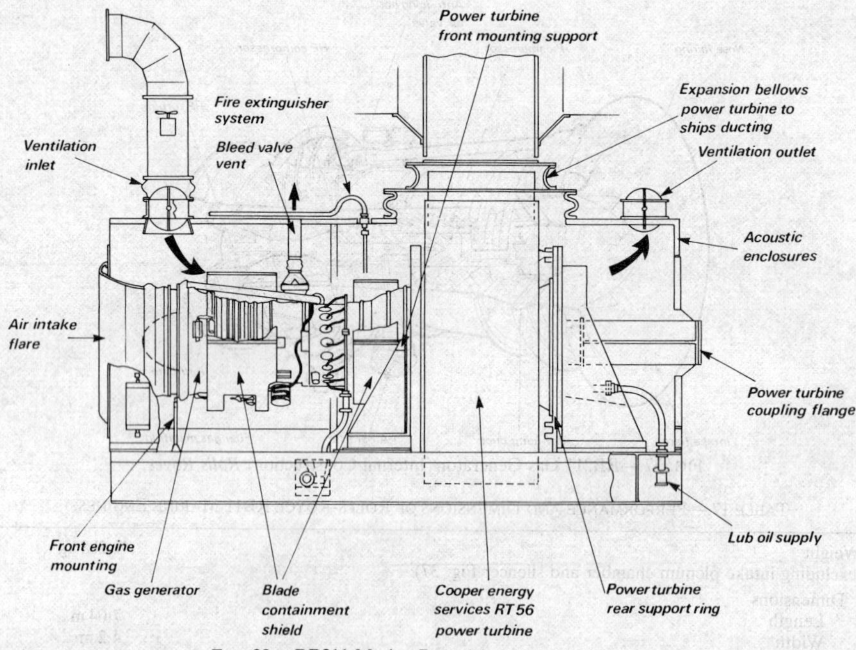

FIG. 38.—RB211 Marine Propulsion Unit *Rolls Royce.*

AUXILIARY POWER SUPPLY AND DEMAND

Before the sudden oil price rise in 1973 fuel accounted for only about 11% of the shipowner's costs, and there was, therefore, little incentive to increase the fuel efficiency of engines at the expense of first cost, or to fit fuel saving or power recovery devices at the expense of plant complexity. Nowadays, however, fuel accounts for over 50% of operating costs, and in addition to improved fuel efficiency of engines, some attention is now given to satisfying auxiliary heat and electrical power requirements using waste heat rejected by the main engine.

The distribution of power as a percentage of the total available from combusion of the fuel is as follows.—

Fuel 100%	0·5%	Radiation
	9·6%	Air cooler
	29%	Exhaust gas
	7·1%	Jacket water
	4·6%	L.O. cooler
	49·2%	Propulsion power

In a modern engine, almost 50% of the energy in the fuel is converted to shaft work. Depending on the particular application, it is possible to use part of the exhaust gas waste heat to generate electrical power and to recover some of the charge air and jacket water waste heat as auxiliary heat sources.

Auxiliary power requirements vary greatly from ship type to ship type: a refrigerated cargo ship, for example, will have an exceptionally high auxiliary power consumption compared to a general cargo ship, and in addition to the technical aspects, the economic viability of some power recovery or power saving schemes may be governed (inter alia) by the ratio of time spent at sea to time spent in port, proportion of time spent in temperate waters and the degree of reduction in operational flexibility which can be accepted.

Jacket Water Heat Utilisation.—At a typical temperature of only around 80°C, jacket water is the lowest temperature heat source. For this reason it is not usually possible to utilise it for any purpose other than the well established generation of fresh water, although there have been proposals to provide accommodation heating and fuel bunker tank heating from the jacket water. A recent proposal to provide electrical power using a freon Rankine cycle and jacket water heat was shown to be economically unattractive.

Charge Air Cooling Water Heat Utilisation.—The turbocharger compressor air discharge temperature may be as high as 150°C and in some applications, charge air cooling water can be used to satisfy various heating requirements which would otherwise be met by saturated steam generated in the exhaust gas boiler. The more useful high temperature (300°C) exhaust gas waste heat is thus able to supply more superheated steam to a turbogenerator set to provide increased electrical power. A disadvantage of charge air heat recovery is that the quantity of heat available is considerably reduced at main engine part load: at 85% full power the available charge air heat may be only half that available at full power.

Exhaust Gas Waste Heat Recovery.—The traditional exhaust gas boiler, used to provide saturated steam for domestic services, bunker tank heating etc is well established, but at an exhaust temperature of around 300°C there exists the possibility of using exhaust gas heat and a low pressure (typically 8 bar) steam Rankine cycle to provide electrical power. In some cases, the electrical power available is sufficient to satisfy all the at-sea auxiliary load.

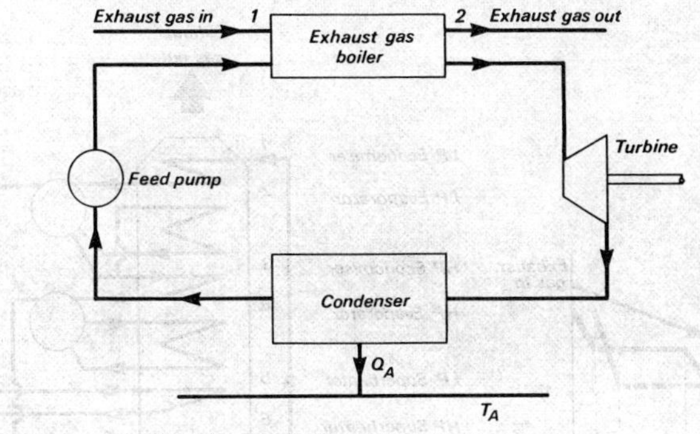

FIG. 39.—Basic Waste Heat Recovery Cycle.

Fundamentally, the cycle is as shown in Fig. 39. Thermodynamic availability theory provides an immediate calculation of the maximum available work obtainable from a system undergoing an irreversible process between specified end states ((1) and (2)) in an environment at temperature T_A. The ideal efficiency η of the above system, in terms of work output as a percentage of the heat transferred from the exhaust gases between states (1) and (2) can thus be shown to be

$$\eta = 1 - \frac{T_A \ln \dfrac{T_1}{T_2}}{T_1 - T_2}$$

Using typical figures of $T_A = 18°C$, $T_1 = 310°C$, $T_2 = 160°C$, then ideal efficiency $\eta = 42\%$.

In practice, irreversibilities due to the finite temperature differences in the waste heat boiler and the low efficiency of steam turbines in the power range 500–1,000 kW reduce the overall efficiency to around 15–18%.

Single and dual pressure cycles.—Figure 40 shows a simple single pressure steam cycle where it can be seen

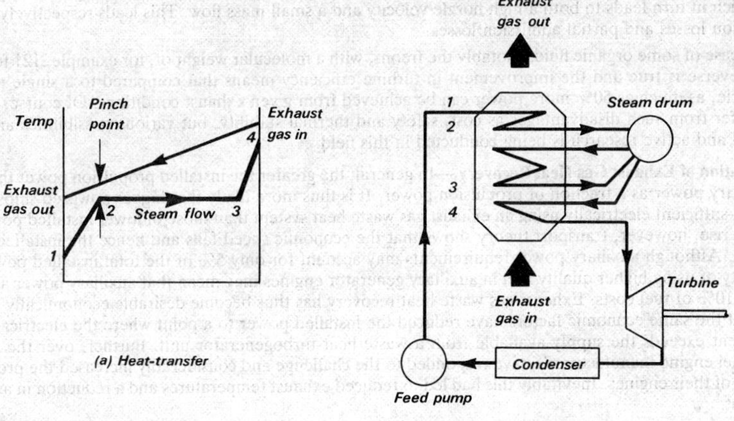

FIG. 40.—Single Pressure Cycle.

that at points other than the pinch point, heat transfer in the boiler takes place across the substantial temperature difference. In selecting the steam pressure it should be noted that lower pressures require high steam flows and large flow areas, but boiler design is straightforward, applying the minimum restrictions to the selection of materials. Higher pressures (20–30 bar) result in lower steam flows and small condensers, and the relatively high speed small diameter turbines usually require partial admission in the first stages incurring turbine efficiency penalties. Boiler costs also increase due to the more sophisticated design requiring higher grade materials. On balance single pressure systems usually operate at 7 to 9 bars.

In order to match the rise in temperature of the steam more closely to the fall in temperature of the exhaust gas, and thus achieve a higher cycle efficiency, dual pressure cycles have been examined. Fig. 41.

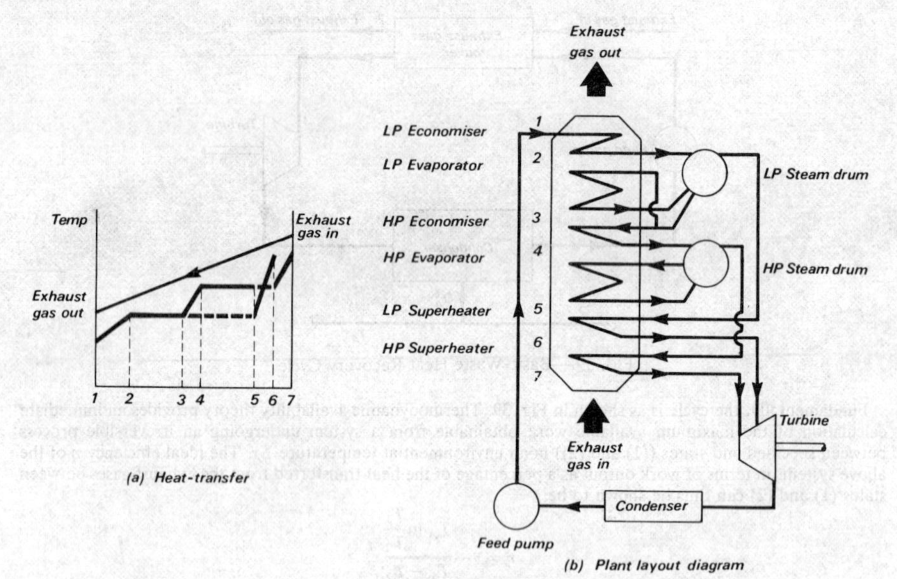

FIG. 41.—Typical Dual Pressure Cycle.

Typically, a dual pressure cycle will operate at 8 bar and 24 bar.

The low turbine efficiency (55–65%) arises from the nature of steam as a working fluid in power cycles. Its low molecular weight and, therefore, high gas constant leads to a large enthalpy drop for a given temperature drop, which in turn leads to both a high nozzle velocity and a small mass flow. This leads respectively to high disk friction losses and partial admission losses.

In the case of some organic fluids, notably the freons, with a molecular weight of, for example, 121 for freon 12, the reverse is true and the improvement in turbine efficiency means that compared to a single pressure steam cycle, as much as 50% more power can be achieved from given exhaust conditions. Of course, organic fluids suffer from such disadvantages as cost, safety and thermal stability, but various possibilities are being examined and active research is being conducted in this field.

Application of Exhaust Gas Heat Recovery.—In general, the greater the installed propulsion power the lower the auxiliary power as a fraction of propulsion power. It is thus more likely that higher powered ships can be made self-sufficient electrically using an exhaust gas waste heat system than those of lower installed power. As fuel costs rise, however, transport theory shows that the economic speed falls and hence the installed power decreases. Although auxiliary power requirements may account for only 5% of the total installed power, the desirability of using higher quality fuel in auxiliary generator engines may mean that auxiliary power accounts for up to 10% of fuel costs. Exhaust gas waste heat recovery has thus become desirable economically but it is ironic that the same economic factors have reduced the installed power to a point where the electrical power requirement exceeds the supply available from a waste heat turbogenerator unit. Further, over the last ten years diesel engine manufacturer's have responded to the challenge and considerably increased the propulsive efficiency of their engines. Inevitably this had led to reduced exhaust temperatures and a reduction in available waste heat.

In a recent study of the auxiliary power consumption of a 70,000 dwt Panamax bulk carrier, it was found that the at-sea auxiliary electrical load totalled 425 kW, of which 53% was accounted for by the main engine pumps, engine room vent fans, galley and air conditioning compressor. By employing various power saving devices, this consumption could be reduced by around 9% to 386 kW.

In calculating the electrical power available from the optimum 9000 kW propulsion slow speed diesel, account was taken of the auxiliary steam heating requirement of 724 kW. The more the steam heating requirement can be reduced, the greater the quantity of steam available for electrical power generation. Charge air cooling may be utilised for part of this duty, particularly in the lower temperature ranges which suffice for double bottom, settling and service tank heating. The effect of reducing the steam heating load on available electrical power is shown in Table 19.

TABLE 19.—STEAM HEATING LOAD/AVAILABLE ELECTRIC POWER.

	Auxiliary steam consumption kW	Electrical power available kW
(1) No charge air heat recovery	724	263
(2) DB, settling and service tank on charge air heat recovery	478	304
(3) All steam requirement satisfied by charge air cooling	0	384

In practice, a margin of 40–50% excess electrical capacity should be allowed so that large intermittently used items (such as compressors) can be started without starting an auxiliary diesel generator. It can, therefore, be seen from Table 19 that there is insufficient electrical power available from the waste heat unit to satisfy an electrical demand of 386 kW or 425 kW. Calculations in this example were, however, based on a moderate level of installed power, and on an engine which reflects the latest propulsion efficiency technology and hence the minimum of available waste heat.

ACKNOWLEDGEMENTS

The authors wish to record their thanks to the following for their assistance in the preparation of this chapter:—

Babock Power Limited
Stal Laval (Great Britain) Limited
NEI APE Limited
Vosper Thorneycroft (UK) Limited
Sulzer Bros (UK) Limited
MAN GHH (Great Britain) Limited
Rolls Royce Limited
MAN-B & W Ltd.

BIBLIOGRAPHY

LARSEN, G. A. *Steam Turbine Propulsion Systems.* I.Mar.E. Victoria (Aust) branch, March 1975.
HODGKIN, A. F. *Marine Boiler Development Over the Past Ten Years*, Trans I.Mar.E., 1973, Vol. 85.
I.Mar.E. Conference on Steam Propulsion for Ships in the Changing Economic Environment, January 1978.
LARSEN, G.A. *VAP Turbine Plant and its Economy.*
HODGKIN, A. F. *Marine Boilers for Very Advanced Purposes.*
NORTAG, L. *The VAP Turbine Machine.*
HODGKIN, A. F. *Marine Applications of the Fluidised Bed*, Marine Engineers Review, June 1982.
WATSON, D. E. V. *Marine Steam Propulsion and the Fluidised Bed*, Marine Engineers Review, August 1978.
HODGKIN, A. F. *Steaming with Fuels of the Future*, Shipbuilding and Marine Engineering International, March 1982.
HODGKIN, A. F. *Coal Fired Marine Boiler Plant*, Proc. Second International Coal Fired Ships Conference, New York, October 1980.
ARMSTRONG, G. *The Influence of Type of Fuel on Ship and Engine Design*, Paper A2 Fifth WEGEMT Graduate School, W. Berlin, 1981.
LUTJE-SCHIPHOLT, LT.CDR. R.M., R.N.N., *Marinisation of Aero Gas Turbines*, Trans I.Mar.E., Vol 87, 1975.
PRESTON, C. E. M. *Naval Gas Turbines for the 1980's*, Rolls Royce Publication.
MCKENNA, M. N. and ROGERS, D. *HMS 'Invicible' Propulsion Machinery from Concept to Fulfilment*, Trans I.Mar.E., Vol 94, 1982.
THORPE, I. and ARMSTRONG, G. *The Economic Selection of Main and Auxiliary Machinery*, Trans I.Mar.E., Vol 95, 1982.

Mid-March 1984
What's new in Industry
The guide to products & equipment
In this issue on page
Mechanical components and sub-assemblies 7
Factory equipment 10
Office equipment and services 18
Inspection and measurement 20
Computer systems and equipment 24
Safety, security and welfare 34
Production machines and tools 36
Environmental control 40
Process plant and control 43
Plant maintenance 48
Handling and storage 51
Finishing and materials 56
Electrical components and sub-assemblies 59
Packaging 63
Buildings and maintenance 66
Hand Tools 71
Free literature 77
Product feature: Valves & Pumps Page 26

INDEX

A

AGR

AIR

C

CON

COP

E

ELE

ELE

I

INT

J

K

M

MEC

MET

N

O

P

Q

R

THE

TIM

W

KEMPES ENGINEERS YEAR-BOOK
INDEX TO ADVERTISERS 1989

Printed in Great Britain by Page Bros (Norwich) Ltd.